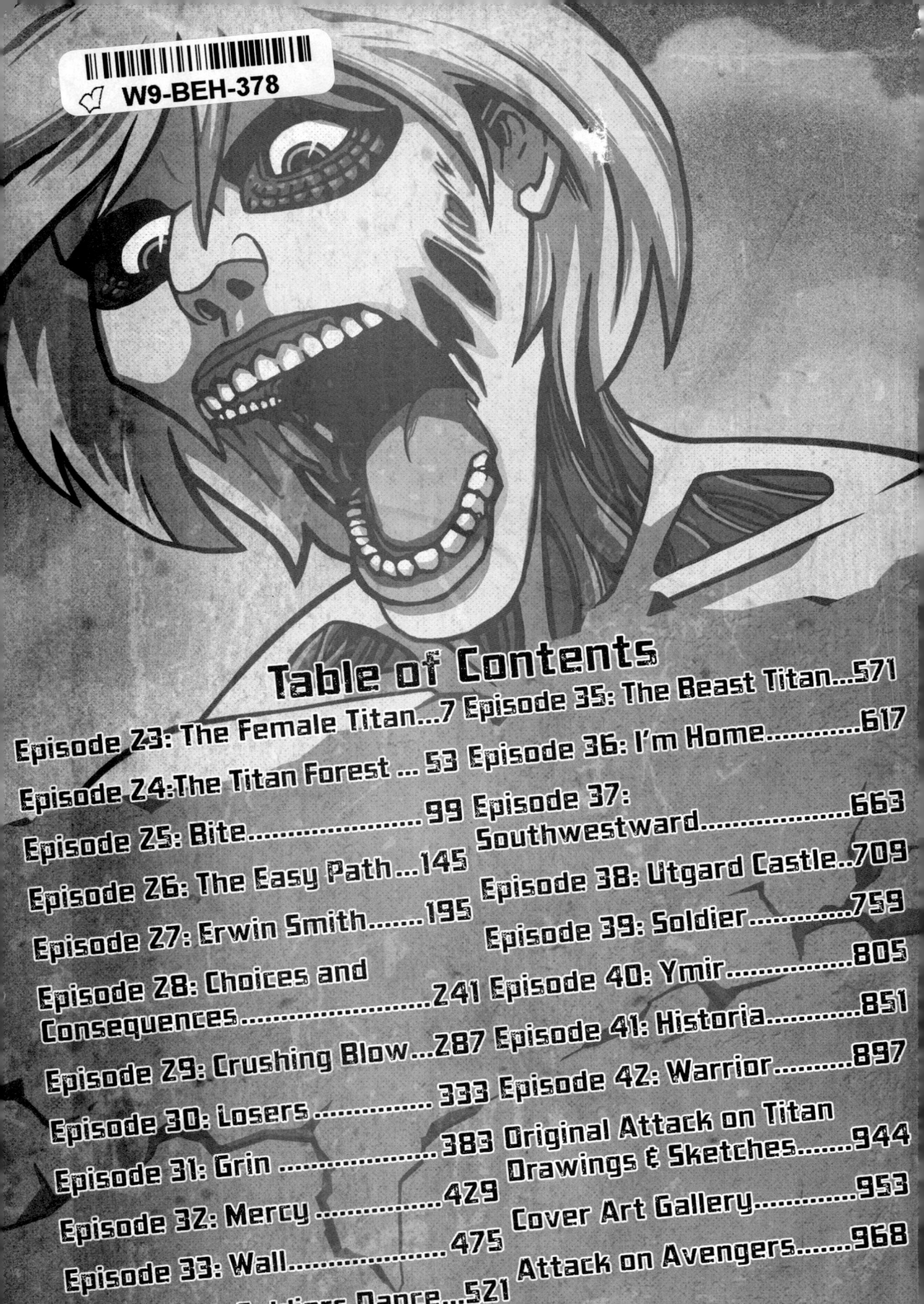

Table of Contents

A Kodansha Comics Trade Paperback Original

Attack on Titan: Colossal Edition 2 copyright © 2011-2013 Hajime Isayama
English translation copyright © 2013-2015 Hajime Isayama

Published in the United States by Kodansha Comics, an imprint of Kodansha USA Publishing, LLC, New York.

Publication rights for this English edition arranged through Kodansha Ltd., Tokyo.

First published in Japan in 2011-2013 by Kodansha Ltd., Tokyo as *Shingeki no kyojin*, volumes 6-10.

ISBN 978-1-63236-181-3

Printed in the United States of America.

www.kodanshacomics.com

9 8 7 6 5 4
Translation, volumes 6-7: Sheldon Drzka
Translation, volumes 8-10: Ko Ransom
Lettering: Steve Wands
Compiled by: Nathalie Kent
Editing: Ben Applegate

Cover designed and illustrated by Phil Balsman

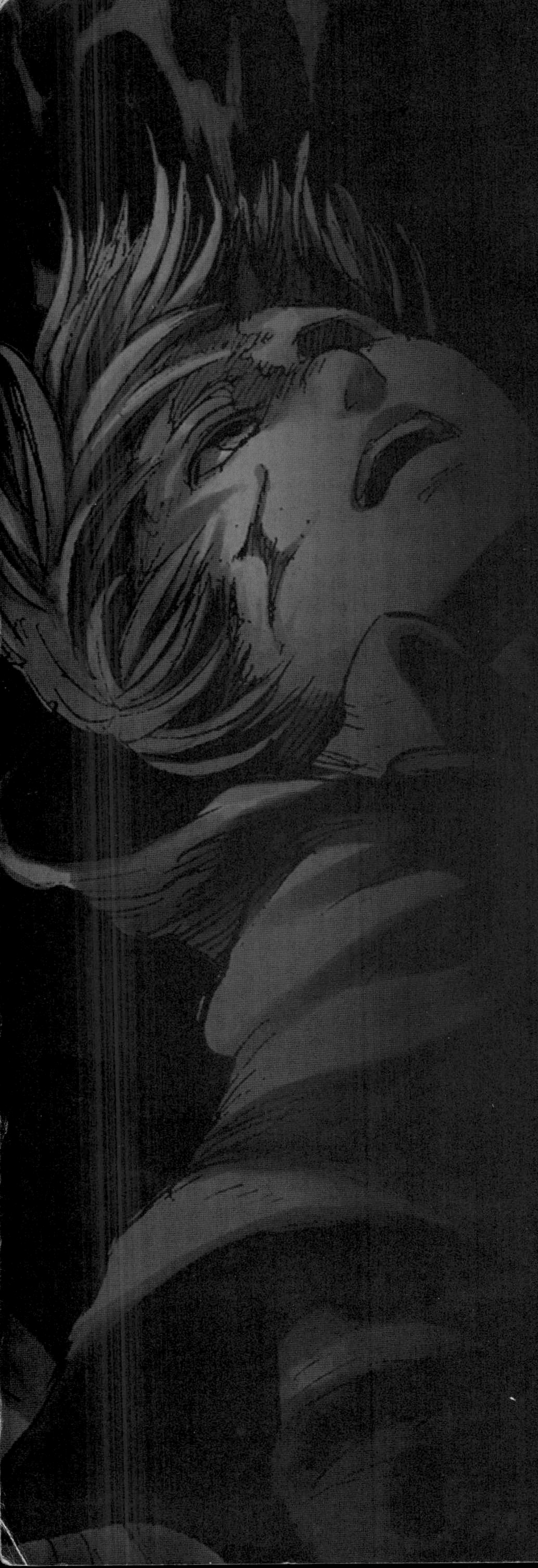

ATTACK ON TITAN

HAJIME ISAYAMA

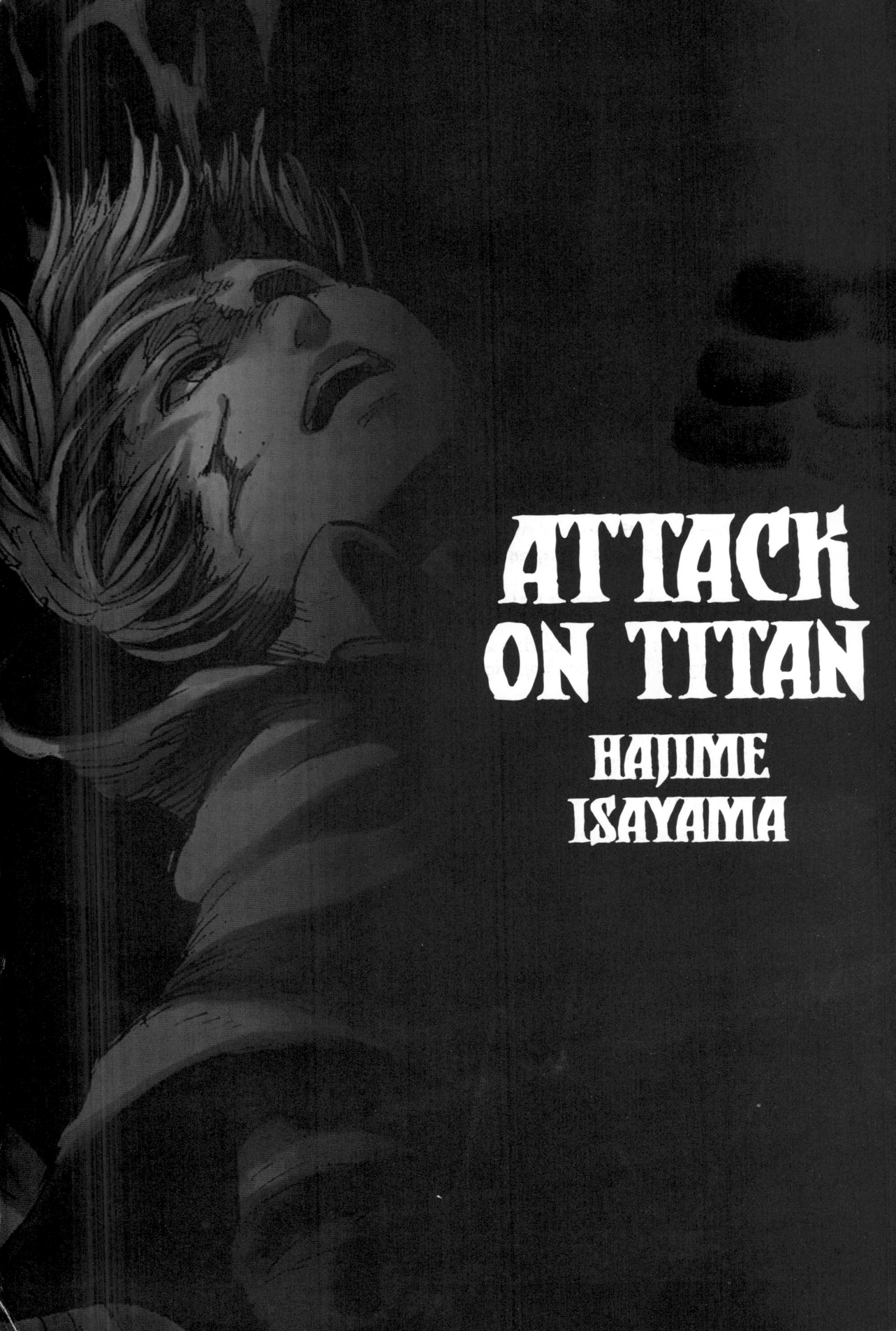

"Attack on Titan" Character Introductions

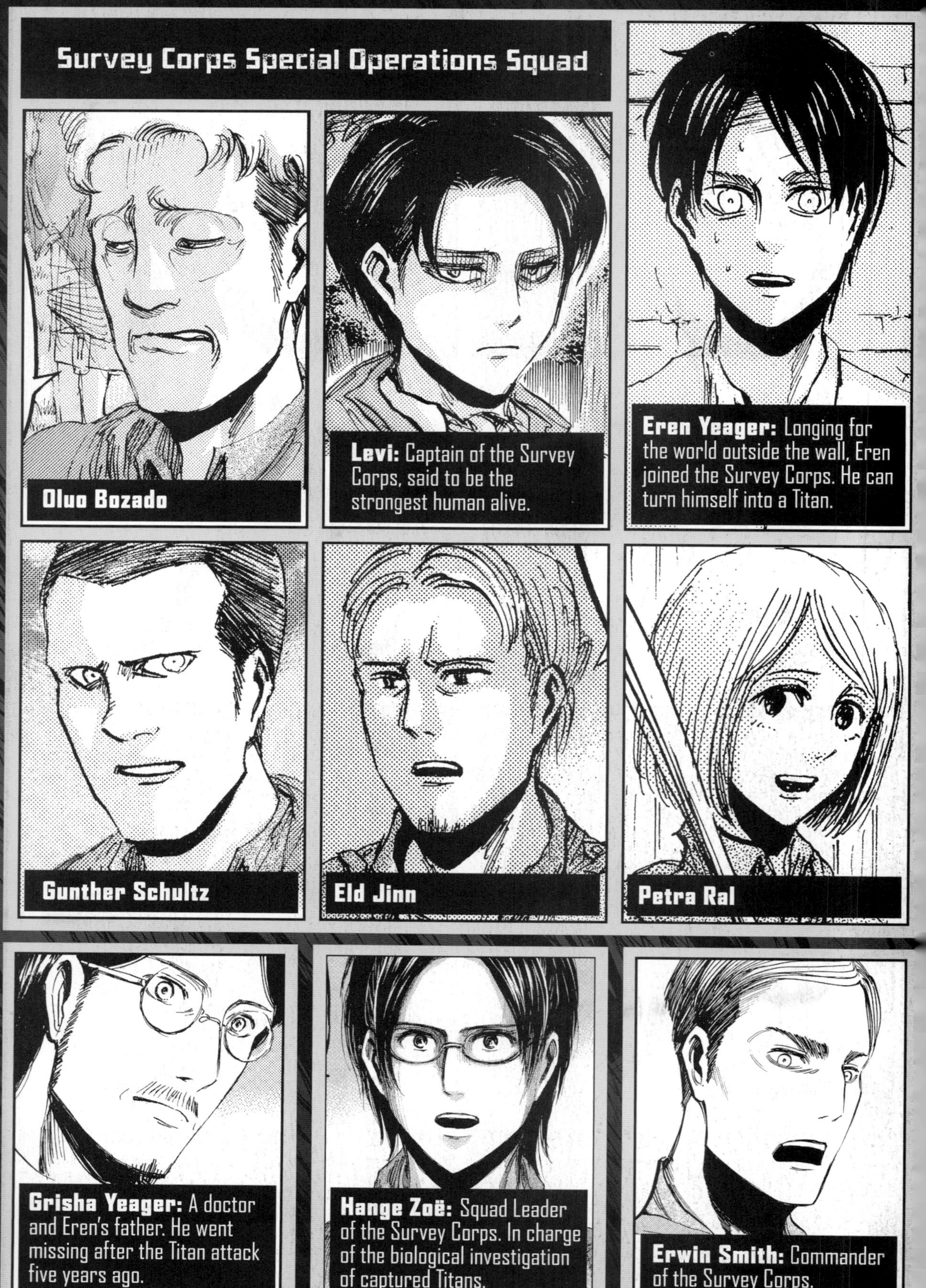
Survey Corps Special Operations Squad
Oluo Bozado
Levi: Captain of the Survey Corps, said to be the strongest human alive.
Eren Yeager: Longing for the world outside the wall, Eren joined the Survey Corps. He can turn himself into a Titan.
Gunther Schultz
Eld Jinn
Petra Ral
Grisha Yeager: A doctor and Eren's father. He went missing after the Titan attack five years ago.
Hange Zoë: Squad Leader of the Survey Corps. In charge of the biological investigation of captured Titans.
Erwin Smith: Commander of the Survey Corps.

104th Corps

Armin Arlert:
Eren and Mikasa's childhood friend. Though Armin isn't athletic in the least, he is an excellent thinker and can produce unique ideas. A member of the Survey Corps.

Mikasa Ackerman:
Mikasa graduated at the top of her training corps. Her parents were murdered before her eyes when she was a child. After that, she was raised alongside Eren, whom she tenaciously tries to protect.

Connie Springer: Effective at vertical maneuvering, but is slow on the uptake, so his comprehension of tactics is less than stellar. A member of the Survey Corps.

Jean Kirstein: Superior at vertical maneuvering. Jean is honest to a fault, which often puts him at odds with other people. A member of the Survey Corps.

Bertolt Hoover: Has a high degree of skill in everything he's been taught, but is indecisive and lacks initiative. A member of the Survey Corps.

Reiner Braun: Graduated second in his training corps. Reiner is as strong as an ox and has the will to match. His comrades have a great deal of trust in him. A member of the Survey Corps.

Marco Bott: Yearned to join the Military Police Brigade so he could serve the king. Marco died during the Titan mop-up operation.

Annie Leonhart: Annie's small stature belies her great skill in the art of hand-to-hand combat. She's a realist through and through, and tends to be a loner. A member of the Military Police Brigade.

Krista Lenz: Extremely short, with a friendly, warm-hearted personality. A member of the Survey Corps.

Sasha Blouse: Sasha is very agile and has remarkable instincts. Owing to her unconventionality, she isn't suited for organized activity. A member of the Survey Corps.

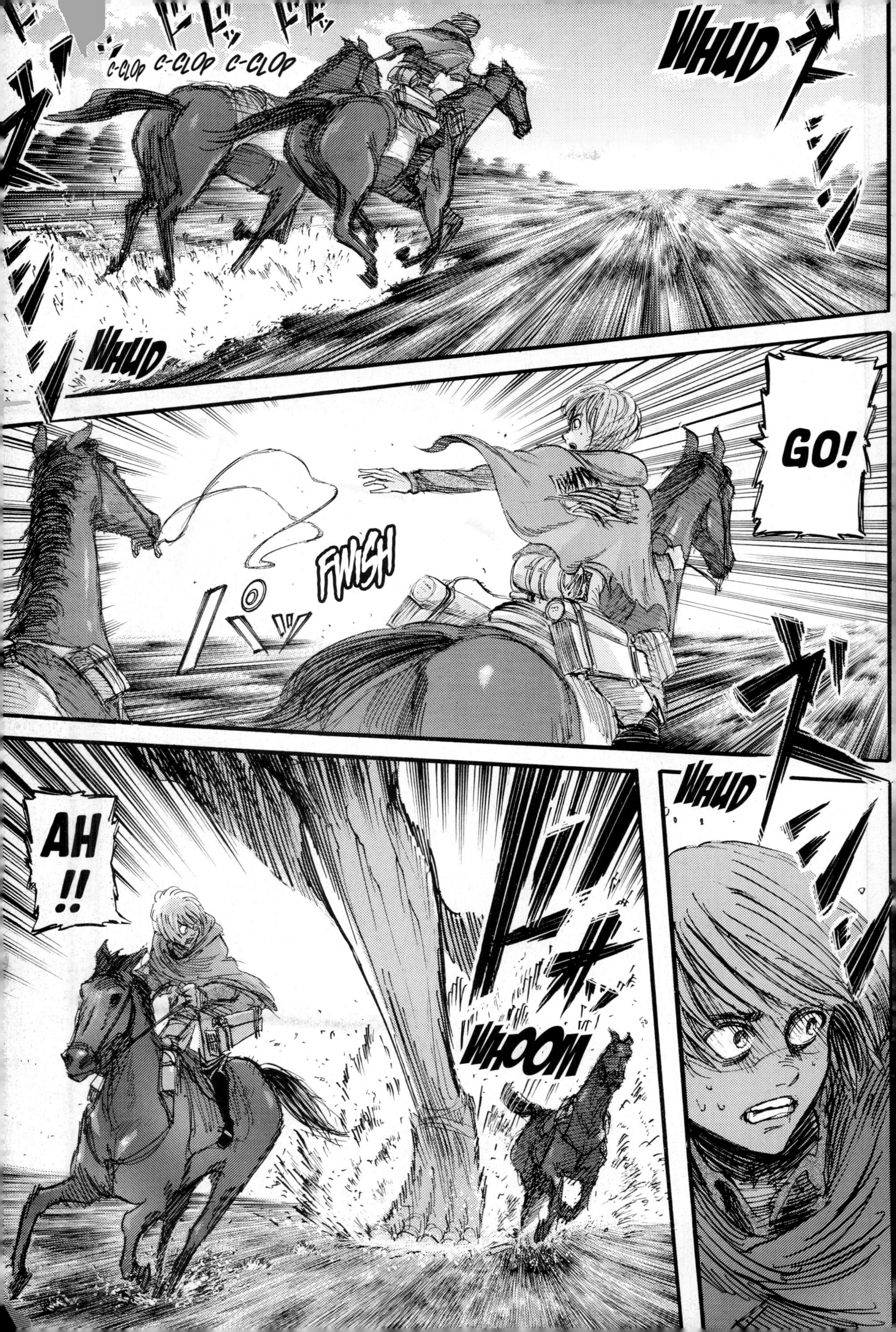
WHUD
C-CLOP C-CLOP C-CLOP
WHUD
GO!
FWISH
WHUD
WHOOM
AH !!

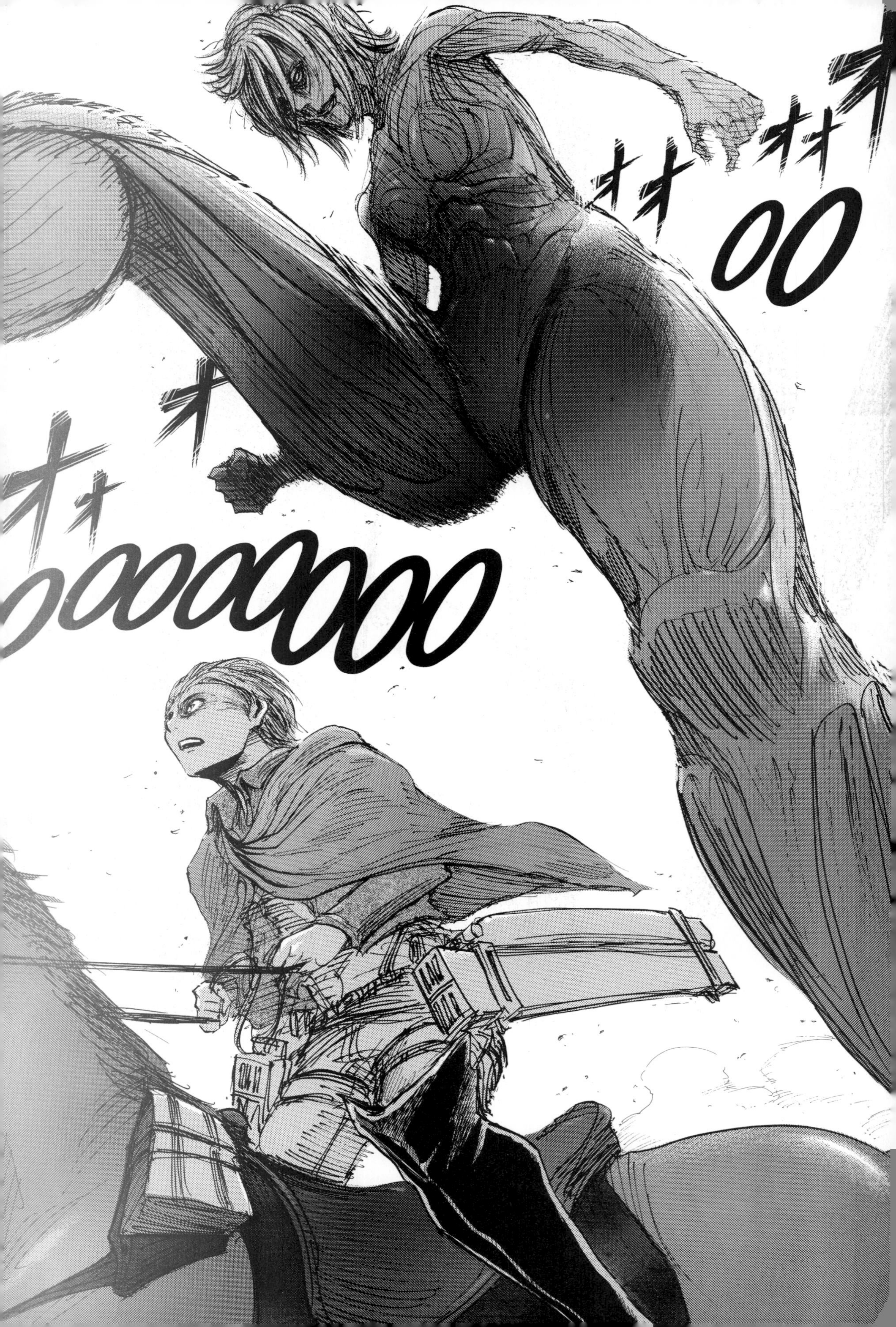

オオオオオ
OO
オオオ
OOOOOOO

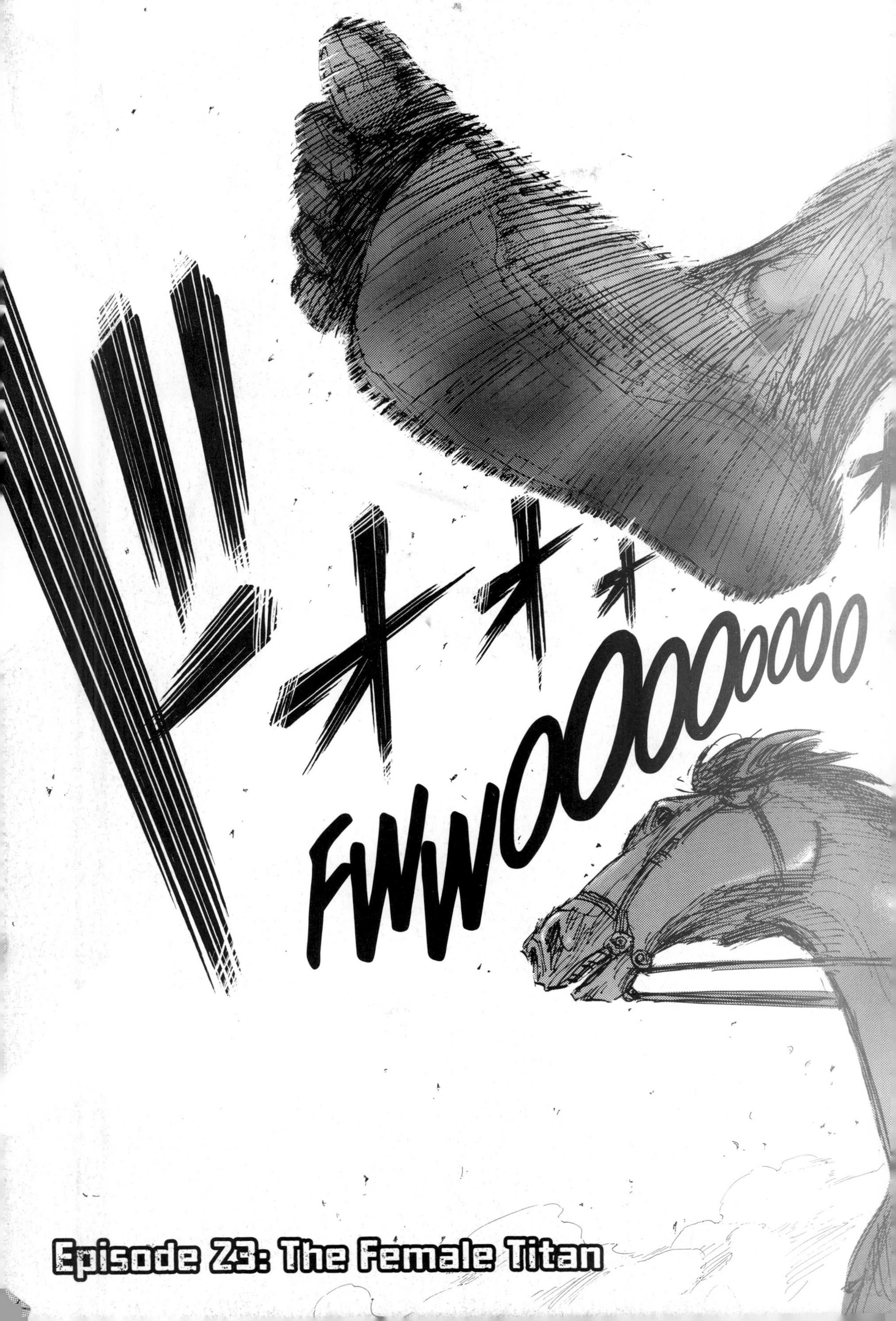
ドオオオ
FWWOOOOOOOO

Episode 23: The Female Titan

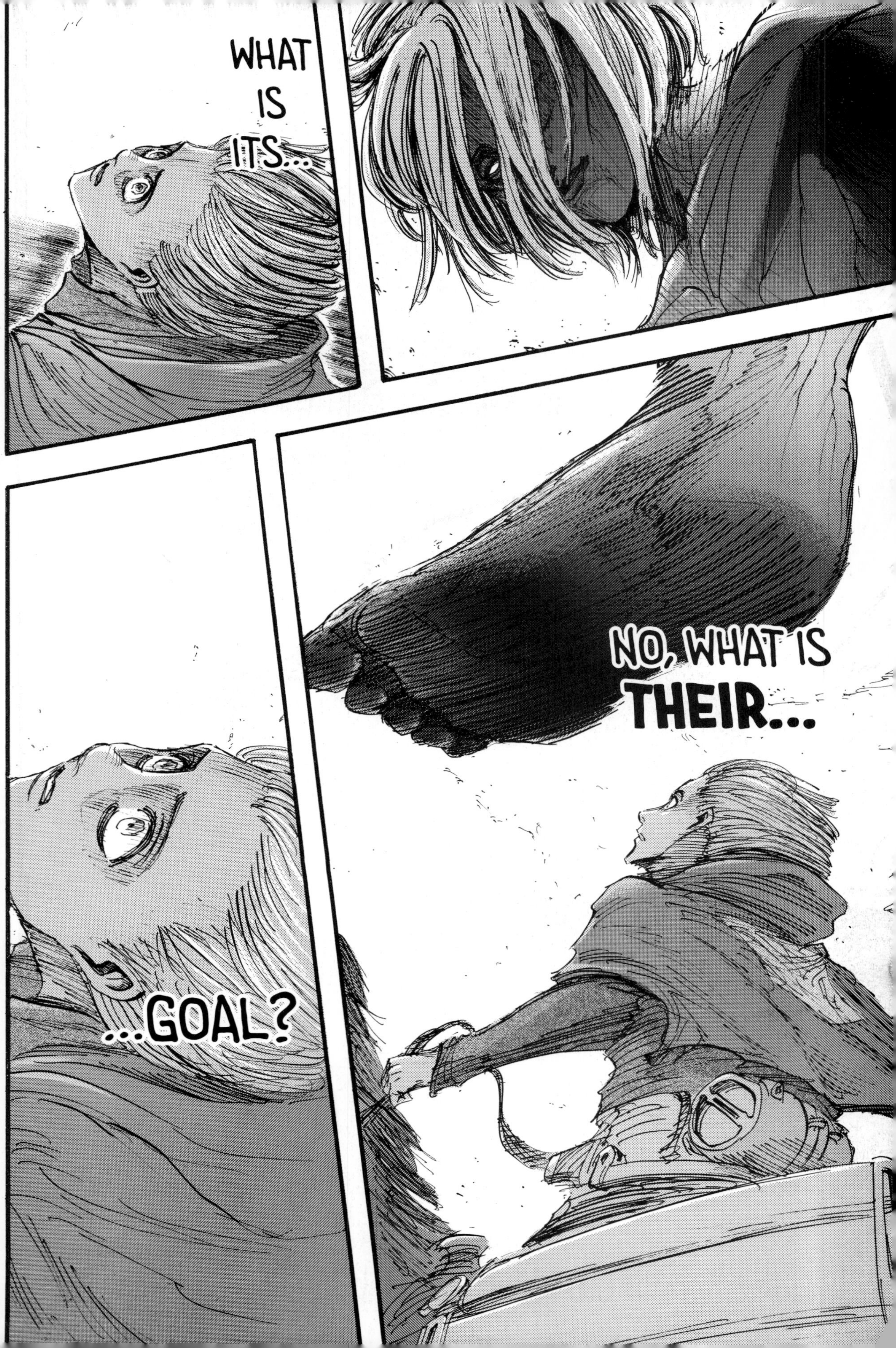
WHAT IS ITS...
NO, WHAT IS THEIR...
...GOAL?

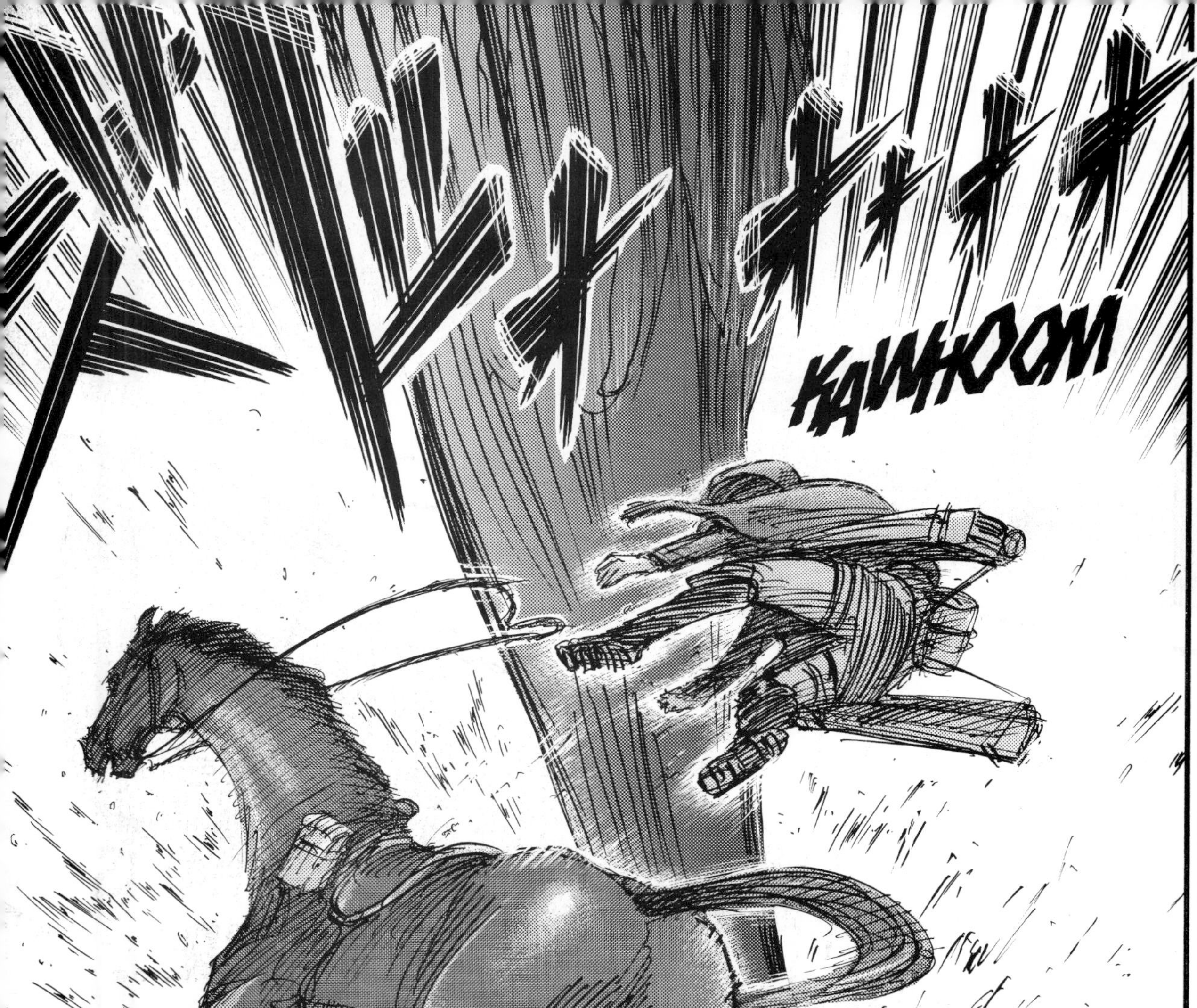
KAWHOOM
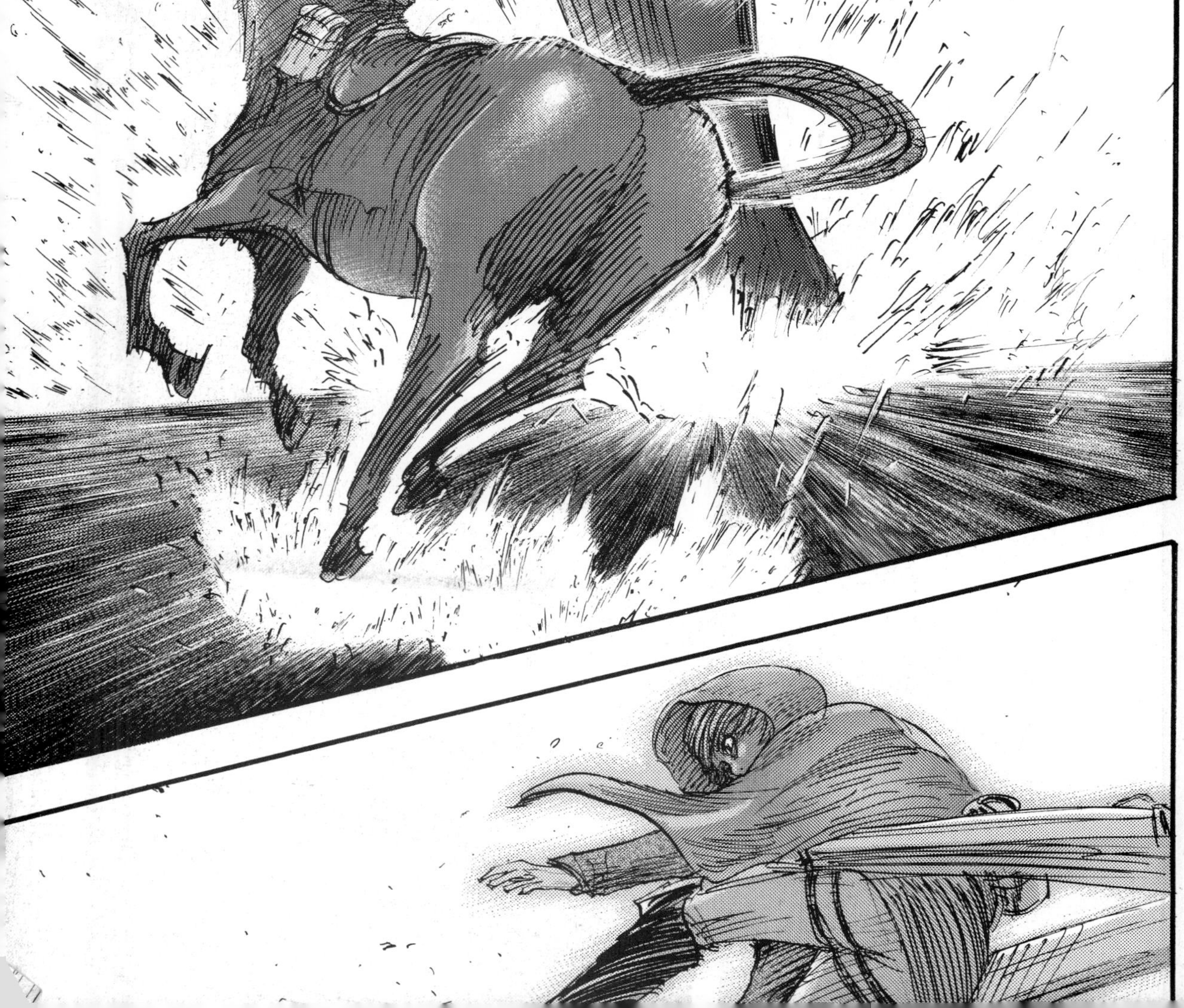

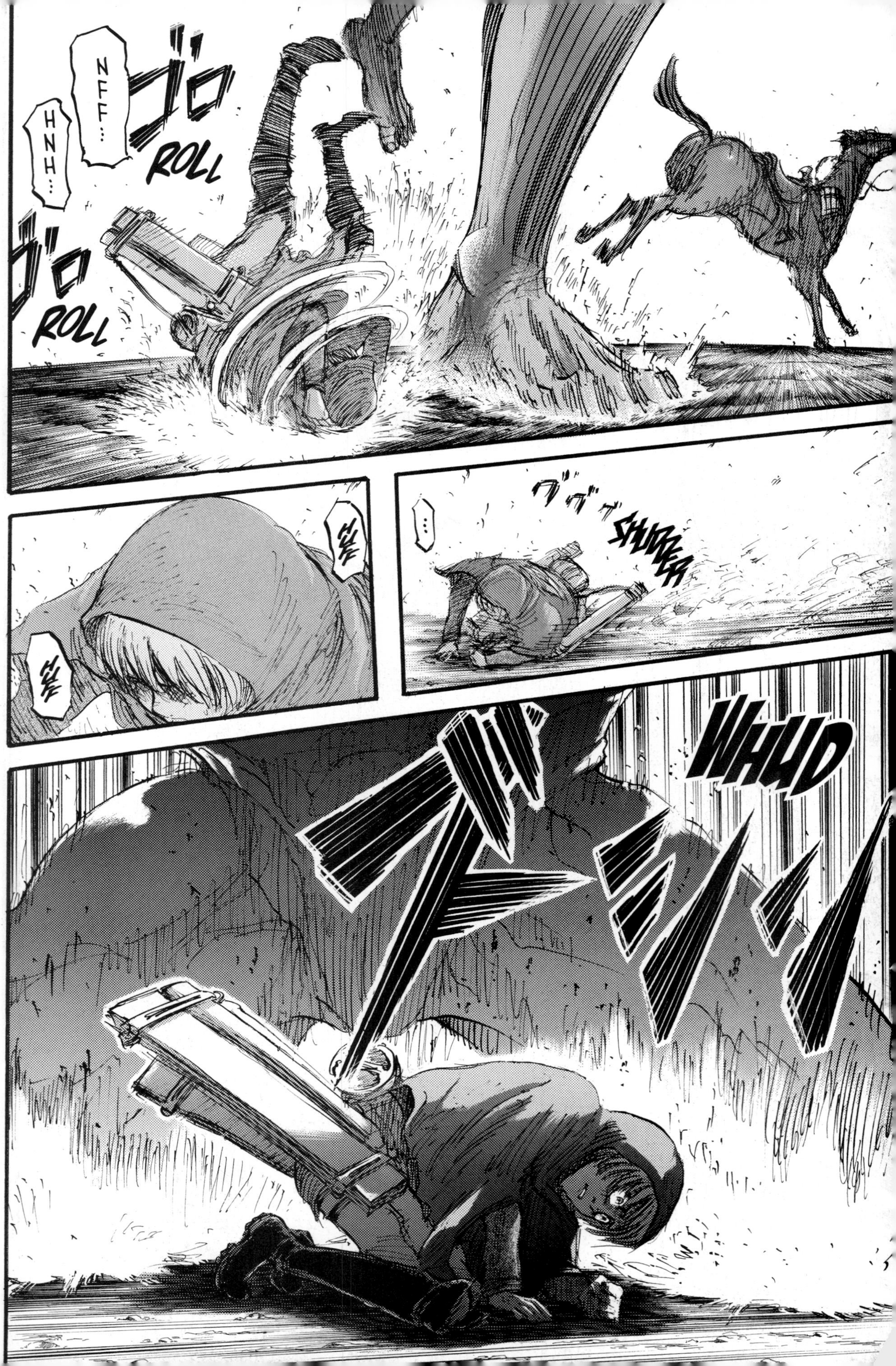

NFF...
ROLL
HNH...
ROLL
...
SHUDDER
HEE
HEE
WHUD

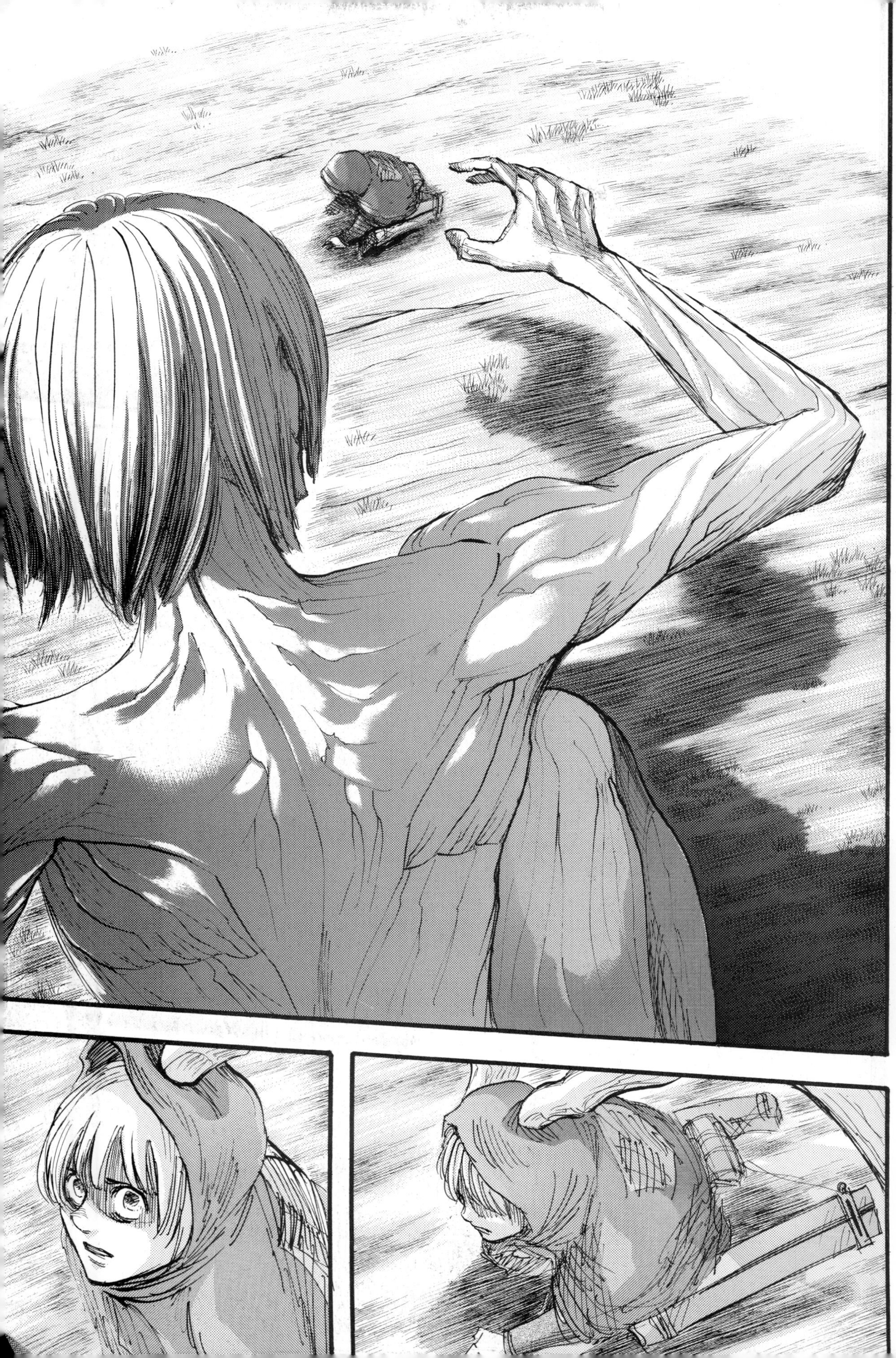

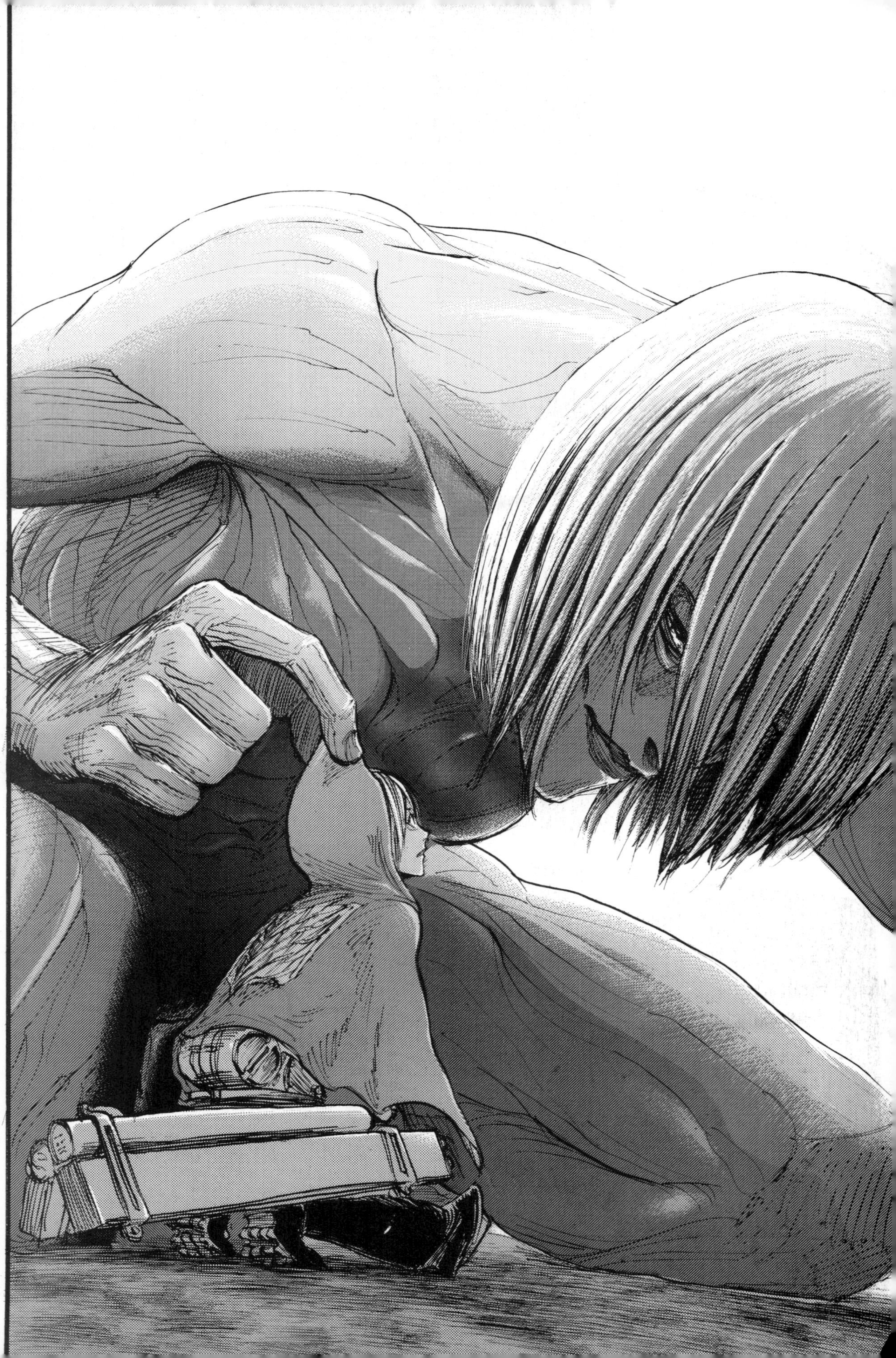

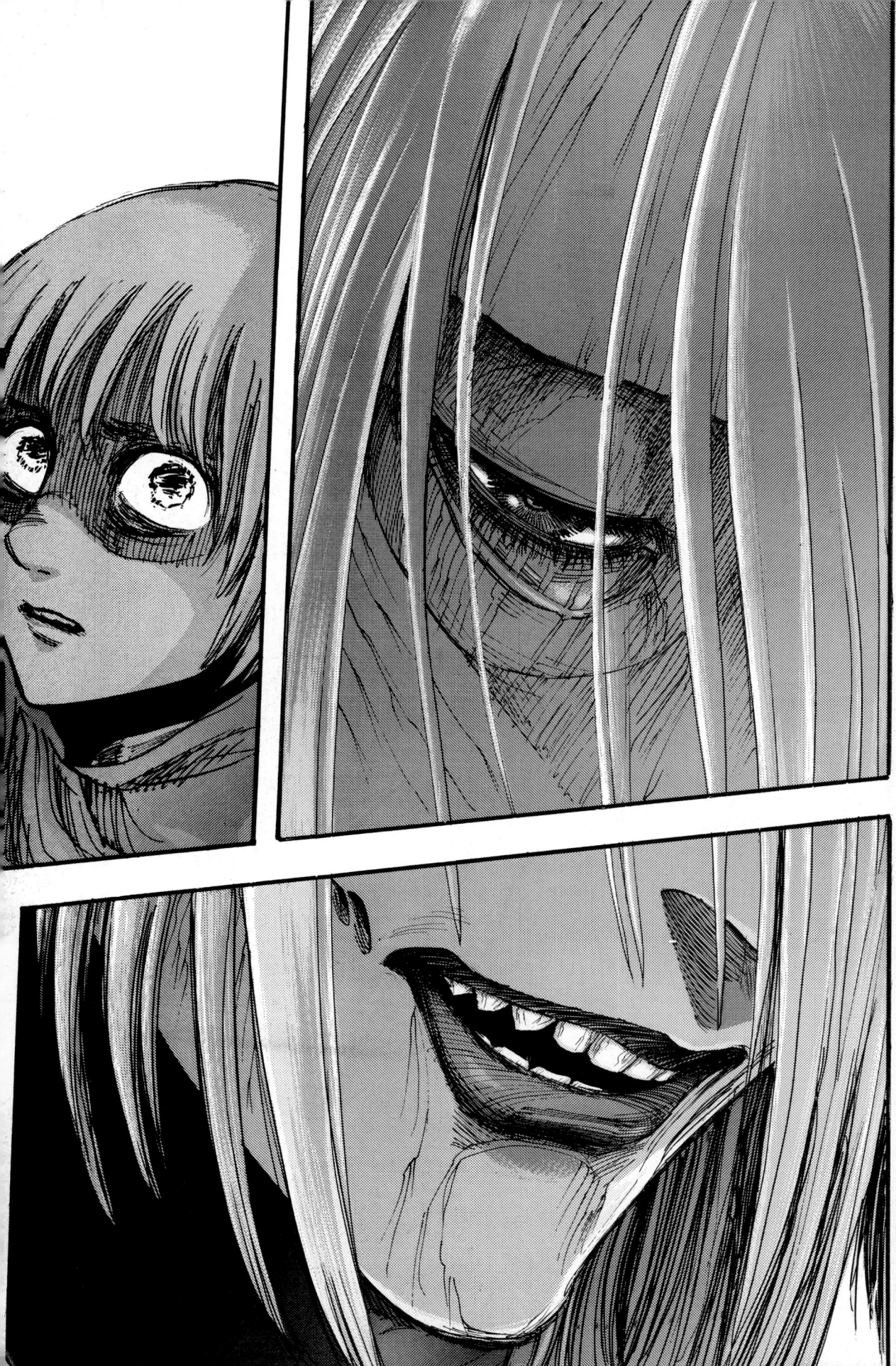

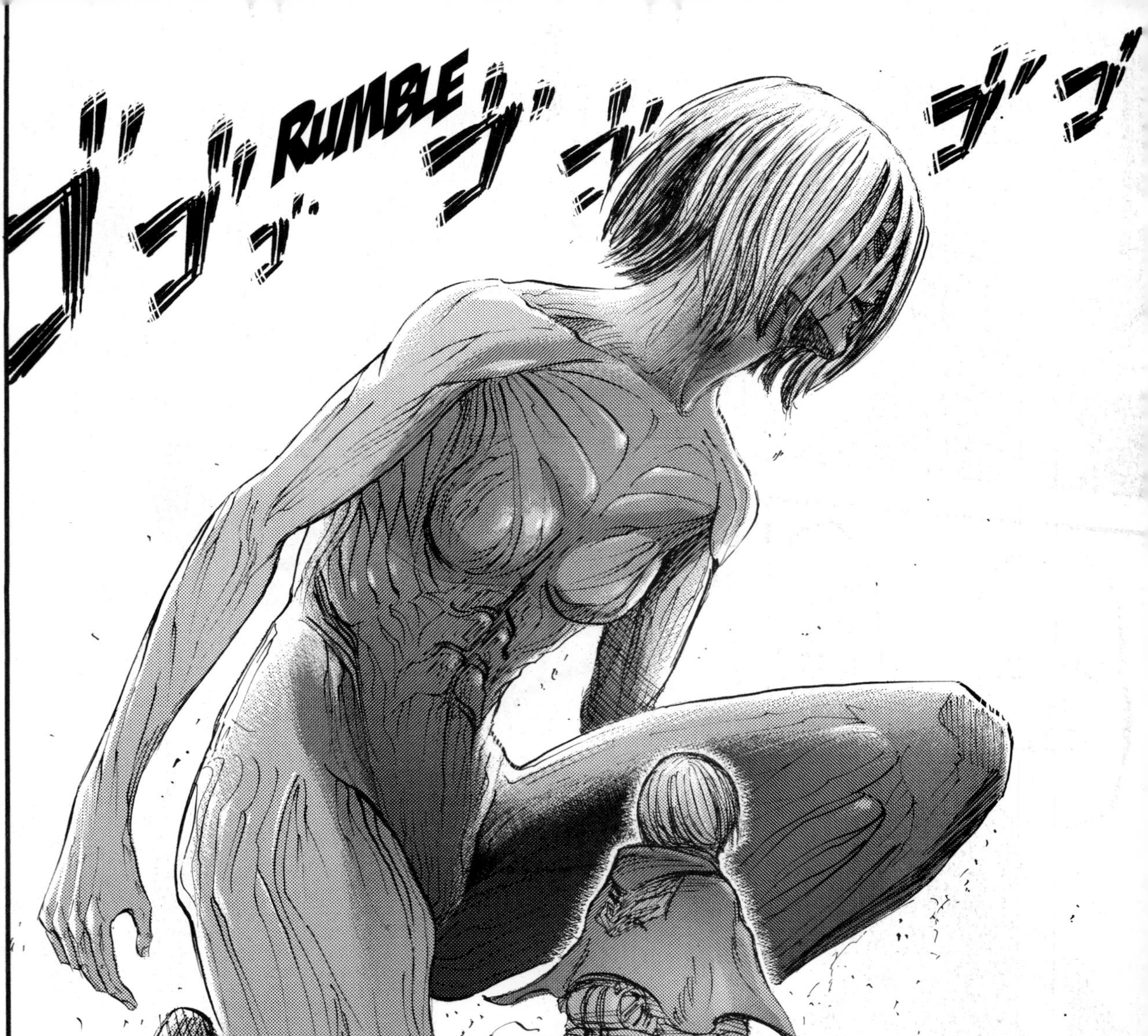
RUMBLE
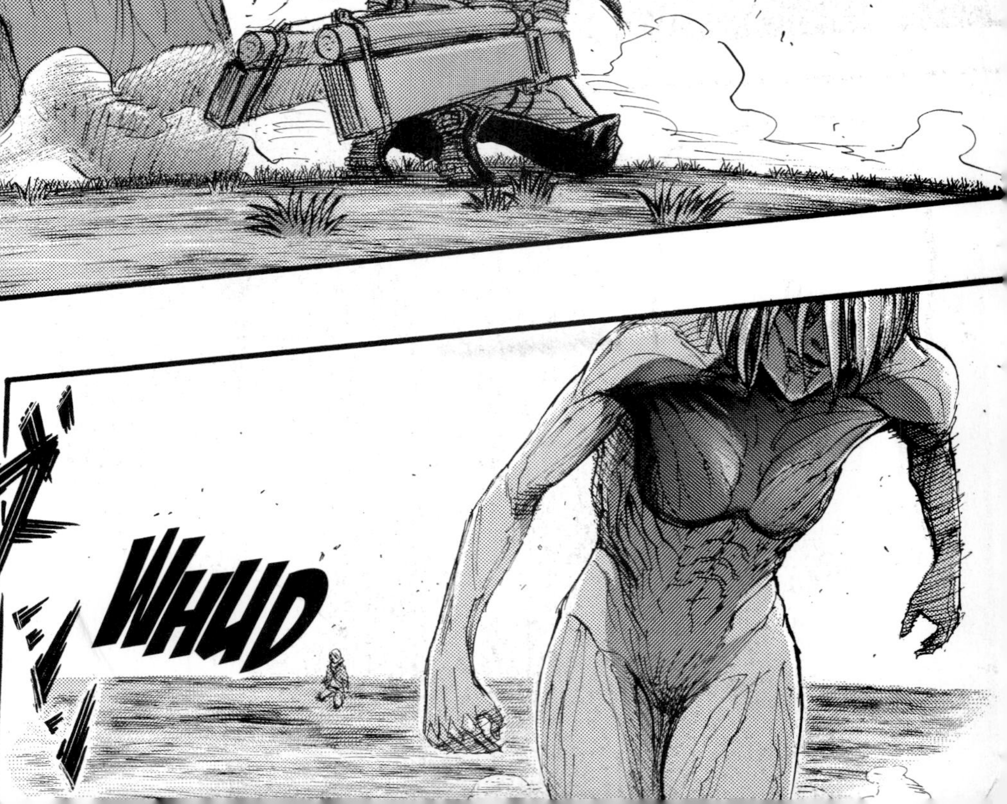
WHUD

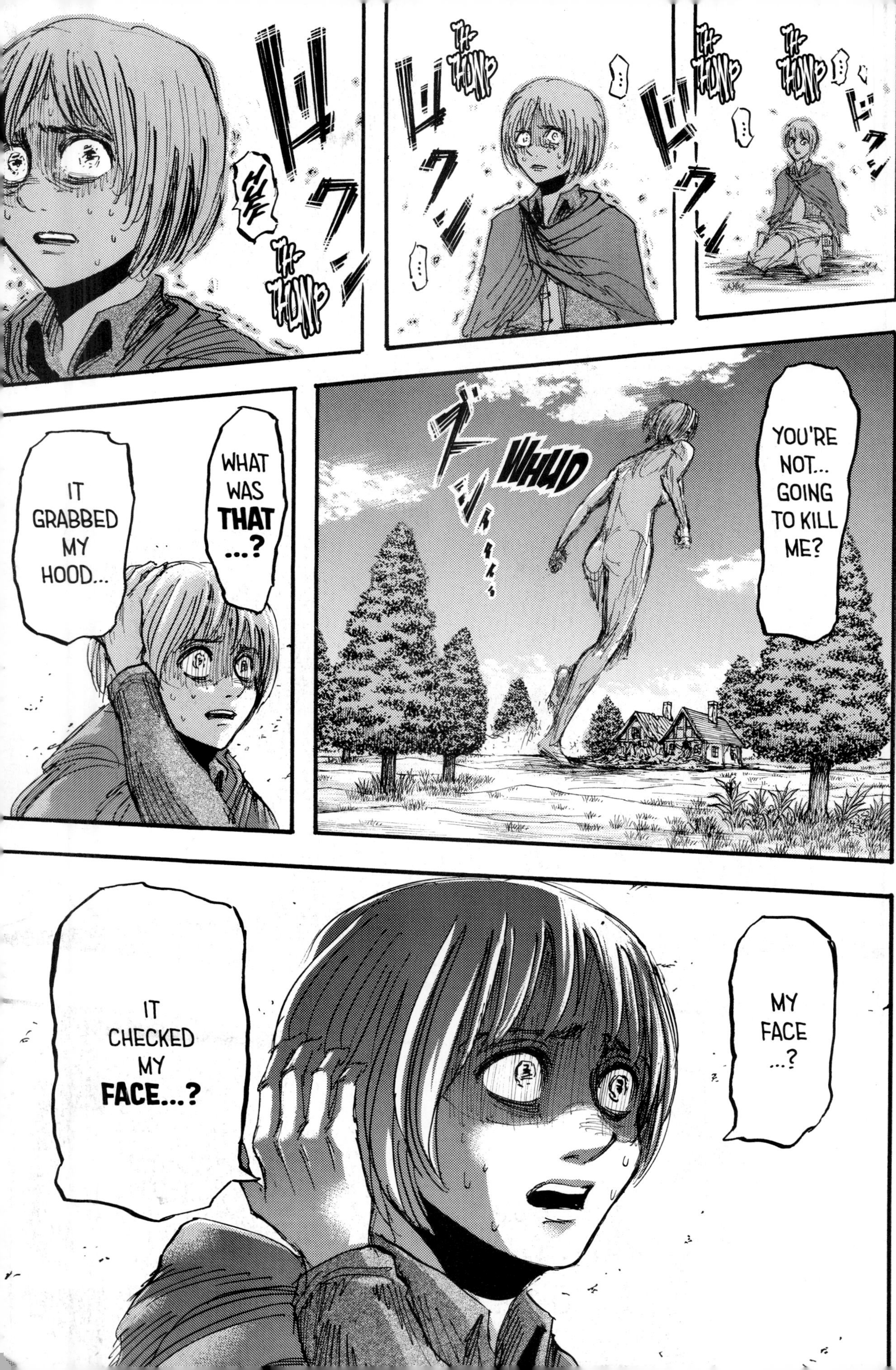
TH-THOMP
...
...
TH-THOMP
TH-THOMP
...
...
TH-THOMP
YOU'RE NOT... GOING TO KILL ME?
WHUD
WHAT WAS **THAT** ...?
IT GRABBED MY HOOD...
MY FACE ...?
IT CHECKED MY **FACE...?**

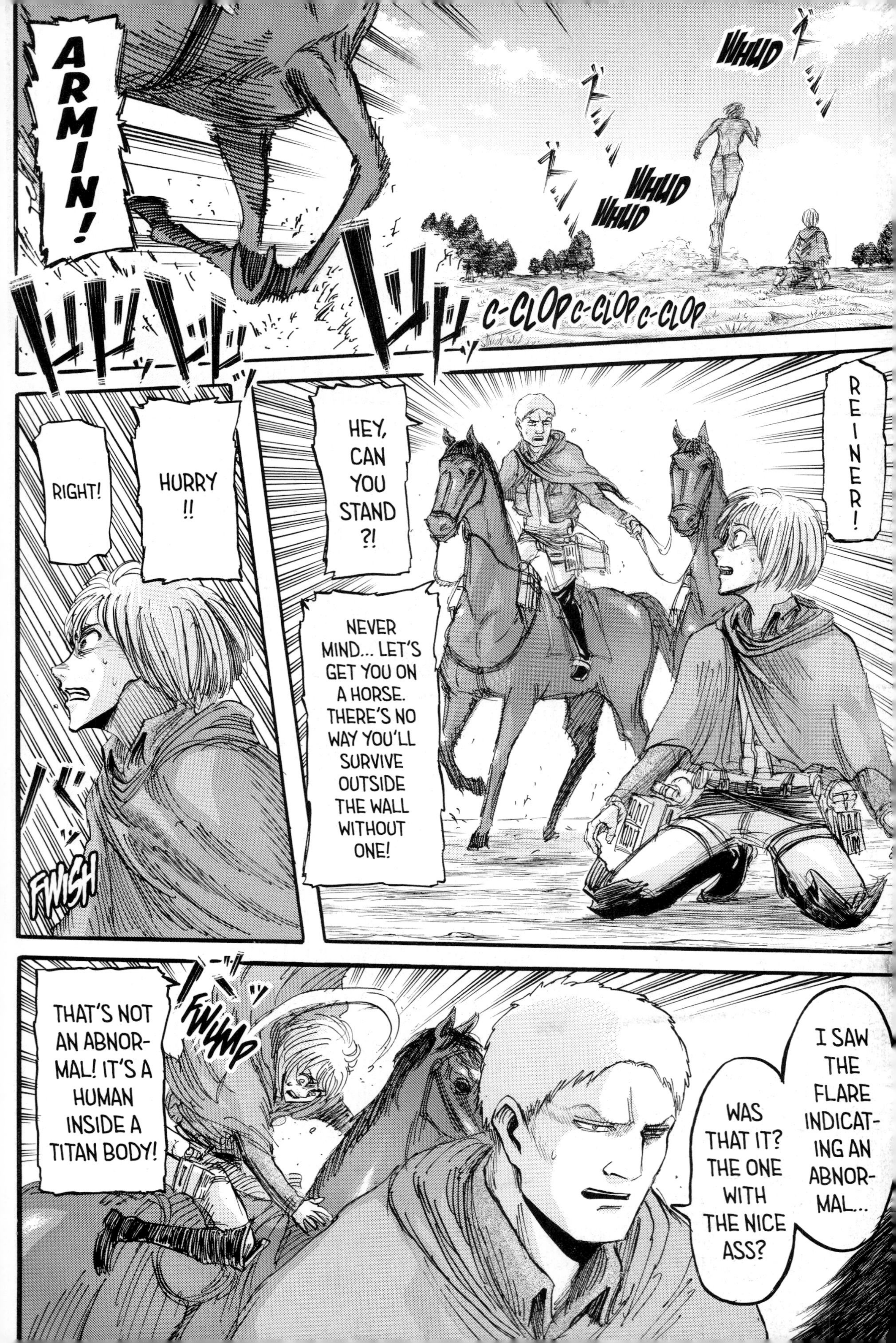
WHUD
WHUD
WHUD
C-CLOP C-CLOP C-CLOP
ARMIN!
REINER!
HEY, CAN YOU STAND?!
NEVER MIND... LET'S GET YOU ON A HORSE. THERE'S NO WAY YOU'LL SURVIVE OUTSIDE THE WALL WITHOUT ONE!
HURRY!!
RIGHT!
FWISH
I SAW THE FLARE INDICATING AN ABNORMAL...
WAS THAT IT? THE ONE WITH THE NICE ASS?
FWUMP
THAT'S NOT AN ABNORMAL! IT'S A HUMAN INSIDE A TITAN BODY!

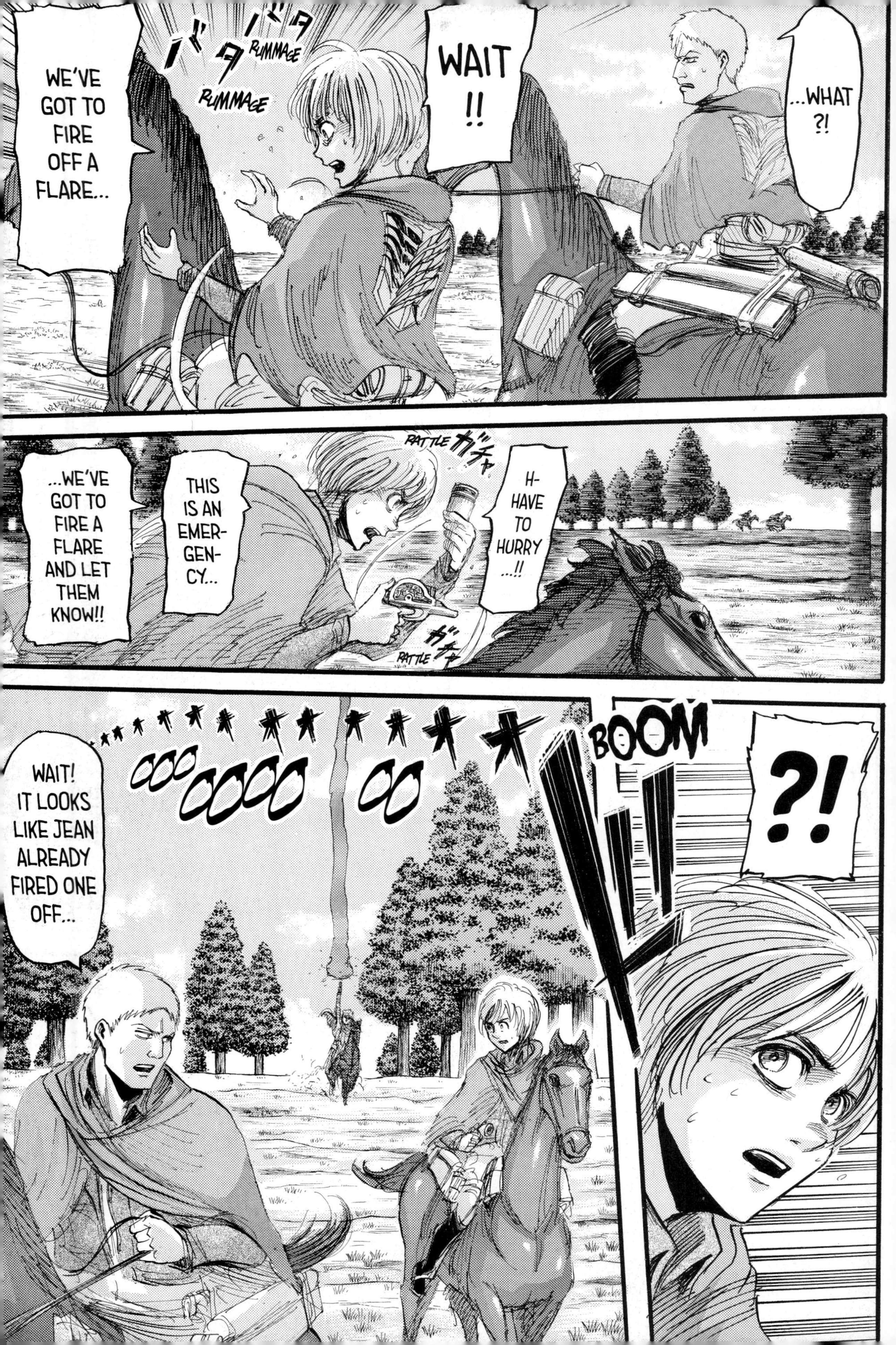

...WHAT ?!
WAIT !!
RUMMAGE
RUMMAGE
WE'VE GOT TO FIRE OFF A FLARE...
RATTLE
H-HAVE TO HURRY...!!
THIS IS AN EMER-GEN-CY...
...WE'VE GOT TO FIRE A FLARE AND LET THEM KNOW!!
RATTLE
?!
BOOM
WAIT! IT LOOKS LIKE JEAN ALREADY FIRED ONE OFF...

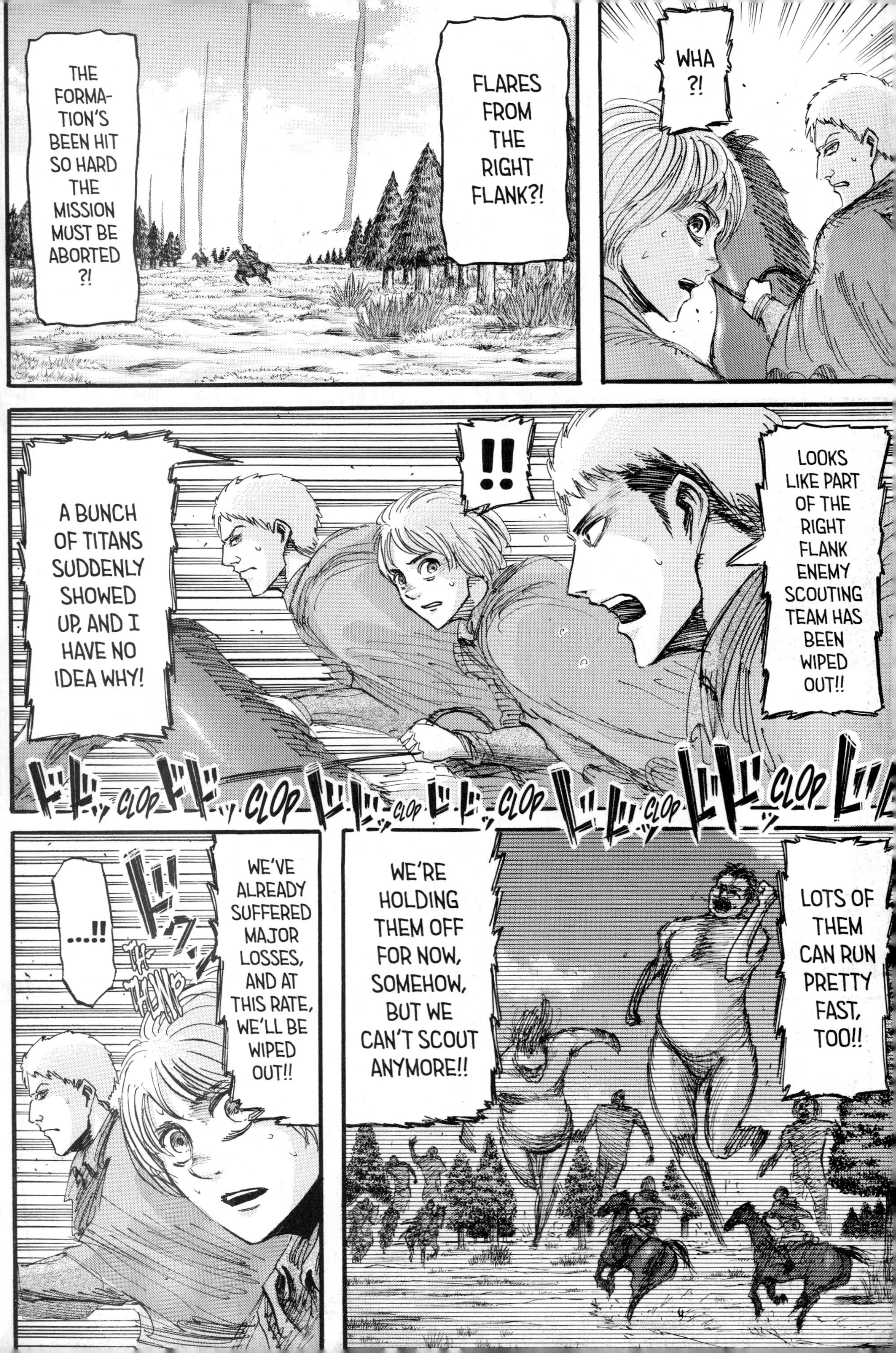
WHA ?!
FLARES FROM THE RIGHT FLANK?!
THE FORMATION'S BEEN HIT SO HARD THE MISSION MUST BE ABORTED ?!
!!
LOOKS LIKE PART OF THE RIGHT FLANK ENEMY SCOUTING TEAM HAS BEEN WIPED OUT!!
A BUNCH OF TITANS SUDDENLY SHOWED UP, AND I HAVE NO IDEA WHY!
CLOP CLOP CLOP CLOP CLOP CLOP
LOTS OF THEM CAN RUN PRETTY FAST, TOO!!
WE'RE HOLDING THEM OFF FOR NOW, SOMEHOW, BUT WE CAN'T SCOUT ANYMORE!!
WE'VE ALREADY SUFFERED MAJOR LOSSES, AND AT THIS RATE, WE'LL BE WIPED OUT!!
...!!

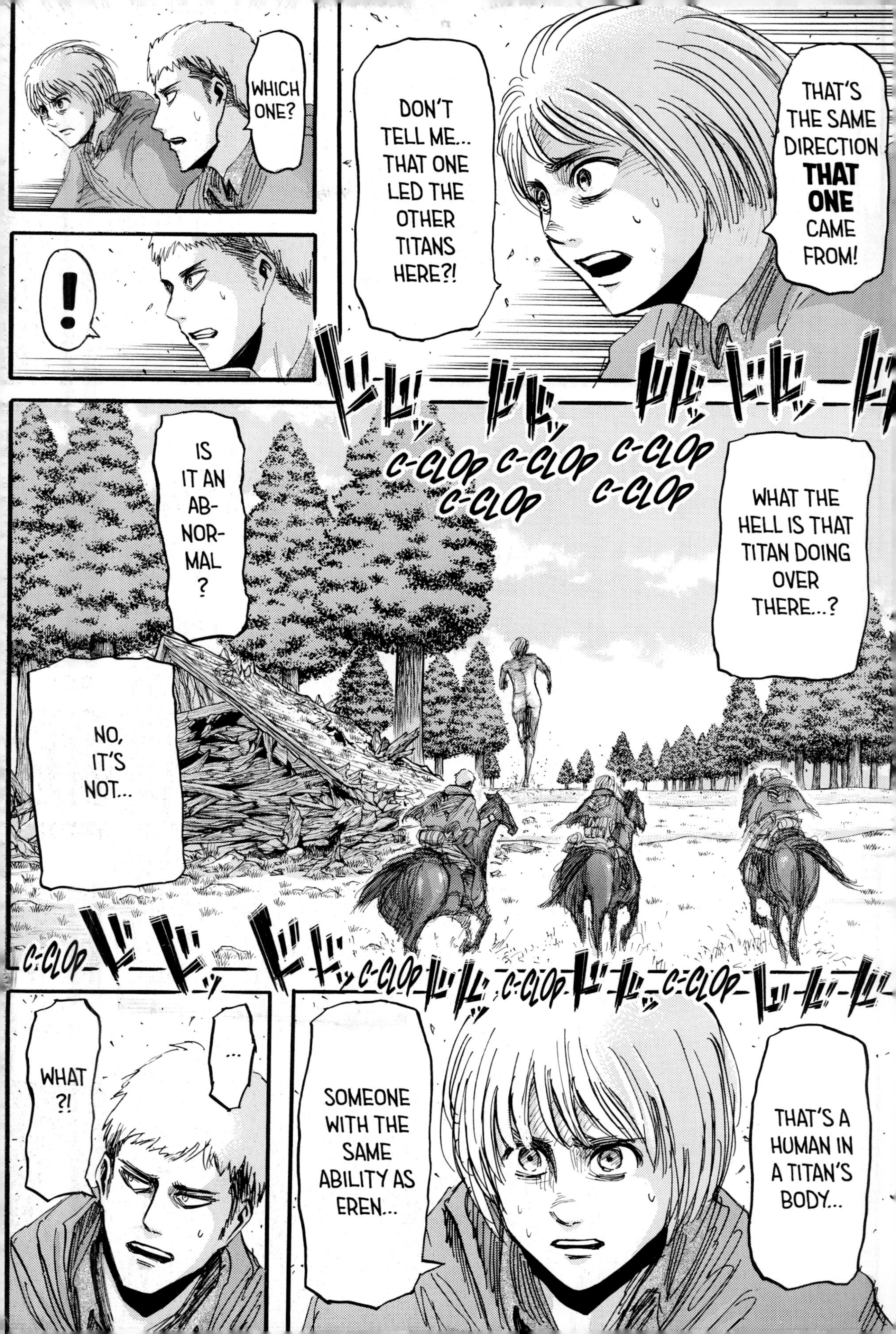
THAT'S THE SAME DIRECTION **THAT ONE** CAME FROM!
DON'T TELL ME... THAT ONE LED THE OTHER TITANS HERE?!
WHICH ONE?
!
C-CLOP C-CLOP C-CLOP C-CLOP C-CLOP
WHAT THE HELL IS THAT TITAN DOING OVER THERE...?
IS IT AN AB-NOR-MAL?
NO, IT'S NOT...
C-CLOP C-CLOP C-CLOP C-CLOP
THAT'S A HUMAN IN A TITAN'S BODY...
SOMEONE WITH THE SAME ABILITY AS EREN...
...
WHAT?!

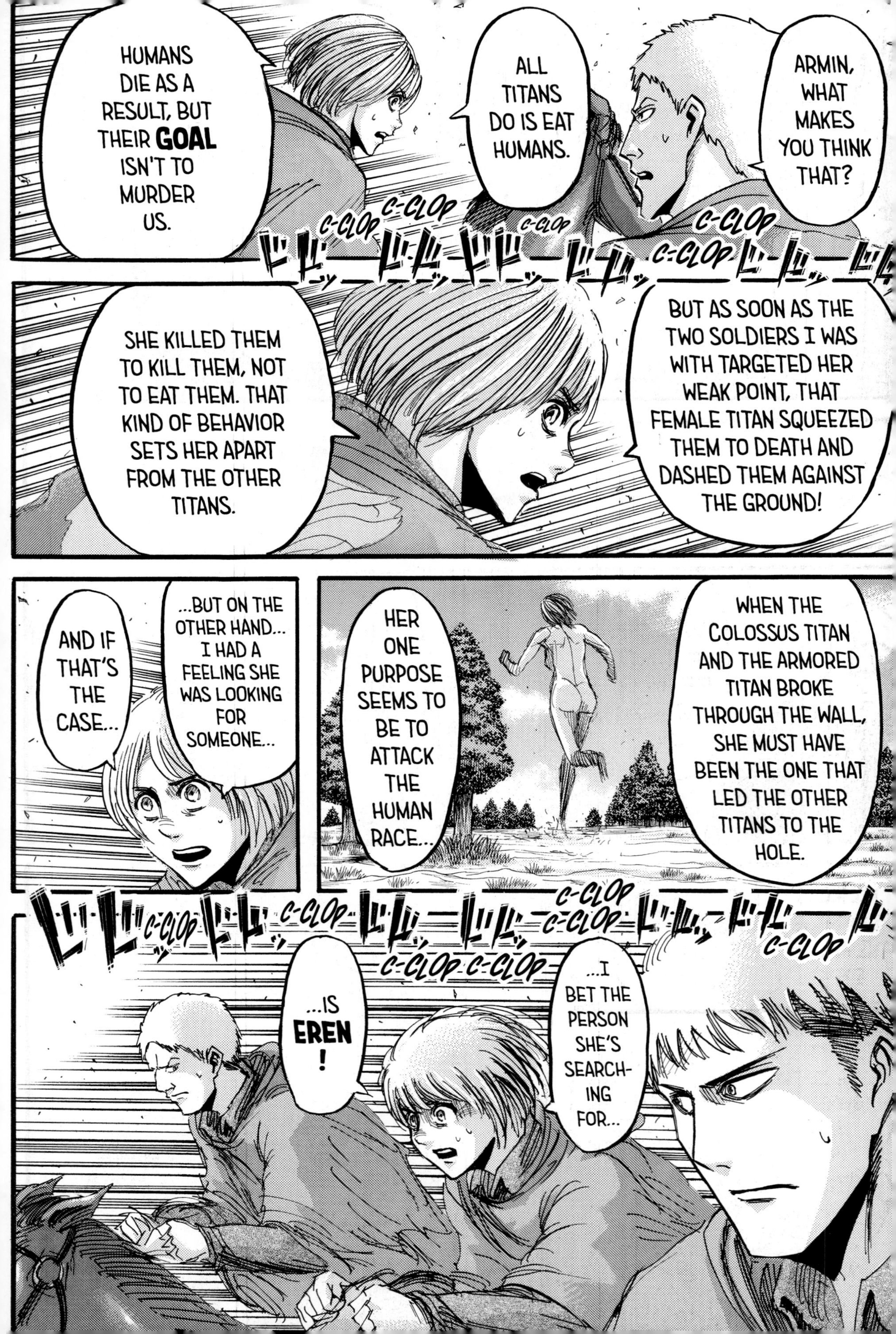
ARMIN, WHAT MAKES YOU THINK THAT?
ALL TITANS DO IS EAT HUMANS.
HUMANS DIE AS A RESULT, BUT THEIR **GOAL** ISN'T TO MURDER US.
C-CLOP C-CLOP C-CLOP C-CLOP C-CLOP
BUT AS SOON AS THE TWO SOLDIERS I WAS WITH TARGETED HER WEAK POINT, THAT FEMALE TITAN SQUEEZED THEM TO DEATH AND DASHED THEM AGAINST THE GROUND!
SHE KILLED THEM TO KILL THEM, NOT TO EAT THEM. THAT KIND OF BEHAVIOR SETS HER APART FROM THE OTHER TITANS.
WHEN THE COLOSSUS TITAN AND THE ARMORED TITAN BROKE THROUGH THE WALL, SHE MUST HAVE BEEN THE ONE THAT LED THE OTHER TITANS TO THE HOLE.
HER ONE PURPOSE SEEMS TO BE TO ATTACK THE HUMAN RACE...
...BUT ON THE OTHER HAND... I HAD A FEELING SHE WAS LOOKING FOR SOMEONE...
AND IF THAT'S THE CASE...
C-CLOP C-CLOP C-CLOP C-CLOP C-CLOP C-CLOP C-CLOP
...I BET THE PERSON SHE'S SEARCHING FOR...
...IS **EREN**!

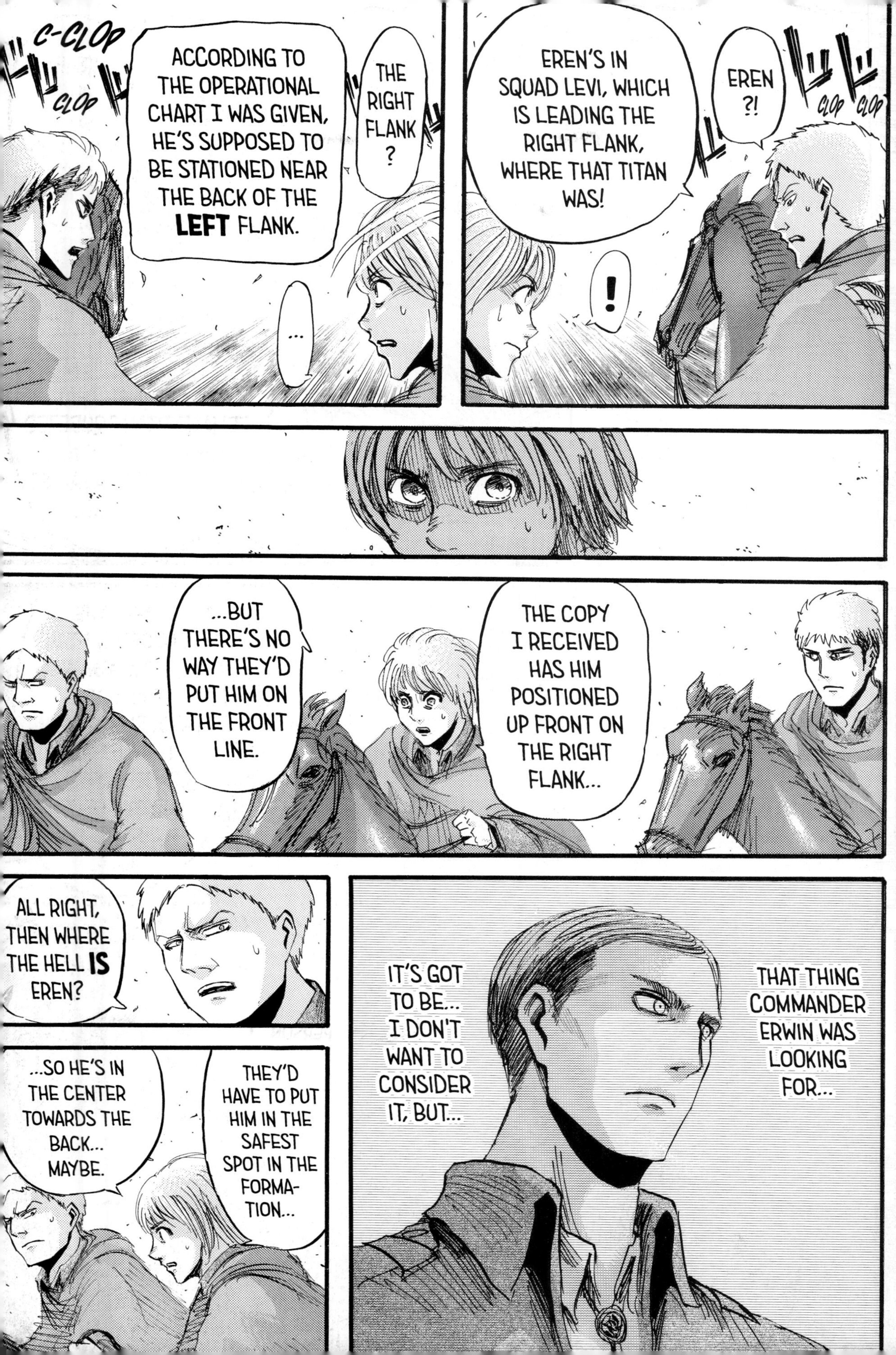
CLOP CLOP
EREN ?!
EREN'S IN SQUAD LEVI, WHICH IS LEADING THE RIGHT FLANK, WHERE THAT TITAN WAS!
!
THE RIGHT FLANK ?
ACCORDING TO THE OPERATIONAL CHART I WAS GIVEN, HE'S SUPPOSED TO BE STATIONED NEAR THE BACK OF THE **LEFT** FLANK.
C-CLOP
CLOP
...
THE COPY I RECEIVED HAS HIM POSITIONED UP FRONT ON THE RIGHT FLANK...
...BUT THERE'S NO WAY THEY'D PUT HIM ON THE FRONT LINE.
THAT THING COMMANDER ERWIN WAS LOOKING FOR...
IT'S GOT TO BE... I DON'T WANT TO CONSIDER IT, BUT...
ALL RIGHT, THEN WHERE THE HELL **IS** EREN?
THEY'D HAVE TO PUT HIM IN THE SAFEST SPOT IN THE FORMATION...
...SO HE'S IN THE CENTER TOWARDS THE BACK... MAYBE.

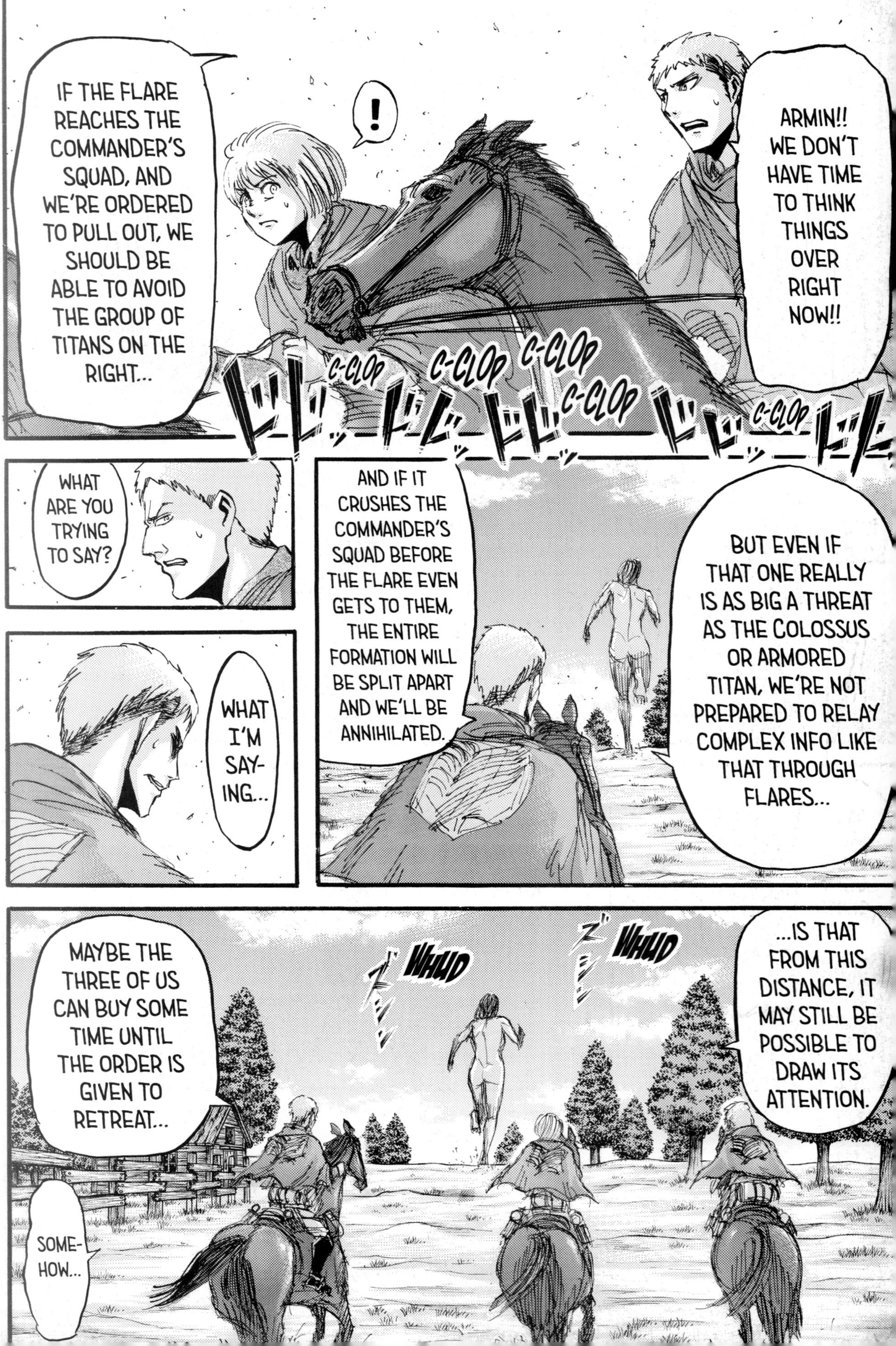
ARMIN!! WE DON'T HAVE TIME TO THINK THINGS OVER RIGHT NOW!!
!
IF THE FLARE REACHES THE COMMANDER'S SQUAD, AND WE'RE ORDERED TO PULL OUT, WE SHOULD BE ABLE TO AVOID THE GROUP OF TITANS ON THE RIGHT...
C-CLOP
C-CLOP
C-CLOP
C-CLOP
C-CLOP
BUT EVEN IF THAT ONE REALLY IS AS BIG A THREAT AS THE COLOSSUS OR ARMORED TITAN, WE'RE NOT PREPARED TO RELAY COMPLEX INFO LIKE THAT THROUGH FLARES...
AND IF IT CRUSHES THE COMMANDER'S SQUAD BEFORE THE FLARE EVEN GETS TO THEM, THE ENTIRE FORMATION WILL BE SPLIT APART AND WE'LL BE ANNIHILATED.
WHAT ARE YOU TRYING TO SAY?
WHAT I'M SAY-ING...
...IS THAT FROM THIS DISTANCE, IT MAY STILL BE POSSIBLE TO DRAW ITS ATTENTION.
WHUD
WHUD
MAYBE THE THREE OF US CAN BUY SOME TIME UNTIL THE ORDER IS GIVEN TO RETREAT...
SOME-HOW...

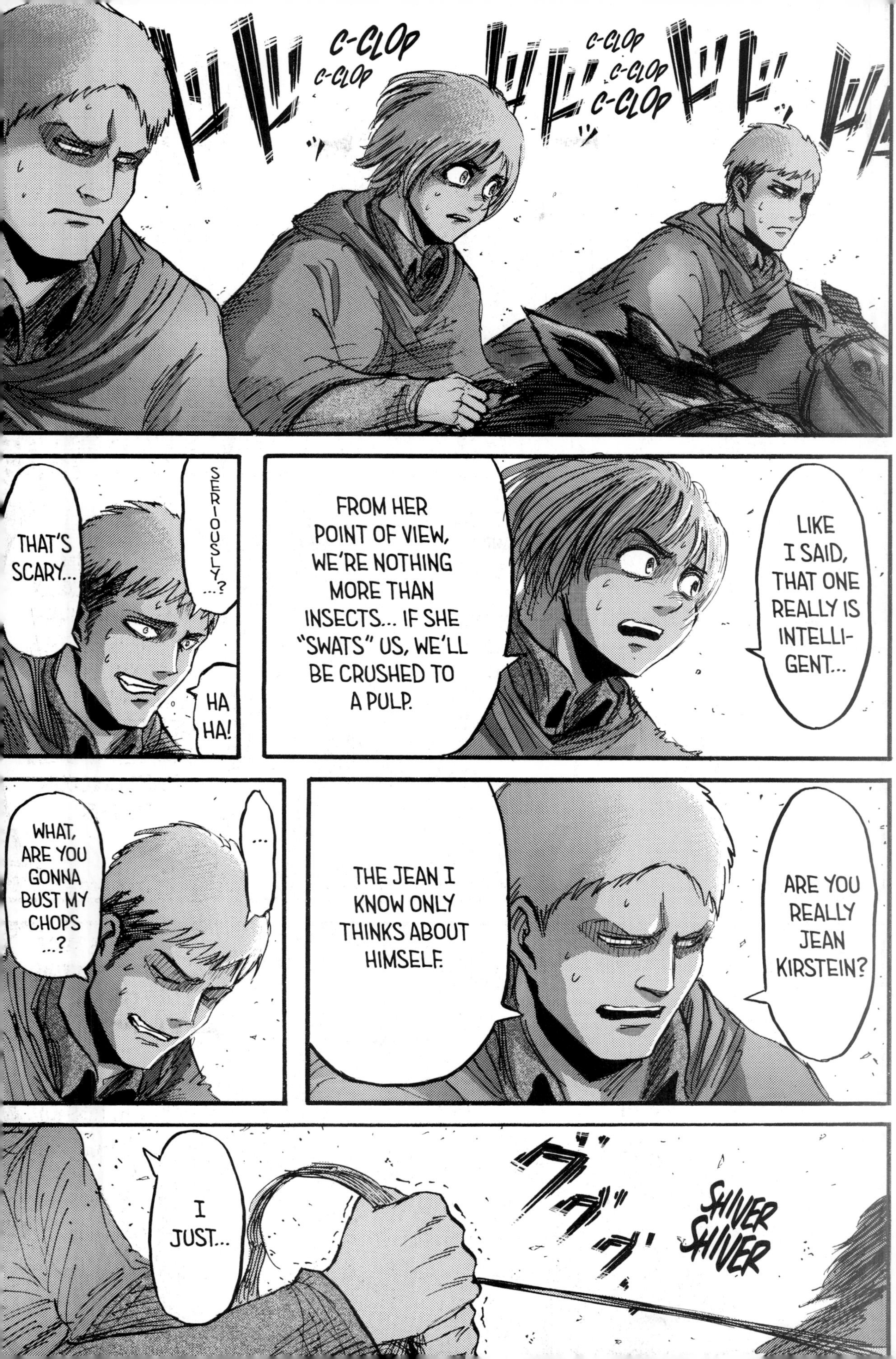
C-CLOP
C-CLOP
C-CLOP
C-CLOP
C-CLOP
LIKE I SAID, THAT ONE REALLY IS INTELLIGENT...
FROM HER POINT OF VIEW, WE'RE NOTHING MORE THAN INSECTS... IF SHE "SWATS" US, WE'LL BE CRUSHED TO A PULP.
SERIOUSLY...?
THAT'S SCARY...
HA HA!
ARE YOU REALLY JEAN KIRSTEIN?
THE JEAN I KNOW ONLY THINKS ABOUT HIMSELF.
...
WHAT, ARE YOU GONNA BUST MY CHOPS ...?
SHIVER SHIVER
I JUST...

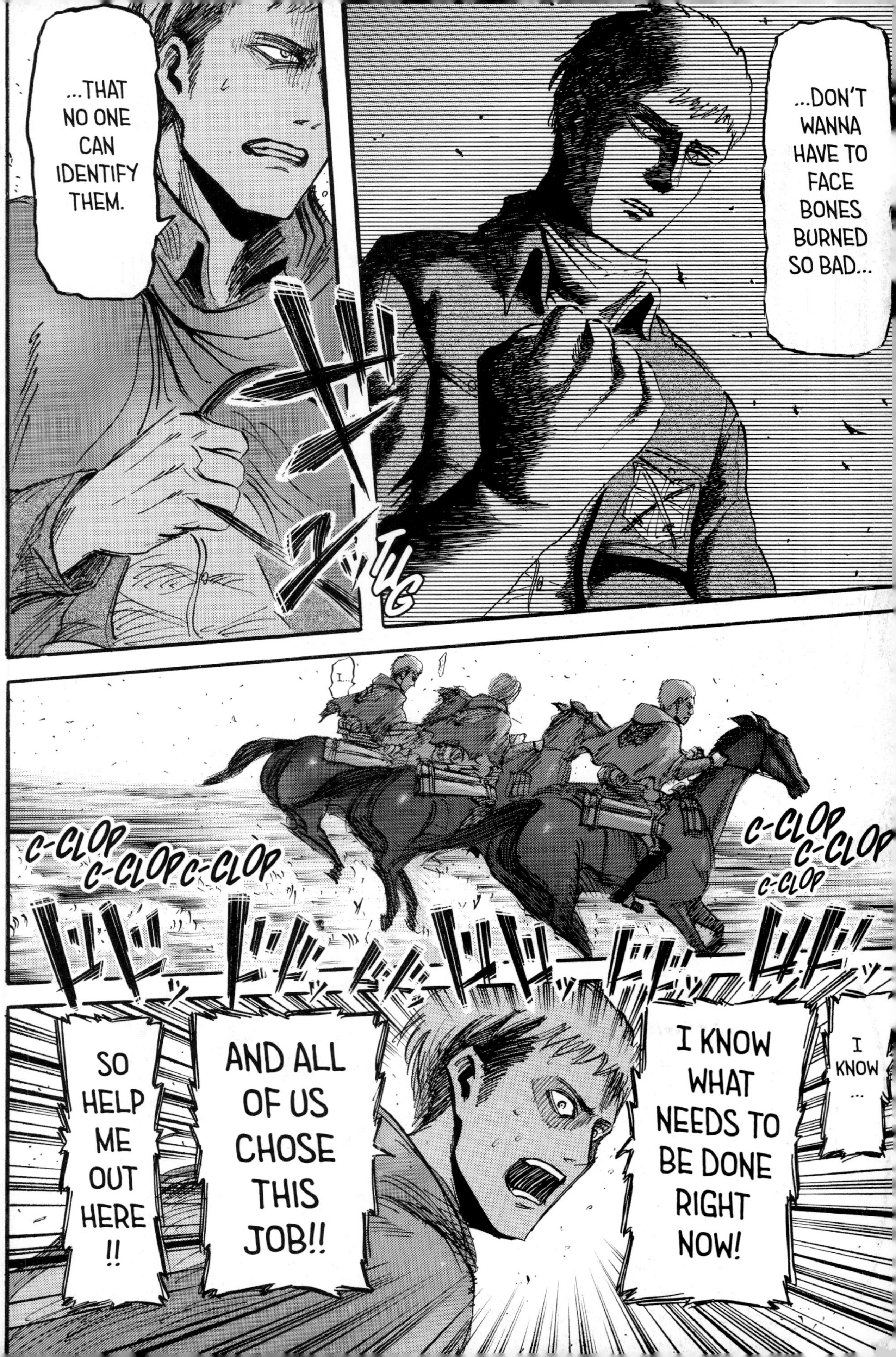
...DON'T WANNA HAVE TO FACE BONES BURNED SO BAD...
...THAT NO ONE CAN IDENTIFY THEM.
TUG
I...
C-CLOP C-CLOP C-CLOP
C-CLOP C-CLOP C-CLOP
I KNOW ...
I KNOW WHAT NEEDS TO BE DONE RIGHT NOW!
AND ALL OF US CHOSE THIS JOB!!
SO HELP ME OUT HERE!!

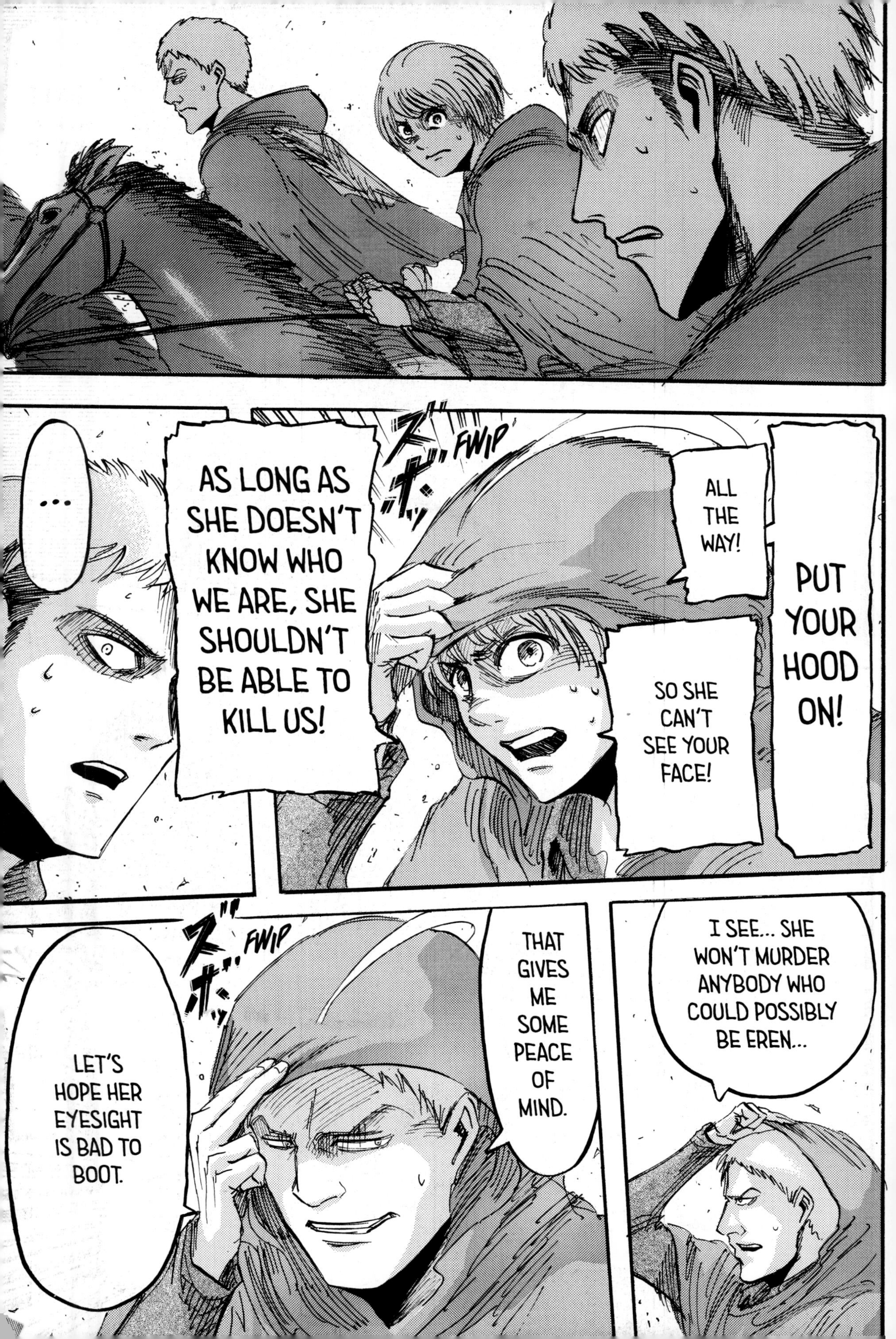
PUT YOUR HOOD ON!
ALL THE WAY!
SO SHE CAN'T SEE YOUR FACE!
FWIP
AS LONG AS SHE DOESN'T KNOW WHO WE ARE, SHE SHOULDN'T BE ABLE TO KILL US!
...
I SEE... SHE WON'T MURDER ANYBODY WHO COULD POSSIBLY BE EREN...
FWIP
THAT GIVES ME SOME PEACE OF MIND.
LET'S HOPE HER EYESIGHT IS BAD TO BOOT.

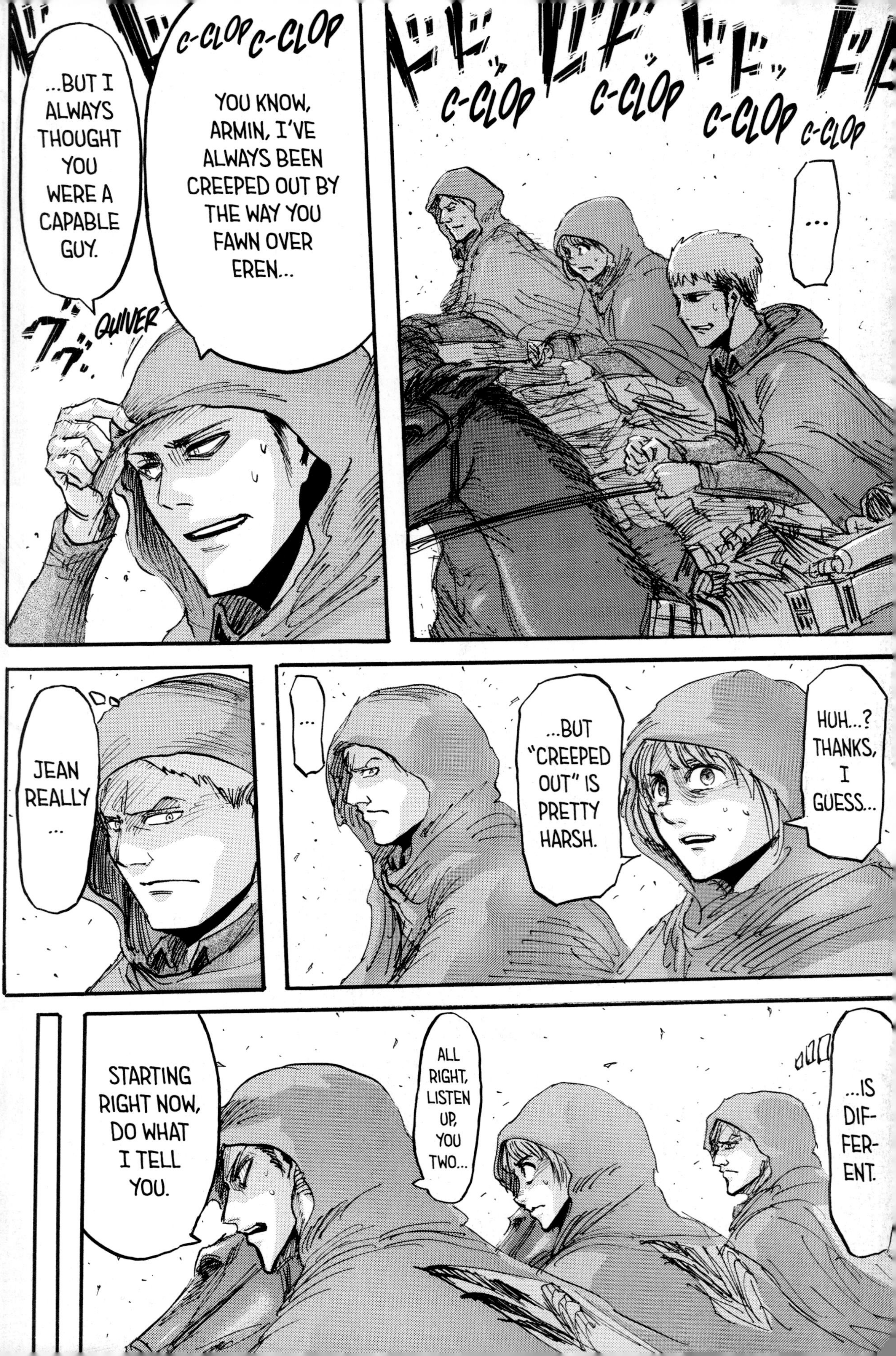
C-CLOP C-CLOP C-CLOP C-CLOP
...
C-CLOP C-CLOP
YOU KNOW, ARMIN, I'VE ALWAYS BEEN CREEPED OUT BY THE WAY YOU FAWN OVER EREN...
...BUT I ALWAYS THOUGHT YOU WERE A CAPABLE GUY.
QUIVER
HUH...? THANKS, I GUESS...
...BUT "CREEPED OUT" IS PRETTY HARSH.
...
JEAN REALLY ...
...IS DIF-FER-ENT.
ALL RIGHT, LISTEN UP, YOU TWO...
STARTING RIGHT NOW, DO WHAT I TELL YOU.

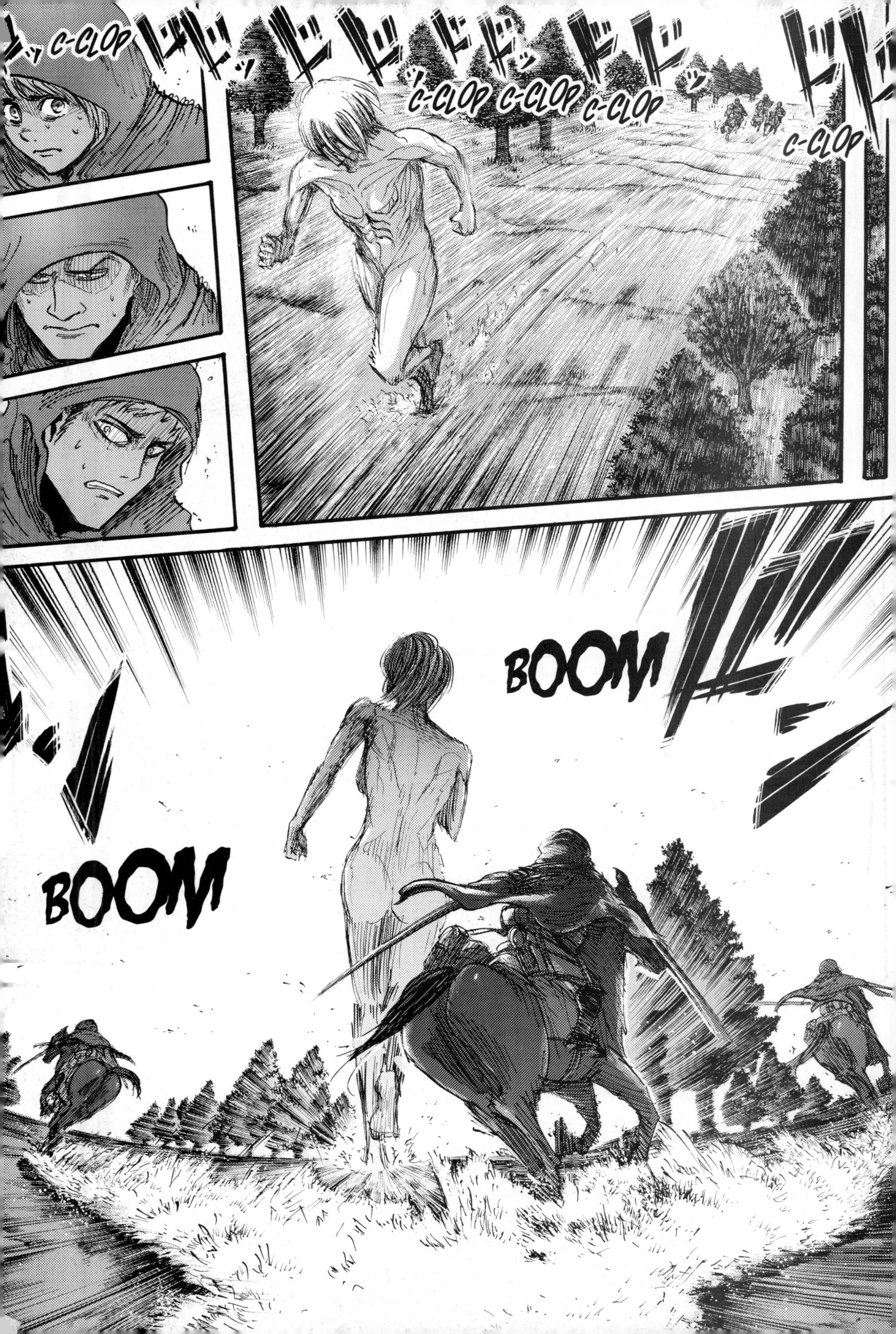
C-CLOP
C-CLOP
C-CLOP
C-CLOP
C-CLOP
BOOM
BOOM

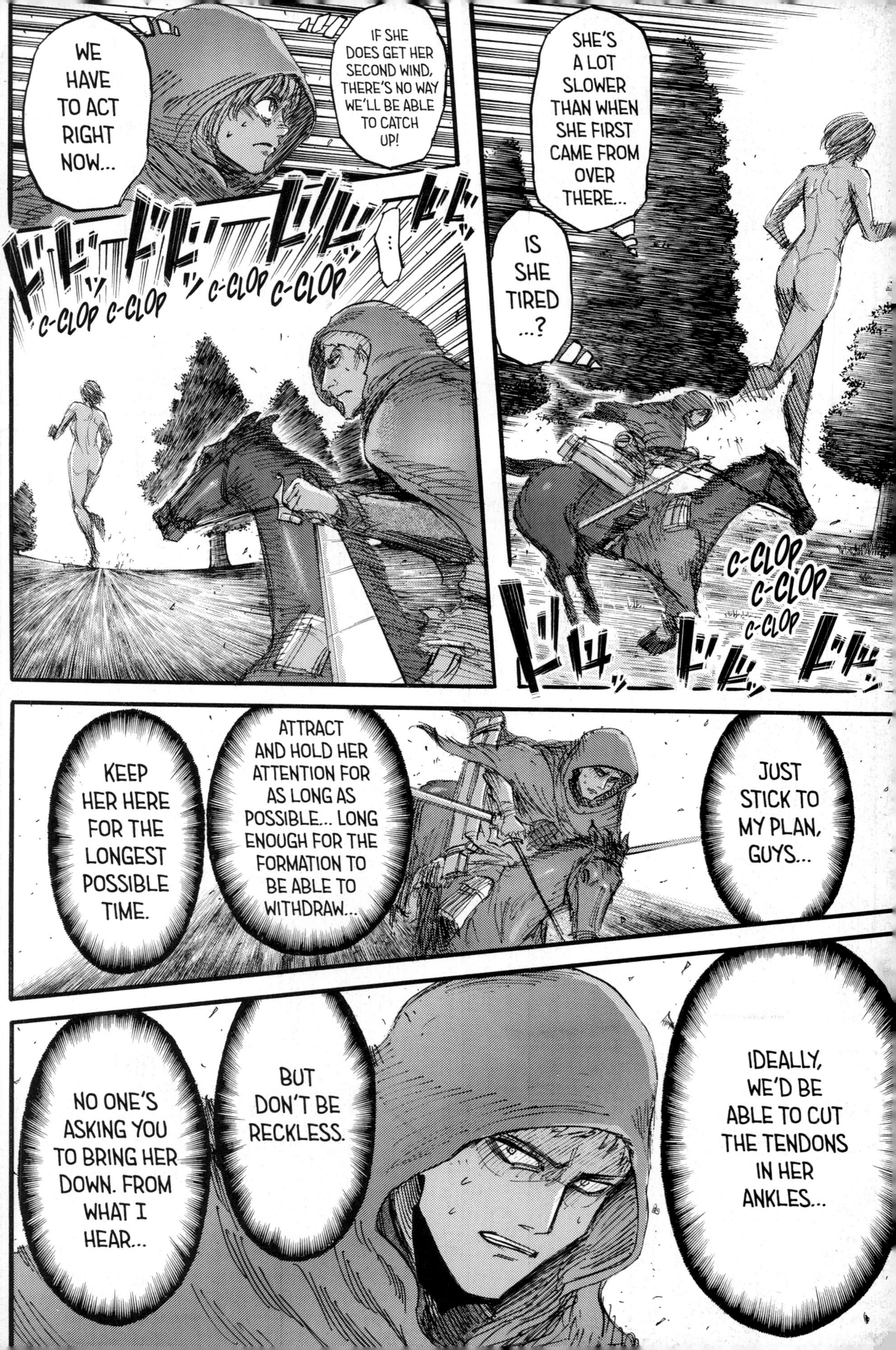
SHE'S A LOT SLOWER THAN WHEN SHE FIRST CAME FROM OVER THERE...
IS SHE TIRED ...?
C-CLOP C-CLOP C-CLOP
IF SHE DOES GET HER SECOND WIND, THERE'S NO WAY WE'LL BE ABLE TO CATCH UP!
WE HAVE TO ACT RIGHT NOW...
C-CLOP C-CLOP C-CLOP C-CLOP
...
JUST STICK TO MY PLAN, GUYS...
ATTRACT AND HOLD HER ATTENTION FOR AS LONG AS POSSIBLE... LONG ENOUGH FOR THE FORMATION TO BE ABLE TO WITHDRAW...
KEEP HER HERE FOR THE LONGEST POSSIBLE TIME.
IDEALLY, WE'D BE ABLE TO CUT THE TENDONS IN HER ANKLES...
BUT DON'T BE RECKLESS.
NO ONE'S ASKING YOU TO BRING HER DOWN. FROM WHAT I HEAR...

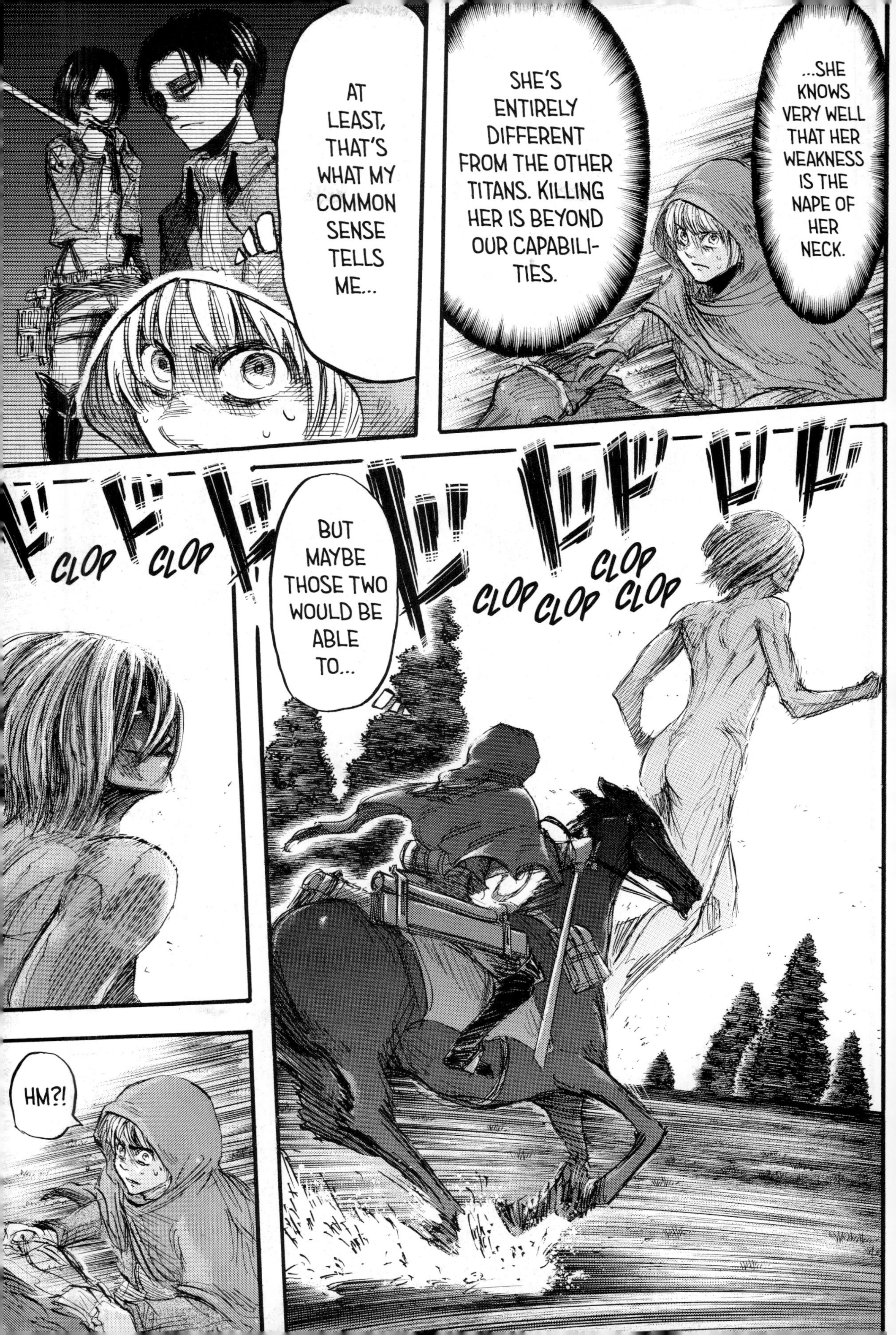
...SHE KNOWS VERY WELL THAT HER WEAKNESS IS THE NAPE OF HER NECK.
SHE'S ENTIRELY DIFFERENT FROM THE OTHER TITANS. KILLING HER IS BEYOND OUR CAPABILI-TIES.
AT LEAST, THAT'S WHAT MY COMMON SENSE TELLS ME...
CLOP CLOP
CLOP CLOP CLOP
BUT MAYBE THOSE TWO WOULD BE ABLE TO...
CLOP CLOP
HM?!

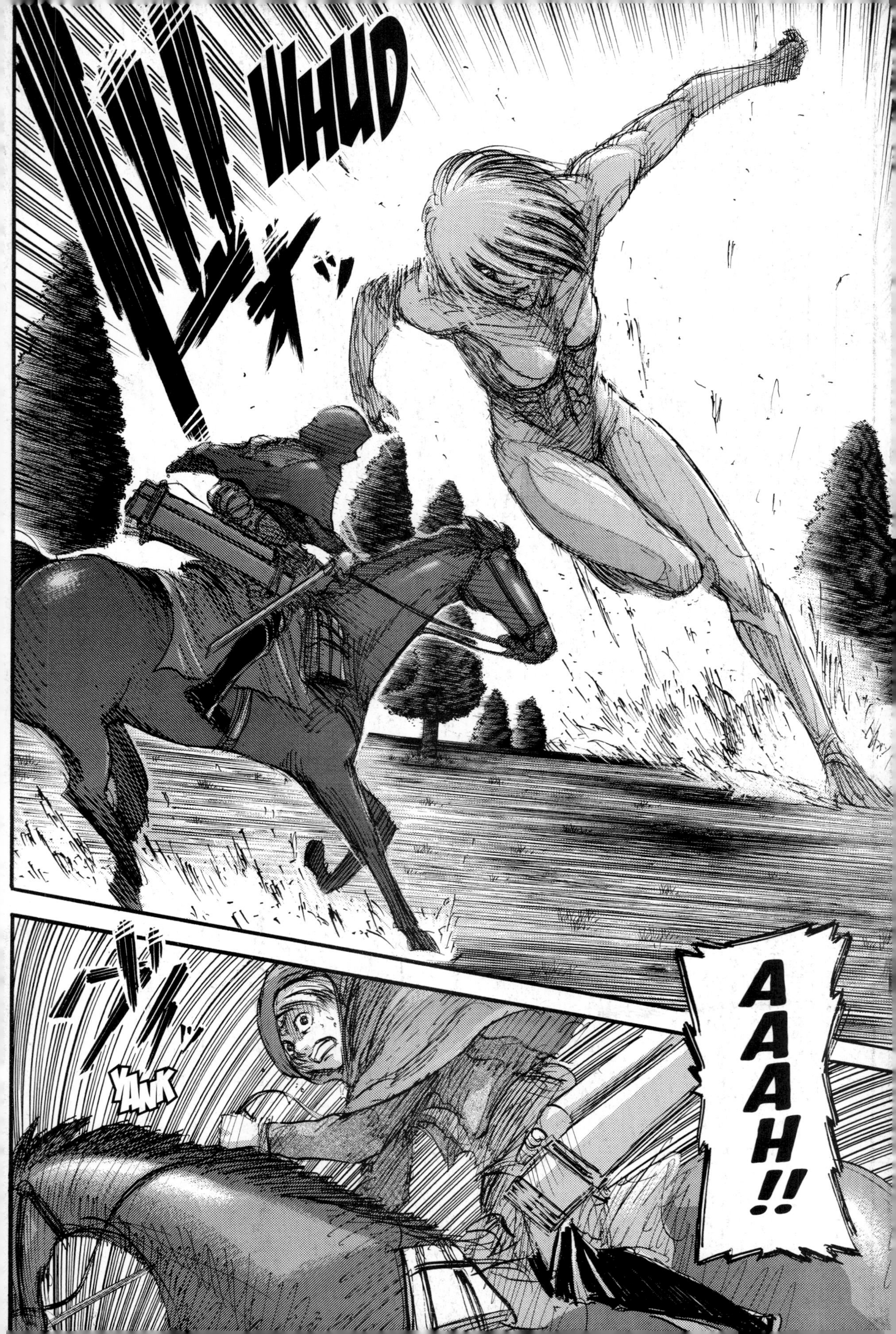
WHUD
AAAAH!!
YANK

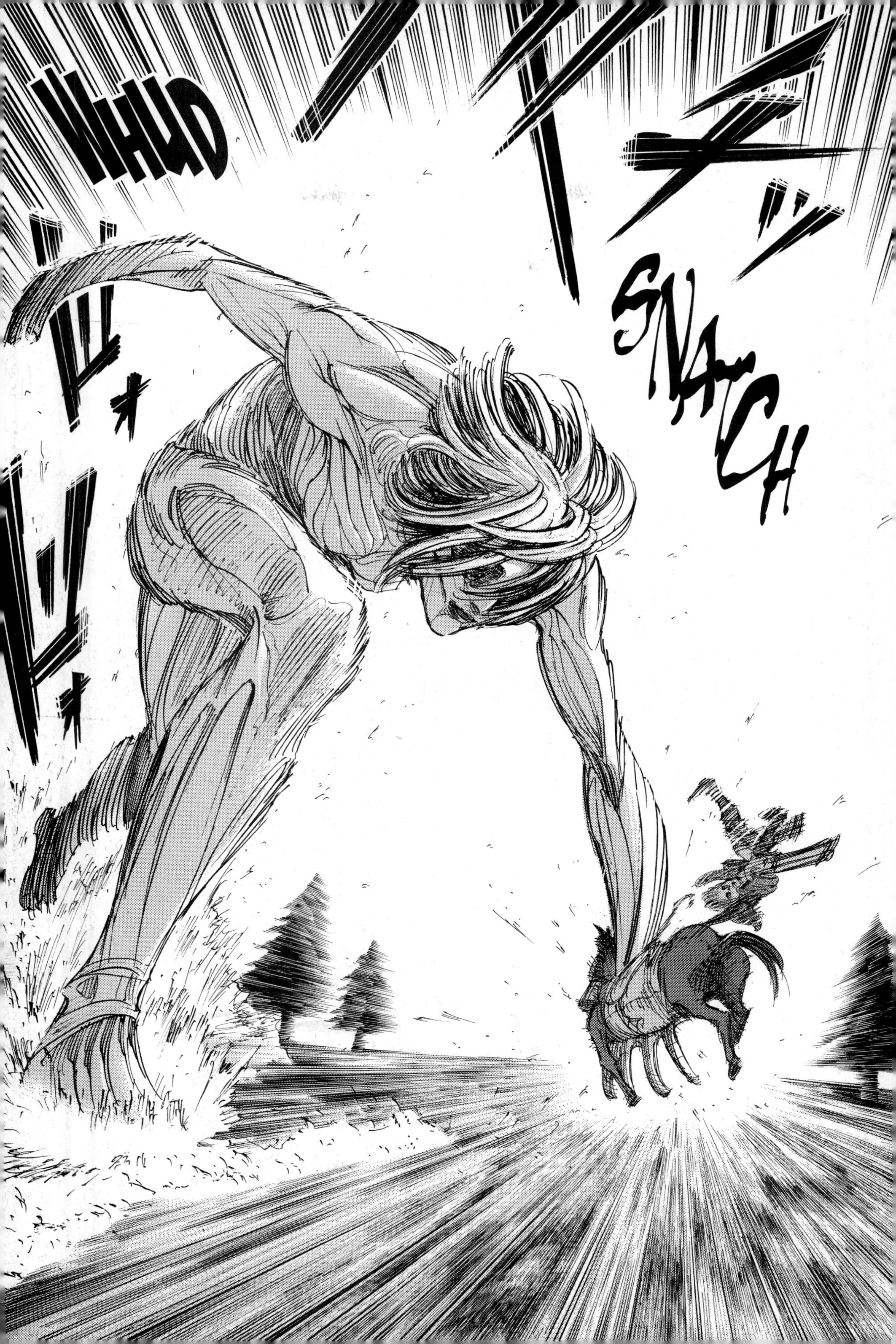
SNATCH
WHUD

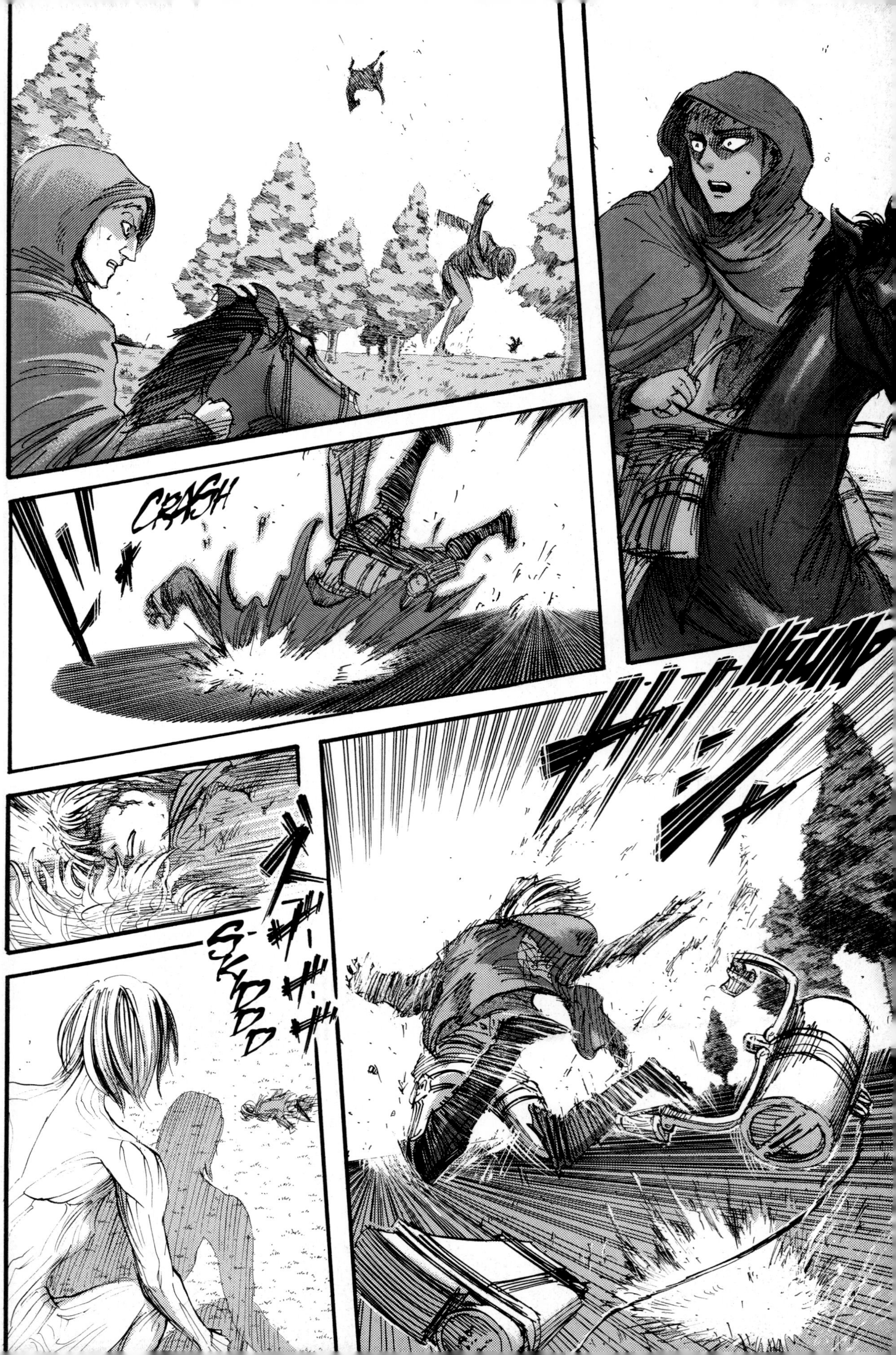
CRASH
WHUMP
SKIDDD

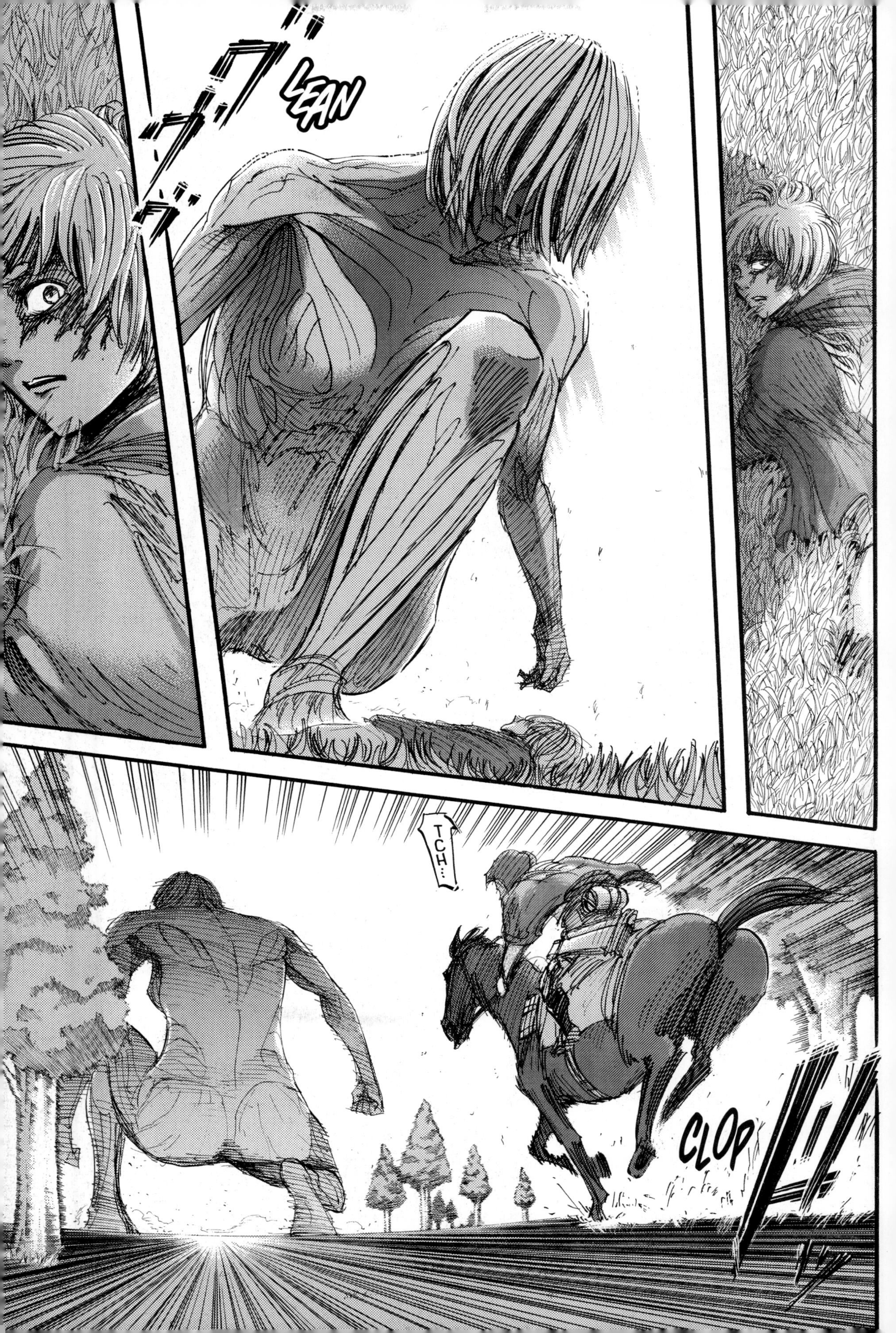
LEAN
TCH...
CLOP

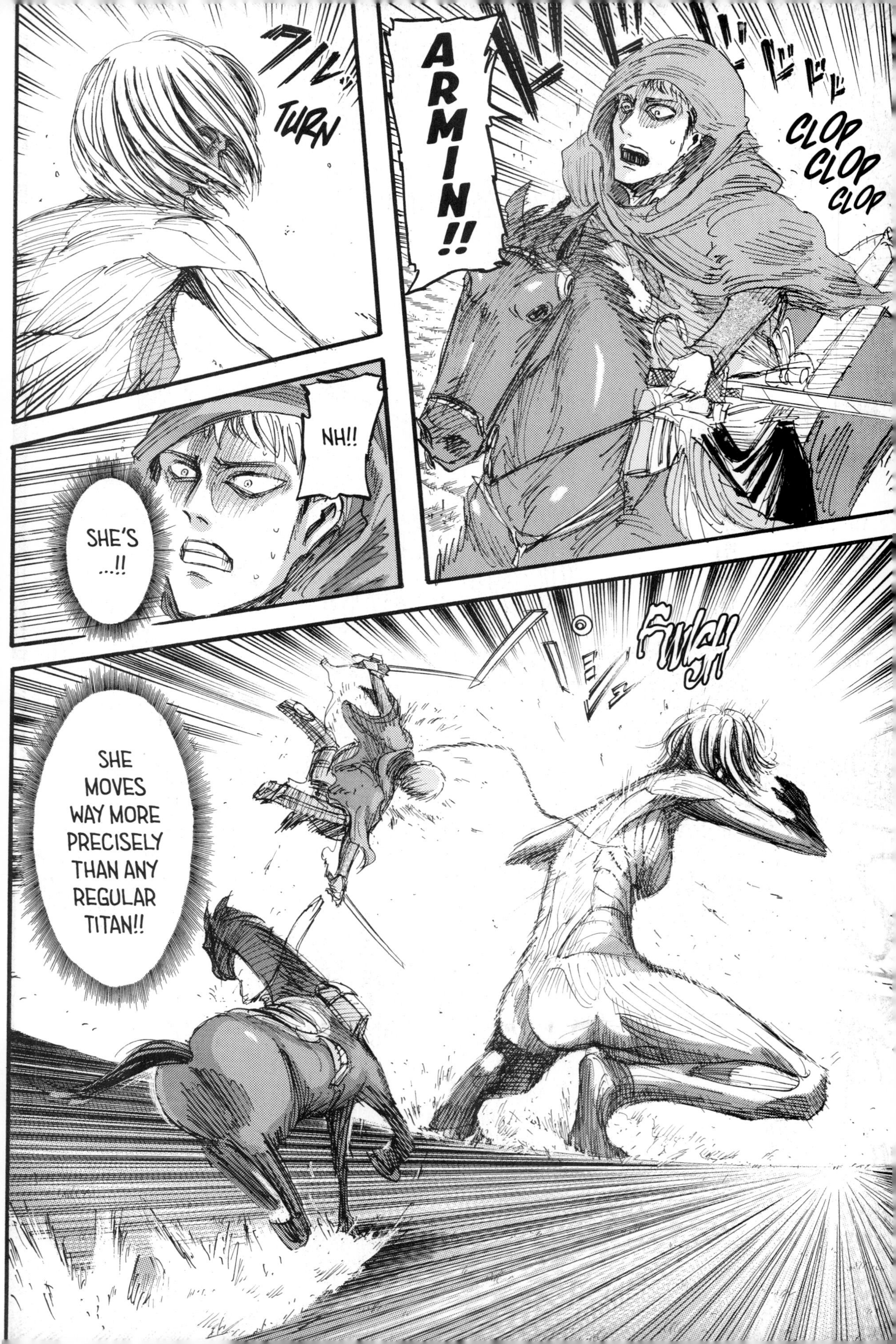
ARMIN!!
CLOP CLOP CLOP
TURN
NH!!
SHE'S ...!!
SHE MOVES WAY MORE PRECISELY THAN ANY REGULAR TITAN!!

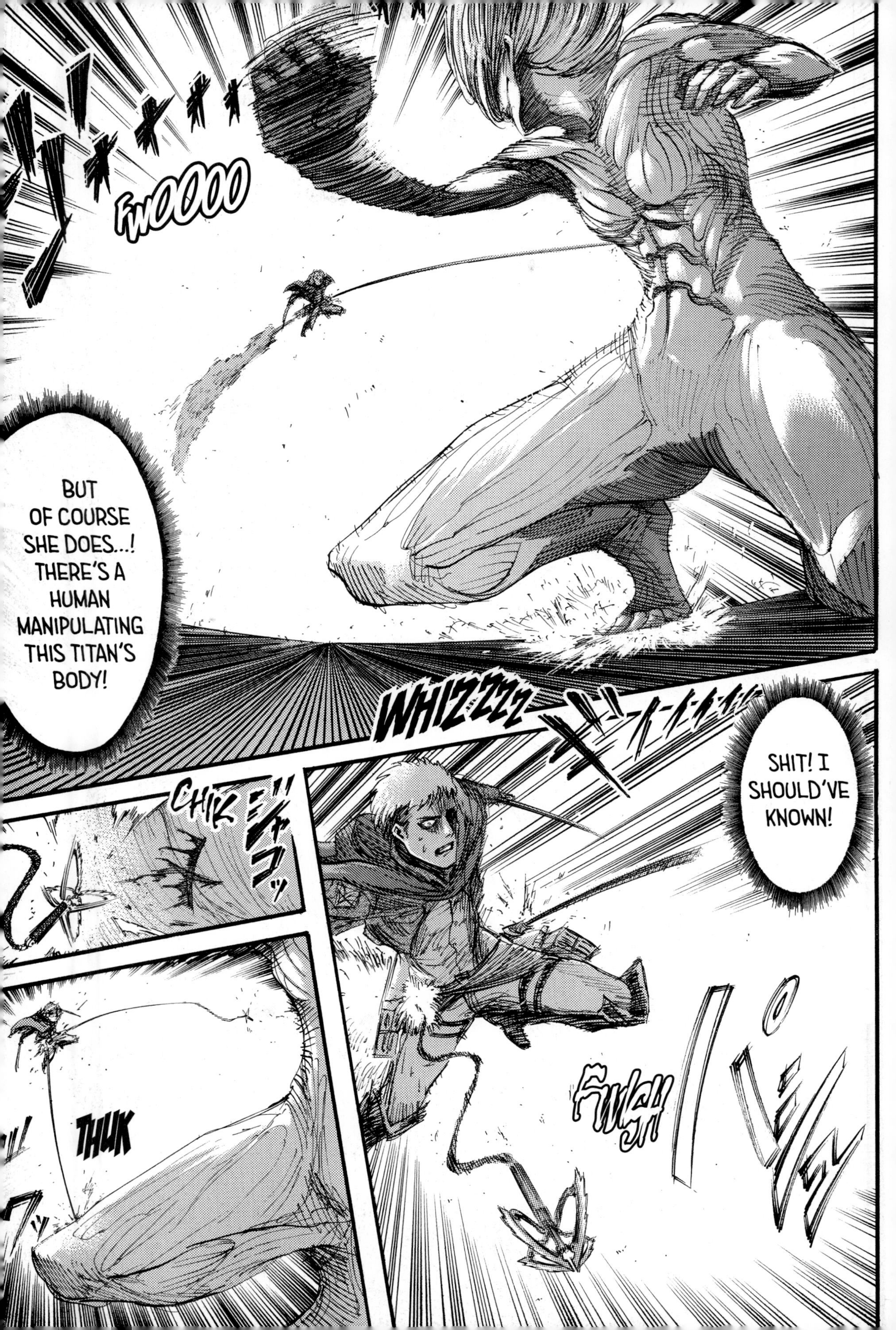
FWOOOO
BUT OF COURSE SHE DOES...! THERE'S A HUMAN MANIPULATING THIS TITAN'S BODY!
WHIZZZZ
SHIT! I SHOULD'VE KNOWN!
CHIK
THUK

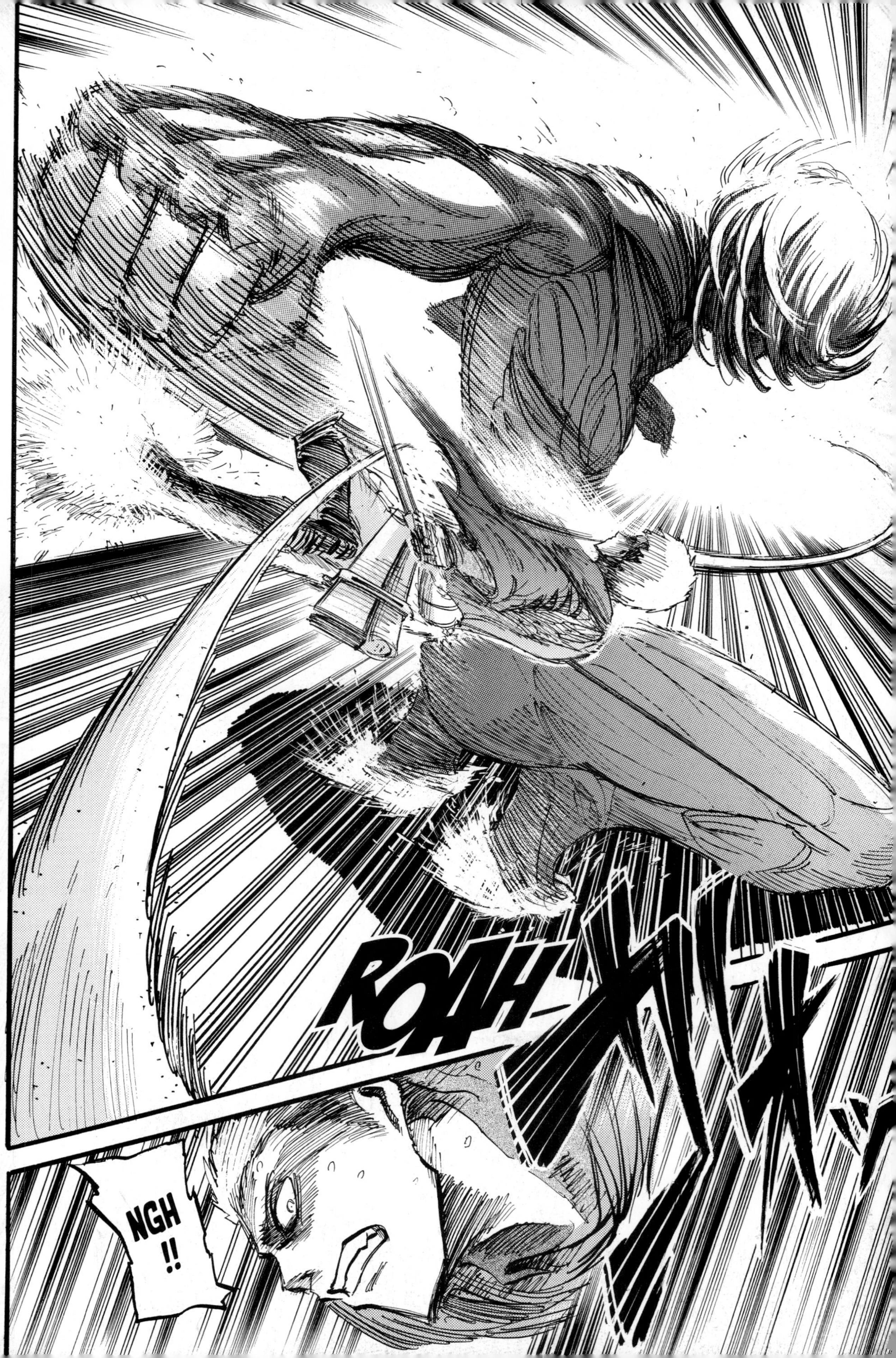
ROAH
NGH !!

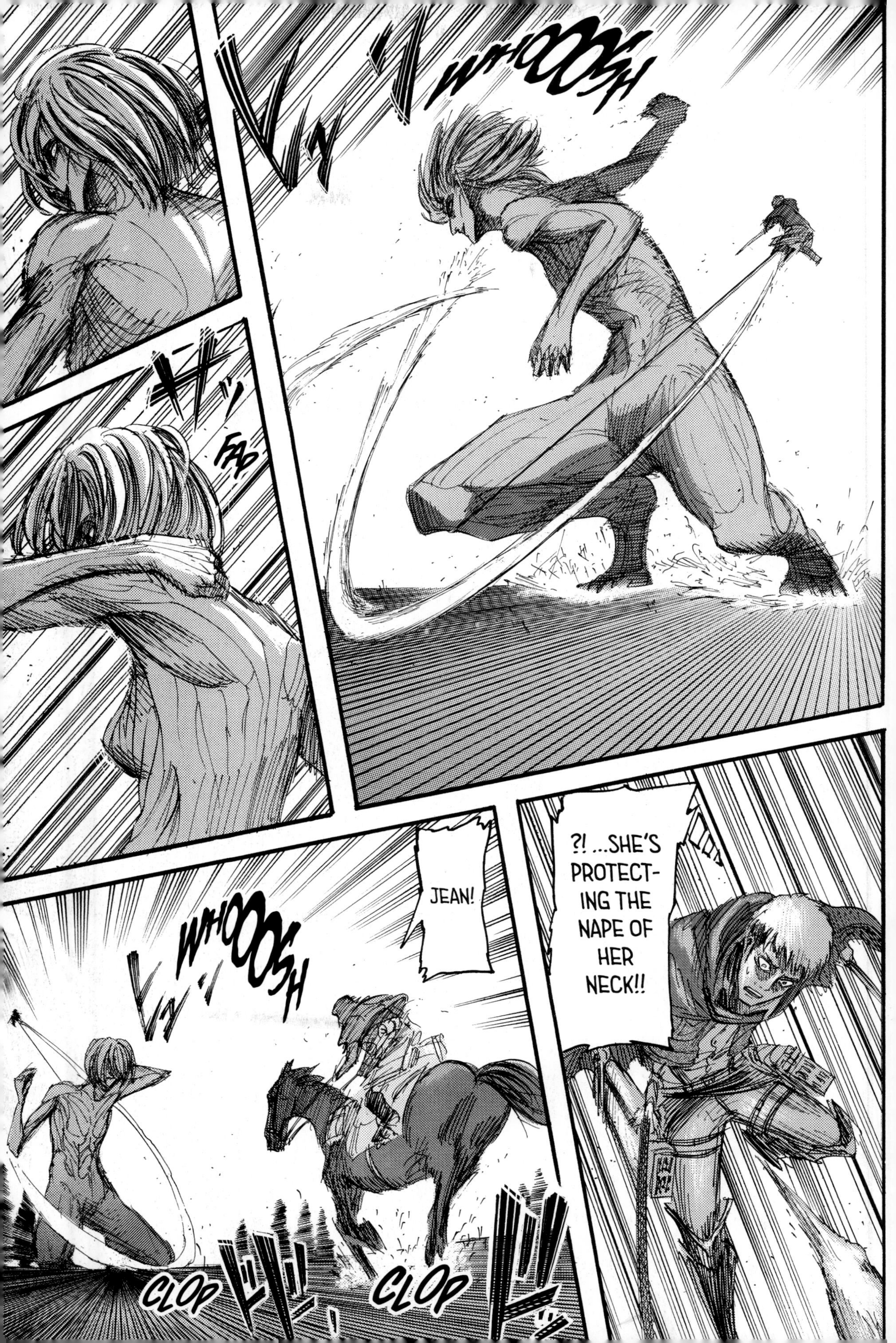
WHOOOSH
?! ...SHE'S PROTECTING THE NAPE OF HER NECK!!
JEAN!
WHOOOSH
CLOP
CLOP

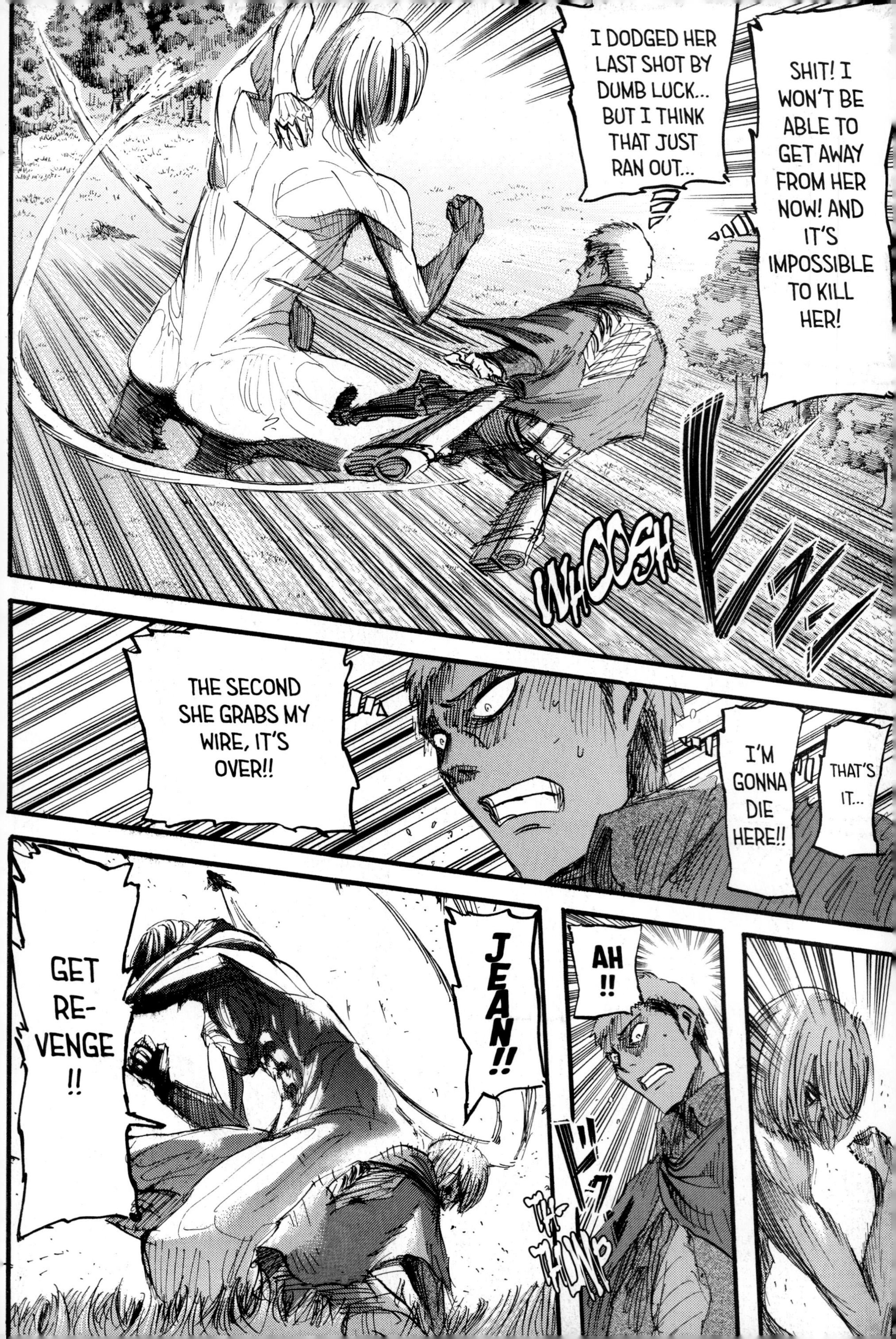
SHIT! I WON'T BE ABLE TO GET AWAY FROM HER NOW! AND IT'S IMPOSSIBLE TO KILL HER!
I DODGED HER LAST SHOT BY DUMB LUCK... BUT I THINK THAT JUST RAN OUT...
WHOOSH
THAT'S IT...
I'M GONNA DIE HERE!!
THE SECOND SHE GRABS MY WIRE, IT'S OVER!!
AH!!
THUMP
JEAN!!
GET RE-VENGE!!

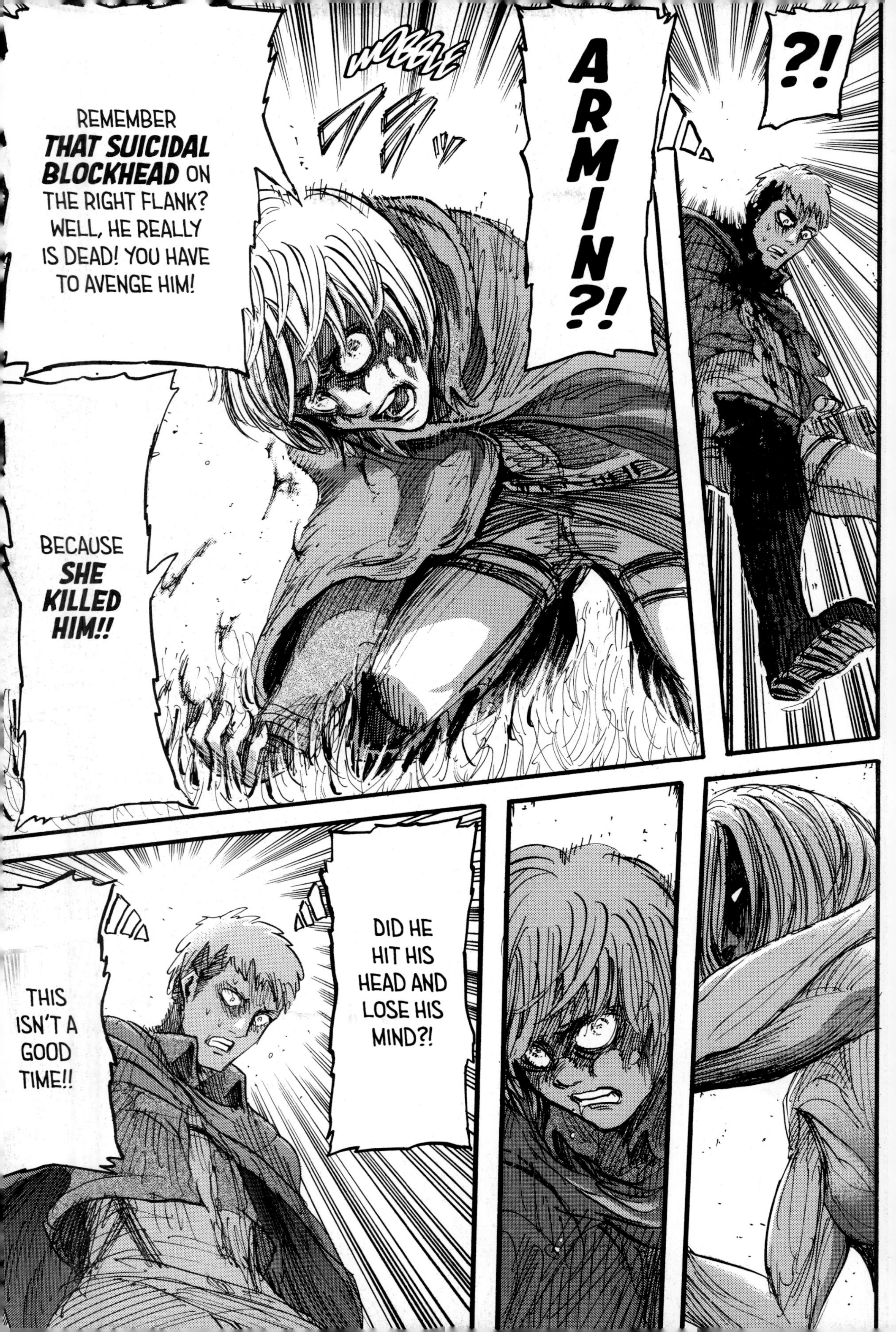
?!
ARMIN?!
WOBBLE
REMEMBER THAT SUICIDAL BLOCKHEAD ON THE RIGHT FLANK? WELL, HE REALLY IS DEAD! YOU HAVE TO AVENGE HIM!
BECAUSE SHE KILLED HIM!!
DID HE HIT HIS HEAD AND LOSE HIS MIND?!
THIS ISN'T A GOOD TIME!!

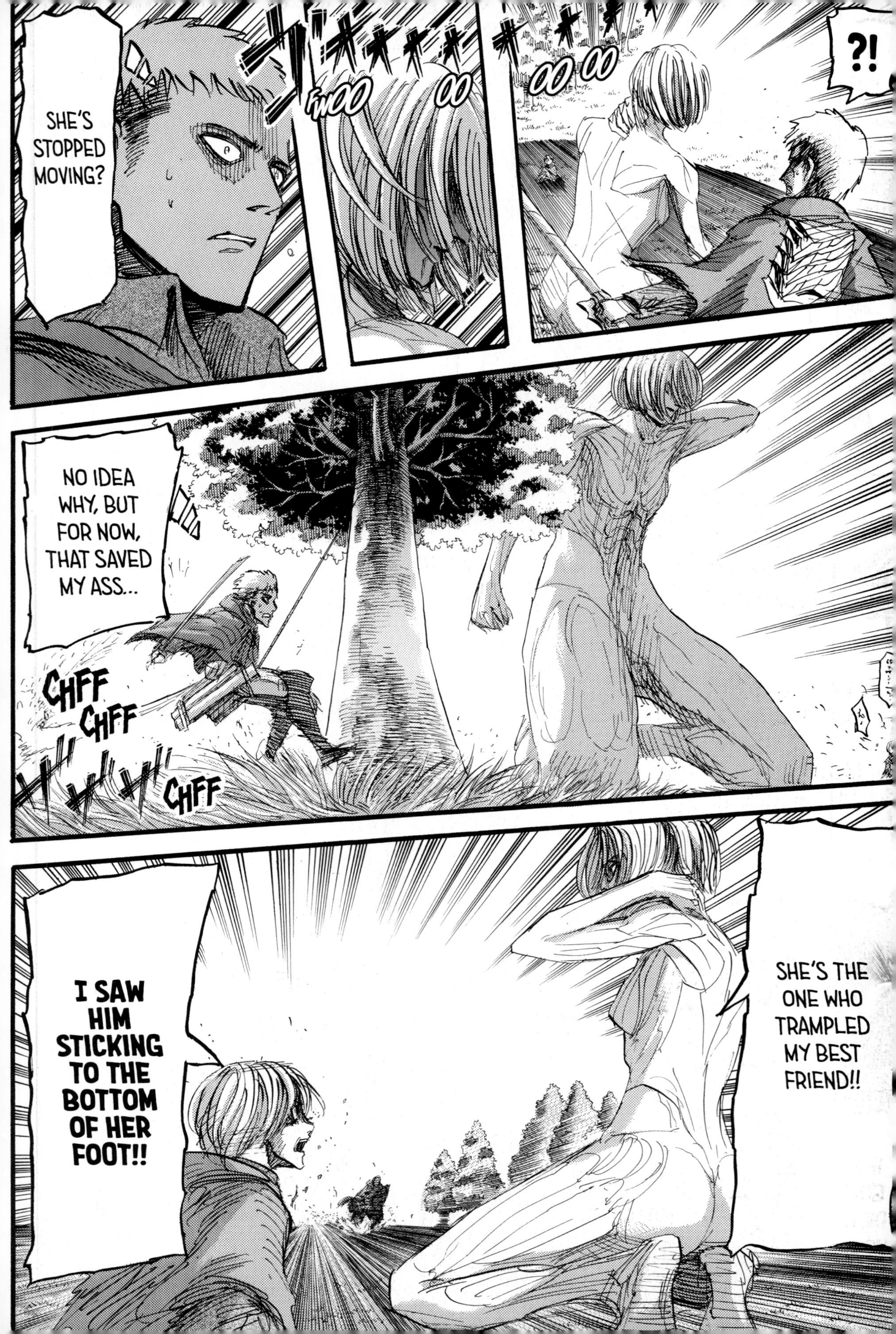
?!
OO OO
OO
FWOO
SHE'S STOPPED MOVING?
?!
NO IDEA WHY, BUT FOR NOW, THAT SAVED MY ASS...
CHFF
CHFF
CHFF
SHE'S THE ONE WHO TRAMPLED MY BEST FRIEND!!
I SAW HIM STICKING TO THE BOTTOM OF HER FOOT!!

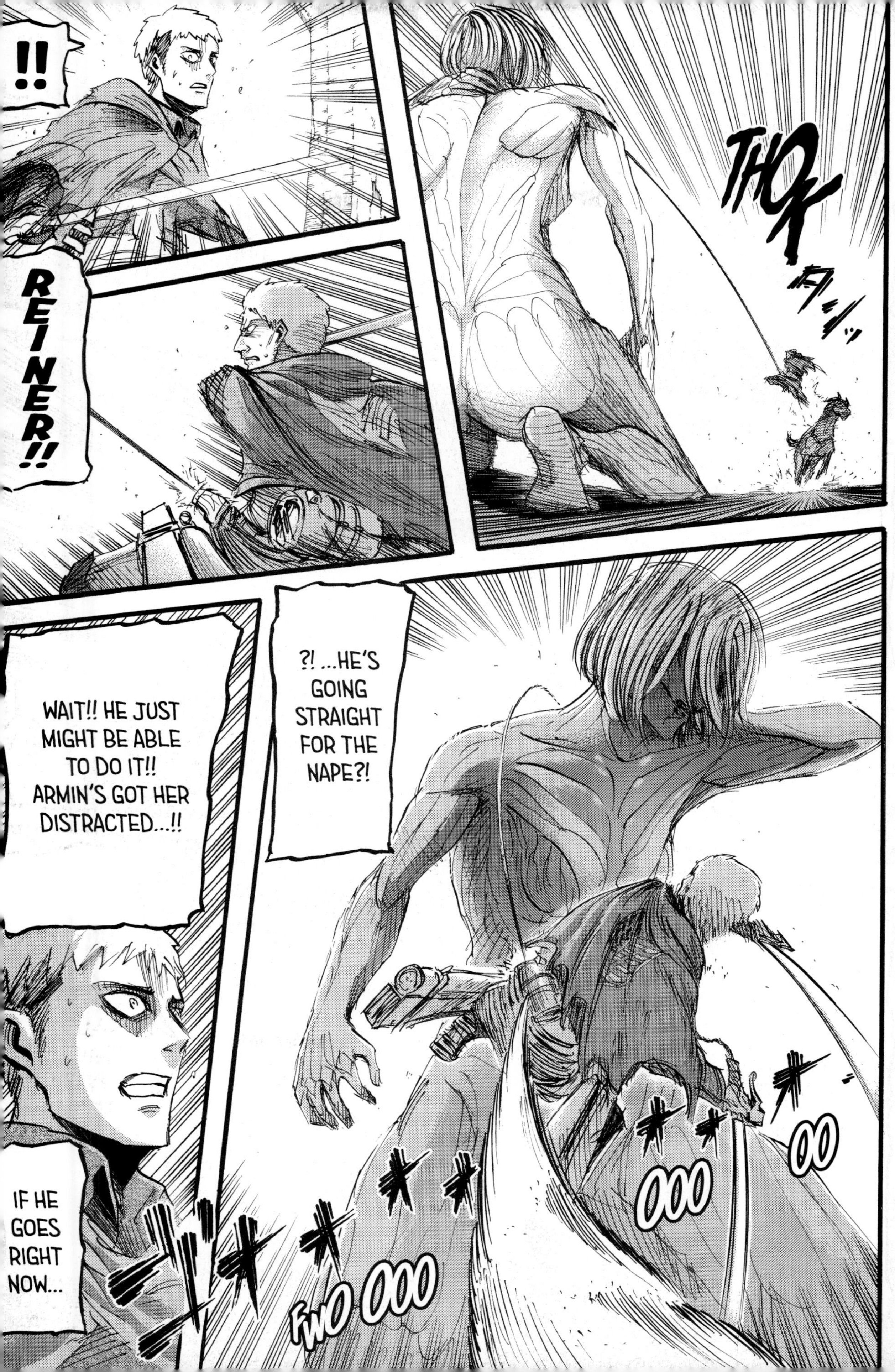
THOK
!!
REINER!!
?! ...HE'S GOING STRAIGHT FOR THE NAPE?!
FWO OOO OOO OO
WAIT!! HE JUST MIGHT BE ABLE TO DO IT!! ARMIN'S GOT HER DISTRACTED...!!
IF HE GOES RIGHT NOW...

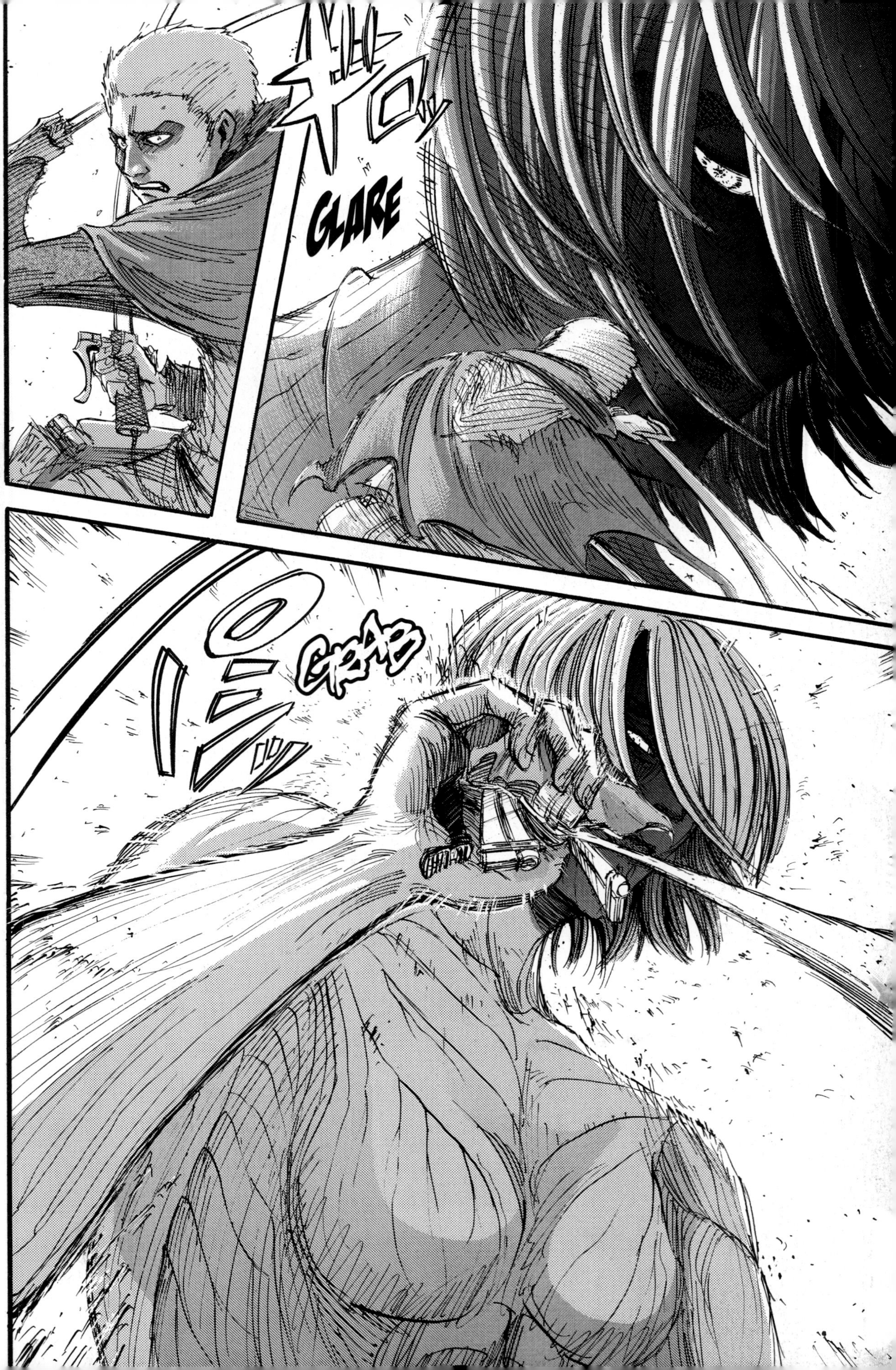
GLARE
GRAB

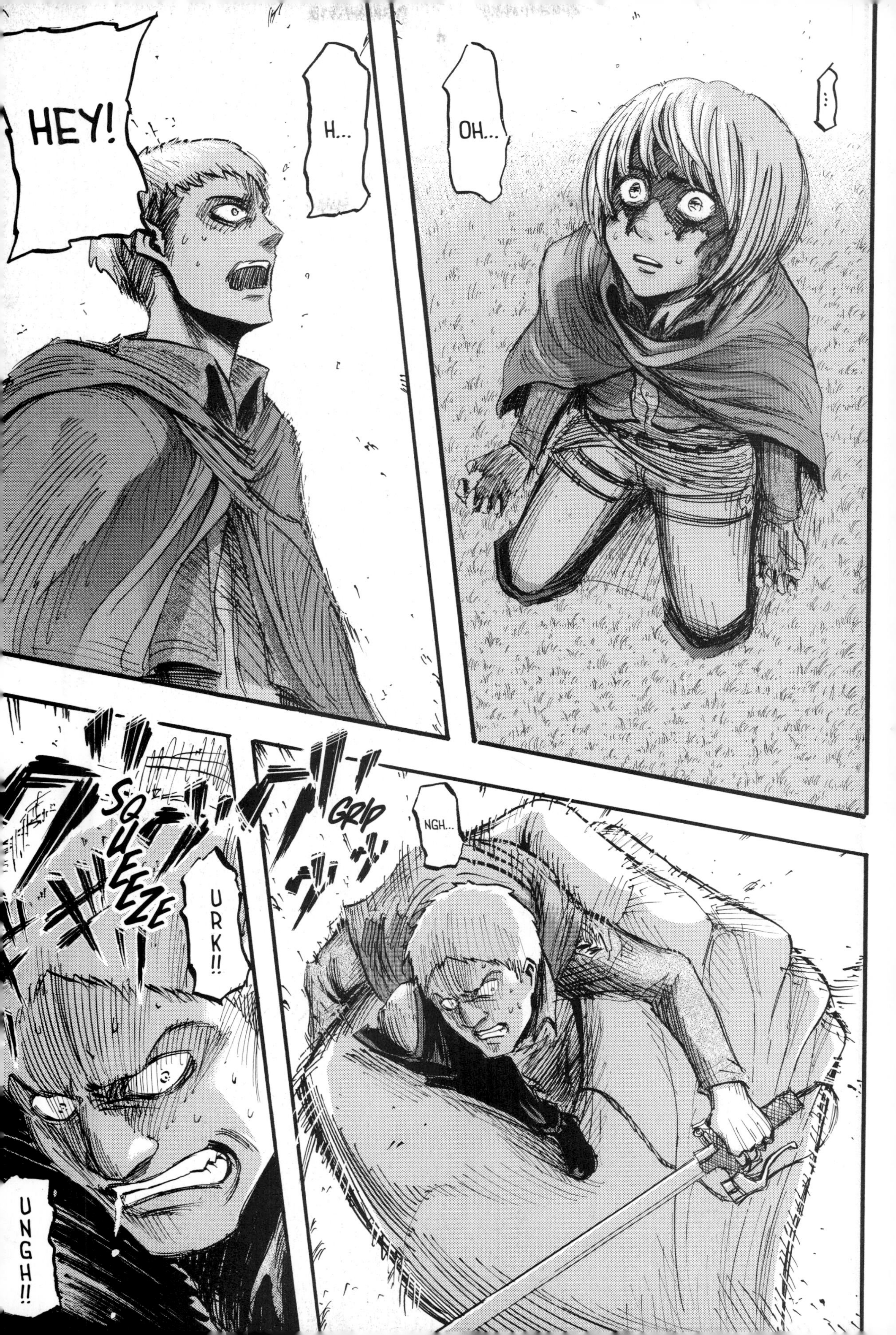
…
OH…
H…
HEY!
GRIP
NGH…
SQUEEZE
URK!!
UNGH!!

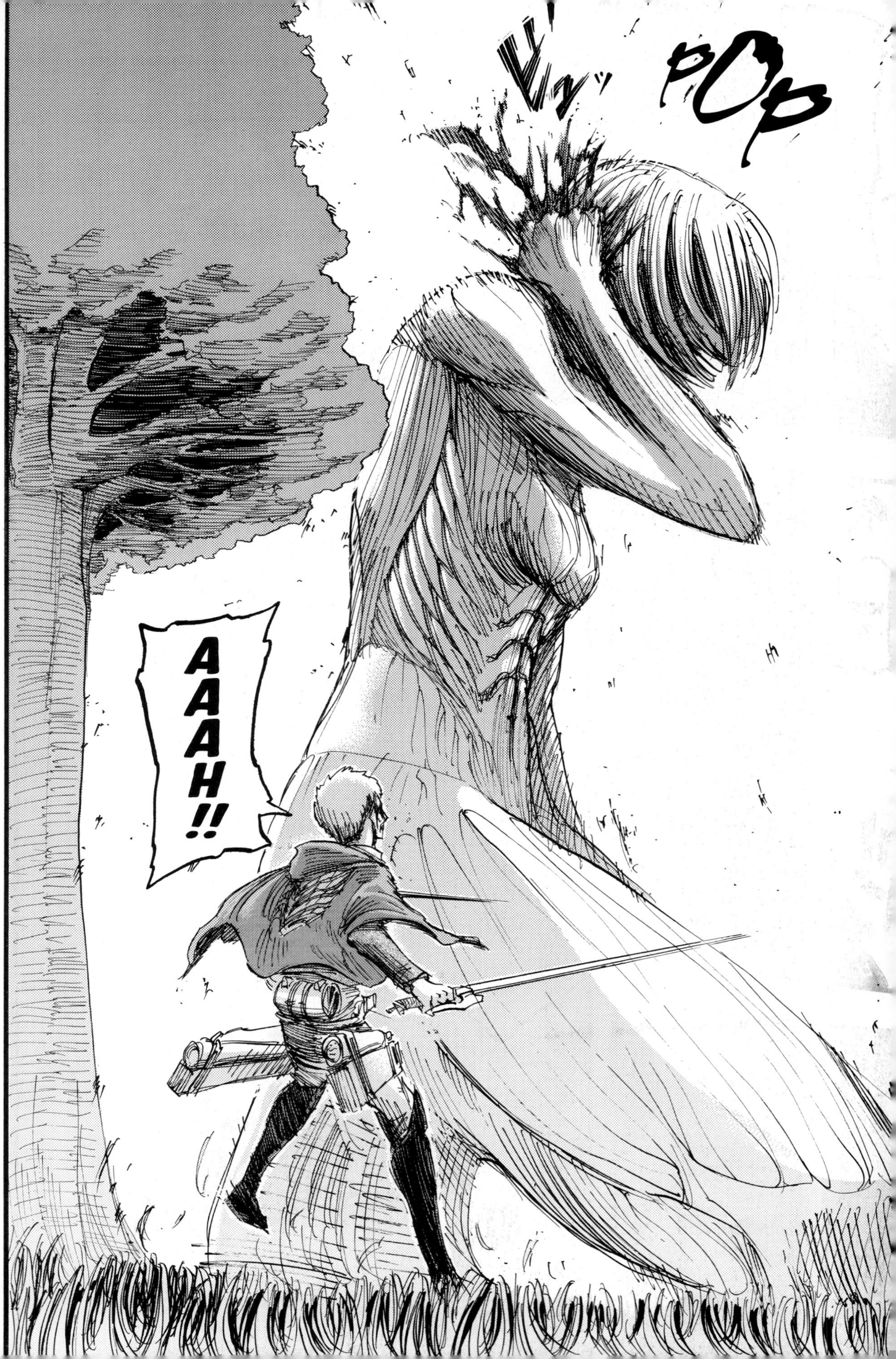
POP
ビュッ
AAAAH!!

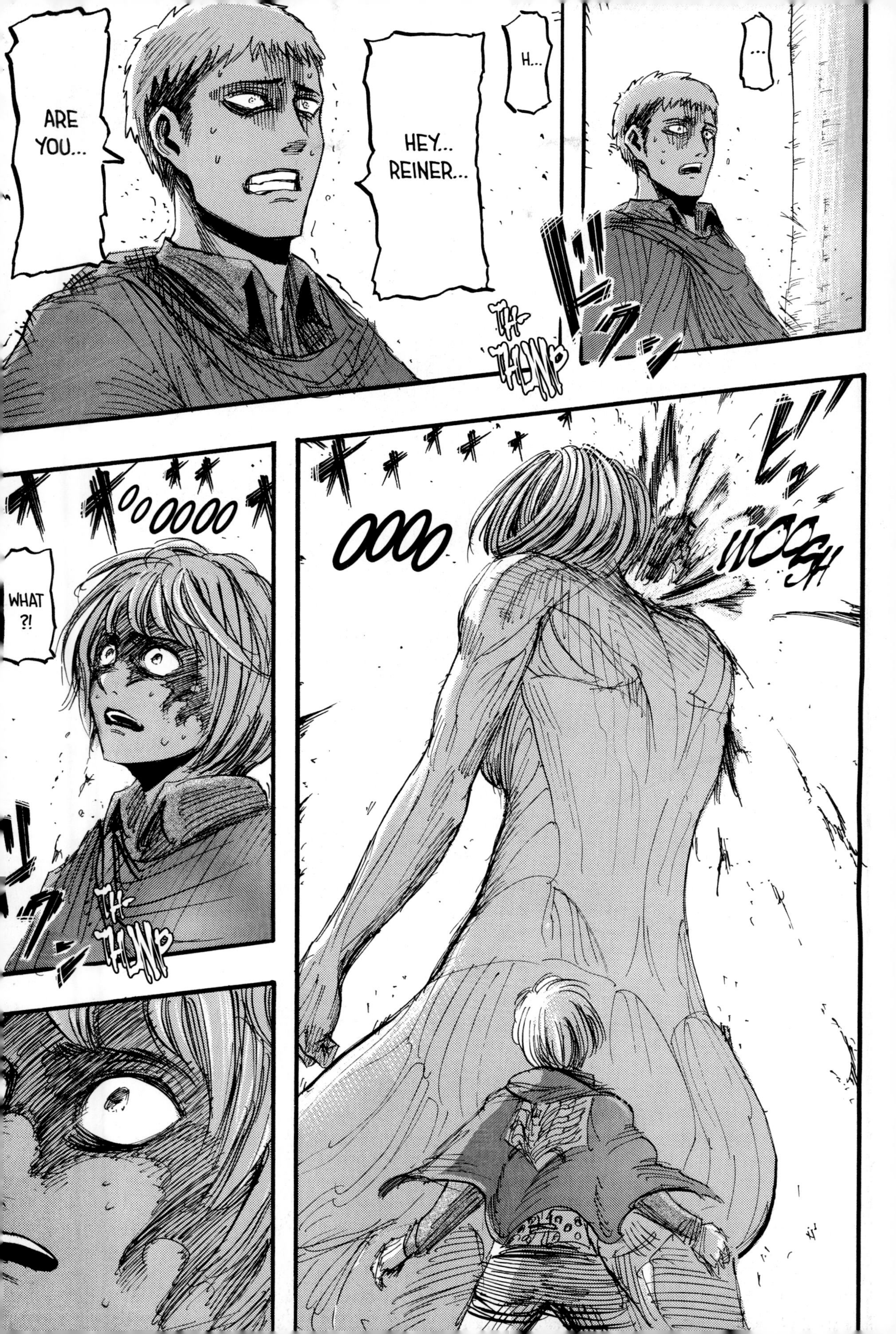
...
TH-THUMP
H...
HEY... REINER...
ARE YOU...
WOOSH
OOOO
ooOOOO
WHAT?!
TH-THUMP

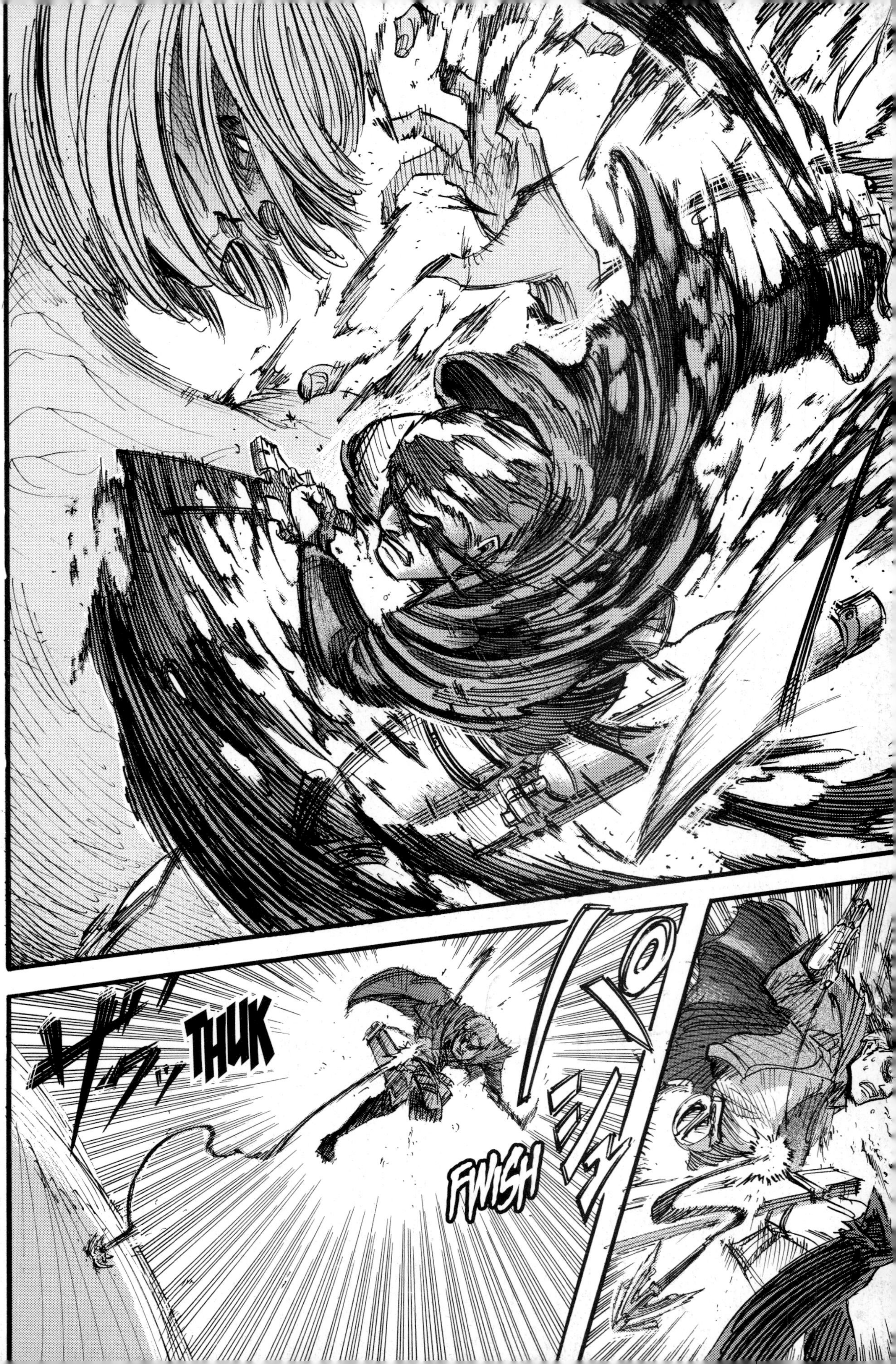
THUK
FWISH

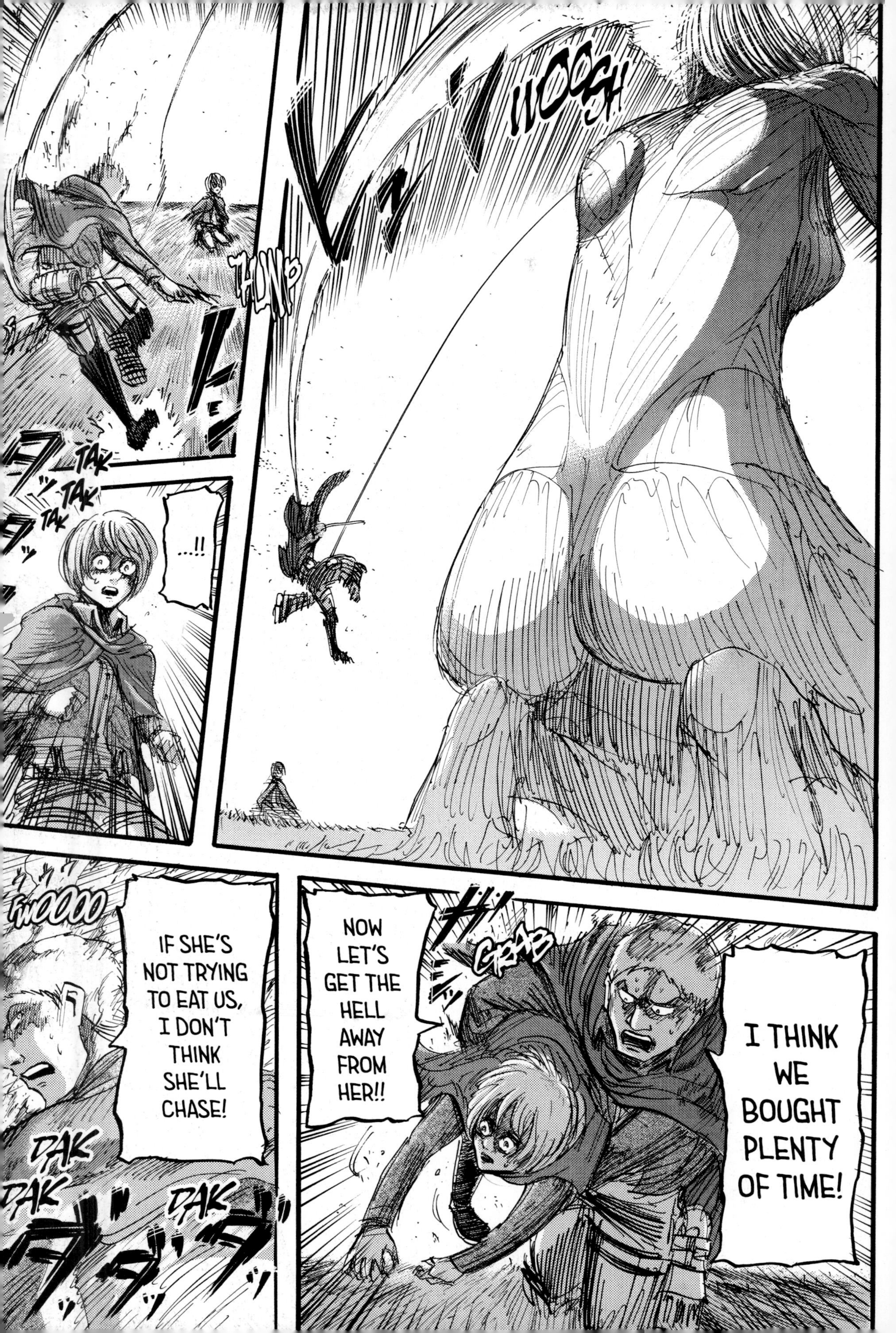
WOOSH!
THUNK
TAK TAK TAK
...!!
GRAB
I THINK WE BOUGHT PLENTY OF TIME!
NOW LET'S GET THE HELL AWAY FROM HER!!
FWOOOO
IF SHE'S NOT TRYING TO EAT US, I DON'T THINK SHE'LL CHASE!
DAK DAK DAK

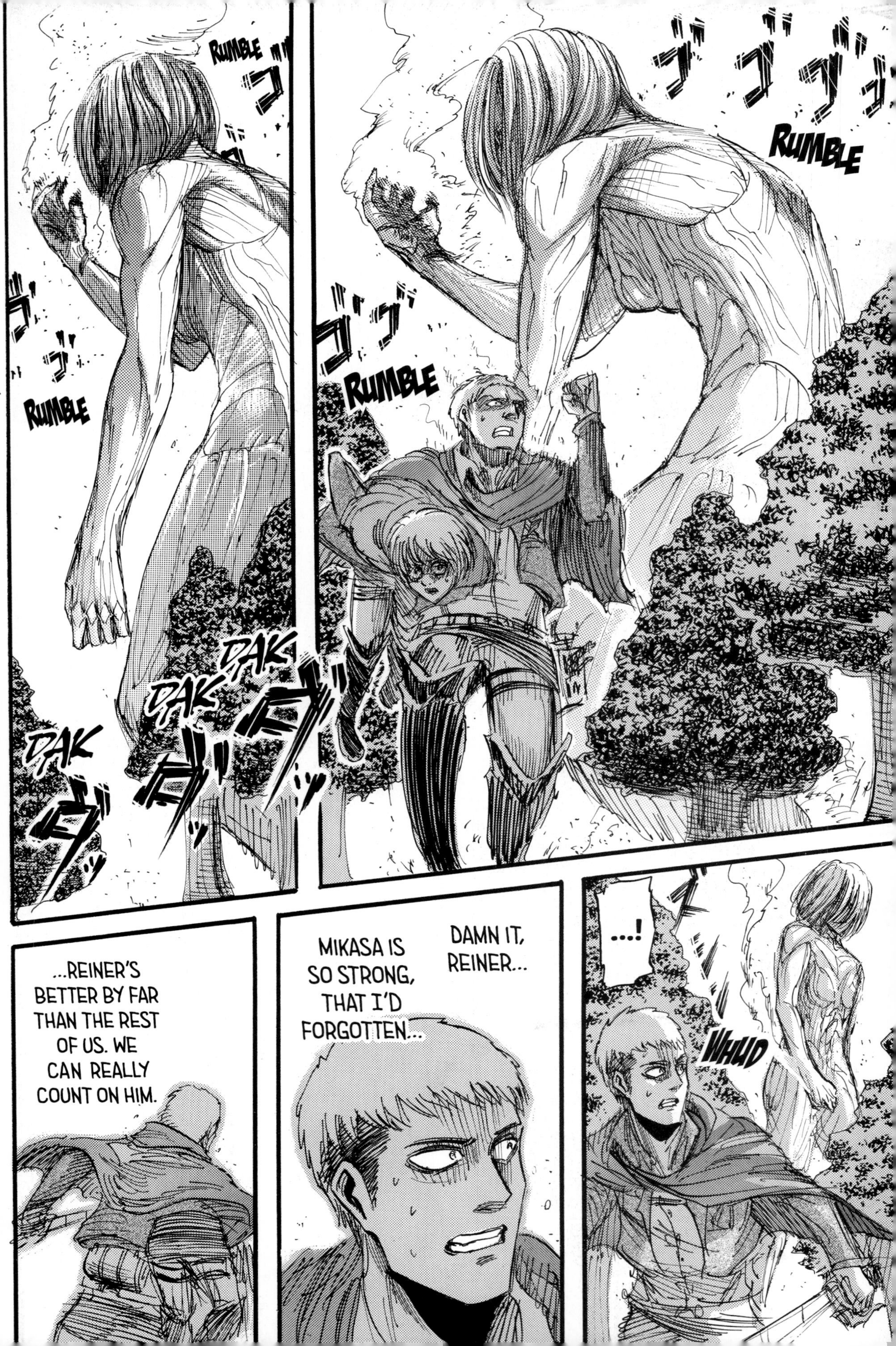
RUMBLE
RUMBLE
RUMBLE
RUMBLE
DAK
DAK
DAK
...!
WHUD
DAMN IT, REINER...
MIKASA IS SO STRONG, THAT I'D FORGOTTEN...
...REINER'S BETTER BY FAR THAN THE REST OF US. WE CAN REALLY COUNT ON HIM.

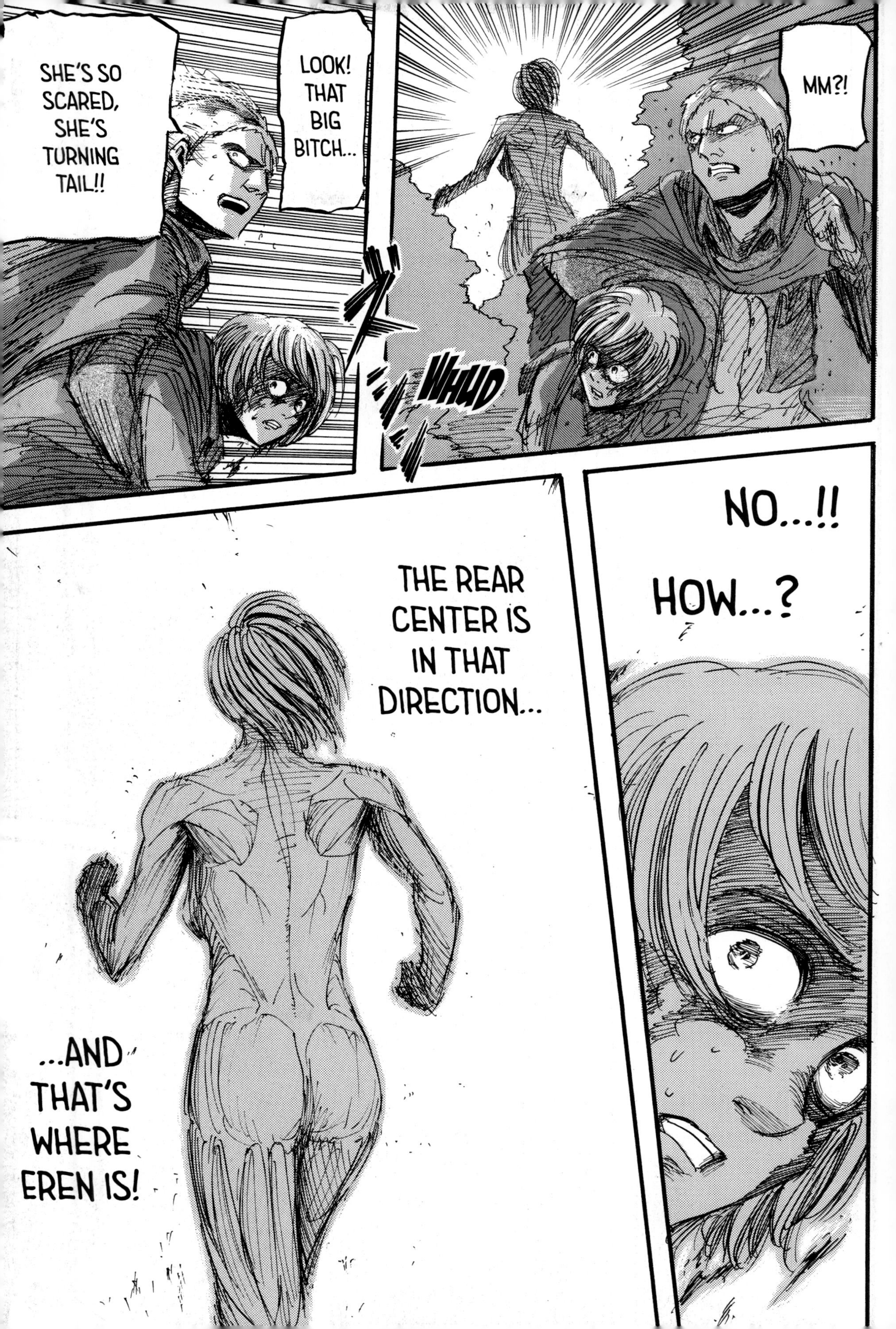
MM?!
WHUD
LOOK! THAT BIG BITCH...
SHE'S SO SCARED, SHE'S TURNING TAIL!!
NO...!!
HOW...?
THE REAR CENTER IS IN THAT DIRECTION...
...AND THAT'S WHERE EREN IS!

Current Publicly Available Information

11. Yeast

A UNIQUE TYPE OF YEAST IS PRODUCED BEHIND WALL SHEENA. AT A GLANCE, IT LOOKS LIKE A LUMP OF FERMENTED SOYBEANS THE SIZE OF A HUMAN HEAD. IT'S A WELL-KNOWN FACT THAT STORING THE YEAST IN SHEDS OR TENTS THAT ALSO CONTAIN FODDER, WHEAT, SOYBEANS, OR DRY-CURED MEAT SLOWS DOWN THE DECOMPOSITION PROCESS IMMENSELY. IT'S A GIVEN THAT THIS YEAST PRESERVES FOOD BY TRANSFORMING IT, ALTHOUGH THERE IS AS YET NO SCIENTIFIC THEORY TO EXPLAIN IT. THE PLACEMENT OF YEAST STORAGE PLANTS IN EVERY AREA SO THAT SUPPLIES CAN BE STOCKPILED IS PART OF THE HUMAN RACE'S STRATEGY TO TAKE BACK WALL MARIA.
(WITH THANKS TO UKYō KODACHI AND KIYOMUNE MIWA)

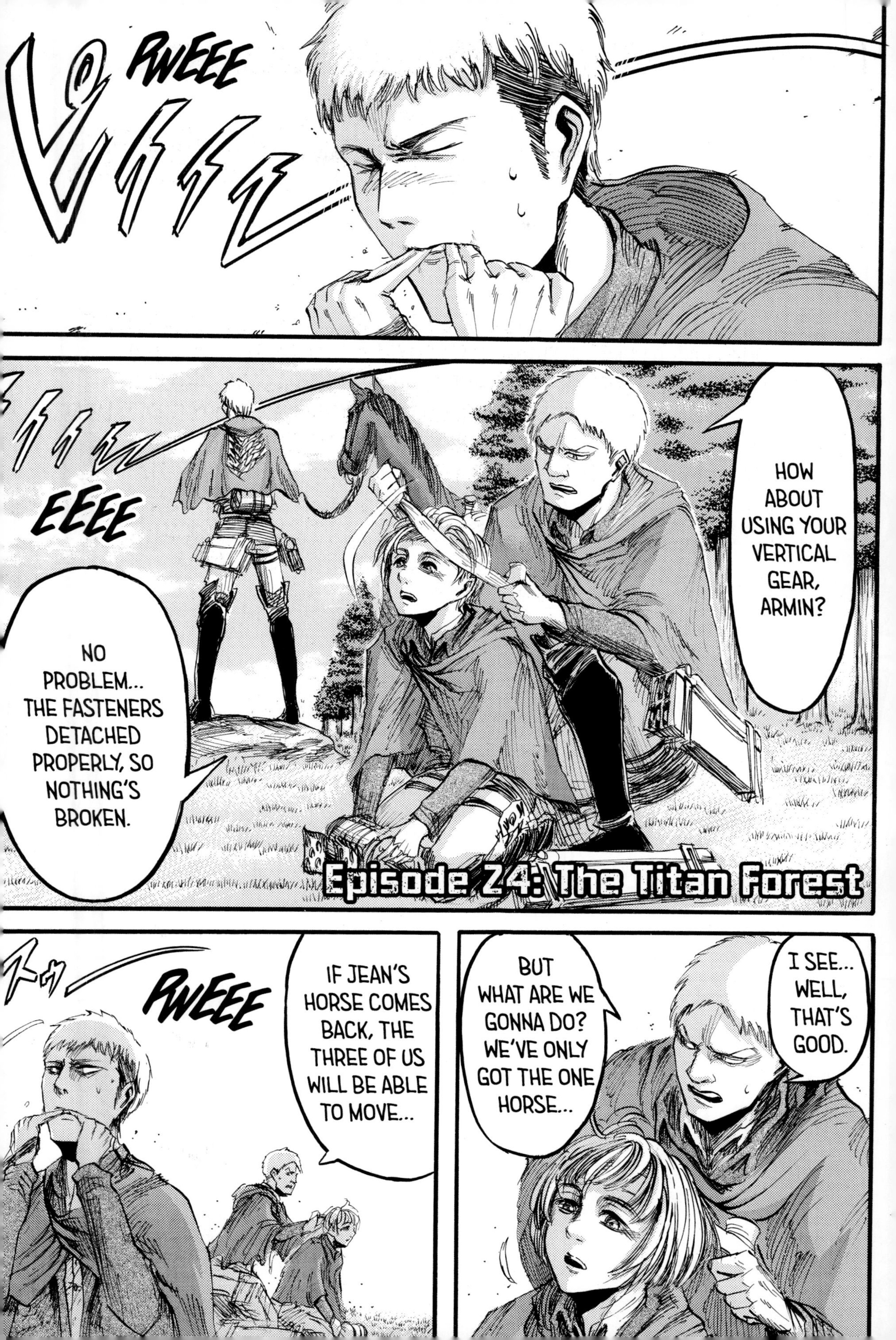
PWEEE
HOW ABOUT USING YOUR VERTICAL GEAR, ARMIN?
EEEE
NO PROBLEM... THE FASTENERS DETACHED PROPERLY, SO NOTHING'S BROKEN.
Episode 24: The Titan Forest
I SEE... WELL, THAT'S GOOD.
BUT WHAT ARE WE GONNA DO? WE'VE ONLY GOT THE ONE HORSE...
IF JEAN'S HORSE COMES BACK, THE THREE OF US WILL BE ABLE TO MOVE...
PWEEE

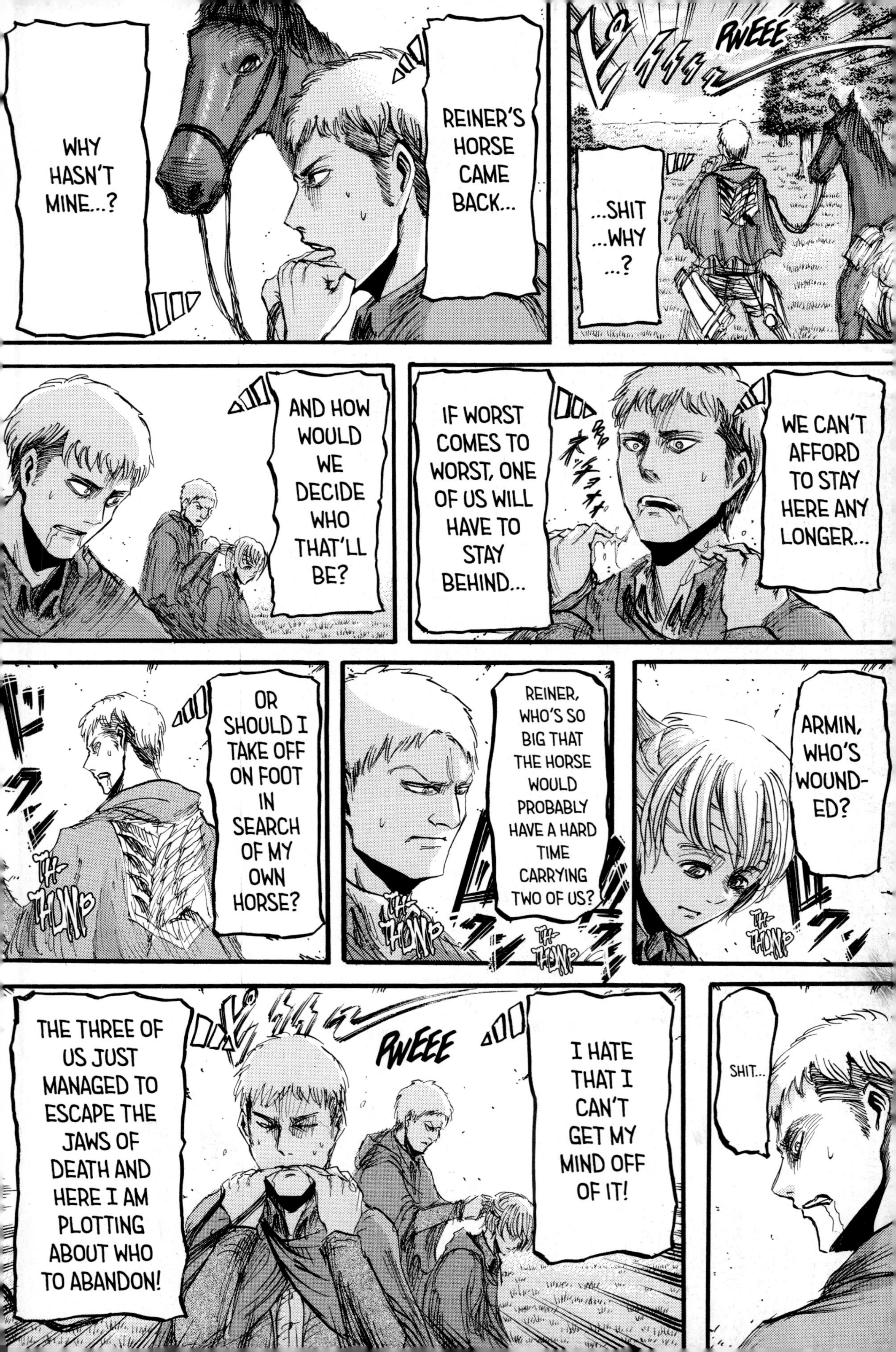
PWEEE
...SHIT ...WHY ...?
REINER'S HORSE CAME BACK...
WHY HASN'T MINE...?
WE CAN'T AFFORD TO STAY HERE ANY LONGER...
IF WORST COMES TO WORST, ONE OF US WILL HAVE TO STAY BEHIND...
AND HOW WOULD WE DECIDE WHO THAT'LL BE?
ARMIN, WHO'S WOUND-ED?
TH-THOMP
REINER, WHO'S SO BIG THAT THE HORSE WOULD PROBABLY HAVE A HARD TIME CARRYING TWO OF US?
TH-THOMP
TH-THOMP
OR SHOULD I TAKE OFF ON FOOT IN SEARCH OF MY OWN HORSE?
TH-THOMP
SHIT...
I HATE THAT I CAN'T GET MY MIND OFF OF IT!
PWEEE
THE THREE OF US JUST MANAGED TO ESCAPE THE JAWS OF DEATH AND HERE I AM PLOTTING ABOUT WHO TO ABANDON!

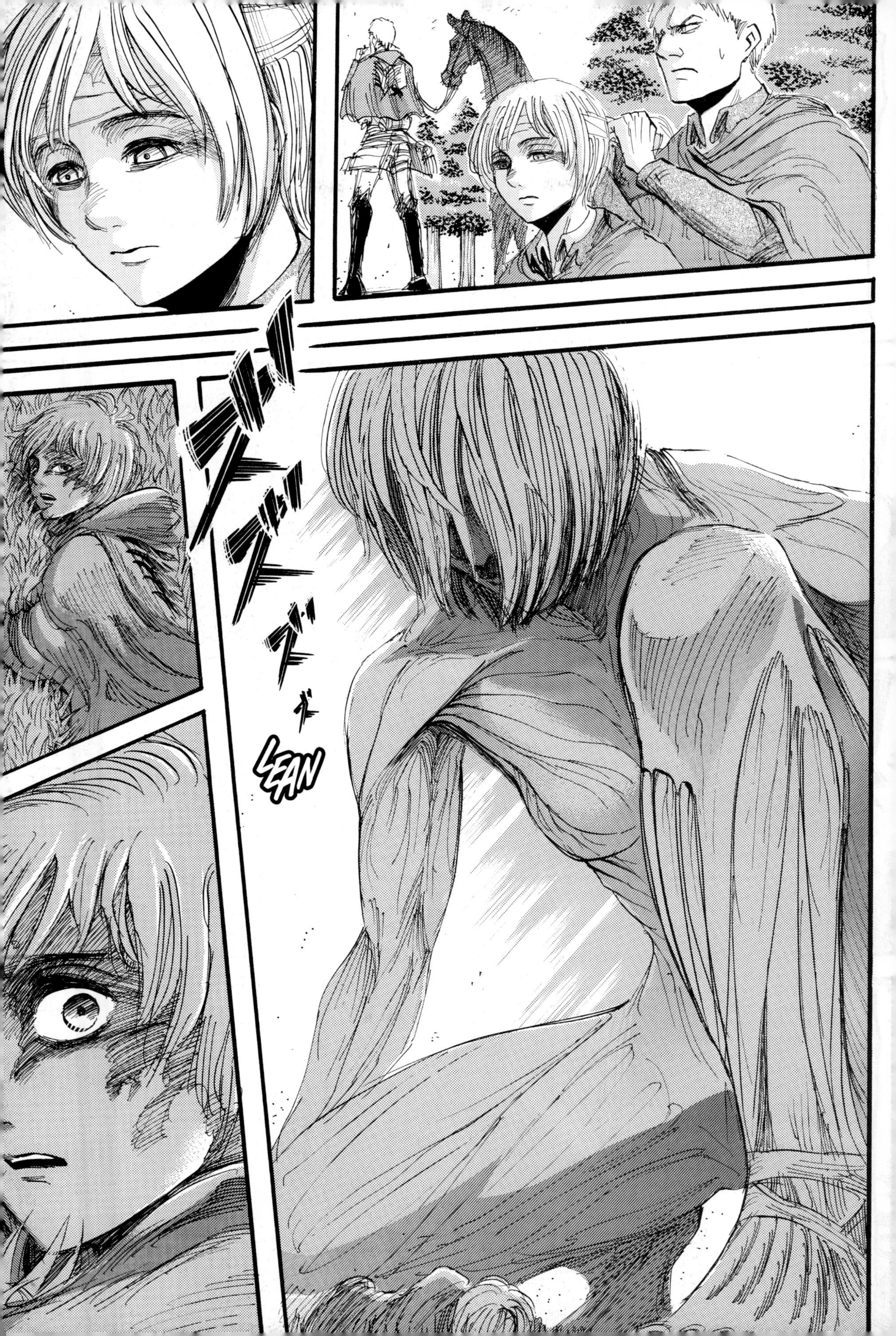
LEAN

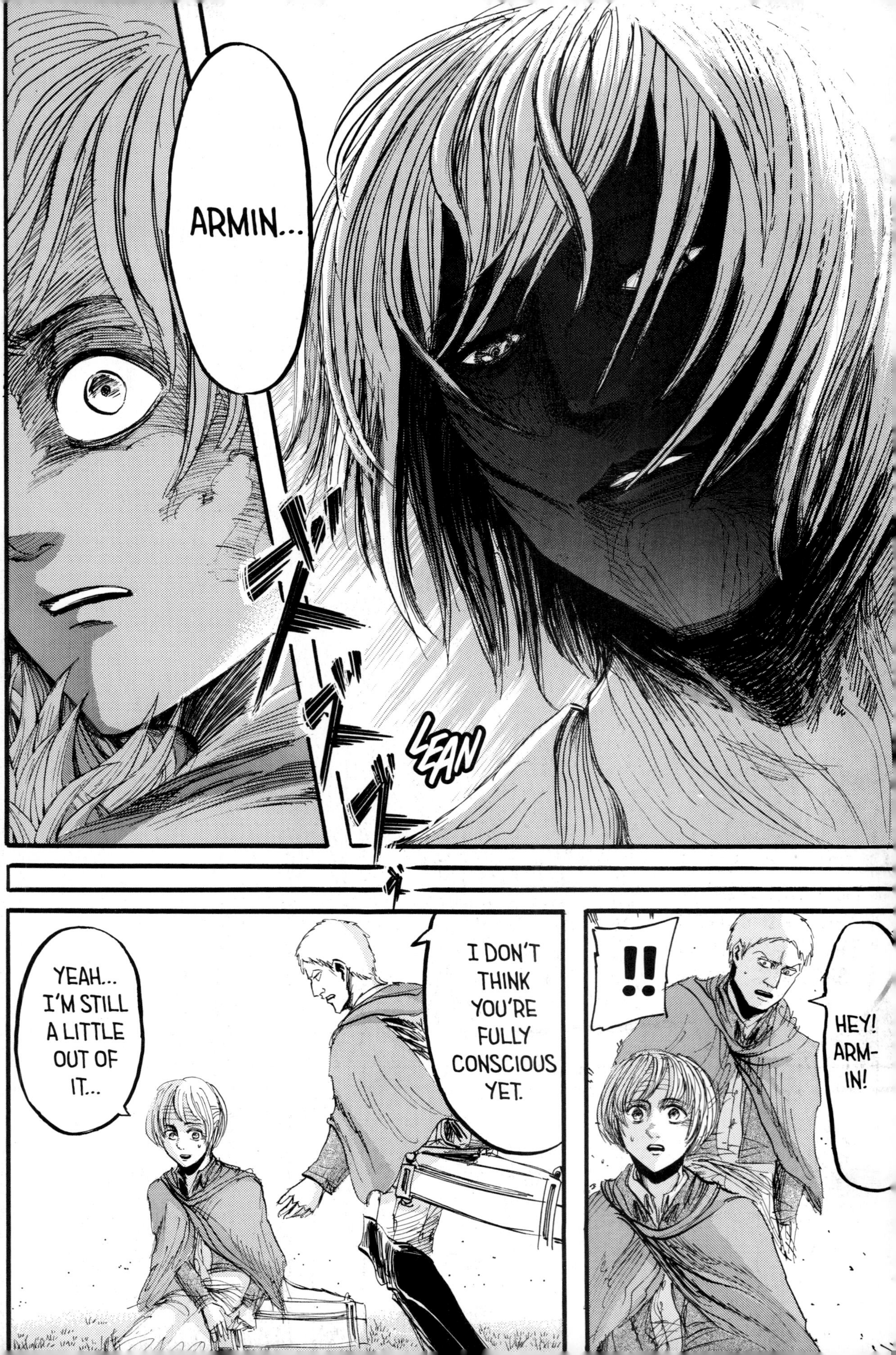
ARMIN...
LEAN
!!
HEY! ARM-IN!
I DON'T THINK YOU'RE FULLY CONSCIOUS YET.
YEAH... I'M STILL A LITTLE OUT OF IT...

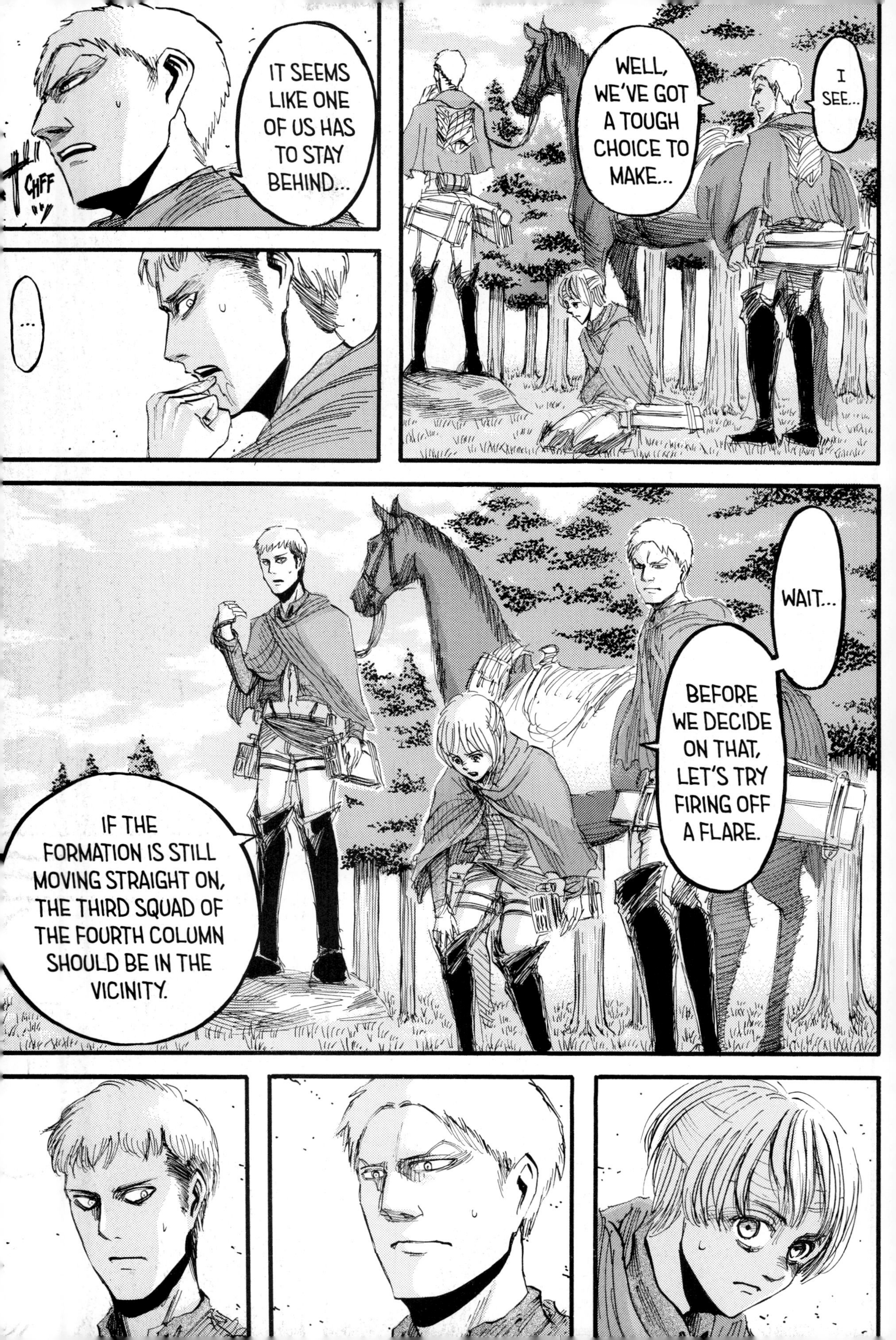

I SEE...
WELL, WE'VE GOT A TOUGH CHOICE TO MAKE...
IT SEEMS LIKE ONE OF US HAS TO STAY BEHIND...
CHFF
...
WAIT...
BEFORE WE DECIDE ON THAT, LET'S TRY FIRING OFF A FLARE.
IF THE FORMATION IS STILL MOVING STRAIGHT ON, THE THIRD SQUAD OF THE FOURTH COLUMN SHOULD BE IN THE VICINITY.

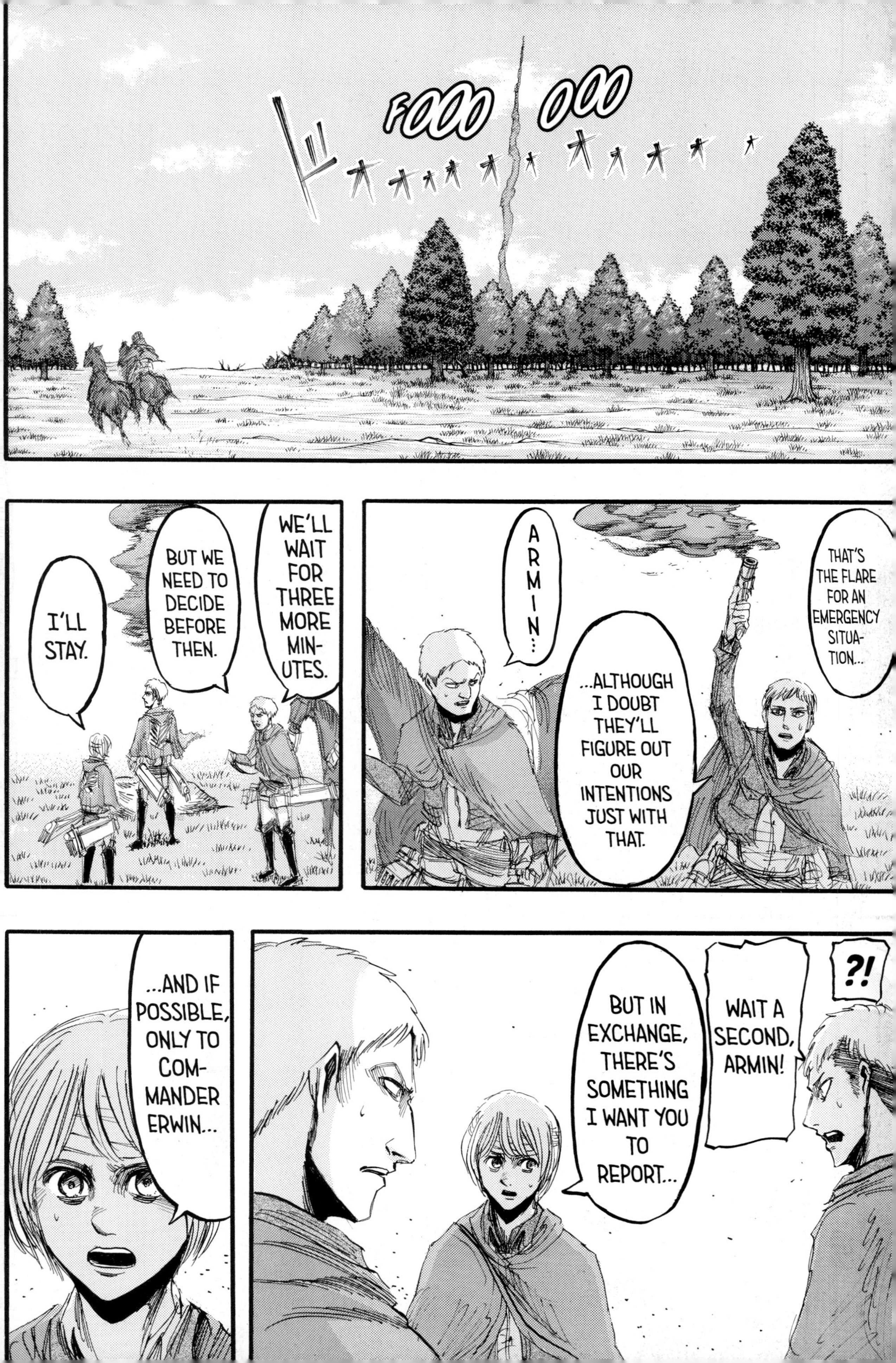

FOOO OOO
THAT'S THE FLARE FOR AN EMERGENCY SITUATION...
...ALTHOUGH I DOUBT THEY'LL FIGURE OUT OUR INTENTIONS JUST WITH THAT.
ARMIN...
WE'LL WAIT FOR THREE MORE MINUTES.
BUT WE NEED TO DECIDE BEFORE THEN.
I'LL STAY.
?!
WAIT A SECOND, ARMIN!
BUT IN EXCHANGE, THERE'S SOMETHING I WANT YOU TO REPORT...
...AND IF POSSIBLE, ONLY TO COMMANDER ERWIN...

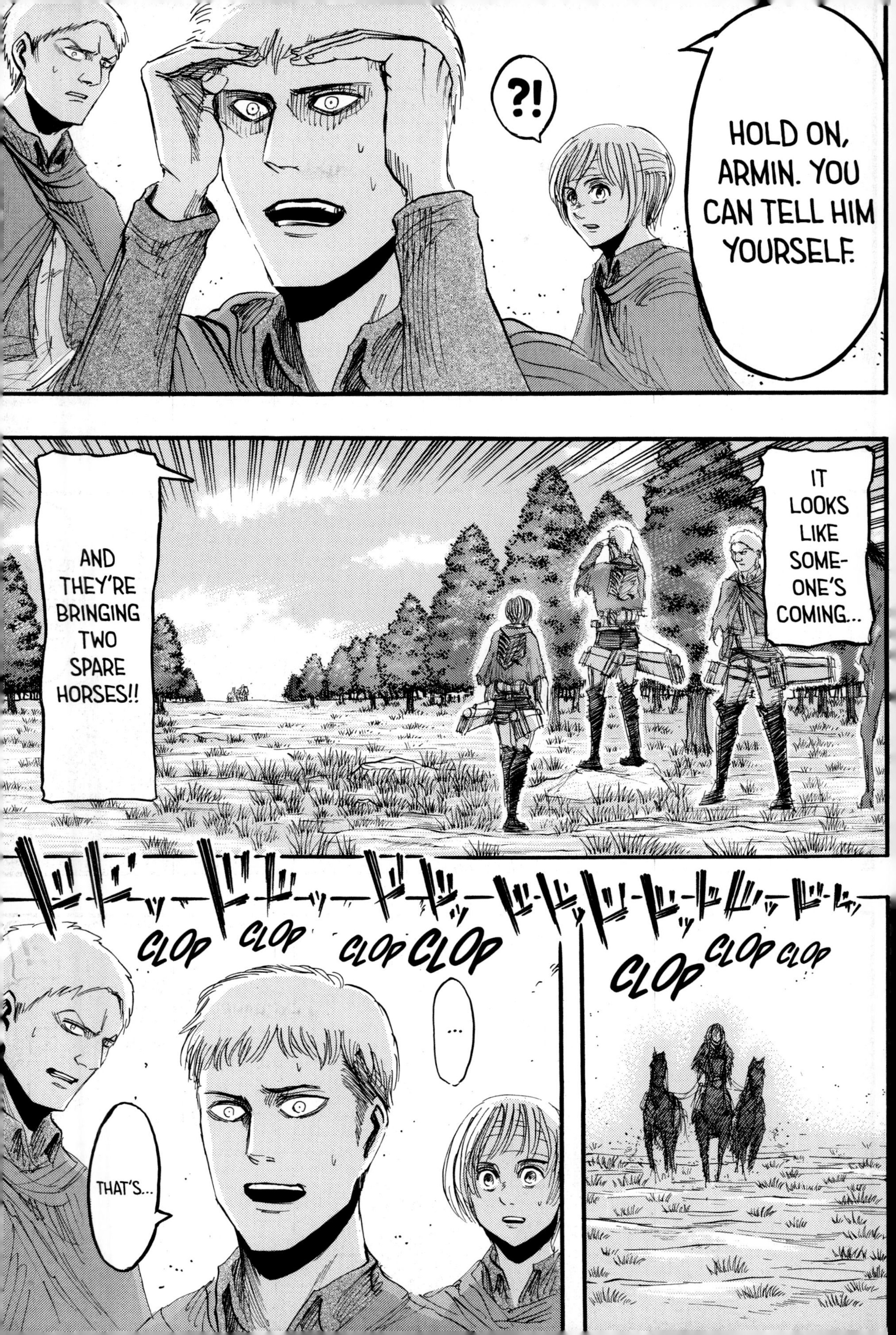
HOLD ON, ARMIN. YOU CAN TELL HIM YOURSELF.
?!
IT LOOKS LIKE SOME-ONE'S COMING...
AND THEY'RE BRINGING TWO SPARE HORSES!!
CLOP CLOP CLOP
CLOP
CLOP CLOP CLOP CLOP
...
THAT'S...

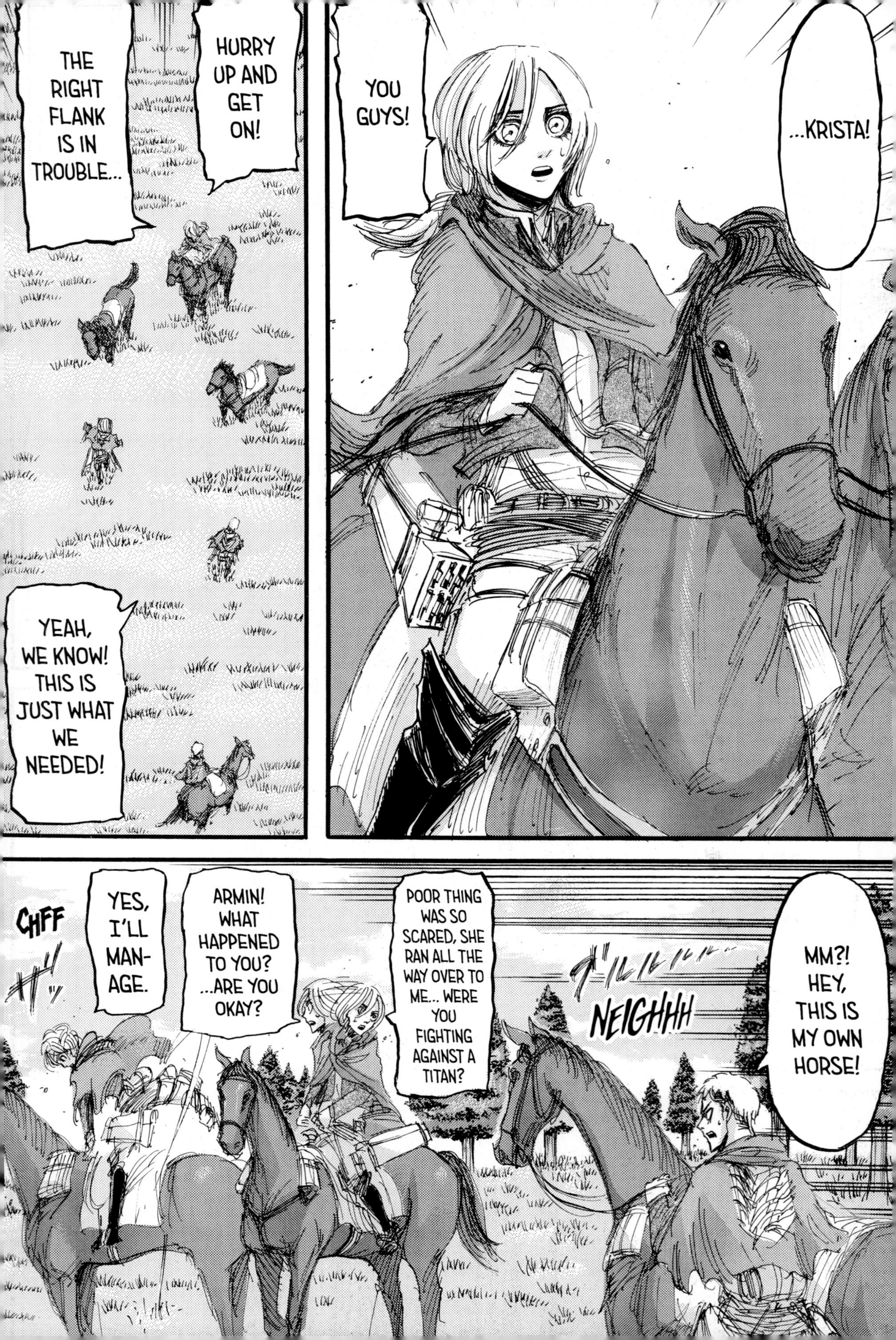
...KRISTA!
YOU GUYS!
HURRY UP AND GET ON!
THE RIGHT FLANK IS IN TROUBLE...
YEAH, WE KNOW! THIS IS JUST WHAT WE NEEDED!
MM?! HEY, THIS IS MY OWN HORSE!
NEIGHHH
POOR THING WAS SO SCARED, SHE RAN ALL THE WAY OVER TO ME... WERE YOU FIGHTING AGAINST A TITAN?
ARMIN! WHAT HAPPENED TO YOU? ...ARE YOU OKAY?
YES, I'LL MAN-AGE.
CHFF

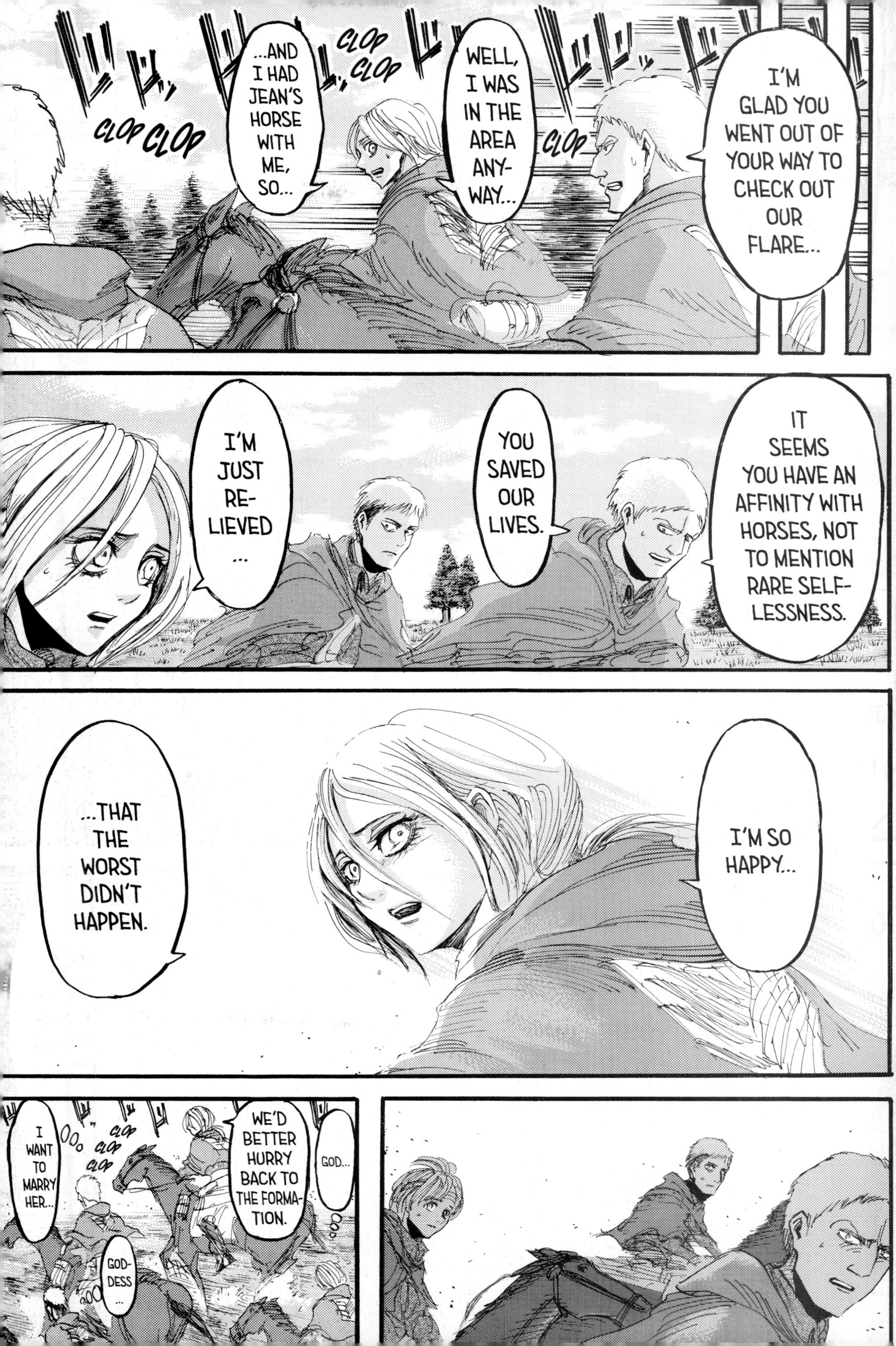
I'M GLAD YOU WENT OUT OF YOUR WAY TO CHECK OUT OUR FLARE...
CLOP
WELL, I WAS IN THE AREA ANYWAY...
CLOP CLOP
...AND I HAD JEAN'S HORSE WITH ME, SO...
CLOP CLOP
IT SEEMS YOU HAVE AN AFFINITY WITH HORSES, NOT TO MENTION RARE SELFLESSNESS.
YOU SAVED OUR LIVES.
I'M JUST RELIEVED...
I'M SO HAPPY...
...THAT THE WORST DIDN'T HAPPEN.
GOD...
WE'D BETTER HURRY BACK TO THE FORMATION.
CLOP CLOP CLOP
I WANT TO MARRY HER...
GODDESS...

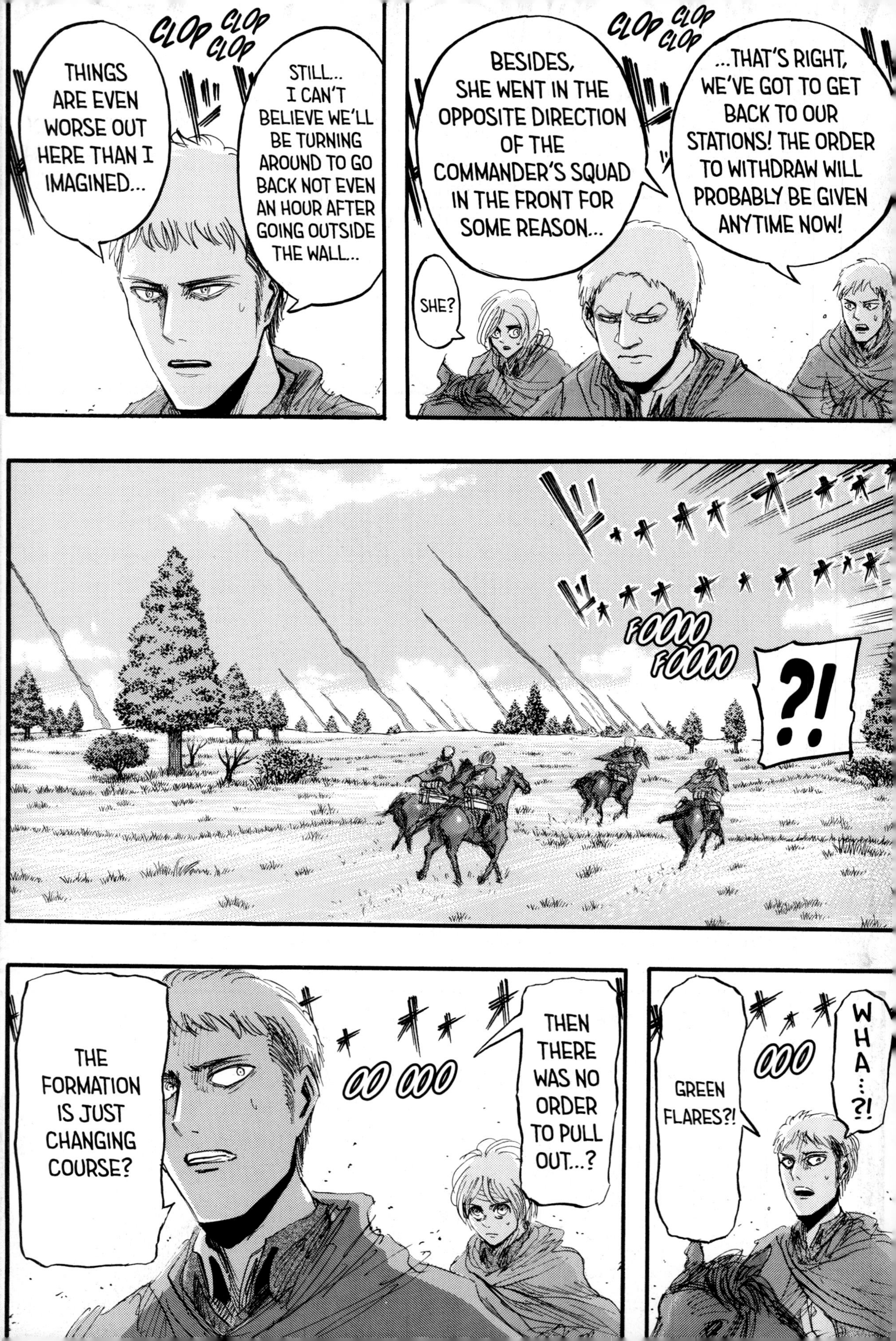
CLOP CLOP CLOP
...THAT'S RIGHT, WE'VE GOT TO GET BACK TO OUR STATIONS! THE ORDER TO WITHDRAW WILL PROBABLY BE GIVEN ANYTIME NOW!
BESIDES, SHE WENT IN THE OPPOSITE DIRECTION OF THE COMMANDER'S SQUAD IN THE FRONT FOR SOME REASON...
SHE?
CLOP CLOP CLOP
STILL... I CAN'T BELIEVE WE'LL BE TURNING AROUND TO GO BACK NOT EVEN AN HOUR AFTER GOING OUTSIDE THE WALL...
THINGS ARE EVEN WORSE OUT HERE THAN I IMAGINED...
FOOOO FOOOO
?!
WHA...?!
OOO
GREEN FLARES?!
THEN THERE WAS NO ORDER TO PULL OUT...?
OO OOO
THE FORMATION IS JUST CHANGING COURSE?

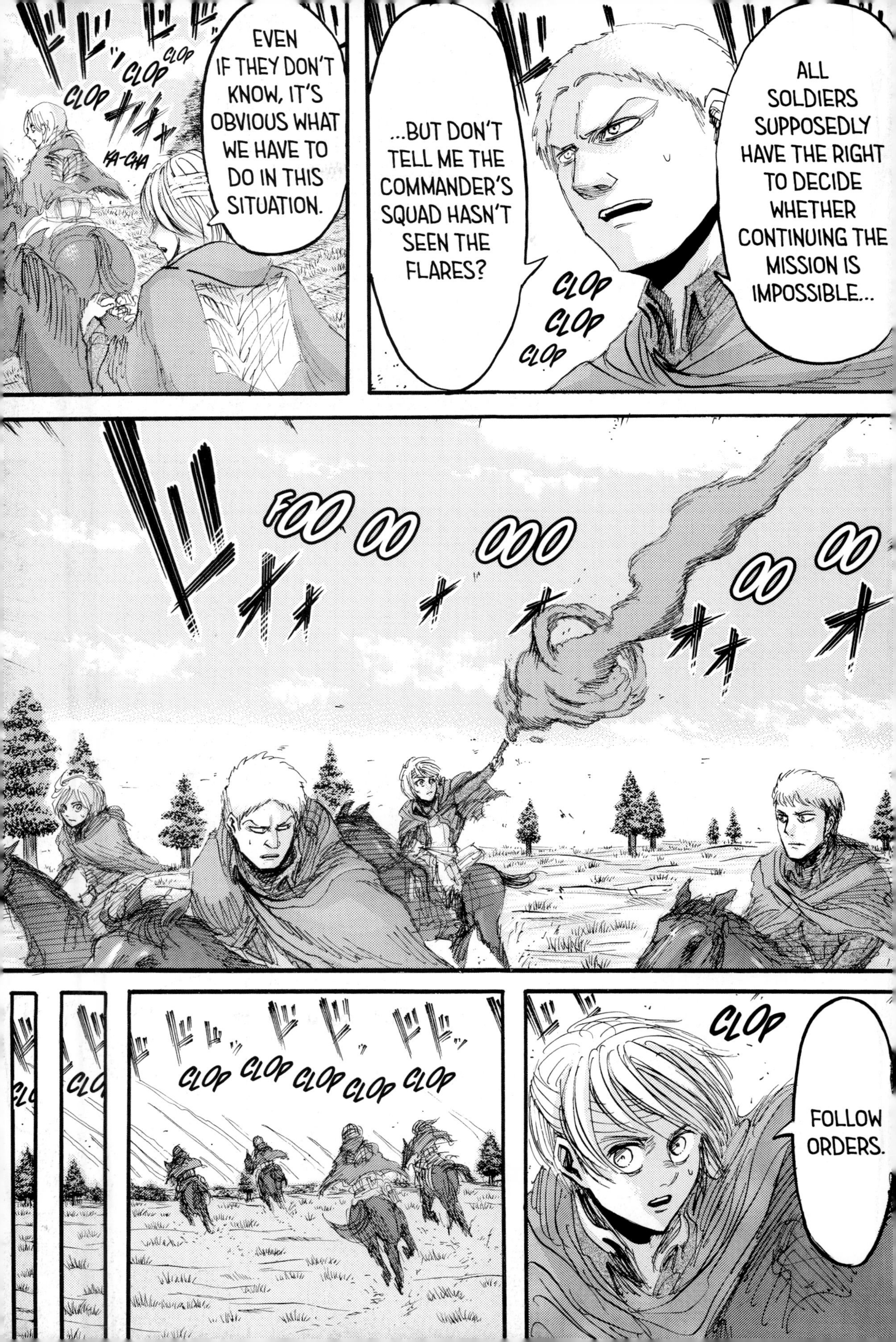
ALL SOLDIERS SUPPOSEDLY HAVE THE RIGHT TO DECIDE WHETHER CONTINUING THE MISSION IS IMPOSSIBLE...
...BUT DON'T TELL ME THE COMMANDER'S SQUAD HASN'T SEEN THE FLARES?
CLOP CLOP CLOP
CLOP CLOP CLOP
KA-CHA
EVEN IF THEY DON'T KNOW, IT'S OBVIOUS WHAT WE HAVE TO DO IN THIS SITUATION.
FOOO OO OOO OO OO
CLOP
FOLLOW ORDERS.
CLOP CLOP CLOP CLOP CLOP
CLO
CL

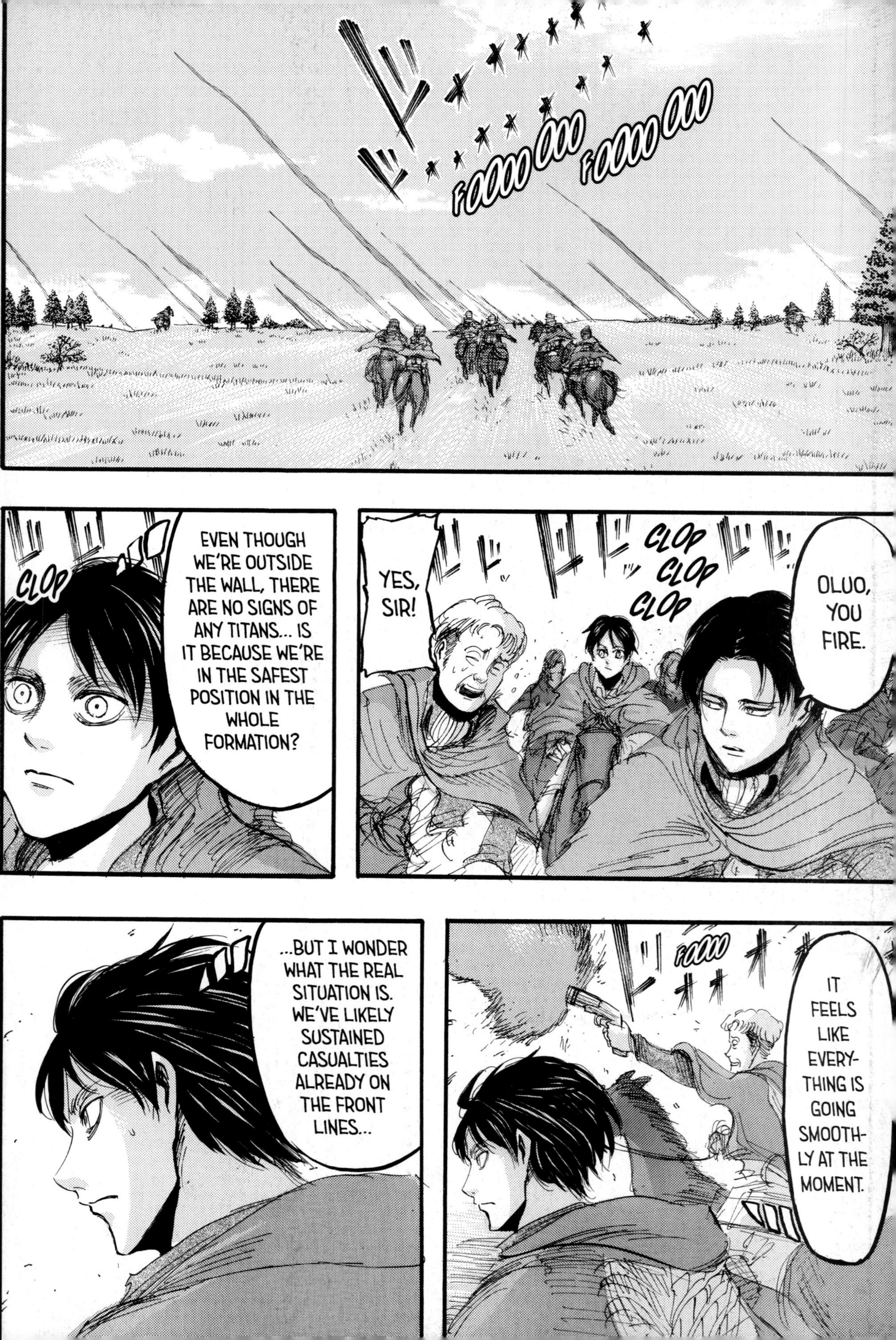

FOOOO OOO
FOOOO OOO
OLUO, YOU FIRE.
CLOP CLOP CLOP
YES, SIR!
CLOP
EVEN THOUGH WE'RE OUTSIDE THE WALL, THERE ARE NO SIGNS OF ANY TITANS... IS IT BECAUSE WE'RE IN THE SAFEST POSITION IN THE WHOLE FORMATION?
FOOOO
IT FEELS LIKE EVERY-THING IS GOING SMOOTH-LY AT THE MOMENT.
...BUT I WONDER WHAT THE REAL SITUATION IS. WE'VE LIKELY SUSTAINED CASUALTIES ALREADY ON THE FRONT LINES...

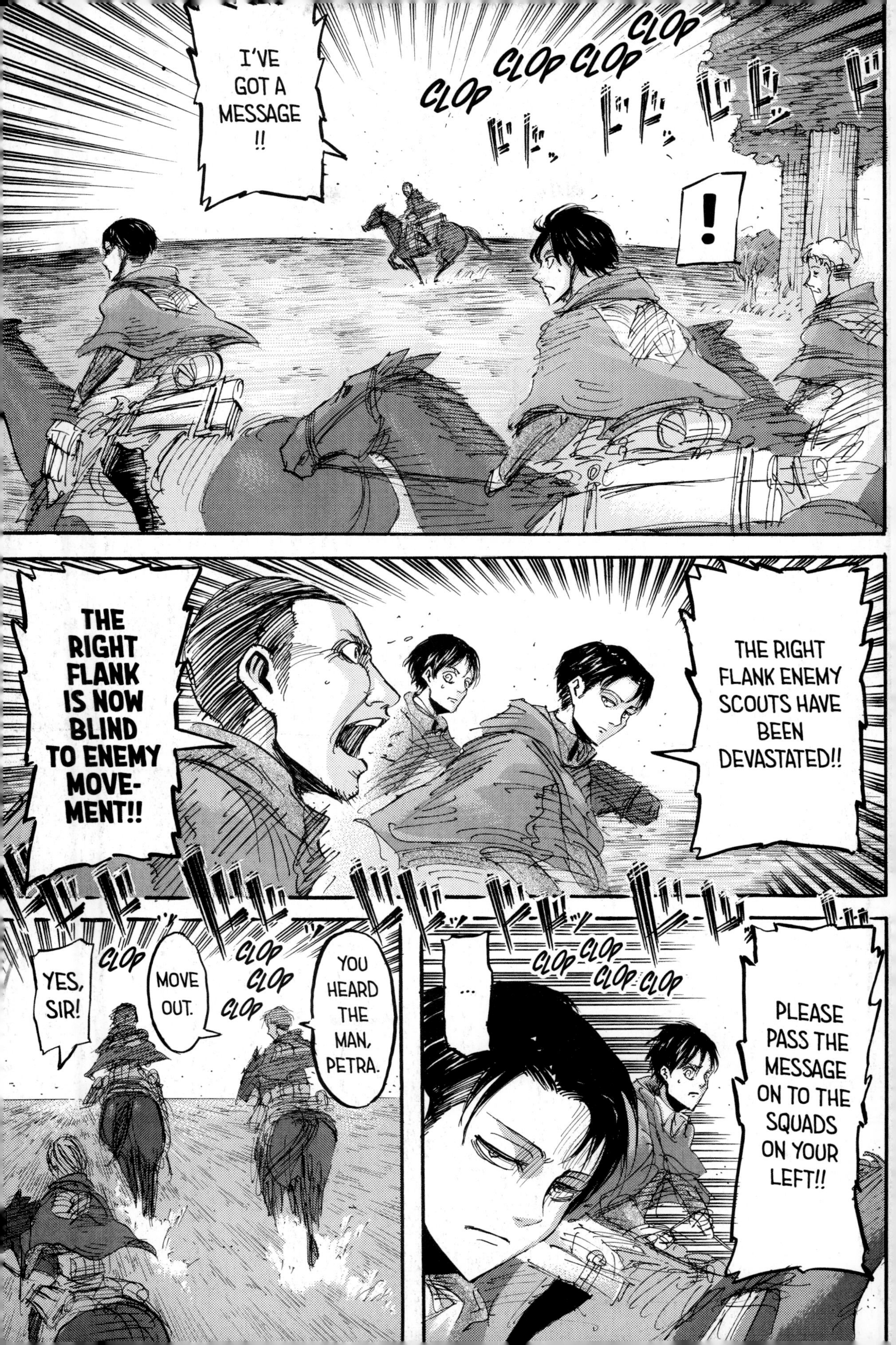
CLOP CLOP CLOP CLOP
I'VE GOT A MESSAGE !!
!
THE RIGHT FLANK ENEMY SCOUTS HAVE BEEN DEVASTATED!!
THE RIGHT FLANK IS NOW BLIND TO ENEMY MOVEMENT!!
PLEASE PASS THE MESSAGE ON TO THE SQUADS ON YOUR LEFT!!
CLOP CLOP CLOP CLOP
...
YOU HEARD THE MAN, PETRA.
CLOP CLOP CLOP
MOVE OUT.
CLOP
YES, SIR!

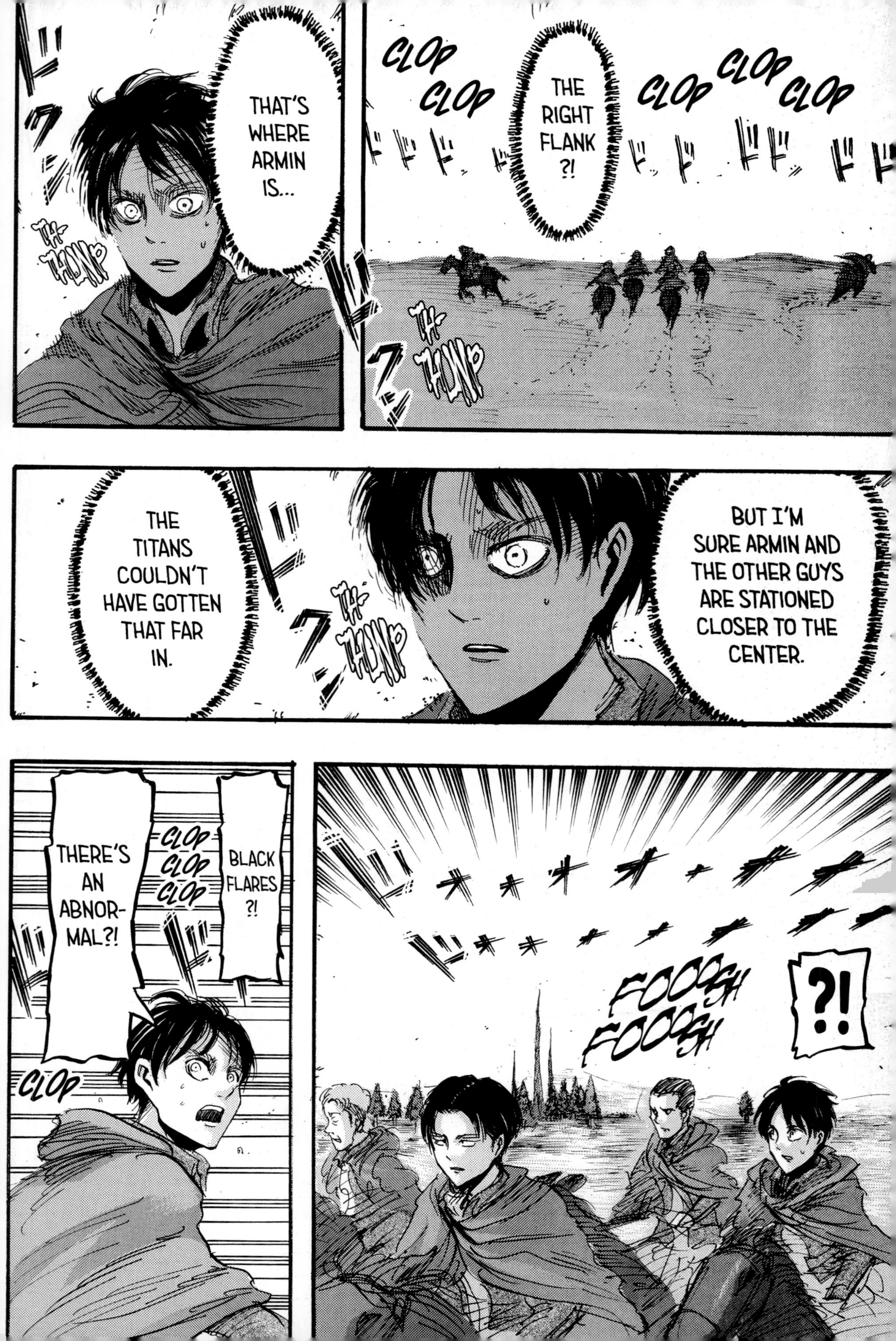

CLOP CLOP
THE RIGHT FLANK?!
CLOP CLOP CLOP
THA THUMP
THAT'S WHERE ARMIN IS...
THA THUMP
BUT I'M SURE ARMIN AND THE OTHER GUYS ARE STATIONED CLOSER TO THE CENTER.
THA THUMP
THE TITANS COULDN'T HAVE GOTTEN THAT FAR IN.
?!
FOOOSH FOOOSH
BLACK FLARES?!
CLOP CLOP CLOP
THERE'S AN ABNORMAL?!
CLOP

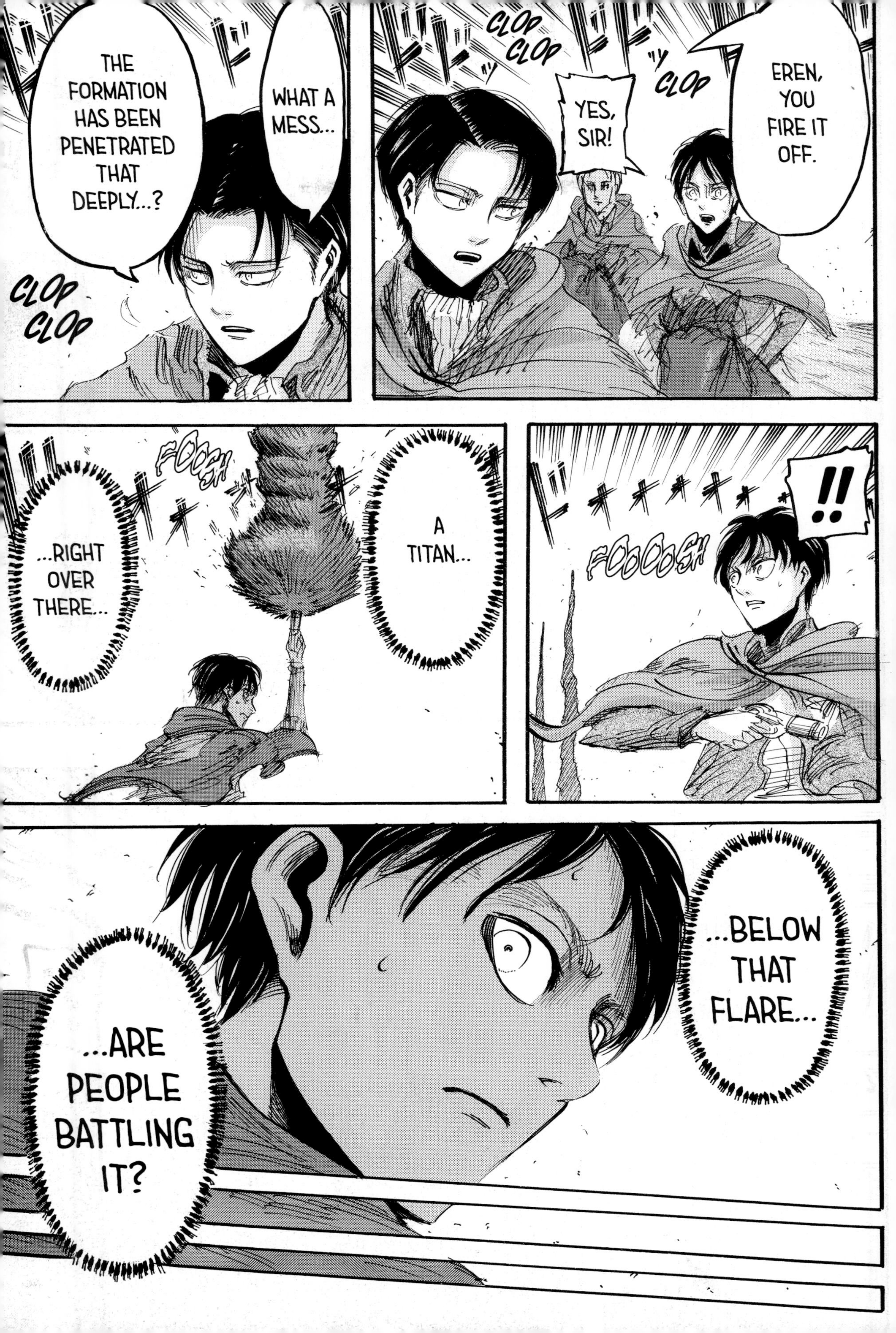
CLOP CLOP
EREN, YOU FIRE IT OFF.
CLOP
YES, SIR!
WHAT A MESS...
THE FORMATION HAS BEEN PENETRATED THAT DEEPLY...?
CLOP CLOP
!!
FOOOOSH
A TITAN...
FOOSH
...RIGHT OVER THERE...
...BELOW THAT FLARE...
...ARE PEOPLE BATTLING IT?

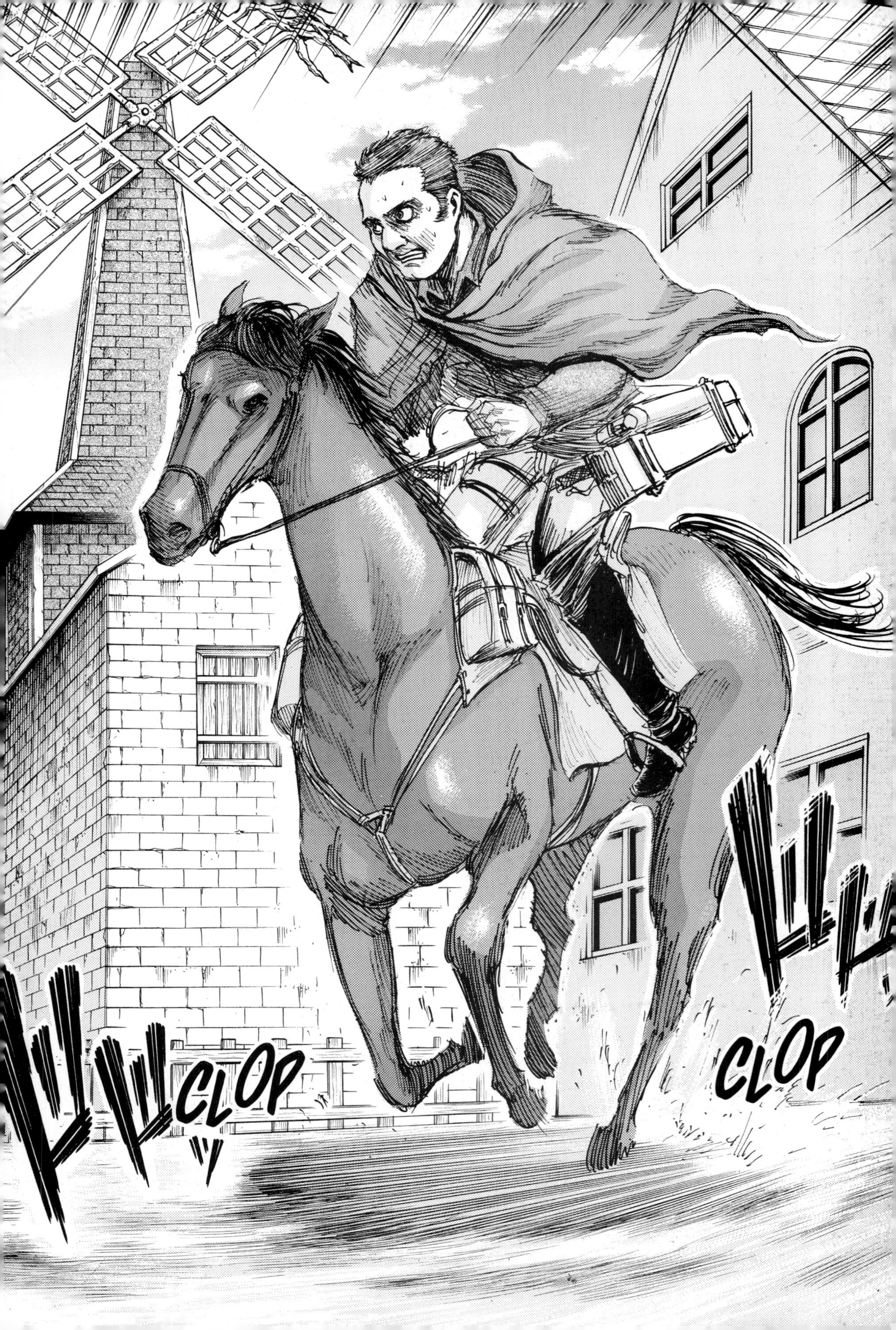
CLOP
CLOP

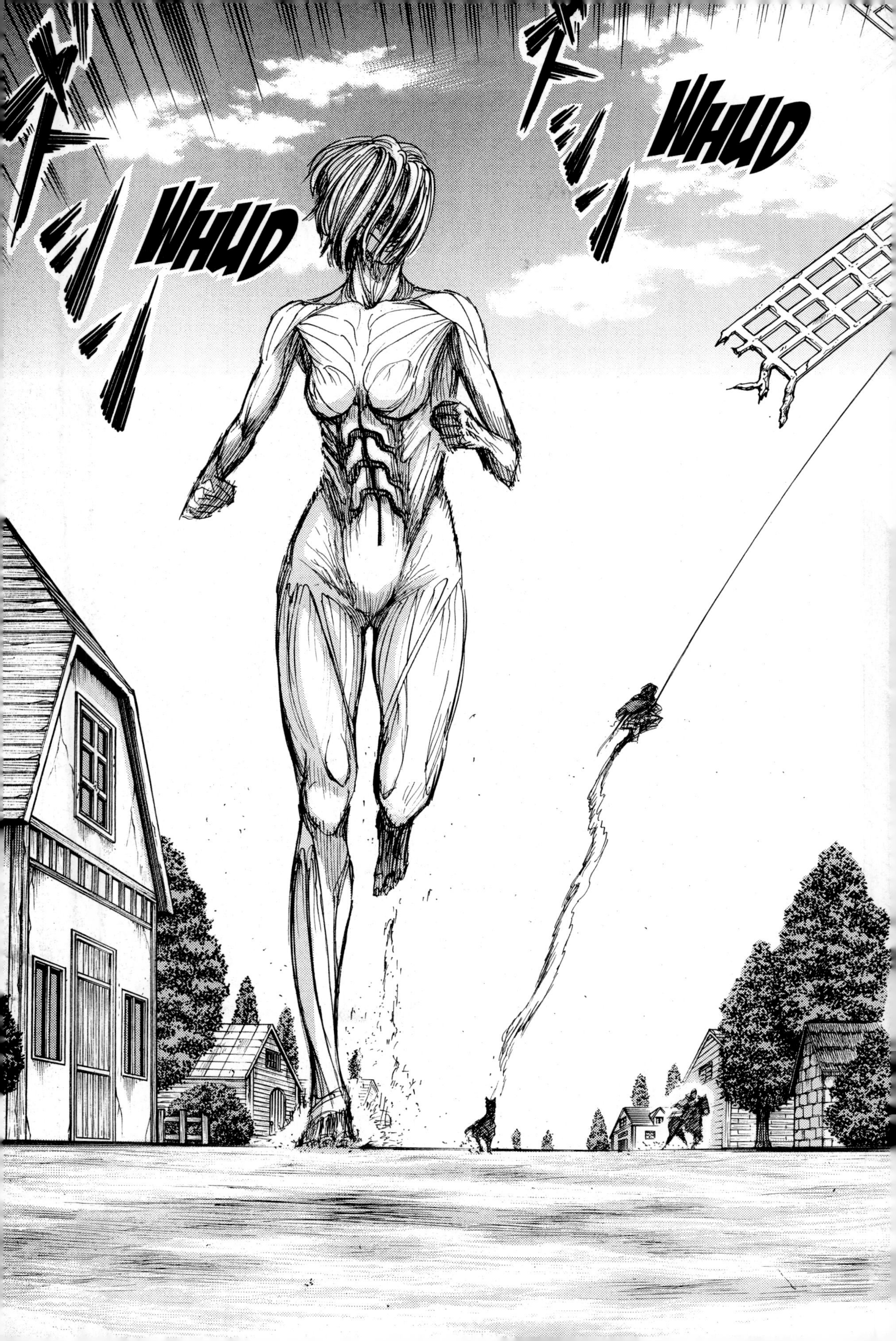
WHUD
WHUD

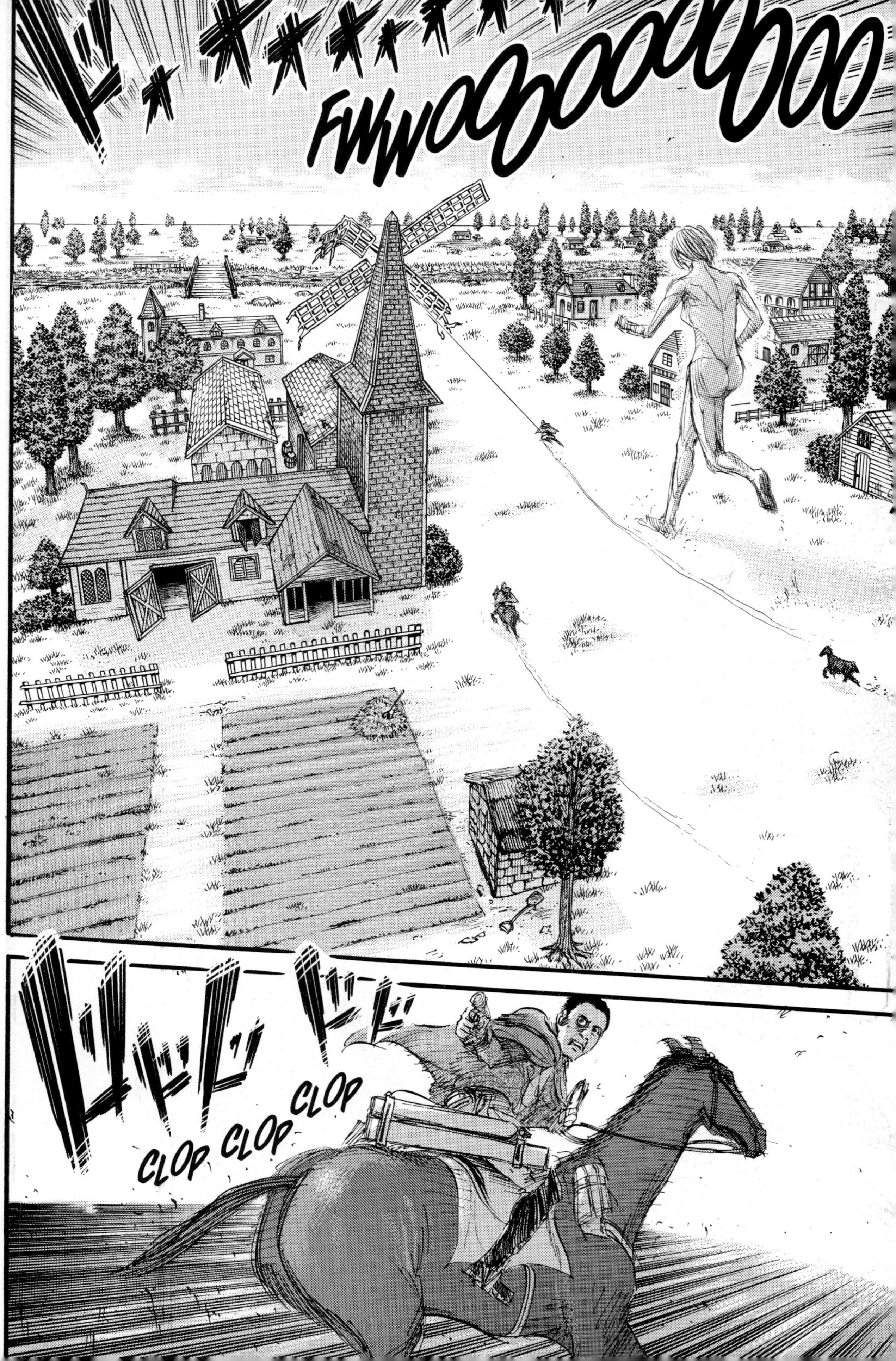
FWWOOOOOOOO
CLOP CLOP CLOP

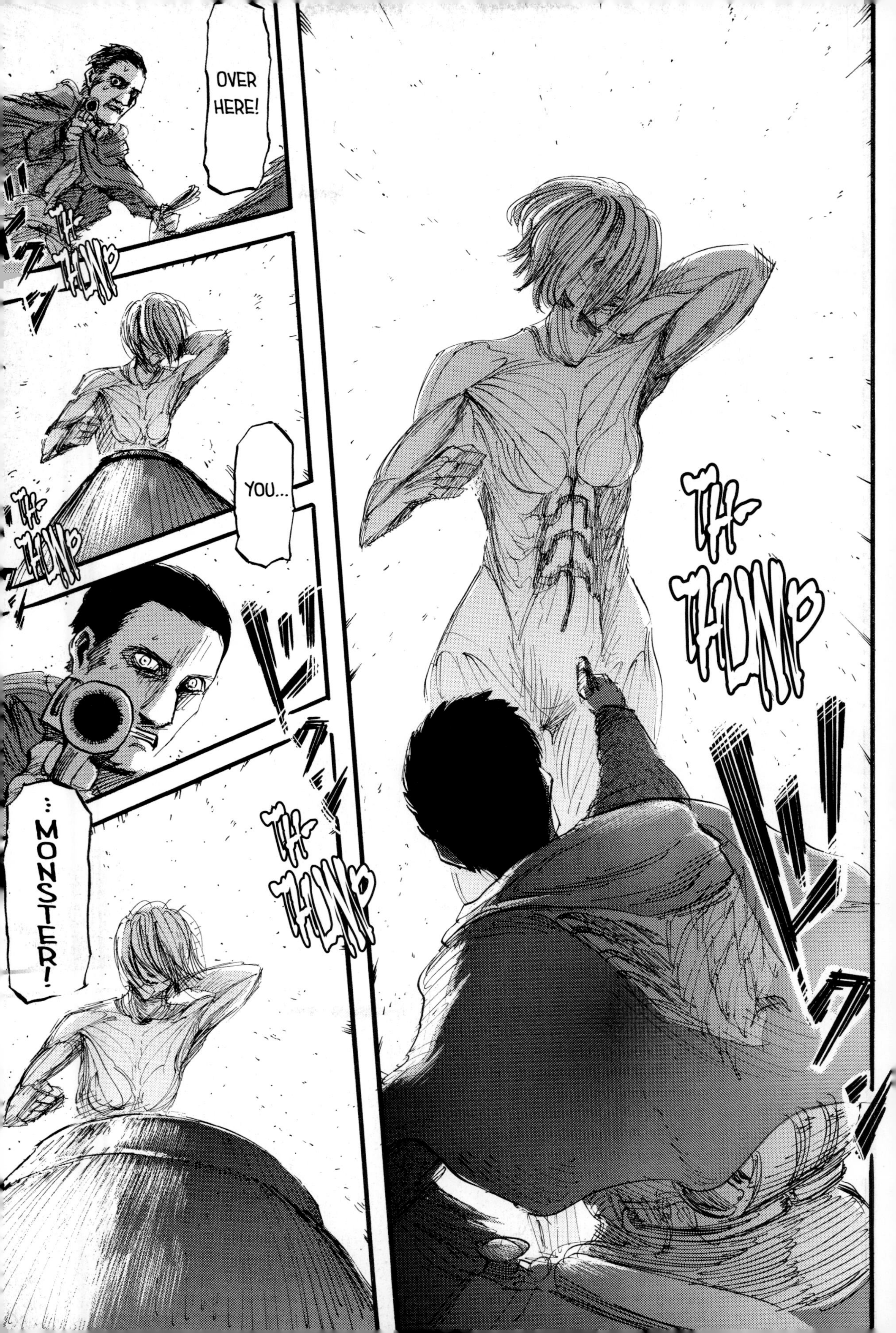
THA-THUMP
OVER HERE!
THA-THUMP
THA-THUMP
YOU...
...MONSTER!
THA-THUMP

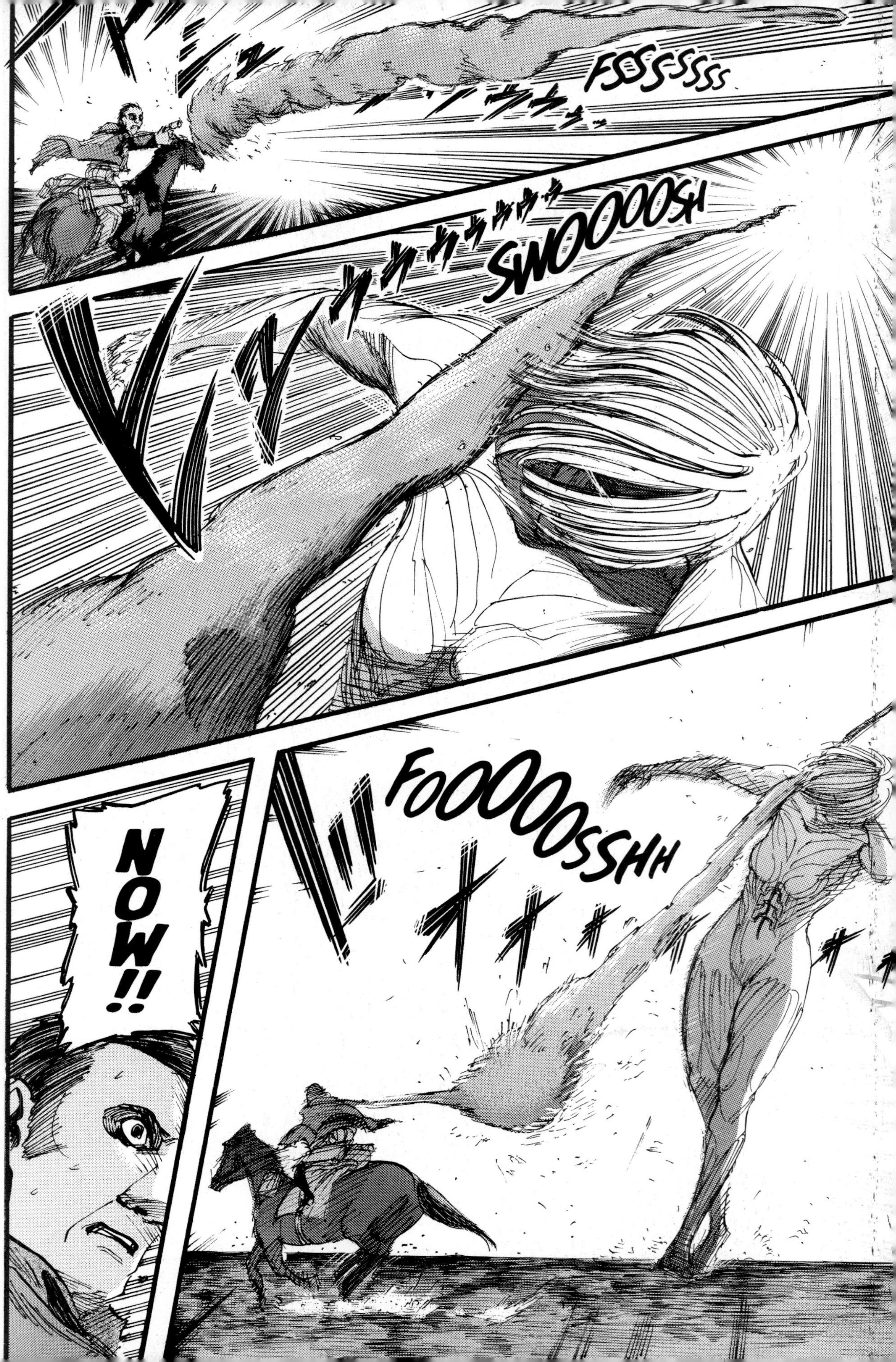
FSSS-SSSS
SWOOOOSH
FOOOOOSSHH
NOW!!

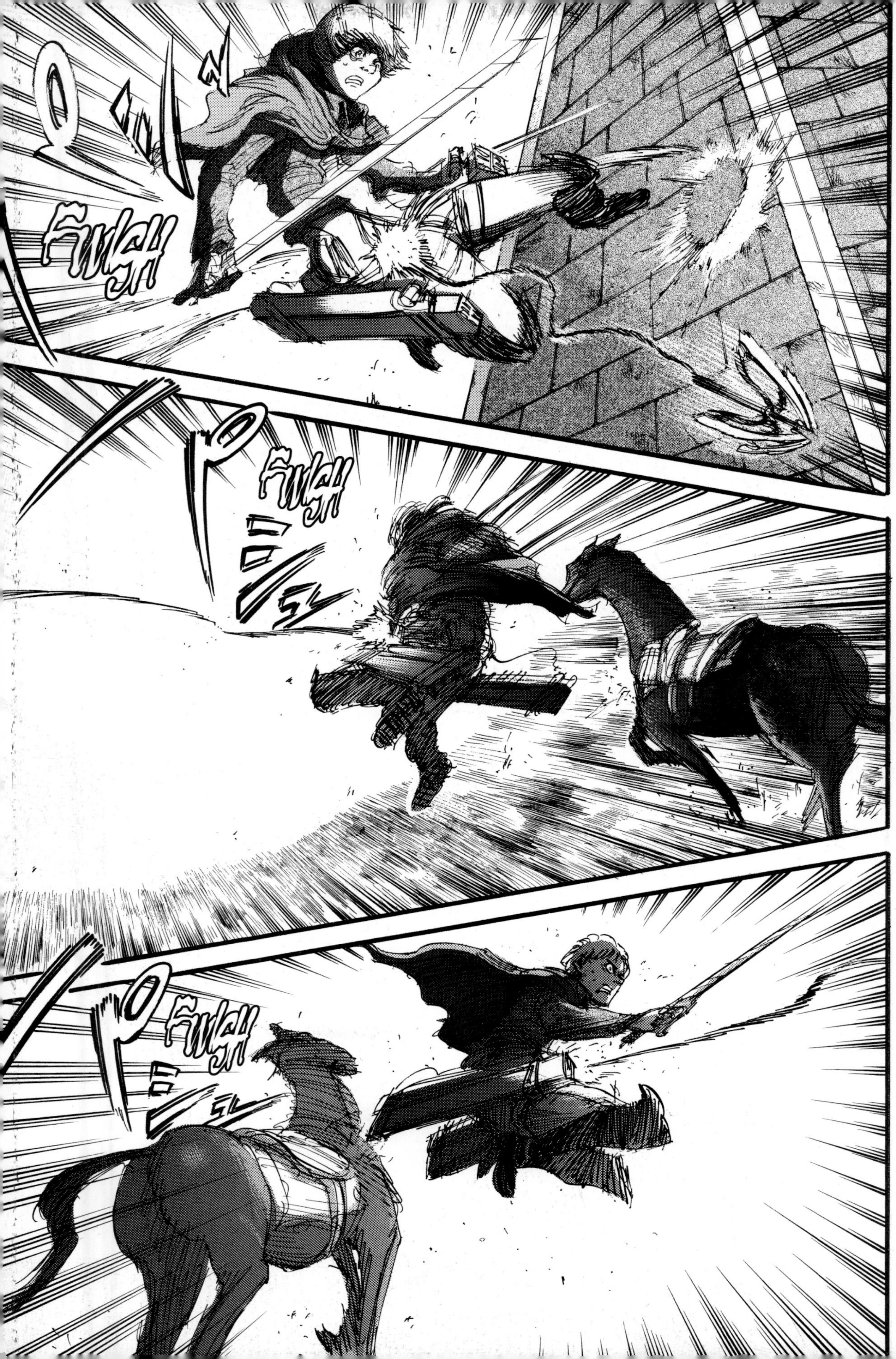
FWISH
FWISH
FWISH

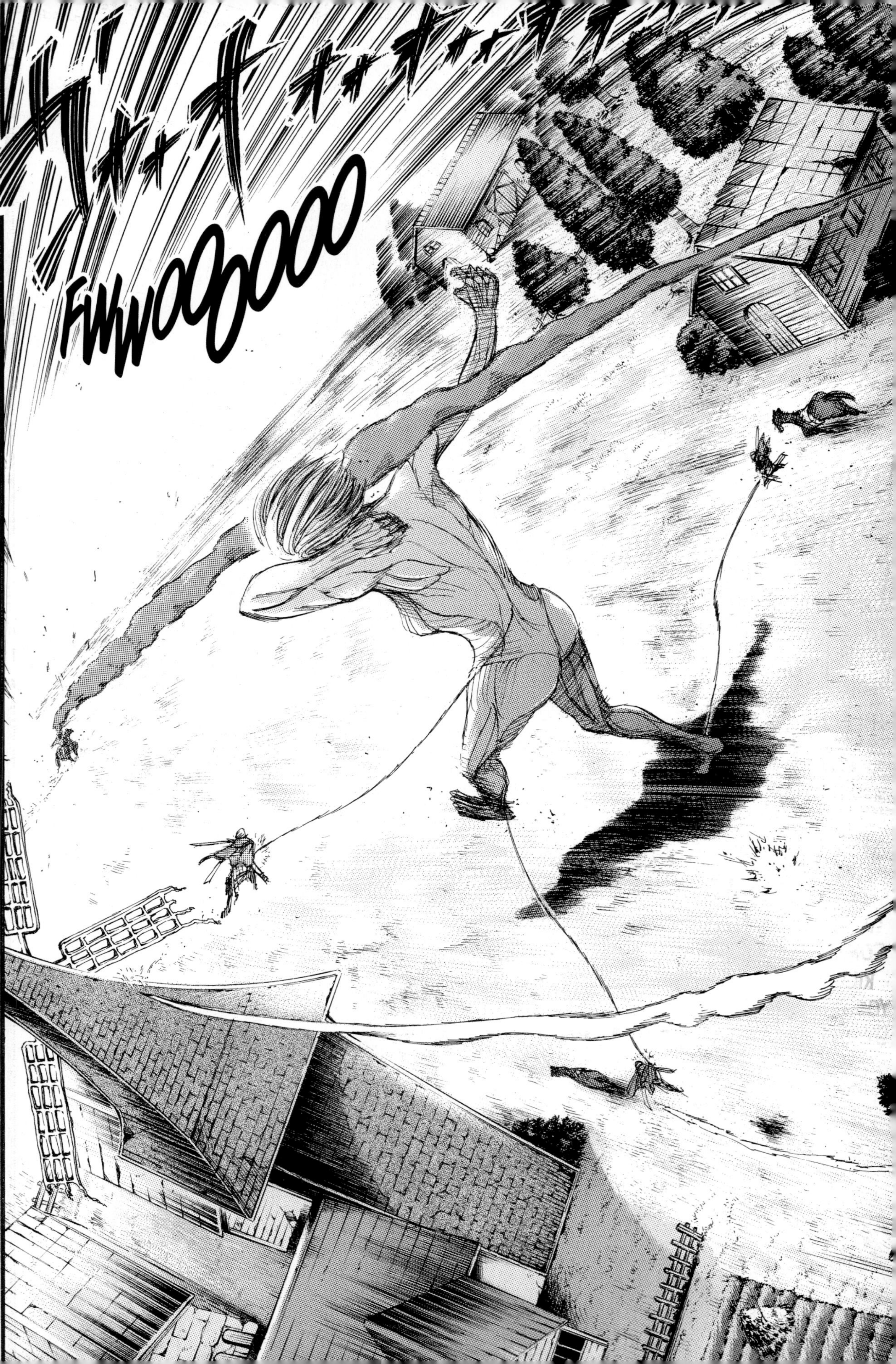
FWOOOOOO

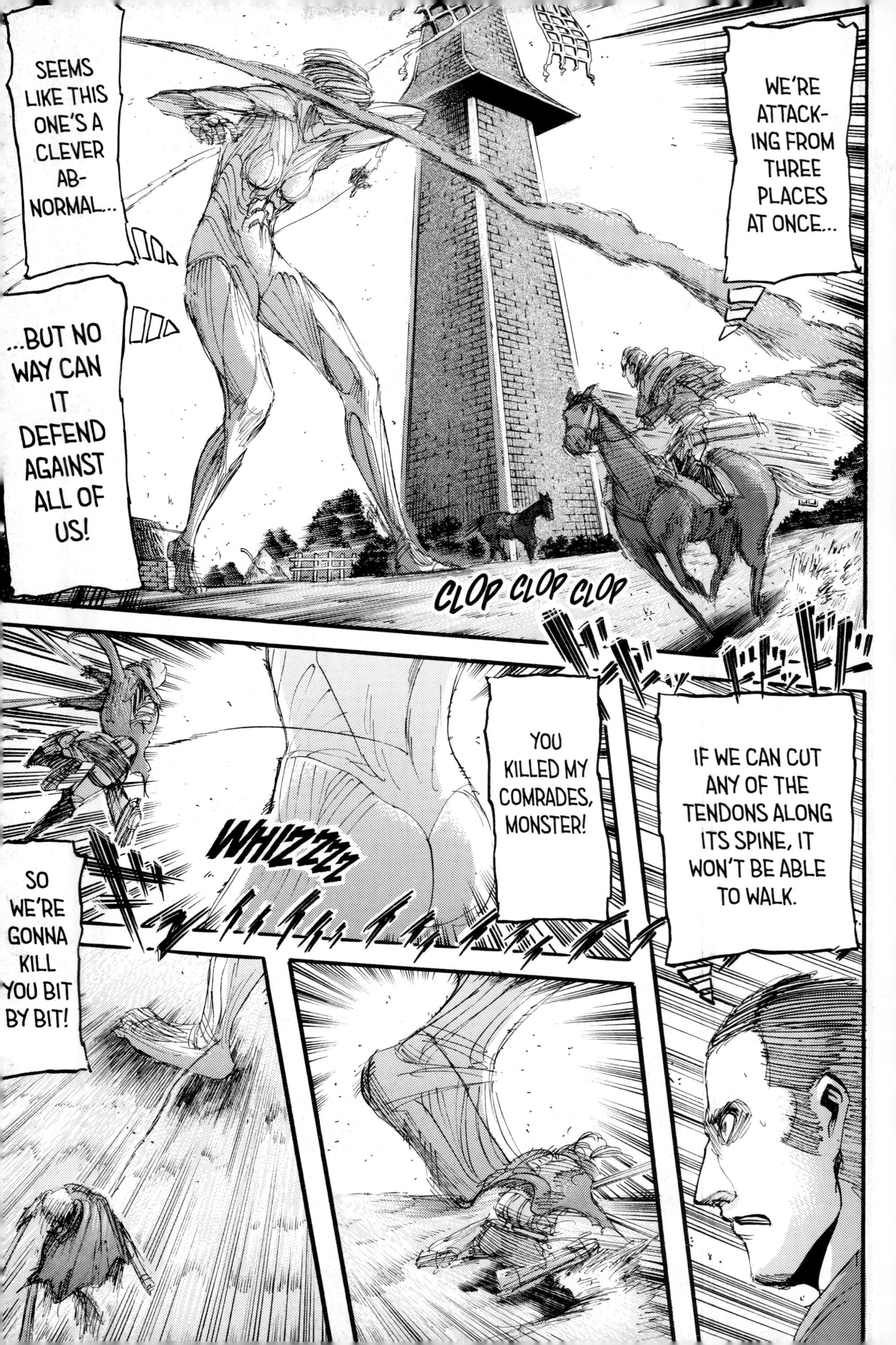
WE'RE ATTACK-ING FROM THREE PLACES AT ONCE...
SEEMS LIKE THIS ONE'S A CLEVER AB-NORMAL...
...BUT NO WAY CAN IT DEFEND AGAINST ALL OF US!
CLOP CLOP CLOP
IF WE CAN CUT ANY OF THE TENDONS ALONG ITS SPINE, IT WON'T BE ABLE TO WALK.
YOU KILLED MY COMRADES, MONSTER!
WHIZZZZ
SO WE'RE GONNA KILL YOU BIT BY BIT!

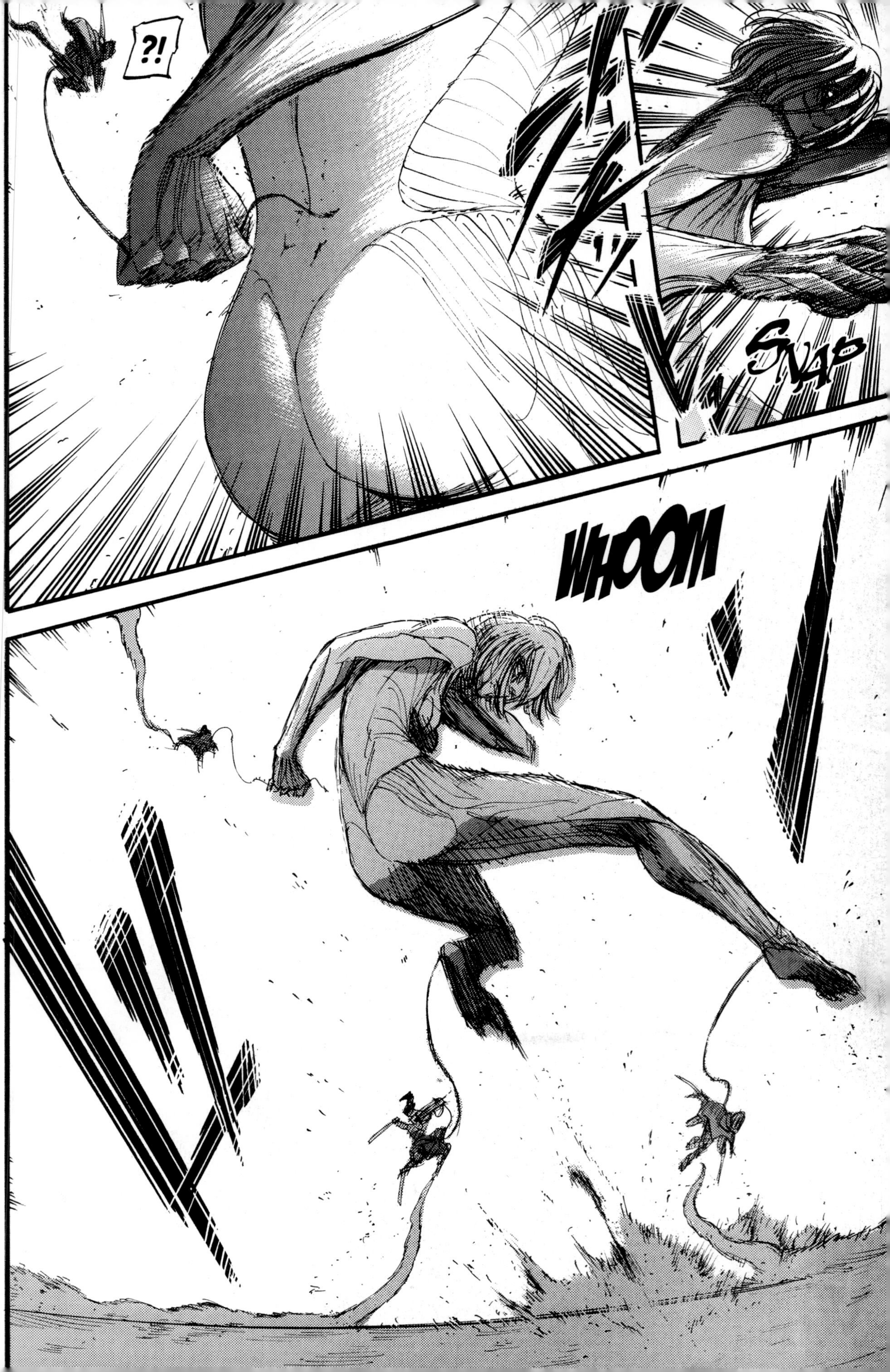
SNAP
?!
WHOOM

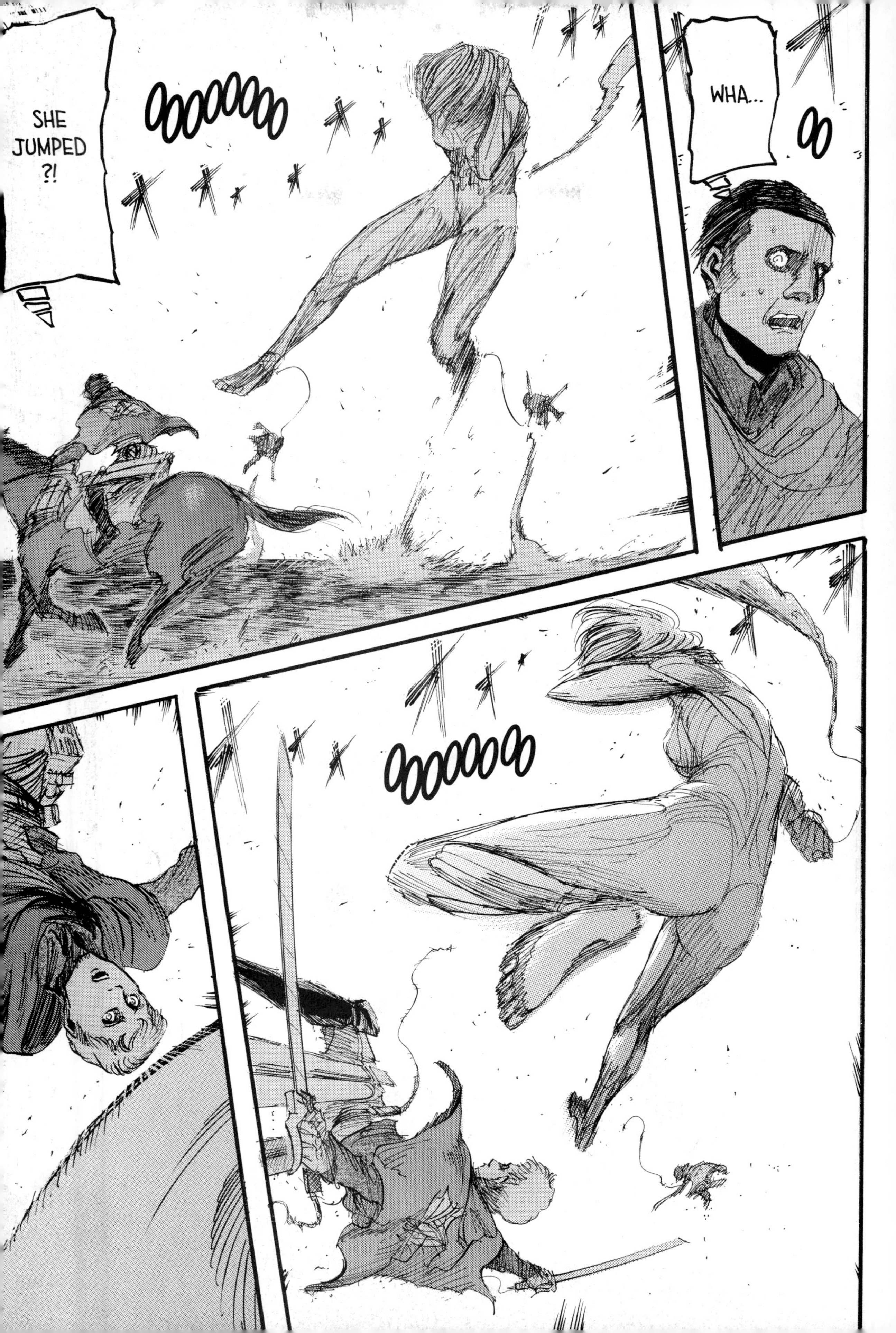
WHA...
OO
SHE JUMPED ?!
OOOOOOOO
OOOOOOO

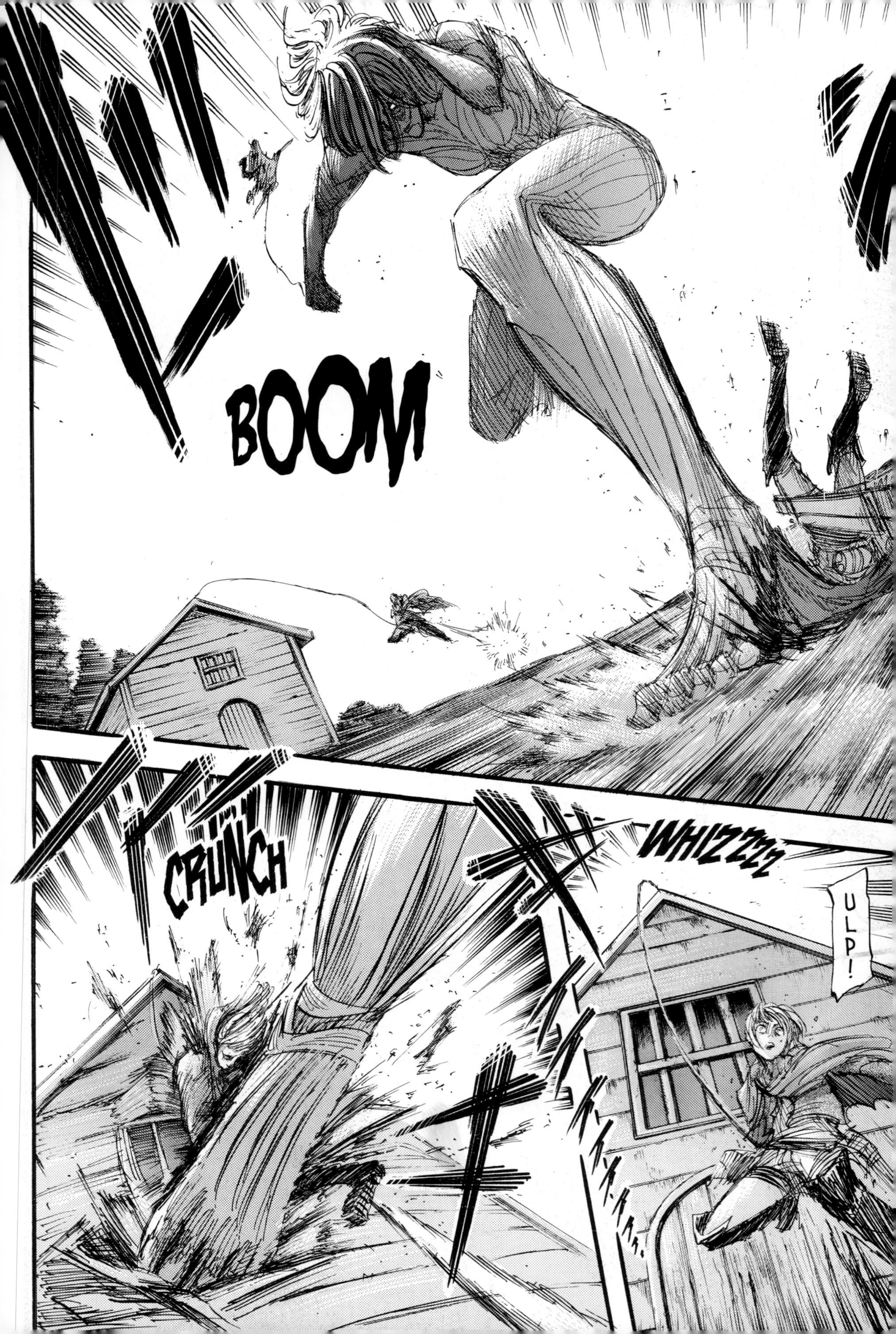
BOOM
WHIZZZZ
ULP!
CRUNCH

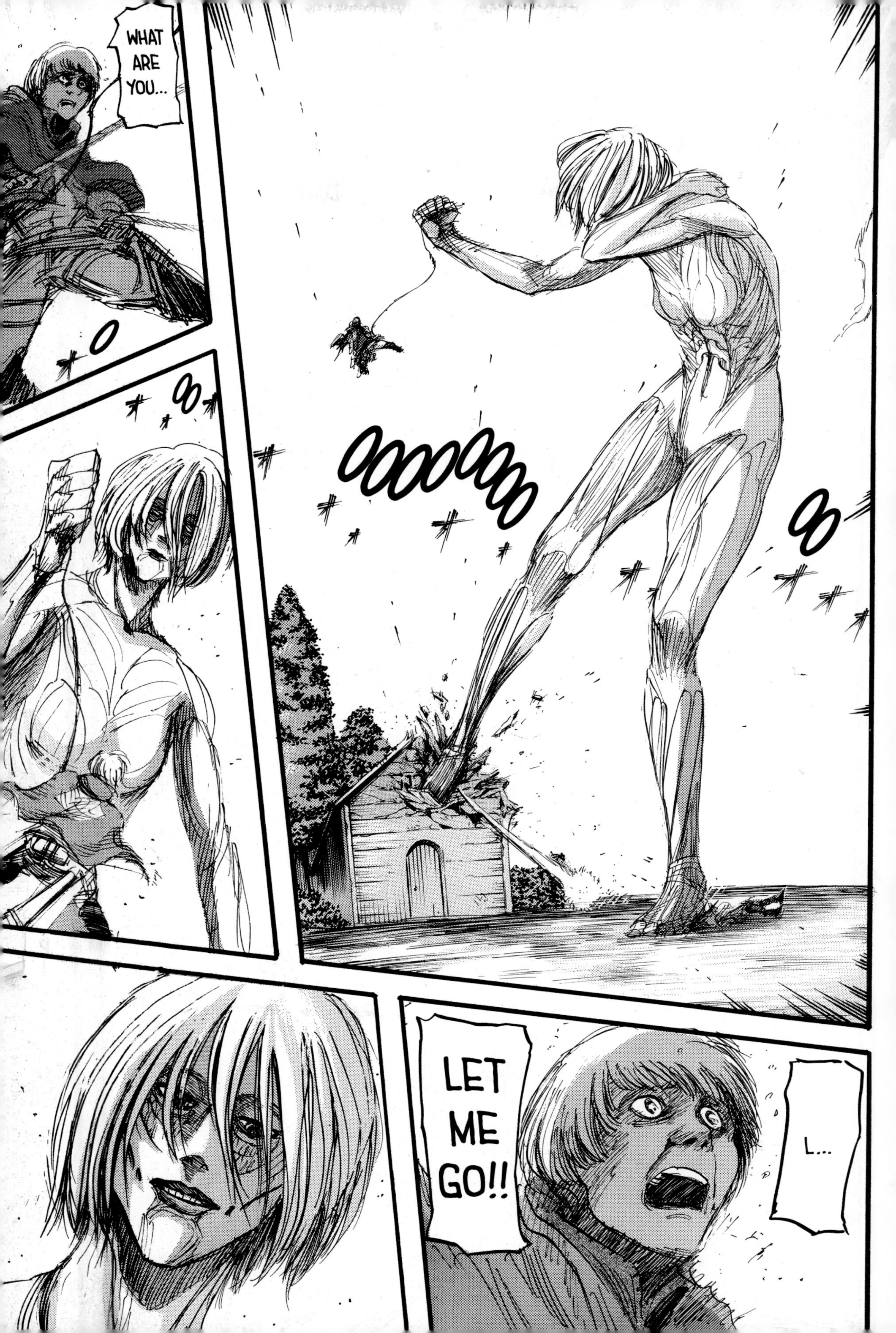
WHAT ARE YOU...
I...
LET ME GO!!

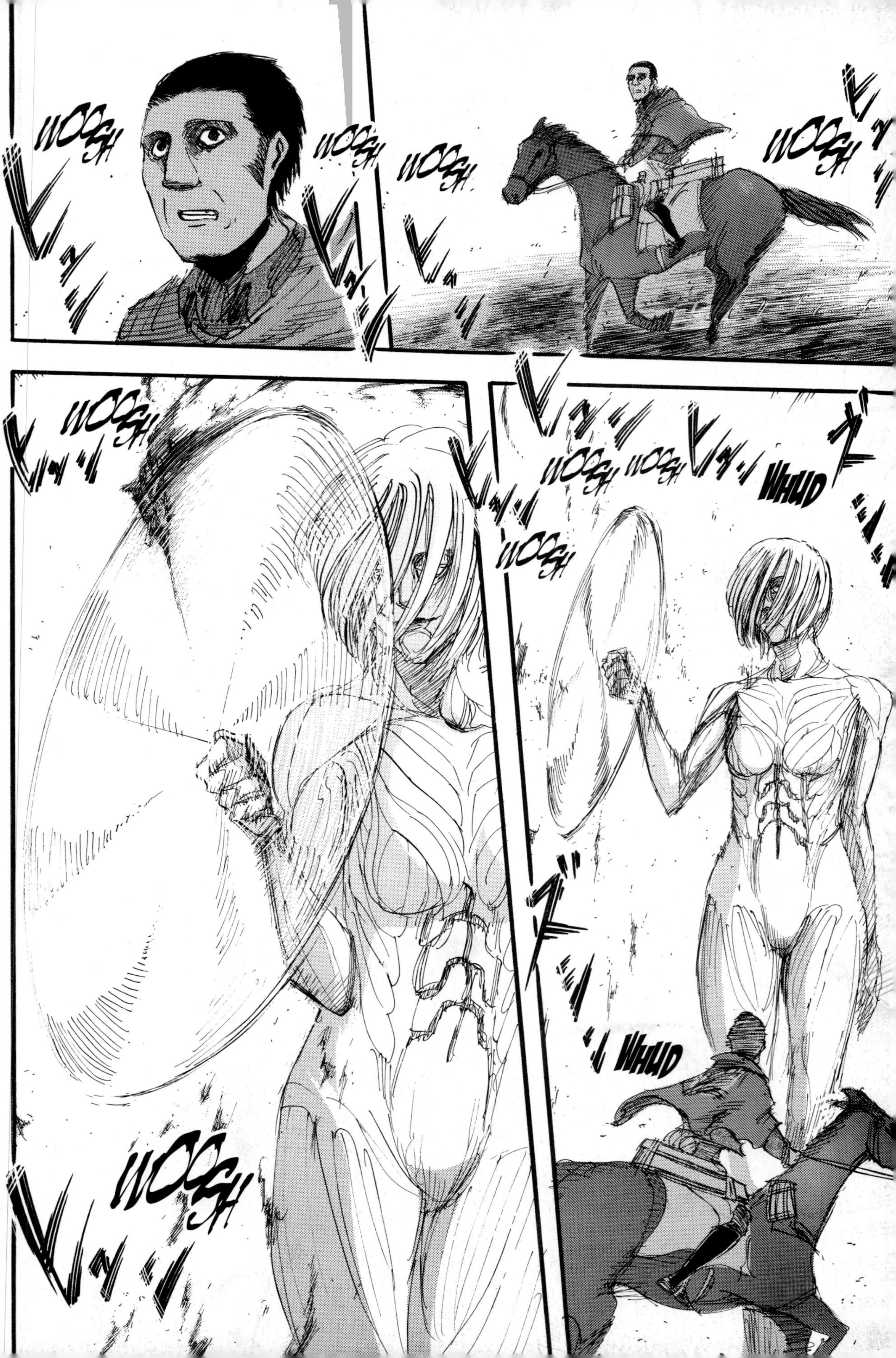

WOOSH
WOOSH
WOOSH
WOOSH
WHUD
WOOSH
WOOSH
WOOSH
WHUD
WOOSH
WOOSH

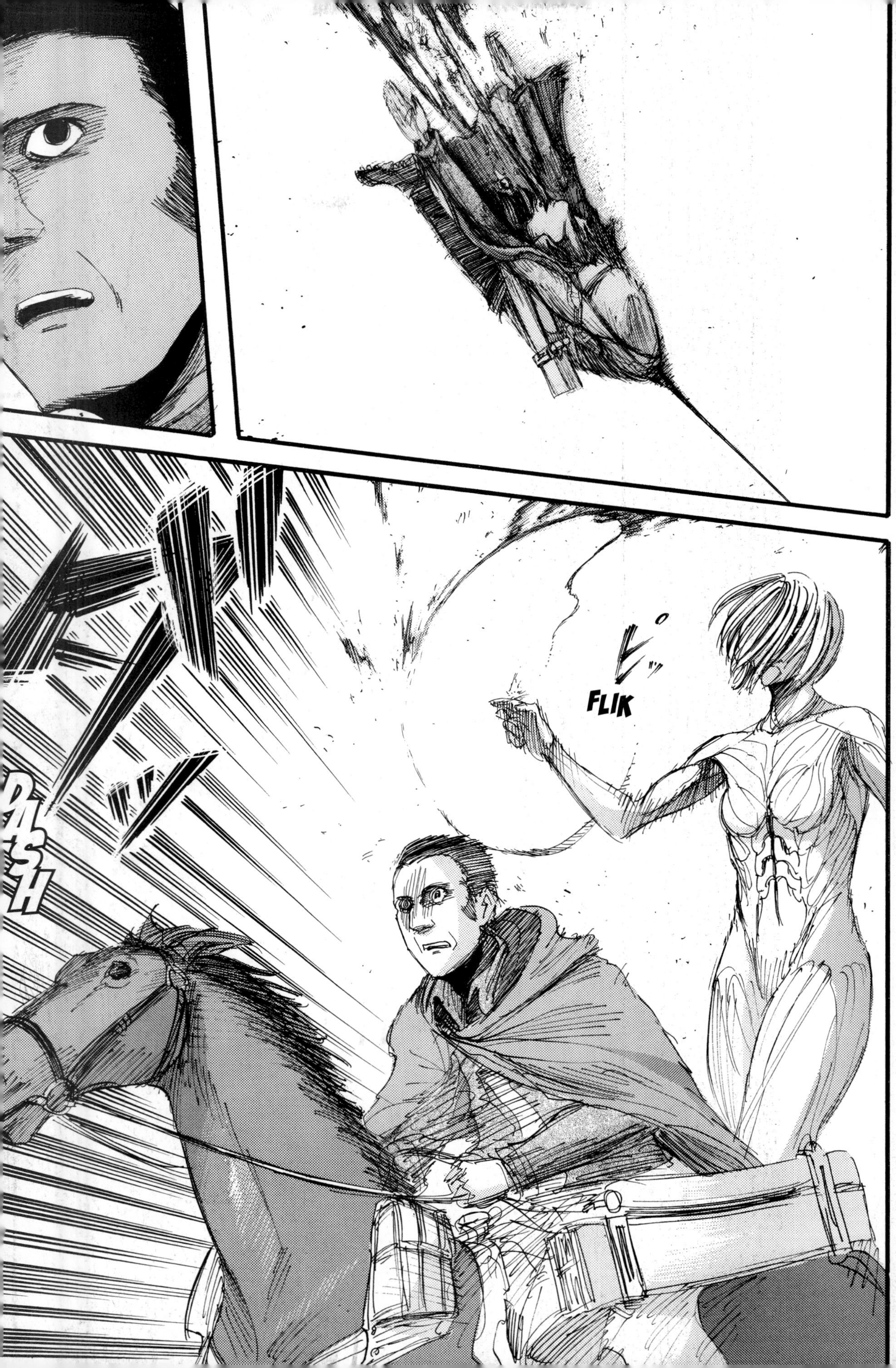
FLIK
DASH

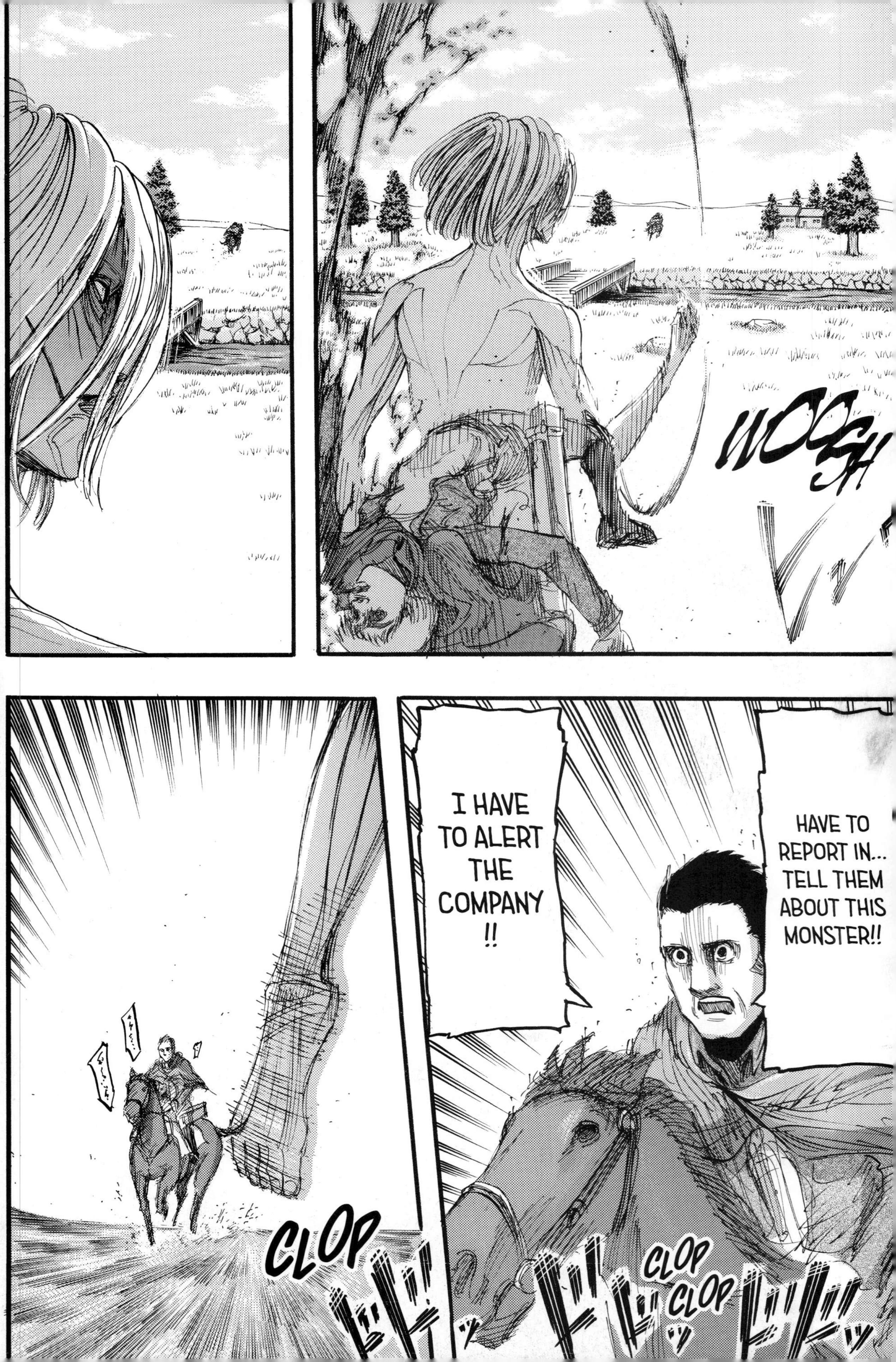
WOOSH
HAVE TO REPORT IN... TELL THEM ABOUT THIS MONSTER!!
I HAVE TO ALERT THE COMPANY!!
CLOP CLOP
CLOP

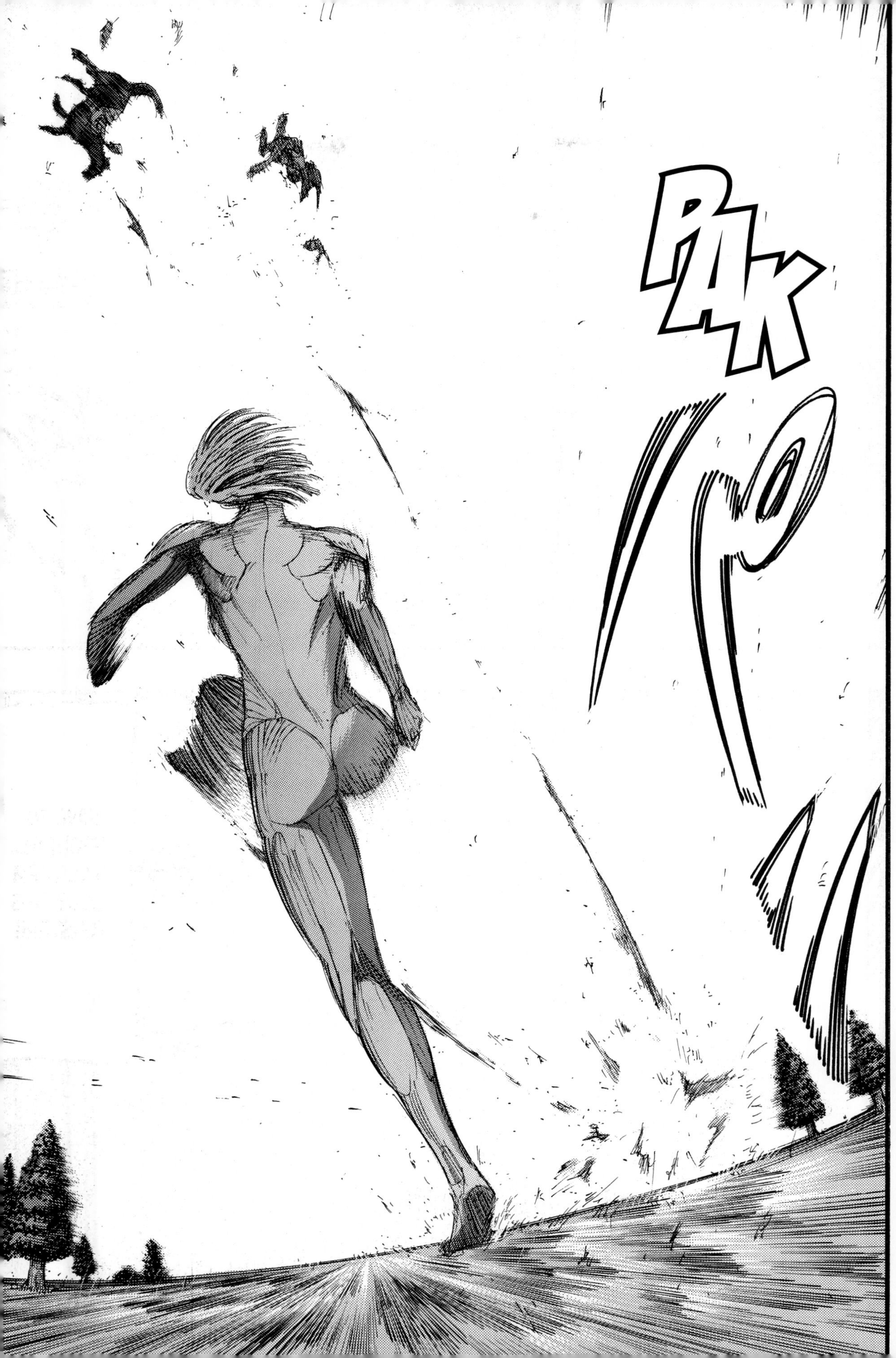
PAK

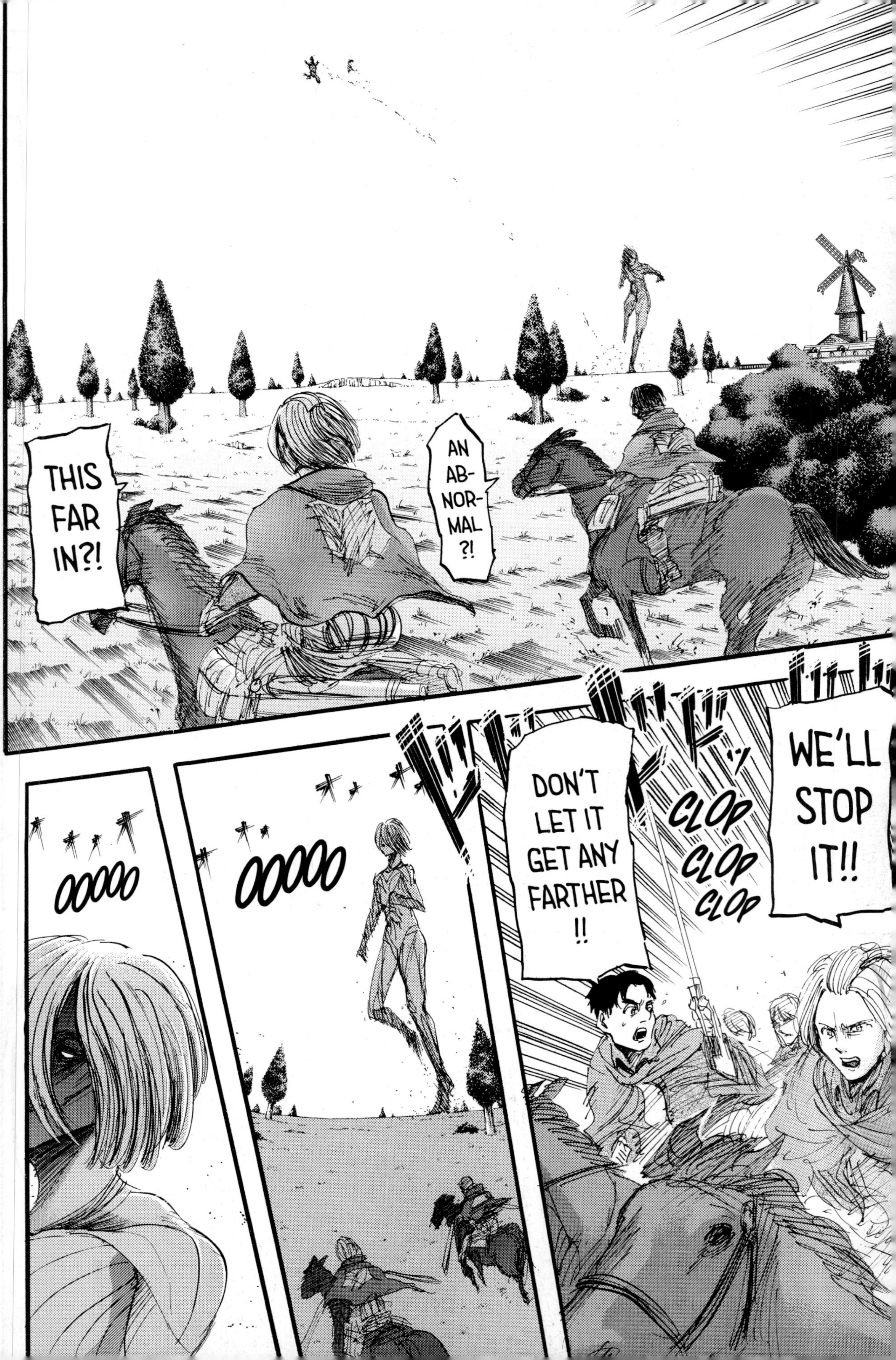
AN AB-NOR-MAL?!
THIS FAR IN?!
WE'LL STOP IT!!
CLOP CLOP CLOP
DON'T LET IT GET ANY FARTHER!!
OOOOO
OOOOO

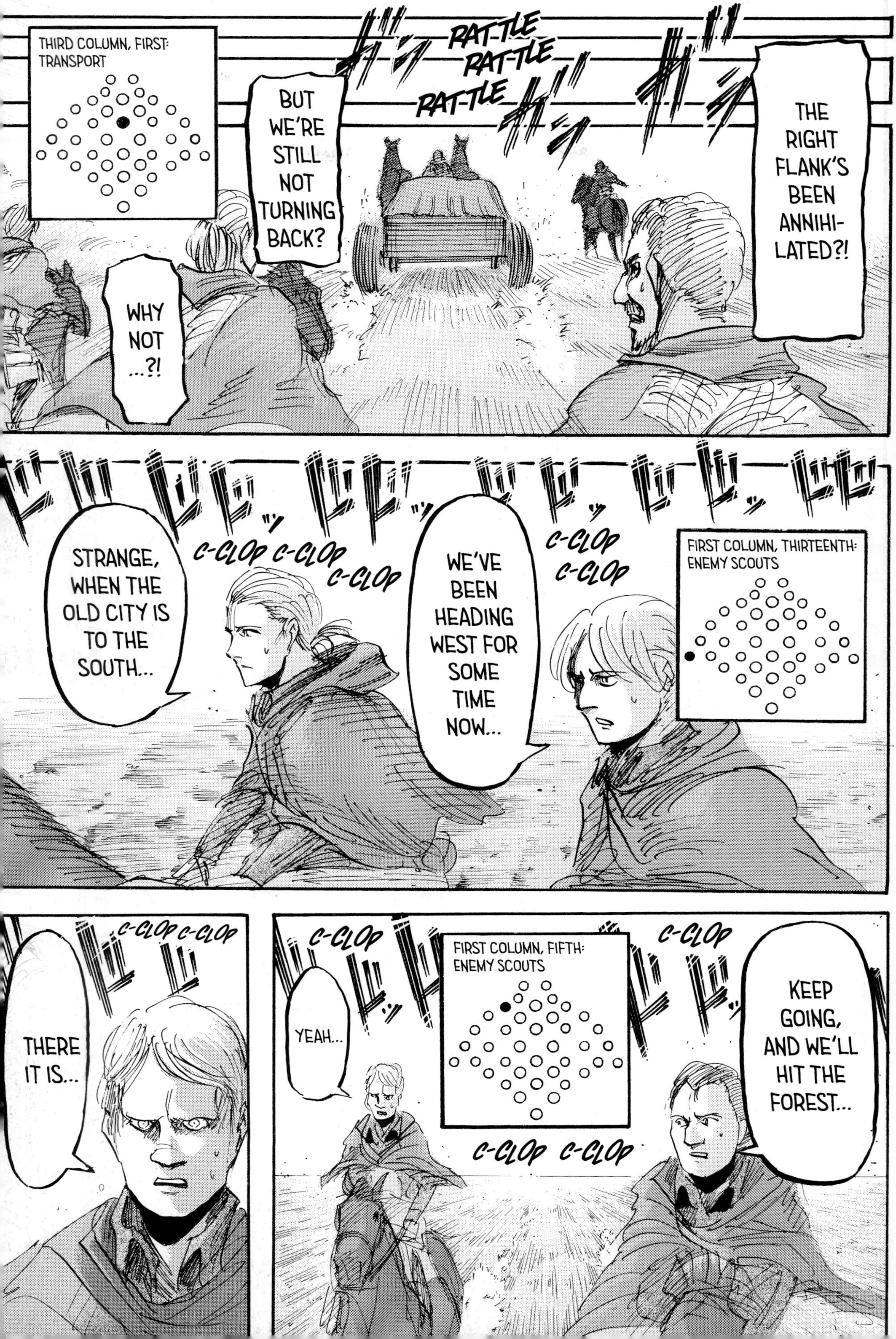
THE RIGHT FLANK'S BEEN ANNIHI-LATED?!
RATTLE RATTLE RATTLE
BUT WE'RE STILL NOT TURNING BACK?
THIRD COLUMN, FIRST: TRANSPORT
WHY NOT ...?!
FIRST COLUMN, THIRTEENTH: ENEMY SCOUTS
C-CLOP C-CLOP
WE'VE BEEN HEADING WEST FOR SOME TIME NOW...
C-CLOP C-CLOP C-CLOP
STRANGE, WHEN THE OLD CITY IS TO THE SOUTH...
C-CLOP
KEEP GOING, AND WE'LL HIT THE FOREST...
FIRST COLUMN, FIFTH: ENEMY SCOUTS
C-CLOP
YEAH...
C-CLOP C-CLOP
C-CLOP C-CLOP
THERE IT IS...

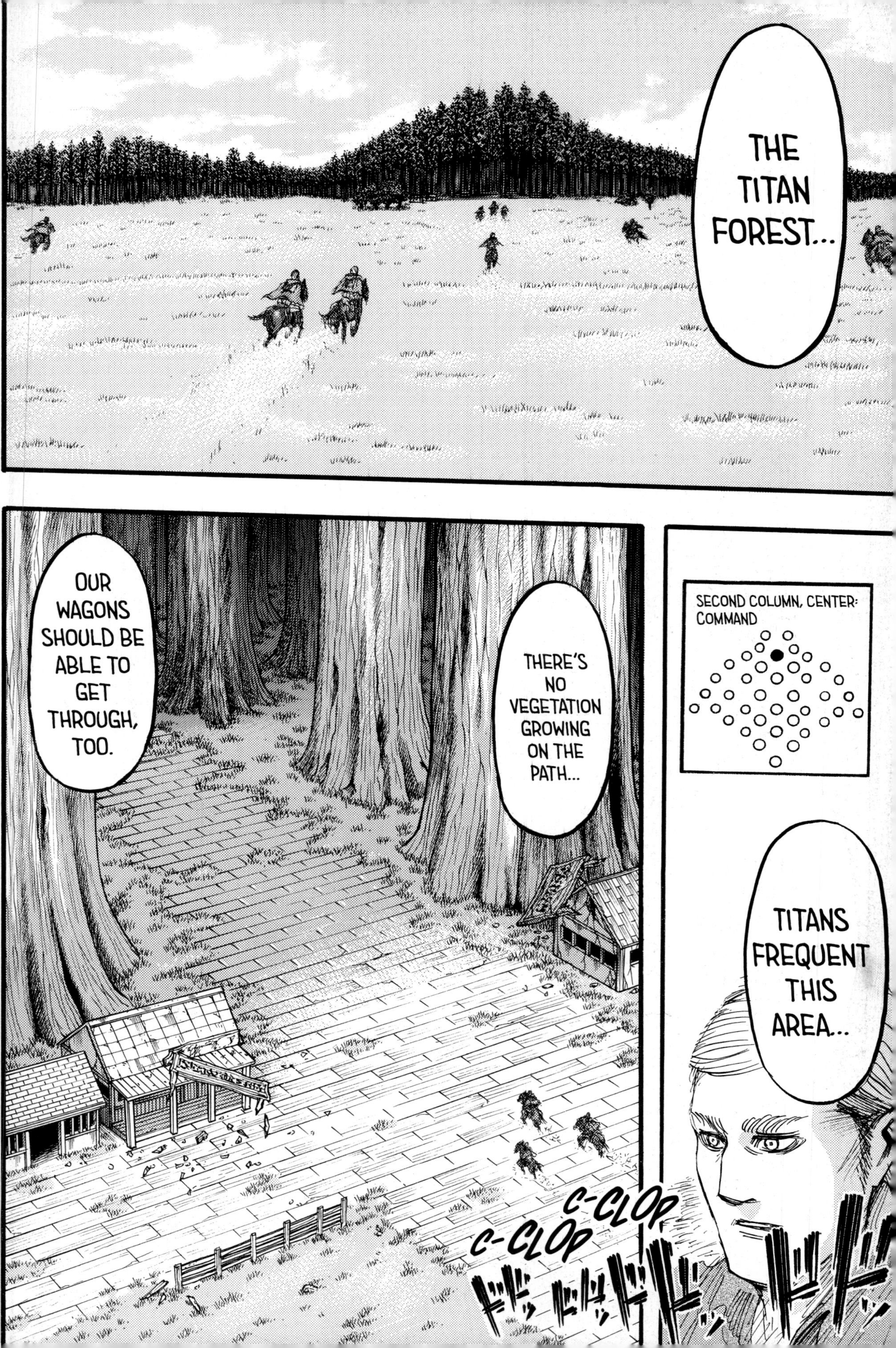
THE TITAN FOREST...
SECOND COLUMN, CENTER: COMMAND
TITANS FREQUENT THIS AREA...
THERE'S NO VEGETATION GROWING ON THE PATH...
OUR WAGONS SHOULD BE ABLE TO GET THROUGH, TOO.
C-CLOP C-CLOP

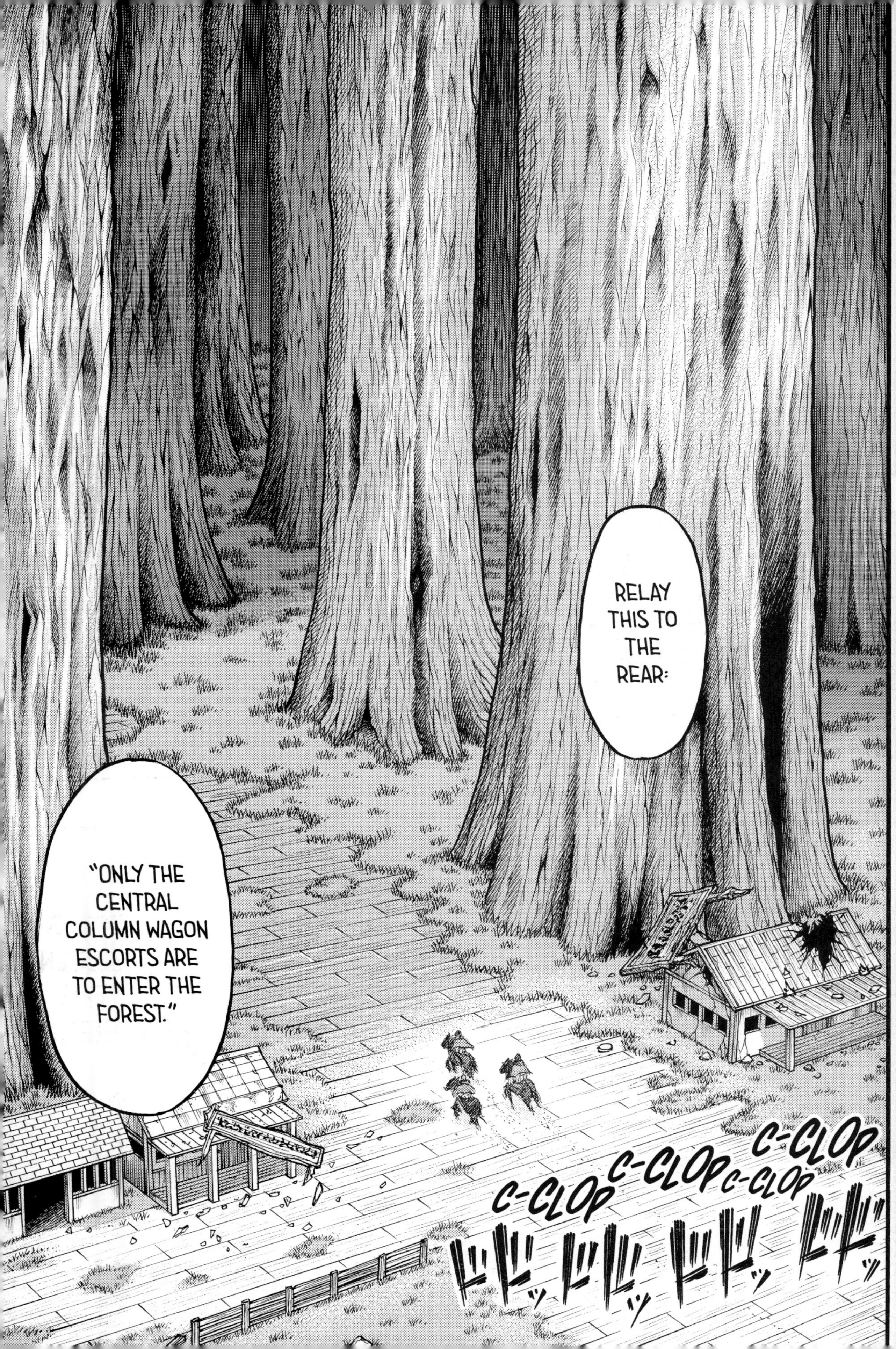
RELAY THIS TO THE REAR:
"ONLY THE CENTRAL COLUMN WAGON ESCORTS ARE TO ENTER THE FOREST."
C-CLOP C-CLOP C-CLOP C-CLOP
ドドッ ドドッ ドドッ ドドッ

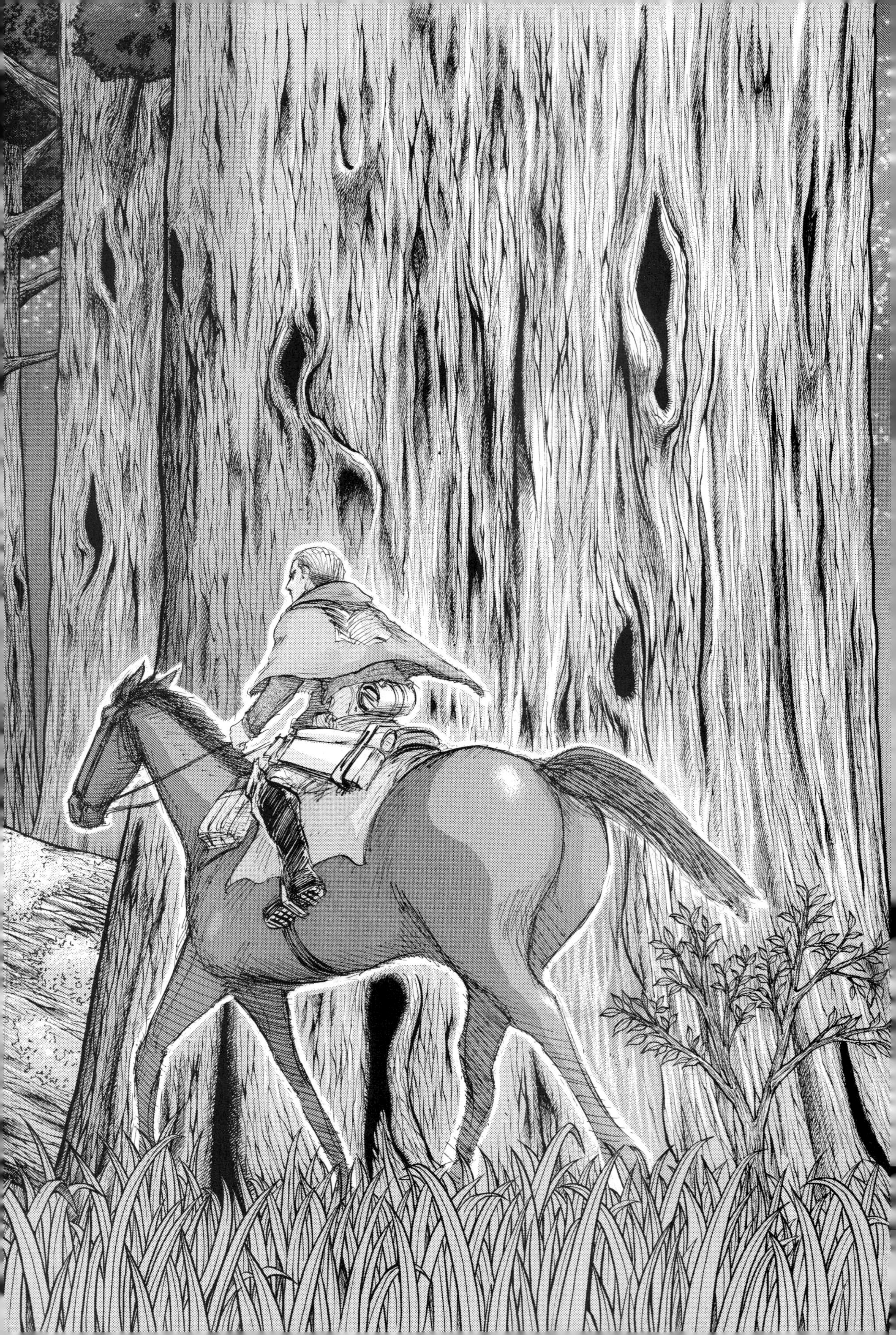

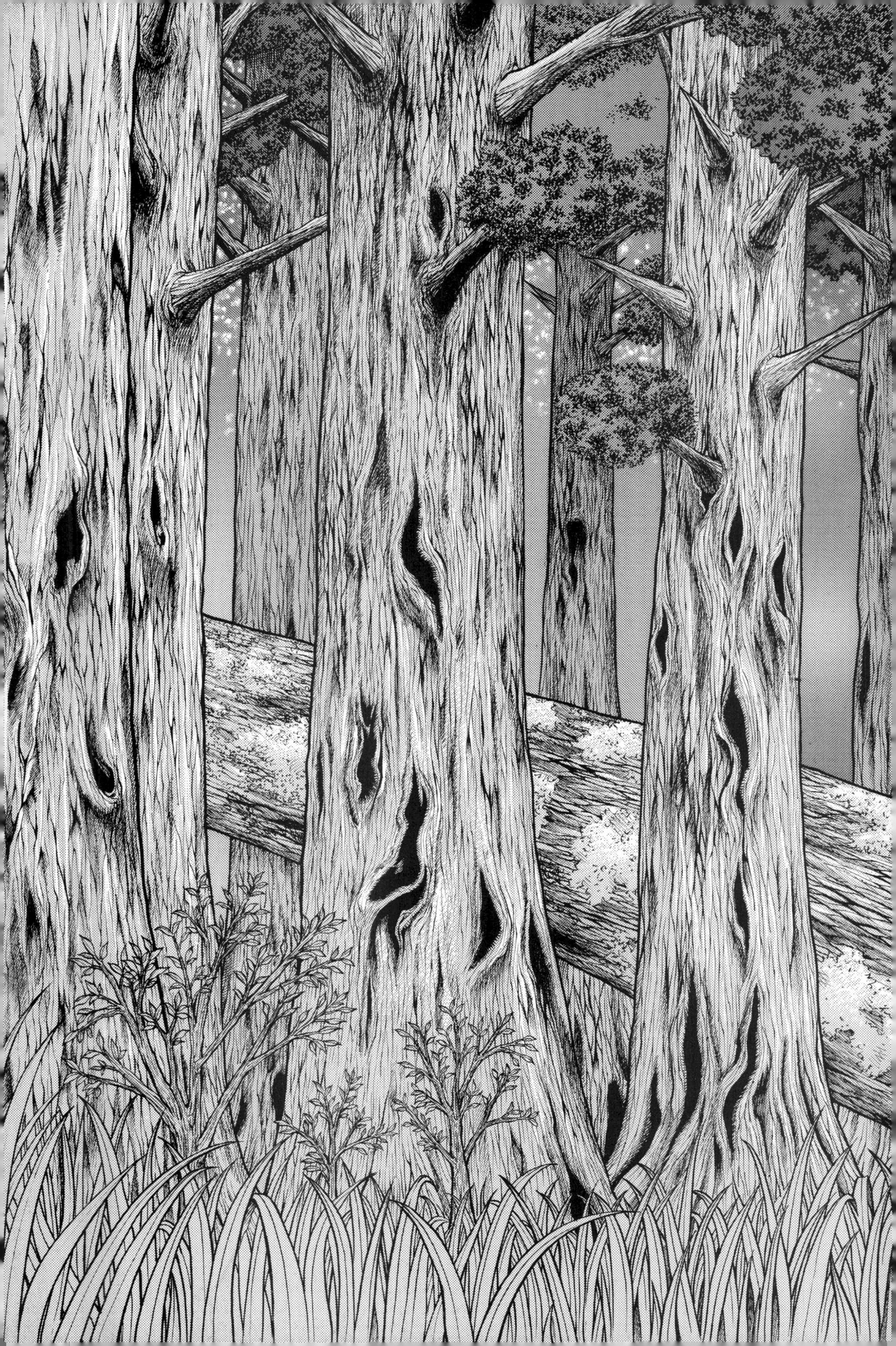

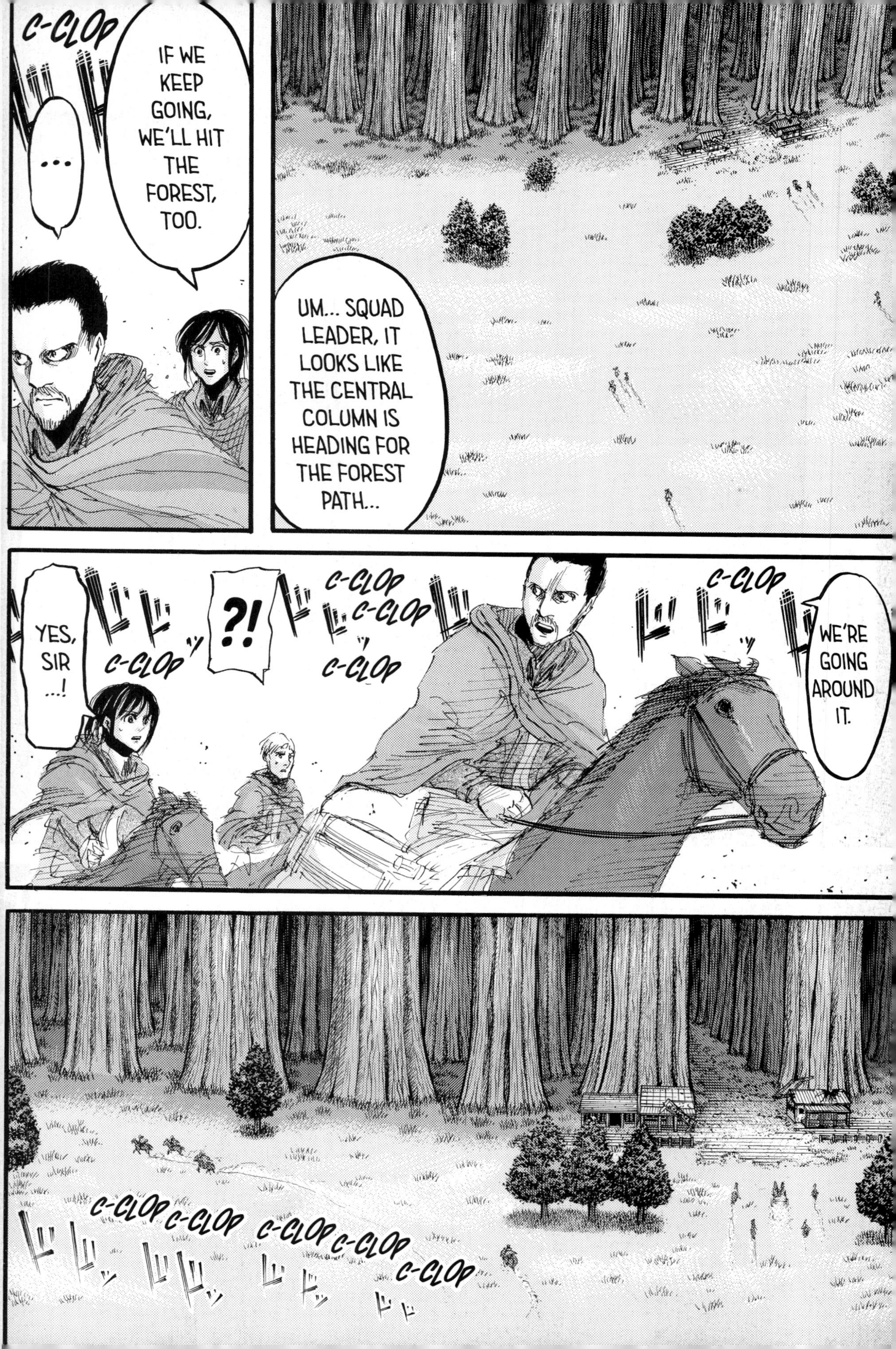
UM... SQUAD LEADER, IT LOOKS LIKE THE CENTRAL COLUMN IS HEADING FOR THE FOREST PATH...
C-CLOP
IF WE KEEP GOING, WE'LL HIT THE FOREST, TOO.
...
C-CLOP
WE'RE GOING AROUND IT.
C-CLOP
C-CLOP
C-CLOP
?!
C-CLOP
YES, SIR ...!
C-CLOP
C-CLOP
C-CLOP
C-CLOP
C-CLOP

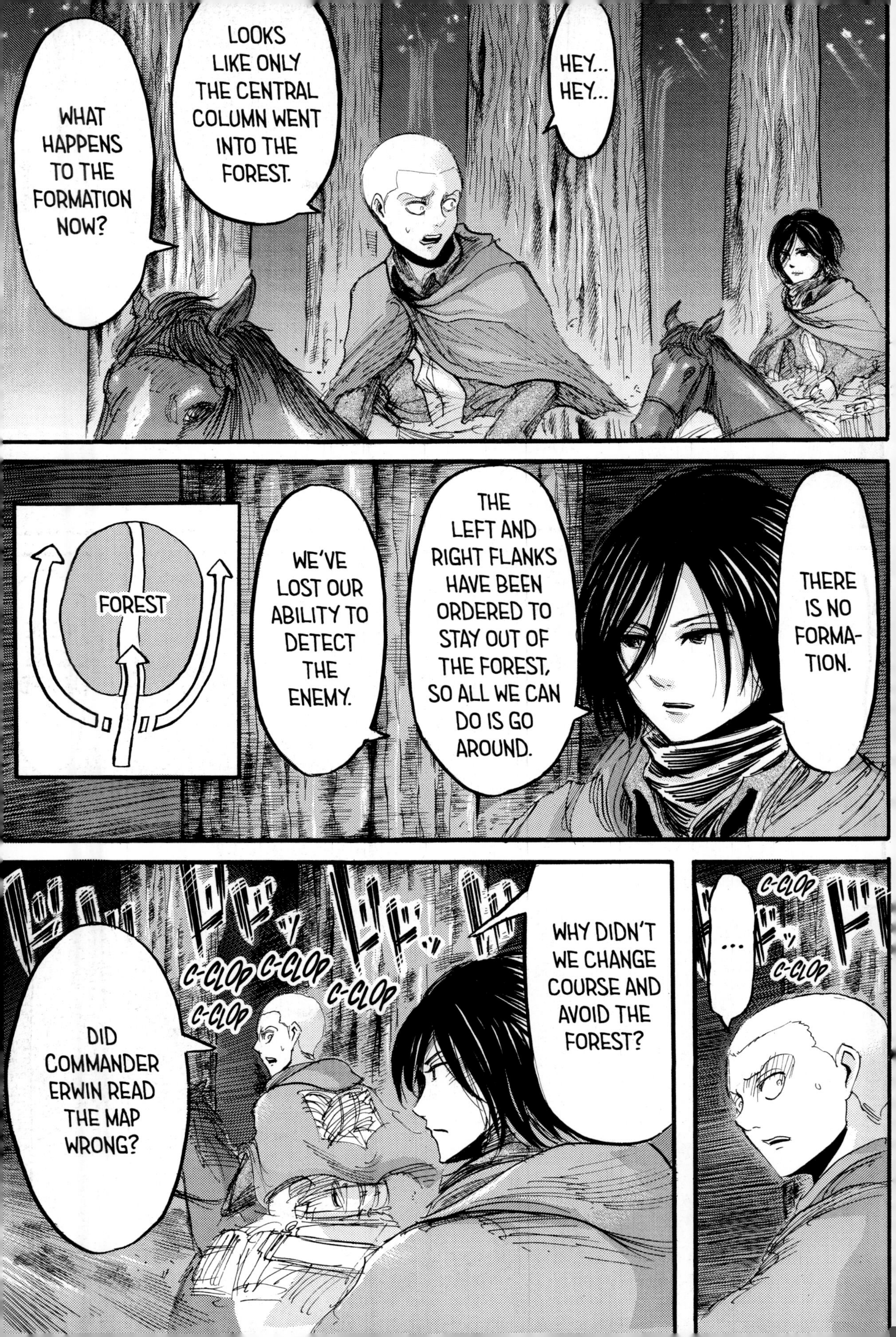
HEY... HEY...
LOOKS LIKE ONLY THE CENTRAL COLUMN WENT INTO THE FOREST.
WHAT HAPPENS TO THE FORMATION NOW?
THERE IS NO FORMA-TION.
THE LEFT AND RIGHT FLANKS HAVE BEEN ORDERED TO STAY OUT OF THE FOREST, SO ALL WE CAN DO IS GO AROUND.
WE'VE LOST OUR ABILITY TO DETECT THE ENEMY.
FOREST
C-CLOP
...
C-CLOP
WHY DIDN'T WE CHANGE COURSE AND AVOID THE FOREST?
C-CLOP C-CLOP
C-CLOP C-CLOP
DID COMMANDER ERWIN READ THE MAP WRONG?

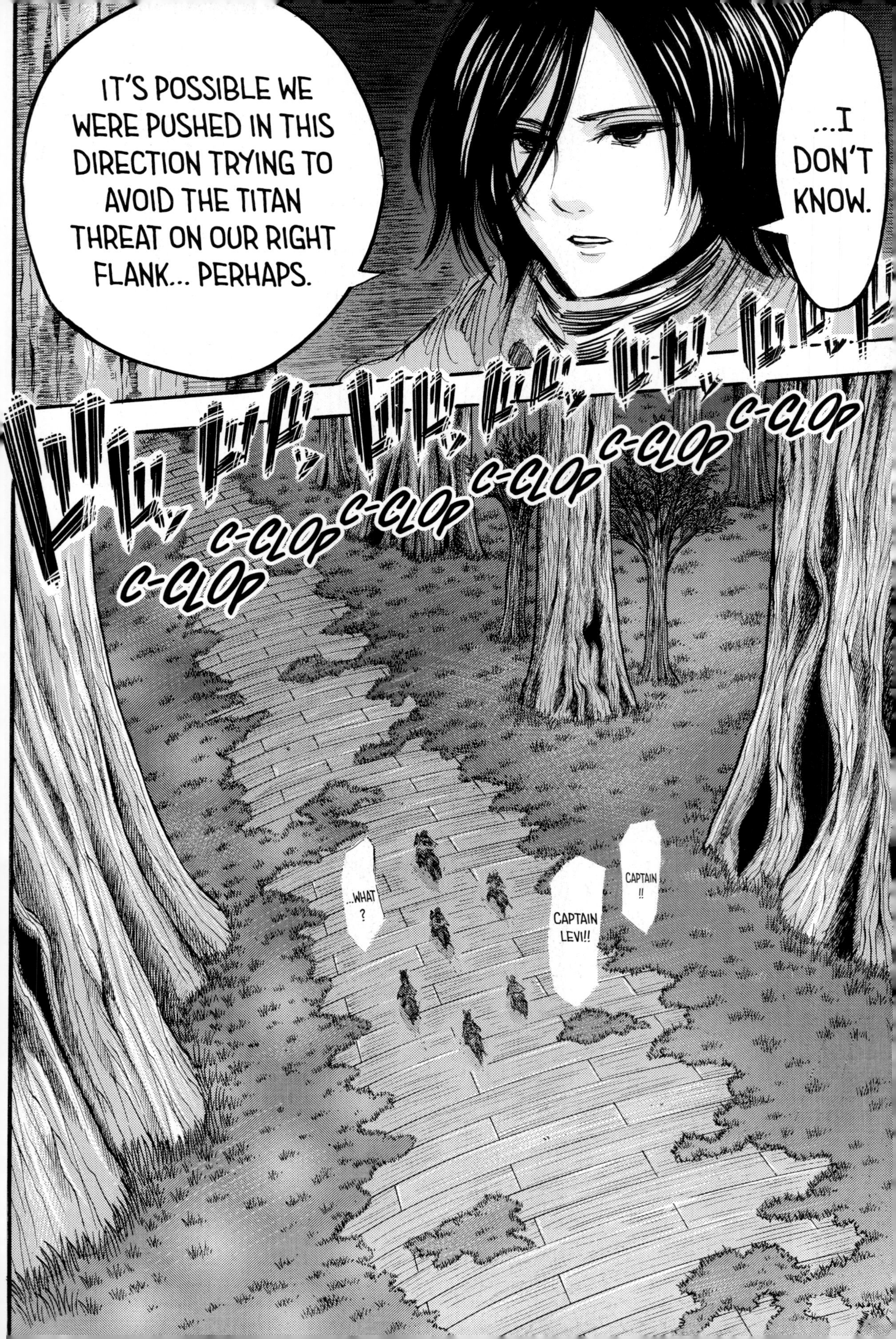
...I DON'T KNOW.
IT'S POSSIBLE WE WERE PUSHED IN THIS DIRECTION TRYING TO AVOID THE TITAN THREAT ON OUR RIGHT FLANK... PERHAPS.
C-CLOP C-CLOP C-CLOP C-CLOP C-CLOP C-CLOP
CAPTAIN !!
CAPTAIN LEVI!!
...WHAT ?

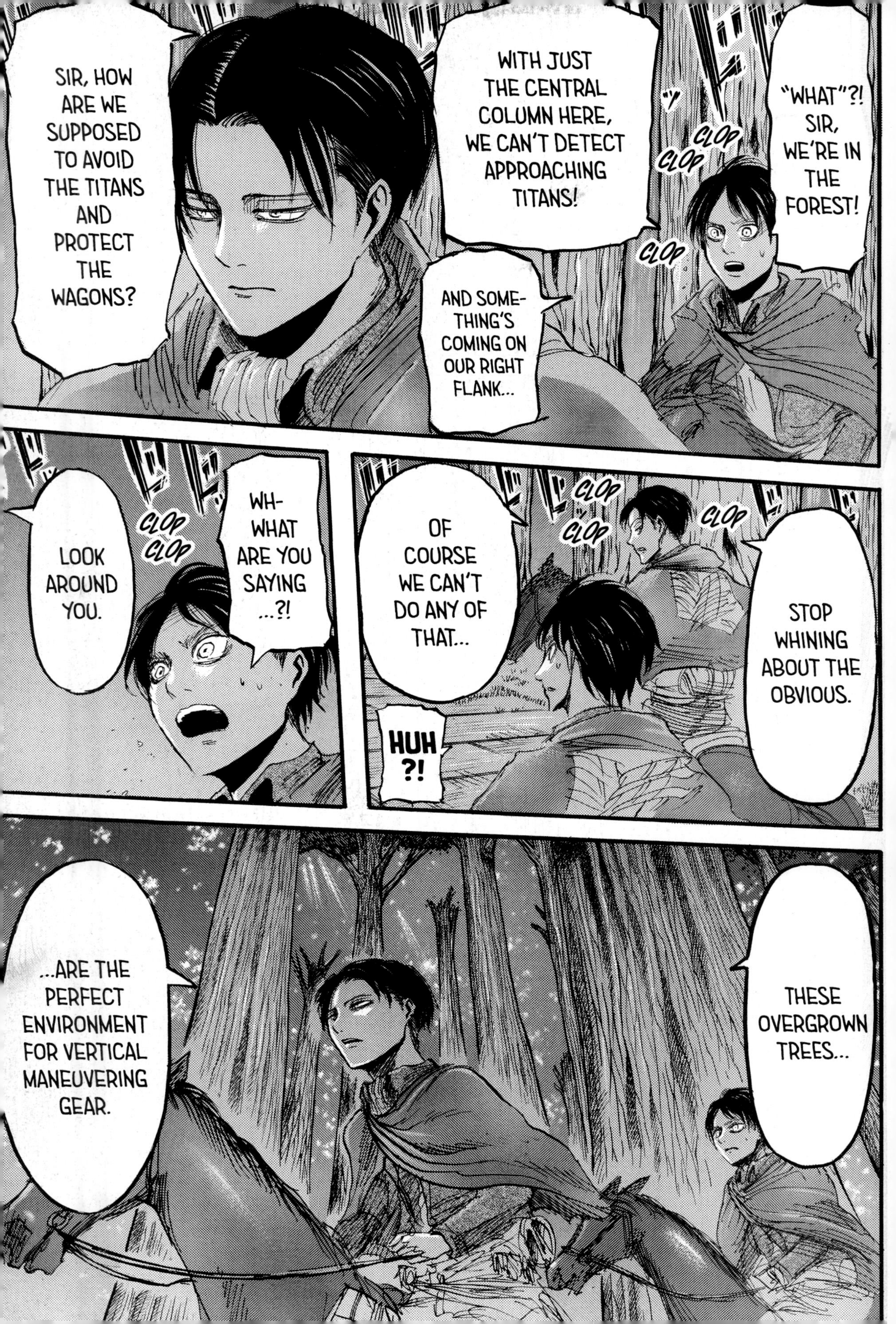
"WHAT"?! SIR, WE'RE IN THE FOREST!
CLOP CLOP
CLOP
WITH JUST THE CENTRAL COLUMN HERE, WE CAN'T DETECT APPROACHING TITANS!
AND SOME-THING'S COMING ON OUR RIGHT FLANK...
SIR, HOW ARE WE SUPPOSED TO AVOID THE TITANS AND PROTECT THE WAGONS?
STOP WHINING ABOUT THE OBVIOUS.
CLOP
CLOP CLOP
HUH?!
OF COURSE WE CAN'T DO ANY OF THAT...
WH-WHAT ARE YOU SAYING...?!
CLOP CLOP
LOOK AROUND YOU.
THESE OVERGROWN TREES...
...ARE THE PERFECT ENVIRONMENT FOR VERTICAL MANEUVERING GEAR.

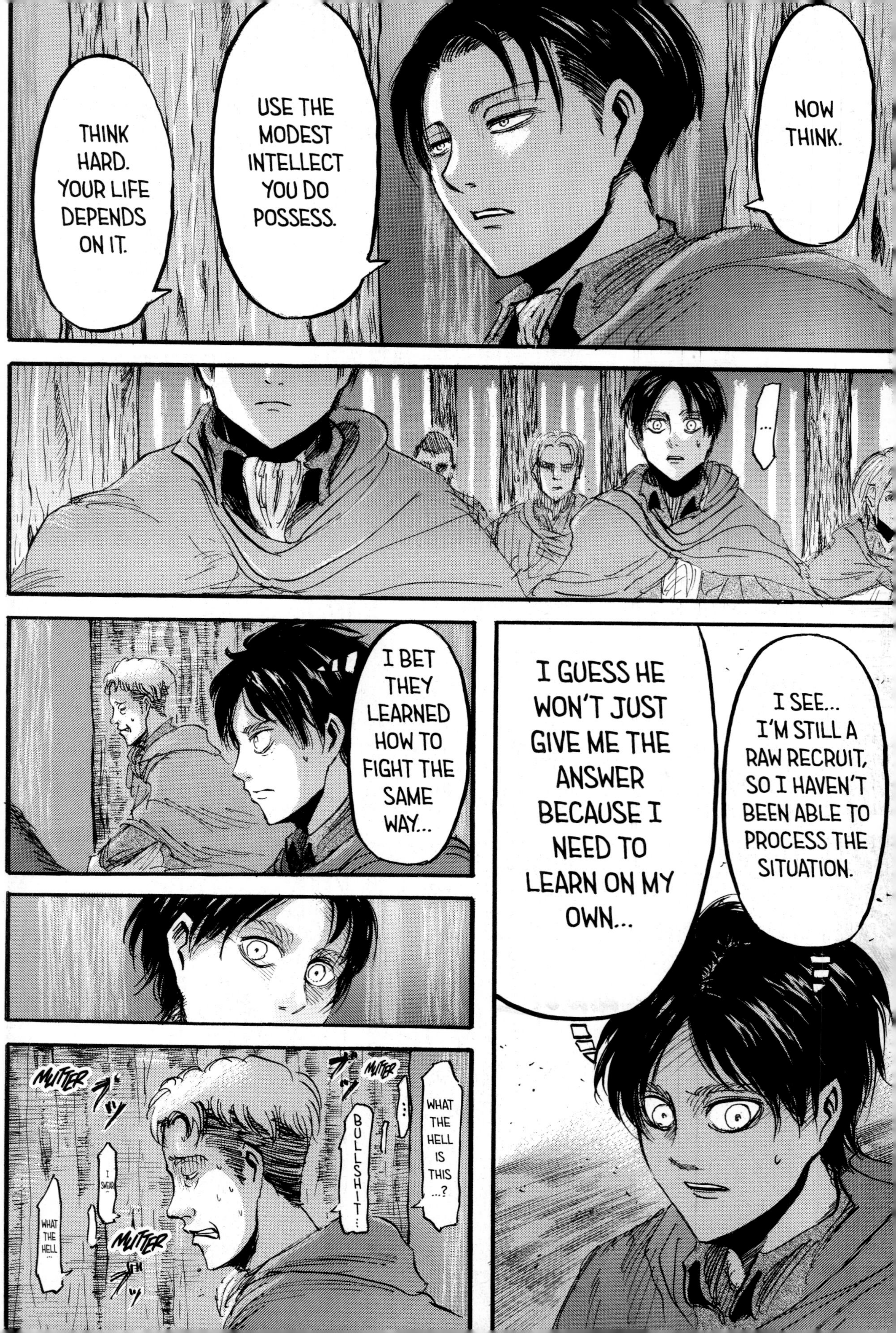
NOW THINK.
USE THE MODEST INTELLECT YOU DO POSSESS.
THINK HARD. YOUR LIFE DEPENDS ON IT.
...
I SEE... I'M STILL A RAW RECRUIT, SO I HAVEN'T BEEN ABLE TO PROCESS THE SITUATION.
I GUESS HE WON'T JUST GIVE ME THE ANSWER BECAUSE I NEED TO LEARN ON MY OWN...
I BET THEY LEARNED HOW TO FIGHT THE SAME WAY...
MUTTER
WHAT THE HELL IS THIS...?
...
BULLSHIT...
MUTTER
I SWEAR...
WHAT THE HELL...
MUTTER

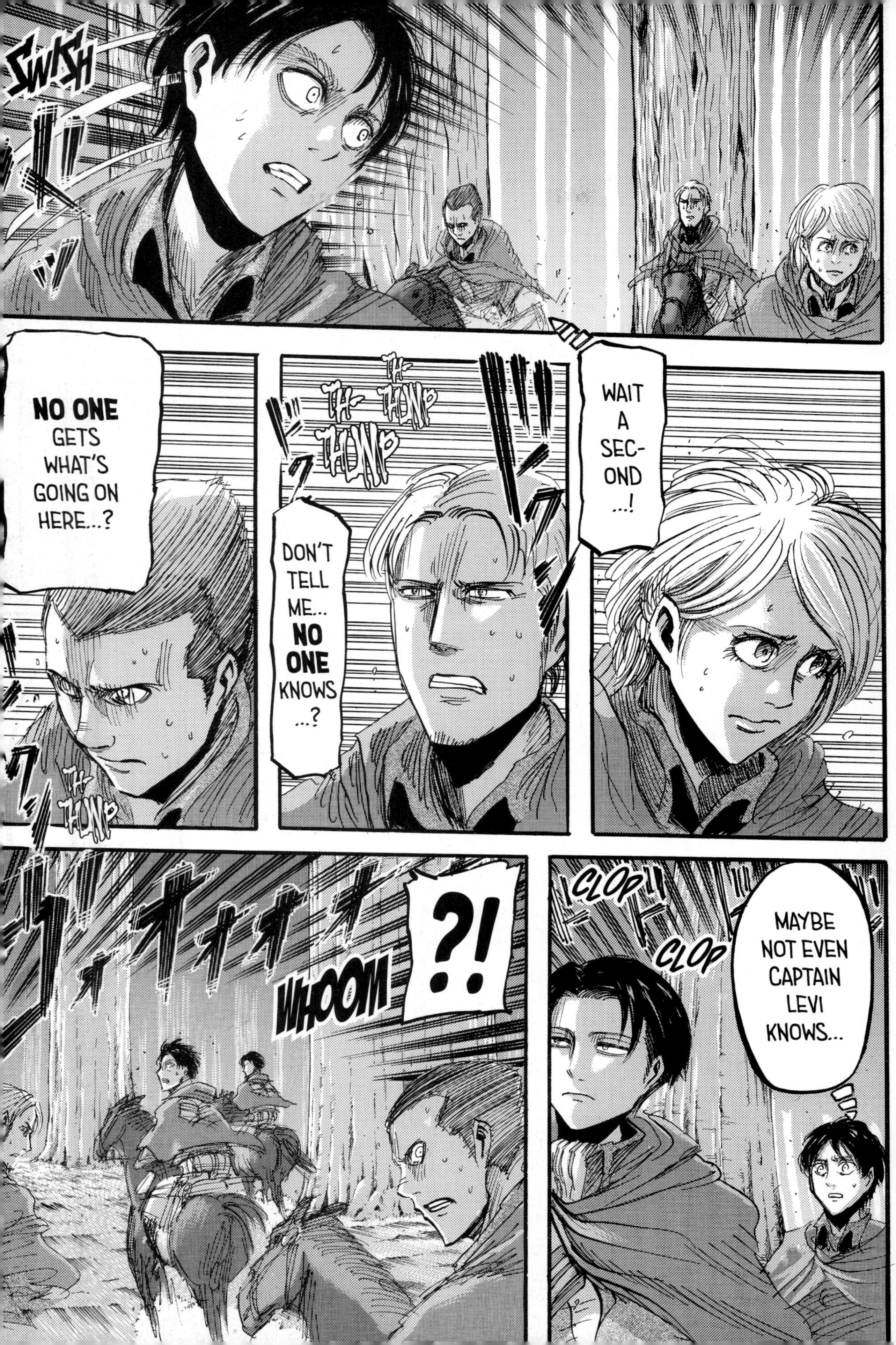

SWISH
WAIT A SEC-OND...!
TH-THUMP
TH-THUMP
DON'T TELL ME... **NO ONE** KNOWS...?
NO ONE GETS WHAT'S GOING ON HERE...?
TH-THUMP
CLOP
CLOP
MAYBE NOT EVEN CAPTAIN LEVI KNOWS...
?!
WHOOM

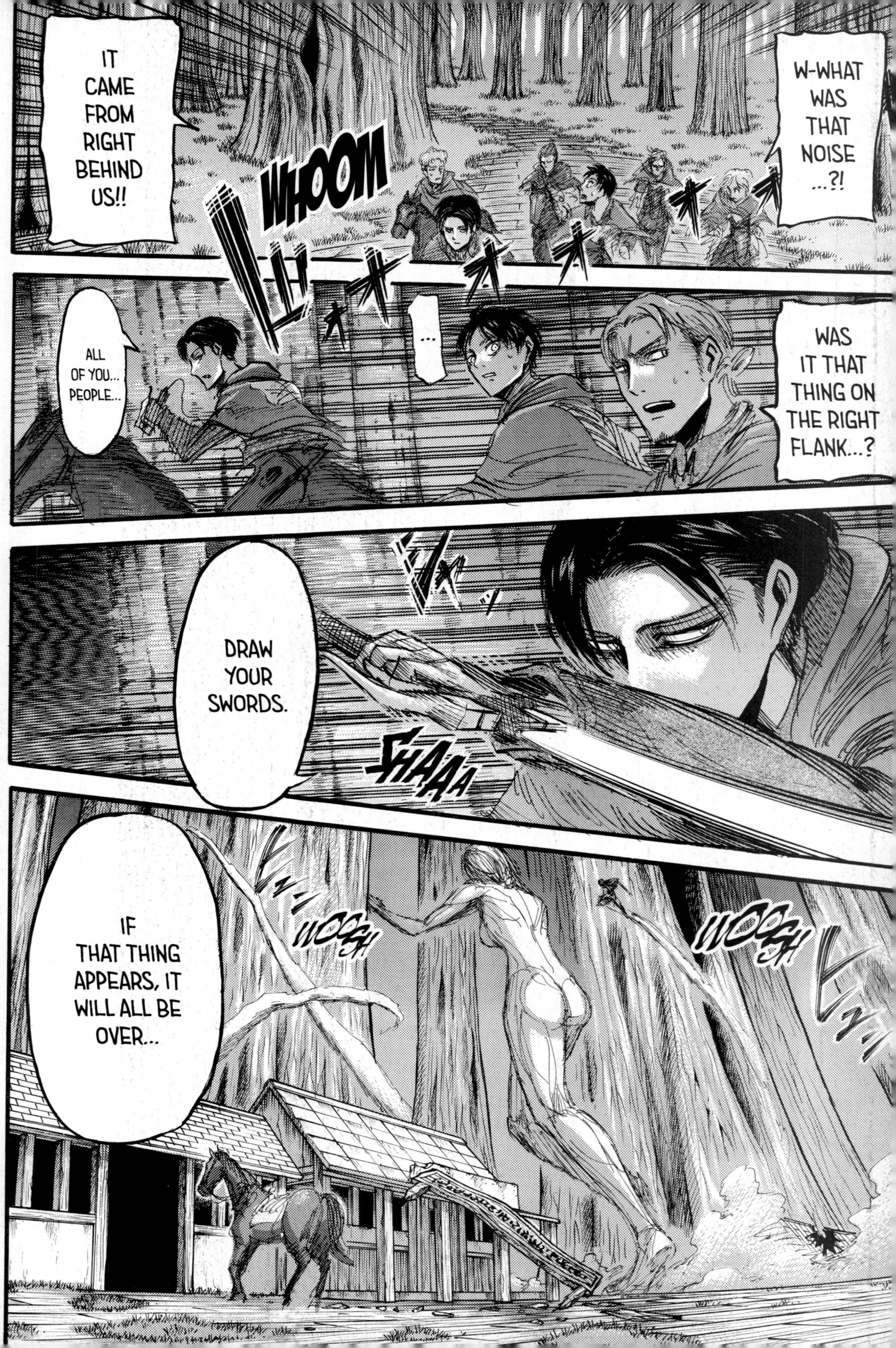
W-WHAT WAS THAT NOISE ...?!
IT CAME FROM RIGHT BEHIND US!!
WHOOM
WAS IT THAT THING ON THE RIGHT FLANK...?
...
ALL OF YOU... PEOPLE...
DRAW YOUR SWORDS.
SHAAA
WOOSH
WOOSH
IF THAT THING APPEARS, IT WILL ALL BE OVER...

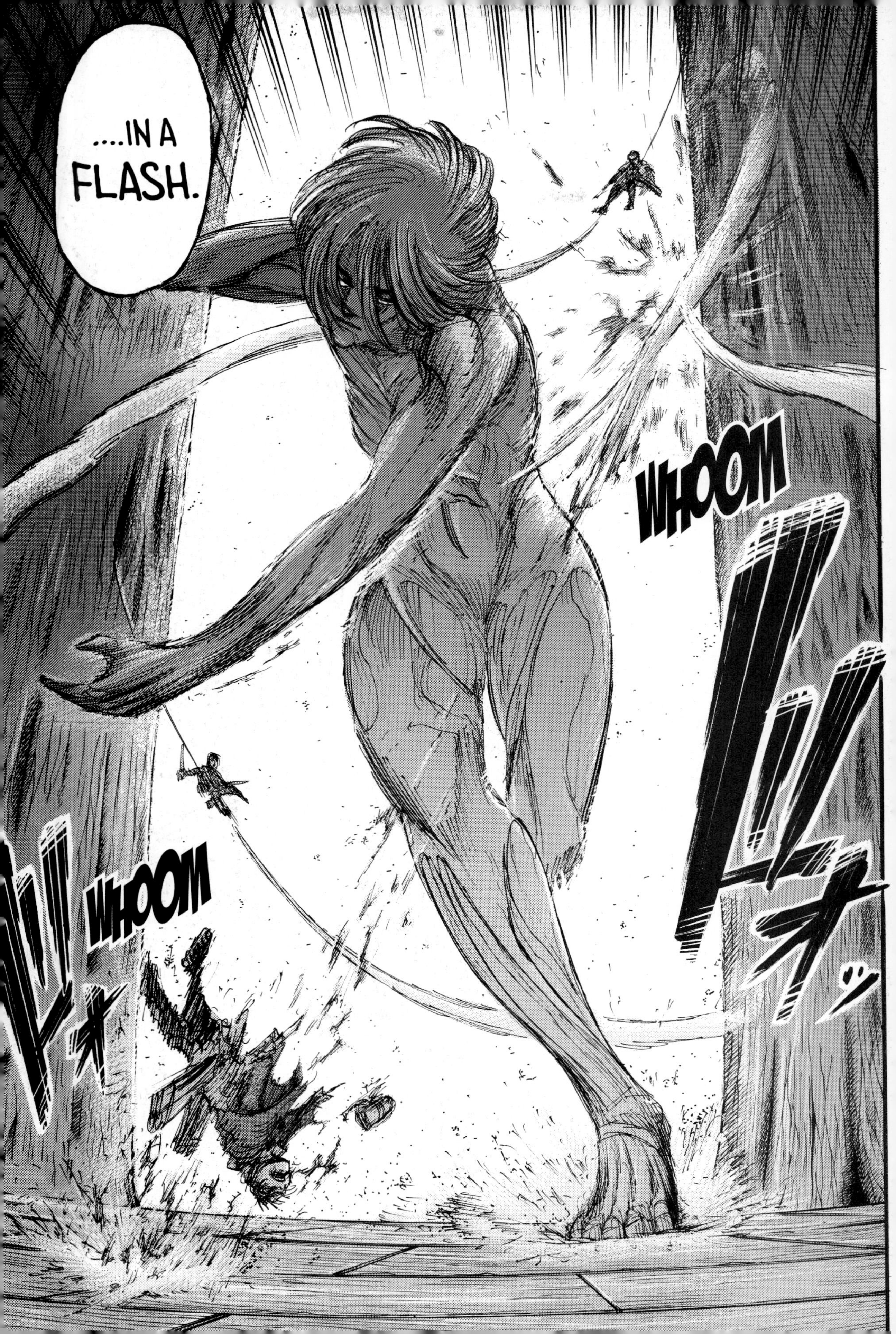
....IN A FLASH.
WHOOM
WHOOM

Current Publicly Available Information

12. The Titan Forest

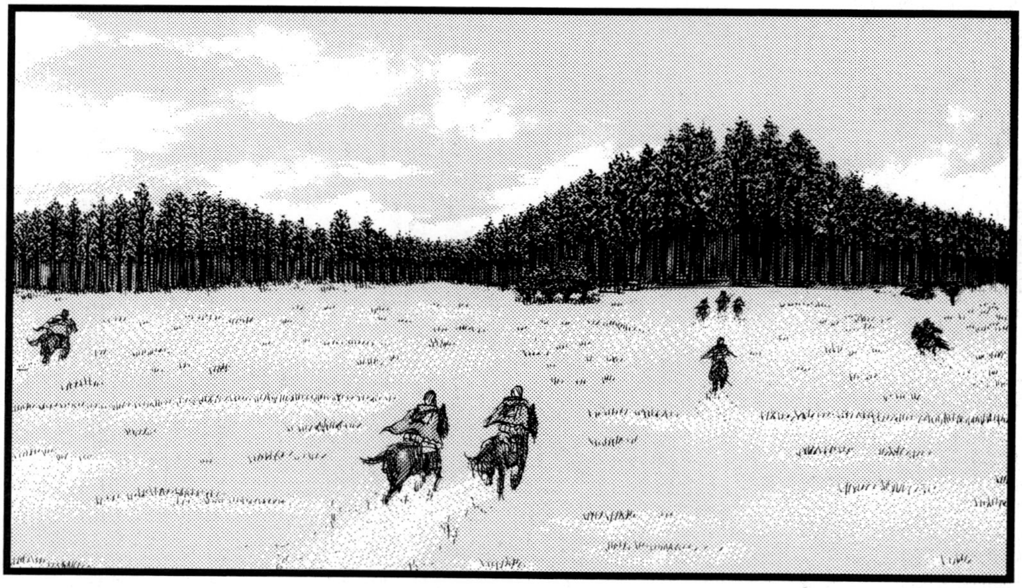

THERE ARE FORESTS OF GIANT TREES BOTH INSIDE AND OUTSIDE THE WALL. THEY GROW WILD ALONG THE BORDER OF ONE DISTRICT, AVERAGING A HEIGHT OF OVER 80 METERS.* NO ONE KNOWS WHY TREES OF THIS SIZE EXIST, BUT SOME HAVE PROPOSED THE NATURE OF THE SOIL AS THE CAUSE. BEFORE THE FALL OF WALL MARIA, PEOPLE MAINTAINED THE FOREST AS A TOURIST ATTRACTION. WITHOUT HUMAN INTERCESSION IN THE LAST SEVERAL YEARS, THE AREA HAS FALLEN INTO RUIN, WITH THE FOREST PATH MOSTLY SWALLOWED UP BY WEEDS AND TREES, ALTHOUGH PARTS OF THE PATH REMAIN INTACT FROM THE COMINGS AND GOINGS OF THE TITANS THROUGH THE WOODS. THE FOREST HAS BECOME AN IMPORTANT BASE FOR THE SURVEY CORPS, USED TO PROTECT THEMSELVES FROM THE TITANS WHILE ON EXPEDITIONS OUTSIDE THE WALL. (WITH THANKS TO UKYŌ KODACHI AND KIYOMUNE MIWA.)

* ABOUT 260 FEET.

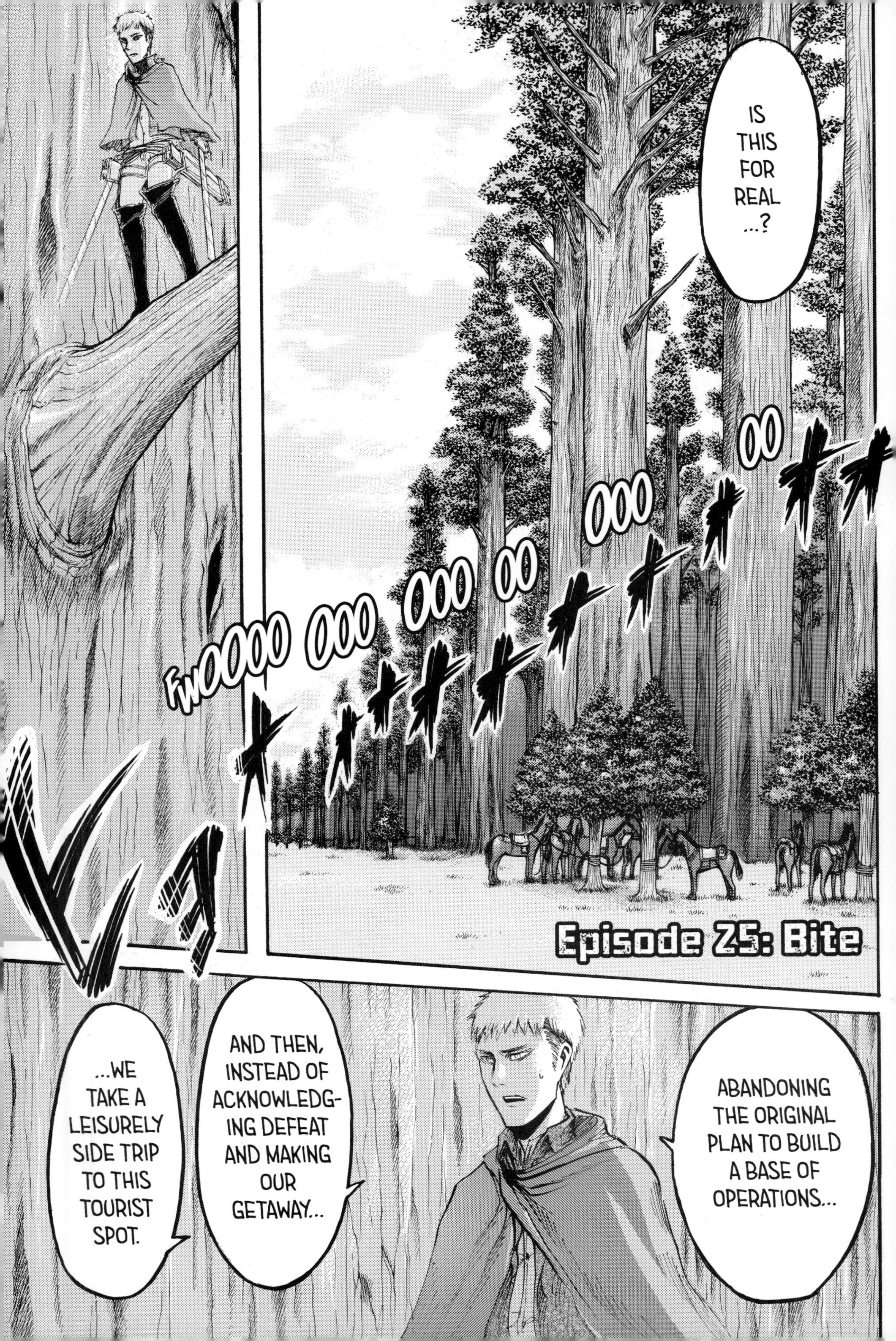
IS THIS FOR REAL ...?
FWOOOO OOO OOO OO OOO OO
Episode 25: Bite
ABANDONING THE ORIGINAL PLAN TO BUILD A BASE OF OPERATIONS...
AND THEN, INSTEAD OF ACKNOWLEDG-ING DEFEAT AND MAKING OUR GETAWAY...
...WE TAKE A LEISURELY SIDE TRIP TO THIS TOURIST SPOT.

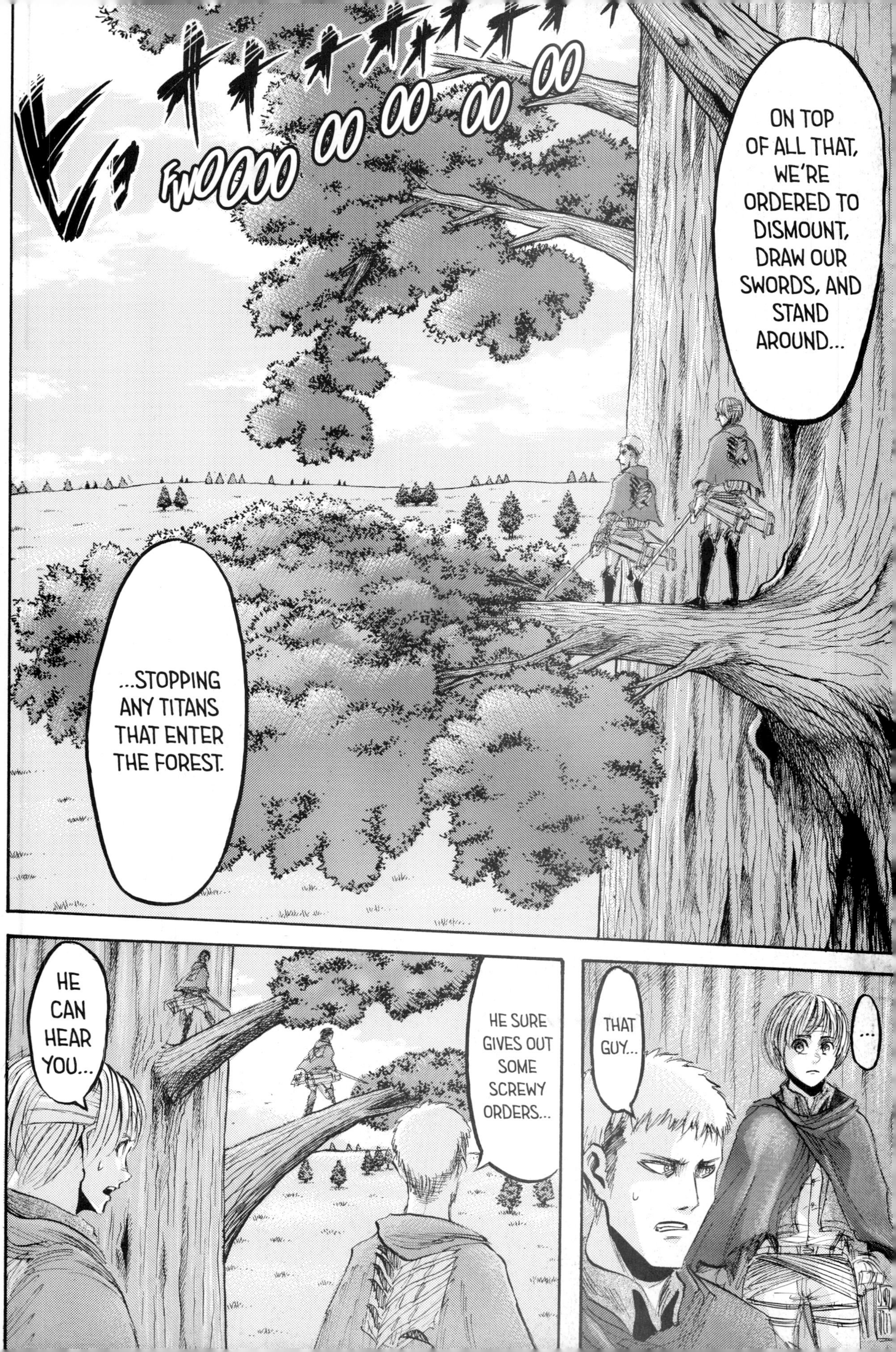
FWOOOO OO OO OO OO
ON TOP OF ALL THAT, WE'RE ORDERED TO DISMOUNT, DRAW OUR SWORDS, AND STAND AROUND...
...STOPPING ANY TITANS THAT ENTER THE FOREST.
...
THAT GUY...
HE SURE GIVES OUT SOME SCREWY ORDERS...
HE CAN HEAR YOU...

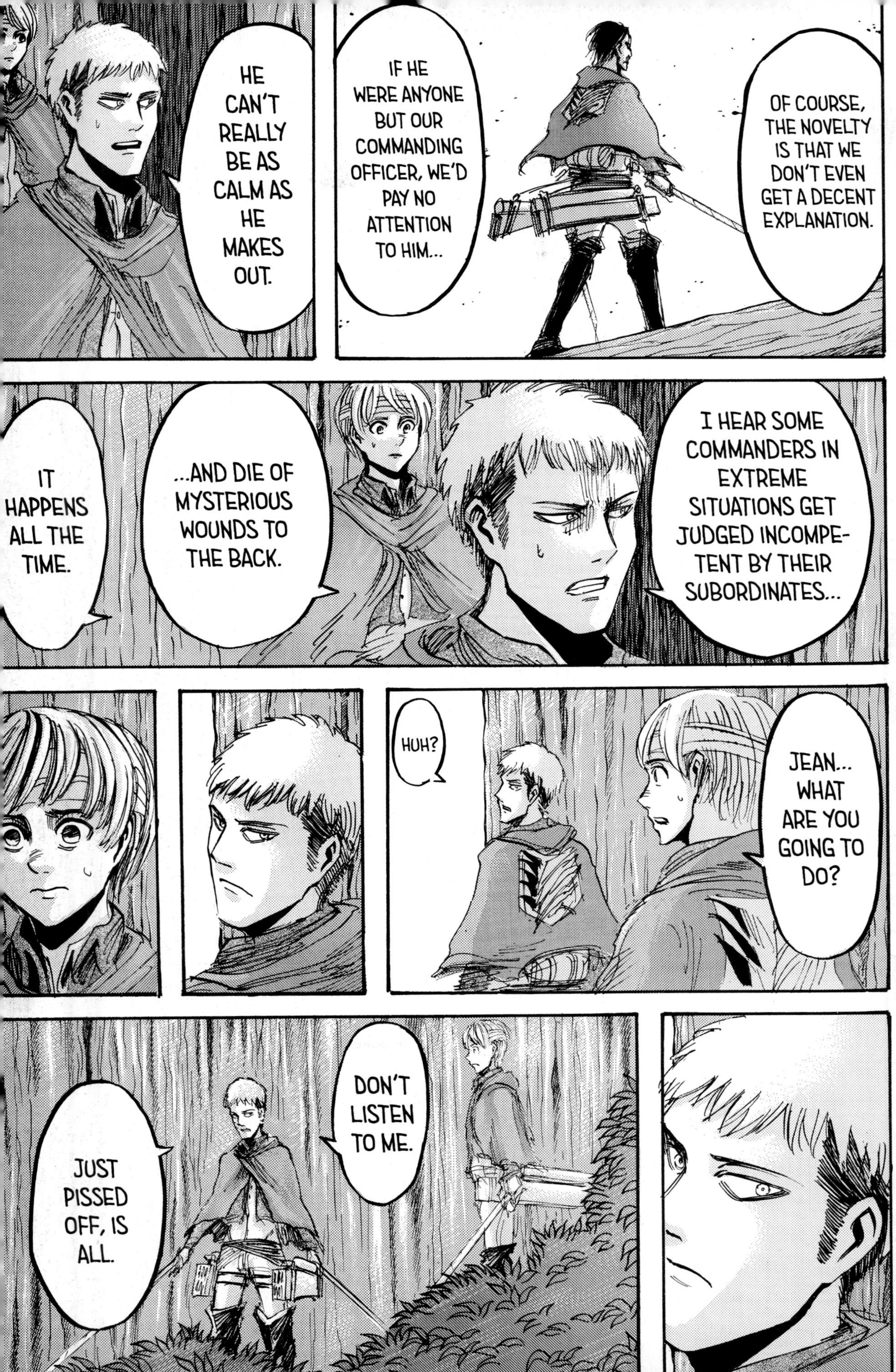
OF COURSE, THE NOVELTY IS THAT WE DON'T EVEN GET A DECENT EXPLANATION.
IF HE WERE ANYONE BUT OUR COMMANDING OFFICER, WE'D PAY NO ATTENTION TO HIM...
HE CAN'T REALLY BE AS CALM AS HE MAKES OUT.
I HEAR SOME COMMANDERS IN EXTREME SITUATIONS GET JUDGED INCOMPETENT BY THEIR SUBORDINATES...
...AND DIE OF MYSTERIOUS WOUNDS TO THE BACK.
IT HAPPENS ALL THE TIME.
JEAN... WHAT ARE YOU GOING TO DO?
HUH?
DON'T LISTEN TO ME.
JUST PISSED OFF, IS ALL.

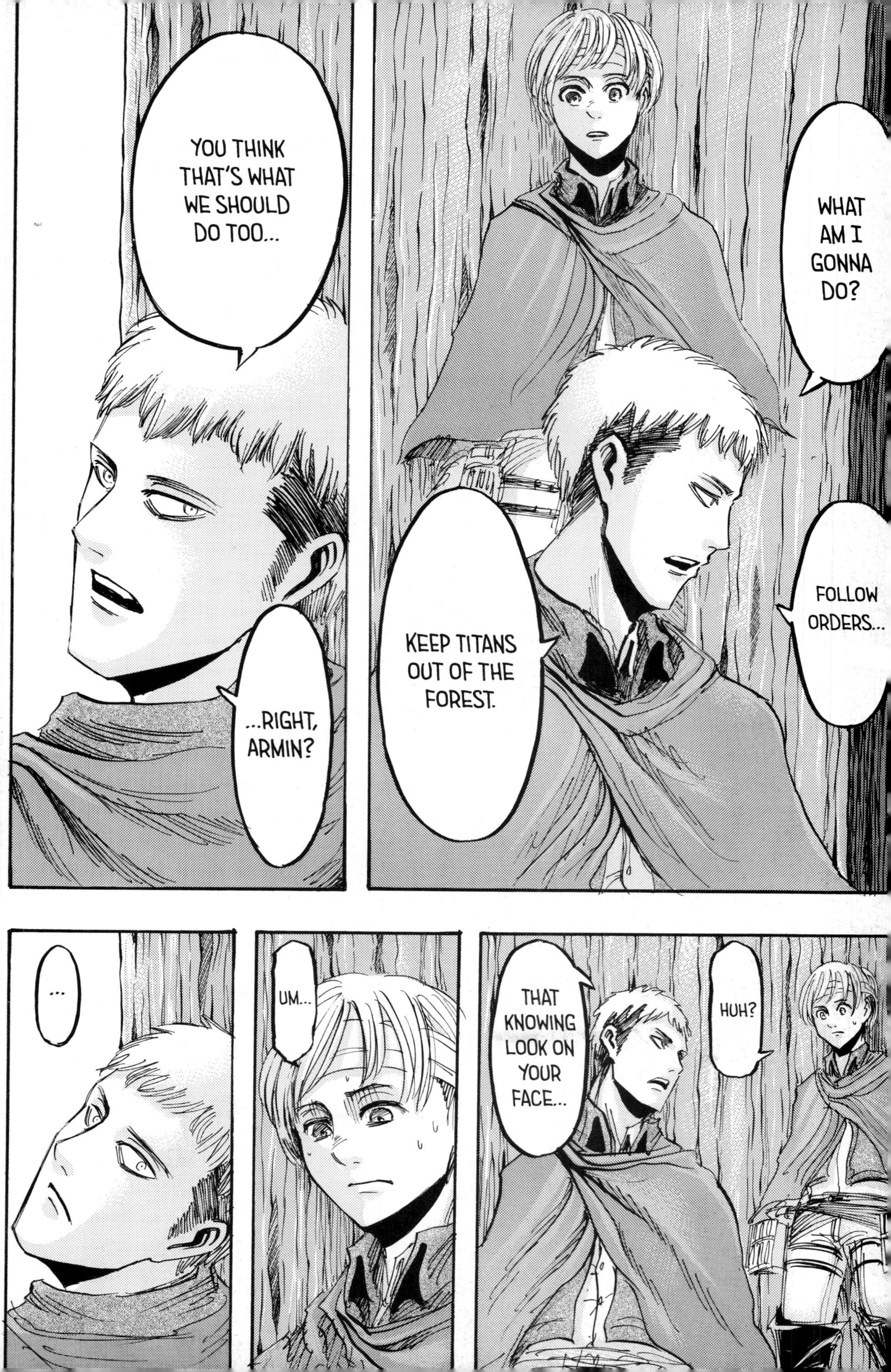
WHAT AM I GONNA DO?
FOLLOW ORDERS...
KEEP TITANS OUT OF THE FOREST.
YOU THINK THAT'S WHAT WE SHOULD DO TOO...
...RIGHT, ARMIN?
HUH?
THAT KNOWING LOOK ON YOUR FACE...
UM...
...

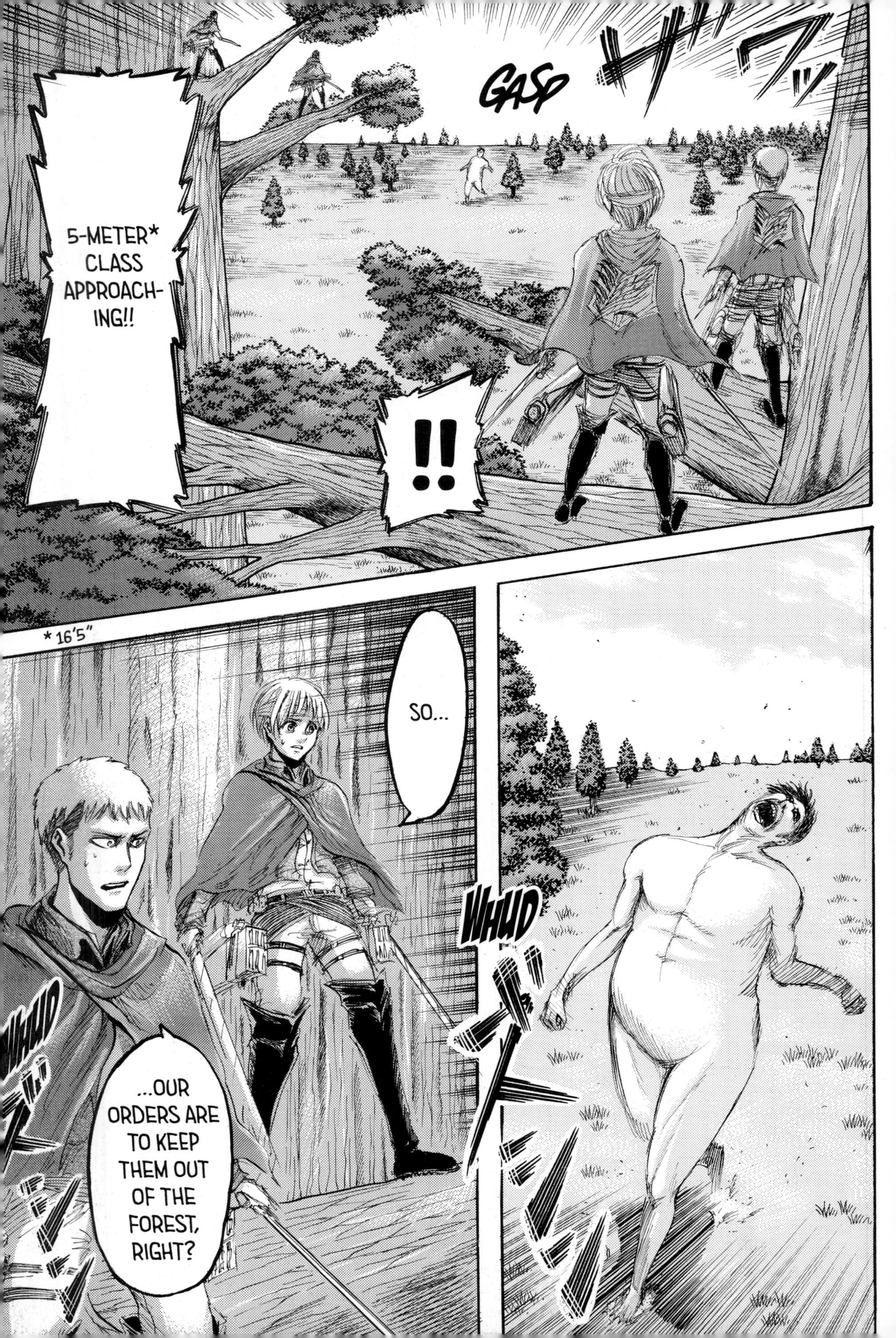
GASP
5-METER* CLASS APPROACHING!!
!!
WHUD
SO...
WHUD
...OUR ORDERS ARE TO KEEP THEM OUT OF THE FOREST, RIGHT?
* 16'5"

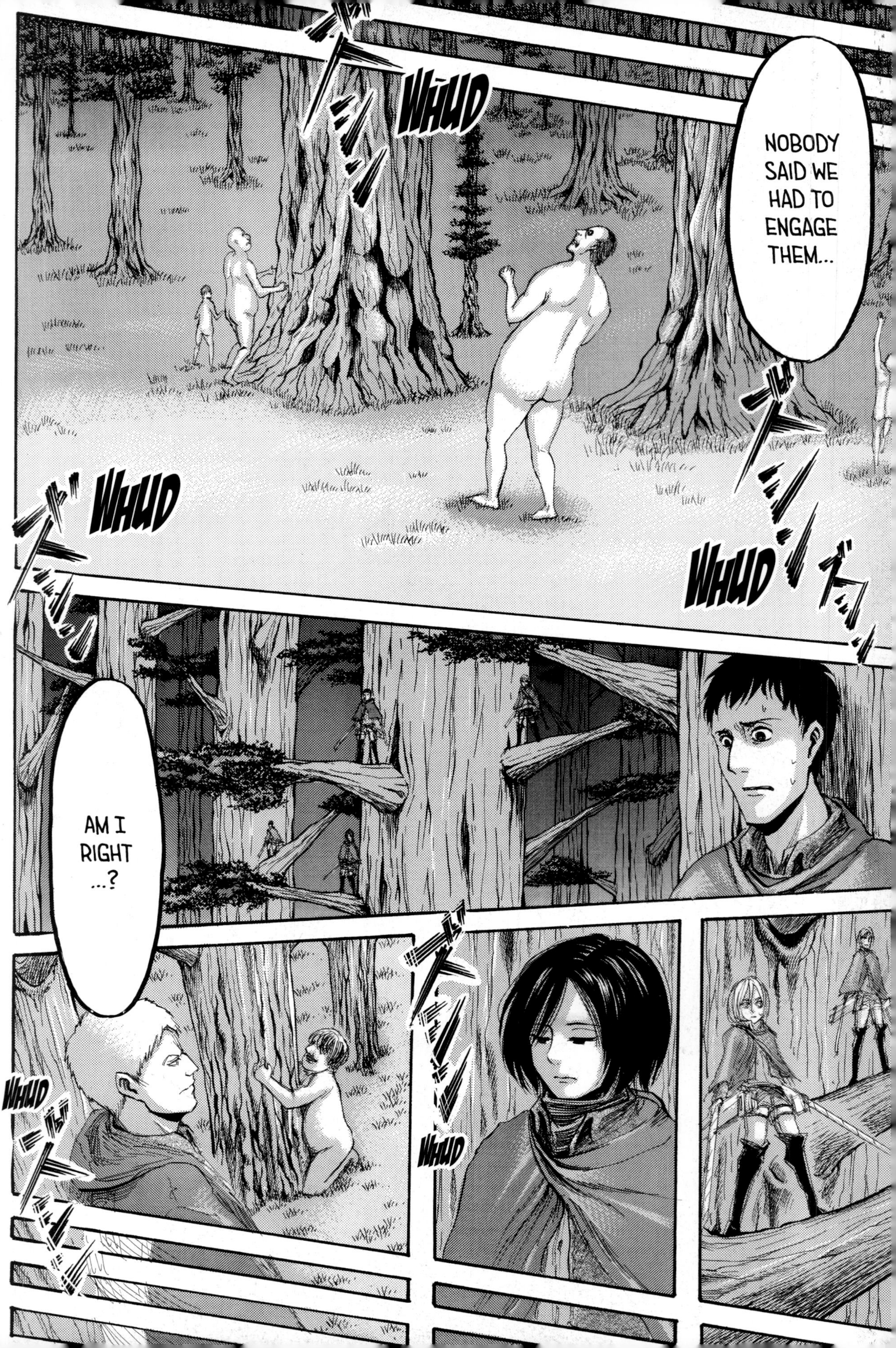
NOBODY SAID WE HAD TO ENGAGE THEM...
WHUD
WHUD
WHUD
AM I RIGHT ...?
WHUD
WHUD

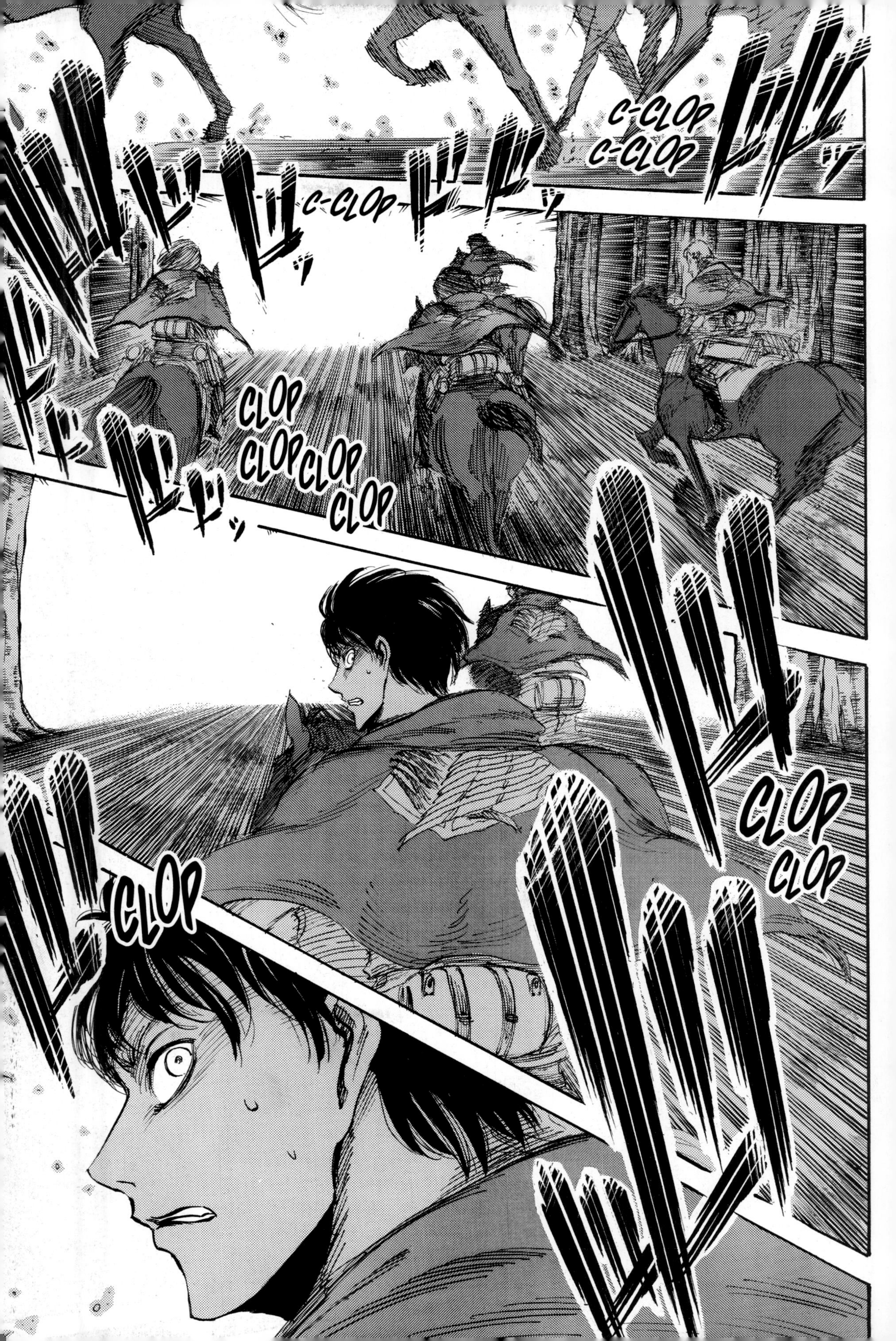
C-CLOP
C-CLOP
C-CLOP
CLOP
CLOP CLOP
CLOP
CLOP
CLOP
CLOP
CLOP

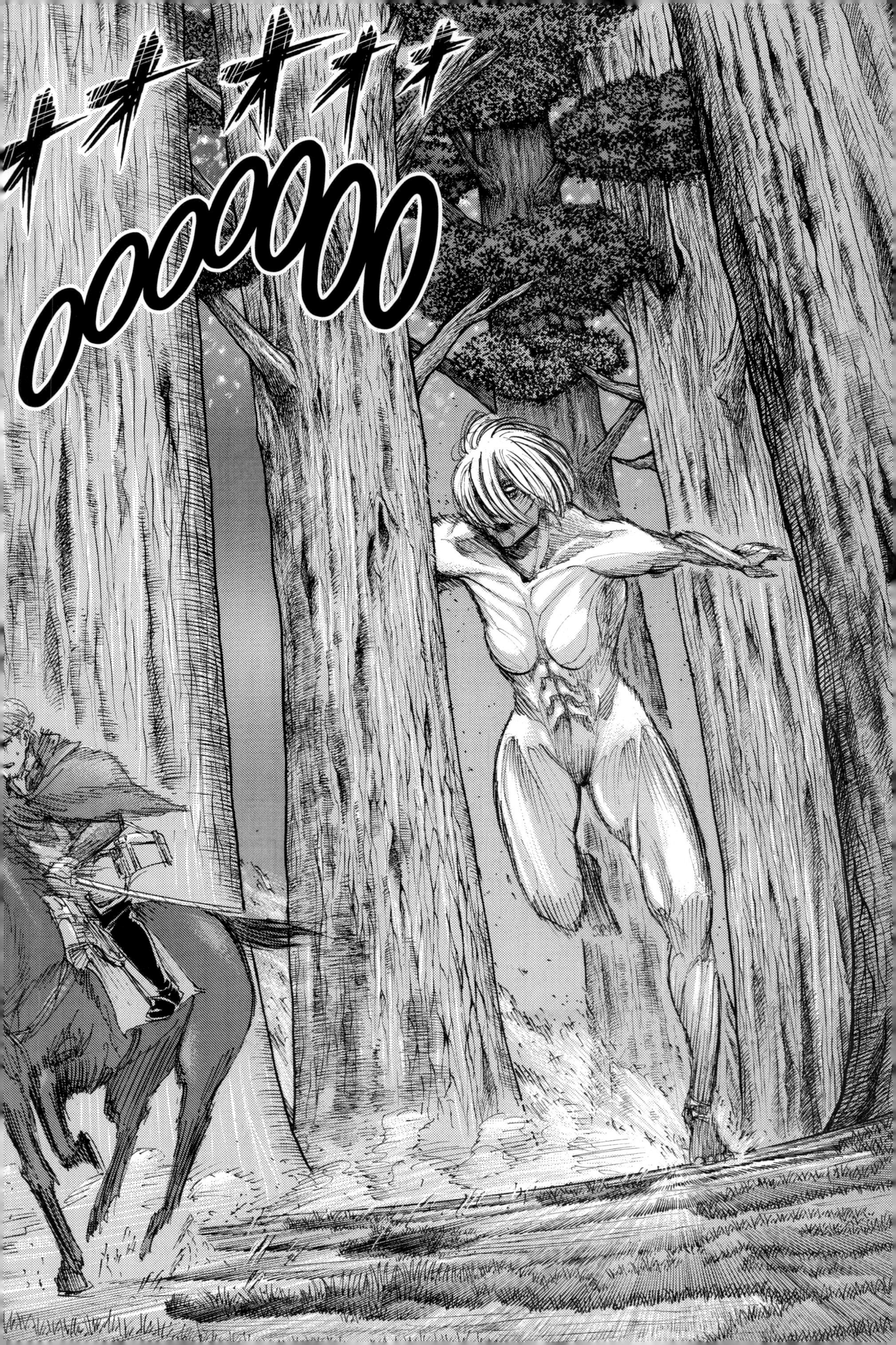
オオオオオ
OOOOOOO

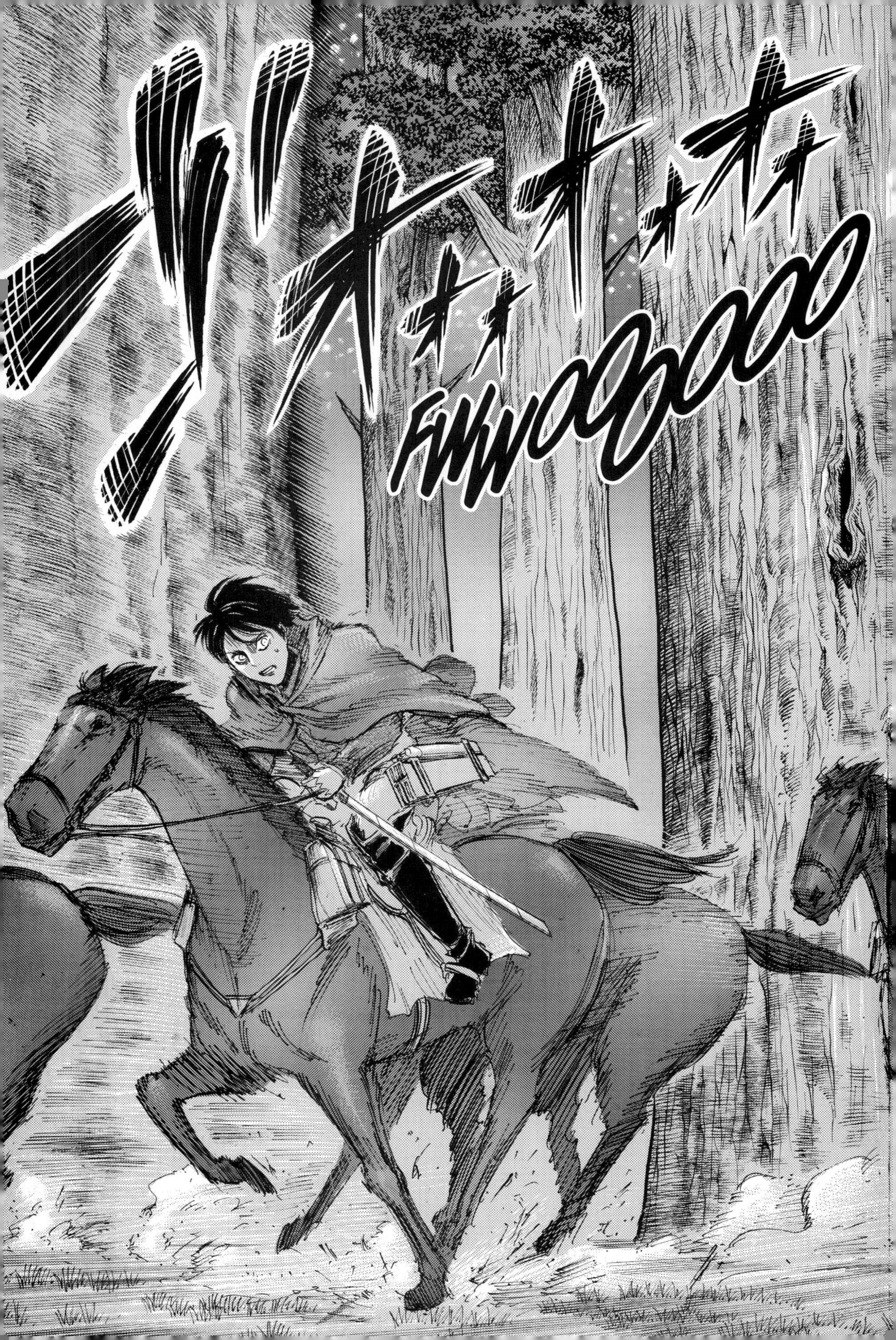
FWOOOOOO

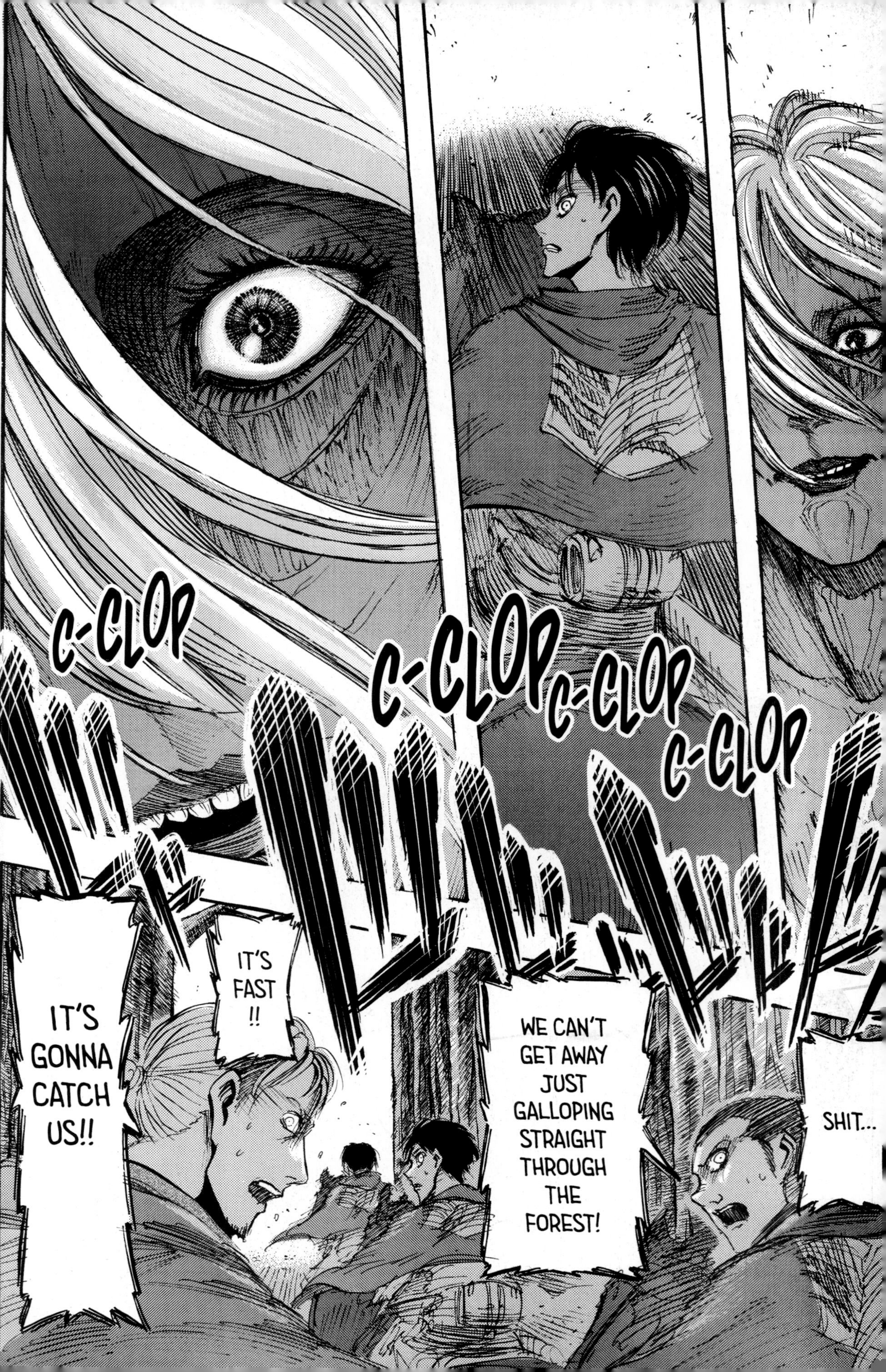
C-CLOP
C-CLOP
C-CLOP
C-CLOP
SHIT...
WE CAN'T GET AWAY JUST GALLOPING STRAIGHT THROUGH THE FOREST!
IT'S FAST!!
IT'S GONNA CATCH US!!

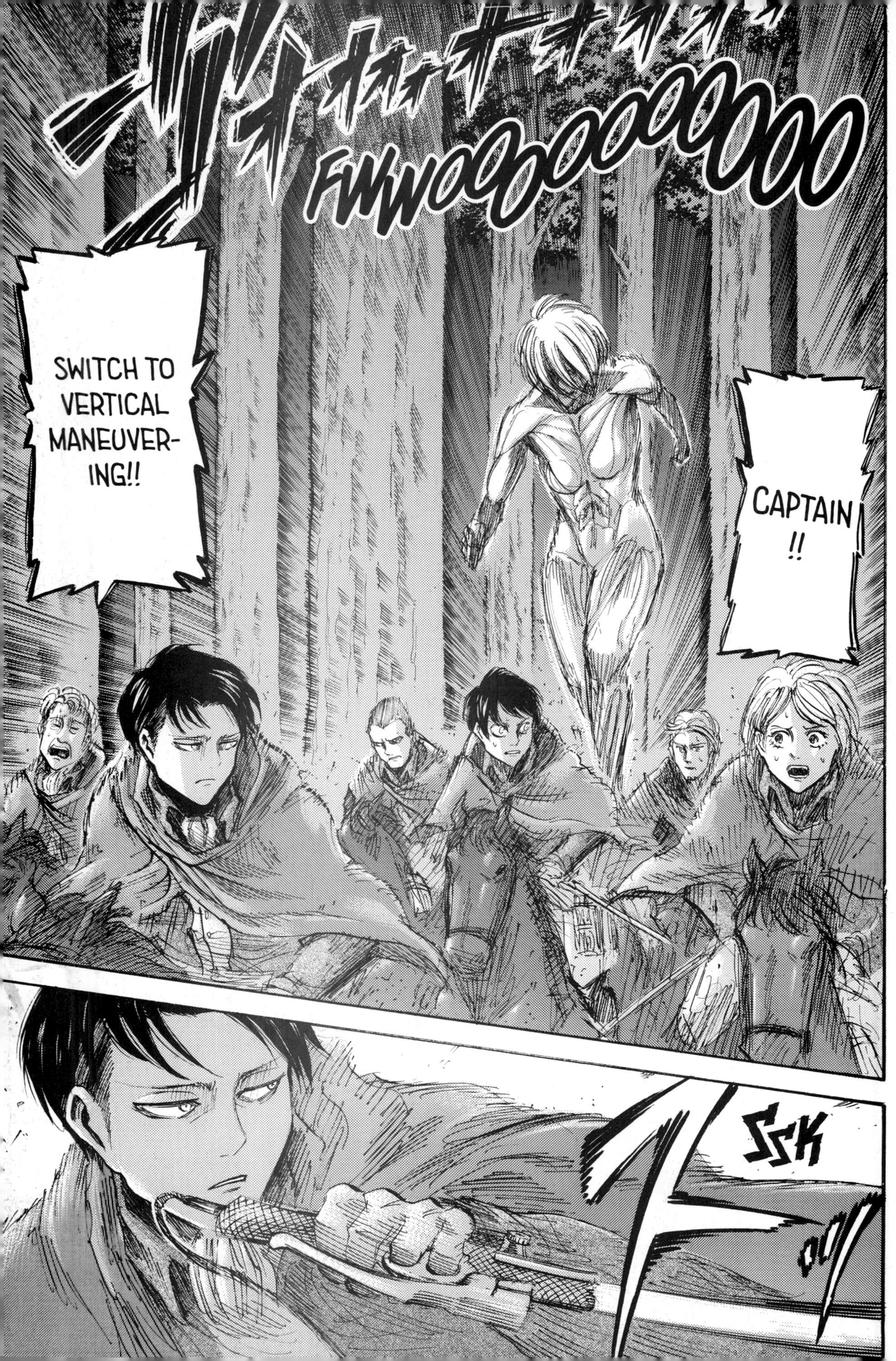
FWWOOOOOOOOOO
CAPTAIN !!
SWITCH TO VERTICAL MANEUVER-ING!!
SSK

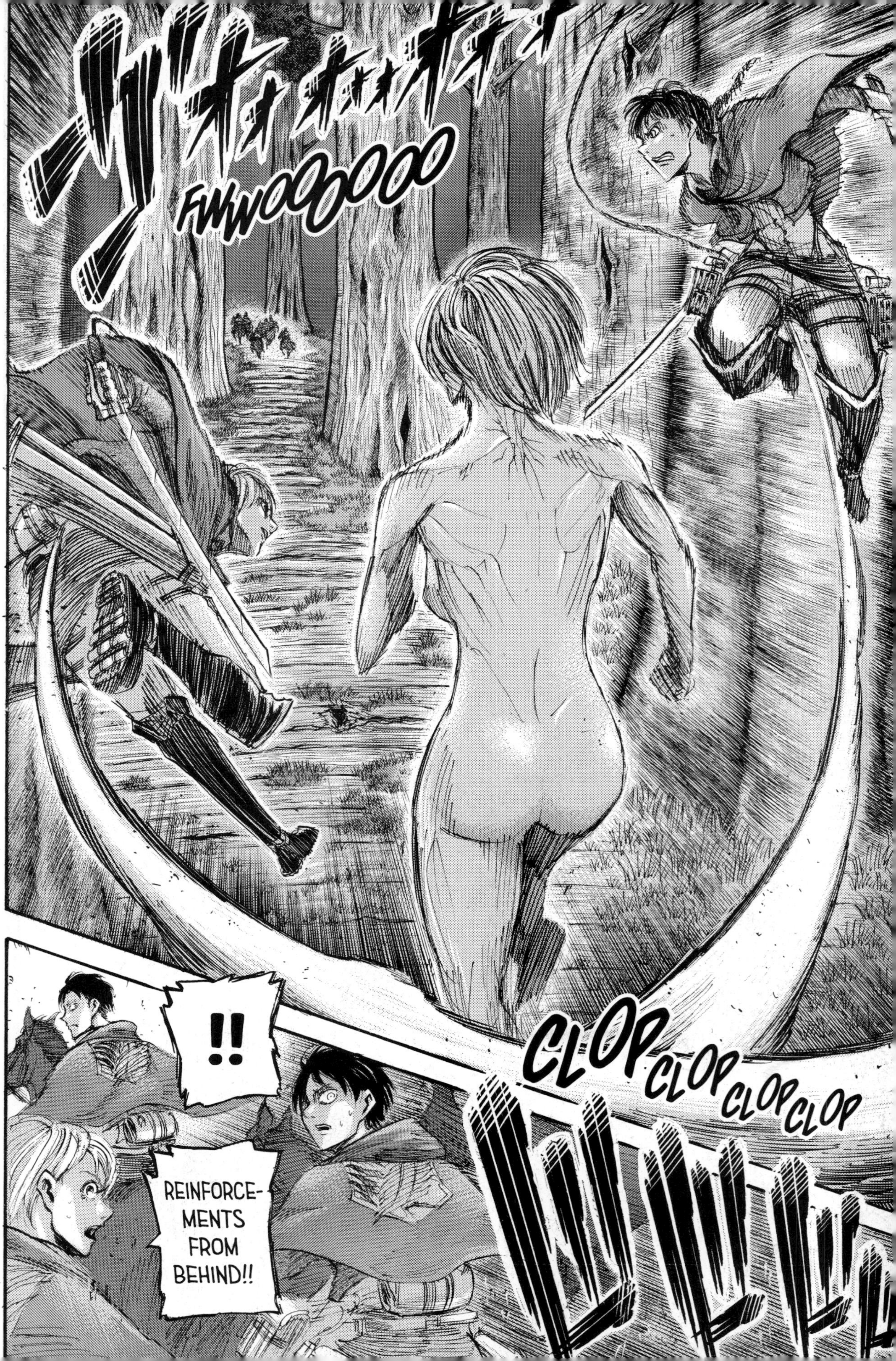
FWWOOOOOOO
CLOP CLOP CLOP CLOP
!!
REINFORCE-
MENTS
FROM
BEHIND!!

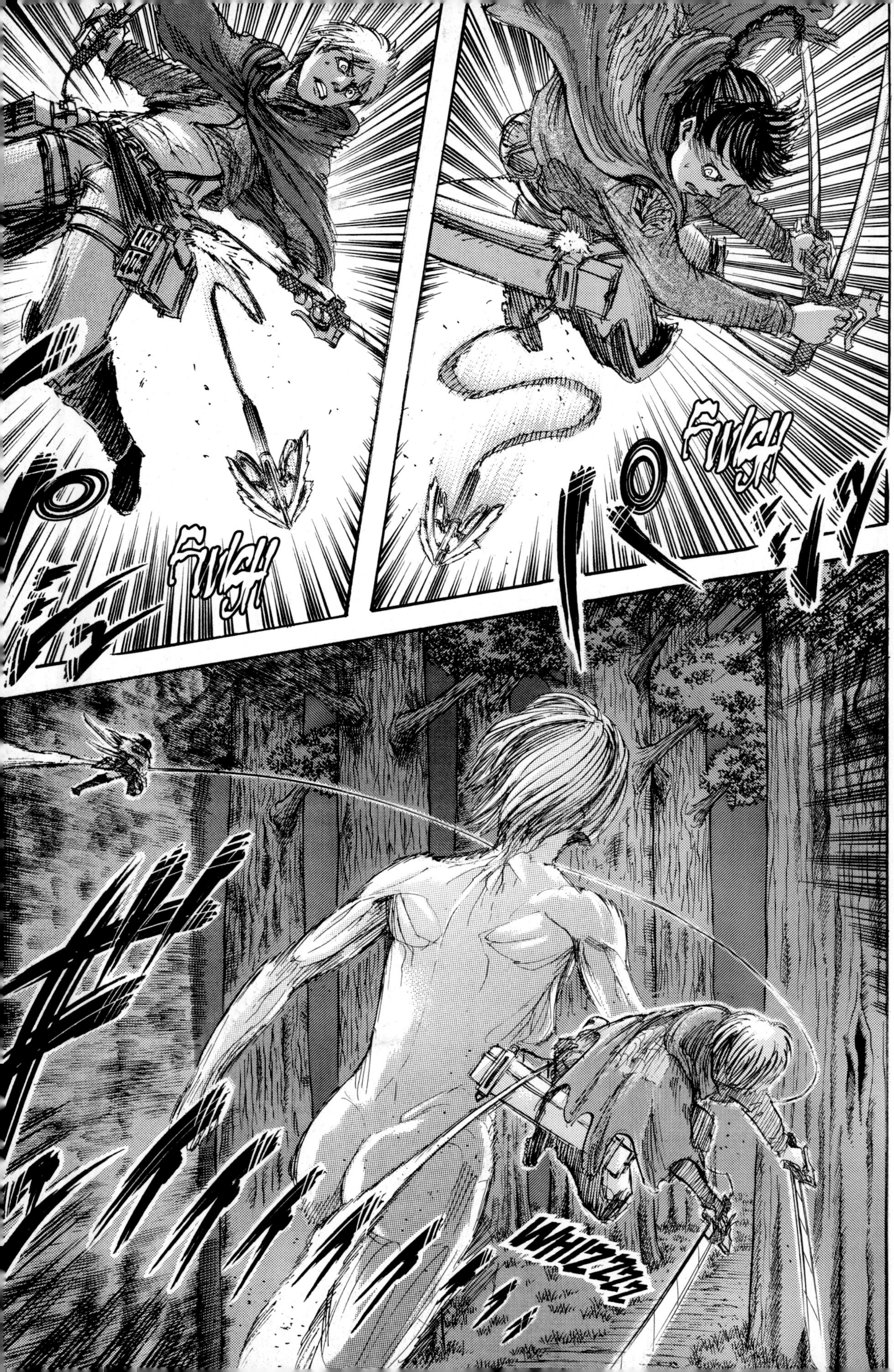
FWISH
FWISH
WHIZZZZ

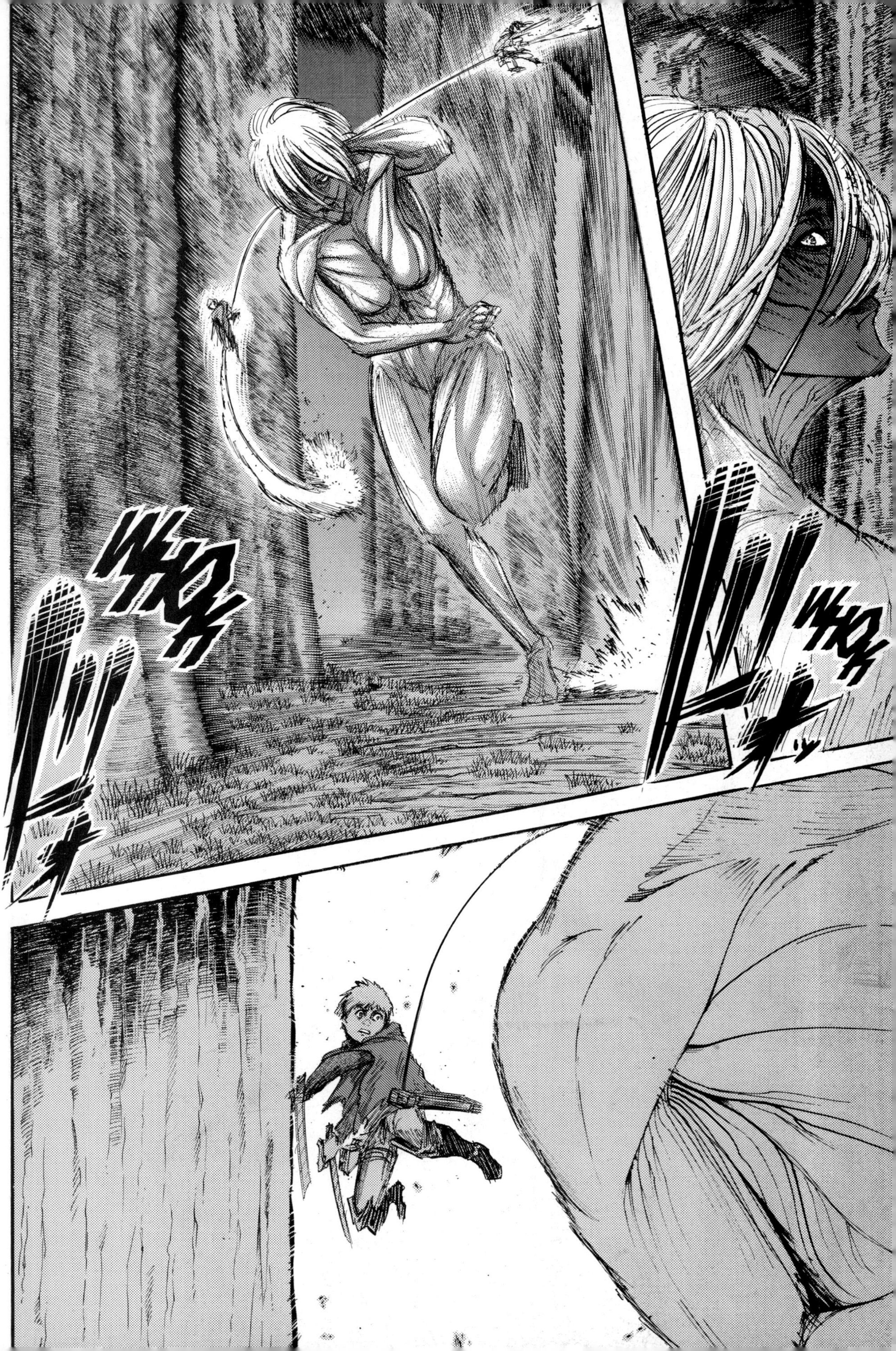

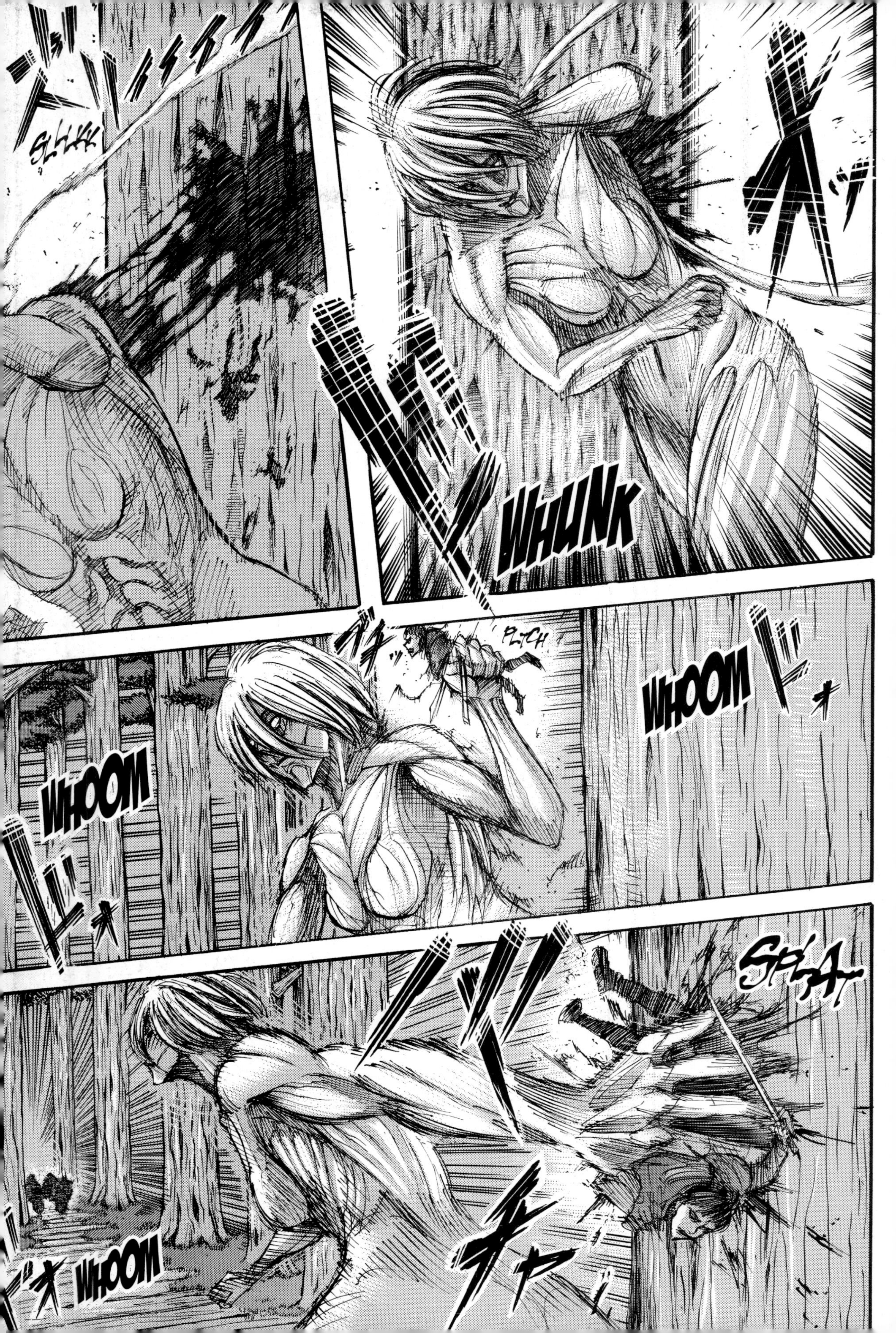
WHUNK
WHOOM
WHOOM
WHOOM

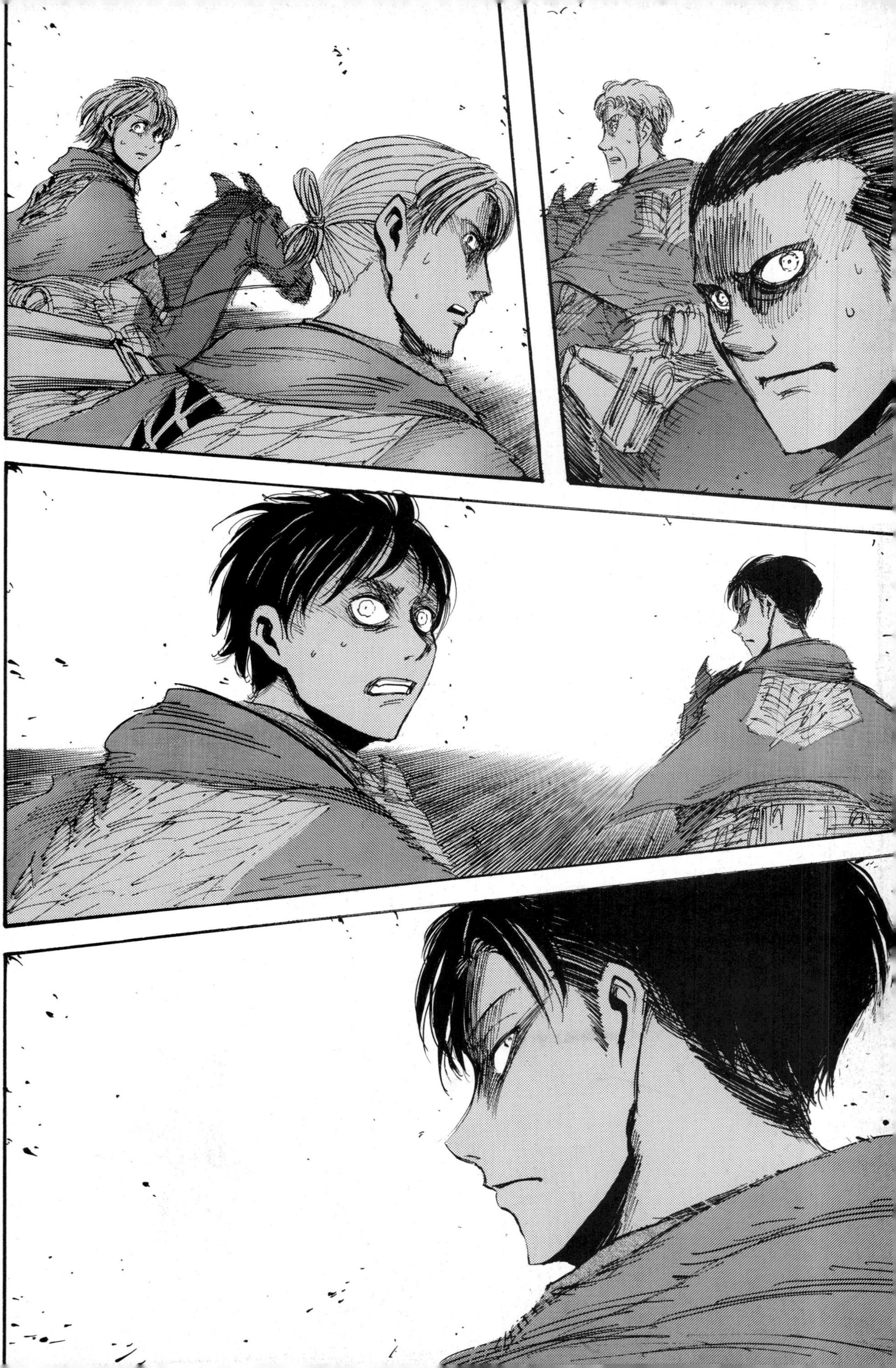

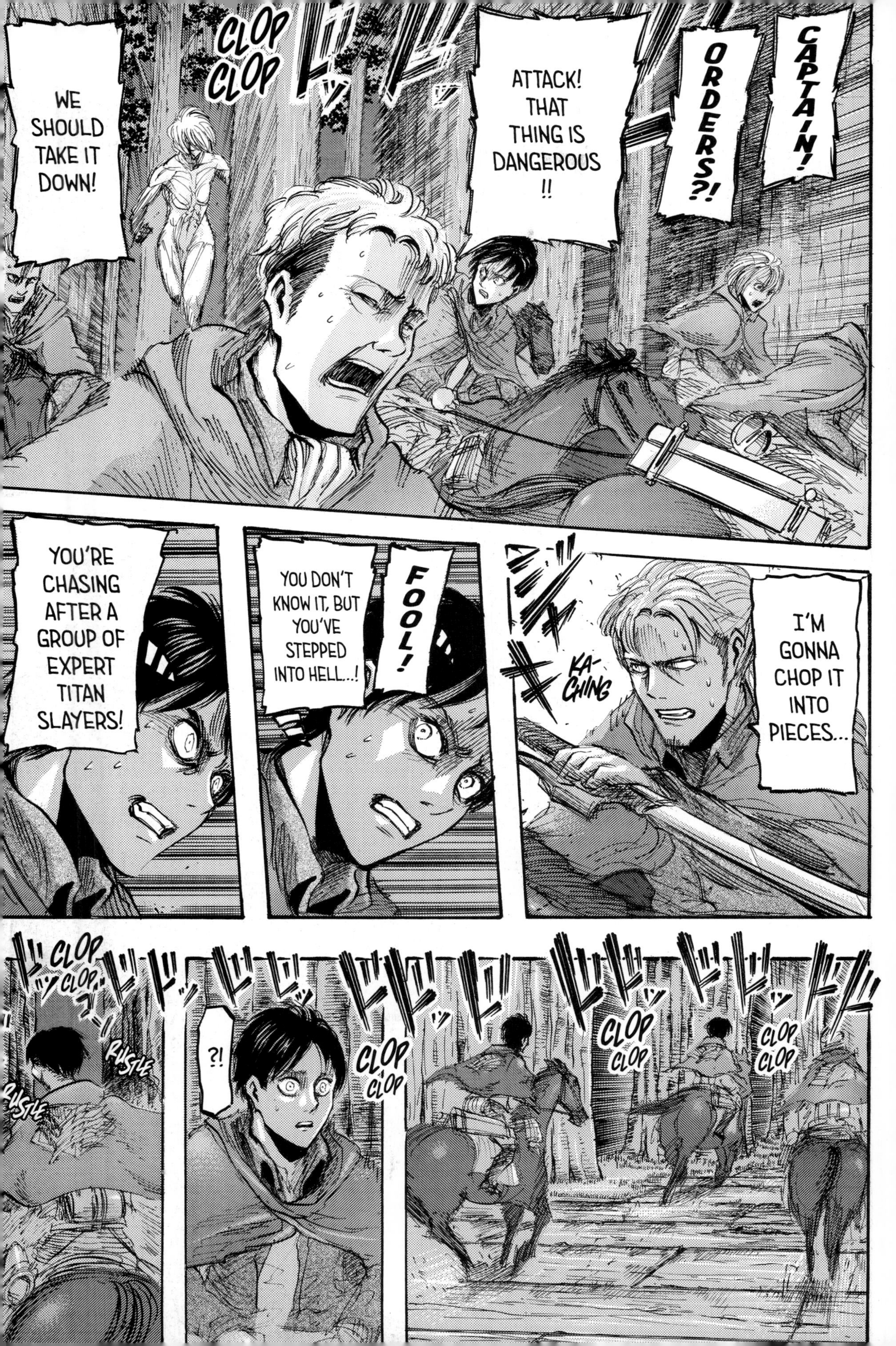
CAPTAIN!
ORDERS?!
ATTACK! THAT THING IS DANGEROUS !!
CLOP CLOP
WE SHOULD TAKE IT DOWN!
I'M GONNA CHOP IT INTO PIECES...
KA-CHING
FOOL!
YOU DON'T KNOW IT, BUT YOU'VE STEPPED INTO HELL...!
YOU'RE CHASING AFTER A GROUP OF EXPERT TITAN SLAYERS!
CLOP CLOP
CLOP CLOP
CLOP CLOP
?!
CLOP CLOP
RUSTLE
RUSTLE

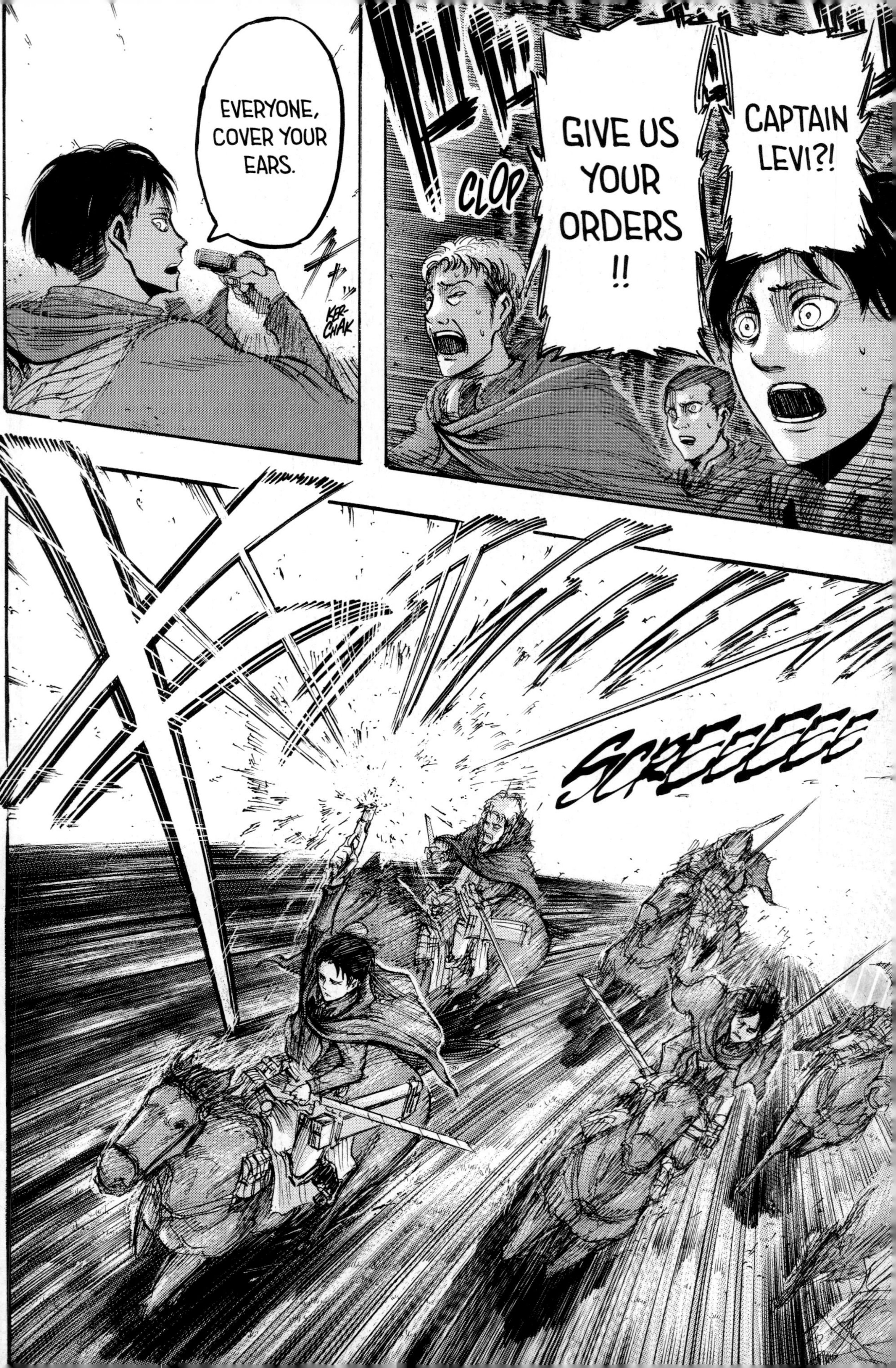
CAPTAIN LEVI?!
GIVE US YOUR ORDERS !!
CLOP
EVERYONE, COVER YOUR EARS.
KER-CHAK
SCREEEEEE

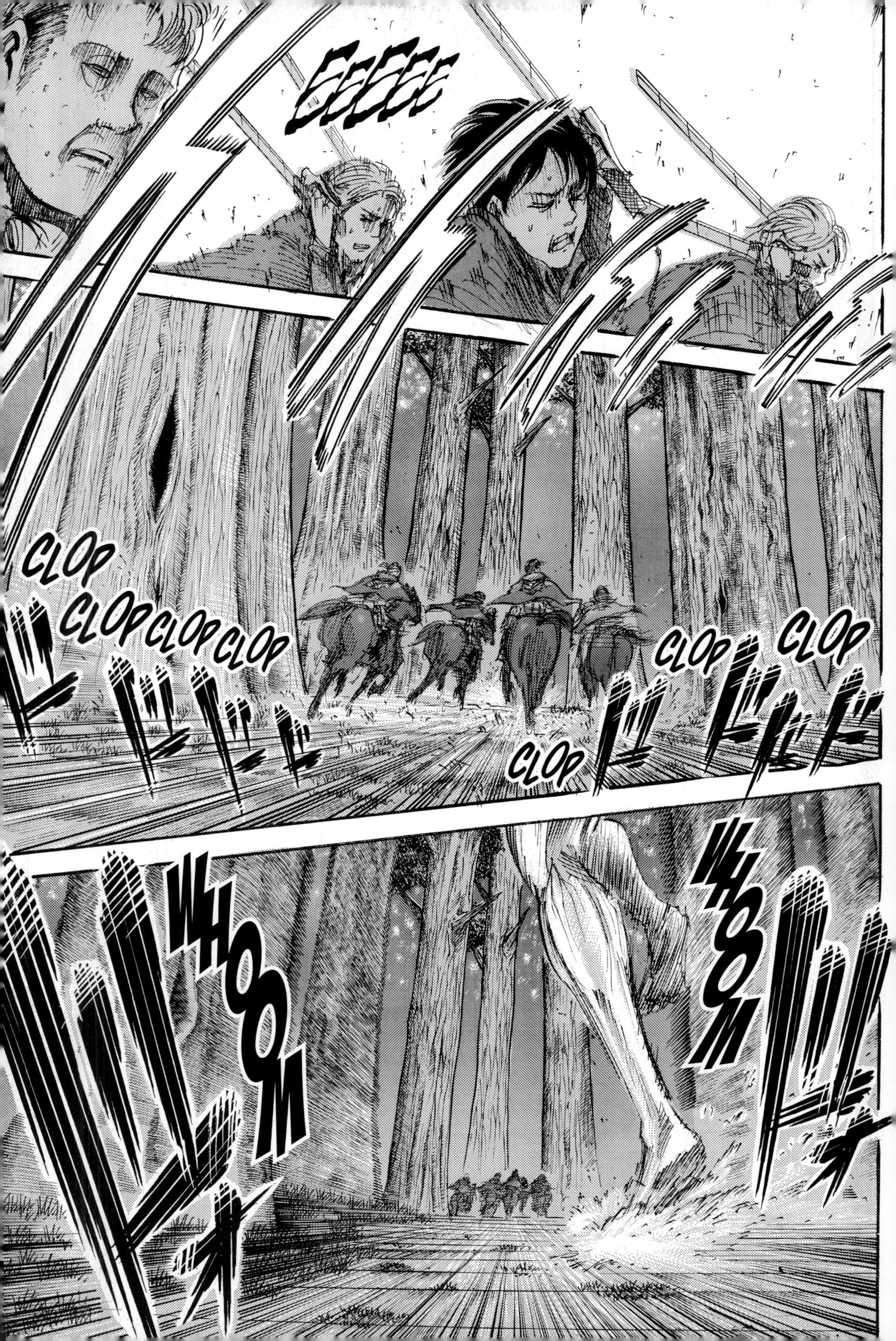
EEEEE
CLOP
CLOP CLOP CLOP
CLOP
CLOP
CLOP CLOP
WHOOM
WHOOM

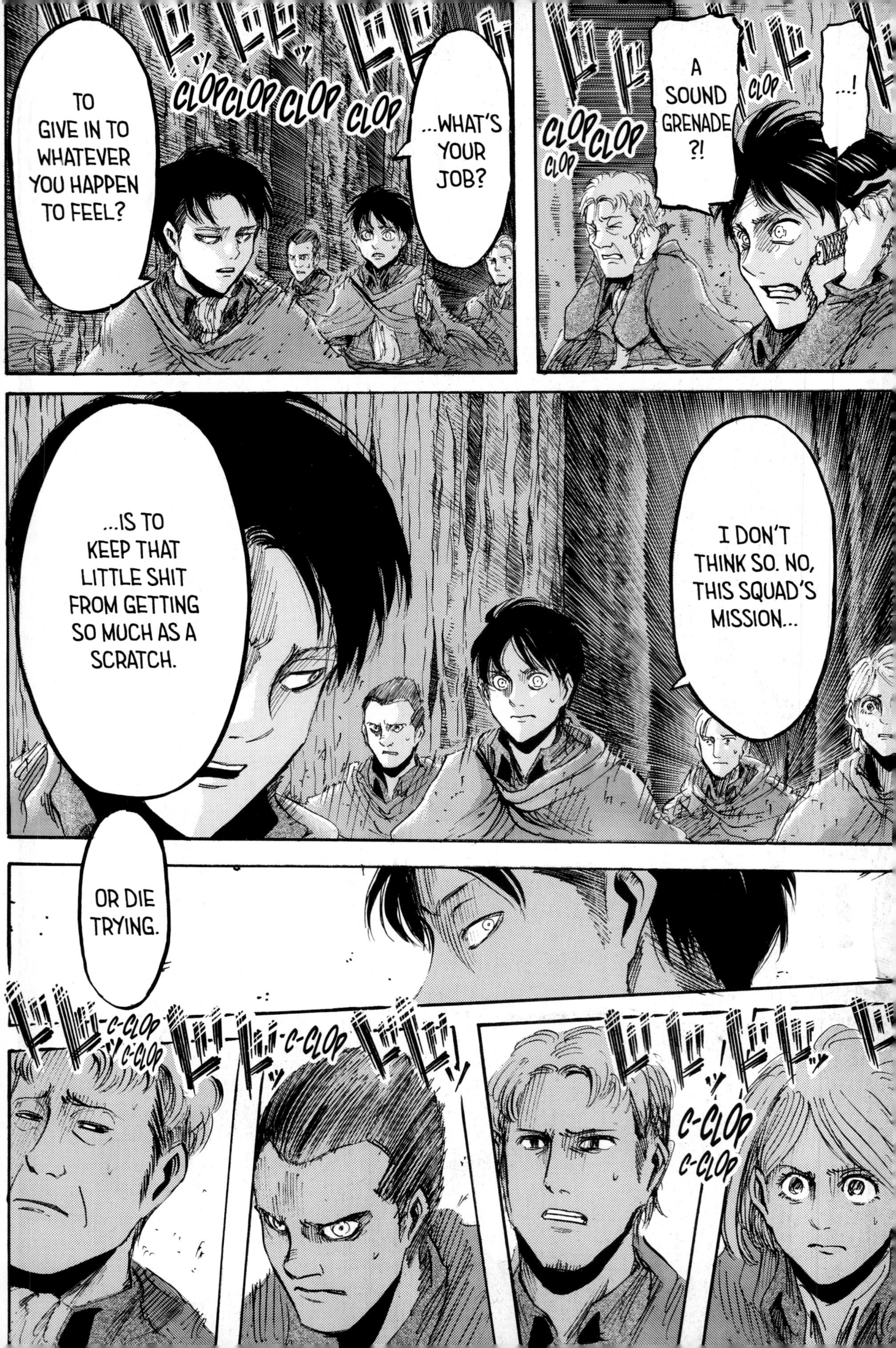

CLOP
CLOP CLOP
CLOP
A SOUND GRENADE ?!
...!
...WHAT'S YOUR JOB?
CLOP
CLOP CLOP CLOP
TO GIVE IN TO WHATEVER YOU HAPPEN TO FEEL?
I DON'T THINK SO. NO, THIS SQUAD'S MISSION...
...IS TO KEEP THAT LITTLE SHIT FROM GETTING SO MUCH AS A SCRATCH.
OR DIE TRYING.
C-CLOP
C-CLOP
C-CLOP
C-CLOP
C-CLOP

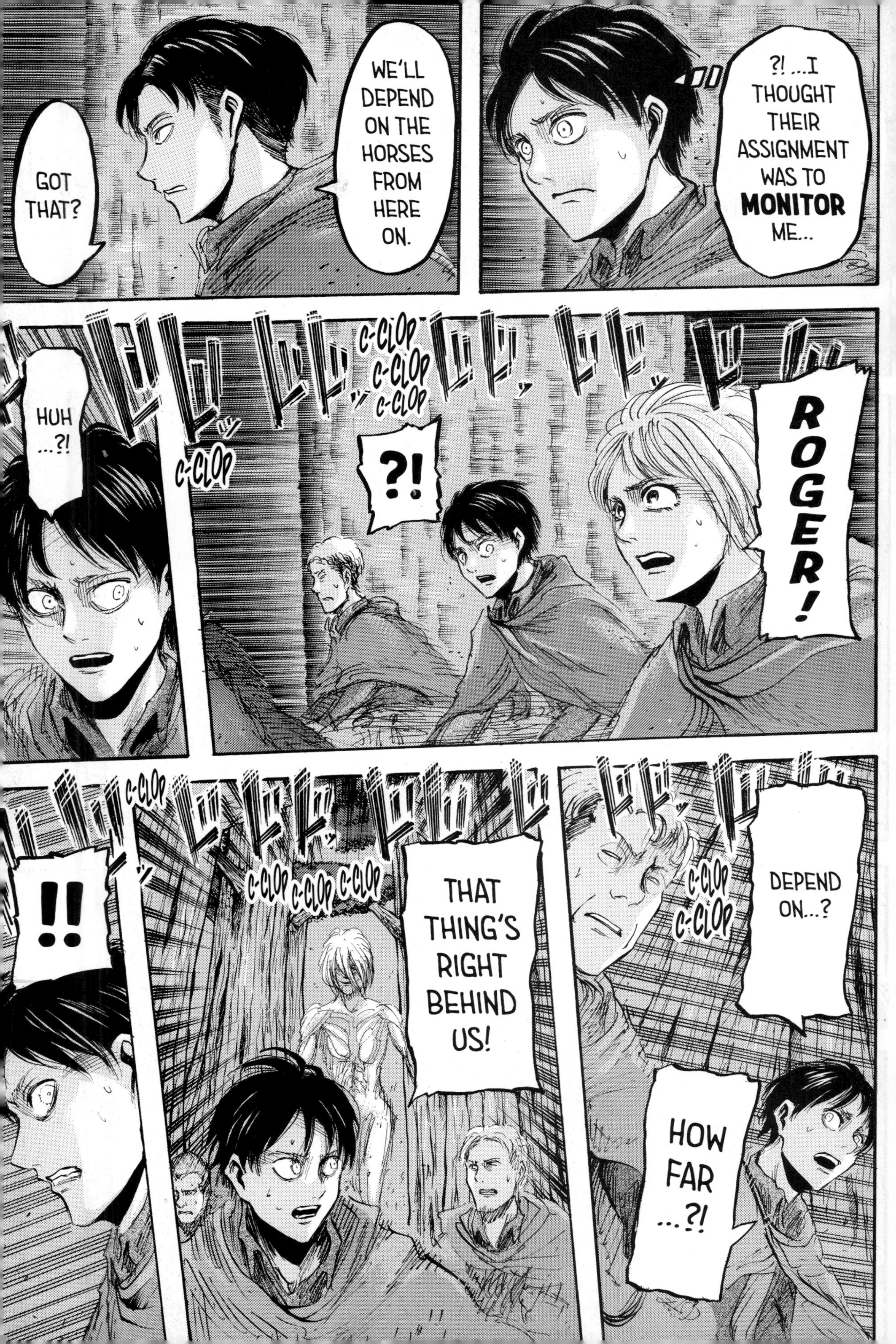
?! ...I THOUGHT THEIR ASSIGNMENT WAS TO **MONITOR** ME...
WE'LL DEPEND ON THE HORSES FROM HERE ON.
GOT THAT?
C-CLOP C-CLOP C-CLOP
ROGER!
?!
HUH ...?!
C-CLOP
C-CLOP C-CLOP
DEPEND ON...?
HOW FAR ...?!
C-CLOP C-CLOP C-CLOP
THAT THING'S RIGHT BEHIND US!
C-CLOP
!!

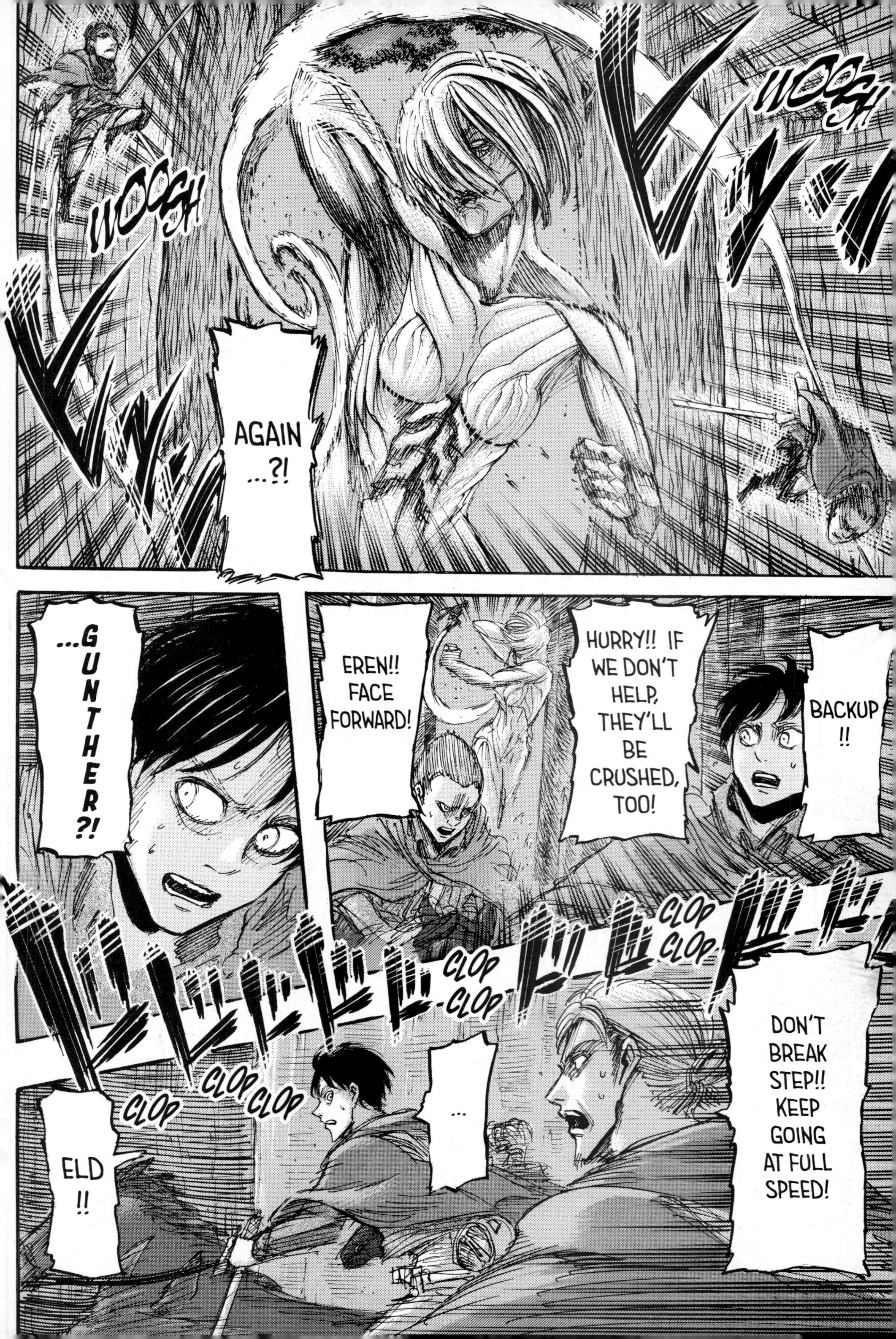
WOOSH
WOOSH!
AGAIN ...?!
BACKUP !!
HURRY!! IF WE DON'T HELP, THEY'LL BE CRUSHED, TOO!
EREN!! FACE FORWARD!
...GUNTHER?!
CLOP CLOP
CLOP CLOP
DON'T BREAK STEP!! KEEP GOING AT FULL SPEED!
...
CLOP CLOP CLOP
ELD !!

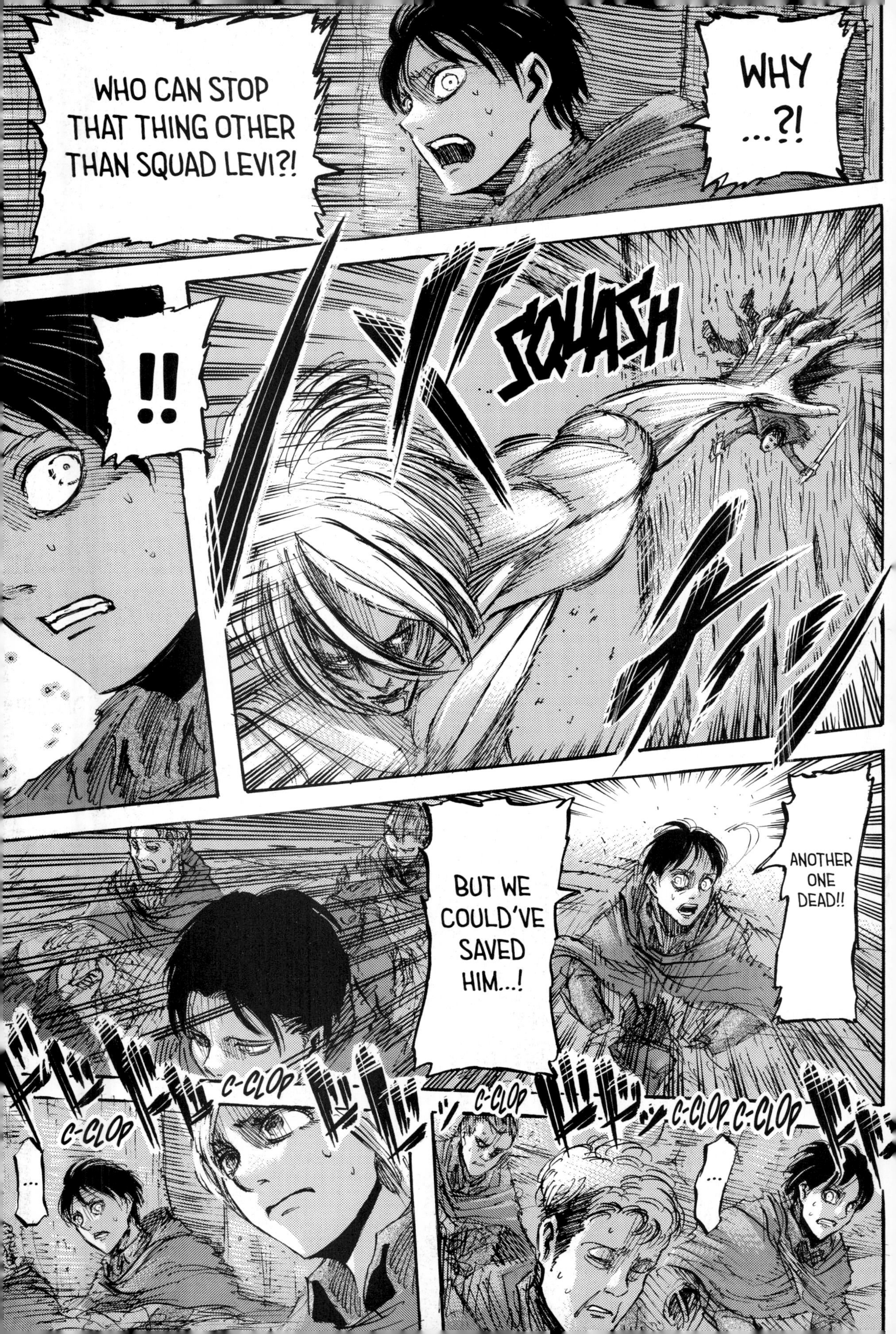
WHY …?!
WHO CAN STOP THAT THING OTHER THAN SQUAD LEVI?!
SQUASH
!!
ANOTHER ONE DEAD!!
BUT WE COULD'VE SAVED HIM…!
C-CLOP C-CLOP
…
C-CLOP
C-CLOP
C-CLOP
…

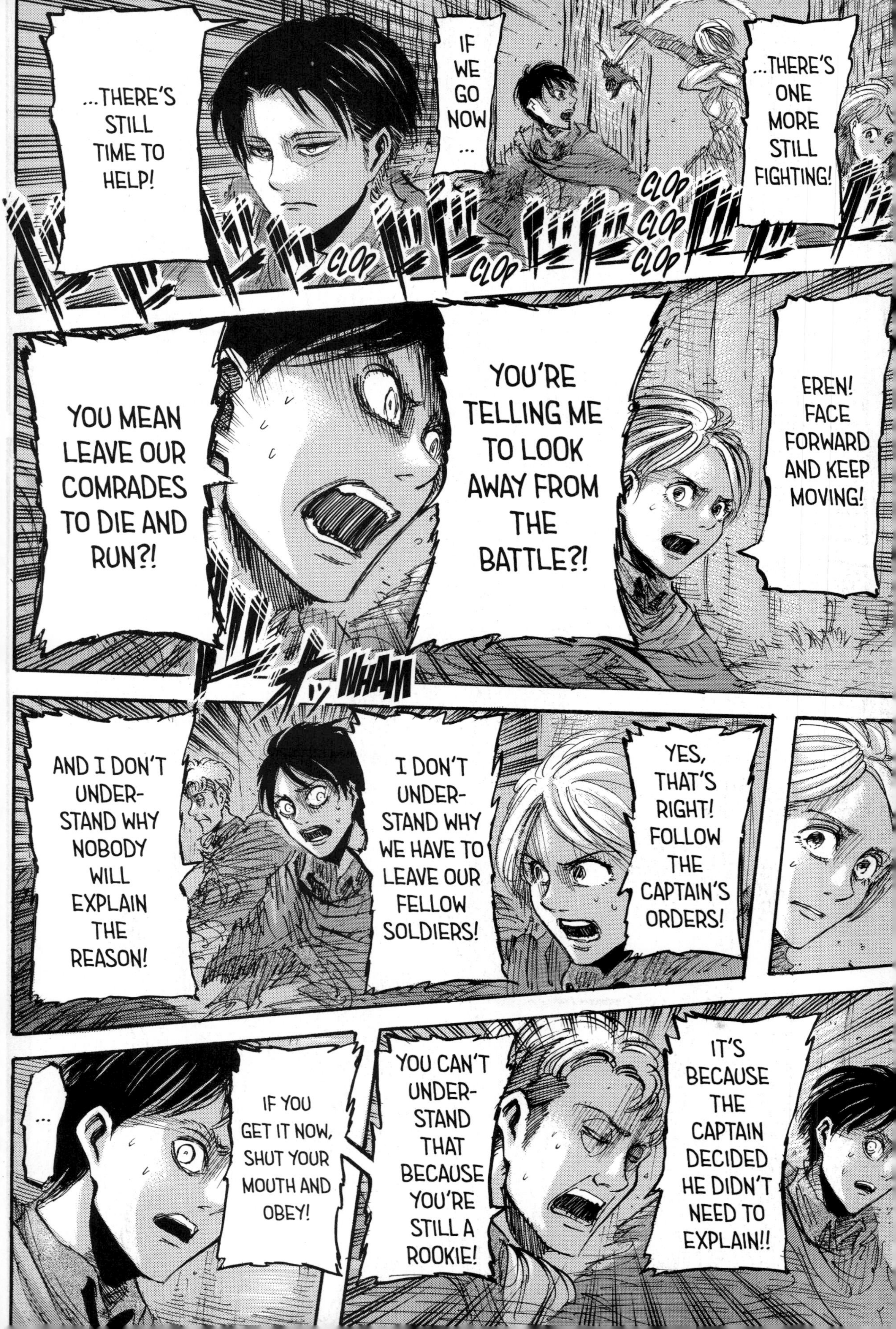
...THERE'S ONE MORE STILL FIGHTING!
IF WE GO NOW ...
CLOP CLOP CLOP
CLOP
...THERE'S STILL TIME TO HELP!
CLOP
EREN! FACE FORWARD AND KEEP MOVING!
YOU'RE TELLING ME TO LOOK AWAY FROM THE BATTLE?!
YOU MEAN LEAVE OUR COMRADES TO DIE AND RUN?!
WHAM
YES, THAT'S RIGHT! FOLLOW THE CAPTAIN'S ORDERS!
I DON'T UNDERSTAND WHY WE HAVE TO LEAVE OUR FELLOW SOLDIERS!
AND I DON'T UNDERSTAND WHY NOBODY WILL EXPLAIN THE REASON!
IT'S BECAUSE THE CAPTAIN DECIDED HE DIDN'T NEED TO EXPLAIN!!
YOU CAN'T UNDERSTAND THAT BECAUSE YOU'RE STILL A ROOKIE!
IF YOU GET IT NOW, SHUT YOUR MOUTH AND OBEY!
...

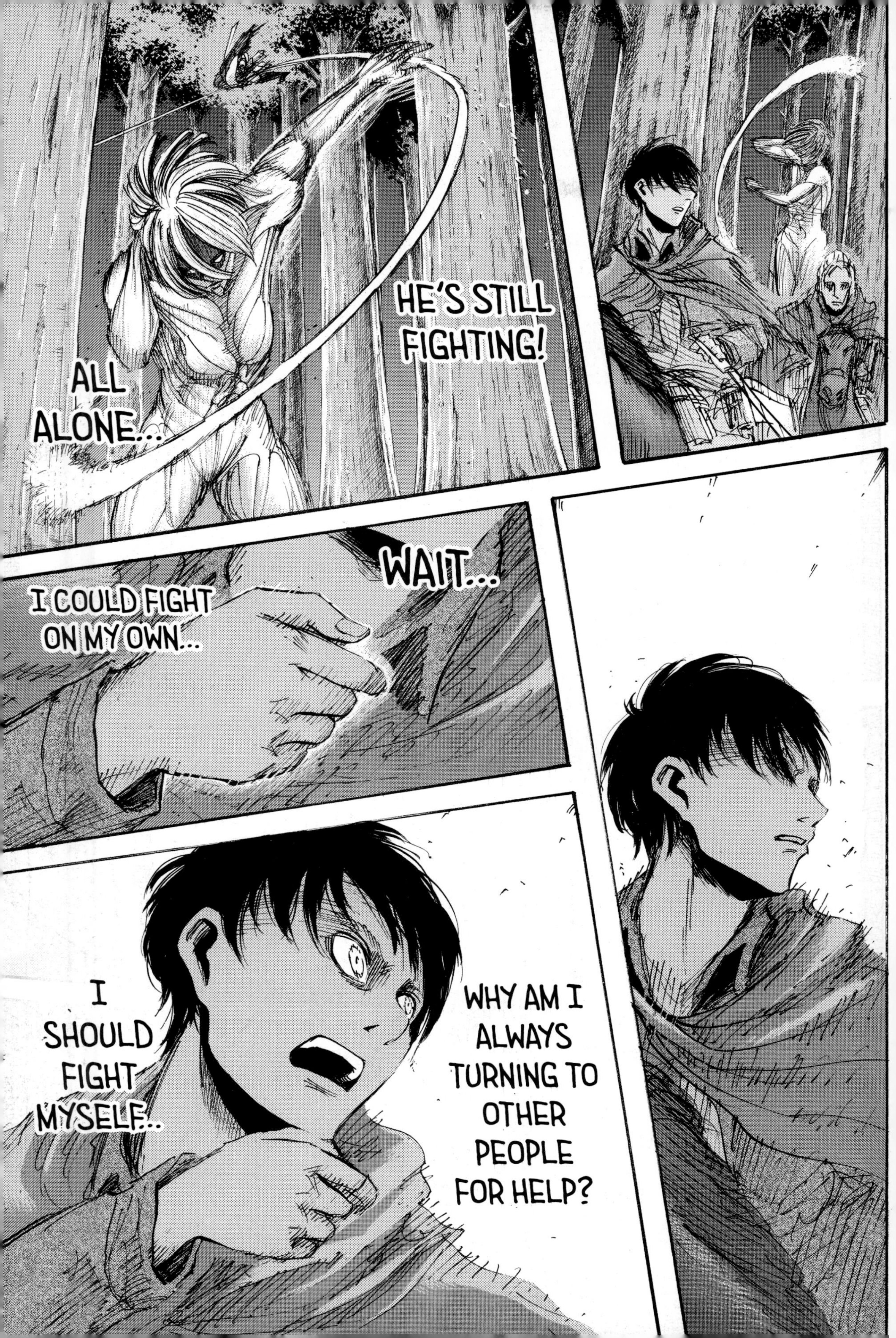
HE'S STILL FIGHTING!
ALL ALONE...
WAIT...
I COULD FIGHT ON MY OWN...
WHY AM I ALWAYS TURNING TO OTHER PEOPLE FOR HELP?
I SHOULD FIGHT MYSELF...

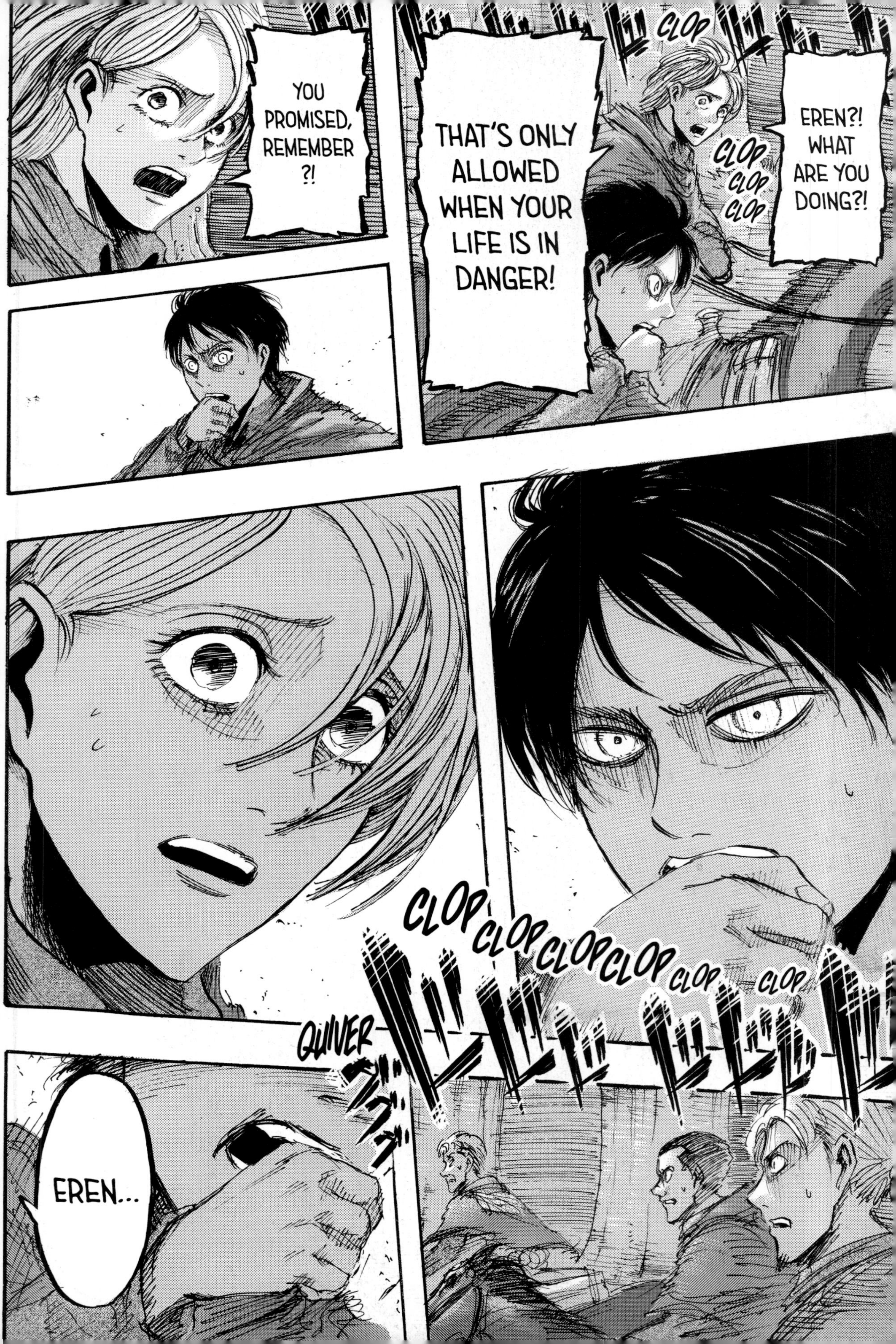

CLOP
EREN?! WHAT ARE YOU DOING?!
CLOP CLOP CLOP
THAT'S ONLY ALLOWED WHEN YOUR LIFE IS IN DANGER!
YOU PROMISED, REMEMBER?!
CLOP CLOP CLOP CLOP CLOP CLOP
QUIVER
EREN...

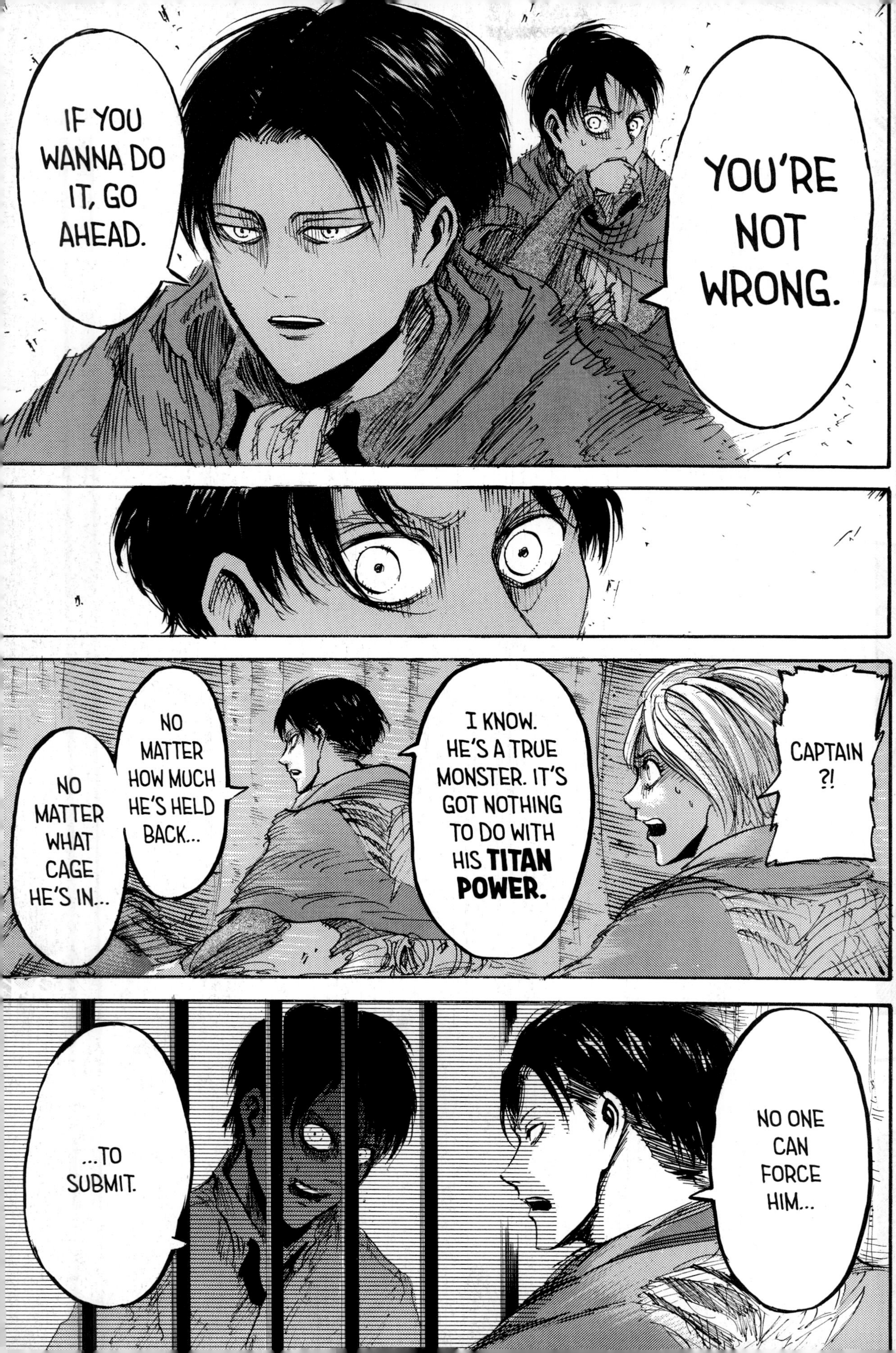
YOU'RE NOT WRONG.
IF YOU WANNA DO IT, GO AHEAD.
CAPTAIN ?!
I KNOW. HE'S A TRUE MONSTER. IT'S GOT NOTHING TO DO WITH HIS TITAN POWER.
NO MATTER HOW MUCH HE'S HELD BACK...
NO MATTER WHAT CAGE HE'S IN...
NO ONE CAN FORCE HIM...
...TO SUBMIT.

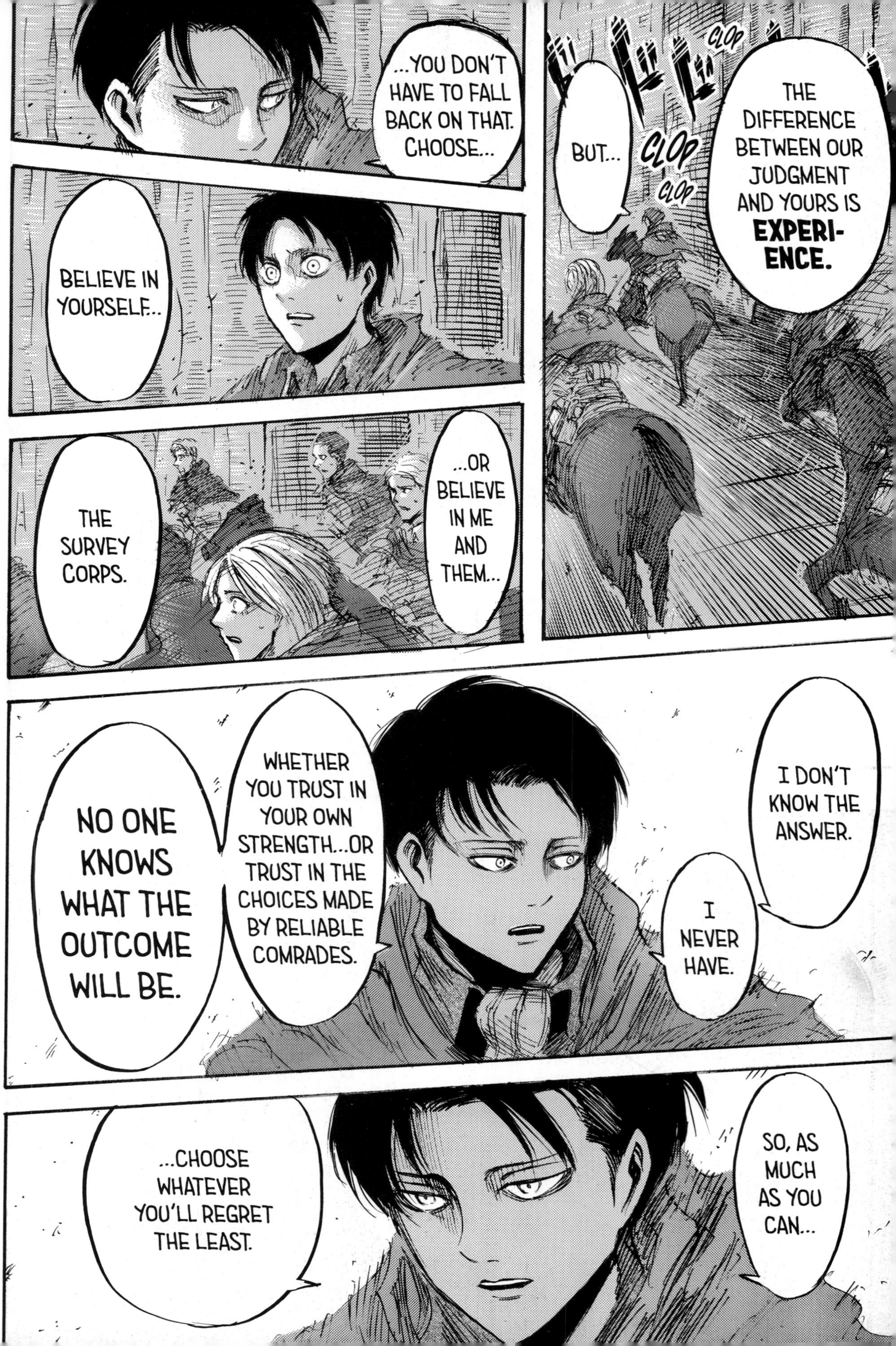
CLOP
THE DIFFERENCE BETWEEN OUR JUDGMENT AND YOURS IS **EXPERIENCE.**
BUT...
CLOP
CLOP
...YOU DON'T HAVE TO FALL BACK ON THAT. CHOOSE...
BELIEVE IN YOURSELF...
...OR BELIEVE IN ME AND THEM...
THE SURVEY CORPS.
I DON'T KNOW THE ANSWER.
I NEVER HAVE.
WHETHER YOU TRUST IN YOUR OWN STRENGTH...OR TRUST IN THE CHOICES MADE BY RELIABLE COMRADES.
NO ONE KNOWS WHAT THE OUTCOME WILL BE.
SO, AS MUCH AS YOU CAN...
...CHOOSE WHATEVER YOU'LL REGRET THE LEAST.

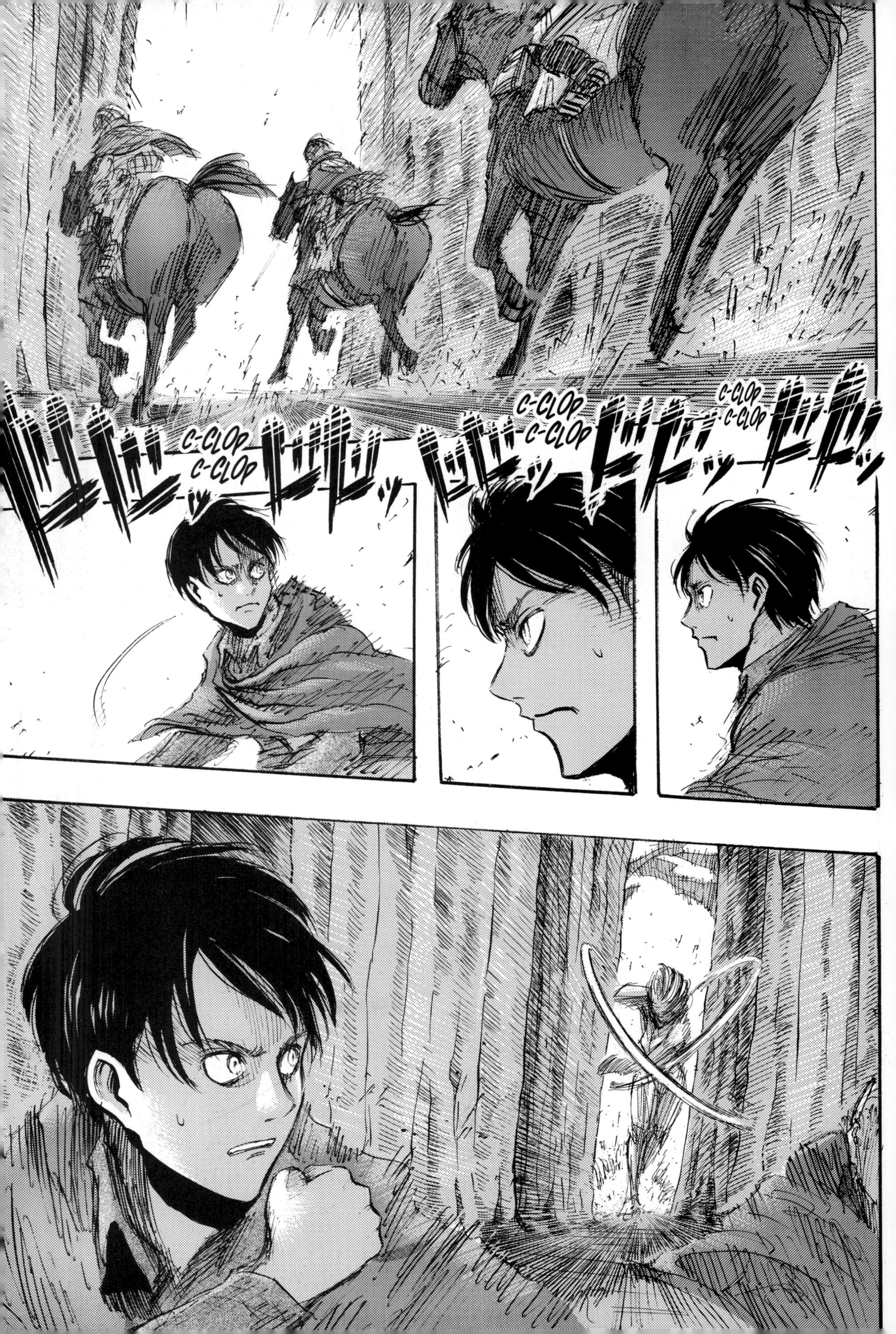
C-CLOP
C-CLOP
C-CLOP
C-CLOP
C-CLOP
C-CLOP

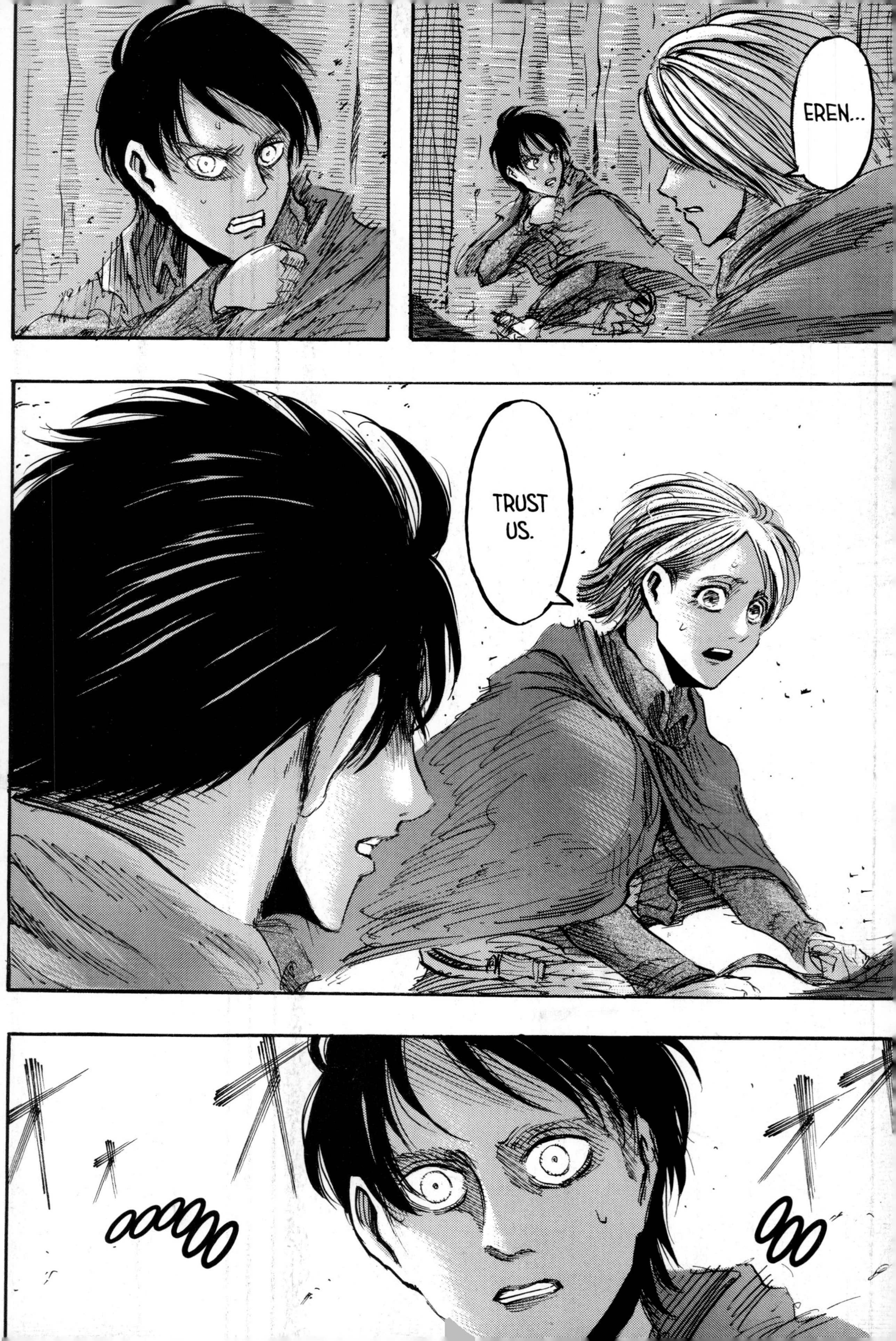
EREN...
TRUST US.

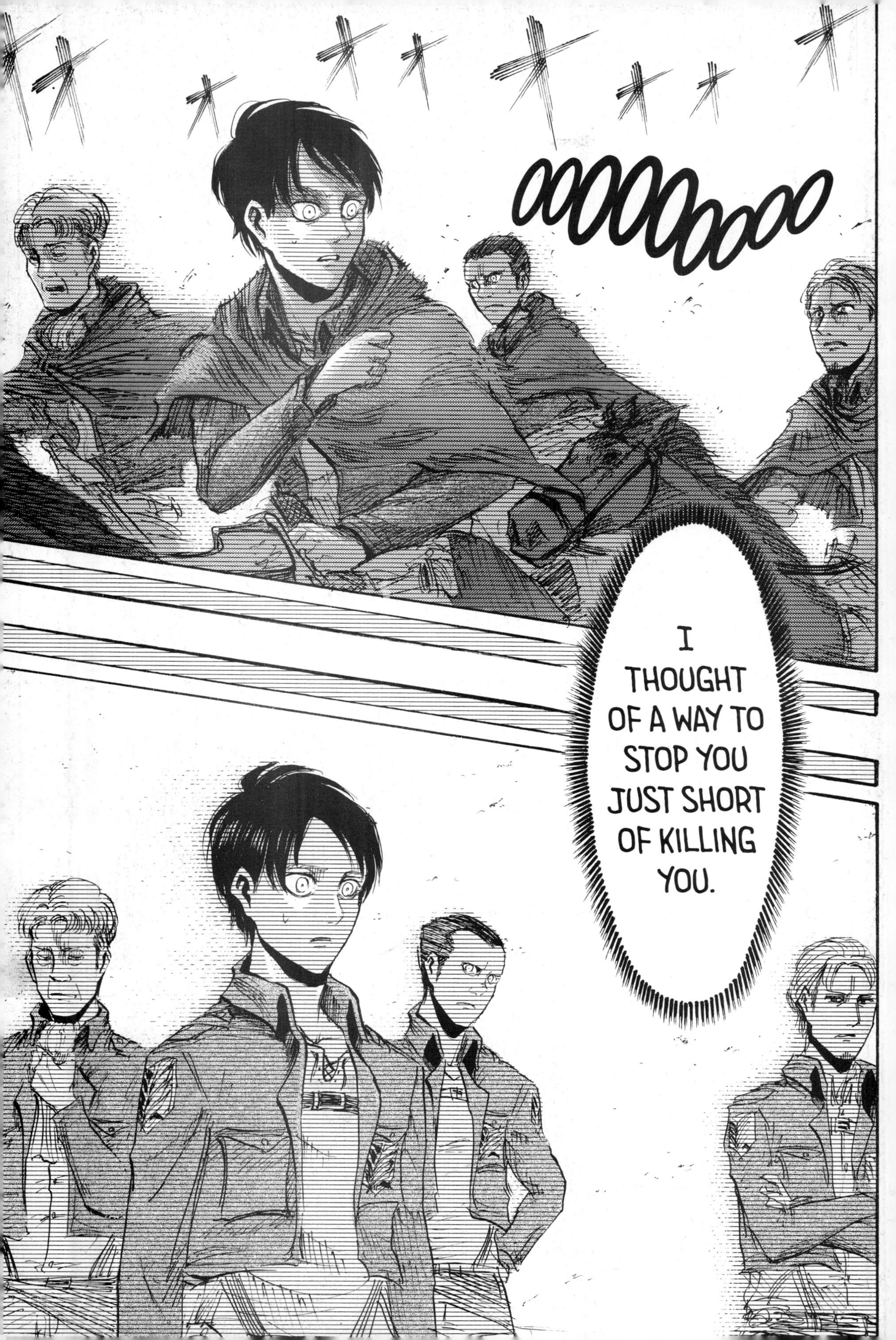
OOOOOOOOOO
I THOUGHT OF A WAY TO STOP YOU JUST SHORT OF KILLING YOU.

...BUT THIS WOULD JUST LEAVE YOU BADLY WOUNDED.

I SAID BEFORE THAT THE ONLY WAY TO STOP YOU IN YOUR TITAN FORM IS TO KILL YOU...

...WHAT?

THAT SAID, IT WOULD RELY ON SEVERAL DIFFERENT SKILLS.

IN SHORT...

THEN WE WOULD CUT OFF YOUR HANDS AND FEET...

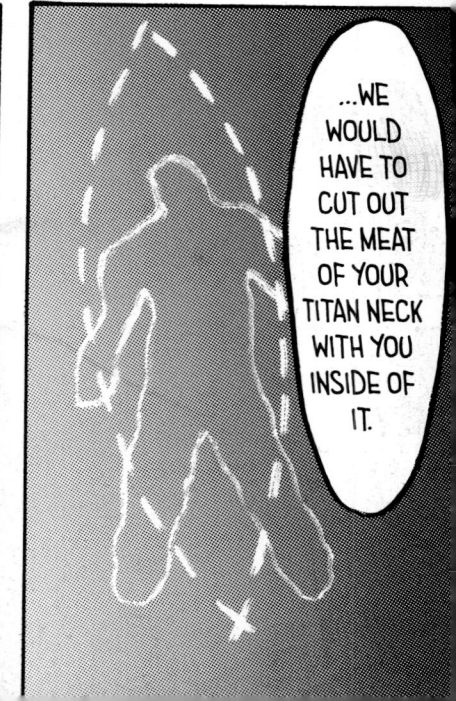

...WE WOULD HAVE TO CUT OUT THE MEAT OF YOUR TITAN NECK WITH YOU INSIDE OF IT.

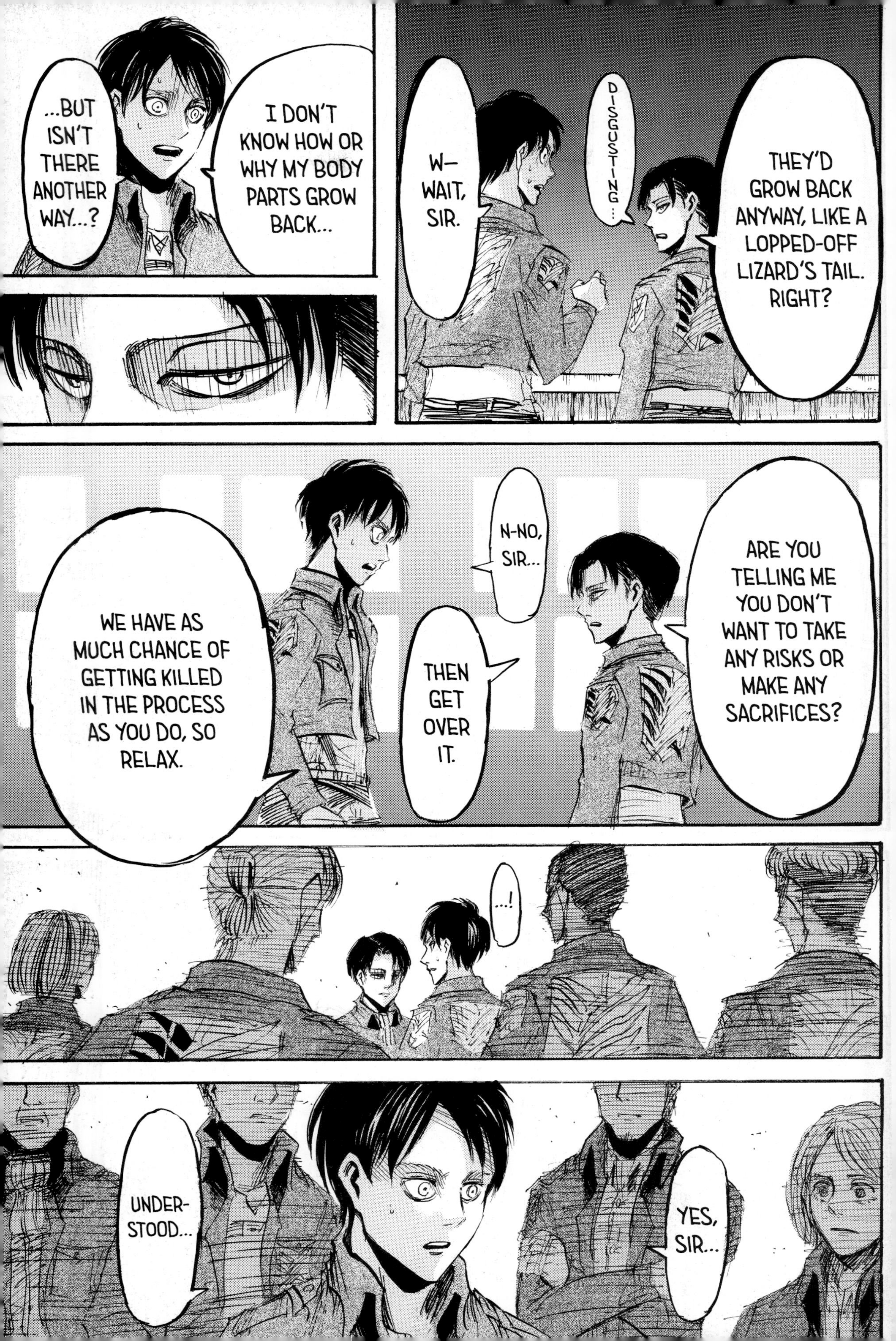

THEY'D GROW BACK ANYWAY, LIKE A LOPPED-OFF LIZARD'S TAIL. RIGHT?
DISGUSTING...
W— WAIT, SIR.
I DON'T KNOW HOW OR WHY MY BODY PARTS GROW BACK...
...BUT ISN'T THERE ANOTHER WAY...?
ARE YOU TELLING ME YOU DON'T WANT TO TAKE ANY RISKS OR MAKE ANY SACRIFICES?
N-NO, SIR...
THEN GET OVER IT.
WE HAVE AS MUCH CHANCE OF GETTING KILLED IN THE PROCESS AS YOU DO, SO RELAX.
...!
YES, SIR...
UNDER-STOOD...

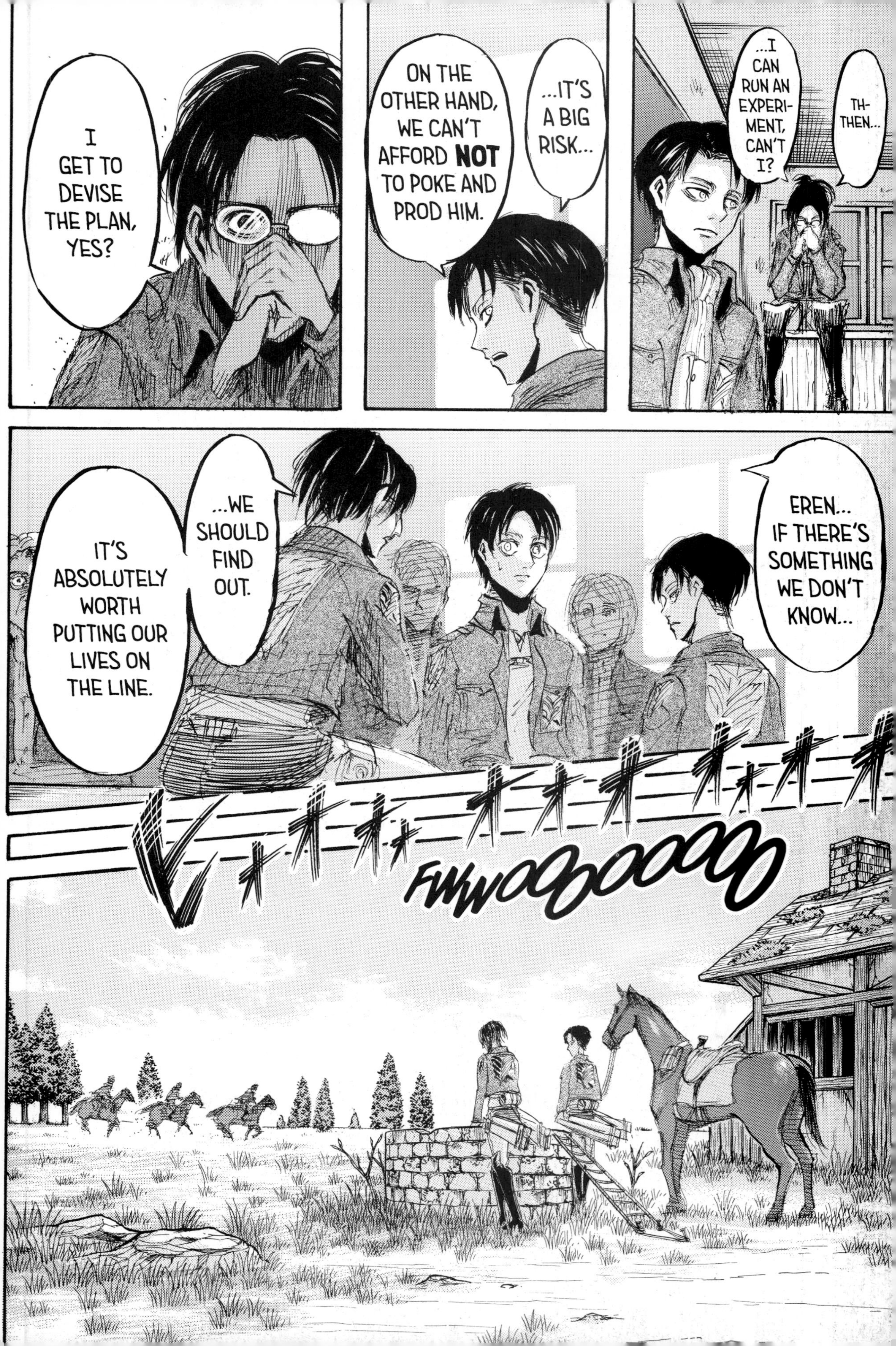
TH-THEN...
...I CAN RUN AN EXPERI-MENT, CAN'T I?
...IT'S A BIG RISK...
ON THE OTHER HAND, WE CAN'T AFFORD **NOT** TO POKE AND PROD HIM.
I GET TO DEVISE THE PLAN, YES?
EREN... IF THERE'S SOMETHING WE DON'T KNOW...
...WE SHOULD FIND OUT.
IT'S ABSOLUTELY WORTH PUTTING OUR LIVES ON THE LINE.
FWWOOOOOOO

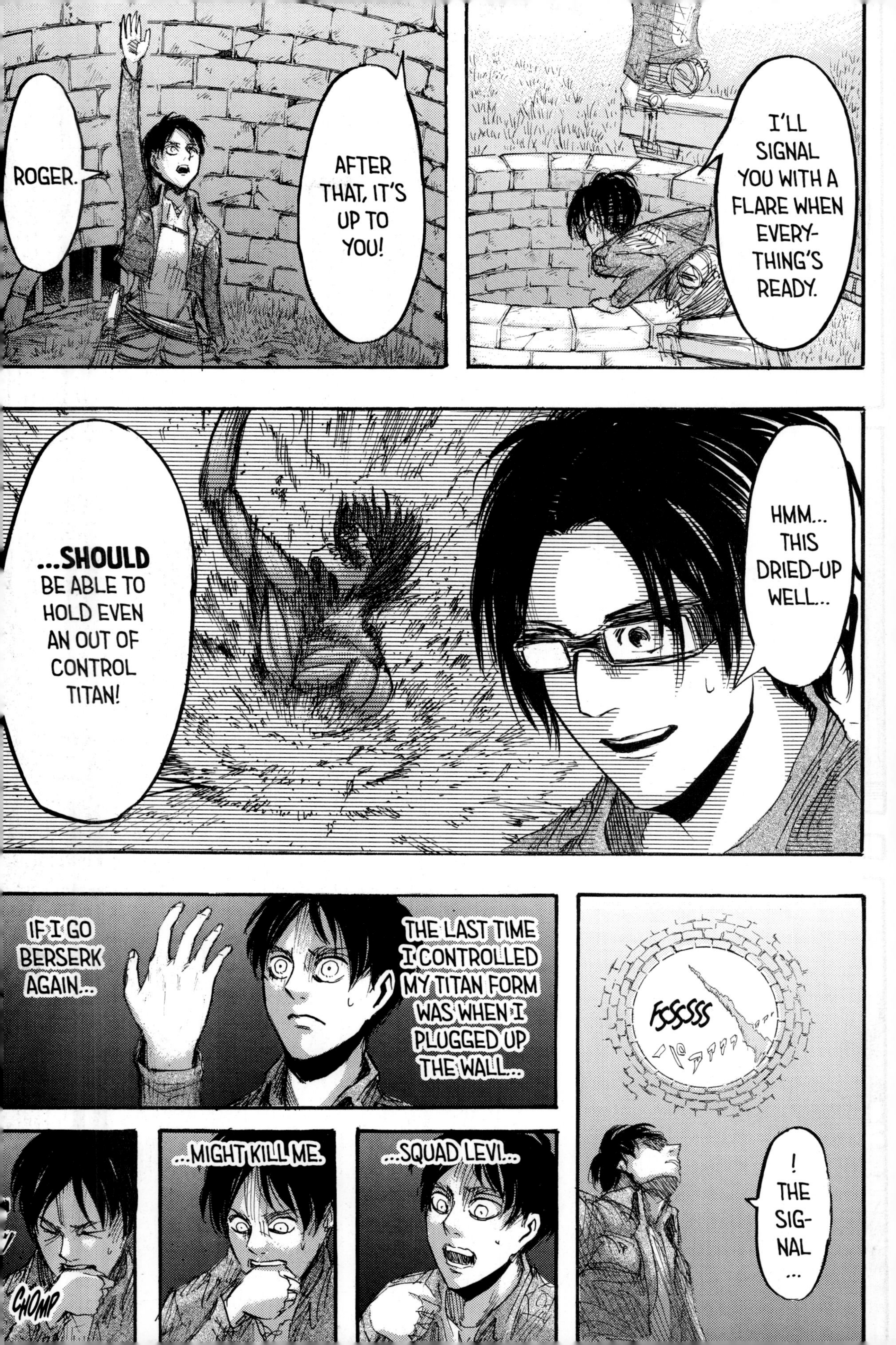
I'LL SIGNAL YOU WITH A FLARE WHEN EVERY-THING'S READY.
AFTER THAT, IT'S UP TO YOU!
ROGER.
HMM... THIS DRIED-UP WELL...
...SHOULD BE ABLE TO HOLD EVEN AN OUT OF CONTROL TITAN!
FSSSSS
パァァァ
! THE SIG-NAL ...
THE LAST TIME I CONTROLLED MY TITAN FORM WAS WHEN I PLUGGED UP THE WALL...
IF I GO BERSERK AGAIN...
...SQUAD LEVI...
...MIGHT KILL ME.
CHOMP

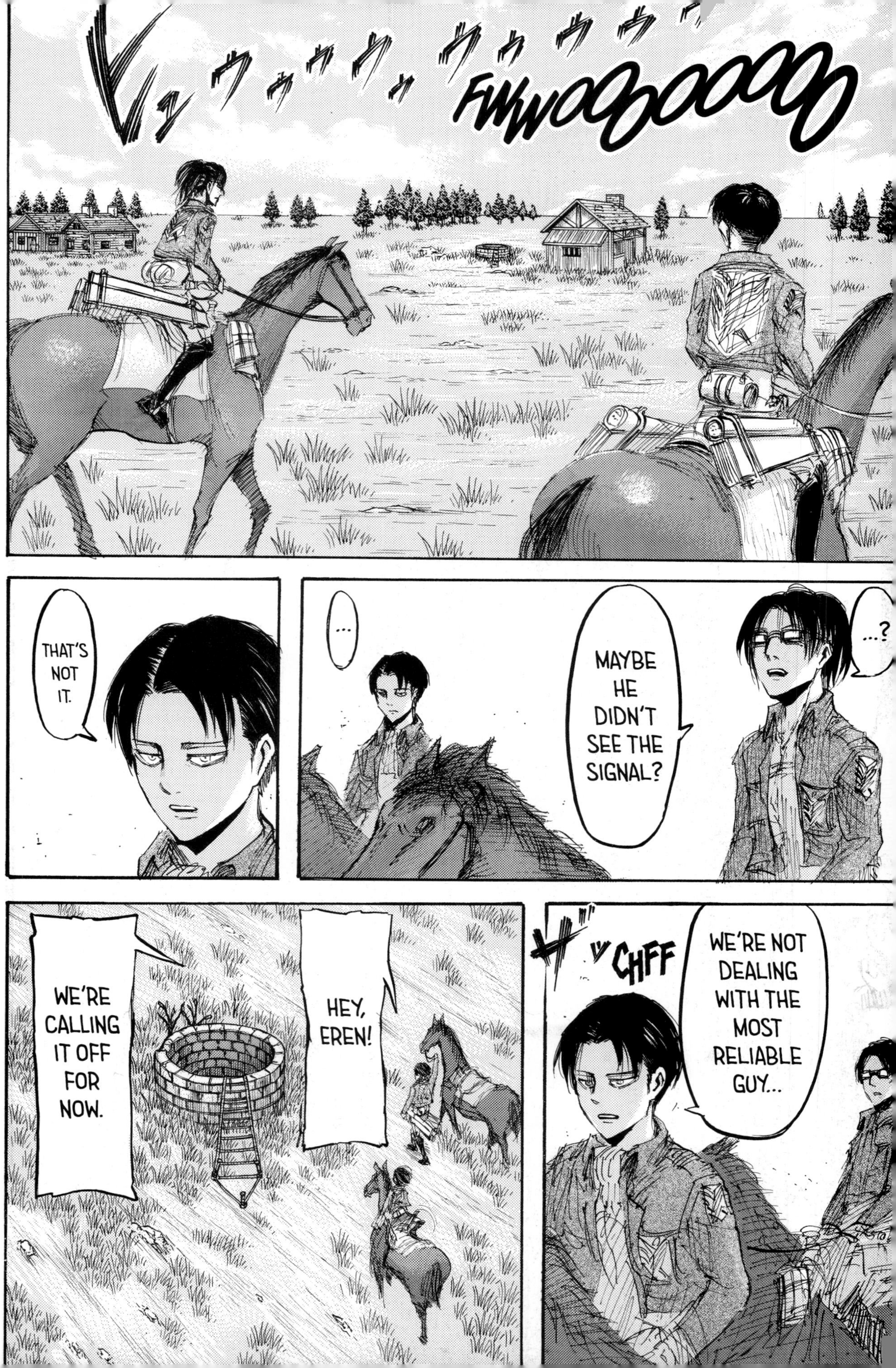
FWWOOOOOOO
...?
MAYBE HE DIDN'T SEE THE SIGNAL?
...
THAT'S NOT IT.
CHFF
WE'RE NOT DEALING WITH THE MOST RELIABLE GUY...
HEY, EREN!
WE'RE CALLING IT OFF FOR NOW.

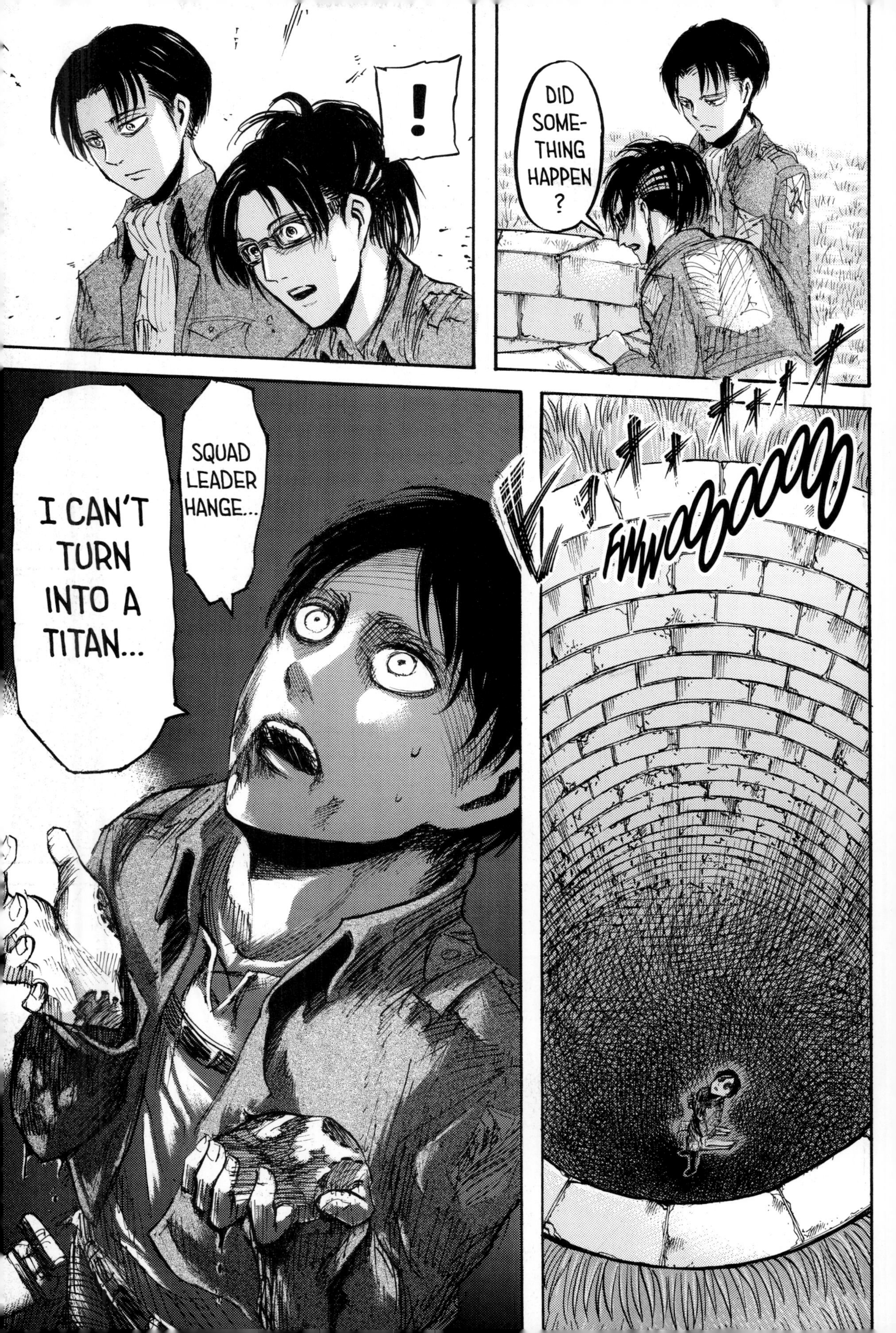
!
DID SOMETHING HAPPEN?
SQUAD LEADER HANGE...
I CAN'T TURN INTO A TITAN...

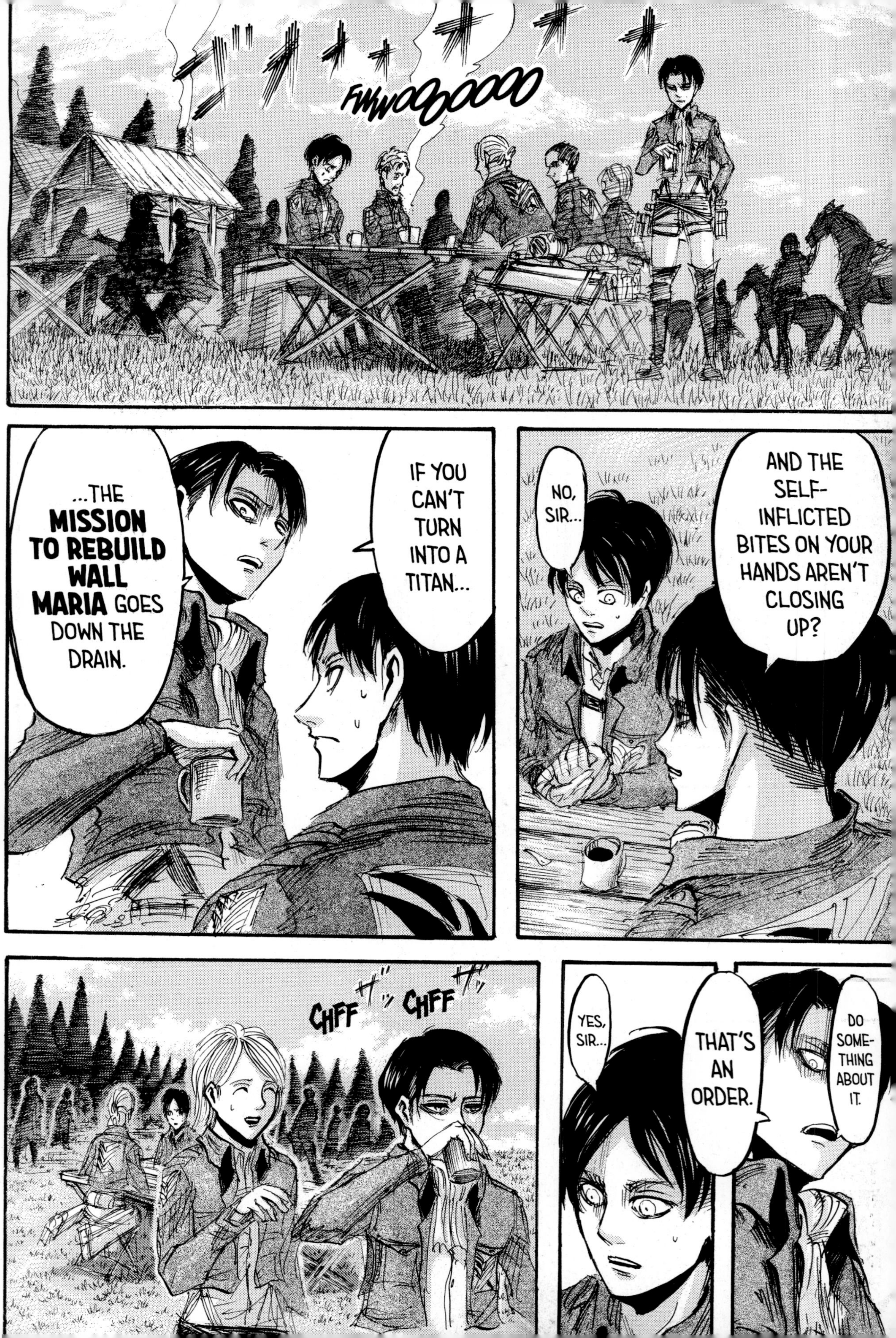
FWOOOOOO
AND THE SELF-INFLICTED BITES ON YOUR HANDS AREN'T CLOSING UP?
NO, SIR...
IF YOU CAN'T TURN INTO A TITAN...
...THE **MISSION TO REBUILD WALL MARIA** GOES DOWN THE DRAIN.
DO SOMETHING ABOUT IT.
THAT'S AN ORDER.
YES, SIR...
CHFF CHFF

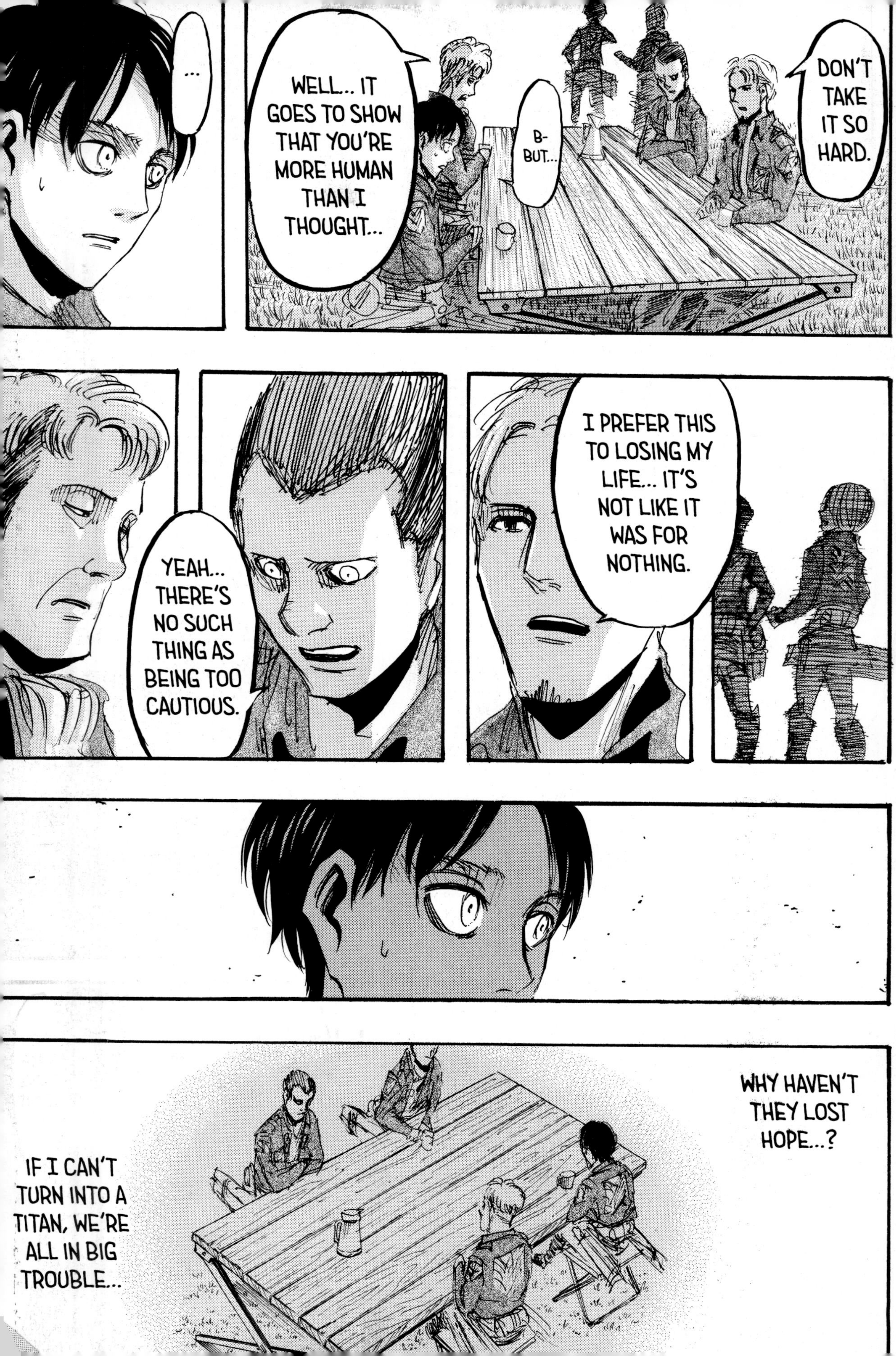
DON'T TAKE IT SO HARD.
B-BUT...
WELL... IT GOES TO SHOW THAT YOU'RE MORE HUMAN THAN I THOUGHT...
...
I PREFER THIS TO LOSING MY LIFE... IT'S NOT LIKE IT WAS FOR NOTHING.
YEAH... THERE'S NO SUCH THING AS BEING TOO CAUTIOUS.
WHY HAVEN'T THEY LOST HOPE...?
IF I CAN'T TURN INTO A TITAN, WE'RE ALL IN BIG TROUBLE...

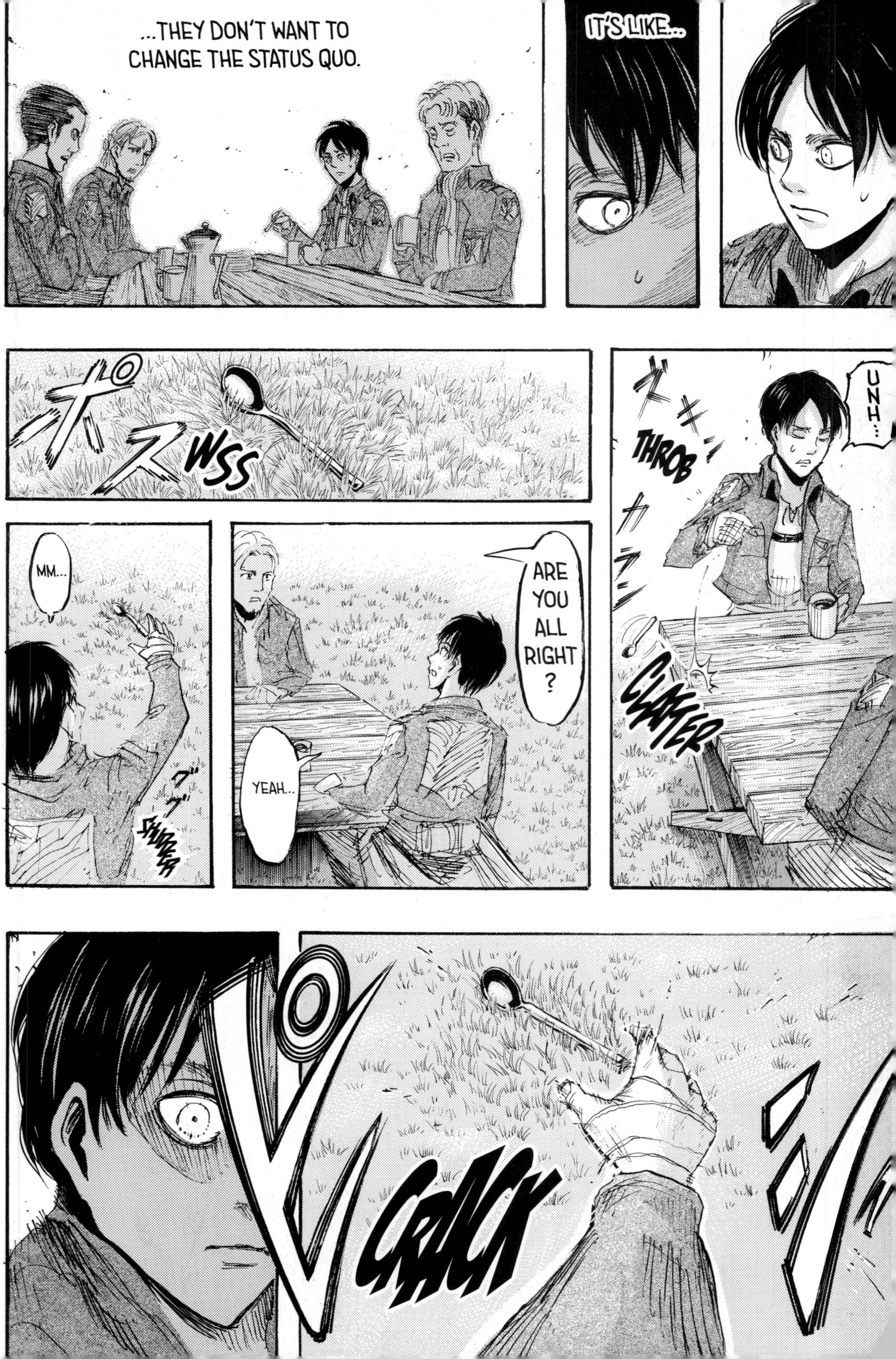
IT'S LIKE...
...THEY DON'T WANT TO CHANGE THE STATUS QUO.
UNH...
THROB
CLATTER
WSS
ARE YOU ALL RIGHT?
YEAH...
MM...
SHUDDER
CRACK

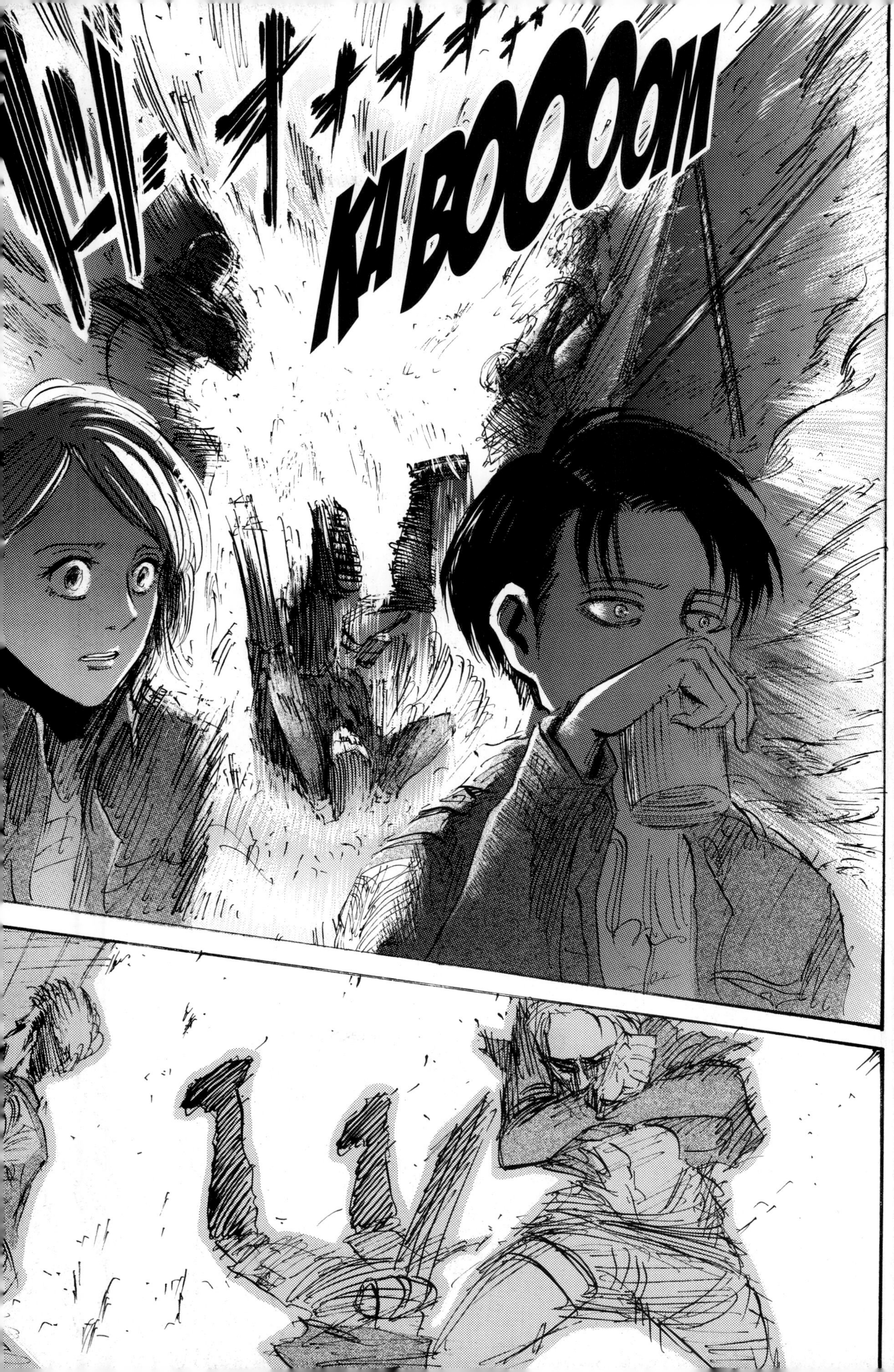
KABOOOOM

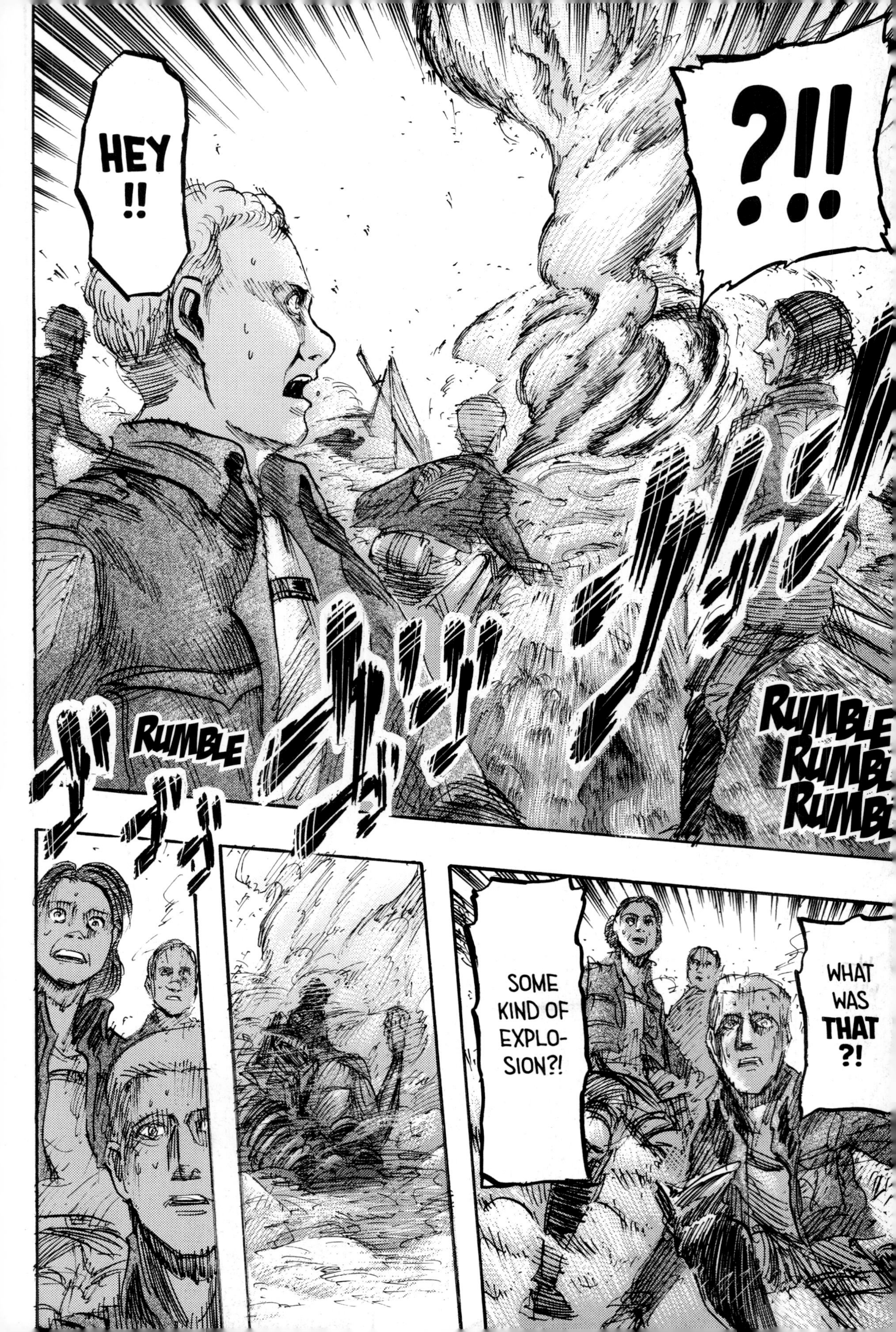
?!!
HEY !!
RUMBLE RUMBLE RUMBLE
RUMBLE
WHAT WAS THAT ?!
SOME KIND OF EXPLOSION?!

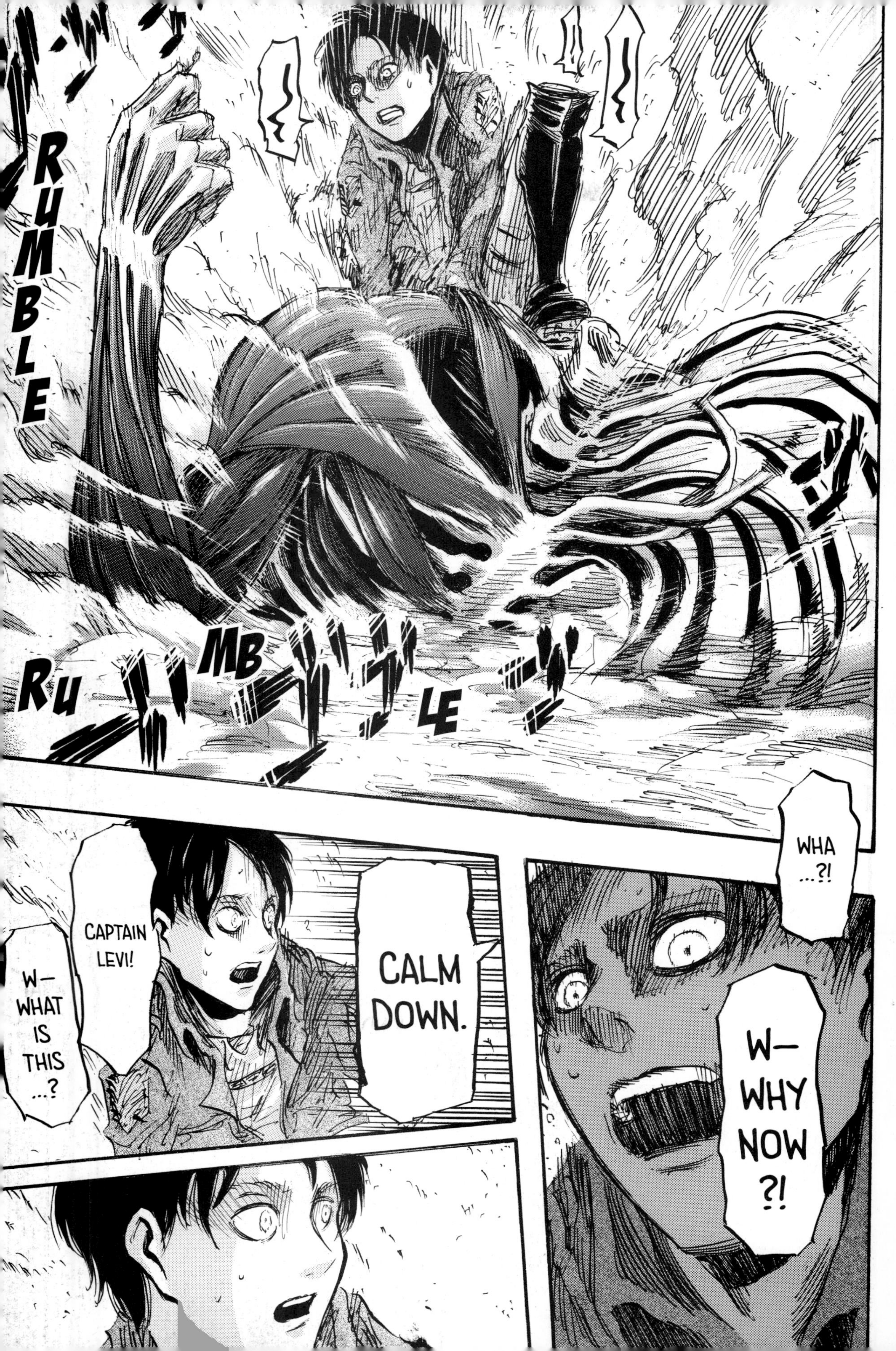
RUMBLE
RuMBLE
WHA ...?!
W— WHY NOW ?!
CALM DOWN.
CAPTAIN LEVI!
W— WHAT IS THIS ...?

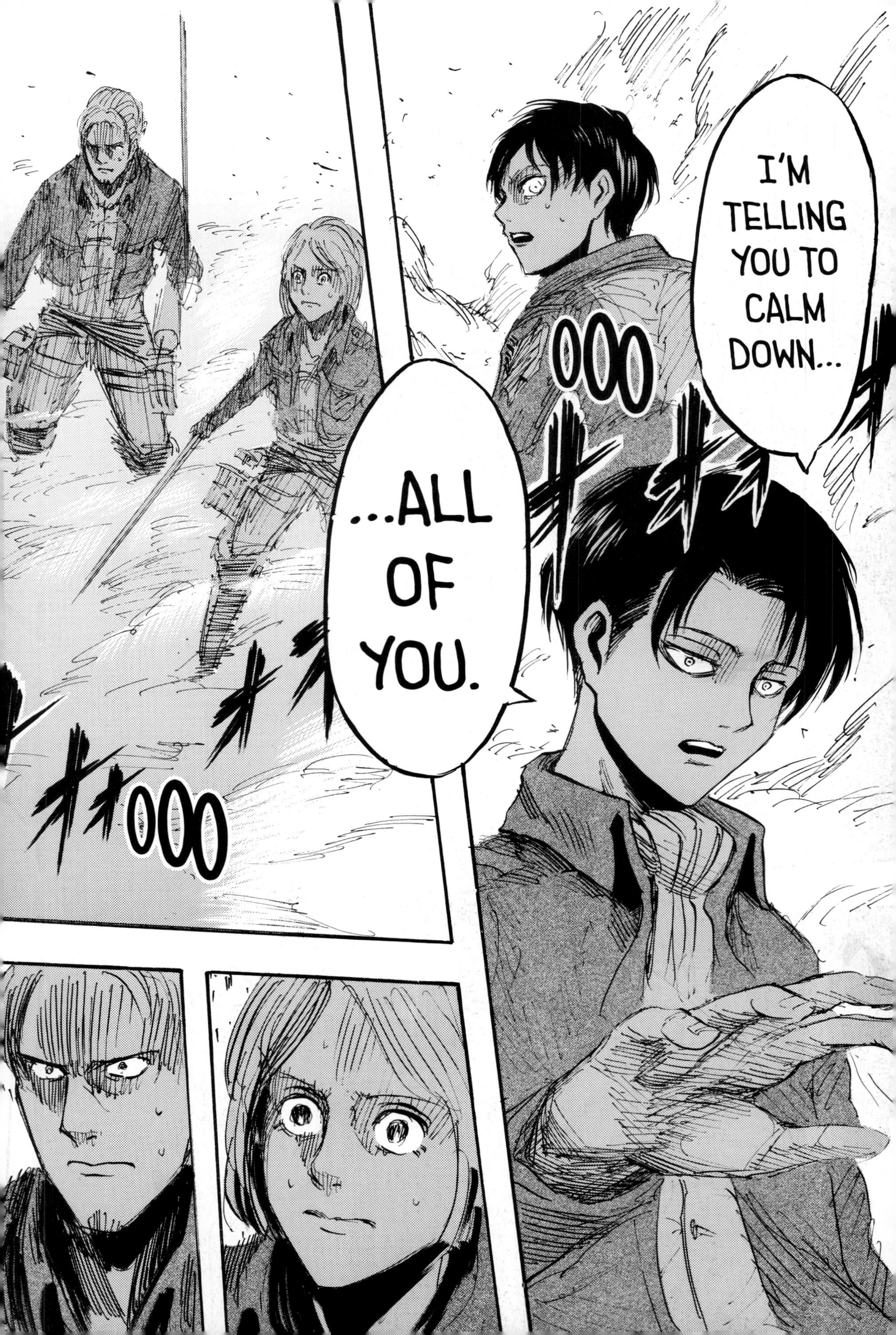
I'M TELLING YOU TO CALM DOWN...
...ALL OF YOU.

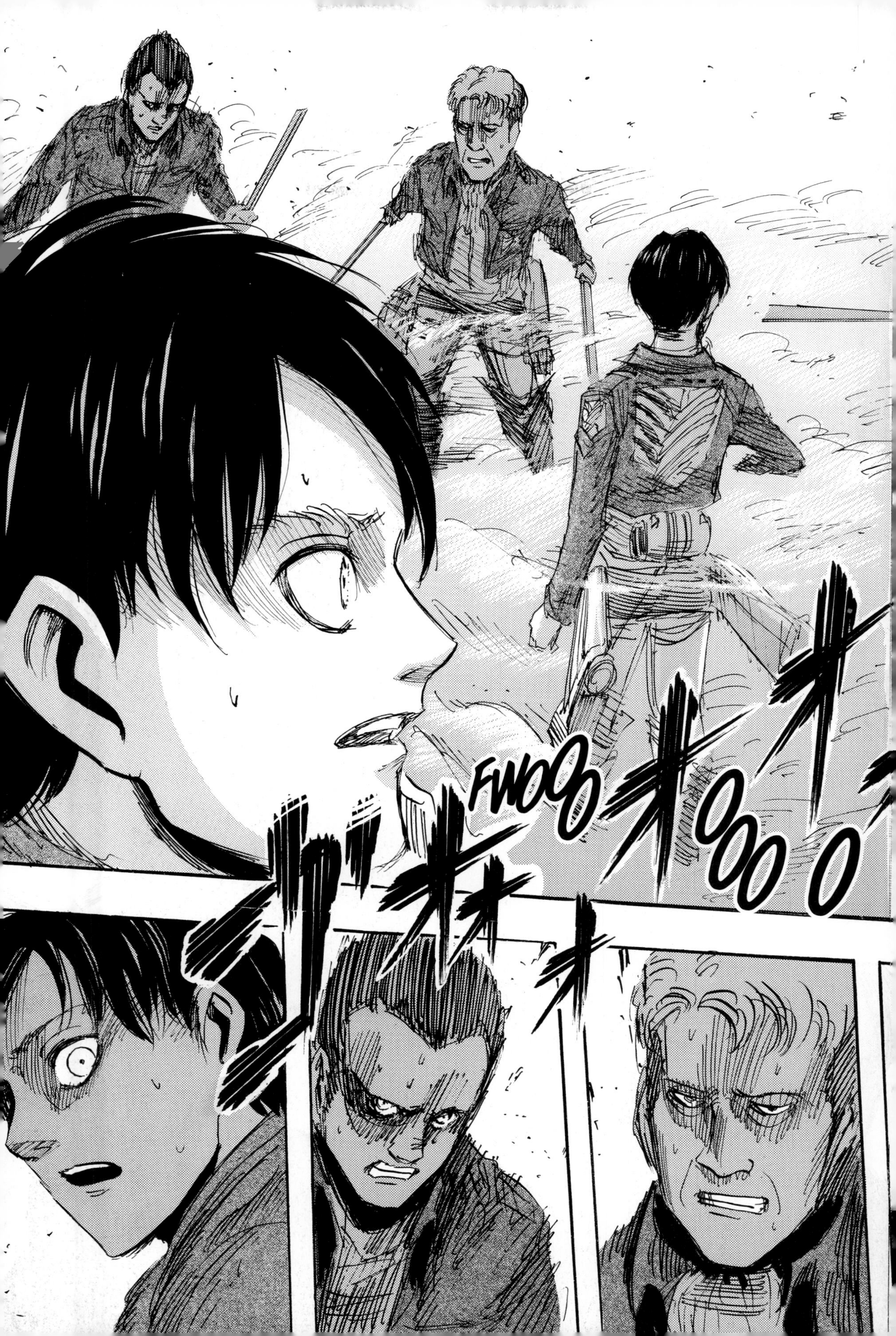
FWOOOOOOO

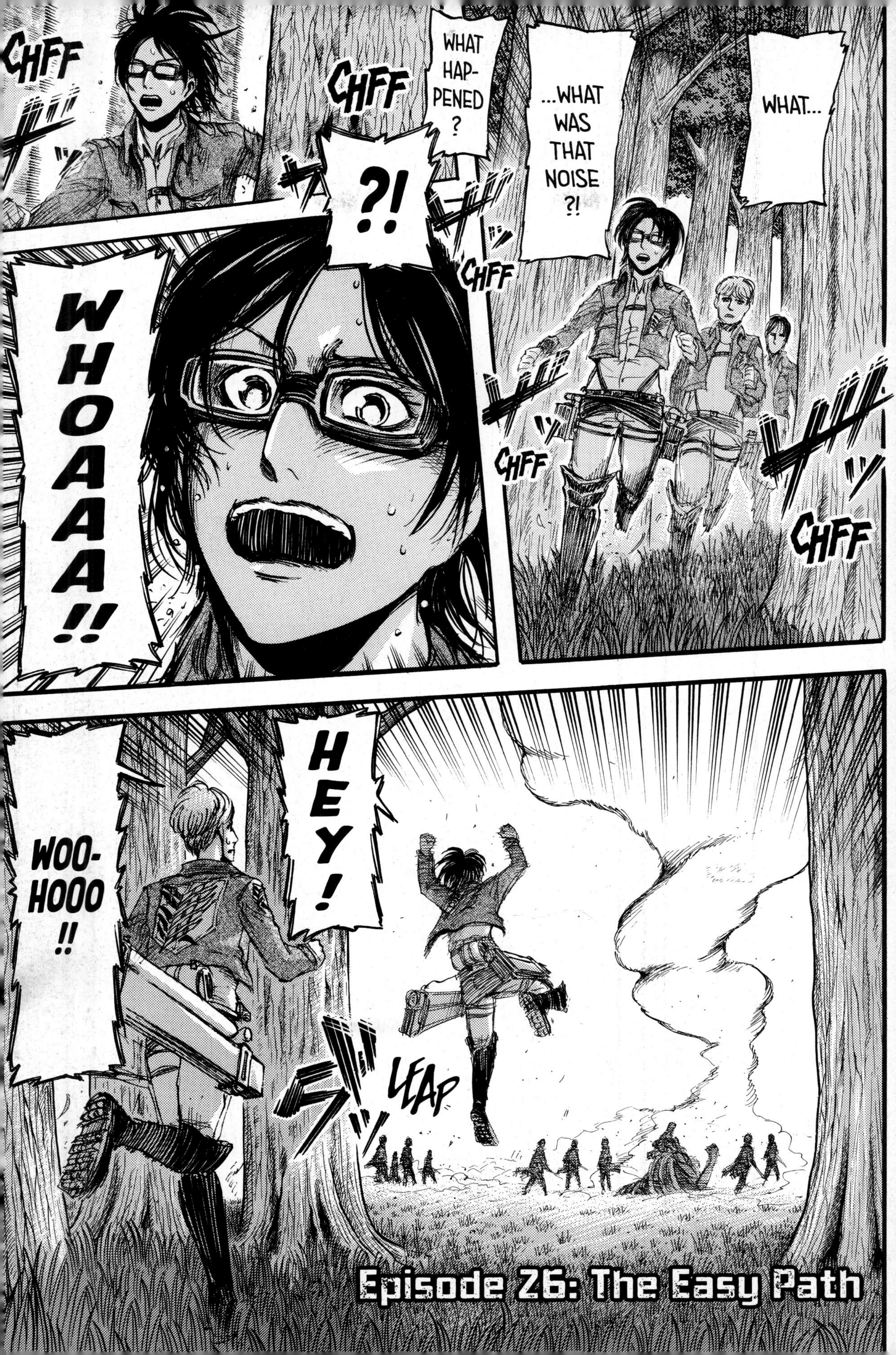
WHAT...
...WHAT WAS THAT NOISE ?!
WHAT HAP- PENED ?
CHFF
CHFF
CHFF
CHFF
CHFF
?!
WHOAAAA!!
HEY!
WOO- HOOO !!
LEAP
Episode 26: The Easy Path

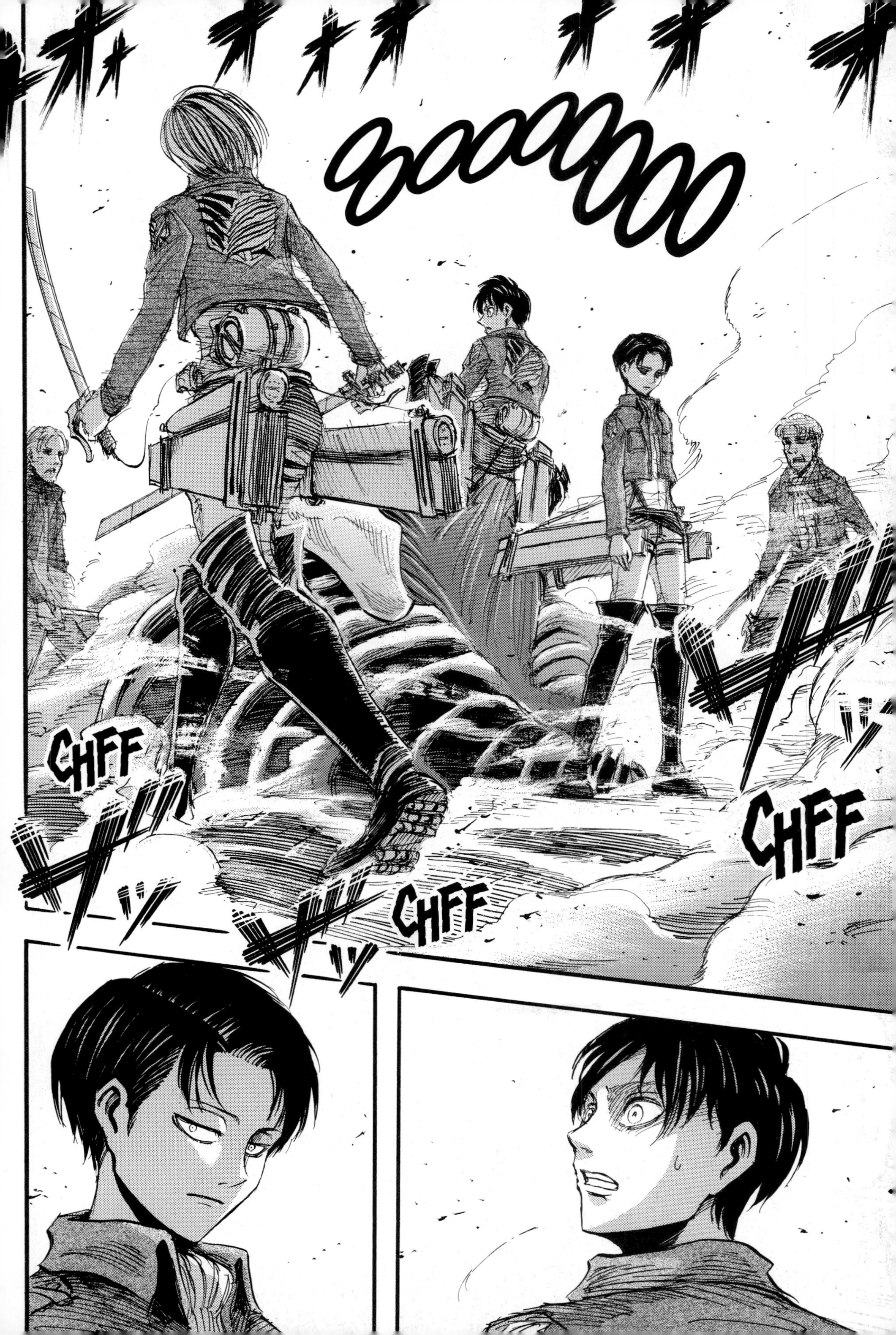
GOOOOOOO
CHFF
CHFF
CHFF

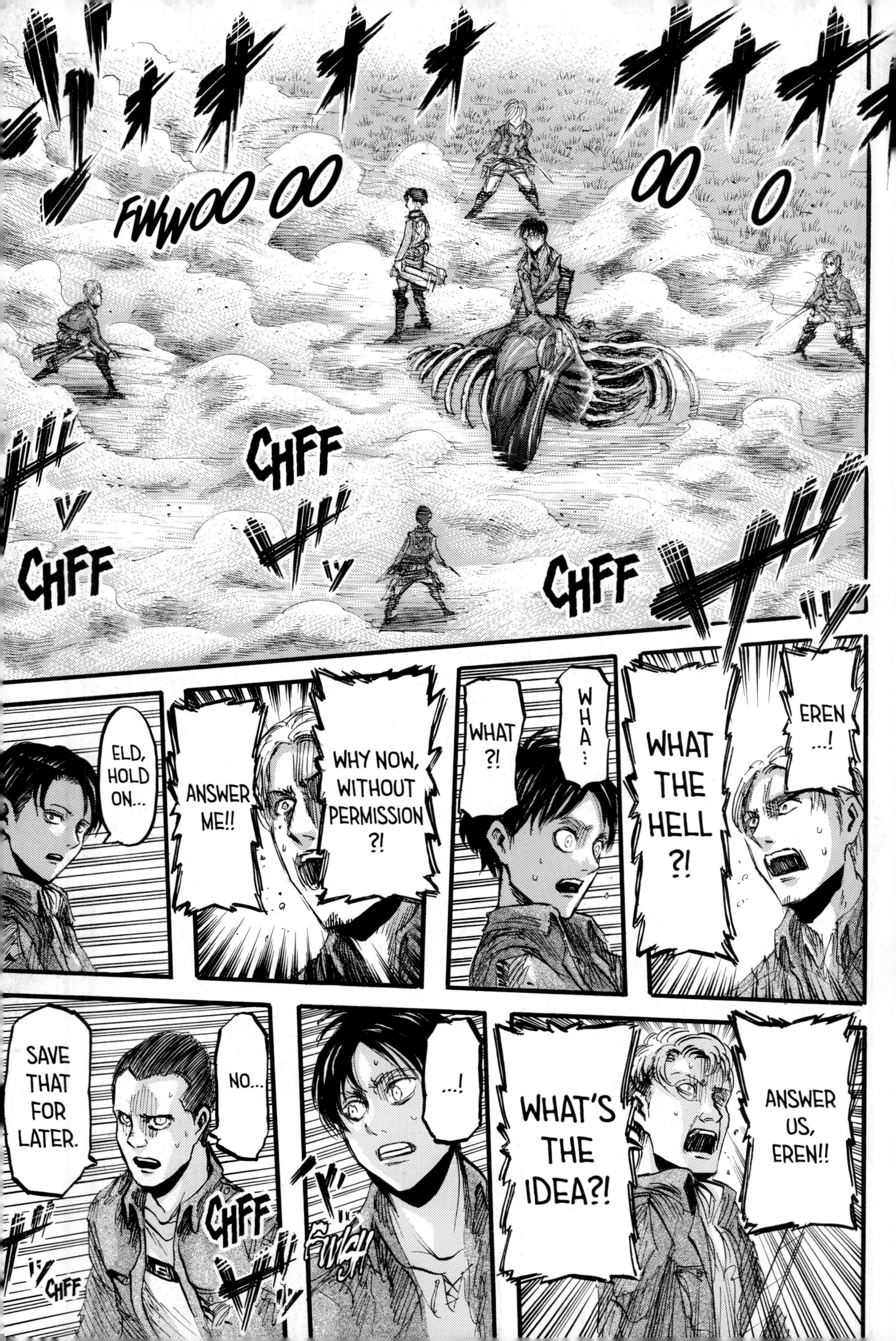
FWWOO OO
OO O
CHFF
CHFF
CHFF
EREN ...!
WHAT THE HELL ?!
WHA...
WHAT ?!
WHY NOW, WITHOUT PERMISSION ?!
ANSWER ME!!
ELD, HOLD ON...
ANSWER US, EREN!!
WHAT'S THE IDEA?!
...!
CHFF
NO...
SAVE THAT FOR LATER.
CHFF

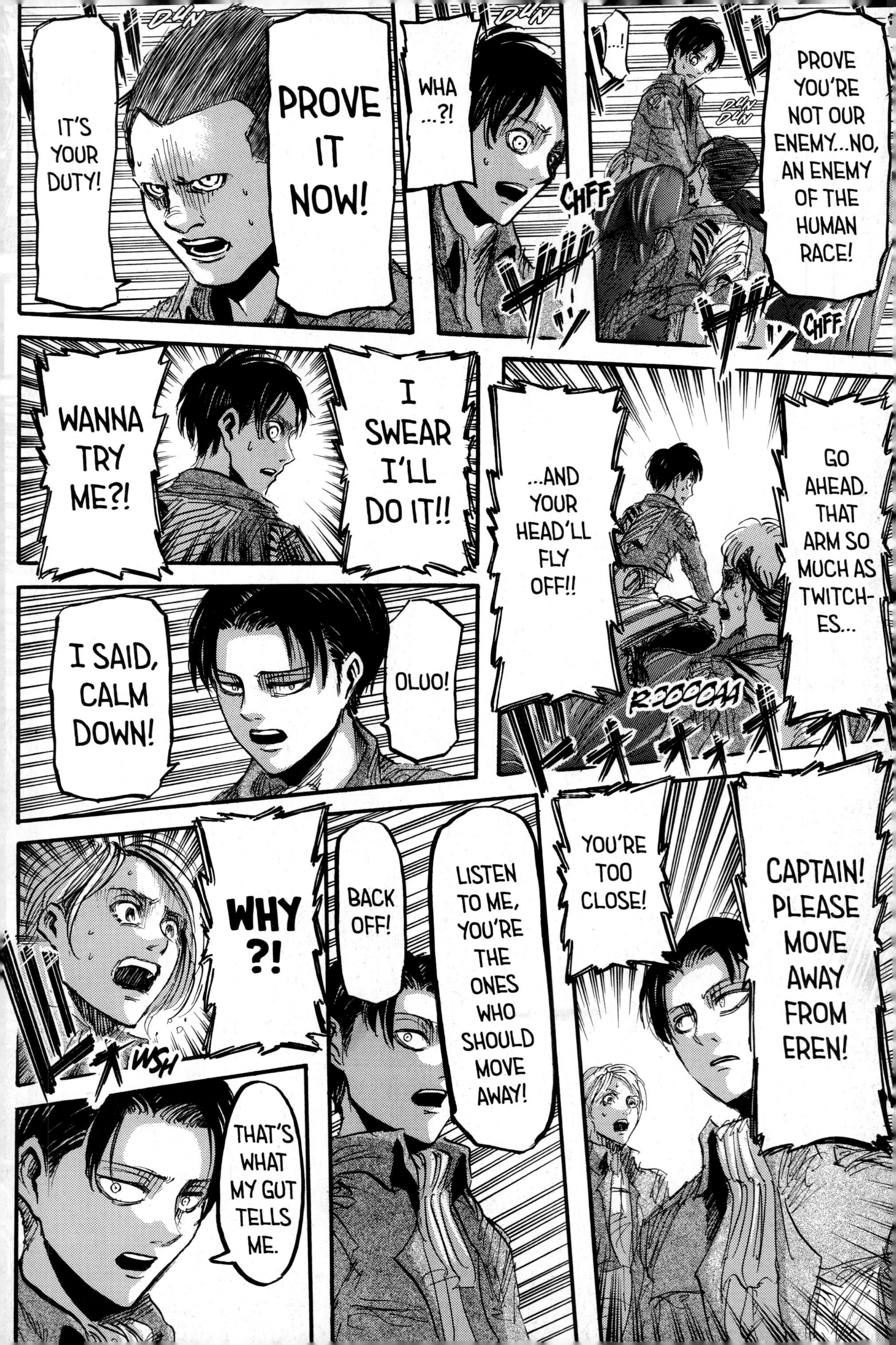
...!
PROVE YOU'RE NOT OUR ENEMY...NO, AN ENEMY OF THE HUMAN RACE!
DUN DUN
CHFF
CHFF
DUN
WHA ...?!
DUN
PROVE IT NOW!
IT'S YOUR DUTY!
GO AHEAD. THAT ARM SO MUCH AS TWITCH-ES...
...AND YOUR HEAD'LL FLY OFF!!
I SWEAR I'LL DO IT!!
WANNA TRY ME?!
OLUO!
I SAID, CALM DOWN!
CAPTAIN! PLEASE MOVE AWAY FROM EREN!
YOU'RE TOO CLOSE!
LISTEN TO ME, YOU'RE THE ONES WHO SHOULD MOVE AWAY!
BACK OFF!
WHY?!
WSH
THAT'S WHAT MY GUT TELLS ME.

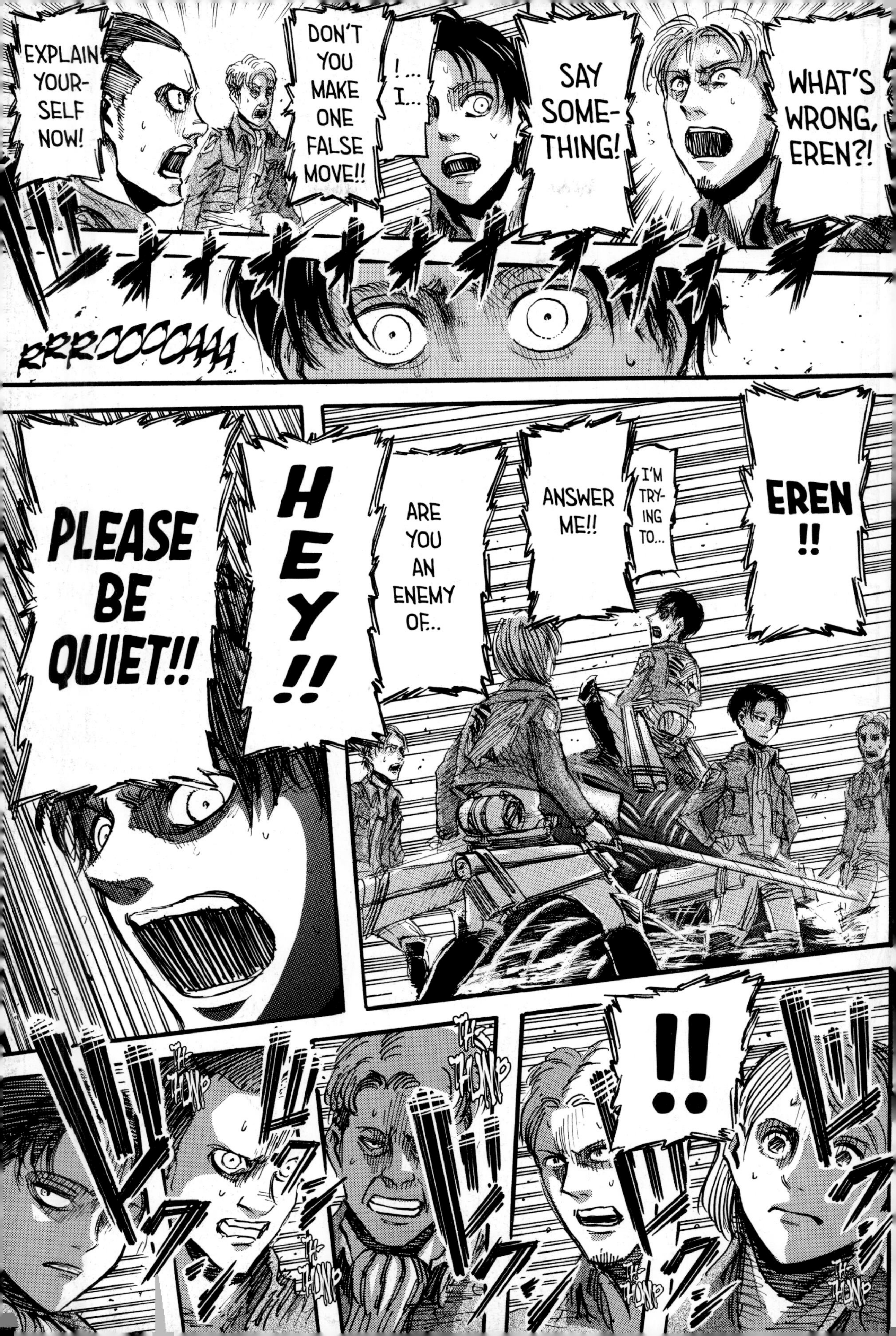
WHAT'S WRONG, EREN?!
SAY SOME-THING!
!... I...
DON'T YOU MAKE ONE FALSE MOVE!!
EXPLAIN YOUR-SELF NOW!
RRROOOOAAA
EREN !!
I'M TRY-ING TO...
ANSWER ME!!
ARE YOU AN ENEMY OF...
HEY!!
PLEASE BE QUIET!!
!!
THOMP
THOMP
THOMP
THOMP
THOMP
THOMP

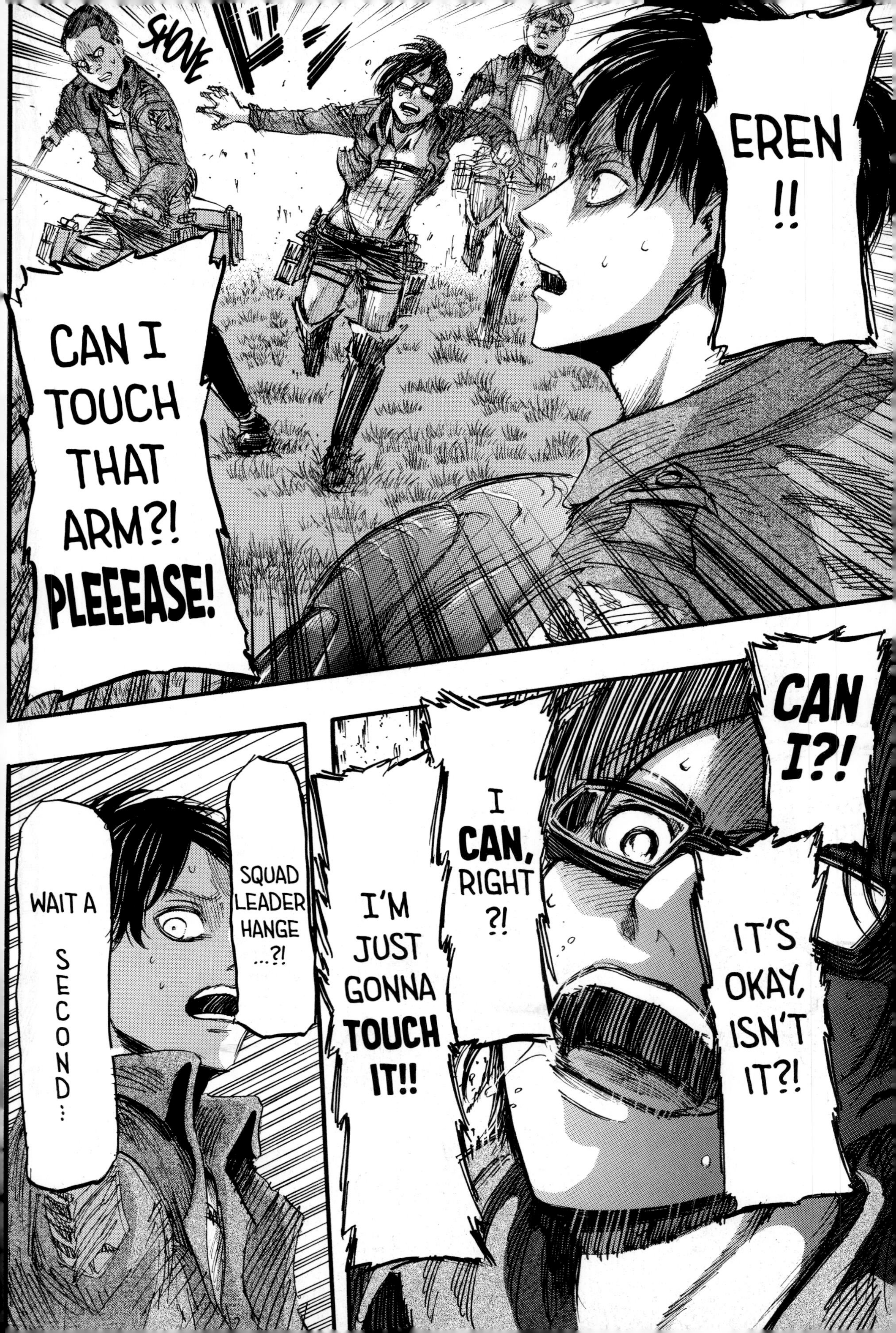
EREN !!
SHOCK
CAN I TOUCH THAT ARM?! PLEEEASE!
CAN I?!
I CAN, RIGHT ?!
IT'S OKAY, ISN'T IT?!
I'M JUST GONNA TOUCH IT!!
SQUAD LEADER HANGE ...?!
WAIT A SECOND...

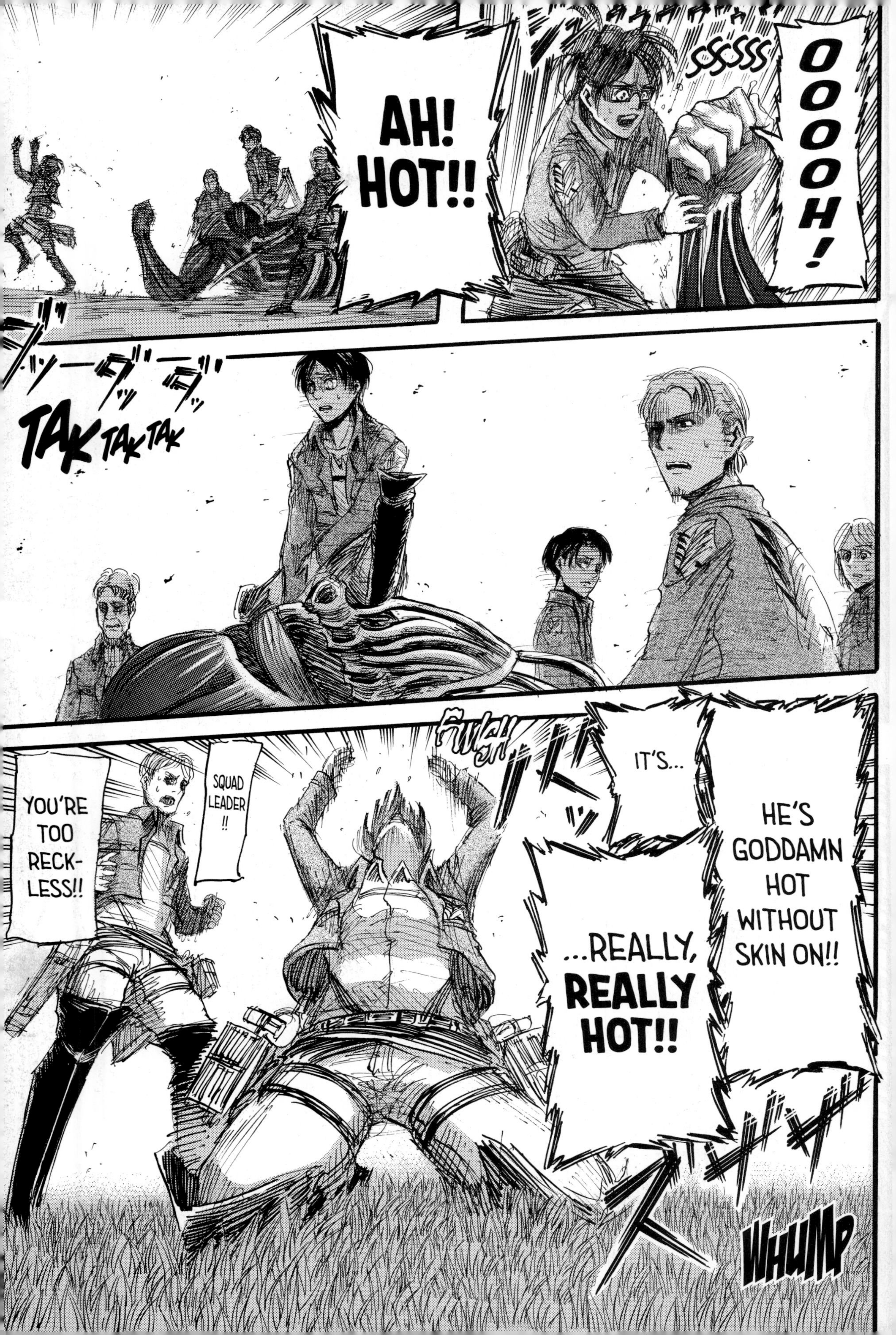
OOOOOH!
SSSSS
AH! HOT!!
TAK TAK TAK
HE'S GODDAMN HOT WITHOUT SKIN ON!!
IT'S...
...REALLY, REALLY HOT!!
FWISH
SQUAD LEADER!!
YOU'RE TOO RECKLESS!!
WHUMP

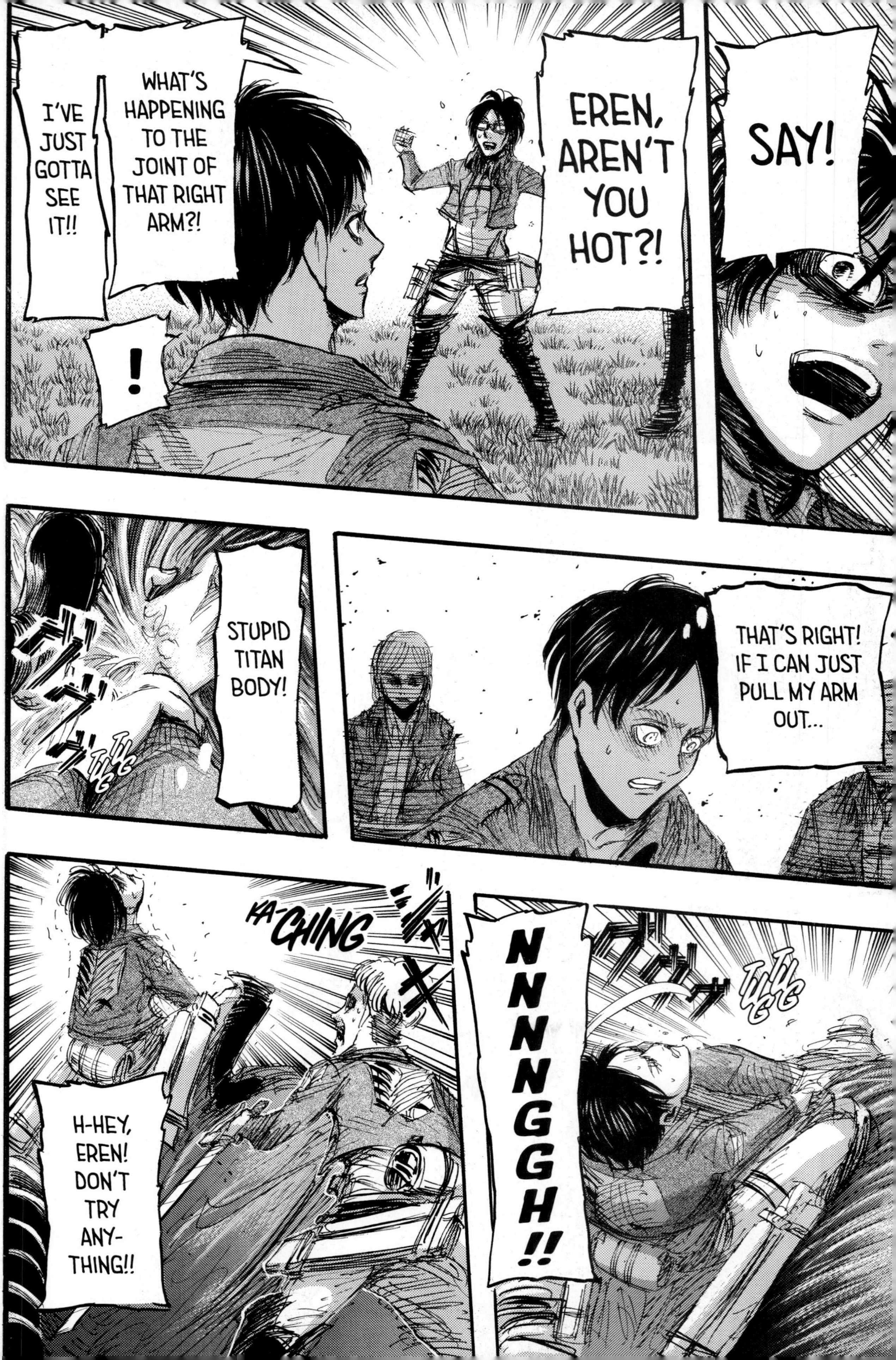
SAY!
EREN, AREN'T YOU HOT?!
WHAT'S HAPPENING TO THE JOINT OF THAT RIGHT ARM?!
I'VE JUST GOTTA SEE IT!!
!
THAT'S RIGHT! IF I CAN JUST PULL MY ARM OUT...
STUPID TITAN BODY!
THUG THUG
NNNNGGH!!
THUG THUG
KA-CHING
H-HEY, EREN! DON'T TRY ANY-THING!!

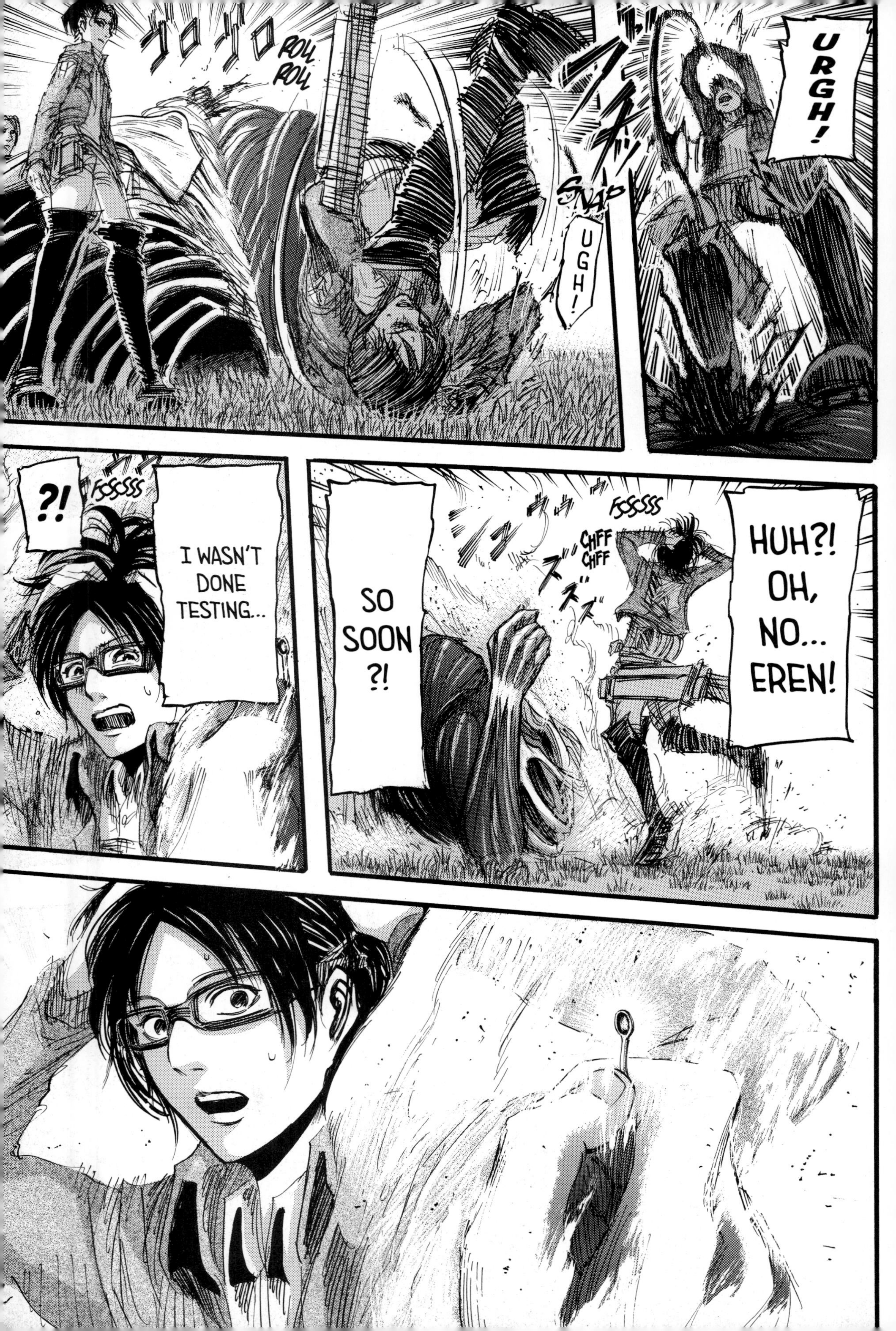
URGH!
SNAP
UGH!
ROLL ROLL
HUH?! OH, NO... EREN!
FSSSSS
CHFF CHFF
SO SOON ?!
I WASN'T DONE TESTING...
FSSSSS
?!

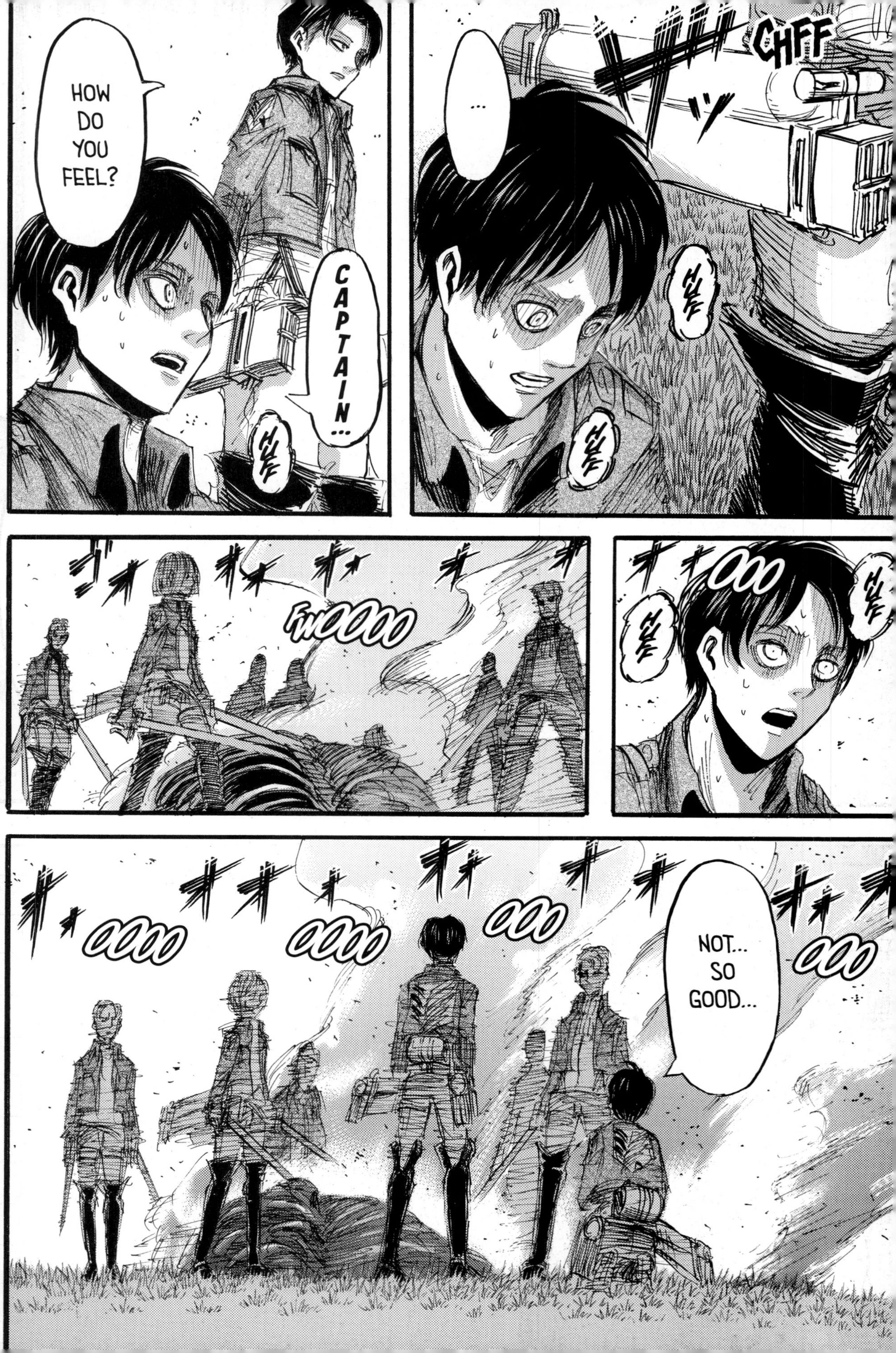
CHFF
...
HUFF
HUFF
HOW DO YOU FEEL?
CAPTAIN...
HUFF
OOO
HUFF
HUFF
FWOOOOO
OOO
NOT... SO GOOD...
OOO
OOOO
OOOO

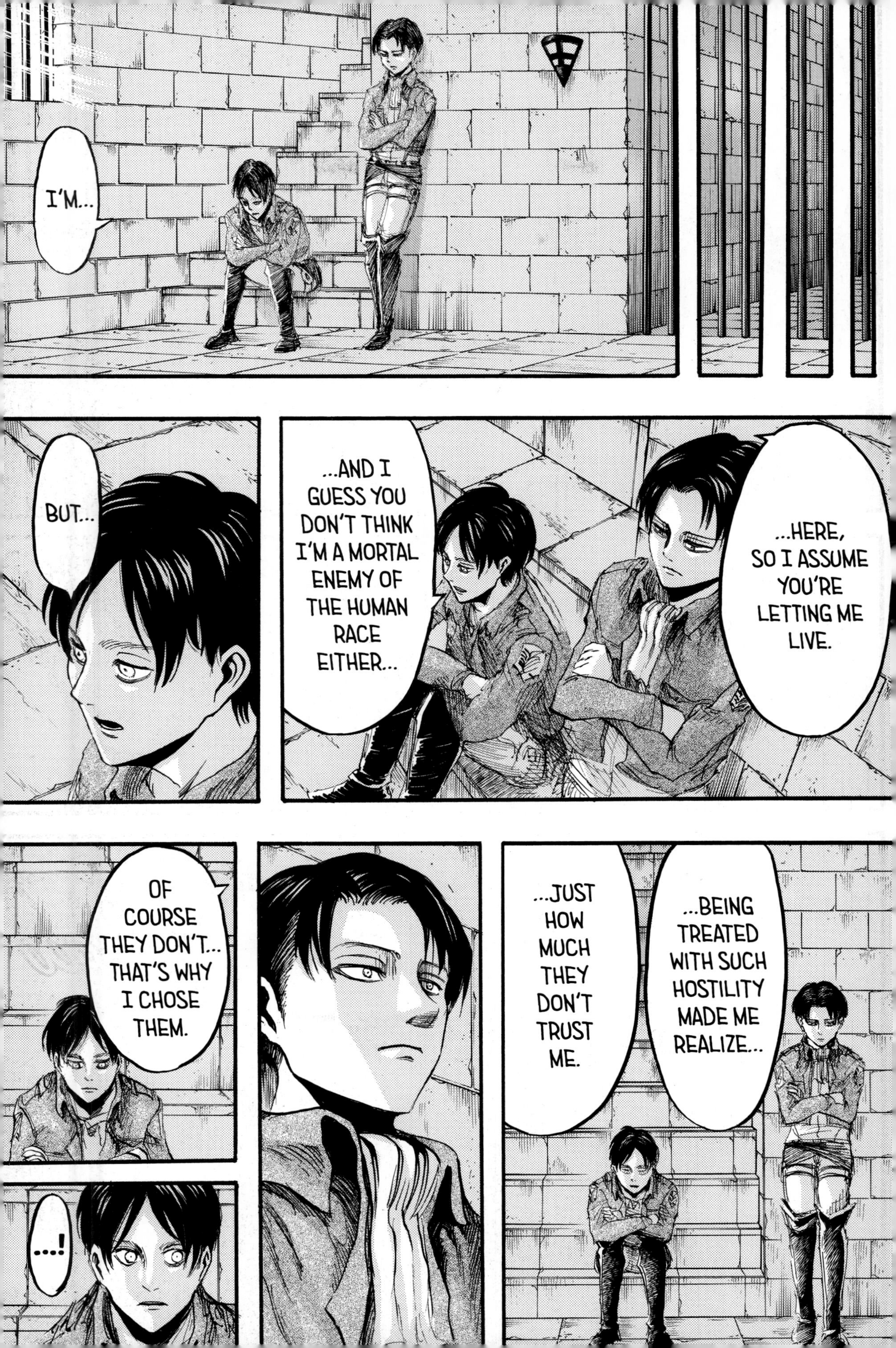

I'M...
...HERE, SO I ASSUME YOU'RE LETTING ME LIVE.
...AND I GUESS YOU DON'T THINK I'M A MORTAL ENEMY OF THE HUMAN RACE EITHER...
BUT...
...BEING TREATED WITH SUCH HOSTILITY MADE ME REALIZE...
...JUST HOW MUCH THEY DON'T TRUST ME.
OF COURSE THEY DON'T... THAT'S WHY I CHOSE THEM.
...!

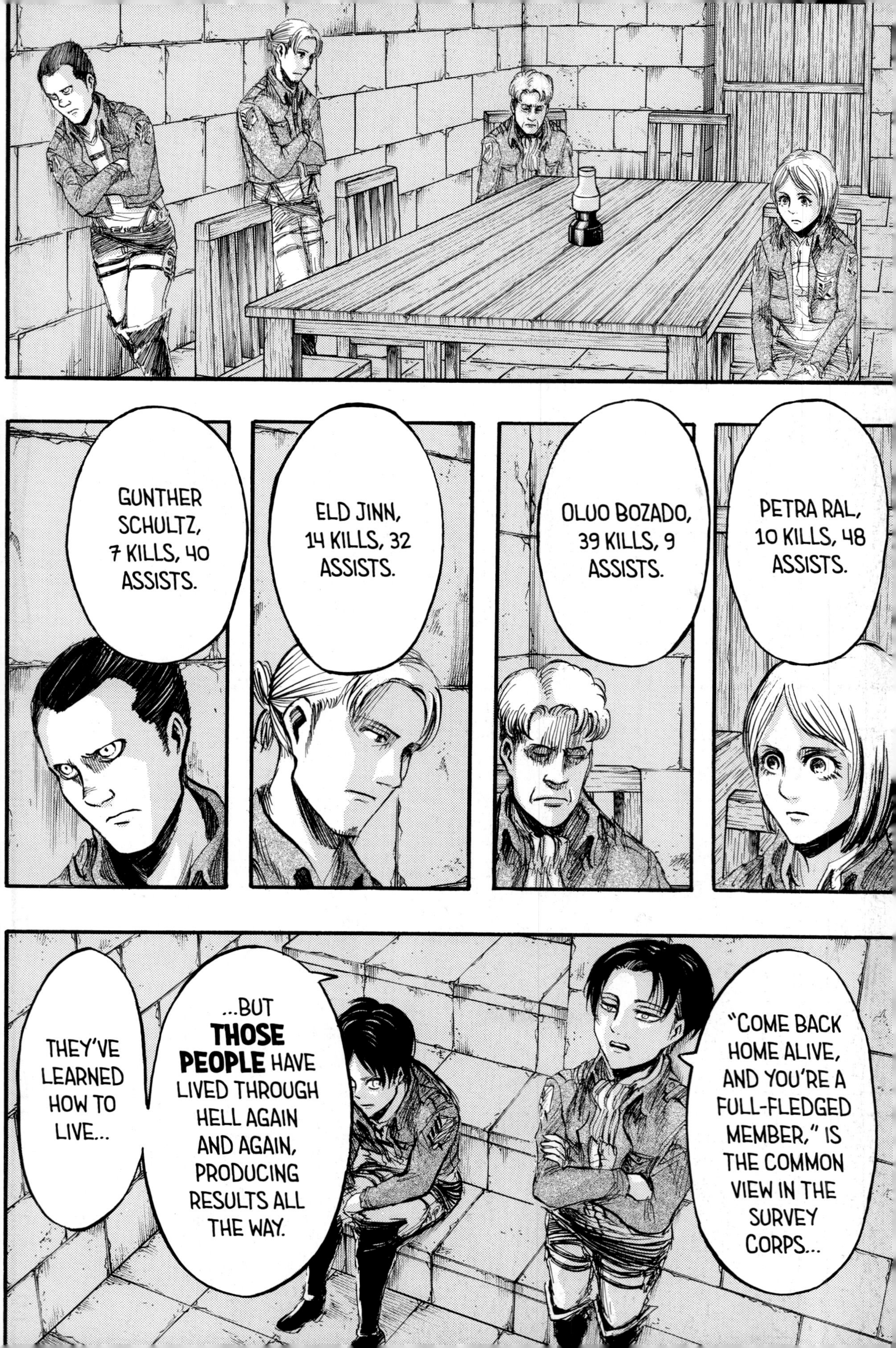
PETRA RAL, 10 KILLS, 48 ASSISTS.
OLUO BOZADO, 39 KILLS, 9 ASSISTS.
ELD JINN, 14 KILLS, 32 ASSISTS.
GUNTHER SCHULTZ, 7 KILLS, 40 ASSISTS.
"COME BACK HOME ALIVE, AND YOU'RE A FULL-FLEDGED MEMBER," IS THE COMMON VIEW IN THE SURVEY CORPS...
...BUT **THOSE PEOPLE** HAVE LIVED THROUGH HELL AGAIN AND AGAIN, PRODUCING RESULTS ALL THE WAY.
THEY'VE LEARNED HOW TO LIVE...

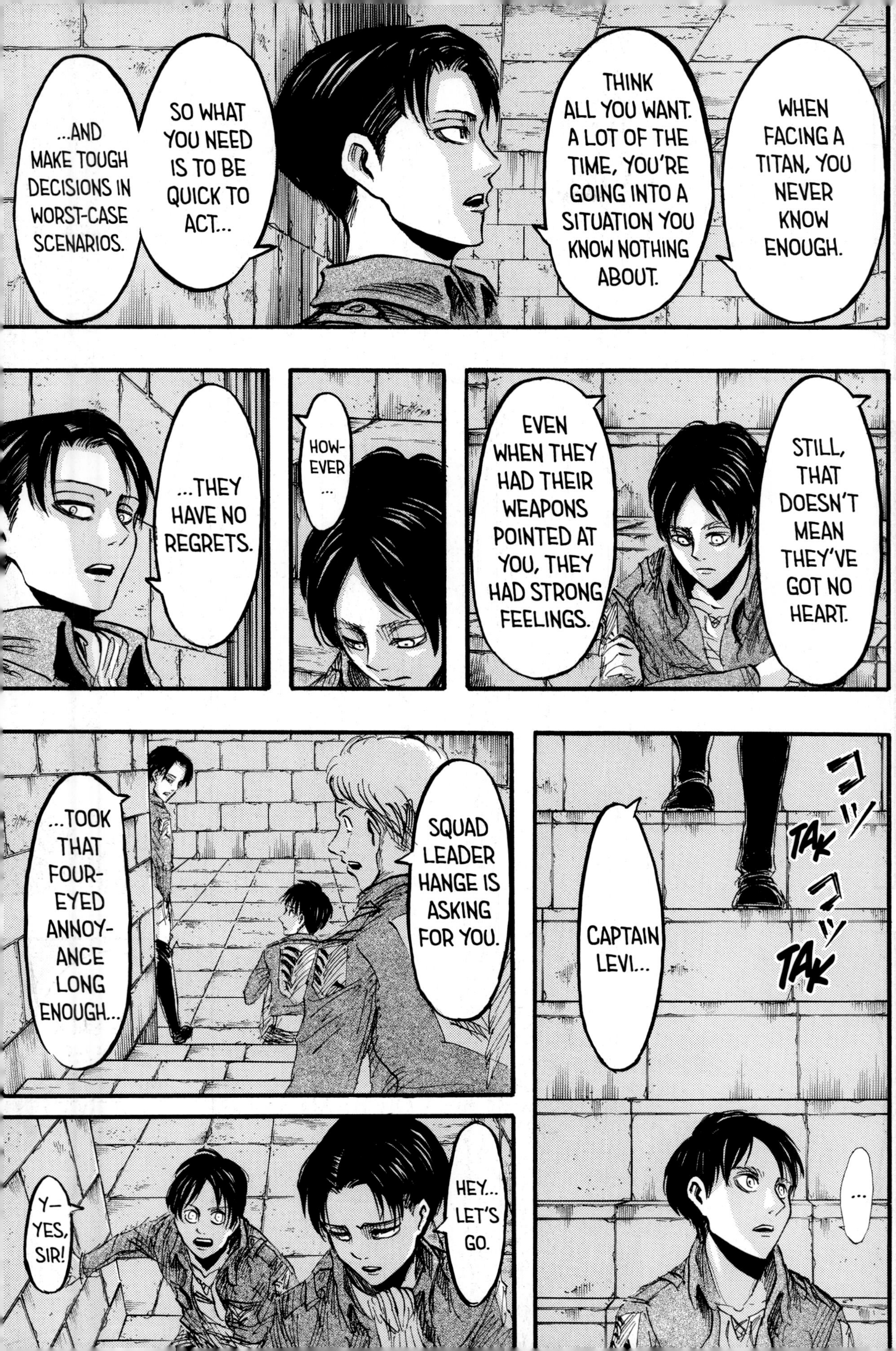
WHEN FACING A TITAN, YOU NEVER KNOW ENOUGH.
THINK ALL YOU WANT. A LOT OF THE TIME, YOU'RE GOING INTO A SITUATION YOU KNOW NOTHING ABOUT.
SO WHAT YOU NEED IS TO BE QUICK TO ACT...
...AND MAKE TOUGH DECISIONS IN WORST-CASE SCENARIOS.
STILL, THAT DOESN'T MEAN THEY'VE GOT NO HEART.
EVEN WHEN THEY HAD THEIR WEAPONS POINTED AT YOU, THEY HAD STRONG FEELINGS.
HOW-EVER...
...THEY HAVE NO REGRETS.
TAK
TAK
CAPTAIN LEVI...
...
SQUAD LEADER HANGE IS ASKING FOR YOU.
...TOOK THAT FOUR-EYED ANNOY-ANCE LONG ENOUGH...
HEY... LET'S GO.
Y— YES, SIR!

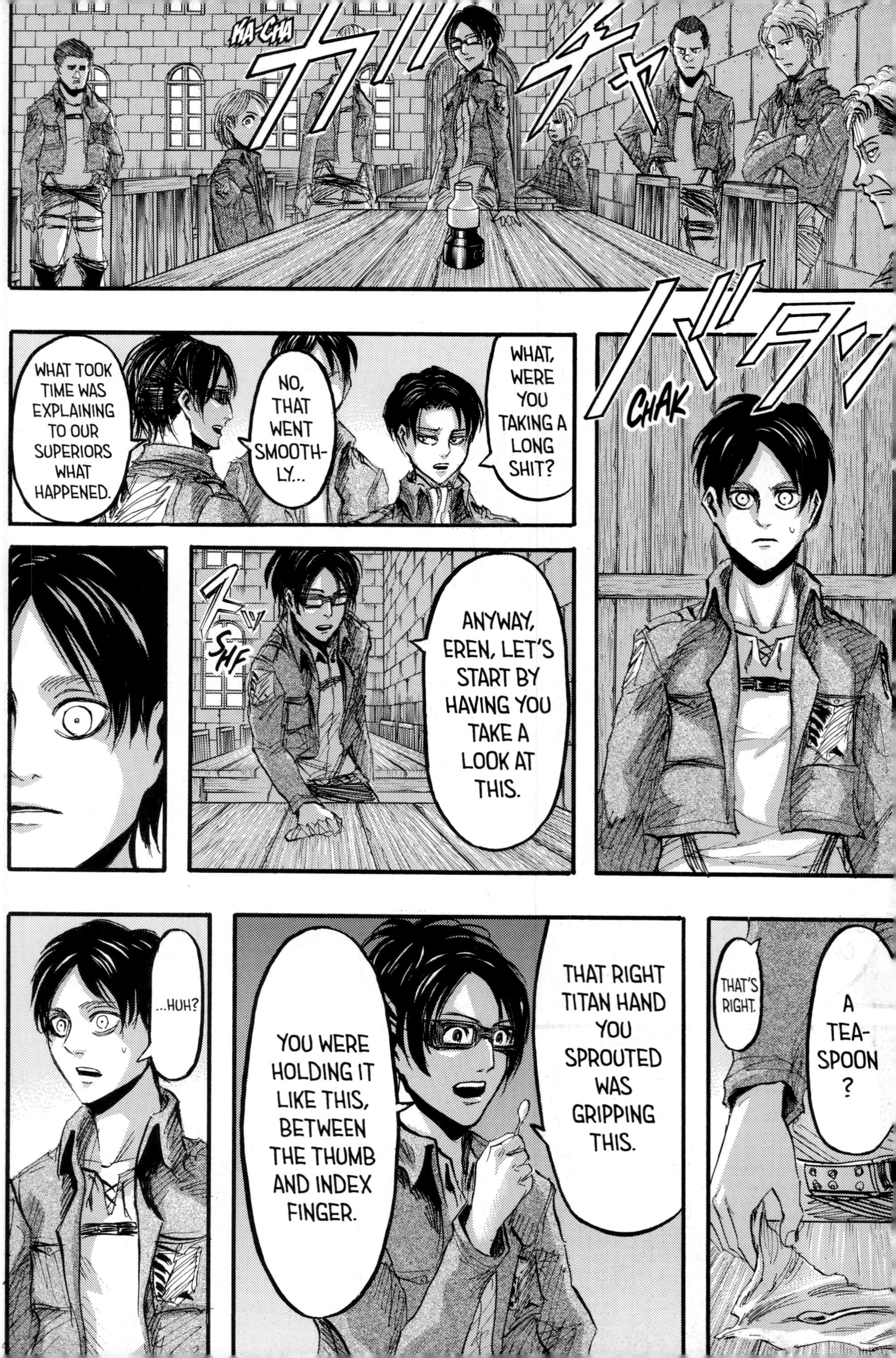
KA-CHA
CHAK
WHAT, WERE YOU TAKING A LONG SHIT?
NO, THAT WENT SMOOTH-LY...
WHAT TOOK TIME WAS EXPLAINING TO OUR SUPERIORS WHAT HAPPENED.
SHF
ANYWAY, EREN, LET'S START BY HAVING YOU TAKE A LOOK AT THIS.
A TEA-SPOON?
THAT'S RIGHT.
THAT RIGHT TITAN HAND YOU SPROUTED WAS GRIPPING THIS.
YOU WERE HOLDING IT LIKE THIS, BETWEEN THE THUMB AND INDEX FINGER.
...HUH?

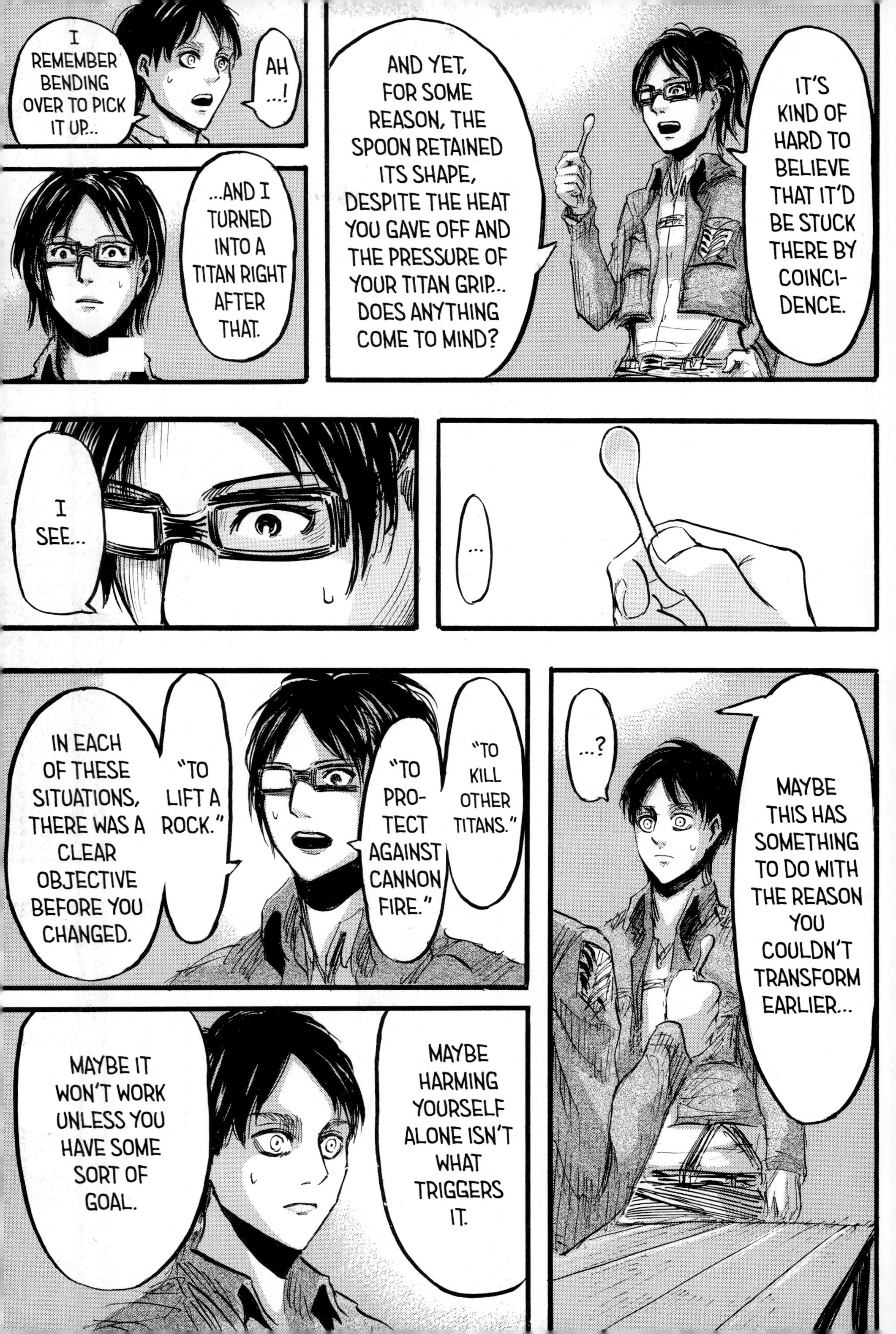
IT'S KIND OF HARD TO BELIEVE THAT IT'D BE STUCK THERE BY COINCIDENCE.
AND YET, FOR SOME REASON, THE SPOON RETAINED ITS SHAPE, DESPITE THE HEAT YOU GAVE OFF AND THE PRESSURE OF YOUR TITAN GRIP... DOES ANYTHING COME TO MIND?
AH ...!
I REMEMBER BENDING OVER TO PICK IT UP...
...AND I TURNED INTO A TITAN RIGHT AFTER THAT.
...
I SEE...
MAYBE THIS HAS SOMETHING TO DO WITH THE REASON YOU COULDN'T TRANSFORM EARLIER...
...?
"TO KILL OTHER TITANS."
"TO PROTECT AGAINST CANNON FIRE."
"TO LIFT A ROCK."
IN EACH OF THESE SITUATIONS, THERE WAS A CLEAR OBJECTIVE BEFORE YOU CHANGED.
MAYBE HARMING YOURSELF ALONE ISN'T WHAT TRIGGERS IT.
MAYBE IT WON'T WORK UNLESS YOU HAVE SOME SORT OF GOAL.

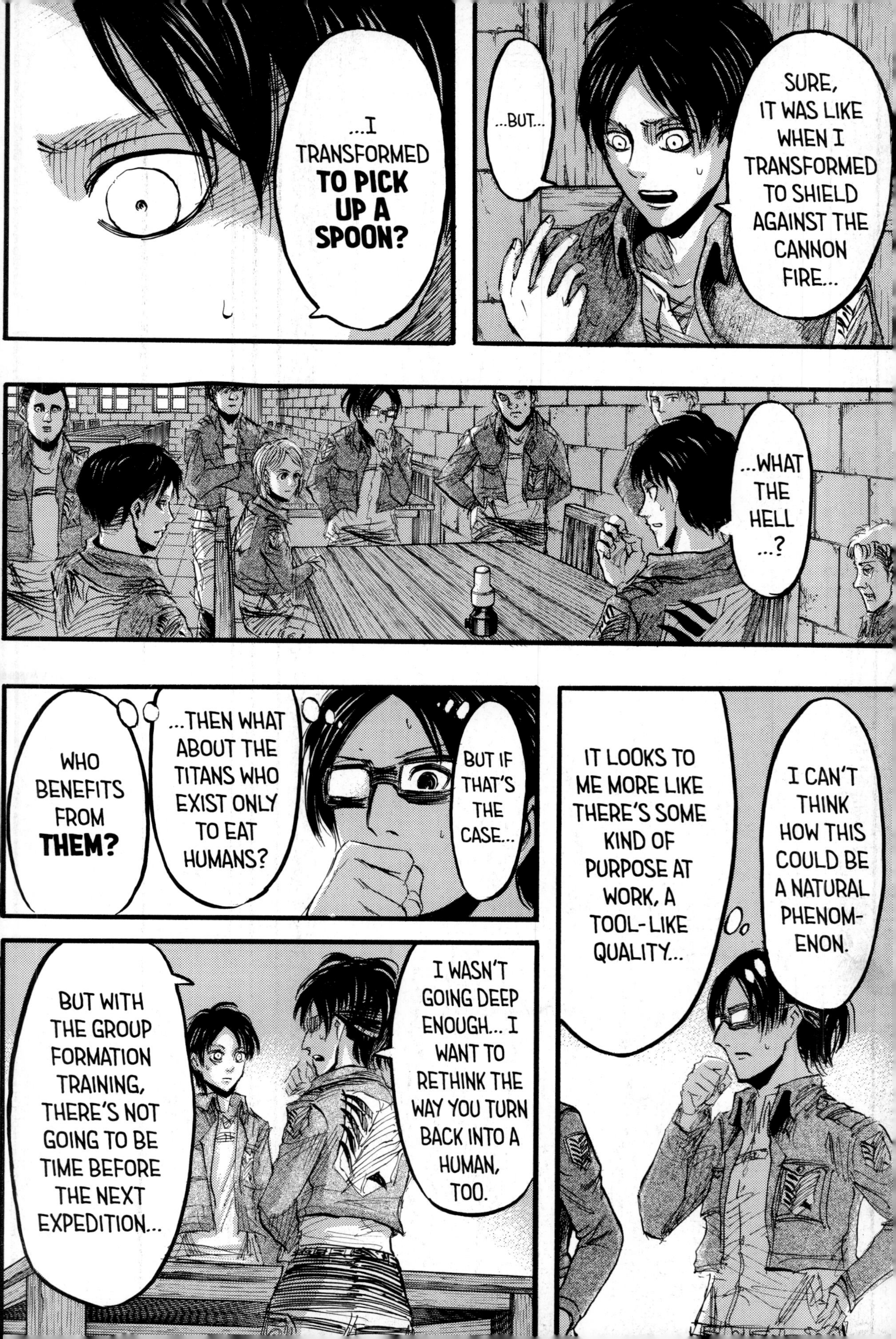
SURE, IT WAS LIKE WHEN I TRANSFORMED TO SHIELD AGAINST THE CANNON FIRE...
...BUT...
...I TRANSFORMED **TO PICK UP A SPOON?**
...WHAT THE HELL ...?
I CAN'T THINK HOW THIS COULD BE A NATURAL PHENOM-ENON.
IT LOOKS TO ME MORE LIKE THERE'S SOME KIND OF PURPOSE AT WORK, A TOOL-LIKE QUALITY...
BUT IF THAT'S THE CASE...
...THEN WHAT ABOUT THE TITANS WHO EXIST ONLY TO EAT HUMANS?
WHO BENEFITS FROM **THEM?**
I WASN'T GOING DEEP ENOUGH... I WANT TO RETHINK THE WAY YOU TURN BACK INTO A HUMAN, TOO.
BUT WITH THE GROUP FORMATION TRAINING, THERE'S NOT GOING TO BE TIME BEFORE THE NEXT EXPEDITION...

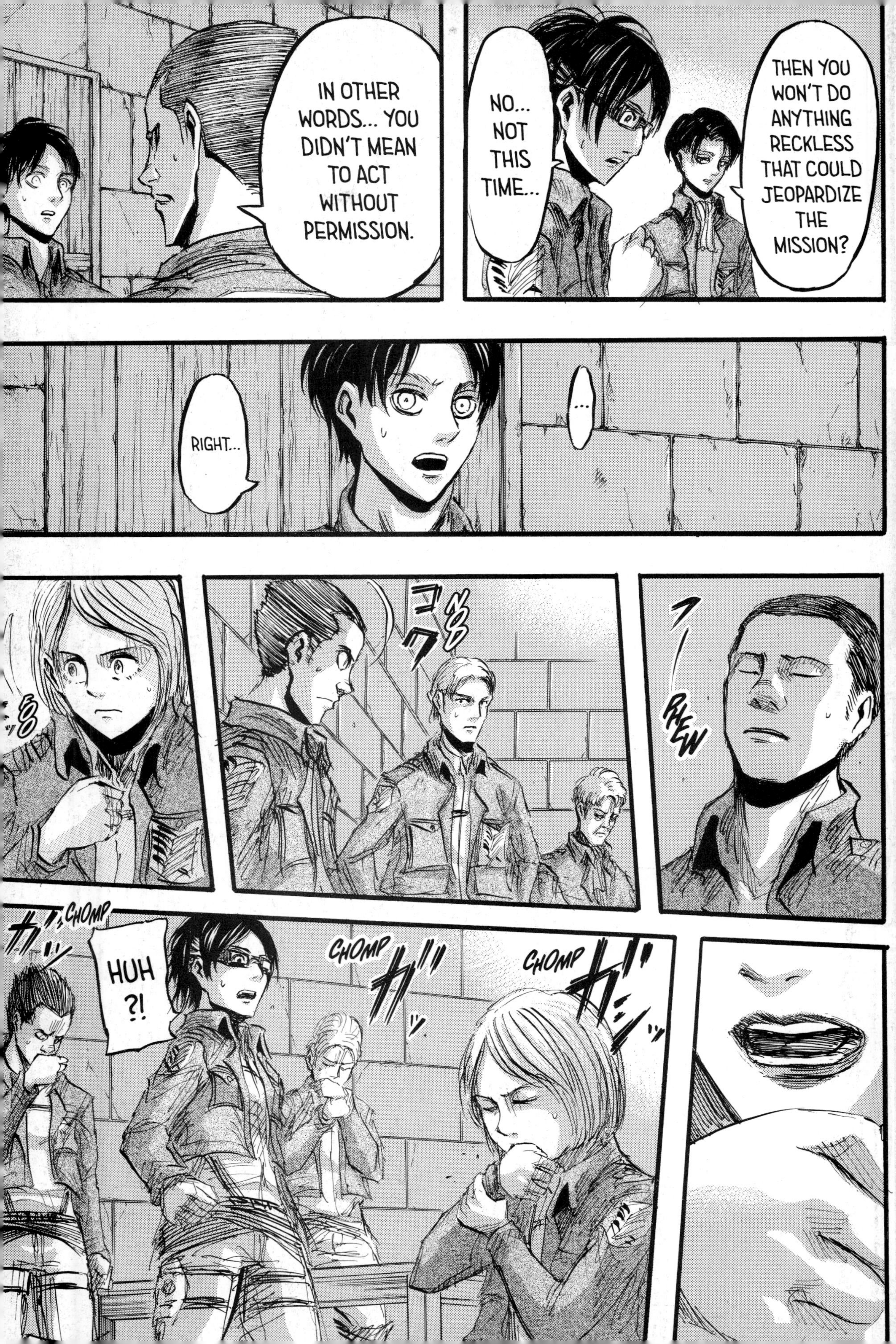
THEN YOU WON'T DO ANYTHING RECKLESS THAT COULD JEOPARDIZE THE MISSION?
NO... NOT THIS TIME...
IN OTHER WORDS... YOU DIDN'T MEAN TO ACT WITHOUT PERMISSION.
...
RIGHT...
PHEW
CHOMP
CHOMP
CHOMP
HUH ?!

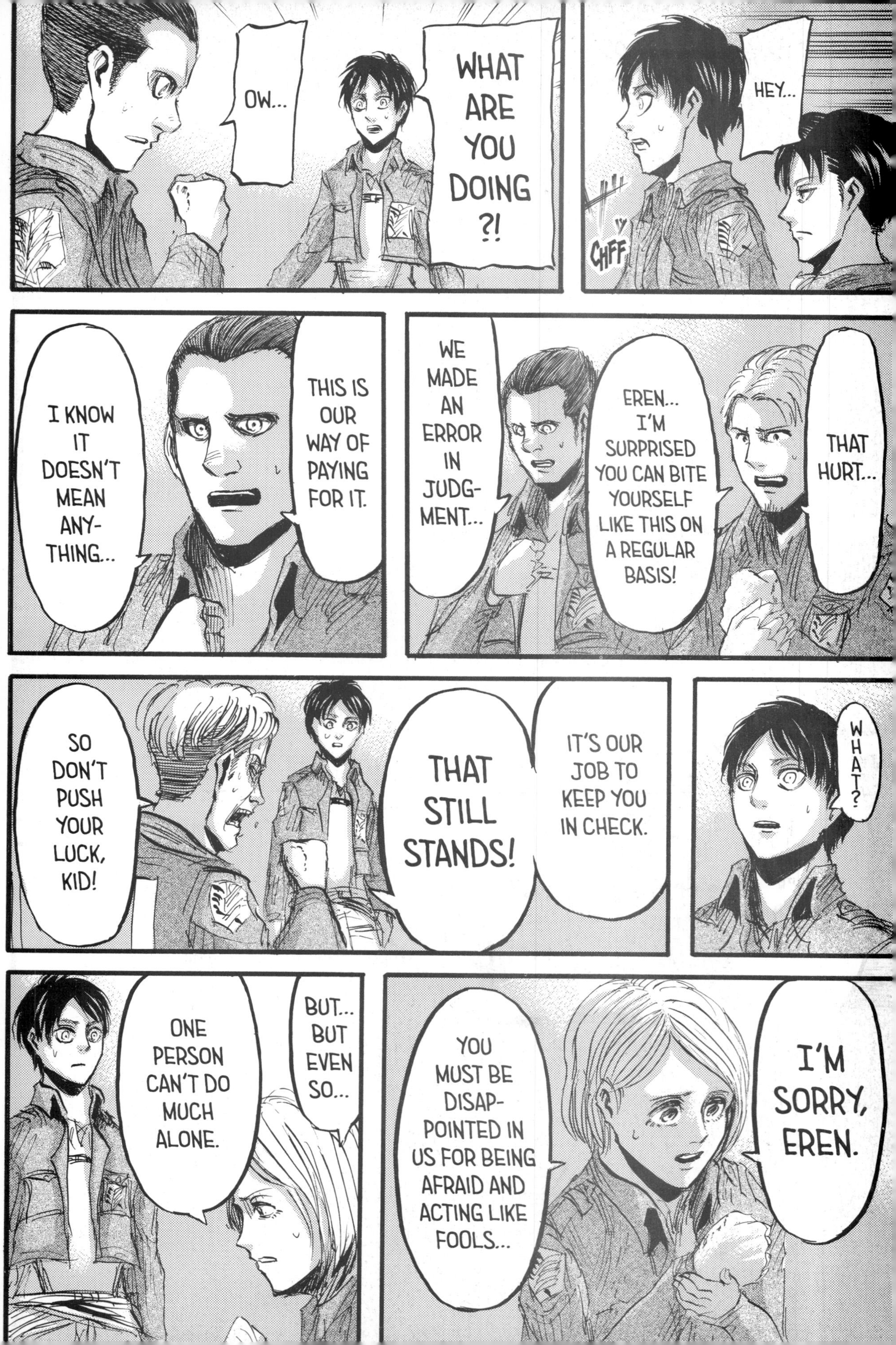
HEY...
CHFF
WHAT ARE YOU DOING ?!
OW...
THAT HURT...
EREN... I'M SURPRISED YOU CAN BITE YOURSELF LIKE THIS ON A REGULAR BASIS!
WE MADE AN ERROR IN JUDGMENT...
THIS IS OUR WAY OF PAYING FOR IT.
I KNOW IT DOESN'T MEAN ANYTHING...
WHAT?
IT'S OUR JOB TO KEEP YOU IN CHECK.
THAT STILL STANDS!
SO DON'T PUSH YOUR LUCK, KID!
I'M SORRY, EREN.
YOU MUST BE DISAPPOINTED IN US FOR BEING AFRAID AND ACTING LIKE FOOLS...
BUT... BUT EVEN SO...
ONE PERSON CAN'T DO MUCH ALONE.

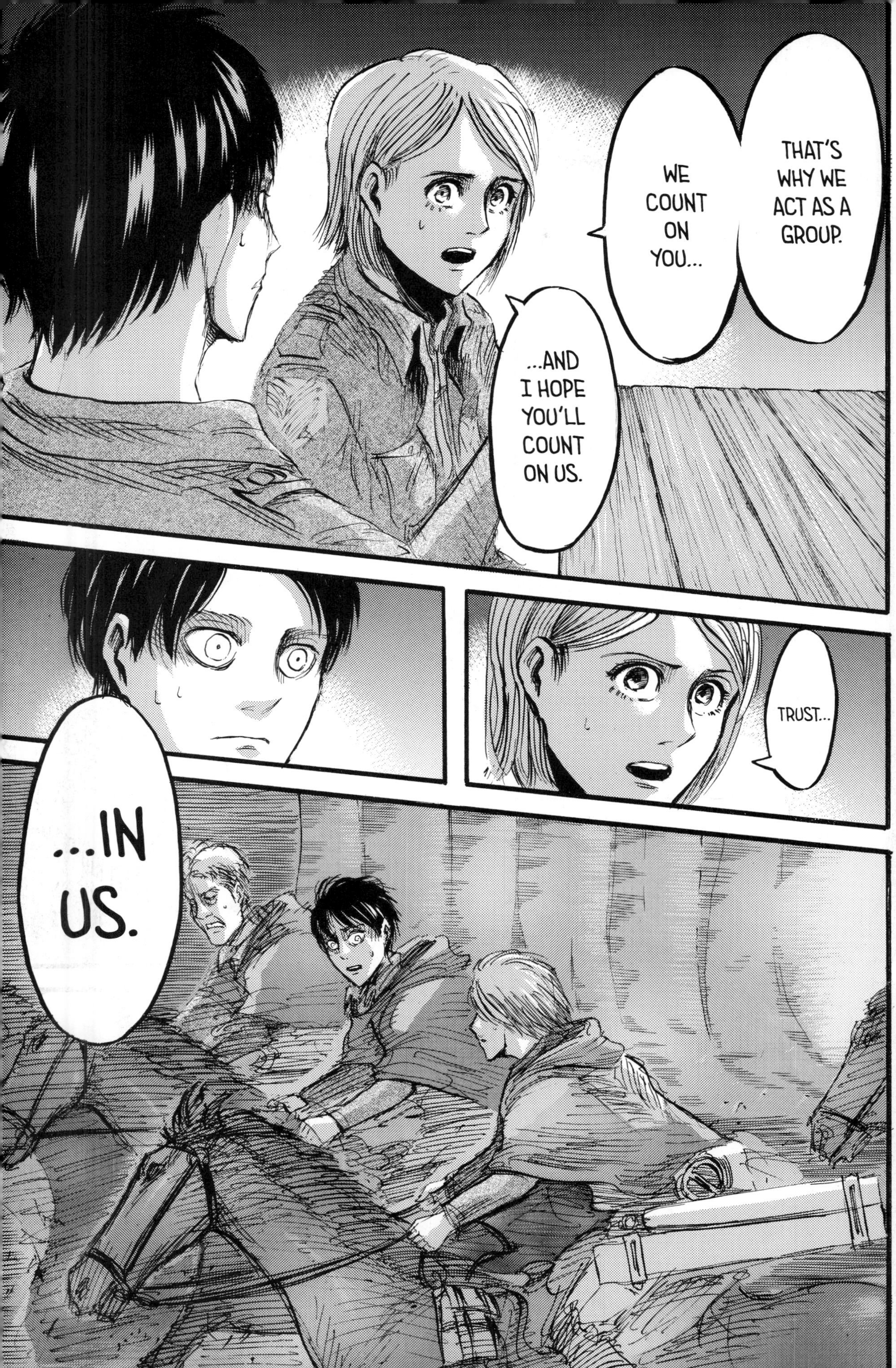
THAT'S WHY WE ACT AS A GROUP.
WE COUNT ON YOU...
...AND I HOPE YOU'LL COUNT ON US.
TRUST...
...IN US.

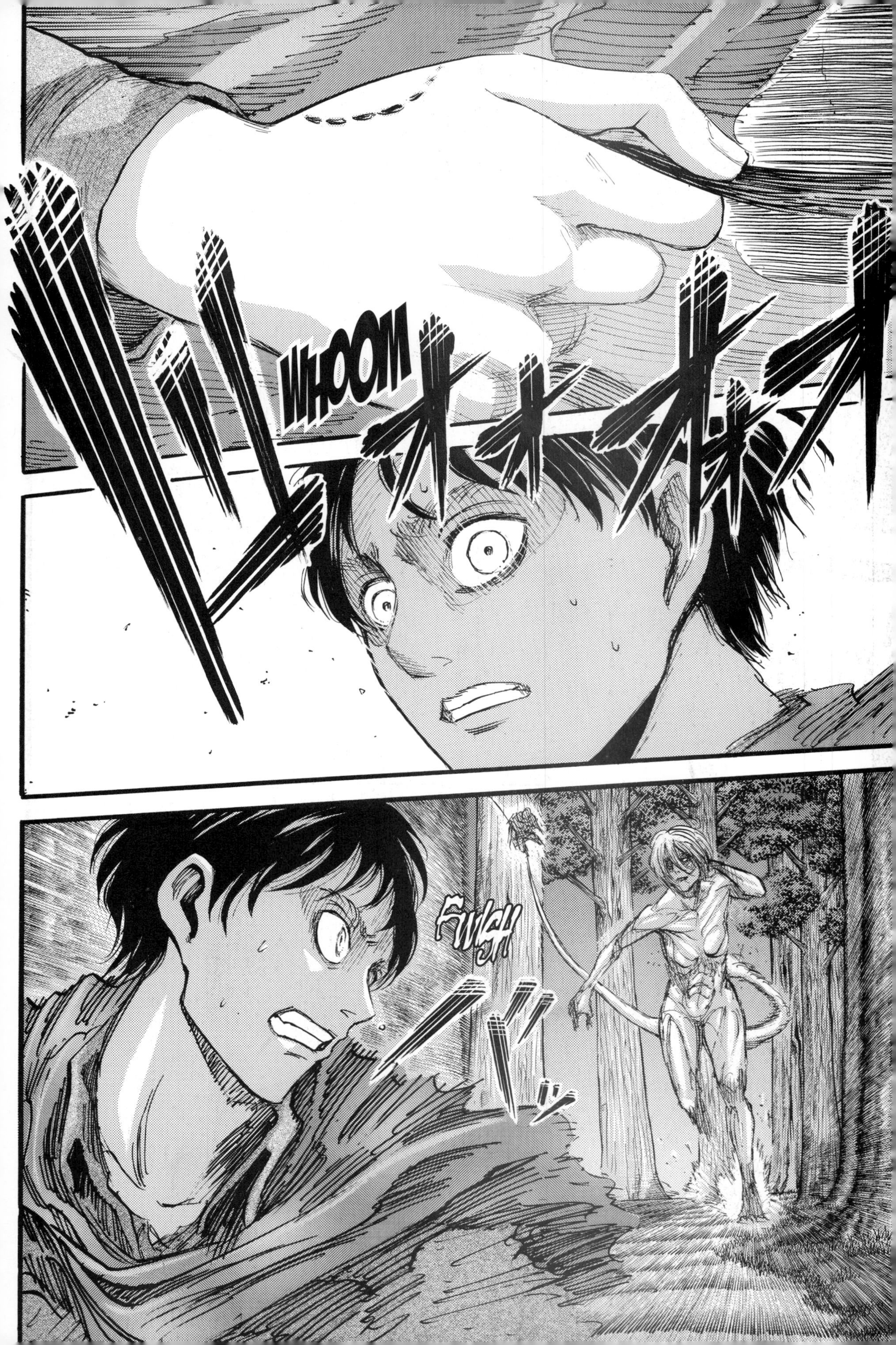
WHOOM
FWISH!

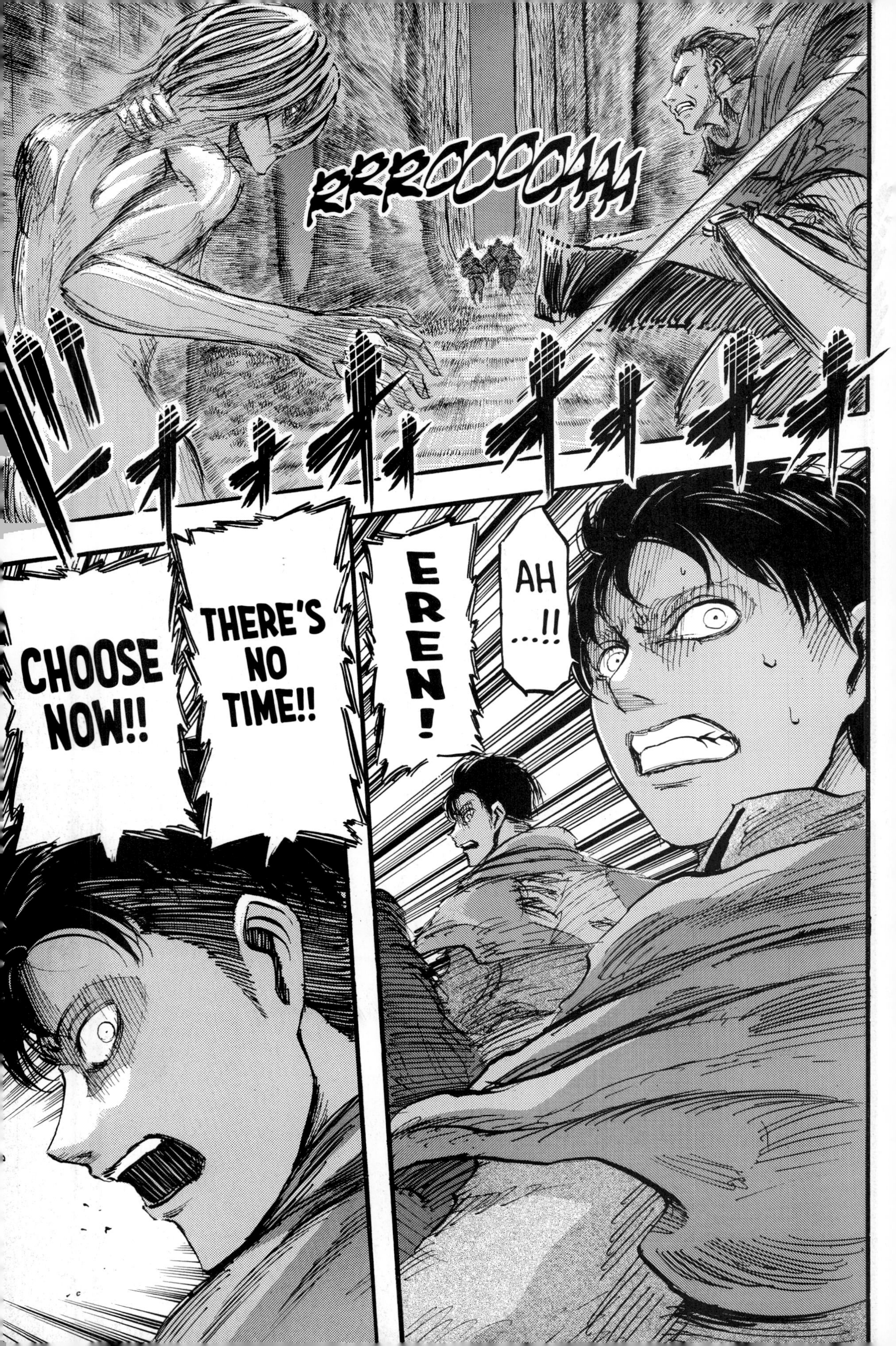
RRROOOOAAA
AH ...!!
EREN!
THERE'S NO TIME!!
CHOOSE NOW!!

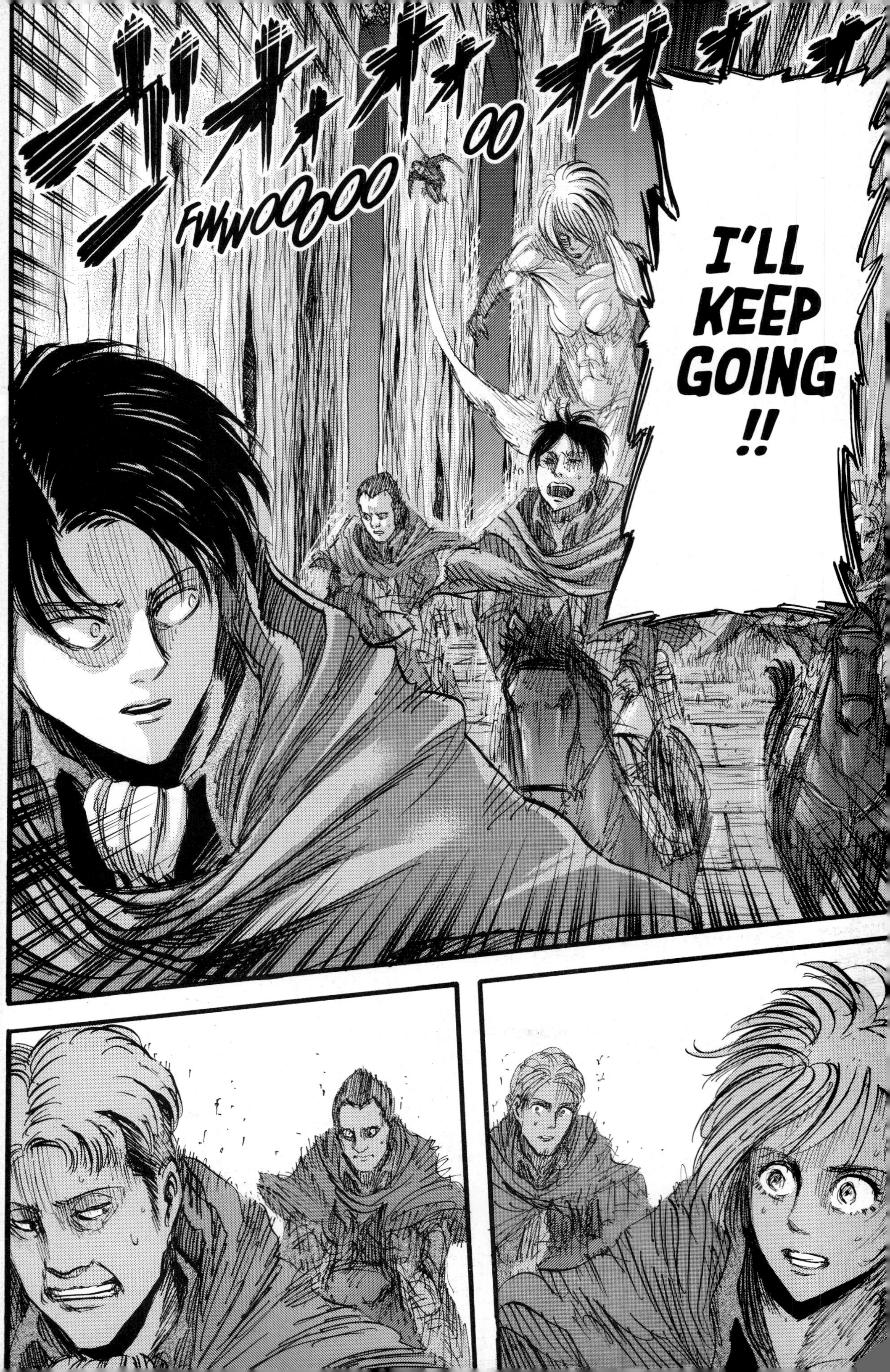
FWWOOOOOOO
I'LL KEEP GOING !!

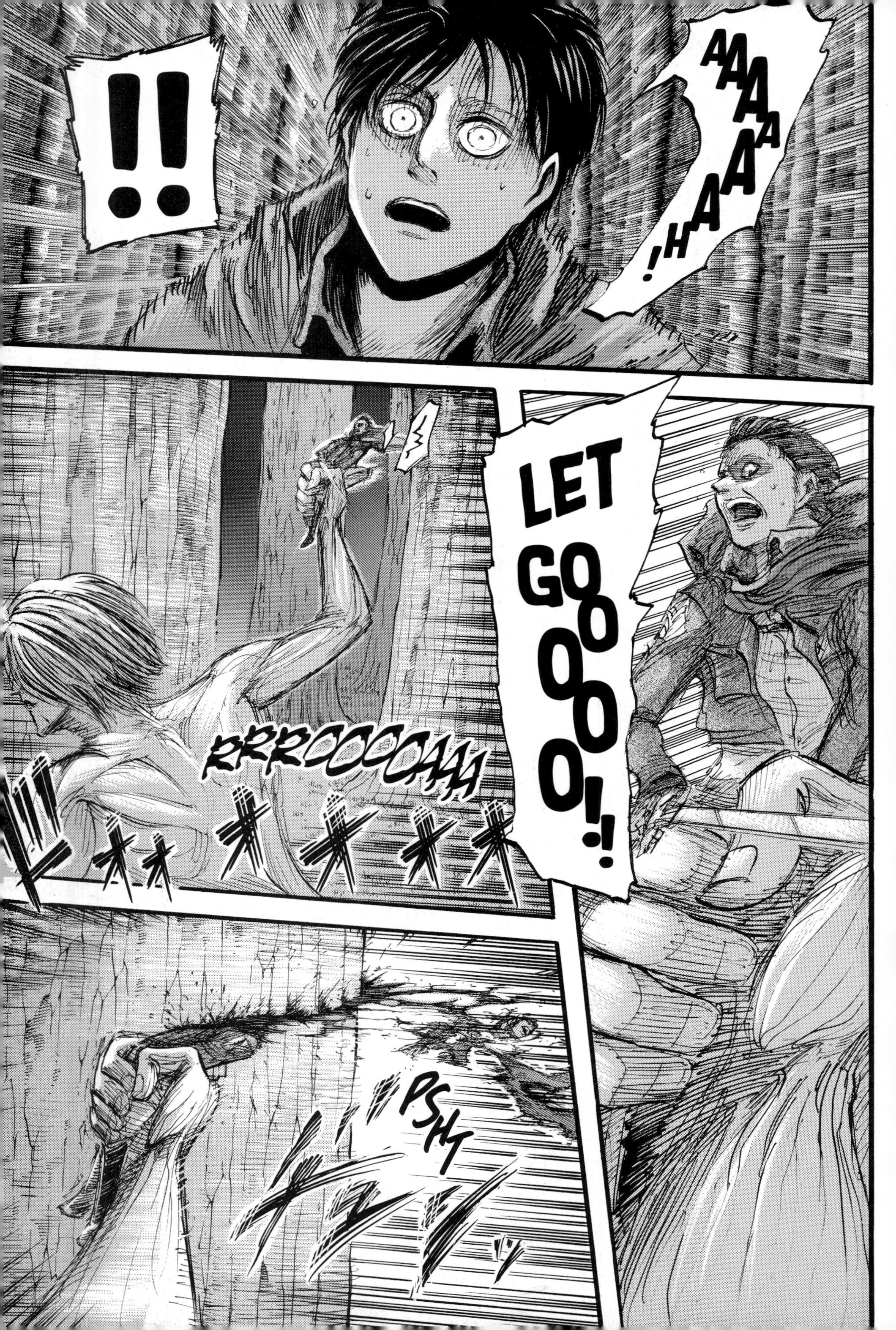

AAAAAAAH!
!!
LET GOOOOOO!!
RRROOOOAAA
PSHT

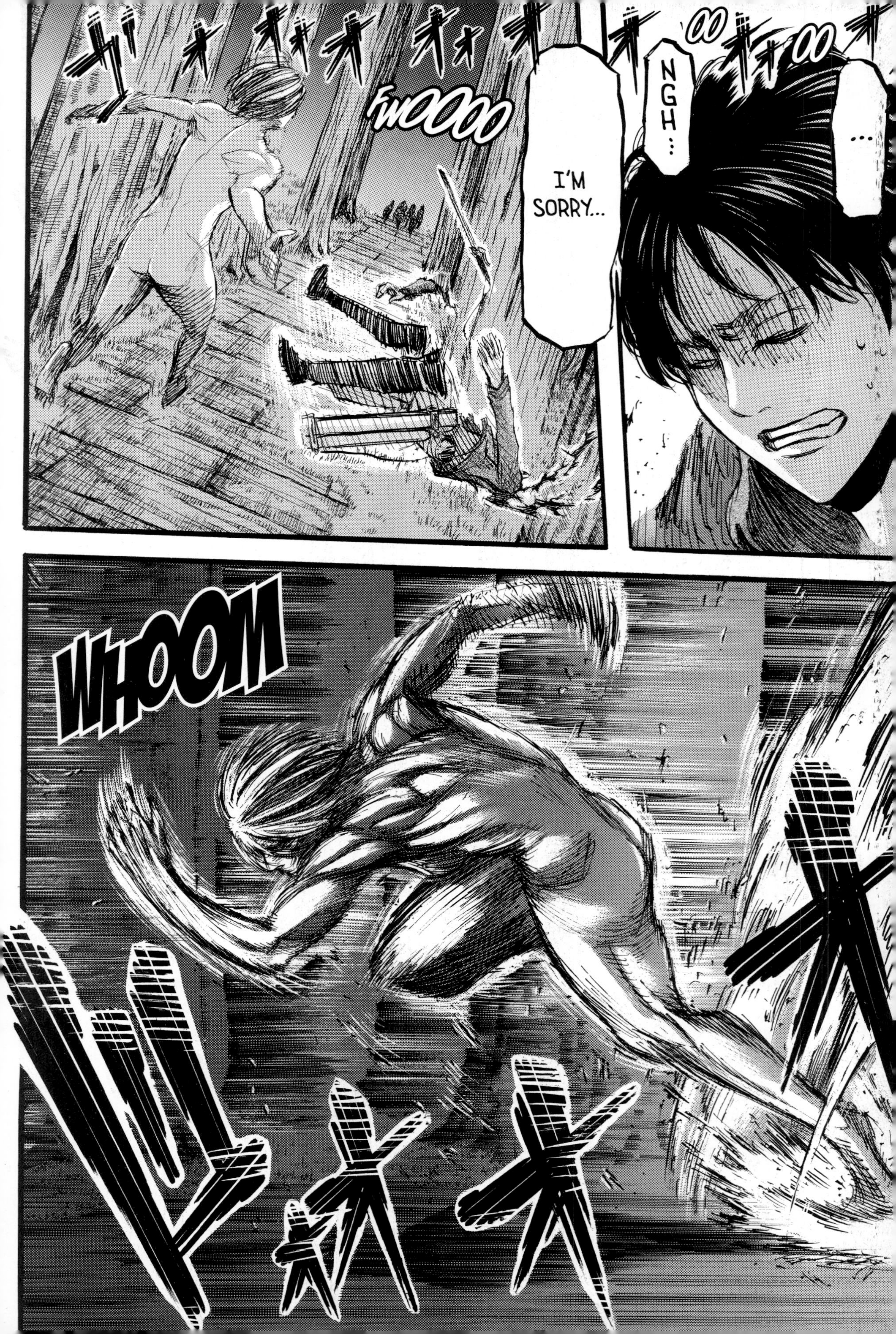
FWOOOO
...
NGH...
I'M SORRY...
WHOOM

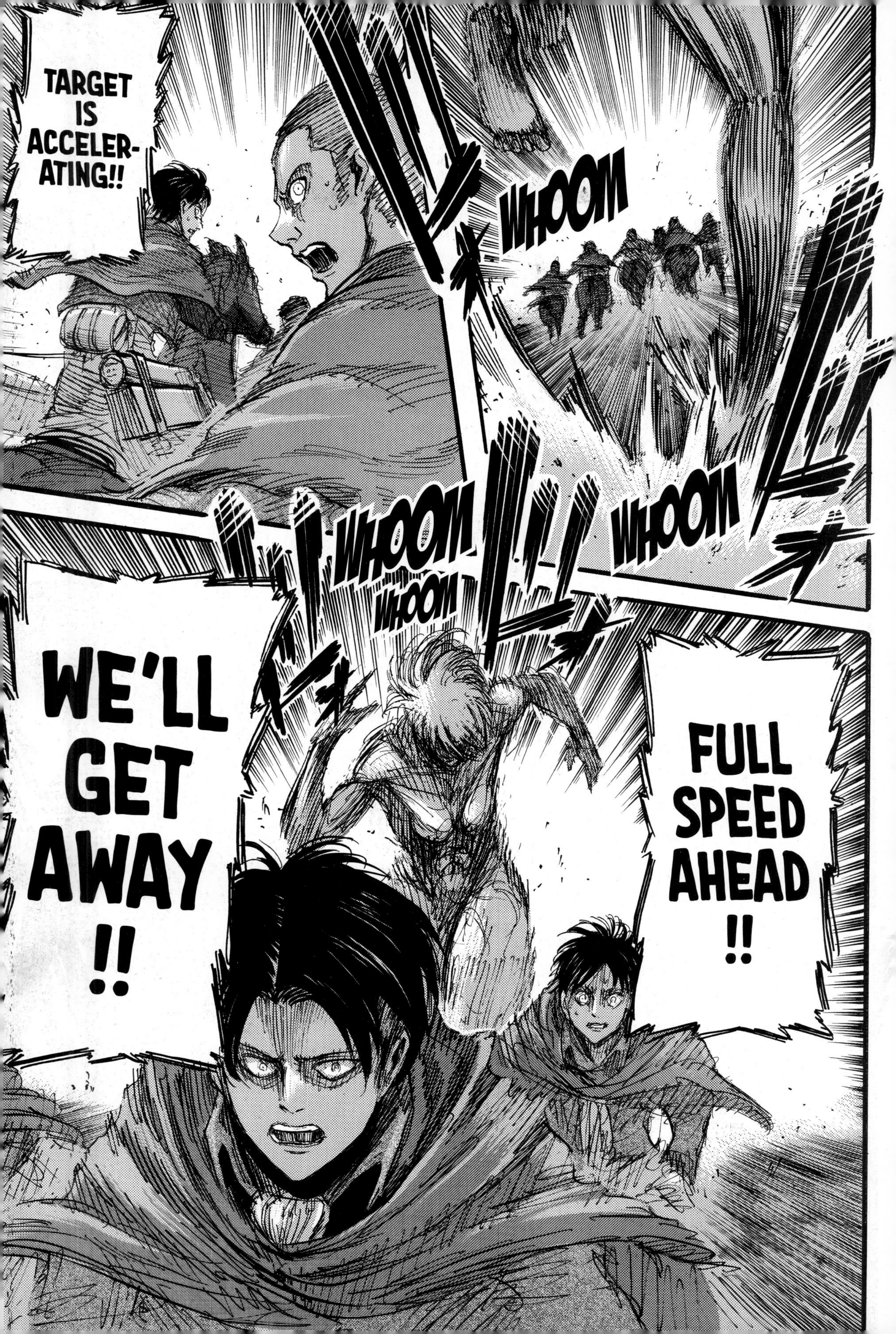
WHOOM
TARGET IS ACCELER-ATING!!
WHOOM
WHOOM
WHOOM
FULL SPEED AHEAD!!
WE'LL GET AWAY!!

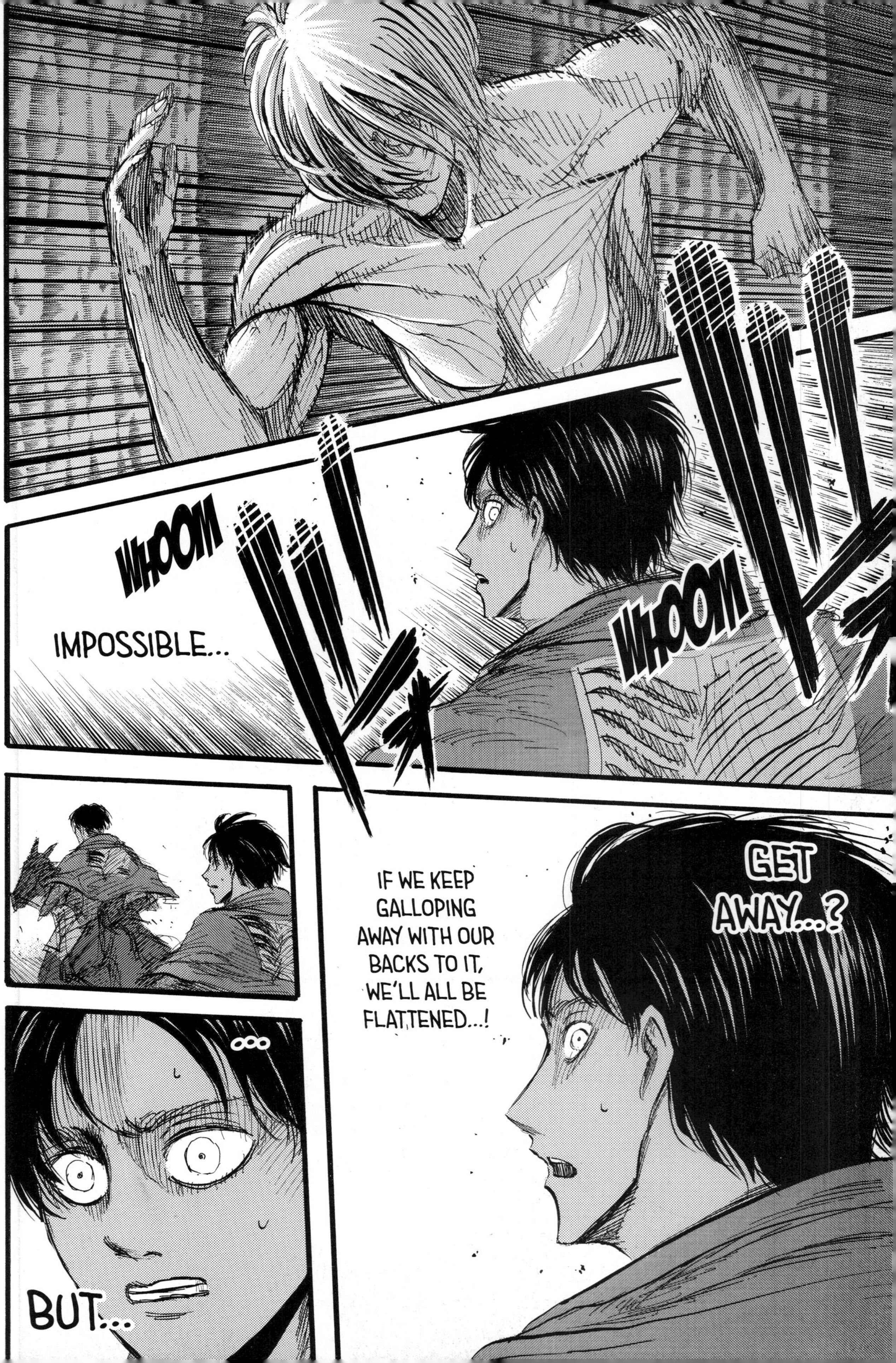
WHOOM
WHOOM
IMPOSSIBLE...
GET AWAY...?
IF WE KEEP GALLOPING AWAY WITH OUR BACKS TO IT, WE'LL ALL BE FLATTENED...!
BUT...

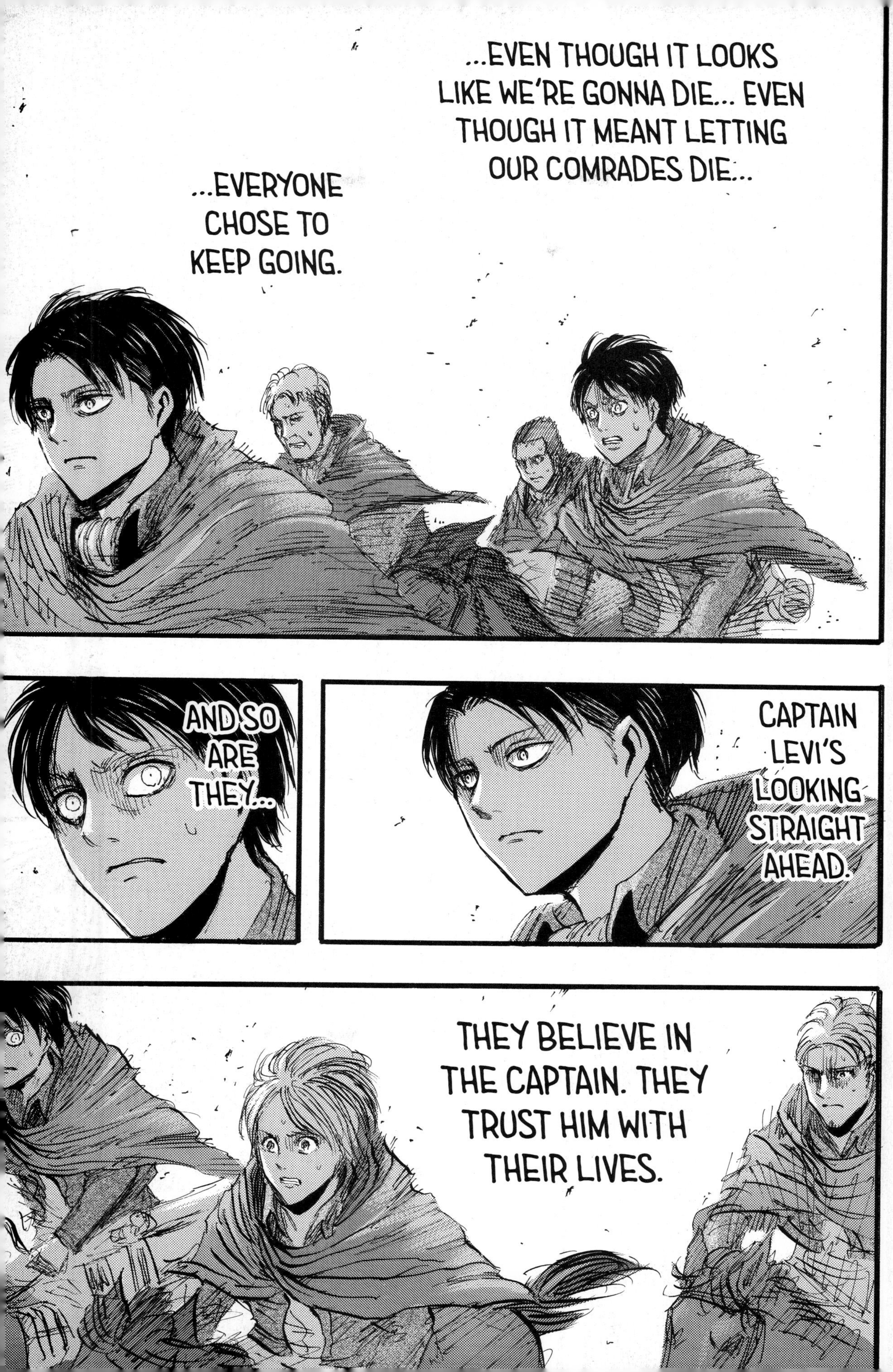
...EVEN THOUGH IT LOOKS LIKE WE'RE GONNA DIE... EVEN THOUGH IT MEANT LETTING OUR COMRADES DIE...
...EVERYONE CHOSE TO KEEP GOING.
CAPTAIN LEVI'S LOOKING STRAIGHT AHEAD.
AND SO ARE THEY...
THEY BELIEVE IN THE CAPTAIN. THEY TRUST HIM WITH THEIR LIVES.

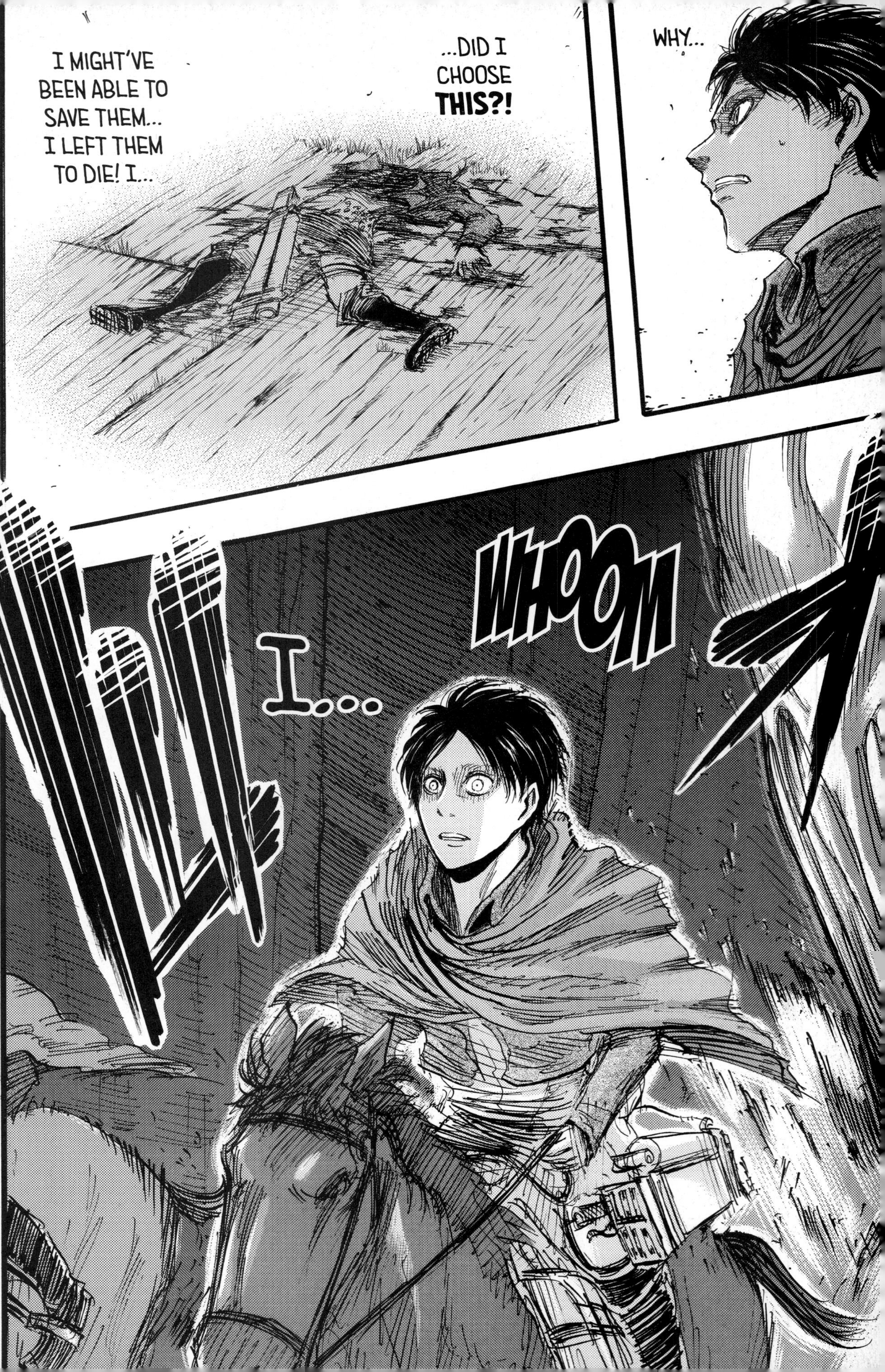
WHY...
...DID I CHOOSE THIS?!
I MIGHT'VE BEEN ABLE TO SAVE THEM... I LEFT THEM TO DIE! I...
WHOOM
I...

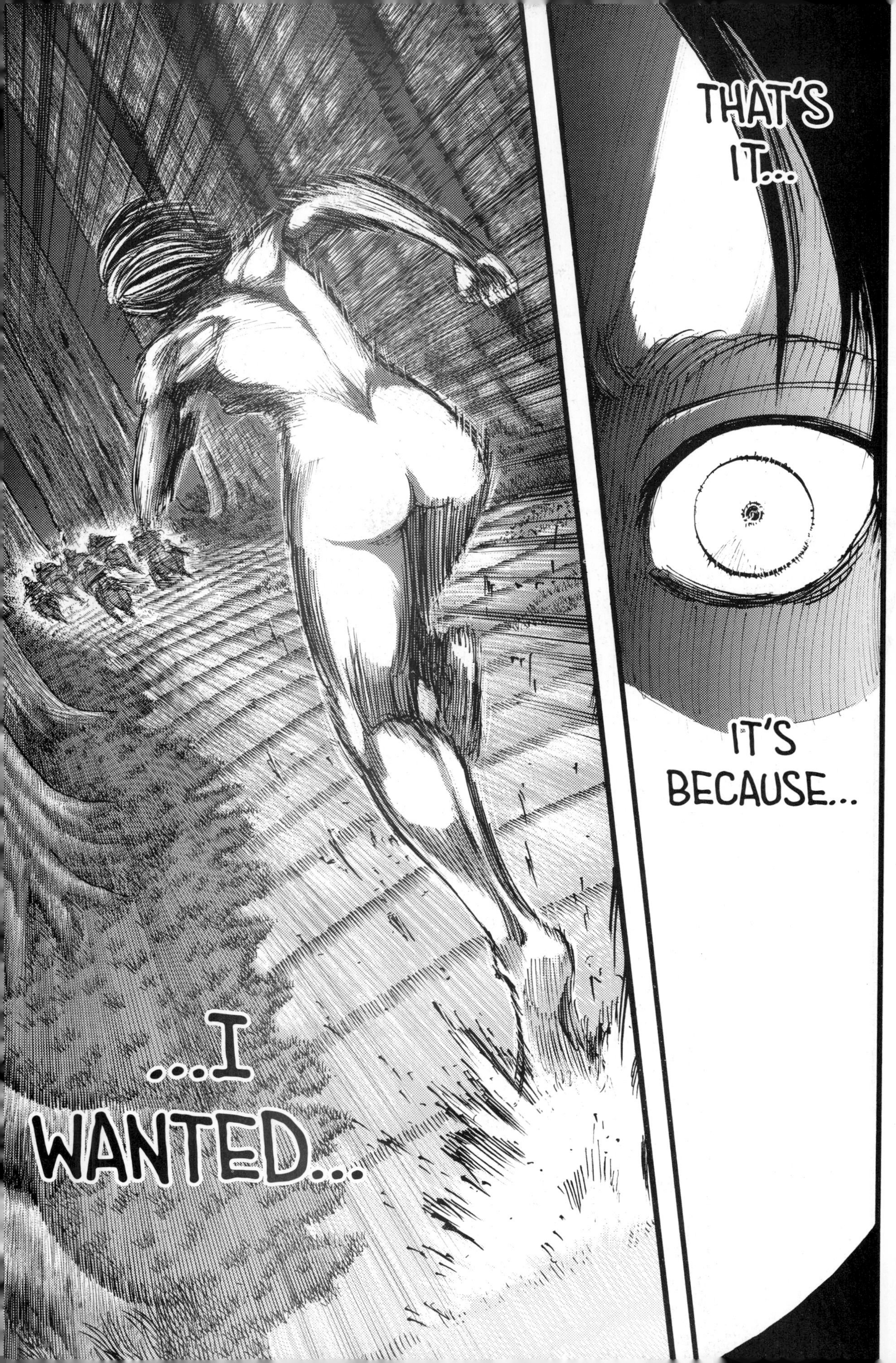
THAT'S IT...
IT'S BECAUSE...
...I WANTED...

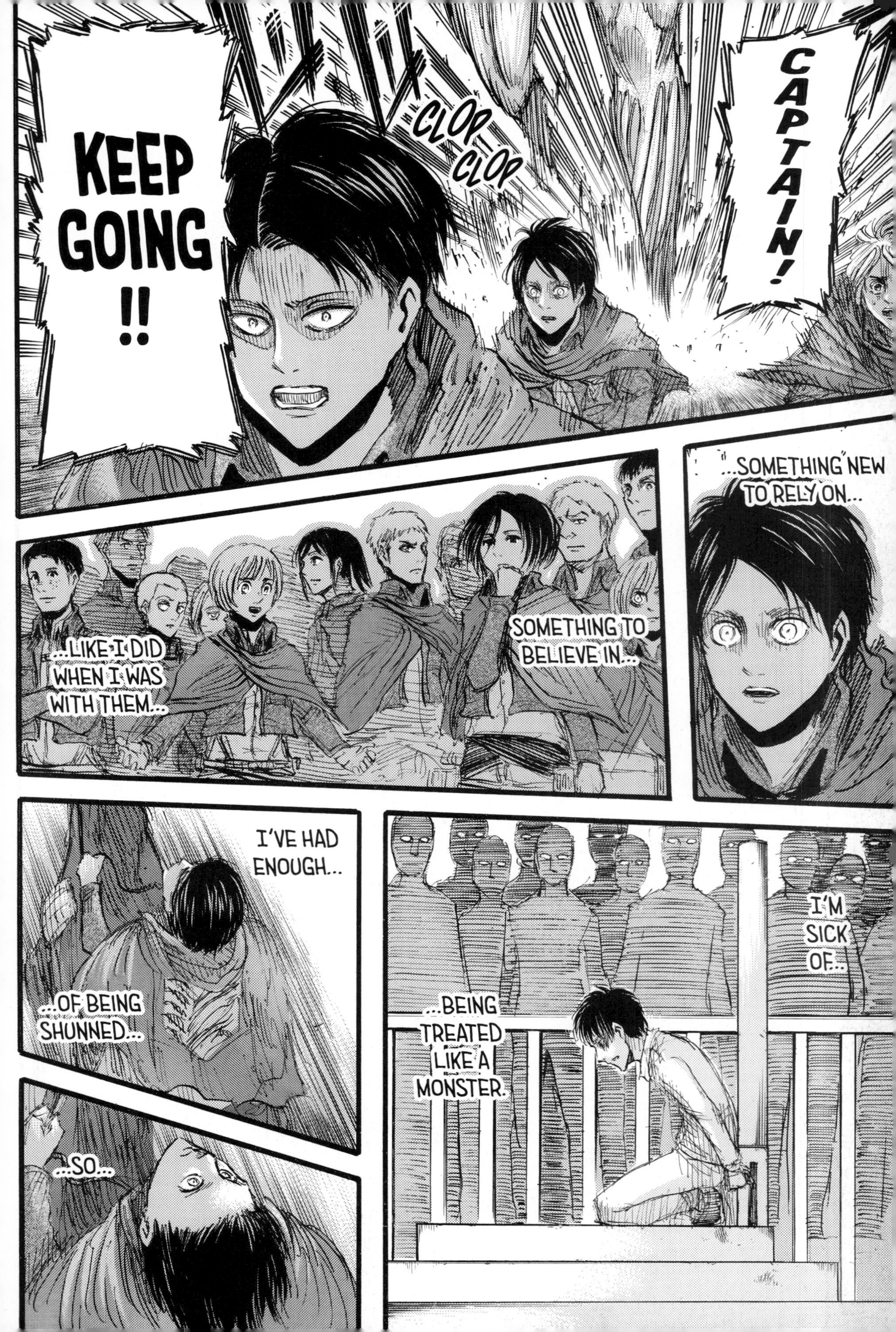
CAPTAIN!
CLOP CLOP
KEEP GOING!!
...SOMETHING NEW TO RELY ON...
SOMETHING TO BELIEVE IN...
...LIKE I DID WHEN I WAS WITH THEM...
I'M SICK OF...
...BEING TREATED LIKE A MONSTER.
I'VE HAD ENOUGH...
...OF BEING SHUNNED...
...SO...

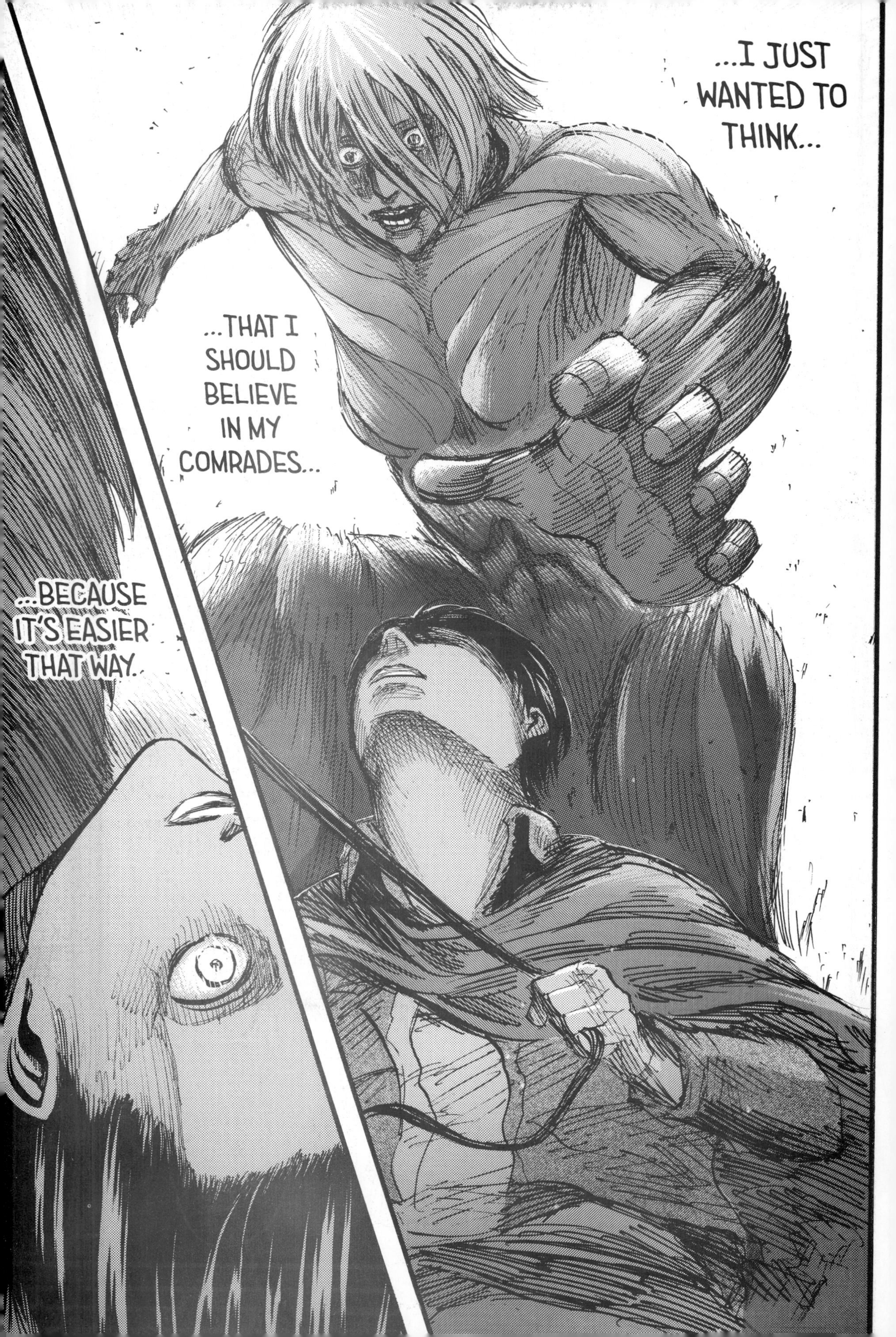
...I JUST WANTED TO THINK...
...THAT I SHOULD BELIEVE IN MY COMRADES...
...BECAUSE IT'S EASIER THAT WAY.

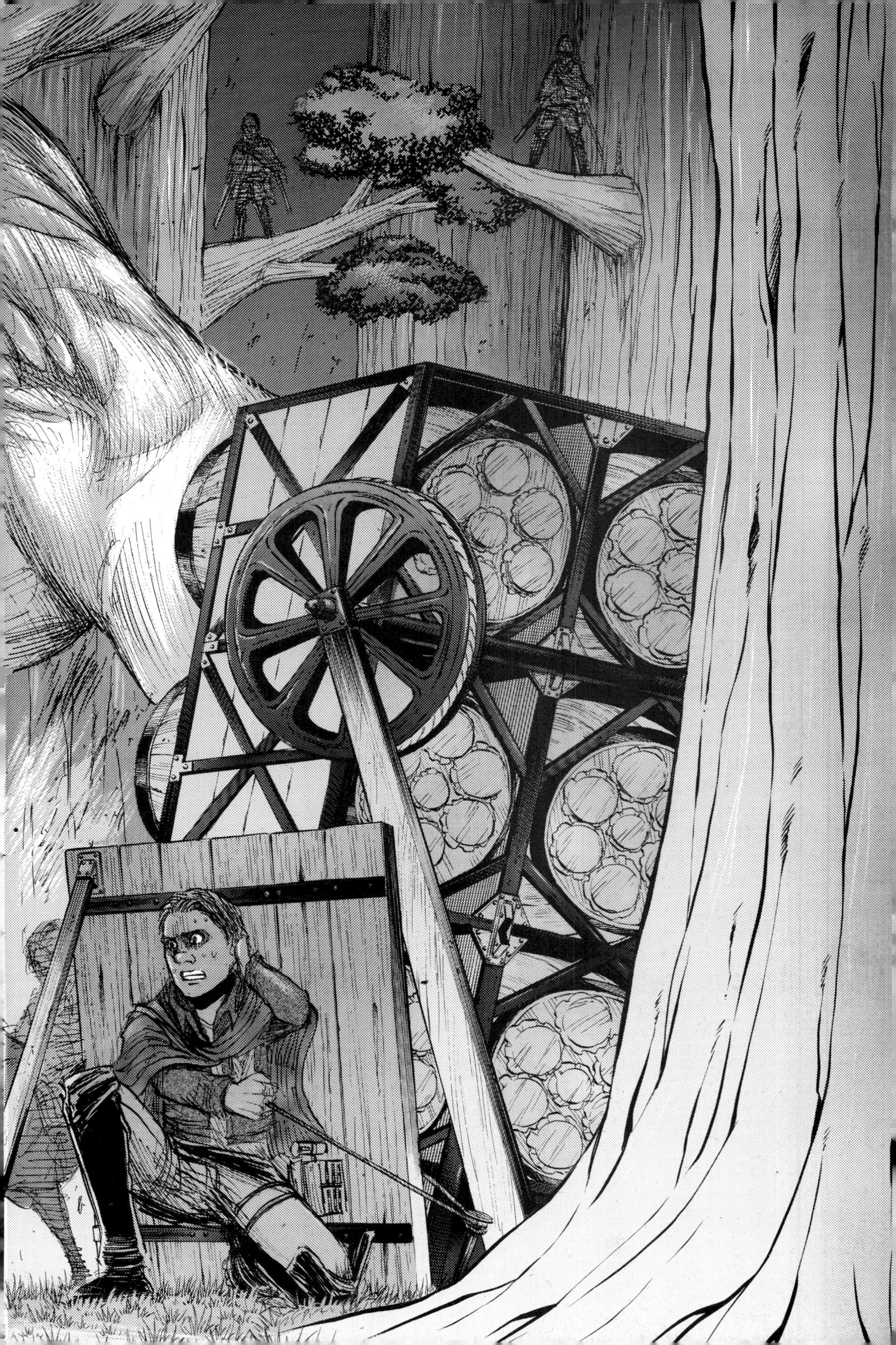

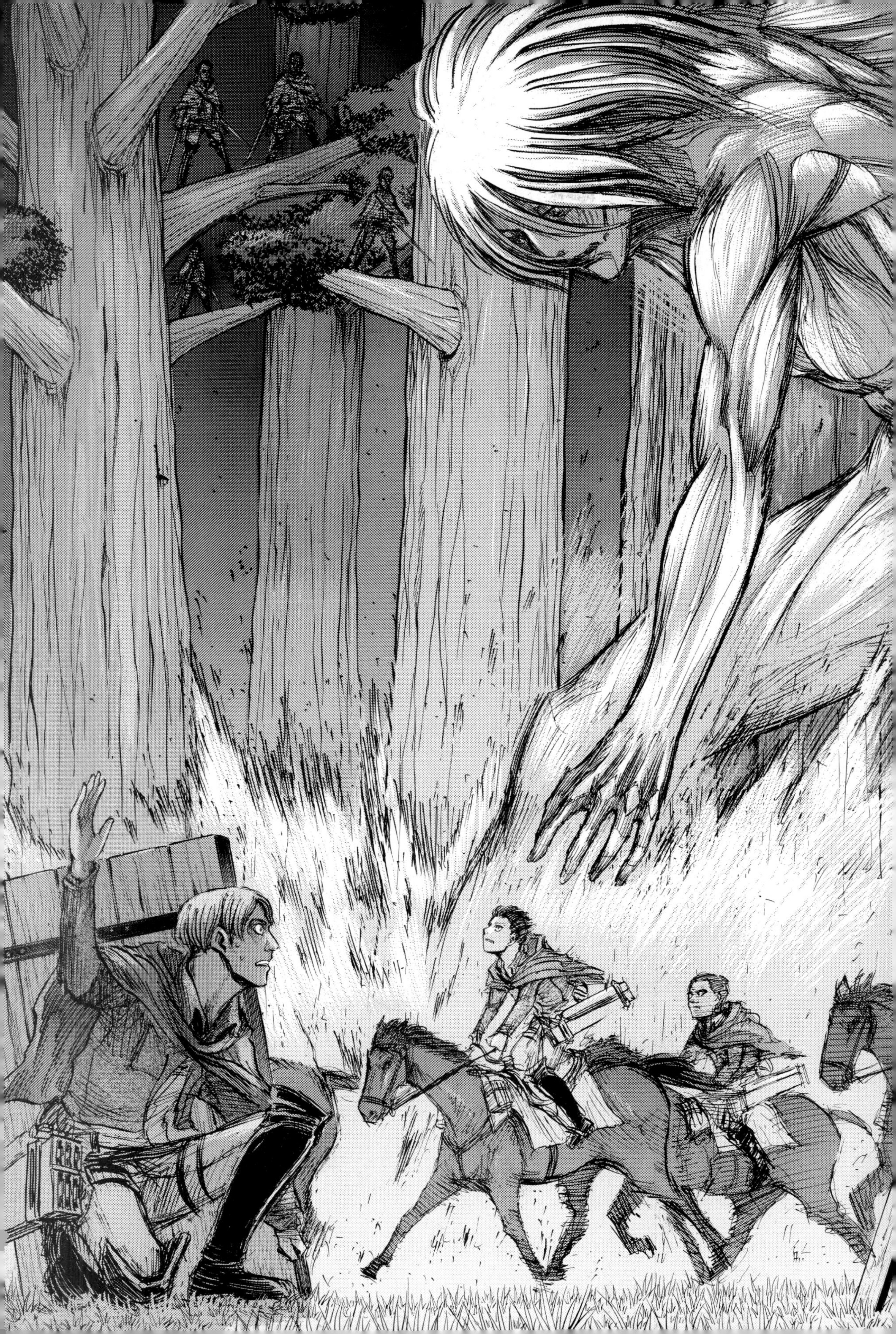

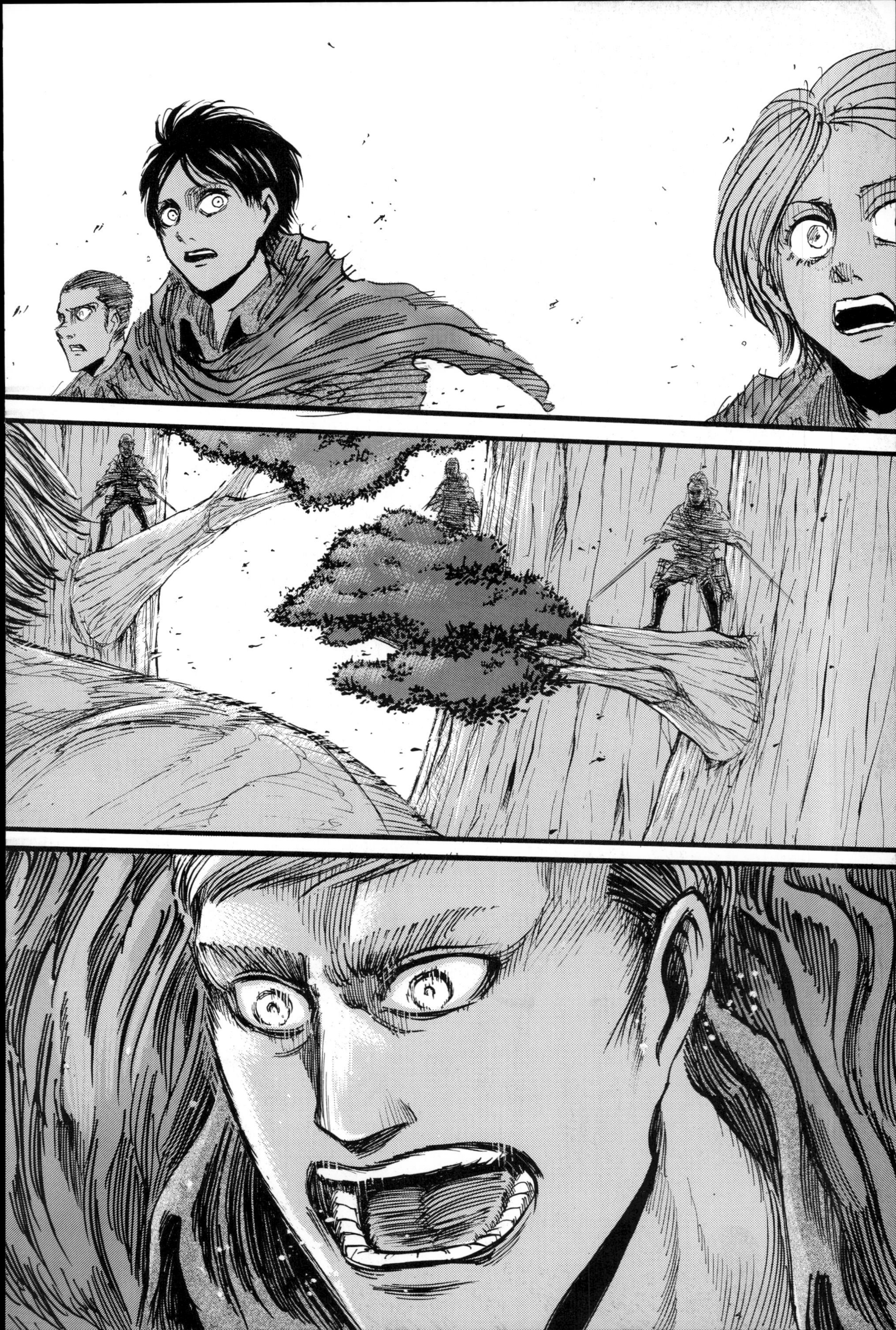

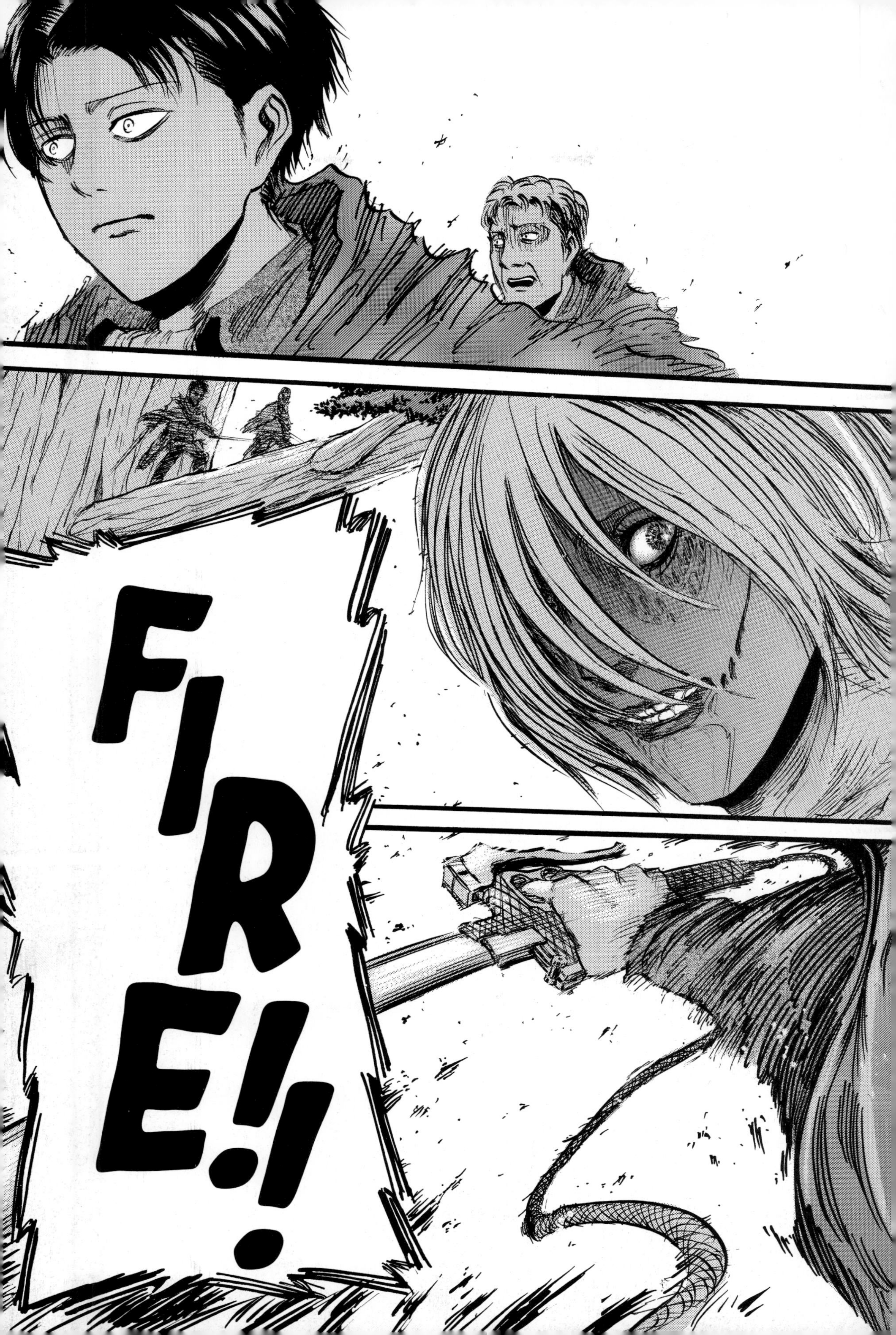
FIRE!!

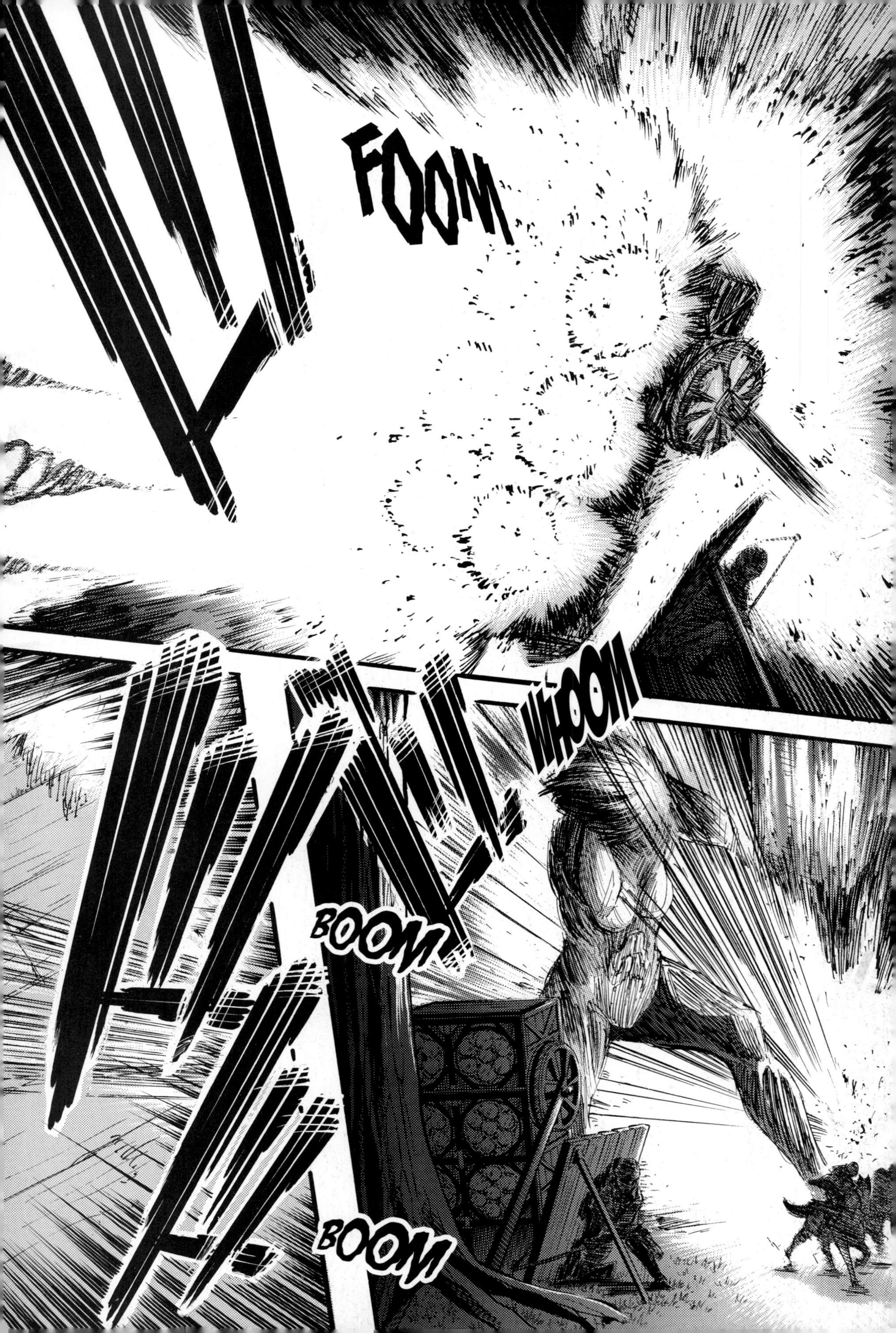
FOOM
WHOOM
BOOM
BOOM

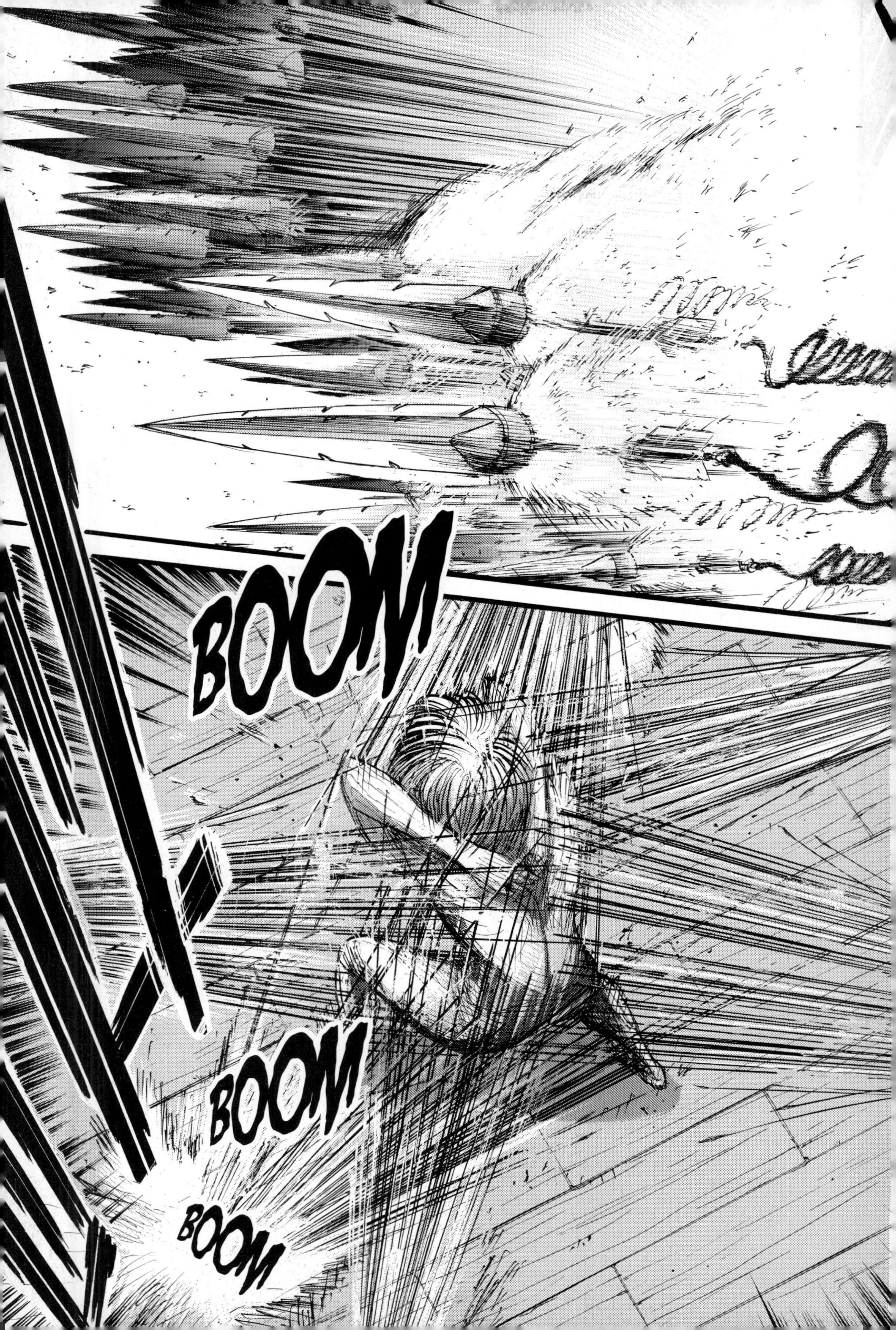
BOOM
BOOM
BOOM

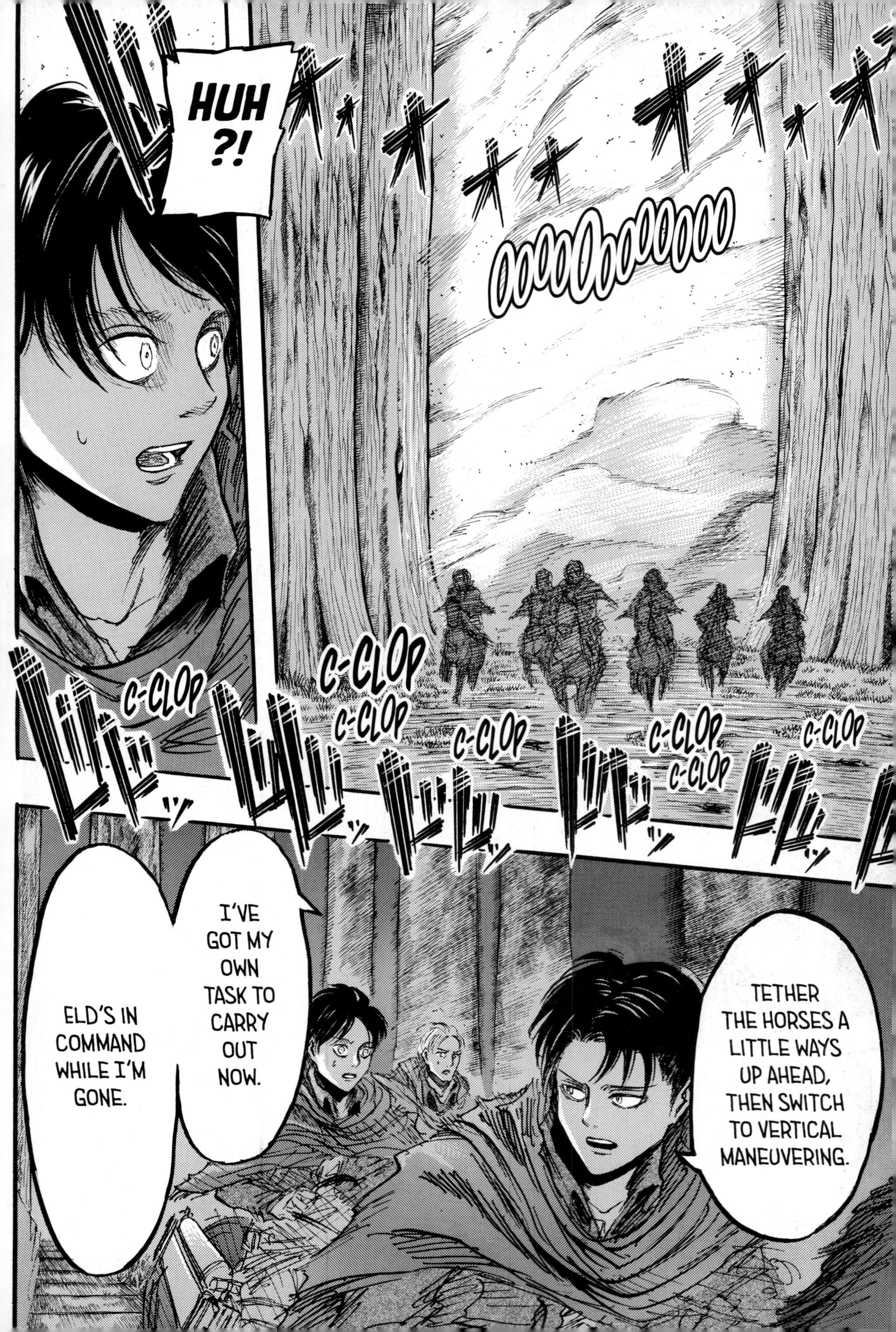
OOOOOOOOOOOO
HUH ?!
C-CLOP
C-CLOP
C-CLOP
C-CLOP
C-CLOP
C-CLOP
C-CLOP
TETHER THE HORSES A LITTLE WAYS UP AHEAD, THEN SWITCH TO VERTICAL MANEUVERING.
I'VE GOT MY OWN TASK TO CARRY OUT NOW.
ELD'S IN COMMAND WHILE I'M GONE.

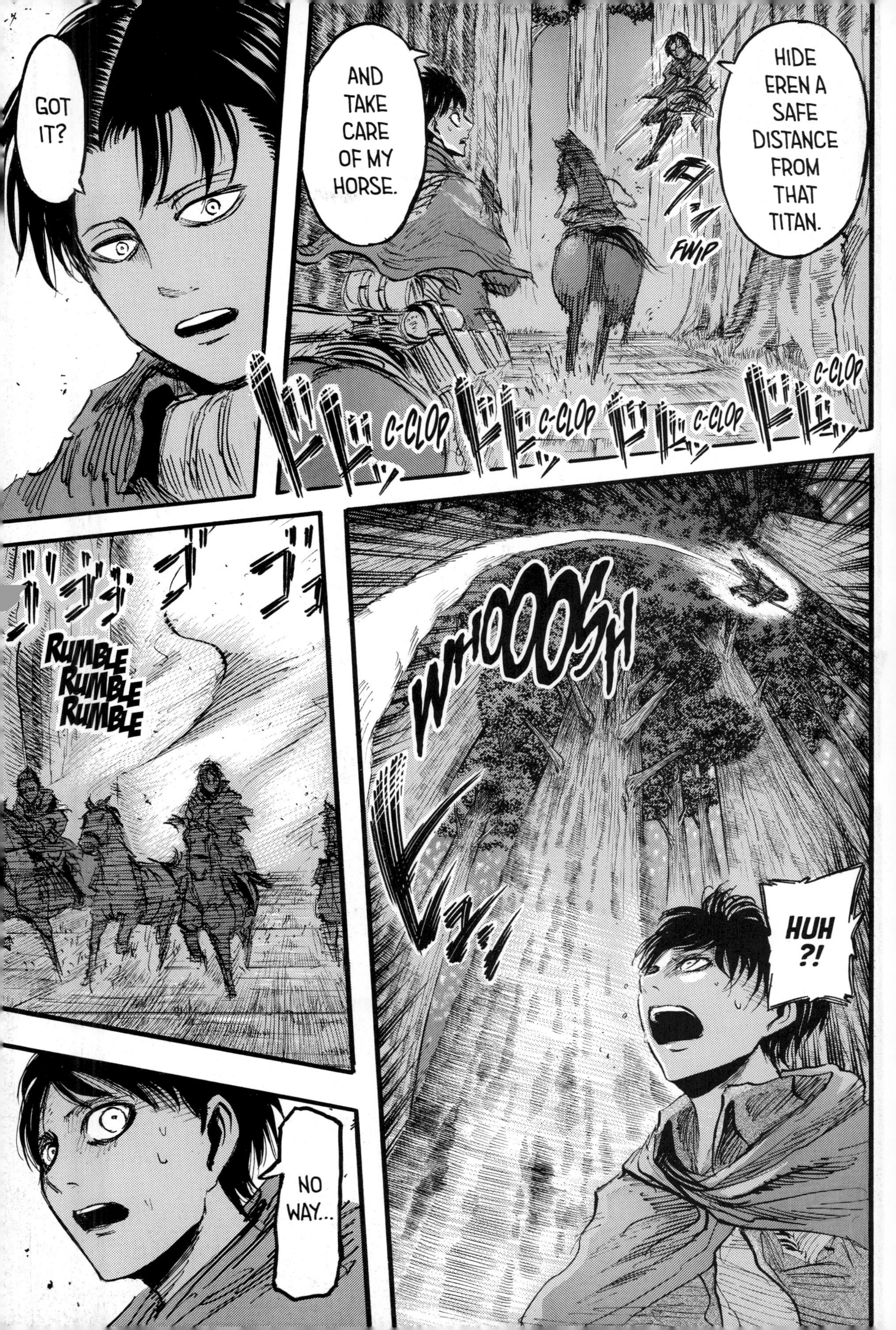
HIDE EREN A SAFE DISTANCE FROM THAT TITAN.
FWIP
AND TAKE CARE OF MY HORSE.
C-CLOP
C-CLOP
C-CLOP
C-CLOP
GOT IT?
WHOOOSH
HUH ?!
RUMBLE RUMBLE RUMBLE
NO WAY...

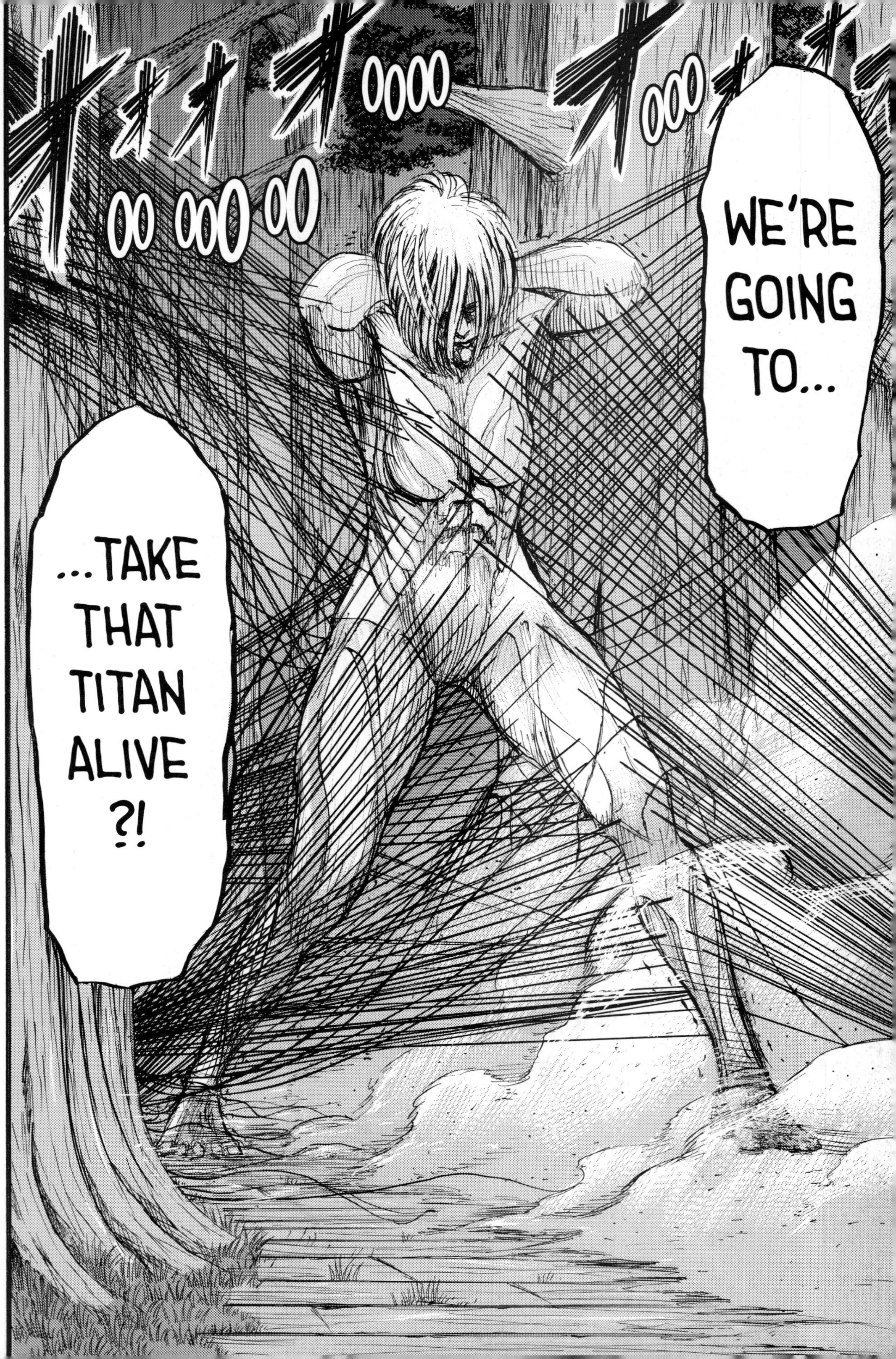
OOO
OOOO
OO OOO OO
WE'RE GOING TO...
...TAKE THAT TITAN ALIVE ?!

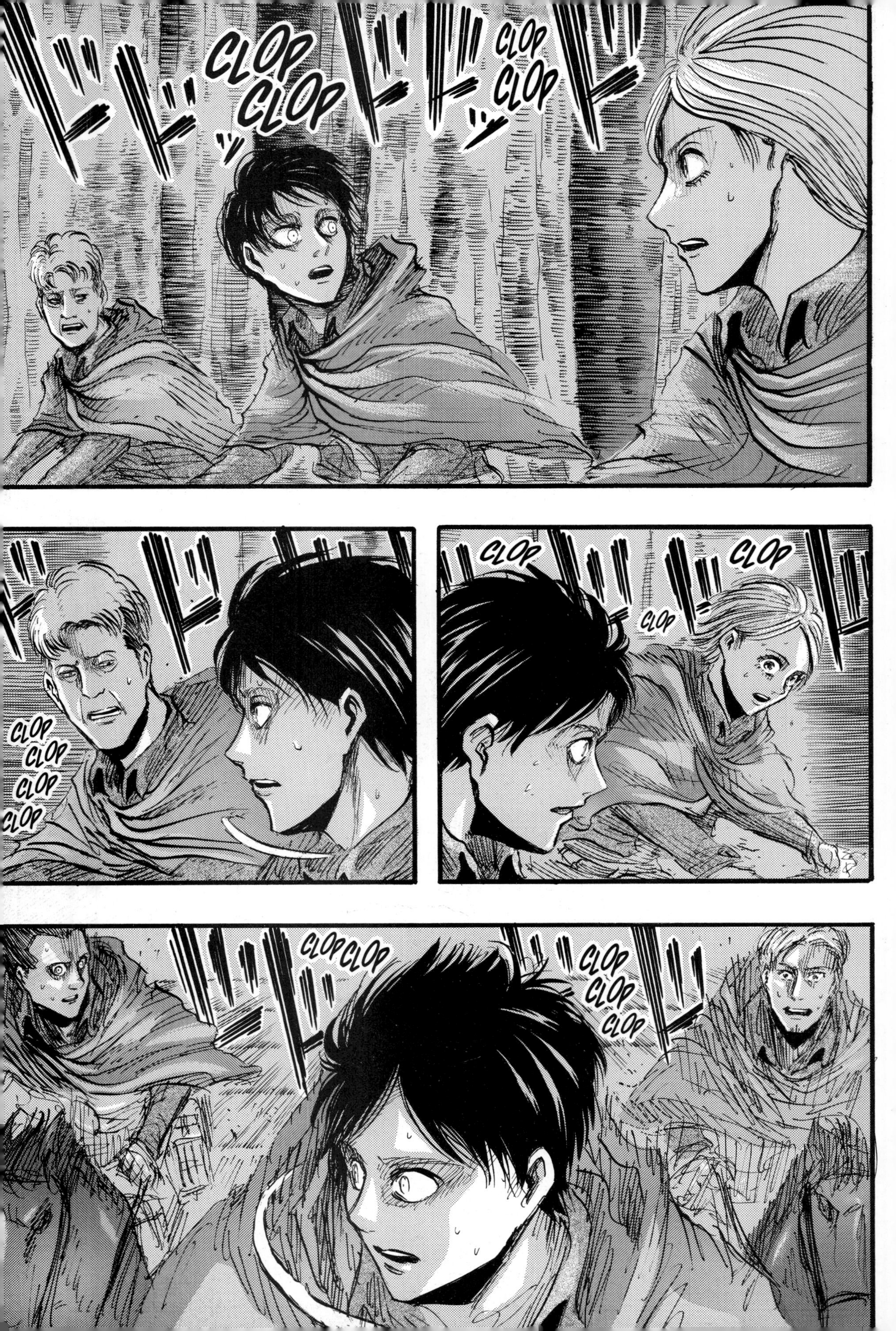

CLOP CLOP
CLOP CLOP
CLOP
CLOP
CLOP
CLOP CLOP CLOP CLOP
CLOP CLOP CLOP
CLOP CLOP

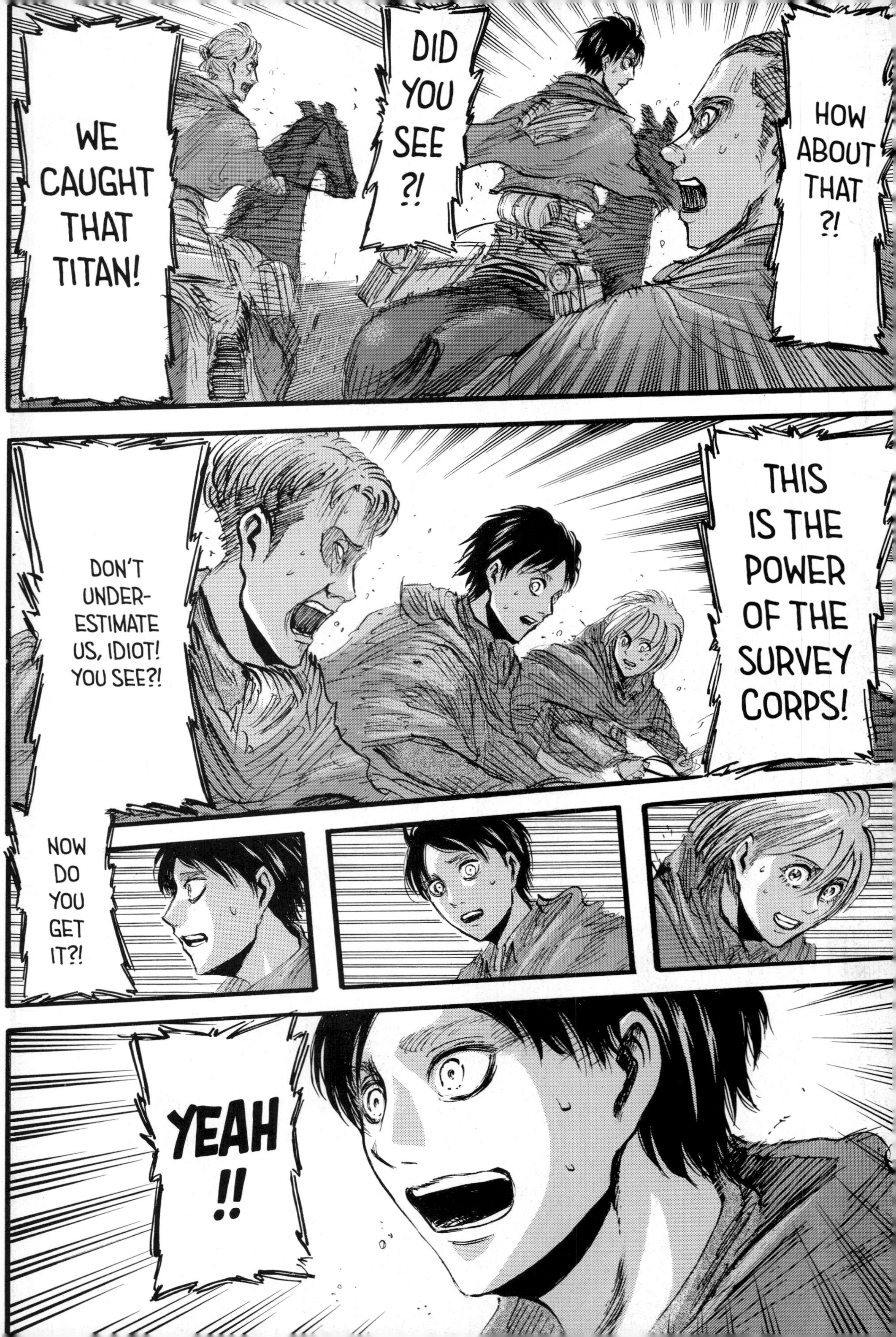
HOW ABOUT THAT?!
DID YOU SEE?!
WE CAUGHT THAT TITAN!
THIS IS THE POWER OF THE SURVEY CORPS!
DON'T UNDER-ESTIMATE US, IDIOT! YOU SEE?!
NOW DO YOU GET IT?!
YEAH!!

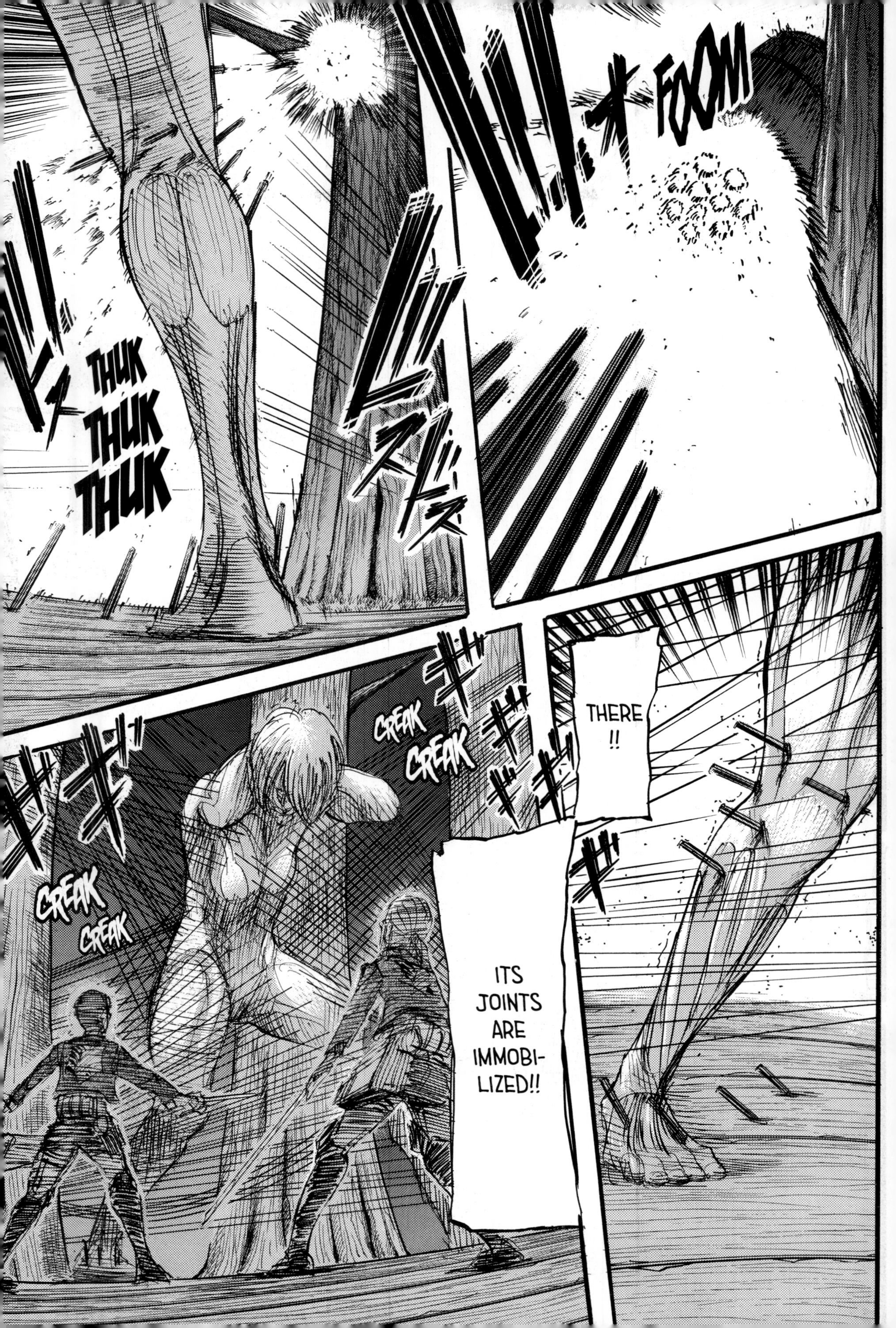
FOOM
THUK
THUK
THUK
THERE !!
ITS JOINTS ARE IMMOBI-LIZED!!
CREAK
CREAK
CREAK
CREAK

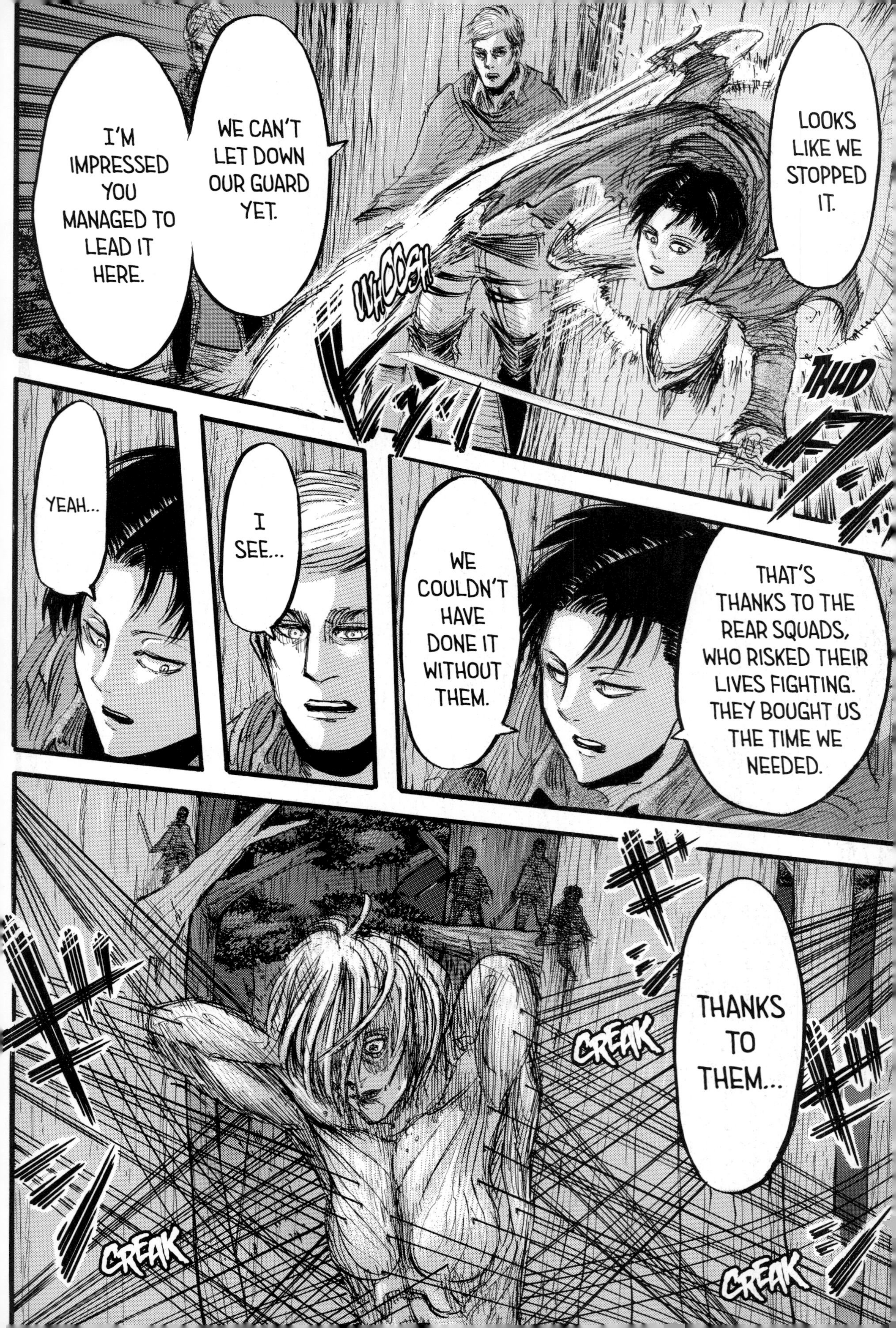
LOOKS LIKE WE STOPPED IT.
WE CAN'T LET DOWN OUR GUARD YET.
I'M IMPRESSED YOU MANAGED TO LEAD IT HERE.
WHOOSH
THUD
THAT'S THANKS TO THE REAR SQUADS, WHO RISKED THEIR LIVES FIGHTING. THEY BOUGHT US THE TIME WE NEEDED.
WE COULDN'T HAVE DONE IT WITHOUT THEM.
I SEE...
YEAH...
THANKS TO THEM...
CREAK
CREAK
CREAK

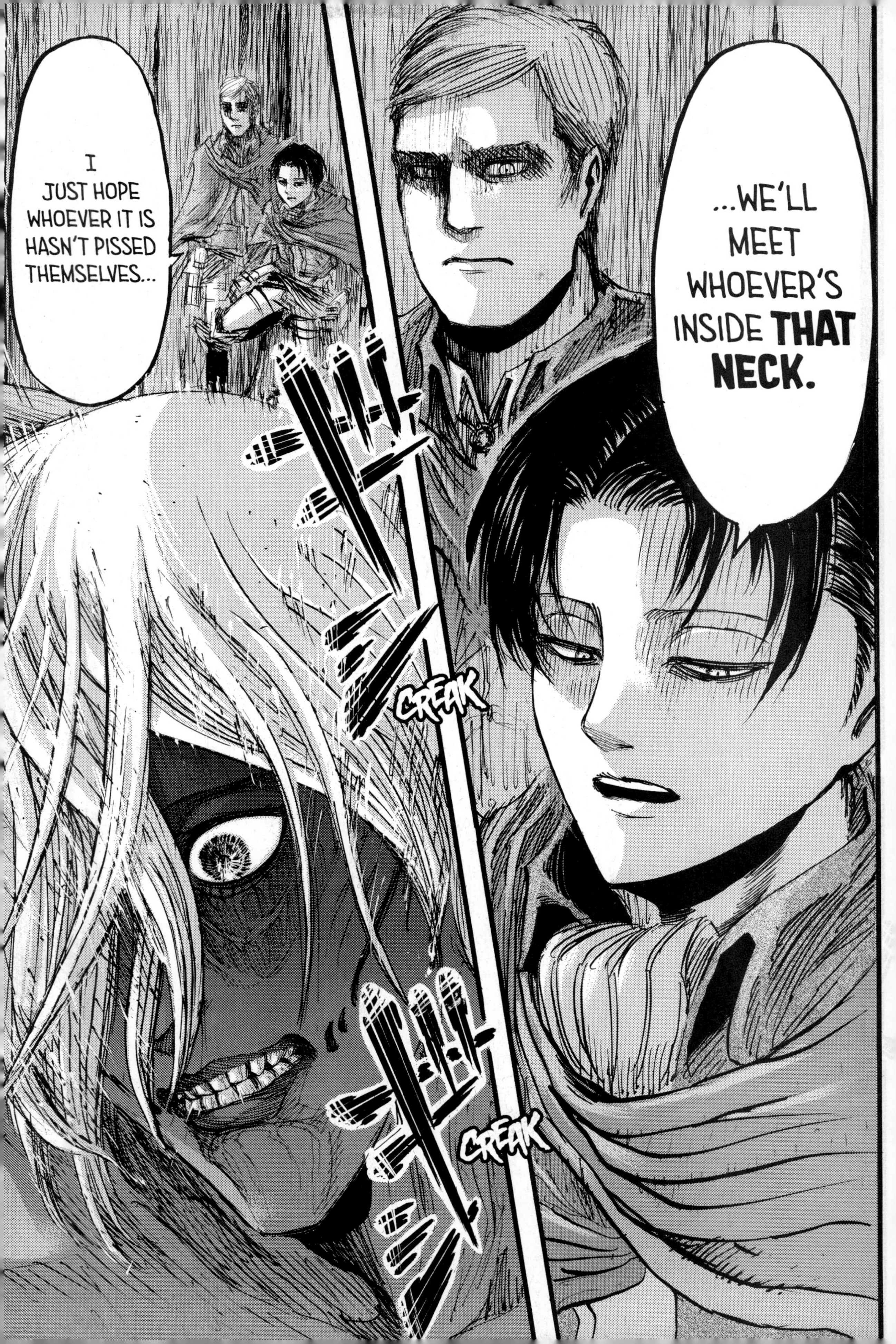
...WE'LL MEET WHOEVER'S INSIDE **THAT NECK.**
I JUST HOPE WHOEVER IT IS HASN'T PISSED THEMSELVES...
CREAK
CREAK

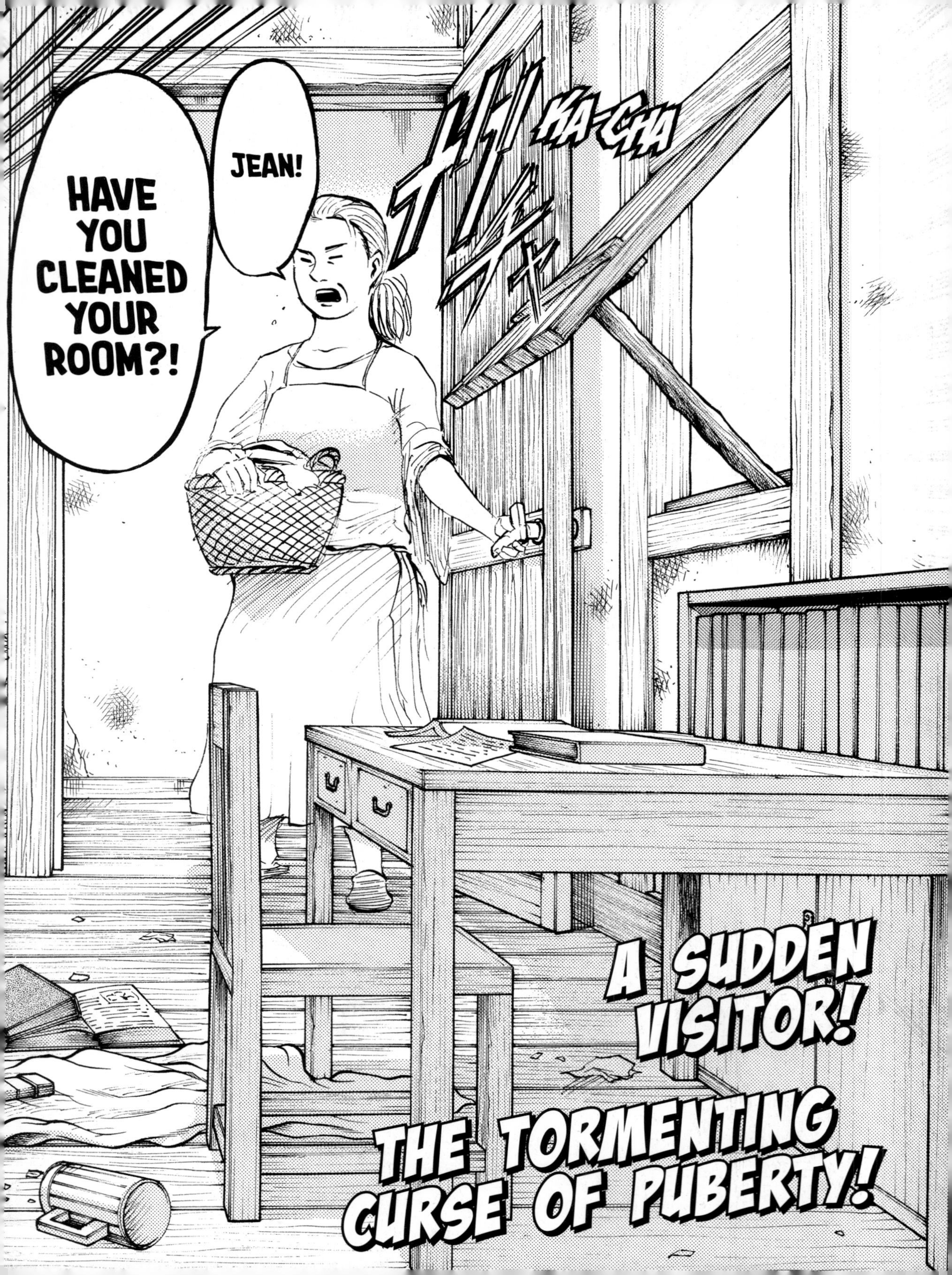
KA-CHA
JEAN!
HAVE YOU CLEANED YOUR ROOM?!
A SUDDEN VISITOR!
THE TORMENTING CURSE OF PUBERTY!

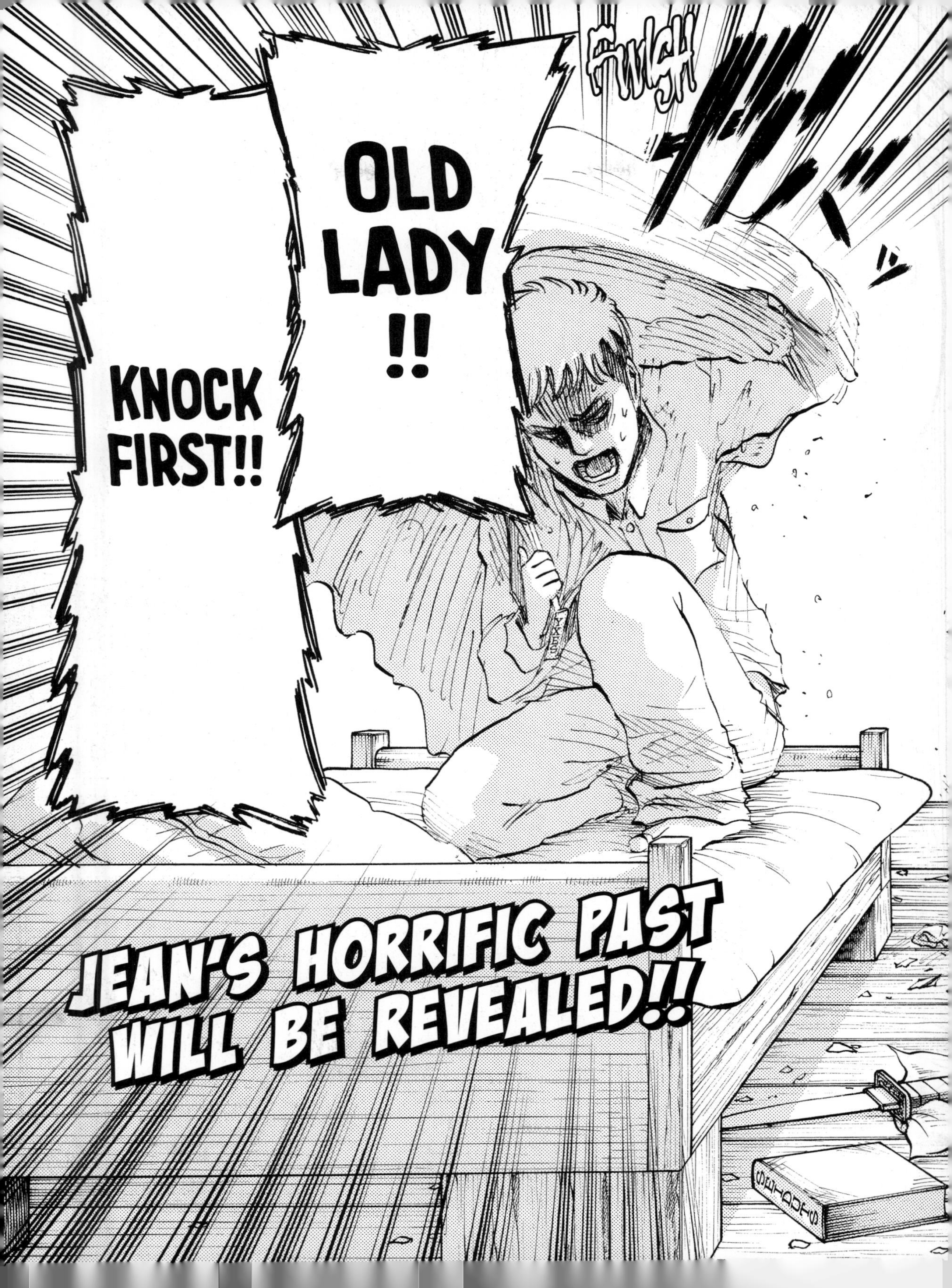
FWISH
OLD LADY!!
KNOCK FIRST!!
JEAN'S HORRIFIC PAST WILL BE REVEALED!!

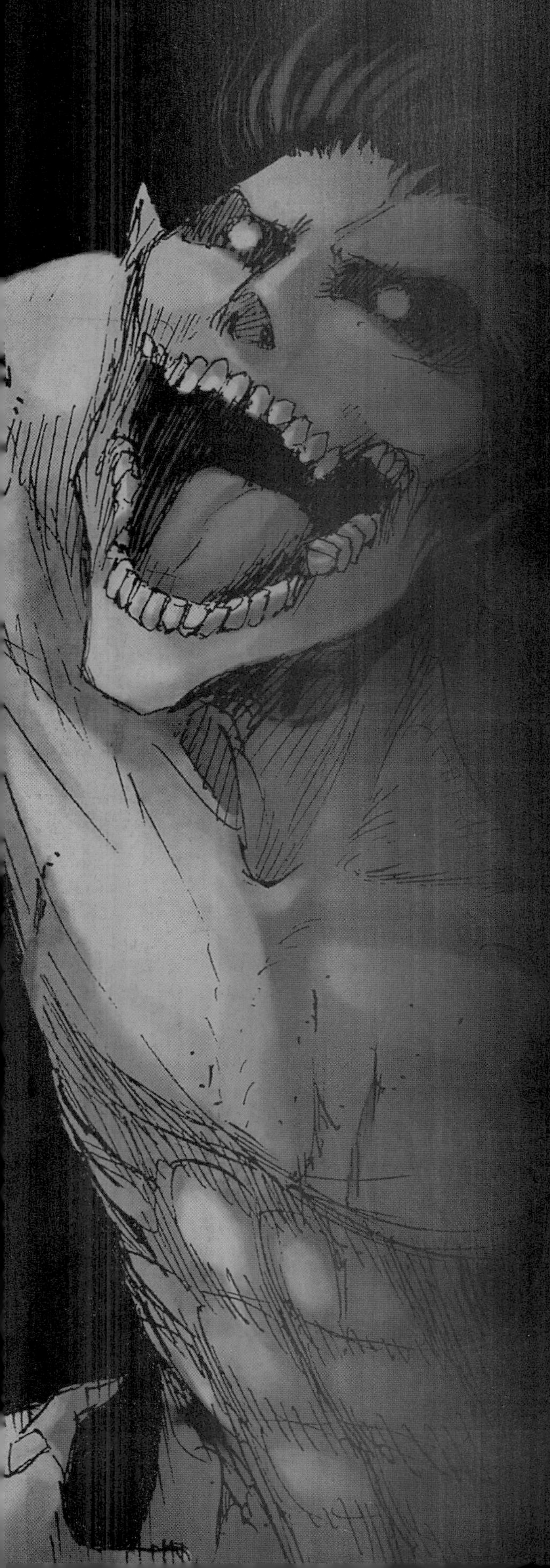

ATTACK ON TITAN

HAJIME ISAYAMA

Episode 27: Erwin Smith

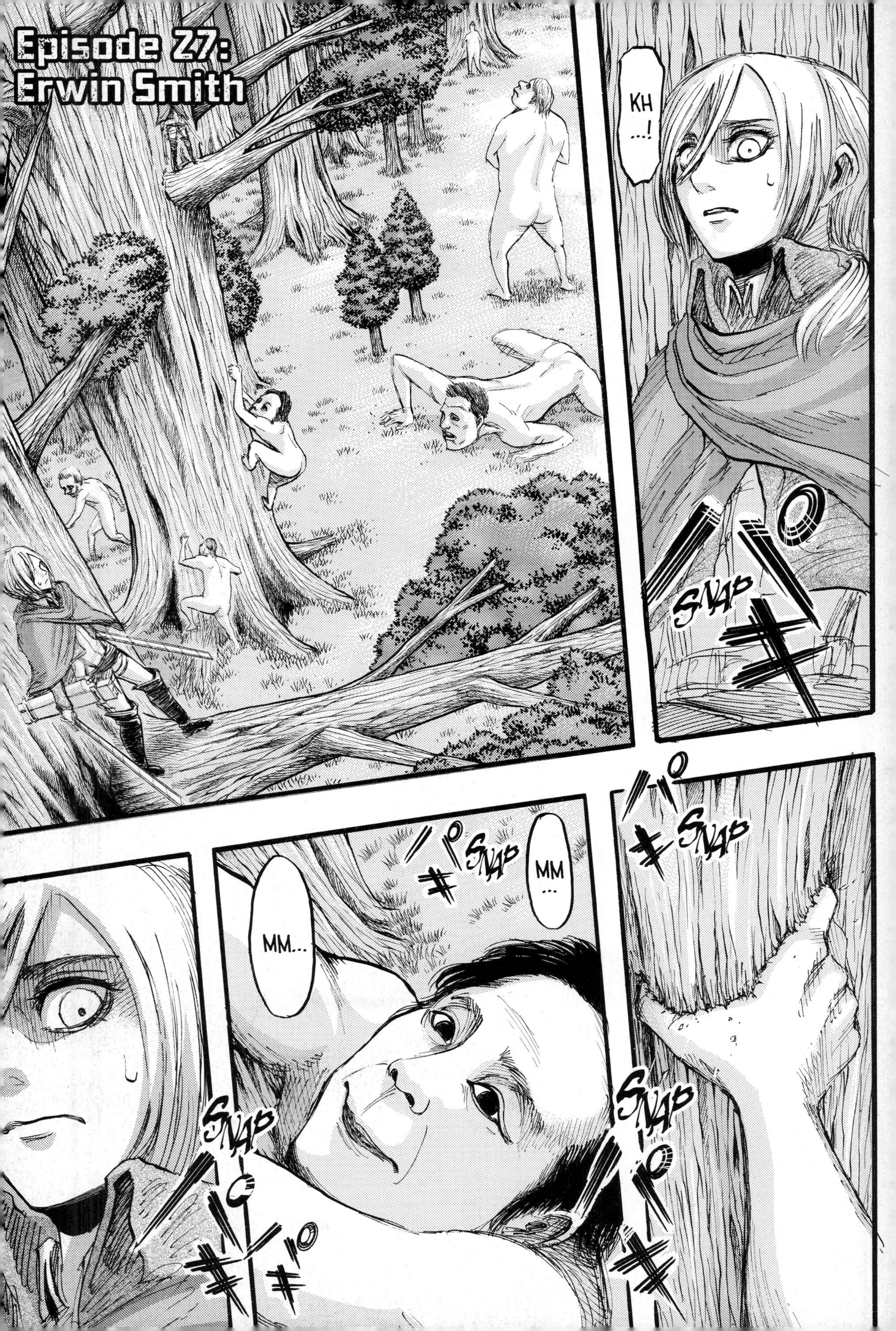
KH ...!
SNAP
SNAP
SNAP
SNAP
MM ...
SNAP
MM...
SNAP

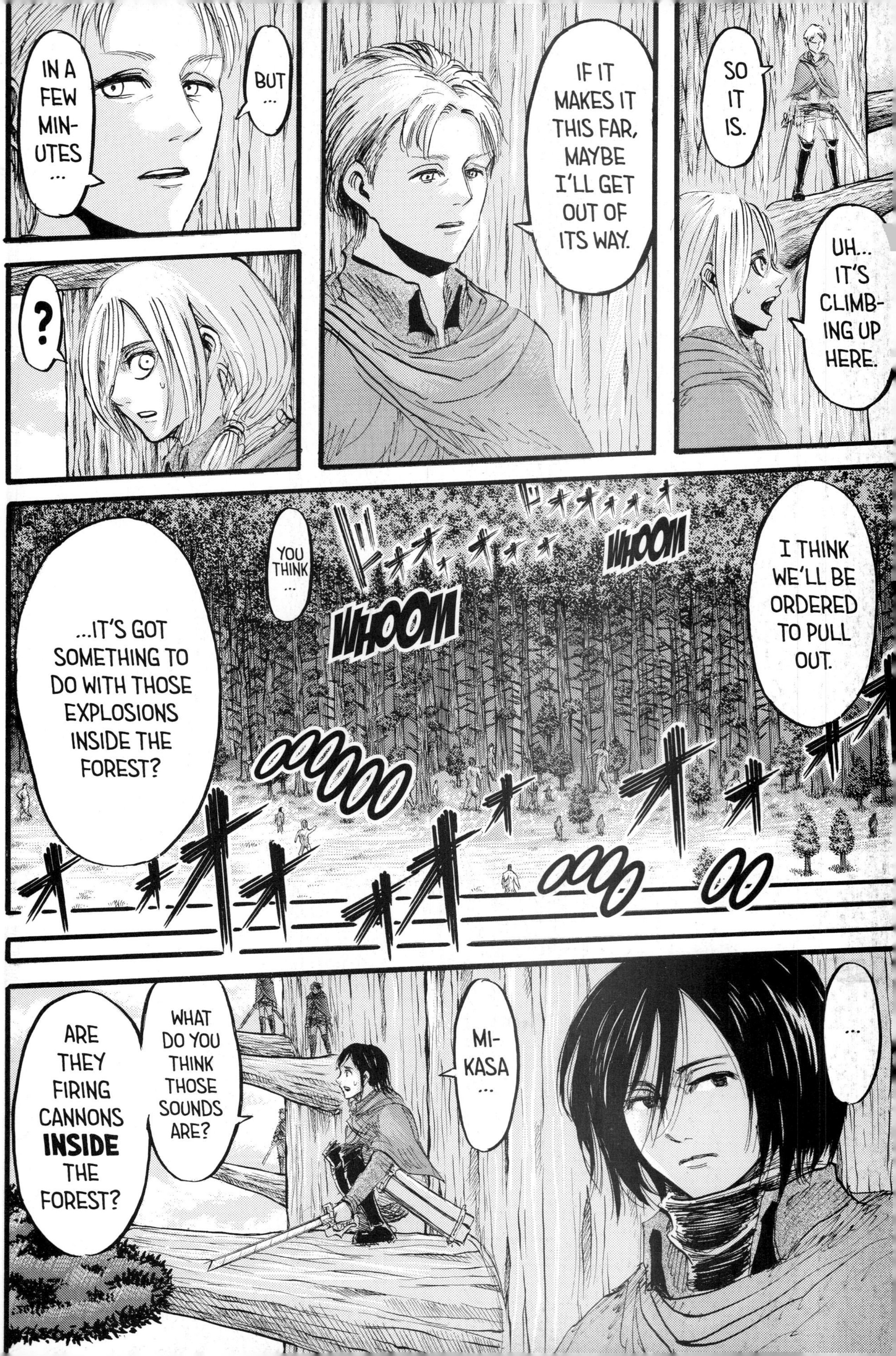
SO IT IS.
UH... IT'S CLIMBING UP HERE.
IF IT MAKES IT THIS FAR, MAYBE I'LL GET OUT OF ITS WAY.
BUT ...
IN A FEW MIN-UTES ...
?
I THINK WE'LL BE ORDERED TO PULL OUT.
WHOOM
YOU THINK ...
WHOOM
...IT'S GOT SOMETHING TO DO WITH THOSE EXPLOSIONS INSIDE THE FOREST?
...
MI-KASA ...
WHAT DO YOU THINK THOSE SOUNDS ARE?
ARE THEY FIRING CANNONS **INSIDE** THE FOREST?

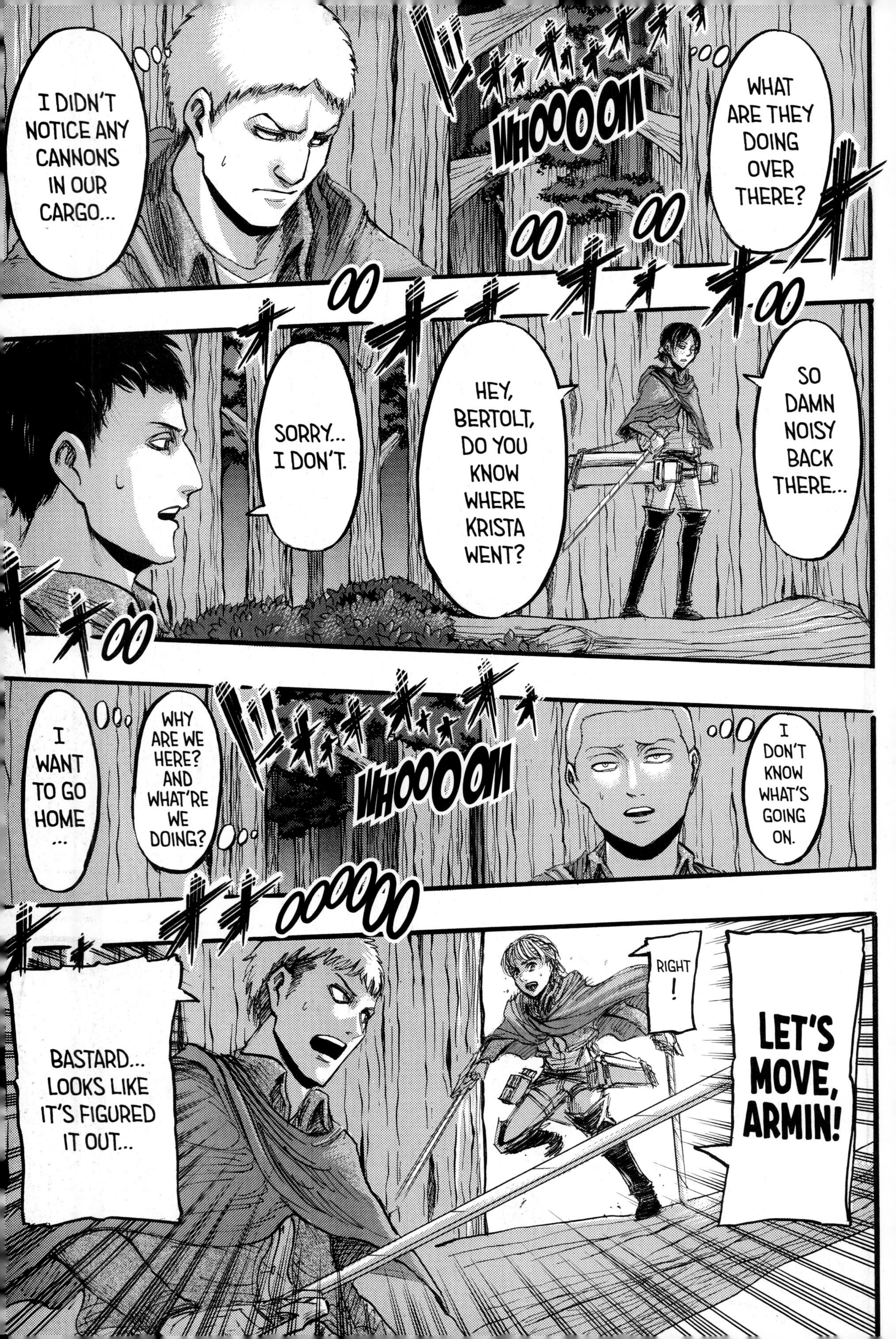
WHAT ARE THEY DOING OVER THERE?
WHOOOOM
OO
OO
I DIDN'T NOTICE ANY CANNONS IN OUR CARGO...
OO
OO
SO DAMN NOISY BACK THERE...
HEY, BERTOLT, DO YOU KNOW WHERE KRISTA WENT?
SORRY... I DON'T.
OO
I DON'T KNOW WHAT'S GOING ON.
WHOOOOM
WHY ARE WE HERE? AND WHAT'RE WE DOING?
I WANT TO GO HOME...
OOOOOO
LET'S MOVE, ARMIN!
RIGHT!
BASTARD... LOOKS LIKE IT'S FIGURED IT OUT...

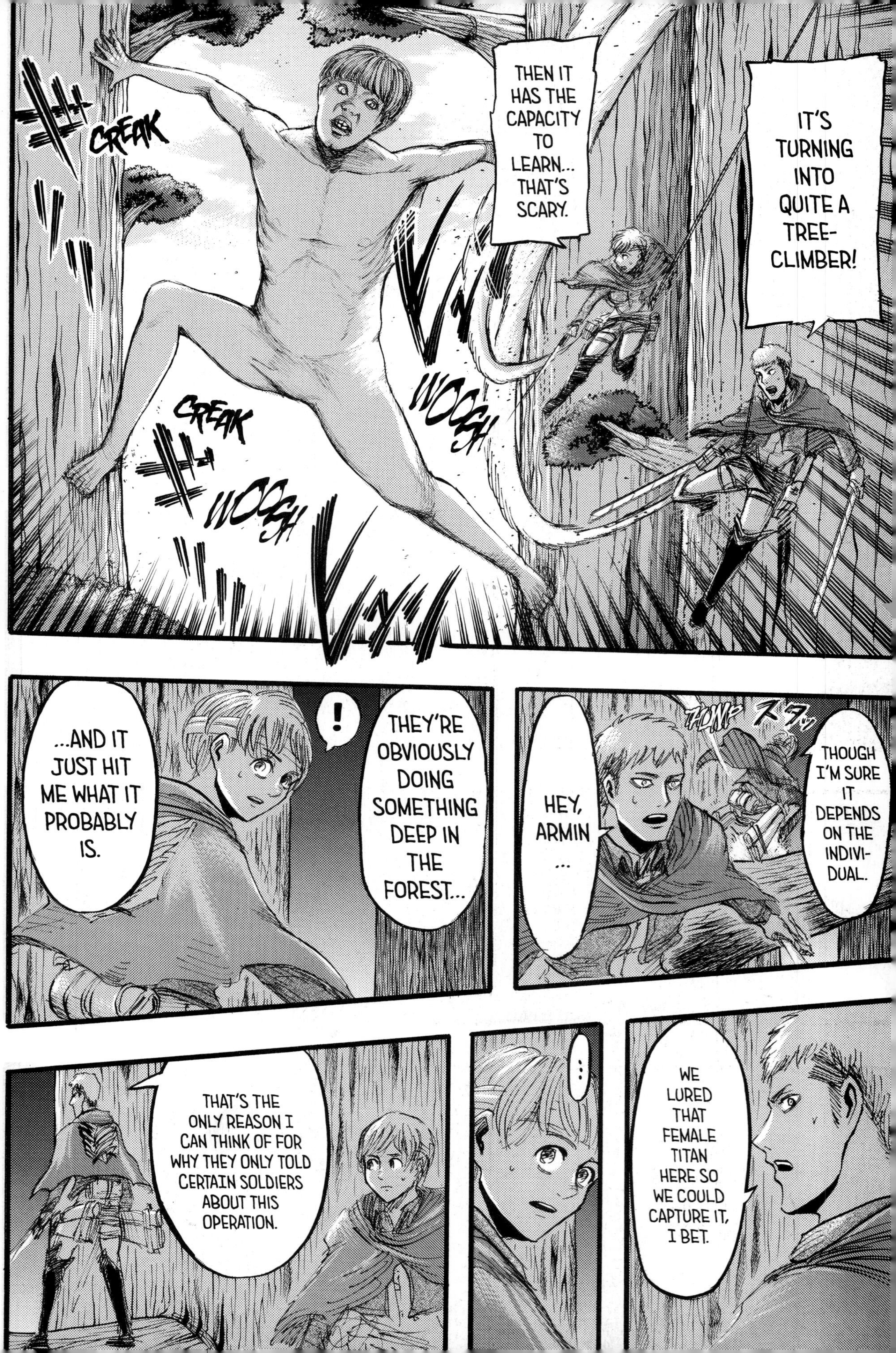
IT'S TURNING INTO QUITE A TREE-CLIMBER!
THEN IT HAS THE CAPACITY TO LEARN... THAT'S SCARY.
CREAK
VWOOSH
CREAK
VWOOSH
THUMP
THOUGH I'M SURE IT DEPENDS ON THE INDIVIDUAL.
HEY, ARMIN...
THEY'RE OBVIOUSLY DOING SOMETHING DEEP IN THE FOREST...
!
...AND IT JUST HIT ME WHAT IT PROBABLY IS.
WE LURED THAT FEMALE TITAN HERE SO WE COULD CAPTURE IT, I BET.
...
THAT'S THE ONLY REASON I CAN THINK OF FOR WHY THEY ONLY TOLD CERTAIN SOLDIERS ABOUT THIS OPERATION.

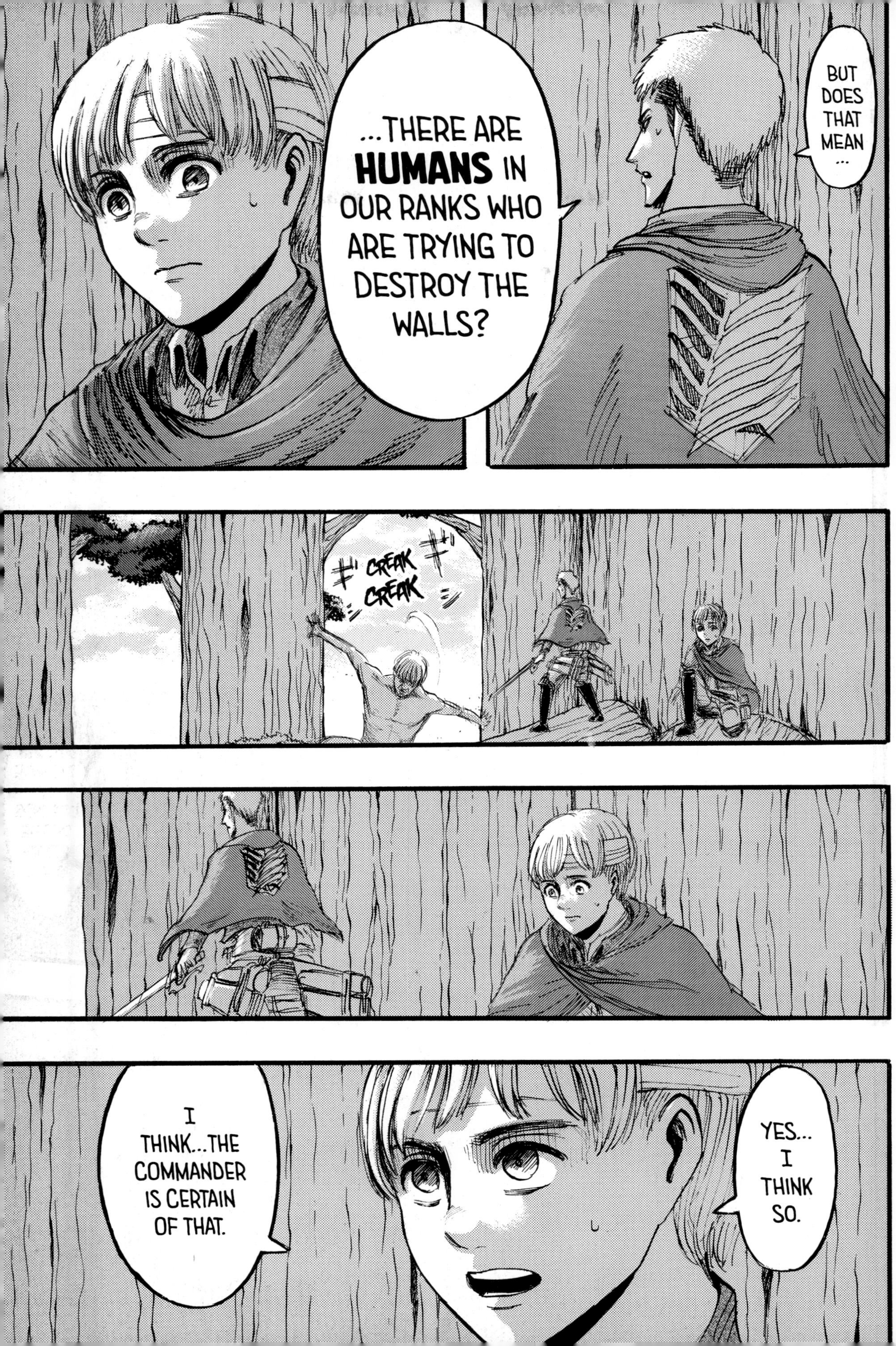
BUT DOES THAT MEAN ...
...THERE ARE **HUMANS** IN OUR RANKS WHO ARE TRYING TO DESTROY THE WALLS?
CREAK CREAK
YES... I THINK SO.
I THINK...THE COMMANDER IS CERTAIN OF THAT.

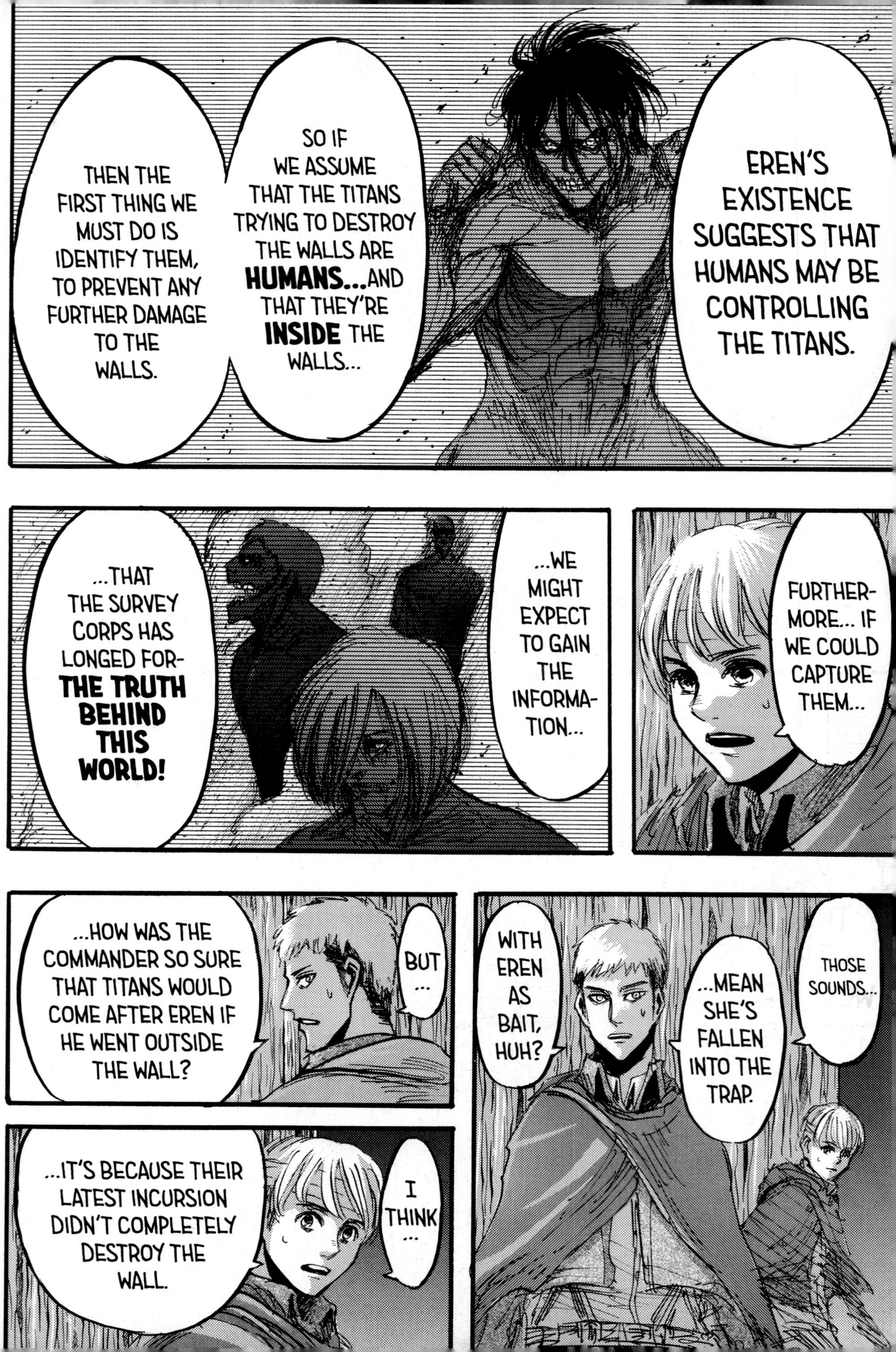
EREN'S EXISTENCE SUGGESTS THAT HUMANS MAY BE CONTROLLING THE TITANS.
SO IF WE ASSUME THAT THE TITANS TRYING TO DESTROY THE WALLS ARE **HUMANS...**AND THAT THEY'RE **INSIDE** THE WALLS...
THEN THE FIRST THING WE MUST DO IS IDENTIFY THEM, TO PREVENT ANY FURTHER DAMAGE TO THE WALLS.
FURTHER-MORE... IF WE COULD CAPTURE THEM...
...WE MIGHT EXPECT TO GAIN THE INFORMA-TION...
...THAT THE SURVEY CORPS HAS LONGED FOR- **THE TRUTH BEHIND THIS WORLD!**
THOSE SOUNDS...
...MEAN SHE'S FALLEN INTO THE TRAP.
WITH EREN AS BAIT, HUH?
BUT...
...HOW WAS THE COMMANDER SO SURE THAT TITANS WOULD COME AFTER EREN IF HE WENT OUTSIDE THE WALL?
I THINK...
...IT'S BECAUSE THEIR LATEST INCURSION DIDN'T COMPLETELY DESTROY THE WALL.

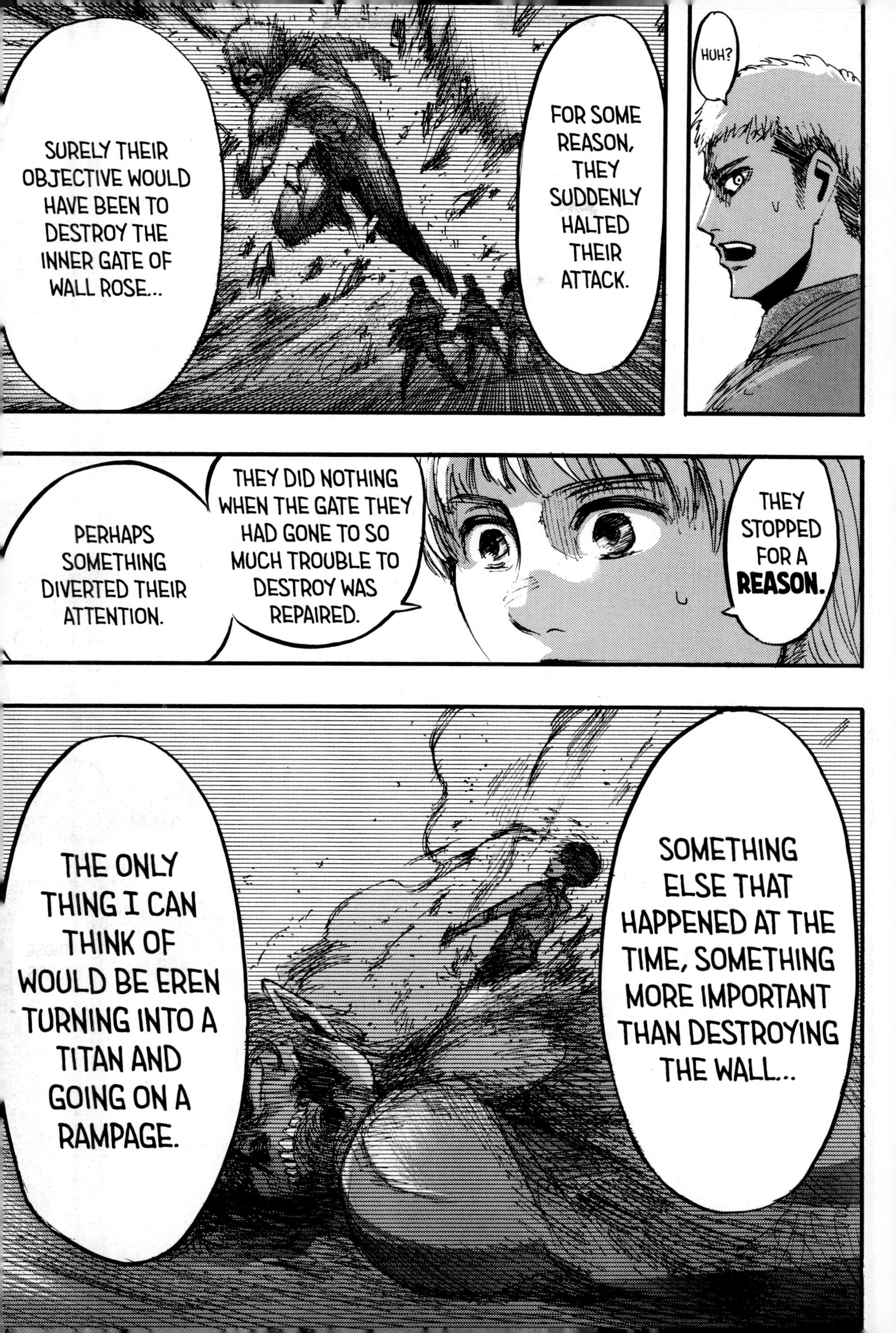
HUH?
FOR SOME REASON, THEY SUDDENLY HALTED THEIR ATTACK.
SURELY THEIR OBJECTIVE WOULD HAVE BEEN TO DESTROY THE INNER GATE OF WALL ROSE...
THEY STOPPED FOR A **REASON.**
THEY DID NOTHING WHEN THE GATE THEY HAD GONE TO SO MUCH TROUBLE TO DESTROY WAS REPAIRED.
PERHAPS SOMETHING DIVERTED THEIR ATTENTION.
SOMETHING ELSE THAT HAPPENED AT THE TIME, SOMETHING MORE IMPORTANT THAN DESTROYING THE WALL...
THE ONLY THING I CAN THINK OF WOULD BE EREN TURNING INTO A TITAN AND GOING ON A RAMPAGE.

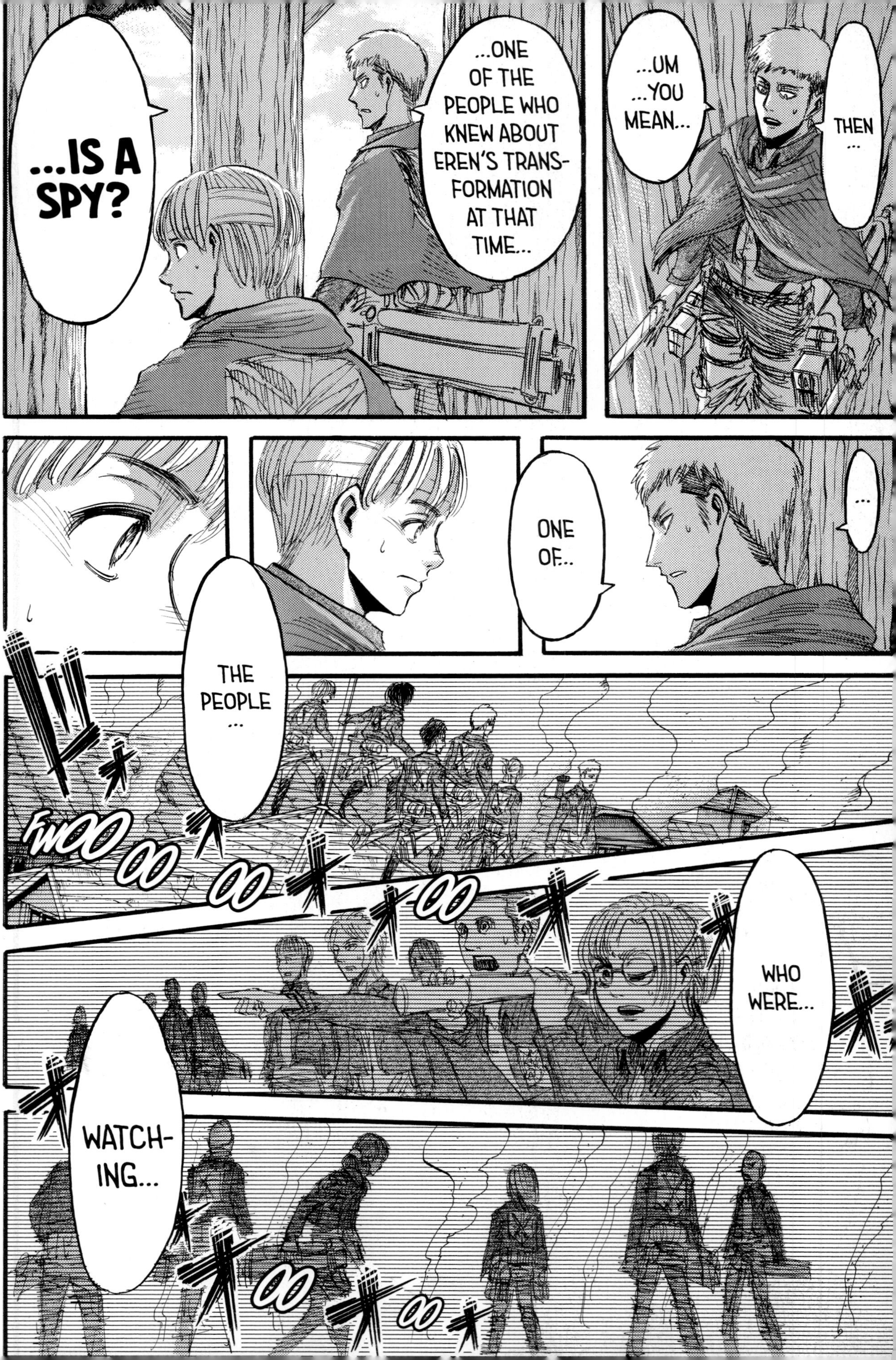
THEN ...
...UM ...YOU MEAN...
...ONE OF THE PEOPLE WHO KNEW ABOUT EREN'S TRANS-FORMATION AT THAT TIME...
...IS A SPY?
...
ONE OF...
THE PEOPLE ...
FWOOOOOOOO
OO
WHO WERE...
WATCHING...
OOOO

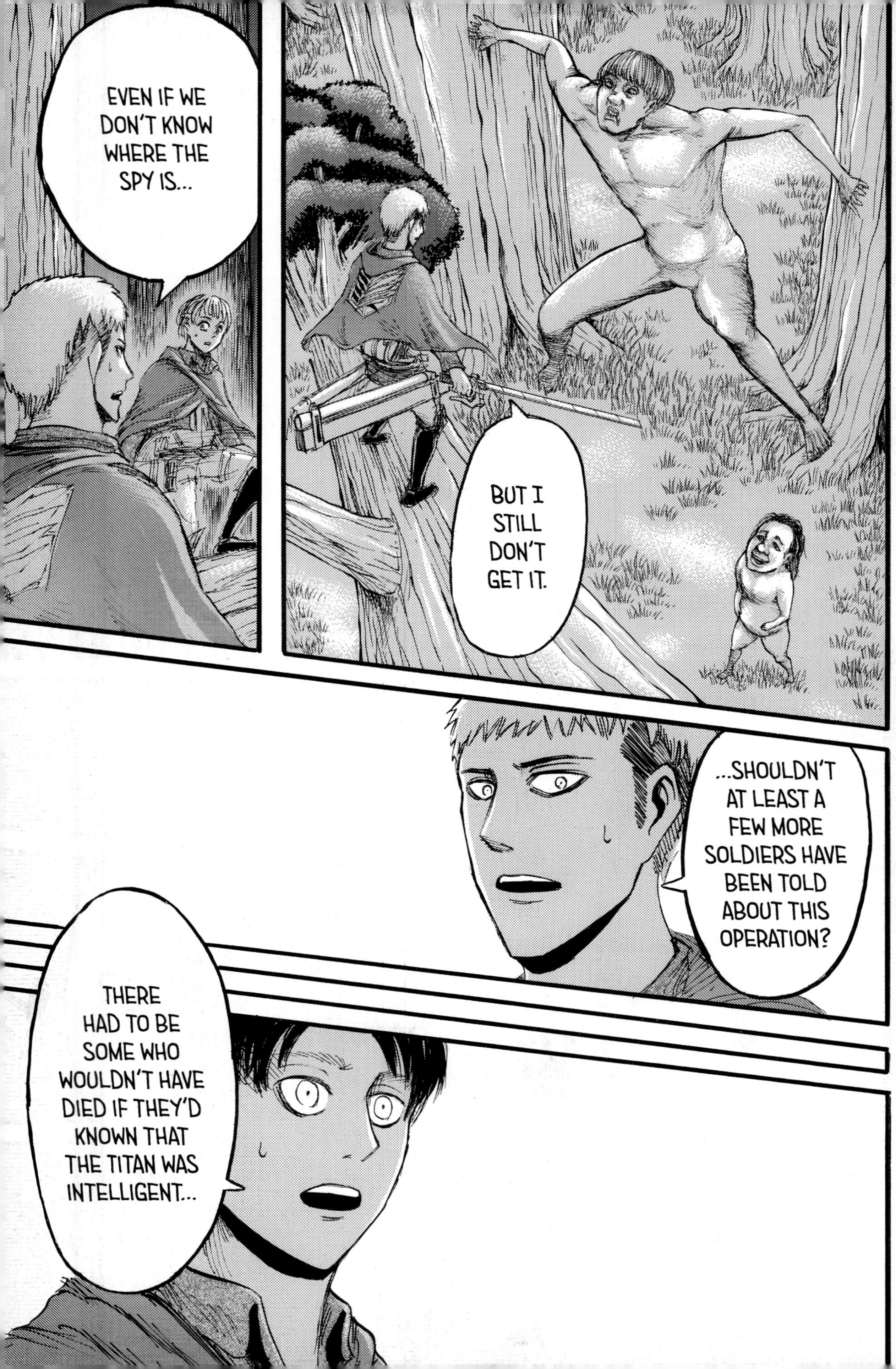
BUT I STILL DON'T GET IT.
EVEN IF WE DON'T KNOW WHERE THE SPY IS...
...SHOULDN'T AT LEAST A FEW MORE SOLDIERS HAVE BEEN TOLD ABOUT THIS OPERATION?
THERE HAD TO BE SOME WHO WOULDN'T HAVE DIED IF THEY'D KNOWN THAT THE TITAN WAS INTELLIGENT...

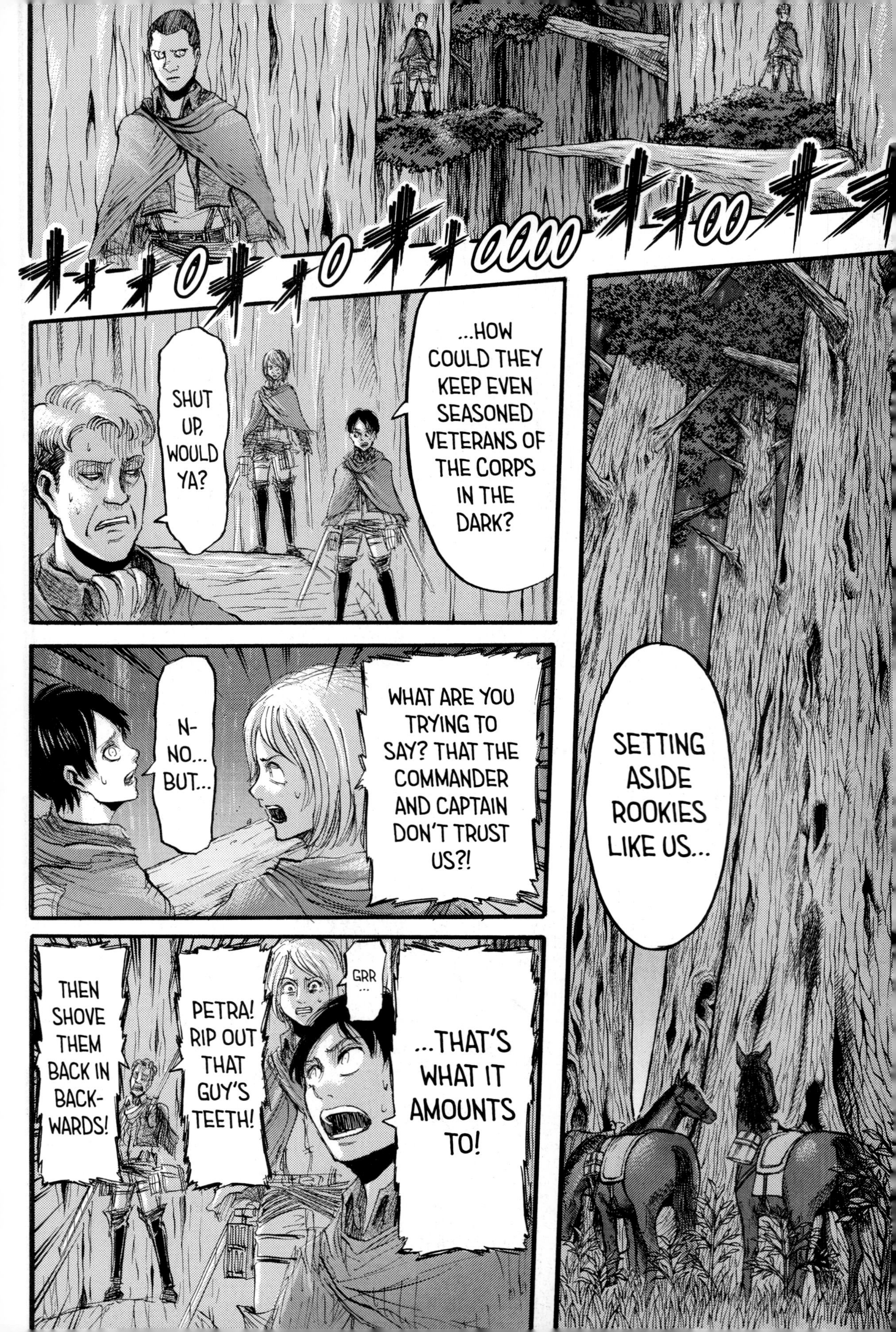
SETTING ASIDE ROOKIES LIKE US...
...HOW COULD THEY KEEP EVEN SEASONED VETERANS OF THE CORPS IN THE DARK?
SHUT UP, WOULD YA?
WHAT ARE YOU TRYING TO SAY? THAT THE COMMANDER AND CAPTAIN DON'T TRUST US?!
N-NO... BUT...
...THAT'S WHAT IT AMOUNTS TO!
GRR...
PETRA! RIP OUT THAT GUY'S TEETH!
THEN SHOVE THEM BACK IN BACK-WARDS!

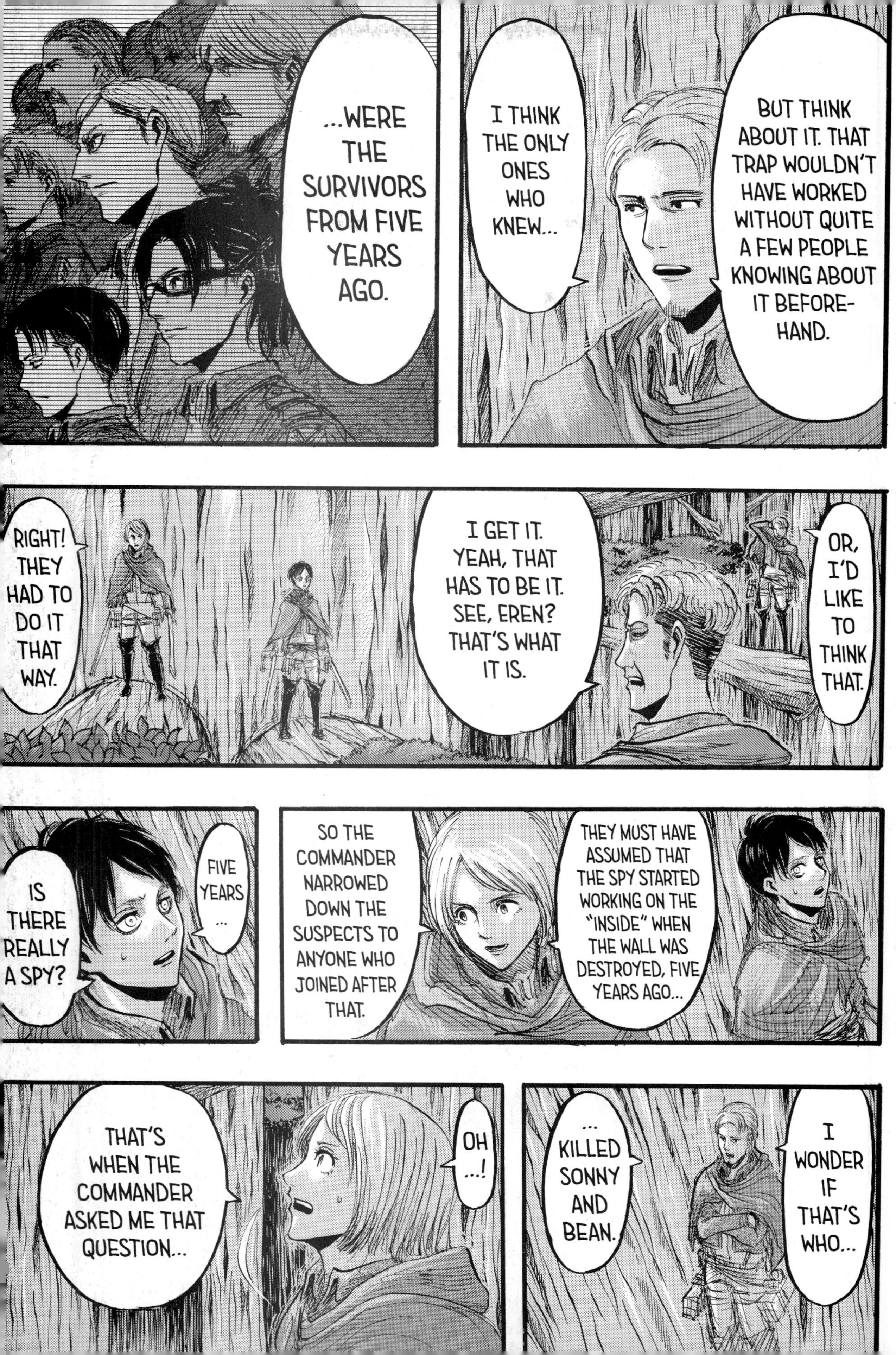
BUT THINK ABOUT IT. THAT TRAP WOULDN'T HAVE WORKED WITHOUT QUITE A FEW PEOPLE KNOWING ABOUT IT BEFORE-HAND.
I THINK THE ONLY ONES WHO KNEW...
...WERE THE SURVIVORS FROM FIVE YEARS AGO.
OR, I'D LIKE TO THINK THAT.
I GET IT. YEAH, THAT HAS TO BE IT. SEE, EREN? THAT'S WHAT IT IS.
RIGHT! THEY HAD TO DO IT THAT WAY.
THEY MUST HAVE ASSUMED THAT THE SPY STARTED WORKING ON THE "INSIDE" WHEN THE WALL WAS DESTROYED, FIVE YEARS AGO...
SO THE COMMANDER NARROWED DOWN THE SUSPECTS TO ANYONE WHO JOINED AFTER THAT.
FIVE YEARS ...
IS THERE REALLY A SPY?
I WONDER IF THAT'S WHO...
...KILLED SONNY AND BEAN.
OH ...!
THAT'S WHEN THE COMMANDER ASKED ME THAT QUESTION...

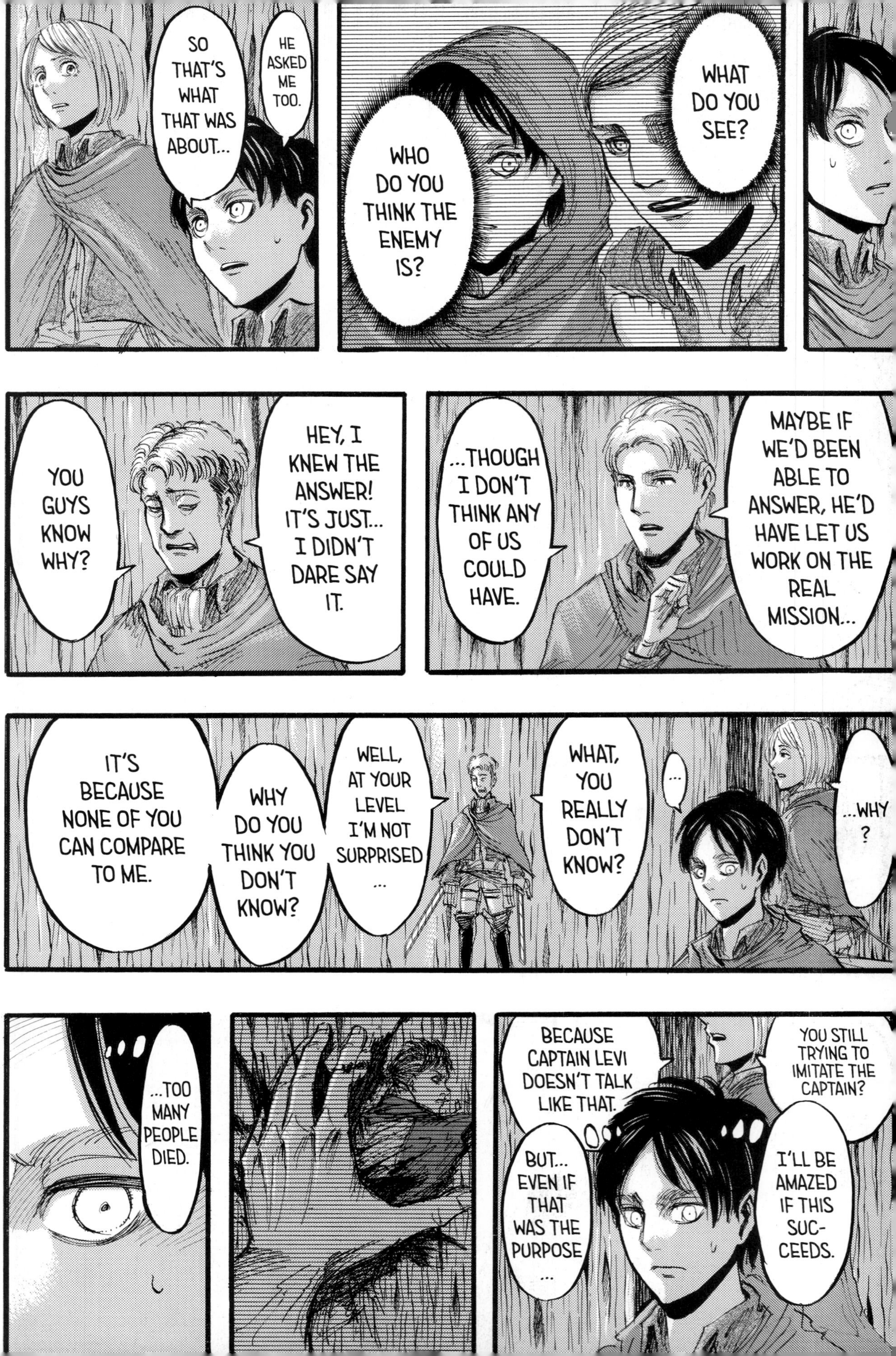
WHAT DO YOU SEE?
WHO DO YOU THINK THE ENEMY IS?
HE ASKED ME TOO.
SO THAT'S WHAT THAT WAS ABOUT...
MAYBE IF WE'D BEEN ABLE TO ANSWER, HE'D HAVE LET US WORK ON THE REAL MISSION...
...THOUGH I DON'T THINK ANY OF US COULD HAVE.
HEY, I KNEW THE ANSWER! IT'S JUST... I DIDN'T DARE SAY IT.
YOU GUYS KNOW WHY?
...WHY?
...
WHAT, YOU REALLY DON'T KNOW?
WELL, AT YOUR LEVEL I'M NOT SURPRISED...
WHY DO YOU THINK YOU DON'T KNOW?
IT'S BECAUSE NONE OF YOU CAN COMPARE TO ME.
YOU STILL TRYING TO IMITATE THE CAPTAIN?
BECAUSE CAPTAIN LEVI DOESN'T TALK LIKE THAT.
I'LL BE AMAZED IF THIS SUC-CEEDS.
BUT... EVEN IF THAT WAS THE PURPOSE...
...TOO MANY PEOPLE DIED.

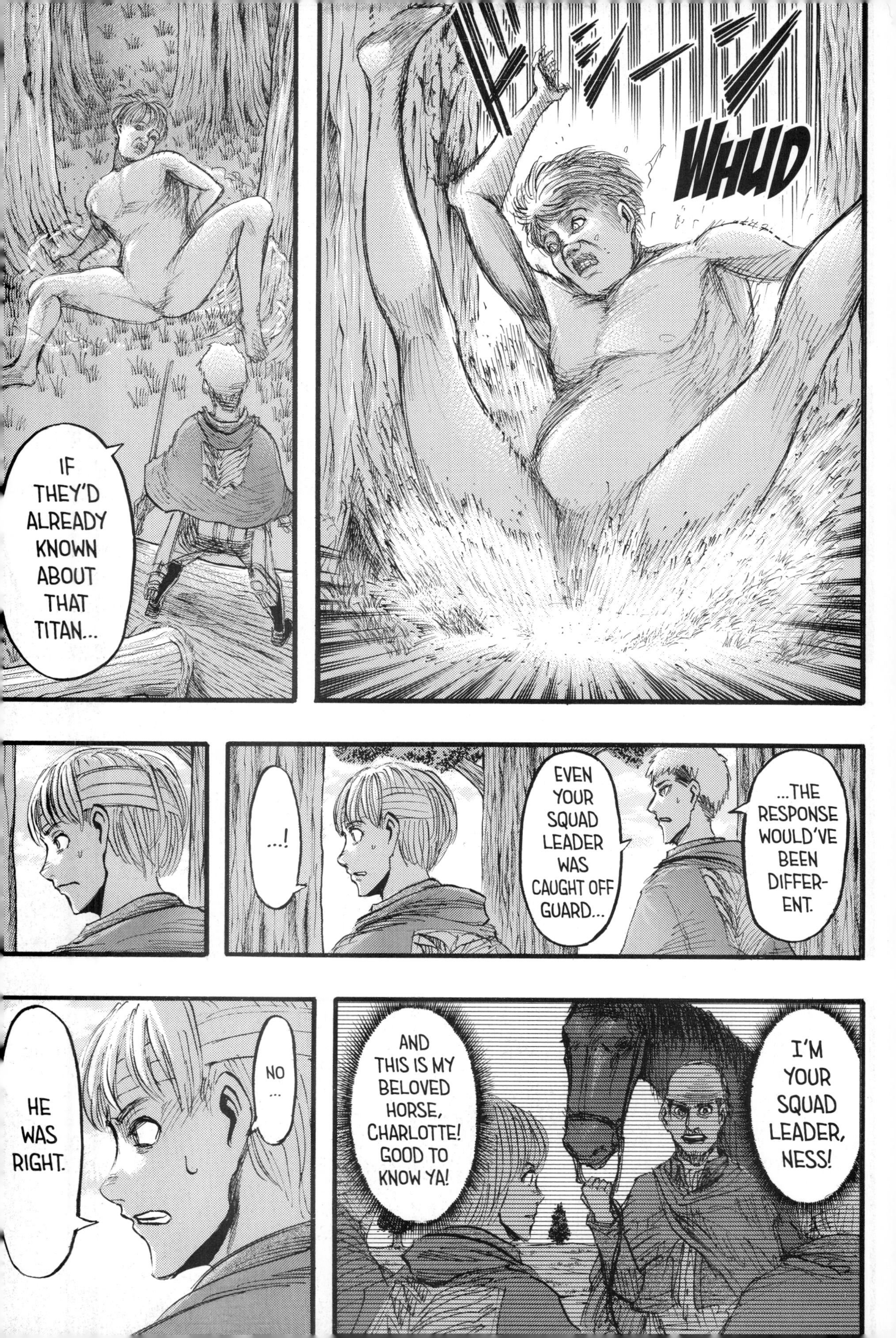
WHUD
IF THEY'D ALREADY KNOWN ABOUT THAT TITAN...
...THE RESPONSE WOULD'VE BEEN DIFFER-ENT.
EVEN YOUR SQUAD LEADER WAS CAUGHT OFF GUARD...
...!
I'M YOUR SQUAD LEADER, NESS!
AND THIS IS MY BELOVED HORSE, CHARLOTTE! GOOD TO KNOW YA!
NO...
HE WAS RIGHT.

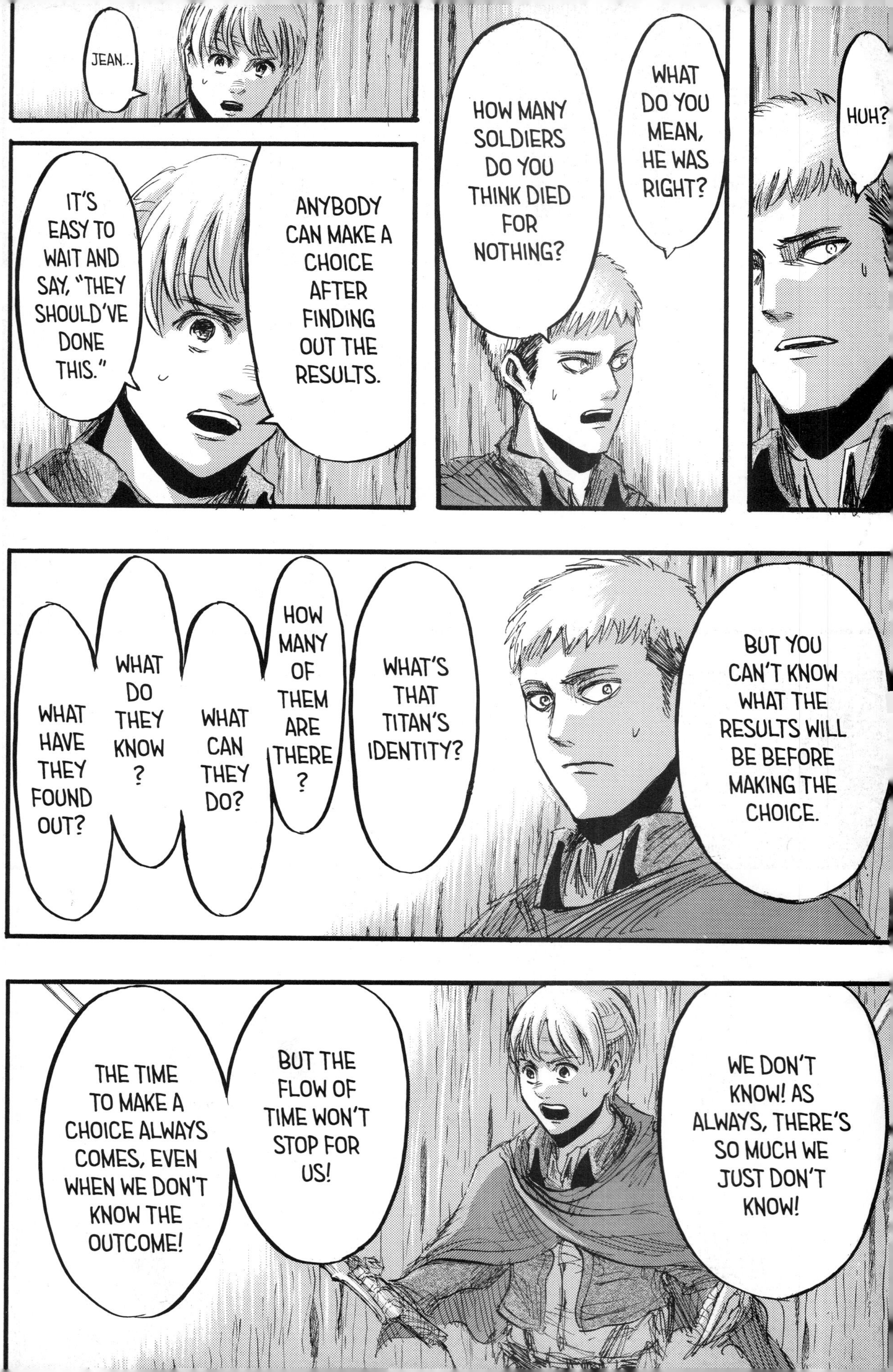
HUH?
WHAT DO YOU MEAN, HE WAS RIGHT?
HOW MANY SOLDIERS DO YOU THINK DIED FOR NOTHING?
JEAN...
ANYBODY CAN MAKE A CHOICE AFTER FINDING OUT THE RESULTS.
IT'S EASY TO WAIT AND SAY, "THEY SHOULD'VE DONE THIS."
BUT YOU CAN'T KNOW WHAT THE RESULTS WILL BE BEFORE MAKING THE CHOICE.
WHAT'S THAT TITAN'S IDENTITY?
HOW MANY OF THEM ARE THERE?
WHAT CAN THEY DO?
WHAT DO THEY KNOW?
WHAT HAVE THEY FOUND OUT?
WE DON'T KNOW! AS ALWAYS, THERE'S SO MUCH WE JUST DON'T KNOW!
BUT THE FLOW OF TIME WON'T STOP FOR US!
THE TIME TO MAKE A CHOICE ALWAYS COMES, EVEN WHEN WE DON'T KNOW THE OUTCOME!

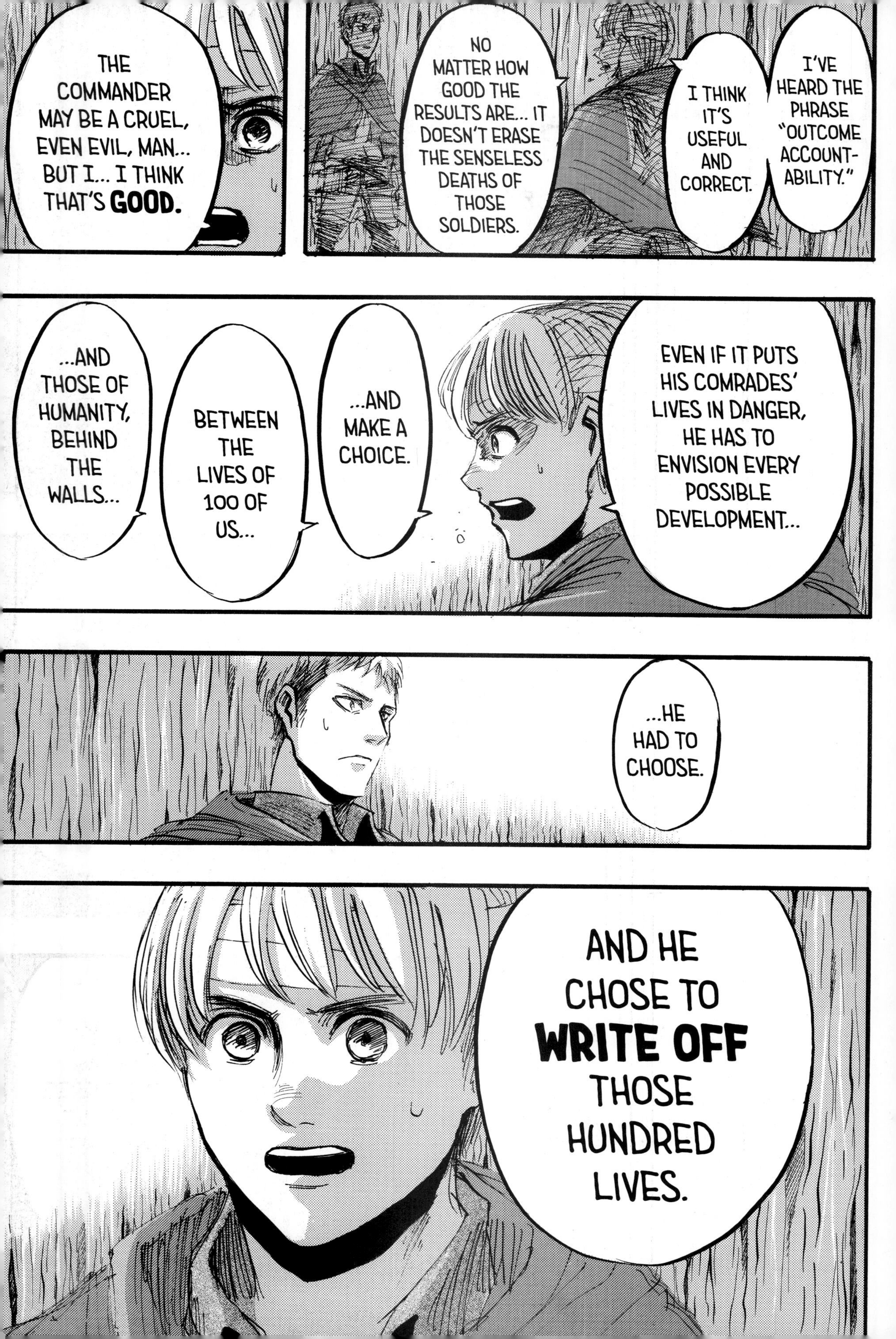
I'VE HEARD THE PHRASE "OUTCOME ACCOUNT-ABILITY."
I THINK IT'S USEFUL AND CORRECT.
NO MATTER HOW GOOD THE RESULTS ARE... IT DOESN'T ERASE THE SENSELESS DEATHS OF THOSE SOLDIERS.
THE COMMANDER MAY BE A CRUEL, EVEN EVIL, MAN... BUT I... I THINK THAT'S **GOOD.**
EVEN IF IT PUTS HIS COMRADES' LIVES IN DANGER, HE HAS TO ENVISION EVERY POSSIBLE DEVELOPMENT...
...AND MAKE A CHOICE.
BETWEEN THE LIVES OF 100 OF US...
...AND THOSE OF HUMANITY, BEHIND THE WALLS...
...HE HAD TO CHOOSE.
AND HE CHOSE TO **WRITE OFF** THOSE HUNDRED LIVES.

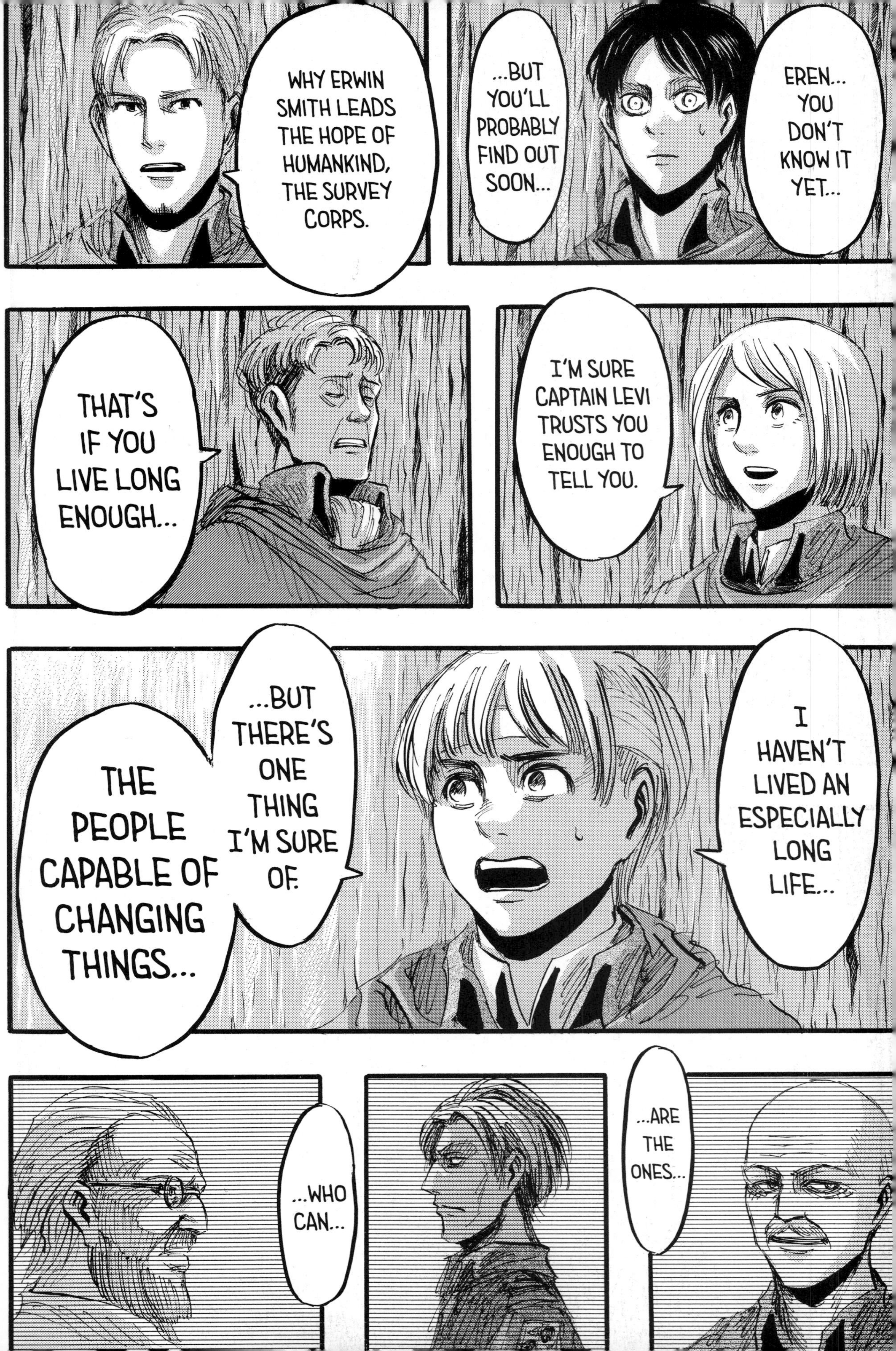
EREN... YOU DON'T KNOW IT YET...
...BUT YOU'LL PROBABLY FIND OUT SOON...
WHY ERWIN SMITH LEADS THE HOPE OF HUMANKIND, THE SURVEY CORPS.
I'M SURE CAPTAIN LEVI TRUSTS YOU ENOUGH TO TELL YOU.
THAT'S IF YOU LIVE LONG ENOUGH...
I HAVEN'T LIVED AN ESPECIALLY LONG LIFE...
...BUT THERE'S ONE THING I'M SURE OF.
THE PEOPLE CAPABLE OF CHANGING THINGS...
...ARE THE ONES...
...WHO CAN...

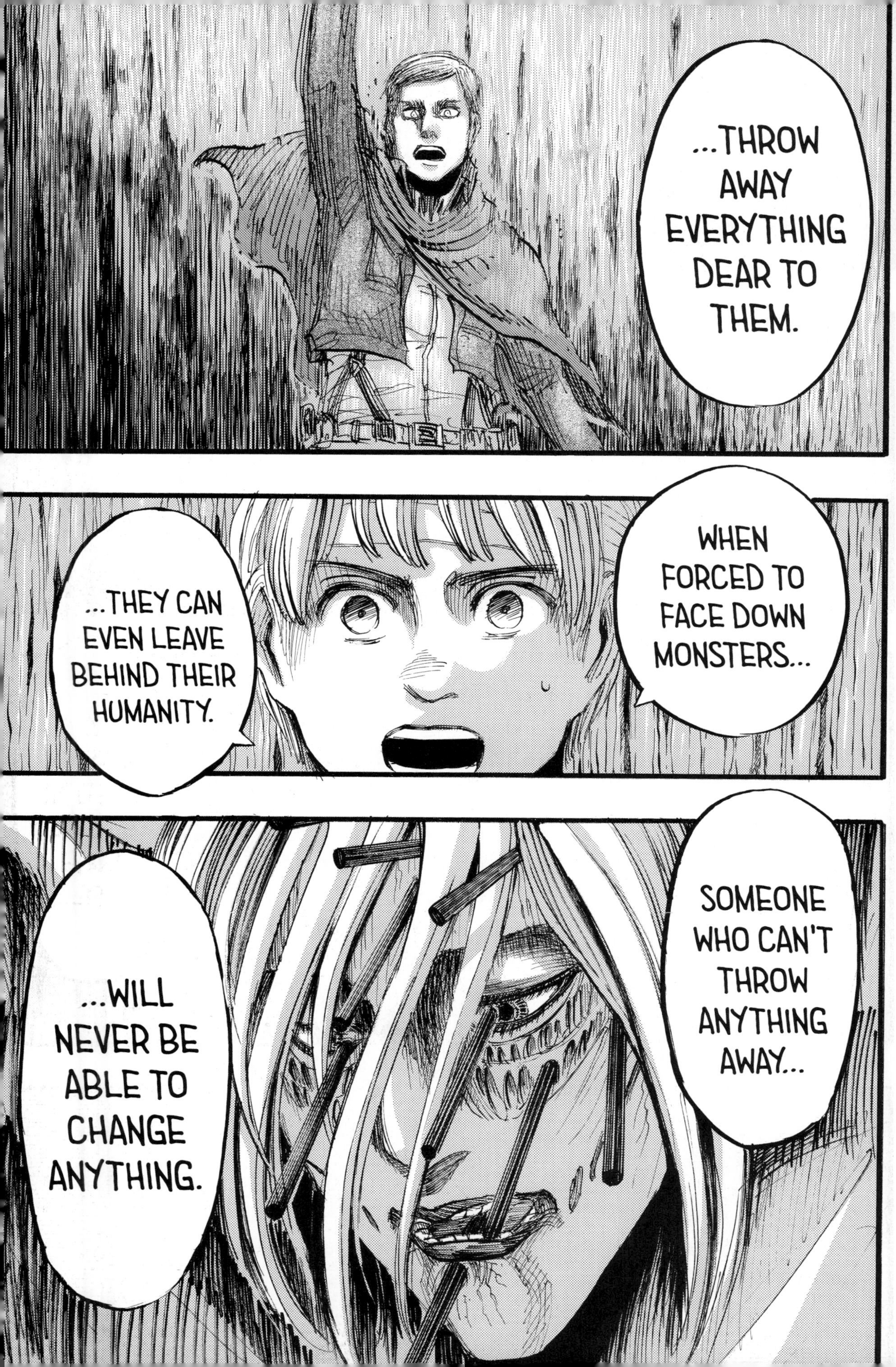
...THROW AWAY EVERYTHING DEAR TO THEM.
WHEN FORCED TO FACE DOWN MONSTERS...
...THEY CAN EVEN LEAVE BEHIND THEIR HUMANITY.
SOMEONE WHO CAN'T THROW ANYTHING AWAY...
...WILL NEVER BE ABLE TO CHANGE ANYTHING.

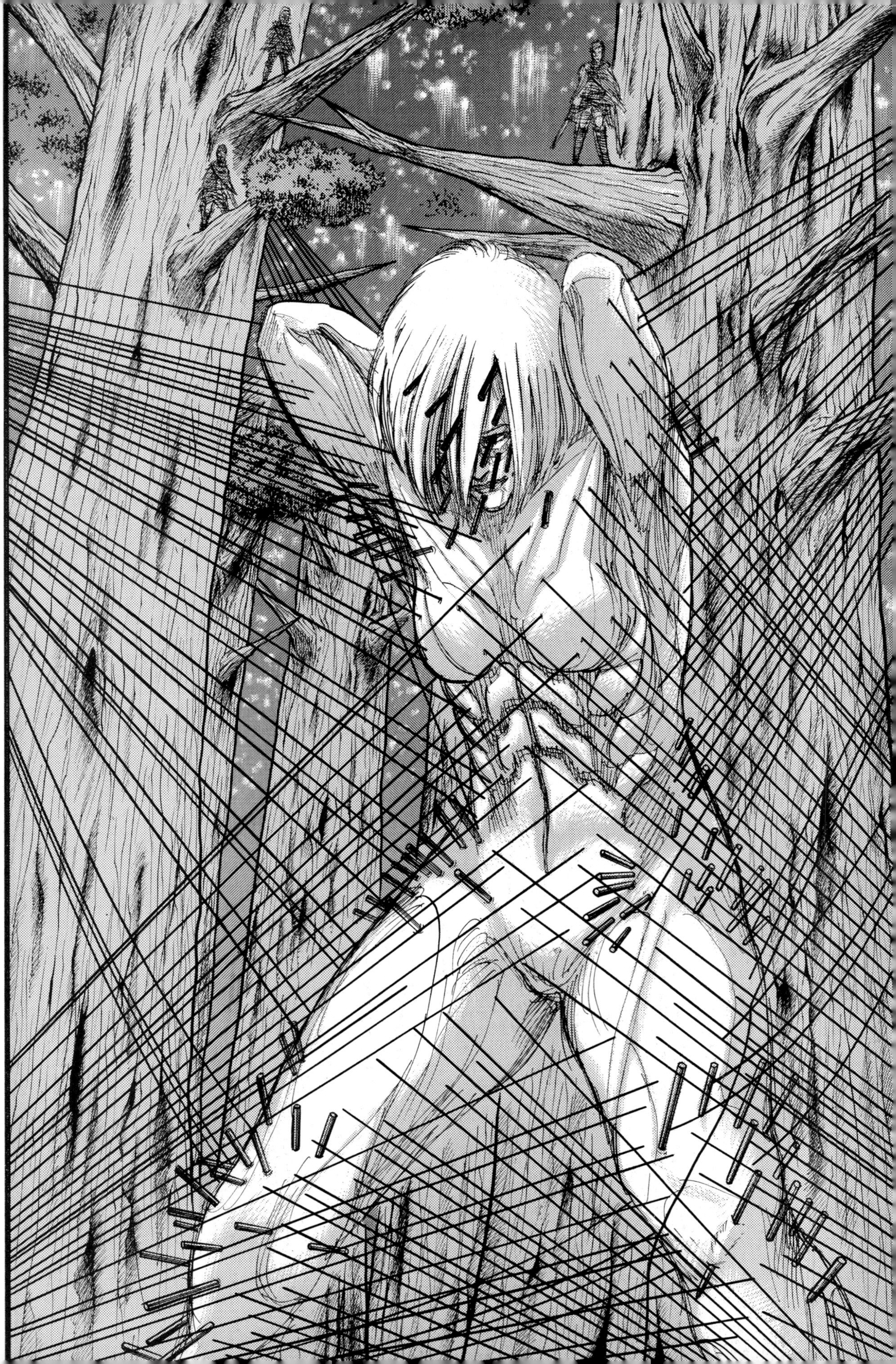

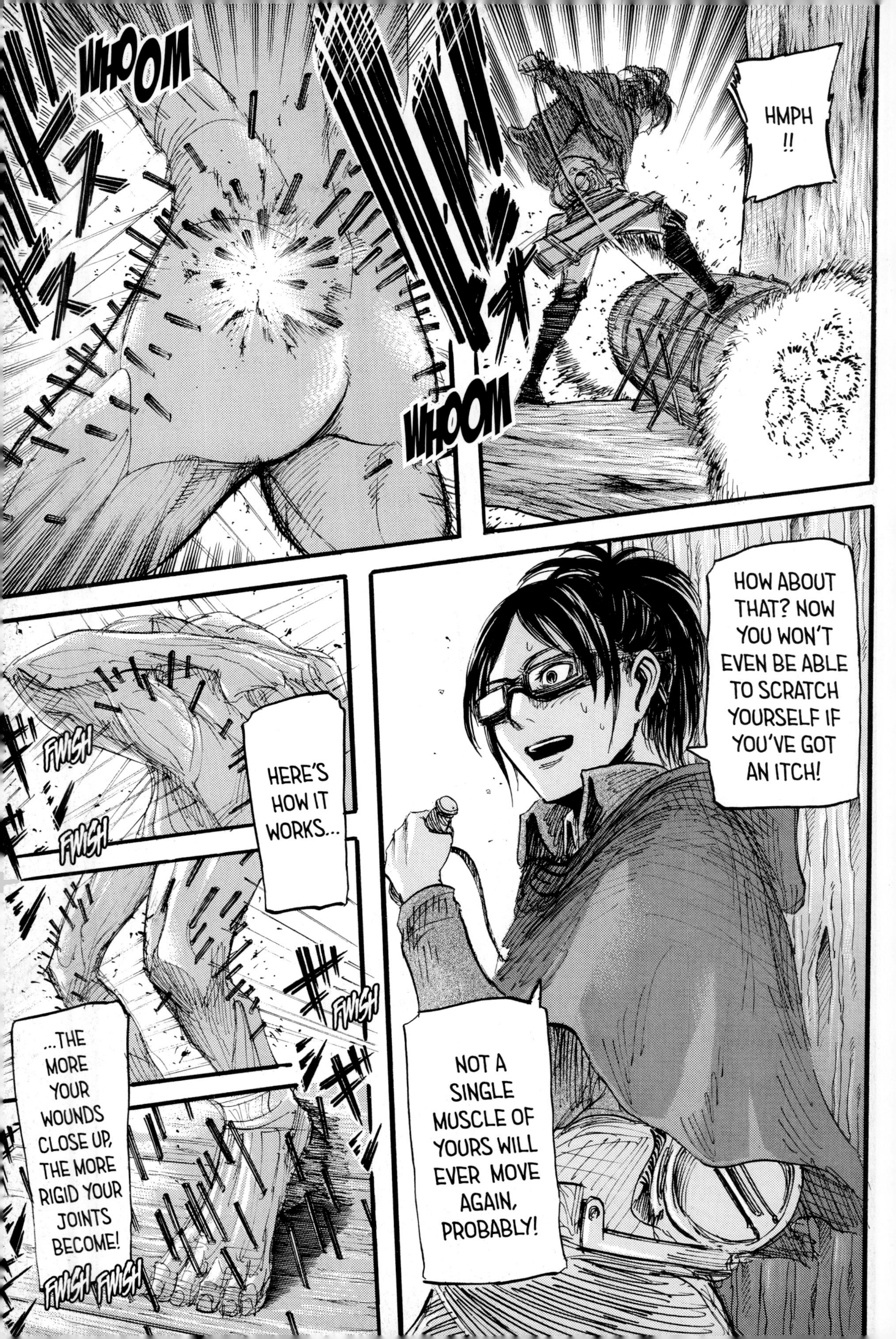
HMPH !!
WHOOM
WHOOM
HOW ABOUT THAT? NOW YOU WON'T EVEN BE ABLE TO SCRATCH YOURSELF IF YOU'VE GOT AN ITCH!
NOT A SINGLE MUSCLE OF YOURS WILL EVER MOVE AGAIN, PROBABLY!
HERE'S HOW IT WORKS...
FWISH
FWISH
FWISH
...THE MORE YOUR WOUNDS CLOSE UP, THE MORE RIGID YOUR JOINTS BECOME!
FWISH FWISH

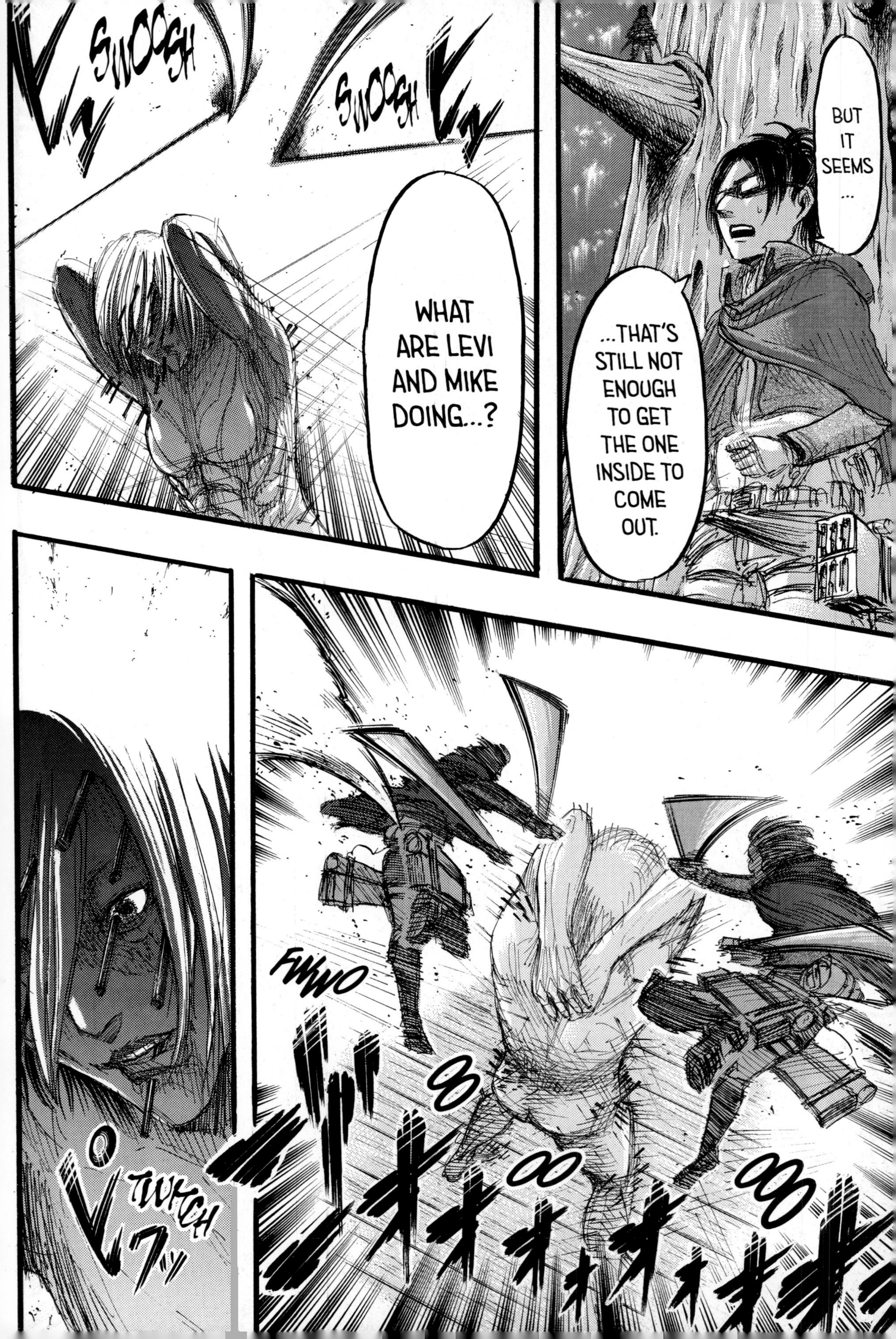
BUT IT SEEMS...
...THAT'S STILL NOT ENOUGH TO GET THE ONE INSIDE TO COME OUT.
SWOOSH
SWOOSH
WHAT ARE LEVI AND MIKE DOING...?
FWWO
TWITCH

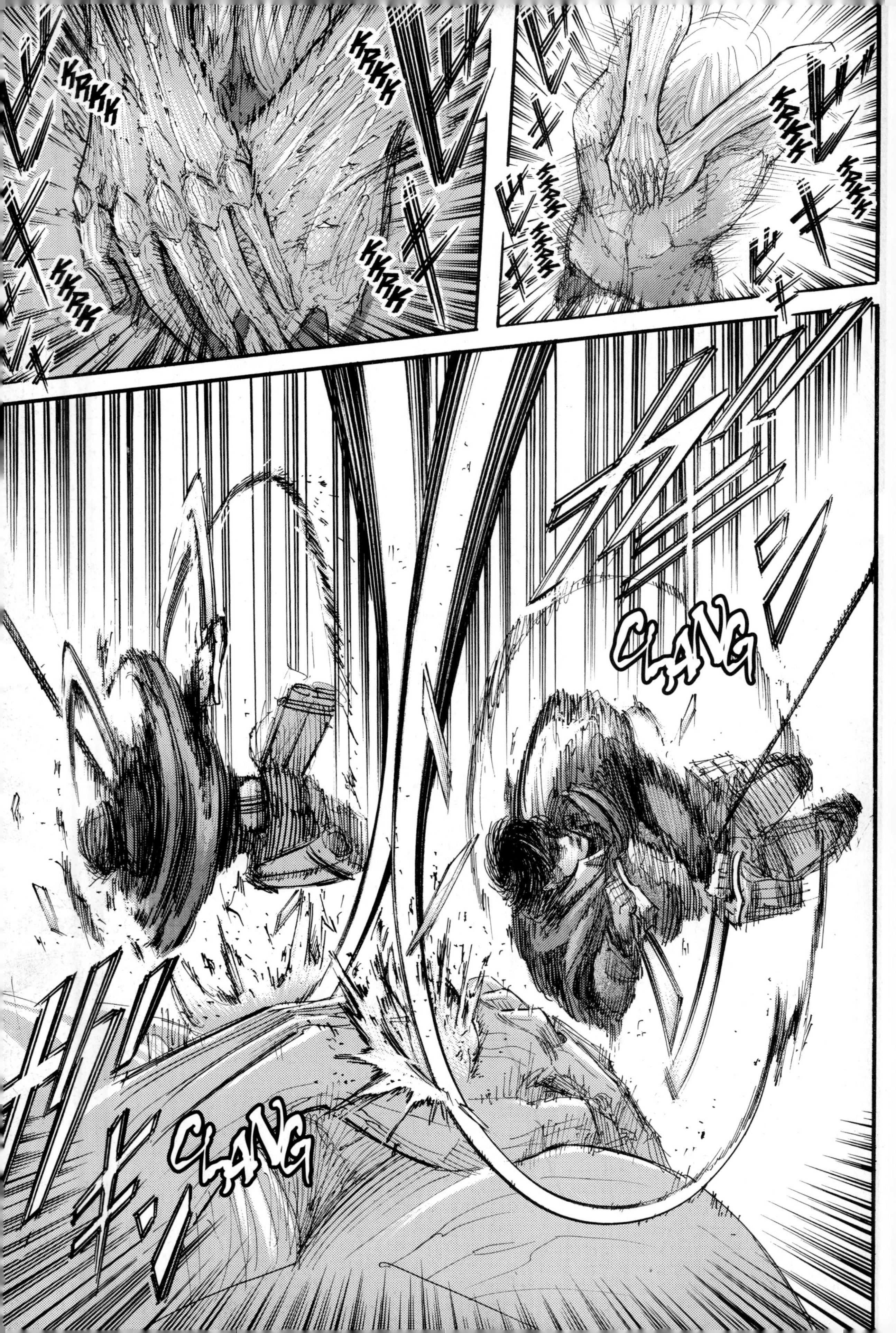
KRKKK
KRKKK
KKRKK
KKRKK
KRKK
KRKK
KKRK
KKRK
CLANG
CLANG

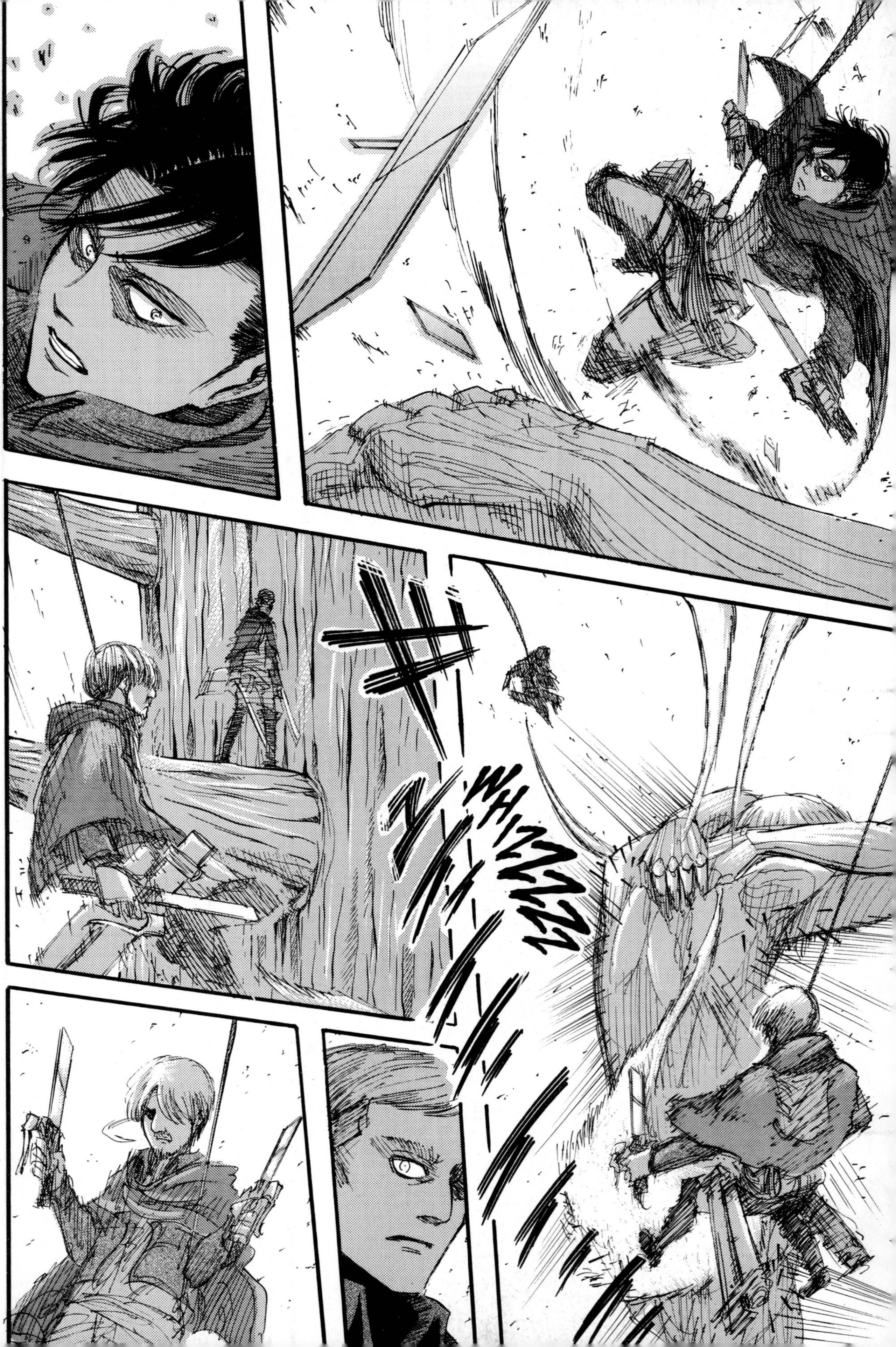
WHIZZZZZ

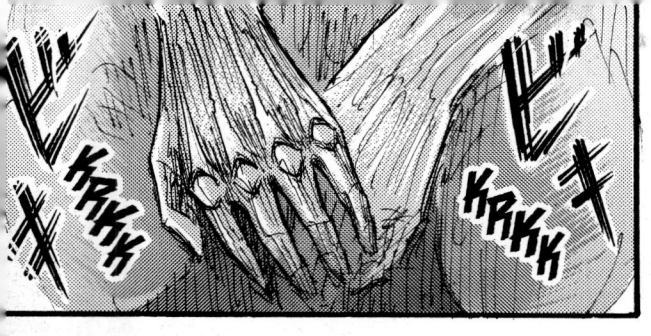

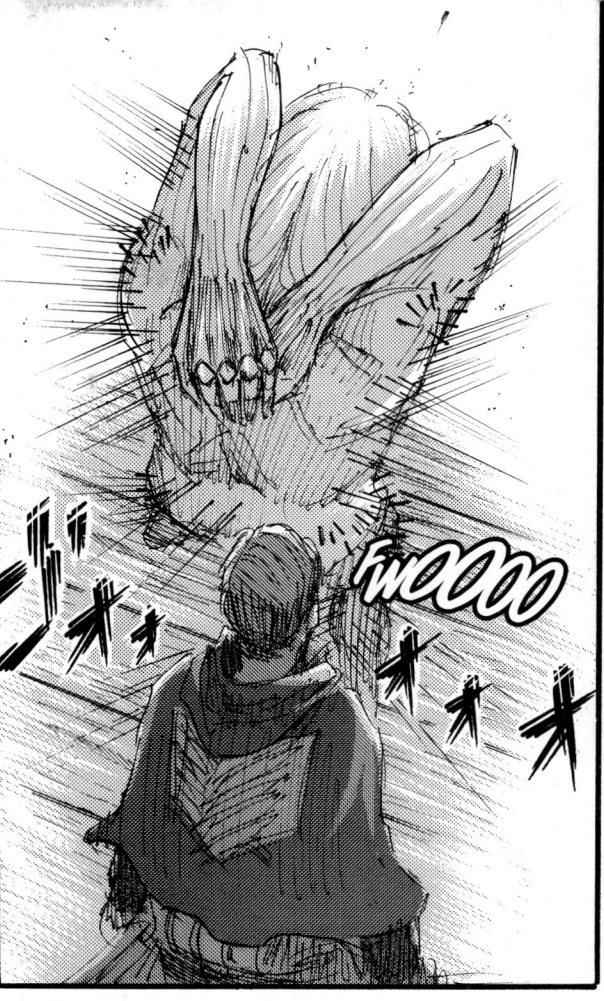

FWOOOO
KRKK
KRKK
LOOKS LIKE SHE CAN OVERLAY PART OF HER BODY WITH A TOUGH LAYER OF SKIN...
A CHARACTER-ISTIC THAT CLOSELY RESEMBLES THE SO-CALLED **ARMORED TITAN...**
CRUMBLE
CRUMBLE
BUT UNLIKE THE ARMORED TITAN, IT SEEMS SHE CAN'T MAINTAIN THAT TOUGHNESS...
WILL SHE WEAKEN IF WE KEEP ATTACKING HER WITH VERTICAL MANEUVERING GEAR AND SWORDS?
THERE'S NO TIME TO TEST IT.
THEREFORE...

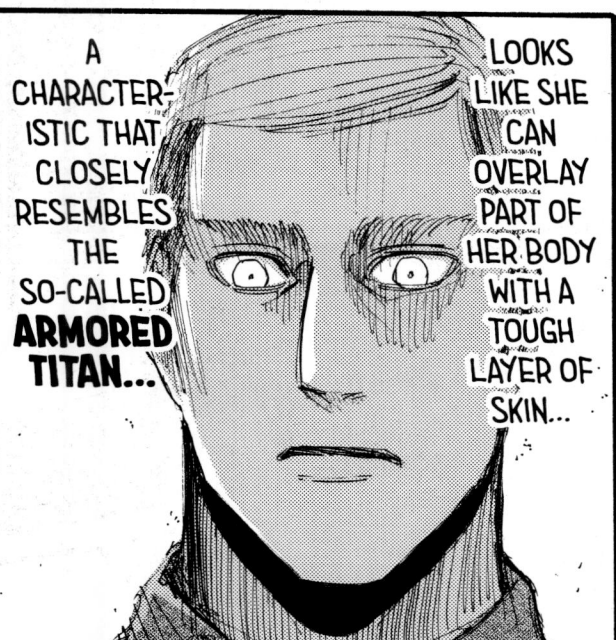

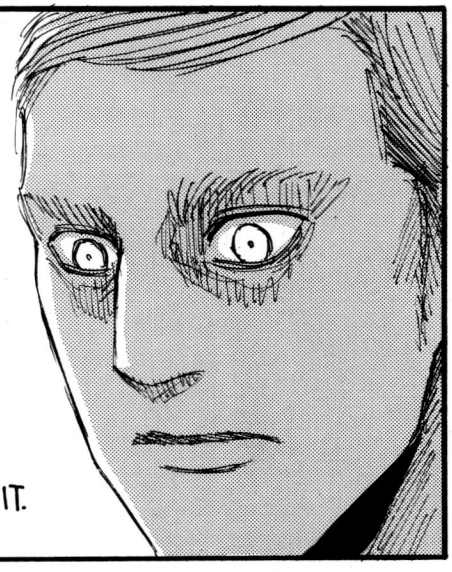

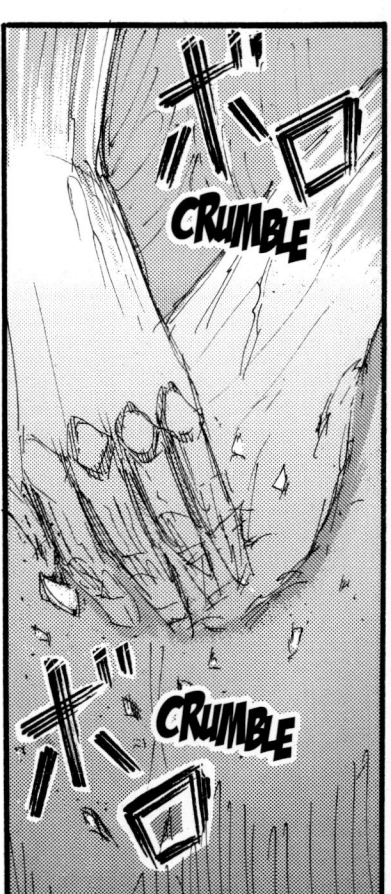

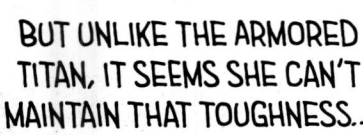

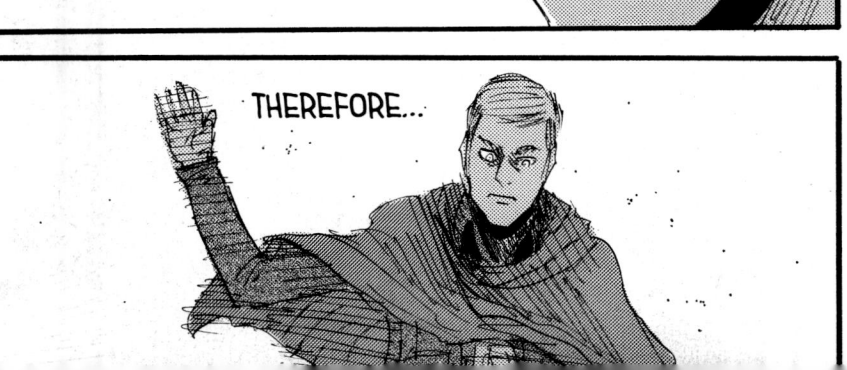

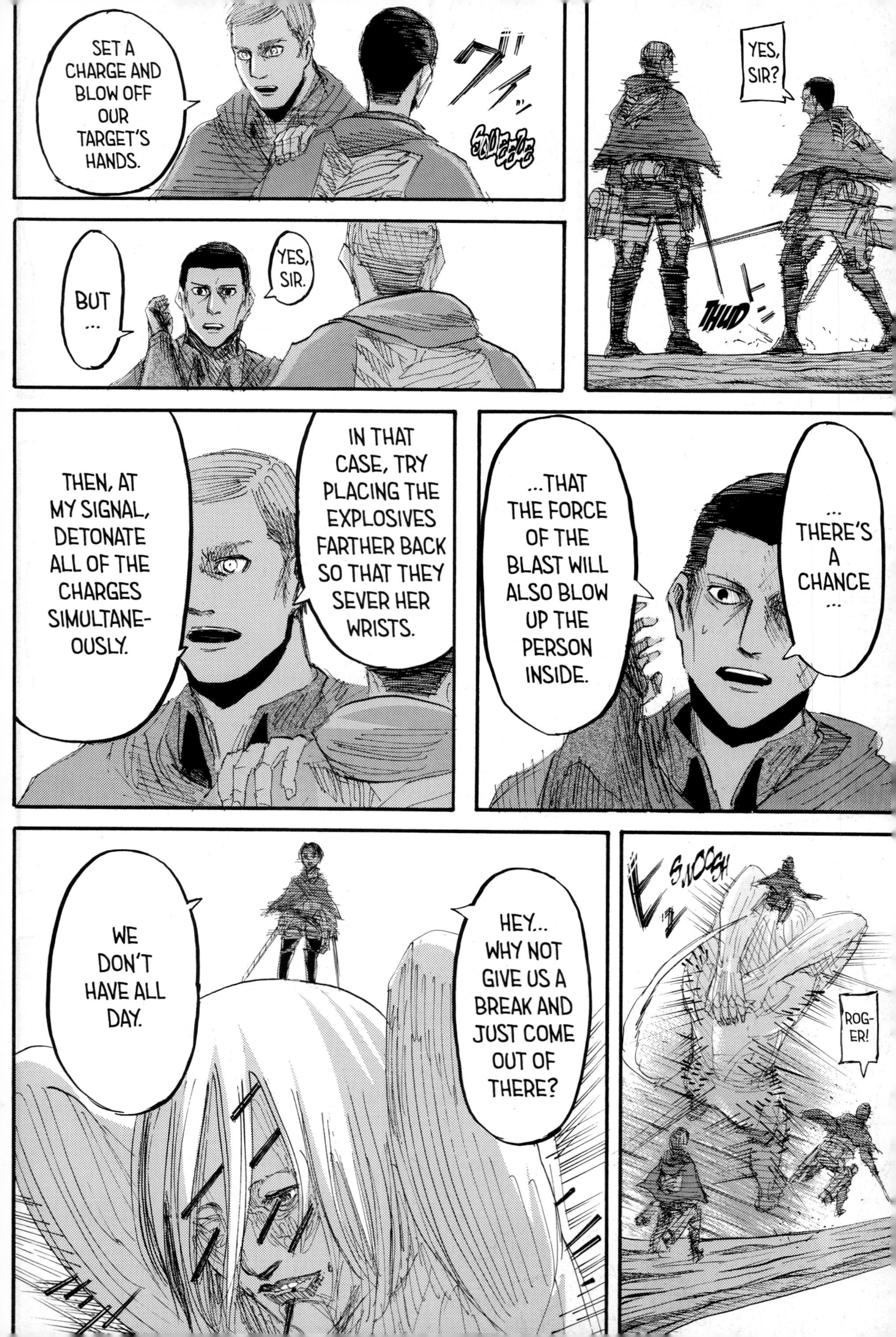
YES, SIR?
THUD
SET A CHARGE AND BLOW OFF OUR TARGET'S HANDS.
SQUEEZE
YES, SIR.
BUT ...
... THERE'S A CHANCE ...
...THAT THE FORCE OF THE BLAST WILL ALSO BLOW UP THE PERSON INSIDE.
IN THAT CASE, TRY PLACING THE EXPLOSIVES FARTHER BACK SO THAT THEY SEVER HER WRISTS.
THEN, AT MY SIGNAL, DETONATE ALL OF THE CHARGES SIMULTANEOUSLY.
SWOOSH
ROGER!
HEY... WHY NOT GIVE US A BREAK AND JUST COME OUT OF THERE?
WE DON'T HAVE ALL DAY.

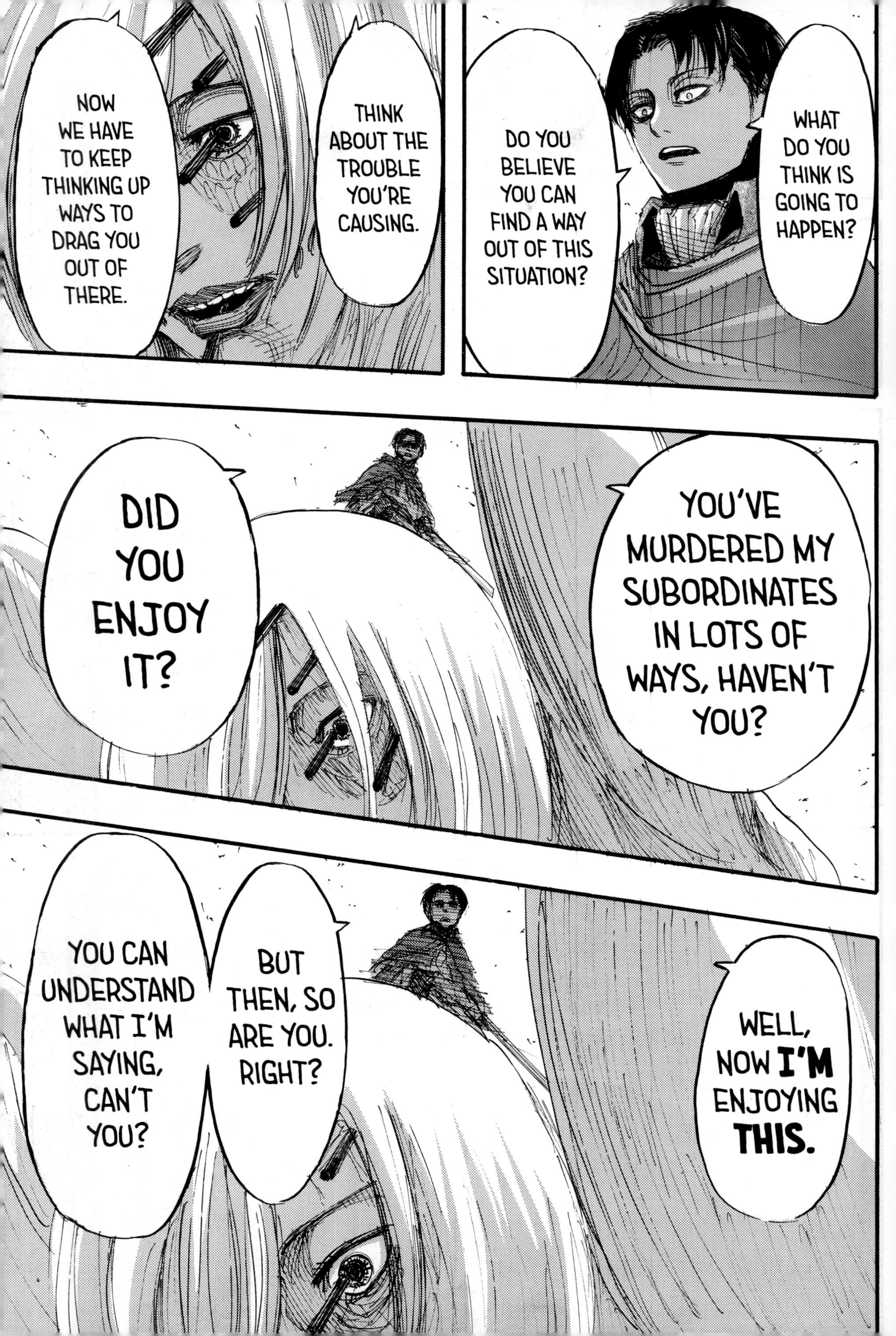
WHAT DO YOU THINK IS GOING TO HAPPEN?
DO YOU BELIEVE YOU CAN FIND A WAY OUT OF THIS SITUATION?
THINK ABOUT THE TROUBLE YOU'RE CAUSING.
NOW WE HAVE TO KEEP THINKING UP WAYS TO DRAG YOU OUT OF THERE.
YOU'VE MURDERED MY SUBORDINATES IN LOTS OF WAYS, HAVEN'T YOU?
DID YOU ENJOY IT?
WELL, NOW **I'M** ENJOYING **THIS.**
BUT THEN, SO ARE YOU. RIGHT?
YOU CAN UNDERSTAND WHAT I'M SAYING, CAN'T YOU?

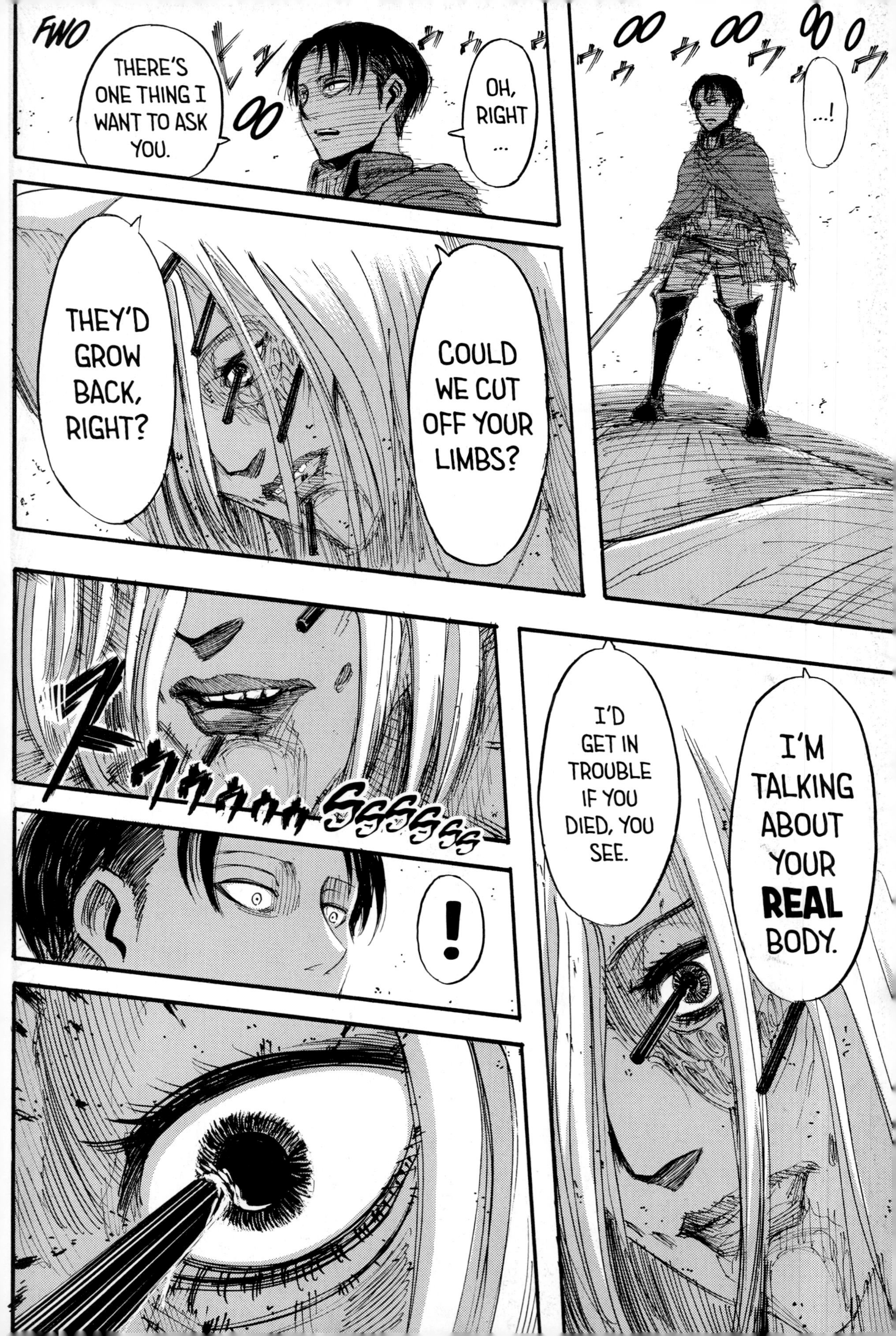
...!
FWO
OH, RIGHT ...
THERE'S ONE THING I WANT TO ASK YOU.
COULD WE CUT OFF YOUR LIMBS?
THEY'D GROW BACK, RIGHT?
I'M TALKING ABOUT YOUR **REAL** BODY.
I'D GET IN TROUBLE IF YOU DIED, YOU SEE.
SSSSSSS
!

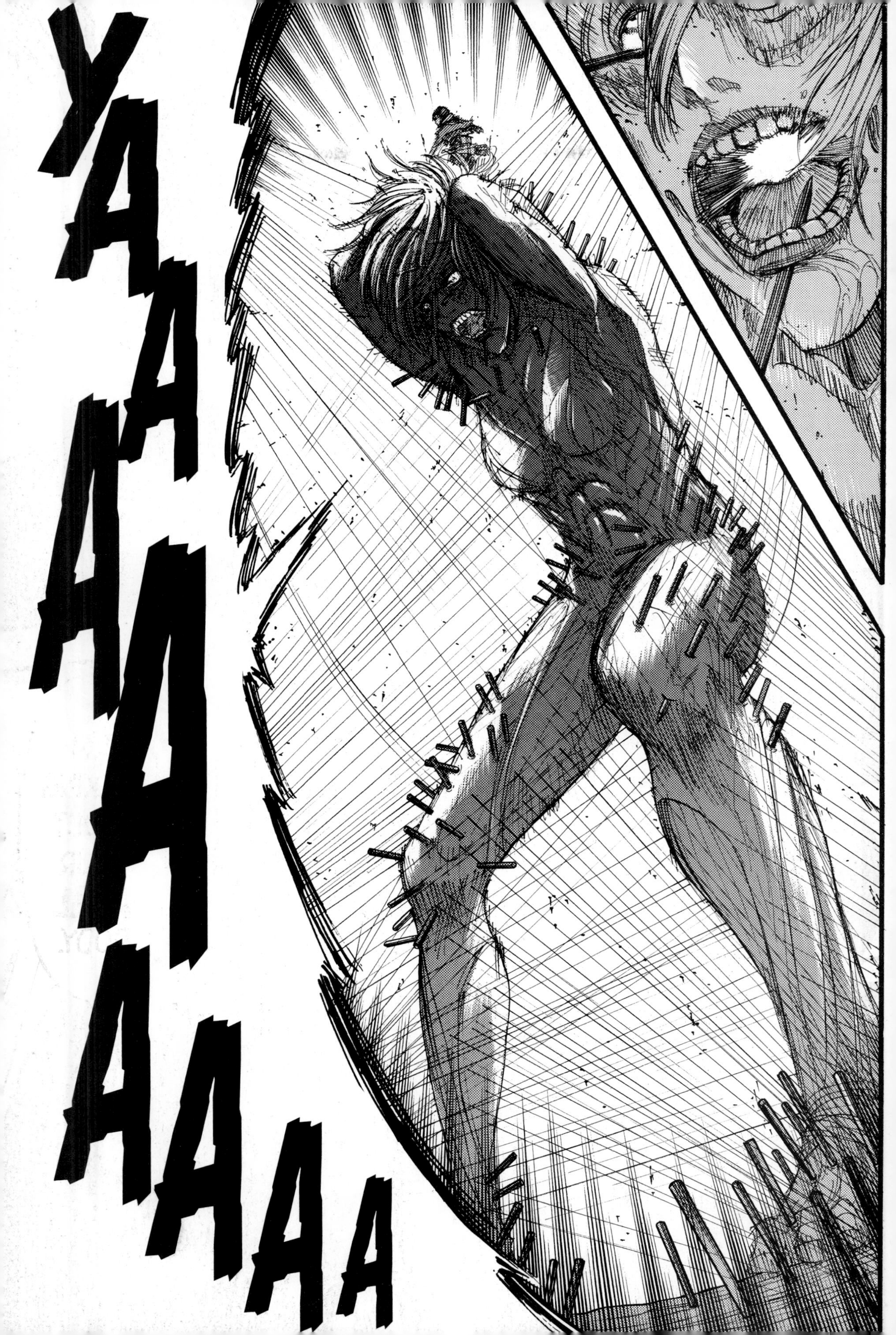
YAAAAAAAAAA

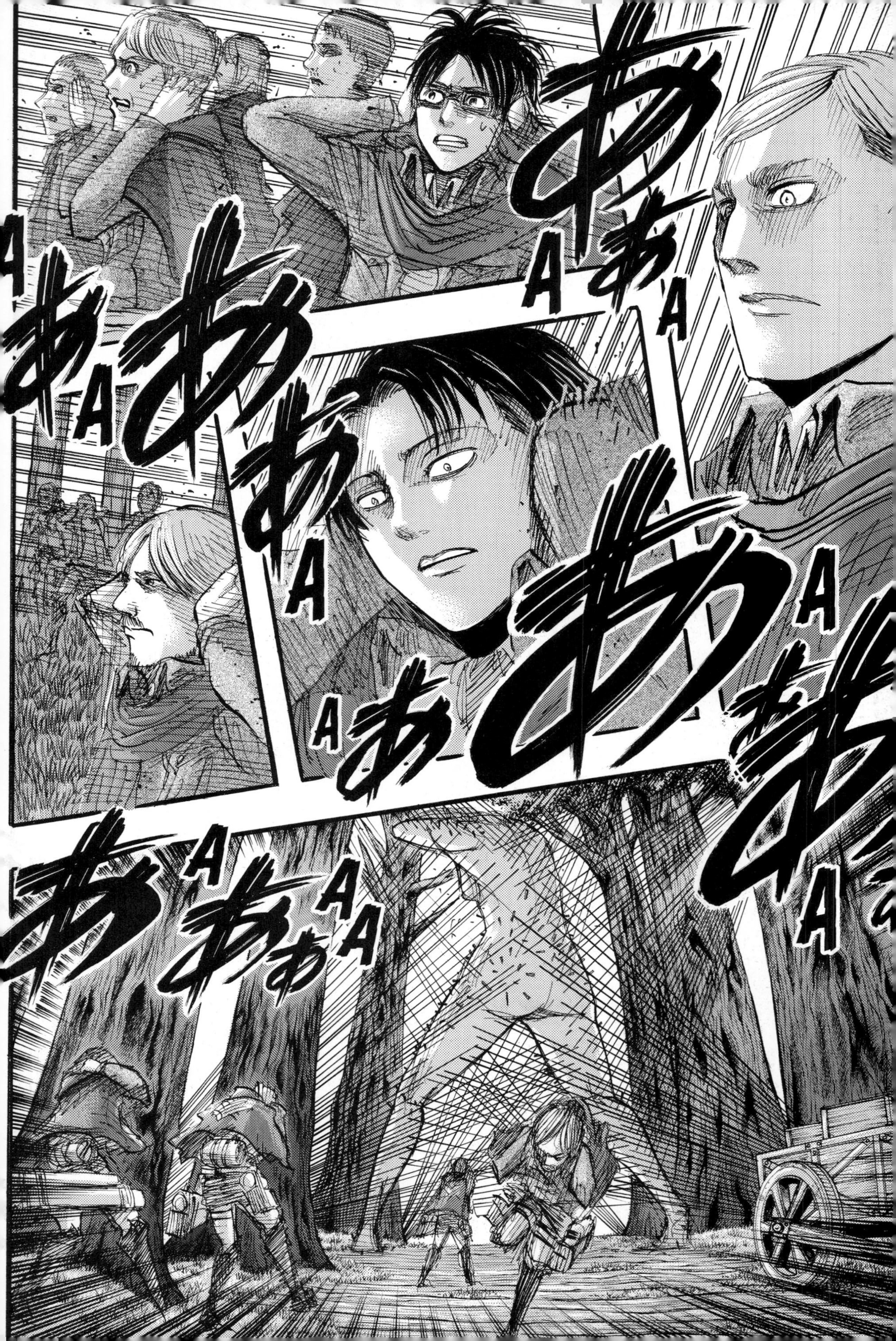

あ A あ A A
あ A あ A A
あ A あ A
あ A あ A A A
あ A あ あ A A A

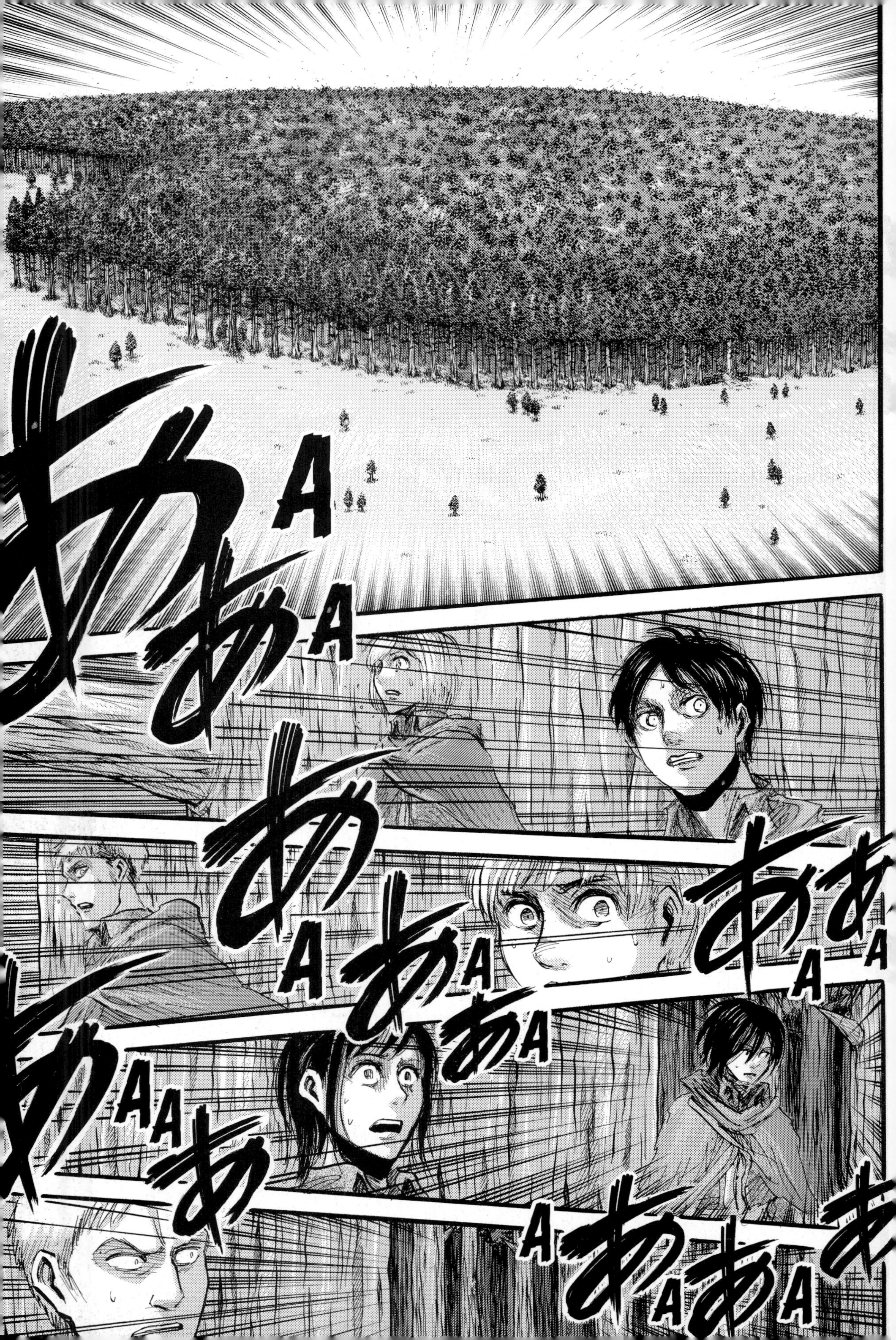
あ A
あ A
あ A
あ A
あ A
あ A
あ A
あ A
あ A
A あ A あ A あ

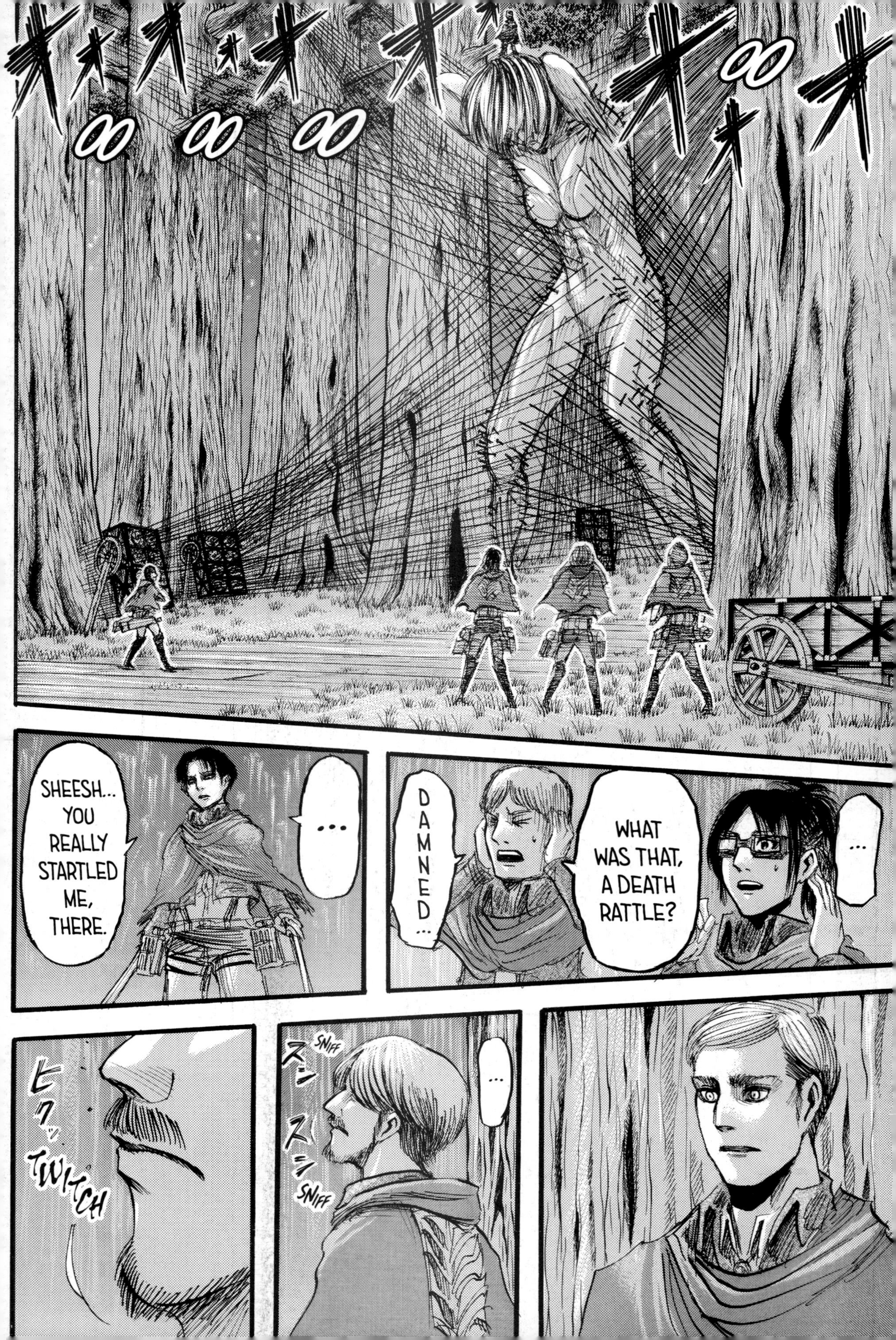
OO
OO
OO
OO
...
WHAT WAS THAT, A DEATH RATTLE?
DAMNED...
...
SHEESH... YOU REALLY STARTLED ME, THERE.
...
SNIFF
SNIFF
TWITCH

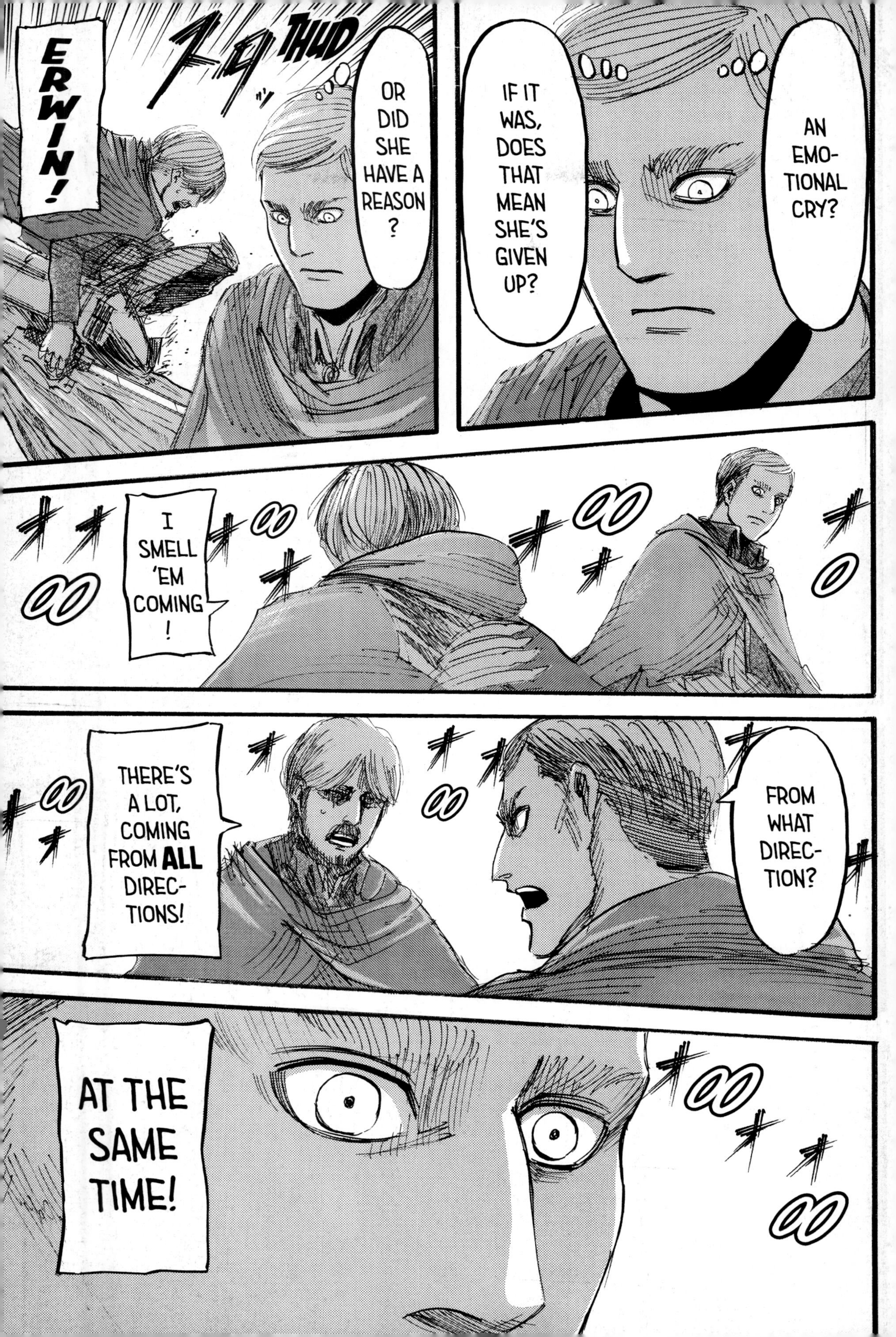
AN EMOTIONAL CRY?
IF IT WAS, DOES THAT MEAN SHE'S GIVEN UP?
OR DID SHE HAVE A REASON?
THUD
ERWIN!
I SMELL 'EM COMING!
FROM WHAT DIRECTION?
THERE'S A LOT, COMING FROM **ALL** DIRECTIONS!
AT THE SAME TIME!

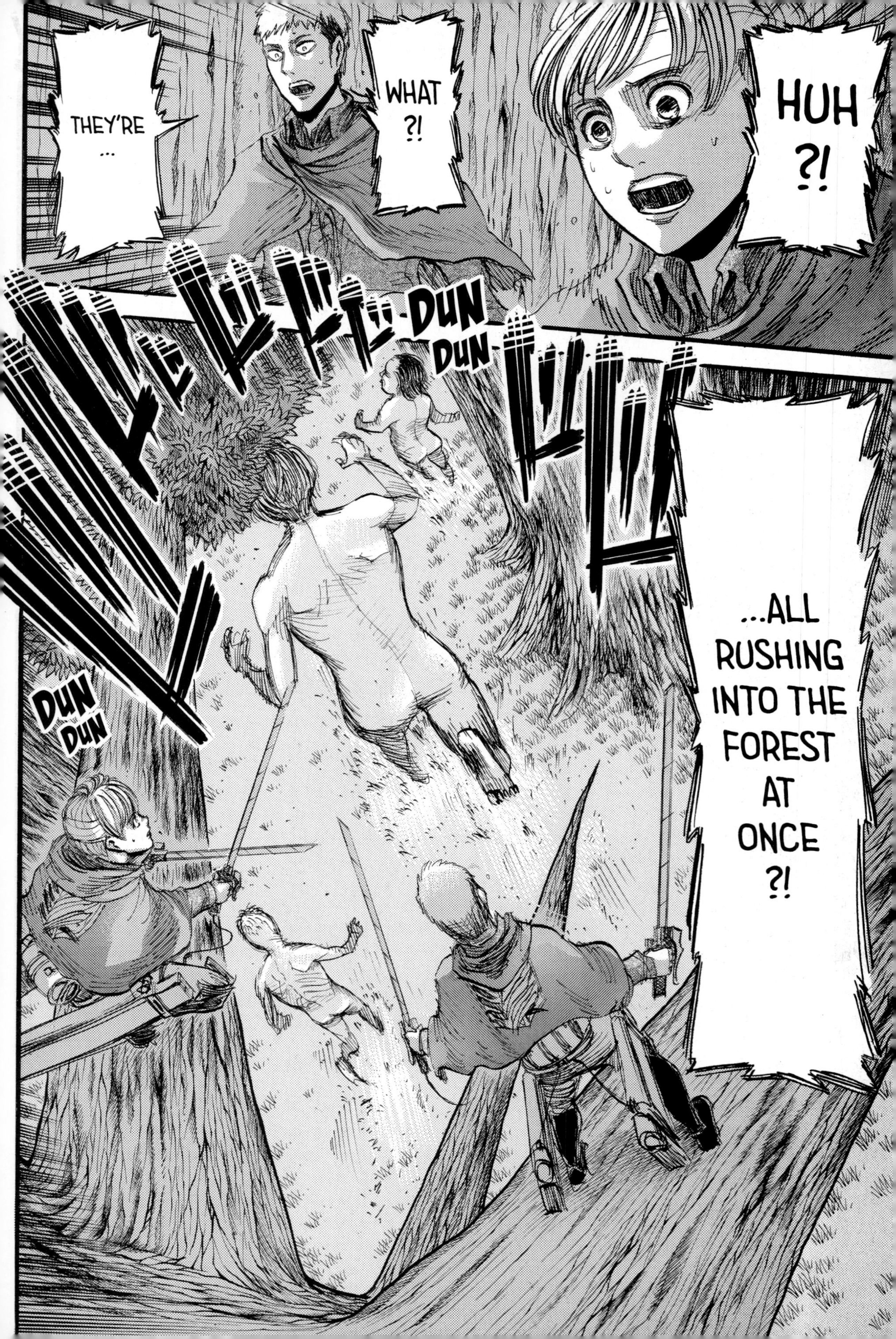
HUH ?!
WHAT ?!
THEY'RE ...
DUN DUN
...ALL RUSHING INTO THE FOREST AT ONCE ?!
DUN DUN

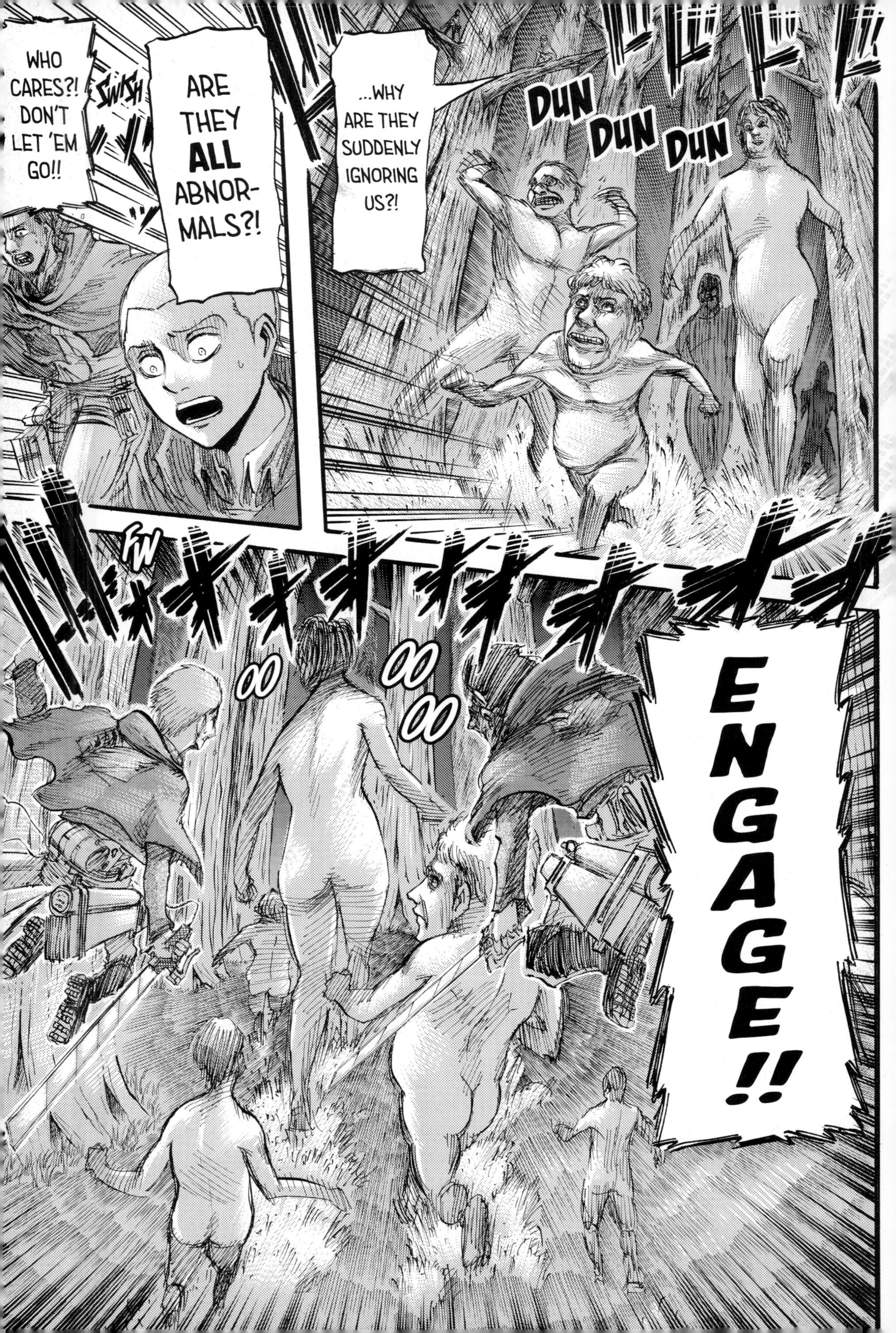
DUN
DUN
DUN
...WHY ARE THEY SUDDENLY IGNORING US?!
ARE THEY **ALL** ABNORMALS?!
SWISH
WHO CARES?! DON'T LET 'EM GO!!
ENGAGE!!
OO
OO
OO
FW

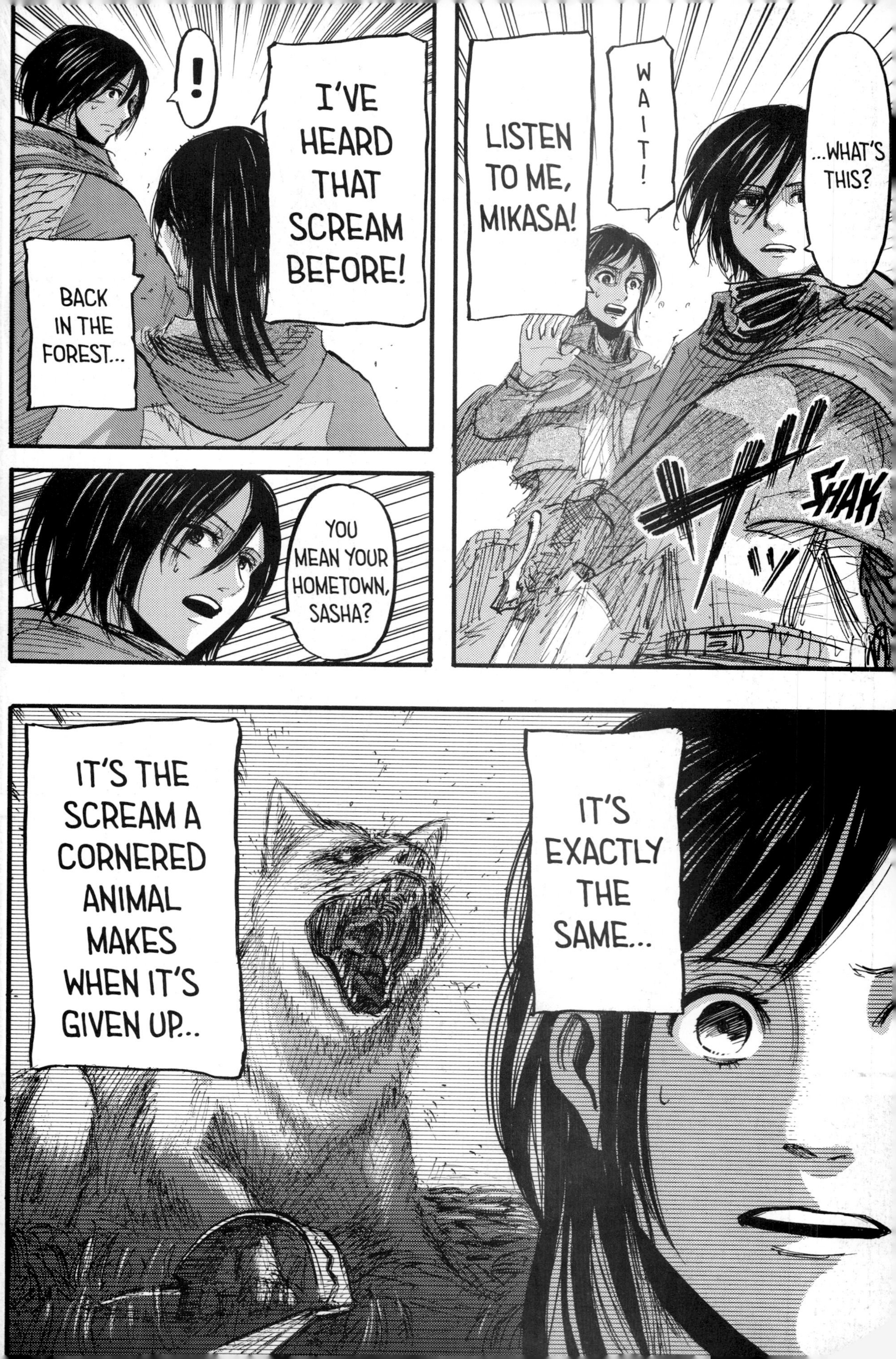
...WHAT'S THIS?
WAIT!
LISTEN TO ME, MIKASA!
SHAK
!
I'VE HEARD THAT SCREAM BEFORE!
BACK IN THE FOREST...
YOU MEAN YOUR HOMETOWN, SASHA?
IT'S EXACTLY THE SAME...
IT'S THE SCREAM A CORNERED ANIMAL MAKES WHEN IT'S GIVEN UP...

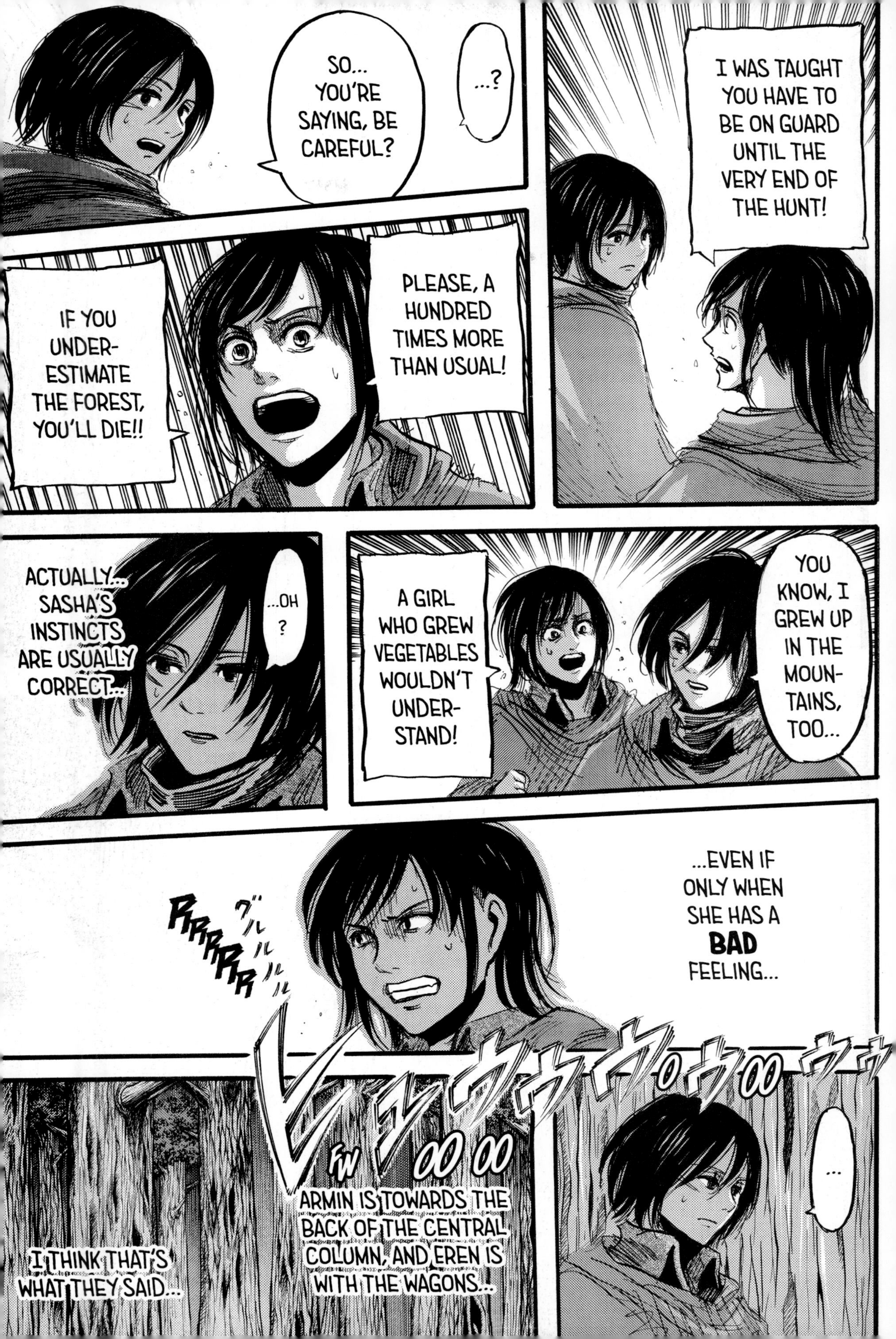
I WAS TAUGHT YOU HAVE TO BE ON GUARD UNTIL THE VERY END OF THE HUNT!
...?
SO... YOU'RE SAYING, BE CAREFUL?
PLEASE, A HUNDRED TIMES MORE THAN USUAL!
IF YOU UNDER-ESTIMATE THE FOREST, YOU'LL DIE!!
YOU KNOW, I GREW UP IN THE MOUN-TAINS, TOO...
A GIRL WHO GREW VEGETABLES WOULDN'T UNDER-STAND!
...OH ?
ACTUALLY... SASHA'S INSTINCTS ARE USUALLY CORRECT...
...EVEN IF ONLY WHEN SHE HAS A **BAD** FEELING...
ヴルルルル
RRRRRRR
FW OO OO
...
ARMIN IS TOWARDS THE BACK OF THE CENTRAL COLUMN, AND EREN IS WITH THE WAGONS...
I THINK THAT'S WHAT THEY SAID...

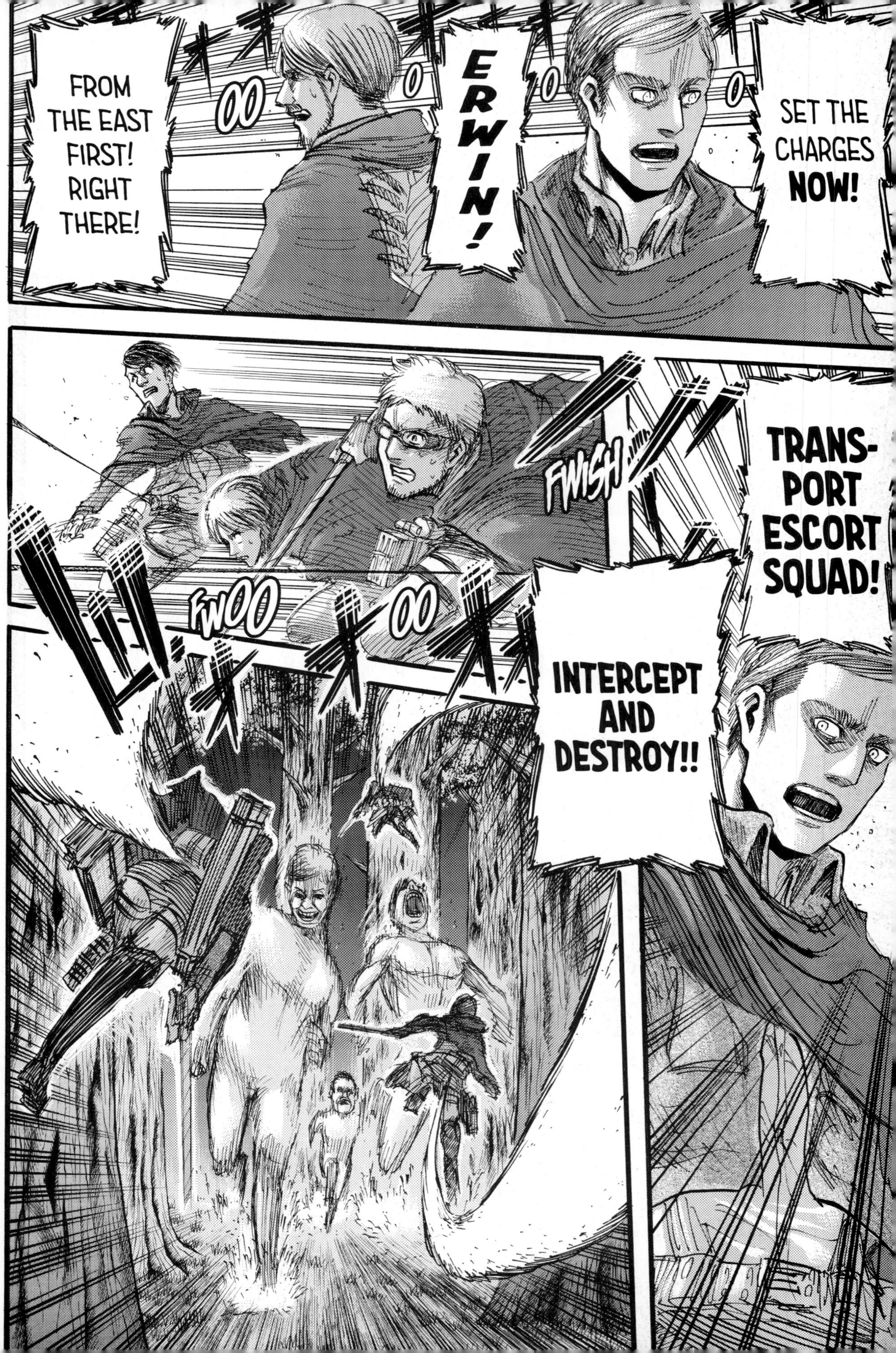
SET THE CHARGES NOW!
ERWIN!
FROM THE EAST FIRST! RIGHT THERE!
OO
TRANS-PORT ESCORT SQUAD!
INTERCEPT AND DESTROY!!
FWISH
FWOO
OO

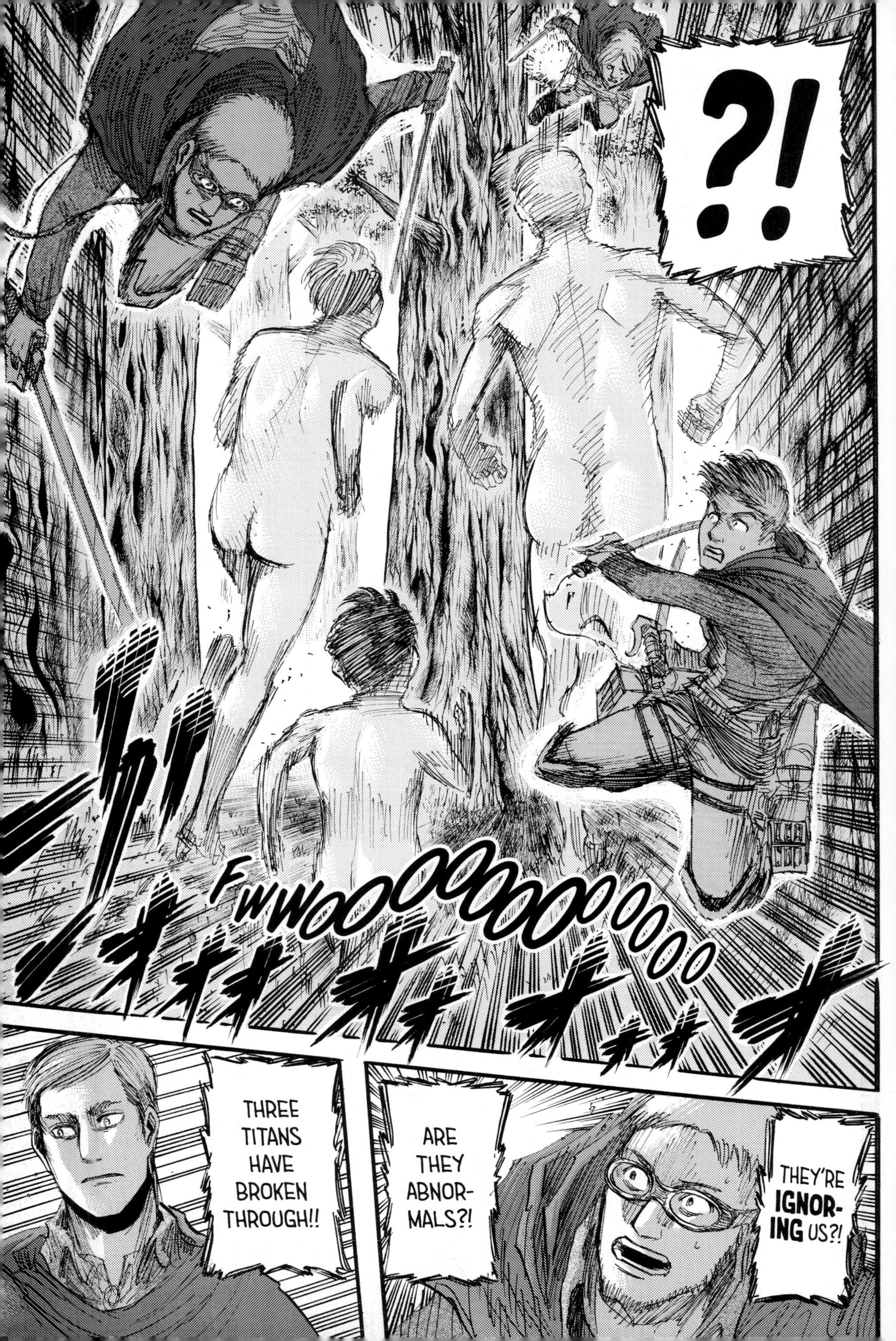
?!
FWWOOOOOOOOOOOOOOOOO
THEY'RE IGNORING US?!
ARE THEY ABNORMALS?!
THREE TITANS HAVE BROKEN THROUGH!!

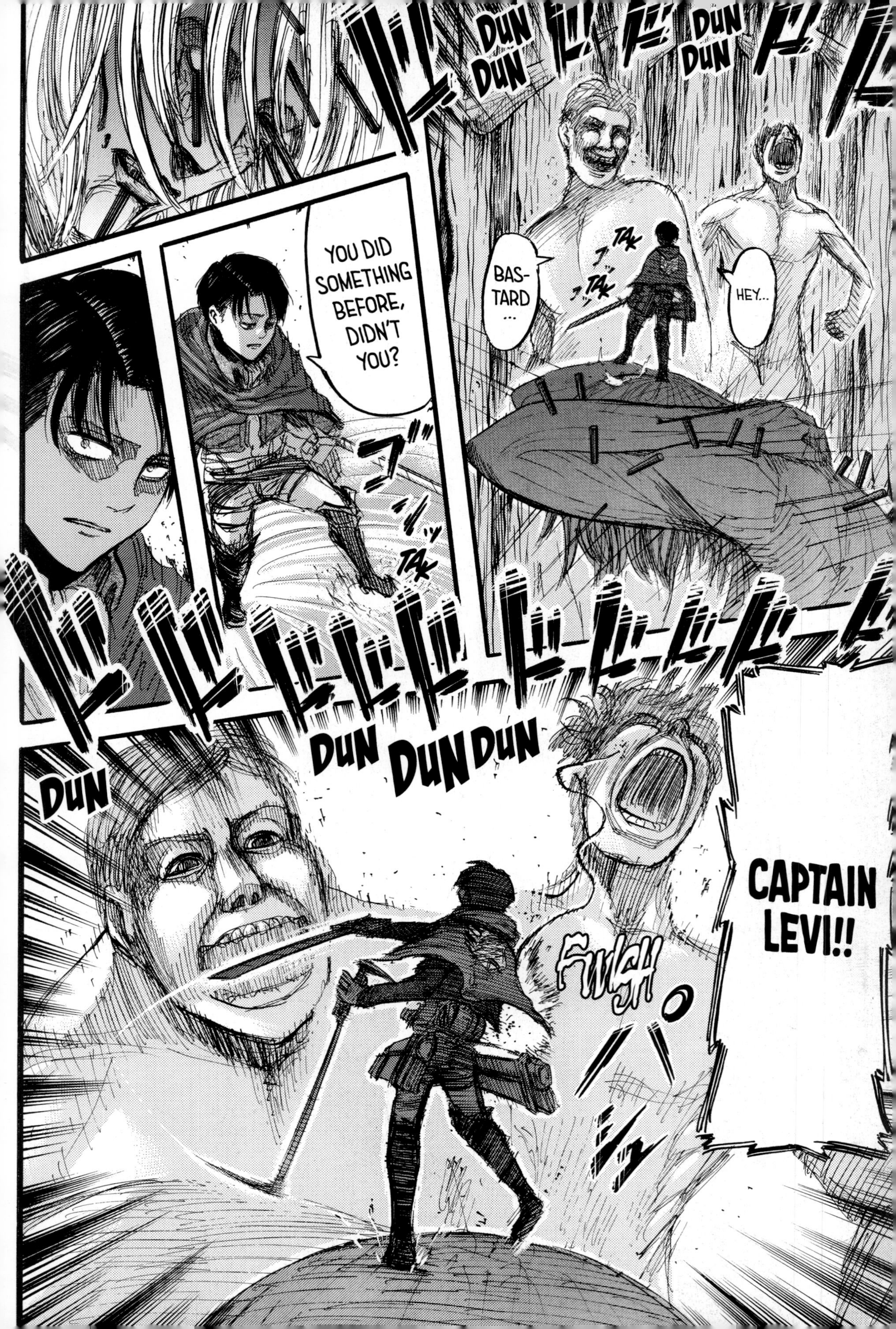
DUN DUN
DUN DUN
HEY...
TAK TAK
BAS-TARD...
YOU DID SOMETHING BEFORE, DIDN'T YOU?
TAK
CAPTAIN LEVI!!
DUN DUN DUN
DUN
FWUSH

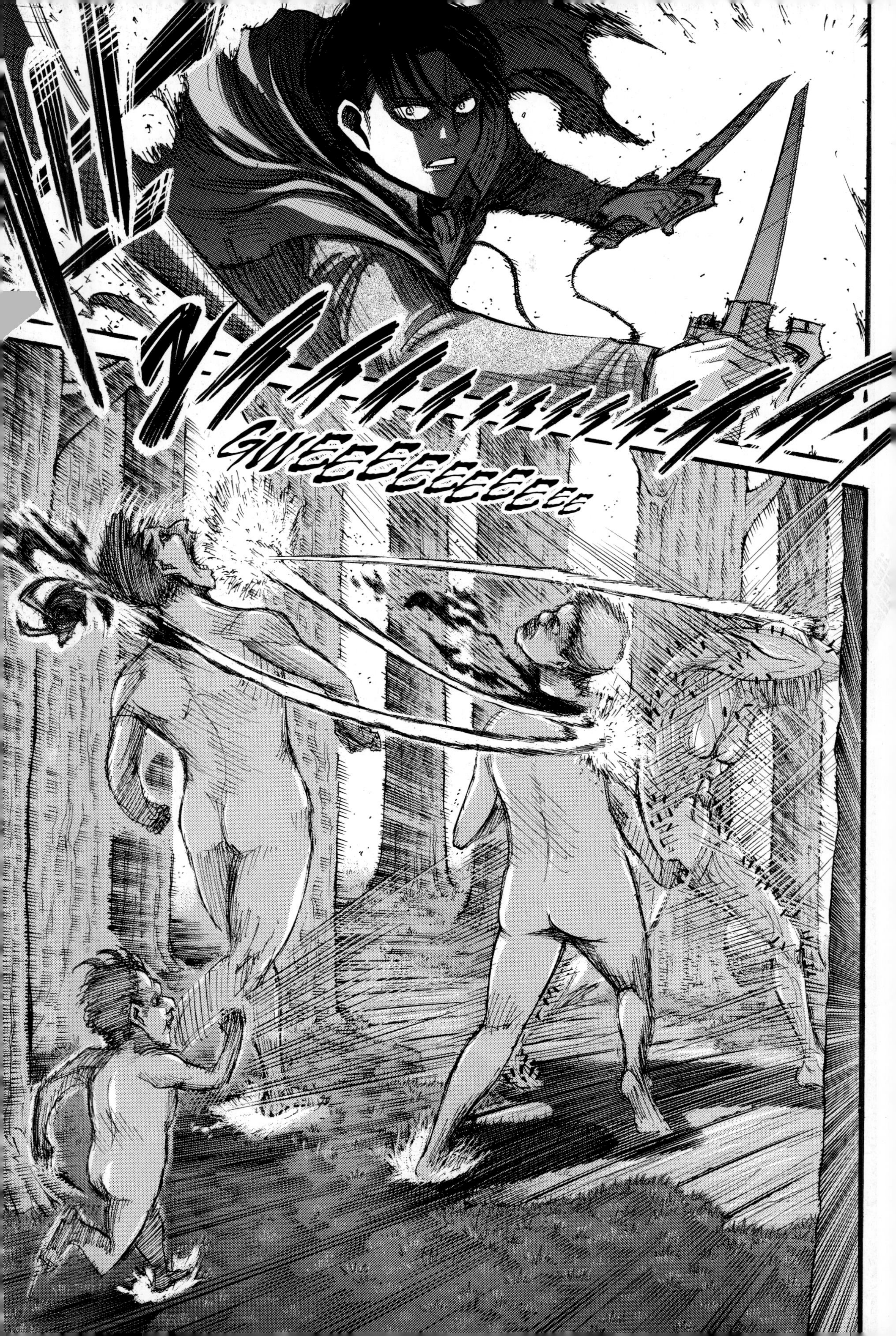
GWEEEEEEEEEEEE

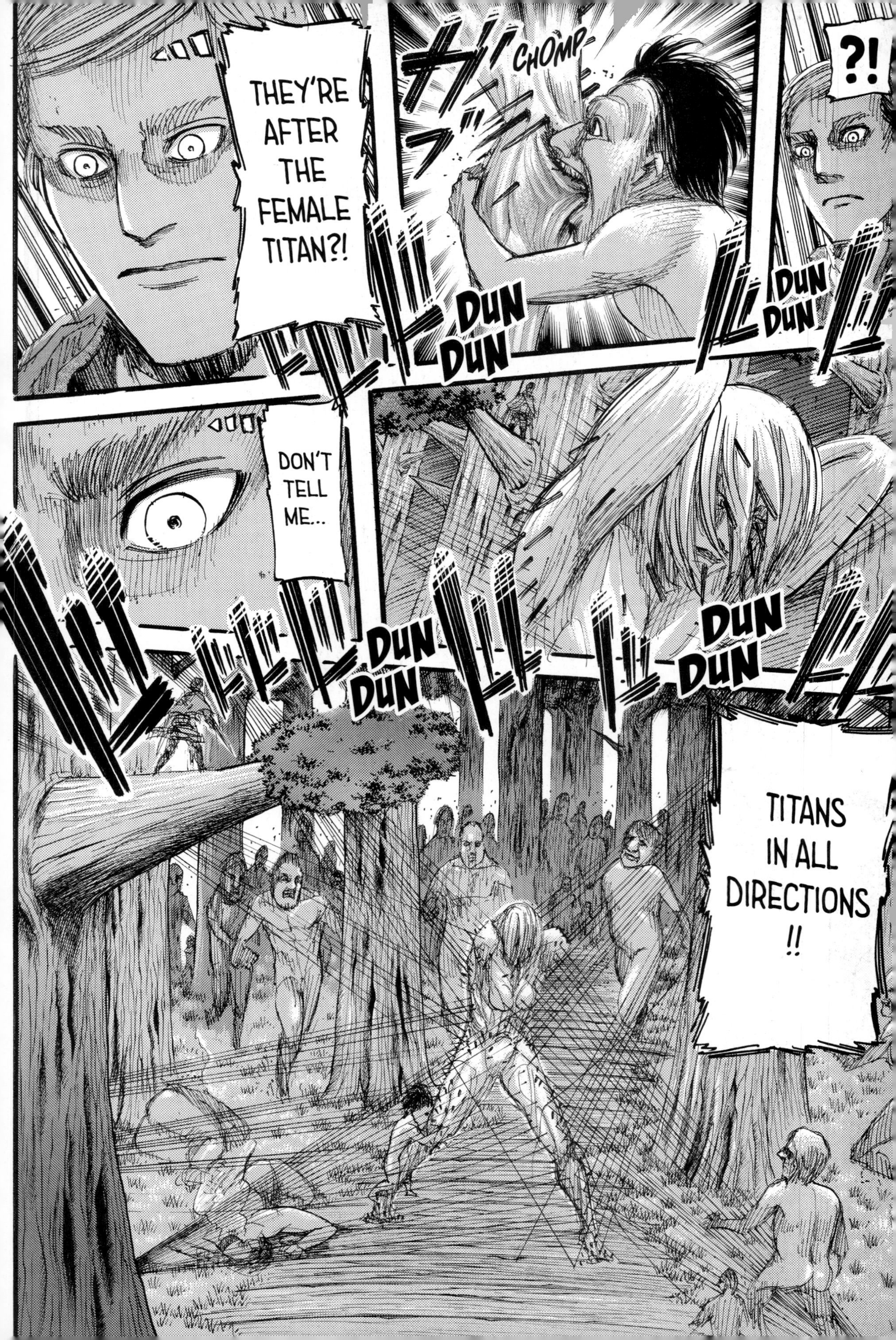
?!
DUN DUN
CHOMP
DUN DUN
THEY'RE AFTER THE FEMALE TITAN?!
DUN DUN
DON'T TELL ME...
DUN DUN
TITANS IN ALL DIRECTIONS !!

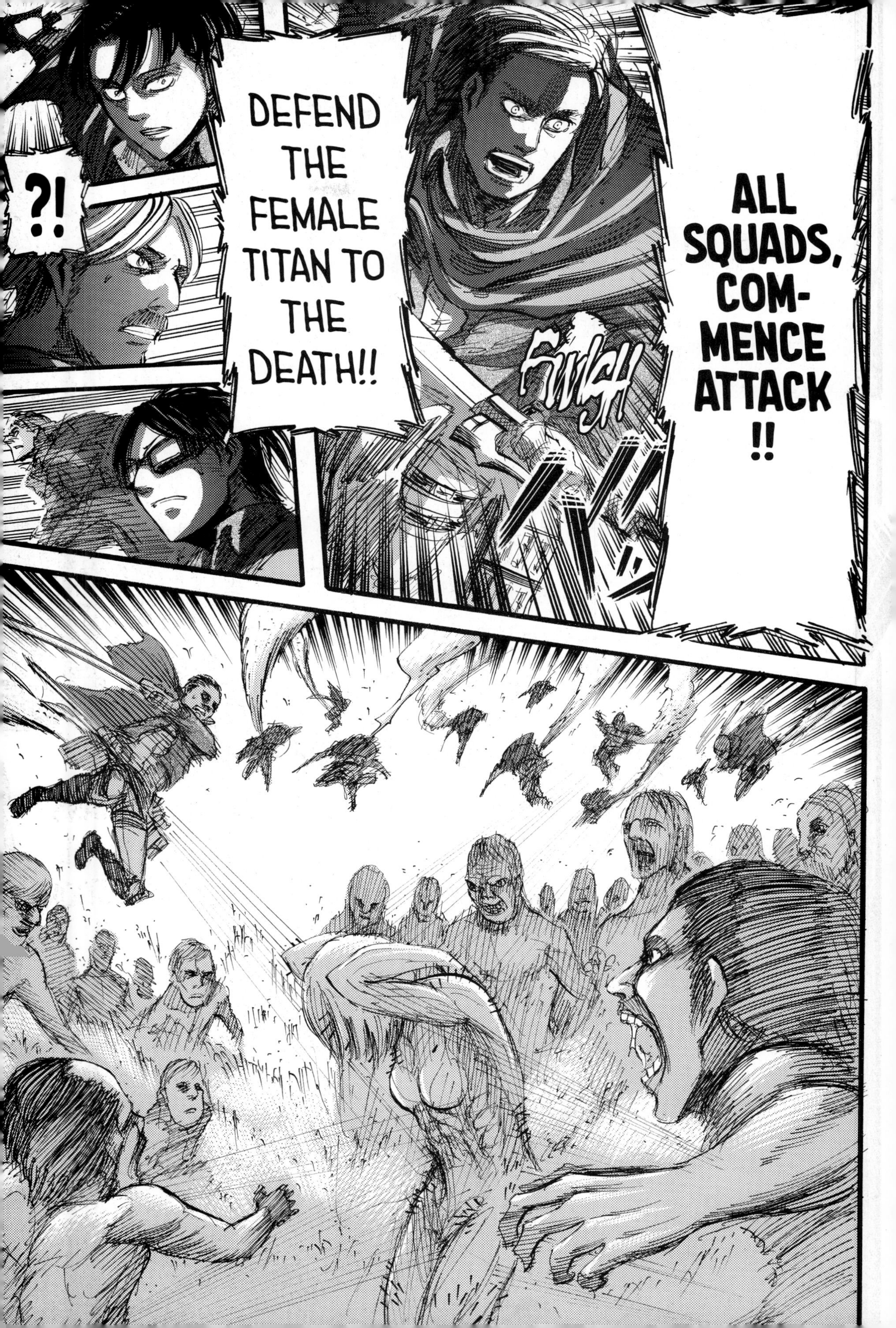
ALL SQUADS, COM-MENCE ATTACK !!
FWISH
DEFEND THE FEMALE TITAN TO THE DEATH!!
?!

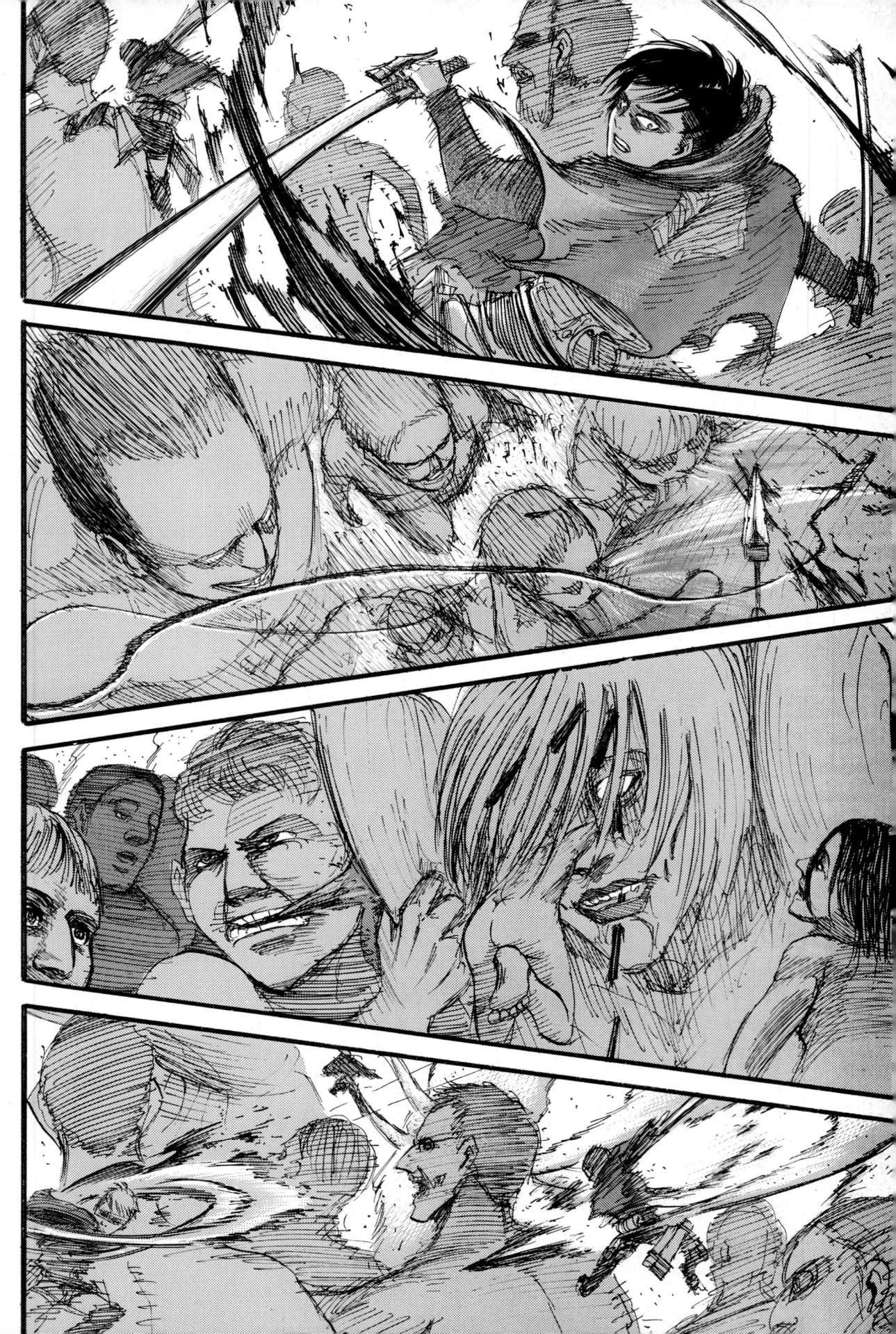

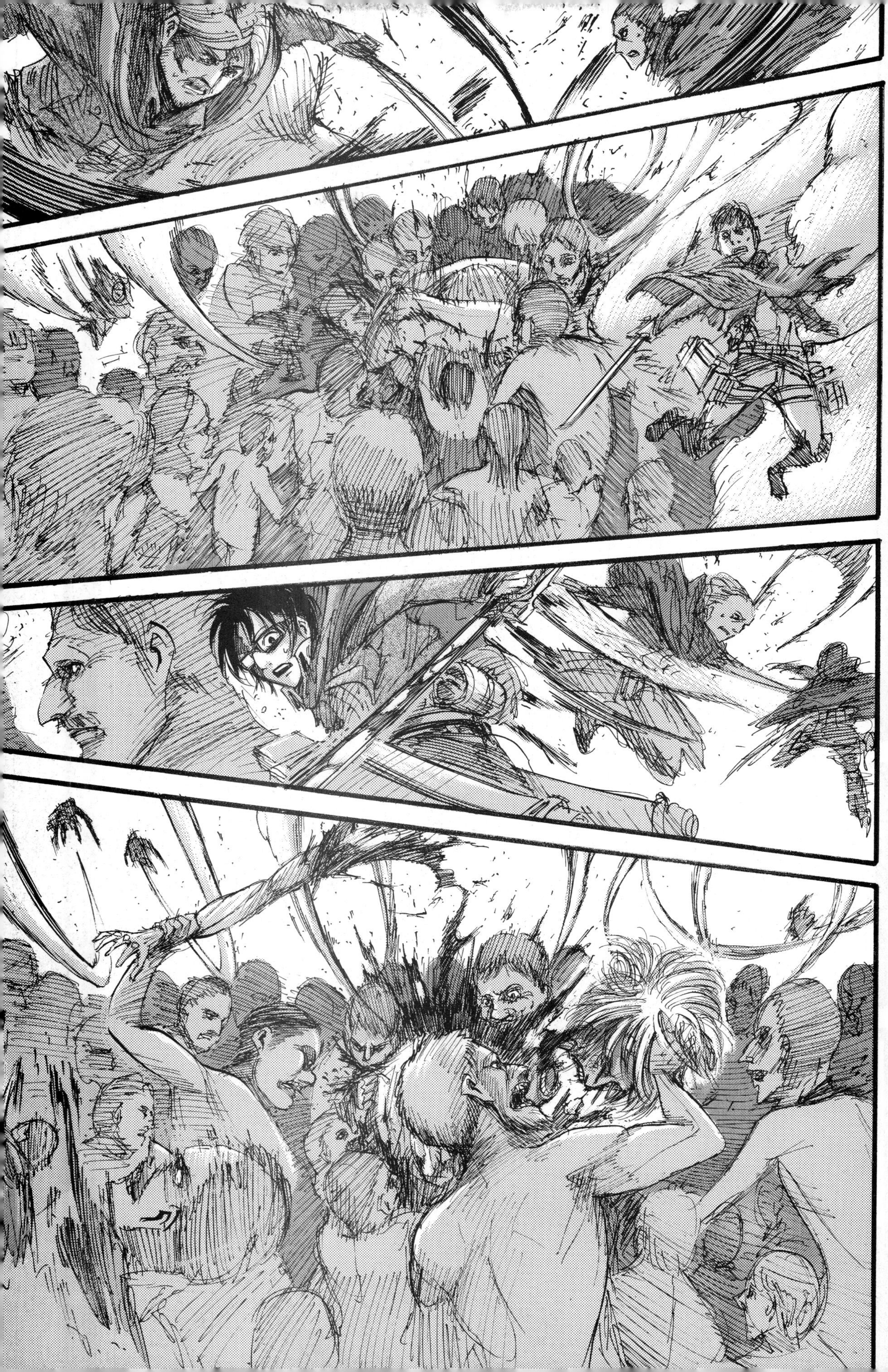

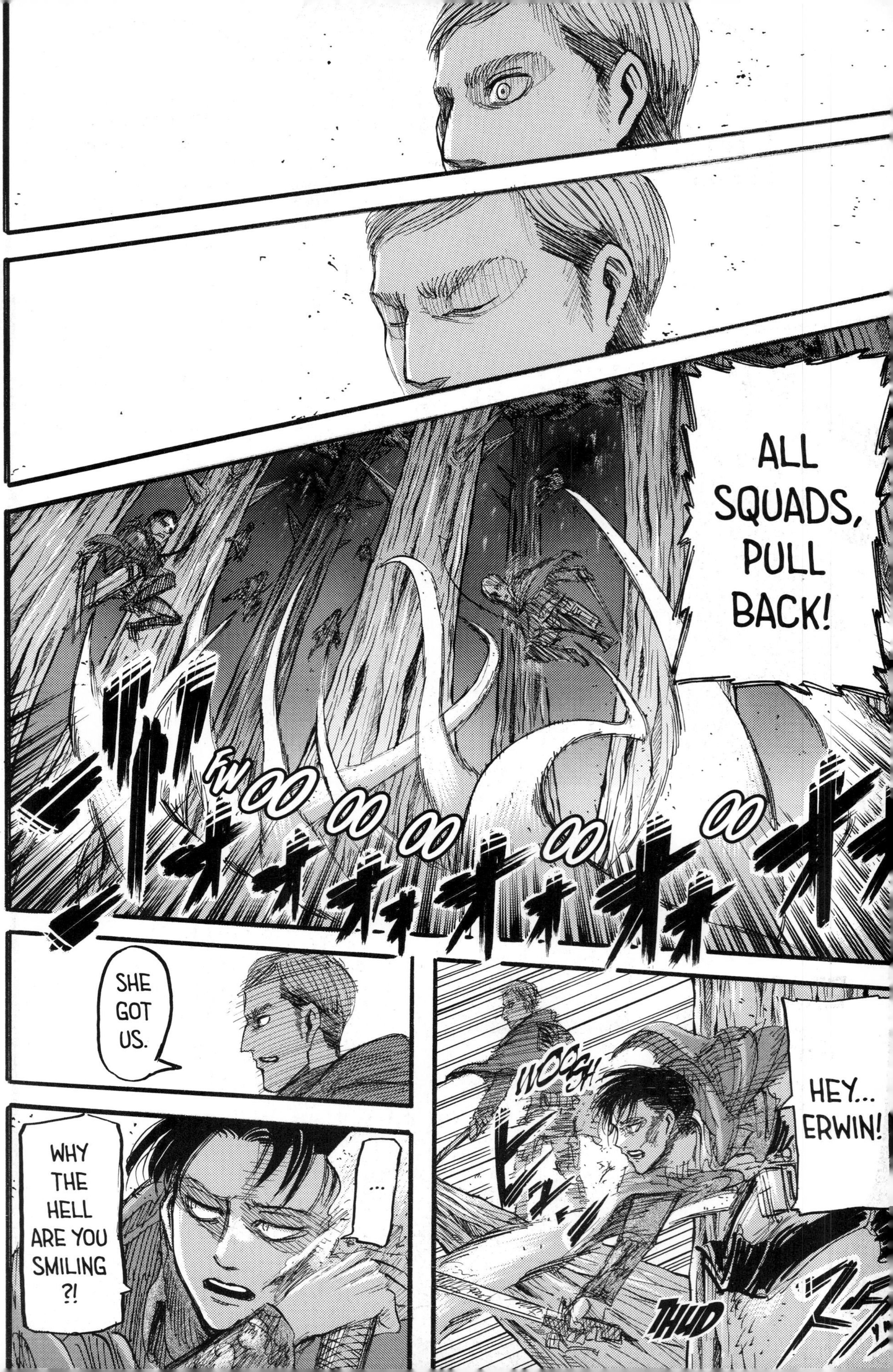
ALL SQUADS, PULL BACK!
FWOO OO OO OO OO OO
HEY... ERWIN!
WOOSH
THUD
SHE GOT US.
...
WHY THE HELL ARE YOU SMILING ?!

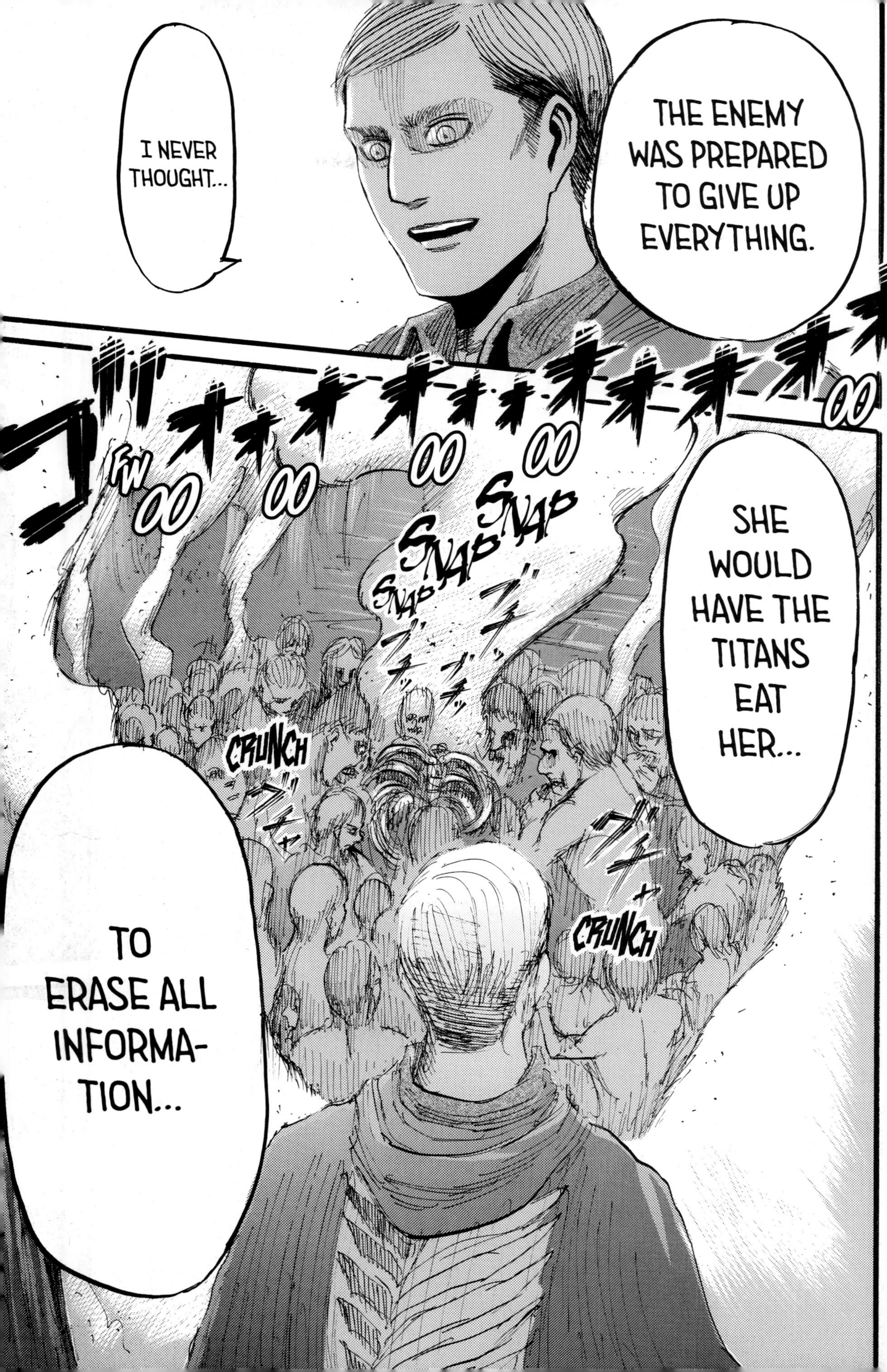
THE ENEMY WAS PREPARED TO GIVE UP EVERYTHING.
I NEVER THOUGHT...
FWOO
OO
OO
OO
SNAP
SNAP
SNAP
SHE WOULD HAVE THE TITANS EAT HER...
CRUNCH
CRUNCH
TO ERASE ALL INFORMATION...

13. Special Target Restraining Weapons

THE SURVEY CORPS HAS DEVELOPED A NEW WEAPON IN ORDER TO RESTRAIN SPECIFIC TITANS. TO THE UNTRAINED EYE, IT LOOKS LIKE A NORMAL WAGON CARRYING BARRELS, BUT INSIDE EACH BARREL ARE SEVEN IRON TUBES CONTAINING COILED WIRES WITH ARROWHEADS ATTACHED AT BOTH ENDS.

THE WIRES ARE STRONG AND SPECIALLY MADE TO BECOME ELASTIC AFTER BEING EJECTED FROM THE BARRELS. WHEN THE DEVICE IS ACTIVATED, ARROWHEADS ARE FIRED FROM BOTH ENDS OF THE TUBES. THE ARROWHEADS ON ONE SIDE HEAD FOR THE TARGETED TITAN, WHILE THE ONES AT THE OTHER SIDE BECOME LODGED IN A TREE TRUNK, SO IF THE TIP PIERCES THE TITAN'S FLESH, IT'S POSSIBLE TO TETHER THE TITAN TO THE TREE WITH THE WIRE. THE PURPOSE OF THIS WEAPON IS TO IMMOBILIZE THE TARGET, ANCHORING IT WITH HUNDREDS OF ARROWHEADS FIRED FROM SEVERAL DIRECTIONS AND WIRES WITH GREAT TENSILE STRENGTH.

DEVELOPMENT OF THIS WEAPON REQUIRED A SIGNIFICANT CAPITAL OUTLAY, SO THE SURVEY CORPS HAD TO GUARANTEE POSITIVE RESULTS BEFORE INVESTORS WOULD CONTRIBUTE THE MONEY. TO THAT END, THE CONTINUED EXISTENCE OF THE SURVEY CORPS ITSELF IS AT LEAST PARTIALLY DEPENDENT ON THE RESULTS OF THEIR CURRENT MISSION.

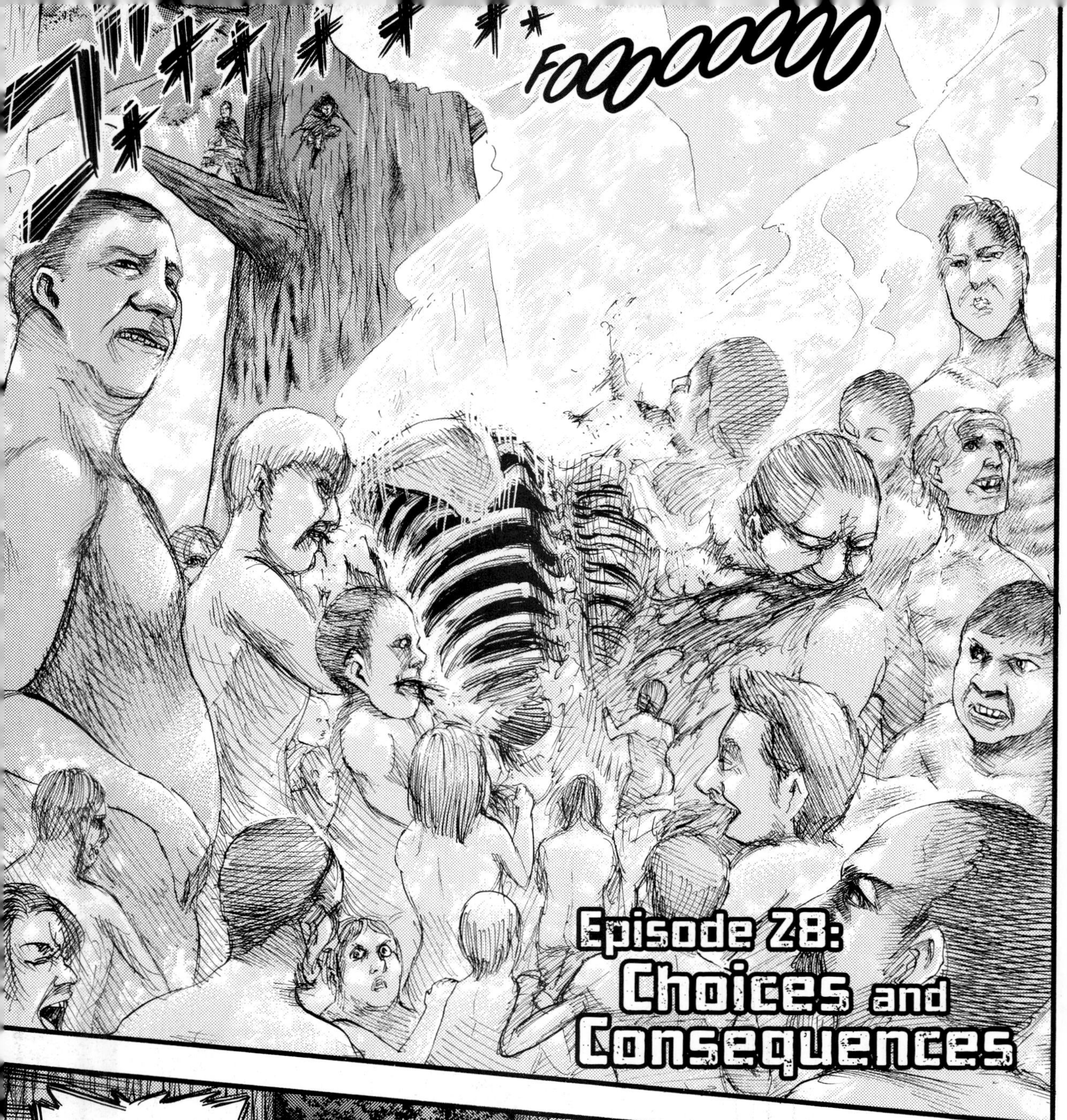
FOOOOOOOO

Episode 28: Choices and Consequences

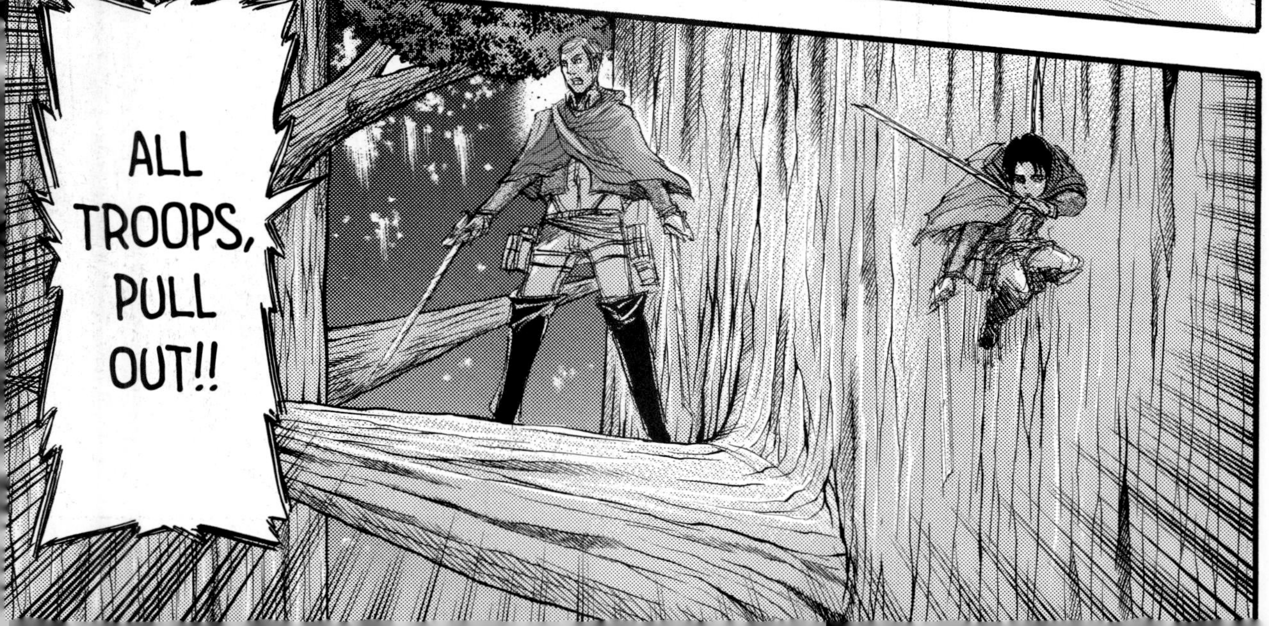
ALL TROOPS, PULL OUT!!

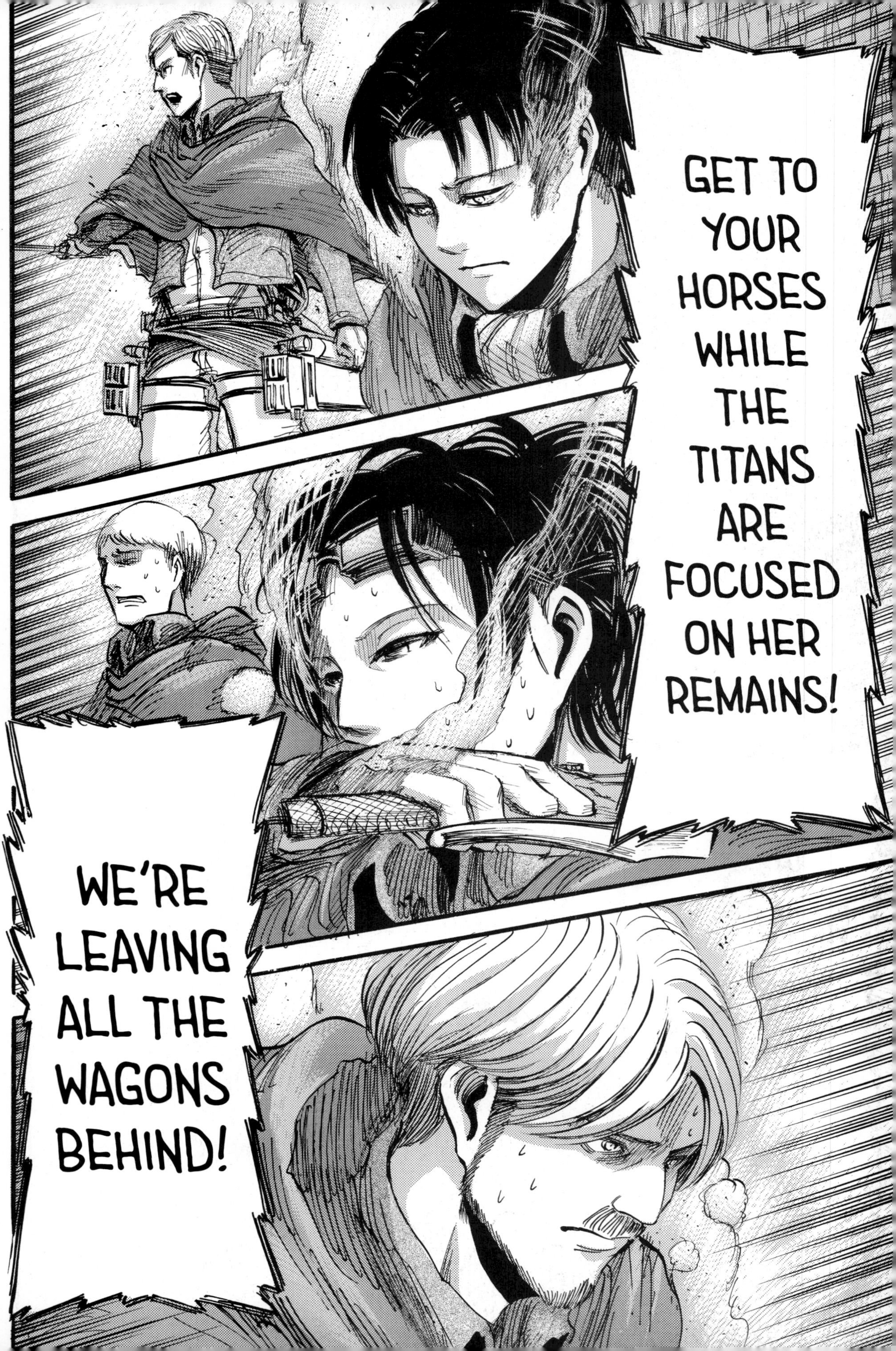
GET TO YOUR HORSES WHILE THE TITANS ARE FOCUSED ON HER REMAINS!
WE'RE LEAVING ALL THE WAGONS BEHIND!

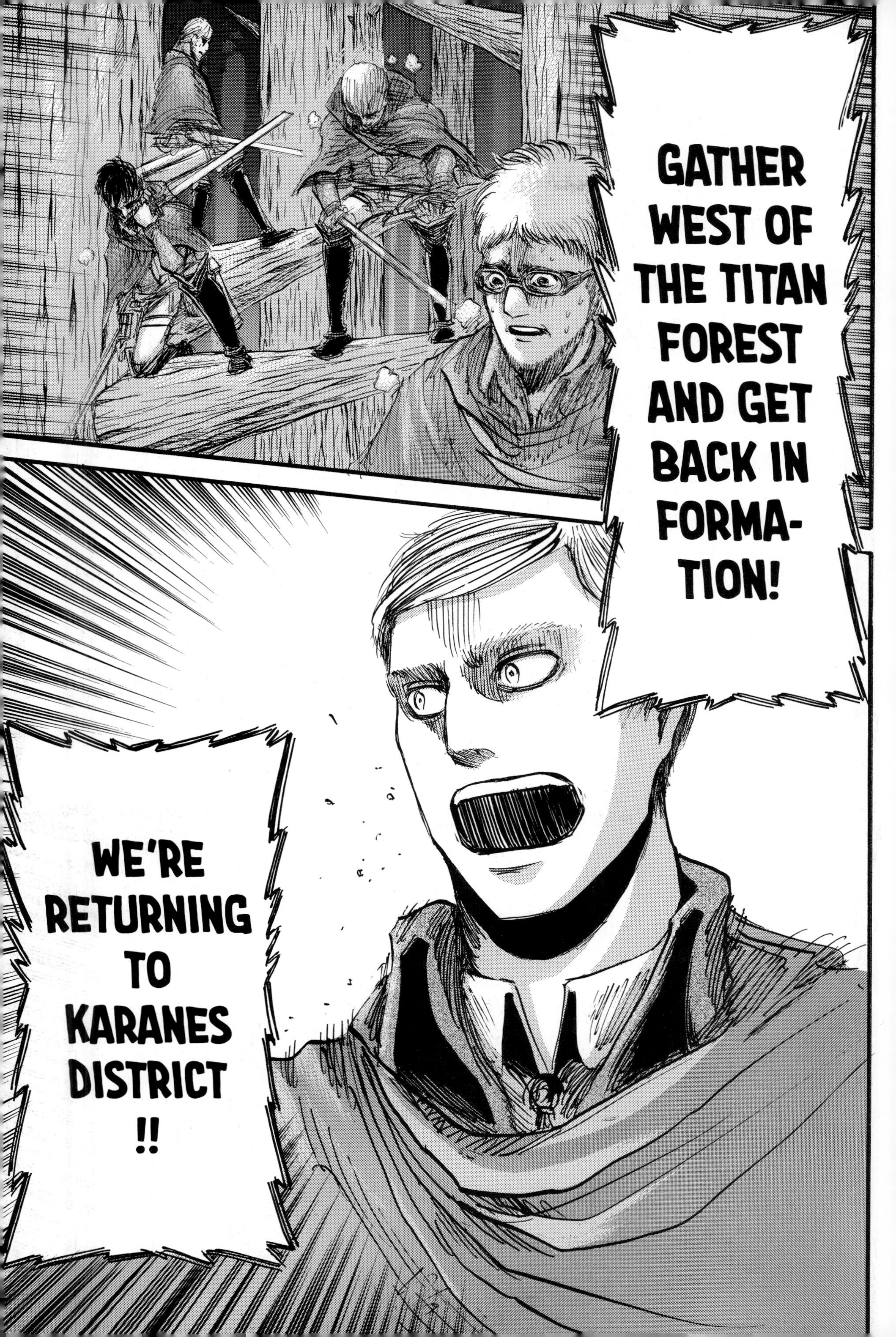
GATHER WEST OF THE TITAN FOREST AND GET BACK IN FORMA-TION!
WE'RE RETURNING TO KARANES DISTRICT !!

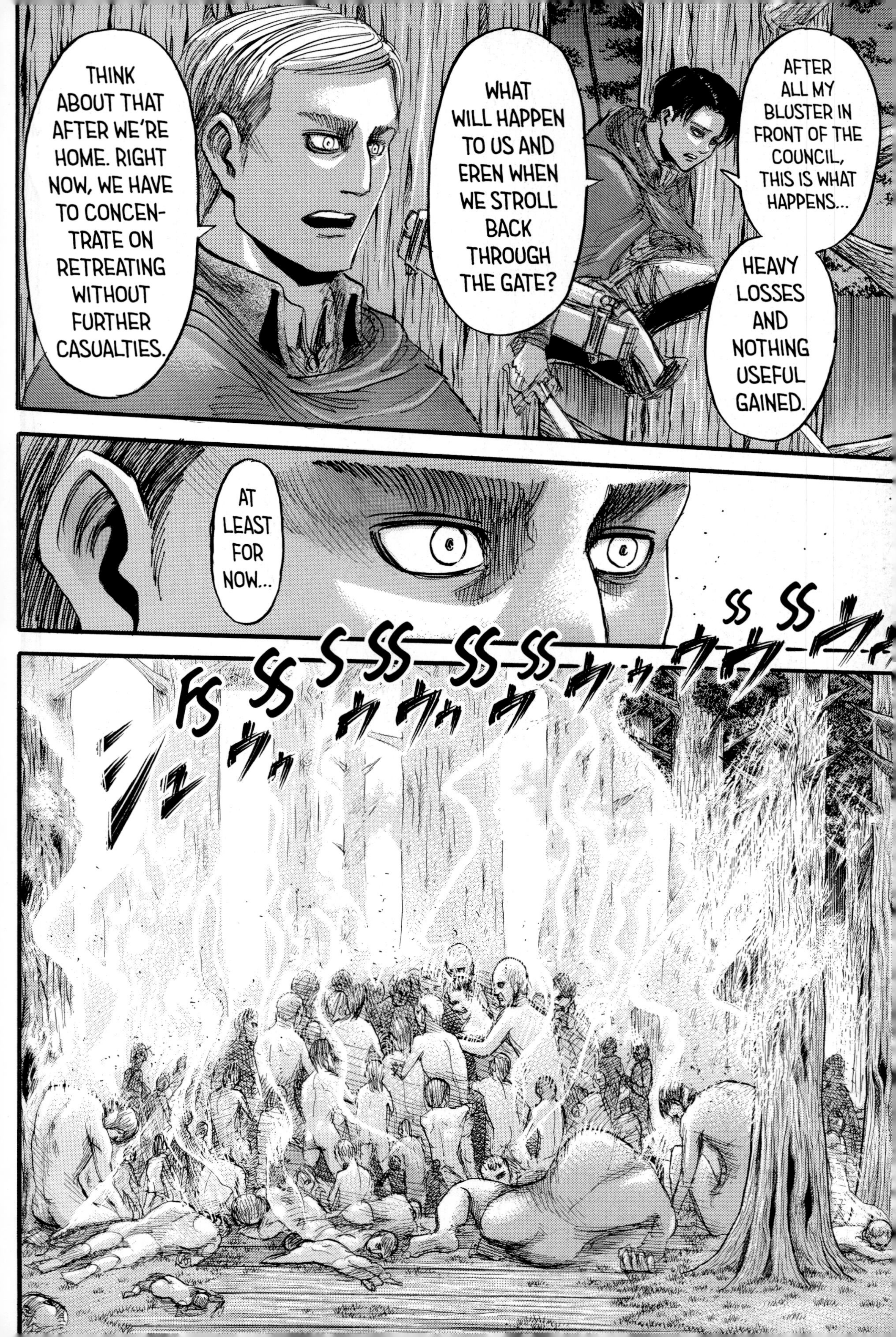
AFTER ALL MY BLUSTER IN FRONT OF THE COUNCIL, THIS IS WHAT HAPPENS...
HEAVY LOSSES AND NOTHING USEFUL GAINED.
WHAT WILL HAPPEN TO US AND EREN WHEN WE STROLL BACK THROUGH THE GATE?
THINK ABOUT THAT AFTER WE'RE HOME. RIGHT NOW, WE HAVE TO CONCEN-TRATE ON RETREATING WITHOUT FURTHER CASUALTIES.
AT LEAST FOR NOW...
FS SS S SS SS SS SS SS

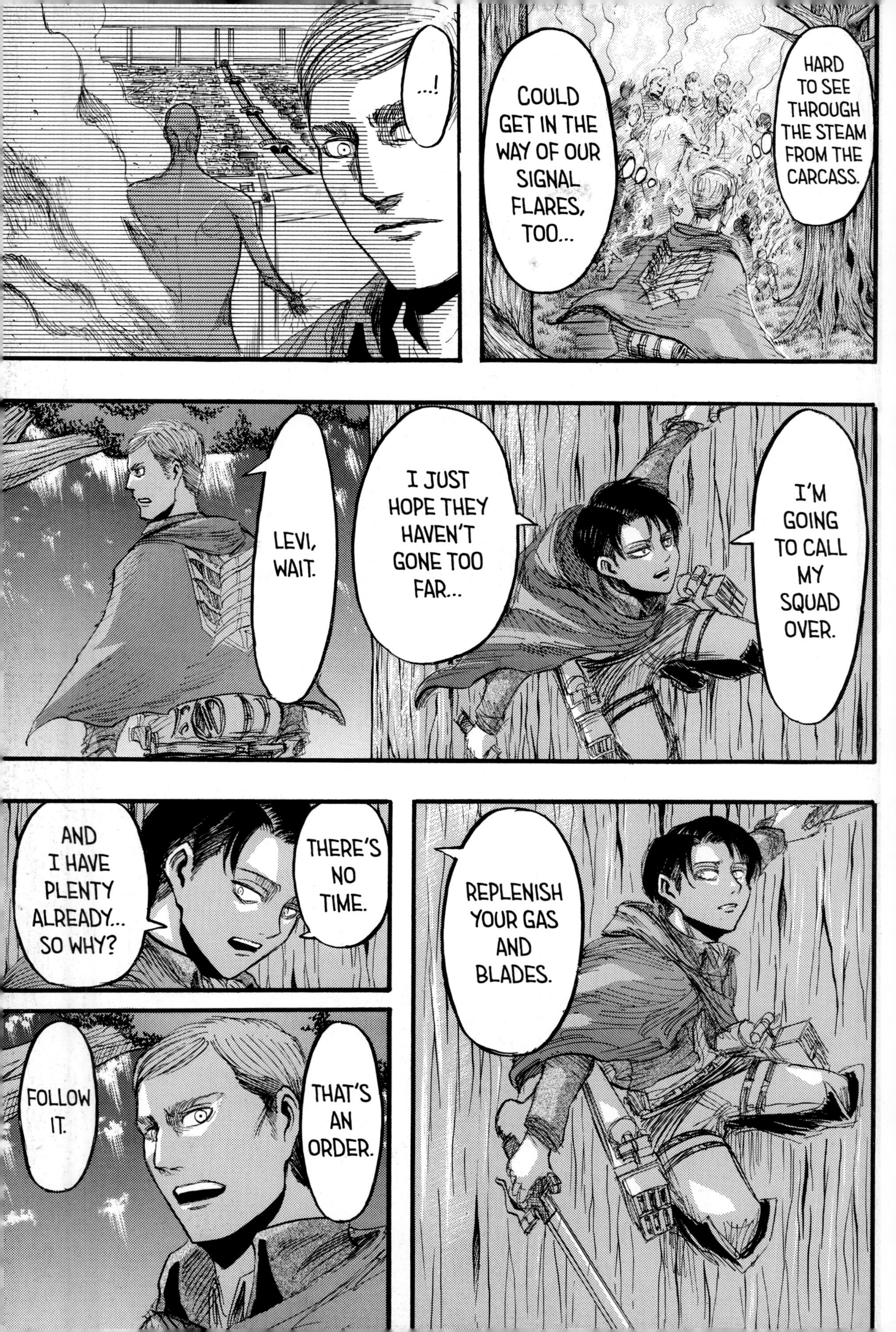
HARD TO SEE THROUGH THE STEAM FROM THE CARCASS.
COULD GET IN THE WAY OF OUR SIGNAL FLARES, TOO...
...!
I'M GOING TO CALL MY SQUAD OVER.
I JUST HOPE THEY HAVEN'T GONE TOO FAR...
LEVI, WAIT.
REPLENISH YOUR GAS AND BLADES.
THERE'S NO TIME.
AND I HAVE PLENTY ALREADY... SO WHY?
THAT'S AN ORDER.
FOLLOW IT.

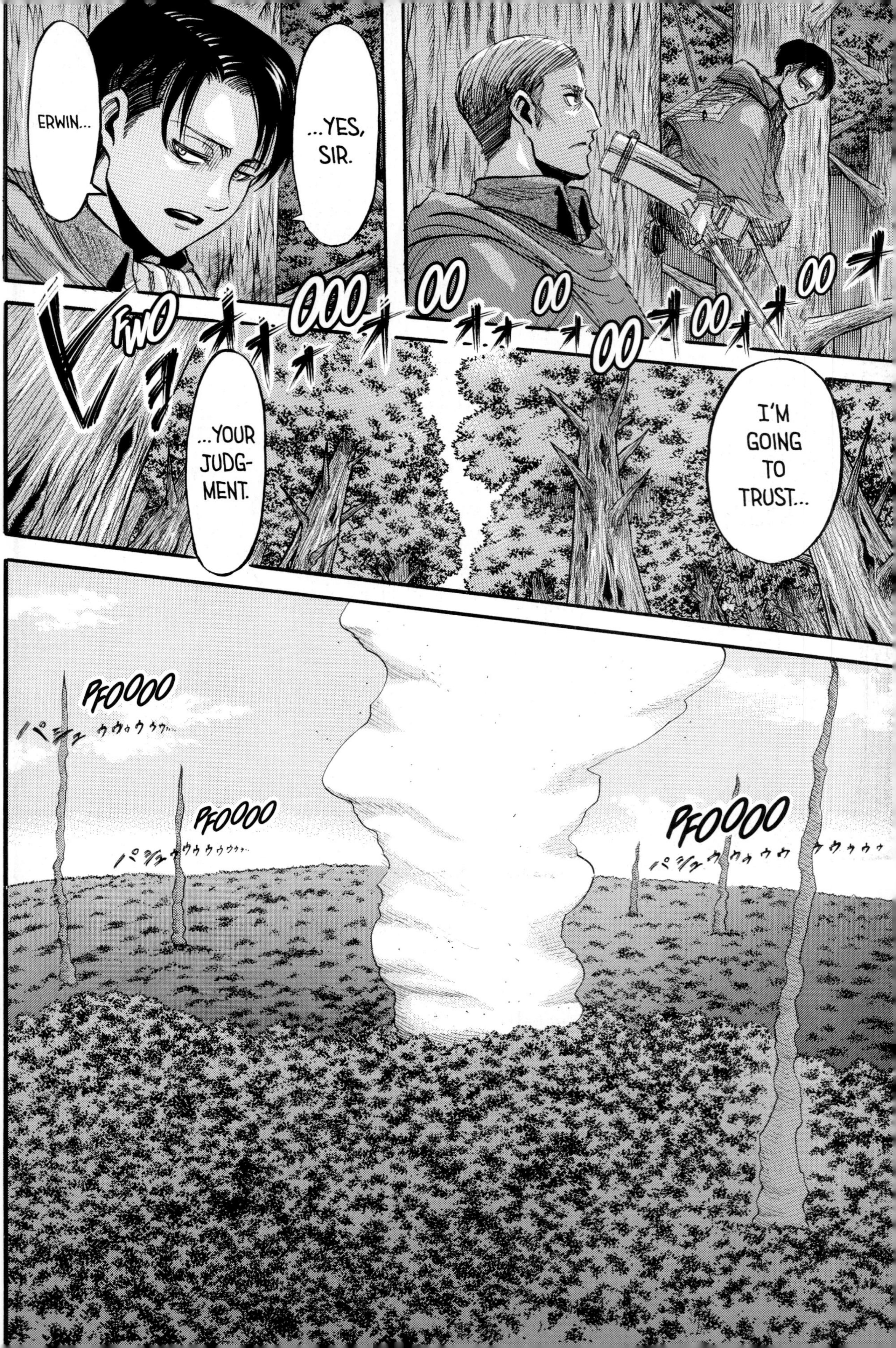
...YES, SIR.
ERWIN...
FWOOOOOOOOOOOOOO
I'M GOING TO TRUST...
...YOUR JUDGMENT.
PFOOOO
PFOOOO
PFOOOO

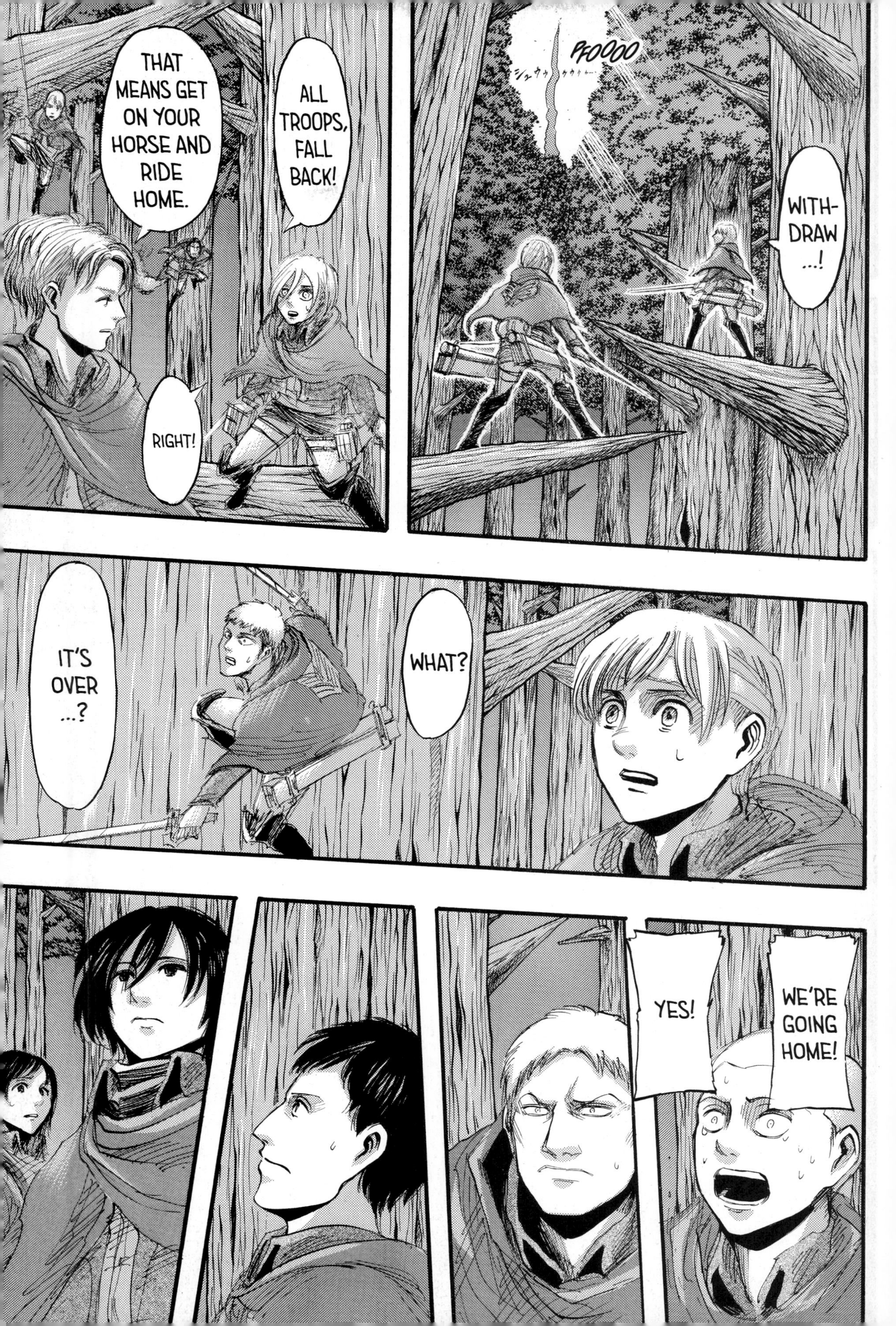
PFOOOO
WITH-DRAW ...!
ALL TROOPS, FALL BACK!
THAT MEANS GET ON YOUR HORSE AND RIDE HOME.
RIGHT!
WHAT?
IT'S OVER ...?
WE'RE GOING HOME!
YES!

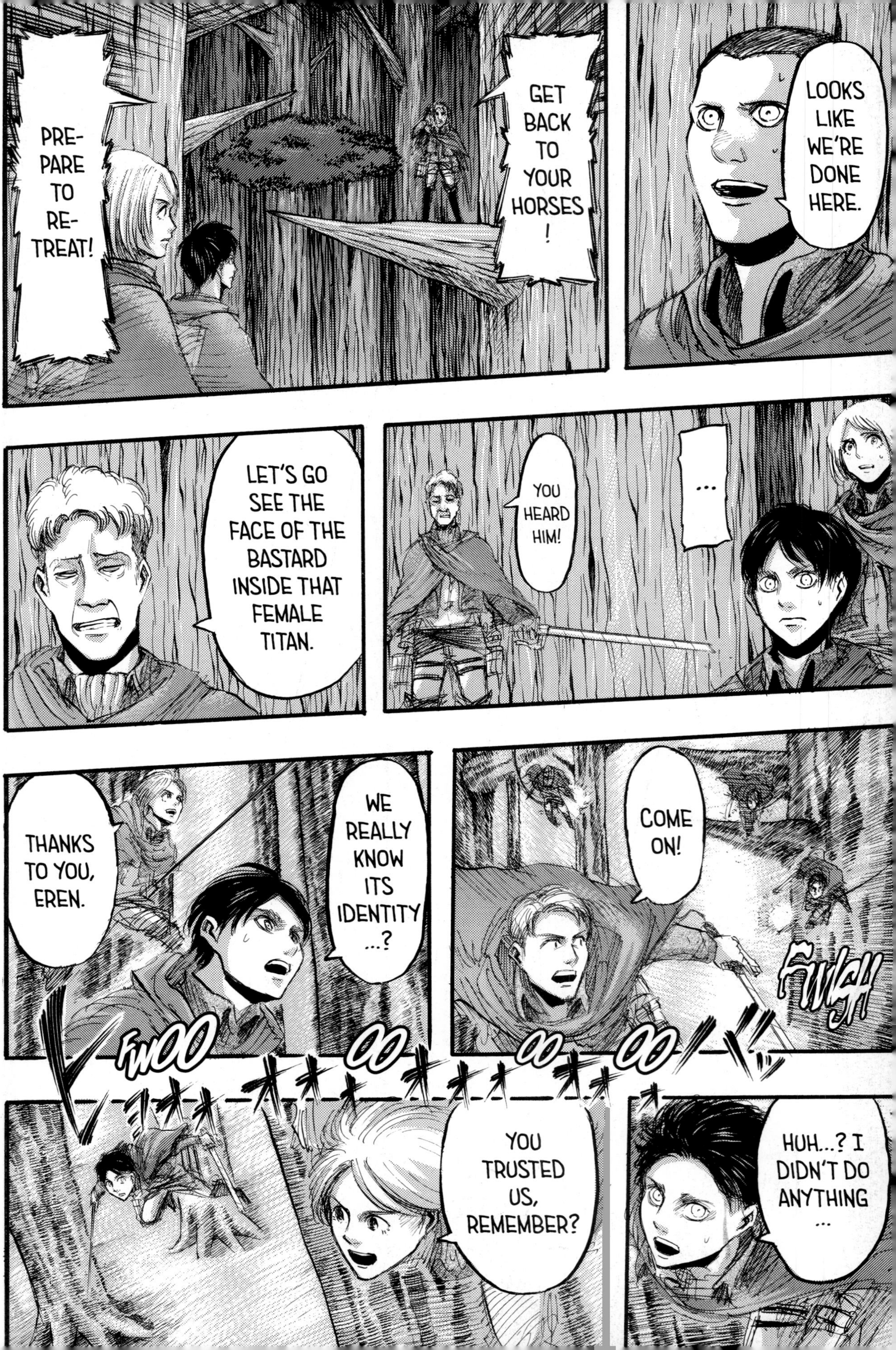
LOOKS LIKE WE'RE DONE HERE.
GET BACK TO YOUR HORSES!
PRE-PARE TO RE-TREAT!
...
YOU HEARD HIM!
LET'S GO SEE THE FACE OF THE BASTARD INSIDE THAT FEMALE TITAN.
COME ON!
WE REALLY KNOW ITS IDENTITY...?
THANKS TO YOU, EREN.
FWOO OO OO OO
HUH...? I DIDN'T DO ANYTHING...
YOU TRUSTED US, REMEMBER?

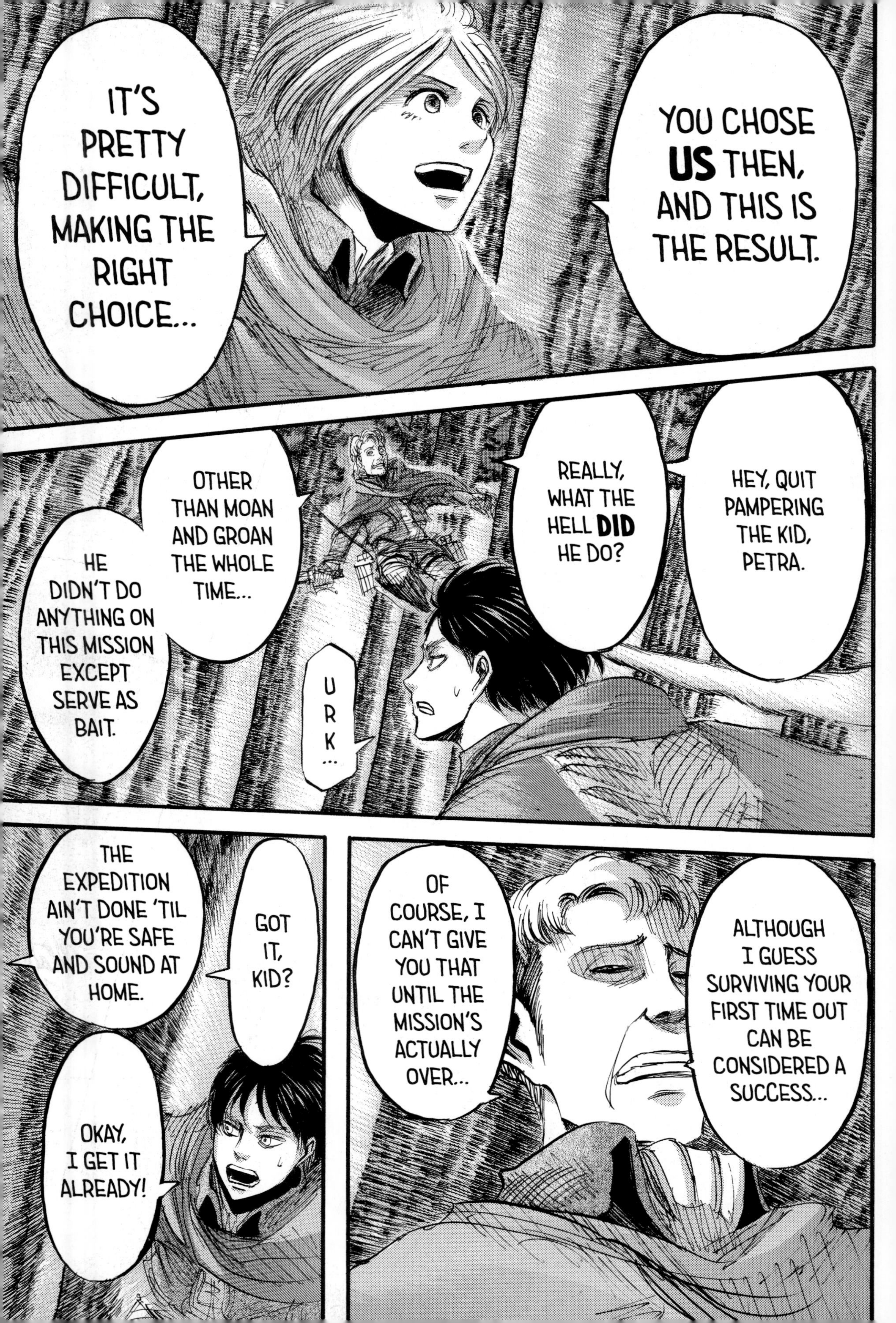
YOU CHOSE **US** THEN, AND THIS IS THE RESULT.
IT'S PRETTY DIFFICULT, MAKING THE RIGHT CHOICE...
HEY, QUIT PAMPERING THE KID, PETRA.
REALLY, WHAT THE HELL **DID** HE DO?
OTHER THAN MOAN AND GROAN THE WHOLE TIME...
URK...
HE DIDN'T DO ANYTHING ON THIS MISSION EXCEPT SERVE AS BAIT.
ALTHOUGH I GUESS SURVIVING YOUR FIRST TIME OUT CAN BE CONSIDERED A SUCCESS...
OF COURSE, I CAN'T GIVE YOU THAT UNTIL THE MISSION'S ACTUALLY OVER...
GOT IT, KID?
THE EXPEDITION AIN'T DONE 'TIL YOU'RE SAFE AND SOUND AT HOME.
OKAY, I GET IT ALREADY!

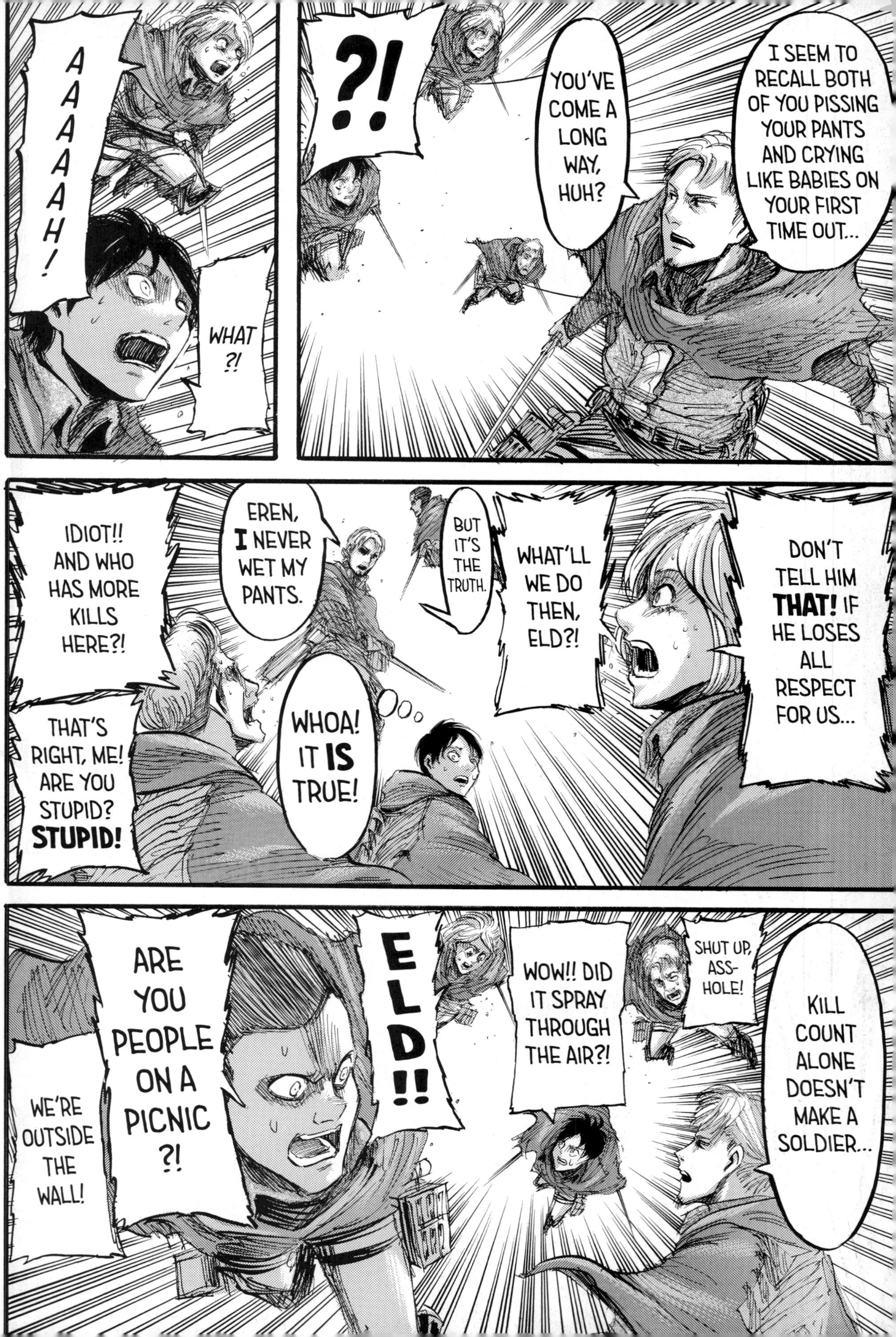
I SEEM TO RECALL BOTH OF YOU PISSING YOUR PANTS AND CRYING LIKE BABIES ON YOUR FIRST TIME OUT...
YOU'VE COME A LONG WAY, HUH?
?!
AAAAAAH!
WHAT ?!
DON'T TELL HIM **THAT!** IF HE LOSES ALL RESPECT FOR US...
WHAT'LL WE DO THEN, ELD?!
BUT IT'S THE TRUTH.
EREN, **I** NEVER WET MY PANTS.
IDIOT!! AND WHO HAS MORE KILLS HERE?!
WHOA! IT **IS** TRUE!
THAT'S RIGHT, ME! ARE YOU STUPID? **STUPID!**
SHUT UP, ASS-HOLE!
KILL COUNT ALONE DOESN'T MAKE A SOLDIER...
WOW!! DID IT SPRAY THROUGH THE AIR?!
ELD!!
ARE YOU PEOPLE ON A PICNIC ?!
WE'RE OUTSIDE THE WALL!

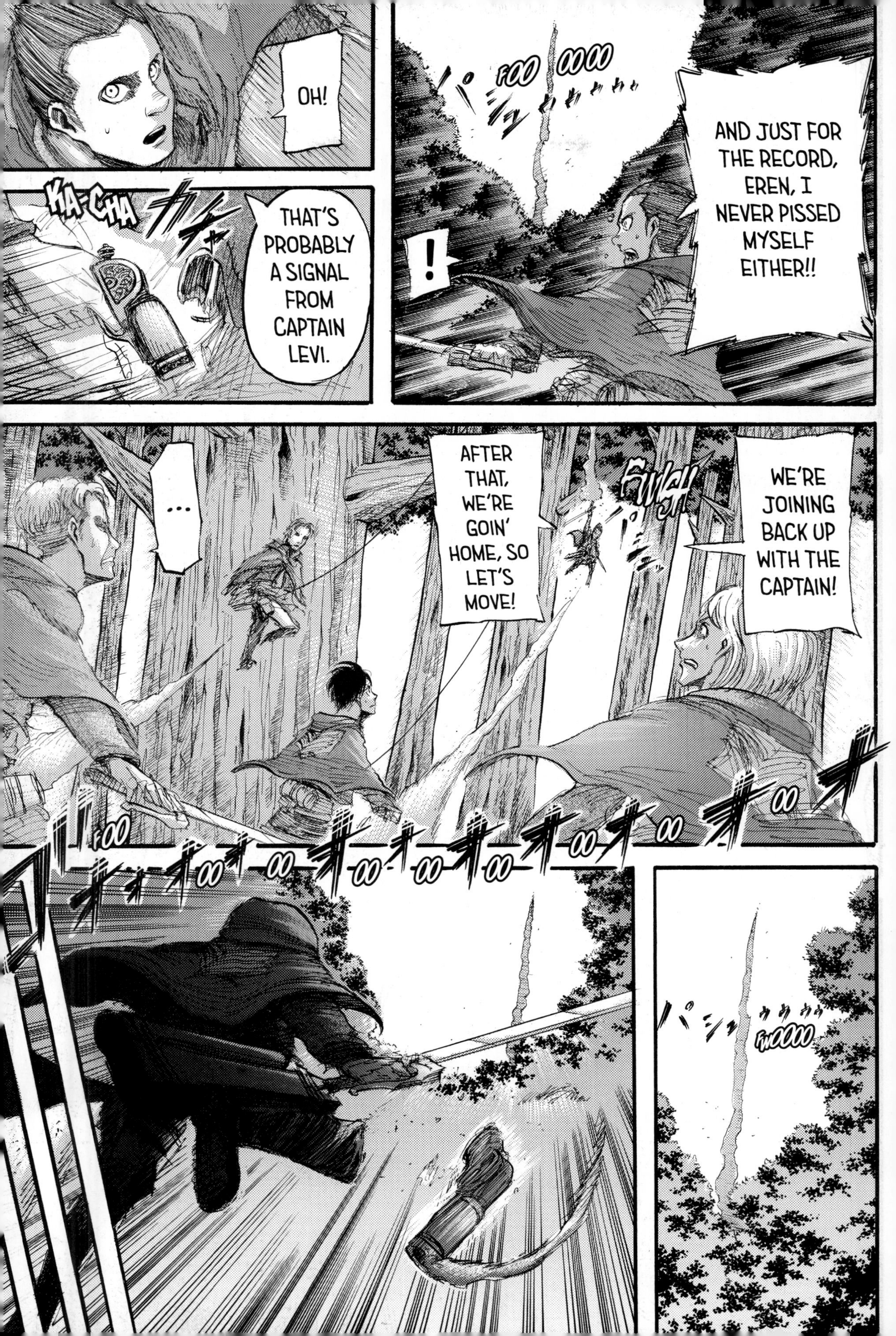

FOO OOOO
!
AND JUST FOR THE RECORD, EREN, I NEVER PISSED MYSELF EITHER!!
OH!
KA-CHA
THAT'S PROBABLY A SIGNAL FROM CAPTAIN LEVI.
WE'RE JOINING BACK UP WITH THE CAPTAIN!
FWSH
AFTER THAT, WE'RE GOIN' HOME, SO LET'S MOVE!
...
FOO OO OO OO OO OO OO OO OO OO OO OO OO
FWOOOO

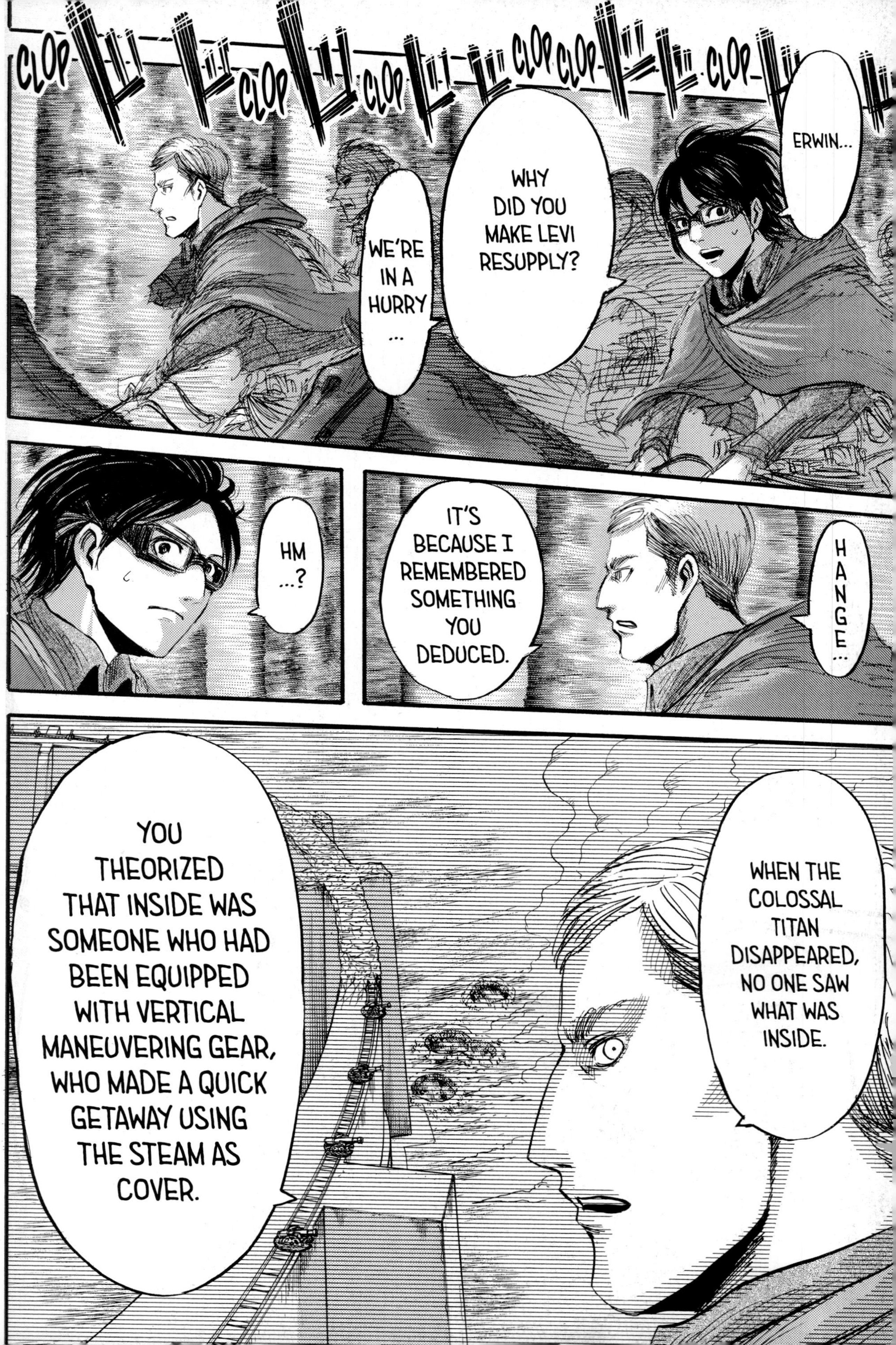
CLOP CLOP CLOP CLOP CLOP CLOP CLOP
ERWIN...
WHY DID YOU MAKE LEVI RESUPPLY?
WE'RE IN A HURRY ...
HANGE...
IT'S BECAUSE I REMEMBERED SOMETHING YOU DEDUCED.
HM ...?
WHEN THE COLOSSAL TITAN DISAPPEARED, NO ONE SAW WHAT WAS INSIDE.
YOU THEORIZED THAT INSIDE WAS SOMEONE WHO HAD BEEN EQUIPPED WITH VERTICAL MANEUVERING GEAR, WHO MADE A QUICK GETAWAY USING THE STEAM AS COVER.

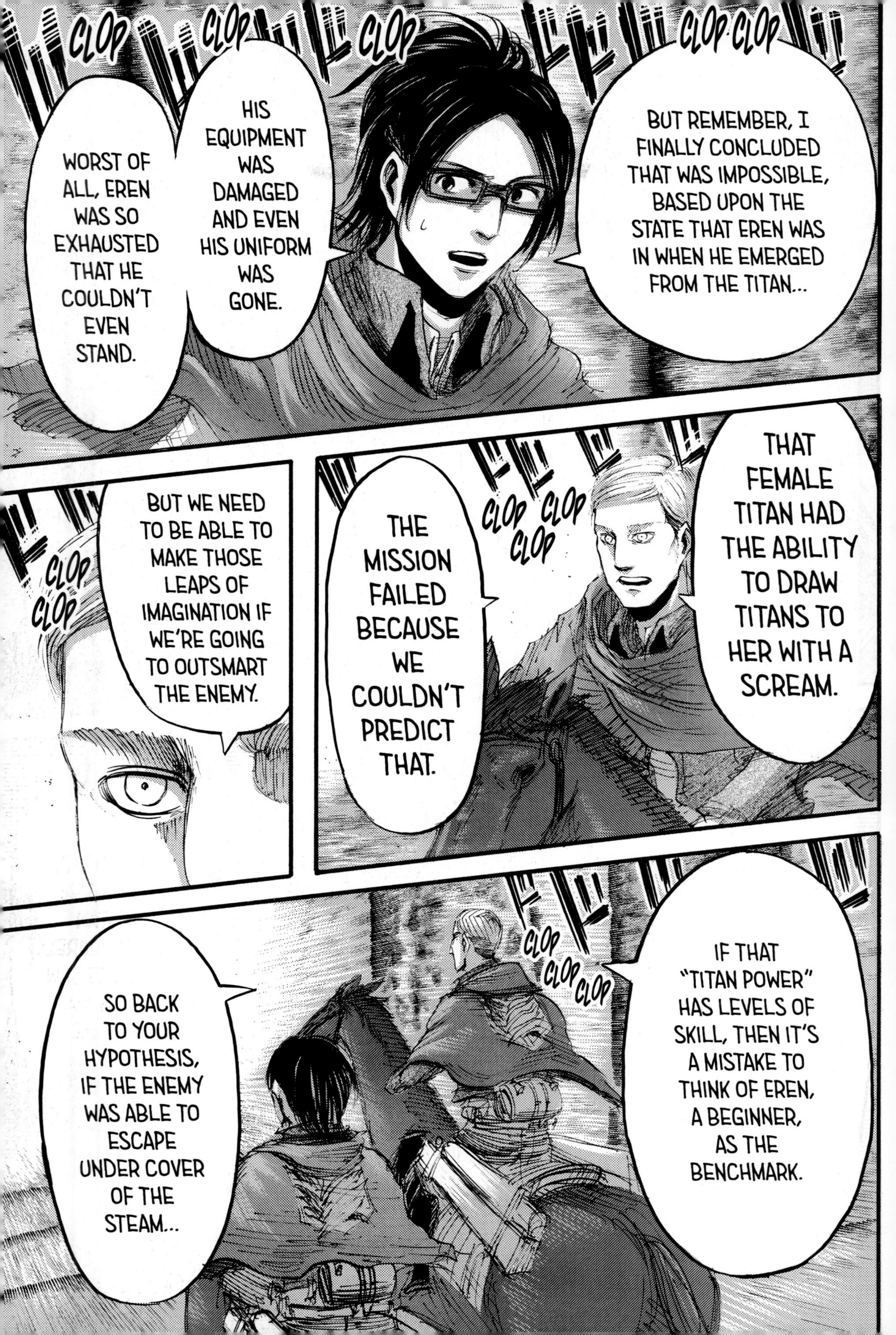
CLOP CLOP
CLOP
CLOP
CLOP
BUT REMEMBER, I FINALLY CONCLUDED THAT WAS IMPOSSIBLE, BASED UPON THE STATE THAT EREN WAS IN WHEN HE EMERGED FROM THE TITAN...
HIS EQUIPMENT WAS DAMAGED AND EVEN HIS UNIFORM WAS GONE.
WORST OF ALL, EREN WAS SO EXHAUSTED THAT HE COULDN'T EVEN STAND.
THAT FEMALE TITAN HAD THE ABILITY TO DRAW TITANS TO HER WITH A SCREAM.
CLOP CLOP CLOP
THE MISSION FAILED BECAUSE WE COULDN'T PREDICT THAT.
BUT WE NEED TO BE ABLE TO MAKE THOSE LEAPS OF IMAGINATION IF WE'RE GOING TO OUTSMART THE ENEMY.
CLOP CLOP
IF THAT "TITAN POWER" HAS LEVELS OF SKILL, THEN IT'S A MISTAKE TO THINK OF EREN, A BEGINNER, AS THE BENCHMARK.
CLOP CLOP CLOP
SO BACK TO YOUR HYPOTHESIS, IF THE ENEMY WAS ABLE TO ESCAPE UNDER COVER OF THE STEAM...

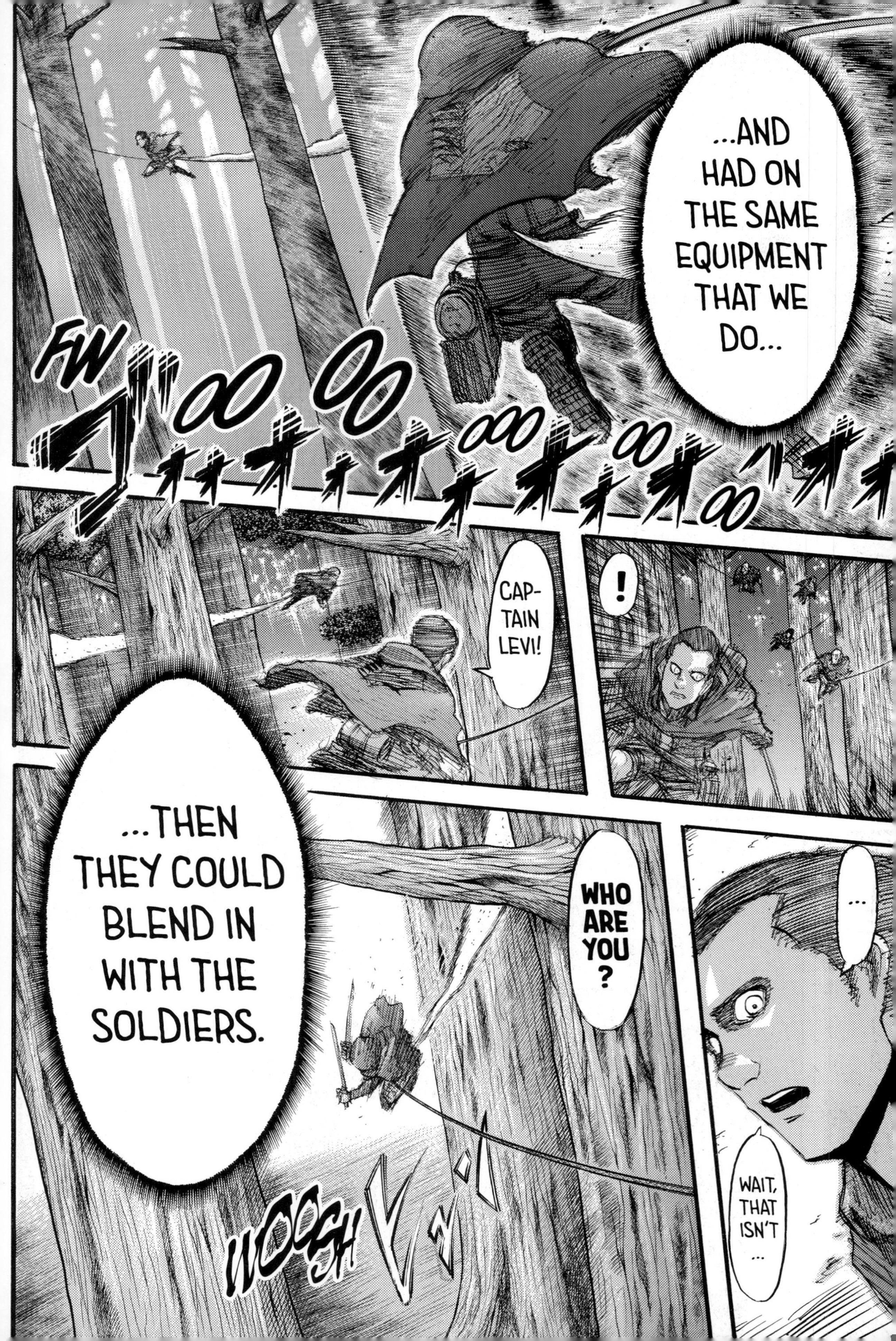

...AND HAD ON THE SAME EQUIPMENT THAT WE DO...
FWOOOOOOOOOOOO
!
CAP-TAIN LEVI!
...
WAIT, THAT ISN'T ...
WHO ARE YOU?
...THEN THEY COULD BLEND IN WITH THE SOLDIERS.
WHOOSH

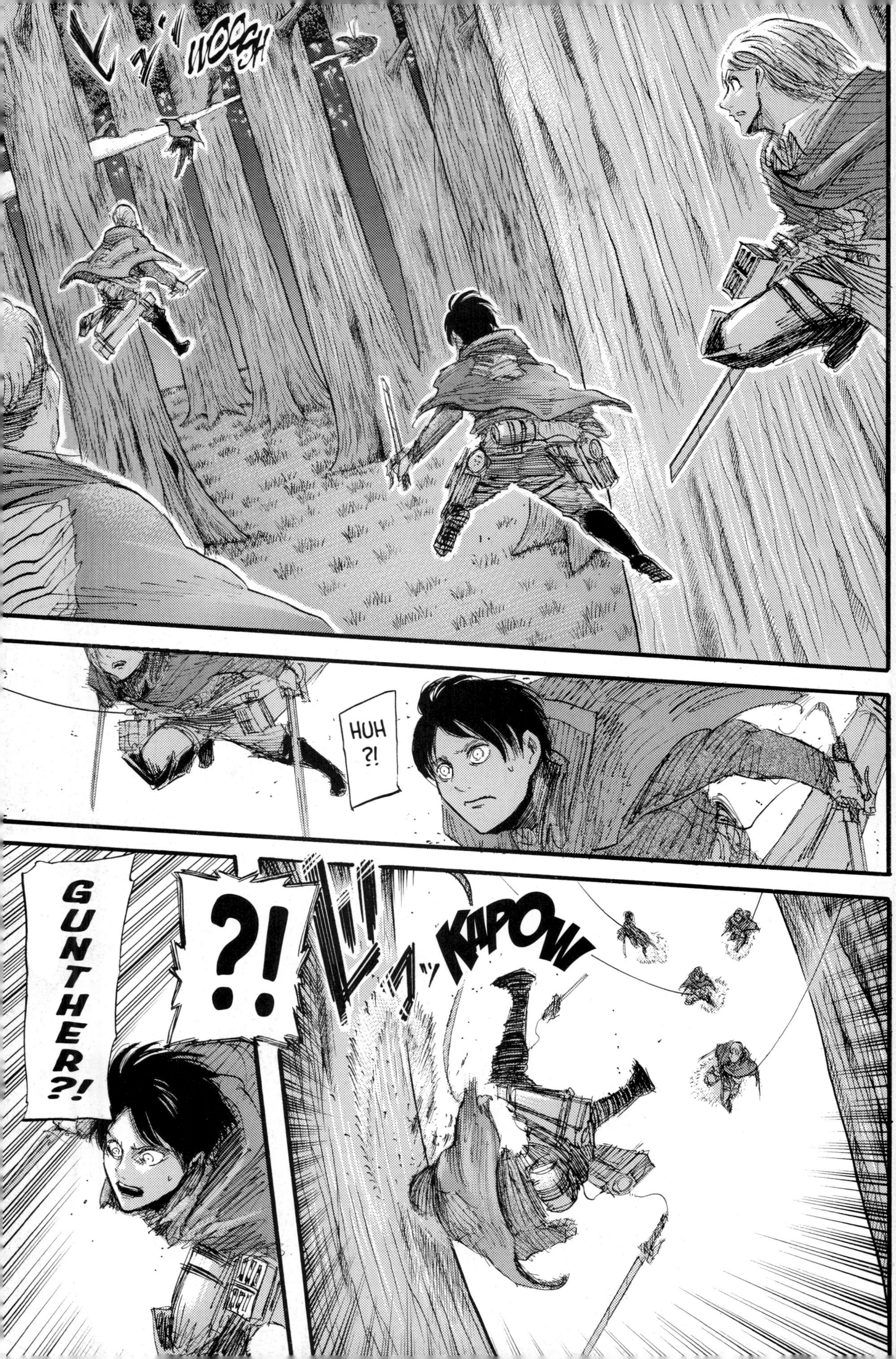

WOOSH
HUH ?!
KAPOW
?!
GUNTHER?!

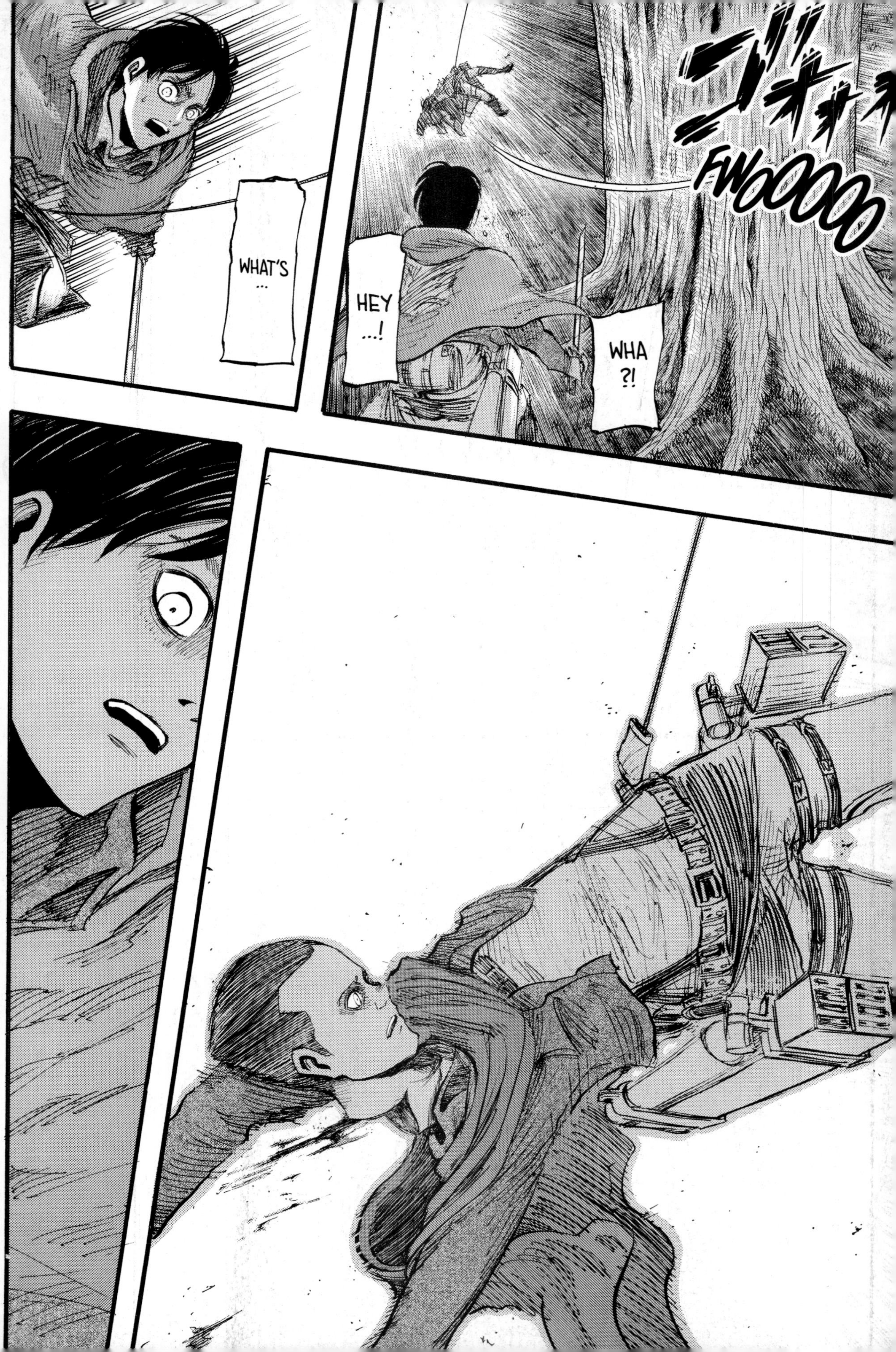
FWOOOOO
WHA ?!
HEY ...!
WHAT'S ...

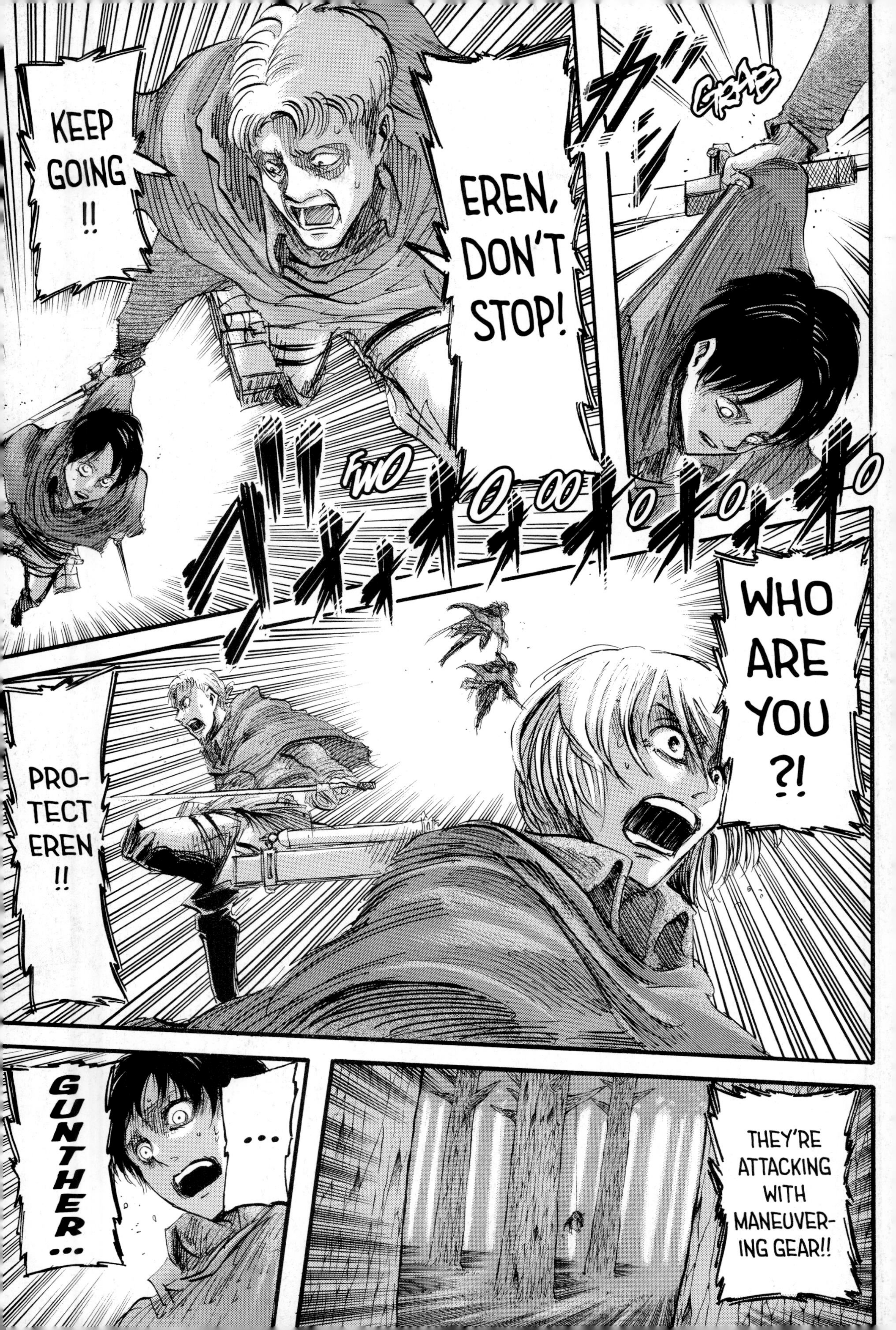
GRAB
EREN, DON'T STOP!
KEEP GOING!!
FWOOOOOOOO
WHO ARE YOU?!
PROTECT EREN!!
THEY'RE ATTACKING WITH MANEUVERING GEAR!!
...
GUNTHER...

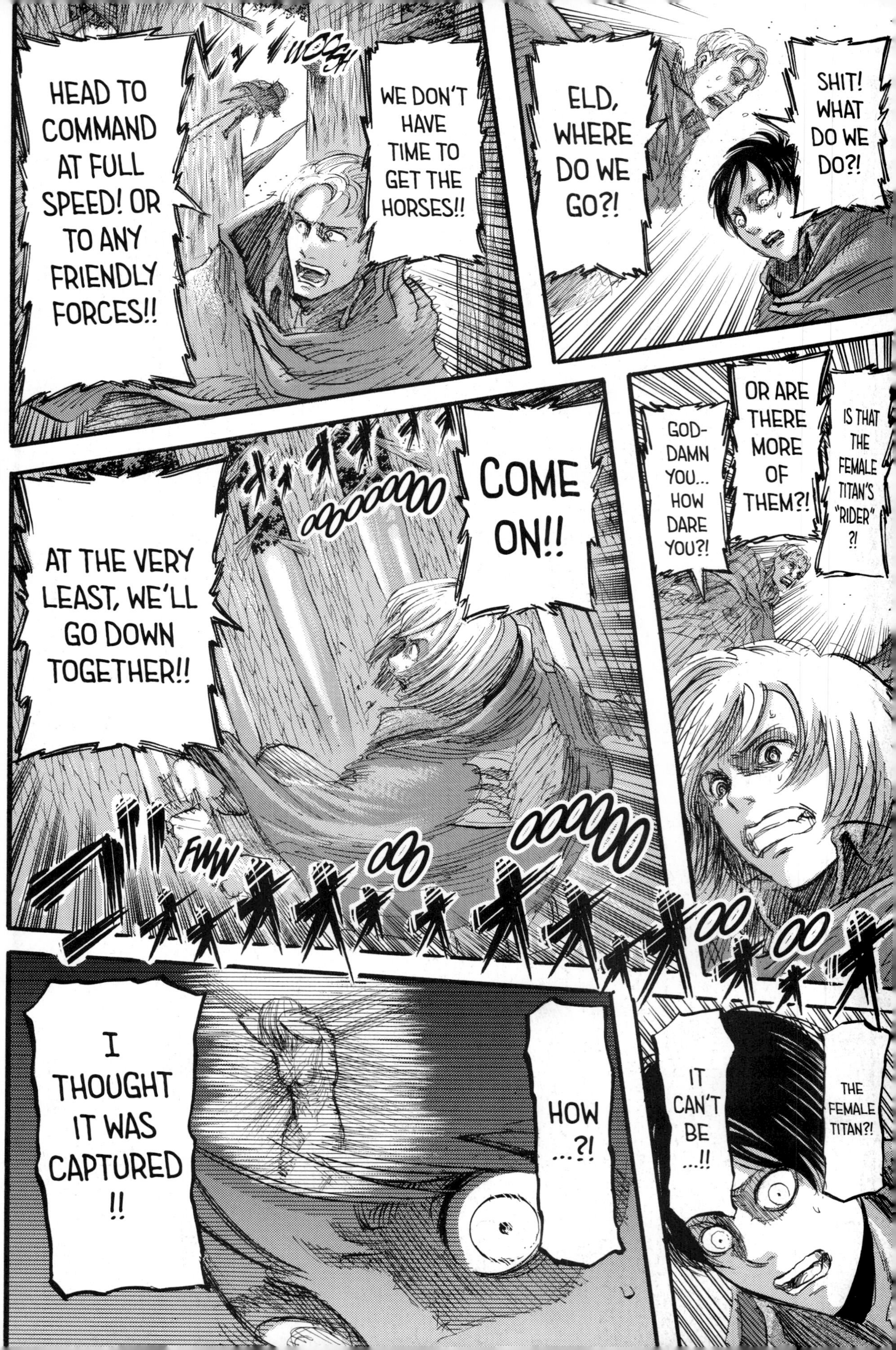
SHIT! WHAT DO WE DO?!
ELD, WHERE DO WE GO?!
WOOSH
WE DON'T HAVE TIME TO GET THE HORSES!!
HEAD TO COMMAND AT FULL SPEED! OR TO ANY FRIENDLY FORCES!!
IS THAT THE FEMALE TITAN'S "RIDER"?!
OR ARE THERE MORE OF THEM?!
GOD-DAMN YOU... HOW DARE YOU?!
COME ON!!
OOOOOOOOOO
AT THE VERY LEAST, WE'LL GO DOWN TOGETHER!!
FWW
OOOOOOO
OO
THE FEMALE TITAN?!
IT CAN'T BE ...!!
HOW ...?!
I THOUGHT IT WAS CAPTURED !!

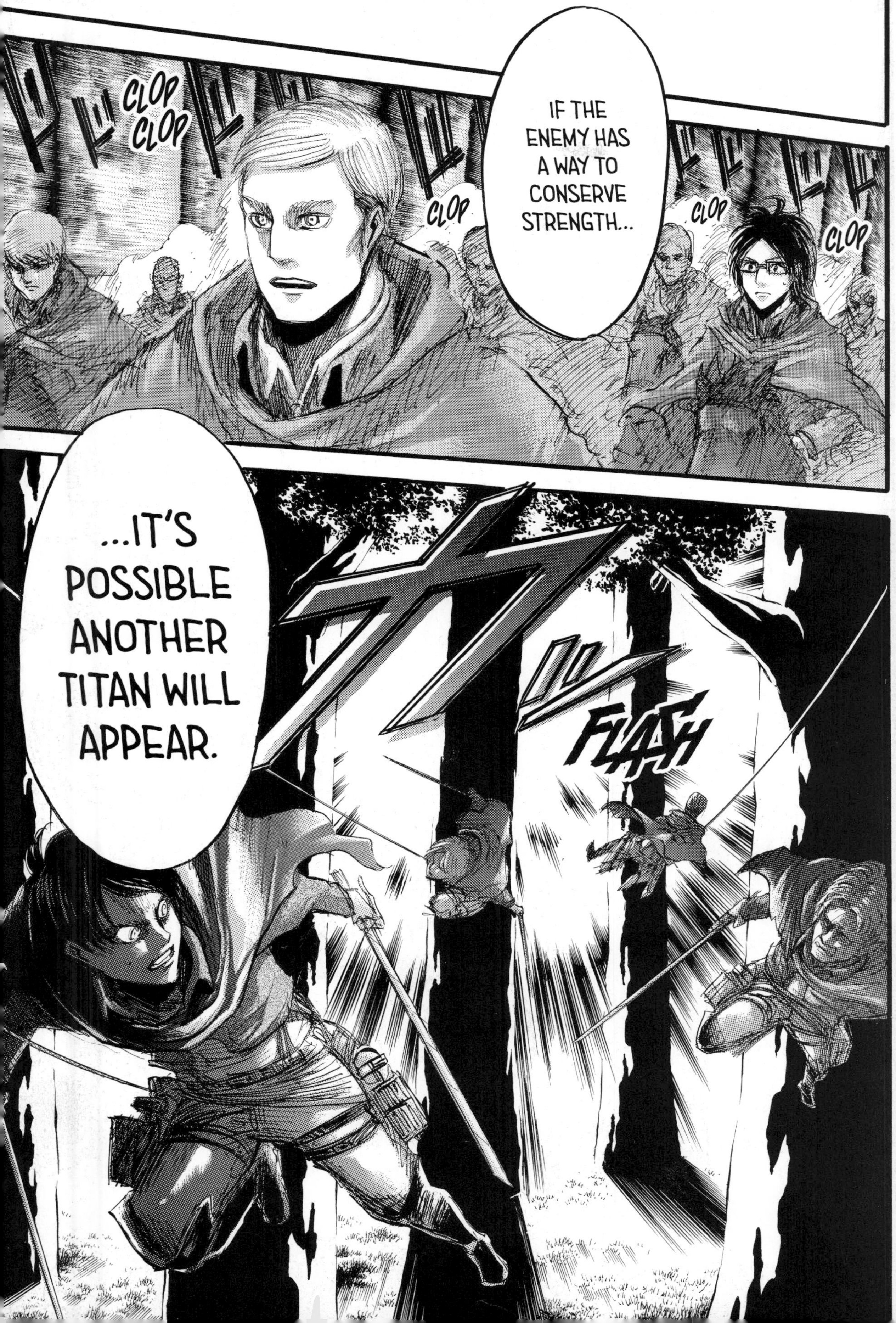
CLOP
CLOP
IF THE ENEMY HAS A WAY TO CONSERVE STRENGTH...
CLOP
CLOP CLOP
...IT'S POSSIBLE ANOTHER TITAN WILL APPEAR.
FLASH

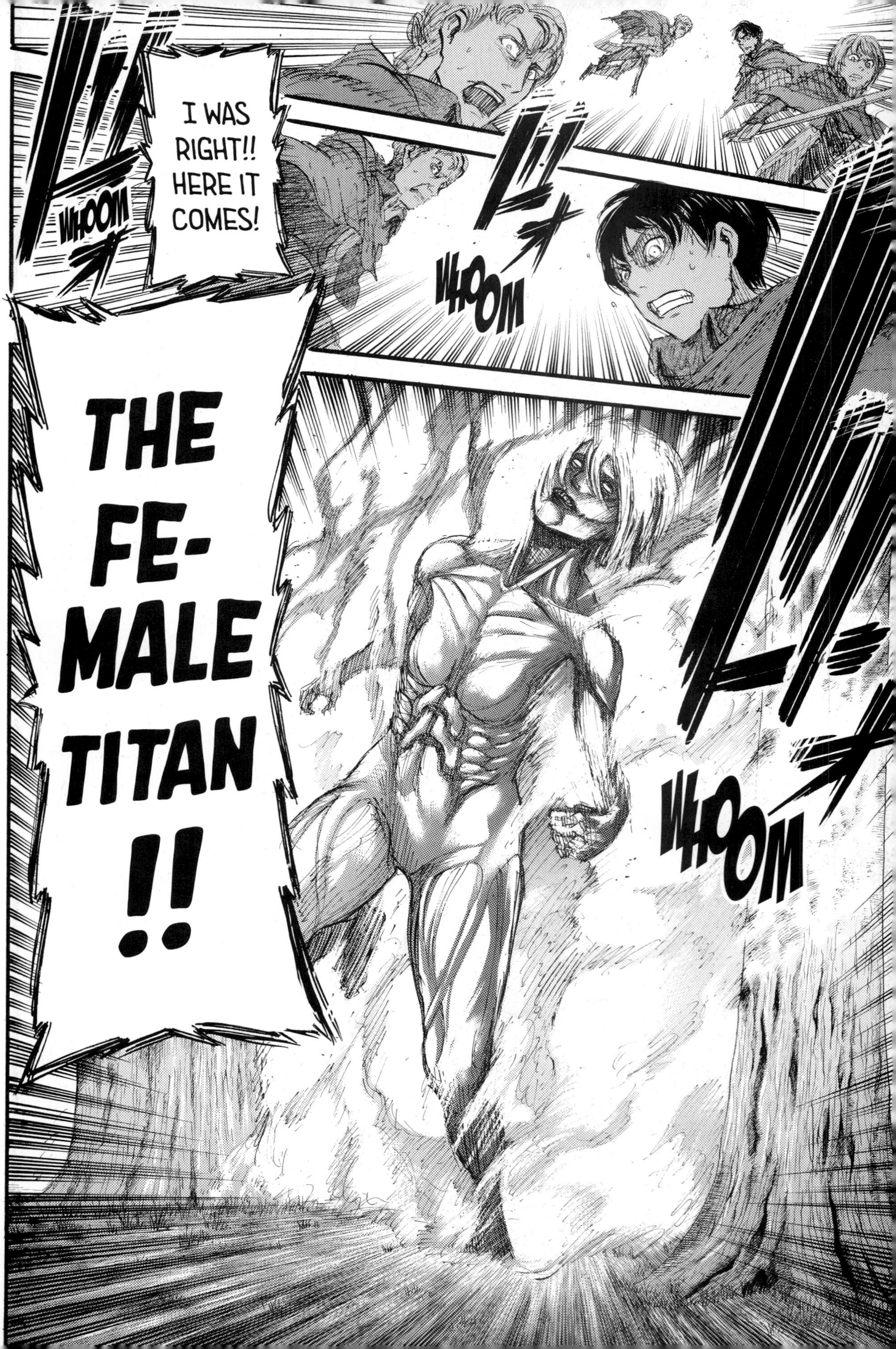
I WAS RIGHT!! HERE IT COMES!
WHOOM
WHOOM
WHOOM
THE FE-MALE TITAN!!

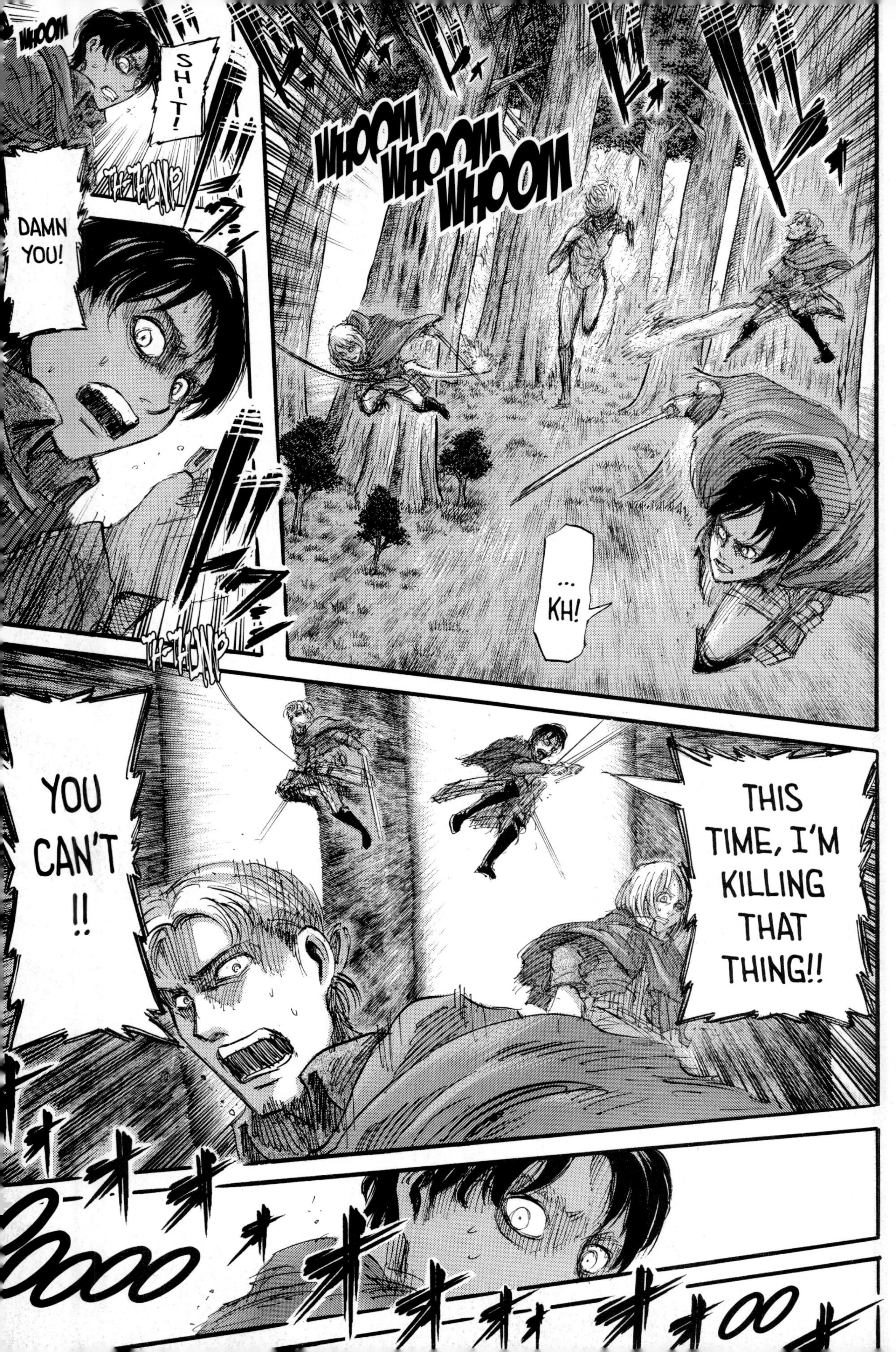
WHOOM WHOOM WHOOM
... KH!
WHOOM
SHIT!
TH-THOMP
DAMN YOU!
TH-THOMP
THIS TIME, I'M KILLING THAT THING!!
YOU CAN'T !!

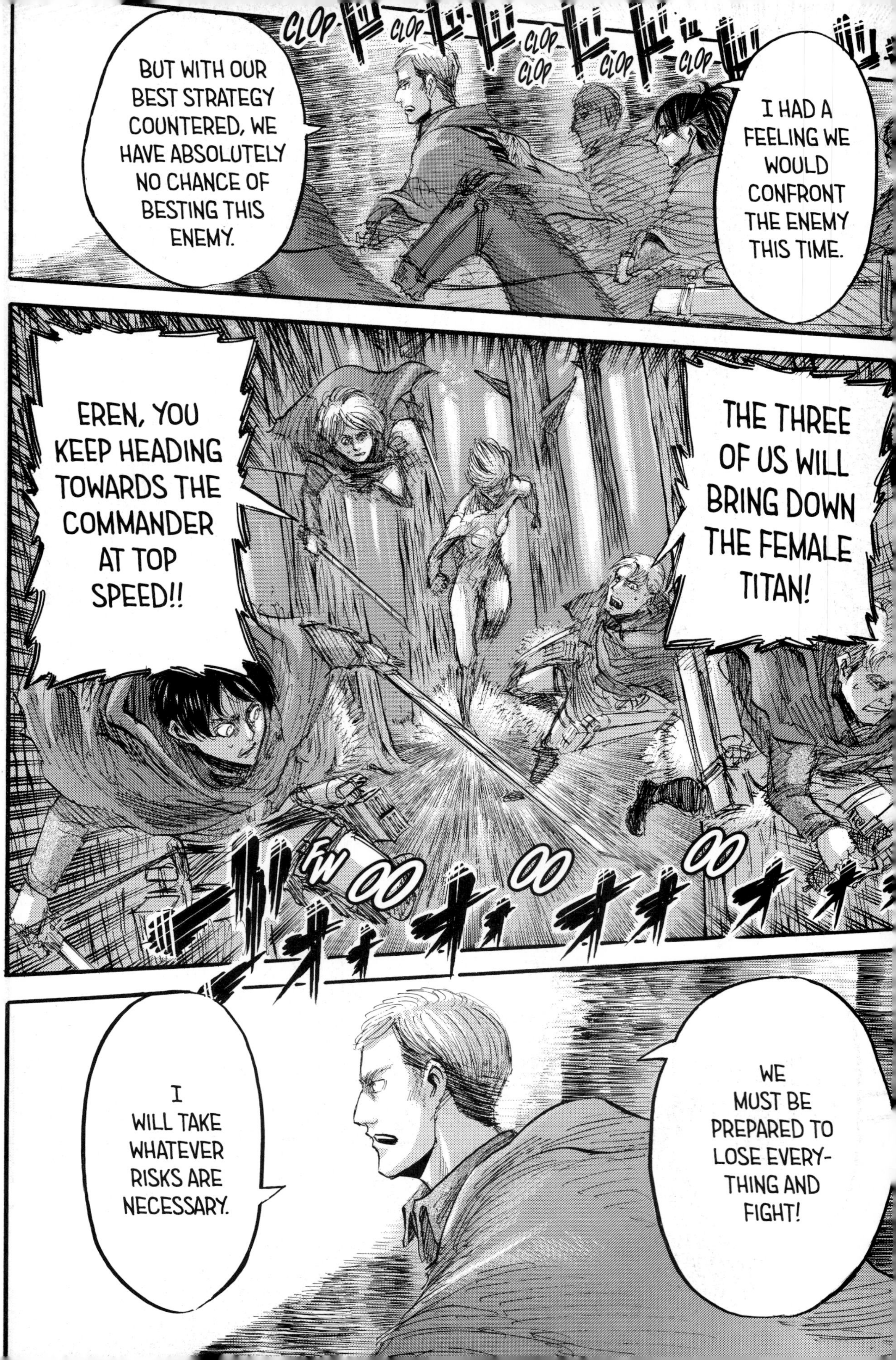
CLOP CLOP CLOP CLOP CLOP CLOP
I HAD A FEELING WE WOULD CONFRONT THE ENEMY THIS TIME.
BUT WITH OUR BEST STRATEGY COUNTERED, WE HAVE ABSOLUTELY NO CHANCE OF BESTING THIS ENEMY.
THE THREE OF US WILL BRING DOWN THE FEMALE TITAN!
EREN, YOU KEEP HEADING TOWARDS THE COMMANDER AT TOP SPEED!!
FWOOOO
WE MUST BE PREPARED TO LOSE EVERY-THING AND FIGHT!
I WILL TAKE WHATEVER RISKS ARE NECESSARY.

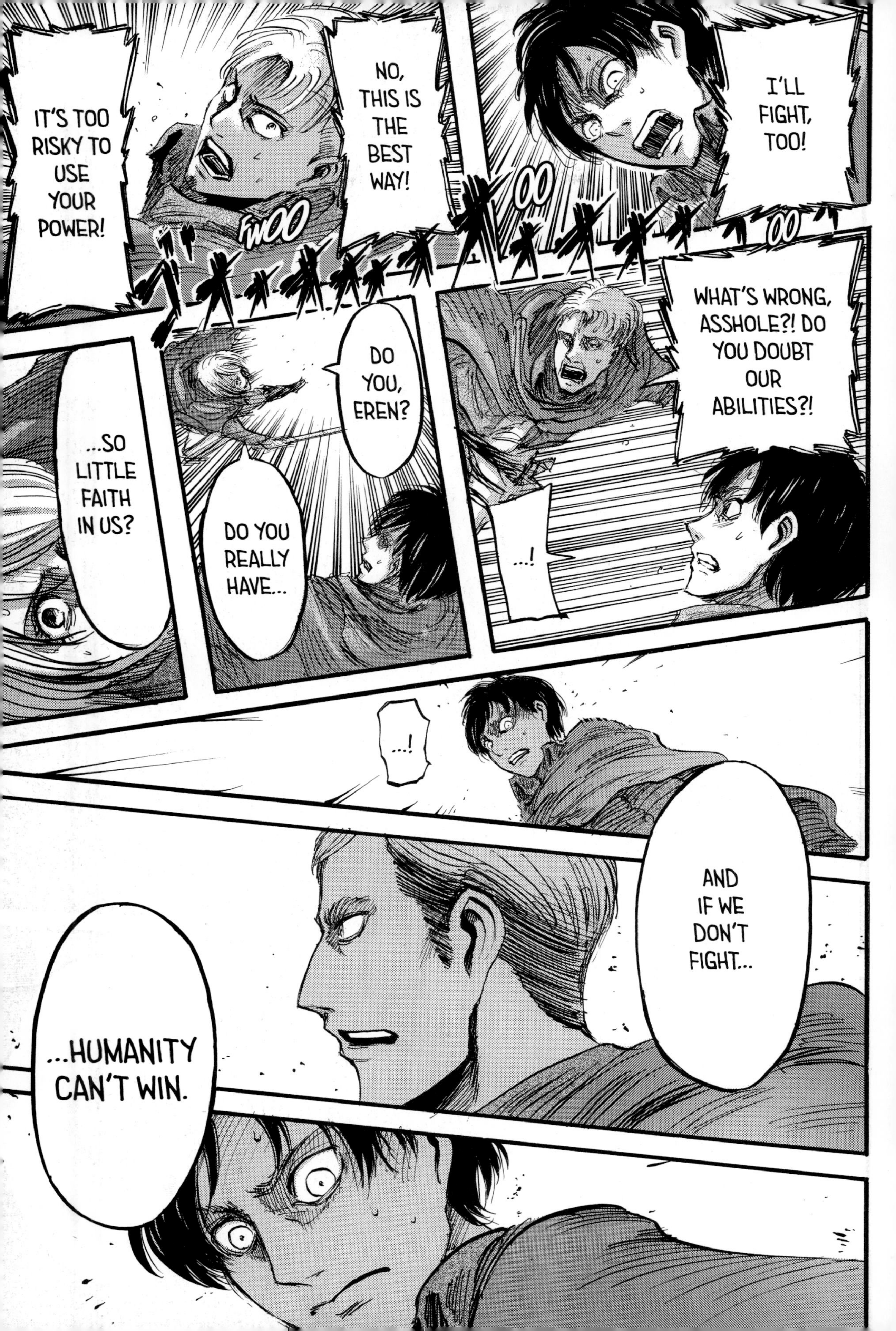
I'LL FIGHT, TOO!
OO
NO, THIS IS THE BEST WAY!
IT'S TOO RISKY TO USE YOUR POWER!
FWOO
OO
WHAT'S WRONG, ASSHOLE?! DO YOU DOUBT OUR ABILITIES?!
...!
DO YOU, EREN?
DO YOU REALLY HAVE...
...SO LITTLE FAITH IN US?
...!
AND IF WE DON'T FIGHT...
...HUMANITY CAN'T WIN.

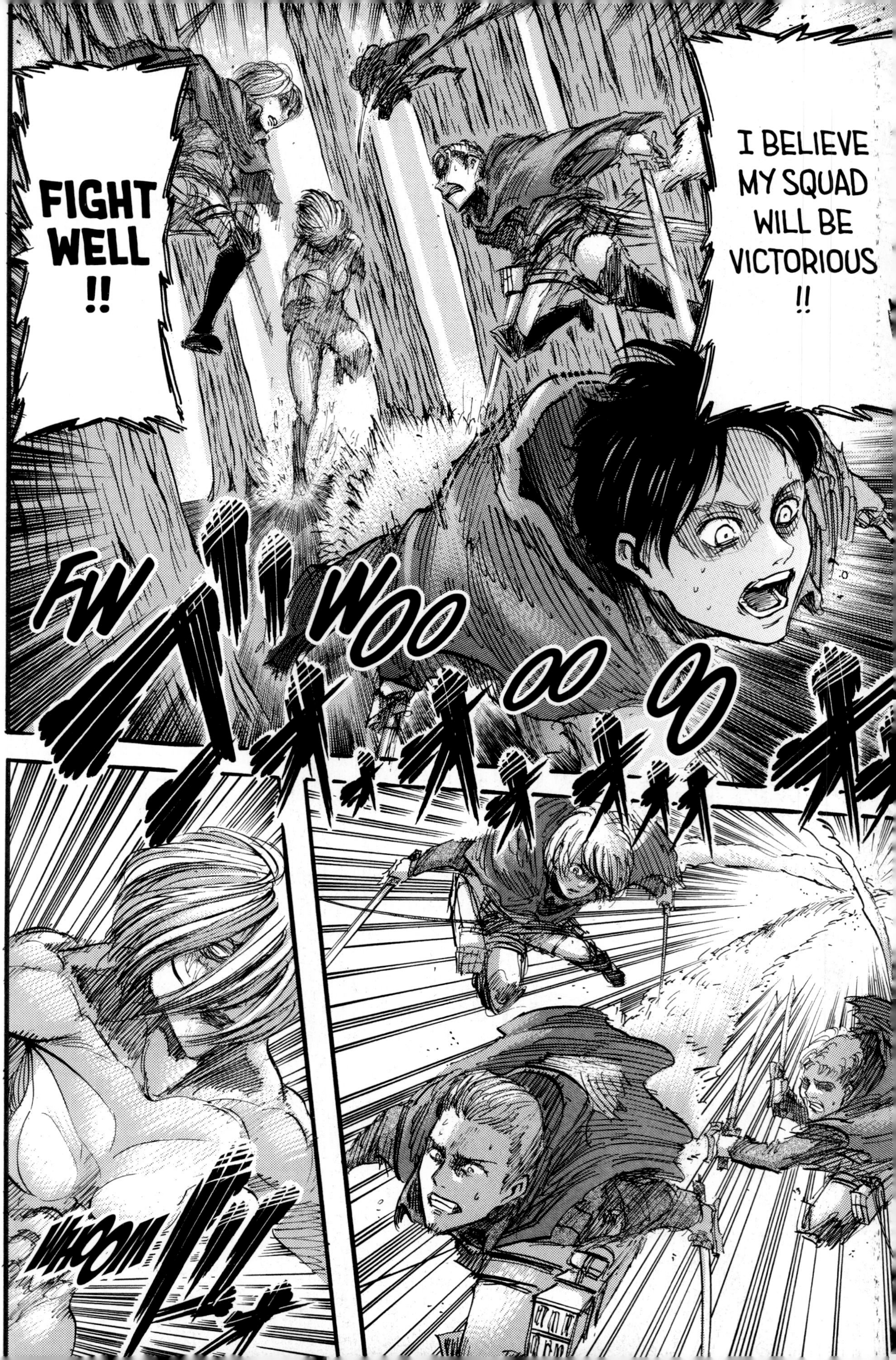
I BELIEVE MY SQUAD WILL BE VICTORIOUS !!
FIGHT WELL !!
FWWOOOOO
WHOOM

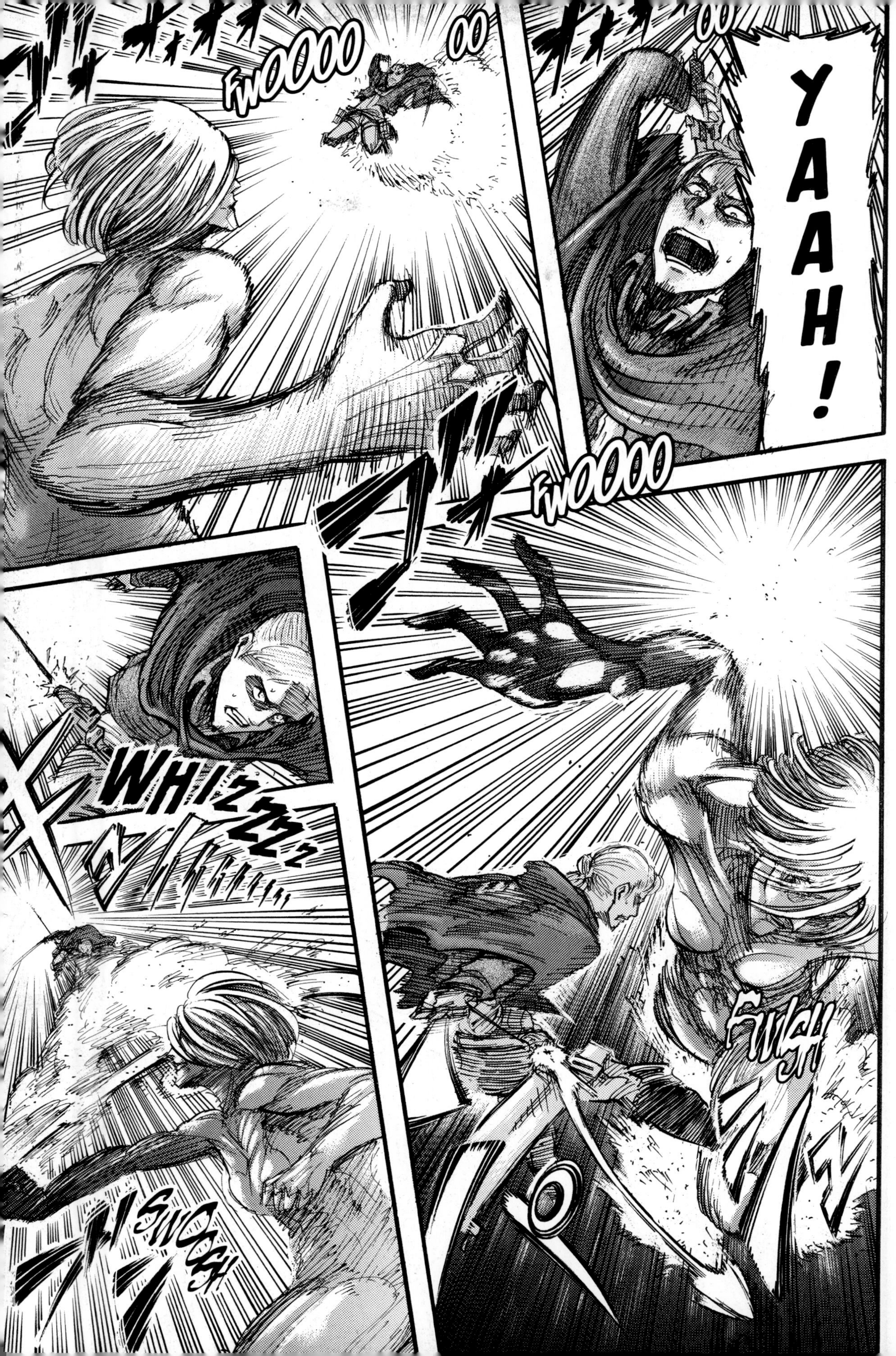
YAAH!
FWOOOO
FWOOOO OO
FWISH!
WHIZZZZ
SWOOSH!

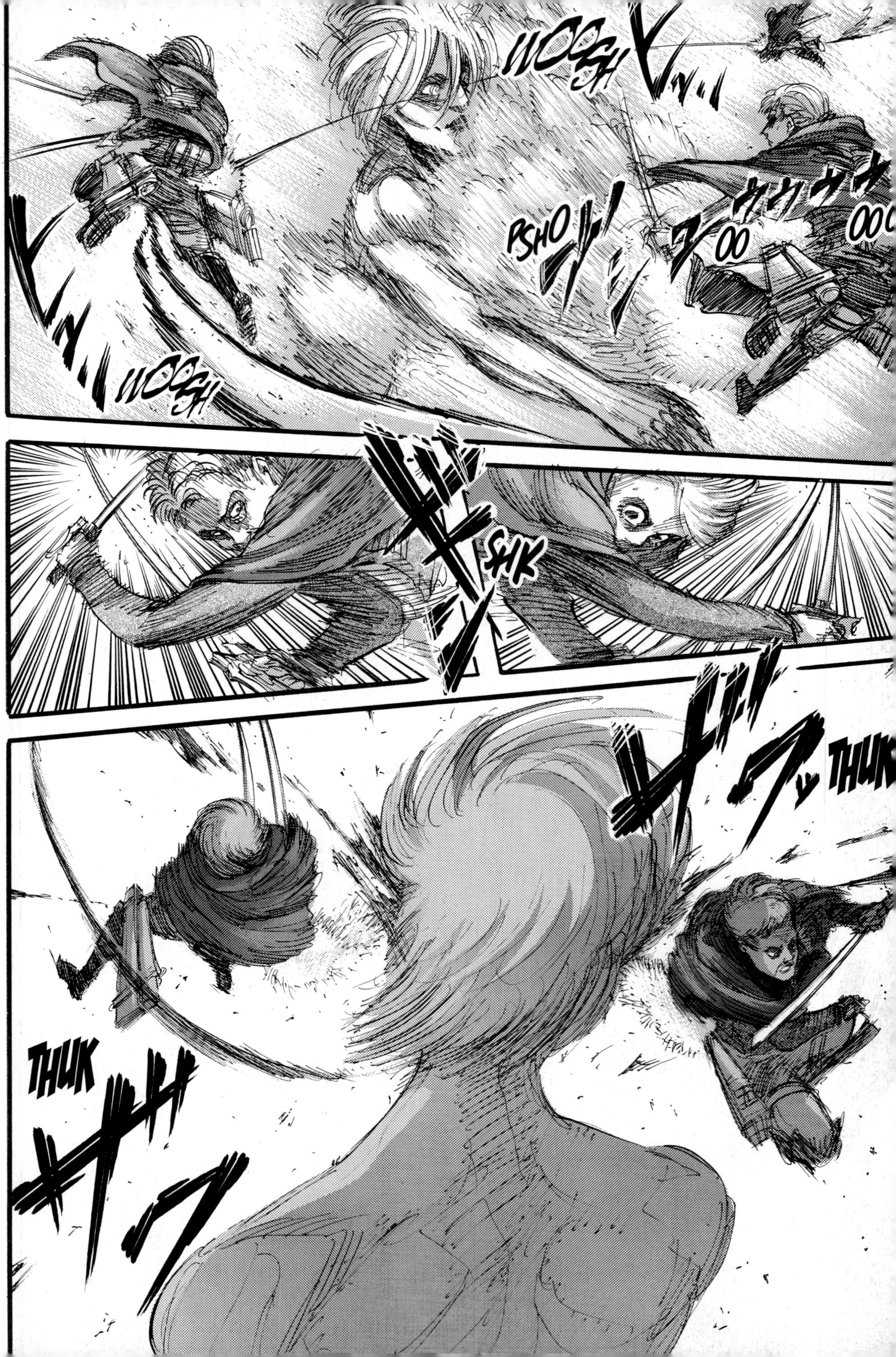

WOOSH
PSHO
OO
WOOSH
SHK
THUK
THUK

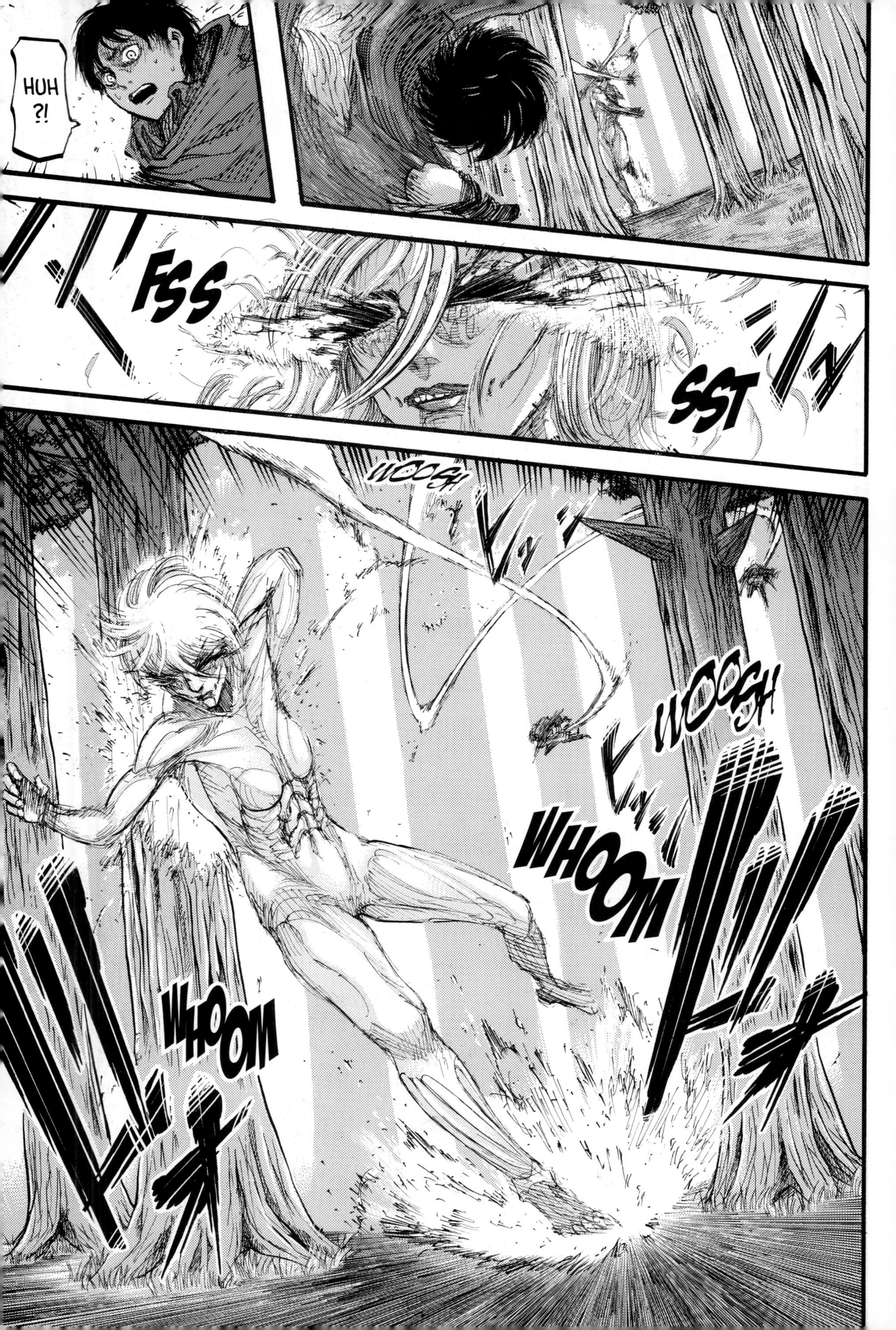

HUH ?!
FSS
SST
WOOSH
WOOSH
WHOOM
WHOOM

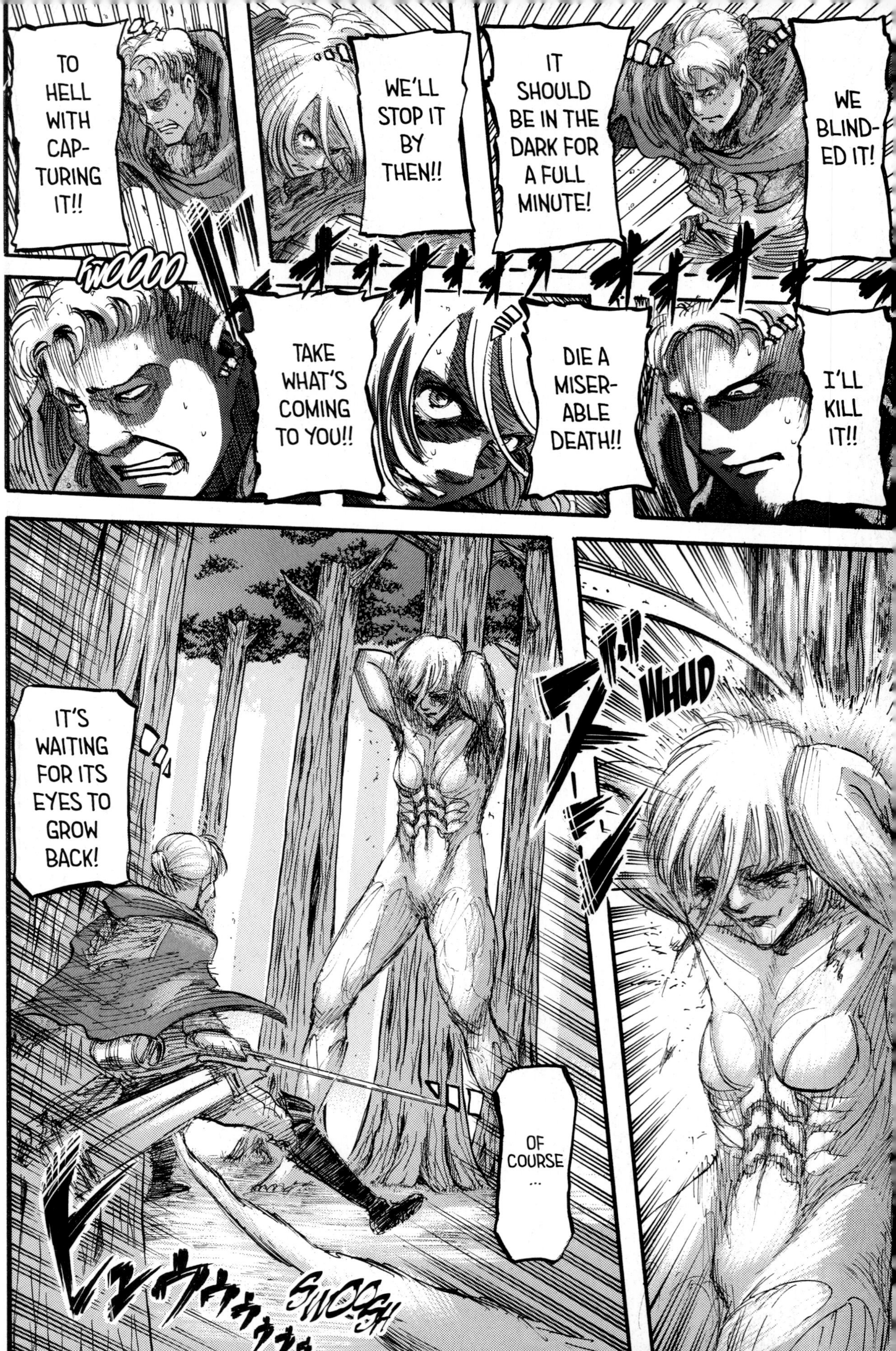
WE BLINDED IT!
IT SHOULD BE IN THE DARK FOR A FULL MINUTE!
WE'LL STOP IT BY THEN!!
TO HELL WITH CAPTURING IT!!
I'LL KILL IT!!
DIE A MISERABLE DEATH!!
TAKE WHAT'S COMING TO YOU!!
FWOOOO
WHUD
IT'S WAITING FOR ITS EYES TO GROW BACK!
OF COURSE...
SWOOSH

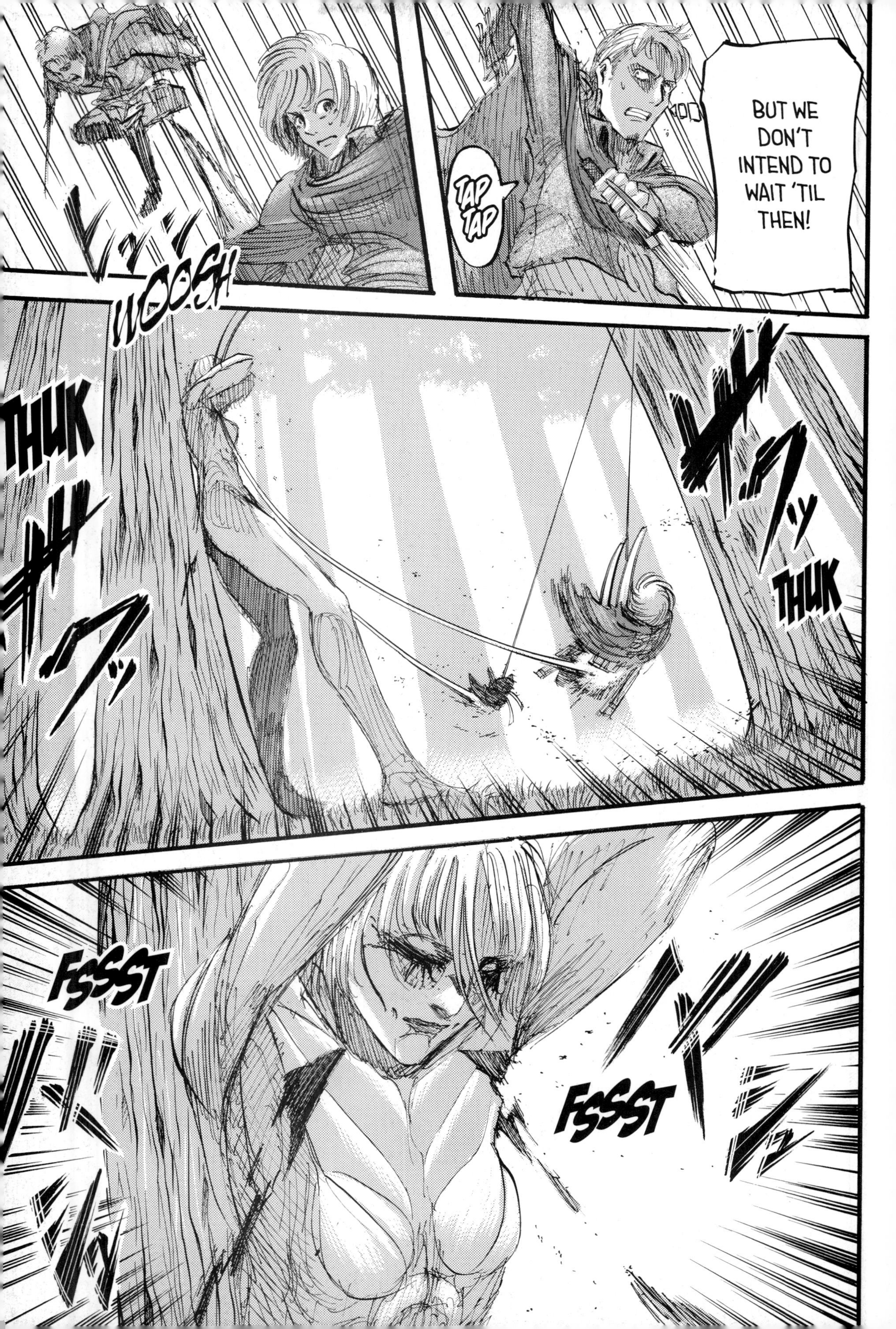
BUT WE DON'T INTEND TO WAIT 'TIL THEN!
TAP TAP
WOOSH
THUK
THUK
FSSST
FSSST

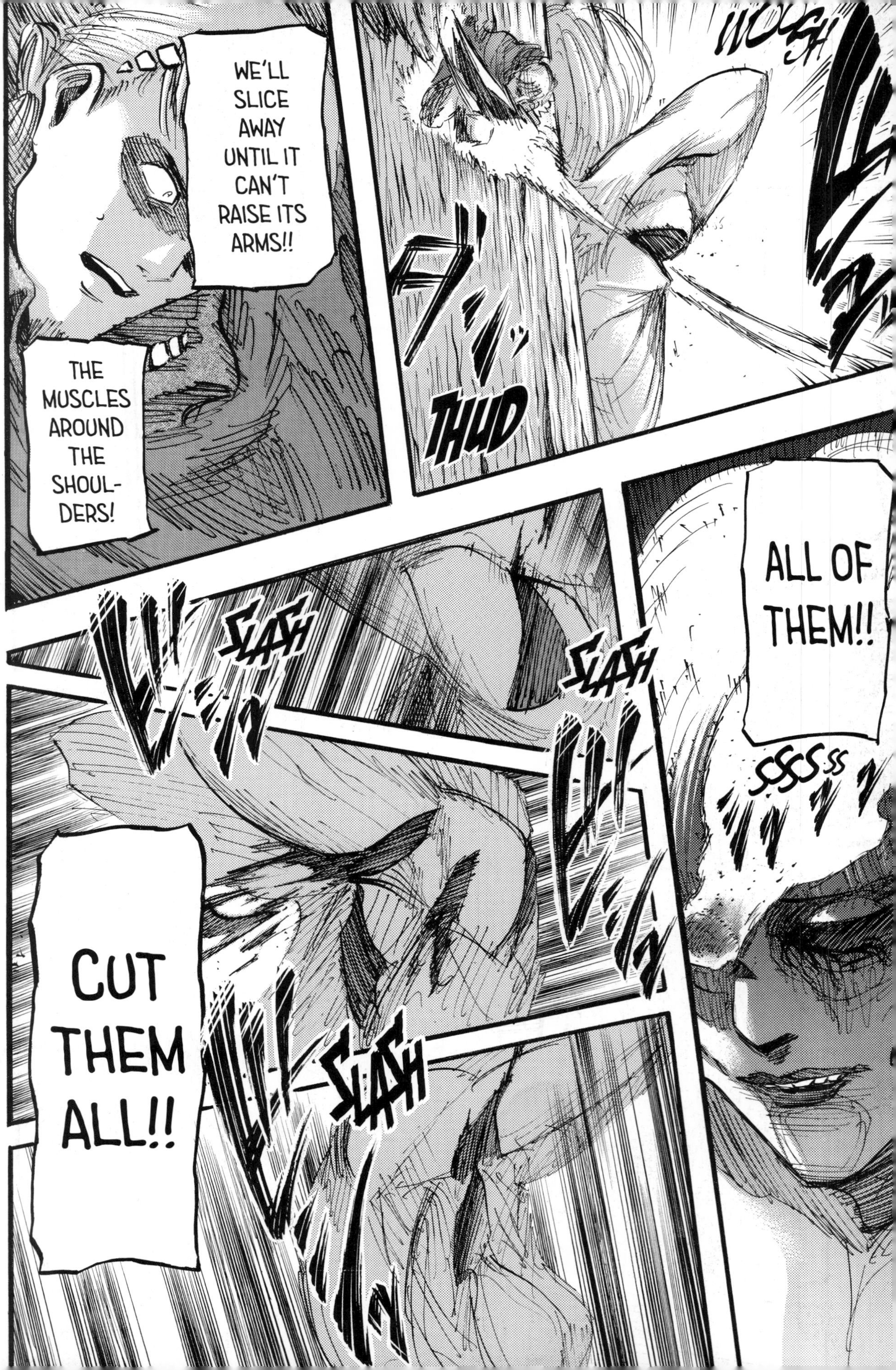
WOOSH!
THUD
WE'LL SLICE AWAY UNTIL IT CAN'T RAISE ITS ARMS!!
THE MUSCLES AROUND THE SHOUL-DERS!
ALL OF THEM!!
SSSS ss
SLASH
SLASH
CUT THEM ALL!!
SLASH

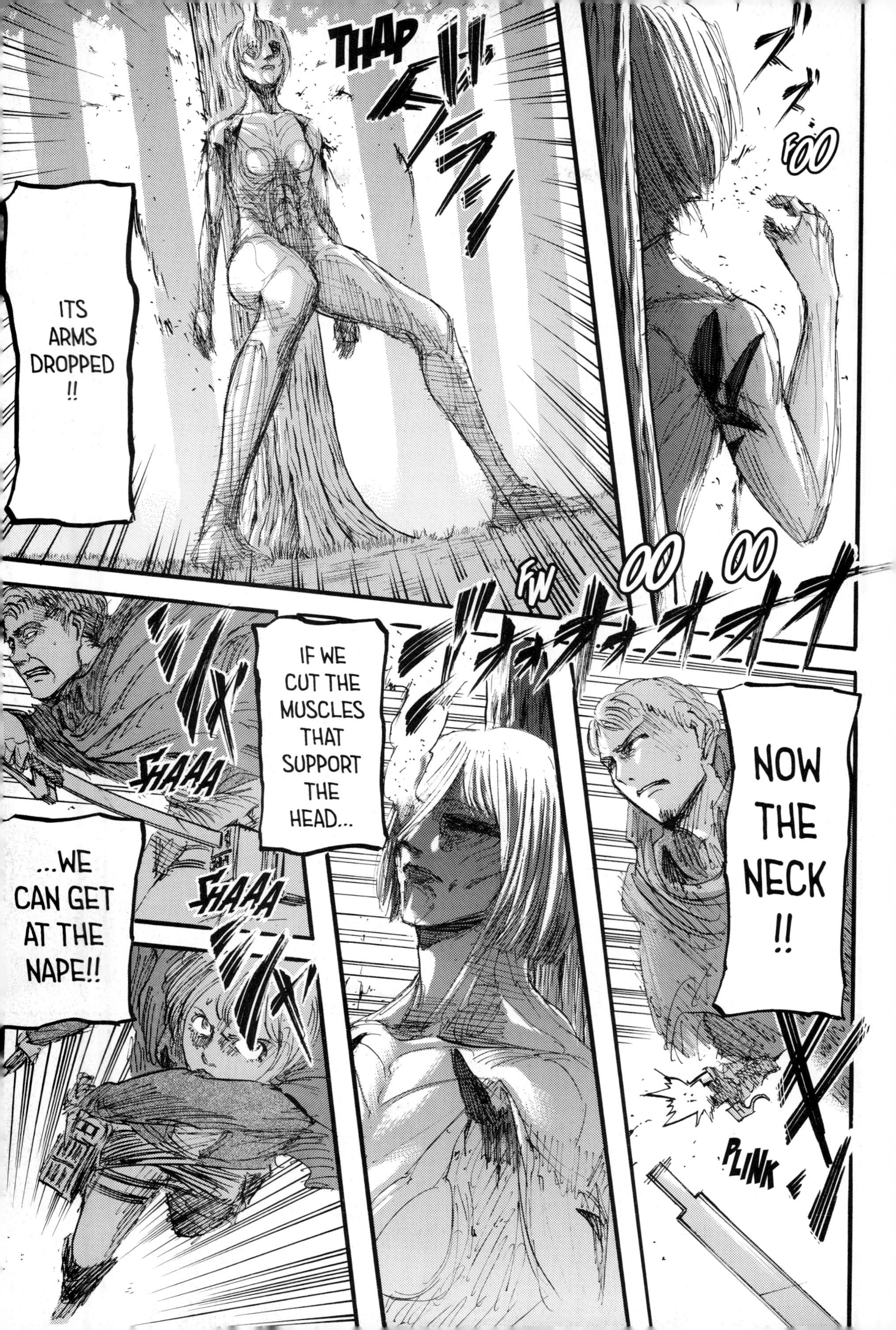

FOO
THAP
ITS ARMS DROPPED !!
FW
OO
OO
NOW THE NECK !!
PLINK
IF WE CUT THE MUSCLES THAT SUPPORT THE HEAD...
SHAAA
...WE CAN GET AT THE NAPE!!
SHAAA

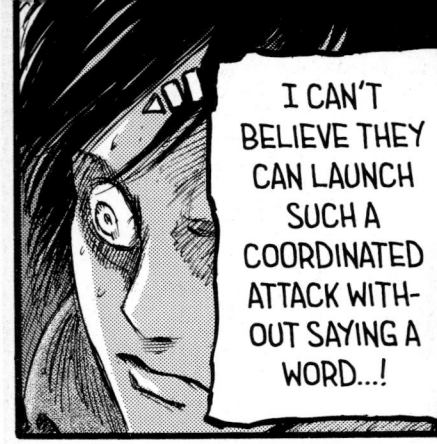

THEY REALLY ARE STRONG ...!!
THEY'RE OVER-WHELMING IT...
I CAN'T BELIEVE THEY CAN LAUNCH SUCH A COORDINATED ATTACK WITH-OUT SAYING A WORD...!
I'M SURE IT'S ONLY POSSIBLE BECAUSE THEY TRUST ONE ANOTHER...
THAT'S HOW THEY'VE BEEN ABLE TO OVERCOME SO MANY CRISES...
AND THAT'S WHY THEY'RE STILL THIS STRONG, EVEN RIGHT AFTER LOSING GUNTHER...
I'LL KEEP MOVING...
KEEP MOVING FORWARD WITHOUT LOOKING BACK, BECAUSE I HAVE FAITH IN THEM... THAT'S THE RIGHT THING TO DO.
I FINALLY UNDERSTAND...
I DON'T KNOW.

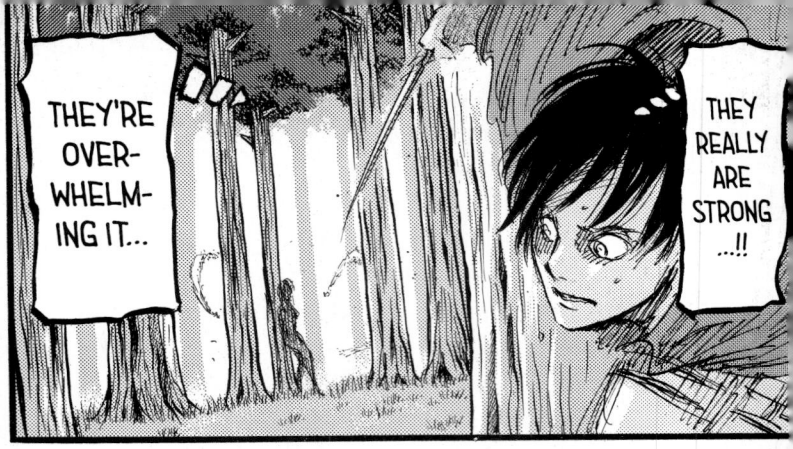

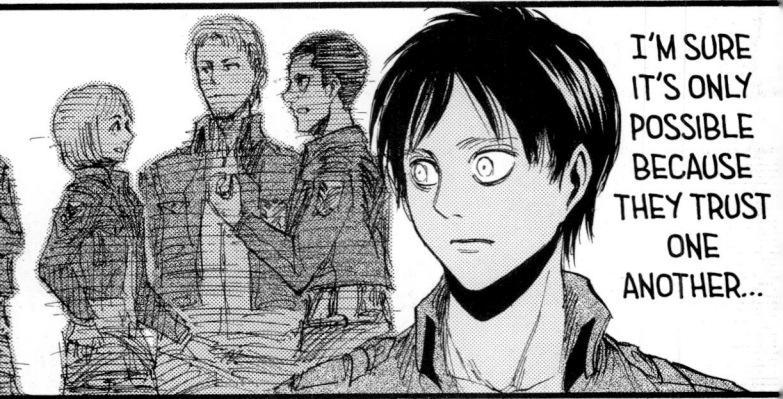

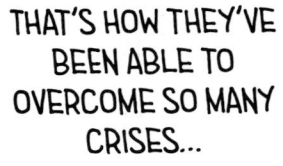

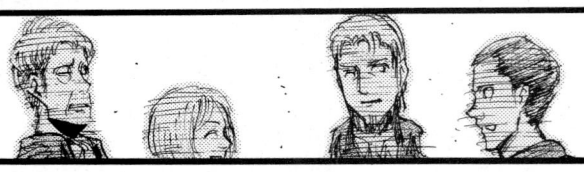

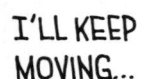

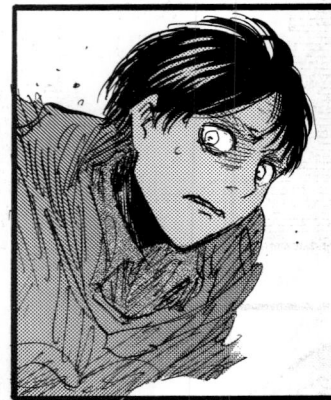

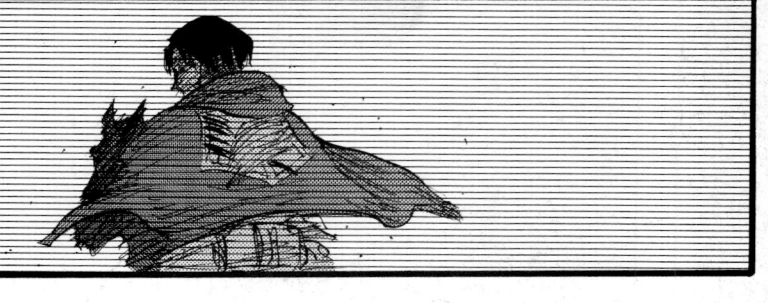

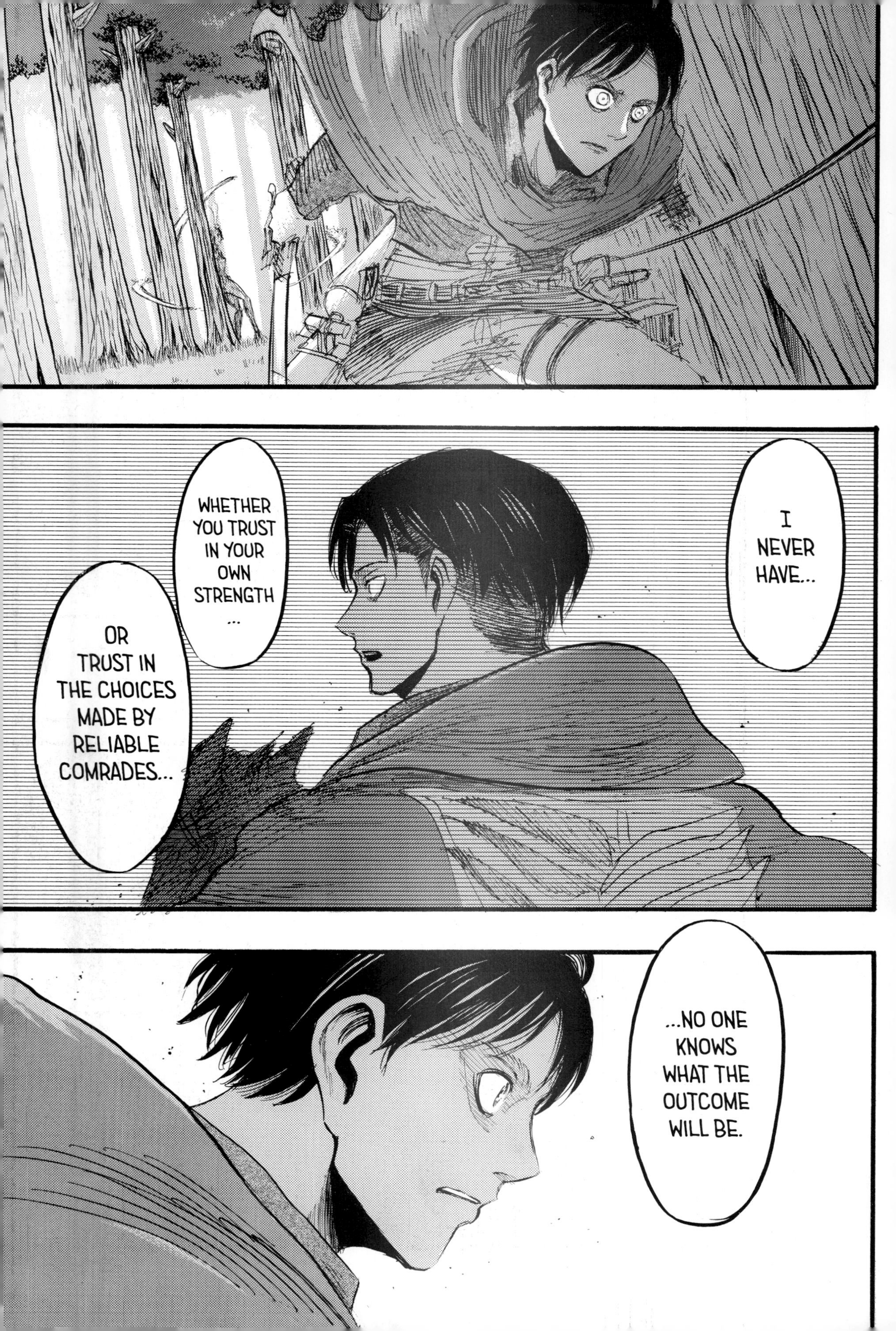
I NEVER HAVE...
WHETHER YOU TRUST IN YOUR OWN STRENGTH ...
OR TRUST IN THE CHOICES MADE BY RELIABLE COMRADES...
...NO ONE KNOWS WHAT THE OUTCOME WILL BE.

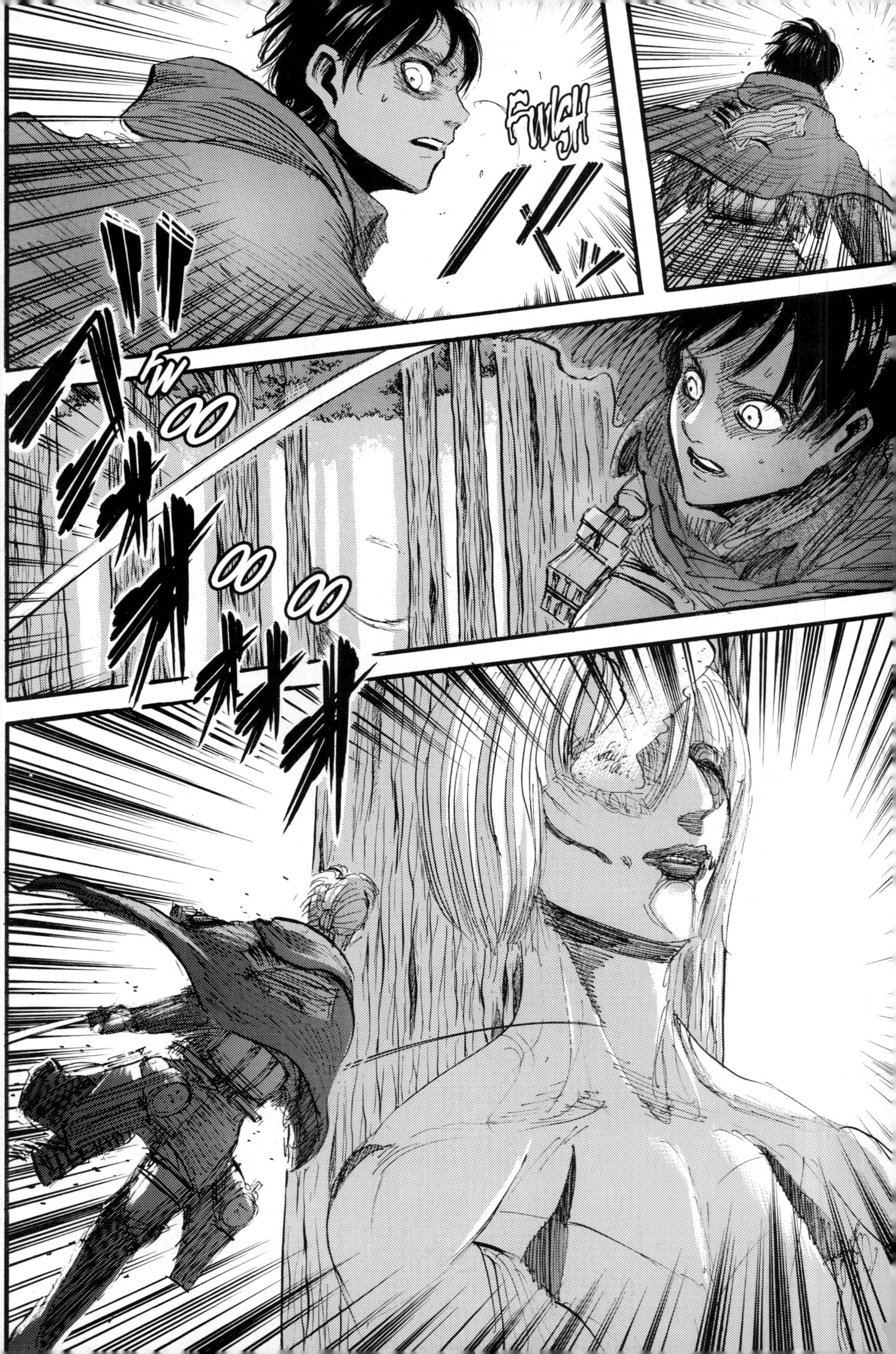
FWISH
Fw OO OO OO

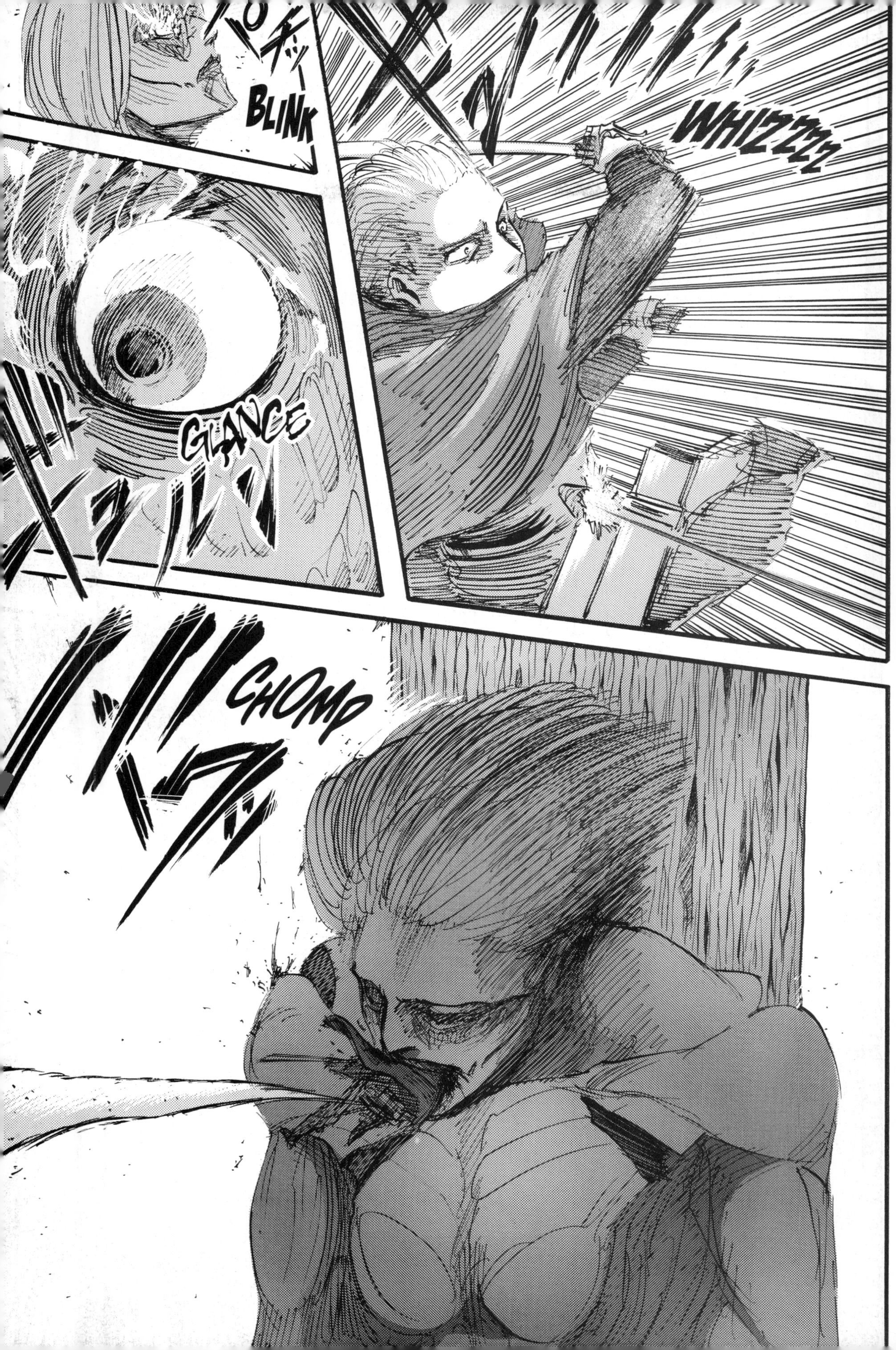
WHIZZZZ
BLINK
GLANCE
CHOMP

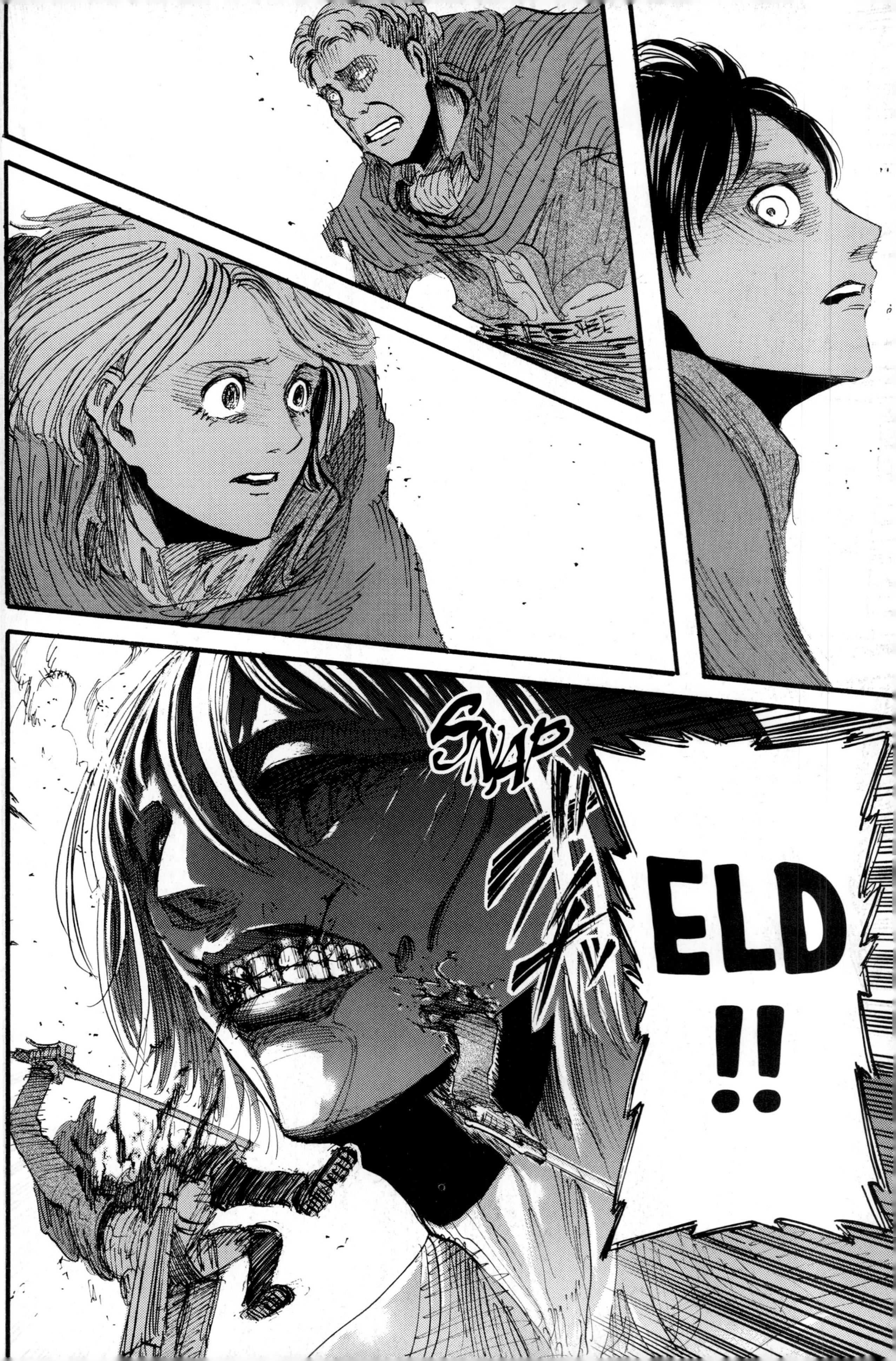
SNAP
ELD!!

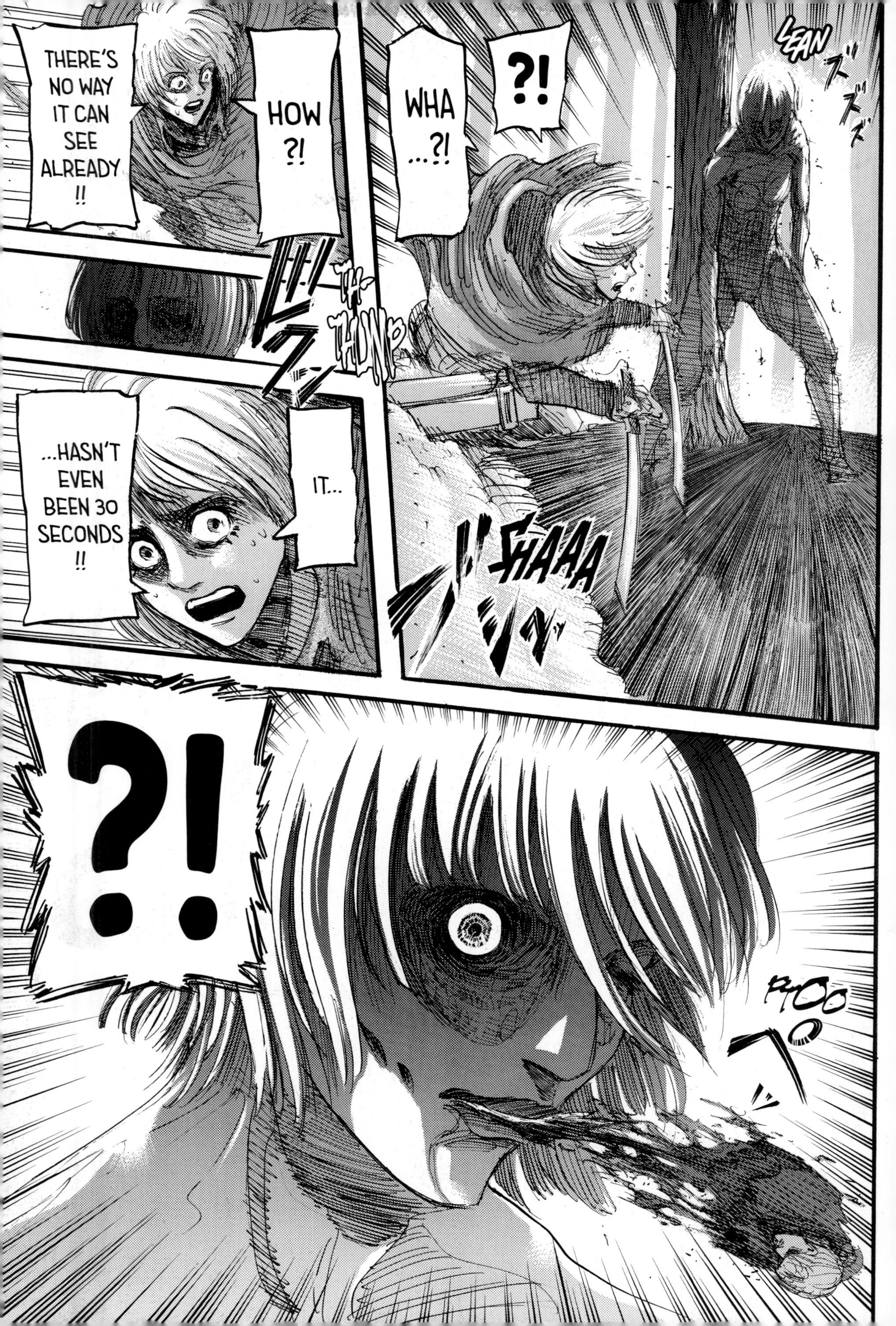
LEAN
?!
WHA...?!
TA-THUMP
SHAAA
HOW?!
THERE'S NO WAY IT CAN SEE ALREADY!!
IT...
...HASN'T EVEN BEEN 30 SECONDS!!
?!
PTOOO

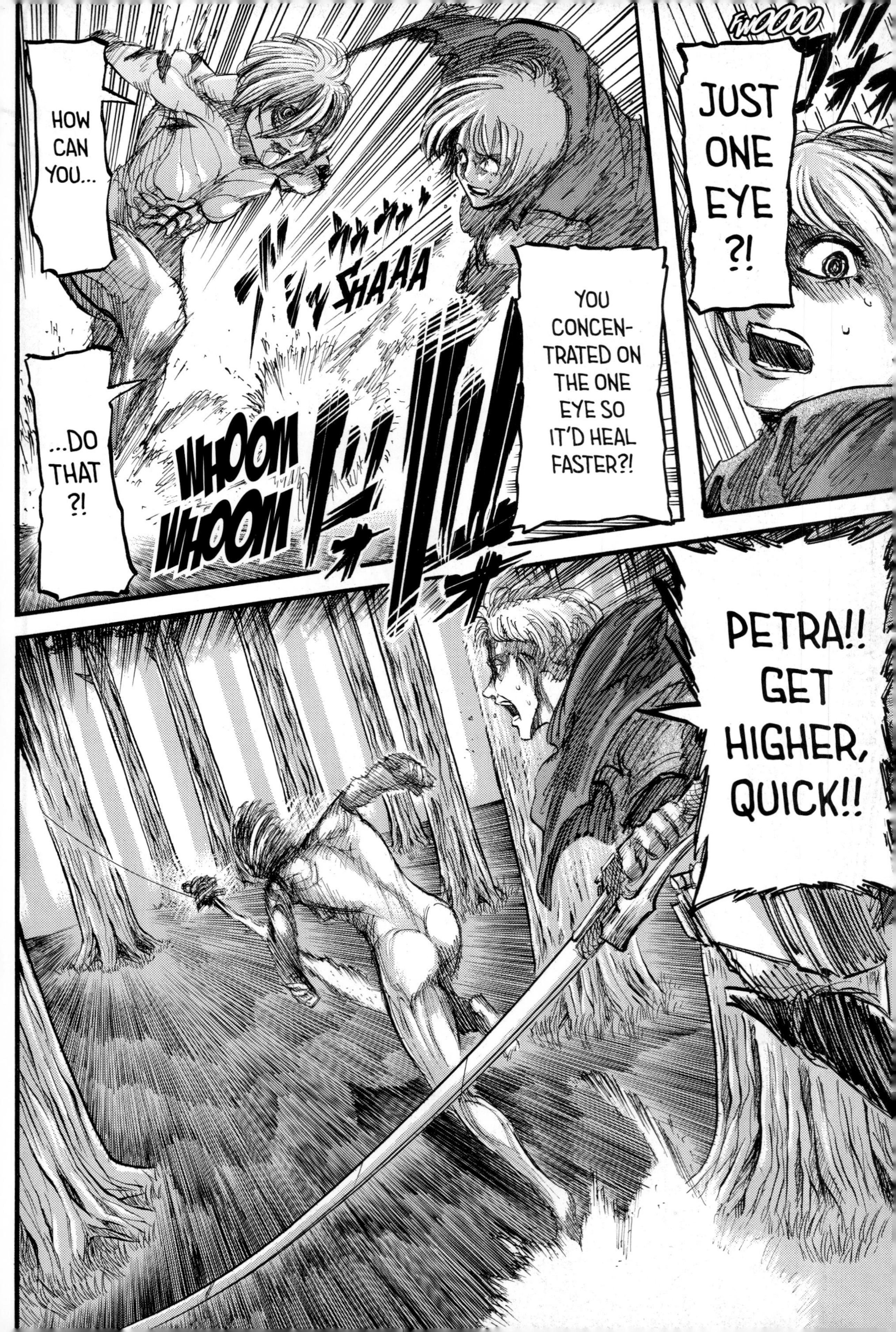
FWOOOO
JUST ONE EYE ?!
YOU CONCEN-TRATED ON THE ONE EYE SO IT'D HEAL FASTER?!
SHAAA
HOW CAN YOU...
...DO THAT ?!
WHOOM WHOOM
PETRA!! GET HIGHER, QUICK!!

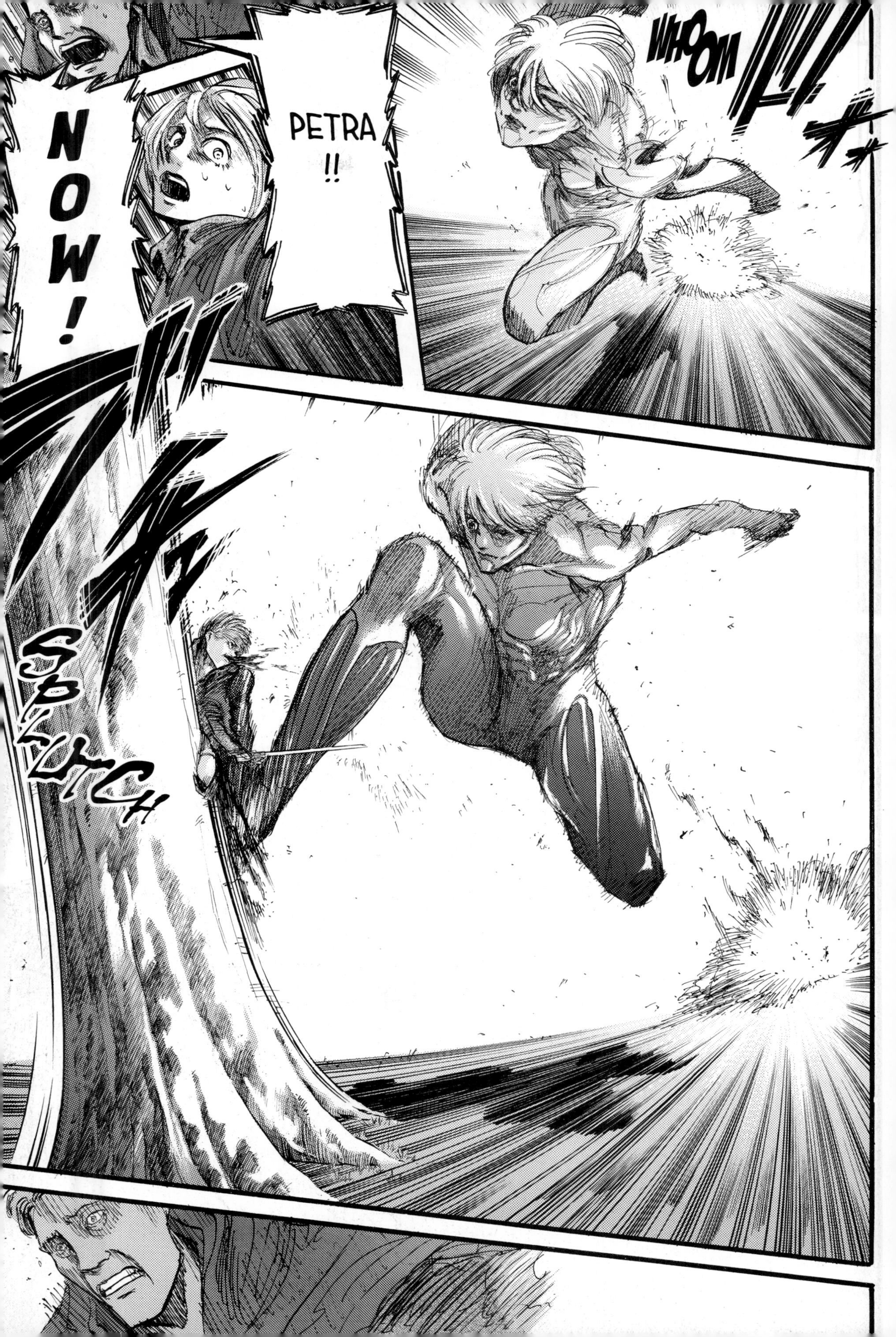
WHOOM
PETRA !!
NOW!
SPLUTCH

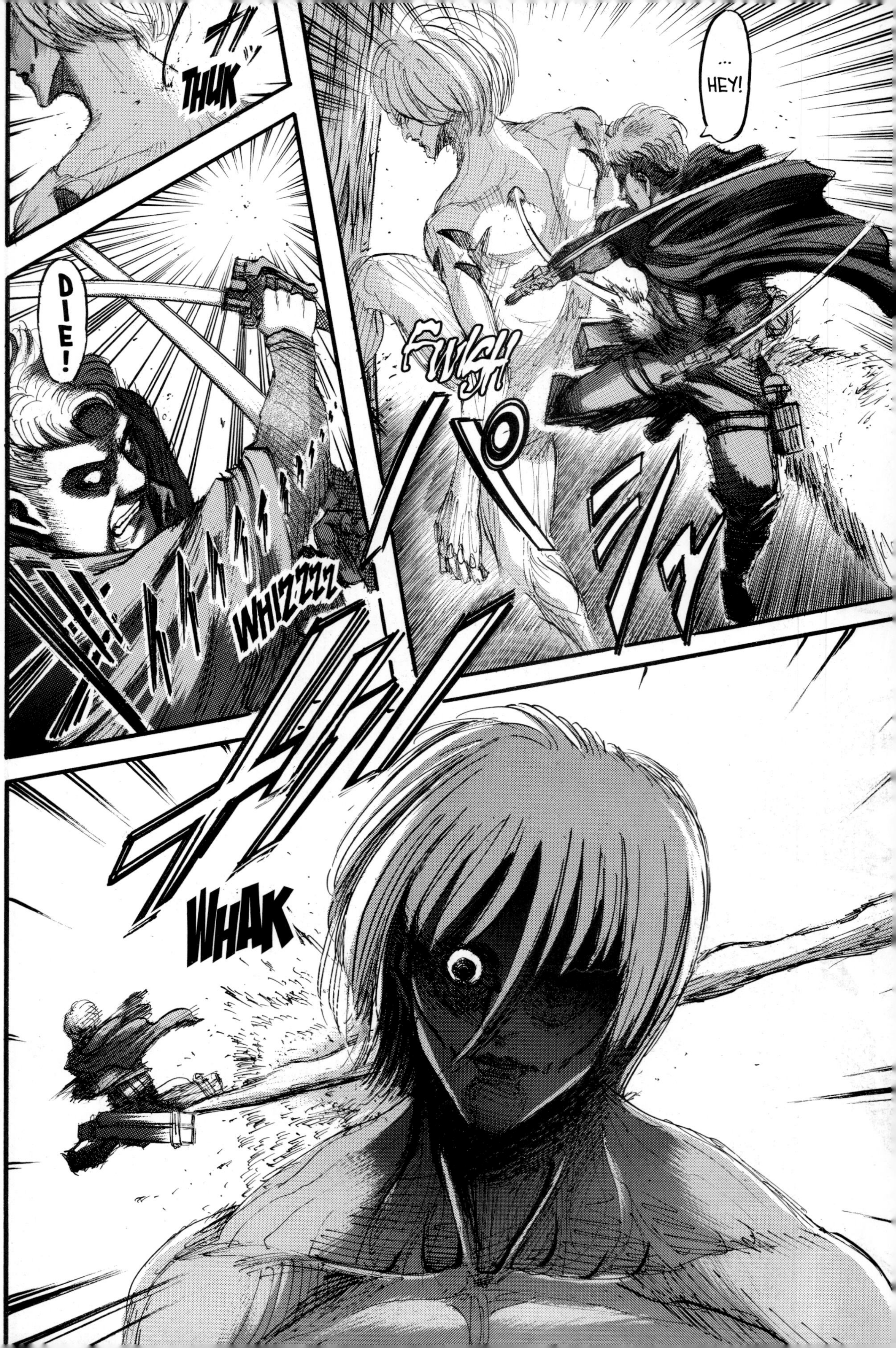
... HEY!
FWISH
THUK
DIE!
WHIZZZZ
WHAK

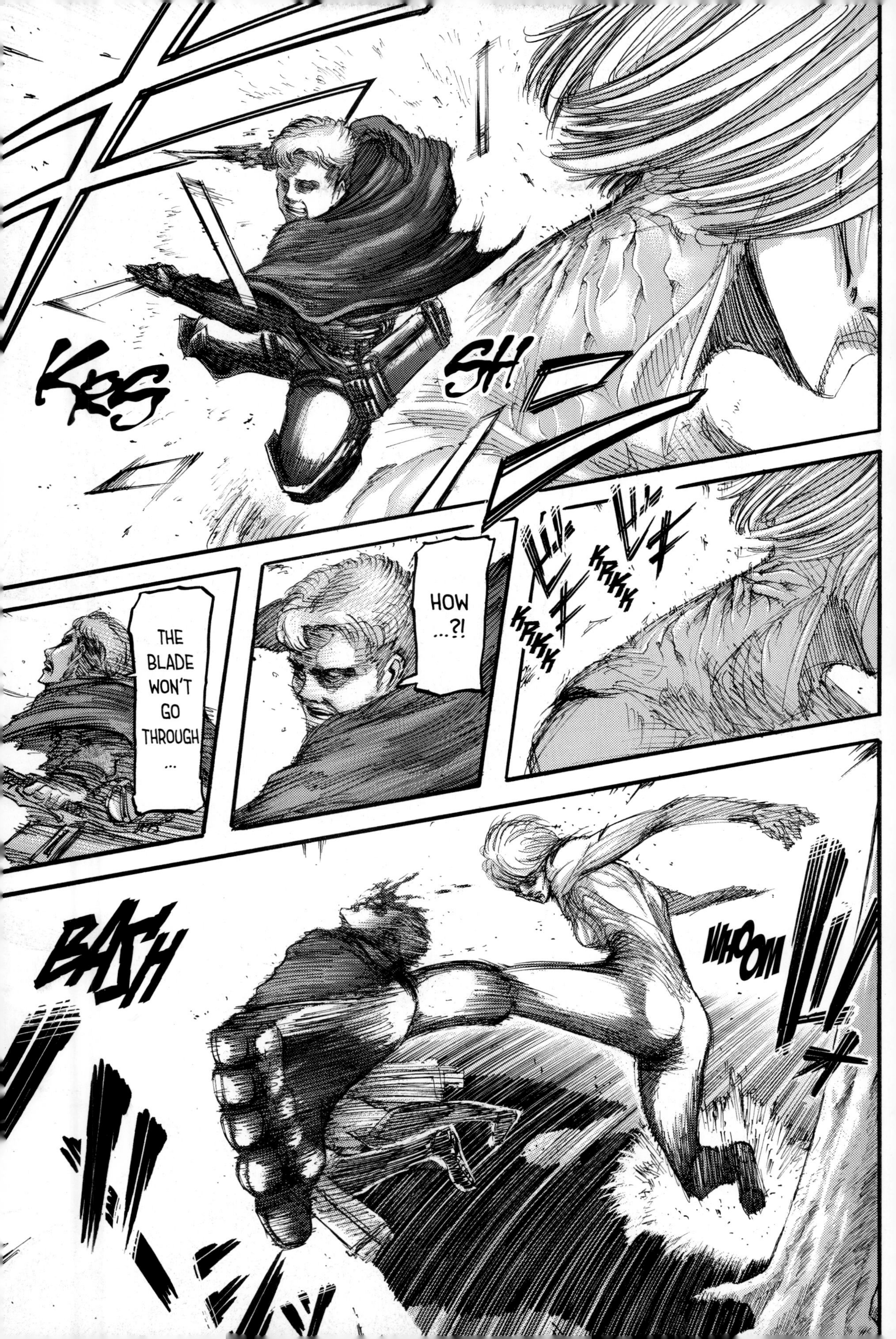
SH
KRIS
KRIKK
KRIKK
HOW ...?!
THE BLADE WON'T GO THROUGH ...
WHOOM
BASH

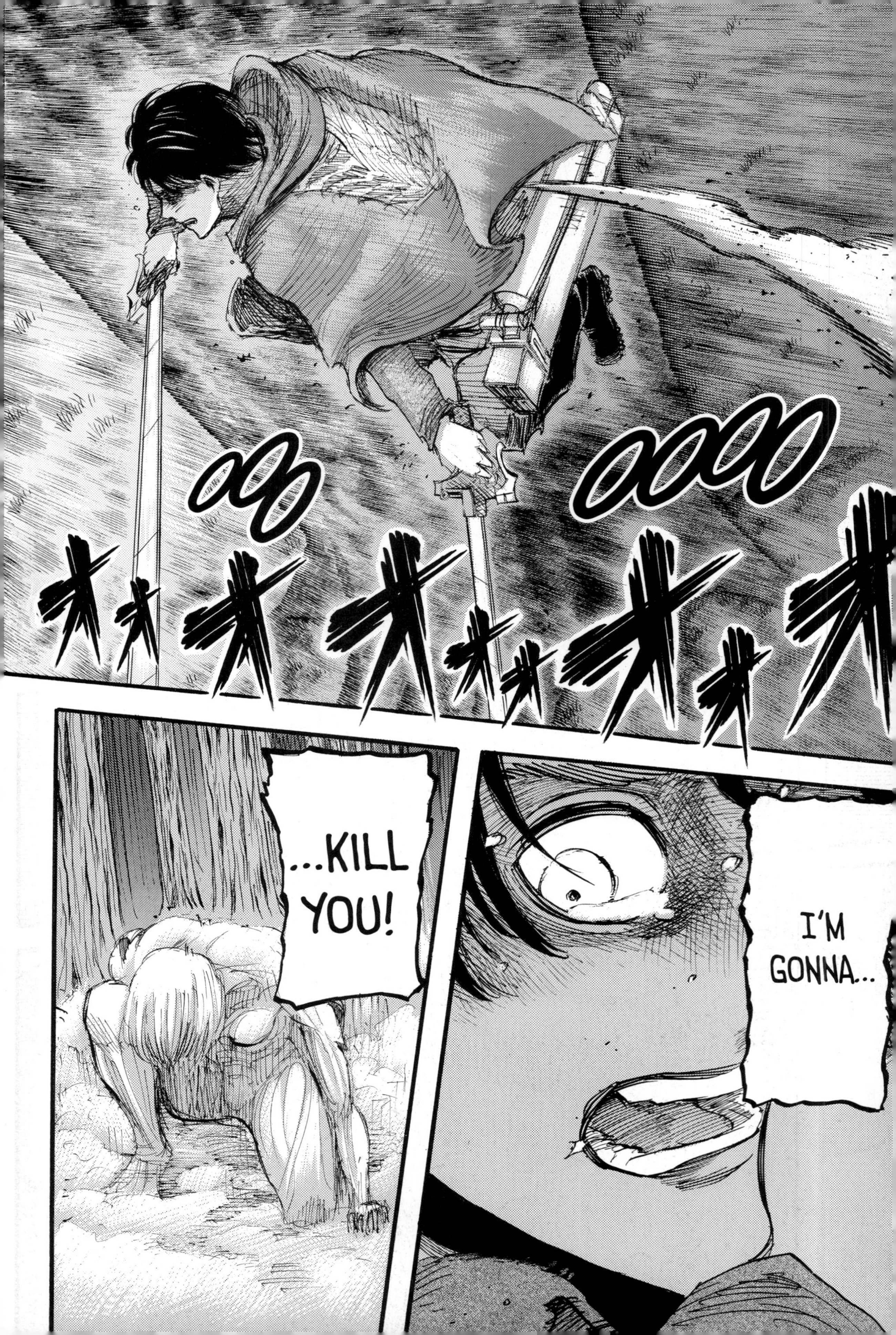
OO
OOOO
I'M GONNA...
...KILL YOU!

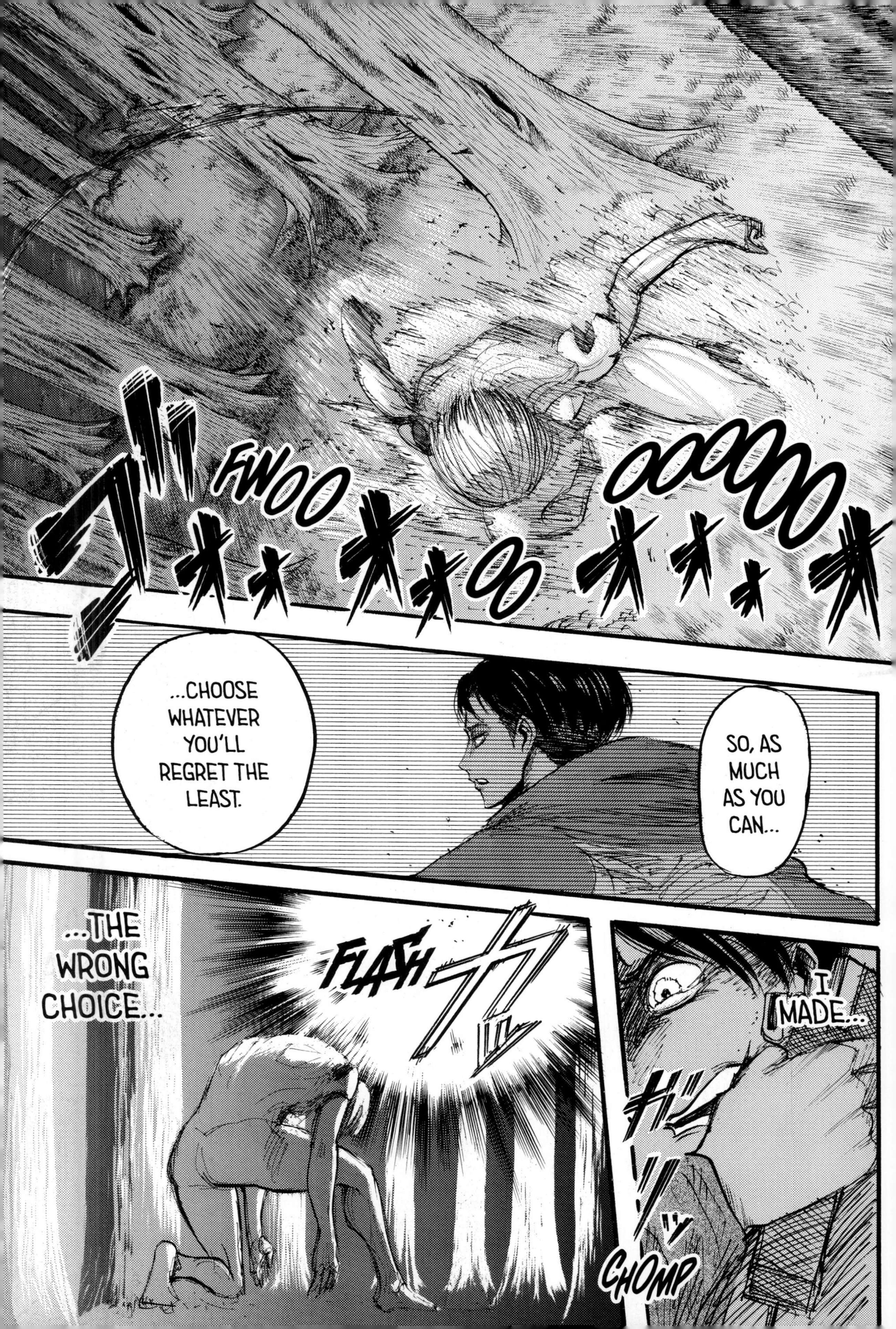
FWOOOOOOOOO
SO, AS MUCH AS YOU CAN...
...CHOOSE WHATEVER YOU'LL REGRET THE LEAST.
I MADE...
CHOMP
FLASH
...THE WRONG CHOICE...

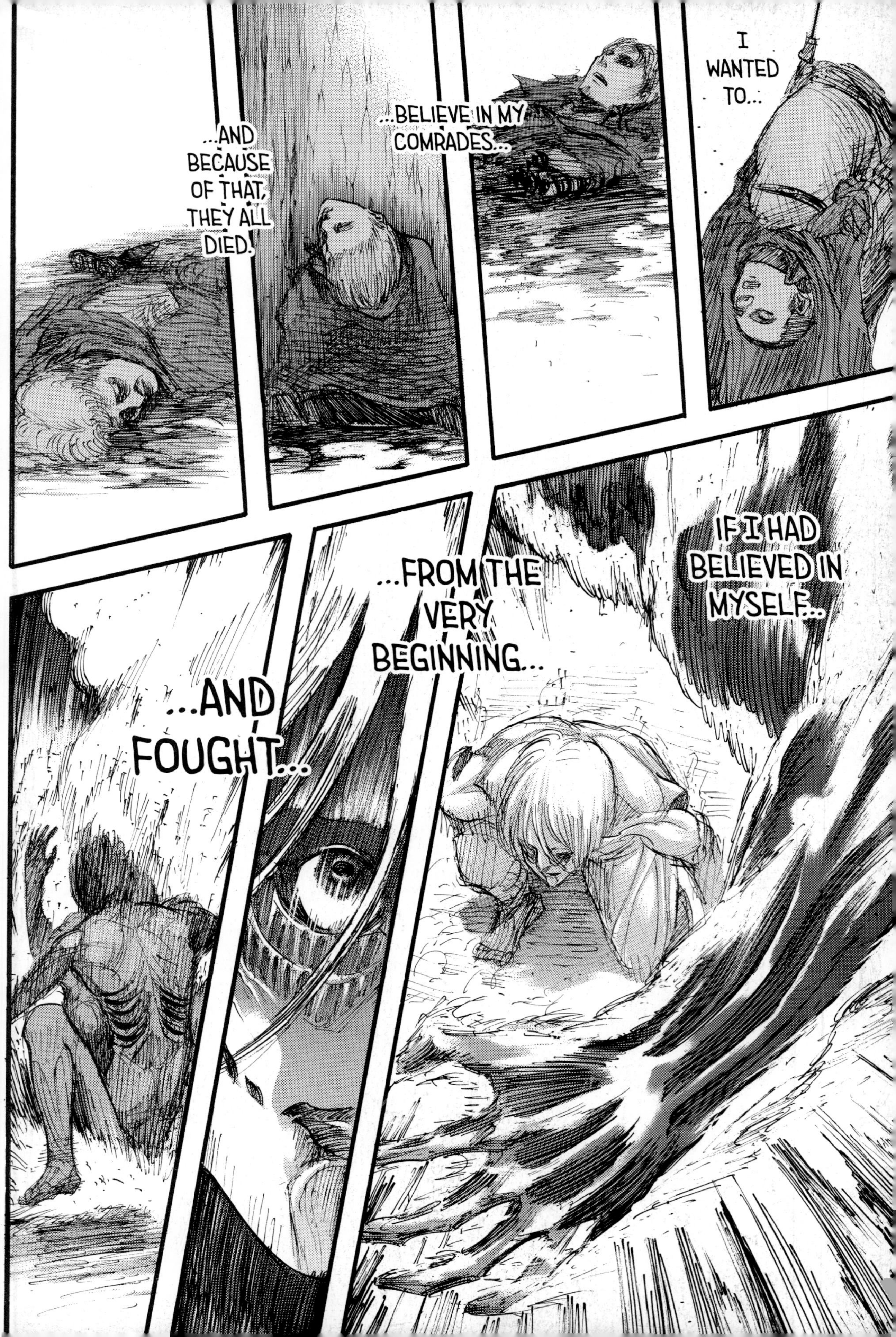
I WANTED TO...
...BELIEVE IN MY COMRADES...
...AND BECAUSE OF THAT, THEY ALL DIED.
IF I HAD BELIEVED IN MYSELF...
...FROM THE VERY BEGINNING...
...AND FOUGHT...

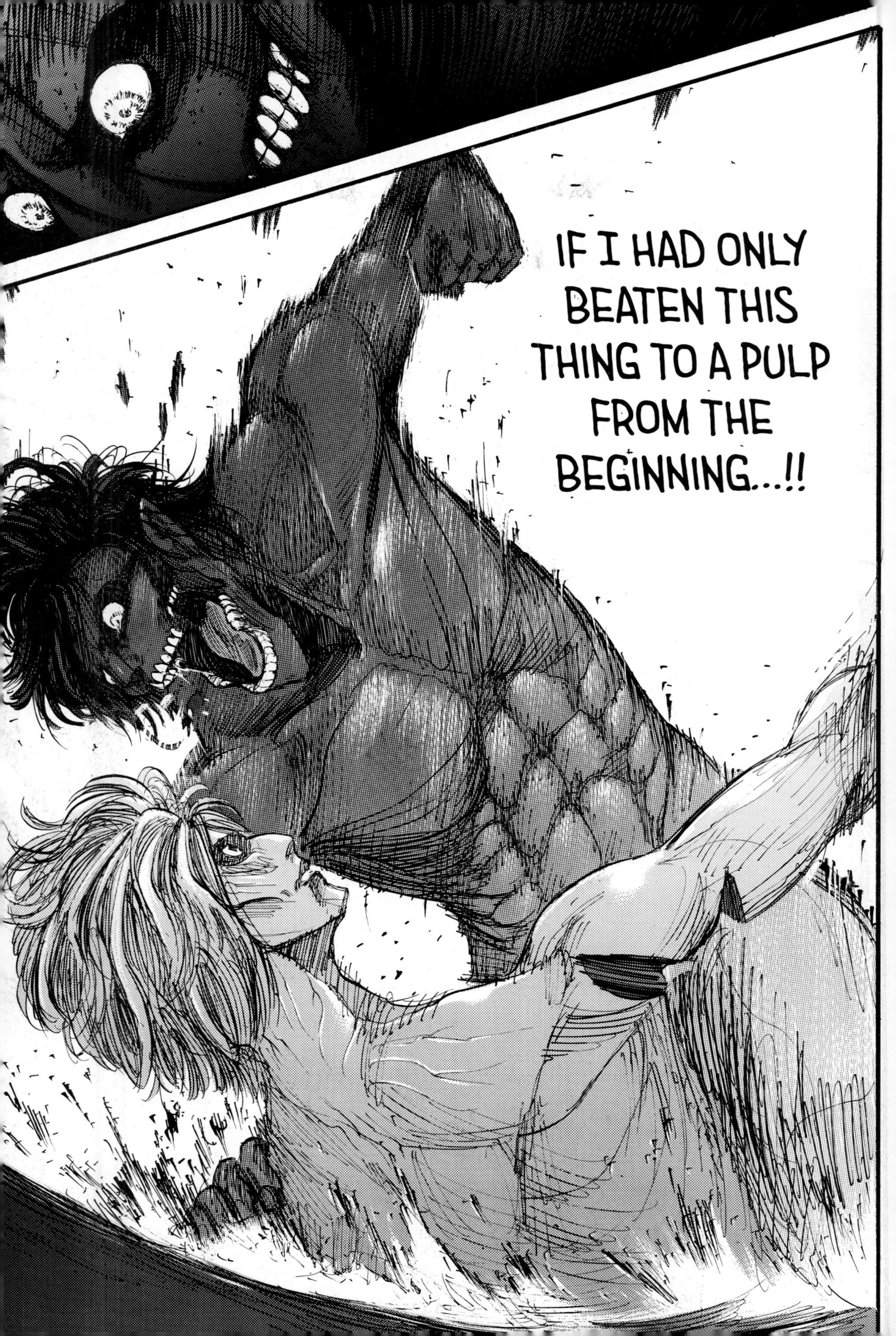
IF I HAD ONLY BEATEN THIS THING TO A PULP FROM THE BEGINNING...!!

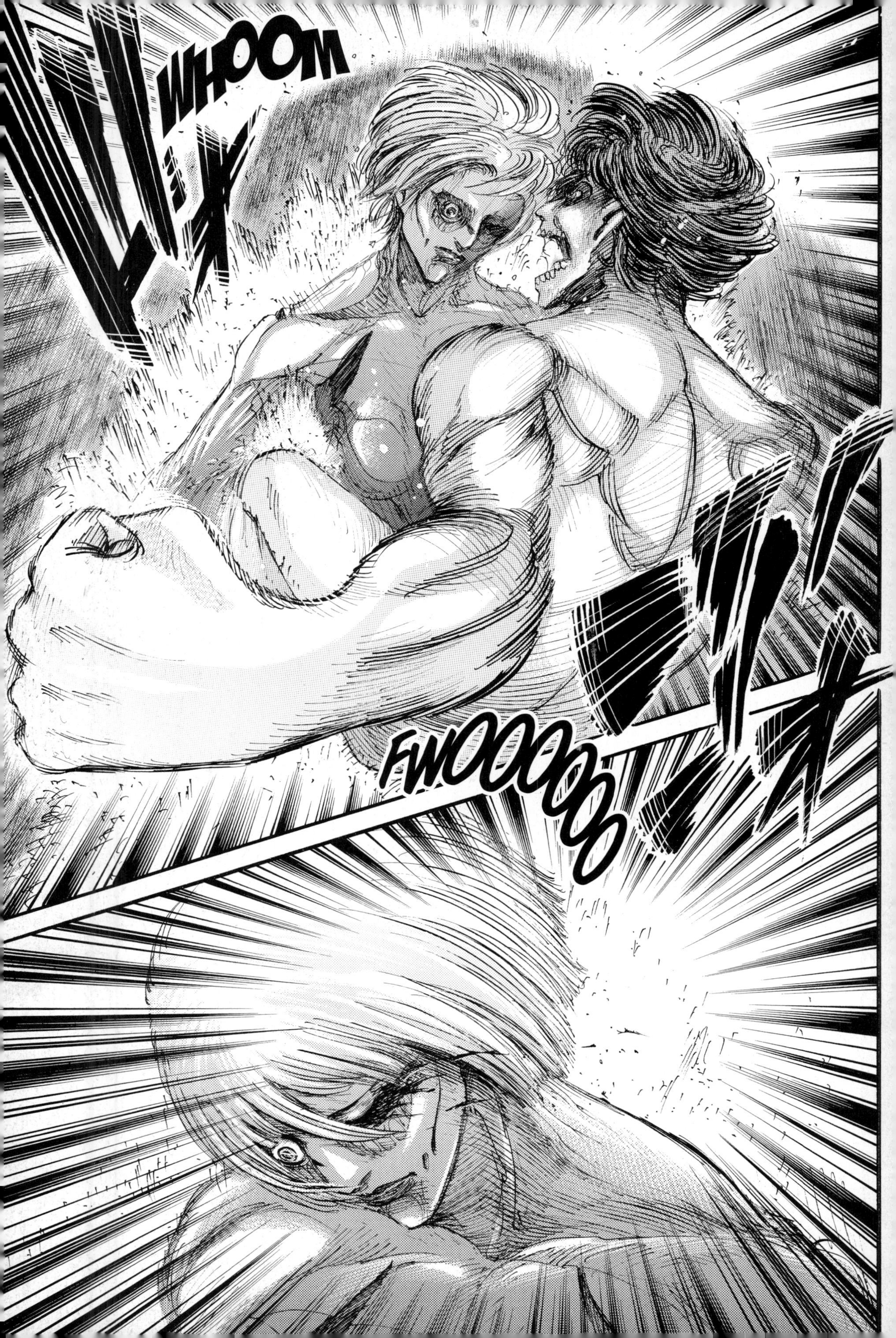
WHOOM
FWOOOOOOO

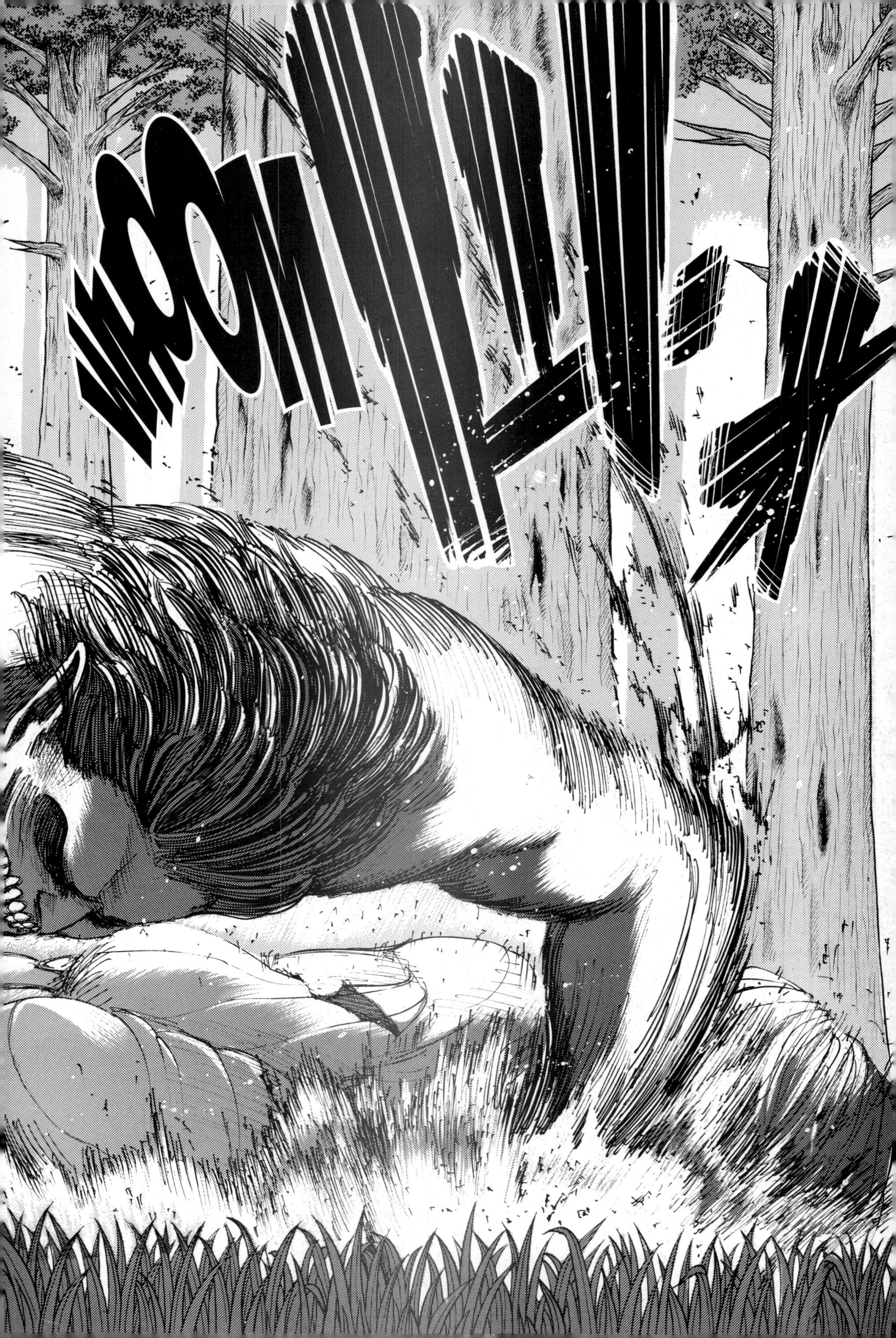
WHOOM

Episode 29: Crushing Blow

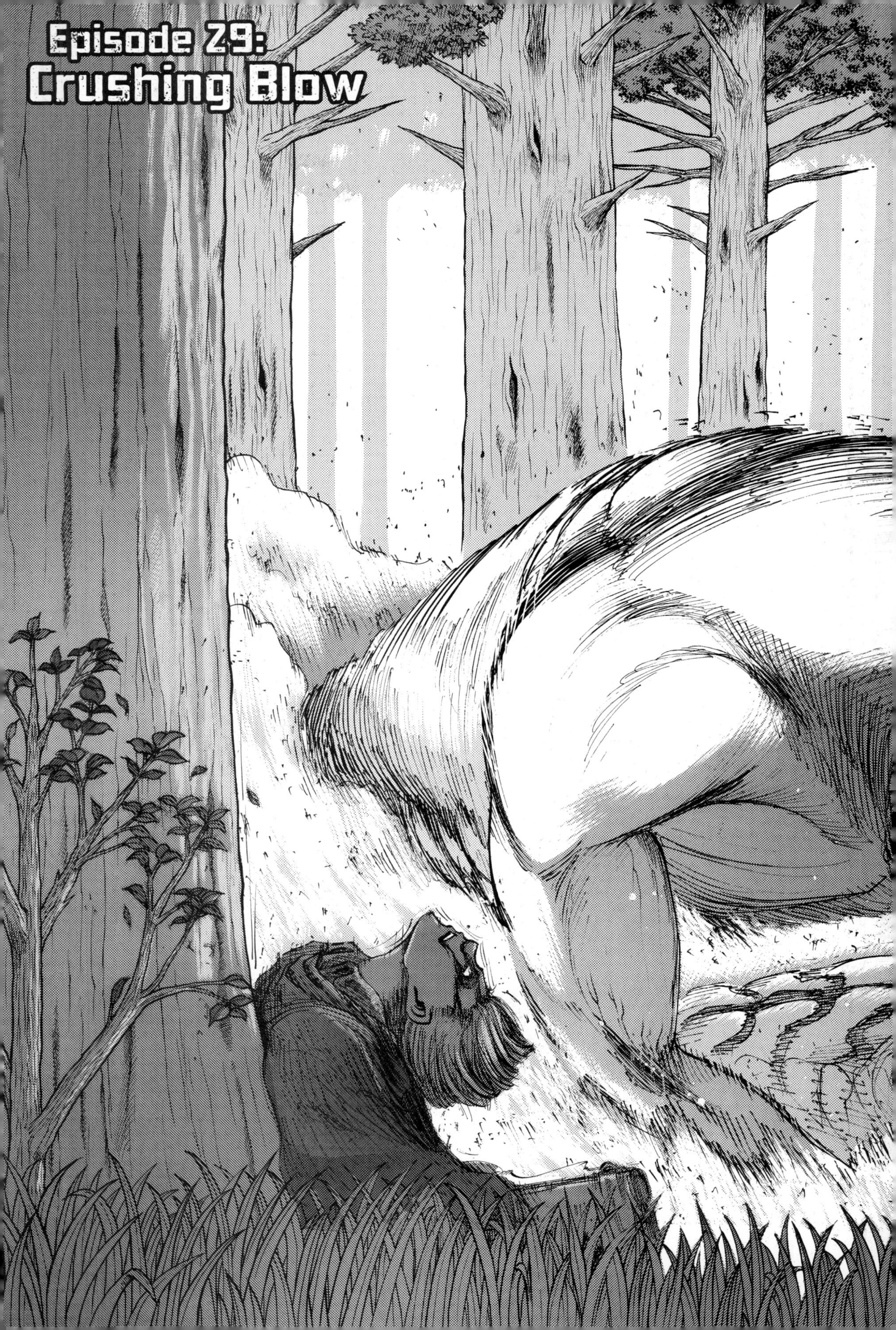

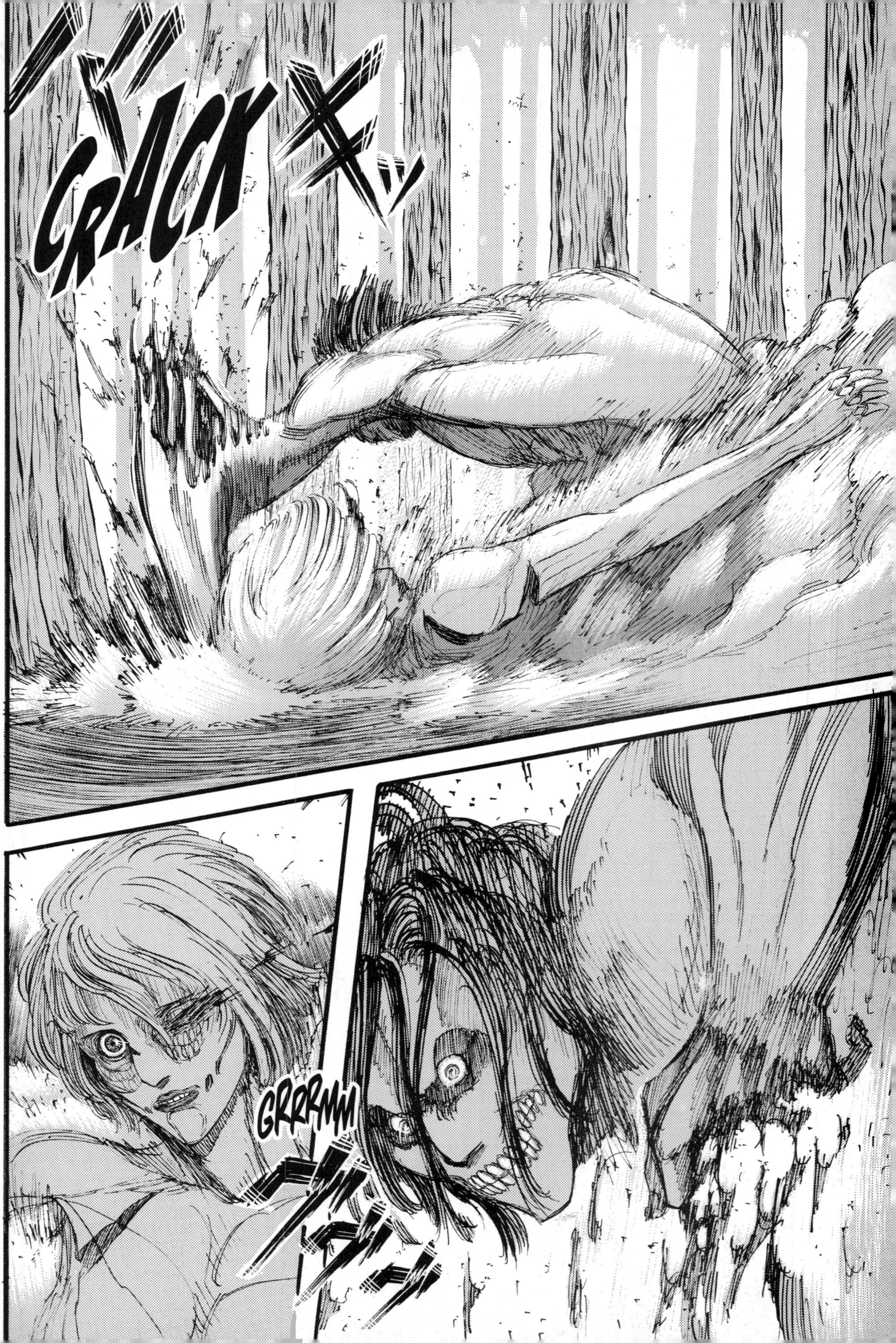
CRACK
GRRRMM

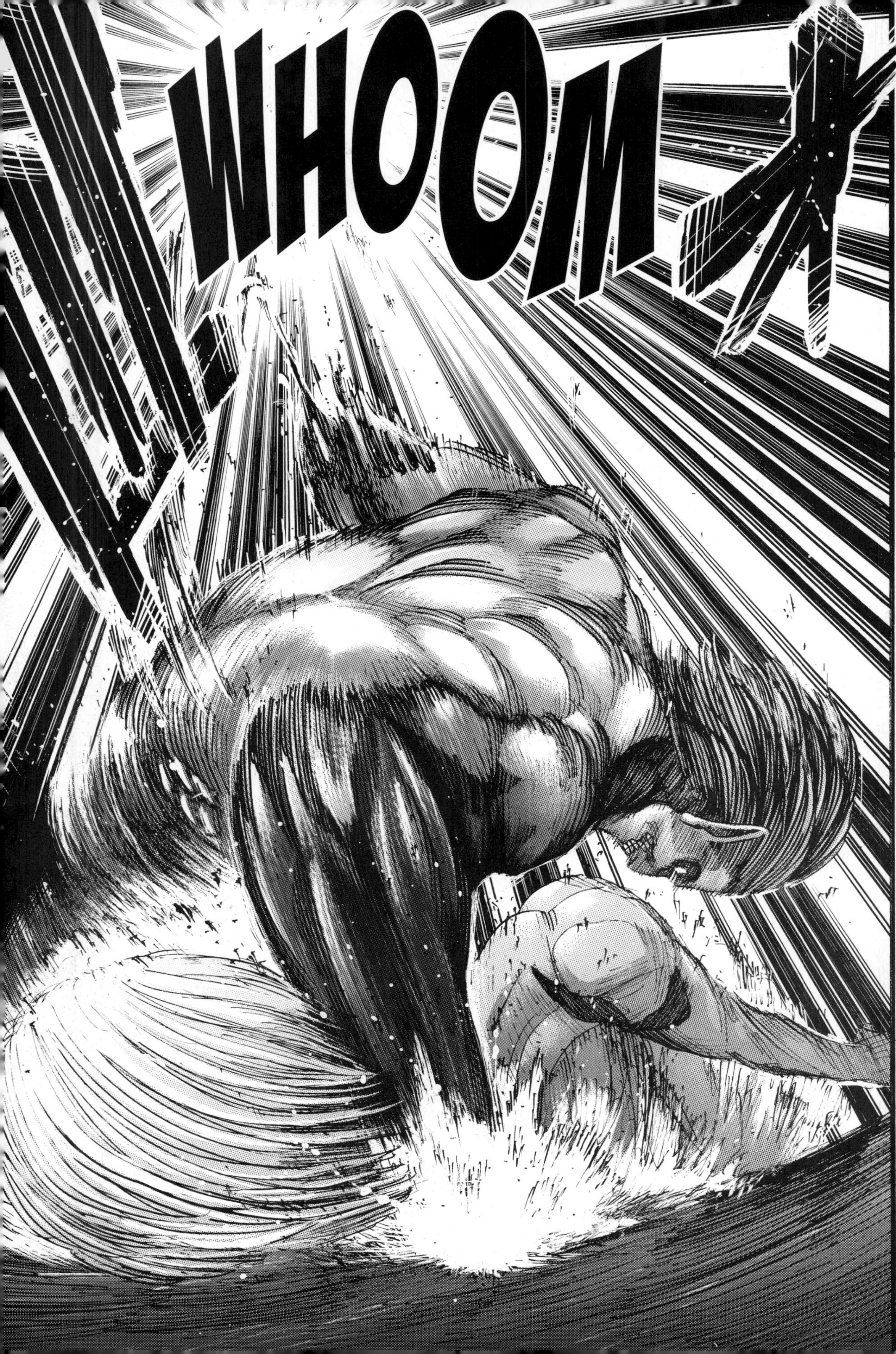
WHOOM

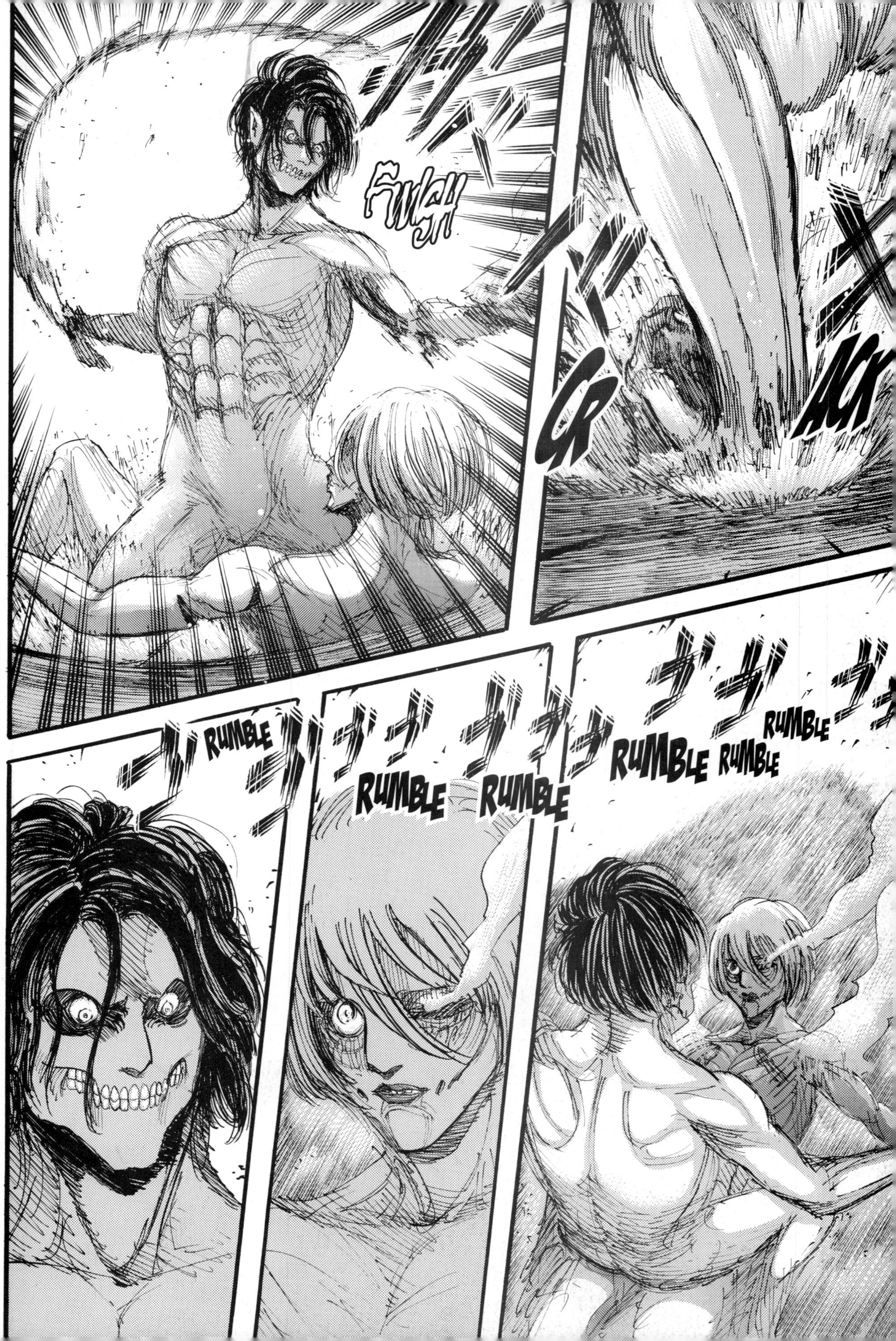

CR
ACK
FWAGH
RUMBLE
RUMBLE
RUMBLE
RUMBLE
RUMBLE
RUMBLE

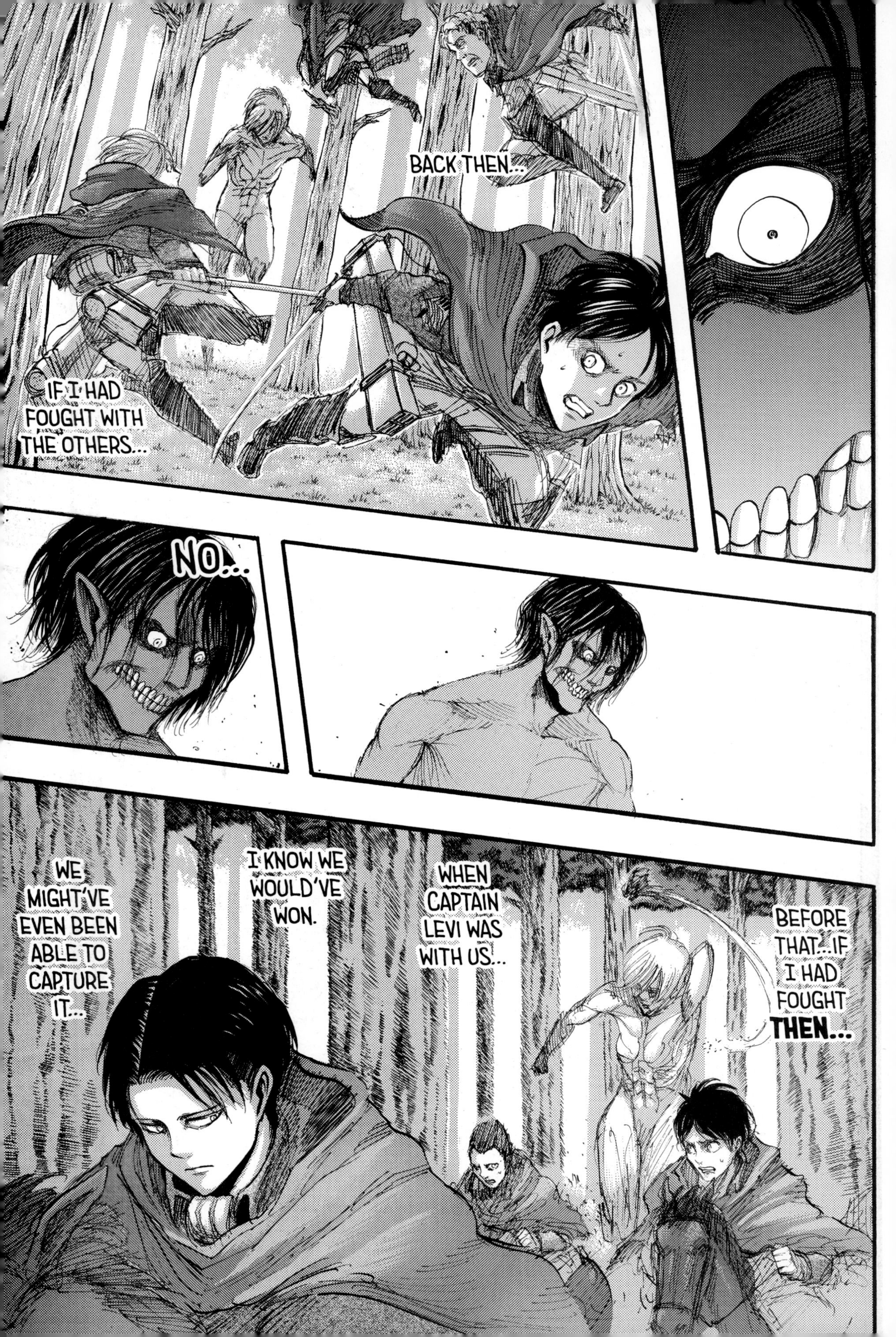
BACK THEN...
IF I HAD FOUGHT WITH THE OTHERS...
NO...
BEFORE THAT...IF I HAD FOUGHT THEN...
WHEN CAPTAIN LEVI WAS WITH US...
I KNOW WE WOULD'VE WON.
WE MIGHT'VE EVEN BEEN ABLE TO CAPTURE IT...

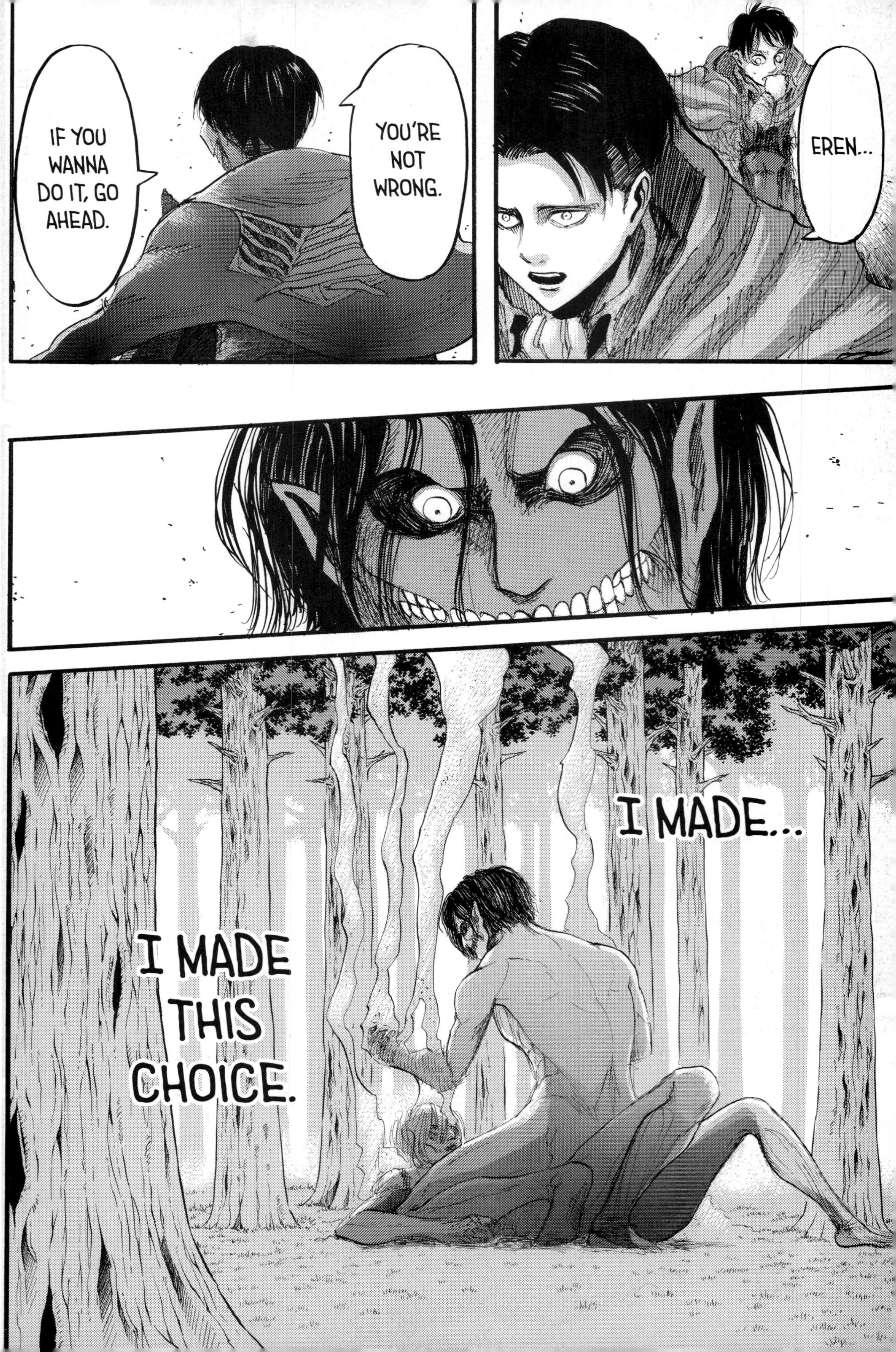
EREN...
YOU'RE NOT WRONG.
IF YOU WANNA DO IT, GO AHEAD.
I MADE...
I MADE THIS CHOICE.

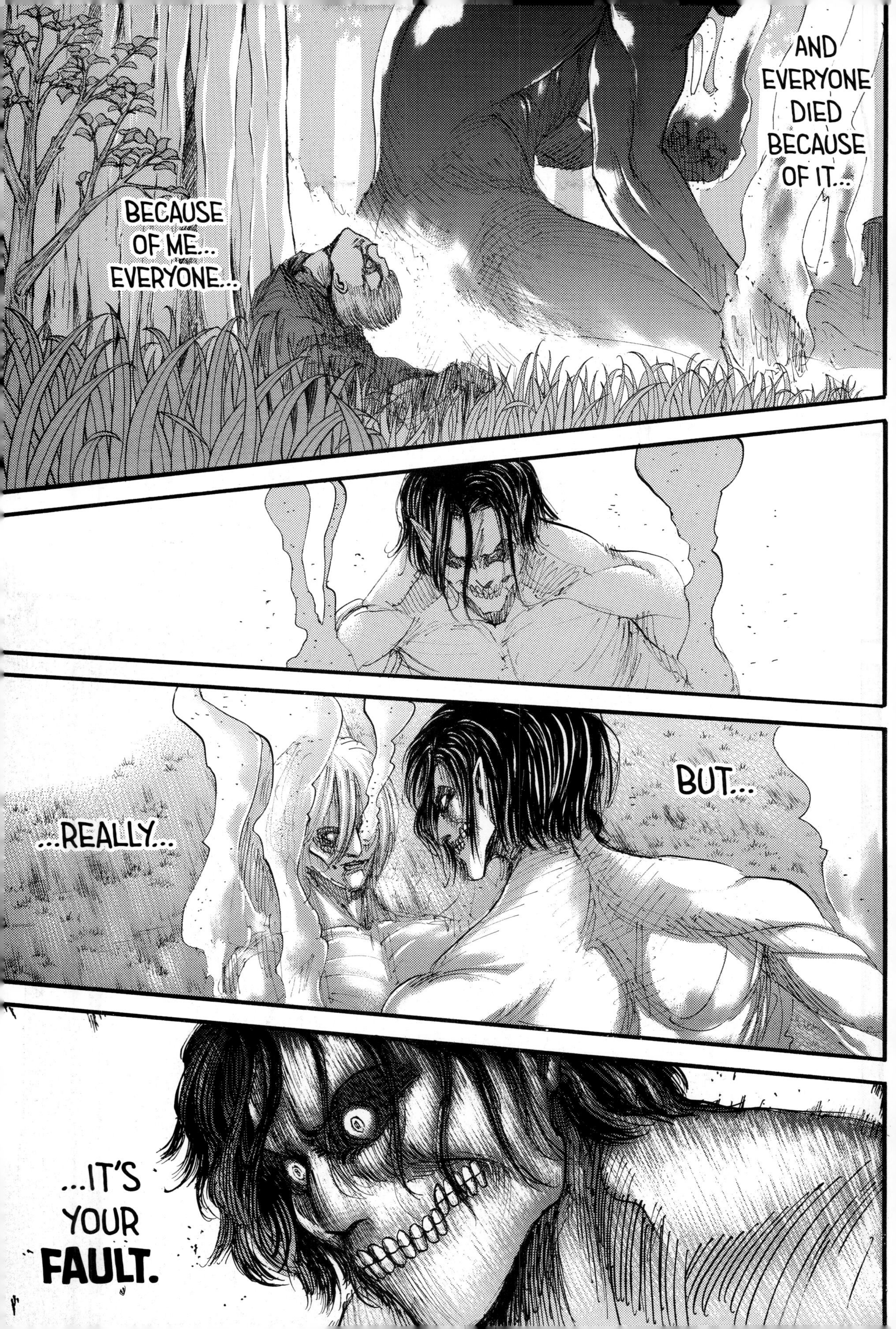
AND EVERYONE DIED BECAUSE OF IT...
BECAUSE OF ME... EVERYONE...
BUT...
...REALLY...
...IT'S YOUR FAULT.

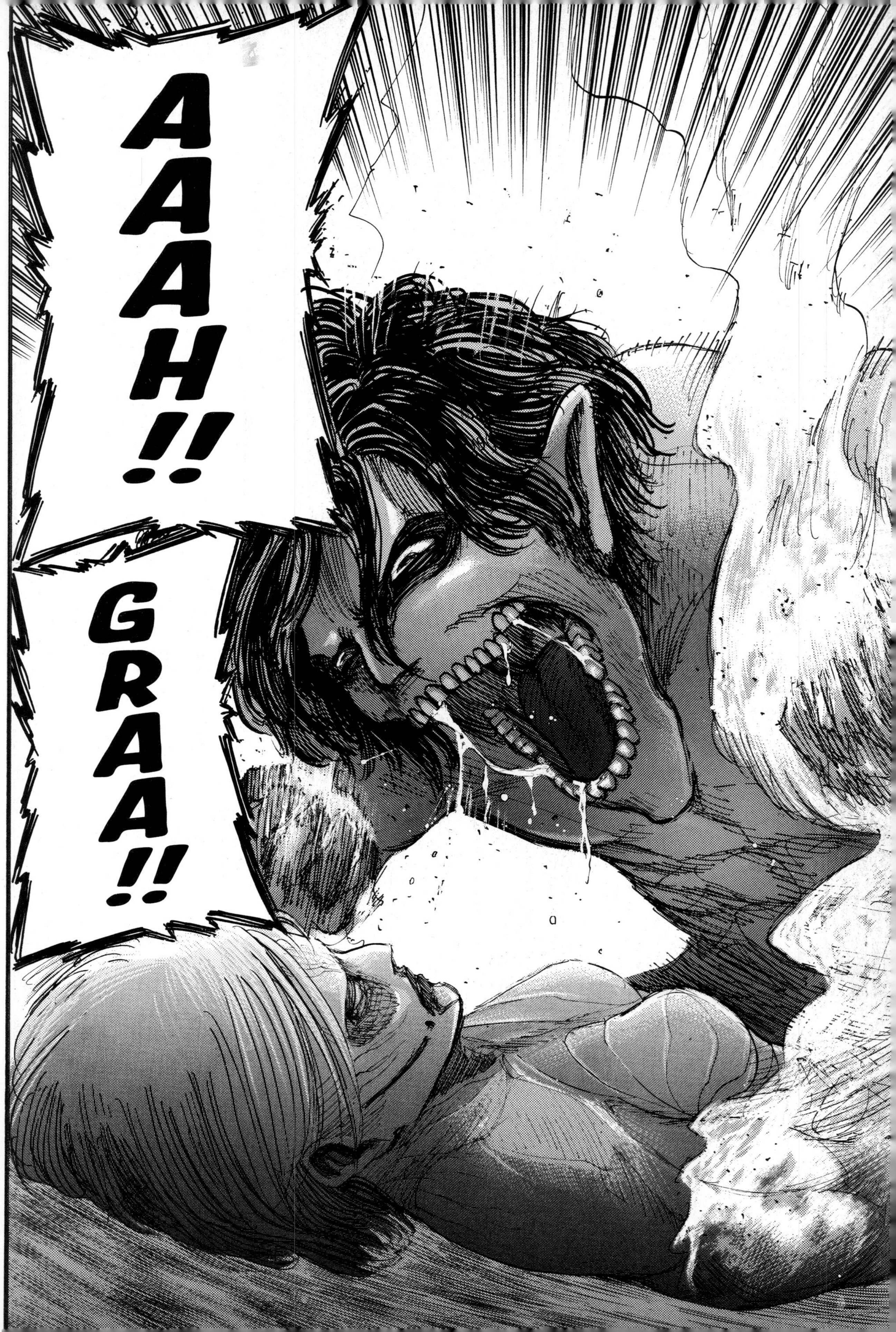
AAAH!!
GRAA!!

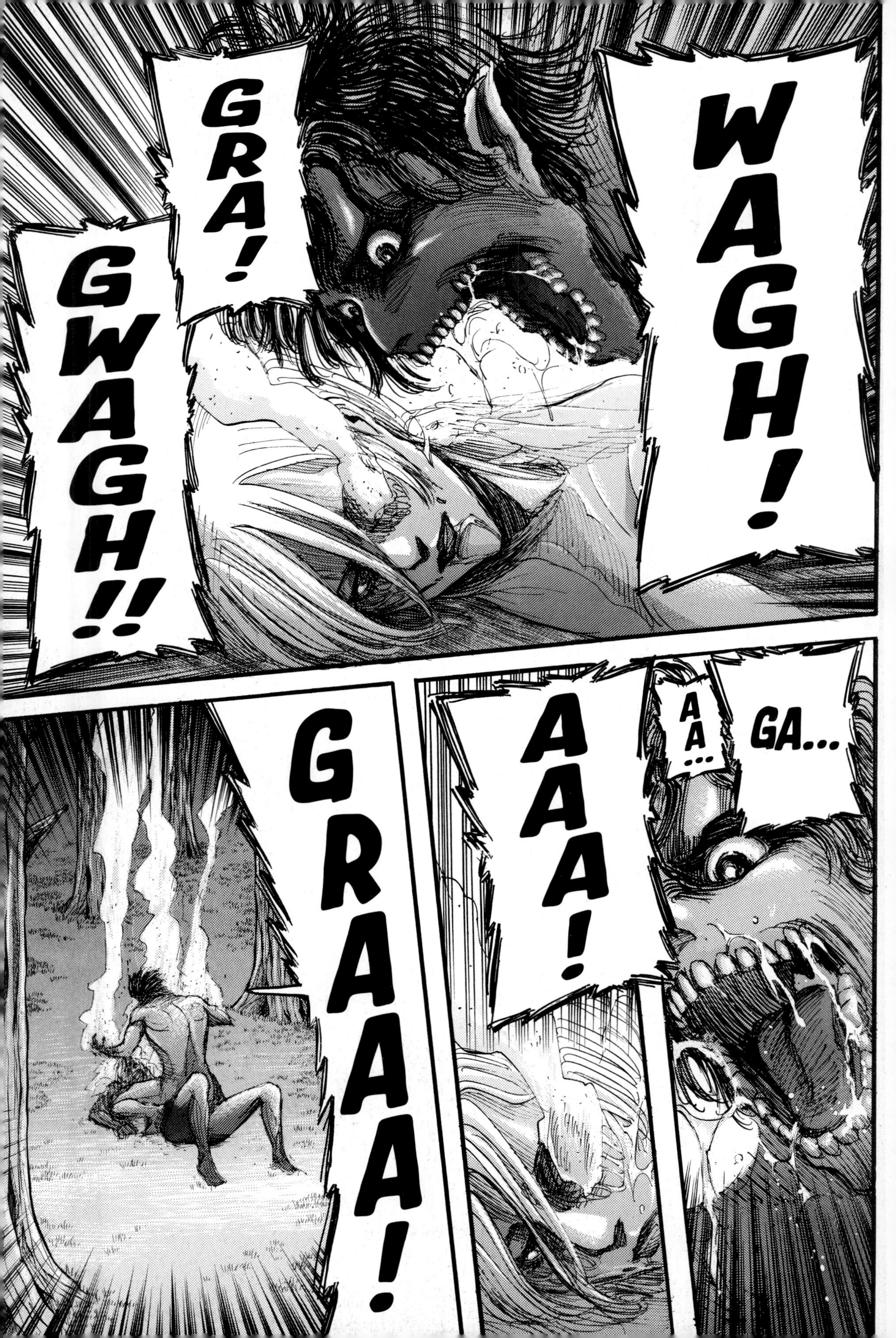
WAGH!
GRA!
GWAGH!!
GA...
AA...
AAA!
GRAAAA!

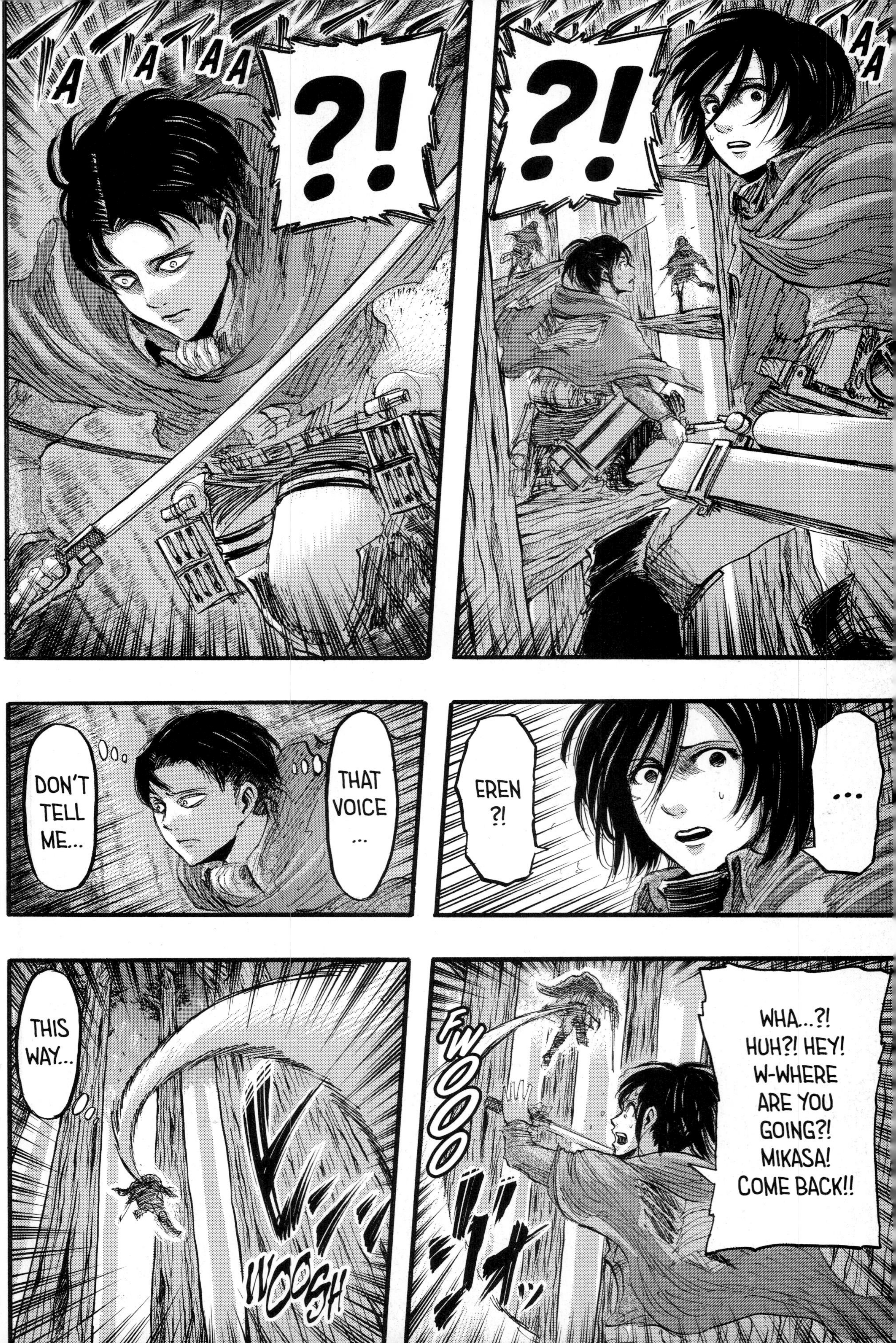
AA
A
?!
A A A AA
?!
...
EREN ?!
THAT VOICE ...
DON'T TELL ME...
WHA...?! HUH?! HEY! W-WHERE ARE YOU GOING?! MIKASA! COME BACK!!
FWOOOO
THIS WAY...
WOOSH

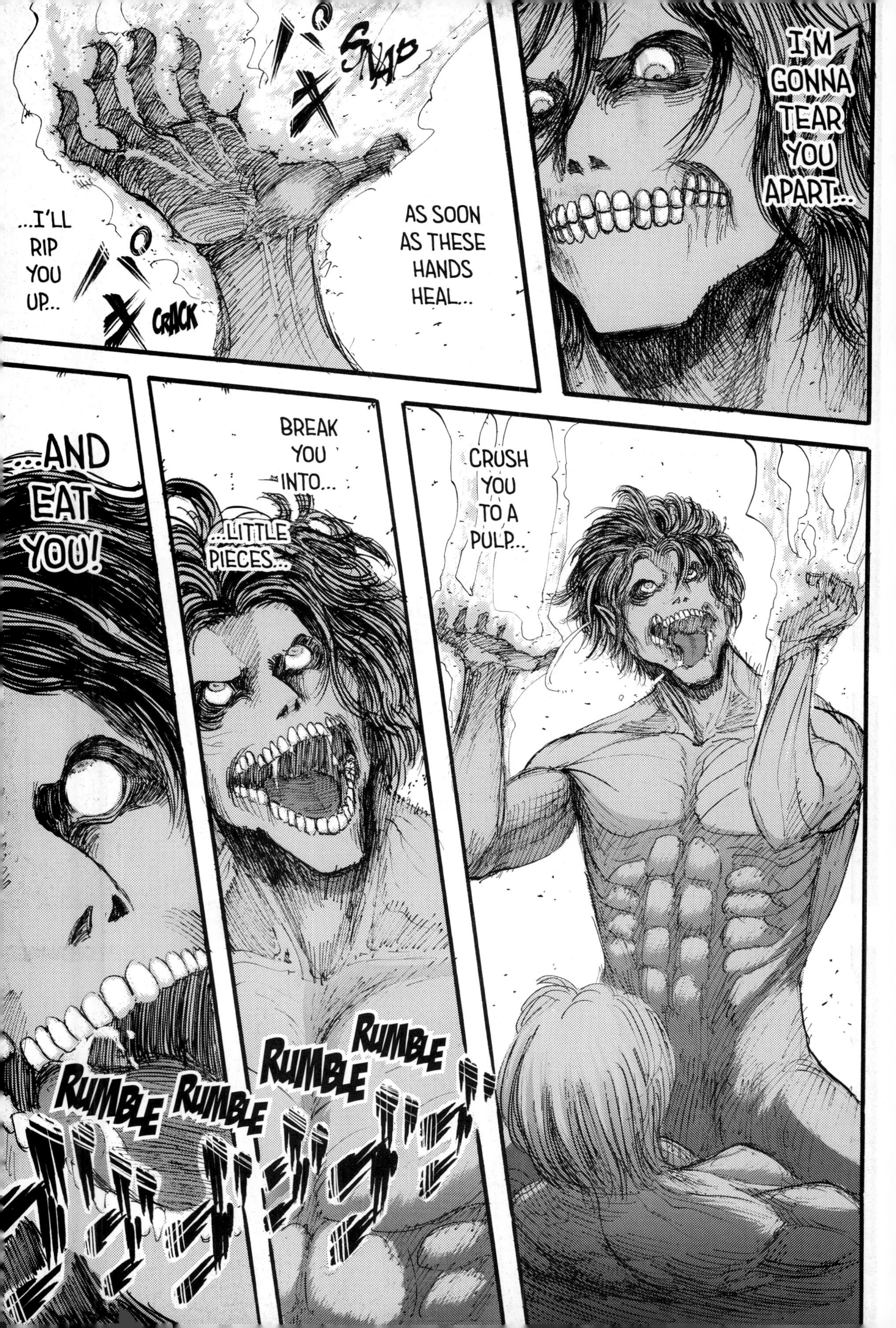
I'M GONNA TEAR YOU APART...
SNAP
AS SOON AS THESE HANDS HEAL...
...I'LL RIP YOU UP...
CRACK
CRUSH YOU TO A PULP...
BREAK YOU INTO...
...LITTLE PIECES...
...AND EAT YOU!
RUMBLE
RUMBLE
RUMBLE
RUMBLE

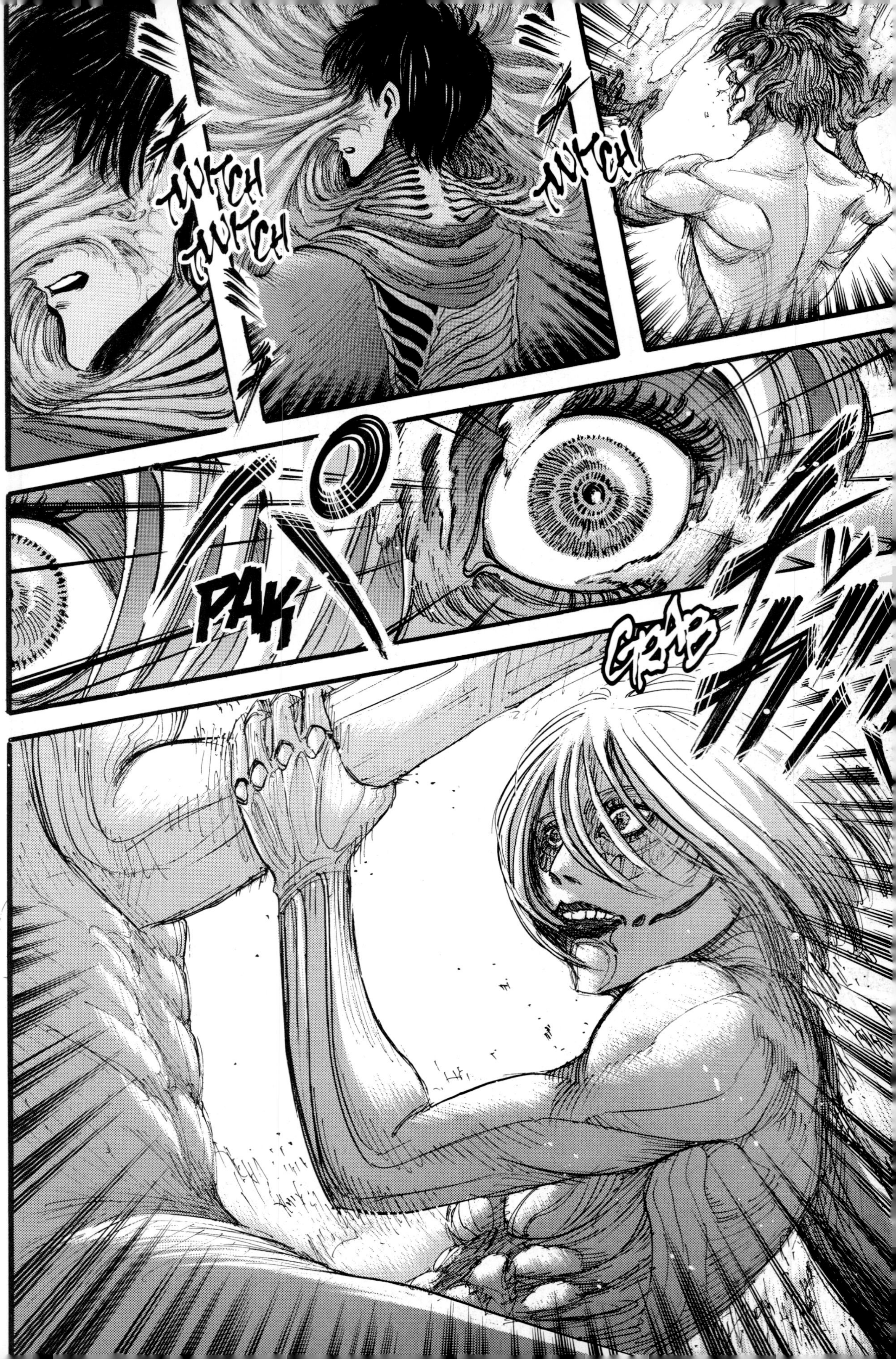
TWITCH
TWITCH
TWITCH
PAK
GRAB

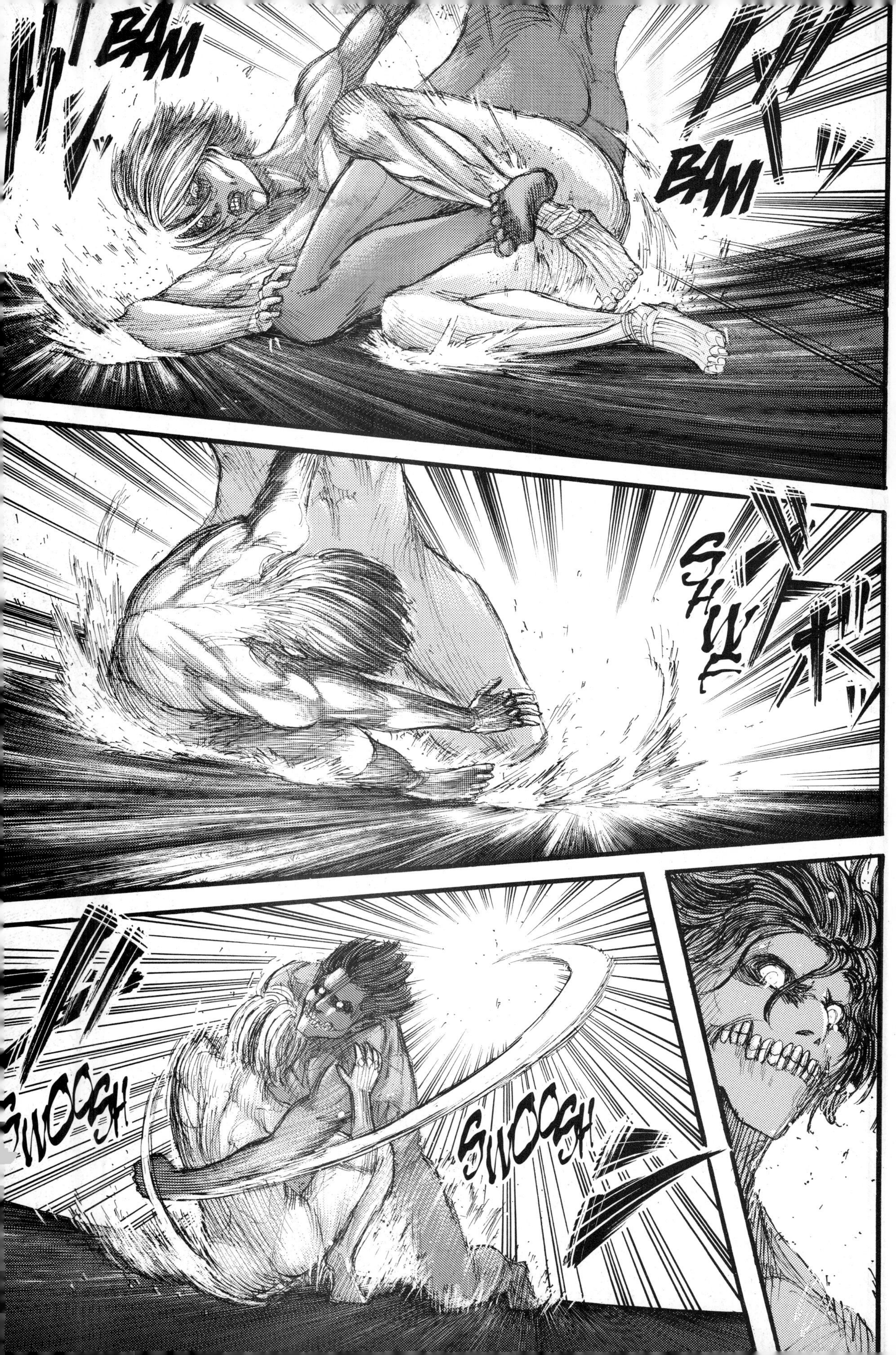

BAM
BAM
SHWF
SWOOSH!
SWOOSH!

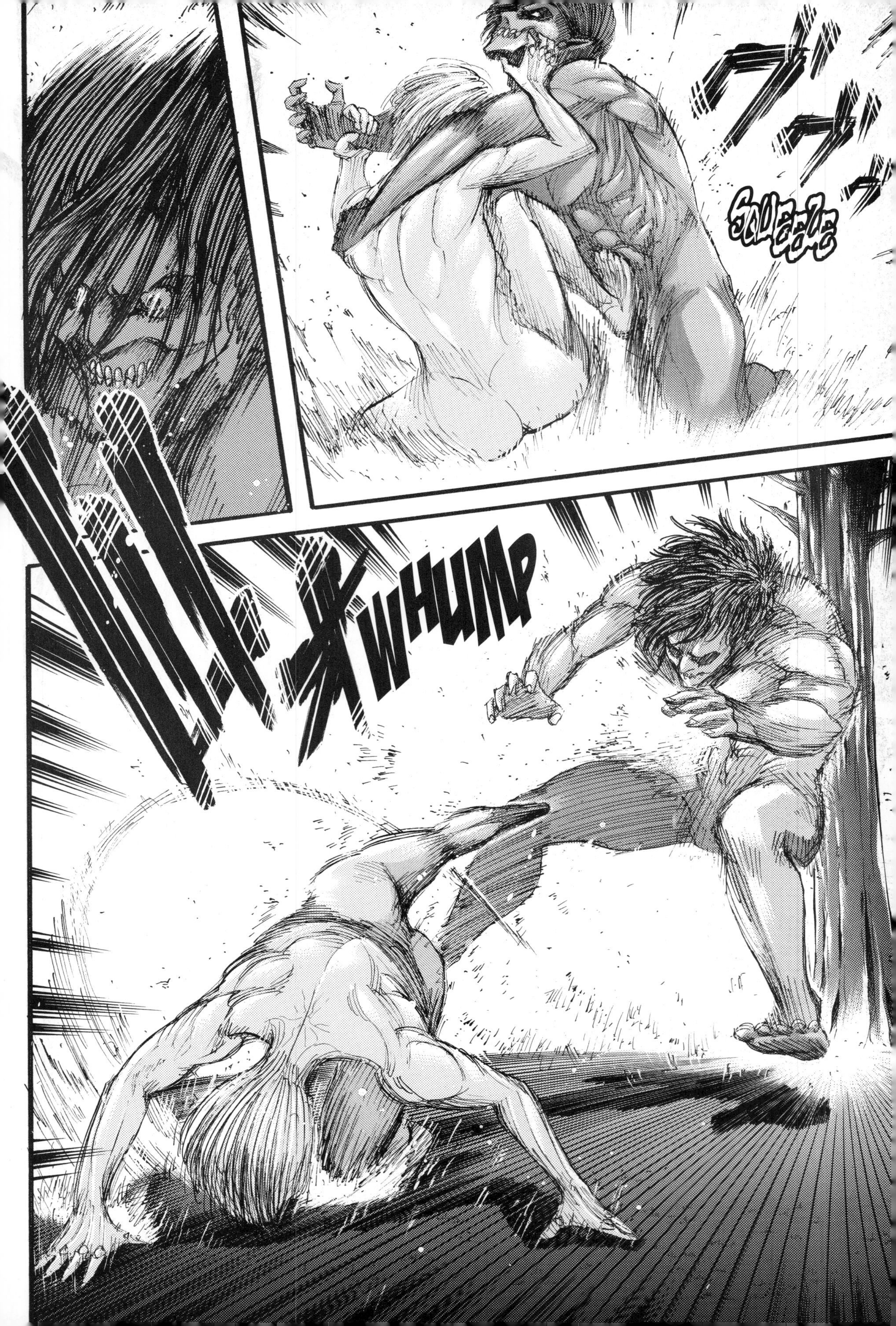
SQUEEZE
WHUMP

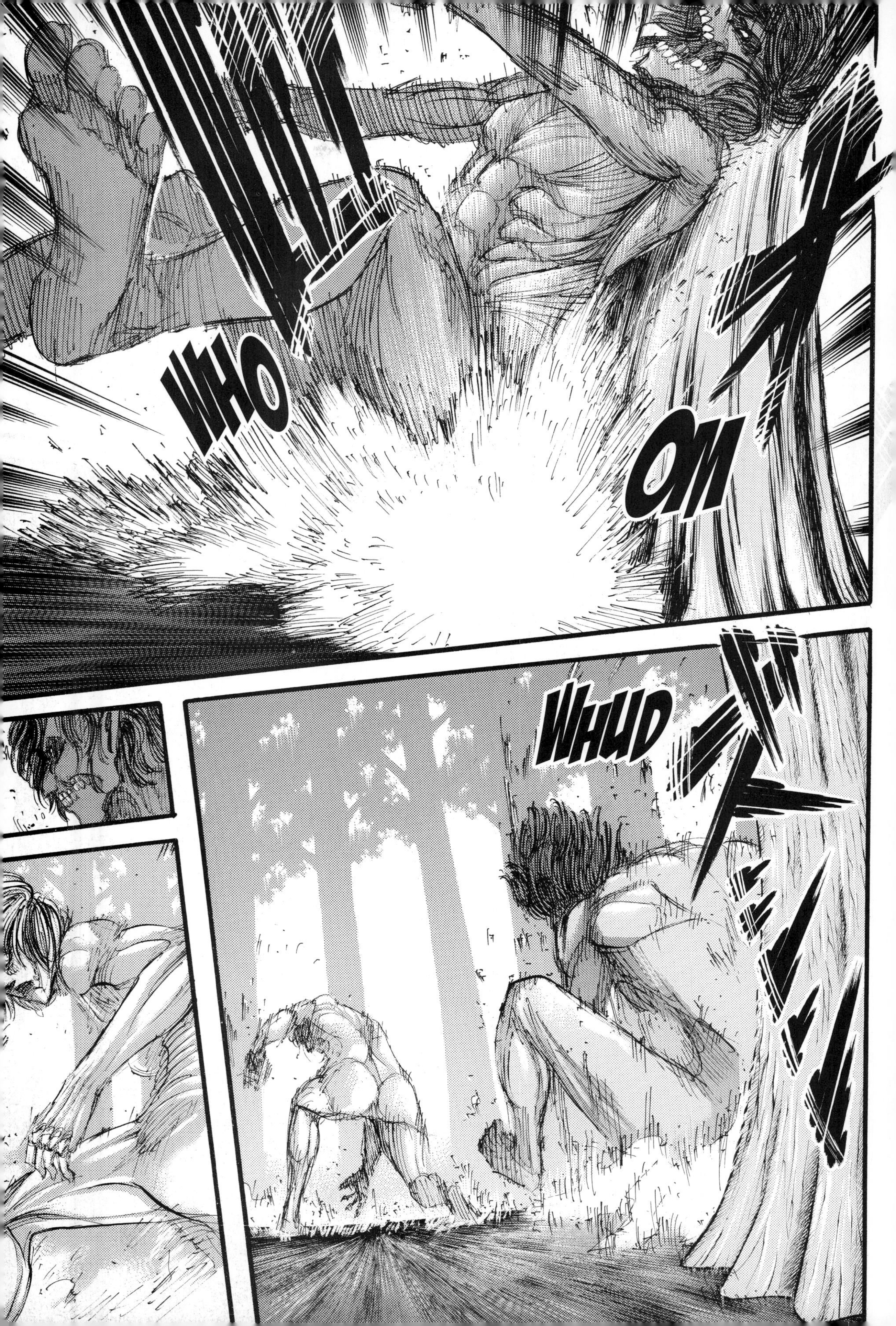
WHO
OM
WHUD

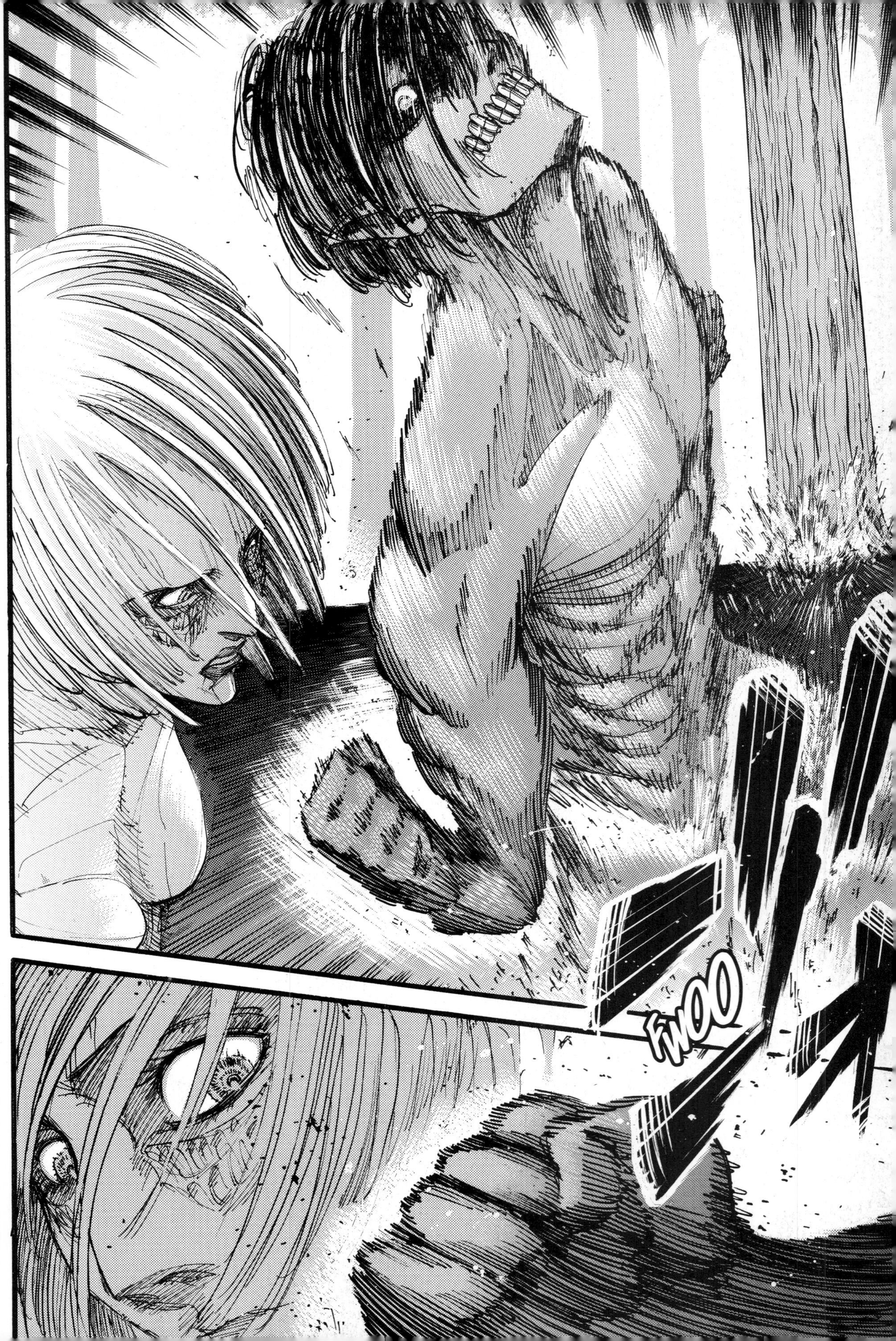
FWOO

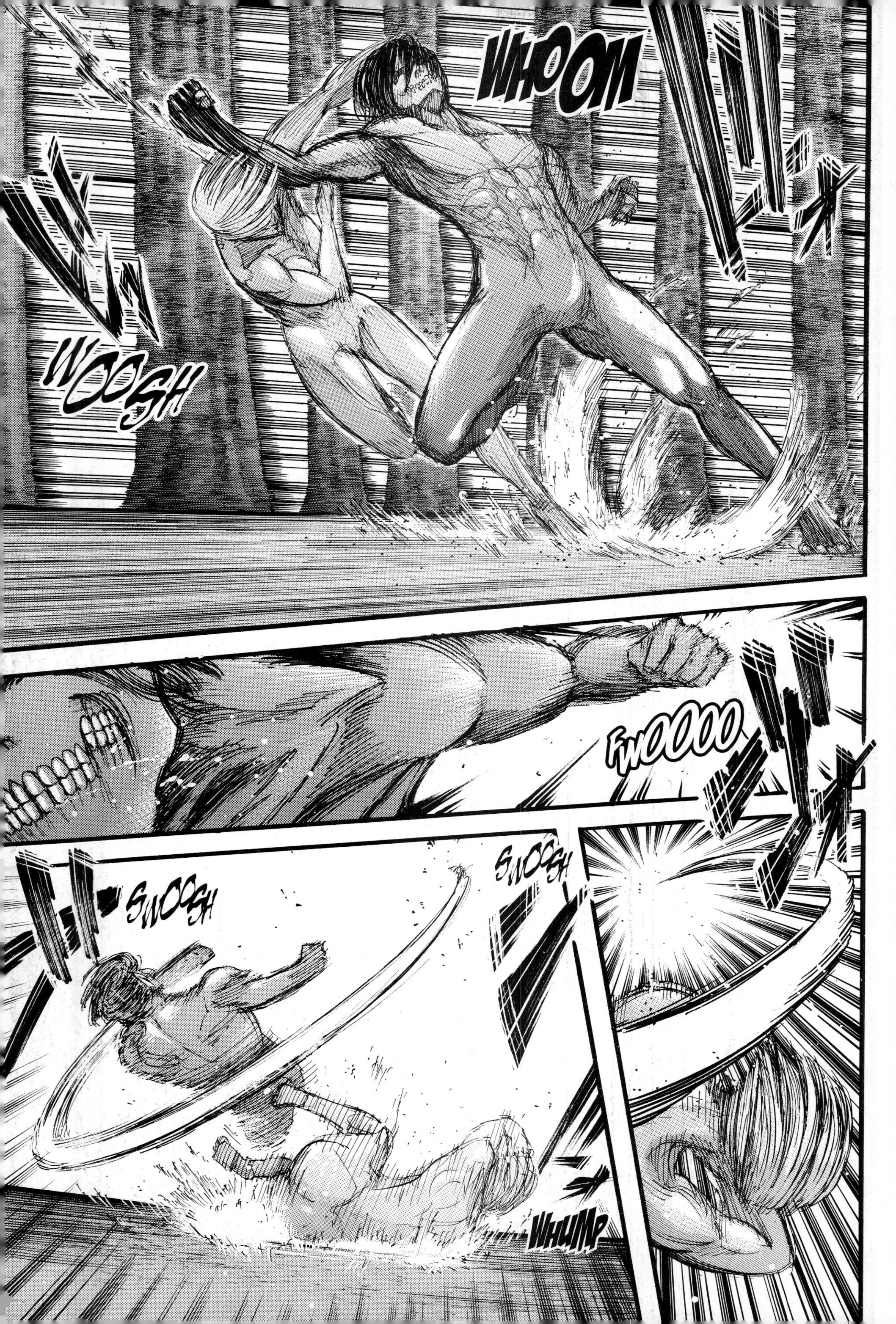
WHOOM
WOOSH
FWOOOO
SWOOSH
SWOOSH
WHUMP

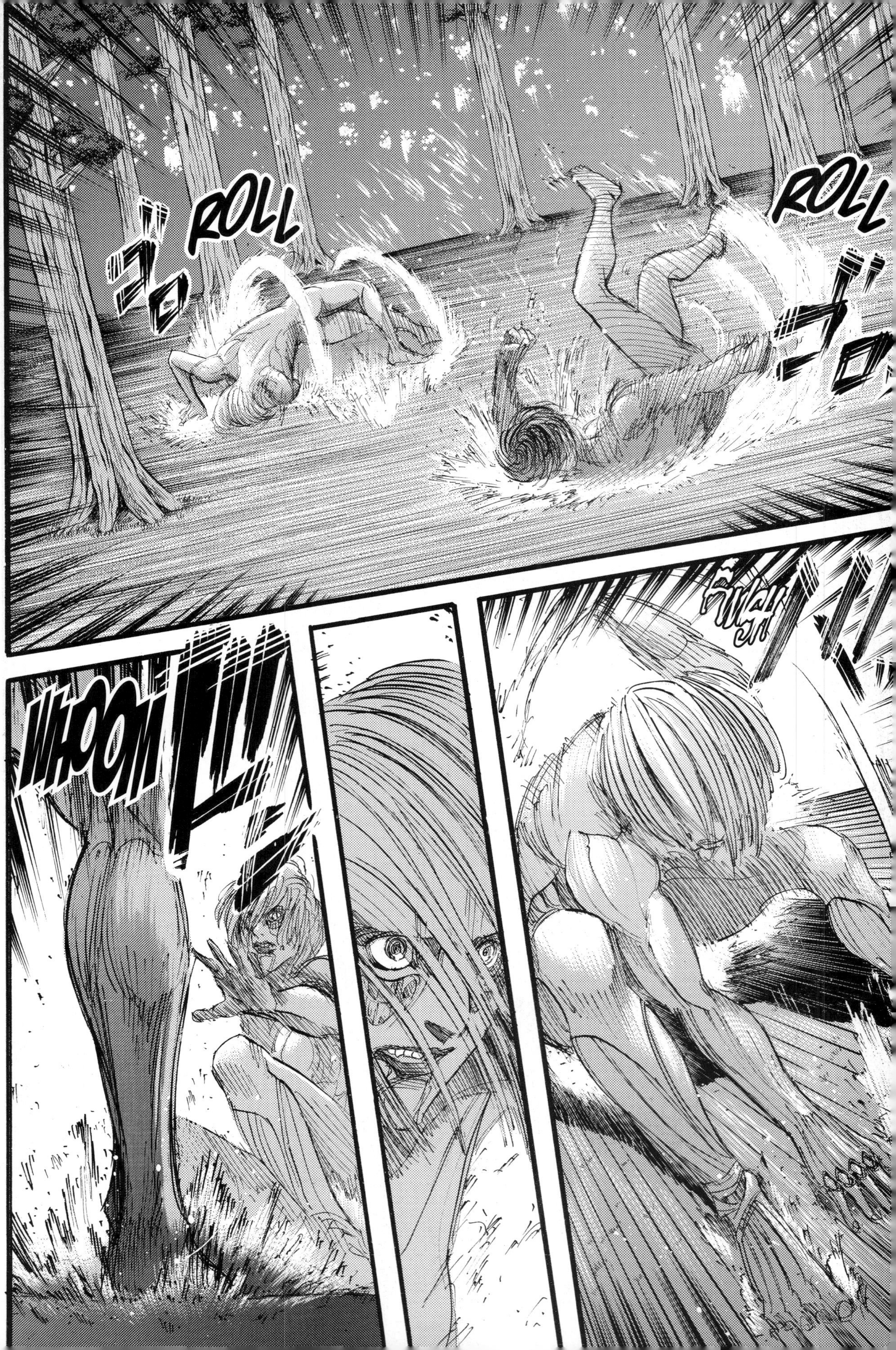
ROLL
ゴロ
ROLL
ゴロ
WHOOM

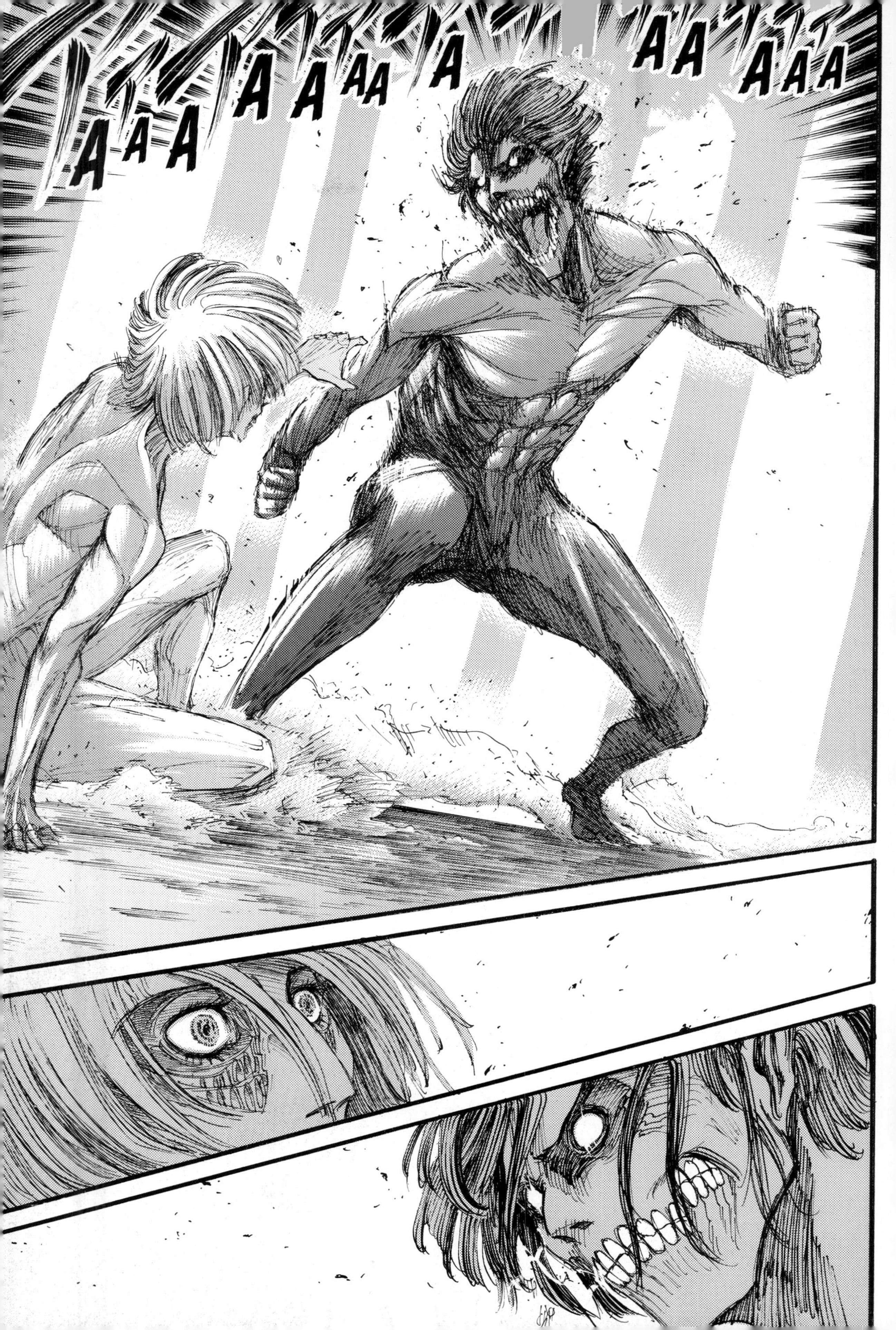
AAAAAAAAAAAAAAA

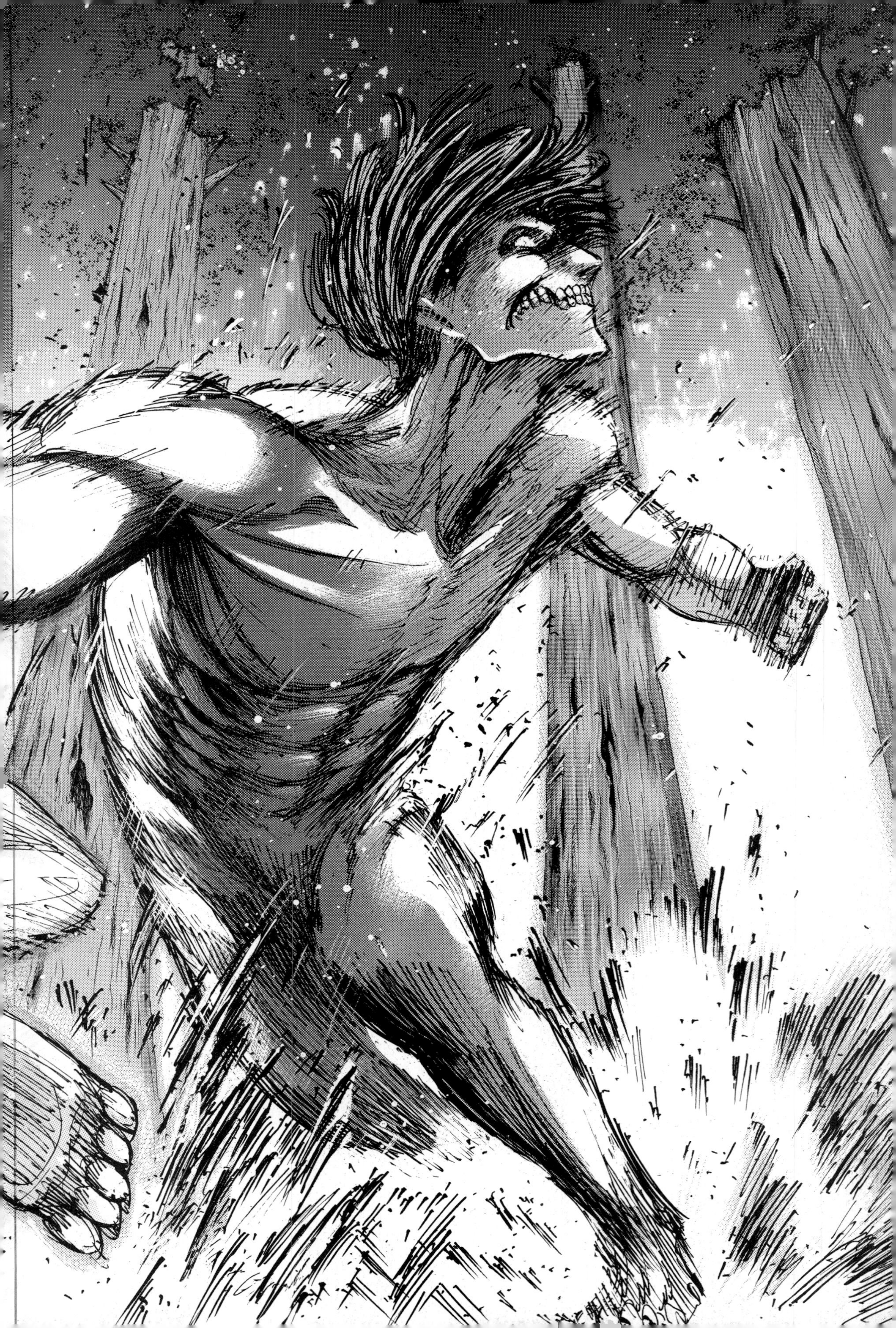

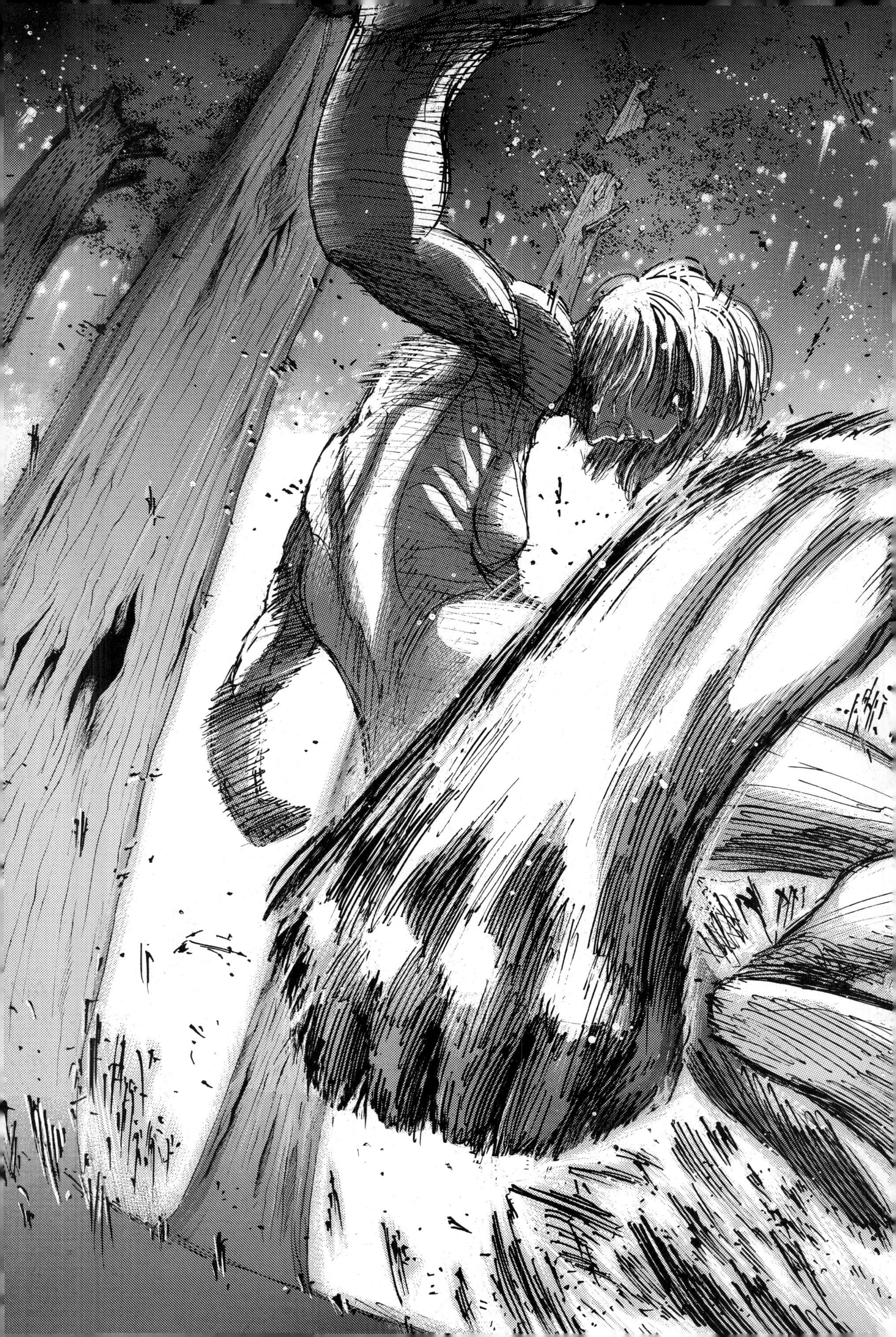

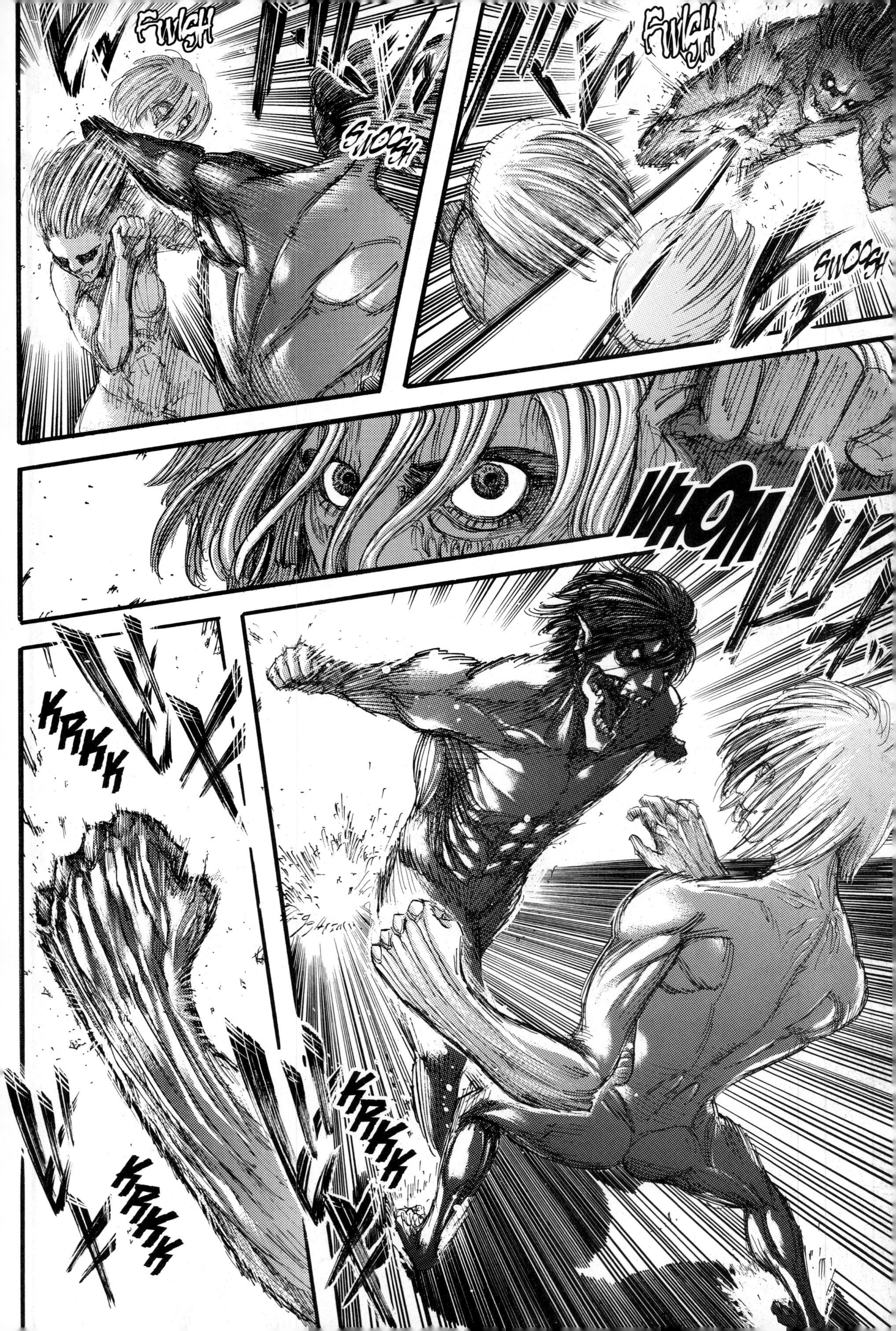
FWISH
SWOOSH
FWISH
SWOOSH
KRKKK
KRKK
KRKK

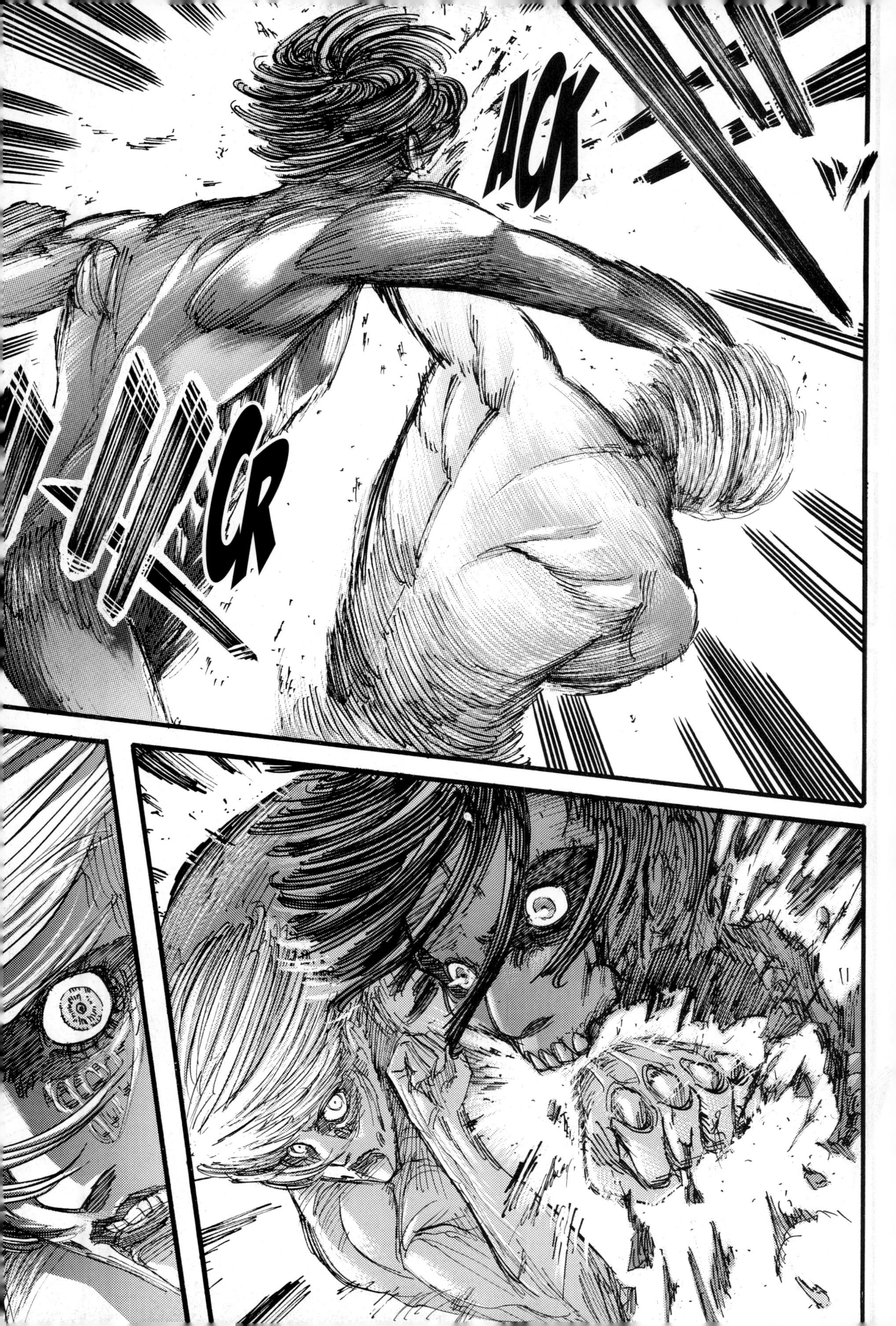
ACK
CR

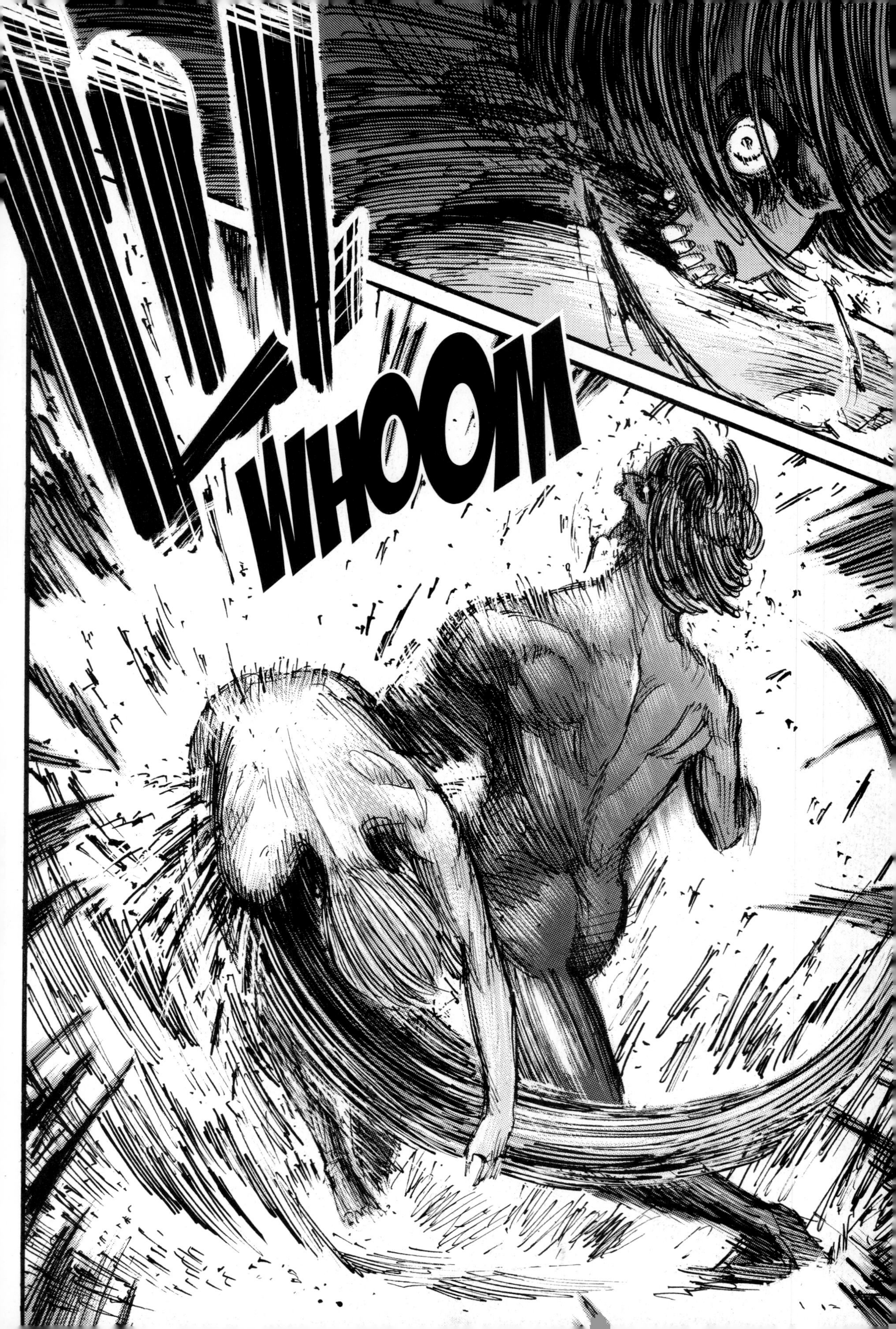
WHOOM

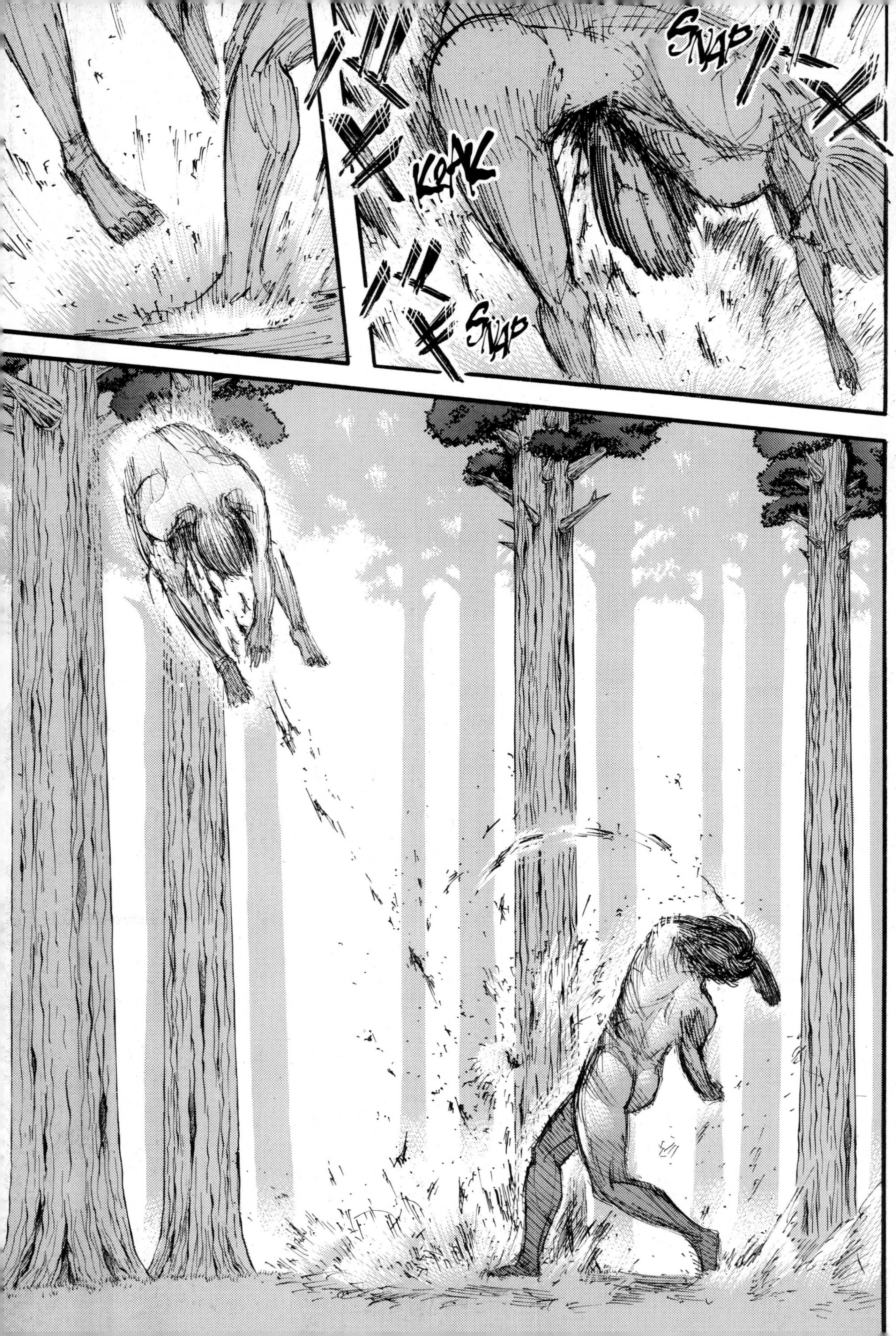
SNAP
KRAK
SNAP

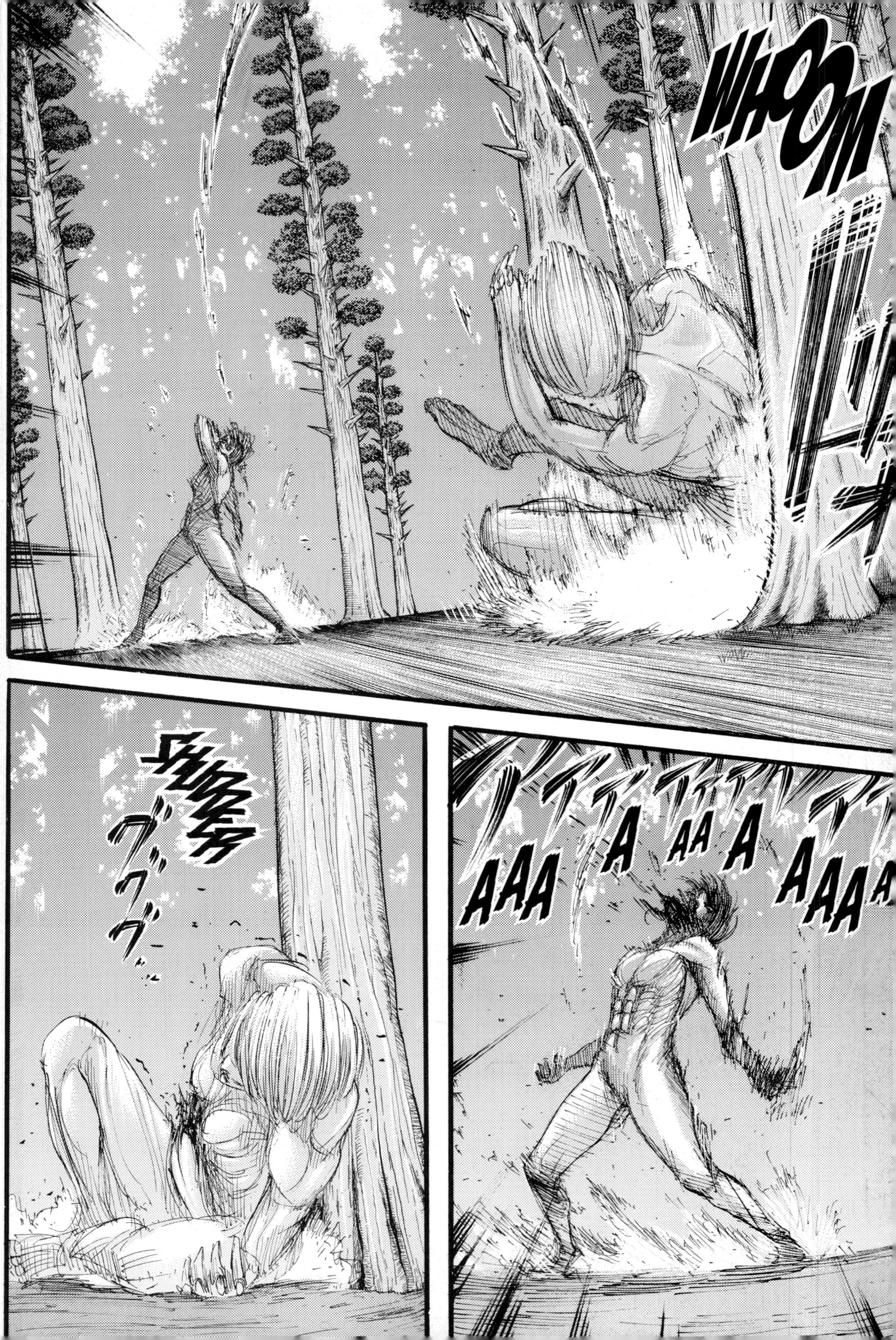
WHOOM
AAA A AA A AAAA
SHUDDER

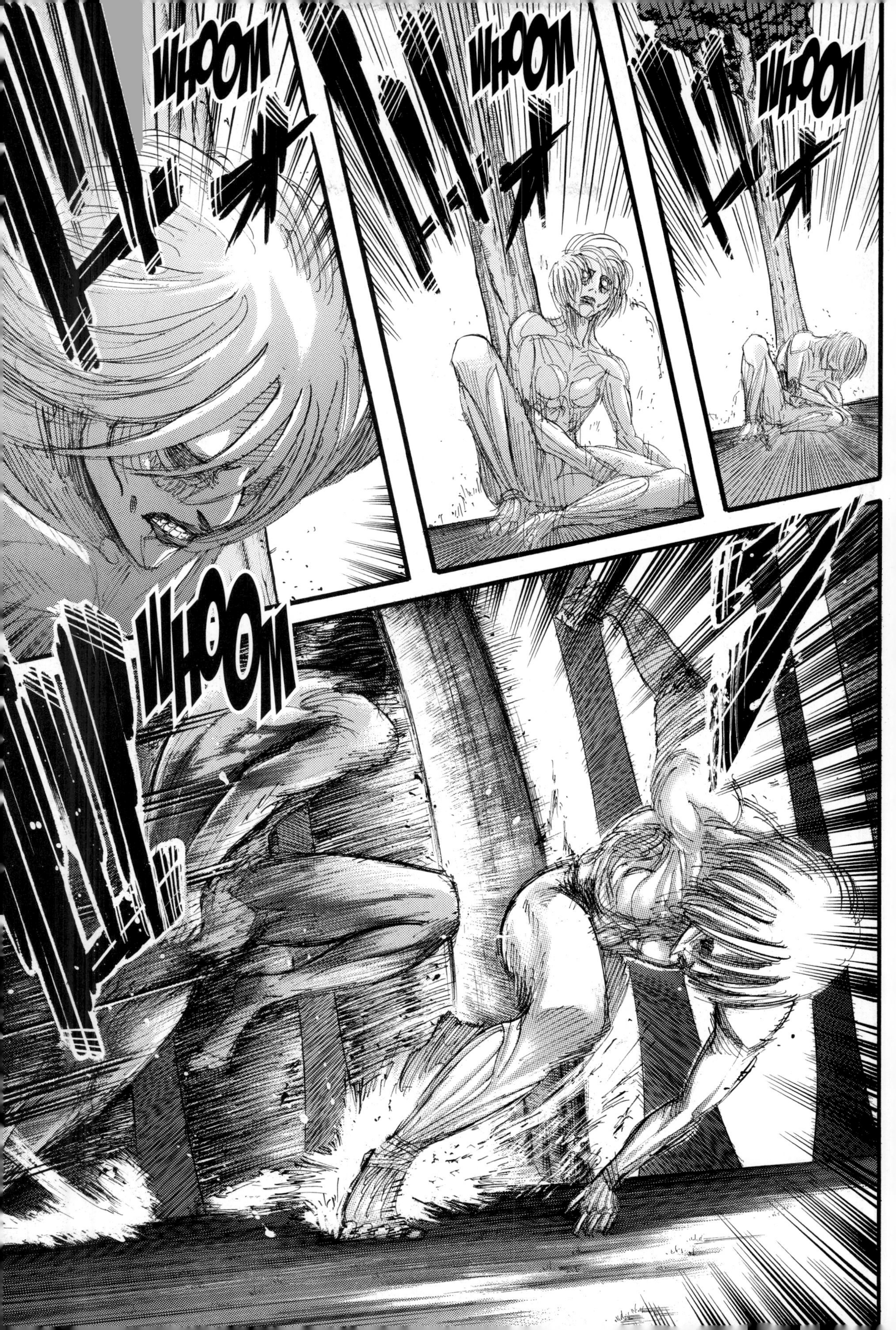
WHOOM
WHOOM
WHOOM
WHOOM

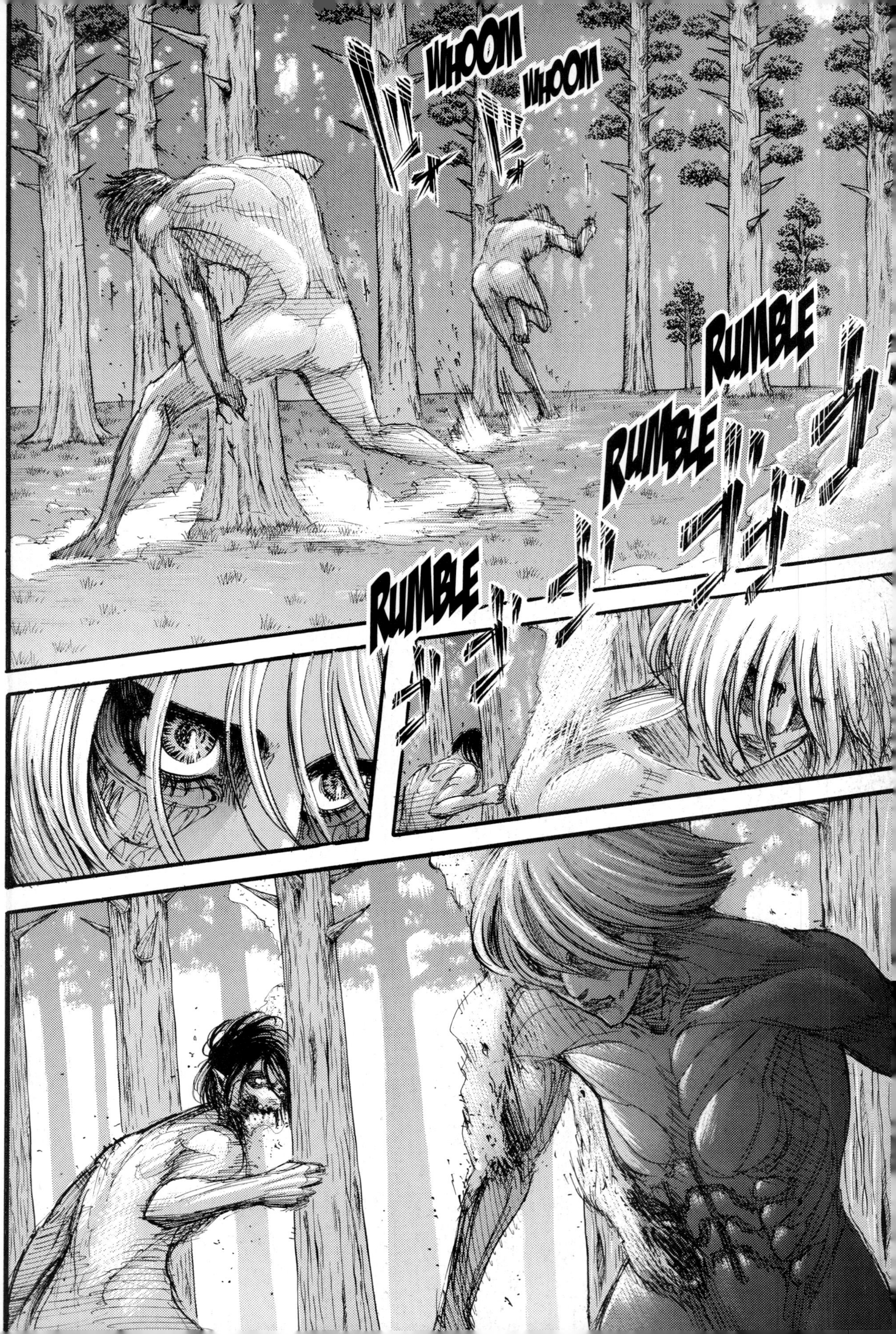
WHOOM
WHOOM
RUMBLE
RUMBLE
RUMBLE
RUMBLE

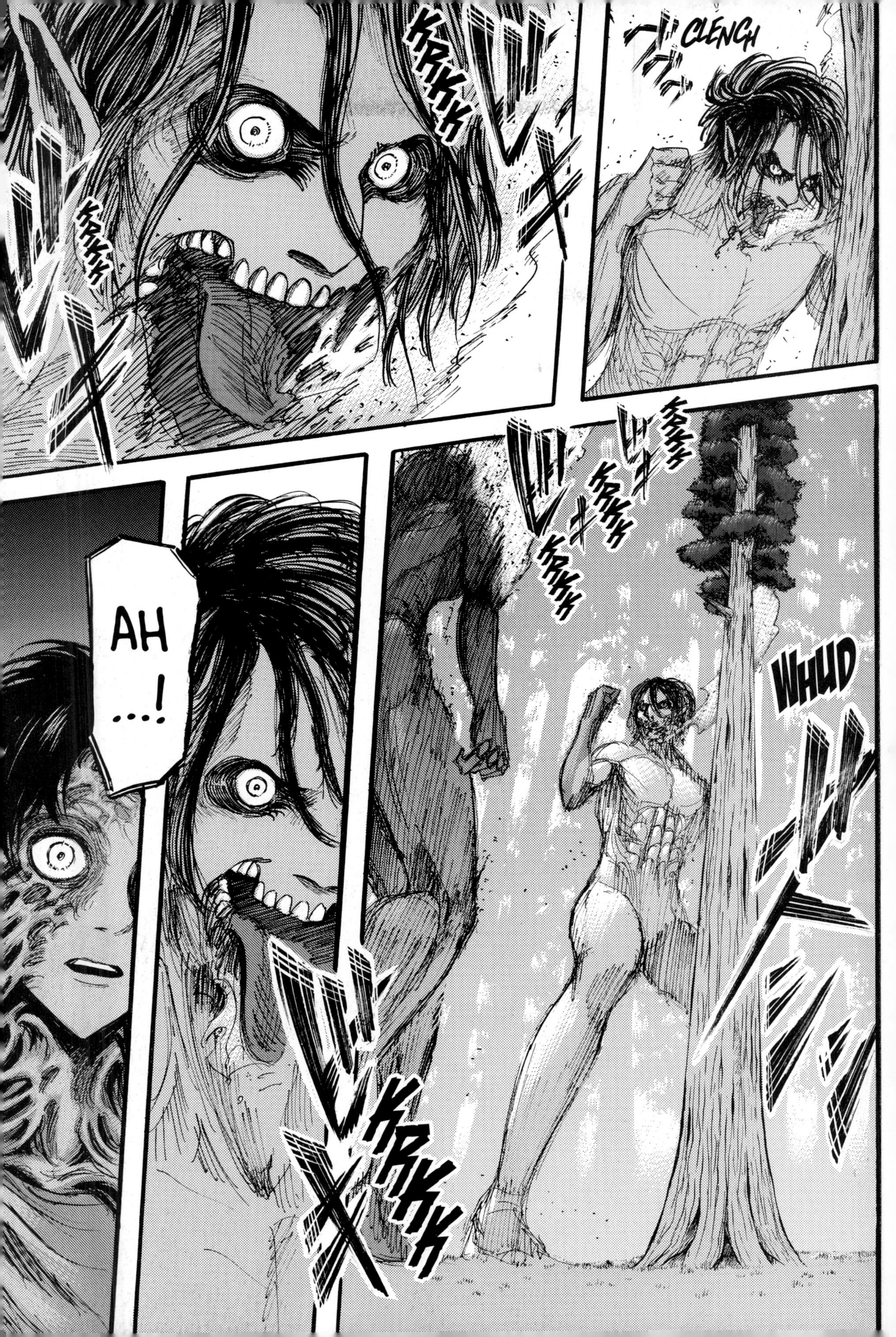
CLENCH
KRKKK
KRKKK
KRKKK
KRKKK
KRKKK
WHUD
KRKKK
AH ...!

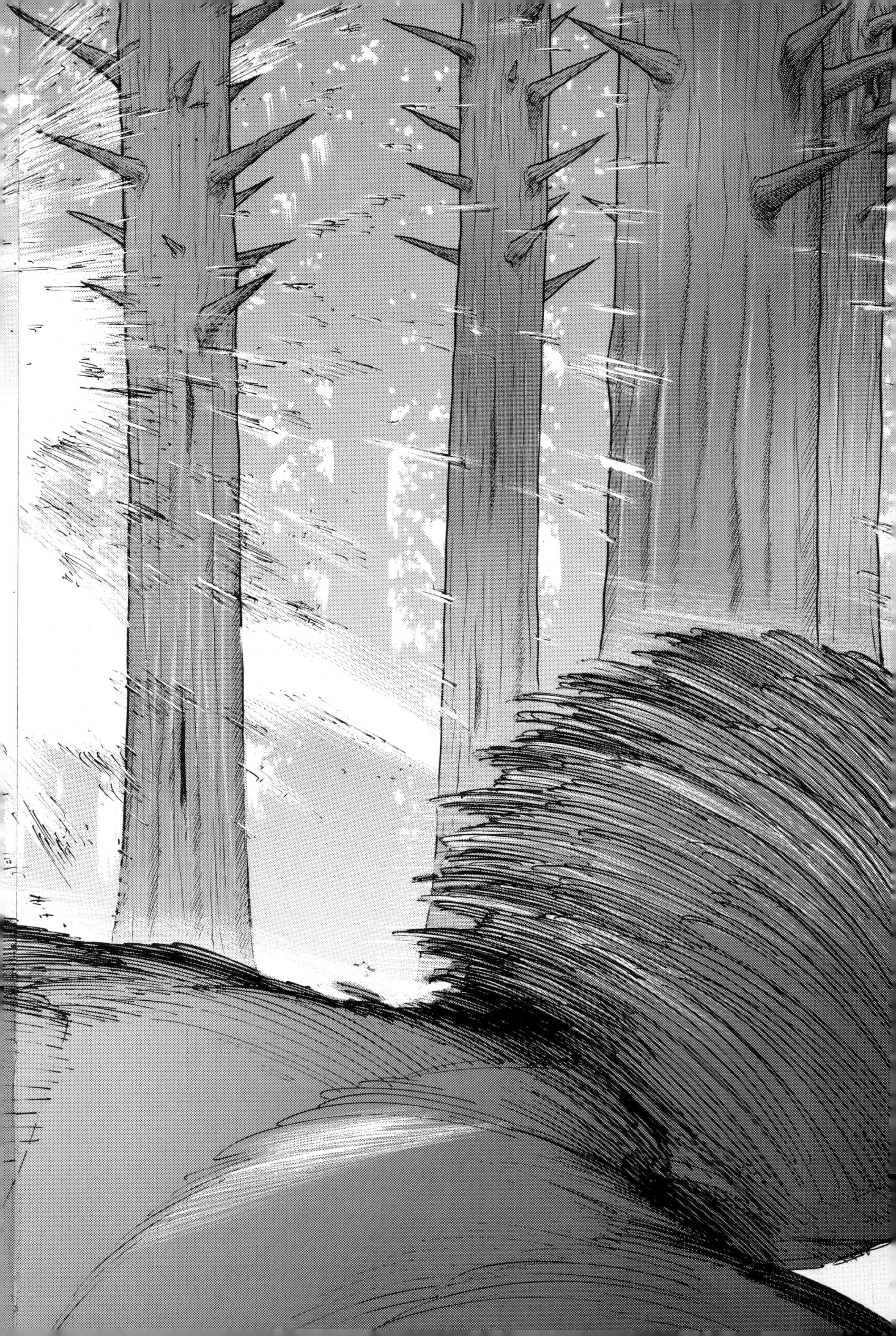

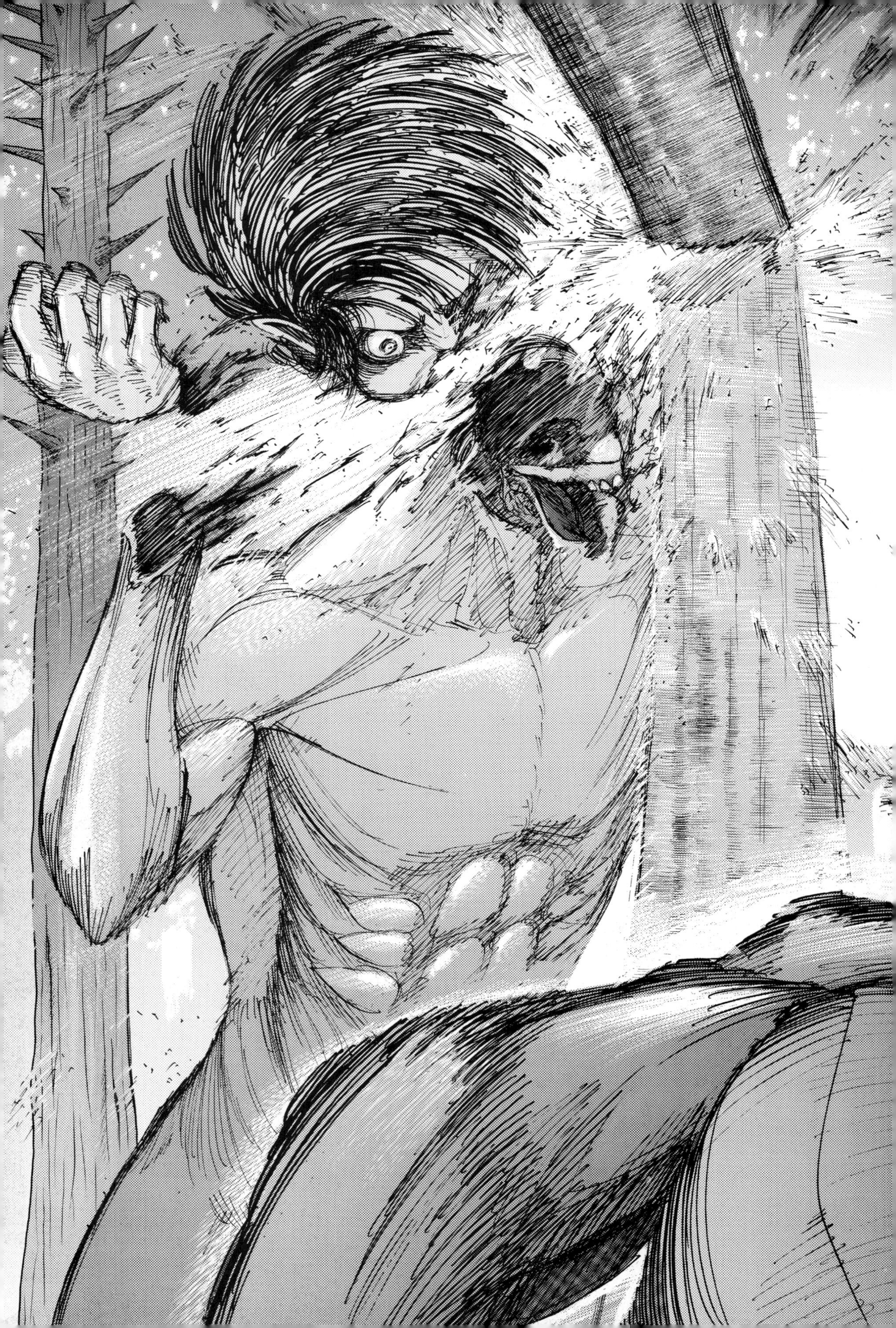

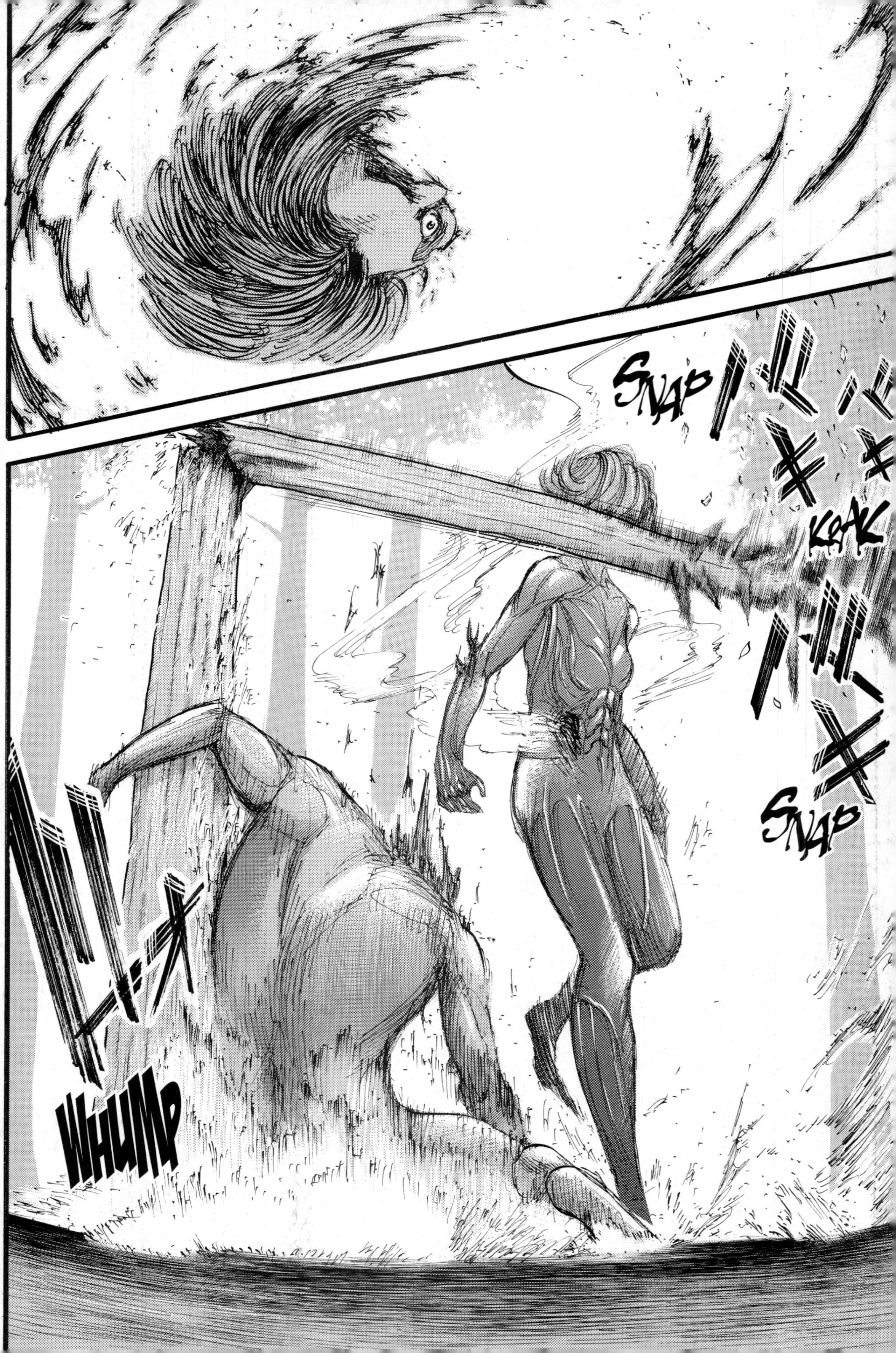
SNAP
KRAK
SNAP
WHUMP

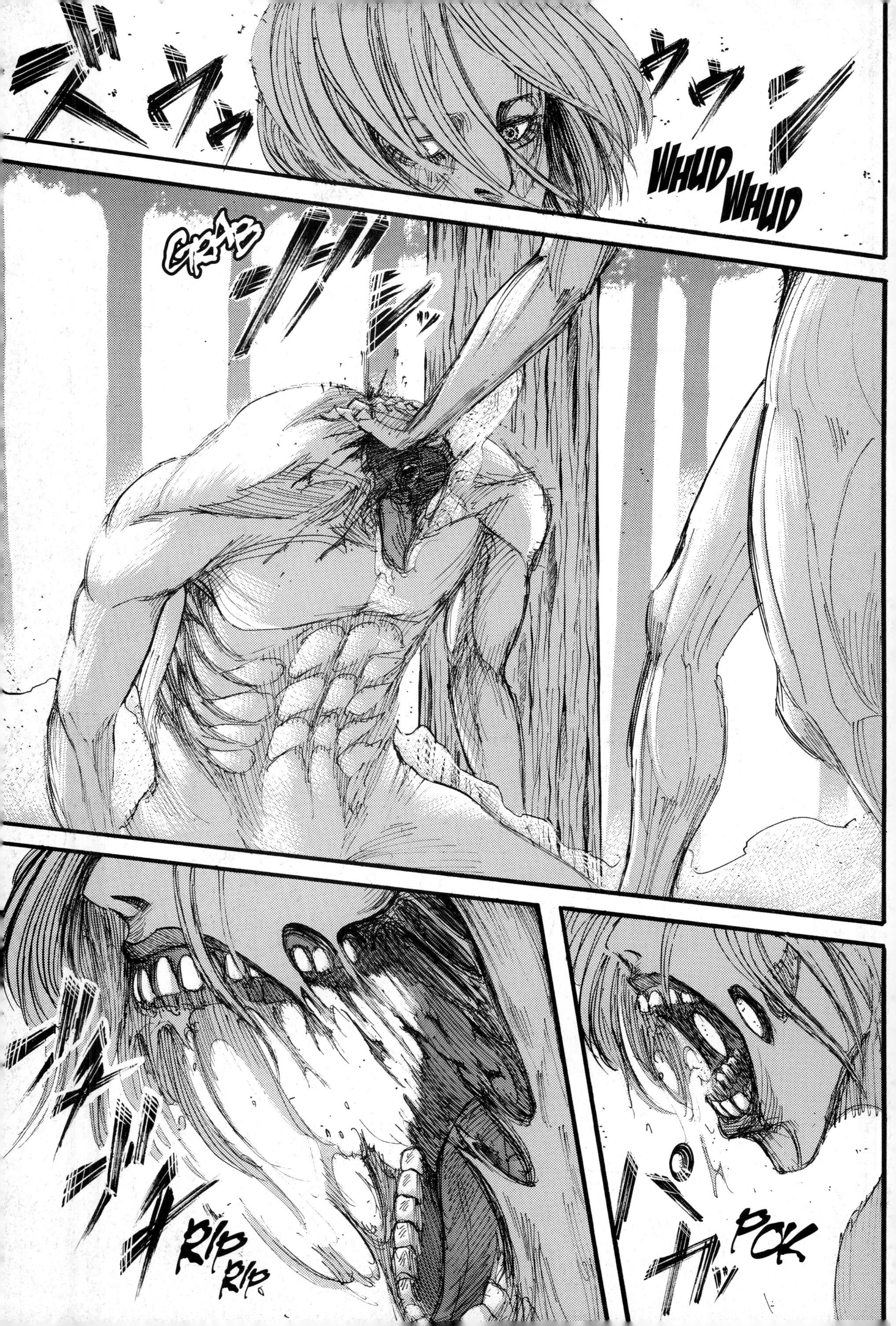
WHUD WHUD
GRAB
RIP RIP
POK

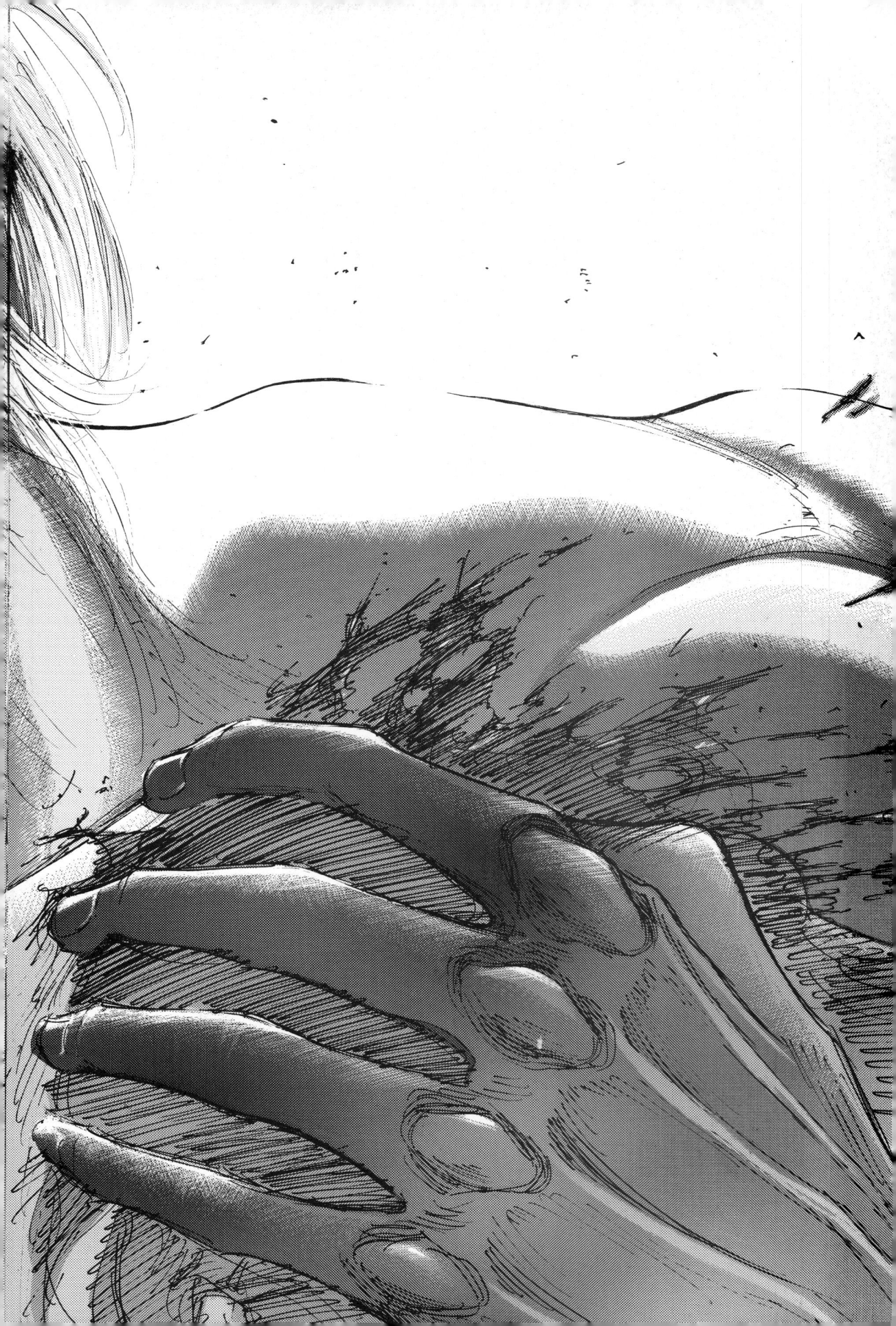

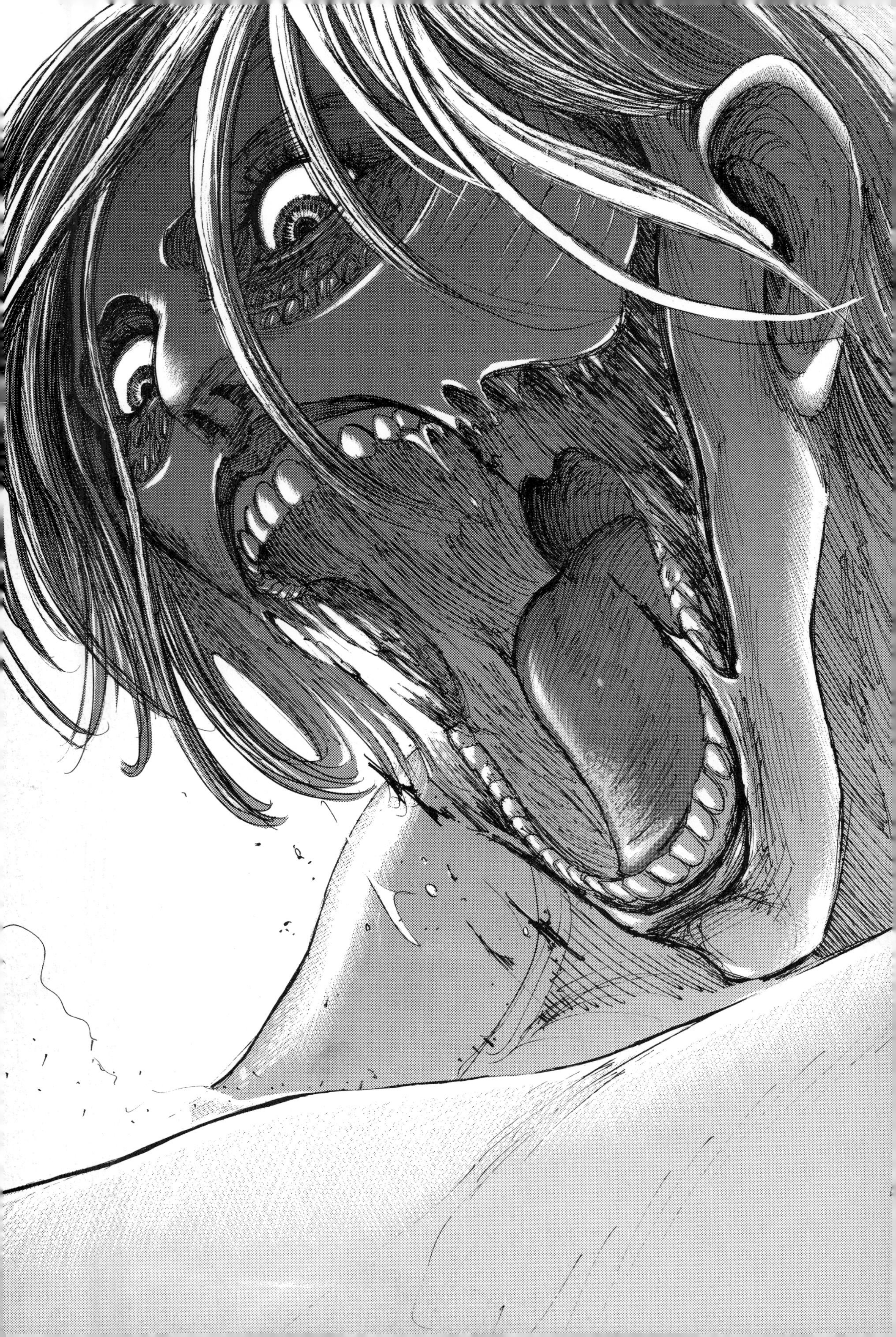

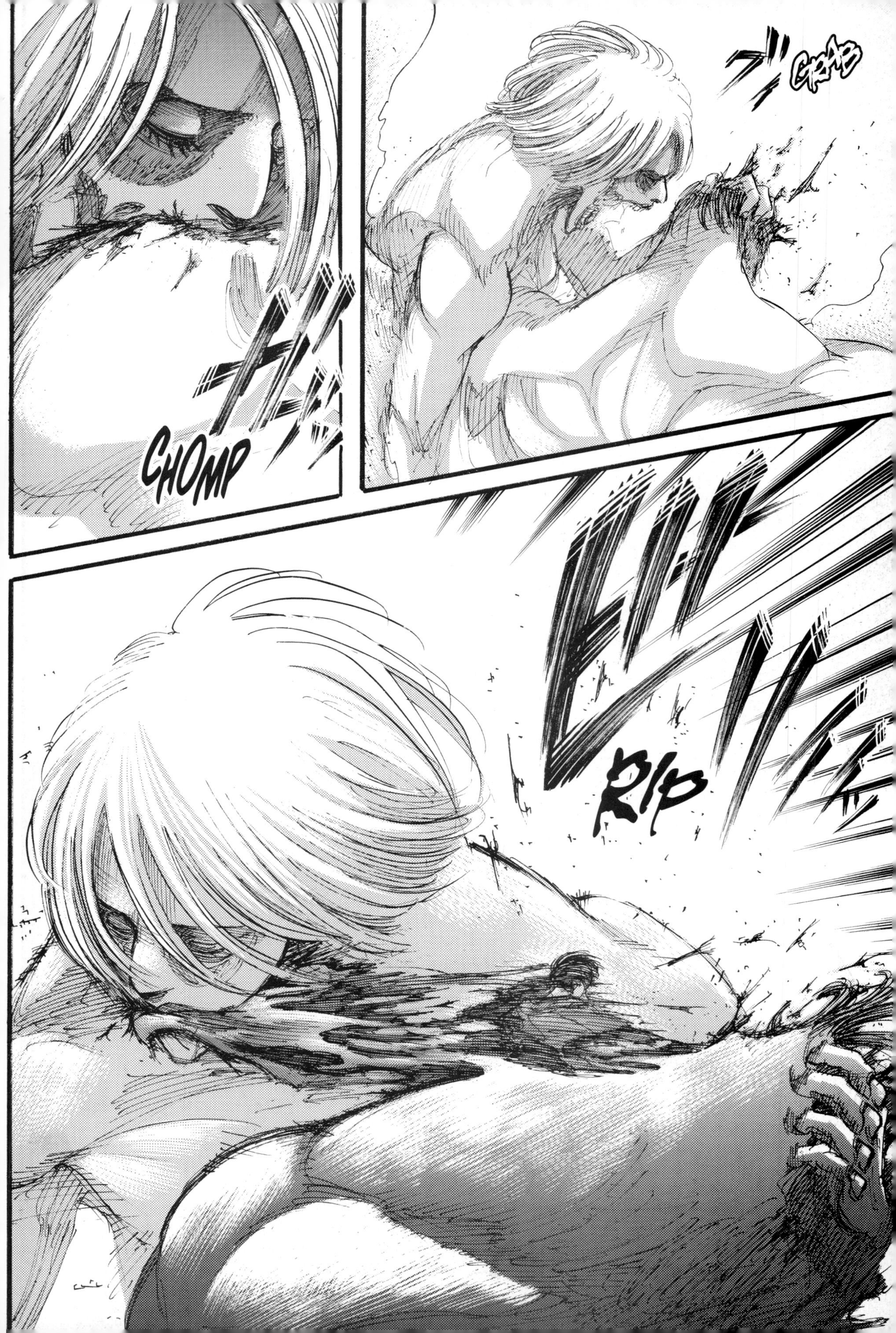
GRAB
CHOMP
RIP

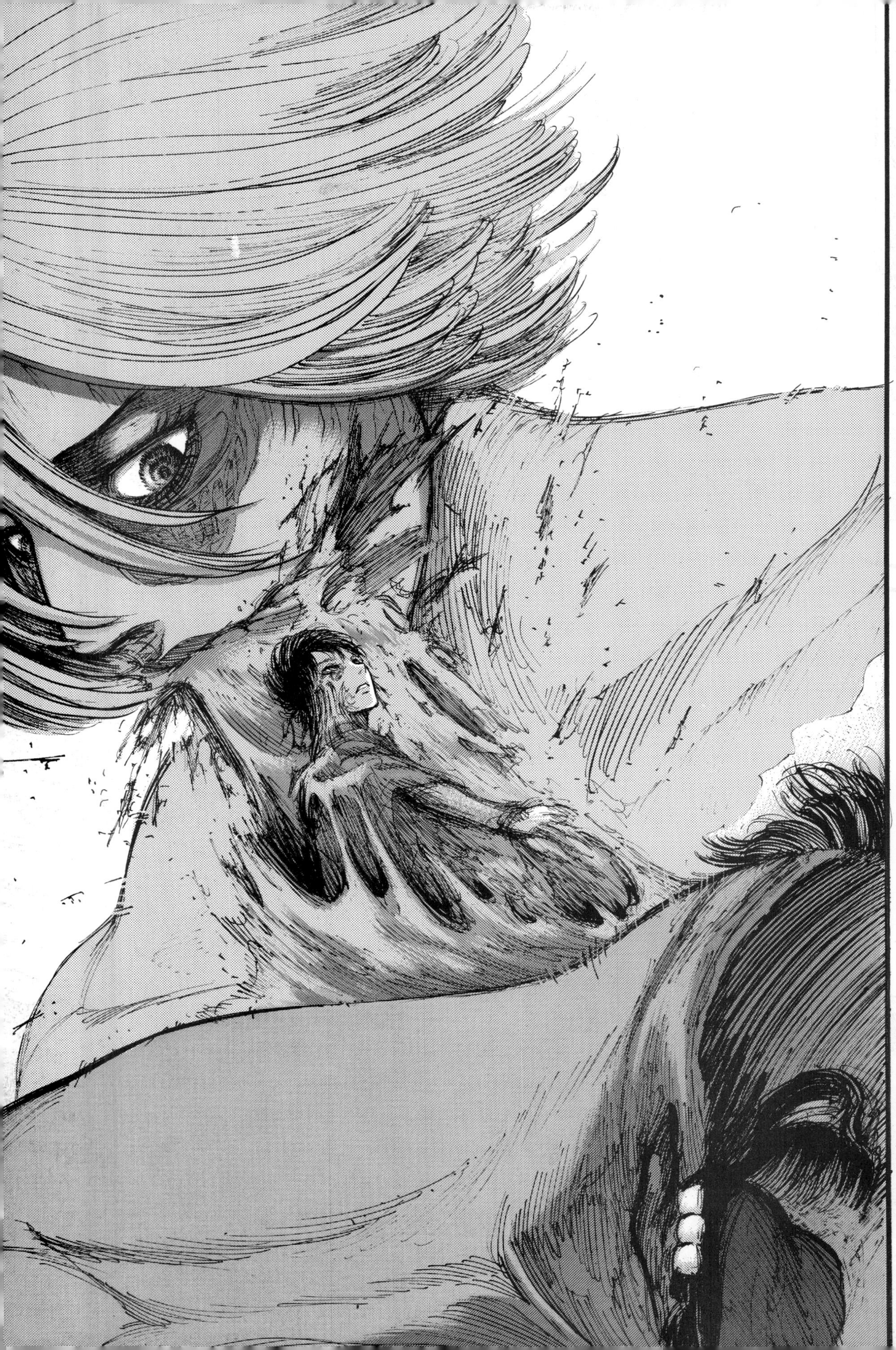

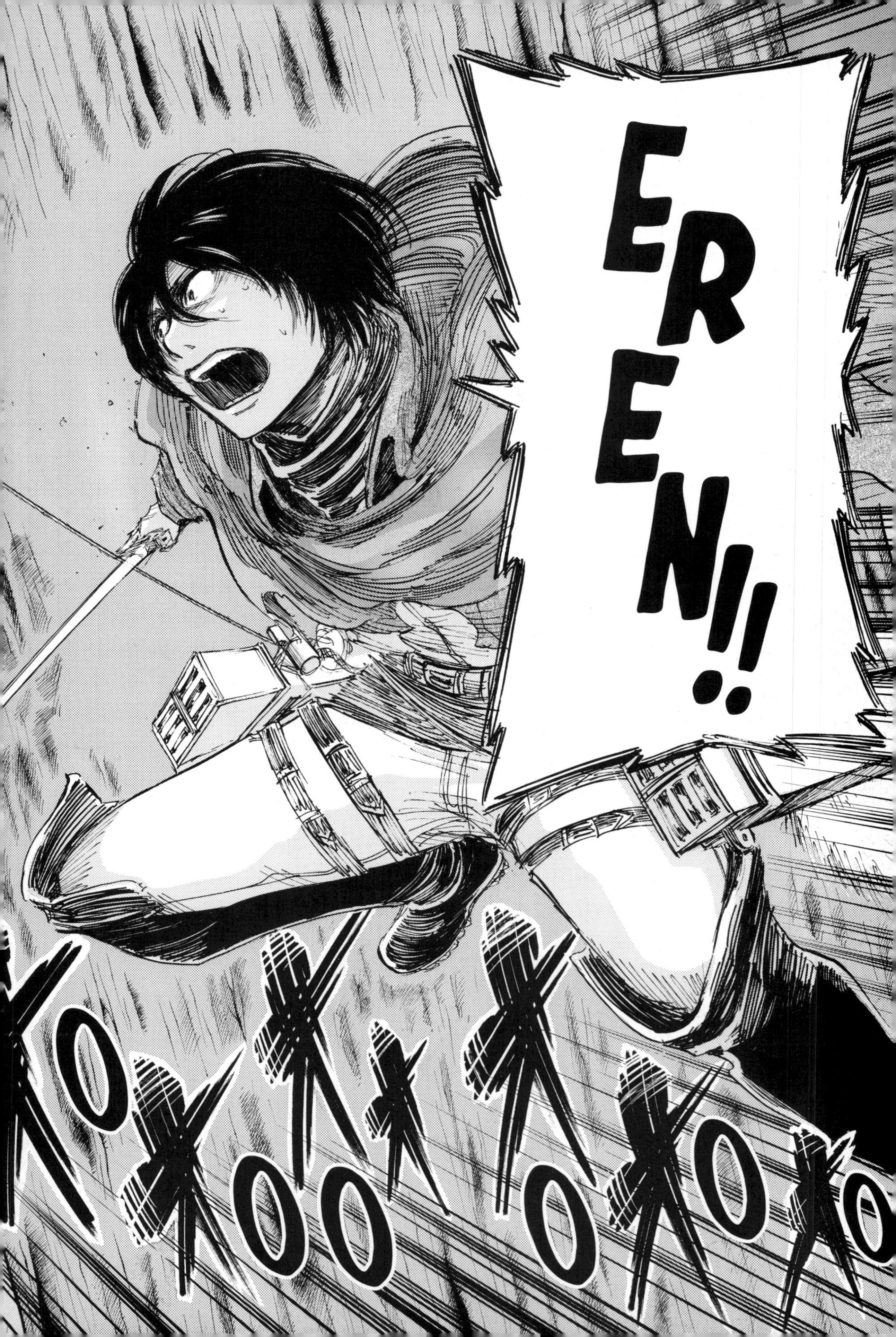
EREN!!

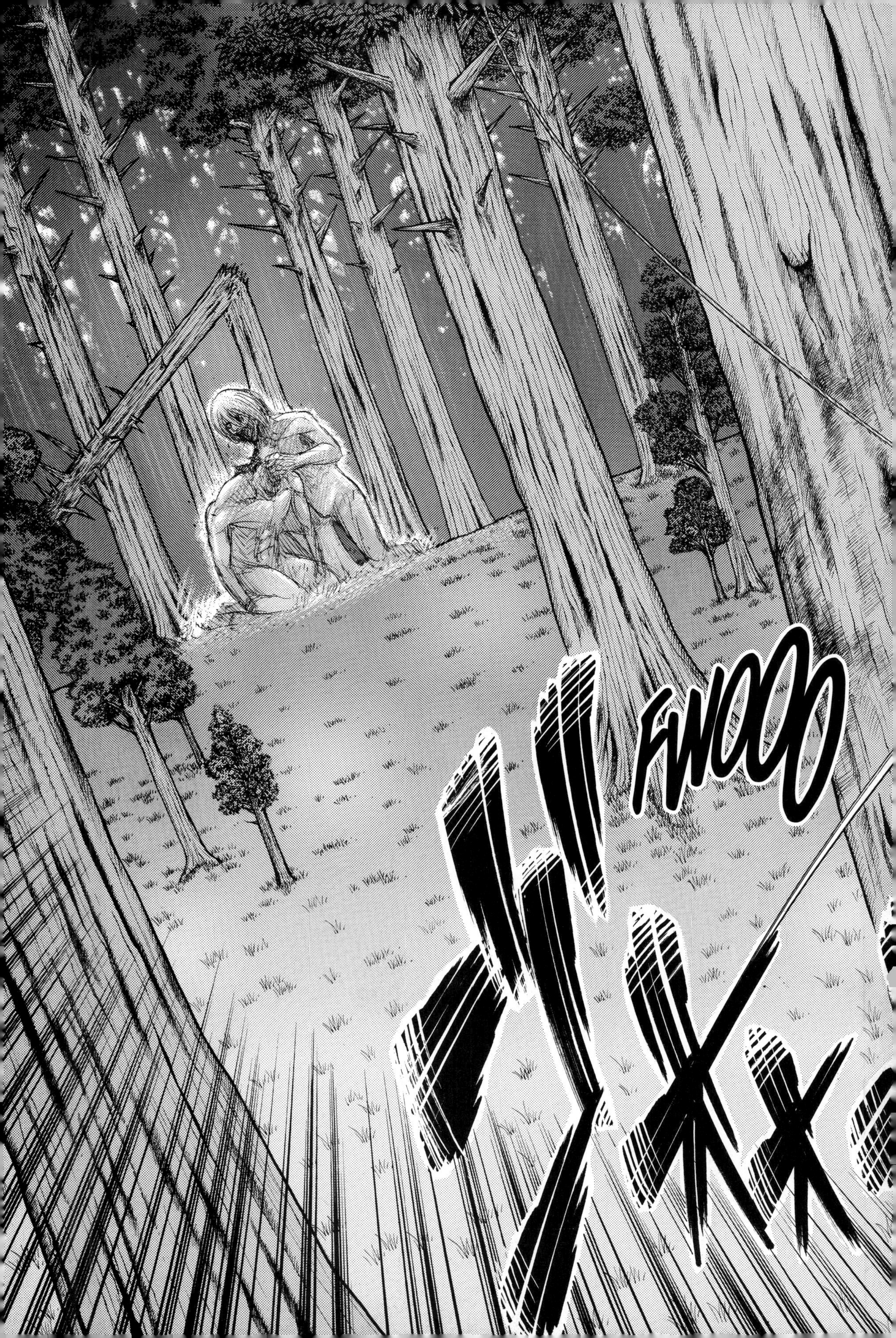
FWOOO

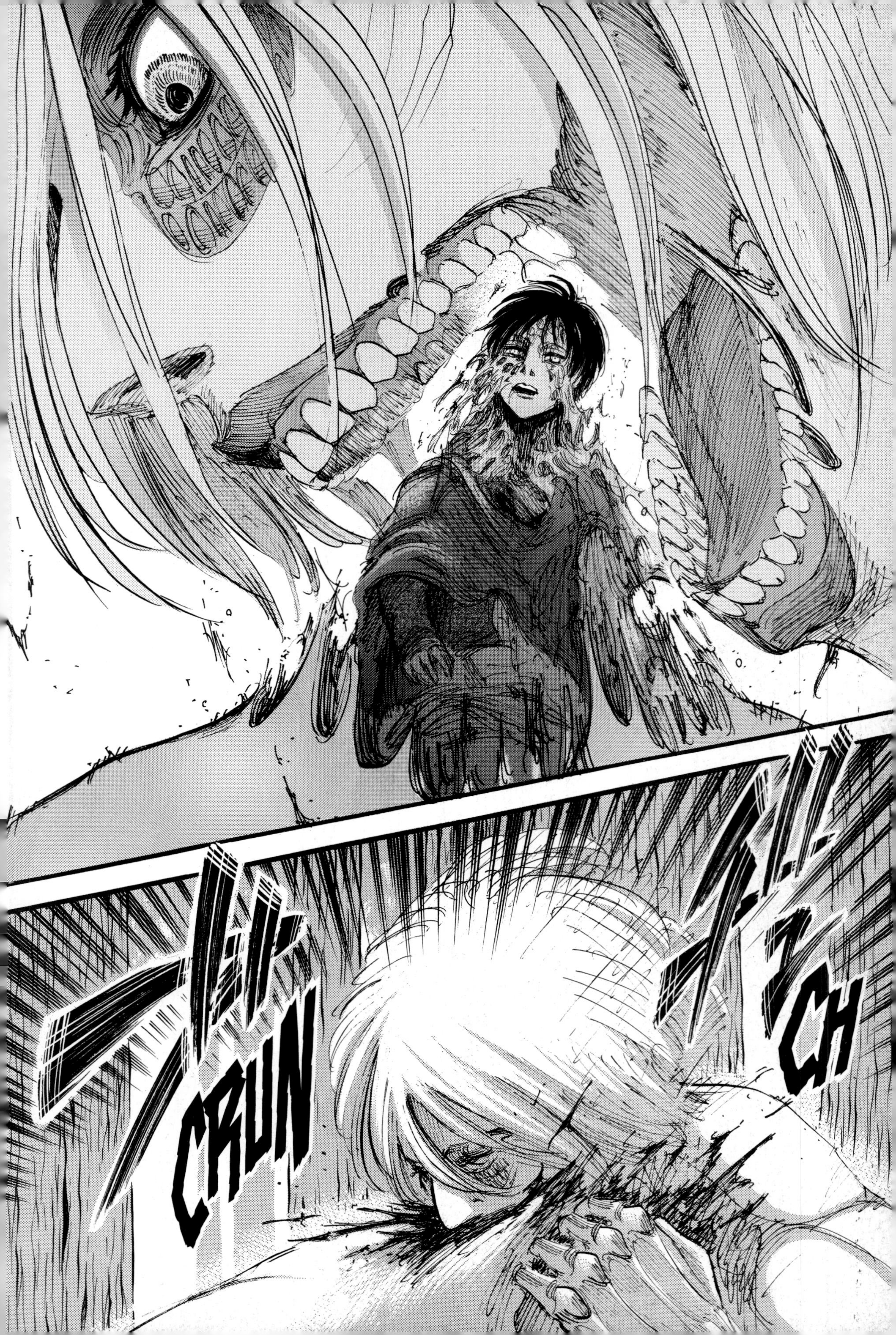
CRUN
CH

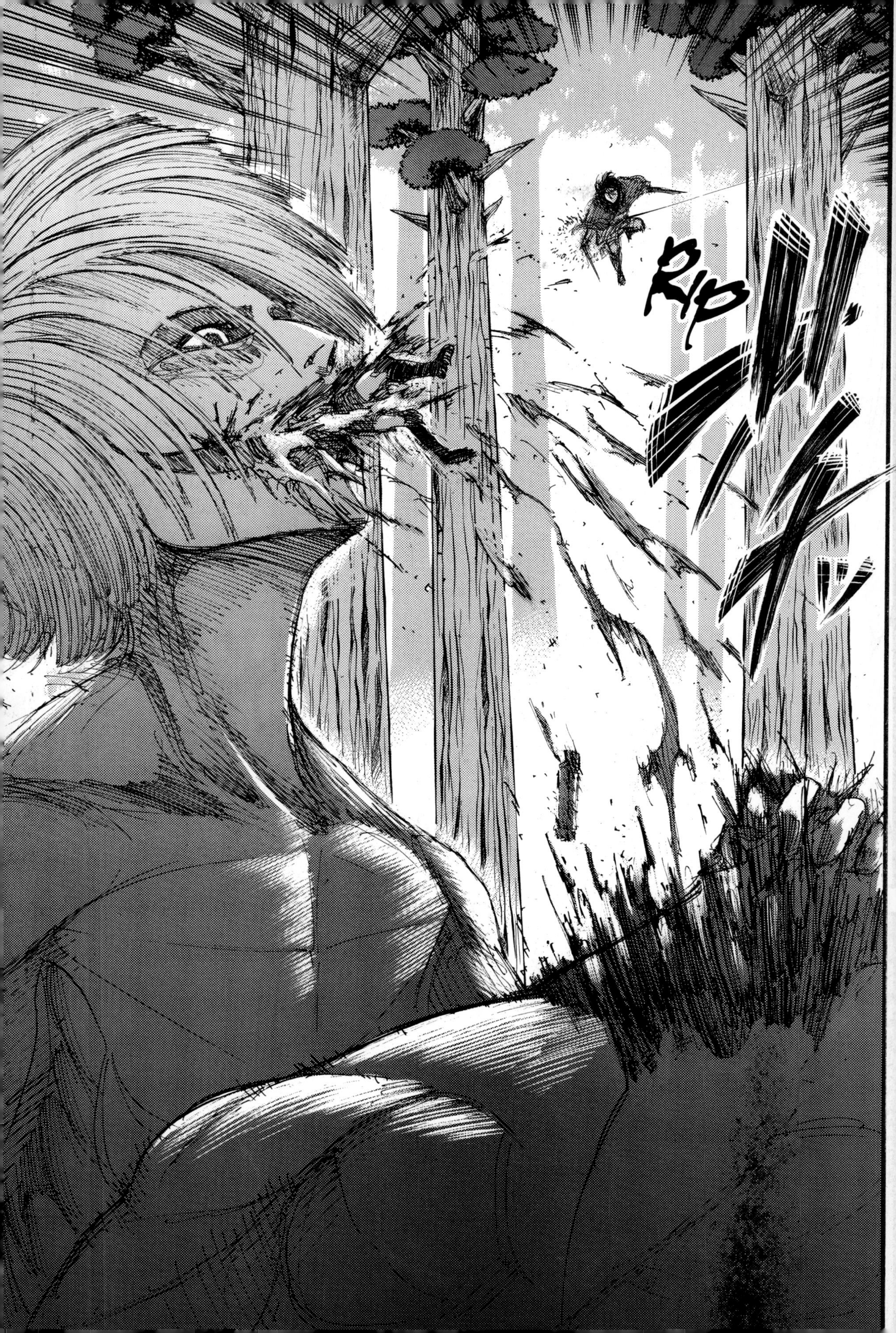
RIP

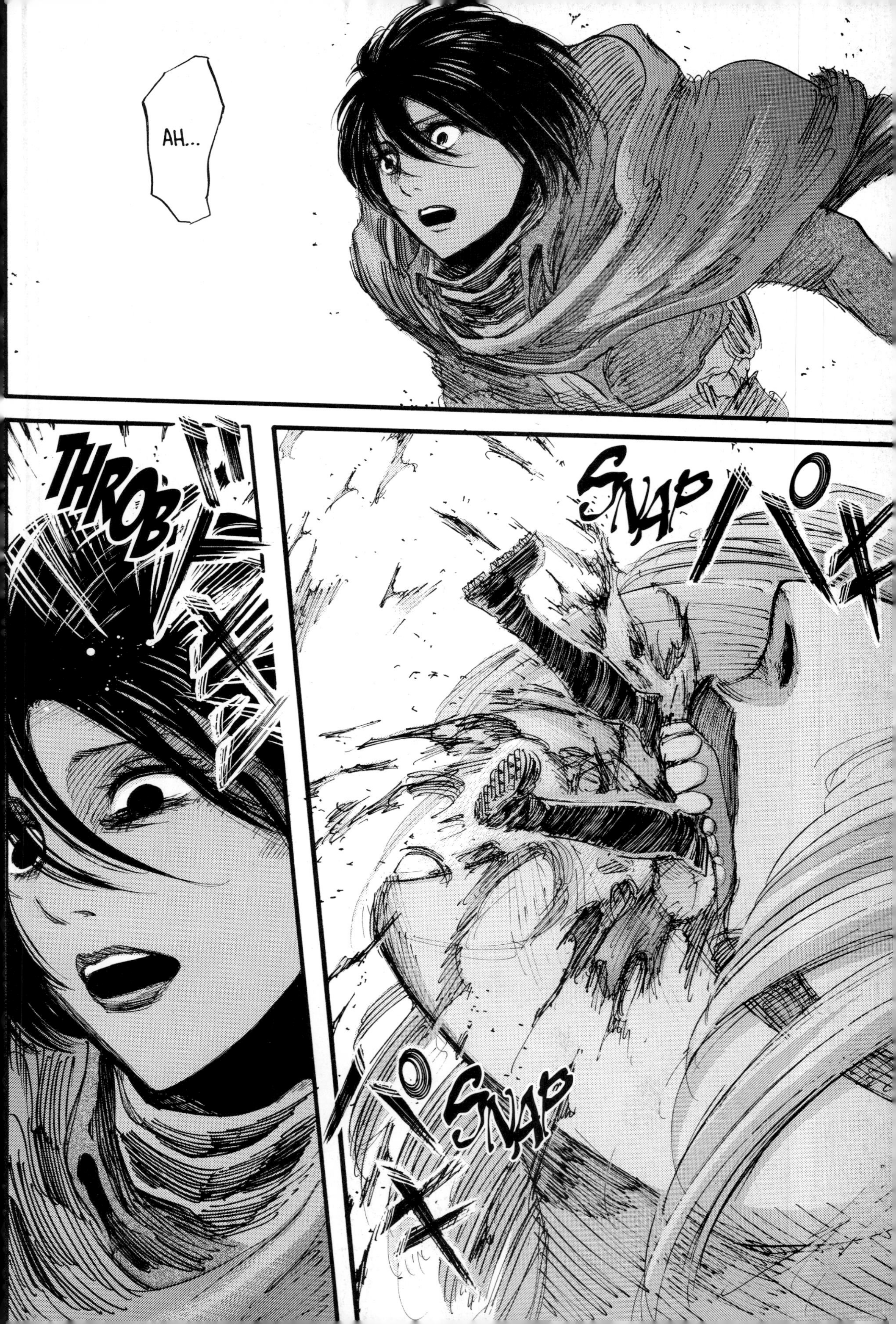
AH...
SNAP
SNAP
THROB!!

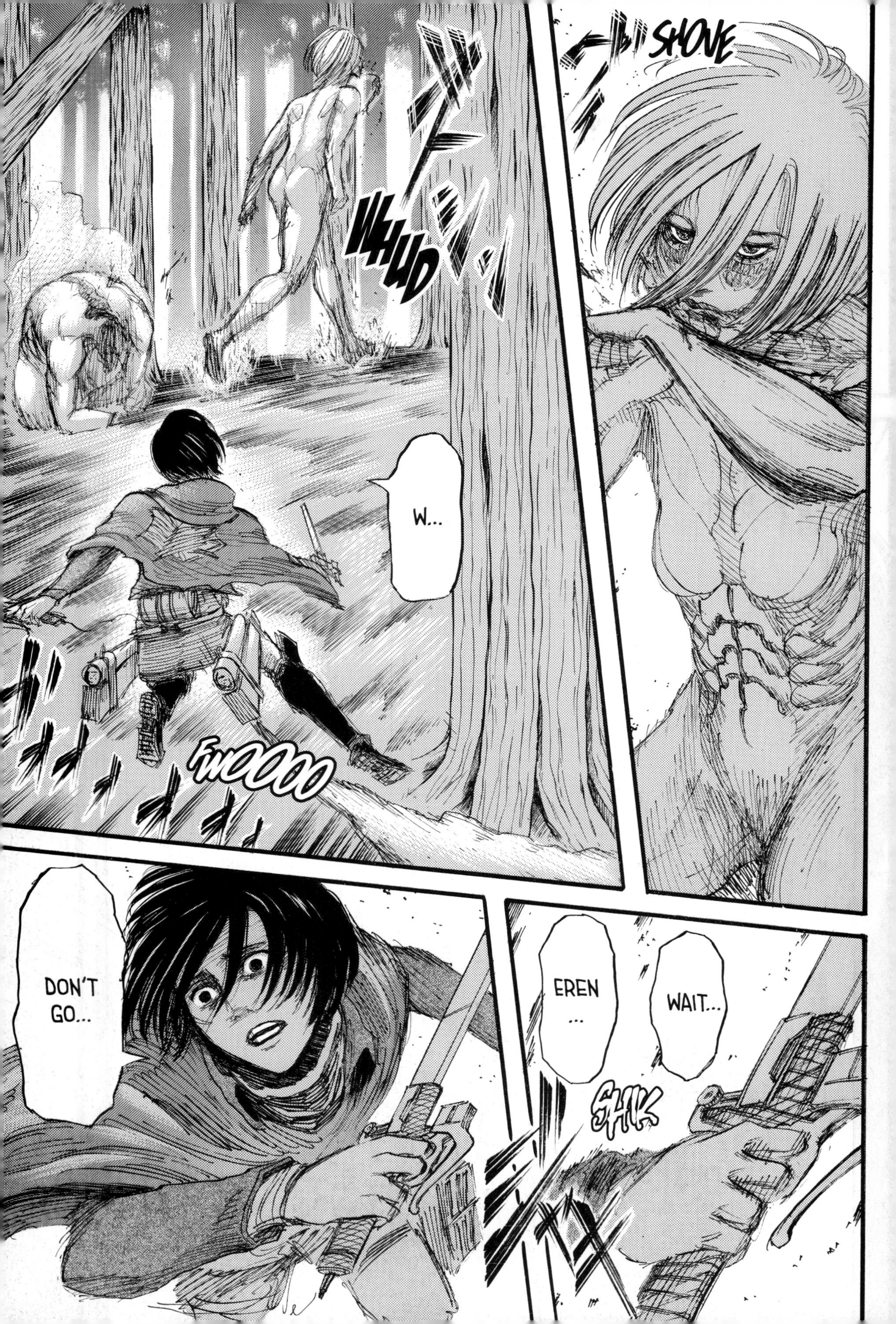
SHOVE
WHUD
W...
FWOOOO
WAIT...
EREN ...
SHIK
DON'T GO...

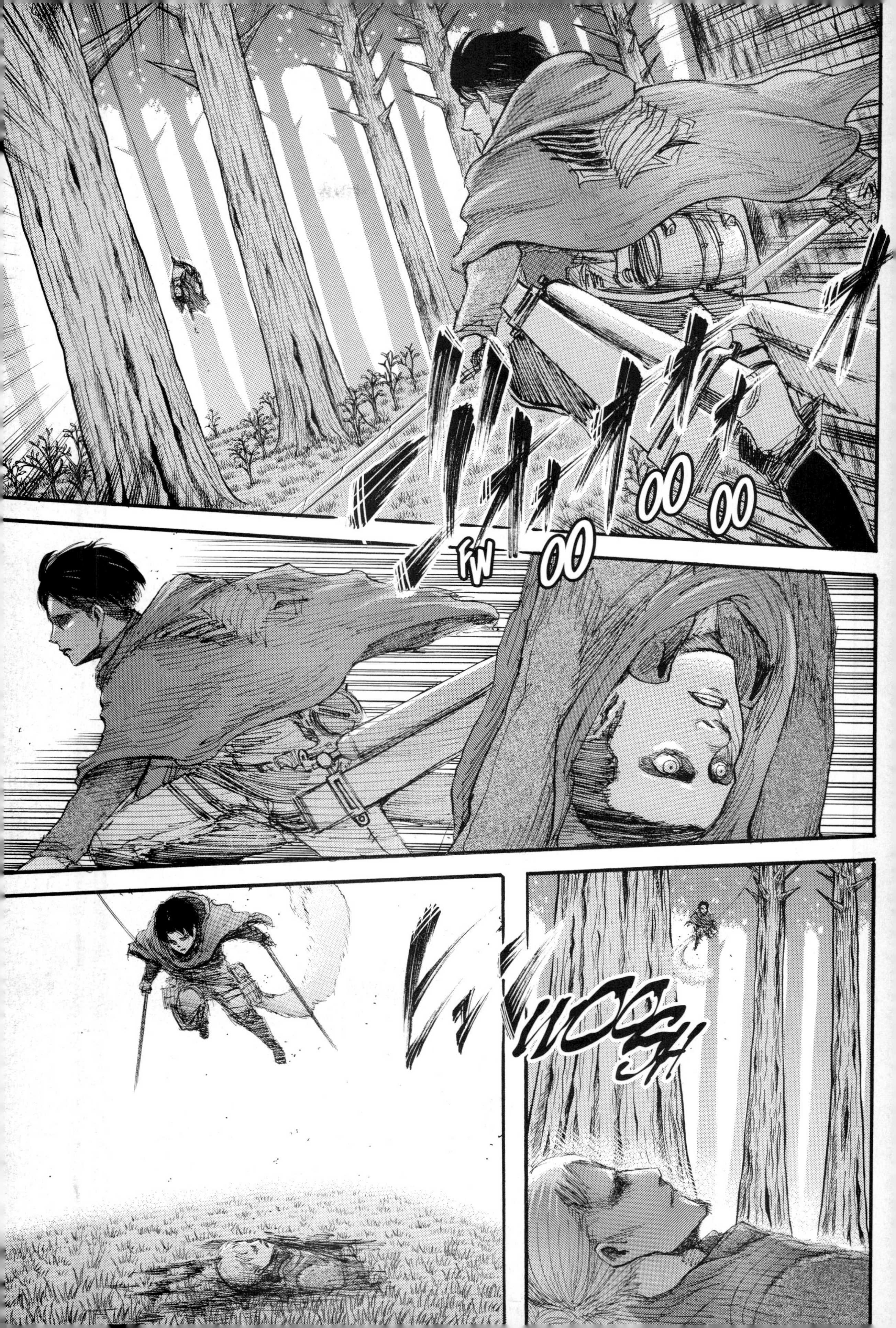
FWOOOOOO
WHOOSH!

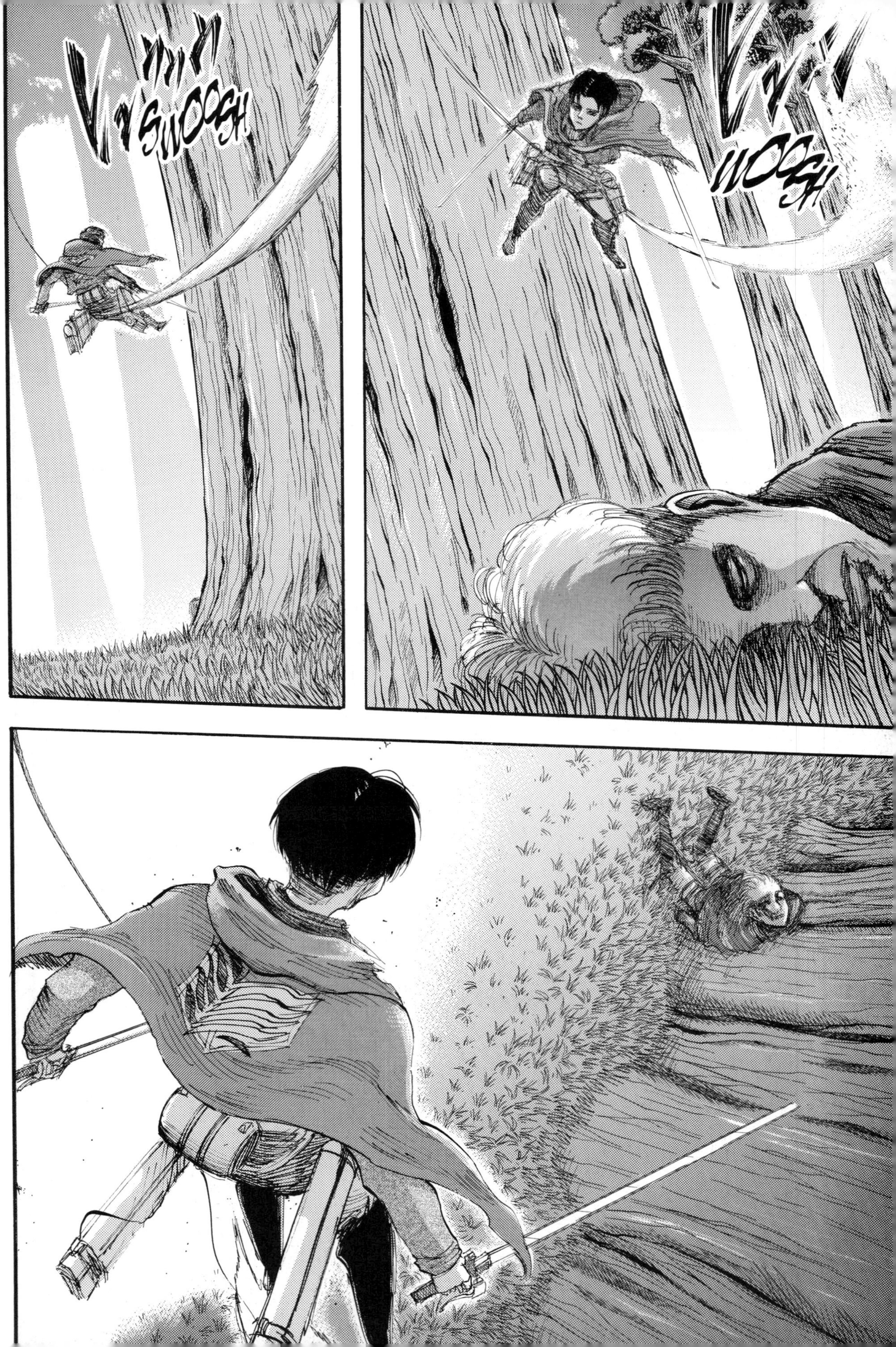
WOOSH
SWOOSH

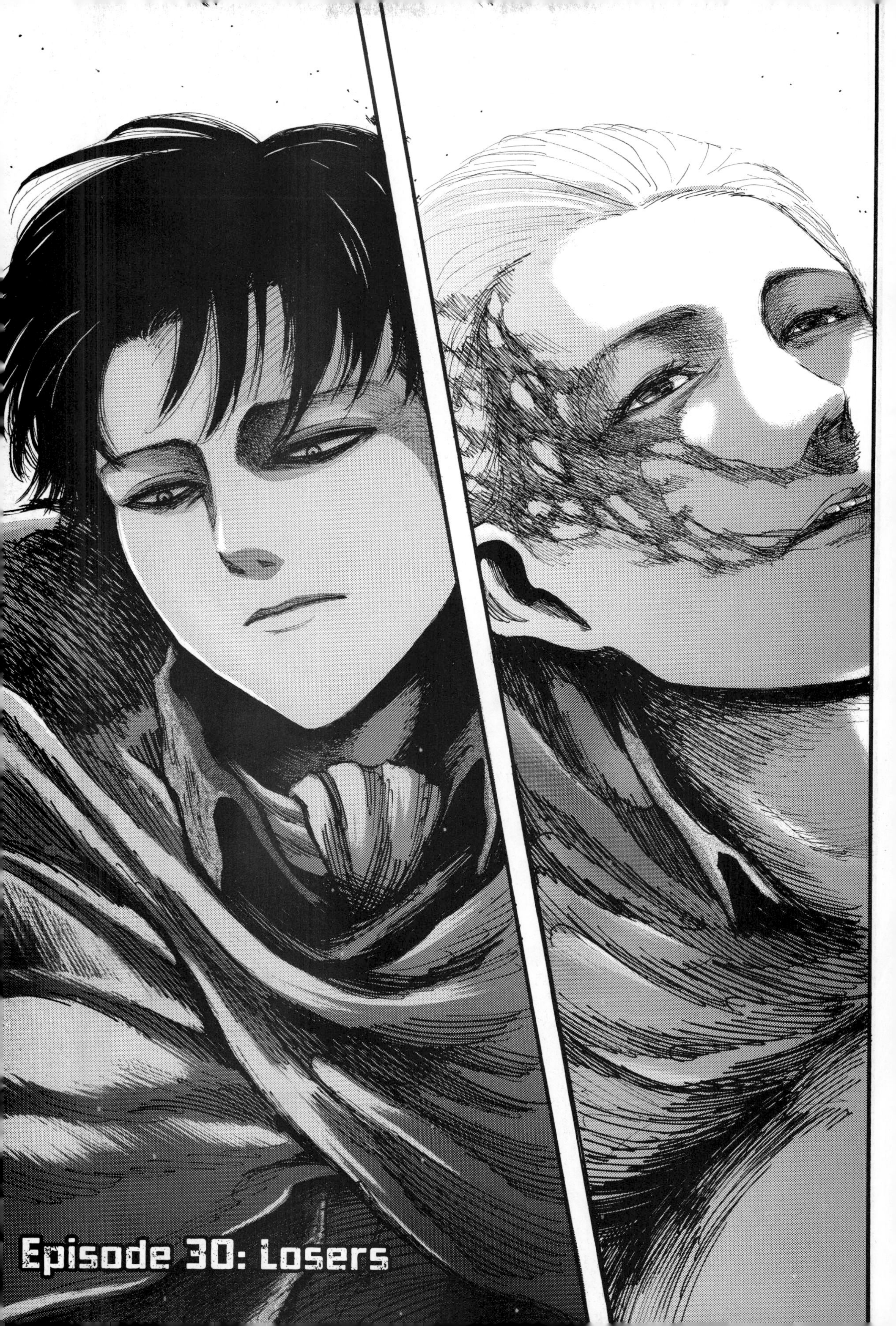
Episode 30: Losers

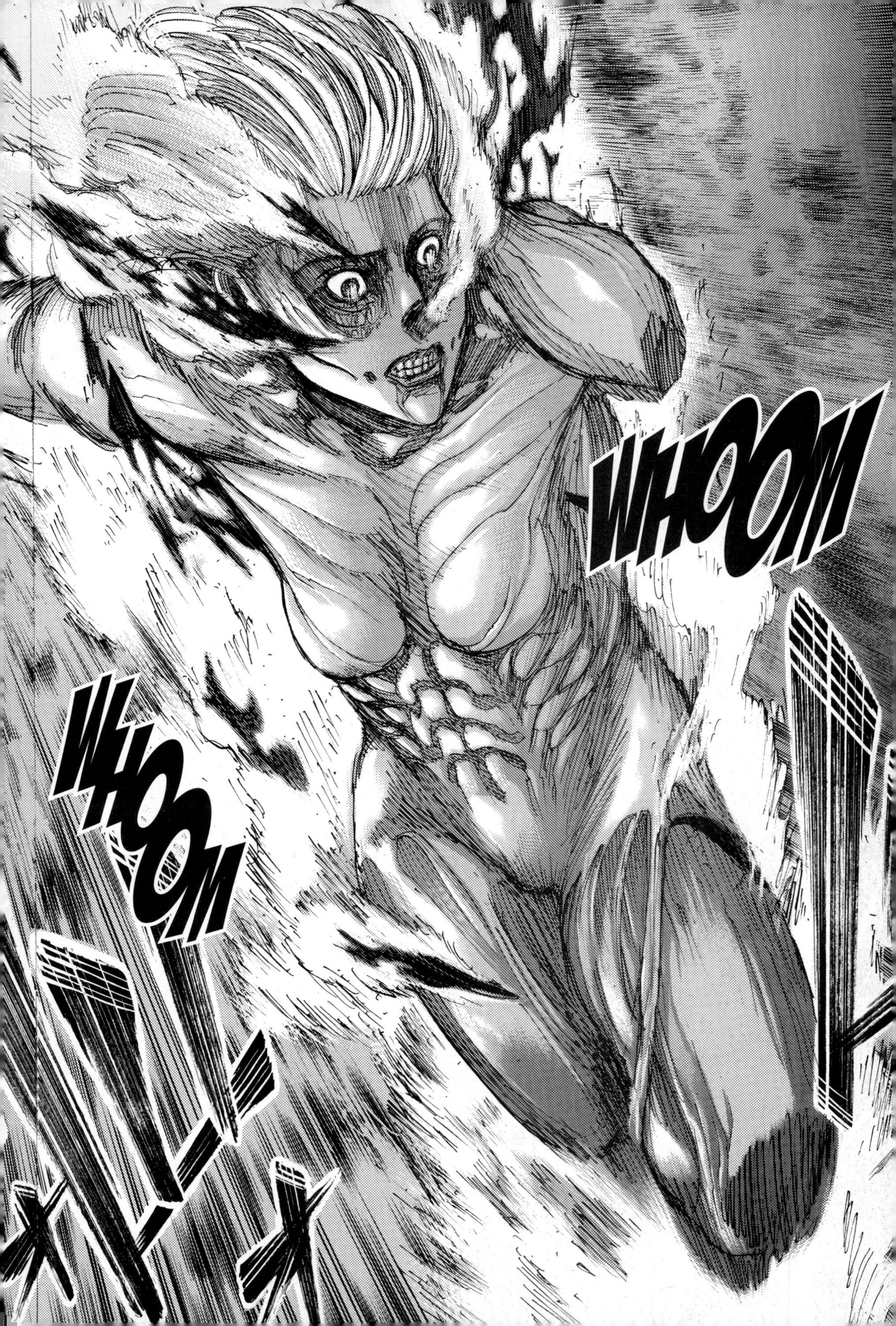
WHOOM
WHOOM

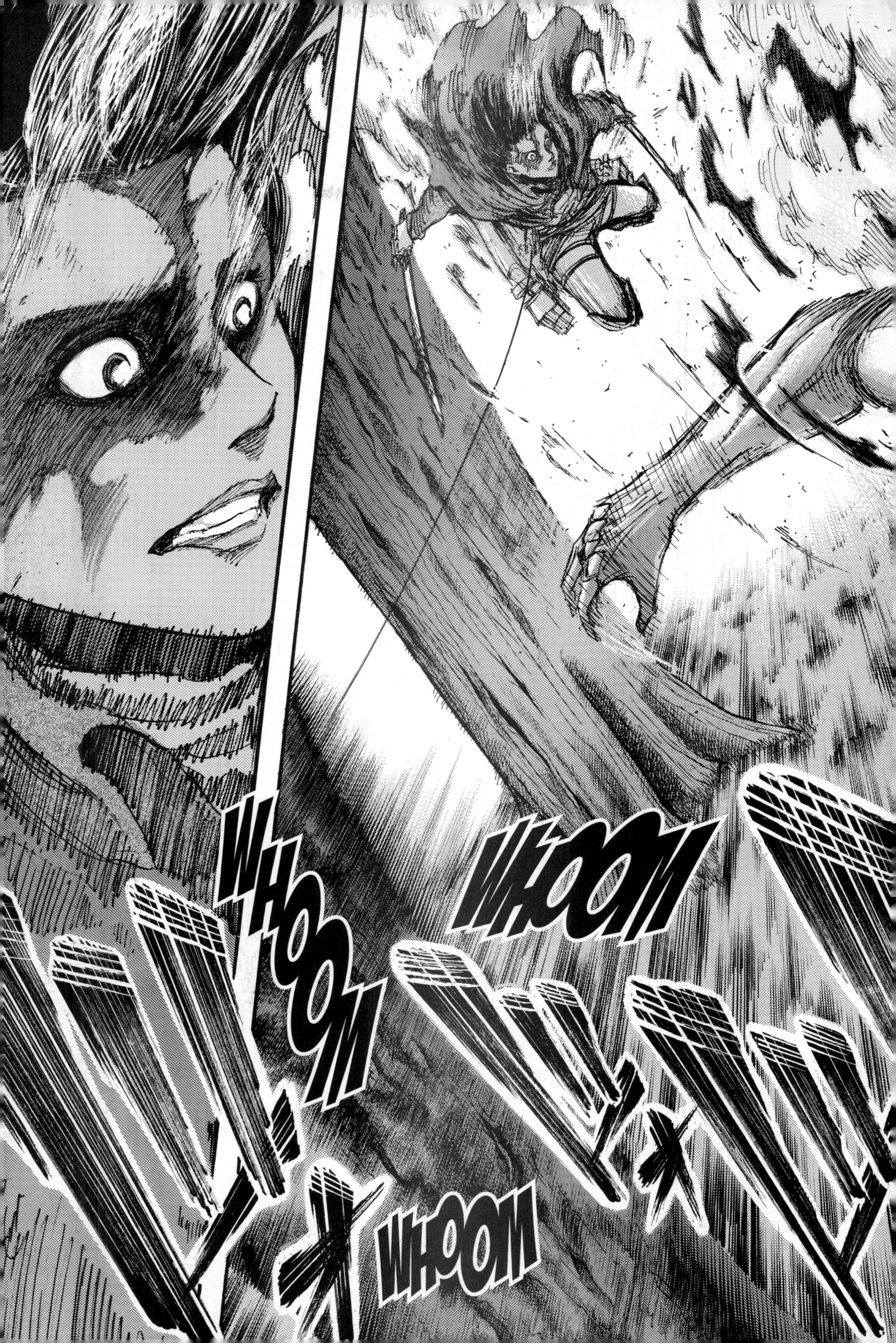
WHOOM
WHOOM
WHOOM

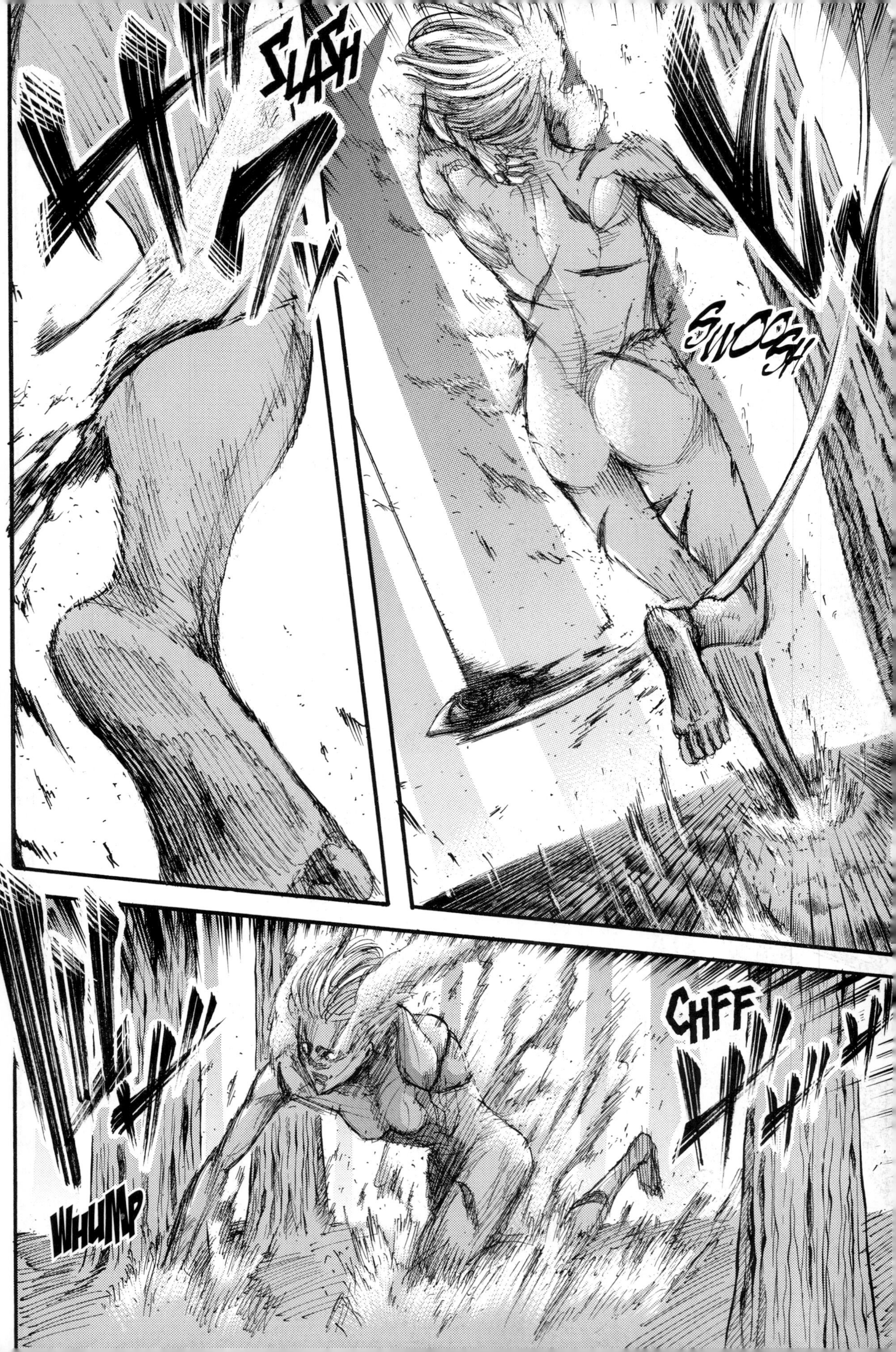

SWOOSH
SLASH
CHFF
WHUMP

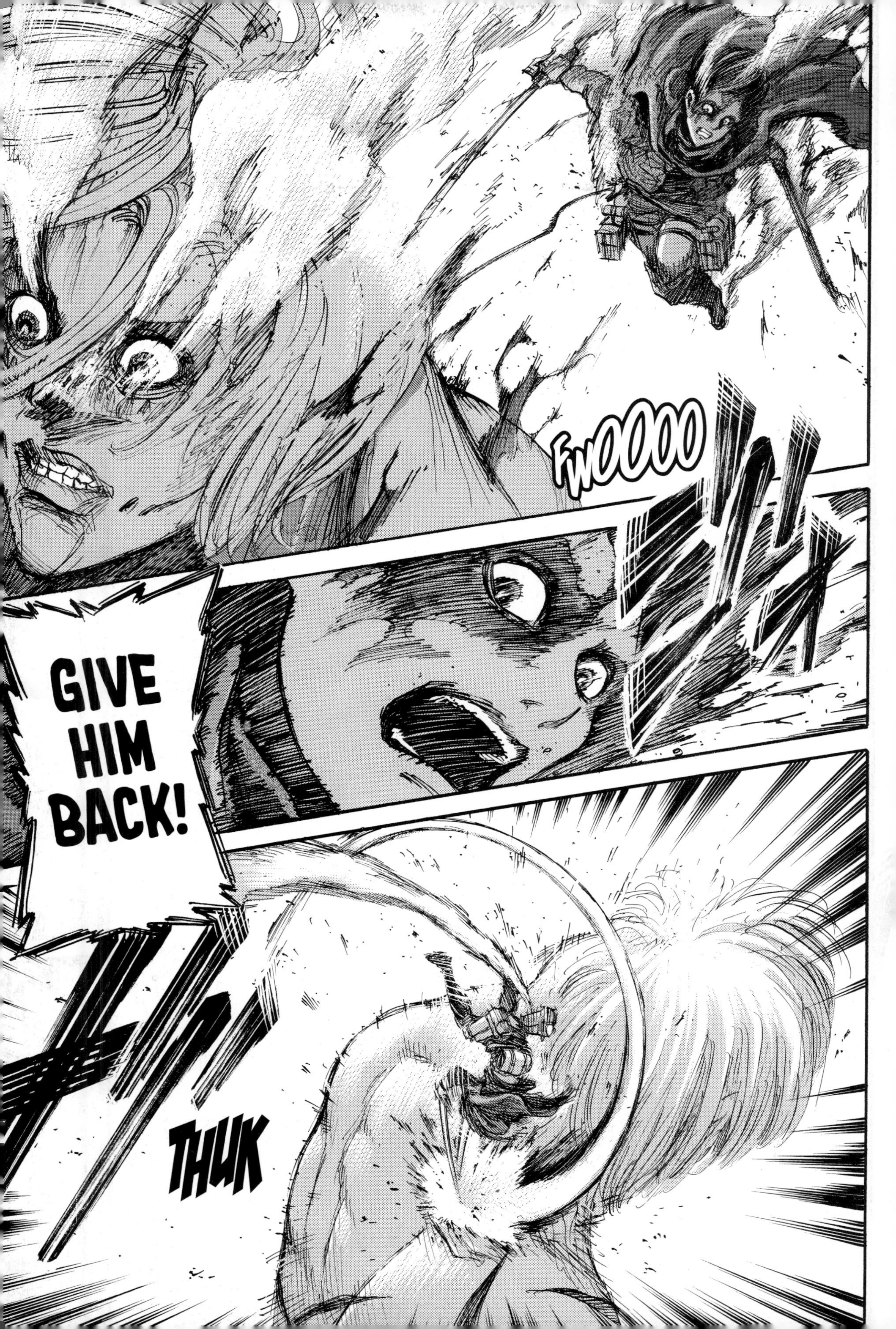
FWOOOO
GIVE HIM BACK!
THUK

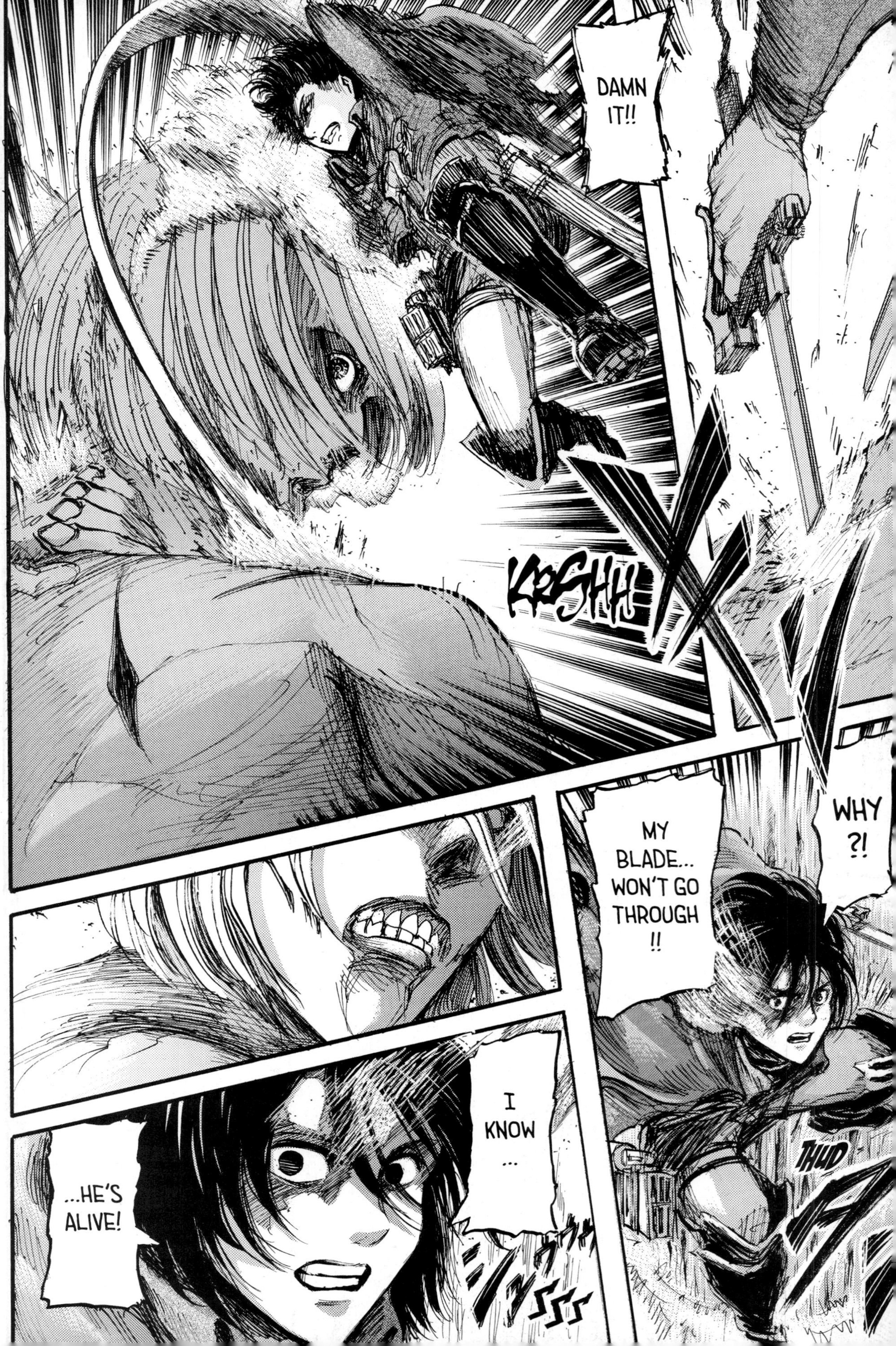
DAMN IT!!
KRSHH
WHY ?!
MY BLADE... WON'T GO THROUGH !!
THUD
I KNOW ...
...HE'S ALIVE!

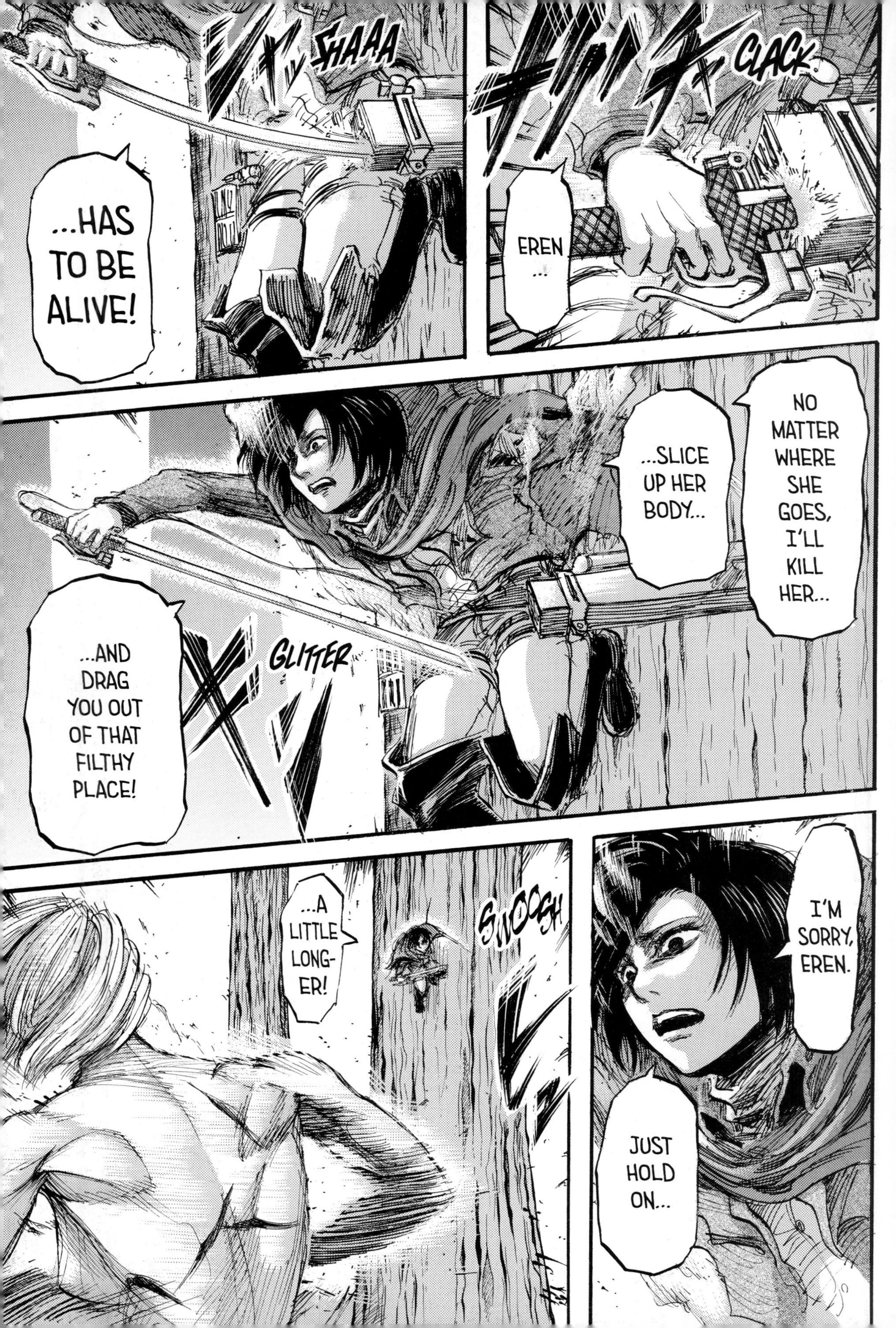
CLACK
EREN...
SHAAA
...HAS TO BE ALIVE!
NO MATTER WHERE SHE GOES, I'LL KILL HER...
...SLICE UP HER BODY...
GLITTER
...AND DRAG YOU OUT OF THAT FILTHY PLACE!
I'M SORRY, EREN.
JUST HOLD ON...
SWOOSH
...A LITTLE LONGER!

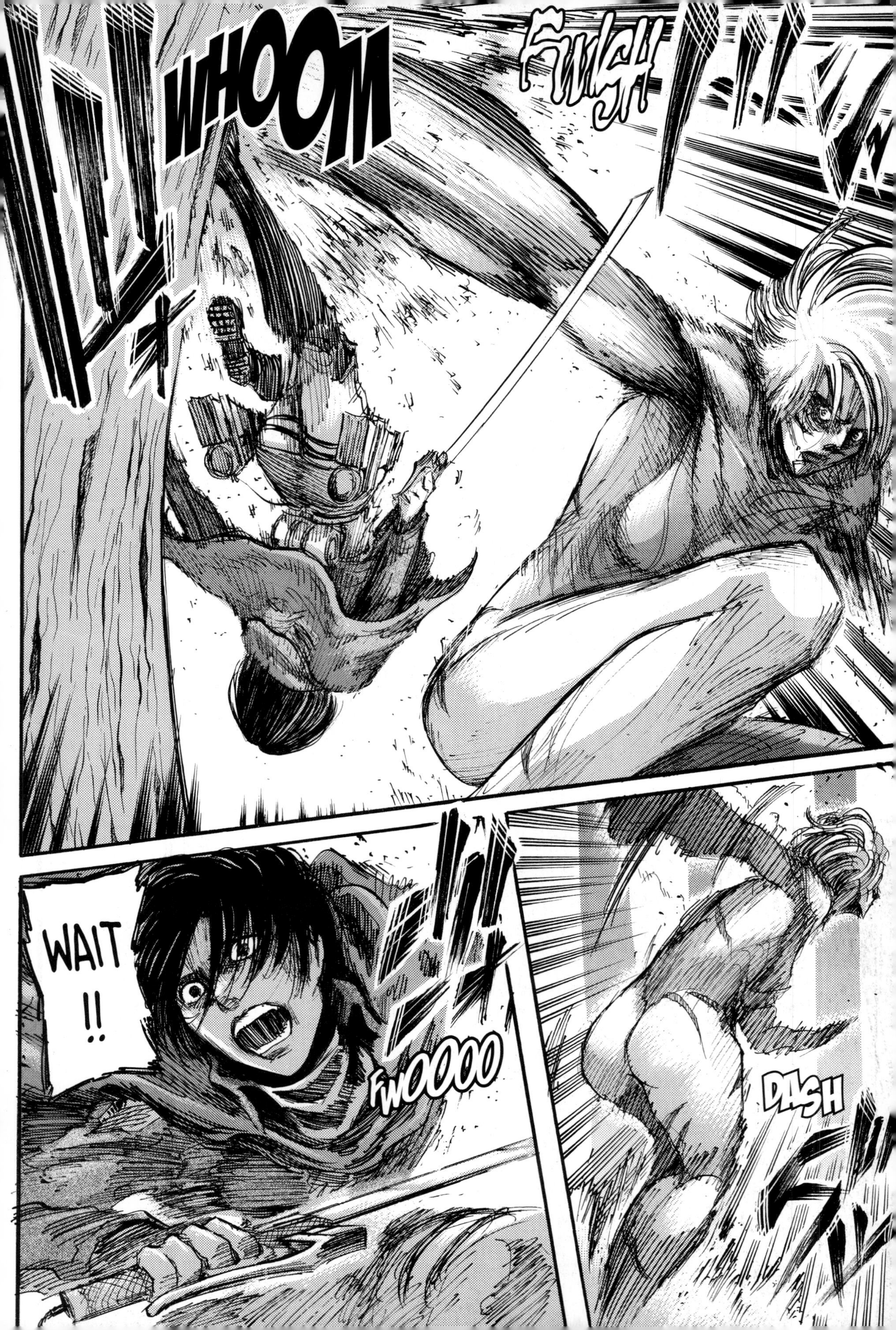
WHOOM
FWISH
DASH
WAIT !!
FWOOOO

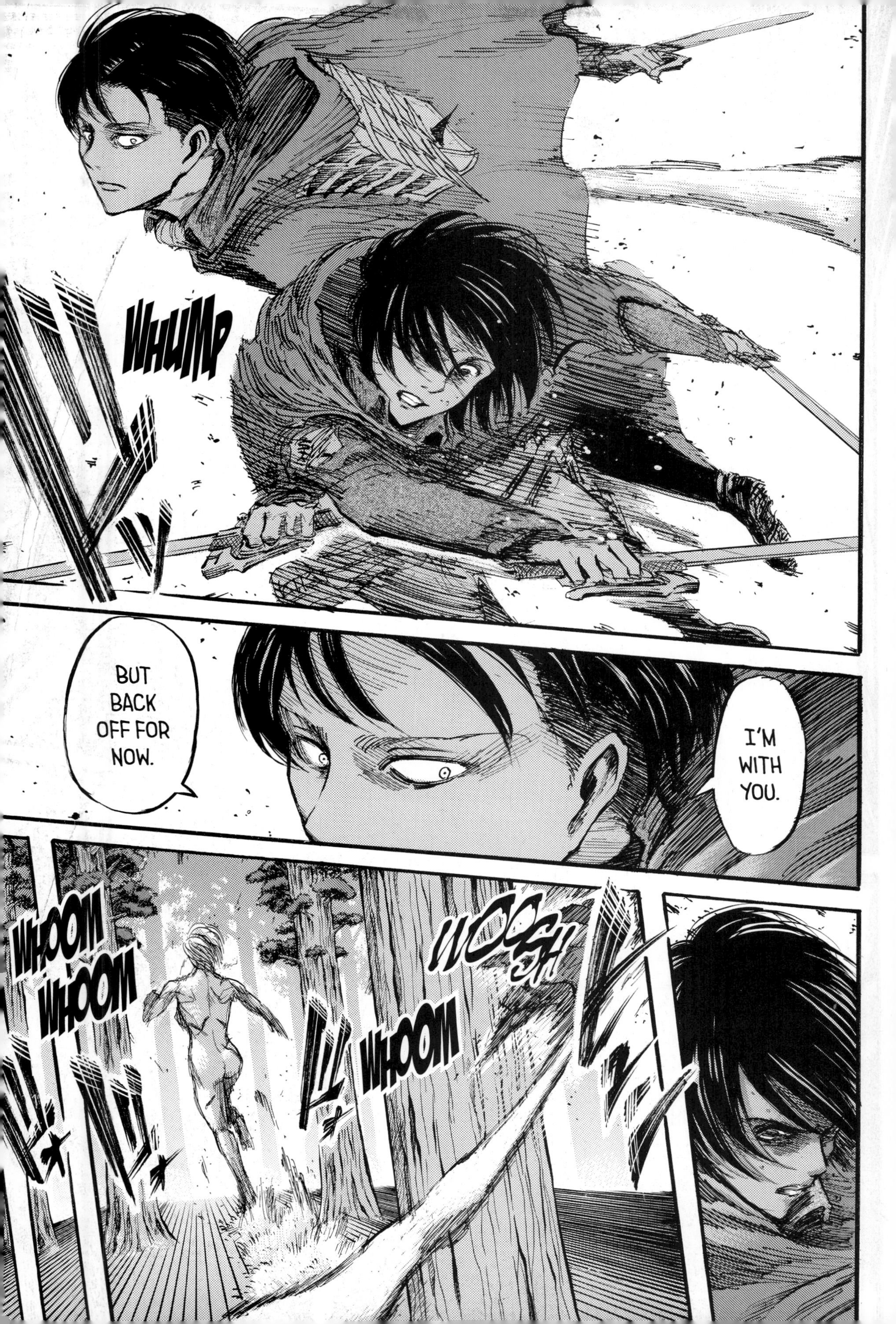
WHUMP
I'M WITH YOU.
BUT BACK OFF FOR NOW.
WOOSH
WHOOM
WHOOM WHOOM

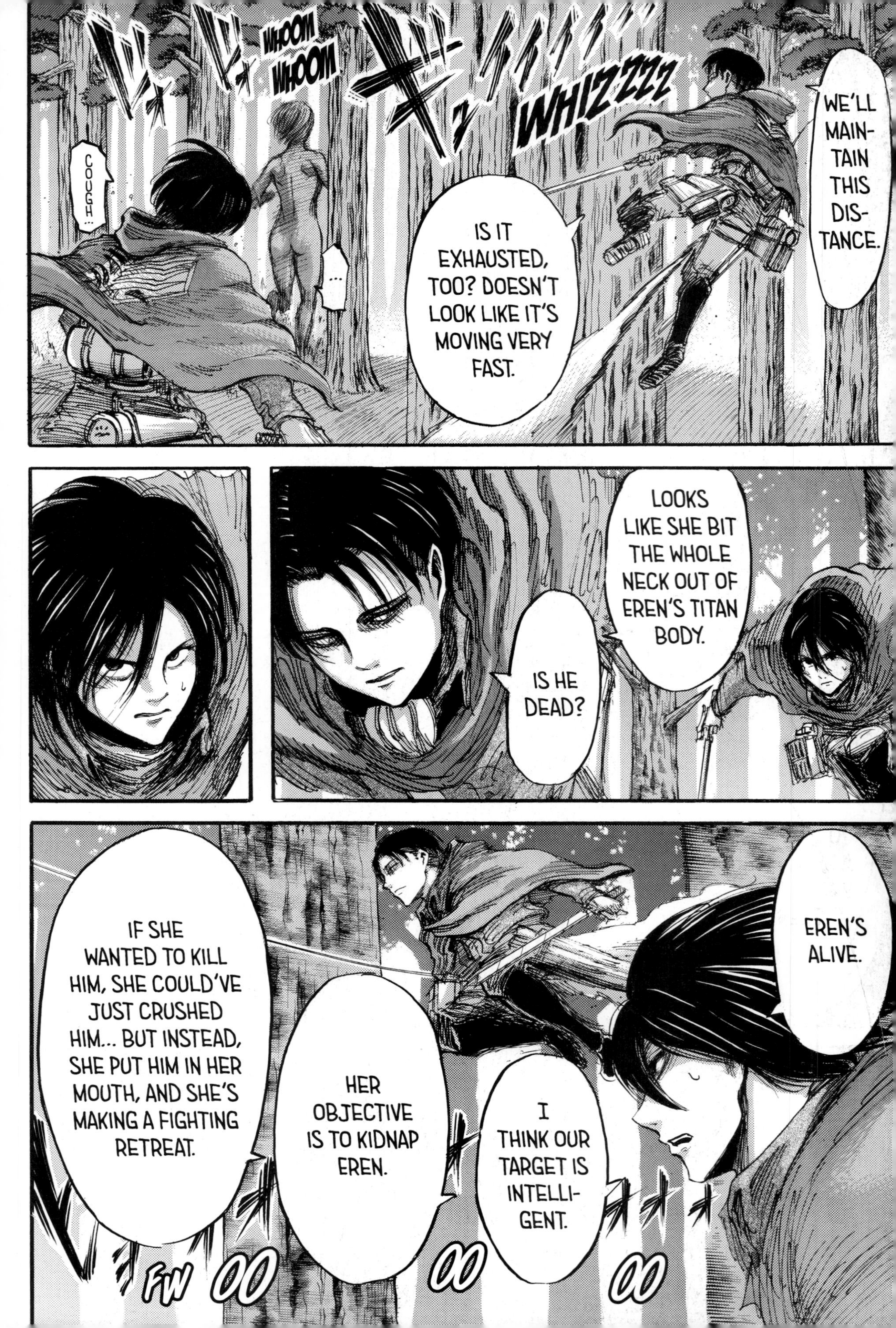
WHIZZZZ
WHOOM WHOOM
WE'LL MAIN-TAIN THIS DIS-TANCE.
IS IT EXHAUSTED, TOO? DOESN'T LOOK LIKE IT'S MOVING VERY FAST.
...
COUGH...
LOOKS LIKE SHE BIT THE WHOLE NECK OUT OF EREN'S TITAN BODY.
IS HE DEAD?
EREN'S ALIVE.
I THINK OUR TARGET IS INTELLI-GENT.
HER OBJECTIVE IS TO KIDNAP EREN.
IF SHE WANTED TO KILL HIM, SHE COULD'VE JUST CRUSHED HIM... BUT INSTEAD, SHE PUT HIM IN HER MOUTH, AND SHE'S MAKING A FIGHTING RETREAT.
FWOOOOOO

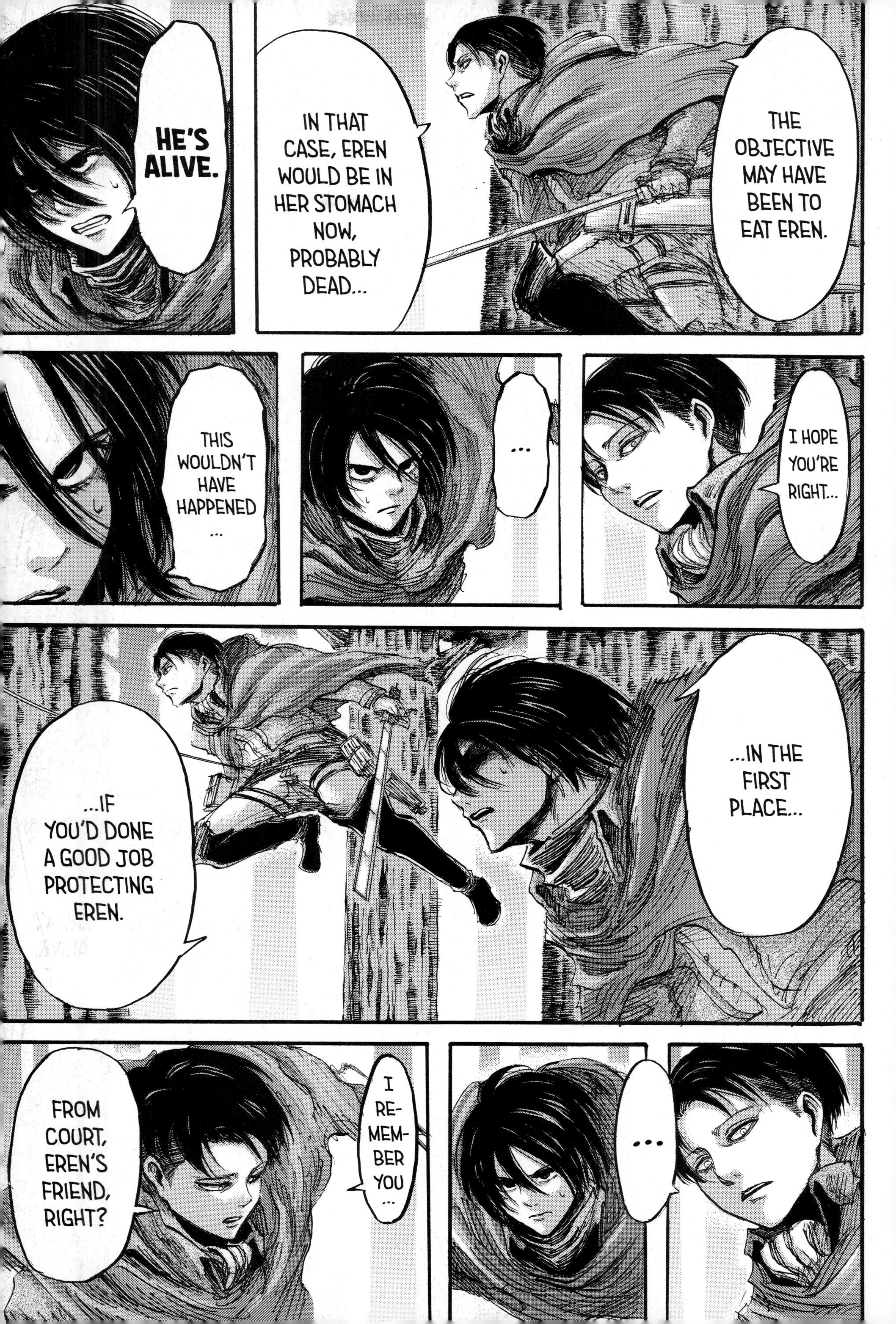
THE OBJECTIVE MAY HAVE BEEN TO EAT EREN.
IN THAT CASE, EREN WOULD BE IN HER STOMACH NOW, PROBABLY DEAD...
HE'S ALIVE.
I HOPE YOU'RE RIGHT...
...
THIS WOULDN'T HAVE HAPPENED ...
...IN THE FIRST PLACE...
...IF YOU'D DONE A GOOD JOB PROTECTING EREN.
...
I RE-MEM-BER YOU ...
FROM COURT, EREN'S FRIEND, RIGHT?

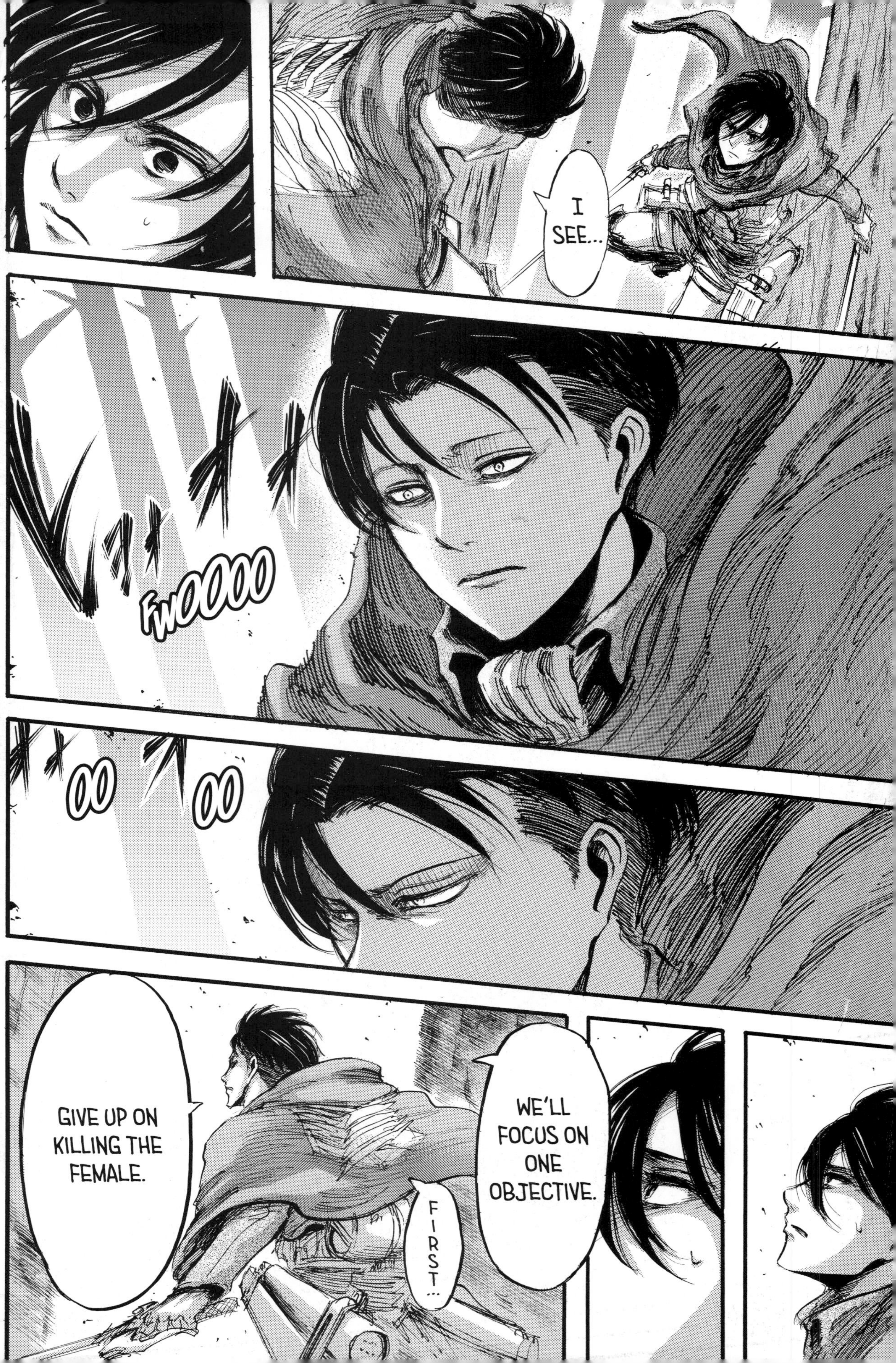
I SEE...
FWOOOO
OO
OO
WE'LL FOCUS ON ONE OBJECTIVE.
FIRST...
GIVE UP ON KILLING THE FEMALE.

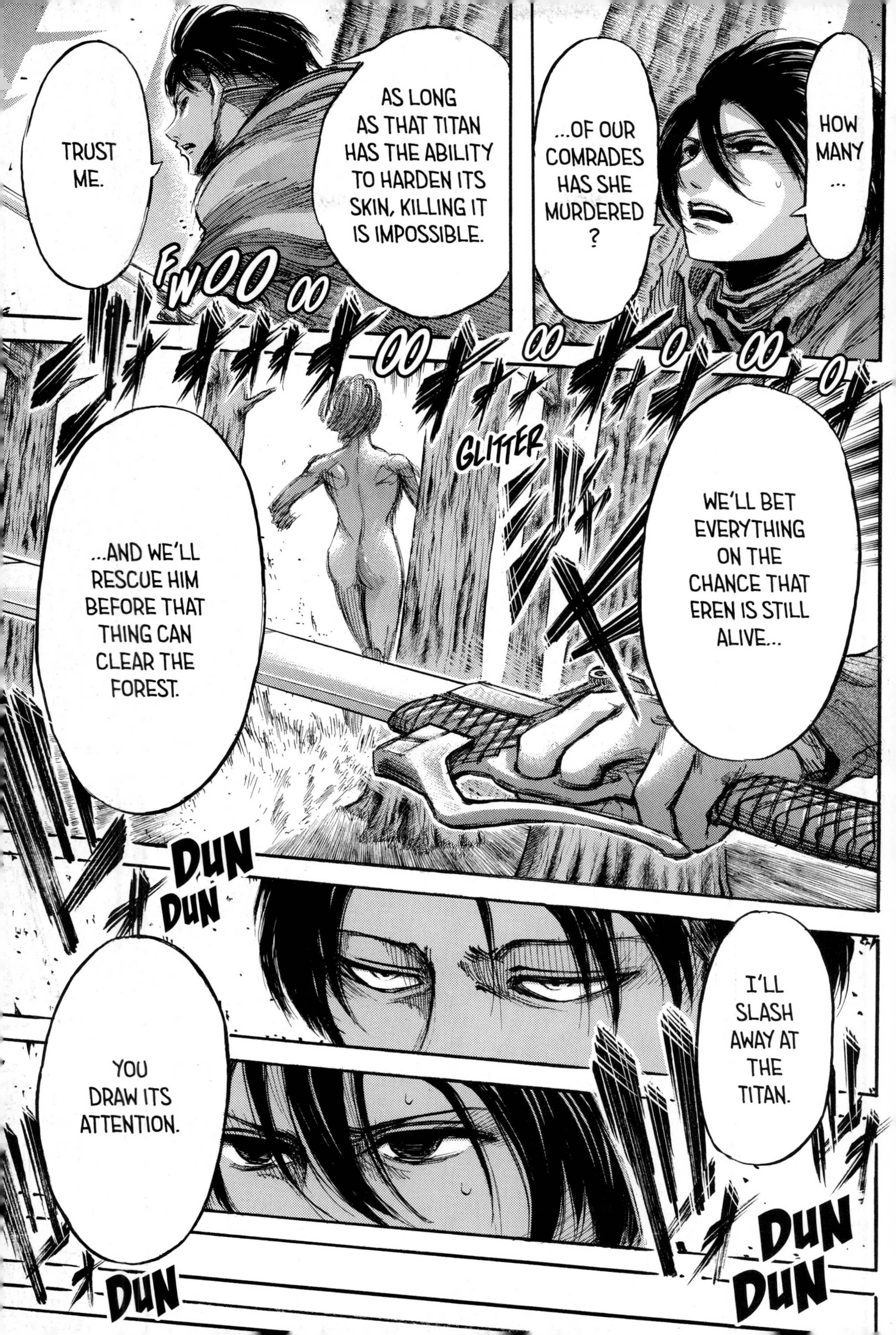
HOW MANY ...
...OF OUR COMRADES HAS SHE MURDERED ?
AS LONG AS THAT TITAN HAS THE ABILITY TO HARDEN ITS SKIN, KILLING IT IS IMPOSSIBLE.
TRUST ME.
FWOOOOOOOOOOOOO
GLITTER
WE'LL BET EVERYTHING ON THE CHANCE THAT EREN IS STILL ALIVE...
...AND WE'LL RESCUE HIM BEFORE THAT THING CAN CLEAR THE FOREST.
DUN DUN
I'LL SLASH AWAY AT THE TITAN.
YOU DRAW ITS ATTENTION.
DUN DUN
DUN

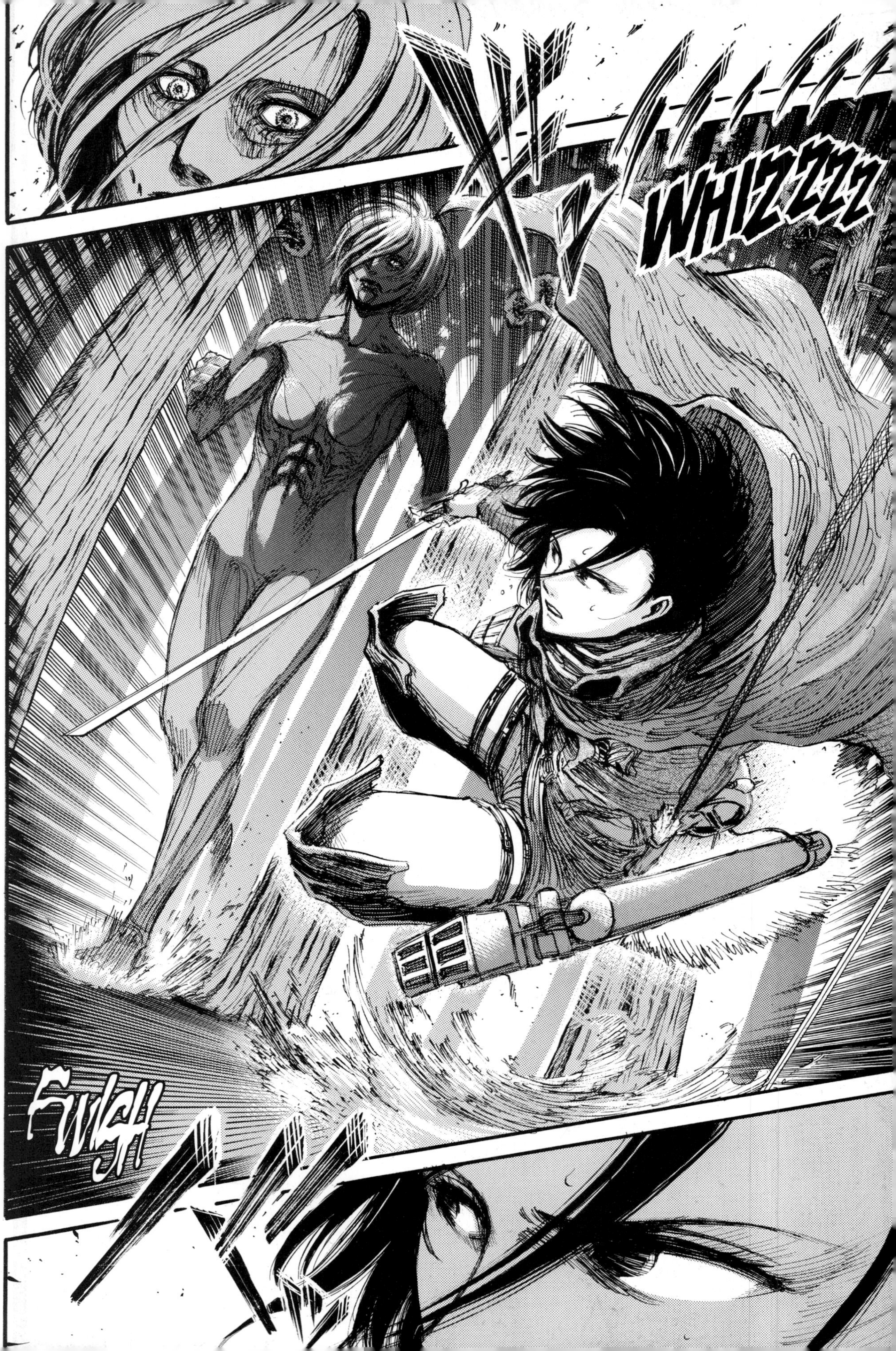
WHIZZZZ
FWISH

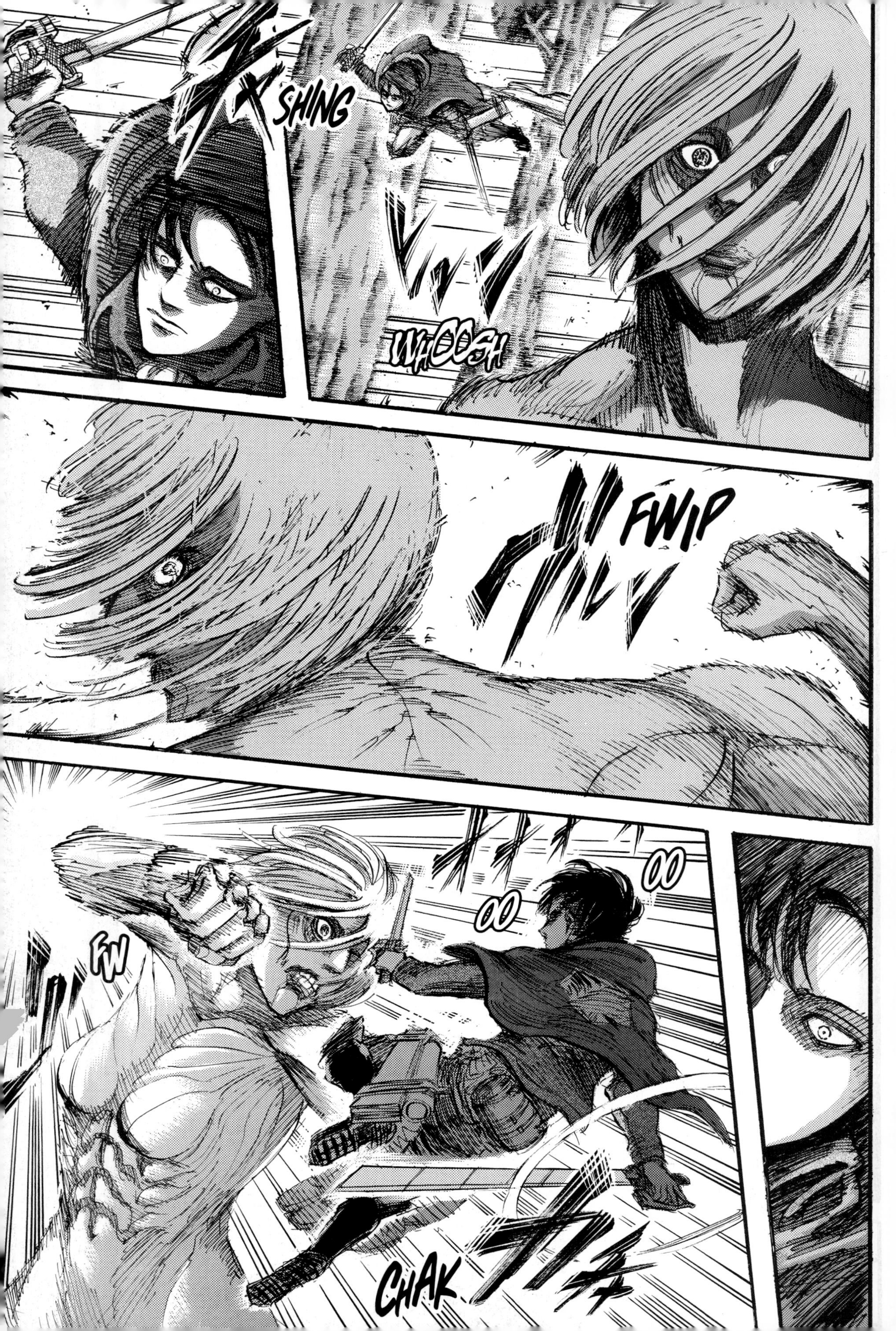
WHOOSH
SHING
FWIP
OO
OO
FW
CHAK

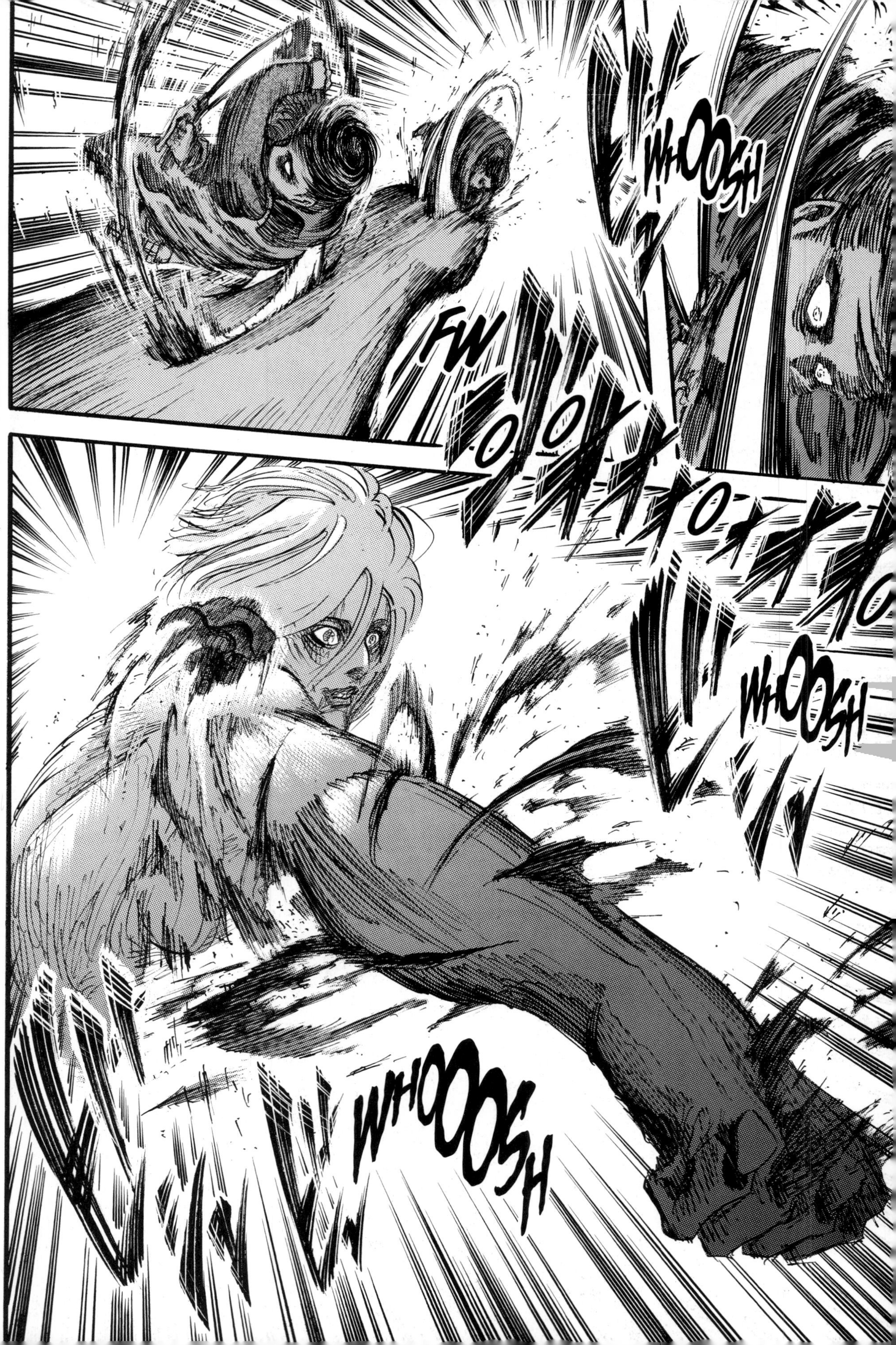
WHOOSH
FWOOOOO
WHOOSH
WHOOOOSH

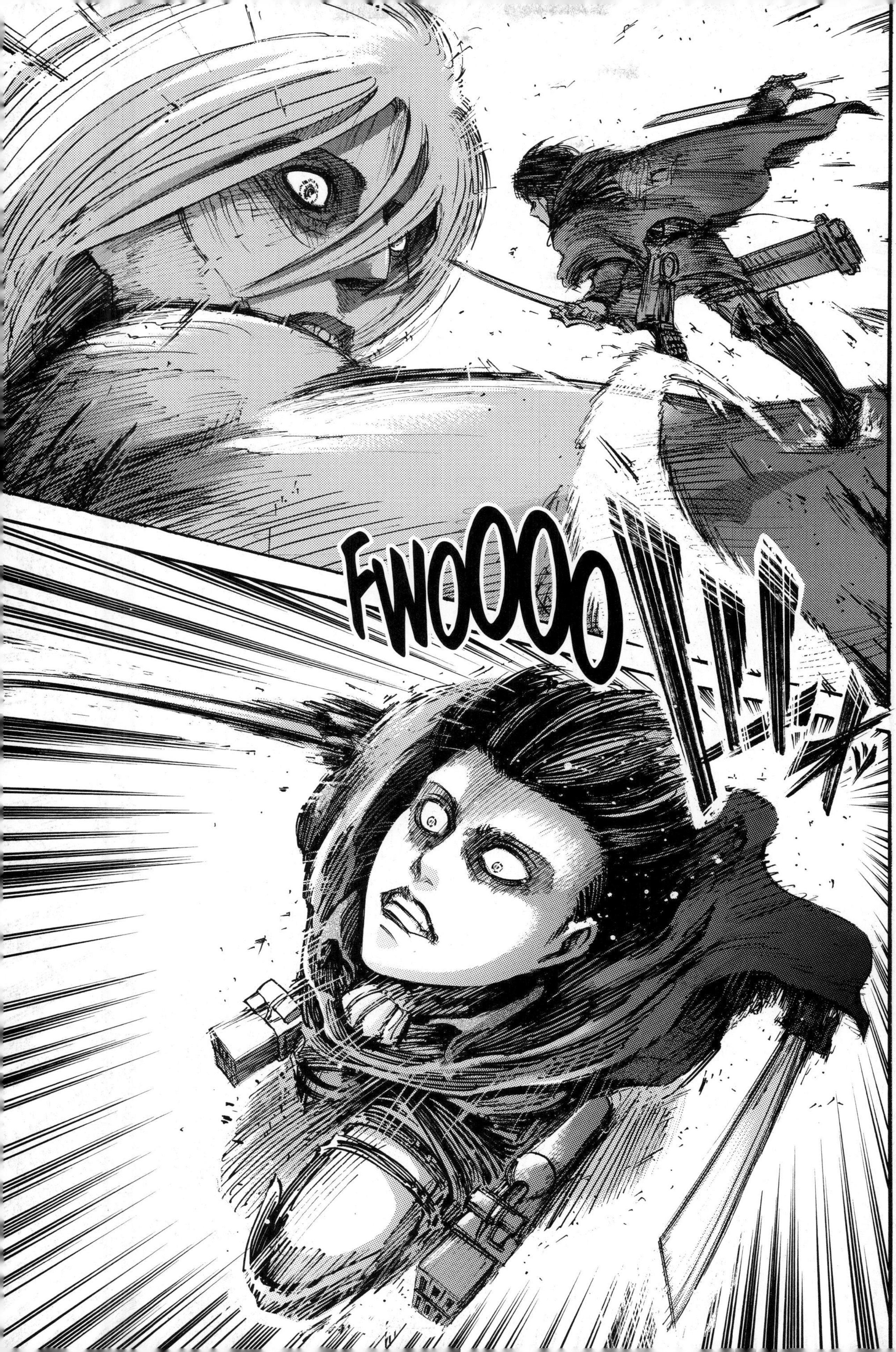
FWOOOO

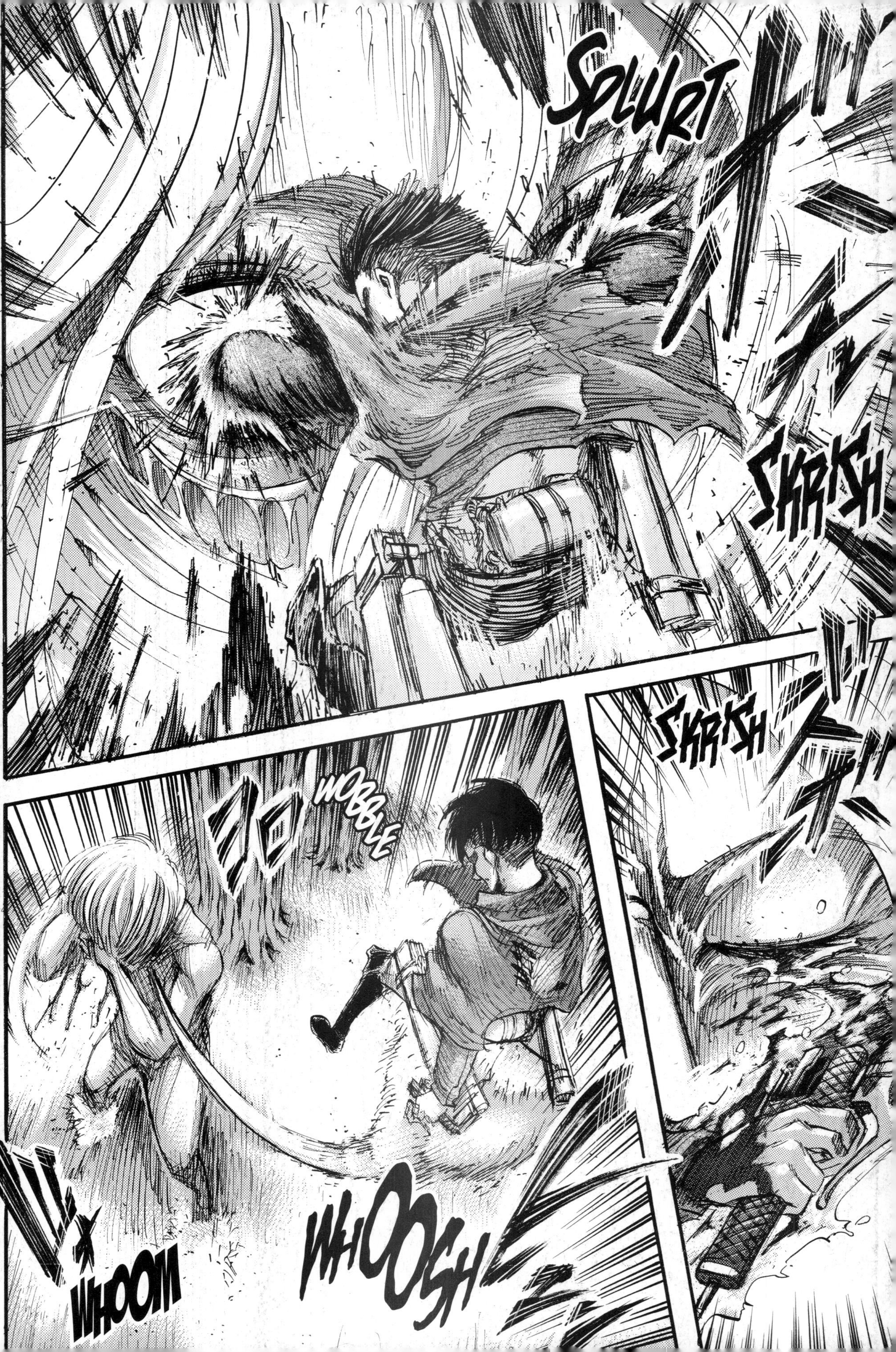
SPLURT
SKRISH
SKRISH
WOBBLE
WHOOSH
WHOOM

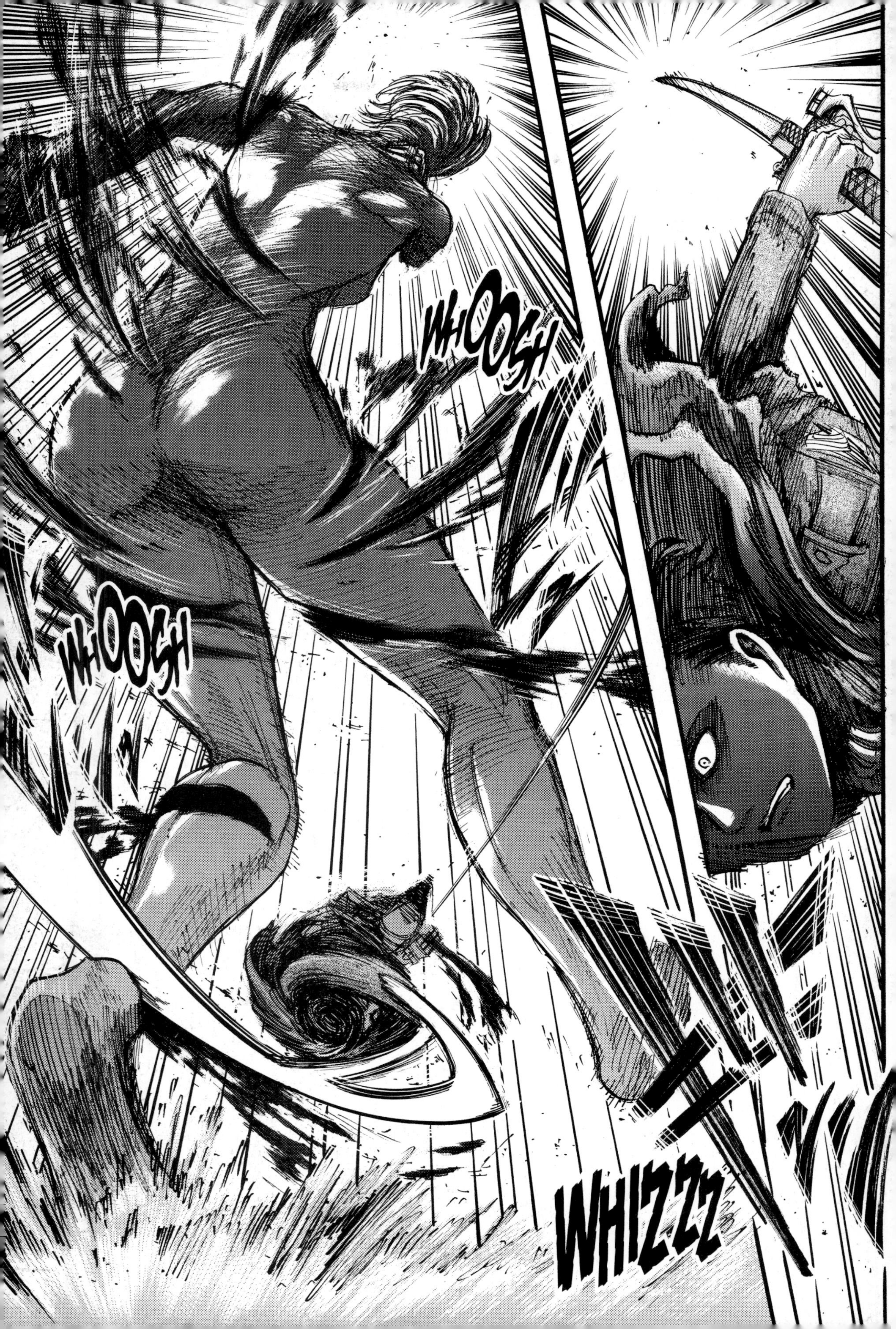
WHOOSH
WHOOSH
WHIZZZ

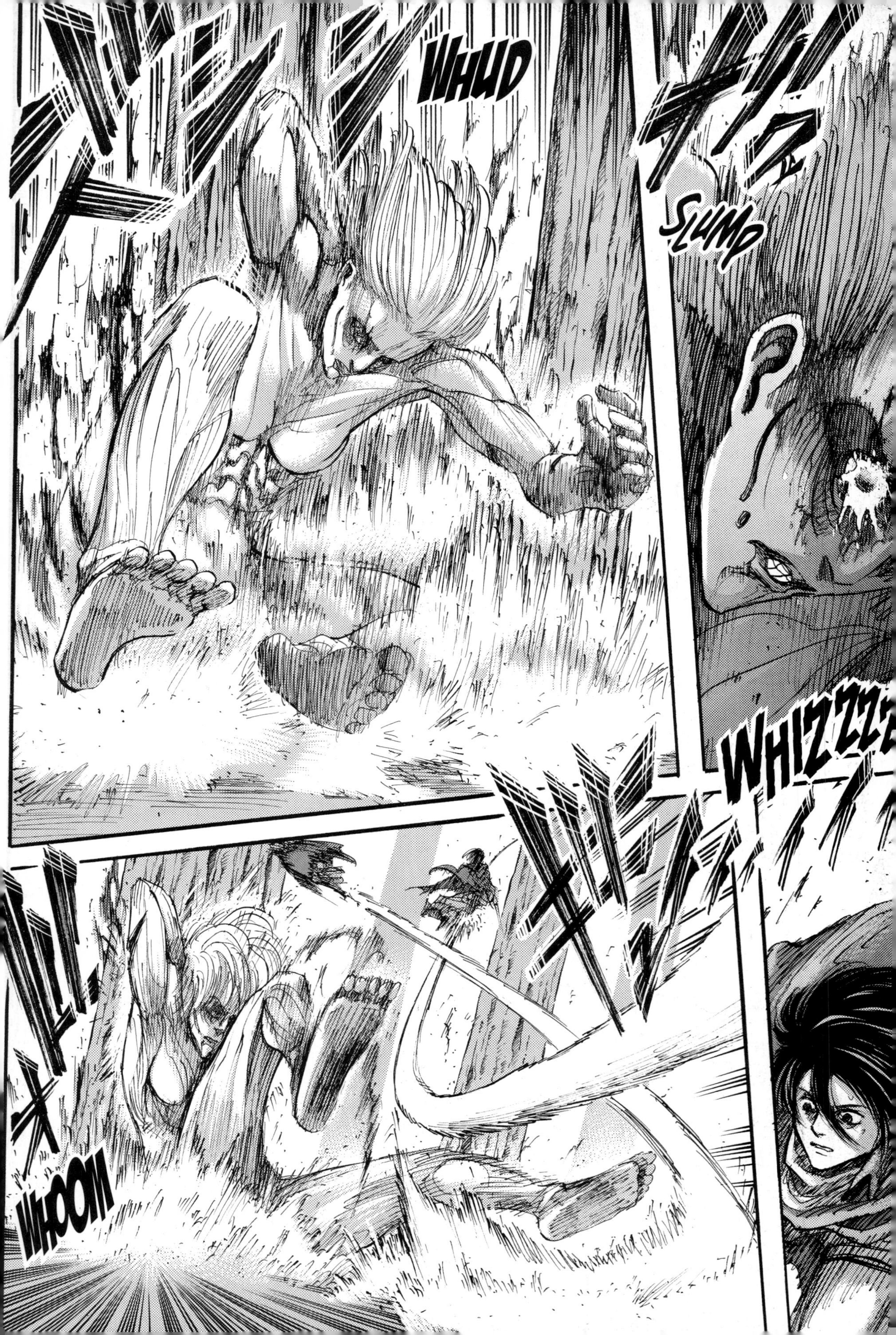
SLUMP
WHUD
WHIZZZ
WHOOM

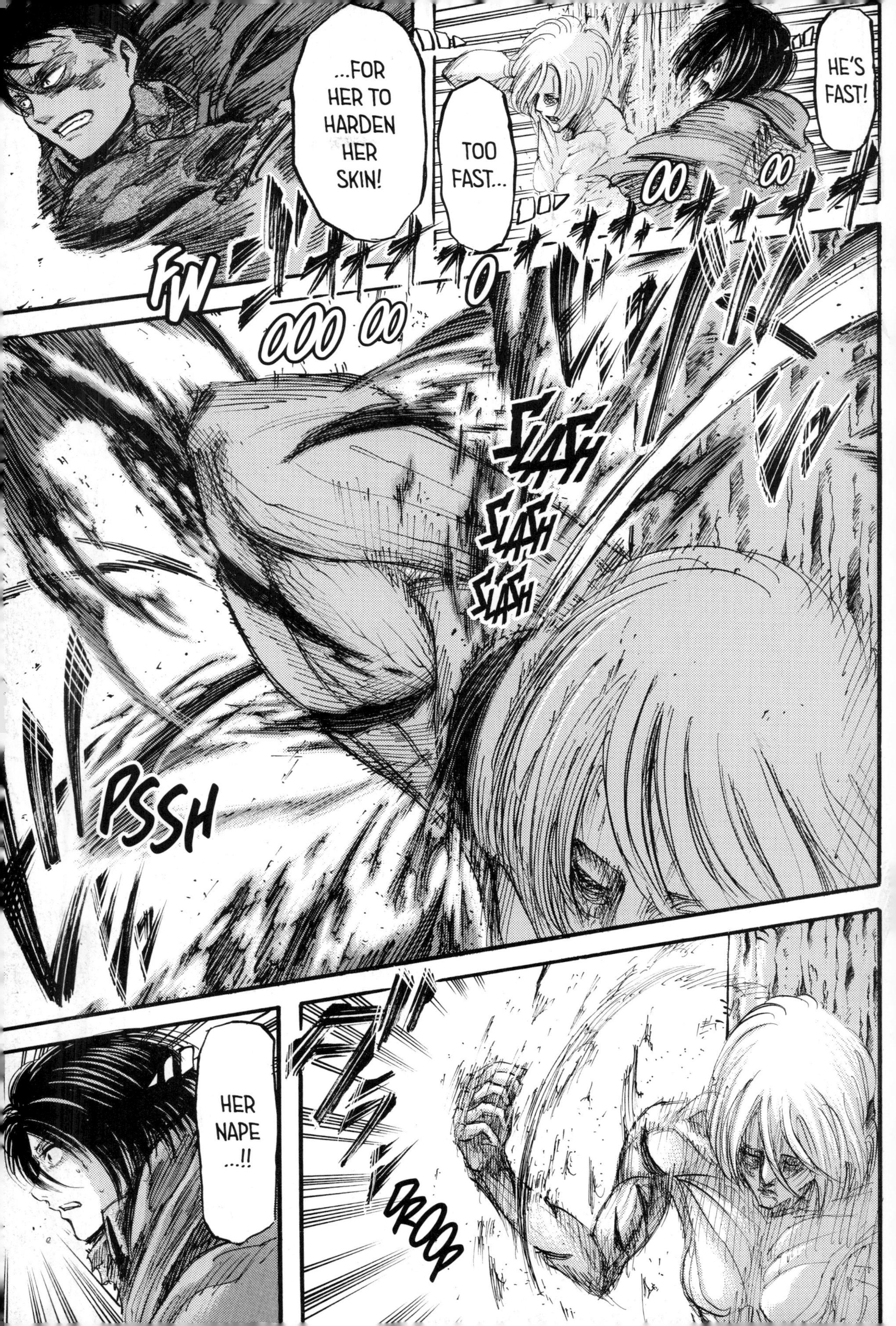
HE'S FAST!
TOO FAST...
...FOR HER TO HARDEN HER SKIN!
FW
OOO OO
O
OO
OO
SLASH
SLASH
SLASH
PSSH
DROOO
HER NAPE ...!!

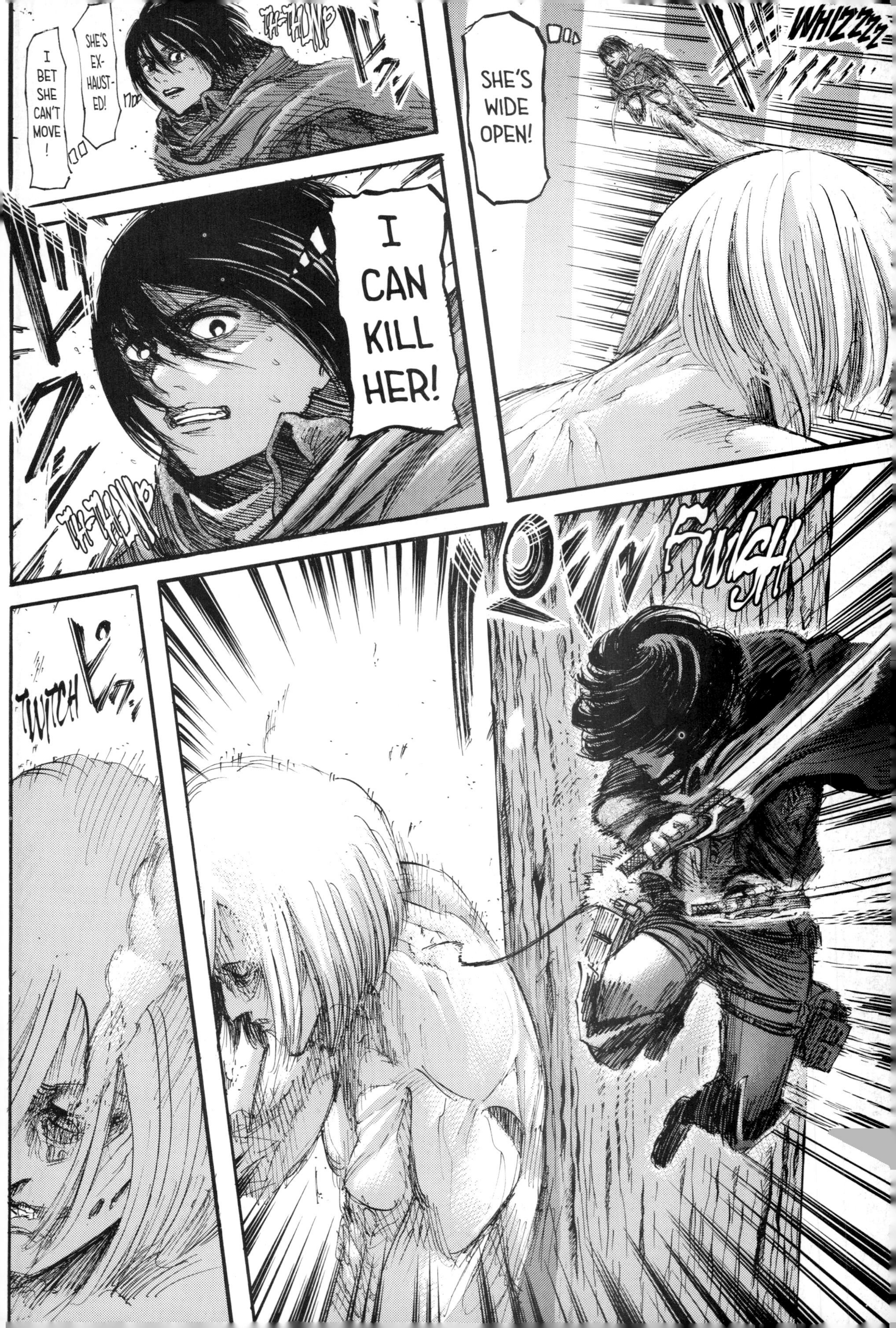
WHIZZZZ
SHE'S WIDE OPEN!
SHE'S EX-HAUSTED!
I BET SHE CAN'T MOVE!
I CAN KILL HER!
FWISH
TWITCH

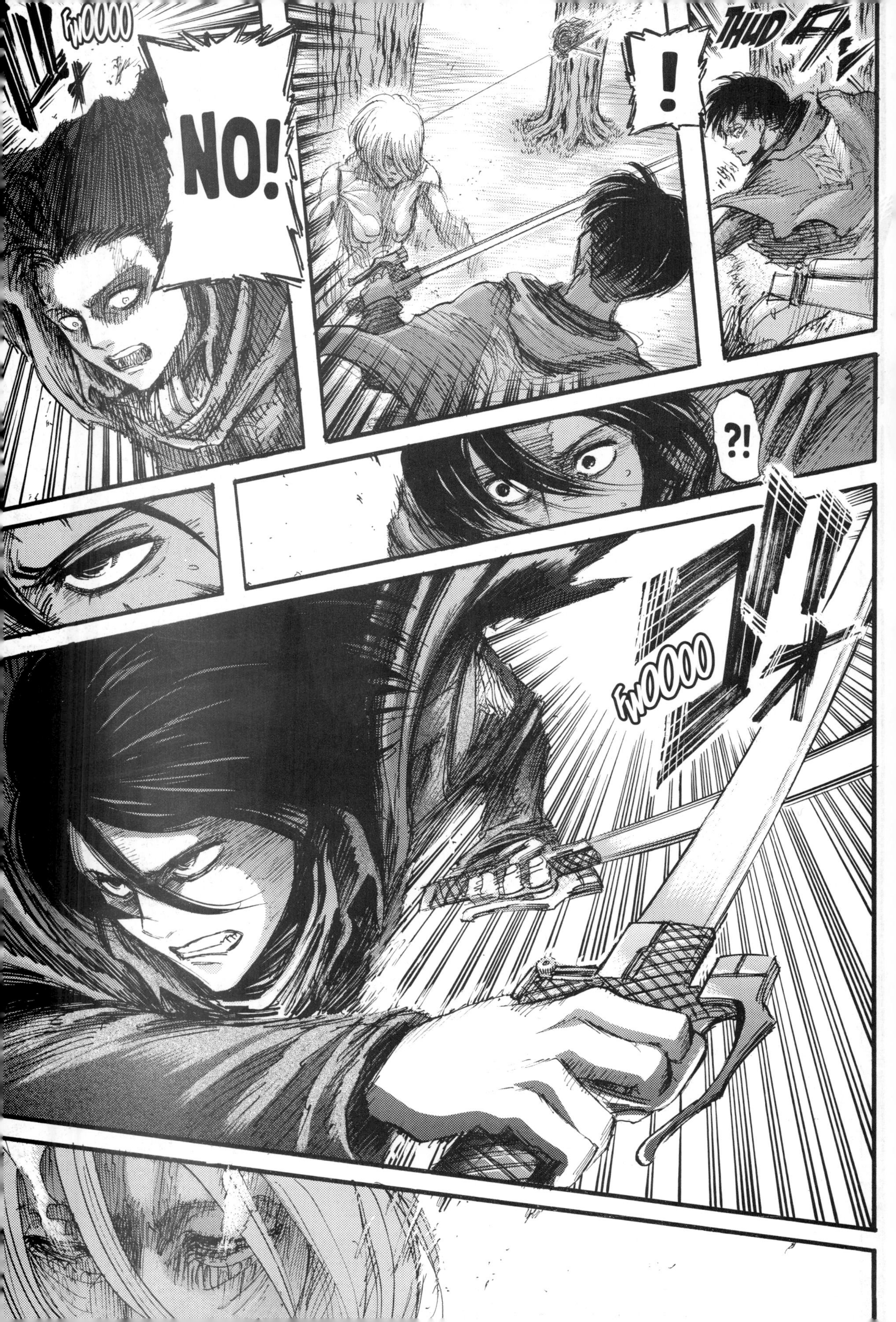
THUD
!
FWOOOO
NO!
?!
FWOOOO

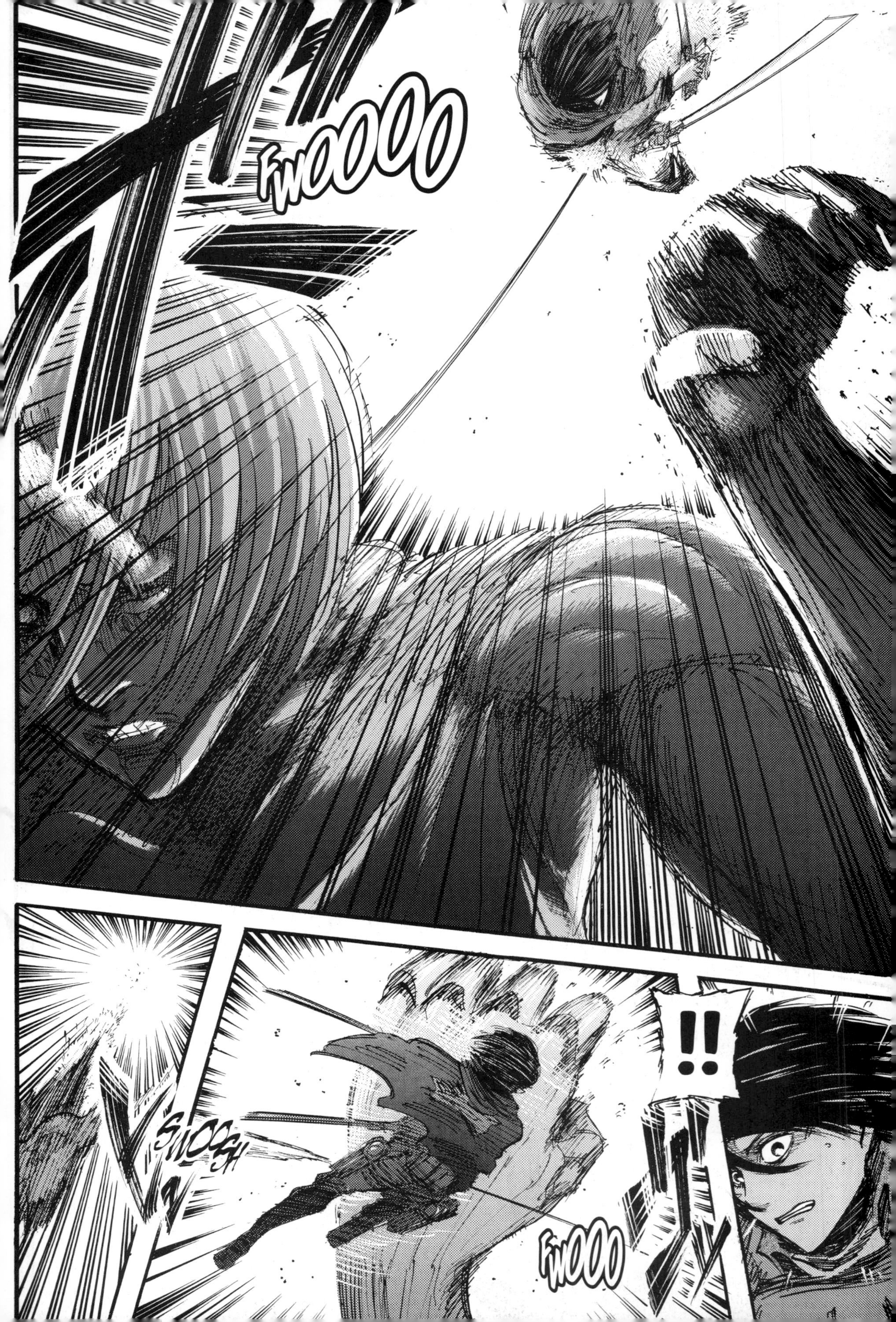
FWOOOO
!!
FWOOO
SHOOSH

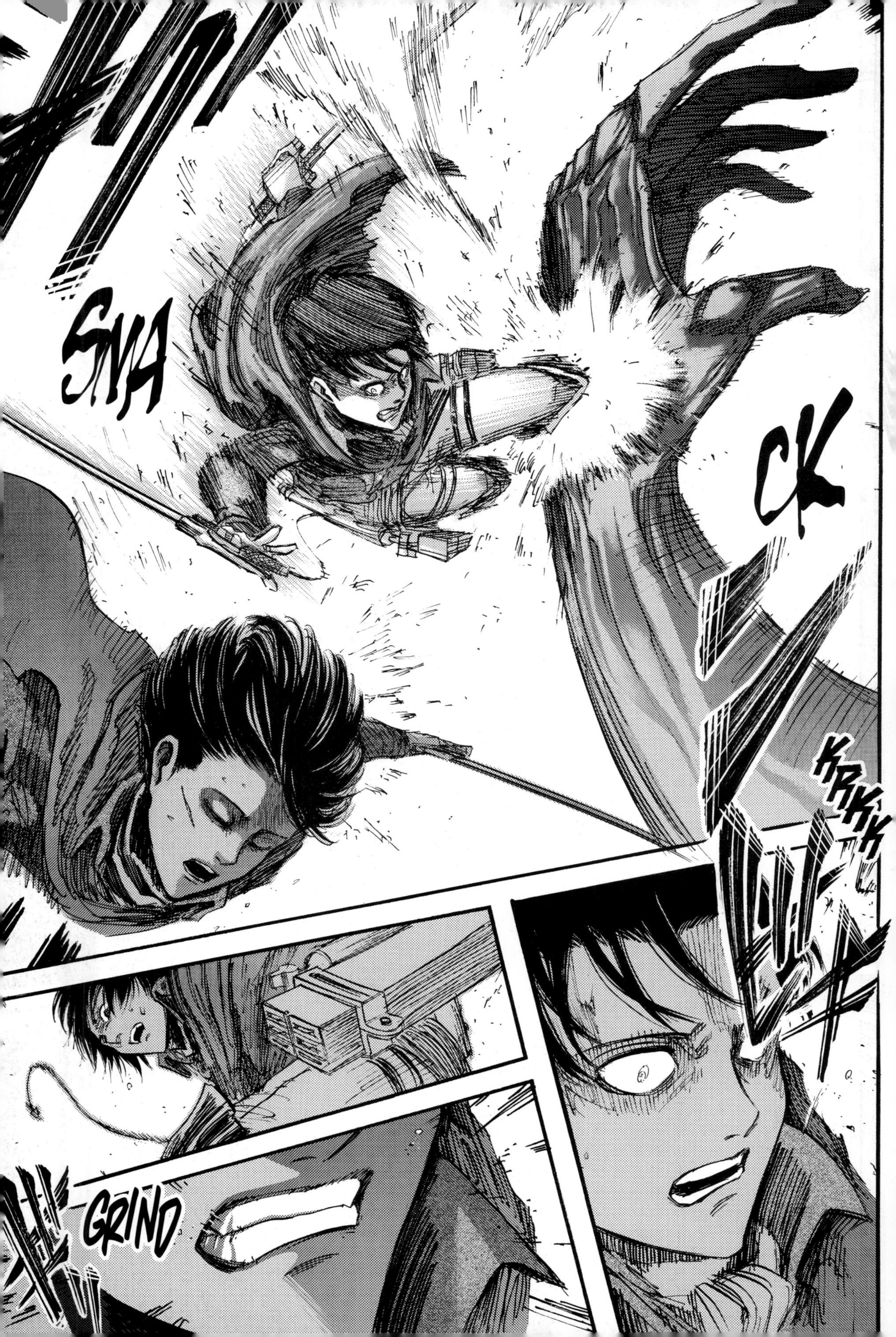
SNA
CK
KRKKK
GRIND

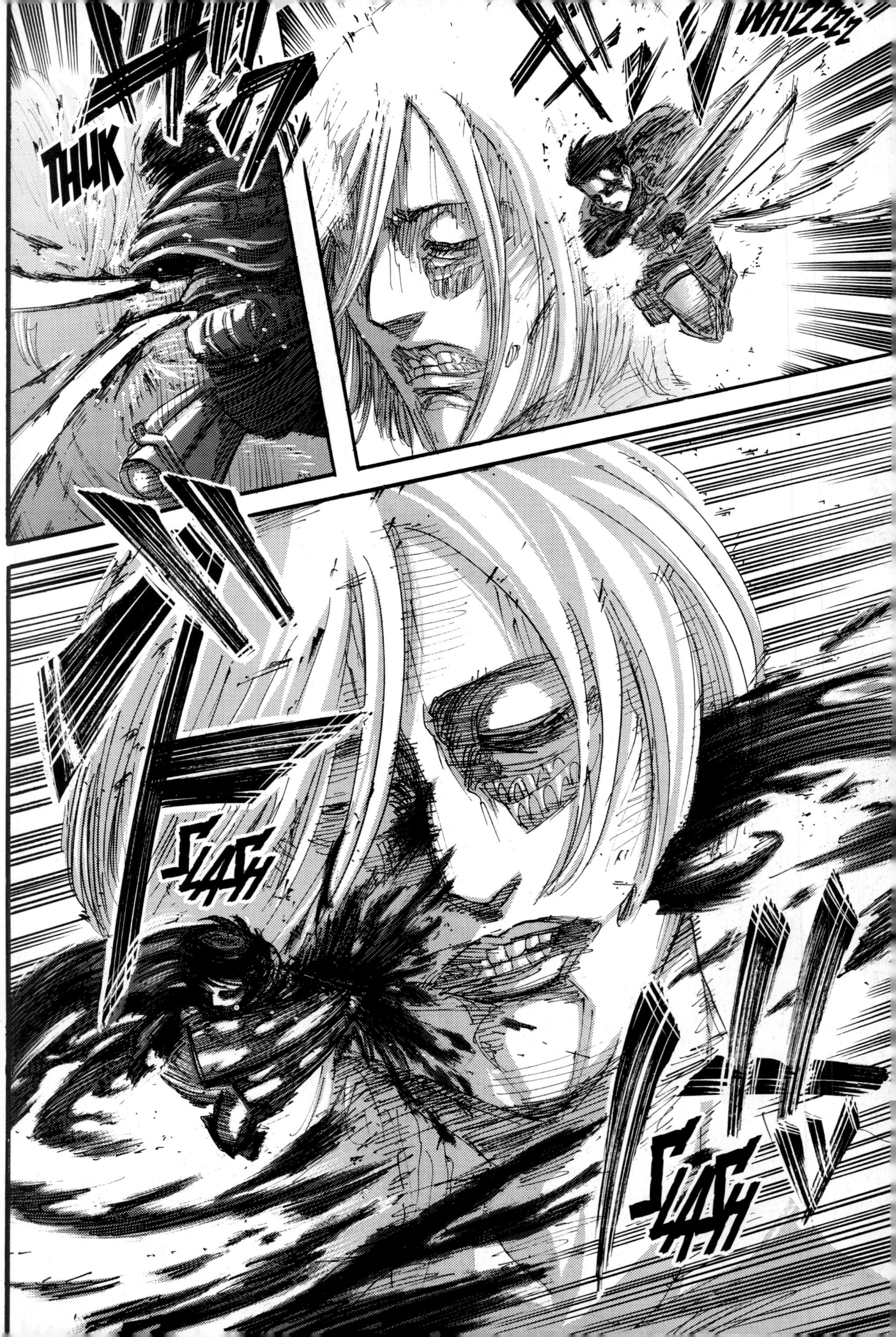
WHIZZZZ
THUK
SLASH
SLASH

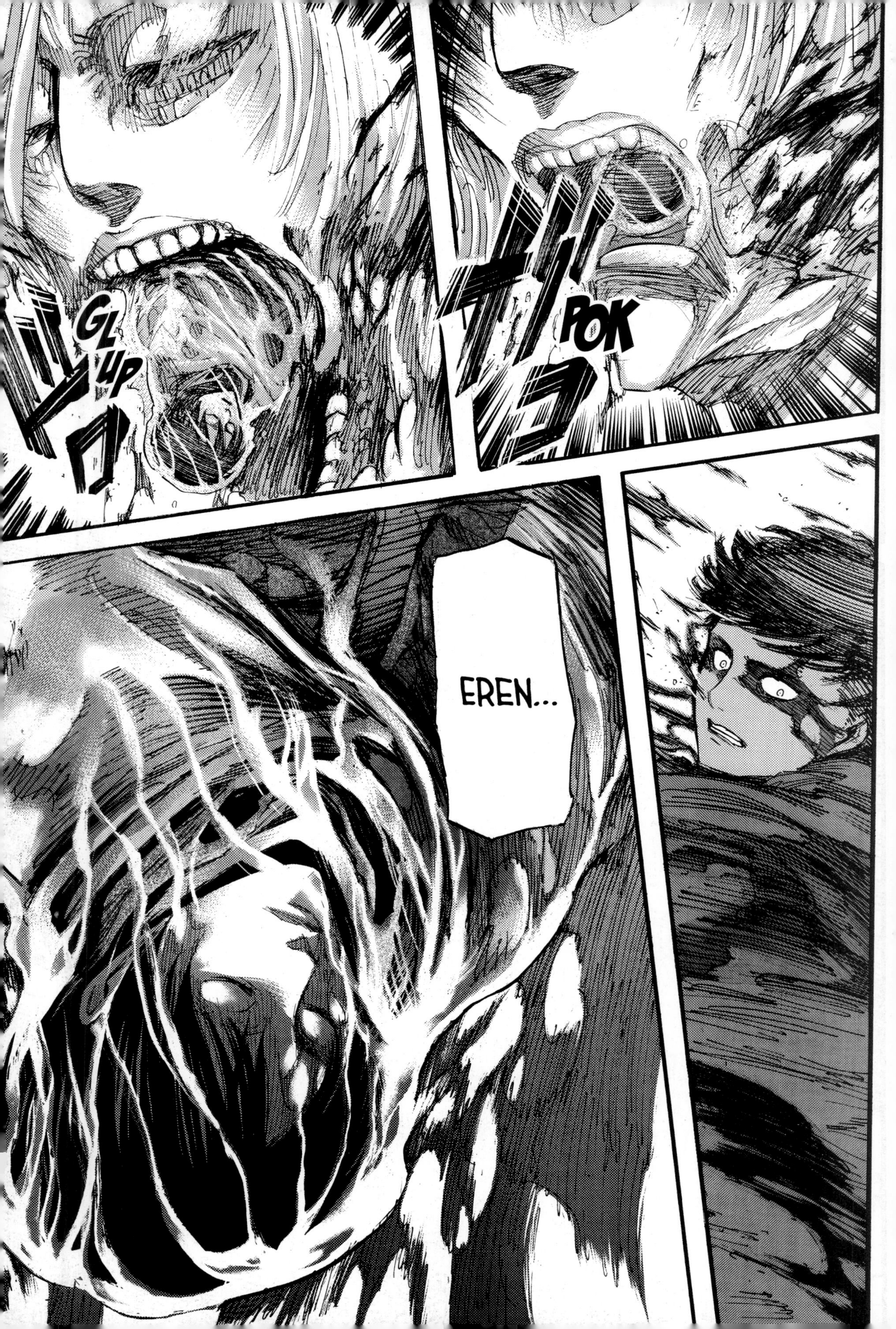
POK
GLUP
EREN...

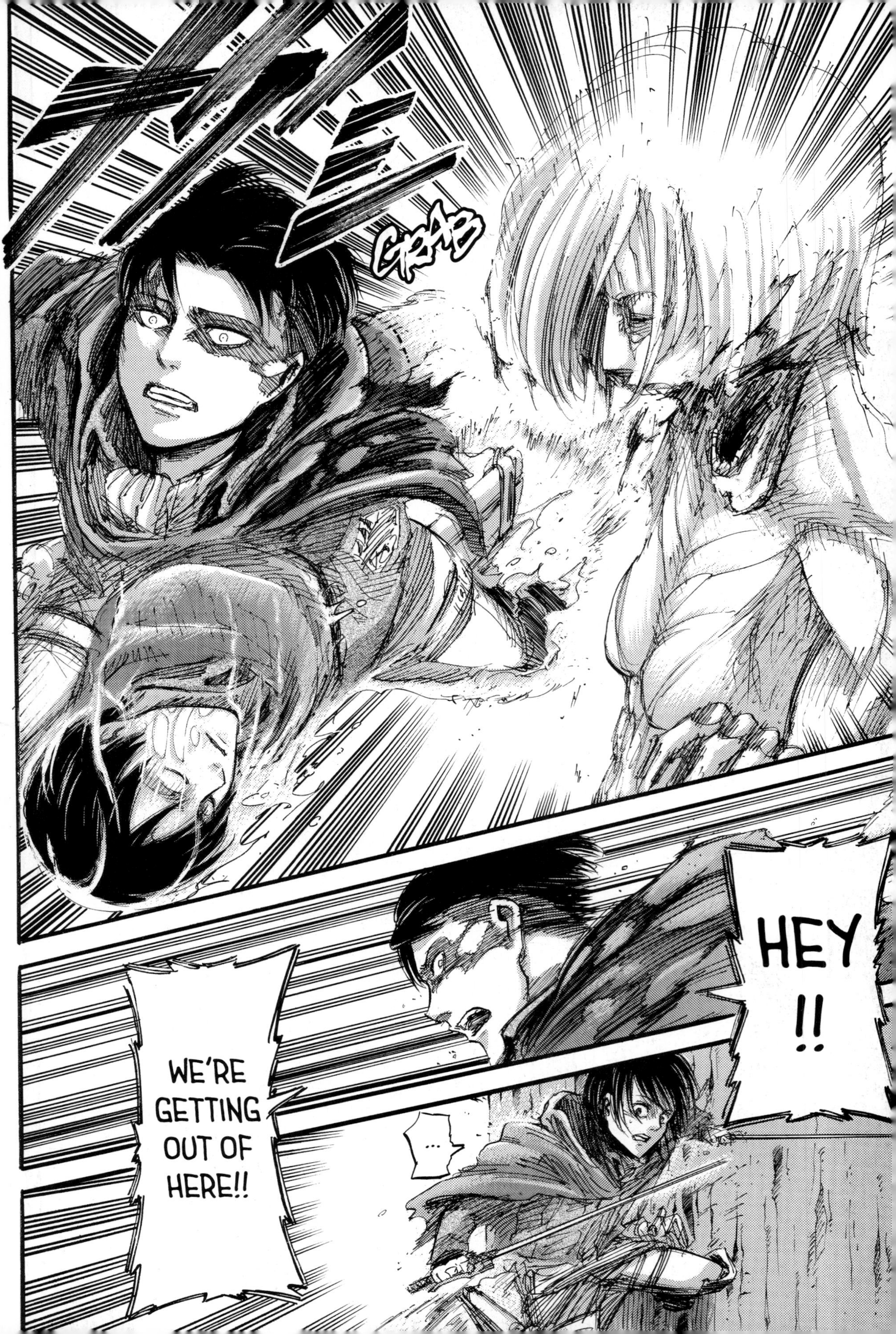
GRAB
HEY !!
WE'RE GETTING OUT OF HERE!!
...

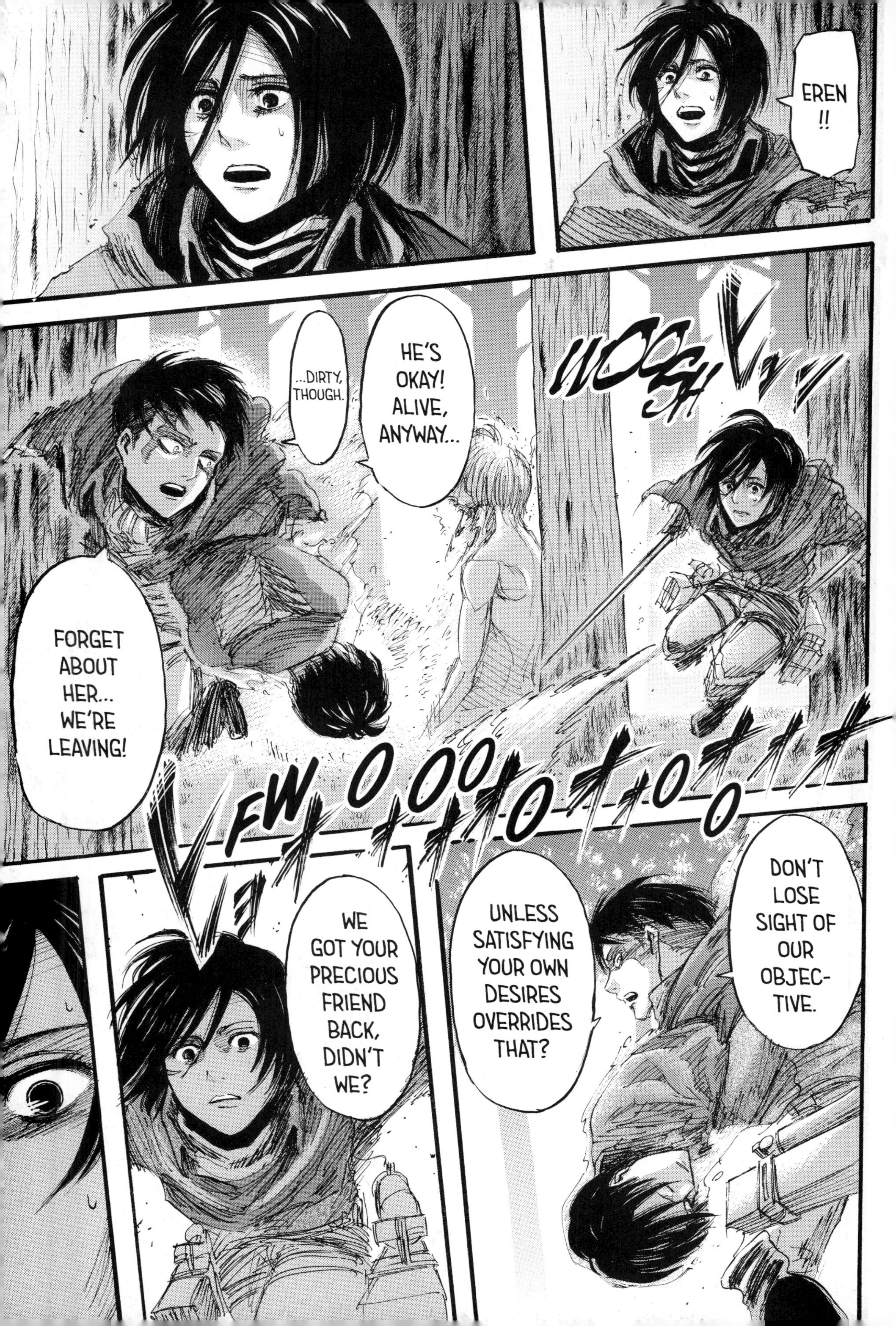
EREN !!
WOOSH
HE'S OKAY! ALIVE, ANYWAY...
...DIRTY, THOUGH.
FORGET ABOUT HER... WE'RE LEAVING!
DON'T LOSE SIGHT OF OUR OBJEC-TIVE.
UNLESS SATISFYING YOUR OWN DESIRES OVERRIDES THAT?
WE GOT YOUR PRECIOUS FRIEND BACK, DIDN'T WE?

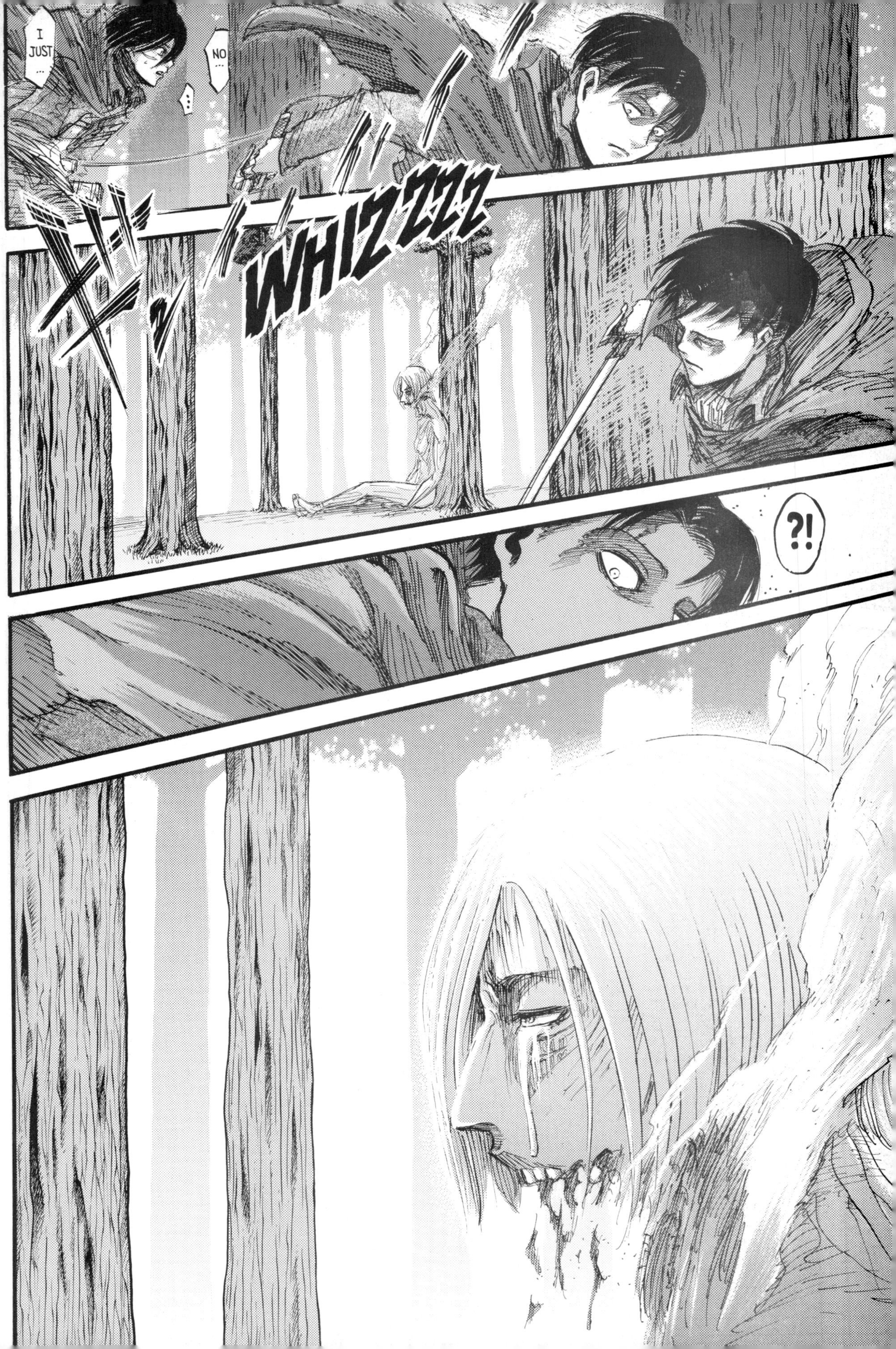
NO ...
I JUST ...
...
WHIZZZZ
?!

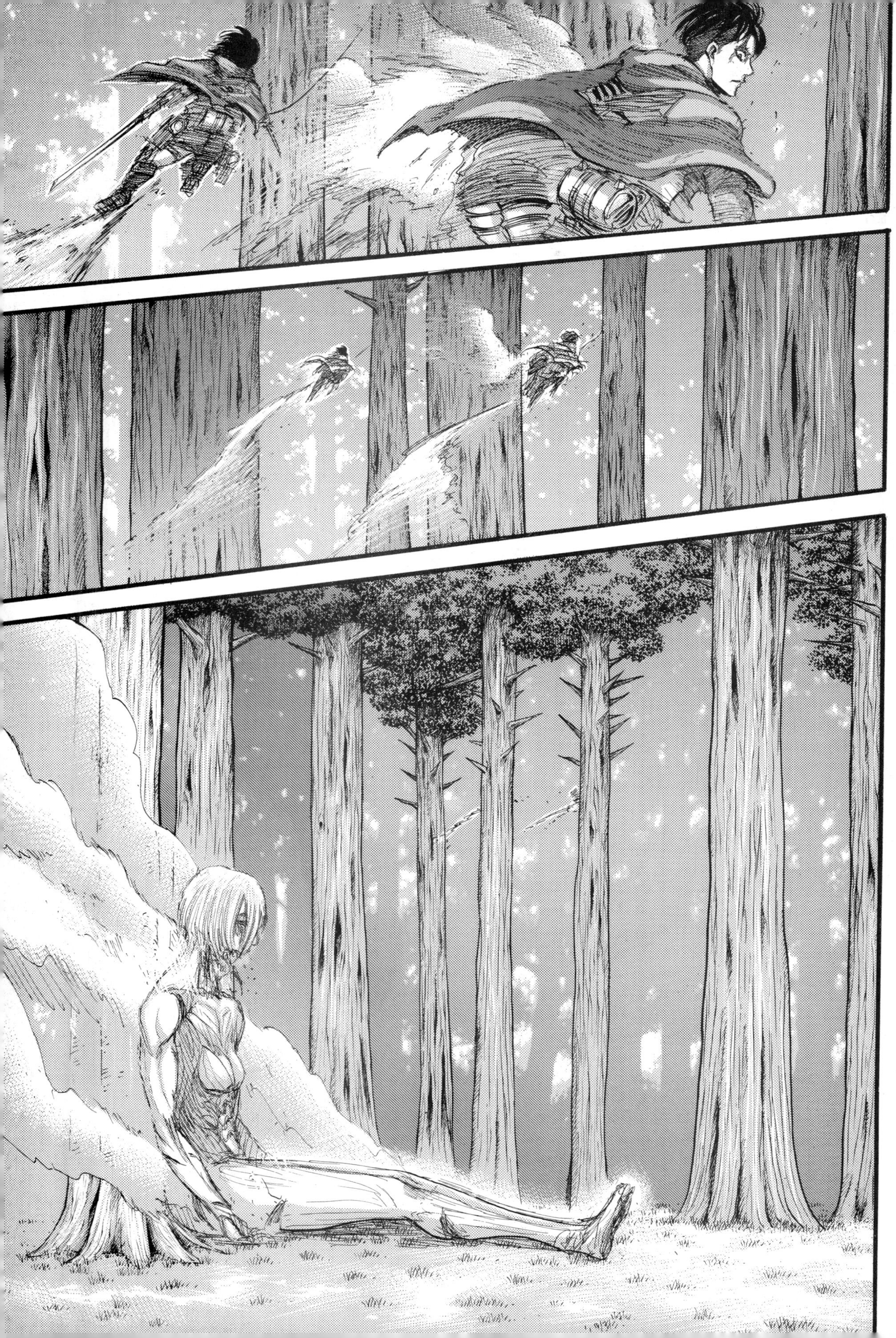

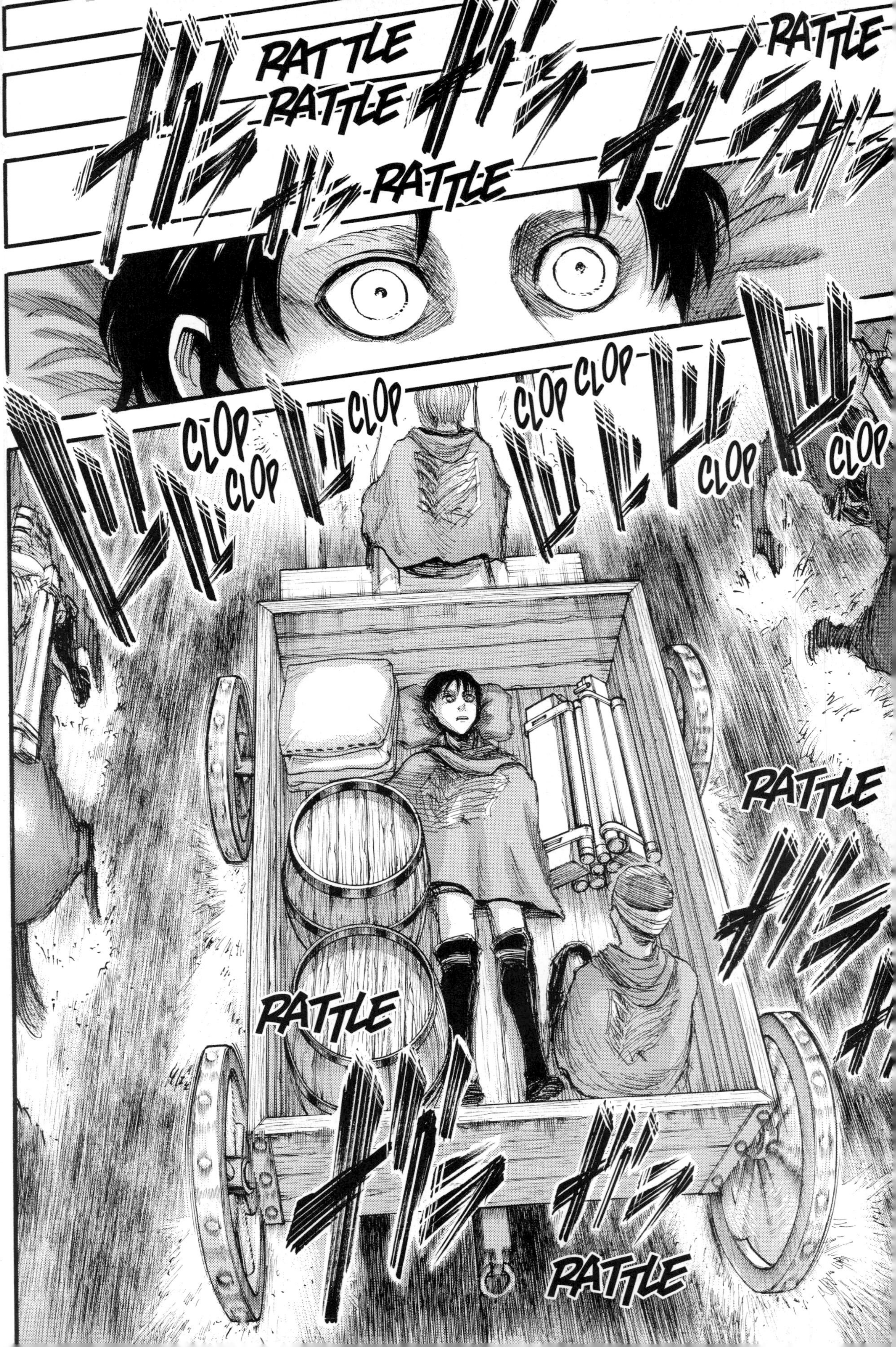
RATTLE
RATTLE
RATTLE
RATTLE
CLOP
CLOP
CLOP CLOP
CLOP
CLOP
CLOP
CLOP
RATTLE
RATTLE
RATTLE

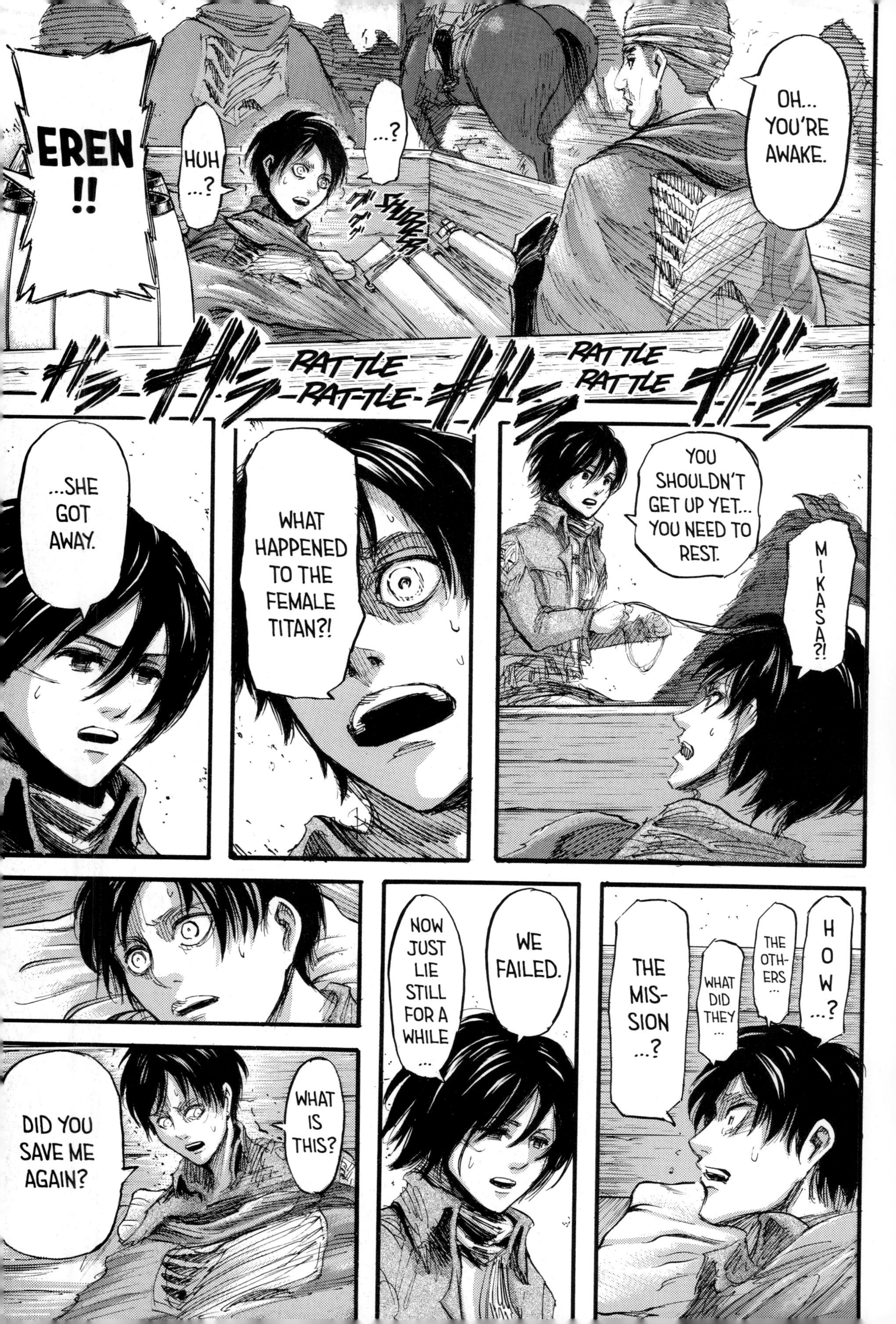
OH... YOU'RE AWAKE.
...?
HUH ...?
EREN !!
RATTLE
RAT-TLE
RATTLE
RATTLE
MIKASA?!
YOU SHOULDN'T GET UP YET... YOU NEED TO REST.
WHAT HAPPENED TO THE FEMALE TITAN?!
...SHE GOT AWAY.
HOW ...?
THE OTHERS ...
WHAT DID THEY ...
THE MIS-SION ...?
WE FAILED.
NOW JUST LIE STILL FOR A WHILE ...
WHAT IS THIS?
DID YOU SAVE ME AGAIN?

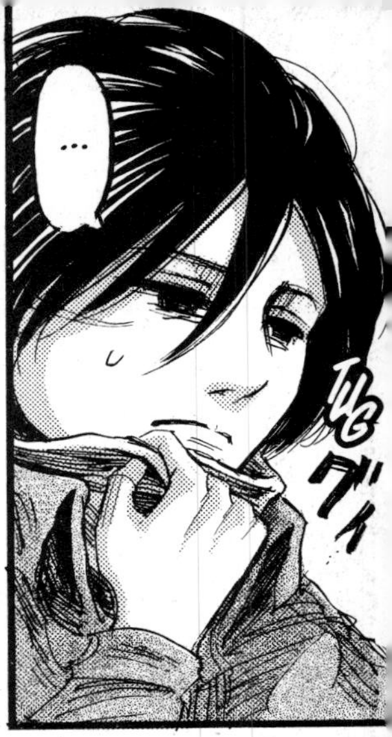
...
TUG
グイ
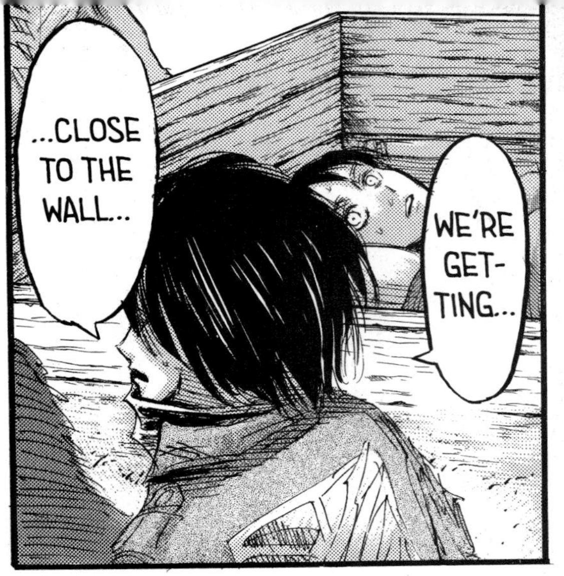
WE'RE GET-
TING...
...CLOSE TO THE WALL...
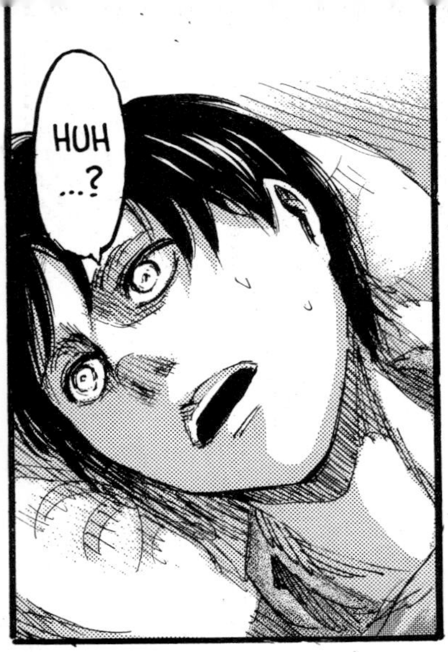
HUH ...?
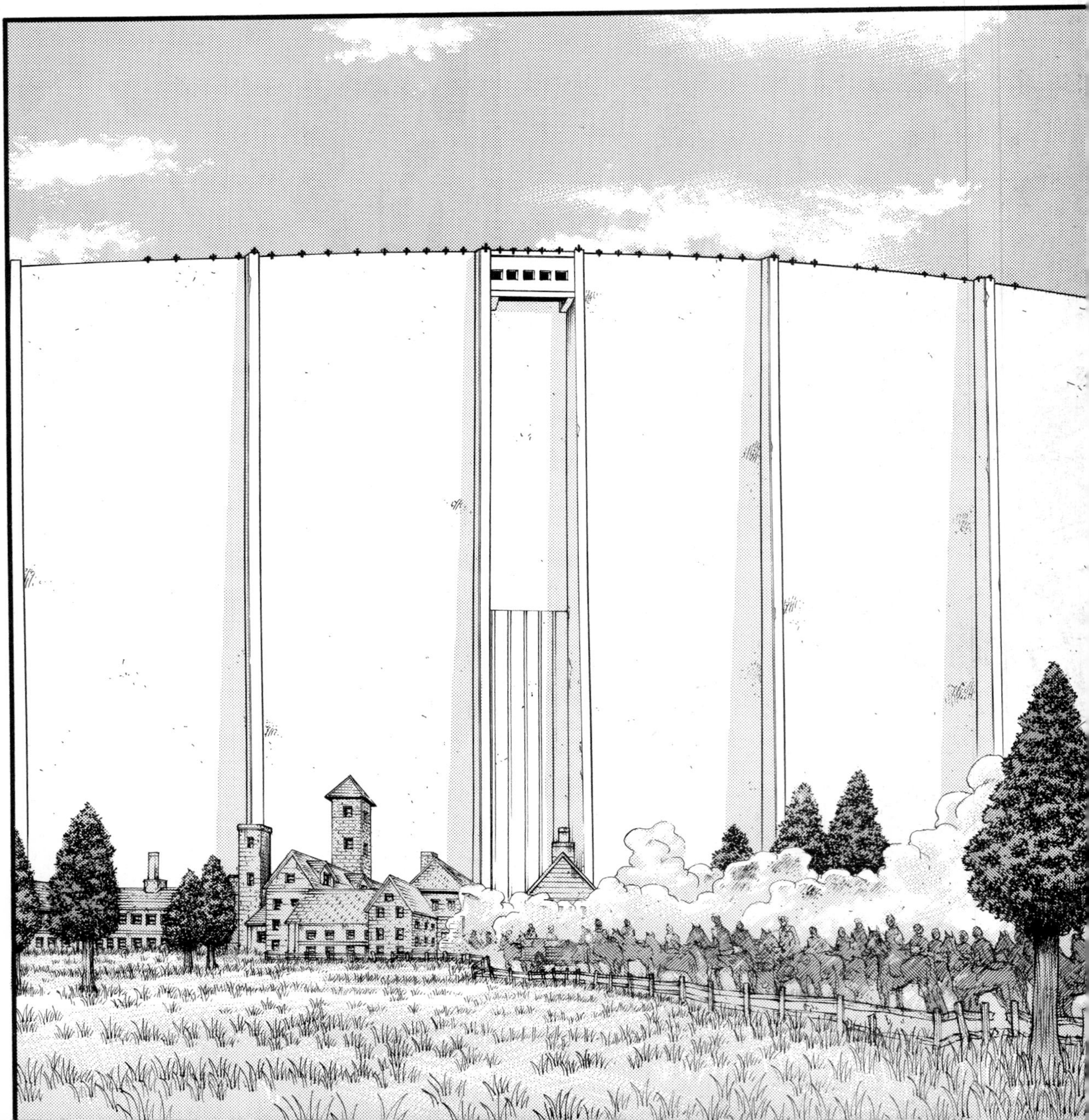

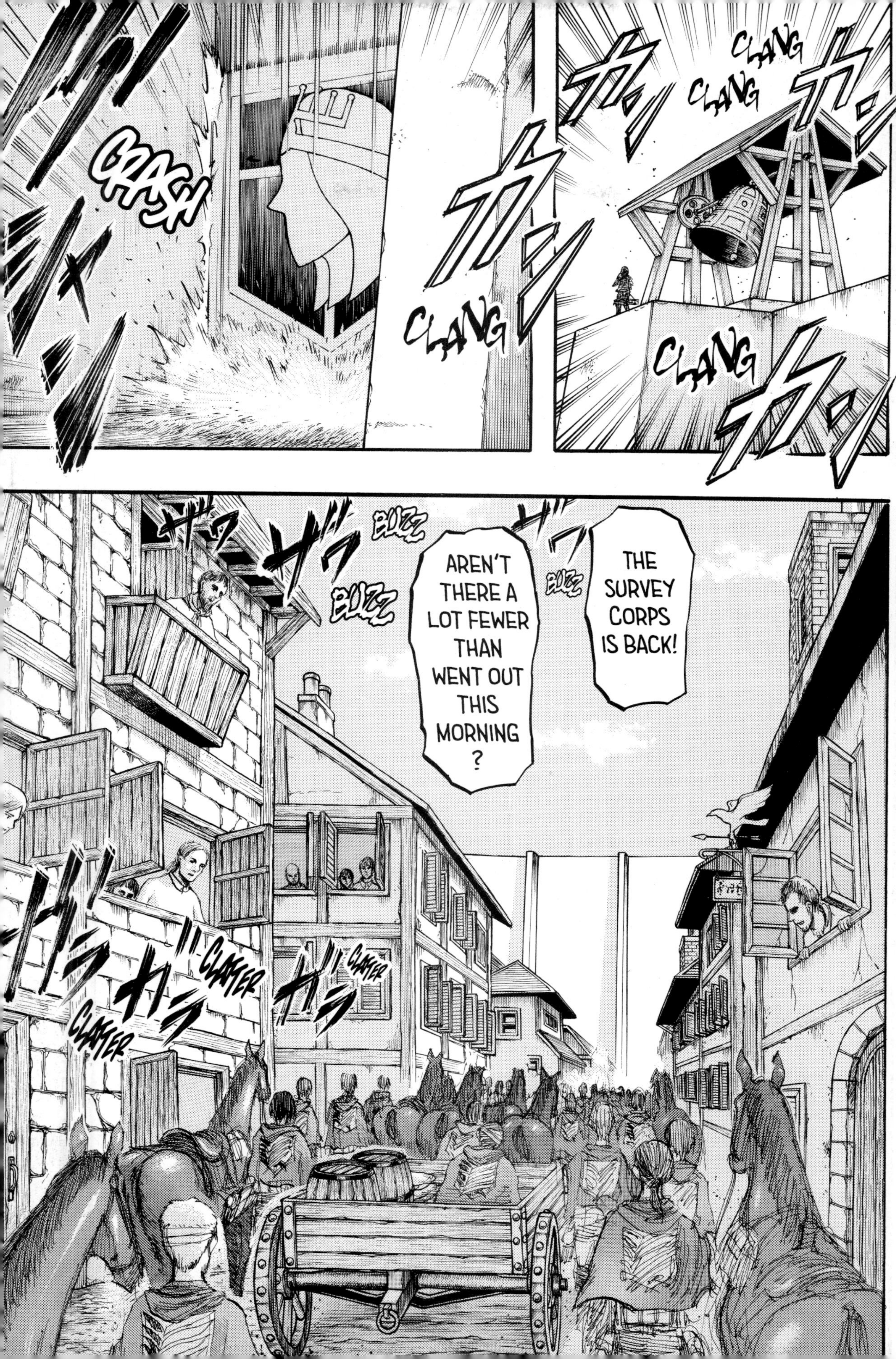
CLANG
CLANG
CLANG
CLANG
CRASH
BUZZ
THE SURVEY CORPS IS BACK!
BUZZ
BUZZ
AREN'T THERE A LOT FEWER THAN WENT OUT THIS MORNING?
CLATTER
CLATTER
CLATTER

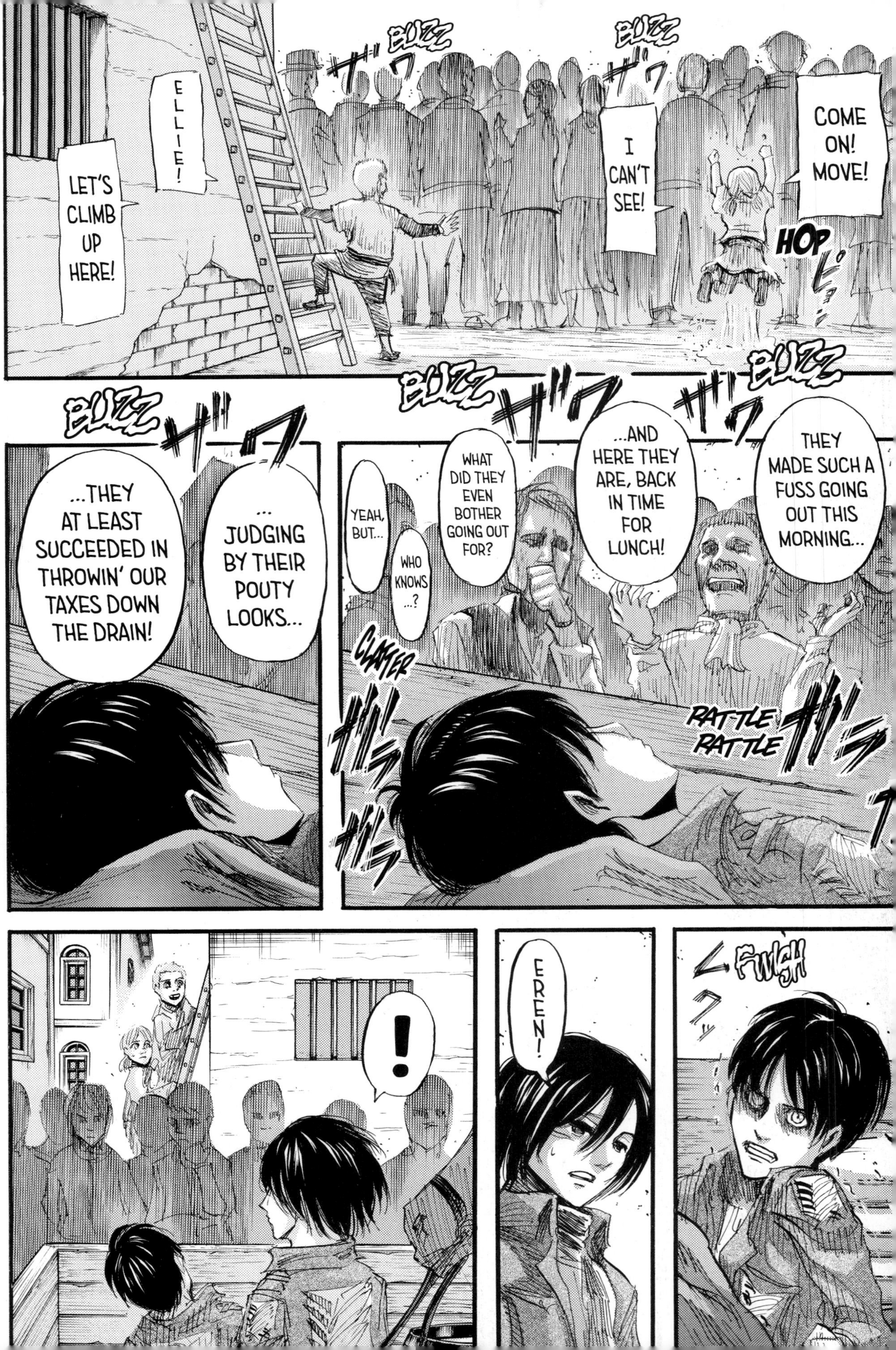
BUZZ
COME ON! MOVE!
HOP
I CAN'T SEE!
BUZZ
ELLIE!
LET'S CLIMB UP HERE!
BUZZ
THEY MADE SUCH A FUSS GOING OUT THIS MORNING...
BUZZ
...AND HERE THEY ARE, BACK IN TIME FOR LUNCH!
WHAT DID THEY EVEN BOTHER GOING OUT FOR?
YEAH, BUT...
WHO KNOWS ...?
RATTLE RATTLE
CLATTER
BUZZ
... JUDGING BY THEIR POUTY LOOKS...
...THEY AT LEAST SUCCEEDED IN THROWIN' OUR TAXES DOWN THE DRAIN!
FWISH
EREN!
!

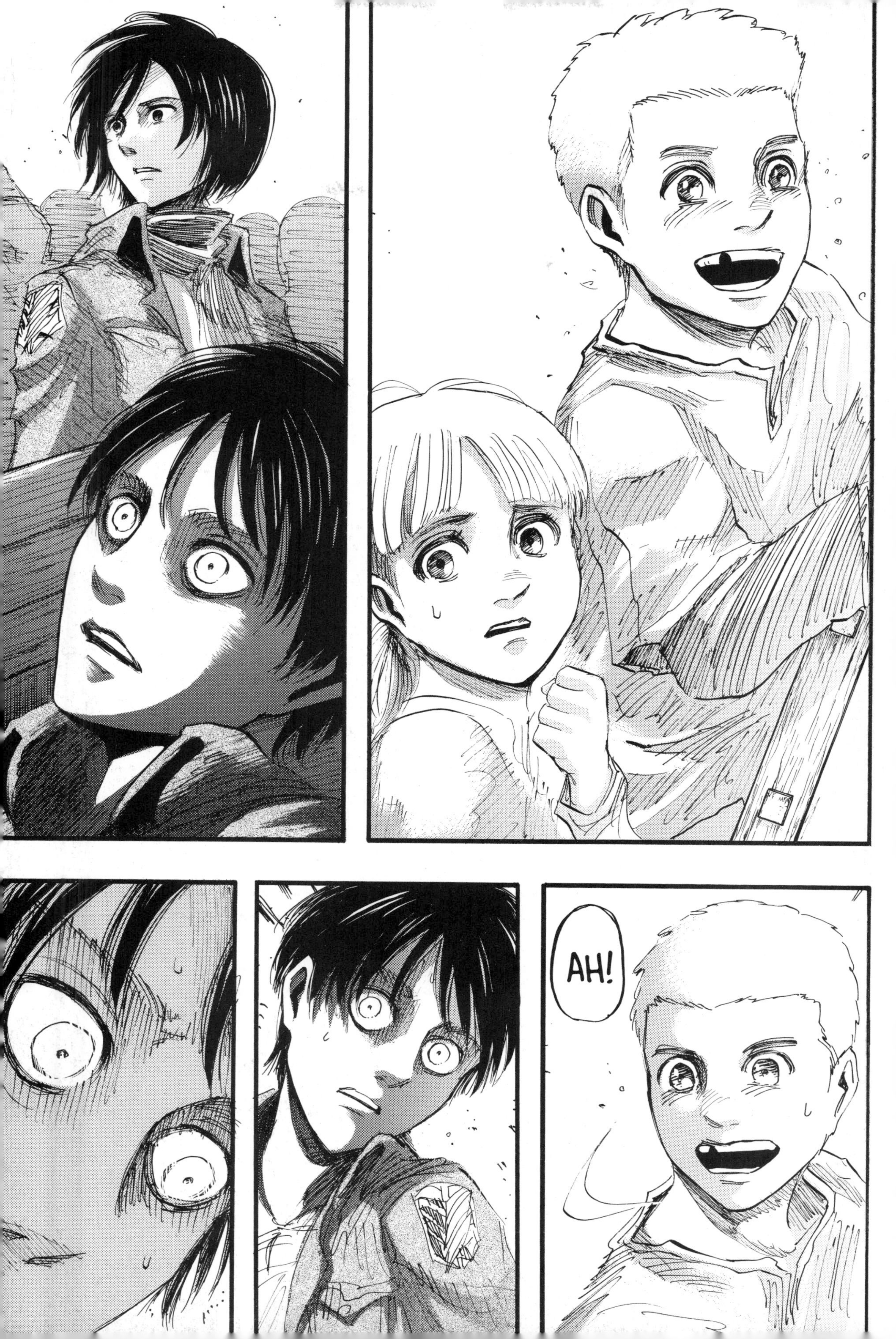
AH!

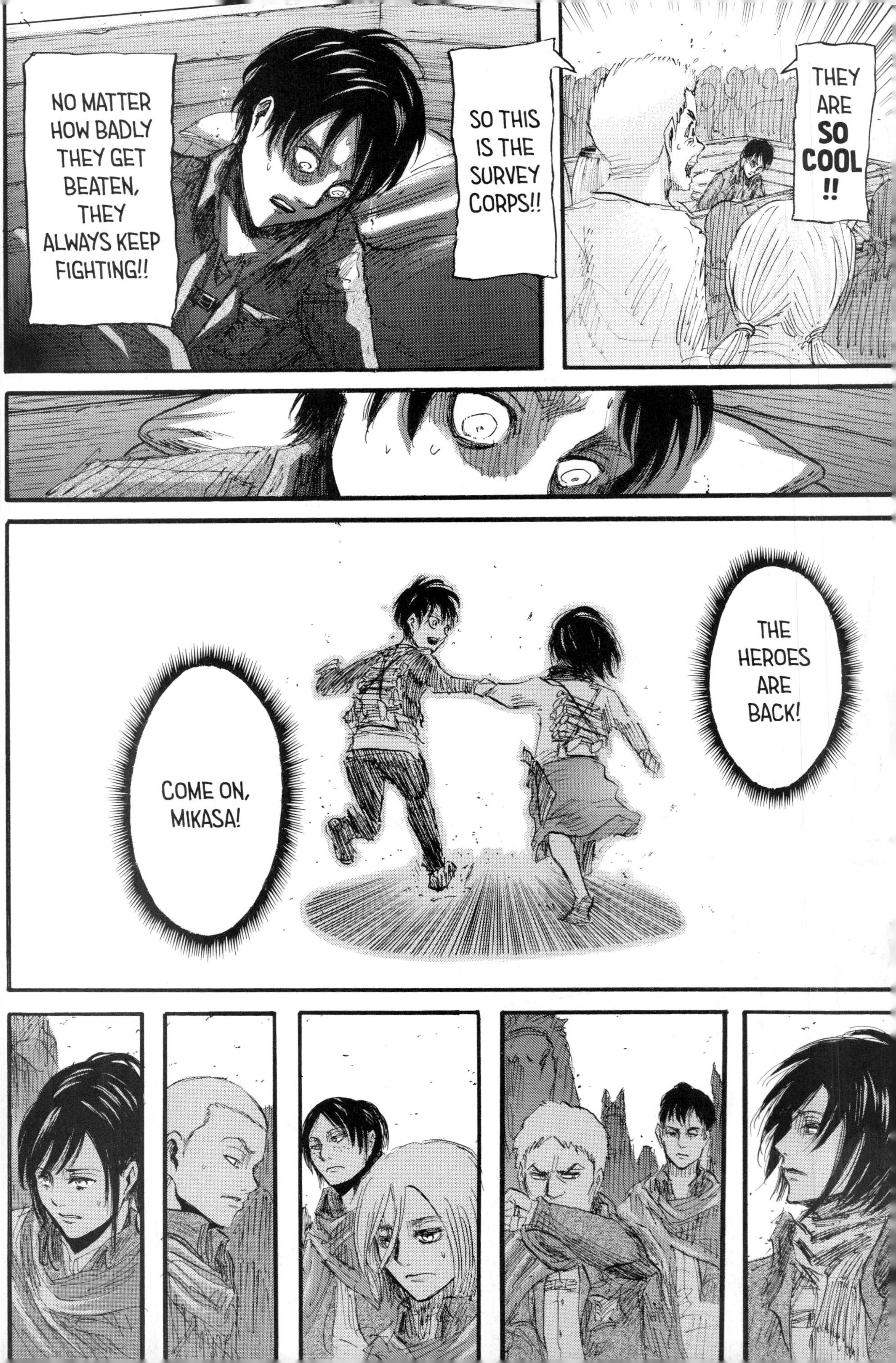
THEY ARE **SO COOL!!**
SO THIS IS THE SURVEY CORPS!!
NO MATTER HOW BADLY THEY GET BEATEN, THEY ALWAYS KEEP FIGHTING!!
THE HEROES ARE BACK!
COME ON, MIKASA!

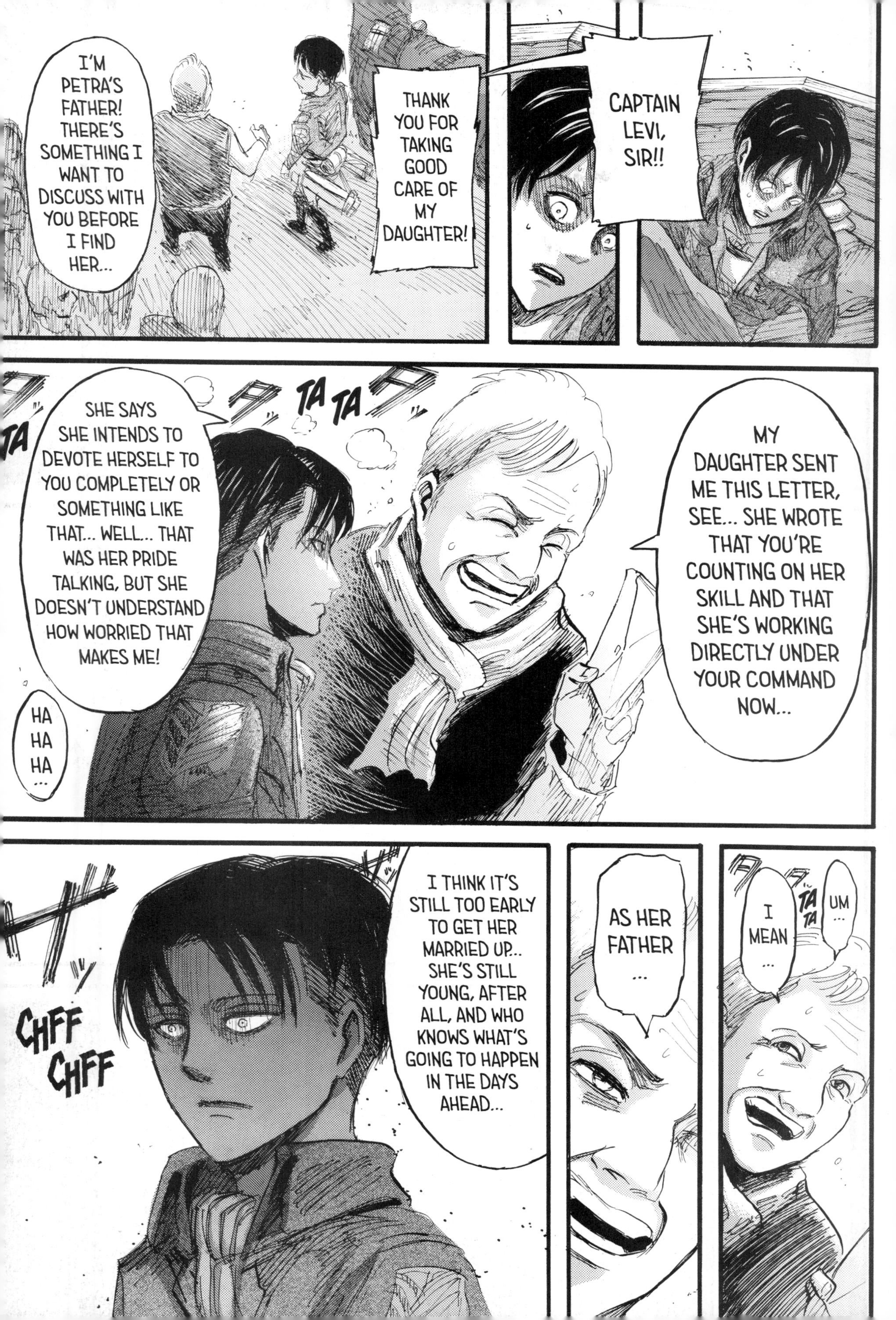
CAPTAIN LEVI, SIR!!
THANK YOU FOR TAKING GOOD CARE OF MY DAUGHTER!
I'M PETRA'S FATHER! THERE'S SOMETHING I WANT TO DISCUSS WITH YOU BEFORE I FIND HER...
MY DAUGHTER SENT ME THIS LETTER, SEE... SHE WROTE THAT YOU'RE COUNTING ON HER SKILL AND THAT SHE'S WORKING DIRECTLY UNDER YOUR COMMAND NOW...
TA TA
SHE SAYS SHE INTENDS TO DEVOTE HERSELF TO YOU COMPLETELY OR SOMETHING LIKE THAT... WELL... THAT WAS HER PRIDE TALKING, BUT SHE DOESN'T UNDERSTAND HOW WORRIED THAT MAKES ME!
HA HA HA ...
UM ...
I MEAN ...
TA TA
AS HER FATHER ...
I THINK IT'S STILL TOO EARLY TO GET HER MARRIED UP... SHE'S STILL YOUNG, AFTER ALL, AND WHO KNOWS WHAT'S GOING TO HAPPEN IN THE DAYS AHEAD...
CHFF CHFF

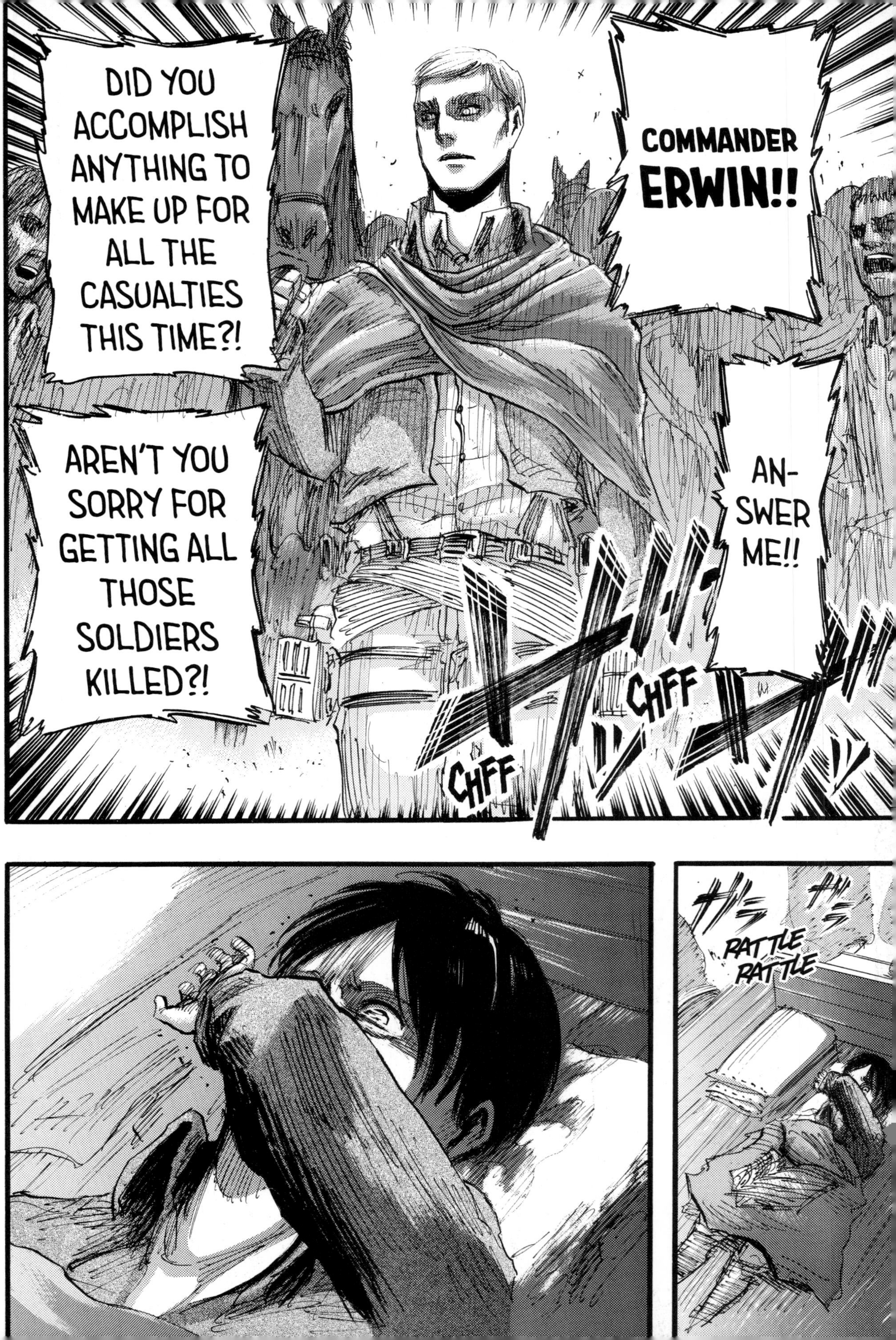
COMMANDER ERWIN!!
DID YOU ACCOMPLISH ANYTHING TO MAKE UP FOR ALL THE CASUALTIES THIS TIME?!
ANSWER ME!!
AREN'T YOU SORRY FOR GETTING ALL THOSE SOLDIERS KILLED?!
CHFF
CHFF
RATTLE RATTLE

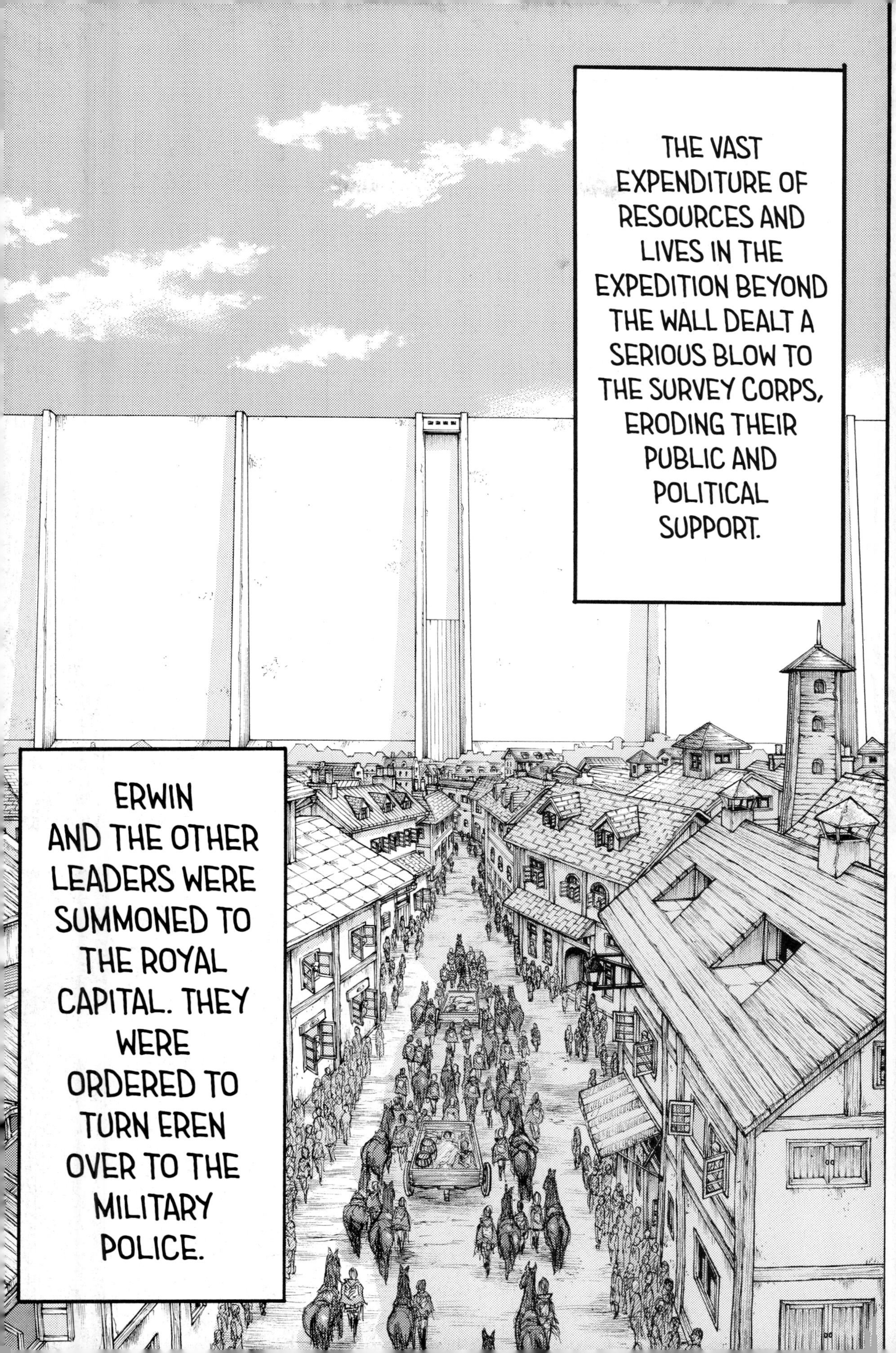
THE VAST EXPENDITURE OF RESOURCES AND LIVES IN THE EXPEDITION BEYOND THE WALL DEALT A SERIOUS BLOW TO THE SURVEY CORPS, ERODING THEIR PUBLIC AND POLITICAL SUPPORT.
ERWIN AND THE OTHER LEADERS WERE SUMMONED TO THE ROYAL CAPITAL. THEY WERE ORDERED TO TURN EREN OVER TO THE MILITARY POLICE.

*Rejected Cover Proposal
The mood just didn't go with the worldview.

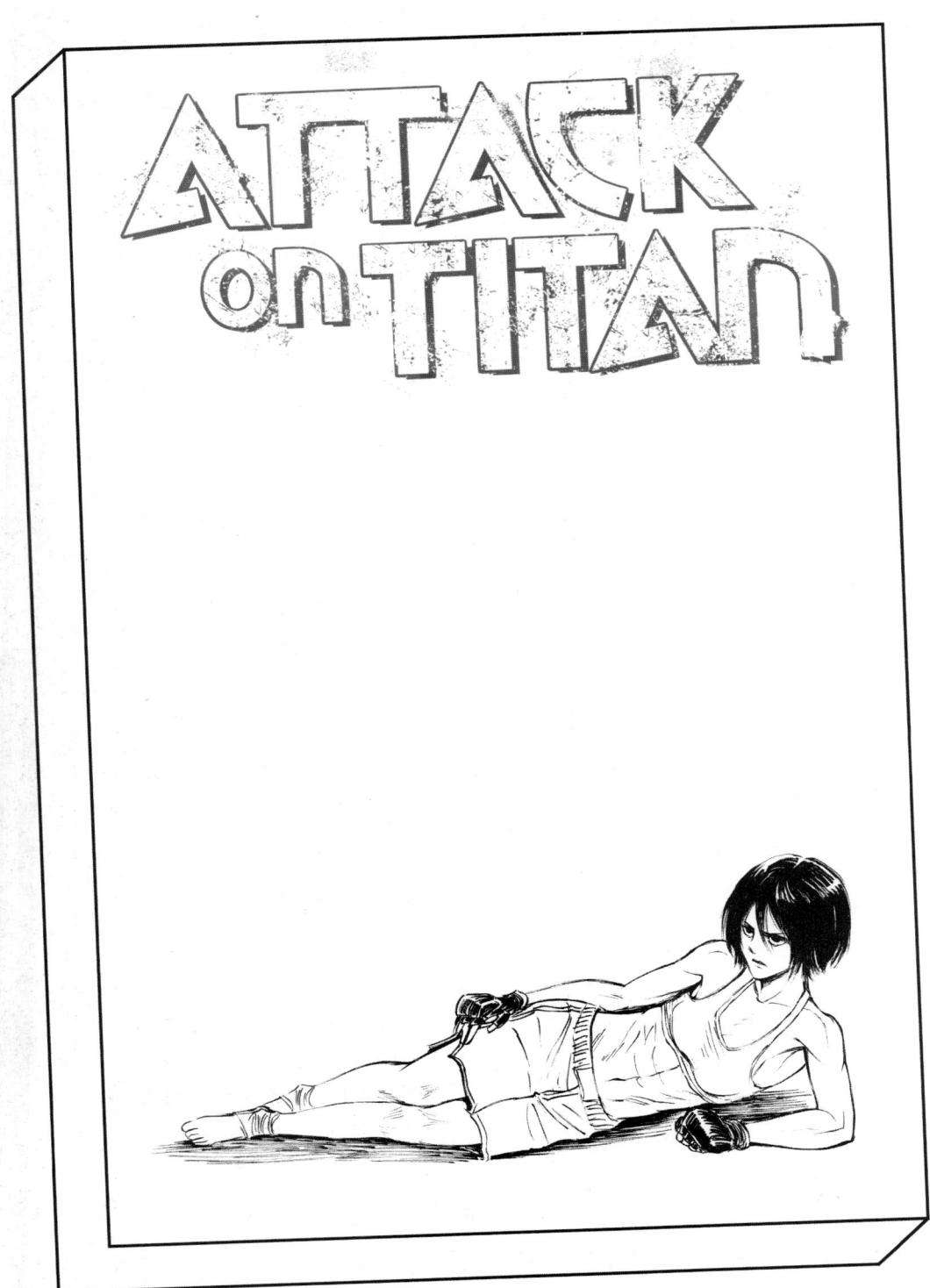

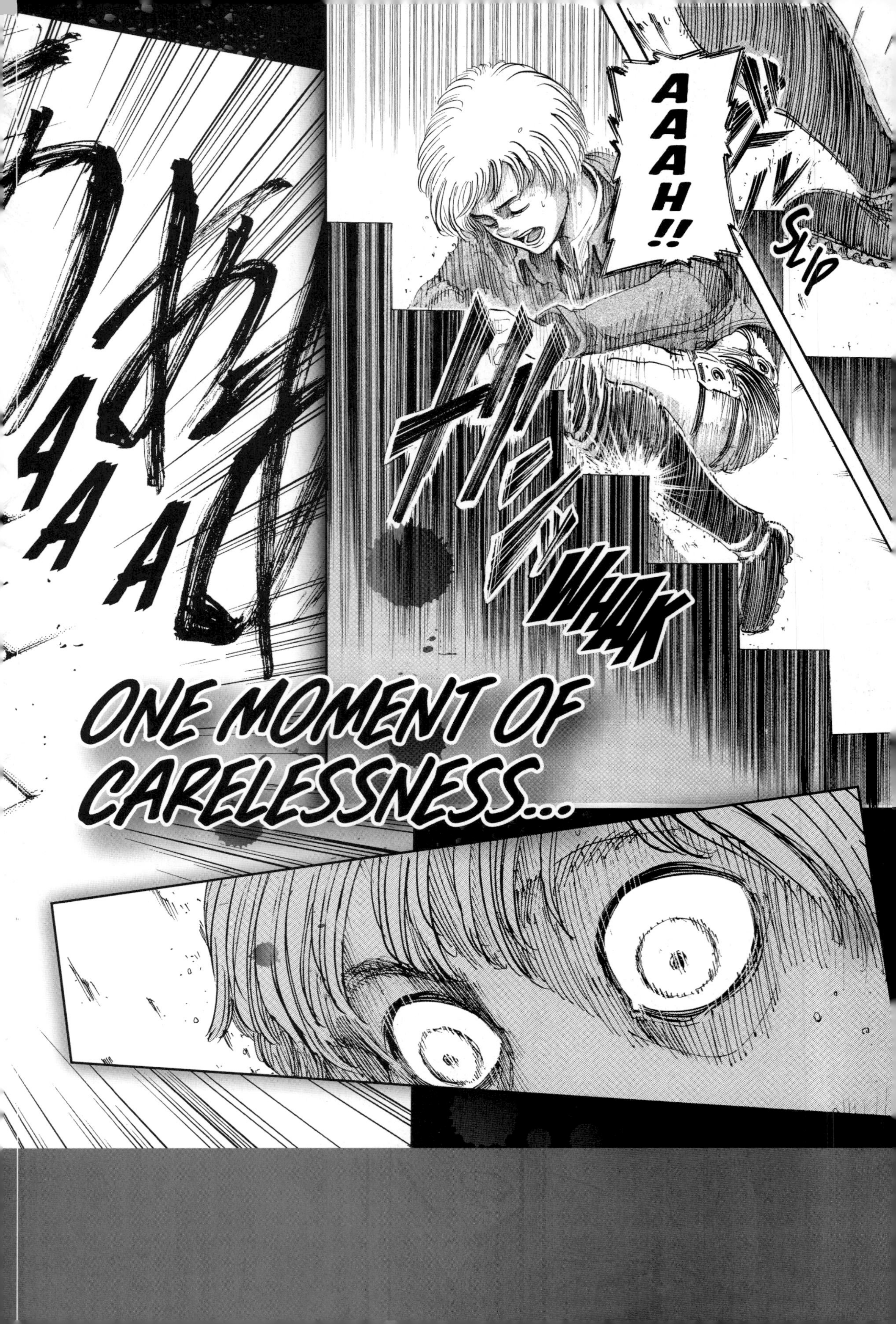
AAAAH!!
SLIP
WHAK
AAAAA
ONE MOMENT OF CARELESSNESS...

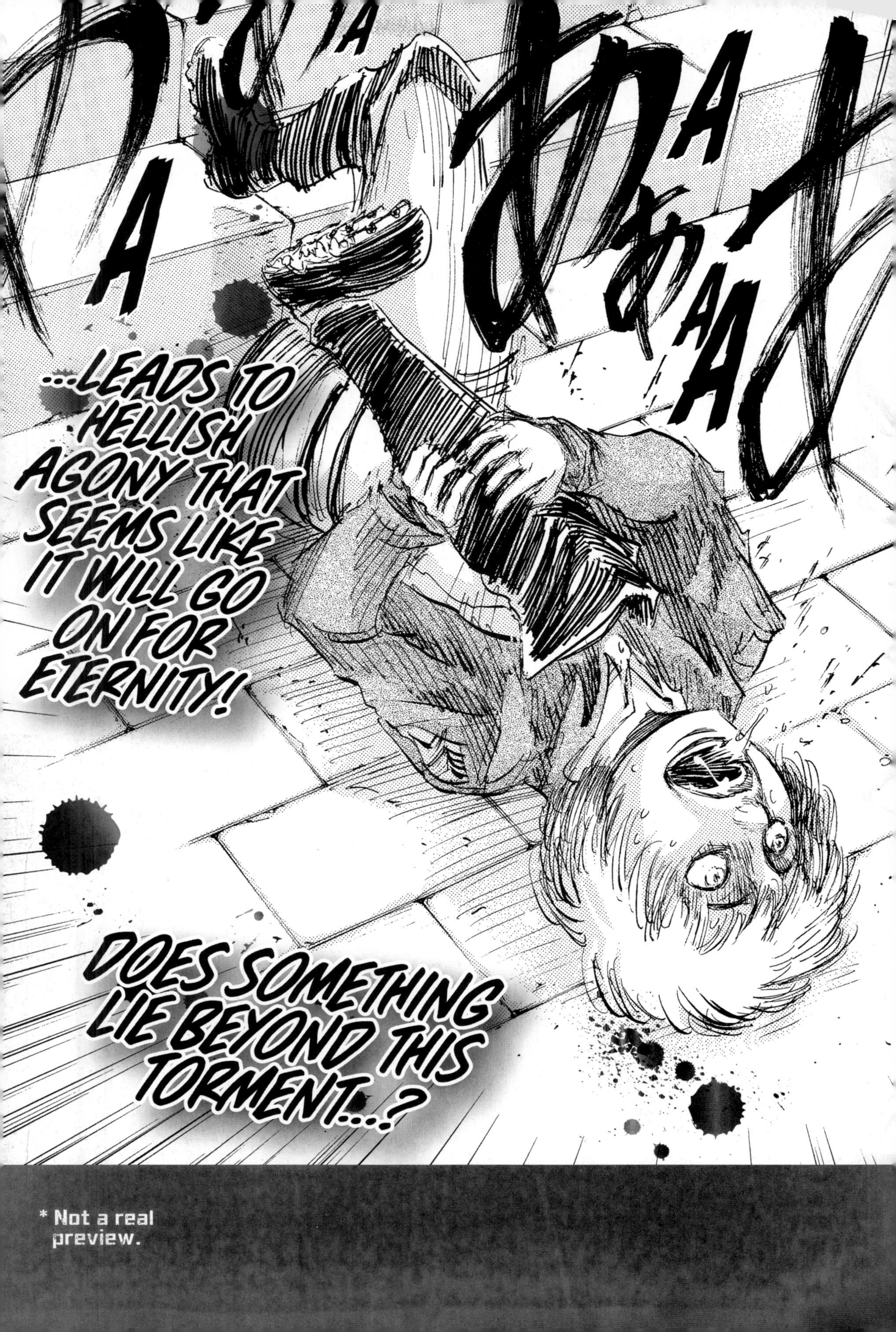

AAAAA
...LEADS TO HELLISH AGONY THAT SEEMS LIKE IT WILL GO ON FOR ETERNITY!
DOES SOMETHING LIE BEYOND THIS TORMENT...?

* Not a real preview.

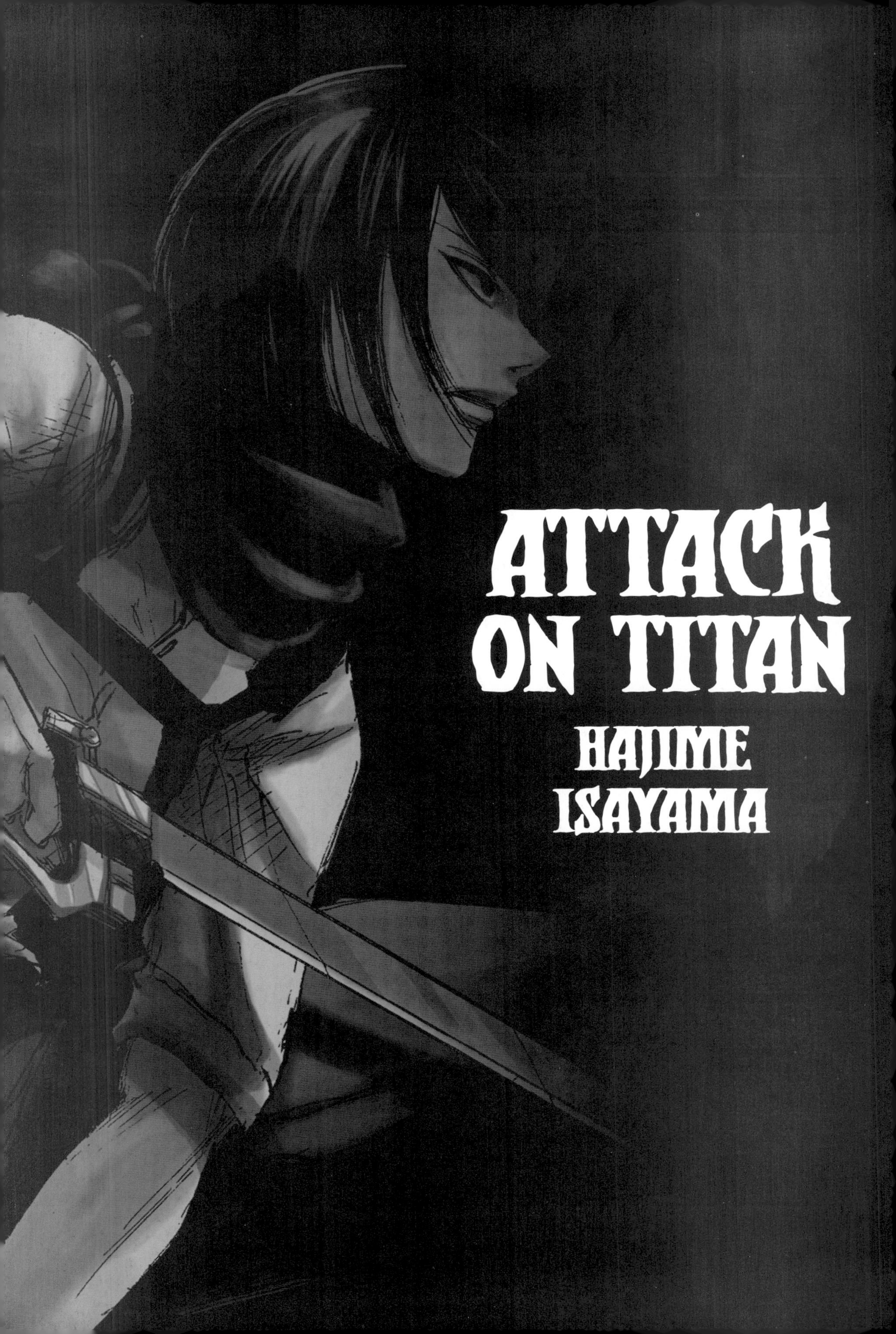
ATTACK ON TITAN
HAJIME ISAYAMA

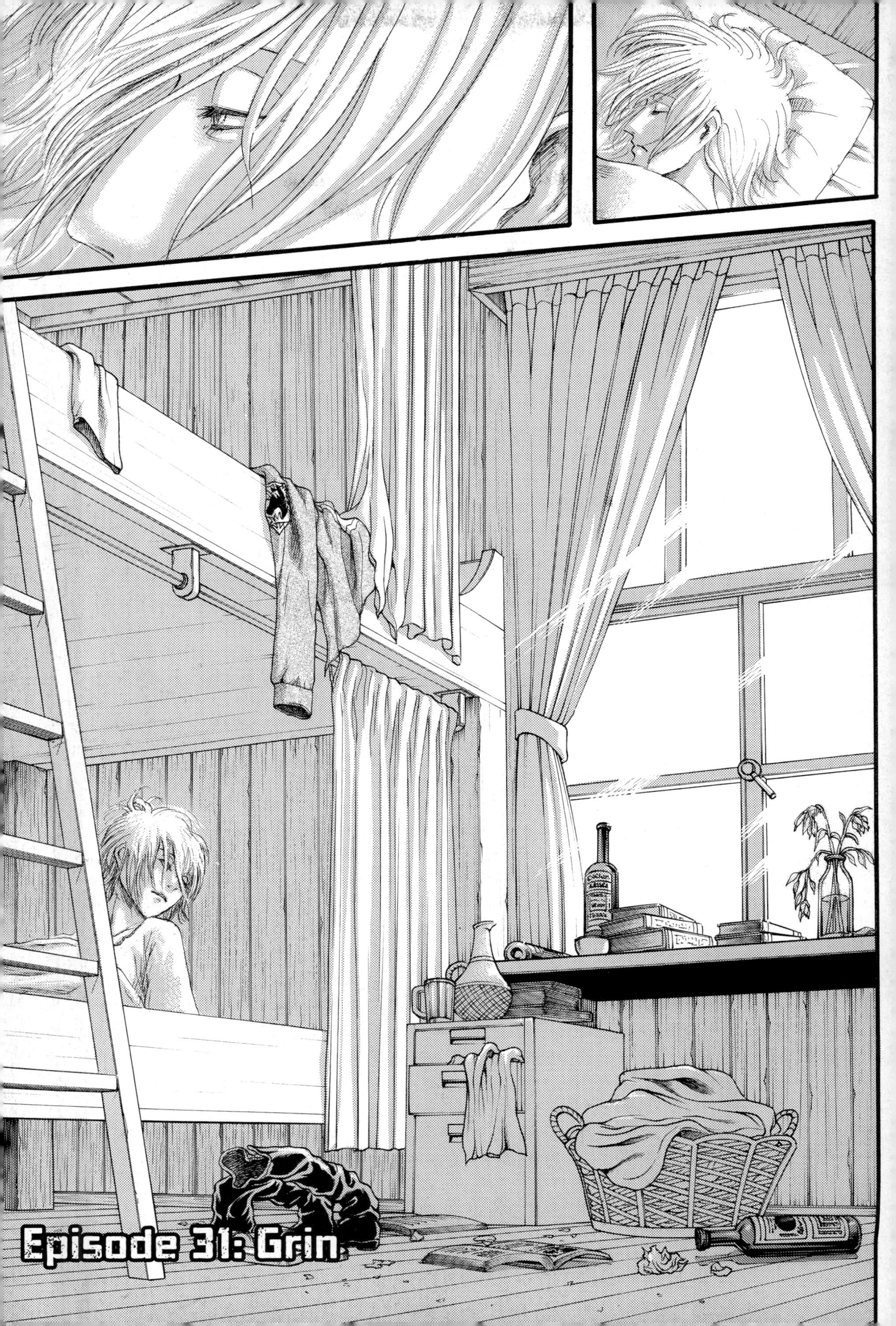
Episode 31: Grin

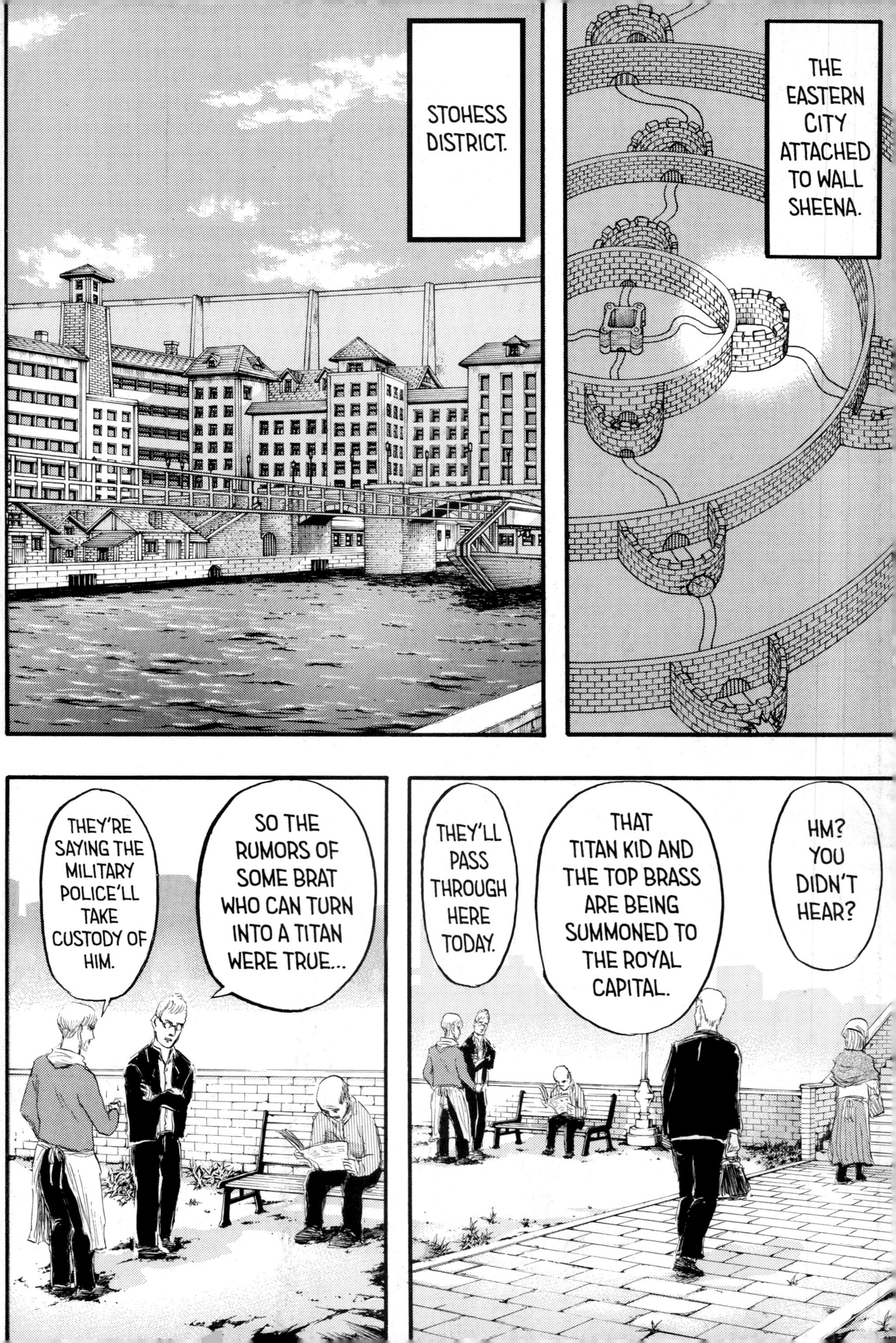
THE EASTERN CITY ATTACHED TO WALL SHEENA.
STOHESS DISTRICT.
HM? YOU DIDN'T HEAR?
THAT TITAN KID AND THE TOP BRASS ARE BEING SUMMONED TO THE ROYAL CAPITAL.
THEY'LL PASS THROUGH HERE TODAY.
SO THE RUMORS OF SOME BRAT WHO CAN TURN INTO A TITAN WERE TRUE...
THEY'RE SAYING THE MILITARY POLICE'LL TAKE CUSTODY OF HIM.

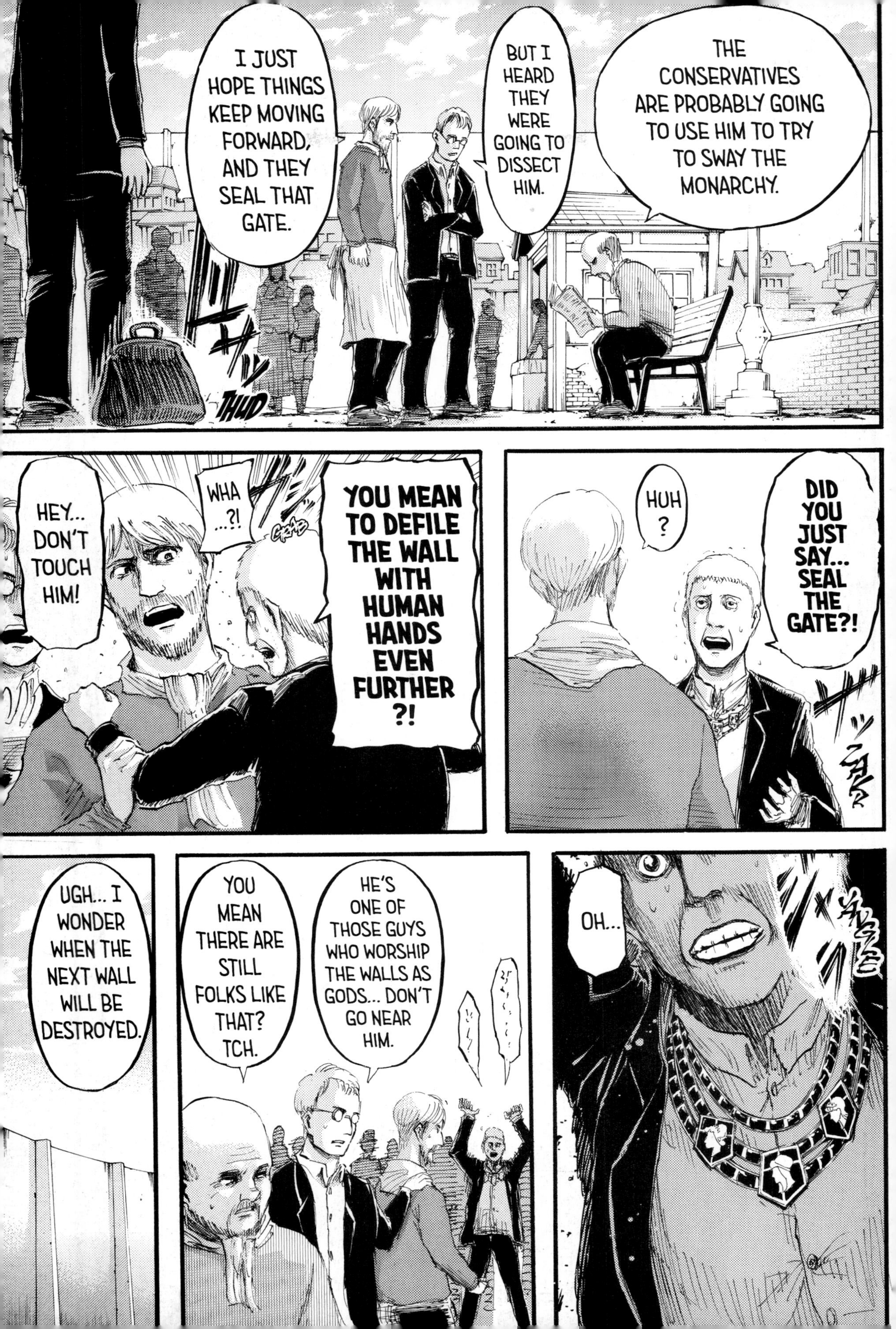
THE CONSERVATIVES ARE PROBABLY GOING TO USE HIM TO TRY TO SWAY THE MONARCHY.
BUT I HEARD THEY WERE GOING TO DISSECT HIM.
I JUST HOPE THINGS KEEP MOVING FORWARD, AND THEY SEAL THAT GATE.
THUD
DID YOU JUST SAY... SEAL THE GATE?!
HUH ?
YOU MEAN TO DEFILE THE WALL WITH HUMAN HANDS EVEN FURTHER ?!
WHA ...?!
HEY... DON'T TOUCH HIM!
OH...
HE'S ONE OF THOSE GUYS WHO WORSHIP THE WALLS AS GODS... DON'T GO NEAR HIM.
YOU MEAN THERE ARE STILL FOLKS LIKE THAT? TCH.
UGH... I WONDER WHEN THE NEXT WALL WILL BE DESTROYED.

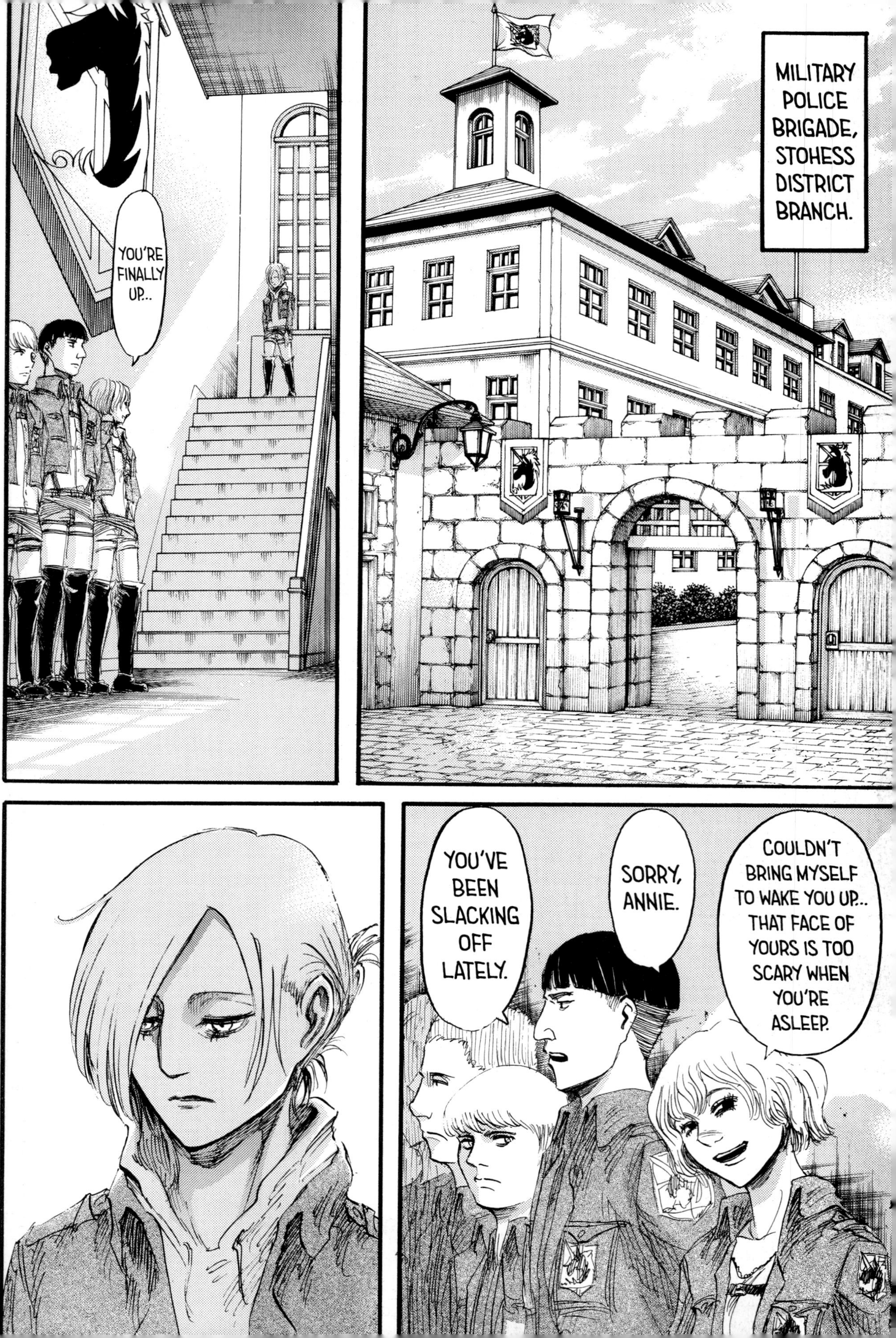
MILITARY POLICE BRIGADE, STOHESS DISTRICT BRANCH.
YOU'RE FINALLY UP...
COULDN'T BRING MYSELF TO WAKE YOU UP... THAT FACE OF YOURS IS TOO SCARY WHEN YOU'RE ASLEEP.
SORRY, ANNIE.
YOU'VE BEEN SLACKING OFF LATELY.

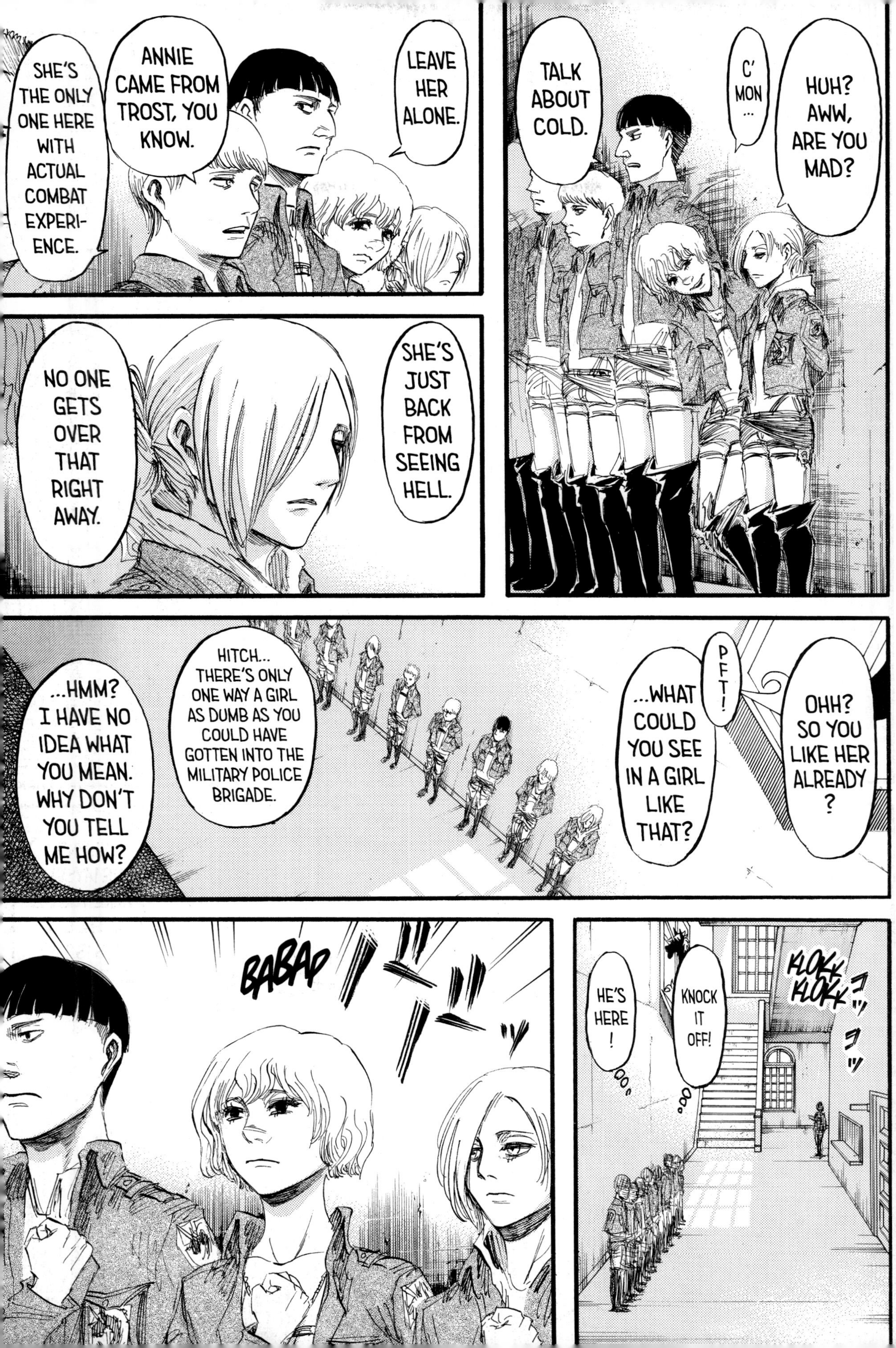
HUH? AWW, ARE YOU MAD?
C'MON...
TALK ABOUT COLD.
LEAVE HER ALONE.
ANNIE CAME FROM TROST, YOU KNOW.
SHE'S THE ONLY ONE HERE WITH ACTUAL COMBAT EXPERIENCE.
SHE'S JUST BACK FROM SEEING HELL.
NO ONE GETS OVER THAT RIGHT AWAY.
OHH? SO YOU LIKE HER ALREADY?
PFT!
...WHAT COULD YOU SEE IN A GIRL LIKE THAT?
HITCH... THERE'S ONLY ONE WAY A GIRL AS DUMB AS YOU COULD HAVE GOTTEN INTO THE MILITARY POLICE BRIGADE.
...HMM? I HAVE NO IDEA WHAT YOU MEAN. WHY DON'T YOU TELL ME HOW?
KLOKK KLOKK
コッ コッ
KNOCK IT OFF!
HE'S HERE!
BABAP

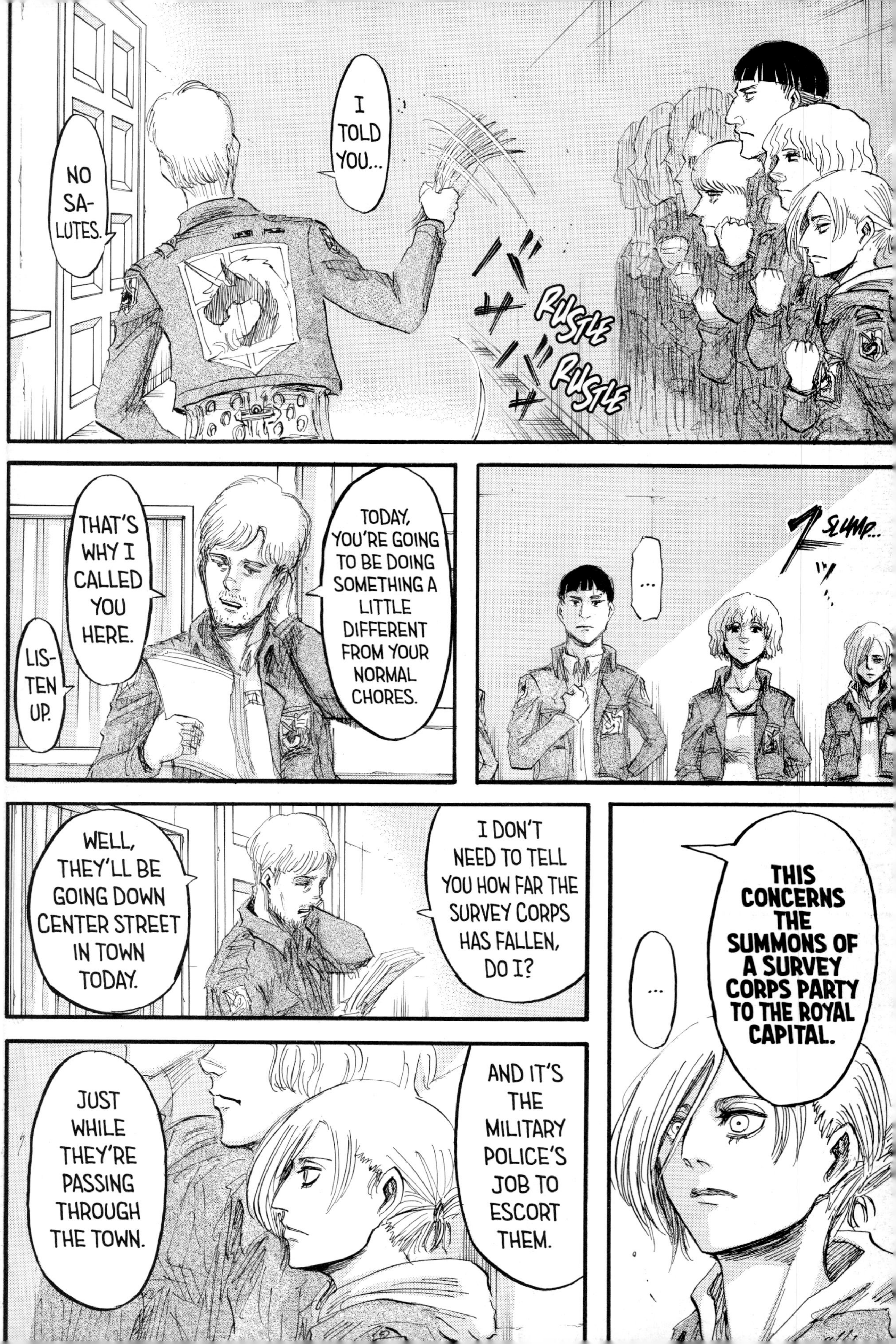
I TOLD YOU...
NO SA-LUTES.
RUSTLE
RUSTLE
SLUMP...
...
TODAY, YOU'RE GOING TO BE DOING SOMETHING A LITTLE DIFFERENT FROM YOUR NORMAL CHORES.
THAT'S WHY I CALLED YOU HERE.
LIS-TEN UP.
THIS CONCERNS THE SUMMONS OF A SURVEY CORPS PARTY TO THE ROYAL CAPITAL.
...
I DON'T NEED TO TELL YOU HOW FAR THE SURVEY CORPS HAS FALLEN, DO I?
WELL, THEY'LL BE GOING DOWN CENTER STREET IN TOWN TODAY.
AND IT'S THE MILITARY POLICE'S JOB TO ESCORT THEM.
JUST WHILE THEY'RE PASSING THROUGH THE TOWN.

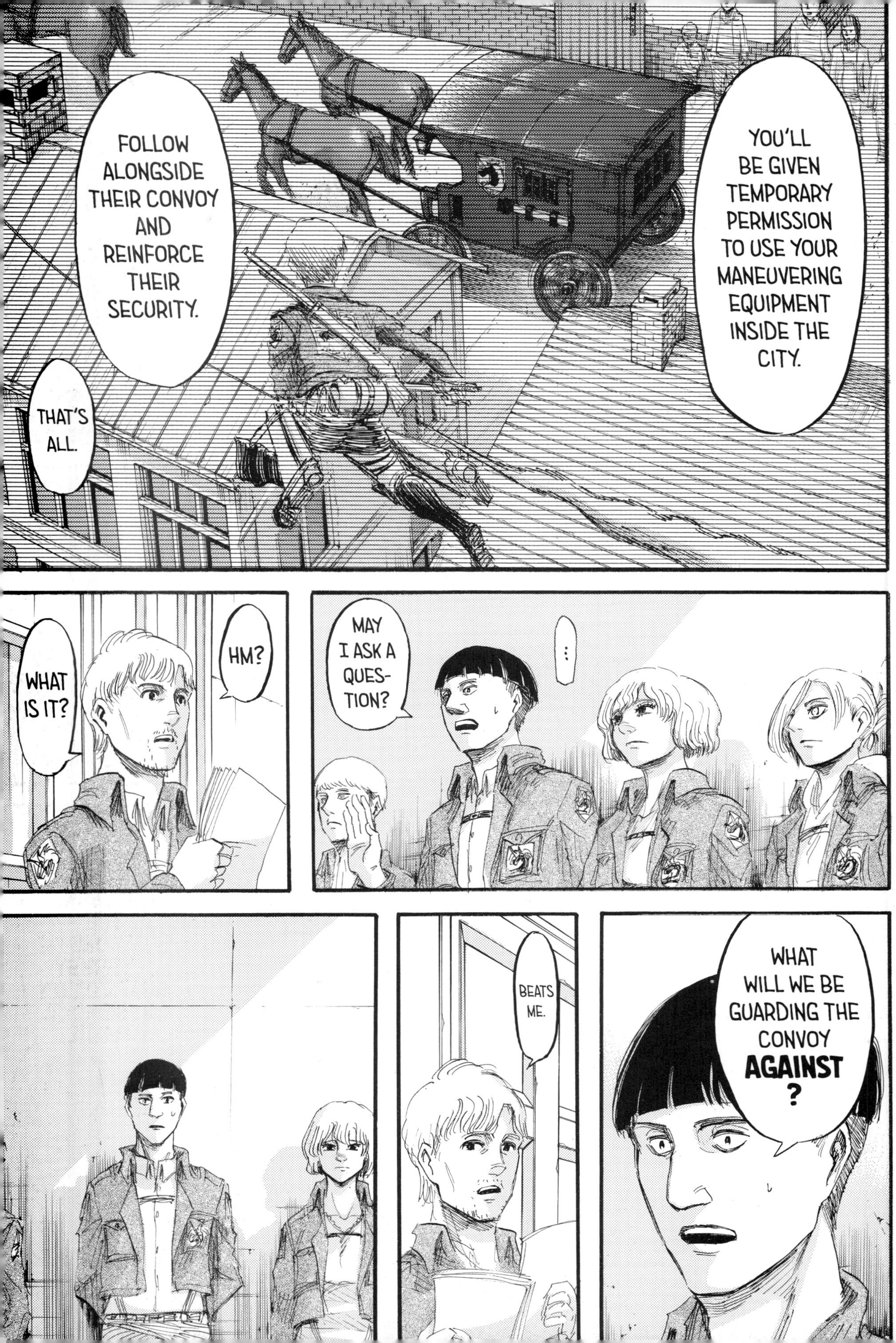
YOU'LL BE GIVEN TEMPORARY PERMISSION TO USE YOUR MANEUVERING EQUIPMENT INSIDE THE CITY.
FOLLOW ALONGSIDE THEIR CONVOY AND REINFORCE THEIR SECURITY.
THAT'S ALL.
...
MAY I ASK A QUES-TION?
HM?
WHAT IS IT?
WHAT WILL WE BE GUARDING THE CONVOY **AGAINST** ?
BEATS ME.

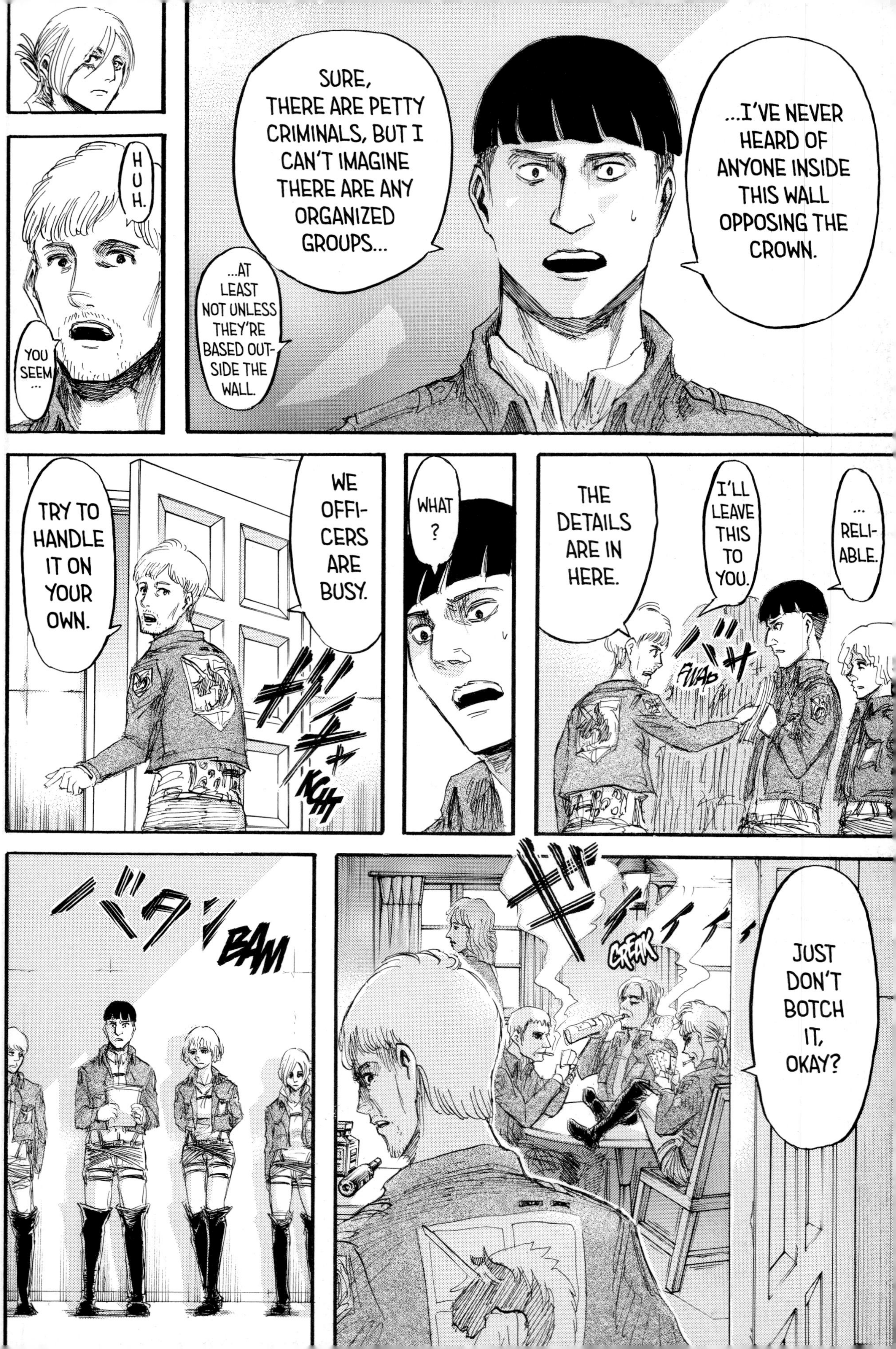
...I'VE NEVER HEARD OF ANYONE INSIDE THIS WALL OPPOSING THE CROWN.
SURE, THERE ARE PETTY CRIMINALS, BUT I CAN'T IMAGINE THERE ARE ANY ORGANIZED GROUPS...
...AT LEAST NOT UNLESS THEY'RE BASED OUT-SIDE THE WALL.
HUH.
YOU SEEM...
...RELI-ABLE.
I'LL LEAVE THIS TO YOU.
THE DETAILS ARE IN HERE.
FWAP
WHAT?
WE OFFI-CERS ARE BUSY.
KCH
TRY TO HANDLE IT ON YOUR OWN.
JUST DON'T BOTCH IT, OKAY?
CREAK
BAM

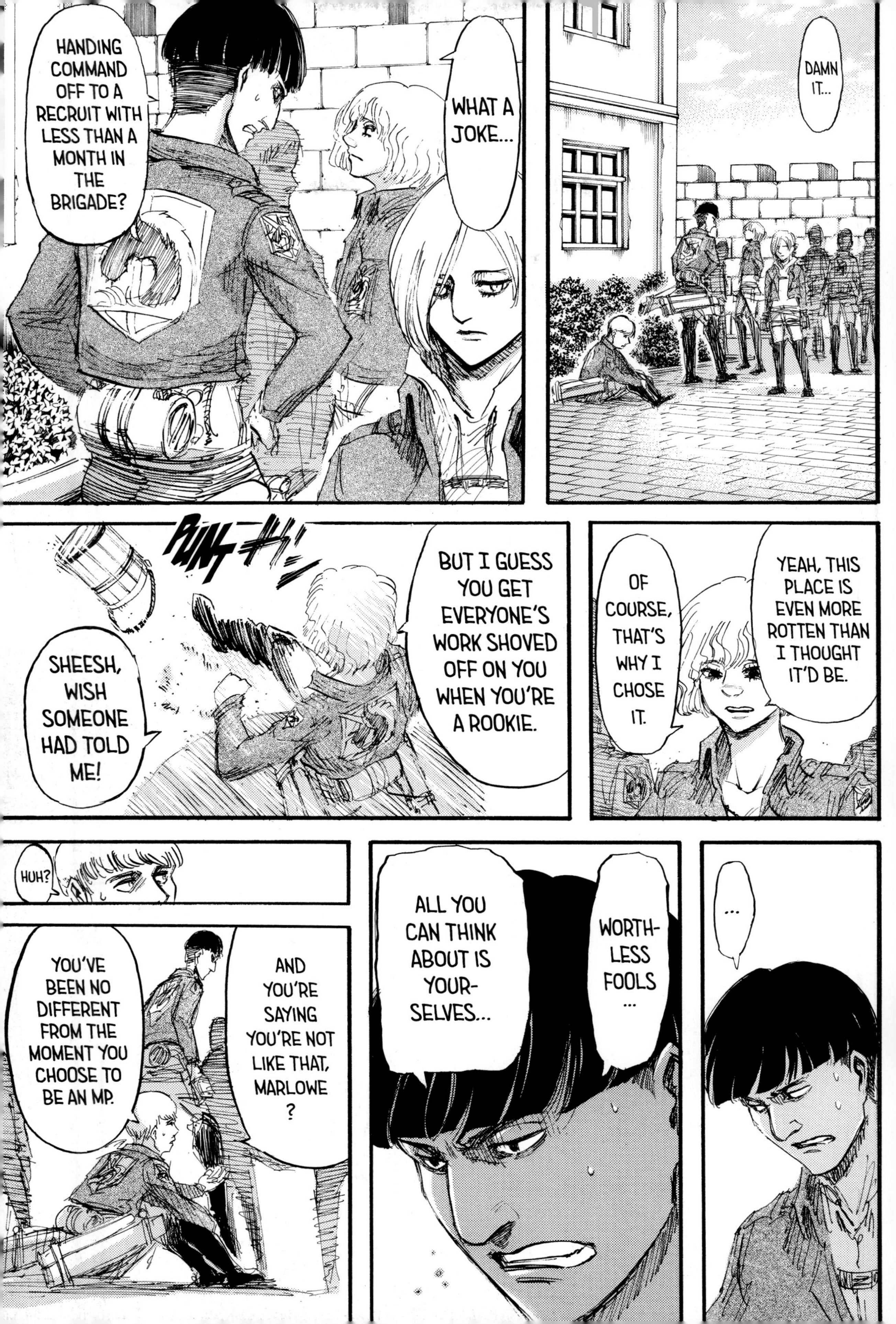
DAMN IT...
WHAT A JOKE...
HANDING COMMAND OFF TO A RECRUIT WITH LESS THAN A MONTH IN THE BRIGADE?
YEAH, THIS PLACE IS EVEN MORE ROTTEN THAN I THOUGHT IT'D BE.
OF COURSE, THAT'S WHY I CHOSE IT.
BUT I GUESS YOU GET EVERYONE'S WORK SHOVED OFF ON YOU WHEN YOU'RE A ROOKIE.
PUNT
SHEESH, WISH SOMEONE HAD TOLD ME!
...
WORTHLESS FOOLS...
ALL YOU CAN THINK ABOUT IS YOURSELVES...
HUH?
AND YOU'RE SAYING YOU'RE NOT LIKE THAT, MARLOWE?
YOU'VE BEEN NO DIFFERENT FROM THE MOMENT YOU CHOOSE TO BE AN MP.

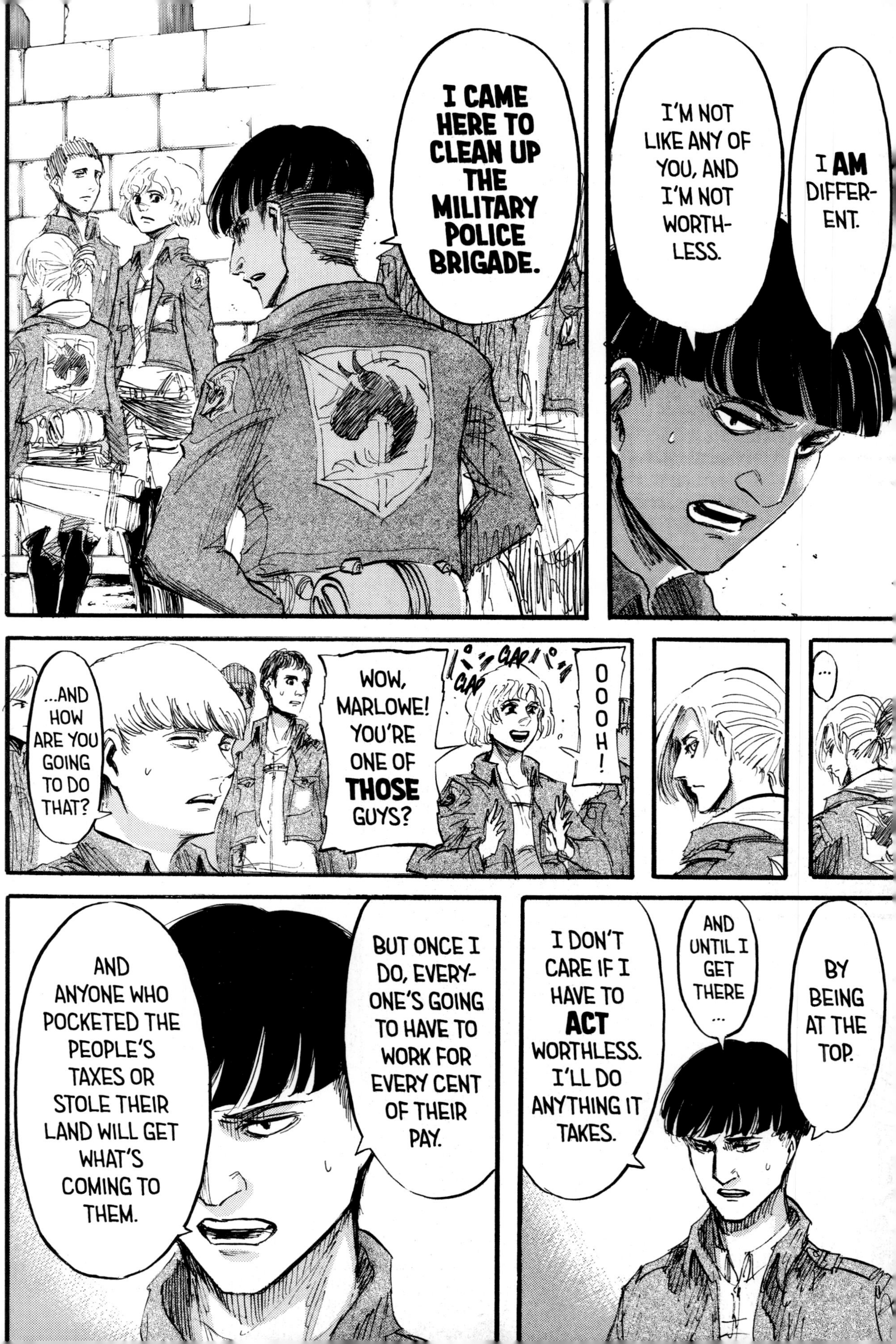
I AM DIFFERENT.
I'M NOT LIKE ANY OF YOU, AND I'M NOT WORTHLESS.
I CAME HERE TO CLEAN UP THE MILITARY POLICE BRIGADE.
...
OOOH!
CLAP CLAP
WOW, MARLOWE! YOU'RE ONE OF THOSE GUYS?
...AND HOW ARE YOU GOING TO DO THAT?
BY BEING AT THE TOP.
AND UNTIL I GET THERE ...
I DON'T CARE IF I HAVE TO ACT WORTHLESS. I'LL DO ANYTHING IT TAKES.
BUT ONCE I DO, EVERYONE'S GOING TO HAVE TO WORK FOR EVERY CENT OF THEIR PAY.
AND ANYONE WHO POCKETED THE PEOPLE'S TAXES OR STOLE THEIR LAND WILL GET WHAT'S COMING TO THEM.

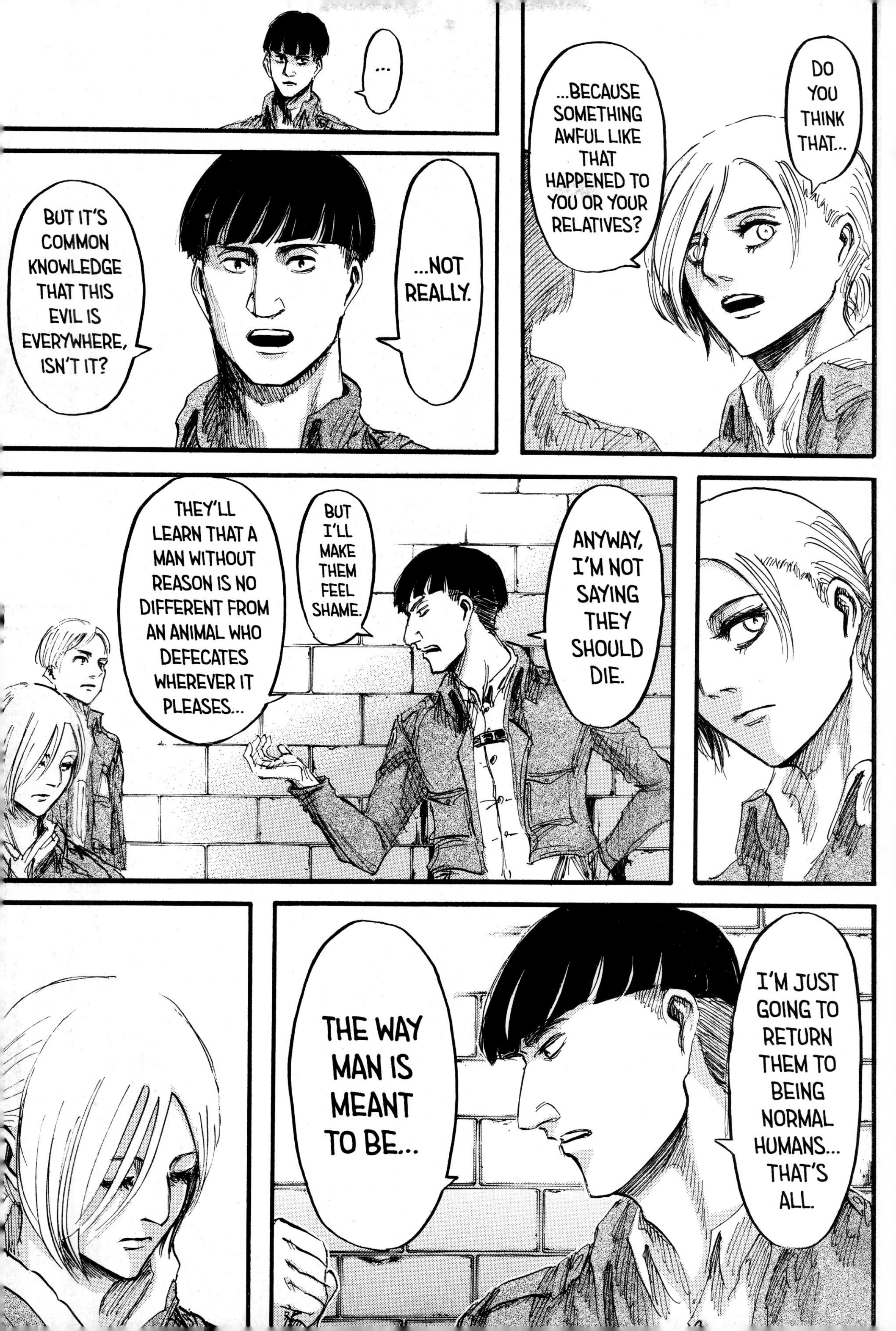
DO YOU THINK THAT...
...BECAUSE SOMETHING AWFUL LIKE THAT HAPPENED TO YOU OR YOUR RELATIVES?
...
...NOT REALLY.
BUT IT'S COMMON KNOWLEDGE THAT THIS EVIL IS EVERYWHERE, ISN'T IT?
ANYWAY, I'M NOT SAYING THEY SHOULD DIE.
BUT I'LL MAKE THEM FEEL SHAME.
THEY'LL LEARN THAT A MAN WITHOUT REASON IS NO DIFFERENT FROM AN ANIMAL WHO DEFECATES WHEREVER IT PLEASES...
I'M JUST GOING TO RETURN THEM TO BEING NORMAL HUMANS... THAT'S ALL.
THE WAY MAN IS MEANT TO BE...

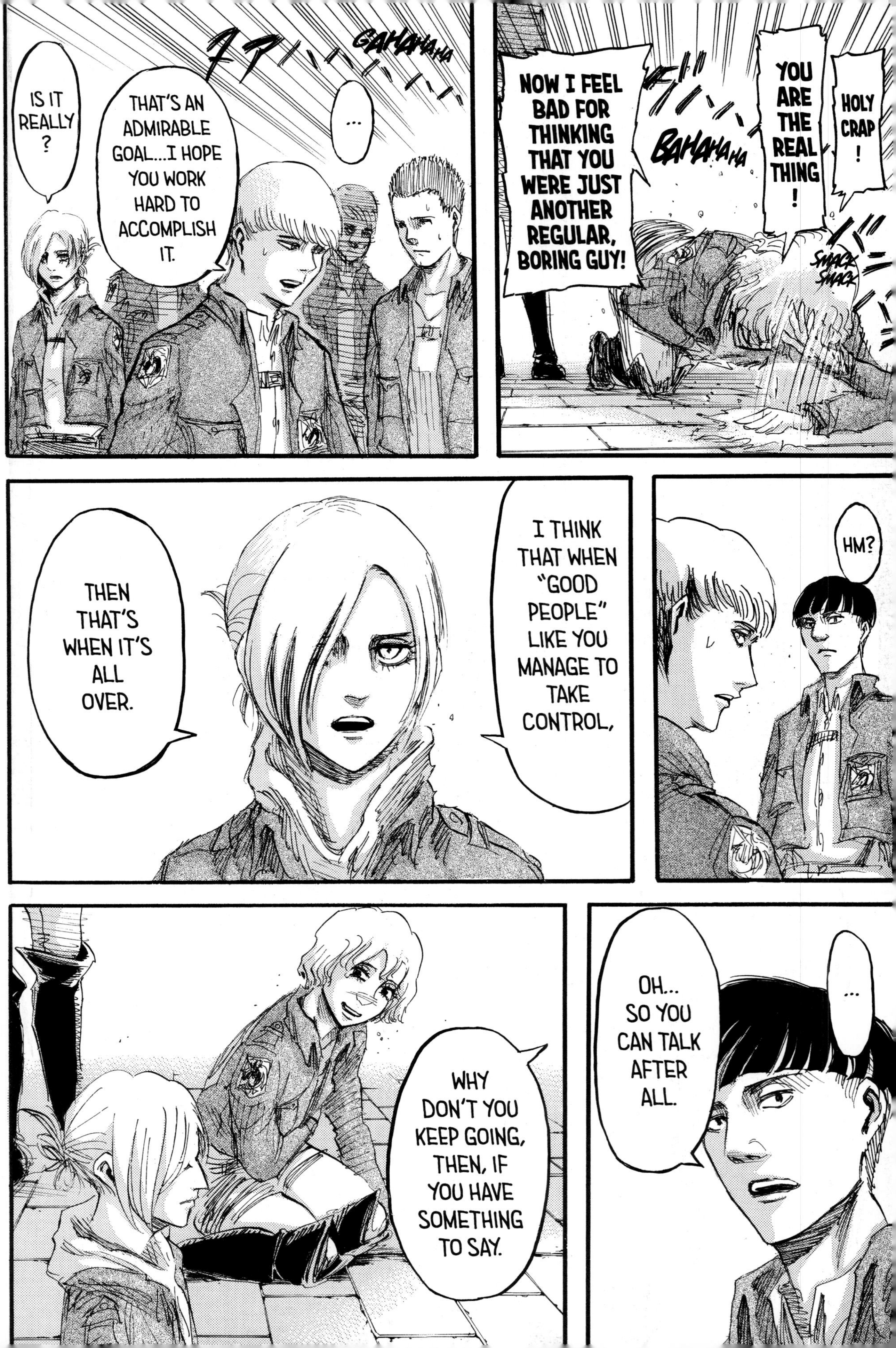
HOLY CRAP!
YOU ARE THE REAL THING!
NOW I FEEL BAD FOR THINKING THAT YOU WERE JUST ANOTHER REGULAR, BORING GUY!
BAHAHAHA
SMACK SMACK
GAHAHAHAHA
...
THAT'S AN ADMIRABLE GOAL...I HOPE YOU WORK HARD TO ACCOMPLISH IT.
IS IT REALLY?
HM?
I THINK THAT WHEN "GOOD PEOPLE" LIKE YOU MANAGE TO TAKE CONTROL,
THEN THAT'S WHEN IT'S ALL OVER.
...
OH... SO YOU CAN TALK AFTER ALL.
WHY DON'T YOU KEEP GOING, THEN, IF YOU HAVE SOMETHING TO SAY.

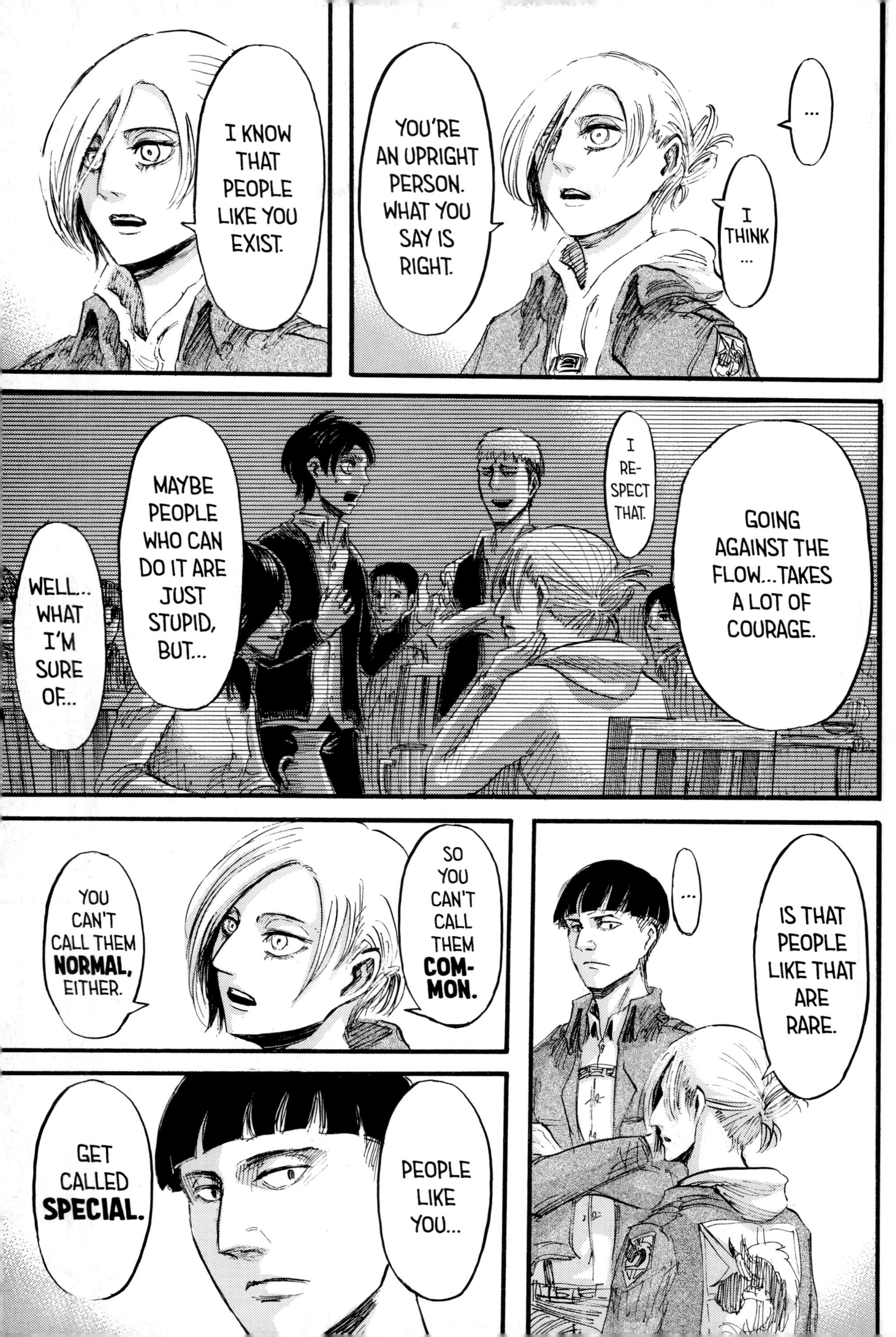
...
I THINK...
YOU'RE AN UPRIGHT PERSON. WHAT YOU SAY IS RIGHT.
I KNOW THAT PEOPLE LIKE YOU EXIST.
I RE-SPECT THAT.
GOING AGAINST THE FLOW...TAKES A LOT OF COURAGE.
MAYBE PEOPLE WHO CAN DO IT ARE JUST STUPID, BUT...
WELL... WHAT I'M SURE OF...
IS THAT PEOPLE LIKE THAT ARE RARE.
...
SO YOU CAN'T CALL THEM **COM-MON.**
YOU CAN'T CALL THEM **NORMAL,** EITHER.
PEOPLE LIKE YOU...
GET CALLED **SPECIAL.**

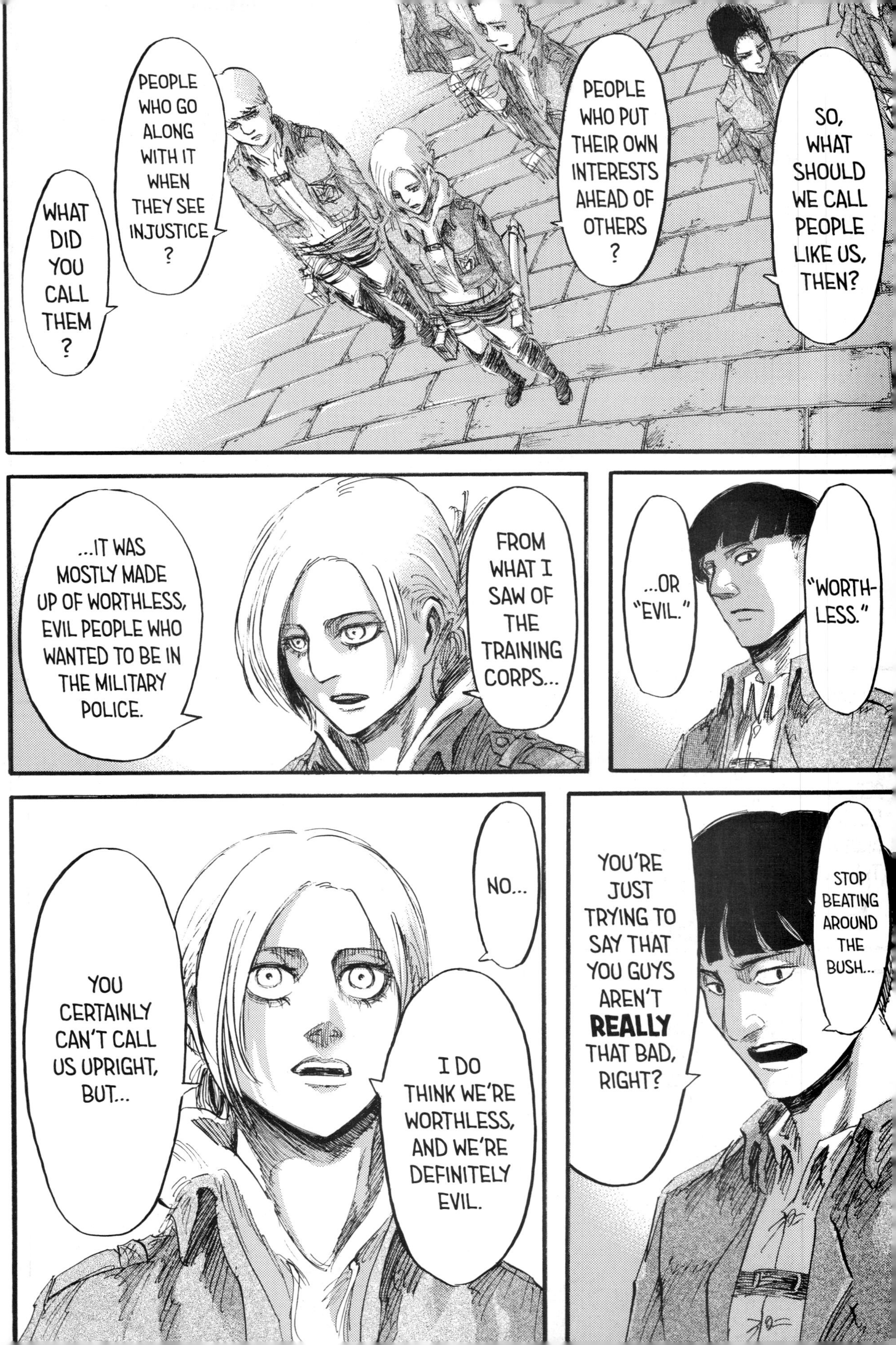
SO, WHAT SHOULD WE CALL PEOPLE LIKE US, THEN?
PEOPLE WHO PUT THEIR OWN INTERESTS AHEAD OF OTHERS?
PEOPLE WHO GO ALONG WITH IT WHEN THEY SEE INJUSTICE?
WHAT DID YOU CALL THEM?
"WORTHLESS."
...OR "EVIL."
FROM WHAT I SAW OF THE TRAINING CORPS...
...IT WAS MOSTLY MADE UP OF WORTHLESS, EVIL PEOPLE WHO WANTED TO BE IN THE MILITARY POLICE.
STOP BEATING AROUND THE BUSH...
YOU'RE JUST TRYING TO SAY THAT YOU GUYS AREN'T **REALLY** THAT BAD, RIGHT?
NO...
I DO THINK WE'RE WORTHLESS, AND WE'RE DEFINITELY EVIL.
YOU CERTAINLY CAN'T CALL US UPRIGHT, BUT...

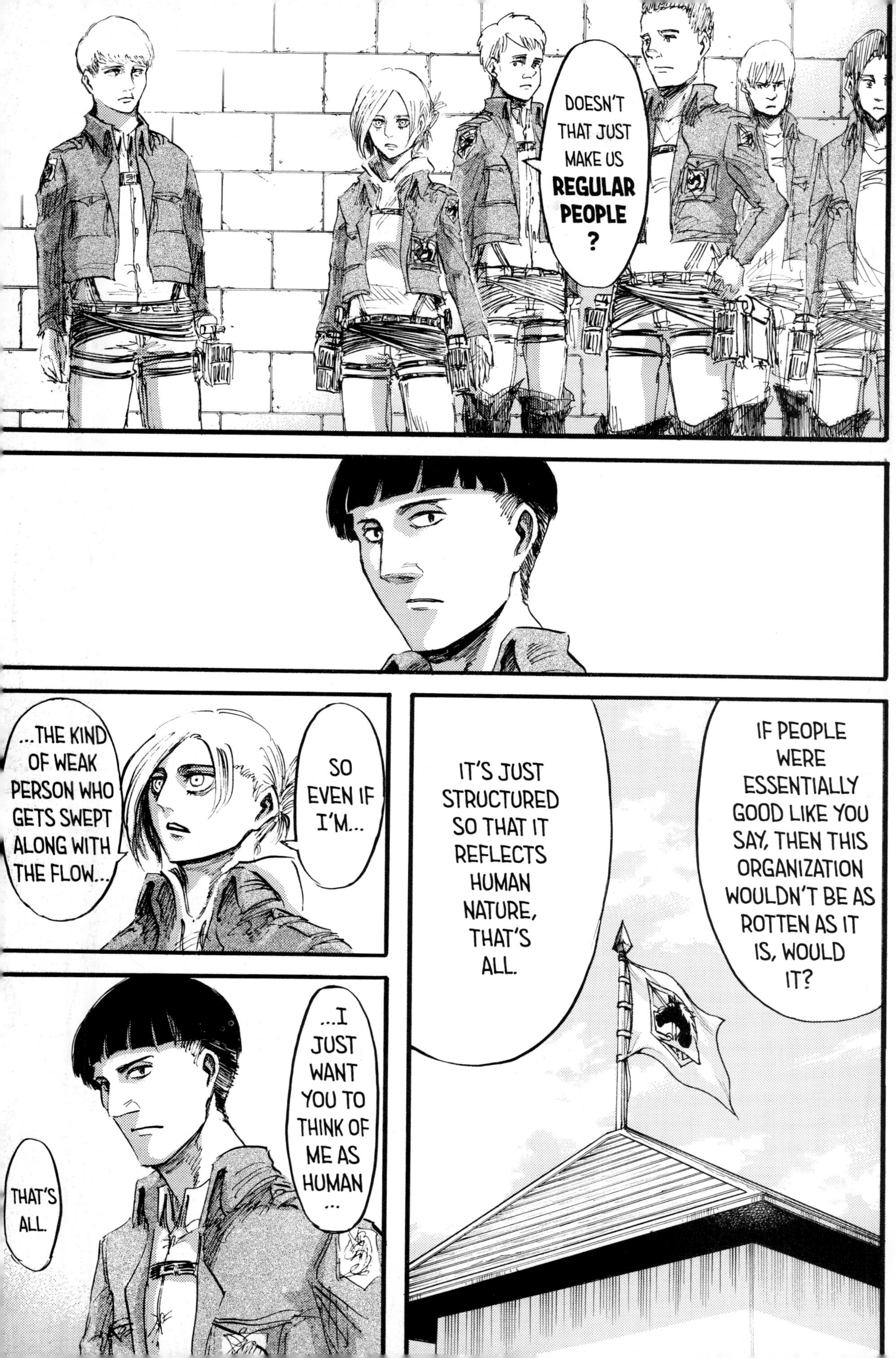
DOESN'T THAT JUST MAKE US **REGULAR PEOPLE** ?
IF PEOPLE WERE ESSENTIALLY GOOD LIKE YOU SAY, THEN THIS ORGANIZATION WOULDN'T BE AS ROTTEN AS IT IS, WOULD IT?
IT'S JUST STRUCTURED SO THAT IT REFLECTS HUMAN NATURE, THAT'S ALL.
SO EVEN IF I'M...
...THE KIND OF WEAK PERSON WHO GETS SWEPT ALONG WITH THE FLOW...
...I JUST WANT YOU TO THINK OF ME AS HUMAN ...
THAT'S ALL.

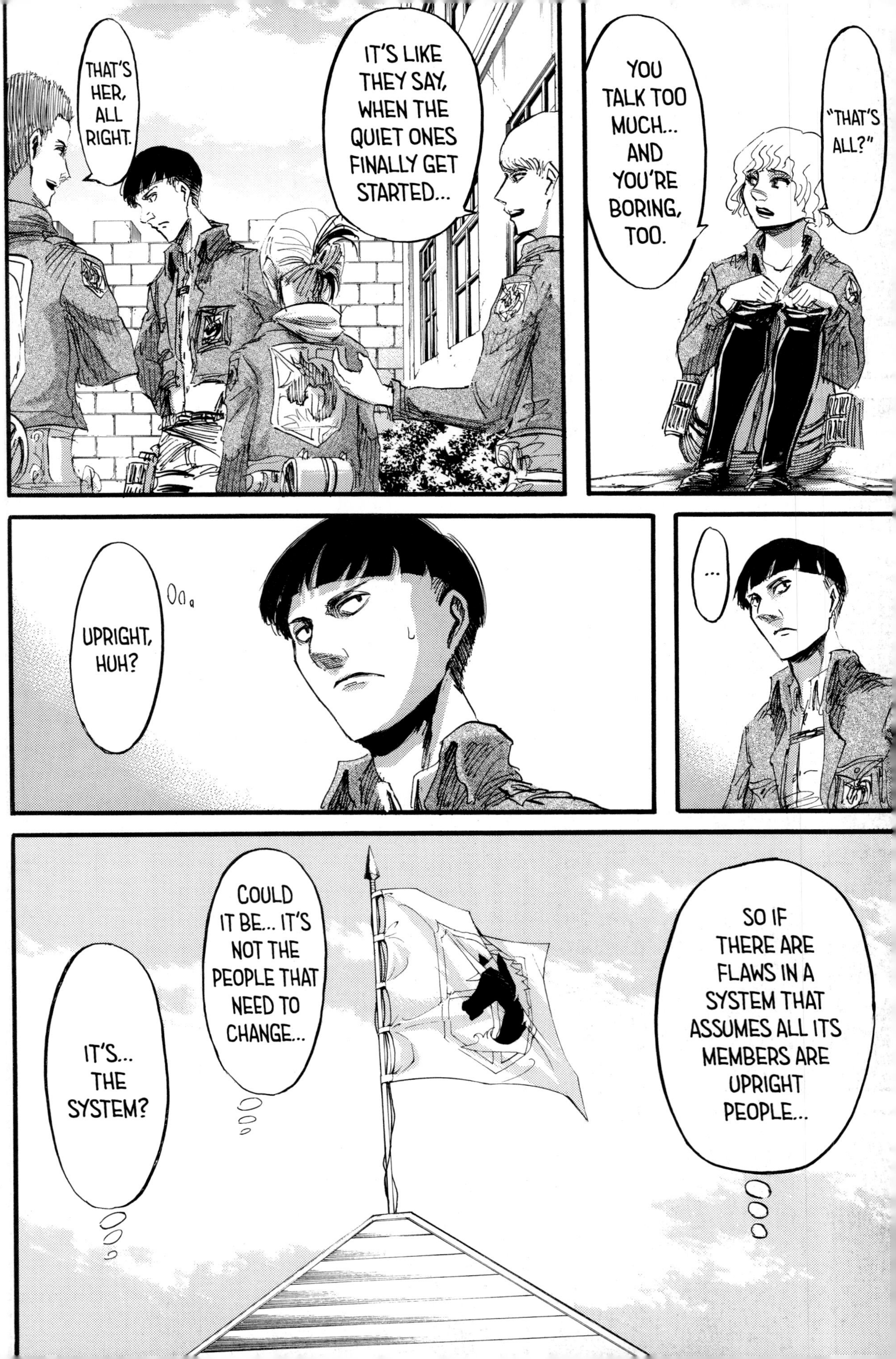
"THAT'S ALL?"
YOU TALK TOO MUCH... AND YOU'RE BORING, TOO.
IT'S LIKE THEY SAY, WHEN THE QUIET ONES FINALLY GET STARTED...
THAT'S HER, ALL RIGHT.
...
UPRIGHT, HUH?
SO IF THERE ARE FLAWS IN A SYSTEM THAT ASSUMES ALL ITS MEMBERS ARE UPRIGHT PEOPLE...
COULD IT BE... IT'S NOT THE PEOPLE THAT NEED TO CHANGE...
IT'S... THE SYSTEM?

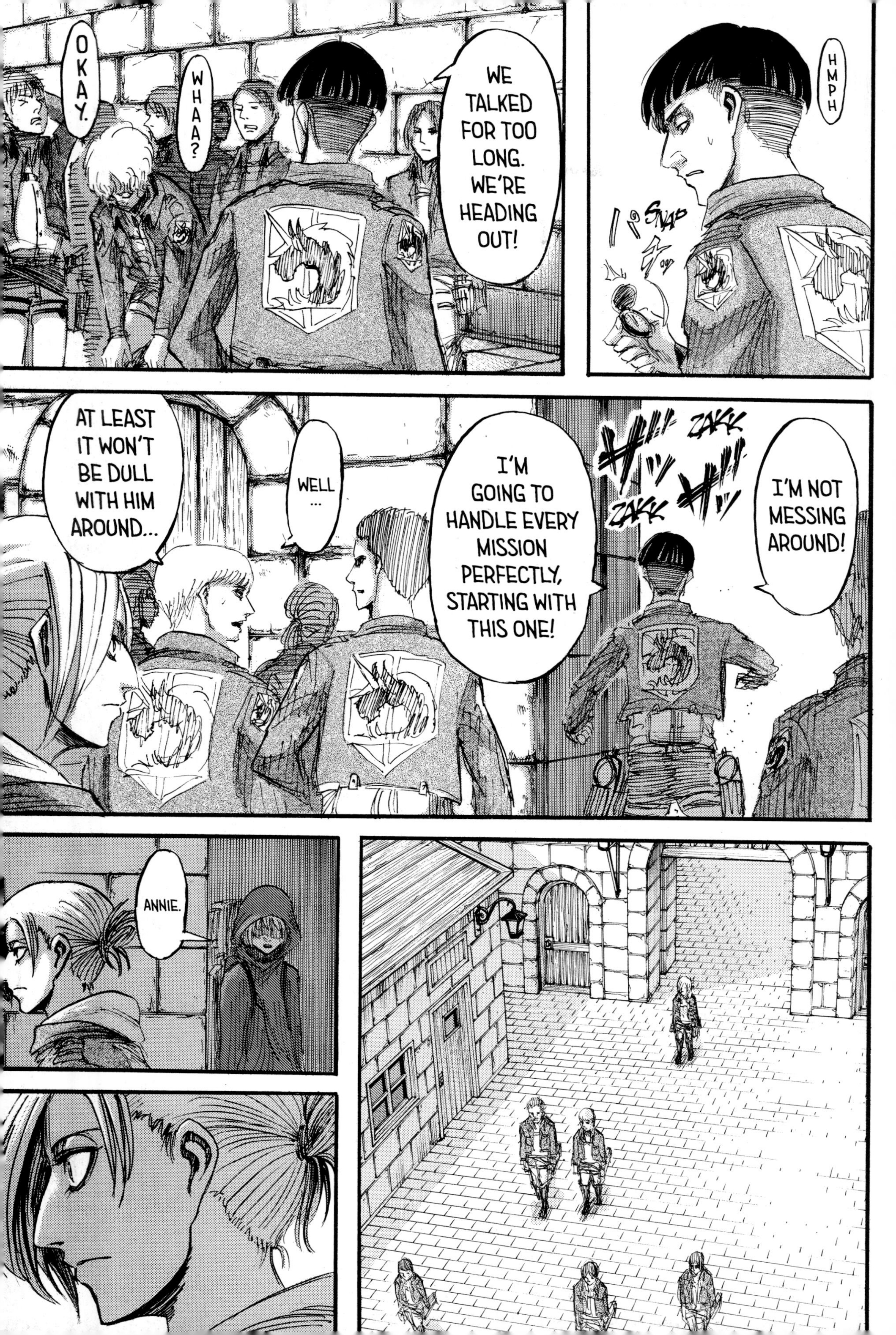
HMPH
SNAP
WE TALKED FOR TOO LONG. WE'RE HEADING OUT!
WHAA?
OKAY.
I'M NOT MESSING AROUND!
ZAKK
ZAKK
I'M GOING TO HANDLE EVERY MISSION PERFECTLY, STARTING WITH THIS ONE!
WELL ...
AT LEAST IT WON'T BE DULL WITH HIM AROUND...
ANNIE.

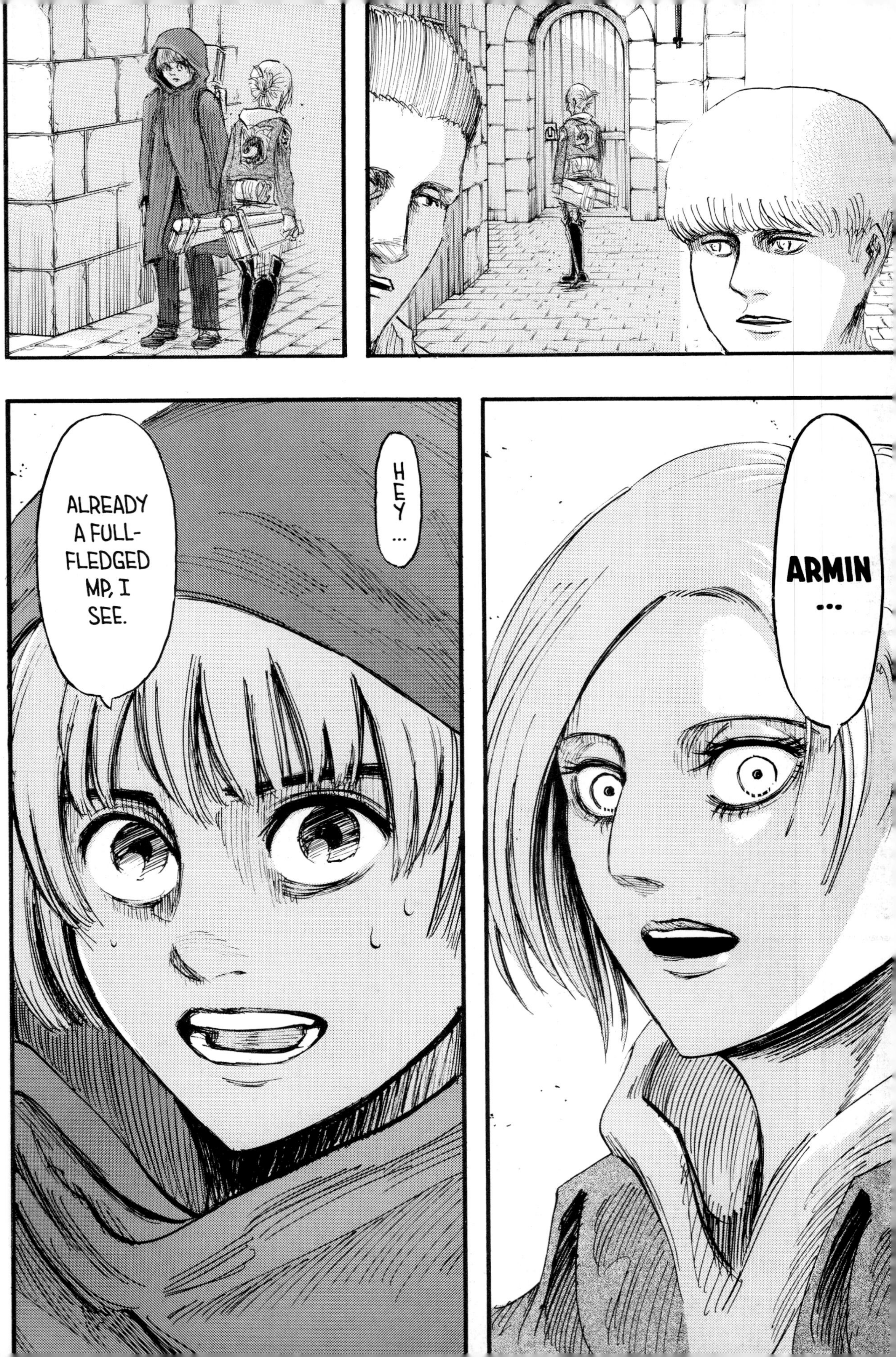
ARMIN ...
HEY ...
ALREADY A FULL-FLEDGED MP, I SEE.

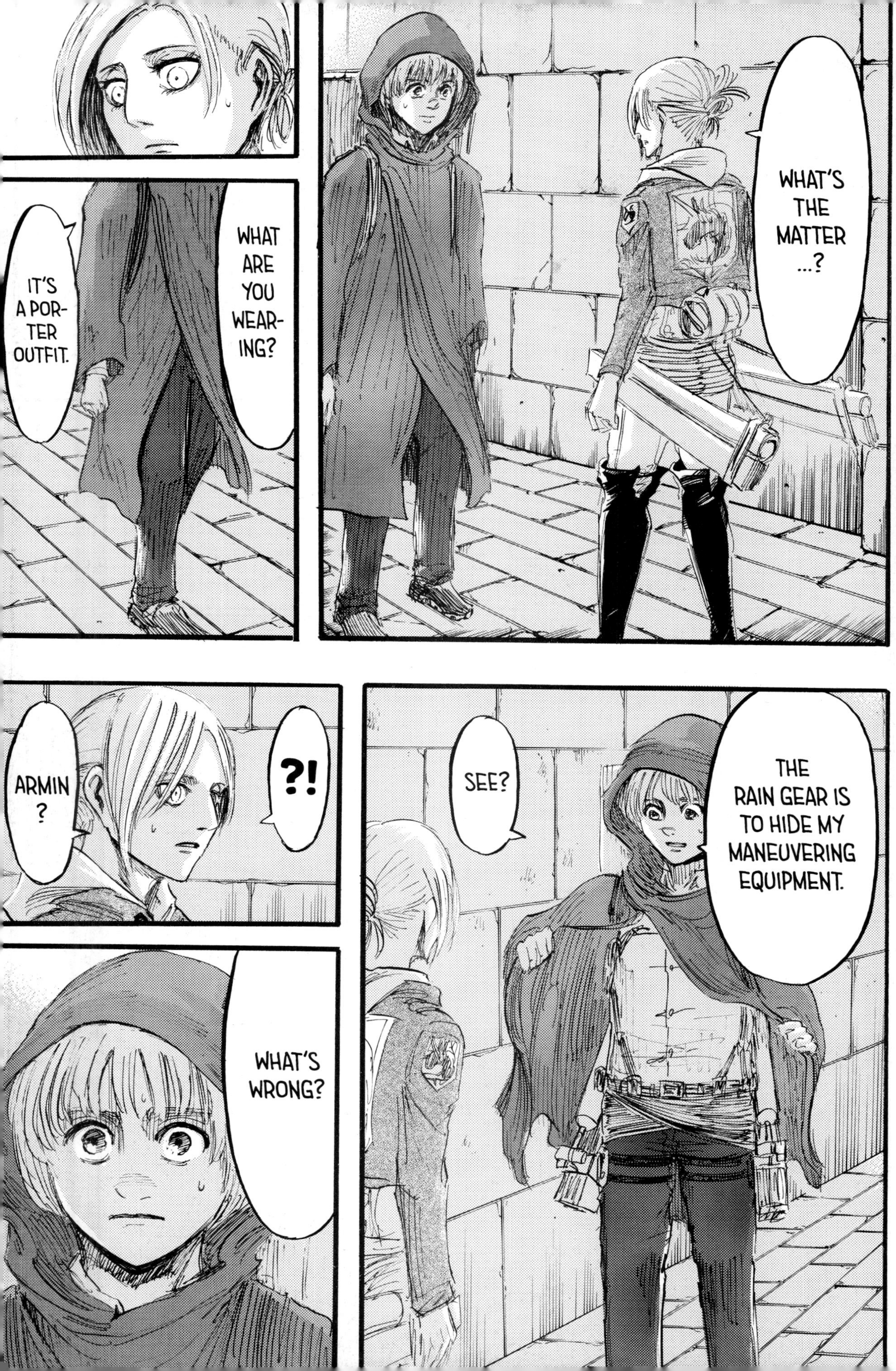
WHAT'S THE MATTER ...?
WHAT ARE YOU WEARING?
IT'S A PORTER OUTFIT.
THE RAIN GEAR IS TO HIDE MY MANEUVERING EQUIPMENT.
SEE?
?!
ARMIN ?
WHAT'S WRONG?

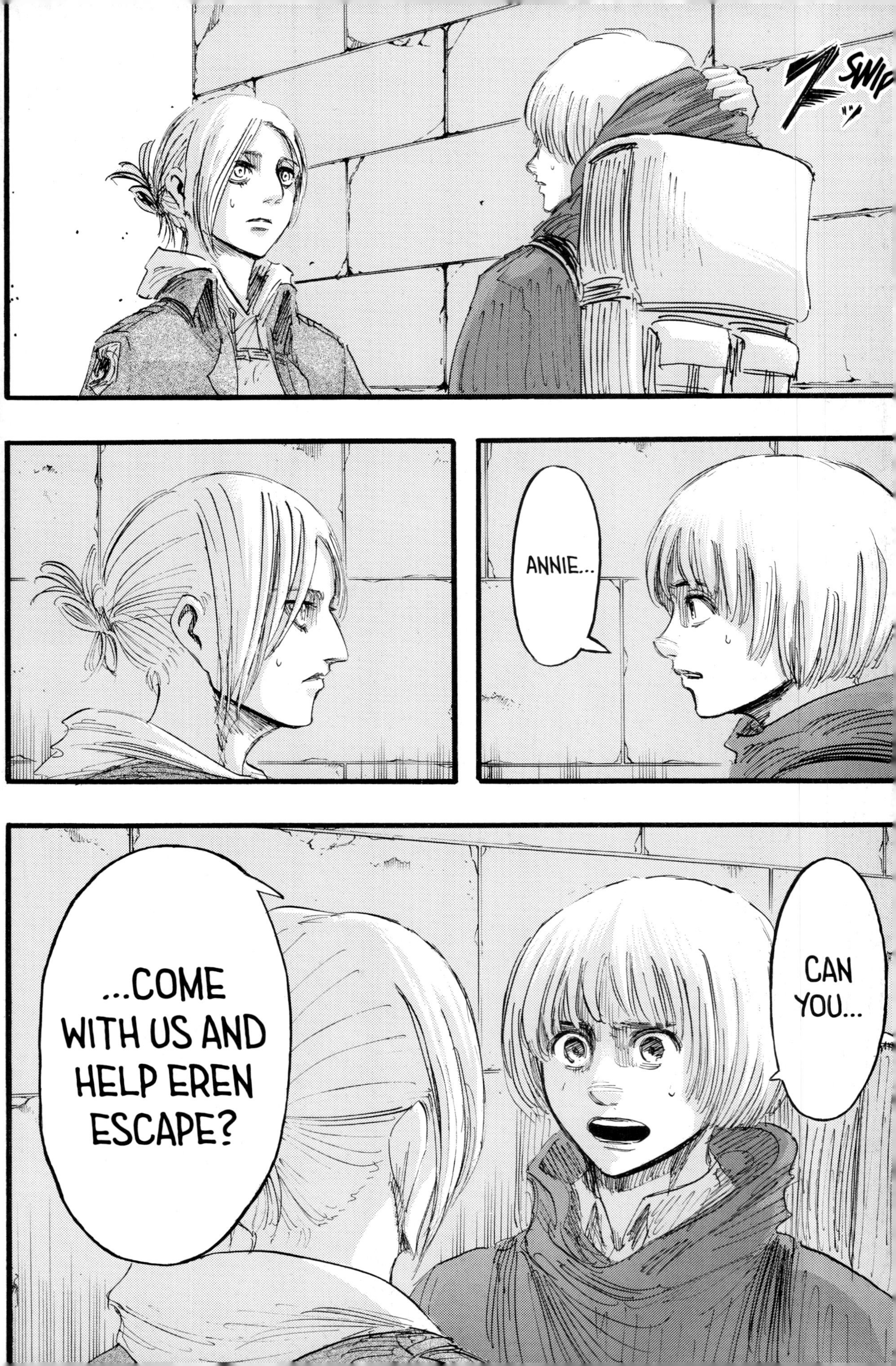
ANNIE...
CAN YOU...
...COME WITH US AND HELP EREN ESCAPE?

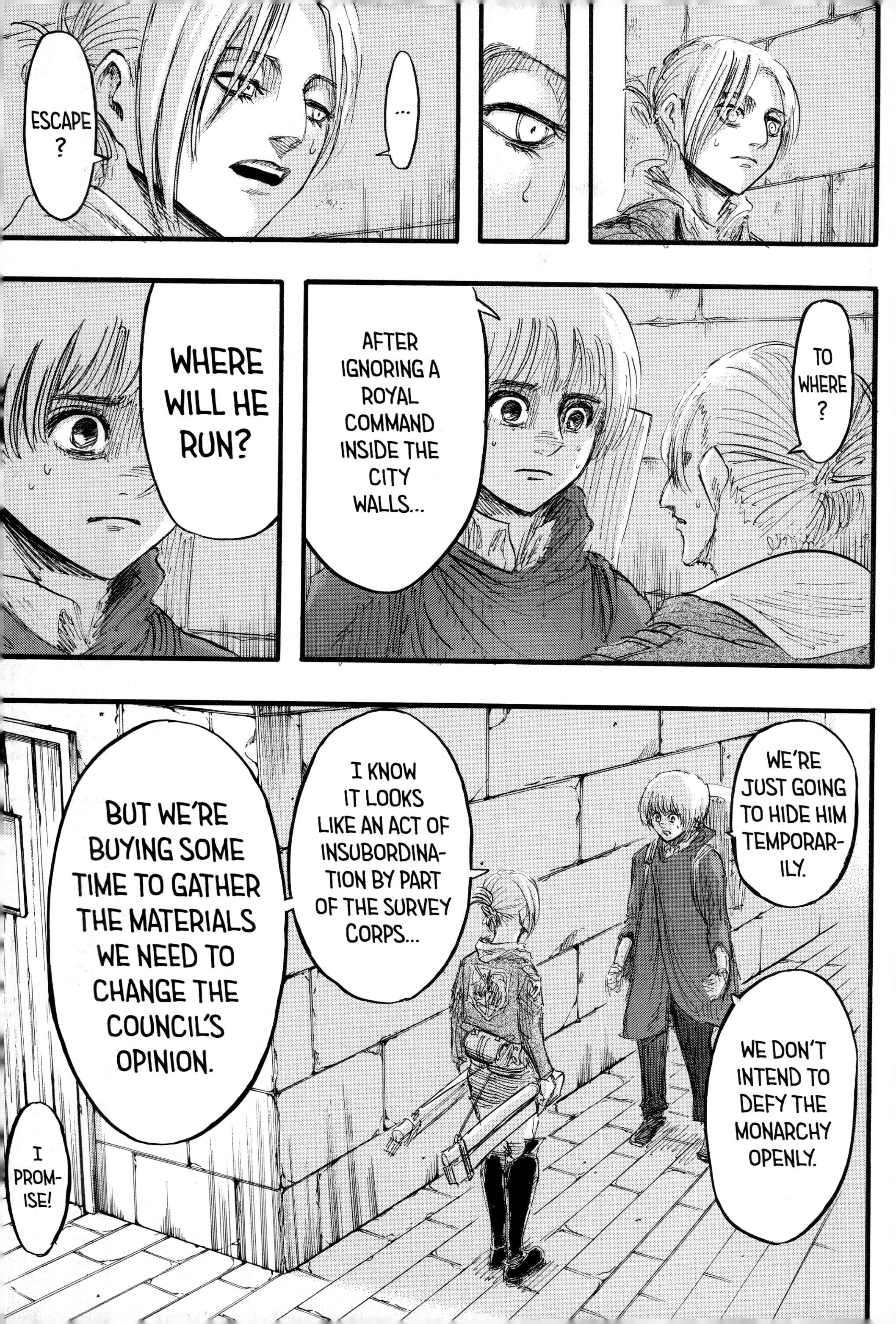
...
ESCAPE?
TO WHERE?
AFTER IGNORING A ROYAL COMMAND INSIDE THE CITY WALLS...
WHERE WILL HE RUN?
WE'RE JUST GOING TO HIDE HIM TEMPORARILY.
WE DON'T INTEND TO DEFY THE MONARCHY OPENLY.
I KNOW IT LOOKS LIKE AN ACT OF INSUBORDINATION BY PART OF THE SURVEY CORPS...
BUT WE'RE BUYING SOME TIME TO GATHER THE MATERIALS WE NEED TO CHANGE THE COUNCIL'S OPINION.
I PROMISE!

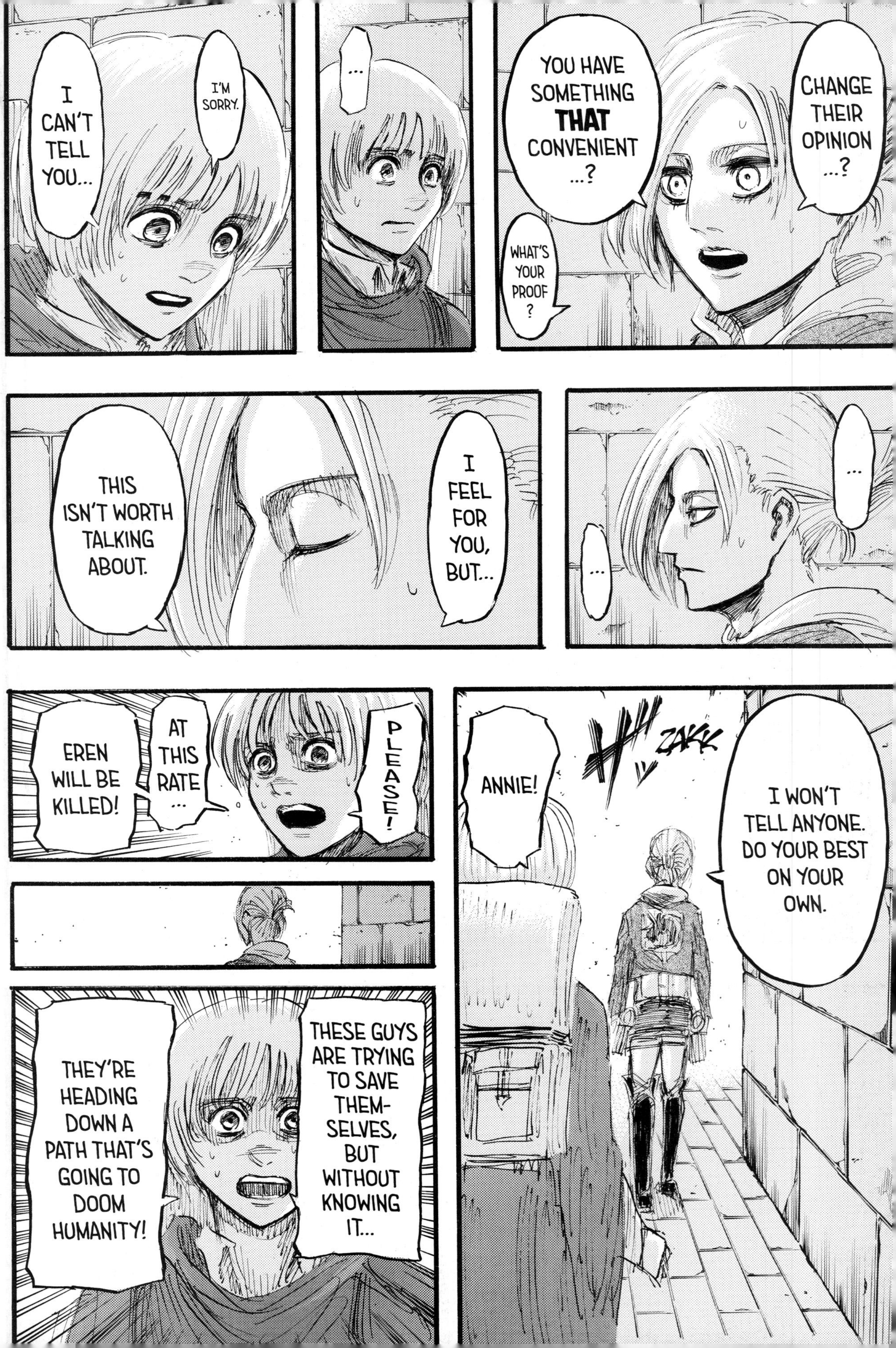
CHANGE THEIR OPINION ...?
YOU HAVE SOMETHING **THAT** CONVENIENT ...?
WHAT'S YOUR PROOF ?
...
I'M SORRY.
I CAN'T TELL YOU...
...
...
I FEEL FOR YOU, BUT...
THIS ISN'T WORTH TALKING ABOUT.
I WON'T TELL ANYONE. DO YOUR BEST ON YOUR OWN.
ZAKK
ANNIE!
PLEASE!
AT THIS RATE ...
EREN WILL BE KILLED!
THESE GUYS ARE TRYING TO SAVE THEM-SELVES, BUT WITHOUT KNOWING IT...
THEY'RE HEADING DOWN A PATH THAT'S GOING TO DOOM HUMANITY!

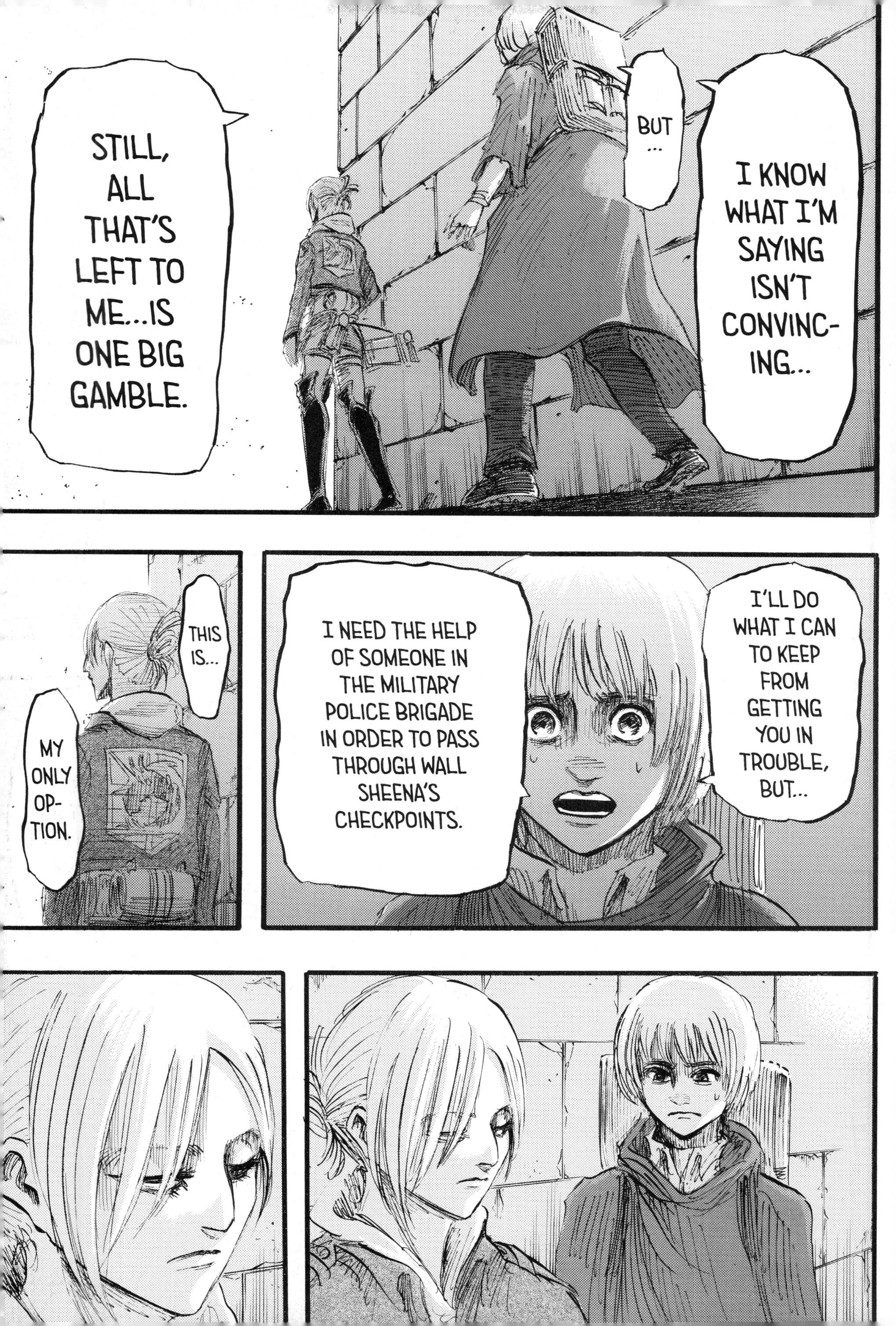
I KNOW WHAT I'M SAYING ISN'T CONVINC-ING...
BUT ...
STILL, ALL THAT'S LEFT TO ME...IS ONE BIG GAMBLE.
I'LL DO WHAT I CAN TO KEEP FROM GETTING YOU IN TROUBLE, BUT...
I NEED THE HELP OF SOMEONE IN THE MILITARY POLICE BRIGADE IN ORDER TO PASS THROUGH WALL SHEENA'S CHECKPOINTS.
THIS IS...
MY ONLY OP-TION.

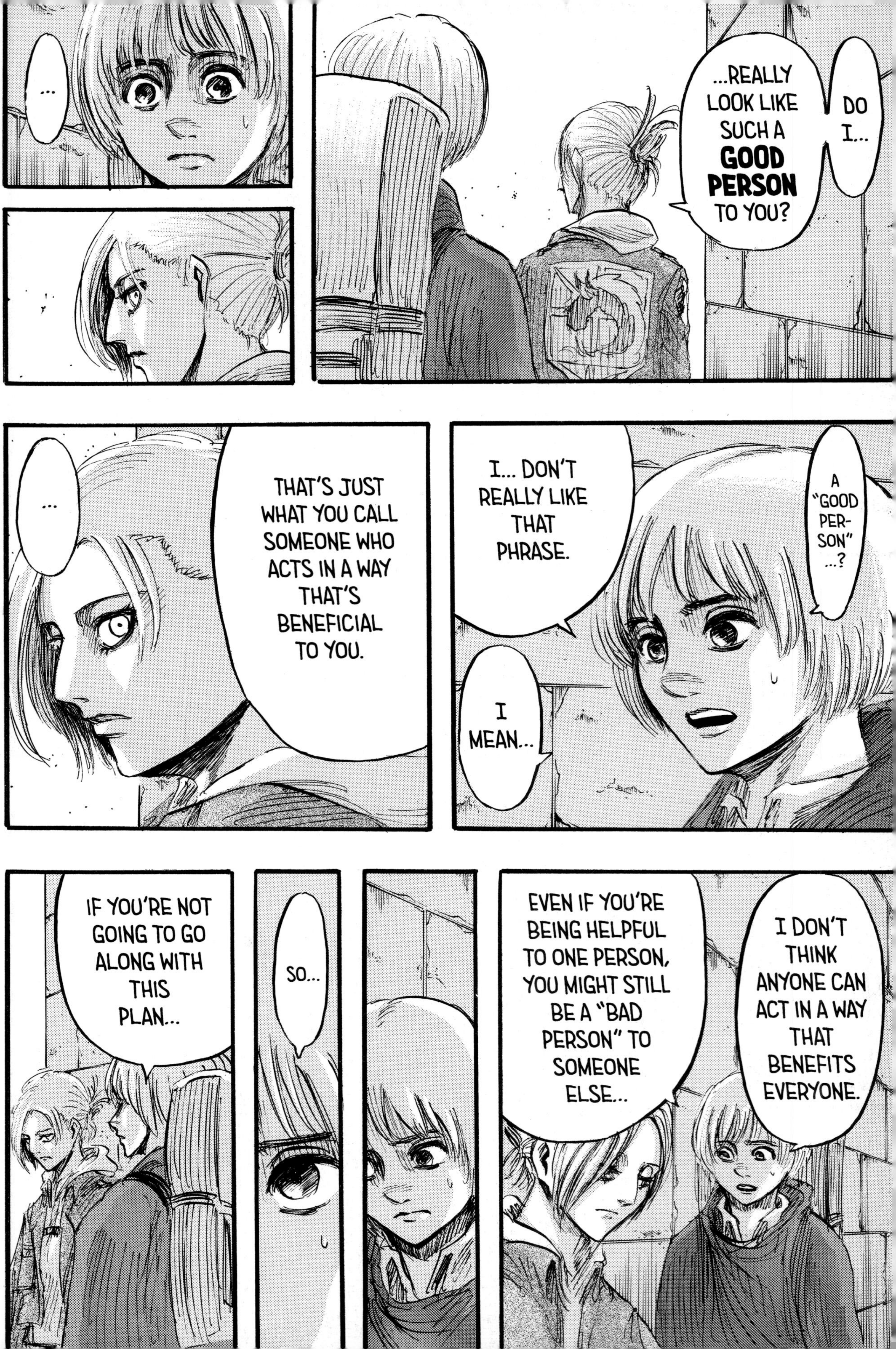
DO I...
...REALLY LOOK LIKE SUCH A **GOOD PERSON** TO YOU?
...
A "GOOD PERSON" ...?
I... DON'T REALLY LIKE THAT PHRASE.
I MEAN...
THAT'S JUST WHAT YOU CALL SOMEONE WHO ACTS IN A WAY THAT'S BENEFICIAL TO YOU.
...
I DON'T THINK ANYONE CAN ACT IN A WAY THAT BENEFITS EVERYONE.
EVEN IF YOU'RE BEING HELPFUL TO ONE PERSON, YOU MIGHT STILL BE A "BAD PERSON" TO SOMEONE ELSE...
SO...
IF YOU'RE NOT GOING TO GO ALONG WITH THIS PLAN...

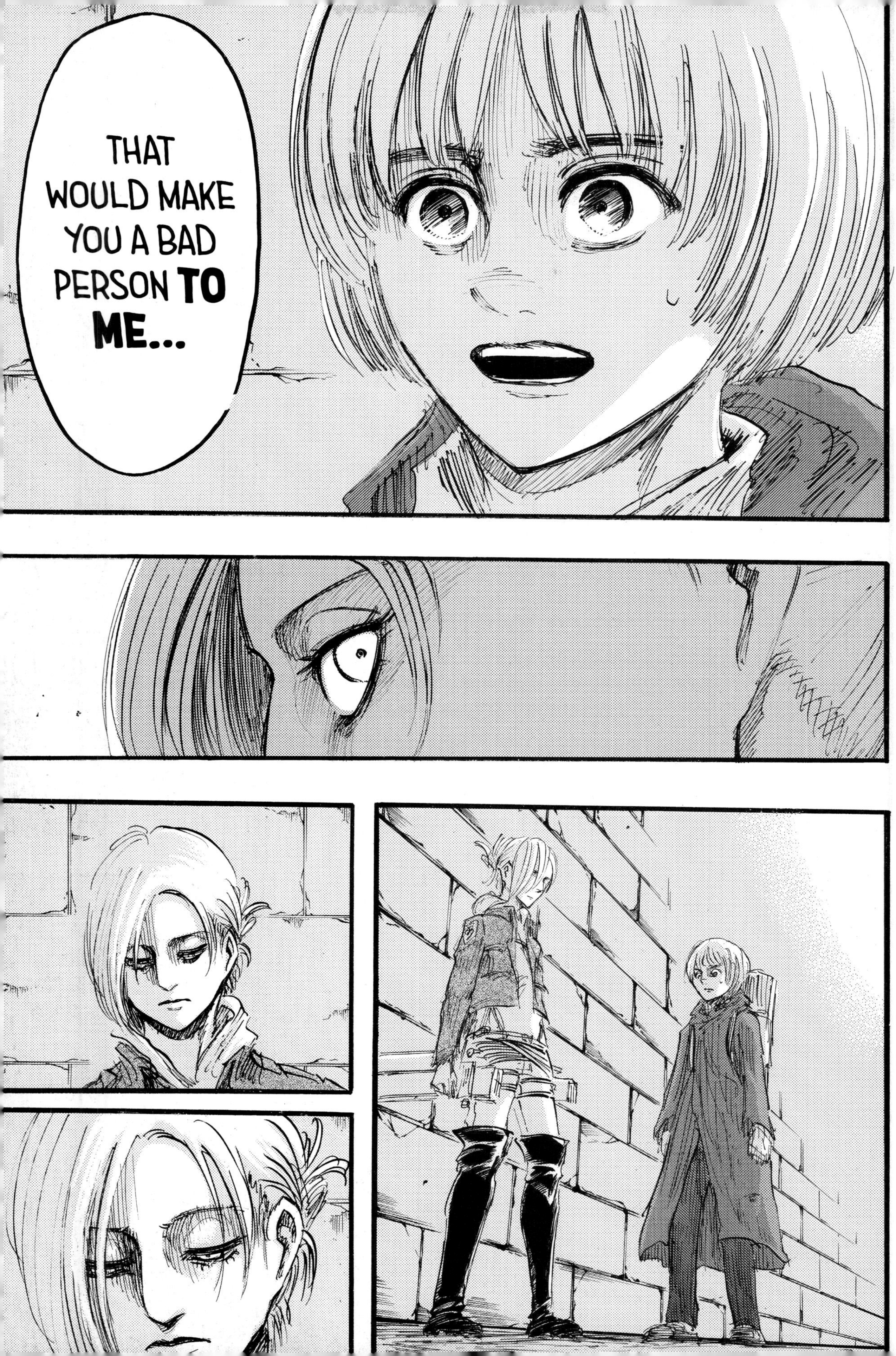
THAT WOULD MAKE YOU A BAD PERSON **TO ME...**

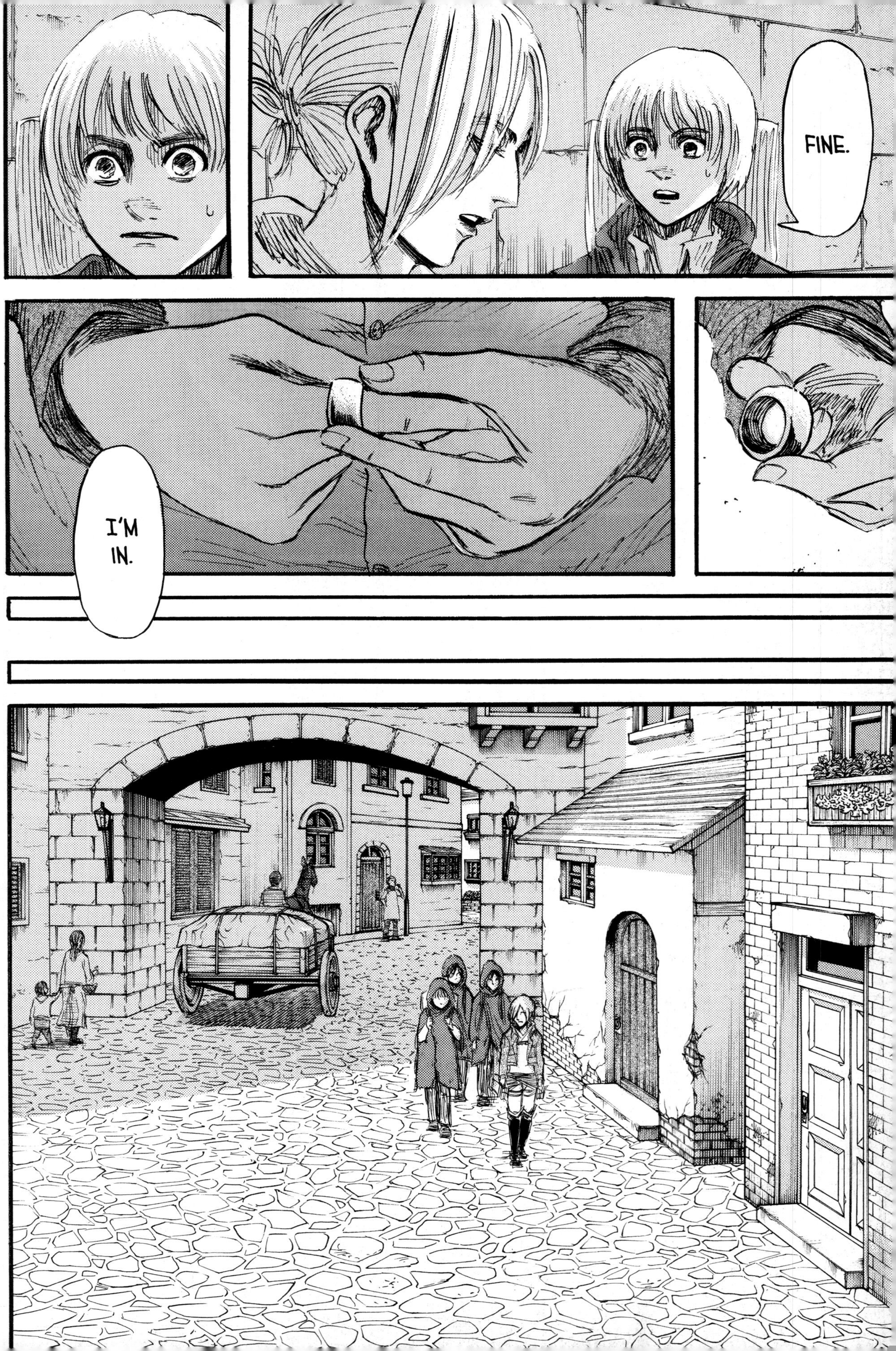
FINE.
I'M IN.

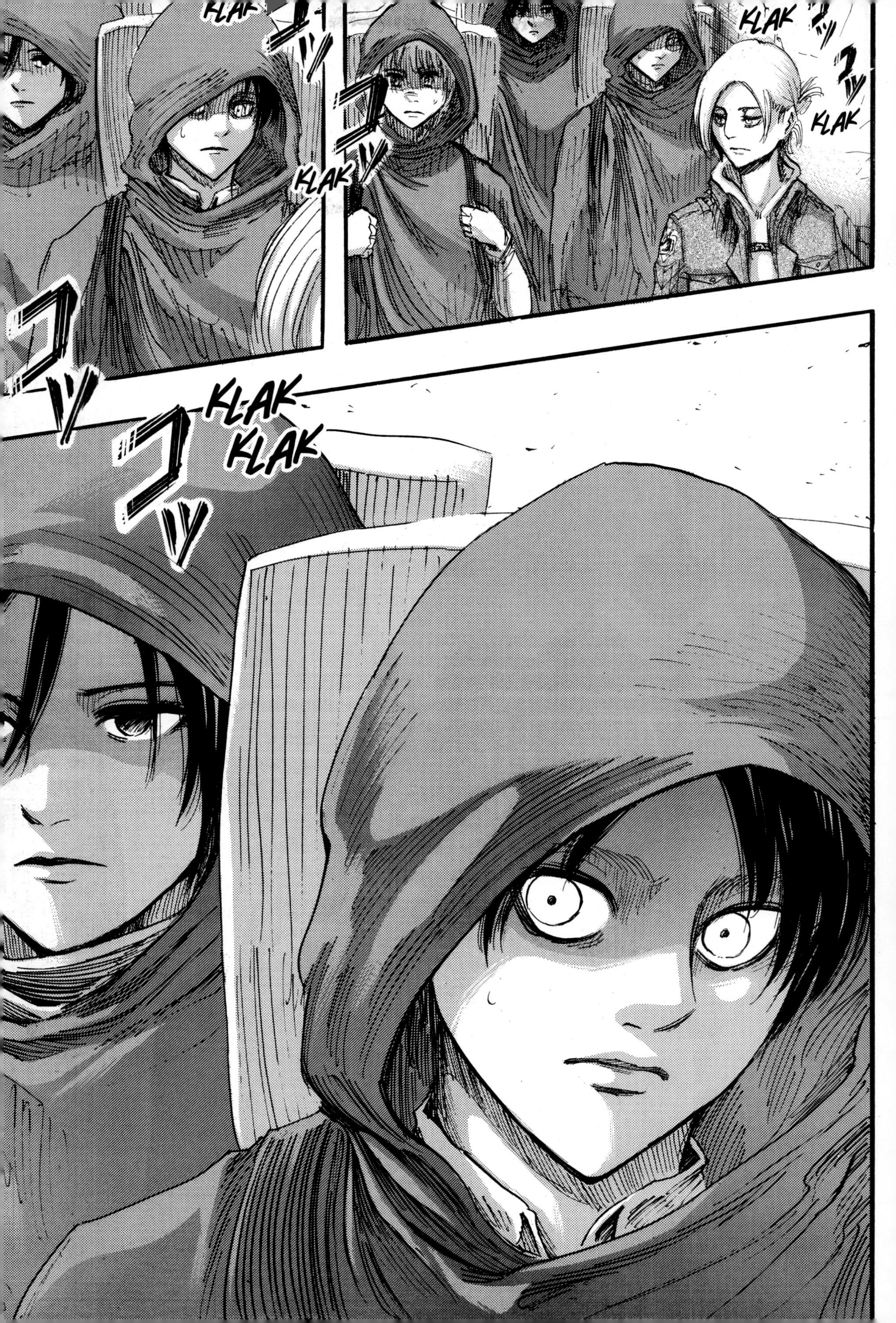

KLAK
KLAK
KLAK
KLAK
KLAK
KLAK

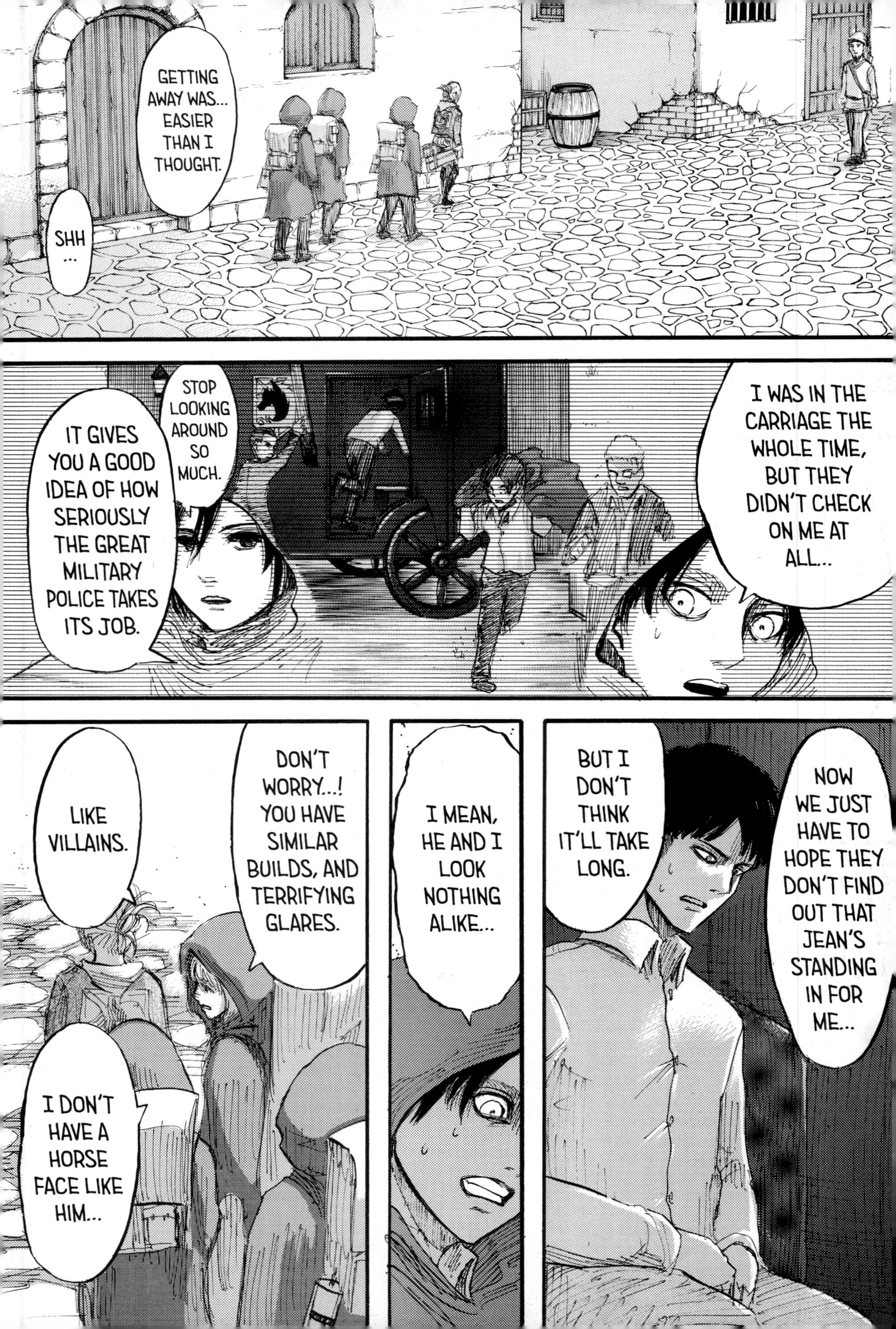
GETTING AWAY WAS... EASIER THAN I THOUGHT.
SHH...
I WAS IN THE CARRIAGE THE WHOLE TIME, BUT THEY DIDN'T CHECK ON ME AT ALL...
STOP LOOKING AROUND SO MUCH.
IT GIVES YOU A GOOD IDEA OF HOW SERIOUSLY THE GREAT MILITARY POLICE TAKES ITS JOB.
NOW WE JUST HAVE TO HOPE THEY DON'T FIND OUT THAT JEAN'S STANDING IN FOR ME...
BUT I DON'T THINK IT'LL TAKE LONG.
I MEAN, HE AND I LOOK NOTHING ALIKE...
DON'T WORRY...! YOU HAVE SIMILAR BUILDS, AND TERRIFYING GLARES.
LIKE VILLAINS.
I DON'T HAVE A HORSE FACE LIKE HIM...

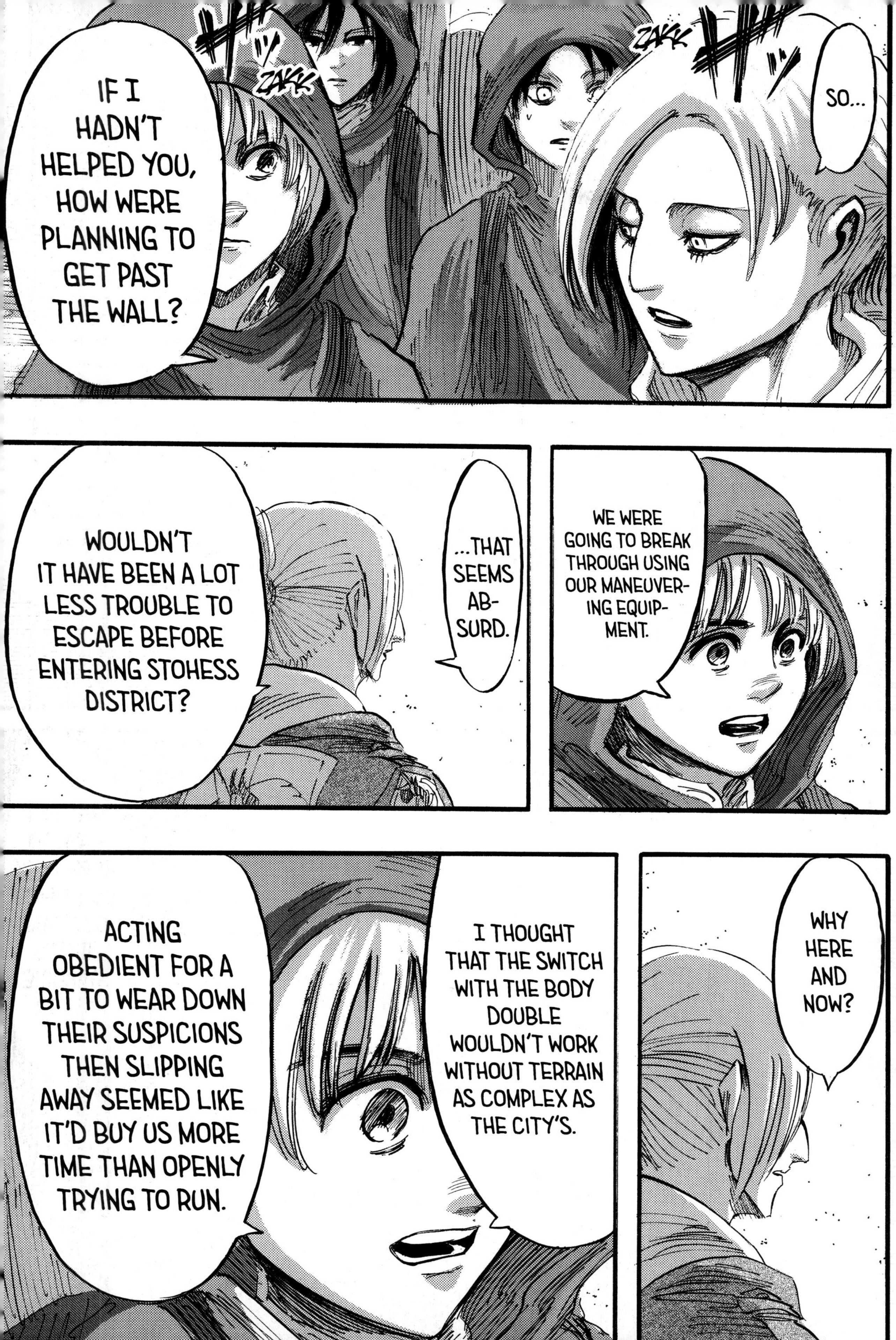
ZAKK
SO...
ZAKK
IF I HADN'T HELPED YOU, HOW WERE PLANNING TO GET PAST THE WALL?
WE WERE GOING TO BREAK THROUGH USING OUR MANEUVERING EQUIPMENT.
...THAT SEEMS ABSURD.
WOULDN'T IT HAVE BEEN A LOT LESS TROUBLE TO ESCAPE BEFORE ENTERING STOHESS DISTRICT?
WHY HERE AND NOW?
I THOUGHT THAT THE SWITCH WITH THE BODY DOUBLE WOULDN'T WORK WITHOUT TERRAIN AS COMPLEX AS THE CITY'S.
ACTING OBEDIENT FOR A BIT TO WEAR DOWN THEIR SUSPICIONS THEN SLIPPING AWAY SEEMED LIKE IT'D BUY US MORE TIME THAN OPENLY TRYING TO RUN.

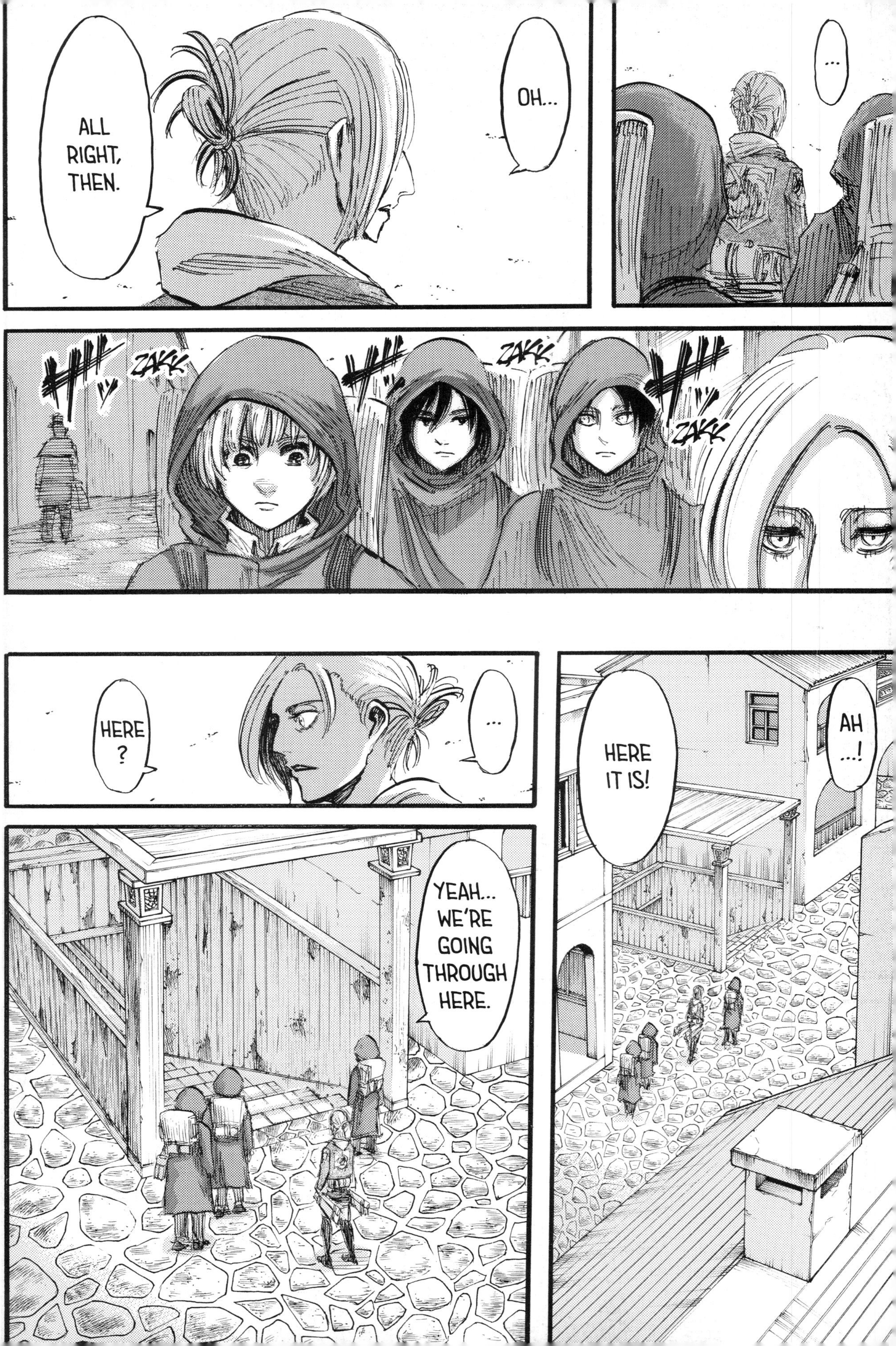
...
OH...
ALL RIGHT, THEN.
ZAKK
ZAKK
ZAKK
AH ...!
HERE IT IS!
...
HERE ?
YEAH... WE'RE GOING THROUGH HERE.

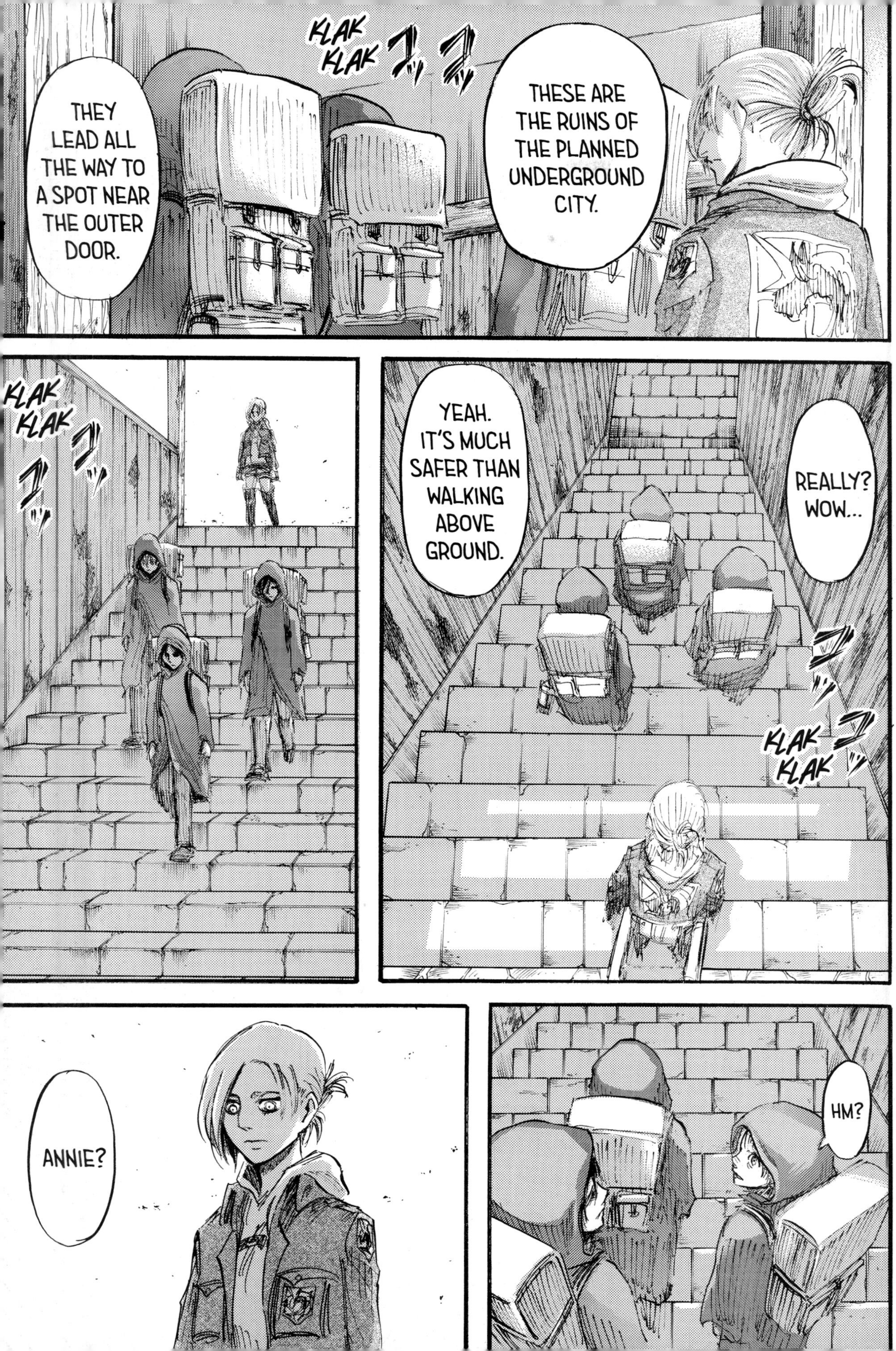
THESE ARE THE RUINS OF THE PLANNED UNDERGROUND CITY.
KLAK KLAK
THEY LEAD ALL THE WAY TO A SPOT NEAR THE OUTER DOOR.
REALLY? WOW...
KLAK KLAK
YEAH. IT'S MUCH SAFER THAN WALKING ABOVE GROUND.
KLAK KLAK
HM?
ANNIE?

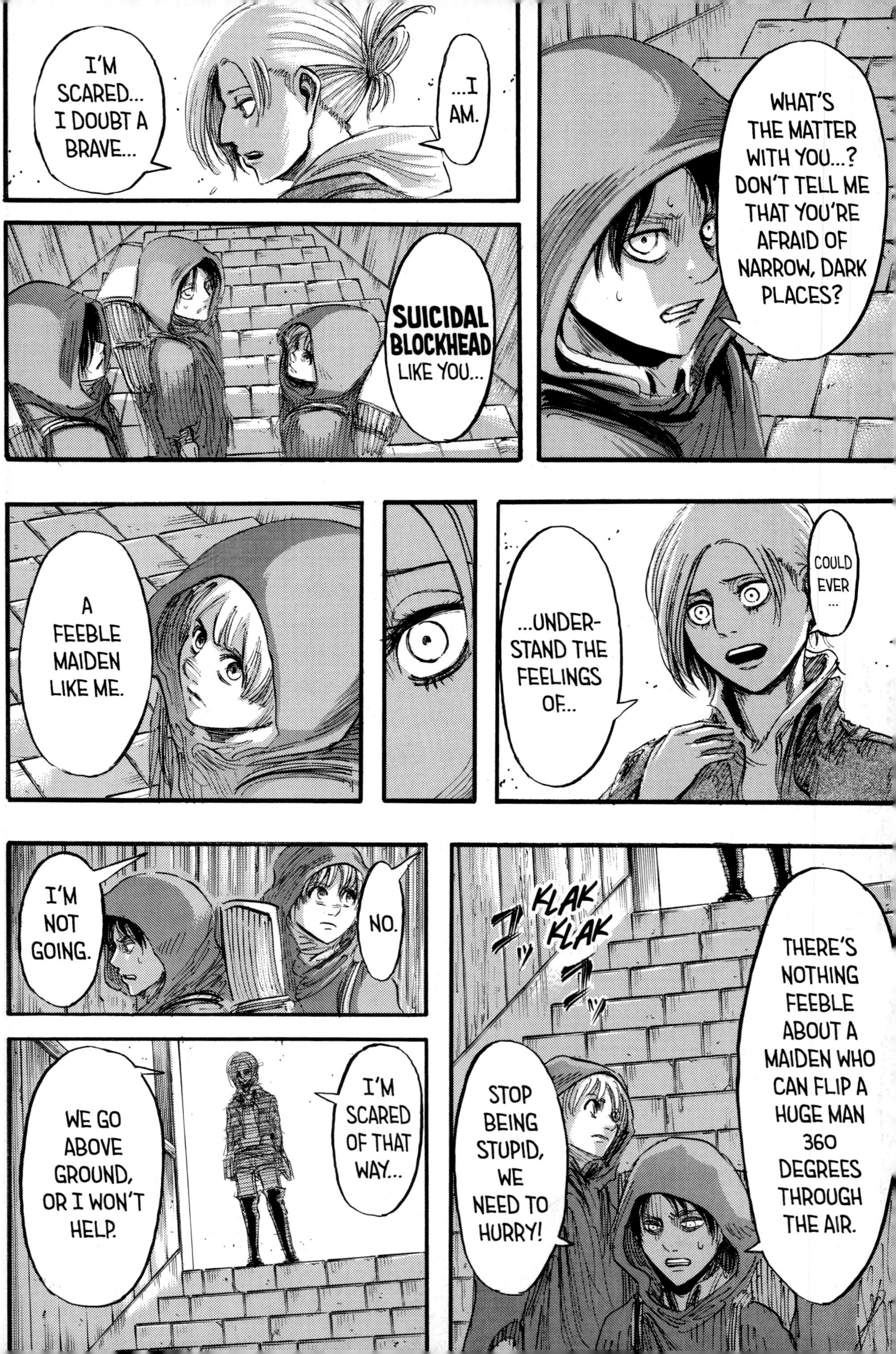
WHAT'S THE MATTER WITH YOU...? DON'T TELL ME THAT YOU'RE AFRAID OF NARROW, DARK PLACES?
...I AM.
I'M SCARED... I DOUBT A BRAVE...
SUICIDAL BLOCKHEAD LIKE YOU...
COULD EVER ...
...UNDER-STAND THE FEELINGS OF...
A FEEBLE MAIDEN LIKE ME.
THERE'S NOTHING FEEBLE ABOUT A MAIDEN WHO CAN FLIP A HUGE MAN 360 DEGREES THROUGH THE AIR.
KLAK KLAK
STOP BEING STUPID, WE NEED TO HURRY!
NO.
I'M NOT GOING.
I'M SCARED OF THAT WAY...
WE GO ABOVE GROUND, OR I WON'T HELP.

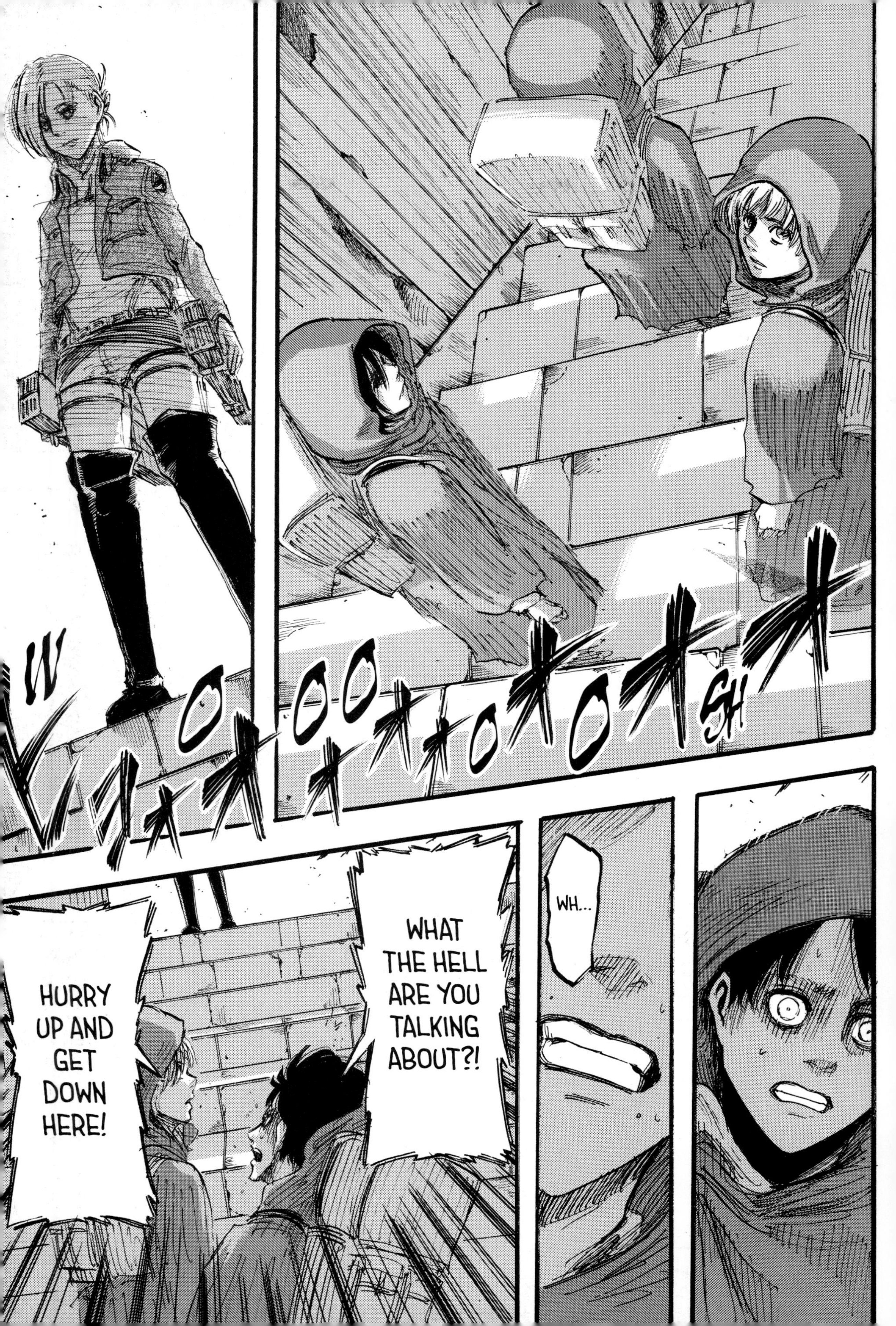
WOOOOOSH
WH...
WHAT THE HELL ARE YOU TALKING ABOUT?!
HURRY UP AND GET DOWN HERE!

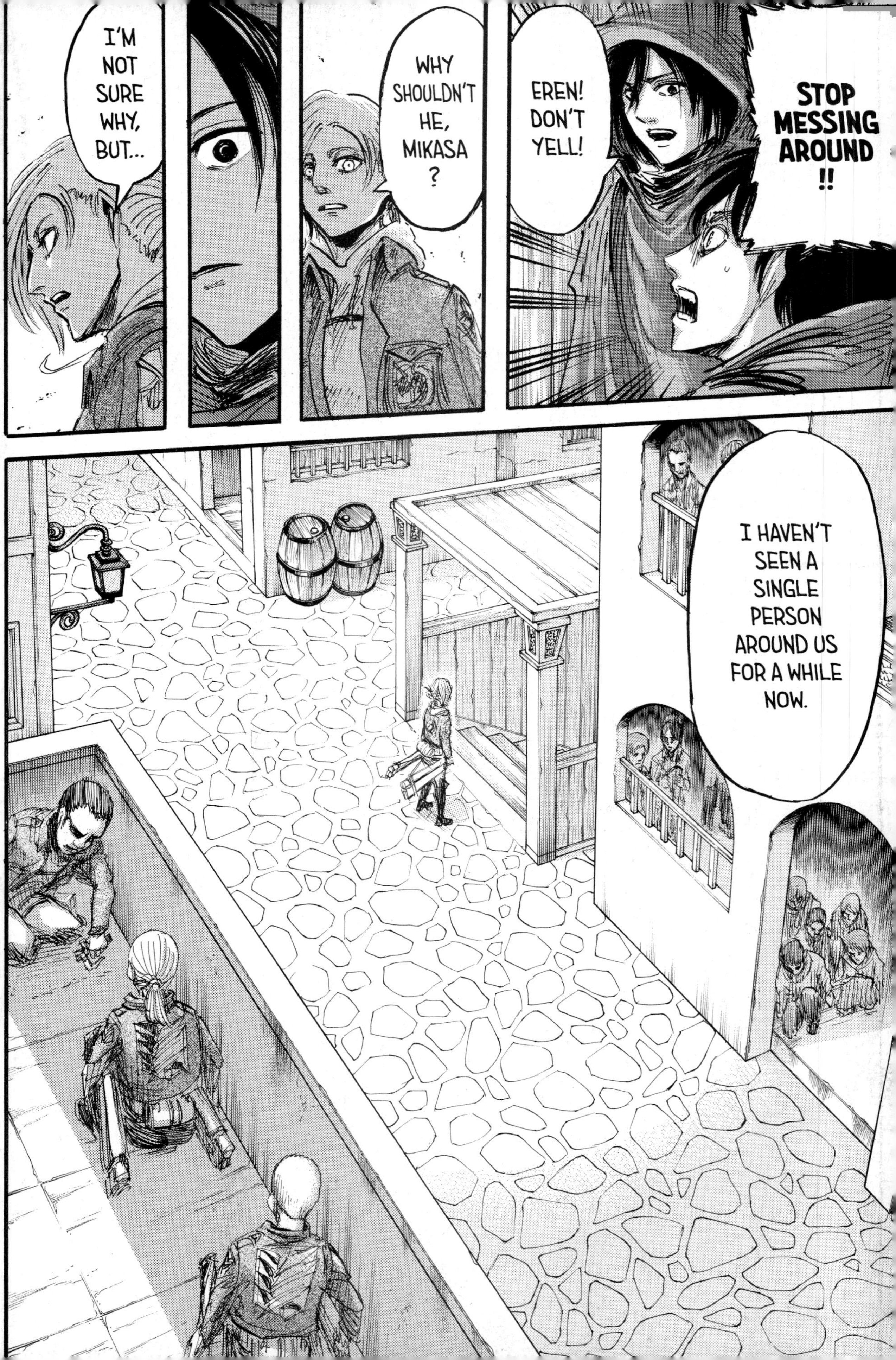
STOP MESSING AROUND !!
EREN! DON'T YELL!
WHY SHOULDN'T HE, MIKASA ?
I'M NOT SURE WHY, BUT...
I HAVEN'T SEEN A SINGLE PERSON AROUND US FOR A WHILE NOW.

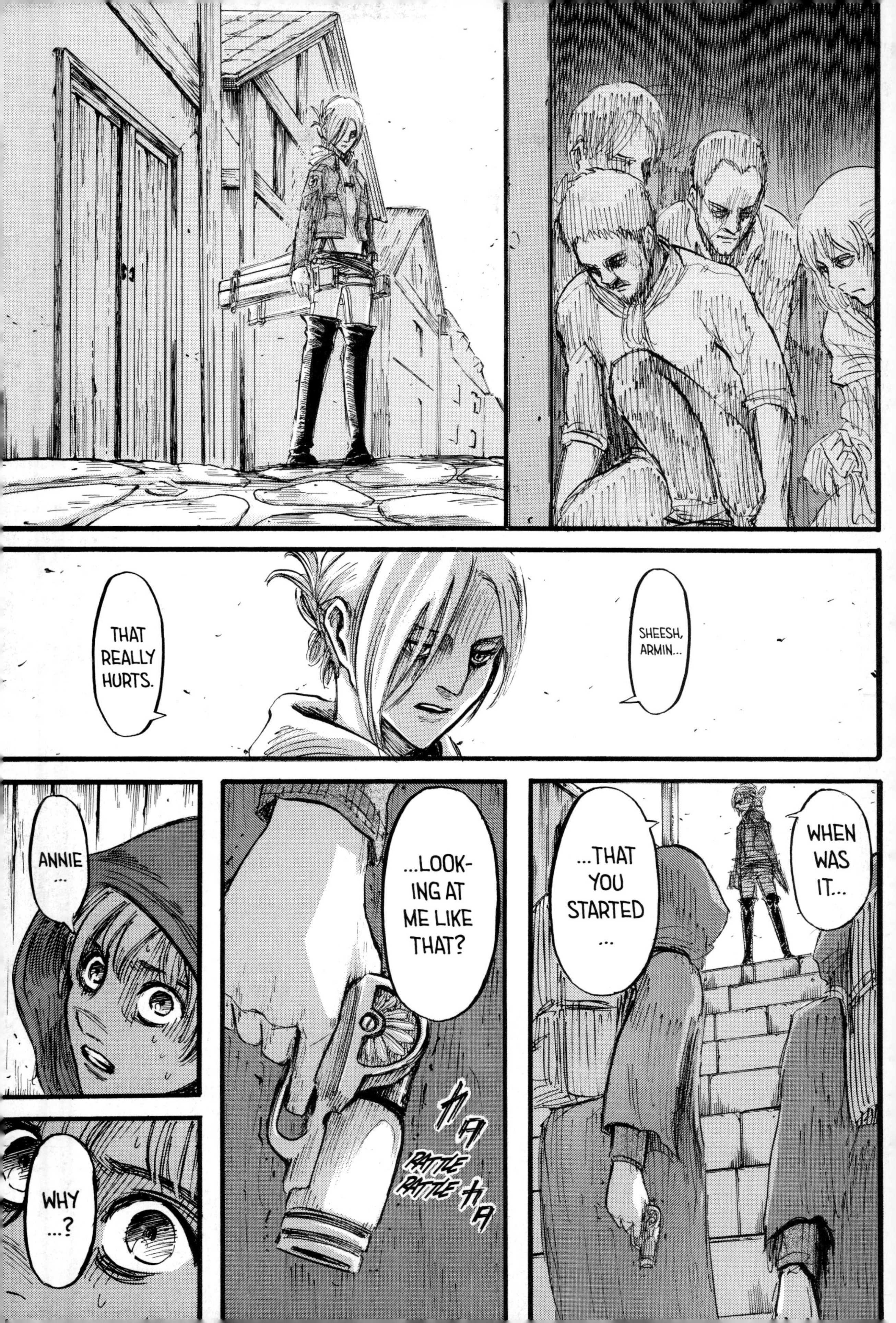
SHEESH, ARMIN...
THAT REALLY HURTS.
WHEN WAS IT...
...THAT YOU STARTED ...
...LOOK-ING AT ME LIKE THAT?
カタ カタ
RATTLE RATTLE
ANNIE ...
WHY ...?

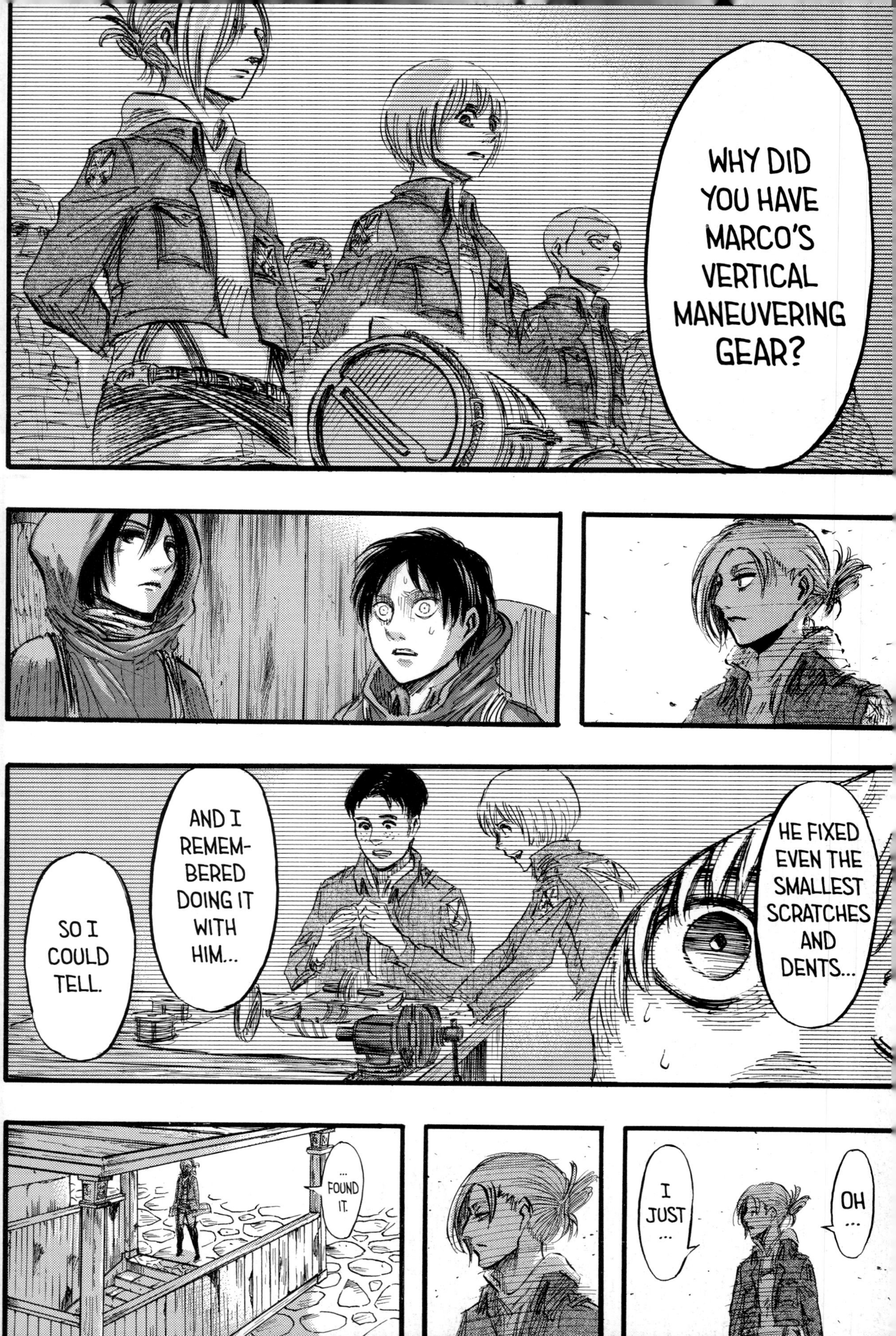
WHY DID YOU HAVE MARCO'S VERTICAL MANEUVERING GEAR?
HE FIXED EVEN THE SMALLEST SCRATCHES AND DENTS...
AND I REMEM-BERED DOING IT WITH HIM...
SO I COULD TELL.
OH ...
I JUST ...
... FOUND IT.

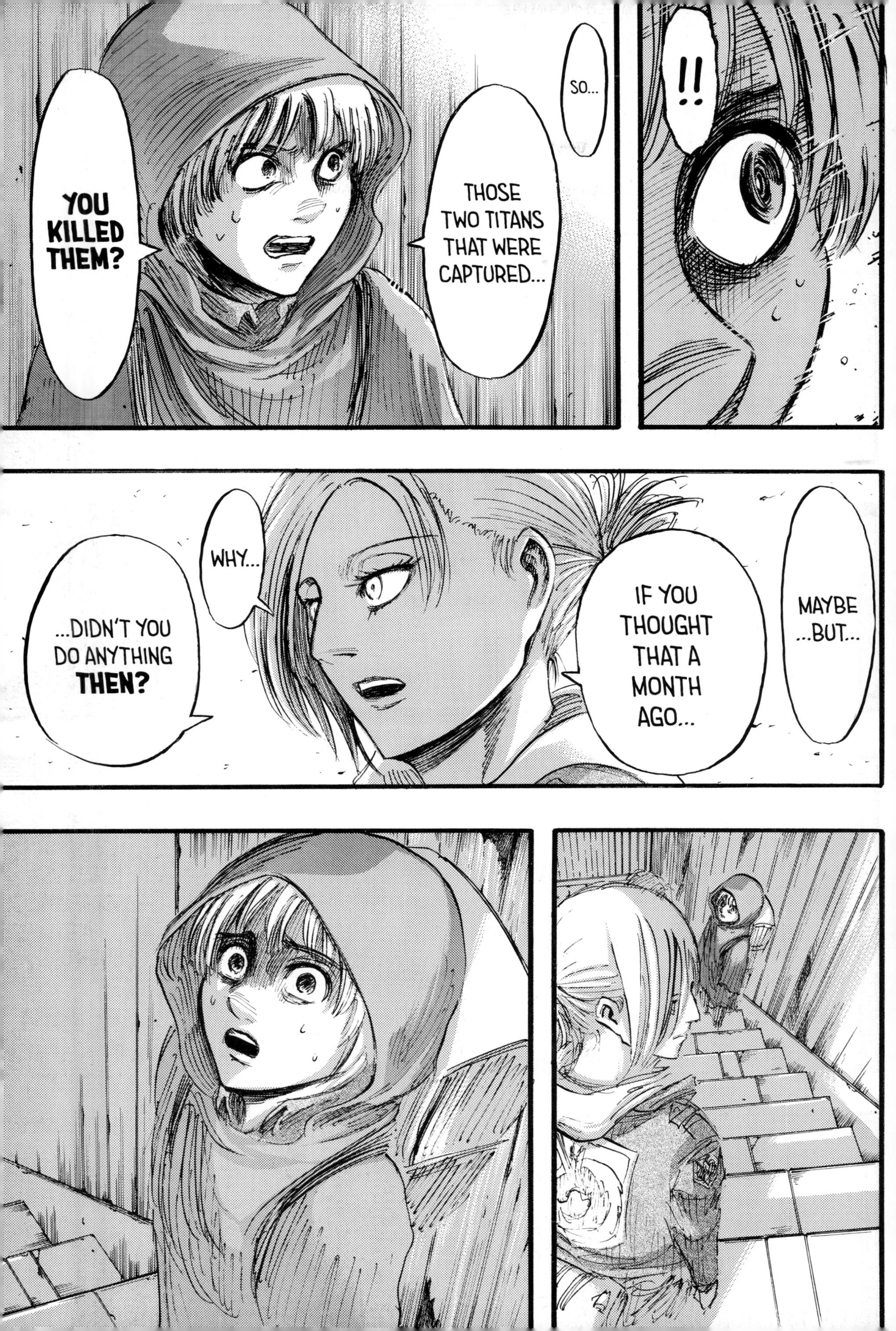
!!
SO...
THOSE TWO TITANS THAT WERE CAPTURED...
YOU KILLED THEM?
MAYBE ...BUT...
IF YOU THOUGHT THAT A MONTH AGO...
WHY...
...DIDN'T YOU DO ANYTHING THEN?

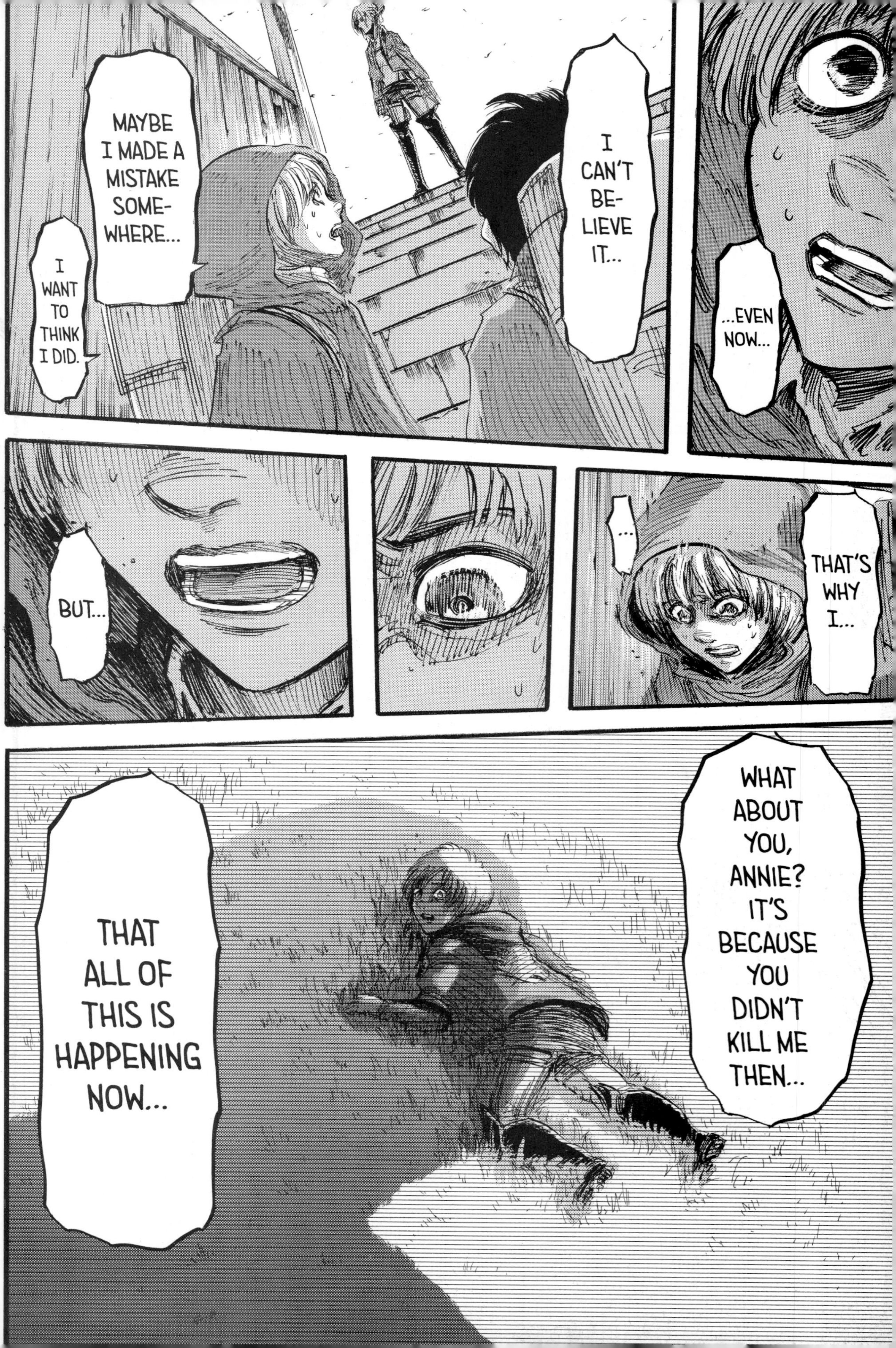
...EVEN NOW...
I CAN'T BE-LIEVE IT...
MAYBE I MADE A MISTAKE SOME-WHERE...
I WANT TO THINK I DID.
THAT'S WHY I...
...
BUT...
WHAT ABOUT YOU, ANNIE? IT'S BECAUSE YOU DIDN'T KILL ME THEN...
THAT ALL OF THIS IS HAPPENING NOW...

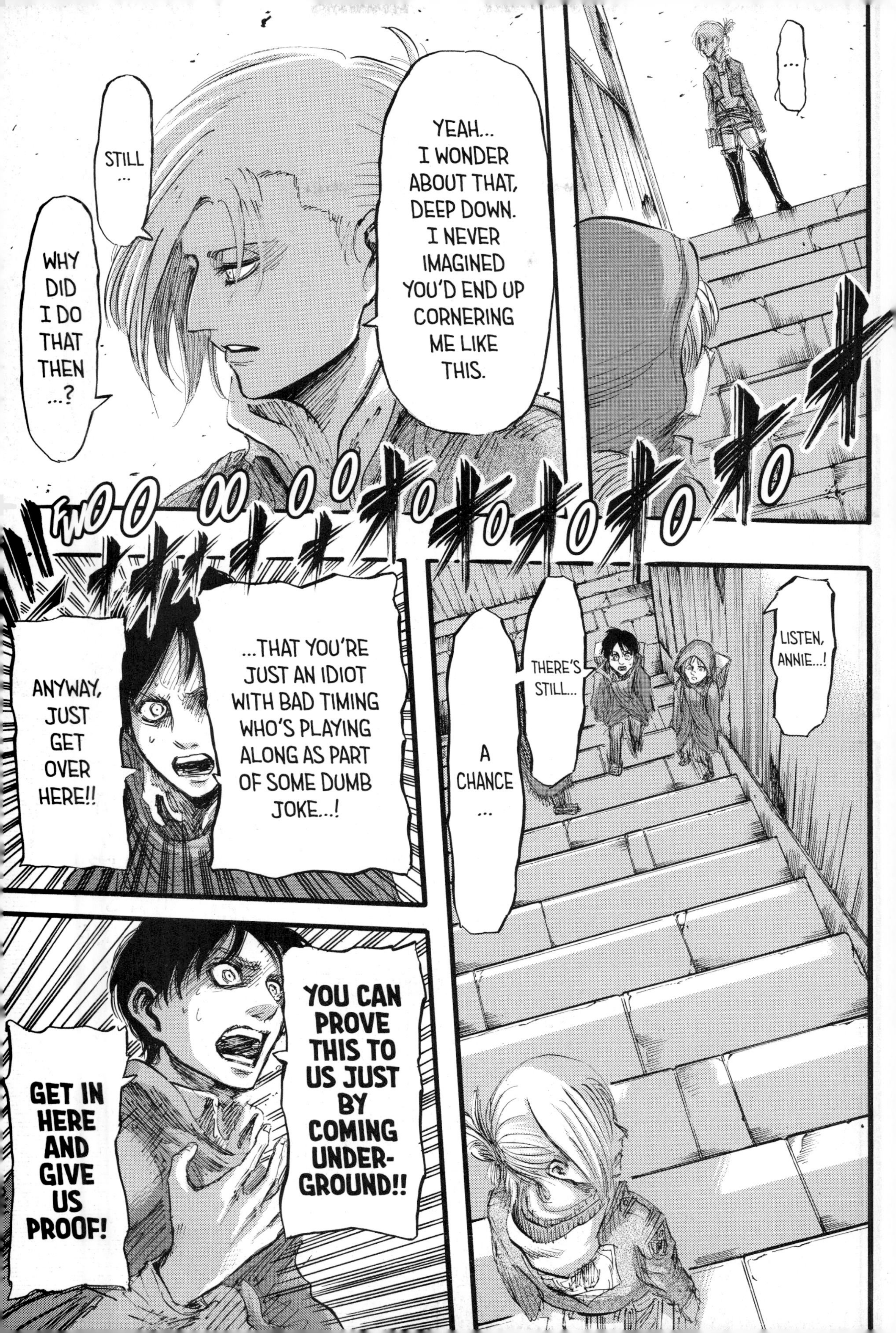
...
YEAH... I WONDER ABOUT THAT, DEEP DOWN. I NEVER IMAGINED YOU'D END UP CORNERING ME LIKE THIS.
STILL...
WHY DID I DO THAT THEN...?
FWOOOOOOOOOOOOOOO
LISTEN, ANNIE...!
THERE'S STILL...
A CHANCE...
...THAT YOU'RE JUST AN IDIOT WITH BAD TIMING WHO'S PLAYING ALONG AS PART OF SOME DUMB JOKE...!
ANYWAY, JUST GET OVER HERE!!
YOU CAN PROVE THIS TO US JUST BY COMING UNDER-GROUND!!
GET IN HERE AND GIVE US PROOF!

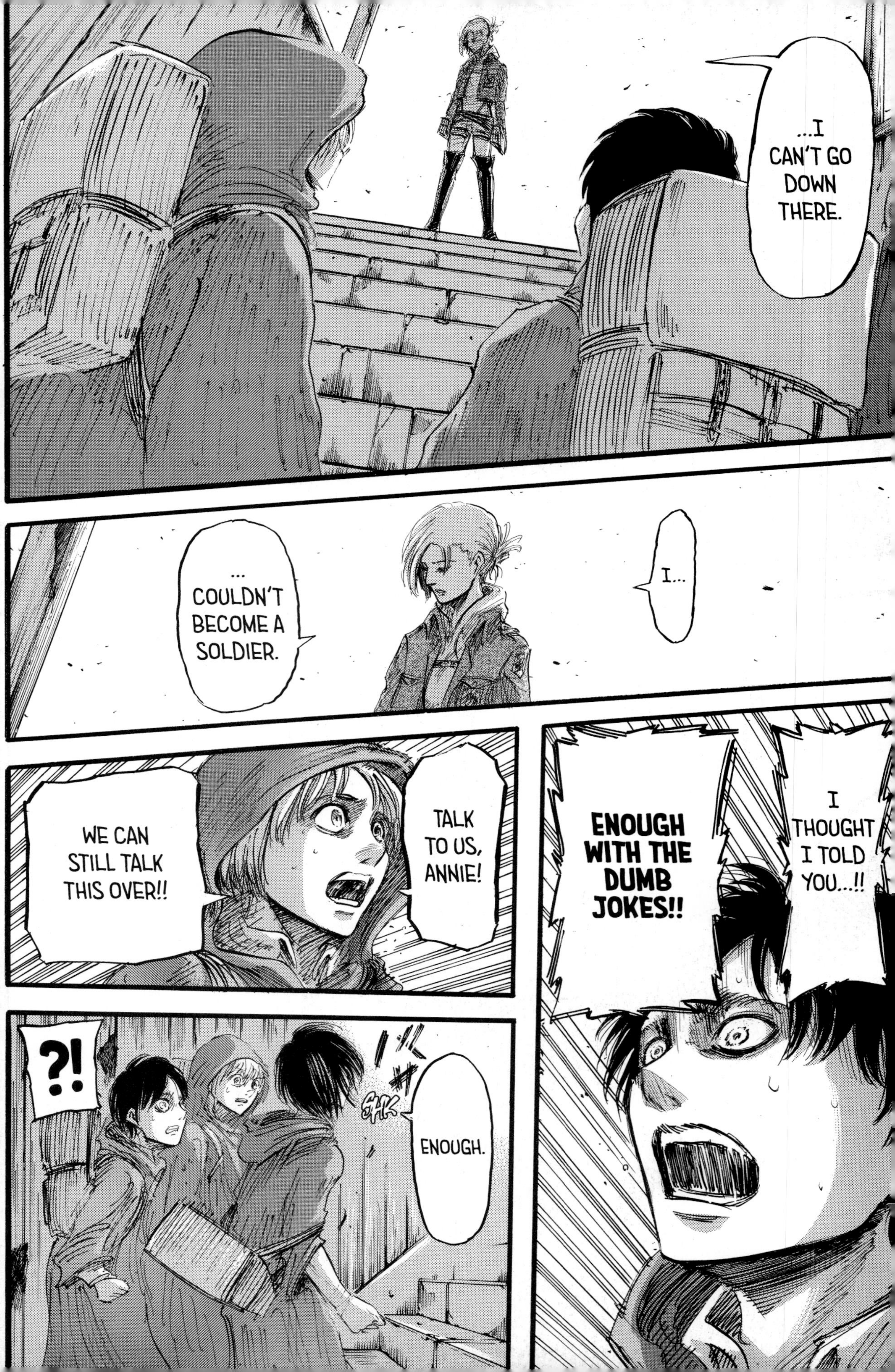
...I CAN'T GO DOWN THERE.
I...
... COULDN'T BECOME A SOLDIER.
I THOUGHT I TOLD YOU...!!
ENOUGH WITH THE DUMB JOKES!!
TALK TO US, ANNIE!
WE CAN STILL TALK THIS OVER!!
ENOUGH.
SHK
?!

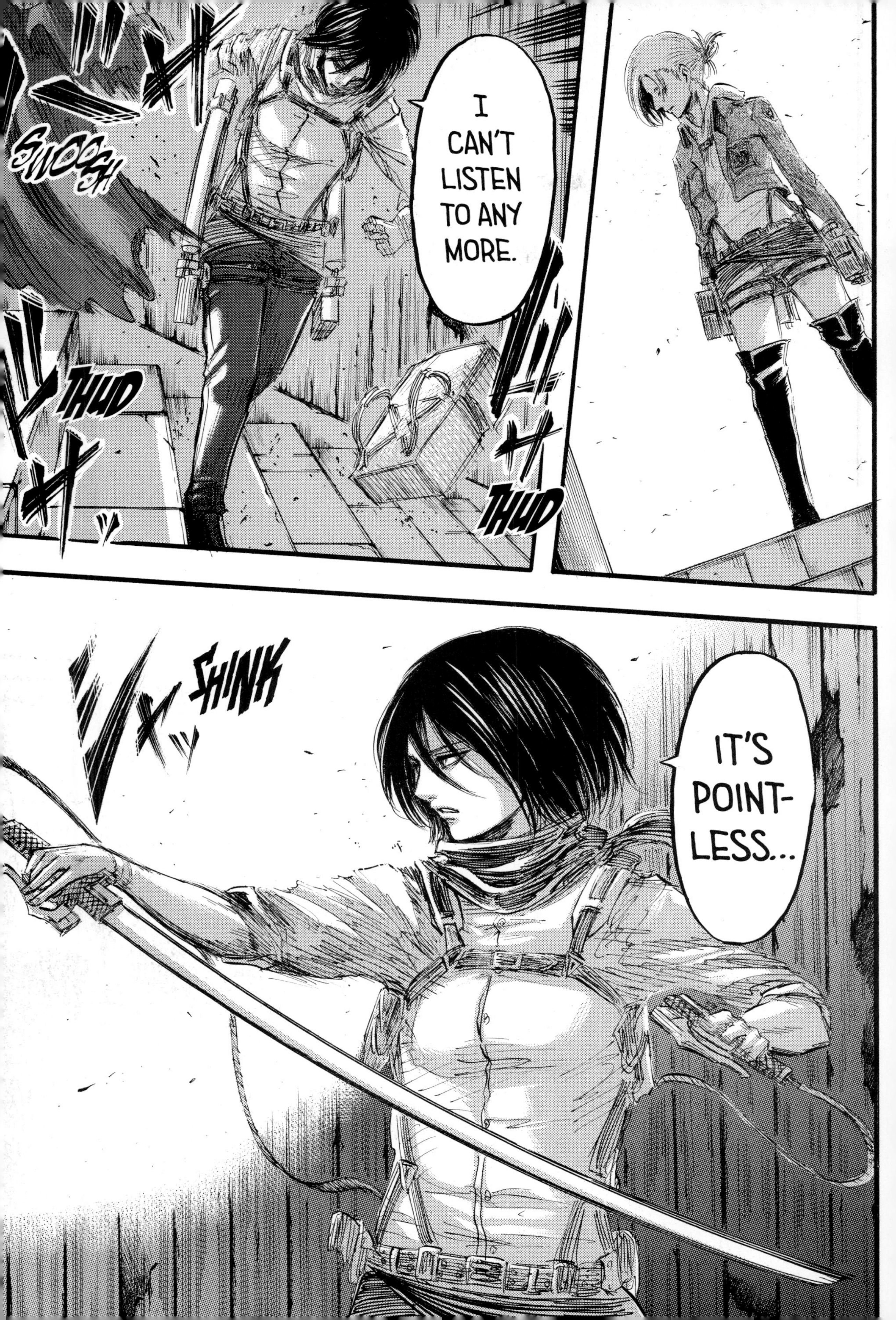
SWOOSH
THUD
I CAN'T LISTEN TO ANY MORE.
THUD
SHINK
IT'S POINT-LESS...

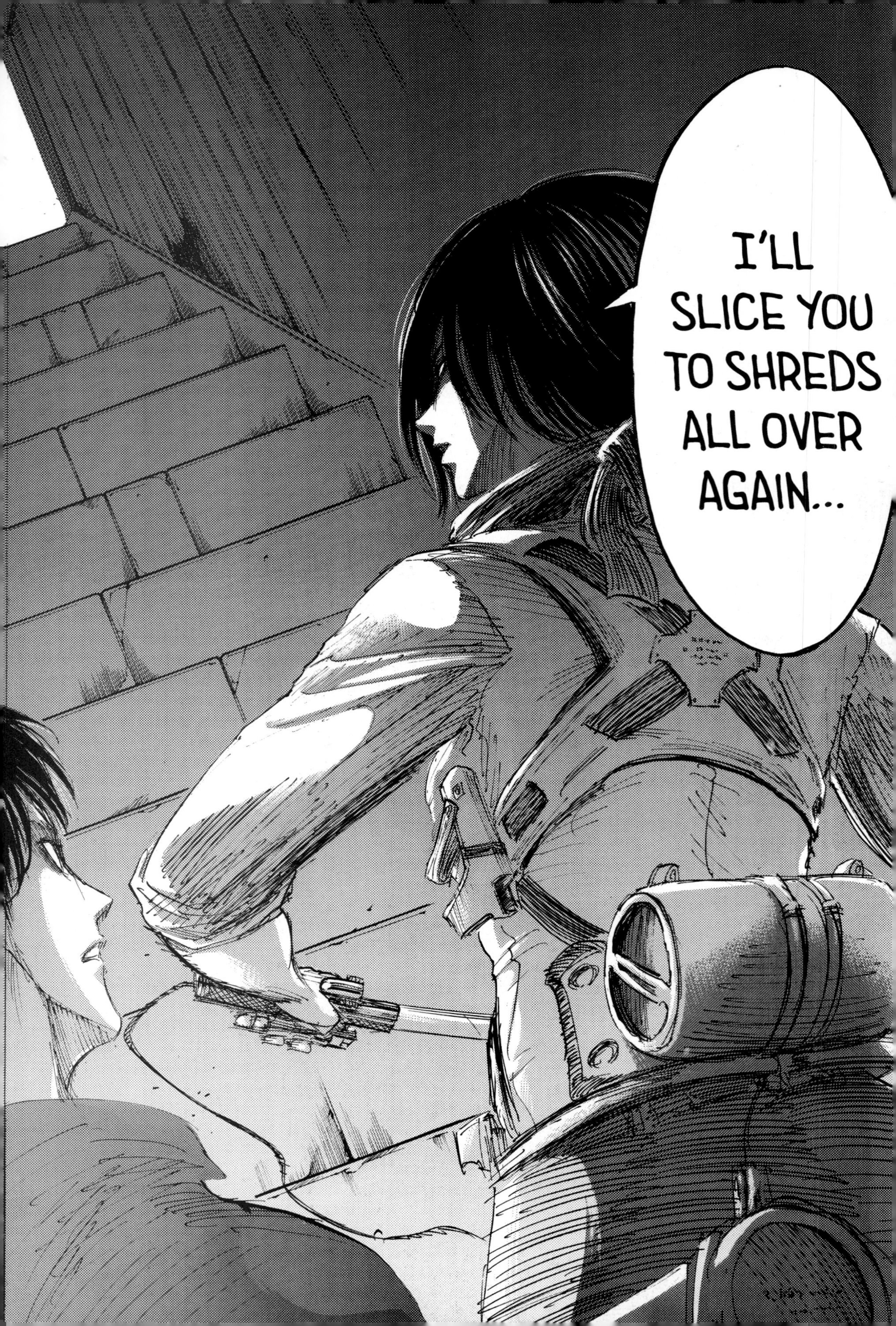
I'LL SLICE YOU TO SHREDS ALL OVER AGAIN...

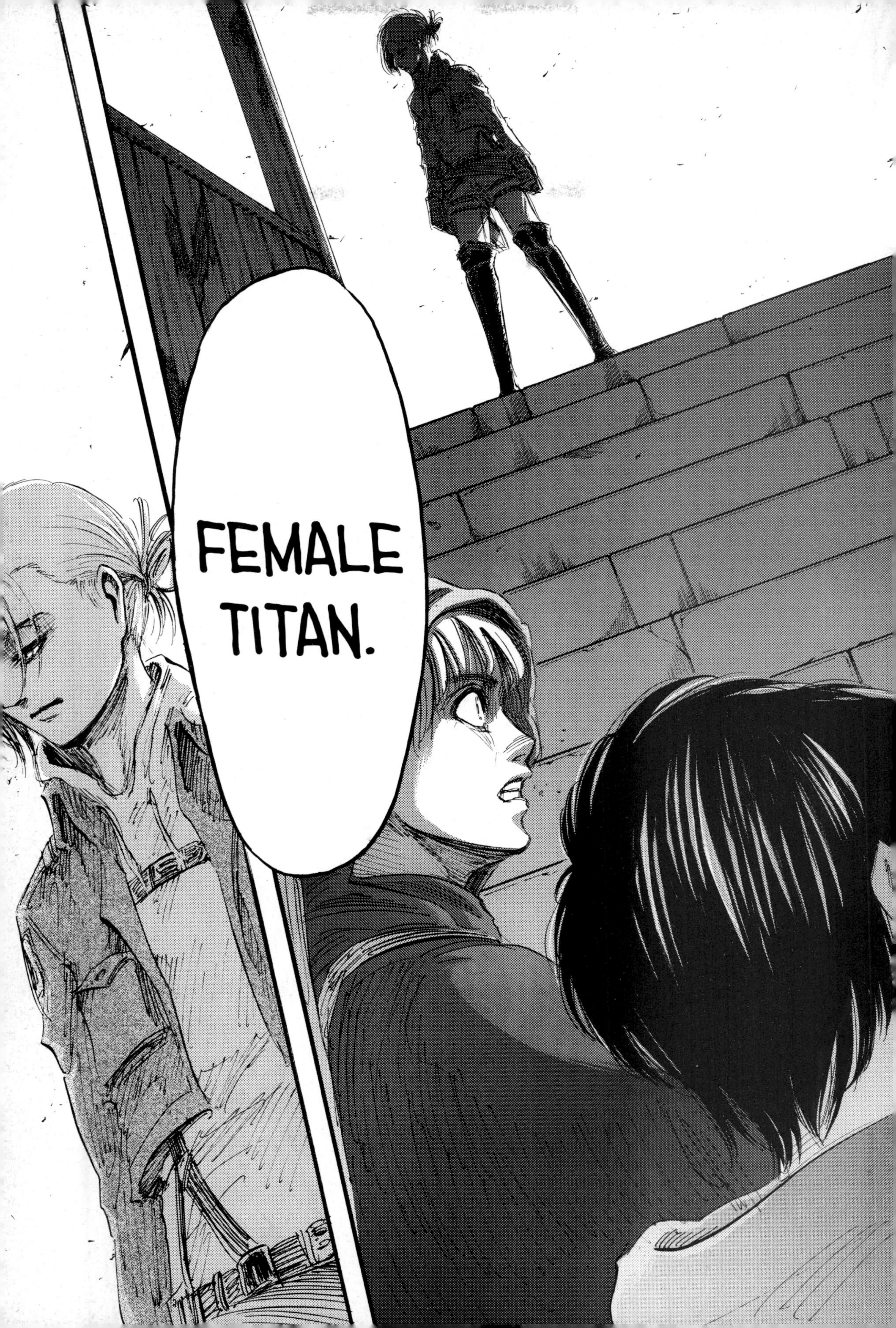
FEMALE TITAN.

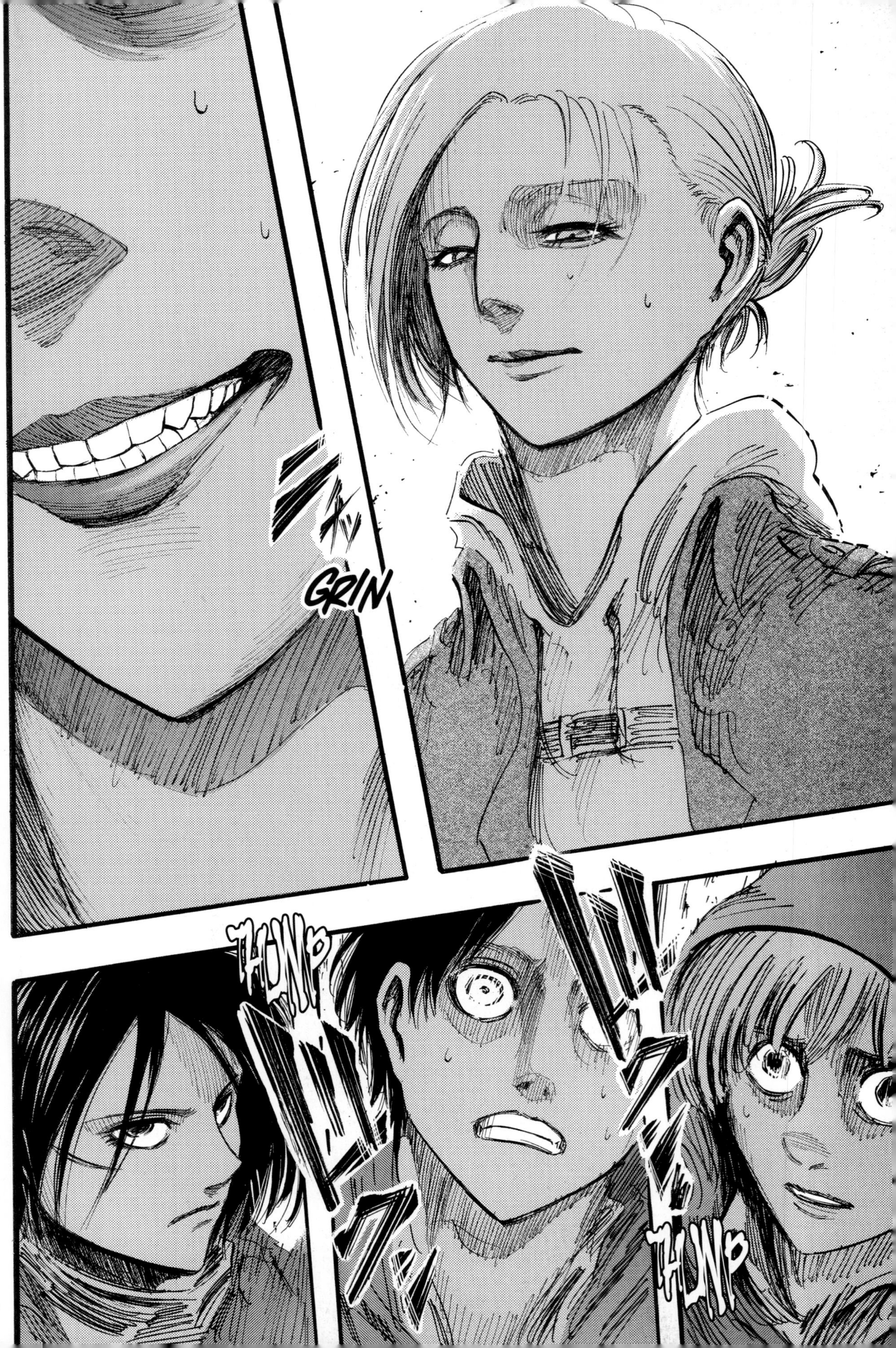

GRIN
THUMP
THUMP

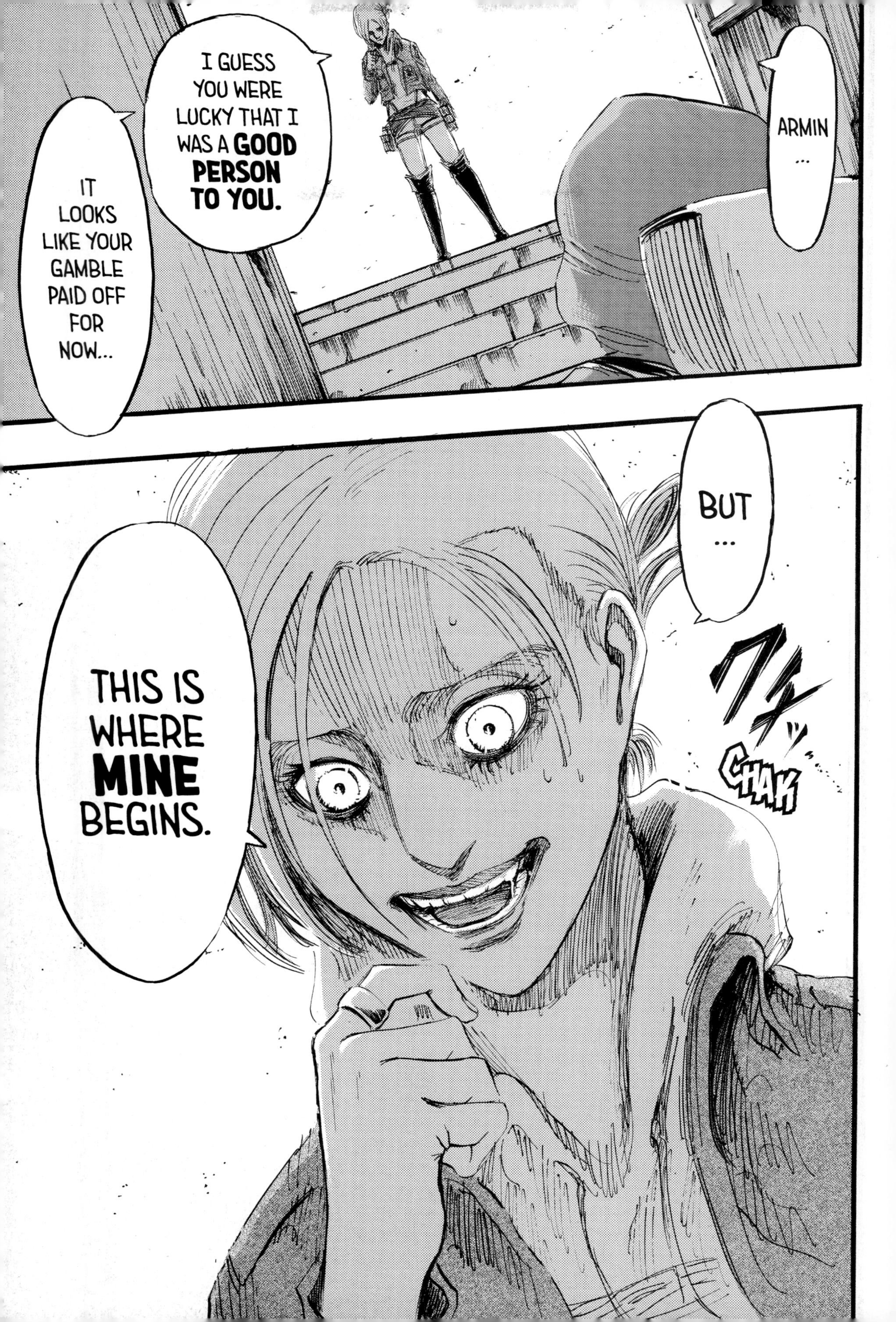
ARMIN ...
I GUESS YOU WERE LUCKY THAT I WAS A **GOOD PERSON** TO YOU.
IT LOOKS LIKE YOUR GAMBLE PAID OFF FOR NOW...
BUT ...
CHAK
THIS IS WHERE **MINE** BEGINS.

Currently Publicly Available Information

14: The Military Police Brigade

ONLY THE TEN INDIVIDUALS WITH THE HIGHEST MARKS IN THEIR YEAR'S TRAINING CORPS MAY APPLY TO THE MILITARY POLICE BRIGADE. ADDITIONAL SOLDIERS JOIN THE BRIGADE IN OTHER WAYS, SUCH AS BY TRANSFER FROM THE GARRISON AFTER GAINING EXPERIENCE THERE.

THE MILITARY POLICE BRIGADE IS ABOUT 2,000 SOLDIERS STRONG, BUT REPORTEDLY HAS AN ACTUAL FIGHTING STRENGTH OF ABOUT 5,000 SOLDIERS INCLUDING THE GARRISON, WHICH IS UNDER ITS COMMAND.

THE BRIGADE ACTS AS THOUGH IT IS ABOVE THE GARRISON, AND BEHIND THE SCENES, IT HAS THE POWER TO INFLUENCE EVERY SECTION OF THE ADMINISTRATION IN THE INTERIOR. AS IT DOES NOT COME INTO CONTACT WITH TITANS ON THE FRONT LINES, IT ALSO SUFFERS NO HUMAN LOSSES.

ABOUT 200 MPS ARE DEPLOYED IN EACH WALLED CITY. THEIR MAIN DUTIES ARE TO PRESIDE OVER THE TRAINING CORPS, SUPERVISE THE GARRISON, AND COMMAND AND CONTROL THE FIRE DEPARTMENTS. THEY ALSO ARREST AND DETAIN POLITICAL CRIMINALS AND MAJOR OFFENDERS. THE MILITARY POLICE BRIGADE IS GIVEN FIRST PRIORITY DURING INVESTIGATIONS THAT INVOLVE NOBILITY OR THE ROYAL FAMILY.

DUE TO ITS CHARACTER, THE BRIGADE OFTEN COMES INTO CONFLICT WITH THE SURVEY CORPS, WHOSE ROOTS ARE DEMOCRATIC IN NATURE.

(WITH THANKS TO UKYŌ KODACHI AND KIYOMUNE MIWA)

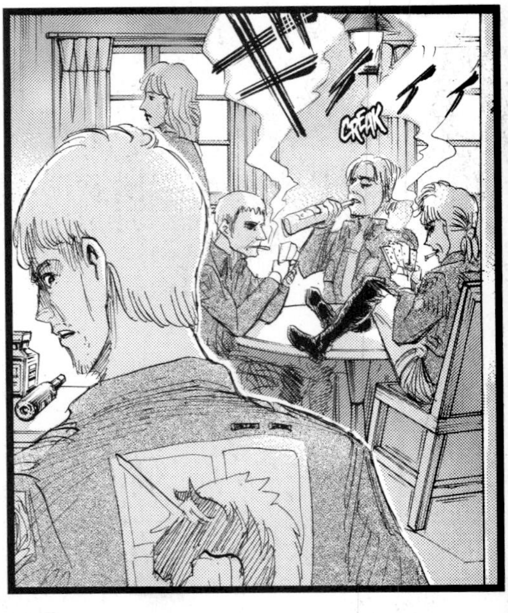
CREAK

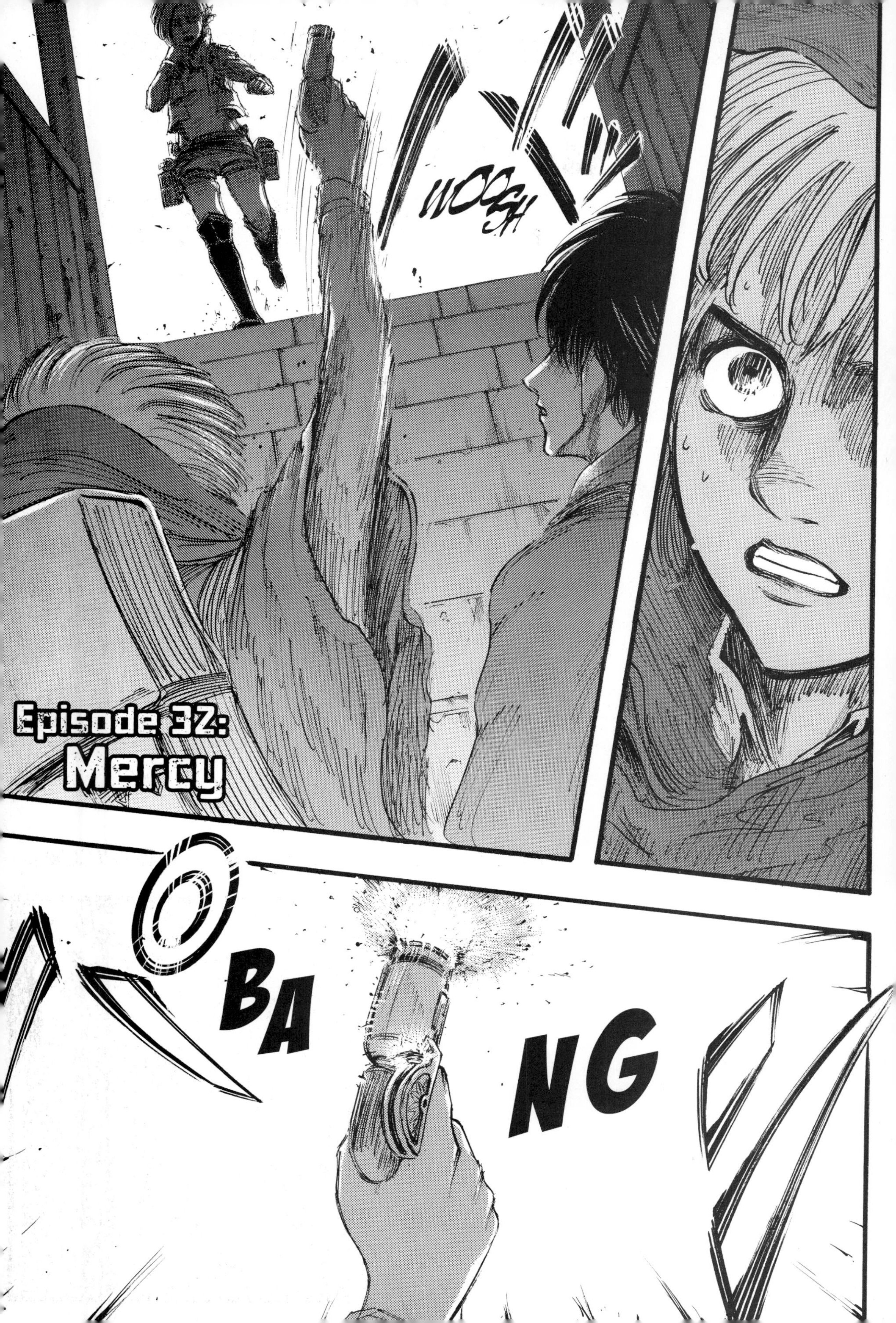
WOOSH
Episode 32:
Mercy
BANG

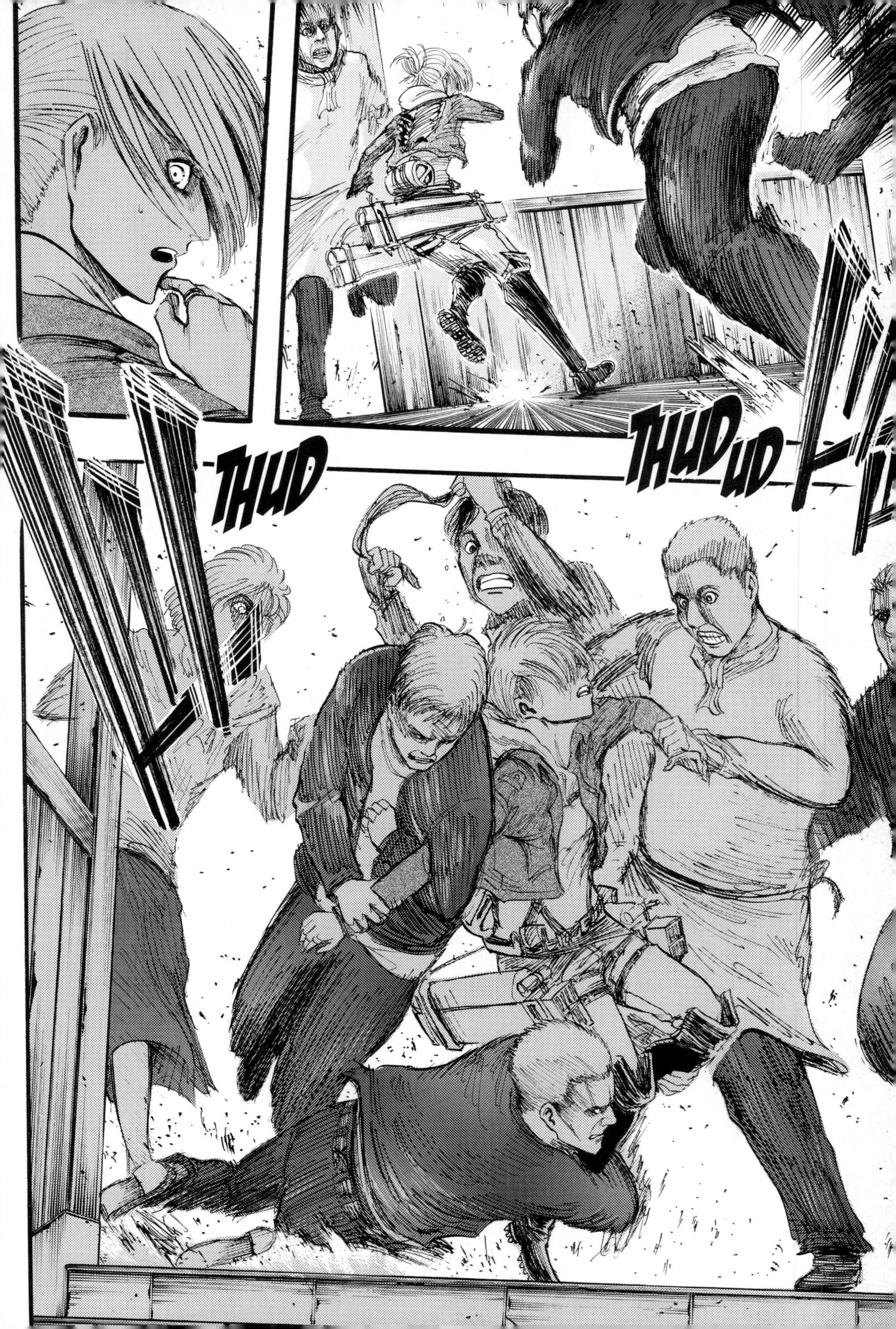
THUDUD
THUD

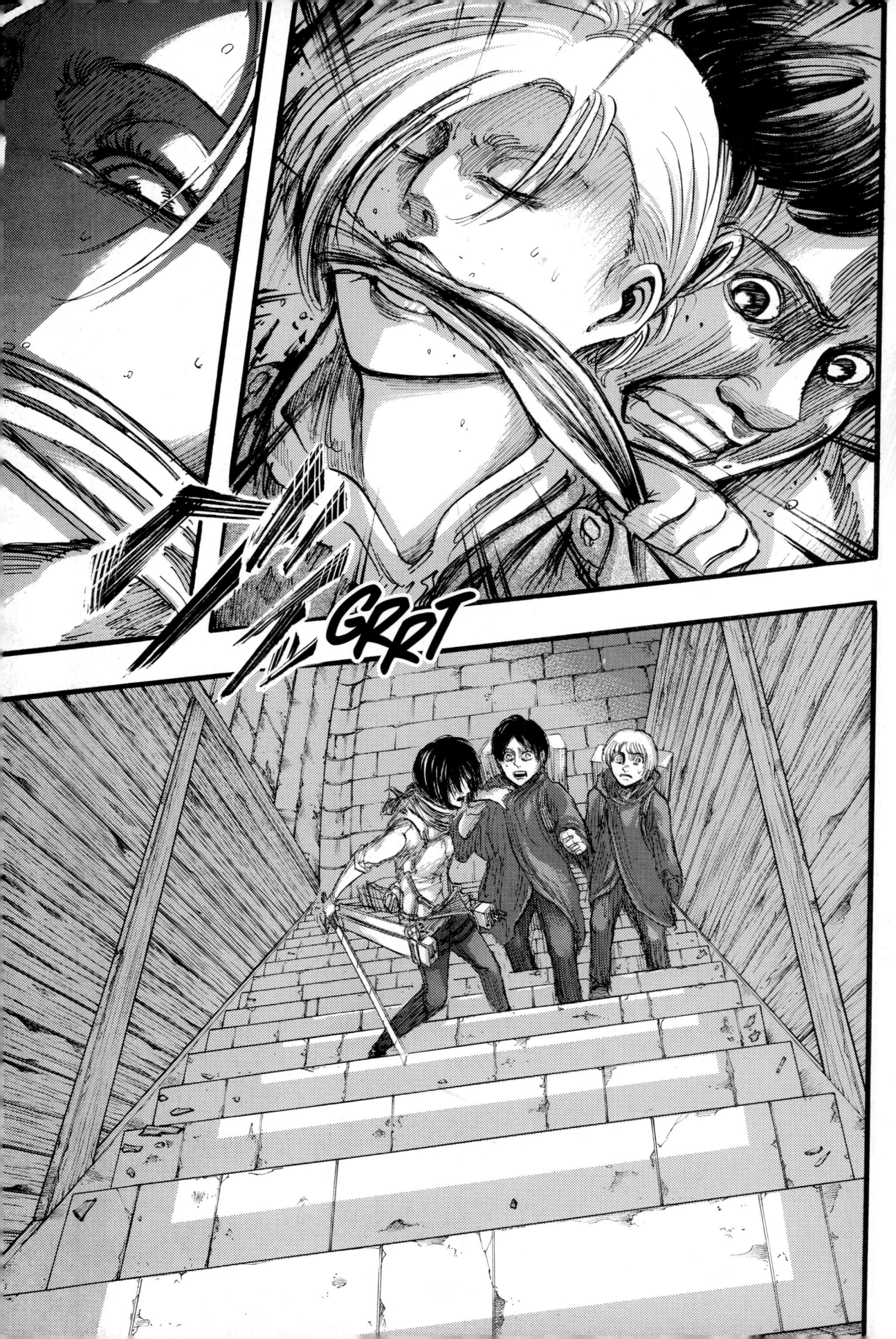

GRRT

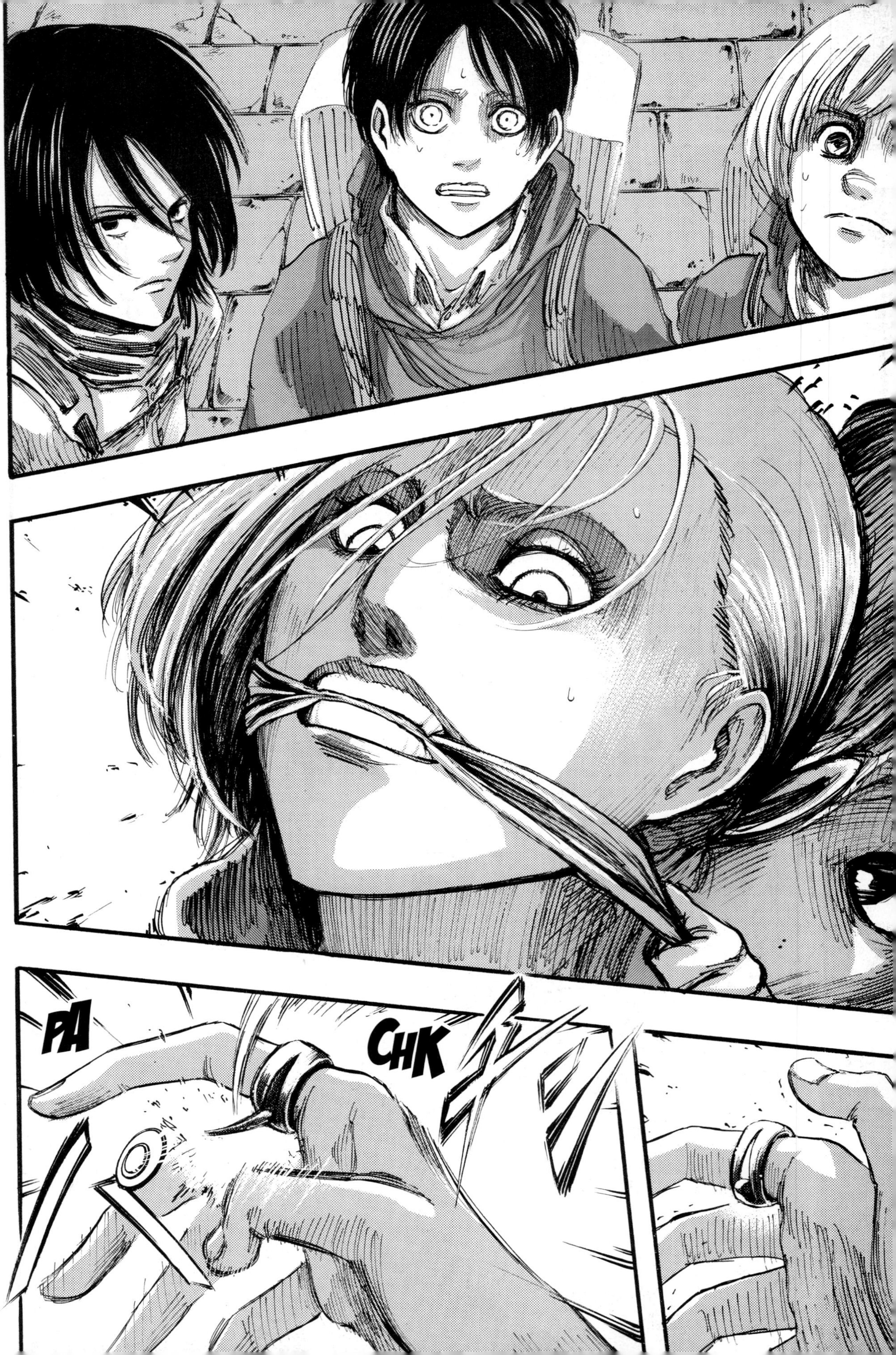
CHK
PA

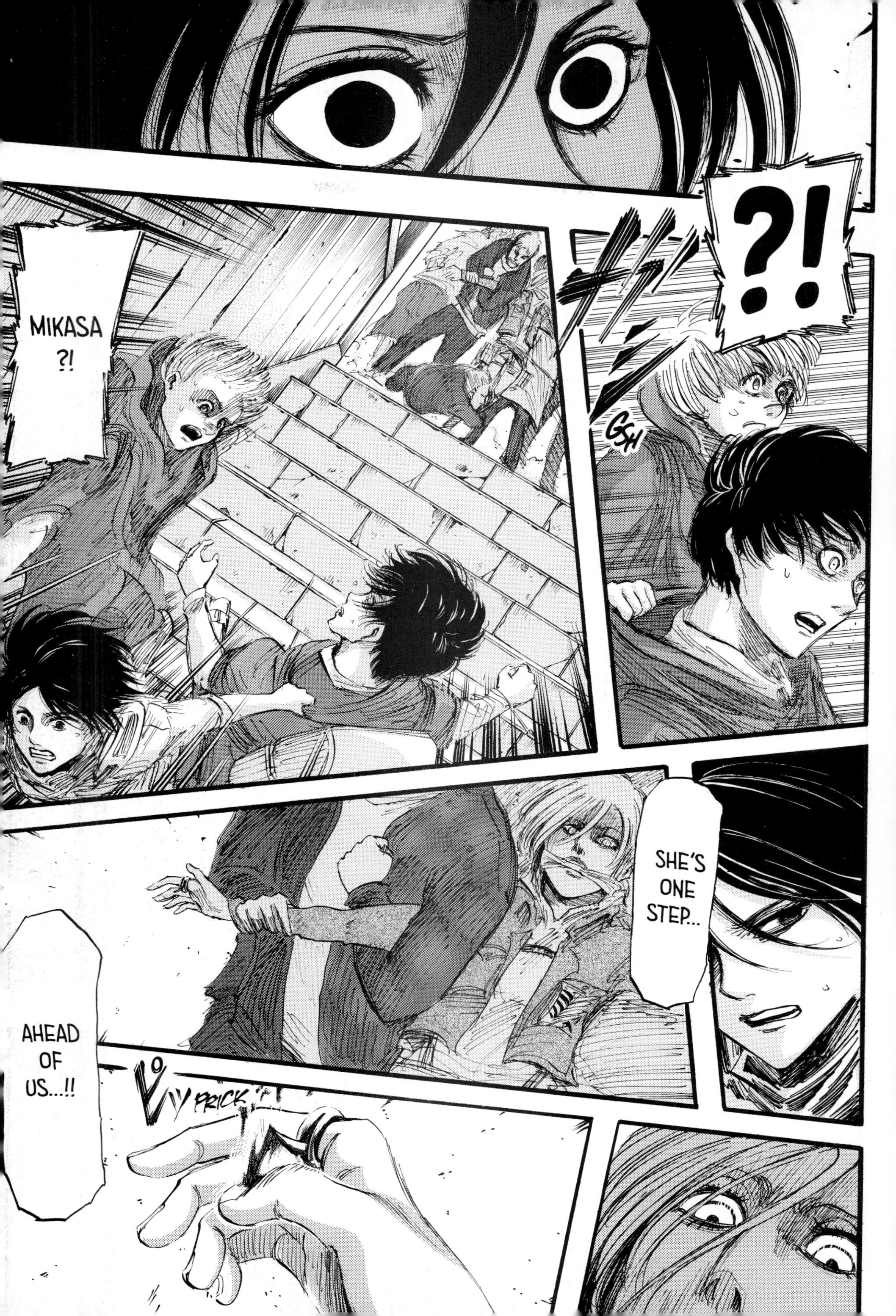
?!
GSH
MIKASA ?!
SHE'S ONE STEP...
AHEAD OF US...!!
PRICK

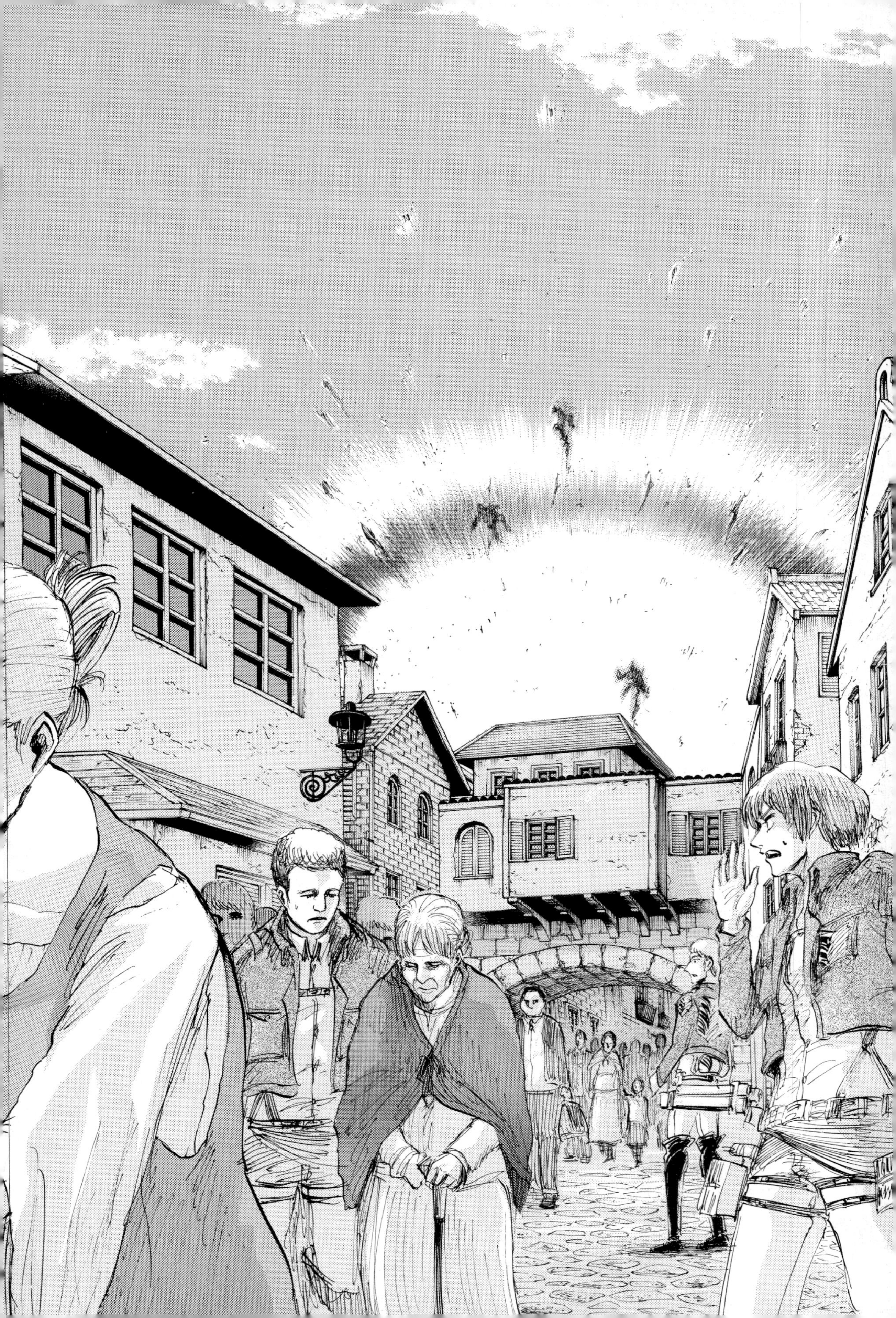

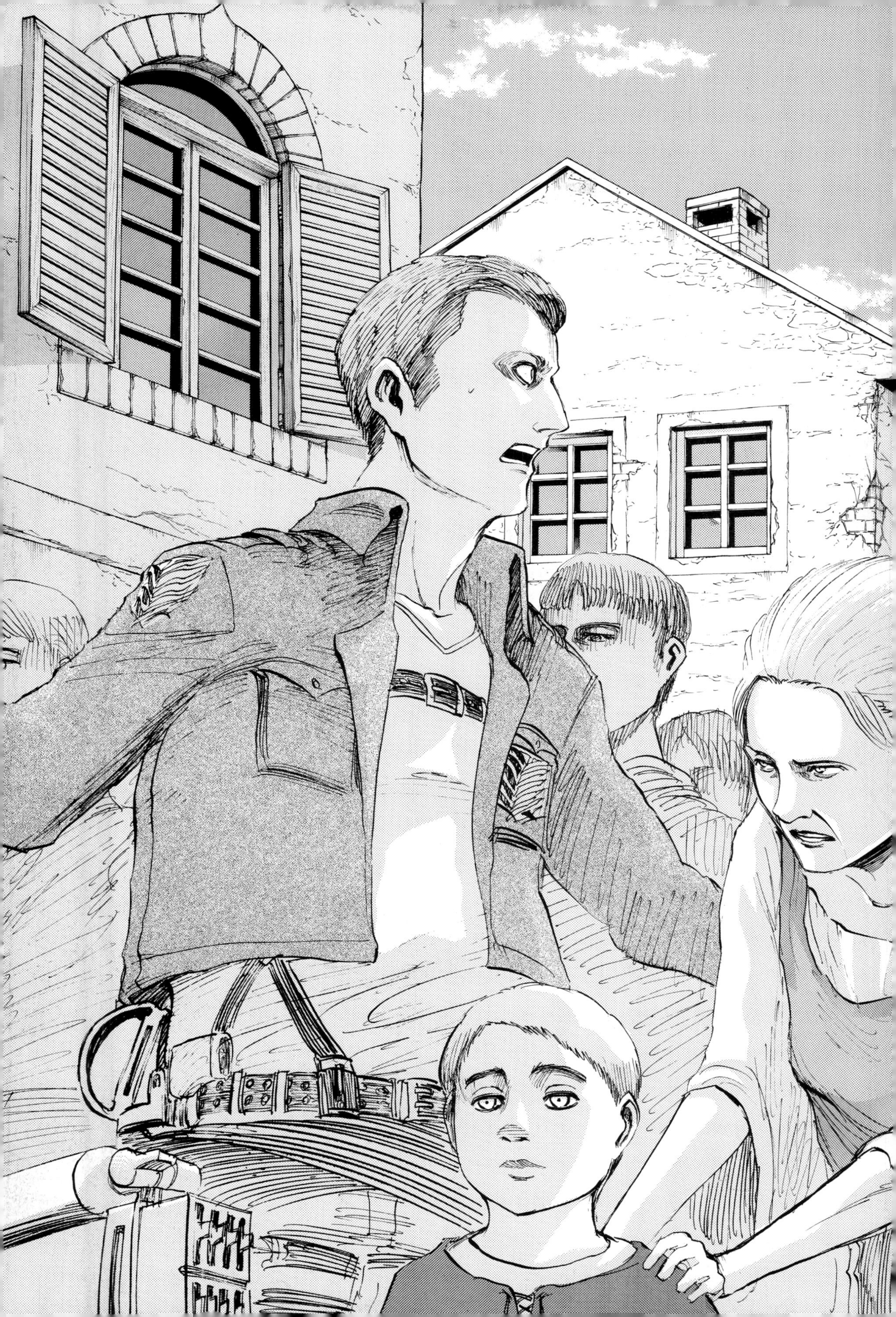

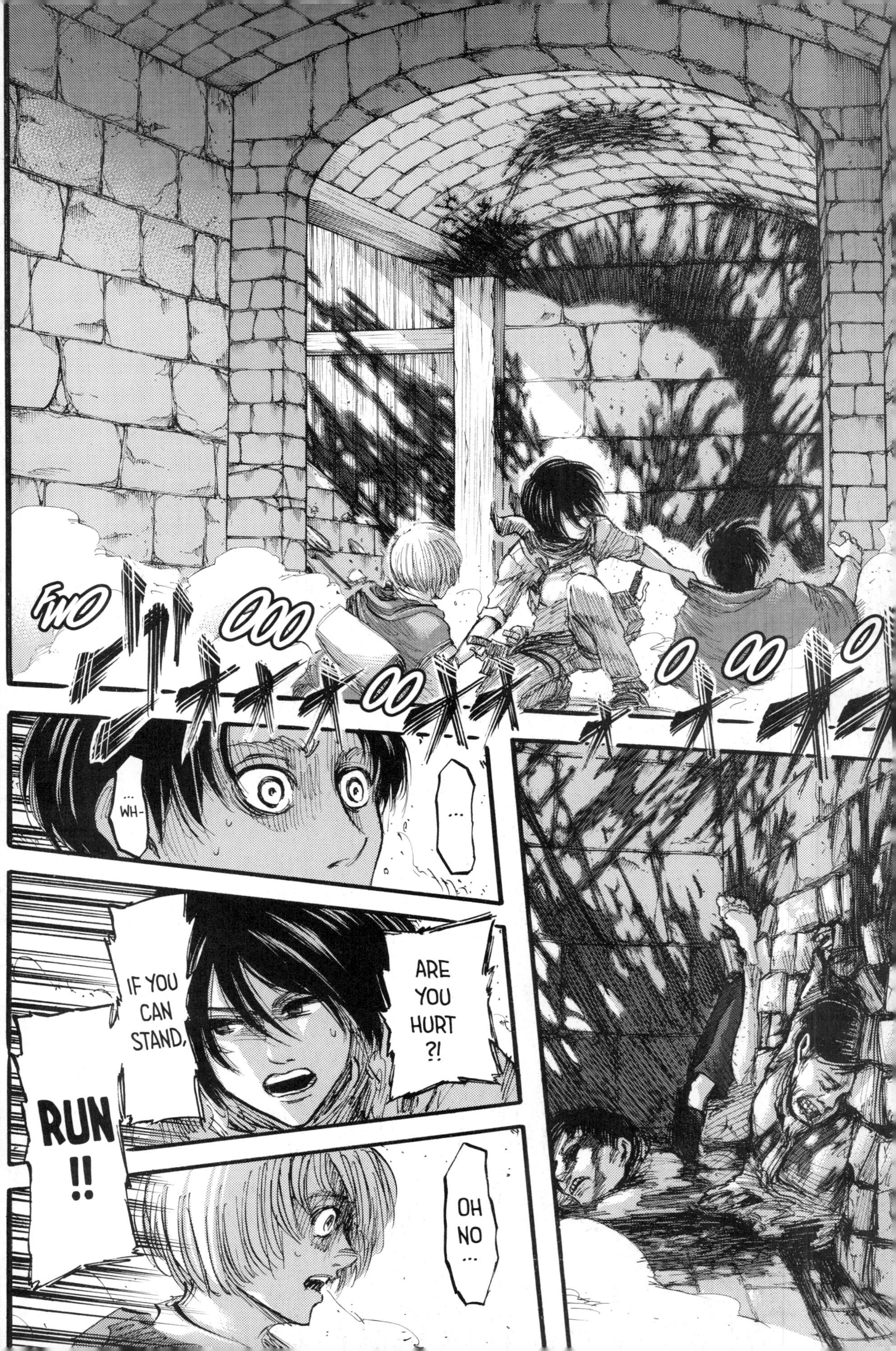
...
... WH-
ARE YOU HURT ?!
IF YOU CAN STAND,
RUN !!
OH NO ...

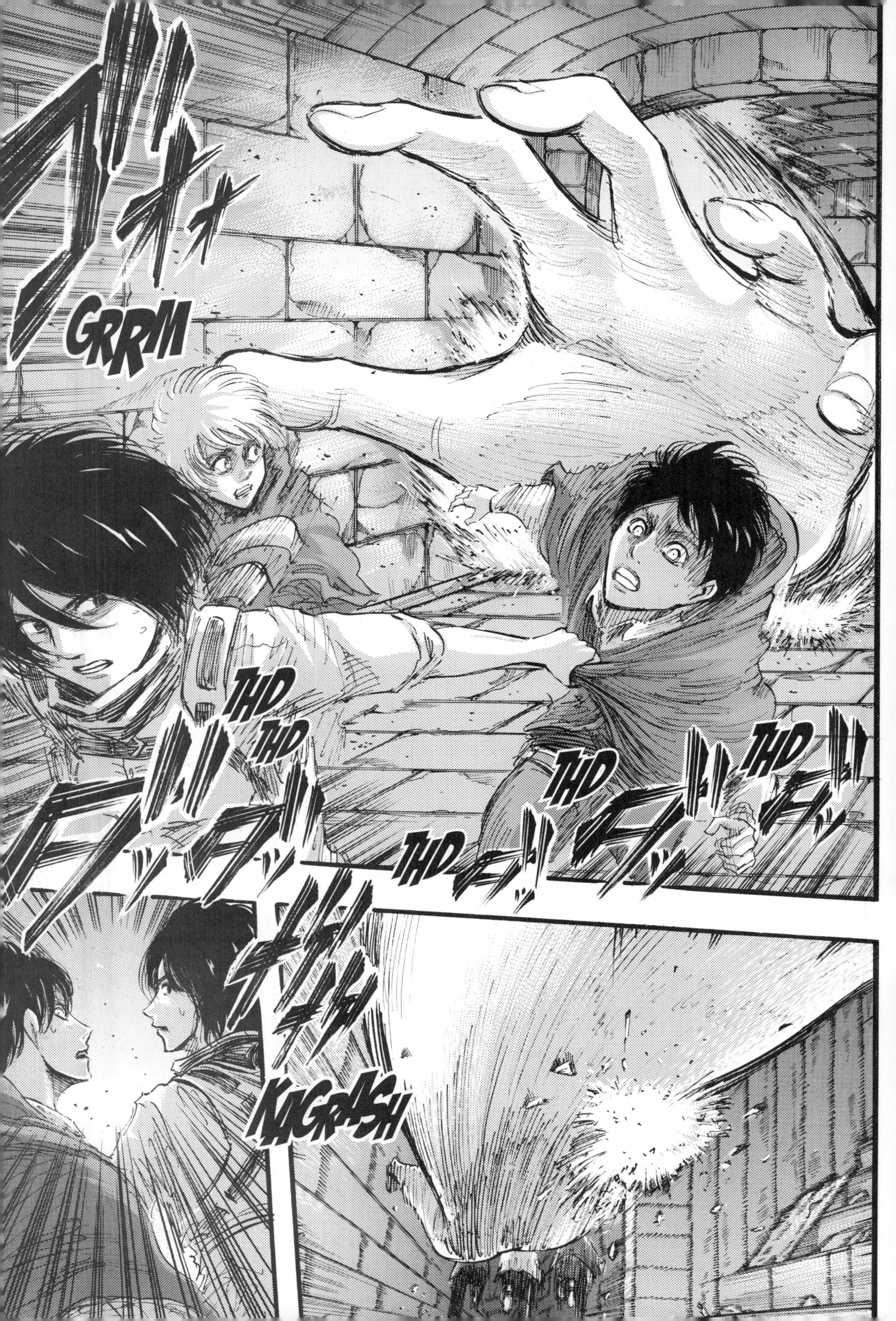
GRRM
THD
THD
THD
THD
THD
KACRASH

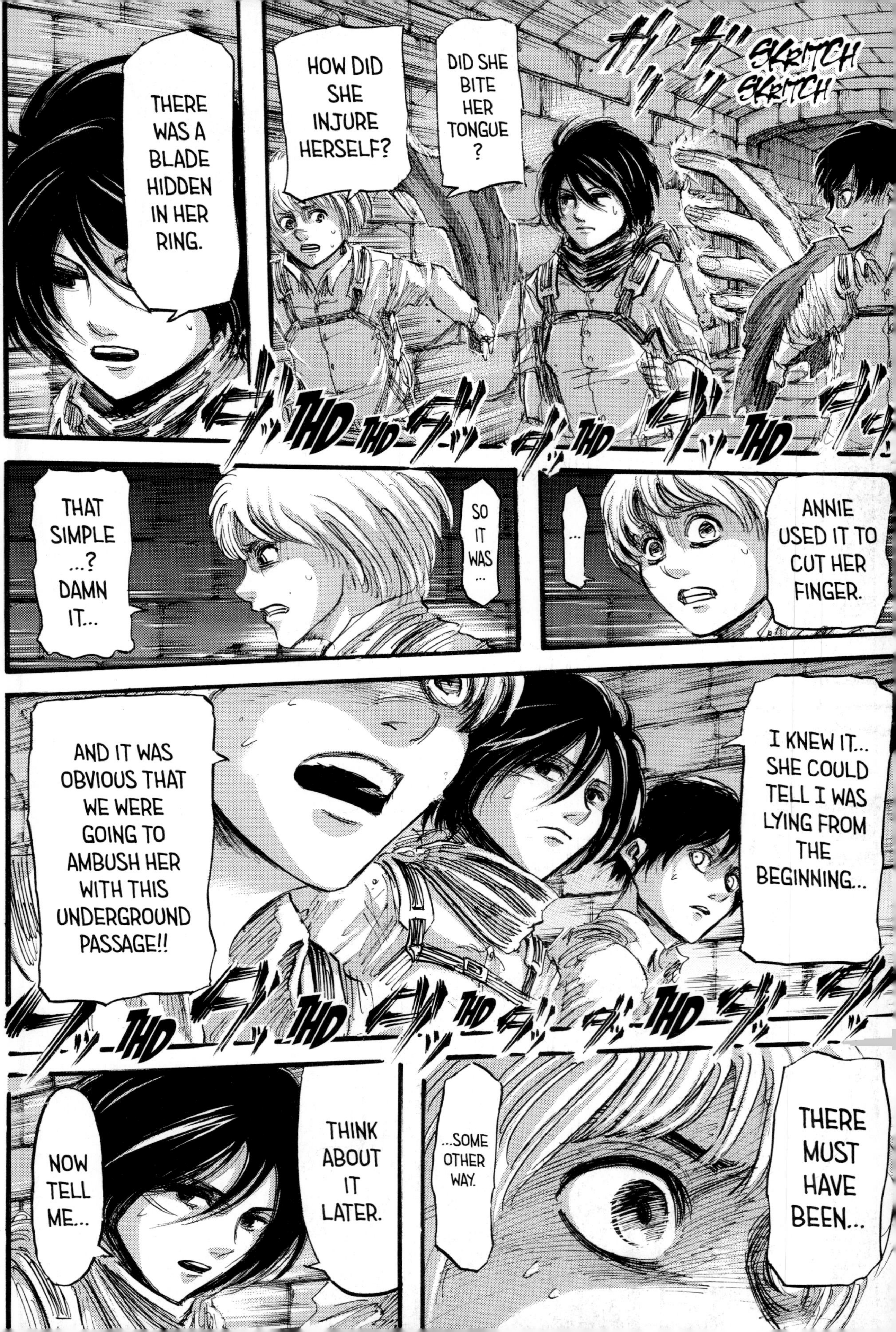
SKRITCH SKRITCH
DID SHE BITE HER TONGUE ?
HOW DID SHE INJURE HERSELF?
THERE WAS A BLADE HIDDEN IN HER RING.
THD THD THD THD
ANNIE USED IT TO CUT HER FINGER.
...
SO IT WAS ...
THAT SIMPLE ...? DAMN IT...
I KNEW IT... SHE COULD TELL I WAS LYING FROM THE BEGINNING...
AND IT WAS OBVIOUS THAT WE WERE GOING TO AMBUSH HER WITH THIS UNDERGROUND PASSAGE!!
THD THD THD THD
THERE MUST HAVE BEEN...
...SOME OTHER WAY.
THINK ABOUT IT LATER.
NOW TELL ME...

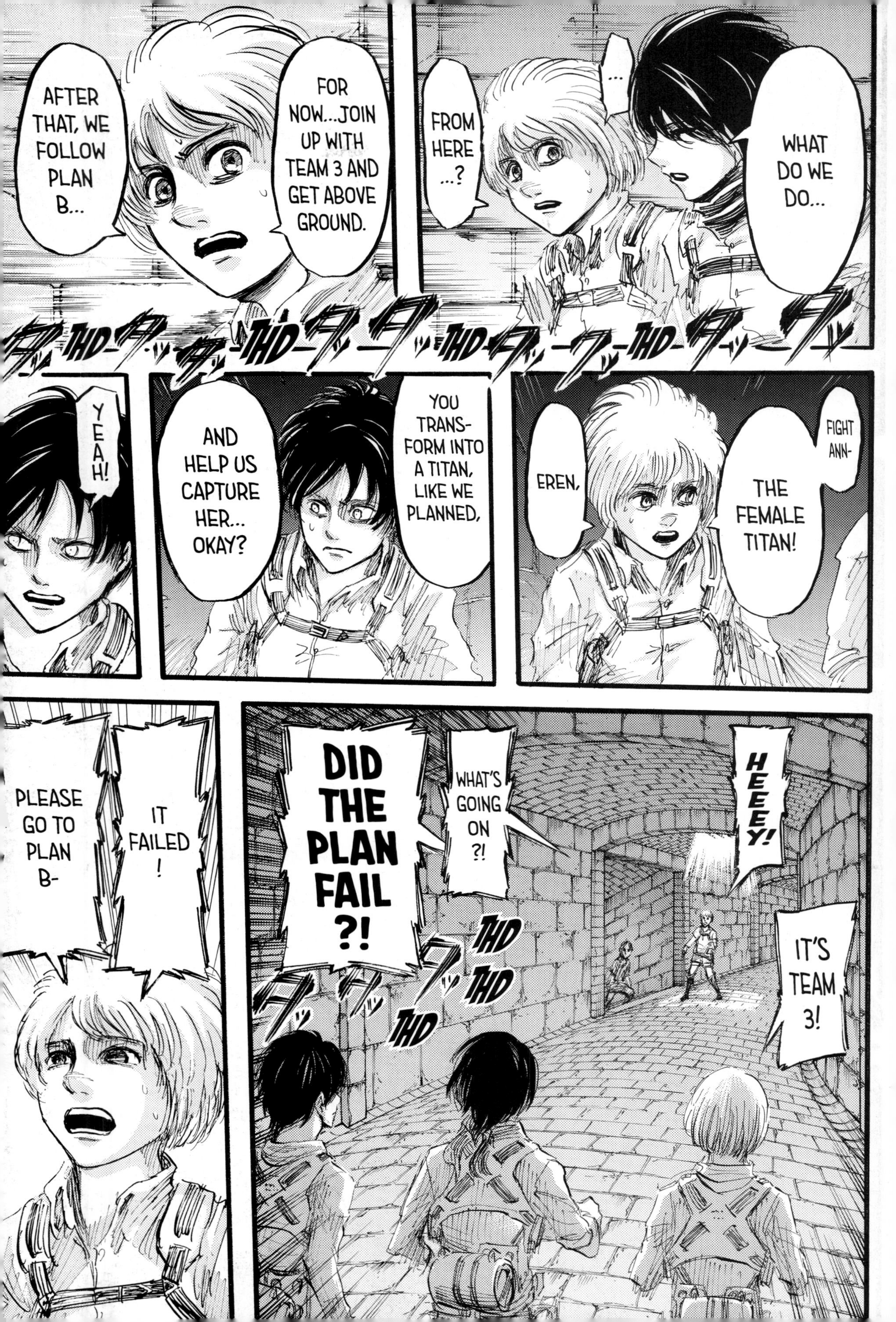
WHAT DO WE DO...
...
FROM HERE ...?
FOR NOW...JOIN UP WITH TEAM 3 AND GET ABOVE GROUND.
AFTER THAT, WE FOLLOW PLAN B...
THD THD THD THD
FIGHT ANN-
THE FEMALE TITAN!
EREN,
YOU TRANS-FORM INTO A TITAN, LIKE WE PLANNED,
AND HELP US CAPTURE HER... OKAY?
YEAH!
HEEEEY!
IT'S TEAM 3!
WHAT'S GOING ON ?!
DID THE PLAN FAIL ?!
THD THD THD
IT FAILED !
PLEASE GO TO PLAN B-

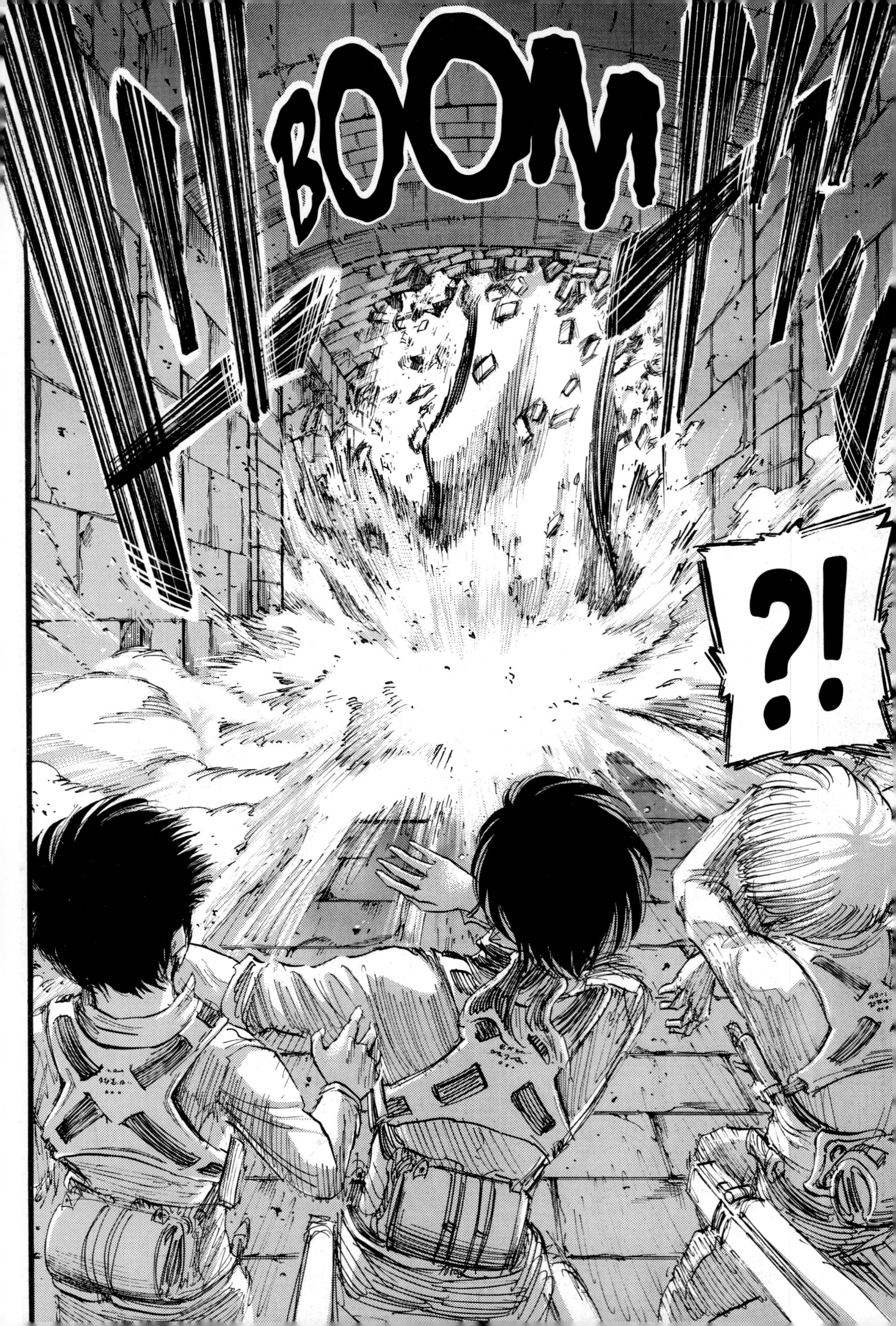
BOOM
?!

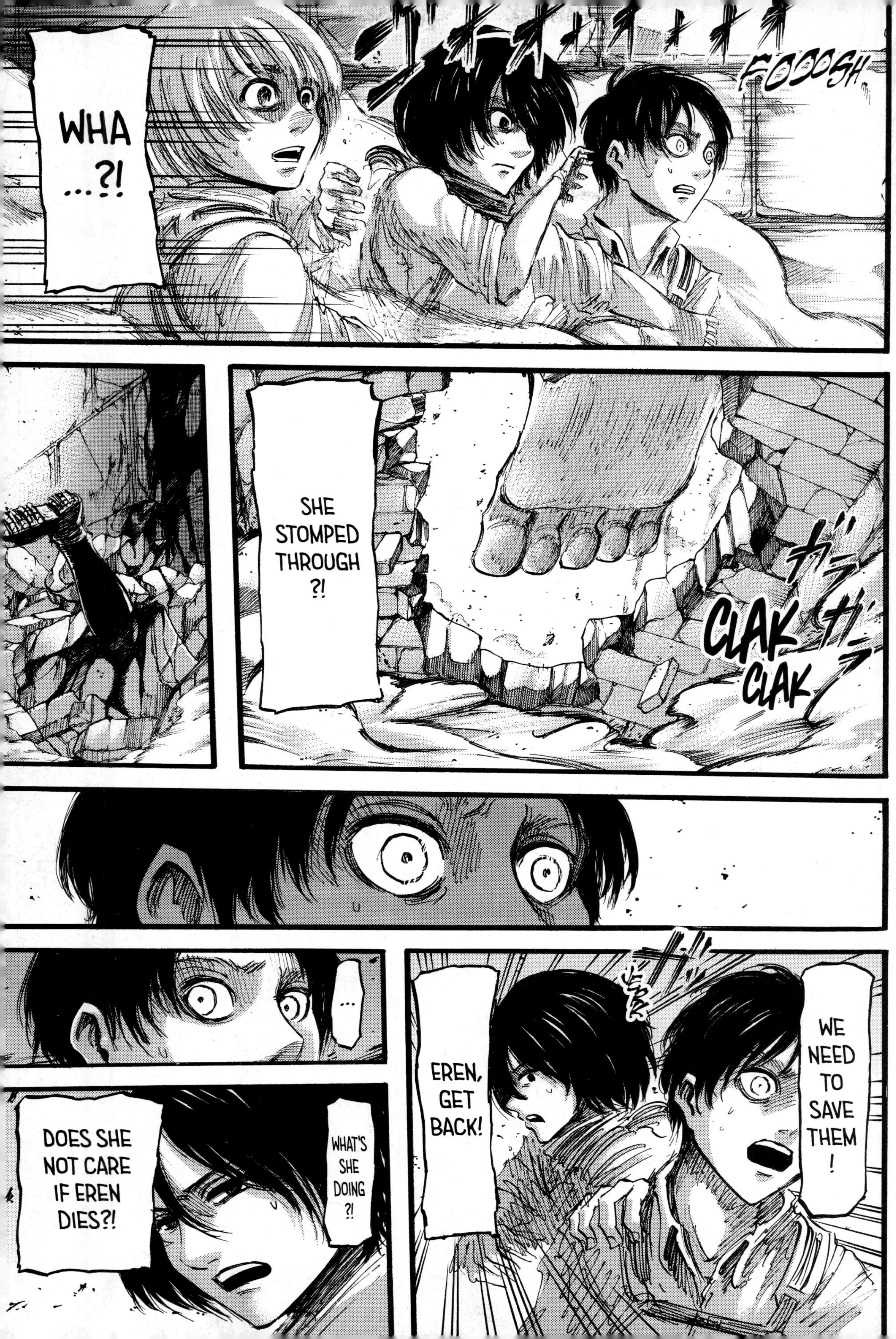
FOOOSH
WHA ...?!
CLAK CLAK
SHE STOMPED THROUGH ?!
WE NEED TO SAVE THEM !
EREN, GET BACK!
...
WHAT'S SHE DOING ?!
DOES SHE NOT CARE IF EREN DIES?!

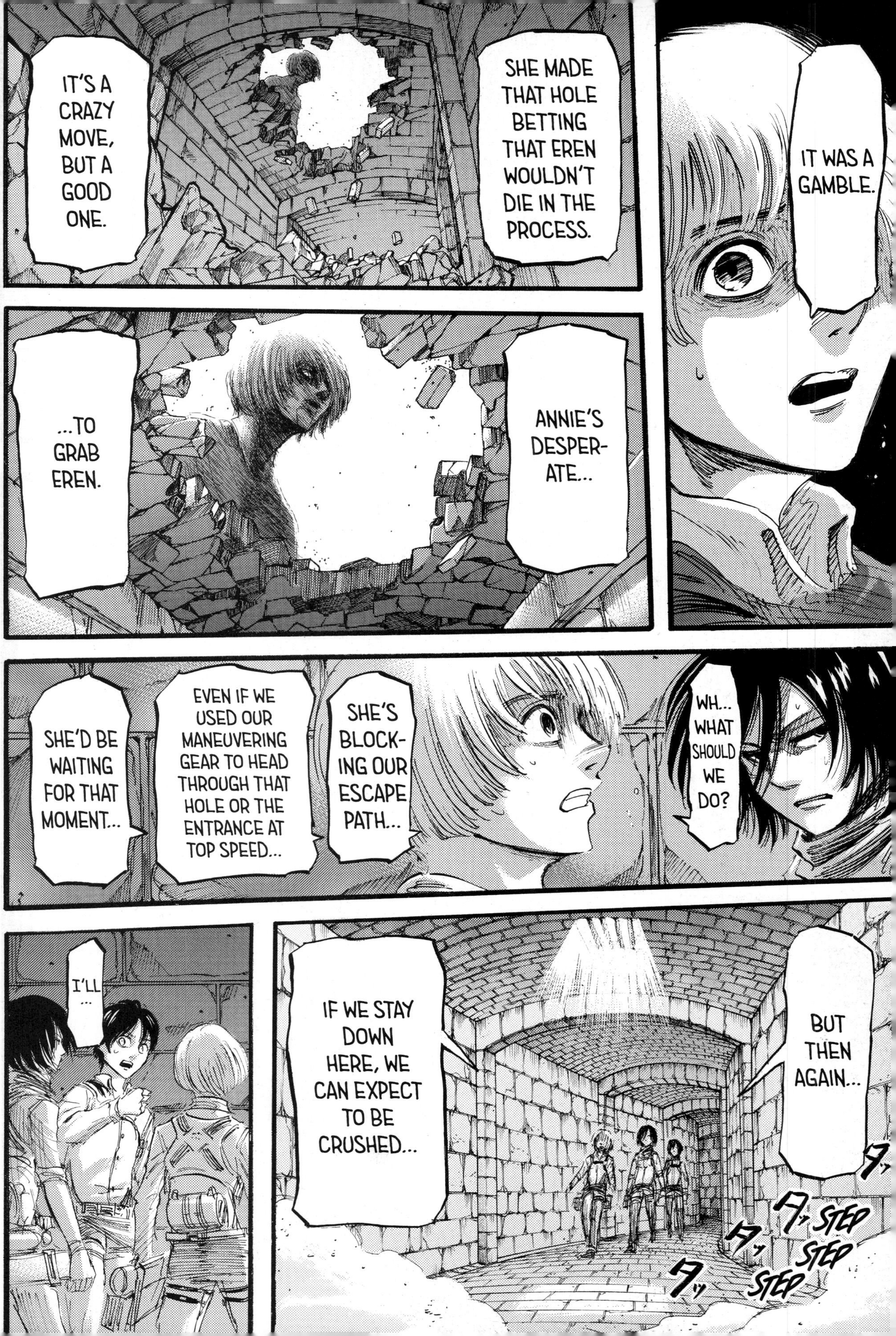
IT WAS A GAMBLE.
SHE MADE THAT HOLE BETTING THAT EREN WOULDN'T DIE IN THE PROCESS.
IT'S A CRAZY MOVE, BUT A GOOD ONE.
ANNIE'S DESPERATE...
...TO GRAB EREN.
WH... WHAT SHOULD WE DO?
SHE'S BLOCKING OUR ESCAPE PATH...
EVEN IF WE USED OUR MANEUVERING GEAR TO HEAD THROUGH THAT HOLE OR THE ENTRANCE AT TOP SPEED...
SHE'D BE WAITING FOR THAT MOMENT...
BUT THEN AGAIN...
IF WE STAY DOWN HERE, WE CAN EXPECT TO BE CRUSHED...
STEP STEP STEP
I'LL ...

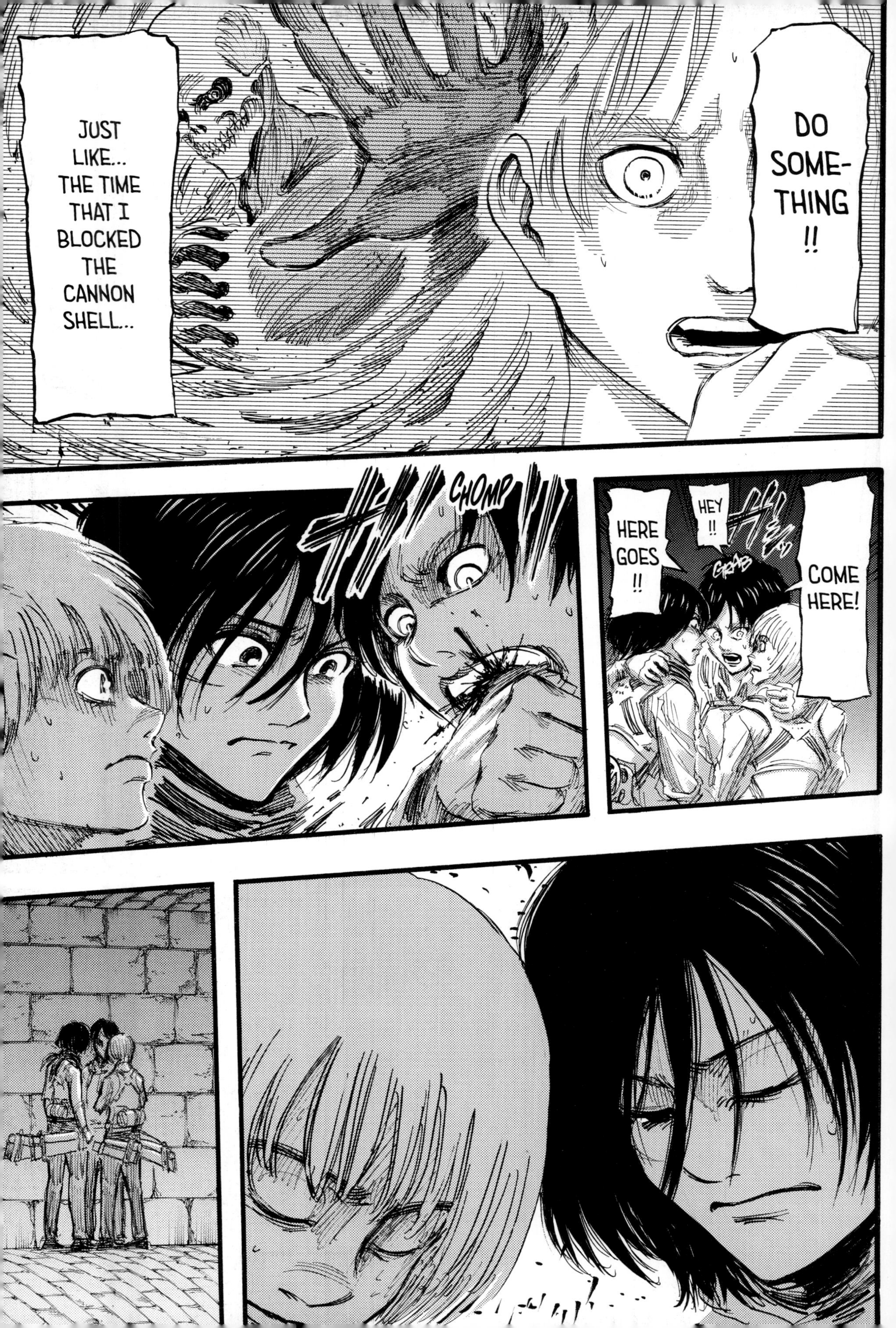
DO SOMETHING!!
JUST LIKE... THE TIME THAT I BLOCKED THE CANNON SHELL...
COME HERE!
HEY!!
GRAB
HERE GOES!!
CHOMP

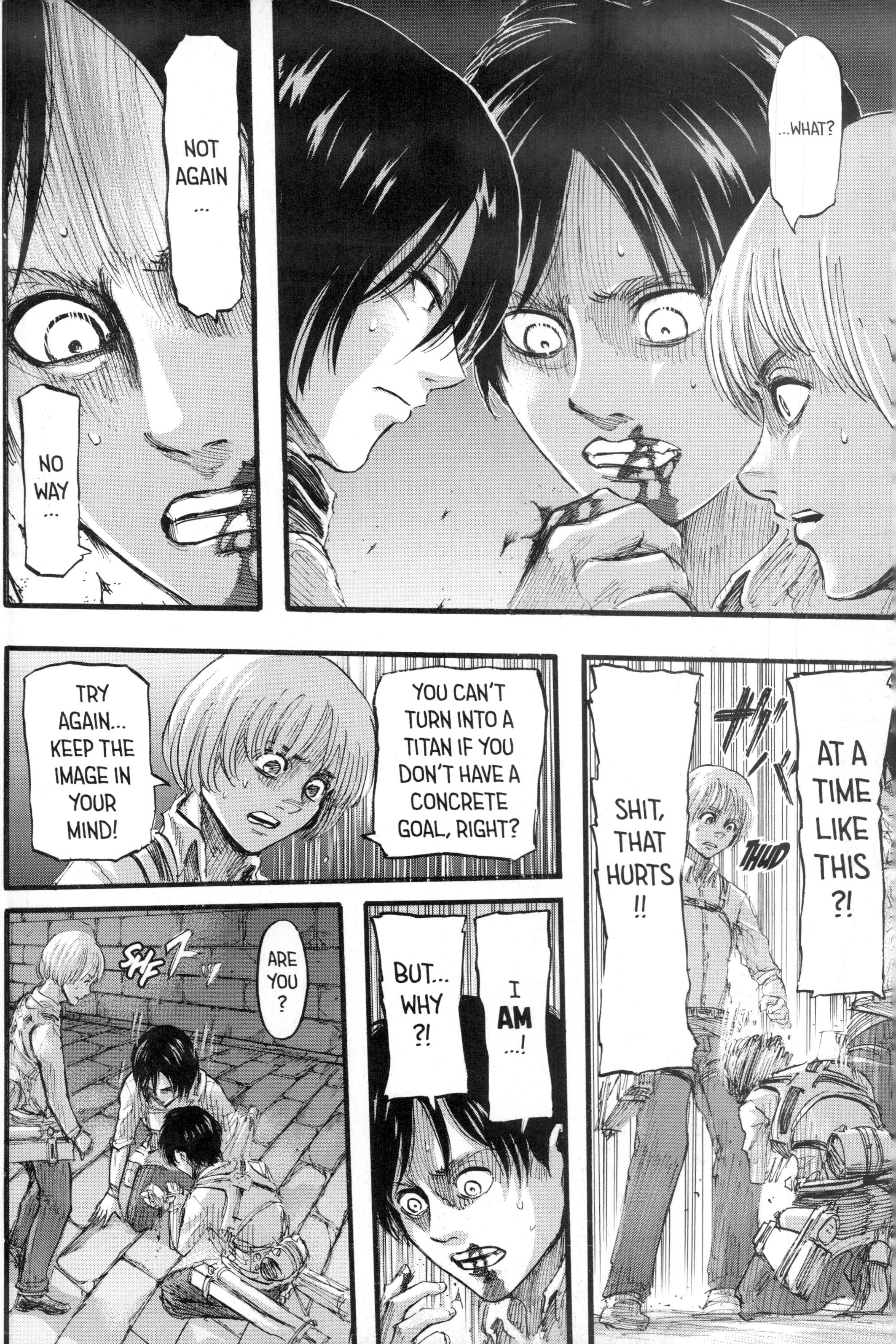
...WHAT?
NOT AGAIN ...
NO WAY ...
AT A TIME LIKE THIS ?!
SHIT, THAT HURTS !!
THUD
YOU CAN'T TURN INTO A TITAN IF YOU DON'T HAVE A CONCRETE GOAL, RIGHT?
TRY AGAIN... KEEP THE IMAGE IN YOUR MIND!
I AM ...!
BUT... WHY ?!
ARE YOU ?
SHF

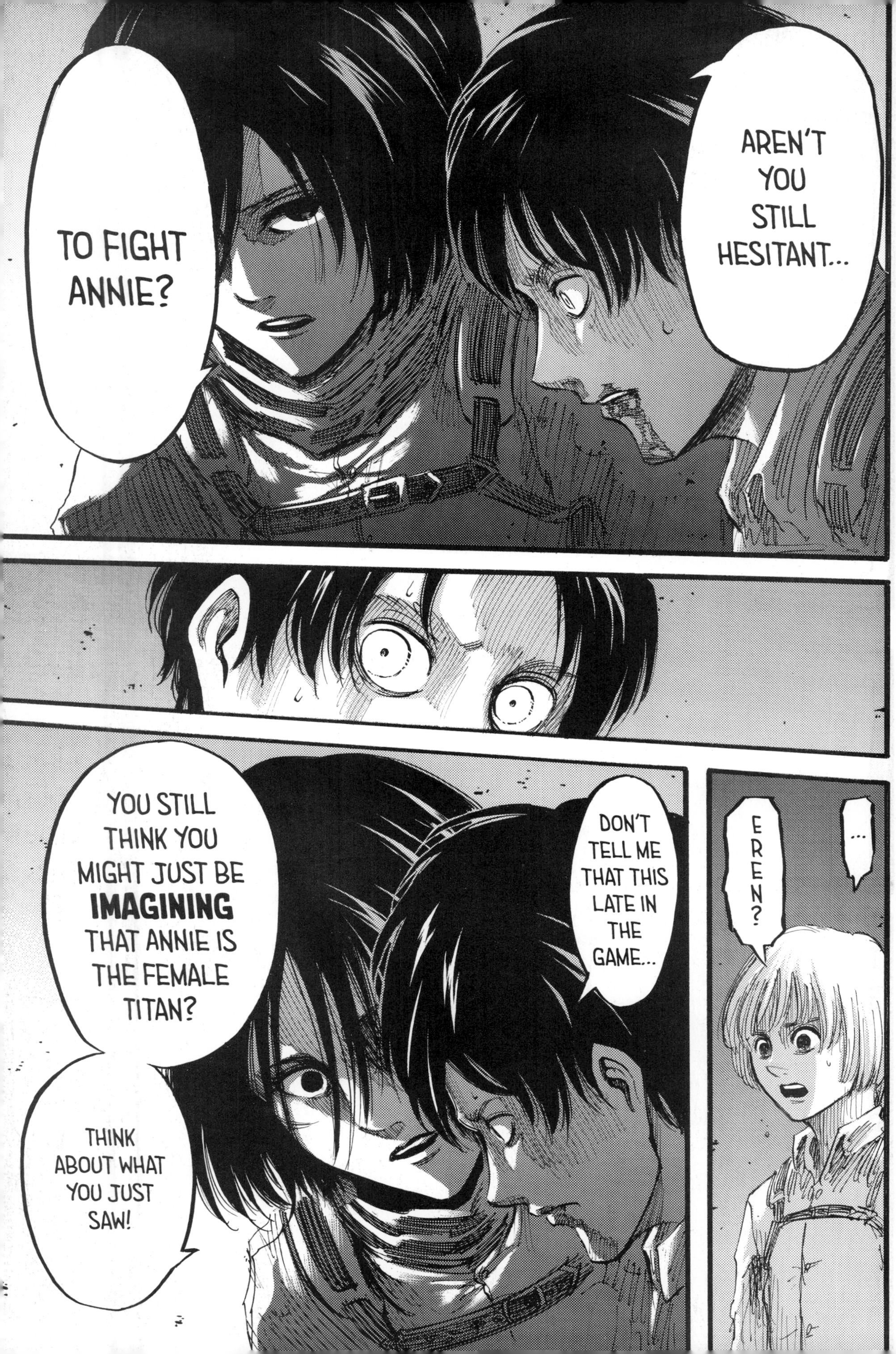
AREN'T YOU STILL HESITANT...
TO FIGHT ANNIE?
...
EREN?
DON'T TELL ME THAT THIS LATE IN THE GAME...
YOU STILL THINK YOU MIGHT JUST BE **IMAGINING** THAT ANNIE IS THE FEMALE TITAN?
THINK ABOUT WHAT YOU JUST SAW!

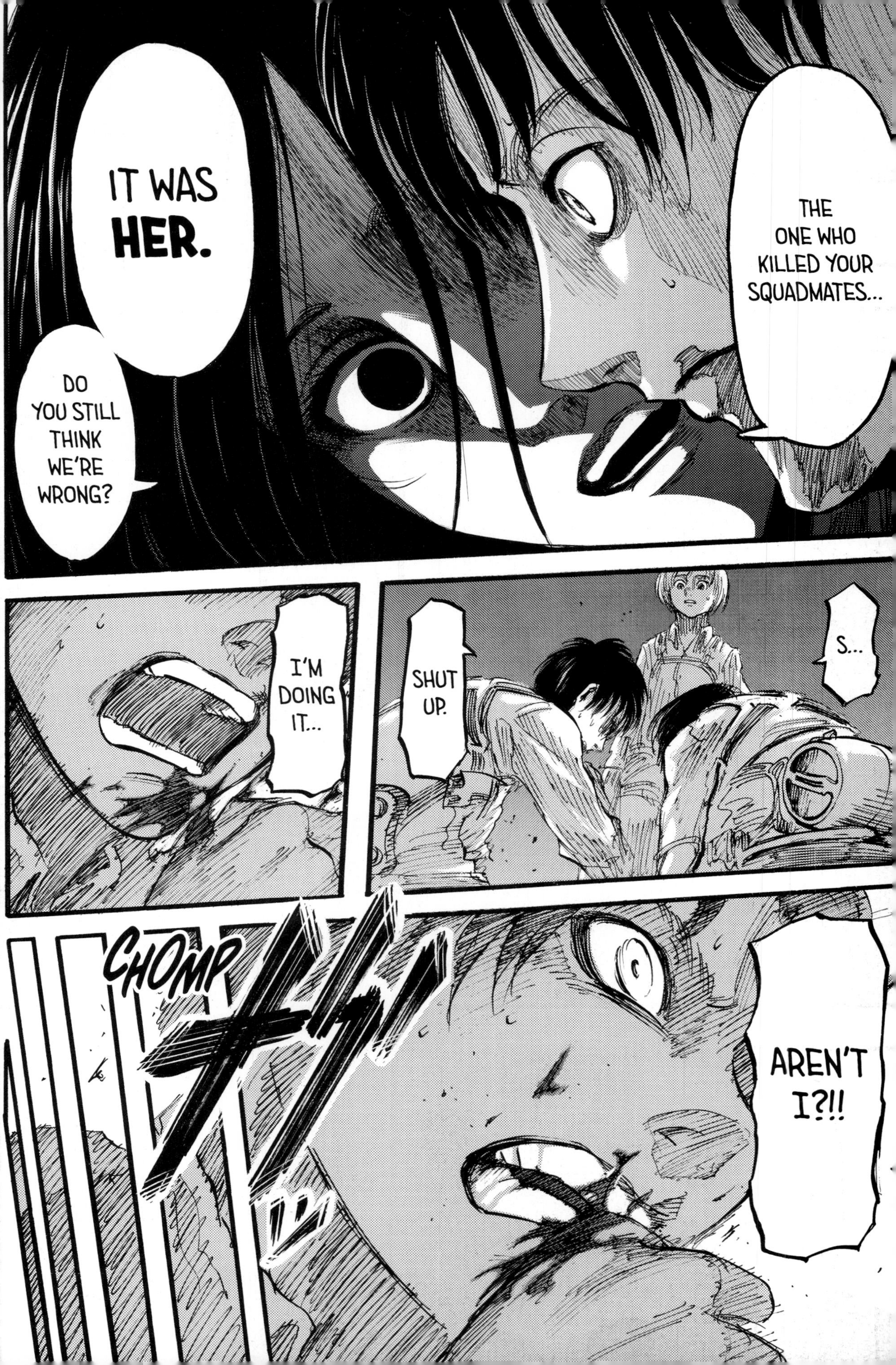
THE ONE WHO KILLED YOUR SQUADMATES...
IT WAS HER.
DO YOU STILL THINK WE'RE WRONG?
S...
SHUT UP.
I'M DOING IT...
AREN'T I?!!
CHOMP

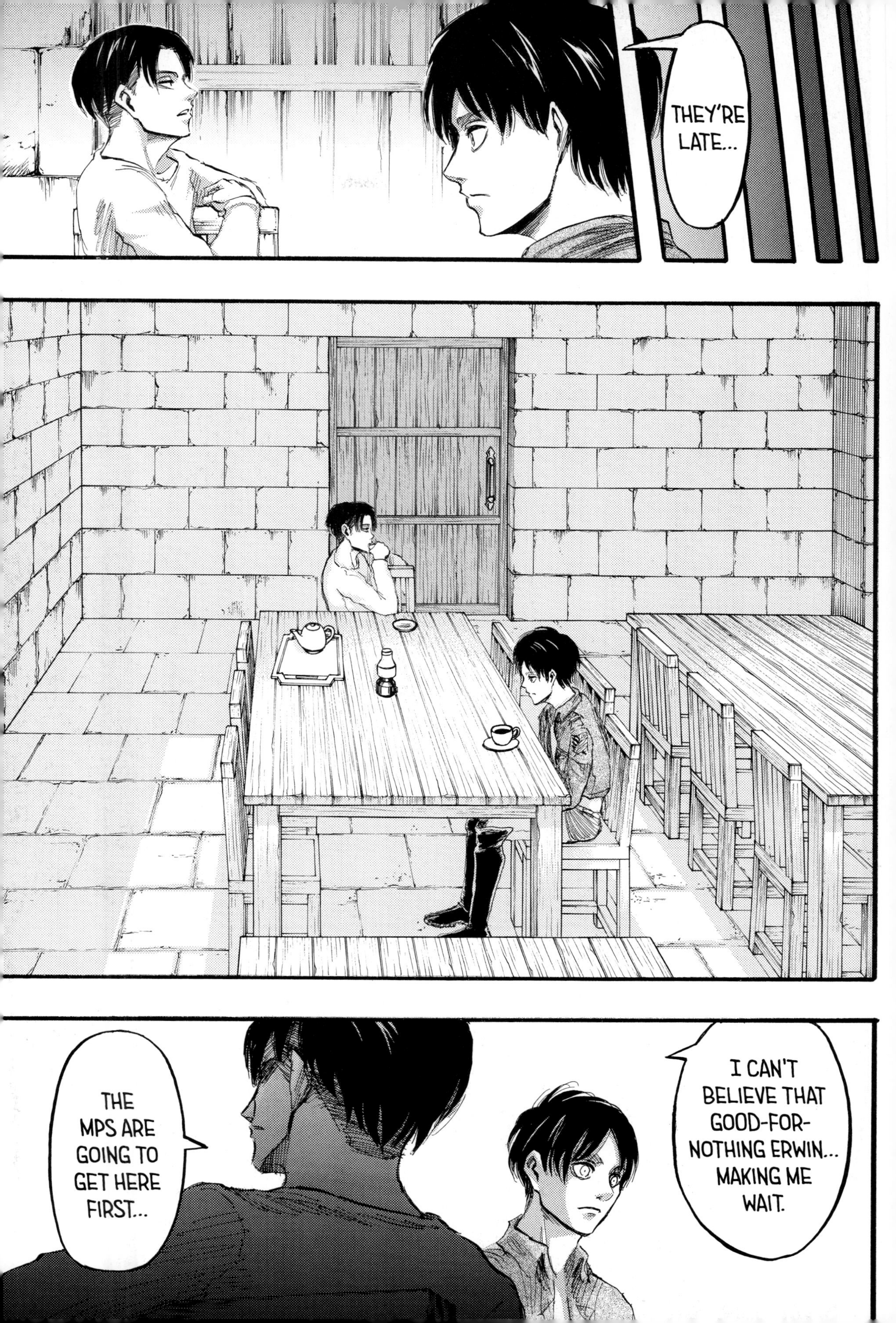
THEY'RE LATE...
I CAN'T BELIEVE THAT GOOD-FOR-NOTHING ERWIN... MAKING ME WAIT.
THE MPS ARE GOING TO GET HERE FIRST...

MOST LIKELY... HE'S HAVING SOME TROUBLE TAKING A SHIT.

SLURP

HA HA...

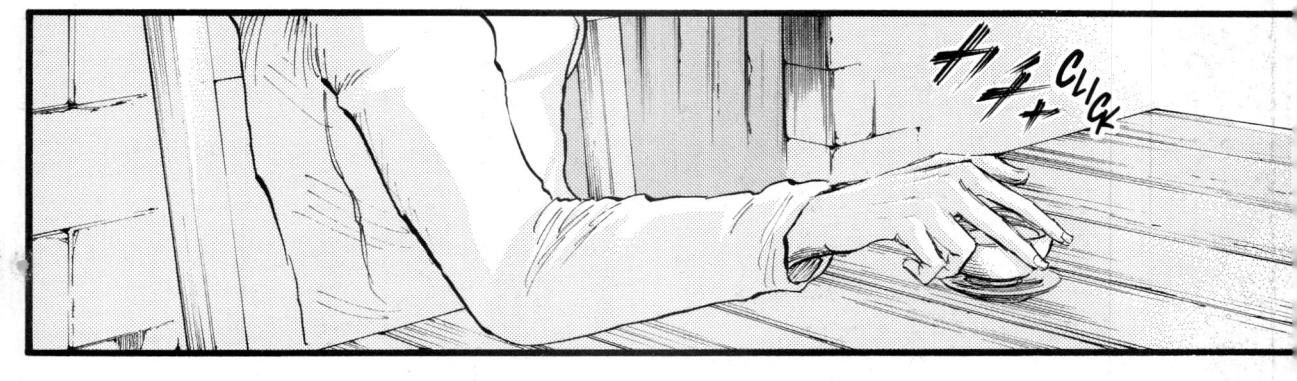

CLICK

...PRETTY TALKATIVE TODAY.

YOU'RE...

CAP-TAIN...

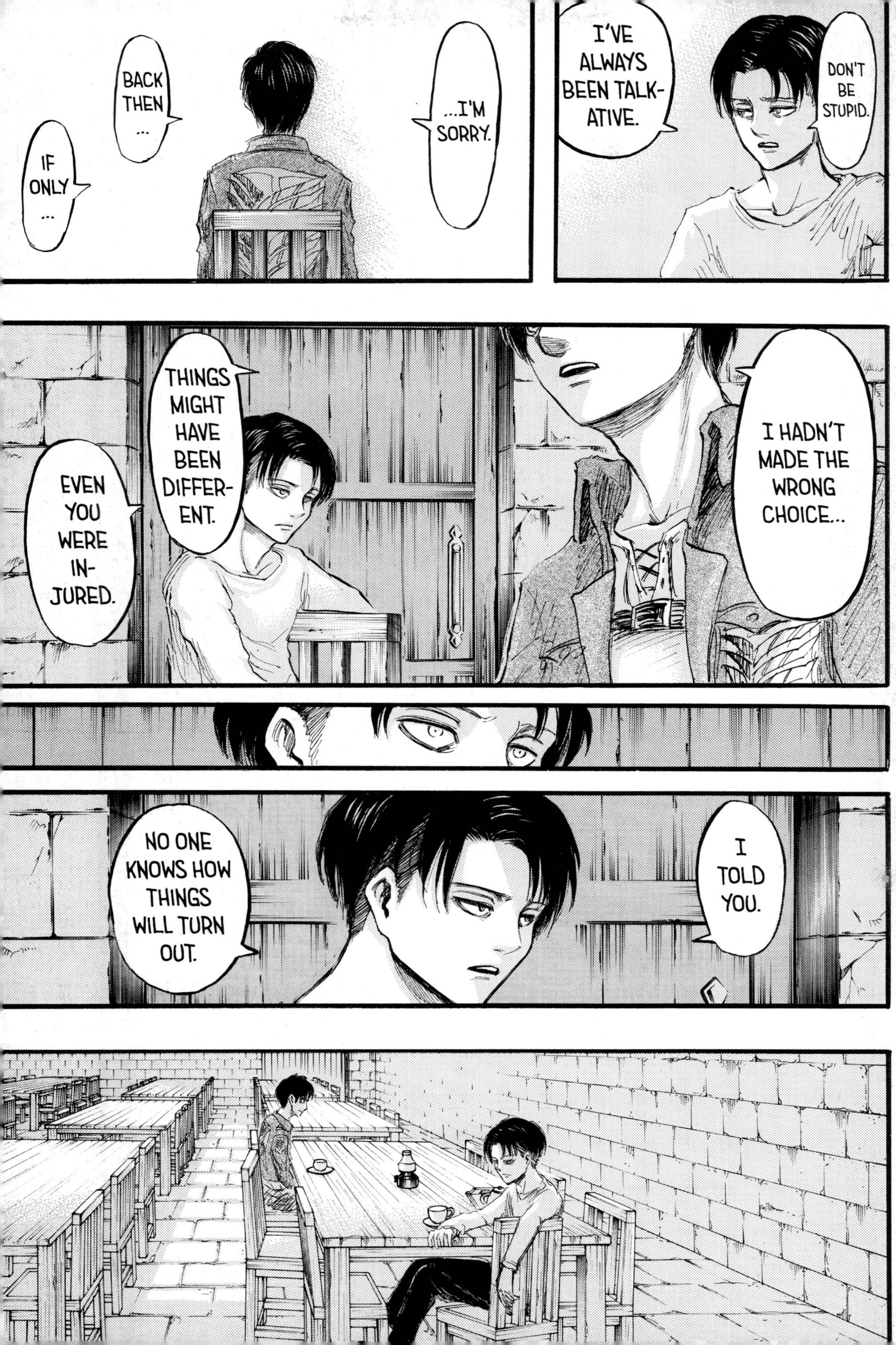
DON'T BE STUPID.
I'VE ALWAYS BEEN TALK-ATIVE.
...I'M SORRY.
BACK THEN ...
IF ONLY ...
I HADN'T MADE THE WRONG CHOICE...
THINGS MIGHT HAVE BEEN DIFFER-ENT.
EVEN YOU WERE IN-JURED.
I TOLD YOU.
NO ONE KNOWS HOW THINGS WILL TURN OUT.

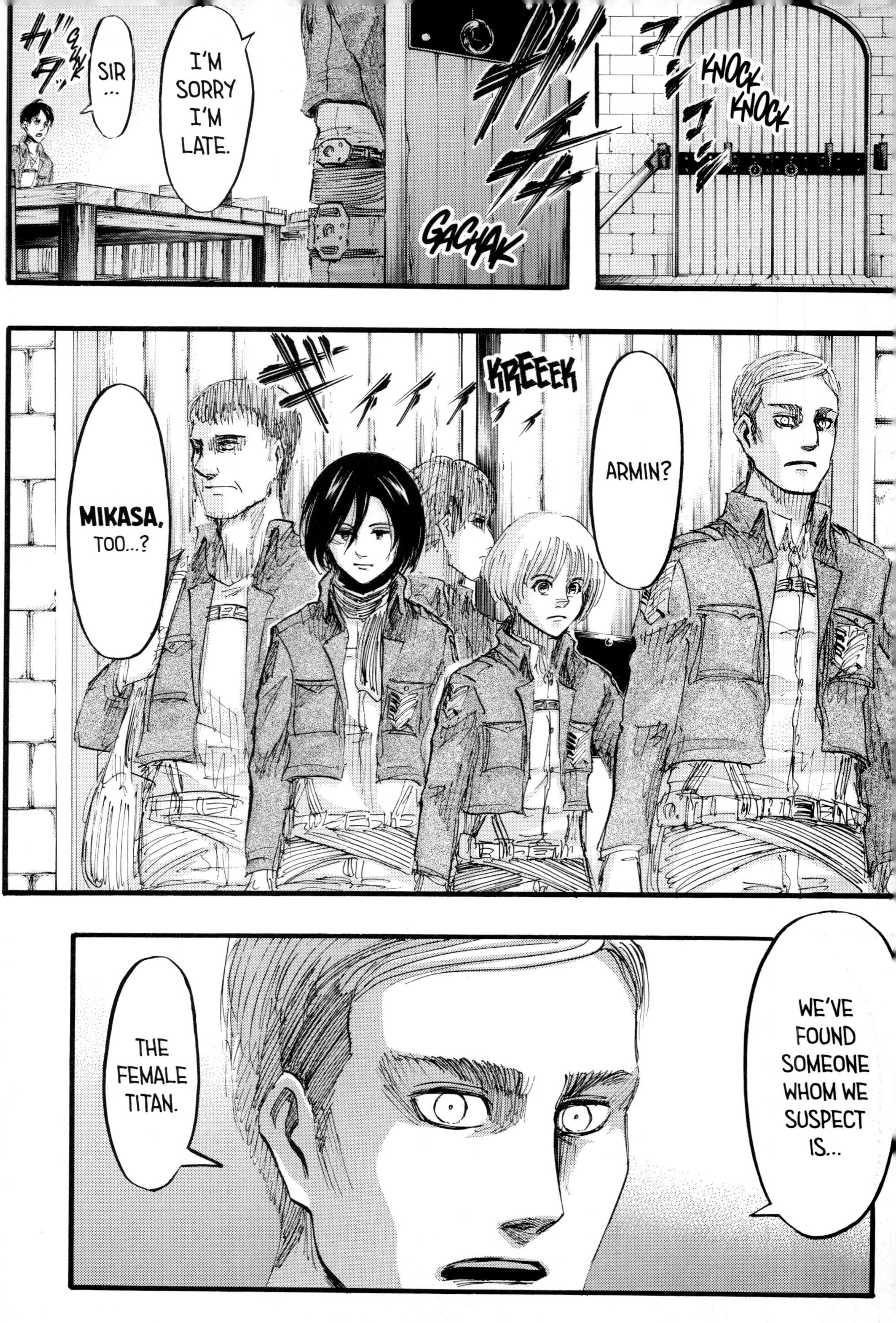
KNOCK KNOCK
GACHAK
I'M SORRY I'M LATE.
SIR ...
CLUNK
KREEEK
ARMIN?
MIKASA, TOO...?
WE'VE FOUND SOMEONE WHOM WE SUSPECT IS...
THE FEMALE TITAN.

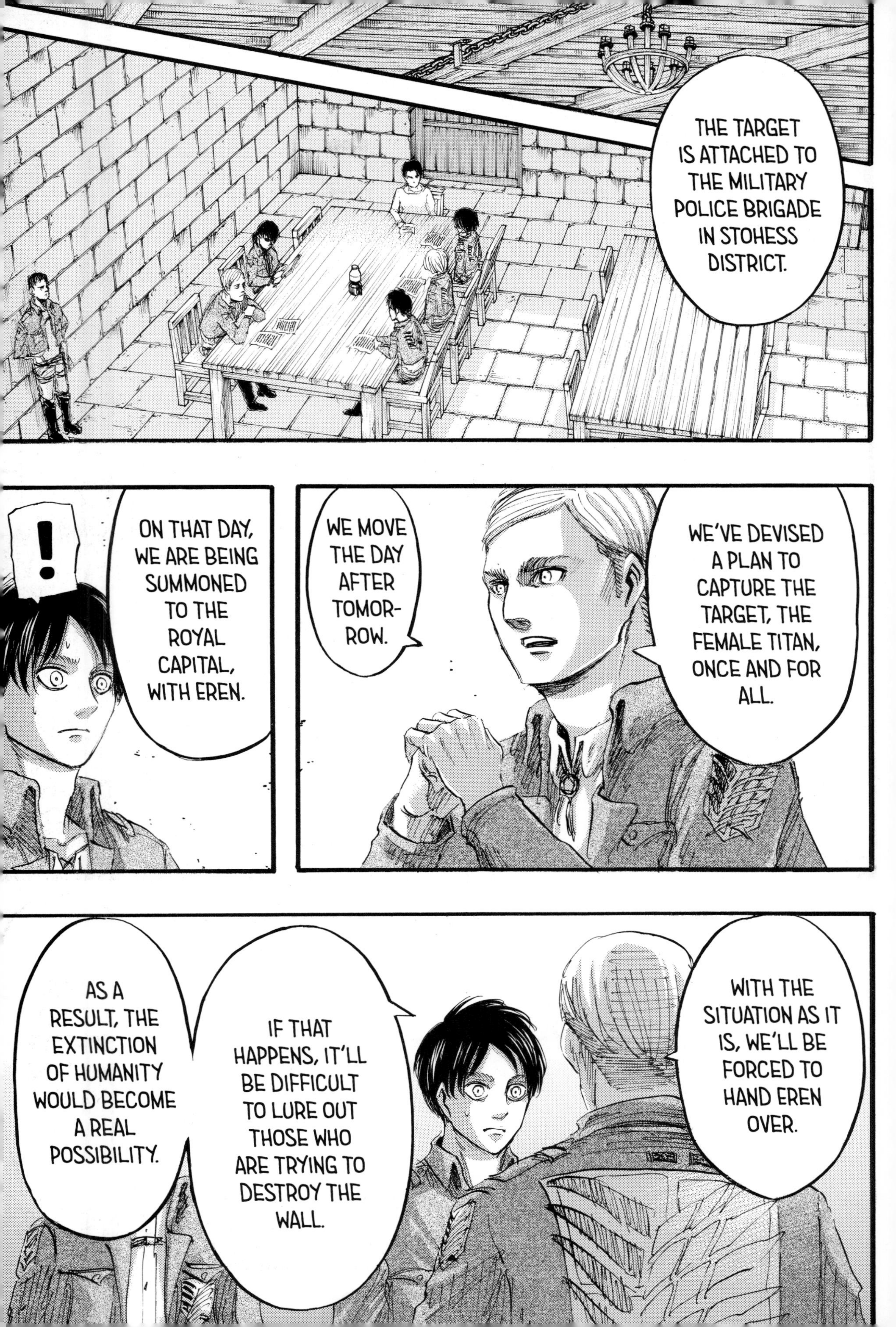
THE TARGET IS ATTACHED TO THE MILITARY POLICE BRIGADE IN STOHESS DISTRICT.
WE'VE DEVISED A PLAN TO CAPTURE THE TARGET, THE FEMALE TITAN, ONCE AND FOR ALL.
WE MOVE THE DAY AFTER TOMOR-ROW.
ON THAT DAY, WE ARE BEING SUMMONED TO THE ROYAL CAPITAL, WITH EREN.
!
WITH THE SITUATION AS IT IS, WE'LL BE FORCED TO HAND EREN OVER.
IF THAT HAPPENS, IT'LL BE DIFFICULT TO LURE OUT THOSE WHO ARE TRYING TO DESTROY THE WALL.
AS A RESULT, THE EXTINCTION OF HUMANITY WOULD BECOME A REAL POSSIBILITY.

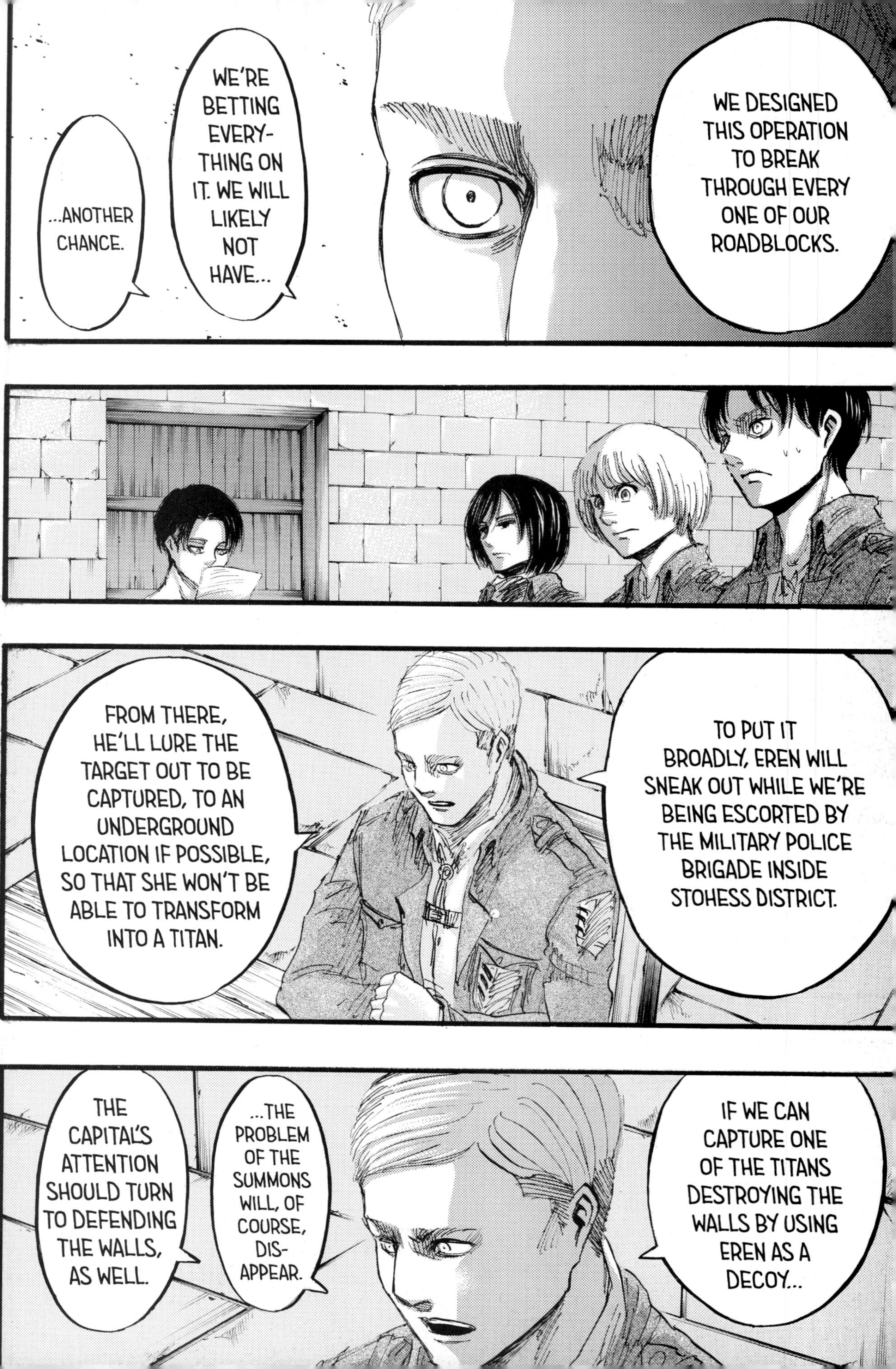
WE DESIGNED THIS OPERATION TO BREAK THROUGH EVERY ONE OF OUR ROADBLOCKS.
WE'RE BETTING EVERY-THING ON IT. WE WILL LIKELY NOT HAVE...
...ANOTHER CHANCE.
TO PUT IT BROADLY, EREN WILL SNEAK OUT WHILE WE'RE BEING ESCORTED BY THE MILITARY POLICE BRIGADE INSIDE STOHESS DISTRICT.
FROM THERE, HE'LL LURE THE TARGET OUT TO BE CAPTURED, TO AN UNDERGROUND LOCATION IF POSSIBLE, SO THAT SHE WON'T BE ABLE TO TRANSFORM INTO A TITAN.
IF WE CAN CAPTURE ONE OF THE TITANS DESTROYING THE WALLS BY USING EREN AS A DECOY...
...THE PROBLEM OF THE SUMMONS WILL, OF COURSE, DIS-APPEAR.
THE CAPITAL'S ATTENTION SHOULD TURN TO DEFENDING THE WALLS, AS WELL.

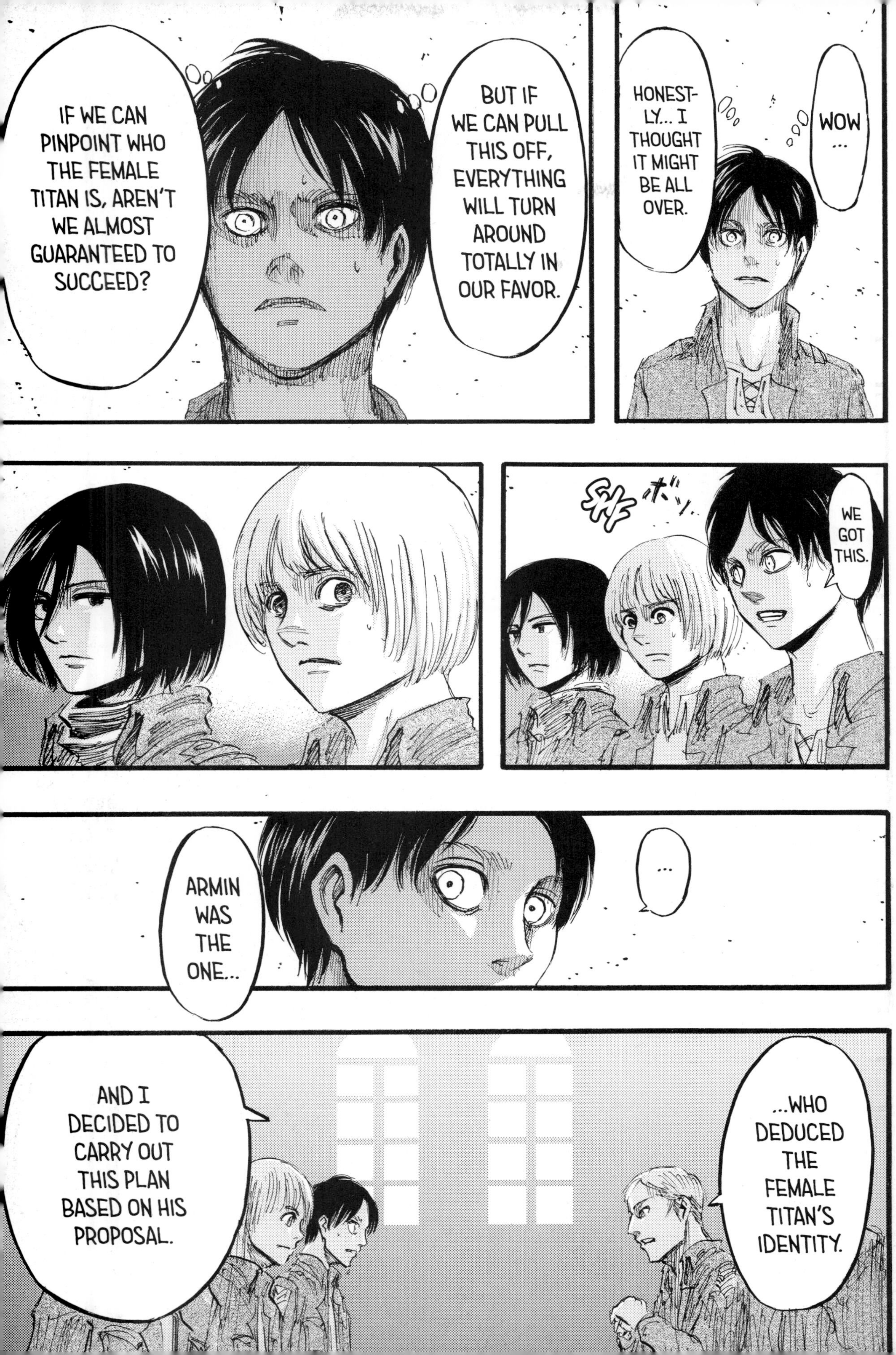
WOW...
HONEST-LY... I THOUGHT IT MIGHT BE ALL OVER.
BUT IF WE CAN PULL THIS OFF, EVERYTHING WILL TURN AROUND TOTALLY IN OUR FAVOR.
IF WE CAN PINPOINT WHO THE FEMALE TITAN IS, AREN'T WE ALMOST GUARANTEED TO SUCCEED?
WE GOT THIS.
SHK
ボッ
...
ARMIN WAS THE ONE...
...WHO DEDUCED THE FEMALE TITAN'S IDENTITY.
AND I DECIDED TO CARRY OUT THIS PLAN BASED ON HIS PROPOSAL.

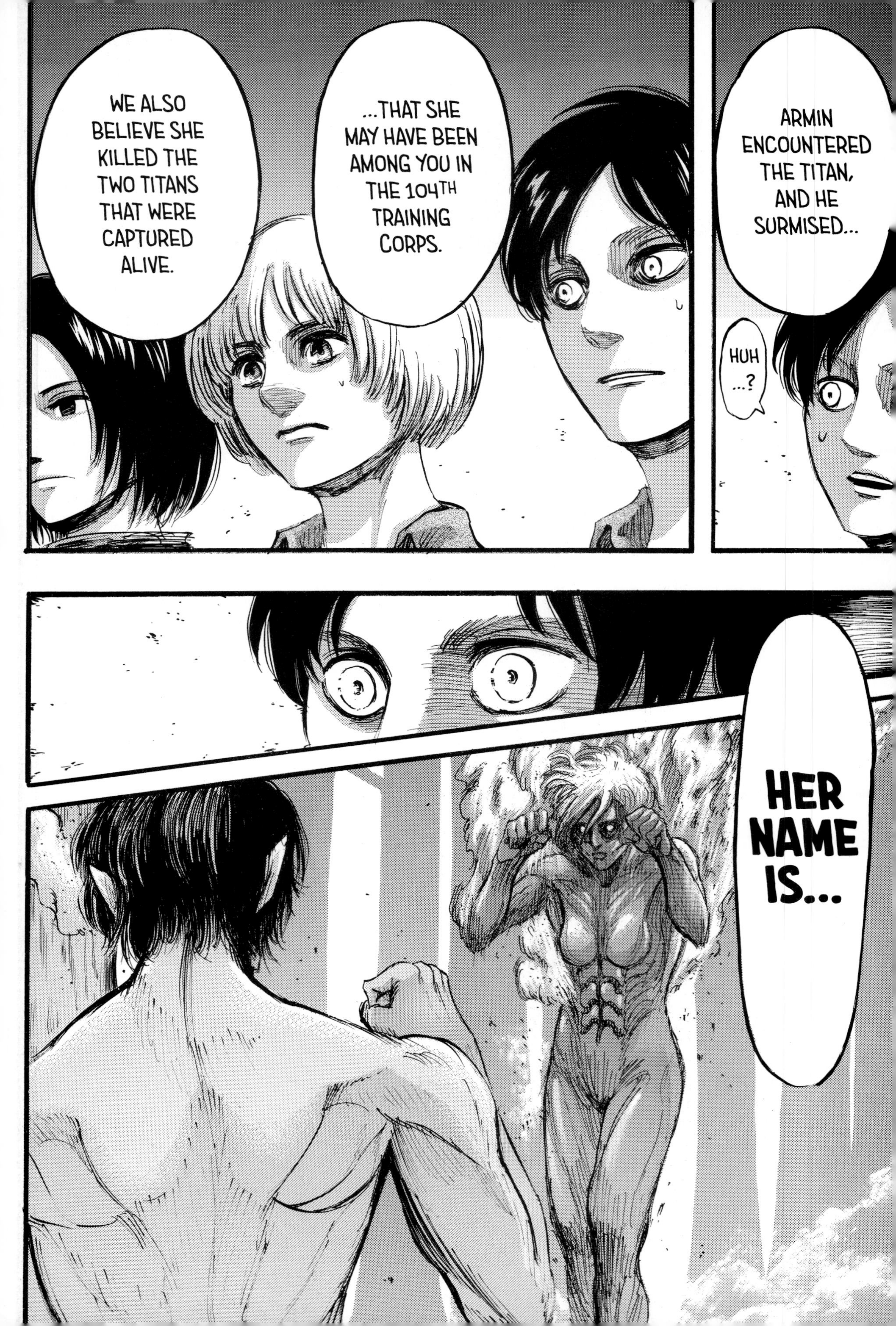
ARMIN ENCOUNTERED THE TITAN, AND HE SURMISED...
HUH ...?
...THAT SHE MAY HAVE BEEN AMONG YOU IN THE 104TH TRAINING CORPS.
WE ALSO BELIEVE SHE KILLED THE TWO TITANS THAT WERE CAPTURED ALIVE.
HER NAME IS...

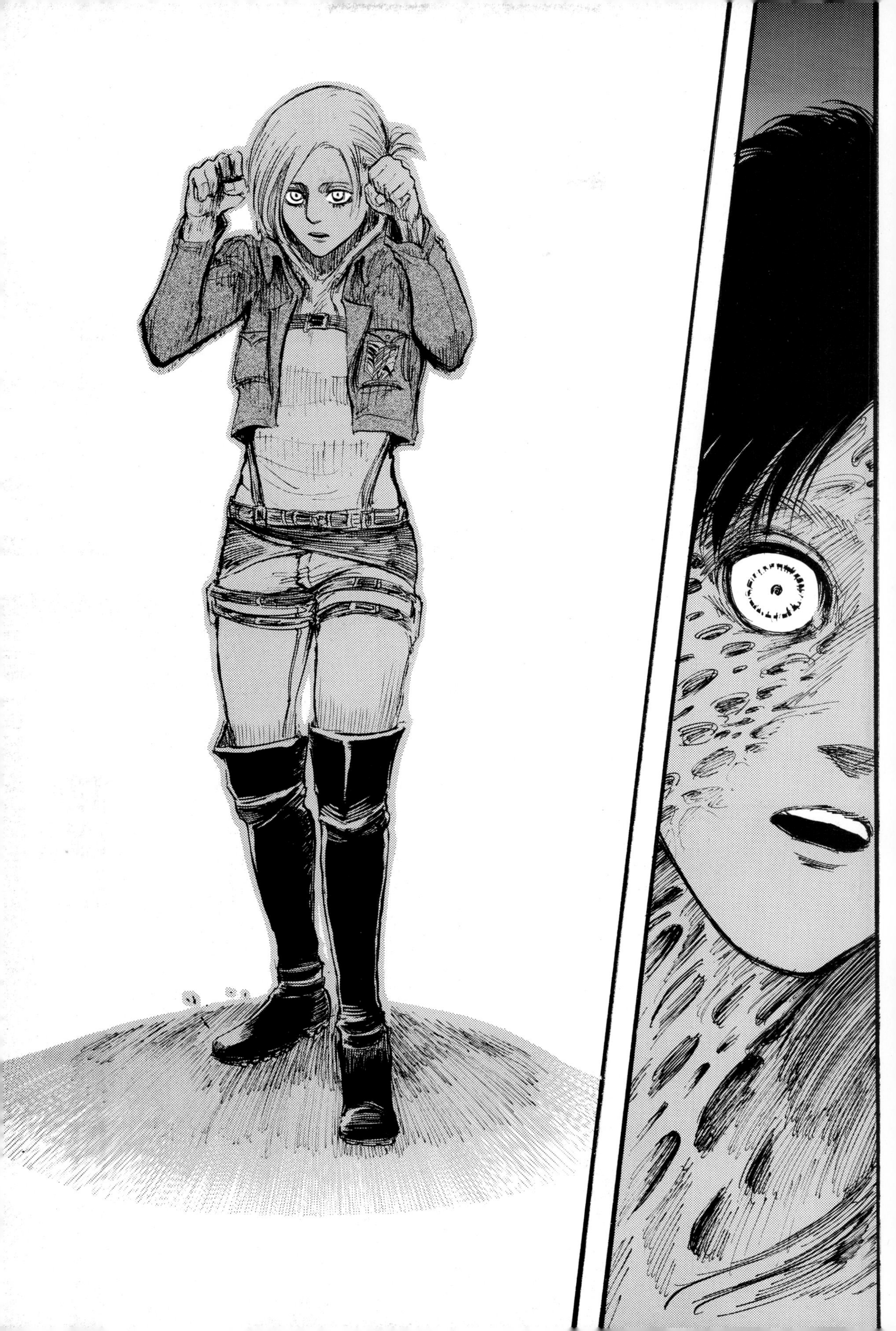

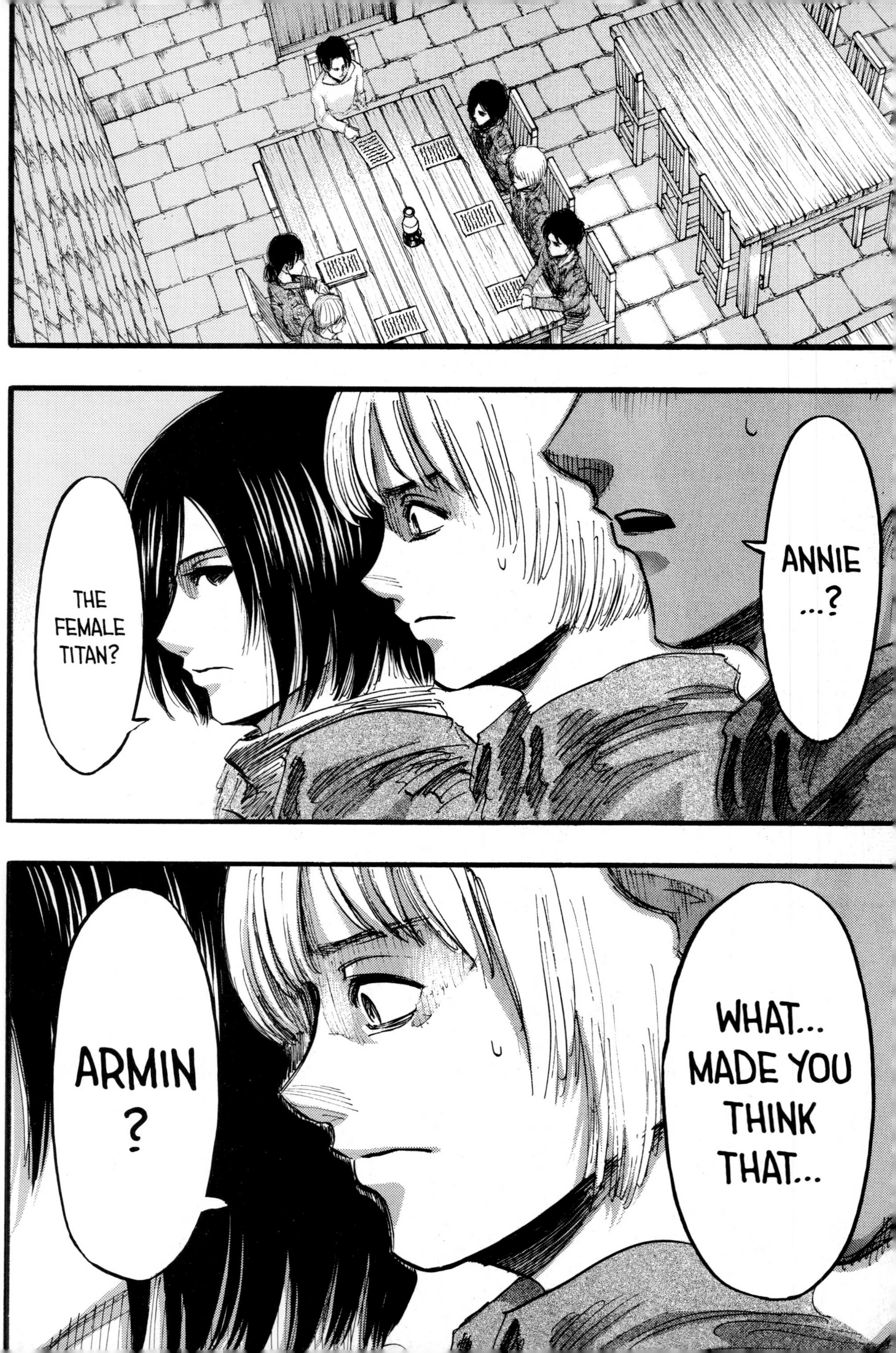
ANNIE ...?
THE FEMALE TITAN?
WHAT... MADE YOU THINK THAT...
ARMIN ?

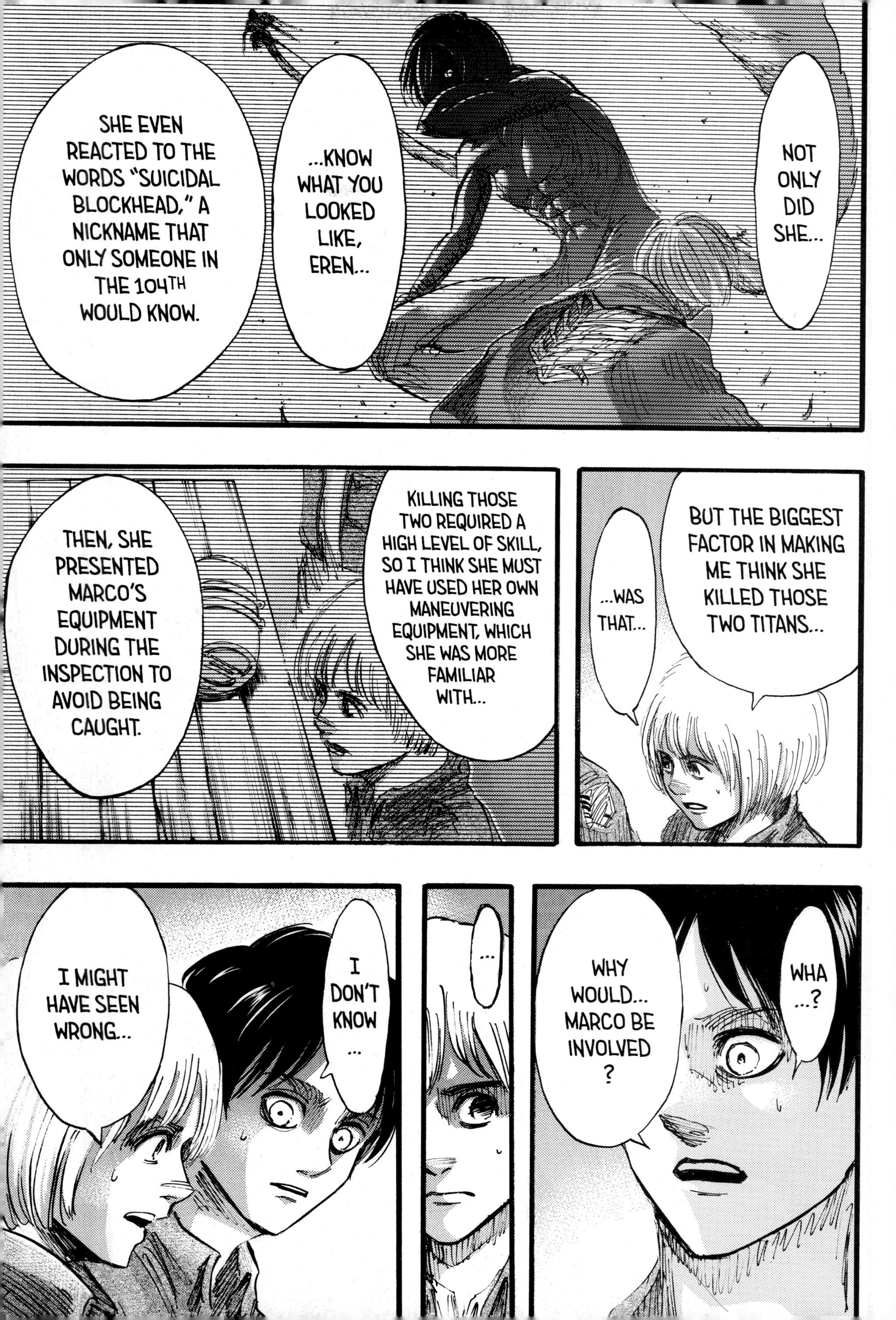
NOT ONLY DID SHE...
...KNOW WHAT YOU LOOKED LIKE, EREN...
SHE EVEN REACTED TO THE WORDS "SUICIDAL BLOCKHEAD," A NICKNAME THAT ONLY SOMEONE IN THE 104TH WOULD KNOW.
BUT THE BIGGEST FACTOR IN MAKING ME THINK SHE KILLED THOSE TWO TITANS...
...WAS THAT...
KILLING THOSE TWO REQUIRED A HIGH LEVEL OF SKILL, SO I THINK SHE MUST HAVE USED HER OWN MANEUVERING EQUIPMENT, WHICH SHE WAS MORE FAMILIAR WITH...
THEN, SHE PRESENTED MARCO'S EQUIPMENT DURING THE INSPECTION TO AVOID BEING CAUGHT.
WHA ...?
WHY WOULD... MARCO BE INVOLVED ?
...
I DON'T KNOW ...
I MIGHT HAVE SEEN WRONG...

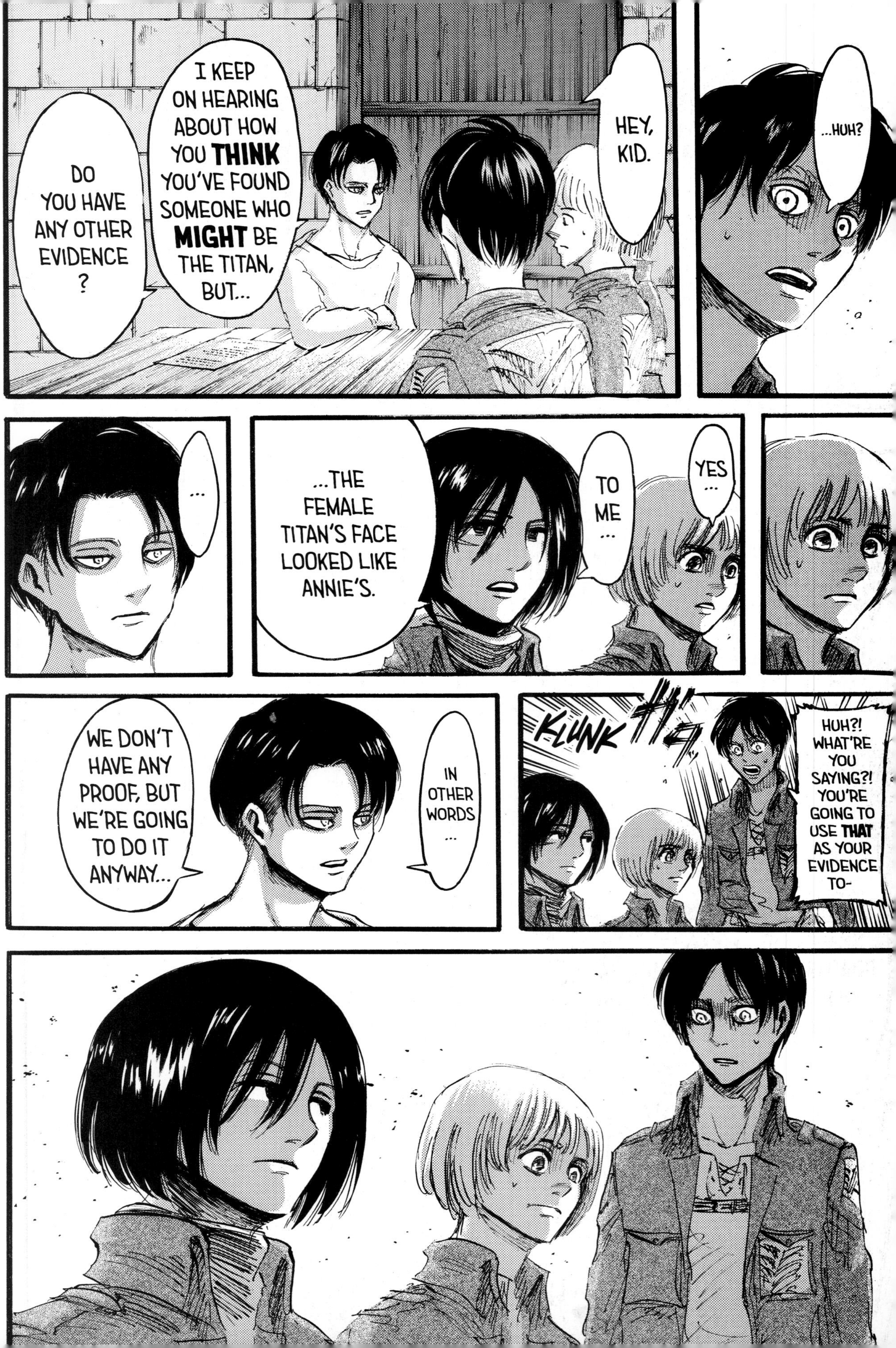
...HUH?
HEY, KID.
I KEEP ON HEARING ABOUT HOW YOU **THINK** YOU'VE FOUND SOMEONE WHO **MIGHT** BE THE TITAN, BUT...
DO YOU HAVE ANY OTHER EVIDENCE ?
YES ...
TO ME ...
...THE FEMALE TITAN'S FACE LOOKED LIKE ANNIE'S.
...
HUH?! WHAT'RE YOU SAYING?! YOU'RE GOING TO USE **THAT** AS YOUR EVIDENCE TO-
KLUNK
IN OTHER WORDS ...
WE DON'T HAVE ANY PROOF, BUT WE'RE GOING TO DO IT ANYWAY...

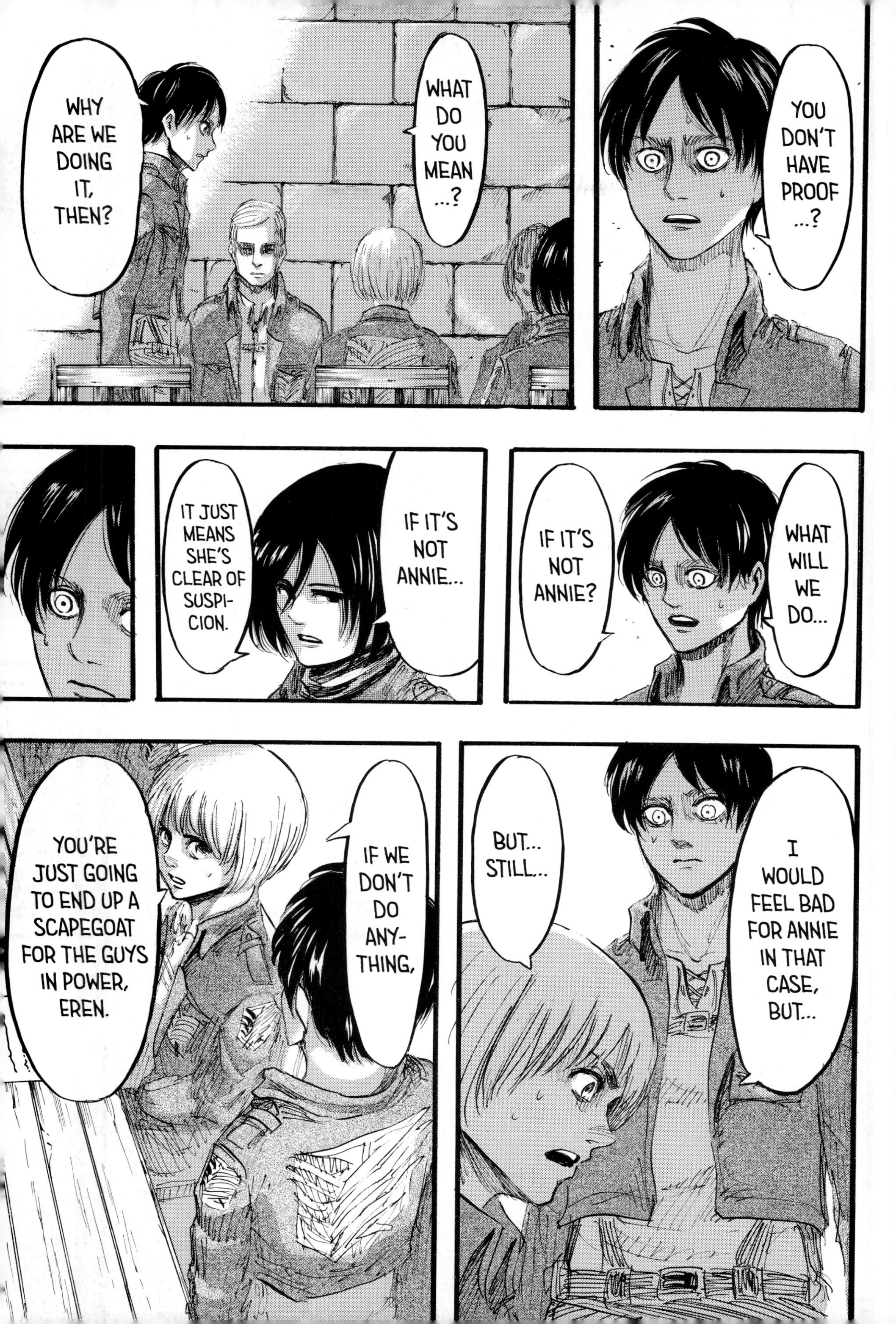
YOU DON'T HAVE PROOF ...?
WHAT DO YOU MEAN ...?
WHY ARE WE DOING IT, THEN?
WHAT WILL WE DO...
IF IT'S NOT ANNIE?
IF IT'S NOT ANNIE...
IT JUST MEANS SHE'S CLEAR OF SUSPI- CION.
I WOULD FEEL BAD FOR ANNIE IN THAT CASE, BUT...
BUT... STILL...
IF WE DON'T DO ANY- THING,
YOU'RE JUST GOING TO END UP A SCAPEGOAT FOR THE GUYS IN POWER, EREN.

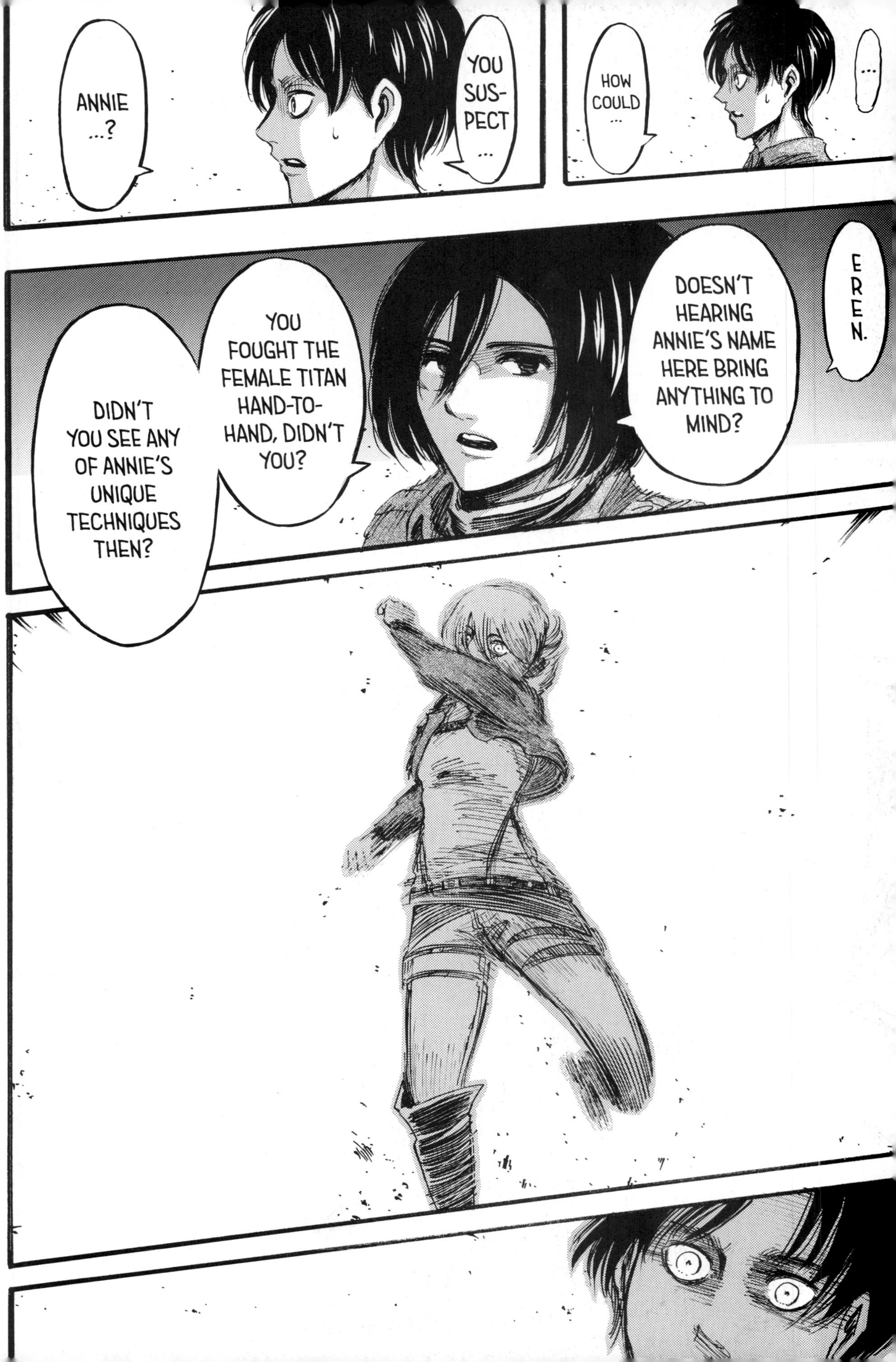
...
HOW COULD ...
YOU SUS-PECT ...
ANNIE ...?
EREN.
DOESN'T HEARING ANNIE'S NAME HERE BRING ANYTHING TO MIND?
YOU FOUGHT THE FEMALE TITAN HAND-TO-HAND, DIDN'T YOU?
DIDN'T YOU SEE ANY OF ANNIE'S UNIQUE TECHNIQUES THEN?

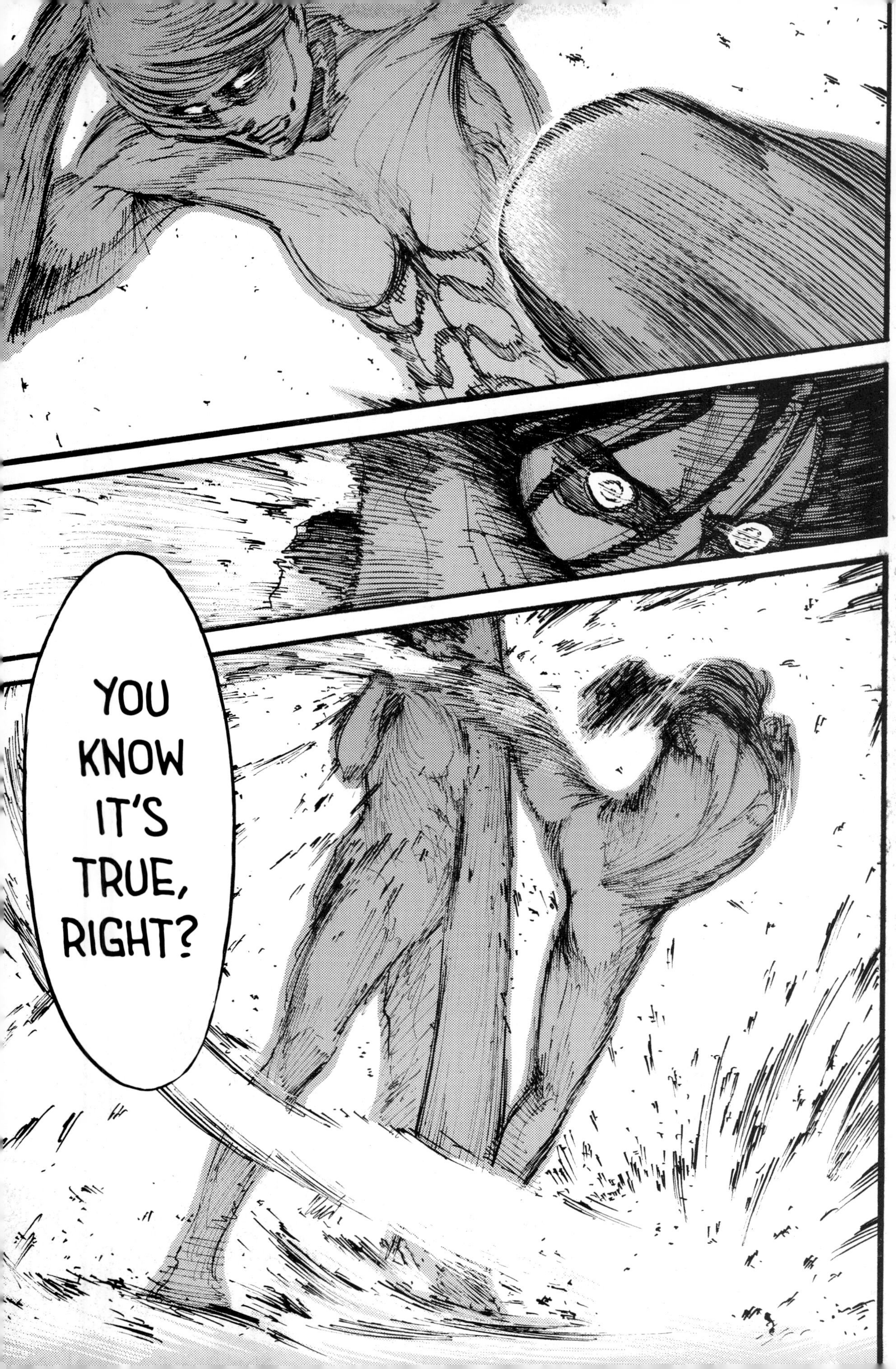
YOU KNOW IT'S TRUE, RIGHT?

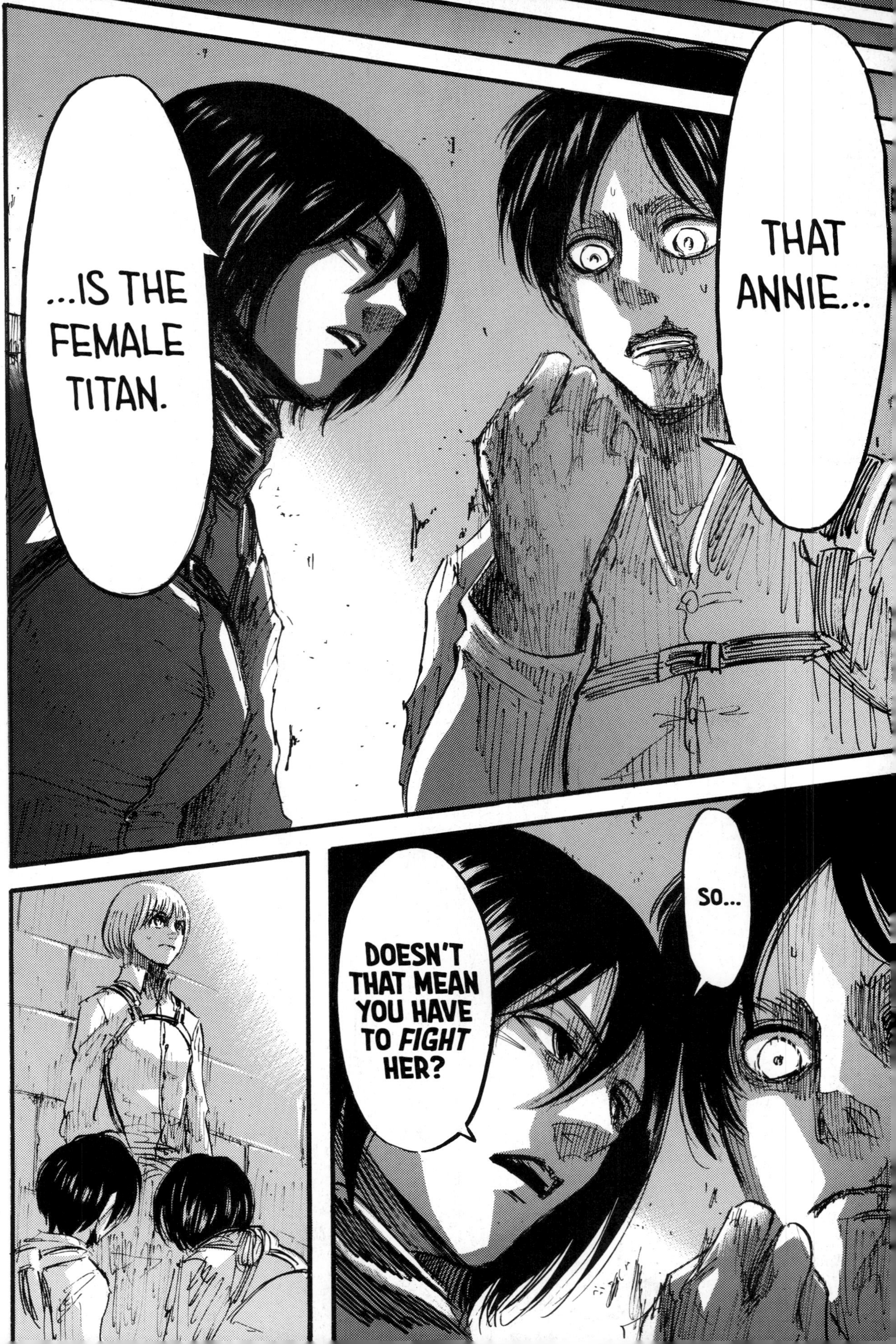
THAT ANNIE...
...IS THE FEMALE TITAN.
SO...
DOESN'T THAT MEAN YOU HAVE TO *FIGHT* HER?

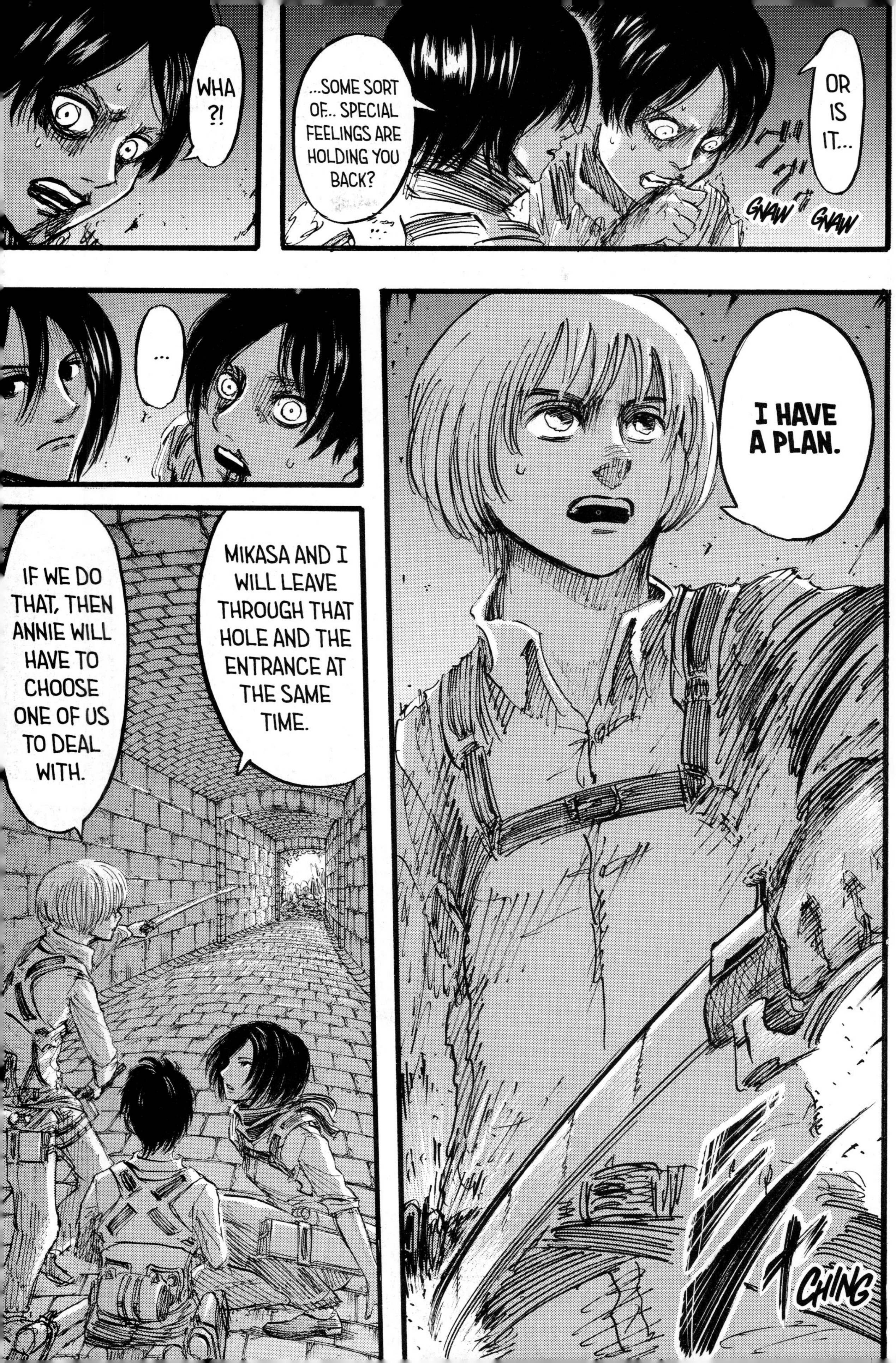

OR IS IT...
GNAW GNAW
...SOME SORT OF... SPECIAL FEELINGS ARE HOLDING YOU BACK?
WHA ?!
I HAVE A PLAN.
CHING
...
MIKASA AND I WILL LEAVE THROUGH THAT HOLE AND THE ENTRANCE AT THE SAME TIME.
IF WE DO THAT, THEN ANNIE WILL HAVE TO CHOOSE ONE OF US TO DEAL WITH.

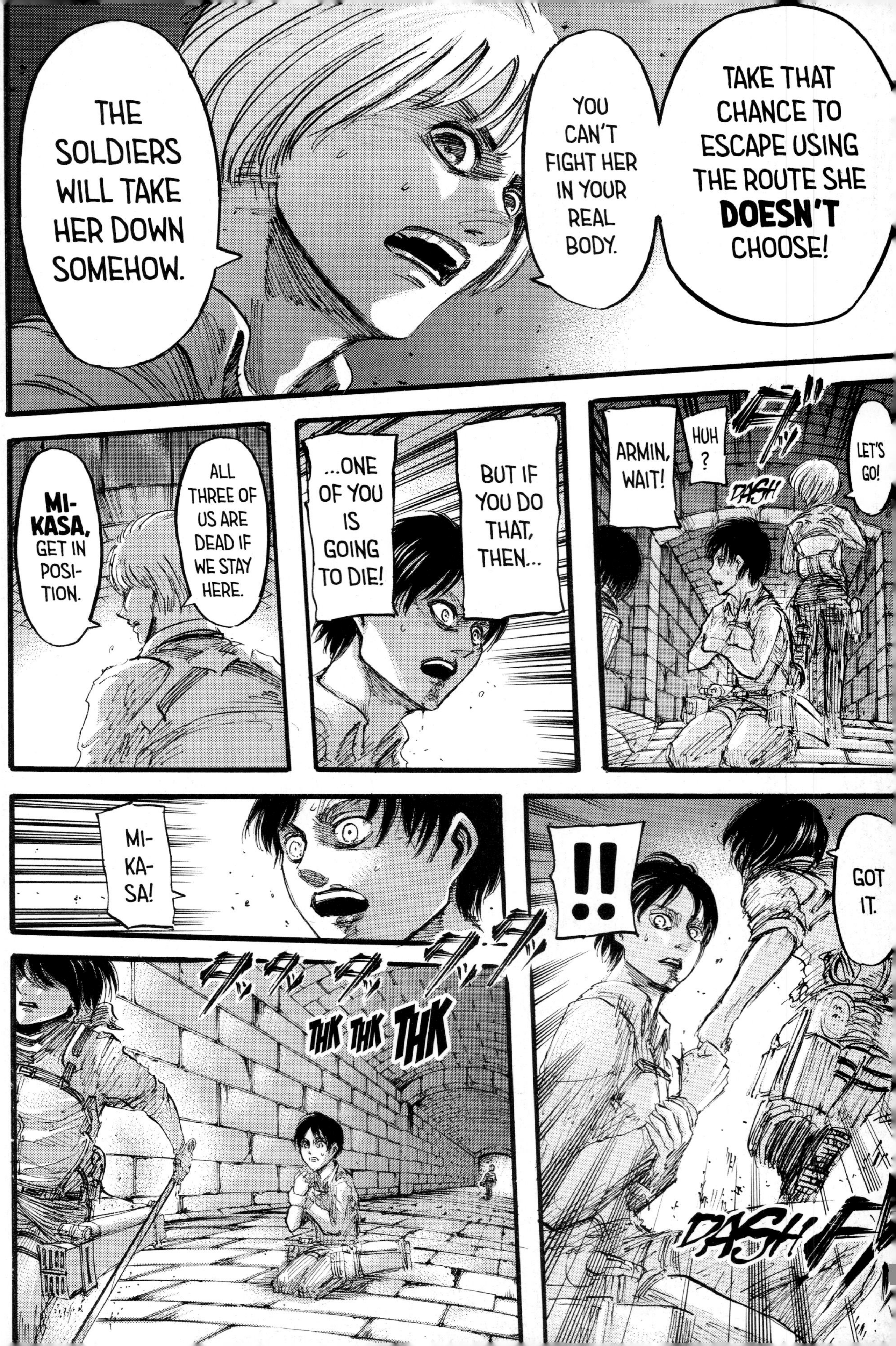
TAKE THAT CHANCE TO ESCAPE USING THE ROUTE SHE **DOESN'T** CHOOSE!
YOU CAN'T FIGHT HER IN YOUR REAL BODY.
THE SOLDIERS WILL TAKE HER DOWN SOMEHOW.
LET'S GO!
DASH
HUH?
ARMIN, WAIT!
BUT IF YOU DO THAT, THEN...
...ONE OF YOU IS GOING TO DIE!
ALL THREE OF US ARE DEAD IF WE STAY HERE.
MI-KASA, GET IN POSI-TION.
GOT IT.
!!
DASH
MI-KA-SA!
THK THK THK

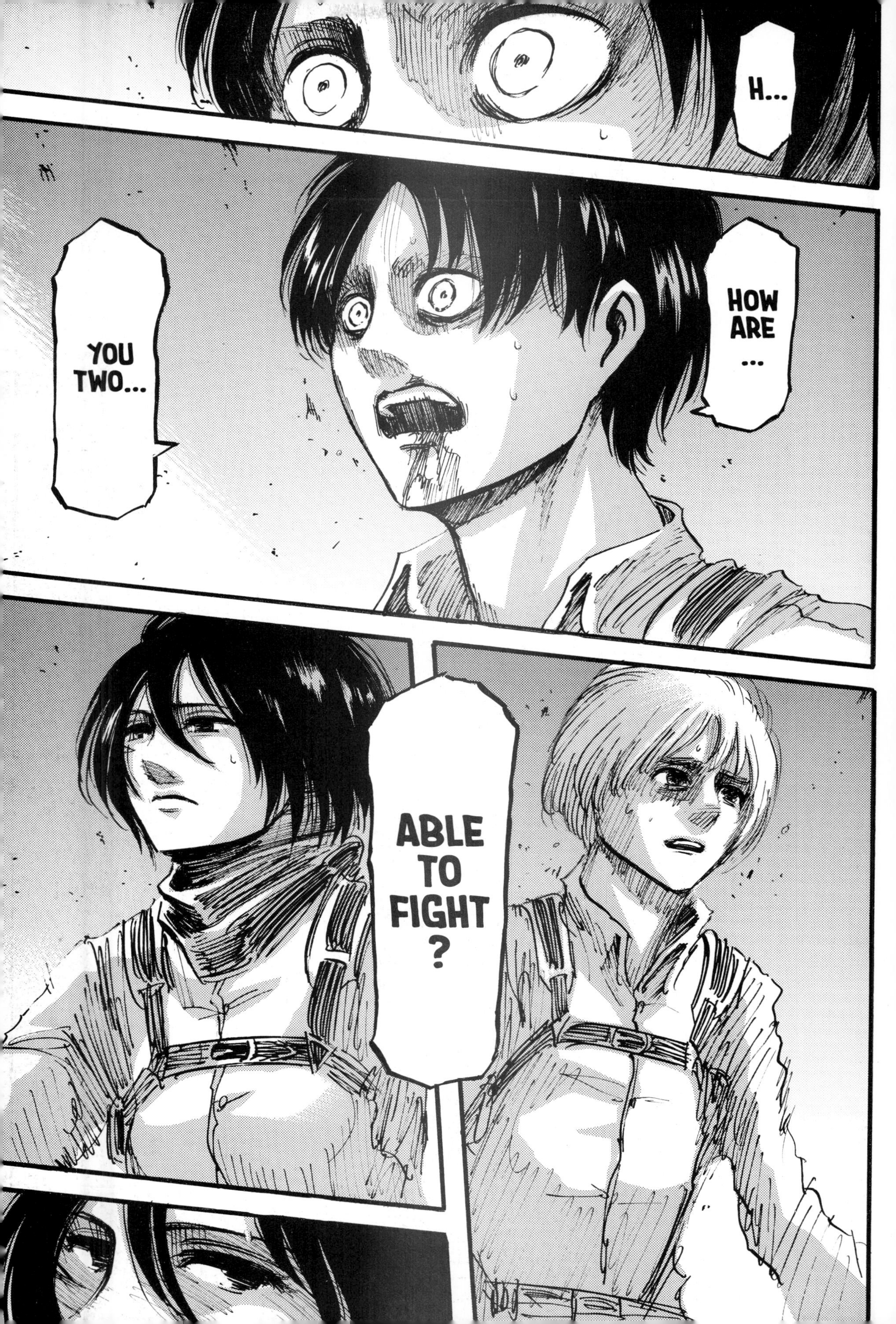
H...
HOW ARE ...
YOU TWO...
ABLE TO FIGHT ?

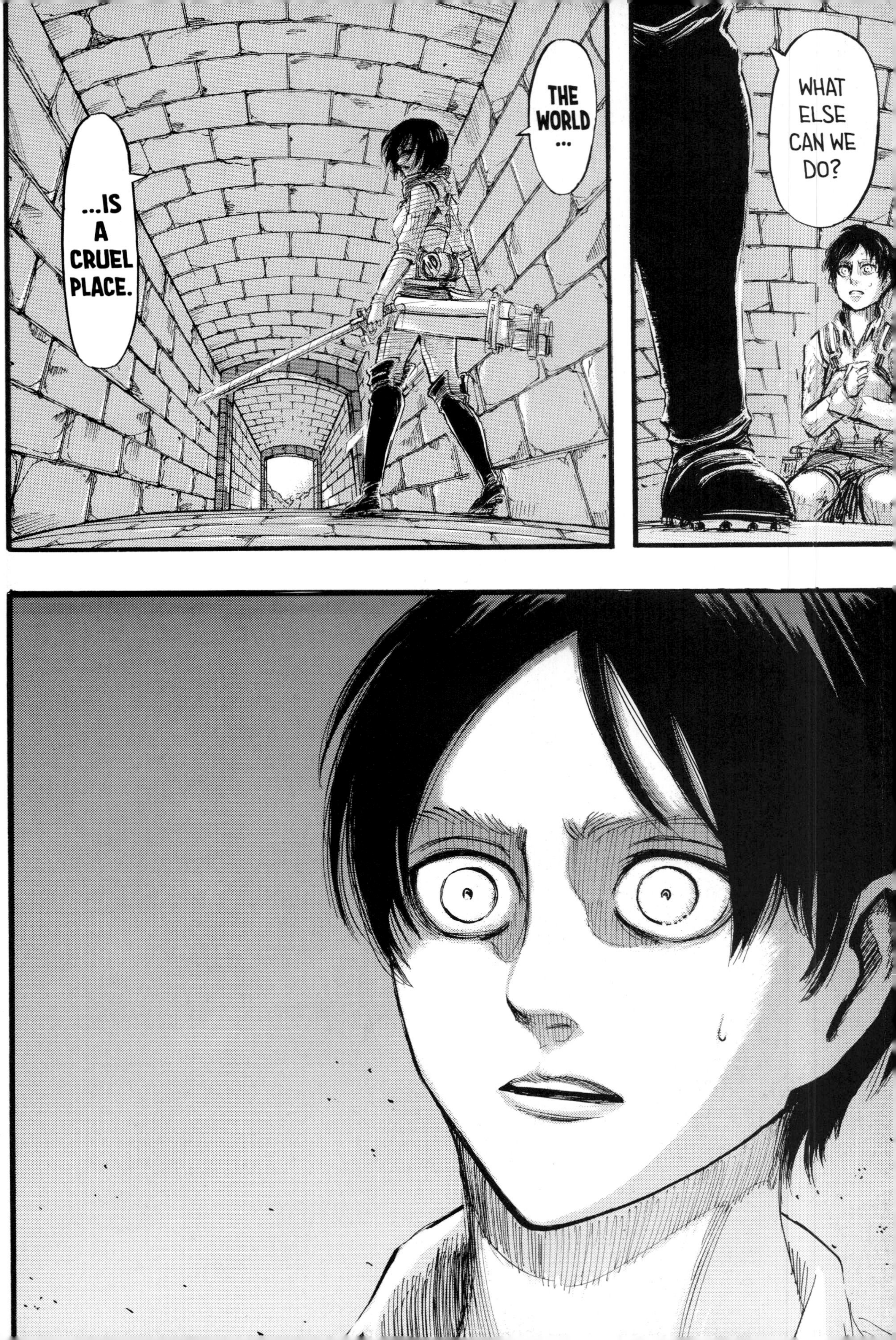
WHAT ELSE CAN WE DO?
THE WORLD ...
...IS A CRUEL PLACE.

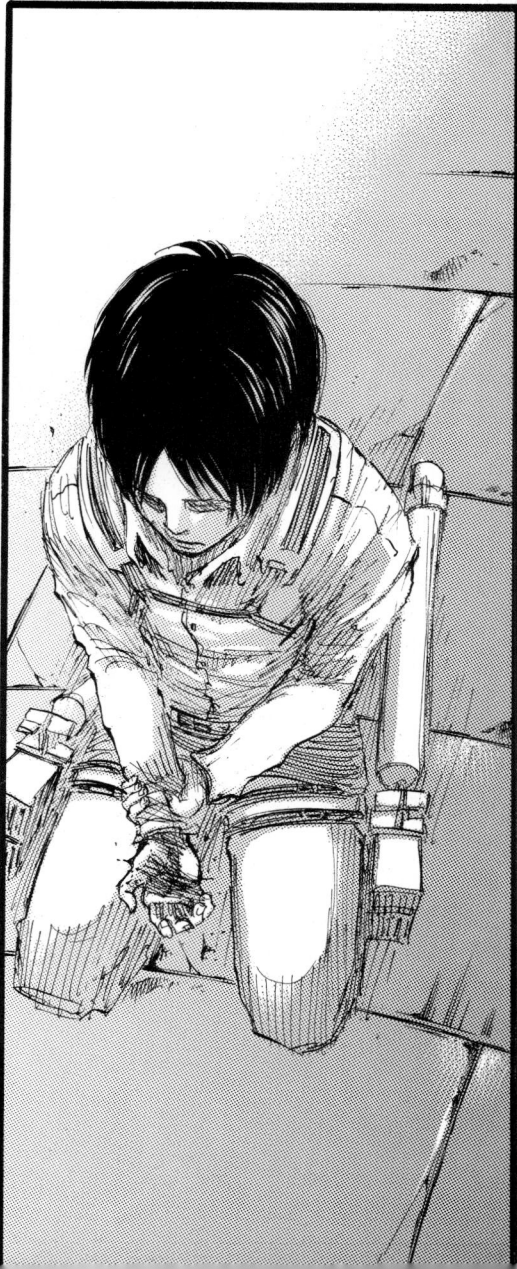

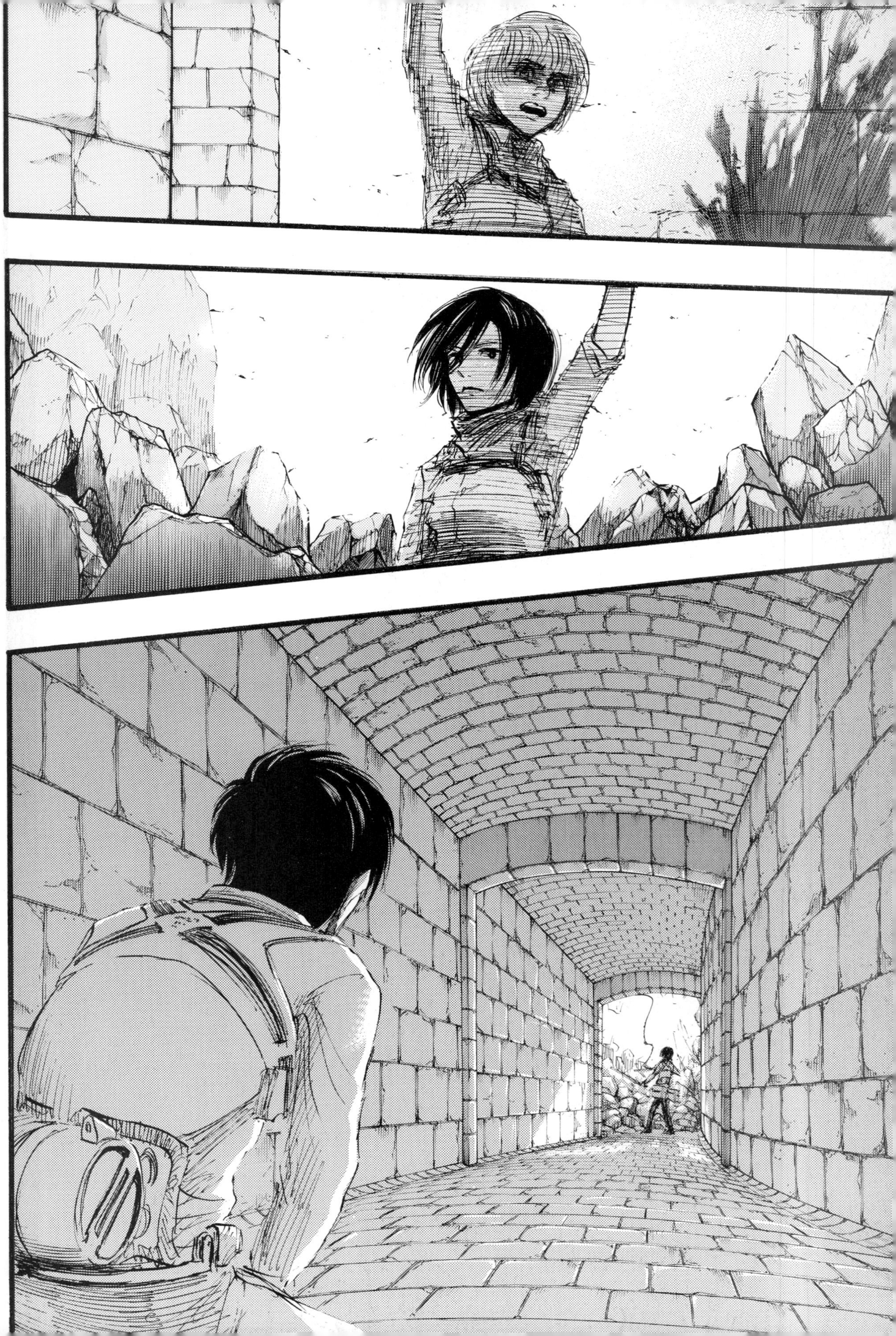

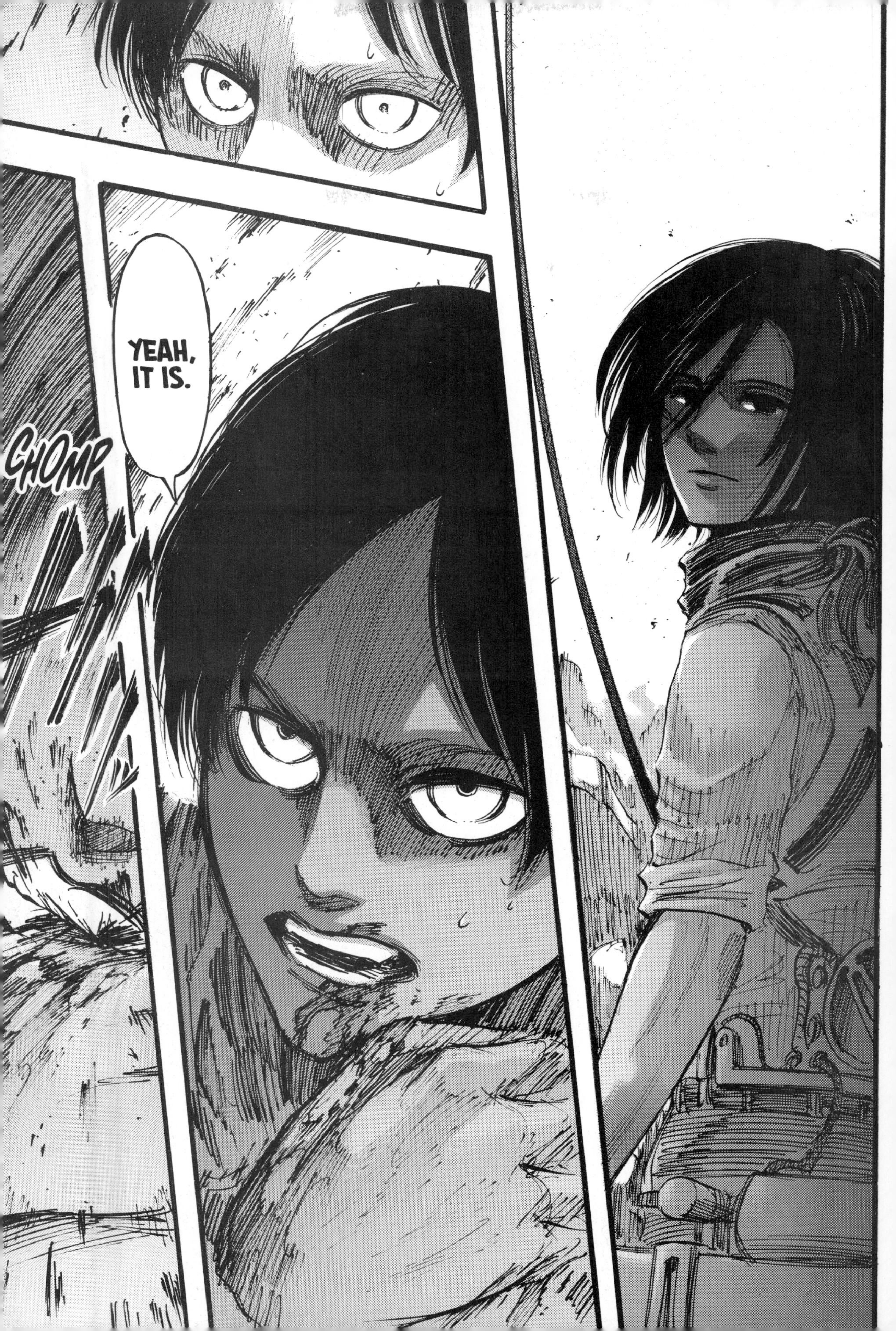
YEAH, IT IS.
CHOMP

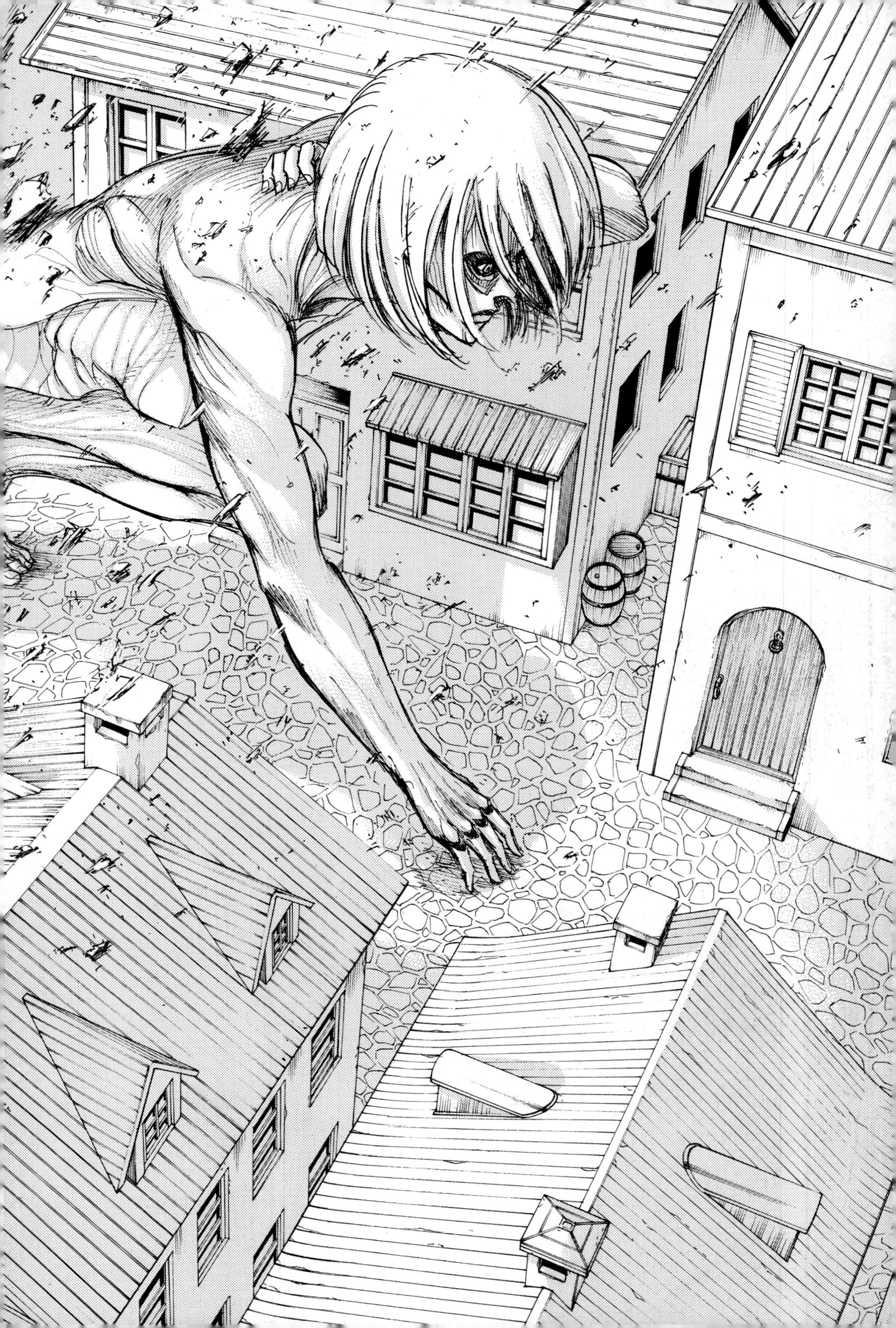

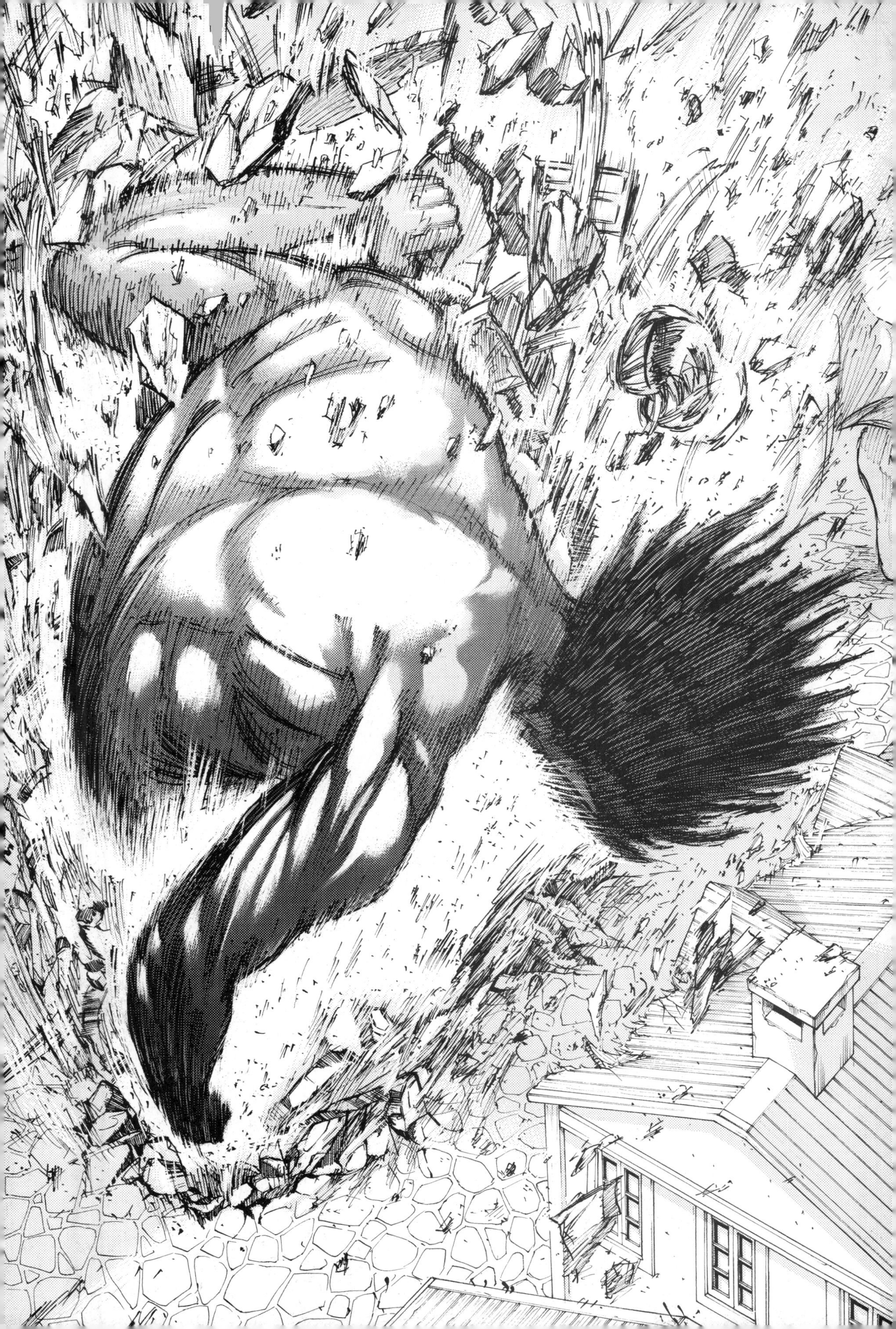

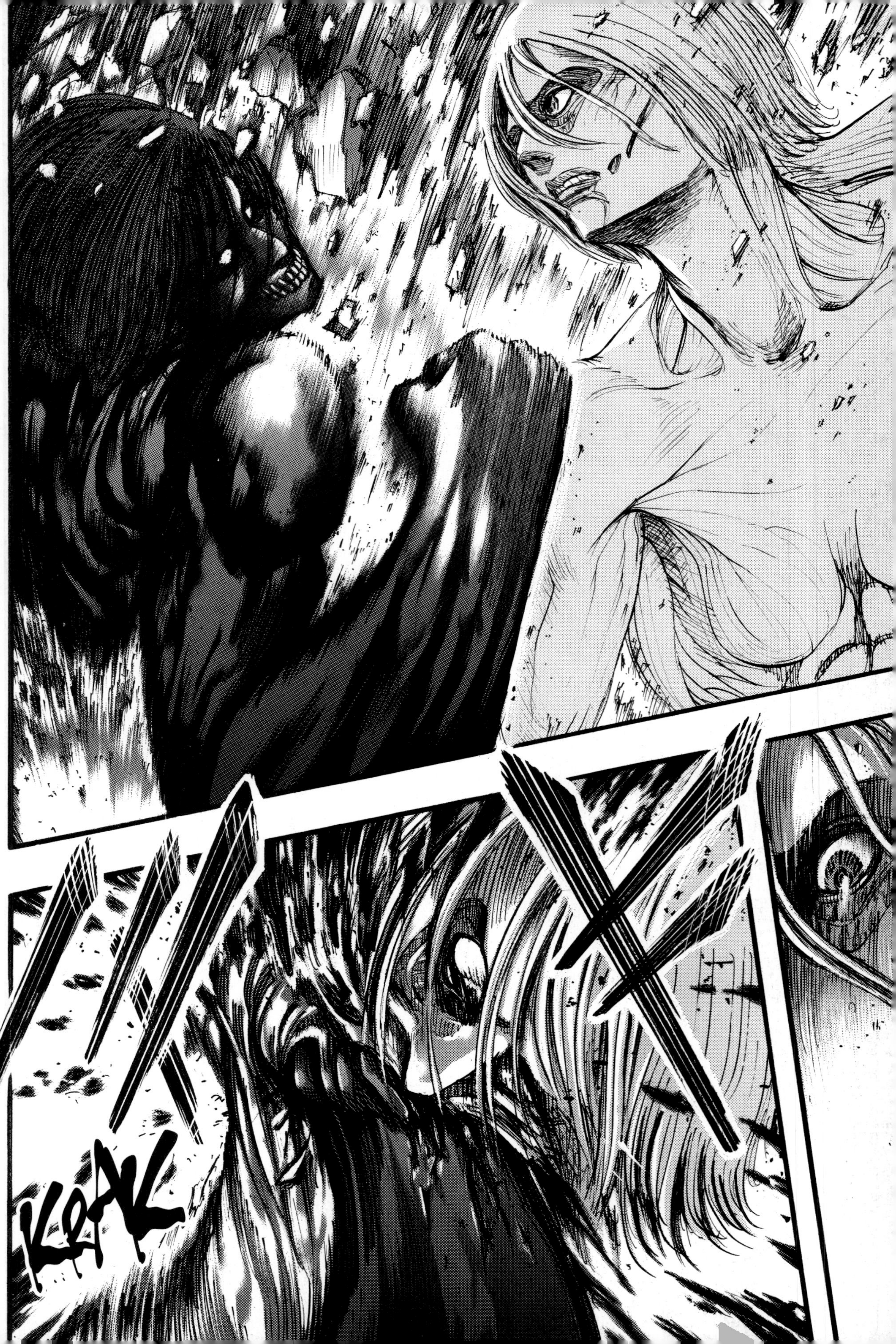
KRAK

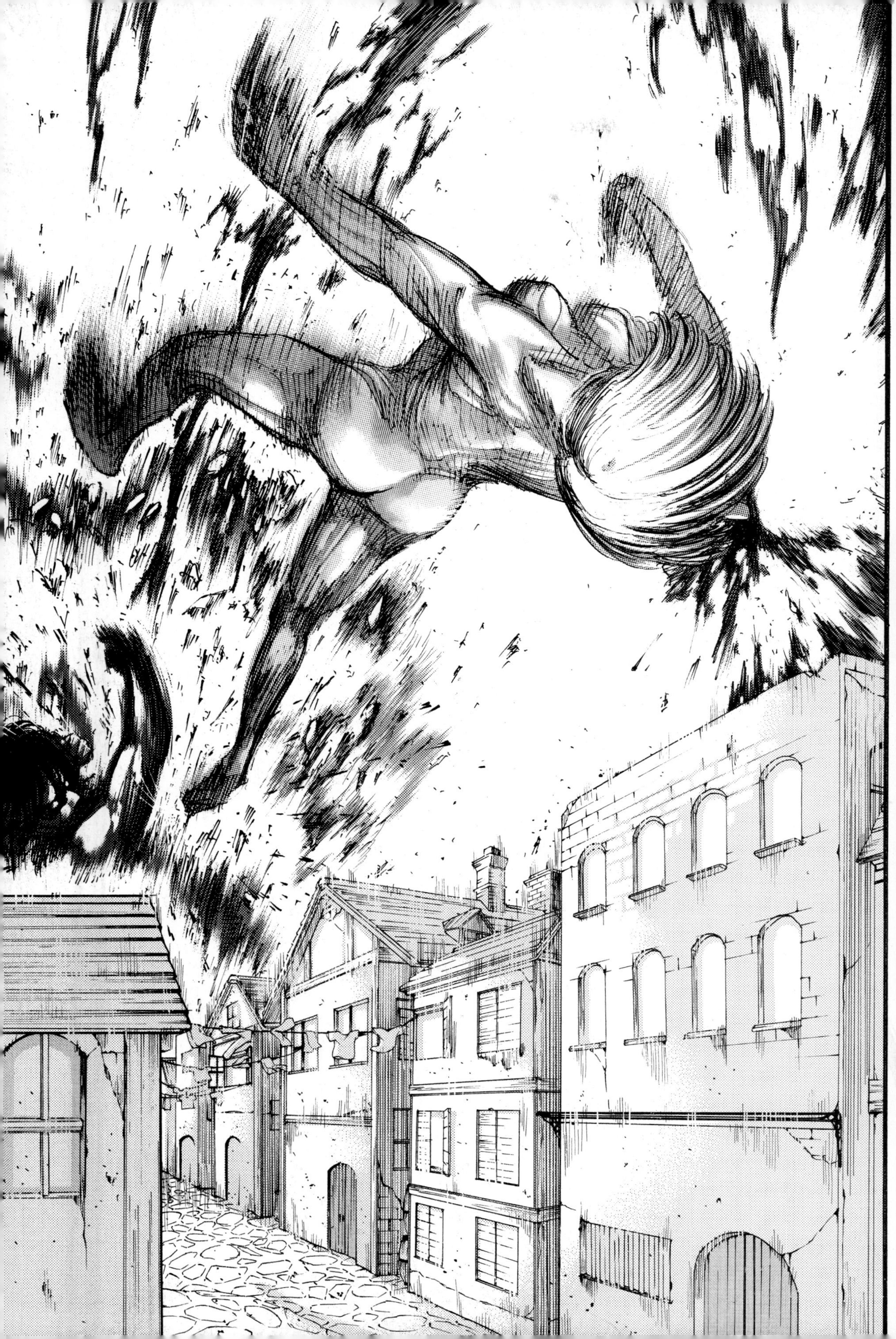

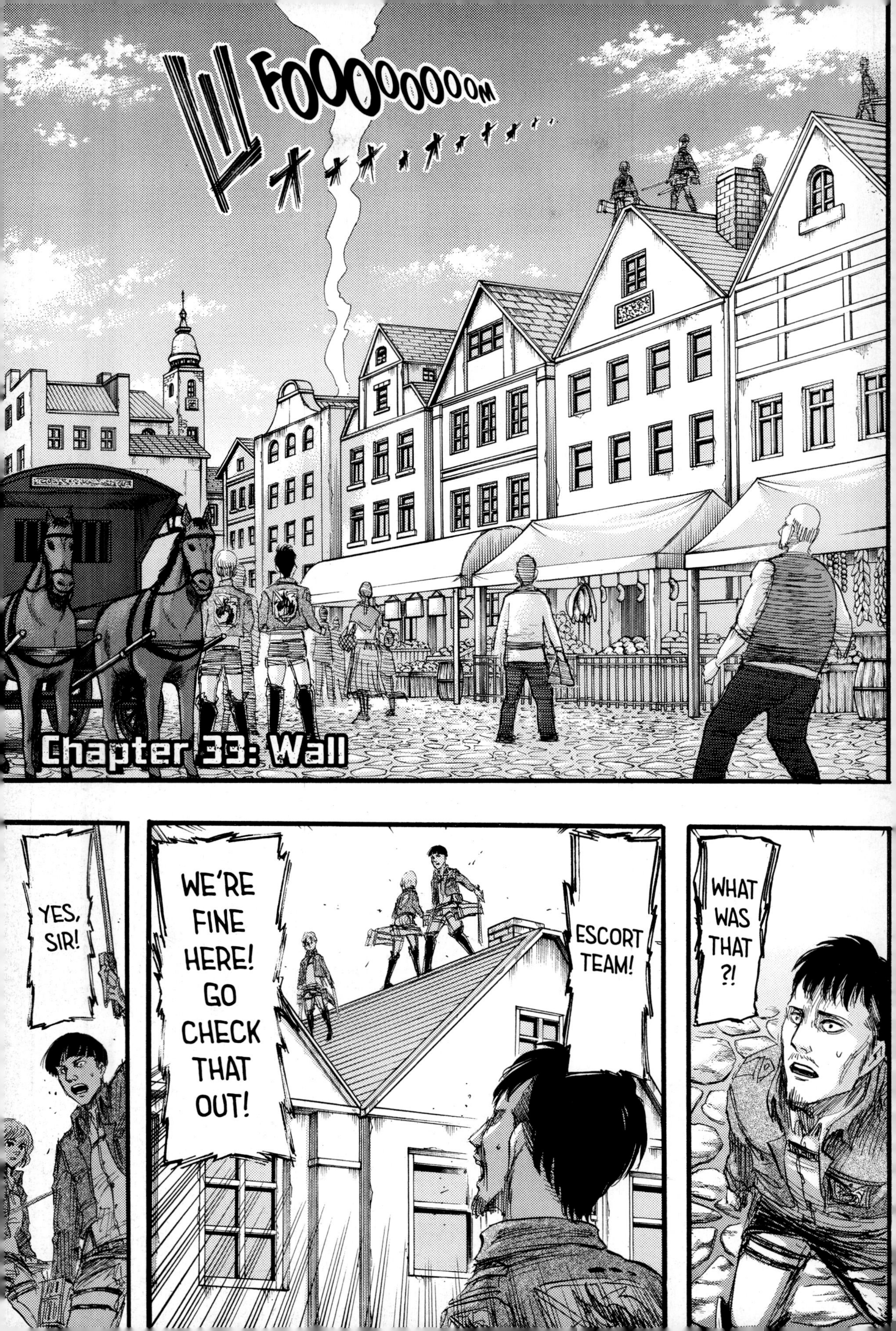
FOOOOOOOOM
Chapter 33: Wall
WHAT WAS THAT?!
ESCORT TEAM!
WE'RE FINE HERE! GO CHECK THAT OUT!
YES, SIR!

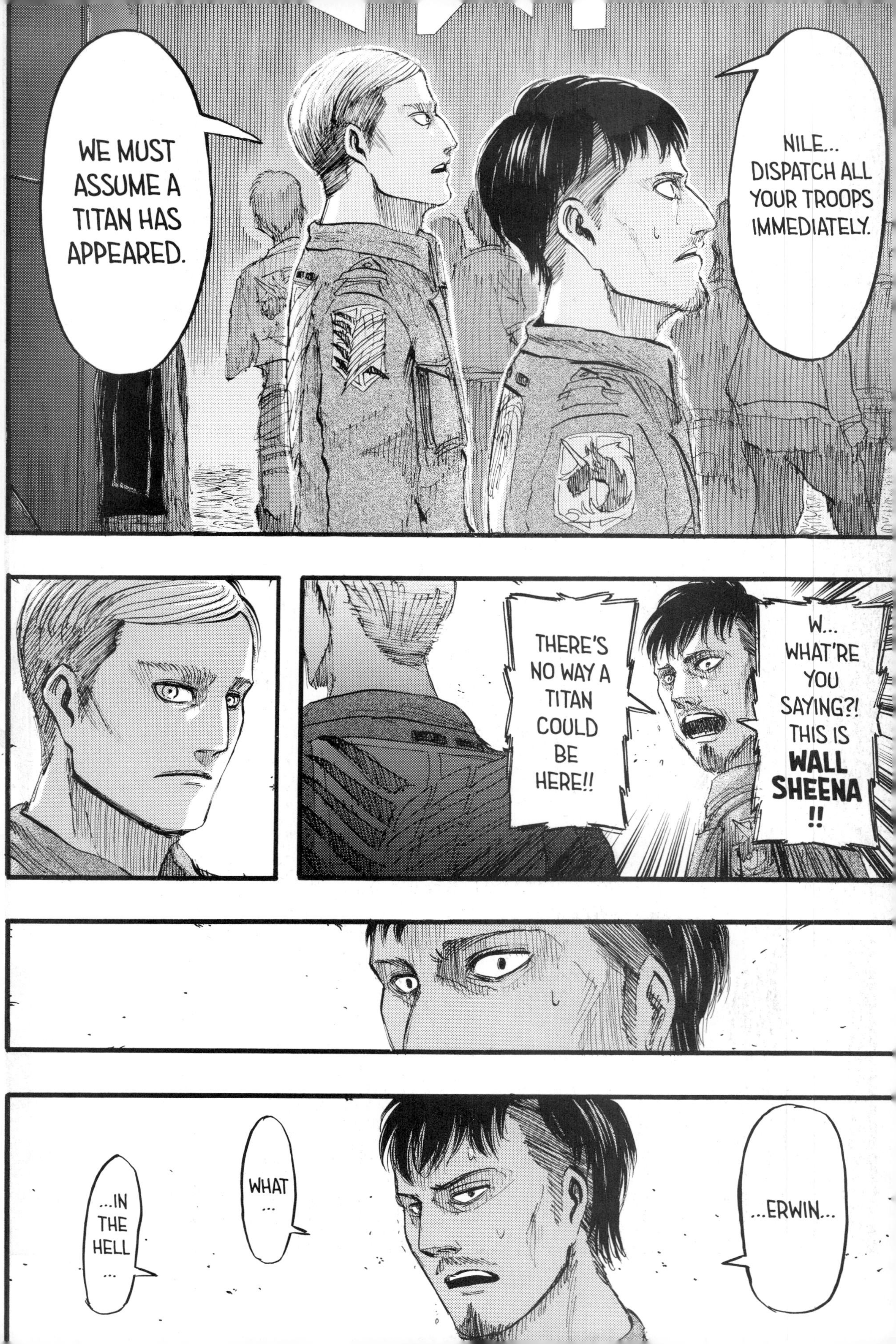
NILE... DISPATCH ALL YOUR TROOPS IMMEDIATELY.
WE MUST ASSUME A TITAN HAS APPEARED.
W... WHAT'RE YOU SAYING?! THIS IS **WALL SHEENA!!**
THERE'S NO WAY A TITAN COULD BE HERE!!
...ERWIN...
WHAT...
...IN THE HELL...

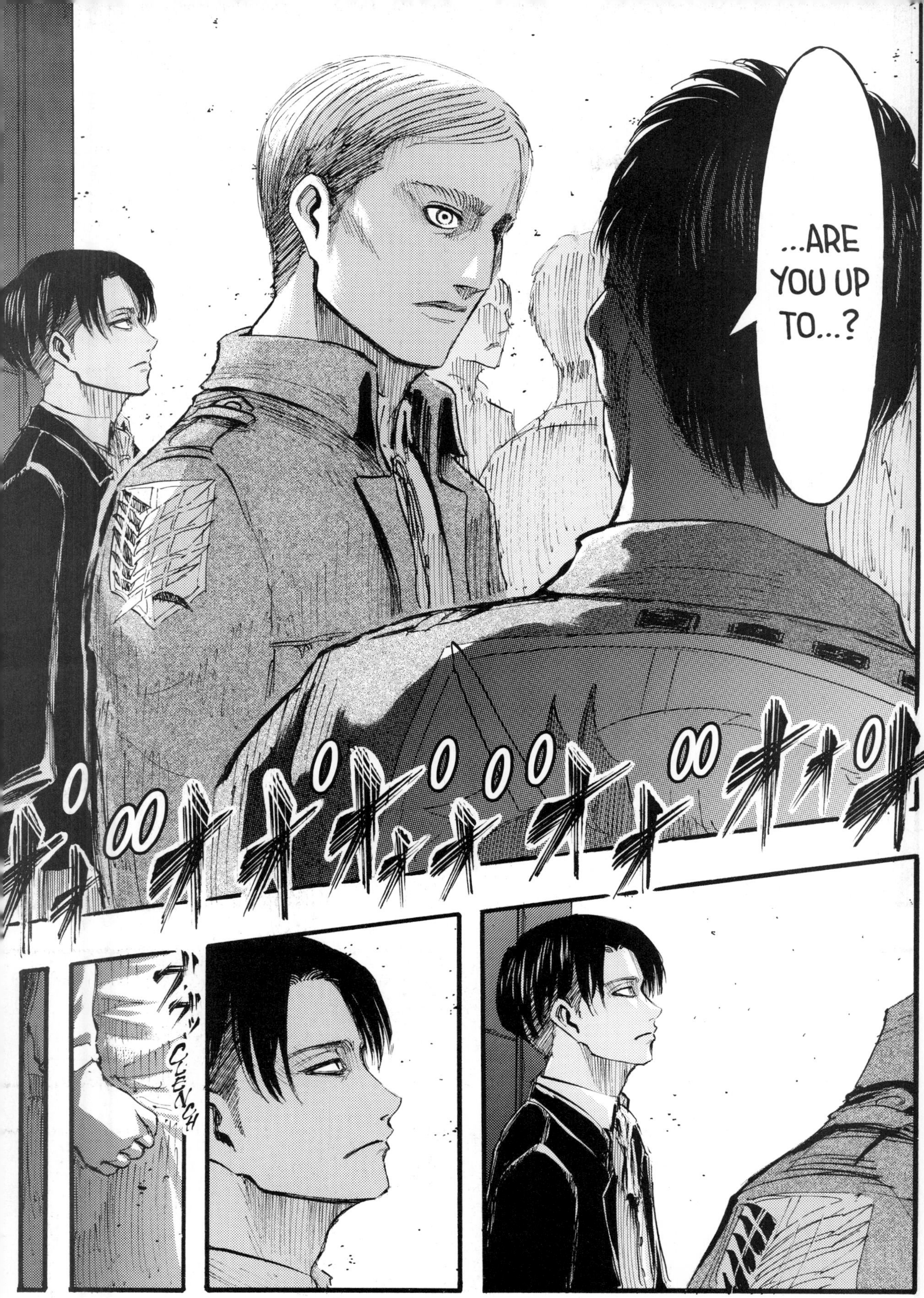
...ARE YOU UP TO...?
CLENCH

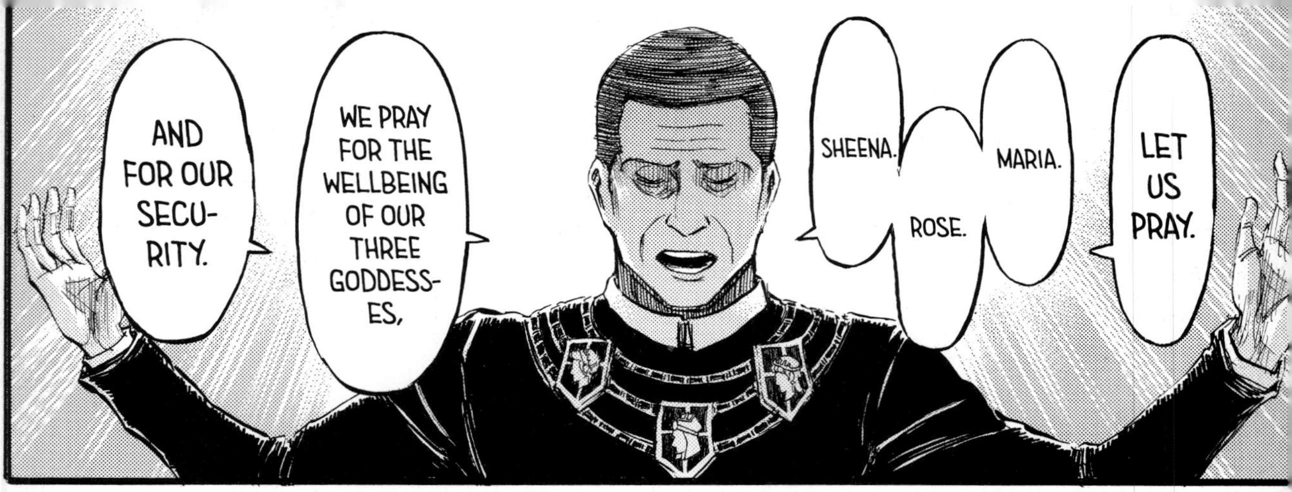
LET US PRAY.
MARIA.
ROSE.
SHEENA.
WE PRAY FOR THE WELLBEING OF OUR THREE GODDESSES,
AND FOR OUR SECURITY.

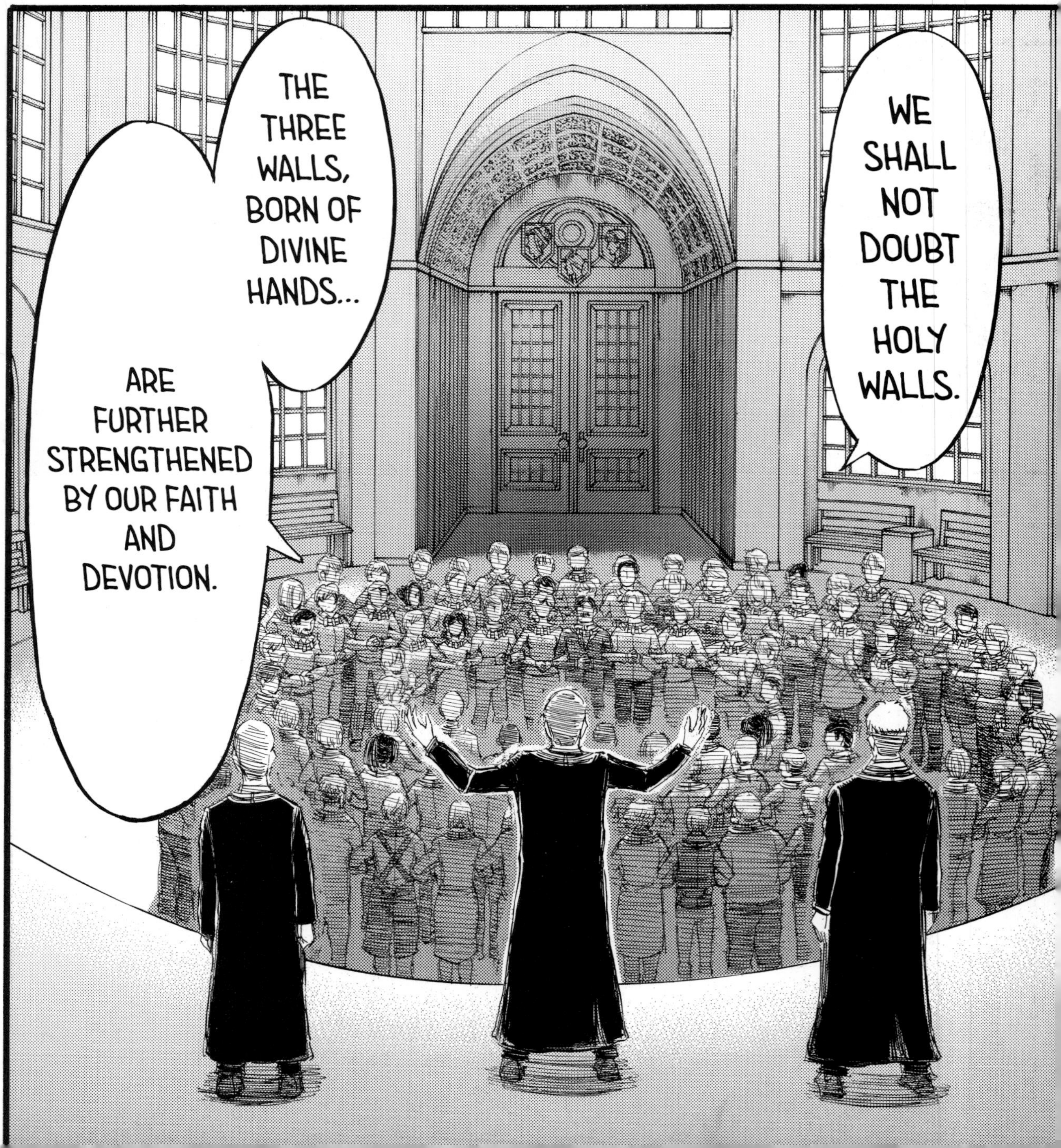
WE SHALL NOT DOUBT THE HOLY WALLS.
THE THREE WALLS, BORN OF DIVINE HANDS...
ARE FURTHER STRENGTHENED BY OUR FAITH AND DEVOTION.

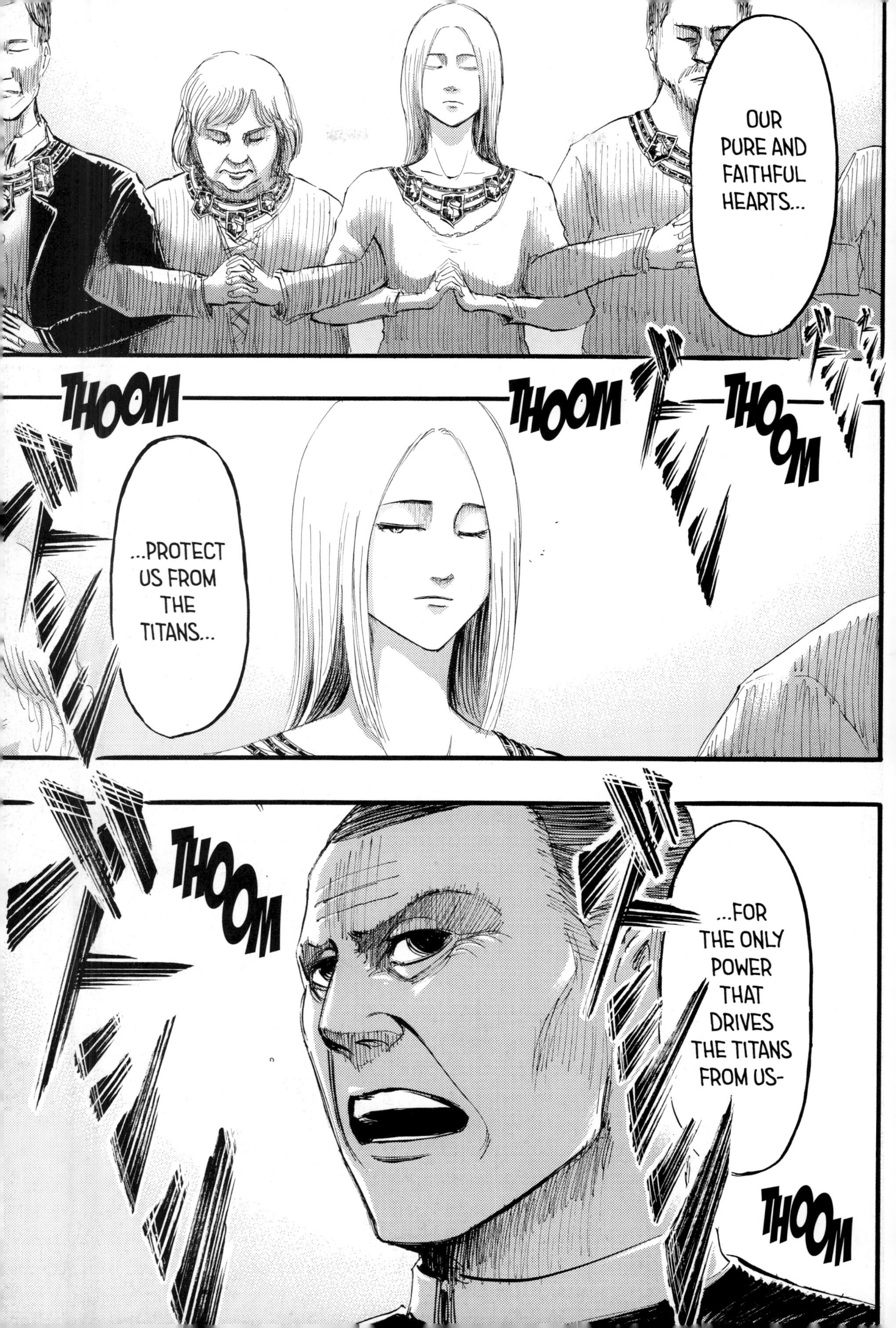
OUR PURE AND FAITHFUL HEARTS...
THOOM
THOOM
THOOM
...PROTECT US FROM THE TITANS...
...FOR THE ONLY POWER THAT DRIVES THE TITANS FROM US-
THOOM
THOOM

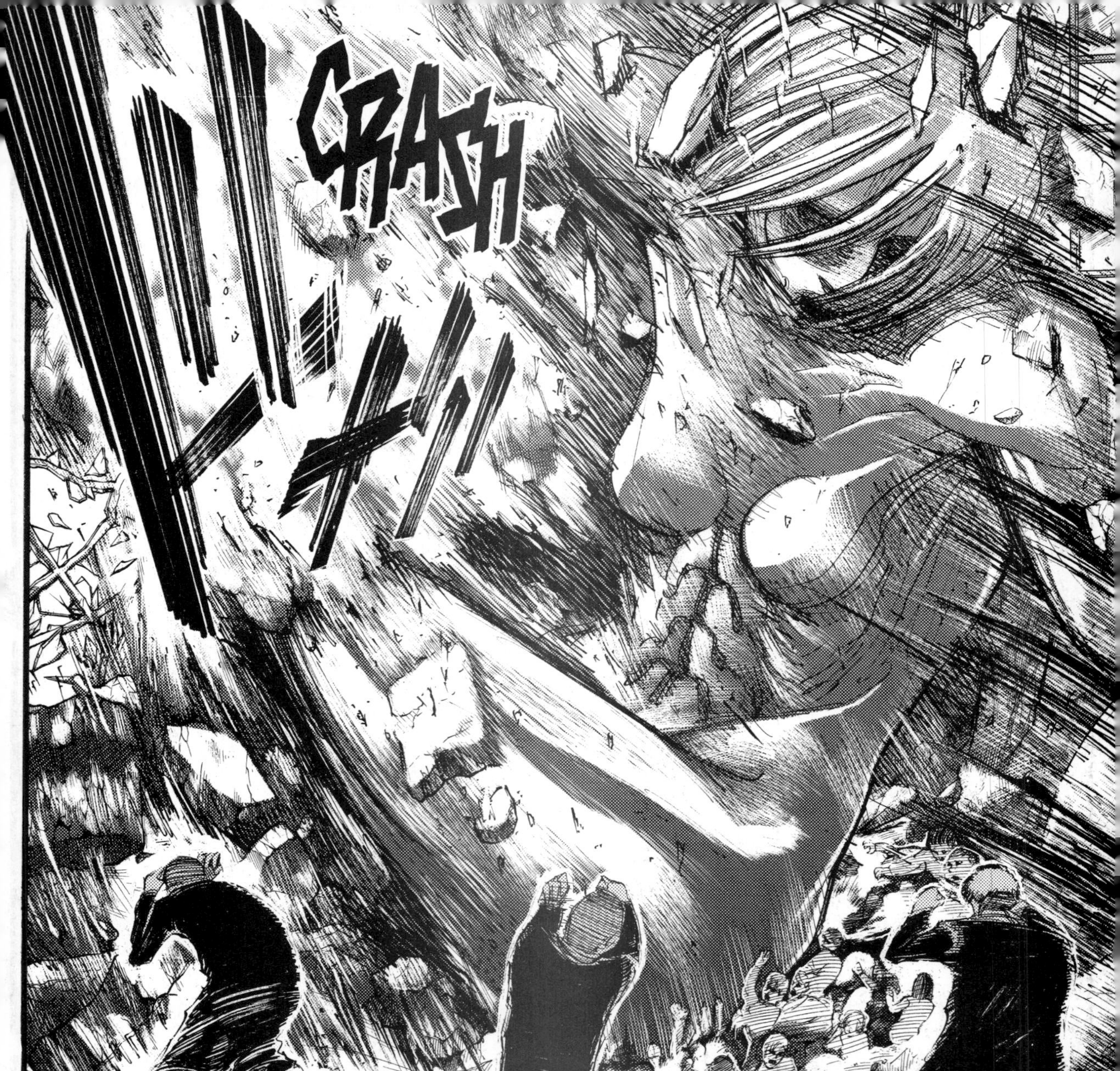
CRASH
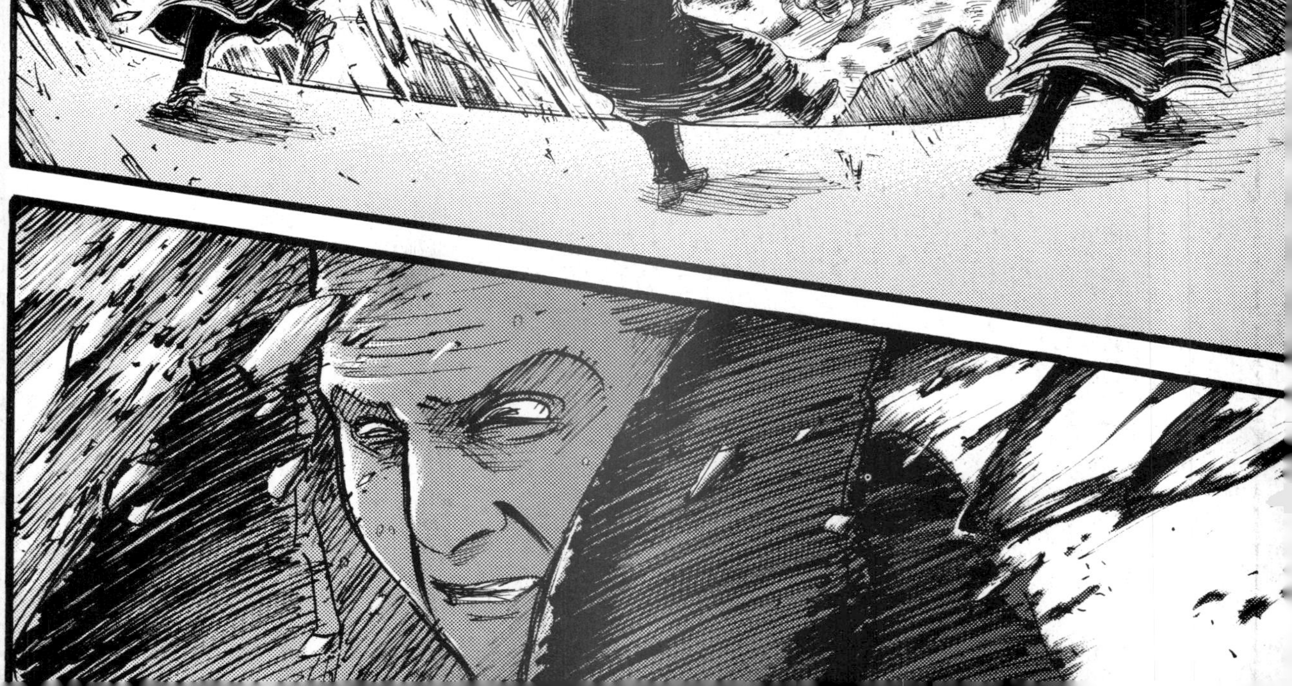

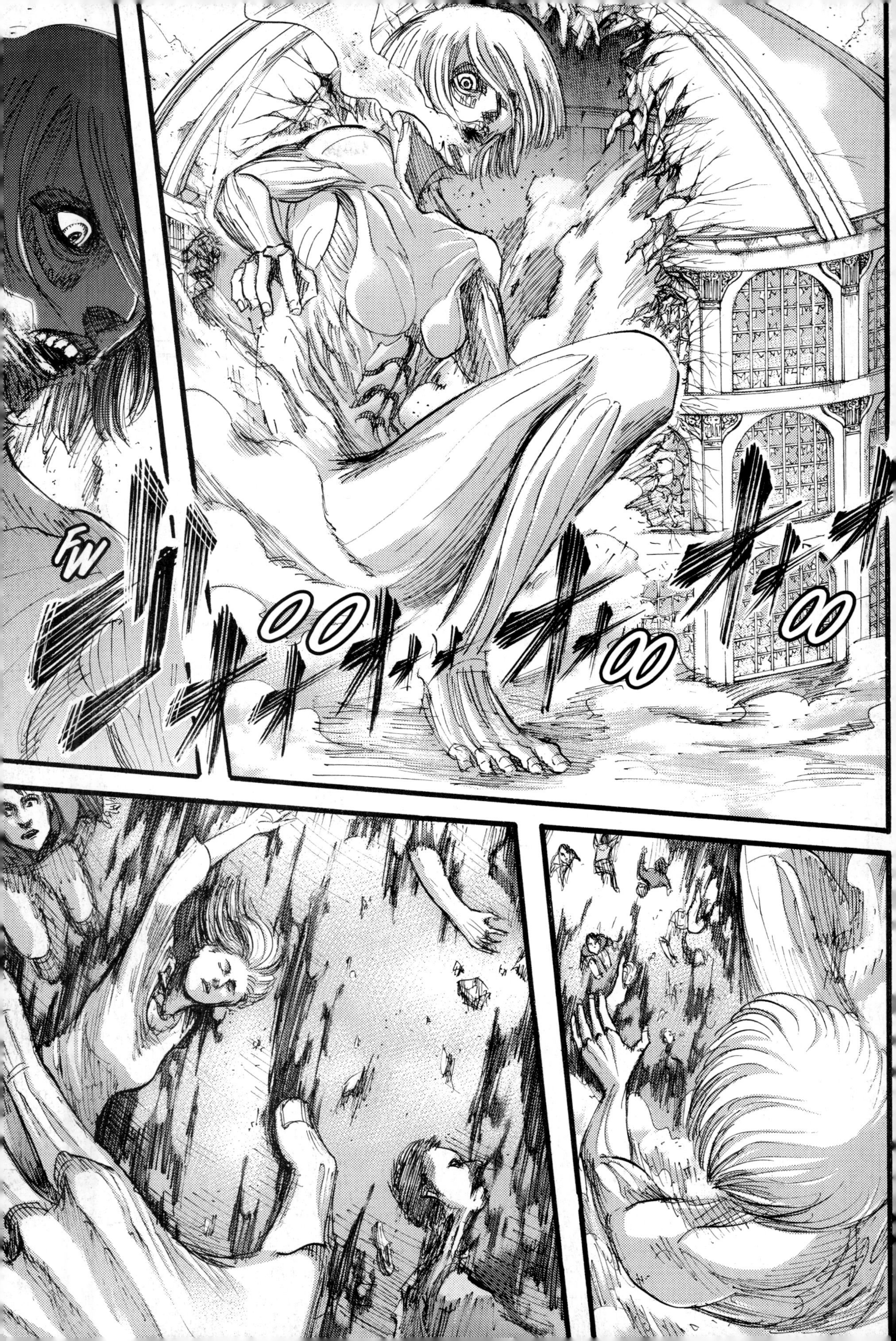
FW
OO
OO
OO

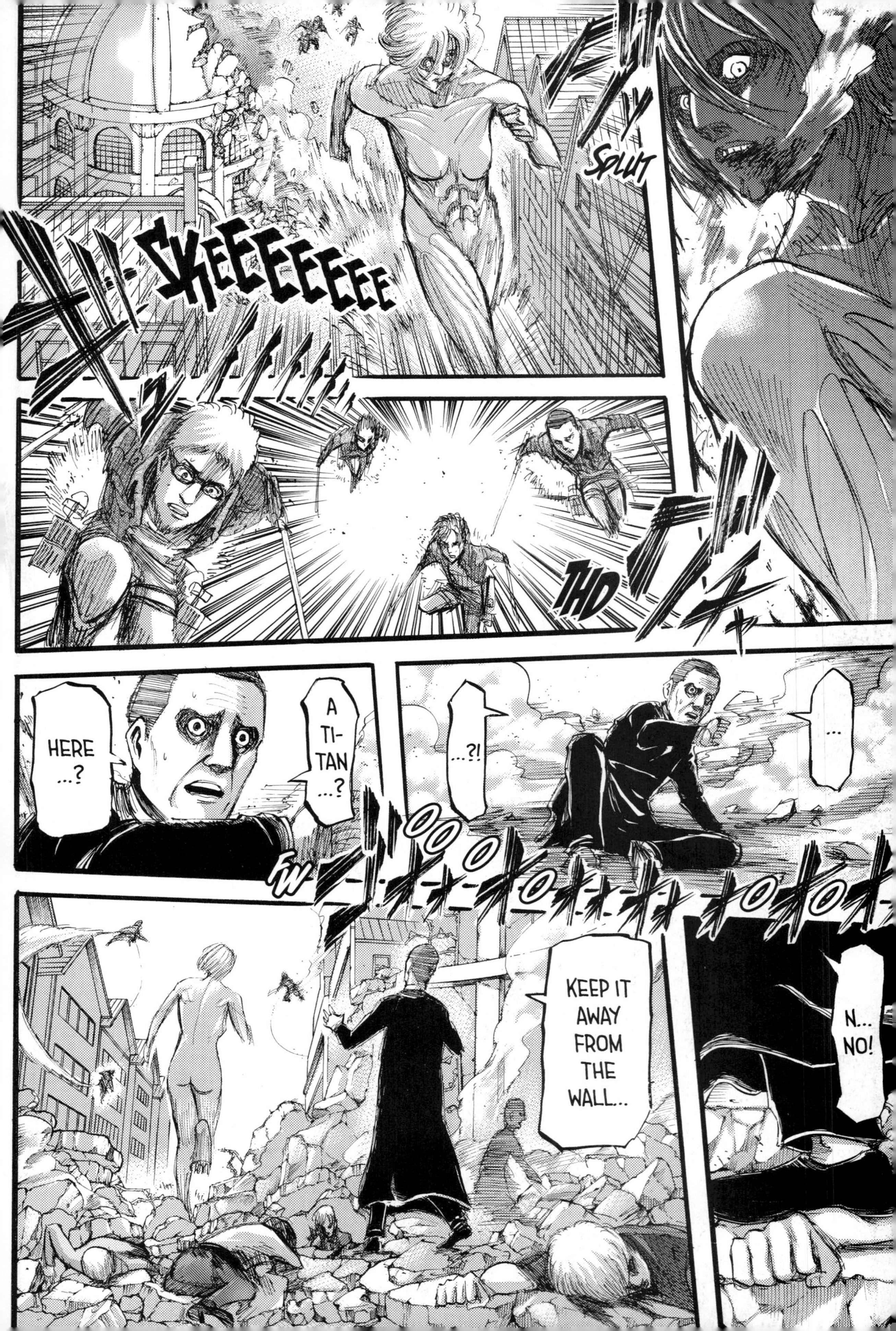
SPLUT
SKEEEEEEEE
THD
...
...?!
A TI-TAN ...?
HERE ...?
FWOOOO
N... NO!
KEEP IT AWAY FROM THE WALL...

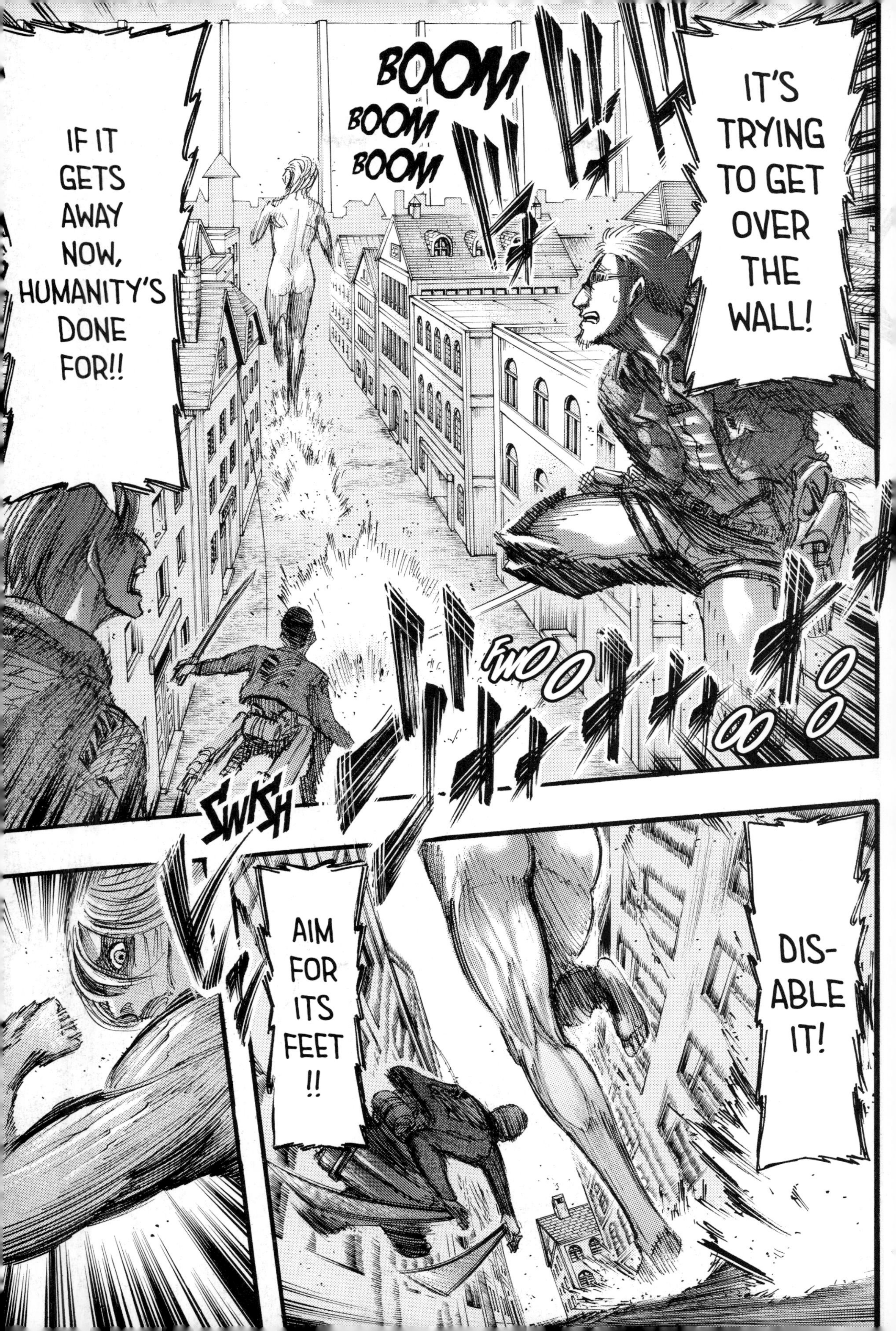
IT'S TRYING TO GET OVER THE WALL!
BOOM BOOM BOOM
IF IT GETS AWAY NOW, HUMANITY'S DONE FOR!!
FWOOOO
SWKSH
DIS-ABLE IT!
AIM FOR ITS FEET !!

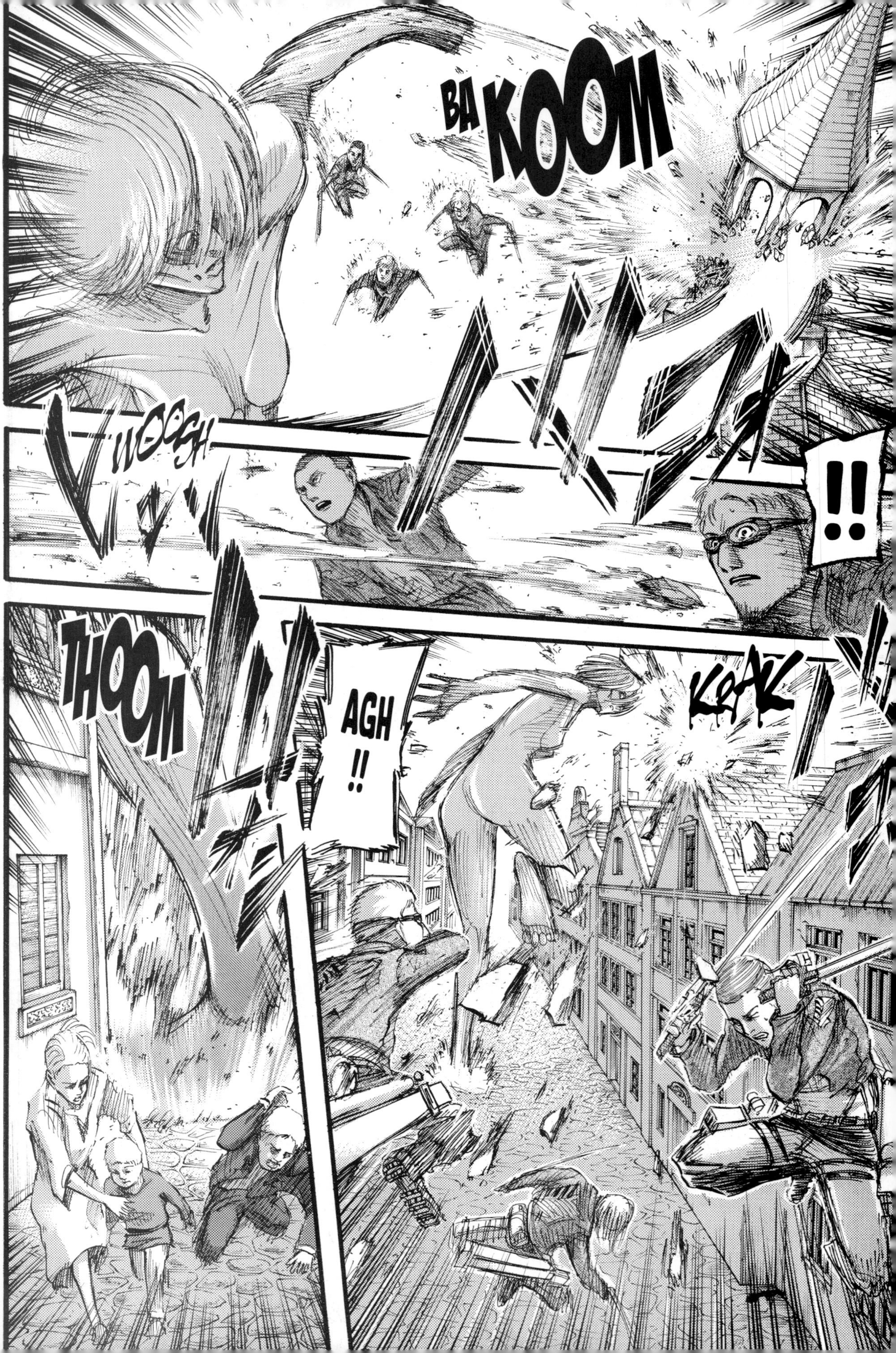
BA KOOM
VWOOSH
!!
KRAK
AGH !!
THOOM

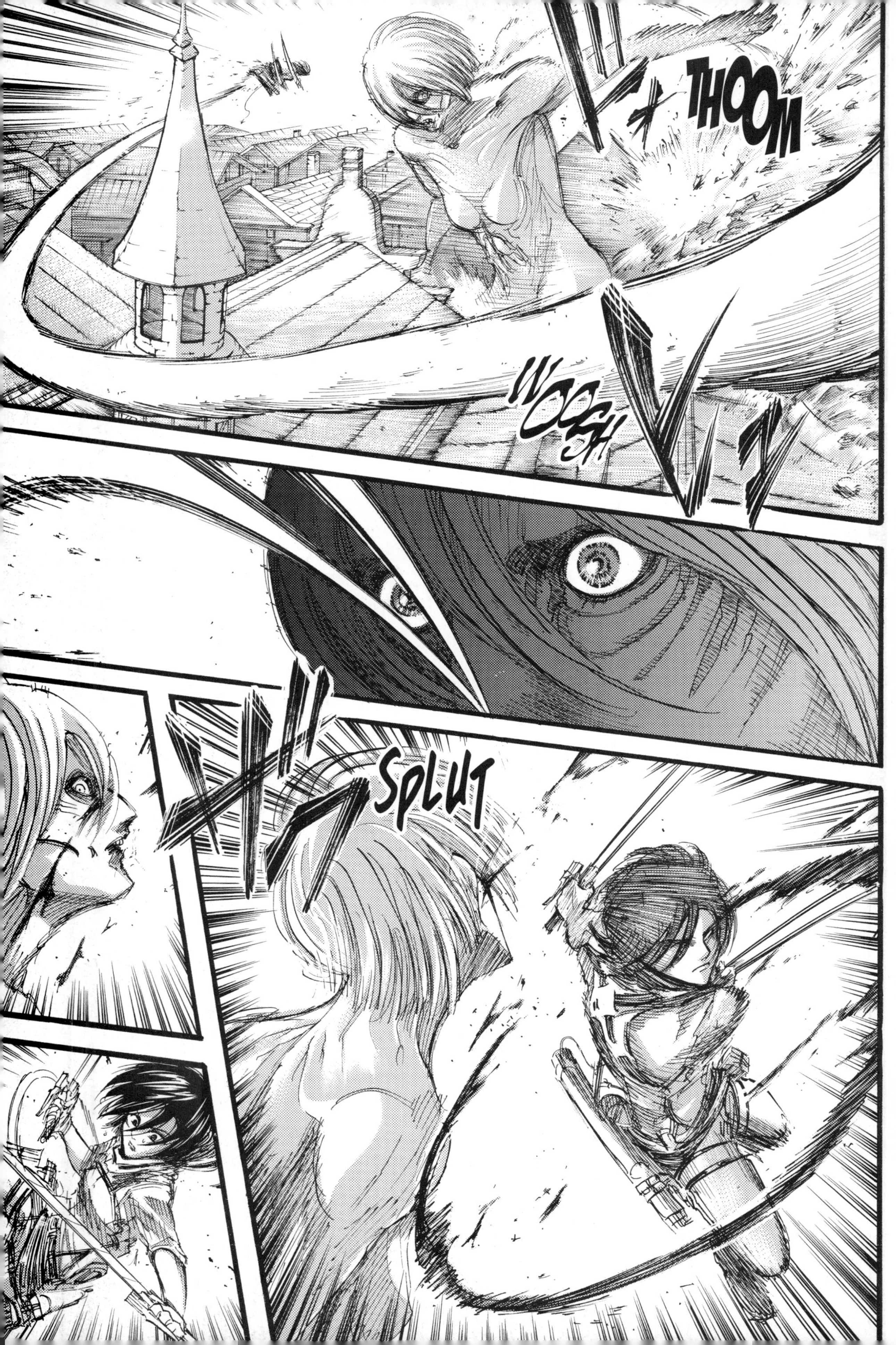
THOOM
WOOSH
SPLUT

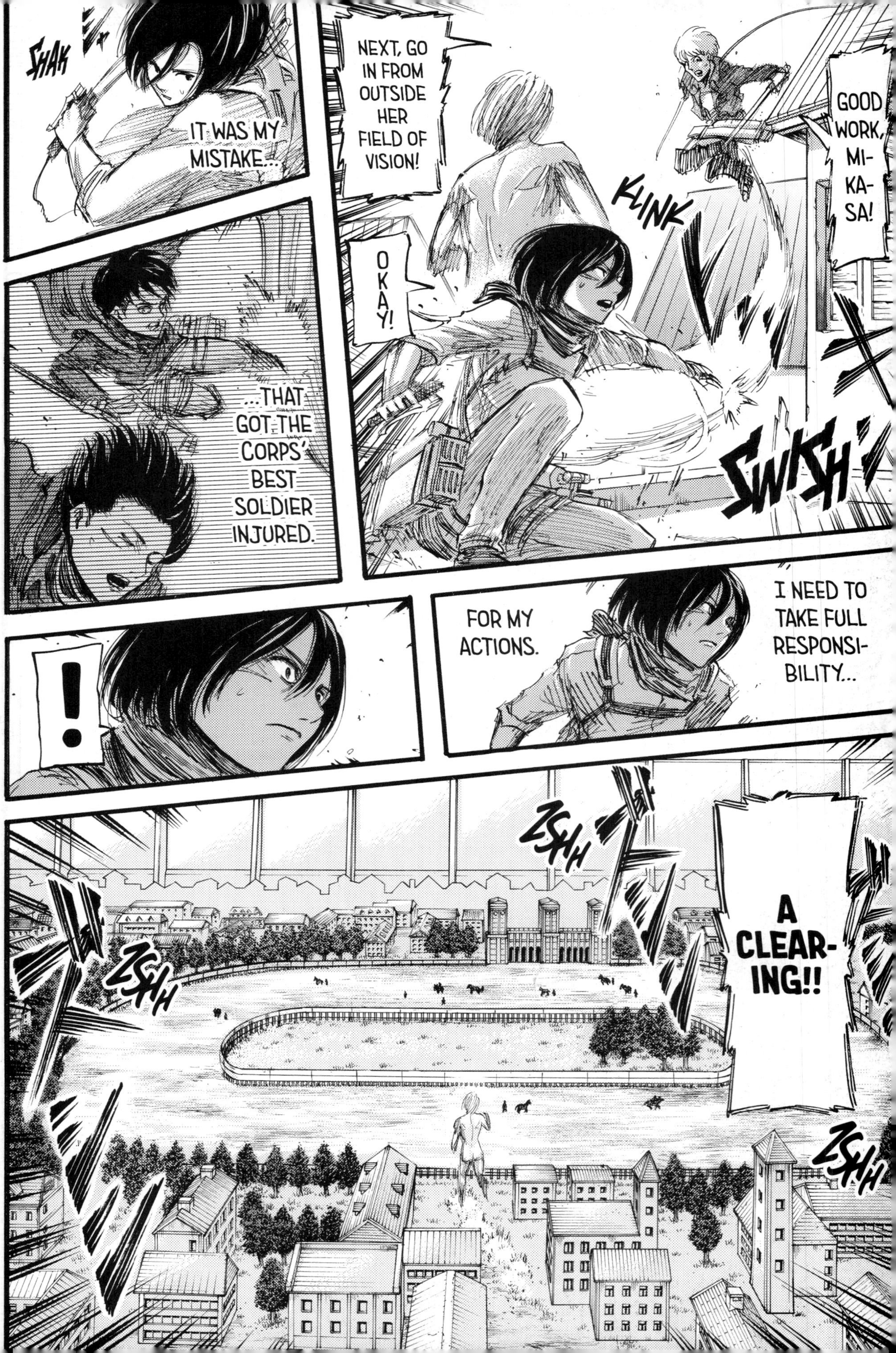
GOOD WORK, MI-KA-SA!
NEXT, GO IN FROM OUTSIDE HER FIELD OF VISION!
KLINK
OKAY!
SWISH
SHAK
IT WAS MY MISTAKE...
...THAT GOT THE CORPS' BEST SOLDIER INJURED.
I NEED TO TAKE FULL RESPONSI-BILITY...
FOR MY ACTIONS.
!
A CLEAR-ING!!
ZSHH
ZSHH
ZSHH

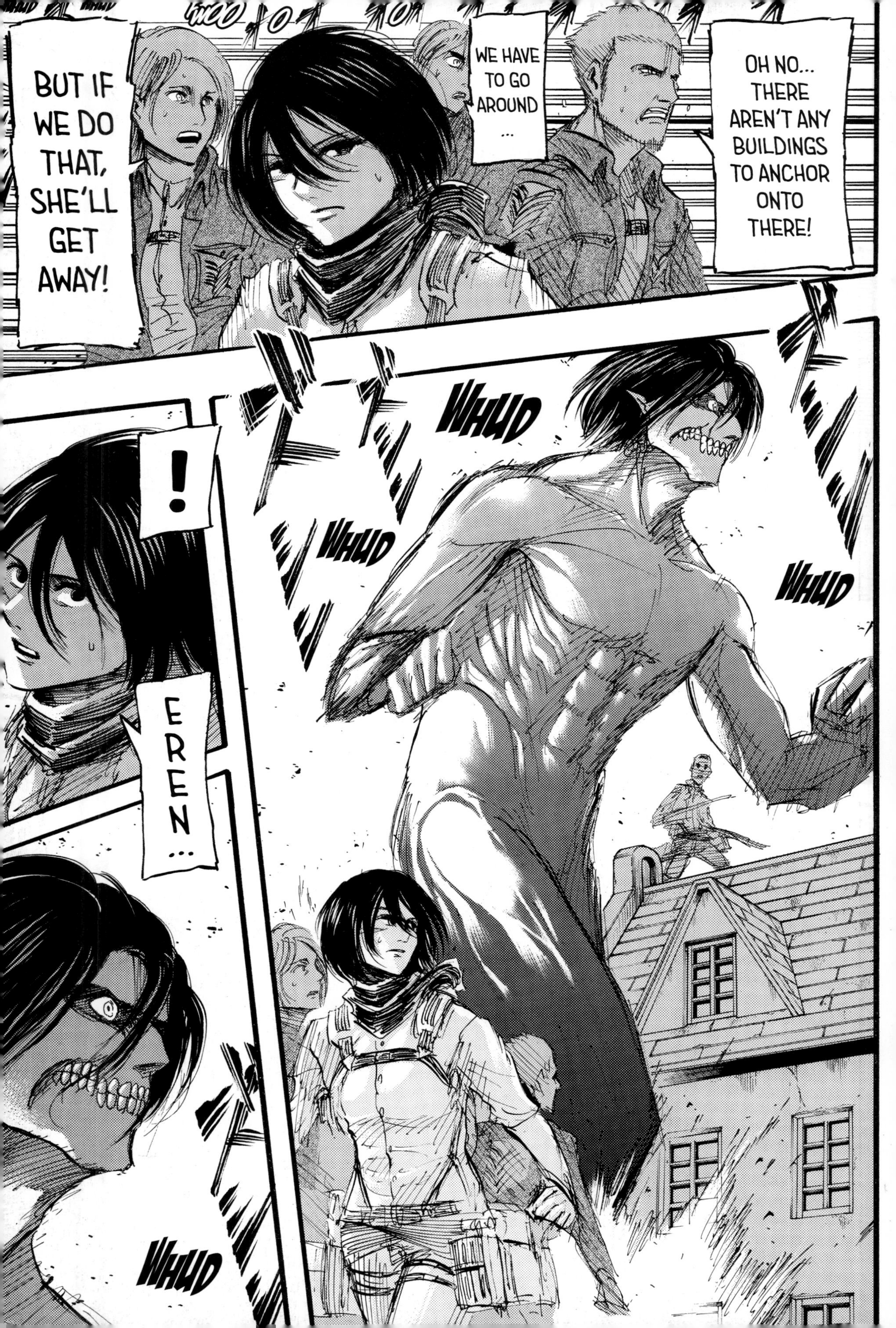
OH NO... THERE AREN'T ANY BUILDINGS TO ANCHOR ONTO THERE!
WE HAVE TO GO AROUND ...
BUT IF WE DO THAT, SHE'LL GET AWAY!
WHUD
WHUD
WHUD
!
EREN ...
WHUD

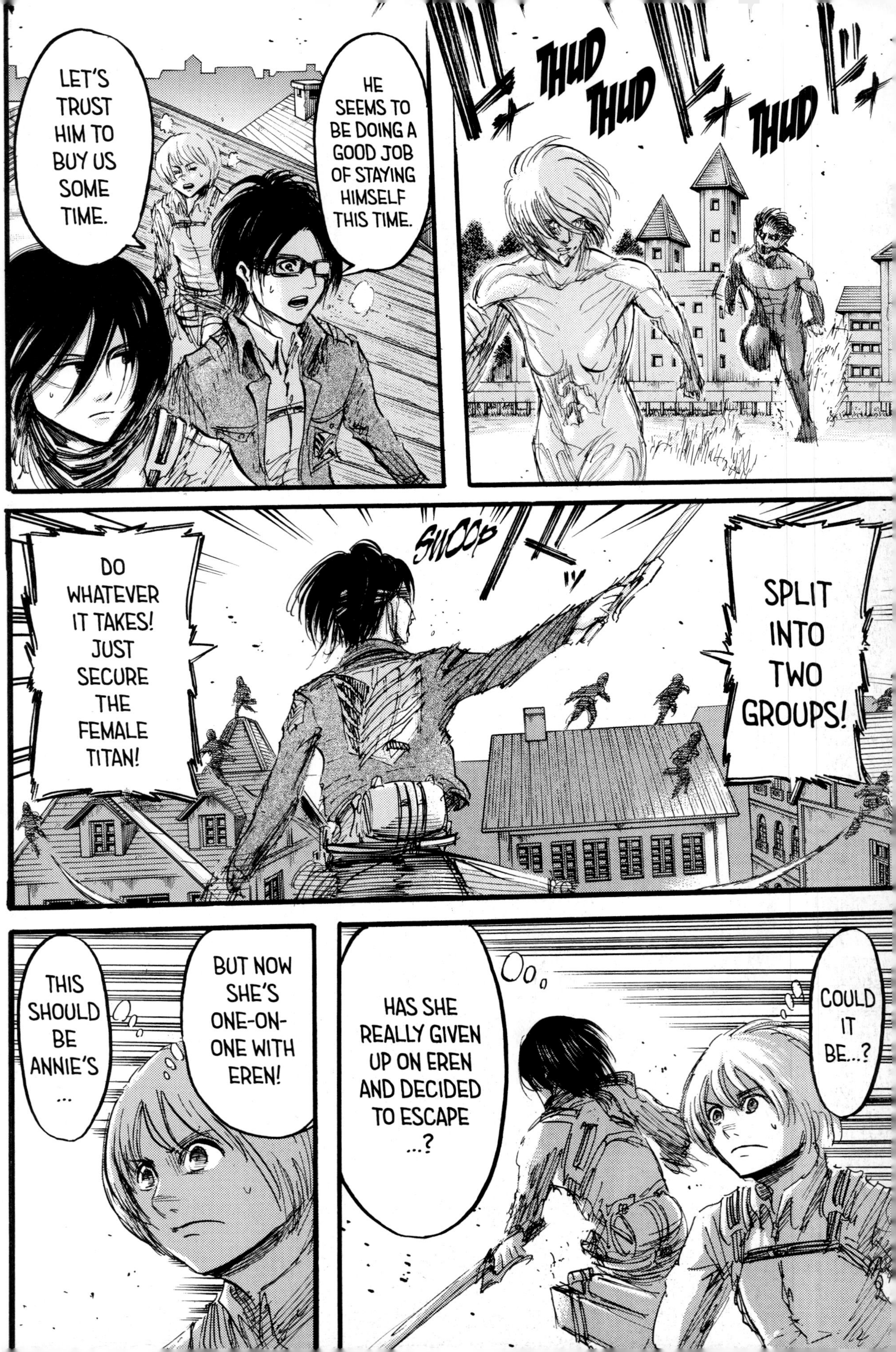
THUD
THUD
THUD
HE SEEMS TO BE DOING A GOOD JOB OF STAYING HIMSELF THIS TIME.
LET'S TRUST HIM TO BUY US SOME TIME.
SWOOP
SPLIT INTO TWO GROUPS!
DO WHATEVER IT TAKES! JUST SECURE THE FEMALE TITAN!
COULD IT BE...?
HAS SHE REALLY GIVEN UP ON EREN AND DECIDED TO ESCAPE ...?
BUT NOW SHE'S ONE-ON-ONE WITH EREN!
THIS SHOULD BE ANNIE'S ...

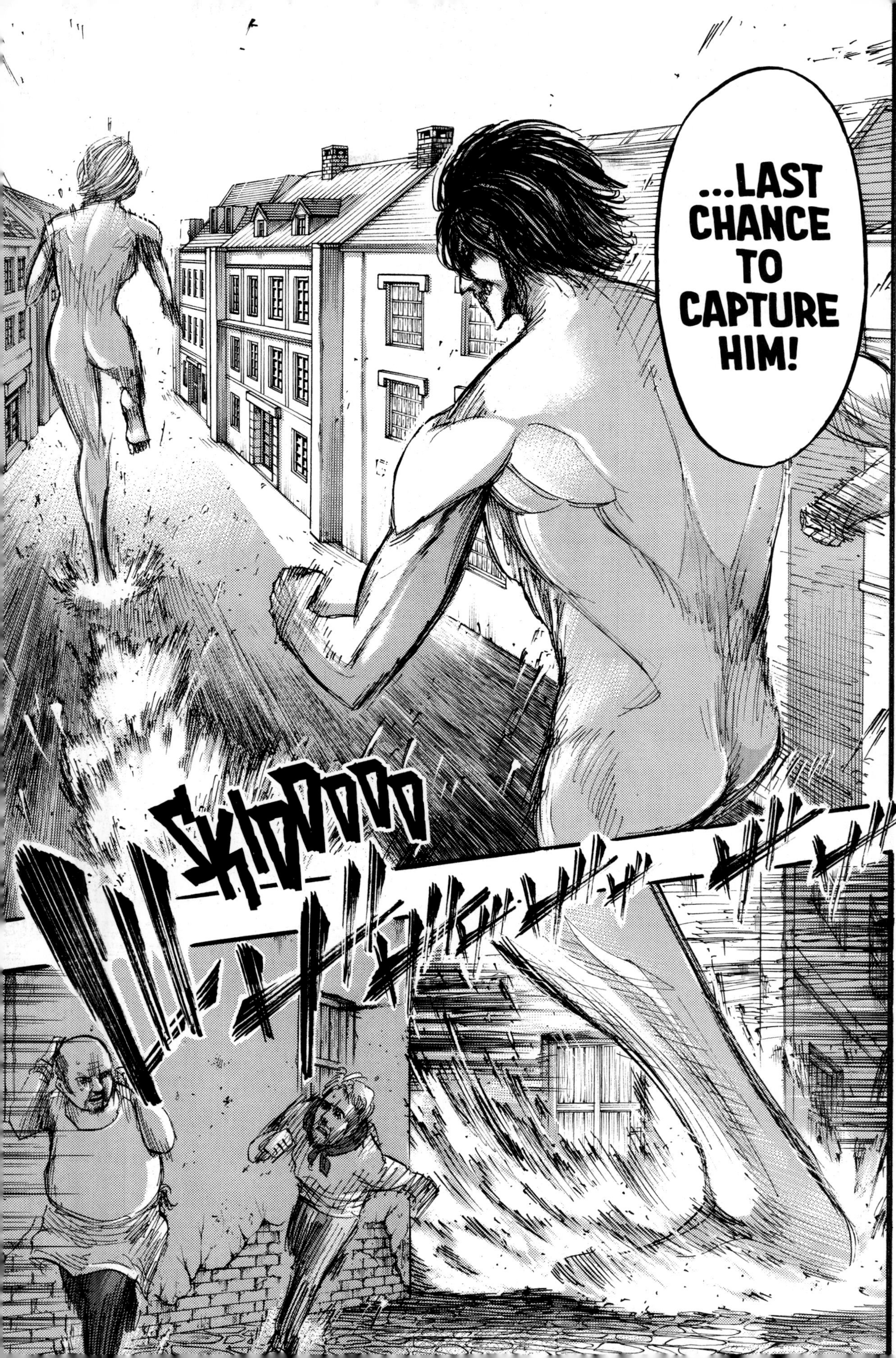
...LAST CHANCE TO CAPTURE HIM!
SKIDDDDD

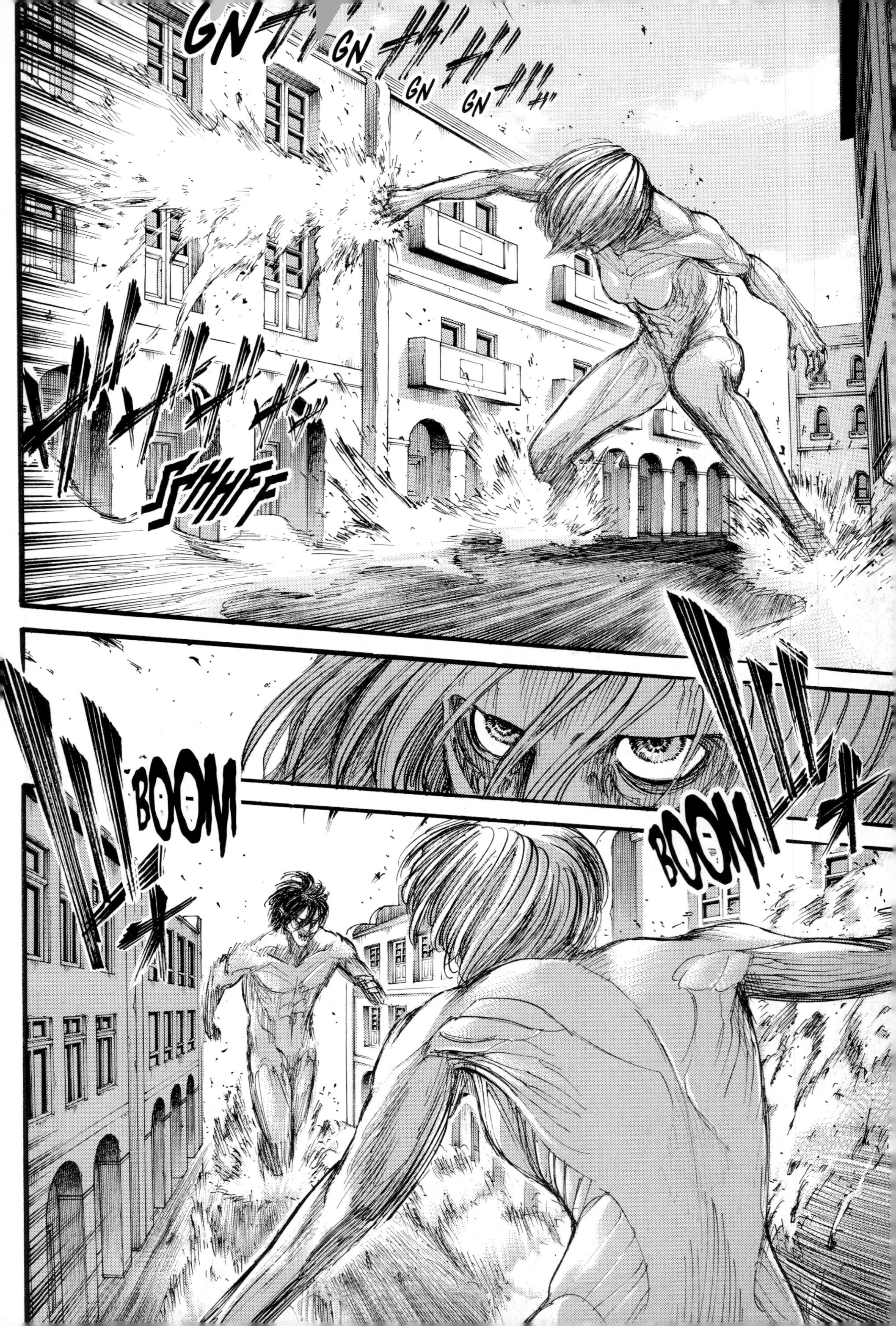
GN
GN
GN
GN
SHHFF
BOOM
BOOM

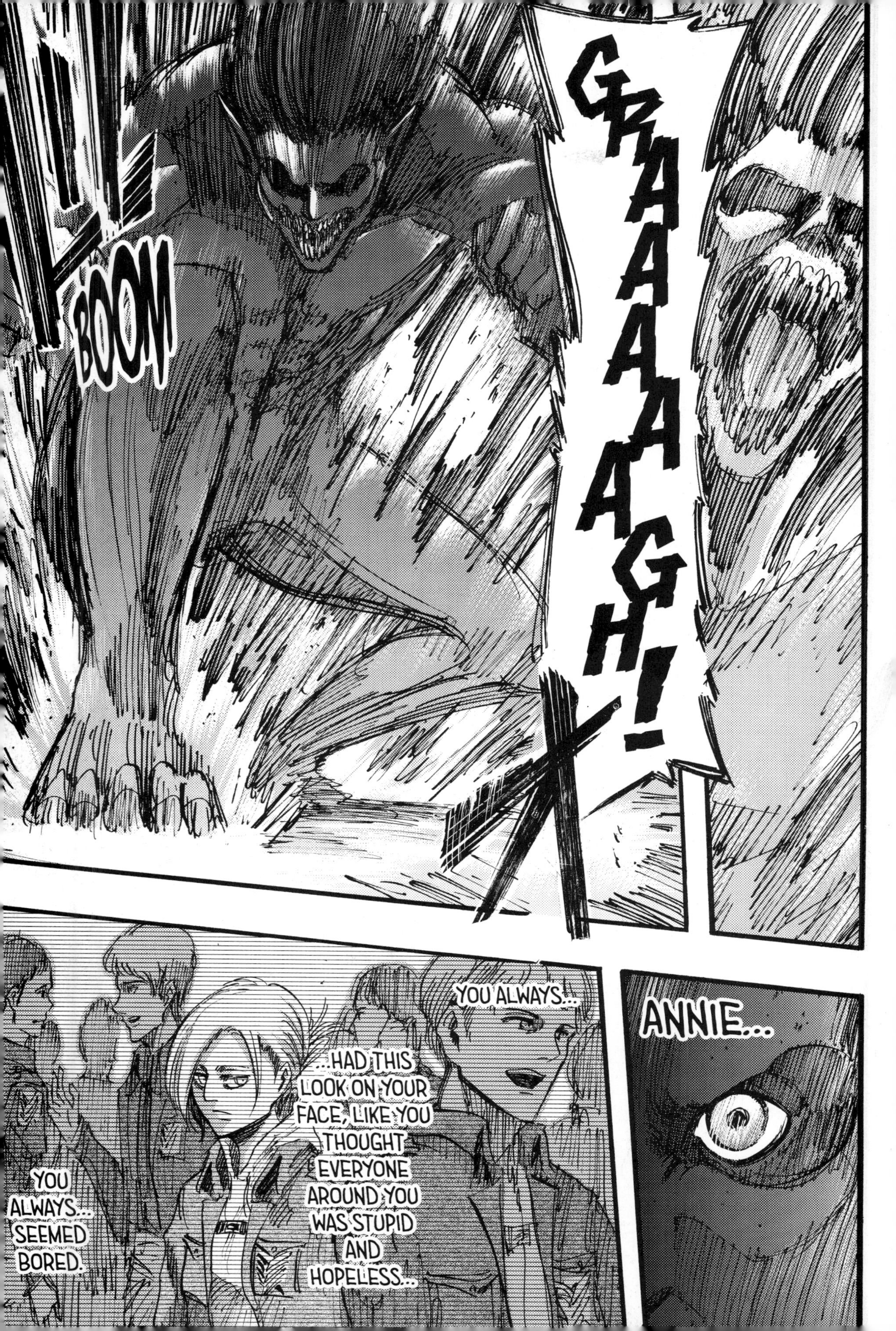
GRAAAAAGH!
BOOM
ANNIE...
YOU ALWAYS...
...HAD THIS LOOK ON YOUR FACE, LIKE YOU THOUGHT EVERYONE AROUND YOU WAS STUPID AND HOPELESS...
YOU ALWAYS... SEEMED BORED.

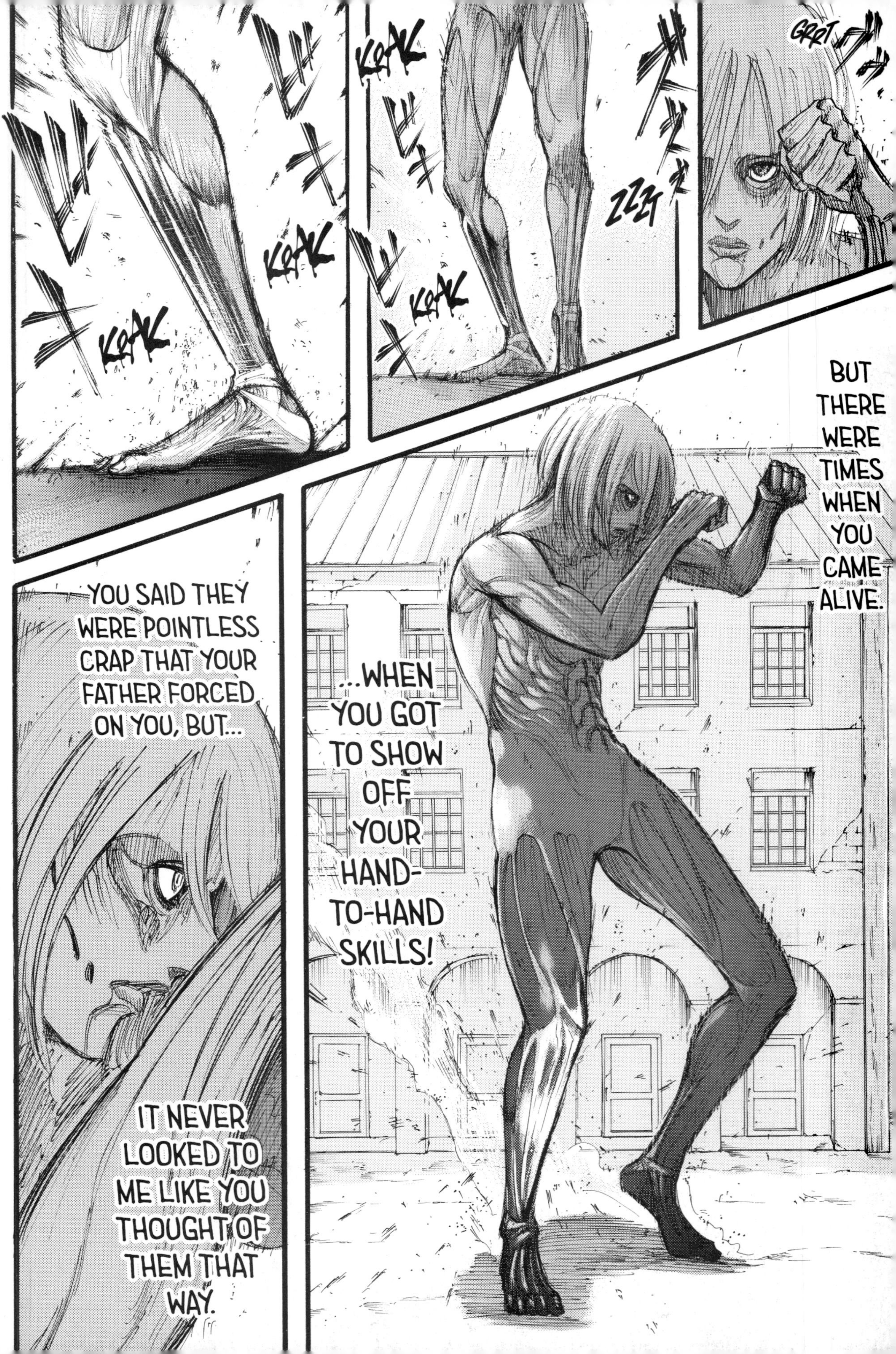
GRRT
ZZZT
KRAK
KRAK
KRAK
KRAK
BUT THERE WERE TIMES WHEN YOU CAME ALIVE.
...WHEN YOU GOT TO SHOW OFF YOUR HAND-TO-HAND SKILLS!
YOU SAID THEY WERE POINTLESS CRAP THAT YOUR FATHER FORCED ON YOU, BUT...
IT NEVER LOOKED TO ME LIKE YOU THOUGHT OF THEM THAT WAY.

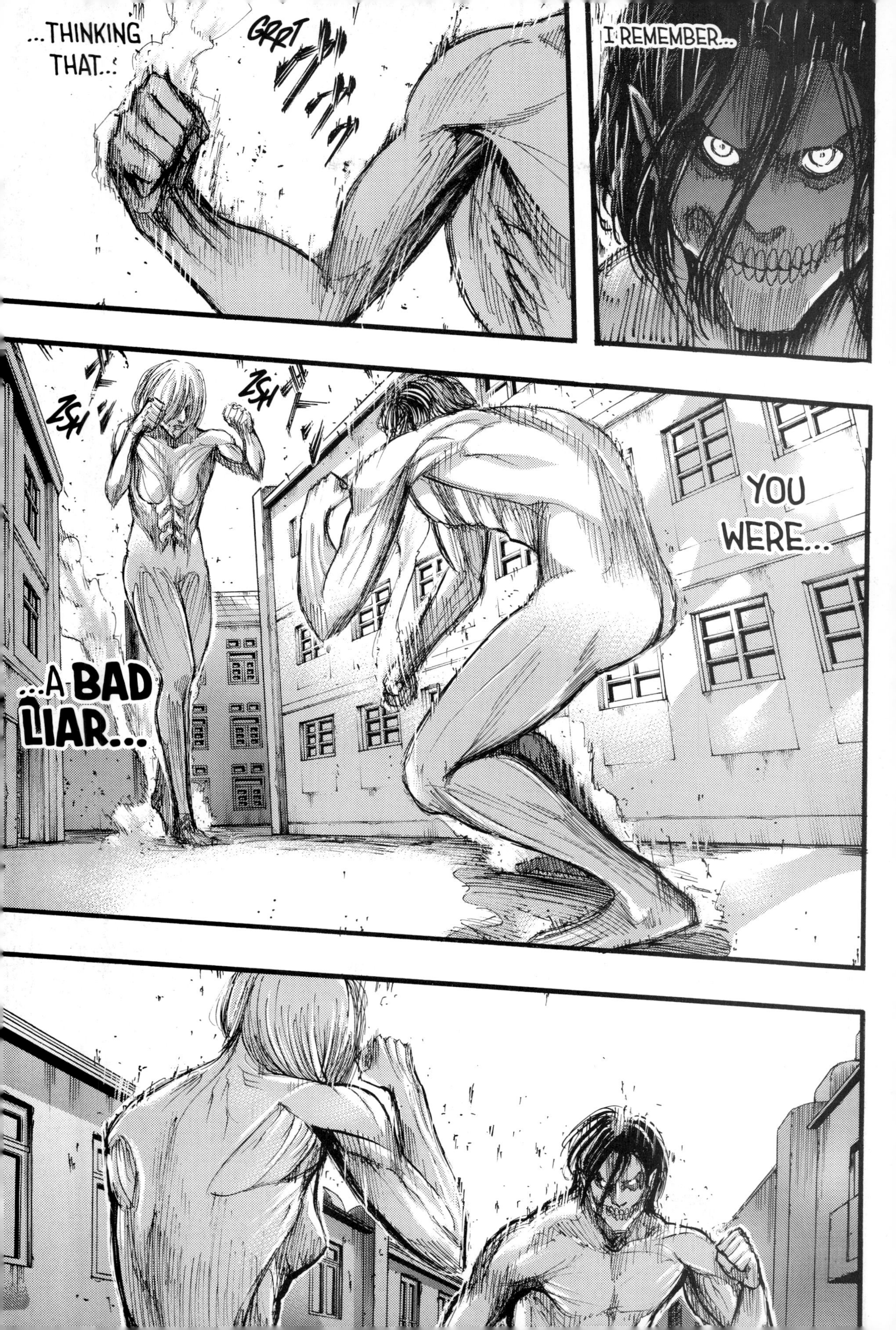

I REMEMBER...
GRRT
...THINKING THAT...
ZSH
ZSH
YOU WERE...
...A BAD LIAR...

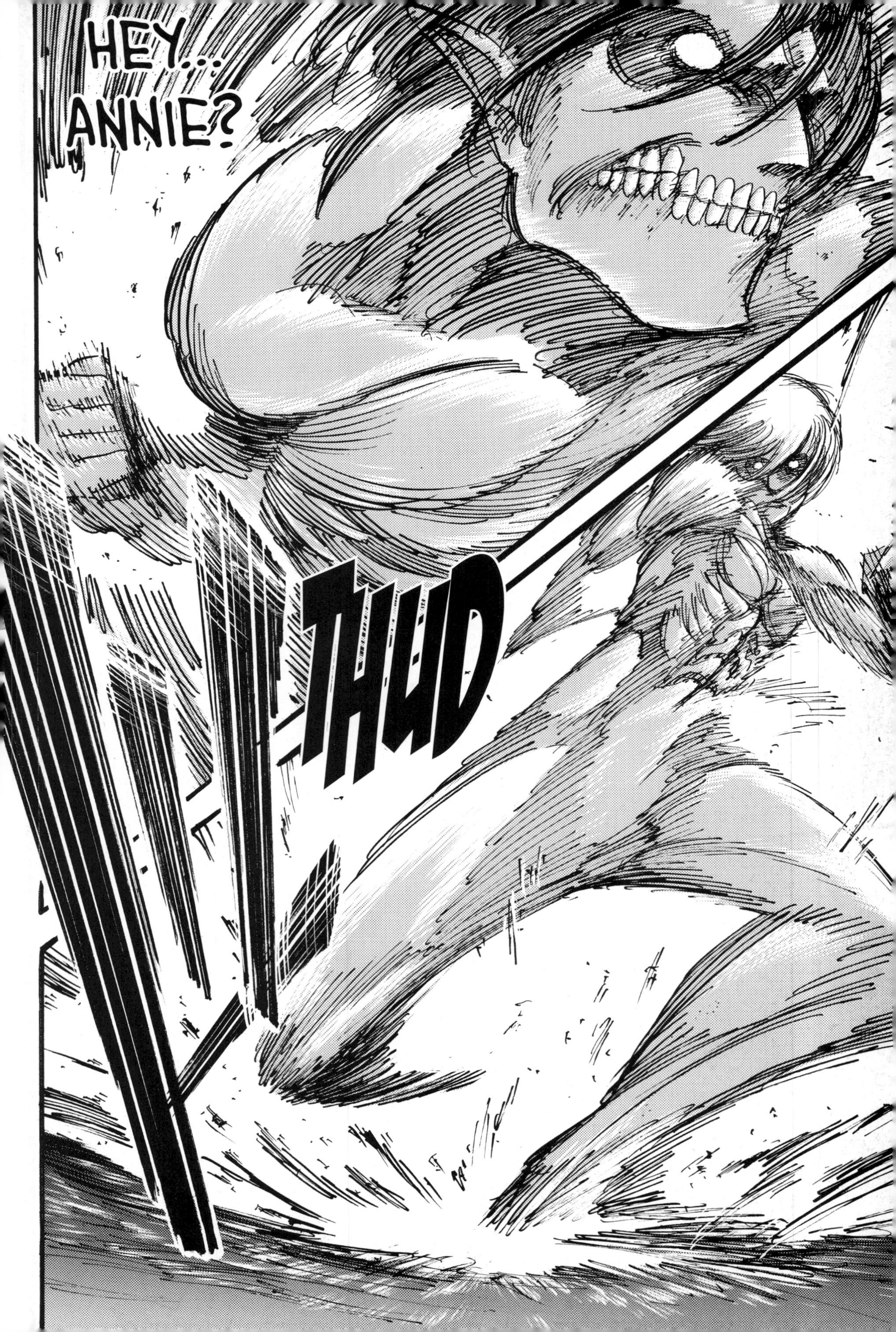
HEY... ANNIE?
THUD

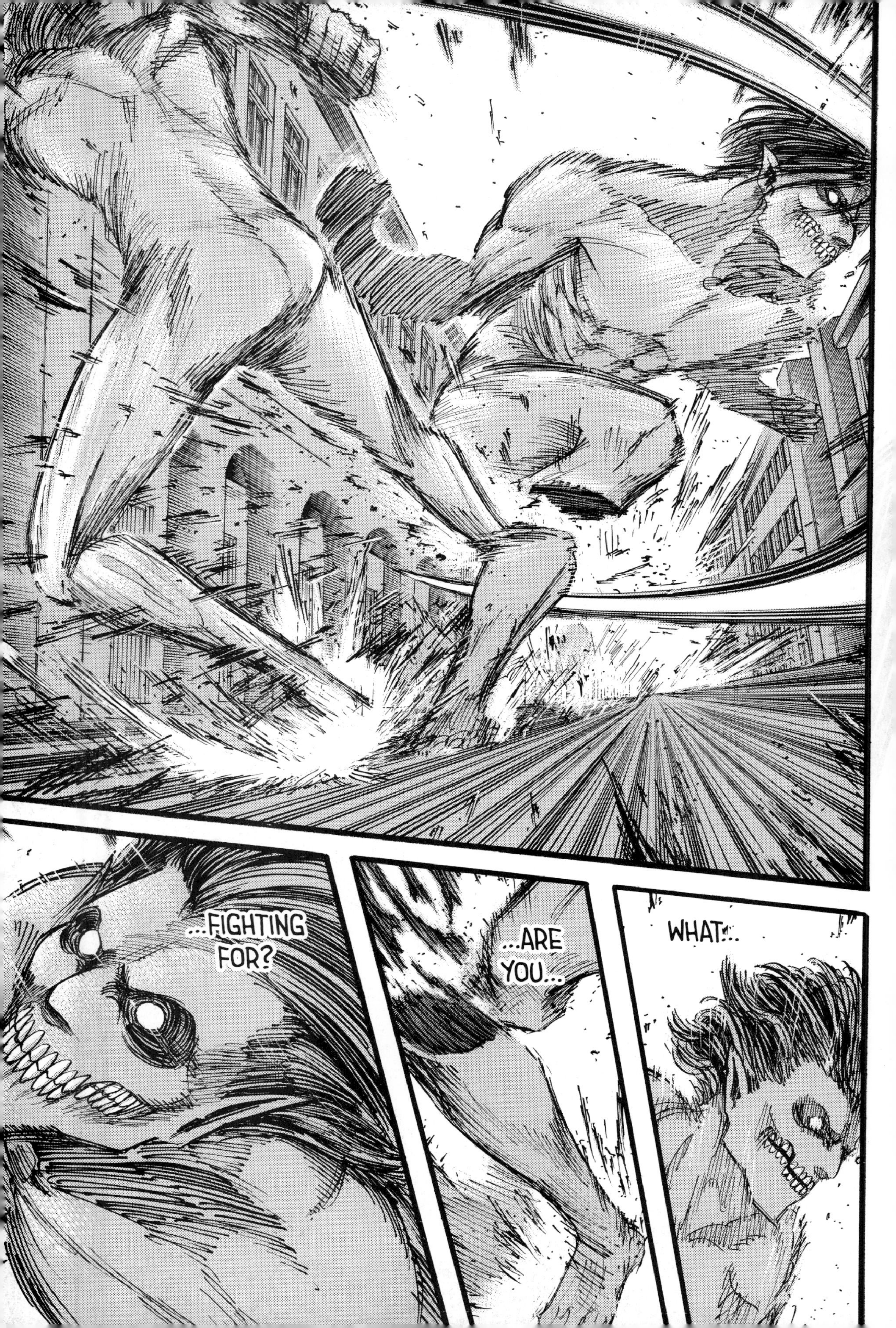
WHAT...
...ARE YOU...
...FIGHTING FOR?

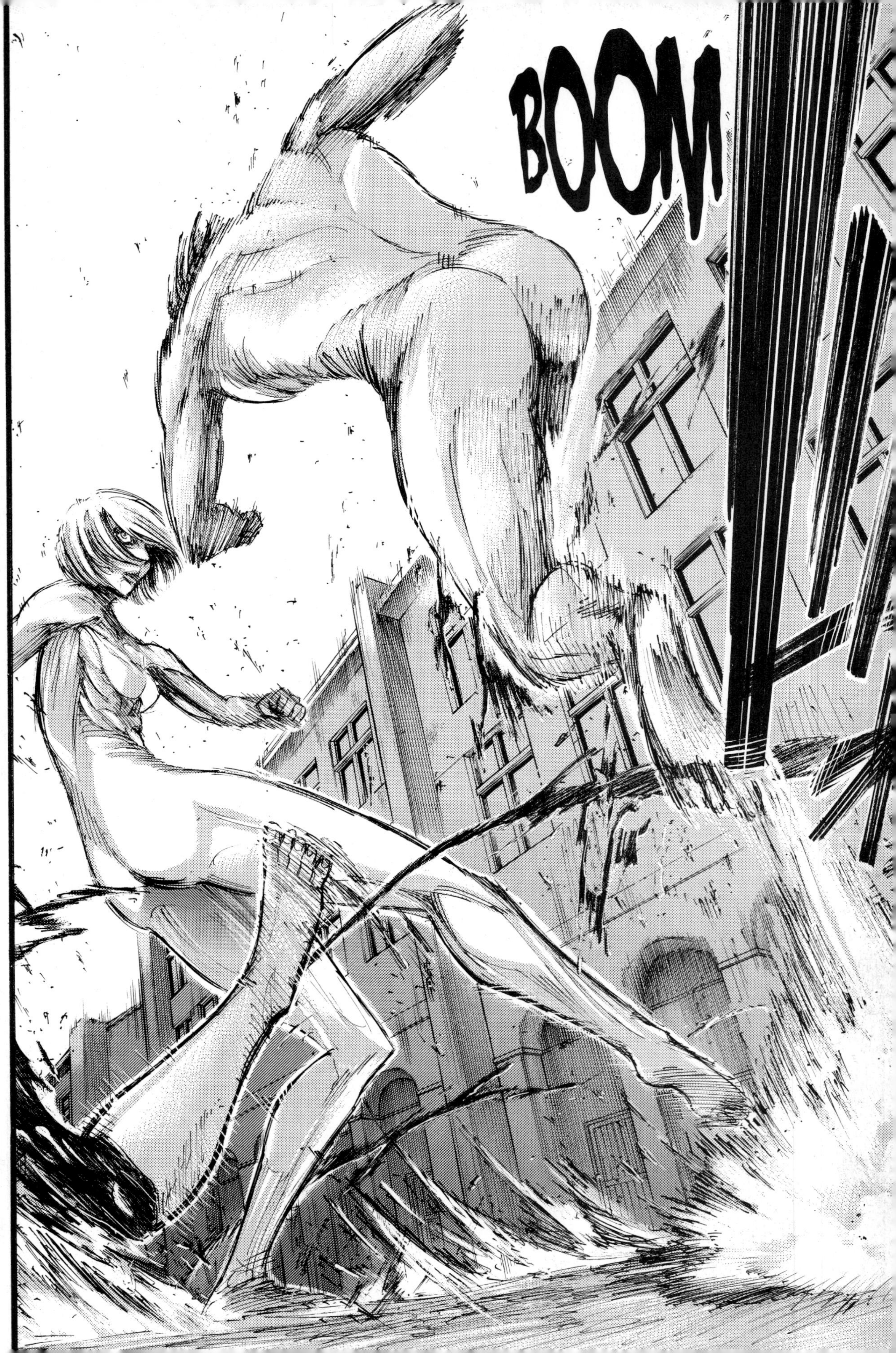
BOOM

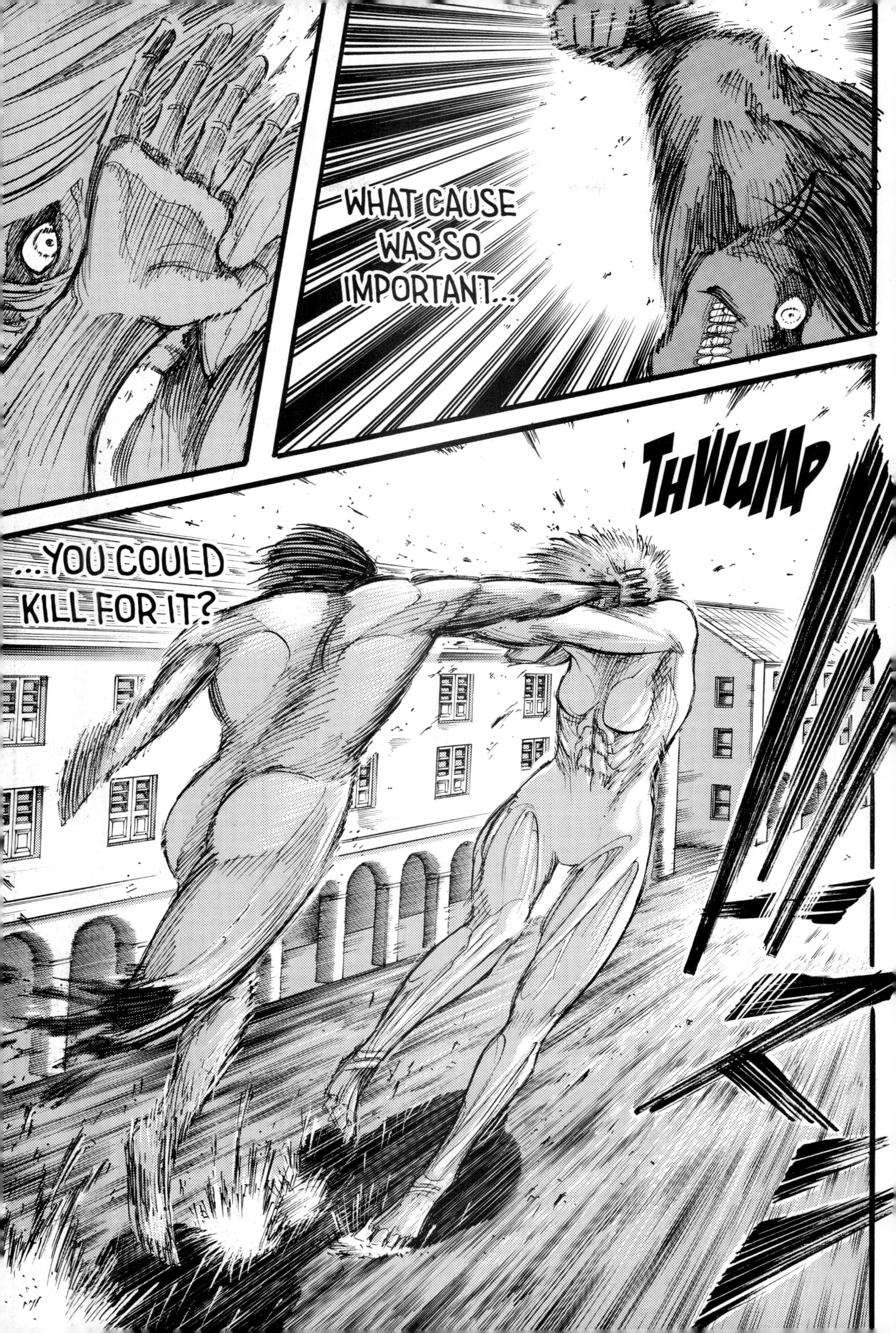
WHAT CAUSE WAS SO IMPORTANT...
THWUMP
...YOU COULD KILL FOR IT?

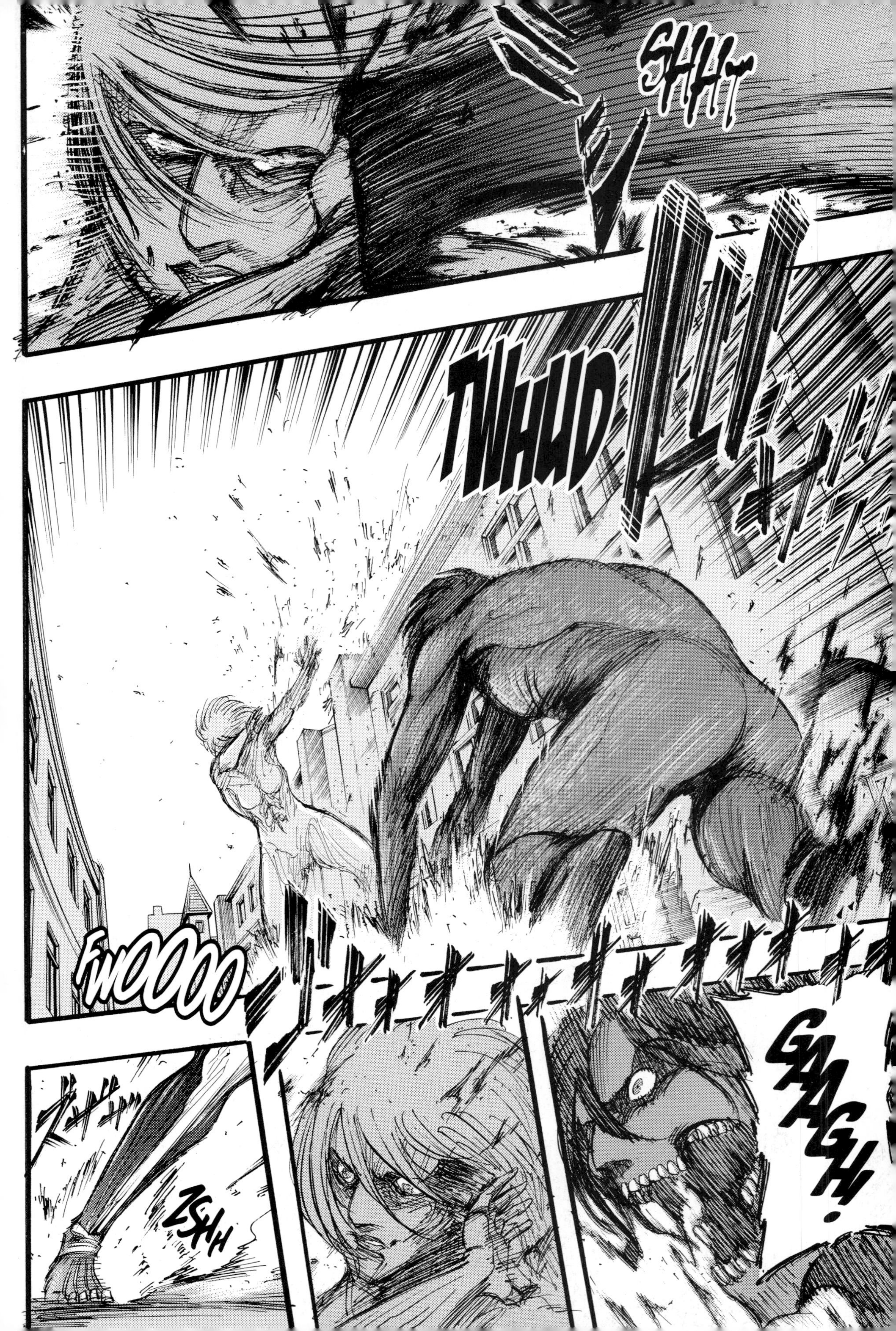
SHHT
THUD
FWOOOOO
GAAGH!
ZSHH

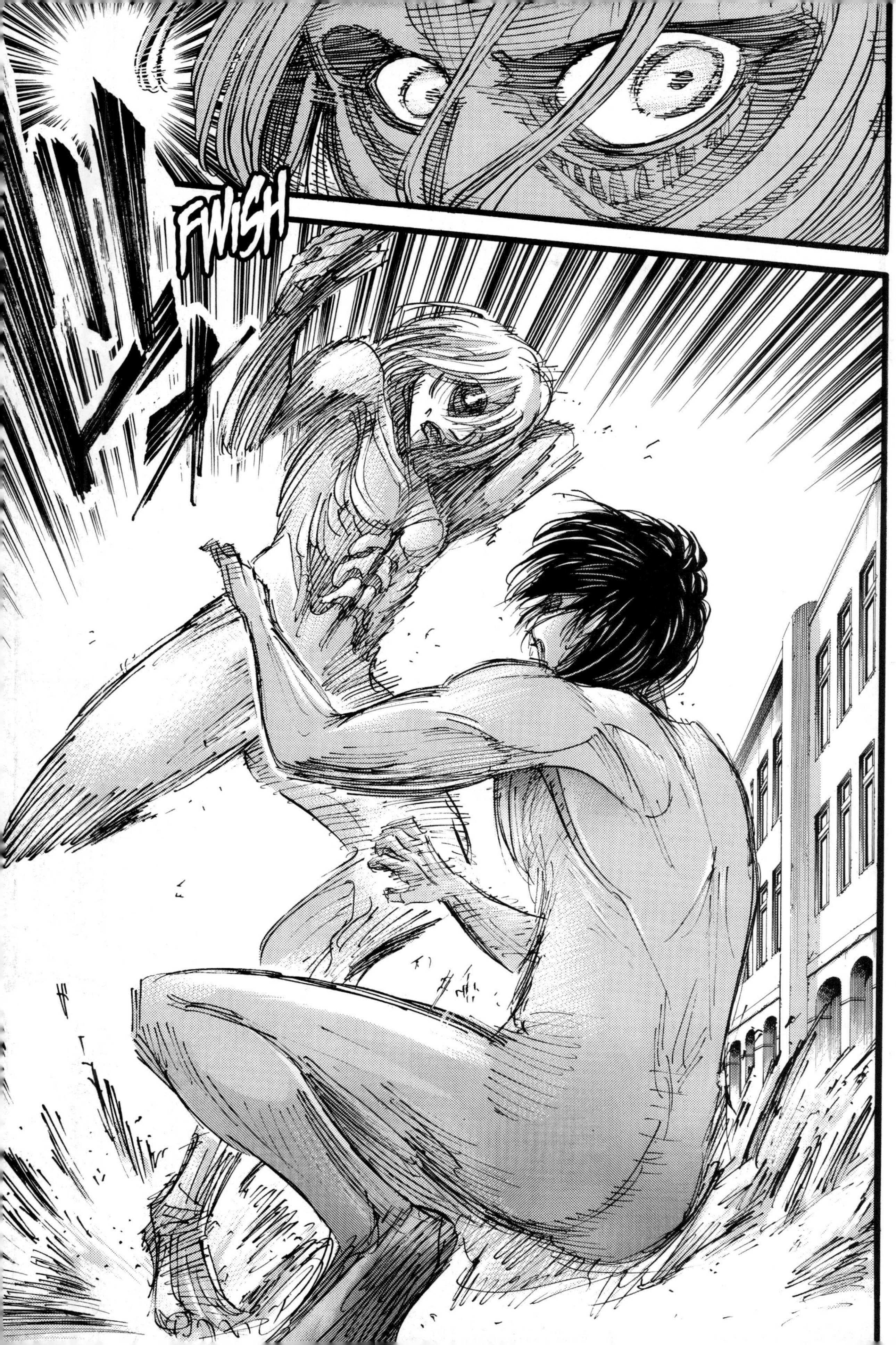
FWISH

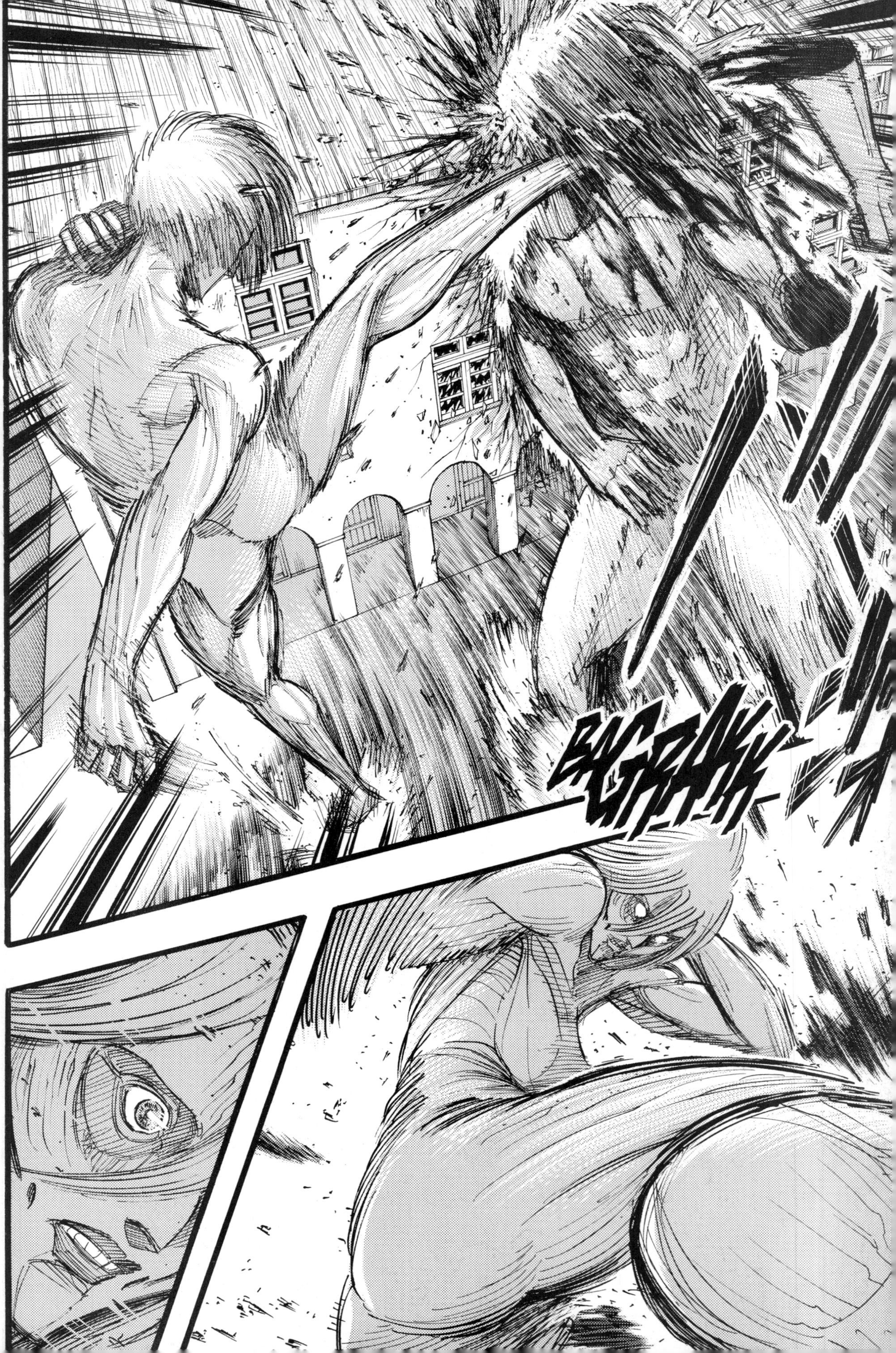
BAGRAKK

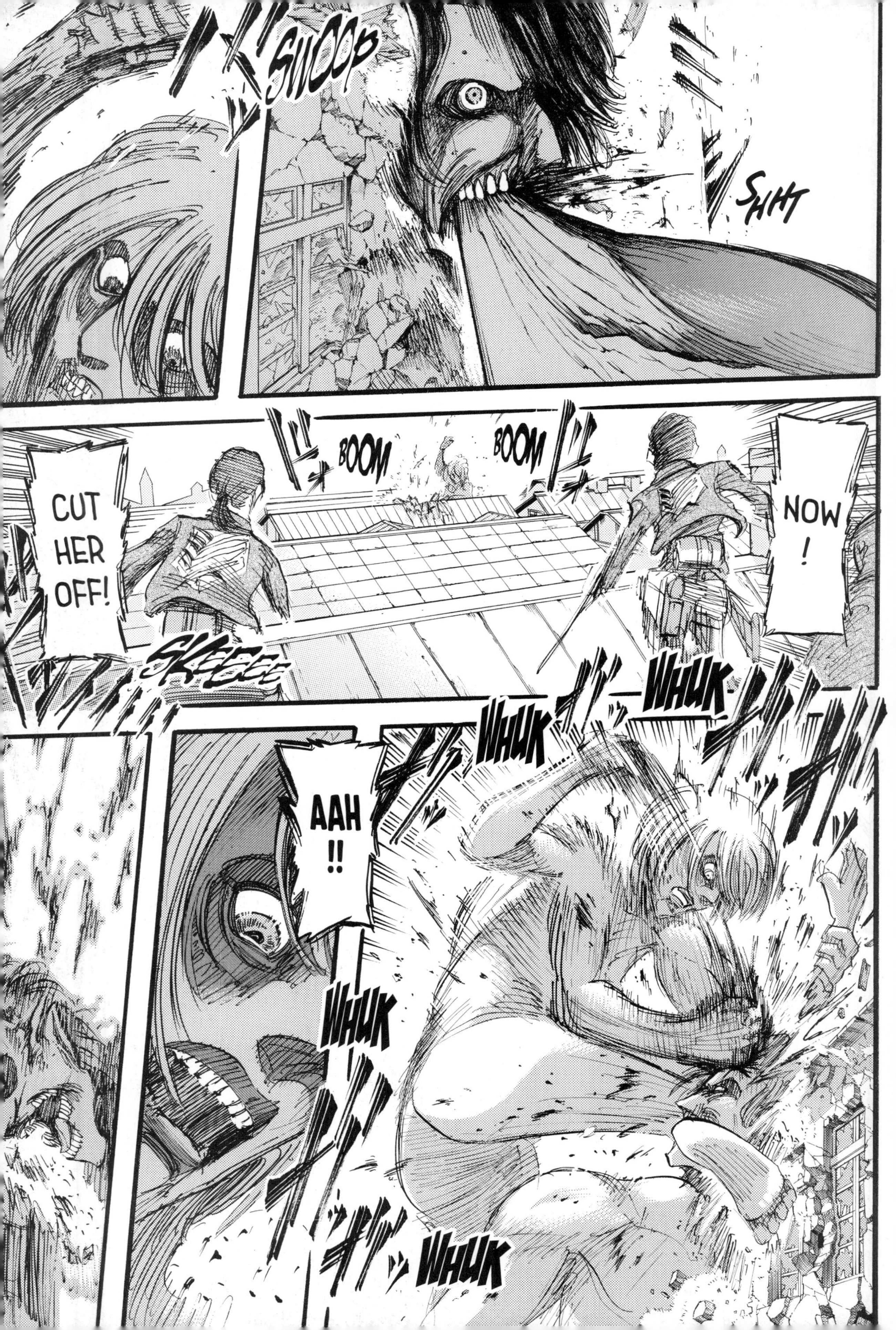
SHHT
SWOOP
NOW!
BOOM
BOOM
CUT HER OFF!
SKEEEE
WHUK
WHUK
AAH!!
WHUK
WHUK

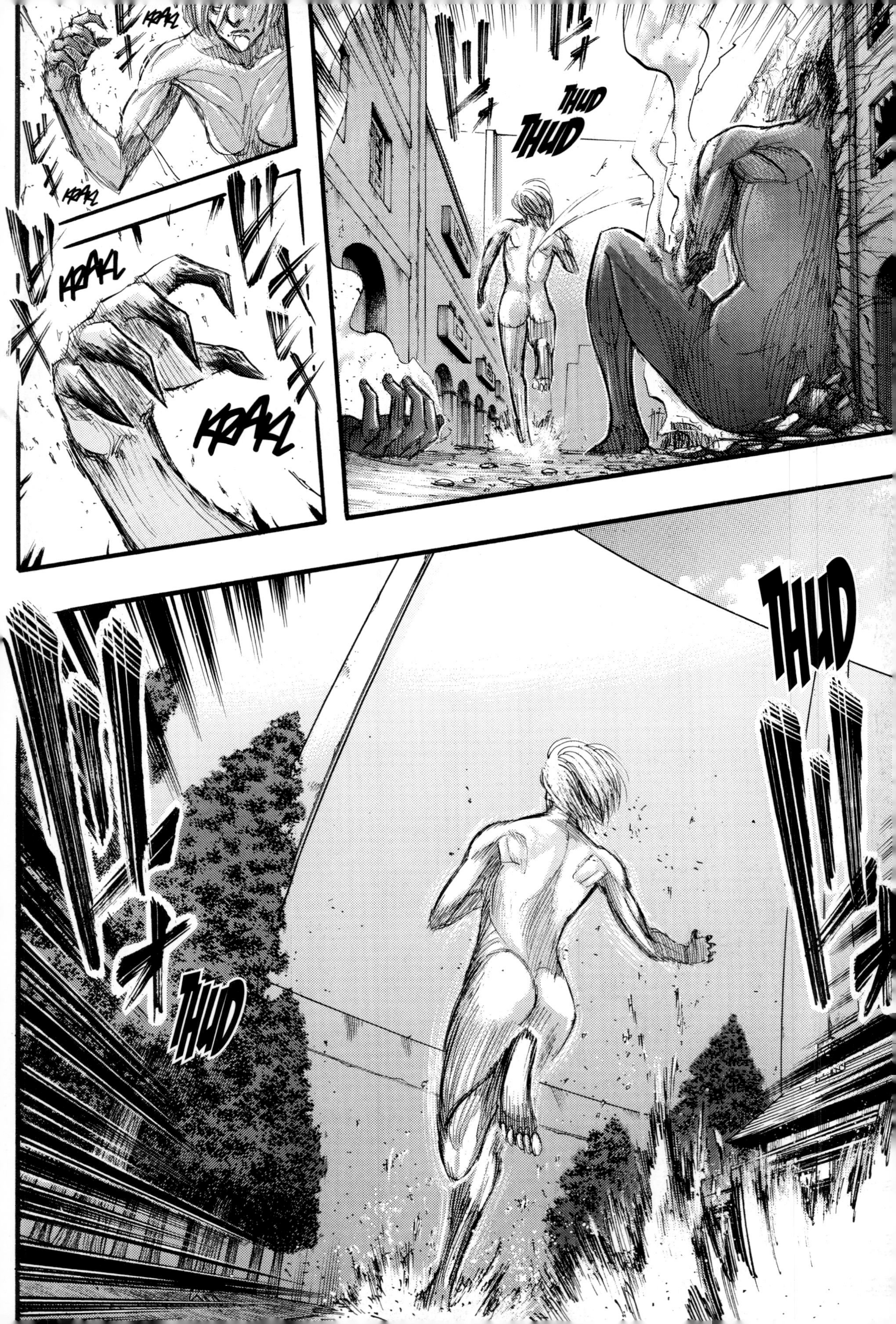
THUD
THUD
KRAK
KRAK
KRAK
KRAK
THUD
THUD

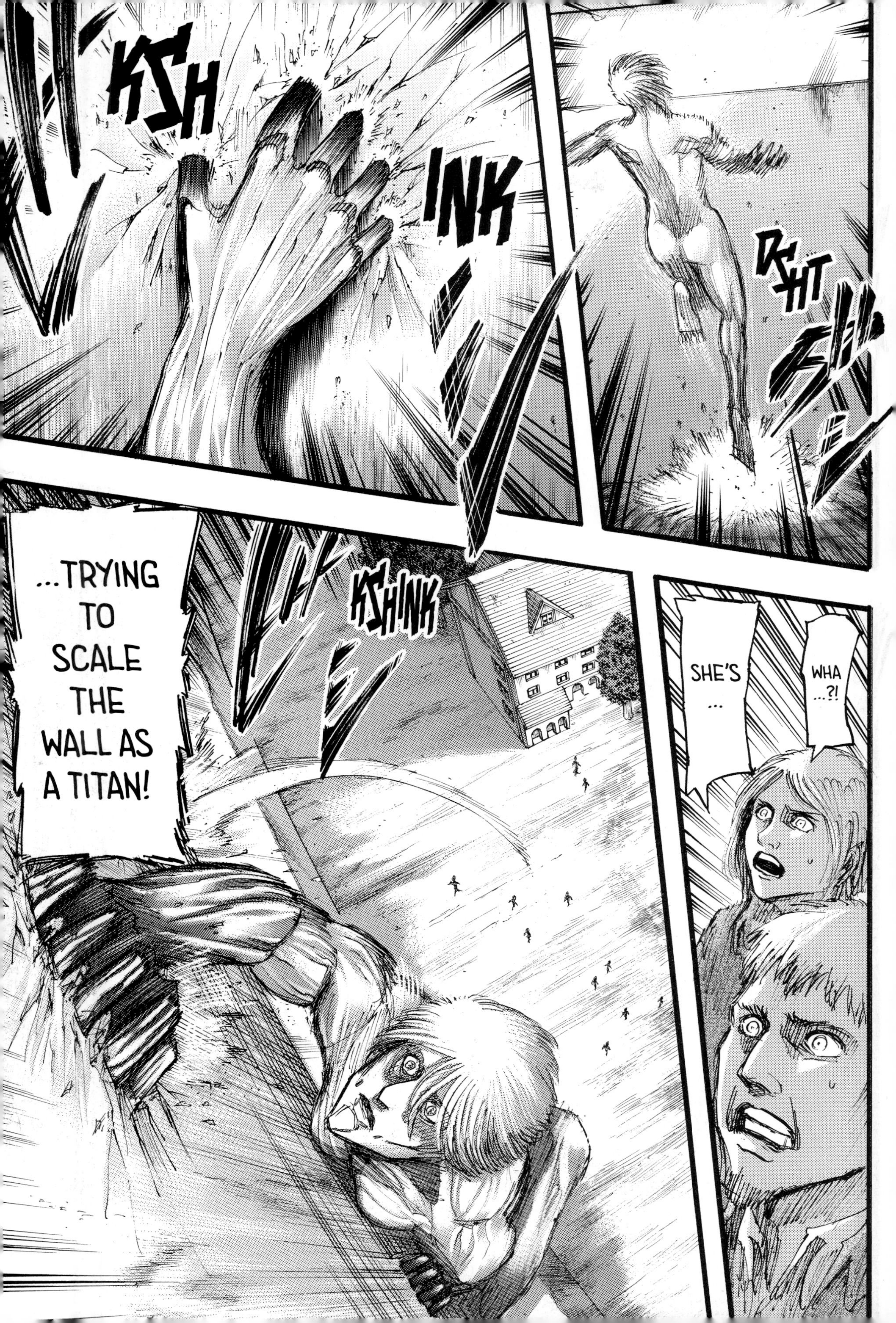
DCHT
KSH
INK
WHA ...?!
SHE'S ...
KSHINK
...TRYING TO SCALE THE WALL AS A TITAN!

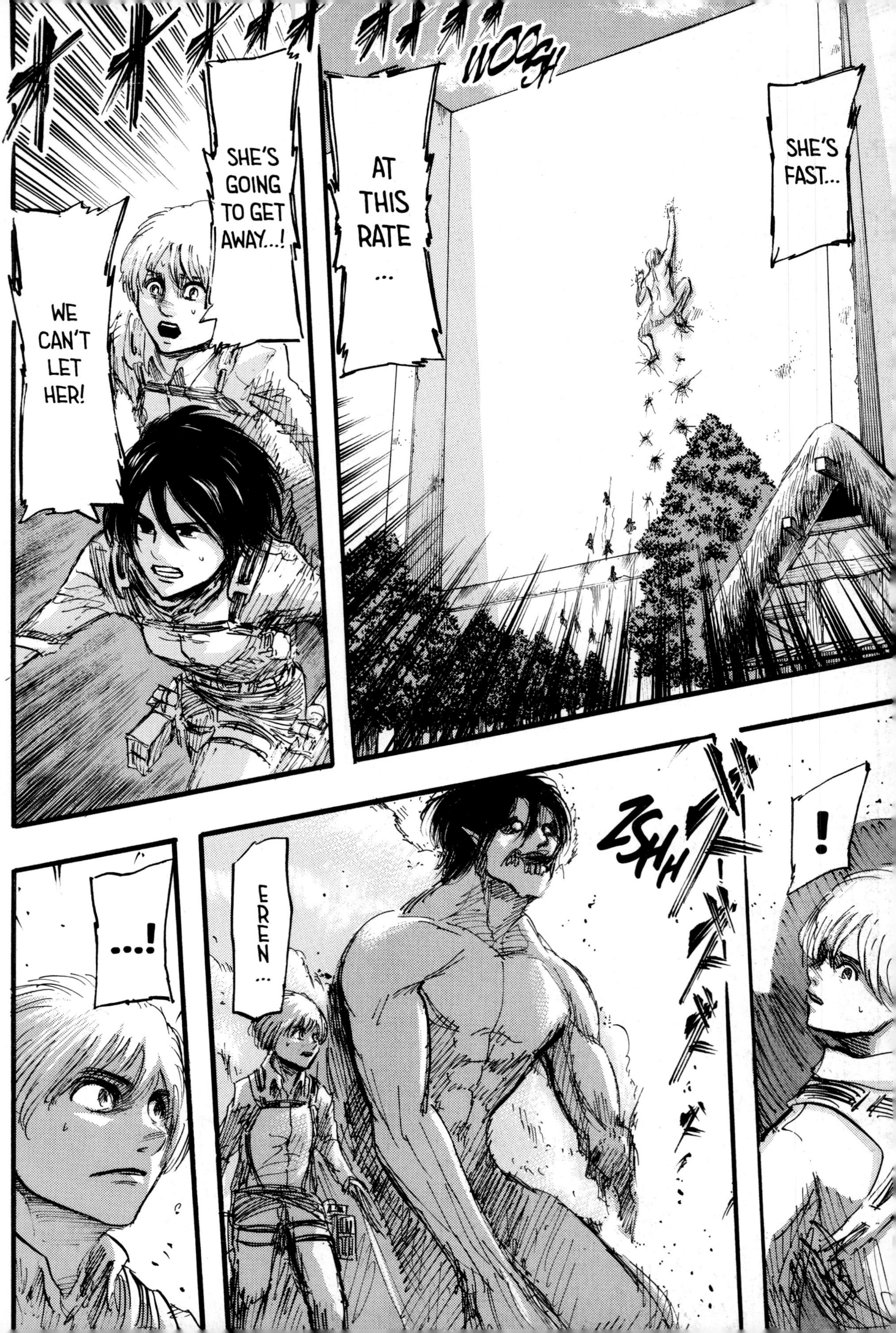
SHE'S FAST...
WOOSH
AT THIS RATE ...
SHE'S GOING TO GET AWAY...!
WE CAN'T LET HER!
!
ZSHH
EREN ...
...!

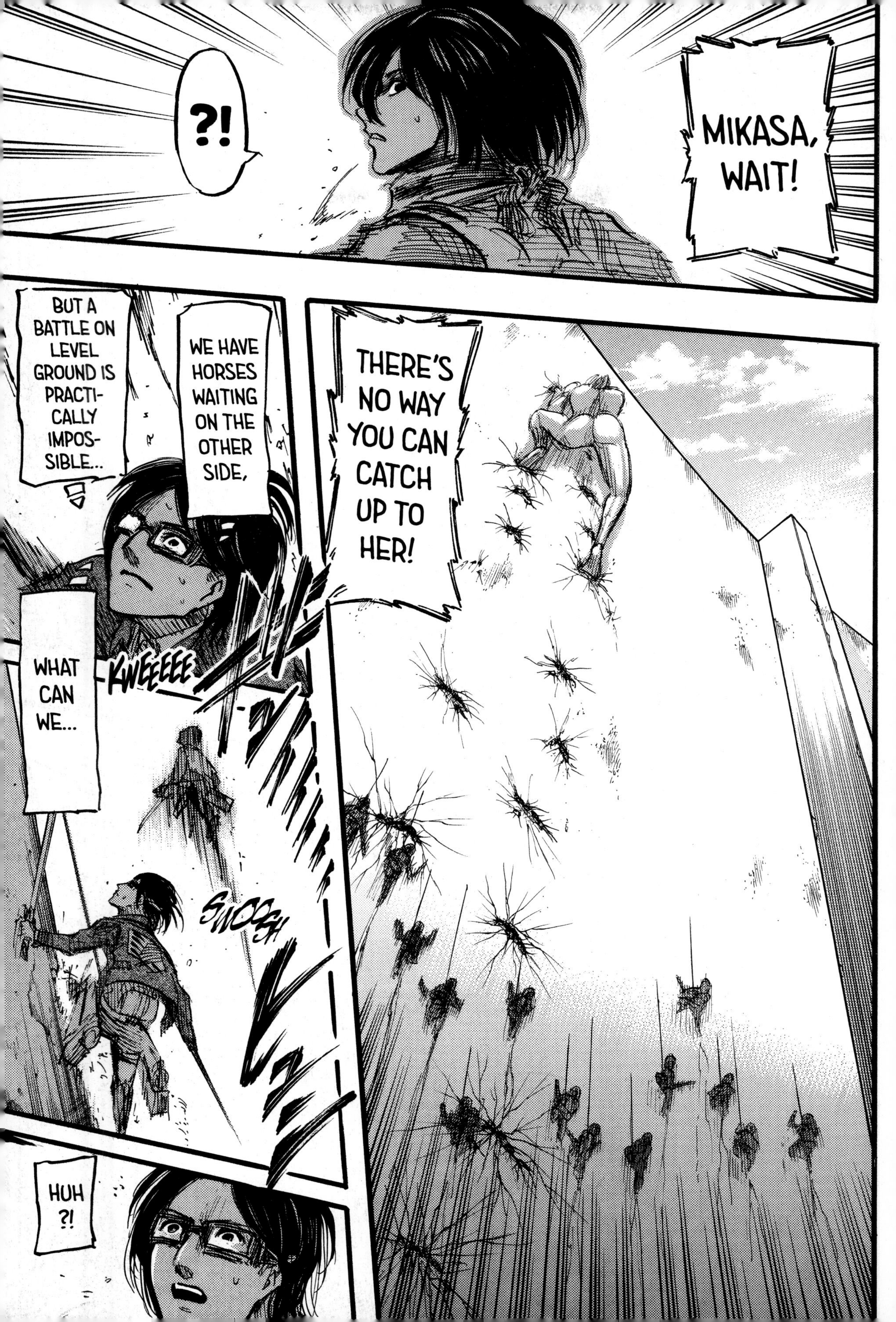
MIKASA, WAIT!
?!
THERE'S NO WAY YOU CAN CATCH UP TO HER!
WE HAVE HORSES WAITING ON THE OTHER SIDE,
BUT A BATTLE ON LEVEL GROUND IS PRACTICALLY IMPOSSIBLE...
WHAT CAN WE...
KWEEEEE
SWOOSH
HUH?!

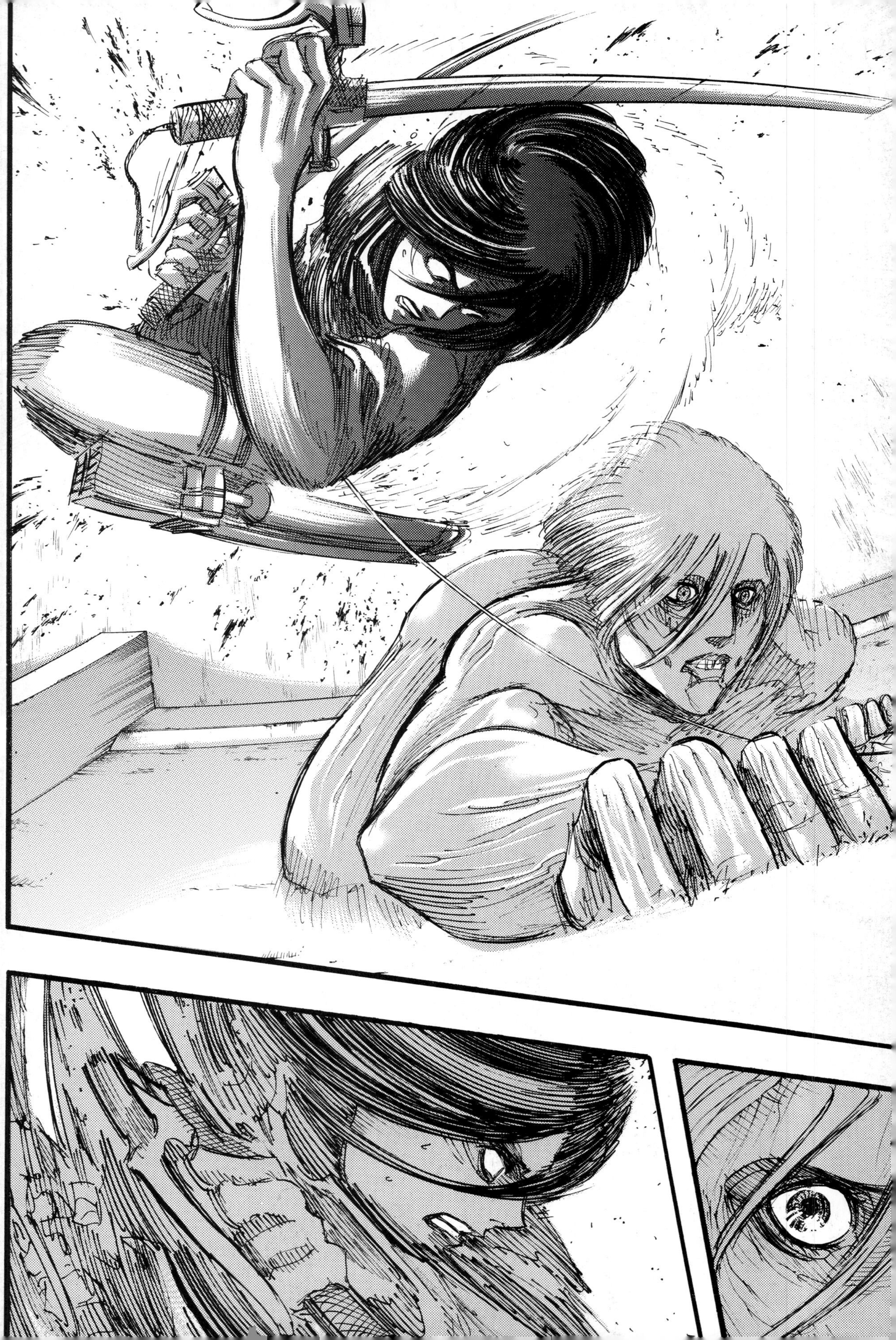

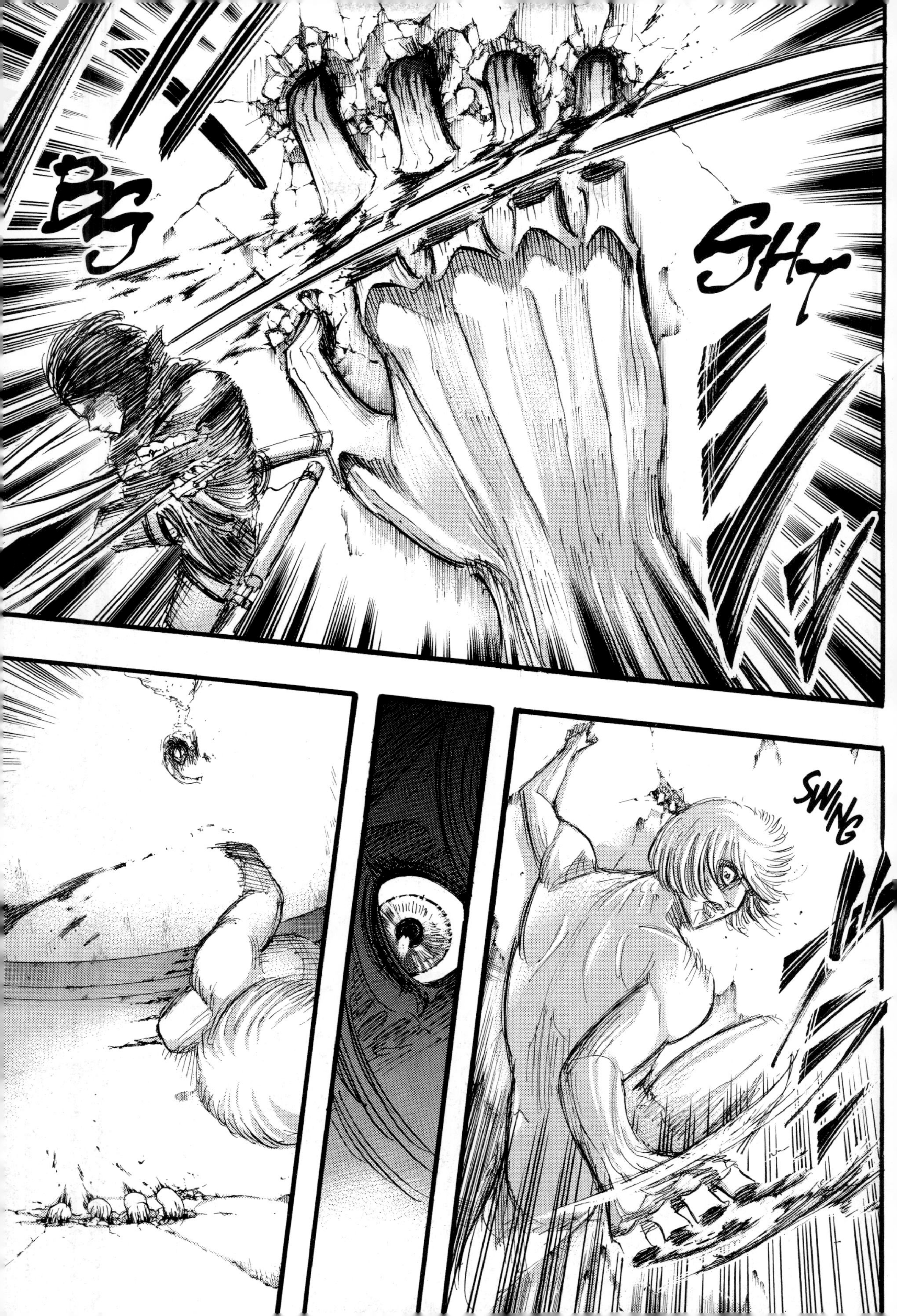
SWING

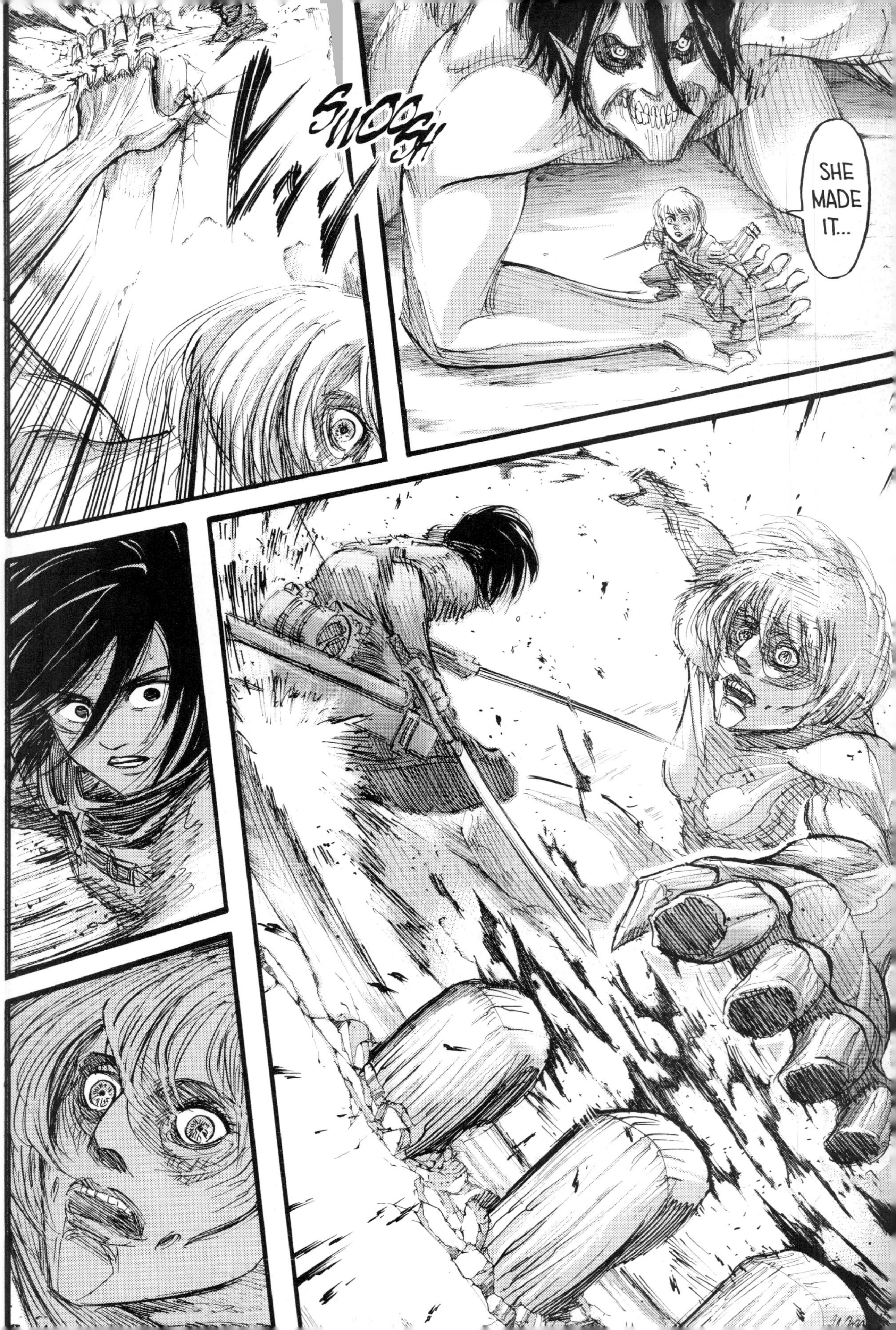
SHE MADE IT...
SWOOSH

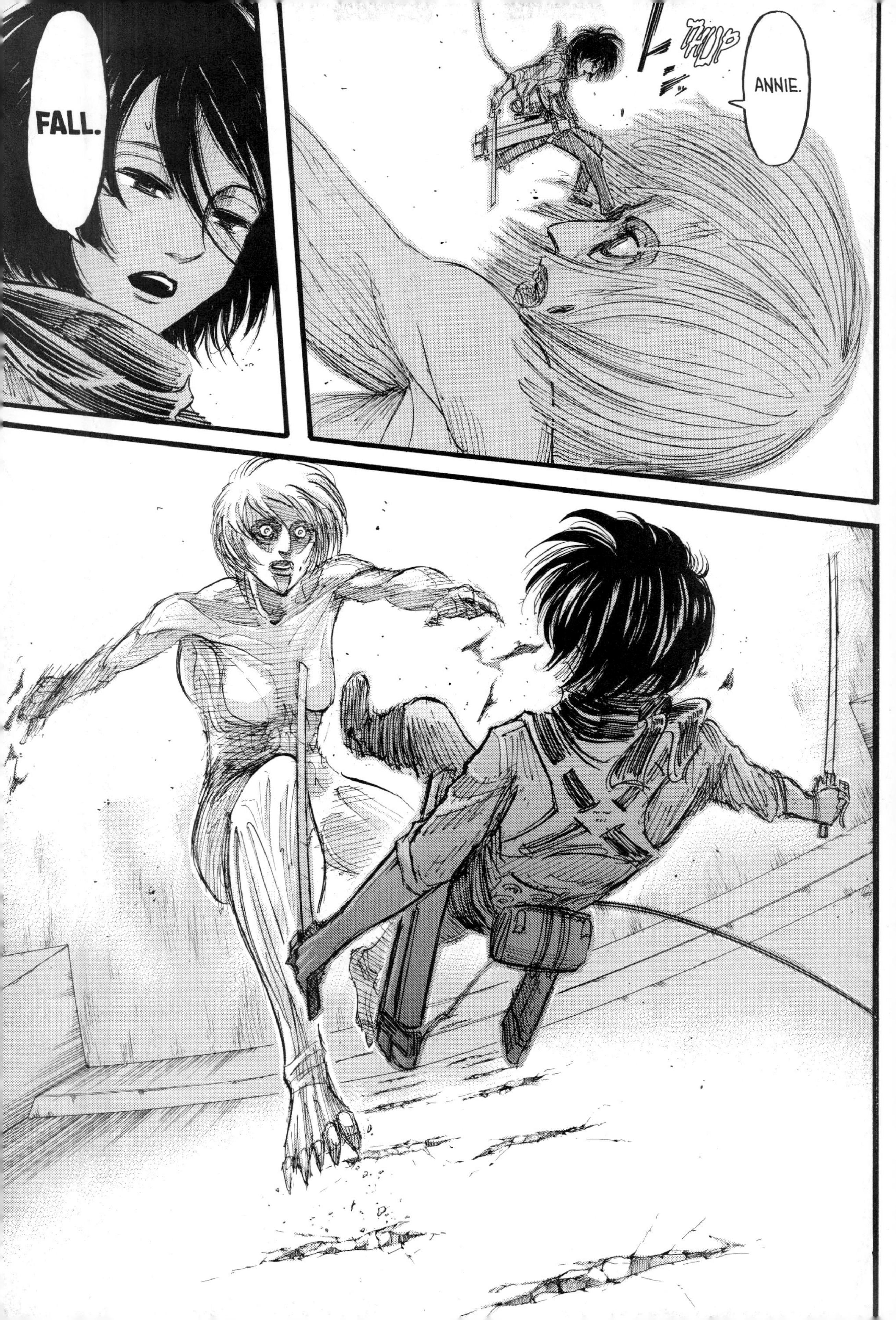
ANNIE.
FALL.

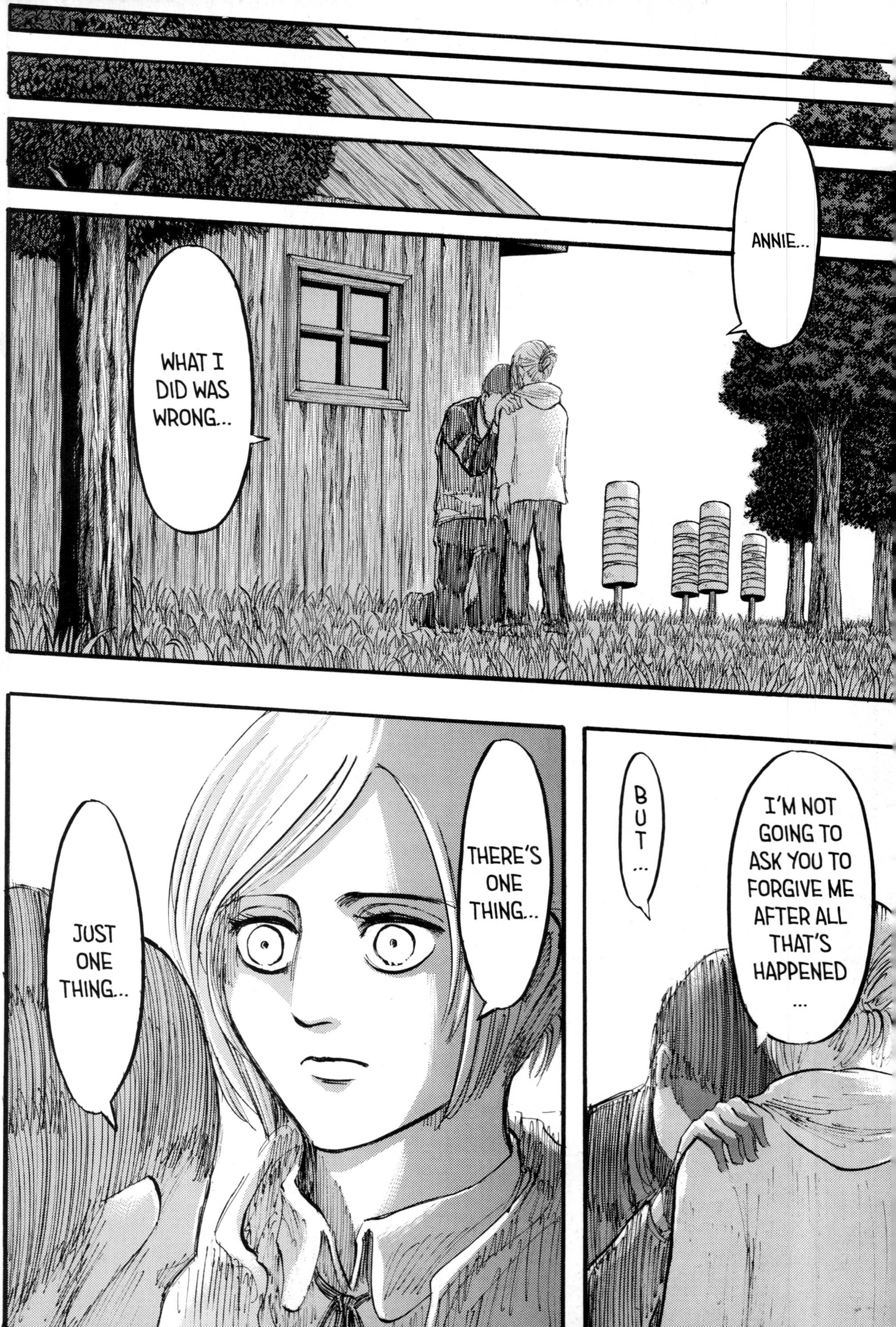
ANNIE...
WHAT I DID WAS WRONG...
I'M NOT GOING TO ASK YOU TO FORGIVE ME AFTER ALL THAT'S HAPPENED ...
BUT ...
THERE'S ONE THING...
JUST ONE THING...

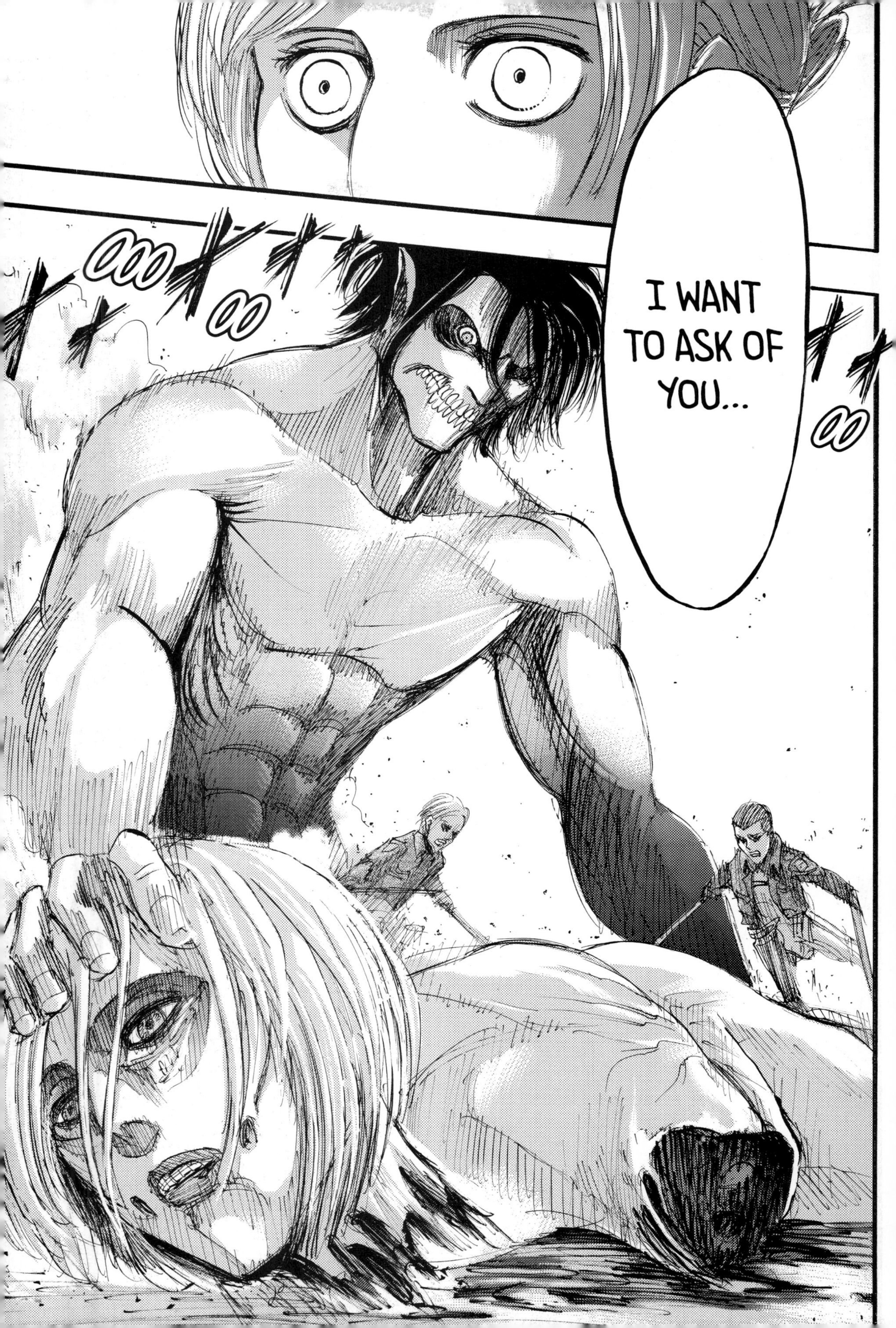
I WANT TO ASK OF YOU...

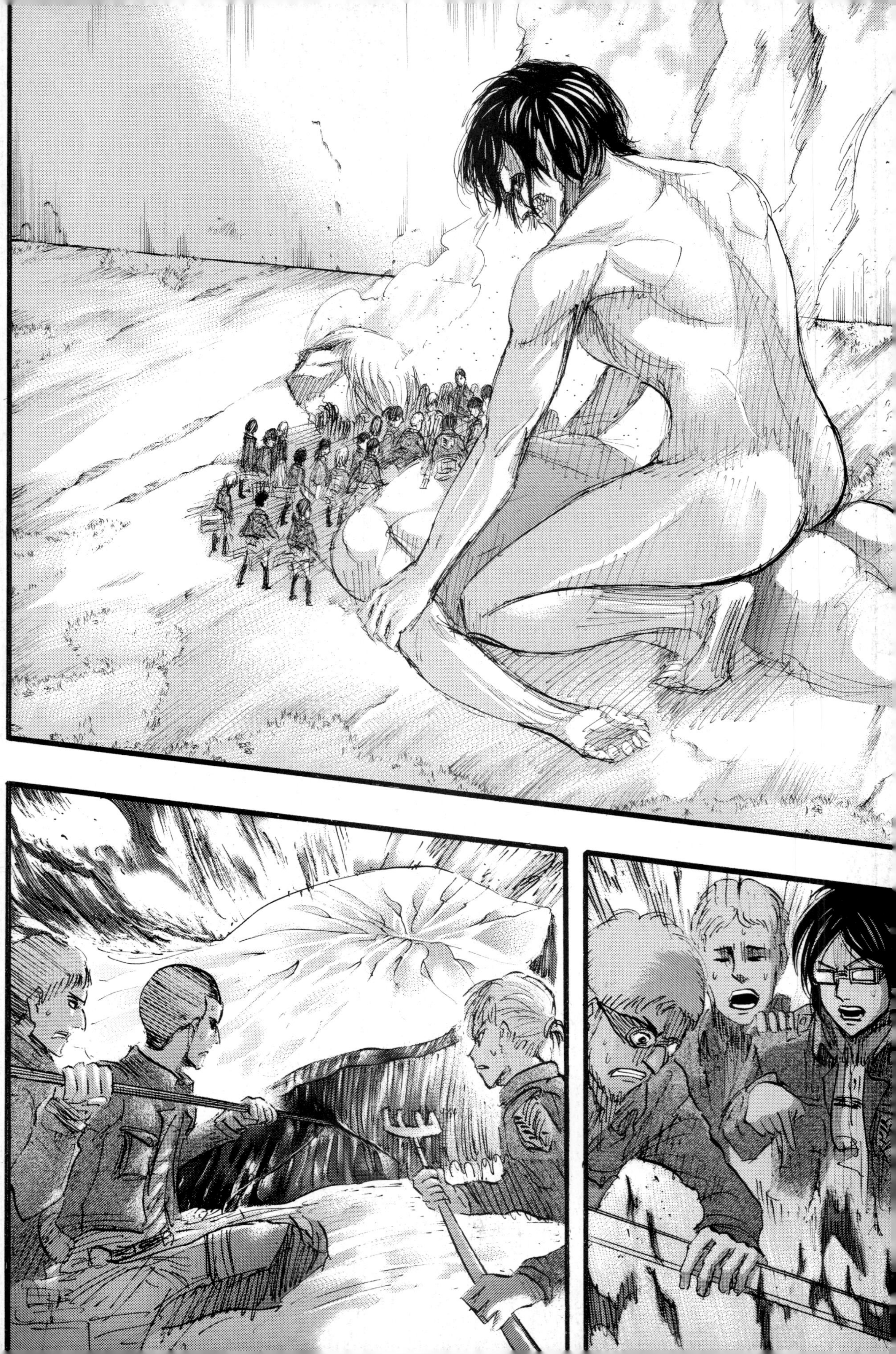

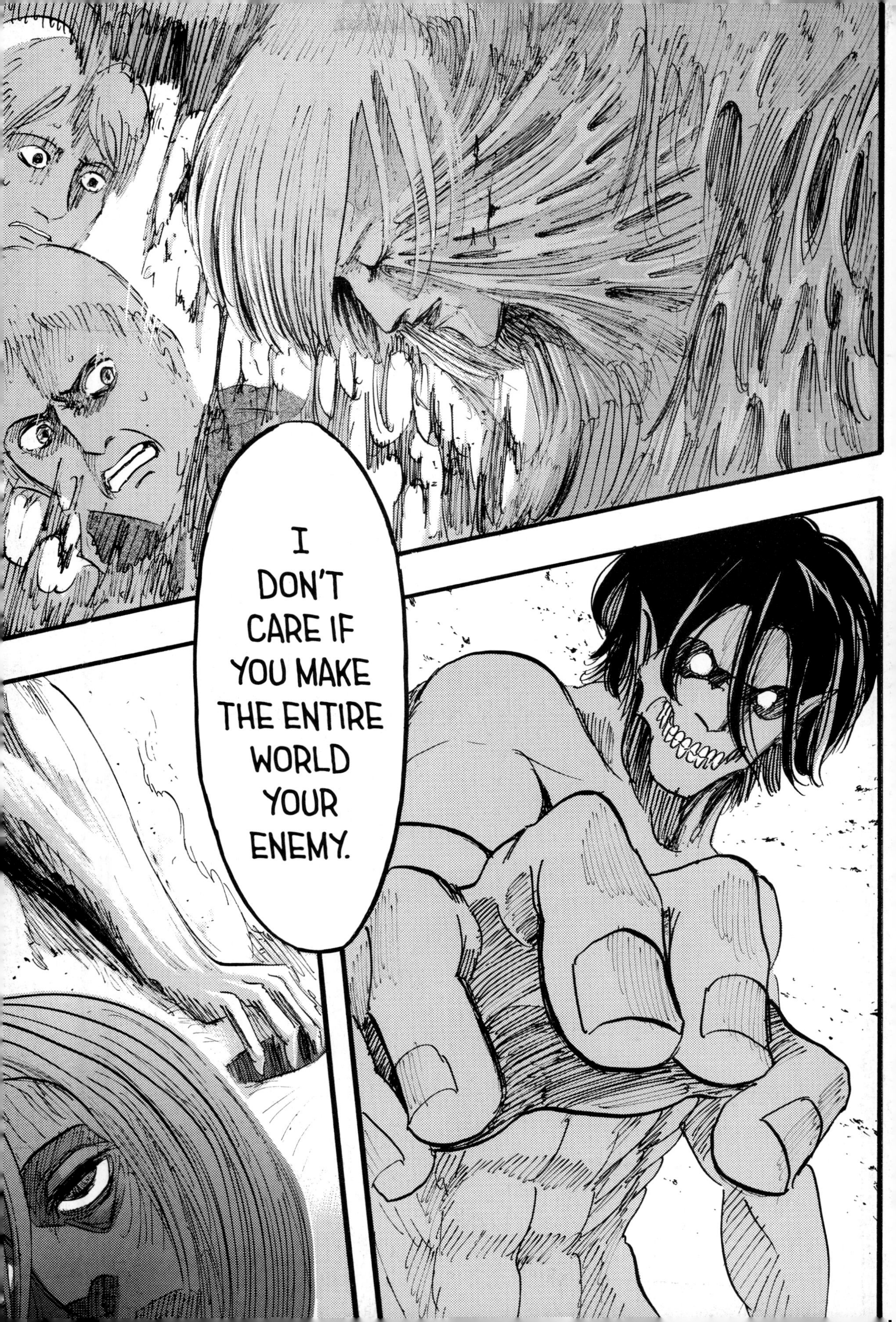
I DON'T CARE IF YOU MAKE THE ENTIRE WORLD YOUR ENEMY.

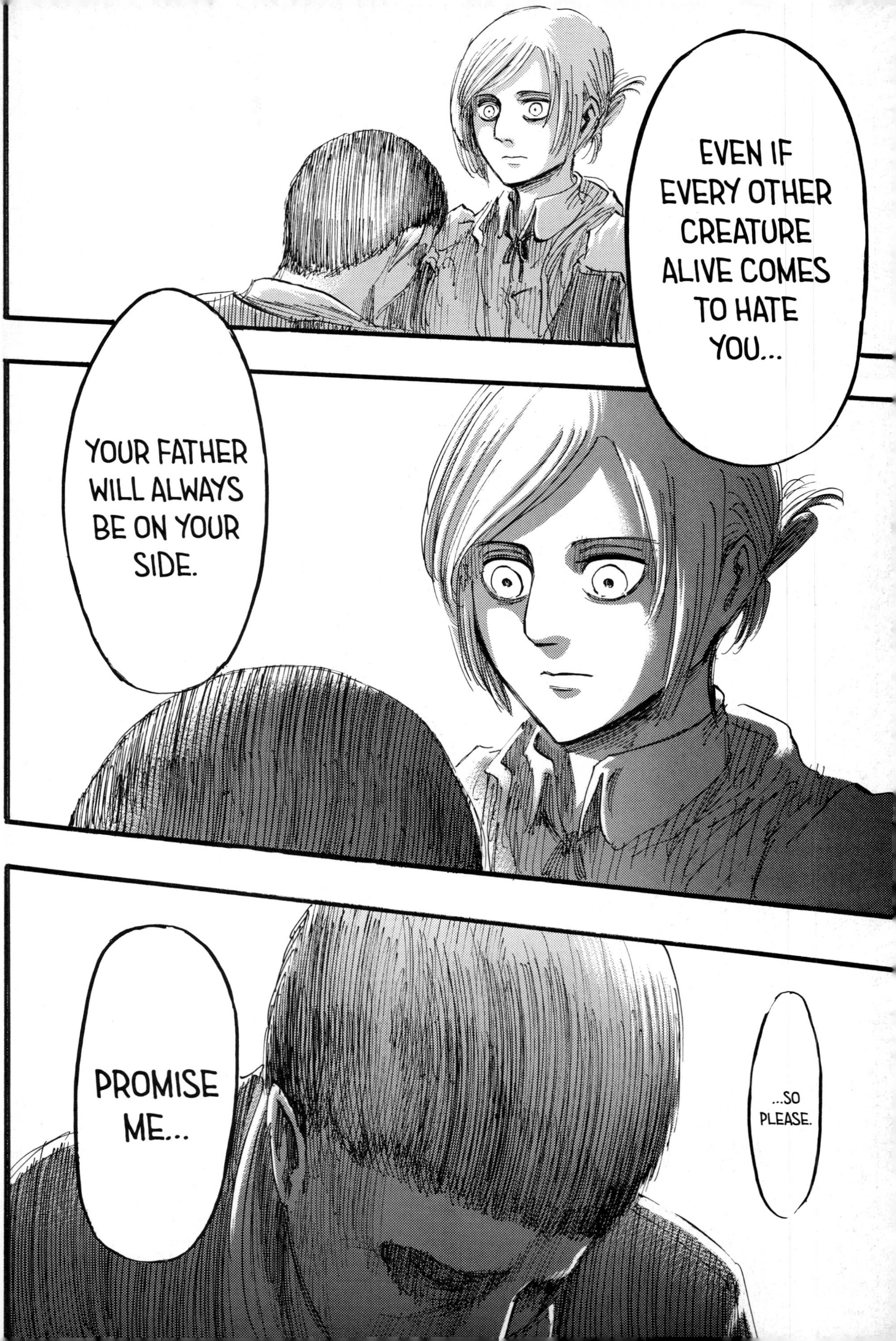
EVEN IF EVERY OTHER CREATURE ALIVE COMES TO HATE YOU...
YOUR FATHER WILL ALWAYS BE ON YOUR SIDE.
...SO PLEASE.
PROMISE ME...

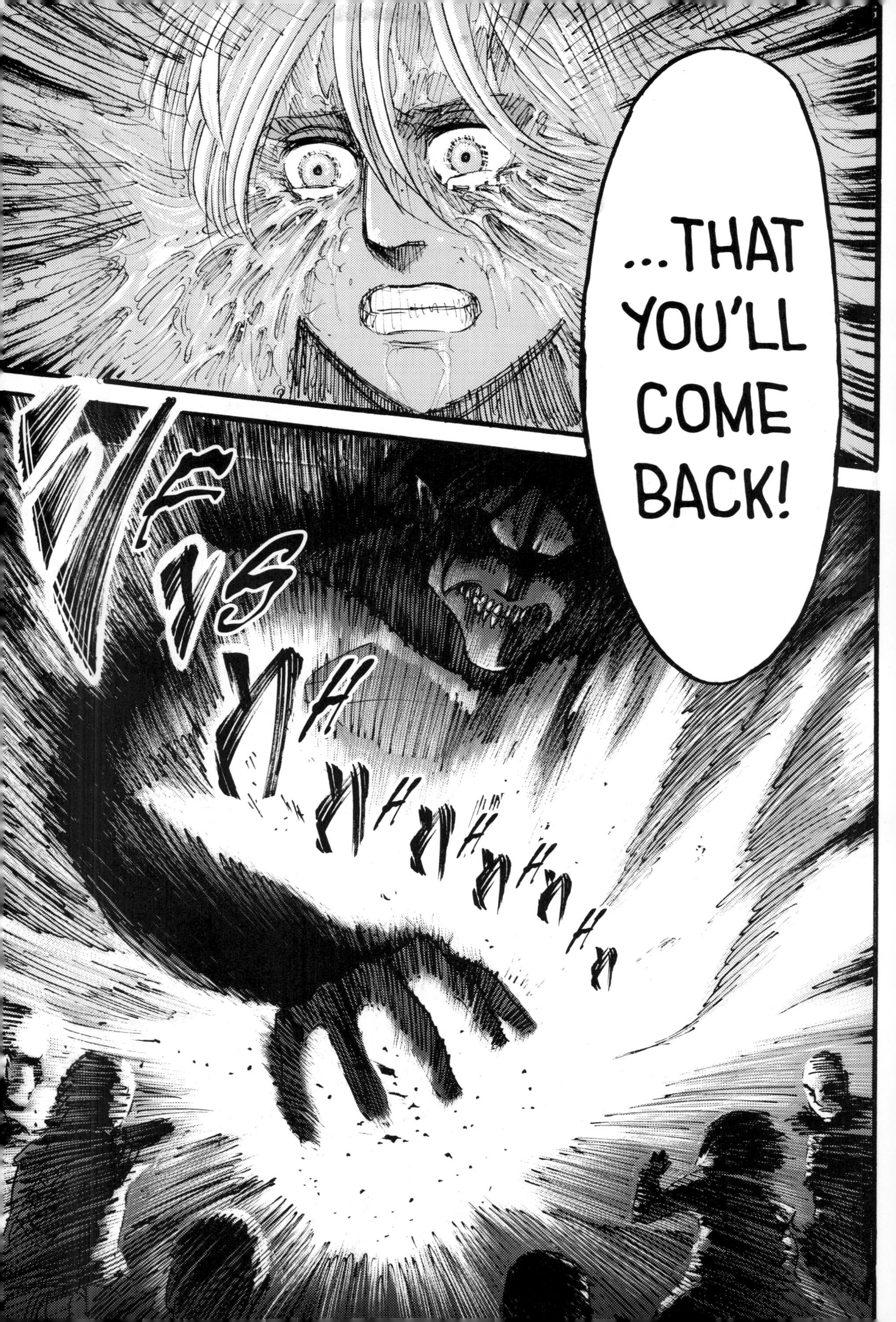
...THAT YOU'LL COME BACK!

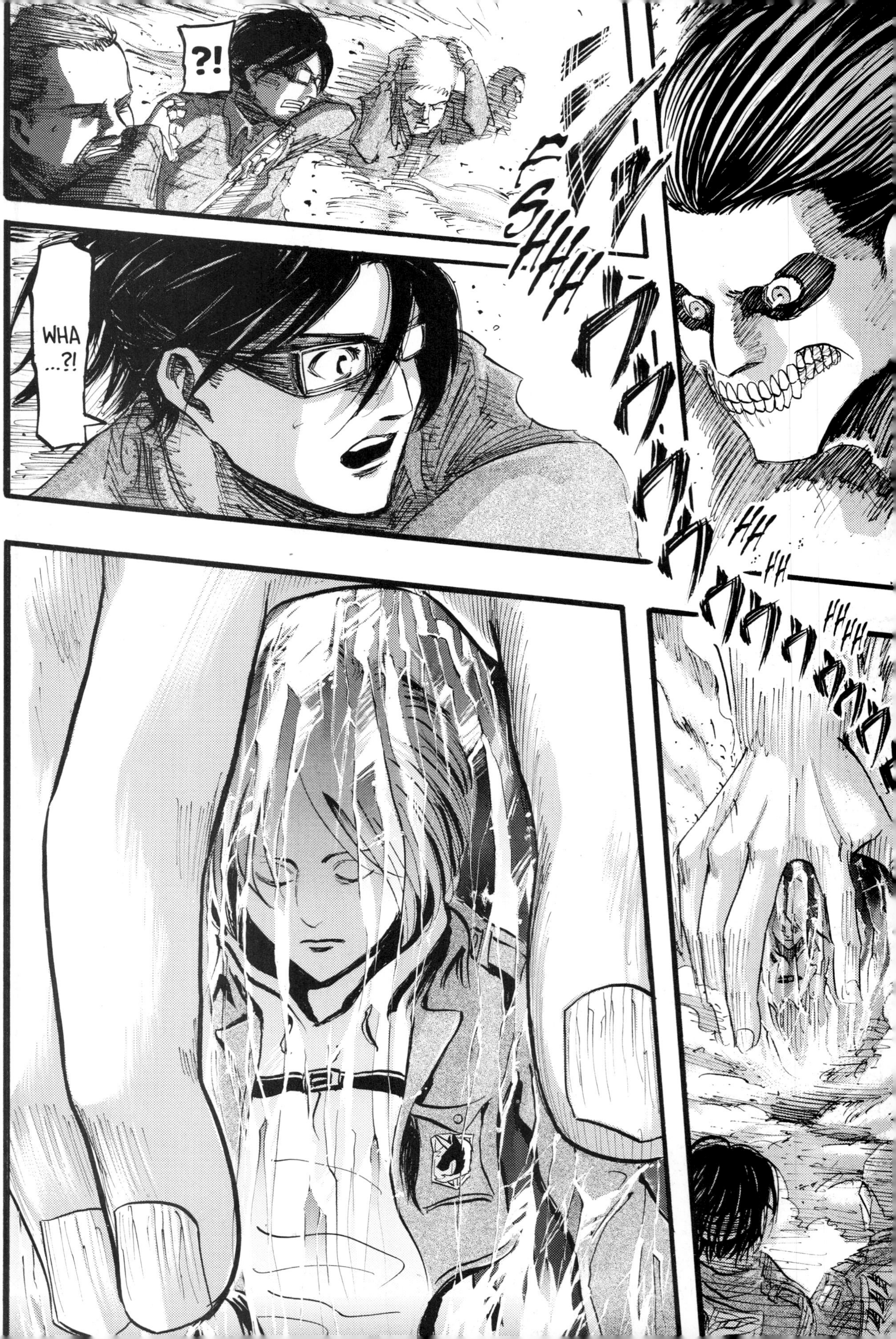
FSHHH
?!
WHA ...?!
HH
HH
HHH

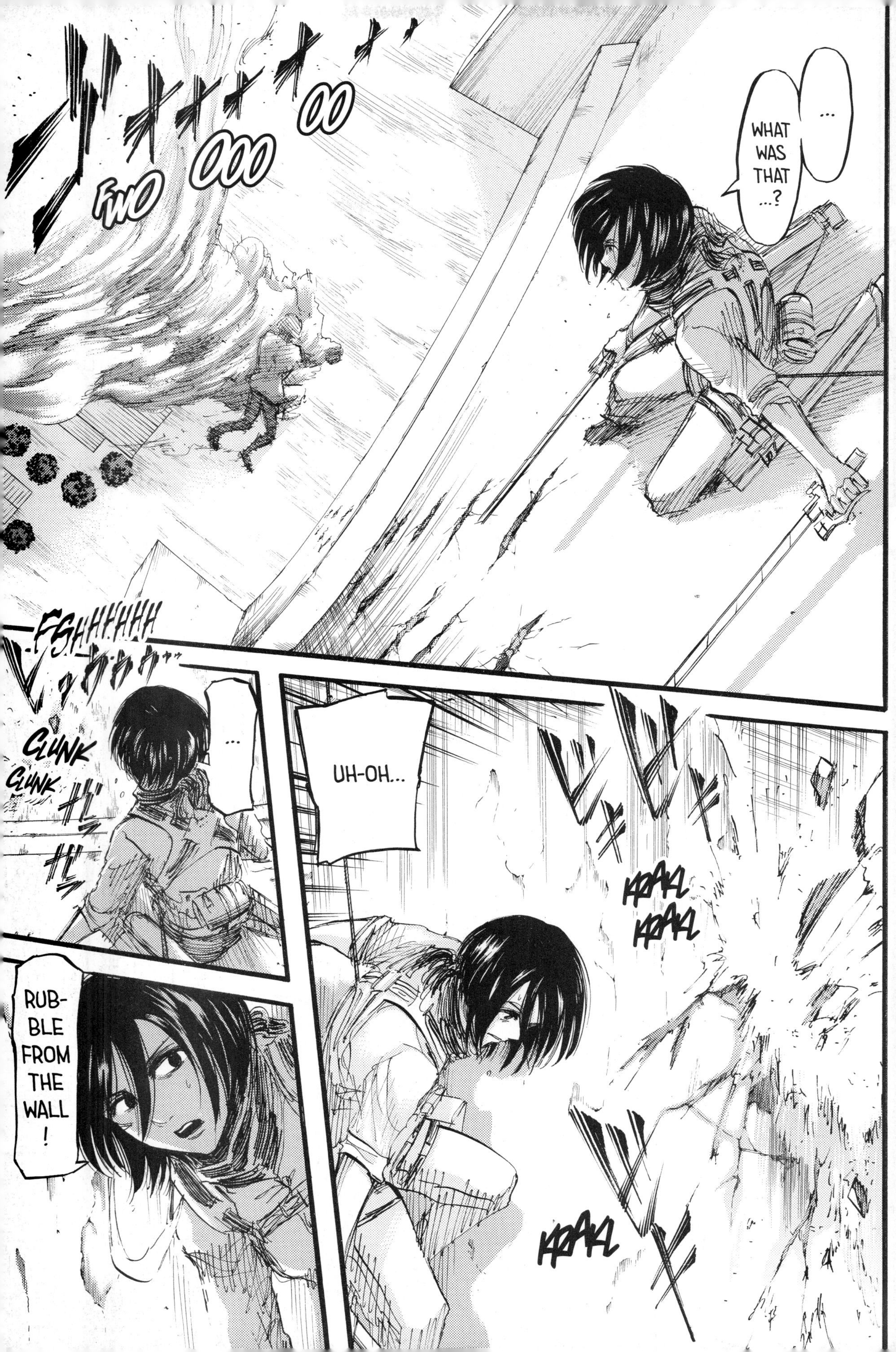
...
WHAT WAS THAT ...?
FWO OOO OO
FSHHHHHH
UH-OH...
KRAK KRAK
KRAK
...
CLUNK CLUNK
RUBBLE FROM THE WALL!

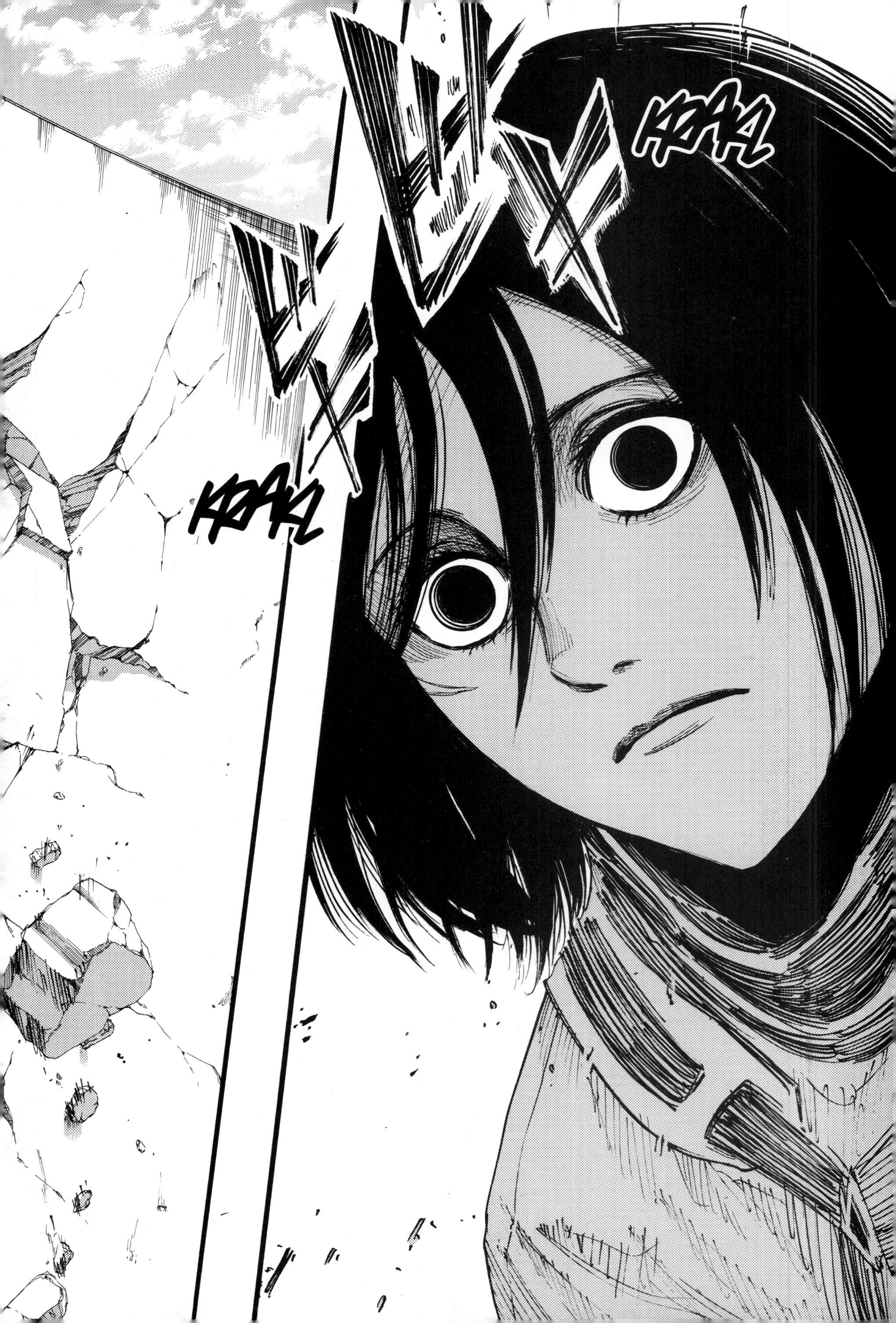
KRAK
KRAK

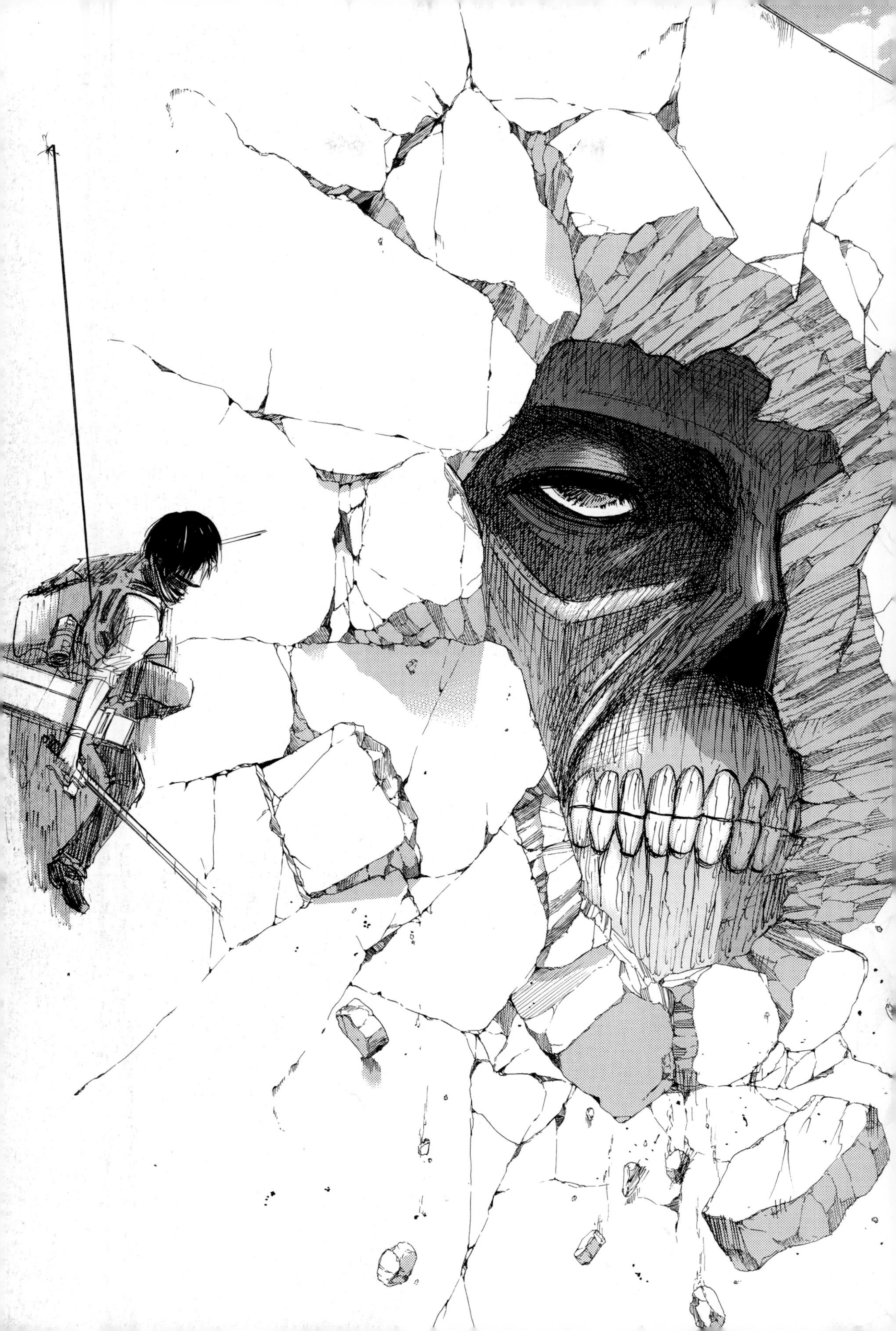

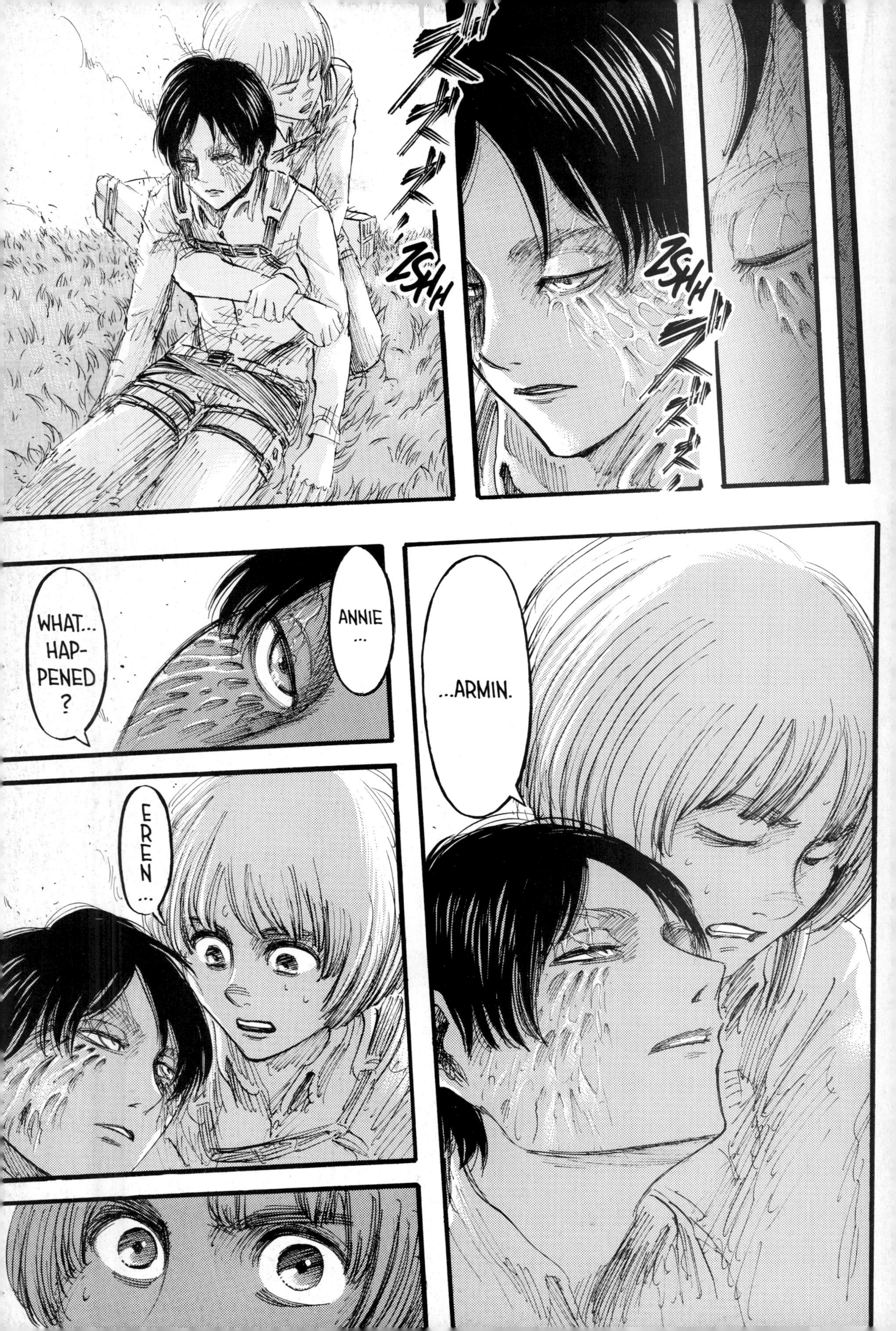

ZSHH
ZSHH
...ARMIN.
ANNIE ...
WHAT... HAP-PENED ?
EREN ...

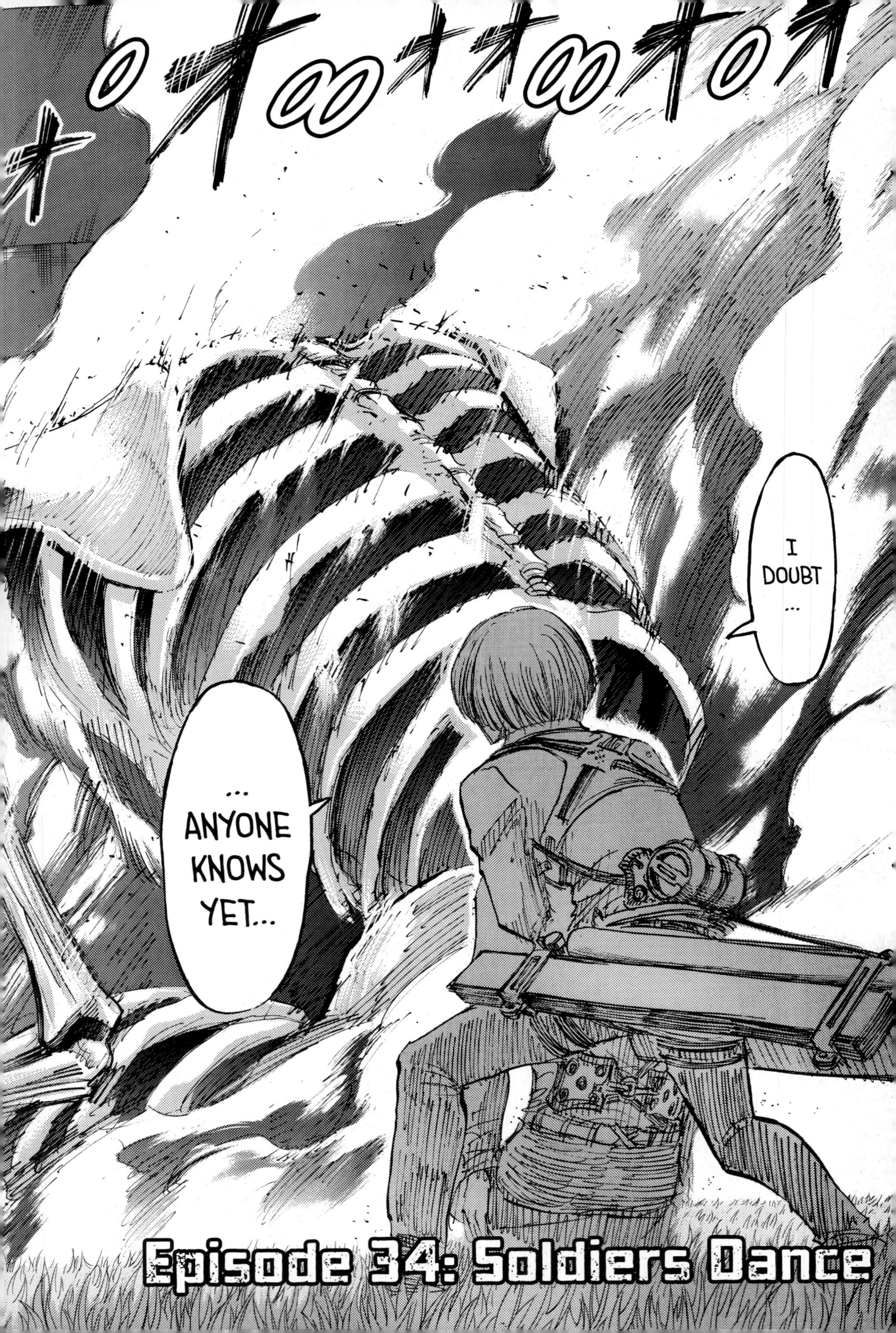
I DOUBT ...
... ANYONE KNOWS YET...
Episode 34: Soldiers Dance

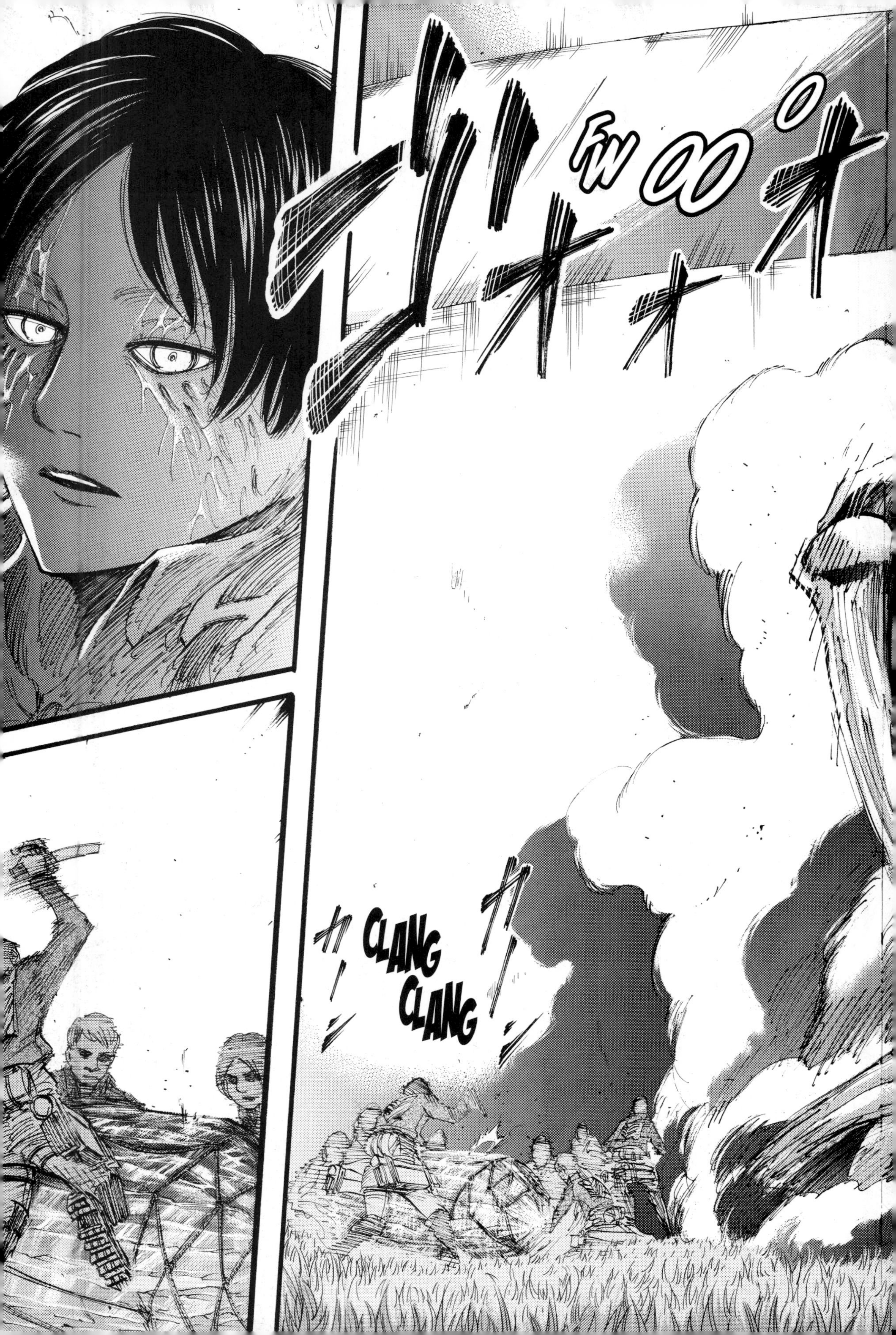
FWOOM
CLANG
CLANG

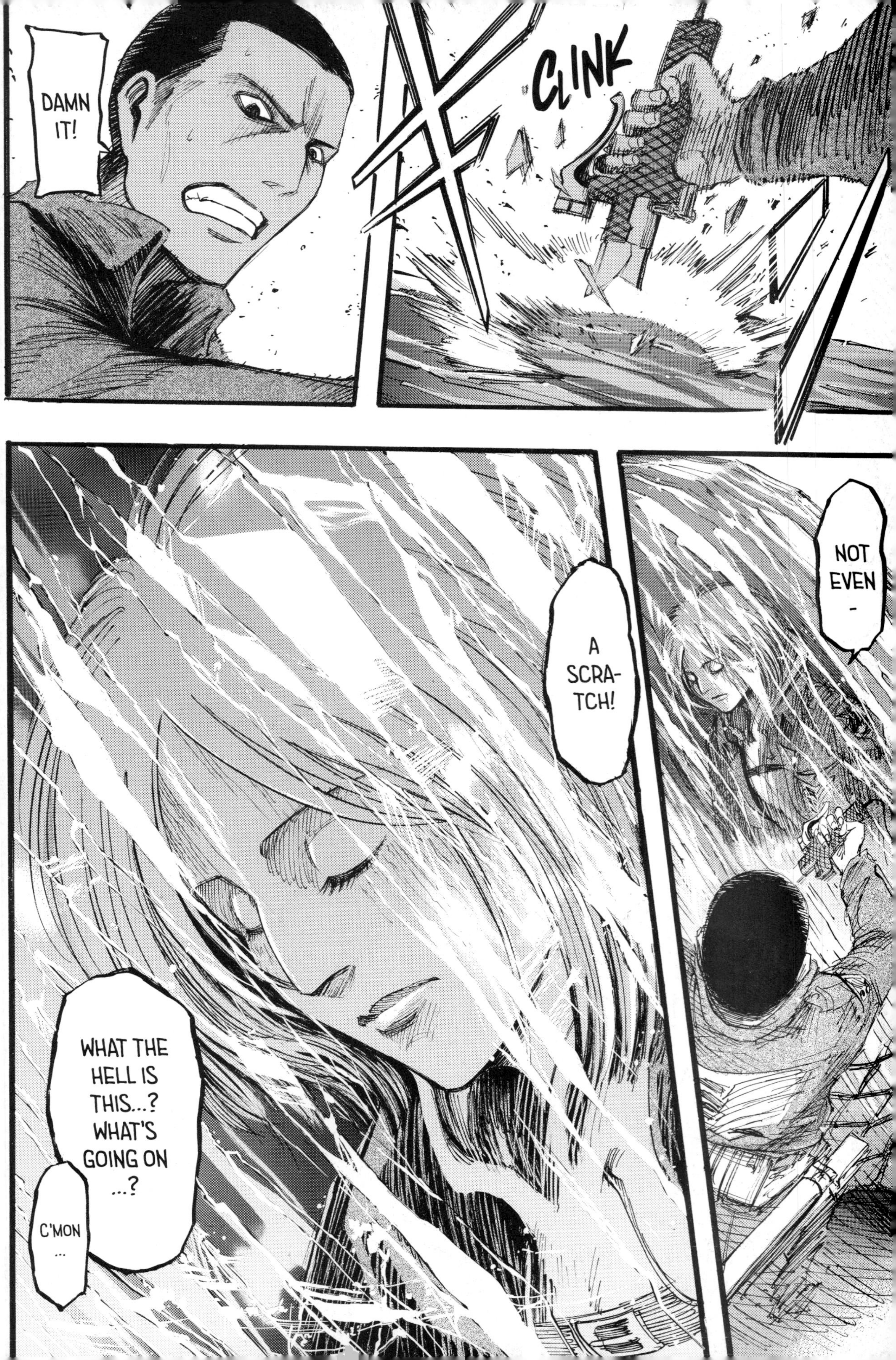
CLINK
DAMN IT!
NOT EVEN -
A SCRA-TCH!
WHAT THE HELL IS THIS...? WHAT'S GOING ON ...?
C'MON ...

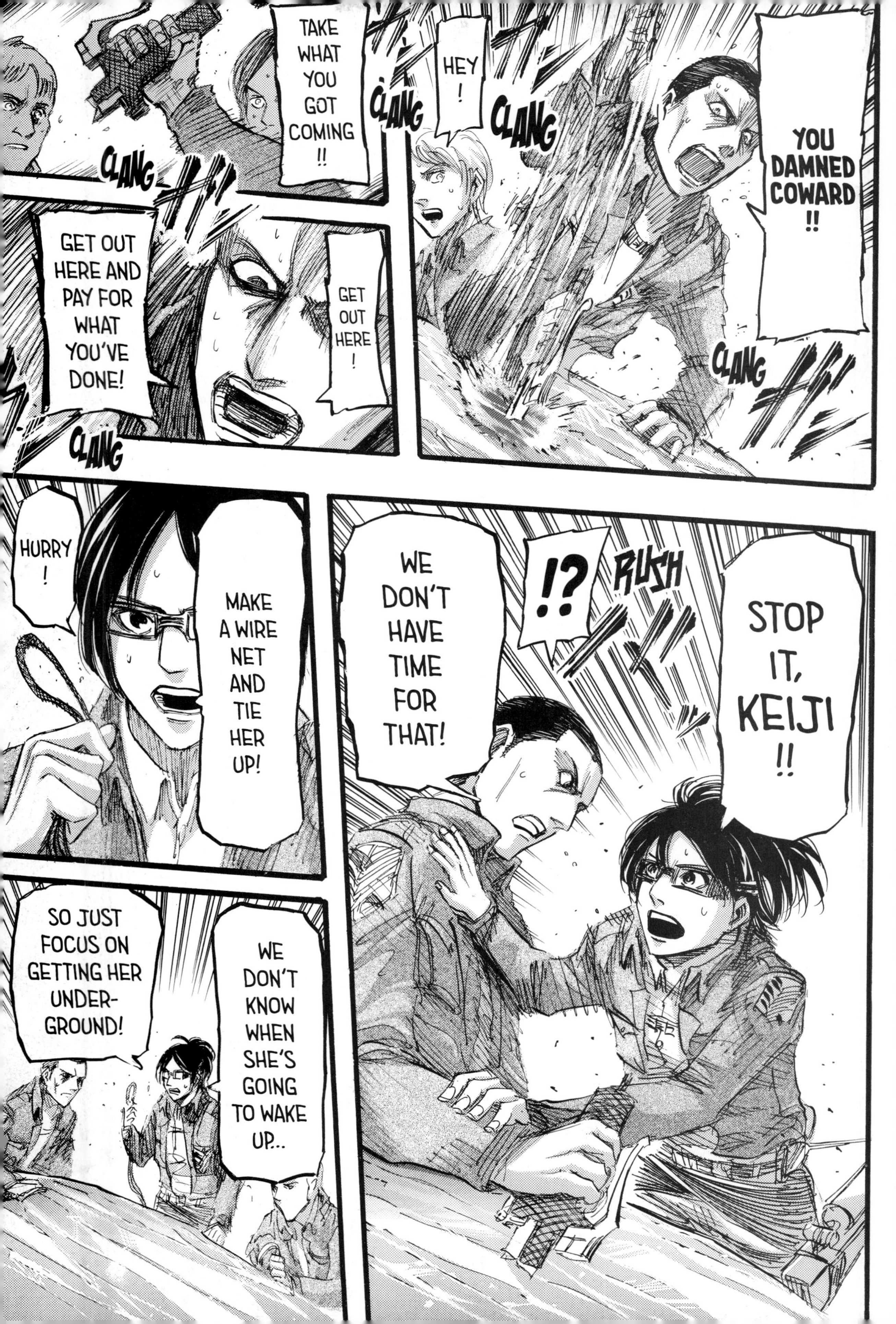
YOU DAMNED COWARD!!
HEY!
CLANG
CLANG
CLANG
TAKE WHAT YOU GOT COMING!!
CLANG
GET OUT HERE!
GET OUT HERE AND PAY FOR WHAT YOU'VE DONE!
CLANG
STOP IT, KEIJI!!
RUSH
!?
WE DON'T HAVE TIME FOR THAT!
MAKE A WIRE NET AND TIE HER UP!
HURRY!
WE DON'T KNOW WHEN SHE'S GOING TO WAKE UP...
SO JUST FOCUS ON GETTING HER UNDER-GROUND!

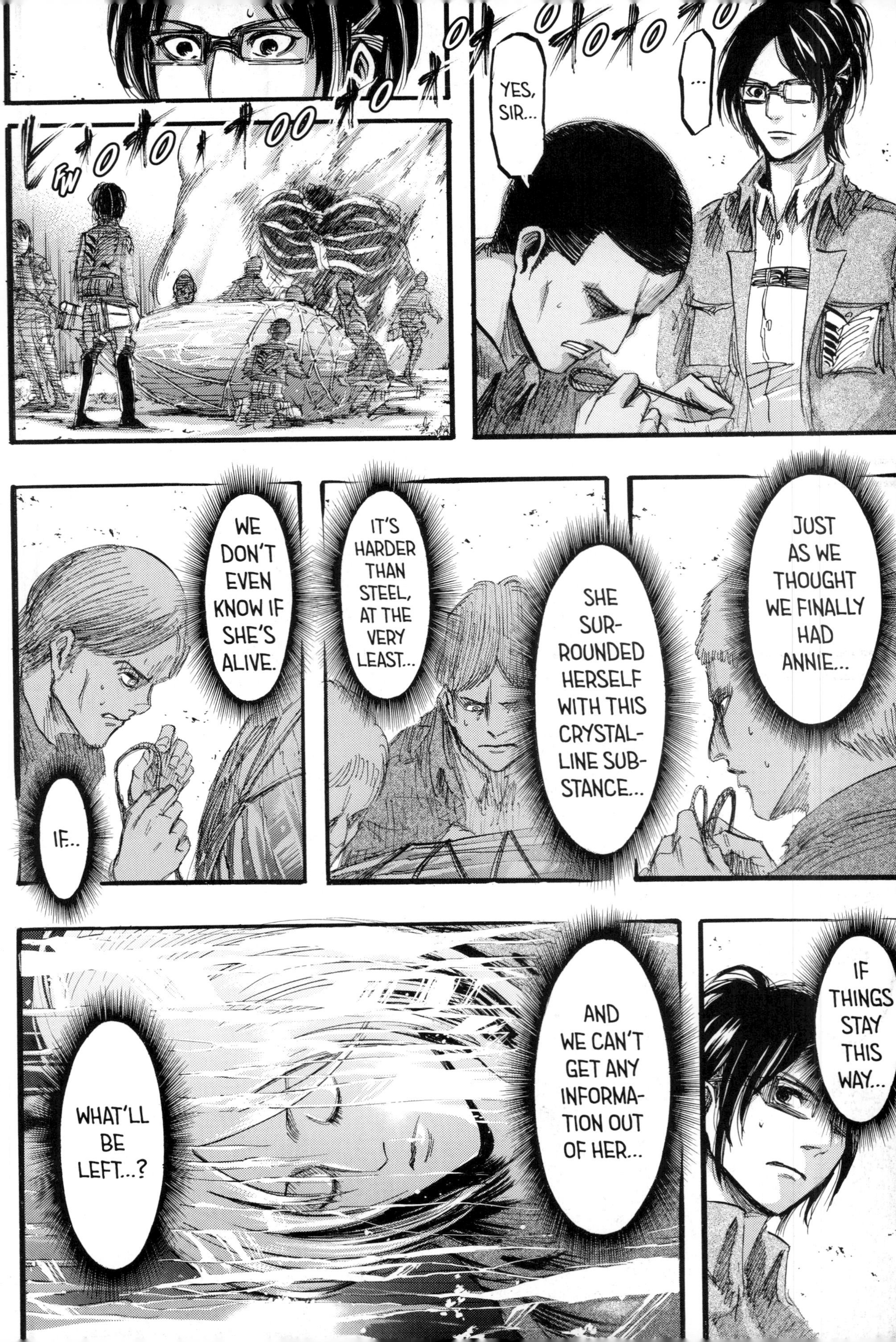
...
YES, SIR...
FWOOOOOO
JUST AS WE THOUGHT WE FINALLY HAD ANNIE...
SHE SUR-ROUNDED HERSELF WITH THIS CRYSTAL-LINE SUB-STANCE...
IT'S HARDER THAN STEEL, AT THE VERY LEAST...
WE DON'T EVEN KNOW IF SHE'S ALIVE.
IF...
IF THINGS STAY THIS WAY...
AND WE CAN'T GET ANY INFORMA-TION OUT OF HER...
WHAT'LL BE LEFT...?

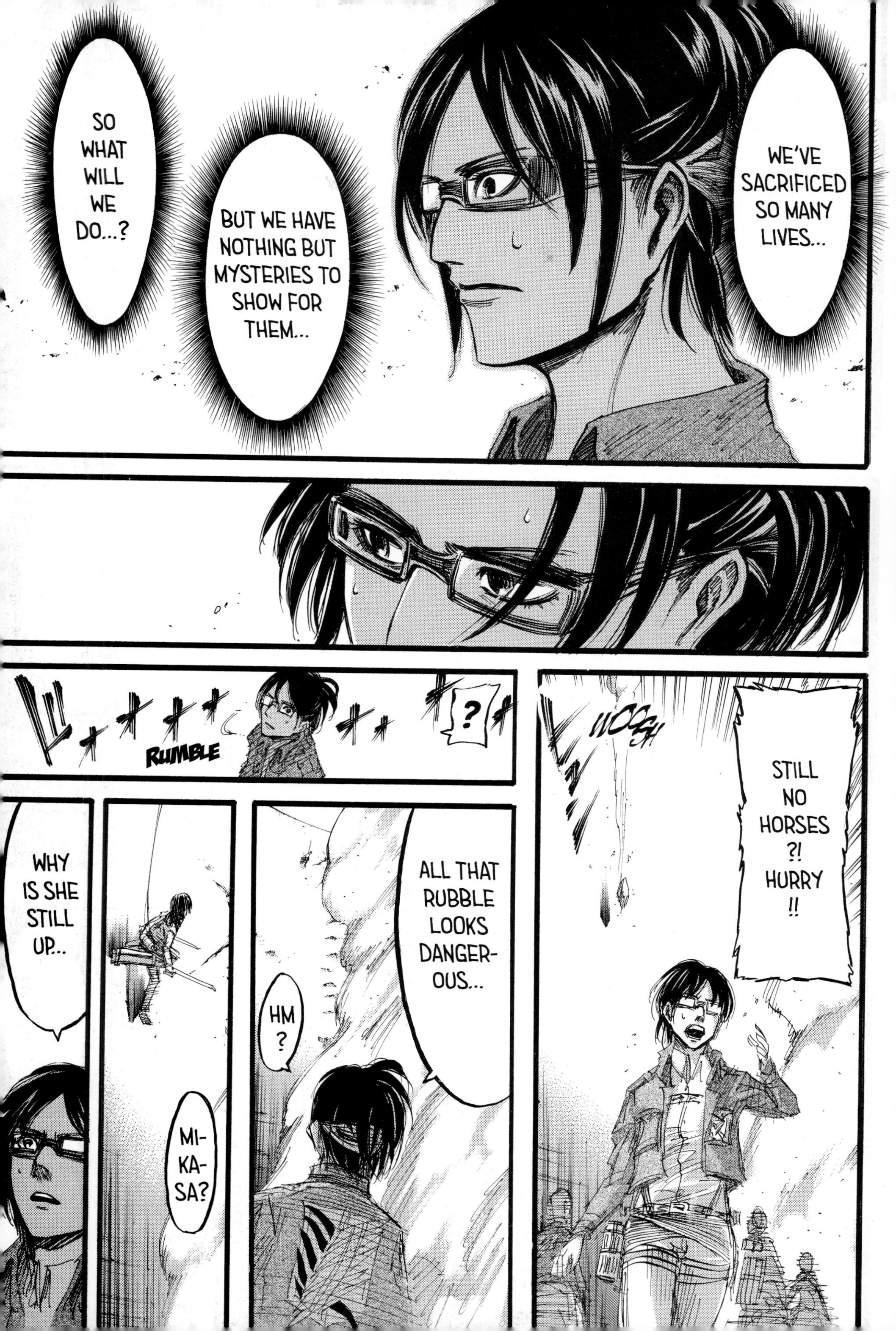
WE'VE SACRIFICED SO MANY LIVES...
BUT WE HAVE NOTHING BUT MYSTERIES TO SHOW FOR THEM...
SO WHAT WILL WE DO...?
WOOSH
STILL NO HORSES?! HURRY!!
?
RUMBLE
ALL THAT RUBBLE LOOKS DANGER-OUS...
HM?
WHY IS SHE STILL UP...
MI-KA-SA?

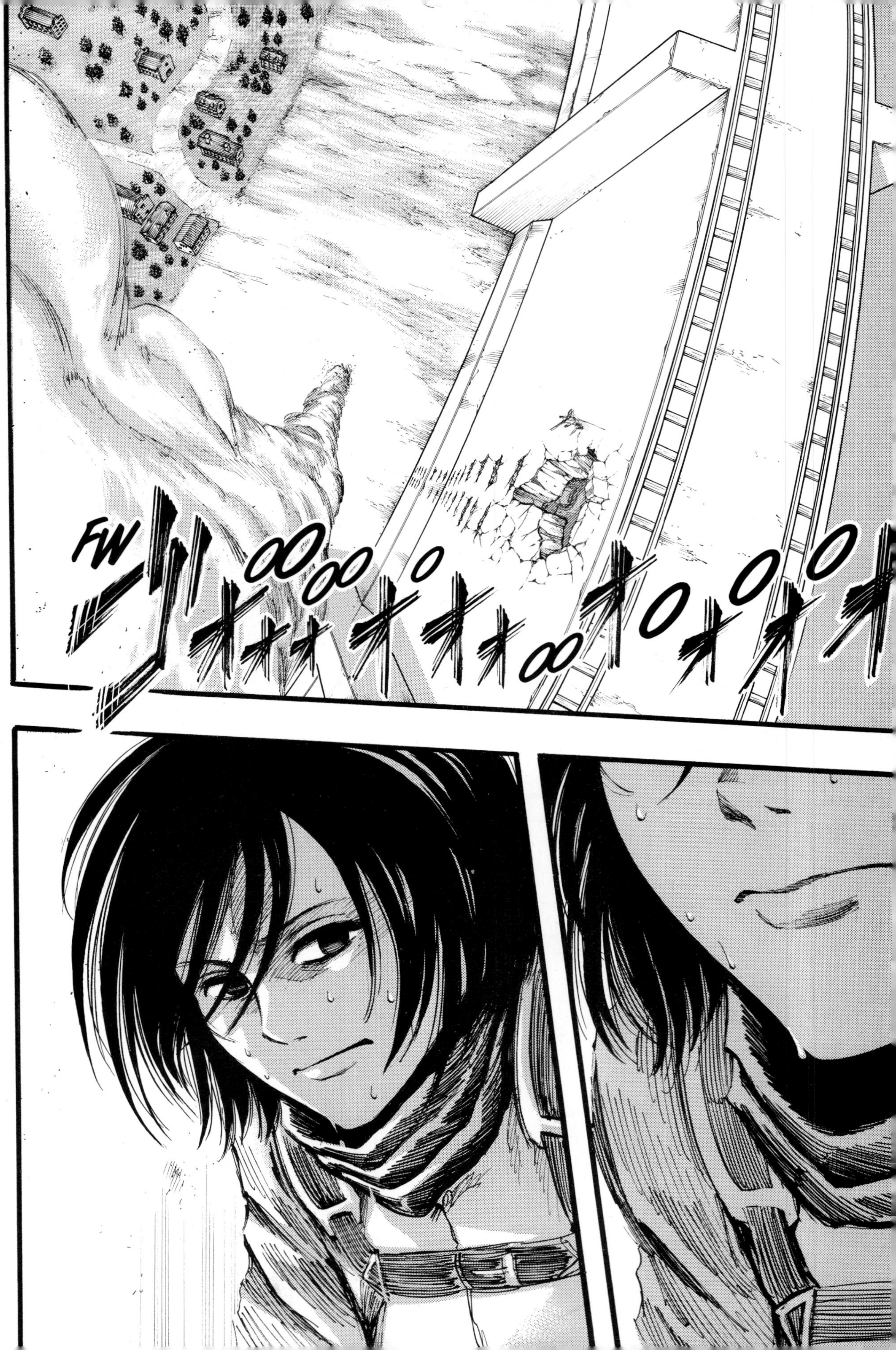
FWOOOOOOOOOO

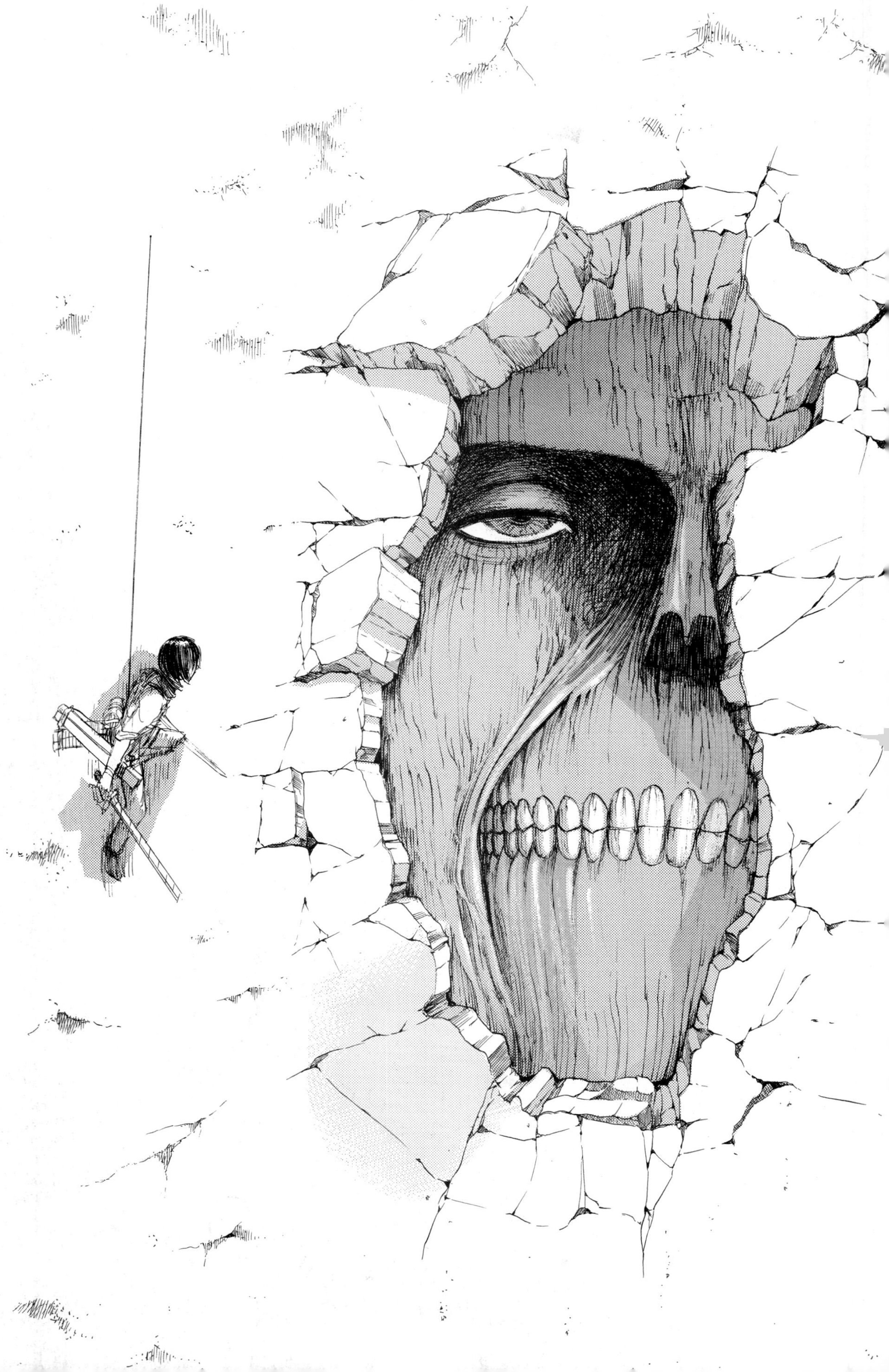

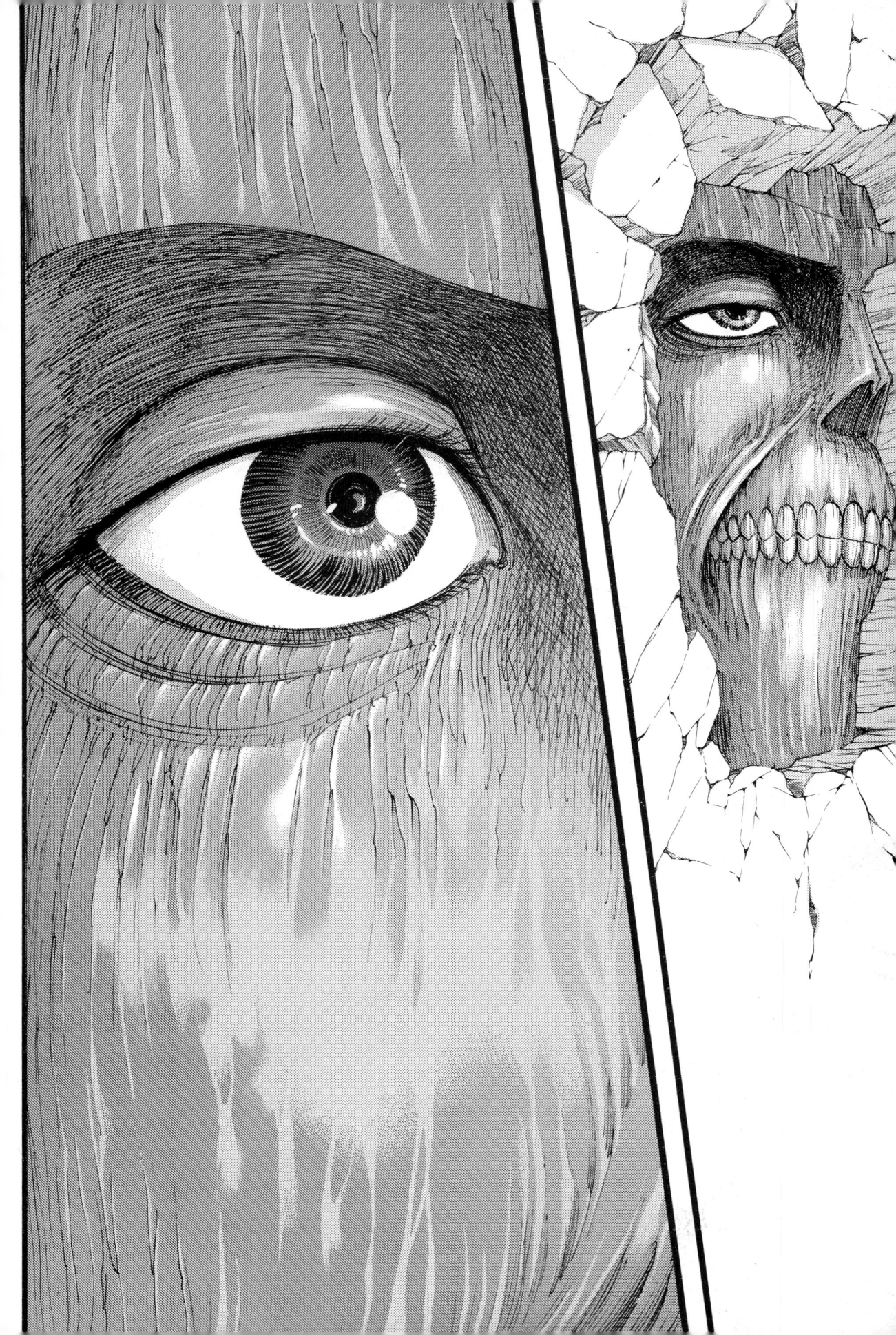

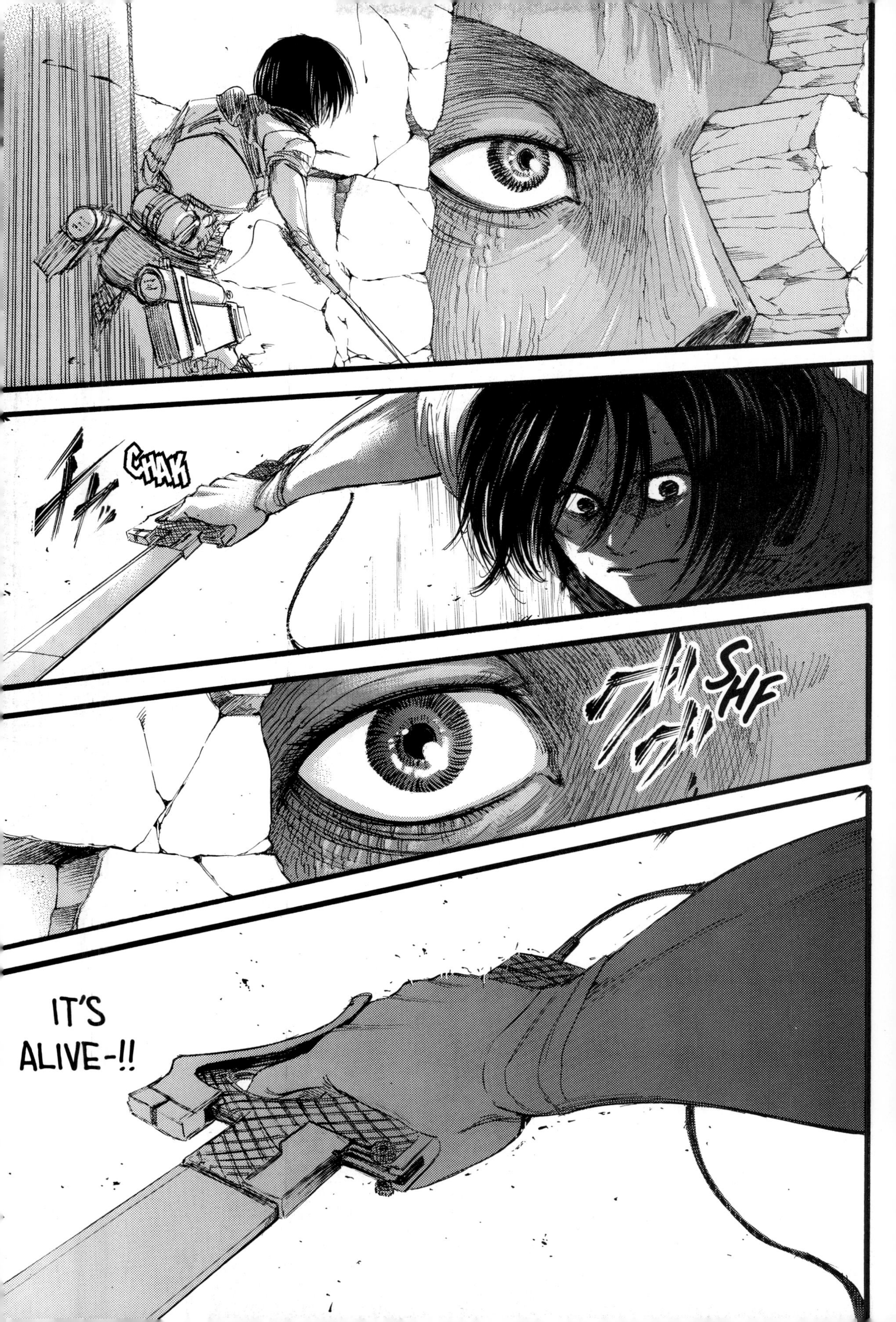
CHAK
SHF
IT'S ALIVE-!!

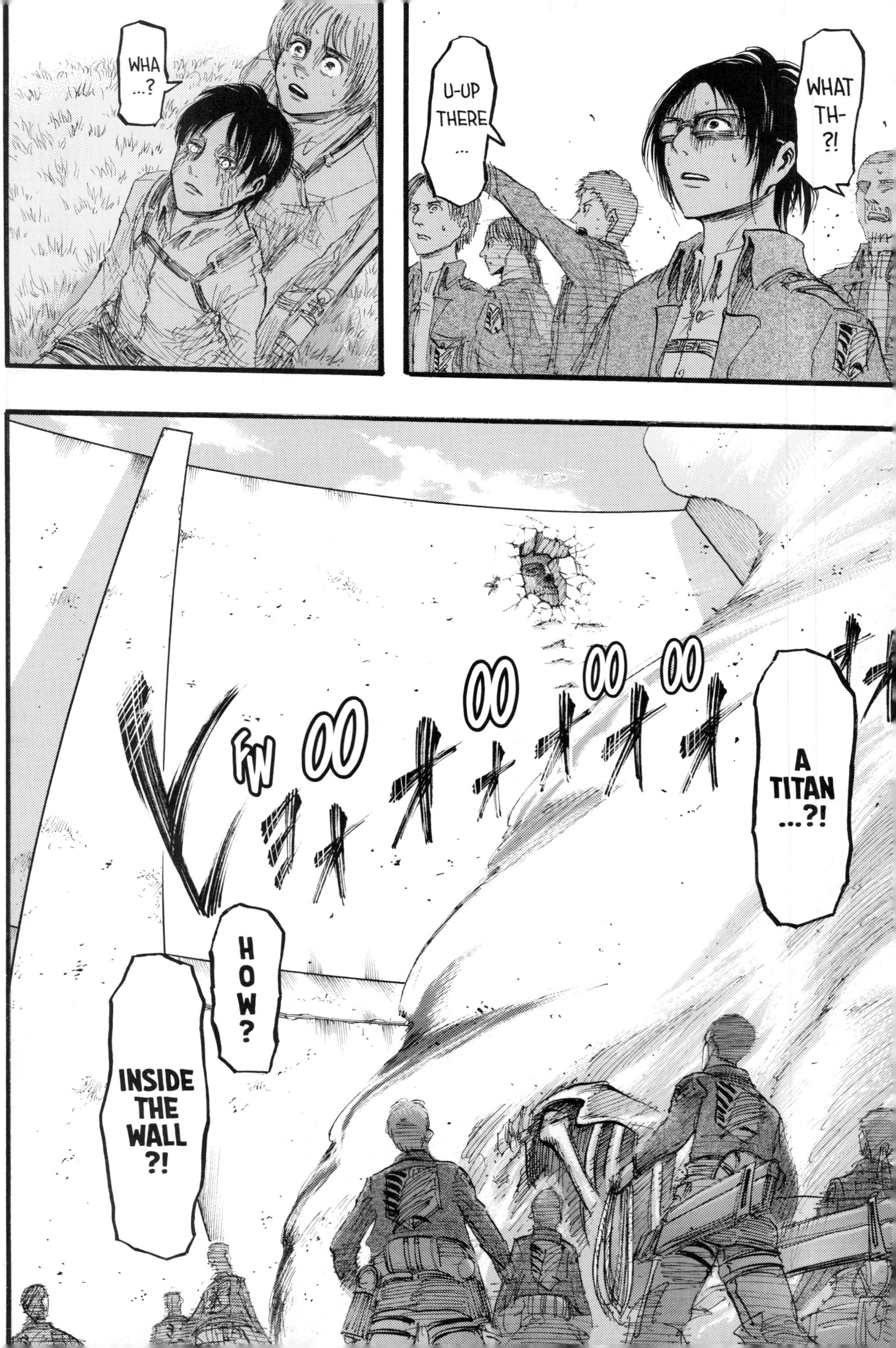

WHAT TH-?!
U-UP THERE ...
WHA ...?
A TITAN ...?!
FWOOOOOOOO
HOW?
INSIDE THE WALL ?!

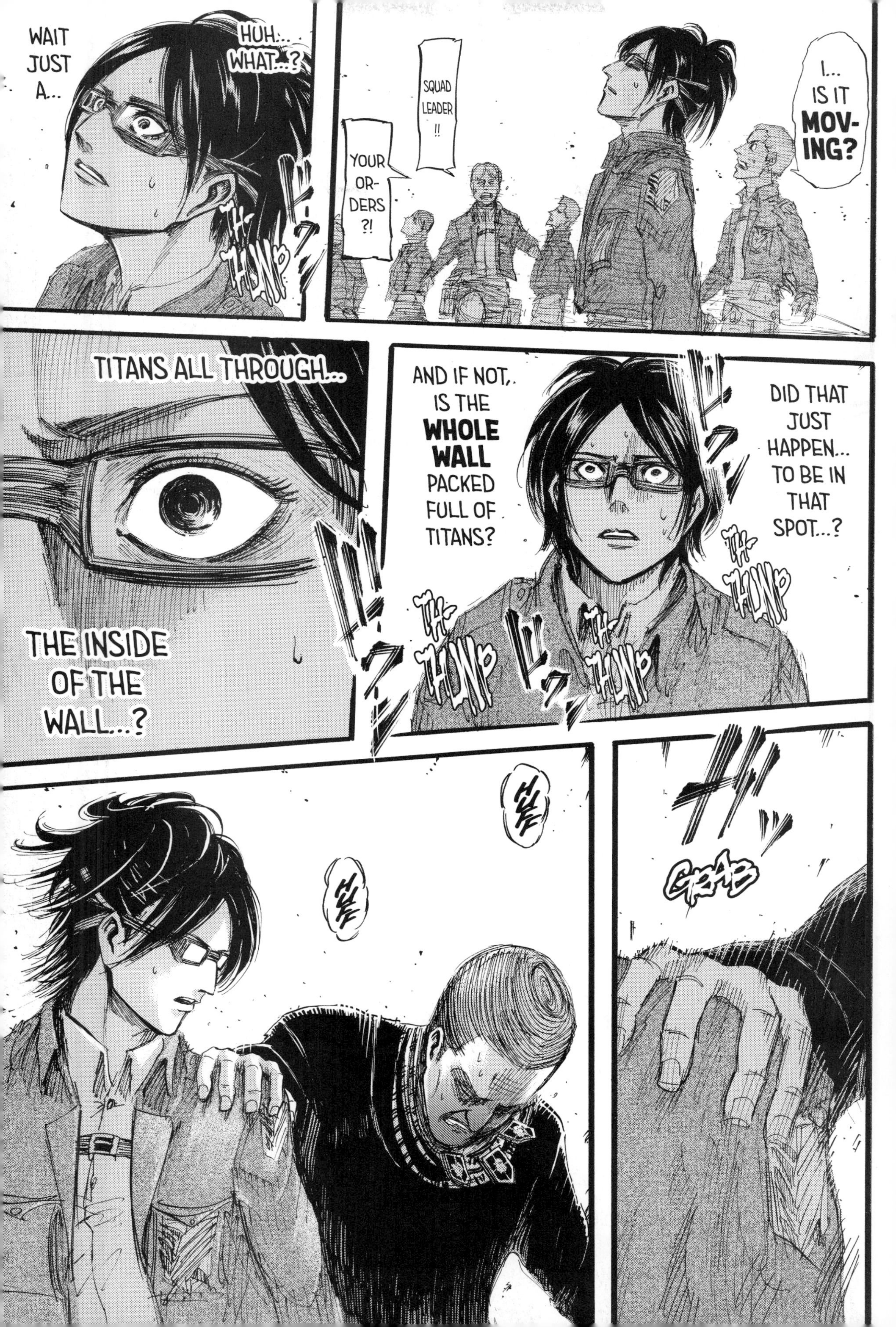
I... IS IT MOVING?
SQUAD LEADER !!
YOUR ORDERS ?!
HUH... WHAT...?
WAIT JUST A...
THA THUMP
DID THAT JUST HAPPEN... TO BE IN THAT SPOT...?
AND IF NOT, IS THE WHOLE WALL PACKED FULL OF TITANS?
THA THUMP
THA THUMP
THA THUMP
TITANS ALL THROUGH...
THE INSIDE OF THE WALL...?
GRAB

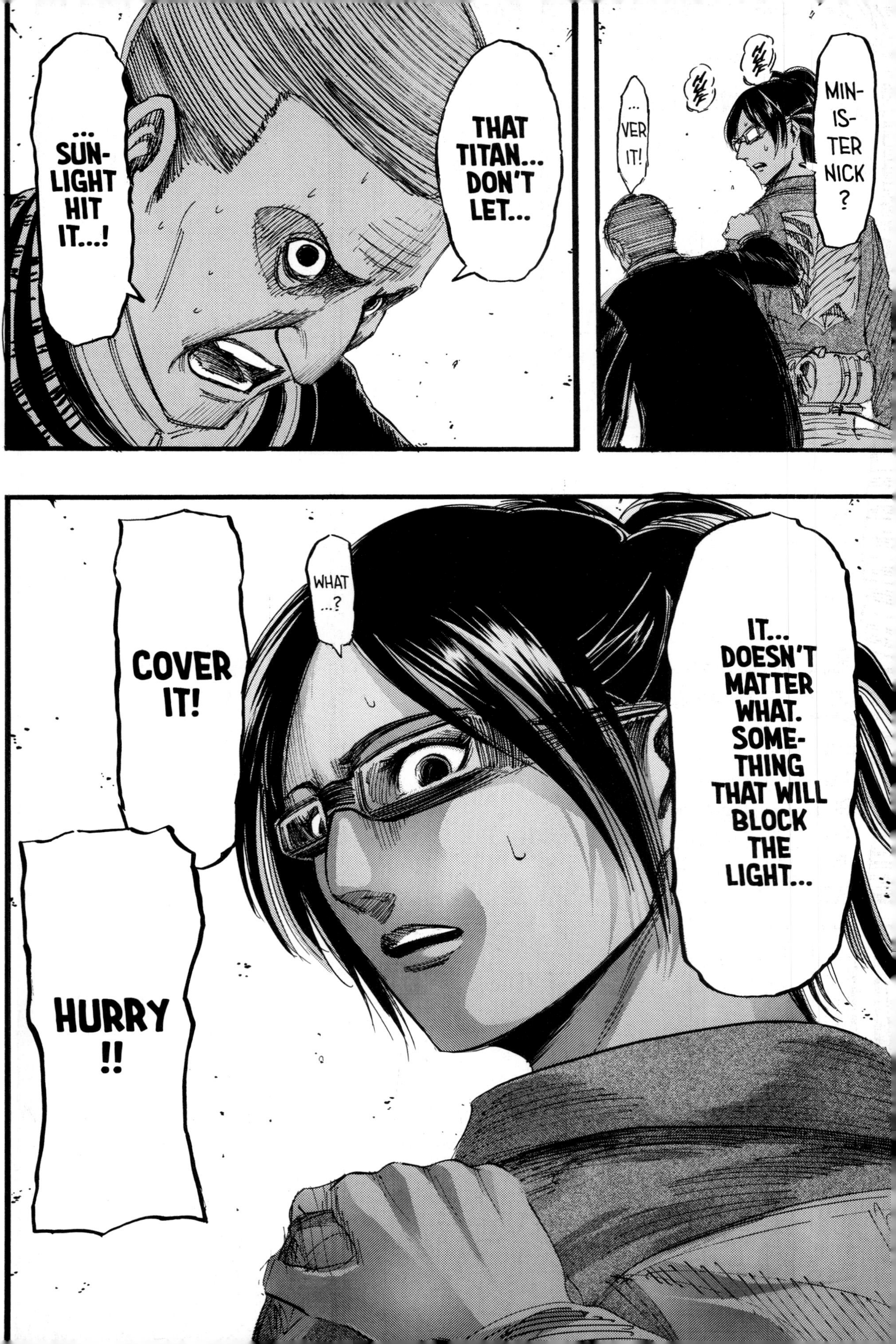
MIN-IS-TER NICK?
...VER IT!
THAT TITAN... DON'T LET...
...SUN-LIGHT HIT IT...!
IT... DOESN'T MATTER WHAT. SOME-THING THAT WILL BLOCK THE LIGHT...
WHAT ...?
COVER IT!
HURRY!!

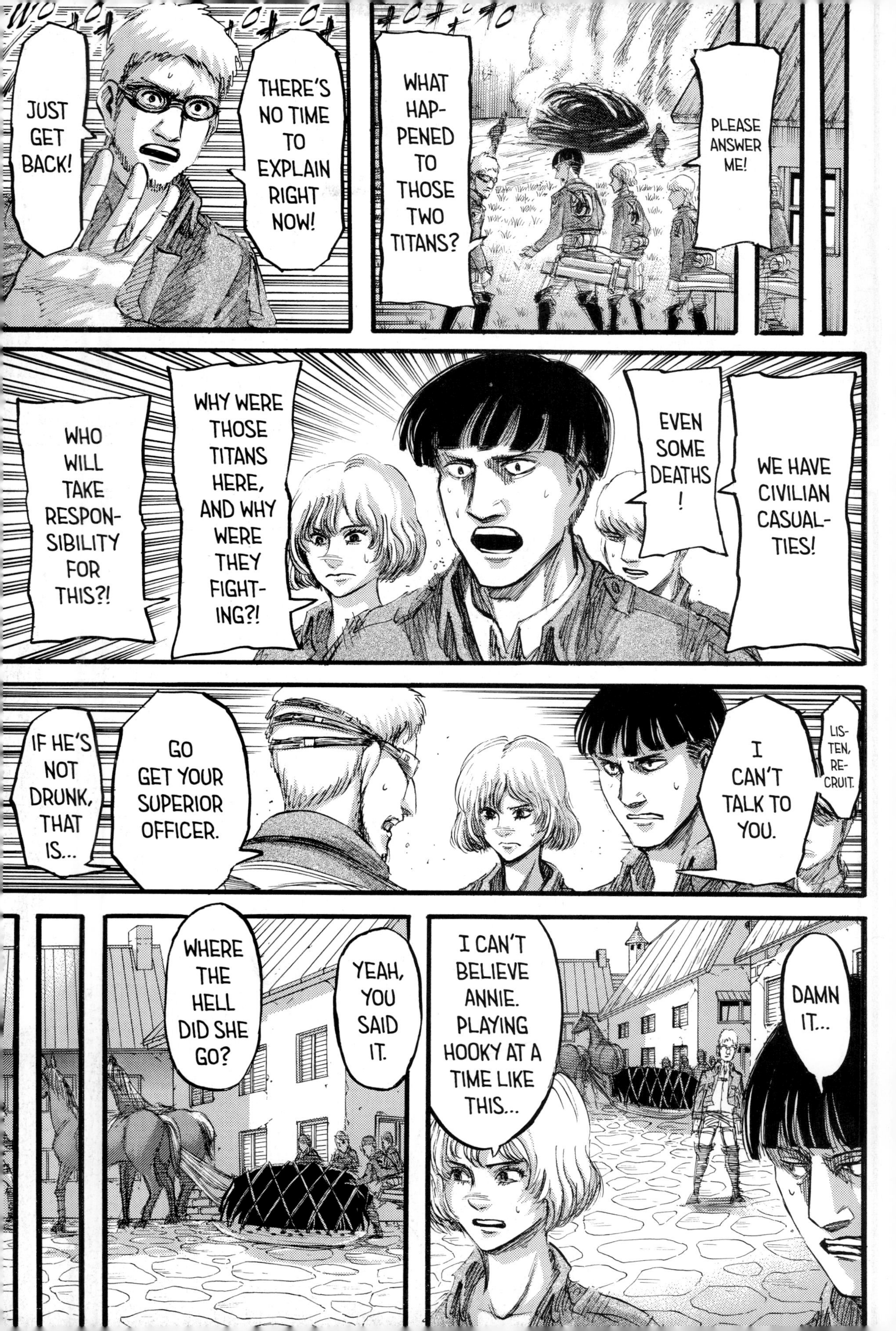
PLEASE ANSWER ME!
WHAT HAPPENED TO THOSE TWO TITANS?
THERE'S NO TIME TO EXPLAIN RIGHT NOW!
JUST GET BACK!
WE HAVE CIVILIAN CASUALTIES!
EVEN SOME DEATHS!
WHY WERE THOSE TITANS HERE, AND WHY WERE THEY FIGHTING?!
WHO WILL TAKE RESPONSIBILITY FOR THIS?!
LISTEN, RECRUIT.
I CAN'T TALK TO YOU.
GO GET YOUR SUPERIOR OFFICER.
IF HE'S NOT DRUNK, THAT IS...
DAMN IT...
I CAN'T BELIEVE ANNIE. PLAYING HOOKY AT A TIME LIKE THIS...
YEAH, YOU SAID IT.
WHERE THE HELL DID SHE GO?

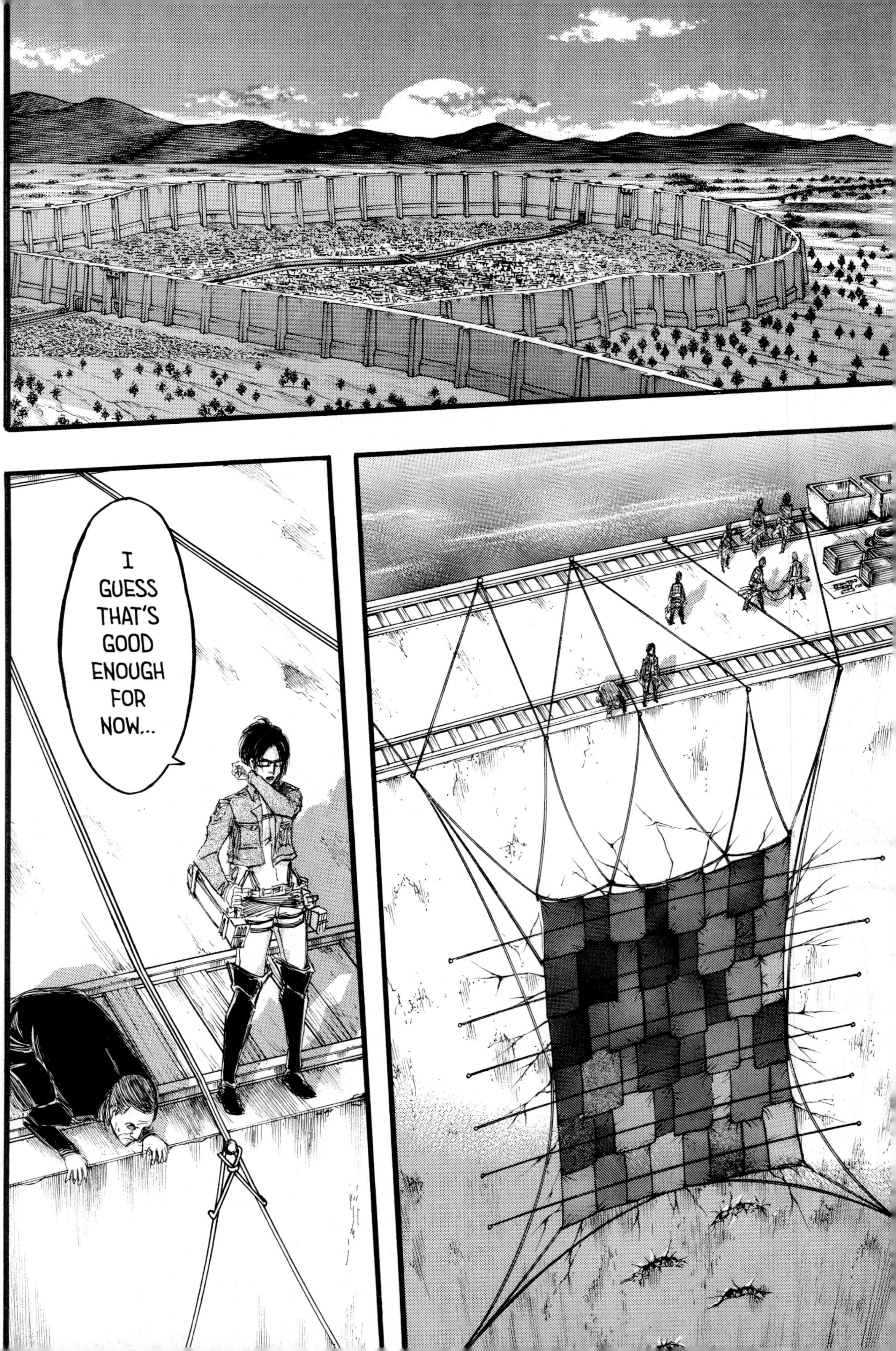
I GUESS THAT'S GOOD ENOUGH FOR NOW...

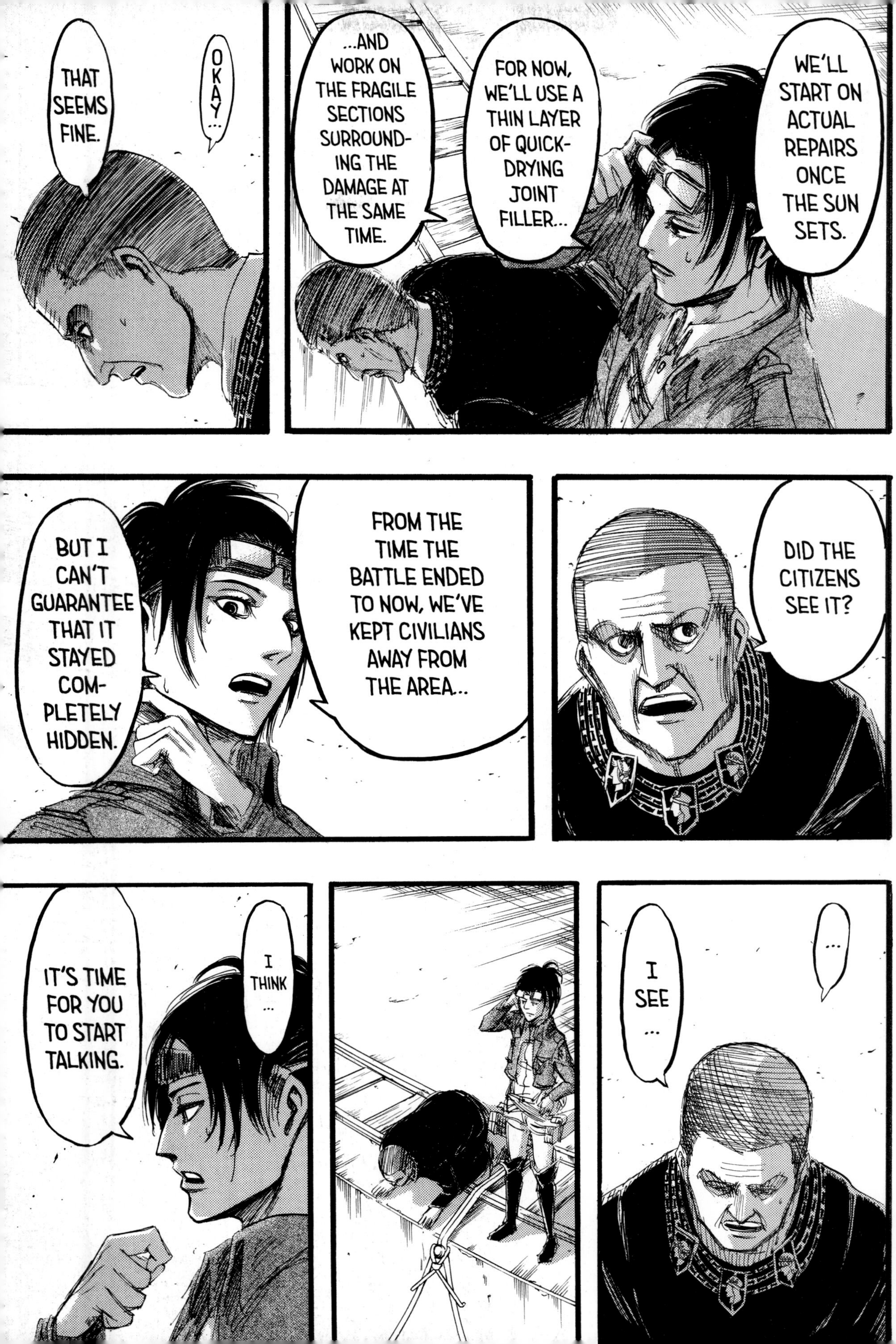
WE'LL START ON ACTUAL REPAIRS ONCE THE SUN SETS.
FOR NOW, WE'LL USE A THIN LAYER OF QUICK-DRYING JOINT FILLER...
...AND WORK ON THE FRAGILE SECTIONS SURROUNDING THE DAMAGE AT THE SAME TIME.
OKAY...
THAT SEEMS FINE.
DID THE CITIZENS SEE IT?
FROM THE TIME THE BATTLE ENDED TO NOW, WE'VE KEPT CIVILIANS AWAY FROM THE AREA...
BUT I CAN'T GUARANTEE THAT IT STAYED COMPLETELY HIDDEN.
...
I SEE...
I THINK...
IT'S TIME FOR YOU TO START TALKING.

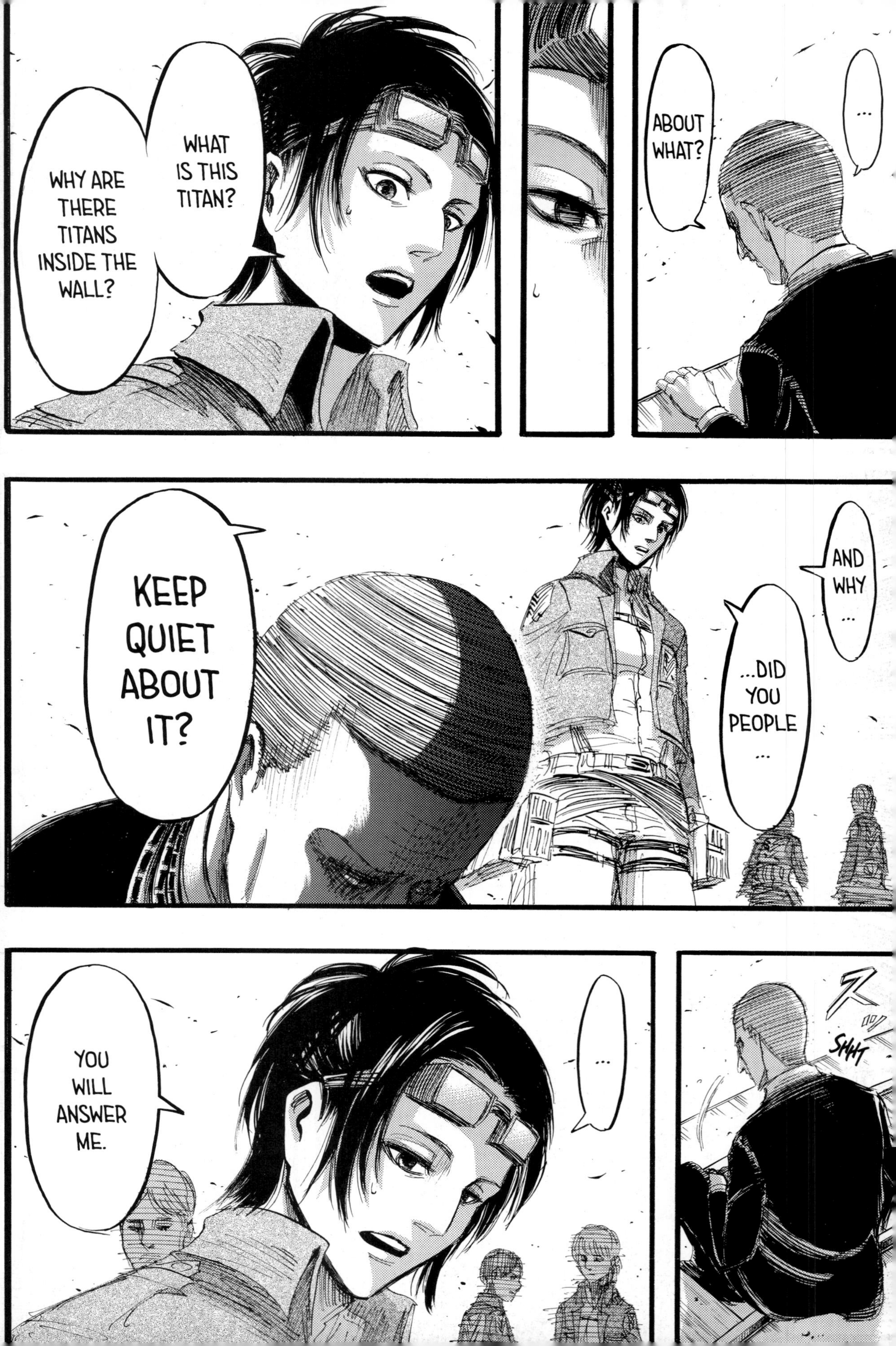
...
ABOUT WHAT?
WHAT IS THIS TITAN?
WHY ARE THERE TITANS INSIDE THE WALL?
AND WHY ...
...DID YOU PEOPLE ...
KEEP QUIET ABOUT IT?
SHHT
...
YOU WILL ANSWER ME.

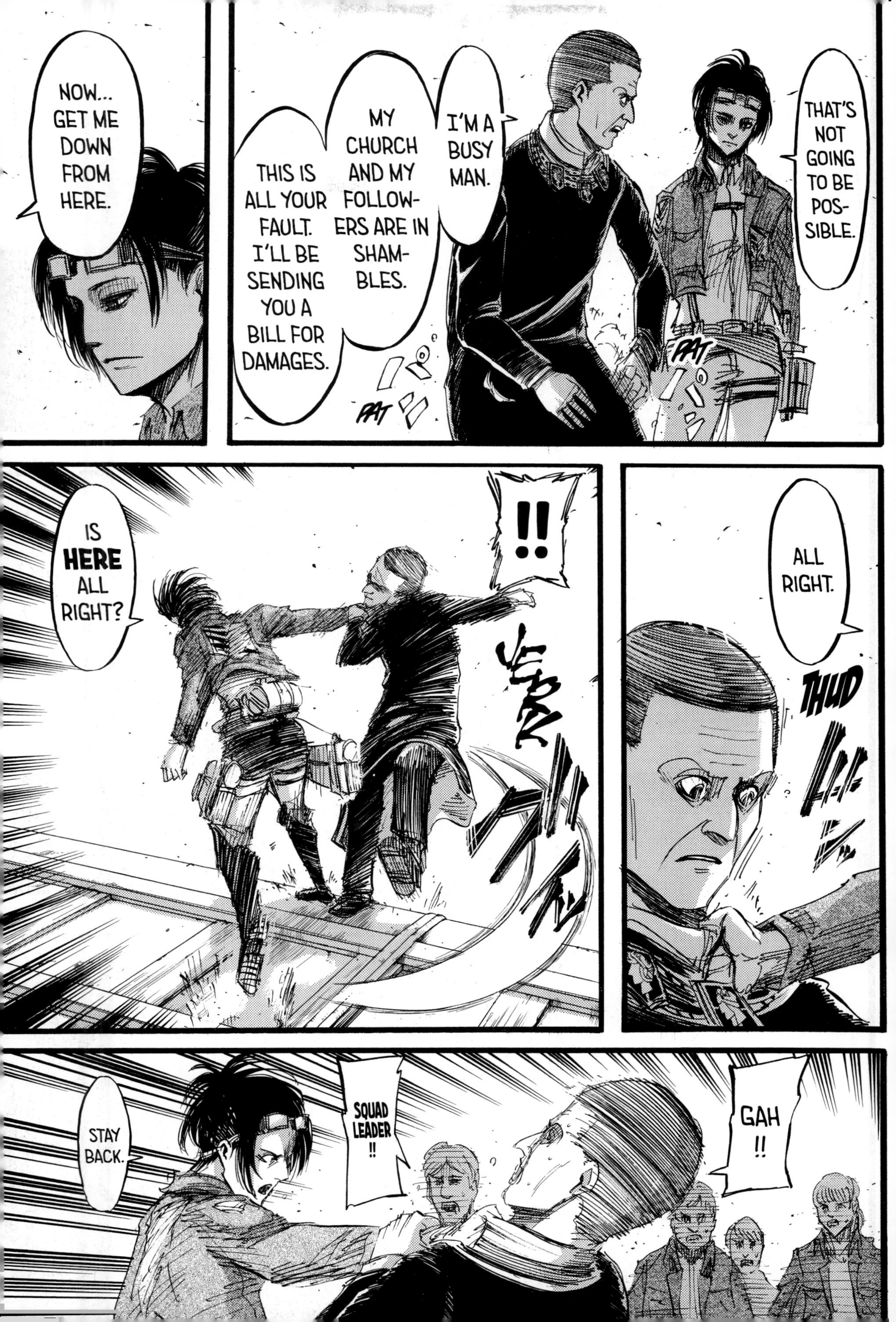
THAT'S NOT GOING TO BE POSSIBLE.
PAT
I'M A BUSY MAN.
MY CHURCH AND MY FOLLOWERS ARE IN SHAMBLES.
THIS IS ALL YOUR FAULT. I'LL BE SENDING YOU A BILL FOR DAMAGES.
PAT
NOW... GET ME DOWN FROM HERE.
ALL RIGHT.
THUD
!!
IS **HERE** ALL RIGHT?
GAH !!
SQUAD LEADER !!
STAY BACK.

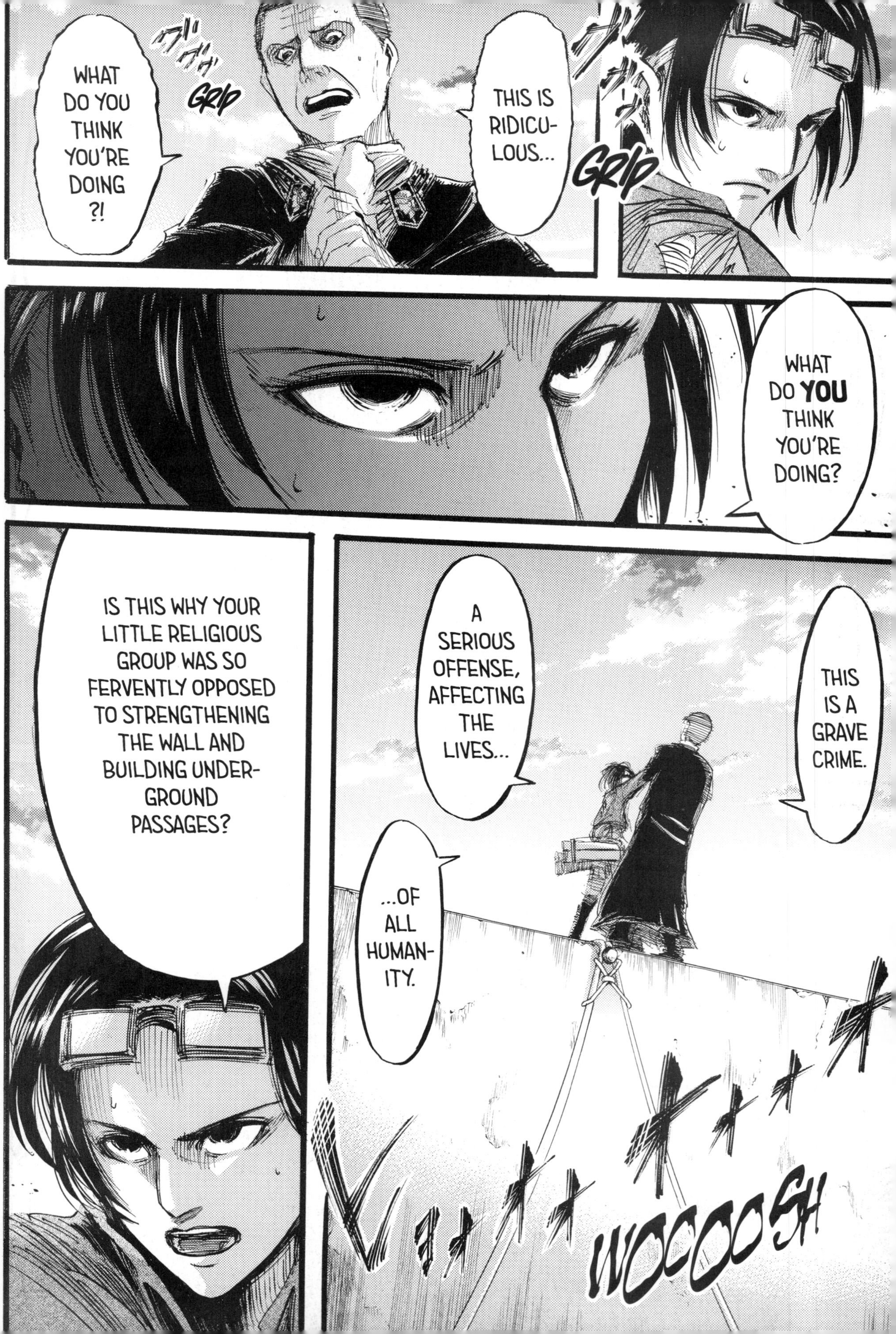
GRIP
THIS IS RIDICULOUS...
GRIP
WHAT DO YOU THINK YOU'RE DOING?!
WHAT DO YOU THINK YOU'RE DOING?
THIS IS A GRAVE CRIME.
A SERIOUS OFFENSE, AFFECTING THE LIVES...
...OF ALL HUMANITY.
WOOOOSH
IS THIS WHY YOUR LITTLE RELIGIOUS GROUP WAS SO FERVENTLY OPPOSED TO STRENGTHENING THE WALL AND BUILDING UNDERGROUND PASSAGES?

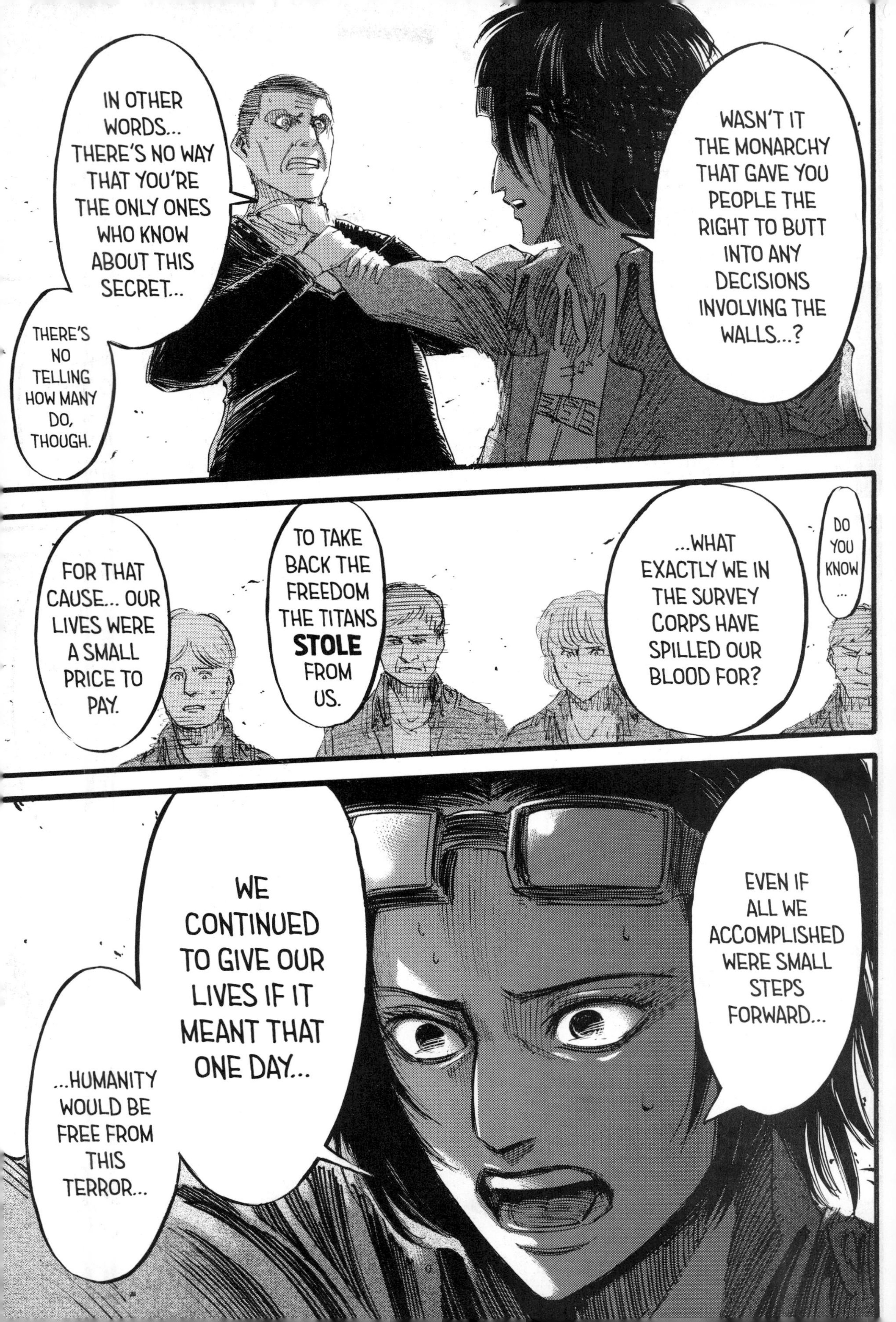
WASN'T IT THE MONARCHY THAT GAVE YOU PEOPLE THE RIGHT TO BUTT INTO ANY DECISIONS INVOLVING THE WALLS...?
IN OTHER WORDS... THERE'S NO WAY THAT YOU'RE THE ONLY ONES WHO KNOW ABOUT THIS SECRET...
THERE'S NO TELLING HOW MANY DO, THOUGH.
DO YOU KNOW...
...WHAT EXACTLY WE IN THE SURVEY CORPS HAVE SPILLED OUR BLOOD FOR?
TO TAKE BACK THE FREEDOM THE TITANS **STOLE** FROM US.
FOR THAT CAUSE... OUR LIVES WERE A SMALL PRICE TO PAY.
EVEN IF ALL WE ACCOMPLISHED WERE SMALL STEPS FORWARD...
WE CONTINUED TO GIVE OUR LIVES IF IT MEANT THAT ONE DAY...
...HUMANITY WOULD BE FREE FROM THIS TERROR...

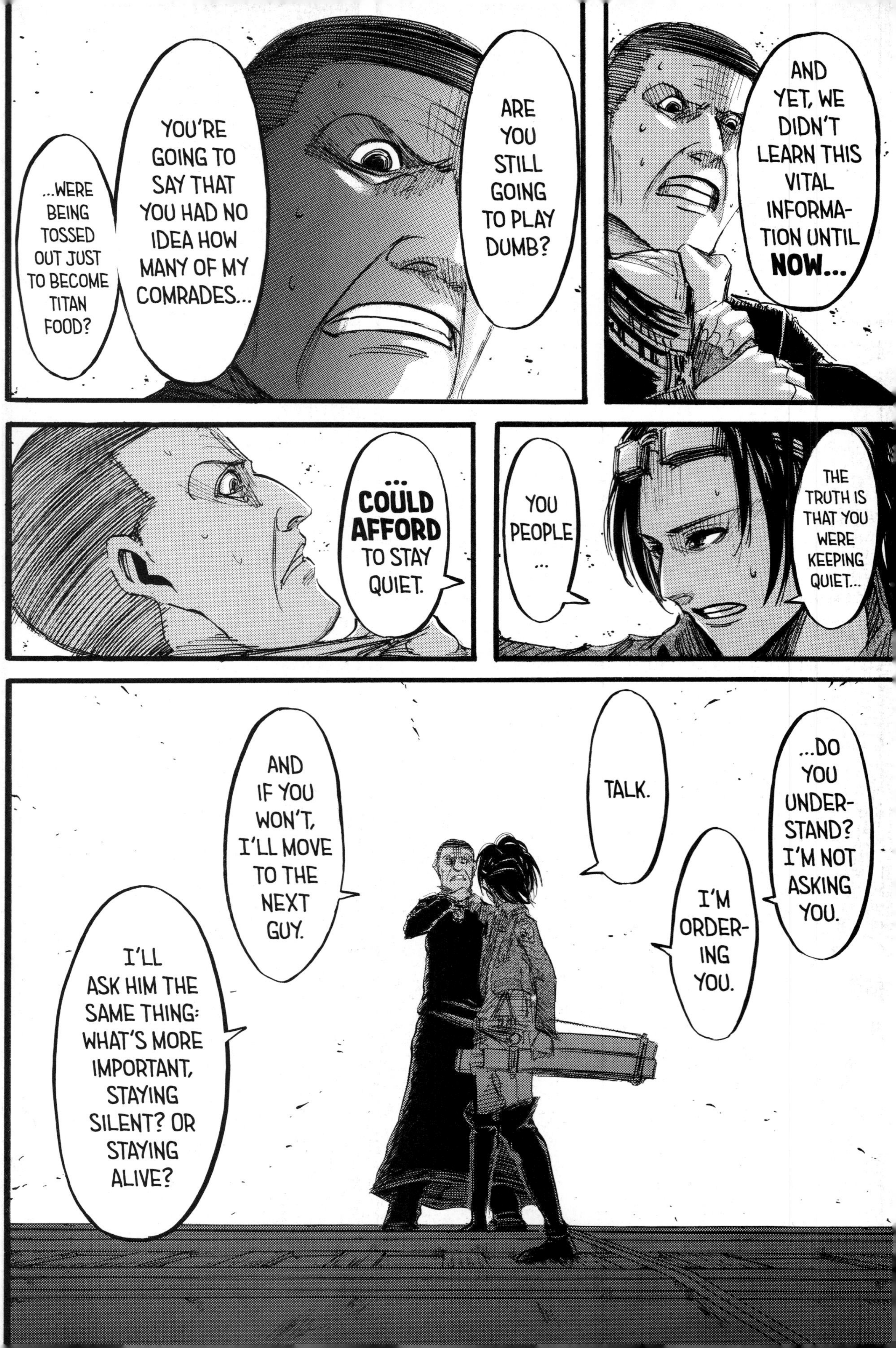
AND YET, WE DIDN'T LEARN THIS VITAL INFORMATION UNTIL **NOW...**
ARE YOU STILL GOING TO PLAY DUMB?
YOU'RE GOING TO SAY THAT YOU HAD NO IDEA HOW MANY OF MY COMRADES...
...WERE BEING TOSSED OUT JUST TO BECOME TITAN FOOD?
THE TRUTH IS THAT YOU WERE KEEPING QUIET...
YOU PEOPLE ...
...COULD AFFORD TO STAY QUIET.
...DO YOU UNDERSTAND? I'M NOT ASKING YOU.
I'M ORDERING YOU.
TALK.
AND IF YOU WON'T, I'LL MOVE TO THE NEXT GUY.
I'LL ASK HIM THE SAME THING: WHAT'S MORE IMPORTANT, STAYING SILENT? OR STAYING ALIVE?

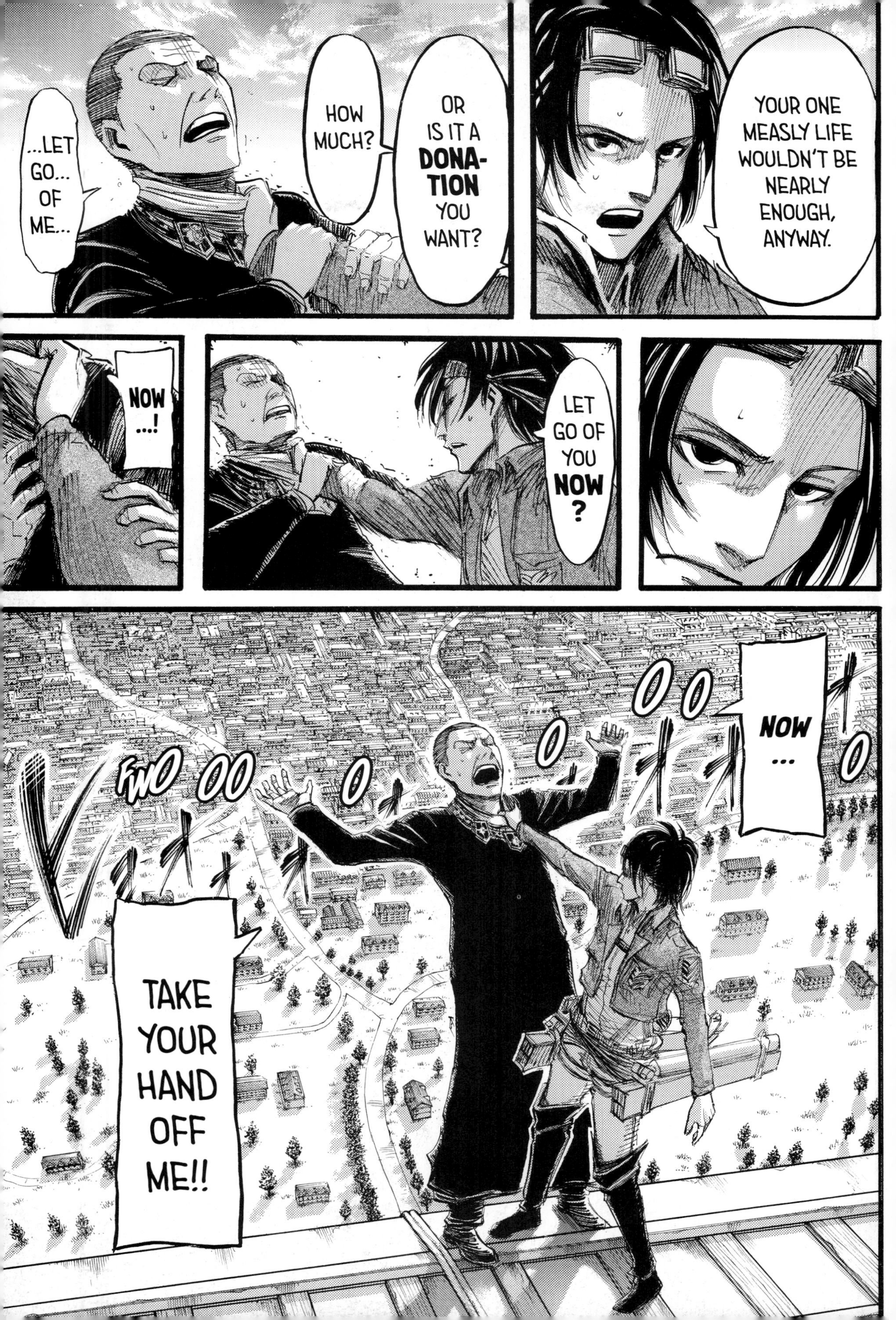

YOUR ONE MEASLY LIFE WOULDN'T BE NEARLY ENOUGH, ANYWAY.
OR IS IT A **DONATION** YOU WANT?
HOW MUCH?
...LET GO... OF ME...
LET GO OF YOU **NOW?**
NOW ...!
NOW ...
FWO OO O O OO OO O
TAKE YOUR HAND OFF ME!!

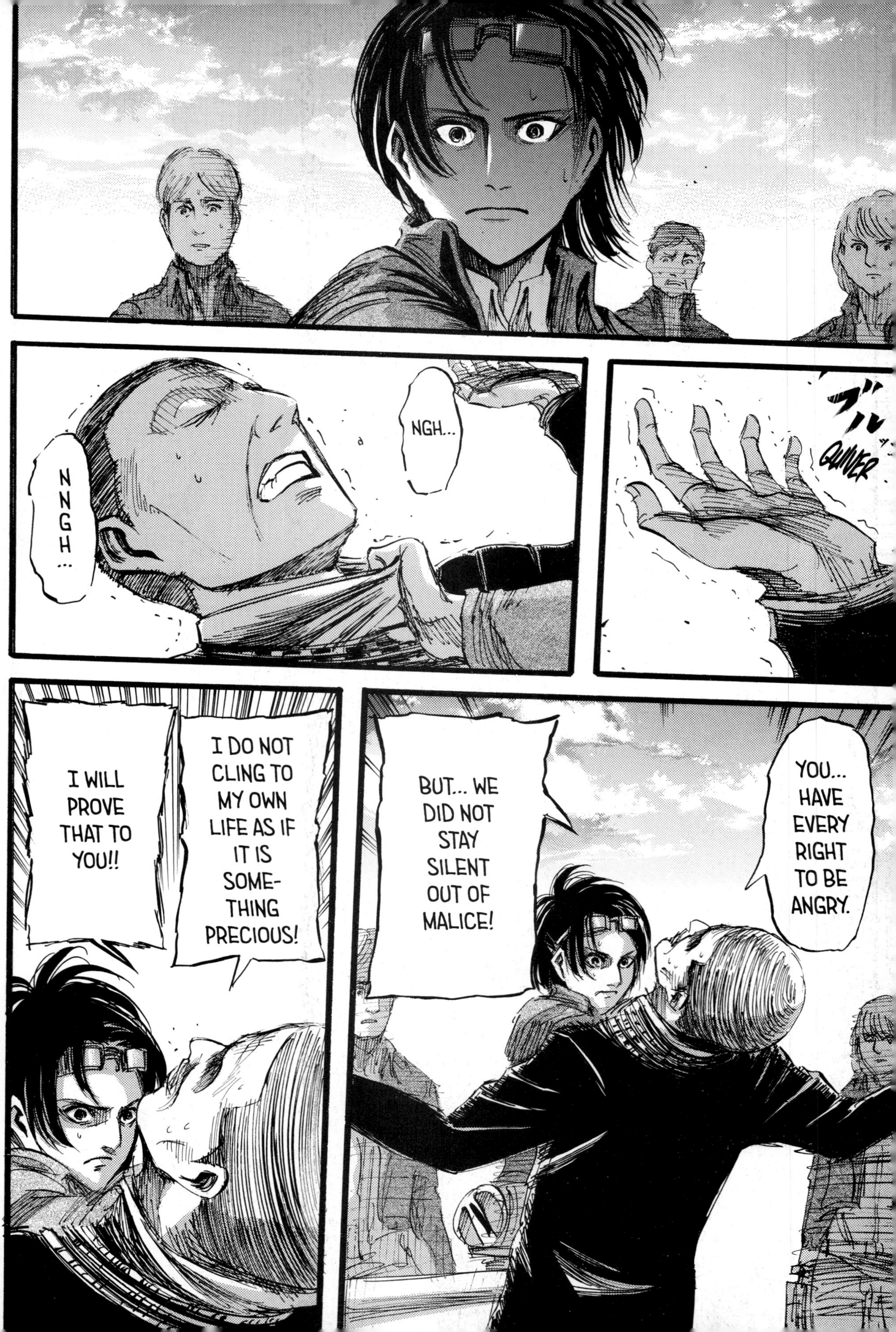

ブルッ
QUIVER
NGH...
NNGH...
YOU... HAVE EVERY RIGHT TO BE ANGRY.
BUT... WE DID NOT STAY SILENT OUT OF MALICE!
I DO NOT CLING TO MY OWN LIFE AS IF IT IS SOME-THING PRECIOUS!
I WILL PROVE THAT TO YOU!!

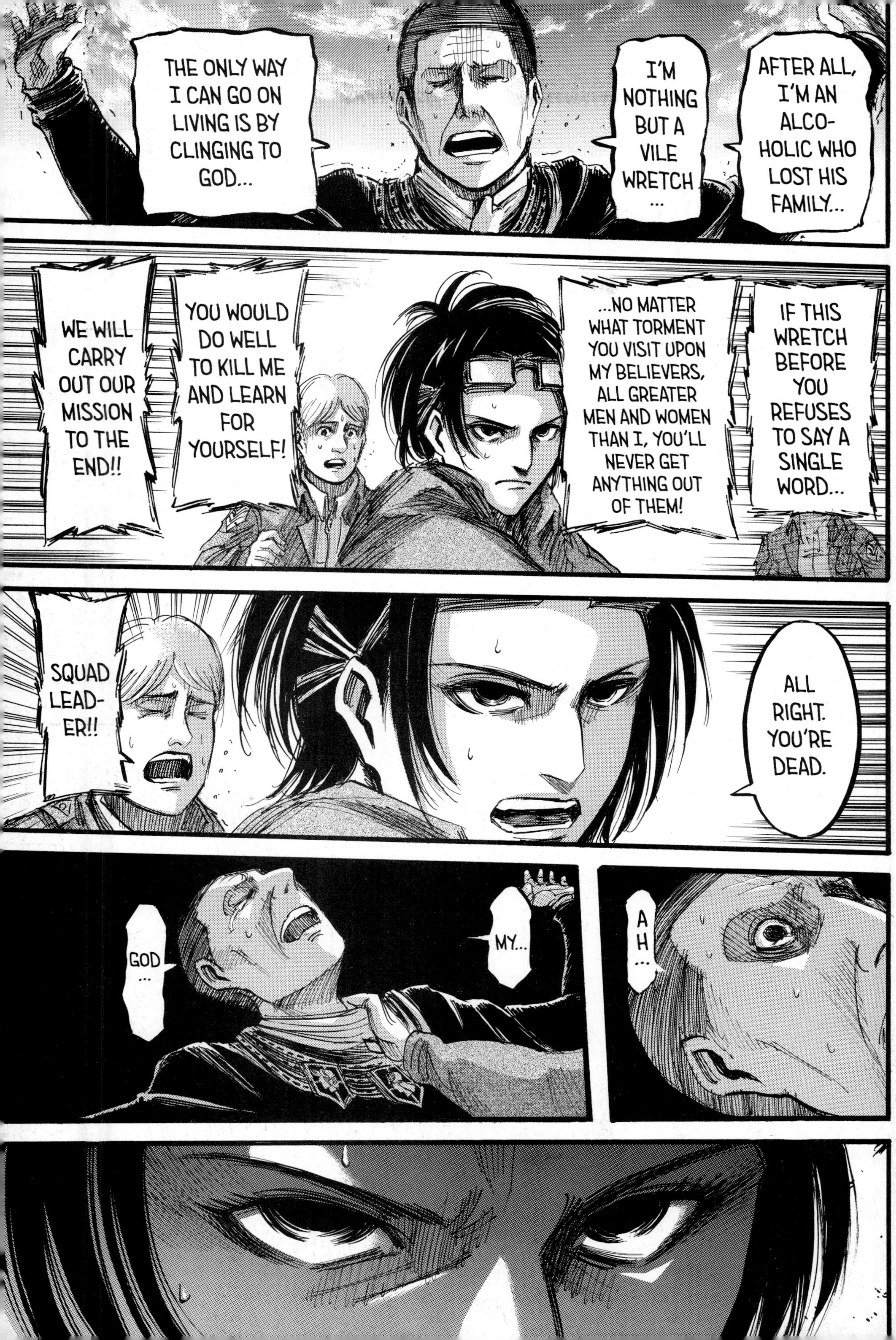
AFTER ALL, I'M AN ALCOHOLIC WHO LOST HIS FAMILY...
I'M NOTHING BUT A VILE WRETCH...
THE ONLY WAY I CAN GO ON LIVING IS BY CLINGING TO GOD...
IF THIS WRETCH BEFORE YOU REFUSES TO SAY A SINGLE WORD...
...NO MATTER WHAT TORMENT YOU VISIT UPON MY BELIEVERS, ALL GREATER MEN AND WOMEN THAN I, YOU'LL NEVER GET ANYTHING OUT OF THEM!
YOU WOULD DO WELL TO KILL ME AND LEARN FOR YOURSELF!
WE WILL CARRY OUT OUR MISSION TO THE END!!
ALL RIGHT. YOU'RE DEAD.
SQUAD LEADER!!
AH...
MY...
GOD...

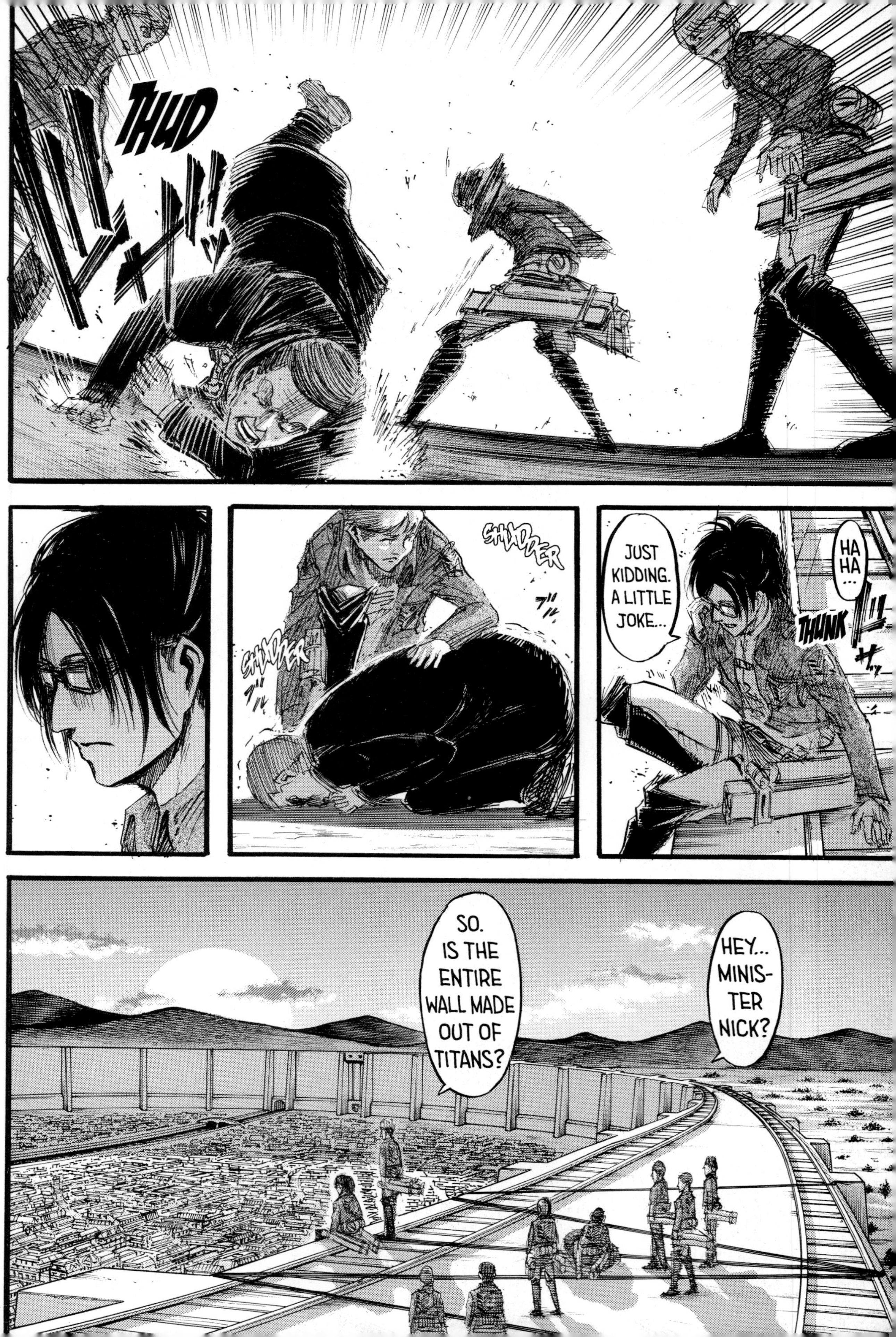
THUD
HA HA...
JUST KIDDING. A LITTLE JOKE...
THUNK
SHUDDER
SHUDDER
HEY... MINISTER NICK?
SO. IS THE ENTIRE WALL MADE OUT OF TITANS?

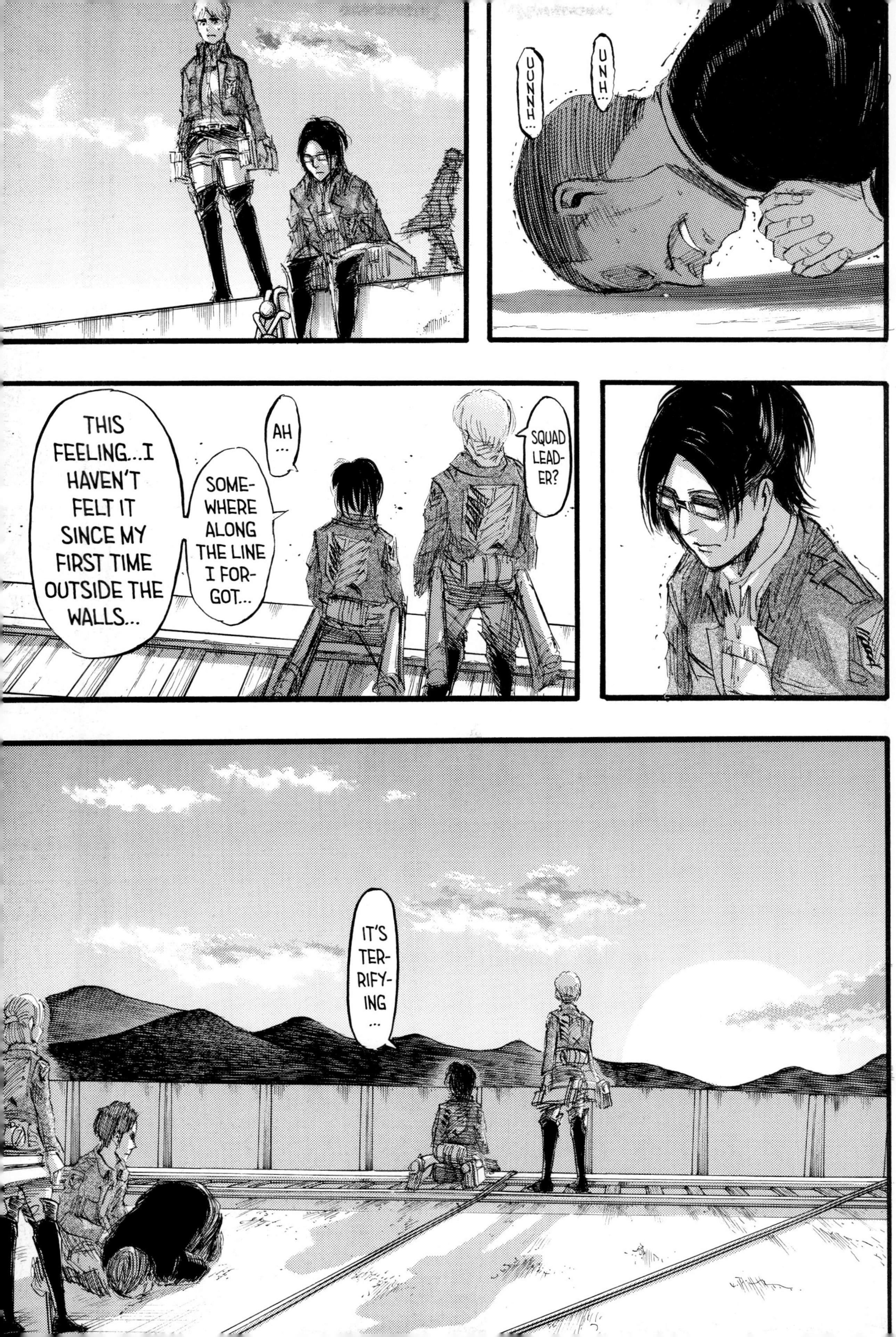
UNH...
UUNNH...
SQUAD LEADER?
AH...
SOMEWHERE ALONG THE LINE I FORGOT...
THIS FEELING...I HAVEN'T FELT IT SINCE MY FIRST TIME OUTSIDE THE WALLS...
IT'S TERRIFYING...

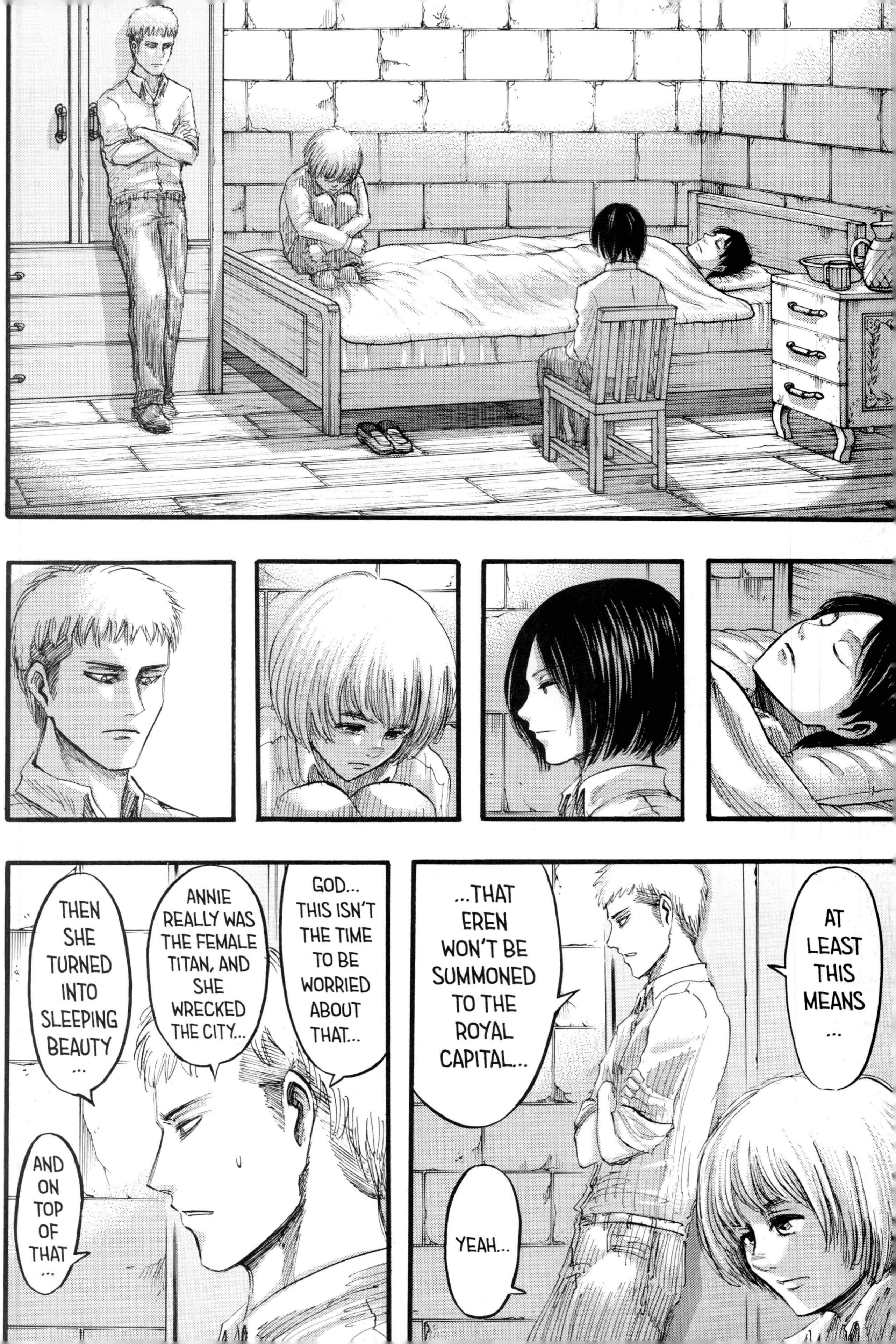
AT LEAST THIS MEANS ...
...THAT EREN WON'T BE SUMMONED TO THE ROYAL CAPITAL...
YEAH...
GOD... THIS ISN'T THE TIME TO BE WORRIED ABOUT THAT...
ANNIE REALLY WAS THE FEMALE TITAN, AND SHE WRECKED THE CITY...
THEN SHE TURNED INTO SLEEPING BEAUTY ...
AND ON TOP OF THAT ...

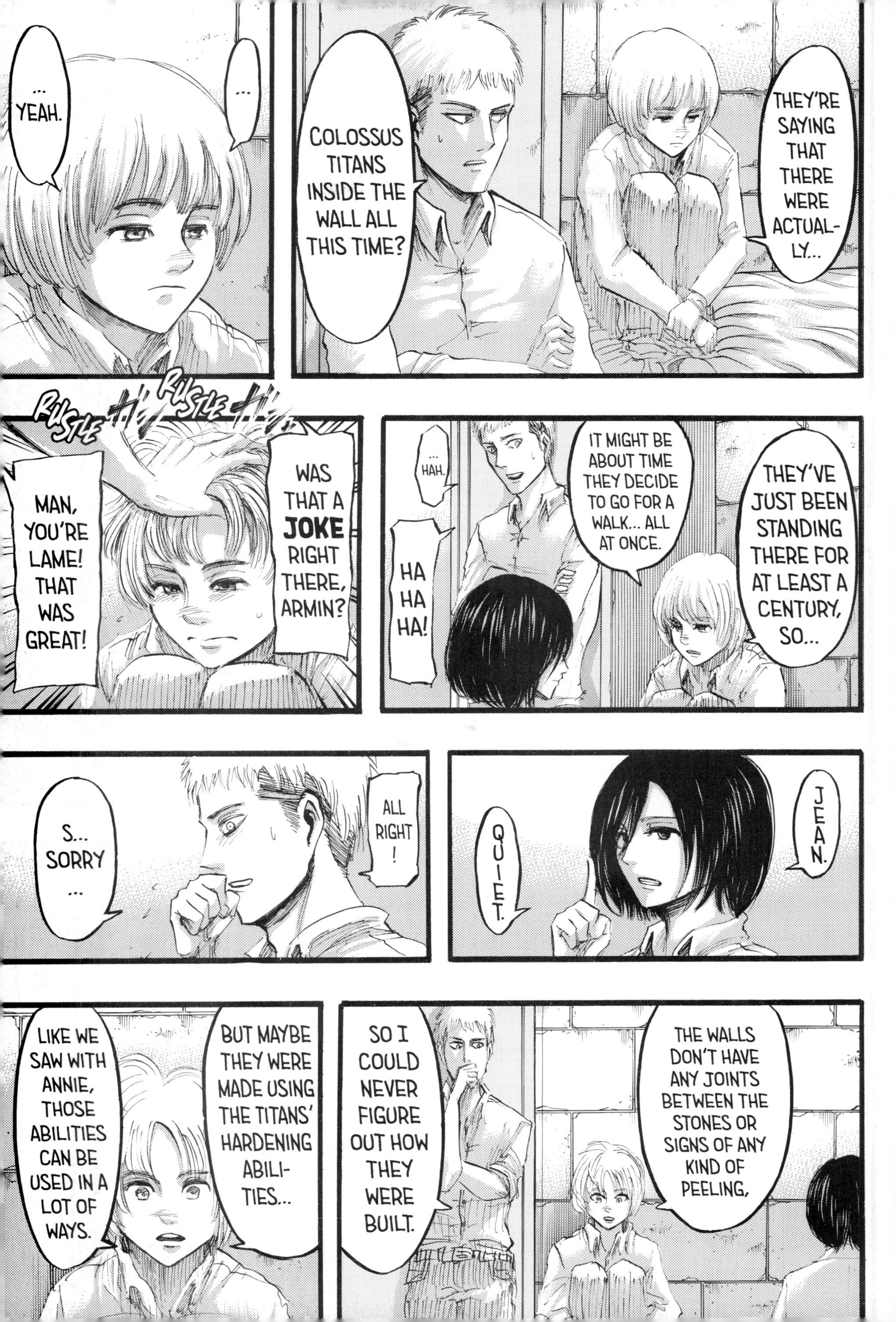
THEY'RE SAYING THAT THERE WERE ACTUAL-LY...
COLOSSUS TITANS INSIDE THE WALL ALL THIS TIME?
...
... YEAH.
THEY'VE JUST BEEN STANDING THERE FOR AT LEAST A CENTURY, SO...
IT MIGHT BE ABOUT TIME THEY DECIDE TO GO FOR A WALK... ALL AT ONCE.
... HAH.
HA HA HA!
RUSTLE RUSTLE
WAS THAT A **JOKE** RIGHT THERE, ARMIN?
MAN, YOU'RE LAME! THAT WAS GREAT!
JEAN.
QUIET.
ALL RIGHT!
S... SORRY...
THE WALLS DON'T HAVE ANY JOINTS BETWEEN THE STONES OR SIGNS OF ANY KIND OF PEELING,
SO I COULD NEVER FIGURE OUT HOW THEY WERE BUILT.
BUT MAYBE THEY WERE MADE USING THE TITANS' HARDENING ABILI-TIES...
LIKE WE SAW WITH ANNIE, THOSE ABILITIES CAN BE USED IN A LOT OF WAYS.

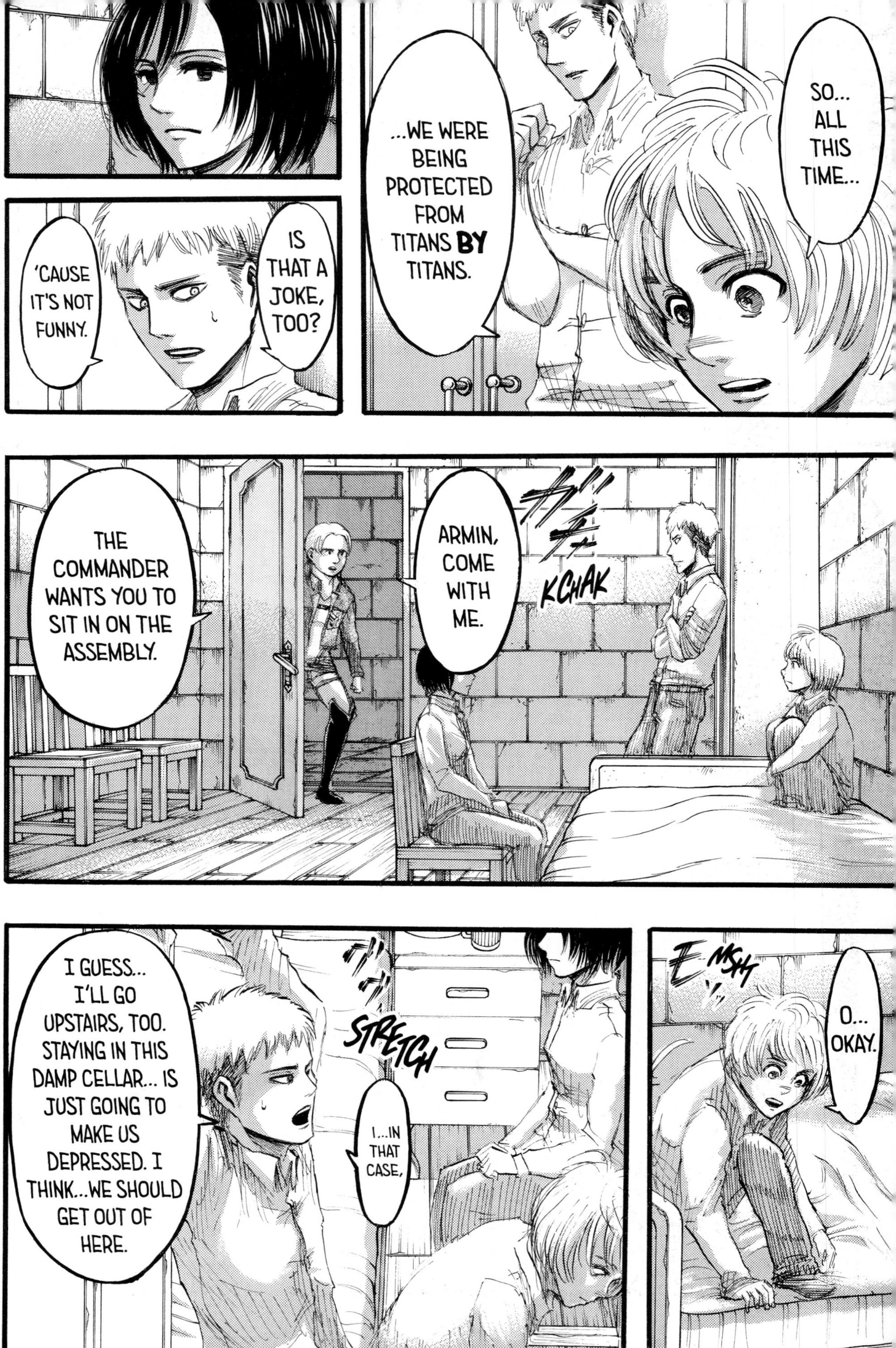
SO... ALL THIS TIME...
...WE WERE BEING PROTECTED FROM TITANS **BY** TITANS.
IS THAT A JOKE, TOO?
'CAUSE IT'S NOT FUNNY.
KCHAK
ARMIN, COME WITH ME.
THE COMMANDER WANTS YOU TO SIT IN ON THE ASSEMBLY.
MSH
O... OKAY.
STRETCH
I...IN THAT CASE,
I GUESS... I'LL GO UPSTAIRS, TOO. STAYING IN THIS DAMP CELLAR... IS JUST GOING TO MAKE US DEPRESSED. I THINK...WE SHOULD GET OUT OF HERE.

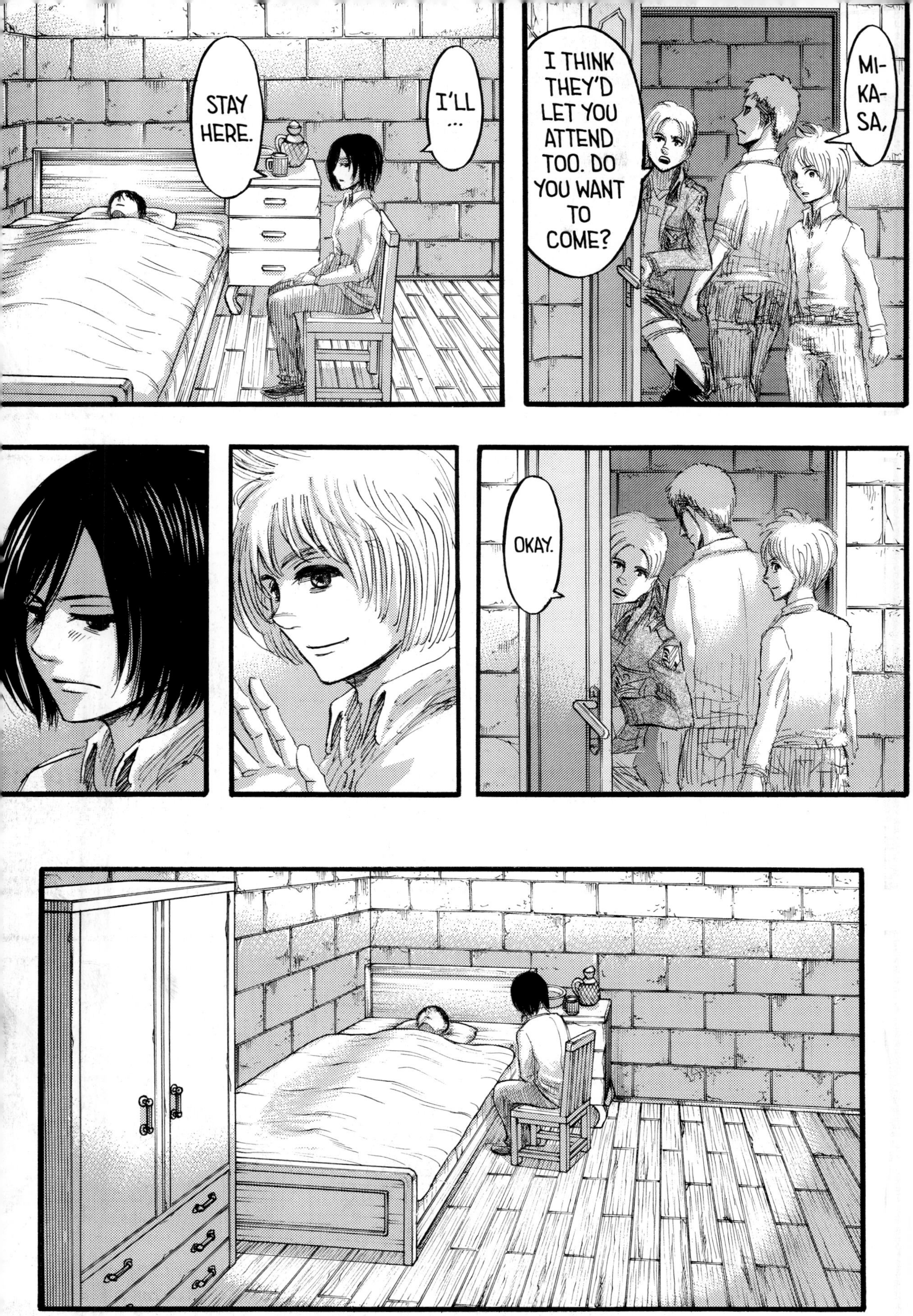
MI-KA-SA,
I THINK THEY'D LET YOU ATTEND TOO. DO YOU WANT TO COME?
I'LL ...
STAY HERE.
OKAY.

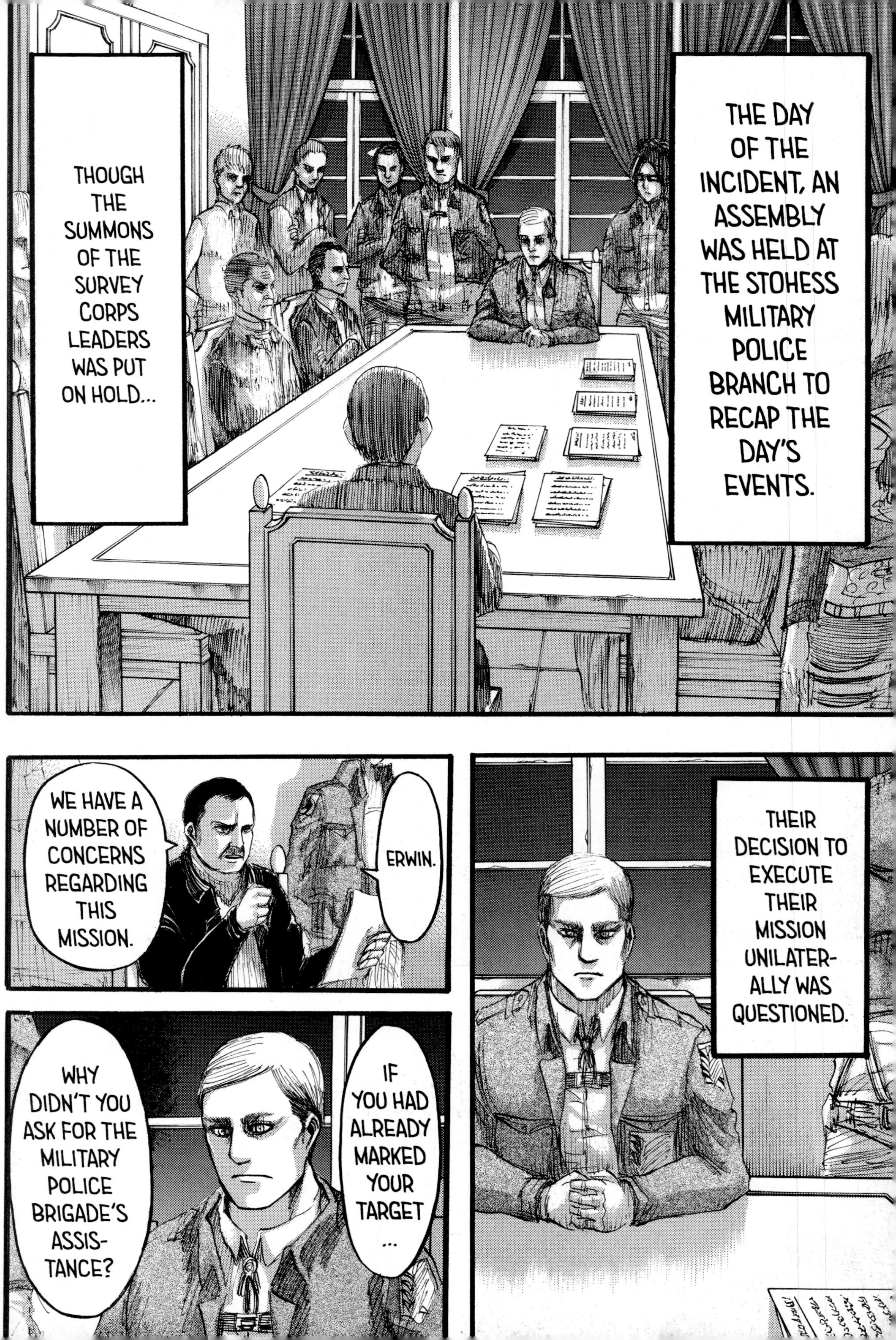
THE DAY OF THE INCIDENT, AN ASSEMBLY WAS HELD AT THE STOHESS MILITARY POLICE BRANCH TO RECAP THE DAY'S EVENTS.
THOUGH THE SUMMONS OF THE SURVEY CORPS LEADERS WAS PUT ON HOLD...
THEIR DECISION TO EXECUTE THEIR MISSION UNILATERALLY WAS QUESTIONED.
ERWIN.
WE HAVE A NUMBER OF CONCERNS REGARDING THIS MISSION.
IF YOU HAD ALREADY MARKED YOUR TARGET...
WHY DIDN'T YOU ASK FOR THE MILITARY POLICE BRIGADE'S ASSISTANCE?

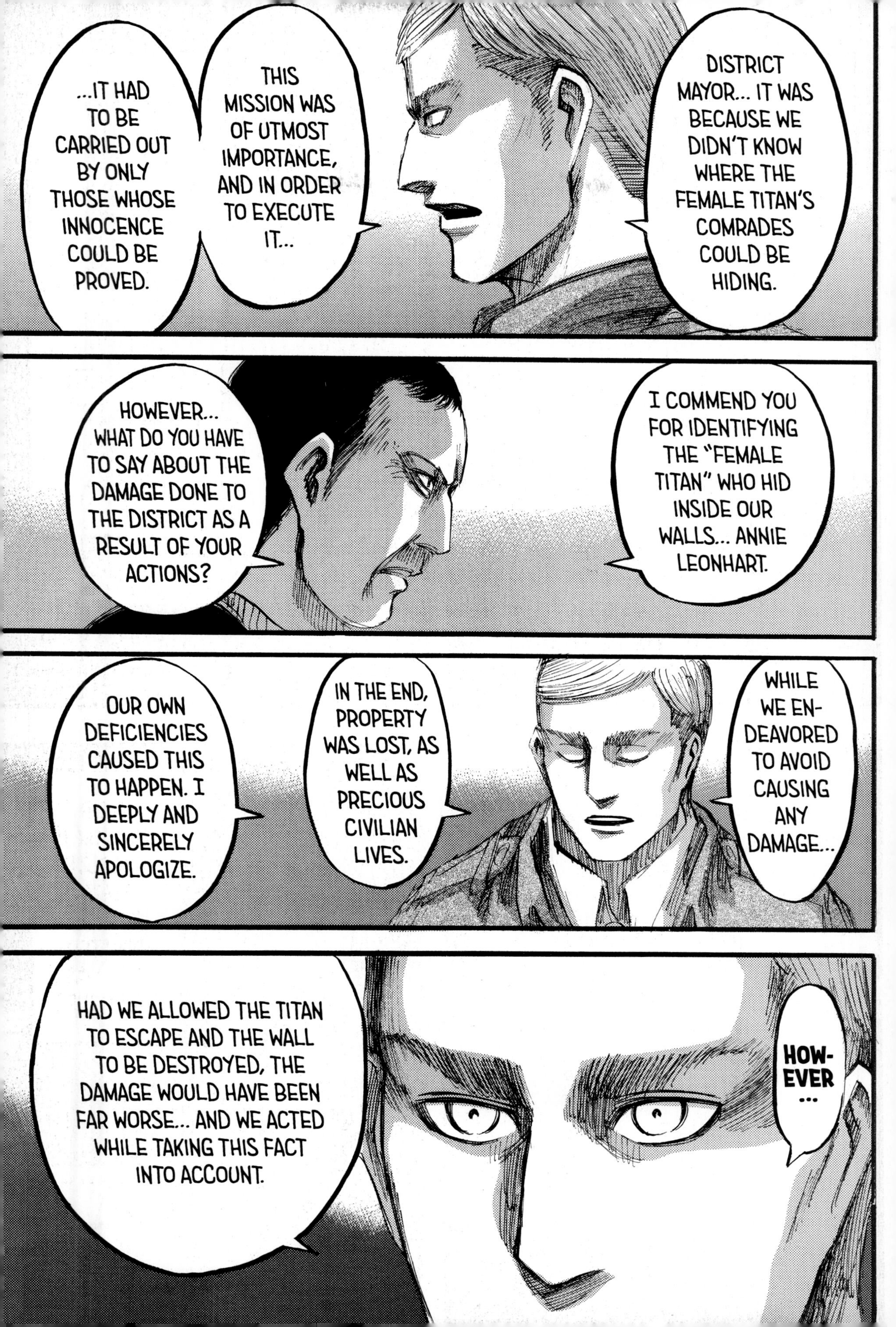
DISTRICT MAYOR... IT WAS BECAUSE WE DIDN'T KNOW WHERE THE FEMALE TITAN'S COMRADES COULD BE HIDING.
THIS MISSION WAS OF UTMOST IMPORTANCE, AND IN ORDER TO EXECUTE IT...
...IT HAD TO BE CARRIED OUT BY ONLY THOSE WHOSE INNOCENCE COULD BE PROVED.
I COMMEND YOU FOR IDENTIFYING THE "FEMALE TITAN" WHO HID INSIDE OUR WALLS... ANNIE LEONHART.
HOWEVER... WHAT DO YOU HAVE TO SAY ABOUT THE DAMAGE DONE TO THE DISTRICT AS A RESULT OF YOUR ACTIONS?
WHILE WE EN-DEAVORED TO AVOID CAUSING ANY DAMAGE...
IN THE END, PROPERTY WAS LOST, AS WELL AS PRECIOUS CIVILIAN LIVES.
OUR OWN DEFICIENCIES CAUSED THIS TO HAPPEN. I DEEPLY AND SINCERELY APOLOGIZE.
HOW-EVER...
HAD WE ALLOWED THE TITAN TO ESCAPE AND THE WALL TO BE DESTROYED, THE DAMAGE WOULD HAVE BEEN FAR WORSE... AND WE ACTED WHILE TAKING THIS FACT INTO ACCOUNT.

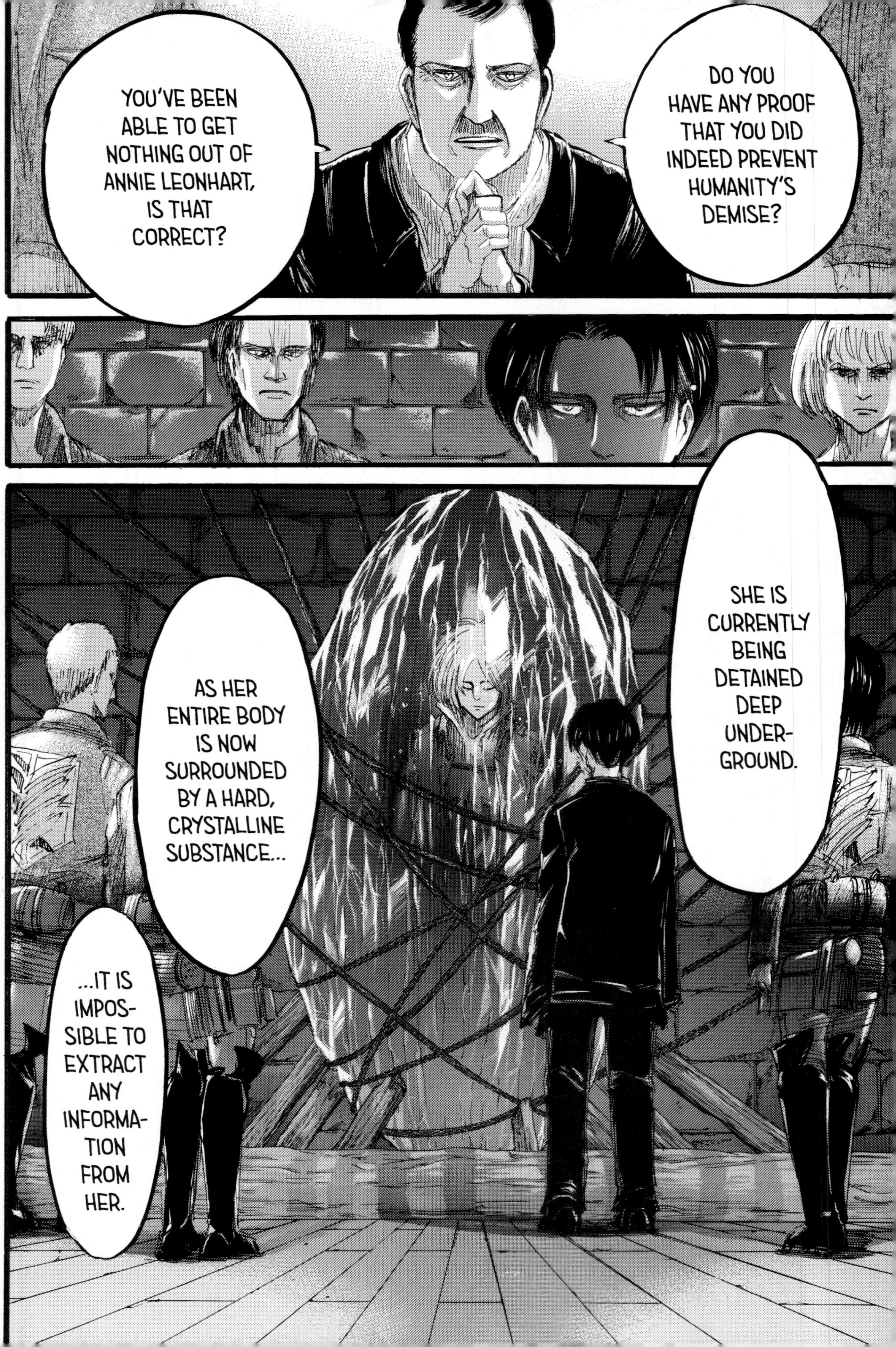
DO YOU HAVE ANY PROOF THAT YOU DID INDEED PREVENT HUMANITY'S DEMISE?
YOU'VE BEEN ABLE TO GET NOTHING OUT OF ANNIE LEONHART, IS THAT CORRECT?
SHE IS CURRENTLY BEING DETAINED DEEP UNDER-GROUND.
AS HER ENTIRE BODY IS NOW SURROUNDED BY A HARD, CRYSTALLINE SUBSTANCE...
...IT IS IMPOS-SIBLE TO EXTRACT ANY INFORMA-TION FROM HER.

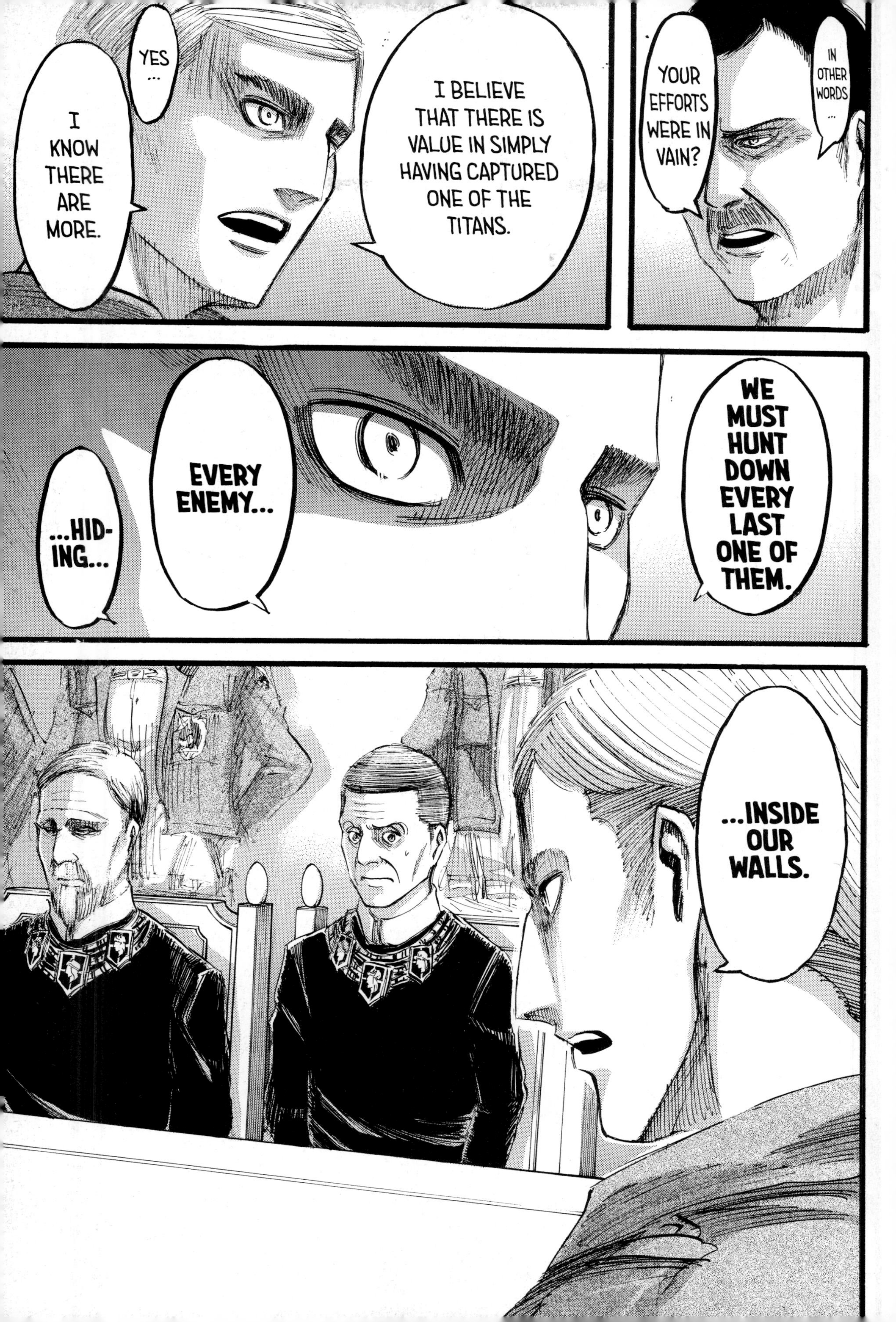
IN OTHER WORDS...
YOUR EFFORTS WERE IN VAIN?
I BELIEVE THAT THERE IS VALUE IN SIMPLY HAVING CAPTURED ONE OF THE TITANS.
YES...
I KNOW THERE ARE MORE.
WE MUST HUNT DOWN EVERY LAST ONE OF THEM.
EVERY ENEMY...
...HID-ING...
...INSIDE OUR WALLS.

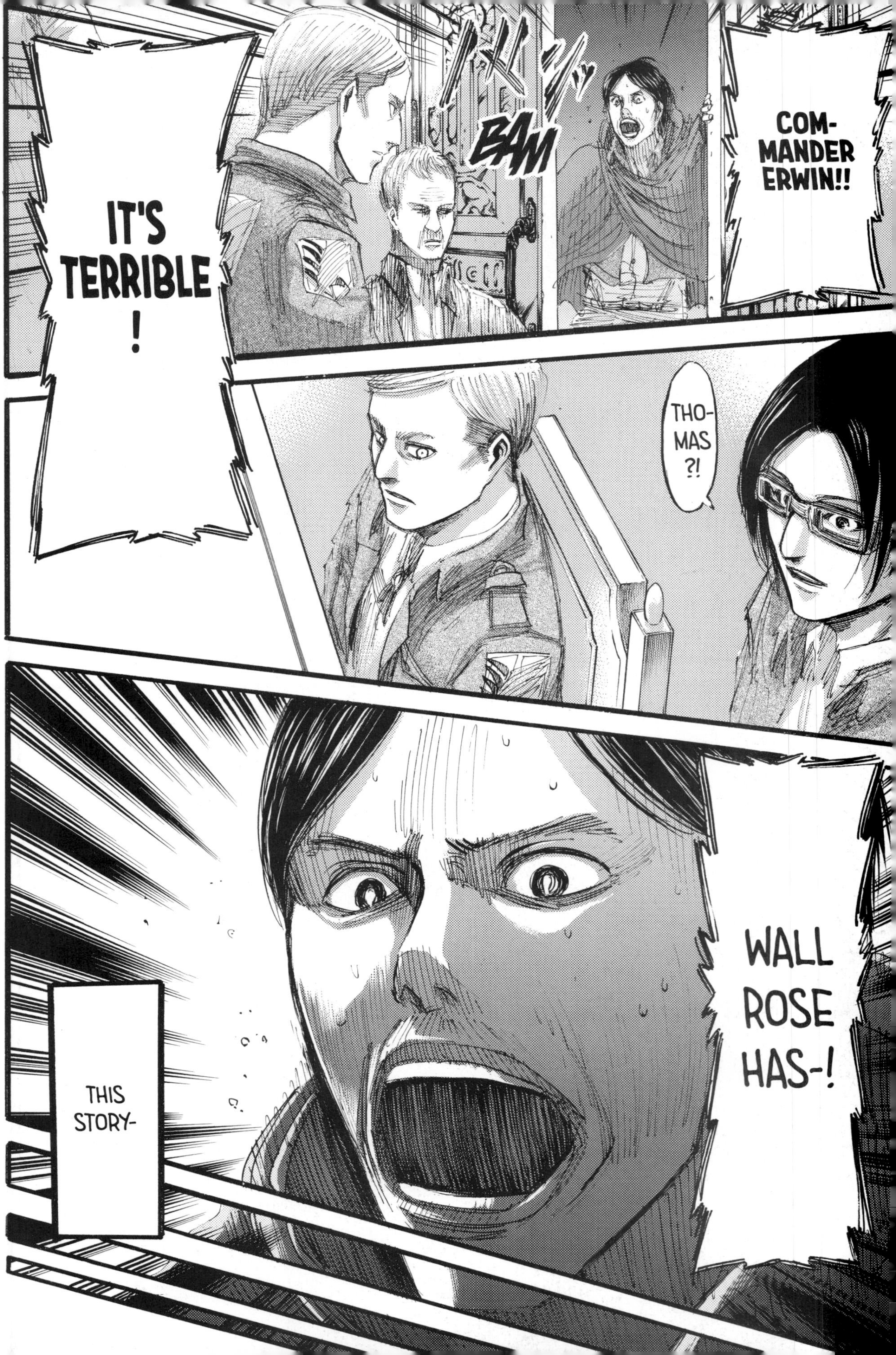
COM-
MANDER
ERWIN!!
BAM
IT'S
TERRIBLE
!
THO-
MAS
?!
WALL
ROSE
HAS-!
THIS
STORY-

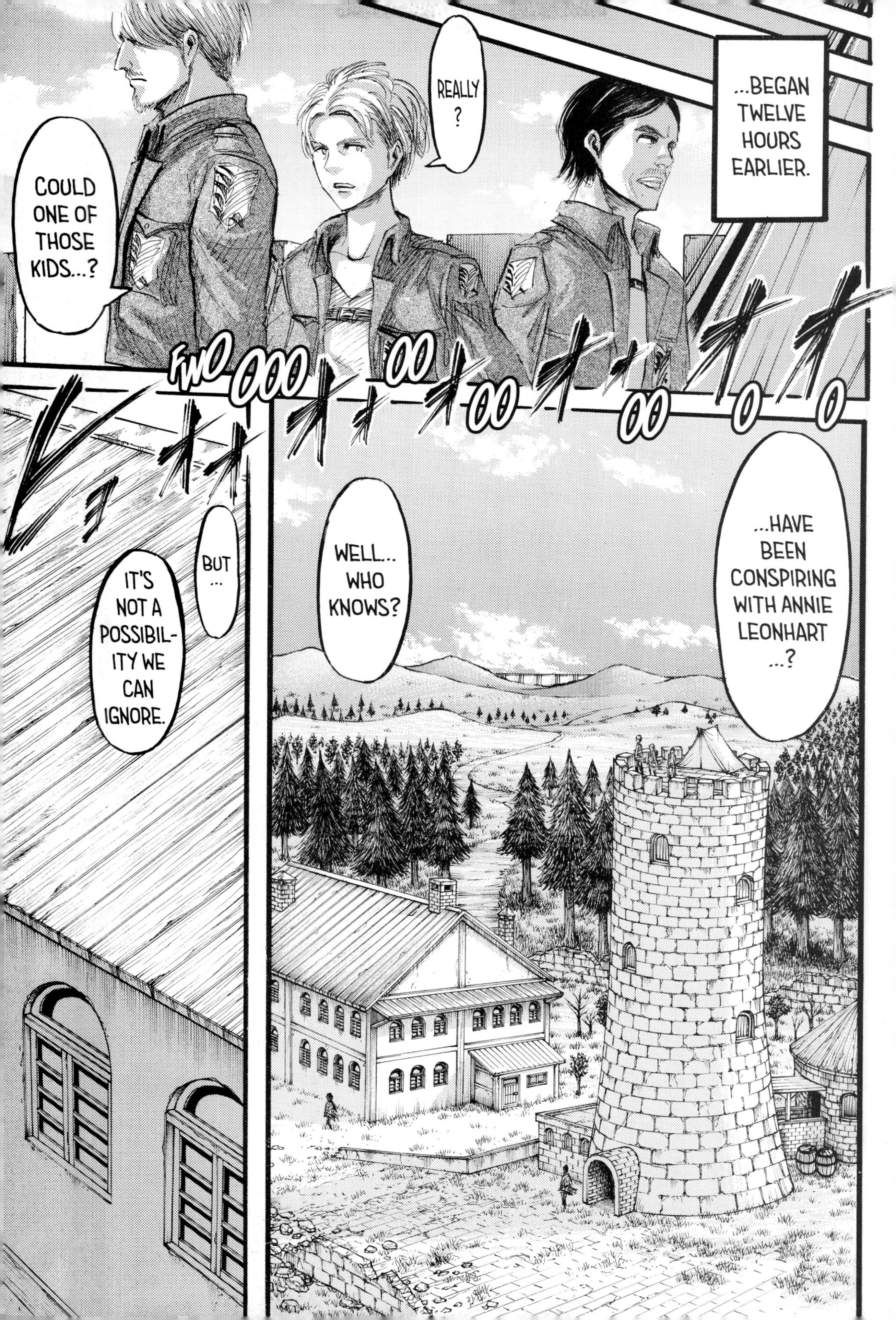
...BEGAN TWELVE HOURS EARLIER.
REALLY?
COULD ONE OF THOSE KIDS...?
FWOOOOOOOOOOOO
...HAVE BEEN CONSPIRING WITH ANNIE LEONHART...?
WELL... WHO KNOWS?
BUT...
IT'S NOT A POSSIBIL-ITY WE CAN IGNORE.

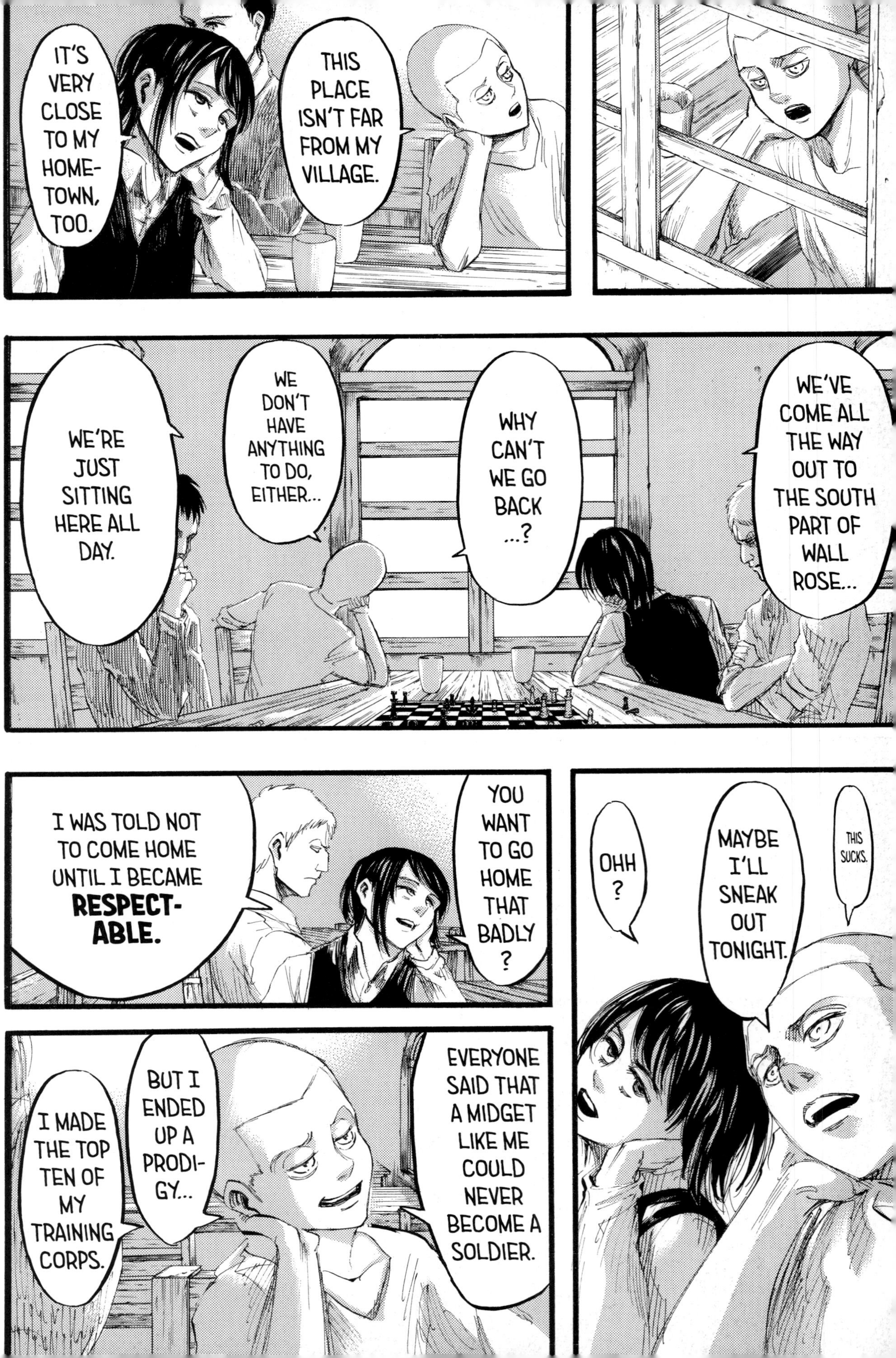
THIS PLACE ISN'T FAR FROM MY VILLAGE.
IT'S VERY CLOSE TO MY HOMETOWN, TOO.
WE'VE COME ALL THE WAY OUT TO THE SOUTH PART OF WALL ROSE...
WHY CAN'T WE GO BACK ...?
WE DON'T HAVE ANYTHING TO DO, EITHER...
WE'RE JUST SITTING HERE ALL DAY.
THIS SUCKS.
MAYBE I'LL SNEAK OUT TONIGHT.
OHH?
YOU WANT TO GO HOME THAT BADLY?
I WAS TOLD NOT TO COME HOME UNTIL I BECAME **RESPECTABLE.**
EVERYONE SAID THAT A MIDGET LIKE ME COULD NEVER BECOME A SOLDIER.
BUT I ENDED UP A PRODIGY...
I MADE THE TOP TEN OF MY TRAINING CORPS.

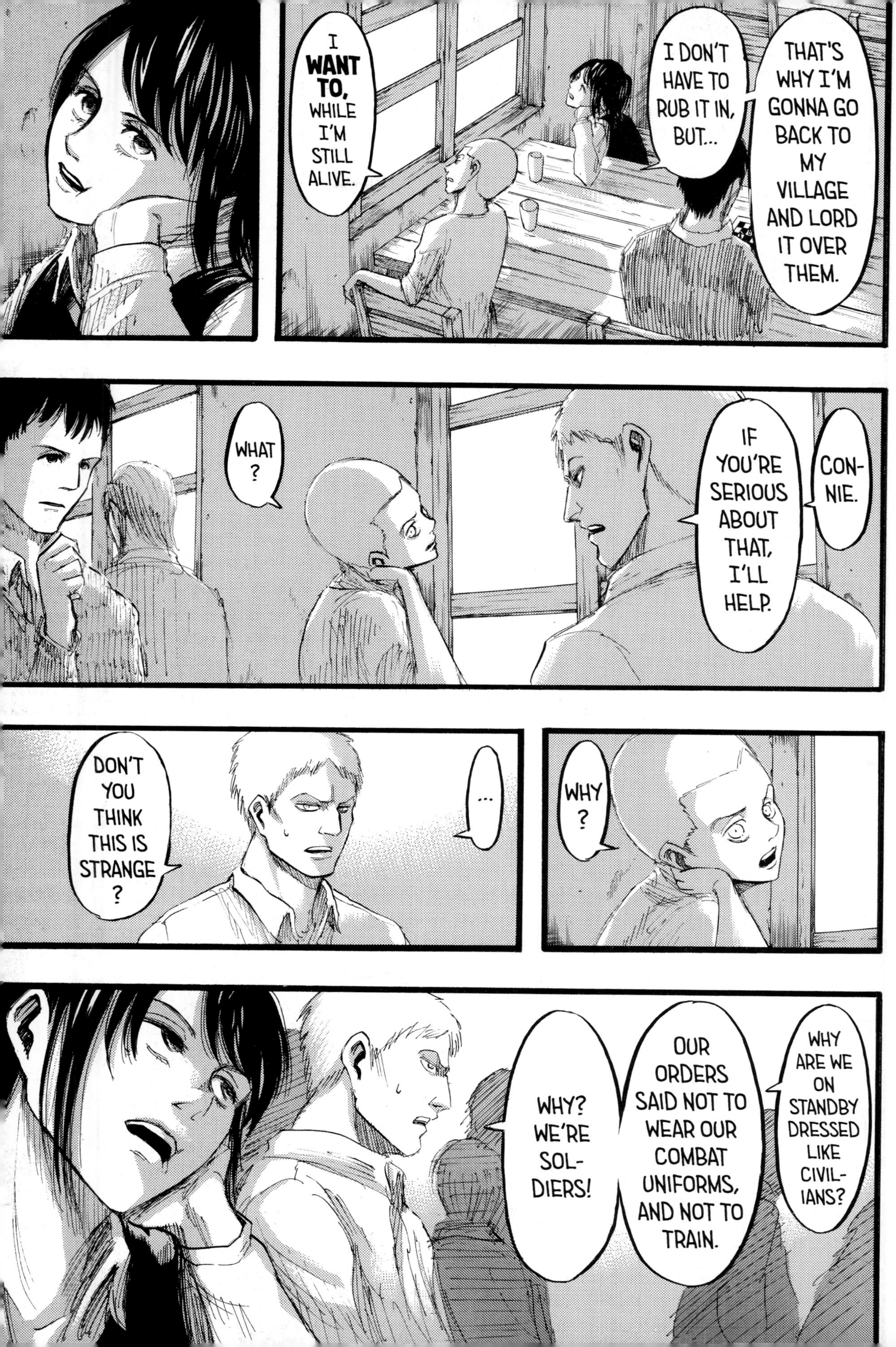
THAT'S WHY I'M GONNA GO BACK TO MY VILLAGE AND LORD IT OVER THEM.
I DON'T HAVE TO RUB IT IN, BUT...
I **WANT TO,** WHILE I'M STILL ALIVE.
CON-NIE.
IF YOU'RE SERIOUS ABOUT THAT, I'LL HELP.
WHAT?
WHY?
...
DON'T YOU THINK THIS IS STRANGE?
WHY ARE WE ON STANDBY DRESSED LIKE CIVIL-IANS?
OUR ORDERS SAID NOT TO WEAR OUR COMBAT UNIFORMS, AND NOT TO TRAIN.
WHY? WE'RE SOL-DIERS!

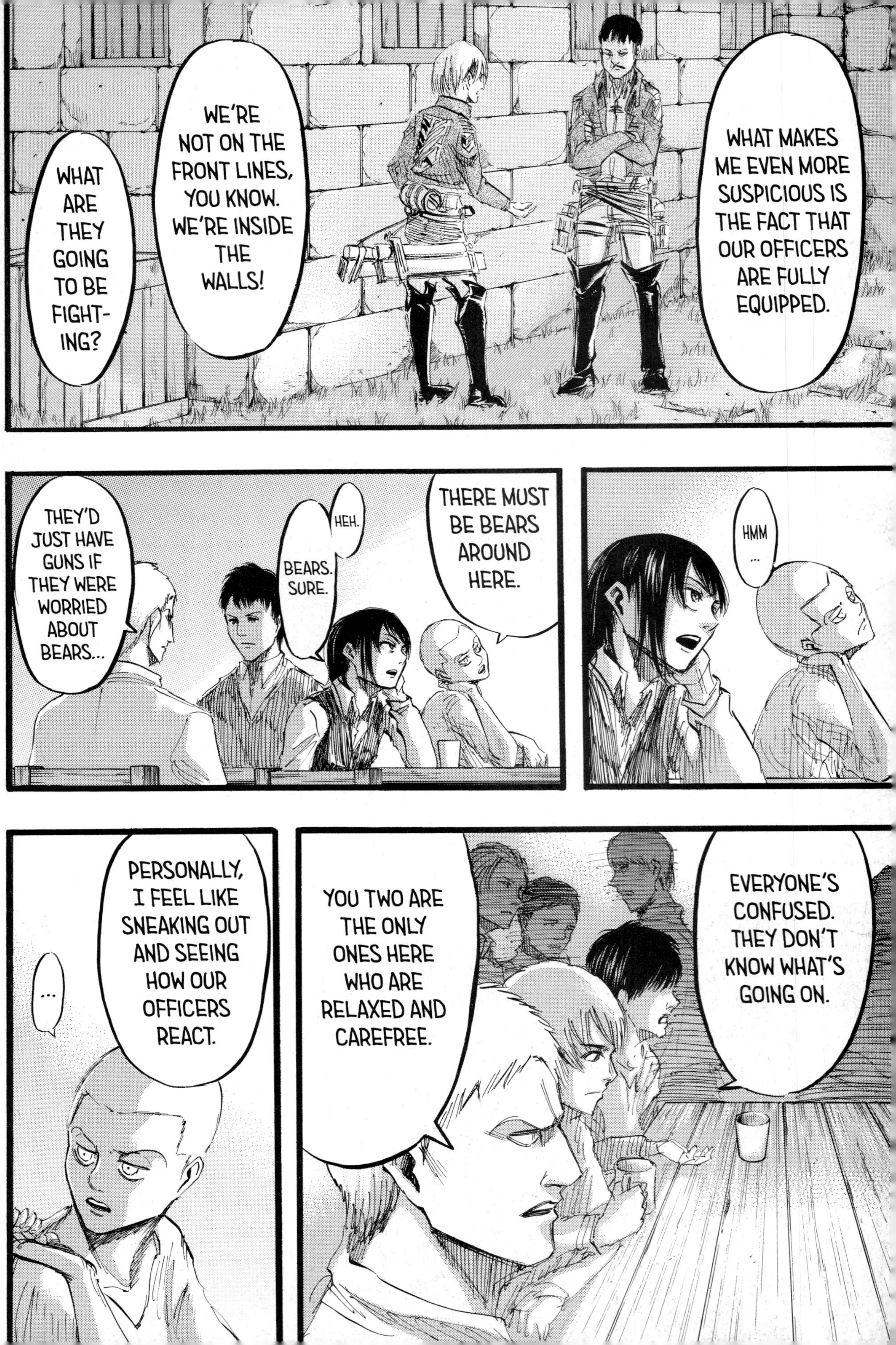
WHAT MAKES ME EVEN MORE SUSPICIOUS IS THE FACT THAT OUR OFFICERS ARE FULLY EQUIPPED.
WE'RE NOT ON THE FRONT LINES, YOU KNOW. WE'RE INSIDE THE WALLS!
WHAT ARE THEY GOING TO BE FIGHT-ING?
HMM...
THERE MUST BE BEARS AROUND HERE.
HEH.
BEARS. SURE.
THEY'D JUST HAVE GUNS IF THEY WERE WORRIED ABOUT BEARS...
EVERYONE'S CONFUSED. THEY DON'T KNOW WHAT'S GOING ON.
YOU TWO ARE THE ONLY ONES HERE WHO ARE RELAXED AND CAREFREE.
PERSONALLY, I FEEL LIKE SNEAKING OUT AND SEEING HOW OUR OFFICERS REACT.
...

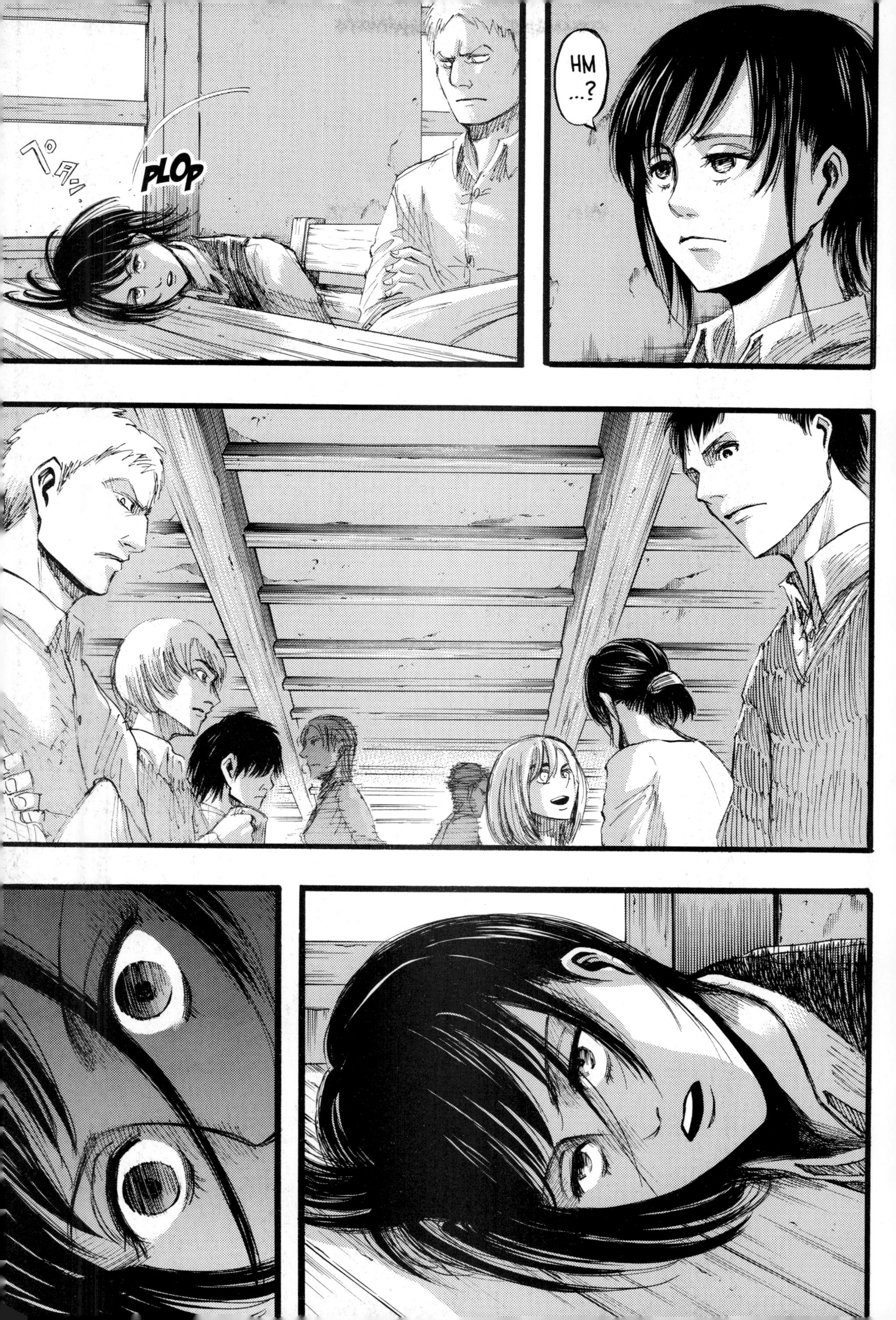
HM ...?
PLOP
ペタン

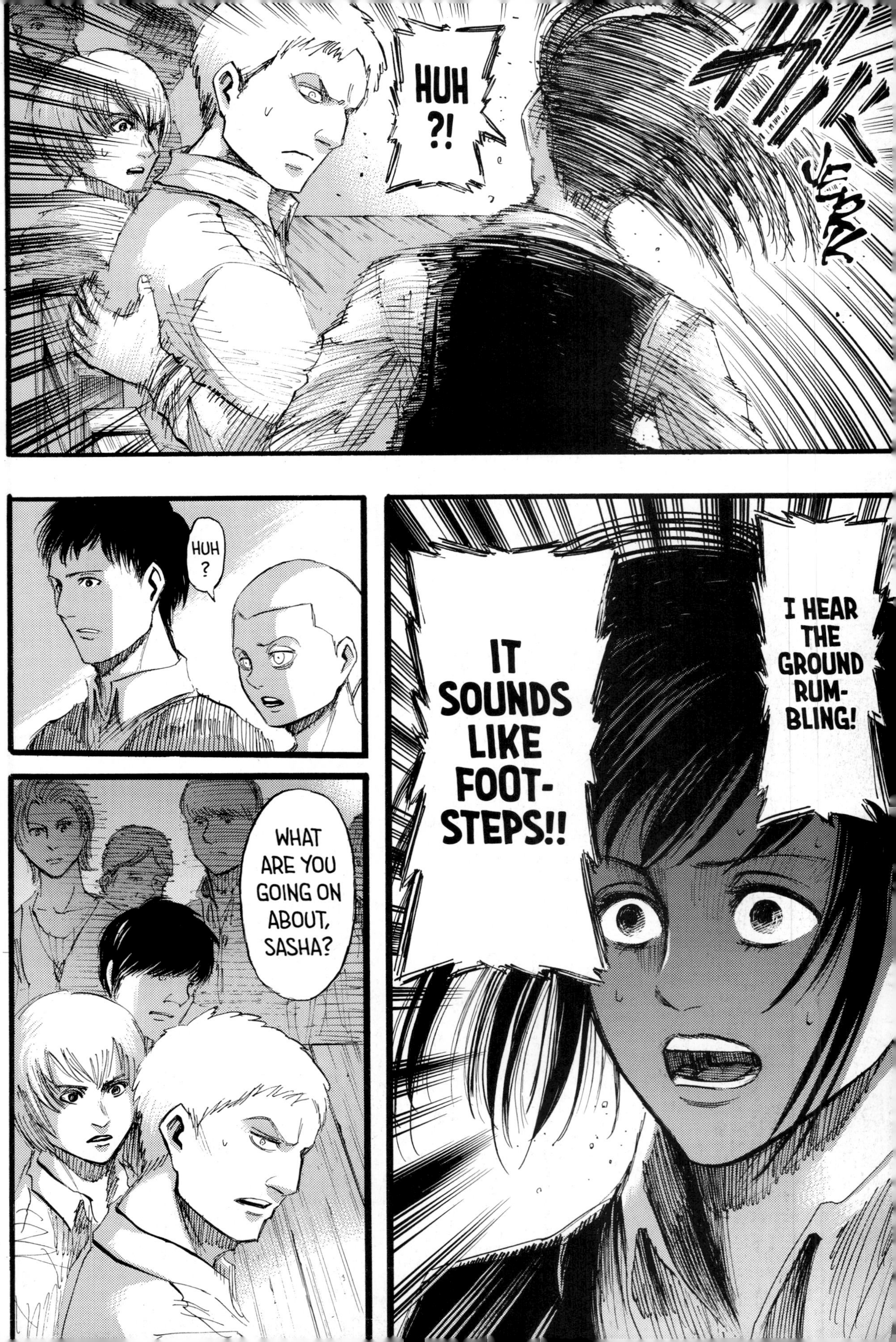
JERK
HUH ?!
I HEAR THE GROUND RUM-BLING!
IT SOUNDS LIKE FOOT-STEPS!!
HUH ?
WHAT ARE YOU GOING ON ABOUT, SASHA?

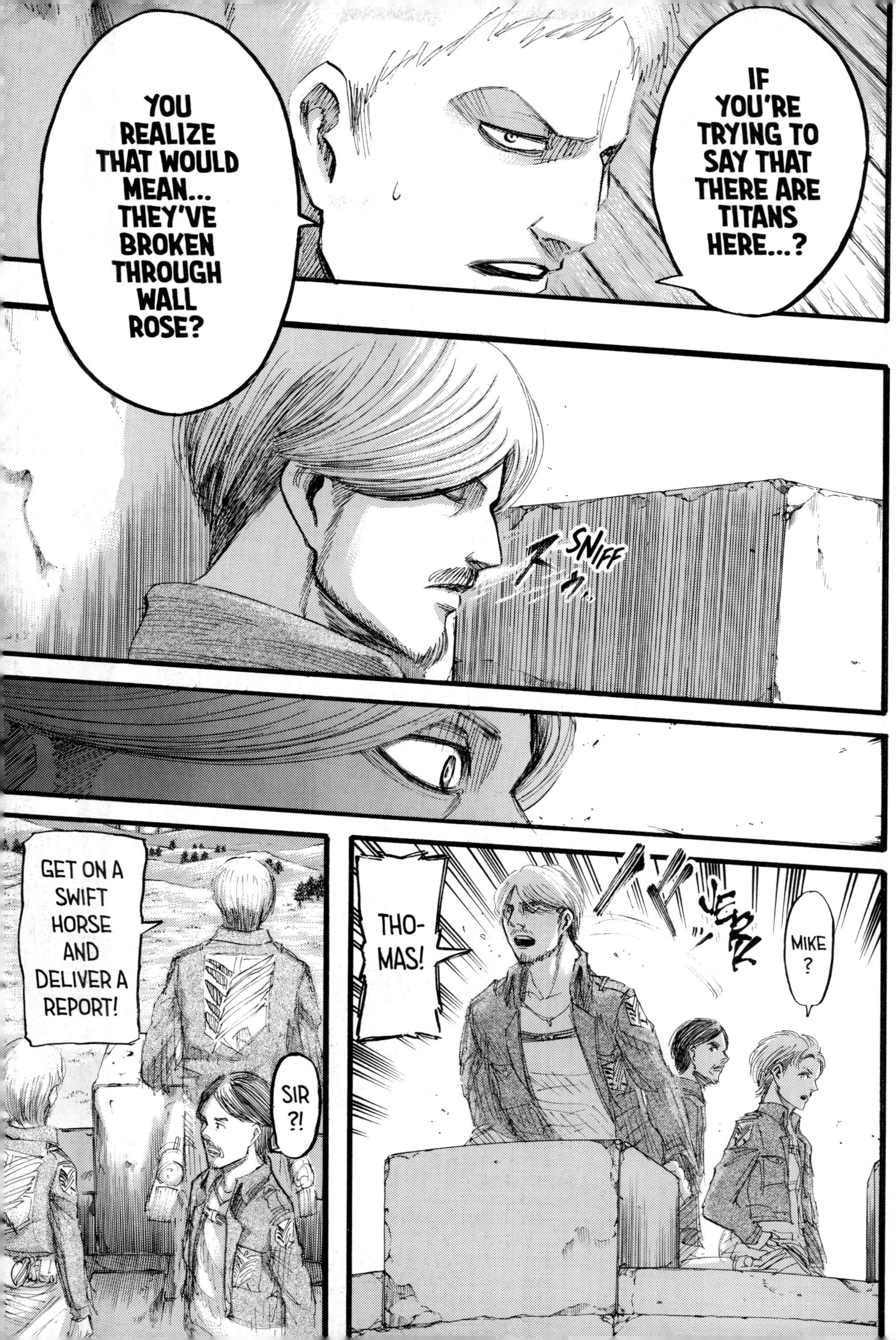
IF YOU'RE TRYING TO SAY THAT THERE ARE TITANS HERE...?
YOU REALIZE THAT WOULD MEAN... THEY'VE BROKEN THROUGH WALL ROSE?
SNIFF
JERK
MIKE ?
THO-MAS!
GET ON A SWIFT HORSE AND DELIVER A REPORT!
SIR ?!

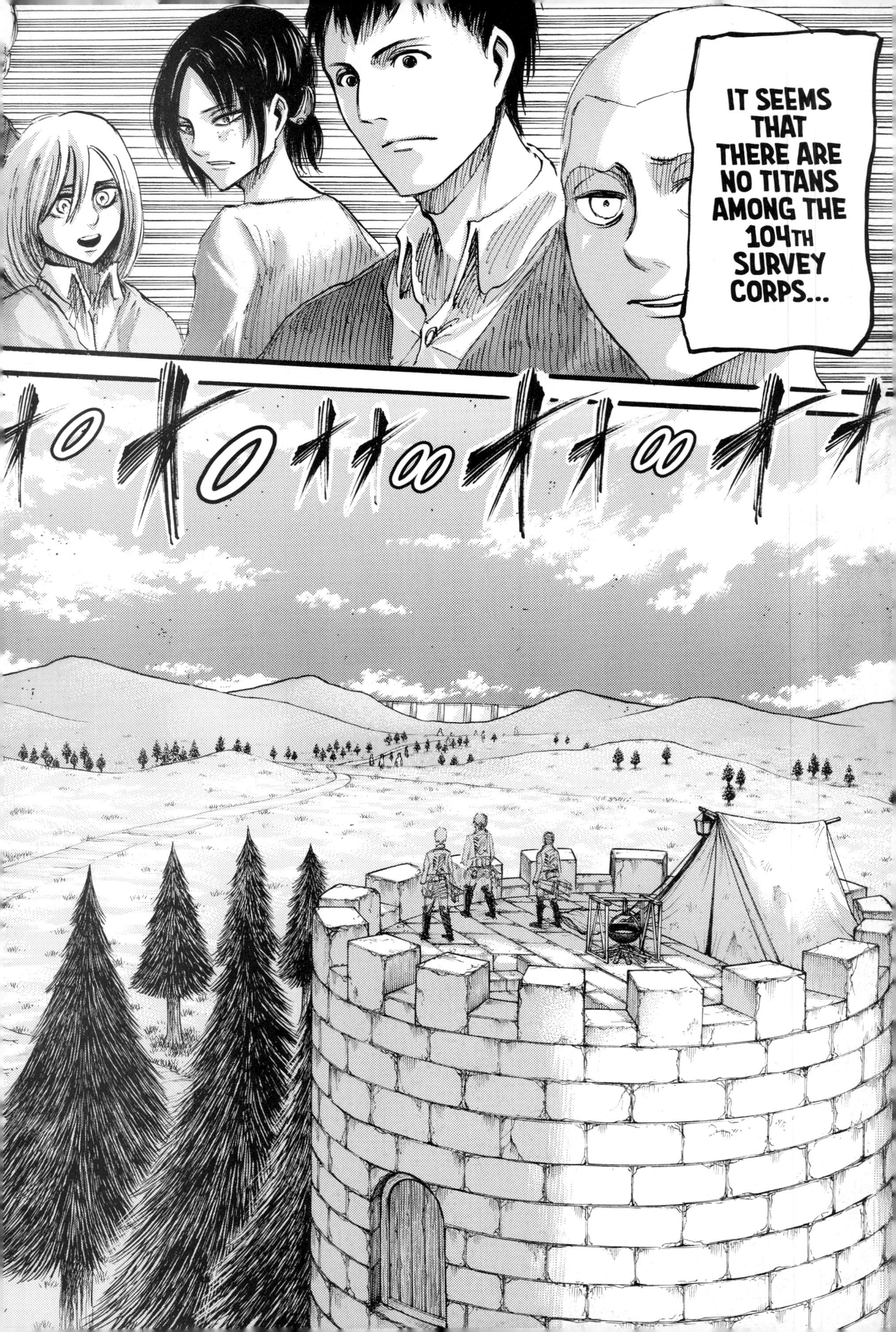
IT SEEMS THAT THERE ARE NO TITANS AMONG THE 104TH SURVEY CORPS...

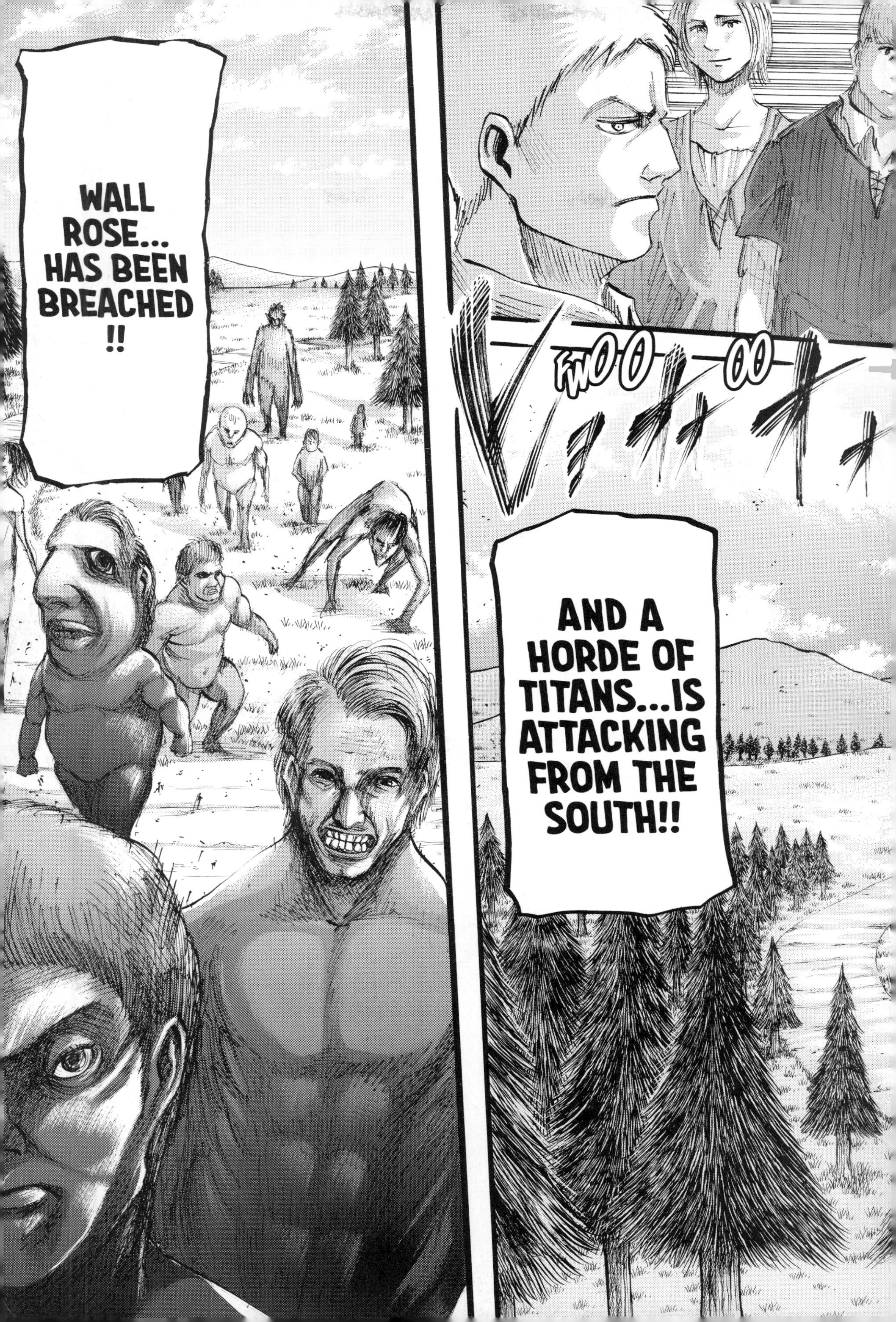
WALL ROSE... HAS BEEN BREACHED !!
FWOOO—OO
AND A HORDE OF TITANS...IS ATTACKING FROM THE SOUTH!!

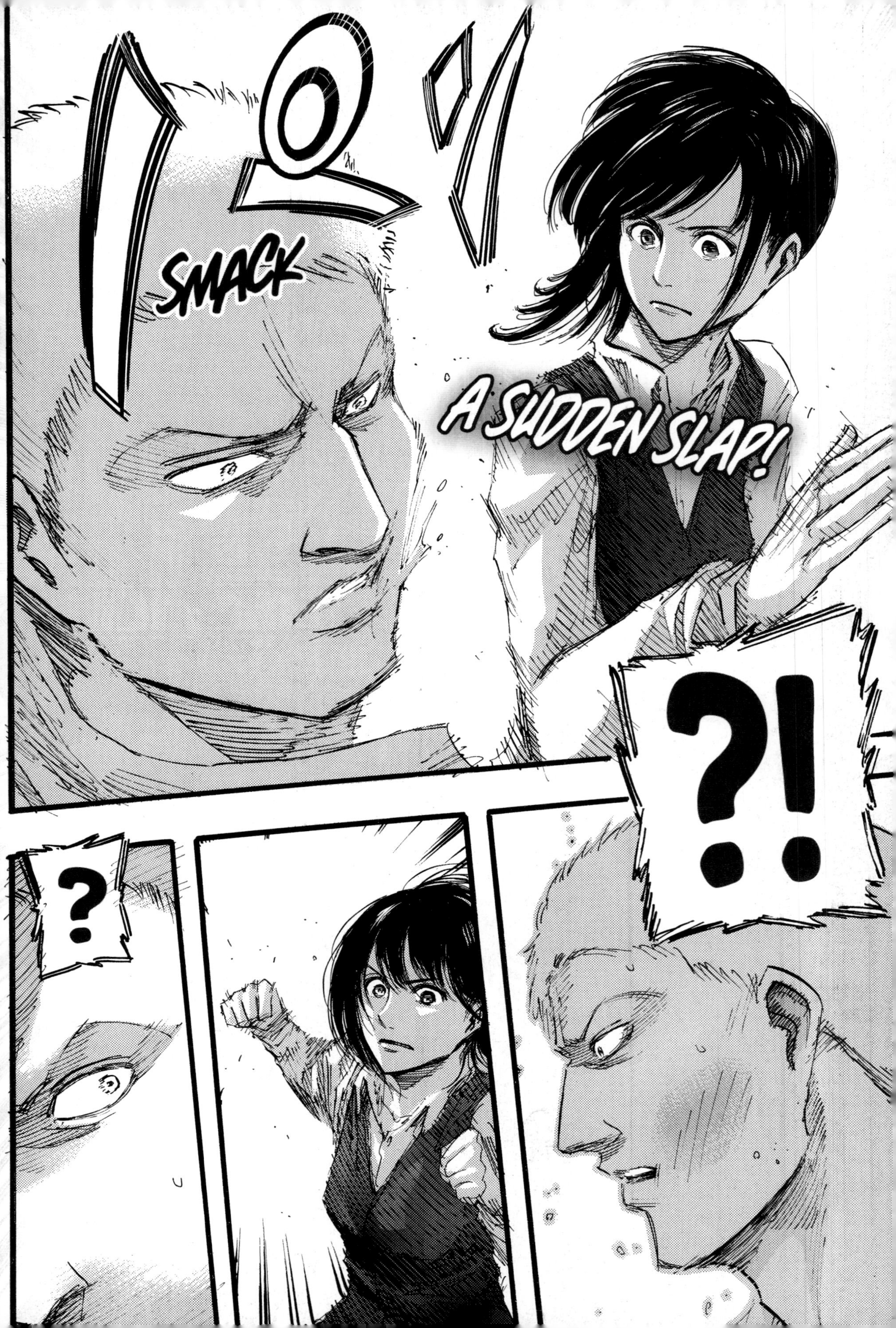
SMACK
A SUDDEN SLAP!
?!
?

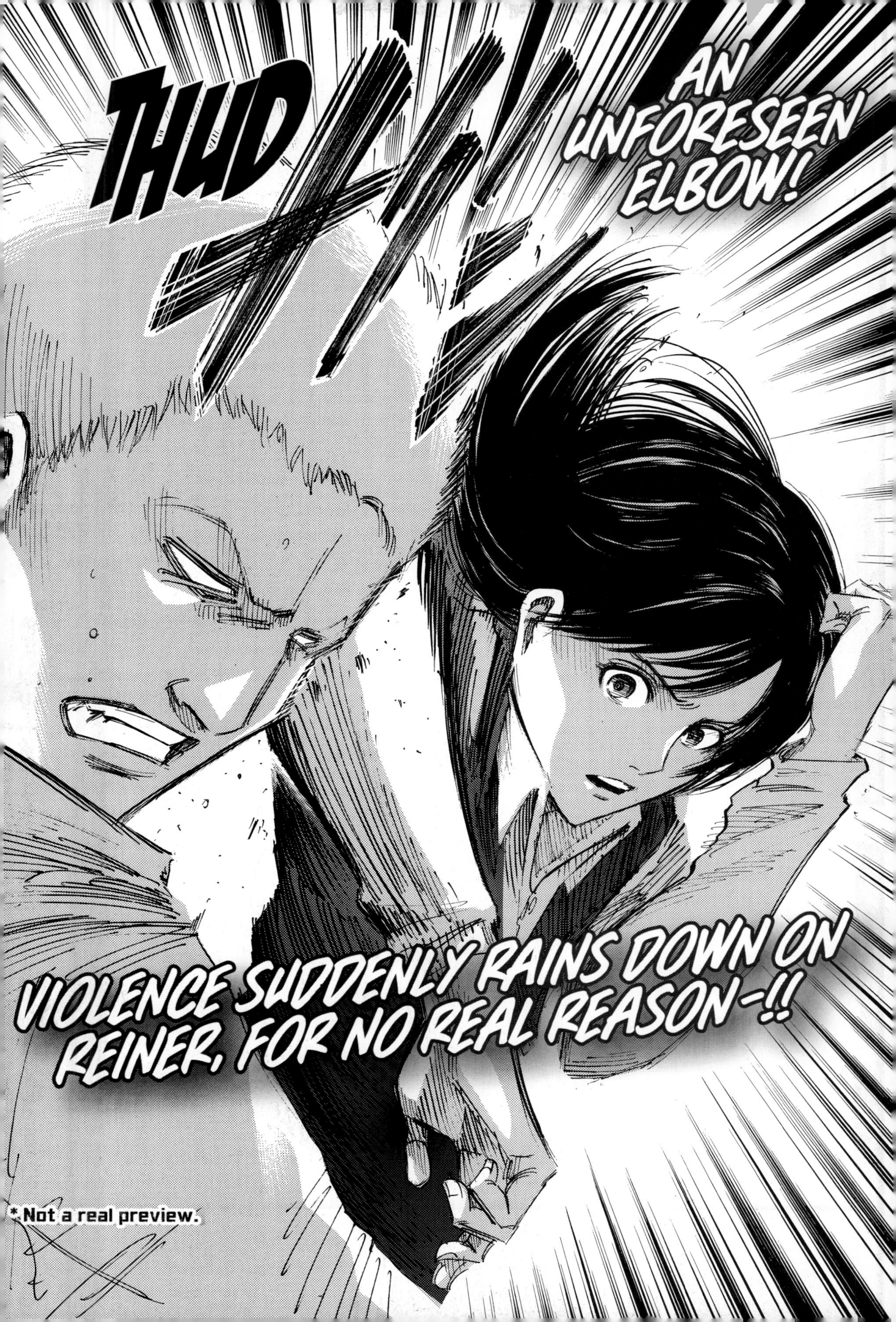
THUD
AN UNFORESEEN ELBOW!
VIOLENCE SUDDENLY RAINS DOWN ON REINER, FOR NO REAL REASON--!!
*Not a real preview.

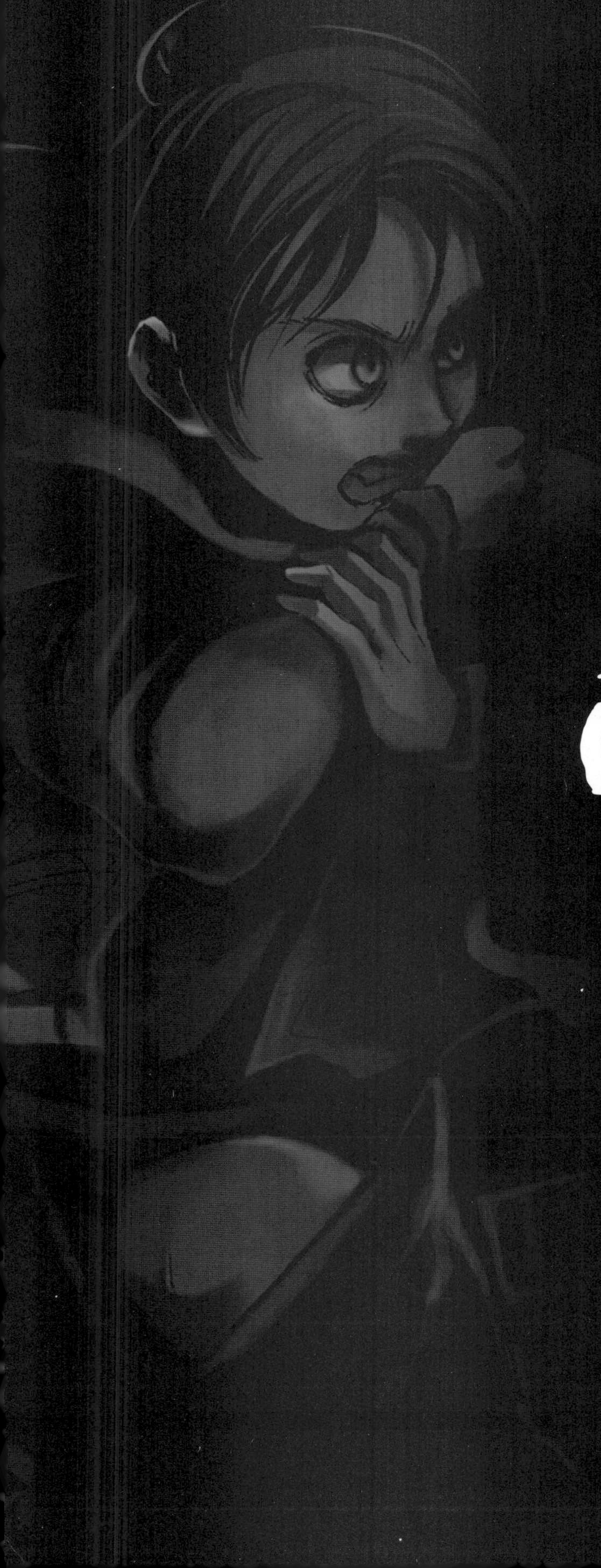

ATTACK ON TITAN

HAJIME ISAYAMA

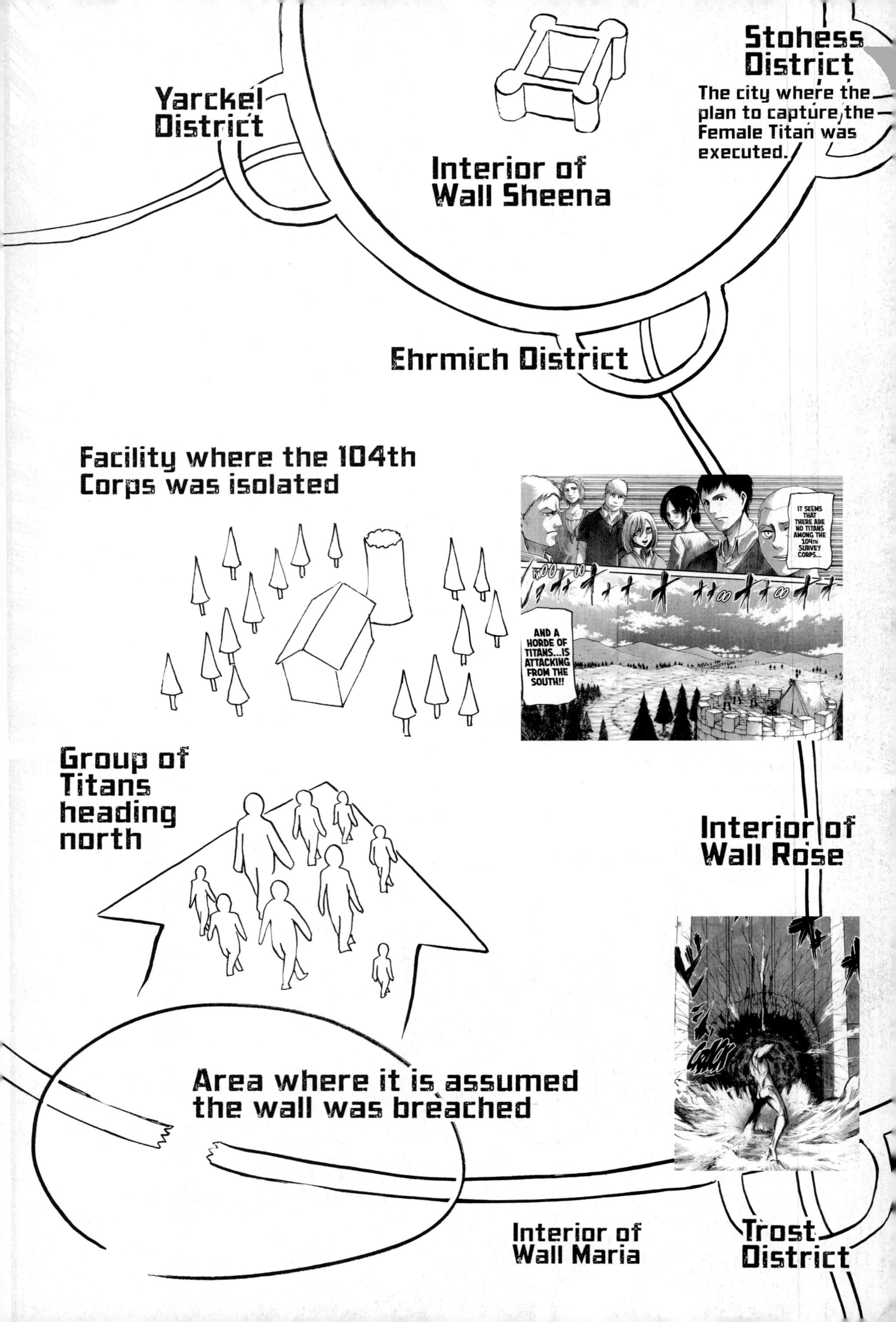
Stohess District
The city where the plan to capture the Female Titan was executed.
Yarckel District
Interior of Wall Sheena
Ehrmich District
Facility where the 104th Corps was isolated
IT SEEMS THAT THERE ARE NO TITANS AMONG THE 104TH SURVEY CORPS...
AND A HORDE OF TITANS...IS ATTACKING FROM THE SOUTH!!
Group of Titans heading north
Interior of Wall Rose
Area where it is assumed the wall was breached
Interior of Wall Maria
Trost District

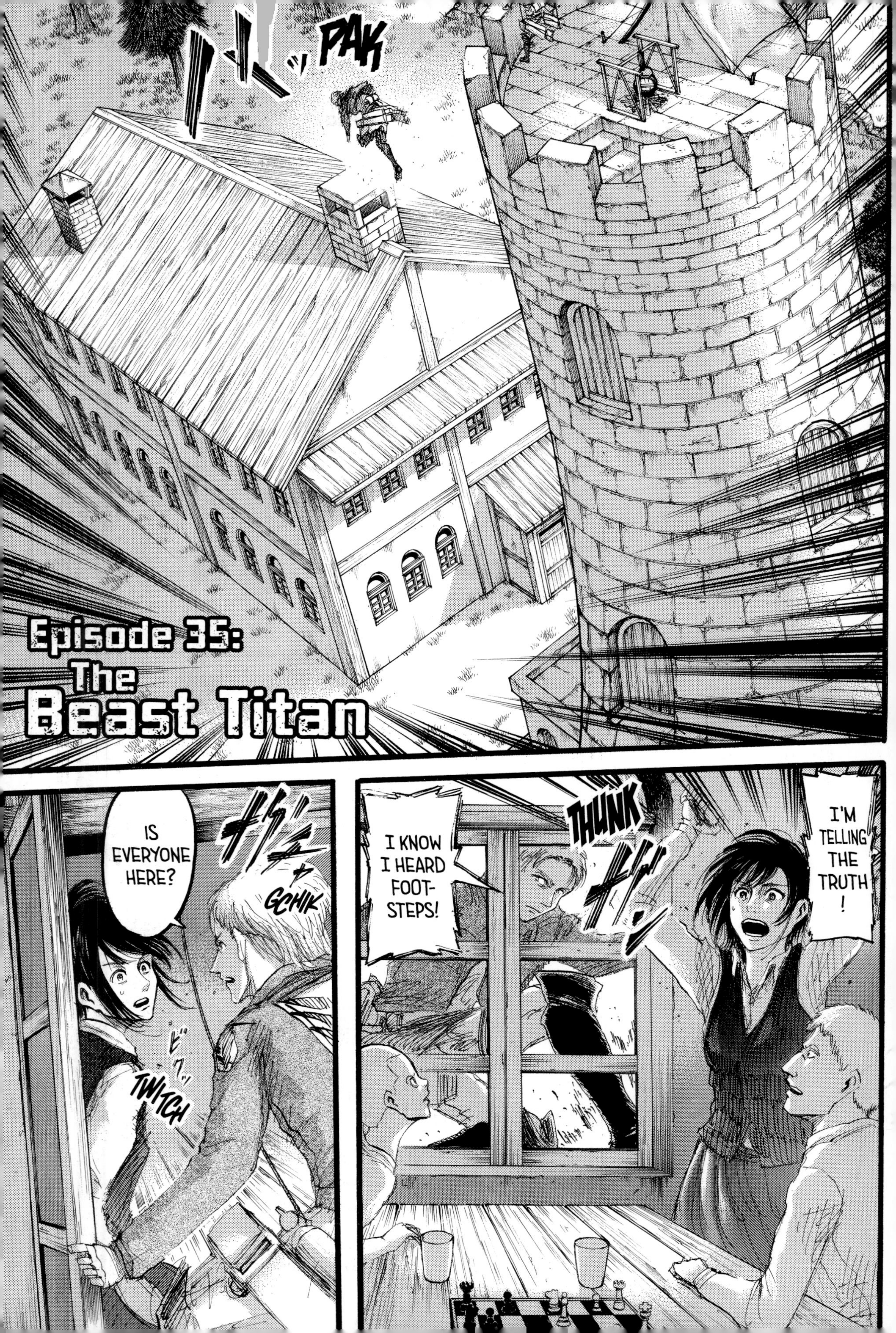
PAK
Episode 35:
The
Beast Titan
THUNK
I'M TELLING THE TRUTH!
I KNOW I HEARD FOOT-STEPS!
GCHIK
IS EVERYONE HERE?
TWITCH

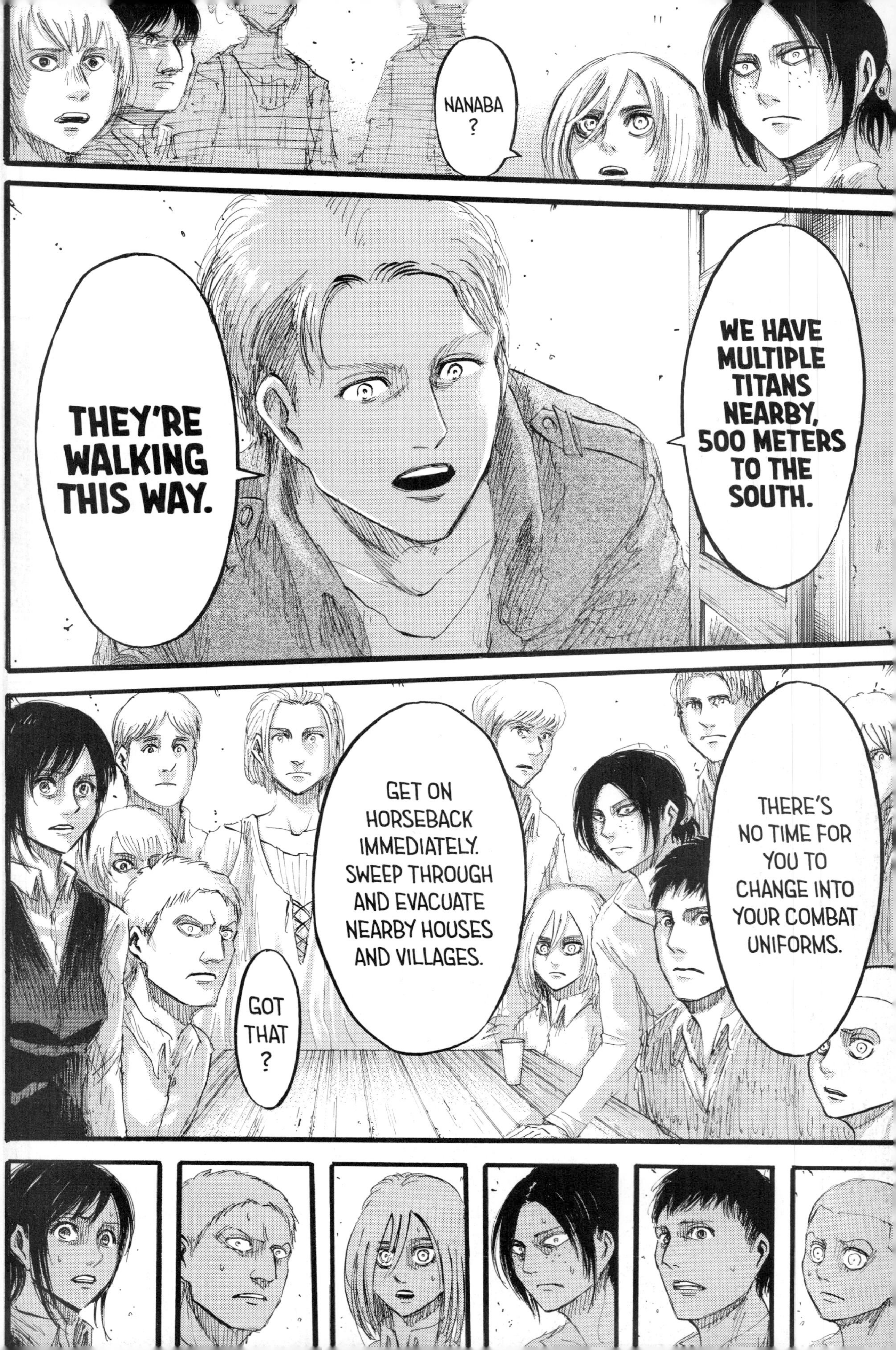
NANABA ?
WE HAVE MULTIPLE TITANS NEARBY, 500 METERS TO THE SOUTH.
THEY'RE WALKING THIS WAY.
THERE'S NO TIME FOR YOU TO CHANGE INTO YOUR COMBAT UNIFORMS.
GET ON HORSEBACK IMMEDIATELY. SWEEP THROUGH AND EVACUATE NEARBY HOUSES AND VILLAGES.
GOT THAT ?

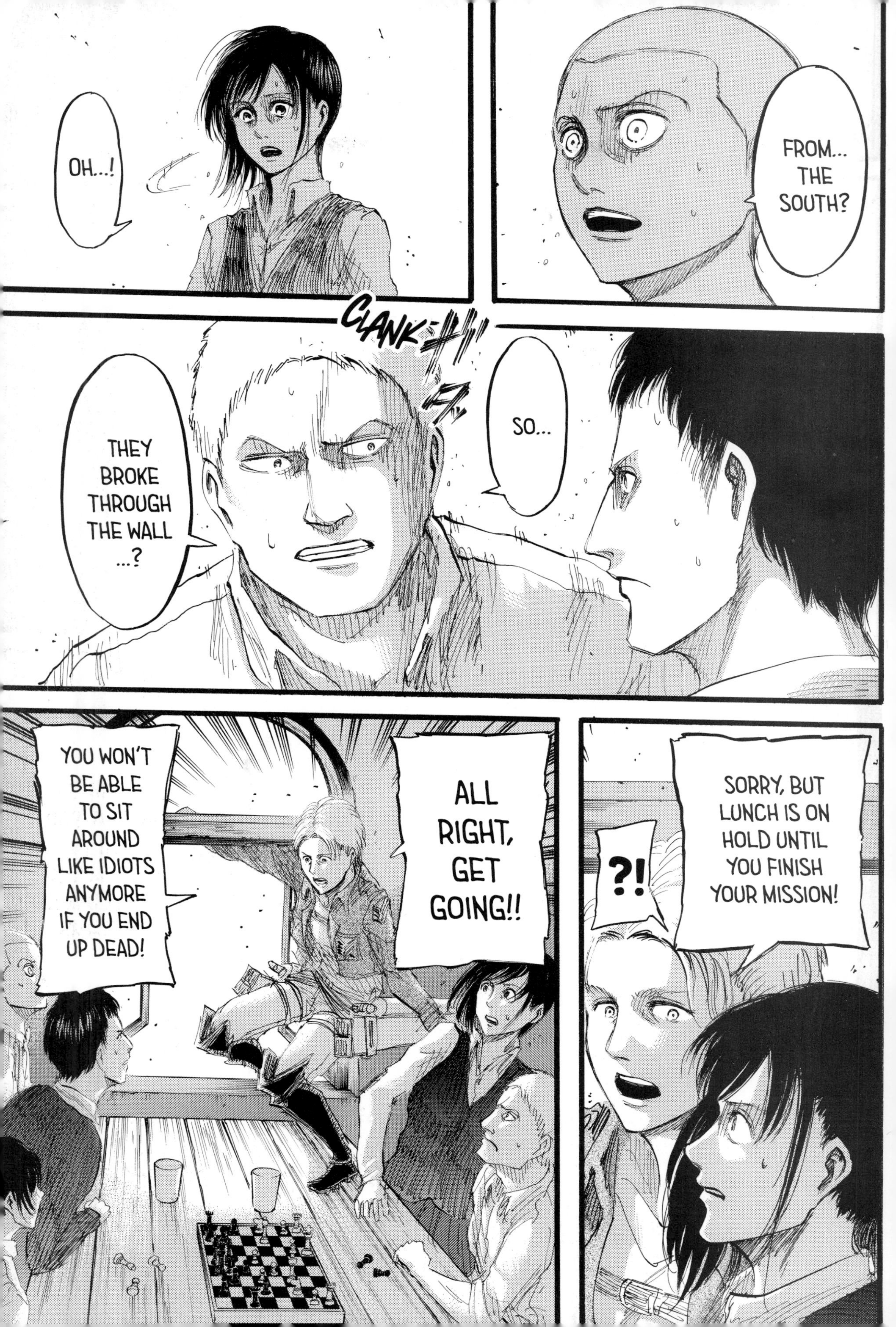
FROM... THE SOUTH?
OH...!
CLANK
SO...
THEY BROKE THROUGH THE WALL ...?
SORRY, BUT LUNCH IS ON HOLD UNTIL YOU FINISH YOUR MISSION!
?!
ALL RIGHT, GET GOING!!
YOU WON'T BE ABLE TO SIT AROUND LIKE IDIOTS ANYMORE IF YOU END UP DEAD!

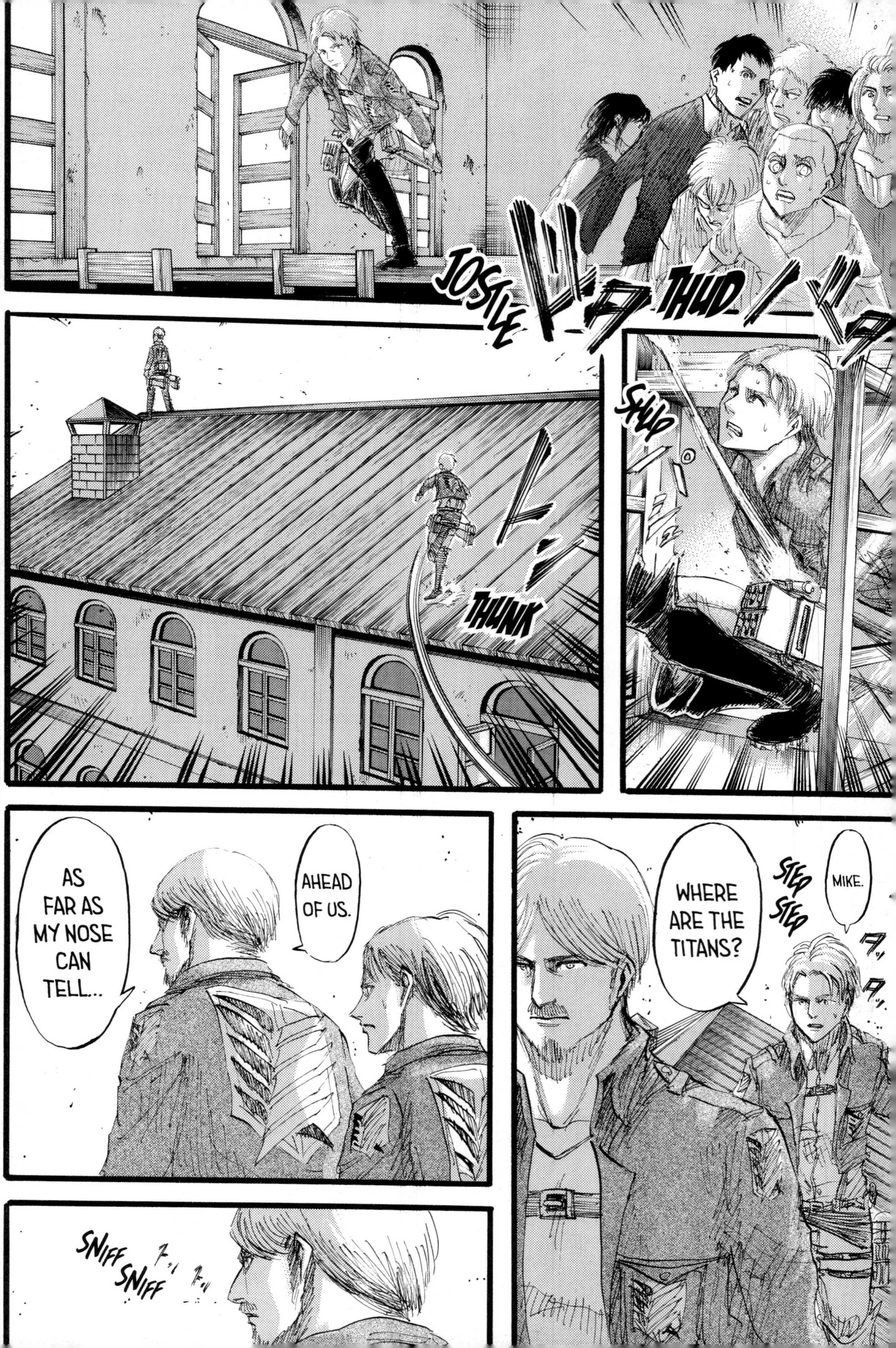
JOSTLE
THUD
SNAP
THUNK
MIKE.
STEP STEP
WHERE ARE THE TITANS?
AHEAD OF US.
AS FAR AS MY NOSE CAN TELL...
SNIFF SNIFF

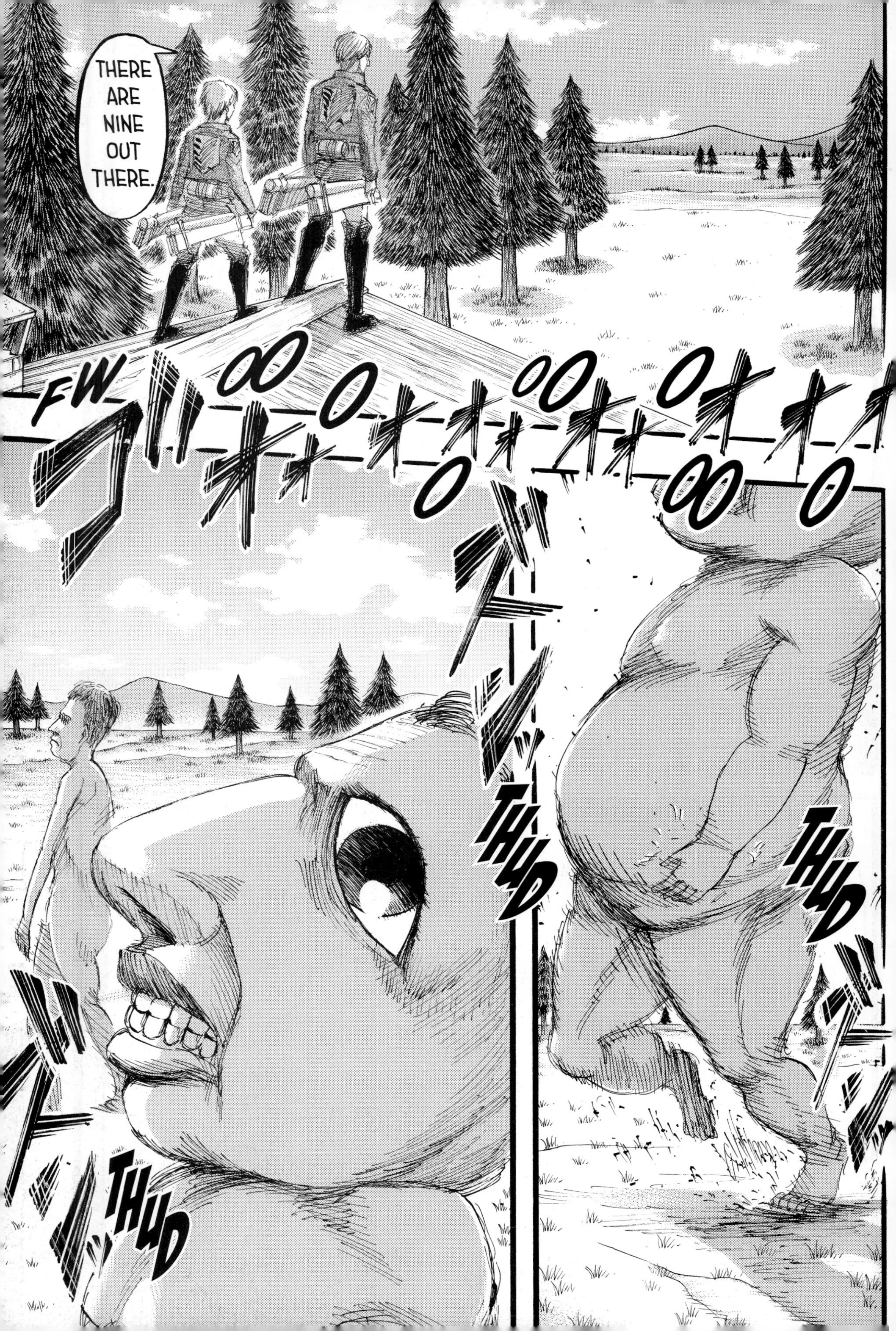
THERE ARE NINE OUT THERE.
FWOOOOOOOOOO
THUD
THUD
THUD

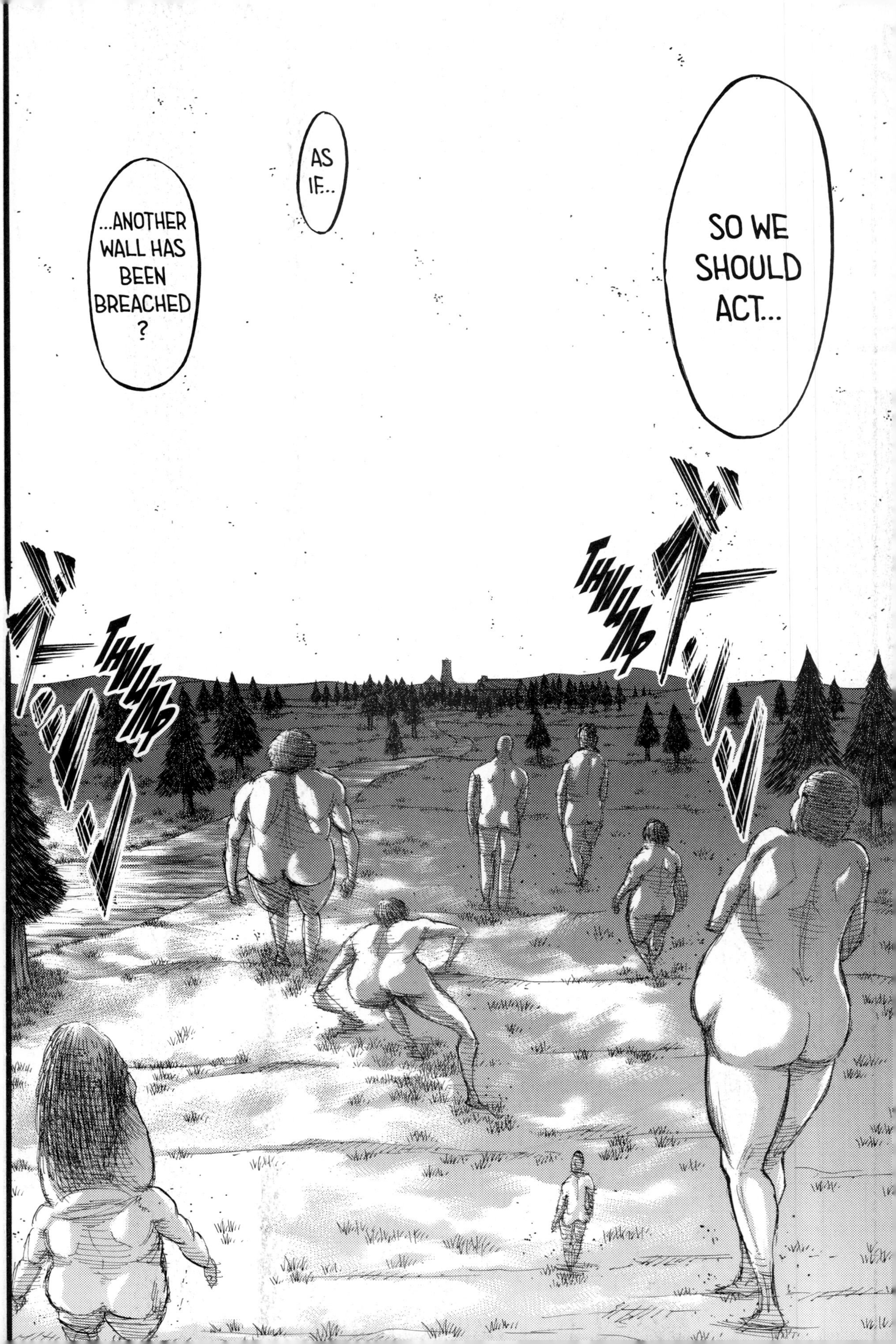
SO WE SHOULD ACT...
AS IF...
...ANOTHER WALL HAS BEEN BREACHED?
THWUMP
THWUMP

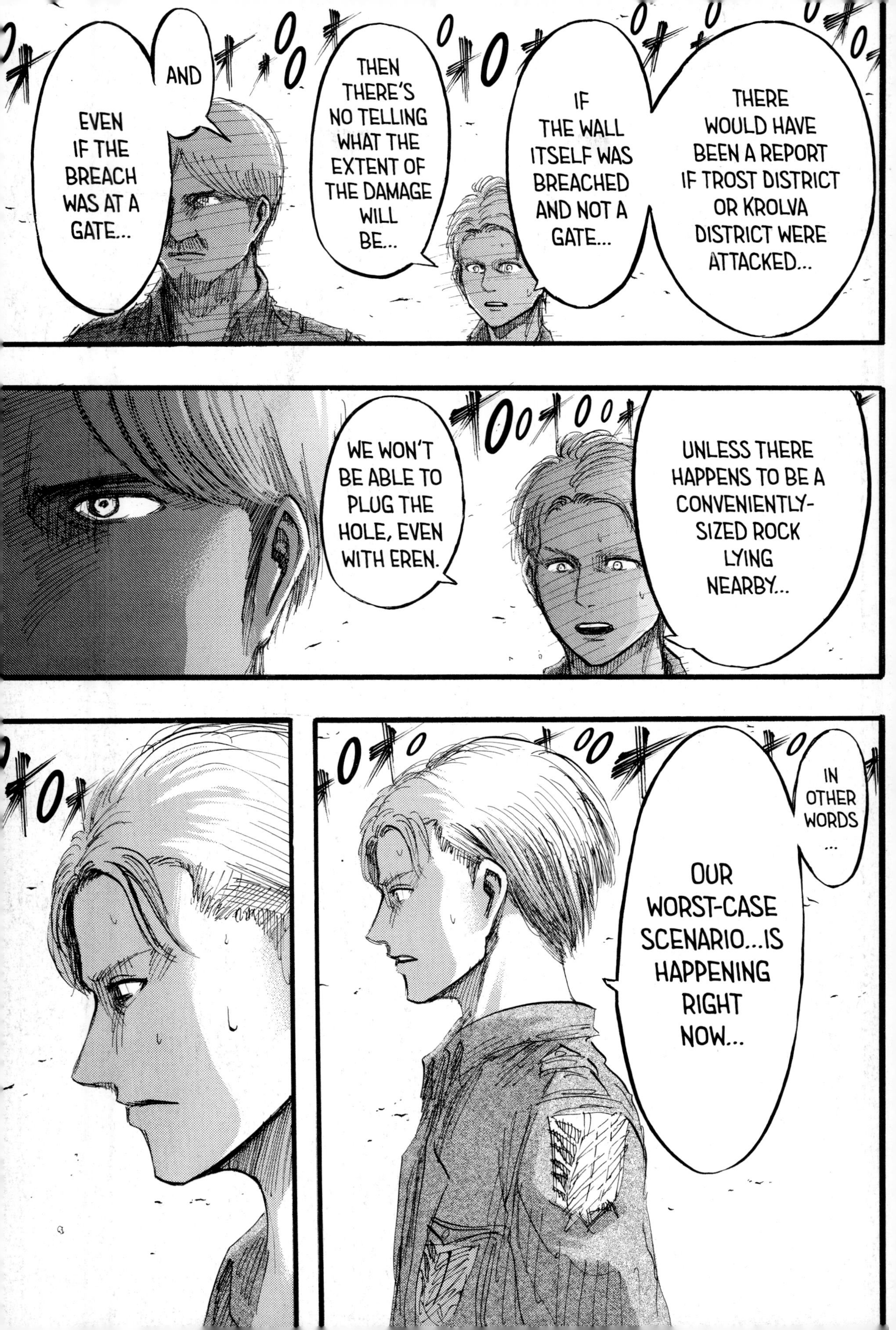
THERE WOULD HAVE BEEN A REPORT IF TROST DISTRICT OR KROLVA DISTRICT WERE ATTACKED...
IF THE WALL ITSELF WAS BREACHED AND NOT A GATE...
THEN THERE'S NO TELLING WHAT THE EXTENT OF THE DAMAGE WILL BE...
AND
EVEN IF THE BREACH WAS AT A GATE...
UNLESS THERE HAPPENS TO BE A CONVENIENTLY-SIZED ROCK LYING NEARBY...
WE WON'T BE ABLE TO PLUG THE HOLE, EVEN WITH EREN.
IN OTHER WORDS...
OUR WORST-CASE SCENARIO...IS HAPPENING RIGHT NOW...

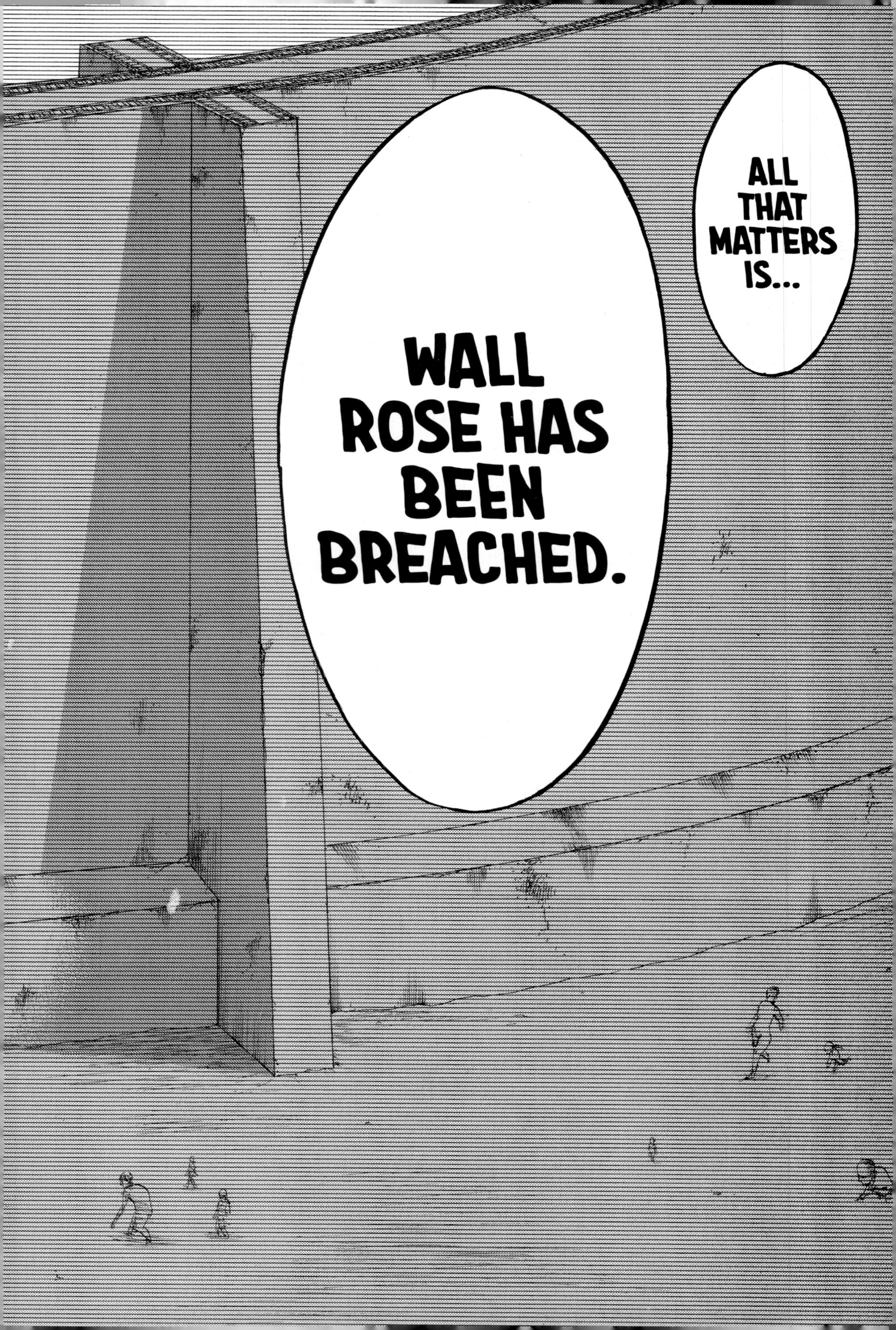
ALL THAT MATTERS IS...
WALL ROSE HAS BEEN BREACHED.

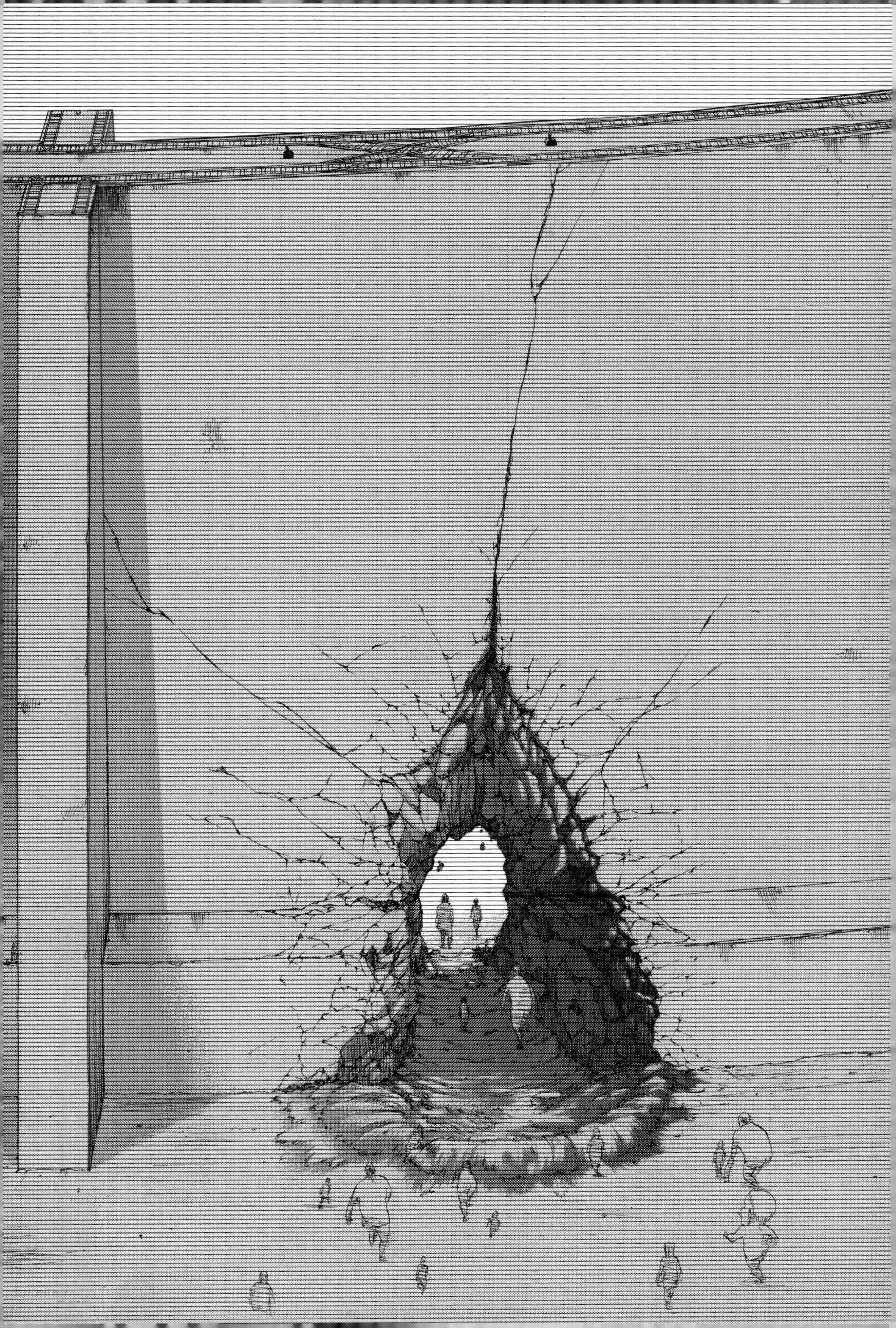

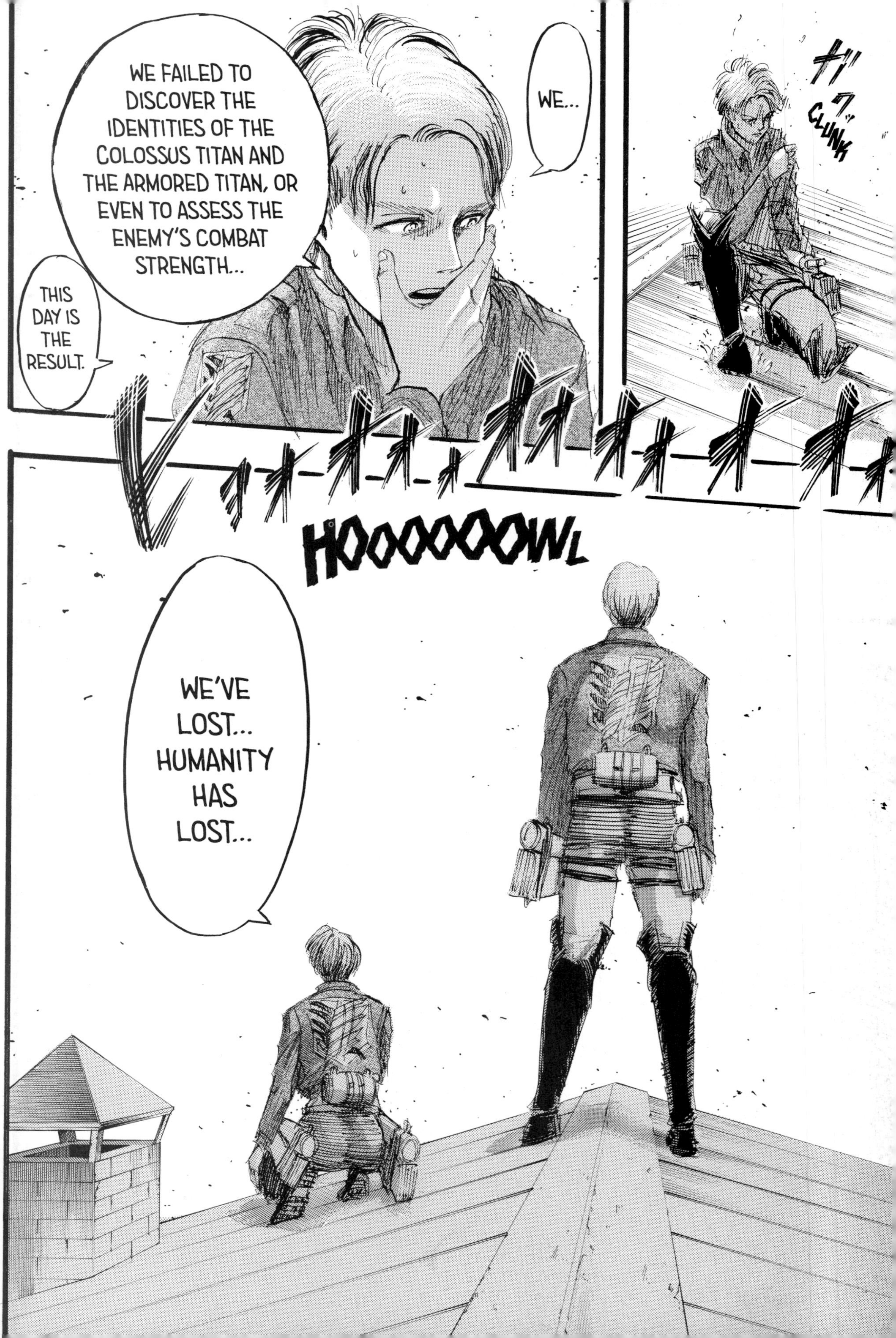
CLUNK
WE...
WE FAILED TO DISCOVER THE IDENTITIES OF THE COLOSSUS TITAN AND THE ARMORED TITAN, OR EVEN TO ASSESS THE ENEMY'S COMBAT STRENGTH...
THIS DAY IS THE RESULT.
HOOOOOOWL
WE'VE LOST... HUMANITY HAS LOST...

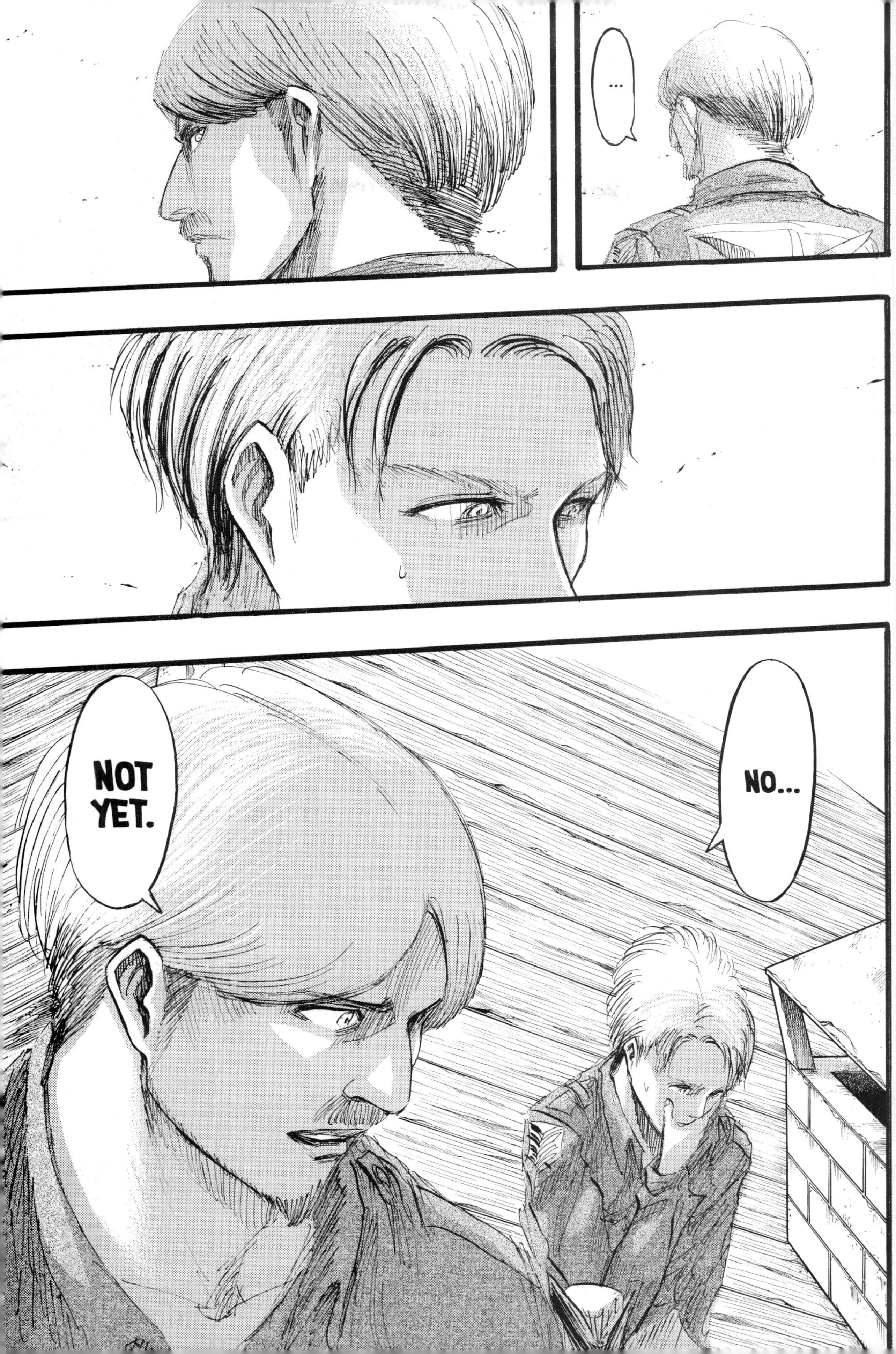
...
NO...
NOT YET.

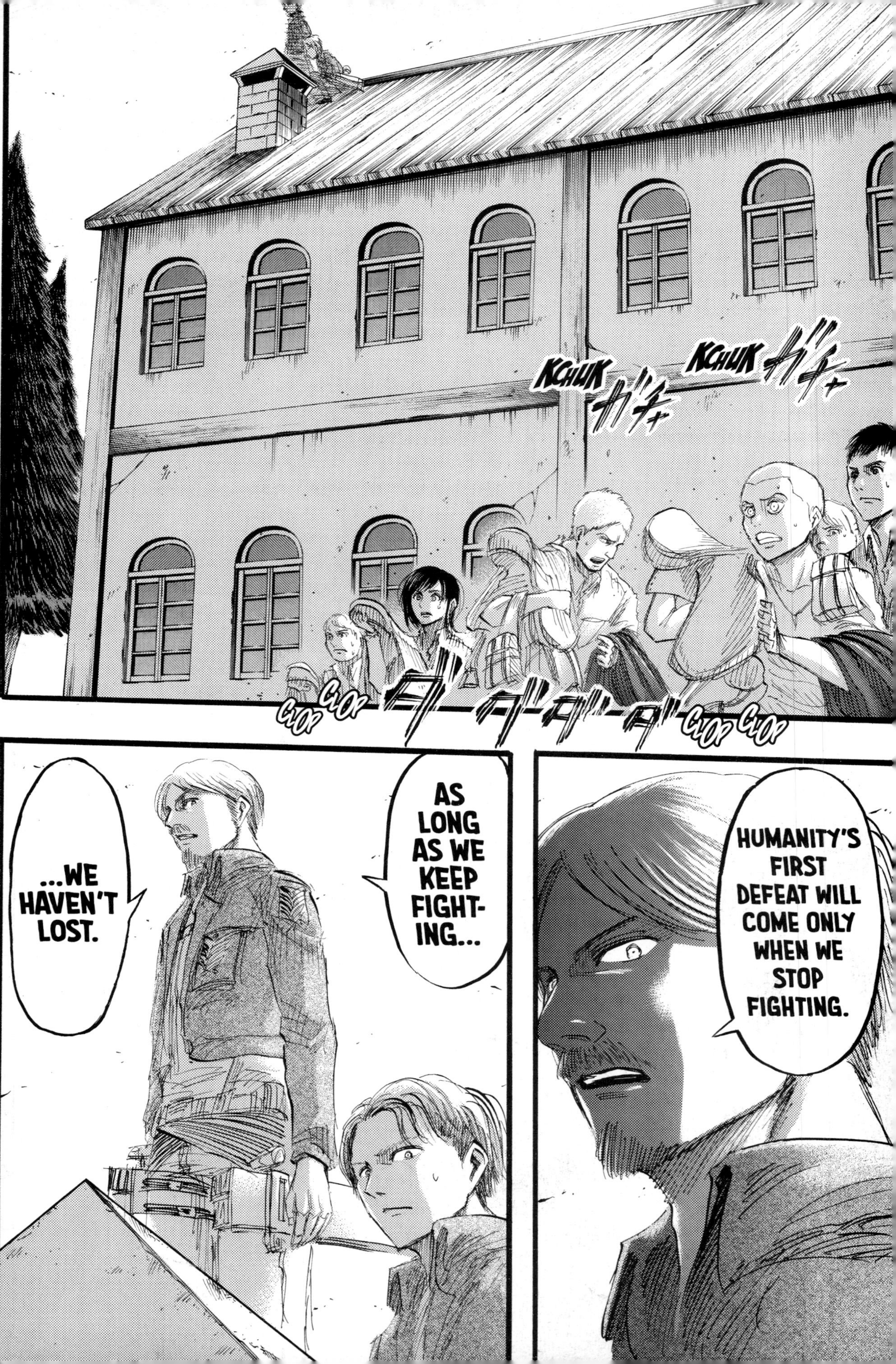
KCHUK
KCHUK
CLOP CLOP
CLOP CLOP
HUMANITY'S FIRST DEFEAT WILL COME ONLY WHEN WE STOP FIGHTING.
AS LONG AS WE KEEP FIGHT-ING...
...WE HAVEN'T LOST.

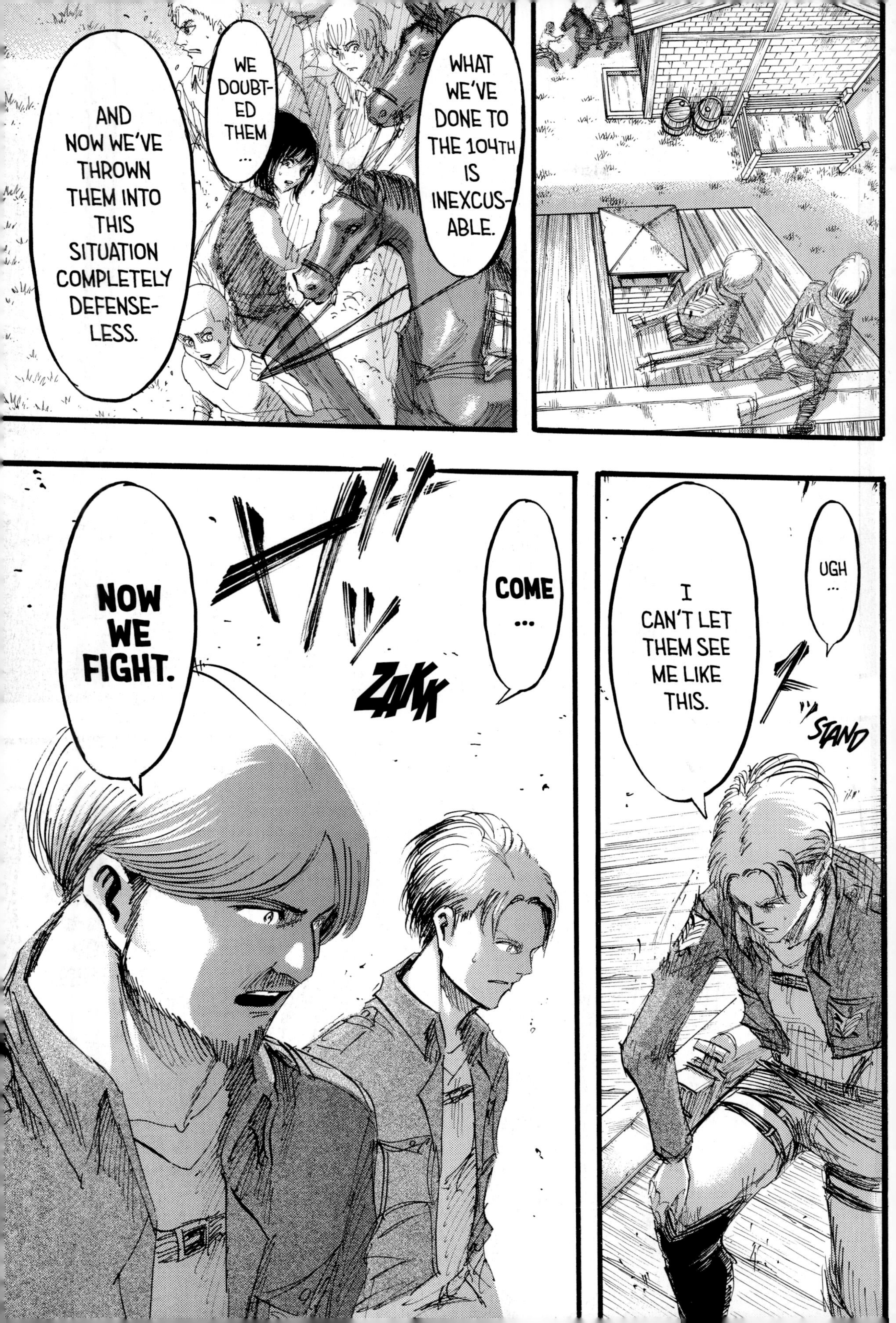
WHAT WE'VE DONE TO THE 104TH IS INEXCUSABLE.
WE DOUBTED THEM ...
AND NOW WE'VE THROWN THEM INTO THIS SITUATION COMPLETELY DEFENSELESS.
UGH ...
I CAN'T LET THEM SEE ME LIKE THIS.
STAND
COME ...
ZAKK
NOW WE FIGHT.

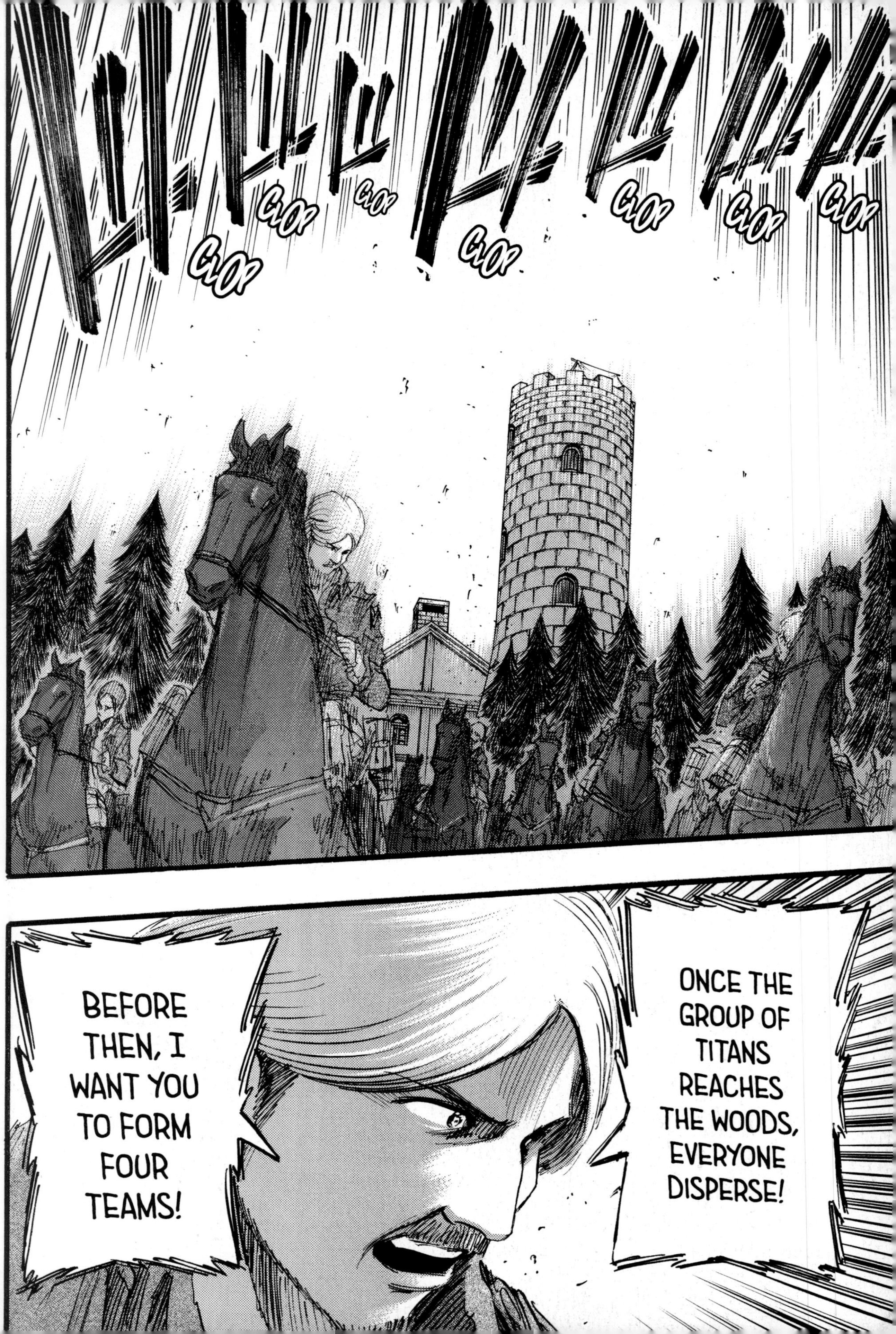
CLOP
CLOP
CLOP
CLOP
CLOP
CLOP
CLOP
ONCE THE GROUP OF TITANS REACHES THE WOODS, EVERYONE DISPERSE!
BEFORE THEN, I WANT YOU TO FORM FOUR TEAMS!

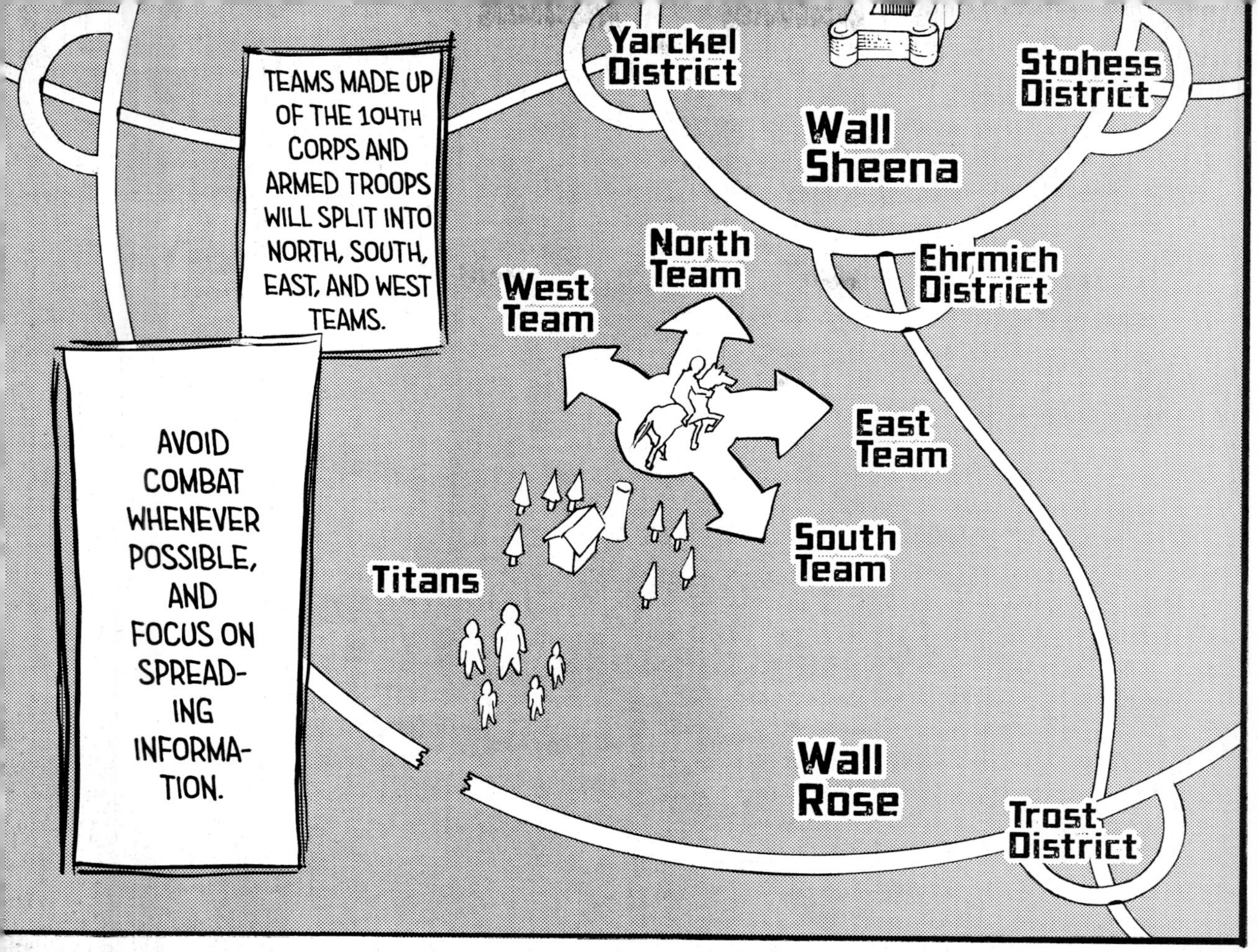
Stohess District
Yarckel District
Wall Sheena
Ehrmich District
TEAMS MADE UP OF THE 104TH CORPS AND ARMED TROOPS WILL SPLIT INTO NORTH, SOUTH, EAST, AND WEST TEAMS.
North Team
West Team
East Team
South Team
AVOID COMBAT WHENEVER POSSIBLE, AND FOCUS ON SPREADING INFORMATION.
Titans
Wall Rose
Trost District

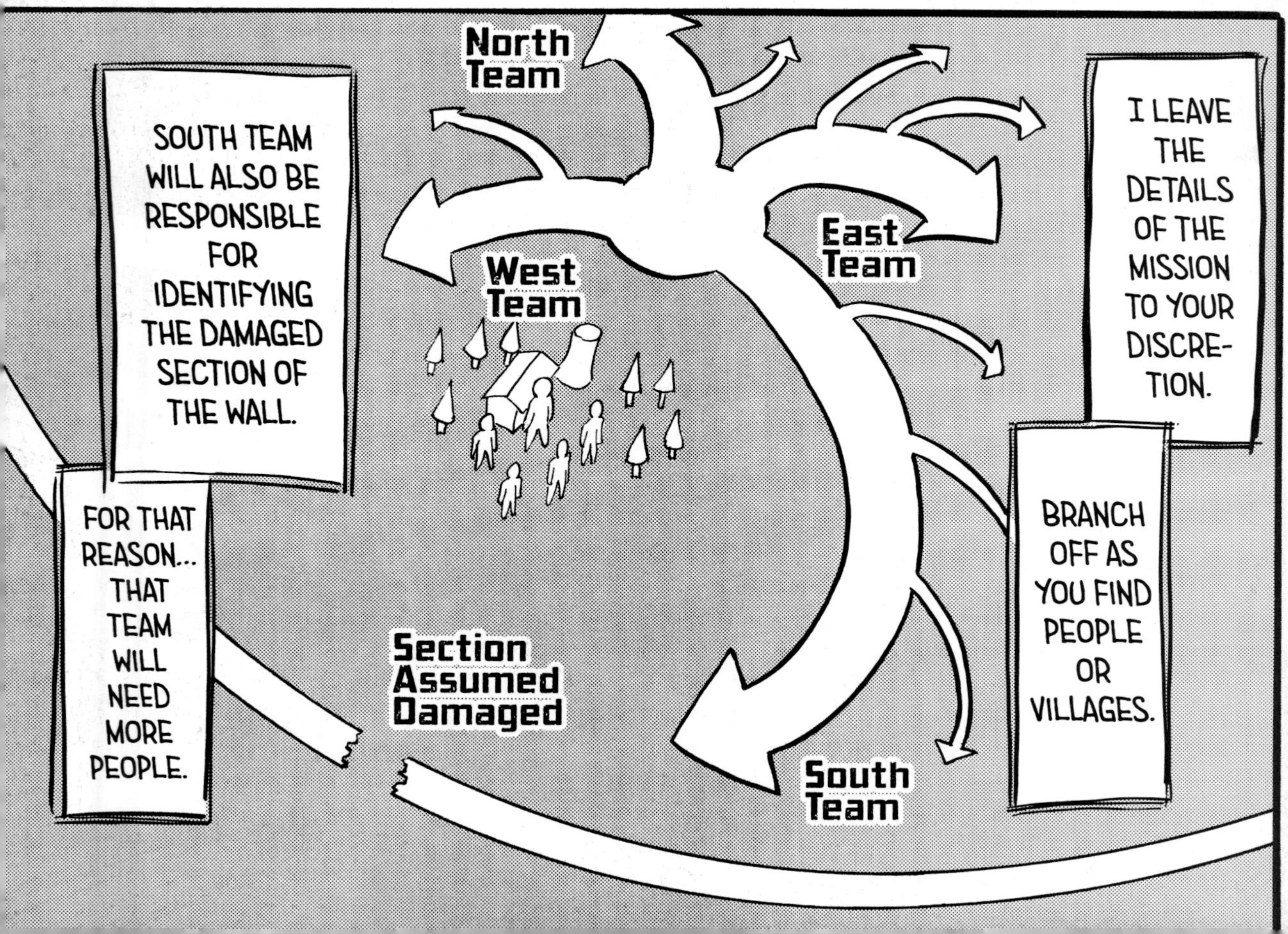
I LEAVE THE DETAILS OF THE MISSION TO YOUR DISCRETION.
BRANCH OFF AS YOU FIND PEOPLE OR VILLAGES.
North Team
East Team
SOUTH TEAM WILL ALSO BE RESPONSIBLE FOR IDENTIFYING THE DAMAGED SECTION OF THE WALL.
West Team
FOR THAT REASON... THAT TEAM WILL NEED MORE PEOPLE.
Section Assumed Damaged
South Team

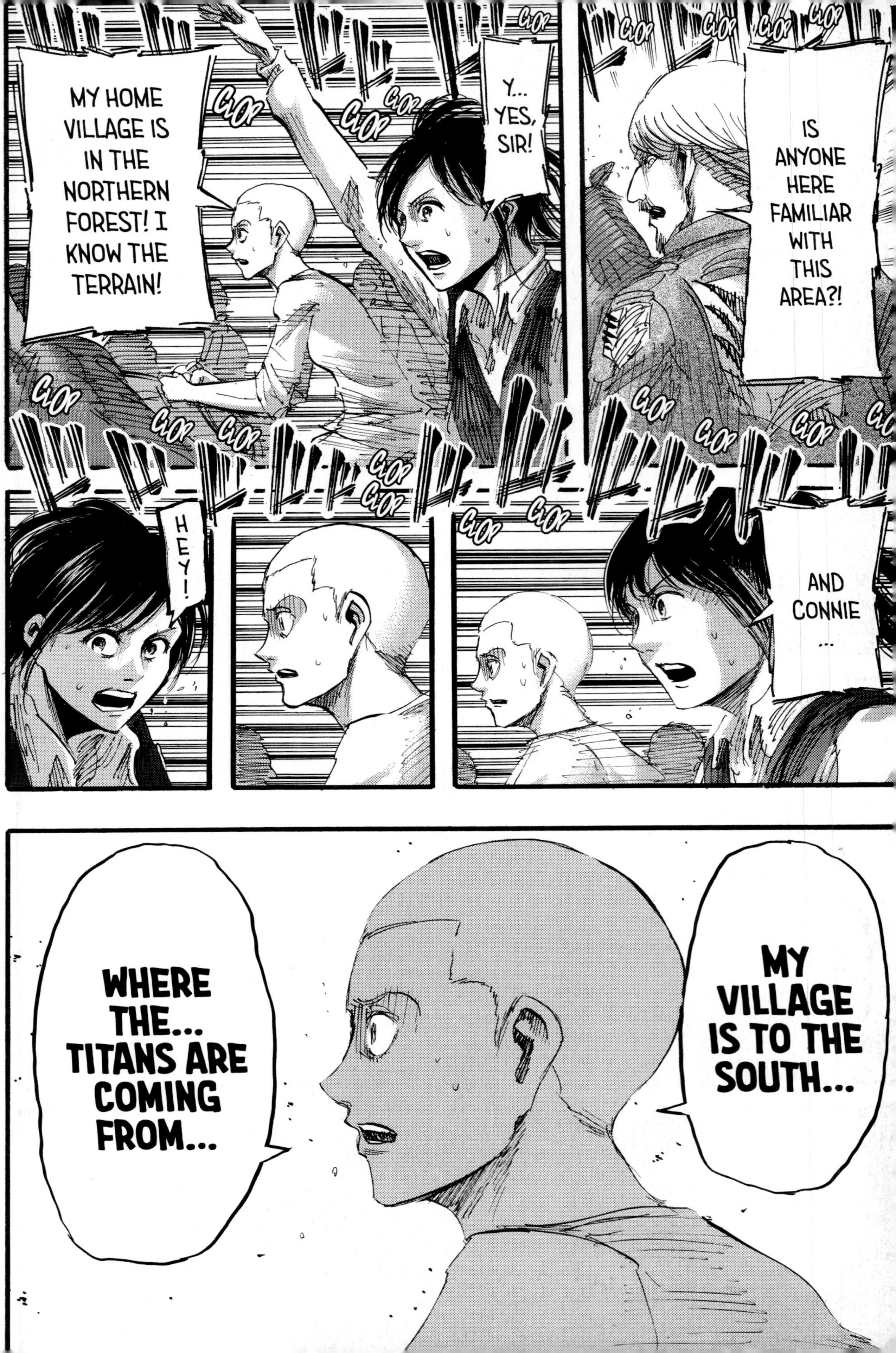
CLOP CLOP CLOP CLOP
IS ANYONE HERE FAMILIAR WITH THIS AREA?!
CLOP CLOP
Y... YES, SIR!
MY HOME VILLAGE IS IN THE NORTHERN FOREST! I KNOW THE TERRAIN!
CLOP CLOP CLOP CLOP CLOP CLOP CLOP CLOP CLOP CLOP CLOP
AND CONNIE ...
CLOP CLOP
HEY!
MY VILLAGE IS TO THE SOUTH...
WHERE THE... TITANS ARE COMING FROM...

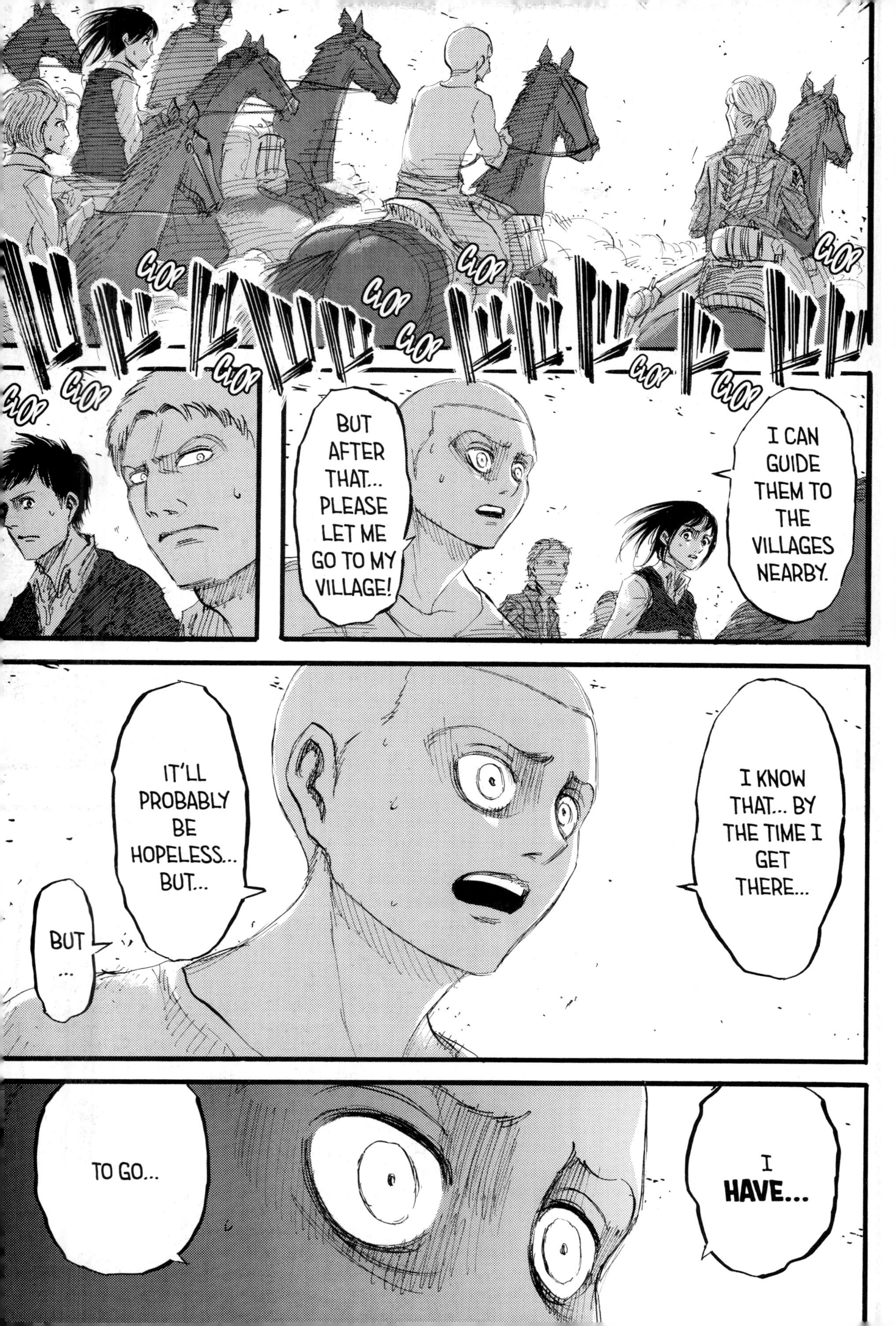
CLOP
CLOP
CLOP
CLOP
CLOP
CLOP
CLOP
CLOP
CLOP
CLOP
I CAN GUIDE THEM TO THE VILLAGES NEARBY.
BUT AFTER THAT... PLEASE LET ME GO TO MY VILLAGE!
I KNOW THAT... BY THE TIME I GET THERE...
IT'LL PROBABLY BE HOPELESS... BUT...
BUT ...
I **HAVE...**
TO GO...

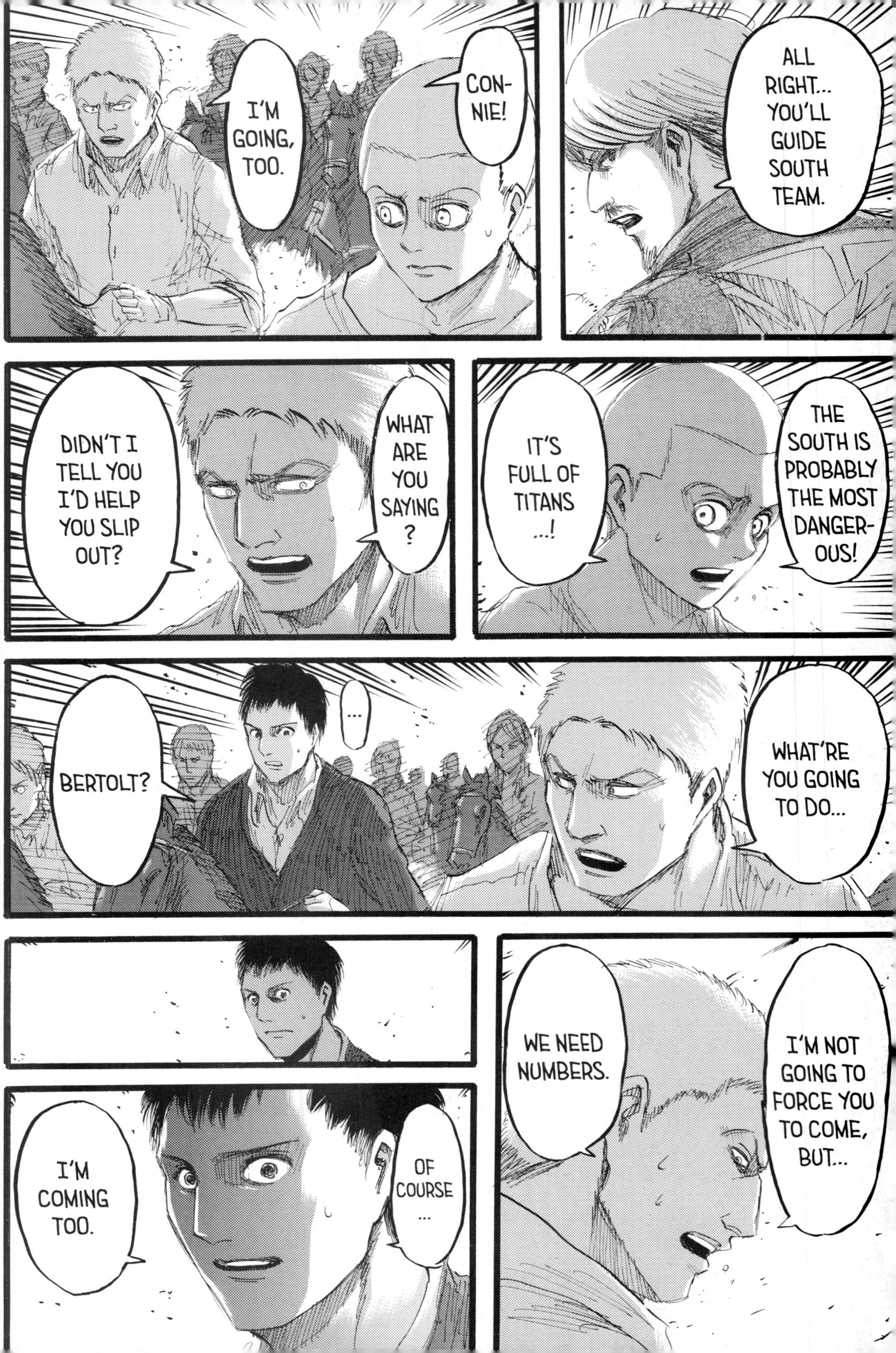
ALL RIGHT... YOU'LL GUIDE SOUTH TEAM.
CON-NIE!
I'M GOING, TOO.
THE SOUTH IS PROBABLY THE MOST DANGER-OUS!
IT'S FULL OF TITANS...!
WHAT ARE YOU SAYING?
DIDN'T I TELL YOU I'D HELP YOU SLIP OUT?
WHAT'RE YOU GOING TO DO...
...
BERTOLT?
I'M NOT GOING TO FORCE YOU TO COME, BUT...
WE NEED NUMBERS.
OF COURSE...
I'M COMING TOO.

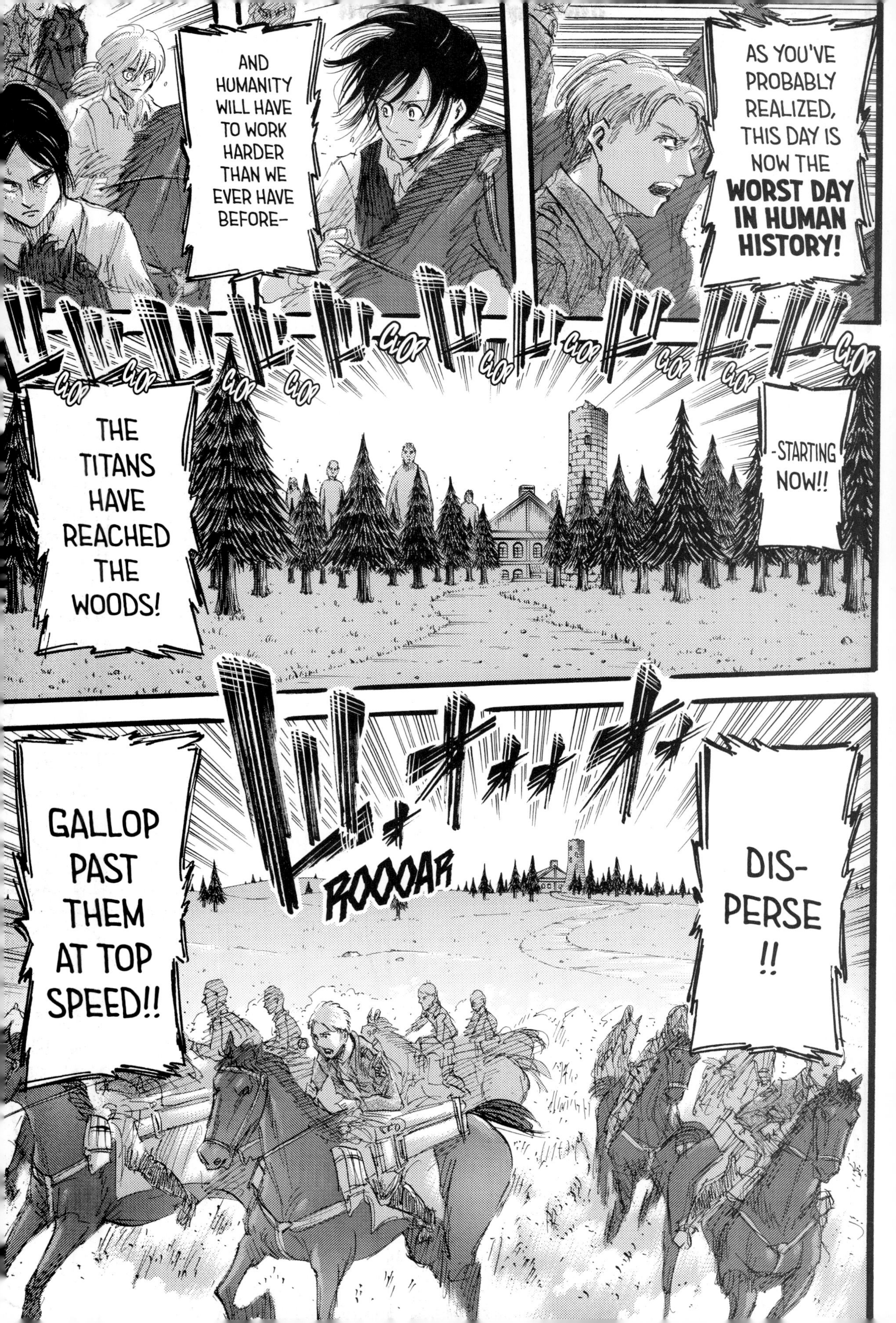
AS YOU'VE PROBABLY REALIZED, THIS DAY IS NOW THE **WORST DAY IN HUMAN HISTORY!**
AND HUMANITY WILL HAVE TO WORK HARDER THAN WE EVER HAVE BEFORE-
CLOP CLOP CLOP CLOP CLOP CLOP CLOP CLOP CLOP CLOP
-STARTING NOW!!
THE TITANS HAVE REACHED THE WOODS!
DIS-PERSE!!
ROOOAR
GALLOP PAST THEM AT TOP SPEED!!

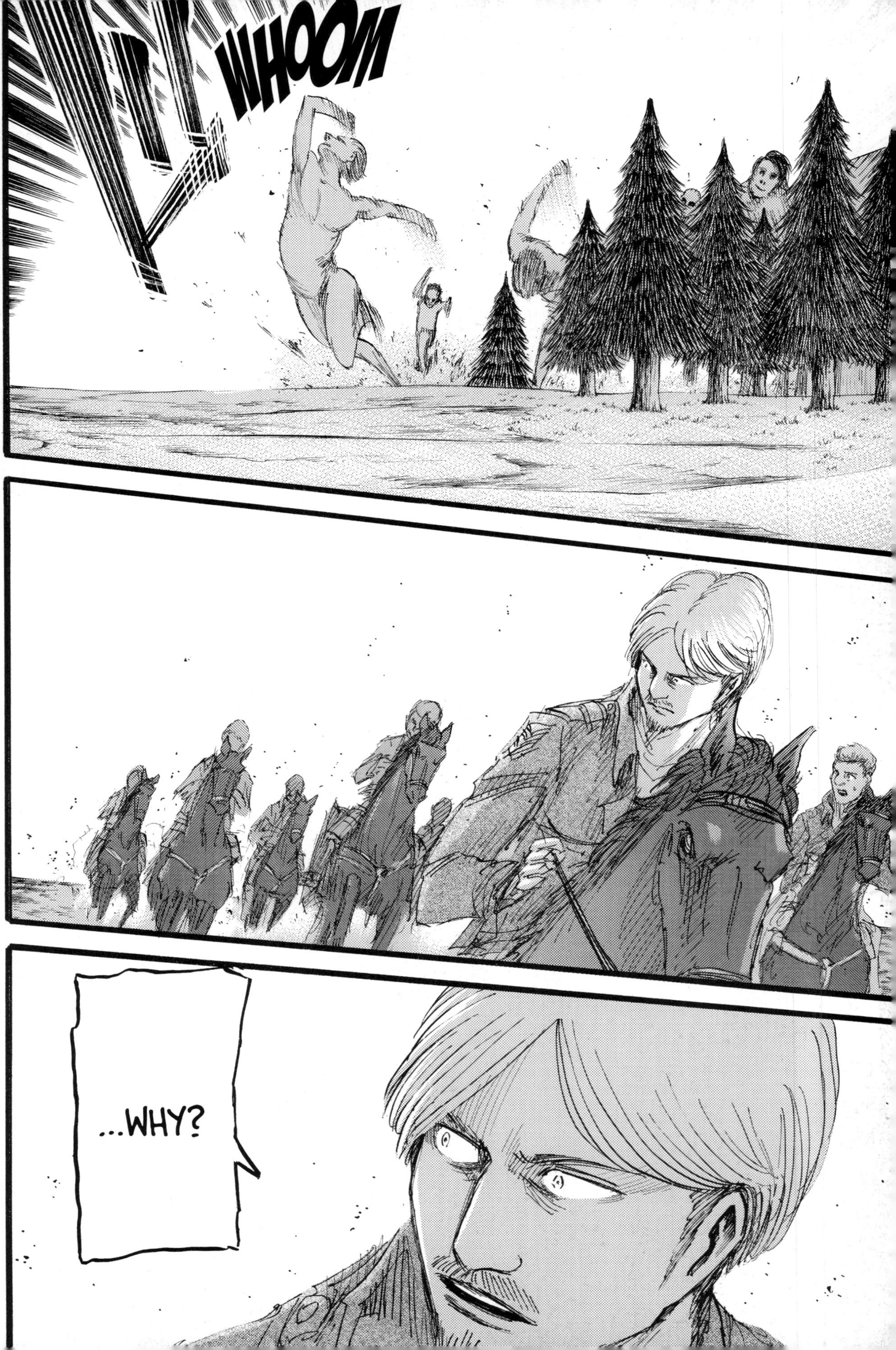
WHOOM
...WHY?

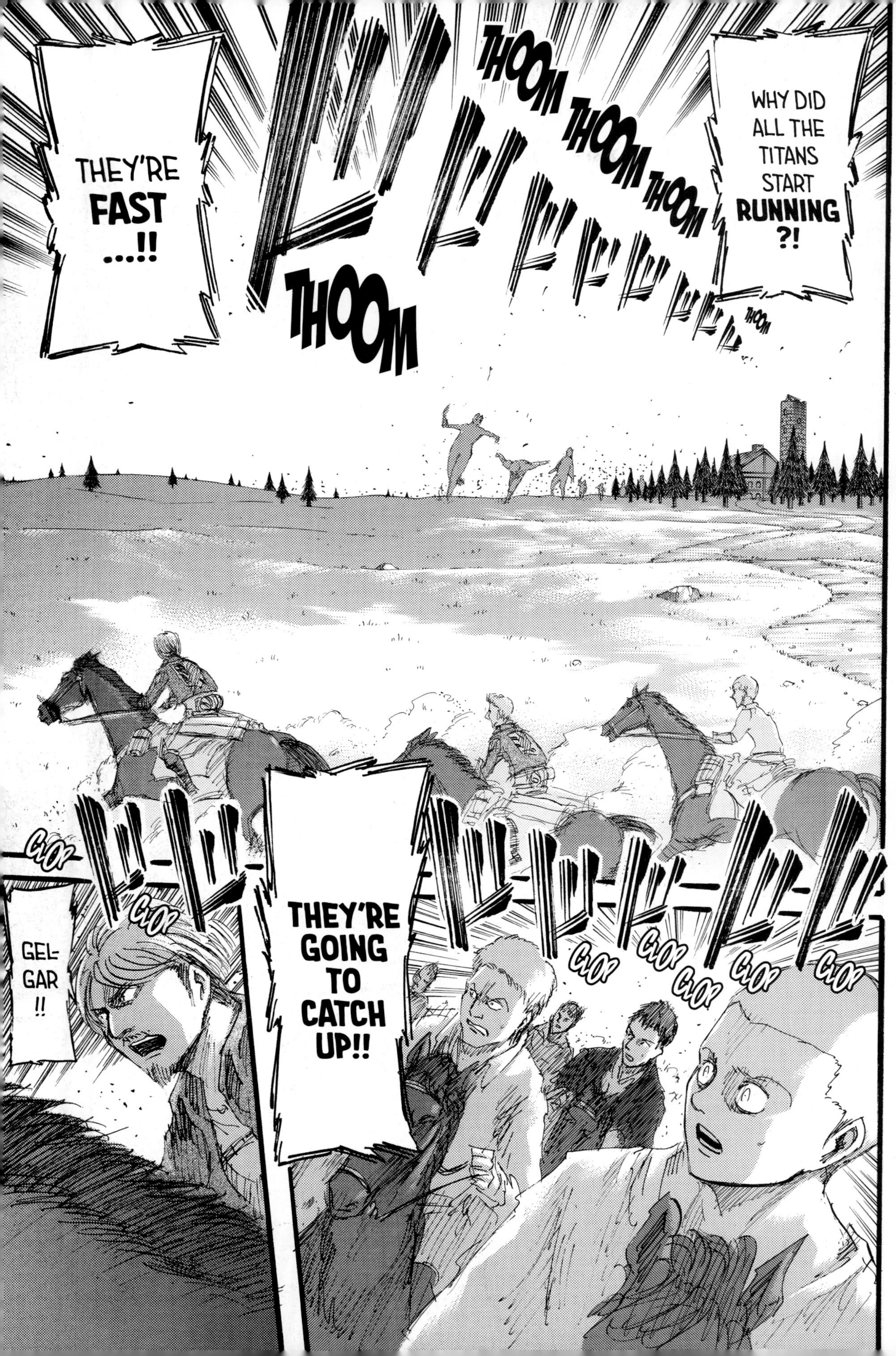
WHY DID ALL THE TITANS START RUNNING ?!
THOOM THOOM THOOM
THOOM
THOOM
THEY'RE FAST ...!!
CLOP CLOP CLOP CLOP CLOP
THEY'RE GOING TO CATCH UP!!
CLOP CLOP
GEL-GAR !!

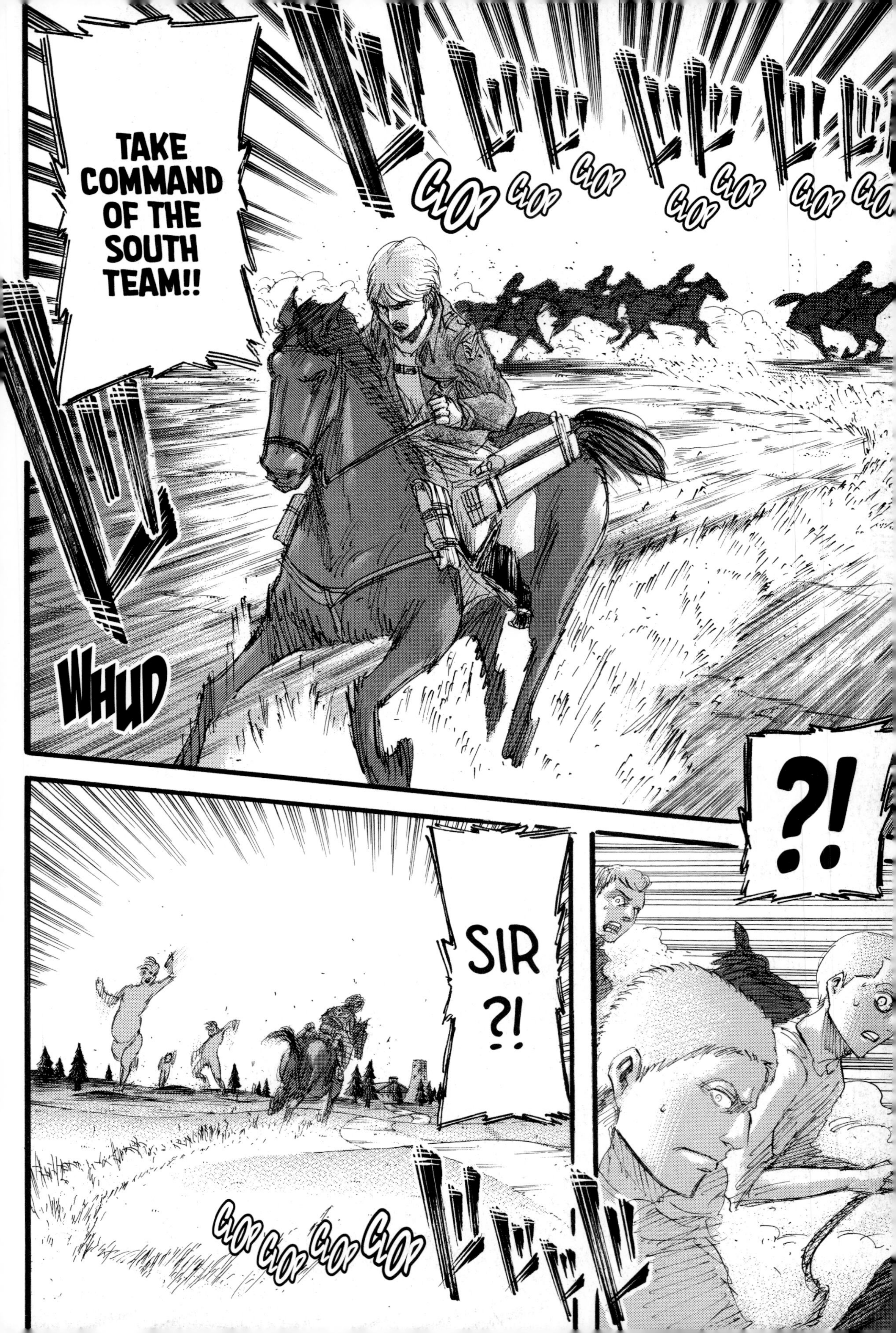
CLOP CLOP CLOP CLOP CLOP CLOP CLOP
TAKE COMMAND OF THE SOUTH TEAM!!
WHUD
?!
SIR ?!
CLOP CLOP CLOP CLOP

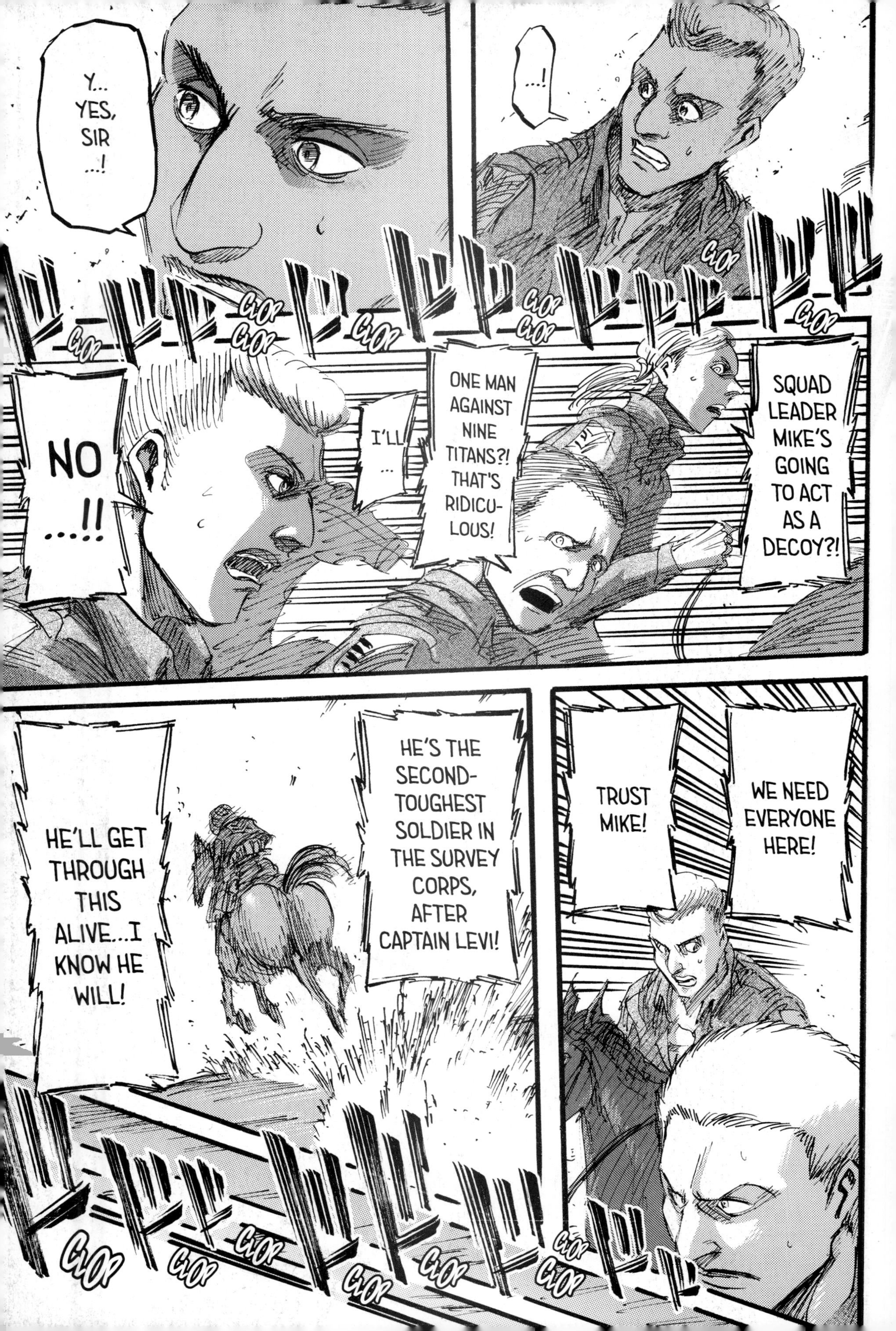
...!
Y... YES, SIR ...!
CLOP CLOP CLOP CLOP CLOP CLOP CLOP
SQUAD LEADER MIKE'S GOING TO ACT AS A DECOY?!
ONE MAN AGAINST NINE TITANS?! THAT'S RIDICULOUS!
I'LL ...
NO ...!!
WE NEED EVERYONE HERE!
TRUST MIKE!
HE'S THE SECOND-TOUGHEST SOLDIER IN THE SURVEY CORPS, AFTER CAPTAIN LEVI!
HE'LL GET THROUGH THIS ALIVE...I KNOW HE WILL!
CLOP CLOP CLOP CLOP CLOP CLOP CLOP

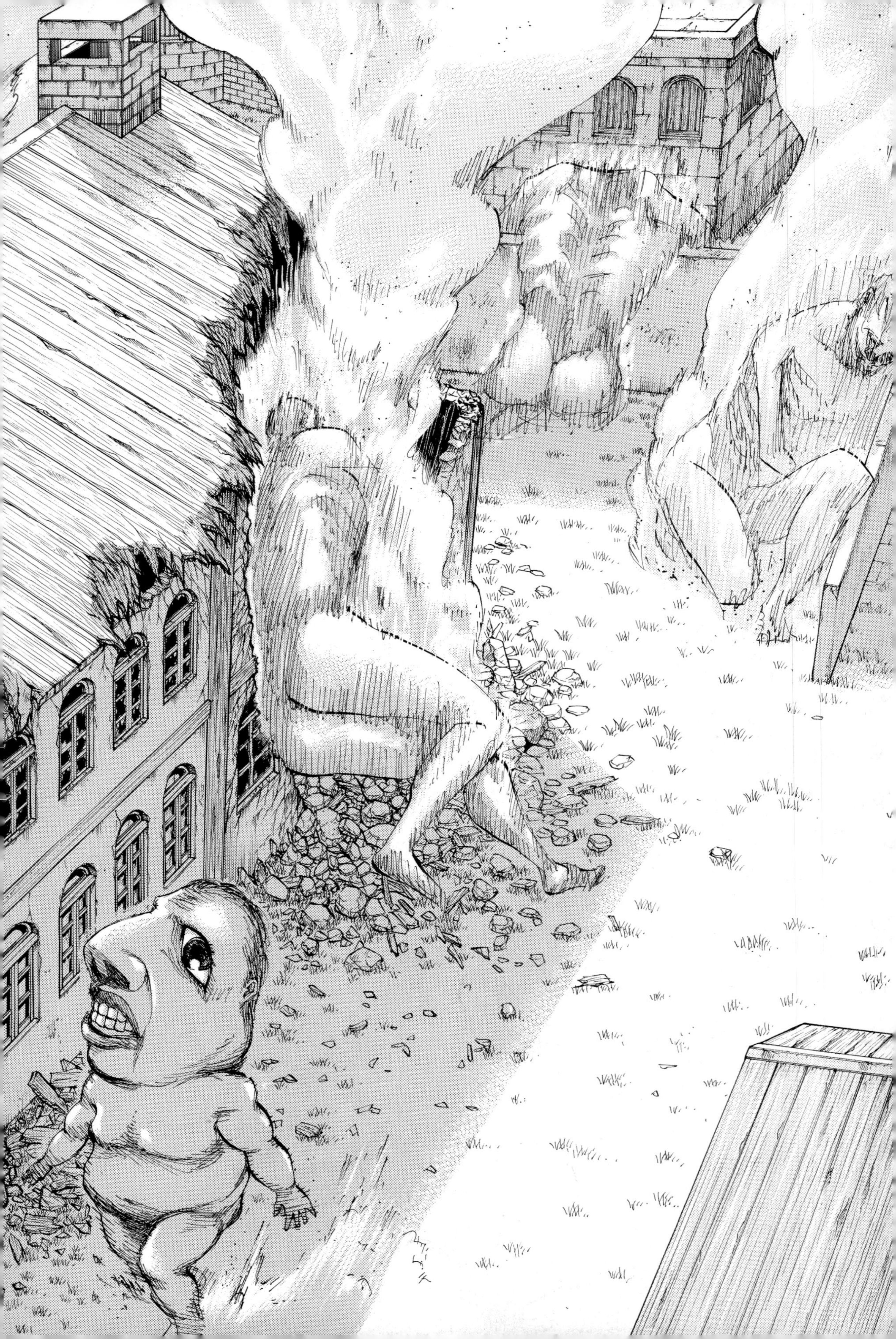

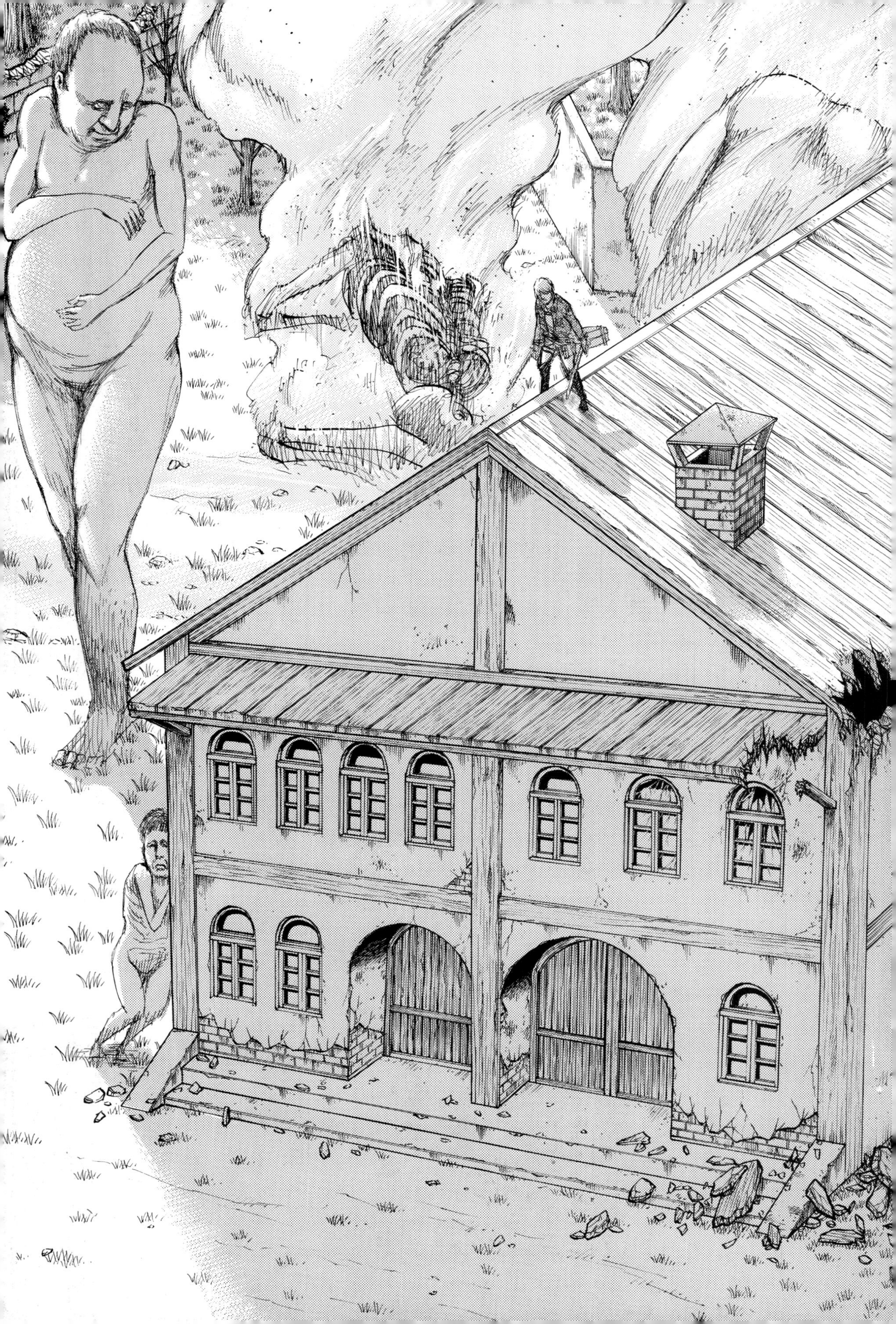

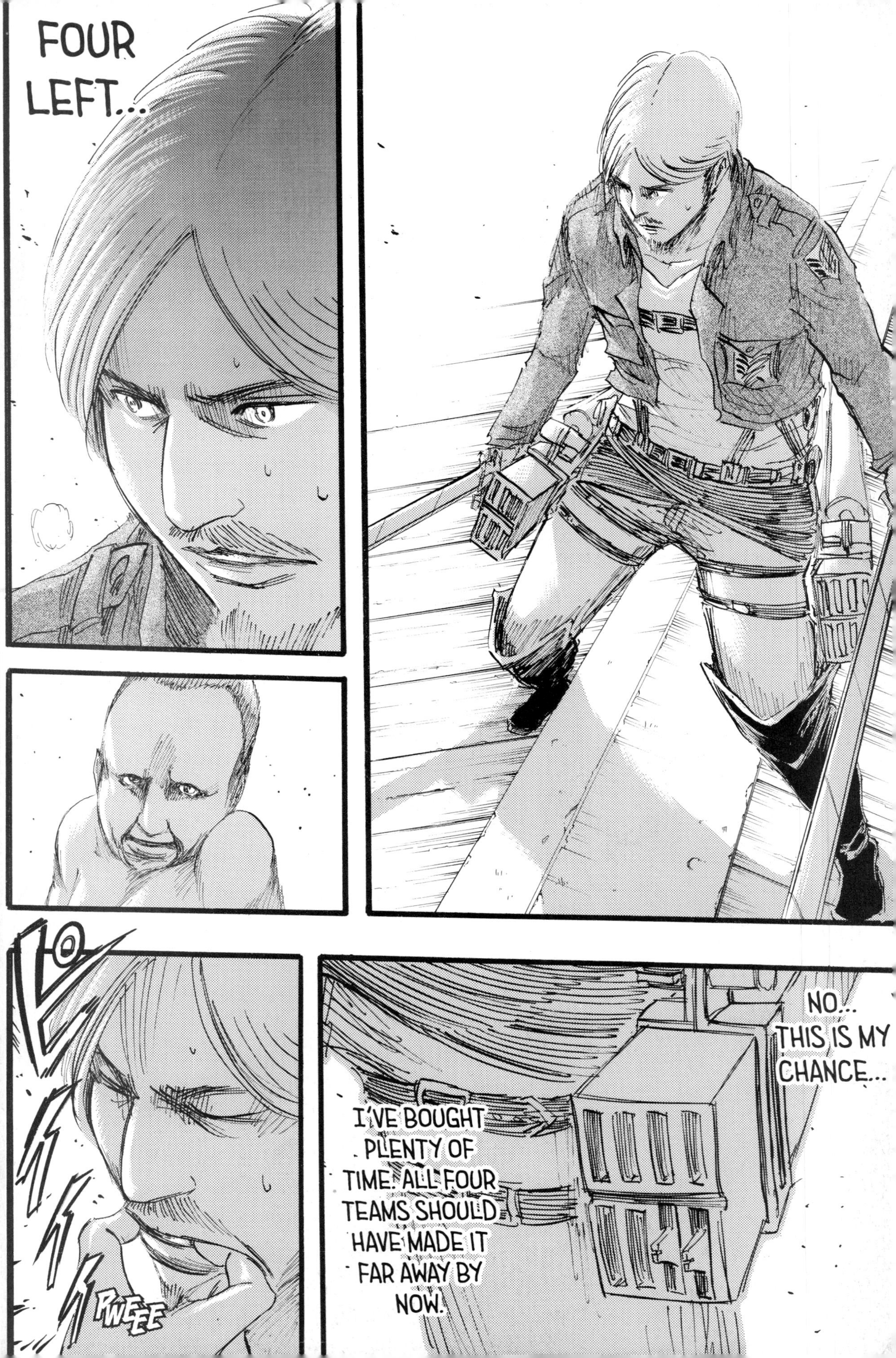
FOUR LEFT...
NO... THIS IS MY CHANCE...
I'VE BOUGHT PLENTY OF TIME. ALL FOUR TEAMS SHOULD HAVE MADE IT FAR AWAY BY NOW.
PWEEE

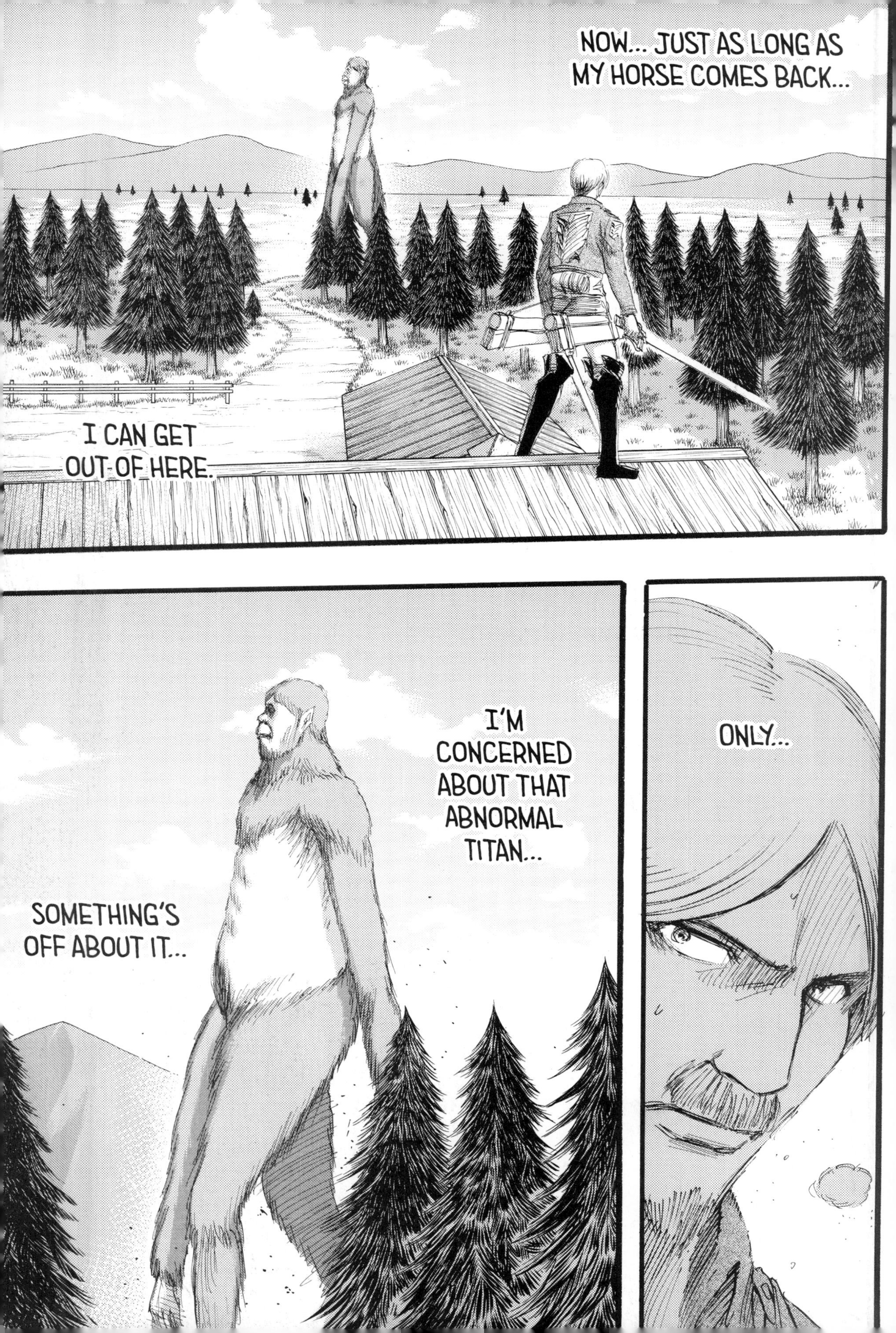
NOW... JUST AS LONG AS MY HORSE COMES BACK...
I CAN GET OUT OF HERE.
ONLY...
I'M CONCERNED ABOUT THAT ABNORMAL TITAN...
SOMETHING'S OFF ABOUT IT...

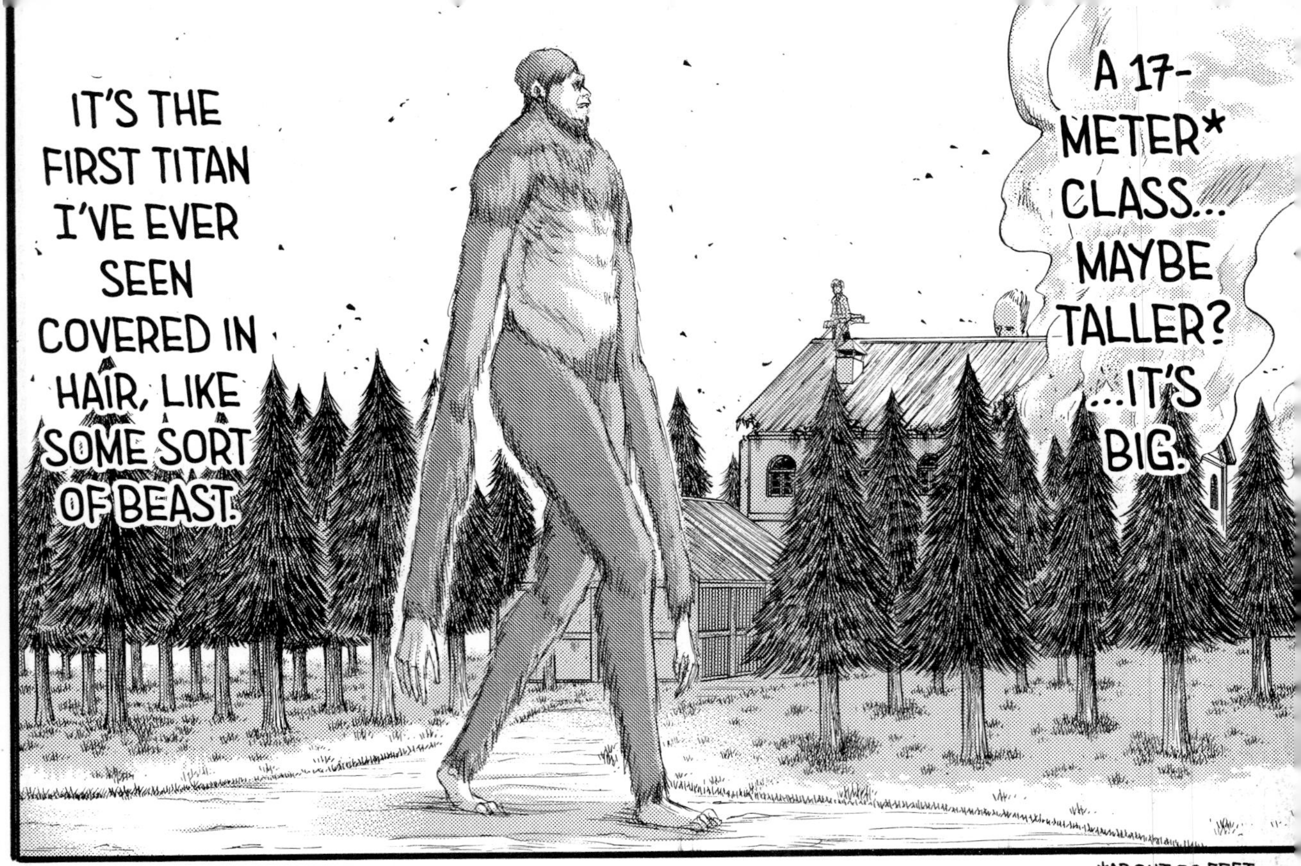
A 17-METER* CLASS... MAYBE TALLER? ...IT'S BIG.
IT'S THE FIRST TITAN I'VE EVER SEEN COVERED IN HAIR, LIKE SOME SORT OF BEAST.

*ABOUT 56 FEET.

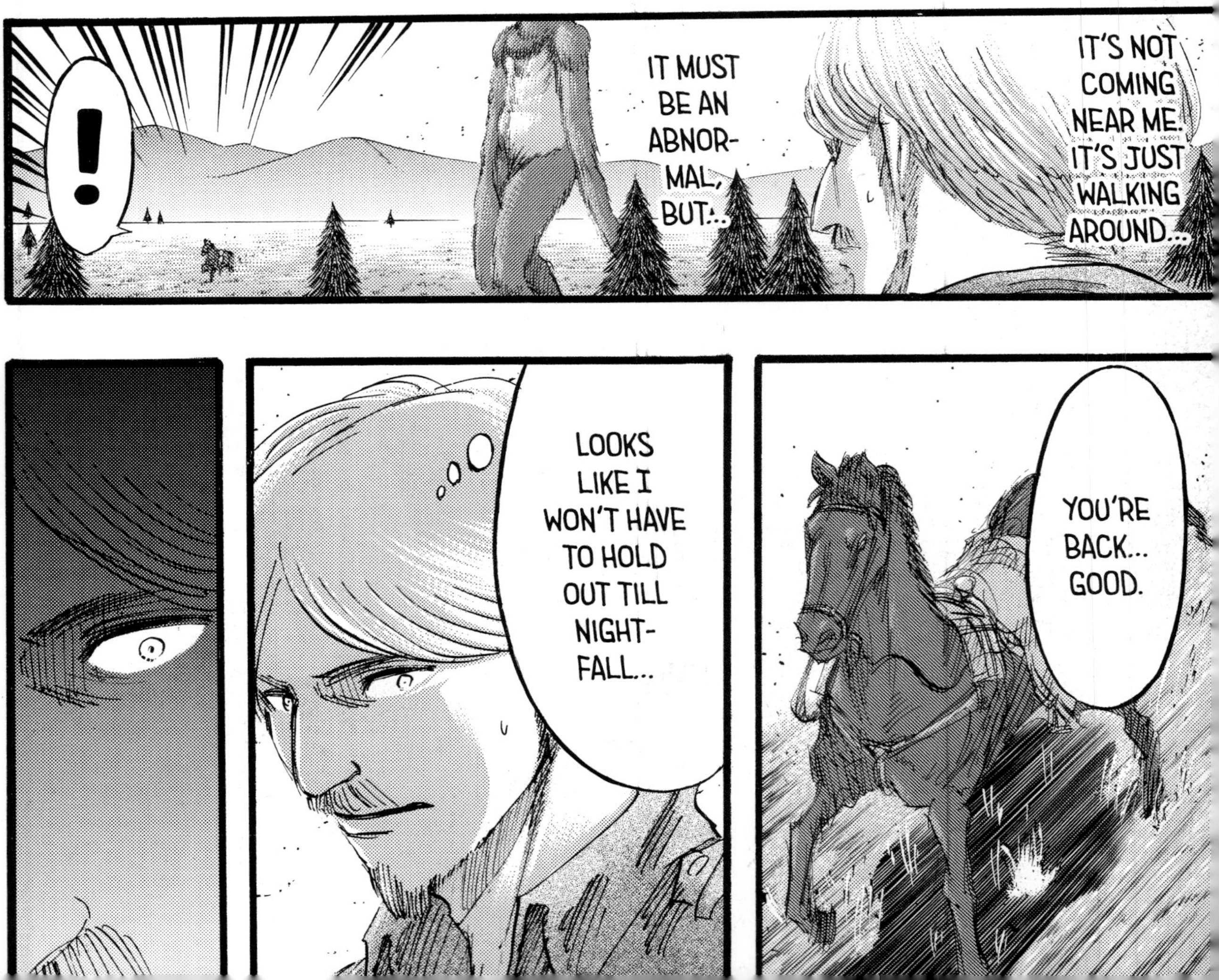
IT'S NOT COMING NEAR ME. IT'S JUST WALKING AROUND...
IT MUST BE AN ABNORMAL, BUT...
!
YOU'RE BACK... GOOD.
LOOKS LIKE I WON'T HAVE TO HOLD OUT TILL NIGHTFALL...

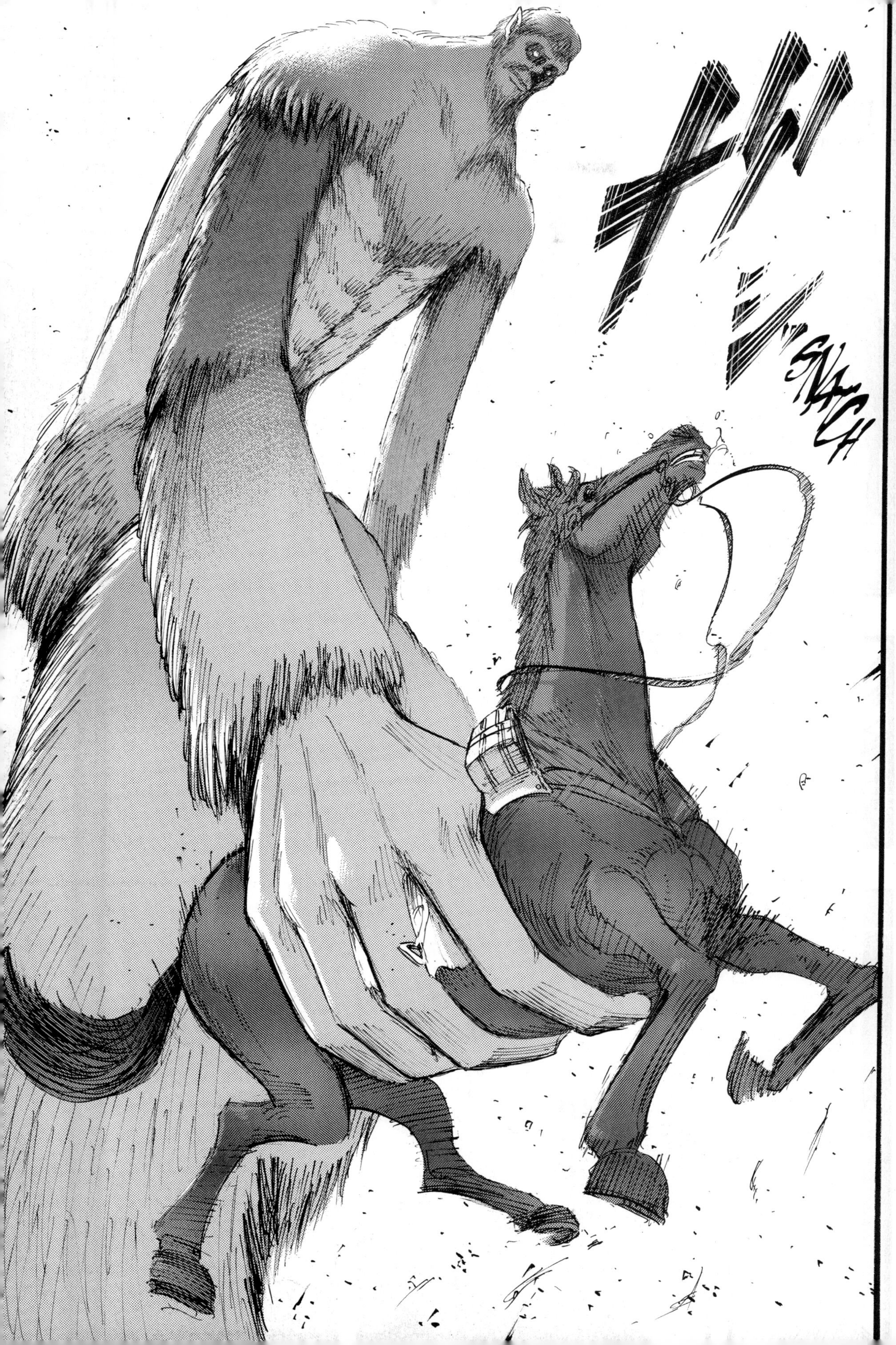
SNATCH

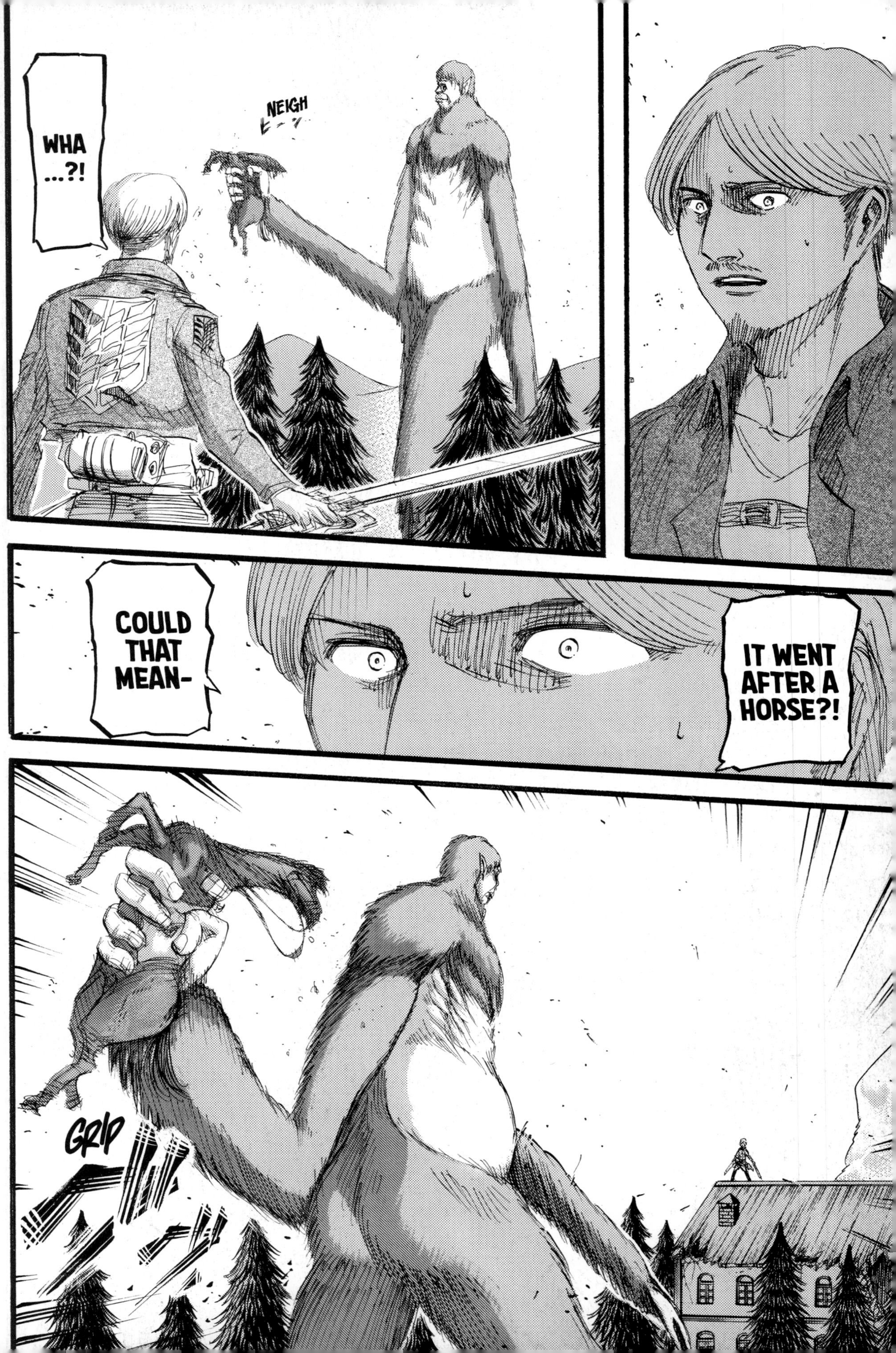
NEIGH
WHA ...?!
IT WENT AFTER A HORSE?!
COULD THAT MEAN-
GRIP

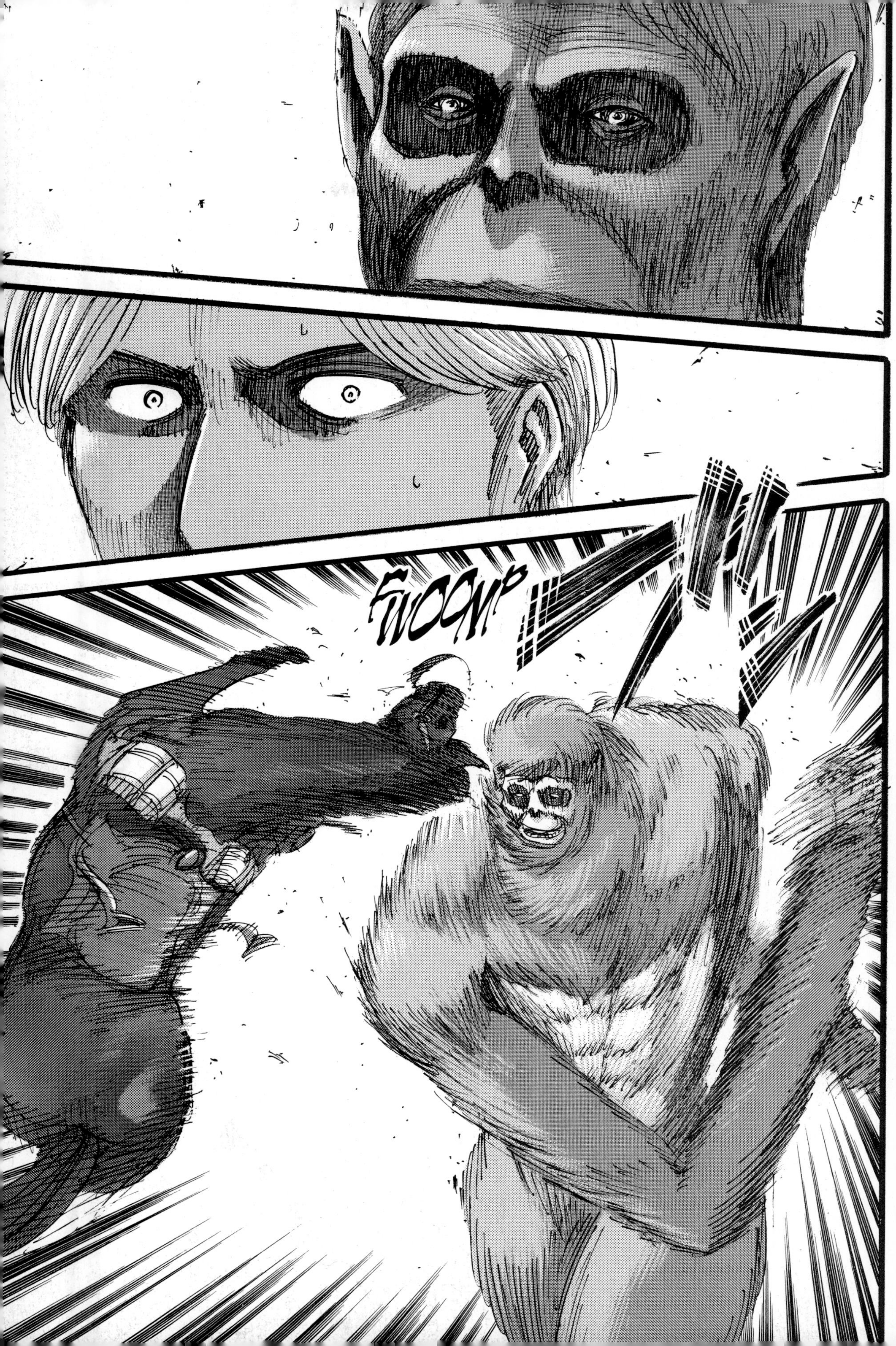
FWOOMP

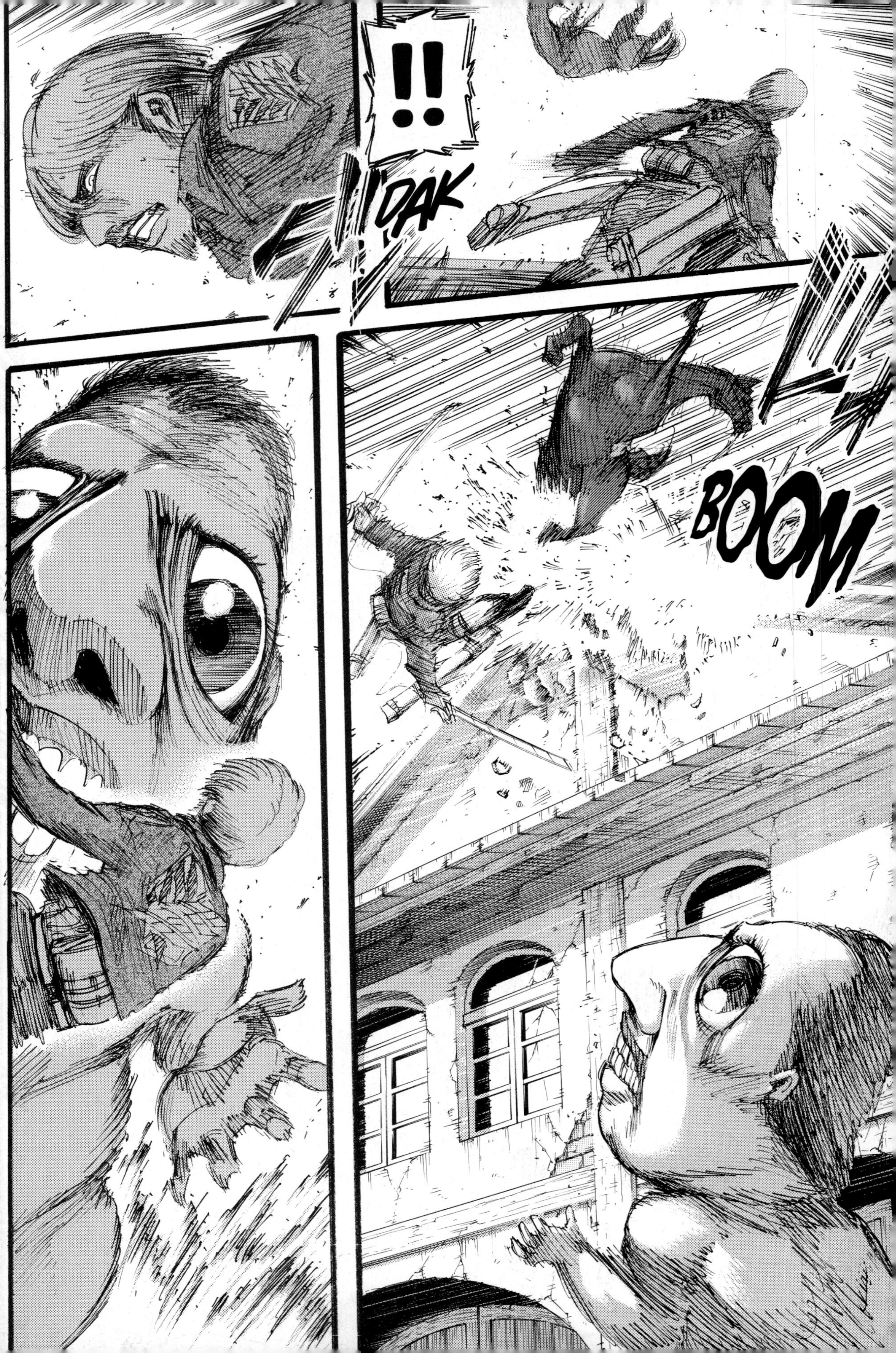
!!
DAK
BOOM

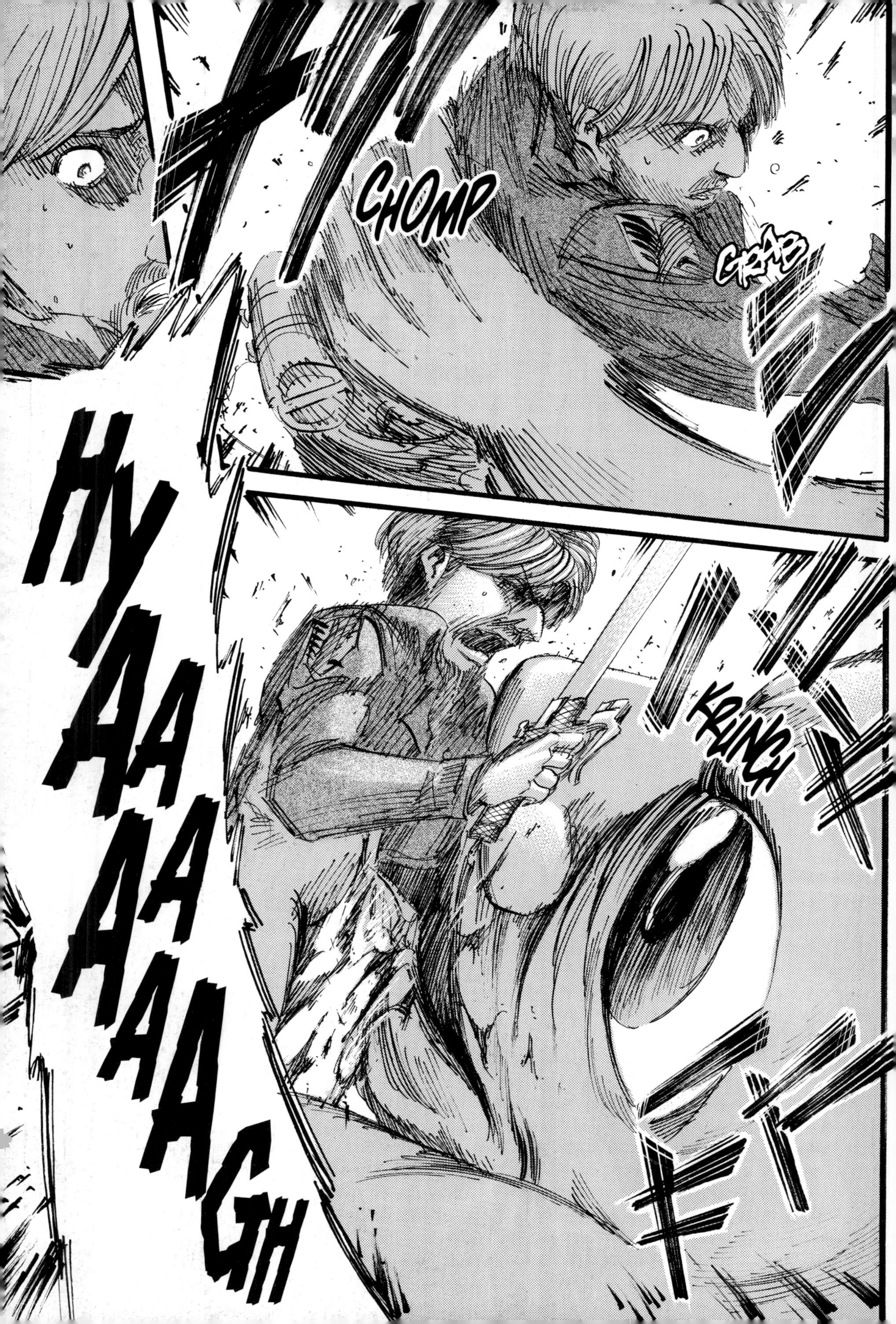
GRAB
CHOMP
KRUNCH
HYAAAAAAAGH

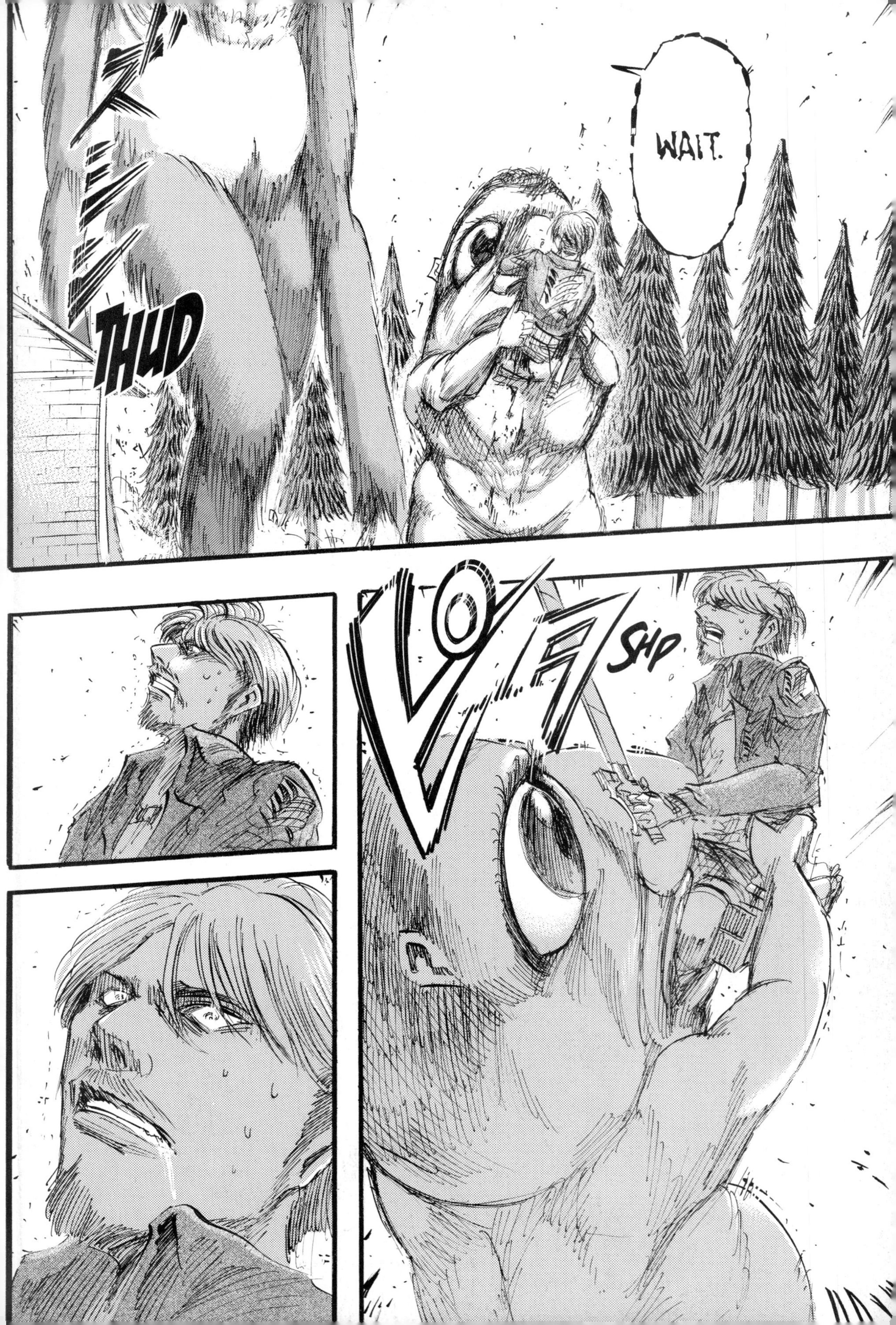
WAIT.
THUD
SHP

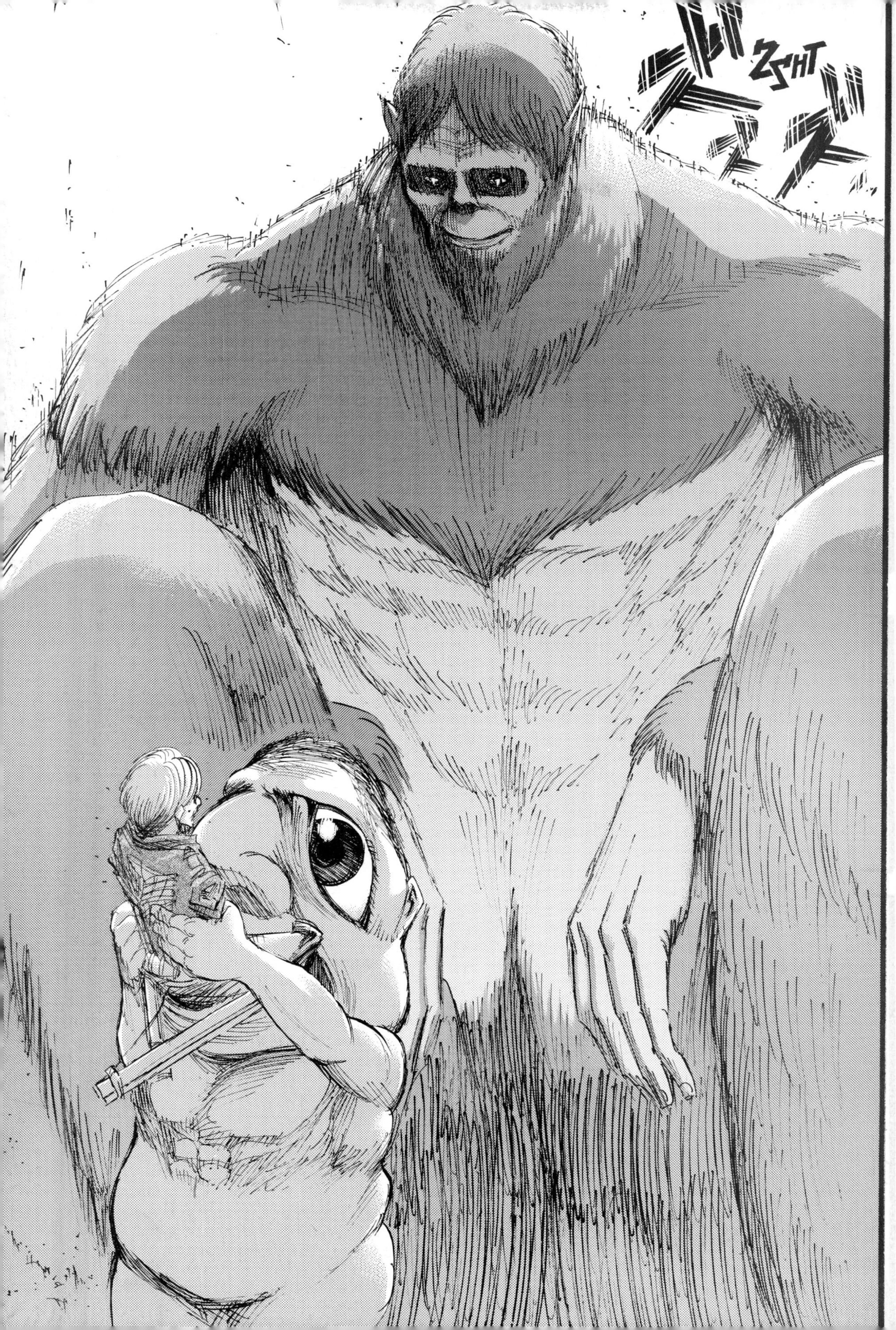
ZSHT

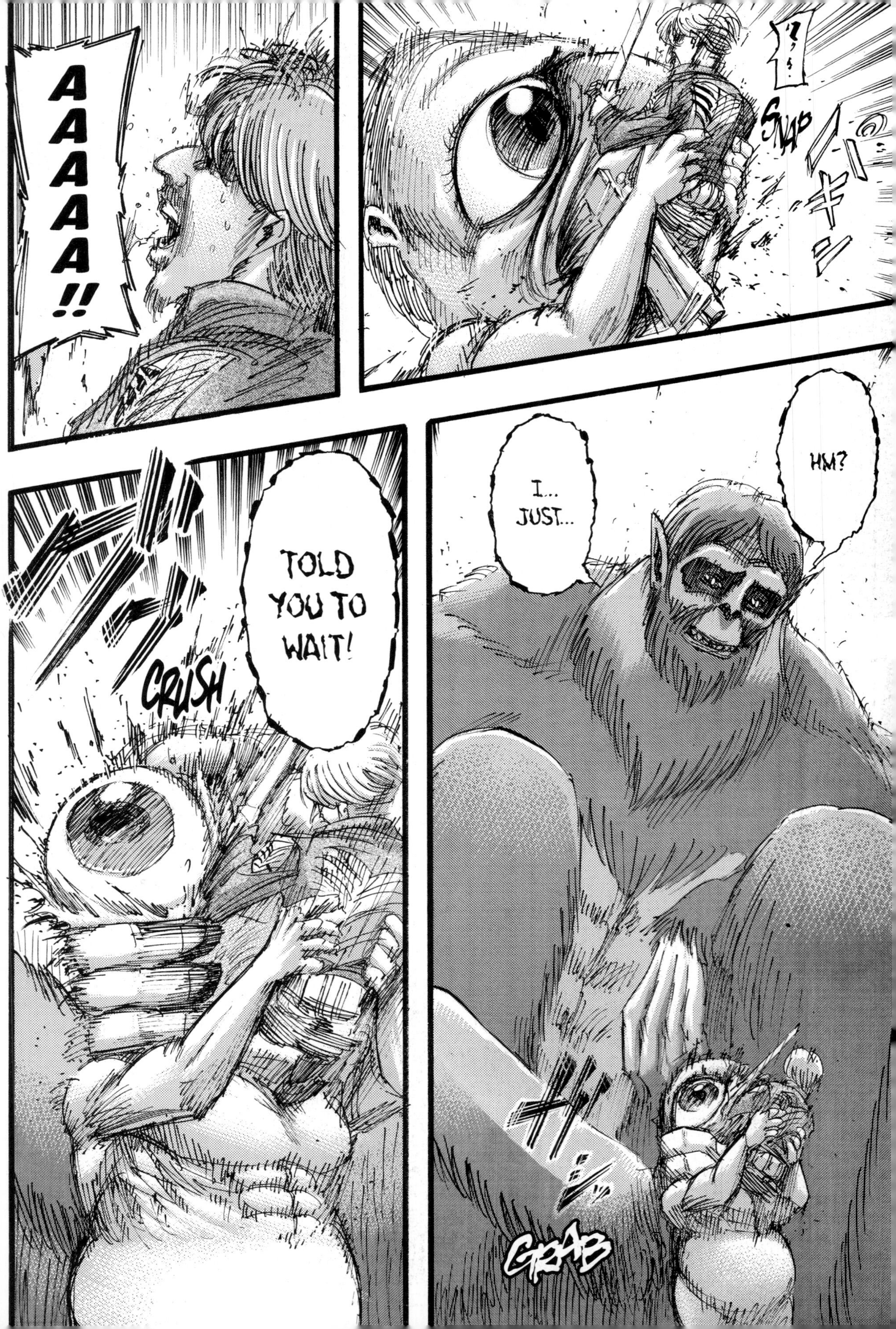
SNAP
AAAAAA!!
HM?
I... JUST...
GRAB
TOLD YOU TO WAIT!
CRUSH

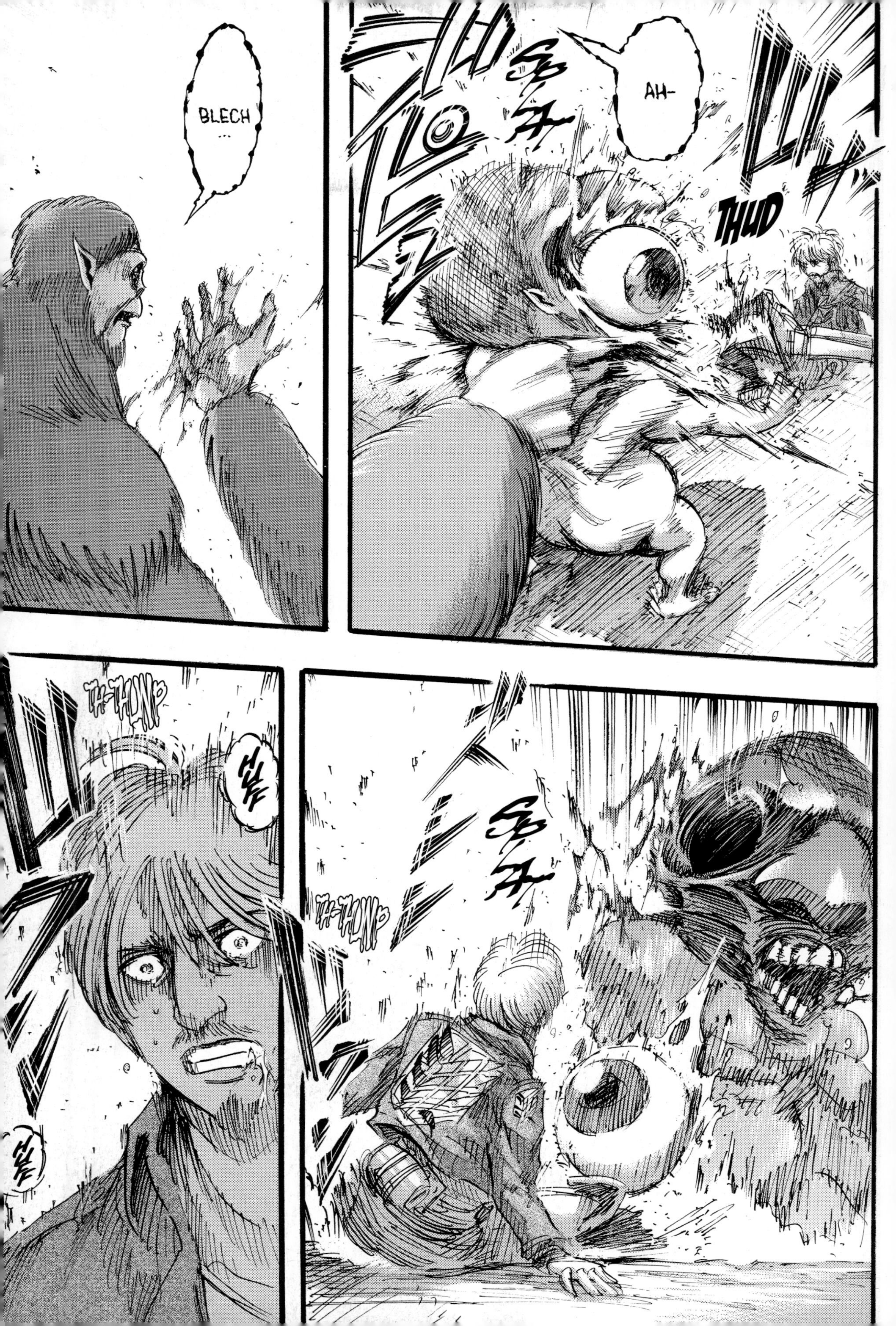
AH-
THUD
BLECH ...
TH-THUMP
TH-THUMP
HUFF
HUFF

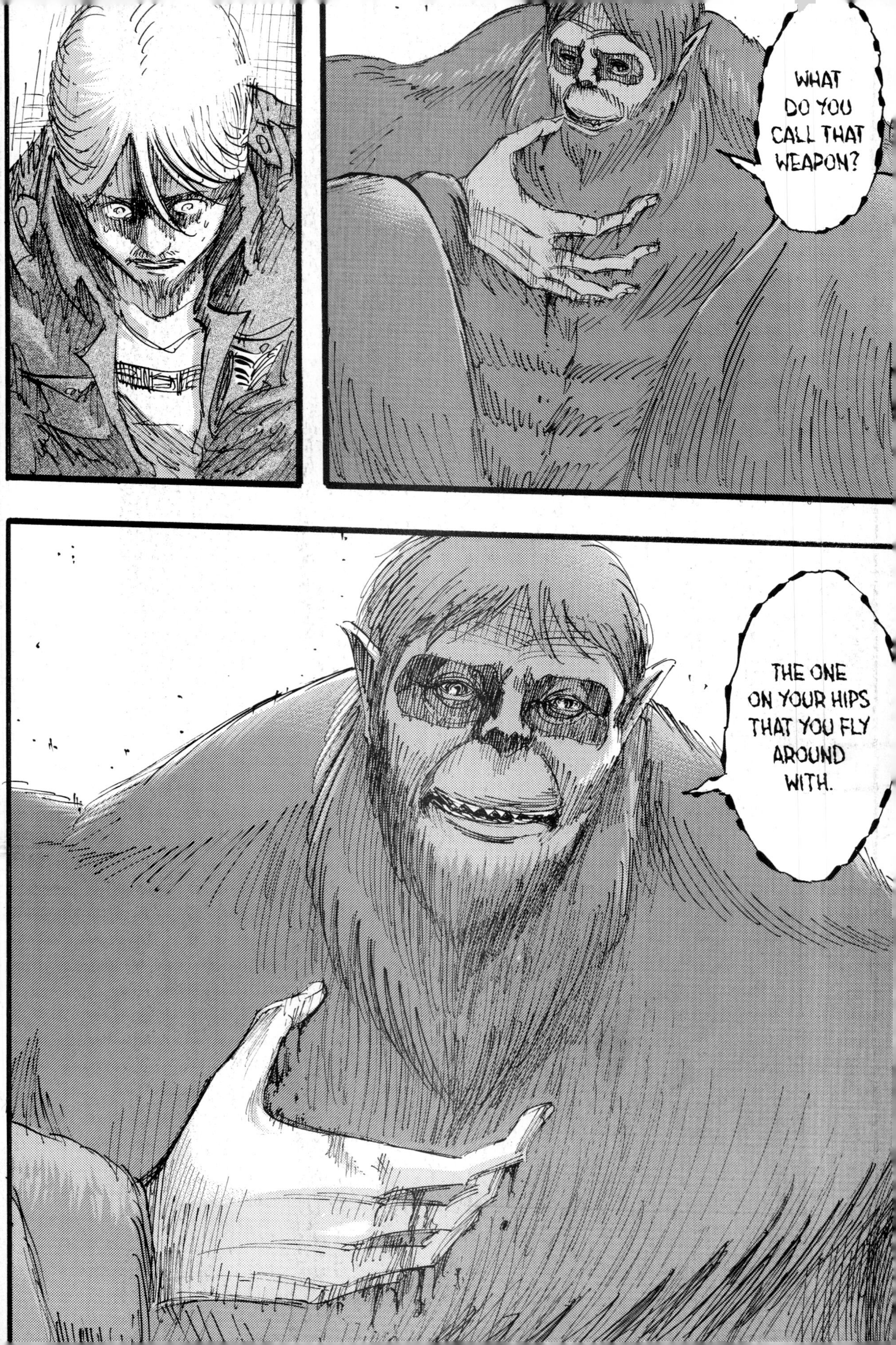
WHAT DO YOU CALL THAT WEAPON?
THE ONE ON YOUR HIPS THAT YOU FLY AROUND WITH.

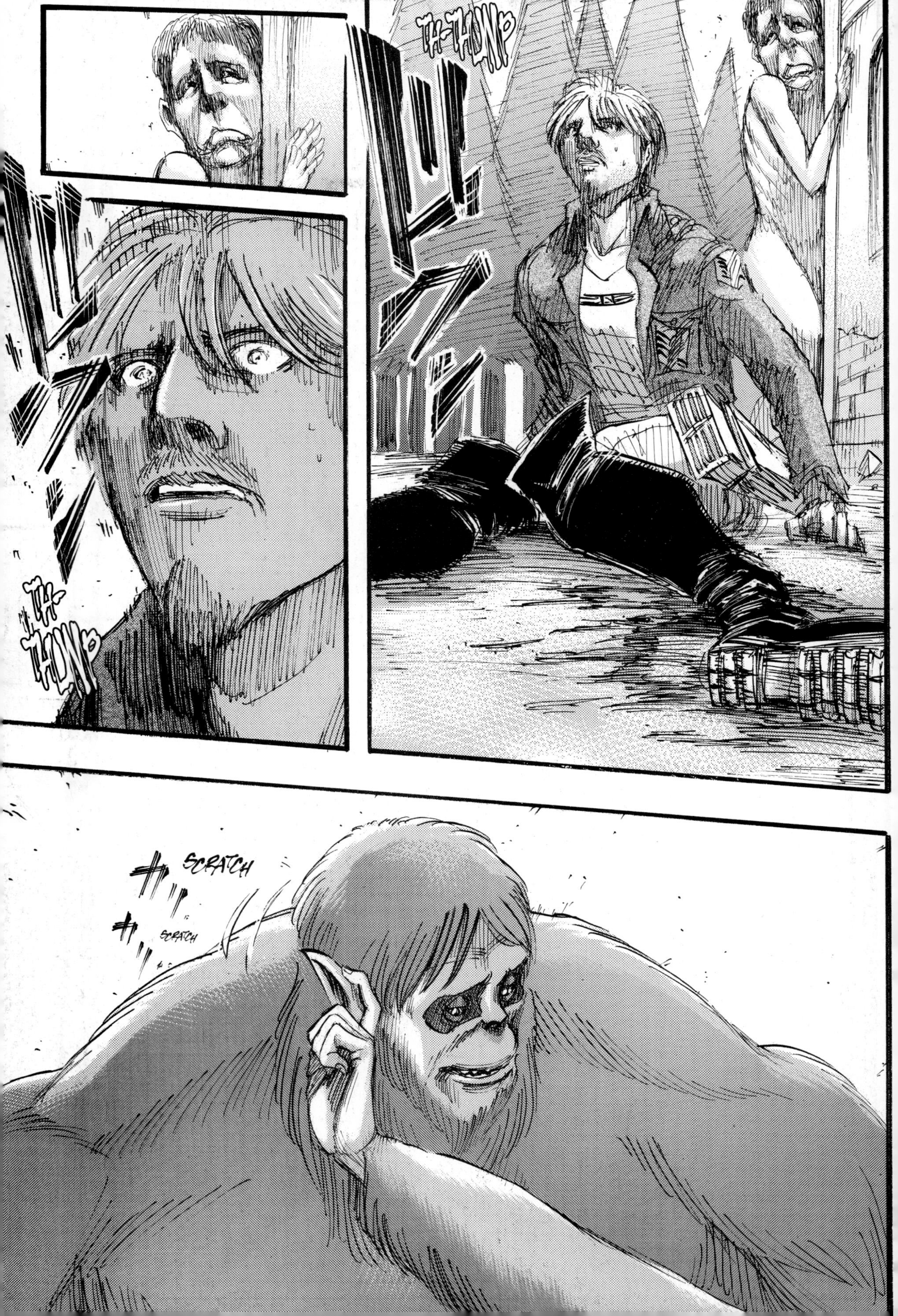

TH-THUMP
TH-THUMP
SCRATCH
SCRATCH

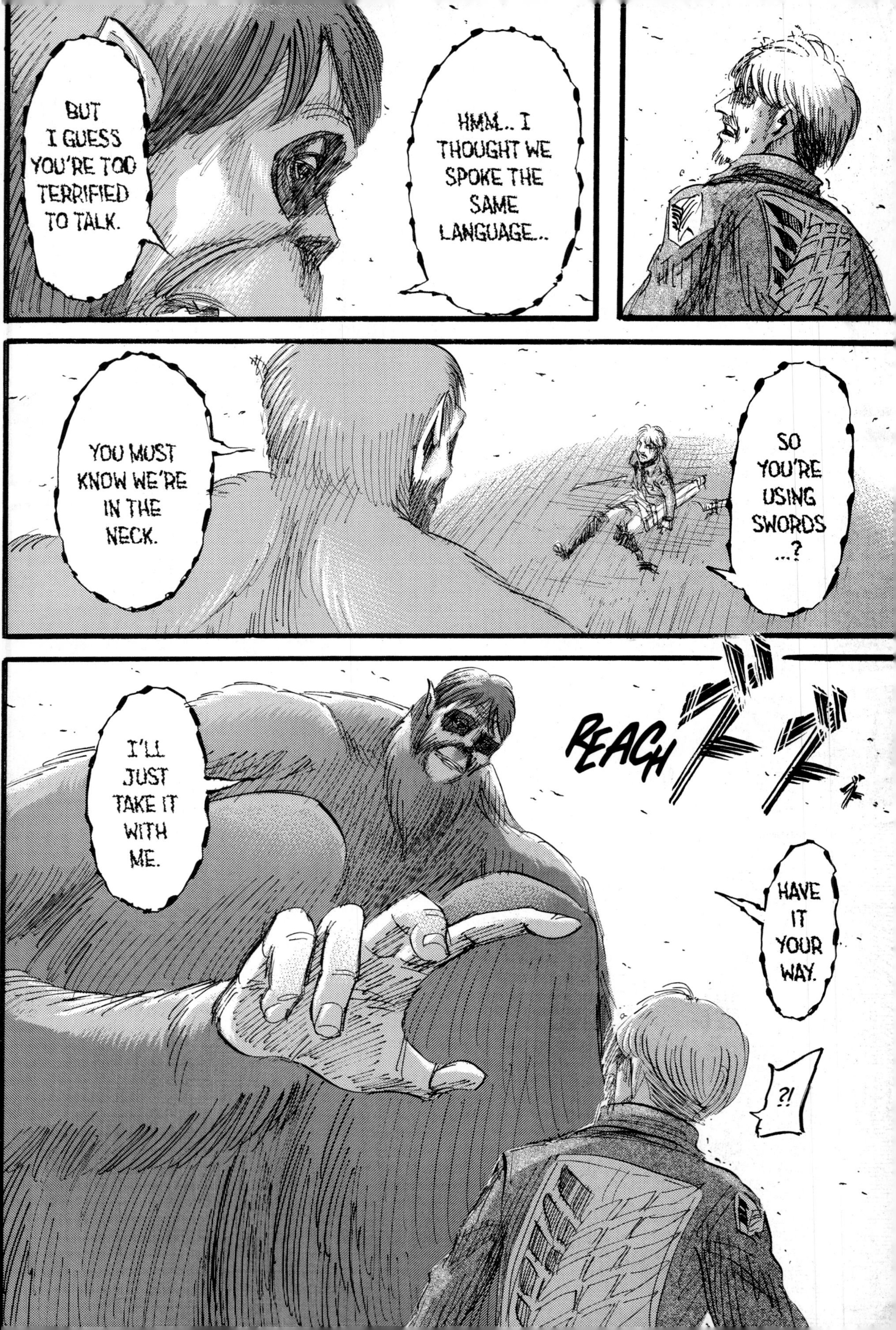
HMM.. I THOUGHT WE SPOKE THE SAME LANGUAGE..
BUT I GUESS YOU'RE TOO TERRIFIED TO TALK.
SO YOU'RE USING SWORDS ...?
YOU MUST KNOW WE'RE IN THE NECK.
REACH
I'LL JUST TAKE IT WITH ME.
HAVE IT YOUR WAY.
?!

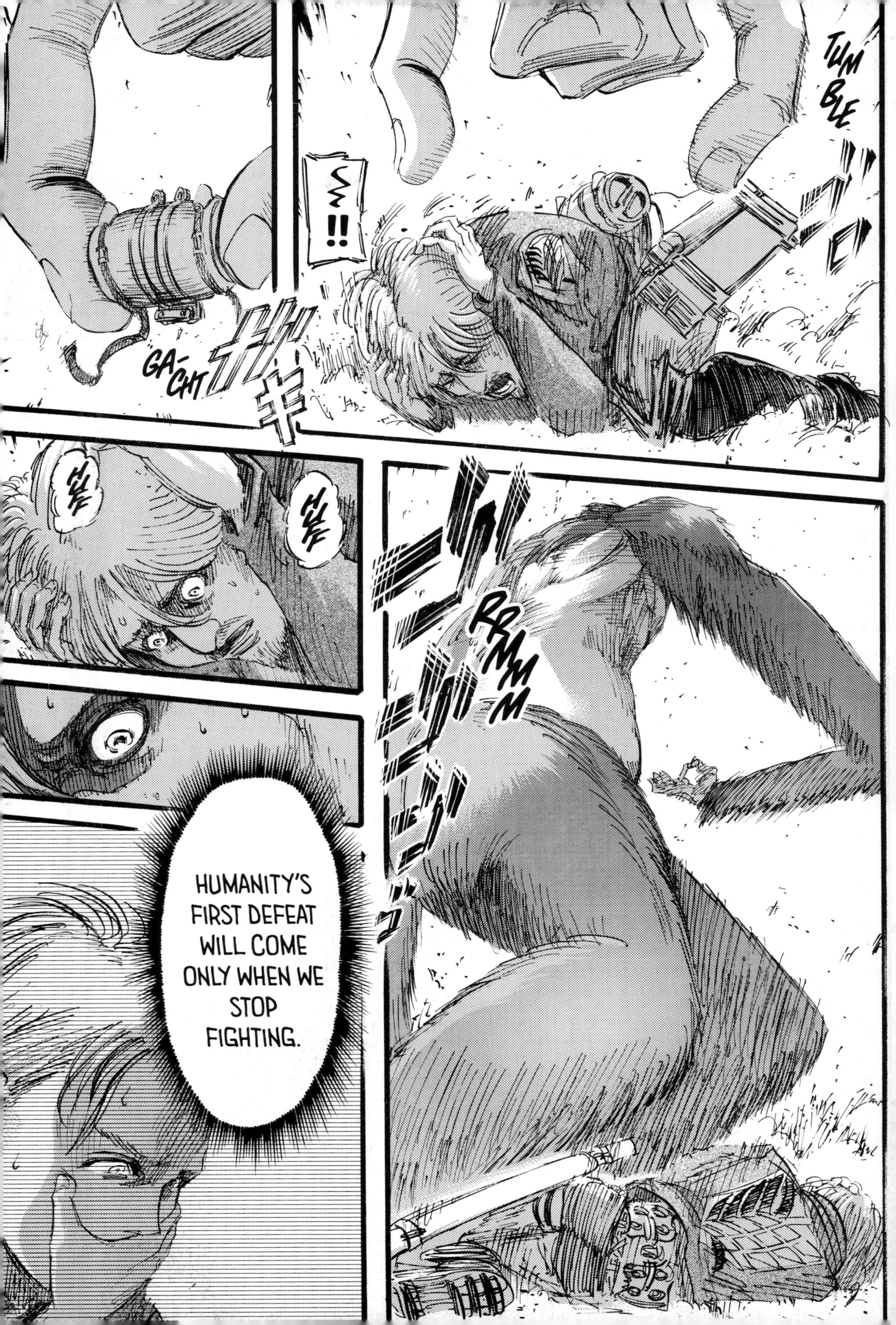

TUMBLE
!!
GA-CHT
RRMMM
HUFF
HUFF
HUMANITY'S FIRST DEFEAT WILL COME ONLY WHEN WE STOP FIGHTING.

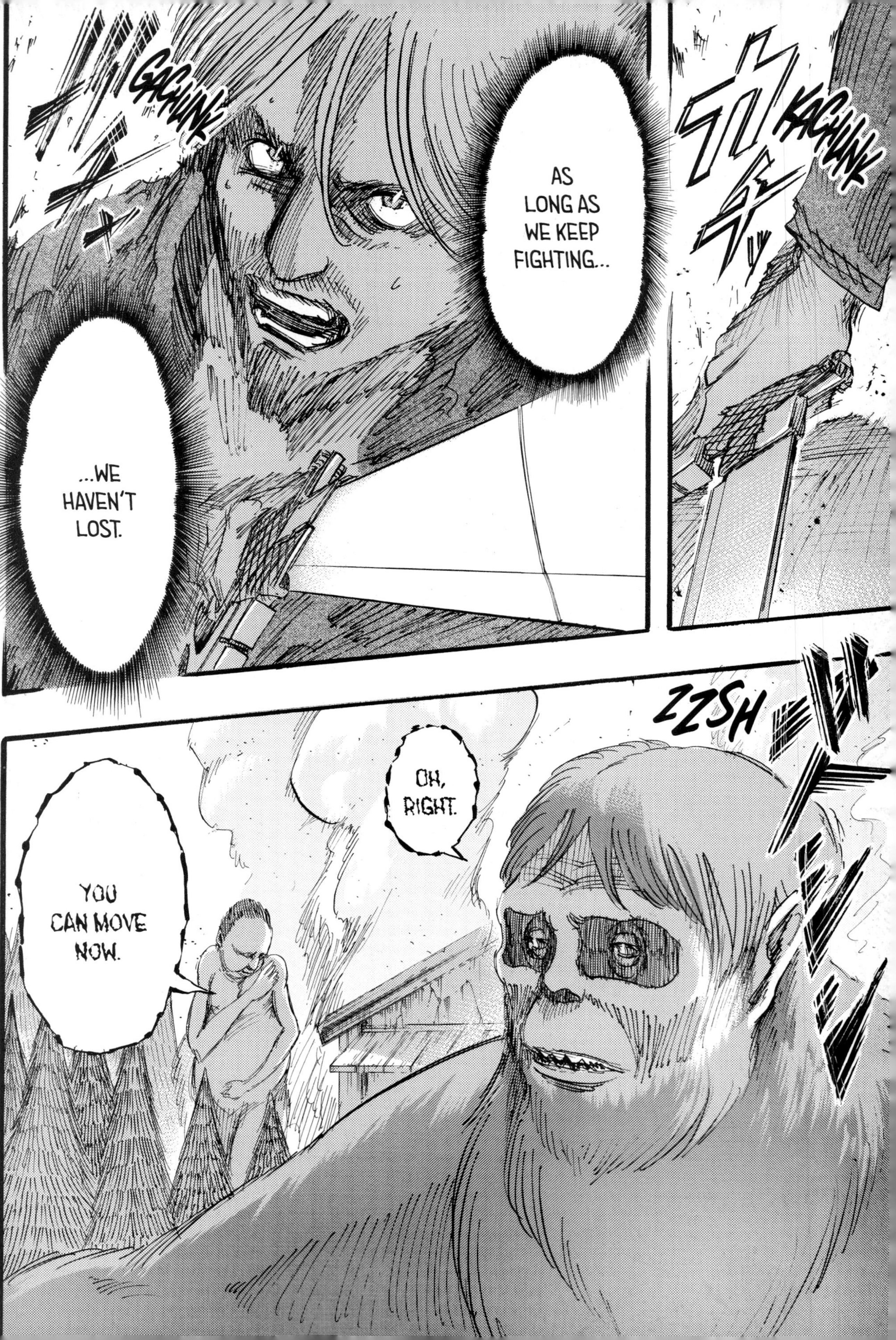
KACHUNK
GACHUNK
AS LONG AS WE KEEP FIGHTING...
...WE HAVEN'T LOST.
ZZSH
OH, RIGHT.
YOU CAN MOVE NOW.

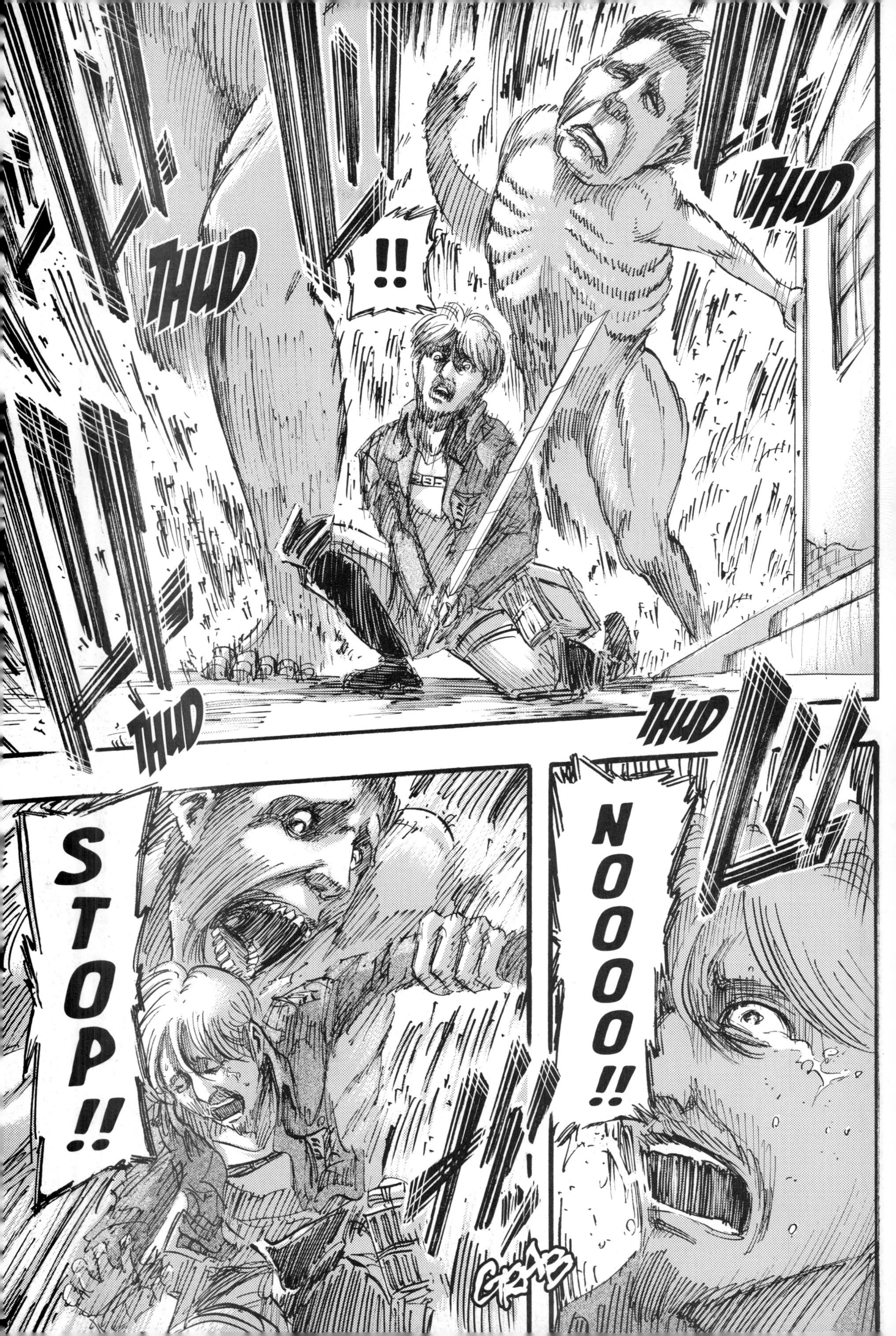
THUD
!!
THUD
THUD
THUD
NOOOOO!!
STOP!!
GRAB

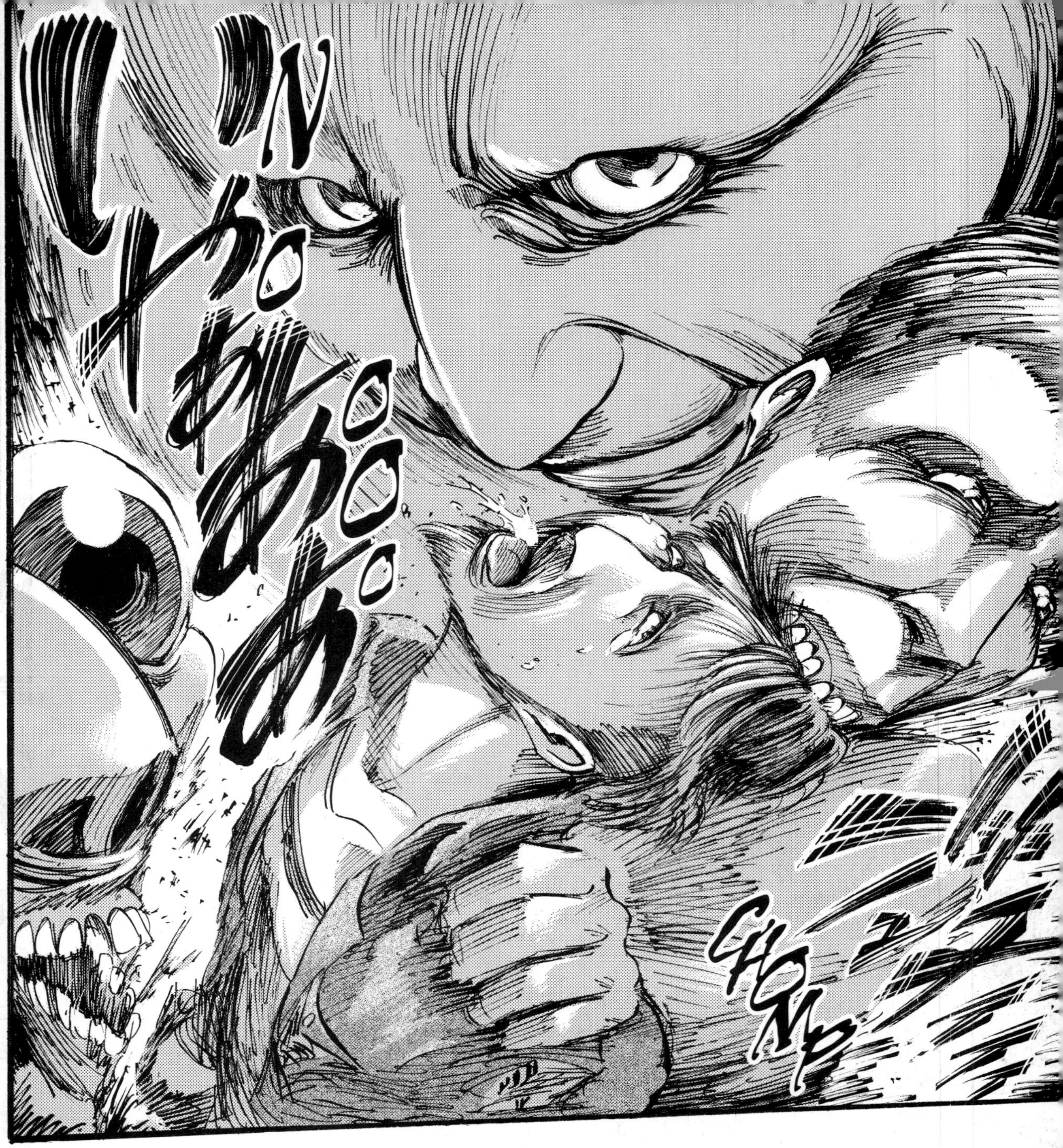
CHOMP
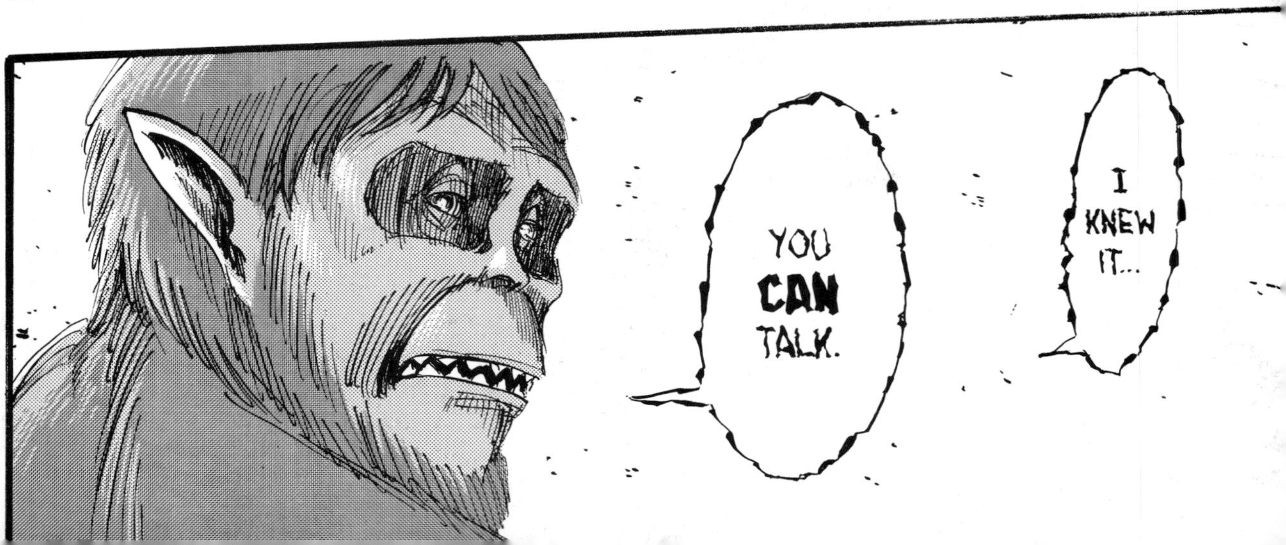
I KNEW IT...
YOU **CAN** TALK.

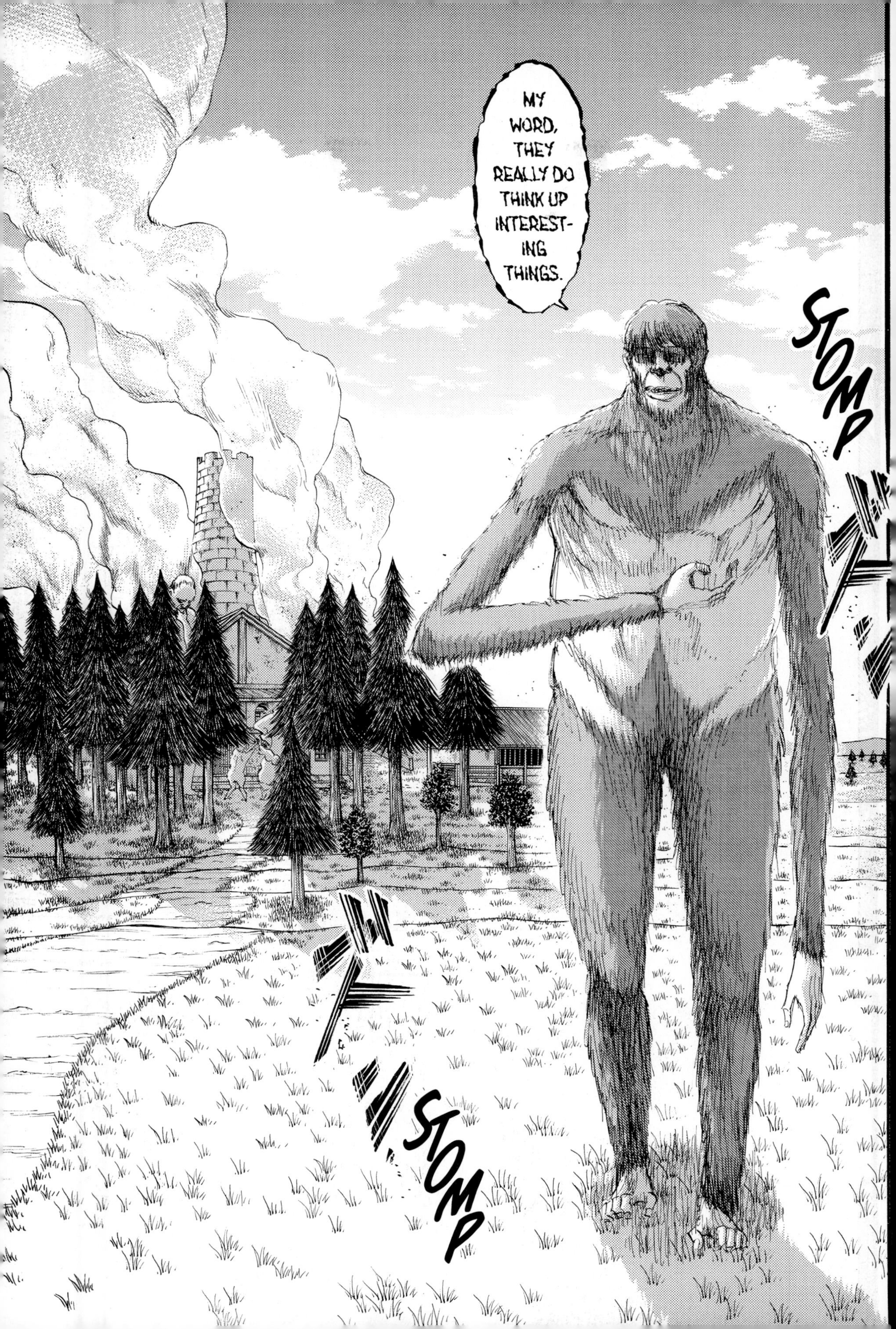
MY WORD, THEY REALLY DO THINK UP INTEREST-ING THINGS.
STOMP
STOMP

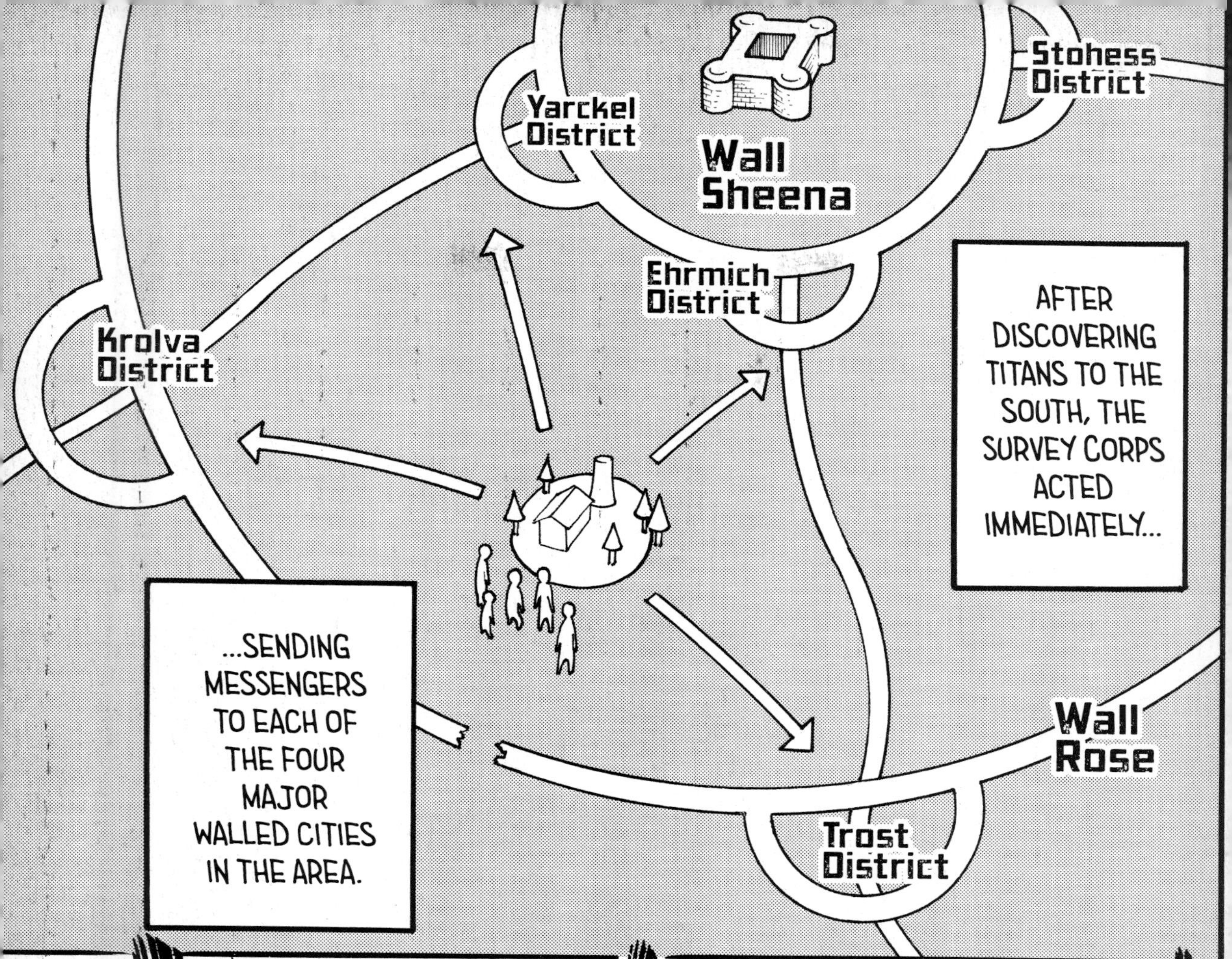
Stohess District
Wall Sheena
Yarckel District
Ehrmich District
Krolva District
Wall Rose
Trost District
AFTER DISCOVERING TITANS TO THE SOUTH, THE SURVEY CORPS ACTED IMMEDIATELY...
...SENDING MESSENGERS TO EACH OF THE FOUR MAJOR WALLED CITIES IN THE AREA.

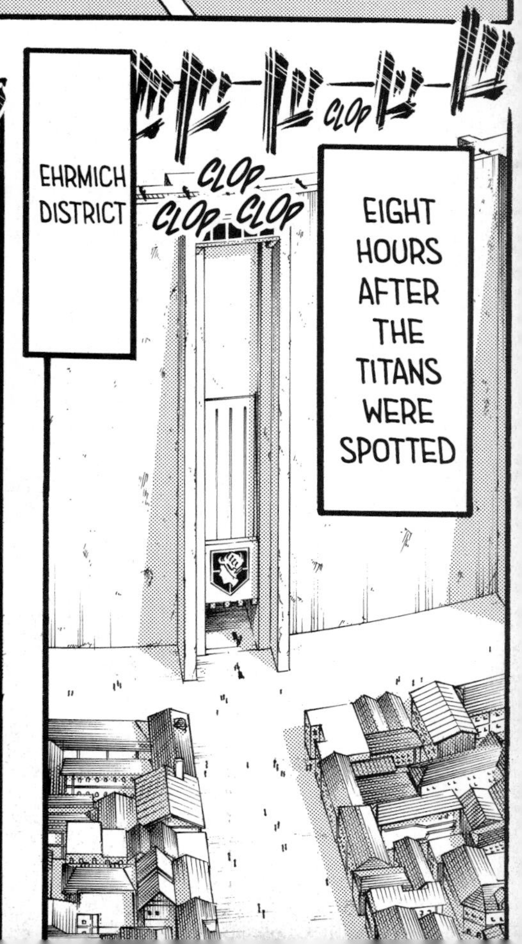
CLOP
EHRMICH DISTRICT
EIGHT HOURS AFTER THE TITANS WERE SPOTTED
CLOP CLOP CLOP

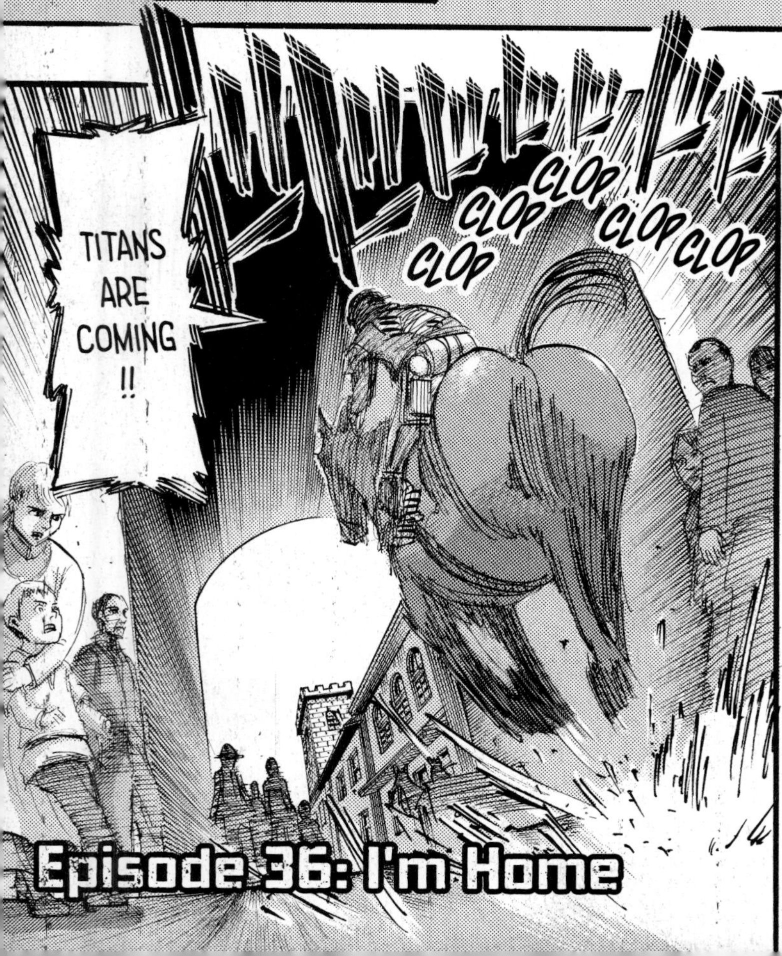
CLOP CLOP CLOP CLOP CLOP CLOP
TITANS ARE COMING !!

Episode 36: I'm Home

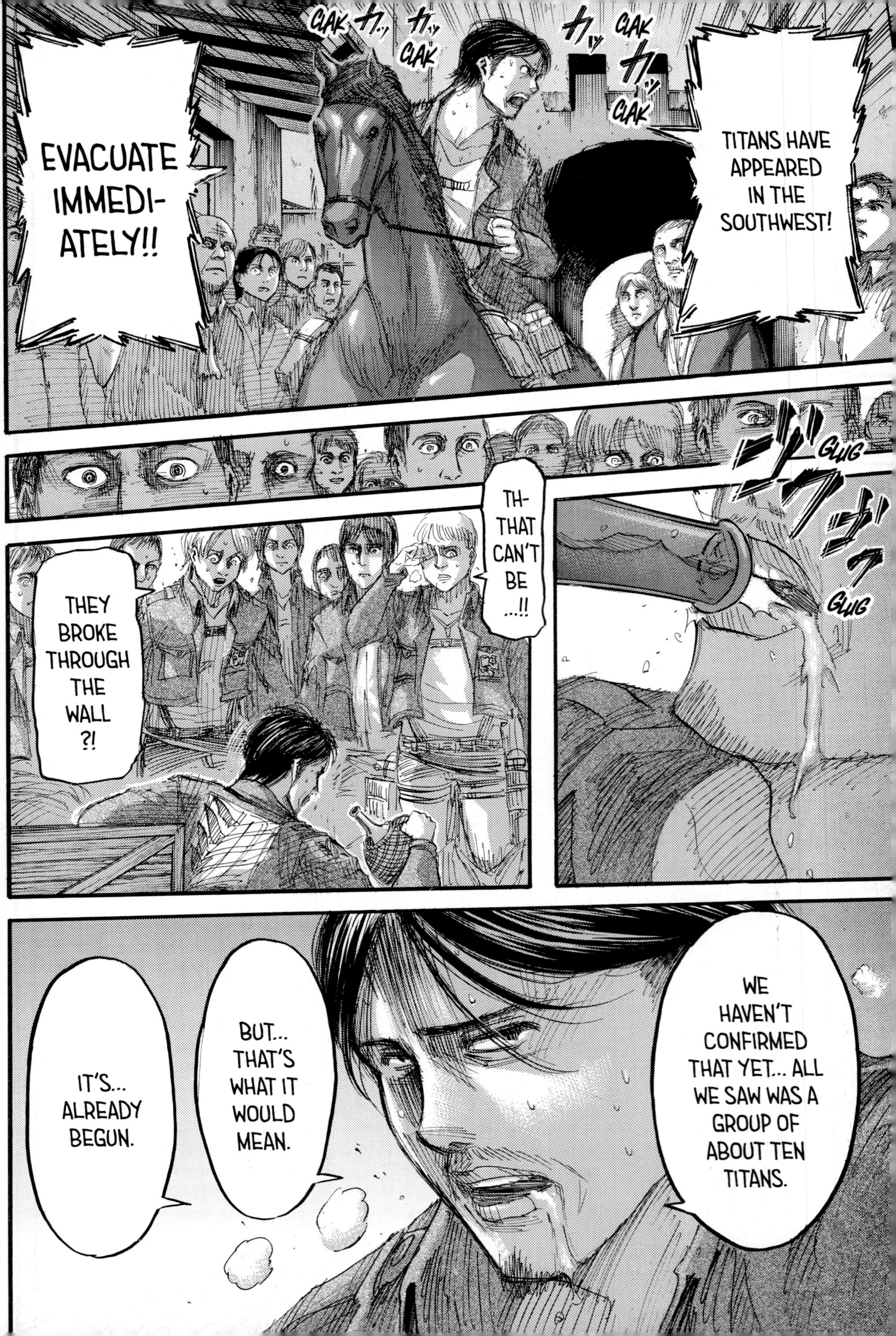
CLAK
CLAK
CLAK
CLAK
TITANS HAVE APPEARED IN THE SOUTHWEST!
EVACUATE IMMEDI-ATELY!!
GLUG
GLUG
TH- THAT CAN'T BE ...!!
THEY BROKE THROUGH THE WALL ?!
WE HAVEN'T CONFIRMED THAT YET... ALL WE SAW WAS A GROUP OF ABOUT TEN TITANS.
BUT... THAT'S WHAT IT WOULD MEAN.
IT'S... ALREADY BEGUN.

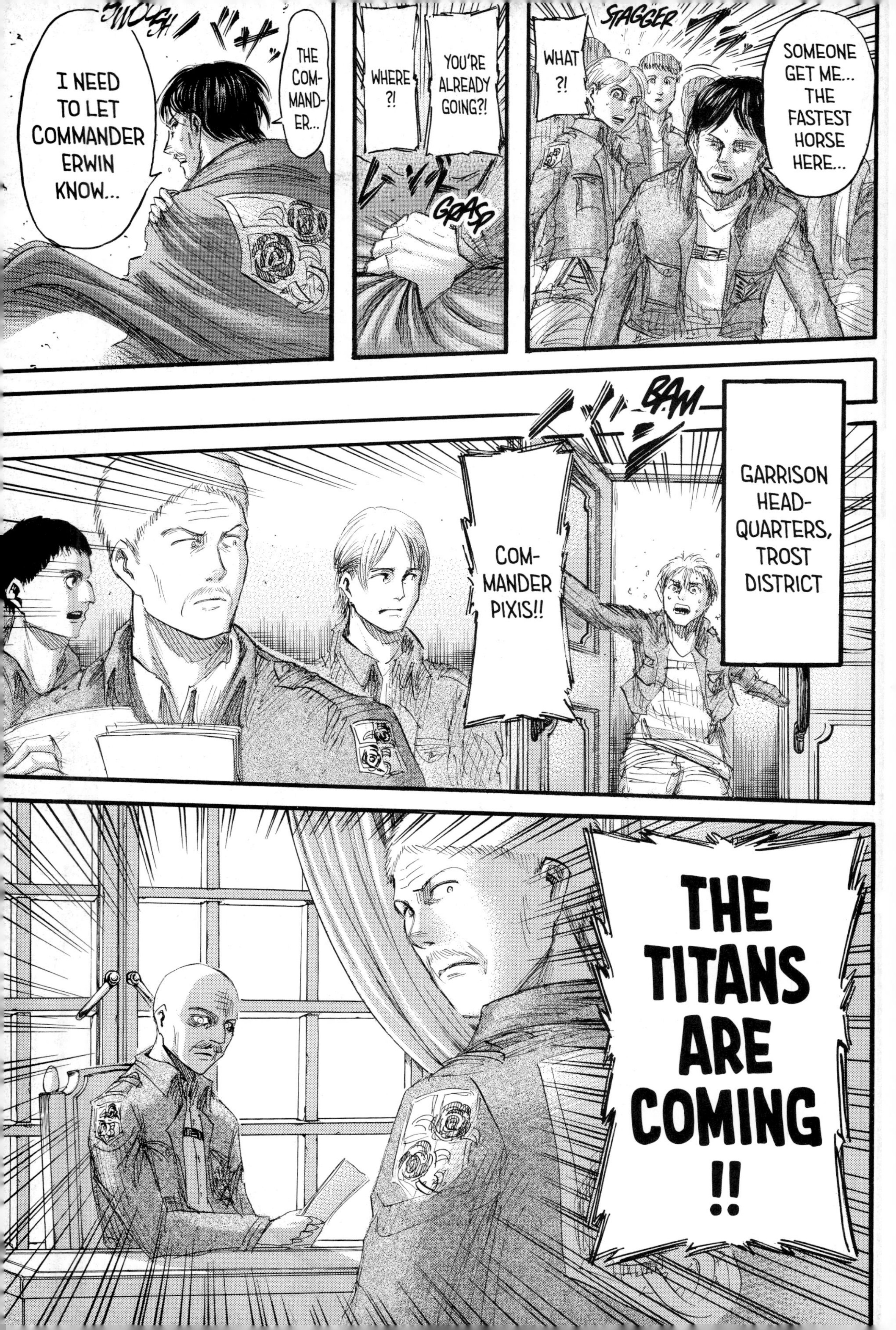
STAGGER
SOMEONE GET ME... THE FASTEST HORSE HERE...
WHAT ?!
YOU'RE ALREADY GOING?!
WHERE ?!
GRASP
THE COM- MAND- ER...
I NEED TO LET COMMANDER ERWIN KNOW...
GARRISON HEAD- QUARTERS, TROST DISTRICT
BAM
COM- MANDER PIXIS!!
THE TITANS ARE COMING !!

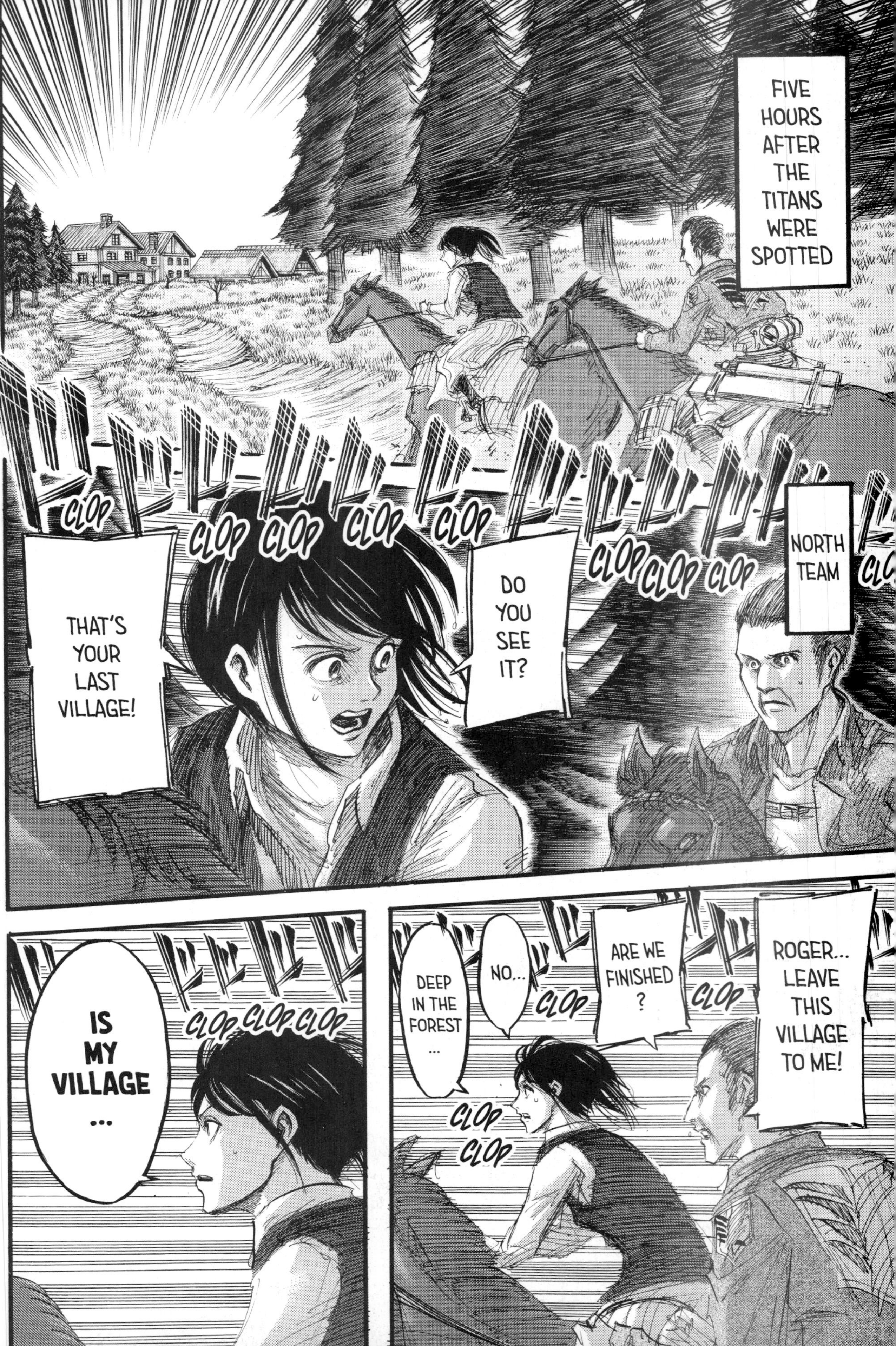
FIVE HOURS AFTER THE TITANS WERE SPOTTED
CLOP CLOP CLOP CLOP CLOP CLOP CLOP CLOP
NORTH TEAM
DO YOU SEE IT?
THAT'S YOUR LAST VILLAGE!
ROGER... LEAVE THIS VILLAGE TO ME!
CLOP
ARE WE FINISHED?
CLOP
NO...
DEEP IN THE FOREST ...
CLOP CLOP
CLOP CLOP CLOP
IS MY VILLAGE ...

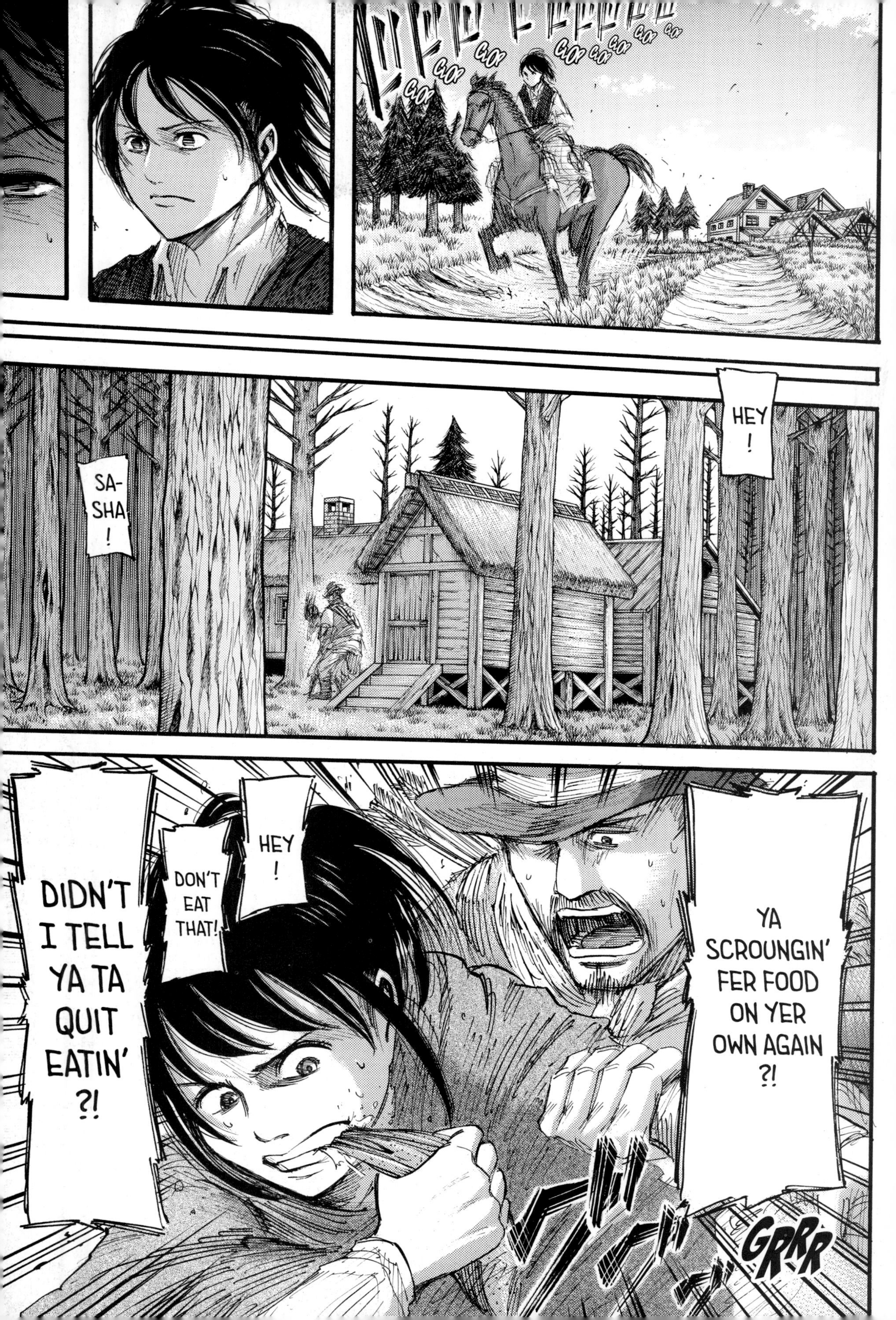
CLOP CLOP CLOP CLOP CLOP CLOP CLOP CLOP
HEY!
SA-SHA!
YA SCROUNGIN' FER FOOD ON YER OWN AGAIN?!
HEY!
DON'T EAT THAT!
DIDN'T I TELL YA TA QUIT EATIN'?!
GRRR

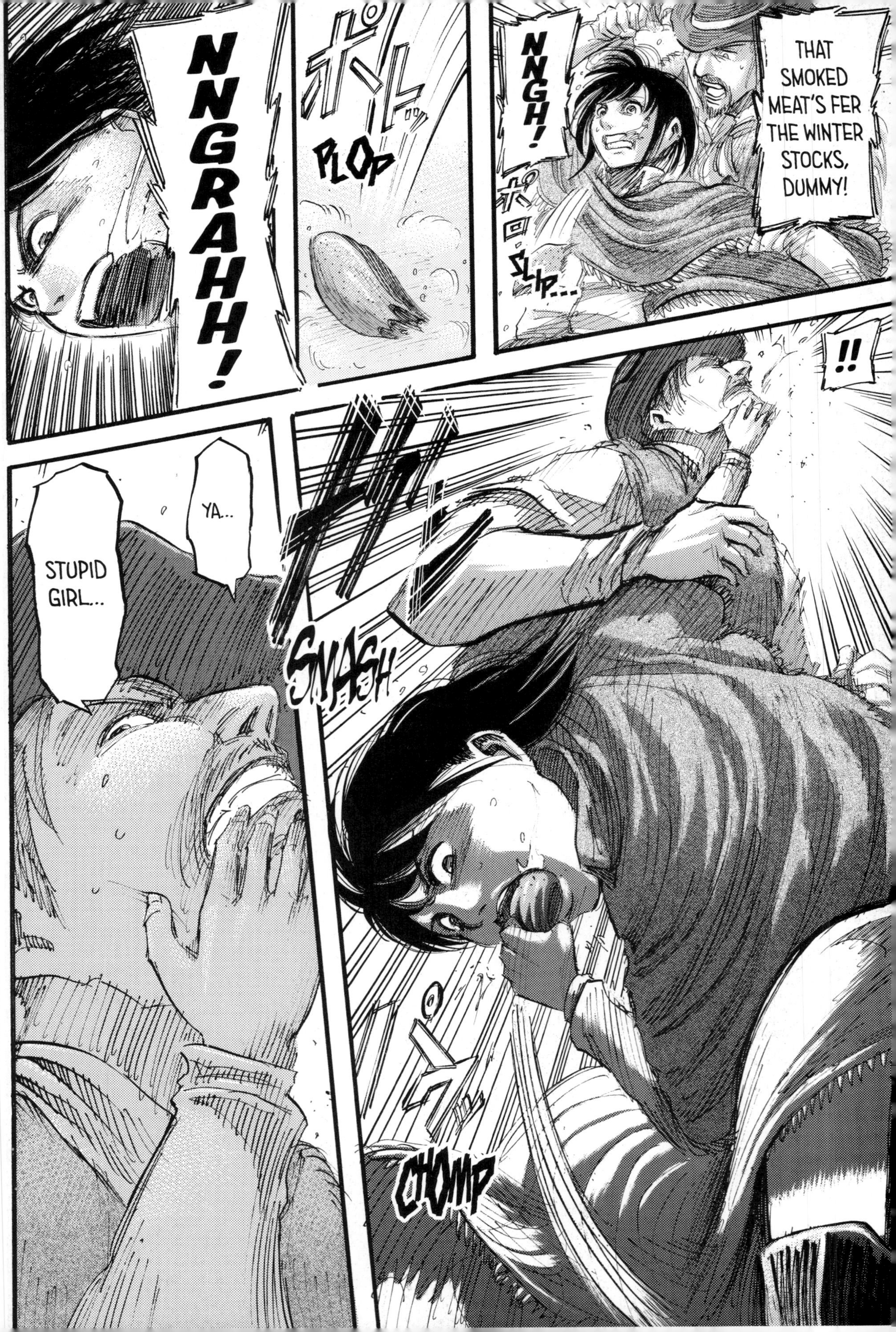
THAT SMOKED MEAT'S FER THE WINTER STOCKS, DUMMY!
NNGH!
SLIP...
PLOP
NNGRAHH!
!!
SMASH
CHOMP
YA...
STUPID GIRL...

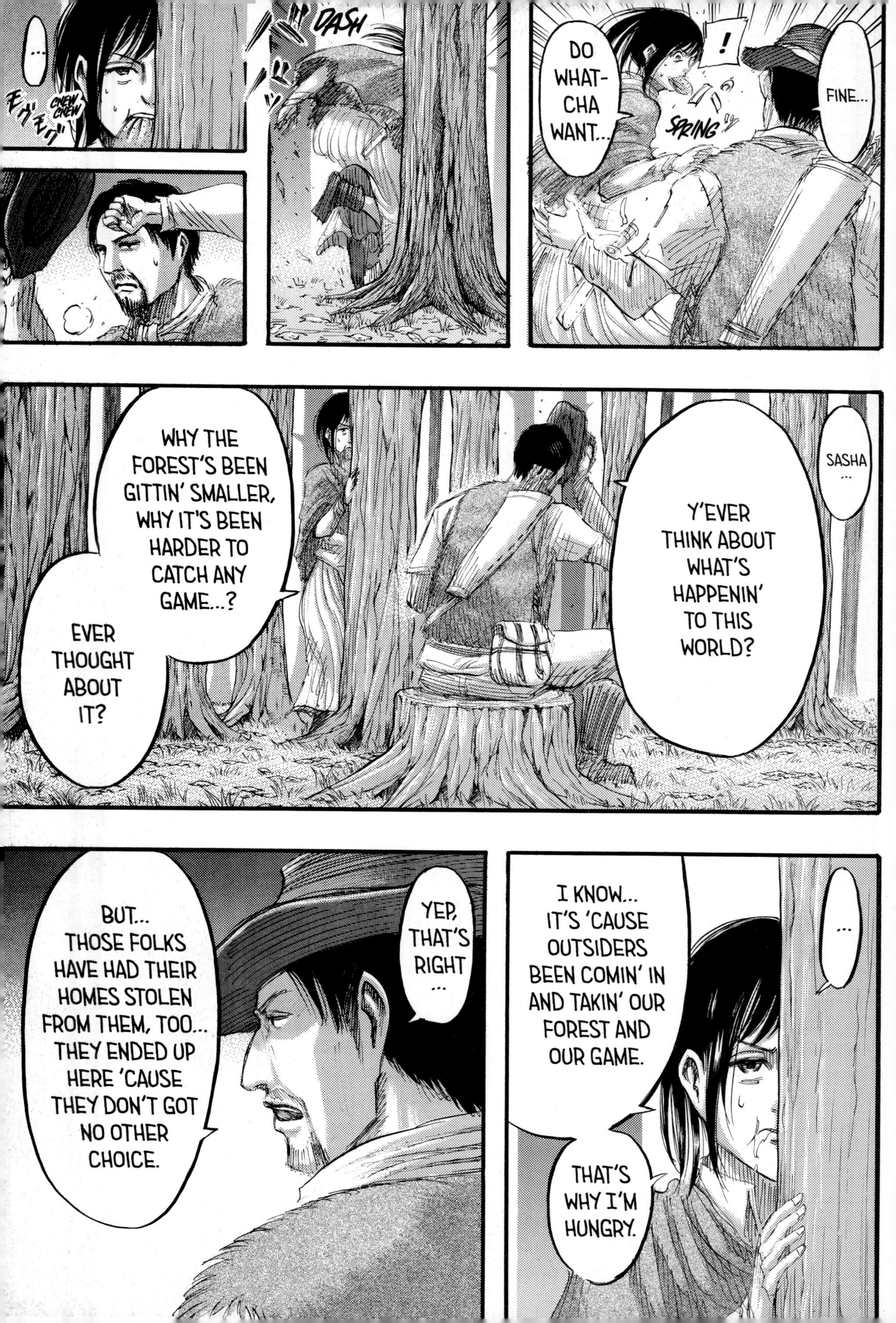
FINE...
!
DO WHAT-CHA WANT...
SPRING
DASH
...
CHEW CHEW
SASHA...
Y'EVER THINK ABOUT WHAT'S HAPPENIN' TO THIS WORLD?
WHY THE FOREST'S BEEN GITTIN' SMALLER, WHY IT'S BEEN HARDER TO CATCH ANY GAME...?
EVER THOUGHT ABOUT IT?
...
I KNOW... IT'S 'CAUSE OUTSIDERS BEEN COMIN' IN AND TAKIN' OUR FOREST AND OUR GAME.
THAT'S WHY I'M HUNGRY.
YEP, THAT'S RIGHT...
BUT... THOSE FOLKS HAVE HAD THEIR HOMES STOLEN FROM THEM, TOO... THEY ENDED UP HERE 'CAUSE THEY DON'T GOT NO OTHER CHOICE.

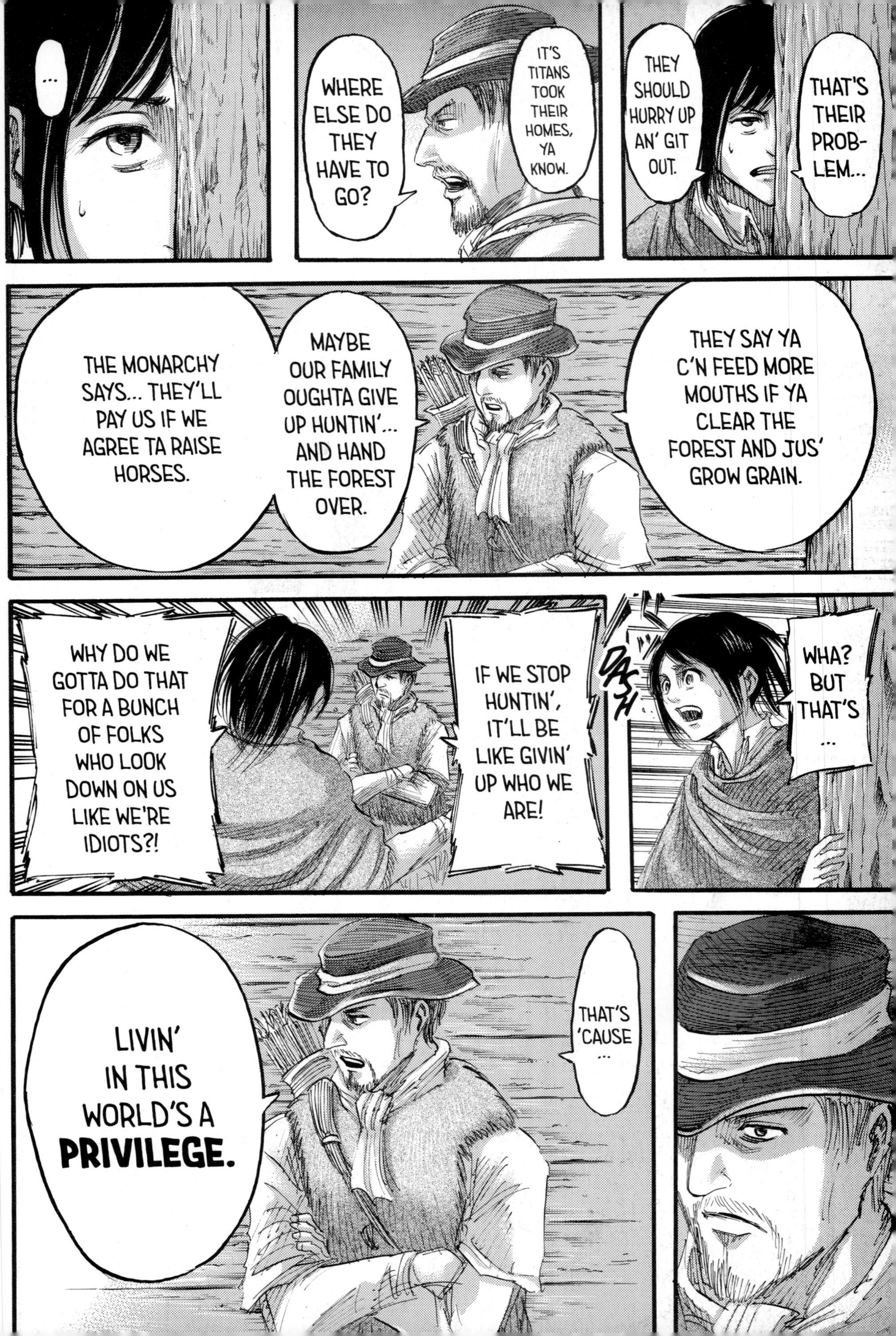
THAT'S THEIR PROB-LEM...
THEY SHOULD HURRY UP AN' GIT OUT.
IT'S TITANS TOOK THEIR HOMES, YA KNOW.
WHERE ELSE DO THEY HAVE TO GO?
...
THEY SAY YA C'N FEED MORE MOUTHS IF YA CLEAR THE FOREST AND JUS' GROW GRAIN.
MAYBE OUR FAMILY OUGHTA GIVE UP HUNTIN'... AND HAND THE FOREST OVER.
THE MONARCHY SAYS... THEY'LL PAY US IF WE AGREE TA RAISE HORSES.
DASH
WHA? BUT THAT'S ...
IF WE STOP HUNTIN', IT'LL BE LIKE GIVIN' UP WHO WE ARE!
WHY DO WE GOTTA DO THAT FOR A BUNCH OF FOLKS WHO LOOK DOWN ON US LIKE WE'RE IDIOTS?!
THAT'S 'CAUSE ...
LIVIN' IN THIS WORLD'S A **PRIVILEGE.**

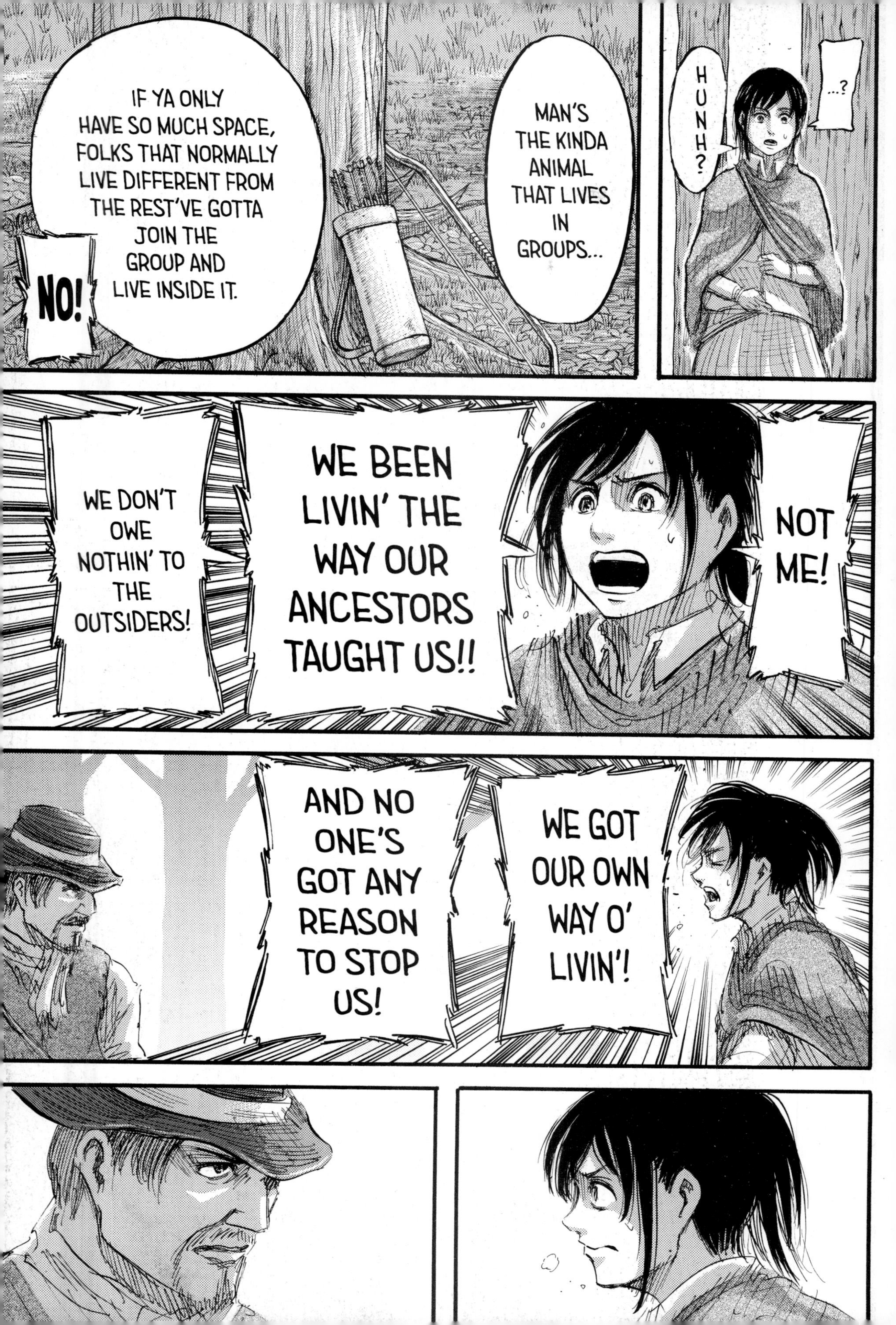
...?
HUNH?
MAN'S THE KINDA ANIMAL THAT LIVES IN GROUPS...
IF YA ONLY HAVE SO MUCH SPACE, FOLKS THAT NORMALLY LIVE DIFFERENT FROM THE REST'VE GOTTA JOIN THE GROUP AND LIVE INSIDE IT.
NO!
NOT ME!
WE BEEN LIVIN' THE WAY OUR ANCESTORS TAUGHT US!!
WE DON'T OWE NOTHIN' TO THE OUTSIDERS!
WE GOT OUR OWN WAY O' LIVIN'!
AND NO ONE'S GOT ANY REASON TO STOP US!

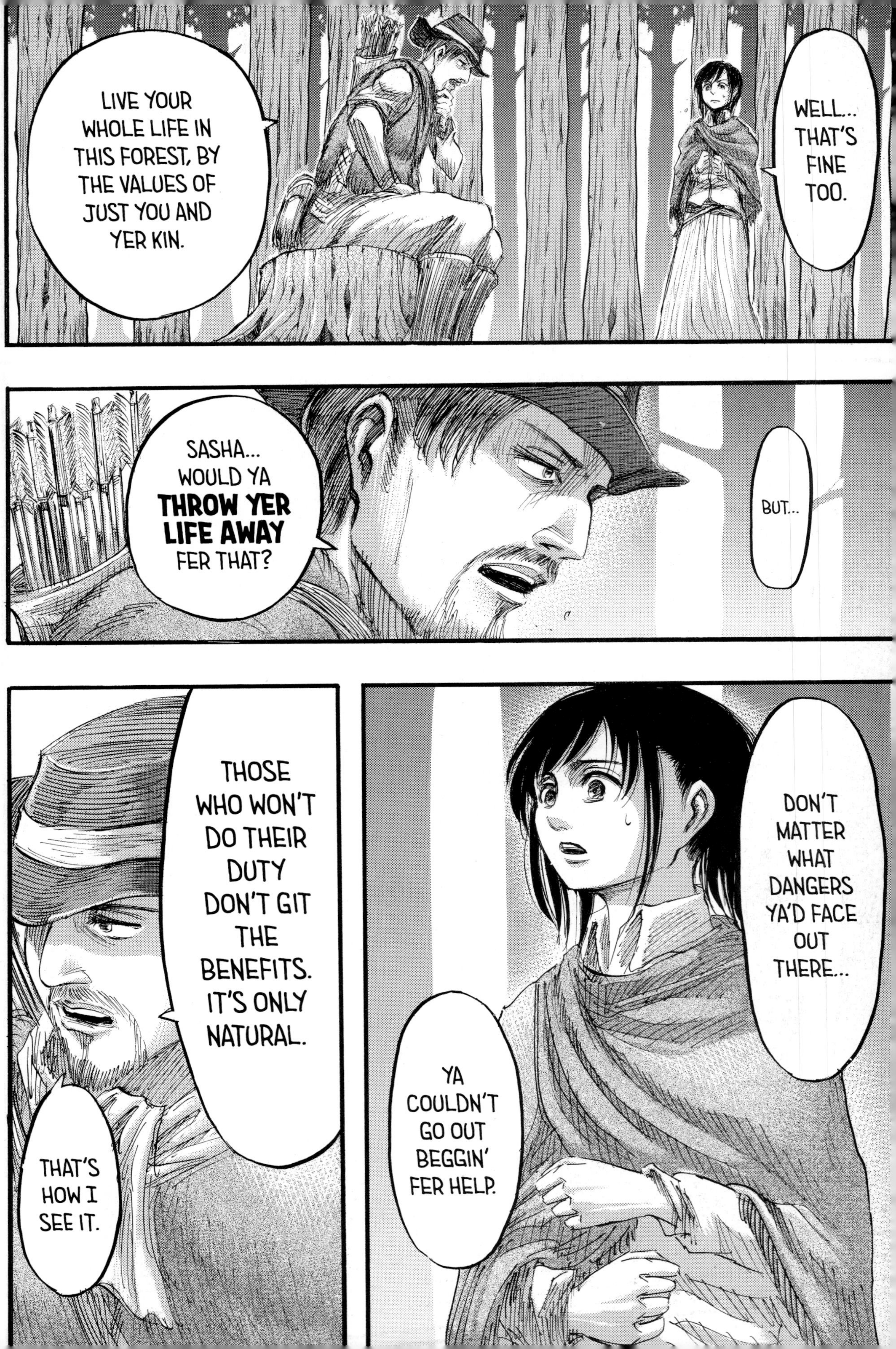
WELL... THAT'S FINE TOO.
LIVE YOUR WHOLE LIFE IN THIS FOREST, BY THE VALUES OF JUST YOU AND YER KIN.
BUT...
SASHA... WOULD YA **THROW YER LIFE AWAY** FER THAT?
DON'T MATTER WHAT DANGERS YA'D FACE OUT THERE...
YA COULDN'T GO OUT BEGGIN' FER HELP.
THOSE WHO WON'T DO THEIR DUTY DON'T GIT THE BENEFITS. IT'S ONLY NATURAL.
THAT'S HOW I SEE IT.

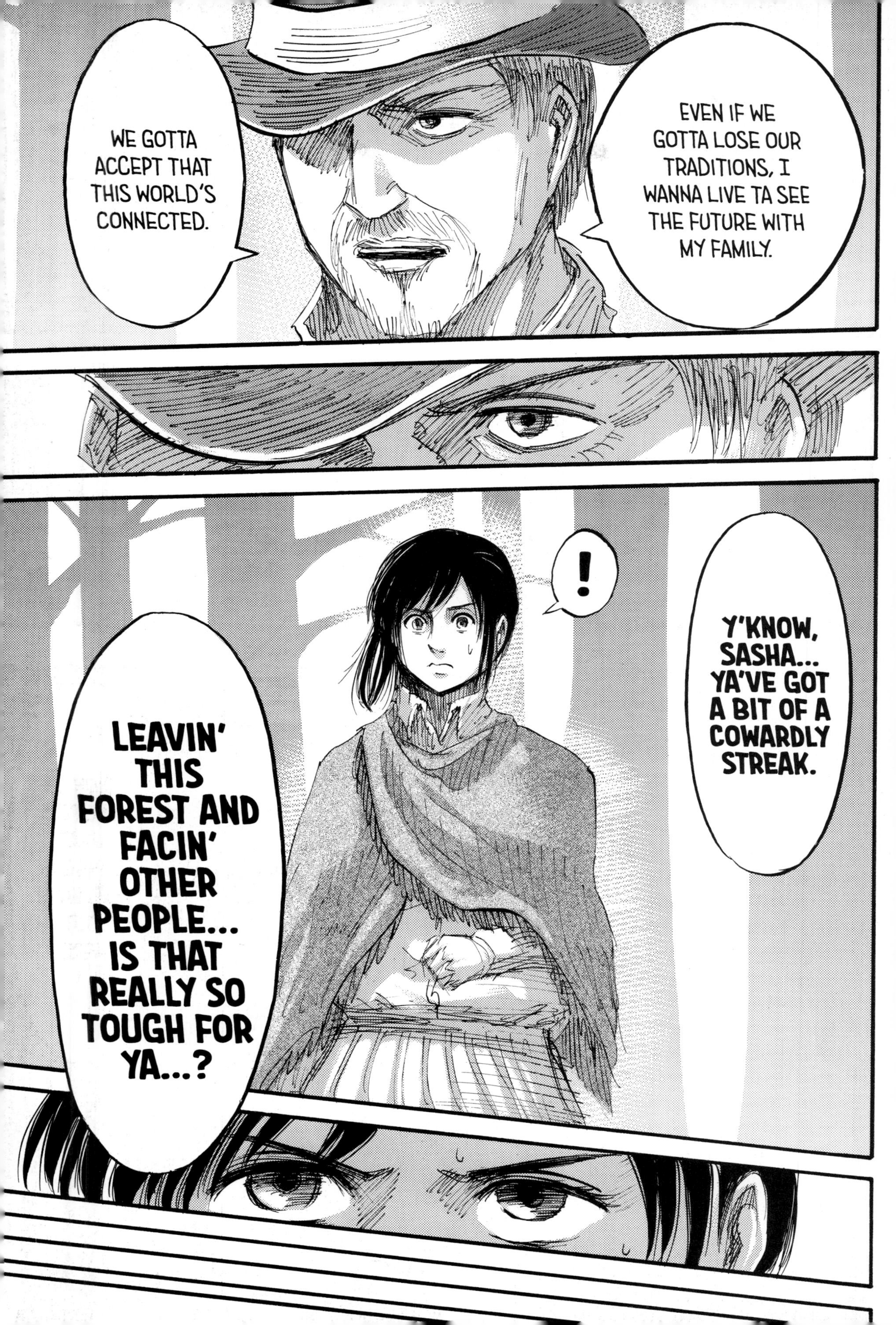
EVEN IF WE GOTTA LOSE OUR TRADITIONS, I WANNA LIVE TA SEE THE FUTURE WITH MY FAMILY.
WE GOTTA ACCEPT THAT THIS WORLD'S CONNECTED.
!
Y'KNOW, SASHA... YA'VE GOT A BIT OF A COWARDLY STREAK.
LEAVIN' THIS FOREST AND FACIN' OTHER PEOPLE... IS THAT REALLY SO TOUGH FOR YA...?

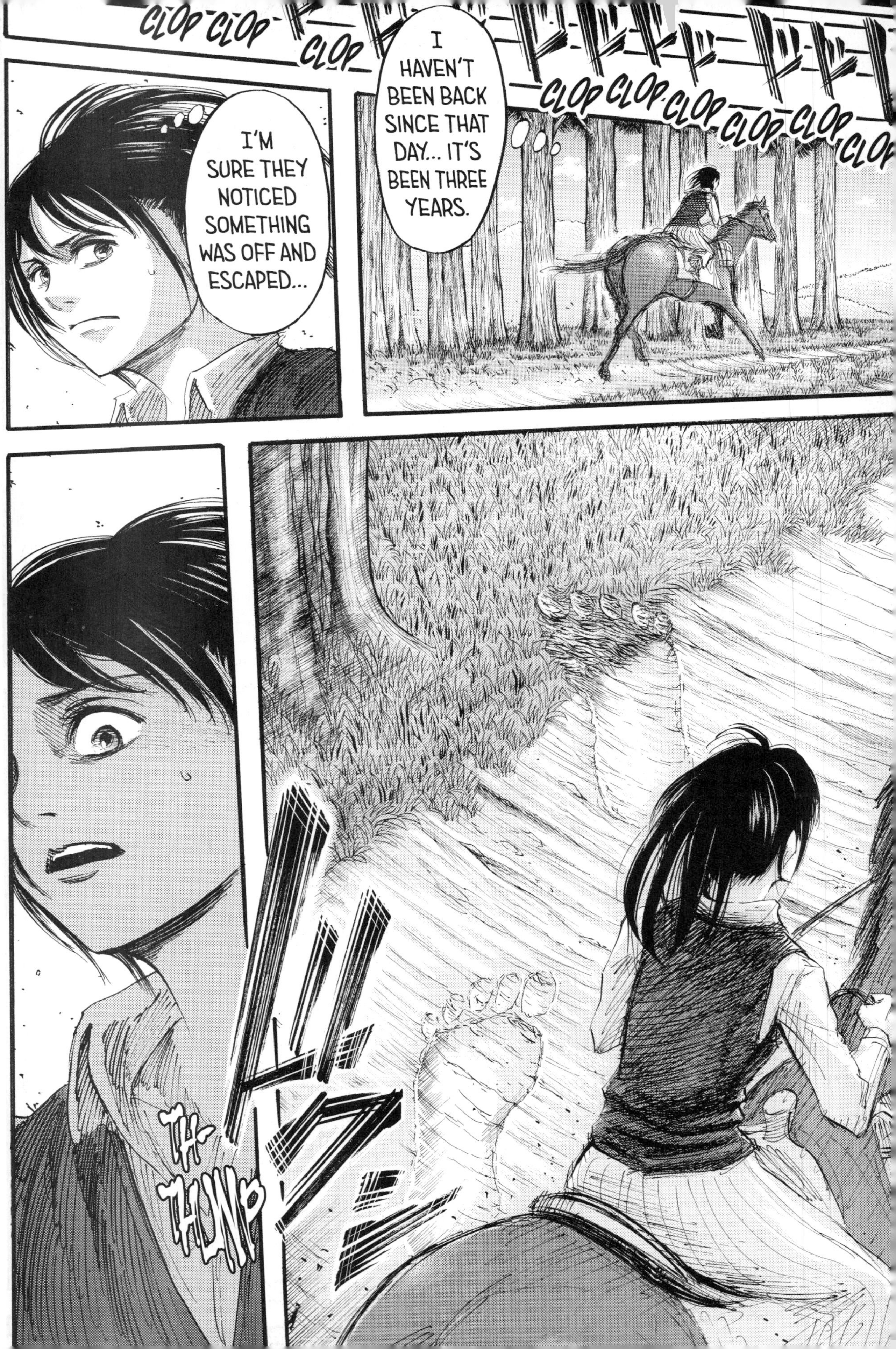
CLOP CLOP CLOP
CLOP CLOP CLOP CLOP CLOP CLOP
I HAVEN'T BEEN BACK SINCE THAT DAY... IT'S BEEN THREE YEARS.
I'M SURE THEY NOTICED SOMETHING WAS OFF AND ESCAPED...
TH-THUMP

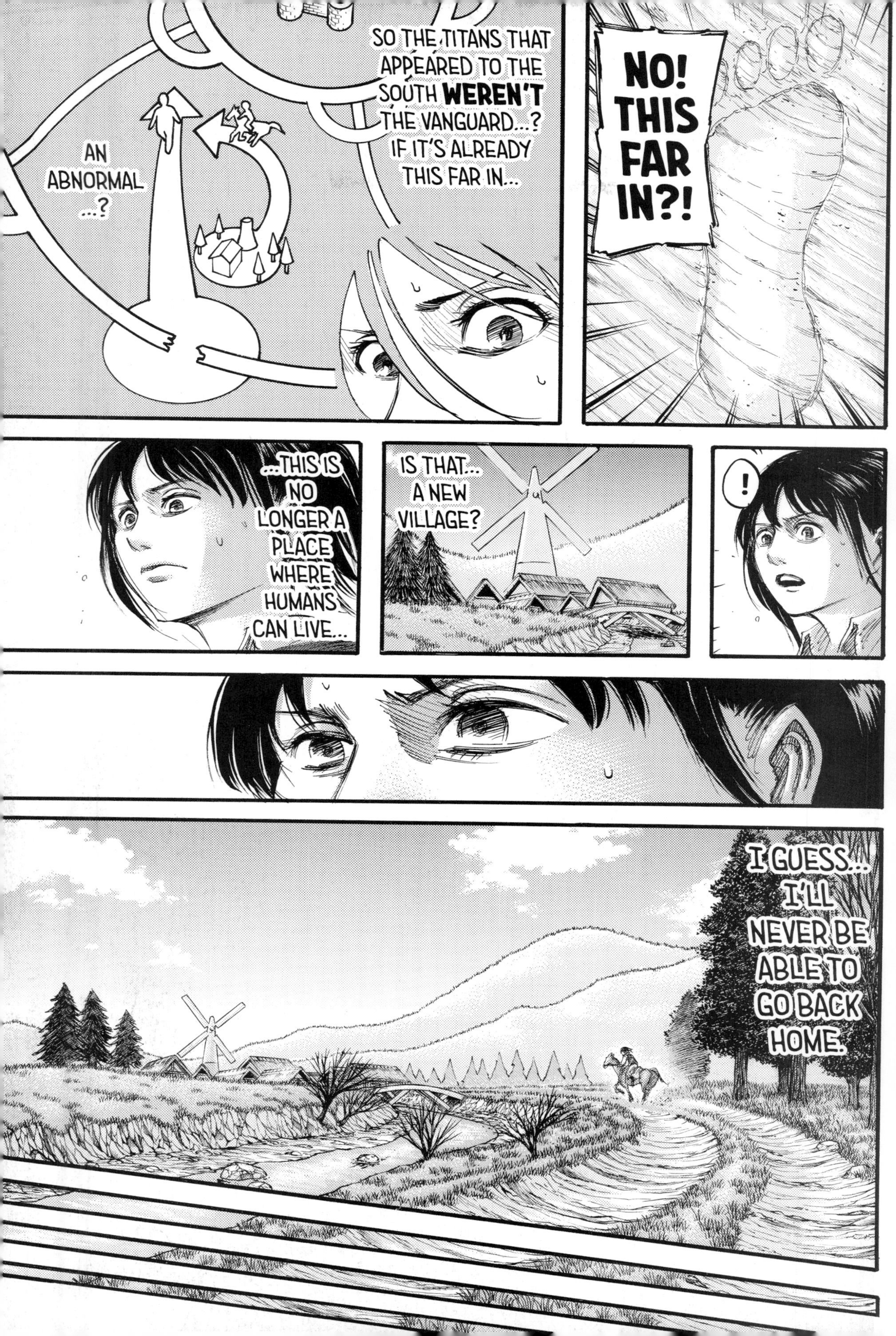
NO! THIS FAR IN?!
SO THE TITANS THAT APPEARED TO THE SOUTH WEREN'T THE VANGUARD...? IF IT'S ALREADY THIS FAR IN...
AN ABNORMAL ...?
!
IS THAT... A NEW VILLAGE?
...THIS IS NO LONGER A PLACE WHERE HUMANS CAN LIVE...
I GUESS... I'LL NEVER BE ABLE TO GO BACK HOME.

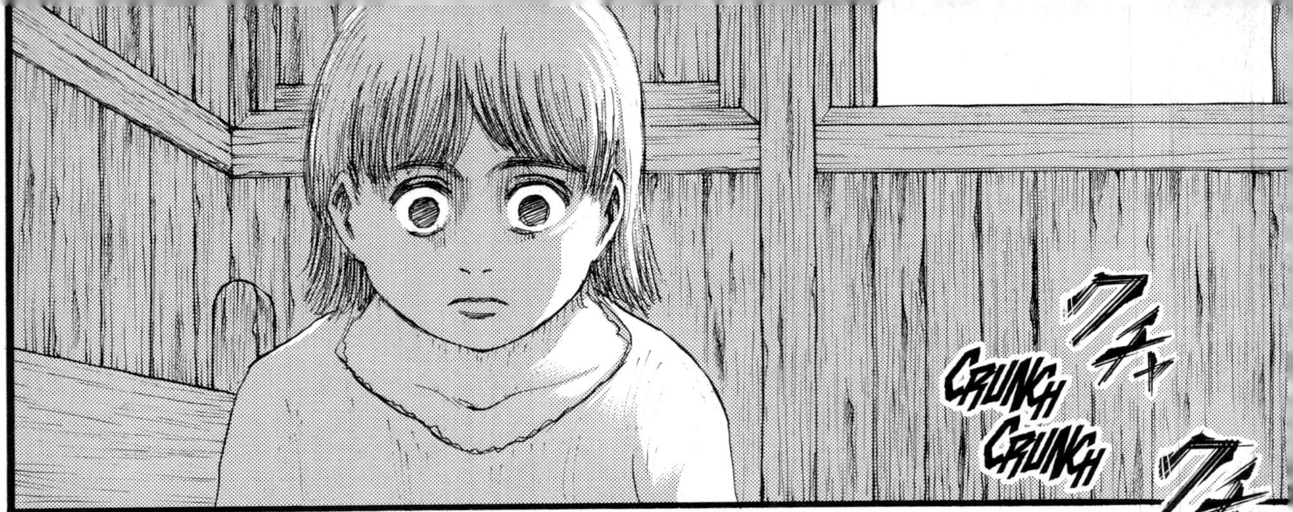
クチャ
CRUNCH
CRUNCH
クチャ

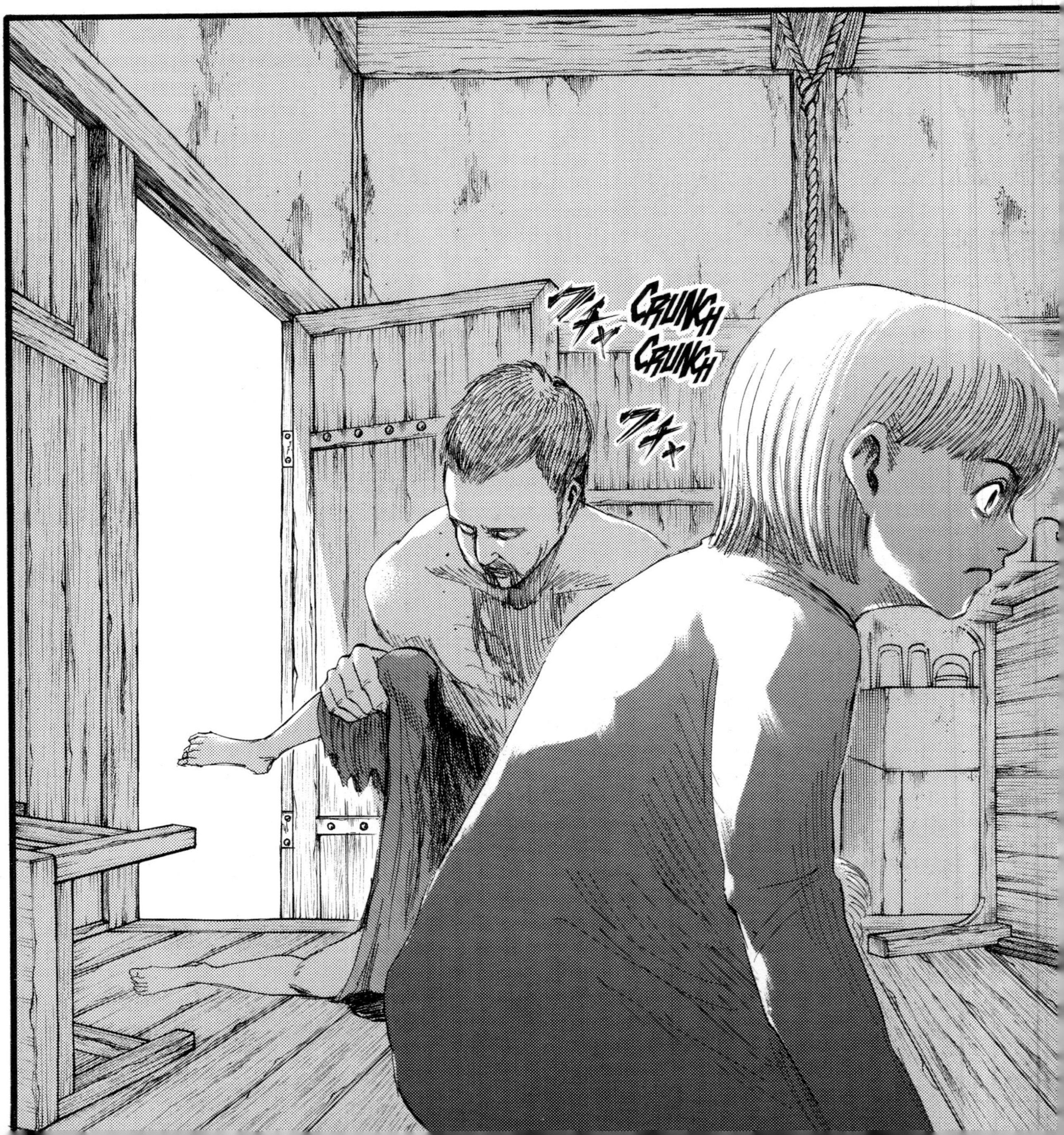
クチャ
CRUNCH
CRUNCH
クチャ

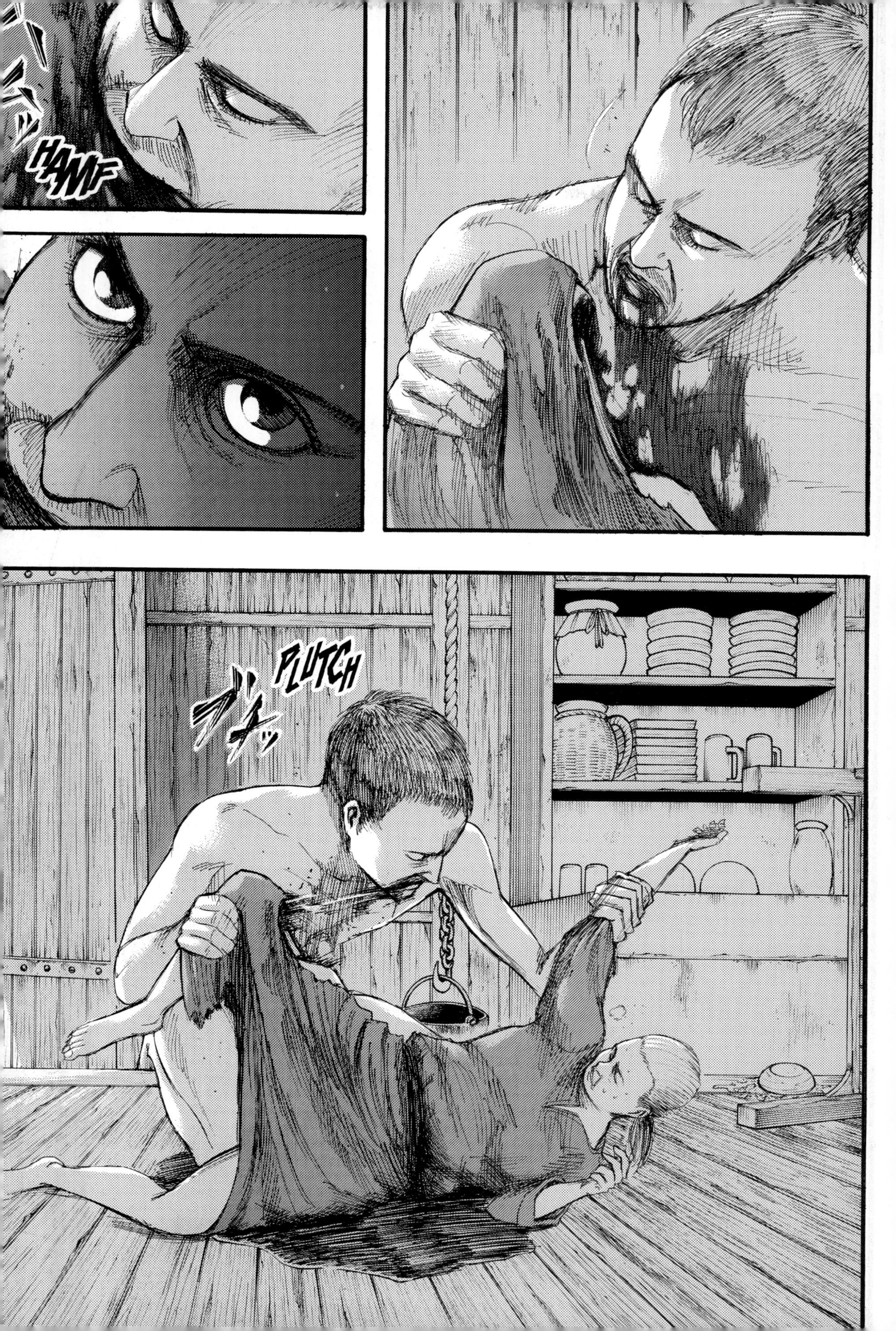
HAMF
PLUTCH

HAAH
HAAH
ゴッ
CLONK
HAAH
HAAH
HAAH
HAAH

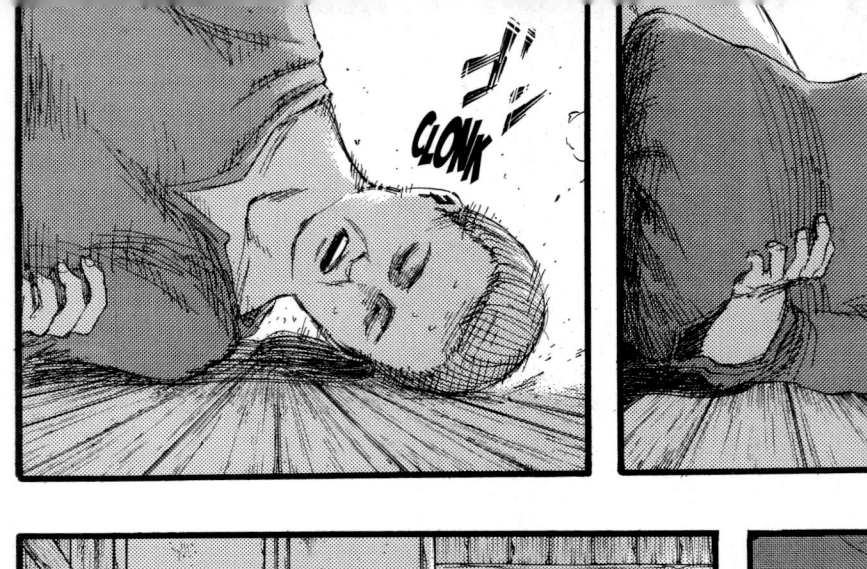

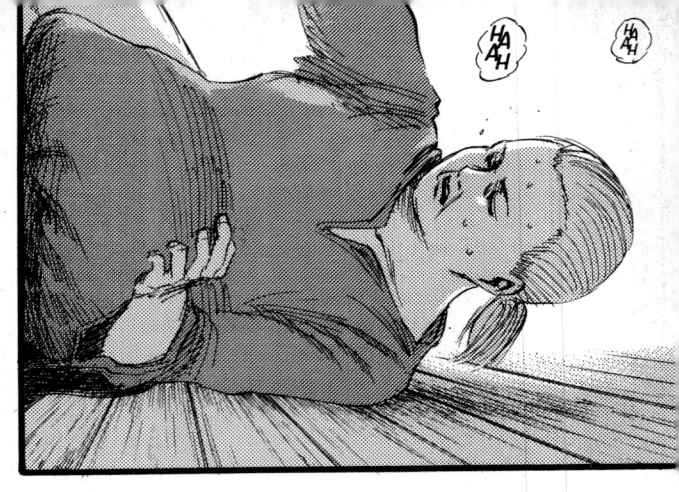

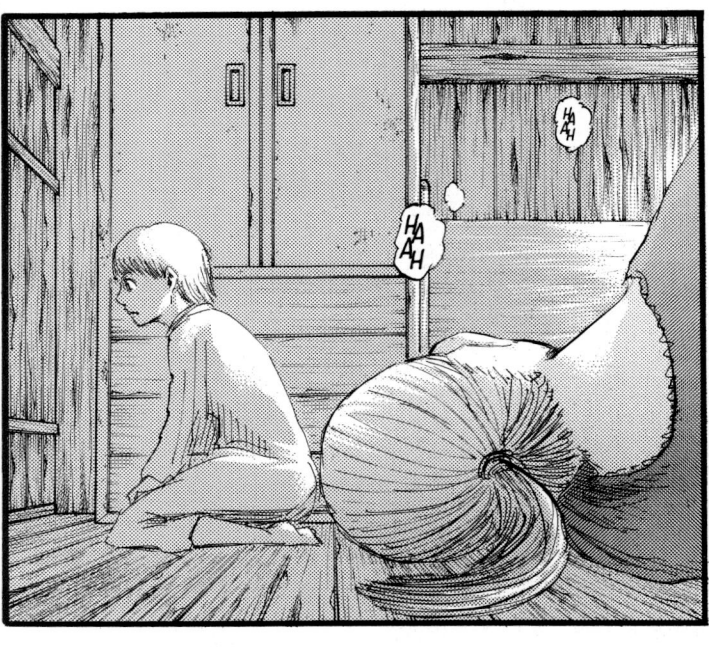

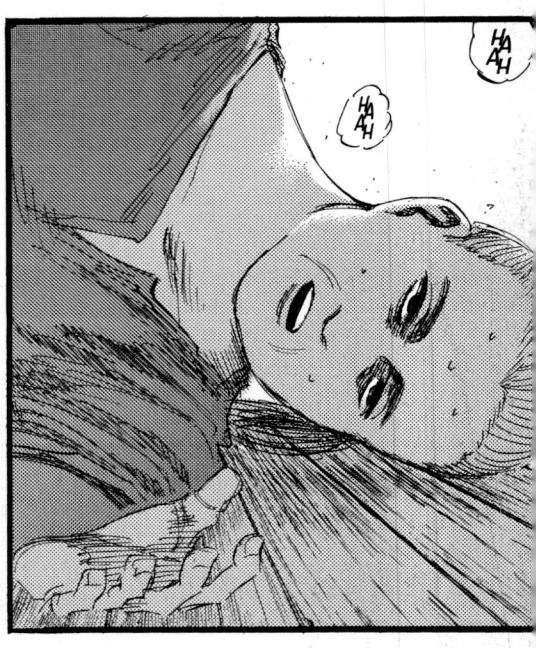

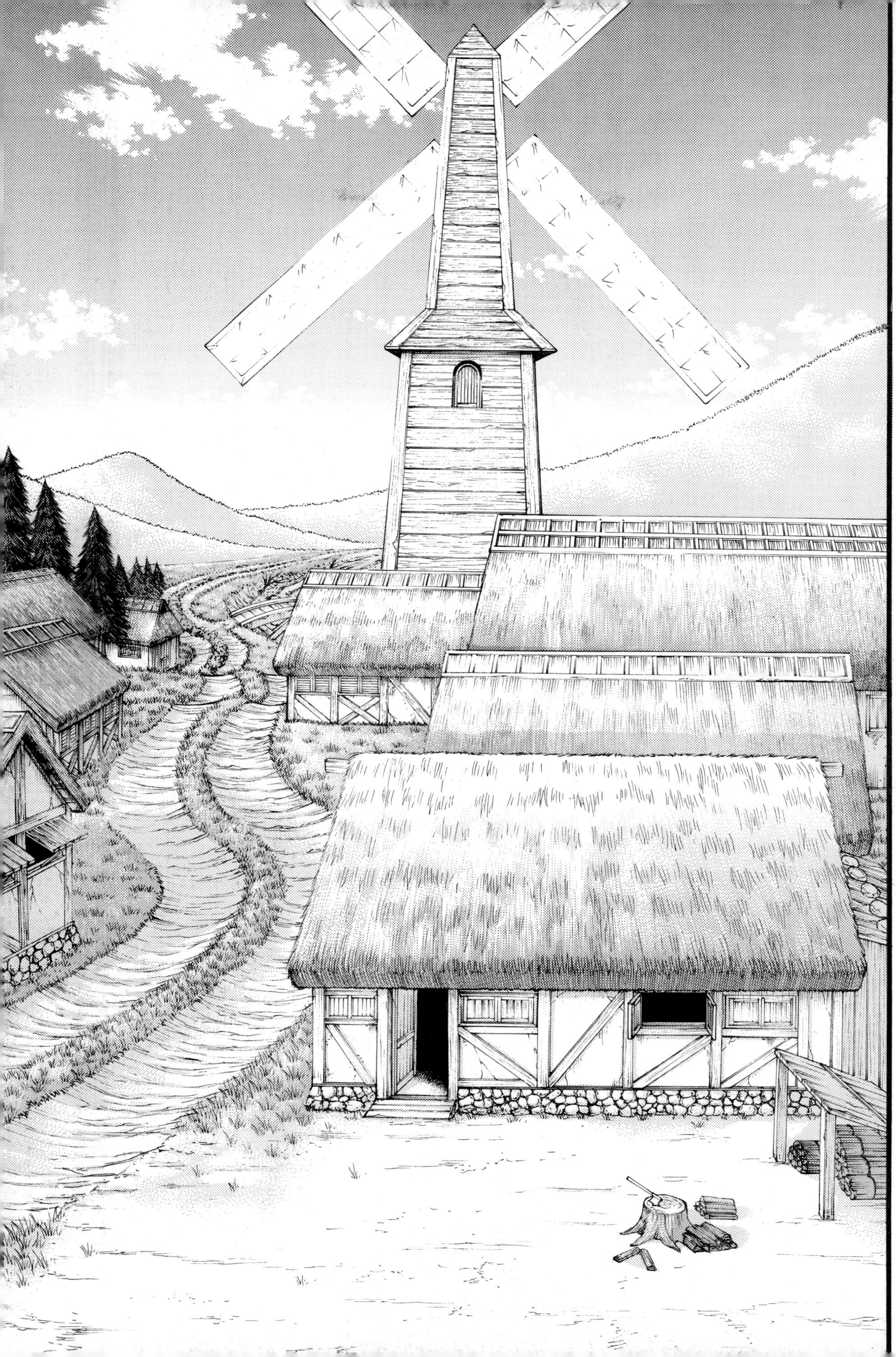

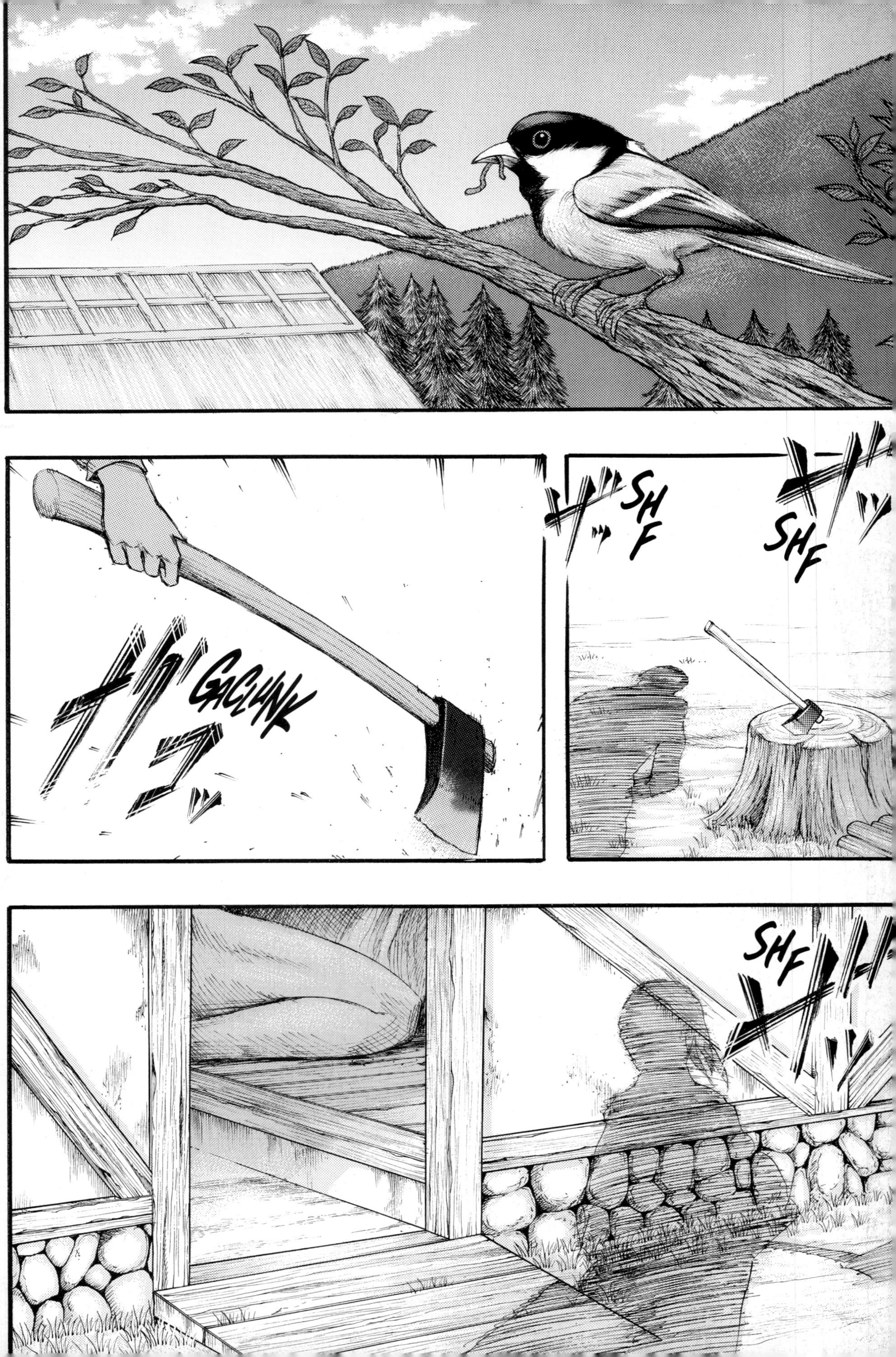

SHF
SHF
GACLUNK
SHF

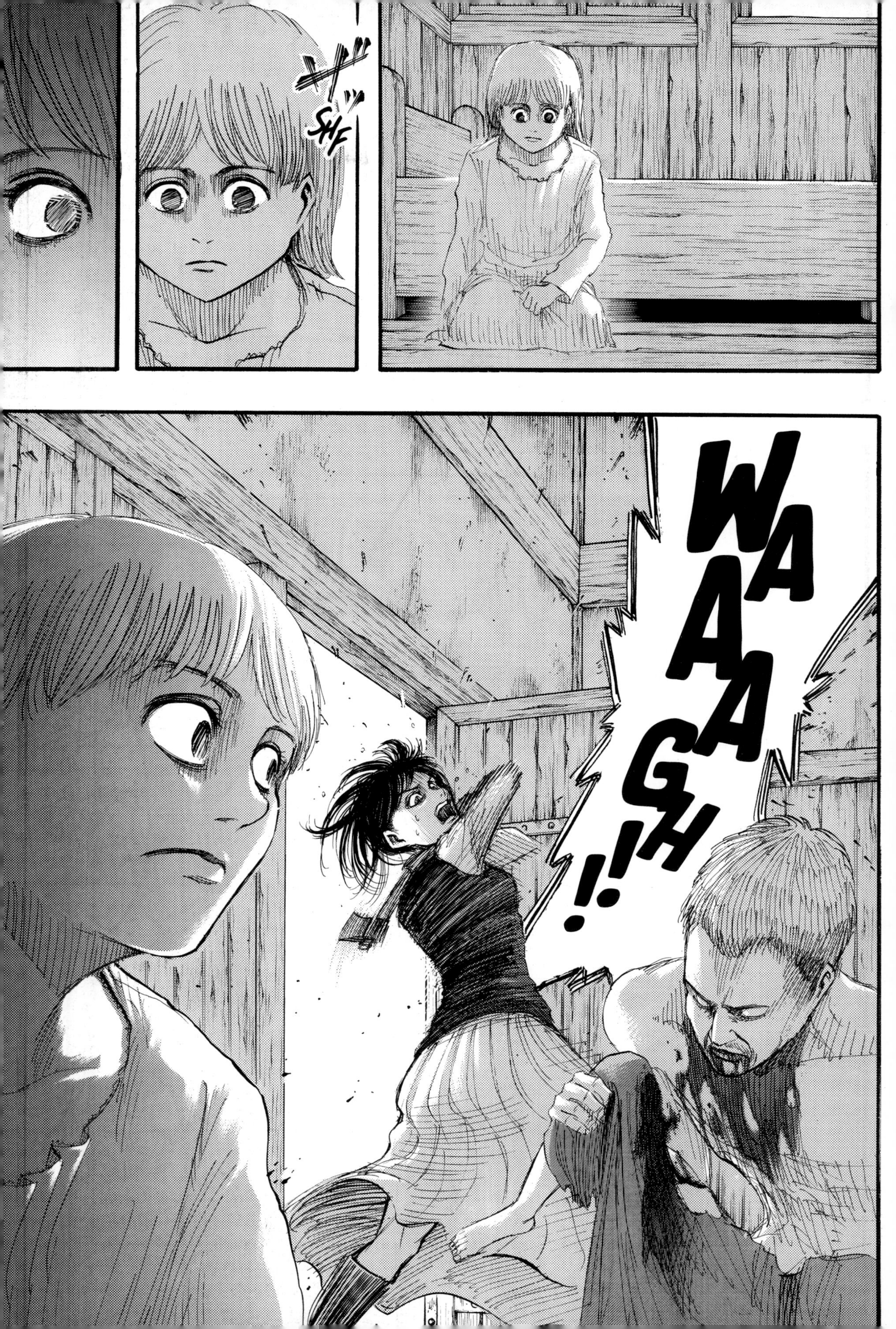
SHF
WAAAGH!!

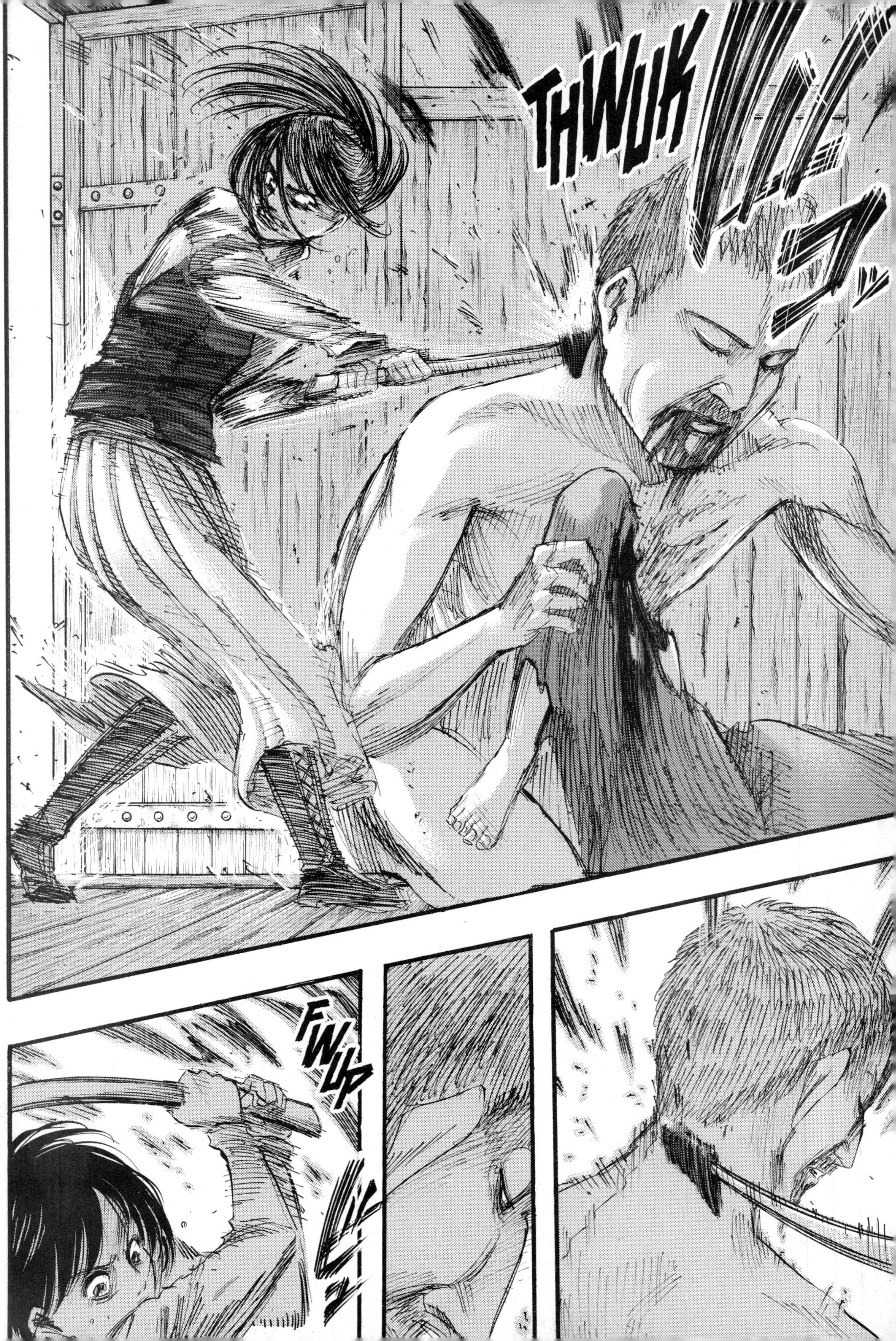
THWUK
FWUP

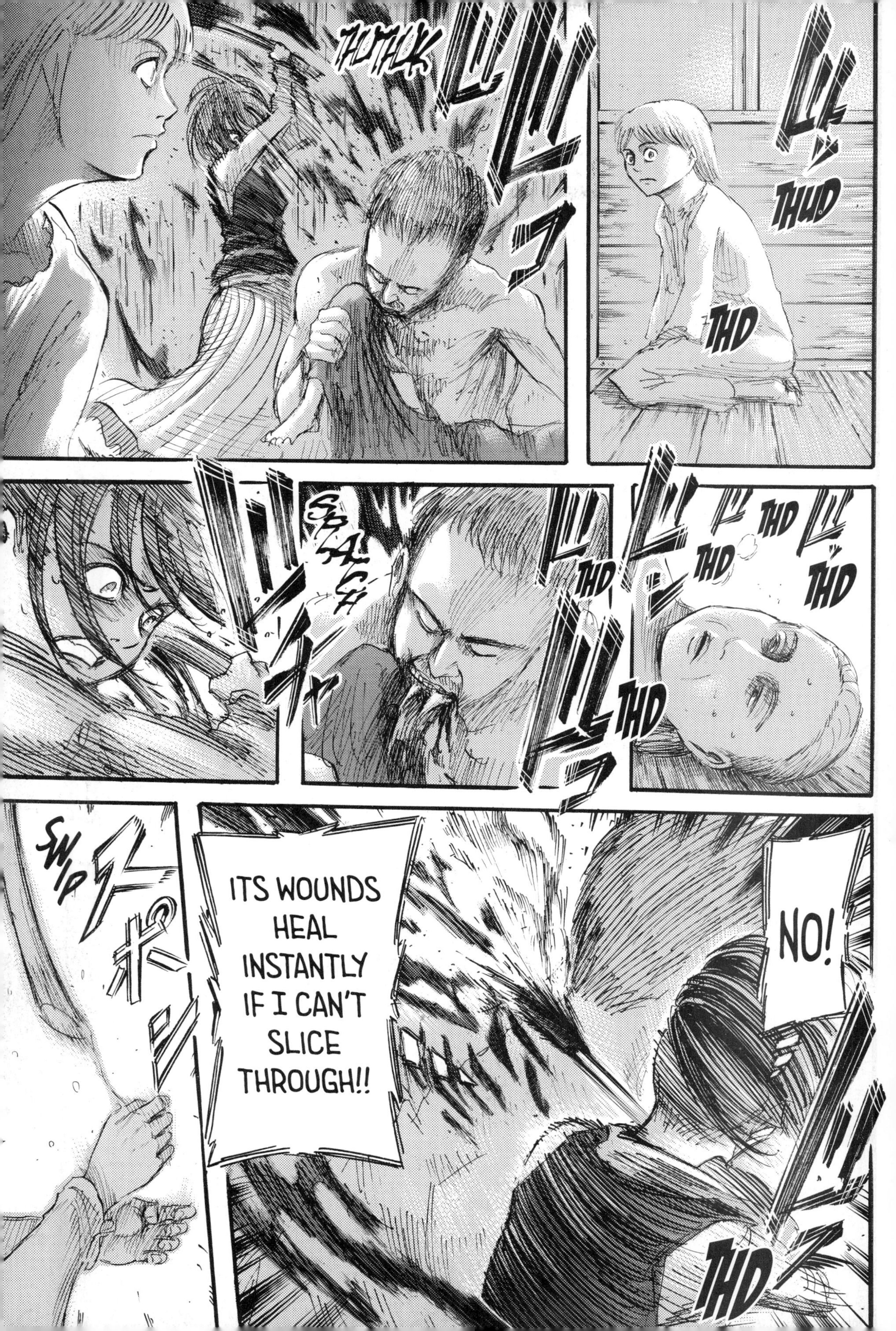
THUD
THD
THTHK
THD
THD
THD
THD
THD
THD
SPLACH
NO!
THD
ITS WOUNDS HEAL INSTANTLY IF I CAN'T SLICE THROUGH!!
SNIP

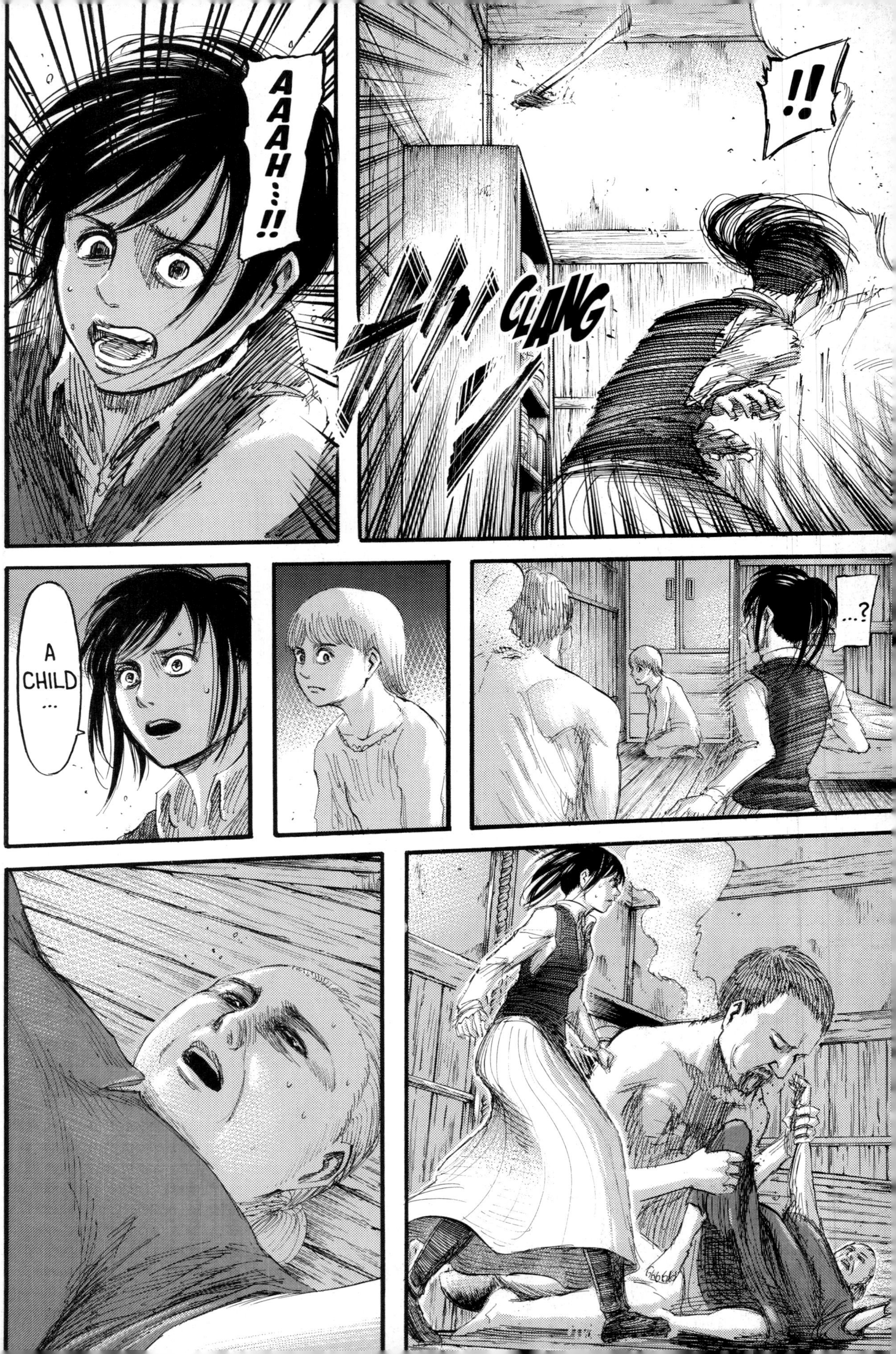
!!
CLANG
AAAH...!!
...?
A CHILD ...

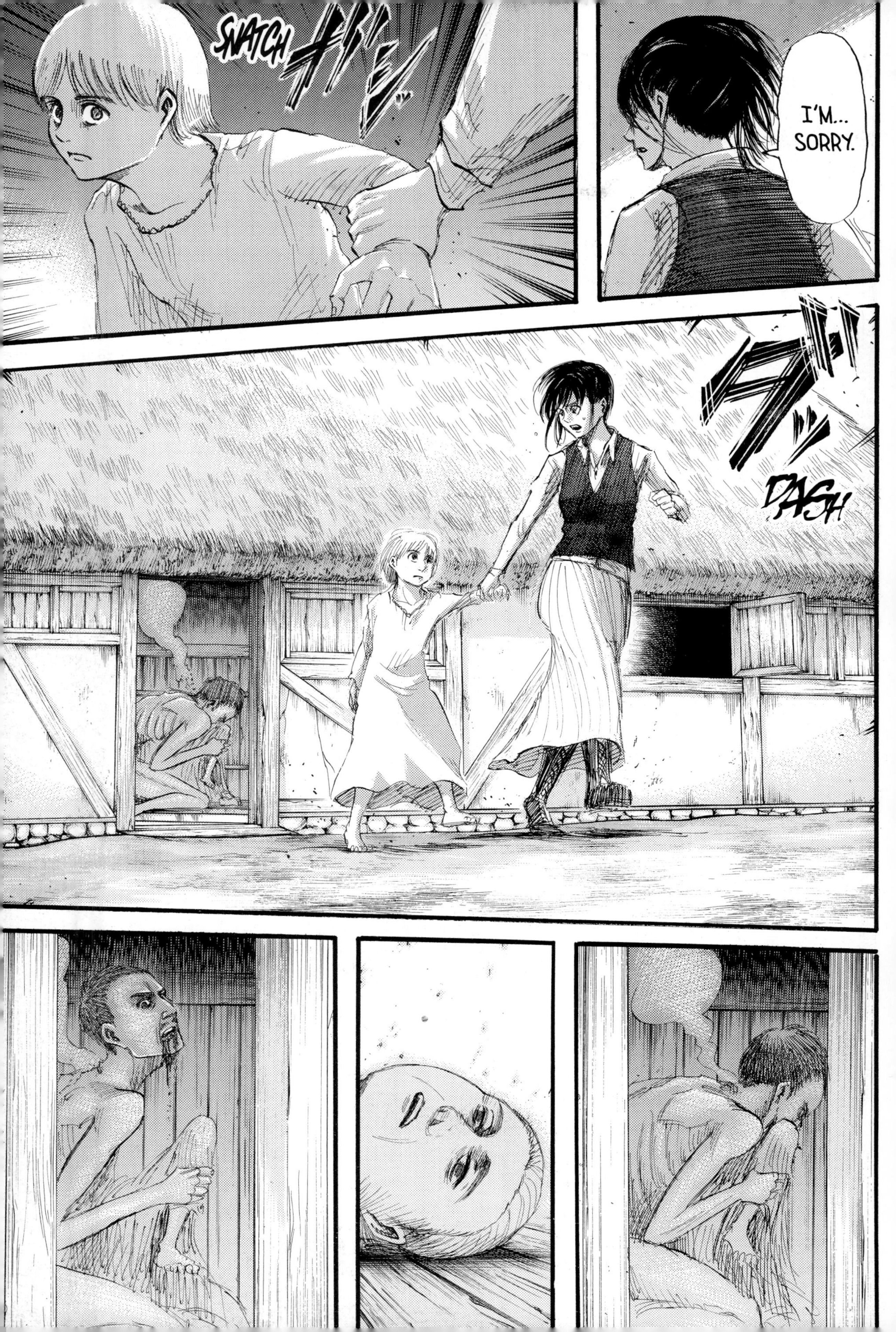
I'M... SORRY.
SNATCH
DASH

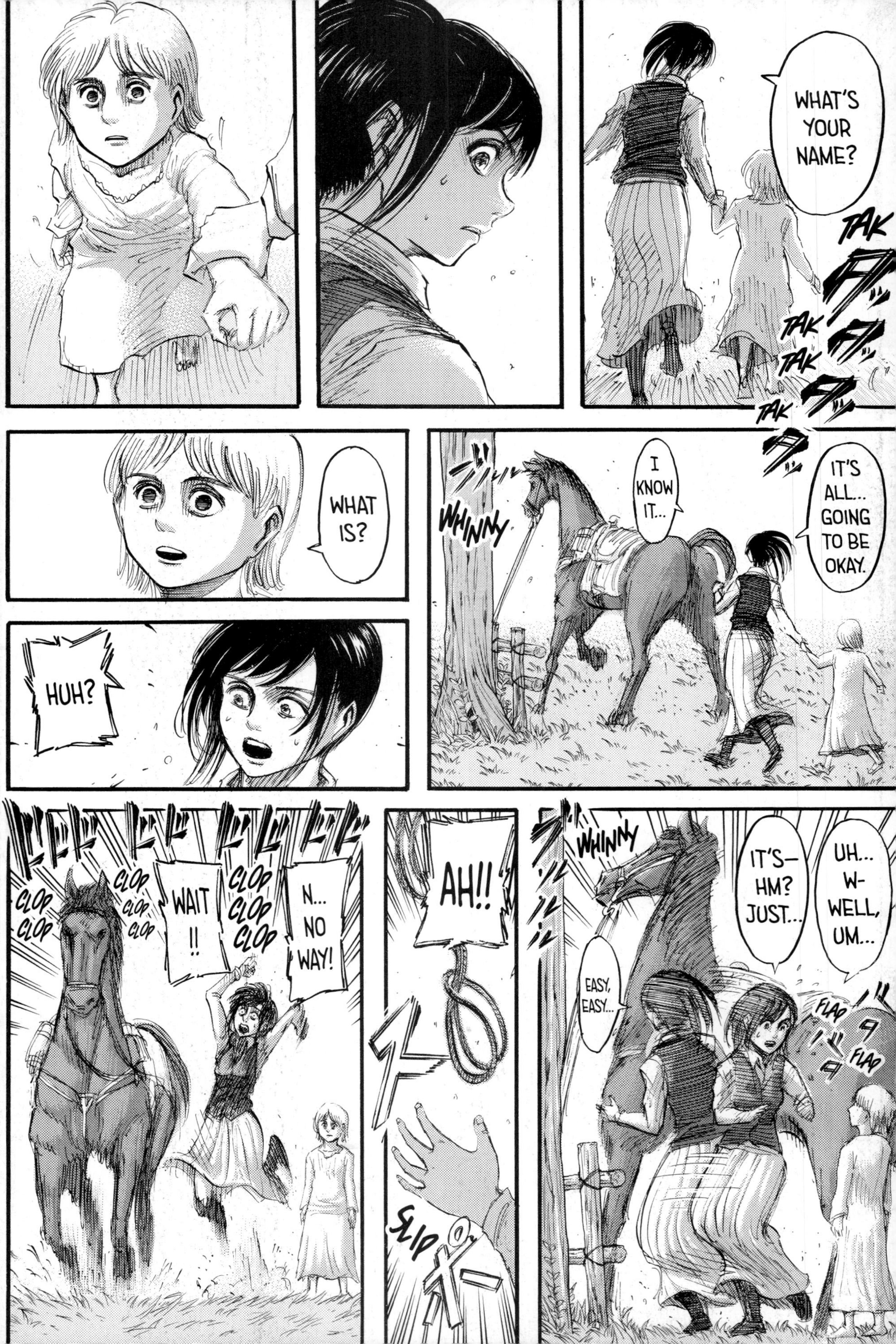
WHAT'S YOUR NAME?
TAK
TAK
TAK
TAK
IT'S ALL... GOING TO BE OKAY.
I KNOW IT...
WHINNY
WHAT IS?
HUH?
UH... W-WELL, UM...
IT'S— HM? JUST...
WHINNY
FLAP
FLAP
EASY, EASY...
AH!!
SLIP
N... NO WAY!
CLOP CLOP CLOP
WAIT!!
CLOP CLOP CLOP
CLOP CLOP

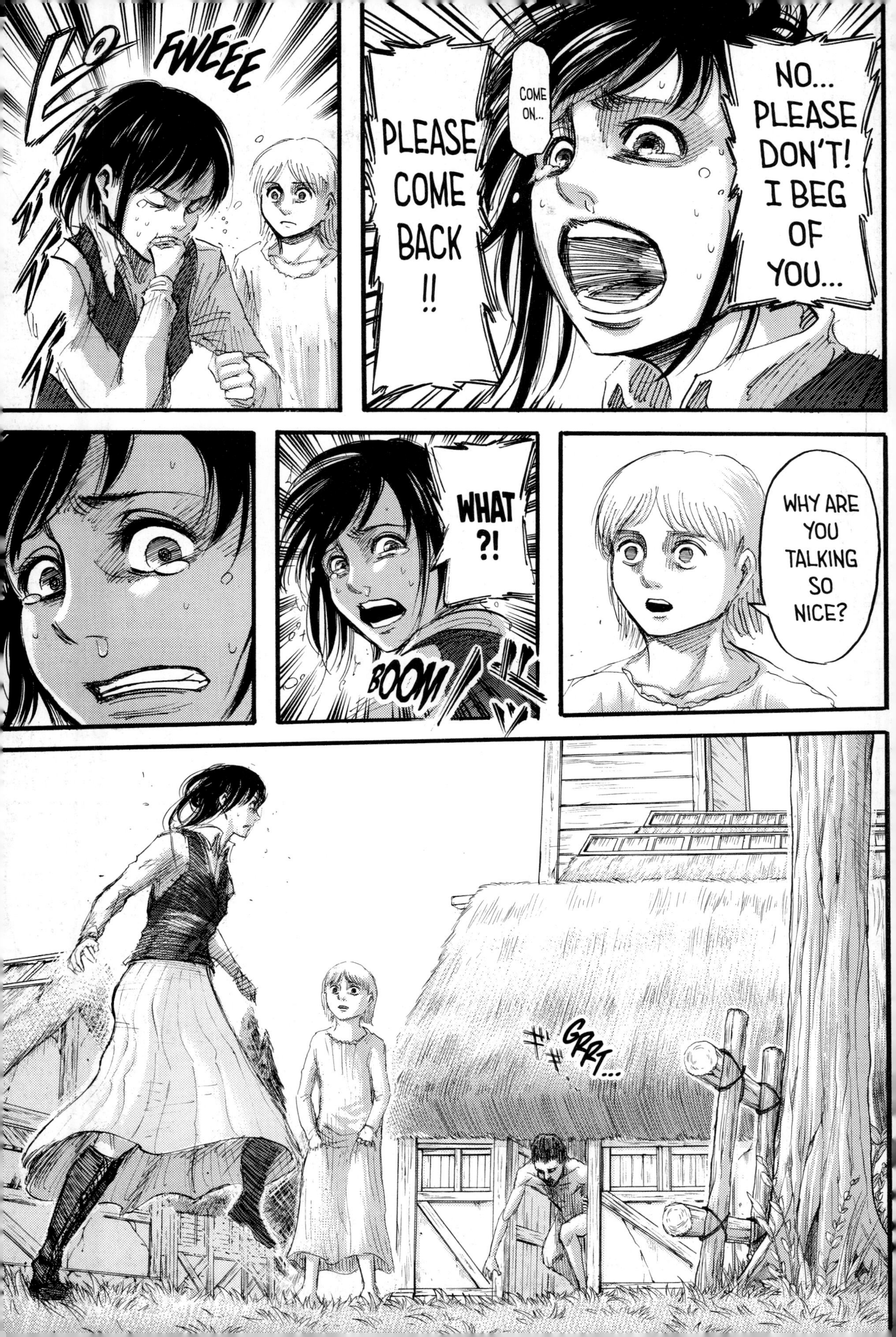
NO... PLEASE DON'T! I BEG OF YOU...
COME ON...
PLEASE COME BACK !!
FWEEE
WHY ARE YOU TALKING SO NICE?
WHAT ?!
BOOM
GRRT...

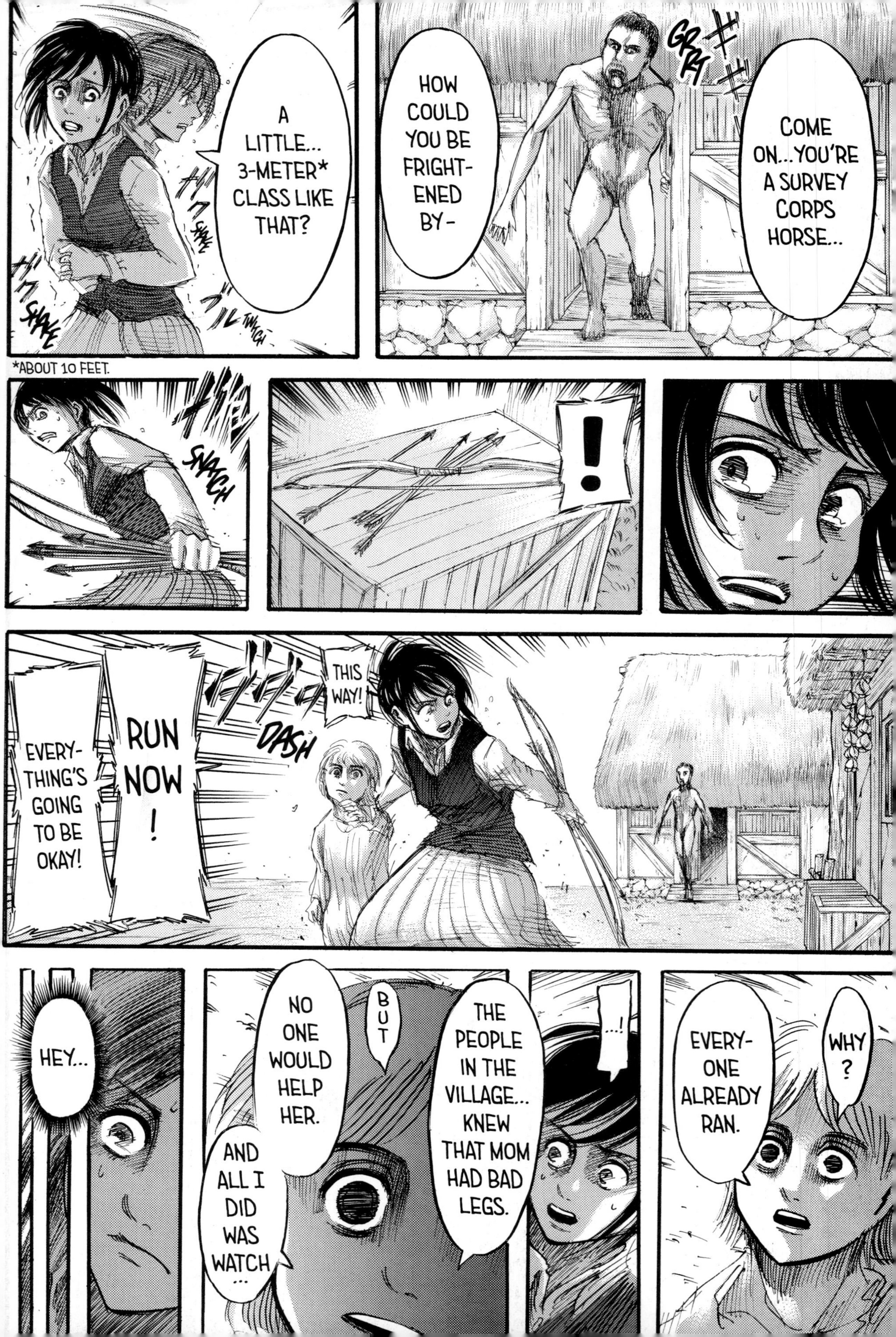
COME ON...YOU'RE A SURVEY CORPS HORSE...
HOW COULD YOU BE FRIGHTENED BY-
SHAKE
A LITTLE... 3-METER* CLASS LIKE THAT?
TWITCH
SHAKE
!
SNATCH
THIS WAY!
DASH
RUN NOW!
EVERYTHING'S GOING TO BE OKAY!
WHY?
EVERYONE ALREADY RAN.
...!
THE PEOPLE IN THE VILLAGE... KNEW THAT MOM HAD BAD LEGS.
BUT
NO ONE WOULD HELP HER.
AND ALL I DID WAS WATCH...
HEY...

*ABOUT 10 FEET.

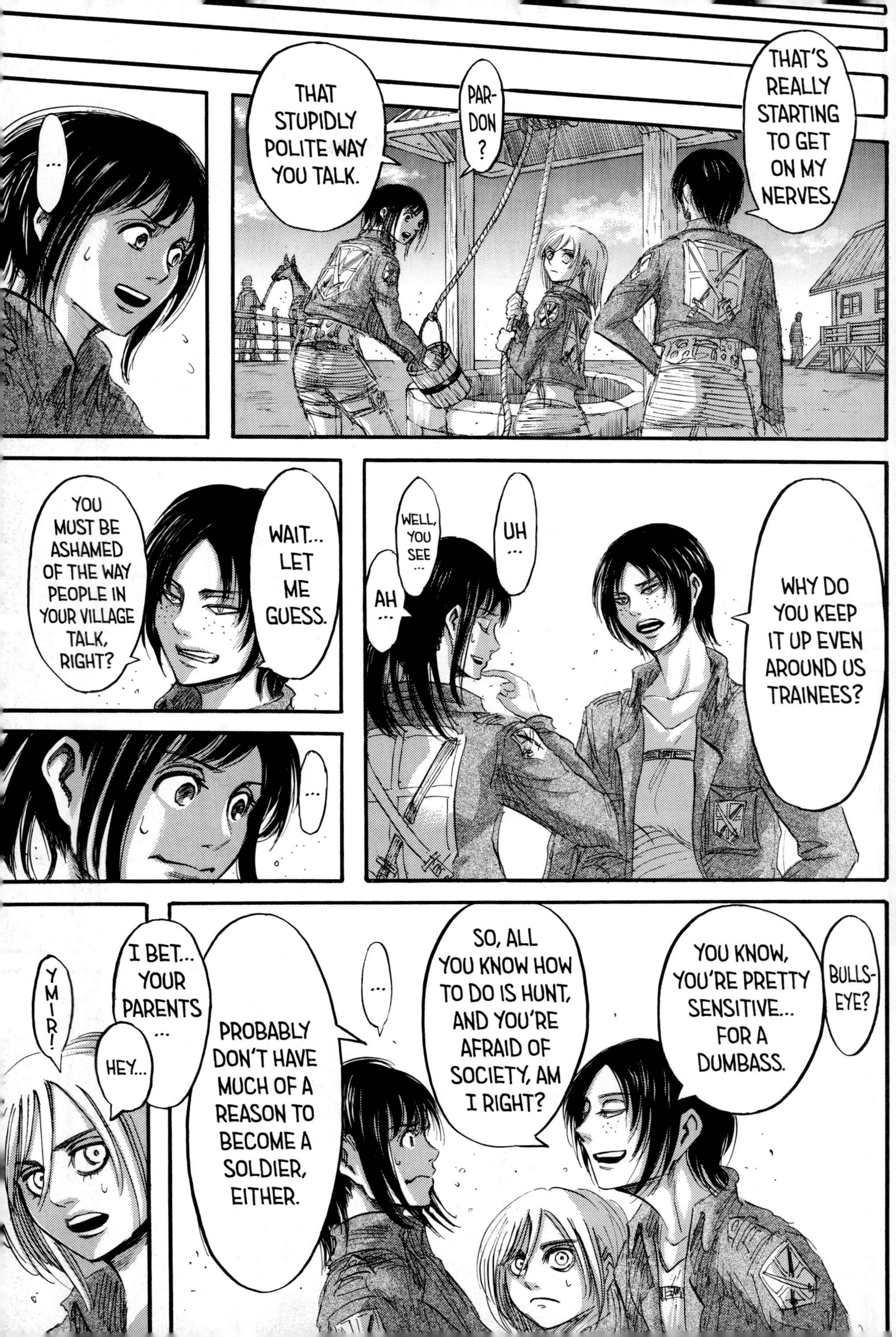
THAT'S REALLY STARTING TO GET ON MY NERVES.
PAR-DON?
THAT STUPIDLY POLITE WAY YOU TALK.
...
WHY DO YOU KEEP IT UP EVEN AROUND US TRAINEES?
UH ...
WELL, YOU SEE ...
AH ...
WAIT... LET ME GUESS.
YOU MUST BE ASHAMED OF THE WAY PEOPLE IN YOUR VILLAGE TALK, RIGHT?
...
BULLS-EYE?
YOU KNOW, YOU'RE PRETTY SENSITIVE... FOR A DUMBASS.
SO, ALL YOU KNOW HOW TO DO IS HUNT, AND YOU'RE AFRAID OF SOCIETY, AM I RIGHT?
...
I BET... YOUR PARENTS ...
PROBABLY DON'T HAVE MUCH OF A REASON TO BECOME A SOLDIER, EITHER.
YMIR!
HEY...

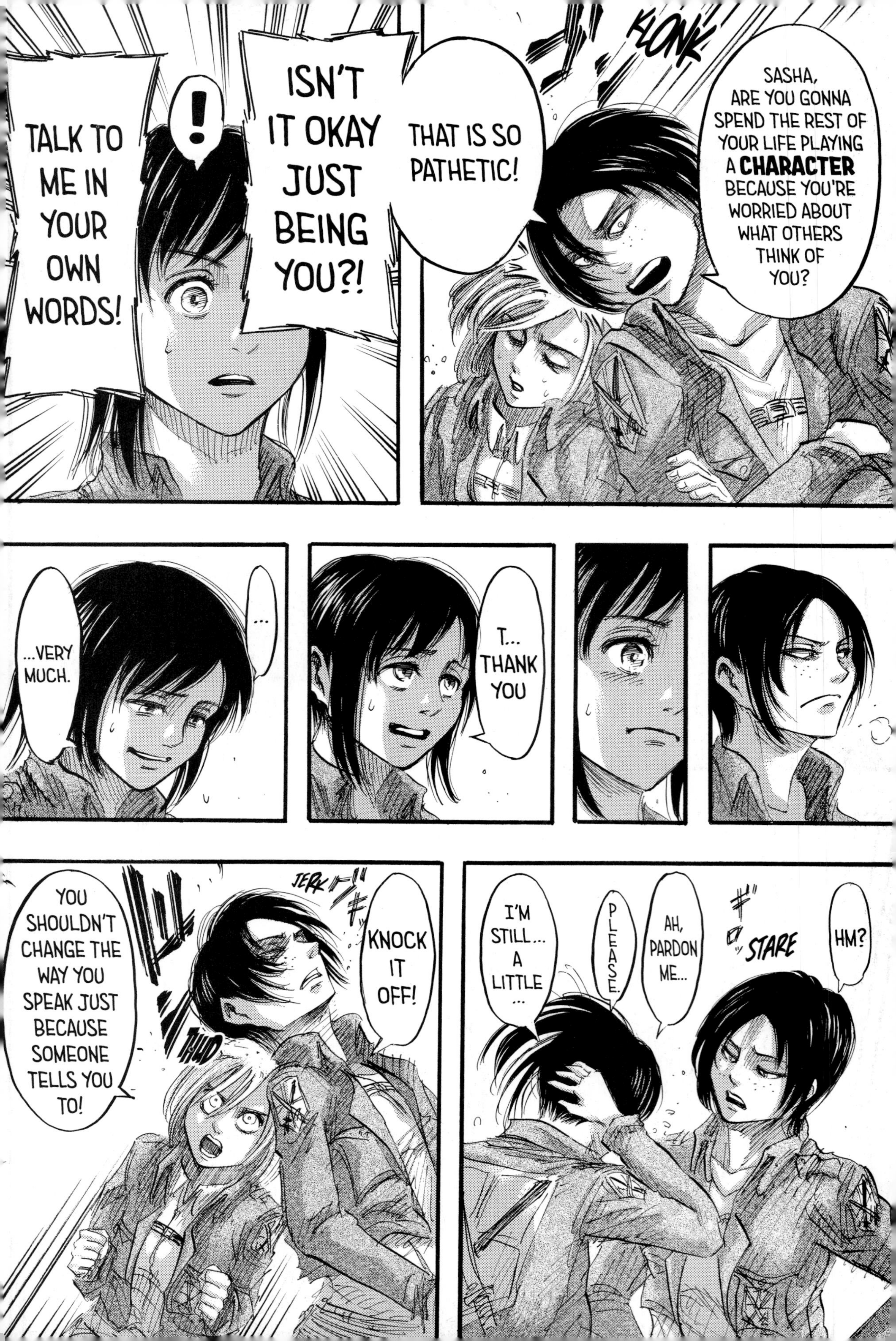
KLONK
SASHA, ARE YOU GONNA SPEND THE REST OF YOUR LIFE PLAYING A **CHARACTER** BECAUSE YOU'RE WORRIED ABOUT WHAT OTHERS THINK OF YOU?
THAT IS SO PATHETIC!
ISN'T IT OKAY JUST BEING YOU?!
!
TALK TO ME IN YOUR OWN WORDS!
T... THANK YOU
...
...VERY MUCH.
HM?
STARE
AH, PARDON ME...
PLEASE.
I'M STILL... A LITTLE ...
JERK
KNOCK IT OFF!
THUD
YOU SHOULDN'T CHANGE THE WAY YOU SPEAK JUST BECAUSE SOMEONE TELLS YOU TO!

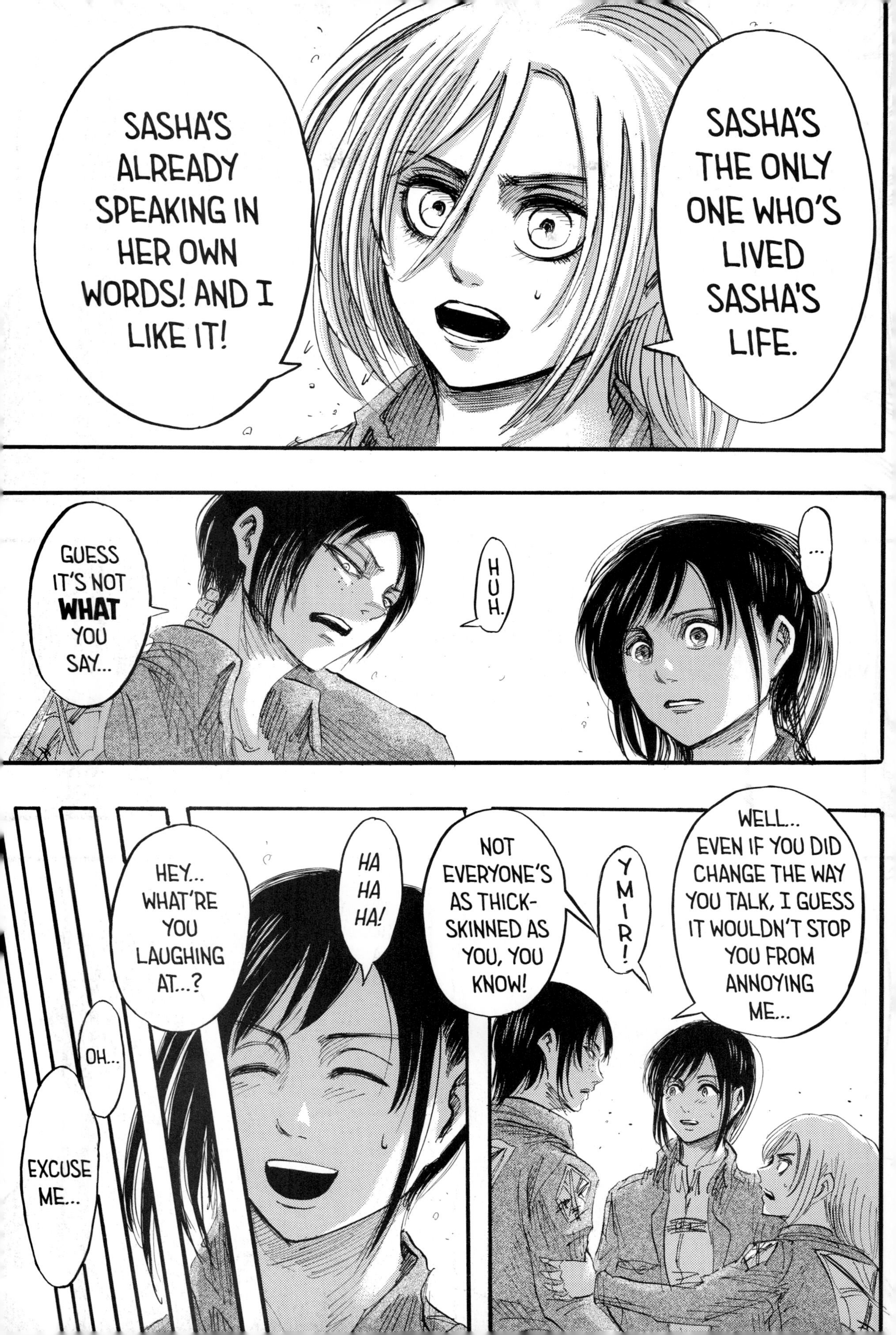
SASHA'S THE ONLY ONE WHO'S LIVED SASHA'S LIFE.
SASHA'S ALREADY SPEAKING IN HER OWN WORDS! AND I LIKE IT!
...
HUH.
GUESS IT'S NOT **WHAT** YOU SAY...
WELL... EVEN IF YOU DID CHANGE THE WAY YOU TALK, I GUESS IT WOULDN'T STOP YOU FROM ANNOYING ME...
YMIR!
NOT EVERYONE'S AS THICK-SKINNED AS YOU, YOU KNOW!
HA HA HA!
HEY... WHAT'RE YOU LAUGHING AT...?
OH...
EXCUSE ME...

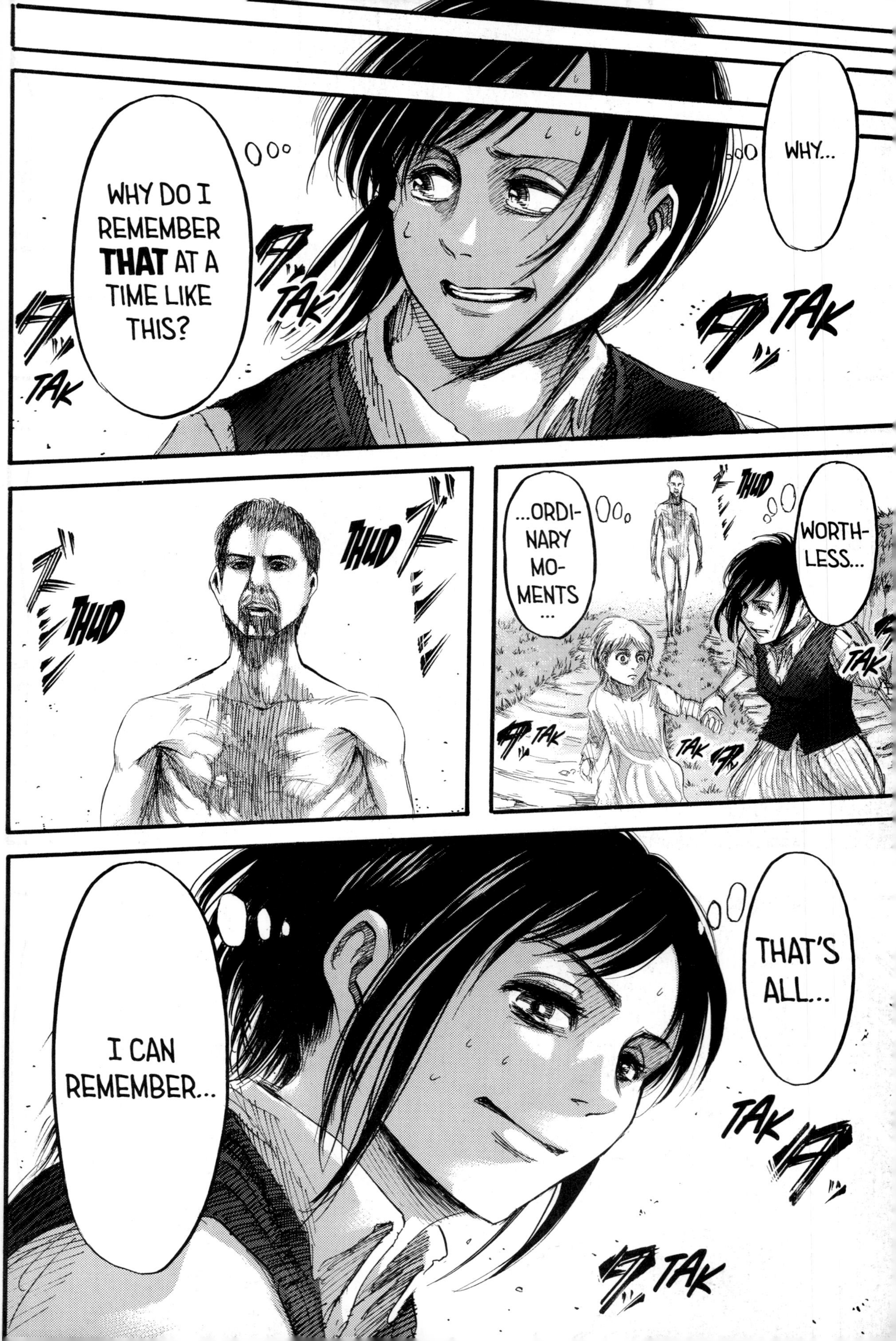
WHY...
WHY DO I REMEMBER **THAT** AT A TIME LIKE THIS?
TAK
TAK
TAK
THUD
WORTH-LESS...
...ORDI-NARY MO-MENTS...
TAK
TAK
TAK
THUD
THUD
THAT'S ALL...
I CAN REMEMBER...
TAK
TAK

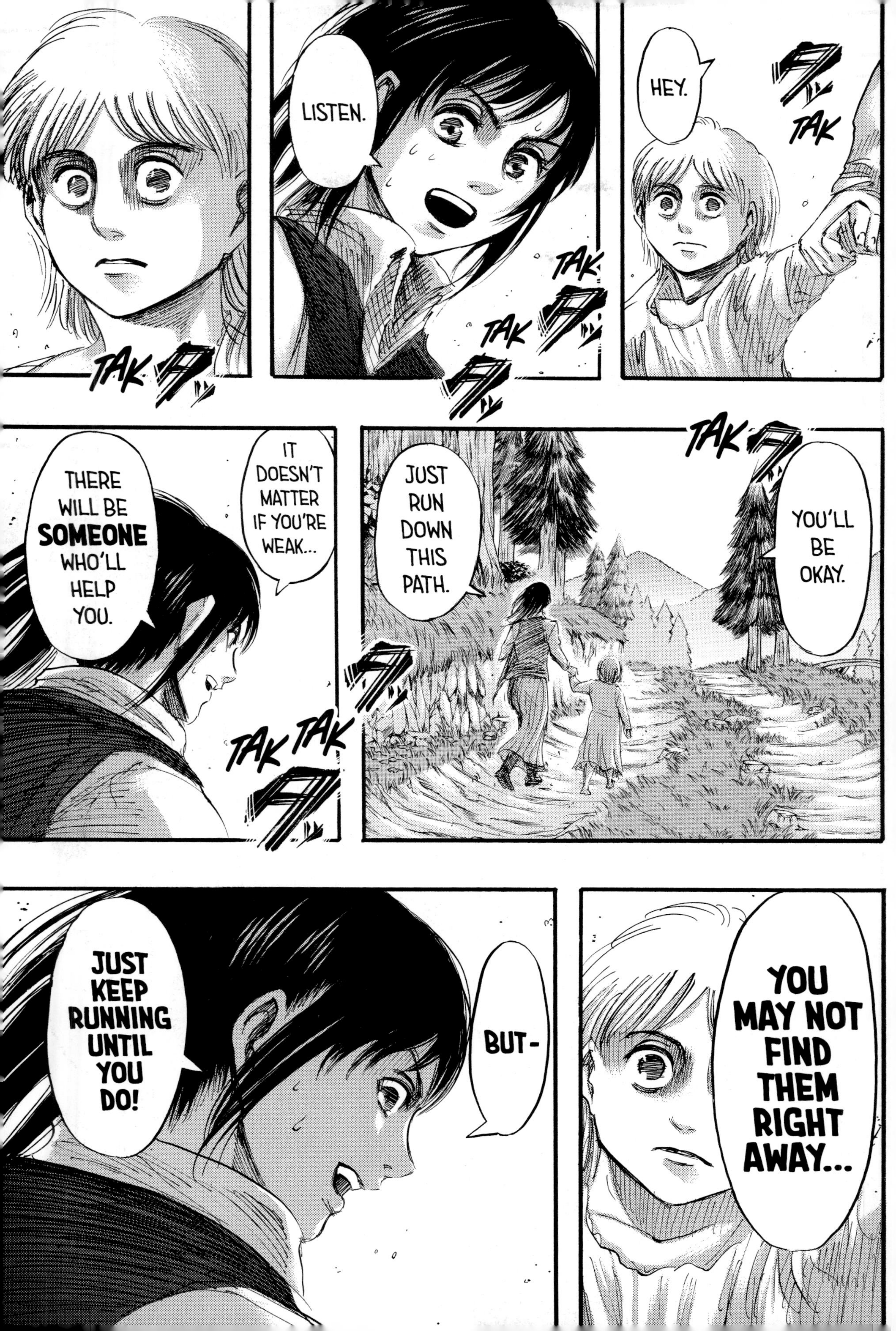
HEY.
TAK
TAK
LISTEN.
TAK
TAK
TAK
YOU'LL BE OKAY.
JUST RUN DOWN THIS PATH.
IT DOESN'T MATTER IF YOU'RE WEAK...
THERE WILL BE **SOMEONE** WHO'LL HELP YOU.
TAK TAK
YOU MAY NOT FIND THEM RIGHT AWAY...
BUT-
JUST KEEP RUNNING UNTIL YOU DO!

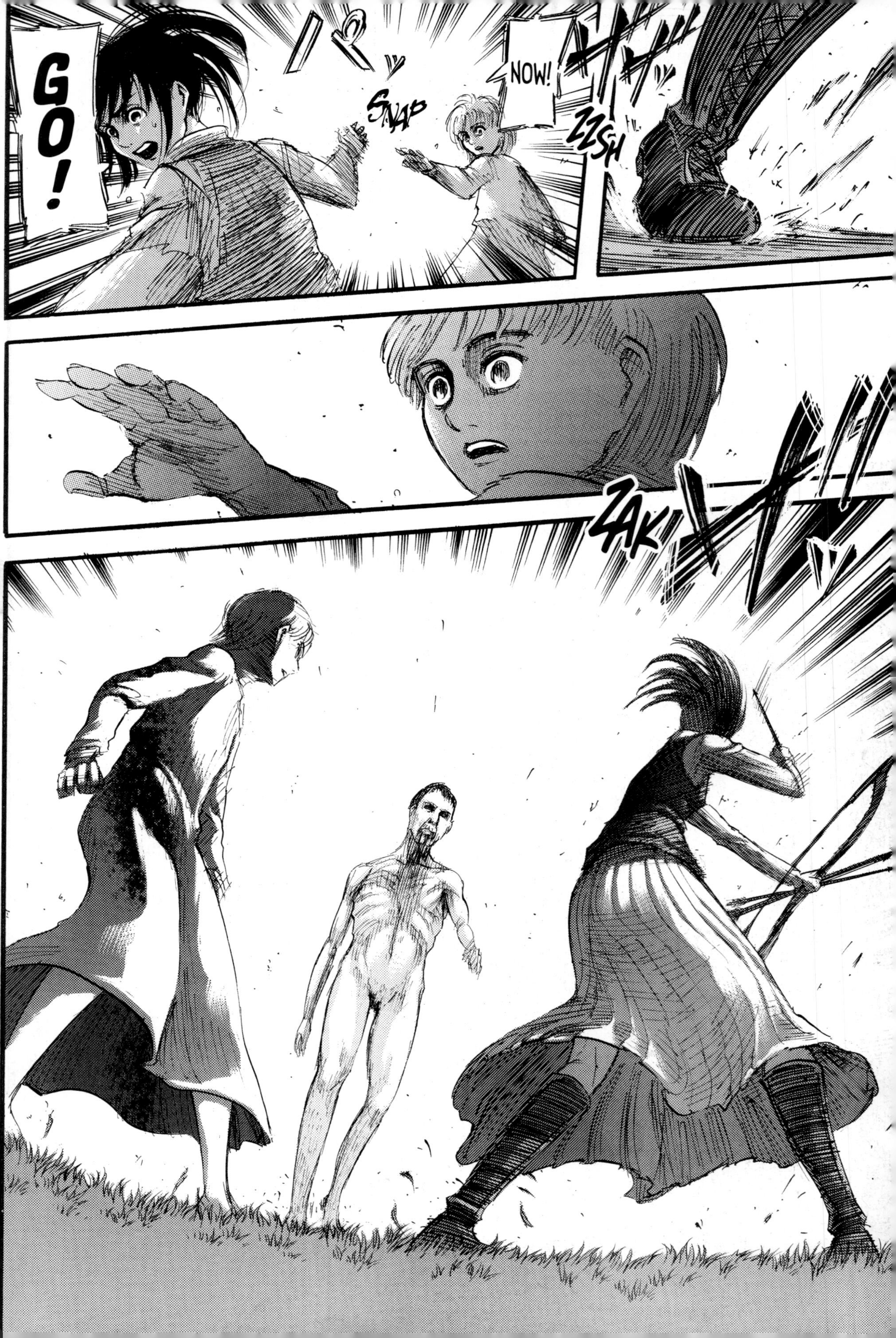
ZZSH
NOW!
SNAP
GO!
ZAK

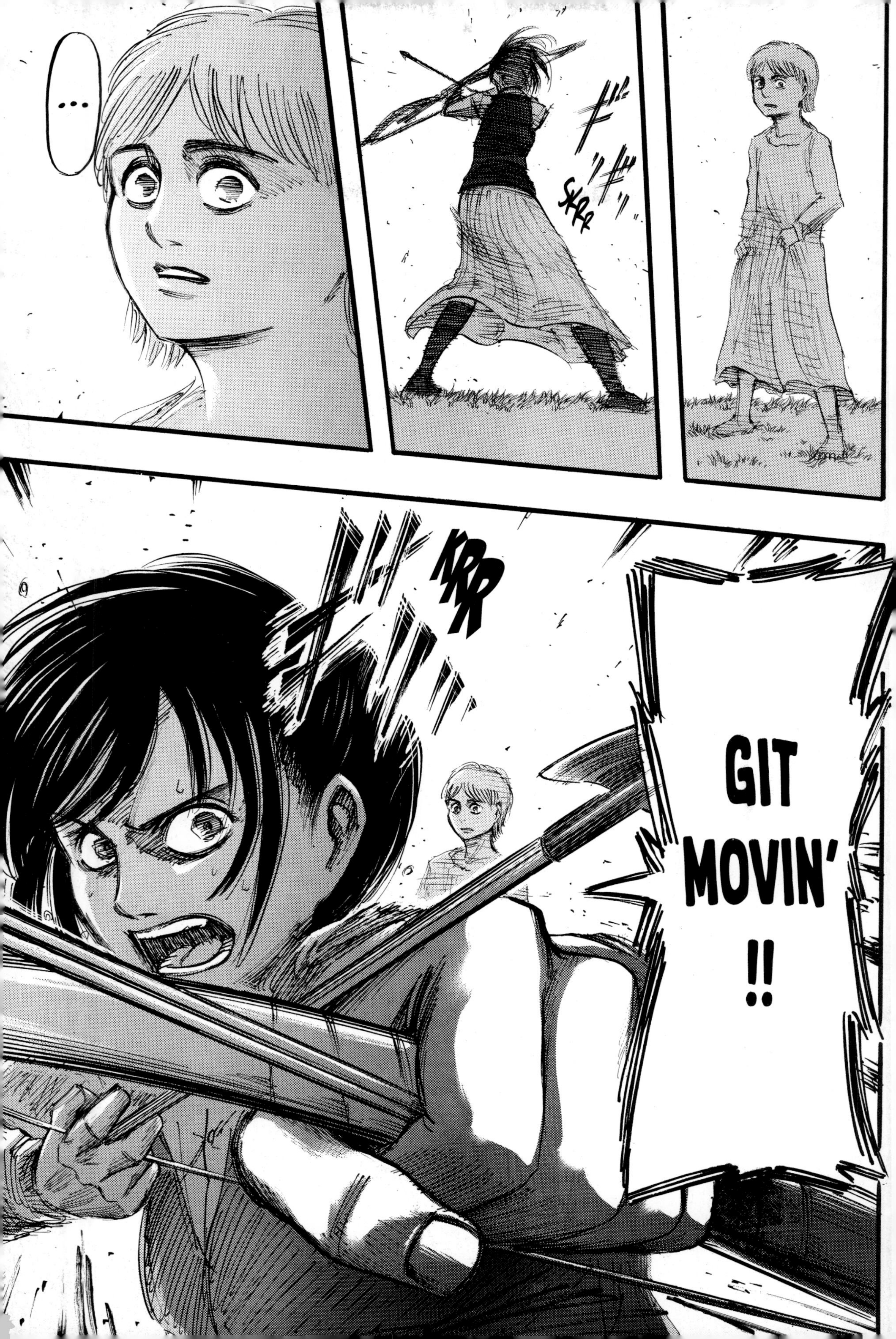
SKRR
...
KRR
GIT MOVIN' !!

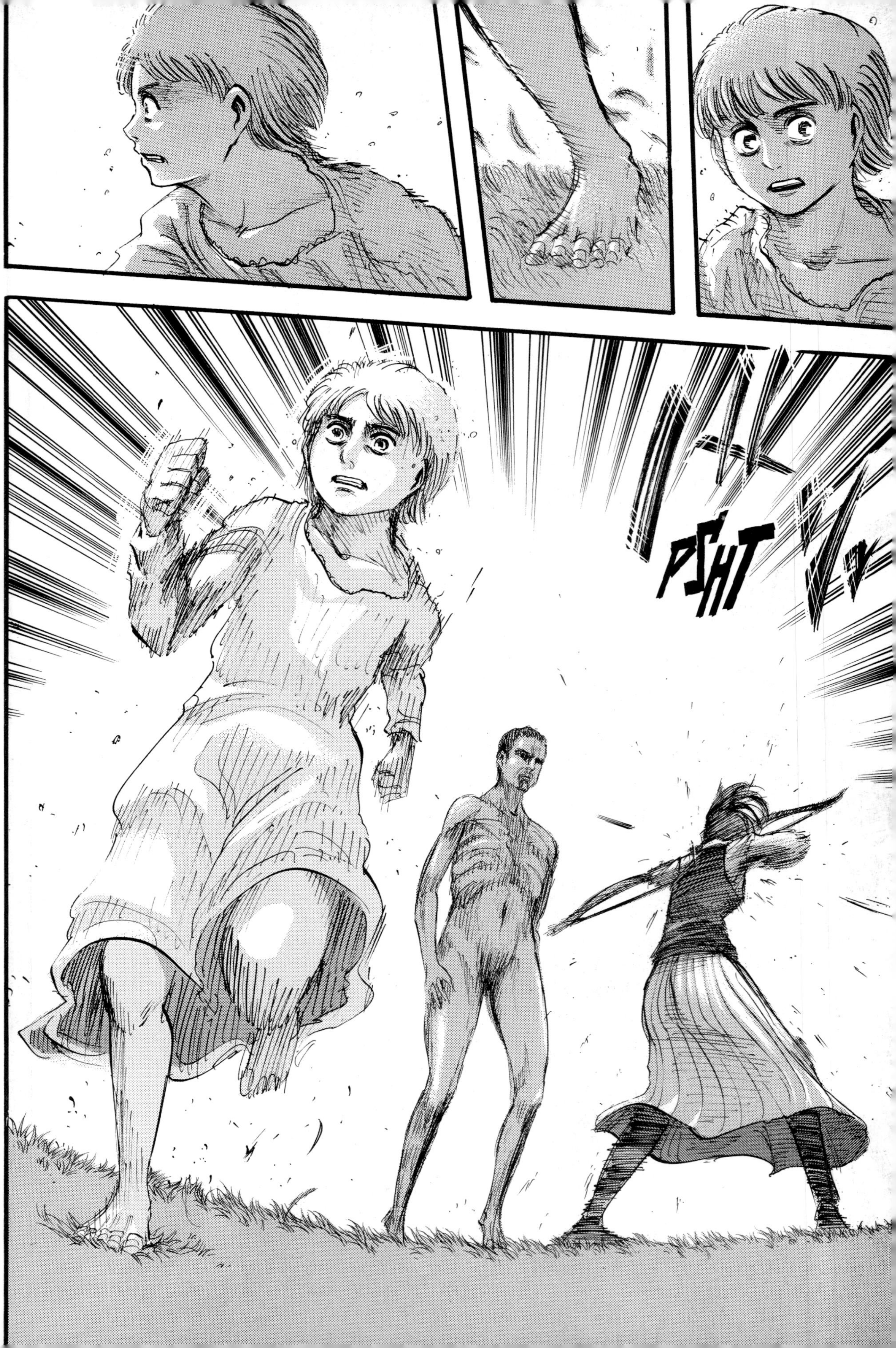
PSHT

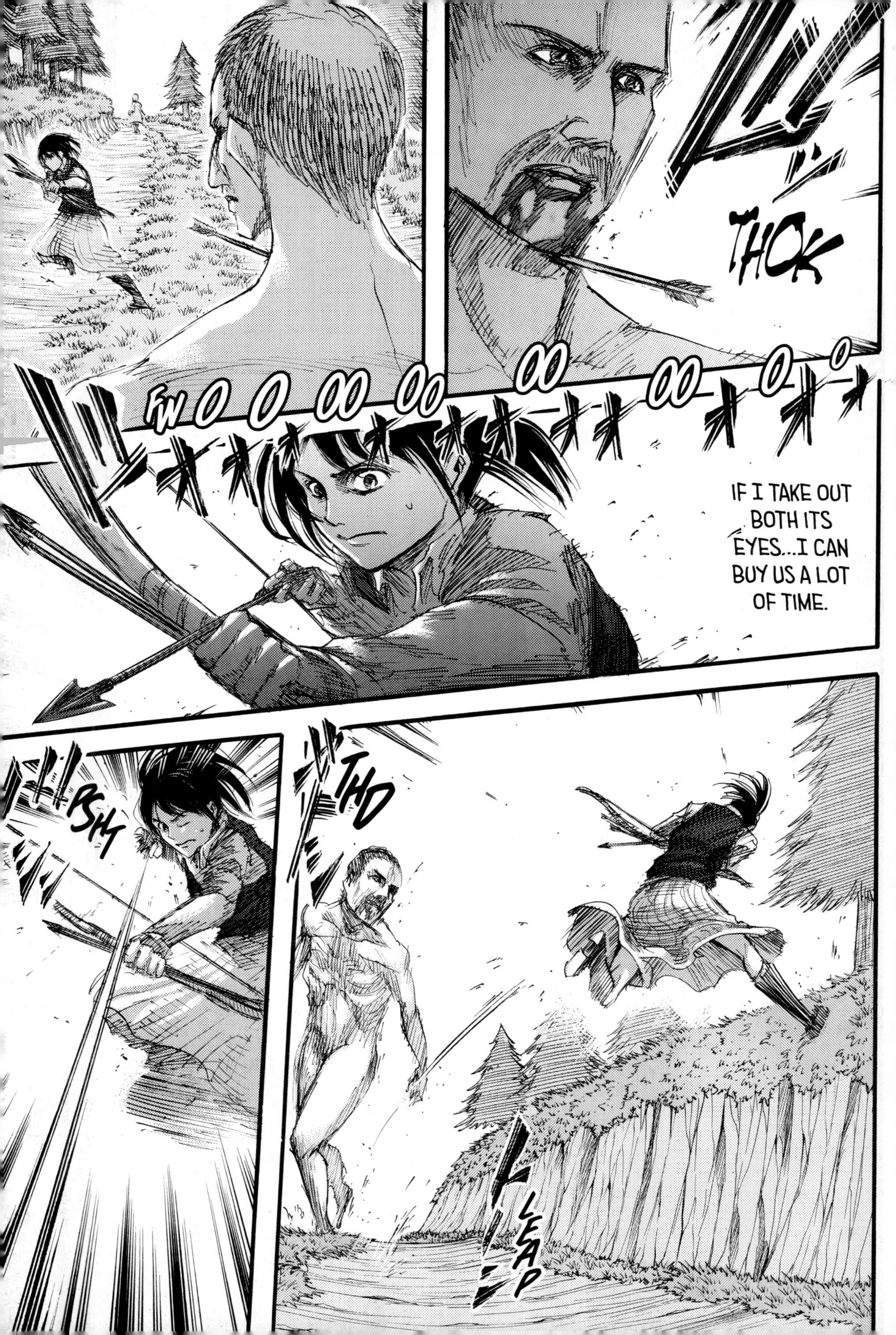
THOK
FWOOOOOOOOOOOOOOOO
IF I TAKE OUT BOTH ITS EYES...I CAN BUY US A LOT OF TIME.
THD
LEAP
PSHY

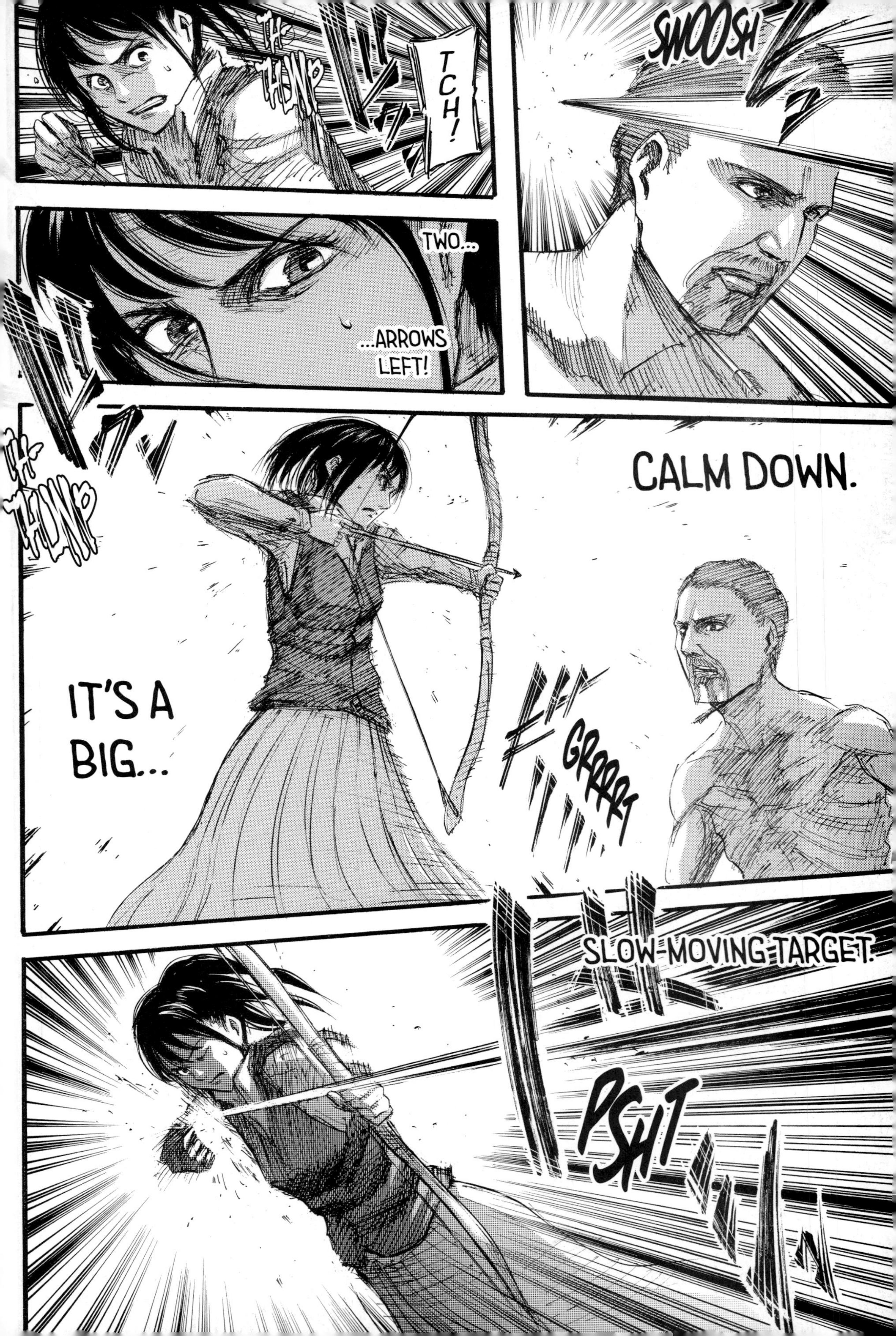
SWOOSH
TCH!
TWO...
...ARROWS LEFT!
CALM DOWN.
IT'S A BIG...
SLOW-MOVING TARGET.
PSHT

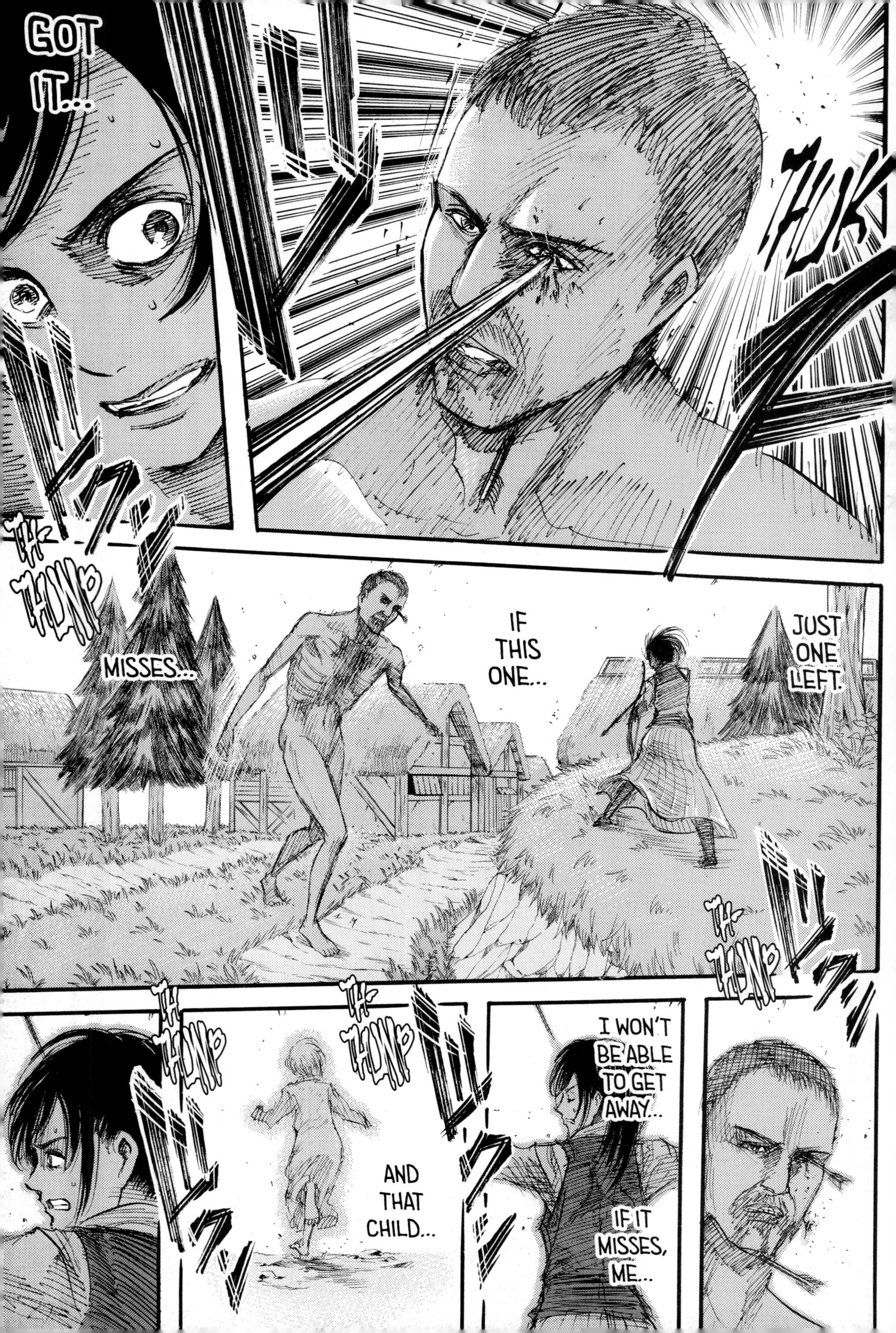
THUK
GOT IT...
TH-THUMP
JUST ONE LEFT.
IF THIS ONE...
MISSES...
TH-THUMP
TH-THUMP
I WON'T BE ABLE TO GET AWAY...
IF IT MISSES, ME...
TH-THUMP
AND THAT CHILD...
TH-THUMP

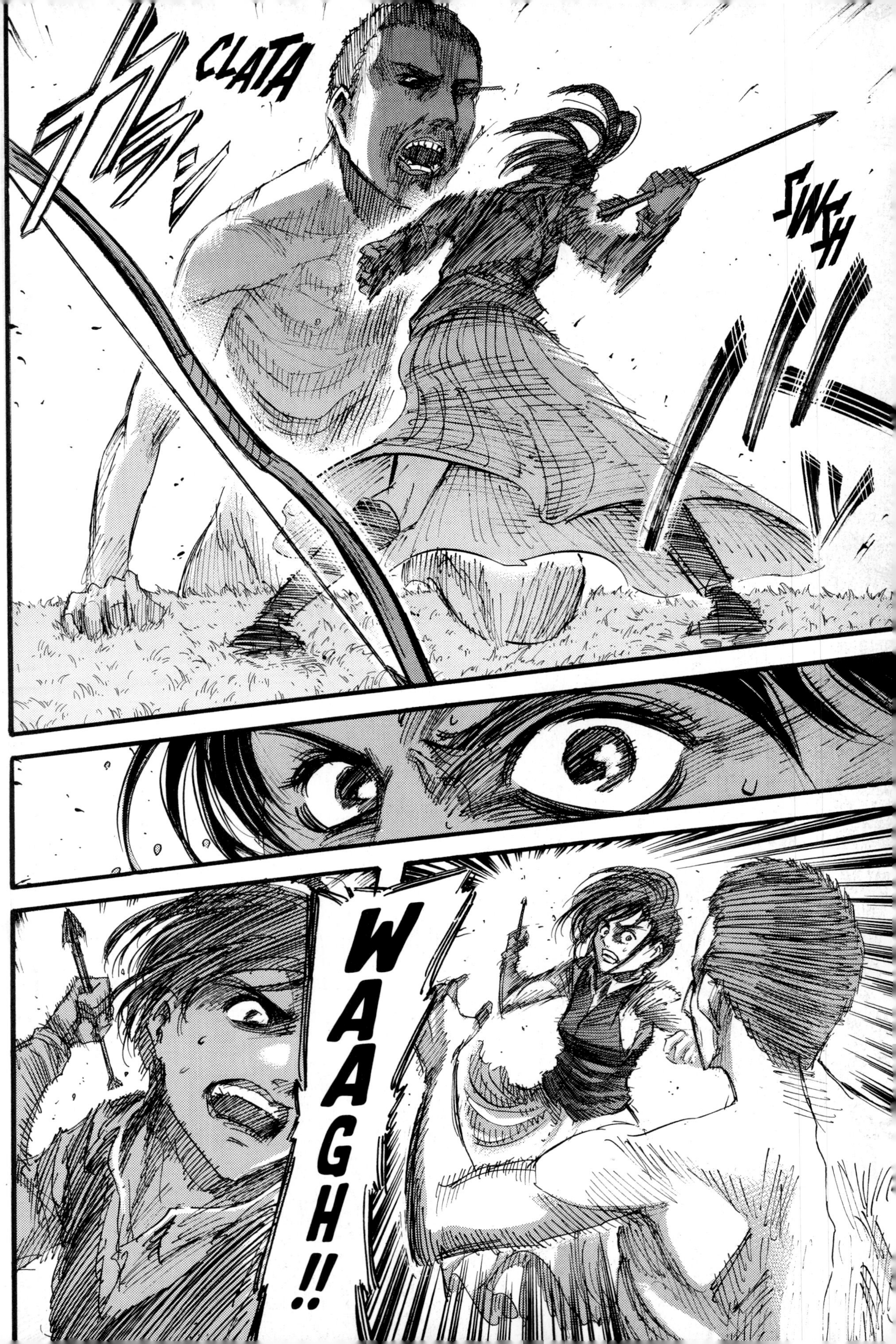
SWISH
CLATA
WAAAGH!!

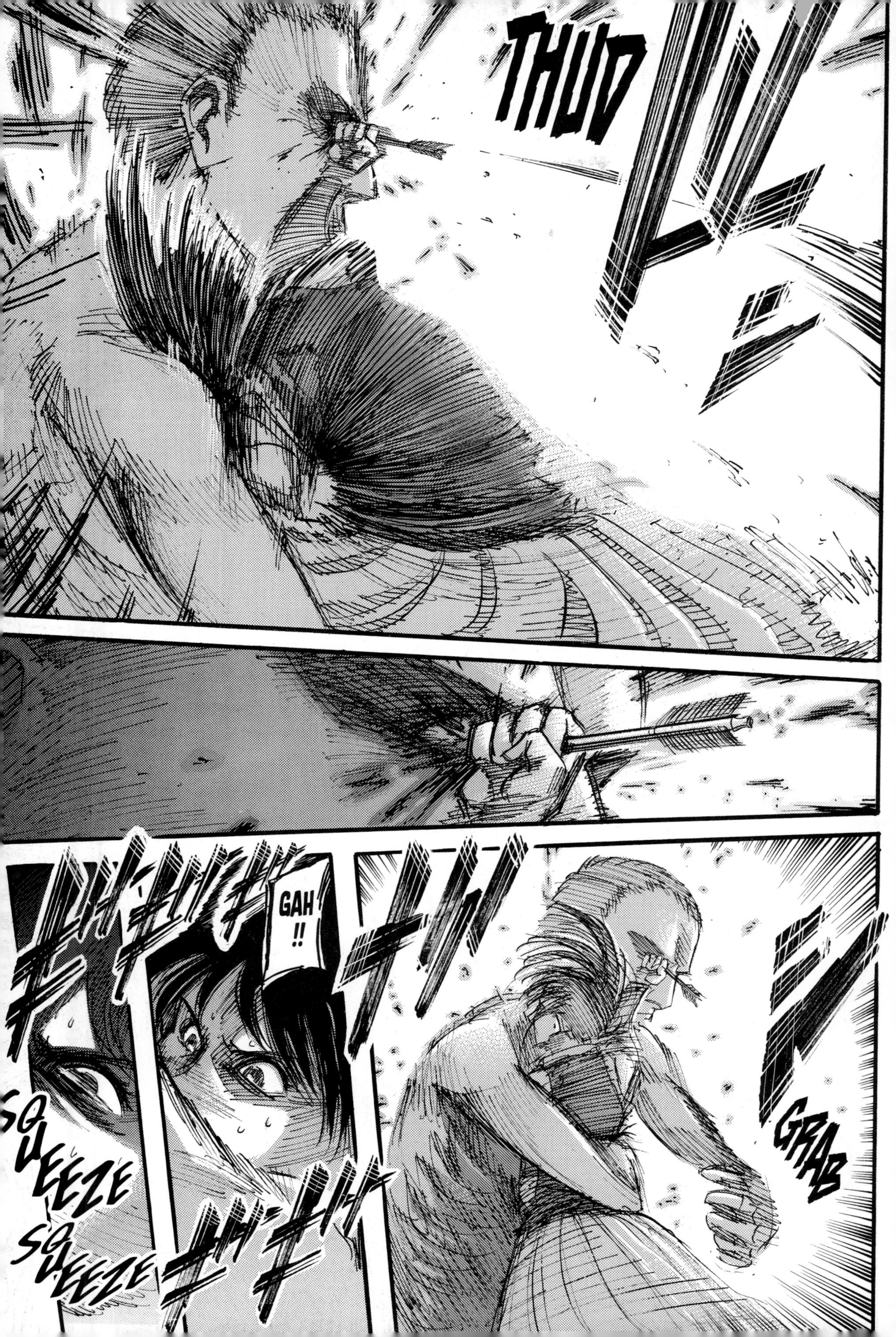
THUD
GRAB
GAH !!
SQUEEZE
SQUEEZE

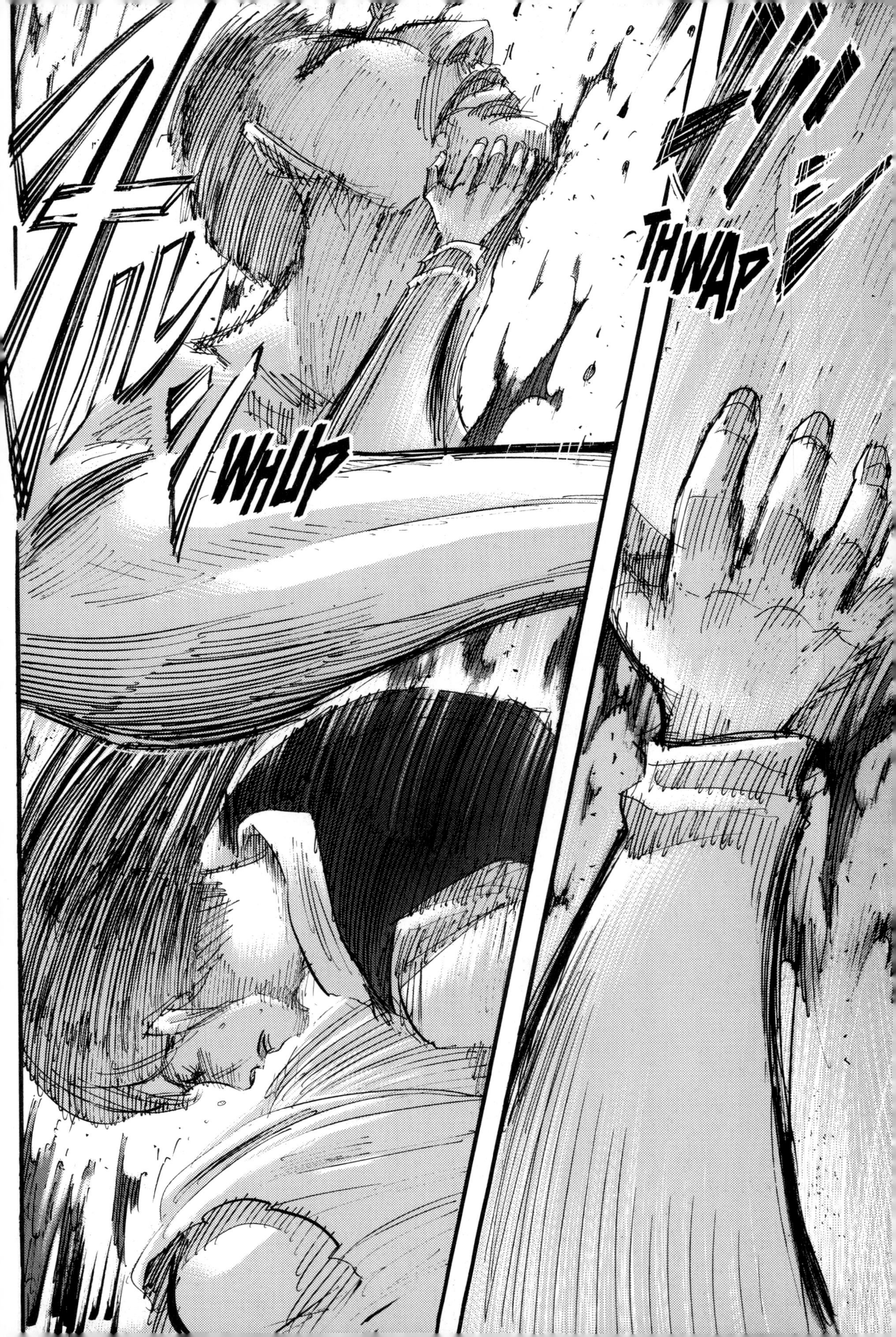
THWAP
WHUP

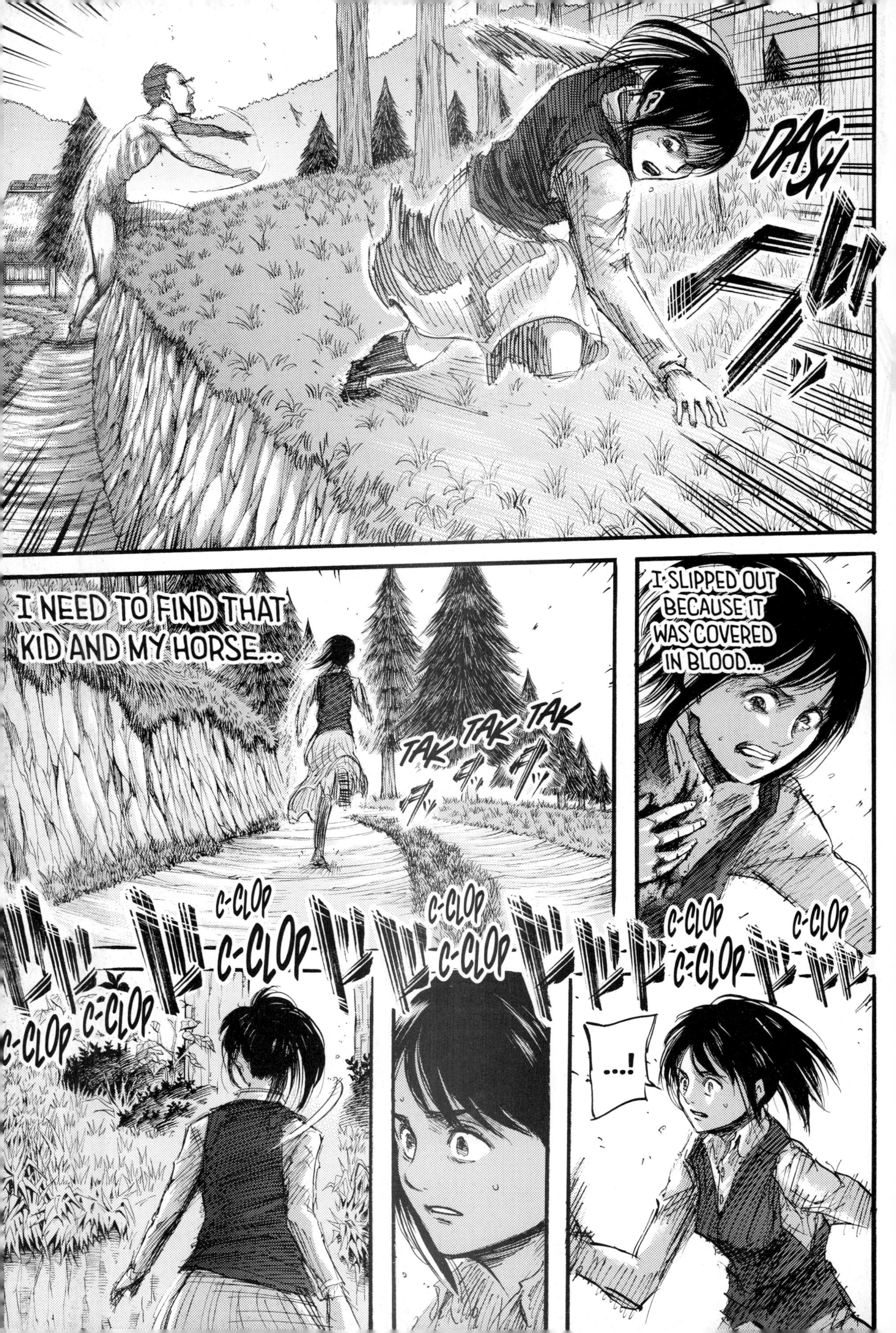
DASH
I SLIPPED OUT BECAUSE IT WAS COVERED IN BLOOD...
I NEED TO FIND THAT KID AND MY HORSE...
TAK TAK TAK
C-CLOP C-CLOP
C-CLOP C-CLOP
C-CLOP C-CLOP
C-CLOP C-CLOP
...!
C-CLOP C-CLOP

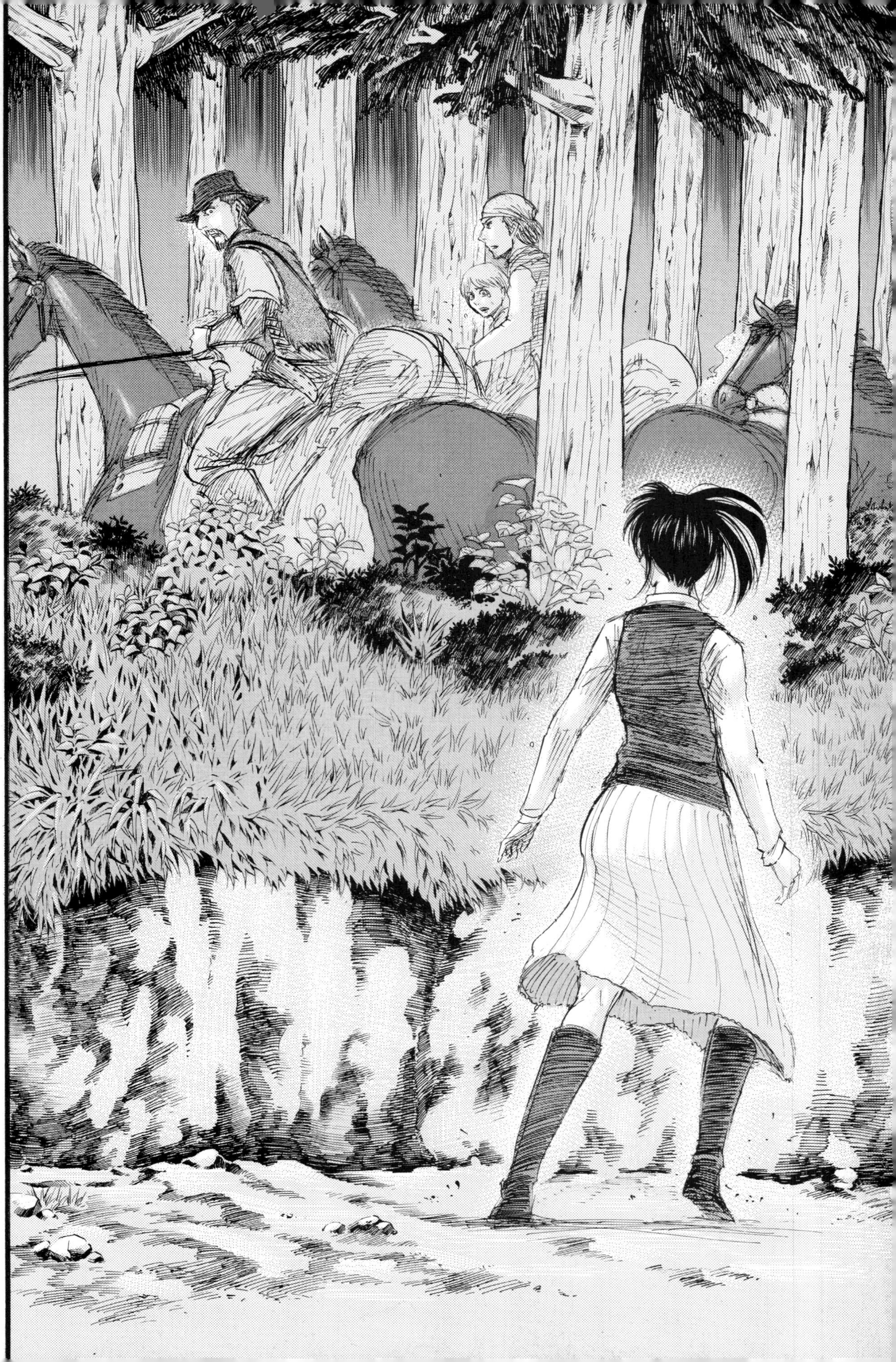

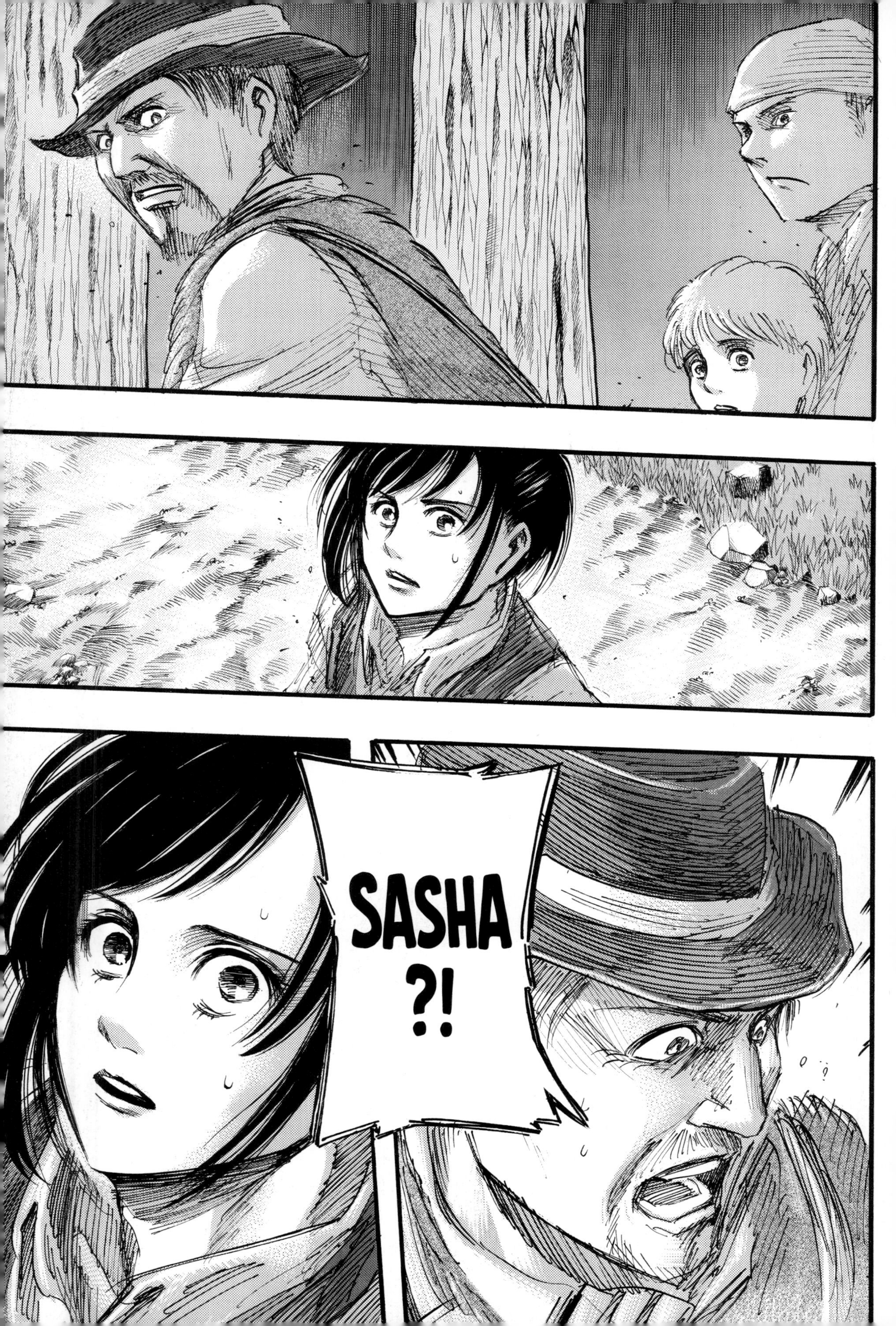
SASHA
?!

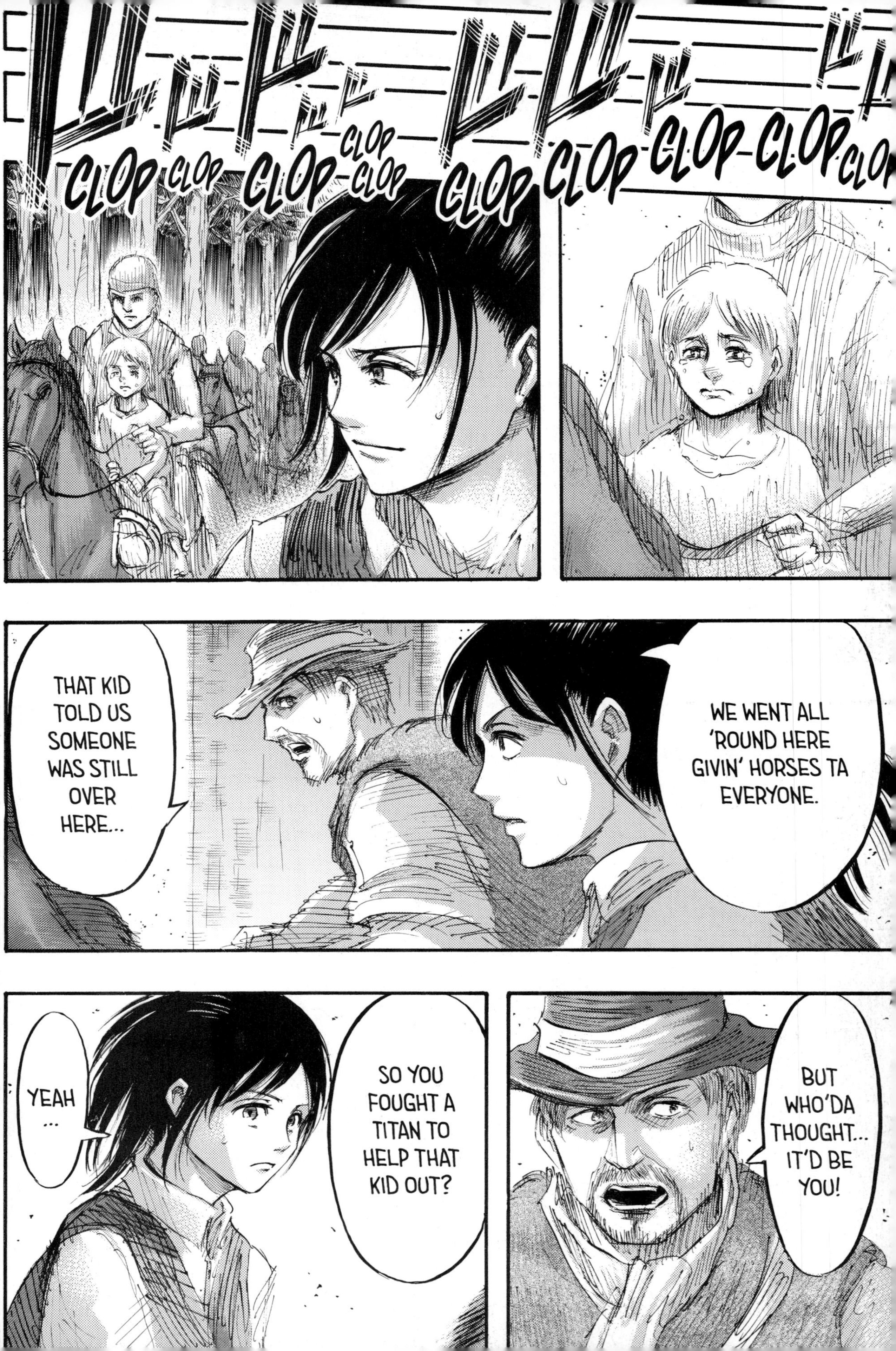
CLOP CLOP CLOP CLOP-CLOP CLOP CLOP-CLOP-CLOP-CLOP
WE WENT ALL 'ROUND HERE GIVIN' HORSES TA EVERYONE.
THAT KID TOLD US SOMEONE WAS STILL OVER HERE...
BUT WHO'DA THOUGHT... IT'D BE YOU!
SO YOU FOUGHT A TITAN TO HELP THAT KID OUT?
YEAH ...

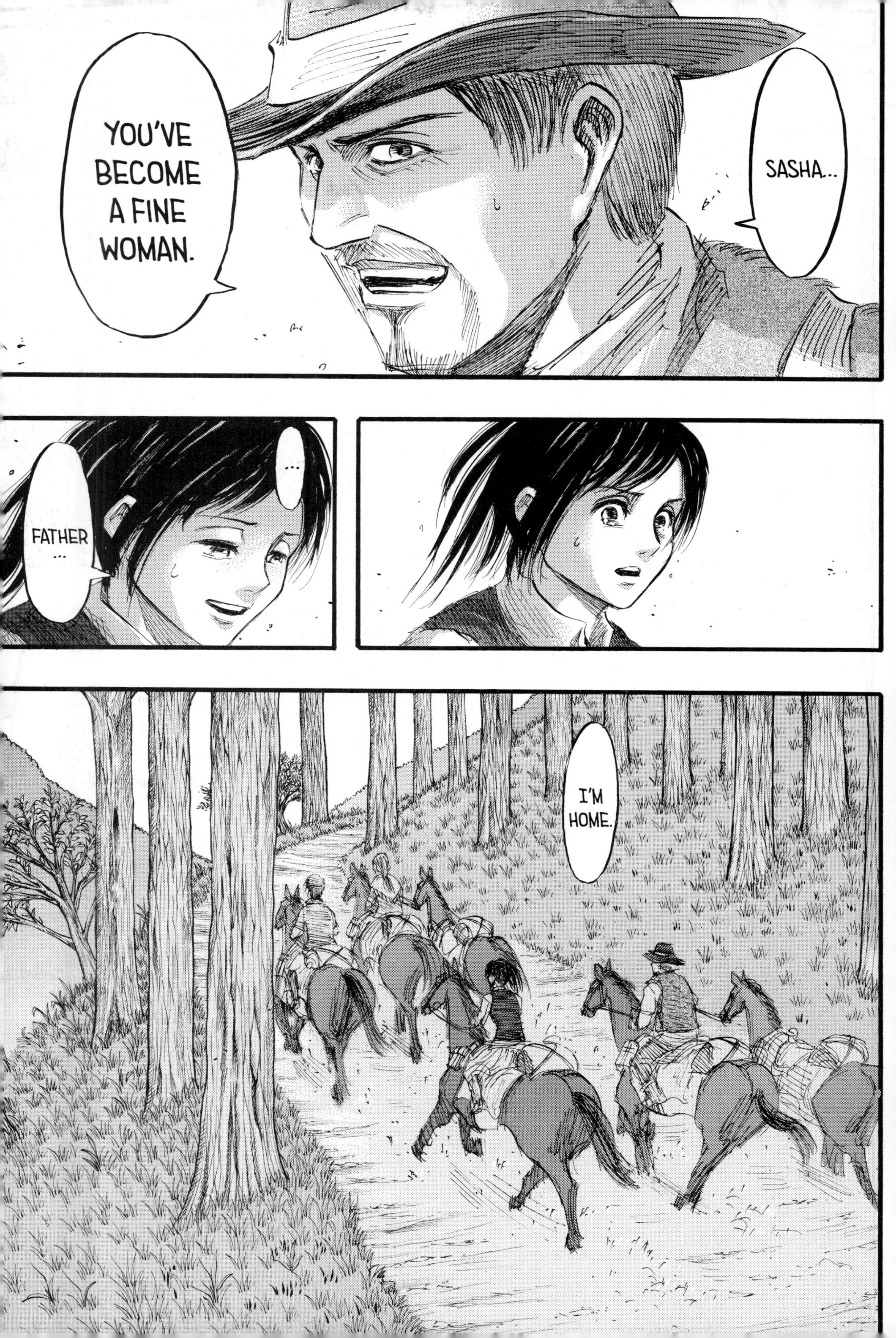
SASHA...
YOU'VE BECOME A FINE WOMAN.
...
FATHER ...
I'M HOME.

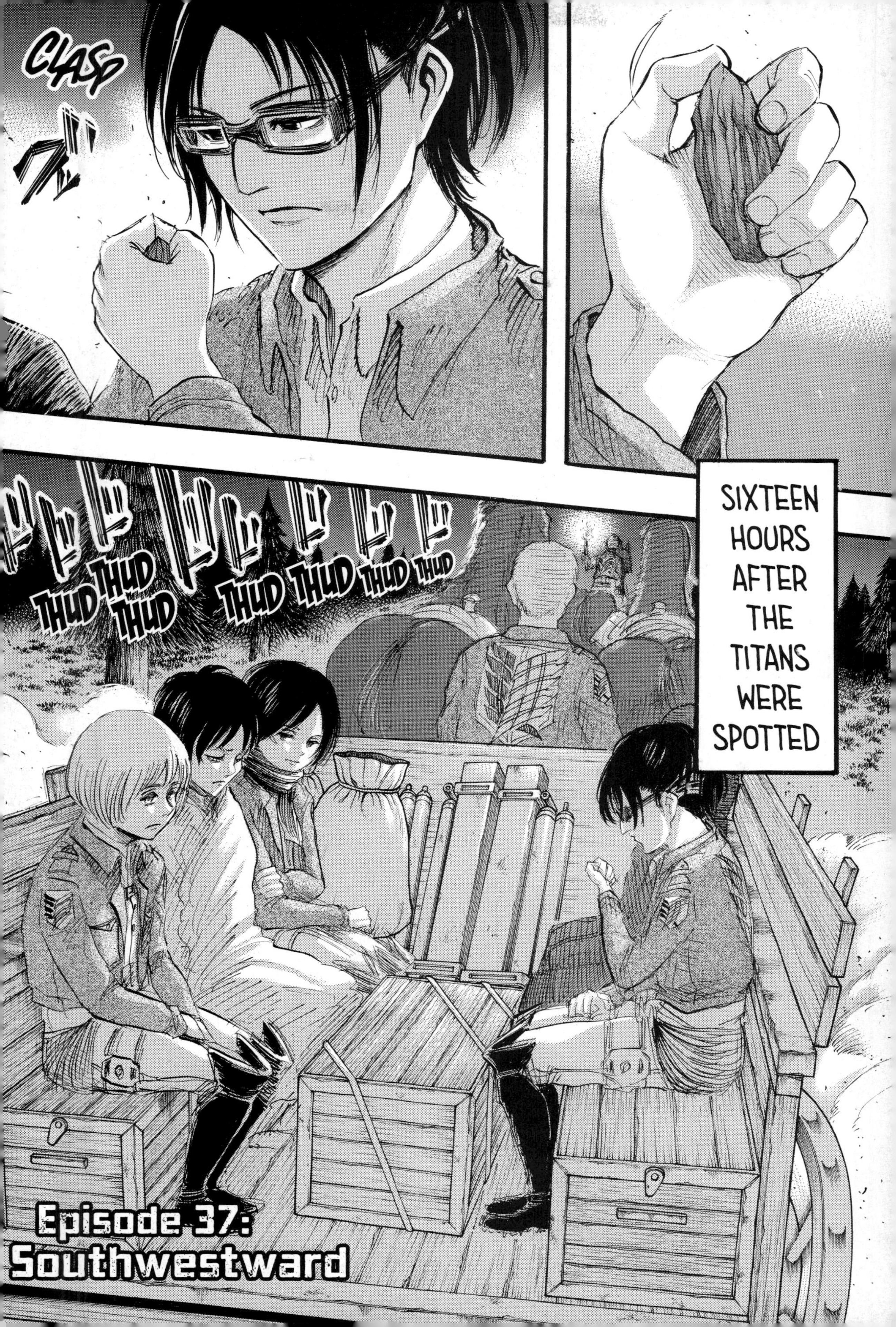
CLASP
SIXTEEN HOURS AFTER THE TITANS WERE SPOTTED
THUD THUD THUD THUD THUD THUD THUD
Episode 37: Southwestward

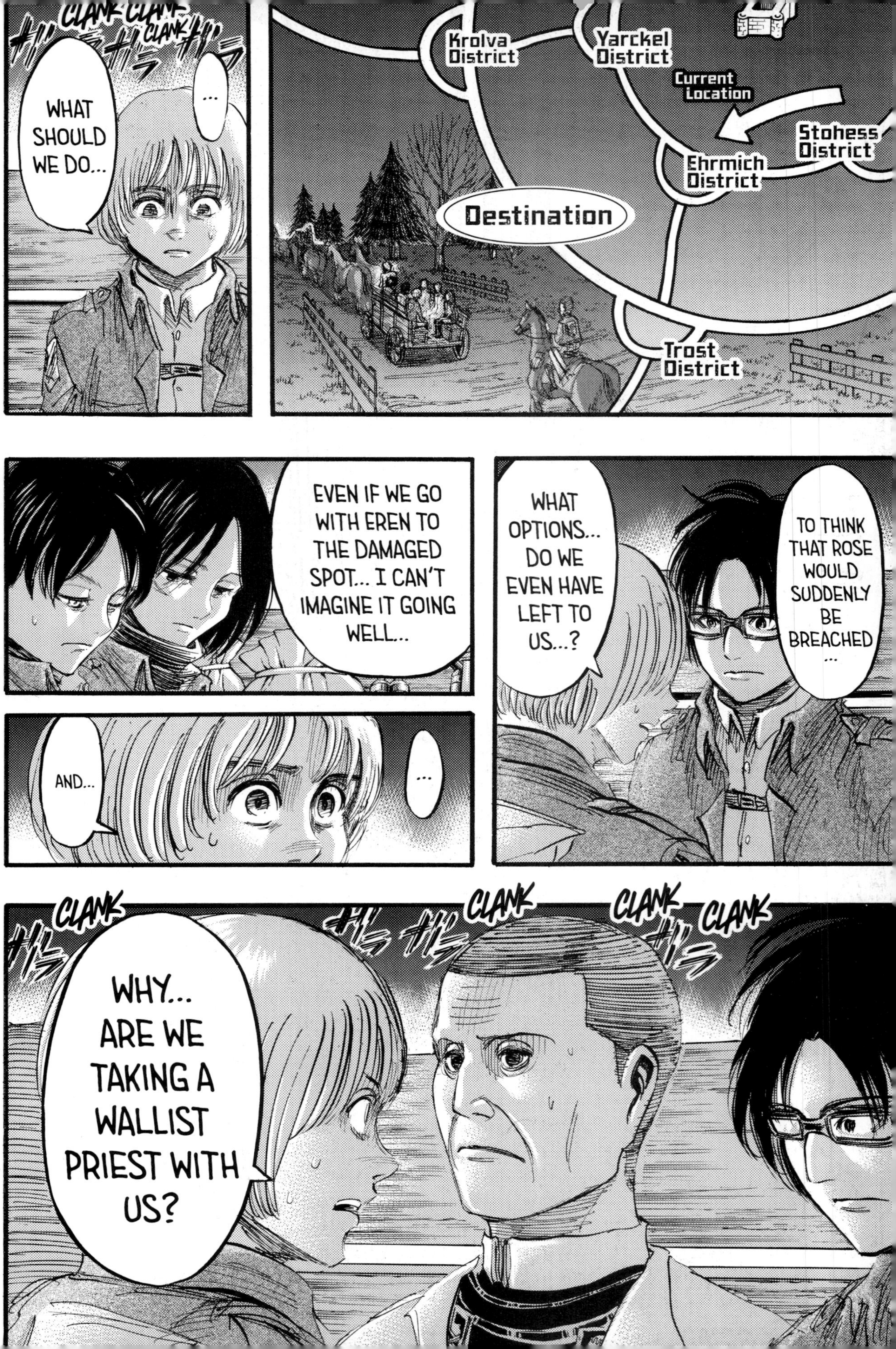
Krolva District
Yarckel District
Current Location
Stohess District
Ehrmich District
Destination
Trost District
CLANK CLANK CLANK
...
WHAT SHOULD WE DO...
TO THINK THAT ROSE WOULD SUDDENLY BE BREACHED...
WHAT OPTIONS... DO WE EVEN HAVE LEFT TO US...?
EVEN IF WE GO WITH EREN TO THE DAMAGED SPOT... I CAN'T IMAGINE IT GOING WELL...
...
AND...
CLANK
CLANK
CLANK
CLANK
WHY... ARE WE TAKING A WALLIST PRIEST WITH US?

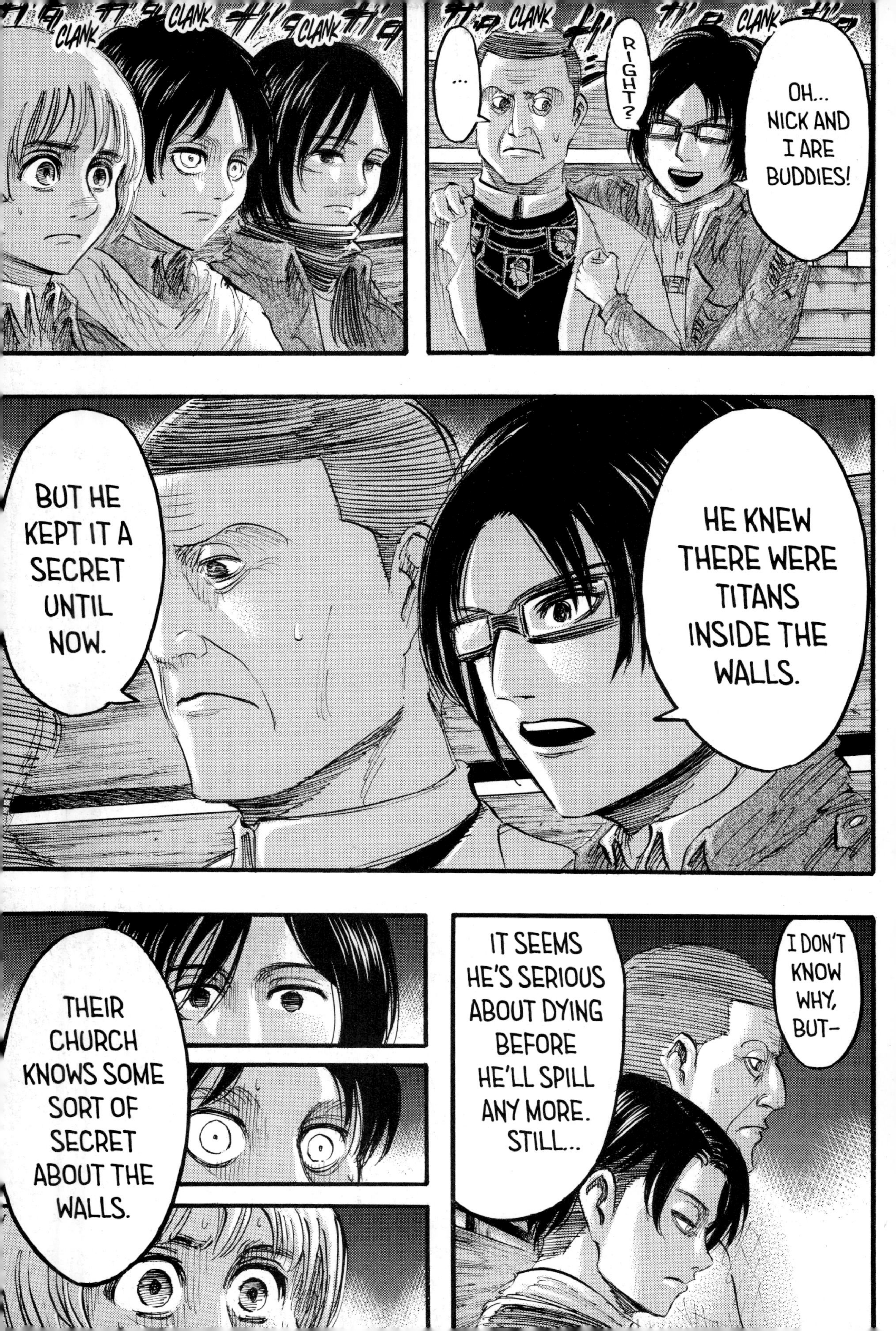
CLANK
CLANK
OH... NICK AND I ARE BUDDIES!
RIGHT?
...
CLANK
CLANK
CLANK
HE KNEW THERE WERE TITANS INSIDE THE WALLS.
BUT HE KEPT IT A SECRET UNTIL NOW.
I DON'T KNOW WHY, BUT-
IT SEEMS HE'S SERIOUS ABOUT DYING BEFORE HE'LL SPILL ANY MORE. STILL...
THEIR CHURCH KNOWS SOME SORT OF SECRET ABOUT THE WALLS.

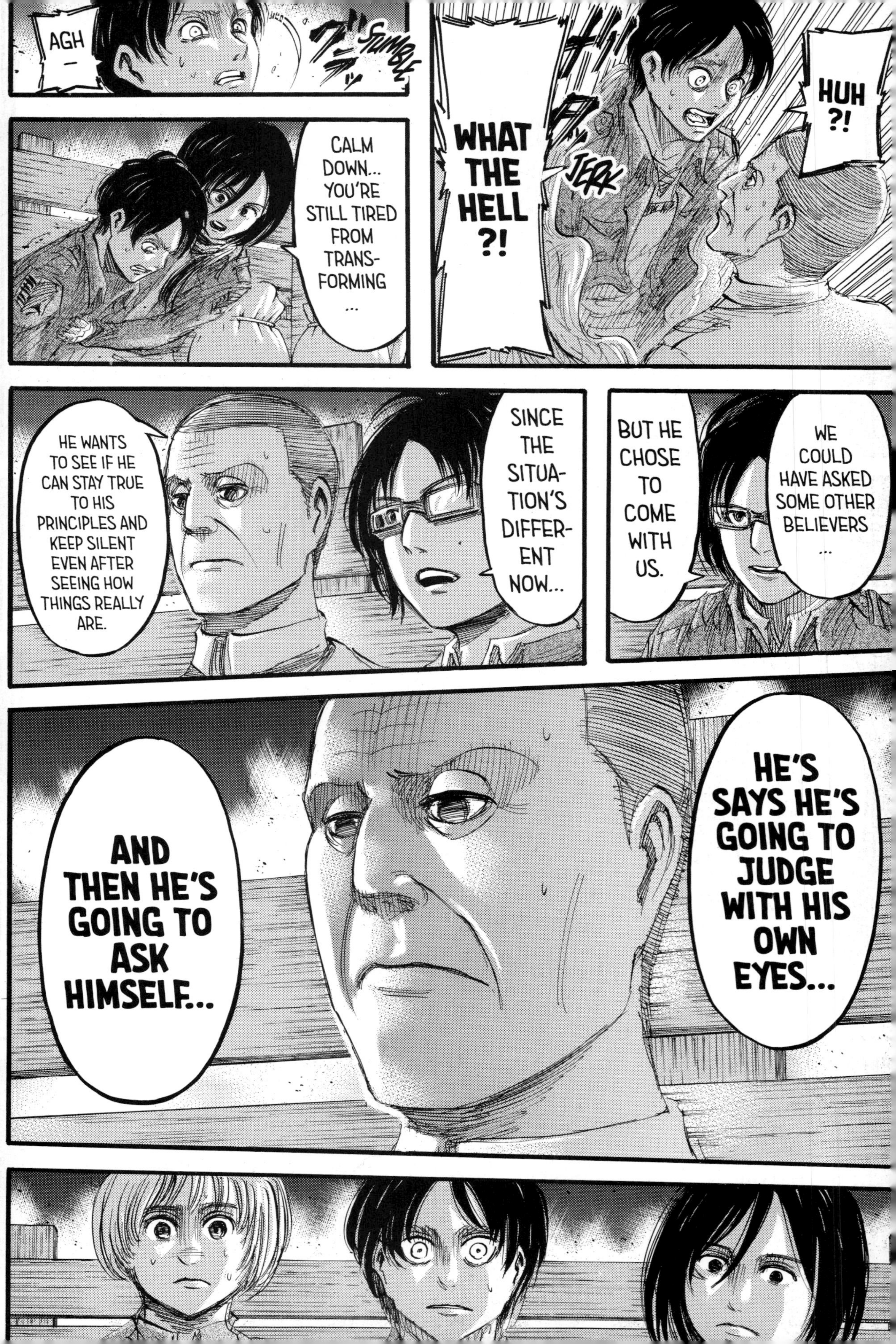
HUH ?!
WHAT THE HELL ?!
JERK
AGH —
STUMBLE
CALM DOWN... YOU'RE STILL TIRED FROM TRANS-FORMING ...
WE COULD HAVE ASKED SOME OTHER BELIEVERS ...
BUT HE CHOSE TO COME WITH US.
SINCE THE SITUA-TION'S DIFFER-ENT NOW...
HE WANTS TO SEE IF HE CAN STAY TRUE TO HIS PRINCIPLES AND KEEP SILENT EVEN AFTER SEEING HOW THINGS REALLY ARE.
HE'S SAYS HE'S GOING TO JUDGE WITH HIS OWN EYES...
AND THEN HE'S GOING TO ASK HIMSELF...

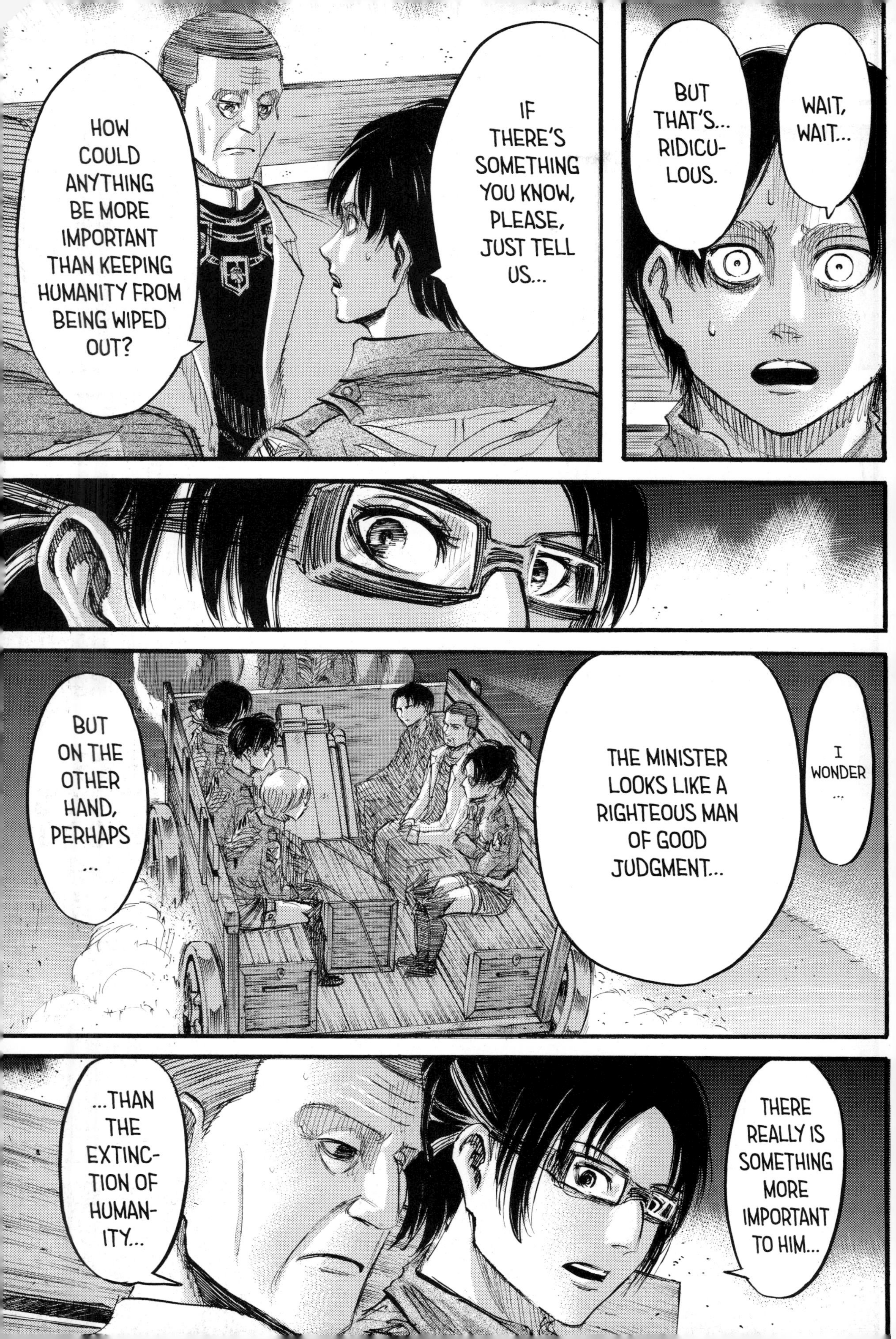
WAIT, WAIT...
BUT THAT'S... RIDICU-LOUS.
IF THERE'S SOMETHING YOU KNOW, PLEASE, JUST TELL US...
HOW COULD ANYTHING BE MORE IMPORTANT THAN KEEPING HUMANITY FROM BEING WIPED OUT?
I WONDER...
THE MINISTER LOOKS LIKE A RIGHTEOUS MAN OF GOOD JUDGMENT...
BUT ON THE OTHER HAND, PERHAPS...
THERE REALLY IS SOMETHING MORE IMPORTANT TO HIM...
...THAN THE EXTINCTION OF HUMAN-ITY...

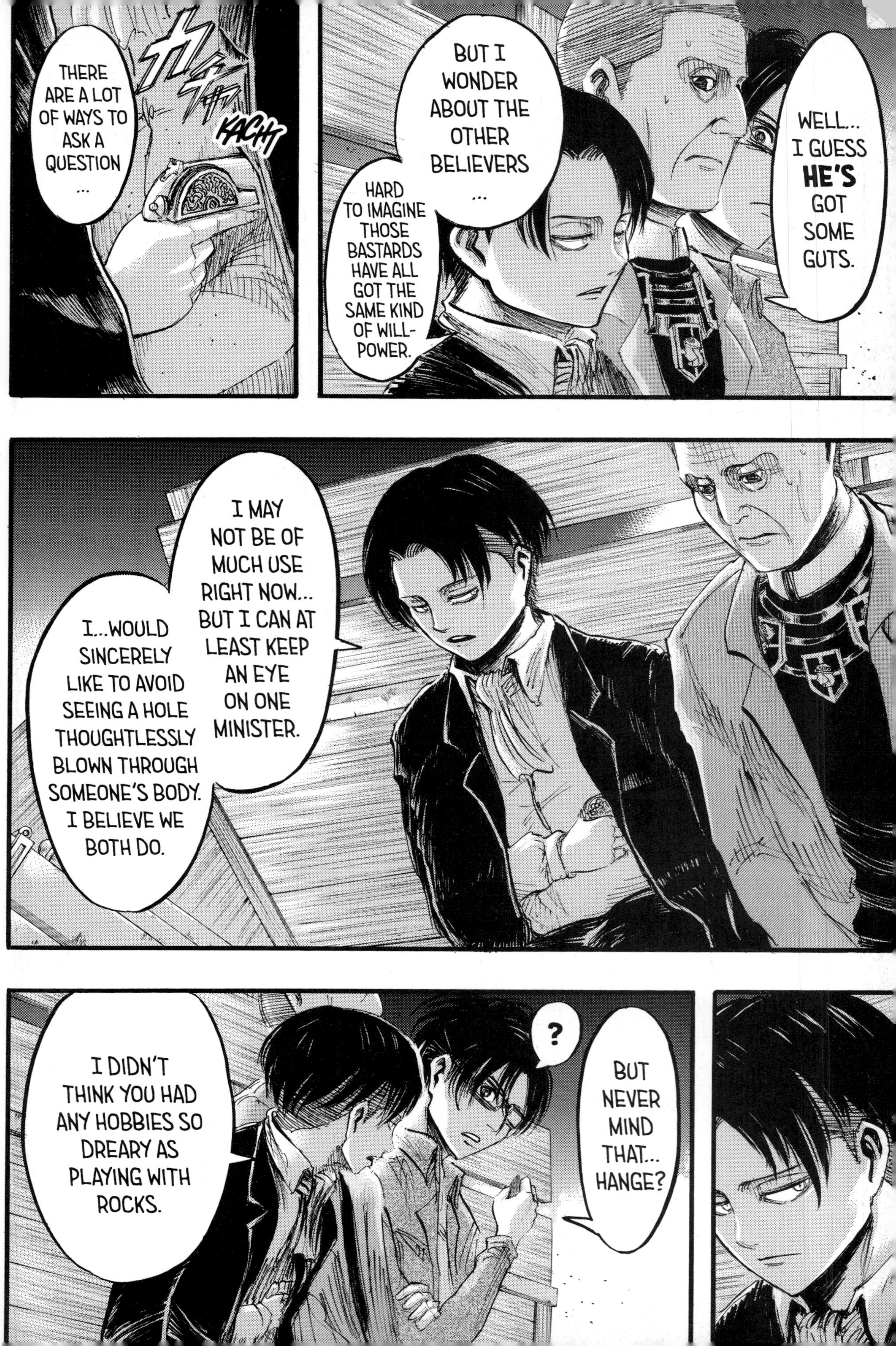
WELL... I GUESS HE'S GOT SOME GUTS.
BUT I WONDER ABOUT THE OTHER BELIEVERS...
HARD TO IMAGINE THOSE BASTARDS HAVE ALL GOT THE SAME KIND OF WILL-POWER.
KACHI
THERE ARE A LOT OF WAYS TO ASK A QUESTION...
I MAY NOT BE OF MUCH USE RIGHT NOW... BUT I CAN AT LEAST KEEP AN EYE ON ONE MINISTER.
I...WOULD SINCERELY LIKE TO AVOID SEEING A HOLE THOUGHTLESSLY BLOWN THROUGH SOMEONE'S BODY. I BELIEVE WE BOTH DO.
?
BUT NEVER MIND THAT... HANGE?
I DIDN'T THINK YOU HAD ANY HOBBIES SO DREARY AS PLAYING WITH ROCKS.

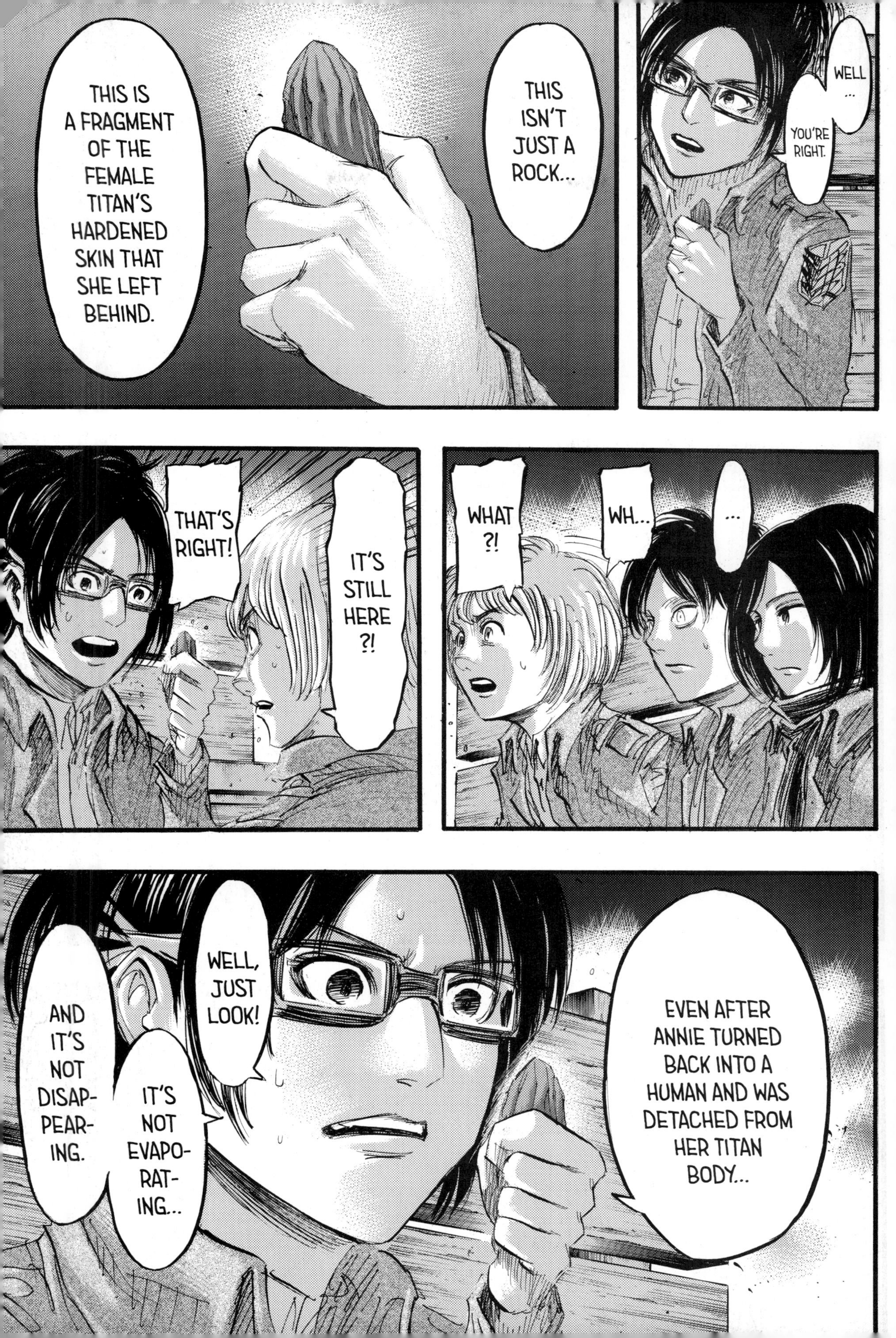
WELL ...
YOU'RE RIGHT.
THIS ISN'T JUST A ROCK...
THIS IS A FRAGMENT OF THE FEMALE TITAN'S HARDENED SKIN THAT SHE LEFT BEHIND.
...
WH...
WHAT ?!
IT'S STILL HERE ?!
THAT'S RIGHT!
EVEN AFTER ANNIE TURNED BACK INTO A HUMAN AND WAS DETACHED FROM HER TITAN BODY...
WELL, JUST LOOK!
IT'S NOT EVAPO-RAT-ING...
AND IT'S NOT DISAP-PEAR-ING.

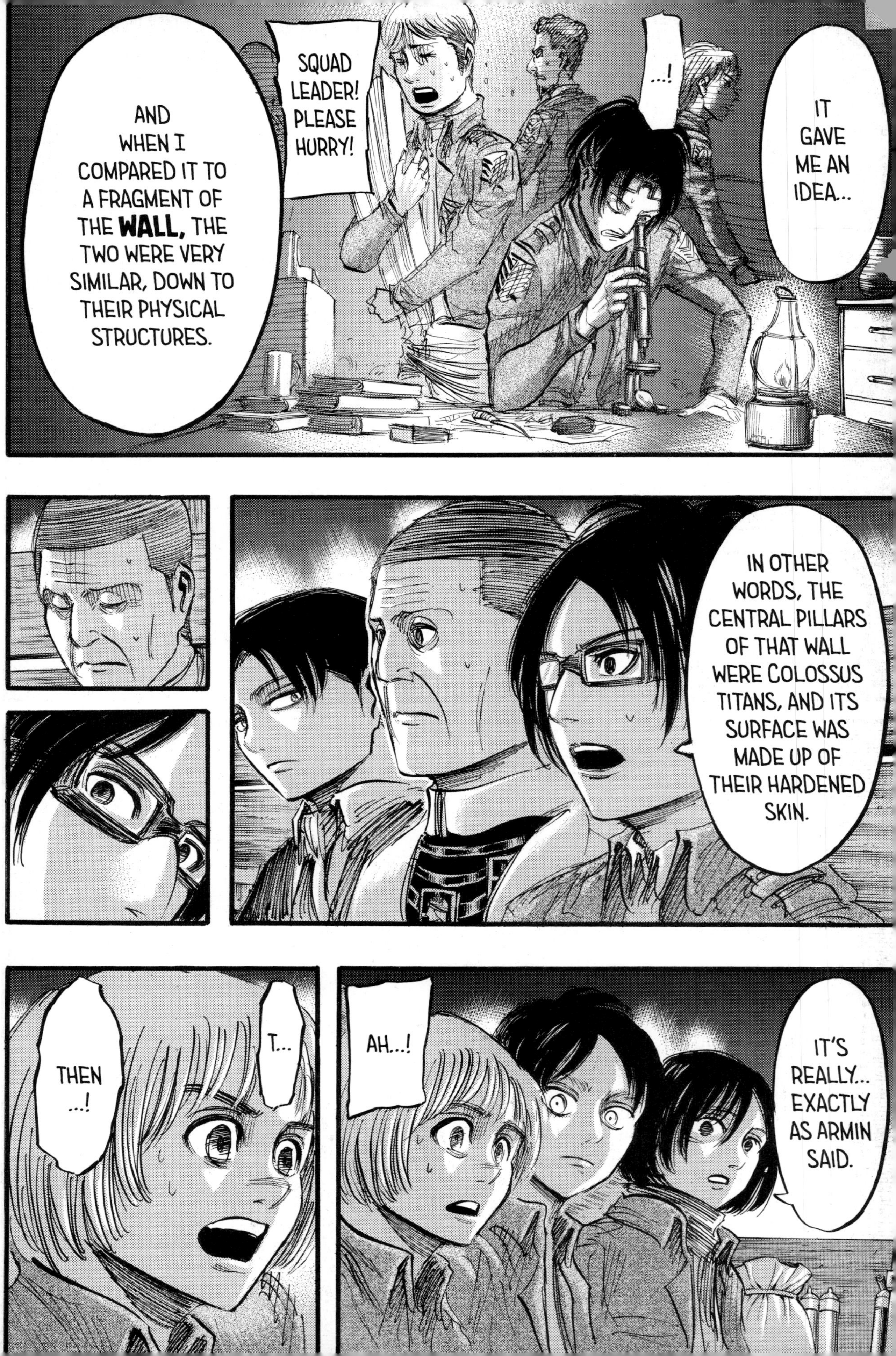
IT GAVE ME AN IDEA...
...!
SQUAD LEADER! PLEASE HURRY!
AND WHEN I COMPARED IT TO A FRAGMENT OF THE WALL, THE TWO WERE VERY SIMILAR, DOWN TO THEIR PHYSICAL STRUCTURES.
IN OTHER WORDS, THE CENTRAL PILLARS OF THAT WALL WERE COLOSSUS TITANS, AND ITS SURFACE WAS MADE UP OF THEIR HARDENED SKIN.
IT'S REALLY... EXACTLY AS ARMIN SAID.
AH...!
T...
THEN ...!

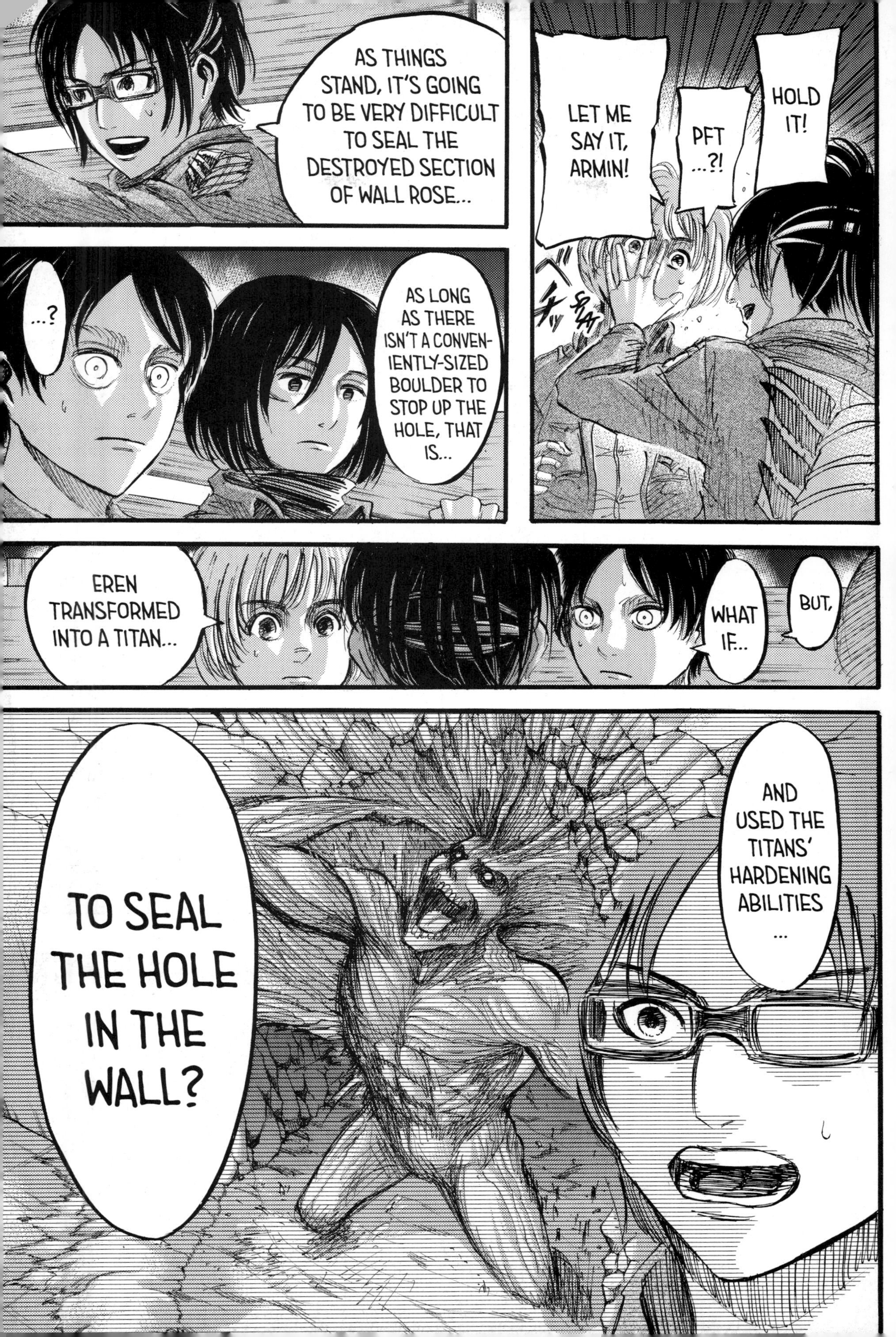
HOLD IT!
PFT ...?!
LET ME SAY IT, ARMIN!
AS THINGS STAND, IT'S GOING TO BE VERY DIFFICULT TO SEAL THE DESTROYED SECTION OF WALL ROSE...
AS LONG AS THERE ISN'T A CONVEN-IENTLY-SIZED BOULDER TO STOP UP THE HOLE, THAT IS...
...?
BUT,
WHAT IF...
EREN TRANSFORMED INTO A TITAN...
AND USED THE TITANS' HARDENING ABILITIES ...
TO SEAL THE HOLE IN THE WALL?

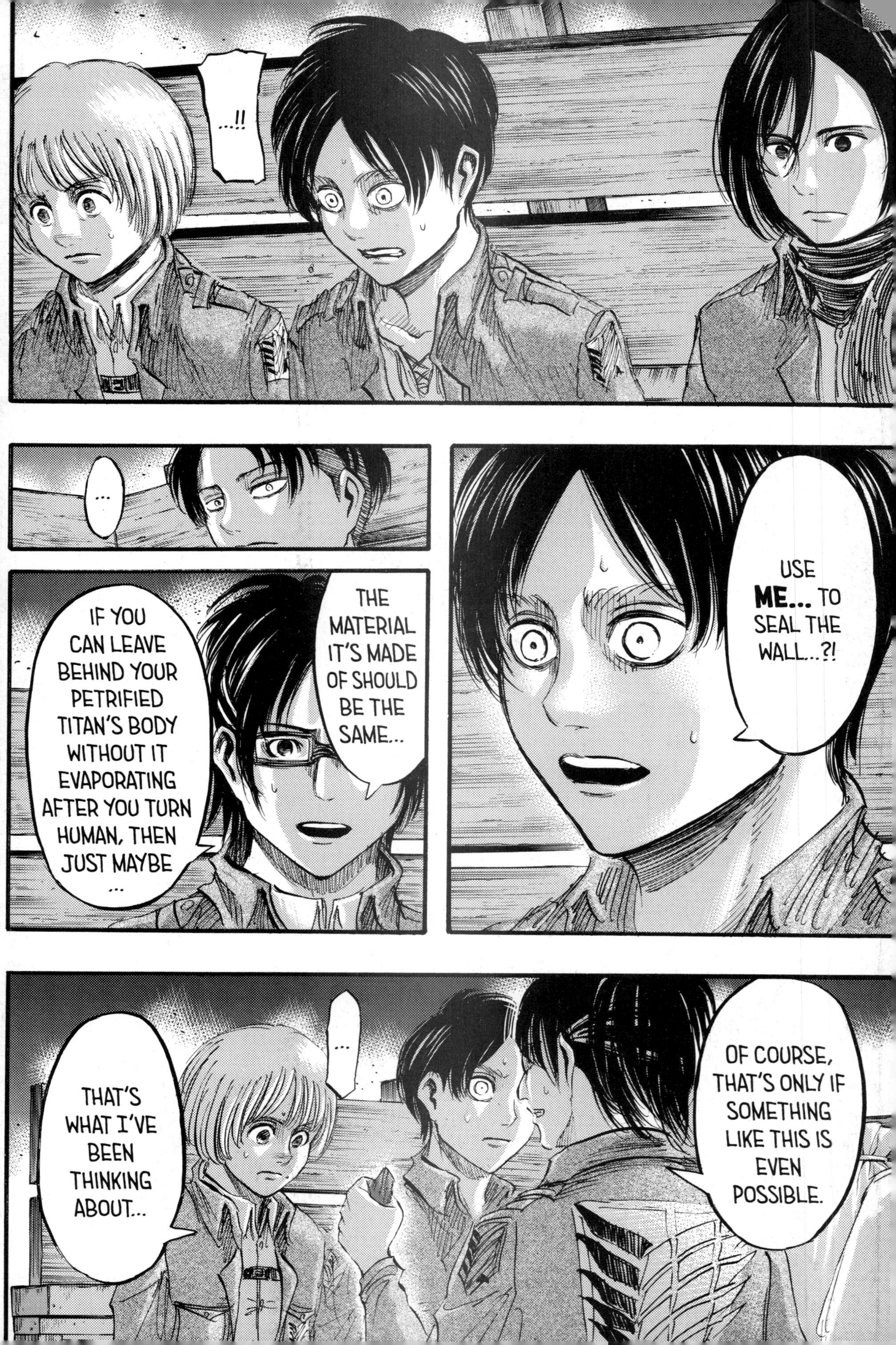
...!!
USE ME... TO SEAL THE WALL...?!
...
THE MATERIAL IT'S MADE OF SHOULD BE THE SAME...
IF YOU CAN LEAVE BEHIND YOUR PETRIFIED TITAN'S BODY WITHOUT IT EVAPORATING AFTER YOU TURN HUMAN, THEN JUST MAYBE ...
OF COURSE, THAT'S ONLY IF SOMETHING LIKE THIS IS EVEN POSSIBLE.
...
THAT'S WHAT I'VE BEEN THINKING ABOUT...

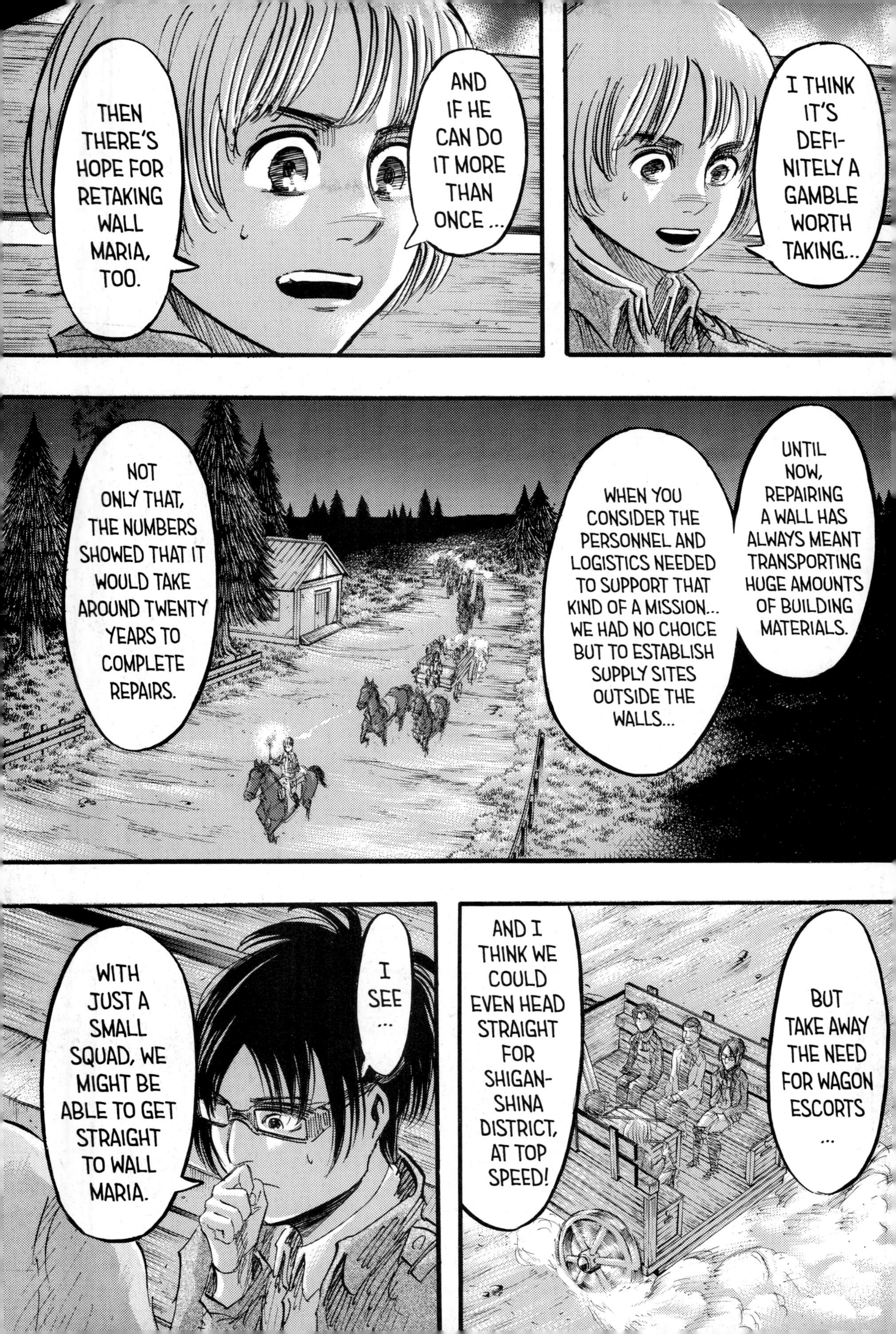
I THINK IT'S DEFINITELY A GAMBLE WORTH TAKING...
AND IF HE CAN DO IT MORE THAN ONCE ...
THEN THERE'S HOPE FOR RETAKING WALL MARIA, TOO.
UNTIL NOW, REPAIRING A WALL HAS ALWAYS MEANT TRANSPORTING HUGE AMOUNTS OF BUILDING MATERIALS.
WHEN YOU CONSIDER THE PERSONNEL AND LOGISTICS NEEDED TO SUPPORT THAT KIND OF A MISSION... WE HAD NO CHOICE BUT TO ESTABLISH SUPPLY SITES OUTSIDE THE WALLS...
NOT ONLY THAT, THE NUMBERS SHOWED THAT IT WOULD TAKE AROUND TWENTY YEARS TO COMPLETE REPAIRS.
BUT TAKE AWAY THE NEED FOR WAGON ESCORTS ...
AND I THINK WE COULD EVEN HEAD STRAIGHT FOR SHIGAN-SHINA DISTRICT, AT TOP SPEED!
I SEE ...
WITH JUST A SMALL SQUAD, WE MIGHT BE ABLE TO GET STRAIGHT TO WALL MARIA.

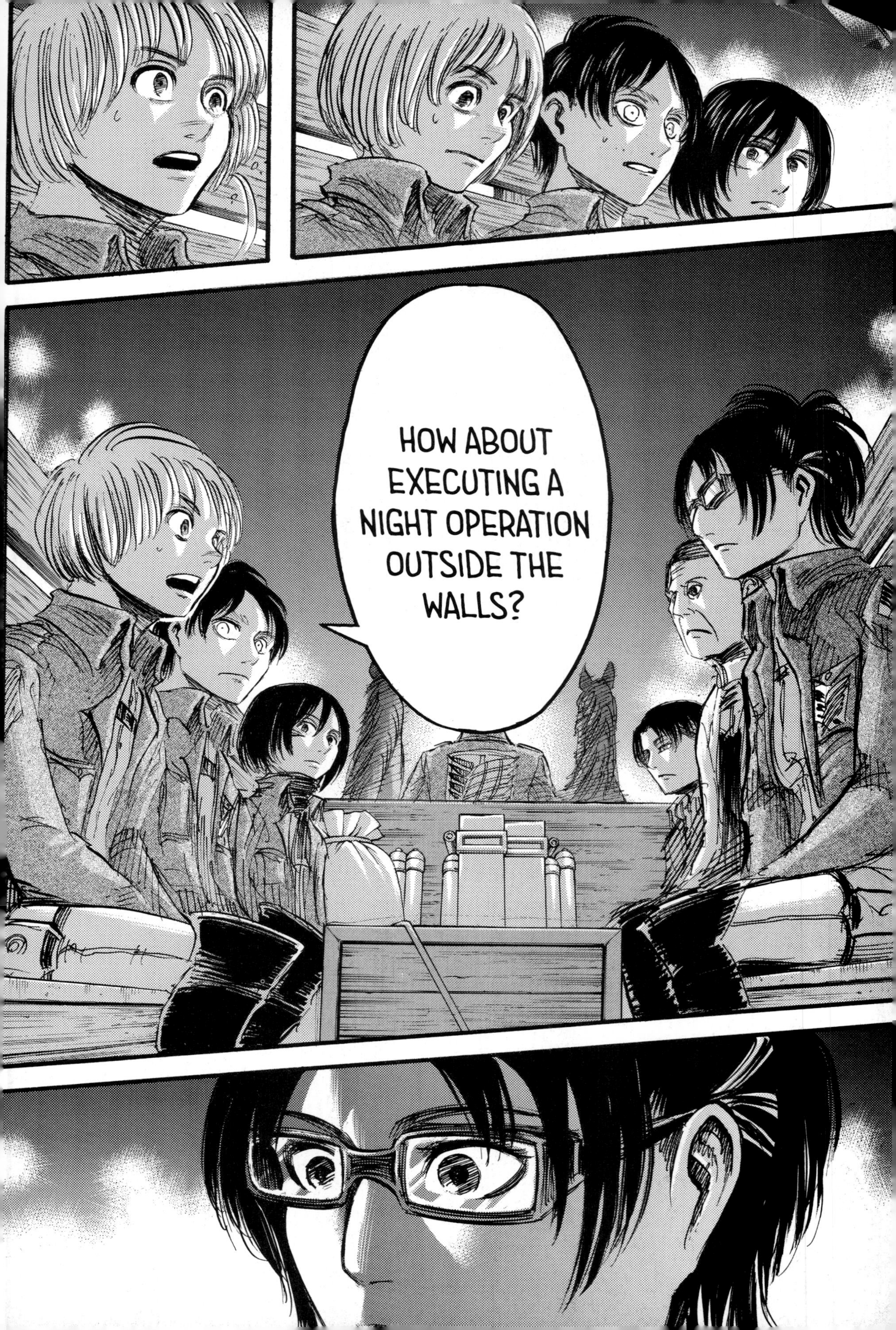
HOW ABOUT EXECUTING A NIGHT OPERATION OUTSIDE THE WALLS?

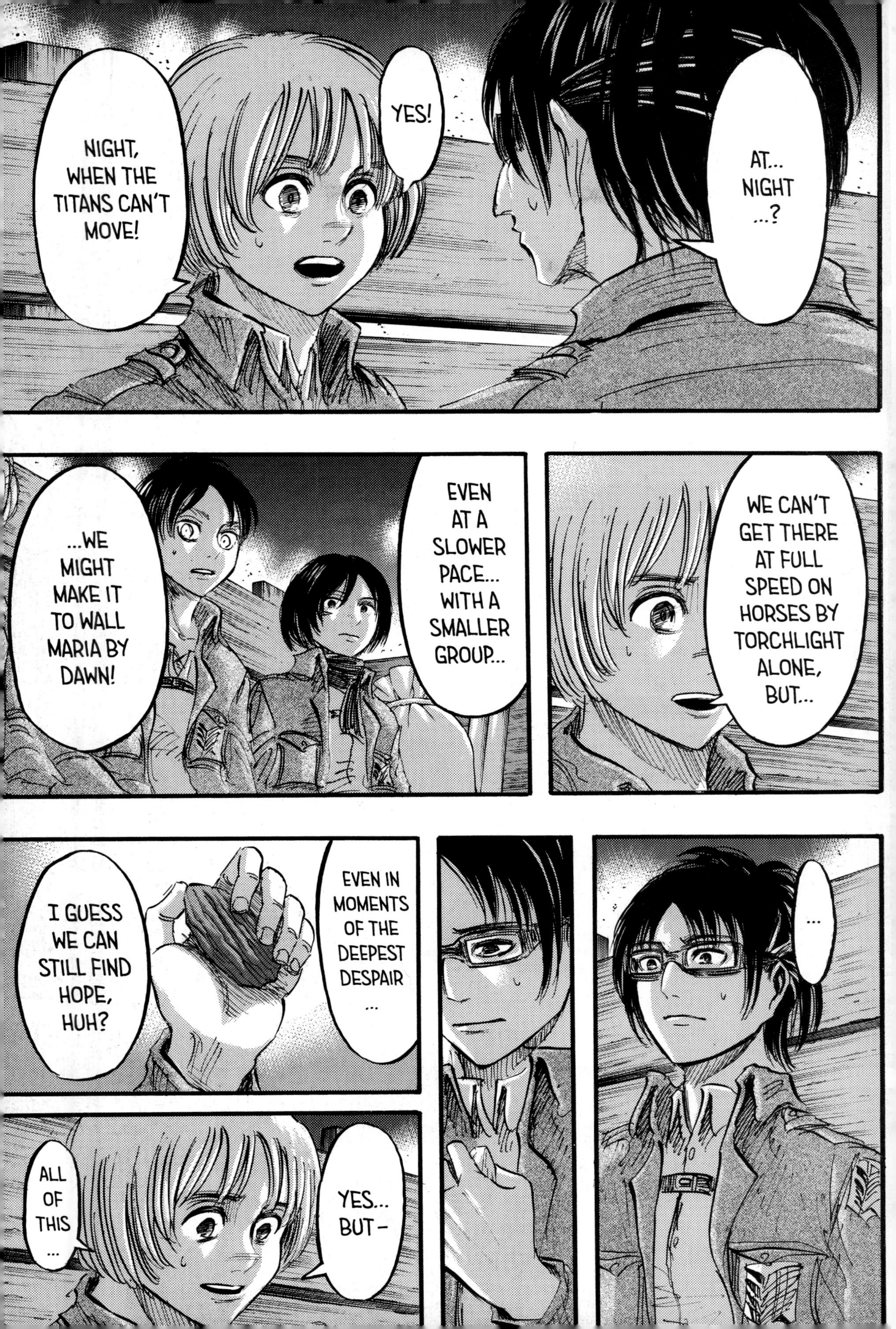
AT... NIGHT ...?
YES!
NIGHT, WHEN THE TITANS CAN'T MOVE!
WE CAN'T GET THERE AT FULL SPEED ON HORSES BY TORCHLIGHT ALONE, BUT...
EVEN AT A SLOWER PACE... WITH A SMALLER GROUP...
...WE MIGHT MAKE IT TO WALL MARIA BY DAWN!
...
EVEN IN MOMENTS OF THE DEEPEST DESPAIR ...
I GUESS WE CAN STILL FIND HOPE, HUH?
YES... BUT–
ALL OF THIS ...

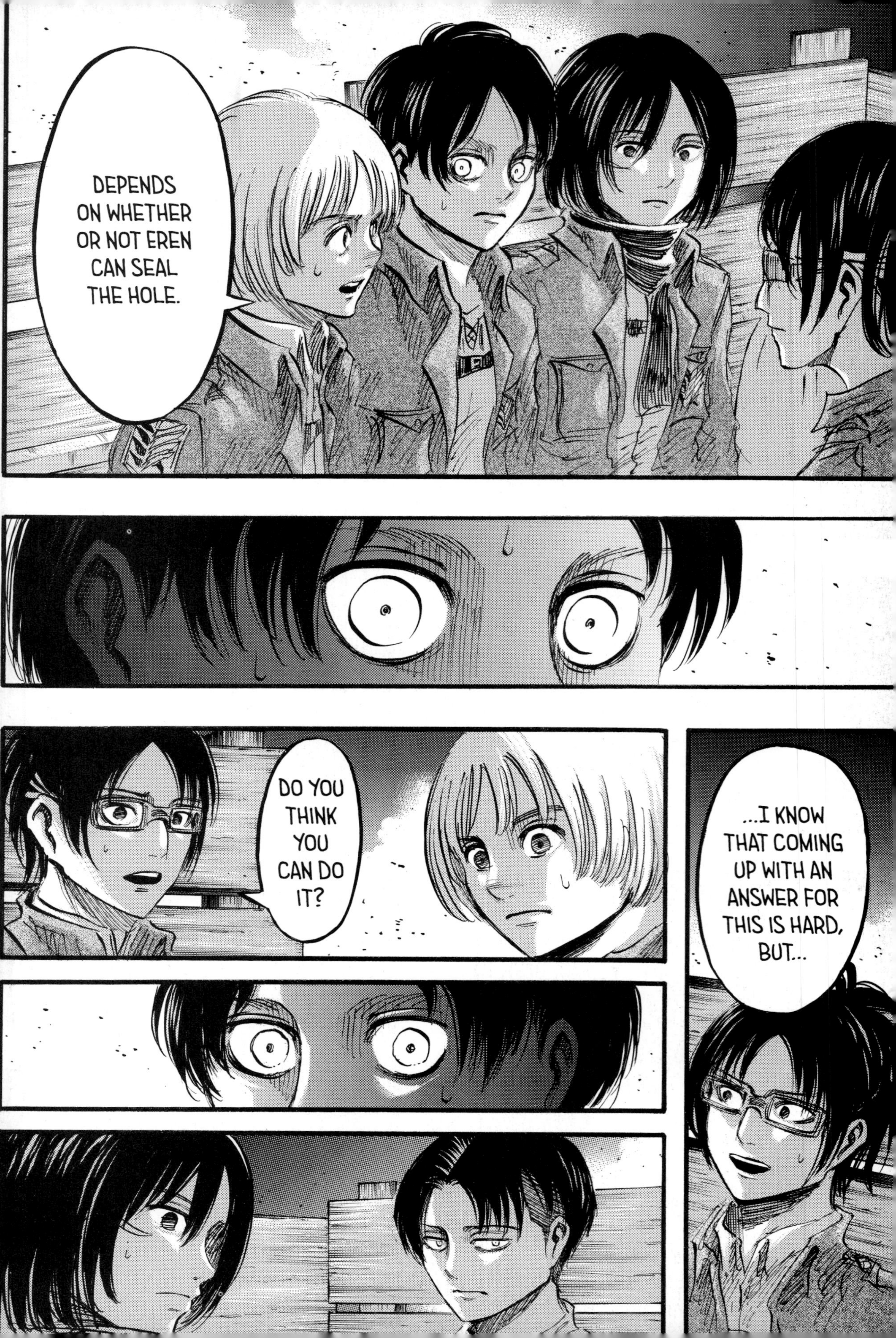
DEPENDS ON WHETHER OR NOT EREN CAN SEAL THE HOLE.
...I KNOW THAT COMING UP WITH AN ANSWER FOR THIS IS HARD, BUT...
DO YOU THINK YOU CAN DO IT?

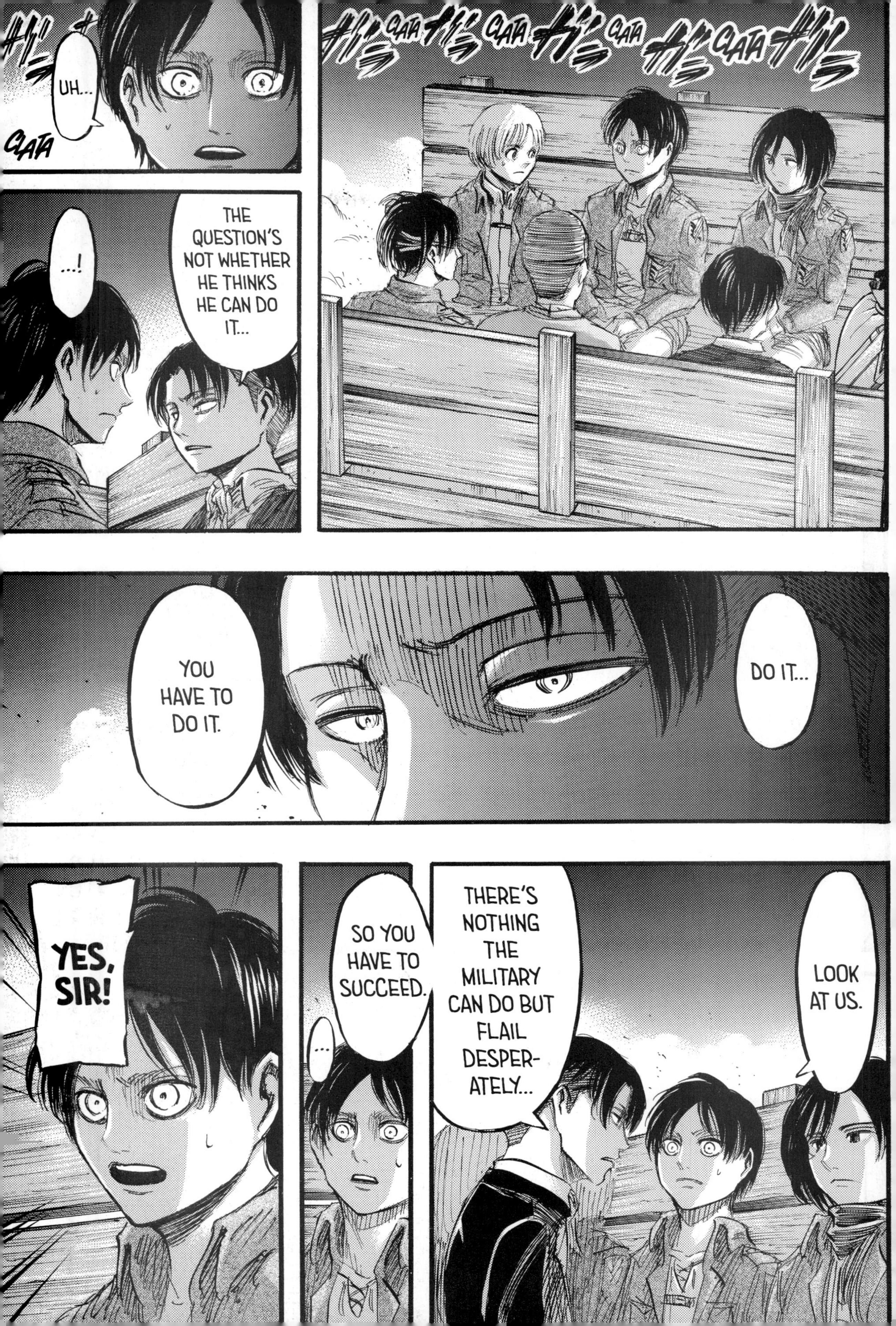
CLATA CLATA CLATA CLATA
UH...
CLATA
THE QUESTION'S NOT WHETHER HE THINKS HE CAN DO IT...
...!
DO IT...
YOU HAVE TO DO IT.
LOOK AT US.
THERE'S NOTHING THE MILITARY CAN DO BUT FLAIL DESPER-ATELY...
SO YOU HAVE TO SUCCEED.
...
YES, SIR!

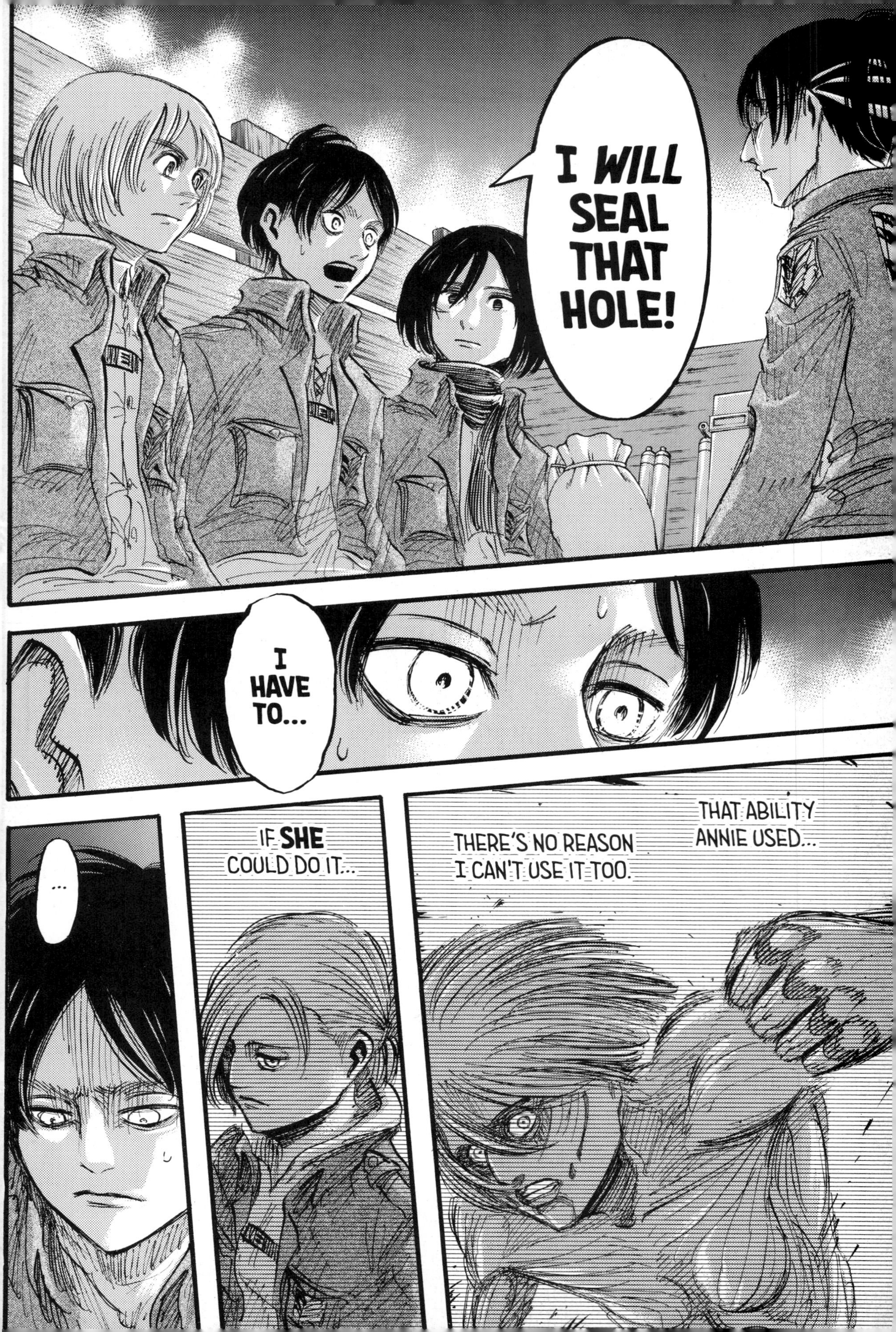
I *WILL* SEAL THAT HOLE!
I HAVE TO...
THAT ABILITY ANNIE USED...
THERE'S NO REASON I CAN'T USE IT TOO.
IF **SHE** COULD DO IT...
...

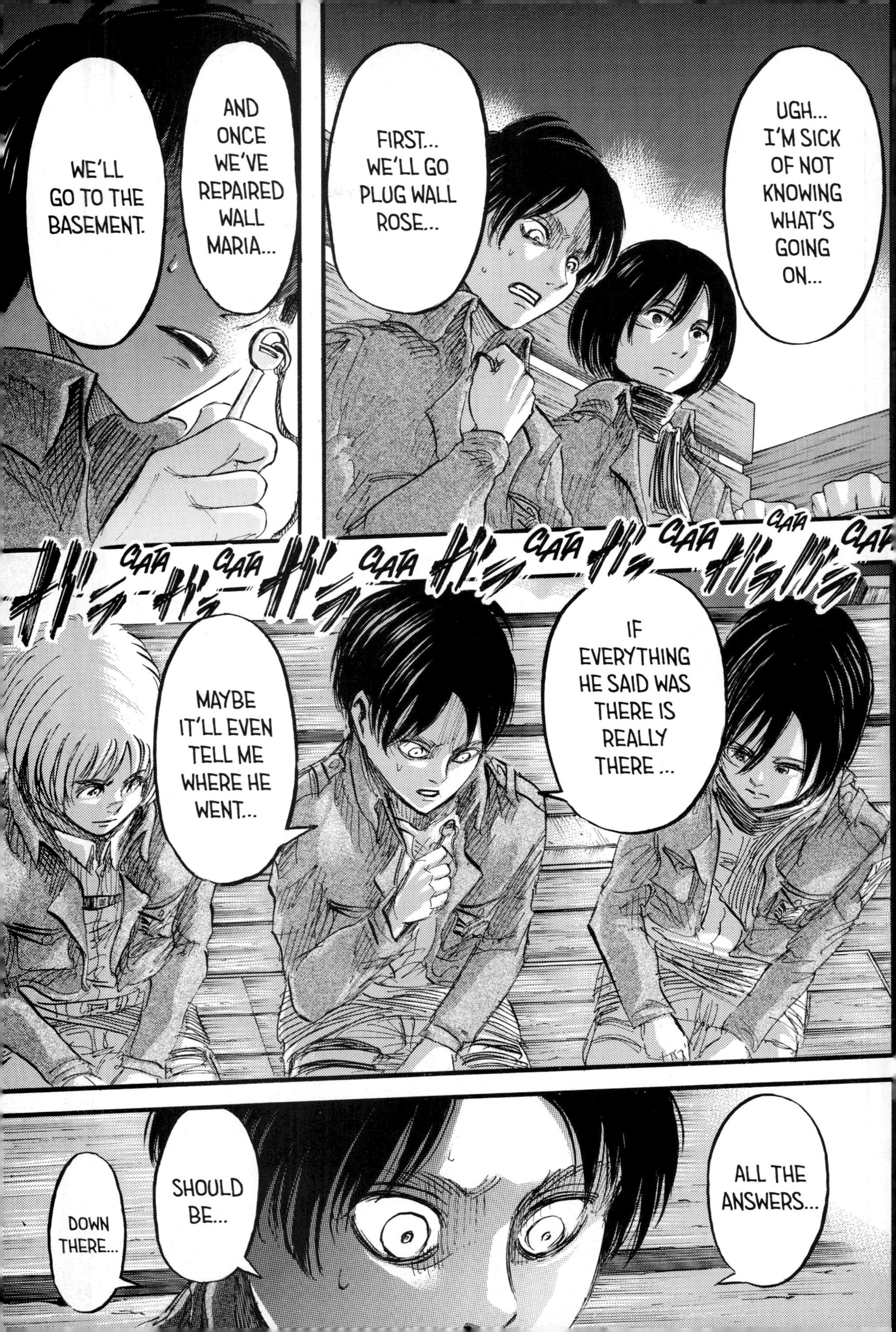
UGH... I'M SICK OF NOT KNOWING WHAT'S GOING ON...
FIRST... WE'LL GO PLUG WALL ROSE...
AND ONCE WE'VE REPAIRED WALL MARIA...
WE'LL GO TO THE BASEMENT.
CLATA
CLATA
CLATA
CLATA
CLATA
CLATA
CLATA
IF EVERYTHING HE SAID WAS THERE IS REALLY THERE ...
MAYBE IT'LL EVEN TELL ME WHERE HE WENT...
ALL THE ANSWERS...
SHOULD BE...
DOWN THERE...

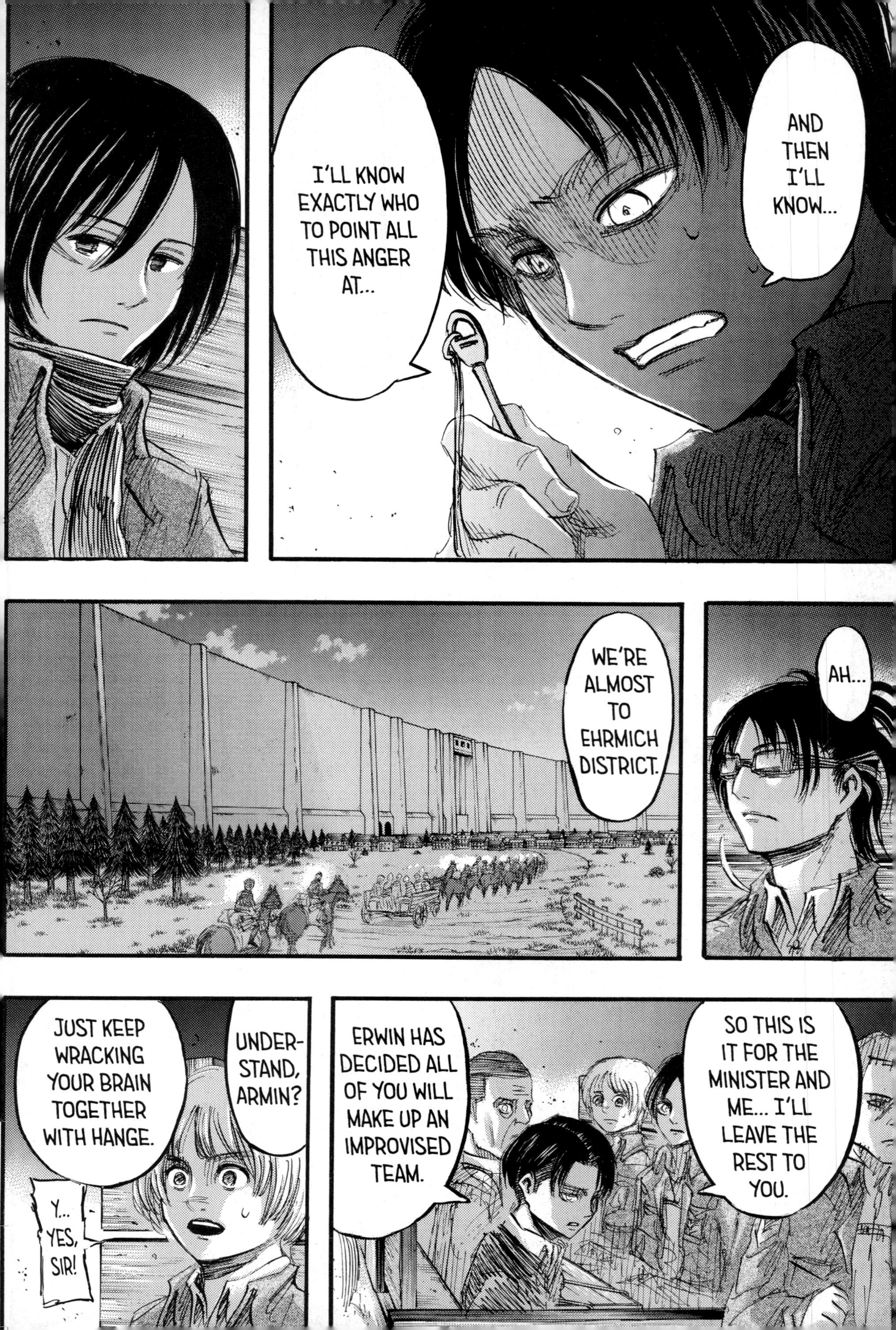
AND THEN I'LL KNOW...
I'LL KNOW EXACTLY WHO TO POINT ALL THIS ANGER AT...
AH...
WE'RE ALMOST TO EHRMICH DISTRICT.
SO THIS IS IT FOR THE MINISTER AND ME... I'LL LEAVE THE REST TO YOU.
ERWIN HAS DECIDED ALL OF YOU WILL MAKE UP AN IMPROVISED TEAM.
UNDER-STAND, ARMIN?
JUST KEEP WRACKING YOUR BRAIN TOGETHER WITH HANGE.
Y... YES, SIR!

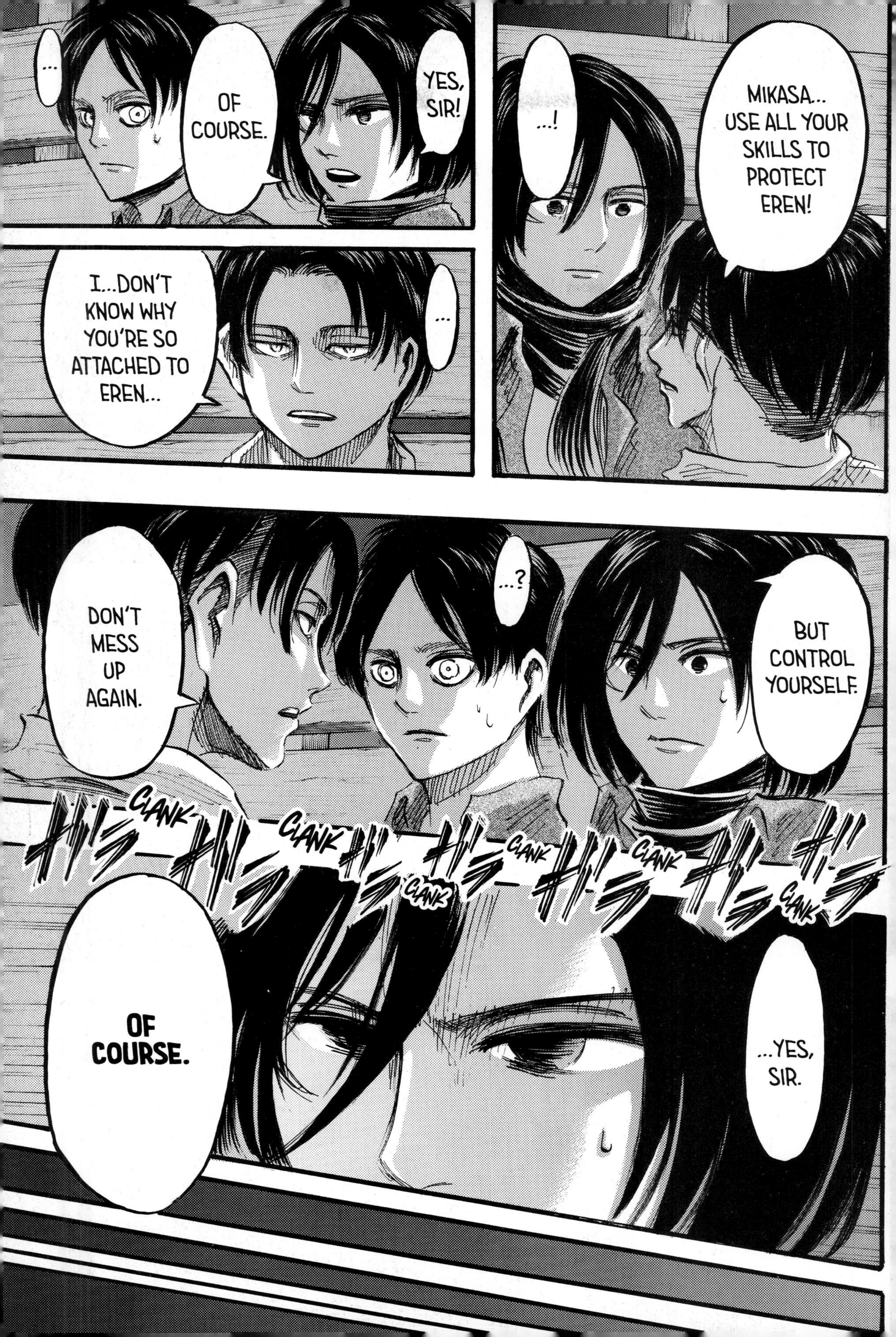
MIKASA... USE ALL YOUR SKILLS TO PROTECT EREN!
...!
YES, SIR!
OF COURSE.
...
...
I...DON'T KNOW WHY YOU'RE SO ATTACHED TO EREN...
BUT CONTROL YOURSELF.
...?
DON'T MESS UP AGAIN.
CLANK CLANK CLANK CLANK CLANK CLANK CLANK
...YES, SIR.
OF COURSE.

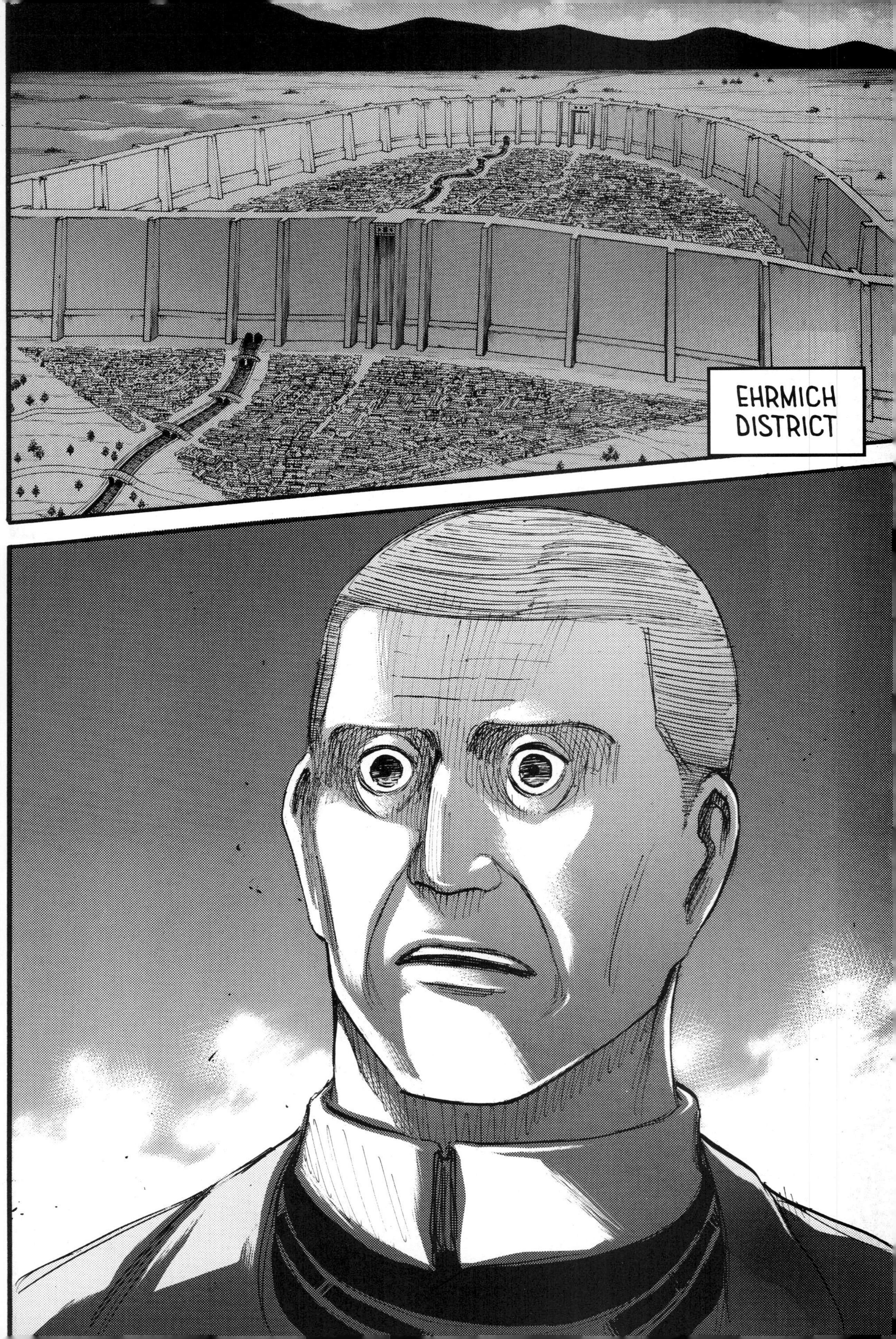
EHRMICH
DISTRICT

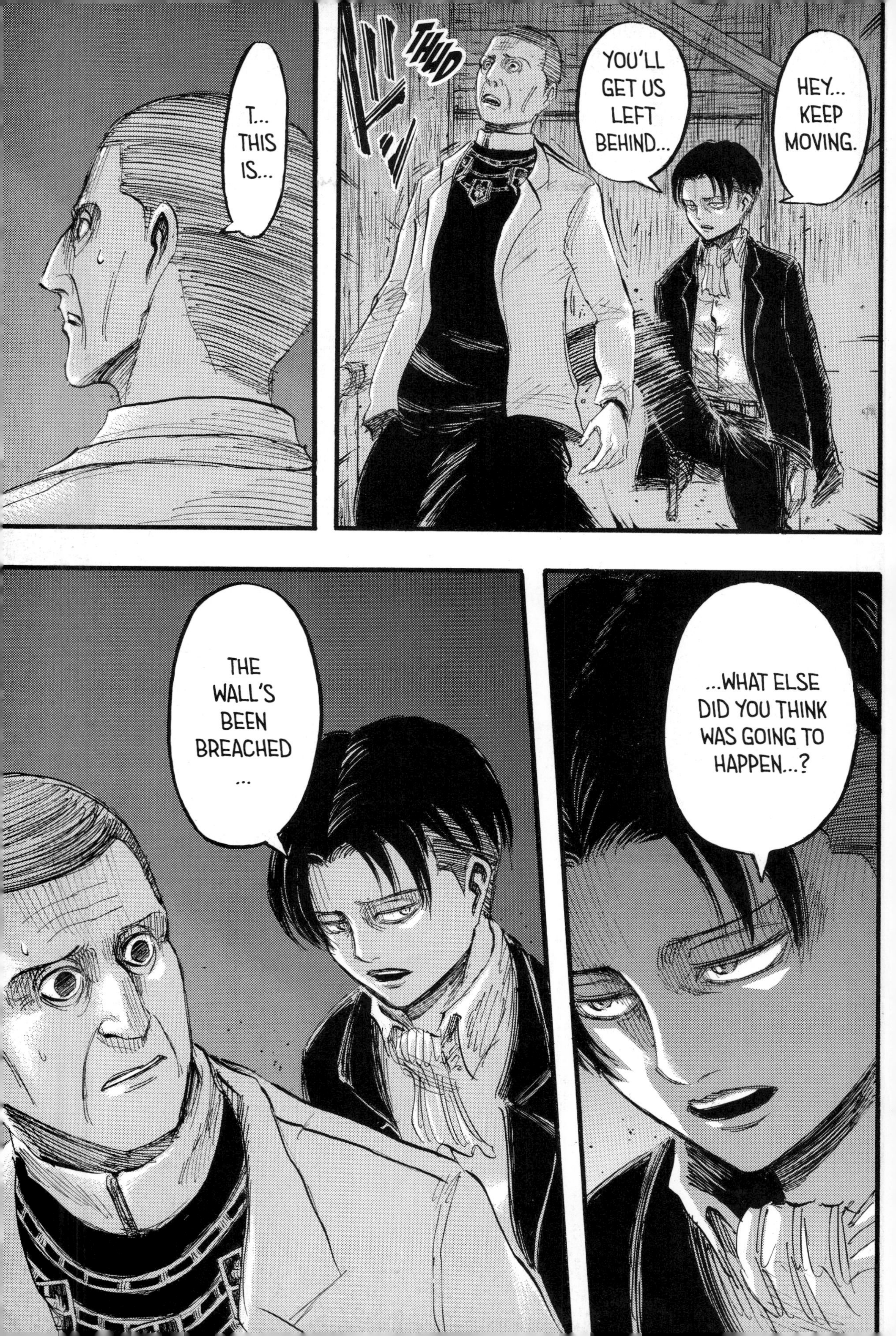
HEY... KEEP MOVING.
YOU'LL GET US LEFT BEHIND...
THUD
T... THIS IS...
...WHAT ELSE DID YOU THINK WAS GOING TO HAPPEN...?
THE WALL'S BEEN BREACHED ...

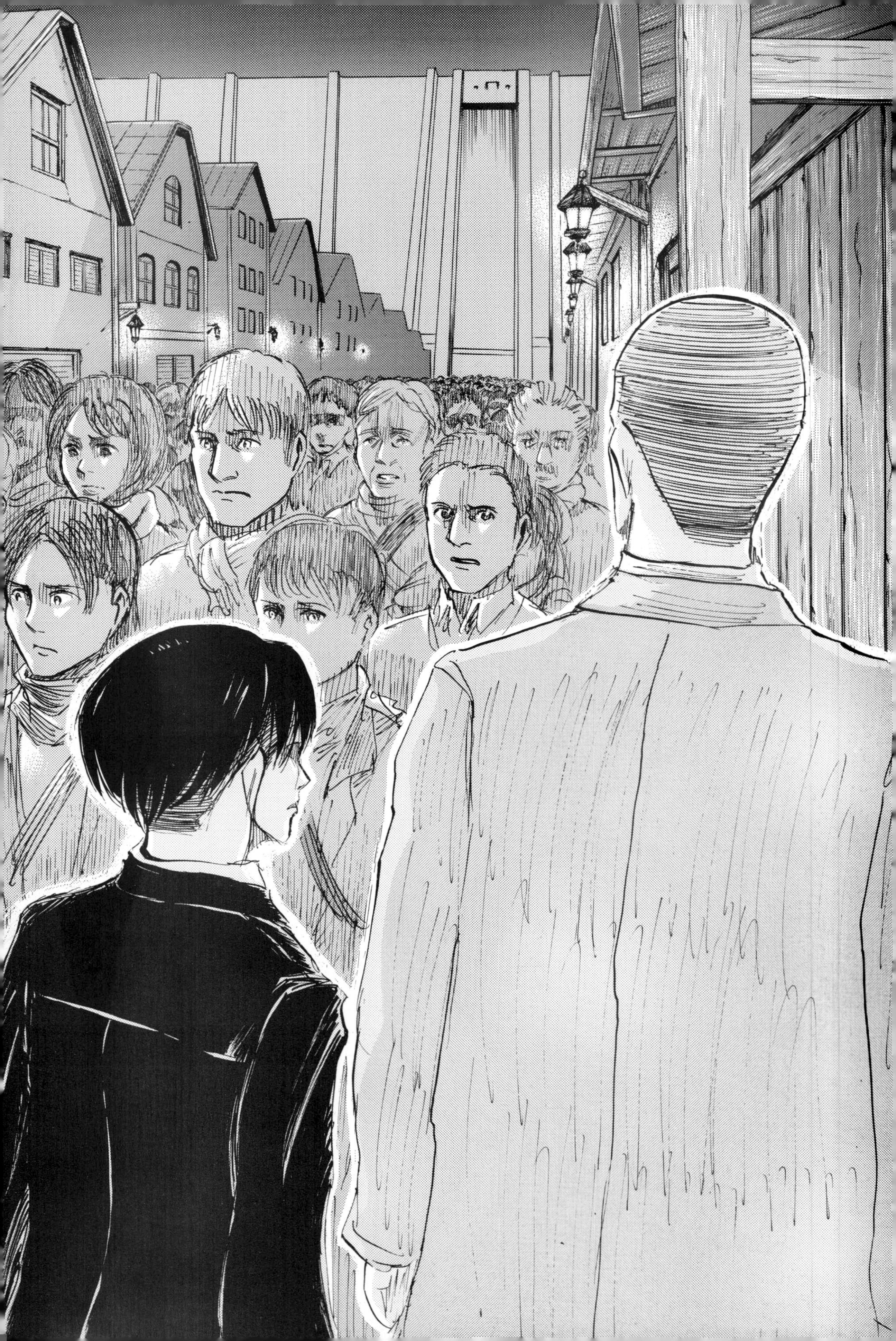

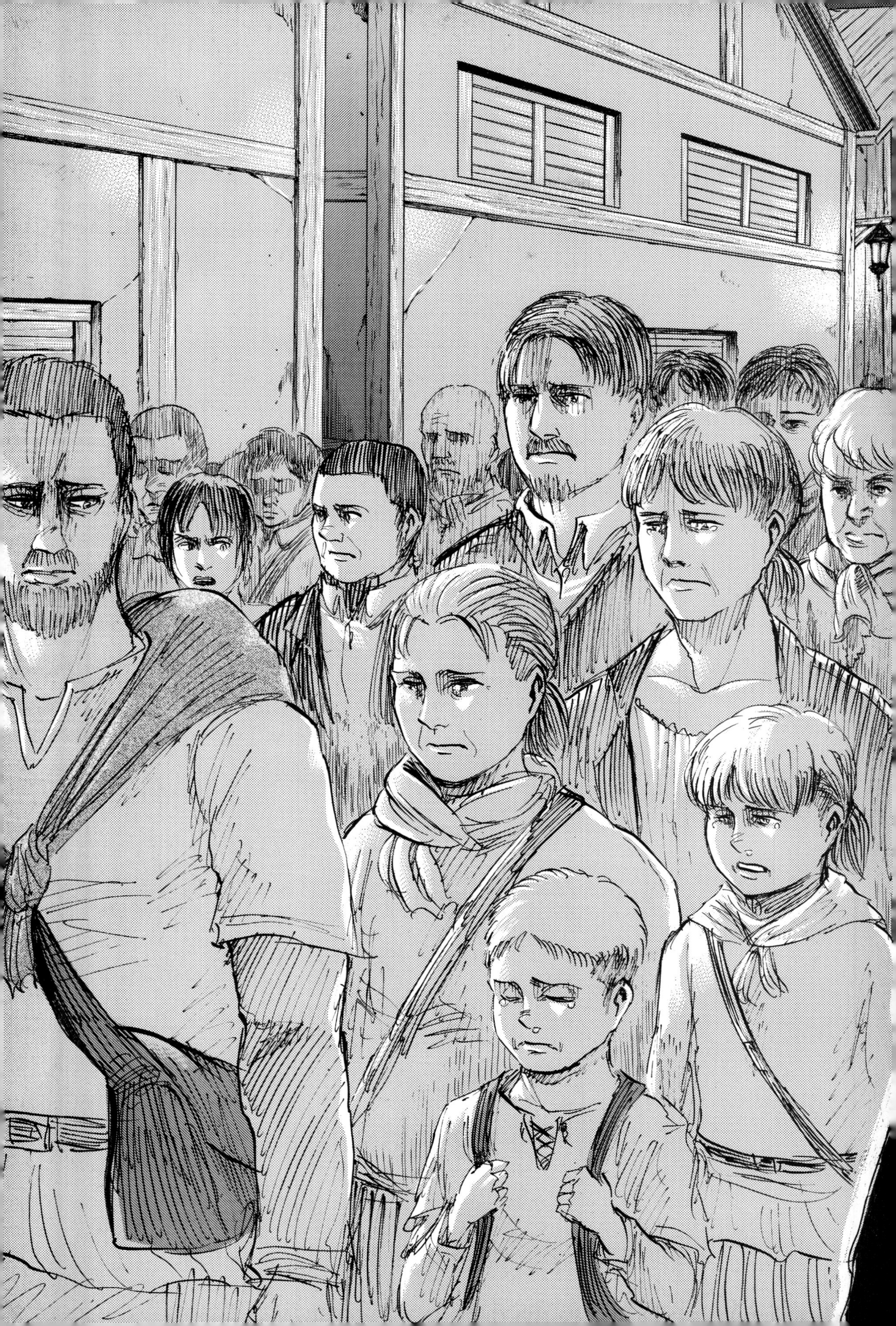

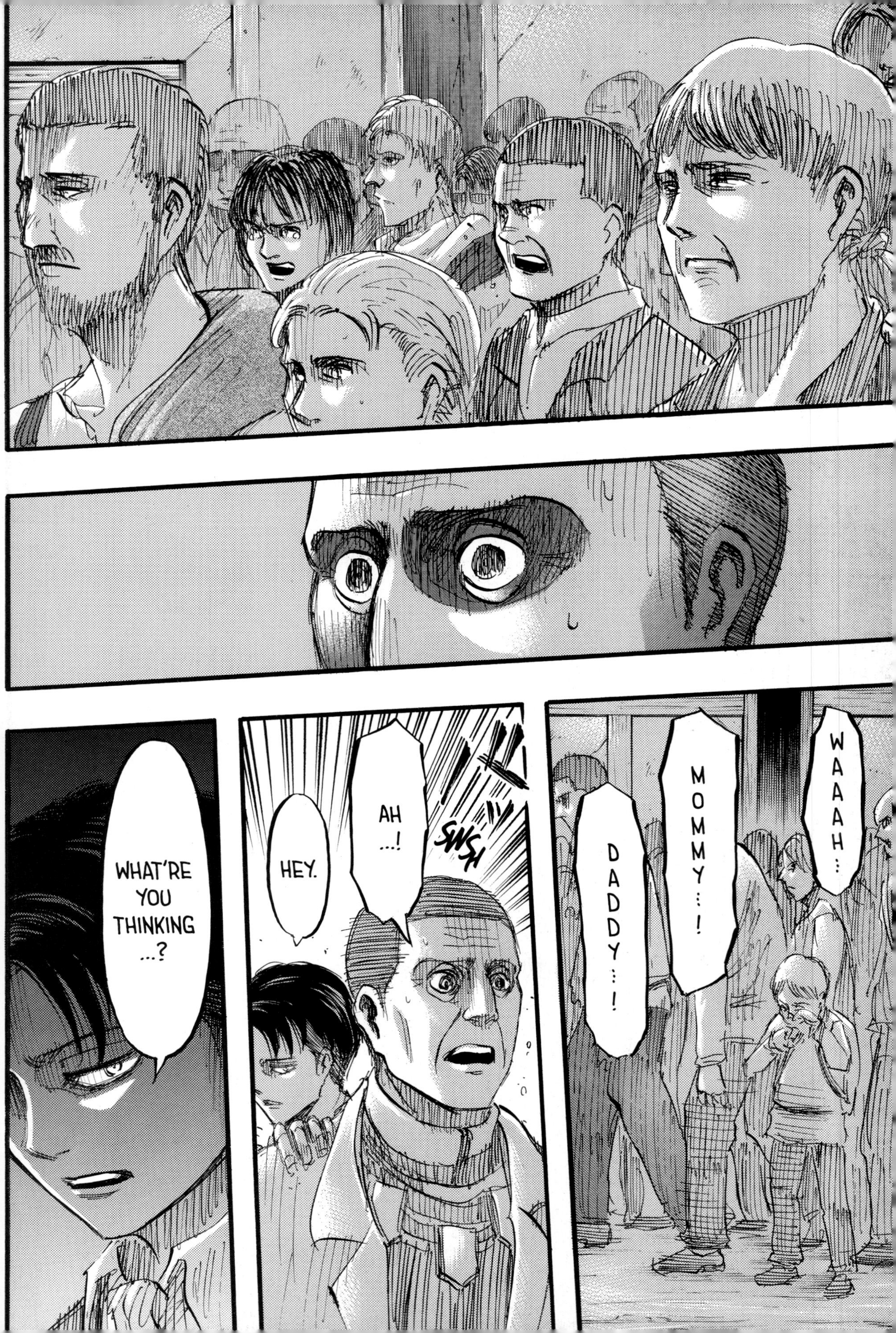
WAAAH...
MOMMY...!
DADDY...!
AH ...!
SWSH
HEY.
WHAT'RE YOU THINKING ...?

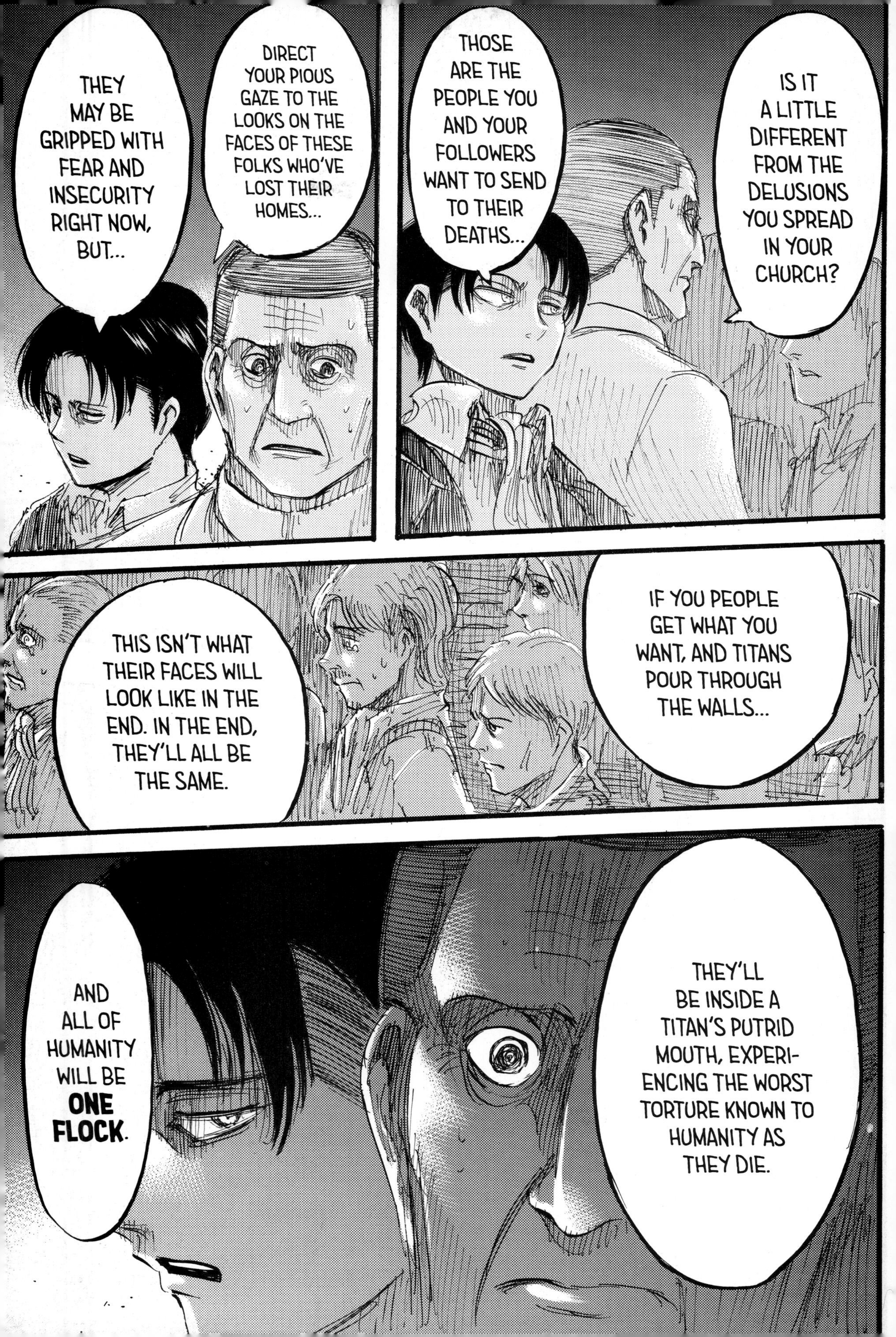
IS IT A LITTLE DIFFERENT FROM THE DELUSIONS YOU SPREAD IN YOUR CHURCH?
THOSE ARE THE PEOPLE YOU AND YOUR FOLLOWERS WANT TO SEND TO THEIR DEATHS...
DIRECT YOUR PIOUS GAZE TO THE LOOKS ON THE FACES OF THESE FOLKS WHO'VE LOST THEIR HOMES...
THEY MAY BE GRIPPED WITH FEAR AND INSECURITY RIGHT NOW, BUT...
IF YOU PEOPLE GET WHAT YOU WANT, AND TITANS POUR THROUGH THE WALLS...
THIS ISN'T WHAT THEIR FACES WILL LOOK LIKE IN THE END. IN THE END, THEY'LL ALL BE THE SAME.
THEY'LL BE INSIDE A TITAN'S PUTRID MOUTH, EXPERIENCING THE WORST TORTURE KNOWN TO HUMANITY AS THEY DIE.
AND ALL OF HUMANITY WILL BE **ONE FLOCK**.

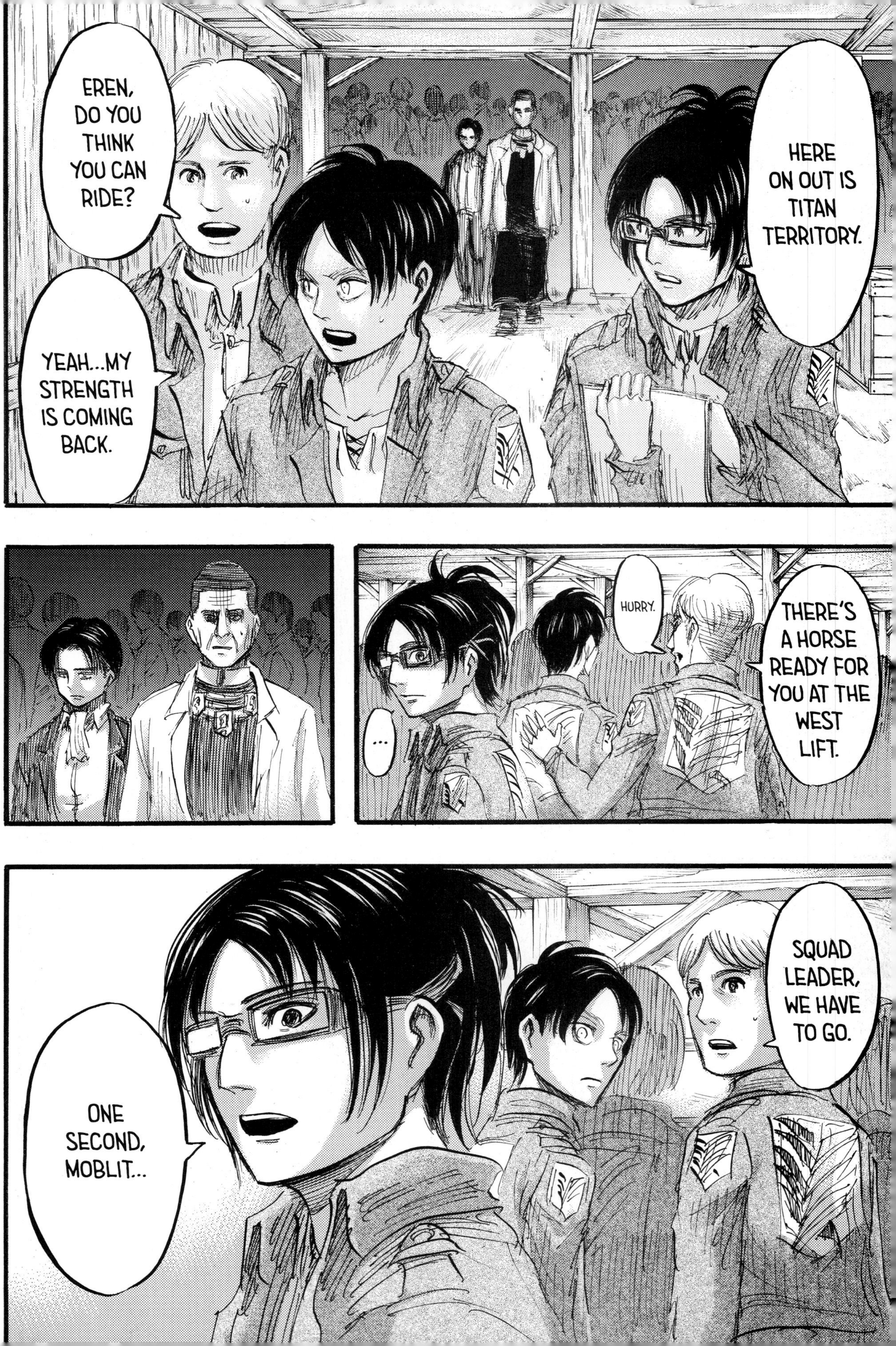
HERE ON OUT IS TITAN TERRITORY.
EREN, DO YOU THINK YOU CAN RIDE?
YEAH...MY STRENGTH IS COMING BACK.
THERE'S A HORSE READY FOR YOU AT THE WEST LIFT.
HURRY.
...
SQUAD LEADER, WE HAVE TO GO.
ONE SECOND, MOBLIT...

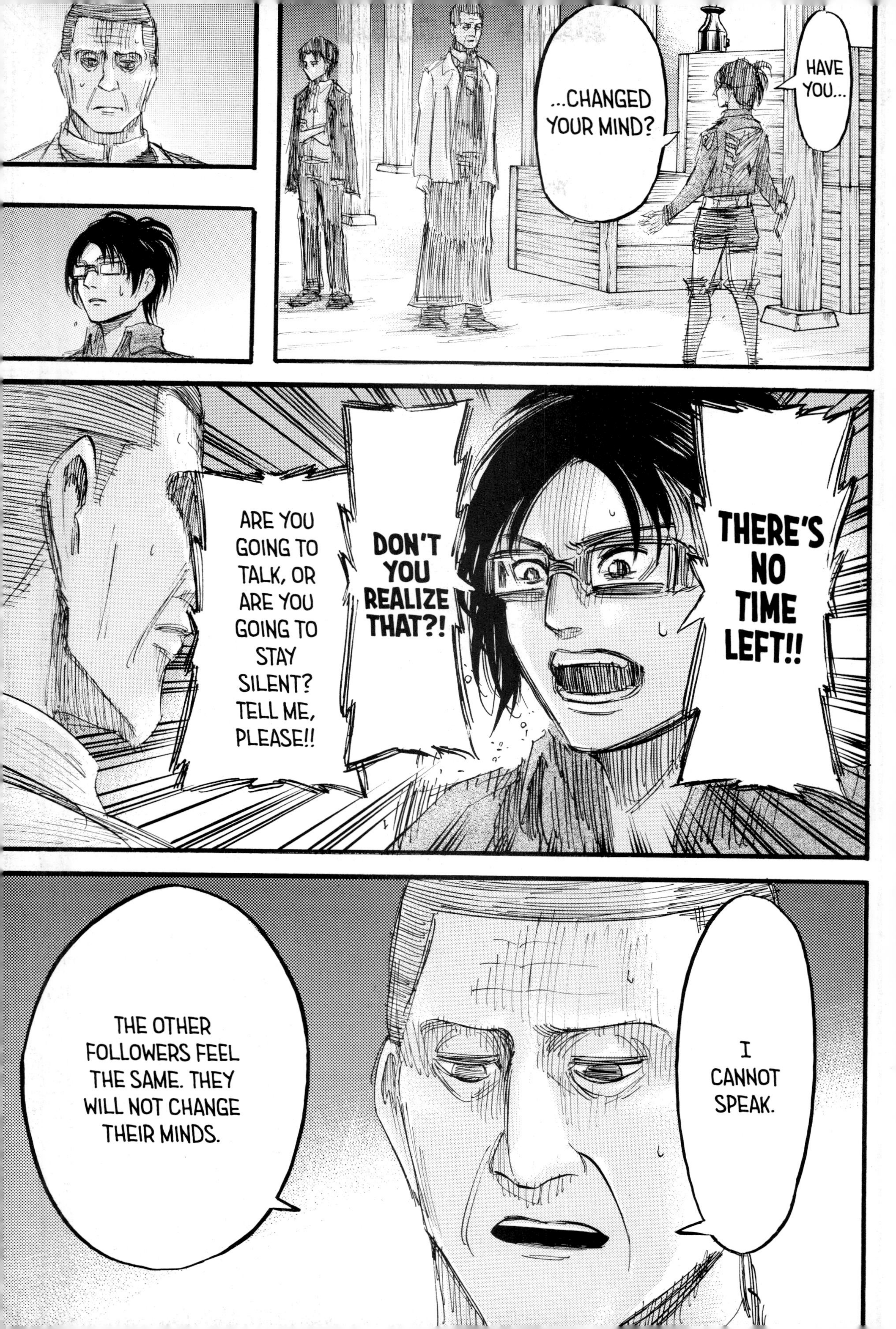
HAVE YOU...
...CHANGED YOUR MIND?
THERE'S NO TIME LEFT!!
DON'T YOU REALIZE THAT?!
ARE YOU GOING TO TALK, OR ARE YOU GOING TO STAY SILENT? TELL ME, PLEASE!!
I CANNOT SPEAK.
THE OTHER FOLLOWERS FEEL THE SAME. THEY WILL NOT CHANGE THEIR MINDS.

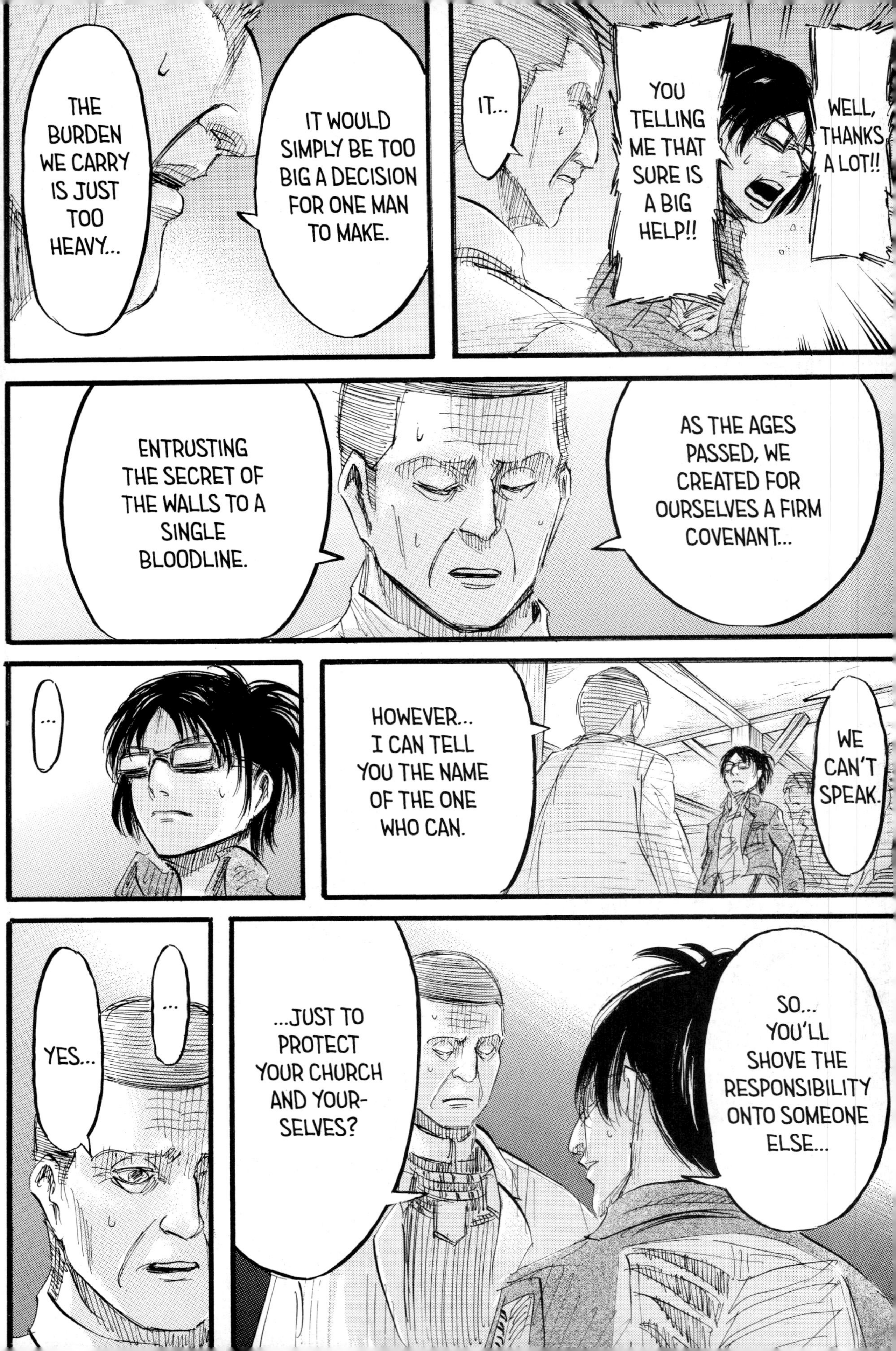

WELL, THANKS A LOT!!
YOU TELLING ME THAT SURE IS A BIG HELP!!
IT...
IT WOULD SIMPLY BE TOO BIG A DECISION FOR ONE MAN TO MAKE.
THE BURDEN WE CARRY IS JUST TOO HEAVY...
AS THE AGES PASSED, WE CREATED FOR OURSELVES A FIRM COVENANT...
ENTRUSTING THE SECRET OF THE WALLS TO A SINGLE BLOODLINE.
WE CAN'T SPEAK.
HOWEVER... I CAN TELL YOU THE NAME OF THE ONE WHO CAN.
...
SO... YOU'LL SHOVE THE RESPONSIBILITY ONTO SOMEONE ELSE...
...JUST TO PROTECT YOUR CHURCH AND YOUR-SELVES?
...
YES...

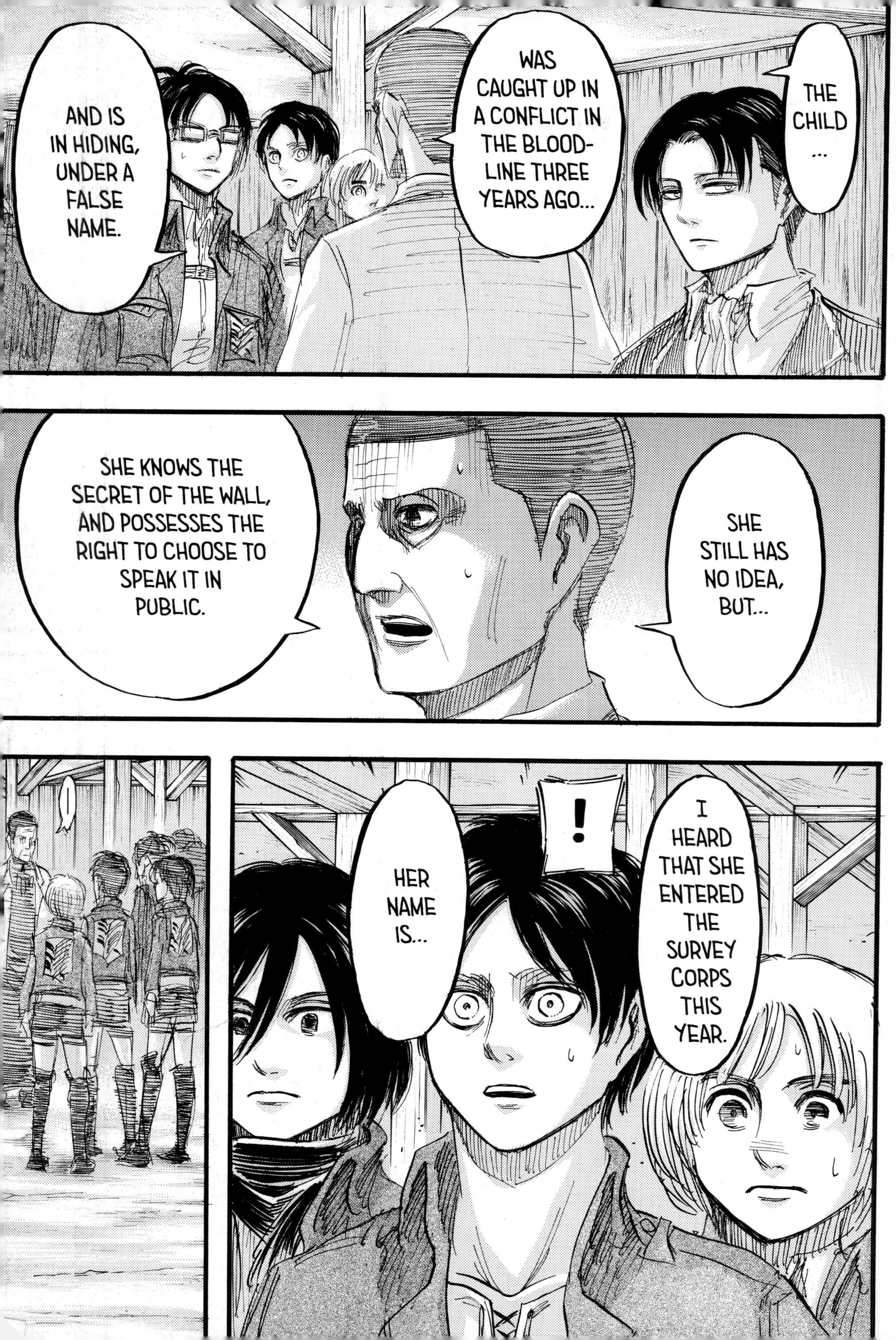
THE CHILD ...
WAS CAUGHT UP IN A CONFLICT IN THE BLOOD-LINE THREE YEARS AGO...
AND IS IN HIDING, UNDER A FALSE NAME.
SHE STILL HAS NO IDEA, BUT...
SHE KNOWS THE SECRET OF THE WALL, AND POSSESSES THE RIGHT TO CHOOSE TO SPEAK IT IN PUBLIC.
I HEARD THAT SHE ENTERED THE SURVEY CORPS THIS YEAR.
!
HER NAME IS...
!

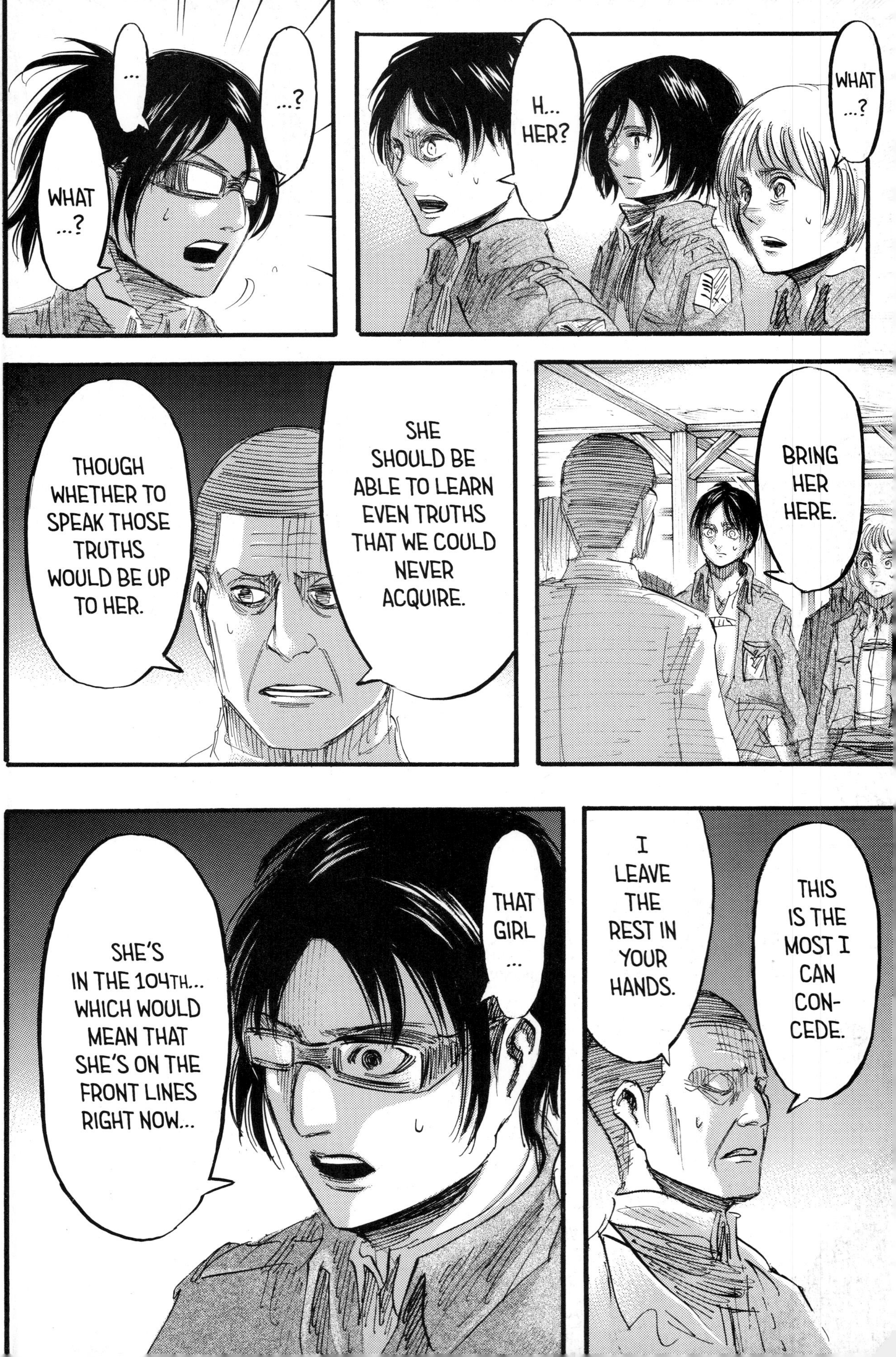
WHAT ...?
H... HER?
...?
...
WHAT ...?
BRING HER HERE.
SHE SHOULD BE ABLE TO LEARN EVEN TRUTHS THAT WE COULD NEVER ACQUIRE.
THOUGH WHETHER TO SPEAK THOSE TRUTHS WOULD BE UP TO HER.
THIS IS THE MOST I CAN CON-CEDE.
I LEAVE THE REST IN YOUR HANDS.
THAT GIRL ...
SHE'S IN THE 104TH... WHICH WOULD MEAN THAT SHE'S ON THE FRONT LINES RIGHT NOW...

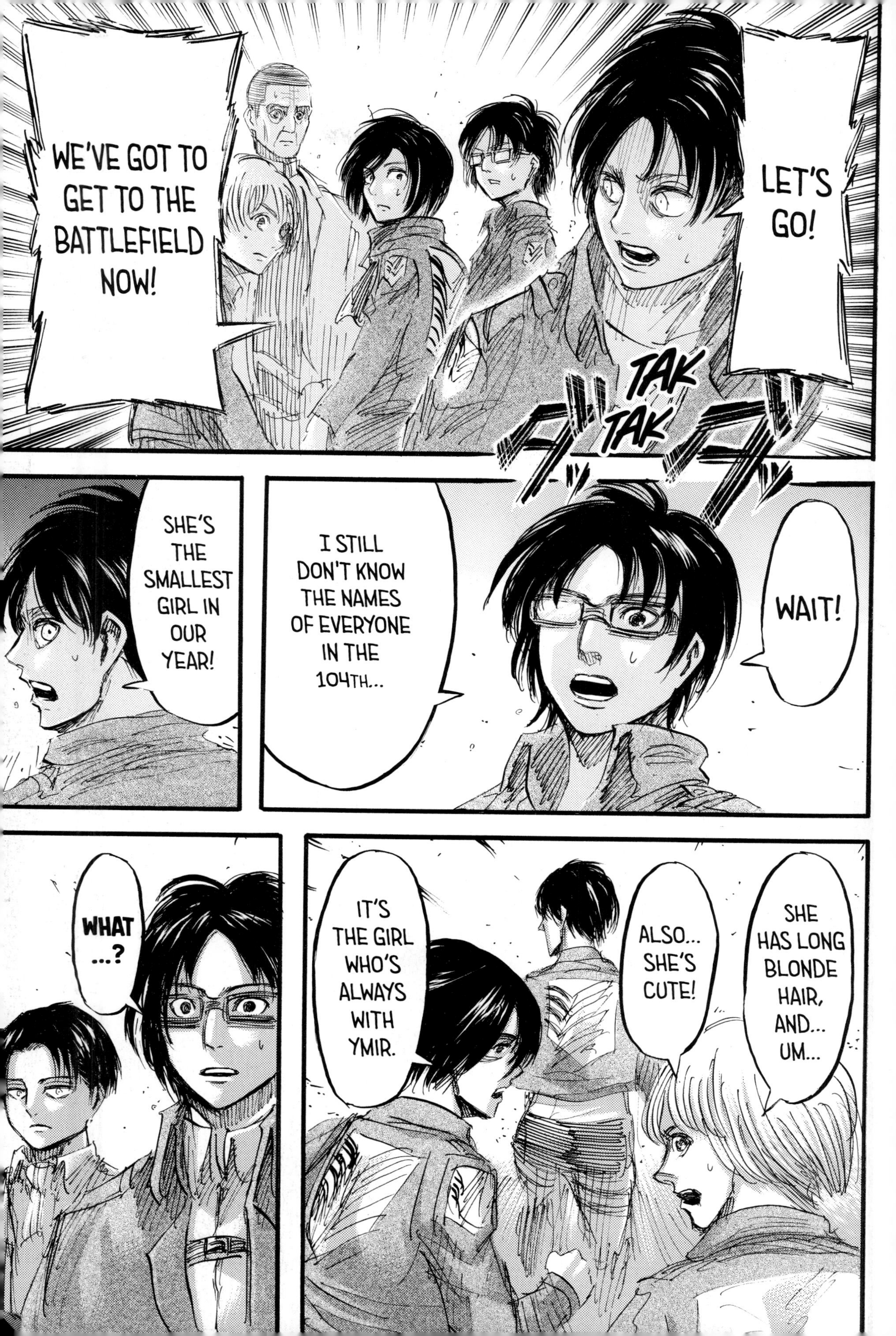
LET'S GO!
WE'VE GOT TO GET TO THE BATTLEFIELD NOW!
TAK TAK
WAIT!
I STILL DON'T KNOW THE NAMES OF EVERYONE IN THE 104TH...
SHE'S THE SMALLEST GIRL IN OUR YEAR!
SHE HAS LONG BLONDE HAIR, AND... UM...
ALSO... SHE'S CUTE!
IT'S THE GIRL WHO'S ALWAYS WITH YMIR.
WHAT ...?

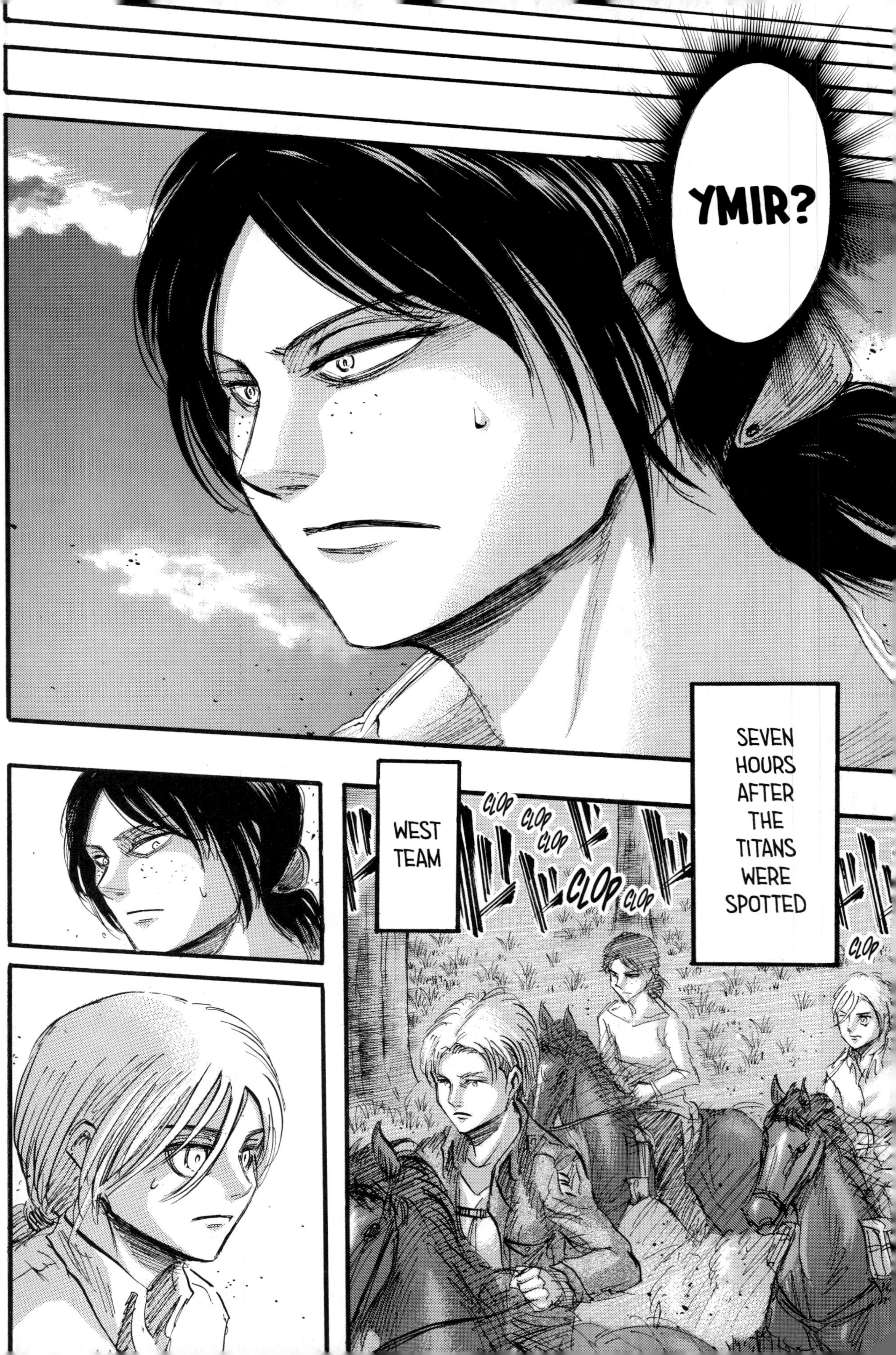
YMIR?
SEVEN HOURS AFTER THE TITANS WERE SPOTTED
WEST TEAM
CLOP
CLOP
CLOP CLOP
CLOP
CLOP
CLOP

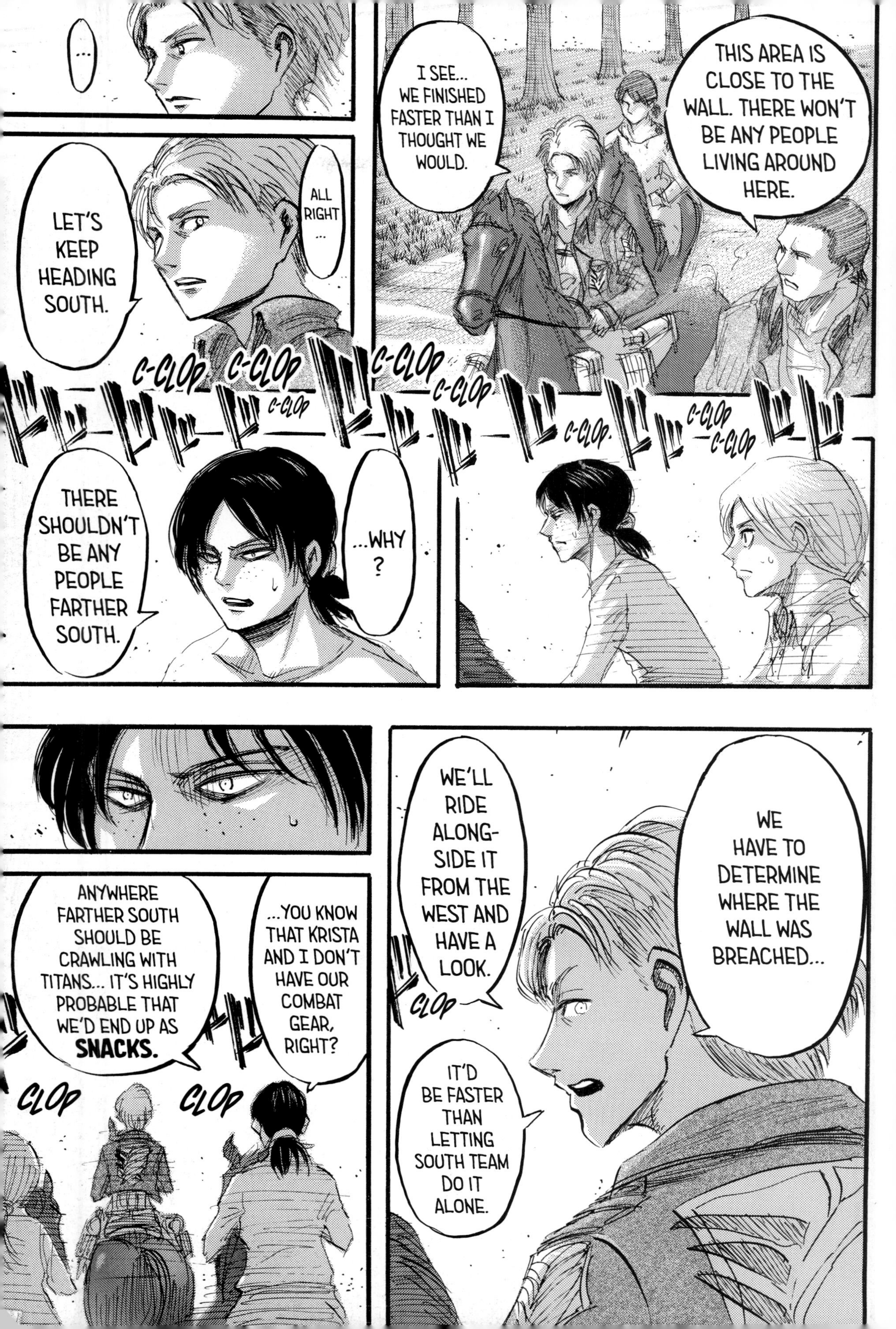

THIS AREA IS CLOSE TO THE WALL. THERE WON'T BE ANY PEOPLE LIVING AROUND HERE.
I SEE... WE FINISHED FASTER THAN I THOUGHT WE WOULD.
...
ALL RIGHT ...
LET'S KEEP HEADING SOUTH.
C-CLOP C-CLOP C-CLOP C-CLOP C-CLOP C-CLOP C-CLOP C-CLOP C-CLOP
...WHY?
THERE SHOULDN'T BE ANY PEOPLE FARTHER SOUTH.
WE HAVE TO DETERMINE WHERE THE WALL WAS BREACHED...
WE'LL RIDE ALONG-SIDE IT FROM THE WEST AND HAVE A LOOK.
CLOP
IT'D BE FASTER THAN LETTING SOUTH TEAM DO IT ALONE.
...YOU KNOW THAT KRISTA AND I DON'T HAVE OUR COMBAT GEAR, RIGHT?
ANYWHERE FARTHER SOUTH SHOULD BE CRAWLING WITH TITANS... IT'S HIGHLY PROBABLE THAT WE'D END UP AS **SNACKS.**
CLOP
CLOP

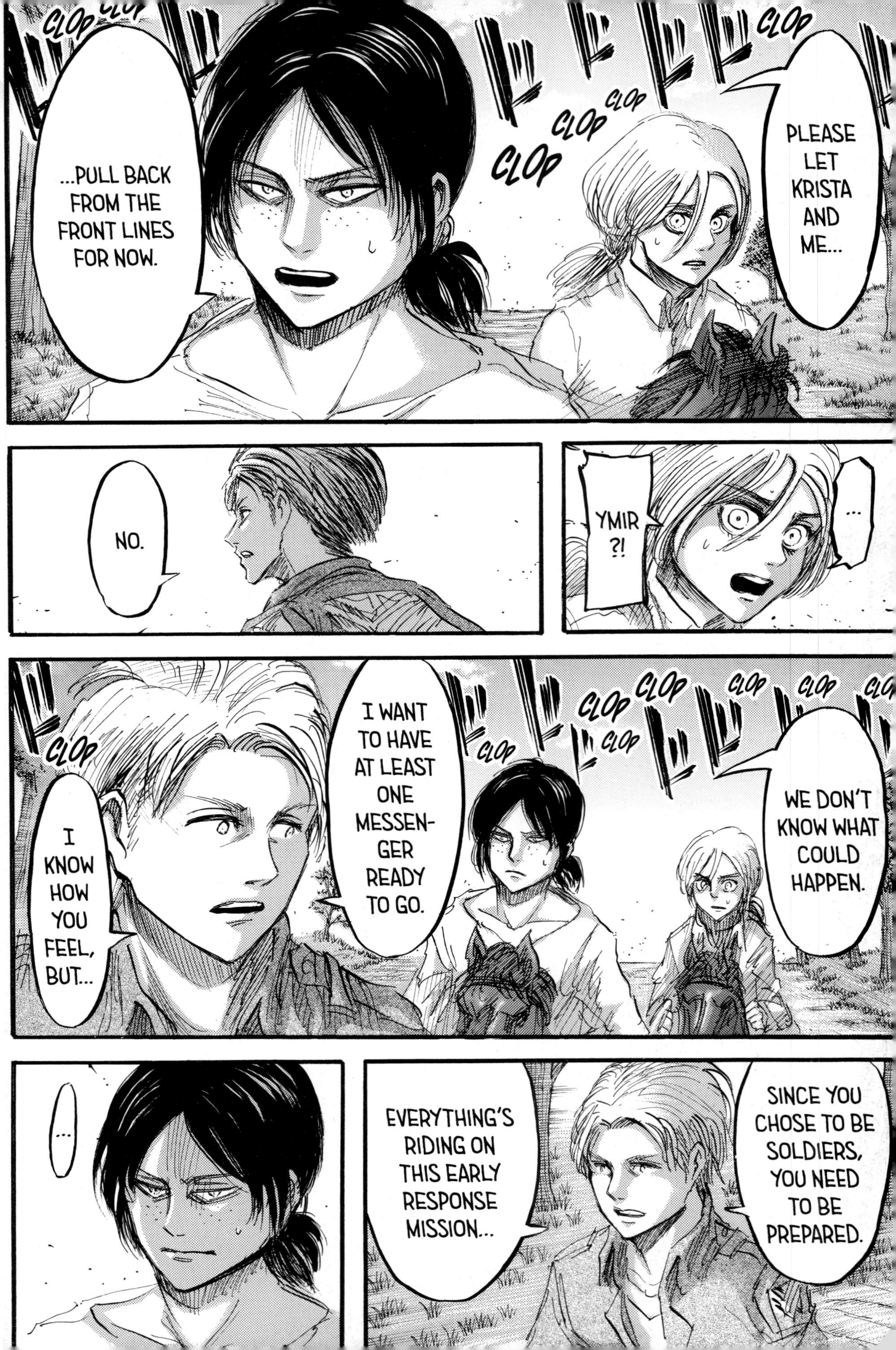
CLOP
CLOP CLOP CLOP
PLEASE LET KRISTA AND ME...
CLOP CLOP
...PULL BACK FROM THE FRONT LINES FOR NOW.
...
YMIR ?!
NO.
CLOP CLOP CLOP CLOP CLOP CLOP
WE DON'T KNOW WHAT COULD HAPPEN.
I WANT TO HAVE AT LEAST ONE MESSENGER READY TO GO.
CLOP
I KNOW HOW YOU FEEL, BUT...
SINCE YOU CHOSE TO BE SOLDIERS, YOU NEED TO BE PREPARED.
EVERYTHING'S RIDING ON THIS EARLY RESPONSE MISSION...
...

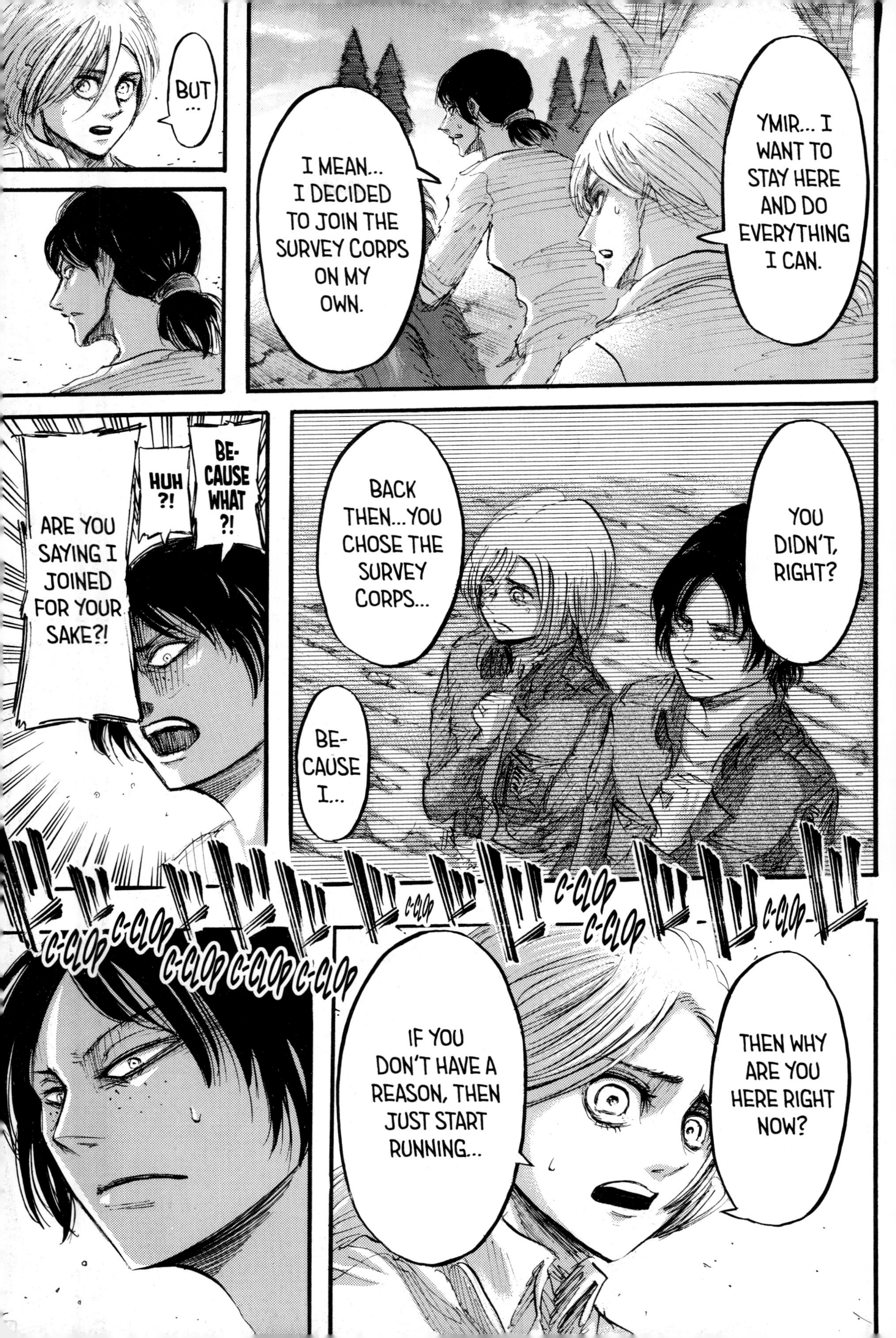
YMIR... I WANT TO STAY HERE AND DO EVERYTHING I CAN.
I MEAN... I DECIDED TO JOIN THE SURVEY CORPS ON MY OWN.
BUT ...
YOU DIDN'T, RIGHT?
BACK THEN...YOU CHOSE THE SURVEY CORPS...
BE-CAUSE I...
BE-CAUSE WHAT ?!
HUH ?!
ARE YOU SAYING I JOINED FOR YOUR SAKE?!
C-CLOP C-CLOP C-CLOP C-CLOP C-CLOP C-CLOP C-CLOP C-CLOP C-CLOP
THEN WHY ARE YOU HERE RIGHT NOW?
IF YOU DON'T HAVE A REASON, THEN JUST START RUNNING...

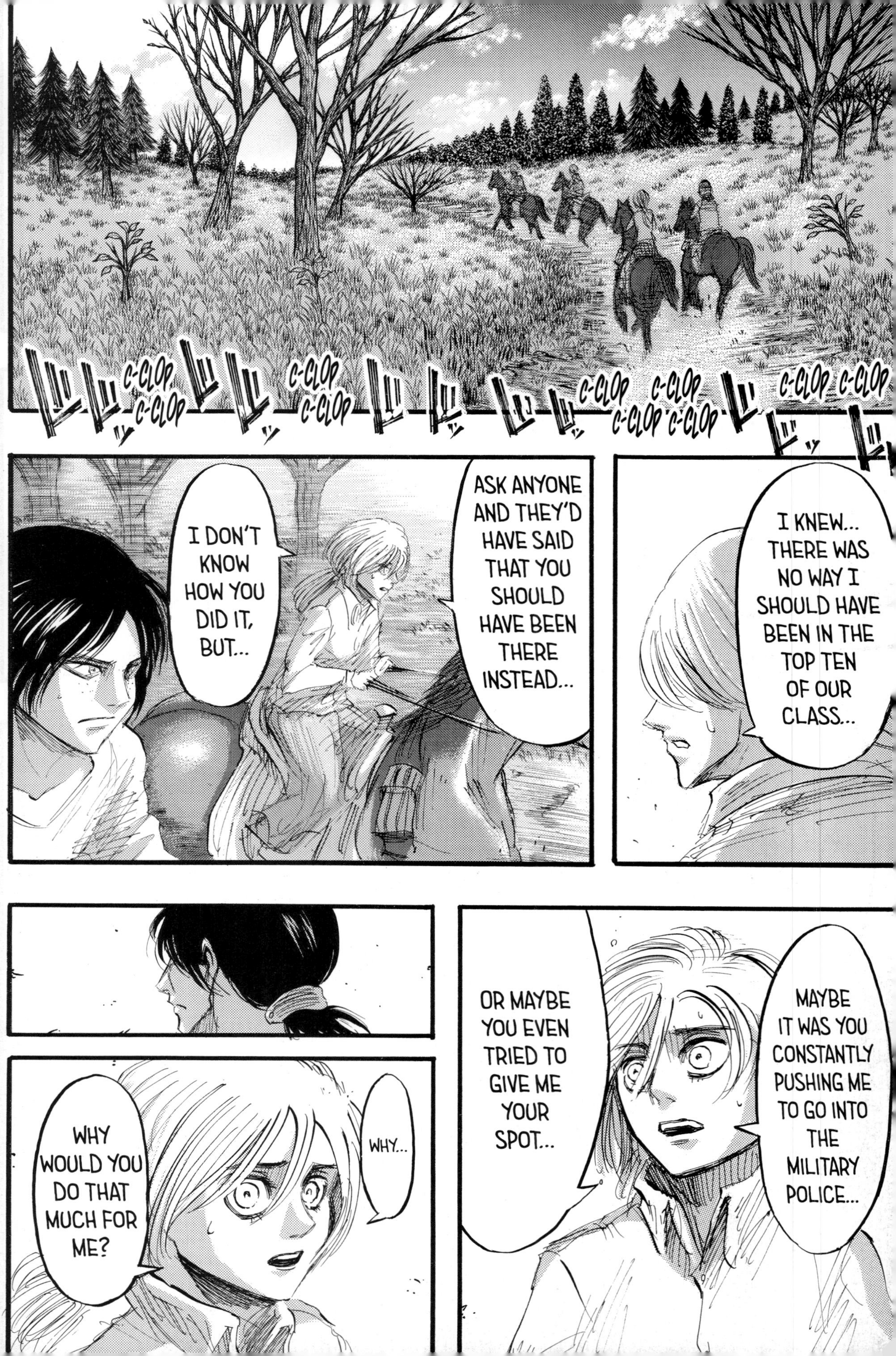

C-CLOP C-CLOP
C-CLOP C-CLOP
C-CLOP C-CLOP
C-CLOP C-CLOP
C-CLOP C-CLOP
I KNEW... THERE WAS NO WAY I SHOULD HAVE BEEN IN THE TOP TEN OF OUR CLASS...
ASK ANYONE AND THEY'D HAVE SAID THAT YOU SHOULD HAVE BEEN THERE INSTEAD...
I DON'T KNOW HOW YOU DID IT, BUT...
MAYBE IT WAS YOU CONSTANTLY PUSHING ME TO GO INTO THE MILITARY POLICE...
OR MAYBE YOU EVEN TRIED TO GIVE ME YOUR SPOT...
WHY...
WHY WOULD YOU DO THAT MUCH FOR ME?

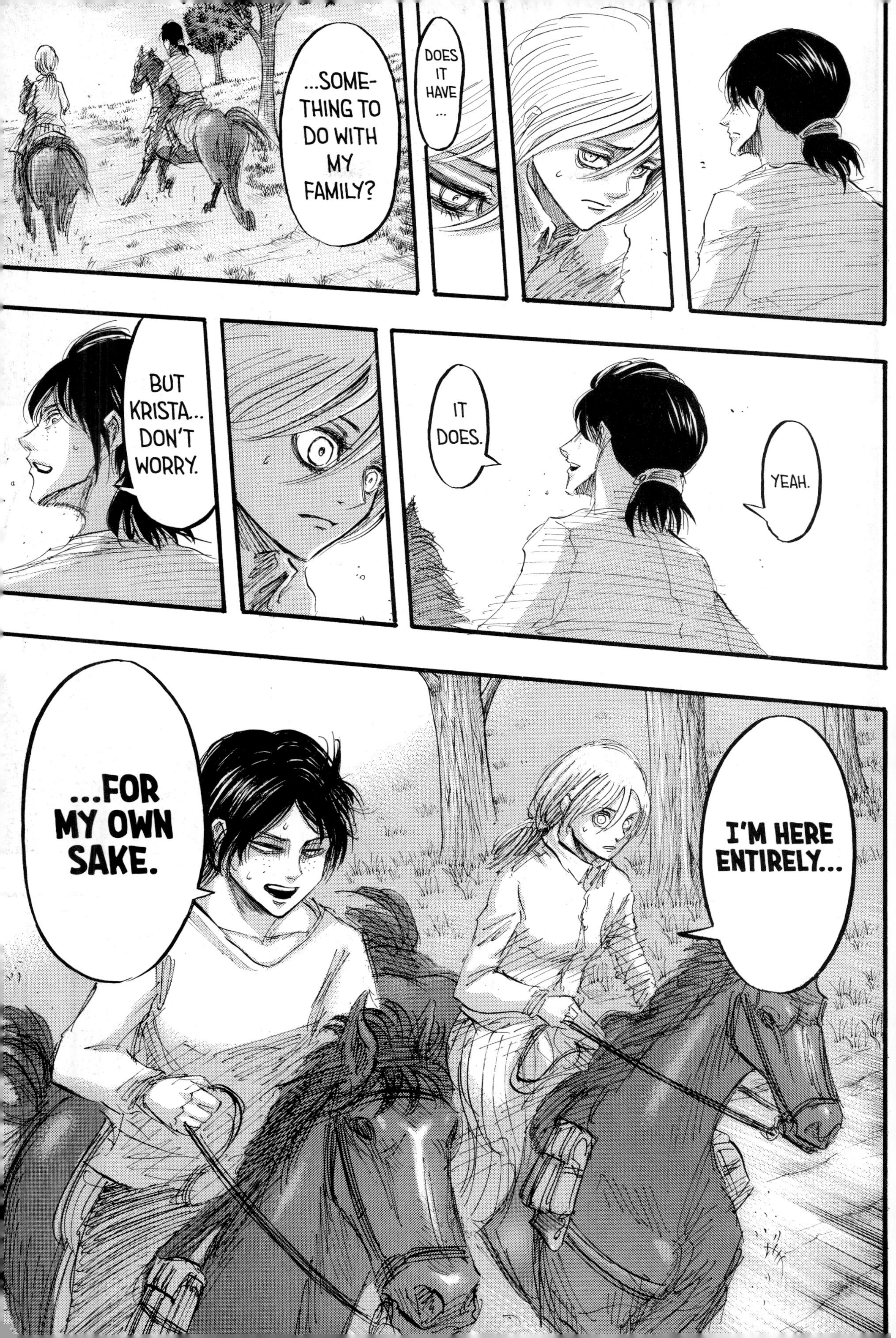
DOES IT HAVE ...
...SOMETHING TO DO WITH MY FAMILY?
YEAH.
IT DOES.
BUT KRISTA... DON'T WORRY.
I'M HERE ENTIRELY...
...FOR MY OWN SAKE.

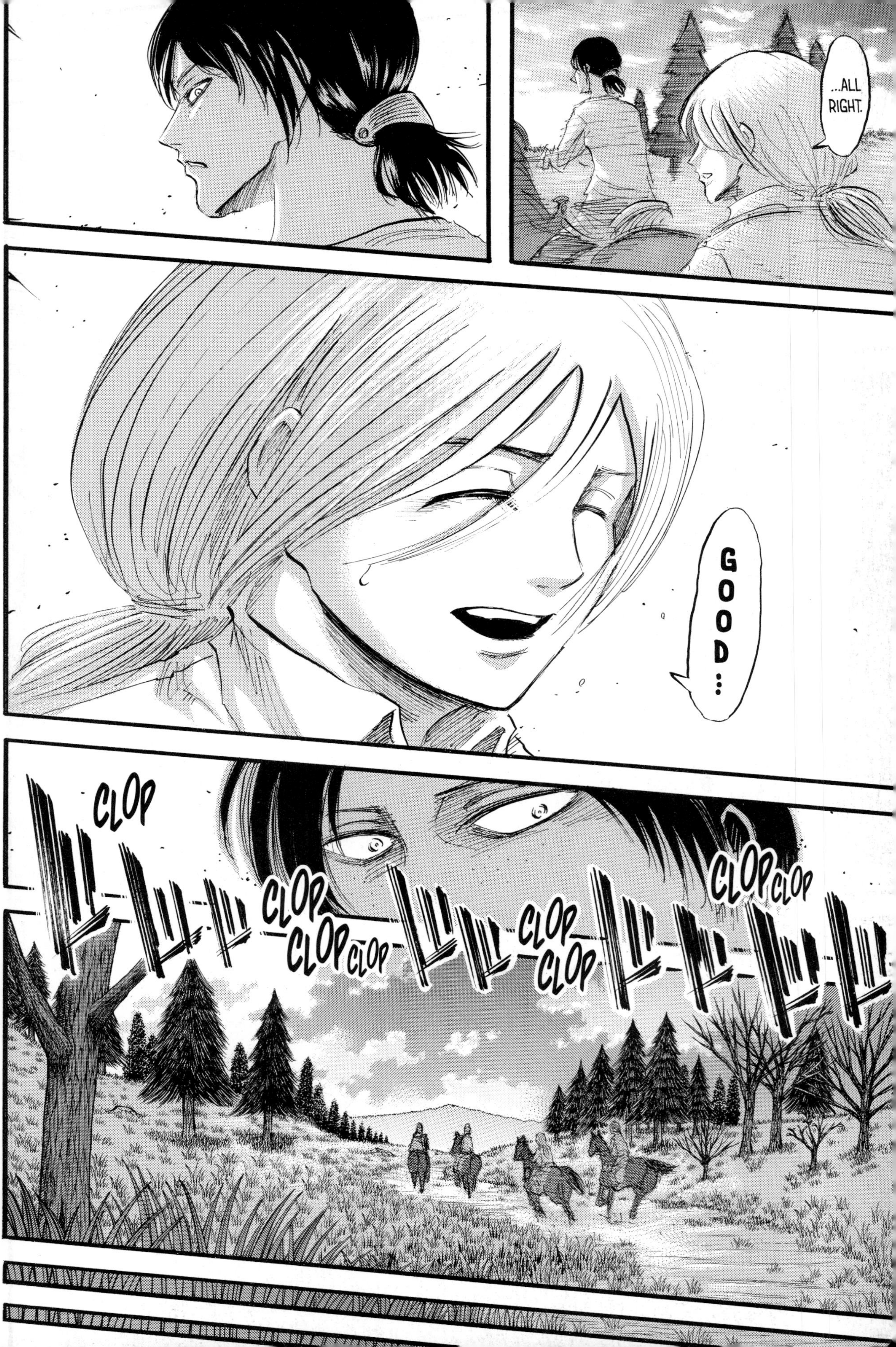
...ALL RIGHT.
GOOD...
CLOP CLOP
CLOP CLOP
CLOP CLOP CLOP
CLOP

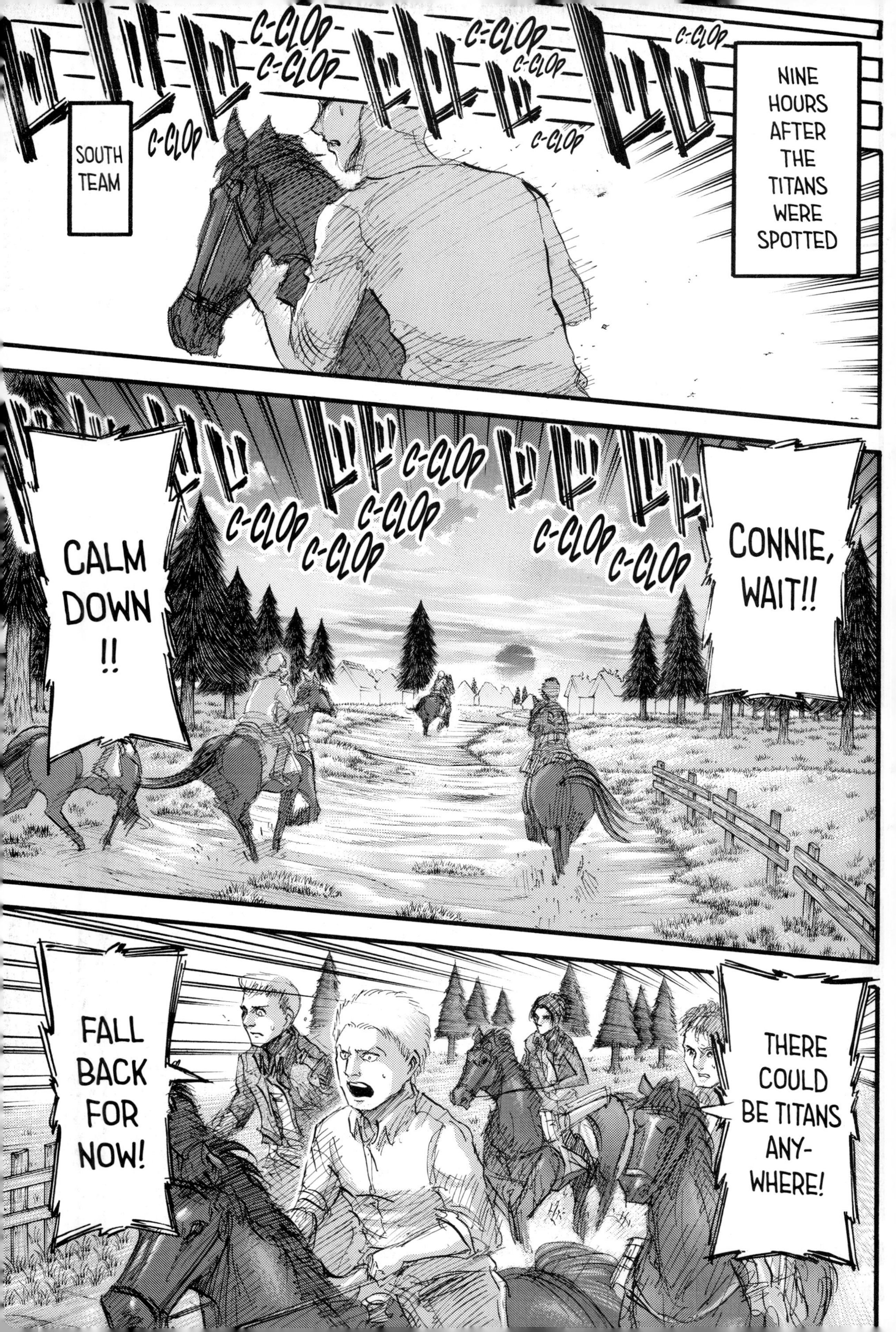
NINE HOURS AFTER THE TITANS WERE SPOTTED
C-CLOP
C-CLOP
C-CLOP
C-CLOP
C-CLOP
C-CLOP
SOUTH TEAM
CONNIE, WAIT!!
C-CLOP
C-CLOP
C-CLOP
C-CLOP
C-CLOP
C-CLOP
CALM DOWN!!
THERE COULD BE TITANS ANY-WHERE!
FALL BACK FOR NOW!

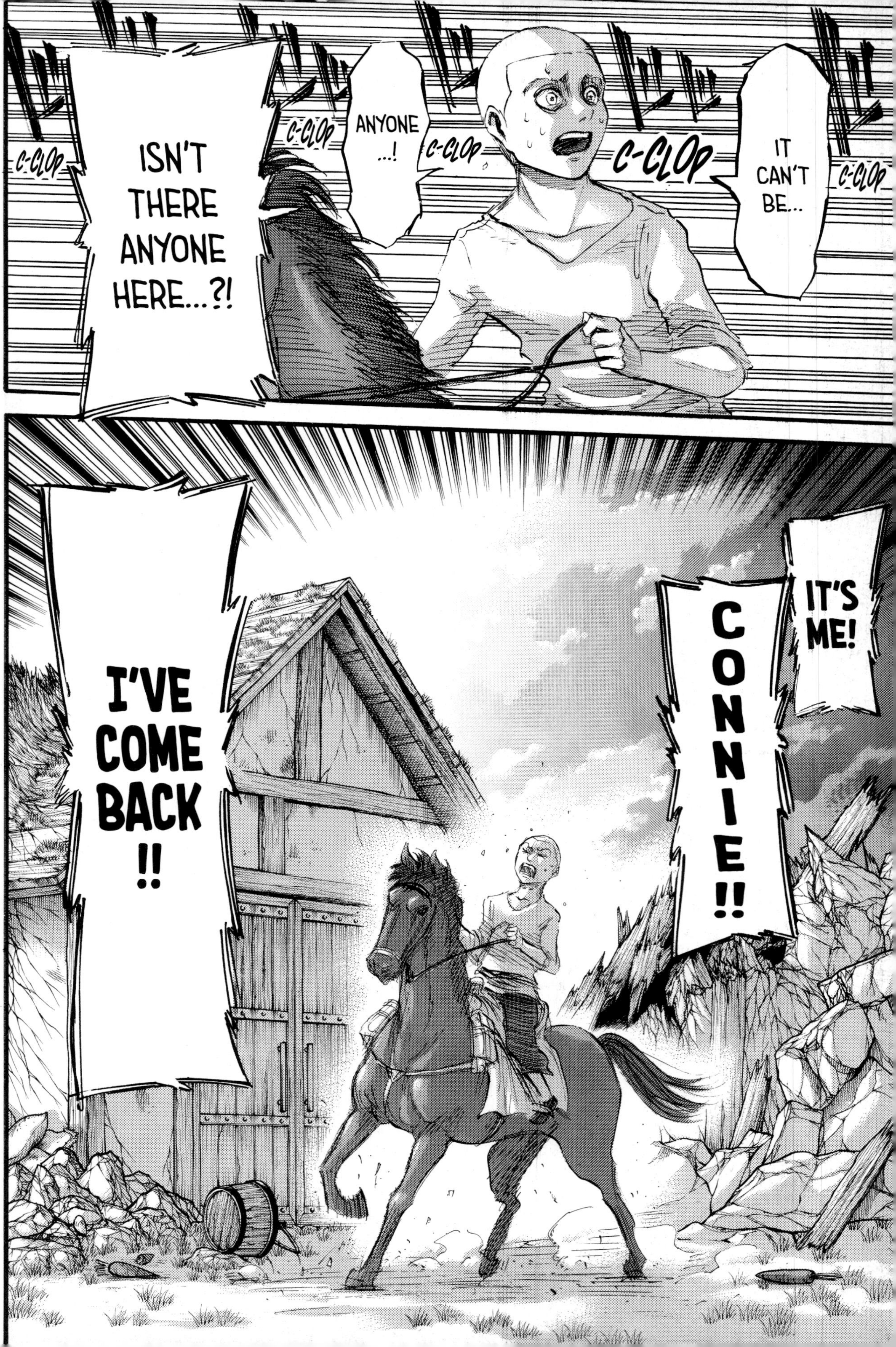
C-CLOP
IT CAN'T BE...
C-CLOP
C-CLOP
ANYONE ...!
C-CLOP
ISN'T THERE ANYONE HERE...?!
C-CLOP
IT'S ME!
CONNIE!!
I'VE COME BACK!!

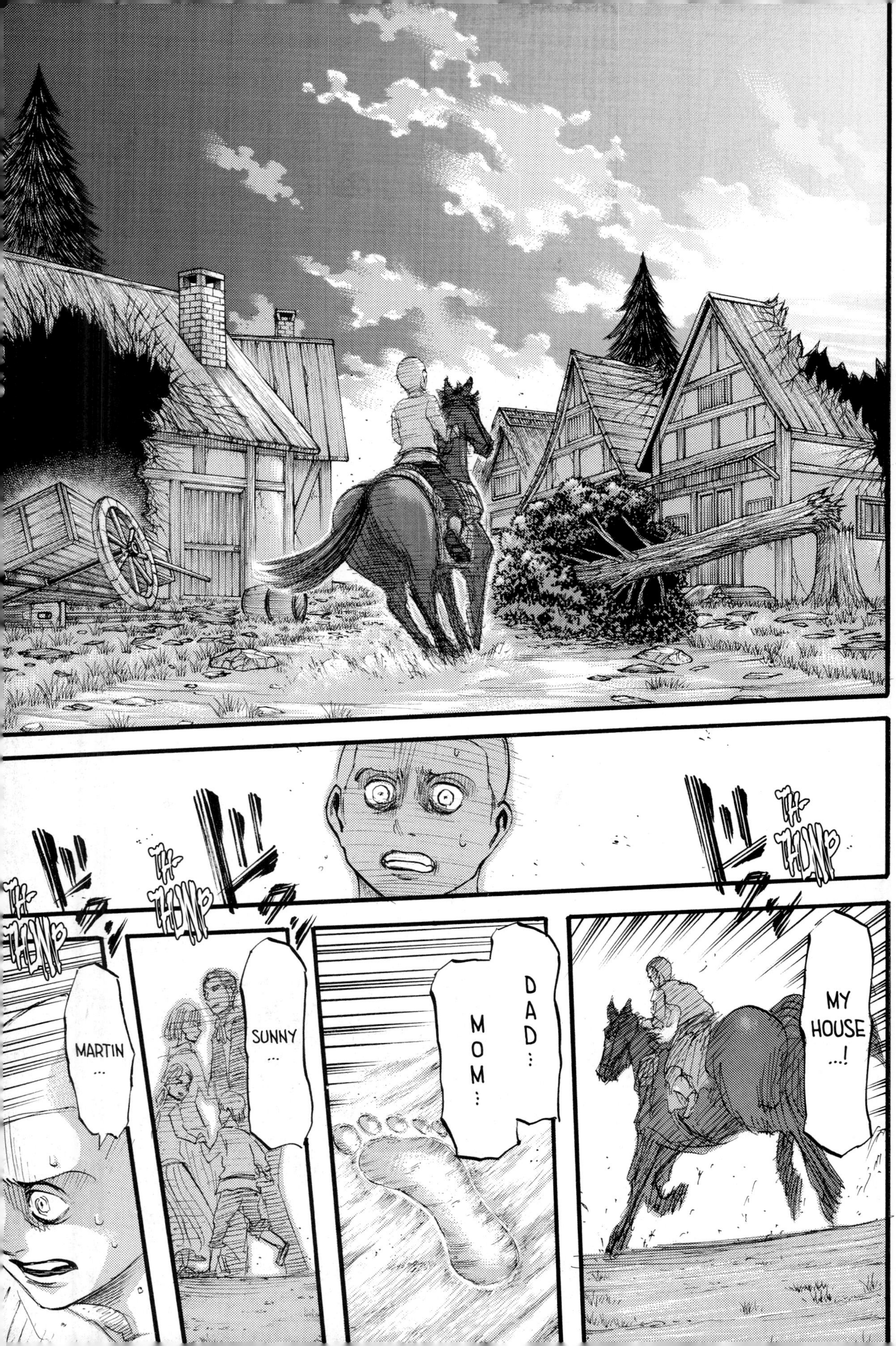
THA THUMP
THA THUMP
THA THUMP
MY HOUSE ...!
DAD... MOM...
SUNNY ...
MARTIN ...

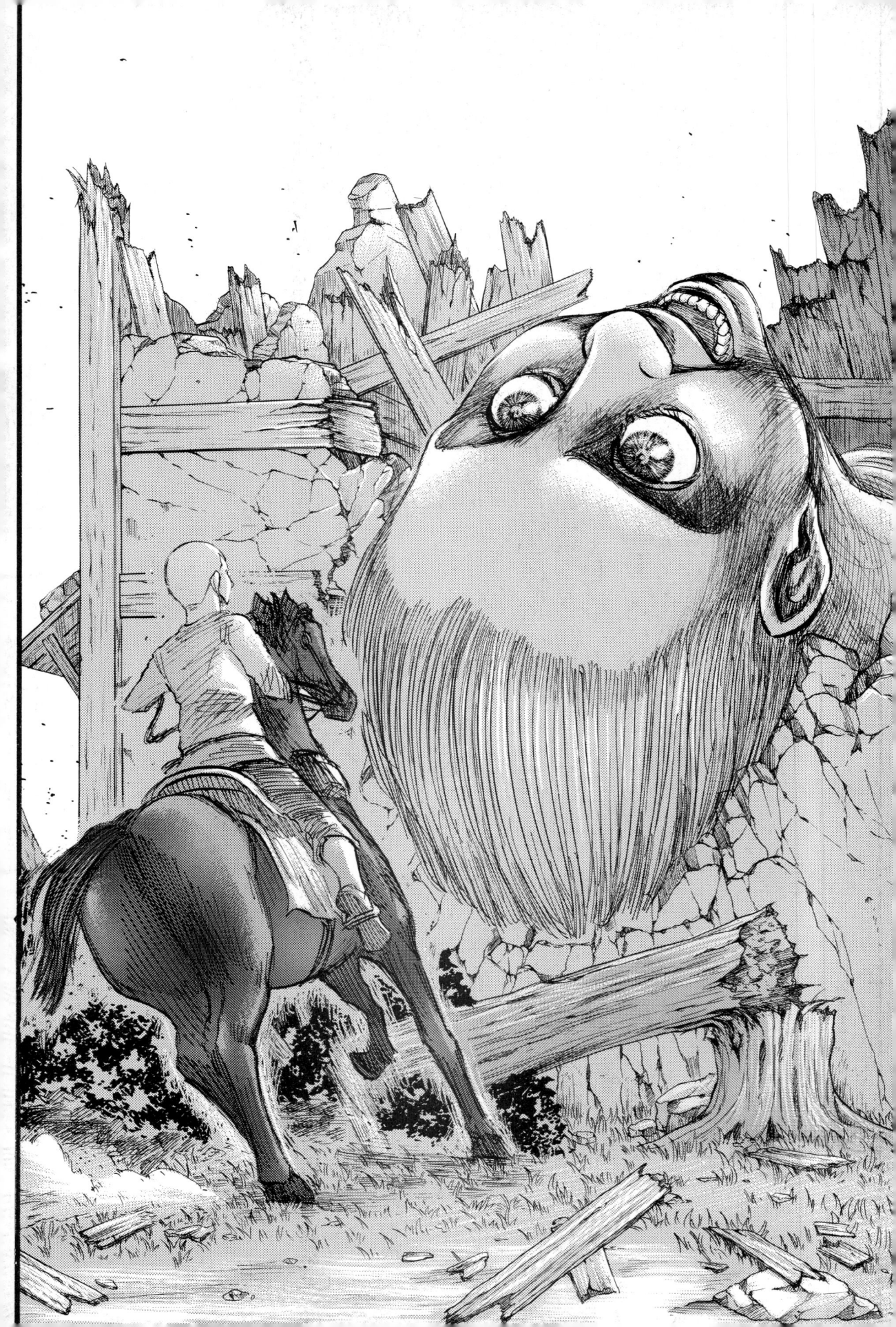

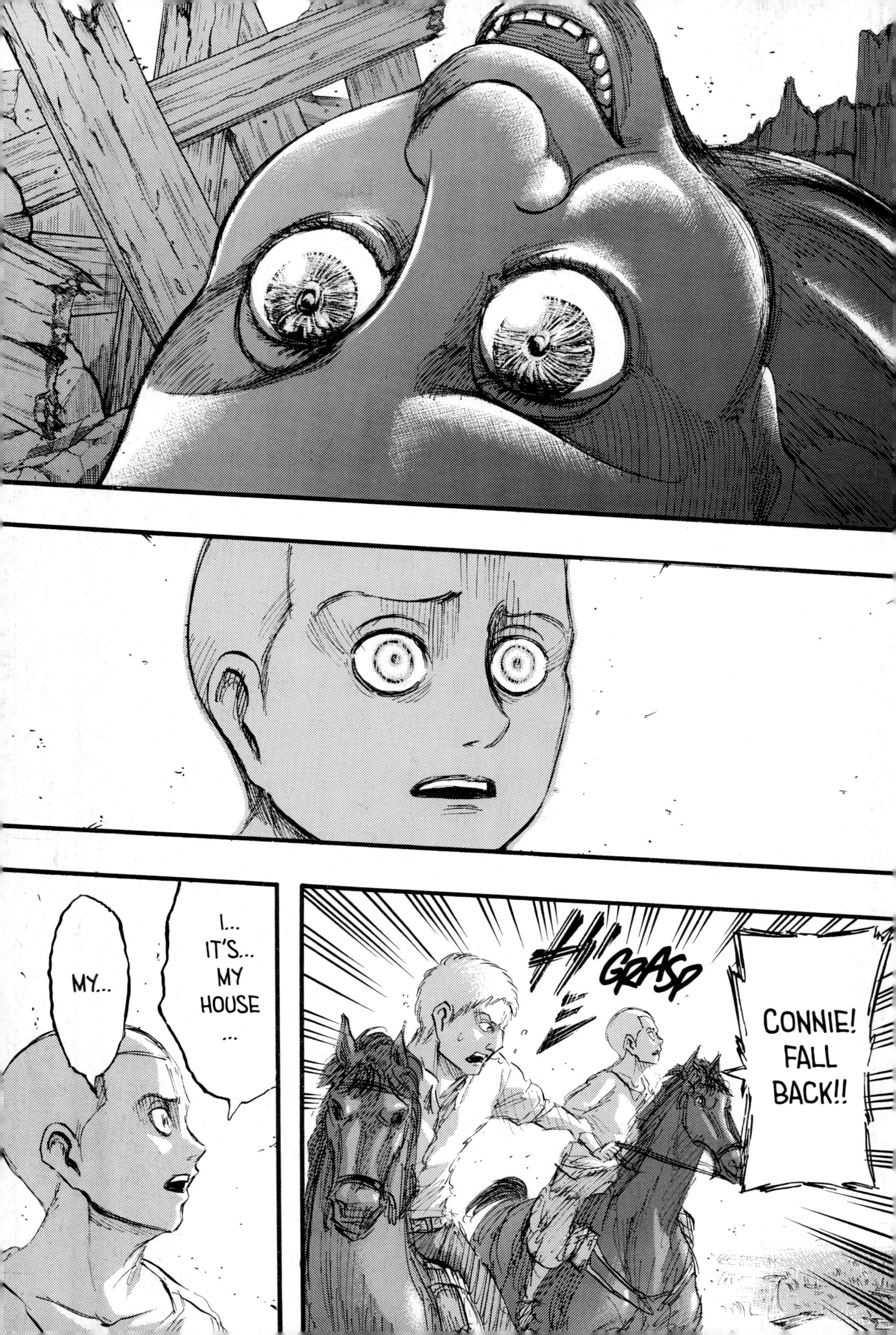
HI
GRASP
CONNIE! FALL BACK!!
I... IT'S... MY HOUSE ...
MY...

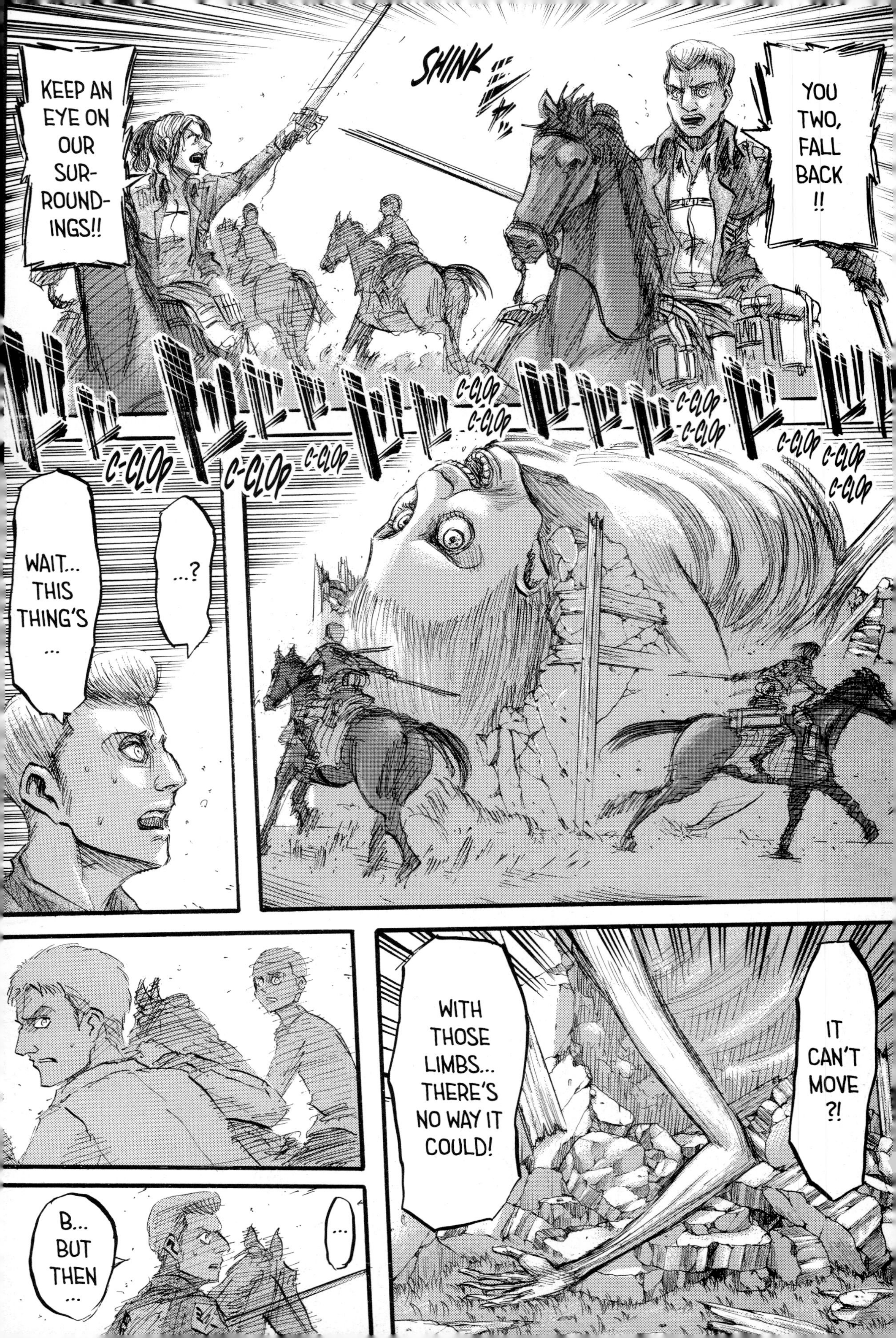
YOU TWO, FALL BACK!!
SHINK
KEEP AN EYE ON OUR SUR-ROUND-INGS!!
C-CLOP C-CLOP
C-CLOP C-CLOP
C-CLOP C-CLOP C-CLOP
C-CLOP C-CLOP
C-CLOP
C-CLOP
C-CLOP
...?
WAIT... THIS THING'S ...
IT CAN'T MOVE?!
WITH THOSE LIMBS... THERE'S NO WAY IT COULD!
...
B... BUT THEN ...

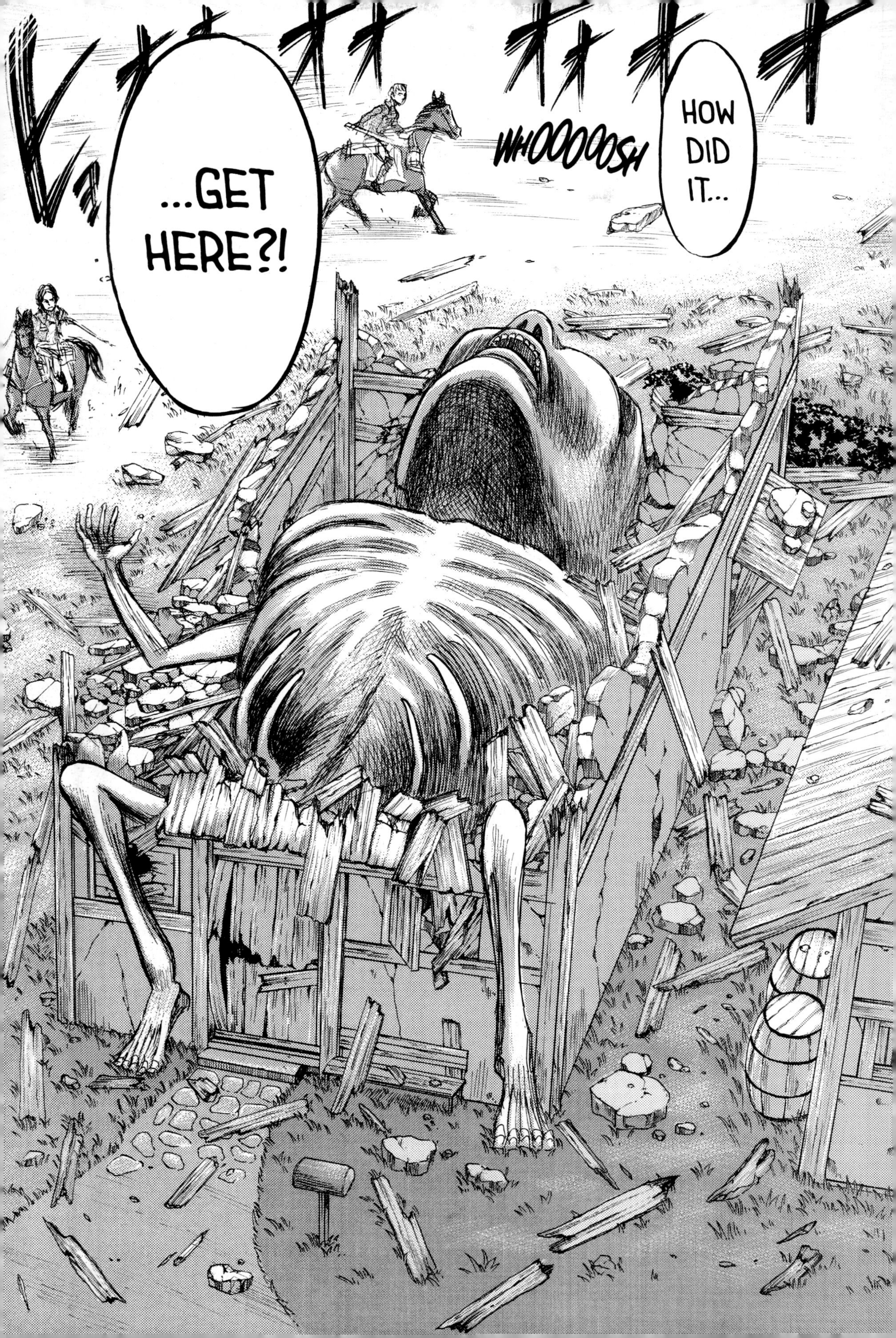
WHOOOOOOSH
HOW DID IT...
...GET HERE?!

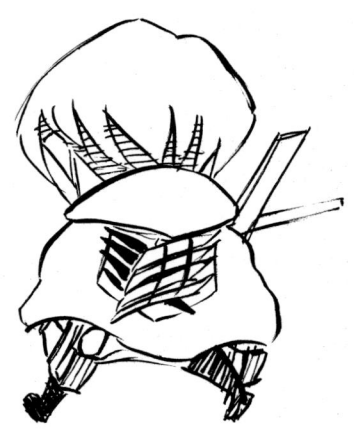

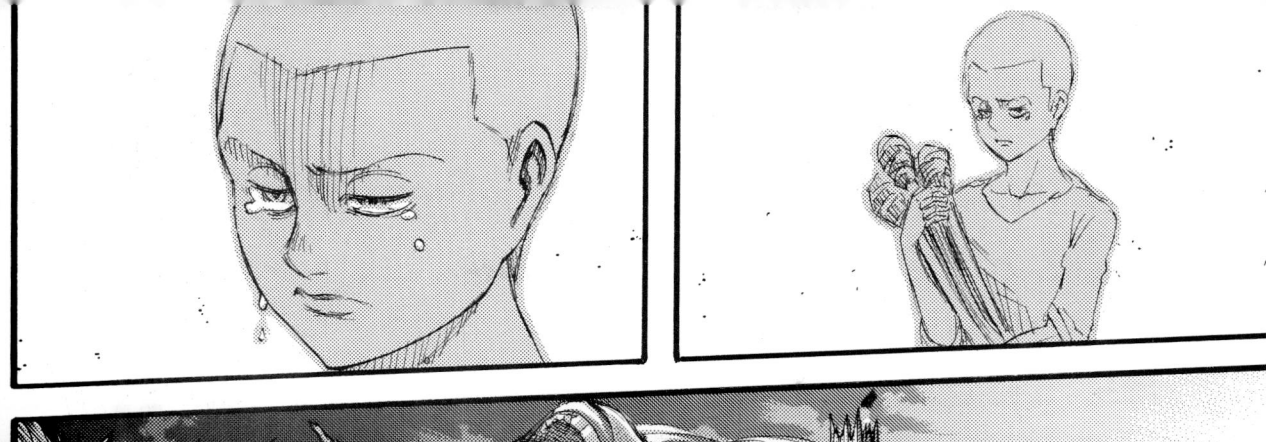

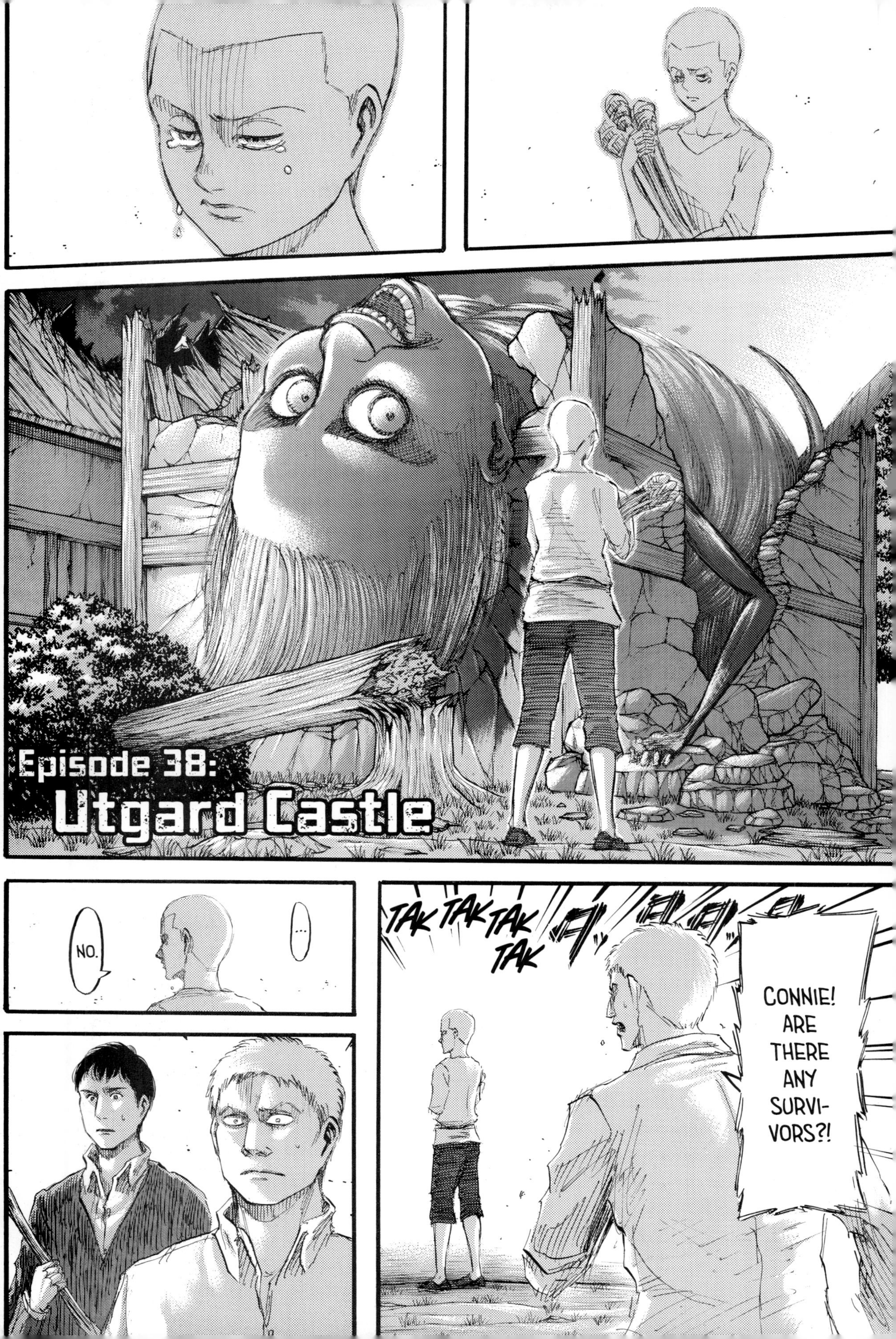

Episode 38:
Utgard Castle

NO.

...

TAK TAK TAK
TAK

CONNIE! ARE THERE ANY SURVIVORS?!

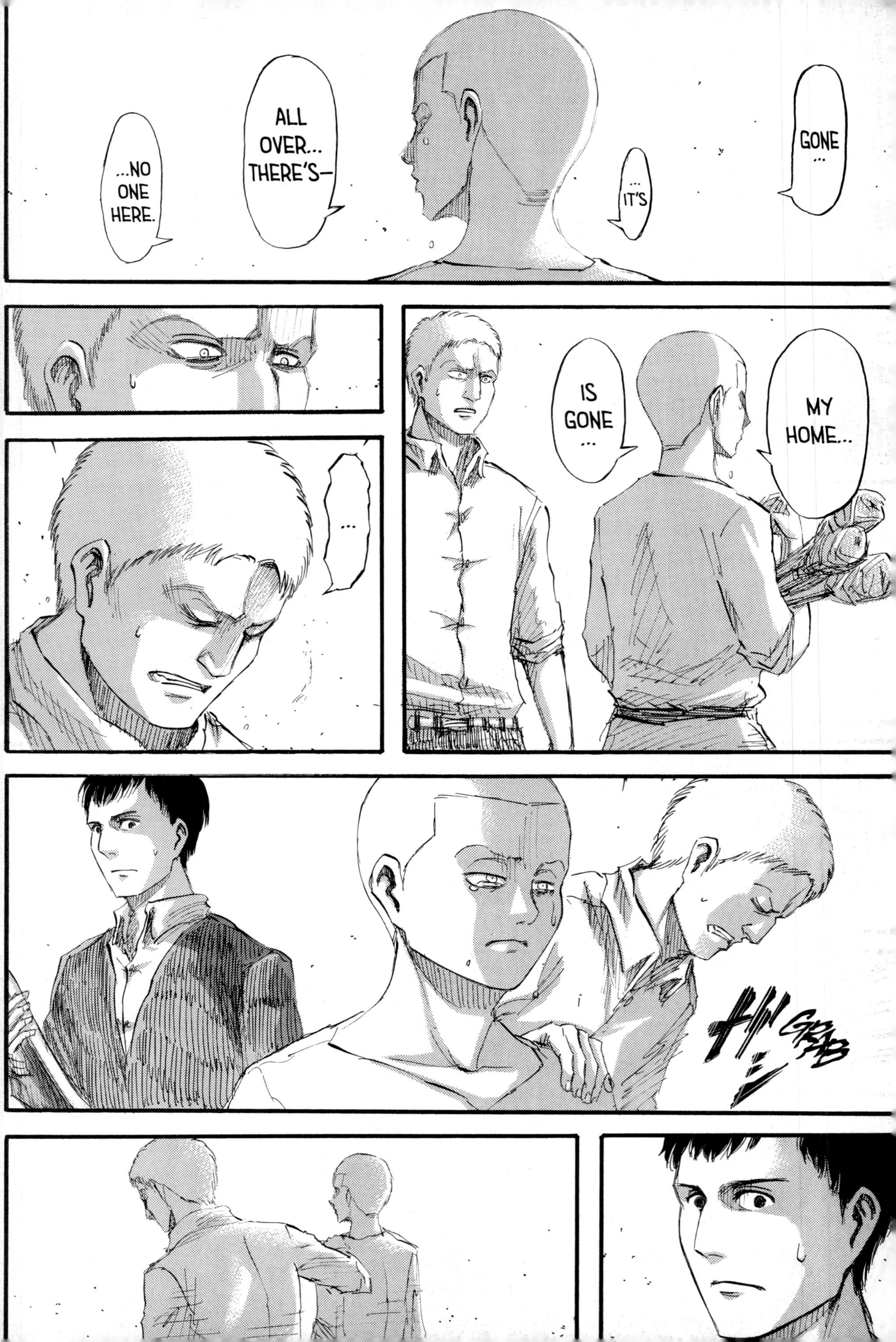
GONE ...
... IT'S
ALL OVER... THERE'S—
...NO ONE HERE.
MY HOME...
IS GONE ...
...
GRAB

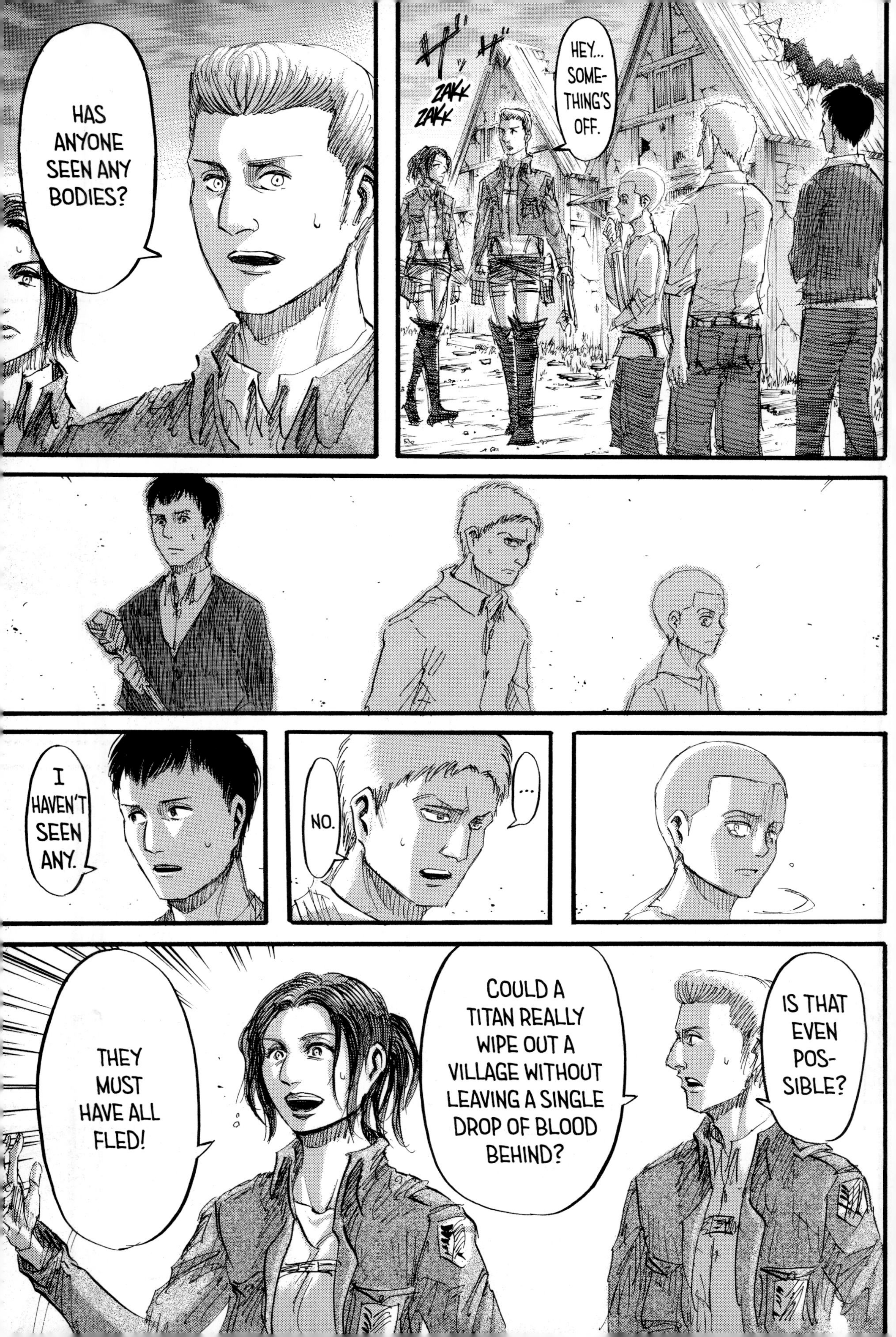
ZAKK
ZAKK
HEY... SOME-THING'S OFF.
HAS ANYONE SEEN ANY BODIES?
...
NO.
I HAVEN'T SEEN ANY.
IS THAT EVEN POS-SIBLE?
COULD A TITAN REALLY WIPE OUT A VILLAGE WITHOUT LEAVING A SINGLE DROP OF BLOOD BEHIND?
THEY MUST HAVE ALL FLED!

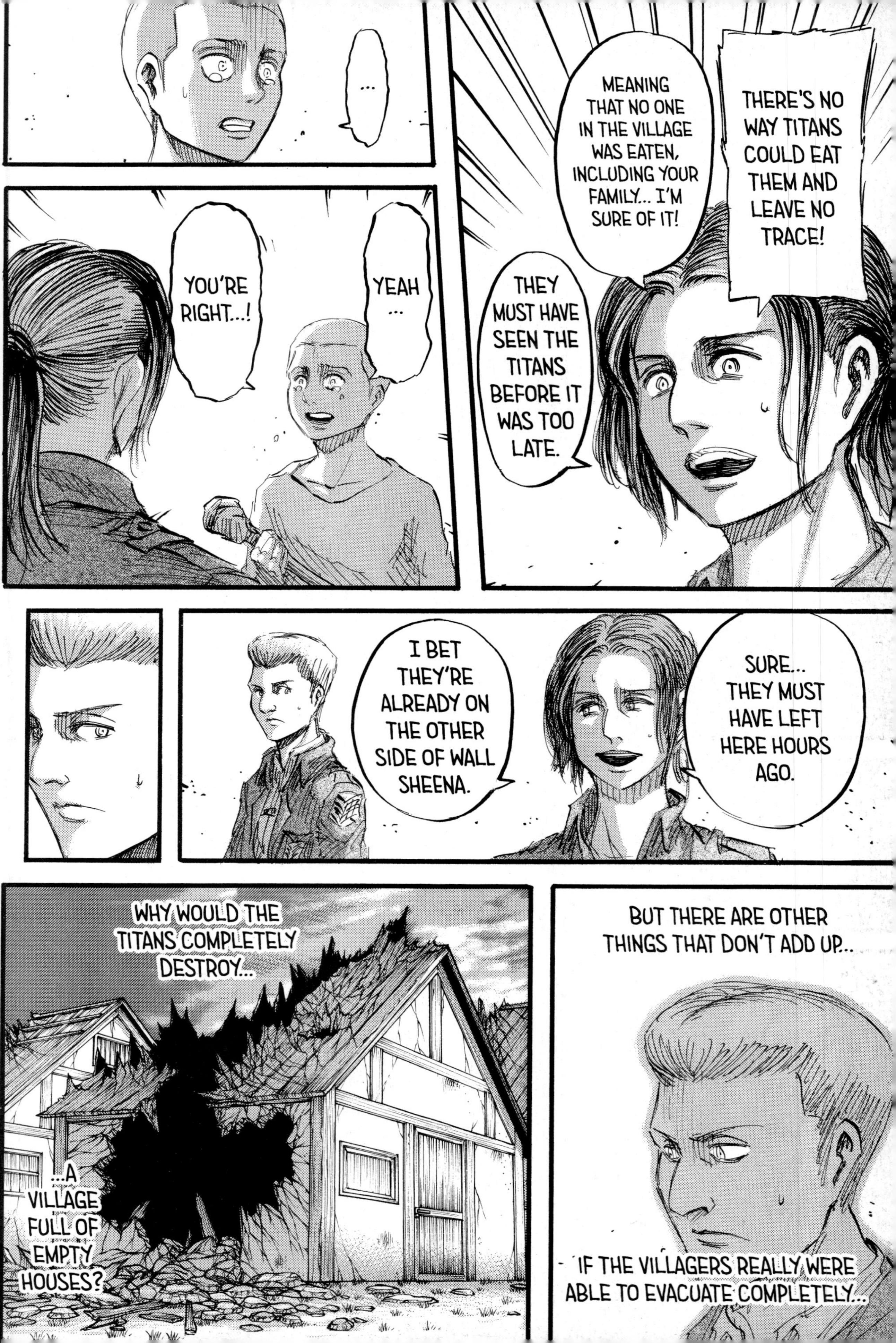
THERE'S NO WAY TITANS COULD EAT THEM AND LEAVE NO TRACE!
MEANING THAT NO ONE IN THE VILLAGE WAS EATEN, INCLUDING YOUR FAMILY... I'M SURE OF IT!
THEY MUST HAVE SEEN THE TITANS BEFORE IT WAS TOO LATE.
...
YEAH ...
YOU'RE RIGHT...!
SURE... THEY MUST HAVE LEFT HERE HOURS AGO.
I BET THEY'RE ALREADY ON THE OTHER SIDE OF WALL SHEENA.
BUT THERE ARE OTHER THINGS THAT DON'T ADD UP...
IF THE VILLAGERS REALLY WERE ABLE TO EVACUATE COMPLETELY...
WHY WOULD THE TITANS COMPLETELY DESTROY...
...A VILLAGE FULL OF EMPTY HOUSES?

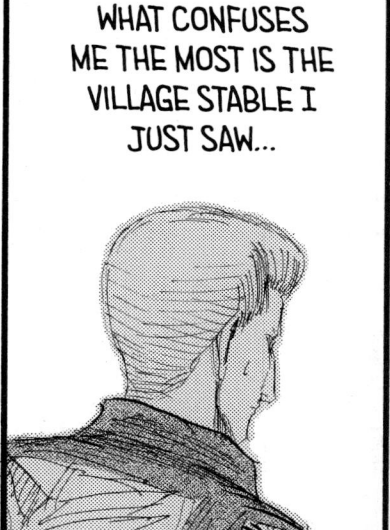

WHAT CONFUSES ME THE MOST IS THE VILLAGE STABLE I JUST SAW...
A LINE OF HORSES, STILL TIED UP...
YOU CAN RUN FROM A TITAN, BUT IF YOU'RE NOT ON HORSEBACK, YOUR CHANCES OF SURVIVAL ARE SLIM...
IN ANY CASE, I CAN'T SHOW THAT STABLE TO CONNIE.
ARE THE TORCHES READY?
WE'RE GOING TO GO FROM HERE TO LOCATE THE DAMAGED AREA OF THE WALL.
WE'RE HEADING OUT.
ZAKK
...
OKAY.
STEP
STEP
KSSH

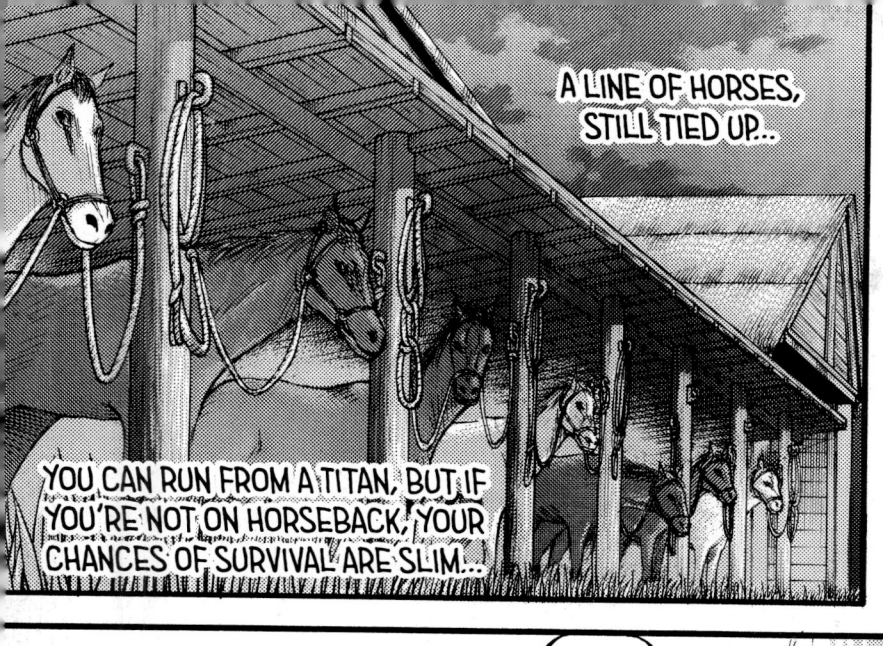

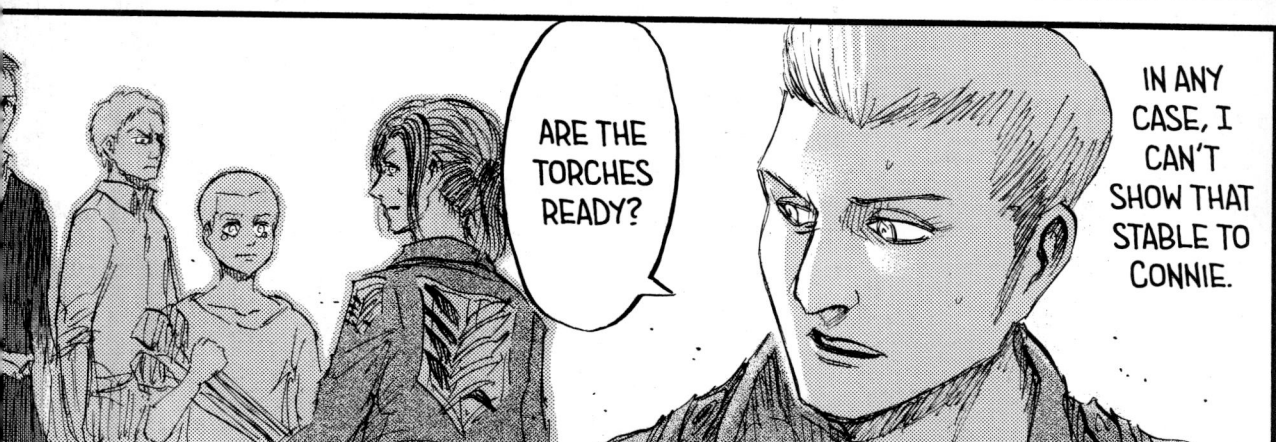

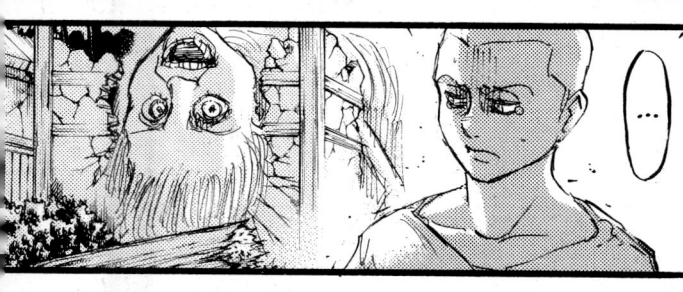

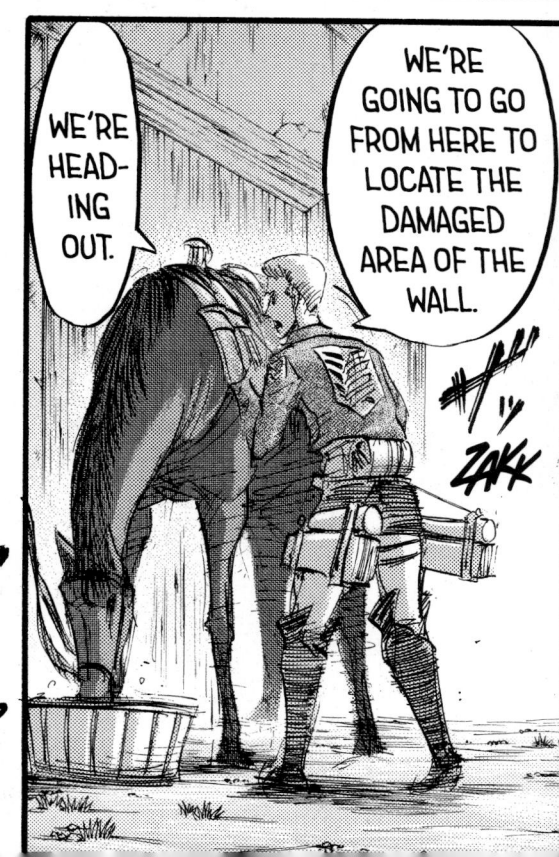

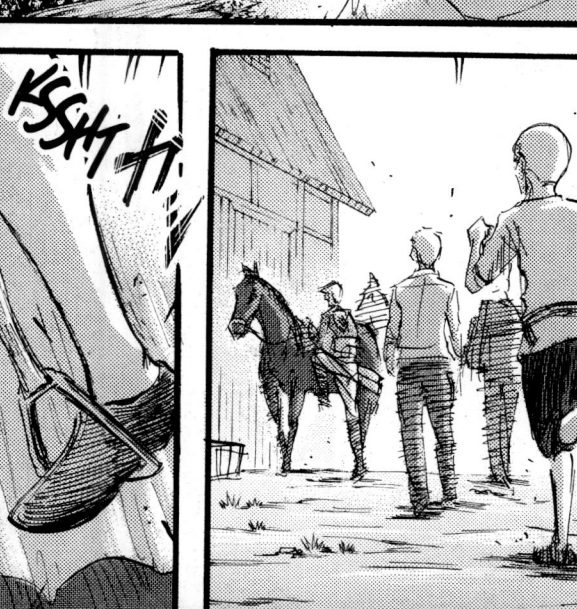

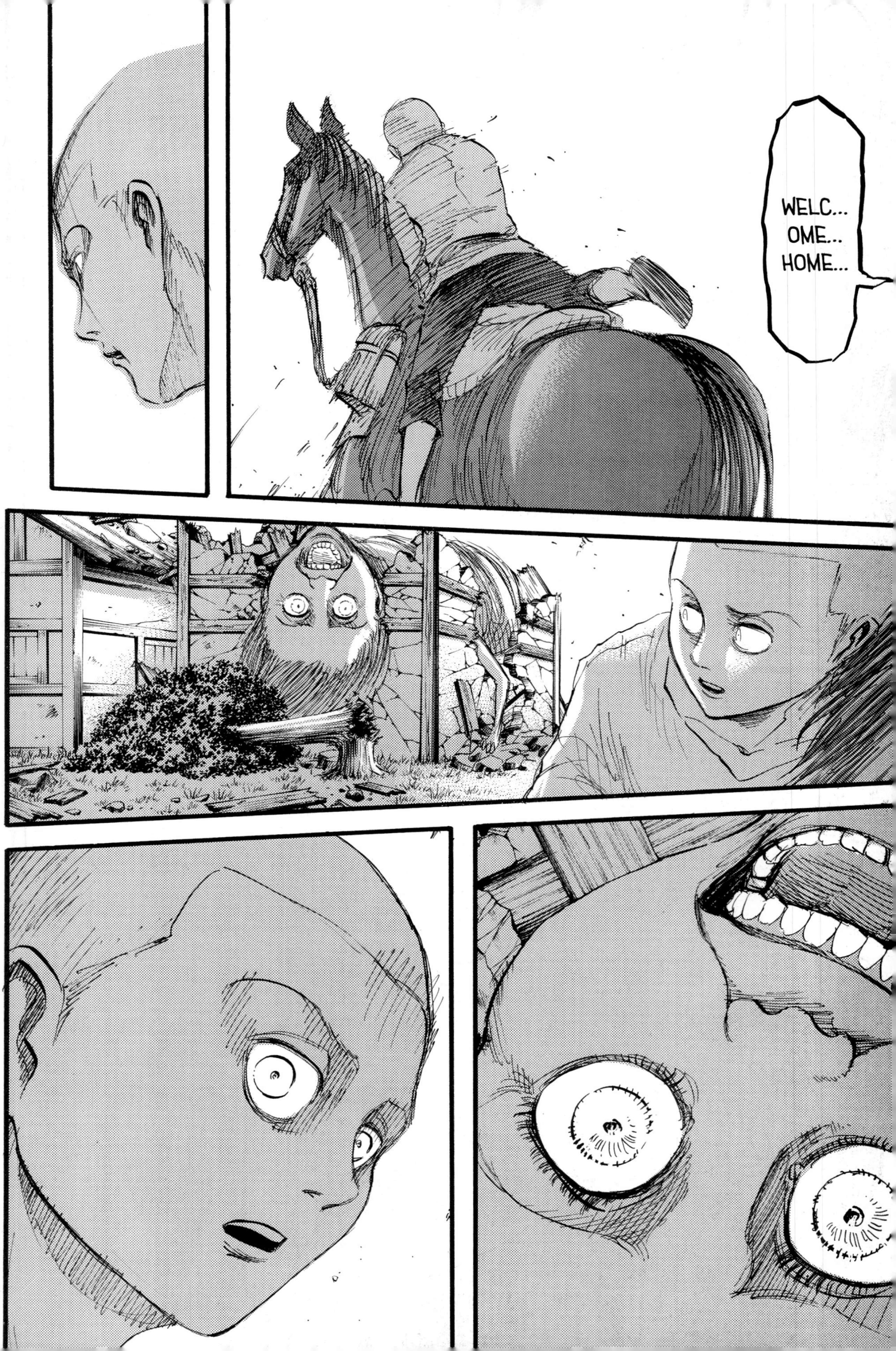
WELC... OME... HOME...

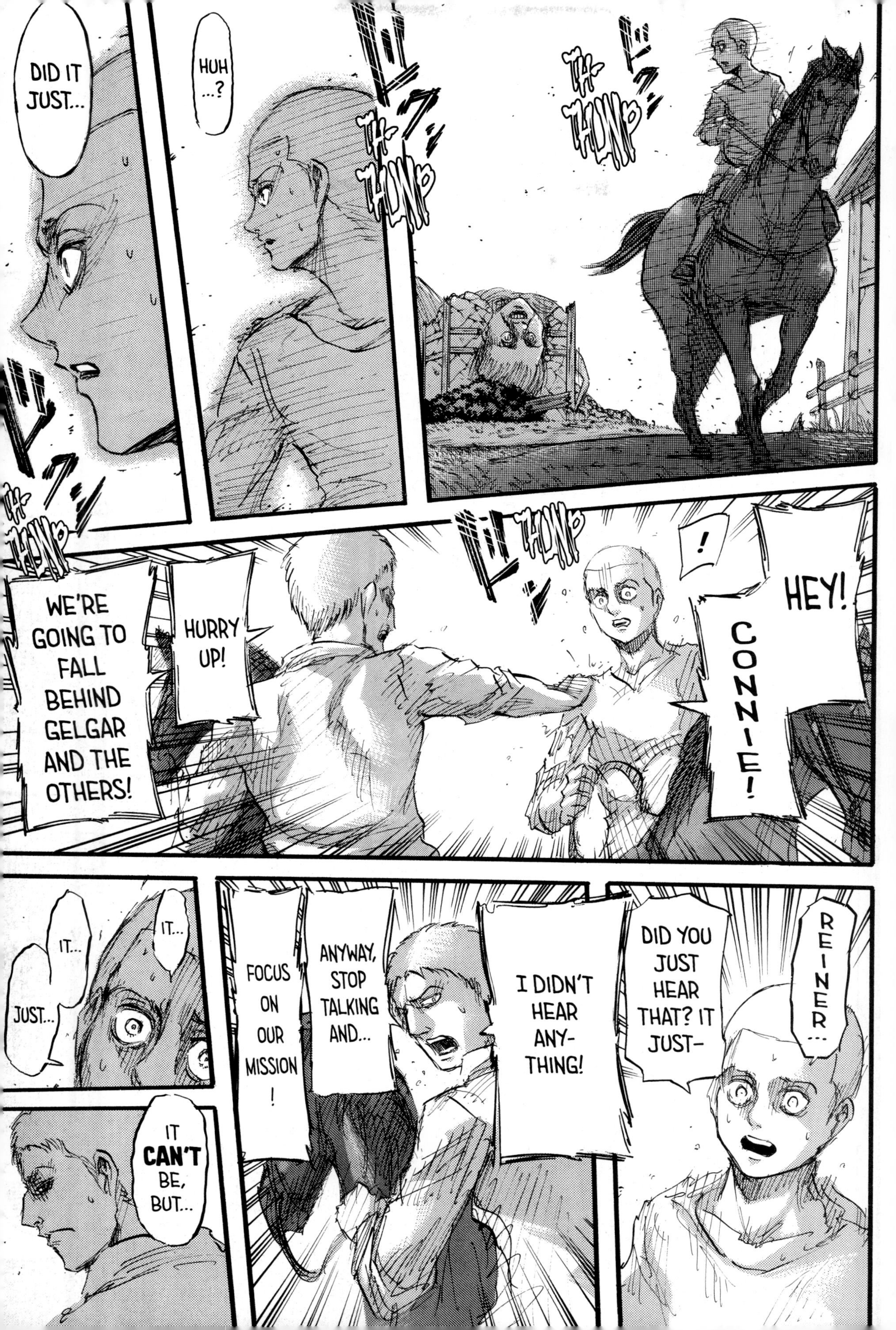
THA-THUMP
HUH...?
THA-THUMP
DID IT JUST...
THA-THUMP
HEY!
CONNIE!
!
THUMP
HURRY UP!
WE'RE GOING TO FALL BEHIND GELGAR AND THE OTHERS!
REINER...
DID YOU JUST HEAR THAT? IT JUST-
I DIDN'T HEAR ANY-THING!
ANYWAY, STOP TALKING AND...
FOCUS ON OUR MISSION!
IT...
IT... JUST...
IT **CAN'T** BE, BUT...

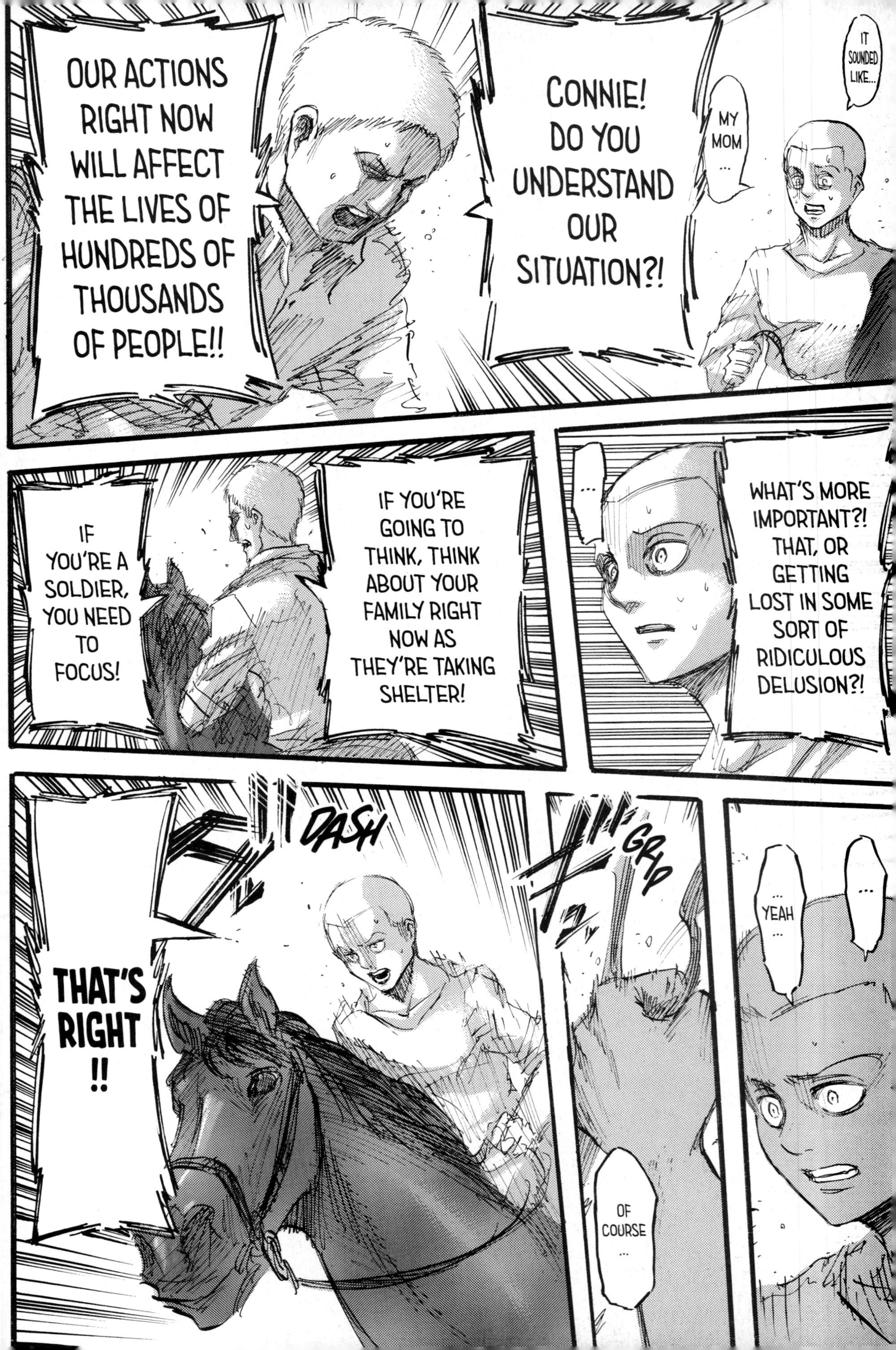
IT SOUNDED LIKE...
MY MOM ...
CONNIE! DO YOU UNDERSTAND OUR SITUATION?!
OUR ACTIONS RIGHT NOW WILL AFFECT THE LIVES OF HUNDREDS OF THOUSANDS OF PEOPLE!!
WHAT'S MORE IMPORTANT?! THAT, OR GETTING LOST IN SOME SORT OF RIDICULOUS DELUSION?!
...
IF YOU'RE GOING TO THINK, THINK ABOUT YOUR FAMILY RIGHT NOW AS THEY'RE TAKING SHELTER!
IF YOU'RE A SOLDIER, YOU NEED TO FOCUS!
...
... YEAH ...
GRAB
OF COURSE ...
DASH
THAT'S RIGHT !!

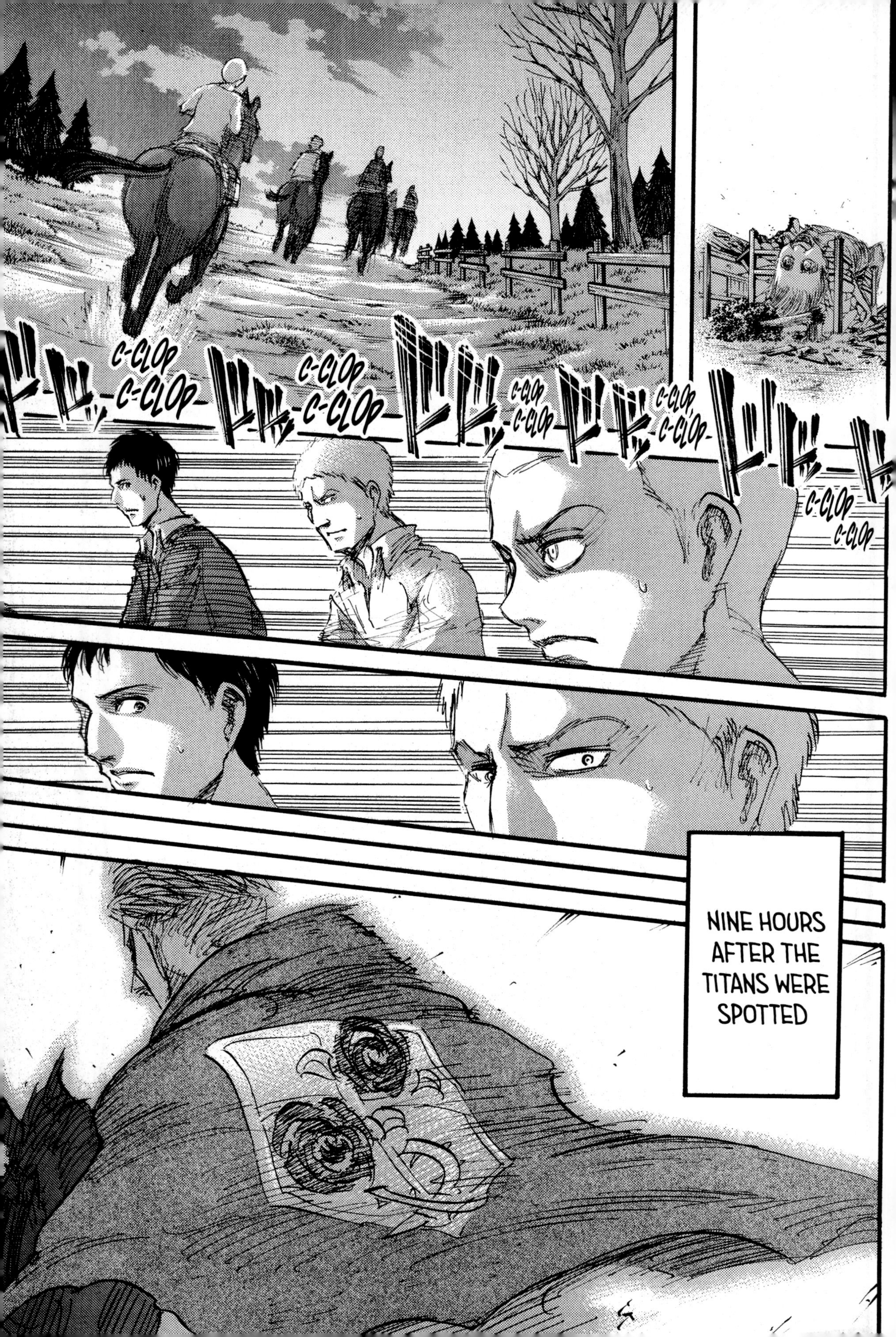
C-CLOP C-CLOP
C-CLOP C-CLOP
C-CLOP C-CLOP
C-CLOP C-CLOP
C-CLOP C-CLOP
NINE HOURS AFTER THE TITANS WERE SPOTTED

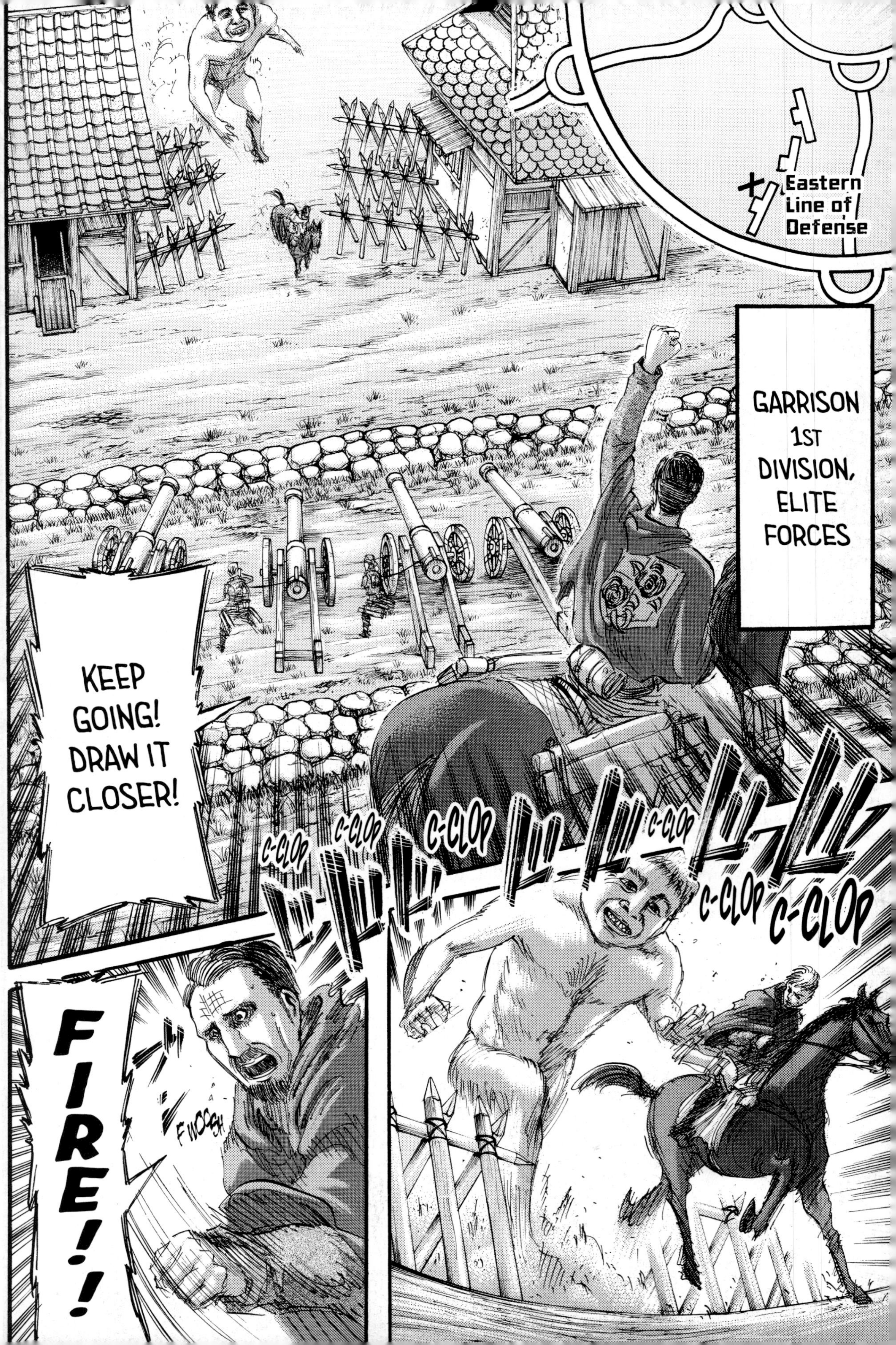

Eastern Line of Defense
GARRISON 1ST DIVISION, ELITE FORCES
KEEP GOING! DRAW IT CLOSER!
C-CLOP
C-CLOP
C-CLOP
C-CLOP
C-CLOP
C-CLOP
C-CLOP
FWOOSH
FIRE!!!

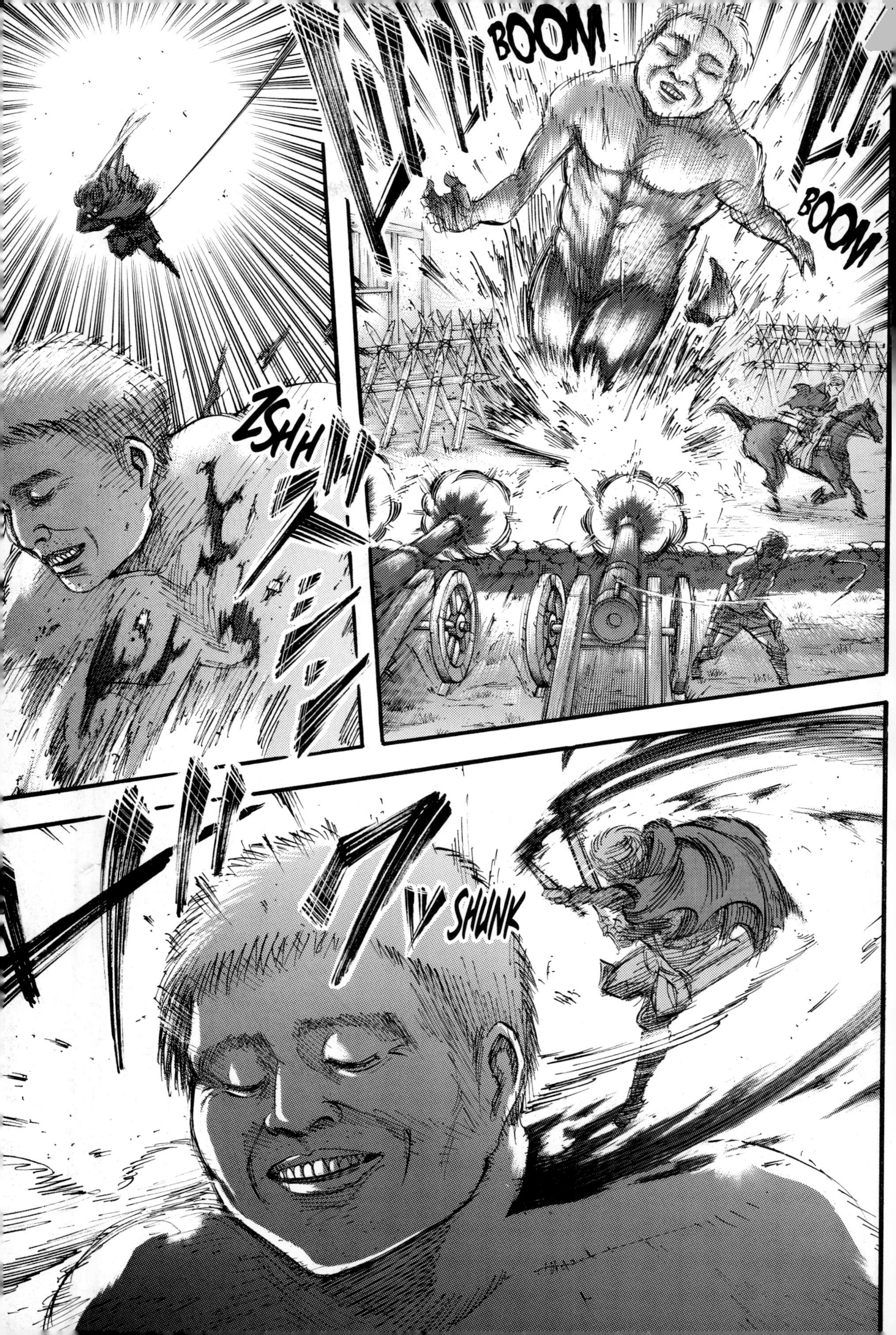
BOOM
BOOM
ZSHH
SHUNK

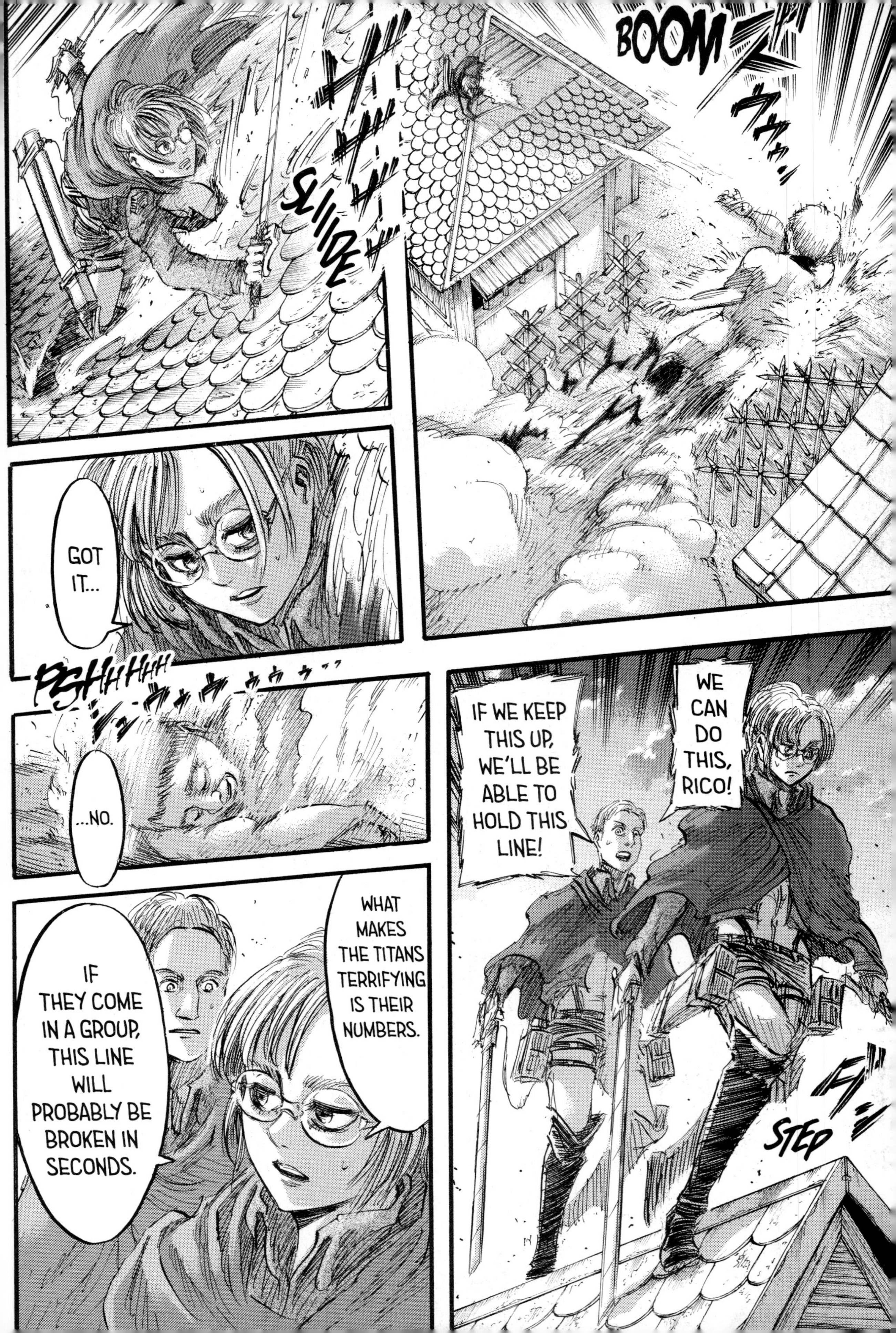
BOOM
SLIIIDE
GOT IT...
WE CAN DO THIS, RICO!
IF WE KEEP THIS UP, WE'LL BE ABLE TO HOLD THIS LINE!
STEP
PSHHHHH
...NO.
WHAT MAKES THE TITANS TERRIFYING IS THEIR NUMBERS.
IF THEY COME IN A GROUP, THIS LINE WILL PROBABLY BE BROKEN IN SECONDS.

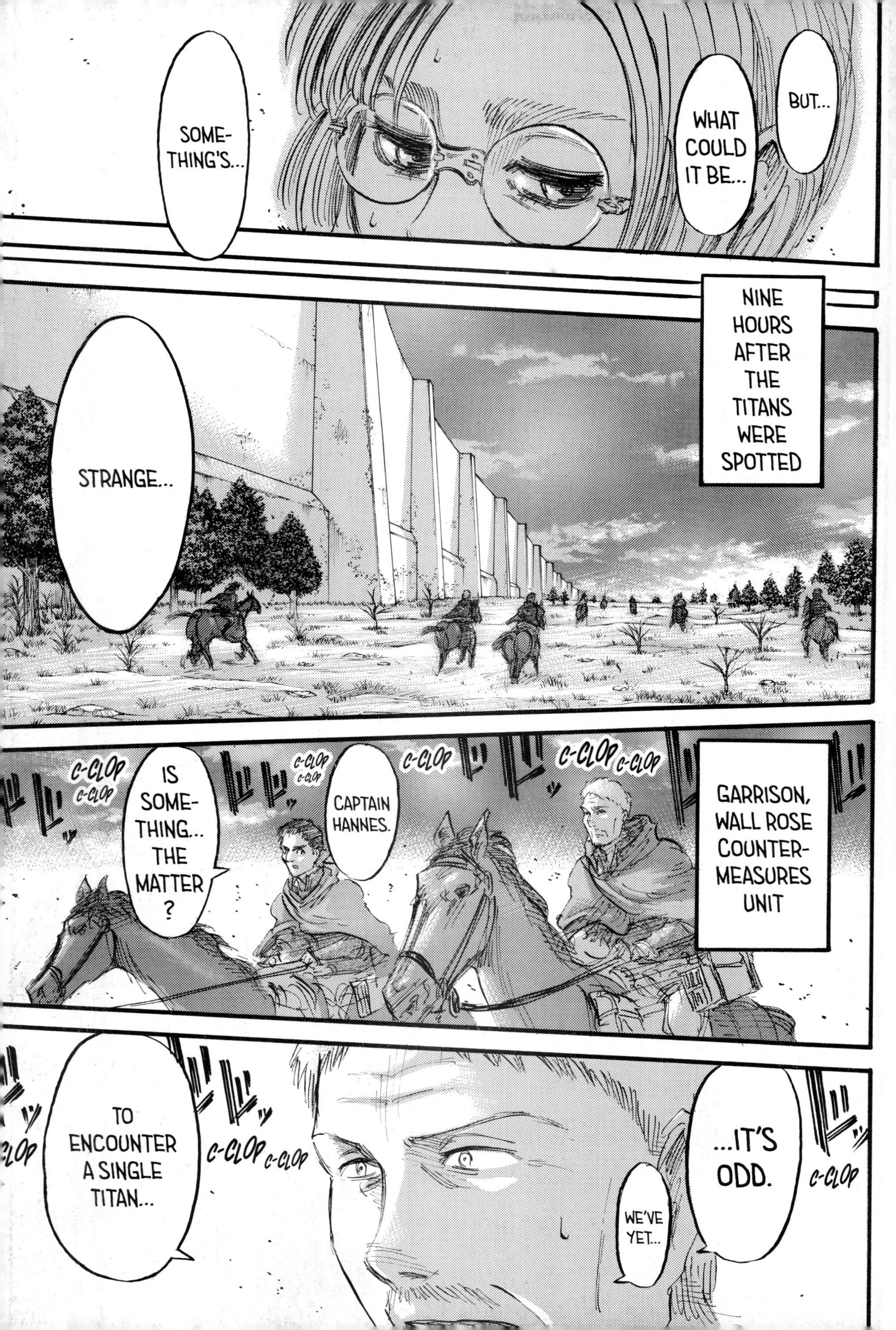
BUT...
WHAT COULD IT BE...
SOME-THING'S...
NINE HOURS AFTER THE TITANS WERE SPOTTED
STRANGE...
GARRISON, WALL ROSE COUNTER-MEASURES UNIT
C-CLOP C-CLOP
C-CLOP
CAPTAIN HANNES.
C-CLOP C-CLOP
IS SOME-THING... THE MATTER?
C-CLOP C-CLOP
C-CLOP
...IT'S ODD.
WE'VE YET...
C-CLOP C-CLOP
TO ENCOUNTER A SINGLE TITAN...
CLOP

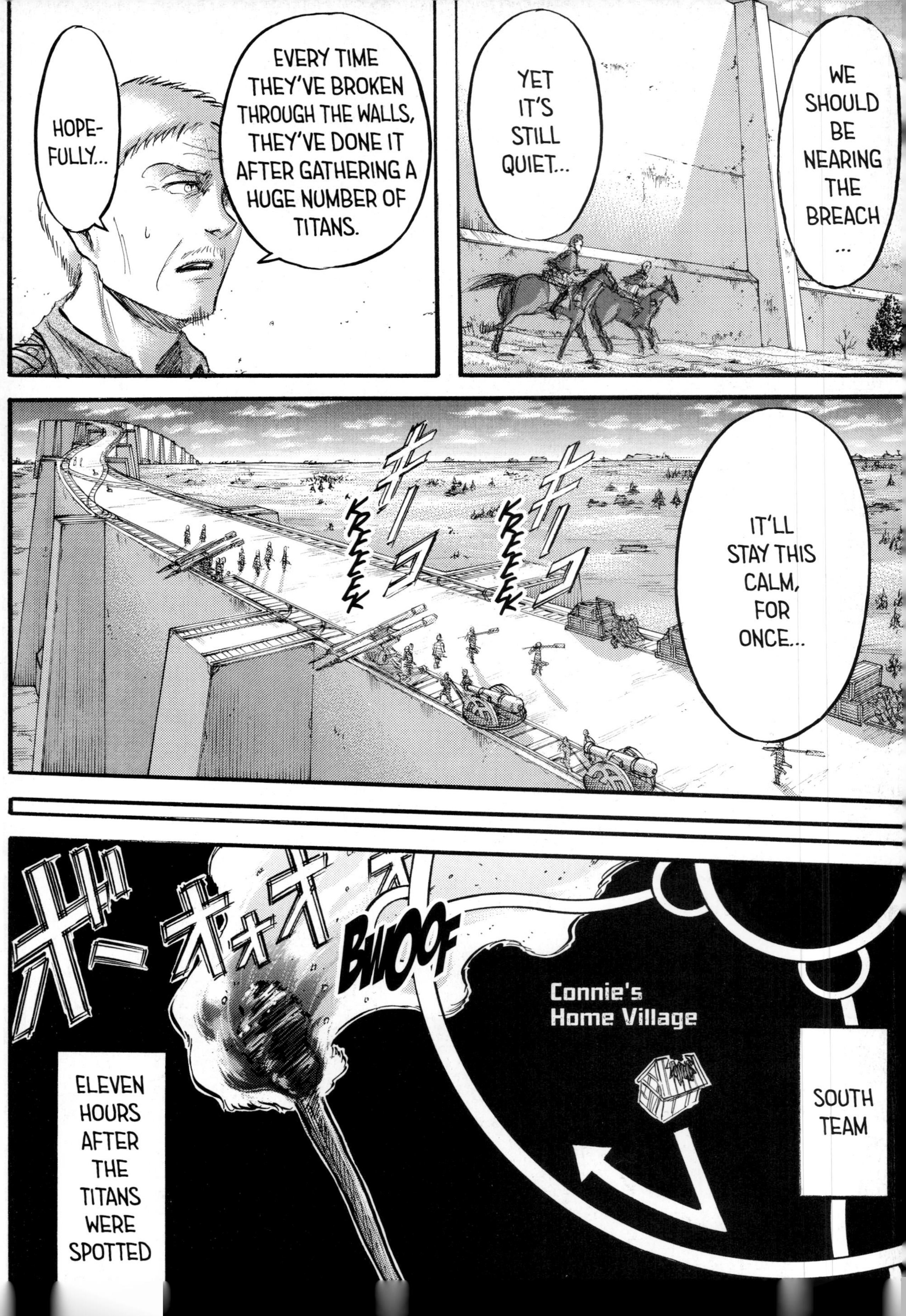
WE SHOULD BE NEARING THE BREACH ...
YET IT'S STILL QUIET...
EVERY TIME THEY'VE BROKEN THROUGH THE WALLS, THEY'VE DONE IT AFTER GATHERING A HUGE NUMBER OF TITANS.
HOPE-FULLY...
IT'LL STAY THIS CALM, FOR ONCE...
KREEEK
KREEEK
BWOOF
Connie's Home Village
SOUTH TEAM
ELEVEN HOURS AFTER THE TITANS WERE SPOTTED

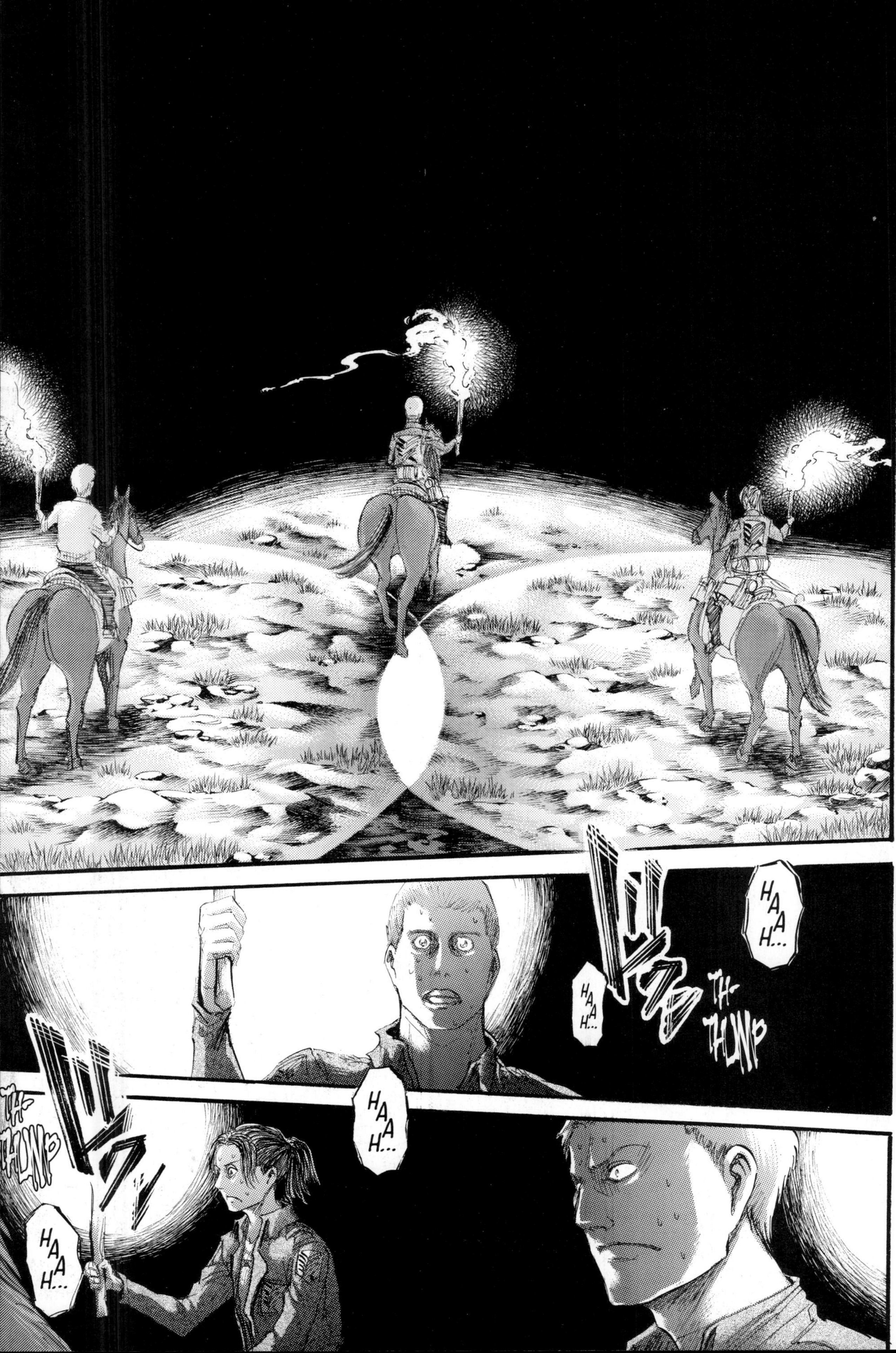
HAAAH...
TH THUMP
HAAH...
HAAAH...
TH THUMP
HAAAH...

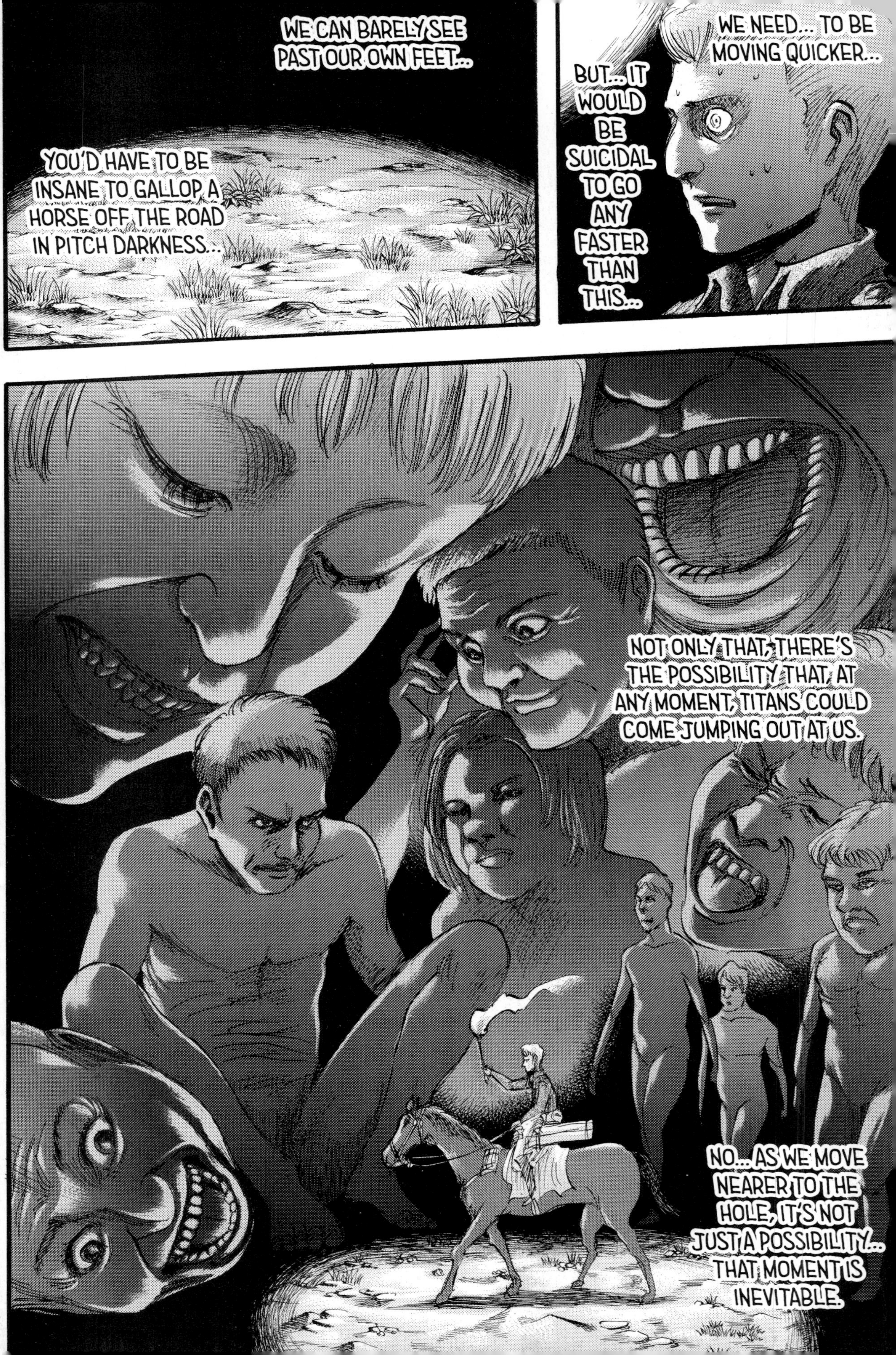
WE NEED... TO BE MOVING QUICKER...
BUT... IT WOULD BE SUICIDAL TO GO ANY FASTER THAN THIS...
WE CAN BARELY SEE PAST OUR OWN FEET...
YOU'D HAVE TO BE INSANE TO GALLOP A HORSE OFF THE ROAD IN PITCH DARKNESS...
NOT ONLY THAT, THERE'S THE POSSIBILITY THAT, AT ANY MOMENT, TITANS COULD COME JUMPING OUT AT US.
NO... AS WE MOVE NEARER TO THE HOLE, IT'S NOT JUST A POSSIBILITY... THAT MOMENT IS INEVITABLE.

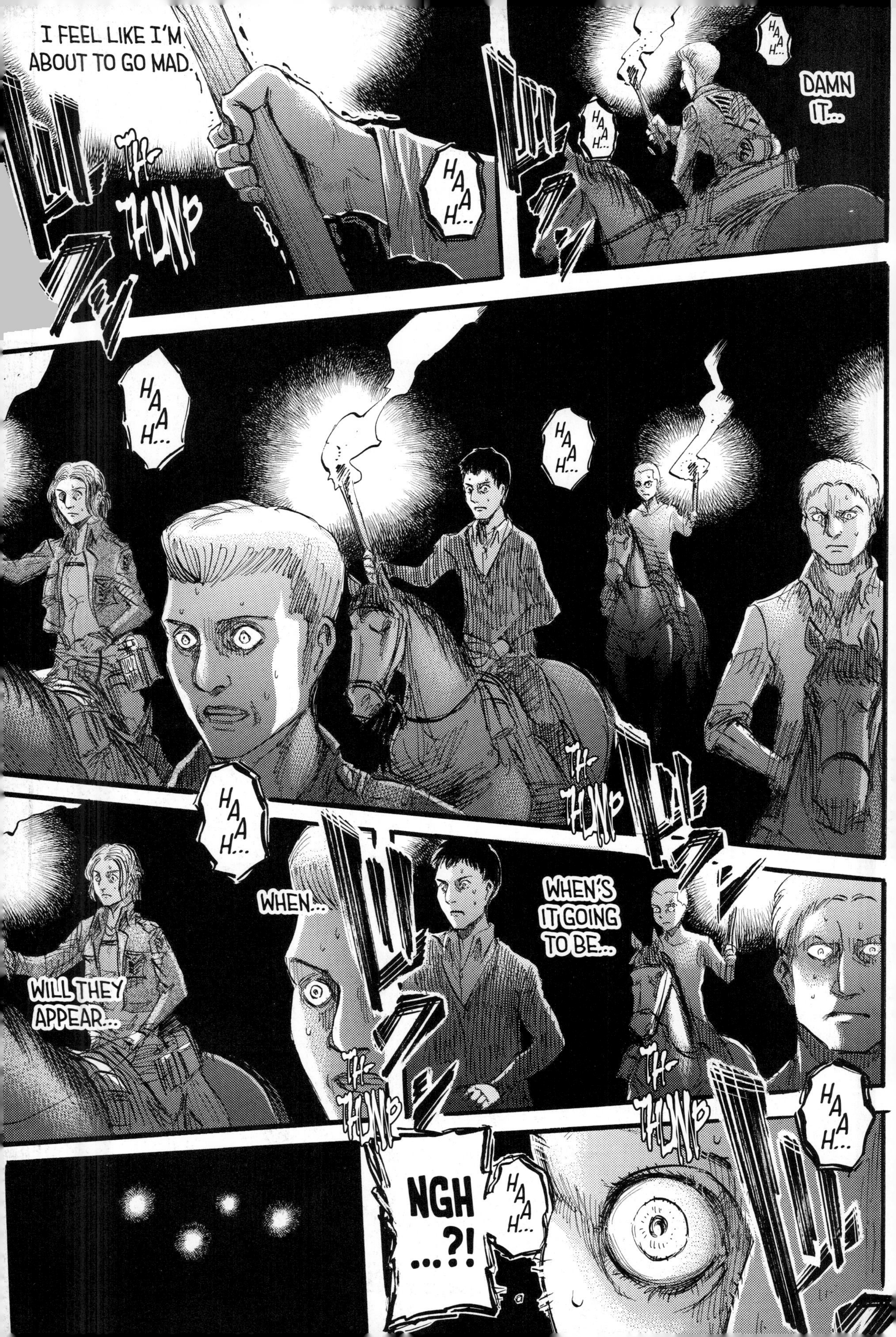
HAA H...
DAMN IT...
HAA H...
I FEEL LIKE I'M ABOUT TO GO MAD.
HAA H...
TH-THUMP
HAA H...
TH-THUMP
HAA H...
WHEN'S IT GOING TO BE...
TH-THUMP
WHEN...
HAA H...
TH-THUMP
WILL THEY APPEAR...
HAA H...
HAA H...
NGH ...?!

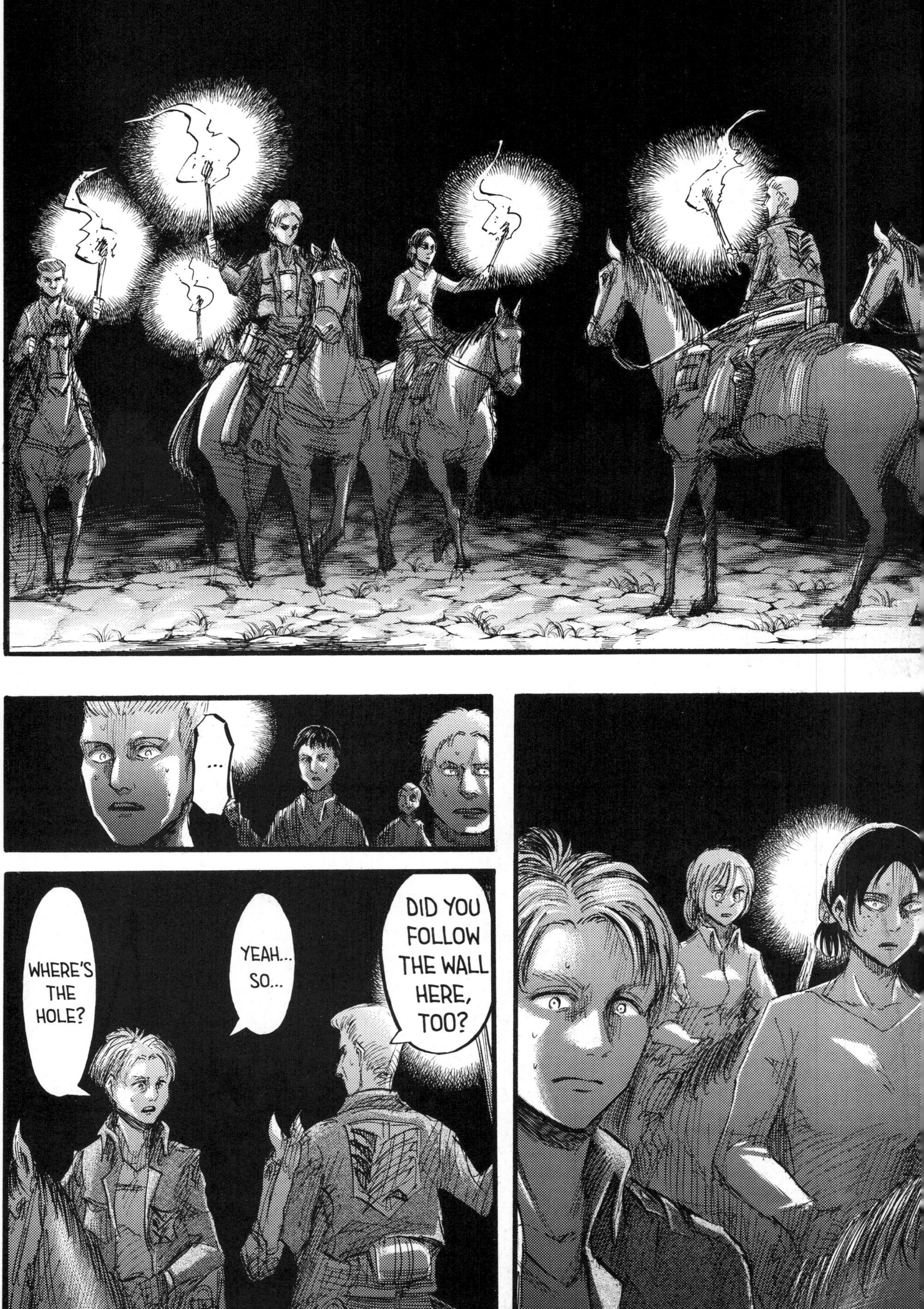
...
DID YOU FOLLOW THE WALL HERE, TOO?
YEAH... SO...
WHERE'S THE HOLE?

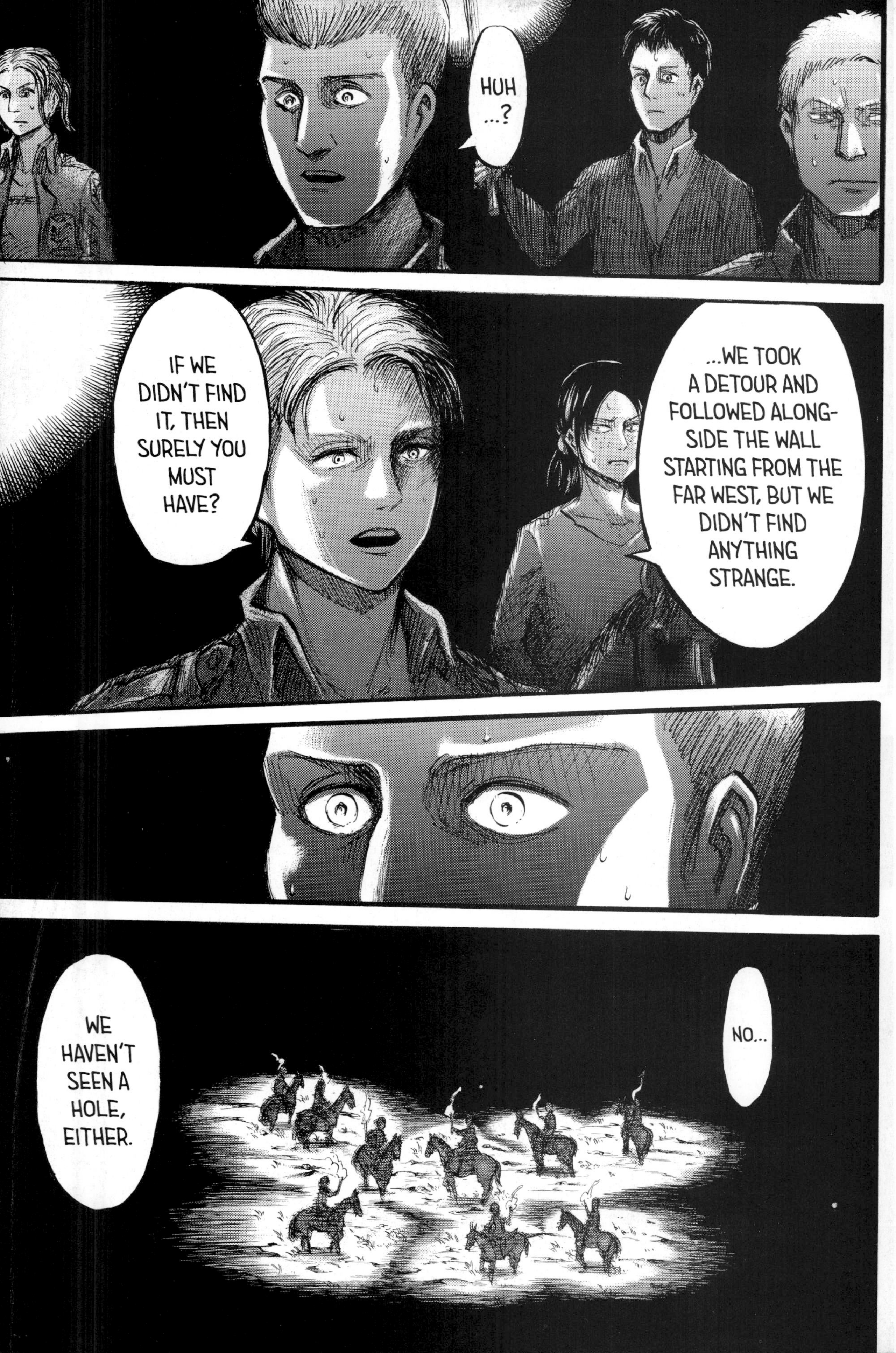
HUH ...?
...WE TOOK A DETOUR AND FOLLOWED ALONG-SIDE THE WALL STARTING FROM THE FAR WEST, BUT WE DIDN'T FIND ANYTHING STRANGE.
IF WE DIDN'T FIND IT, THEN SURELY YOU MUST HAVE?
NO...
WE HAVEN'T SEEN A HOLE, EITHER.

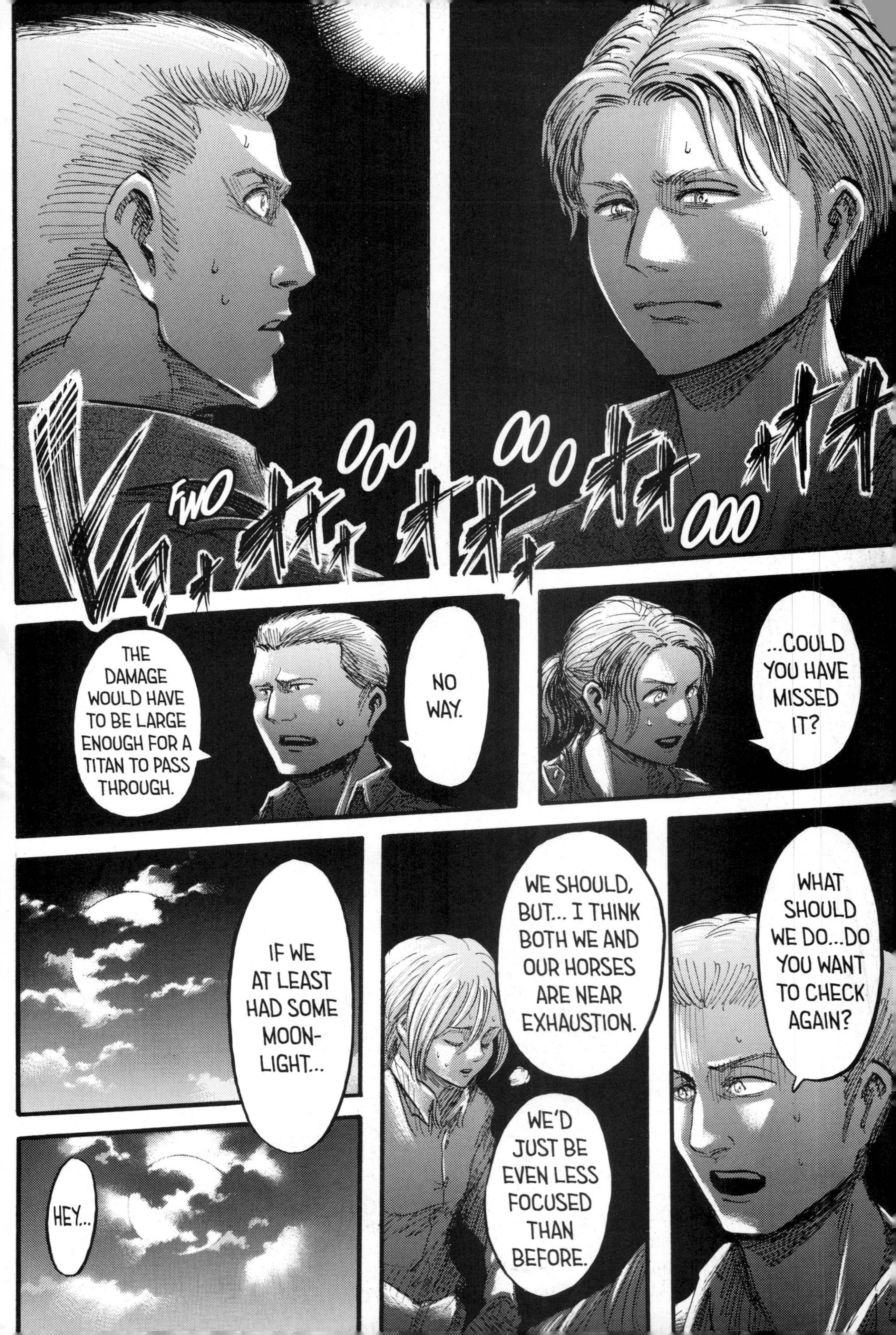
FWOOOOOOOOOOO
...COULD YOU HAVE MISSED IT?
NO WAY.
THE DAMAGE WOULD HAVE TO BE LARGE ENOUGH FOR A TITAN TO PASS THROUGH.
WHAT SHOULD WE DO...DO YOU WANT TO CHECK AGAIN?
WE SHOULD, BUT... I THINK BOTH WE AND OUR HORSES ARE NEAR EXHAUSTION.
WE'D JUST BE EVEN LESS FOCUSED THAN BEFORE.
IF WE AT LEAST HAD SOME MOON-LIGHT...
HEY...

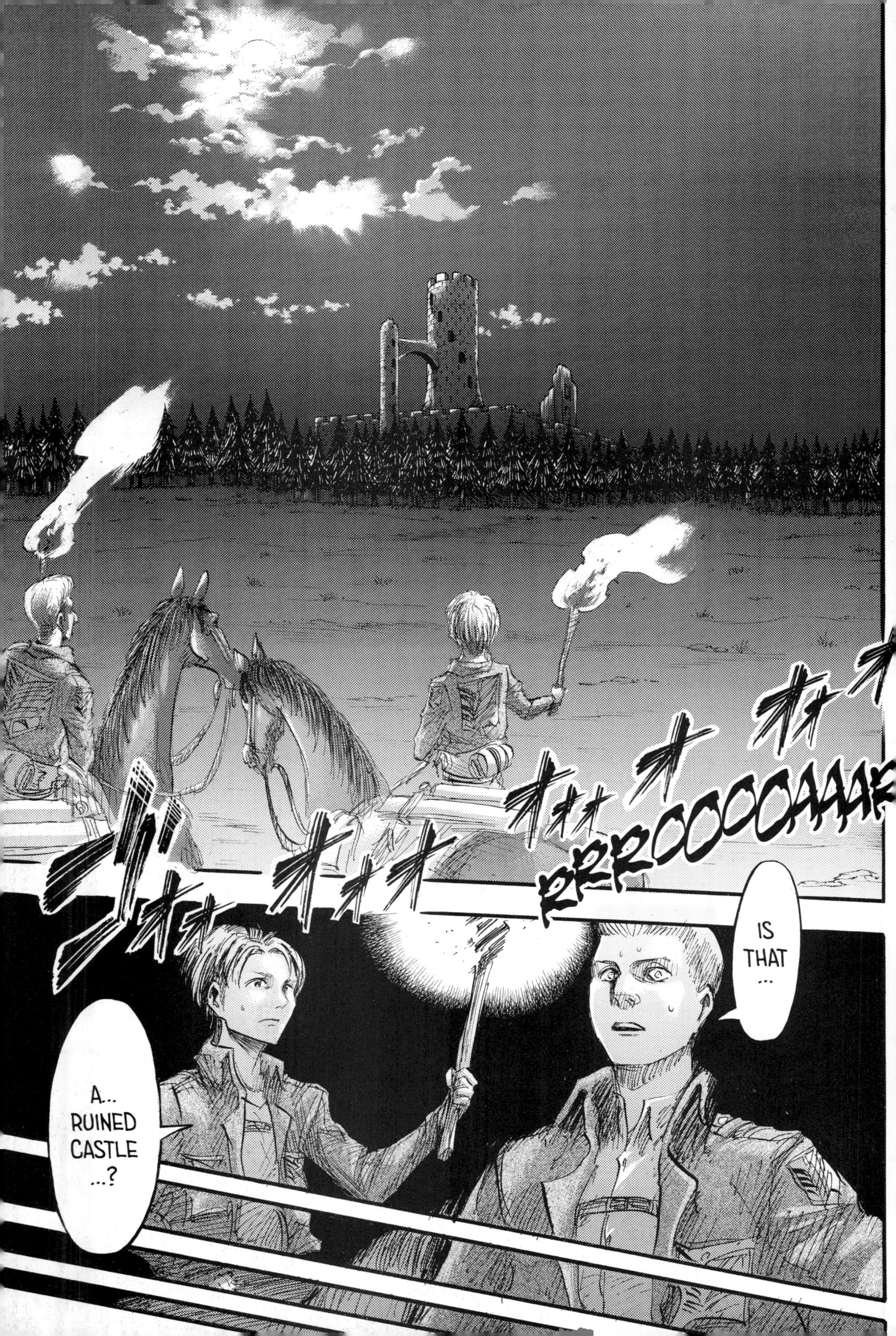
RRROOOOAAAR
IS THAT ...
A... RUINED CASTLE ...?

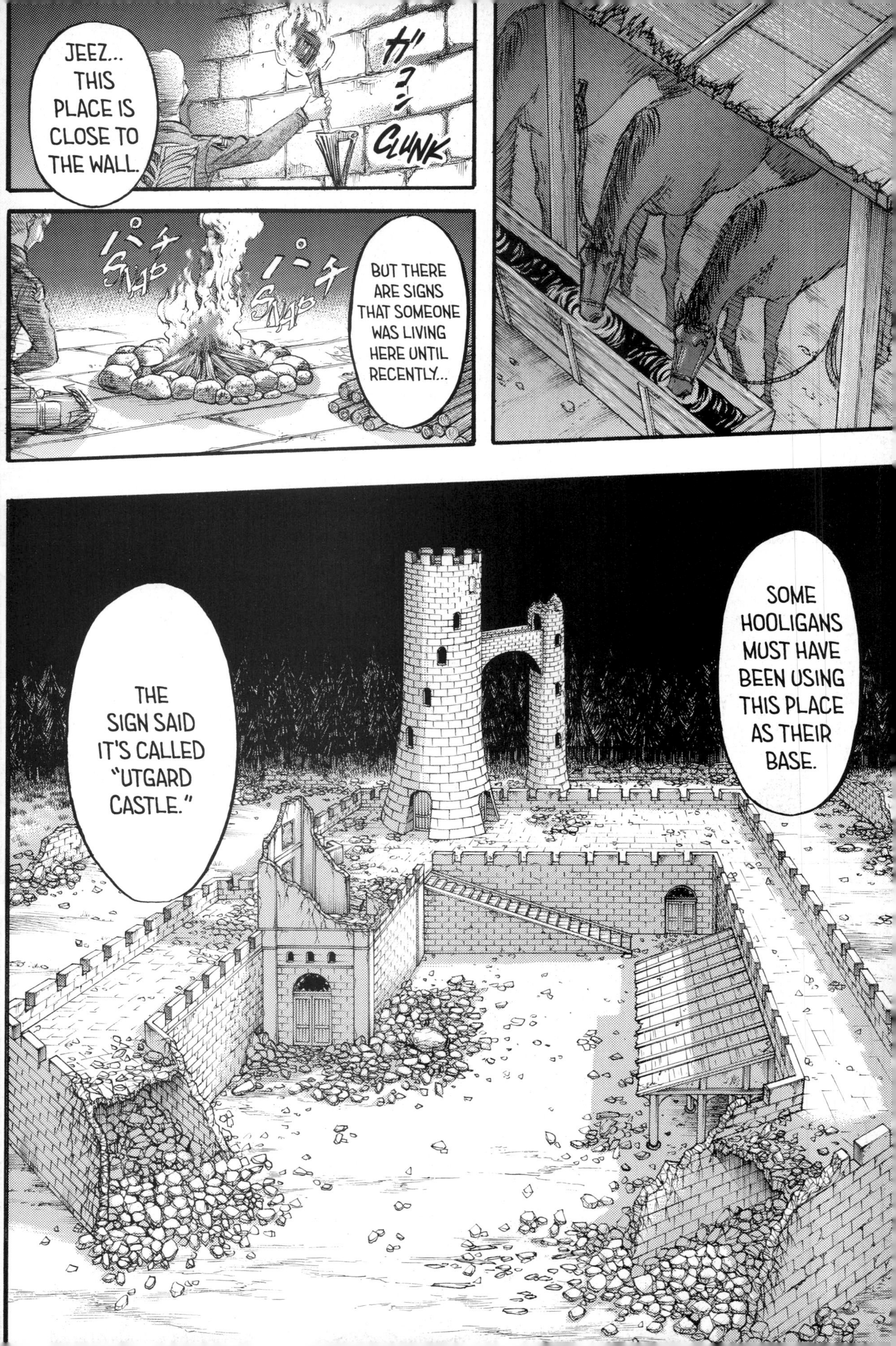

ガコン
CLUNK
JEEZ... THIS PLACE IS CLOSE TO THE WALL.
BUT THERE ARE SIGNS THAT SOMEONE WAS LIVING HERE UNTIL RECENTLY...
パチ
SNAP
パチ
SNAP
SOME HOOLIGANS MUST HAVE BEEN USING THIS PLACE AS THEIR BASE.
THE SIGN SAID IT'S CALLED "UTGARD CASTLE."

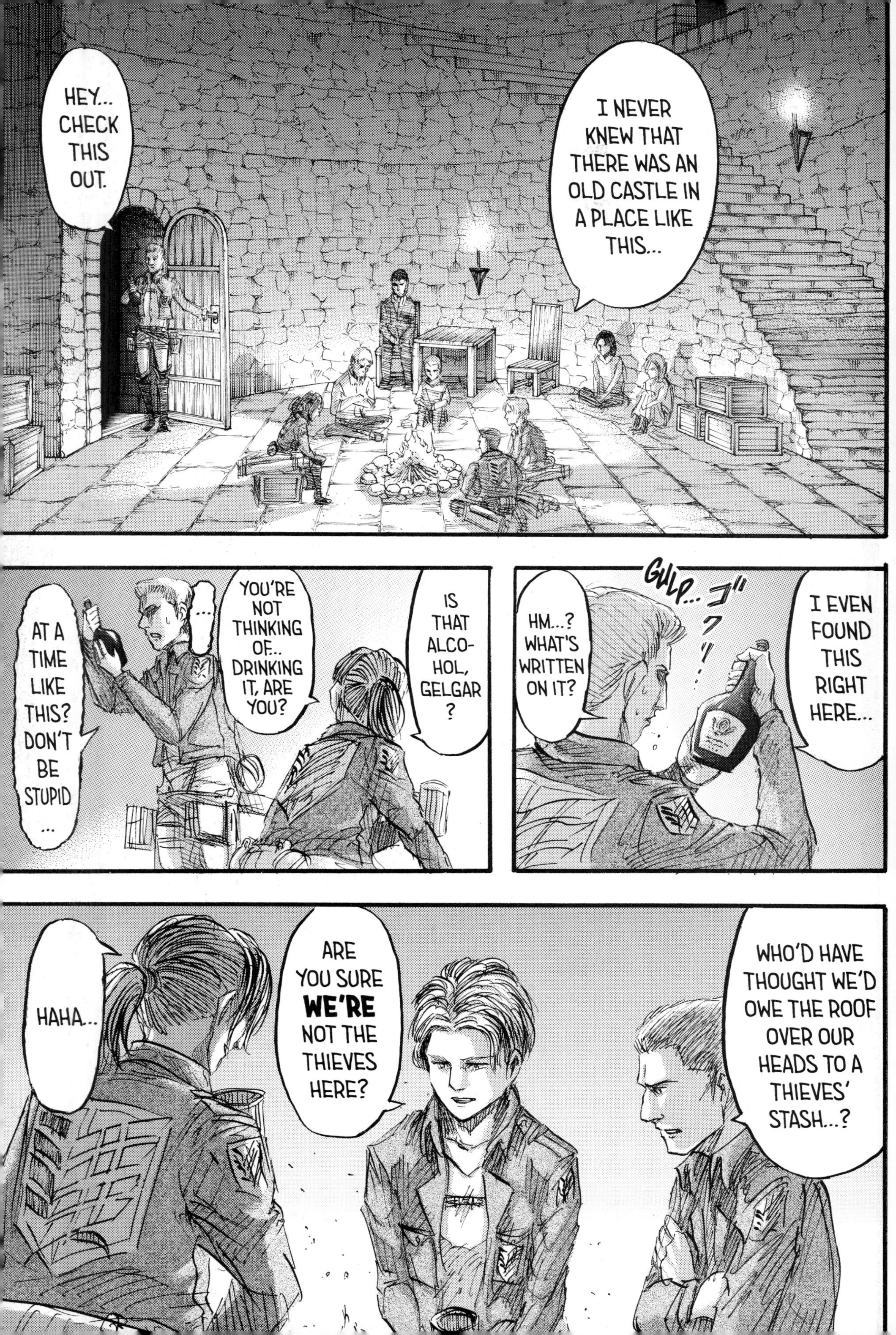
I NEVER KNEW THAT THERE WAS AN OLD CASTLE IN A PLACE LIKE THIS...
HEY... CHECK THIS OUT.
I EVEN FOUND THIS RIGHT HERE...
GULP...
ゴクリ...
HM...? WHAT'S WRITTEN ON IT?
IS THAT ALCO-HOL, GELGAR?
YOU'RE NOT THINKING OF... DRINKING IT, ARE YOU?
...
AT A TIME LIKE THIS? DON'T BE STUPID...
WHO'D HAVE THOUGHT WE'D OWE THE ROOF OVER OUR HEADS TO A THIEVES' STASH...?
ARE YOU SURE **WE'RE** NOT THE THIEVES HERE?
HAHA...

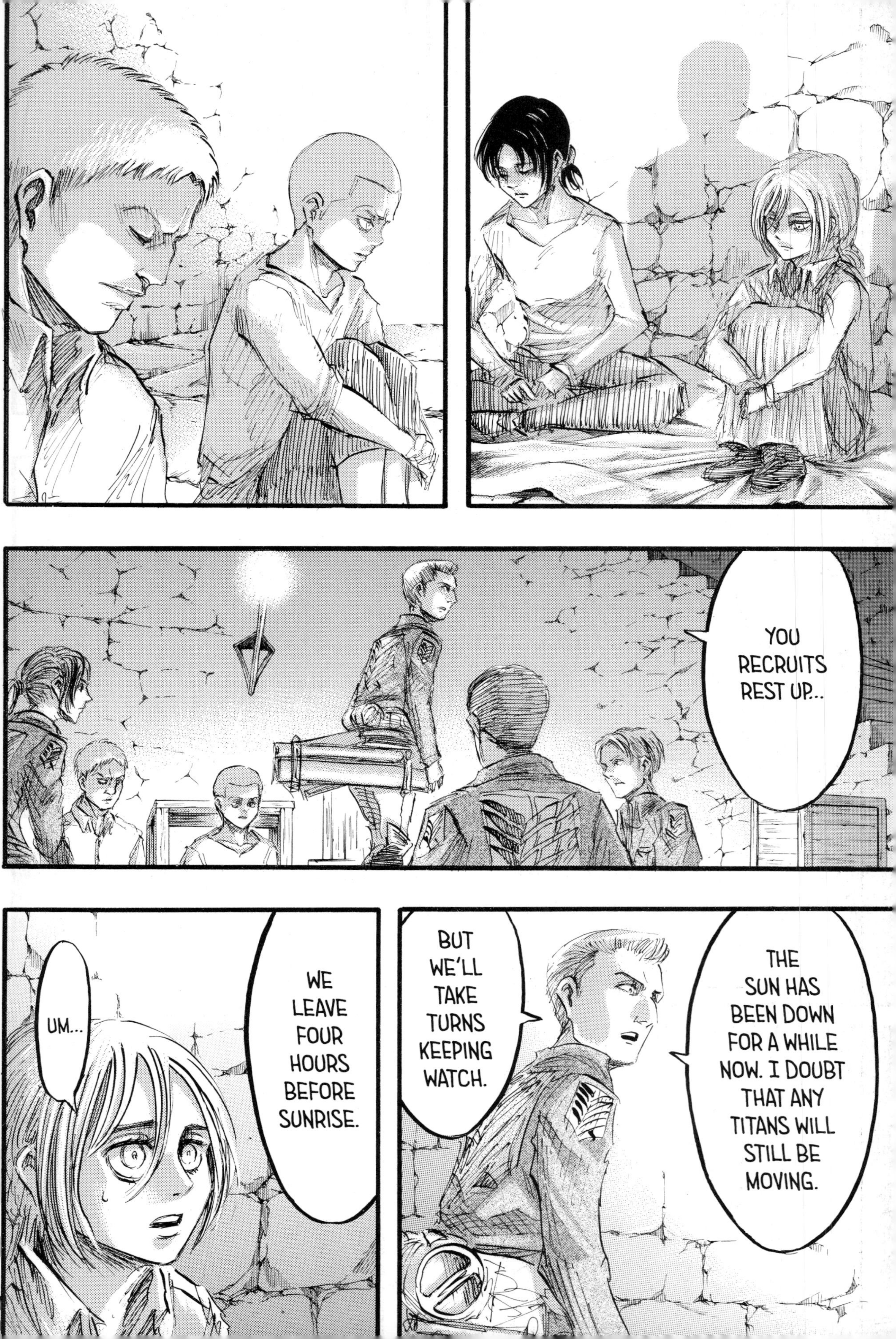
YOU RECRUITS REST UP...
THE SUN HAS BEEN DOWN FOR A WHILE NOW. I DOUBT THAT ANY TITANS WILL STILL BE MOVING.
BUT WE'LL TAKE TURNS KEEPING WATCH.
WE LEAVE FOUR HOURS BEFORE SUNRISE.
UM...

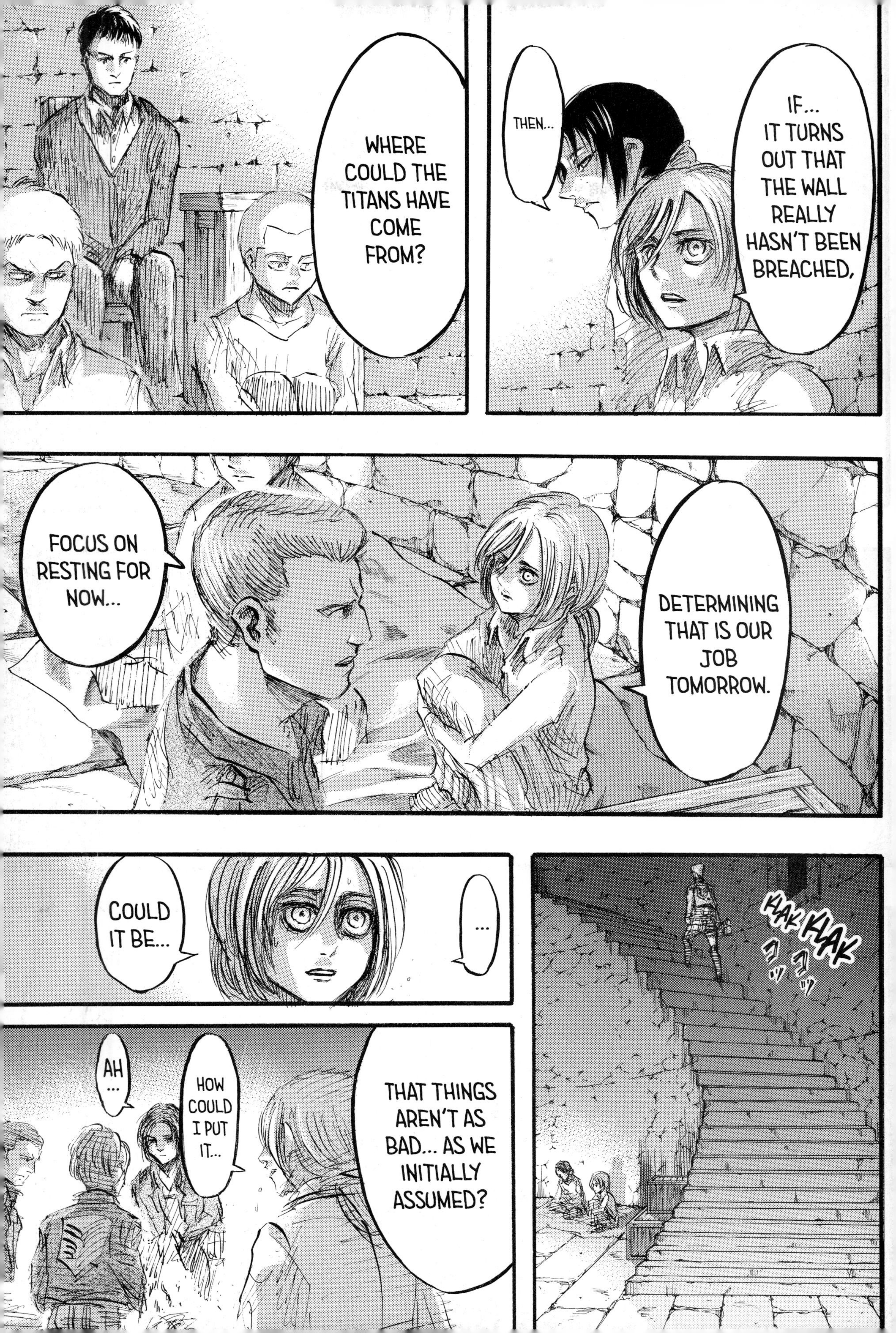
IF... IT TURNS OUT THAT THE WALL REALLY HASN'T BEEN BREACHED,
THEN...
WHERE COULD THE TITANS HAVE COME FROM?
DETERMINING THAT IS OUR JOB TOMORROW.
FOCUS ON RESTING FOR NOW...
KLAK KLAK
...
COULD IT BE...
THAT THINGS AREN'T AS BAD... AS WE INITIALLY ASSUMED?
HOW COULD I PUT IT...
AH...

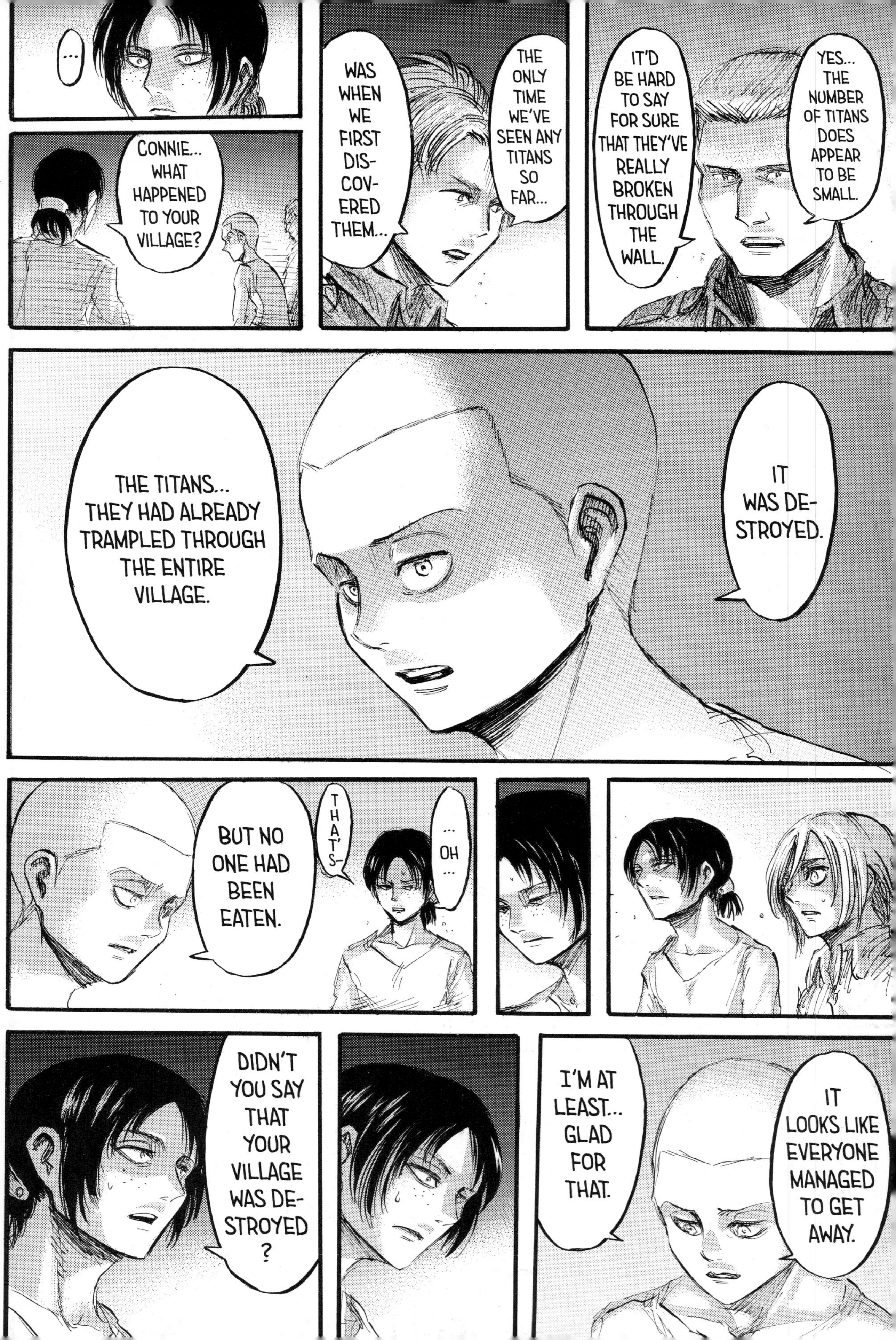
YES... THE NUMBER OF TITANS DOES APPEAR TO BE SMALL.
IT'D BE HARD TO SAY FOR SURE THAT THEY'VE REALLY BROKEN THROUGH THE WALL.
THE ONLY TIME WE'VE SEEN ANY TITANS SO FAR...
WAS WHEN WE FIRST DISCOVERED THEM...
...
CONNIE... WHAT HAPPENED TO YOUR VILLAGE?
IT WAS DESTROYED.
THE TITANS... THEY HAD ALREADY TRAMPLED THROUGH THE ENTIRE VILLAGE.
... OH ...
THAT'S-
BUT NO ONE HAD BEEN EATEN.
IT LOOKS LIKE EVERYONE MANAGED TO GET AWAY.
I'M AT LEAST... GLAD FOR THAT.
DIDN'T YOU SAY THAT YOUR VILLAGE WAS DESTROYED?

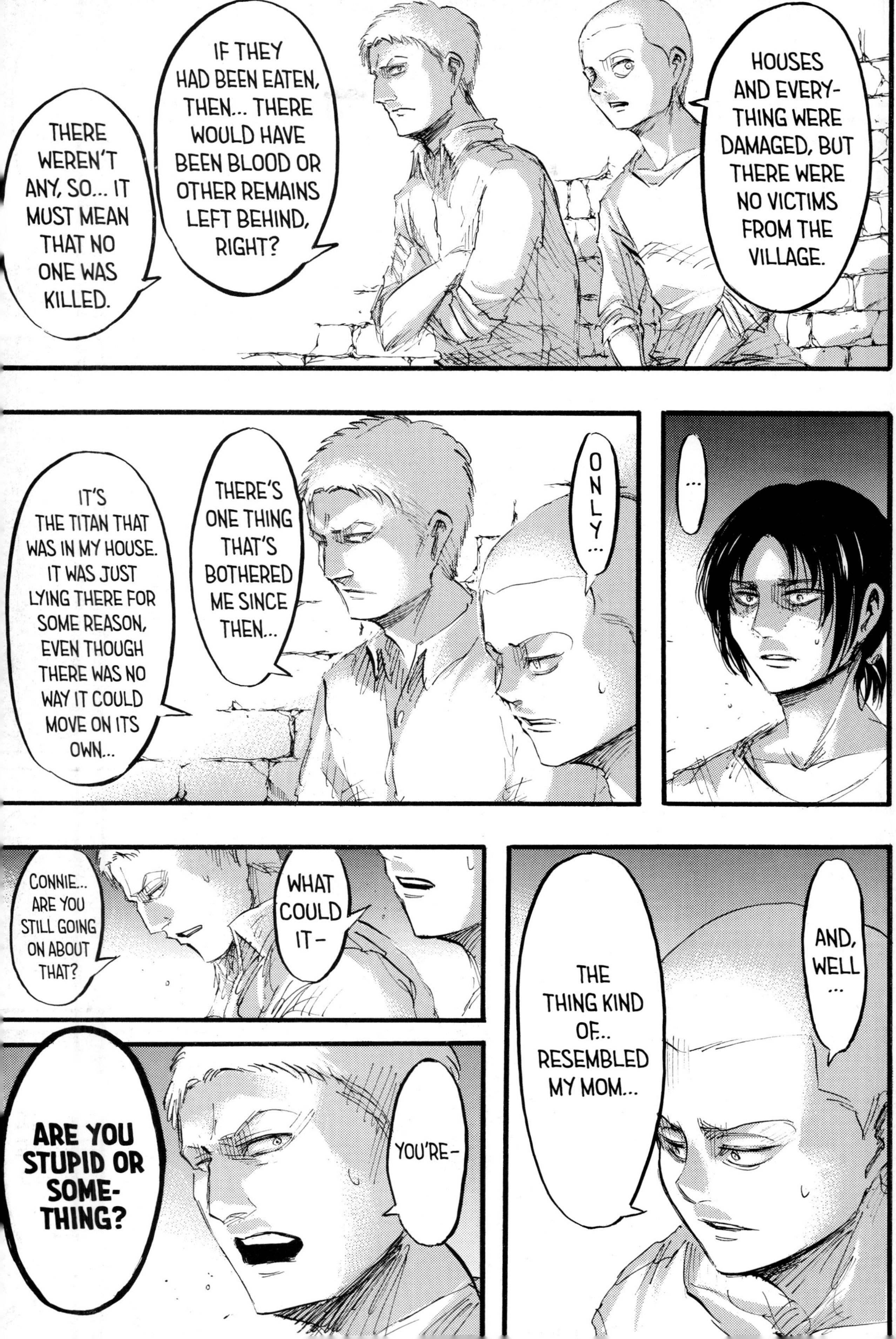
HOUSES AND EVERY-THING WERE DAMAGED, BUT THERE WERE NO VICTIMS FROM THE VILLAGE.
IF THEY HAD BEEN EATEN, THEN... THERE WOULD HAVE BEEN BLOOD OR OTHER REMAINS LEFT BEHIND, RIGHT?
THERE WEREN'T ANY, SO... IT MUST MEAN THAT NO ONE WAS KILLED.
...
ONLY...
THERE'S ONE THING THAT'S BOTHERED ME SINCE THEN...
IT'S THE TITAN THAT WAS IN MY HOUSE. IT WAS JUST LYING THERE FOR SOME REASON, EVEN THOUGH THERE WAS NO WAY IT COULD MOVE ON ITS OWN...
AND, WELL ...
THE THING KIND OF.. RESEMBLED MY MOM...
WHAT COULD IT-
CONNIE... ARE YOU STILL GOING ON ABOUT THAT?
YOU'RE-
ARE YOU STUPID OR SOME-THING?

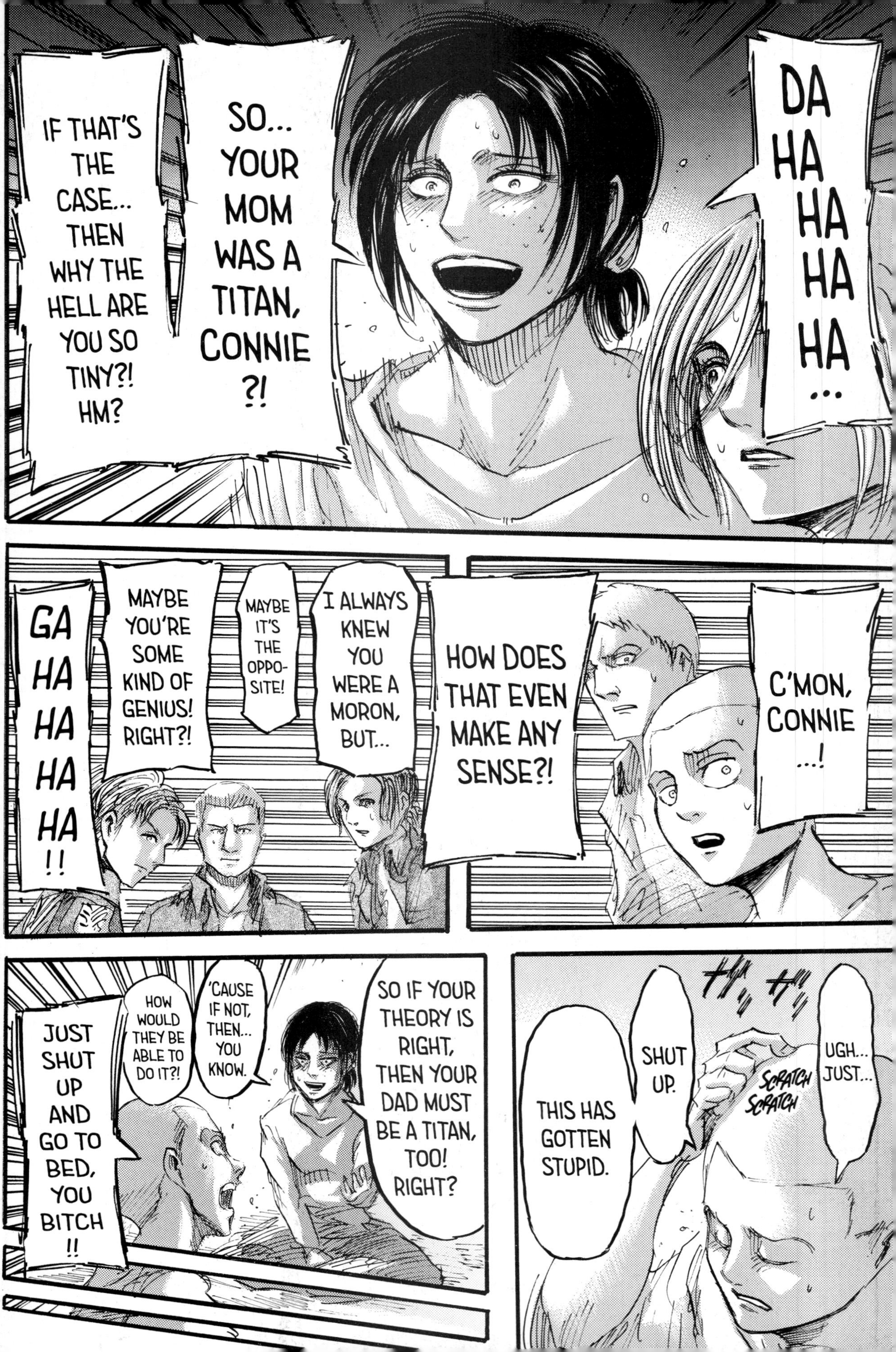
DA HA HA HA HA...
SO... YOUR MOM WAS A TITAN, CONNIE?!
IF THAT'S THE CASE... THEN WHY THE HELL ARE YOU SO TINY?! HM?
C'MON, CONNIE...!
HOW DOES THAT EVEN MAKE ANY SENSE?!
I ALWAYS KNEW YOU WERE A MORON, BUT...
MAYBE IT'S THE OPPOSITE!
MAYBE YOU'RE SOME KIND OF GENIUS! RIGHT?!
GA HA HA HA HA!!
UGH... JUST...
SCRATCH SCRATCH
SHUT UP.
THIS HAS GOTTEN STUPID.
SO IF YOUR THEORY IS RIGHT, THEN YOUR DAD MUST BE A TITAN, TOO! RIGHT?
'CAUSE IF NOT, THEN... YOU KNOW.
HOW WOULD THEY BE ABLE TO DO IT?!
JUST SHUT UP AND GO TO BED, YOU BITCH!!

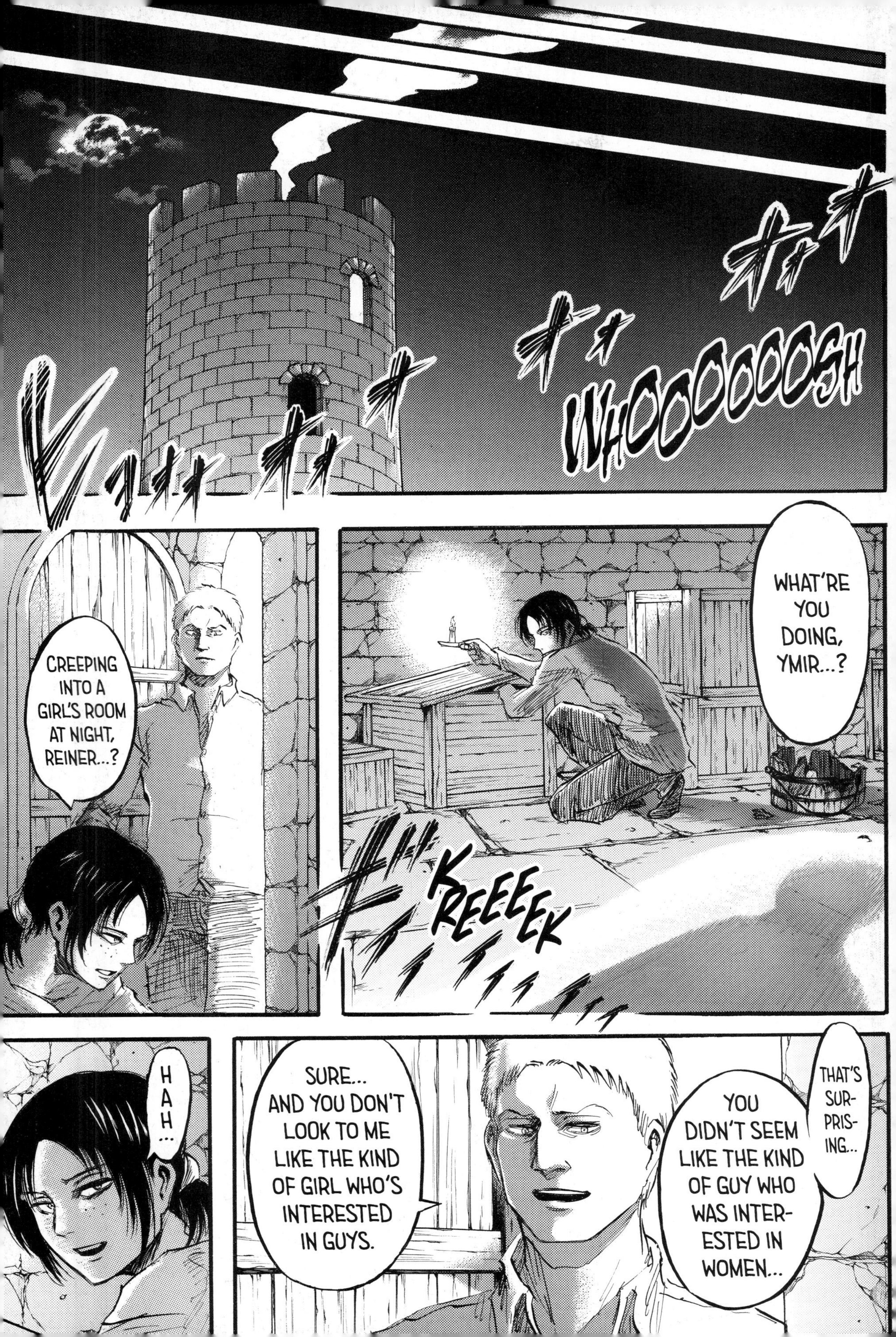
WHOOOOOOOSH
WHAT'RE YOU DOING, YMIR...?
KREEEEK
CREEPING INTO A GIRL'S ROOM AT NIGHT, REINER...?
THAT'S SURPRISING...
YOU DIDN'T SEEM LIKE THE KIND OF GUY WHO WAS INTERESTED IN WOMEN...
SURE... AND YOU DON'T LOOK TO ME LIKE THE KIND OF GIRL WHO'S INTERESTED IN GUYS.
HAH...

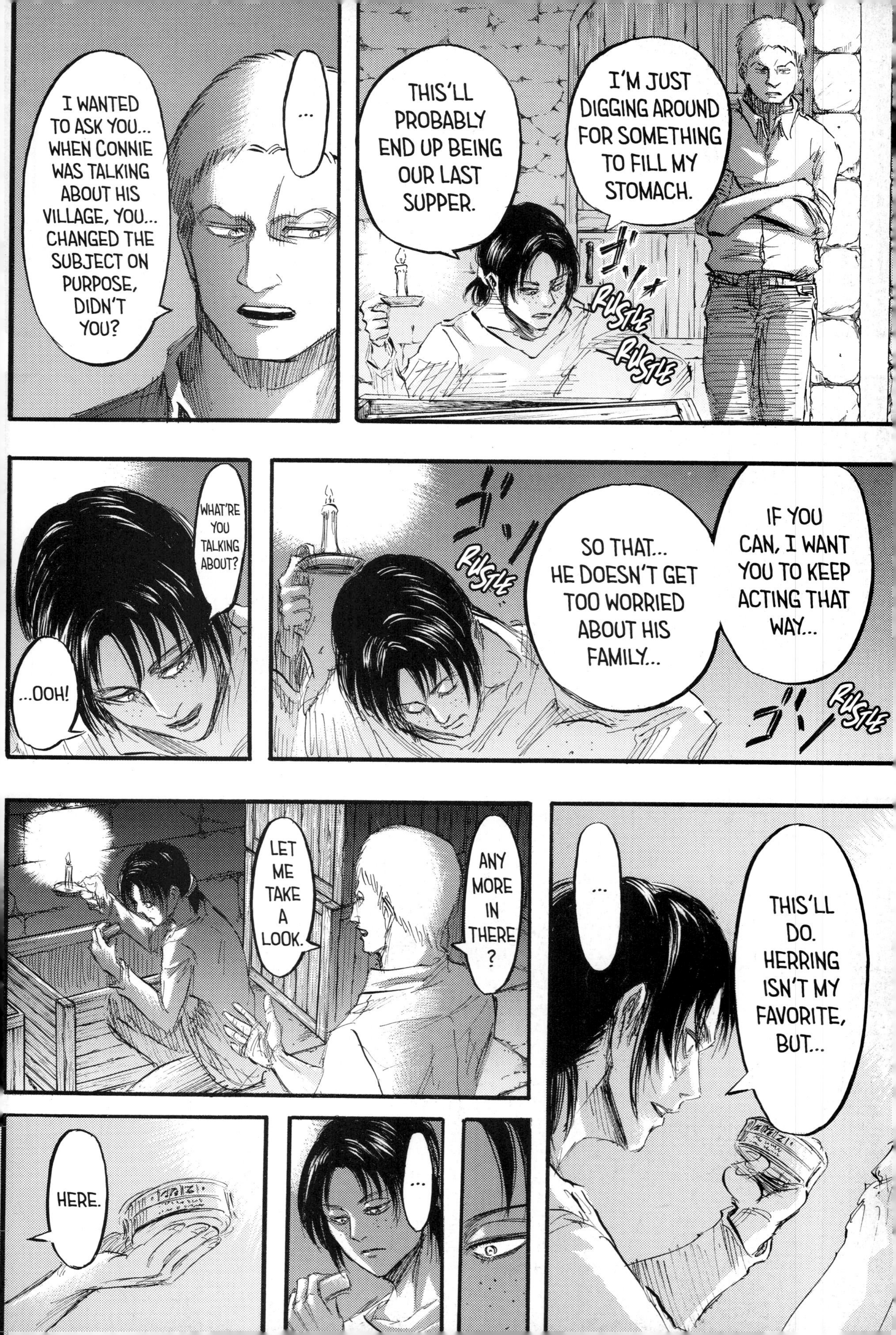
I'M JUST DIGGING AROUND FOR SOMETHING TO FILL MY STOMACH.
THIS'LL PROBABLY END UP BEING OUR LAST SUPPER.
RUSTLE
RUSTLE
...
I WANTED TO ASK YOU... WHEN CONNIE WAS TALKING ABOUT HIS VILLAGE, YOU... CHANGED THE SUBJECT ON PURPOSE, DIDN'T YOU?
IF YOU CAN, I WANT YOU TO KEEP ACTING THAT WAY...
SO THAT... HE DOESN'T GET TOO WORRIED ABOUT HIS FAMILY...
RUSTLE
RUSTLE
WHAT'RE YOU TALKING ABOUT?
...OOH!
...
THIS'LL DO. HERRING ISN'T MY FAVORITE, BUT...
ANY MORE IN THERE?
LET ME TAKE A LOOK.
...
HERE.

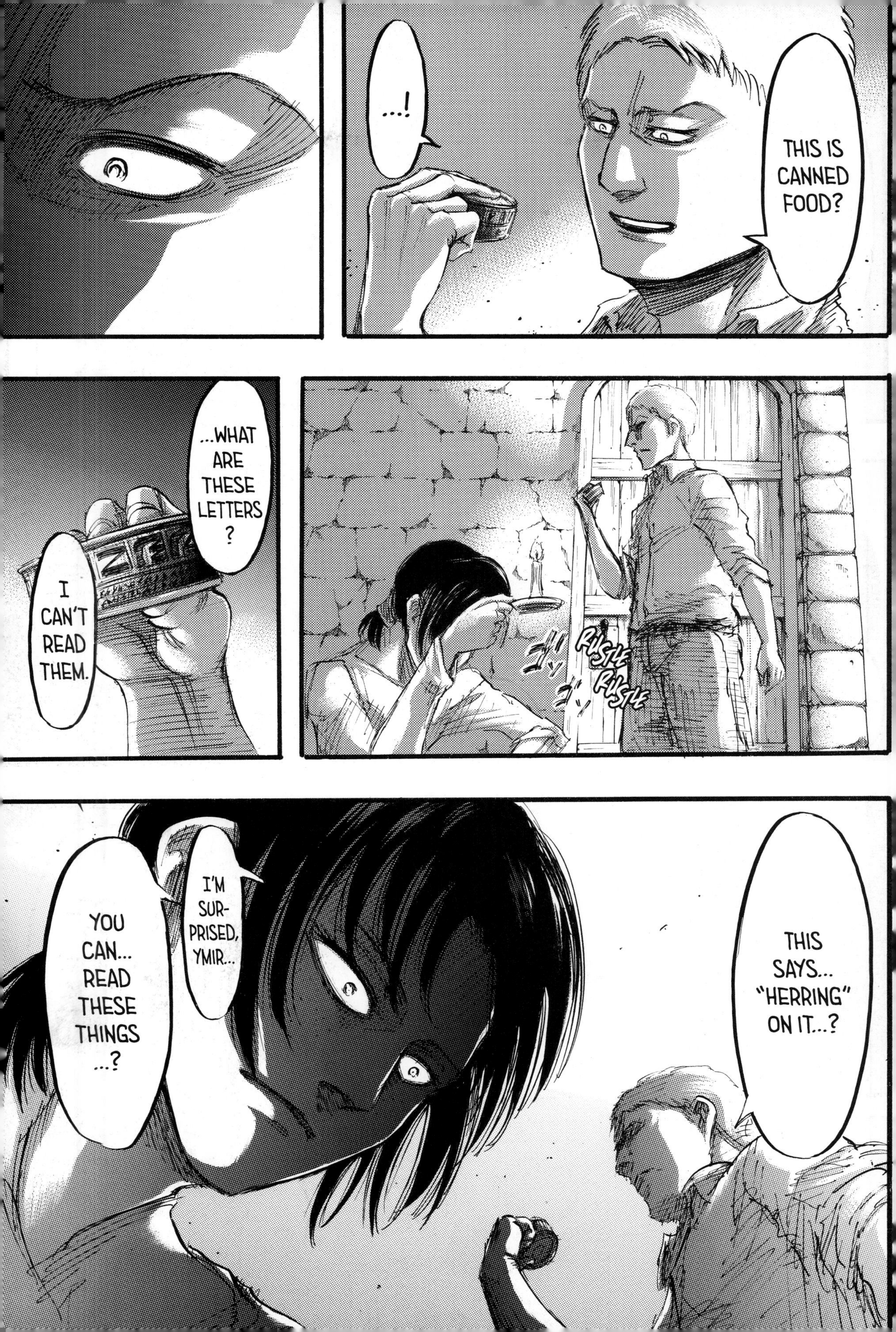
THIS IS CANNED FOOD?
...!
RUSTLE RUSTLE
...WHAT ARE THESE LETTERS?
I CAN'T READ THEM.
THIS SAYS... "HERRING" ON IT...?
I'M SURPRISED, YMIR...
YOU CAN... READ THESE THINGS...?

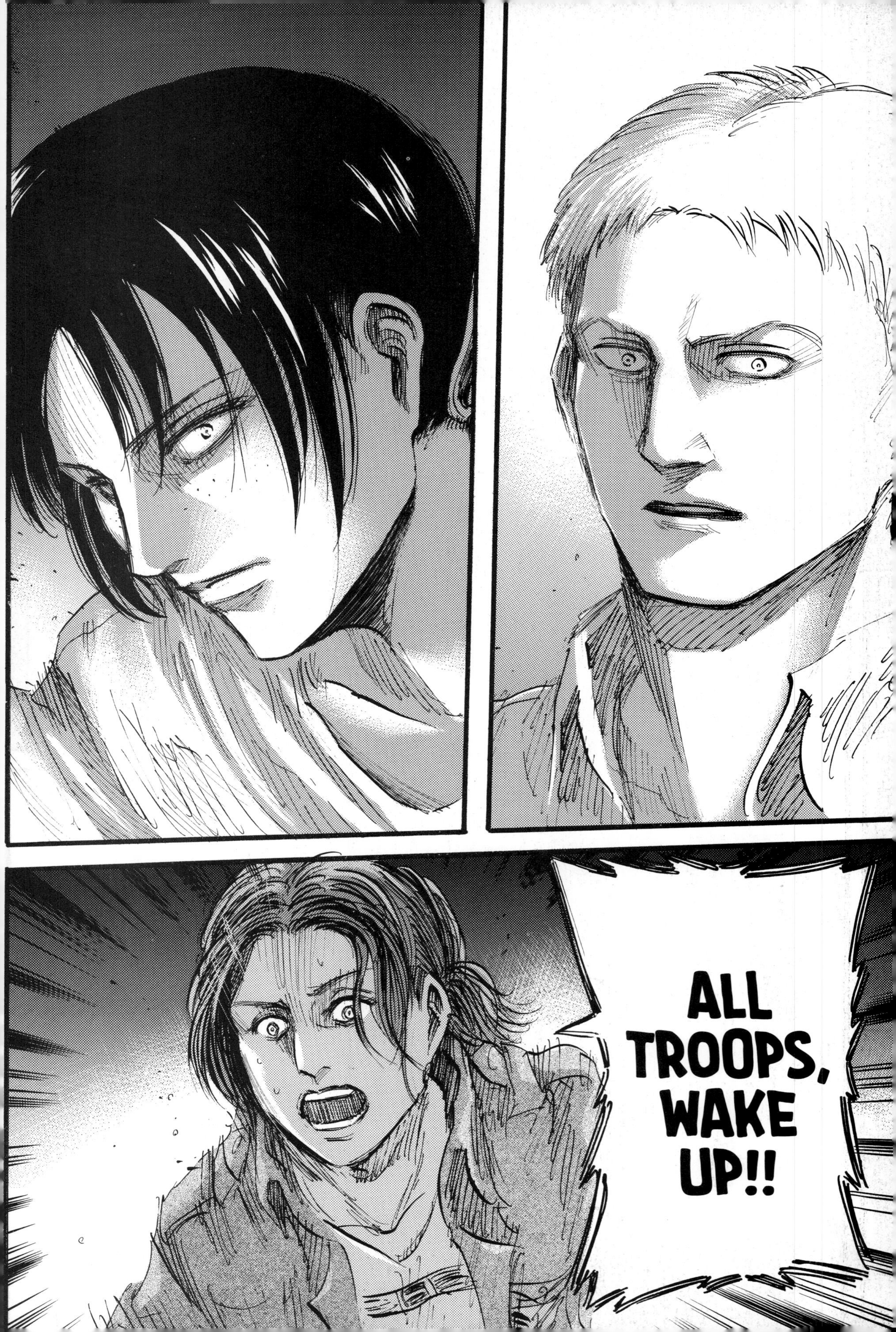
ALL TROOPS, WAKE UP!!

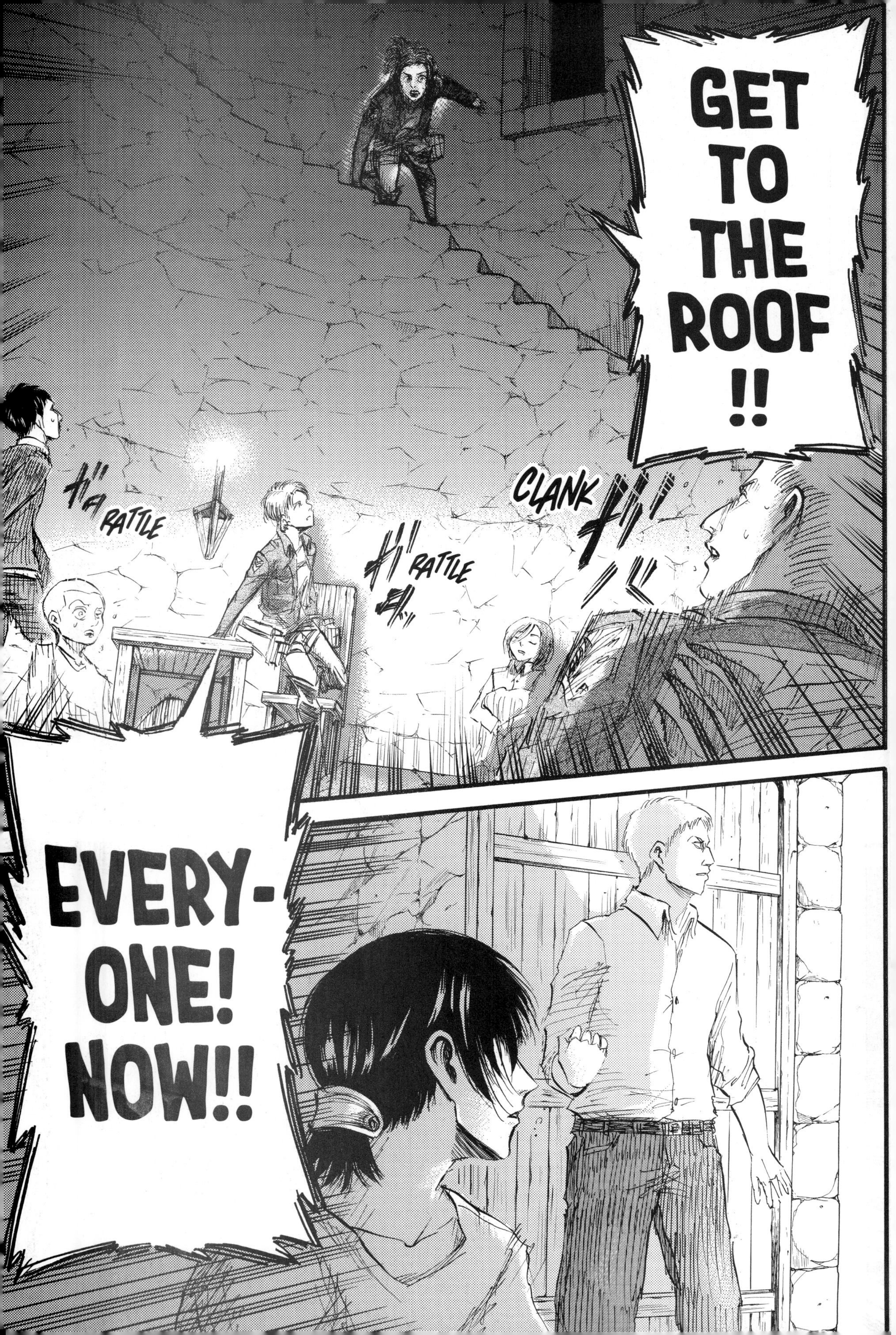
GET TO THE ROOF!!
CLANK
RATTLE
RATTLE
EVERY-ONE! NOW!!

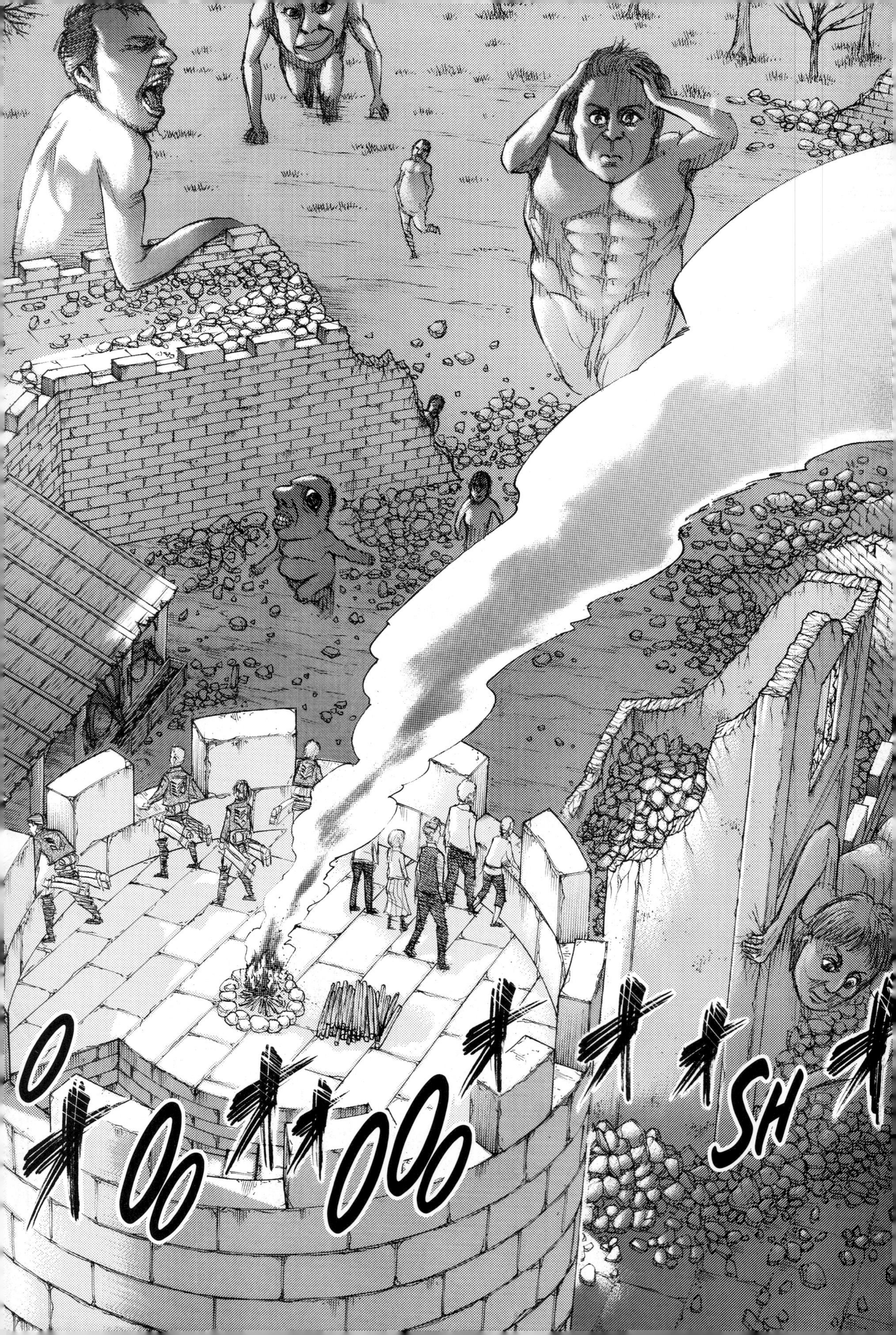
OOOOOOSH

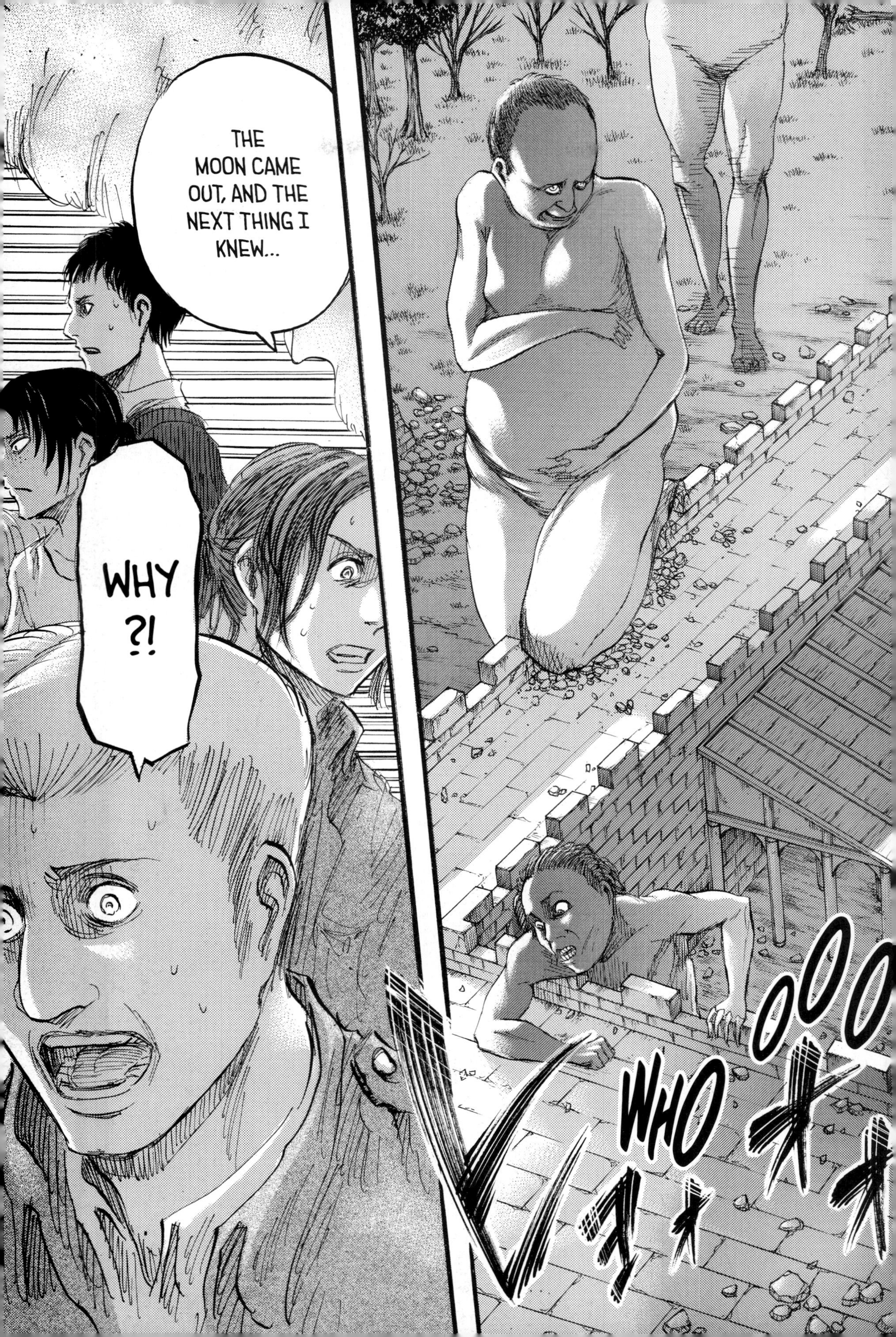
WHOOOO
THE MOON CAME OUT, AND THE NEXT THING I KNEW...
WHY?!

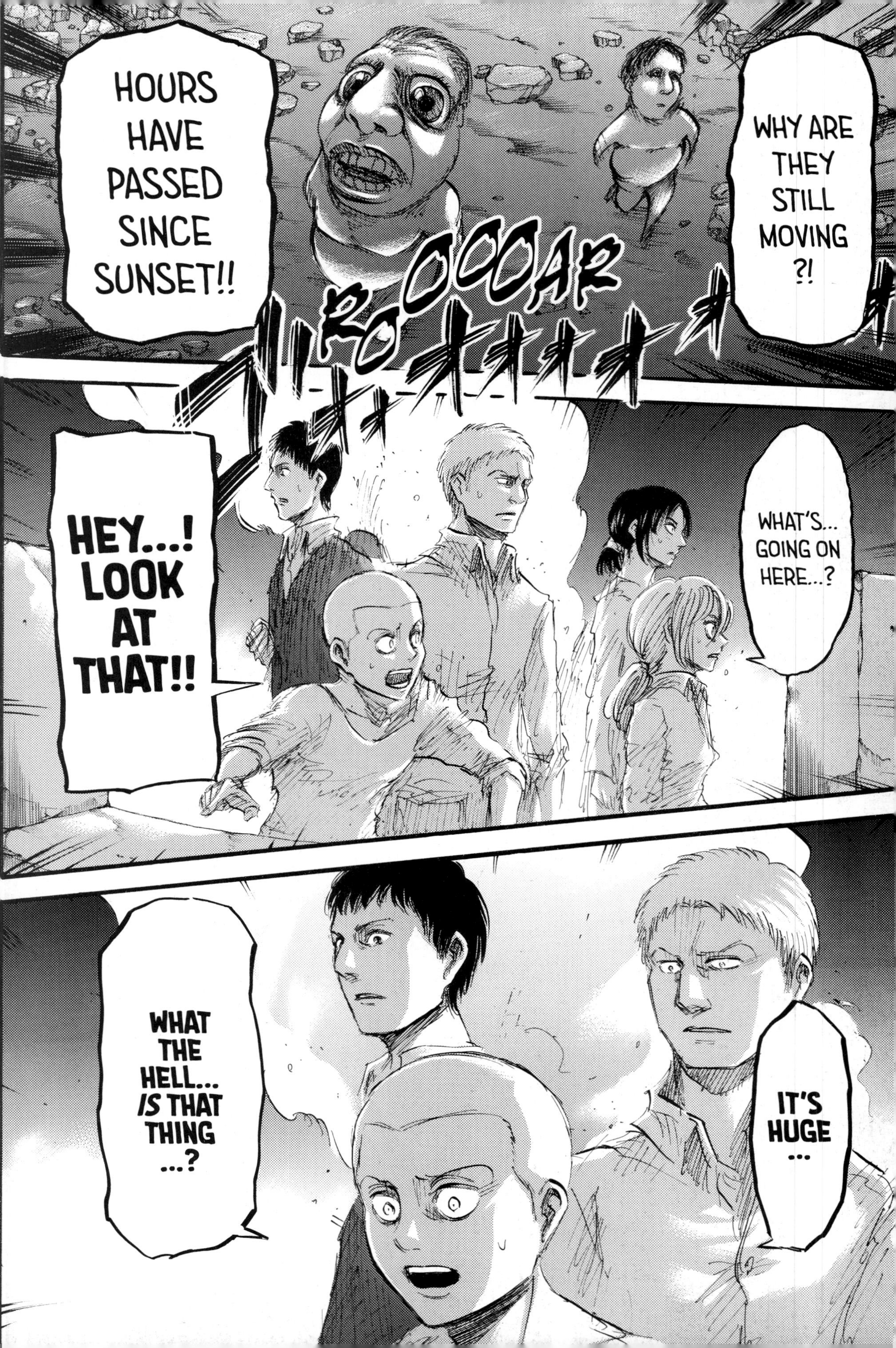
WHY ARE THEY STILL MOVING ?!
HOURS HAVE PASSED SINCE SUNSET!!
ROOOOAR
WHAT'S... GOING ON HERE...?
HEY...! LOOK AT THAT!!
IT'S HUGE ...
WHAT THE HELL... IS THAT THING ...?

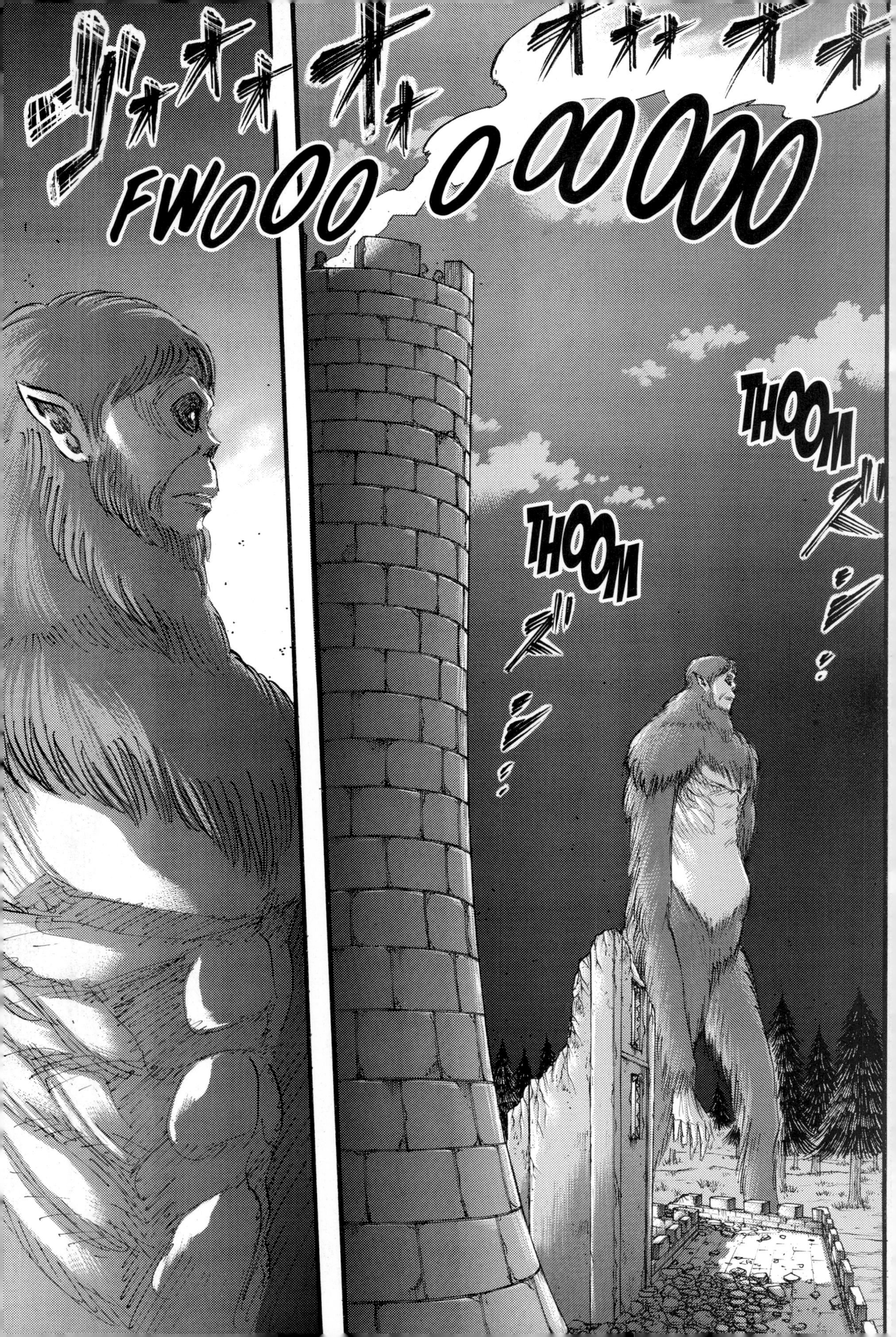
FWOOOOOOOOOO
THOOM
THOOM

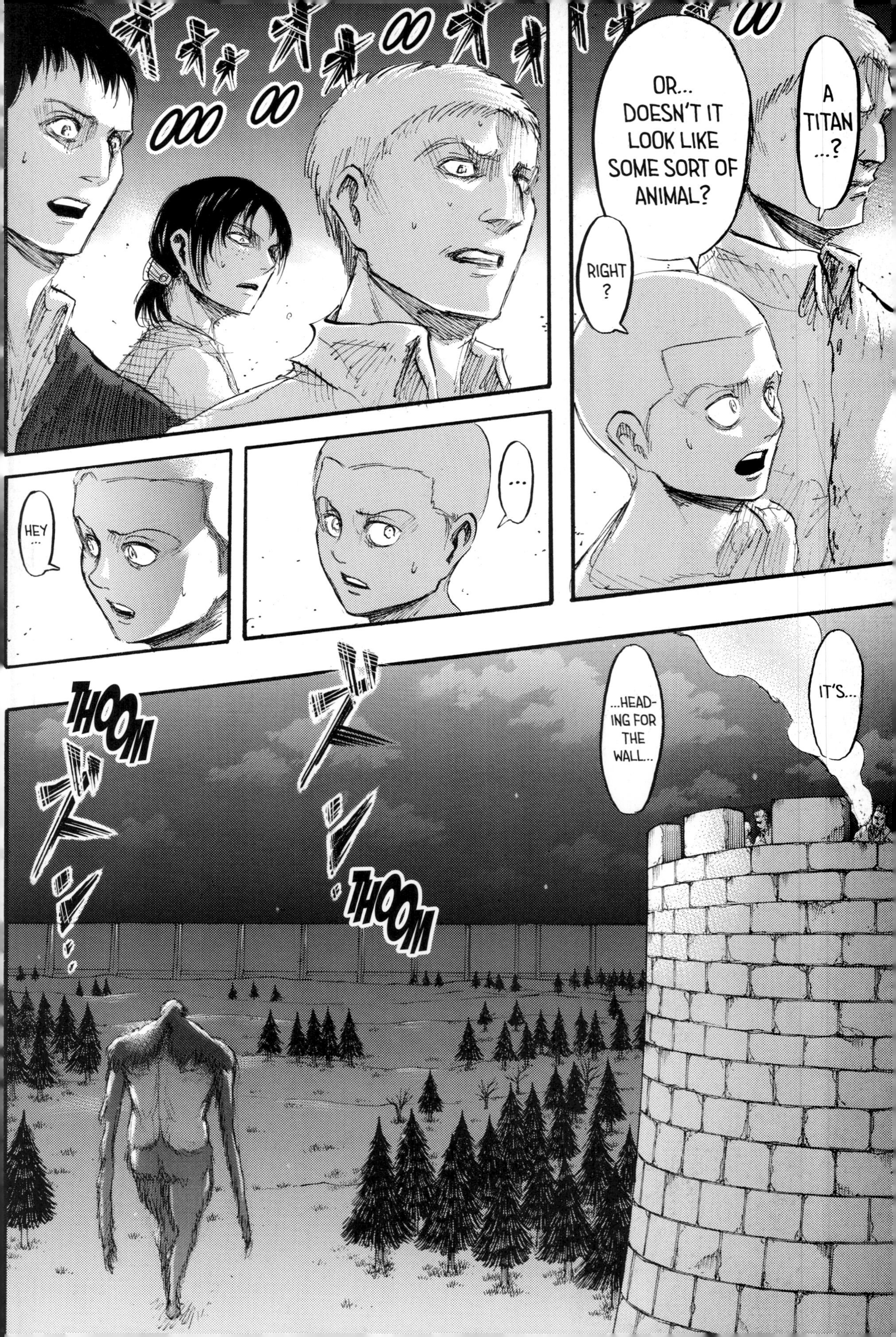
A TITAN ...?
OR... DOESN'T IT LOOK LIKE SOME SORT OF ANIMAL?
RIGHT ?
...
HEY ...
IT'S...
...HEADING FOR THE WALL...
THOOM
THOOM

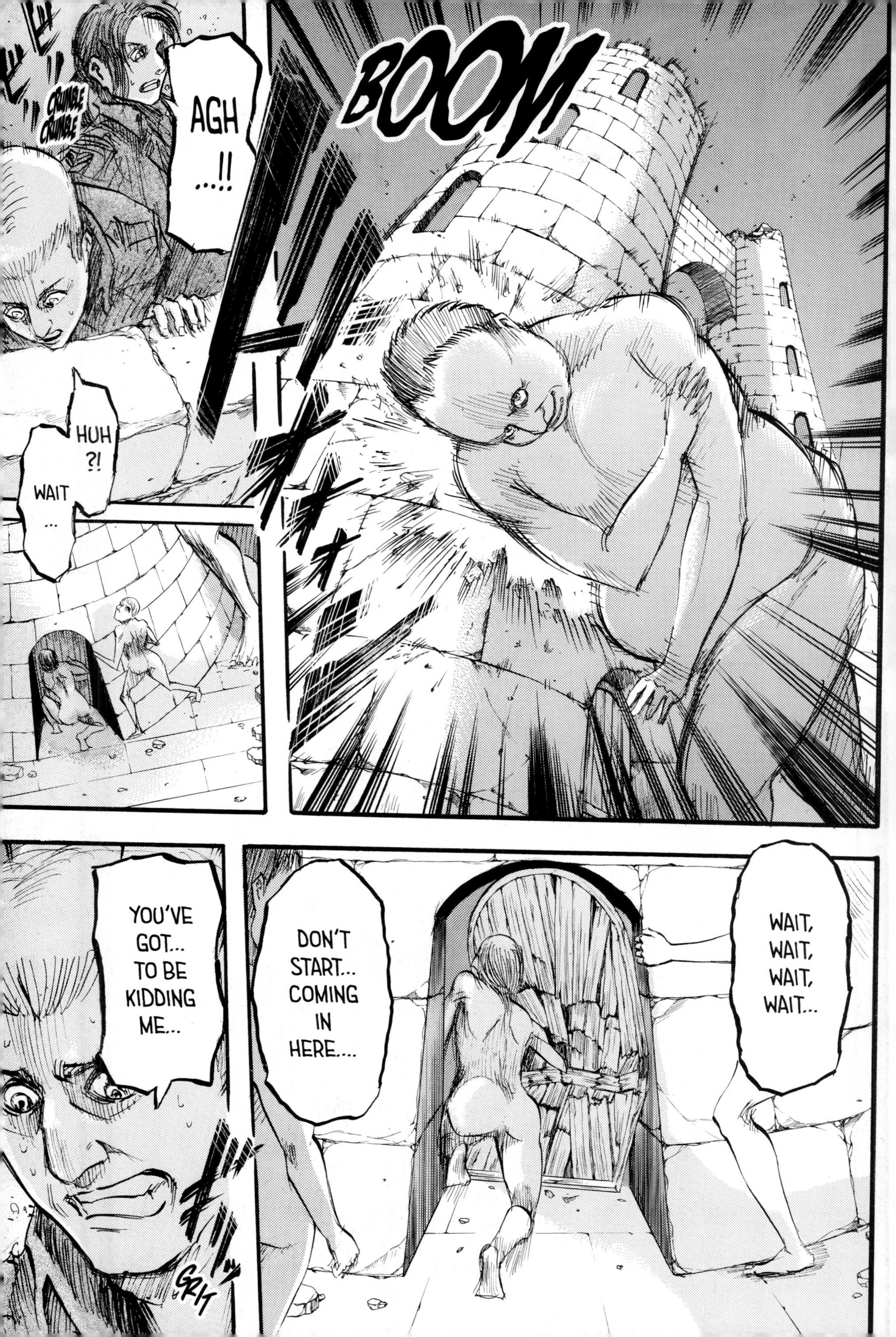
BOOM
CRUMBLE CRUMBLE
AGH ...!!
HUH ?! WAIT ...
WAIT, WAIT, WAIT, WAIT...
DON'T START... COMING IN HERE....
YOU'VE GOT... TO BE KIDDING ME...
GRK

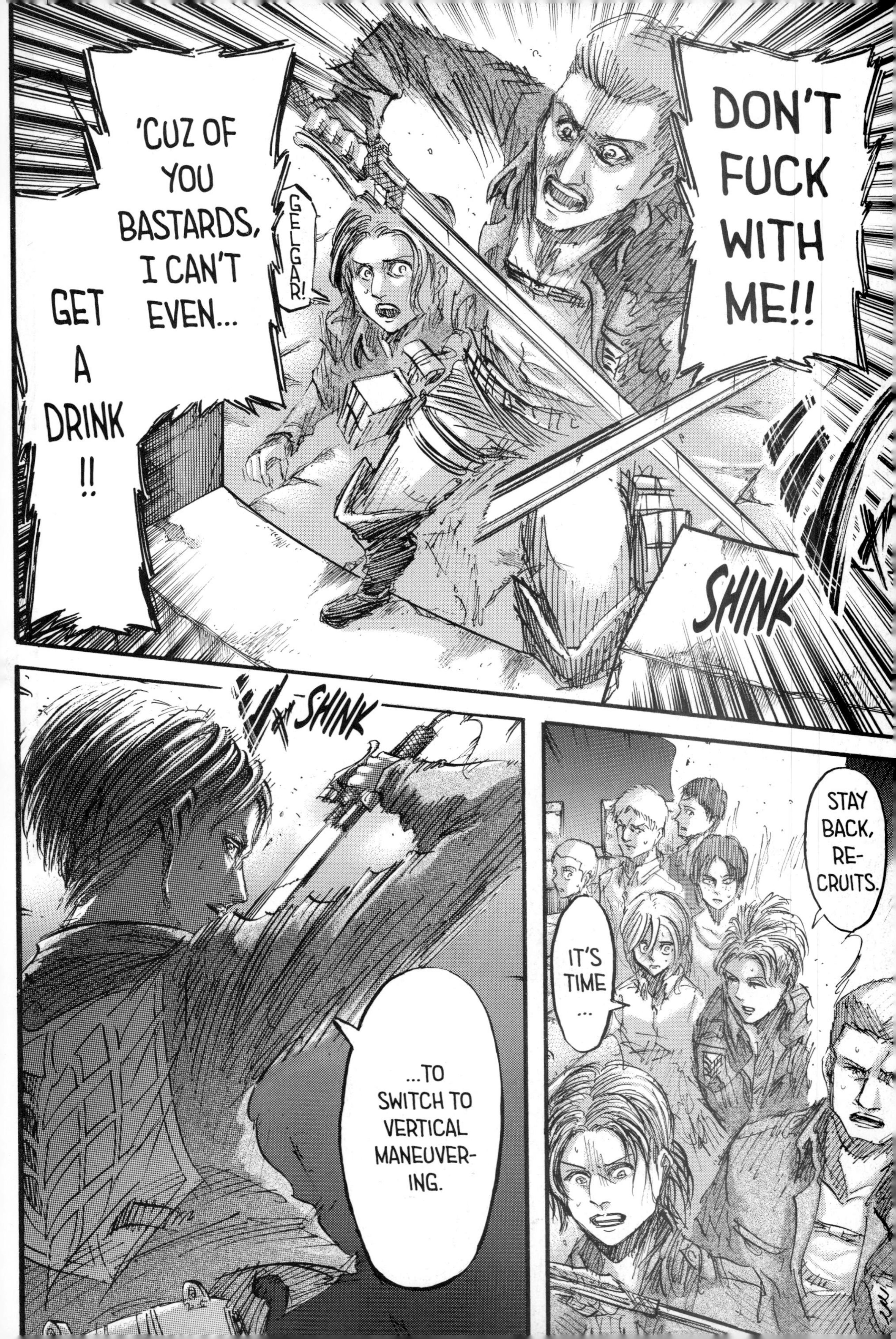
DON'T FUCK WITH ME!!
GELGAR!
'CUZ OF YOU BASTARDS, I CAN'T EVEN...
GET A DRINK!!
SHINK
STAY BACK, RE-CRUITS.
IT'S TIME...
SHINK
...TO SWITCH TO VERTICAL MANEUVER-ING.

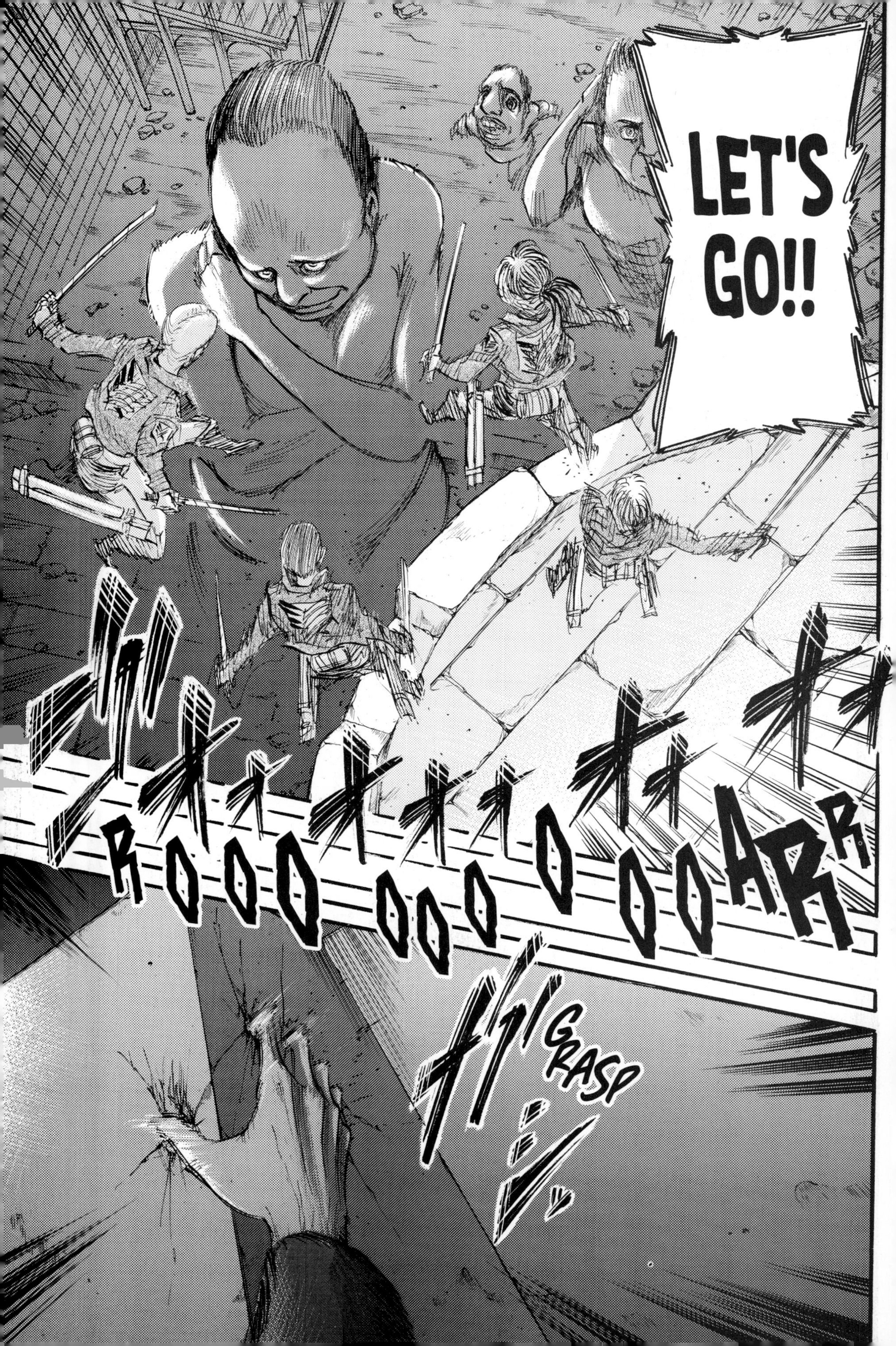
LET'S GO!!
ROOOOOOOOOARR
GRASP

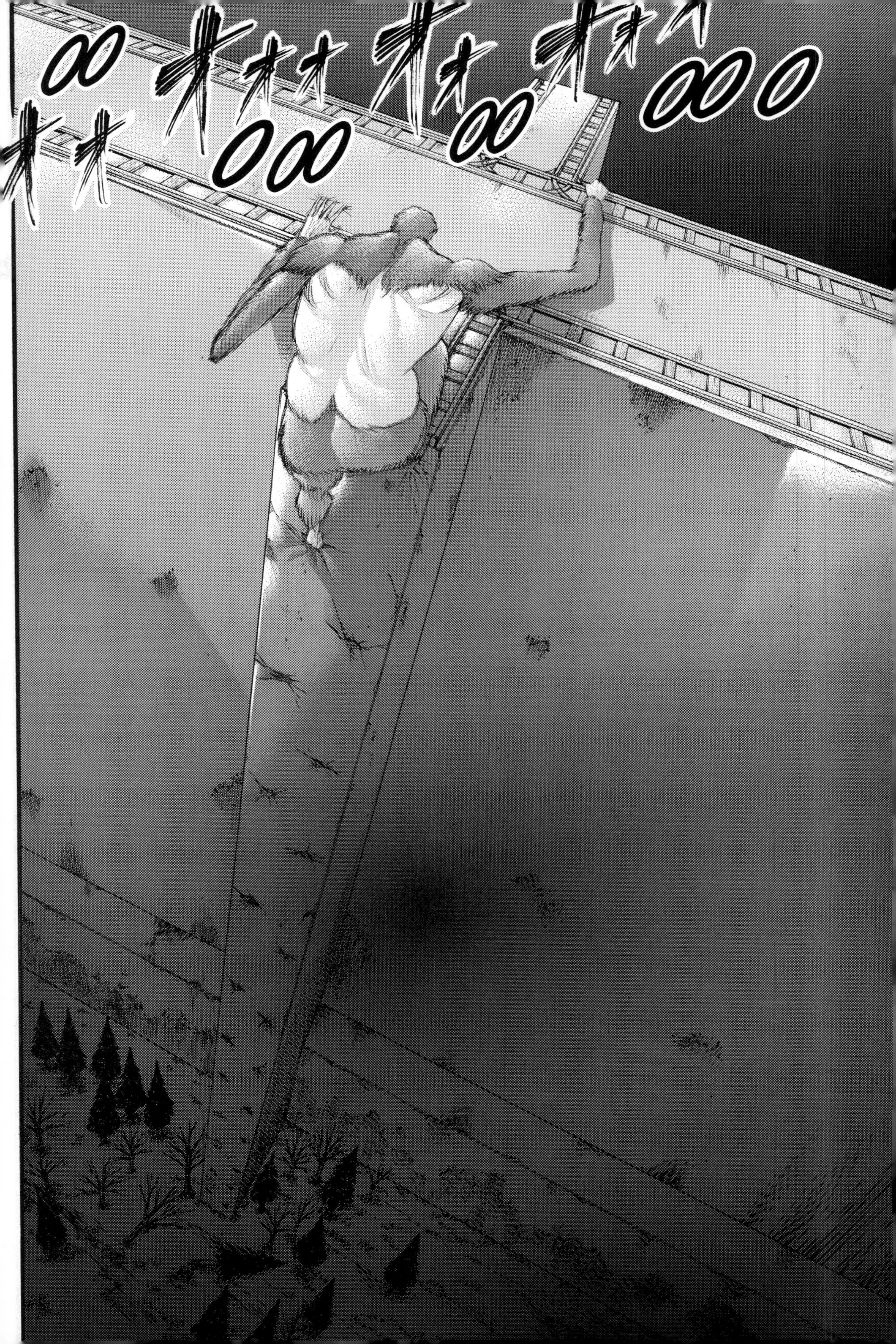
オオオオオオオオオオヘ
OOOOOOOOOO

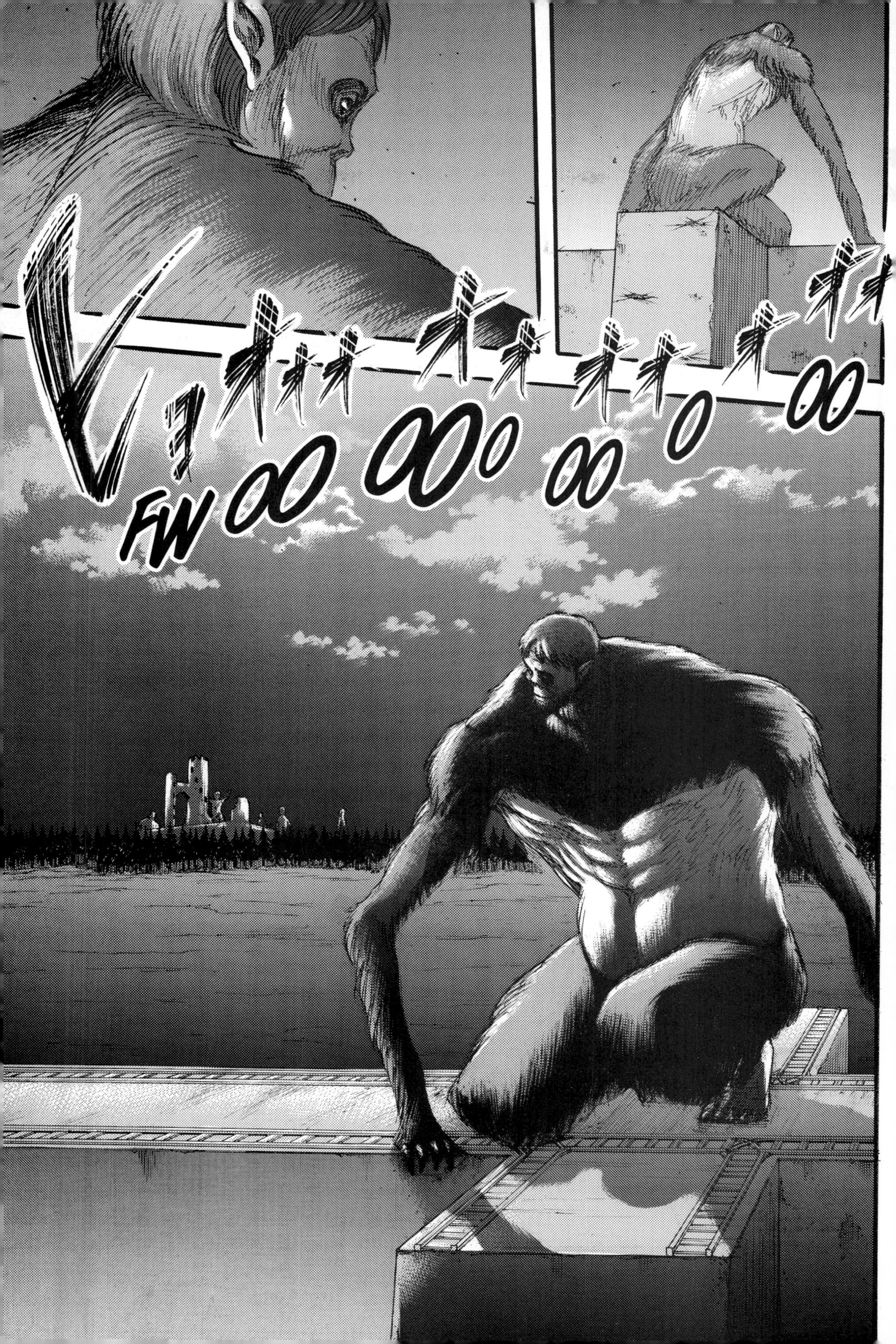
FWOOOOOOOOOO

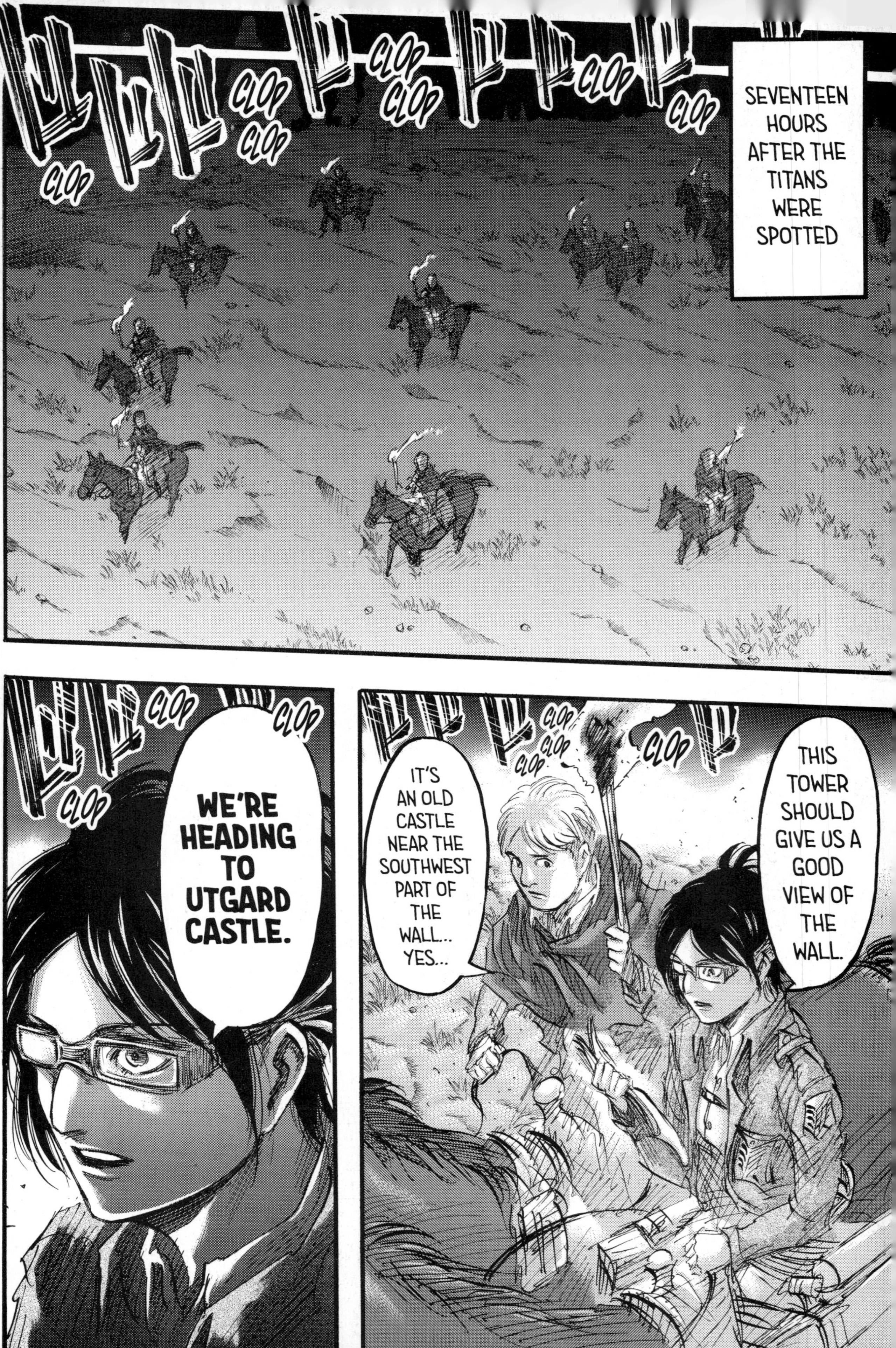
SEVENTEEN HOURS AFTER THE TITANS WERE SPOTTED
CLOP
CLOP
CLOP
CLOP
CLOP
CLOP
CLOP
CLOP
THIS TOWER SHOULD GIVE US A GOOD VIEW OF THE WALL.
CLOP
CLOP
CLOP
CLOP
IT'S AN OLD CASTLE NEAR THE SOUTHWEST PART OF THE WALL... YES...
CLOP
CLOP
CLOP
WE'RE HEADING TO UTGARD CASTLE.

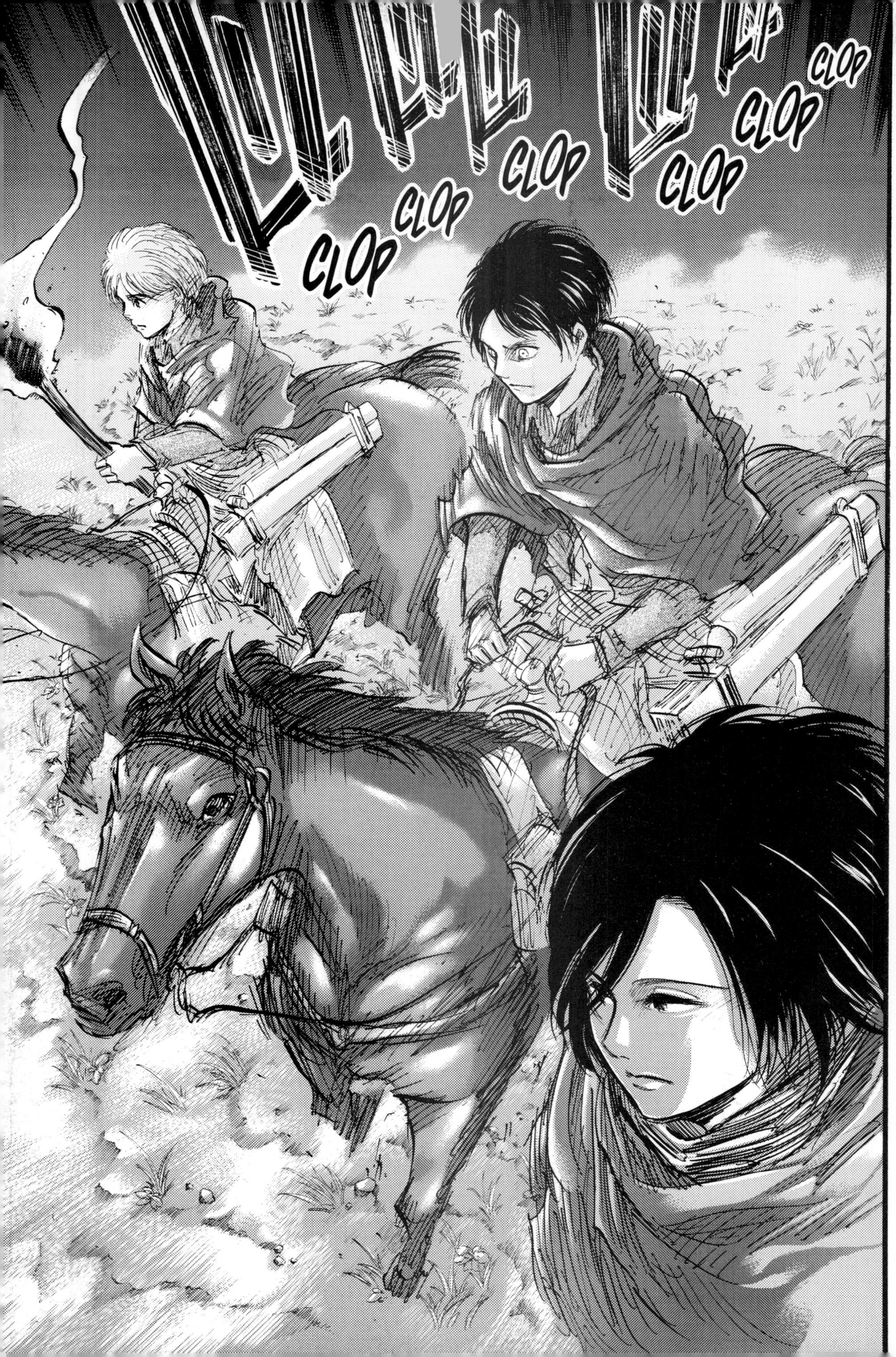
CLOP
CLOP
CLOP
CLOP
CLOP
CLOP

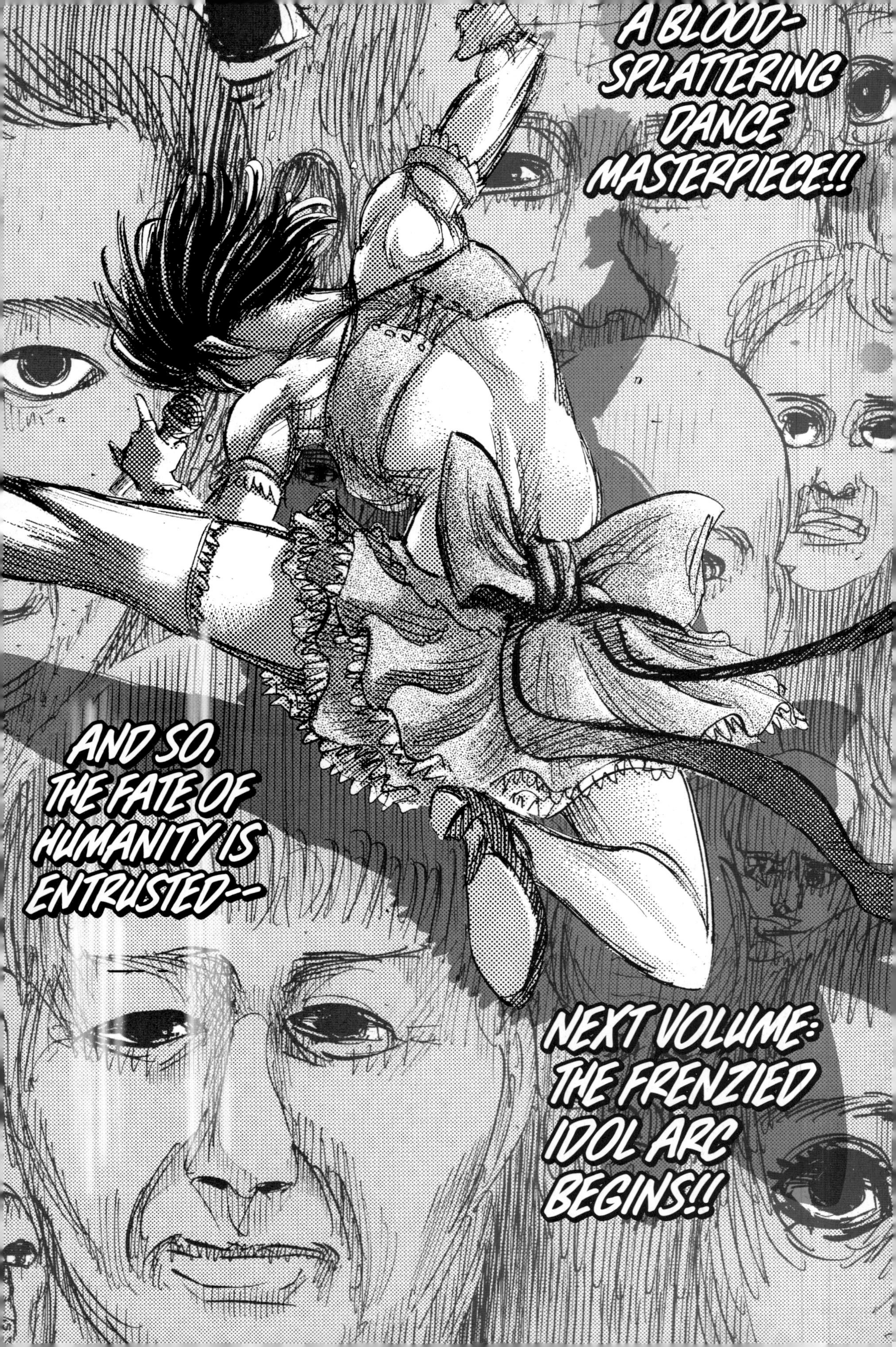
A BLOOD-SPLATTERING DANCE MASTERPIECE!!
AND SO, THE FATE OF HUMANITY IS ENTRUSTED--
NEXT VOLUME: THE FRENZIED IDOL ARC BEGINS!!

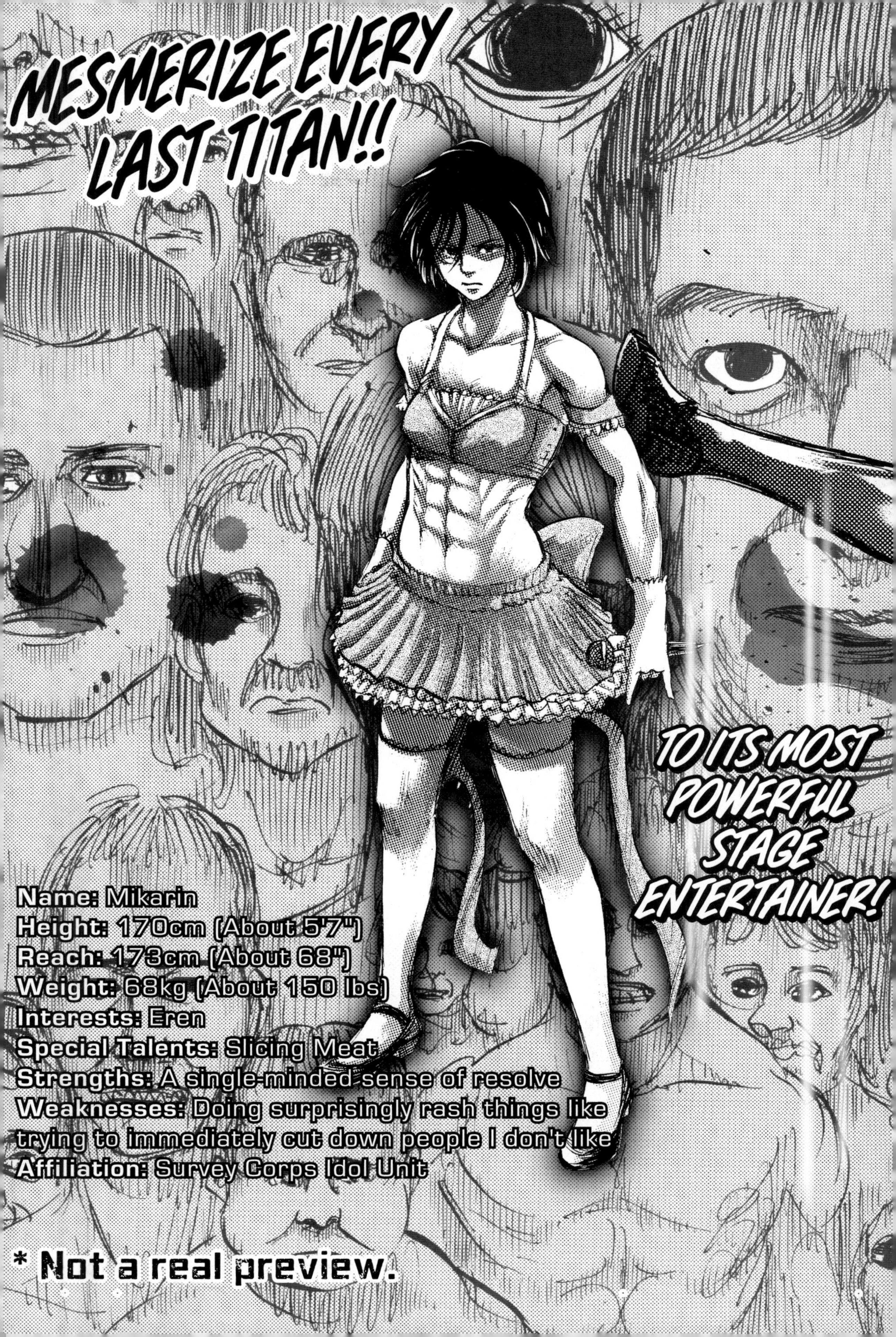
MESMERIZE EVERY LAST TITAN!!
TO ITS MOST POWERFUL STAGE ENTERTAINER!
Name: Mikarin
Height: 170cm (About 5'7")
Reach: 173cm (About 68")
Weight: 68kg (About 150 lbs)
Interests: Eren
Special Talents: Slicing Meat
Strengths: A single-minded sense of resolve
Weaknesses: Doing surprisingly rash things like trying to immediately cut down people I don't like
Affiliation: Survey Corps Idol Unit
* Not a real preview.

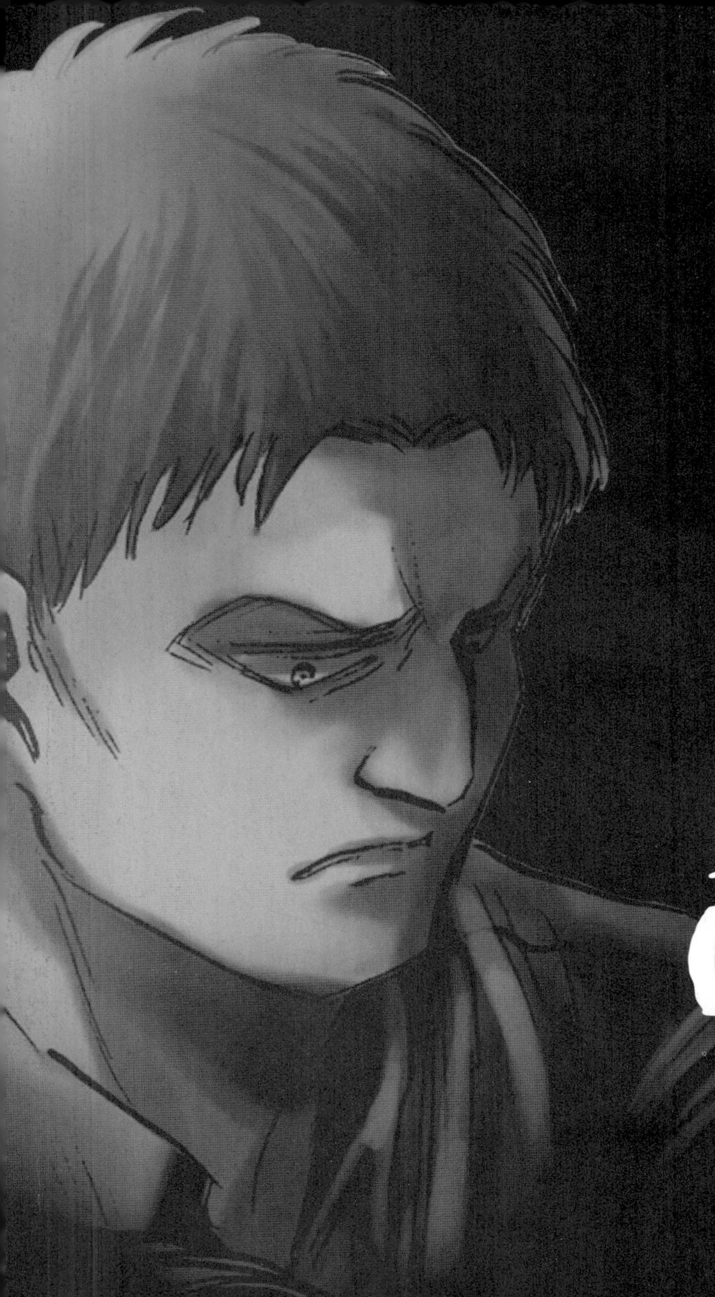

ATTACK ON TITAN

HAJIME ISAYAMA

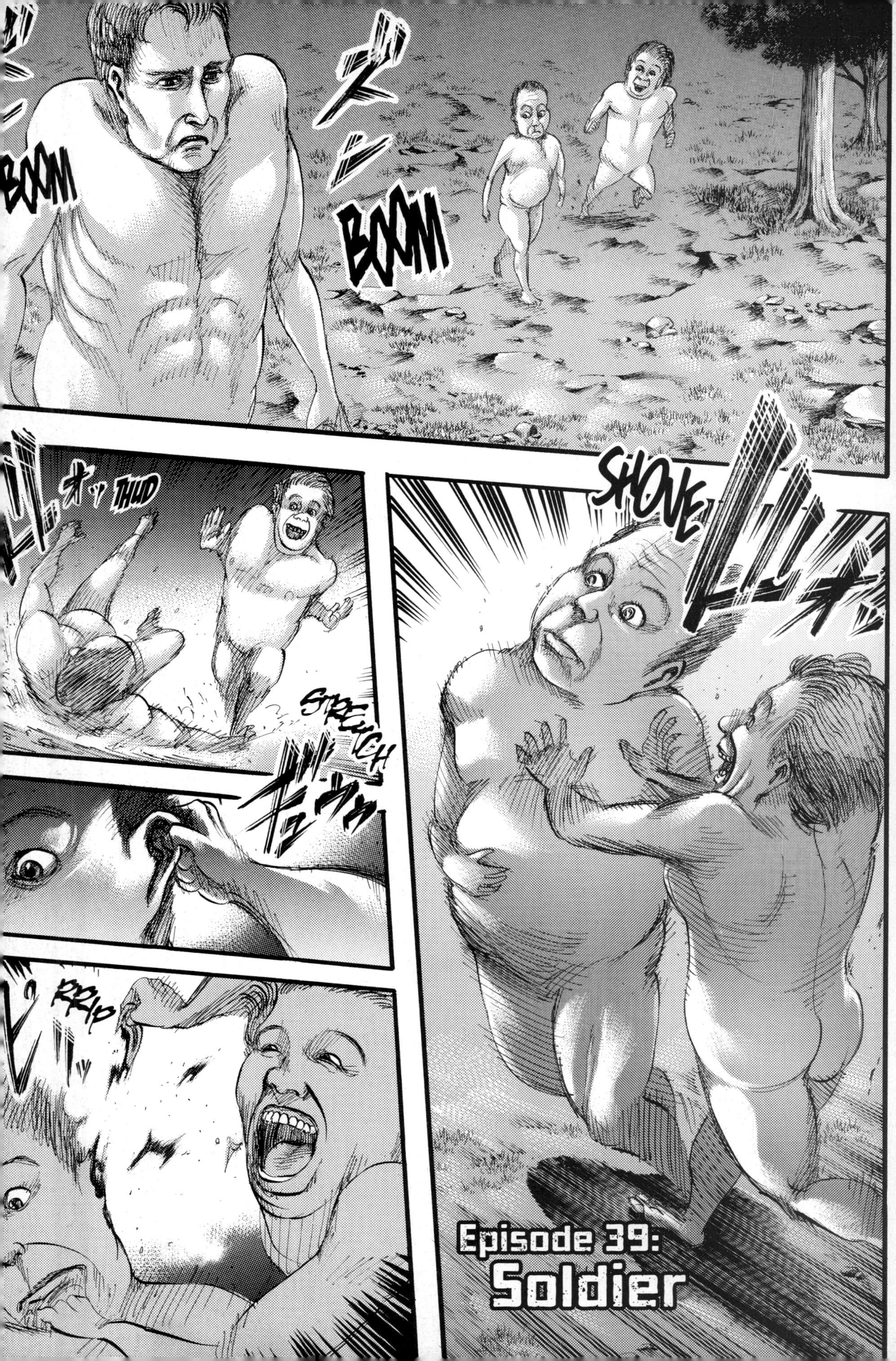
BOOM
BOOM
SHOVE
THUD
STRETCH
RRIP

Episode 39: Soldier

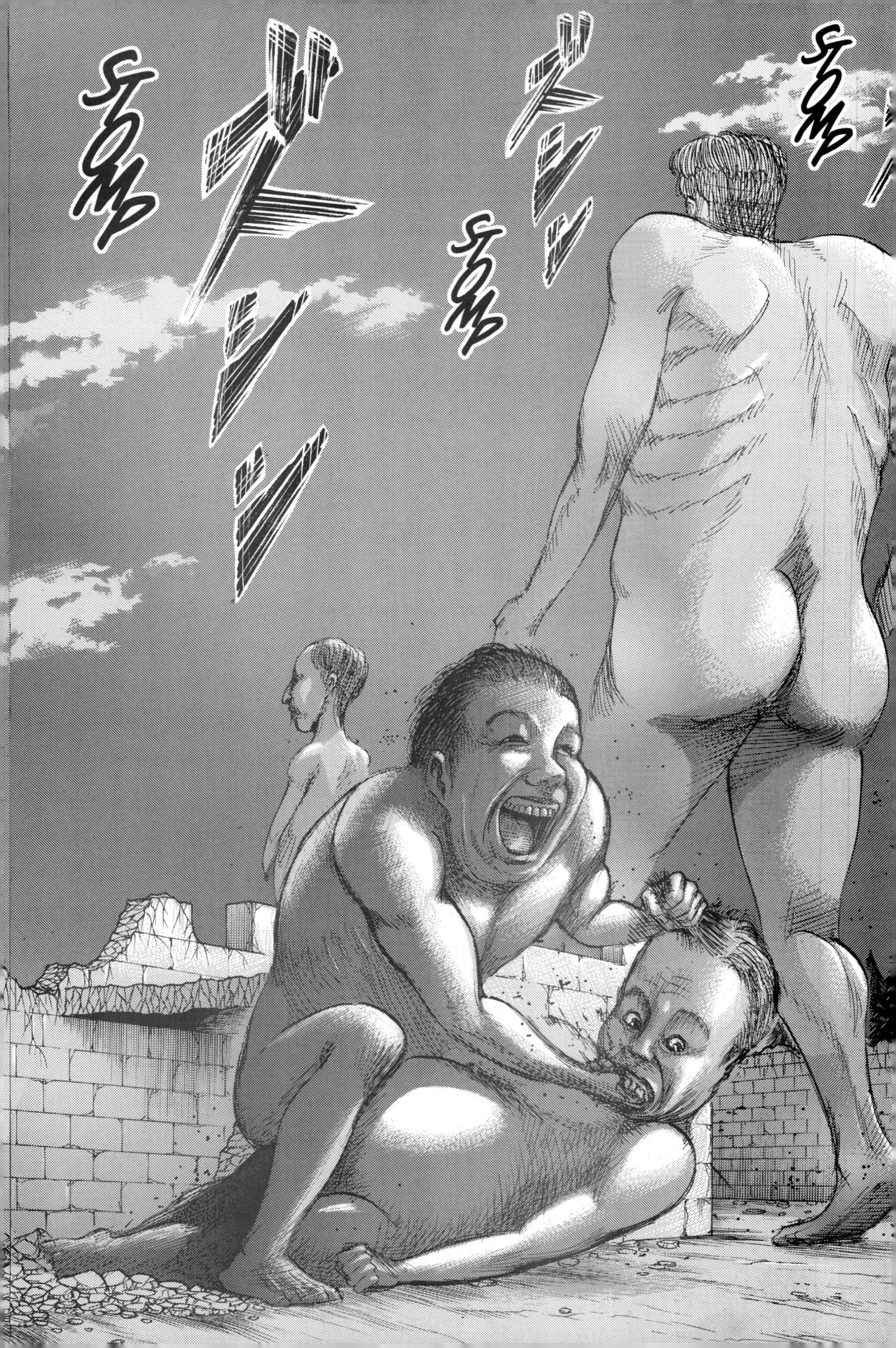
STOMP
STOMP
STOMP

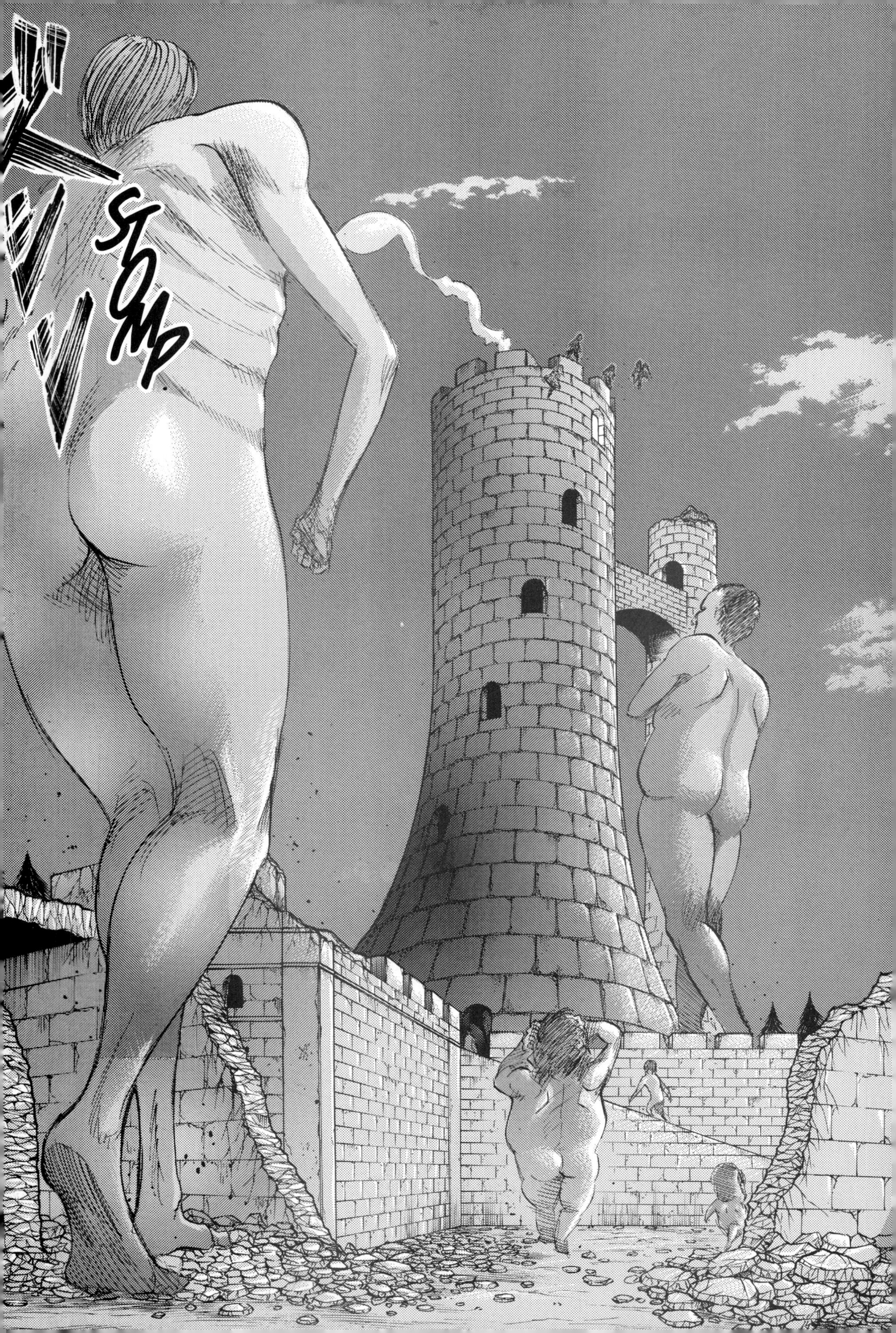
STOMP

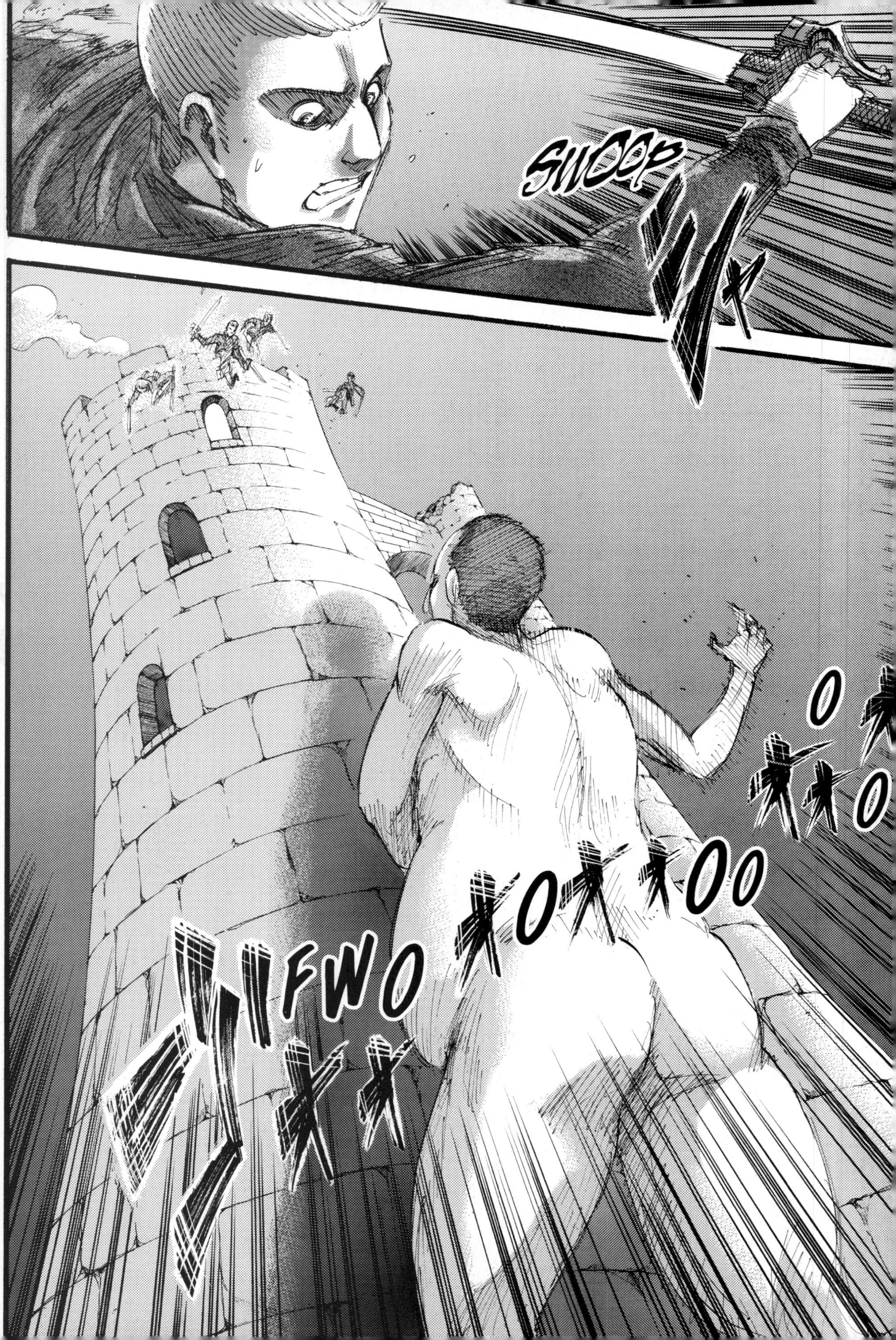
SWOOP
FWOOOOOO

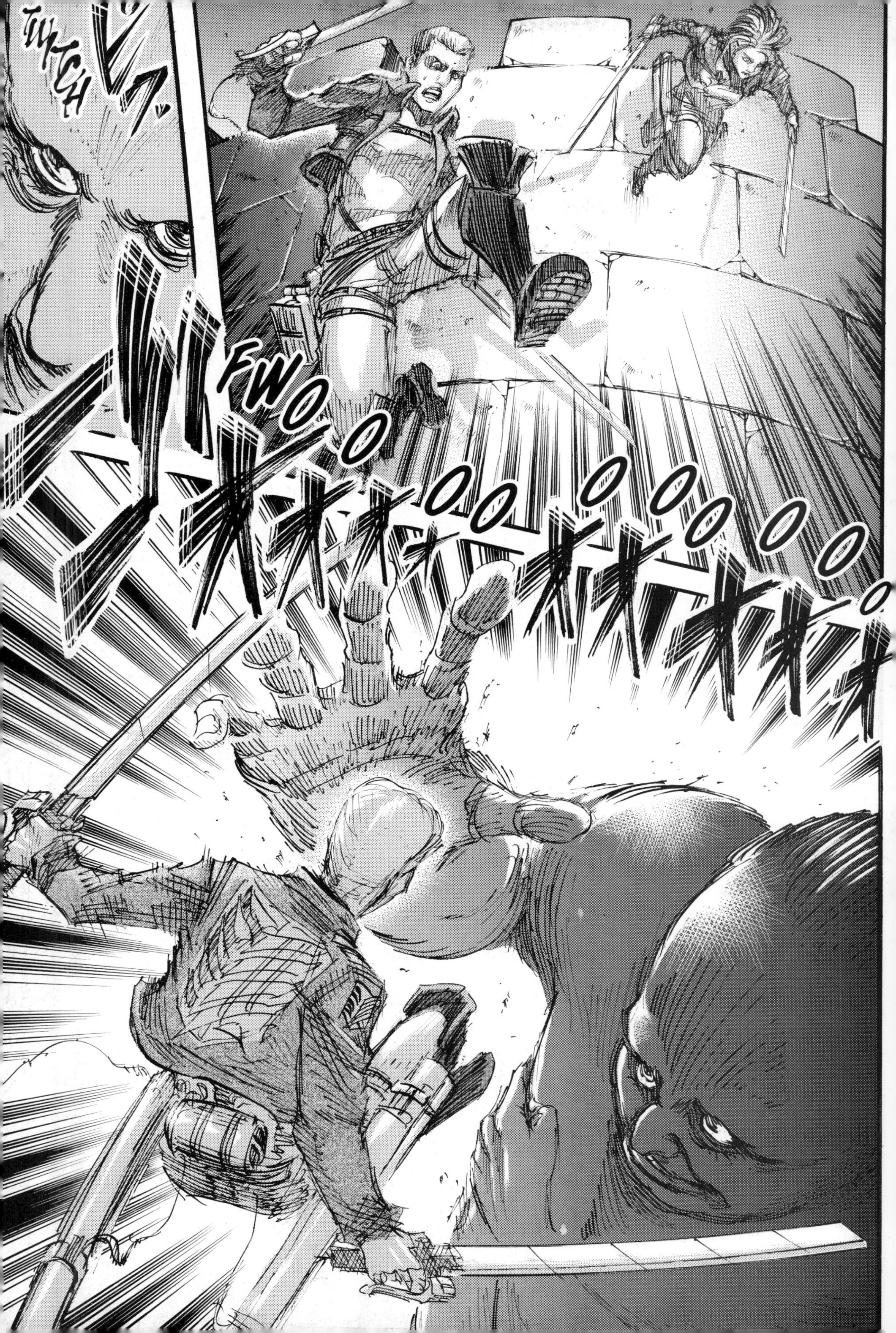
TWITCH
FWOOOOOOOOOOOOO

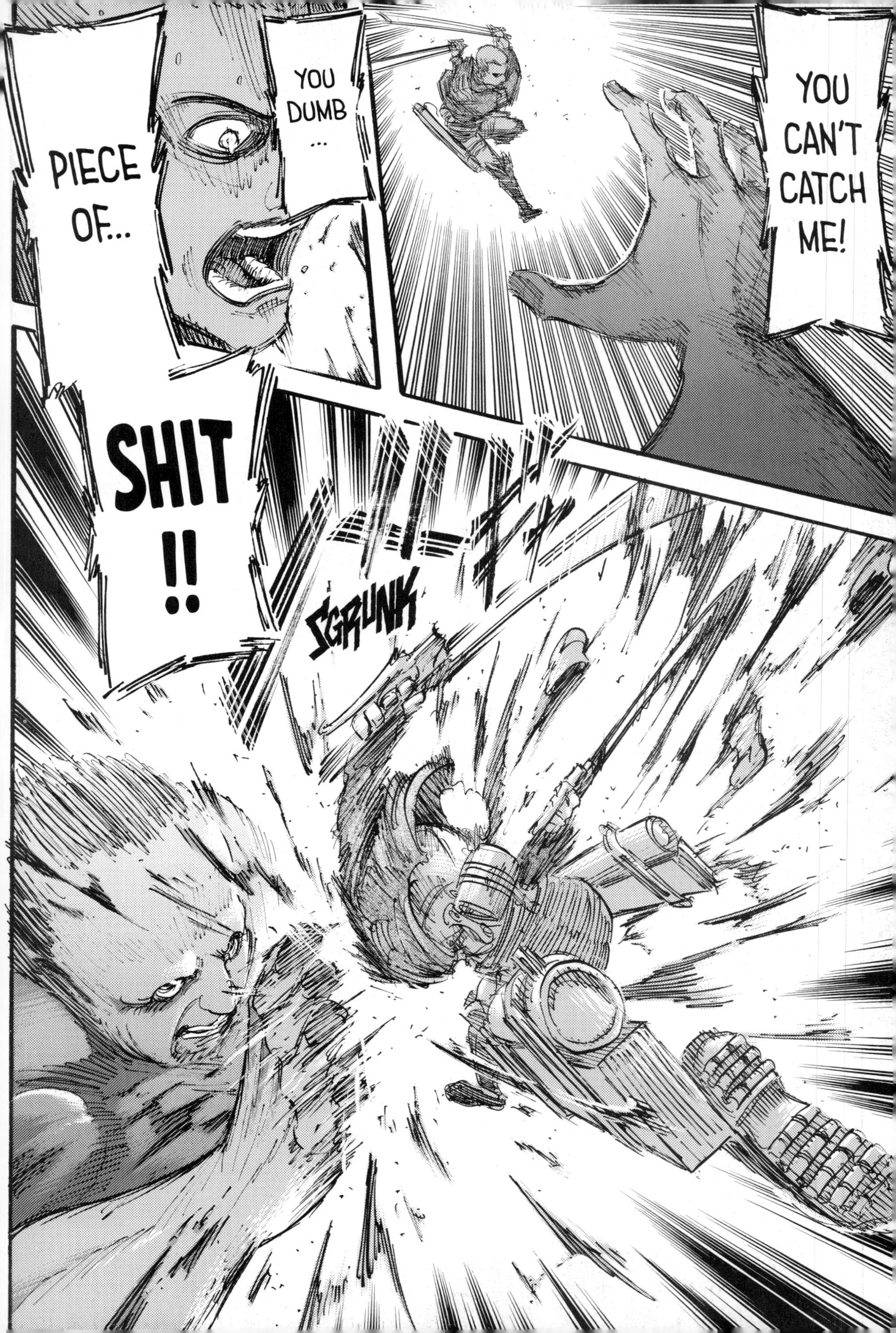
YOU CAN'T CATCH ME!
YOU DUMB ...
PIECE OF...
SHIT !!
SGRUNK

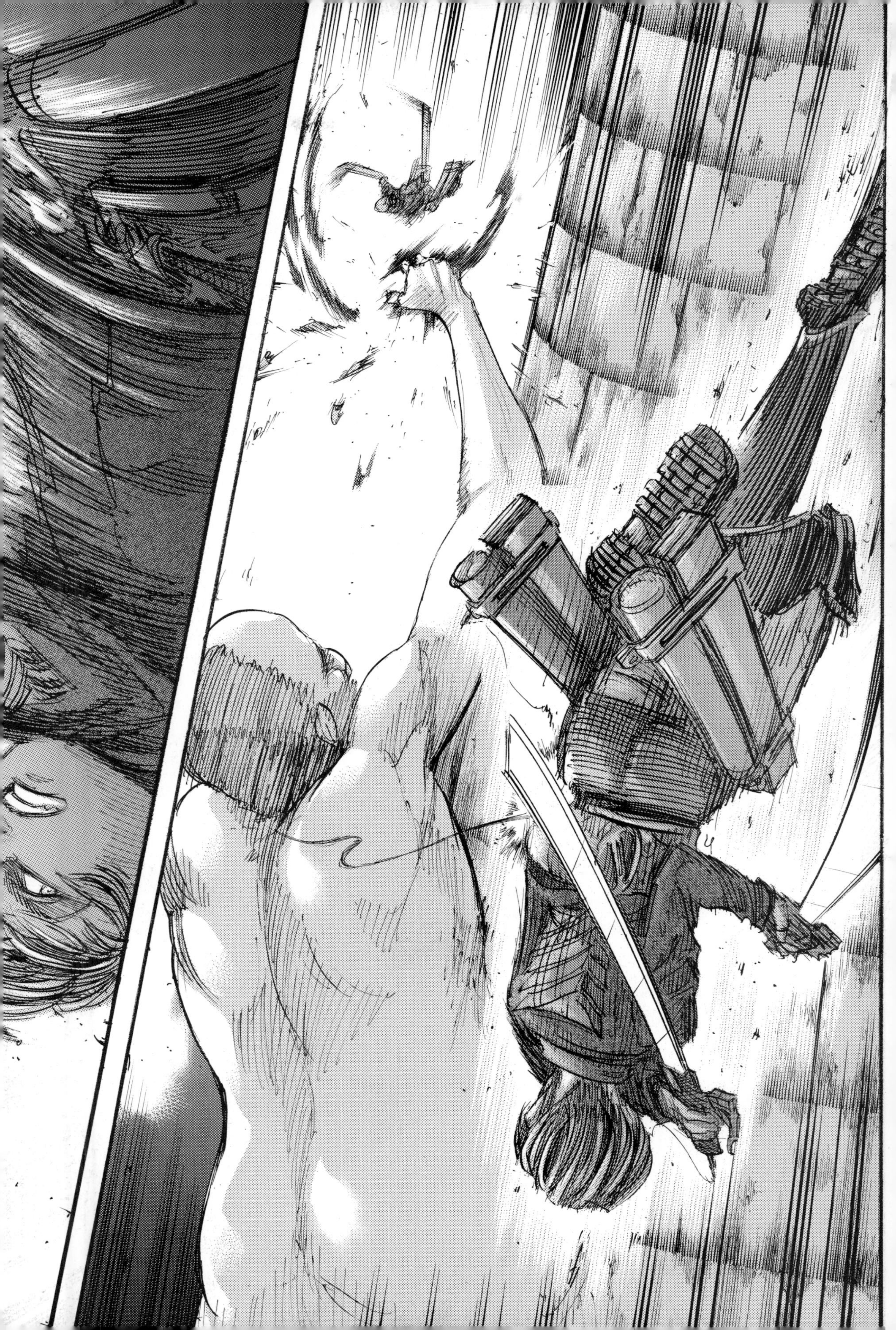

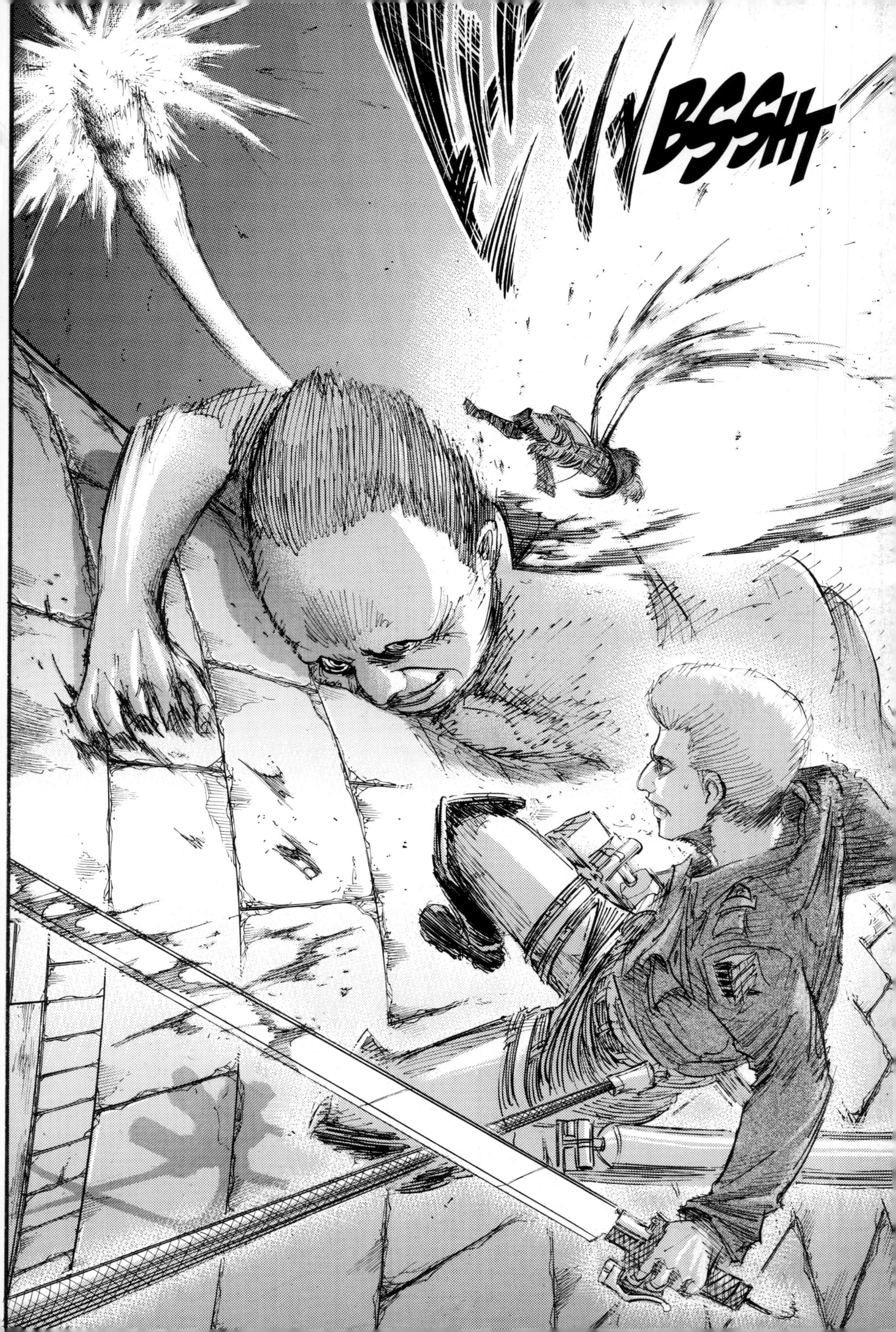
BSSHT

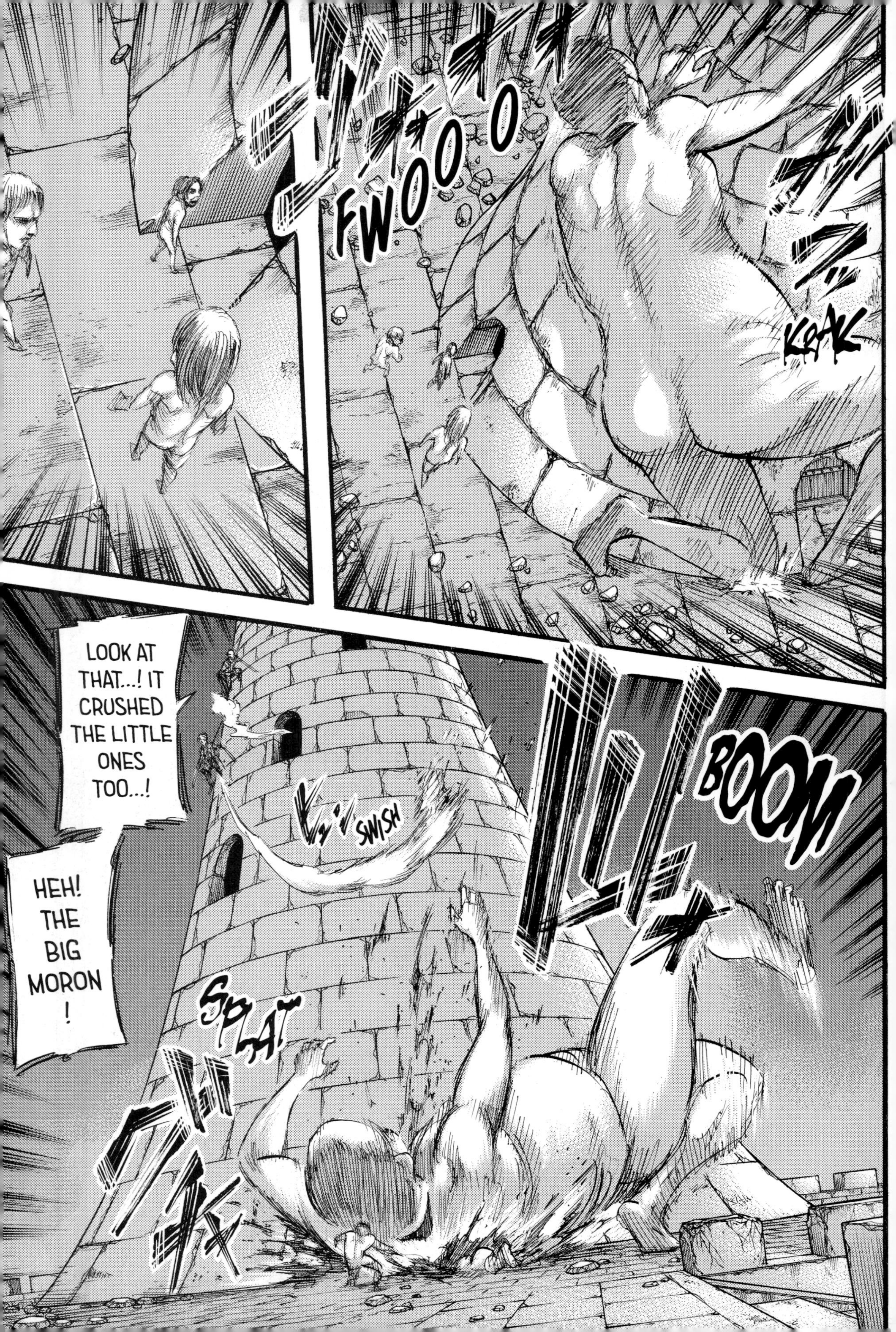
FWOOO
KRAK
BOOM
LOOK AT THAT...! IT CRUSHED THE LITTLE ONES TOO...!
SWISH
HEH! THE BIG MORON!
SPLAT

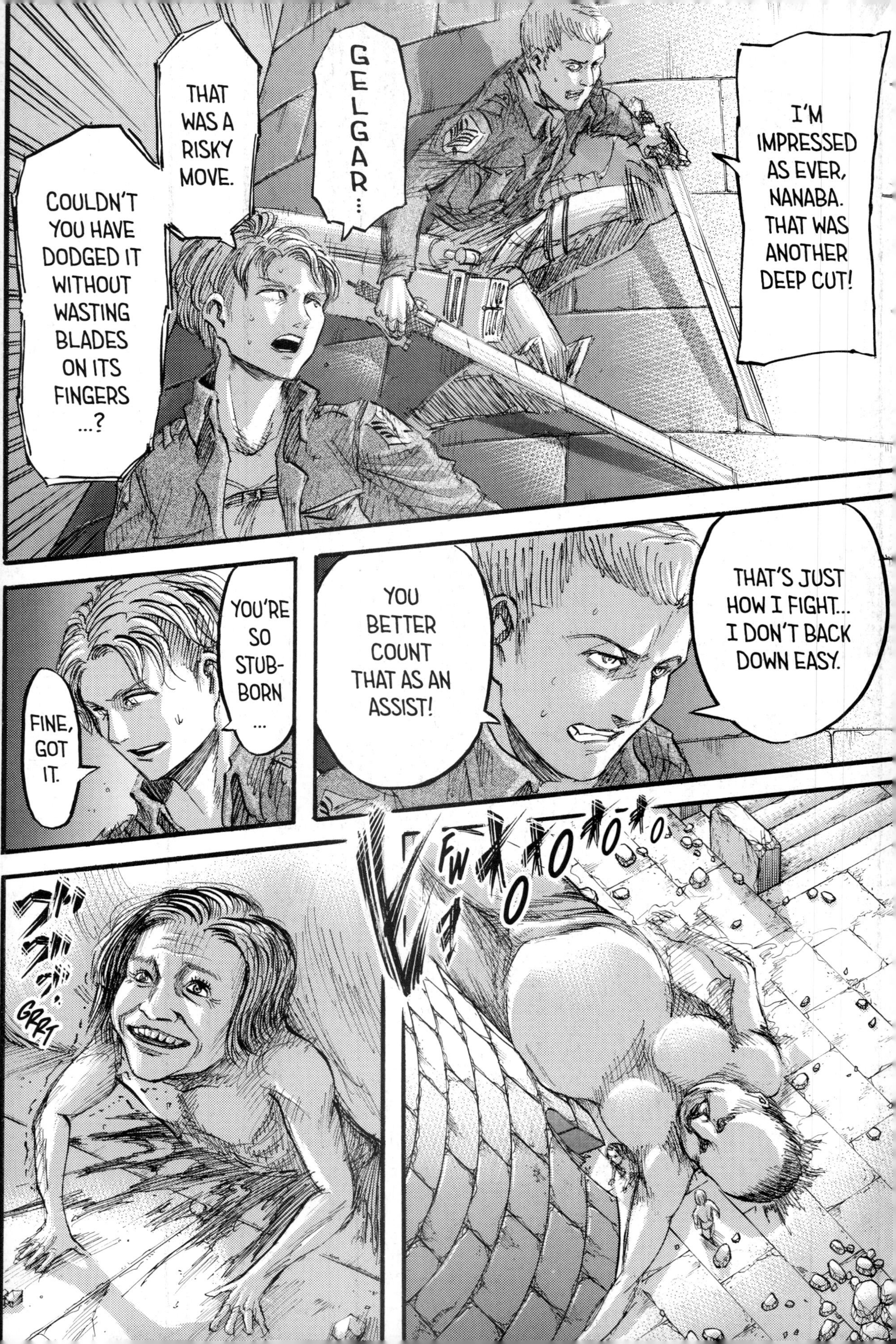
I'M IMPRESSED AS EVER, NANABA. THAT WAS ANOTHER DEEP CUT!
GELGAR...
THAT WAS A RISKY MOVE.
COULDN'T YOU HAVE DODGED IT WITHOUT WASTING BLADES ON ITS FINGERS...?
THAT'S JUST HOW I FIGHT... I DON'T BACK DOWN EASY.
YOU BETTER COUNT THAT AS AN ASSIST!
YOU'RE SO STUB-BORN...
FINE, GOT IT.
FWOOOOOO
GRRT

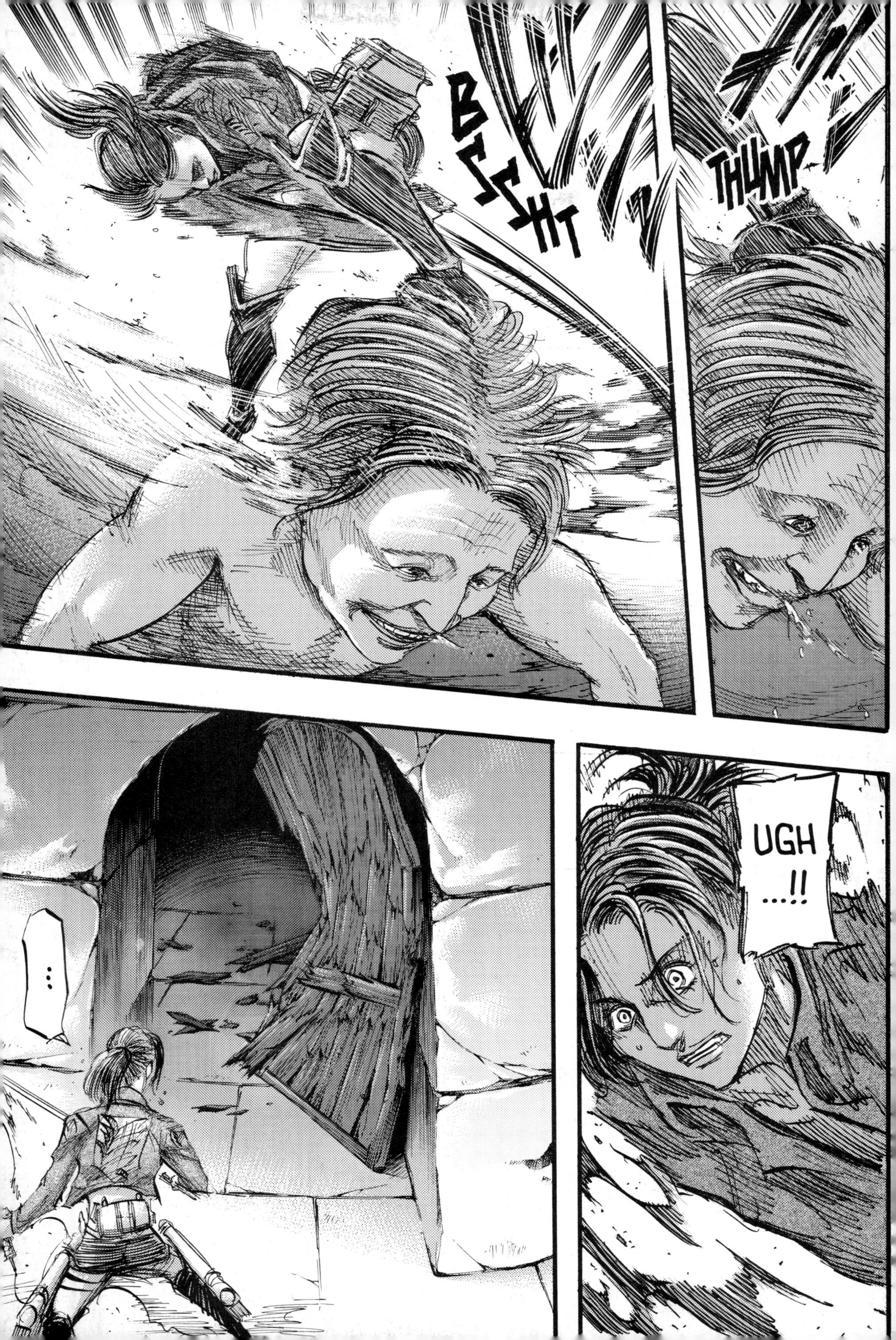
THUMP
BSSHT
UGH ...!!
...

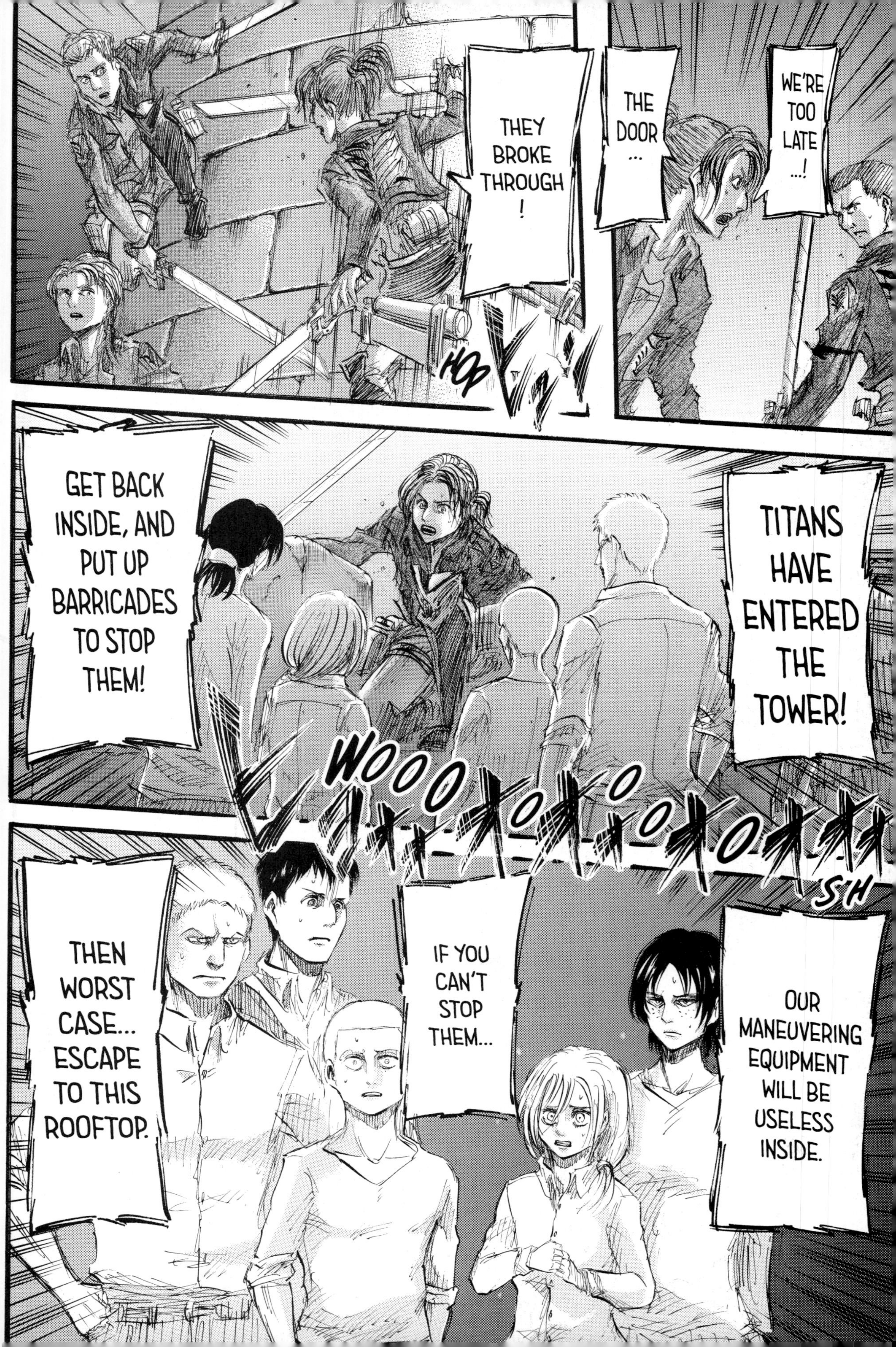
WE'RE TOO LATE...!
THE DOOR...
THEY BROKE THROUGH!
HOP
TITANS HAVE ENTERED THE TOWER!
GET BACK INSIDE, AND PUT UP BARRICADES TO STOP THEM!
WOOOOOO
SH
OUR MANEUVERING EQUIPMENT WILL BE USELESS INSIDE.
IF YOU CAN'T STOP THEM...
THEN WORST CASE... ESCAPE TO THIS ROOFTOP.

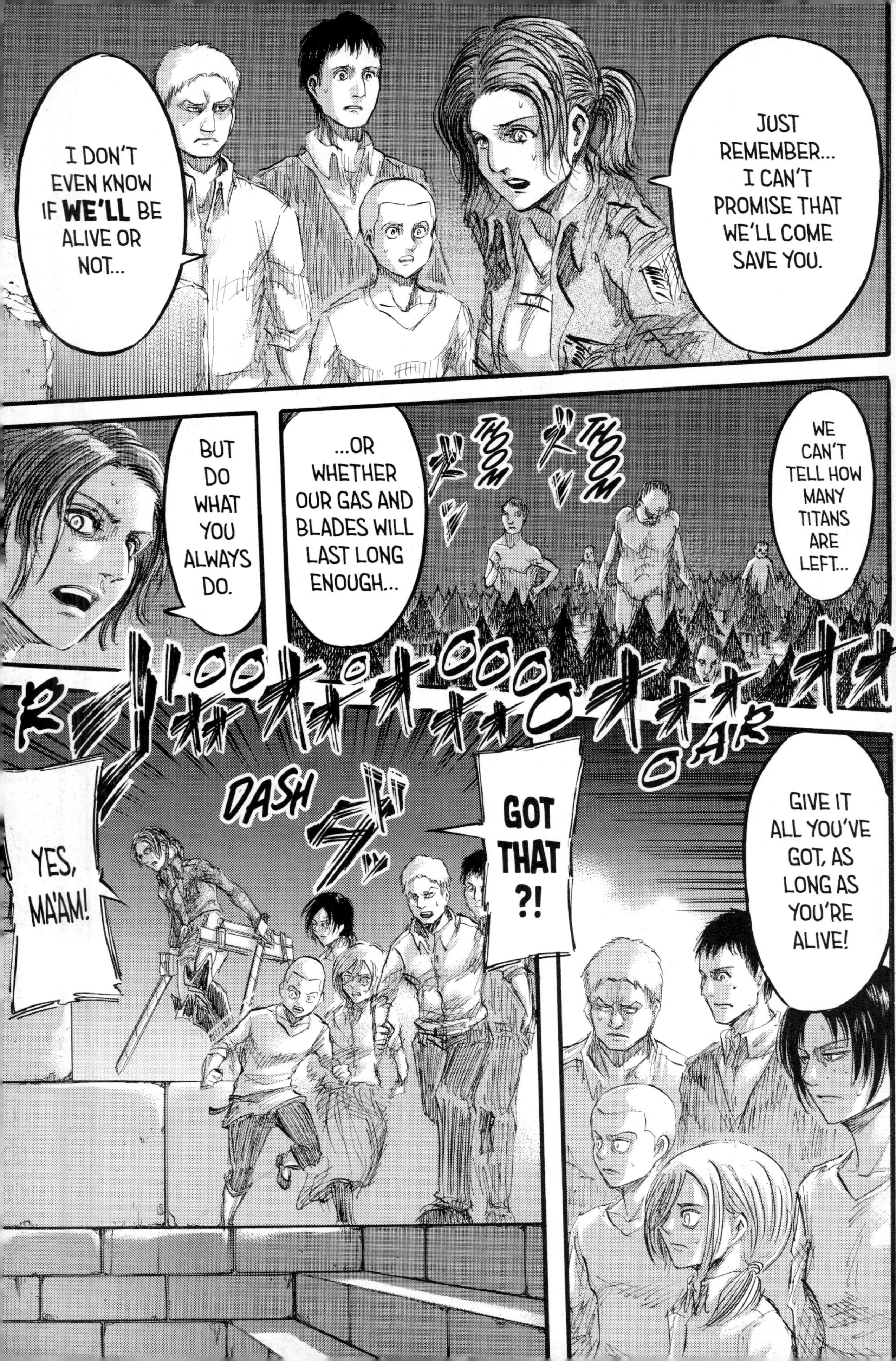
JUST REMEMBER... I CAN'T PROMISE THAT WE'LL COME SAVE YOU.
I DON'T EVEN KNOW IF **WE'LL** BE ALIVE OR NOT...
WE CAN'T TELL HOW MANY TITANS ARE LEFT...
THOOM
THOOM
...OR WHETHER OUR GAS AND BLADES WILL LAST LONG ENOUGH...
BUT DO WHAT YOU ALWAYS DO.
ROAR
GIVE IT ALL YOU'VE GOT, AS LONG AS YOU'RE ALIVE!
GOT THAT?!
DASH
YES, MA'AM!

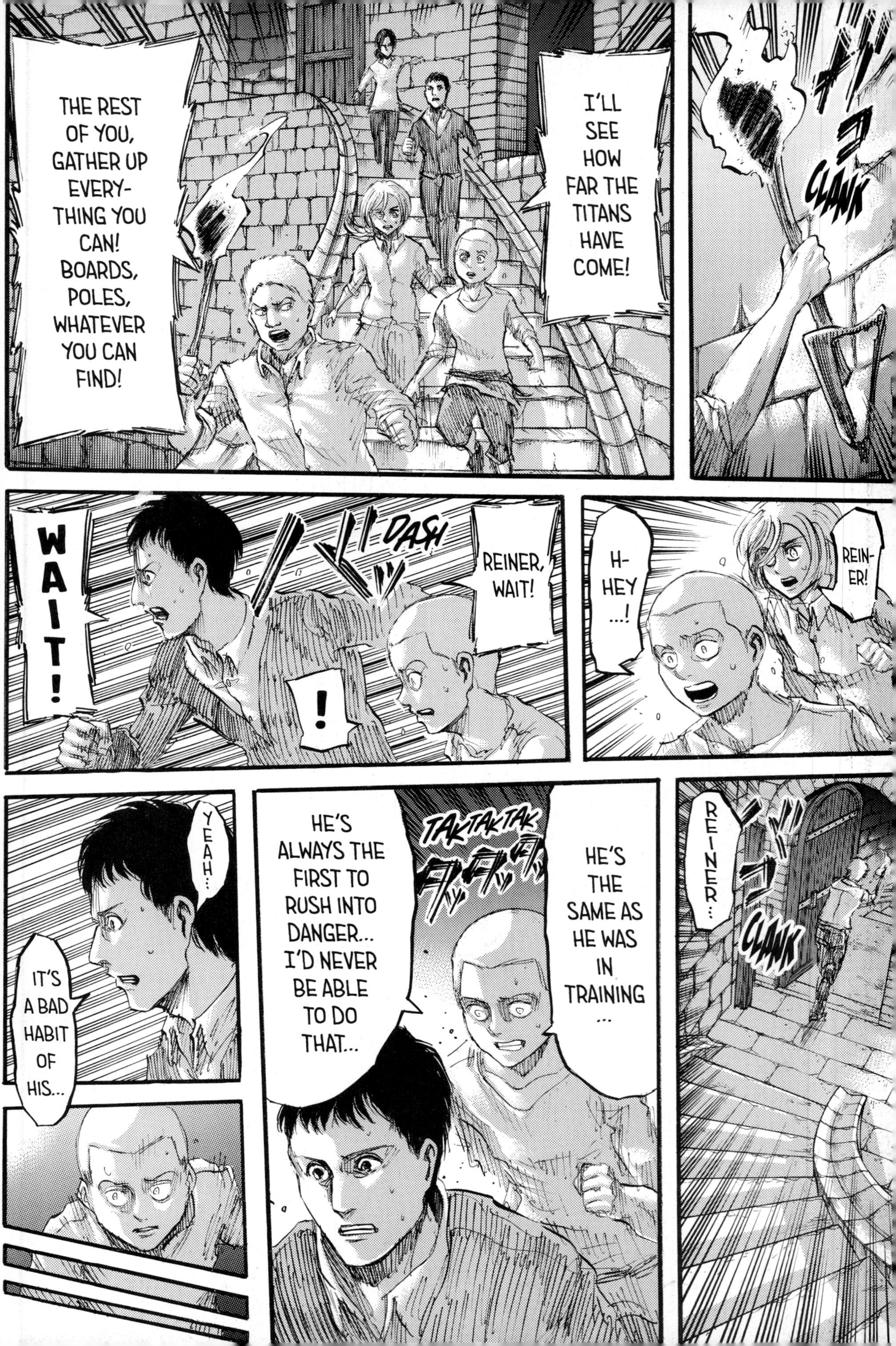
CLANK
I'LL SEE HOW FAR THE TITANS HAVE COME!
THE REST OF YOU, GATHER UP EVERY-THING YOU CAN! BOARDS, POLES, WHATEVER YOU CAN FIND!
REIN-ER!
H-HEY...!
REINER, WAIT!
DASH
!
WAIT!
REINER...
CLANK
HE'S THE SAME AS HE WAS IN TRAINING...
TAKTAKTAK
HE'S ALWAYS THE FIRST TO RUSH INTO DANGER... I'D NEVER BE ABLE TO DO THAT...
YEAH...
IT'S A BAD HABIT OF HIS...

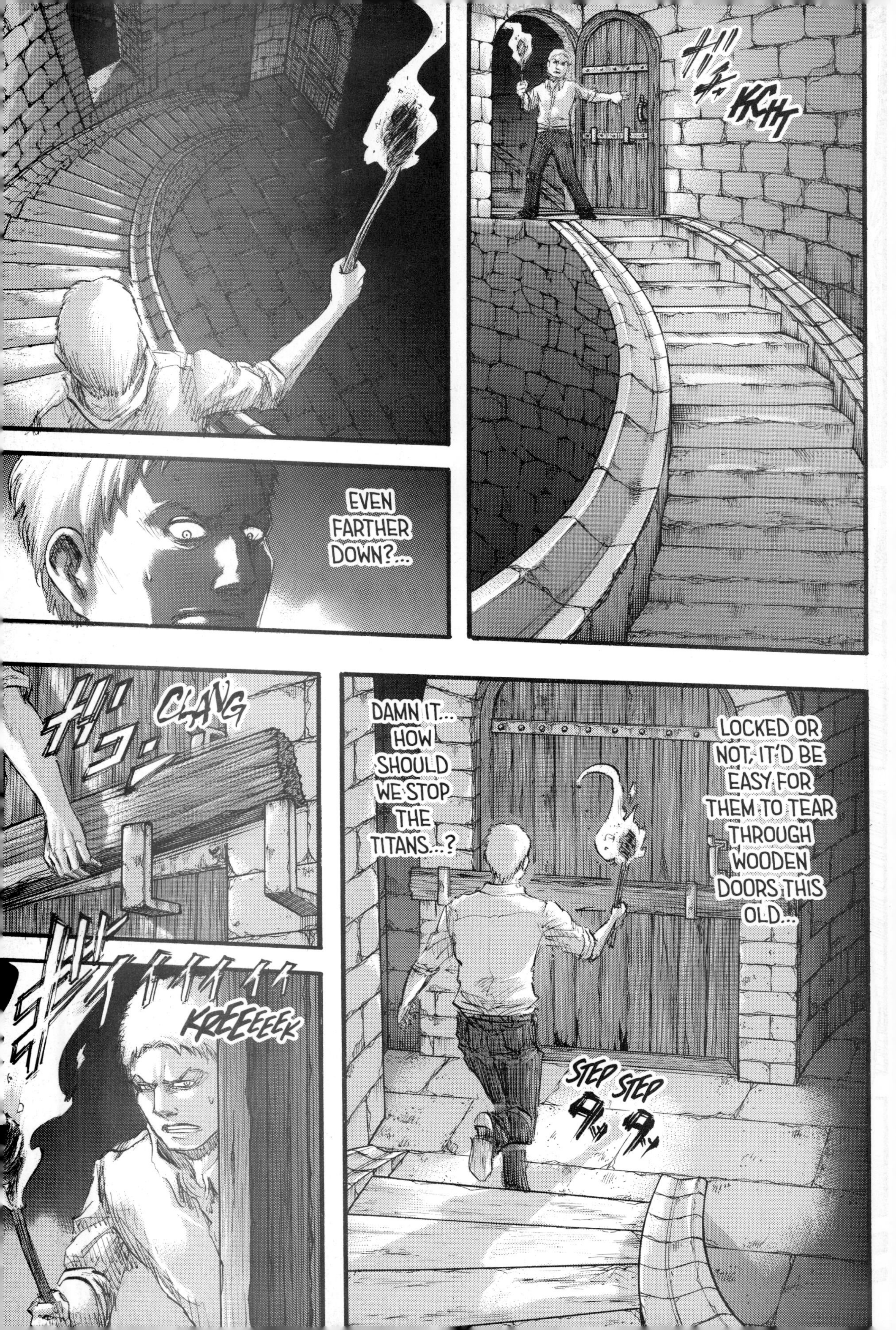
KCHT
EVEN FARTHER DOWN?...
LOCKED OR NOT, IT'D BE EASY FOR THEM TO TEAR THROUGH WOODEN DOORS THIS OLD...
DAMN IT... HOW SHOULD WE STOP THE TITANS...?
STEP STEP
CLANG
KREEEEEK

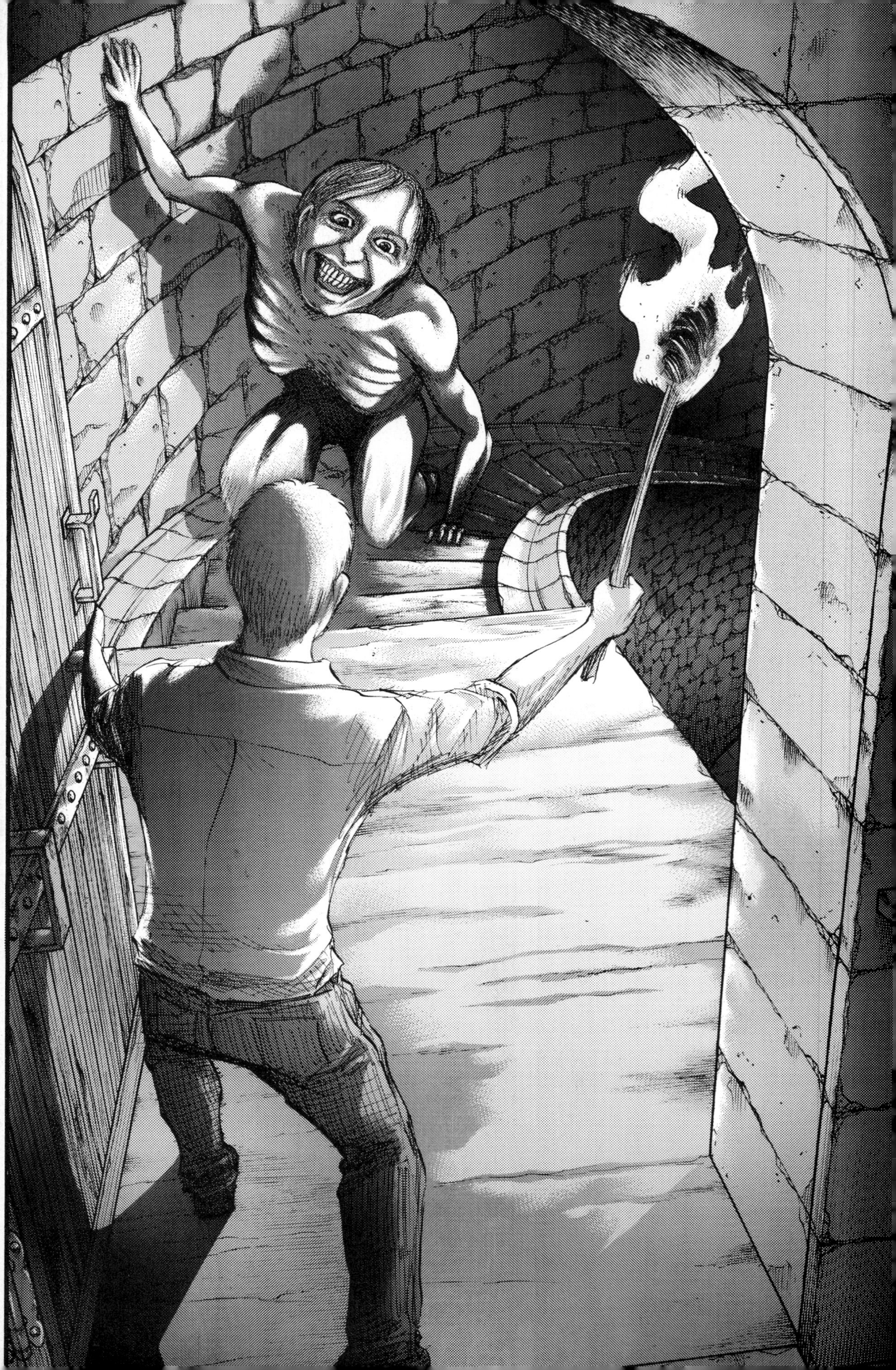

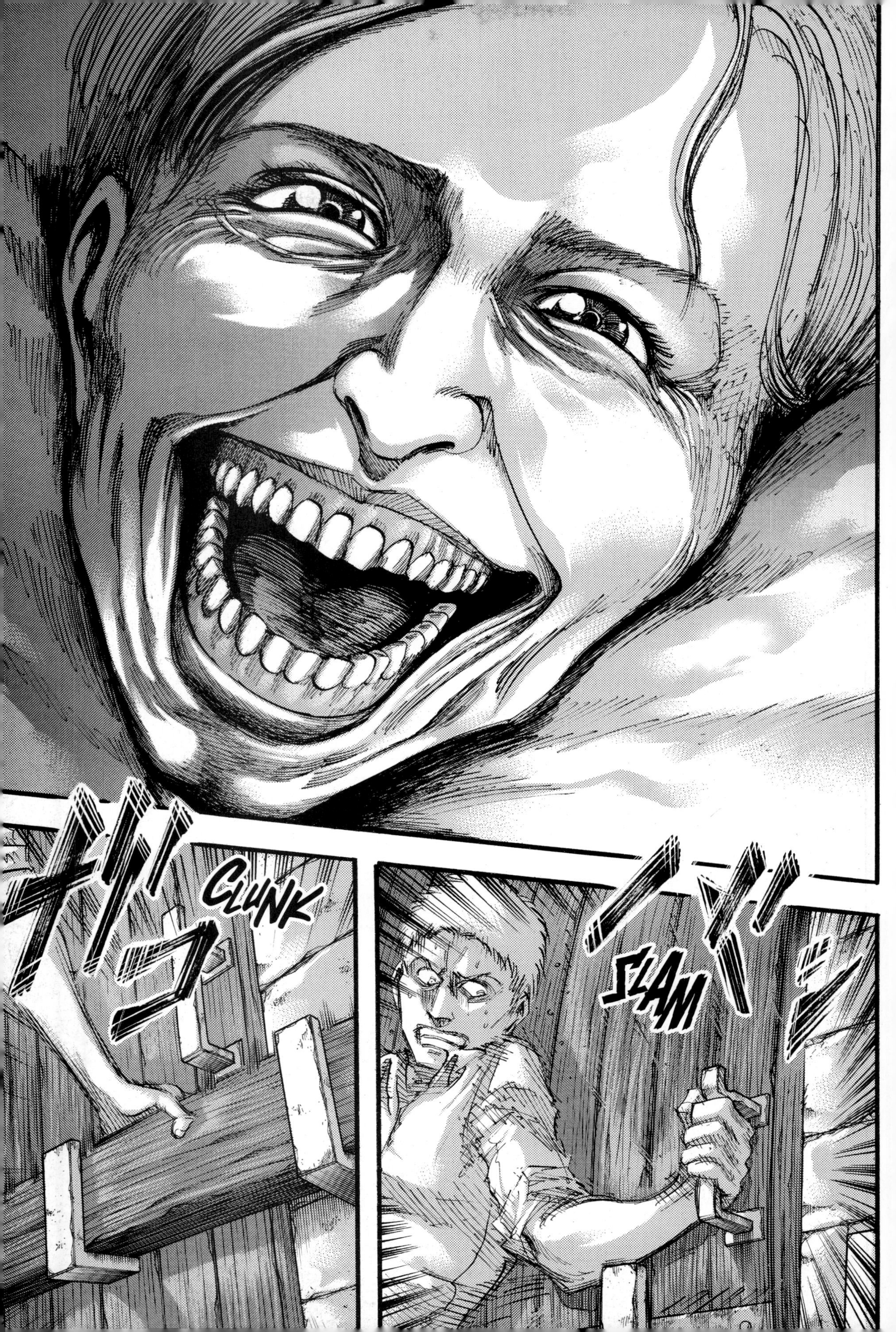
SLAM
CLUNK

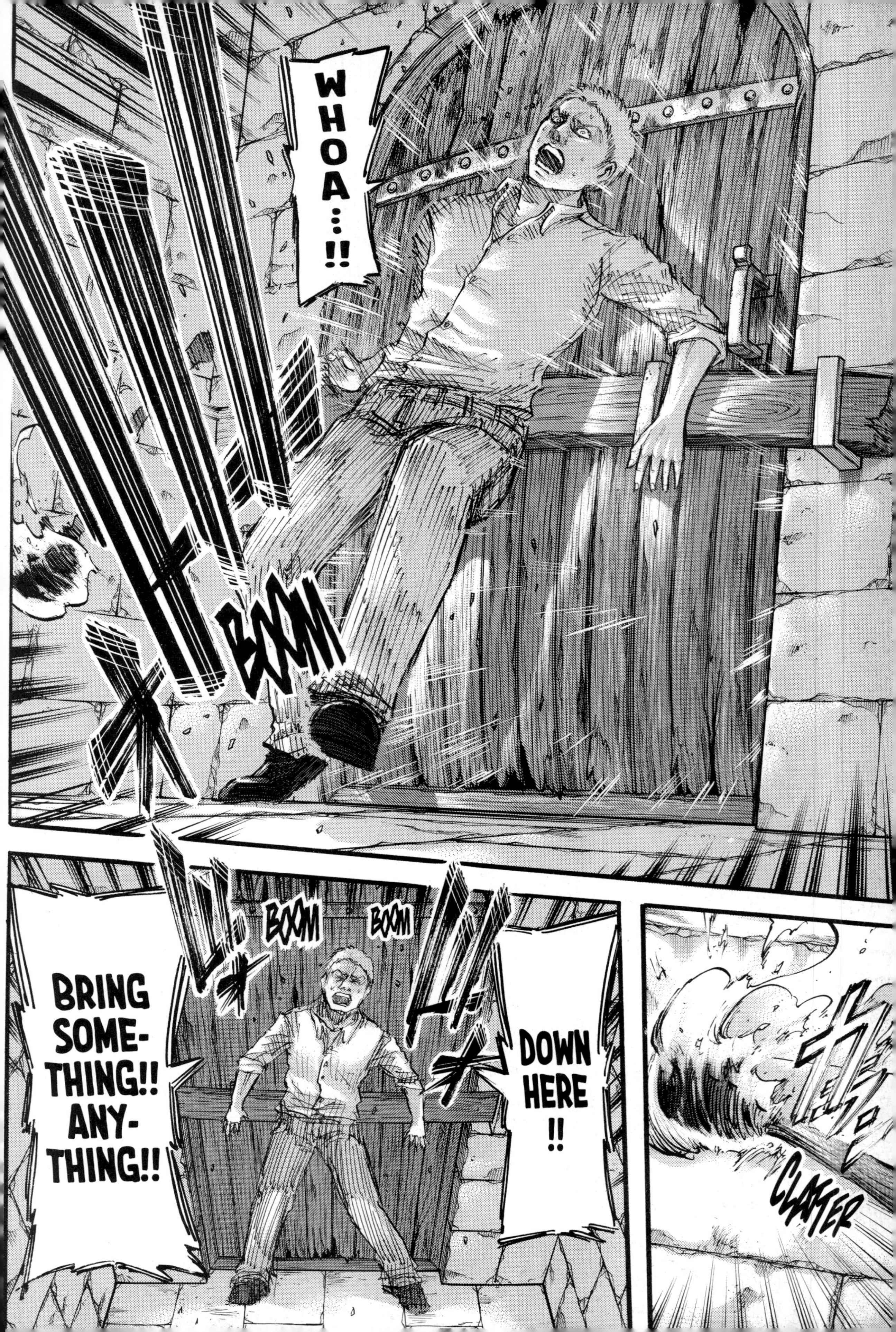
WHOA...!!
BOOM
CLATTER
BOOM
BOOM
DOWN HERE !!
BRING SOME-THING!! ANY-THING!!

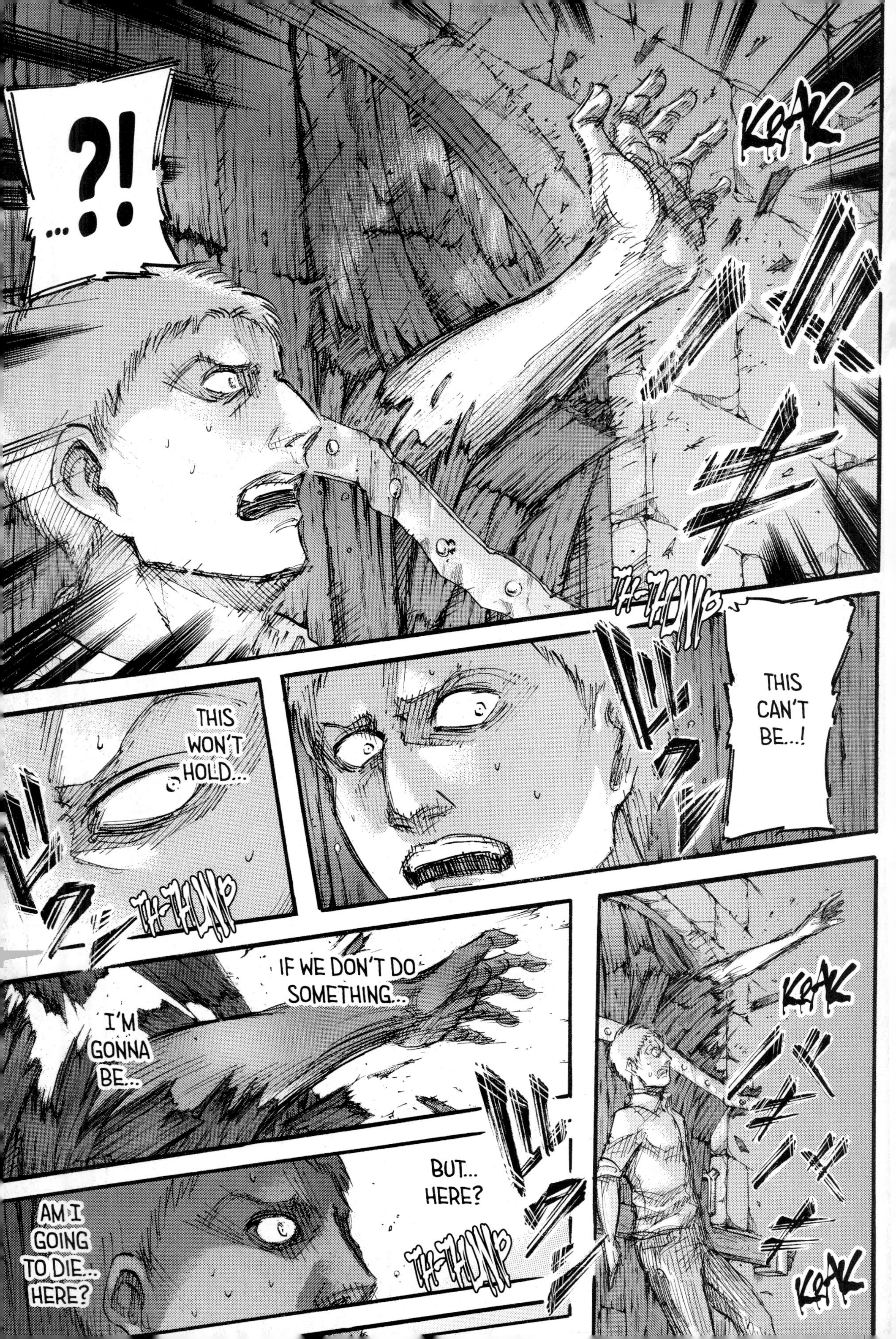
KRAK
...?!
TH-THUMP
THIS CAN'T BE...!
THIS WON'T HOLD...
TH-THUMP
KRAK
KRAK
IF WE DON'T DO SOMETHING...
I'M GONNA BE...
BUT... HERE?
AM I GOING TO DIE... HERE?
TH-THUMP

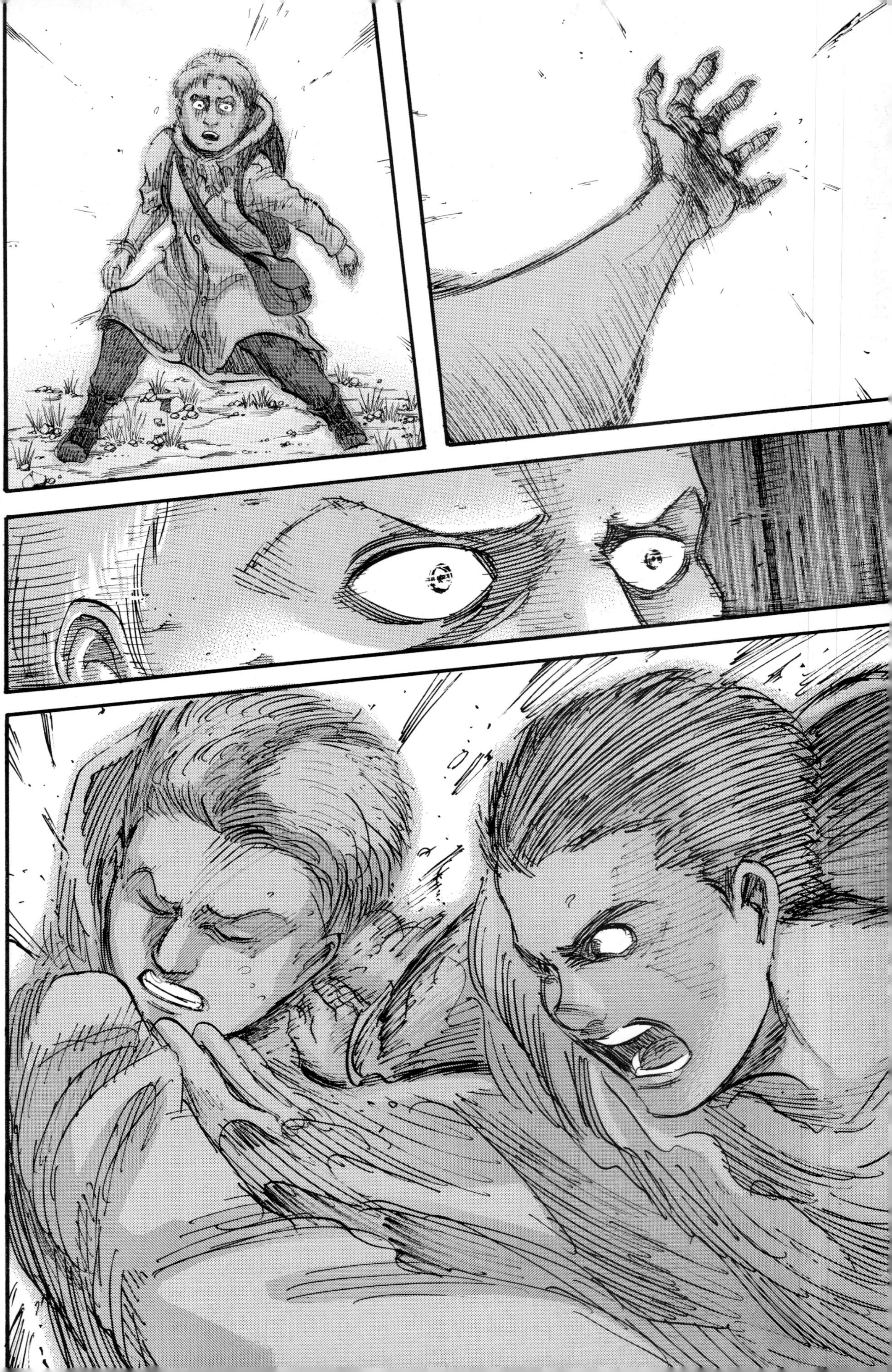

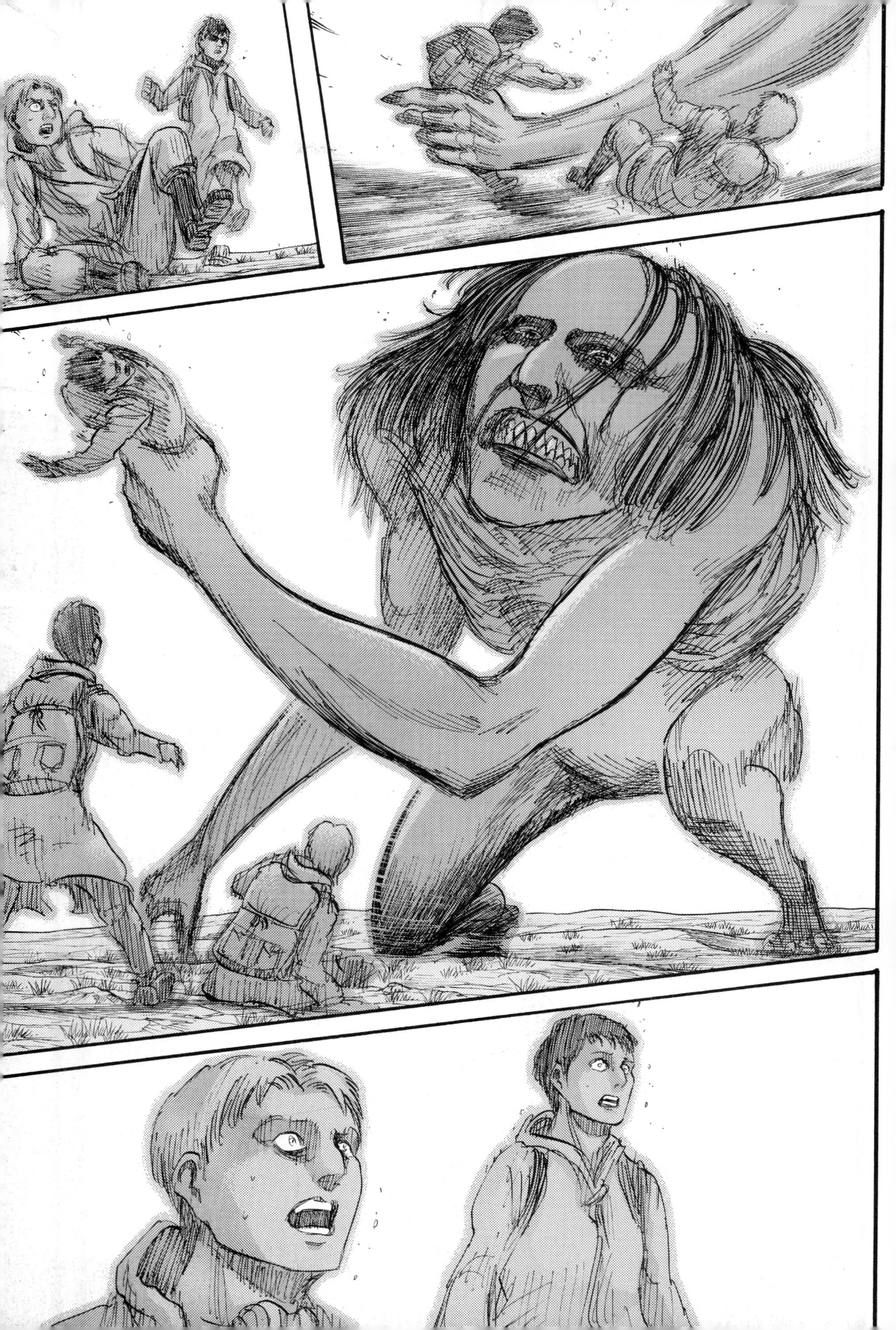

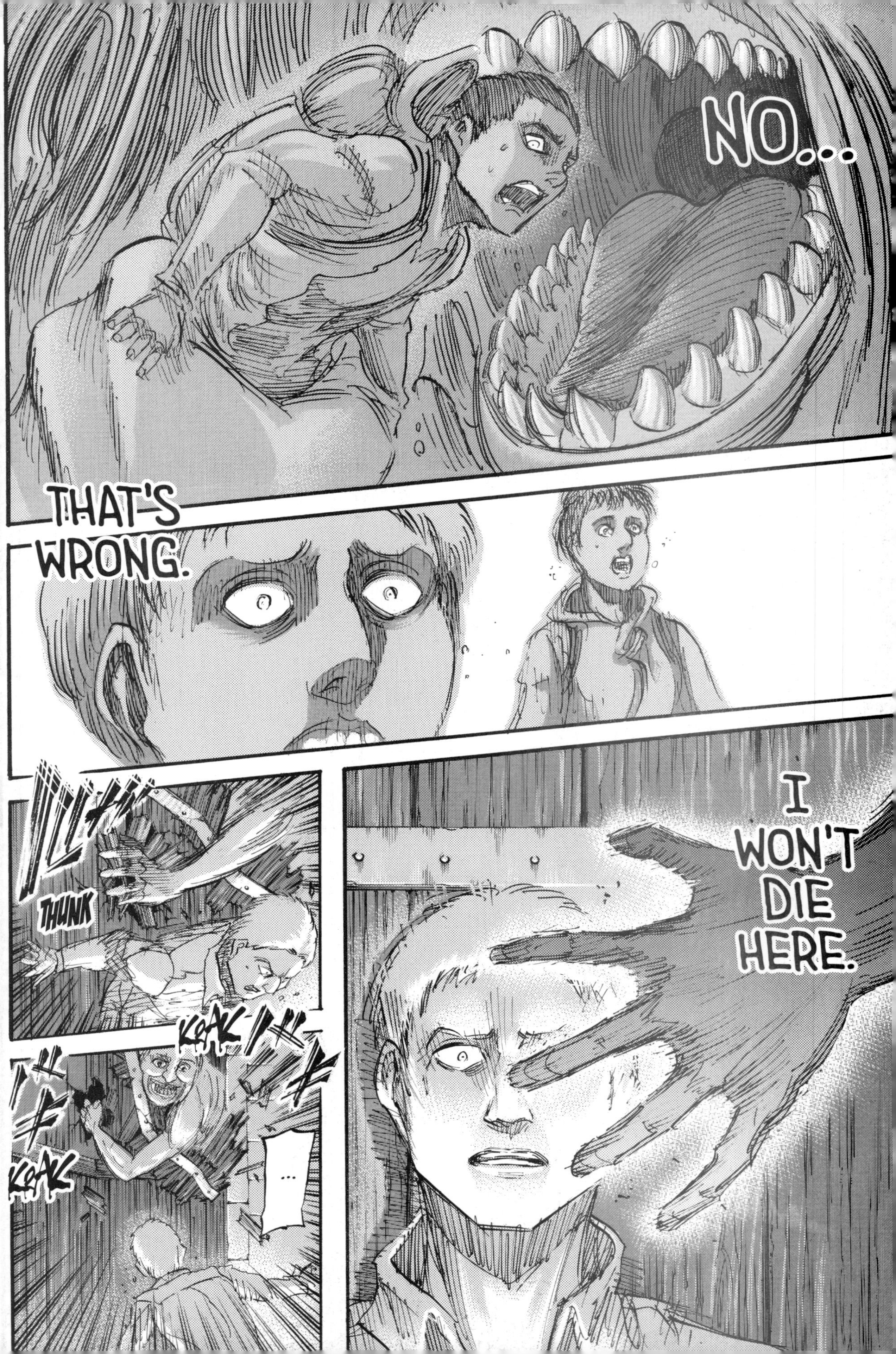
NO...
THAT'S WRONG.
I WON'T DIE HERE.
THUNK
KRAK
KRAK
...

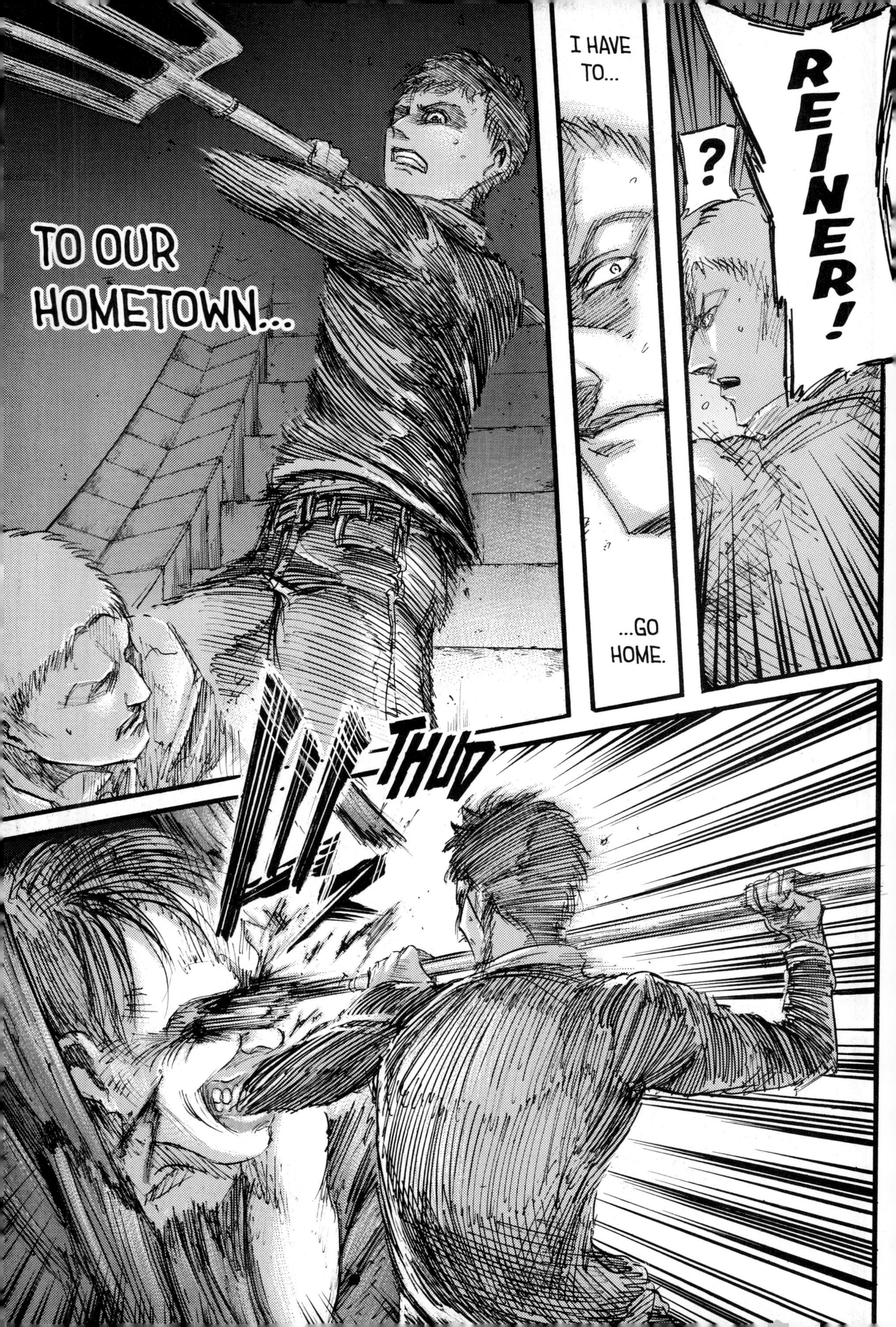
REINER!
?
I HAVE TO...
...GO HOME.
TO OUR HOMETOWN...
THUD

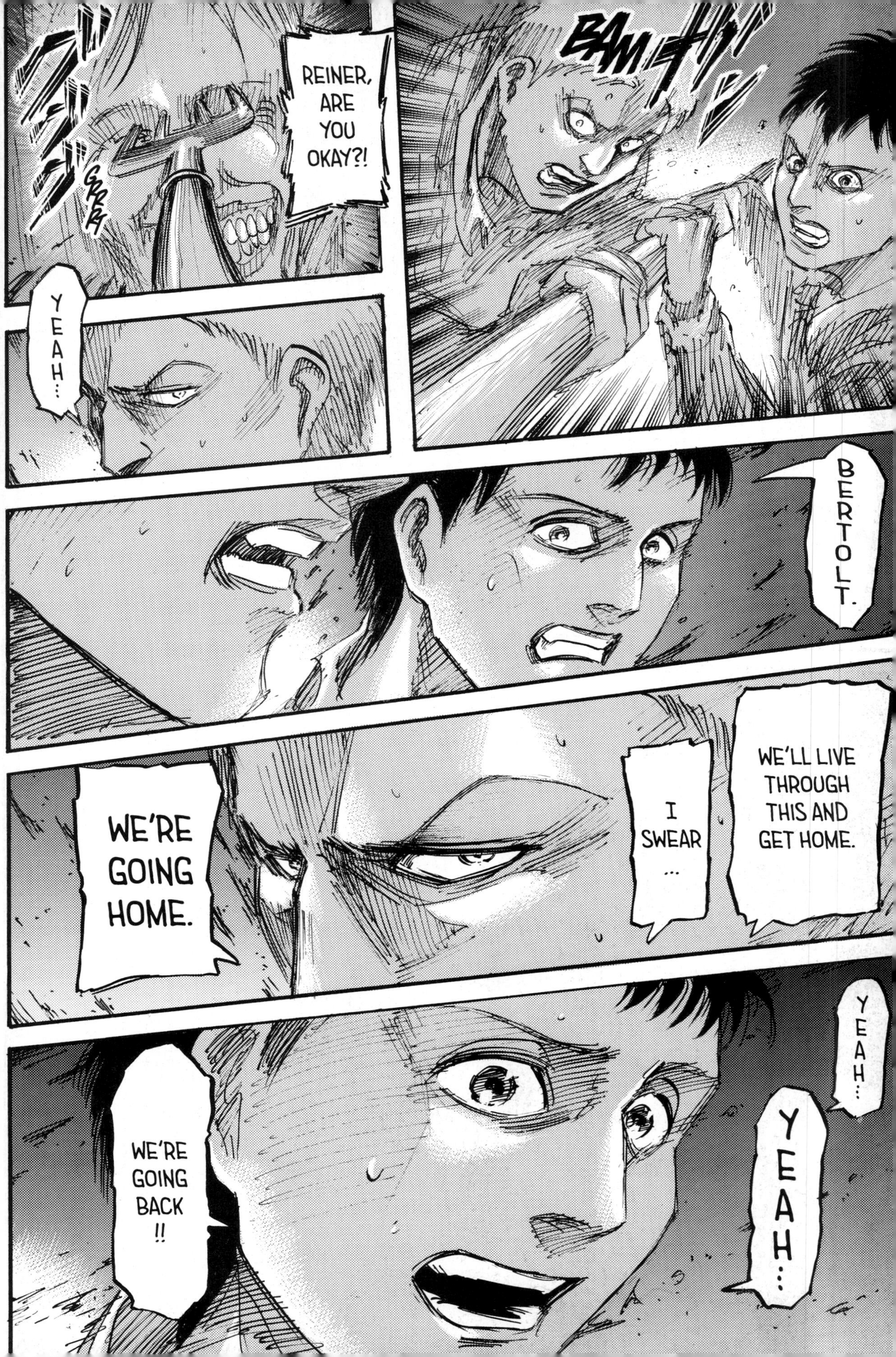
BAM
REINER, ARE YOU OKAY?!
GRRR
YEAH...
BERTOLT.
WE'LL LIVE THROUGH THIS AND GET HOME.
I SWEAR ...
WE'RE GOING HOME.
YEAH...
YEAH...
WE'RE GOING BACK !!

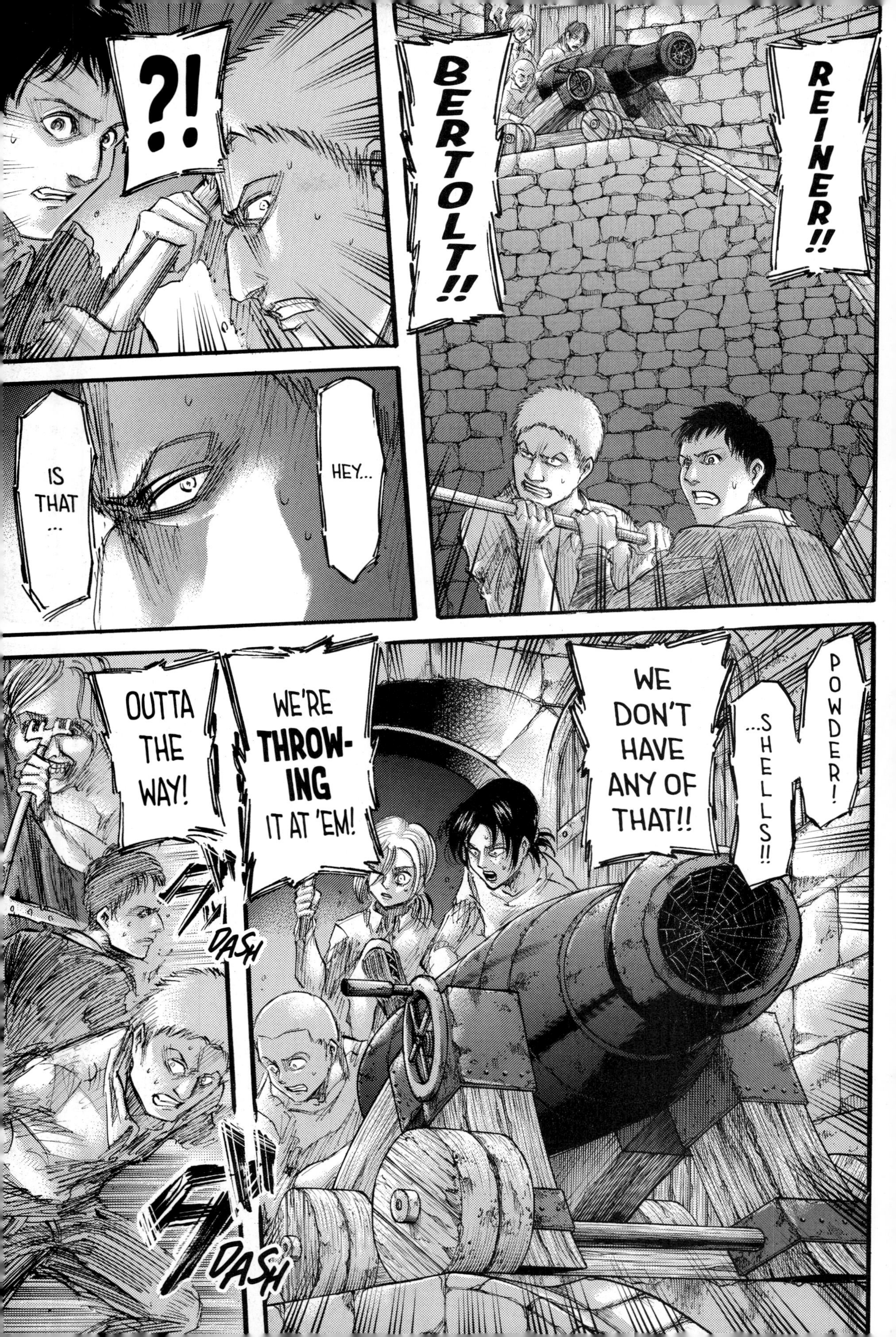
REINER!!
BERTOLT!!
?!
HEY...
IS THAT ...
POWDER!
...SHELLS!!
WE DON'T HAVE ANY OF THAT!!
WE'RE THROWING IT AT 'EM!
OUTTA THE WAY!
DASH
DASH

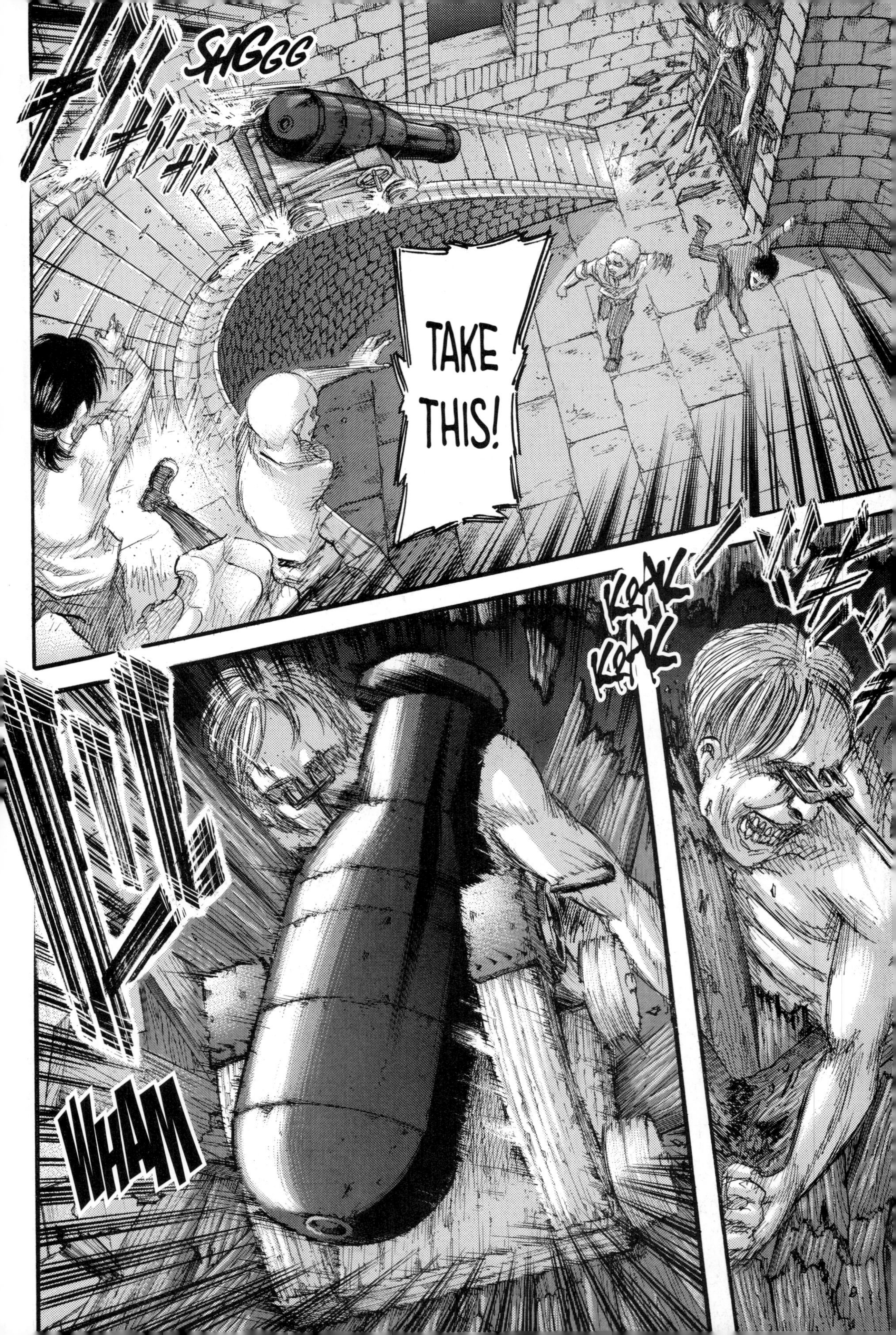
SHGGG
TAKE THIS!
KRAK KRAK
WHAM

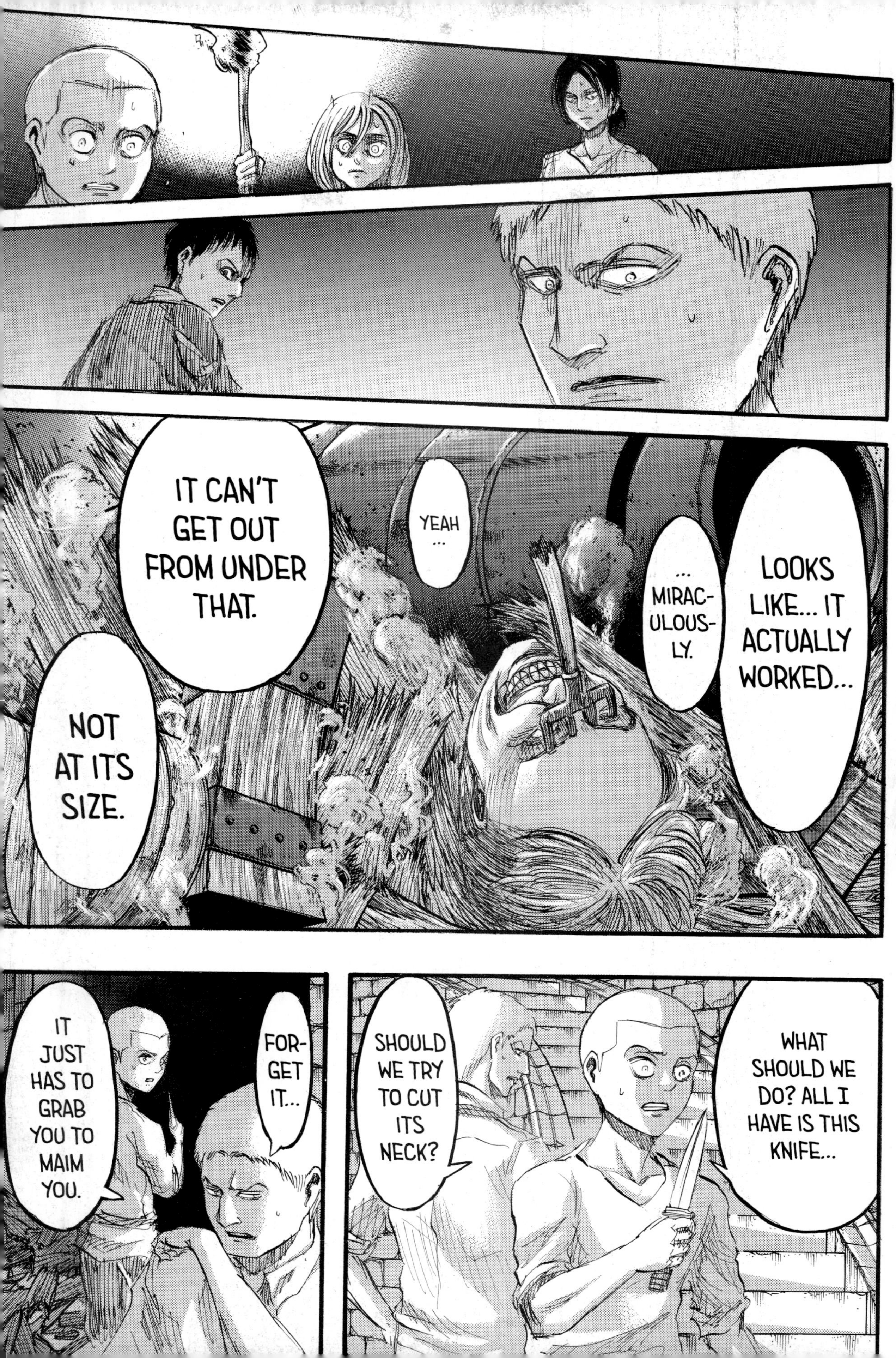
LOOKS LIKE... IT ACTUALLY WORKED...
...MIRACULOUSLY.
YEAH...
IT CAN'T GET OUT FROM UNDER THAT.
NOT AT ITS SIZE.
WHAT SHOULD WE DO? ALL I HAVE IS THIS KNIFE...
SHOULD WE TRY TO CUT ITS NECK?
FORGET IT...
IT JUST HAS TO GRAB YOU TO MAIM YOU.

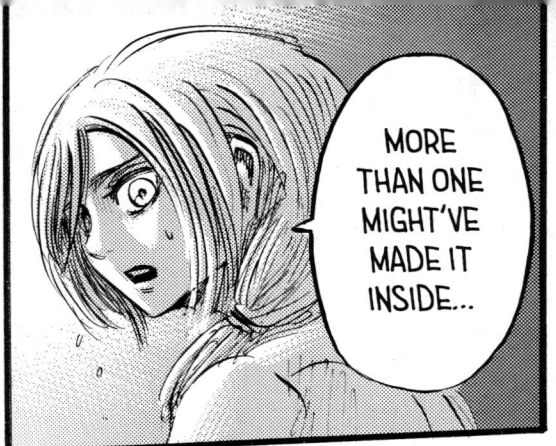

F... FOR NOW...
STEP
LET'S RETREAT BACK UPSTAIRS!
MORE THAN ONE MIGHT'VE MADE IT INSIDE...
GRIP...
POP
RUSH
CONNIE!!

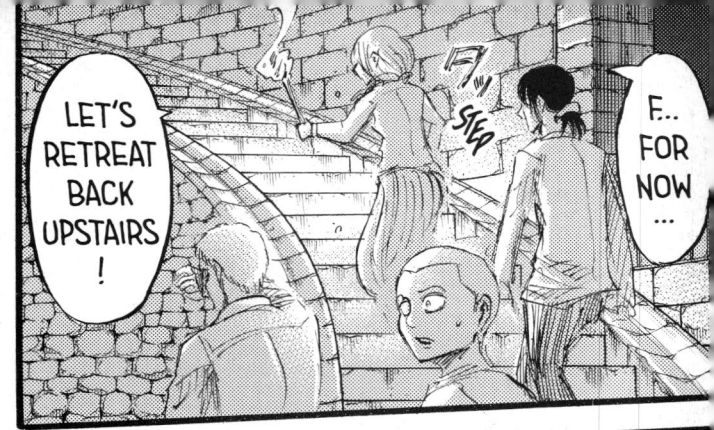

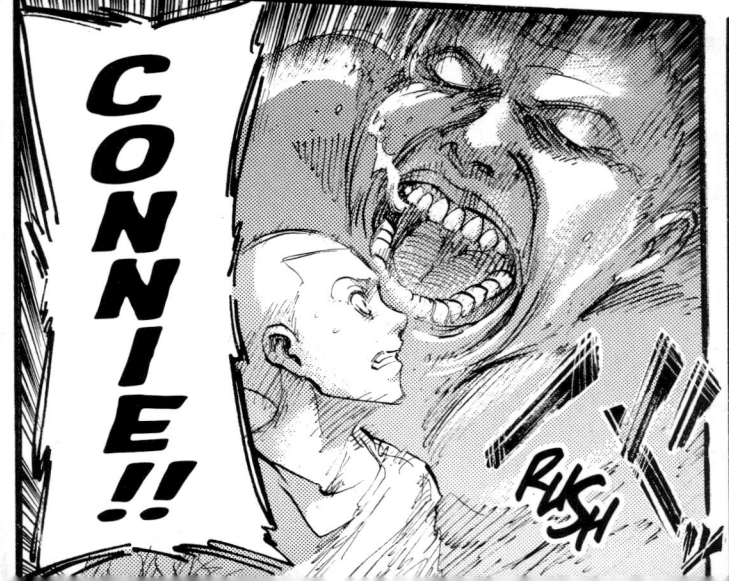

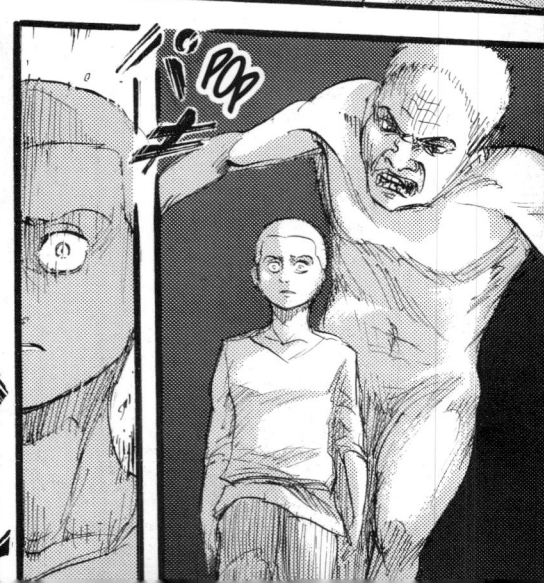

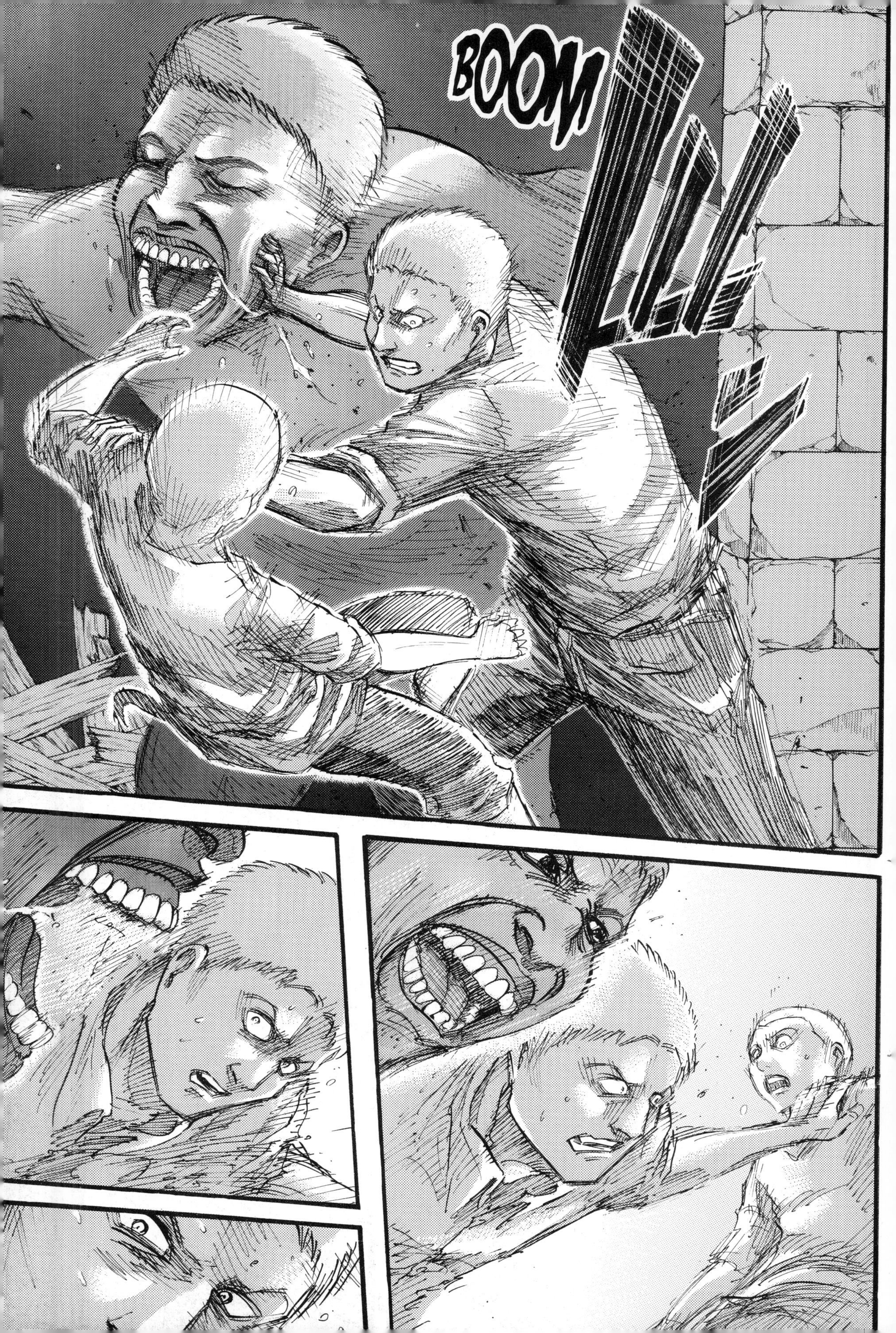
BOOM

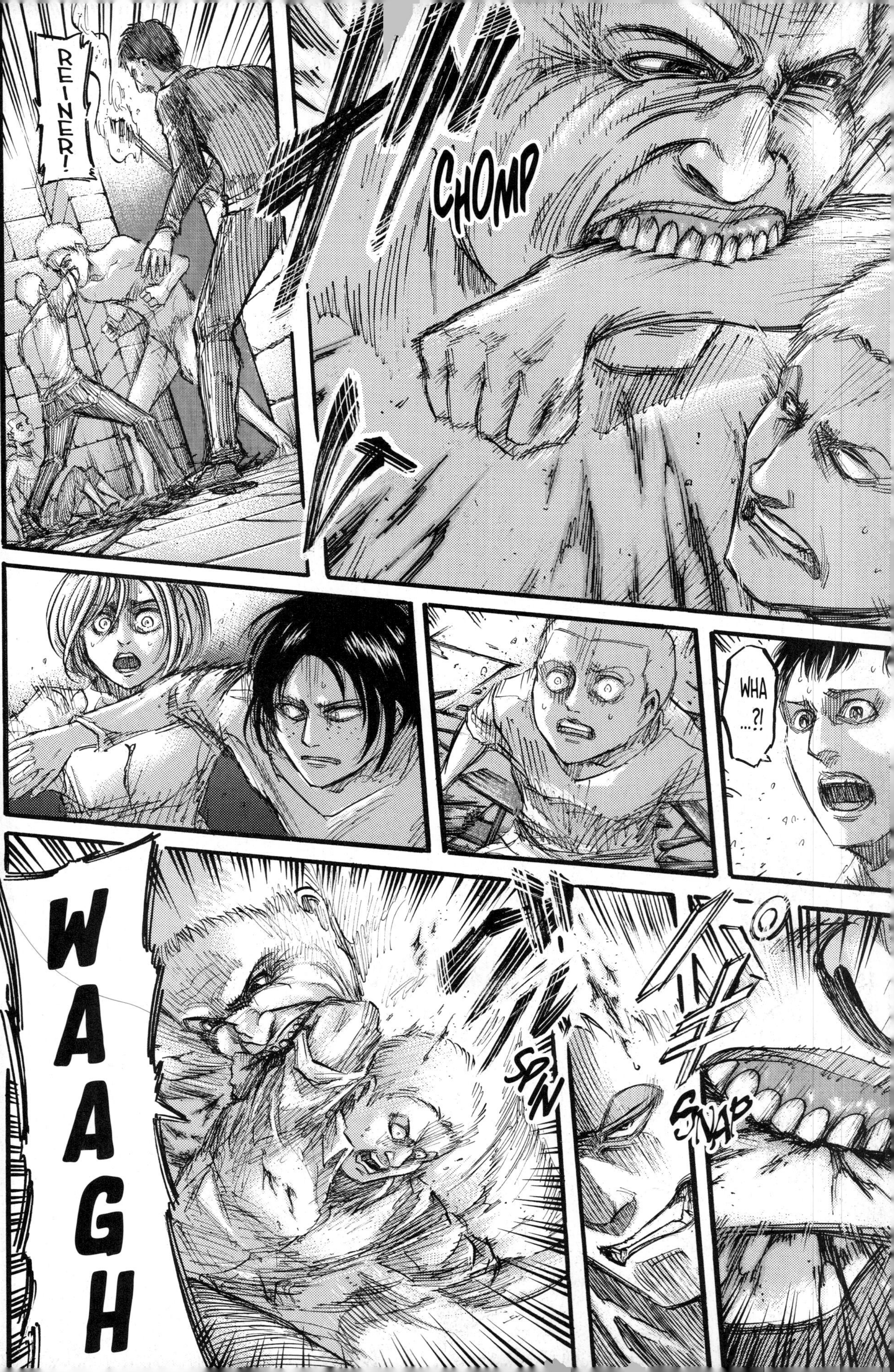

CHOMP
REINER!
WHA ...?!
SNAP
SPIN
WAAGH

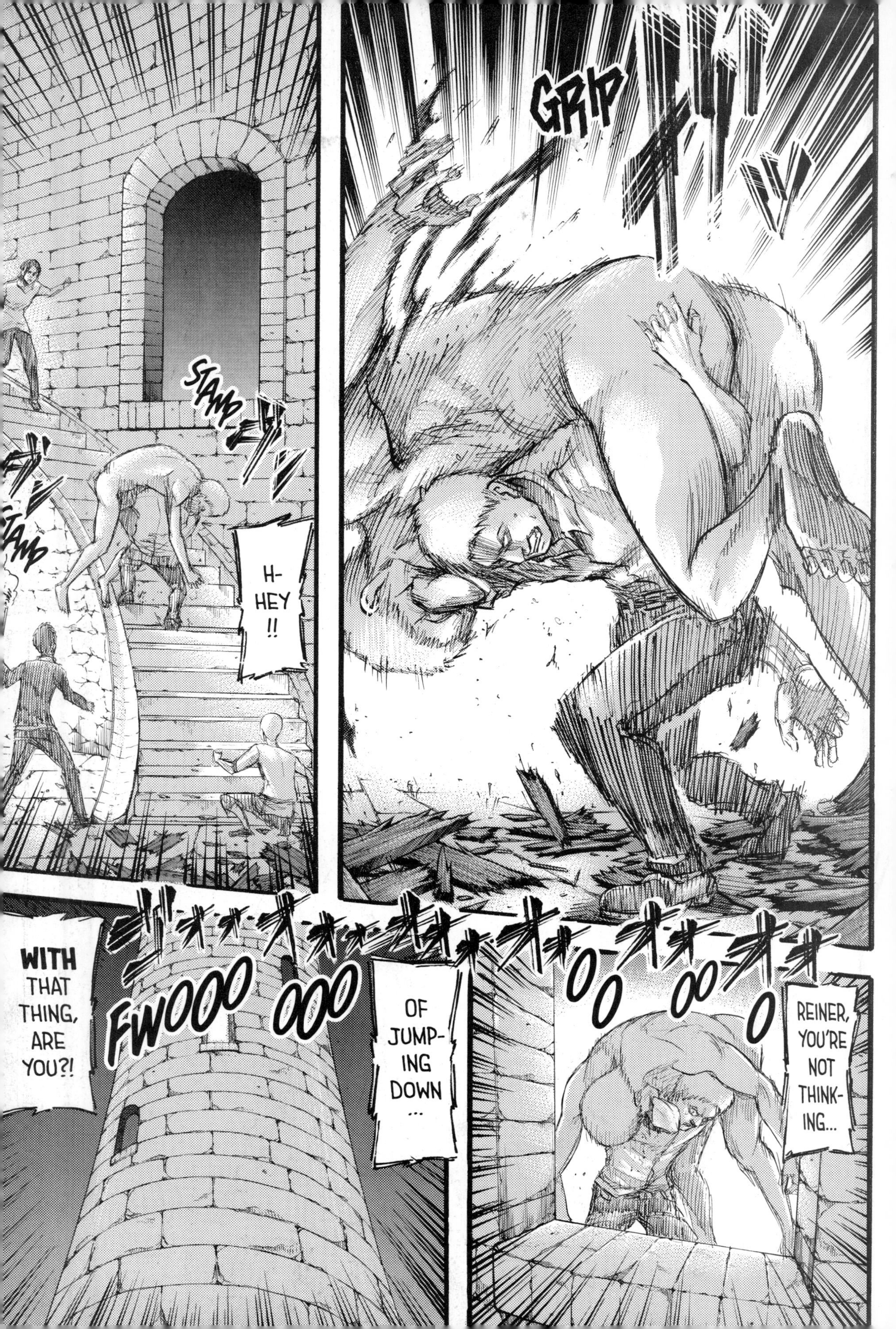

GRIP
STAMP
STAMP
H-HEY!!
REINER, YOU'RE NOT THINKING...
FWOOO OOO OO O OO O
OF JUMPING DOWN...
WITH THAT THING, ARE YOU?!

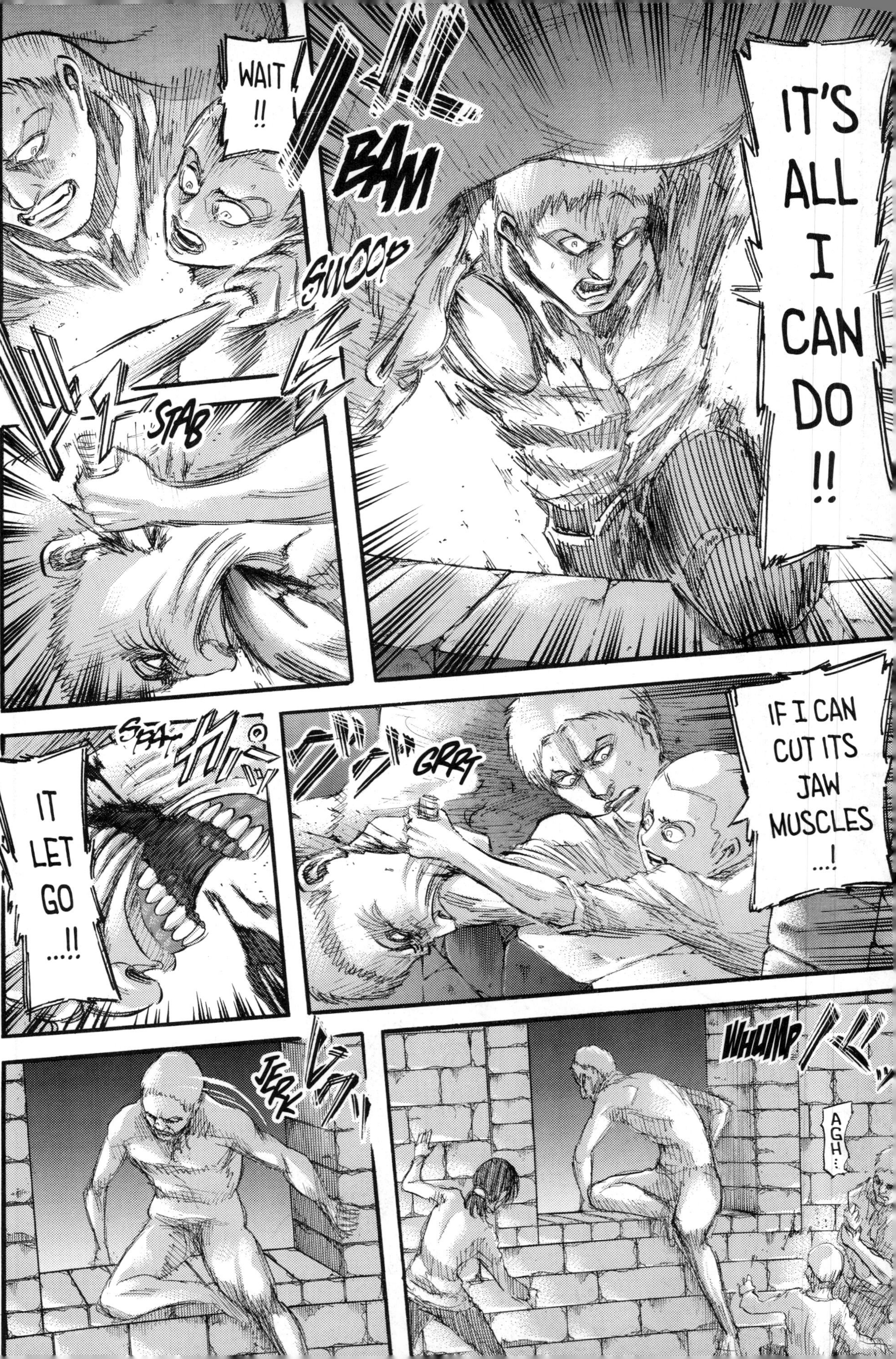
IT'S ALL I CAN DO!!
WAIT!!
BAM
SWOOP
STAB
GRRR
IF I CAN CUT ITS JAW MUSCLES ...!
IT LET GO ...!!
WHUMP
AGH...
JERK

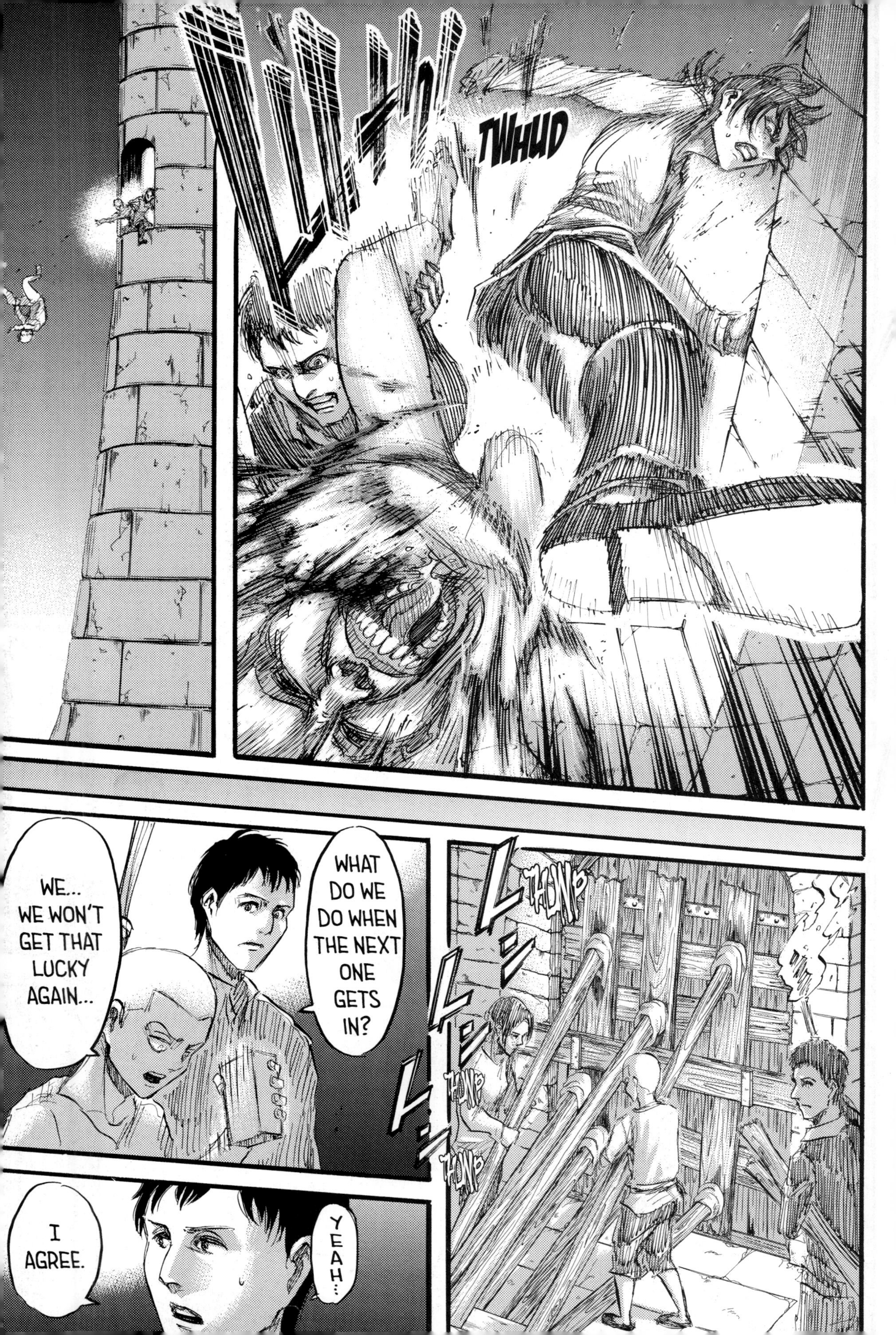
TWHUD
THUMP
THUMP
THUMP
WHAT DO WE DO WHEN THE NEXT ONE GETS IN?
WE... WE WON'T GET THAT LUCKY AGAIN...
YEAH...
I AGREE.

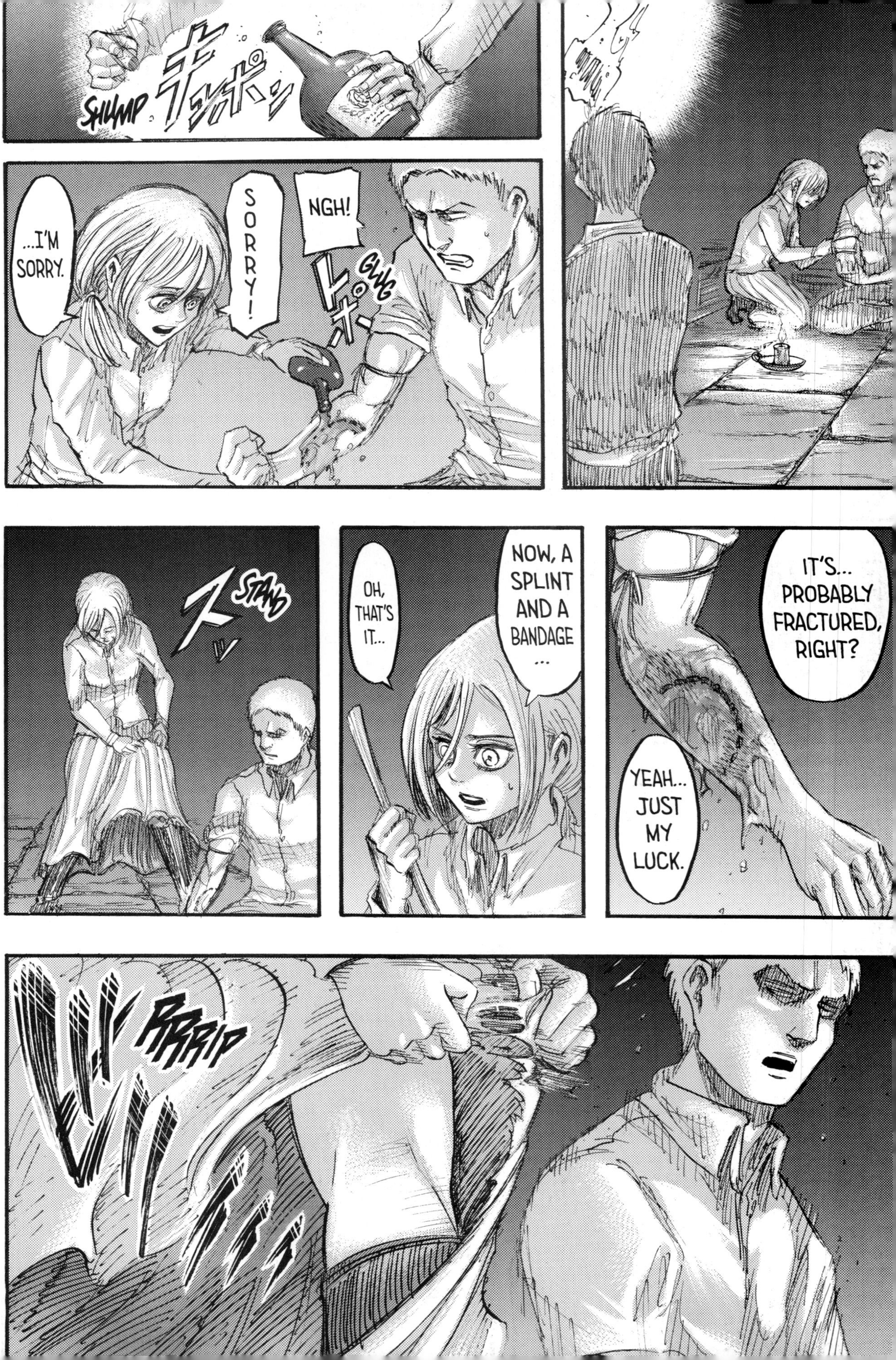

SHUMP
NGH!
SORRY!
...I'M SORRY.
GLUG
IT'S... PROBABLY FRACTURED, RIGHT?
YEAH... JUST MY LUCK.
NOW, A SPLINT AND A BANDAGE ...
OH, THAT'S IT...
STAND
RRRIP

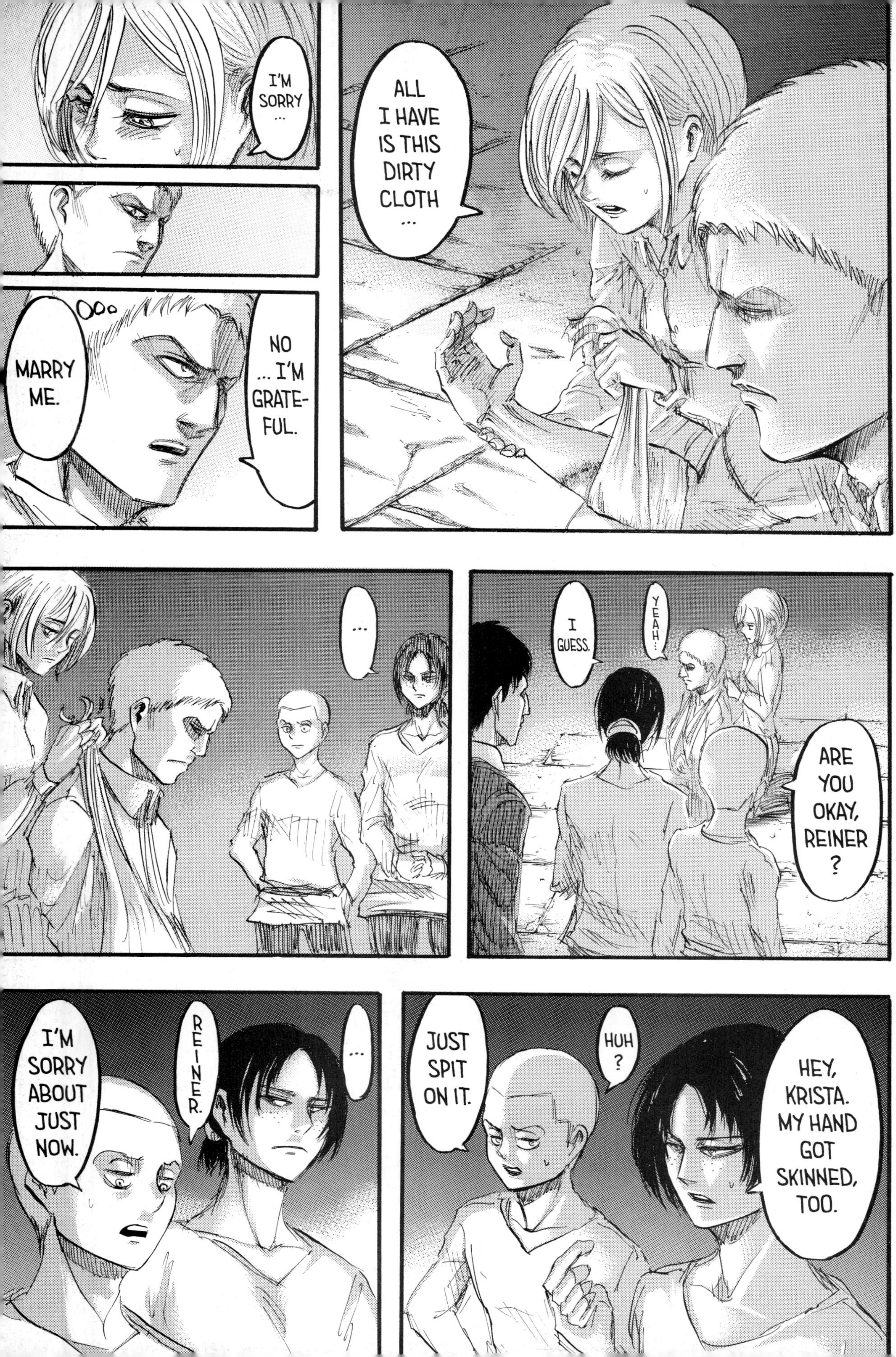
I'M SORRY ...
MARRY ME.
NO ... I'M GRATE-FUL.
ALL I HAVE IS THIS DIRTY CLOTH ...
...
I GUESS.
YEAH...
ARE YOU OKAY, REINER ?
I'M SORRY ABOUT JUST NOW.
REINER.
...
JUST SPIT ON IT.
HUH ?
HEY, KRISTA. MY HAND GOT SKINNED, TOO.

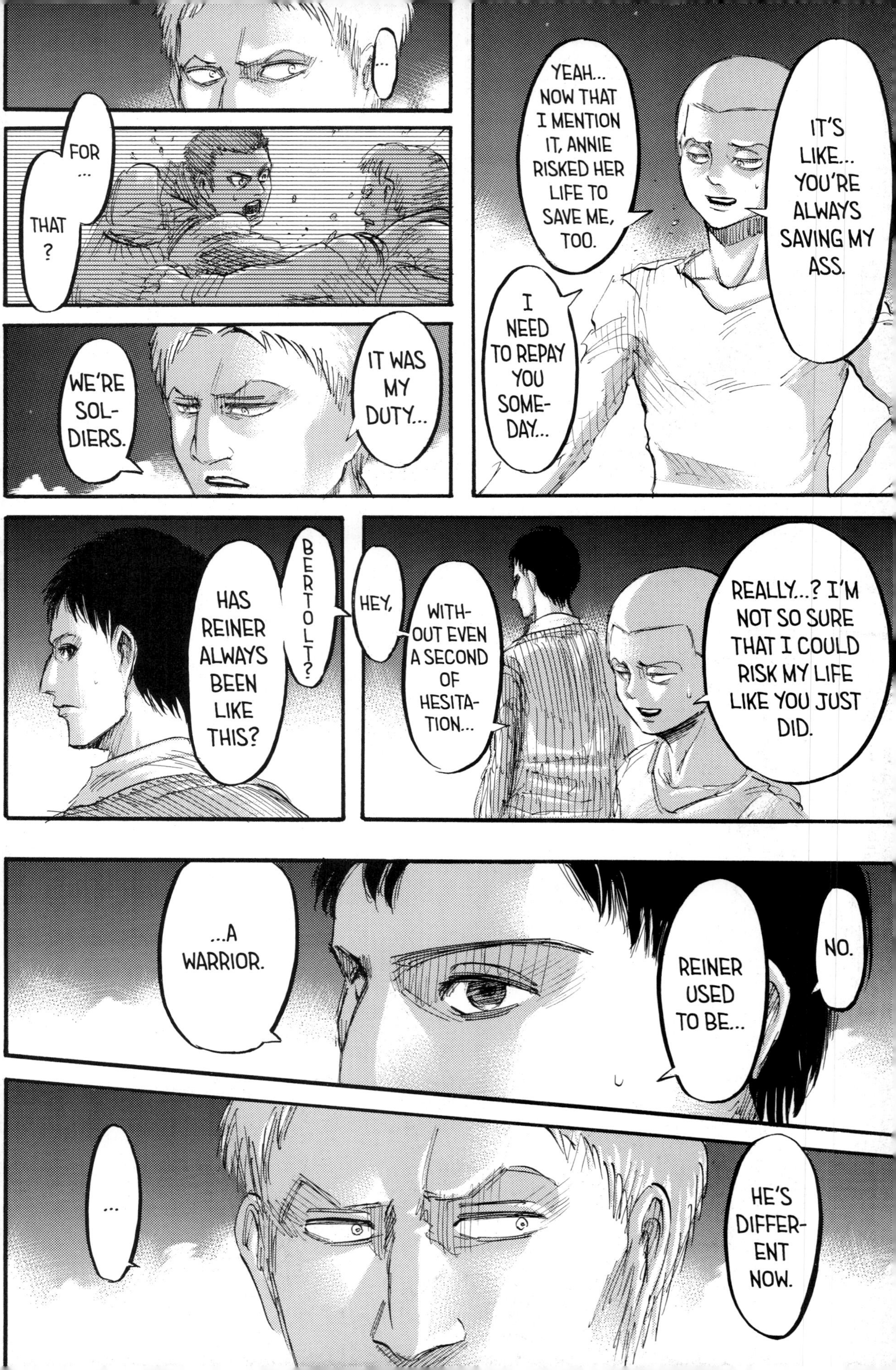
IT'S LIKE... YOU'RE ALWAYS SAVING MY ASS.
YEAH... NOW THAT I MENTION IT, ANNIE RISKED HER LIFE TO SAVE ME, TOO.
I NEED TO REPAY YOU SOMEDAY...
...
FOR ... THAT ?
IT WAS MY DUTY...
WE'RE SOLDIERS.
REALLY...? I'M NOT SO SURE THAT I COULD RISK MY LIFE LIKE YOU JUST DID.
WITHOUT EVEN A SECOND OF HESITATION...
HEY,
BERTOLT?
HAS REINER ALWAYS BEEN LIKE THIS?
NO.
REINER USED TO BE...
...A WARRIOR.
HE'S DIFFERENT NOW.
...

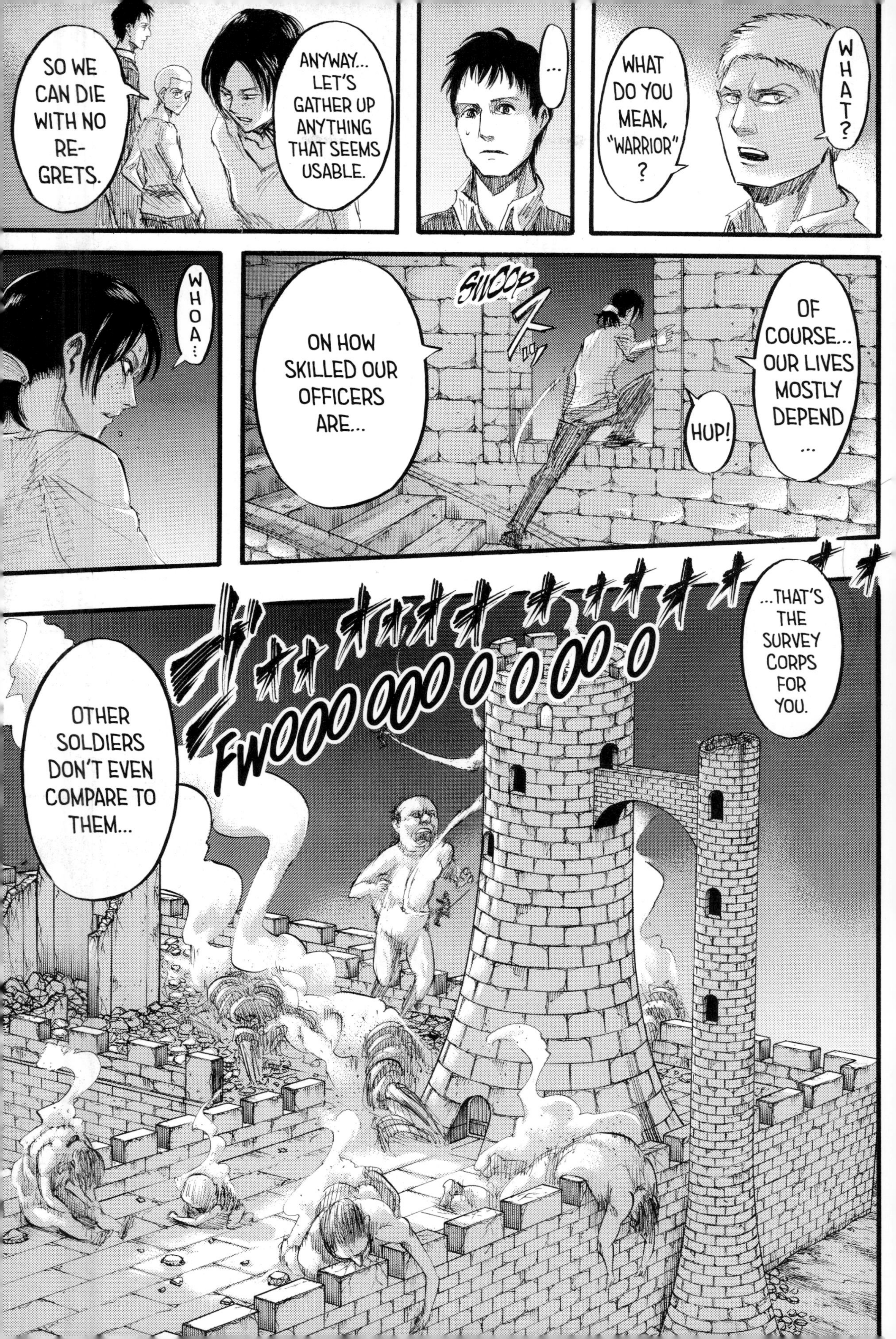
WHAT?
WHAT DO YOU MEAN, "WARRIOR"?
...
ANYWAY... LET'S GATHER UP ANYTHING THAT SEEMS USABLE.
SO WE CAN DIE WITH NO RE-GRETS.
OF COURSE... OUR LIVES MOSTLY DEPEND ...
HUP!
SWOOP
ON HOW SKILLED OUR OFFICERS ARE...
WHOA...
...THAT'S THE SURVEY CORPS FOR YOU.
FWOOO OOO O O OO O
OTHER SOLDIERS DON'T EVEN COMPARE TO THEM...

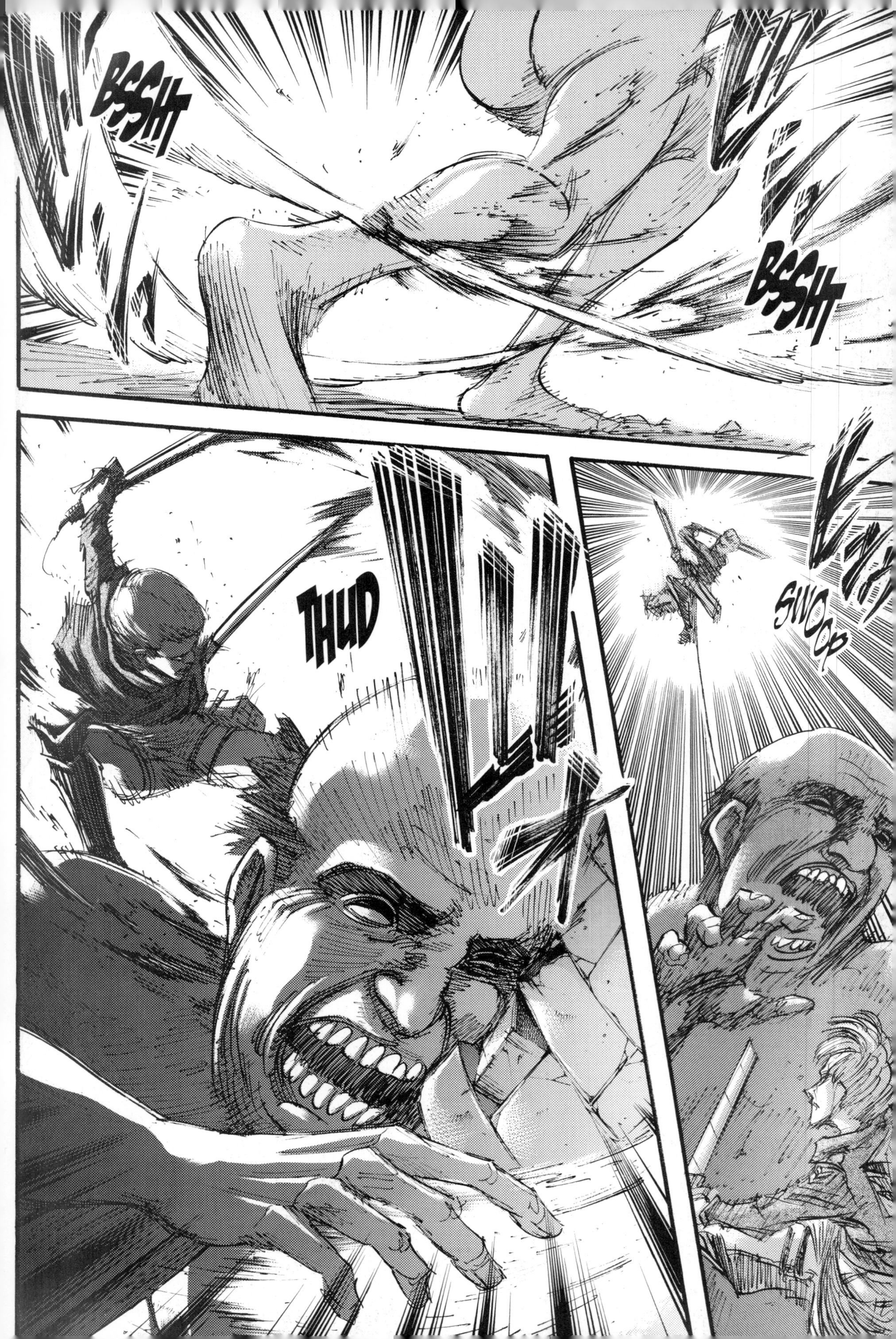
BSSHT
BSSHT
SWOOP
THUD

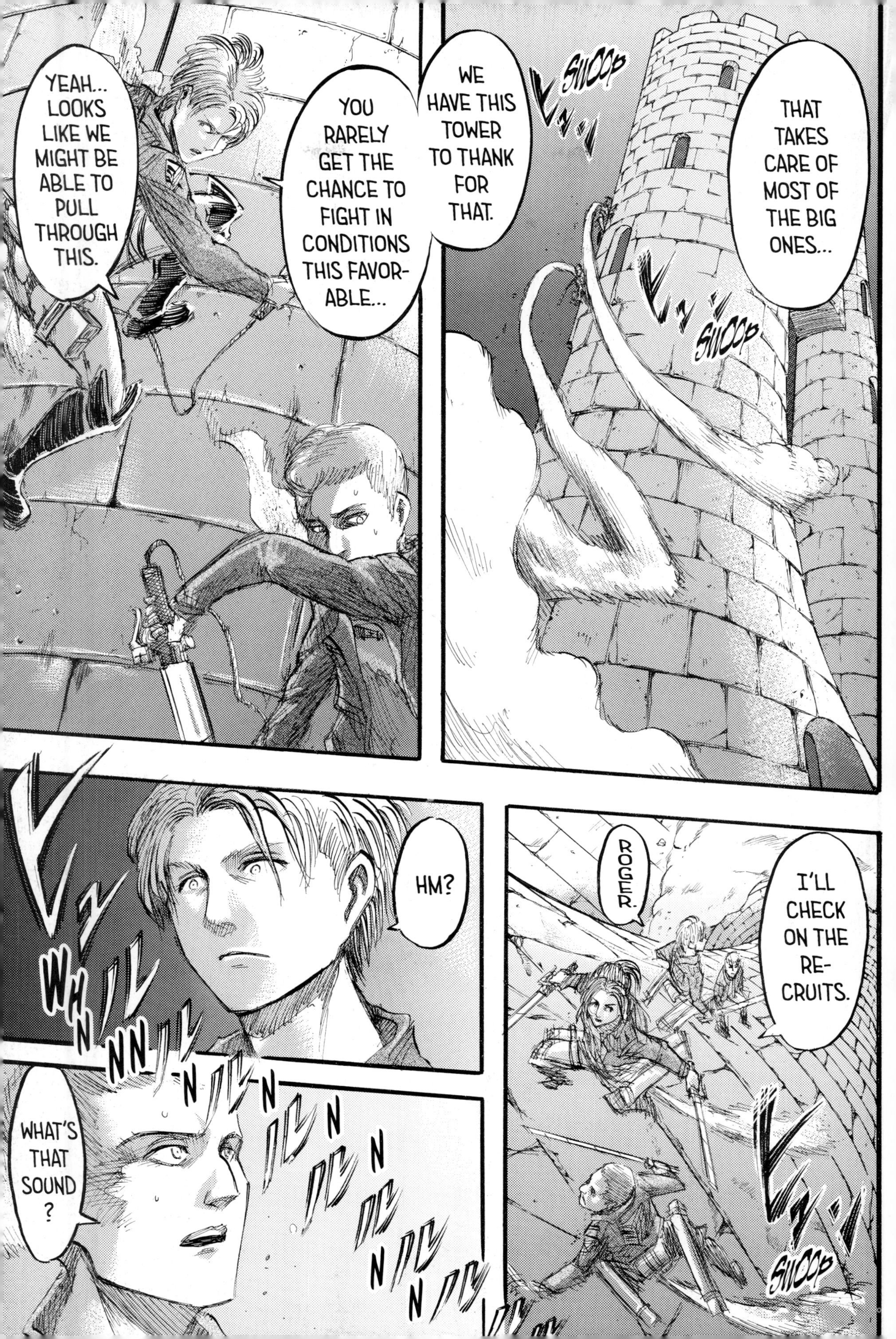
SWOOP
THAT TAKES CARE OF MOST OF THE BIG ONES...
SWOOP
WE HAVE THIS TOWER TO THANK FOR THAT.
YOU RARELY GET THE CHANCE TO FIGHT IN CONDITIONS THIS FAVOR-ABLE...
YEAH... LOOKS LIKE WE MIGHT BE ABLE TO PULL THROUGH THIS.
I'LL CHECK ON THE RE-CRUITS.
ROGER.
SWOOP
HM?
WHNNNNNNNNN
WHAT'S THAT SOUND?

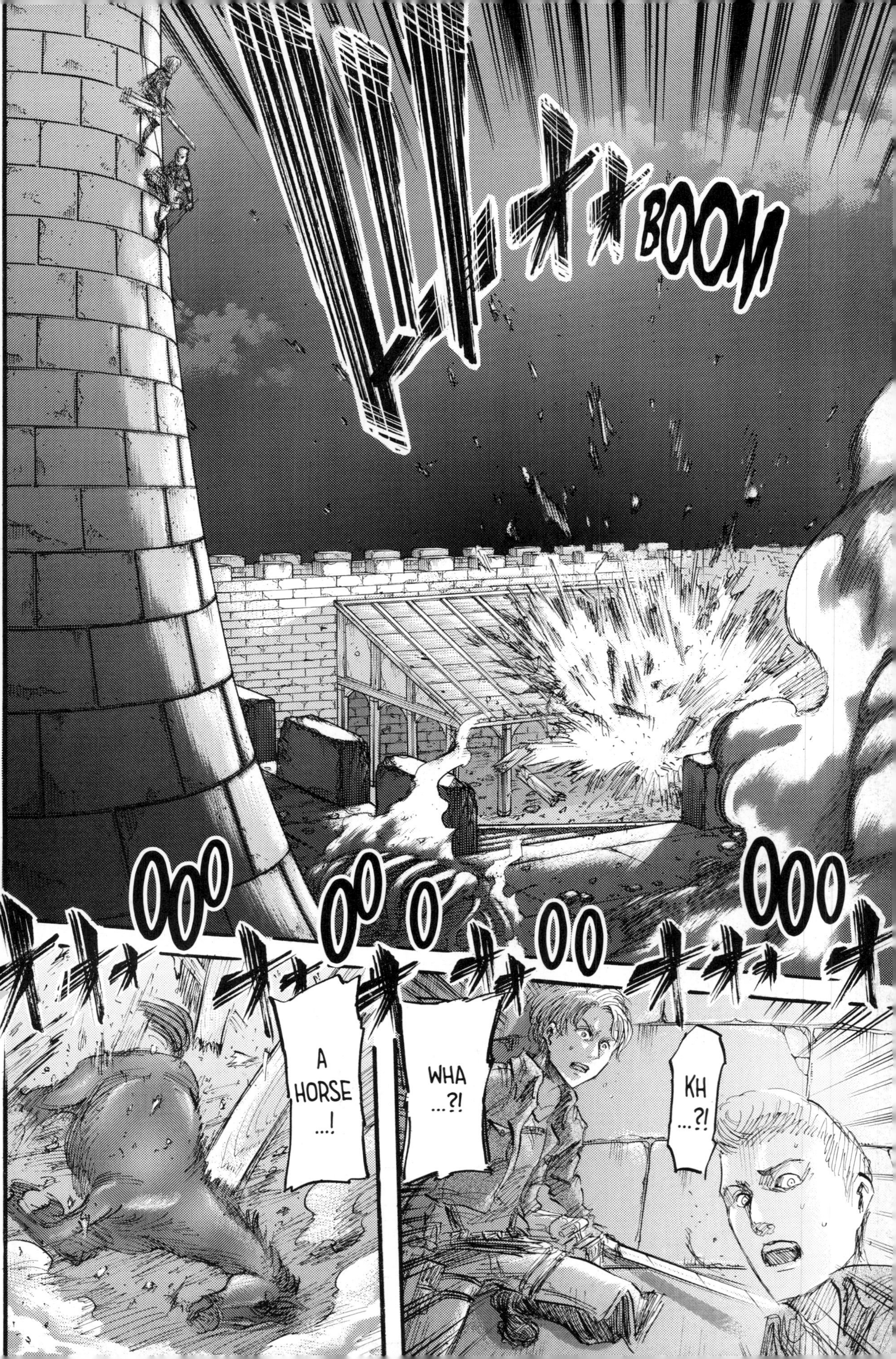
BOOM
OOO OOO OO OOO
KH ...?!
WHA ...?!
A HORSE ...!

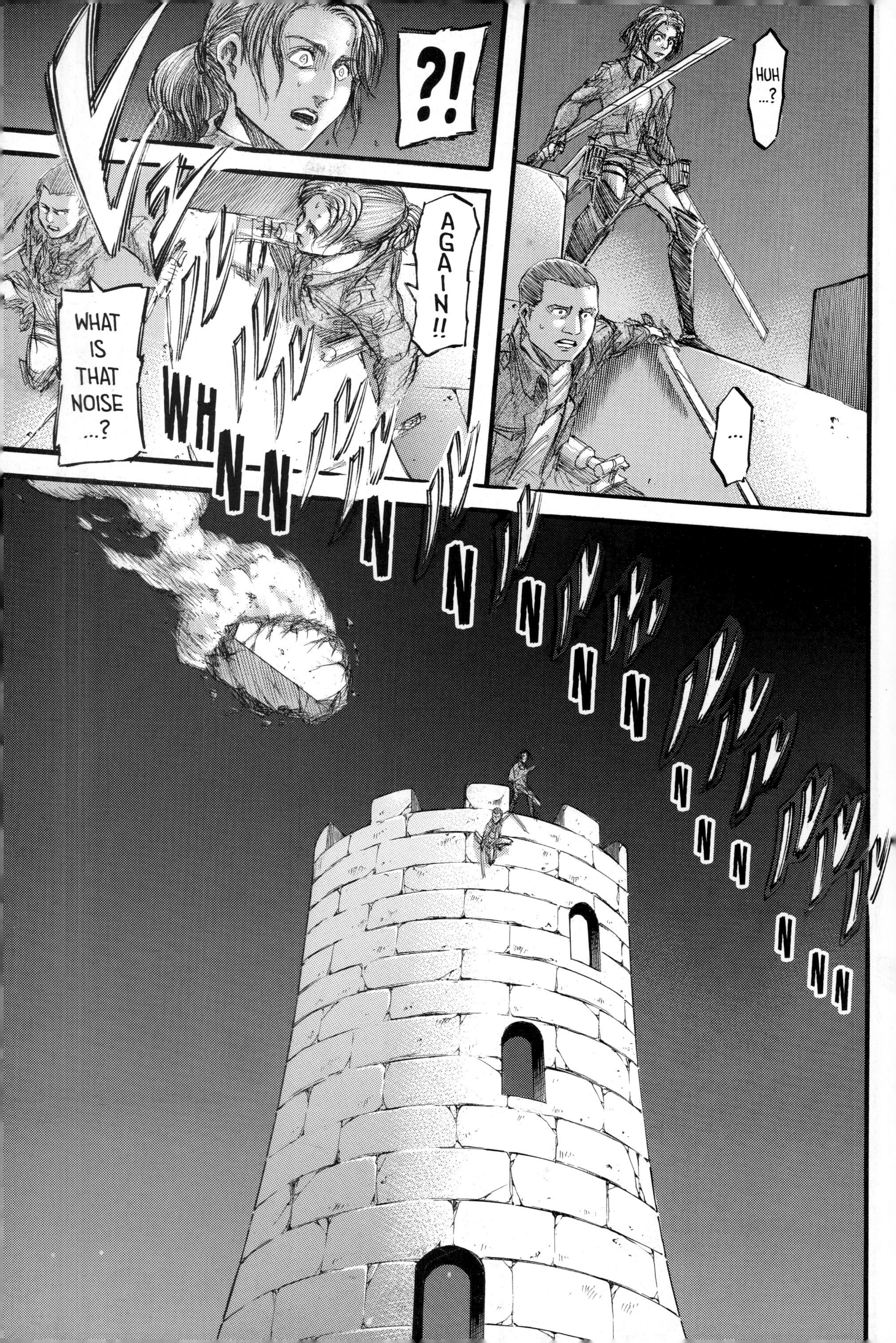
HUH ...?
...
?!
AGAIN!!
WHAT IS THAT NOISE ...?
WHN-N-NNNNNNNNNN

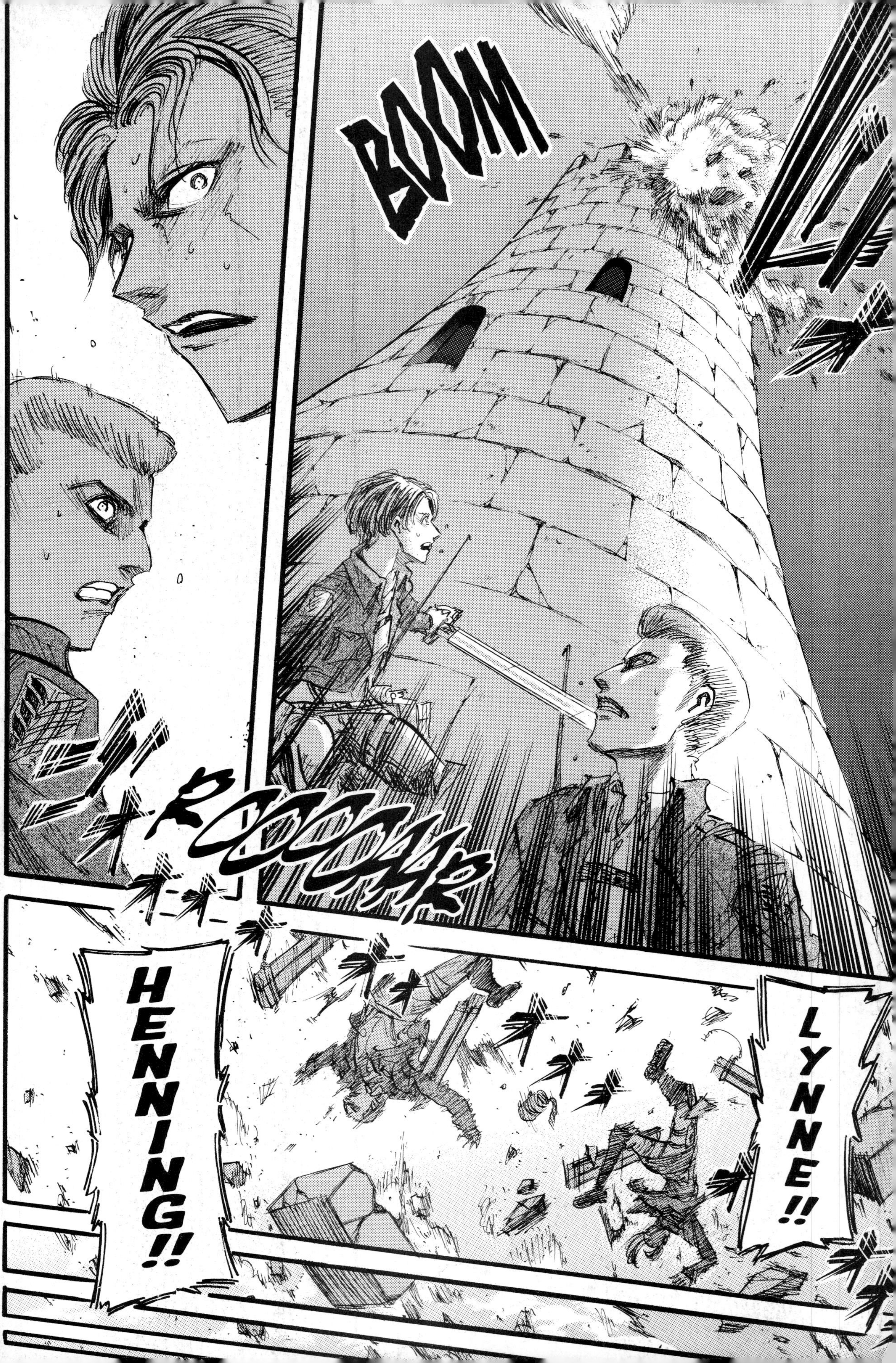
BOOM
ROOOAR
LYNNE!!
HENNING!!

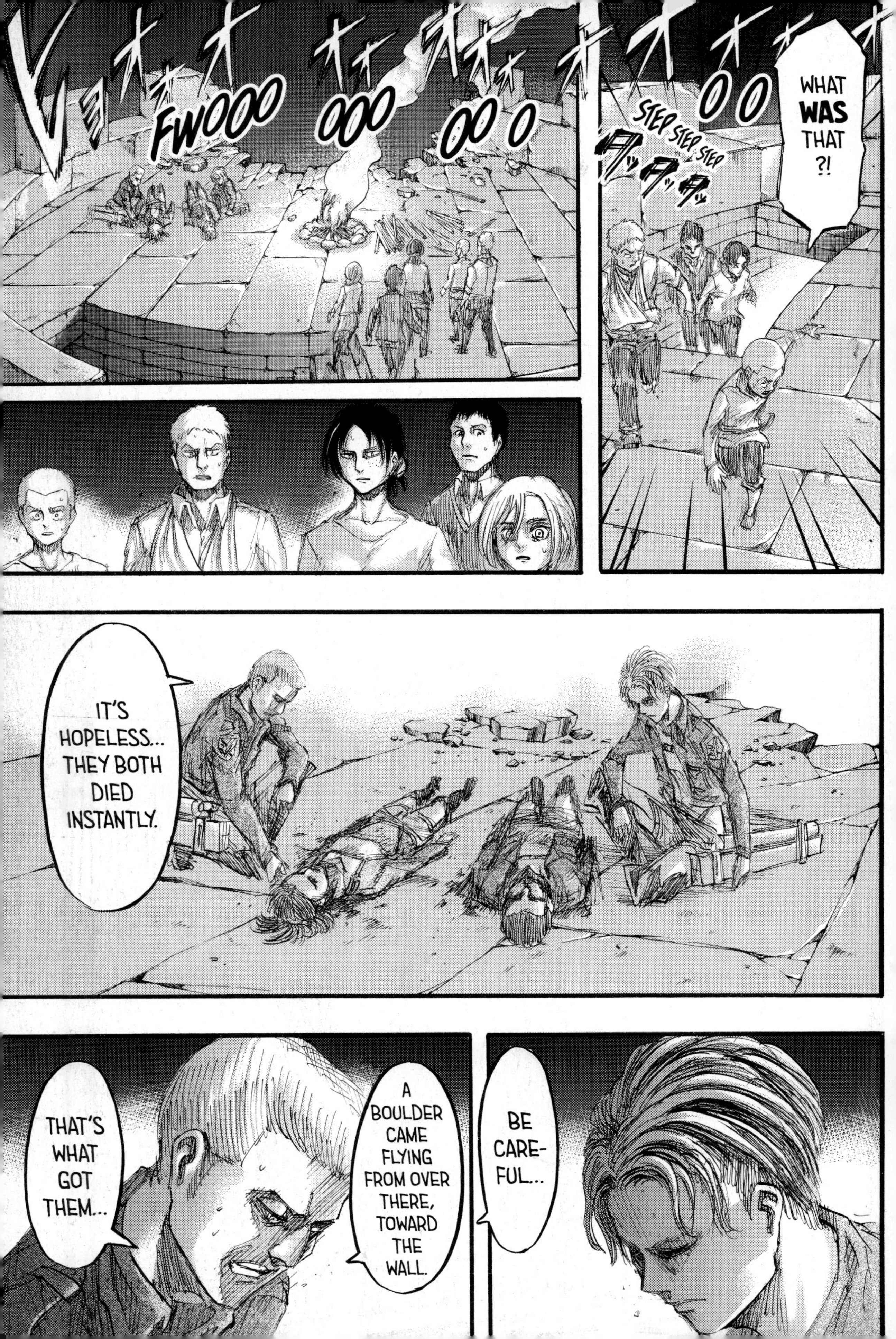
FWOOO OOO OO O OO
WHAT WAS THAT ?!
STEP STEP STEP
IT'S HOPELESS... THEY BOTH DIED INSTANTLY.
BE CARE-FUL...
A BOULDER CAME FLYING FROM OVER THERE, TOWARD THE WALL.
THAT'S WHAT GOT THEM...

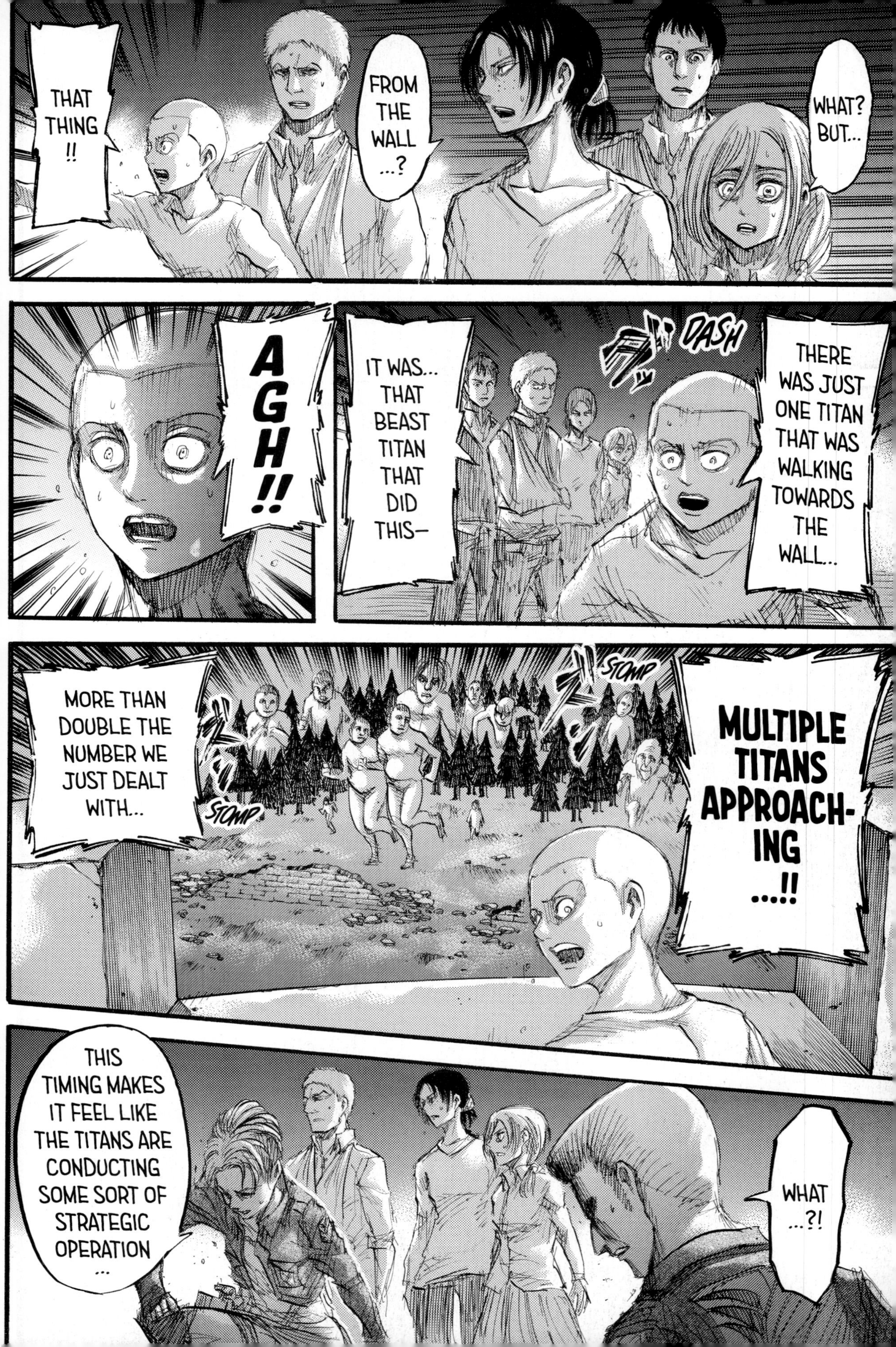
WHAT? BUT...
FROM THE WALL ...?
THAT THING !!
DASH
THERE WAS JUST ONE TITAN THAT WAS WALKING TOWARDS THE WALL...
IT WAS... THAT BEAST TITAN THAT DID THIS—
AGH!!
MULTIPLE TITANS APPROACHING ...!!
STOMP
STOMP
MORE THAN DOUBLE THE NUMBER WE JUST DEALT WITH...
WHAT ...?!
THIS TIMING MAKES IT FEEL LIKE THE TITANS ARE CONDUCTING SOME SORT OF STRATEGIC OPERATION ...

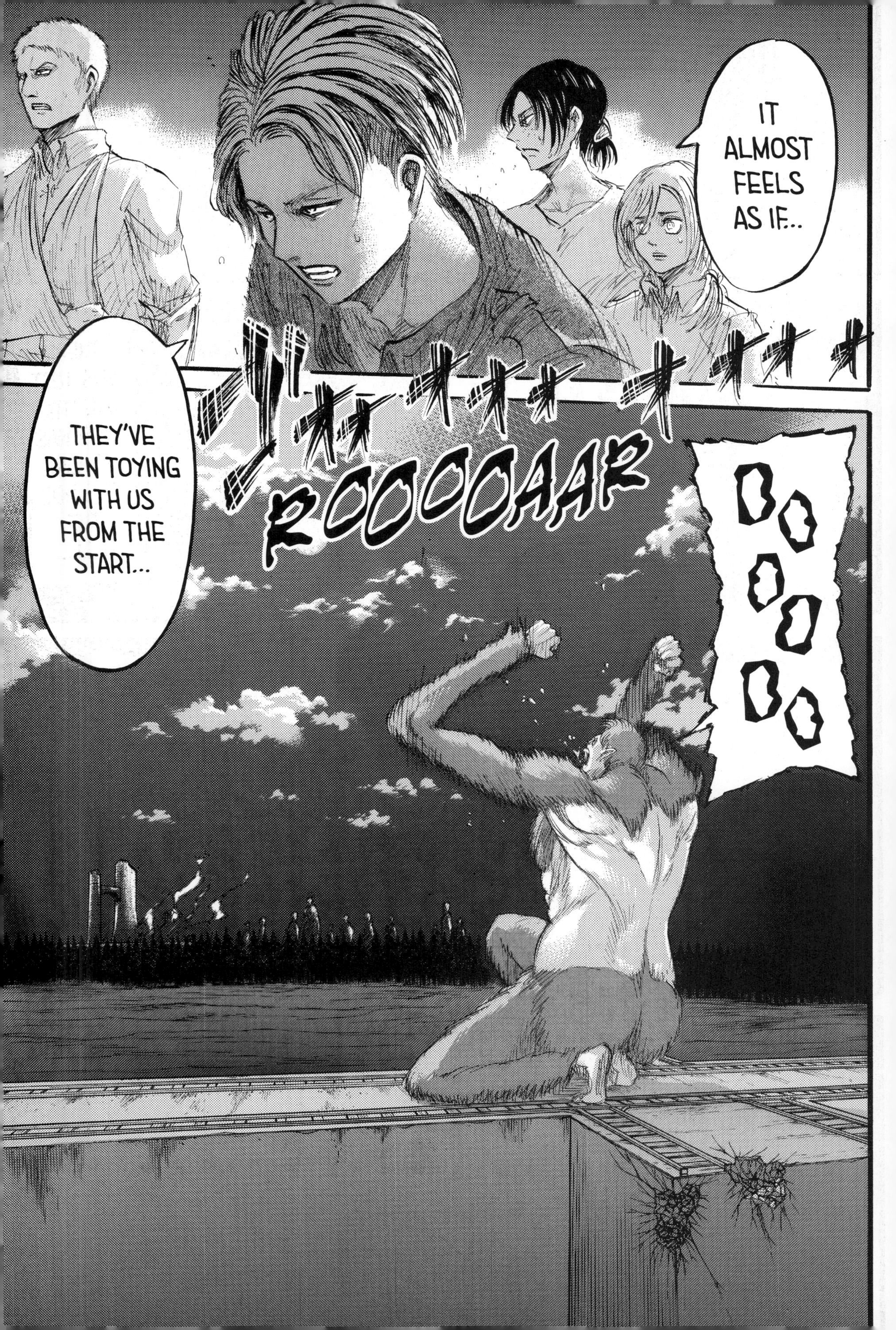
IT ALMOST FEELS AS IF...
THEY'VE BEEN TOYING WITH US FROM THE START...
ROOOOAAR
BOOOOOOO

HOOOOOOOWL

GRASP

GRASP

Episode 40:
Ymir

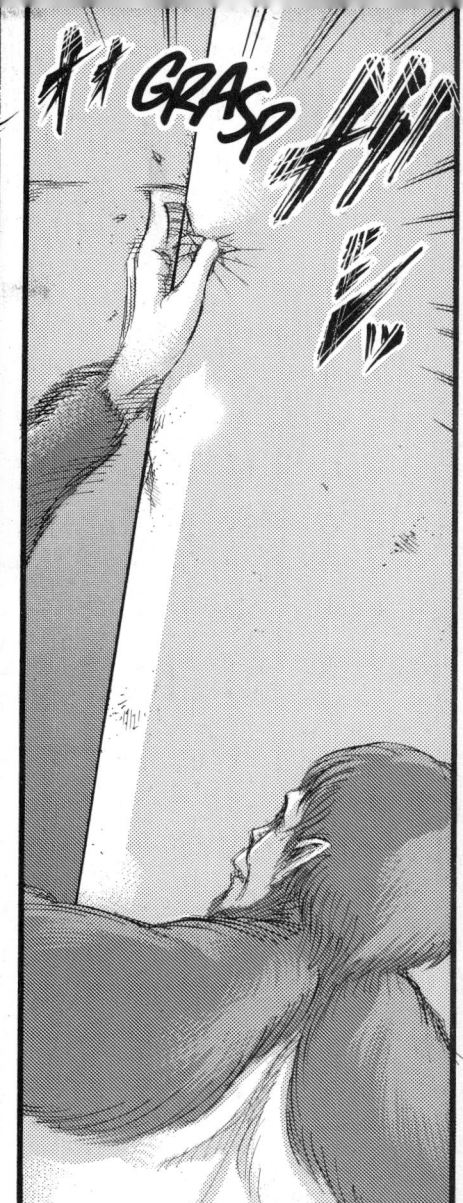

TWENTY
HOURS
AFTER
THE
TITANS
WERE
SPOTTED

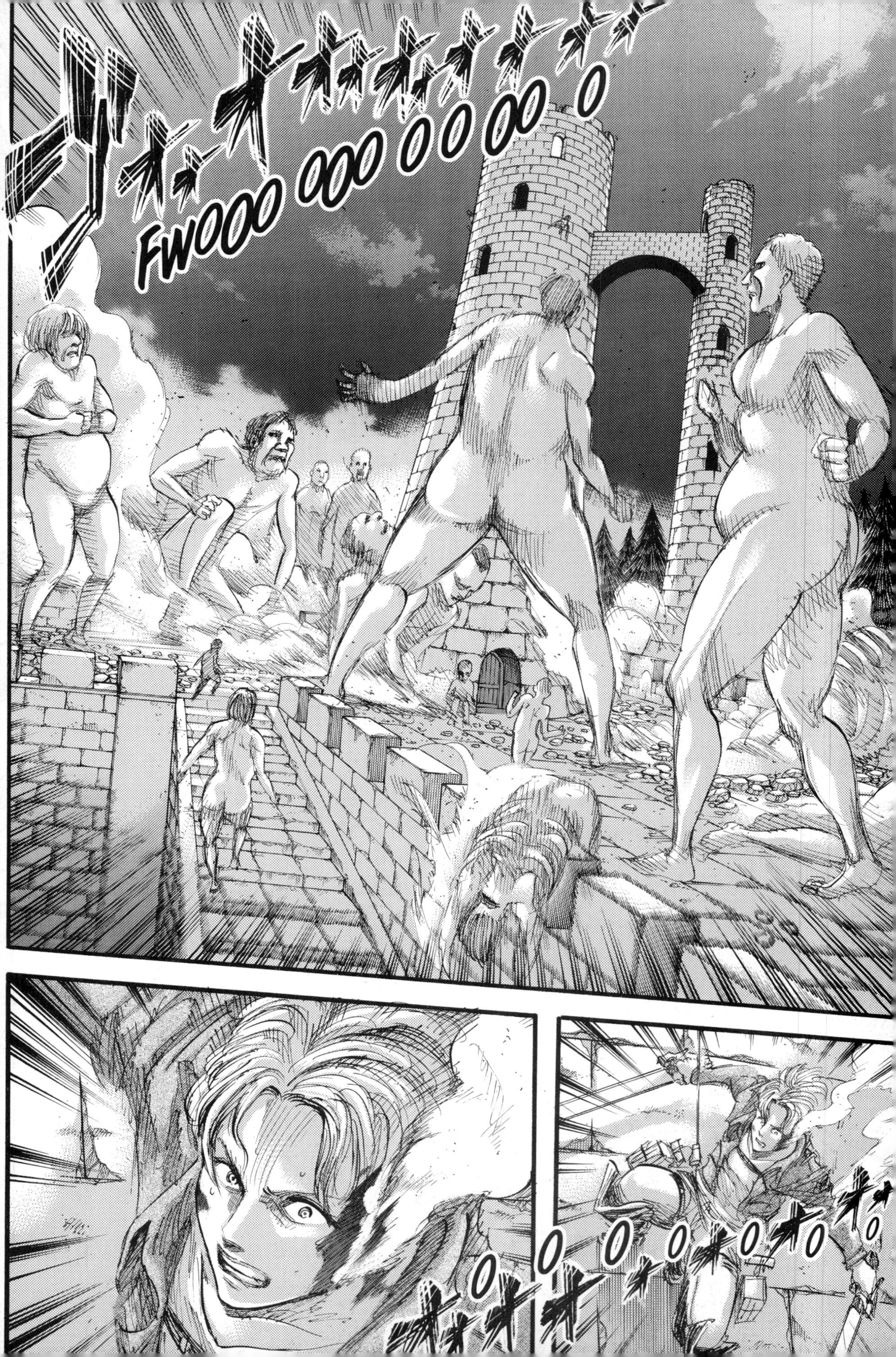
FWOOO OOO O O OO O
O O O O O O O

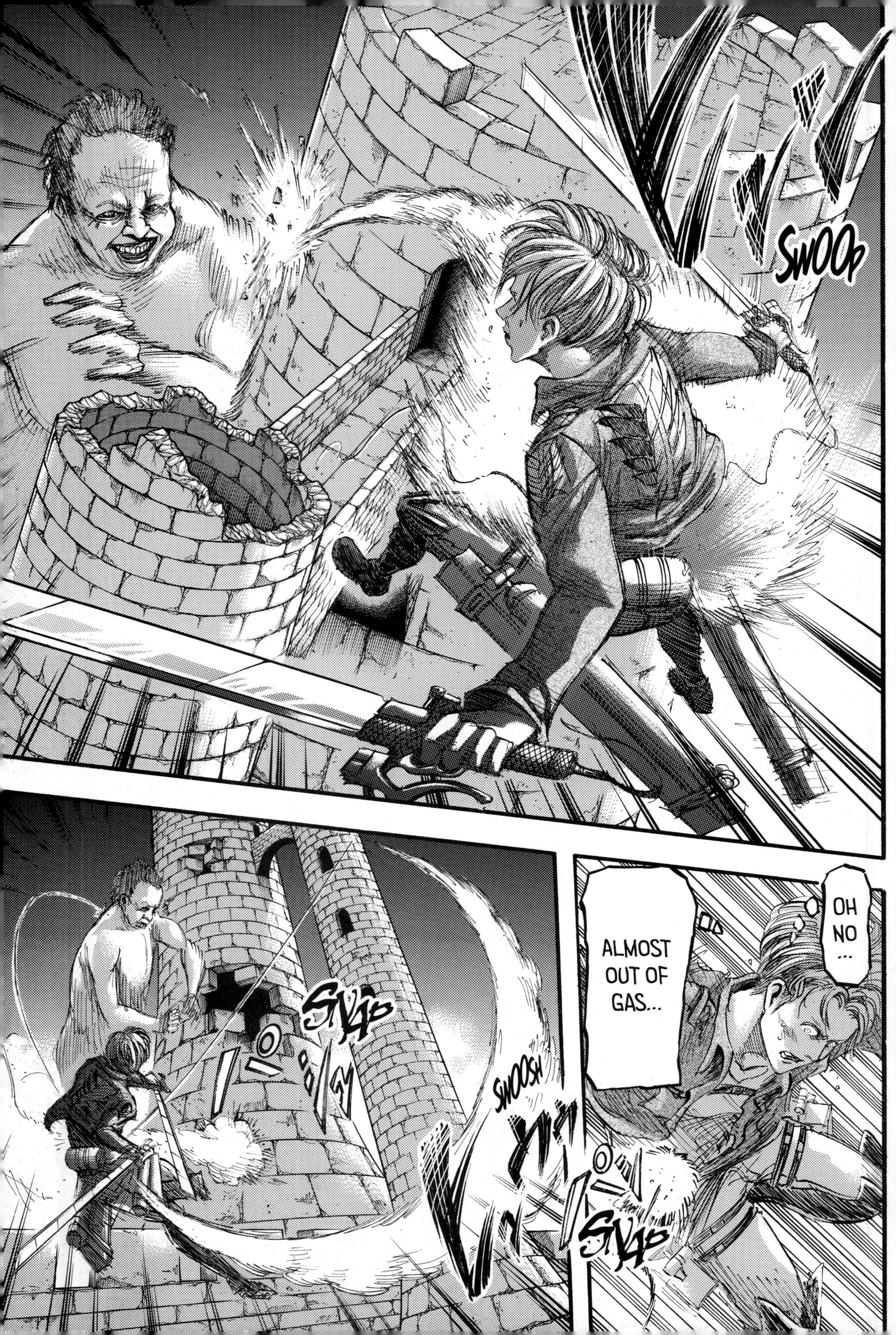
SWOOP
OH NO ...
ALMOST OUT OF GAS...
SWOOSH
SNAP
SNAP

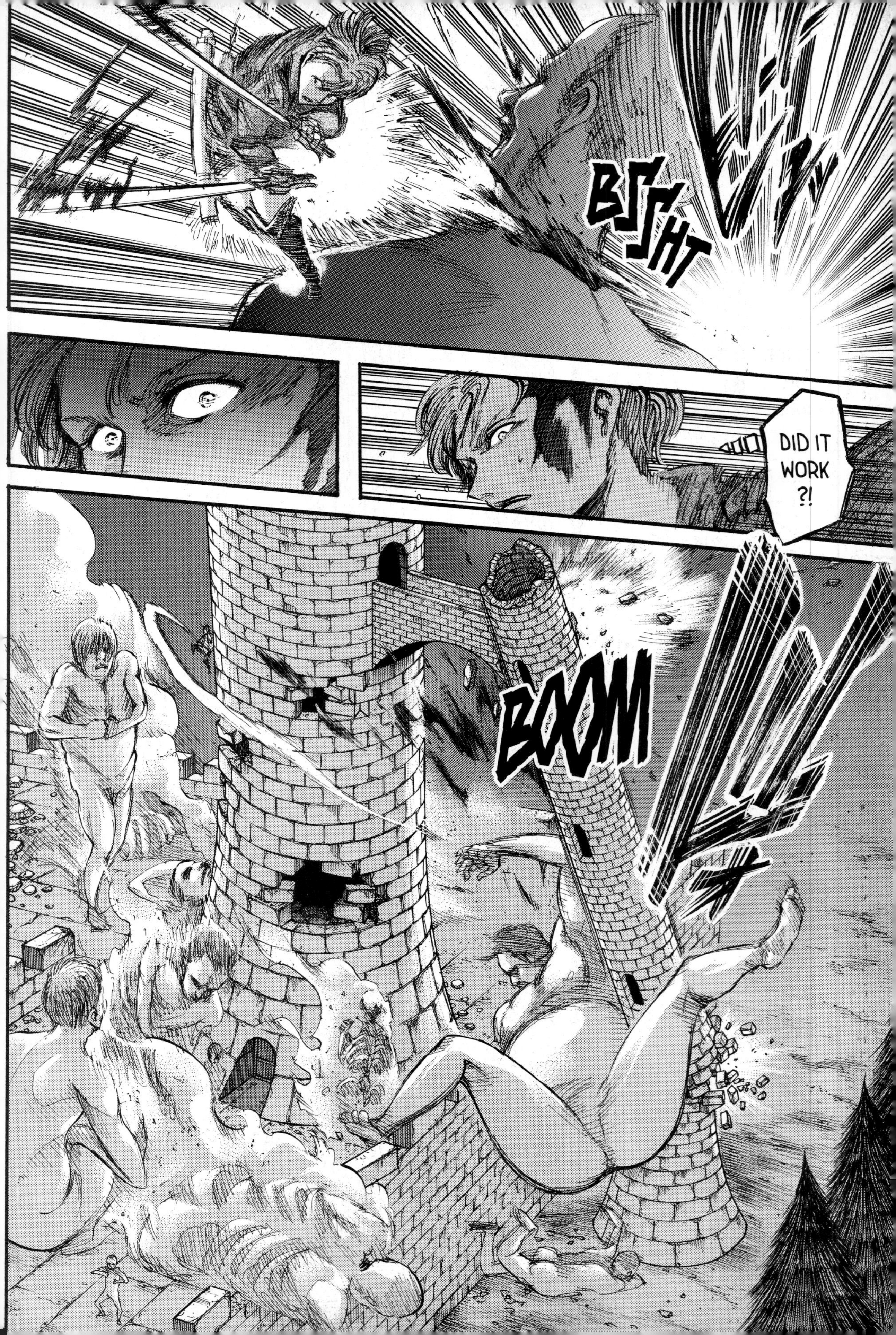
BSHT
DID IT WORK ?!
BOOM

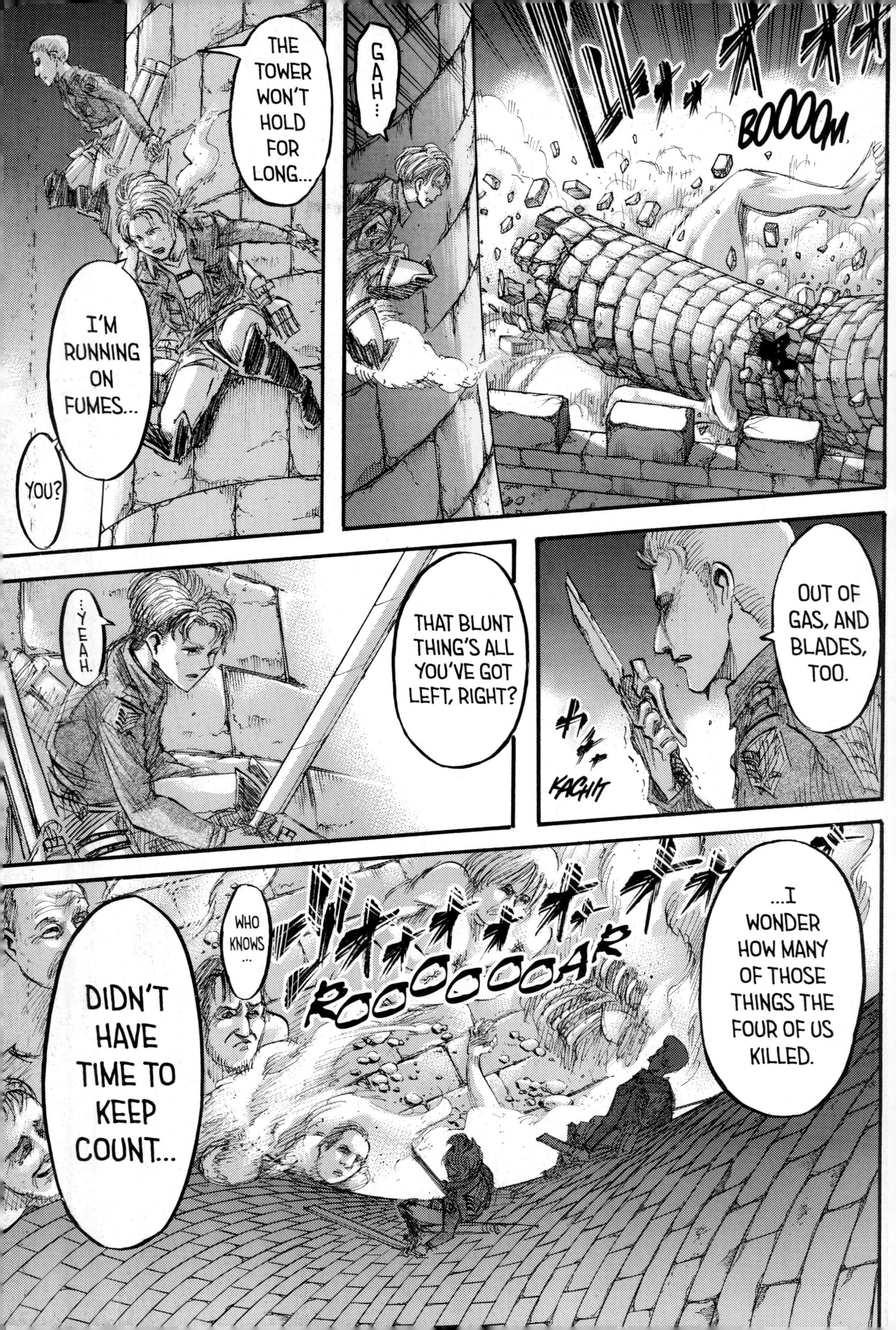
BOOOOM
GAH...
THE TOWER WON'T HOLD FOR LONG...
I'M RUNNING ON FUMES...
YOU?
OUT OF GAS, AND BLADES, TOO.
KACHIT
THAT BLUNT THING'S ALL YOU'VE GOT LEFT, RIGHT?
...YEAH.
...I WONDER HOW MANY OF THOSE THINGS THE FOUR OF US KILLED.
ROOOOOOAR
WHO KNOWS...
DIDN'T HAVE TIME TO KEEP COUNT...

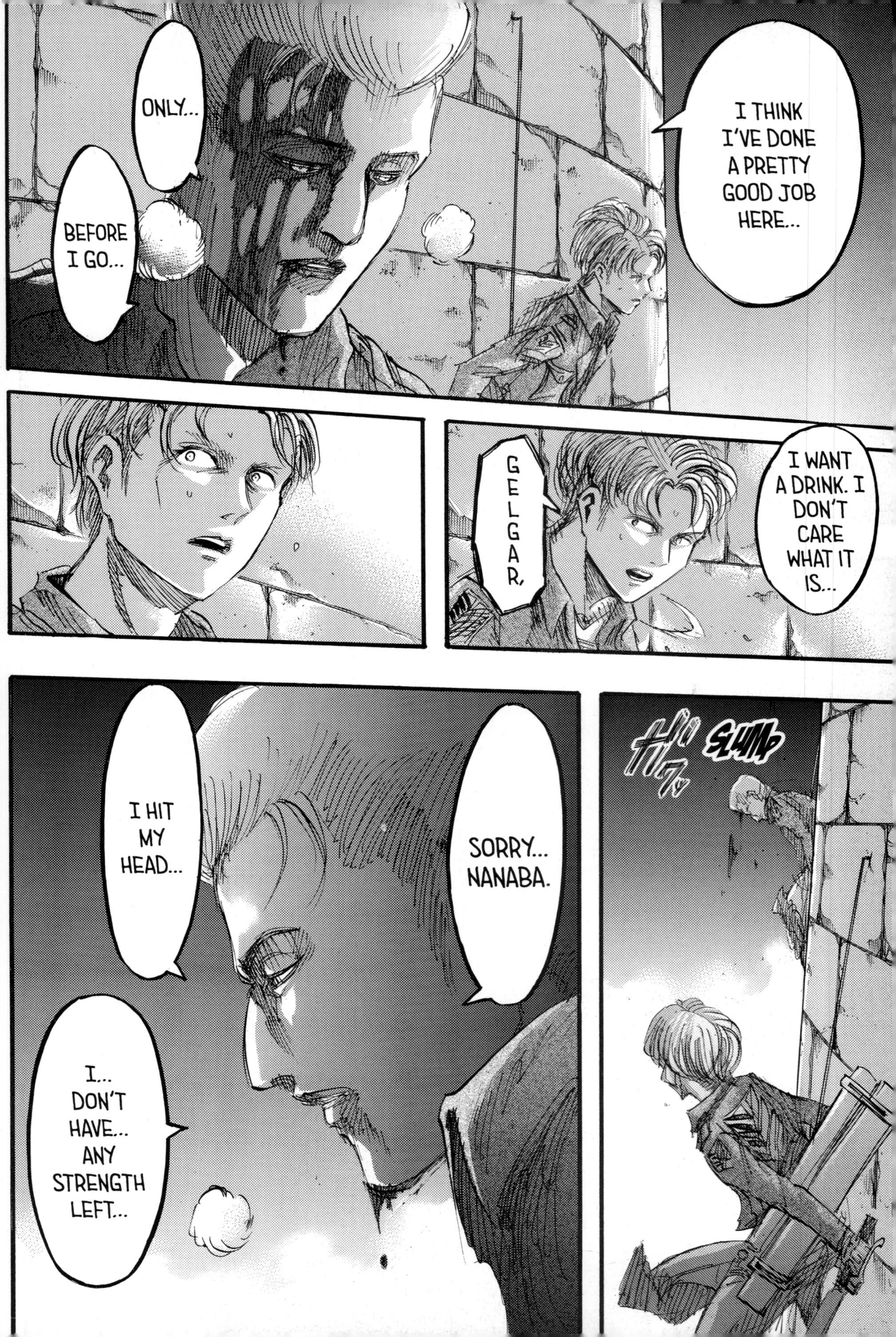
I THINK I'VE DONE A PRETTY GOOD JOB HERE...
ONLY...
BEFORE I GO...
I WANT A DRINK. I DON'T CARE WHAT IT IS...
GELGAR,
SLUMP
SORRY... NANABA.
I HIT MY HEAD...
I... DON'T HAVE... ANY STRENGTH LEFT...

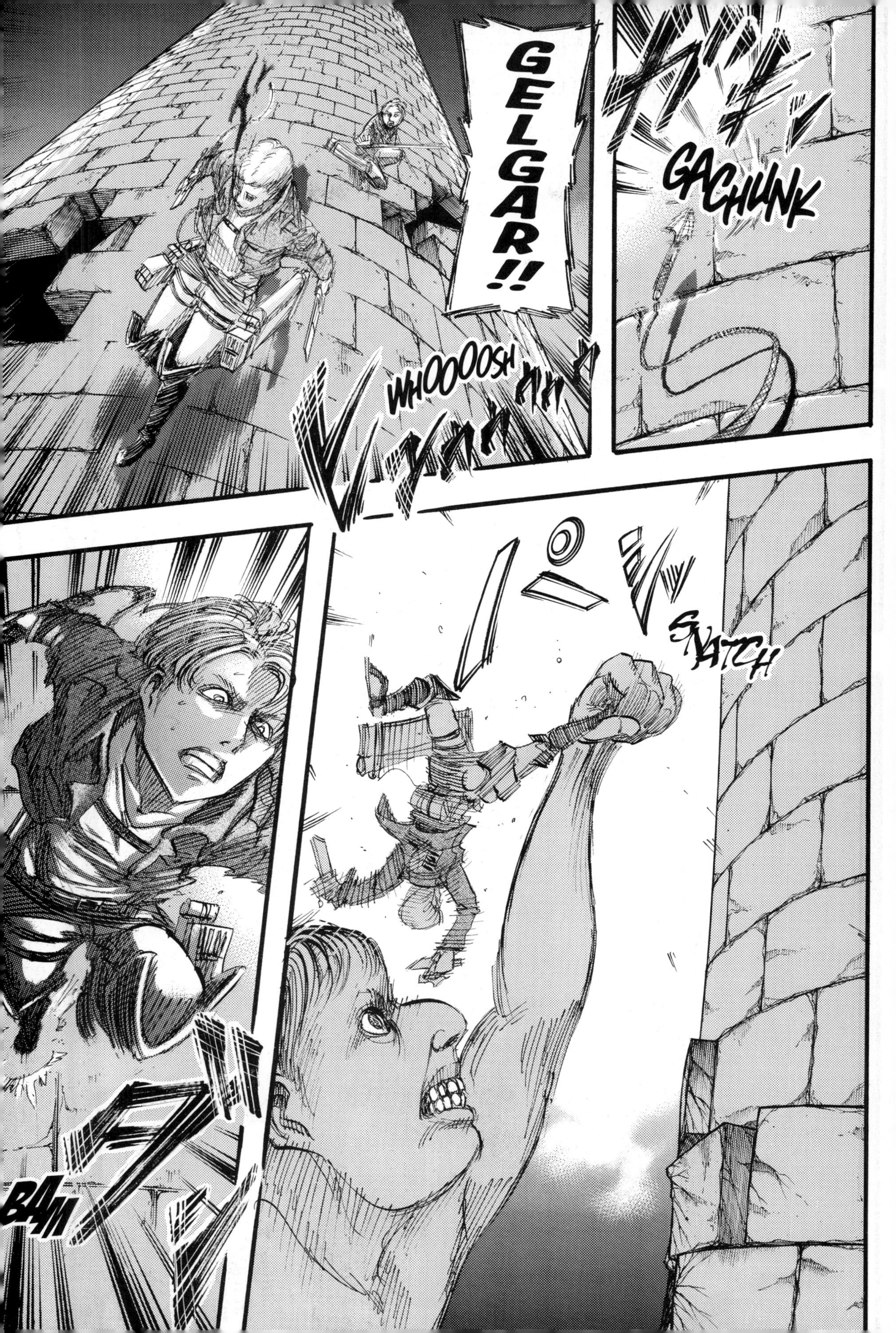
GACHUNK
GELGAR!!
WHOOOOSH
SNATCH
BAM

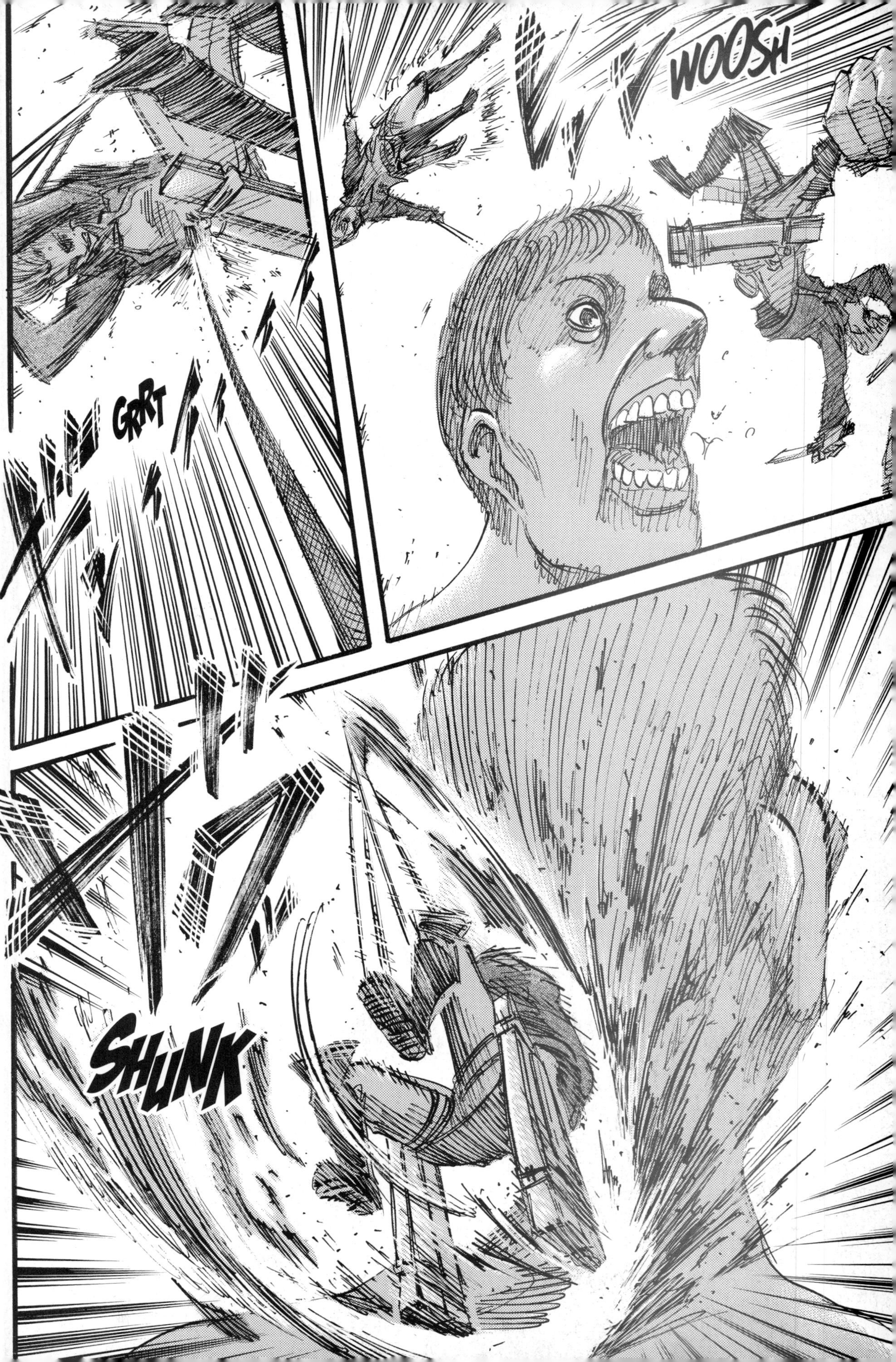
WOOSH
GRRT
SHUNK

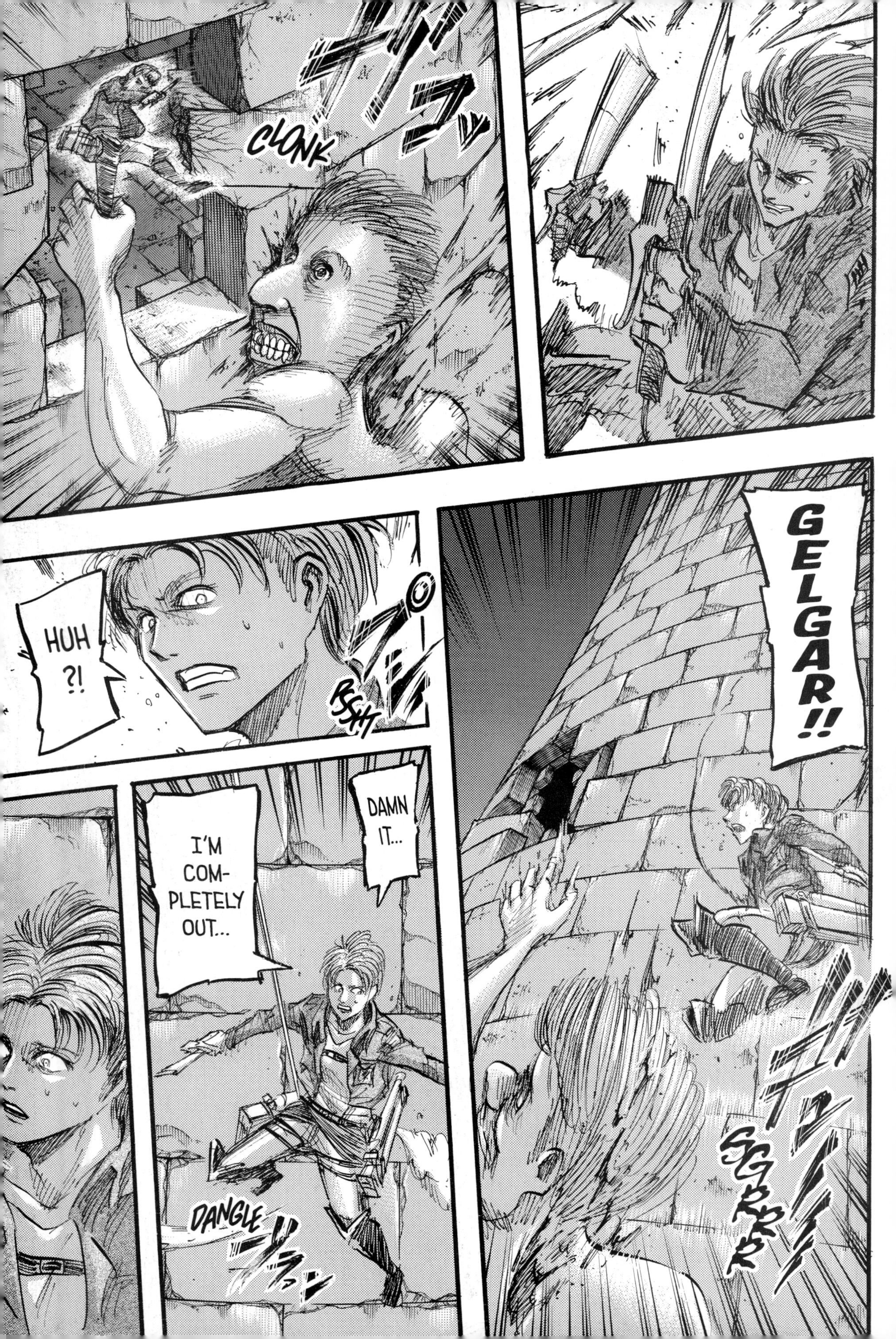
CLONK
GELGAR!!
SCRRRR
HUH ?!
RSSH
DAMN IT...
I'M COM-PLETELY OUT...
DANGLE

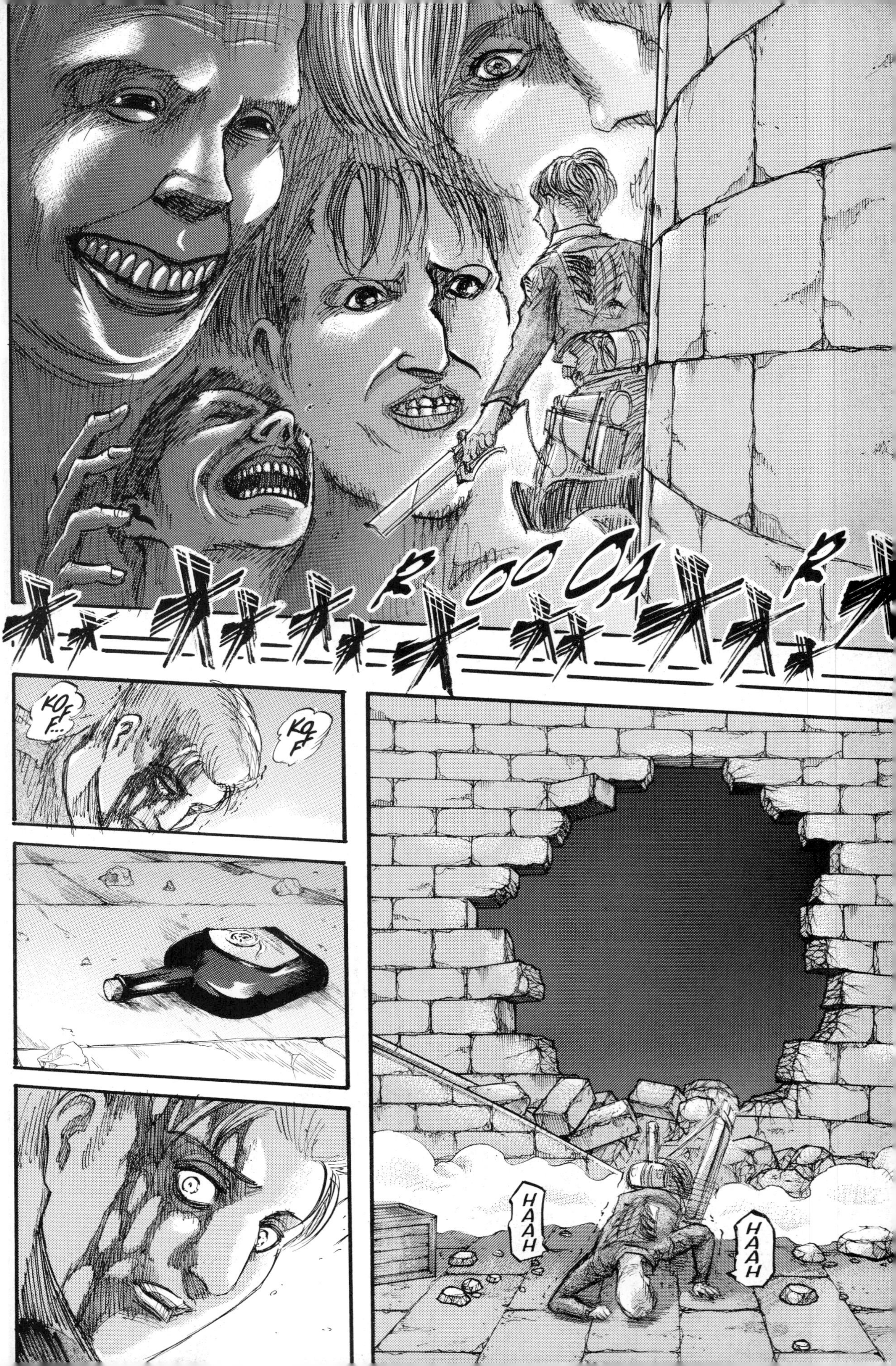
ROOOAR
HAAH
HAAH
KOF
F...
KOF
F

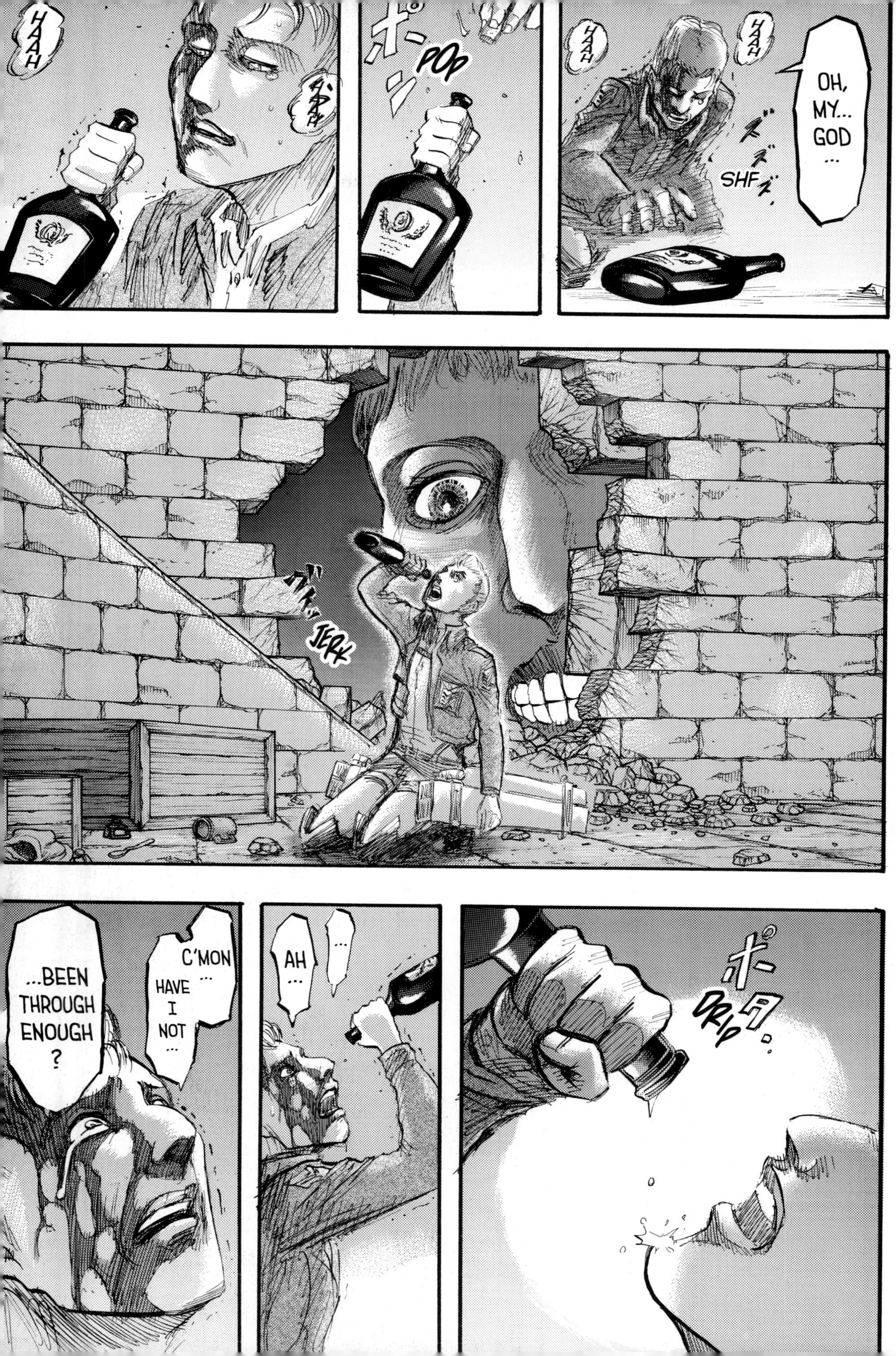
OH, MY... GOD ...
HAAH
HAAH
SHF
POP
HAAH
JERK
DRIP
...
AH ...
C'MON ... HAVE I NOT ...
...BEEN THROUGH ENOUGH ?

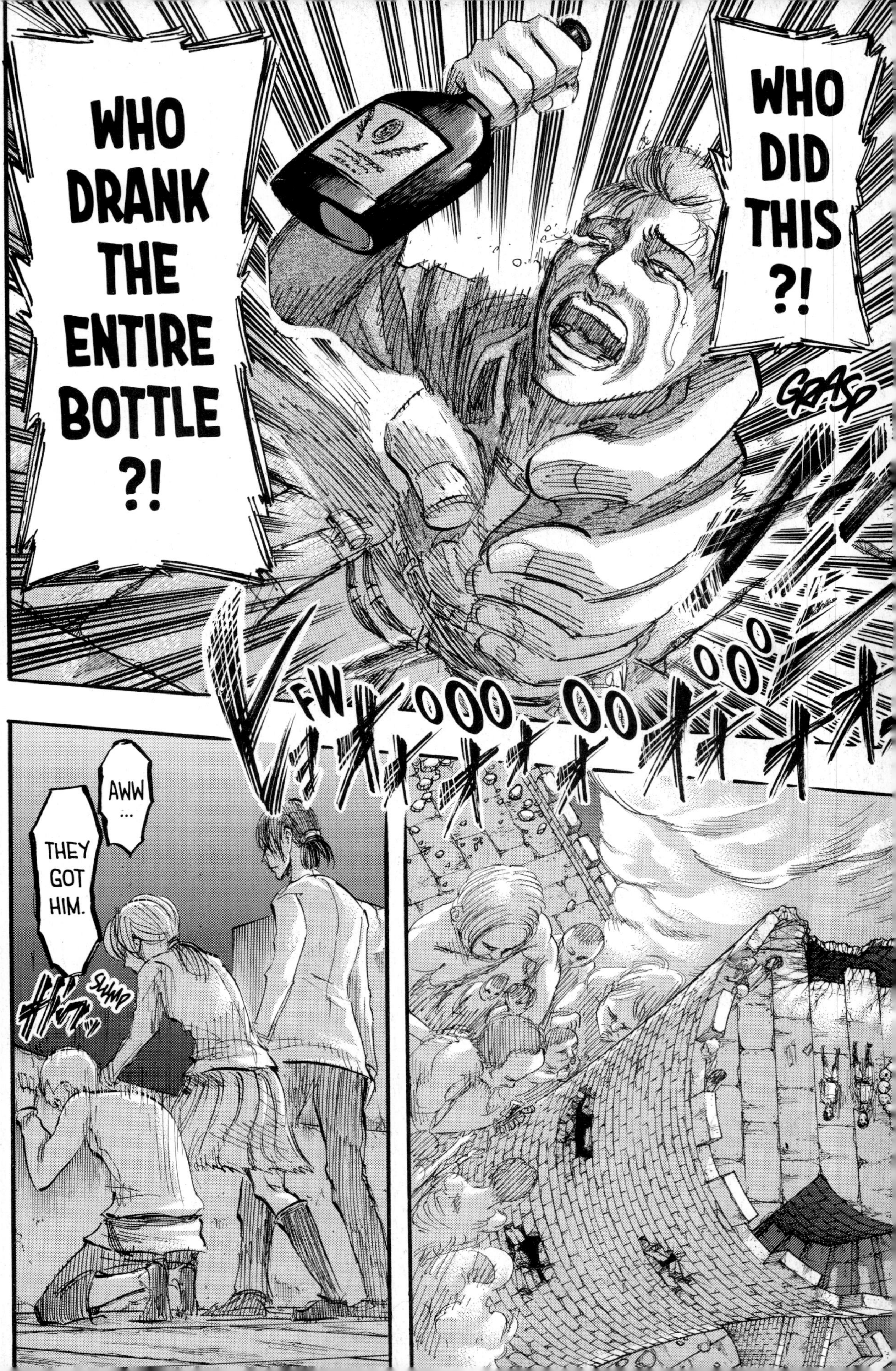
WHO DID THIS ?!
WHO DRANK THE ENTIRE BOTTLE ?!
GRASP
FWOOO-OO-OOO
AWW ...
THEY GOT HIM.
SLUMP

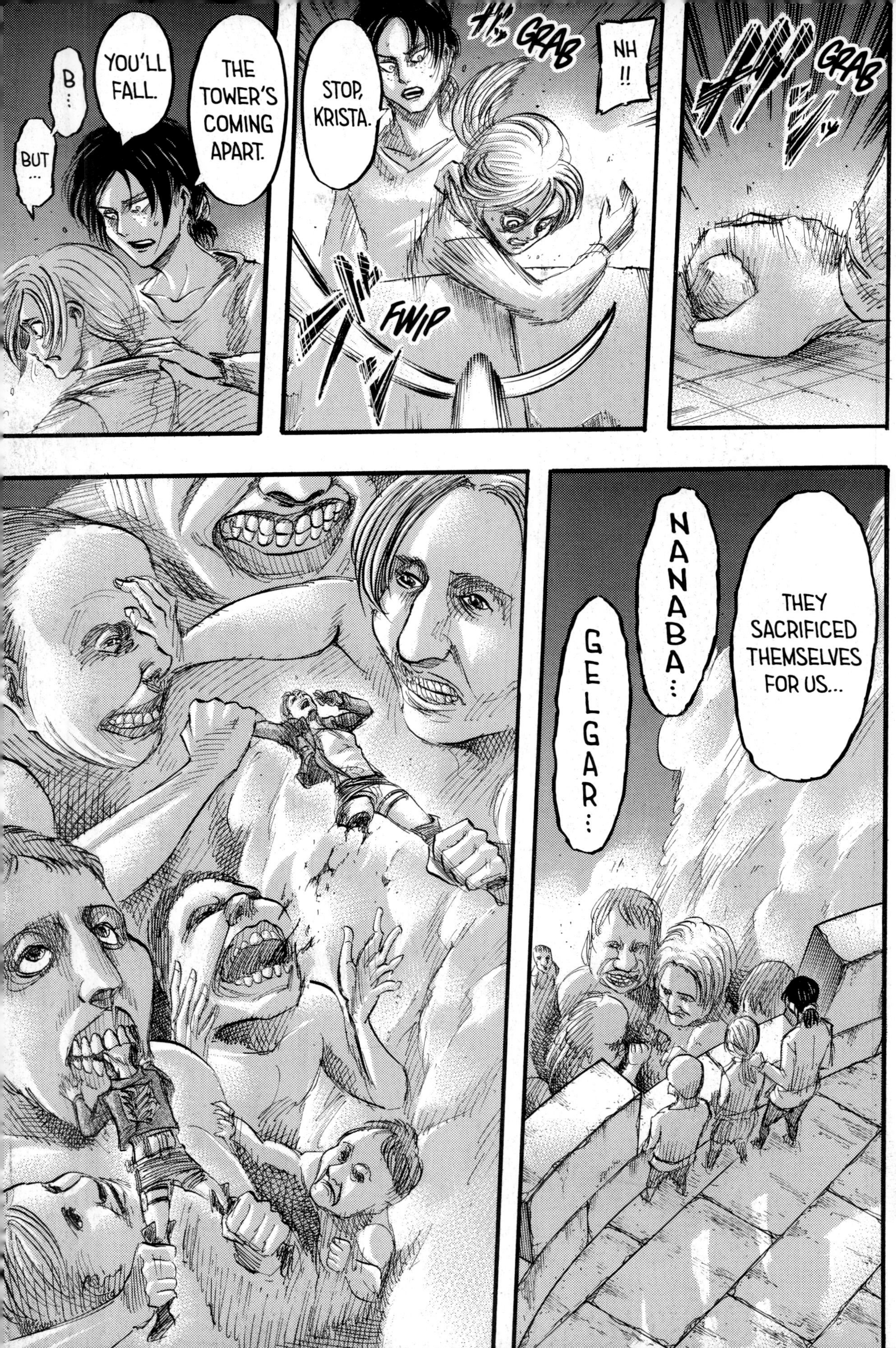

B... BUT...

YOU'LL FALL.

THE TOWER'S COMING APART.

STOP, KRISTA.

NH!!

GRAB

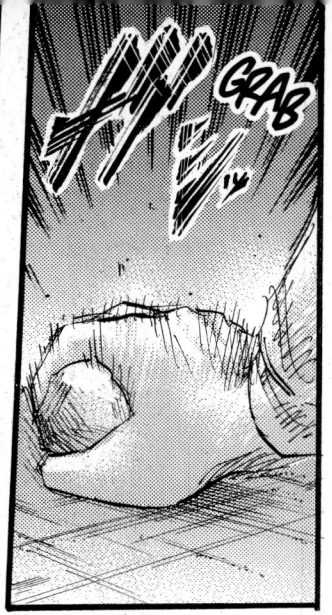

GRAB

GELGAR...

NANABA...

THEY SACRIFICED THEMSELVES FOR US...

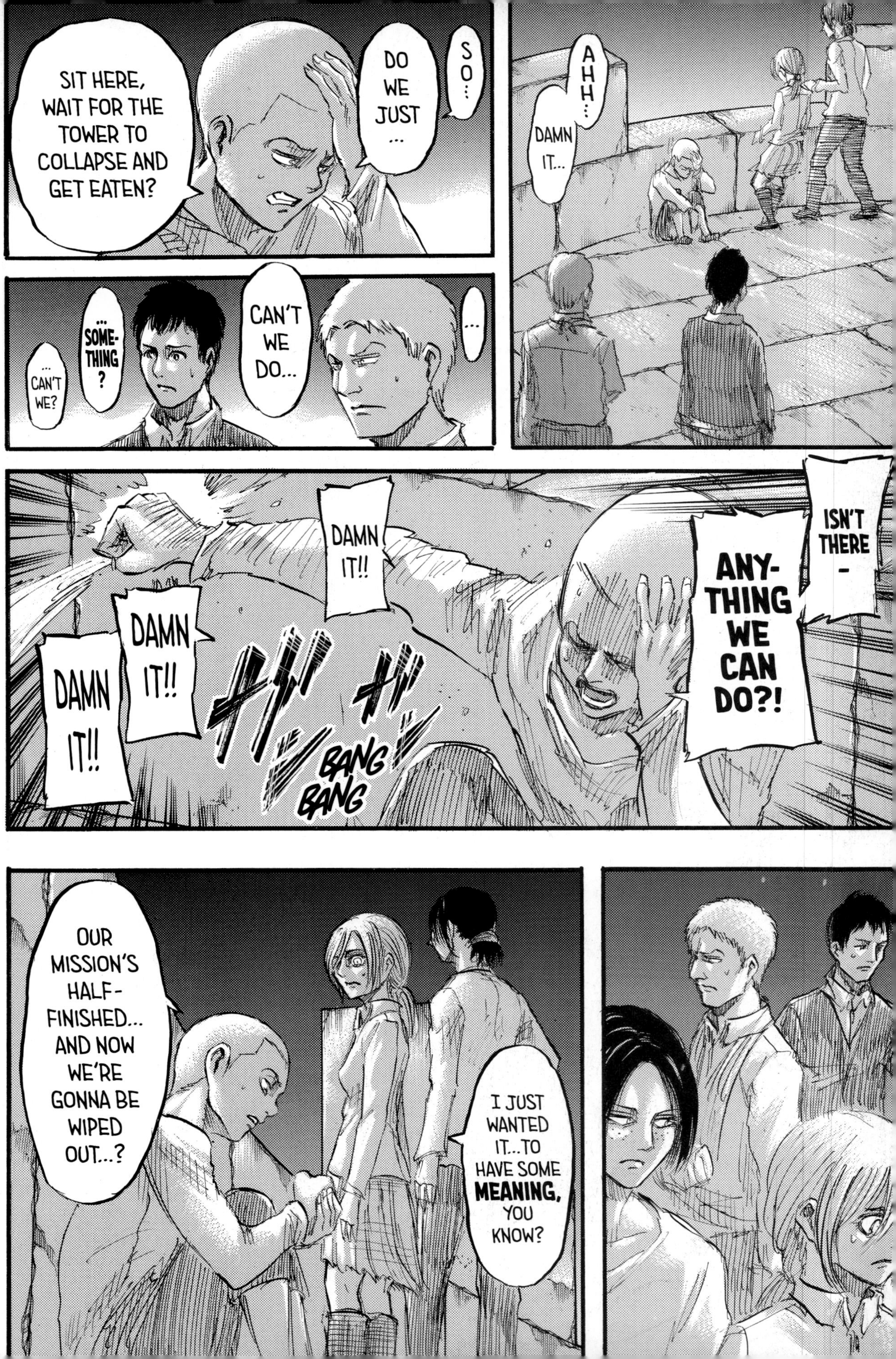
AHH...
DAMN IT...
SO...
DO WE JUST ...
SIT HERE, WAIT FOR THE TOWER TO COLLAPSE AND GET EATEN?
...
CAN'T WE DO...
...SOME-THING?
...CAN'T WE?
ISN'T THERE -
ANY-THING WE CAN DO?!
DAMN IT!!
DAMN IT!!
DAMN IT!!
BANG BANG
OUR MISSION'S HALF-FINISHED... AND NOW WE'RE GONNA BE WIPED OUT...?
I JUST WANTED IT...TO HAVE SOME MEANING, YOU KNOW?

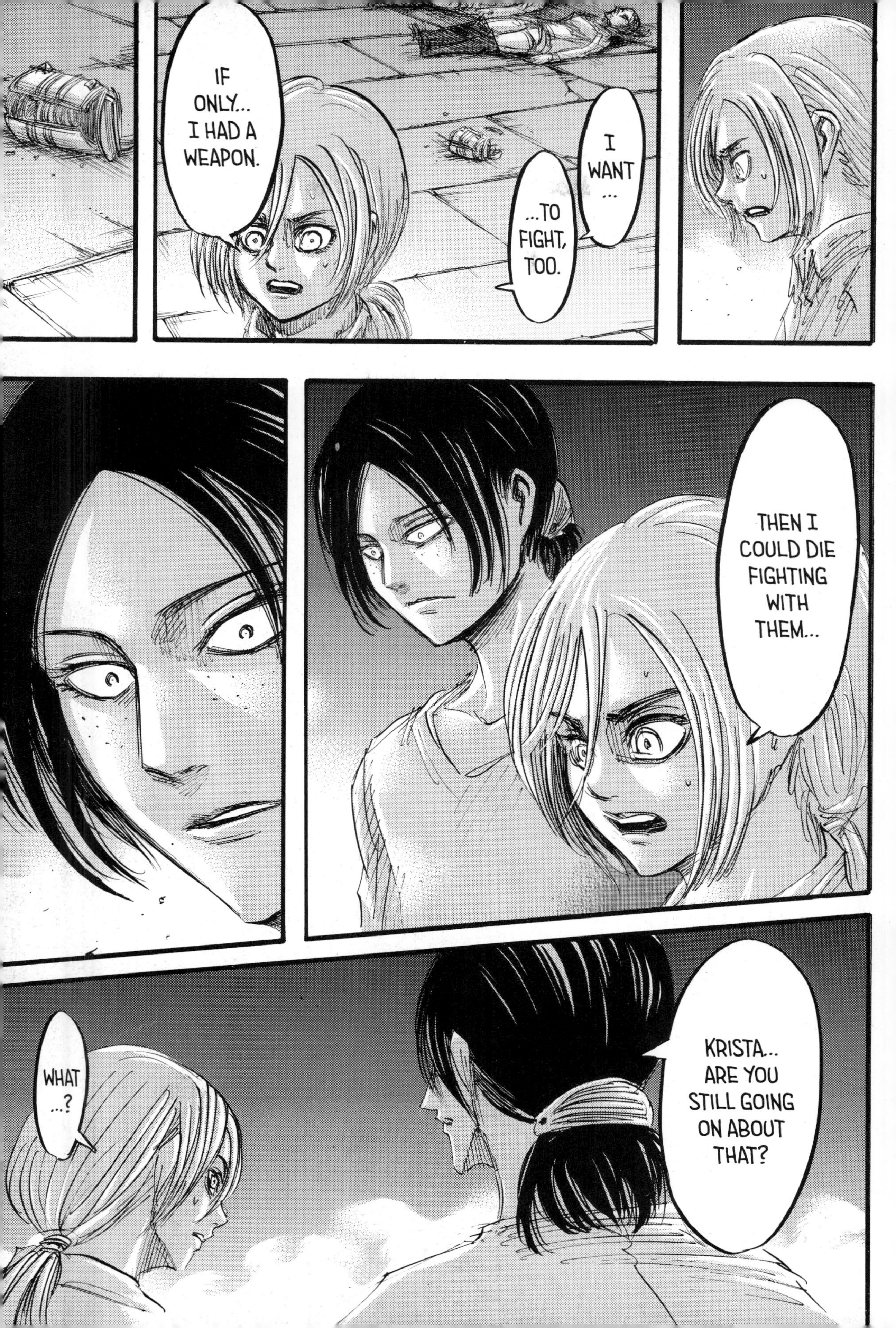
I WANT ...
...TO FIGHT, TOO.
IF ONLY... I HAD A WEAPON.
THEN I COULD DIE FIGHTING WITH THEM...
KRISTA... ARE YOU STILL GOING ON ABOUT THAT?
WHAT ...?

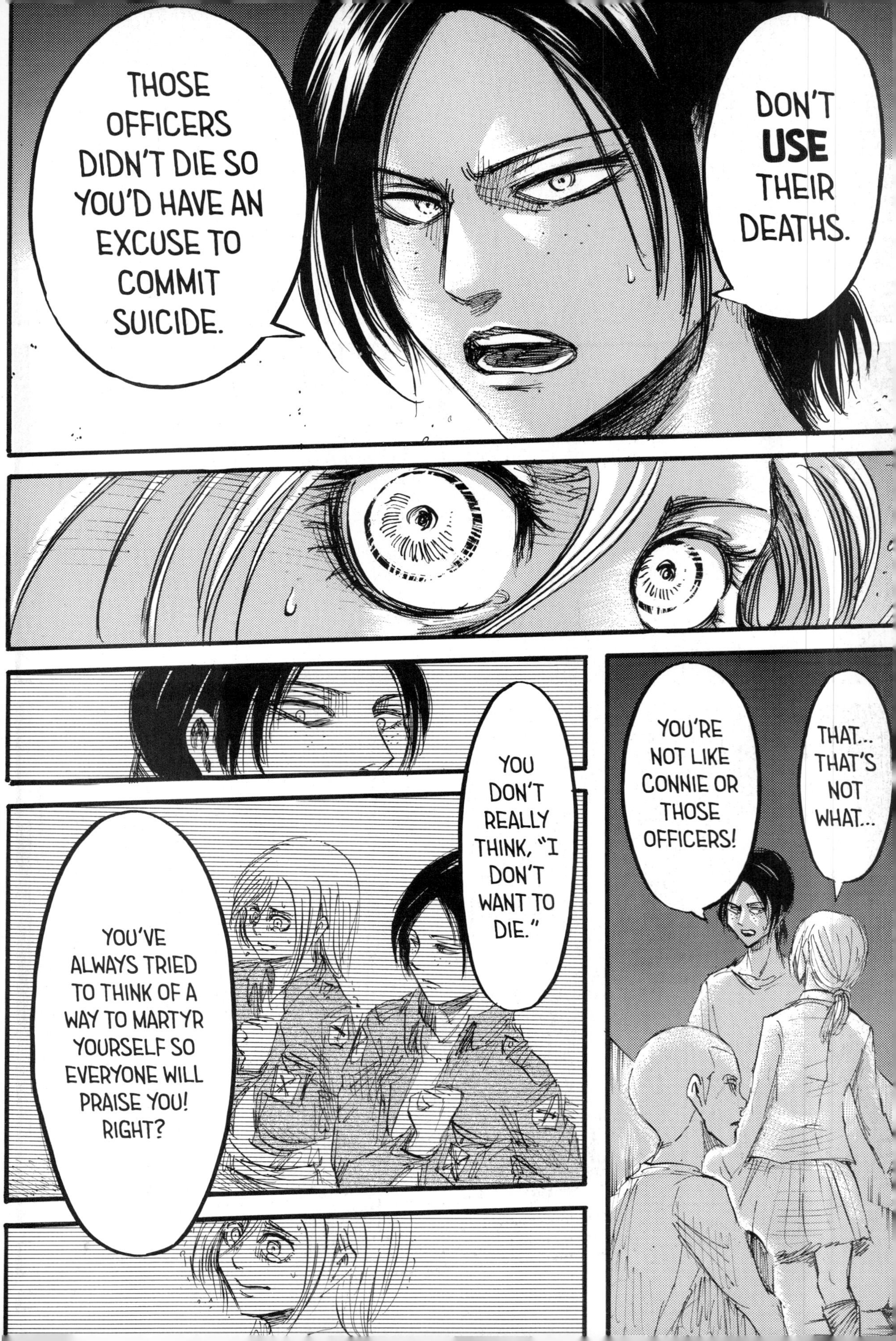
DON'T USE THEIR DEATHS.
THOSE OFFICERS DIDN'T DIE SO YOU'D HAVE AN EXCUSE TO COMMIT SUICIDE.
THAT... THAT'S NOT WHAT...
YOU'RE NOT LIKE CONNIE OR THOSE OFFICERS!
YOU DON'T REALLY THINK, "I DON'T WANT TO DIE."
YOU'VE ALWAYS TRIED TO THINK OF A WAY TO MARTYR YOURSELF SO EVERYONE WILL PRAISE YOU! RIGHT?

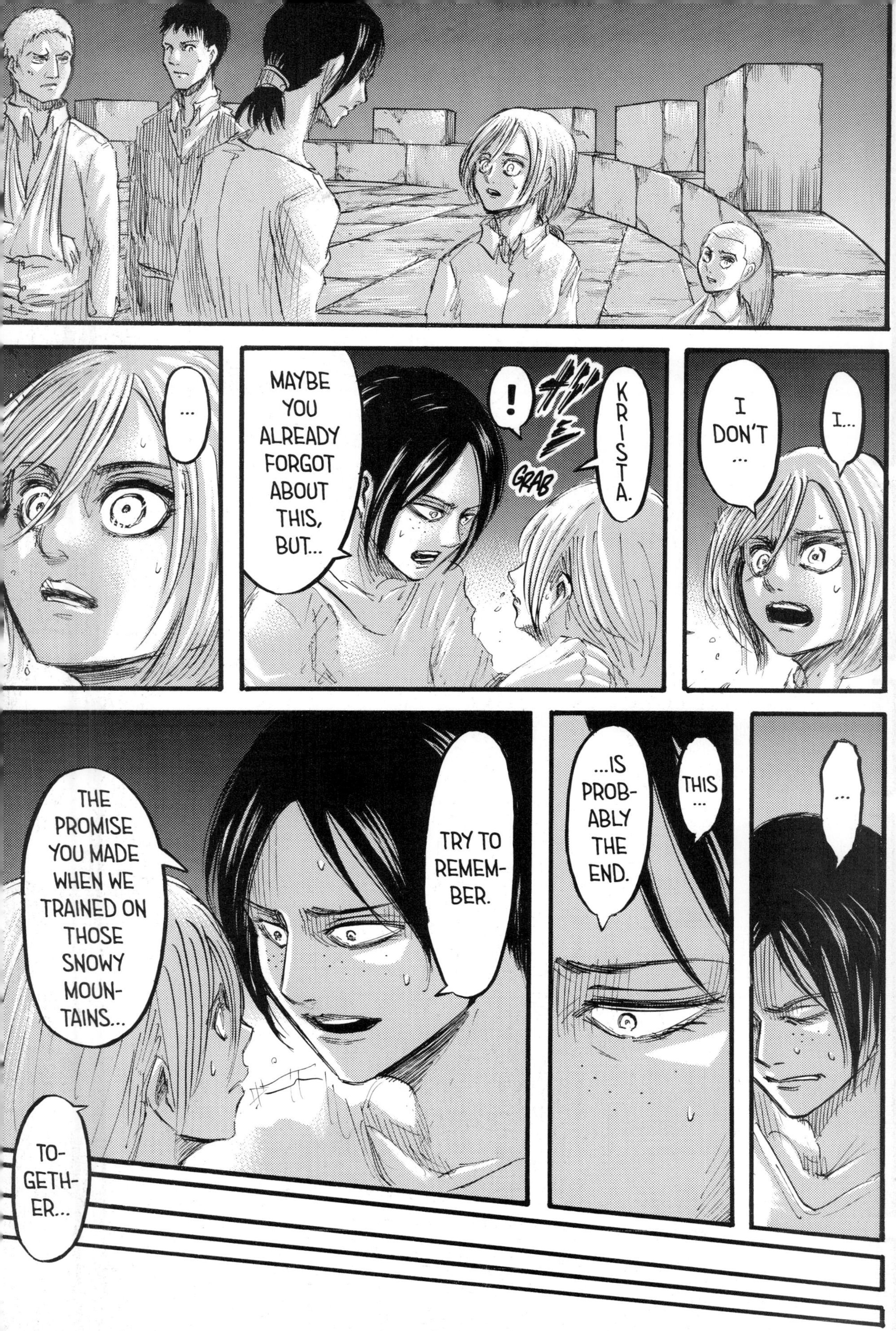
I...
I DON'T ...
KRISTA.
GRAB
!
MAYBE YOU ALREADY FORGOT ABOUT THIS, BUT...
...
...
THIS ...
...IS PROBABLY THE END.
TRY TO REMEMBER.
THE PROMISE YOU MADE WHEN WE TRAINED ON THOSE SNOWY MOUNTAINS...
TOGETHER...

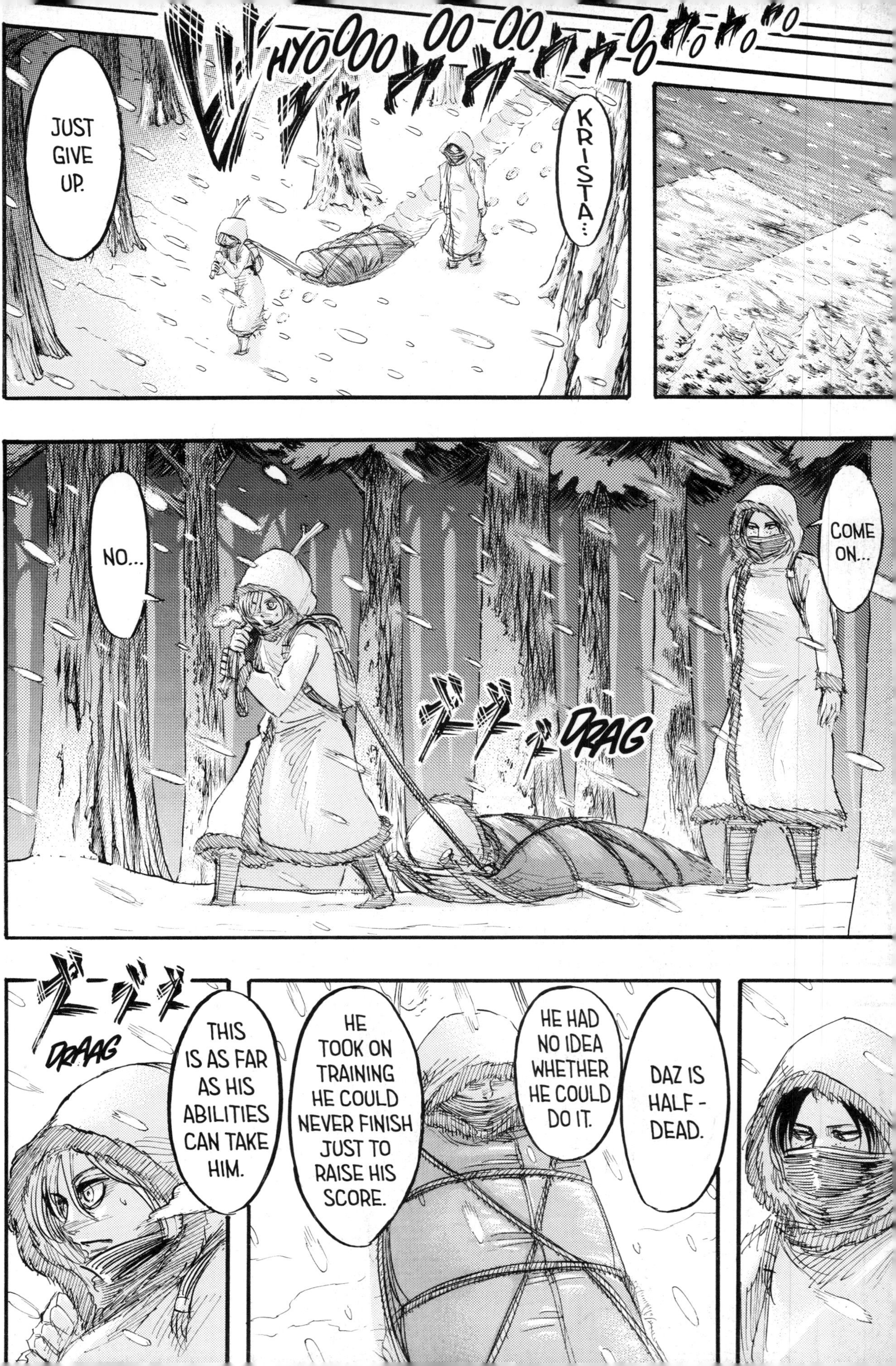
WHYOOOO OO OO
KRISTA...
JUST GIVE UP.
COME ON...
DRAG
NO...
DAZ IS HALF-DEAD.
HE HAD NO IDEA WHETHER HE COULD DO IT.
HE TOOK ON TRAINING HE COULD NEVER FINISH JUST TO RAISE HIS SCORE.
THIS IS AS FAR AS HIS ABILITIES CAN TAKE HIM.
DRAAG

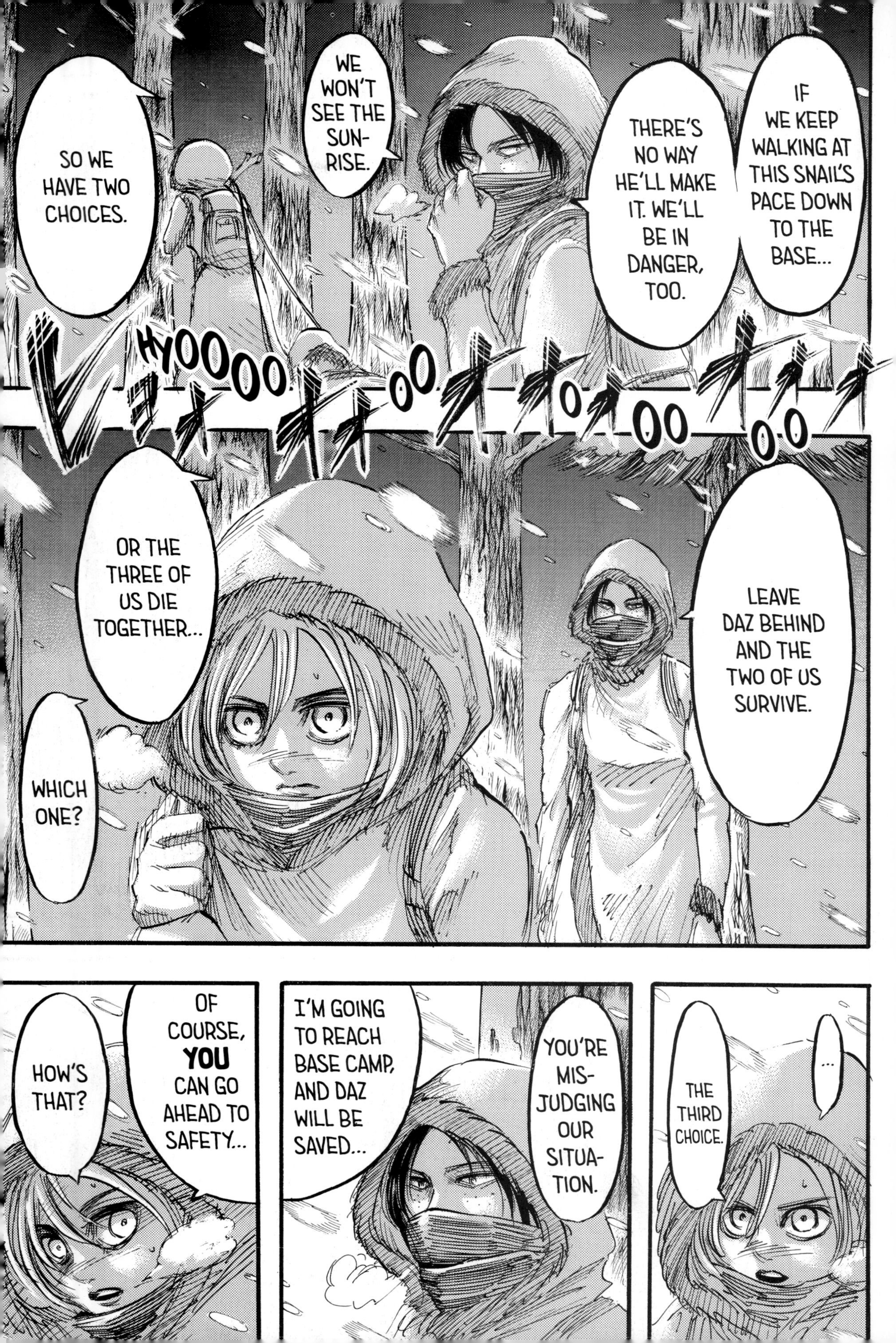

IF WE KEEP WALKING AT THIS SNAIL'S PACE DOWN TO THE BASE...
THERE'S NO WAY HE'LL MAKE IT. WE'LL BE IN DANGER, TOO.
WE WON'T SEE THE SUN-RISE.
SO WE HAVE TWO CHOICES.
HYOOOOOOOOOOOOO
LEAVE DAZ BEHIND AND THE TWO OF US SURVIVE.
OR THE THREE OF US DIE TOGETHER...
WHICH ONE?
...
THE THIRD CHOICE.
YOU'RE MIS-JUDGING OUR SITUA-TION.
I'M GOING TO REACH BASE CAMP, AND DAZ WILL BE SAVED...
OF COURSE, **YOU** CAN GO AHEAD TO SAFETY...
HOW'S THAT?

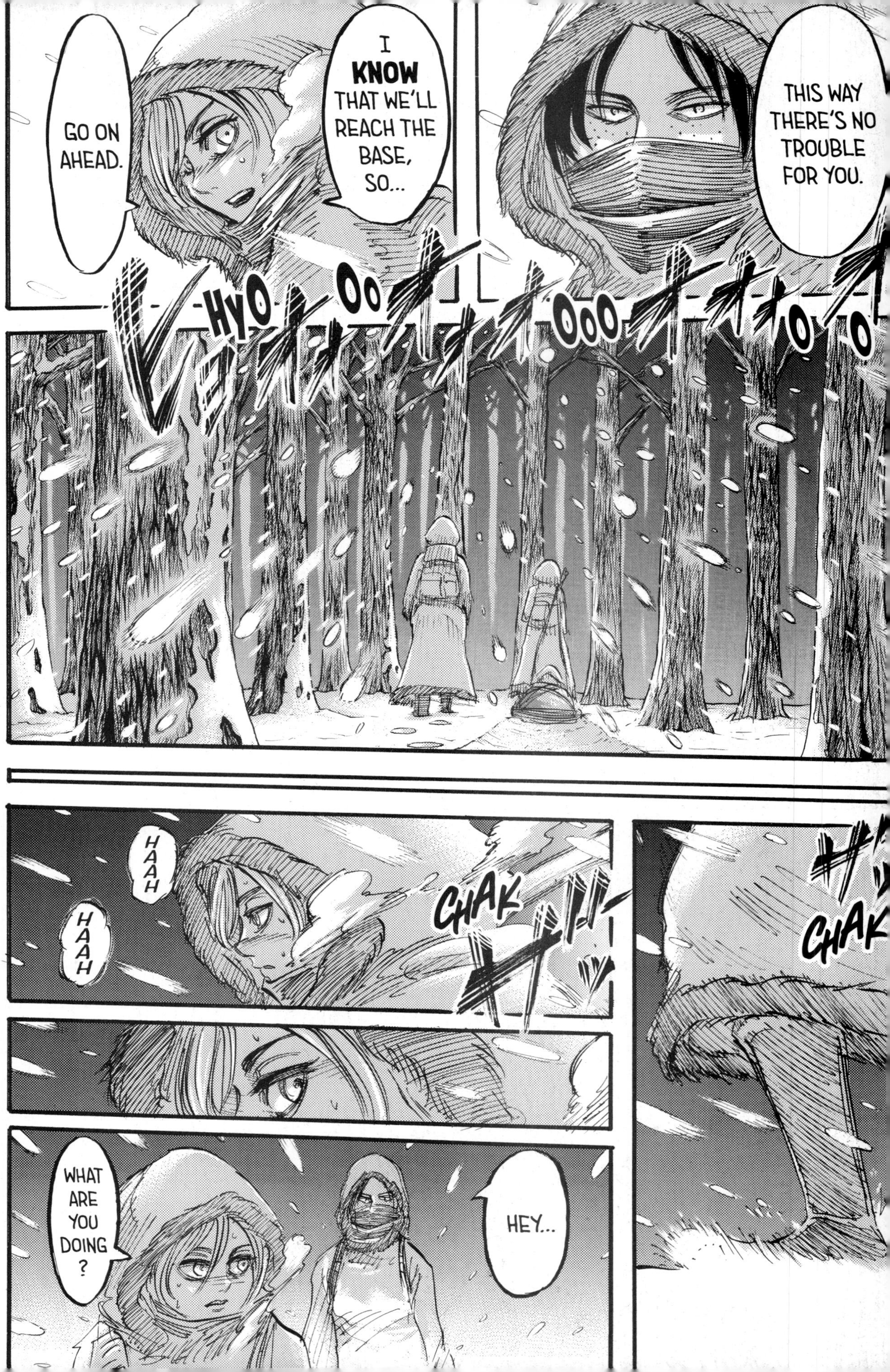
THIS WAY THERE'S NO TROUBLE FOR YOU.
I KNOW THAT WE'LL REACH THE BASE, SO...
GO ON AHEAD.
HYOOOOO
CHAK
HAAH HAAH
CHAK
HEY...
WHAT ARE YOU DOING?

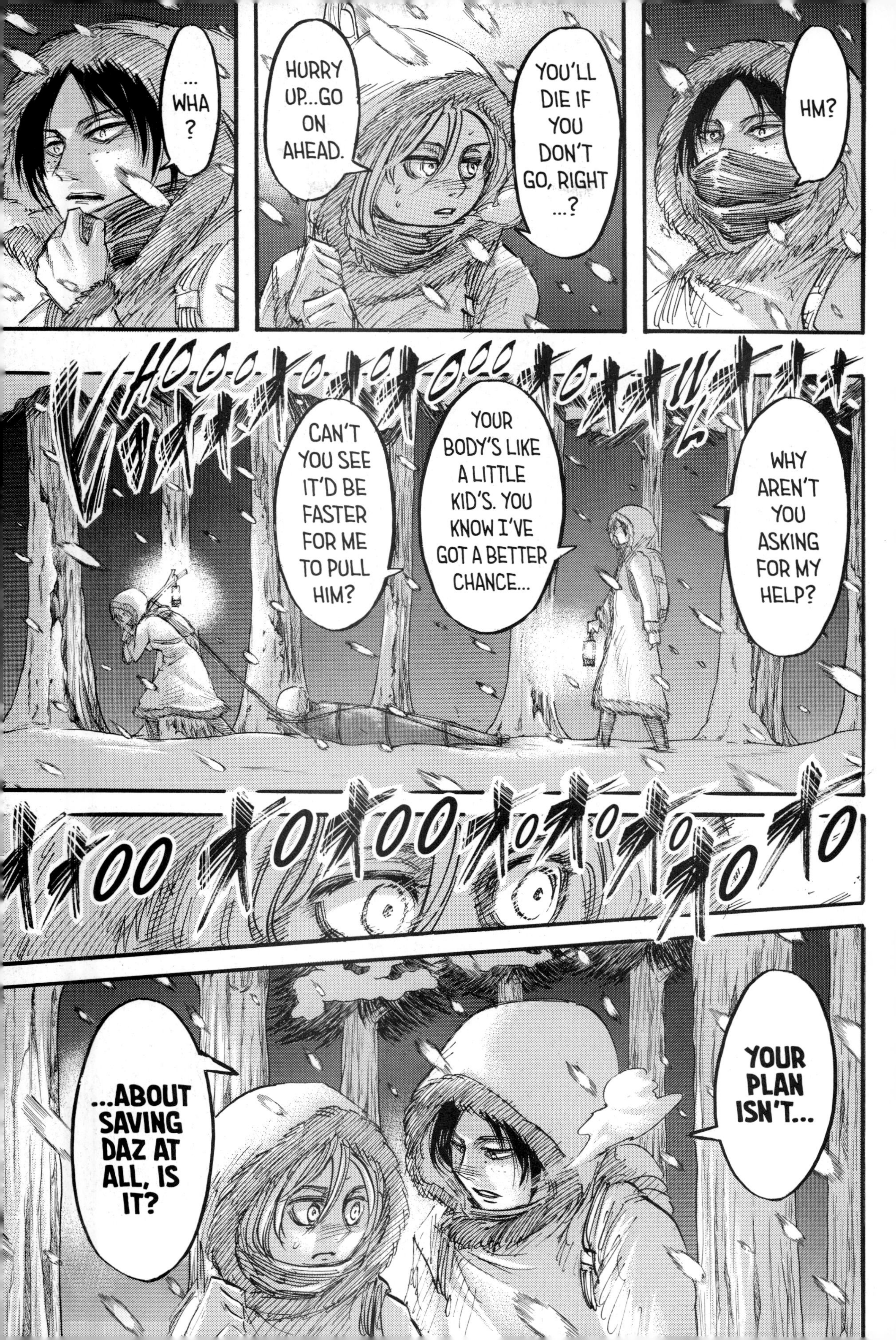
HM?
YOU'LL DIE IF YOU DON'T GO, RIGHT ...?
HURRY UP...GO ON AHEAD.
... WHA ?
WHY AREN'T YOU ASKING FOR MY HELP?
YOUR BODY'S LIKE A LITTLE KID'S. YOU KNOW I'VE GOT A BETTER CHANCE...
CAN'T YOU SEE IT'D BE FASTER FOR ME TO PULL HIM?
YOUR PLAN ISN'T...
...ABOUT SAVING DAZ AT ALL, IS IT?

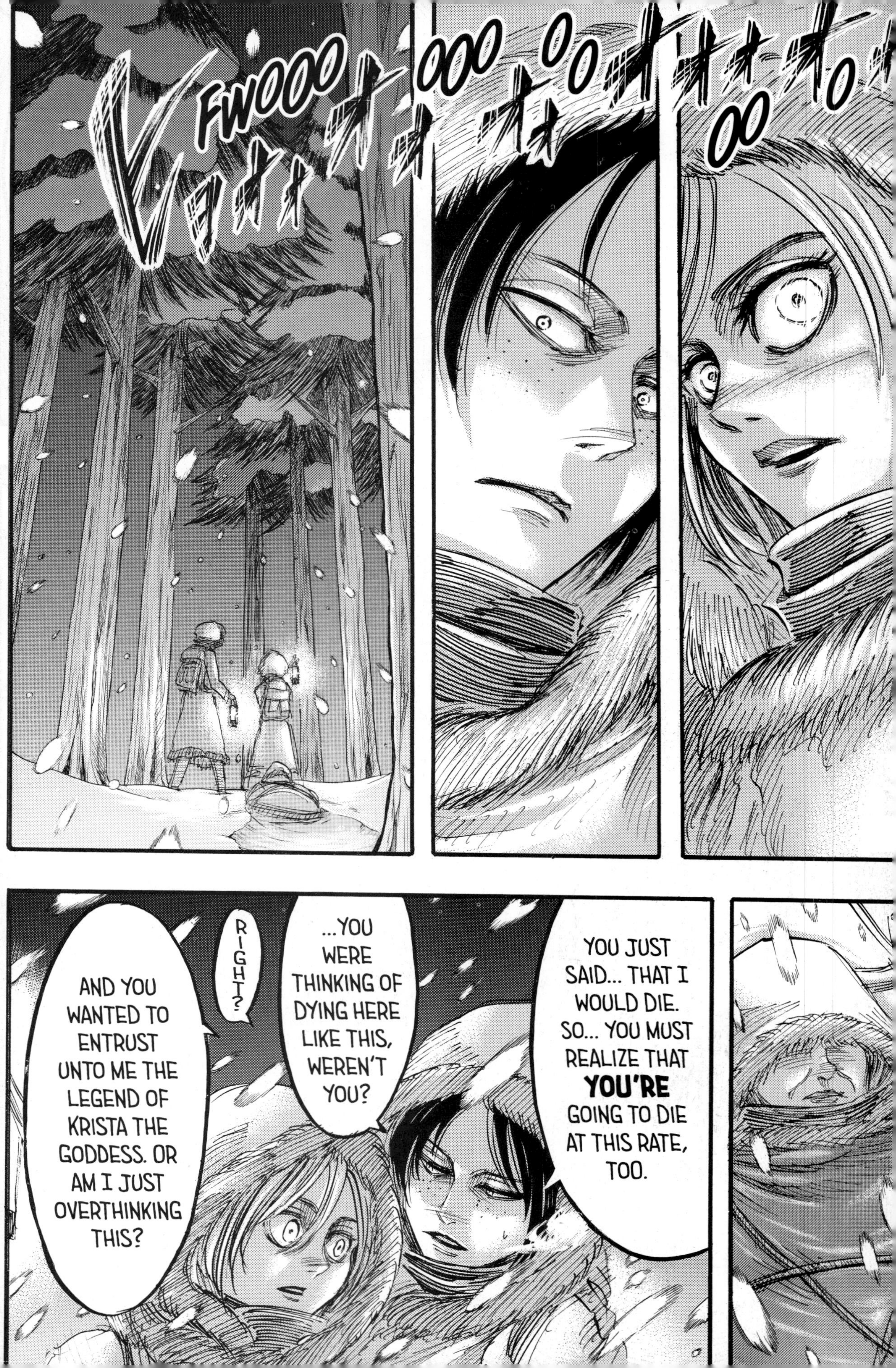
FWOOOOOOOOOOOO
YOU JUST SAID... THAT I WOULD DIE. SO... YOU MUST REALIZE THAT **YOU'RE** GOING TO DIE AT THIS RATE, TOO.
...YOU WERE THINKING OF DYING HERE LIKE THIS, WEREN'T YOU?
RIGHT?
AND YOU WANTED TO ENTRUST UNTO ME THE LEGEND OF KRISTA THE GODDESS. OR AM I JUST OVERTHINKING THIS?

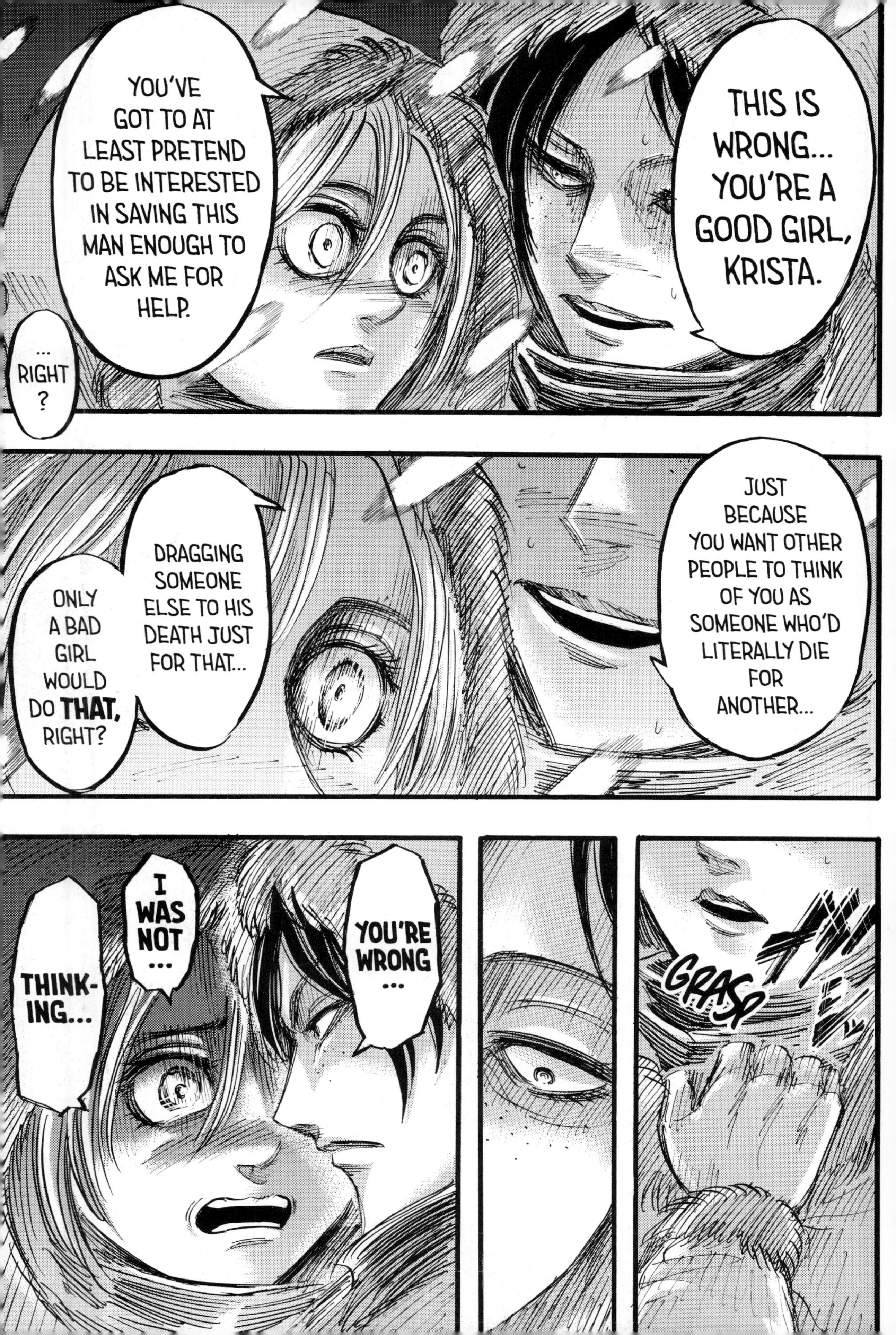
THIS IS WRONG... YOU'RE A GOOD GIRL, KRISTA.
YOU'VE GOT TO AT LEAST PRETEND TO BE INTERESTED IN SAVING THIS MAN ENOUGH TO ASK ME FOR HELP.
...RIGHT?
JUST BECAUSE YOU WANT OTHER PEOPLE TO THINK OF YOU AS SOMEONE WHO'D LITERALLY DIE FOR ANOTHER...
DRAGGING SOMEONE ELSE TO HIS DEATH JUST FOR THAT...
ONLY A BAD GIRL WOULD DO **THAT,** RIGHT?
GRASP
YOU'RE WRONG...
I WAS NOT...
THINKING...

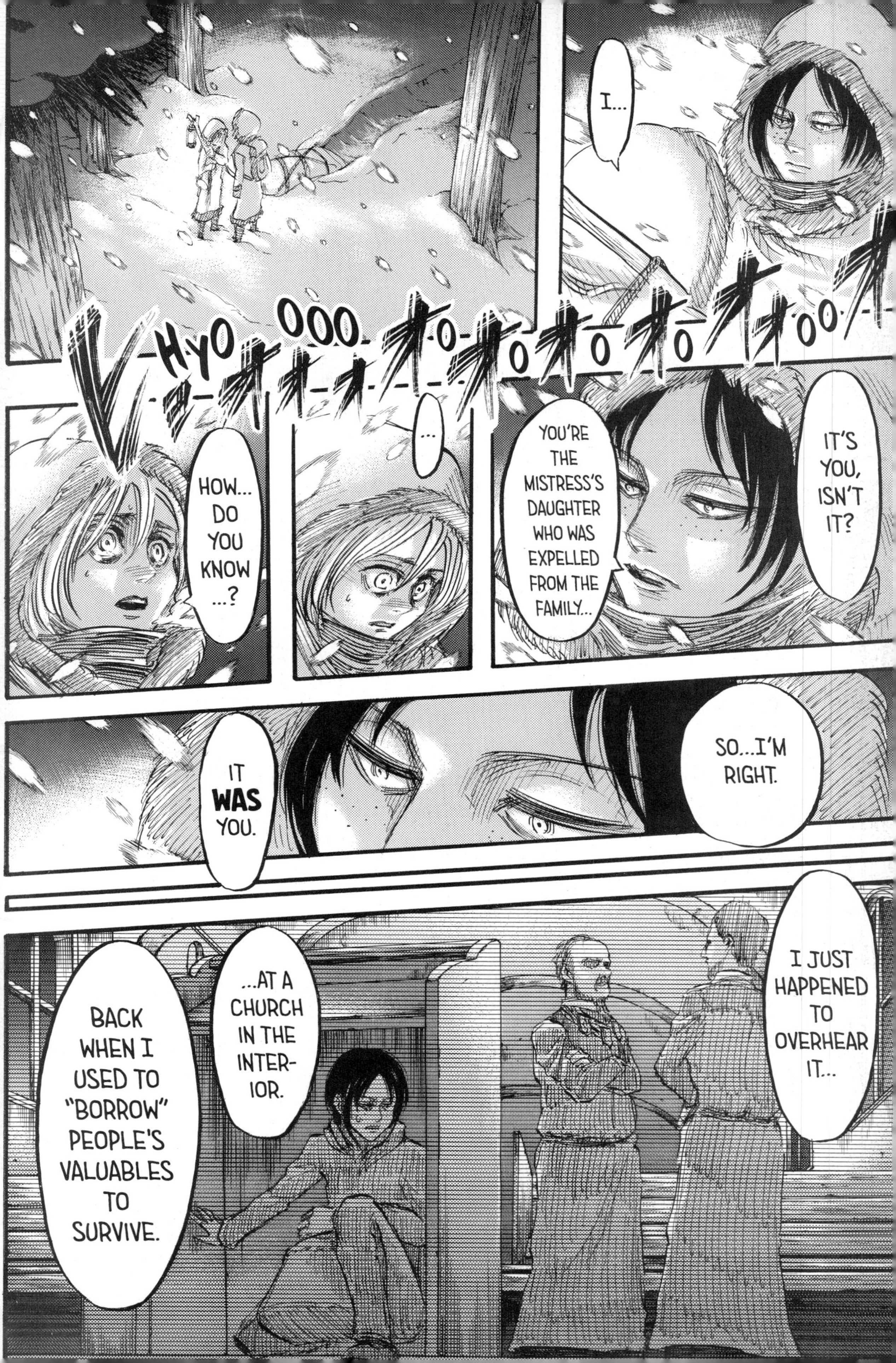
I...
HYOOOOOOOOOOOOO
IT'S YOU, ISN'T IT?
YOU'RE THE MISTRESS'S DAUGHTER WHO WAS EXPELLED FROM THE FAMILY...
...
HOW... DO YOU KNOW ...?
SO...I'M RIGHT.
IT **WAS** YOU.
I JUST HAPPENED TO OVERHEAR IT...
...AT A CHURCH IN THE INTER-IOR.
BACK WHEN I USED TO "BORROW" PEOPLE'S VALUABLES TO SURVIVE.

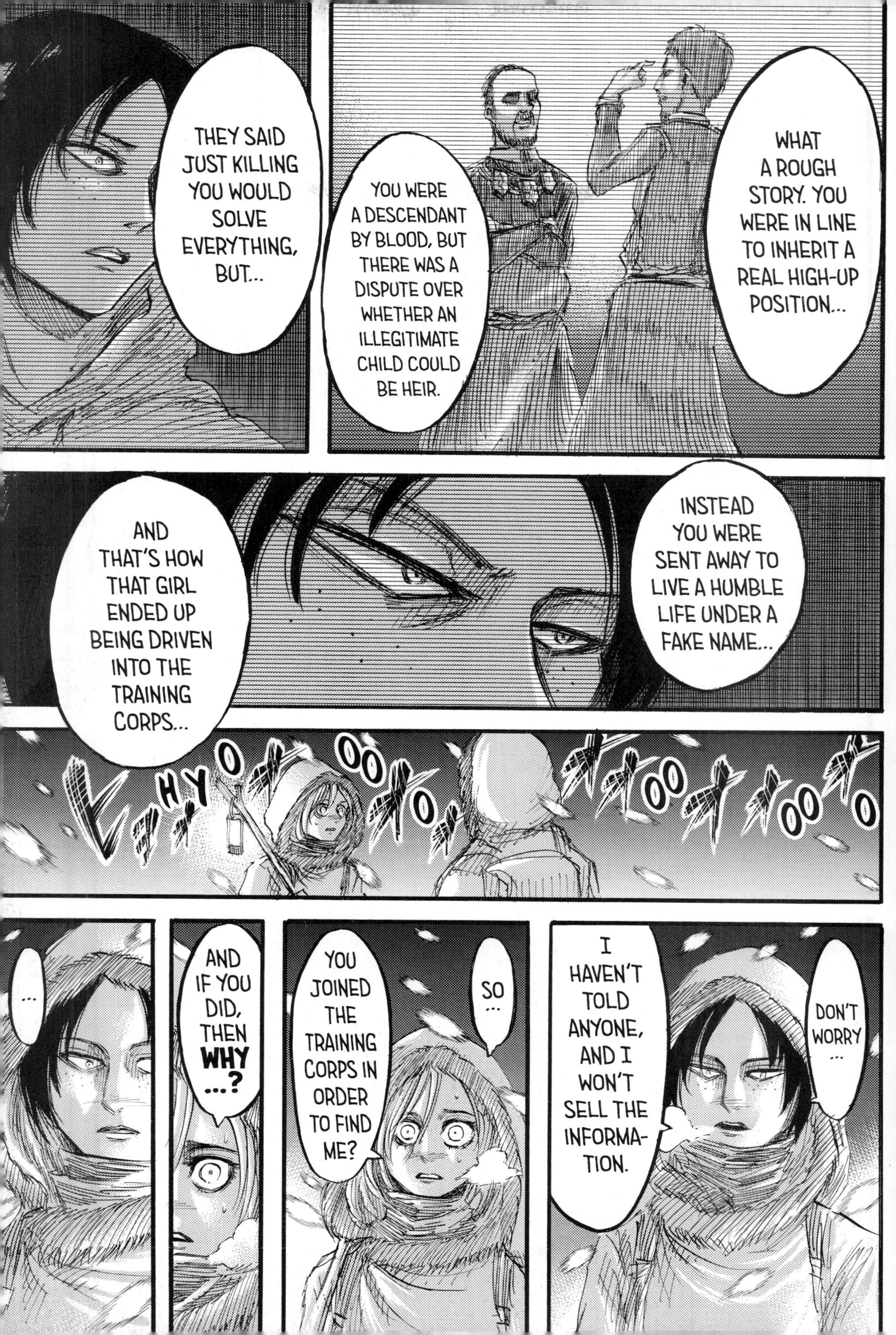
WHAT A ROUGH STORY. YOU WERE IN LINE TO INHERIT A REAL HIGH-UP POSITION...
YOU WERE A DESCENDANT BY BLOOD, BUT THERE WAS A DISPUTE OVER WHETHER AN ILLEGITIMATE CHILD COULD BE HEIR.
THEY SAID JUST KILLING YOU WOULD SOLVE EVERYTHING, BUT...
INSTEAD YOU WERE SENT AWAY TO LIVE A HUMBLE LIFE UNDER A FAKE NAME...
AND THAT'S HOW THAT GIRL ENDED UP BEING DRIVEN INTO THE TRAINING CORPS...
WHYOOOOOOOOOO
DON'T WORRY...
I HAVEN'T TOLD ANYONE, AND I WON'T SELL THE INFORMATION.
SO...
YOU JOINED THE TRAINING CORPS IN ORDER TO FIND ME?
AND IF YOU DID, THEN **WHY**...?
...

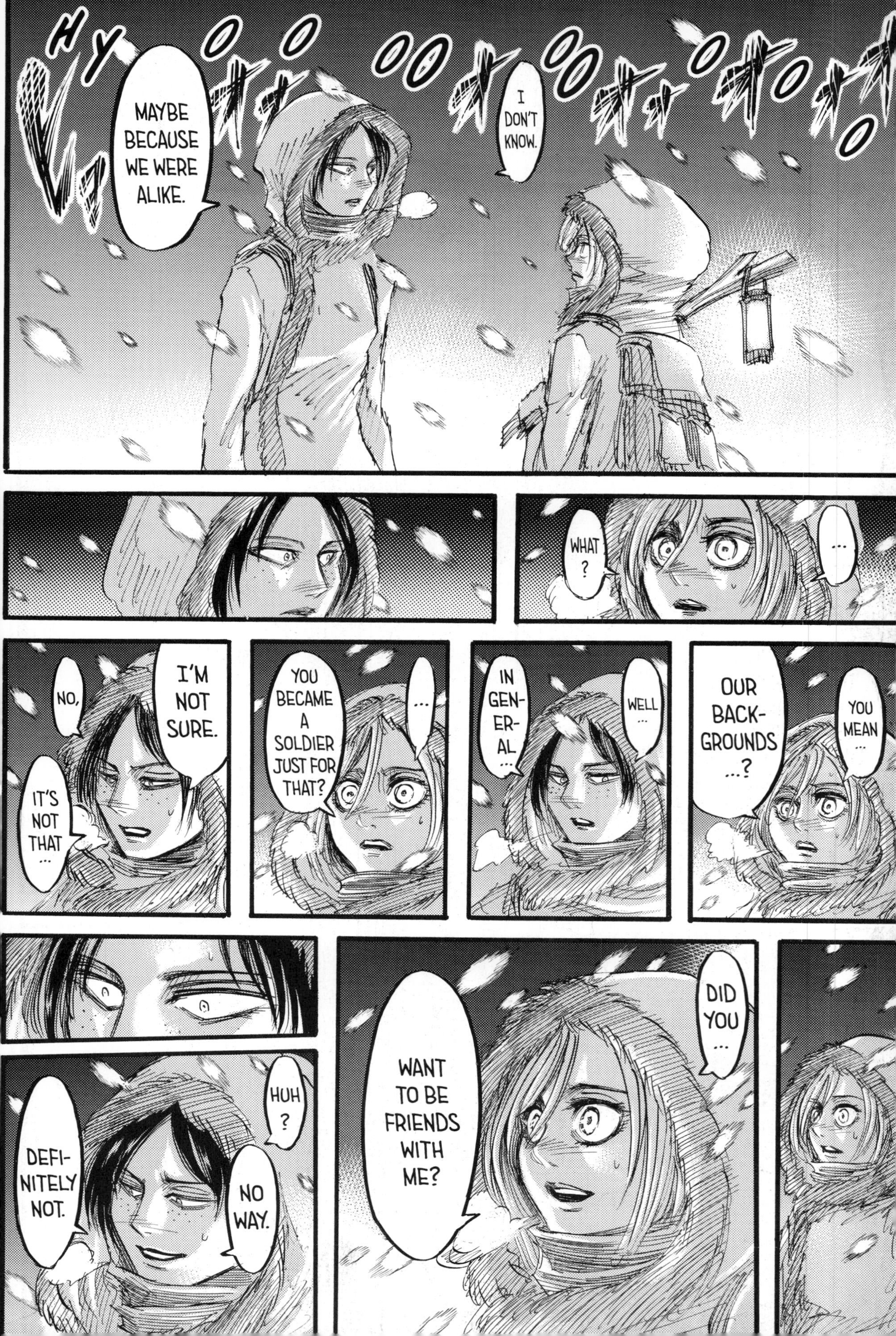
HYOOOOOOOOOOO
I DON'T KNOW.
MAYBE BECAUSE WE WERE ALIKE.
...
WHAT?
YOU MEAN...
OUR BACKGROUNDS...?
WELL...
IN GENERAL...
...
YOU BECAME A SOLDIER JUST FOR THAT?
I'M NOT SURE.
NO,
IT'S NOT THAT...
DID YOU...
WANT TO BE FRIENDS WITH ME?
HUH?
NO WAY.
DEFINITELY NOT.

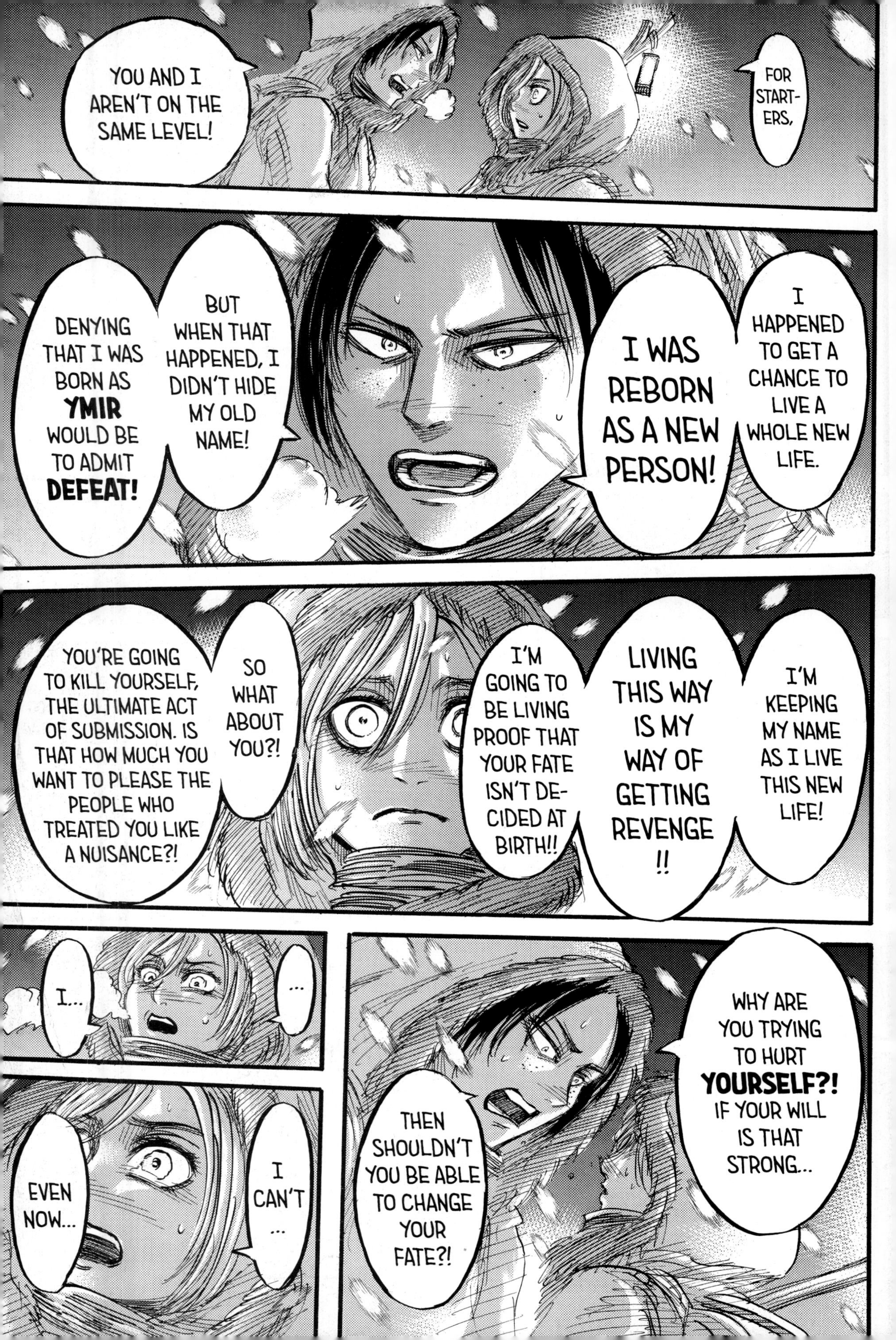
FOR STARTERS,
YOU AND I AREN'T ON THE SAME LEVEL!
I HAPPENED TO GET A CHANCE TO LIVE A WHOLE NEW LIFE.
I WAS REBORN AS A NEW PERSON!
BUT WHEN THAT HAPPENED, I DIDN'T HIDE MY OLD NAME!
DENYING THAT I WAS BORN AS **YMIR** WOULD BE TO ADMIT **DEFEAT!**
I'M KEEPING MY NAME AS I LIVE THIS NEW LIFE!
LIVING THIS WAY IS MY WAY OF GETTING REVENGE!!
I'M GOING TO BE LIVING PROOF THAT YOUR FATE ISN'T DECIDED AT BIRTH!!
SO WHAT ABOUT YOU?!
YOU'RE GOING TO KILL YOURSELF, THE ULTIMATE ACT OF SUBMISSION. IS THAT HOW MUCH YOU WANT TO PLEASE THE PEOPLE WHO TREATED YOU LIKE A NUISANCE?!
WHY ARE YOU TRYING TO HURT **YOURSELF?!** IF YOUR WILL IS THAT STRONG...
THEN SHOULDN'T YOU BE ABLE TO CHANGE YOUR FATE?!
...
I...
I CAN'T ...
EVEN NOW...

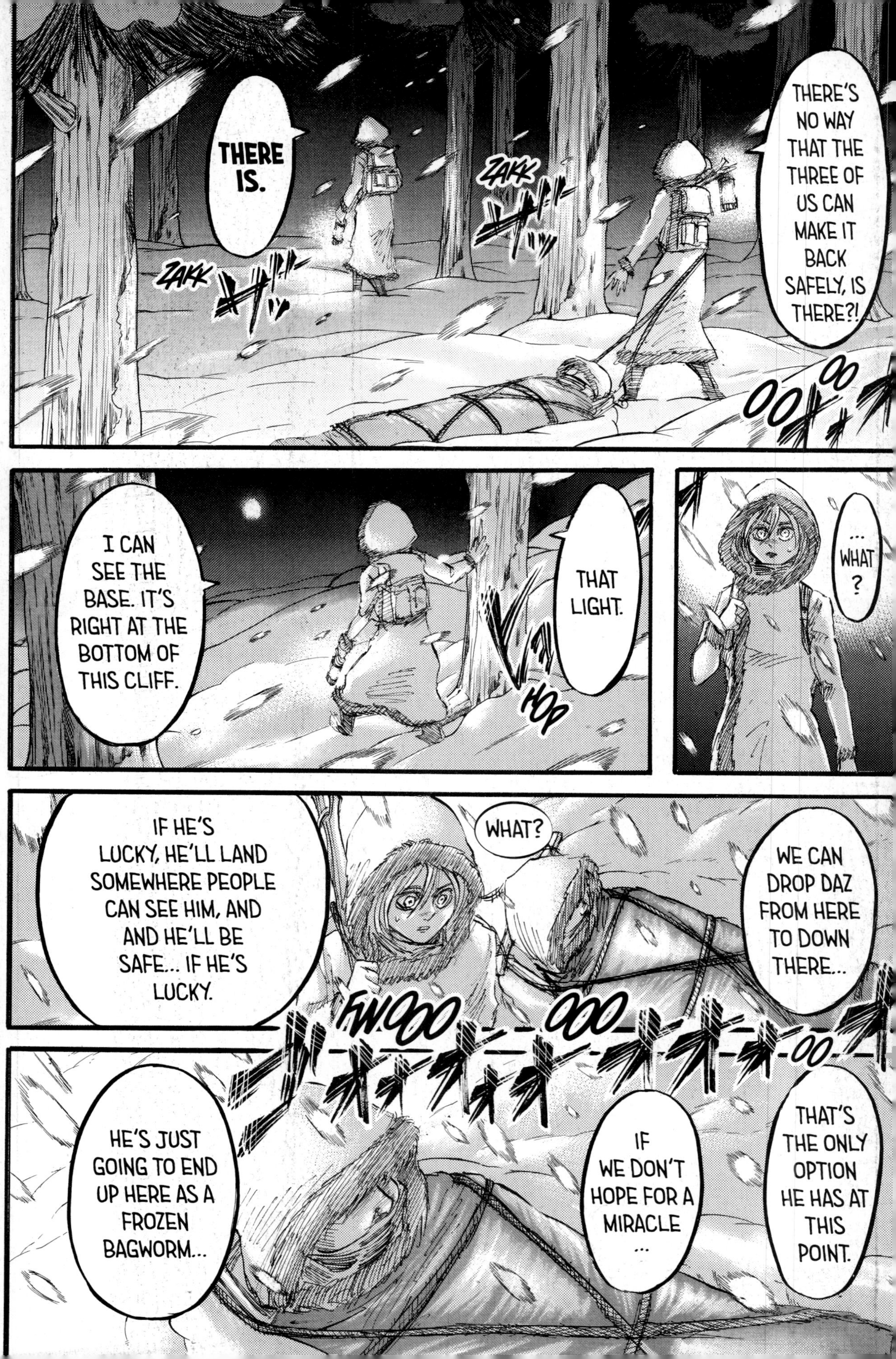
THERE'S NO WAY THAT THE THREE OF US CAN MAKE IT BACK SAFELY, IS THERE?!
OOO
ZAKK
THERE IS.
ZAKK
...WHAT?
THAT LIGHT.
HOP
I CAN SEE THE BASE. IT'S RIGHT AT THE BOTTOM OF THIS CLIFF.
WE CAN DROP DAZ FROM HERE TO DOWN THERE...
WHAT?
IF HE'S LUCKY, HE'LL LAND SOMEWHERE PEOPLE CAN SEE HIM, AND AND HE'LL BE SAFE... IF HE'S LUCKY.
FWOOO OOO OO
THAT'S THE ONLY OPTION HE HAS AT THIS POINT.
IF WE DON'T HOPE FOR A MIRACLE...
HE'S JUST GOING TO END UP HERE AS A FROZEN BAGWORM...

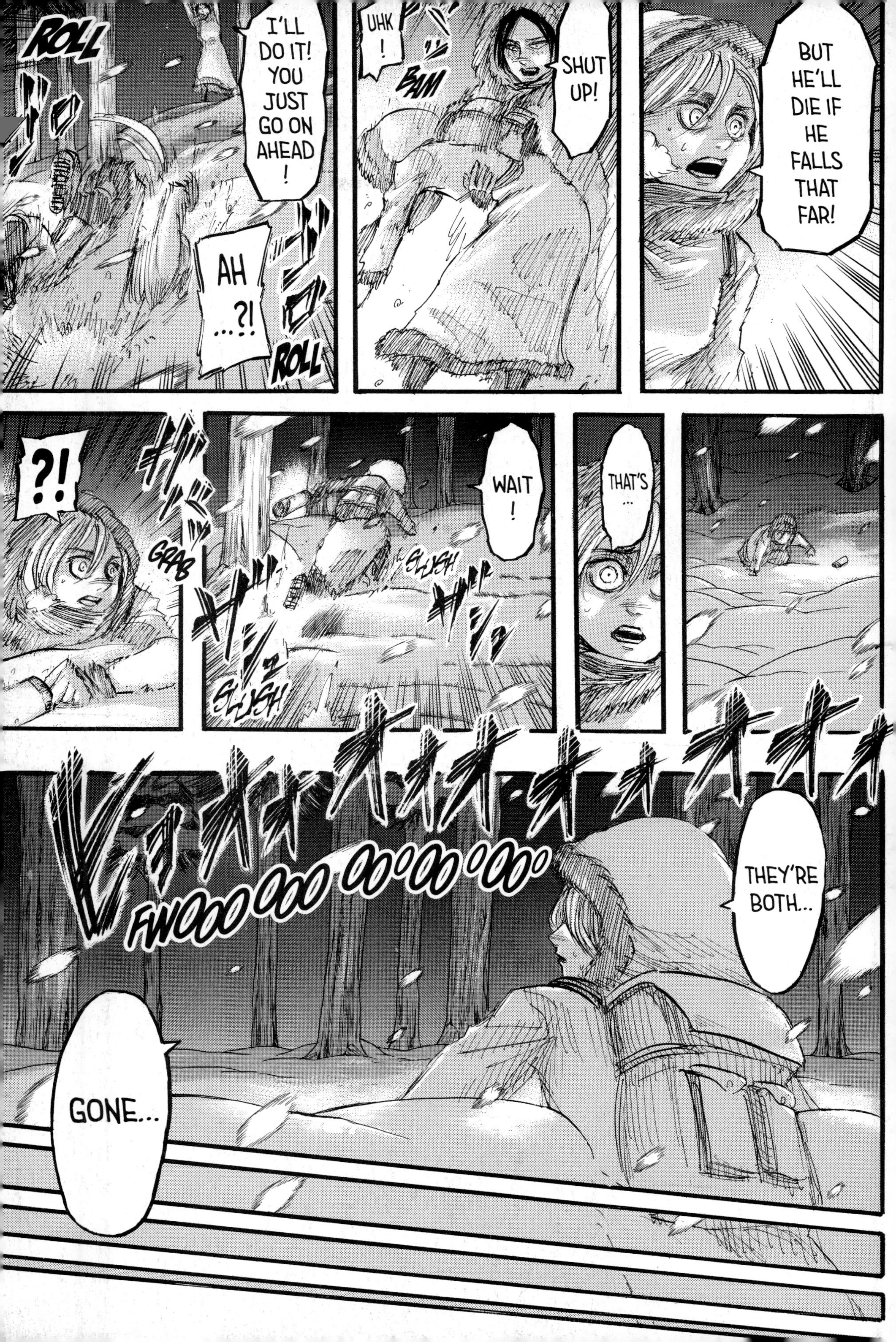

BUT HE'LL DIE IF HE FALLS THAT FAR!
SHUT UP!
UHK!
BAM
I'LL DO IT! YOU JUST GO ON AHEAD!
ROLL
AH...?!
ROLL
THAT'S...
WAIT!
SLUSH
SLUSH
?!
GRAB
FWOOOO OOO OOOOOO OOO
THEY'RE BOTH...
GONE...

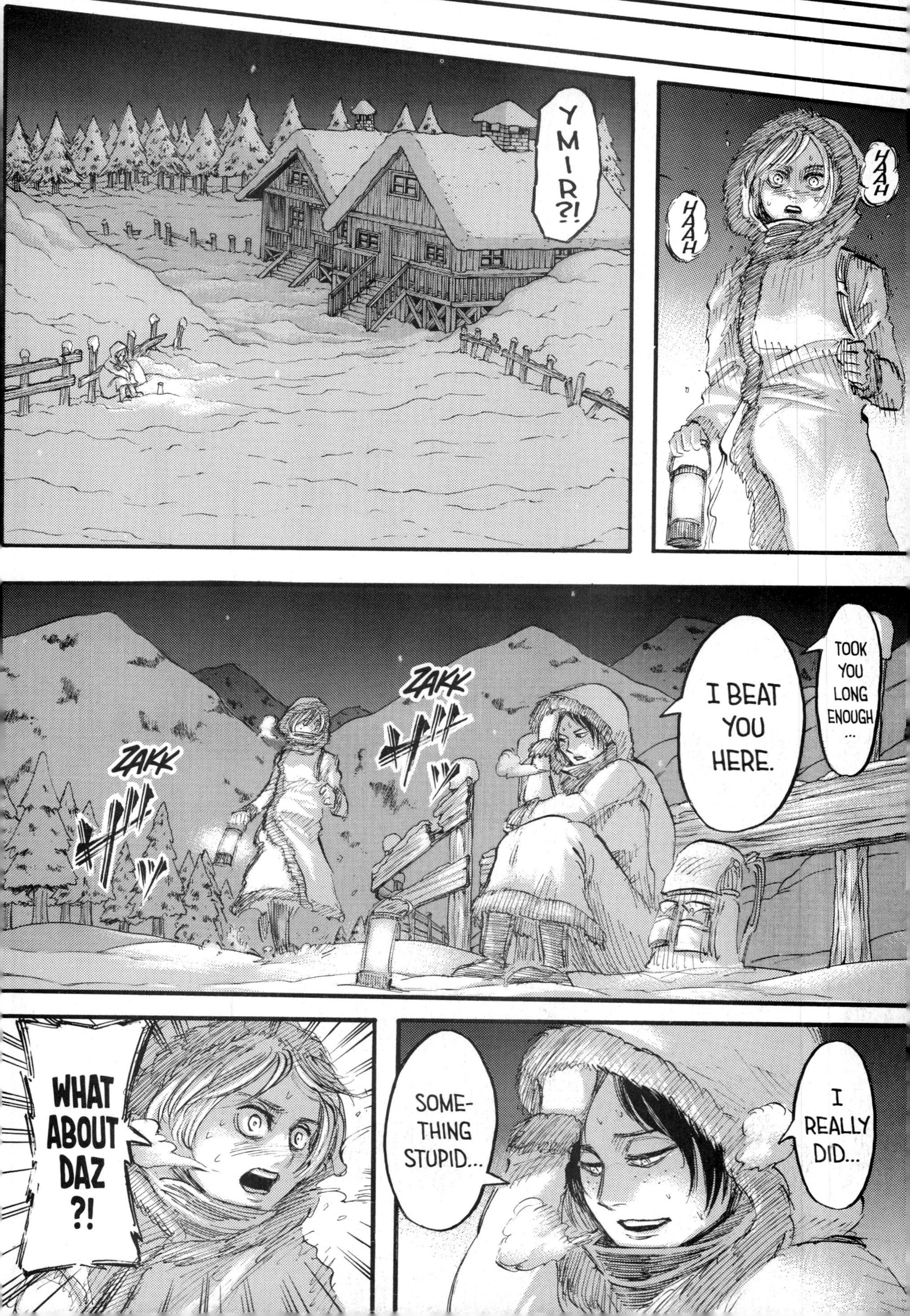
HAAH
HAAH
YMIR?!
TOOK YOU LONG ENOUGH...
I BEAT YOU HERE.
ZAKK
ZAKK
I REALLY DID...
SOME-THING STUPID...
WHAT ABOUT DAZ?!

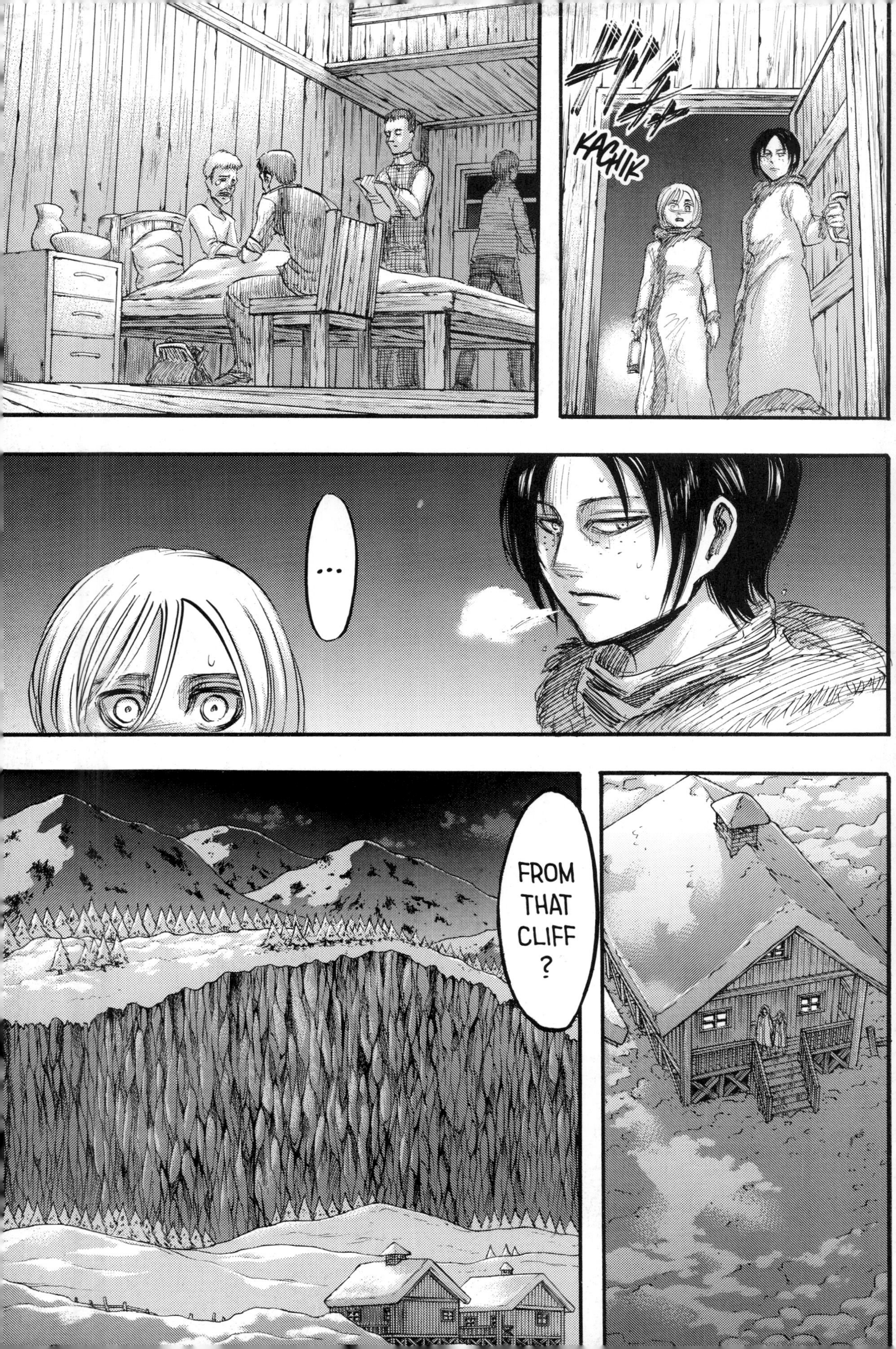
KACHIK
...
FROM THAT CLIFF ?

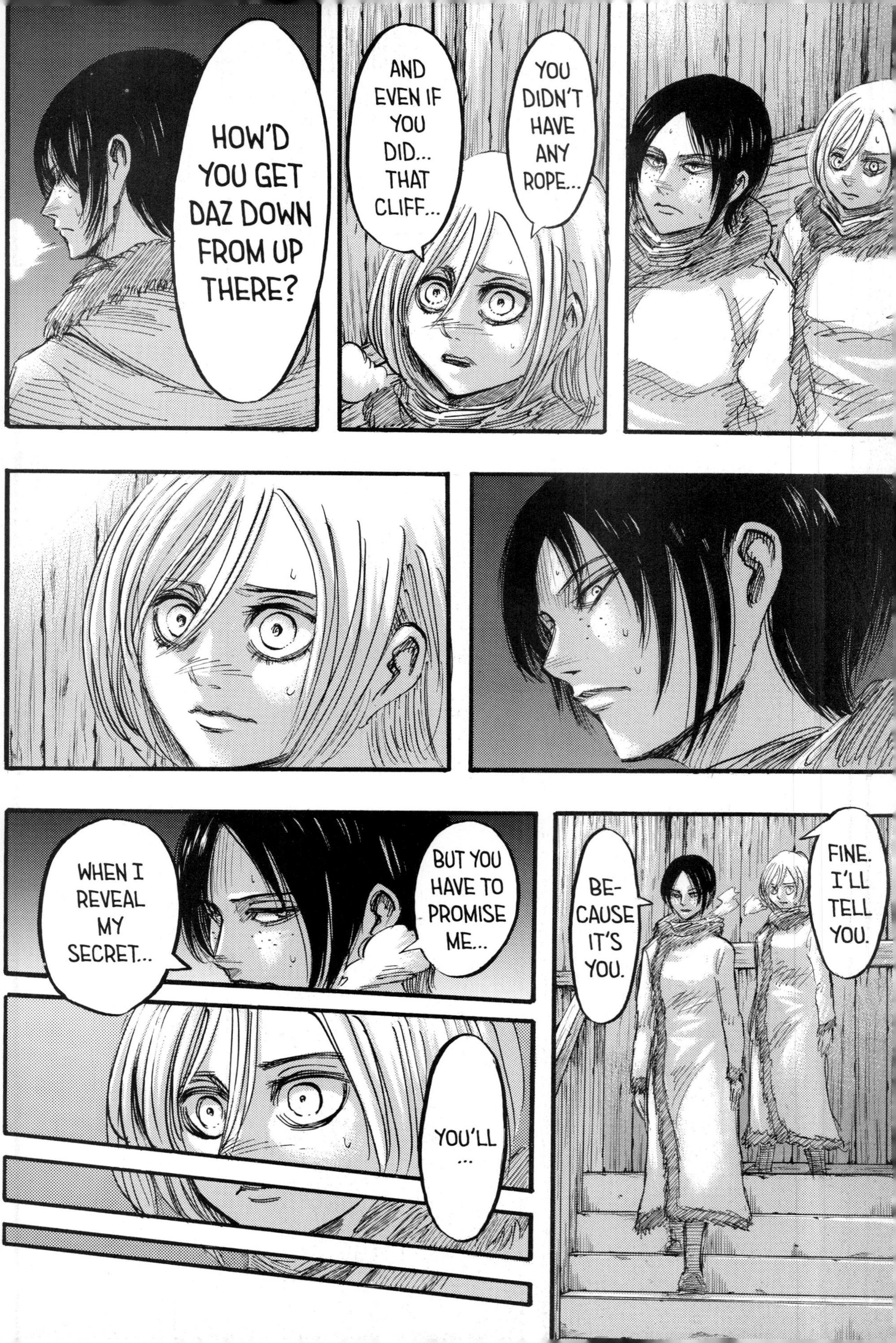
YOU DIDN'T HAVE ANY ROPE...
AND EVEN IF YOU DID... THAT CLIFF...
HOW'D YOU GET DAZ DOWN FROM UP THERE?
FINE. I'LL TELL YOU.
BE-CAUSE IT'S YOU.
BUT YOU HAVE TO PROMISE ME...
WHEN I REVEAL MY SECRET...
YOU'LL ...

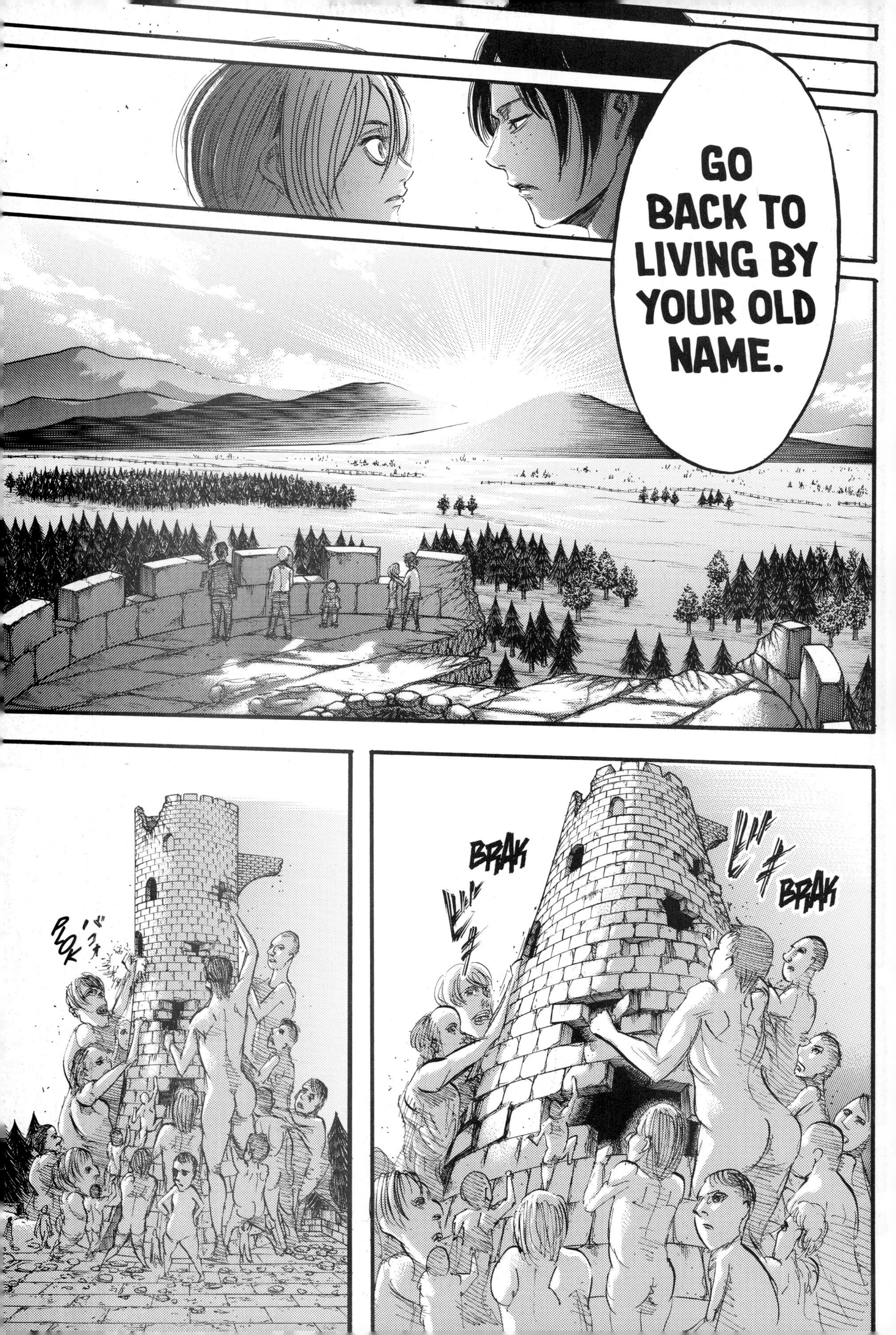
GO BACK TO LIVING BY YOUR OLD NAME.
BRAK
BRAK
PLOK
バコォ

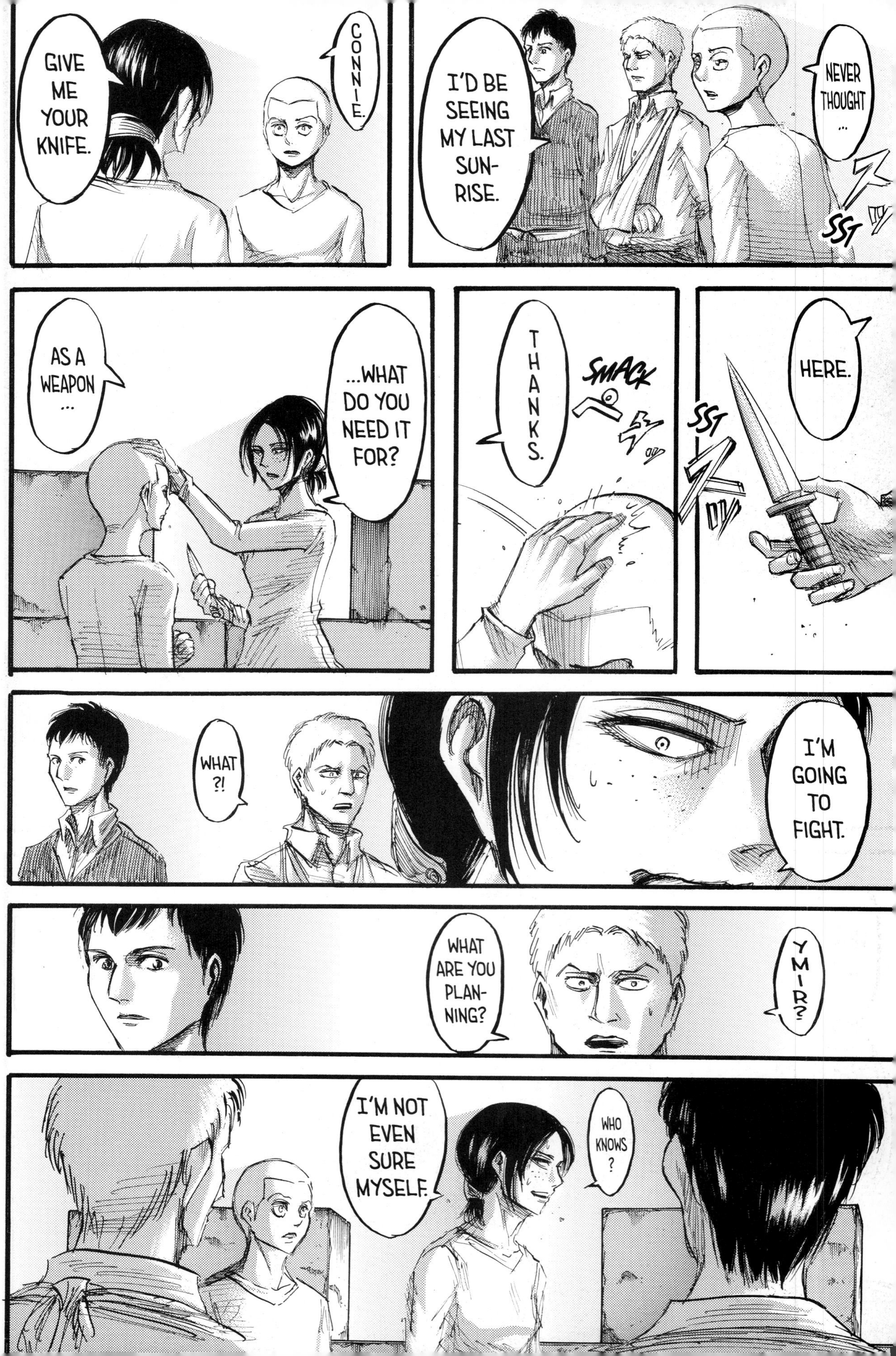
NEVER THOUGHT ...
SST
I'D BE SEEING MY LAST SUN-RISE.
CONNIE.
GIVE ME YOUR KNIFE.
HERE.
SST
SMACK
THANKS.
...WHAT DO YOU NEED IT FOR?
AS A WEAPON ...
I'M GOING TO FIGHT.
WHAT?!
YMIR?
WHAT ARE YOU PLANNING?
WHO KNOWS?
I'M NOT EVEN SURE MYSELF.

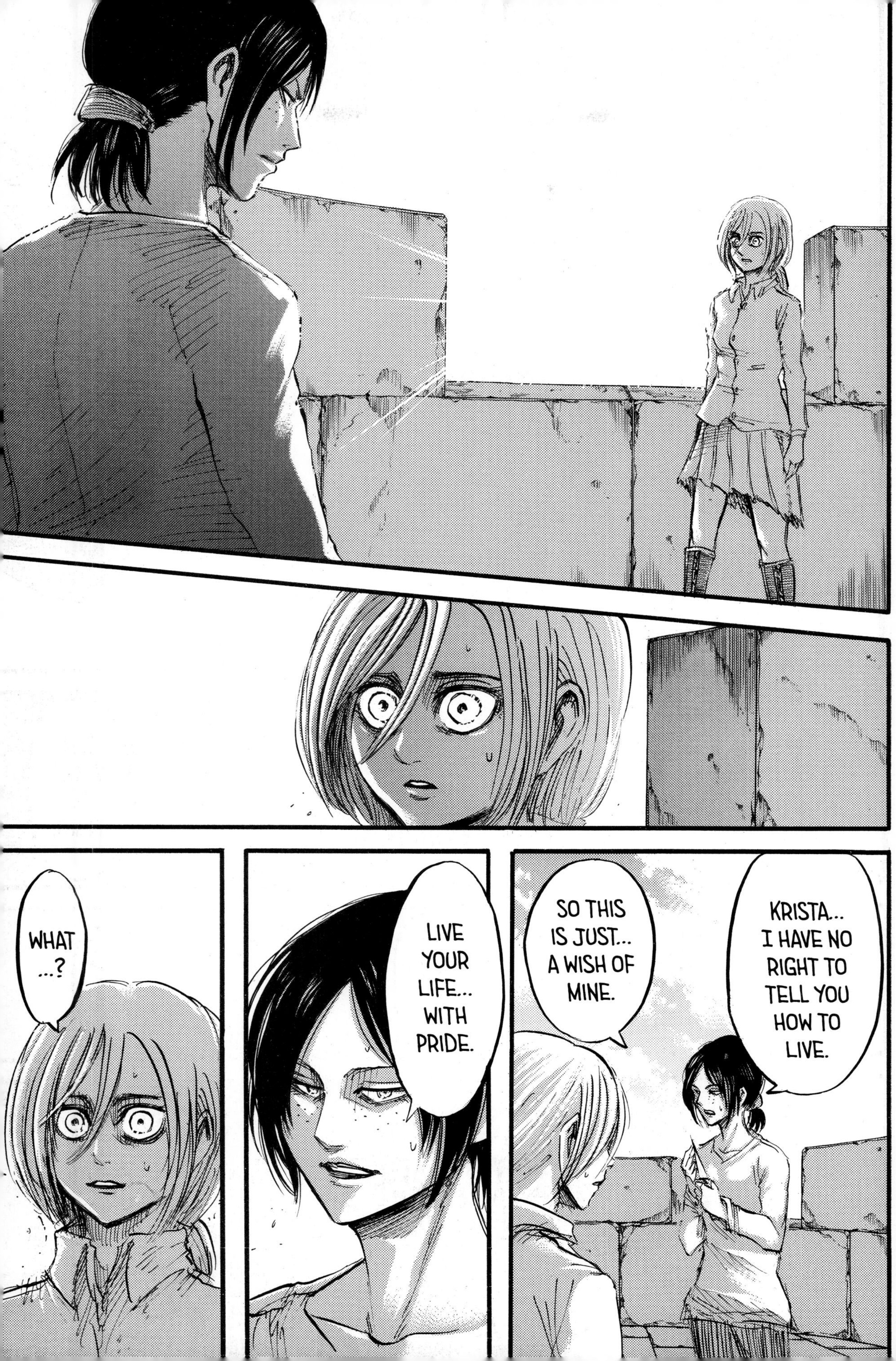
KRISTA... I HAVE NO RIGHT TO TELL YOU HOW TO LIVE.
SO THIS IS JUST... A WISH OF MINE.
LIVE YOUR LIFE... WITH PRIDE.
WHAT ...?

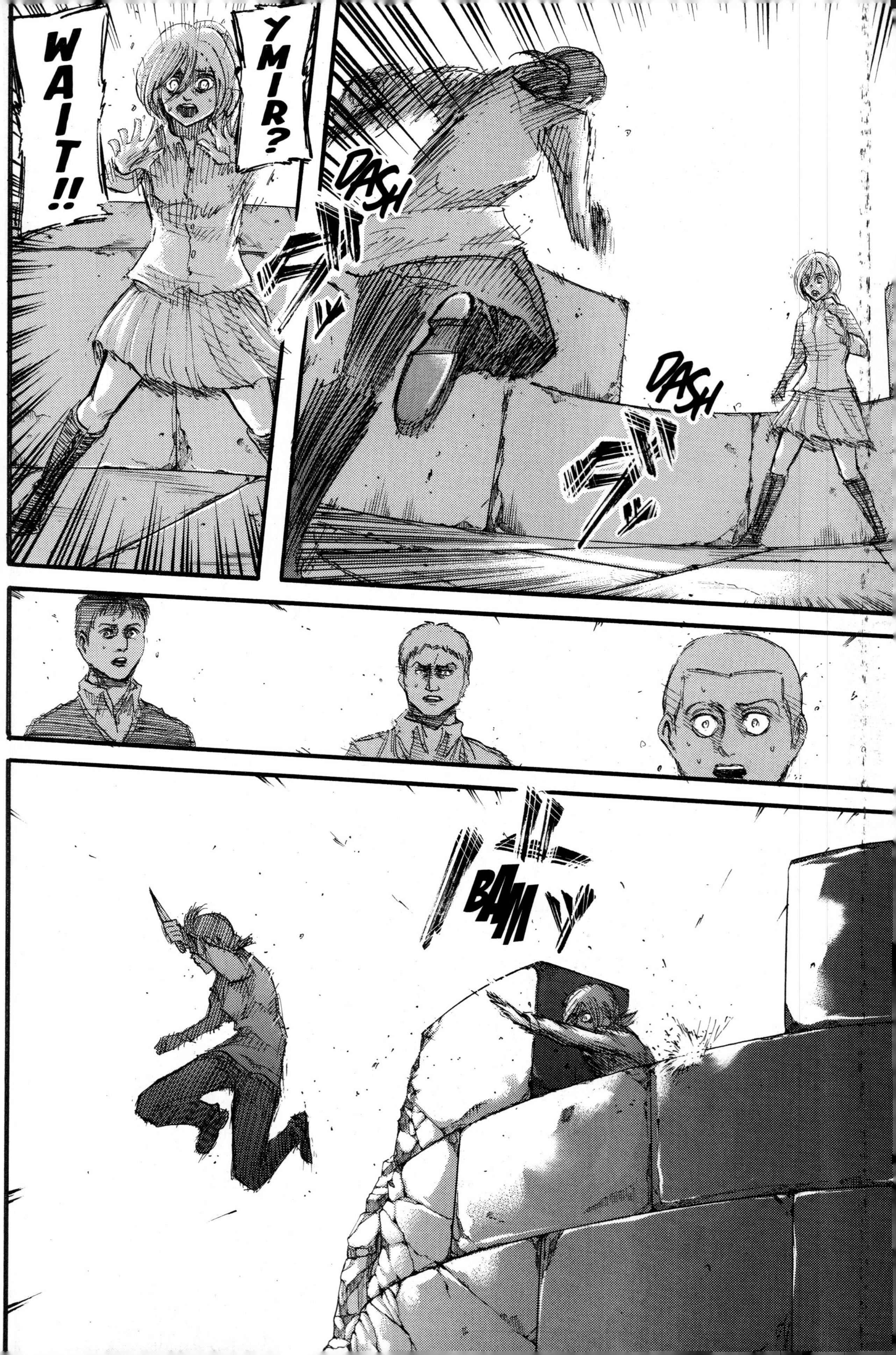
DASH
DASH
YMIR?
WAIT!!
BAM

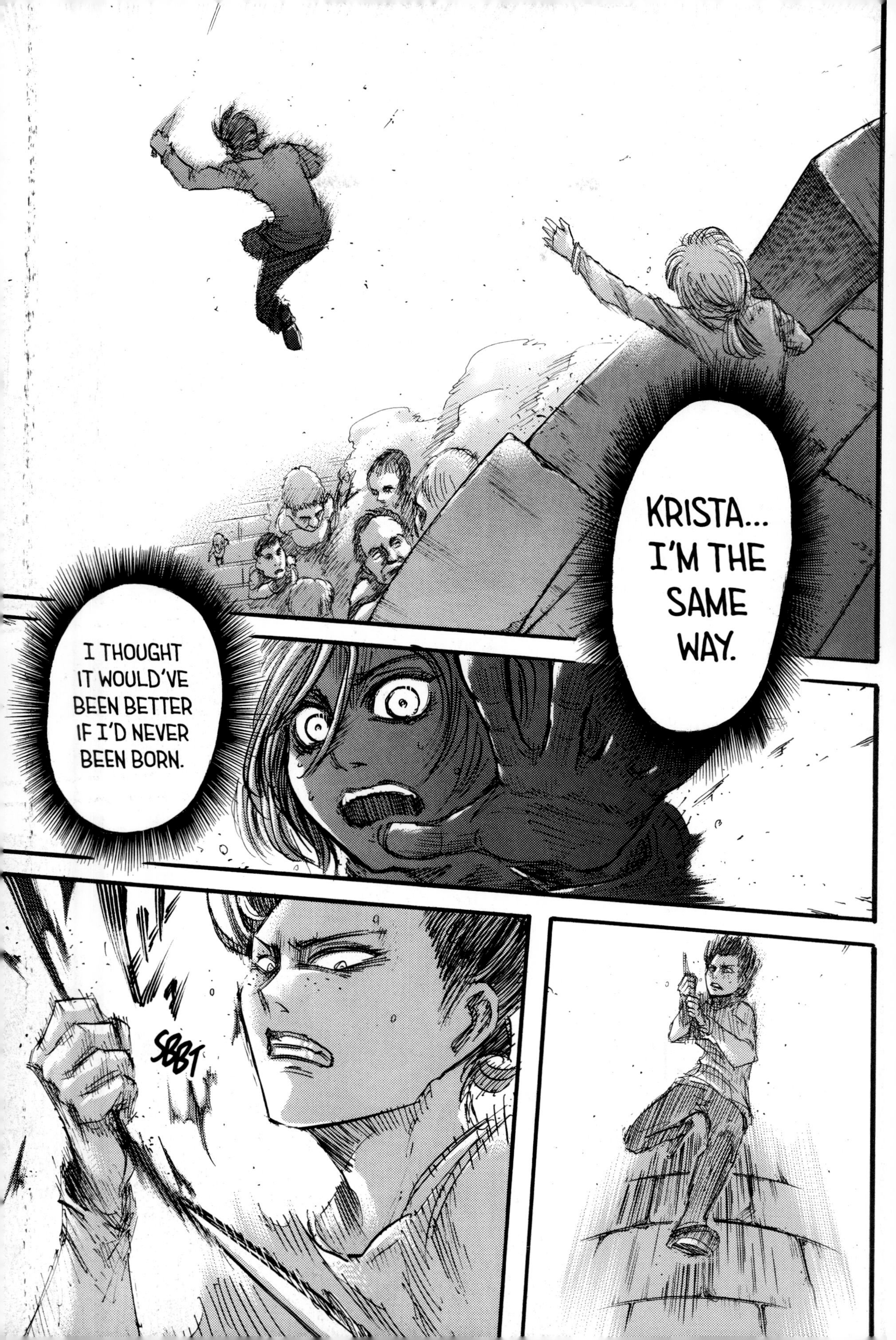
KRISTA... I'M THE SAME WAY.
I THOUGHT IT WOULD'VE BEEN BETTER IF I'D NEVER BEEN BORN.
SBBT

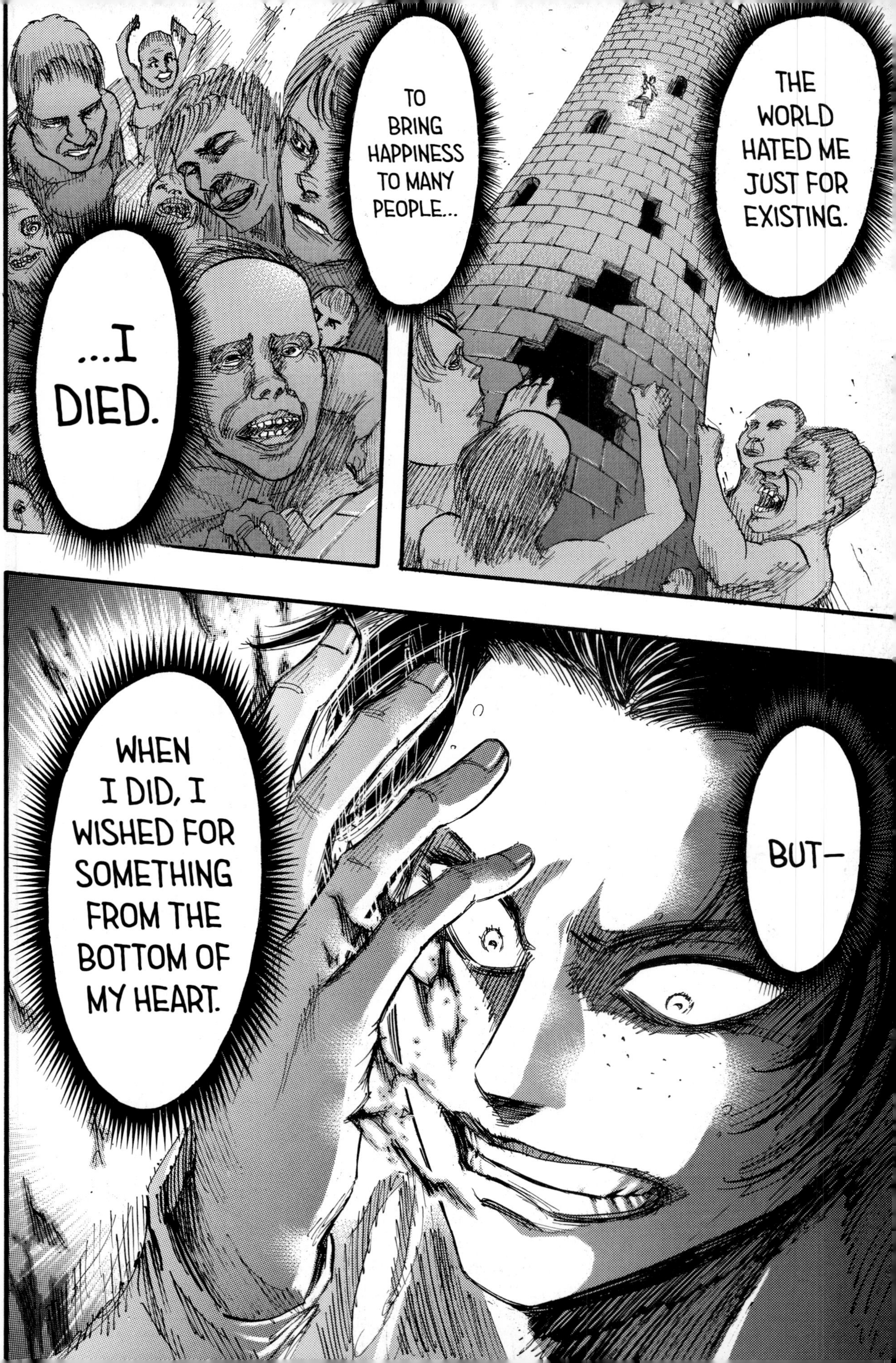
THE WORLD HATED ME JUST FOR EXISTING.
TO BRING HAPPINESS TO MANY PEOPLE...
...I DIED.
BUT—
WHEN I DID, I WISHED FOR SOMETHING FROM THE BOTTOM OF MY HEART.

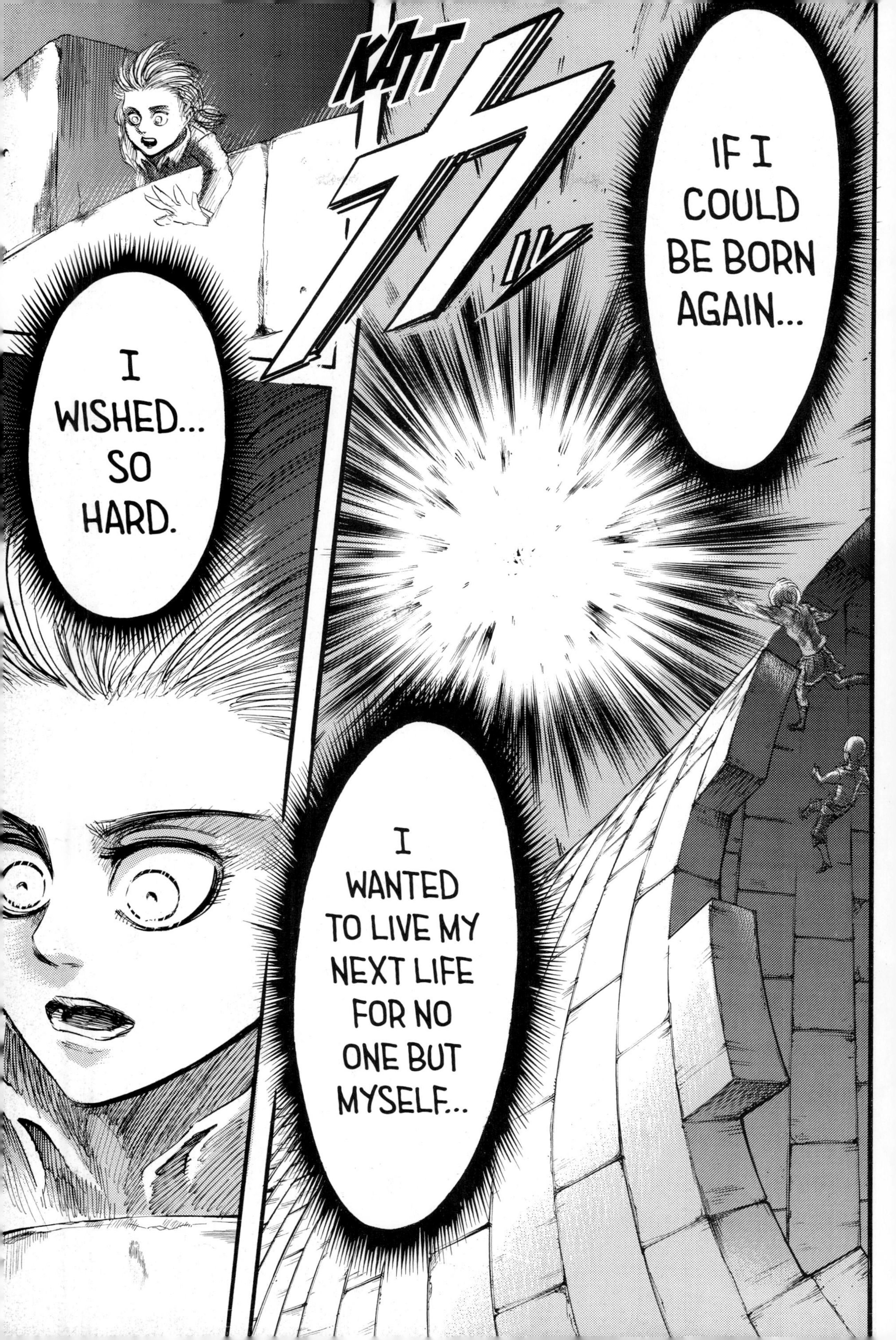
IF I COULD BE BORN AGAIN...
K'ATT
I WISHED... SO HARD.
I WANTED TO LIVE MY NEXT LIFE FOR NO ONE BUT MYSELF...

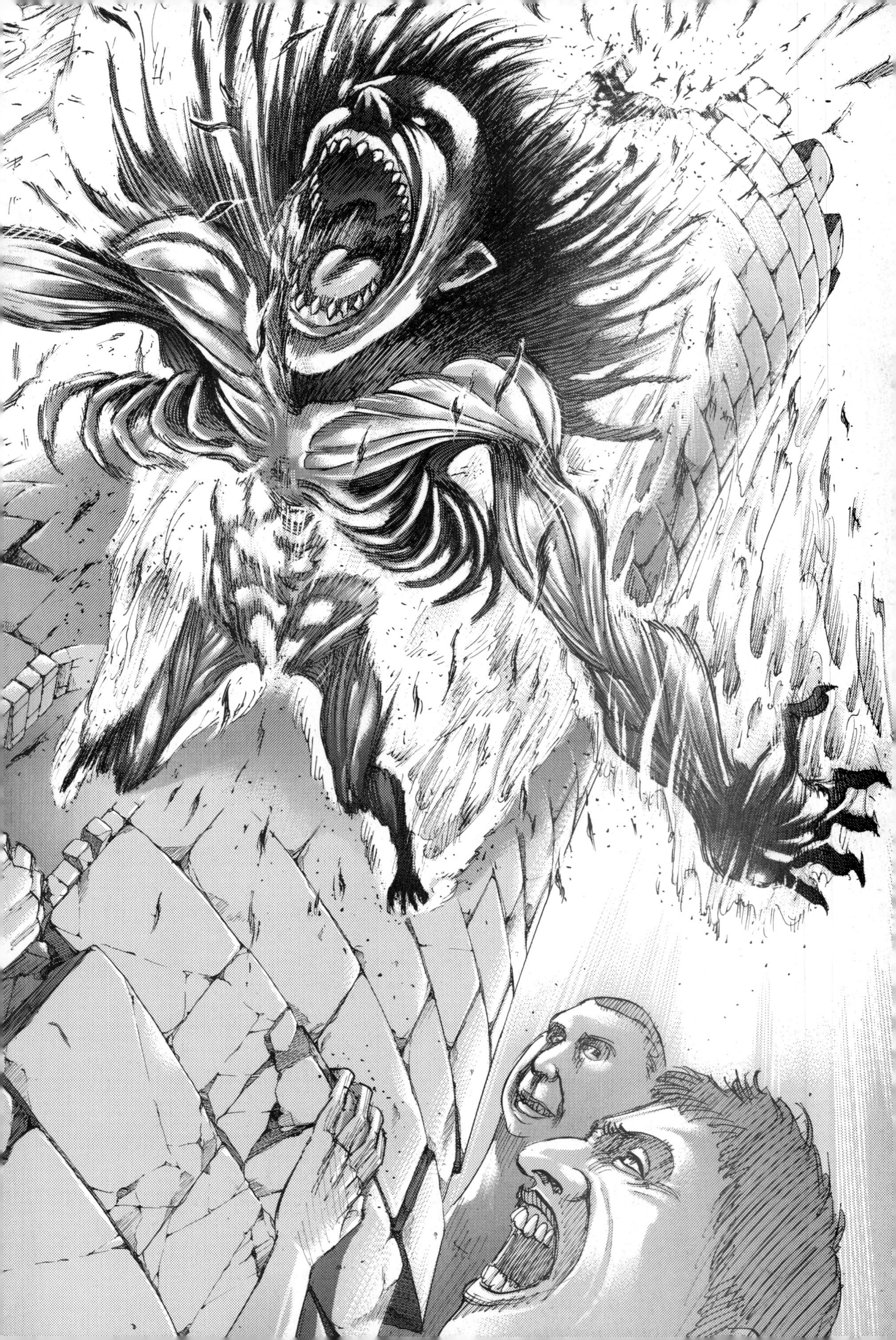

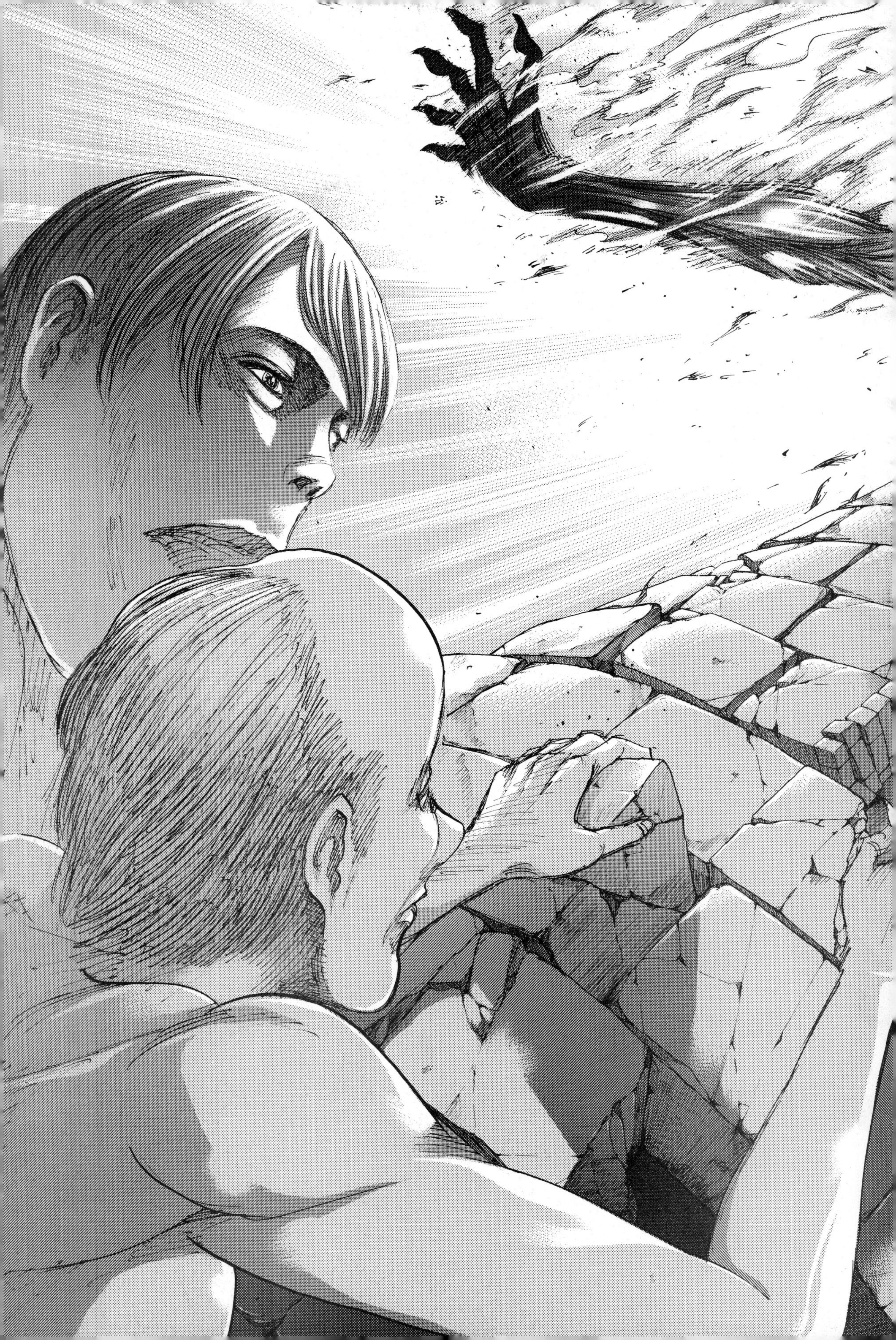

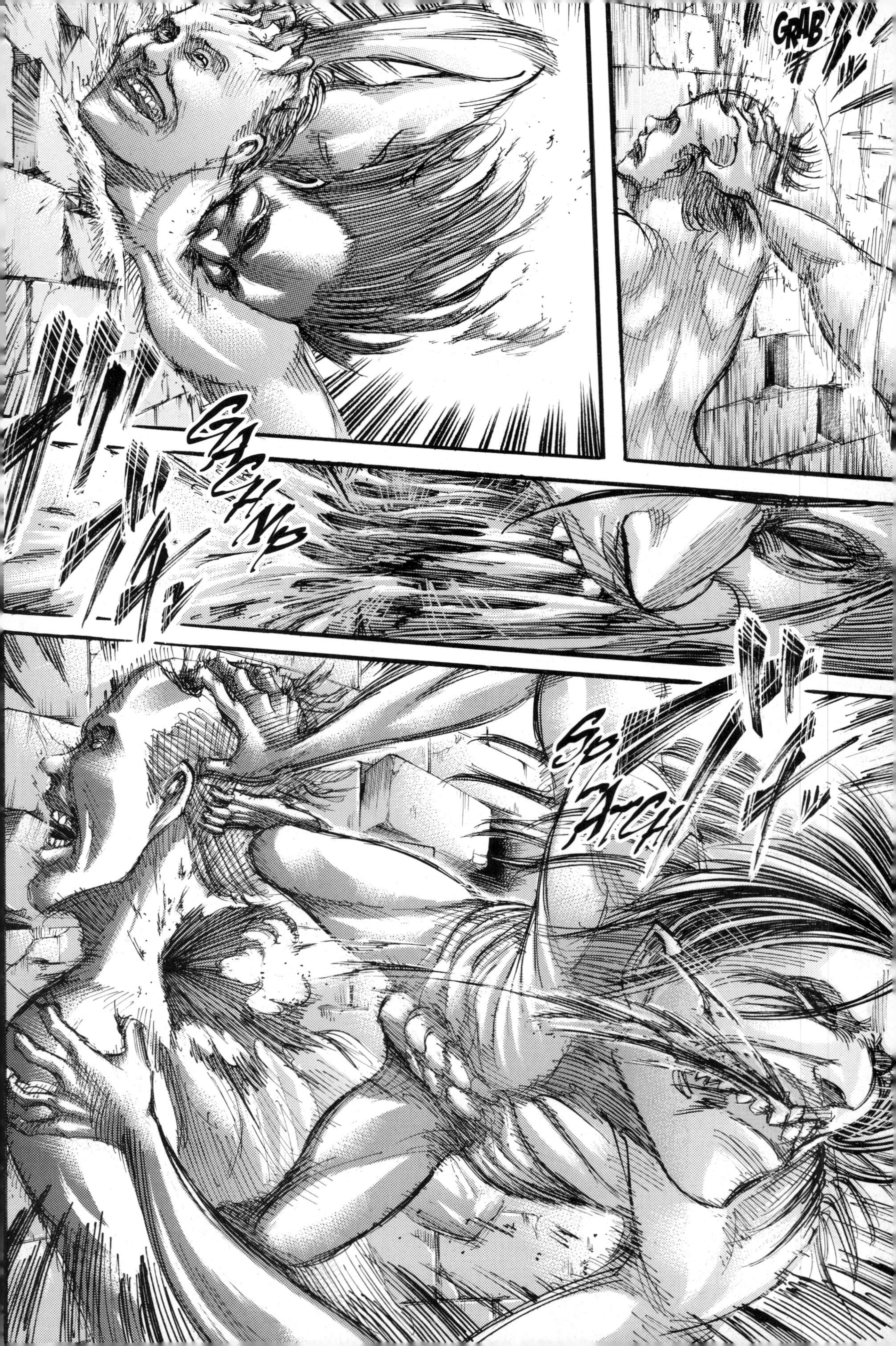
GRAB
GACHNG
SPLATCH

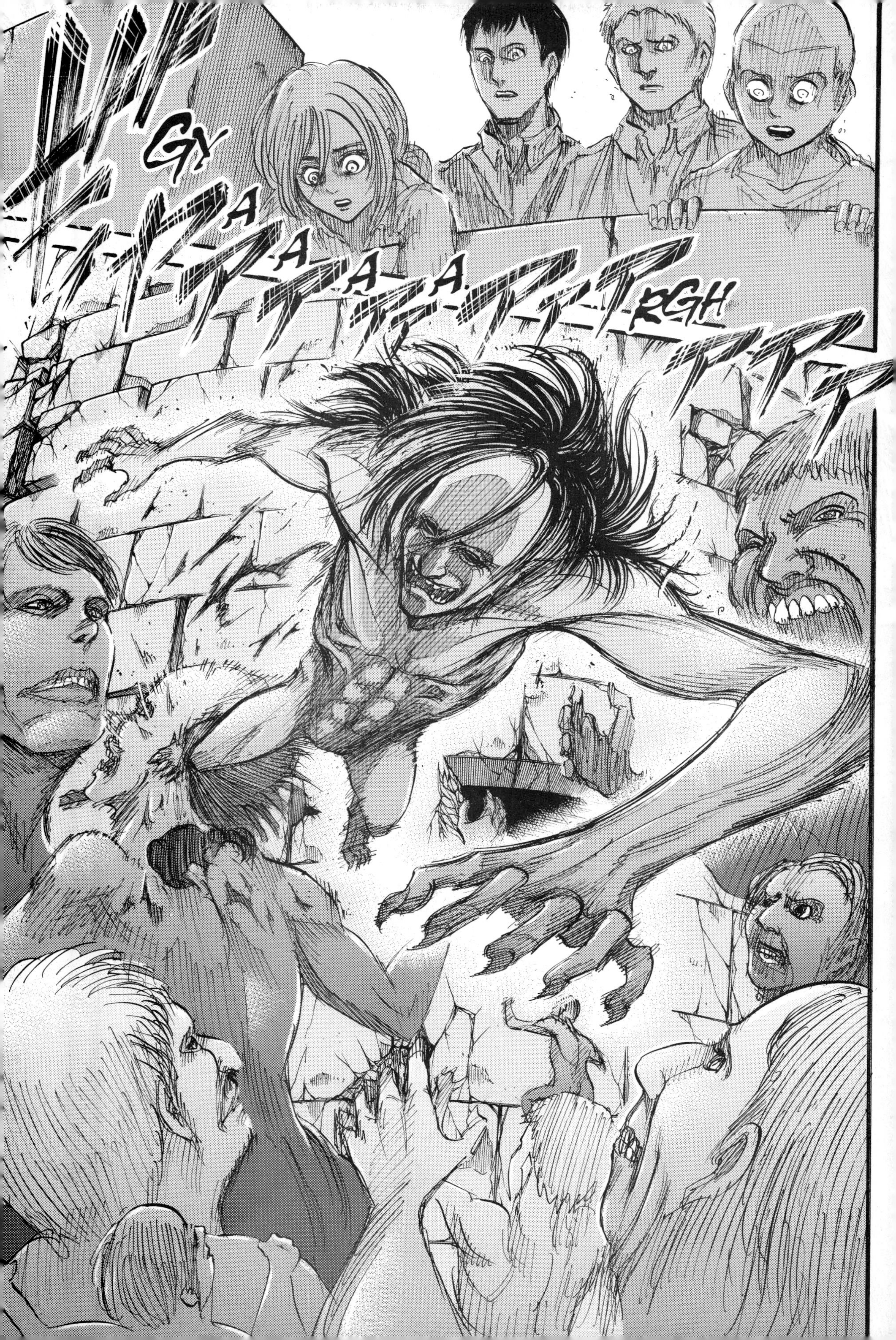
GYAAAAARGH

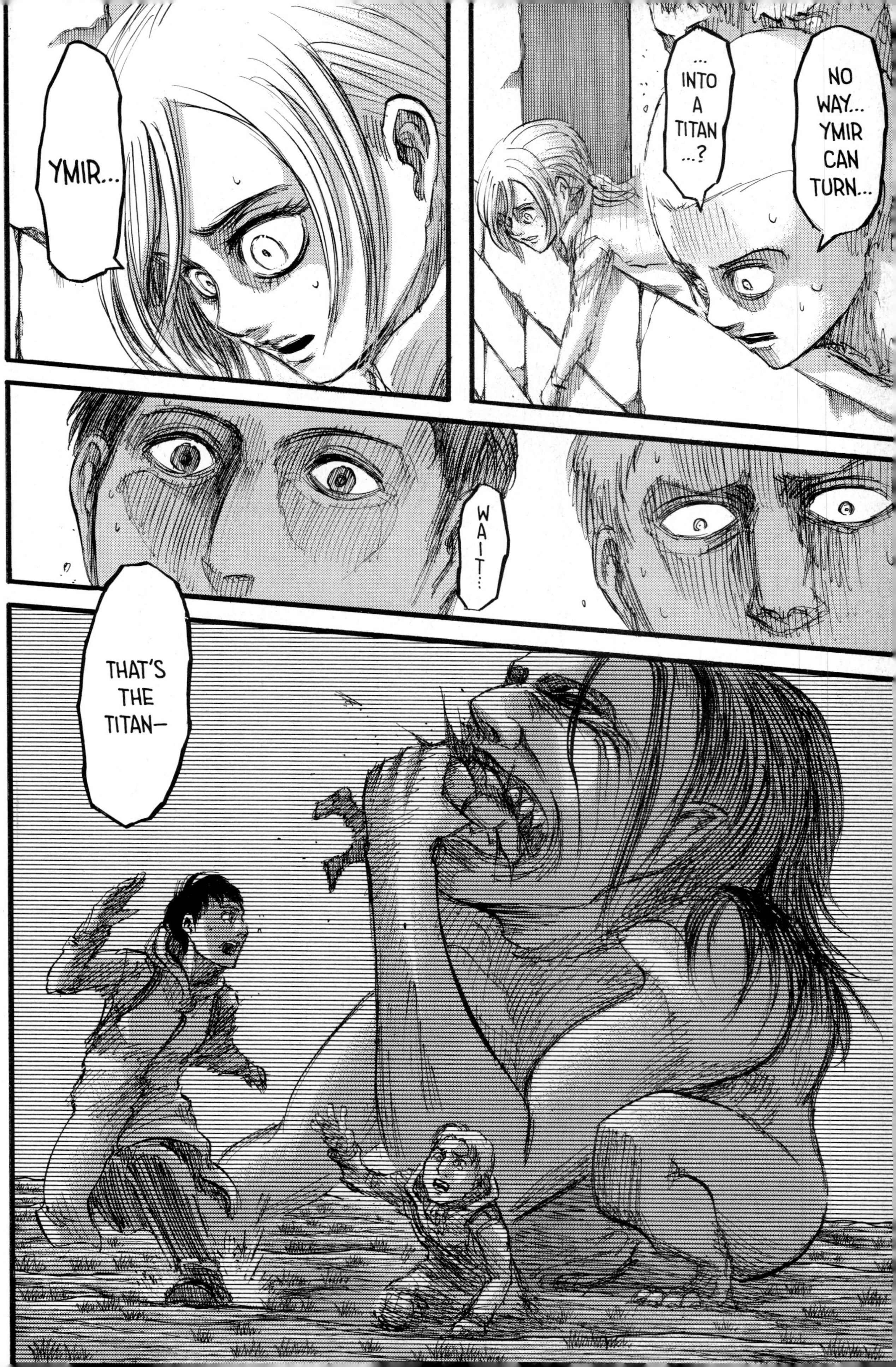
NO WAY... YMIR CAN TURN...
... INTO A TITAN ...?
YMIR...
WAIT...
THAT'S THE TITAN—

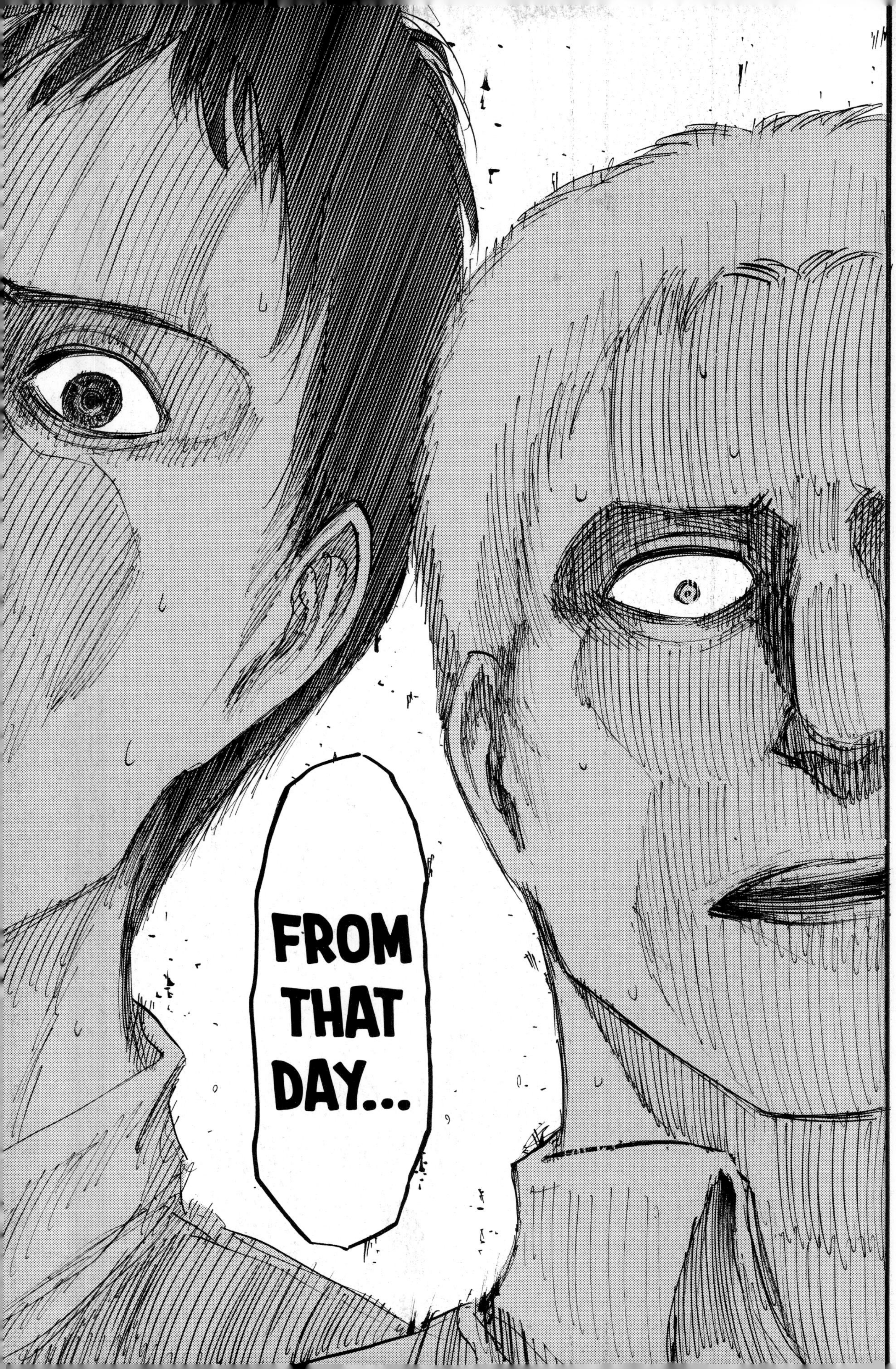
FROM THAT DAY...

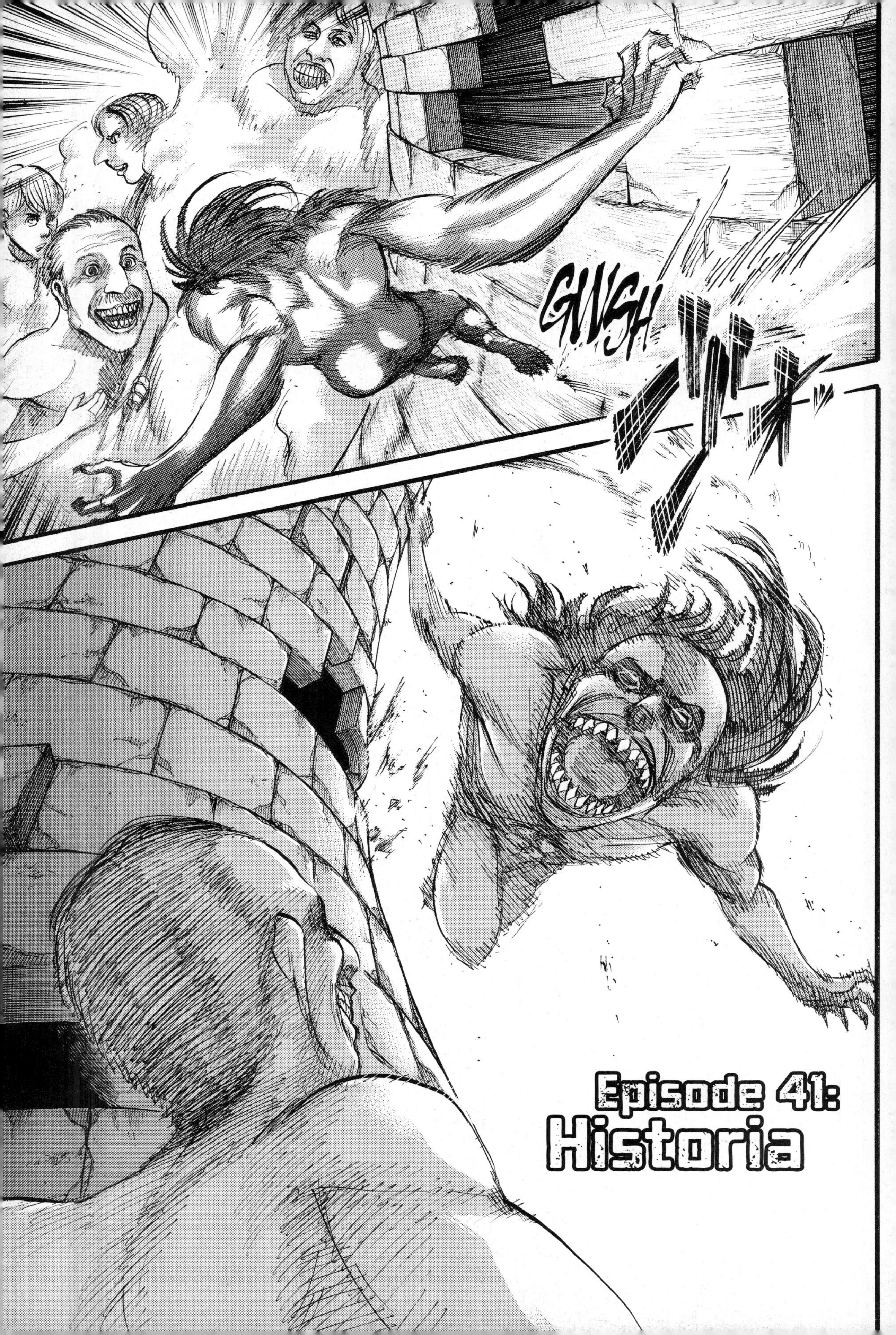
GNNGH
Episode 41:
Historia

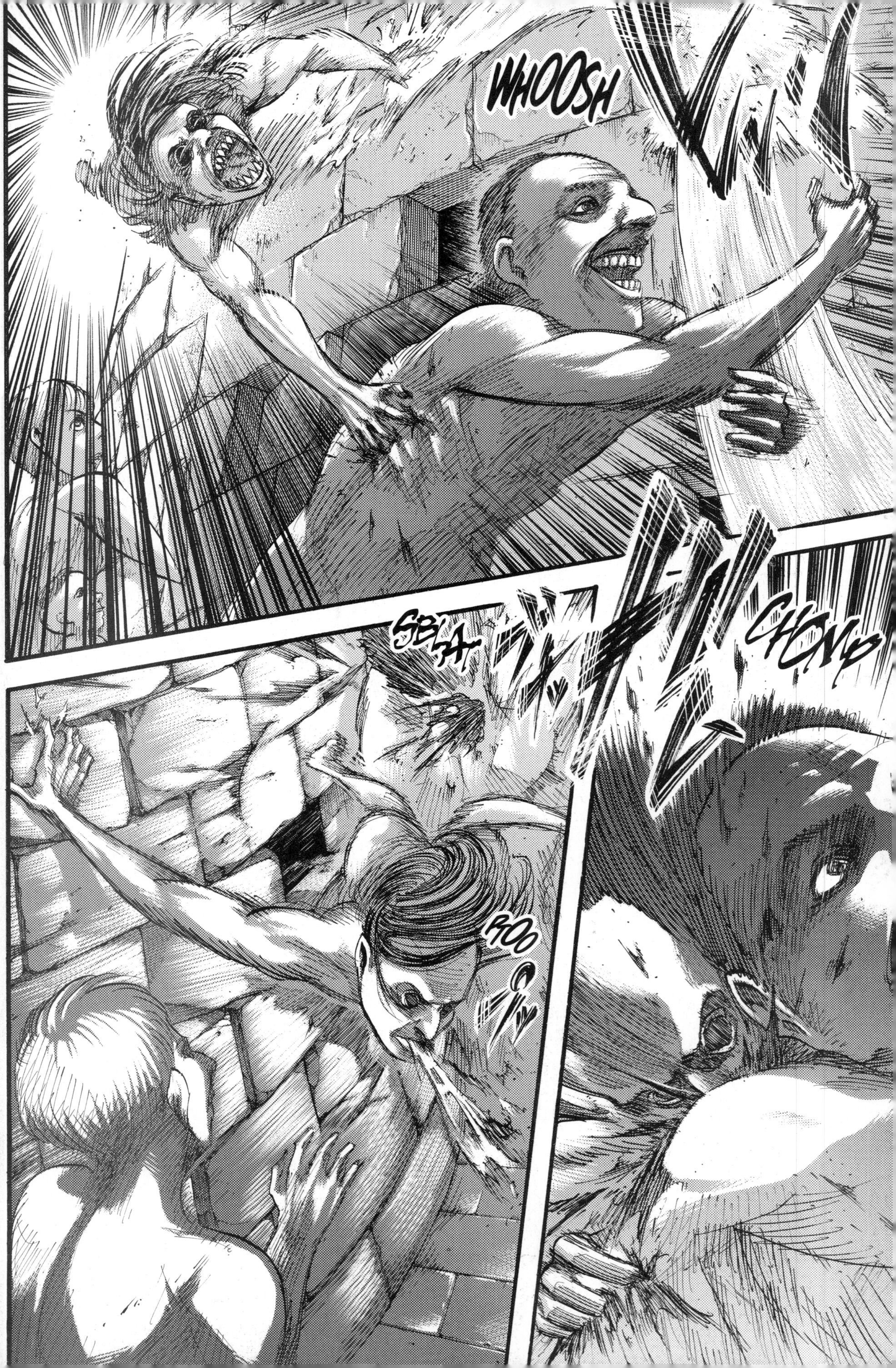
WHOOSH
CHOMP
SBLAT
ROO

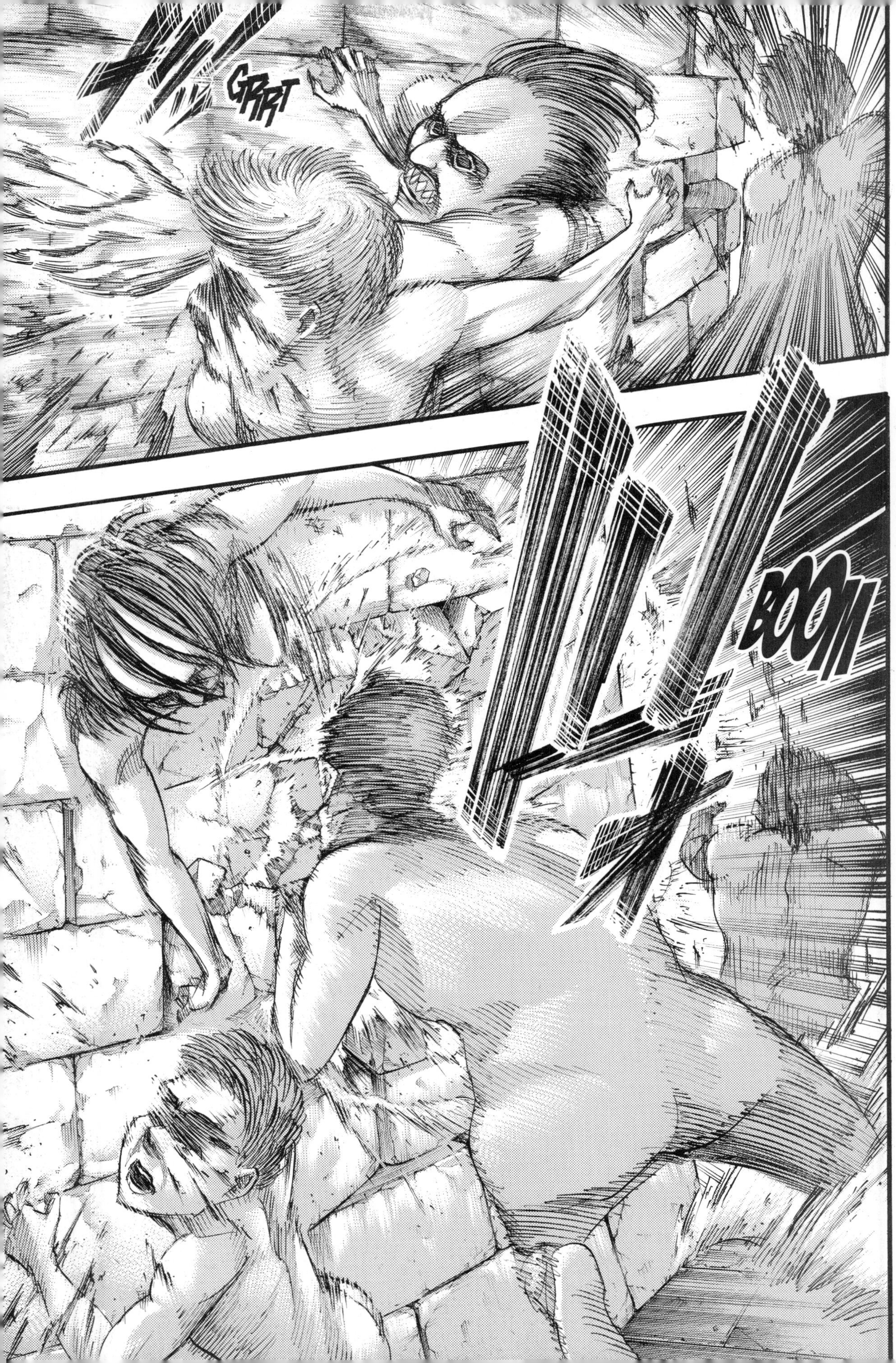
GRRRT
BOOM

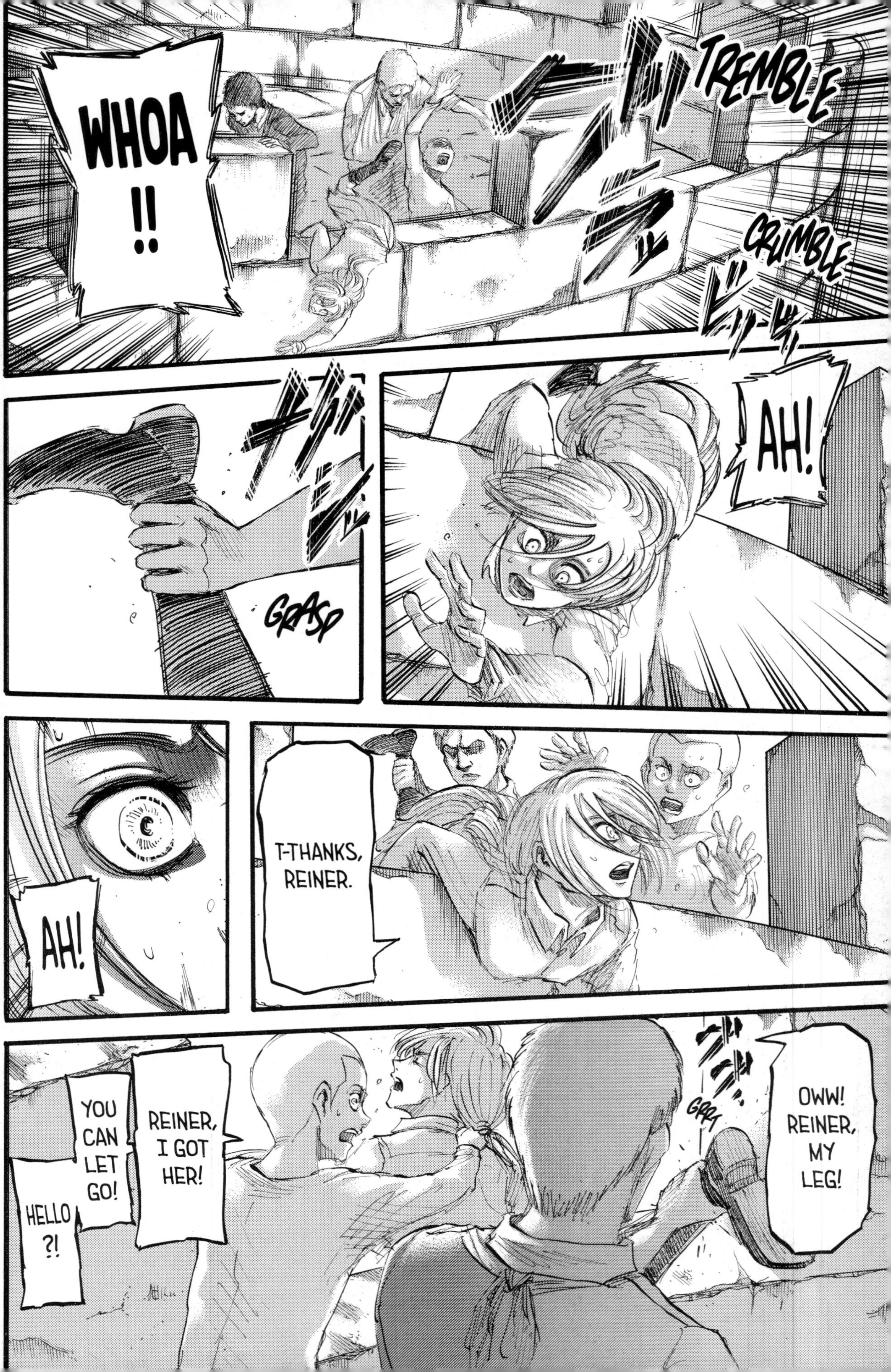
TREMBLE
CRUMBLE
WHOA!!
AH!
GRASP
T-THANKS, REINER.
AH!
OWW! REINER, MY LEG!
GRR
REINER, I GOT HER!
YOU CAN LET GO!
HELLO?!

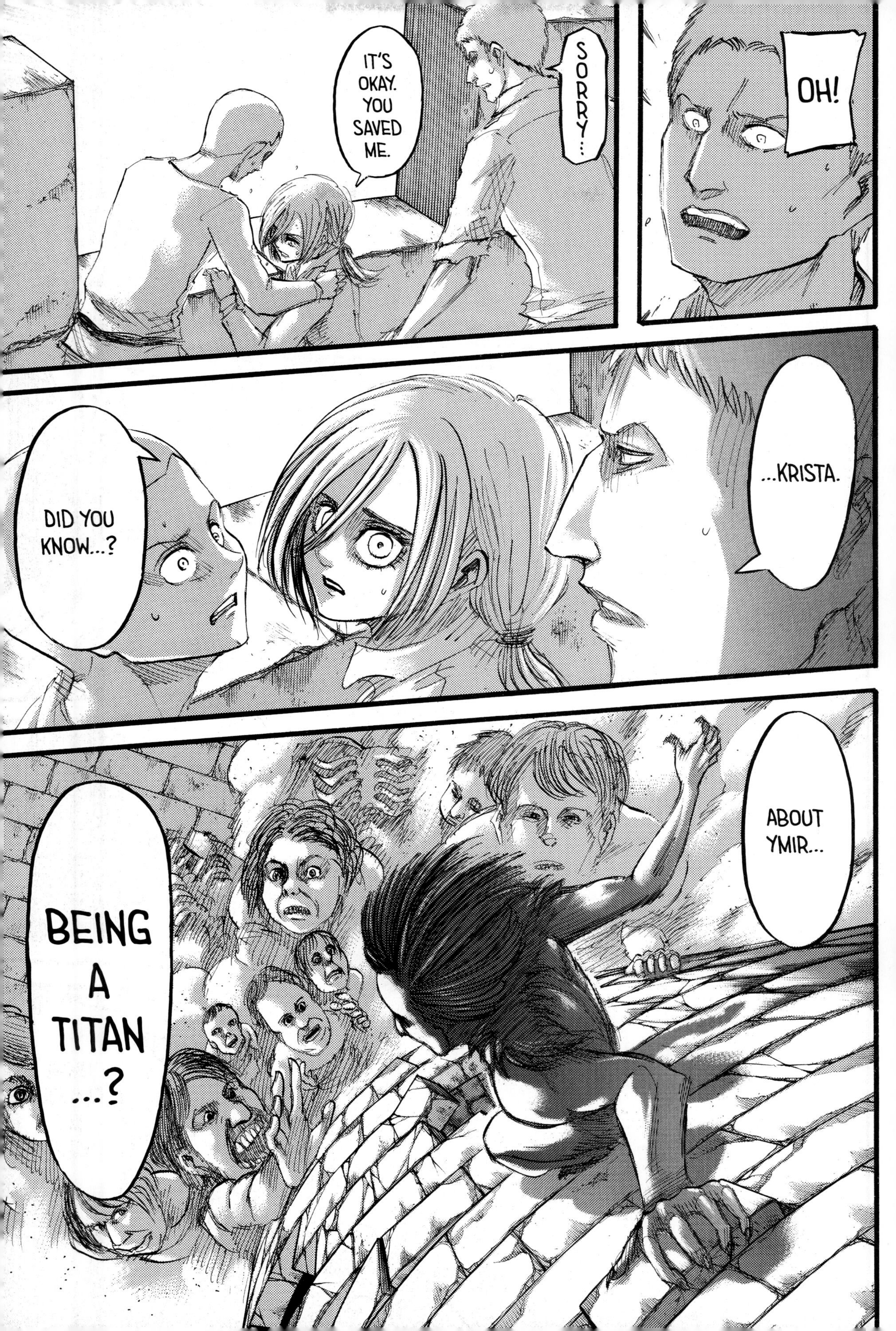
OH!
SORRY...
IT'S OKAY. YOU SAVED ME.
...KRISTA.
DID YOU KNOW...?
ABOUT YMIR...
BEING A TITAN ...?

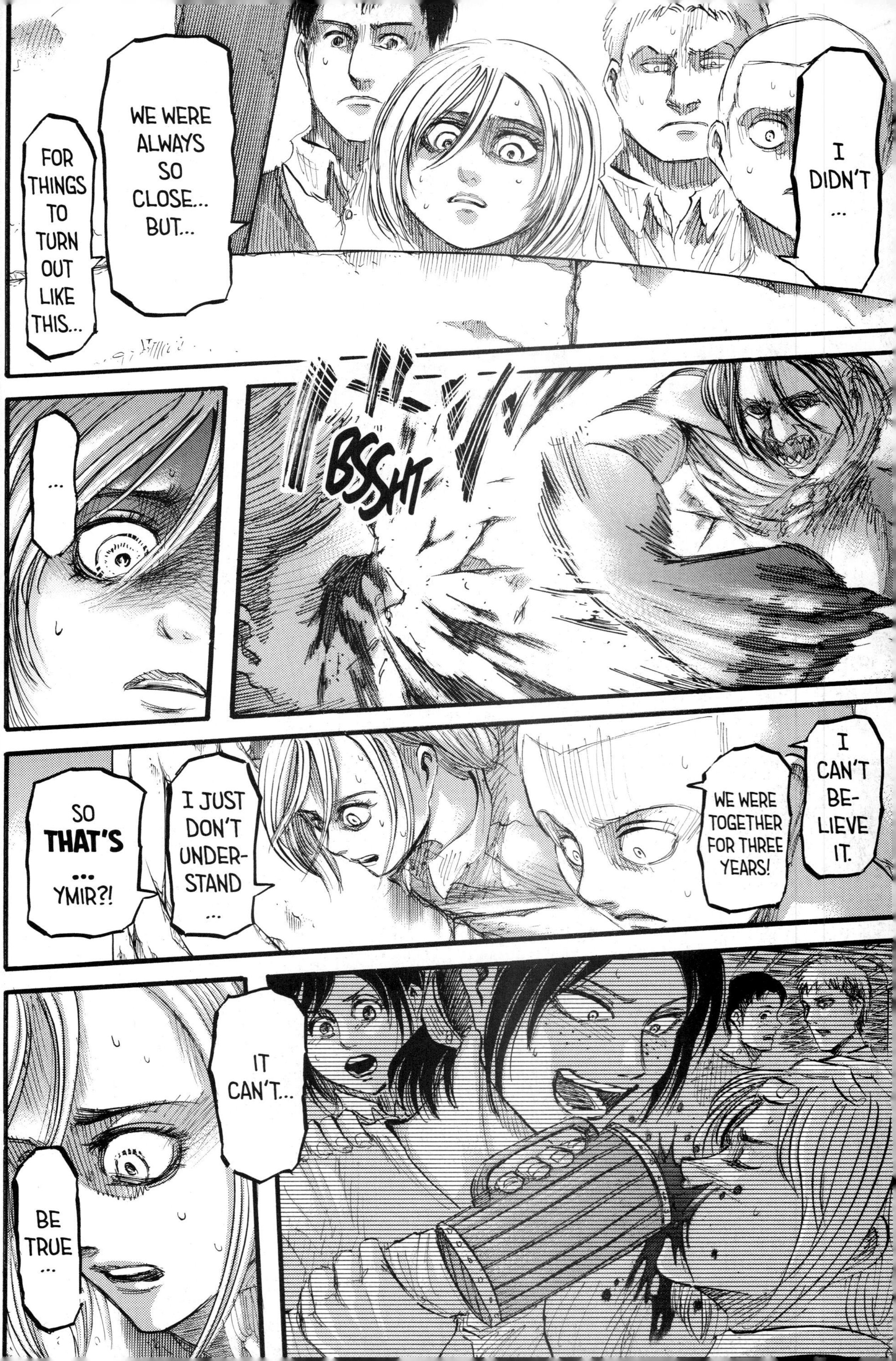
I DIDN'T ...
WE WERE ALWAYS SO CLOSE... BUT...
FOR THINGS TO TURN OUT LIKE THIS...
BSSHT
...
I CAN'T BE-LIEVE IT.
WE WERE TOGETHER FOR THREE YEARS!
I JUST DON'T UNDERSTAND ...
SO **THAT'S** ... YMIR?!
IT CAN'T...
BE TRUE ...

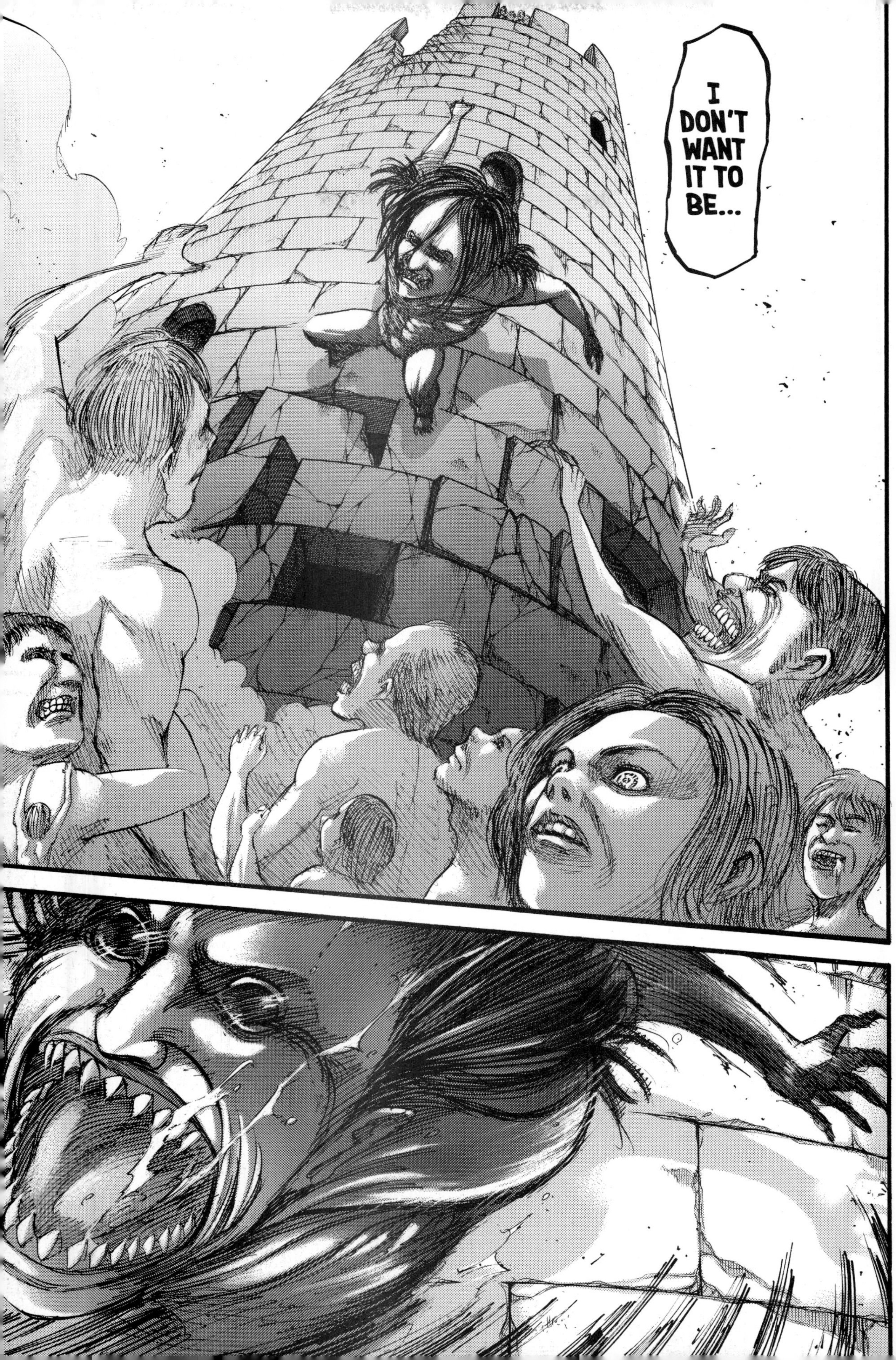
I DON'T WANT IT TO BE...

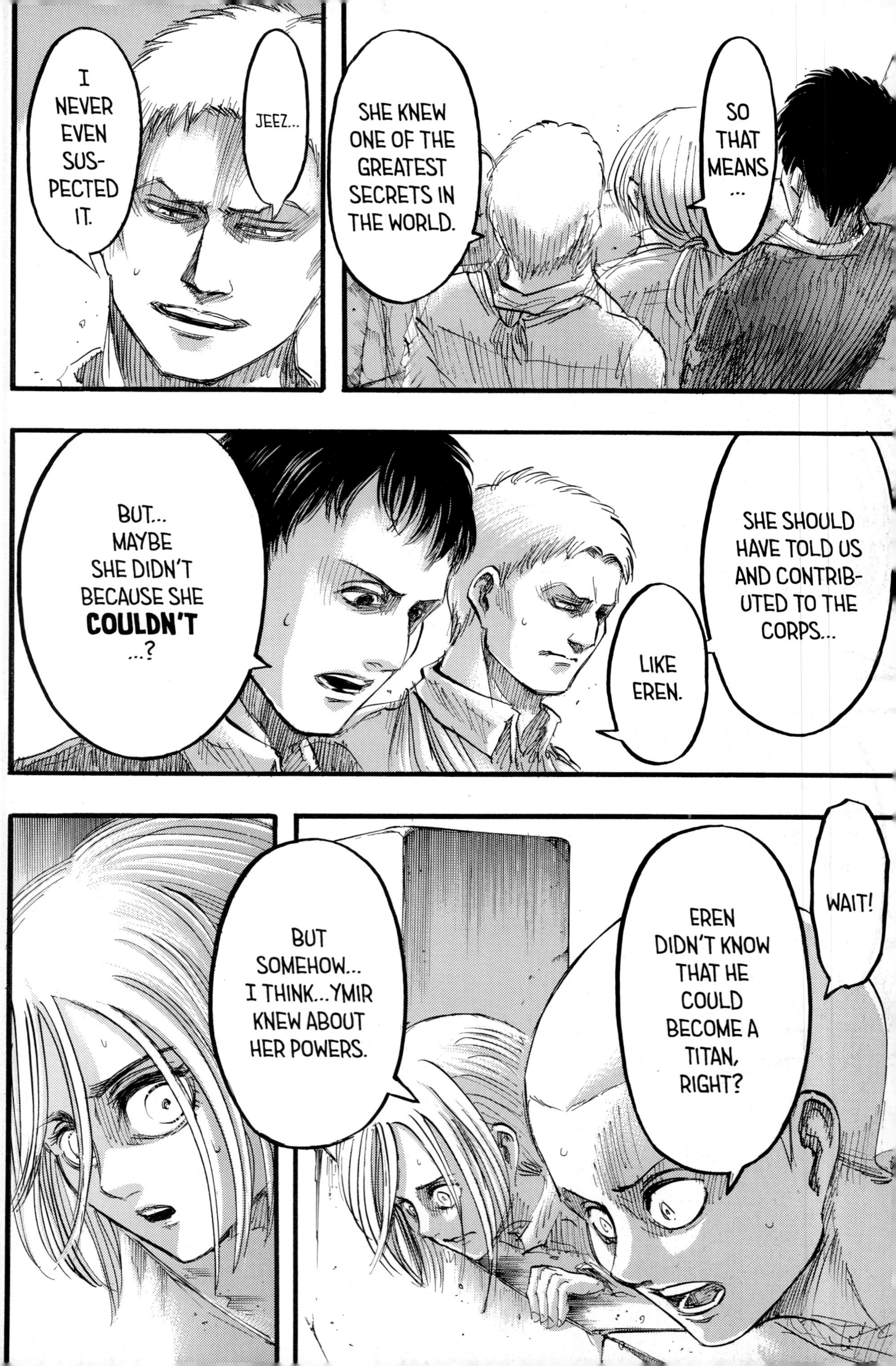
SO THAT MEANS ...
SHE KNEW ONE OF THE GREATEST SECRETS IN THE WORLD.
JEEZ...
I NEVER EVEN SUS-PECTED IT.
SHE SHOULD HAVE TOLD US AND CONTRIB-UTED TO THE CORPS...
LIKE EREN.
BUT... MAYBE SHE DIDN'T BECAUSE SHE **COULDN'T** ...?
WAIT!
EREN DIDN'T KNOW THAT HE COULD BECOME A TITAN, RIGHT?
BUT SOMEHOW... I THINK...YMIR KNEW ABOUT HER POWERS.

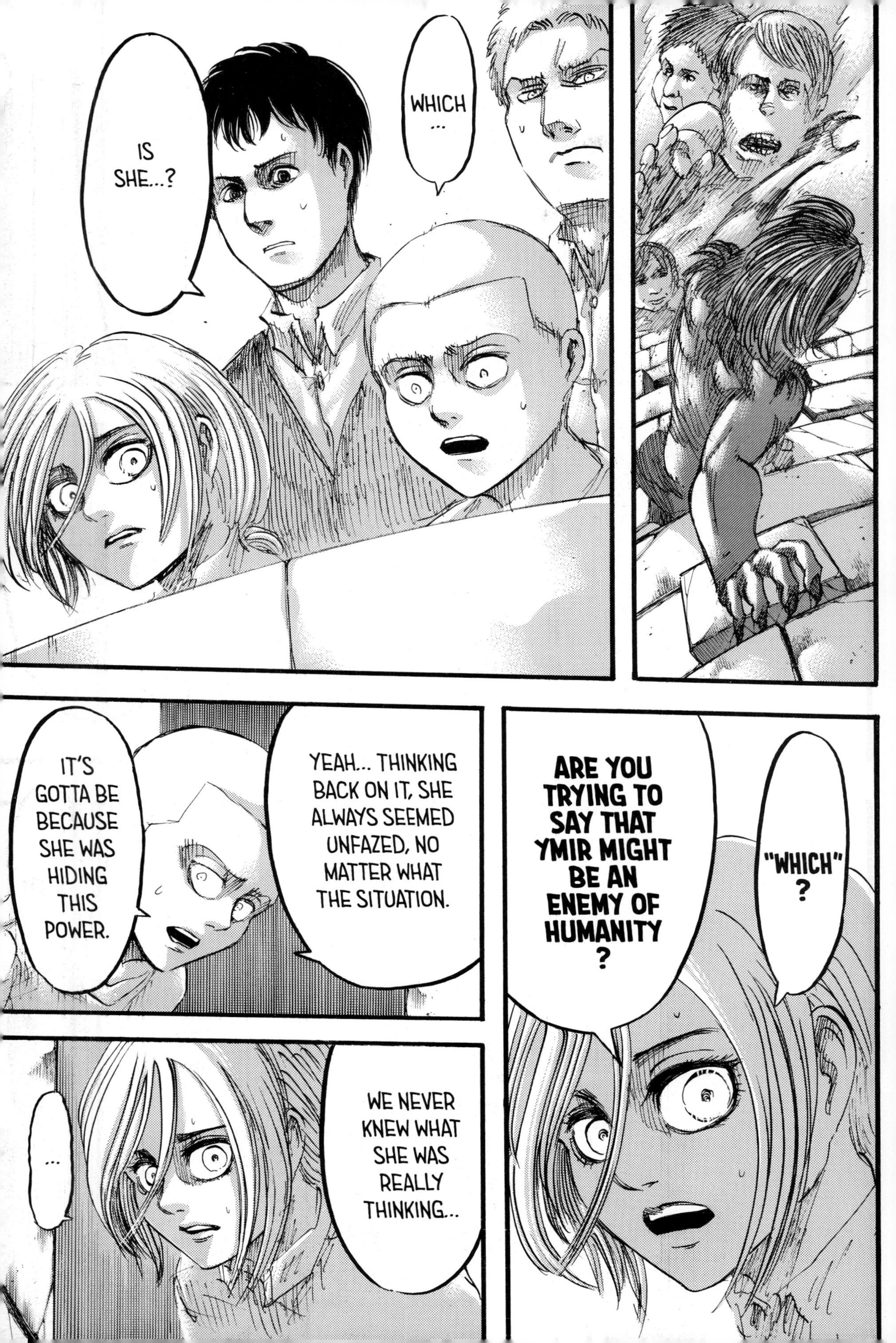
WHICH ...
IS SHE...?
"WHICH"?
ARE YOU TRYING TO SAY THAT YMIR MIGHT BE AN ENEMY OF HUMANITY?
YEAH... THINKING BACK ON IT, SHE ALWAYS SEEMED UNFAZED, NO MATTER WHAT THE SITUATION.
IT'S GOTTA BE BECAUSE SHE WAS HIDING THIS POWER.
WE NEVER KNEW WHAT SHE WAS REALLY THINKING...
...

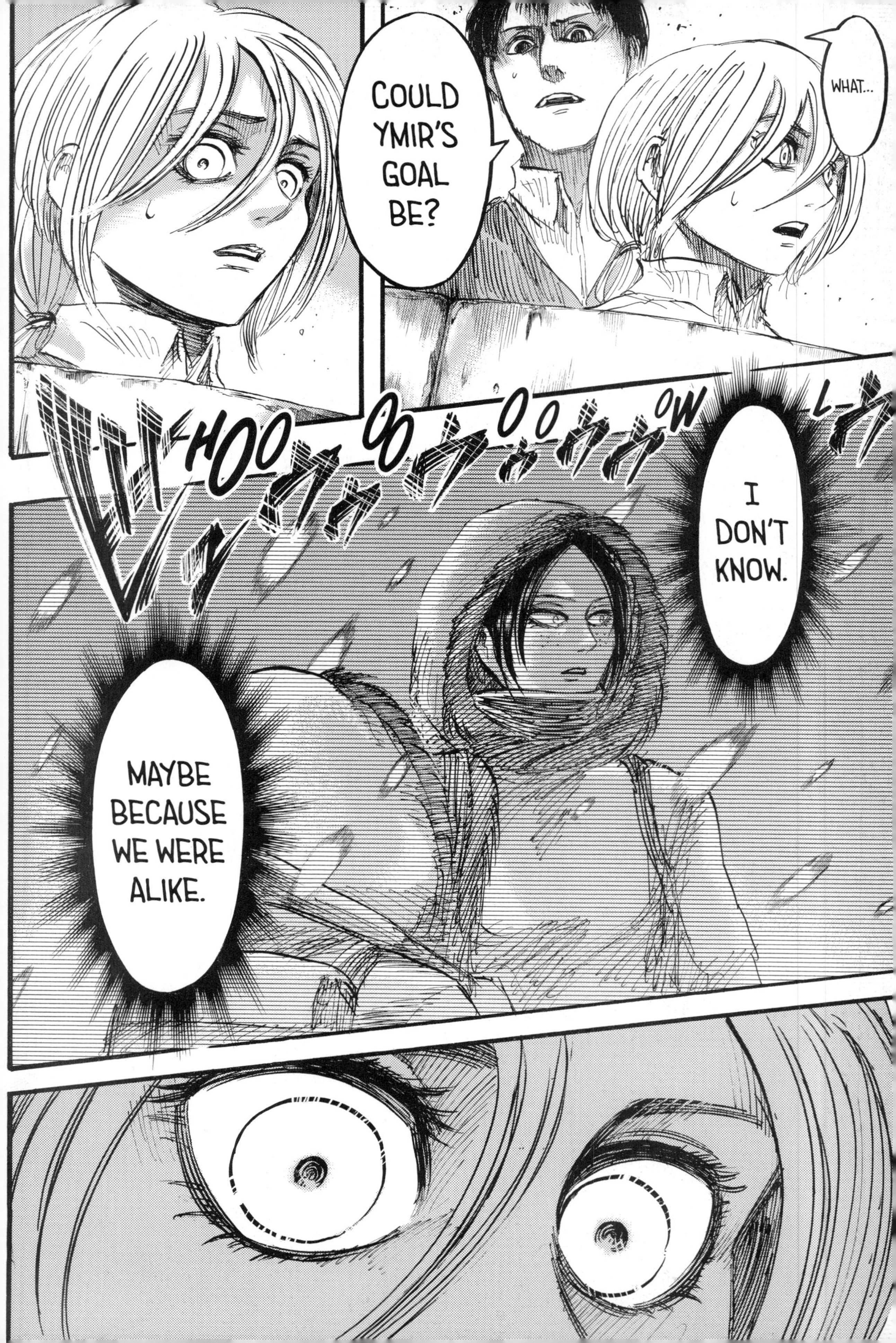
WHAT...
COULD YMIR'S GOAL BE?
WHOOOOOOOW
I DON'T KNOW.
MAYBE BECAUSE WE WERE ALIKE.

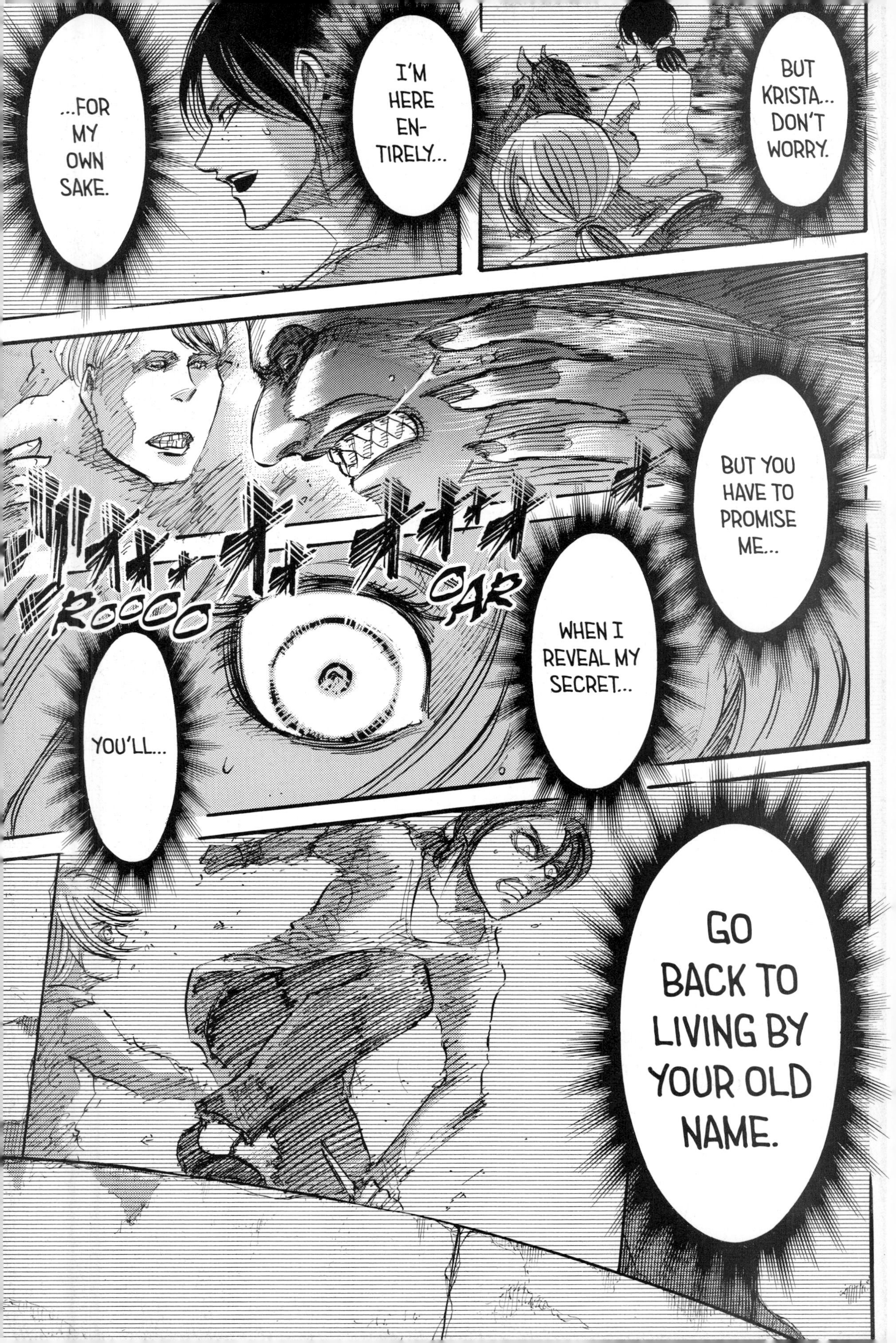
BUT KRISTA... DON'T WORRY.
I'M HERE EN-TIRELY...
...FOR MY OWN SAKE.
BUT YOU HAVE TO PROMISE ME...
WHEN I REVEAL MY SECRET...
ROOOOO
OAR
YOU'LL...
GO BACK TO LIVING BY YOUR OLD NAME.

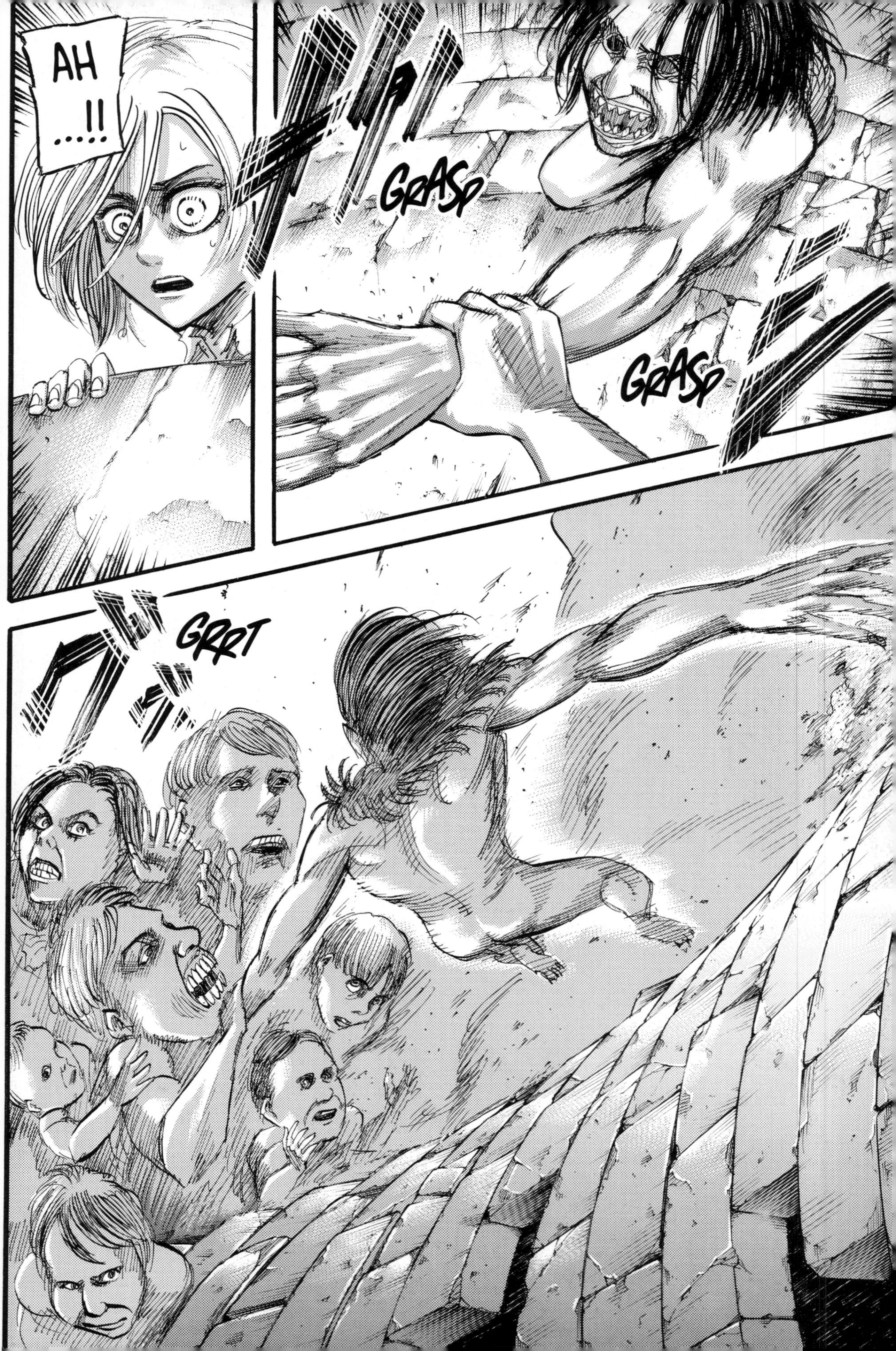
GRASP
GRASP
AH ...!!
GRRT

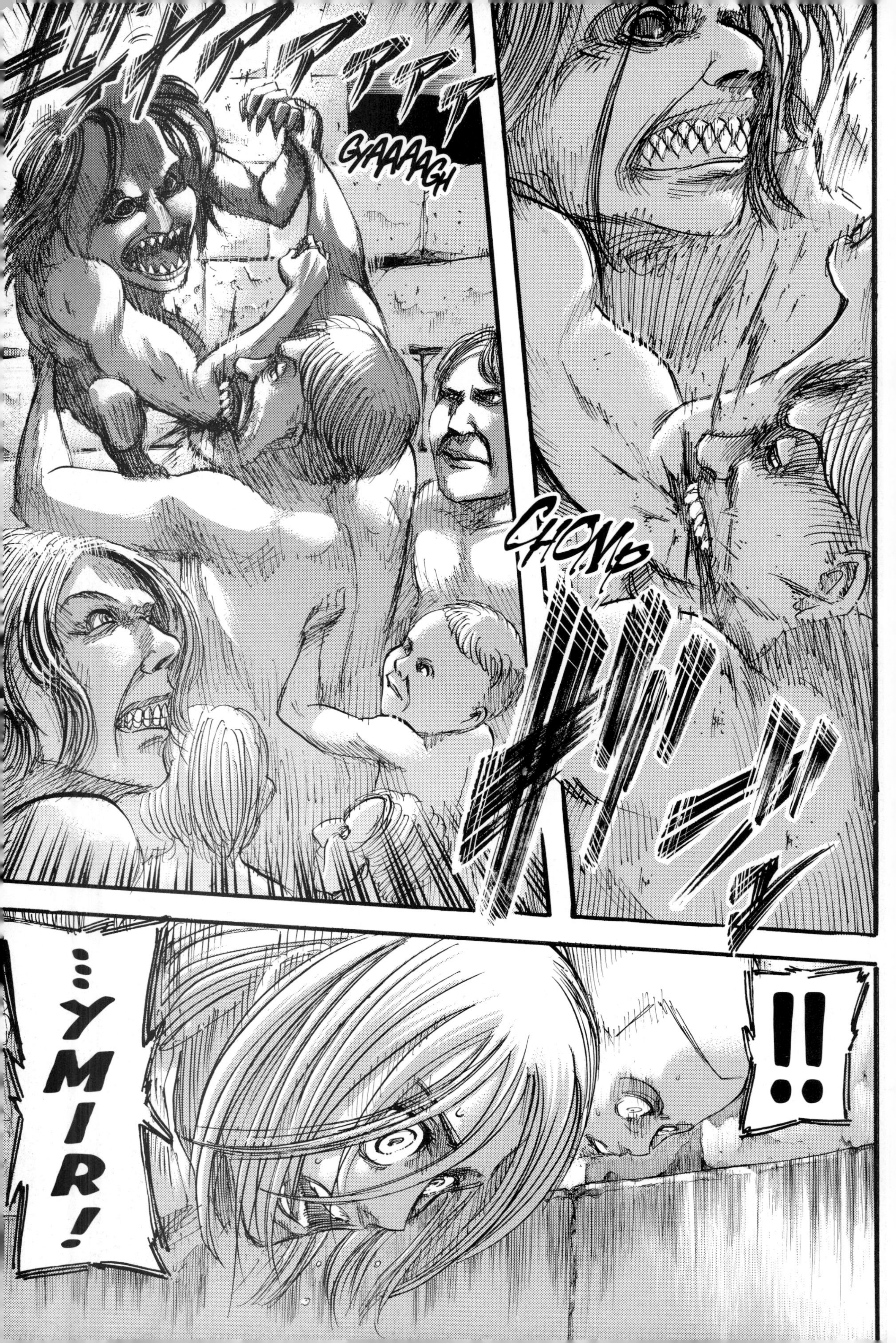
CHOMP
GYAAAAGH
!!
...YMIR!

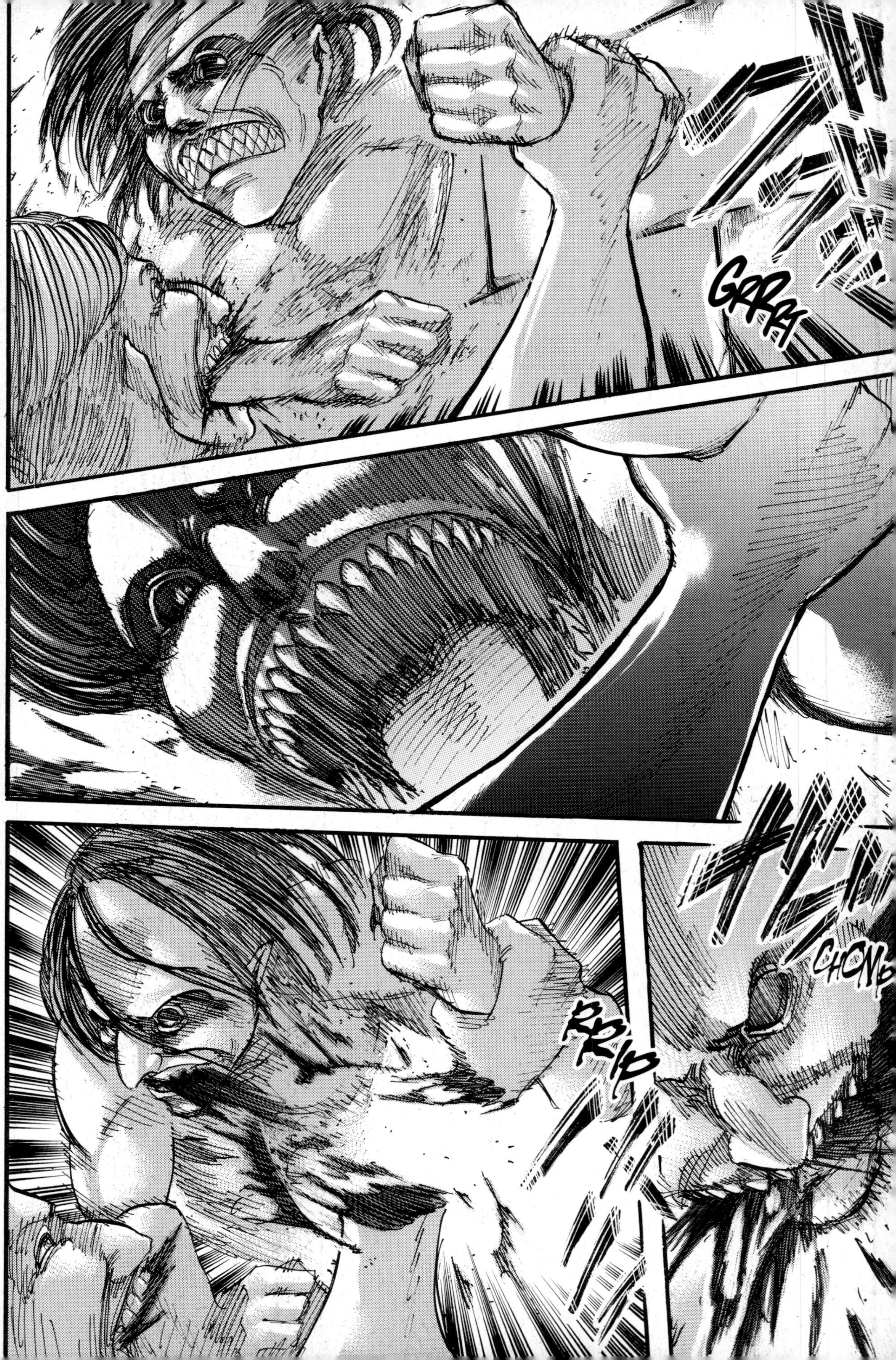
GRRR
CHOMP
RRIP

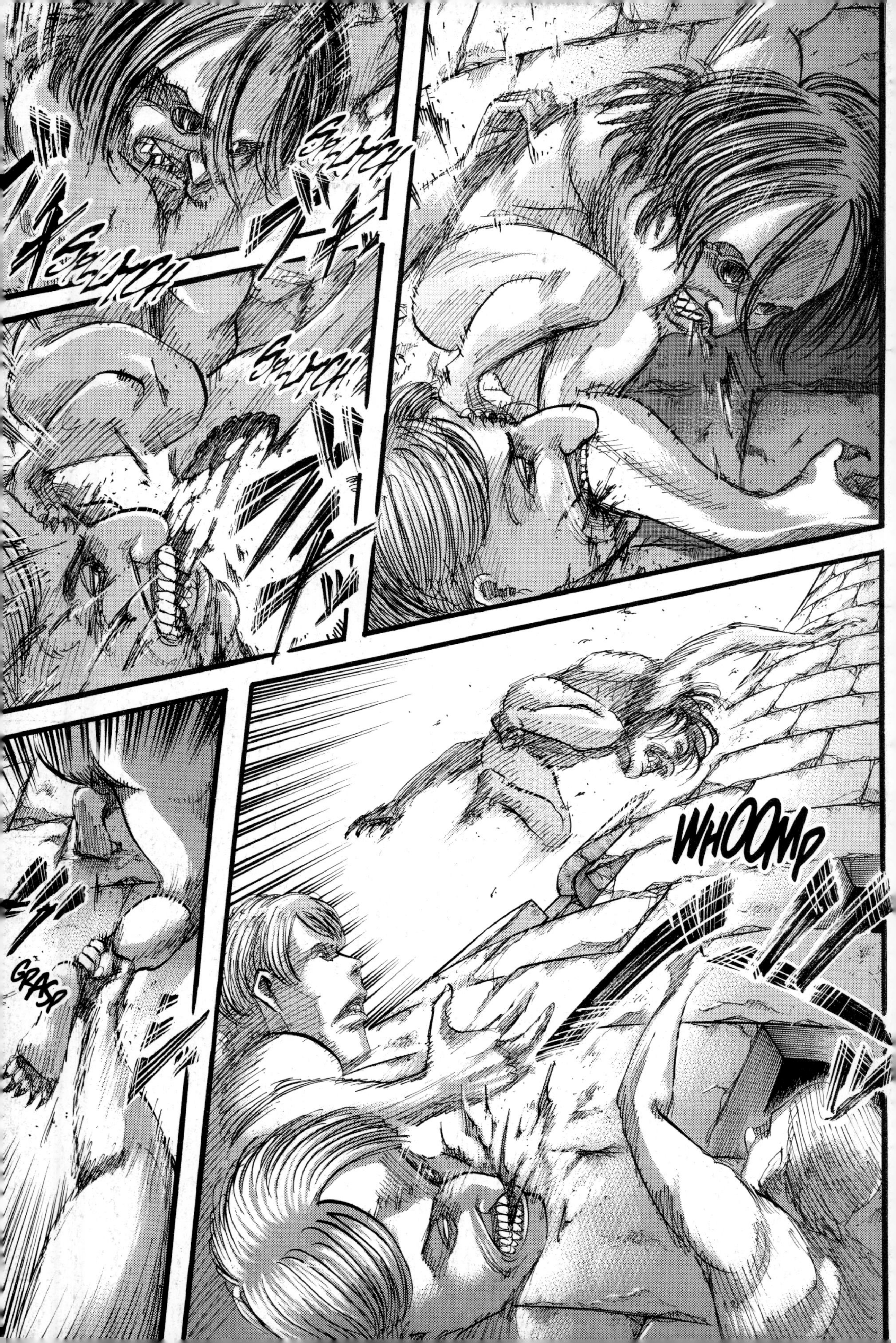
GSHUCH!
GSHUCH!
GSHUCH!
WHOOMP
GRASP

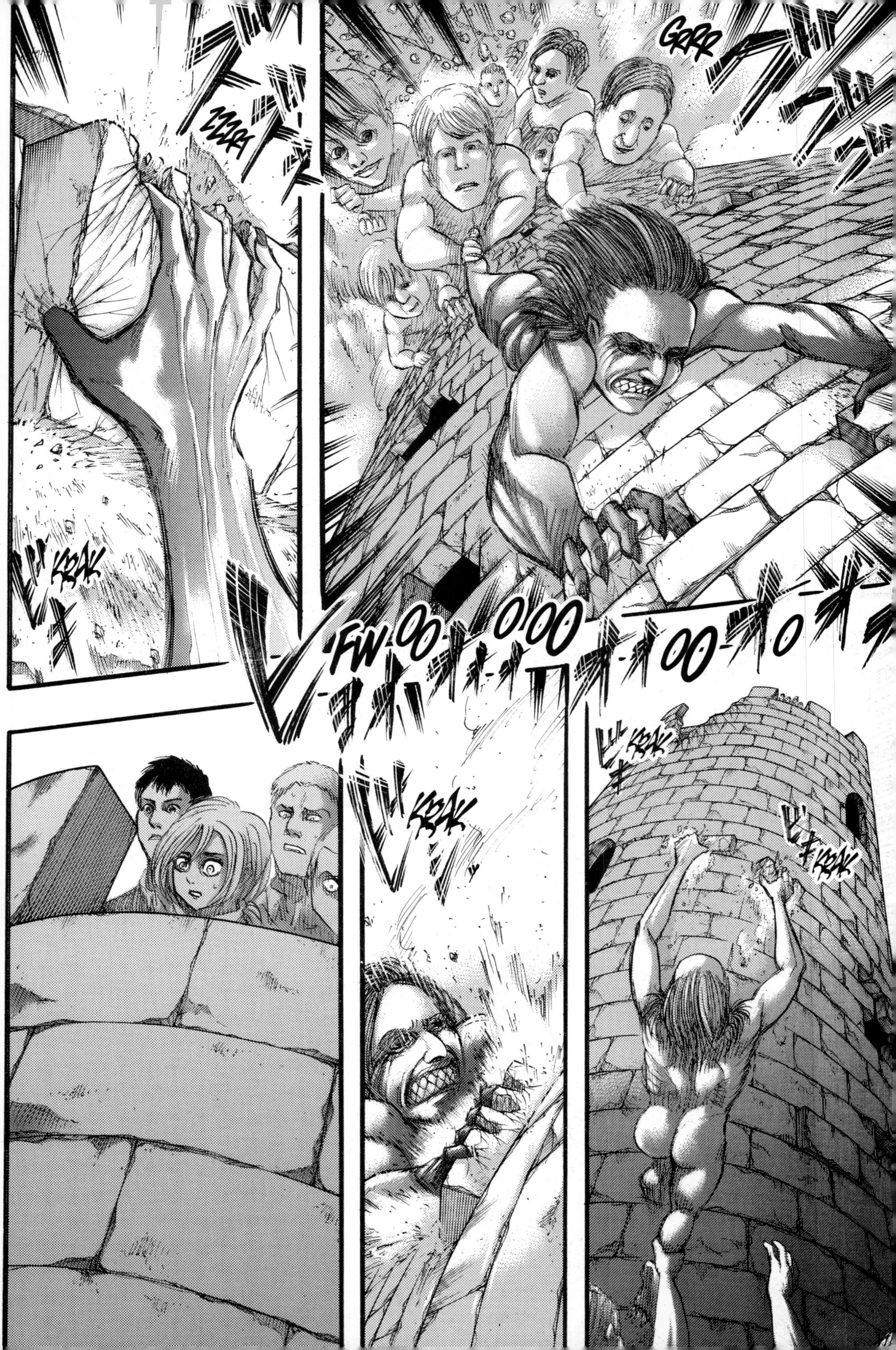
GRRR
FW-OO-O-OO-OO-O
ZZZRK
KRAK
KRAK
KRAK
KRAK

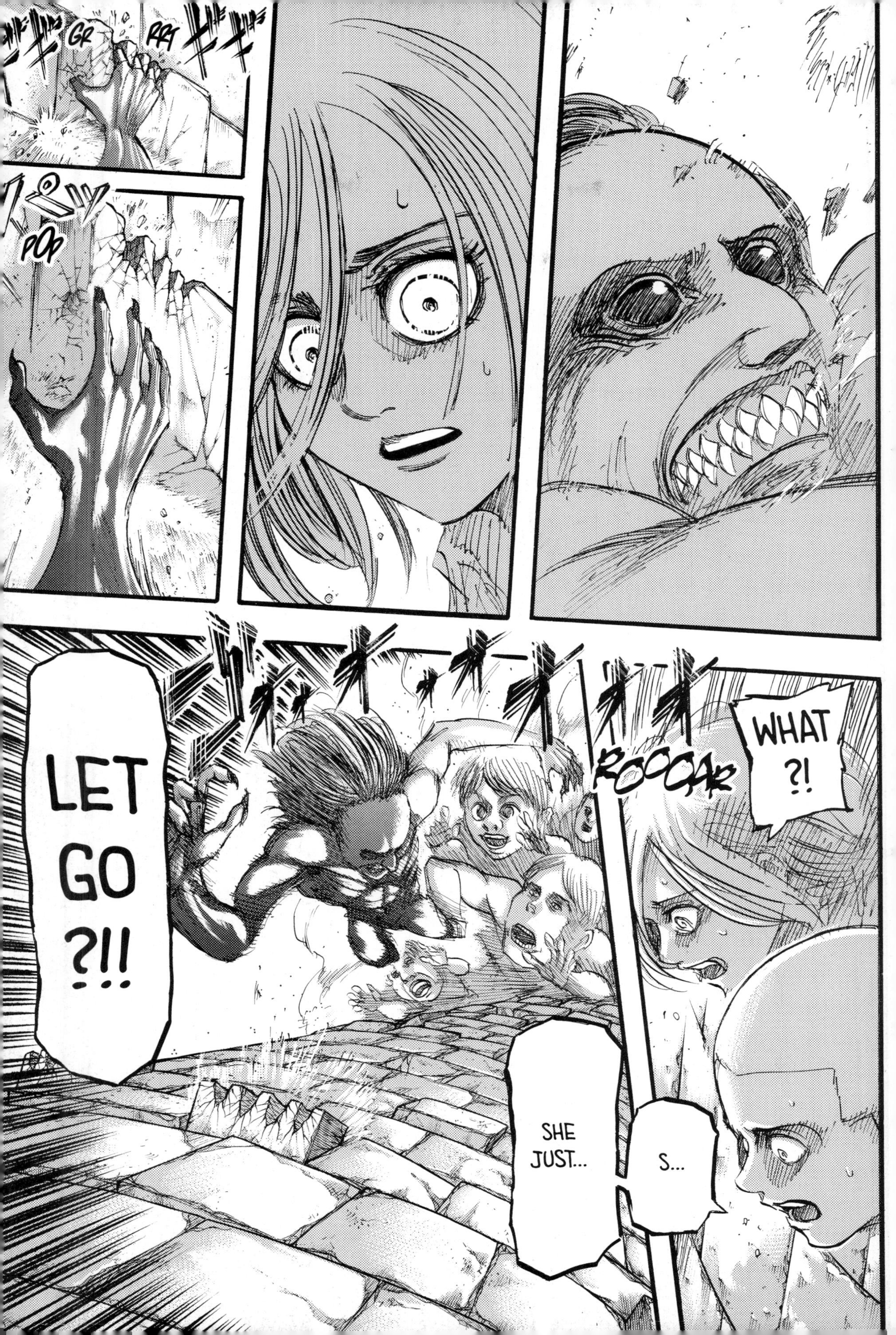
GR
RRT
POP
WHAT ?!
ROOOAR
S...
SHE JUST...
LET GO ?!!

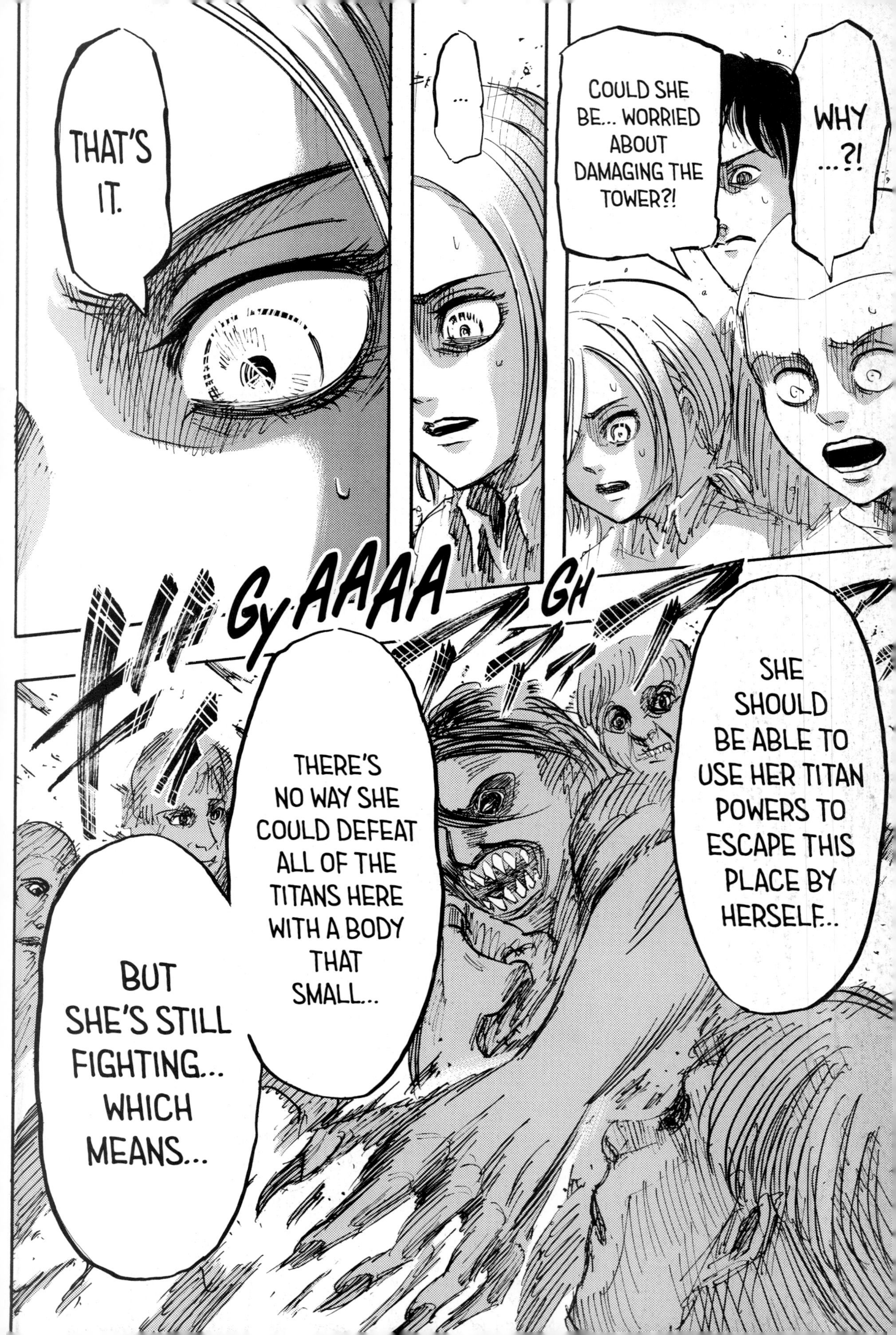
WHY...?!
COULD SHE BE... WORRIED ABOUT DAMAGING THE TOWER?!
...
THAT'S IT.
GYAAAAGH
SHE SHOULD BE ABLE TO USE HER TITAN POWERS TO ESCAPE THIS PLACE BY HERSELF...
THERE'S NO WAY SHE COULD DEFEAT ALL OF THE TITANS HERE WITH A BODY THAT SMALL...
BUT SHE'S STILL FIGHTING... WHICH MEANS...

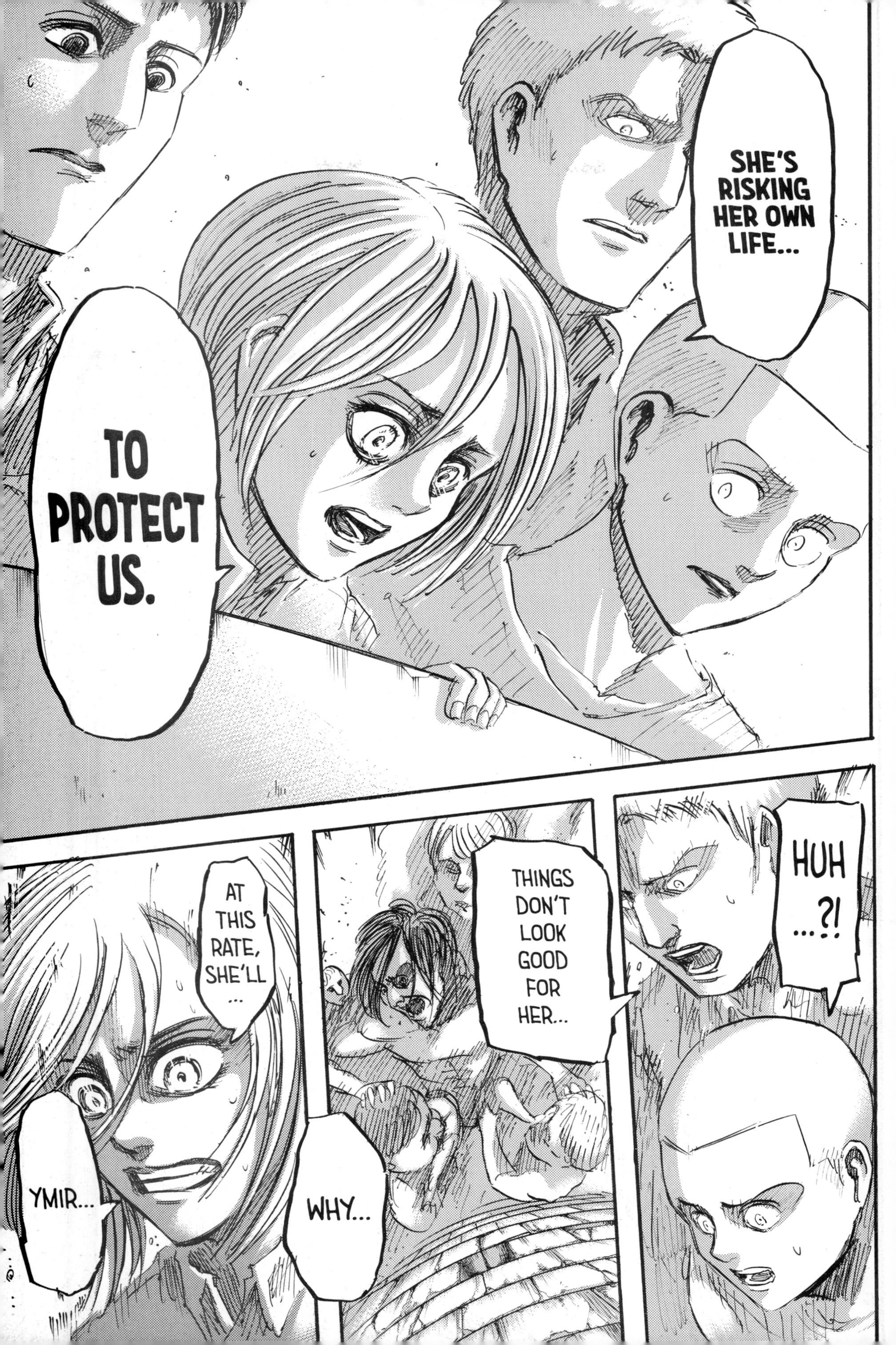
SHE'S RISKING HER OWN LIFE...
TO PROTECT US.
HUH ...?!
THINGS DON'T LOOK GOOD FOR HER...
WHY...
AT THIS RATE, SHE'LL ...
YMIR...

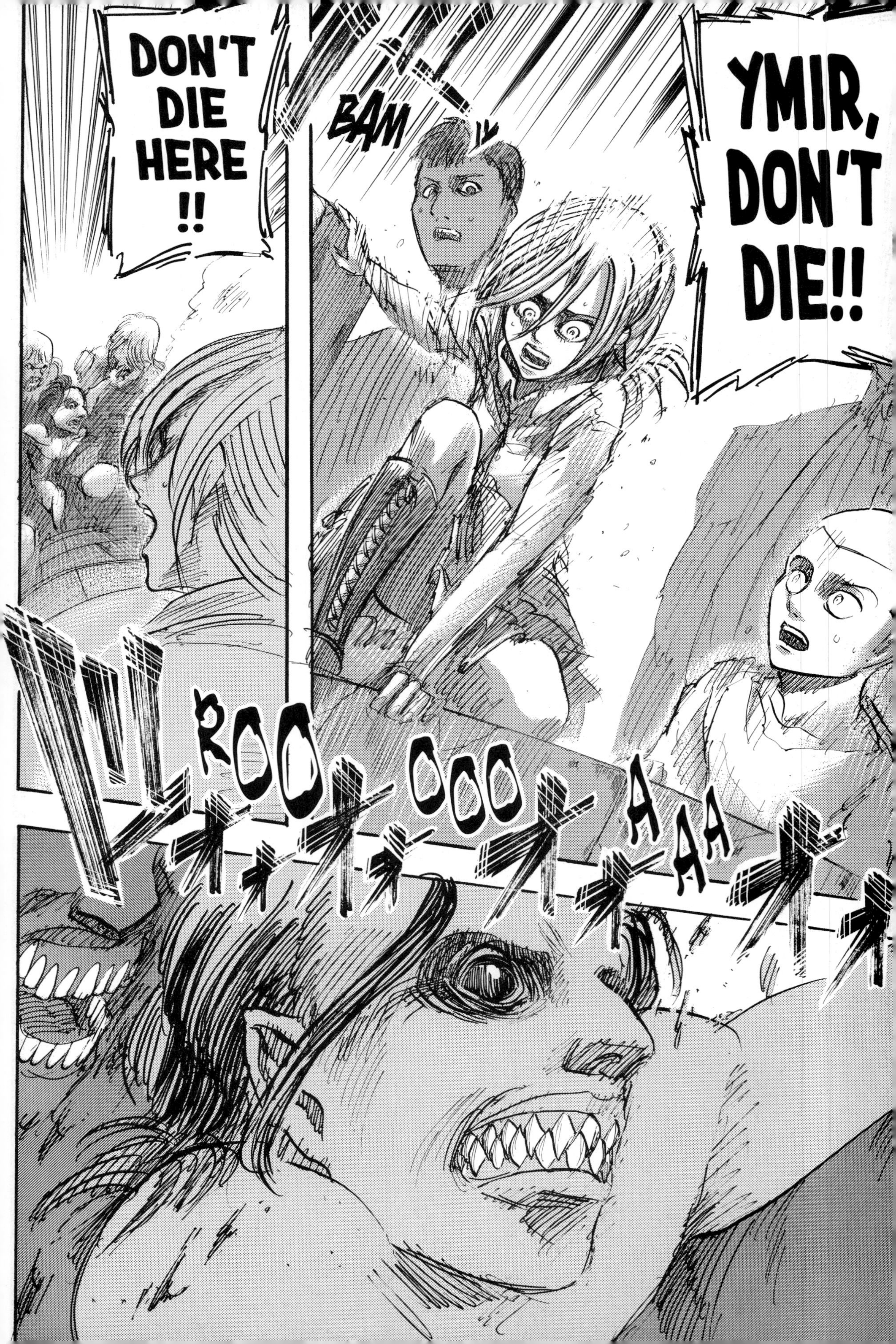
YMIR, DON'T DIE!!
BAM
DON'T DIE HERE!!
ROOOOOOAAA

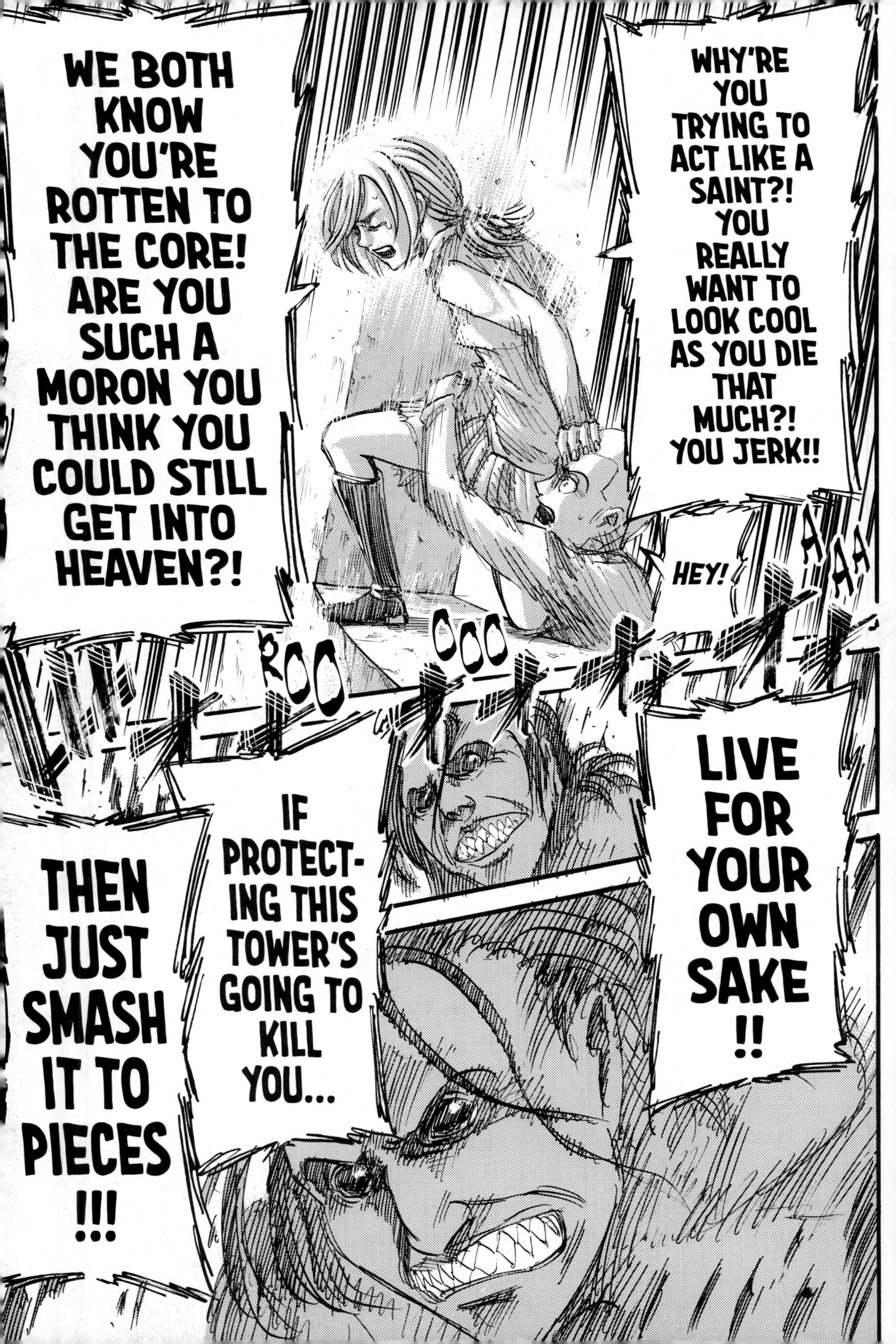
WHY'RE YOU TRYING TO ACT LIKE A SAINT?! YOU REALLY WANT TO LOOK COOL AS YOU DIE THAT MUCH?! YOU JERK!!
HEY!
AAA
WE BOTH KNOW YOU'RE ROTTEN TO THE CORE! ARE YOU SUCH A MORON YOU THINK YOU COULD STILL GET INTO HEAVEN?!
ROOOOO
LIVE FOR YOUR OWN SAKE!!
IF PROTECT-ING THIS TOWER'S GOING TO KILL YOU...
THEN JUST SMASH IT TO PIECES!!!

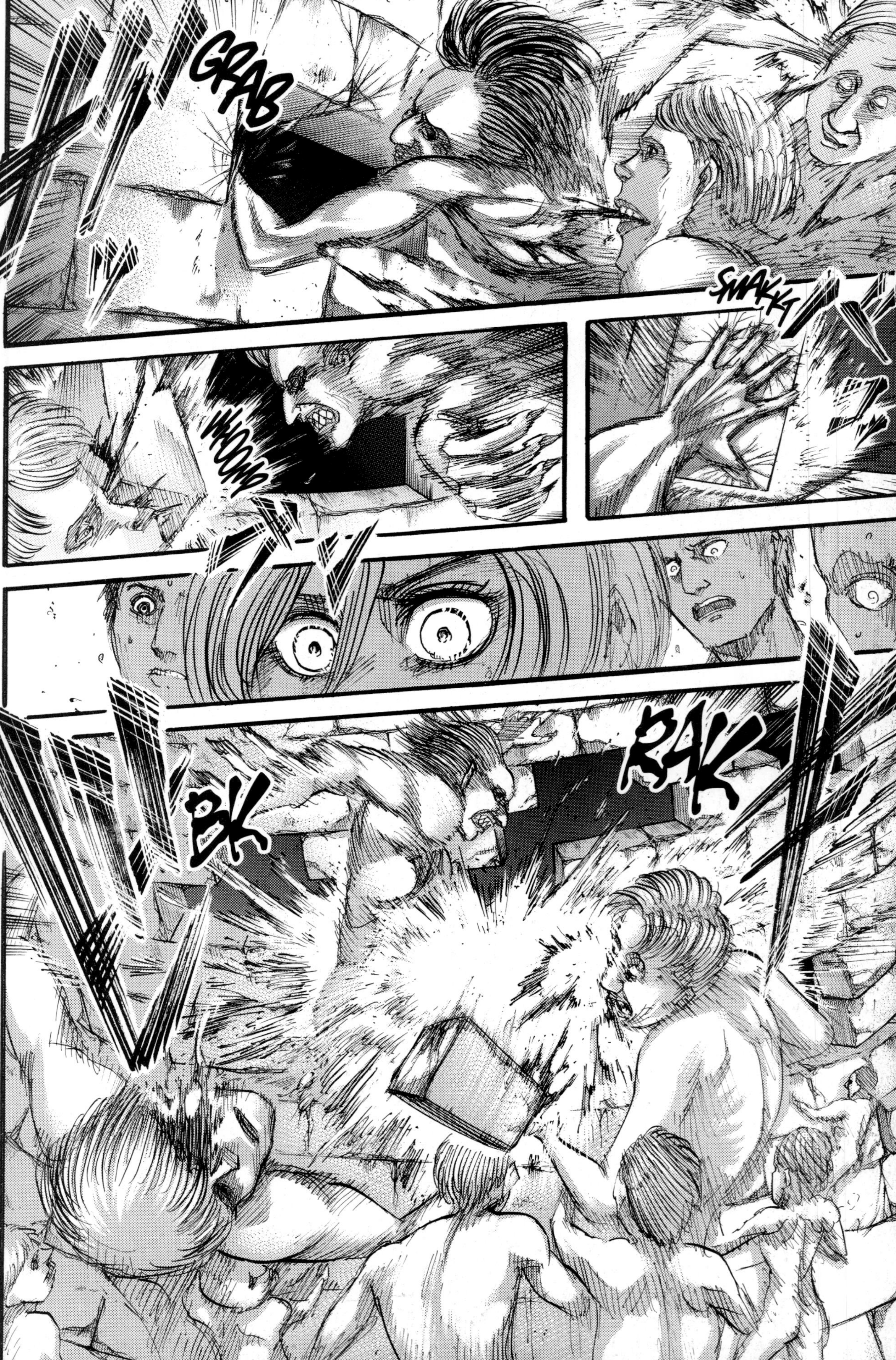
GRAB
SMAKK
WHOOM
RAK
BK

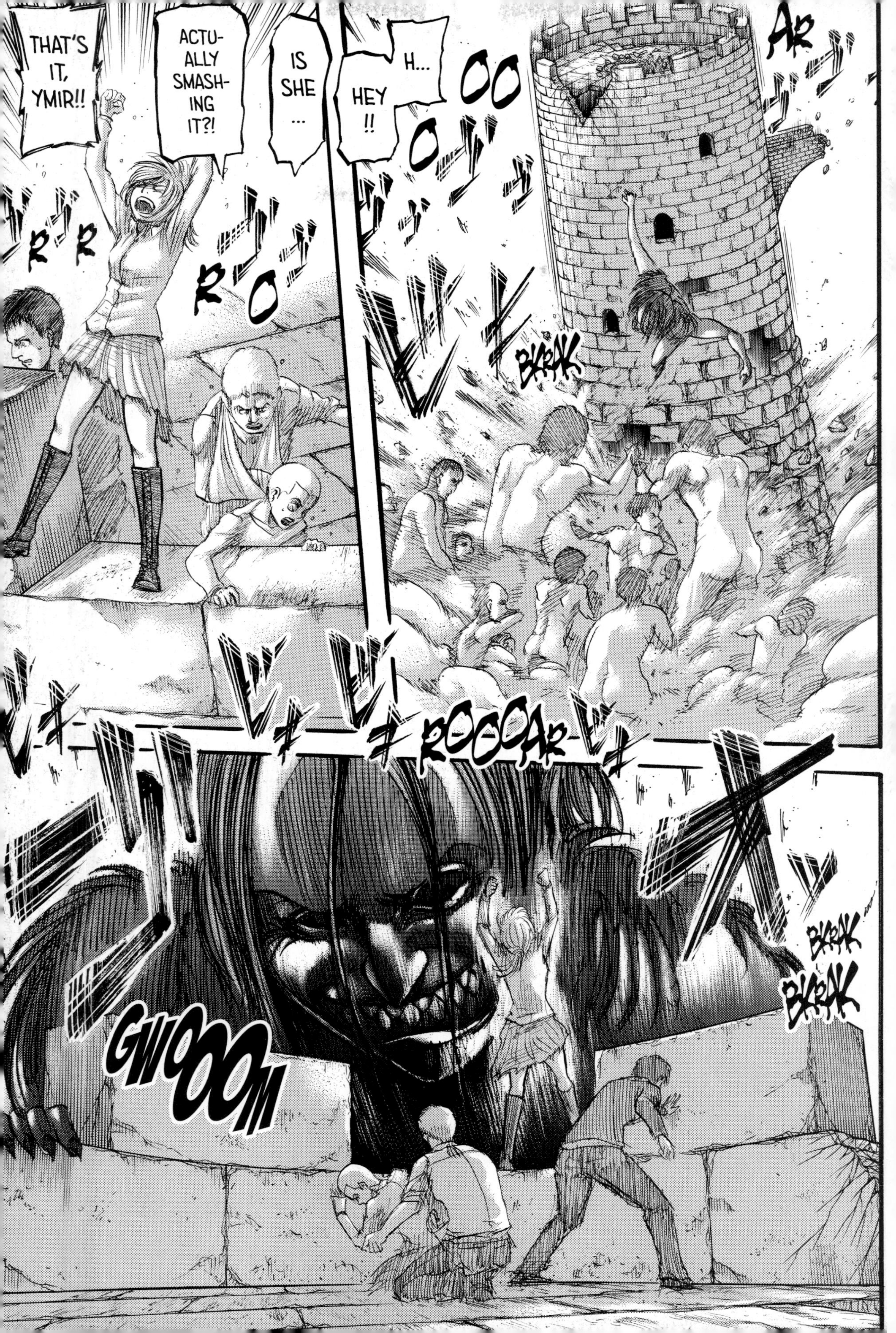

AR
OOO
H...
HEY!!
BKRAK
IS SHE ...
ACTUALLY SMASHING IT?!
THAT'S IT, YMIR!!
RO
RR
ROOOAR
BKRAK
BKRAK
GWOOOM

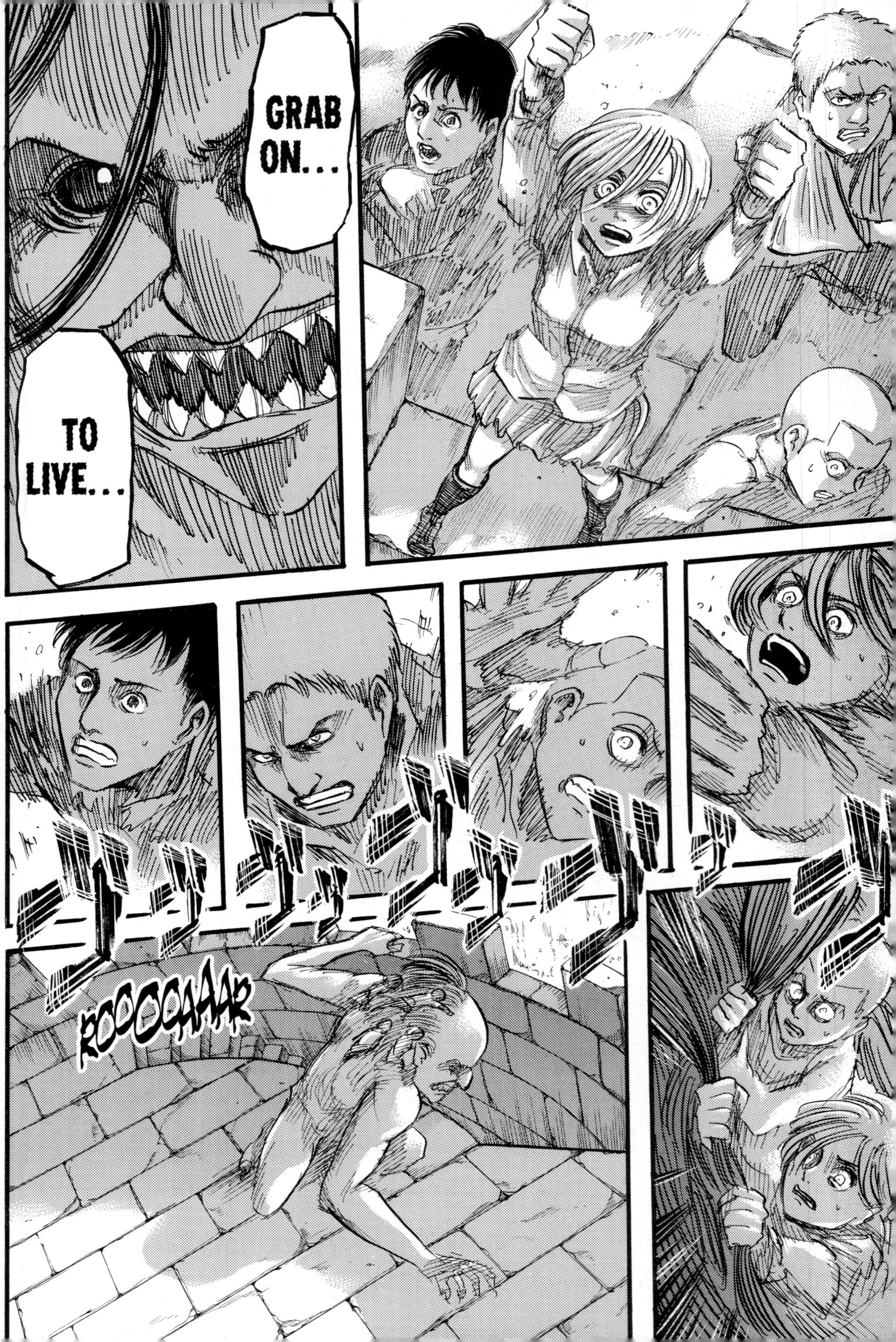
GRAB ON...
TO LIVE...
ROOOAAAR

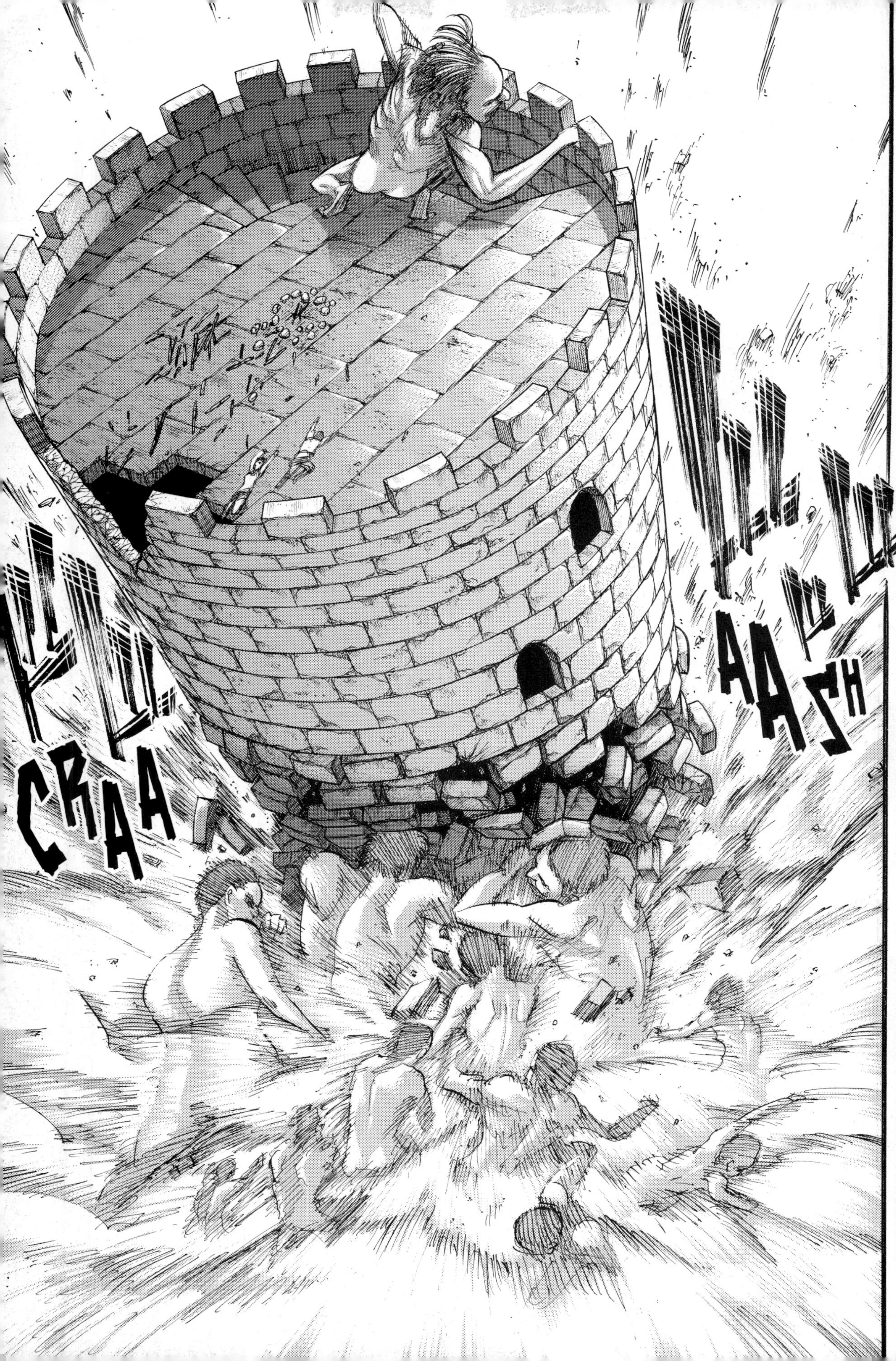
AASH
CRAA

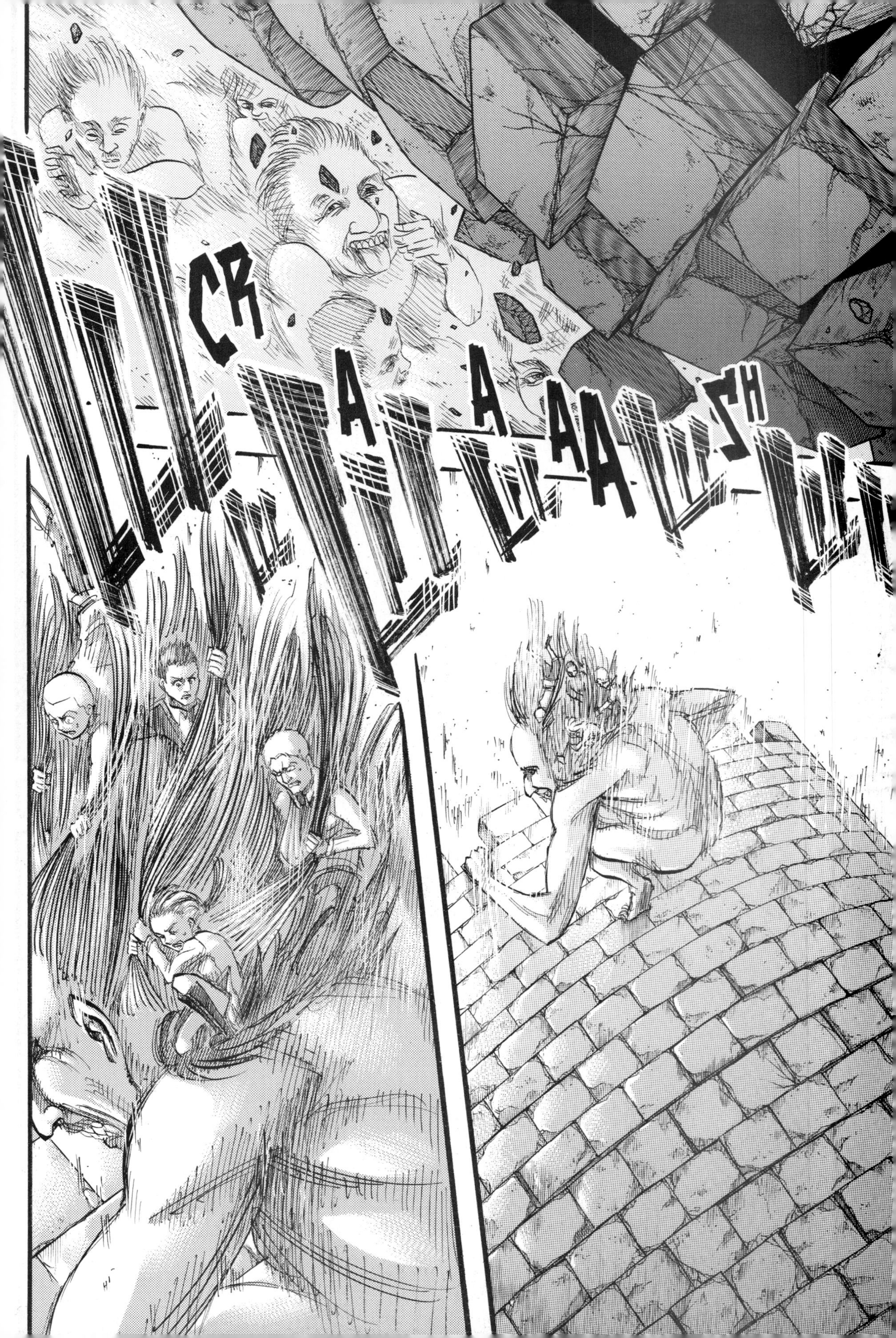
CRAAASH

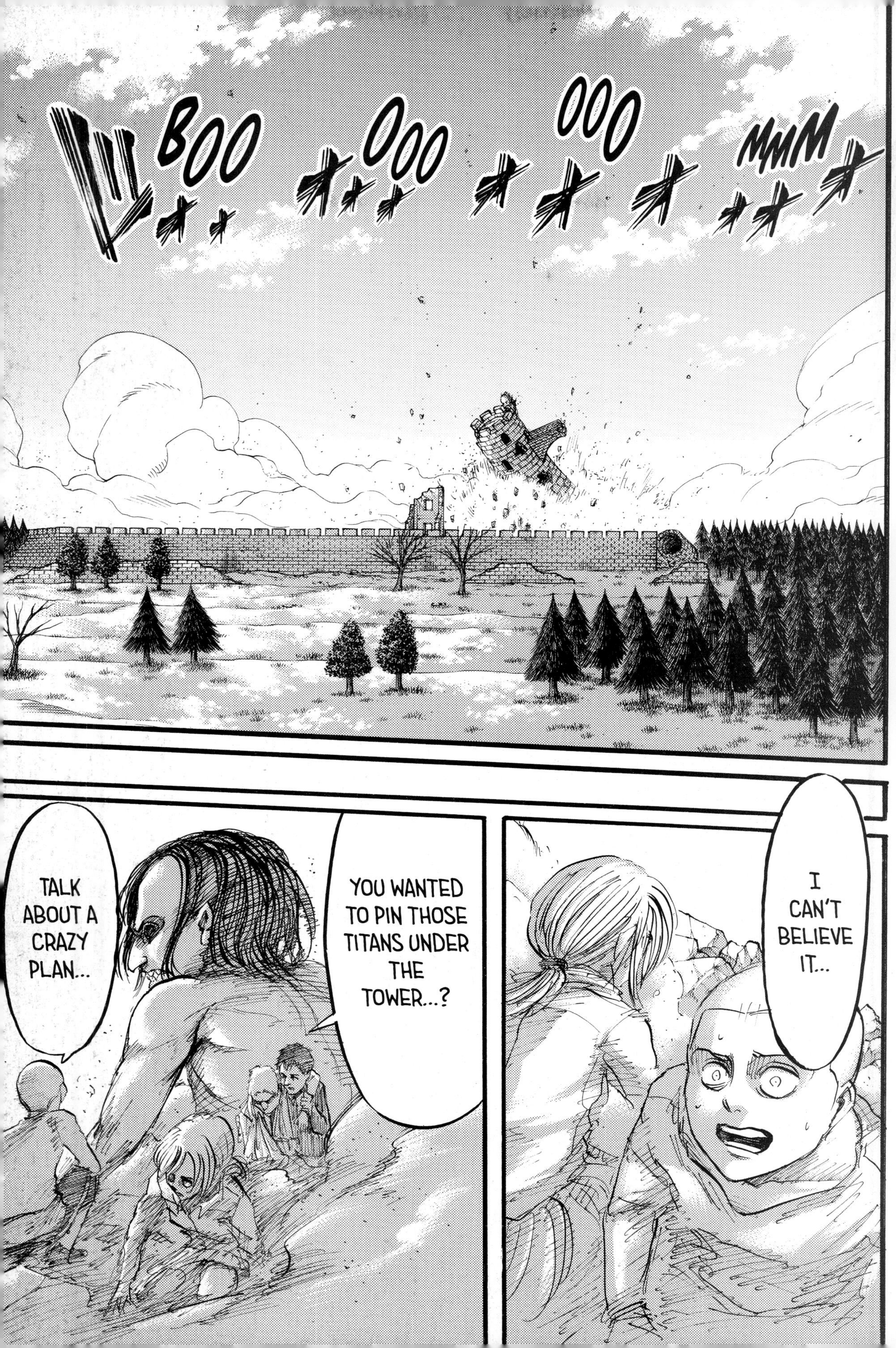

BOOOOOOOOOMMM
I CAN'T BELIEVE IT...
YOU WANTED TO PIN THOSE TITANS UNDER THE TOWER...?
TALK ABOUT A CRAZY PLAN...

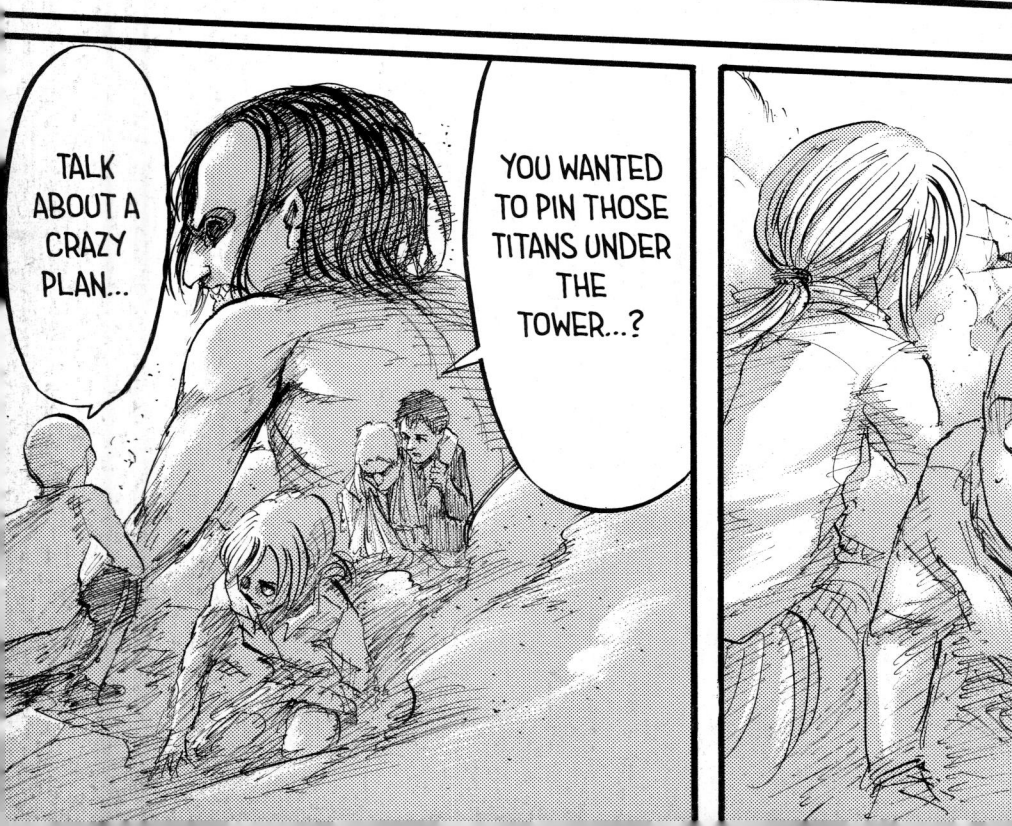

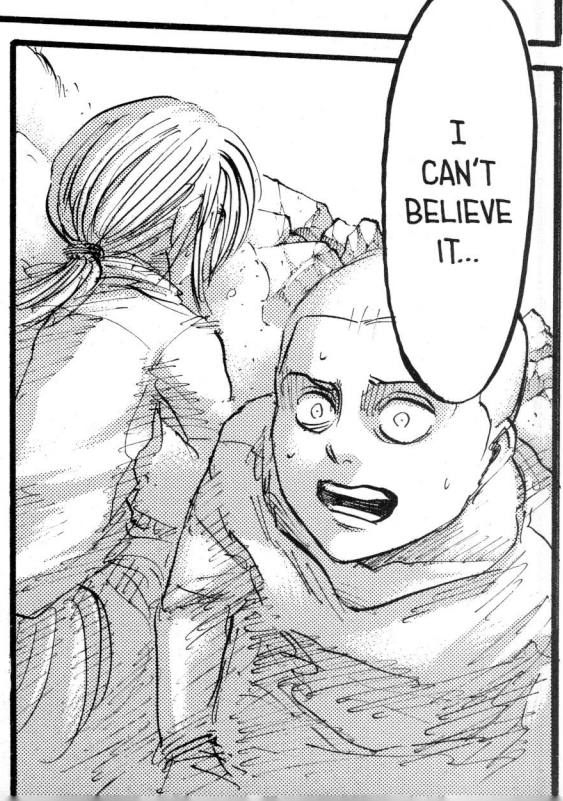

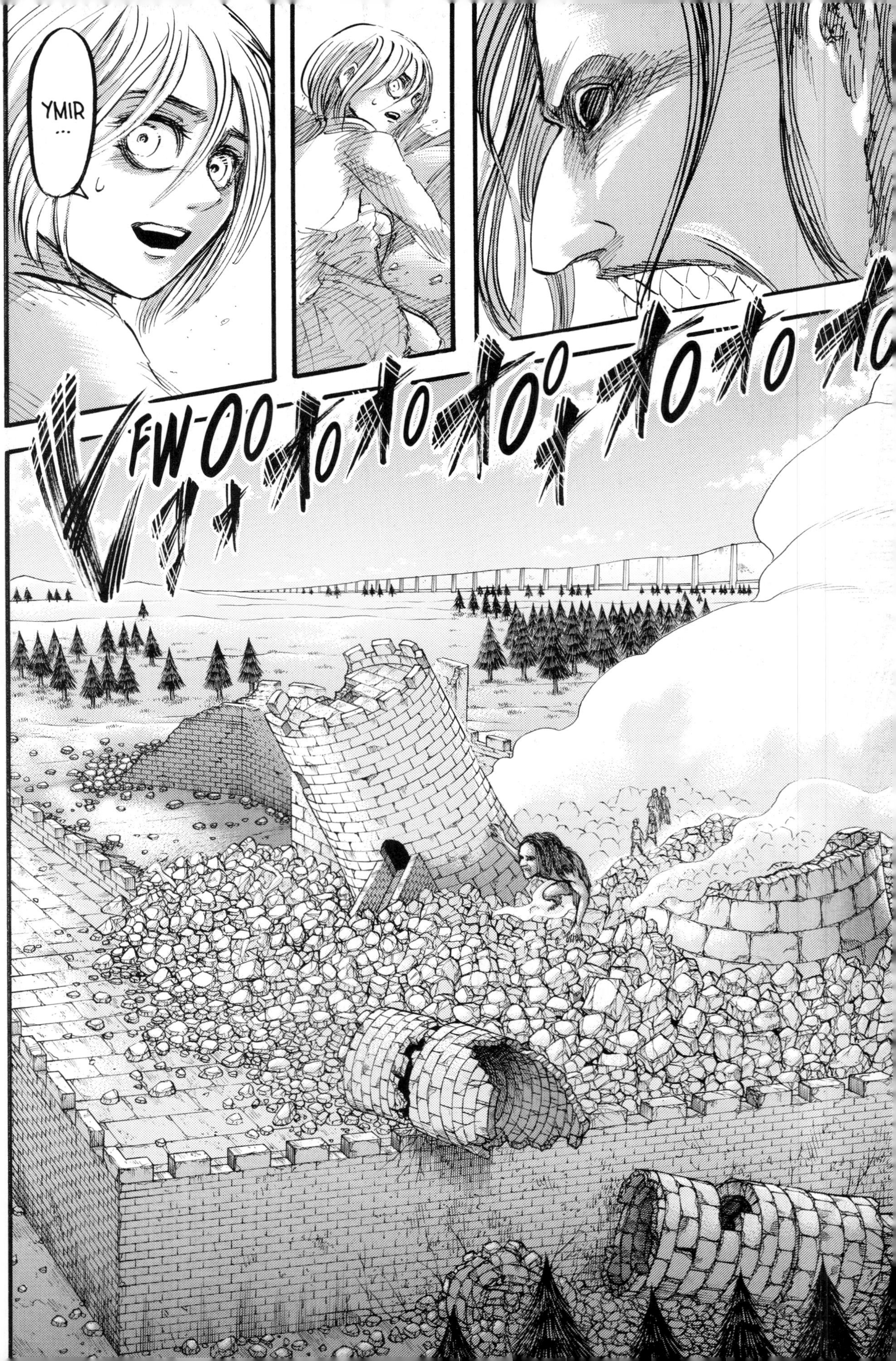
YMIR
...
VFWOOOOOOOOOOO

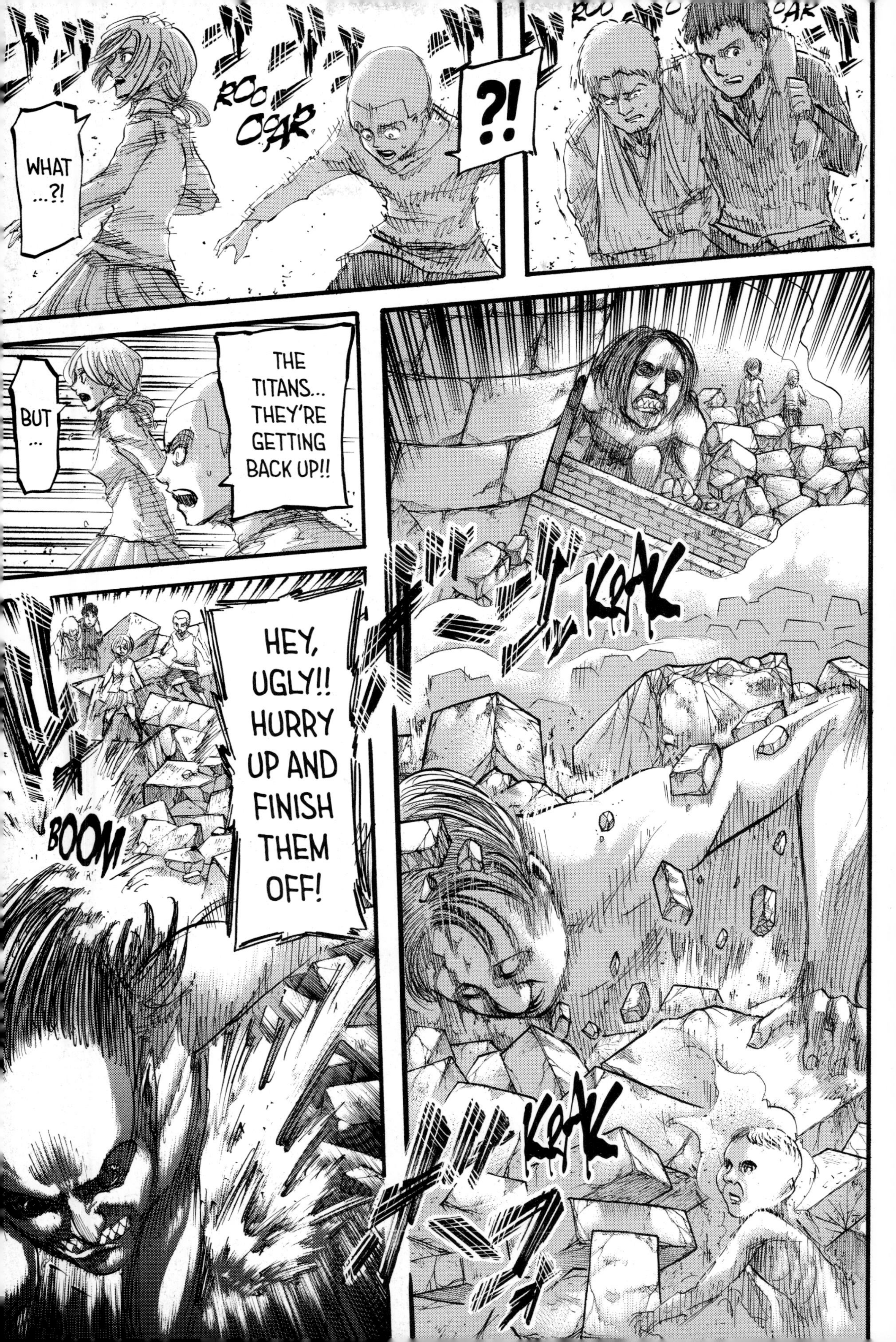
?!
ROO OOAR
WHAT ...?!
KRAK
KRAK
THE TITANS... THEY'RE GETTING BACK UP!!
BUT ...
HEY, UGLY!! HURRY UP AND FINISH THEM OFF!
BOOM

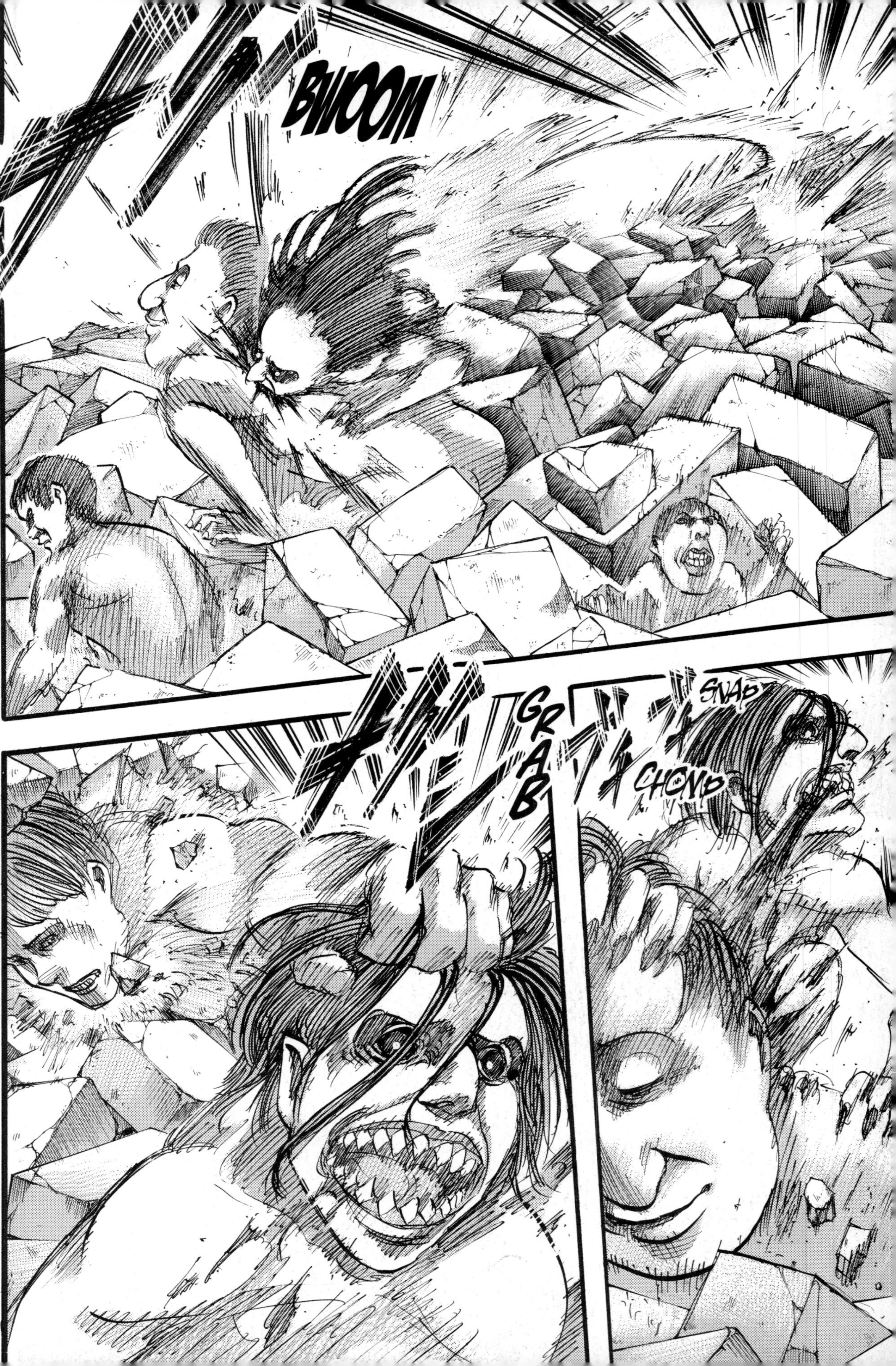
BWOOM
SNAP
CHOMP
GRAB

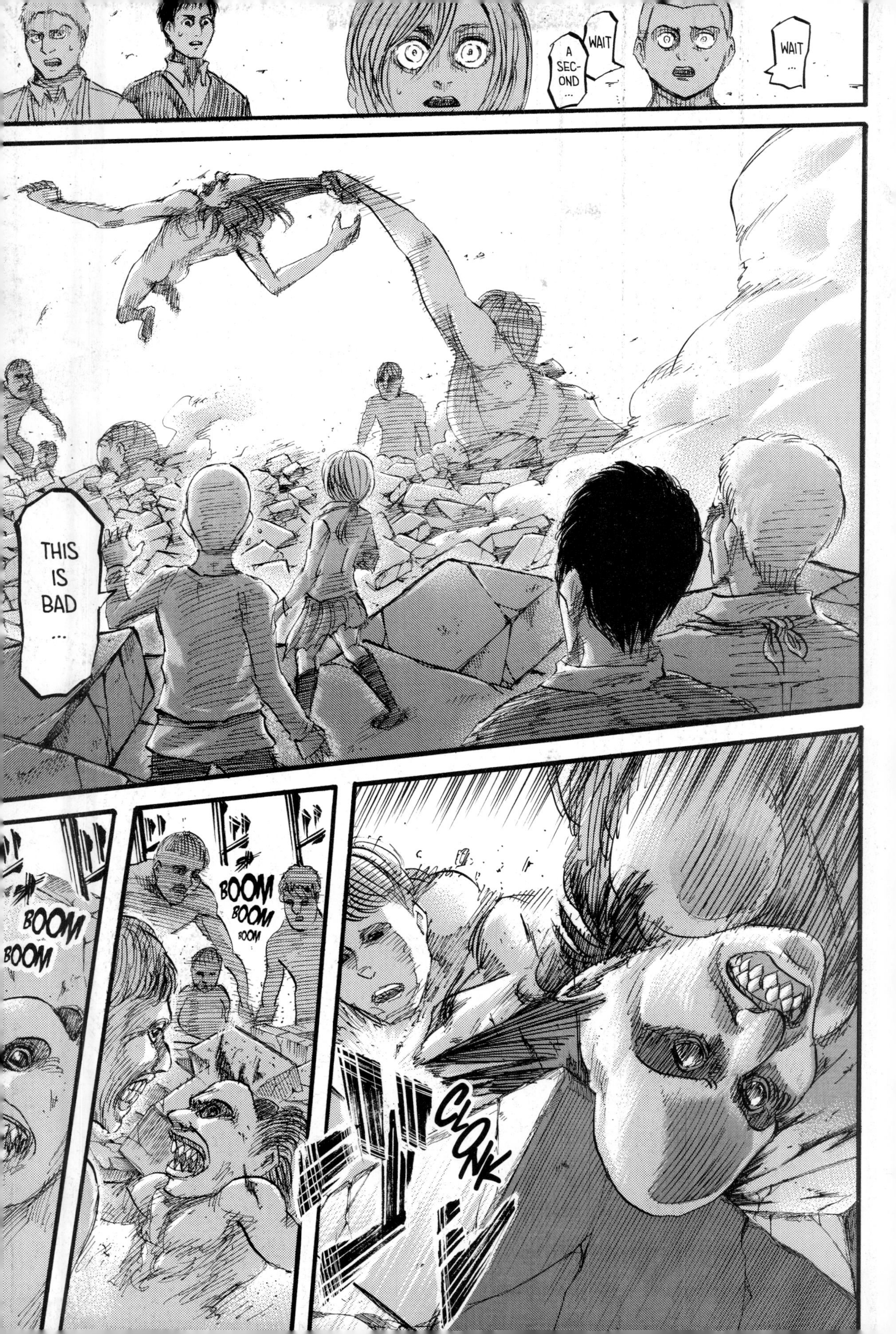
WAIT ...
WAIT A SECOND ...
THIS IS BAD ...
CLONK
BOOM BOOM BOOM
BOOM BOOM

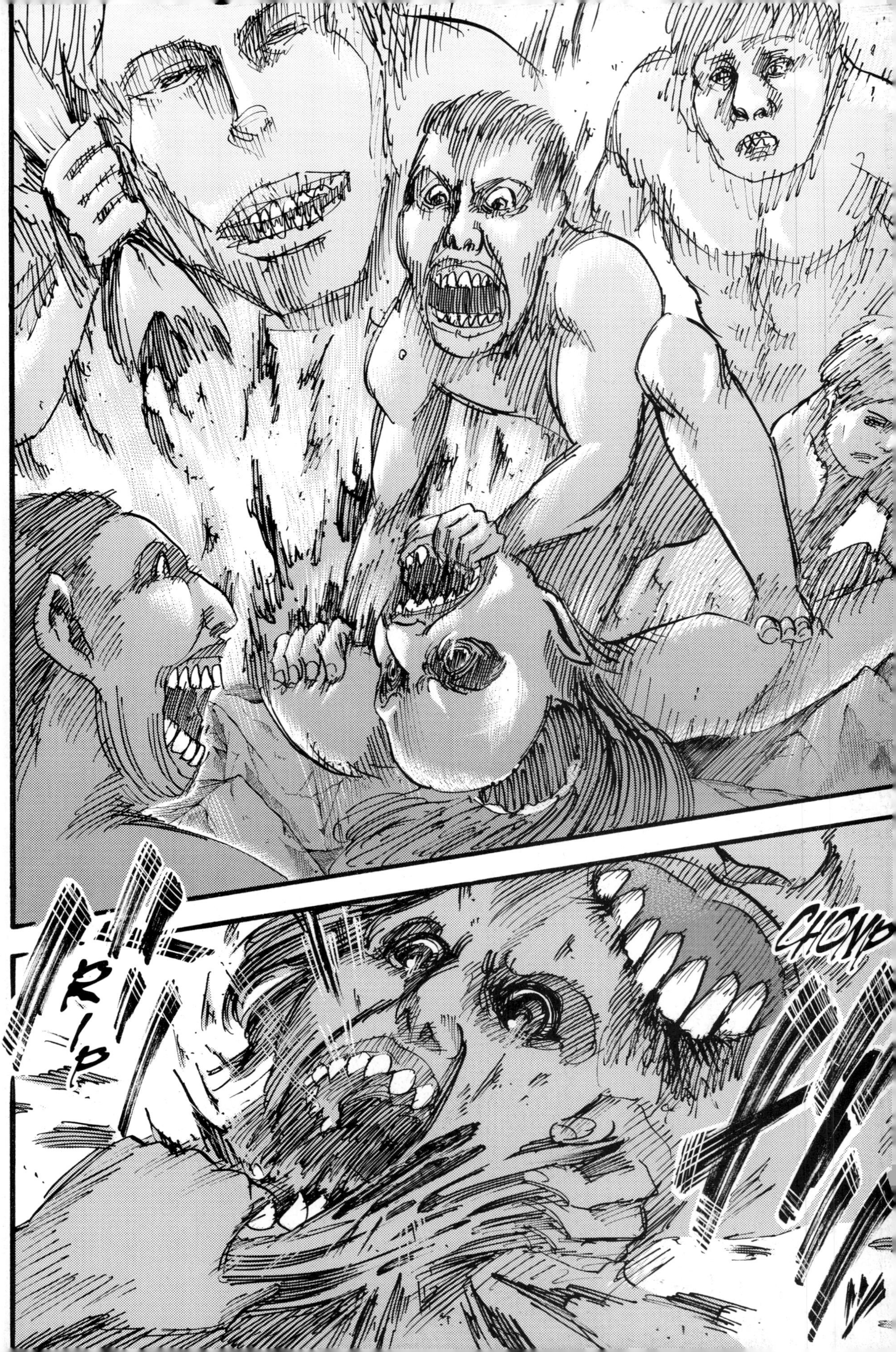
CHOMP
RIP

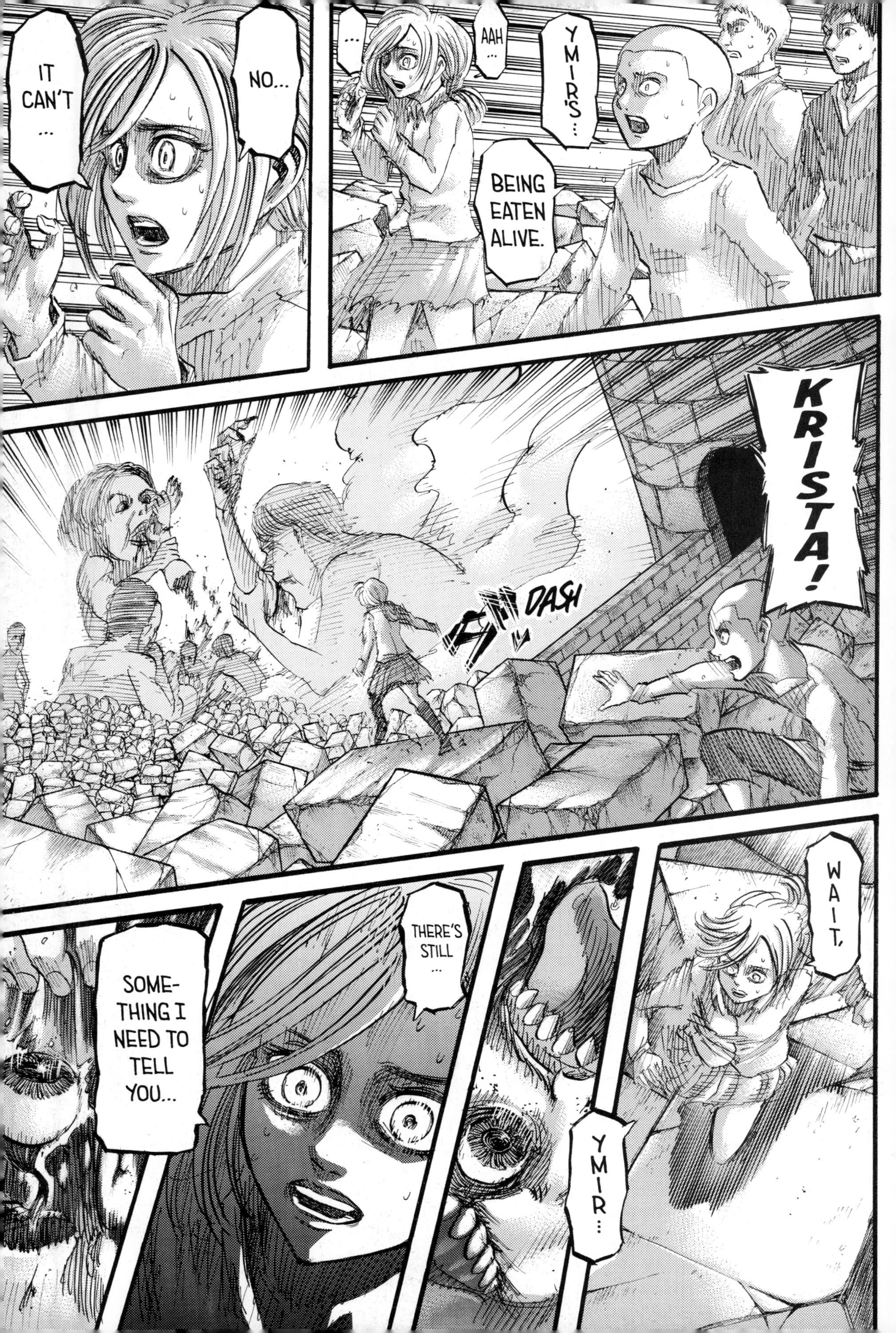
YMIR'S...
AAH...
...
BEING EATEN ALIVE.
NO...
IT CAN'T...
KRISTA!
DASH
WAIT,
YMIR...
THERE'S STILL...
SOME-THING I NEED TO TELL YOU...

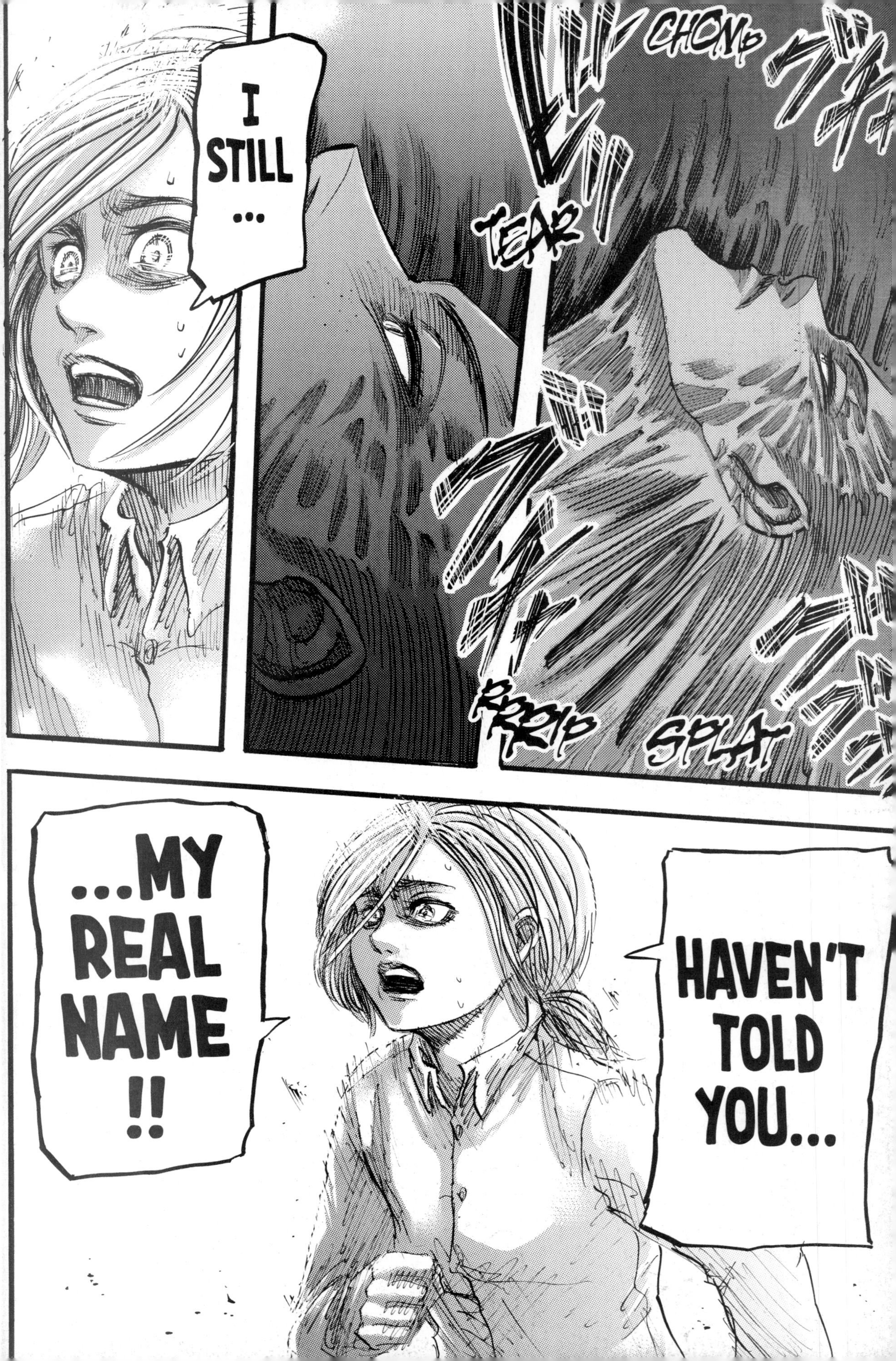
CHOMP
TEAR
RRRIP
SPLAT
I STILL ...
HAVEN'T TOLD YOU...
...MY REAL NAME !!

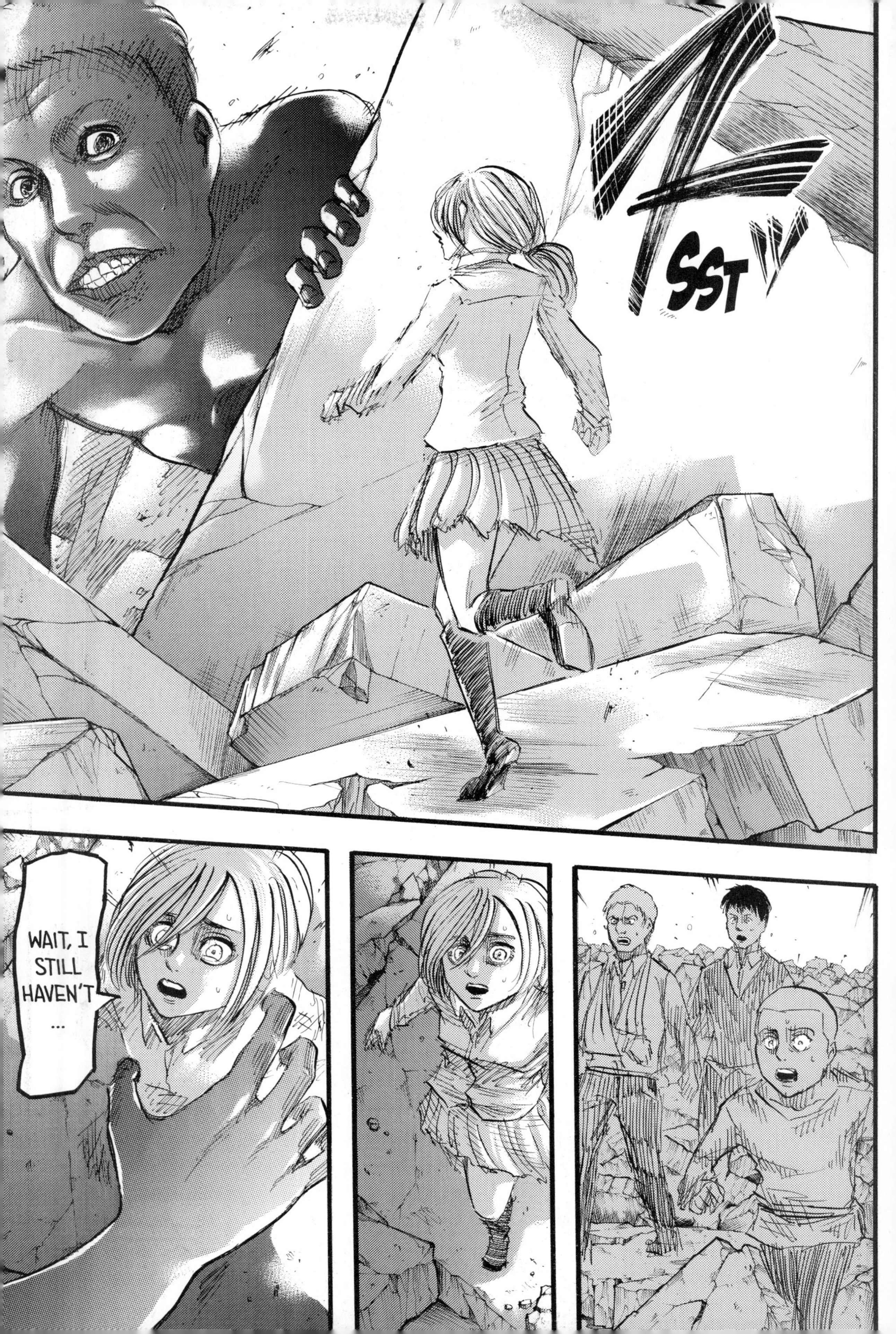
SST
WAIT, I STILL HAVEN'T ...

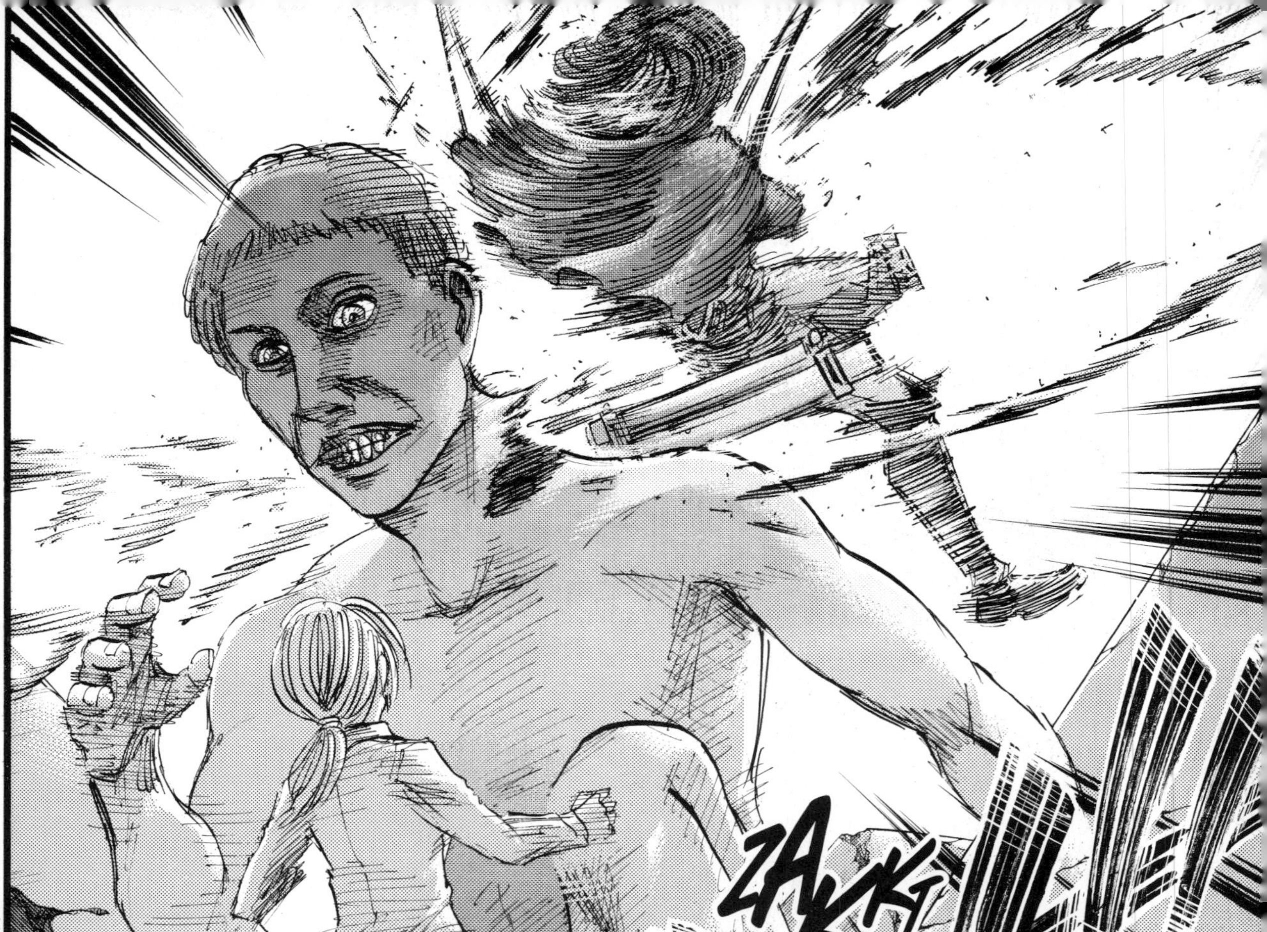
ZAKK
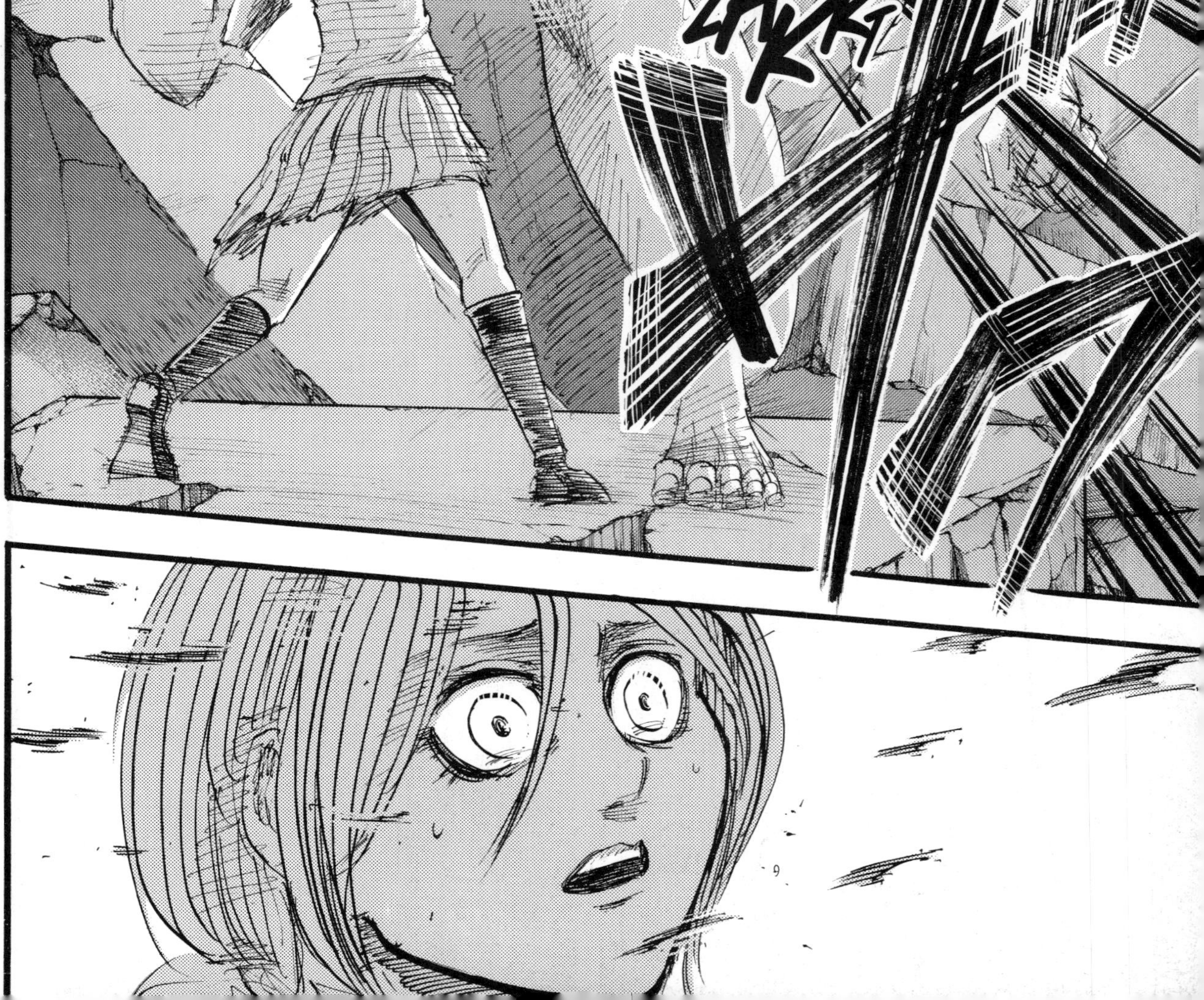

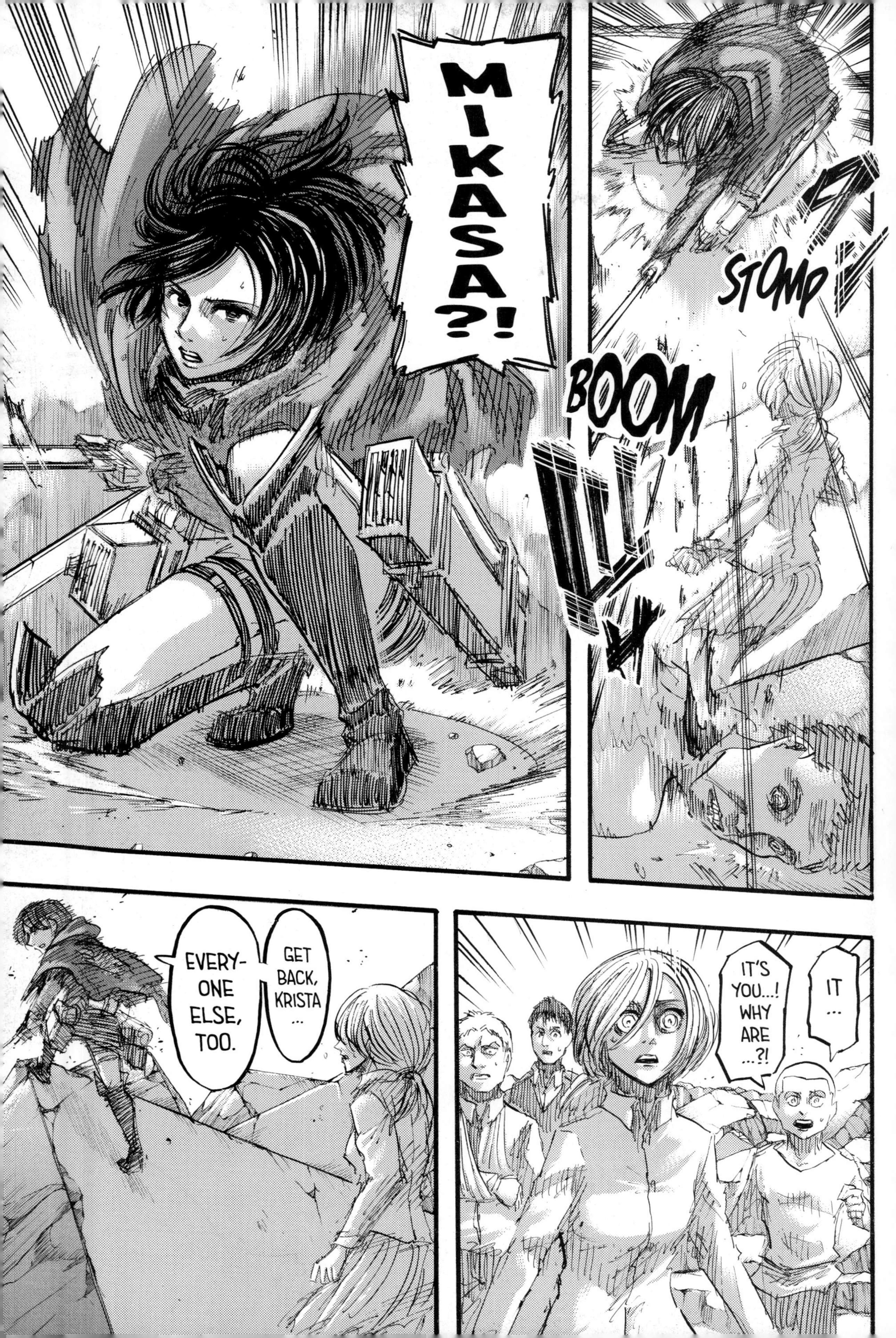
STOMP
BOOM
MIKASA?!
IT ...
IT'S YOU...! WHY ARE ...?!
GET BACK, KRISTA ...
EVERY-ONE ELSE, TOO.

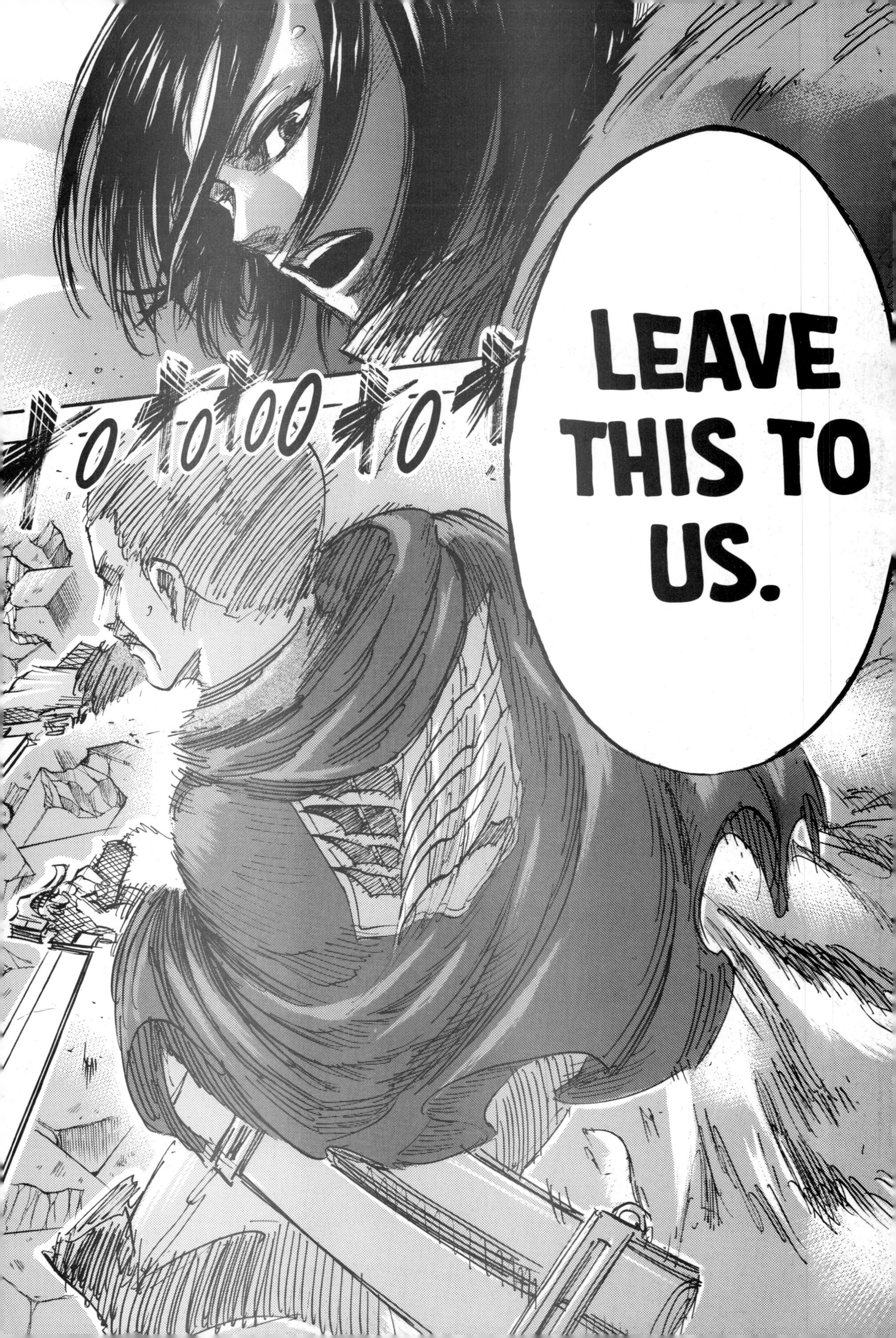
LEAVE THIS TO US.

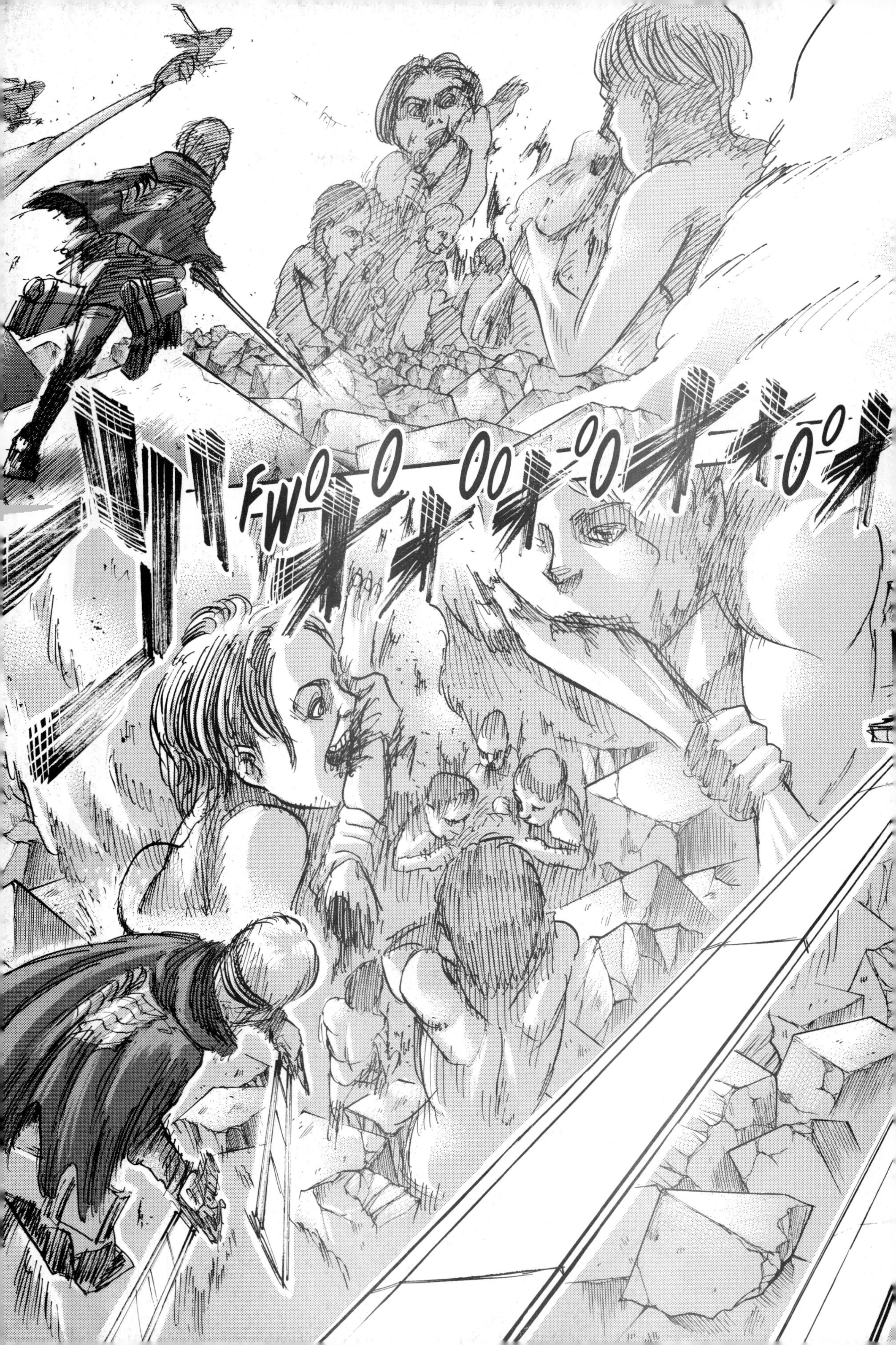
FWOOOOOOOO

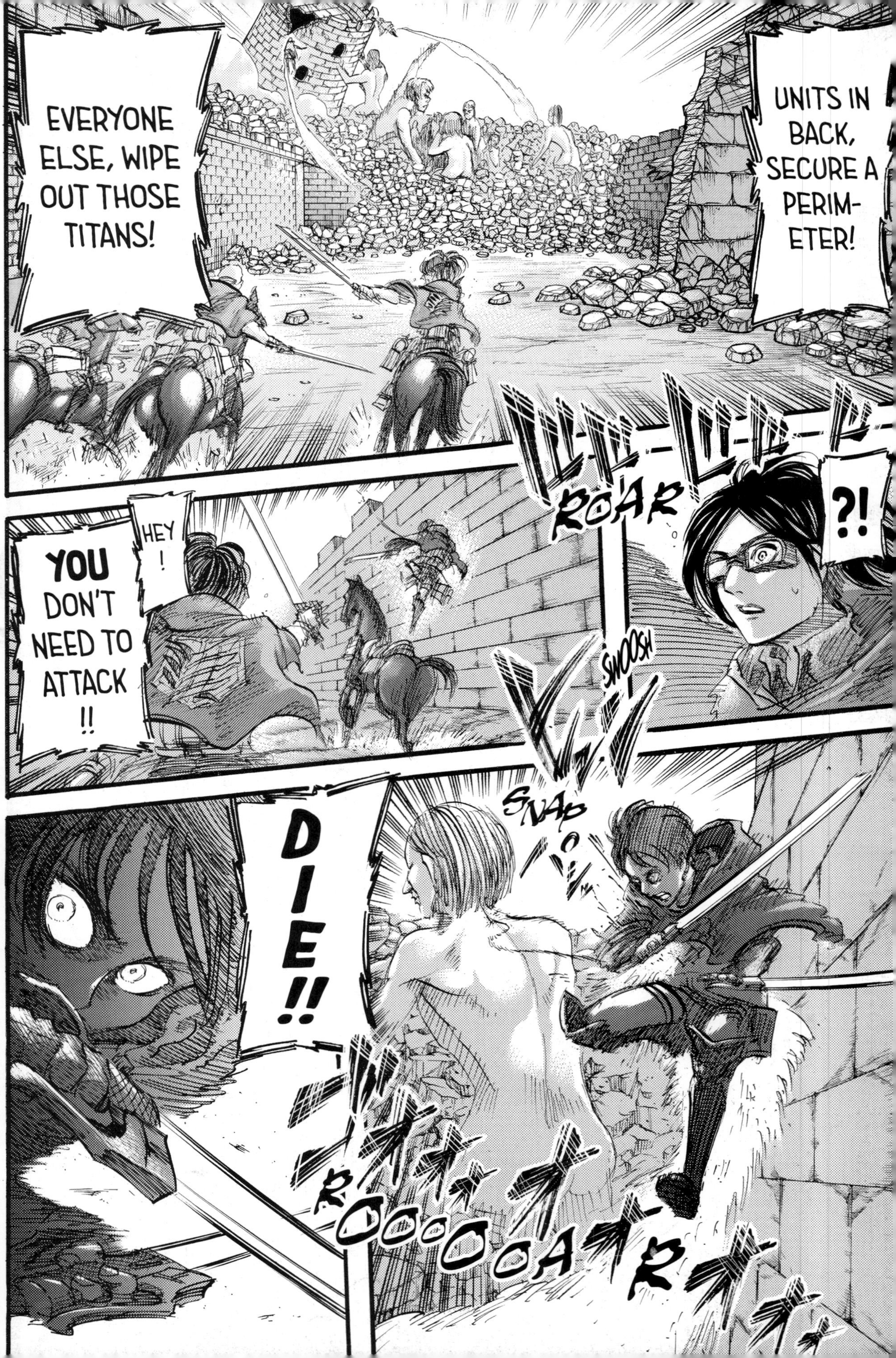
UNITS IN BACK, SECURE A PERIM-ETER!
EVERYONE ELSE, WIPE OUT THOSE TITANS!
ROAR
?!
SWOOSH
HEY!
YOU DON'T NEED TO ATTACK!!
SNAP
DIE!!
ROOOOOAR

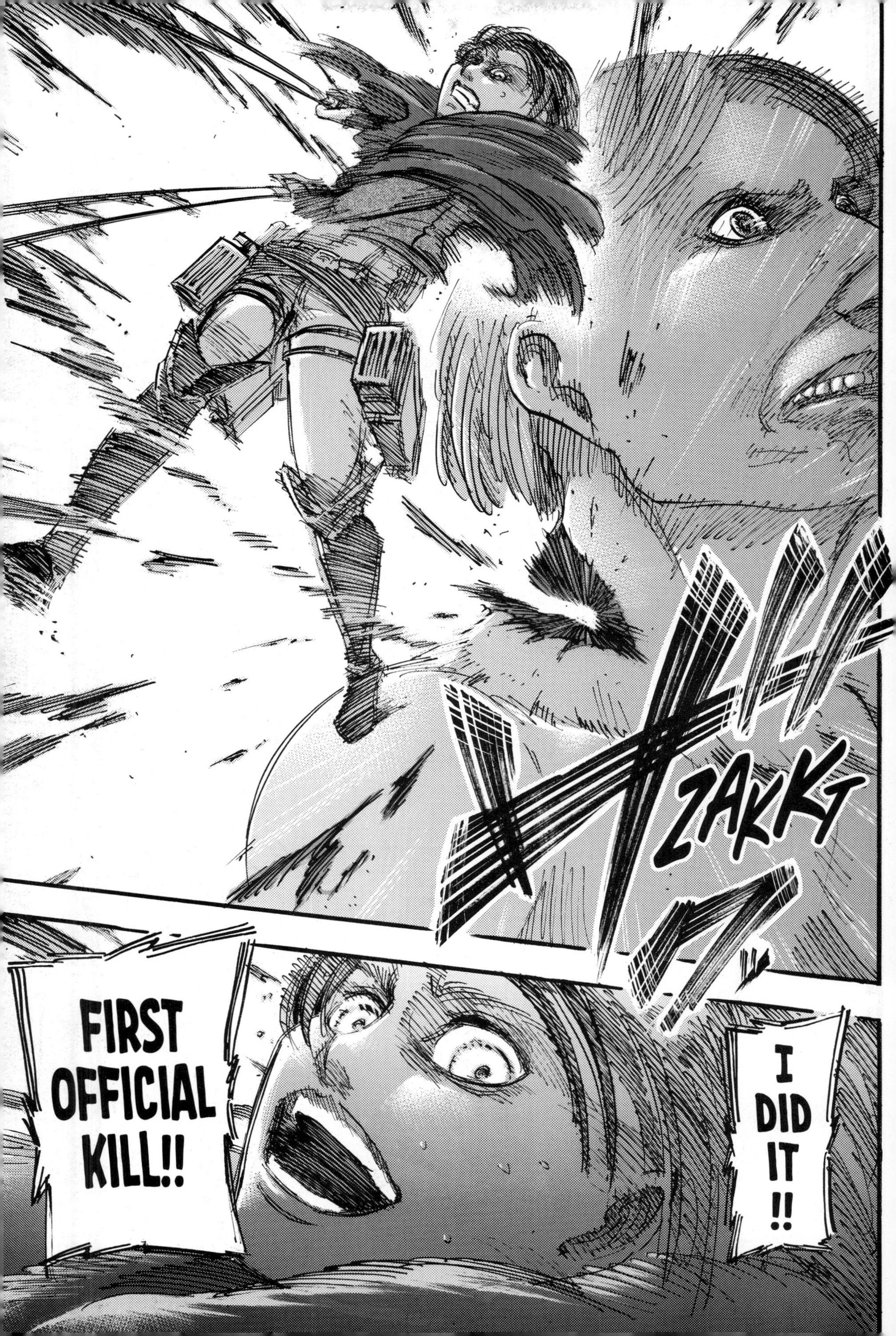
ZAKK
I DID IT!!
FIRST OFFICIAL KILL!!

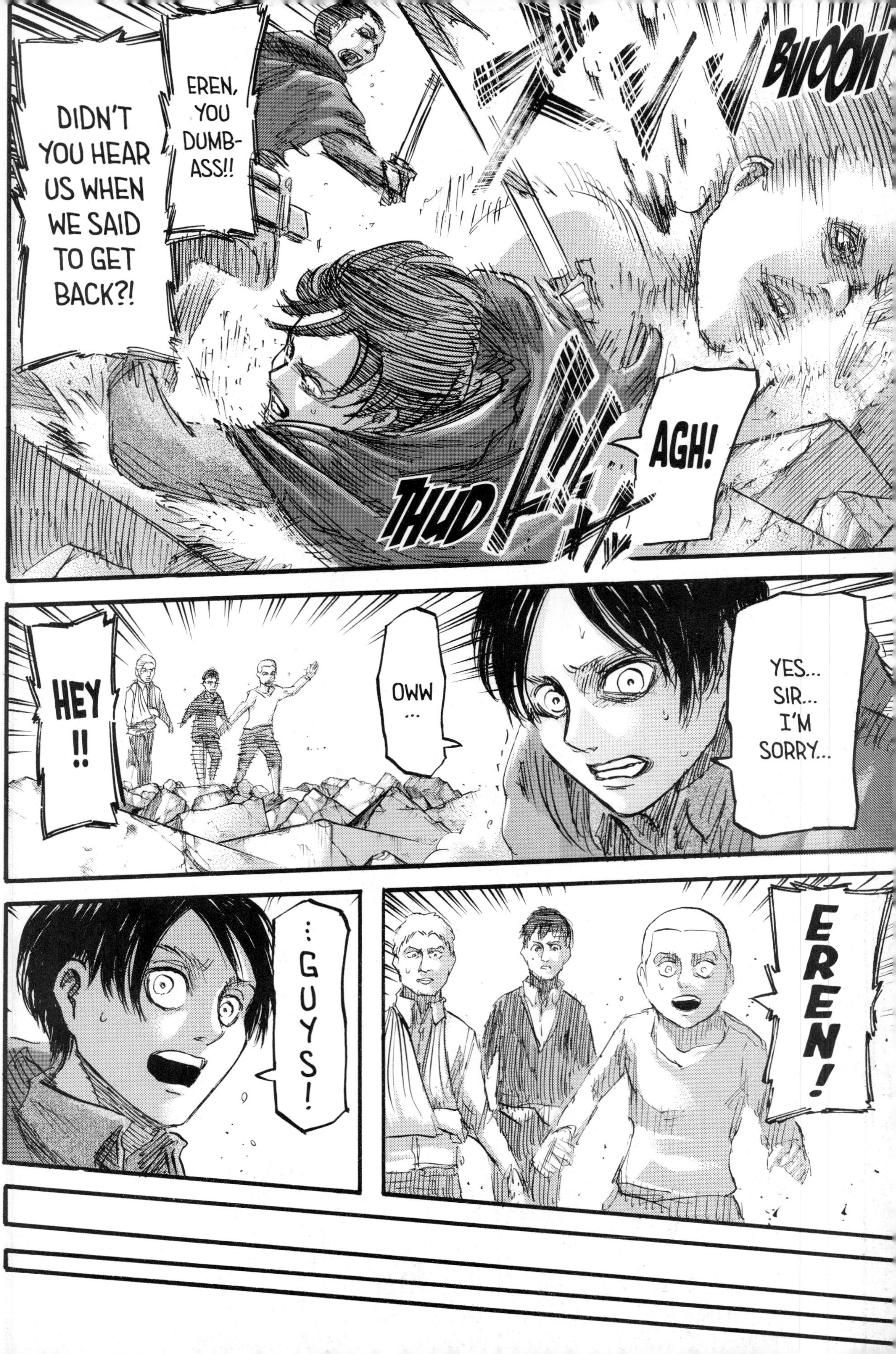

BWOOM
EREN, YOU DUMB-ASS!!
DIDN'T YOU HEAR US WHEN WE SAID TO GET BACK?!
AGH!
THUD
YES... SIR... I'M SORRY...
OWW ...
HEY !!
EREN!
...GUYS!

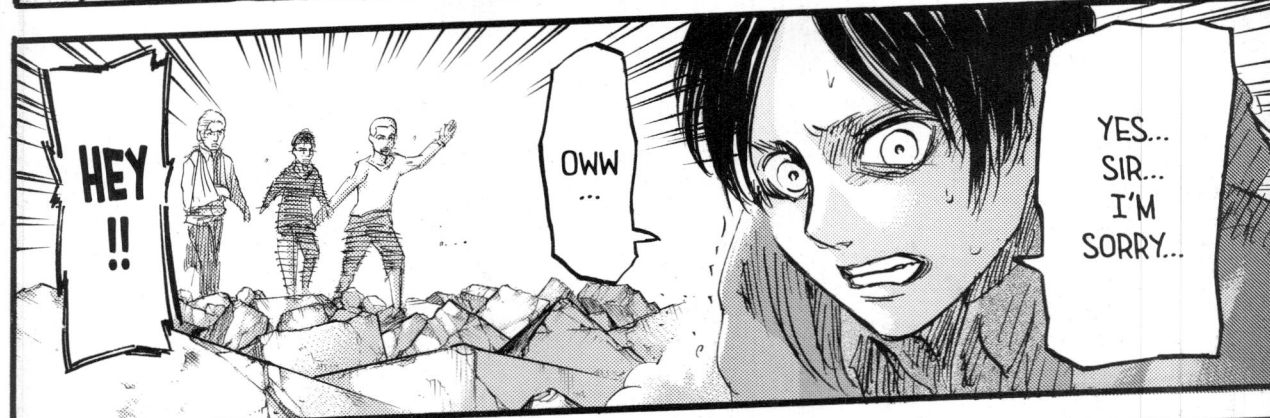

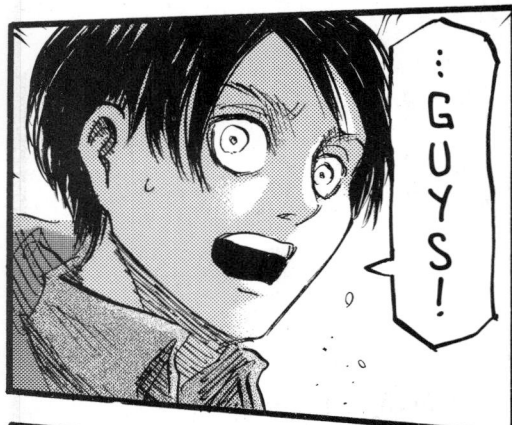

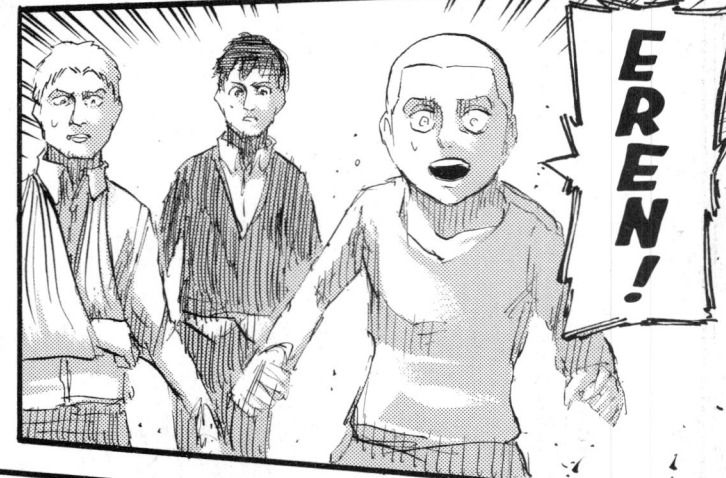

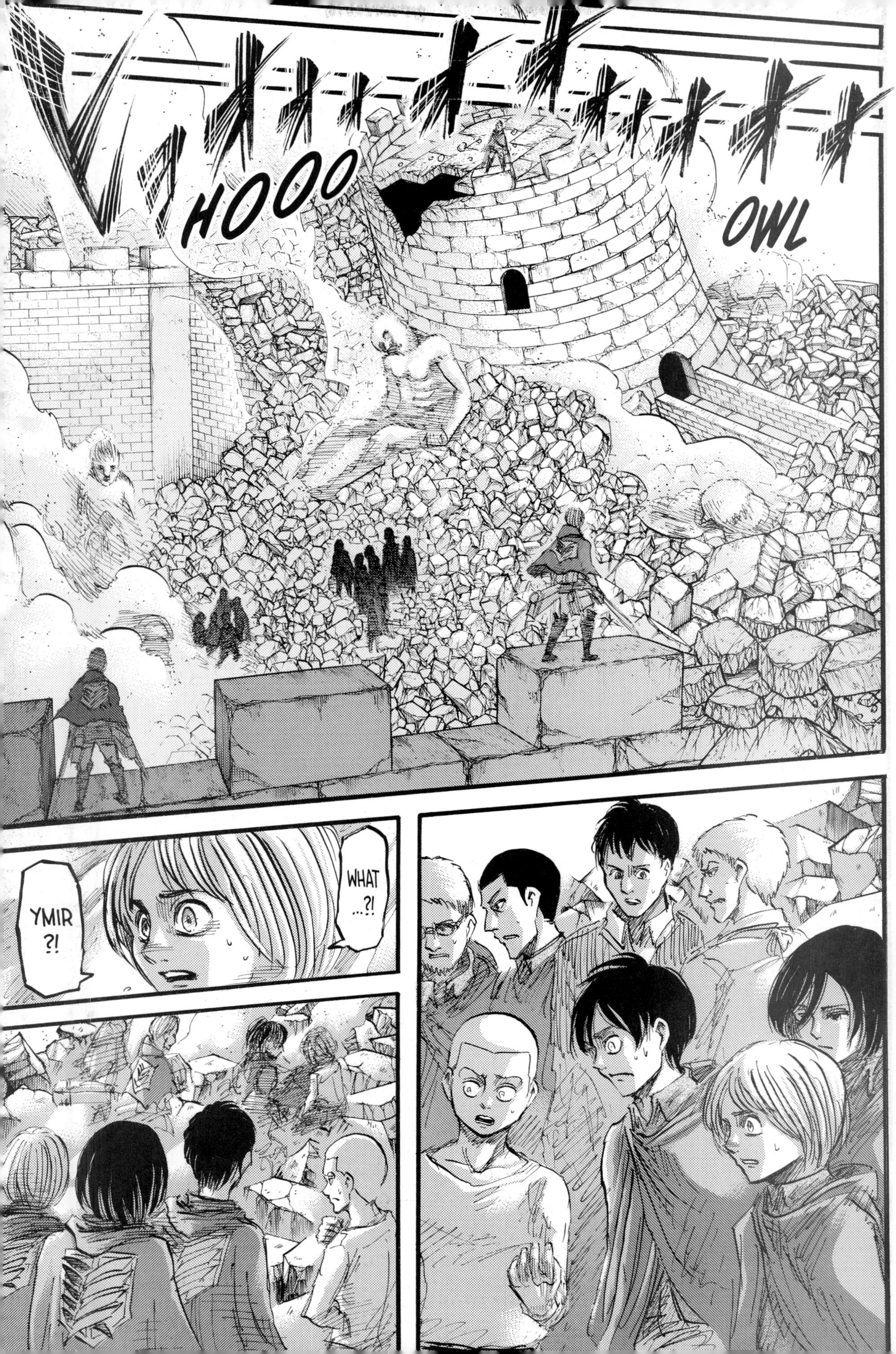
HOOO
OWL
WHAT ...?!
YMIR ?!

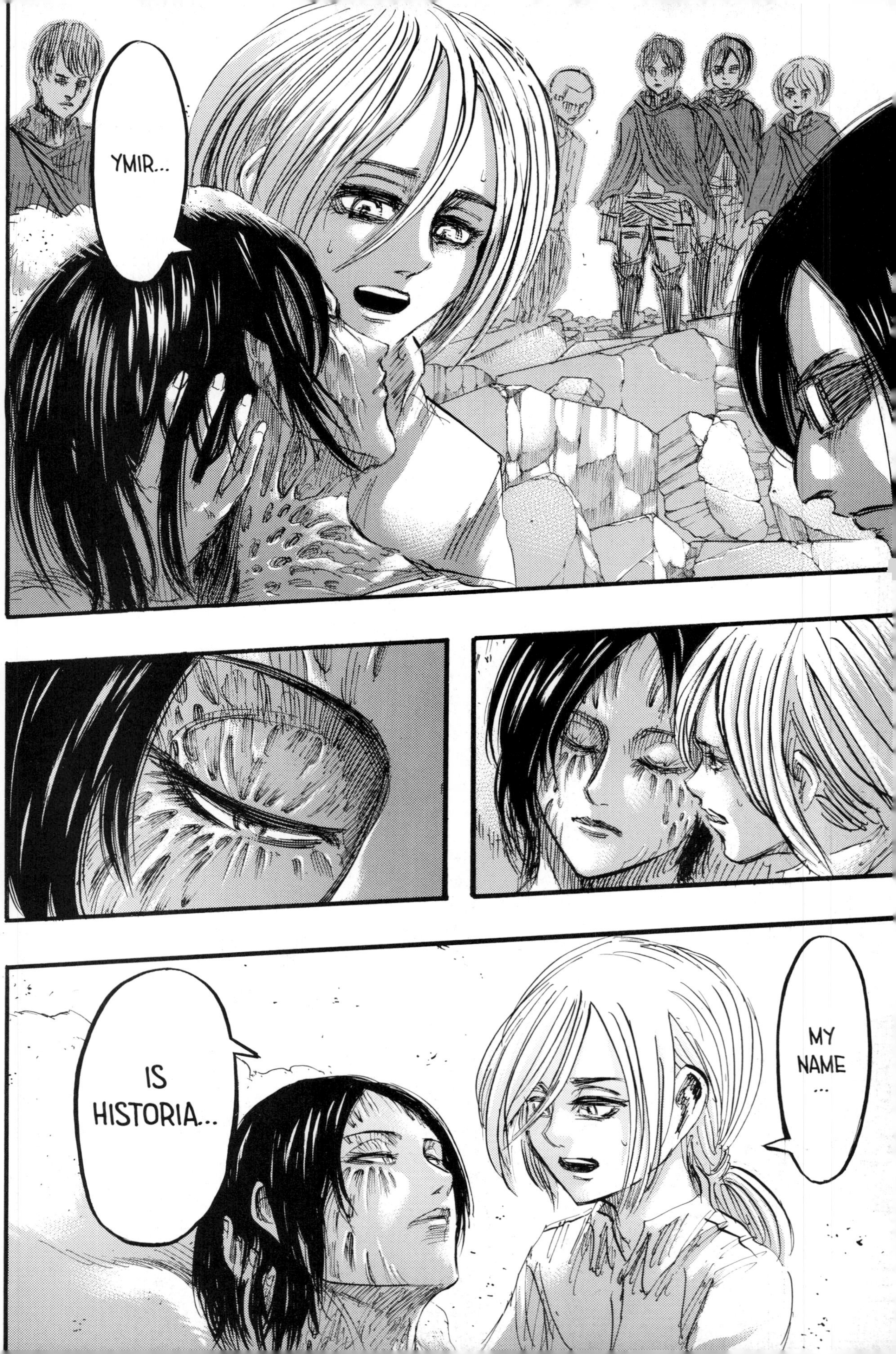

YMIR...

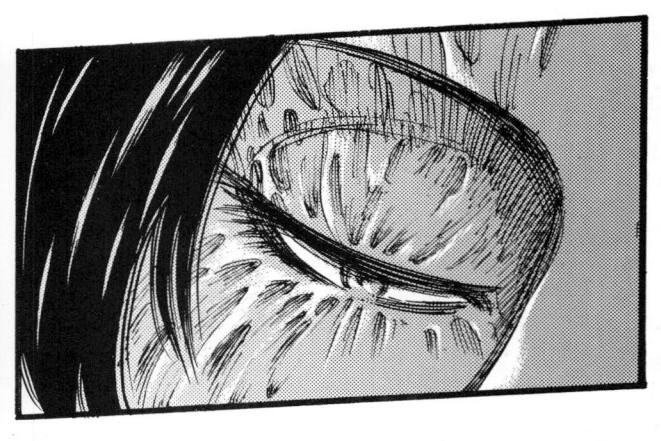

IS HISTORIA...

MY NAME ...

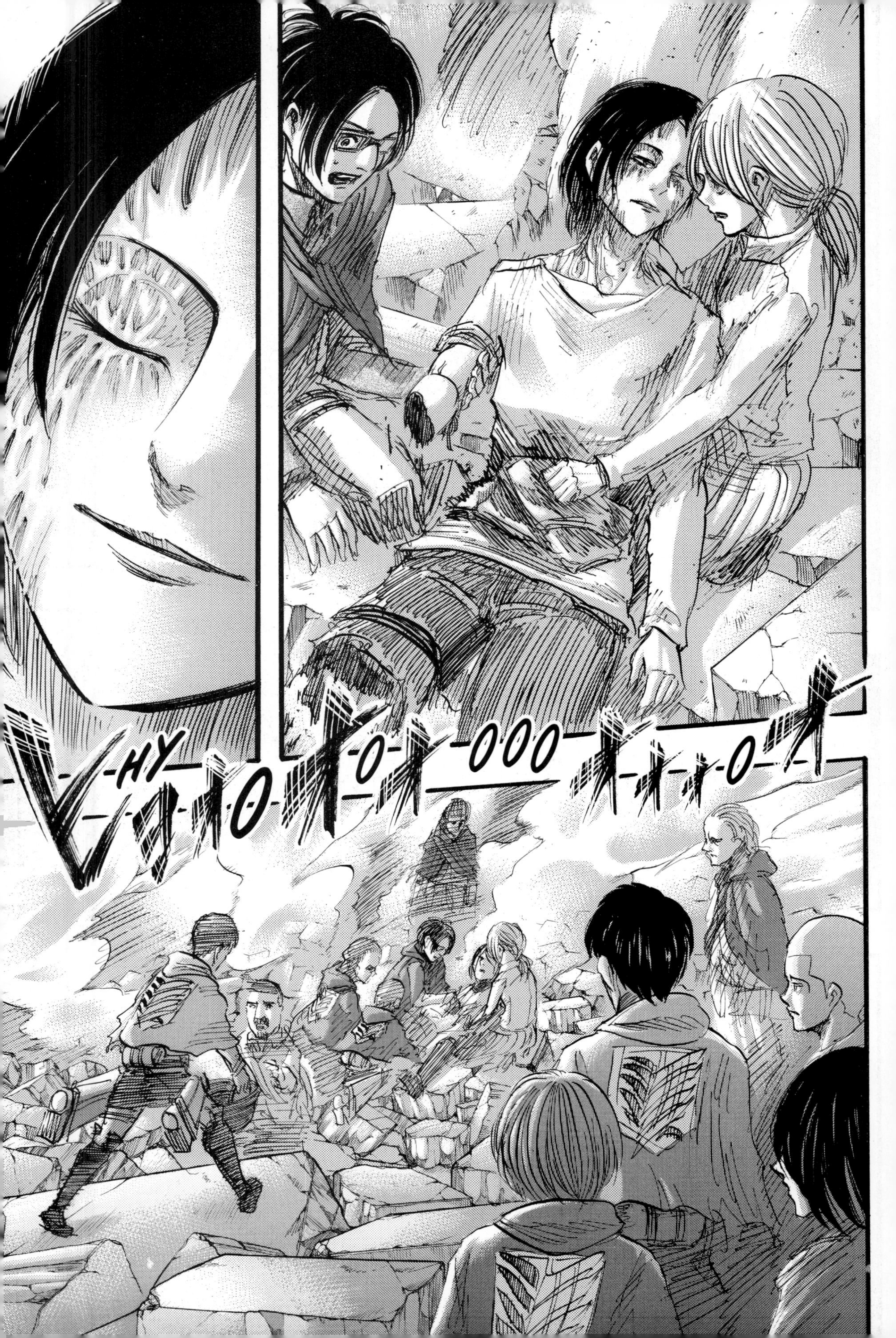
WHY

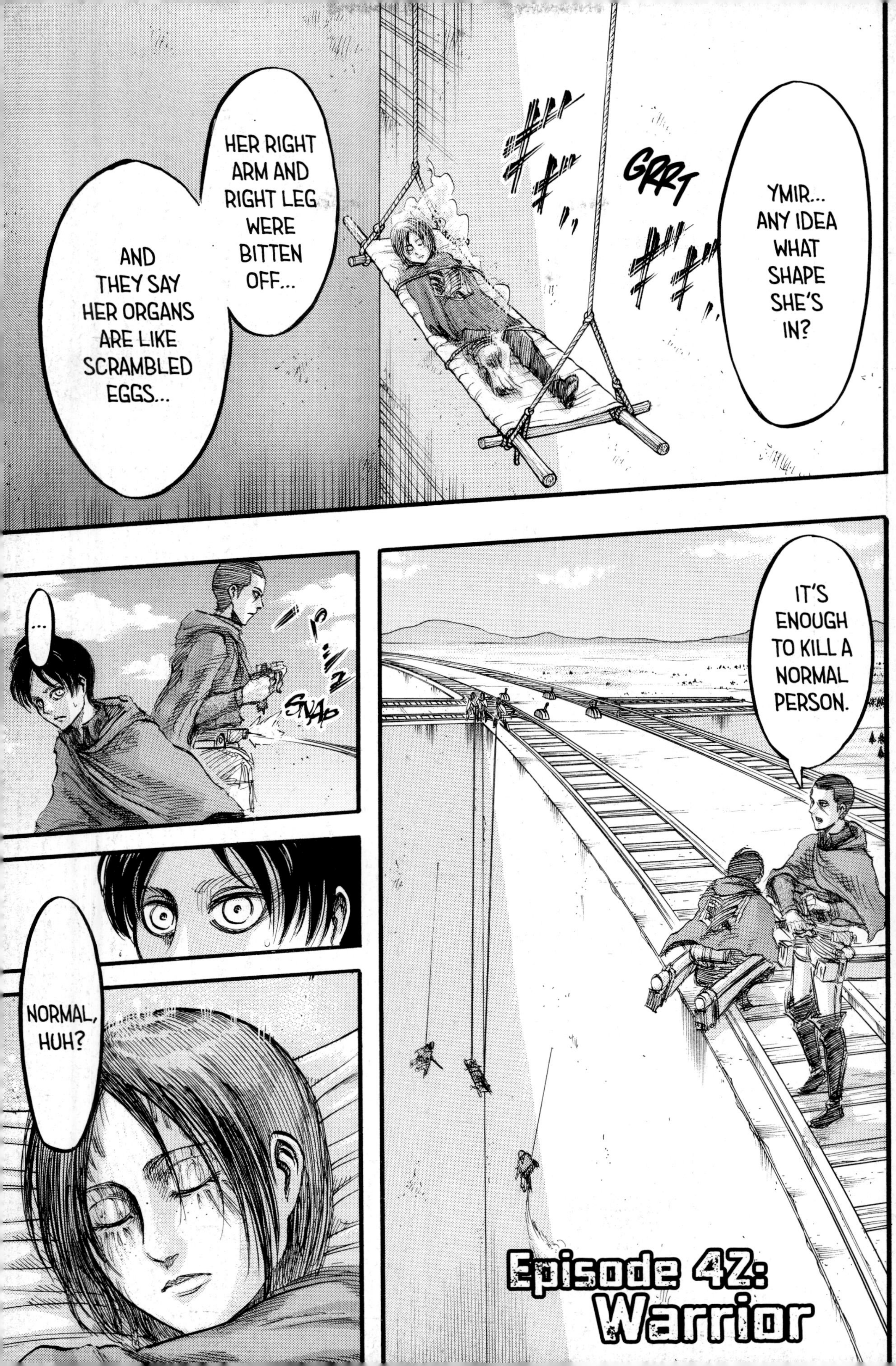
YMIR... ANY IDEA WHAT SHAPE SHE'S IN?
HER RIGHT ARM AND RIGHT LEG WERE BITTEN OFF...
AND THEY SAY HER ORGANS ARE LIKE SCRAMBLED EGGS...
IT'S ENOUGH TO KILL A NORMAL PERSON.
...
SNAP
NORMAL, HUH?
Episode 42:
Warrior

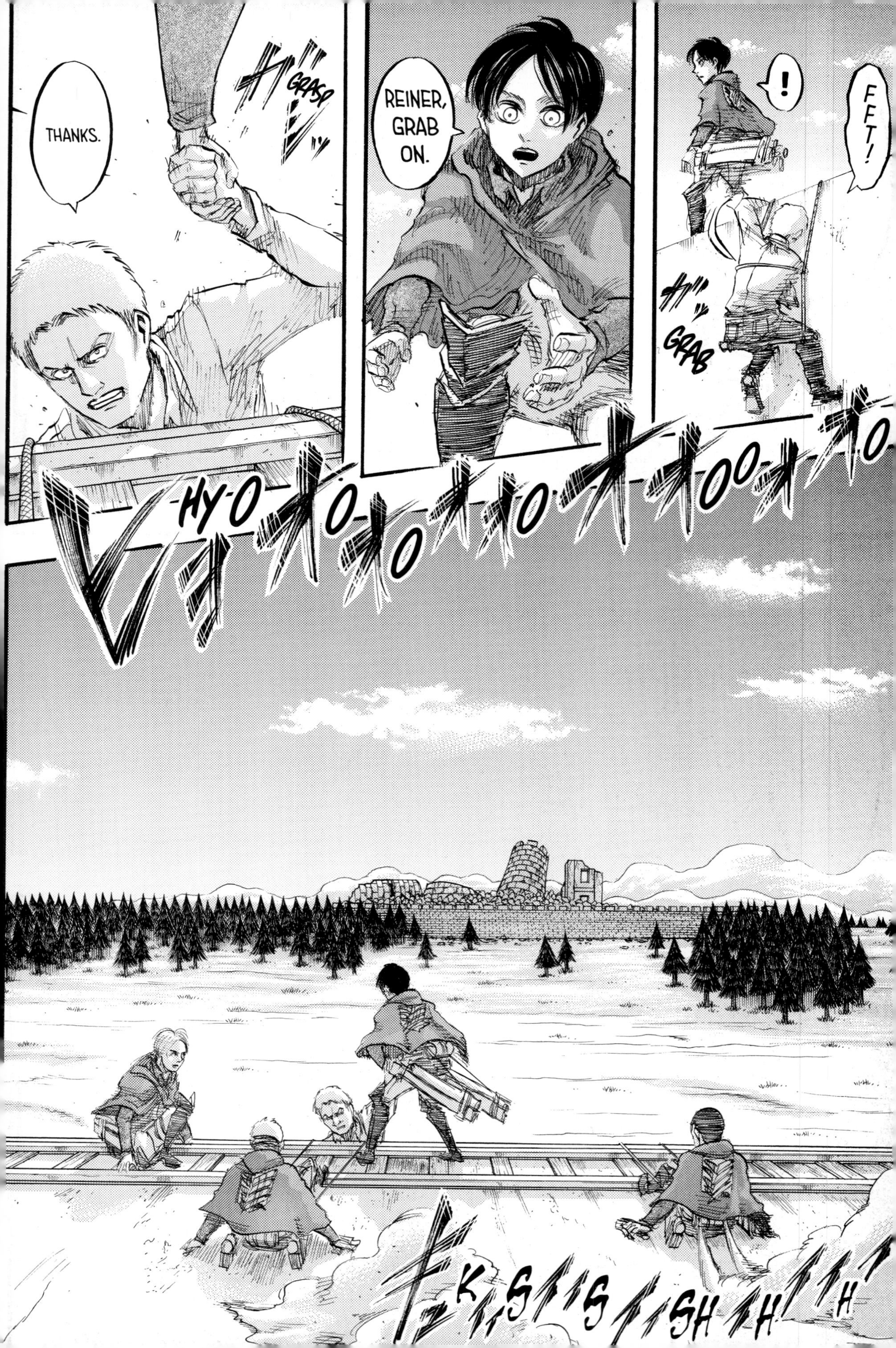
FFT!
!
GRAB
REINER, GRAB ON.
GRASP
THANKS.
HY-O-O-O-O-O-OO-O-O
KSSSHHH

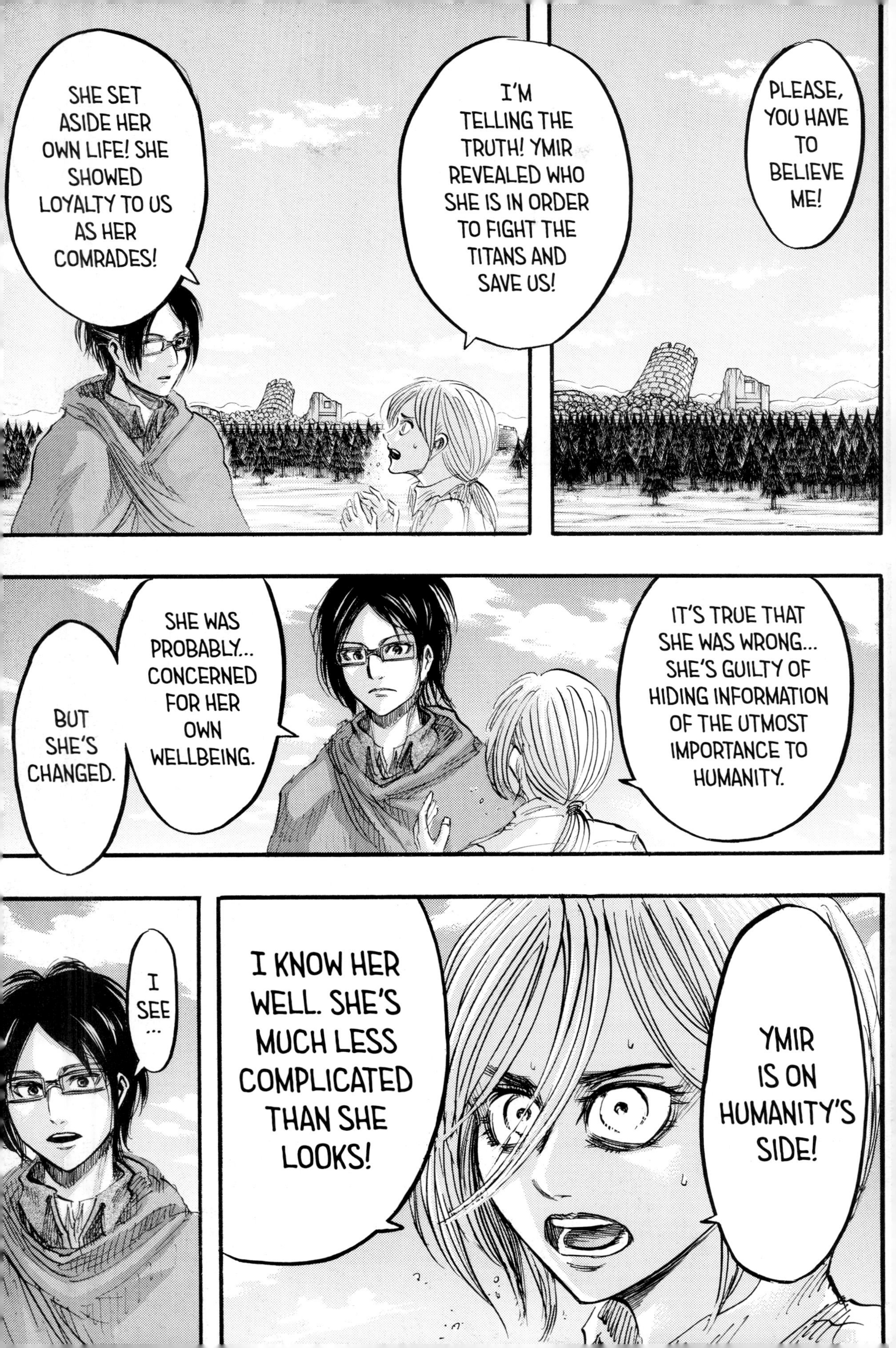
PLEASE, YOU HAVE TO BELIEVE ME!
I'M TELLING THE TRUTH! YMIR REVEALED WHO SHE IS IN ORDER TO FIGHT THE TITANS AND SAVE US!
SHE SET ASIDE HER OWN LIFE! SHE SHOWED LOYALTY TO US AS HER COMRADES!
IT'S TRUE THAT SHE WAS WRONG... SHE'S GUILTY OF HIDING INFORMATION OF THE UTMOST IMPORTANCE TO HUMANITY.
SHE WAS PROBABLY... CONCERNED FOR HER OWN WELLBEING.
BUT SHE'S CHANGED.
YMIR IS ON HUMANITY'S SIDE!
I KNOW HER WELL. SHE'S MUCH LESS COMPLICATED THAN SHE LOOKS!
I SEE...

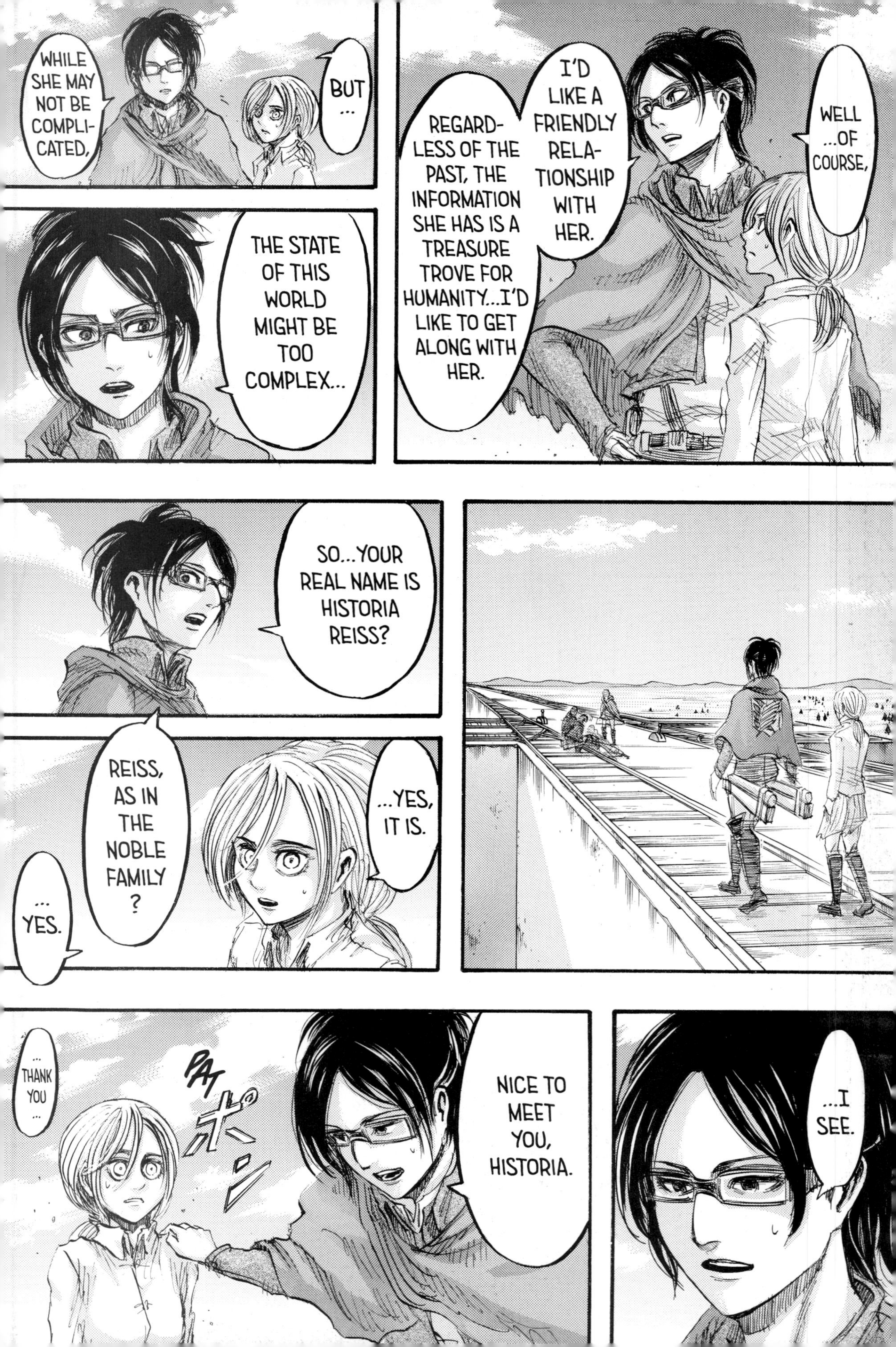
WELL ...OF COURSE,
I'D LIKE A FRIENDLY RELATIONSHIP WITH HER.
REGARDLESS OF THE PAST, THE INFORMATION SHE HAS IS A TREASURE TROVE FOR HUMANITY...I'D LIKE TO GET ALONG WITH HER.
BUT ...
WHILE SHE MAY NOT BE COMPLICATED,
THE STATE OF THIS WORLD MIGHT BE TOO COMPLEX...
SO...YOUR REAL NAME IS HISTORIA REISS?
...YES, IT IS.
REISS, AS IN THE NOBLE FAMILY?
... YES.
...I SEE.
NICE TO MEET YOU, HISTORIA.
PAT
ポン
... THANK YOU ...

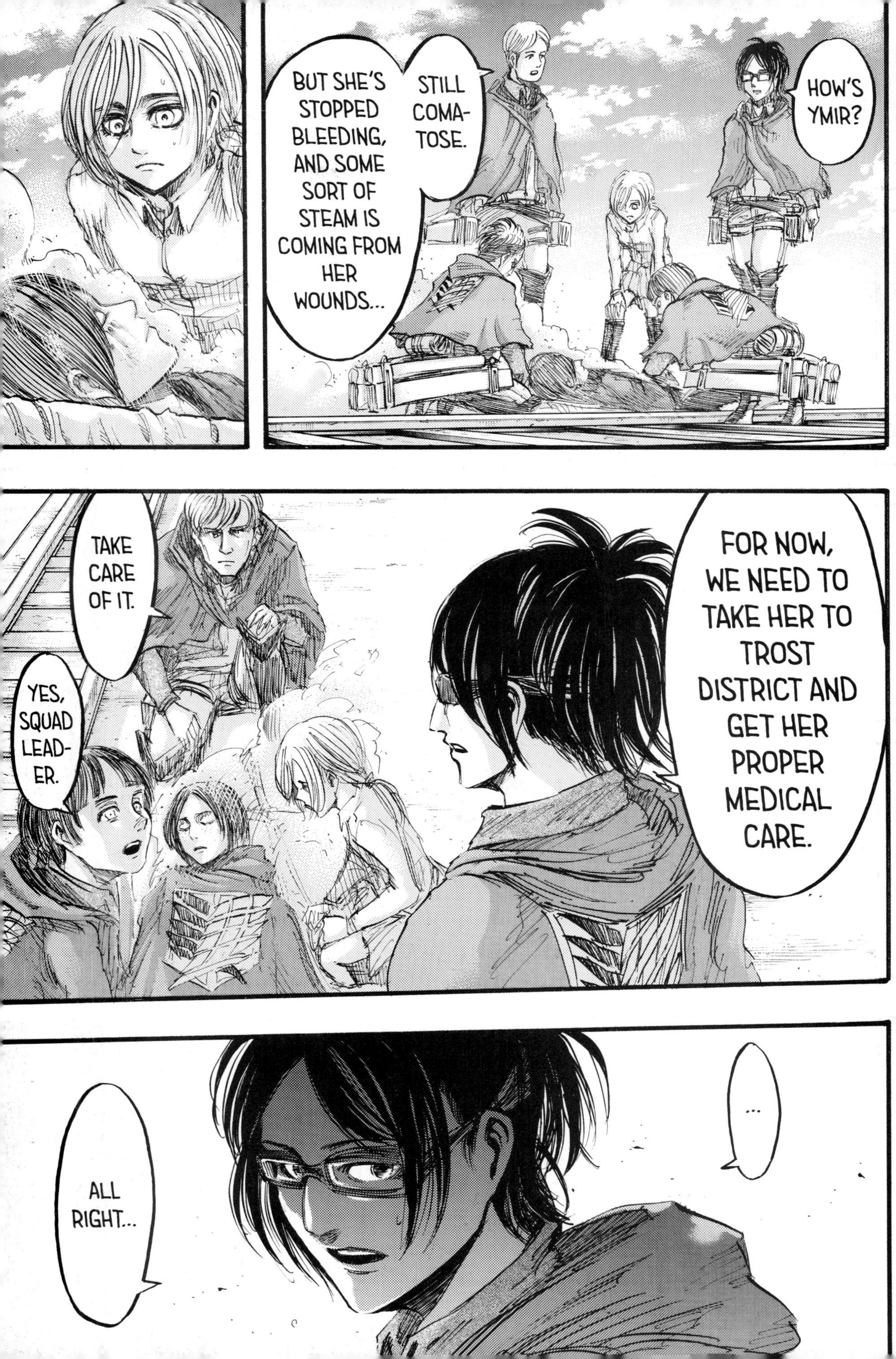
HOW'S YMIR?
STILL COMA-TOSE.
BUT SHE'S STOPPED BLEEDING, AND SOME SORT OF STEAM IS COMING FROM HER WOUNDS...
FOR NOW, WE NEED TO TAKE HER TO TROST DISTRICT AND GET HER PROPER MEDICAL CARE.
TAKE CARE OF IT.
YES, SQUAD LEADER.
...
ALL RIGHT...

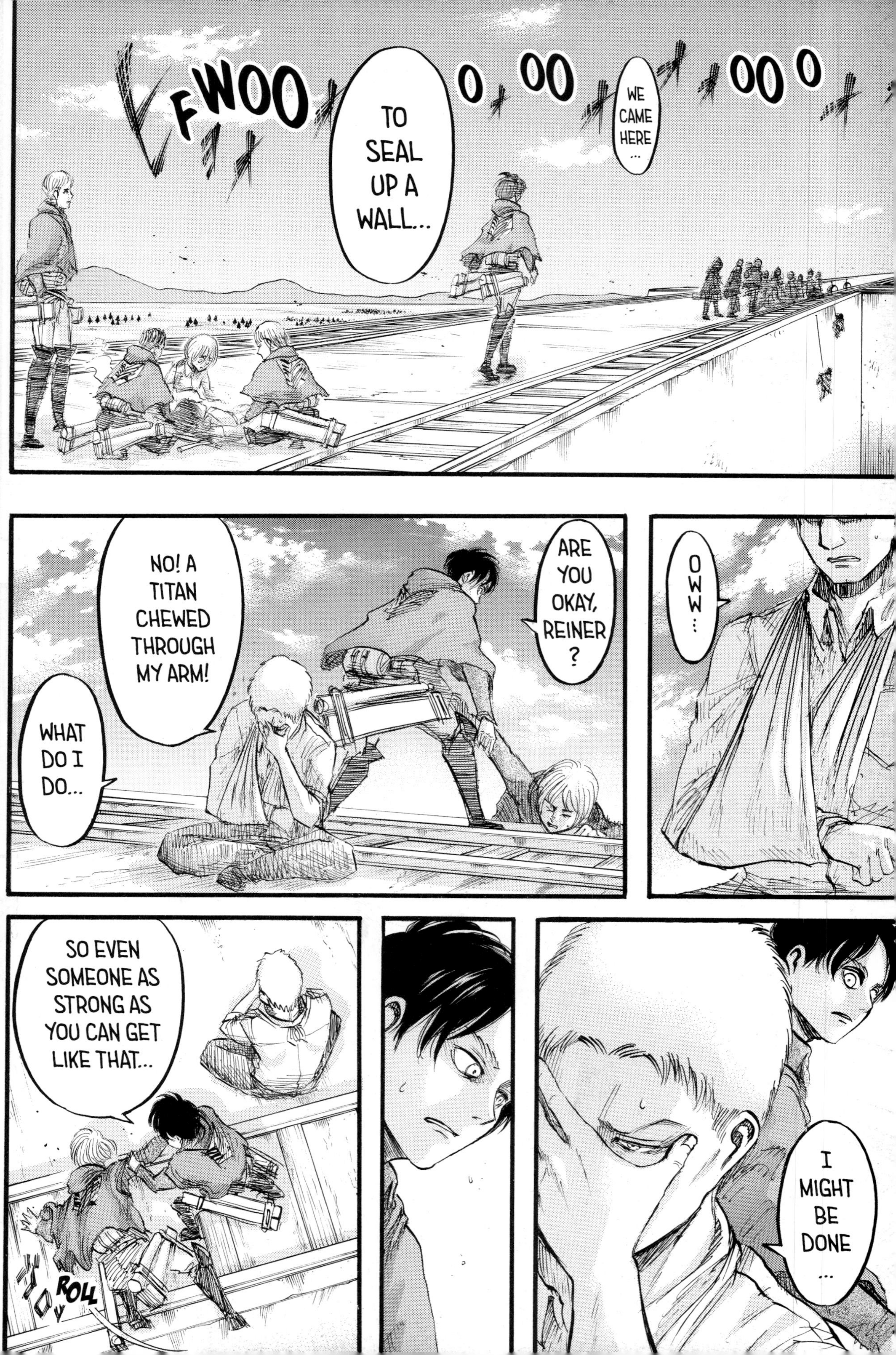
FWOOOOOOOOO
WE CAME HERE...
TO SEAL UP A WALL...
OWW...
ARE YOU OKAY, REINER?
NO! A TITAN CHEWED THROUGH MY ARM!
WHAT DO I DO...
I MIGHT BE DONE...
SO EVEN SOMEONE AS STRONG AS YOU CAN GET LIKE THAT...
ROLL

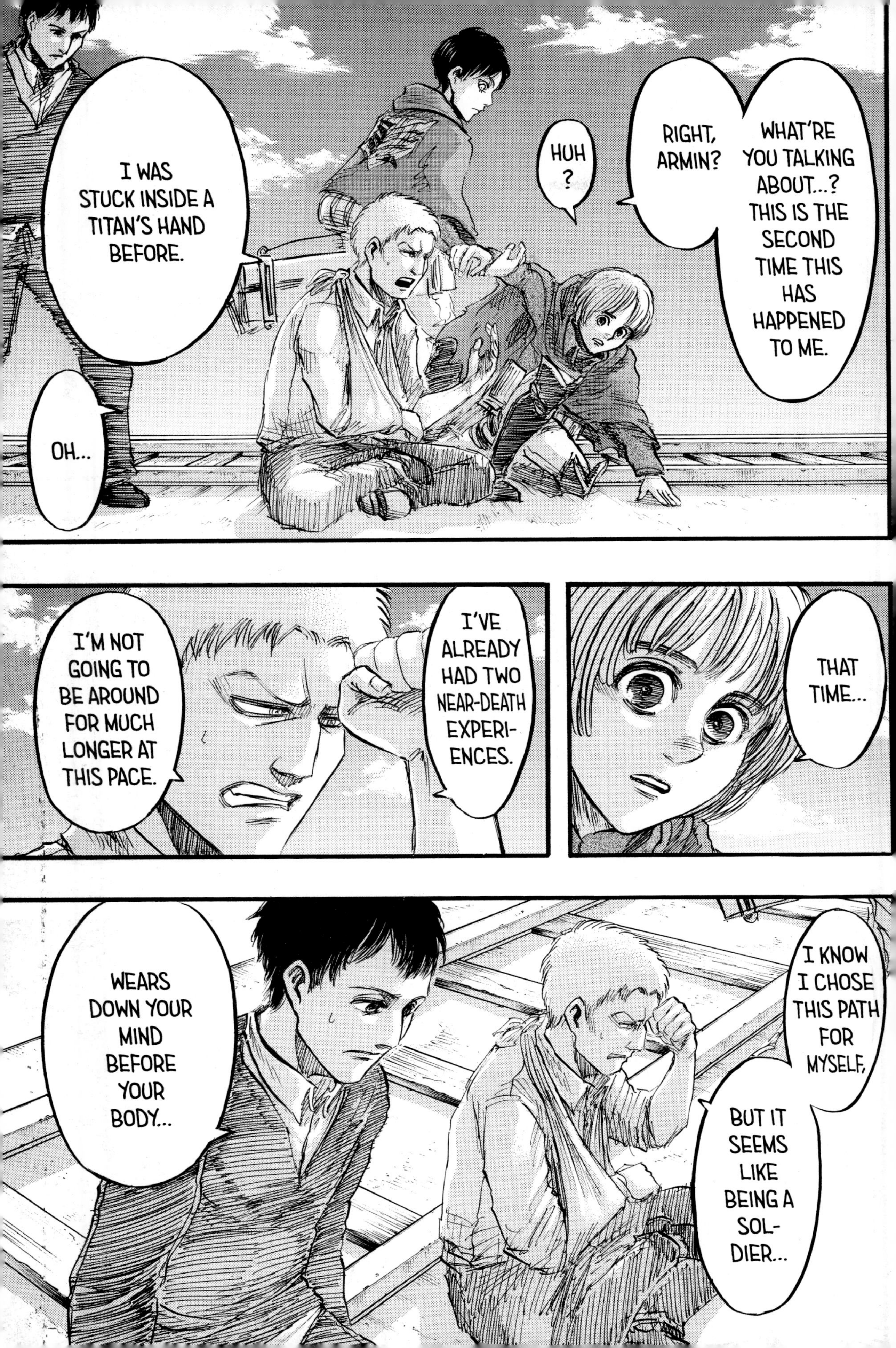
WHAT'RE YOU TALKING ABOUT...? THIS IS THE SECOND TIME THIS HAS HAPPENED TO ME.
RIGHT, ARMIN?
HUH ?
I WAS STUCK INSIDE A TITAN'S HAND BEFORE.
OH...
THAT TIME...
I'VE ALREADY HAD TWO NEAR-DEATH EXPERI-ENCES.
I'M NOT GOING TO BE AROUND FOR MUCH LONGER AT THIS PACE.
I KNOW I CHOSE THIS PATH FOR MYSELF,
BUT IT SEEMS LIKE BEING A SOL-DIER...
WEARS DOWN YOUR MIND BEFORE YOUR BODY...

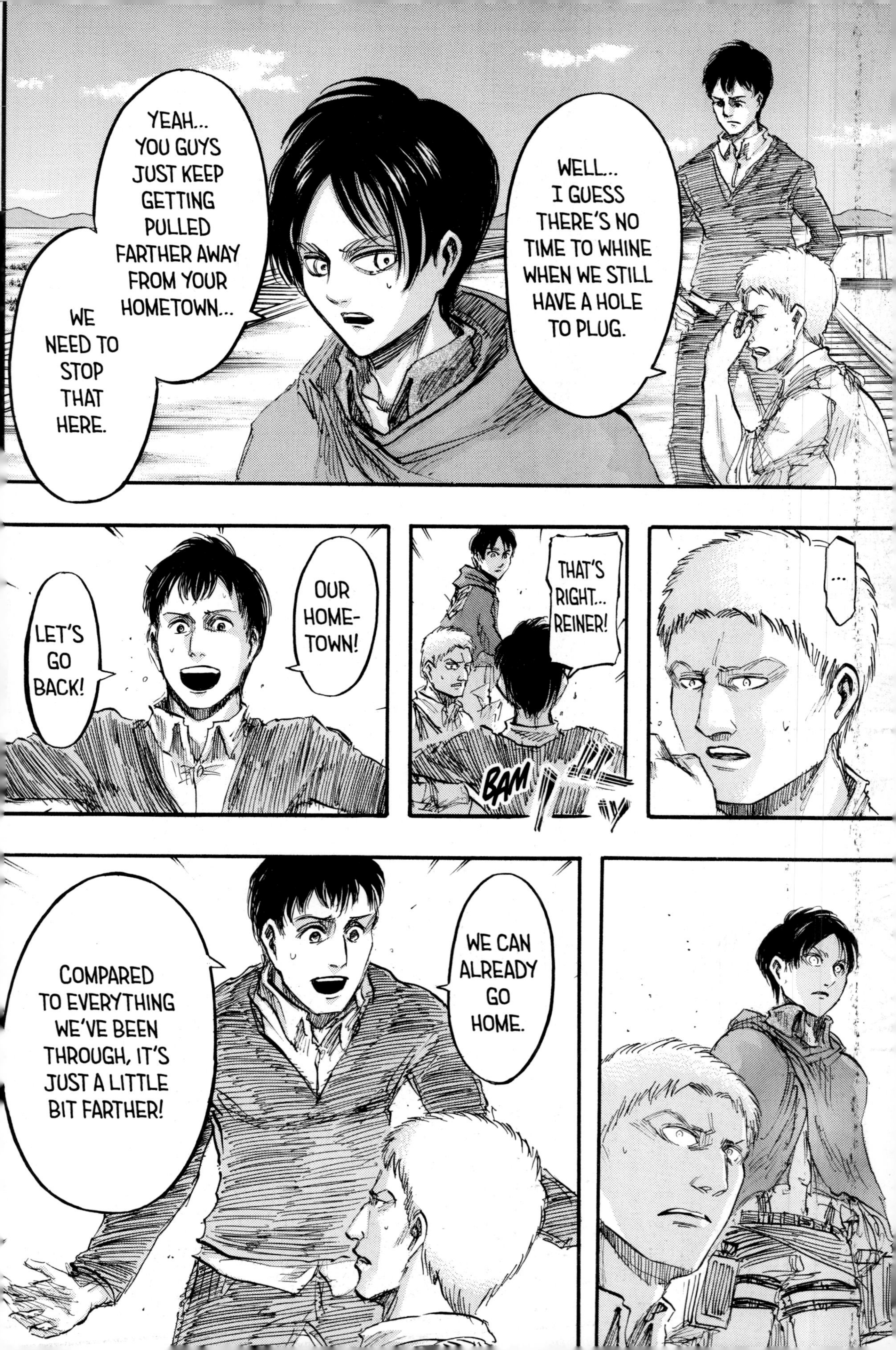
WELL... I GUESS THERE'S NO TIME TO WHINE WHEN WE STILL HAVE A HOLE TO PLUG.
YEAH... YOU GUYS JUST KEEP GETTING PULLED FARTHER AWAY FROM YOUR HOMETOWN...
WE NEED TO STOP THAT HERE.
...
THAT'S RIGHT... REINER!
BAM
OUR HOME-TOWN!
LET'S GO BACK!
WE CAN ALREADY GO HOME.
COMPARED TO EVERYTHING WE'VE BEEN THROUGH, IT'S JUST A LITTLE BIT FARTHER!

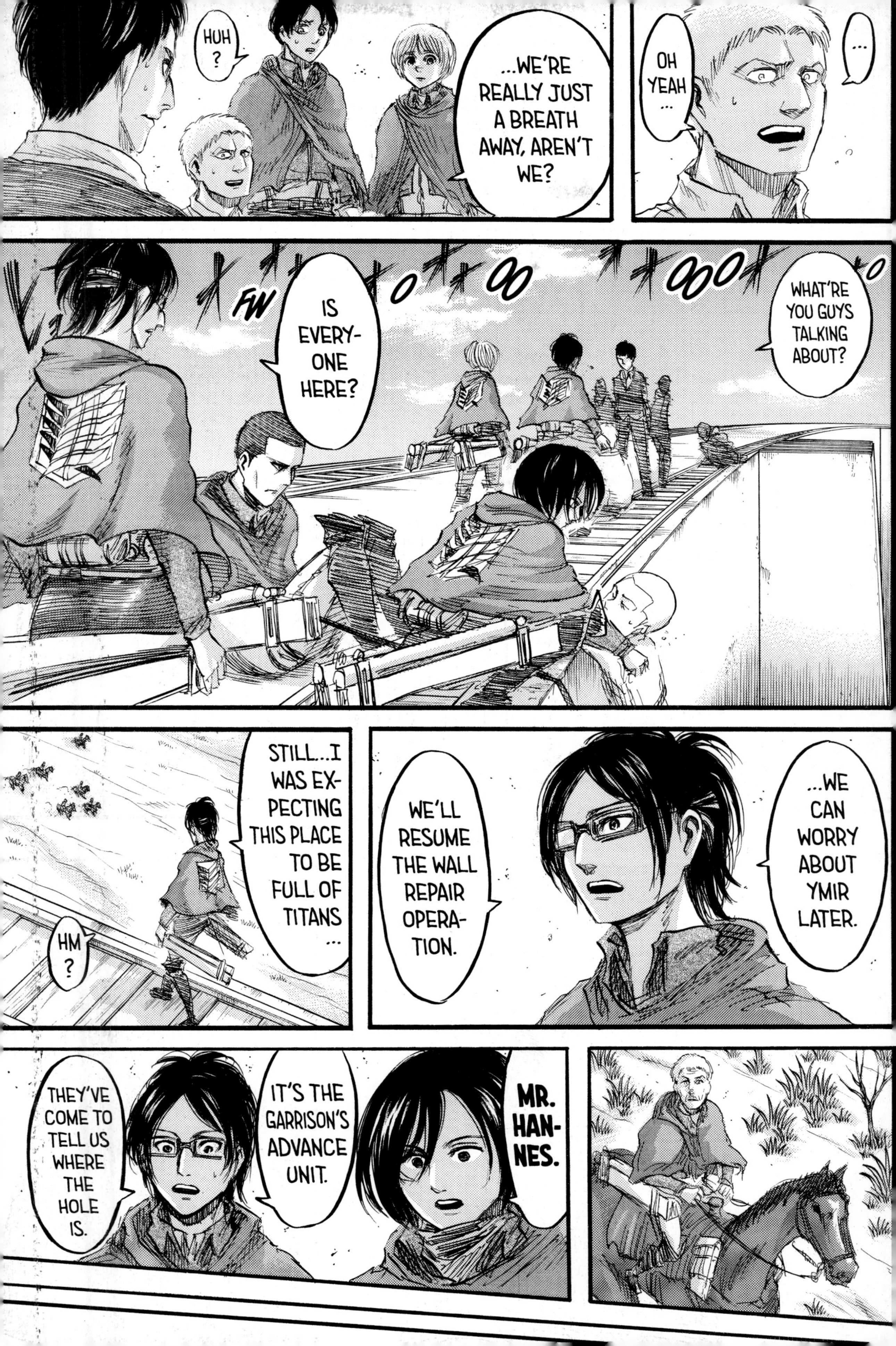
...
OH YEAH ...
...WE'RE REALLY JUST A BREATH AWAY, AREN'T WE?
HUH ?
WHAT'RE YOU GUYS TALKING ABOUT?
FWOOOOOOOO
IS EVERY-ONE HERE?
...WE CAN WORRY ABOUT YMIR LATER.
WE'LL RESUME THE WALL REPAIR OPERA-TION.
STILL...I WAS EX-PECTING THIS PLACE TO BE FULL OF TITANS ...
HM ?
MR. HAN-NES.
IT'S THE GARRISON'S ADVANCE UNIT.
THEY'VE COME TO TELL US WHERE THE HOLE IS.

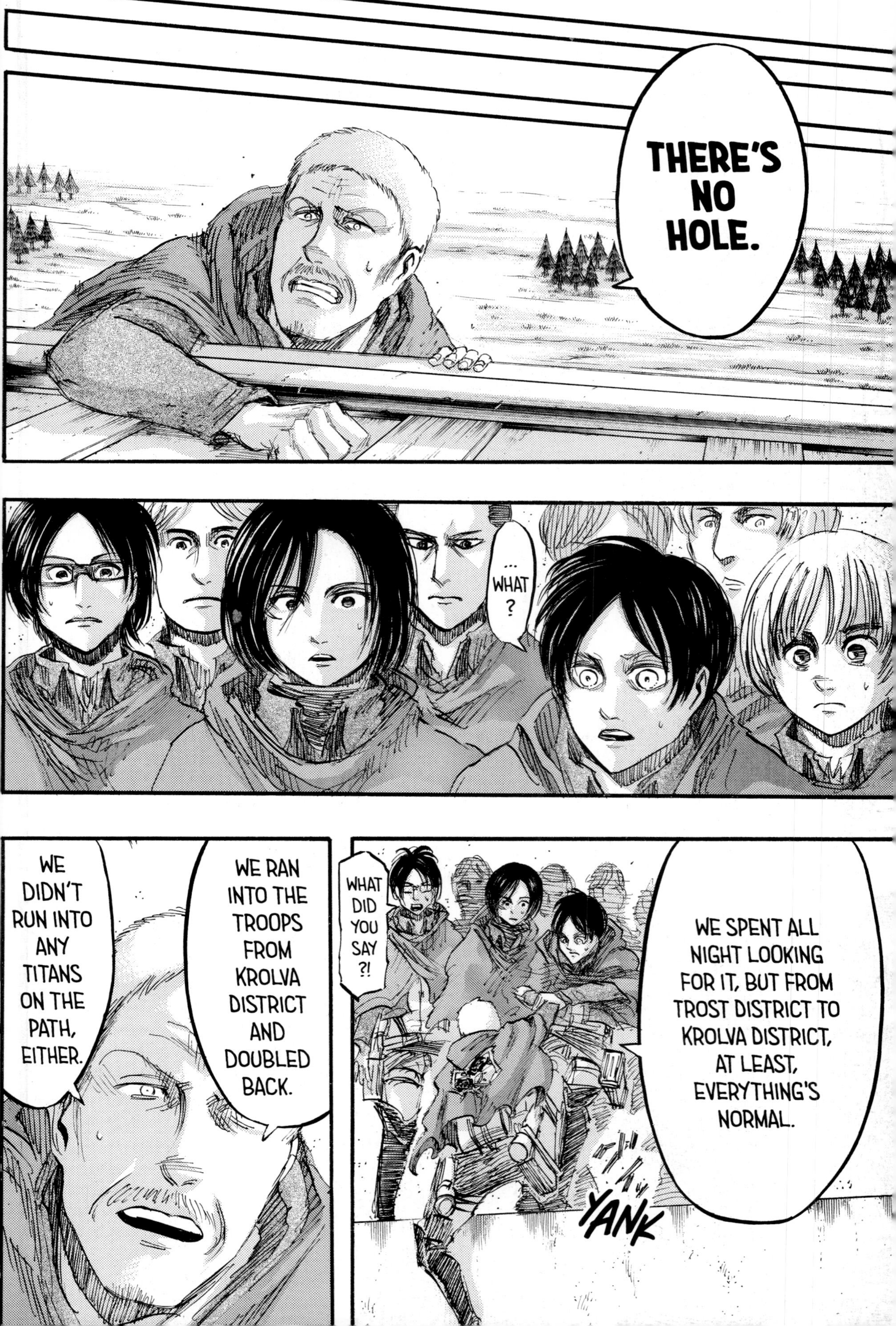
THERE'S NO HOLE.
...WHAT?
WE SPENT ALL NIGHT LOOKING FOR IT, BUT FROM TROST DISTRICT TO KROLVA DISTRICT, AT LEAST, EVERYTHING'S NORMAL.
WHAT DID YOU SAY ?!
YANK
WE RAN INTO THE TROOPS FROM KROLVA DISTRICT AND DOUBLED BACK.
WE DIDN'T RUN INTO ANY TITANS ON THE PATH, EITHER.

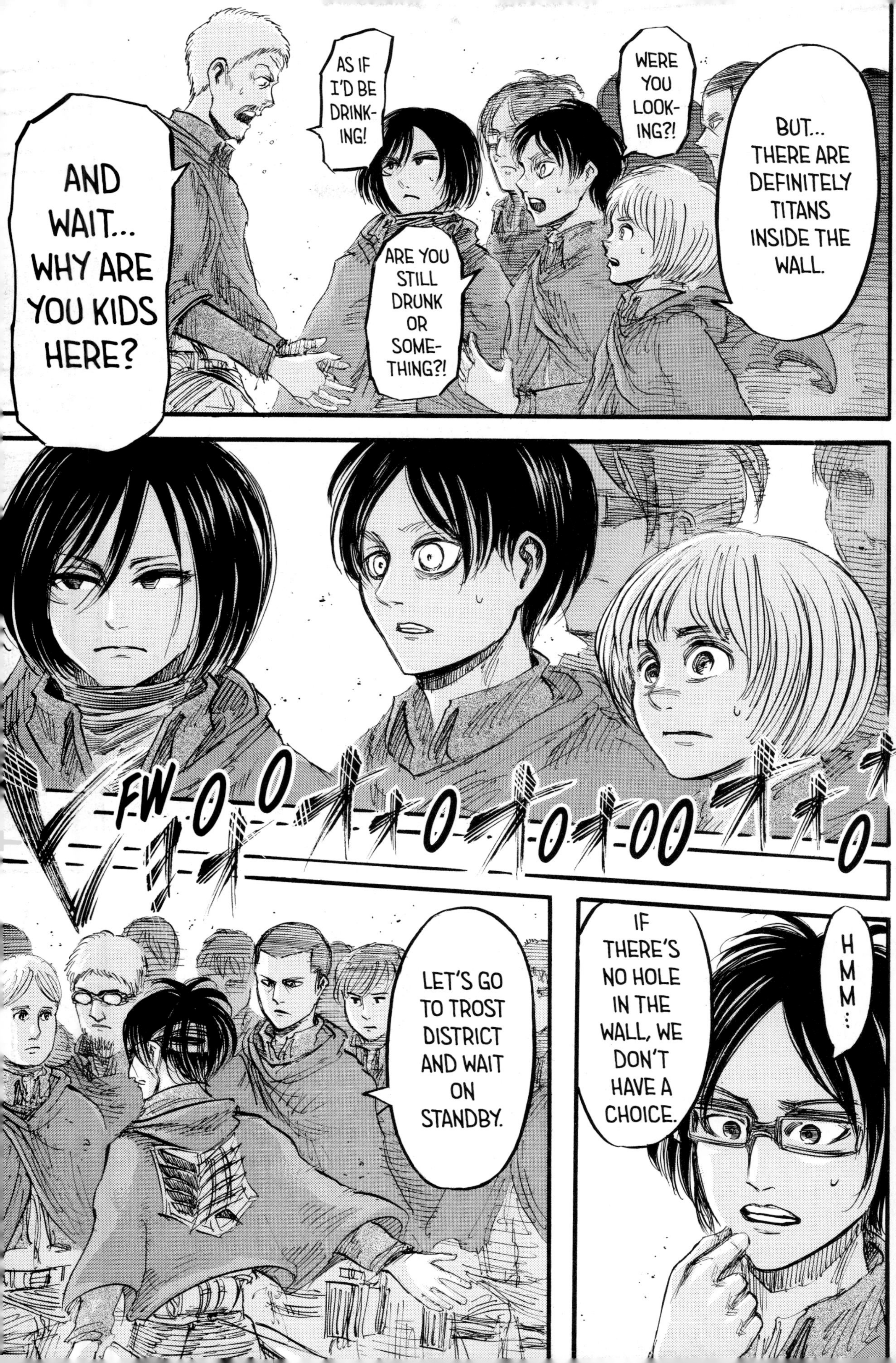
BUT... THERE ARE DEFINITELY TITANS INSIDE THE WALL.
WERE YOU LOOK-ING?!
ARE YOU STILL DRUNK OR SOME-THING?!
AS IF I'D BE DRINK-ING!
AND WAIT... WHY ARE YOU KIDS HERE?
FWOOOOOOOOOO
HMM...
IF THERE'S NO HOLE IN THE WALL, WE DON'T HAVE A CHOICE.
LET'S GO TO TROST DISTRICT AND WAIT ON STANDBY.

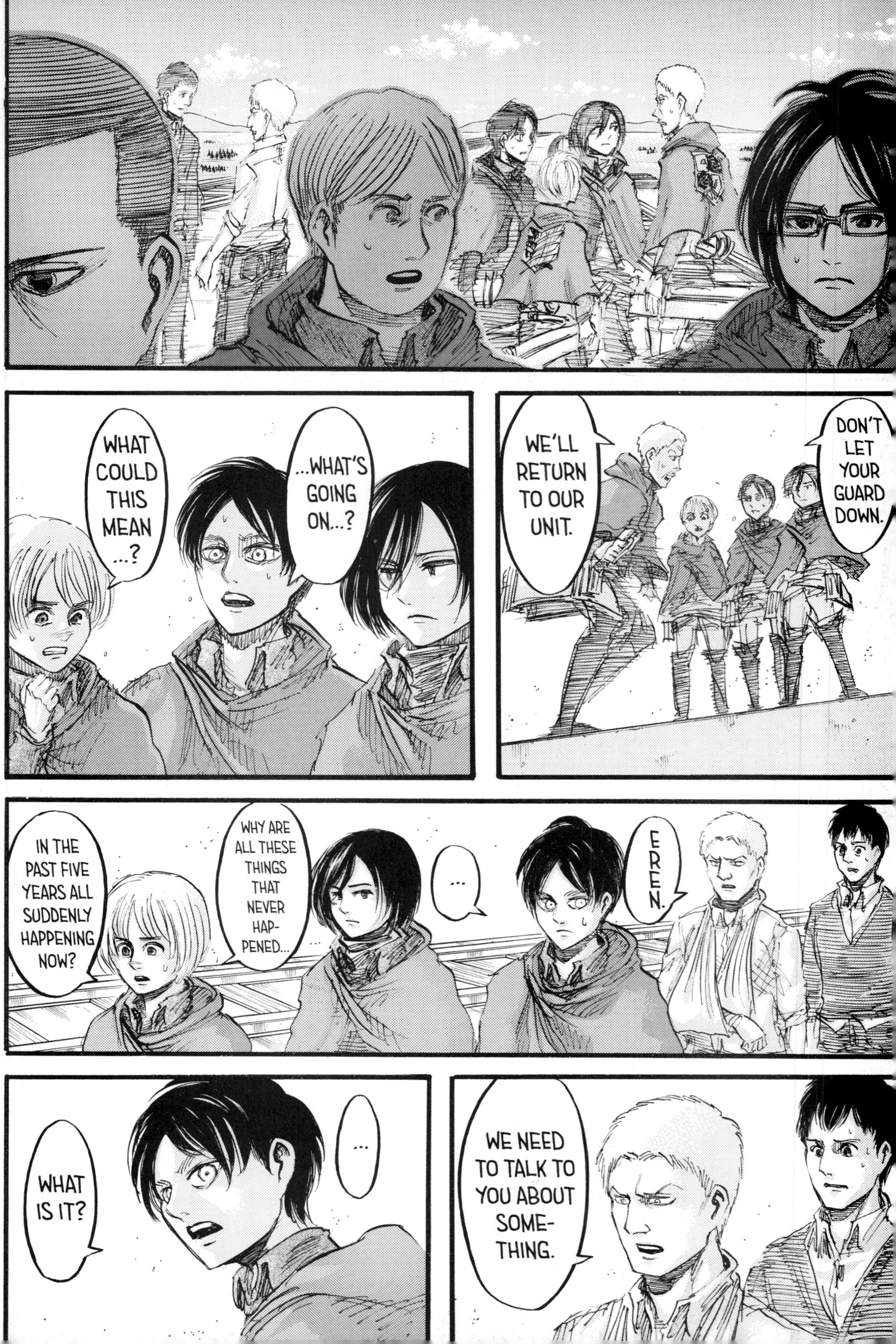
DON'T LET YOUR GUARD DOWN.
WE'LL RETURN TO OUR UNIT.
...WHAT'S GOING ON...?
WHAT COULD THIS MEAN ...?
EREN.
...
WHY ARE ALL THESE THINGS THAT NEVER HAP-PENED...
IN THE PAST FIVE YEARS ALL SUDDENLY HAPPENING NOW?
WE NEED TO TALK TO YOU ABOUT SOME-THING.
...
WHAT IS IT?

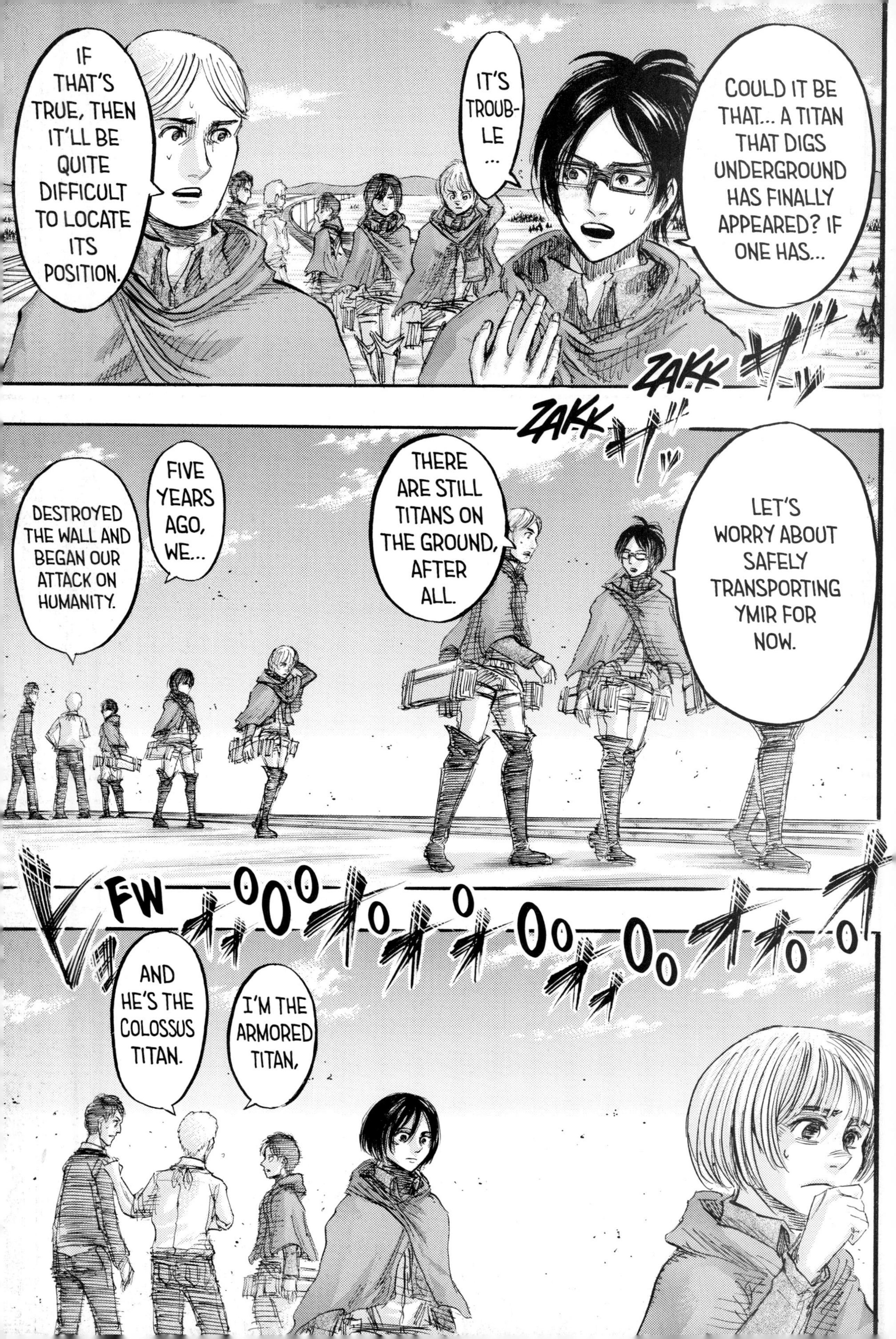
COULD IT BE THAT... A TITAN THAT DIGS UNDERGROUND HAS FINALLY APPEARED? IF ONE HAS...
IT'S TROUB-LE...
IF THAT'S TRUE, THEN IT'LL BE QUITE DIFFICULT TO LOCATE ITS POSITION.
ZAKK
ZAKK
LET'S WORRY ABOUT SAFELY TRANSPORTING YMIR FOR NOW.
THERE ARE STILL TITANS ON THE GROUND, AFTER ALL.
FIVE YEARS AGO, WE...
DESTROYED THE WALL AND BEGAN OUR ATTACK ON HUMANITY.
FWOOOOOOOOOO
I'M THE ARMORED TITAN,
AND HE'S THE COLOSSUS TITAN.

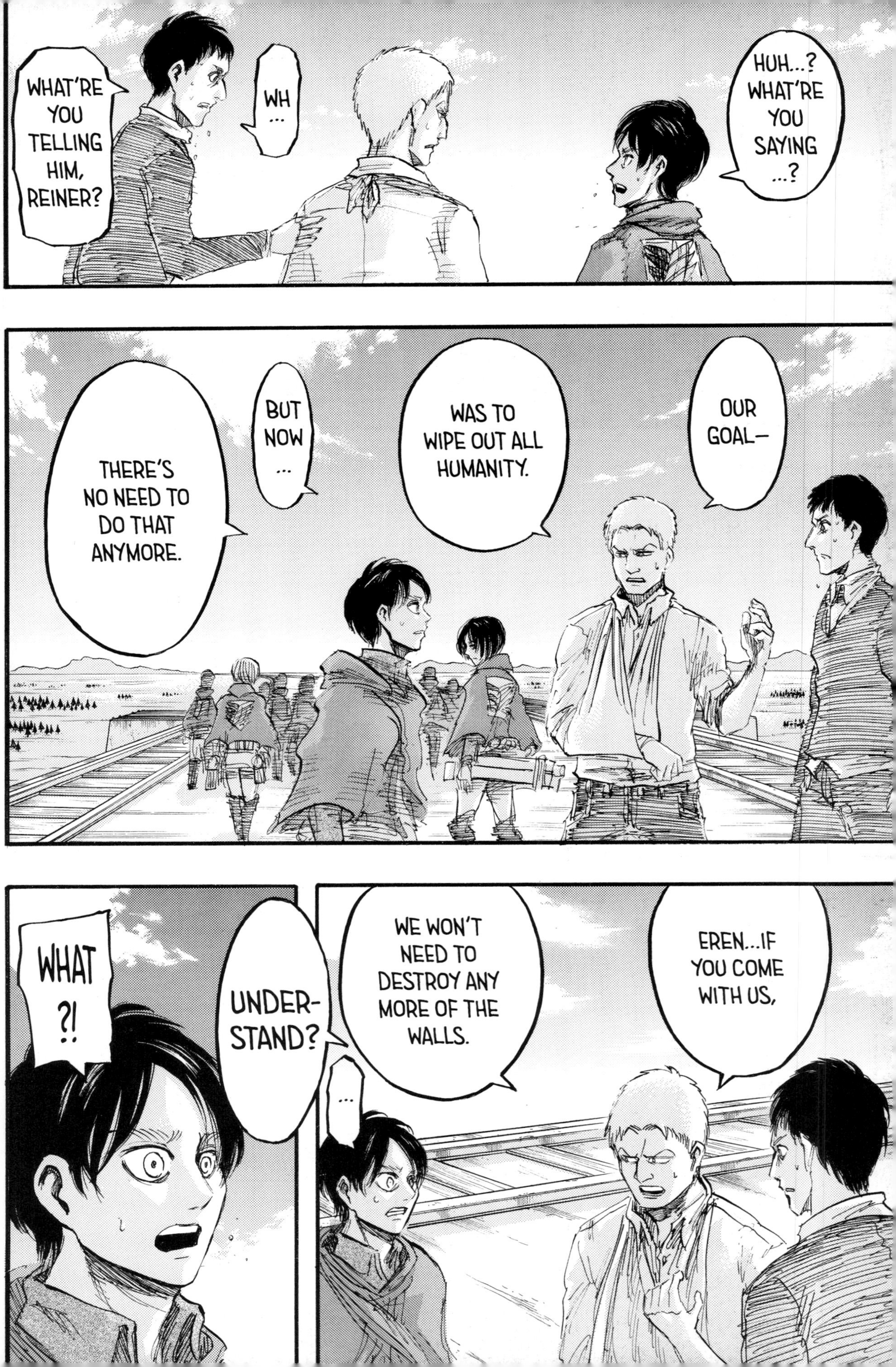
HUH...? WHAT'RE YOU SAYING ...?
WH ...
WHAT'RE YOU TELLING HIM, REINER?
OUR GOAL—
WAS TO WIPE OUT ALL HUMANITY.
BUT NOW ...
THERE'S NO NEED TO DO THAT ANYMORE.
EREN...IF YOU COME WITH US,
WE WON'T NEED TO DESTROY ANY MORE OF THE WALLS.
UNDER-STAND?
...
WHAT ?!

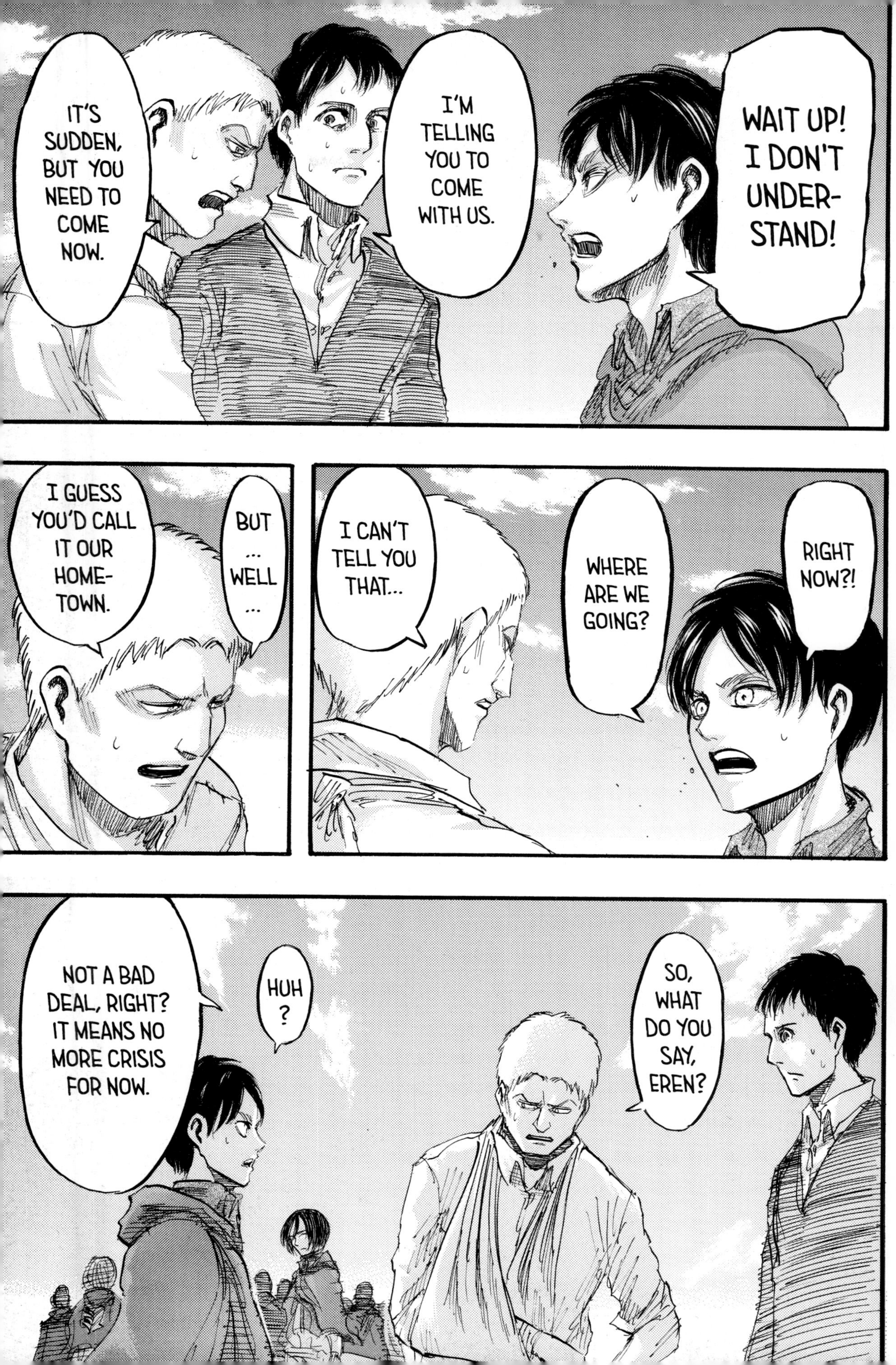
WAIT UP! I DON'T UNDER-STAND!
I'M TELLING YOU TO COME WITH US.
IT'S SUDDEN, BUT YOU NEED TO COME NOW.
RIGHT NOW?!
WHERE ARE WE GOING?
I CAN'T TELL YOU THAT...
BUT ... WELL ...
I GUESS YOU'D CALL IT OUR HOME-TOWN.
SO, WHAT DO YOU SAY, EREN?
HUH?
NOT A BAD DEAL, RIGHT? IT MEANS NO MORE CRISIS FOR NOW.

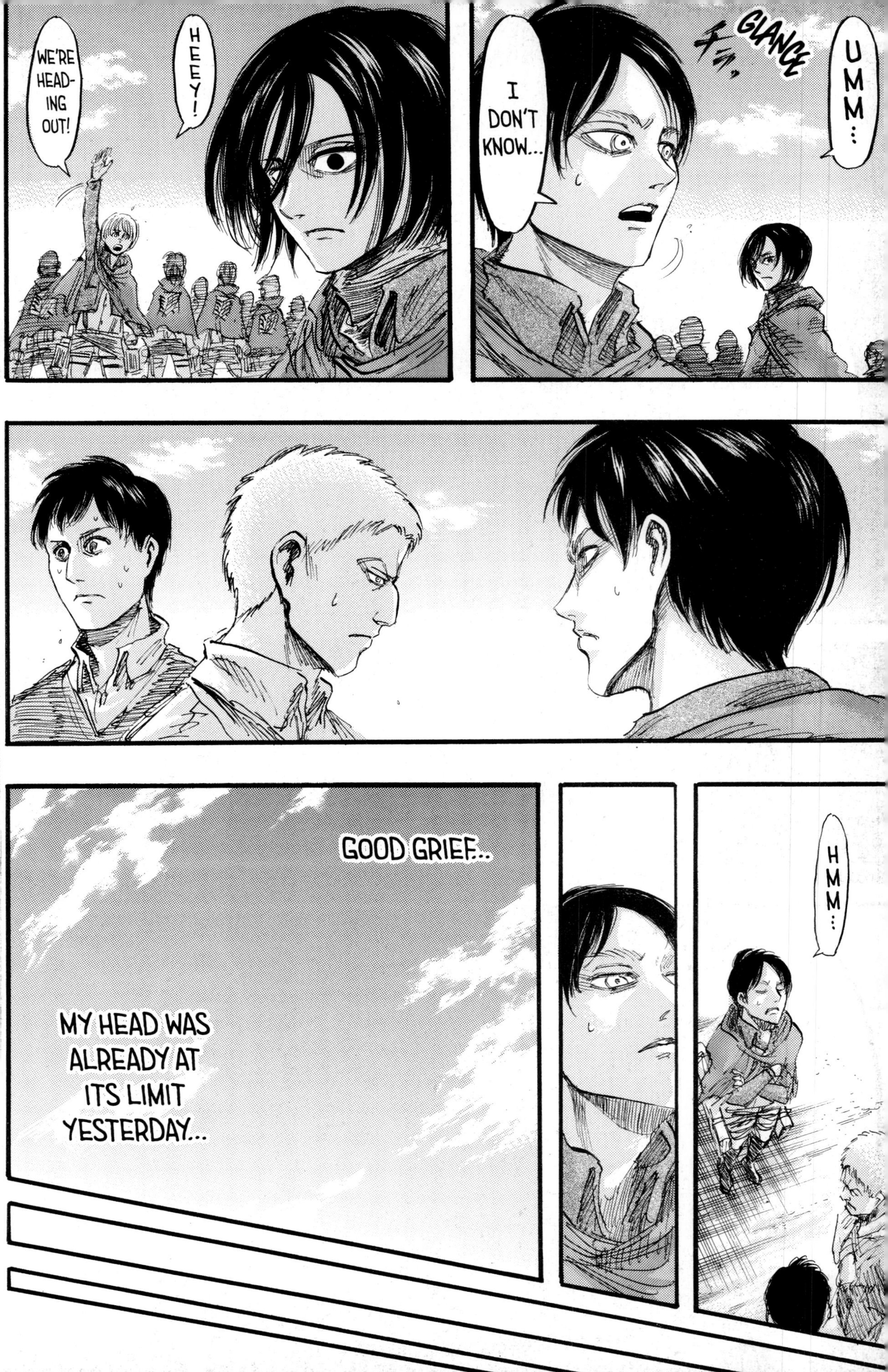

UMM...
チラッ
GLANCE
I DON'T KNOW...
HEEY!
WE'RE HEAD-ING OUT!
HMM...
GOOD GRIEF...
MY HEAD WAS ALREADY AT ITS LIMIT YESTERDAY...

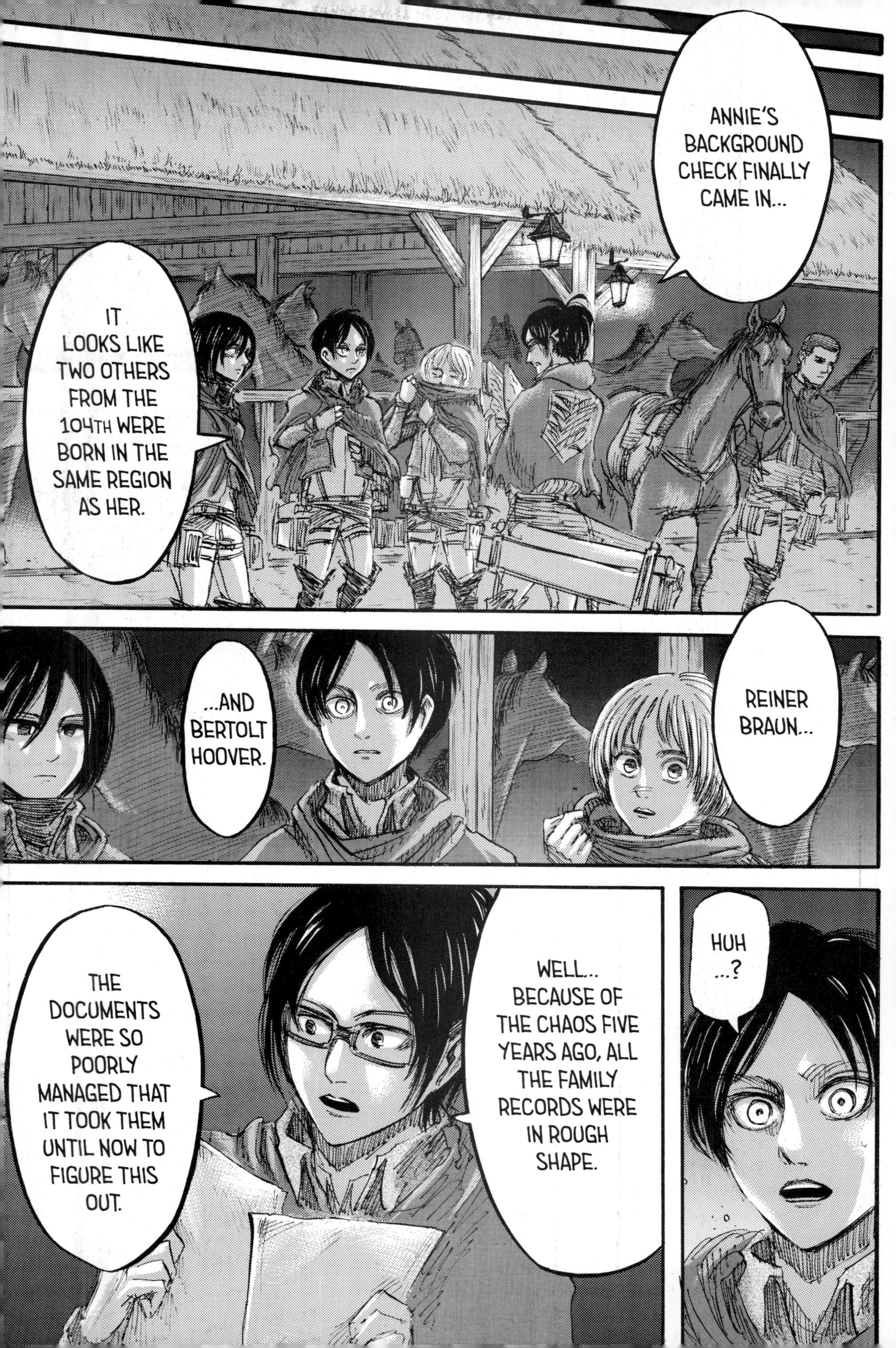
ANNIE'S BACKGROUND CHECK FINALLY CAME IN...
IT LOOKS LIKE TWO OTHERS FROM THE 104TH WERE BORN IN THE SAME REGION AS HER.
REINER BRAUN...
...AND BERTOLT HOOVER.
HUH ...?
WELL... BECAUSE OF THE CHAOS FIVE YEARS AGO, ALL THE FAMILY RECORDS WERE IN ROUGH SHAPE.
THE DOCUMENTS WERE SO POORLY MANAGED THAT IT TOOK THEM UNTIL NOW TO FIGURE THIS OUT.

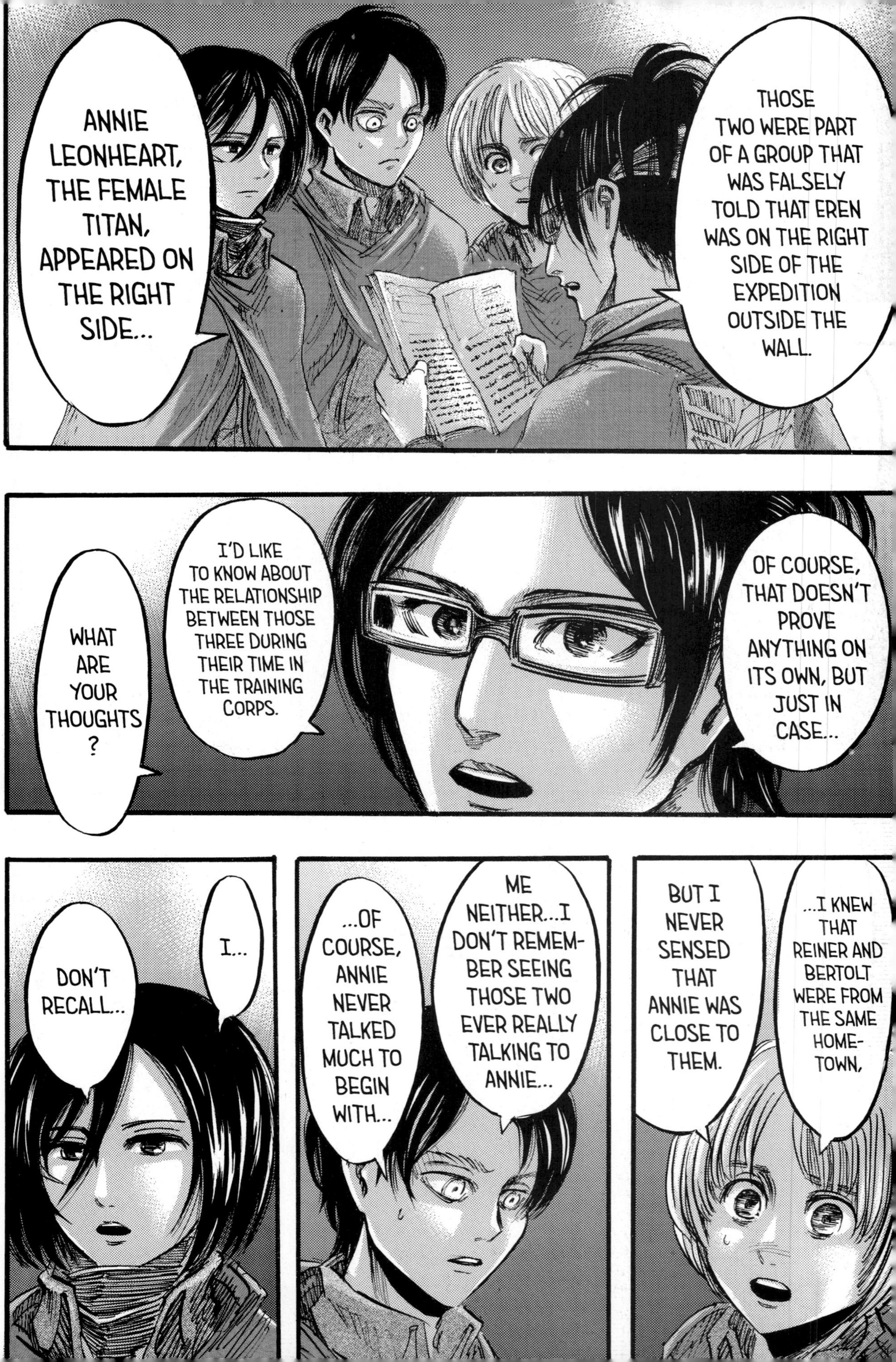
THOSE TWO WERE PART OF A GROUP THAT WAS FALSELY TOLD THAT EREN WAS ON THE RIGHT SIDE OF THE EXPEDITION OUTSIDE THE WALL.
ANNIE LEONHEART, THE FEMALE TITAN, APPEARED ON THE RIGHT SIDE...
OF COURSE, THAT DOESN'T PROVE ANYTHING ON ITS OWN, BUT JUST IN CASE...
I'D LIKE TO KNOW ABOUT THE RELATIONSHIP BETWEEN THOSE THREE DURING THEIR TIME IN THE TRAINING CORPS.
WHAT ARE YOUR THOUGHTS?
...I KNEW THAT REINER AND BERTOLT WERE FROM THE SAME HOME-TOWN,
BUT I NEVER SENSED THAT ANNIE WAS CLOSE TO THEM.
ME NEITHER...I DON'T REMEM-BER SEEING THOSE TWO EVER REALLY TALKING TO ANNIE...
...OF COURSE, ANNIE NEVER TALKED MUCH TO BEGIN WITH...
I...
DON'T RECALL...

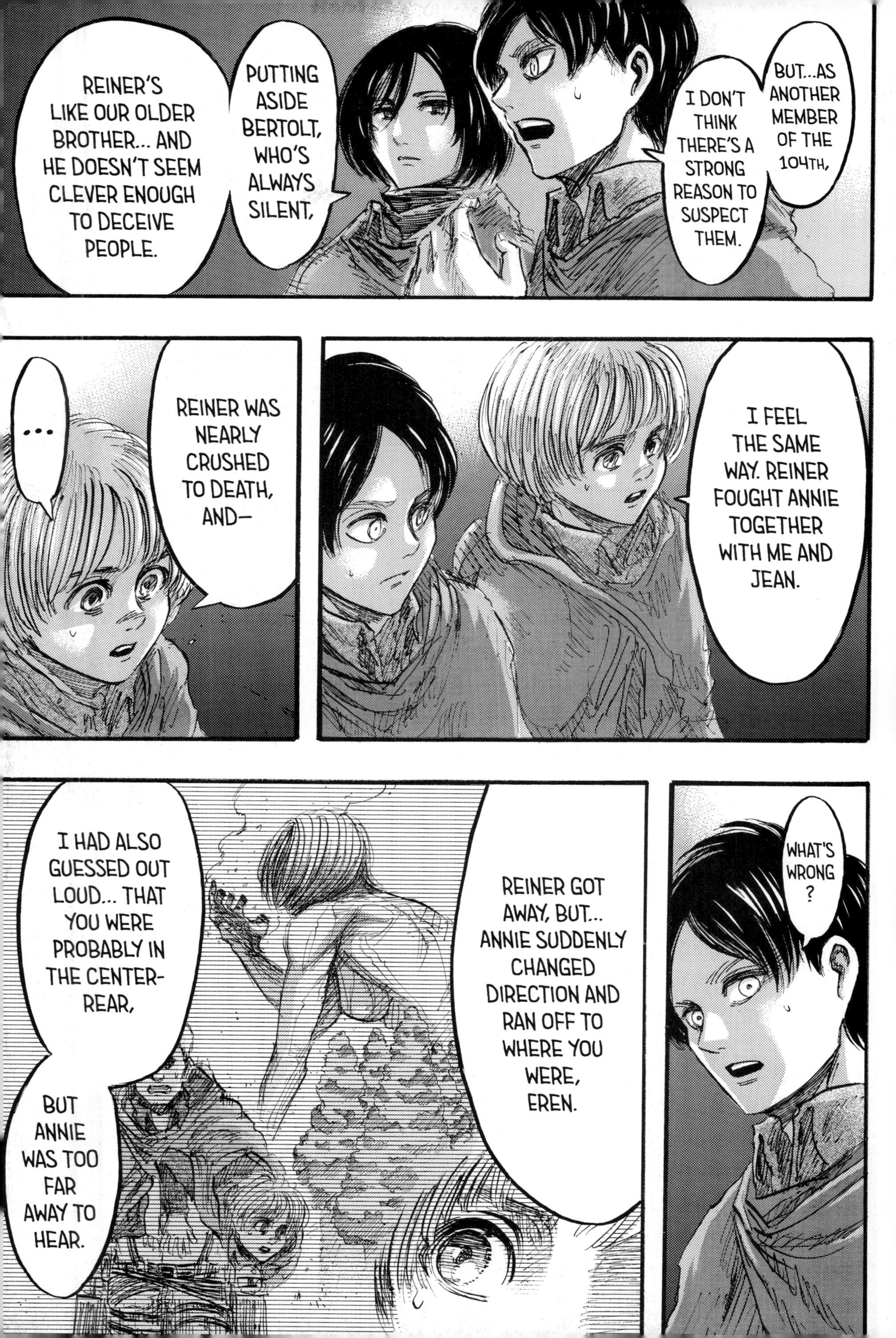
BUT...AS ANOTHER MEMBER OF THE 104TH,
I DON'T THINK THERE'S A STRONG REASON TO SUSPECT THEM.
PUTTING ASIDE BERTOLT, WHO'S ALWAYS SILENT,
REINER'S LIKE OUR OLDER BROTHER... AND HE DOESN'T SEEM CLEVER ENOUGH TO DECEIVE PEOPLE.
I FEEL THE SAME WAY. REINER FOUGHT ANNIE TOGETHER WITH ME AND JEAN.
REINER WAS NEARLY CRUSHED TO DEATH, AND—
...
WHAT'S WRONG ?
REINER GOT AWAY, BUT... ANNIE SUDDENLY CHANGED DIRECTION AND RAN OFF TO WHERE YOU WERE, EREN.
I HAD ALSO GUESSED OUT LOUD... THAT YOU WERE PROBABLY IN THE CENTER-REAR,
BUT ANNIE WAS TOO FAR AWAY TO HEAR.

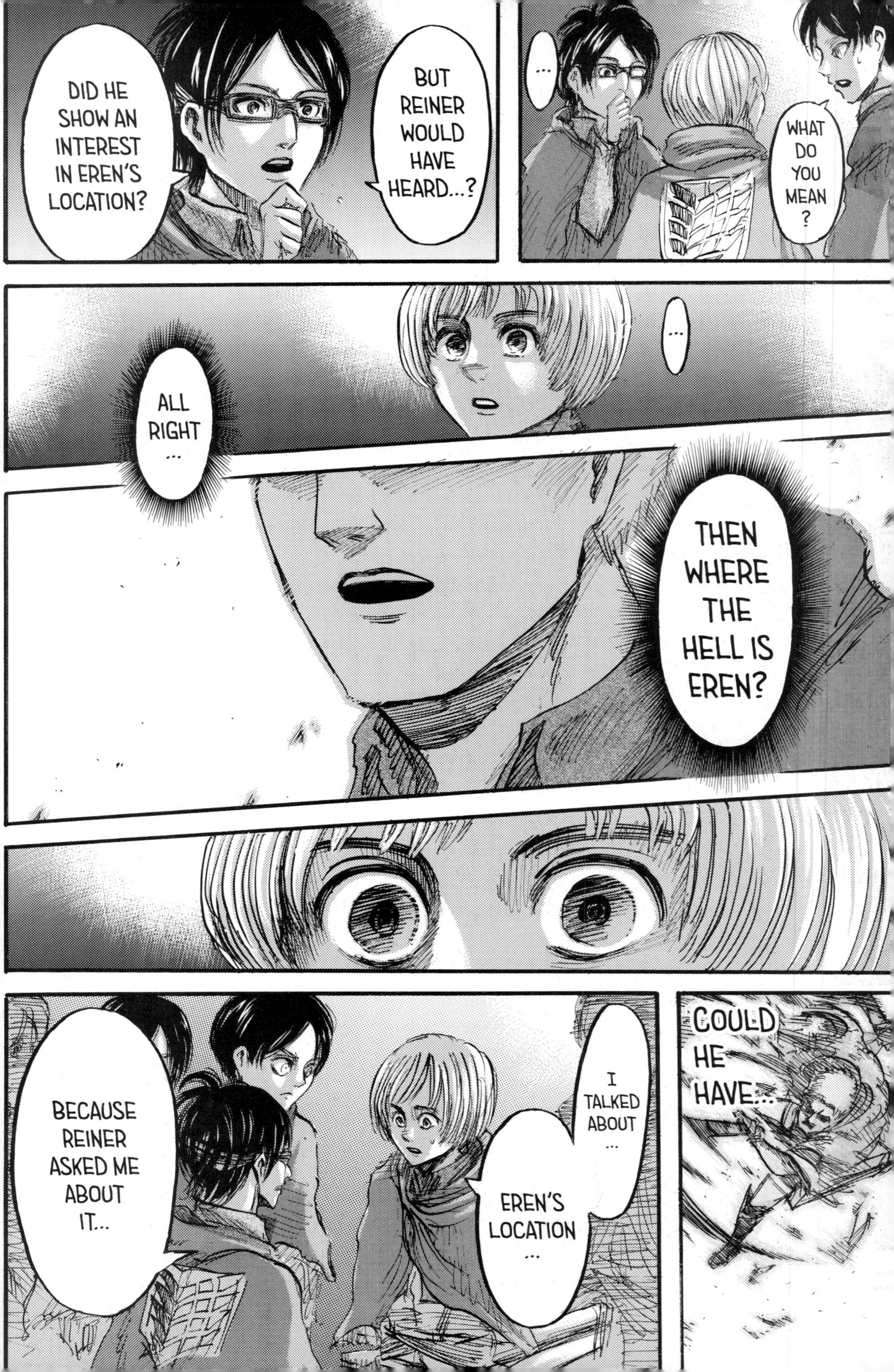
WHAT DO YOU MEAN?
...
BUT REINER WOULD HAVE HEARD...?
DID HE SHOW AN INTEREST IN EREN'S LOCATION?
...
ALL RIGHT...
THEN WHERE THE HELL IS EREN?
COULD HE HAVE...
I TALKED ABOUT...
EREN'S LOCATION...
BECAUSE REINER ASKED ME ABOUT IT...

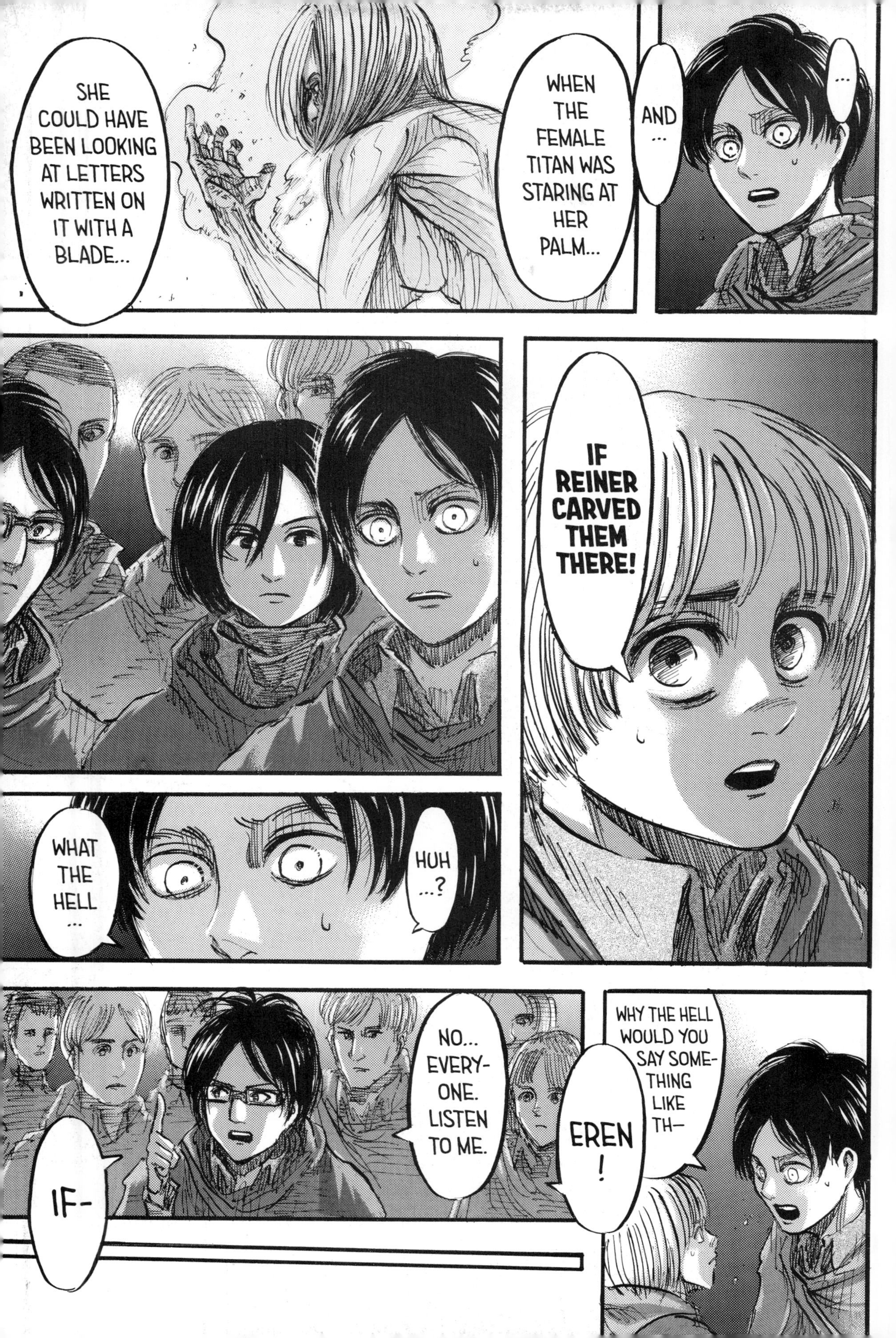
...
AND ...
WHEN THE FEMALE TITAN WAS STARING AT HER PALM...
SHE COULD HAVE BEEN LOOKING AT LETTERS WRITTEN ON IT WITH A BLADE...
IF REINER CARVED THEM THERE!
HUH ...?
WHAT THE HELL ...
WHY THE HELL WOULD YOU SAY SOME-THING LIKE TH—
EREN !
NO... EVERY-ONE. LISTEN TO ME.
IF-

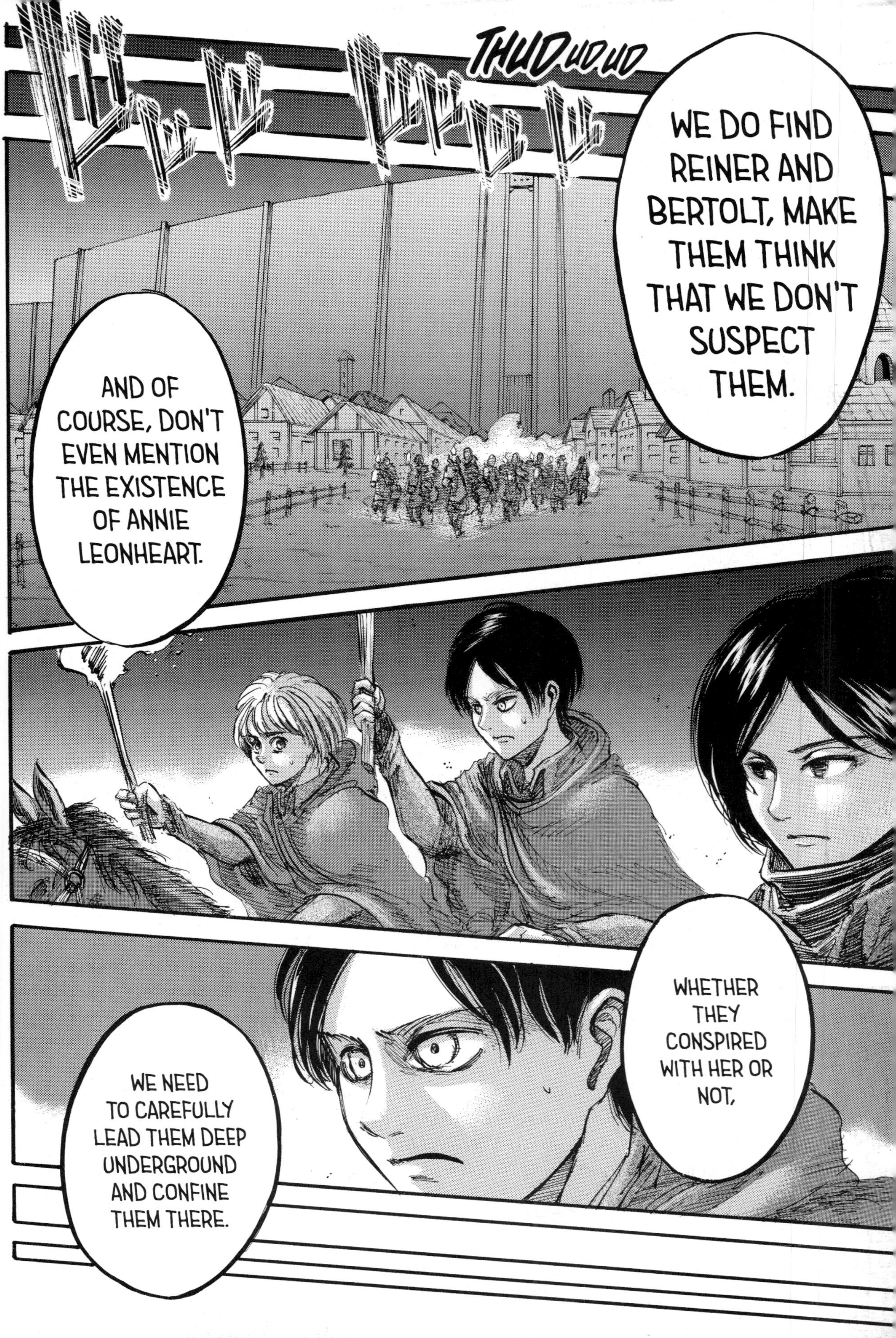
THUDUDUD
WE DO FIND REINER AND BERTOLT, MAKE THEM THINK THAT WE DON'T SUSPECT THEM.
AND OF COURSE, DON'T EVEN MENTION THE EXISTENCE OF ANNIE LEONHEART.
WHETHER THEY CONSPIRED WITH HER OR NOT,
WE NEED TO CAREFULLY LEAD THEM DEEP UNDERGROUND AND CONFINE THEM THERE.

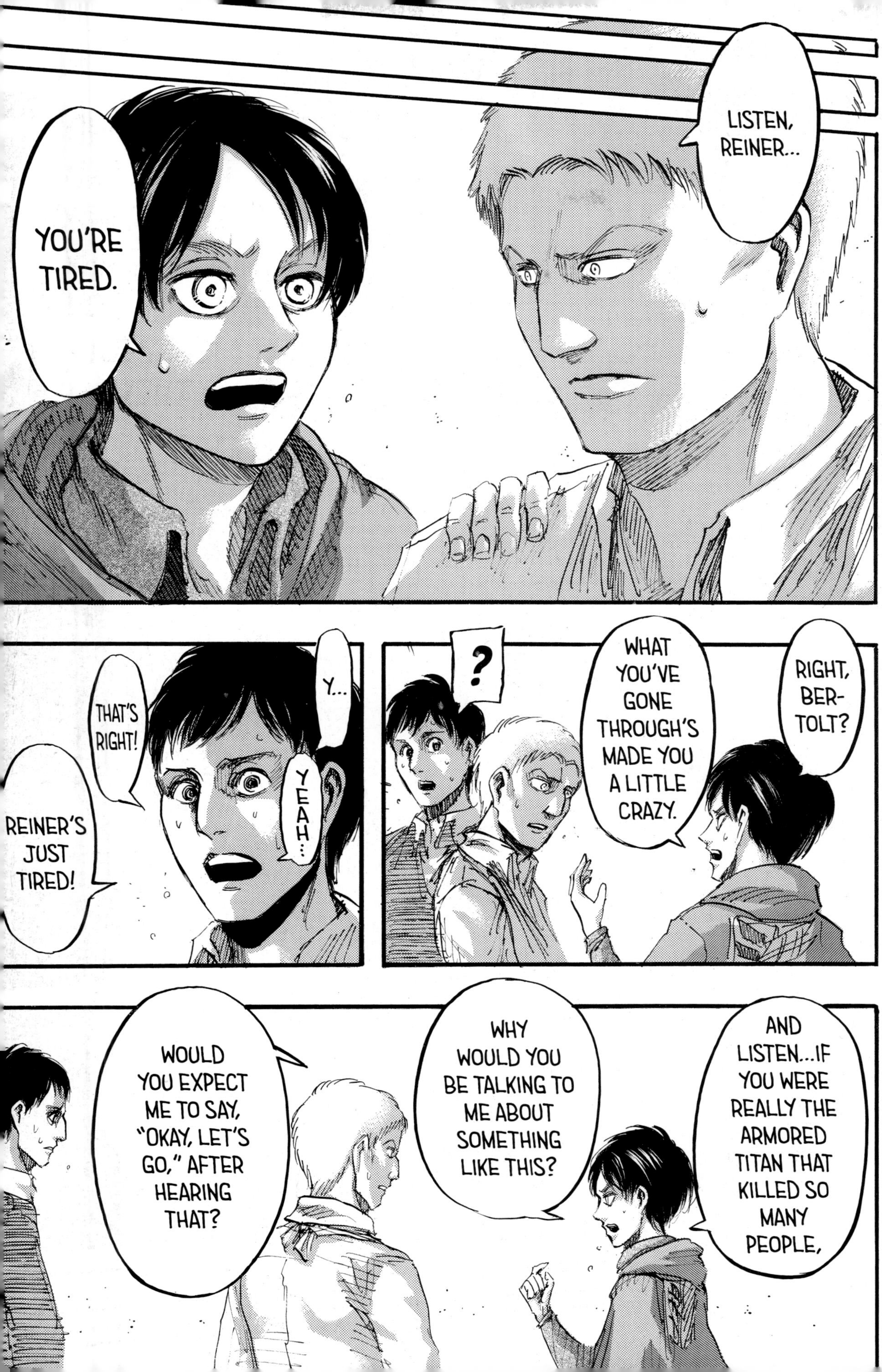
LISTEN, REINER...
YOU'RE TIRED.
RIGHT, BER-TOLT?
WHAT YOU'VE GONE THROUGH'S MADE YOU A LITTLE CRAZY.
?
Y...
YEAH...
THAT'S RIGHT!
REINER'S JUST TIRED!
AND LISTEN...IF YOU WERE REALLY THE ARMORED TITAN THAT KILLED SO MANY PEOPLE,
WHY WOULD YOU BE TALKING TO ME ABOUT SOMETHING LIKE THIS?
WOULD YOU EXPECT ME TO SAY, "OKAY, LET'S GO," AFTER HEARING THAT?

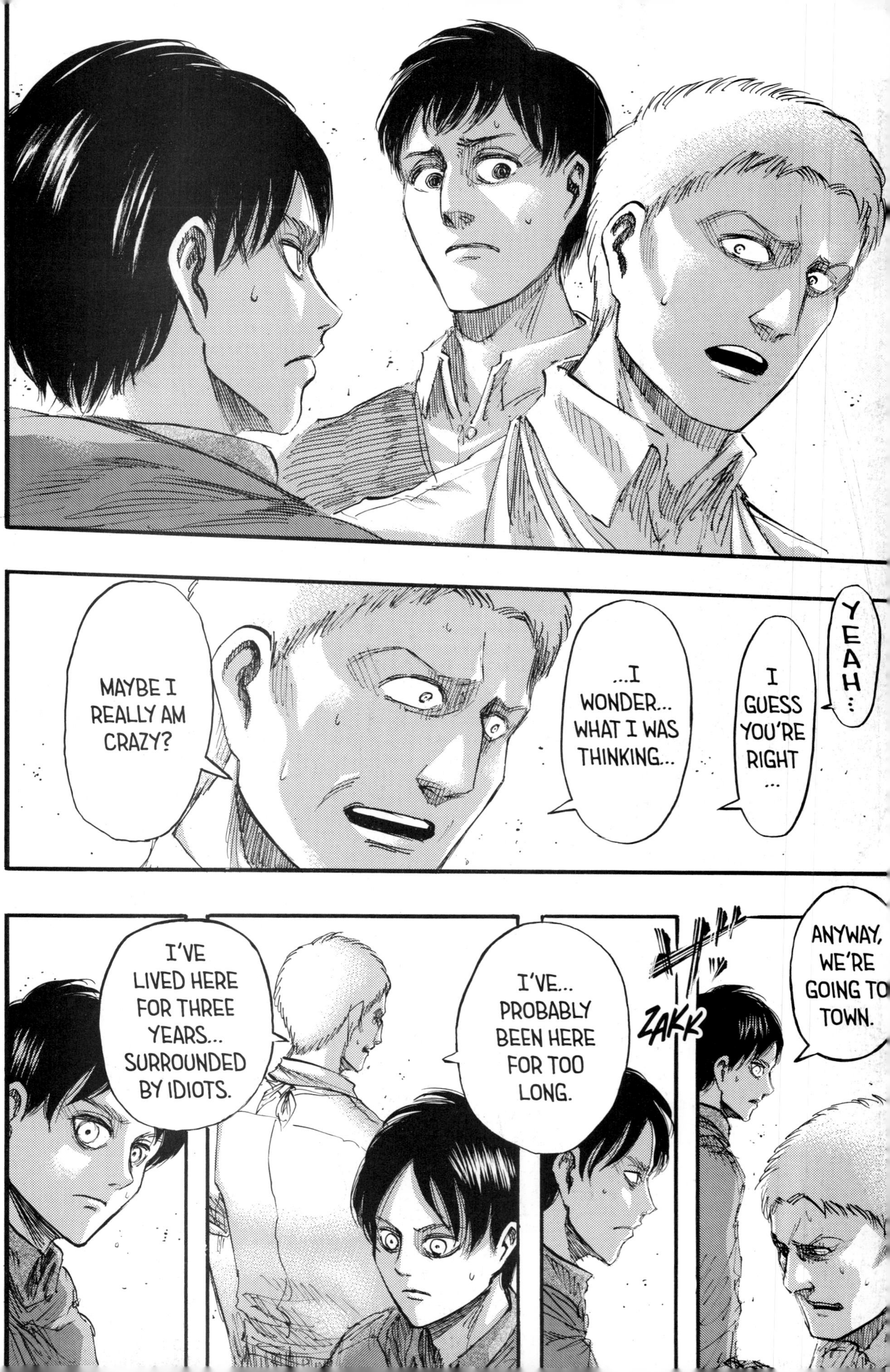
YEAH...
I GUESS YOU'RE RIGHT ...
...I WONDER... WHAT I WAS THINKING...
MAYBE I REALLY AM CRAZY?
ANYWAY, WE'RE GOING TO TOWN.
ZAKK
I'VE... PROBABLY BEEN HERE FOR TOO LONG.
I'VE LIVED HERE FOR THREE YEARS... SURROUNDED BY IDIOTS.

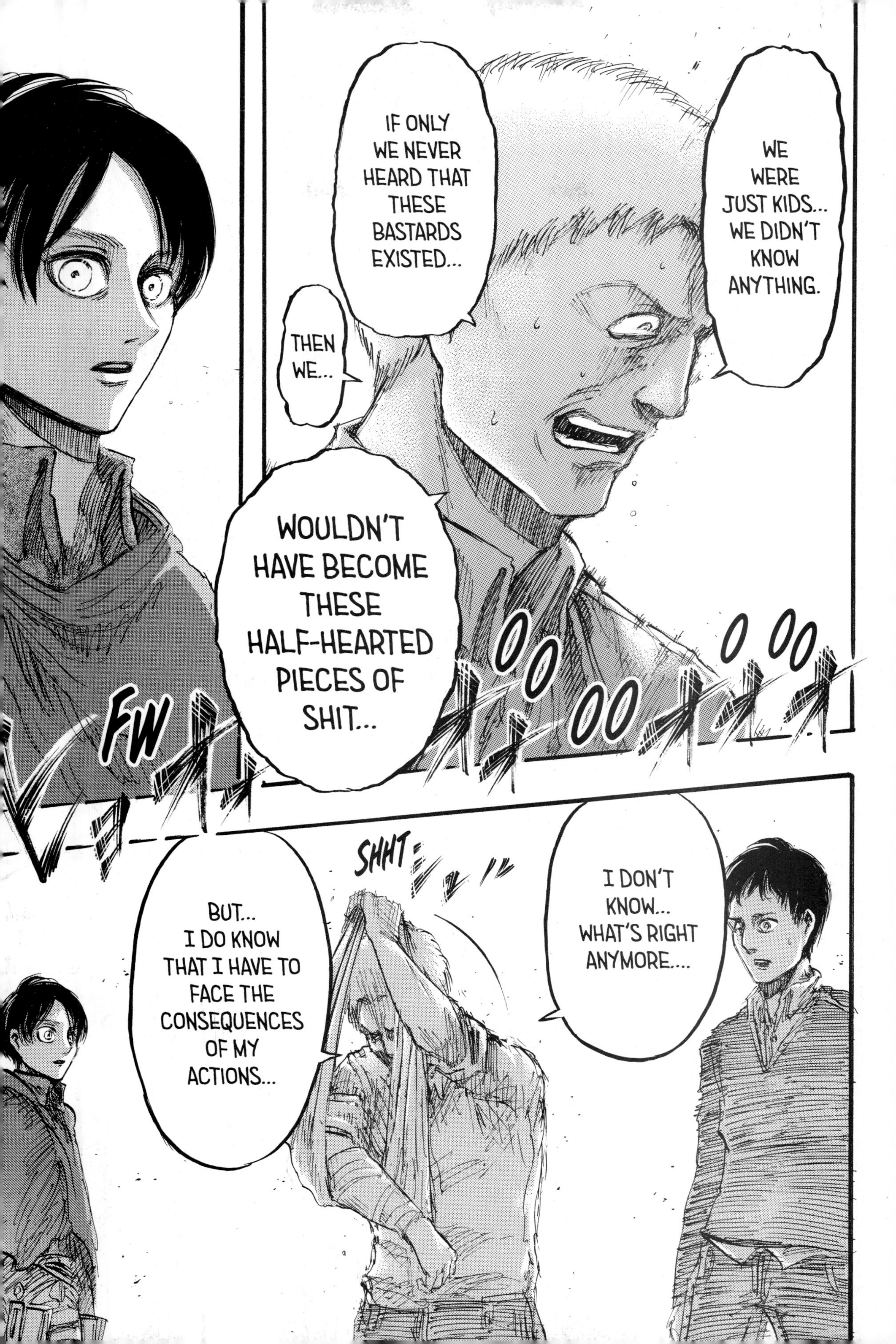
WE WERE JUST KIDS... WE DIDN'T KNOW ANYTHING.
IF ONLY WE NEVER HEARD THAT THESE BASTARDS EXISTED...
THEN WE...
WOULDN'T HAVE BECOME THESE HALF-HEARTED PIECES OF SHIT...
FWOOOOOO
I DON'T KNOW... WHAT'S RIGHT ANYMORE....
SHHT
BUT... I DO KNOW THAT I HAVE TO FACE THE CONSEQUENCES OF MY ACTIONS...

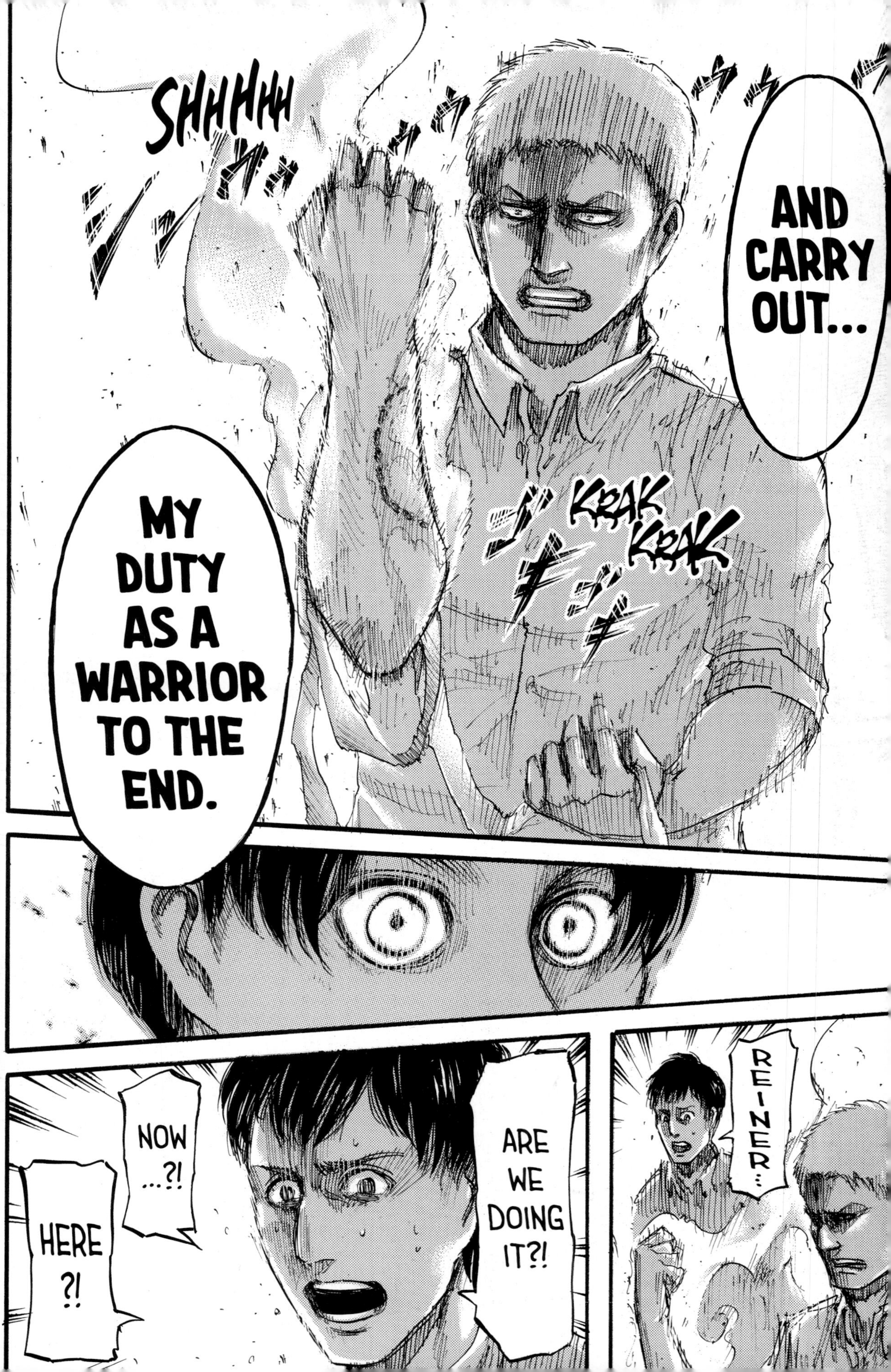
AND CARRY OUT...
SHHHHH
KRAK KRAK
MY DUTY AS A WARRIOR TO THE END.
REINER...
ARE WE DOING IT?!
NOW ...?!
HERE ?!

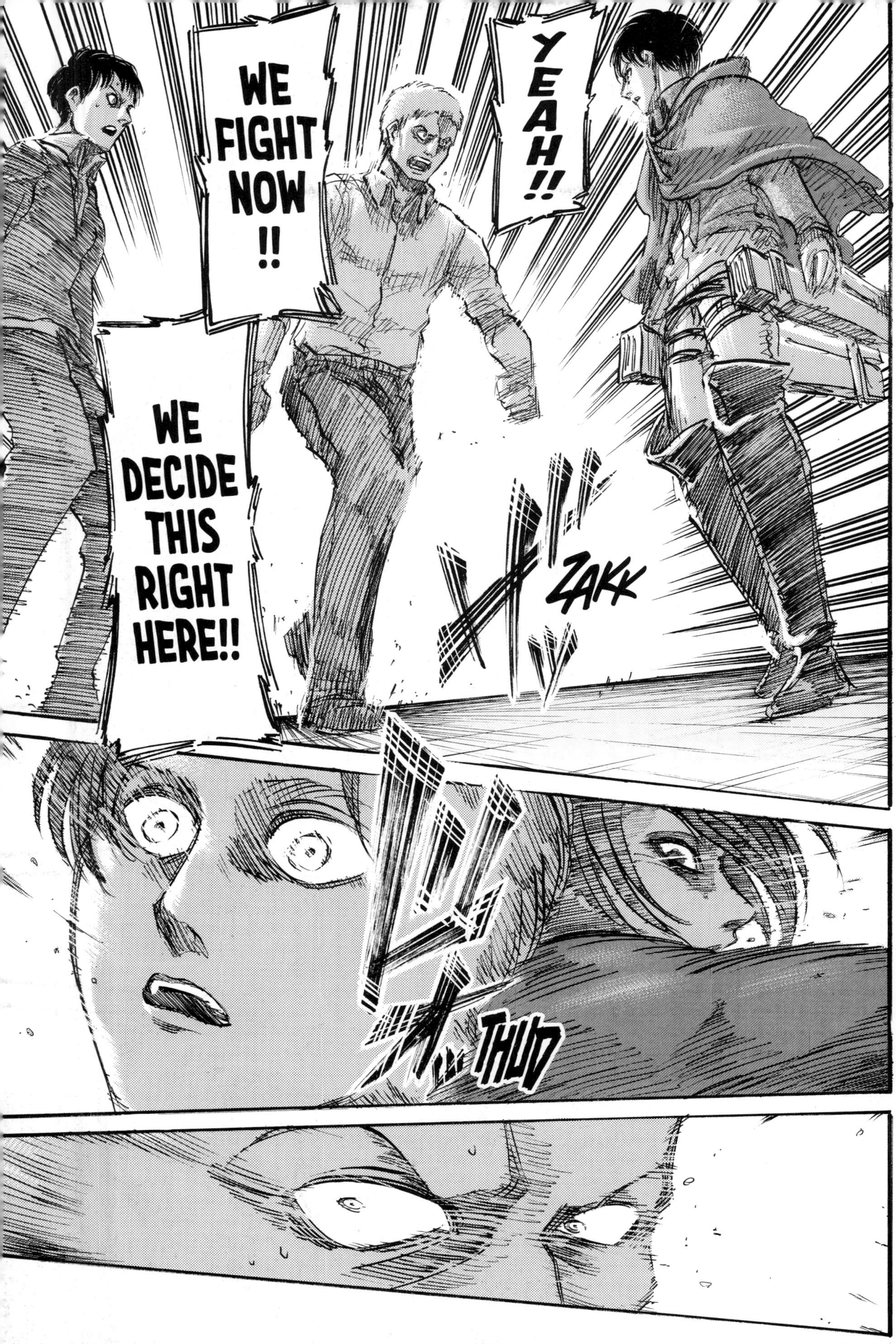
YEAH!!
WE FIGHT NOW !!
WE DECIDE THIS RIGHT HERE!!
ZAKK
THUD

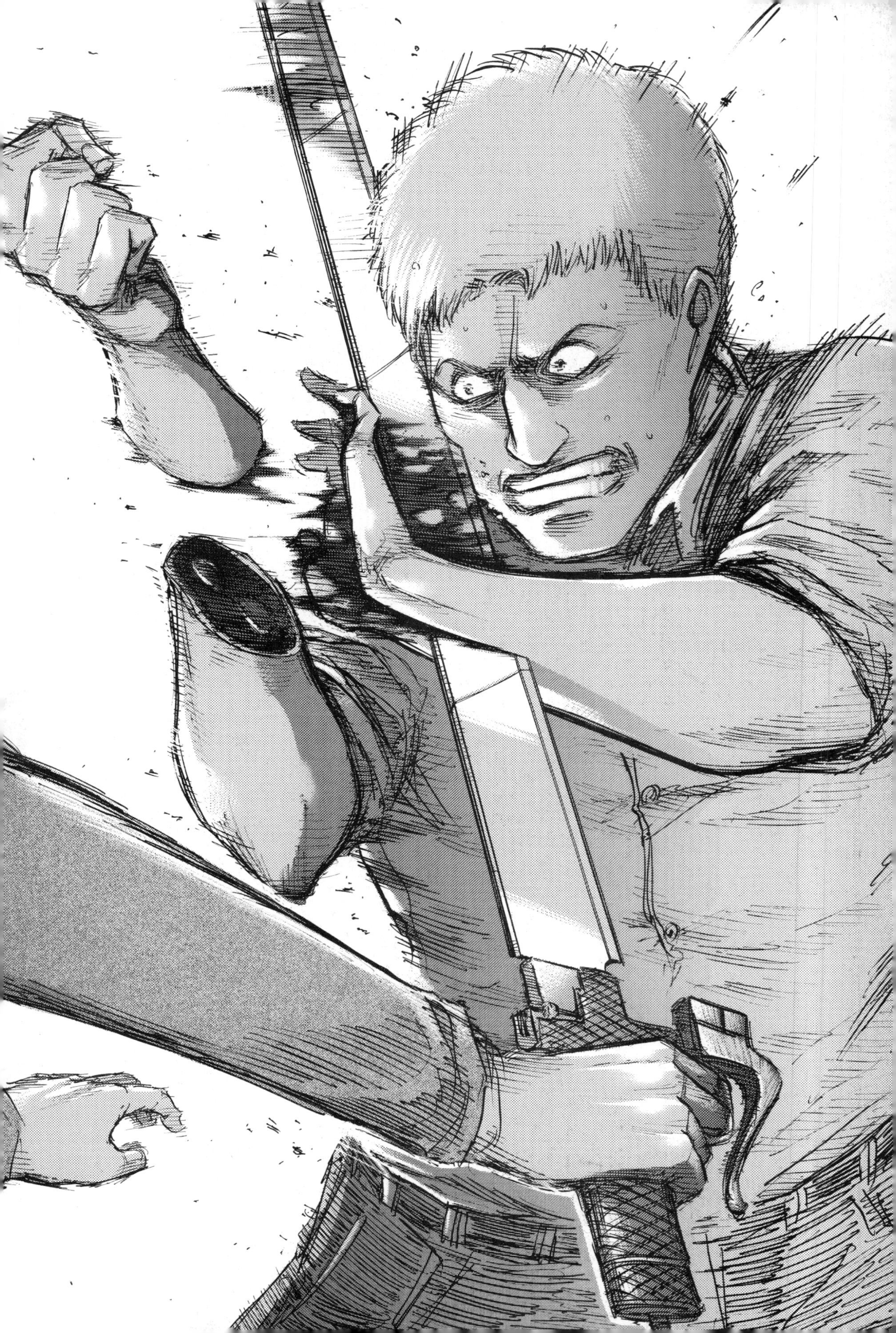

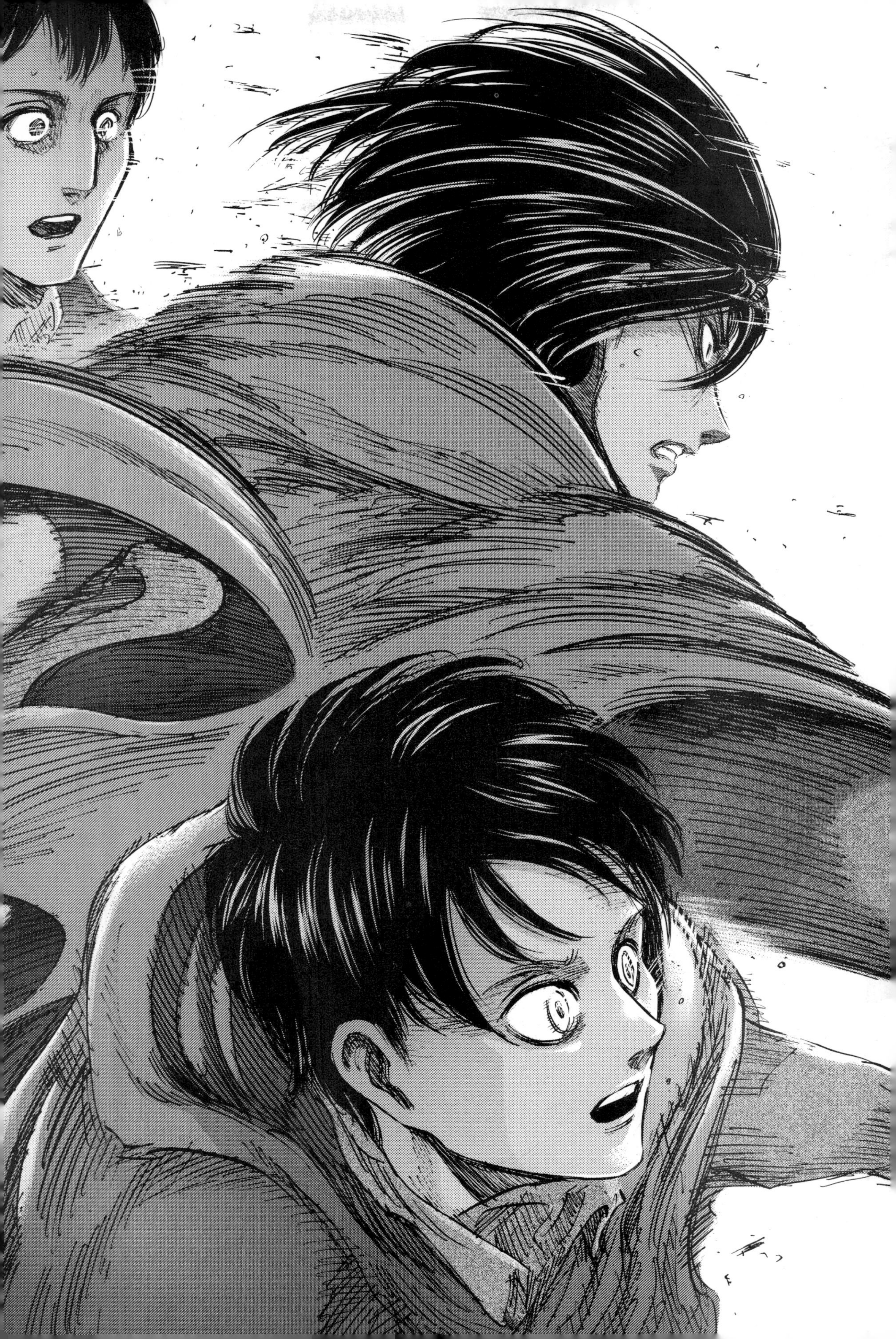

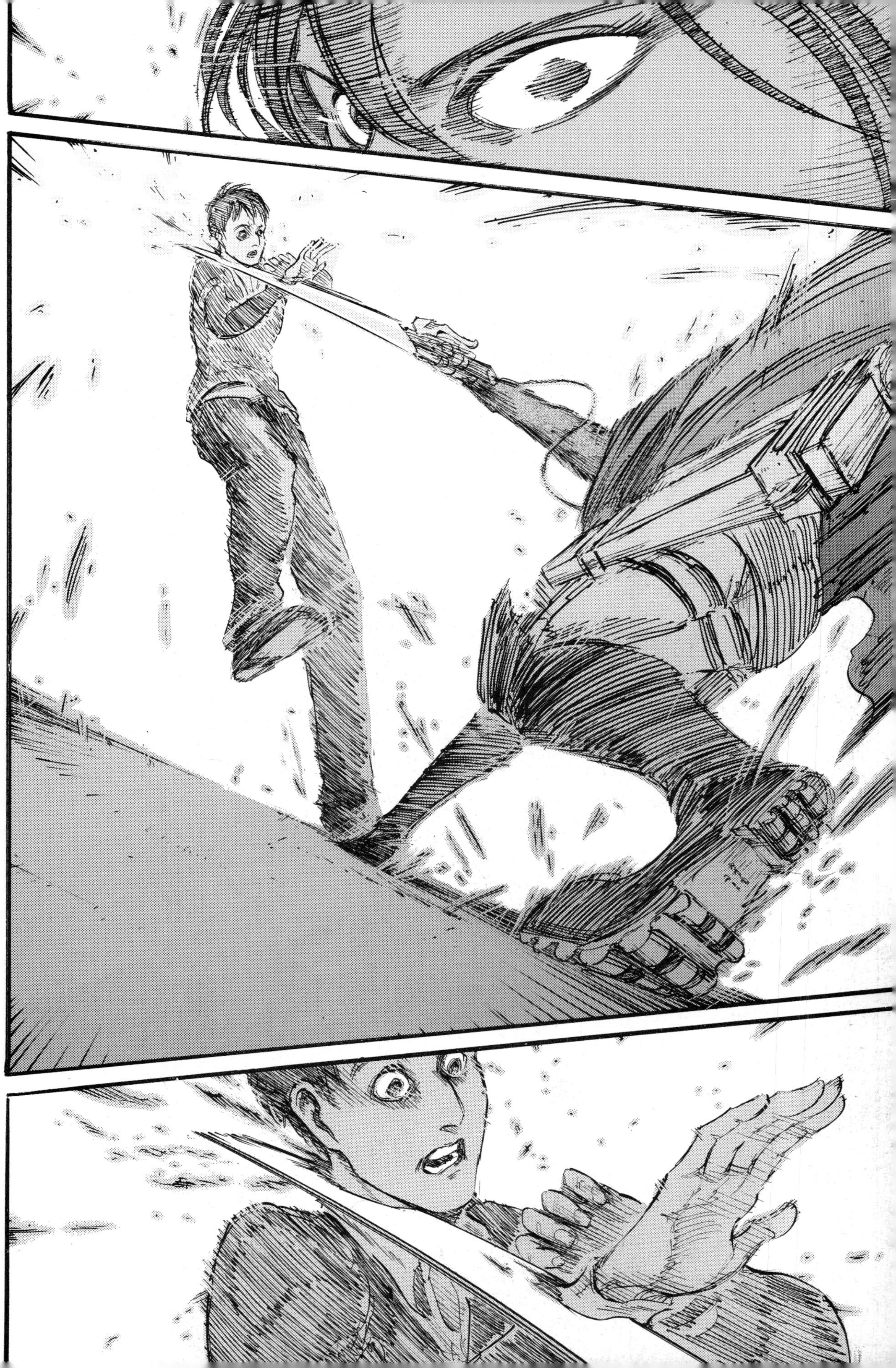

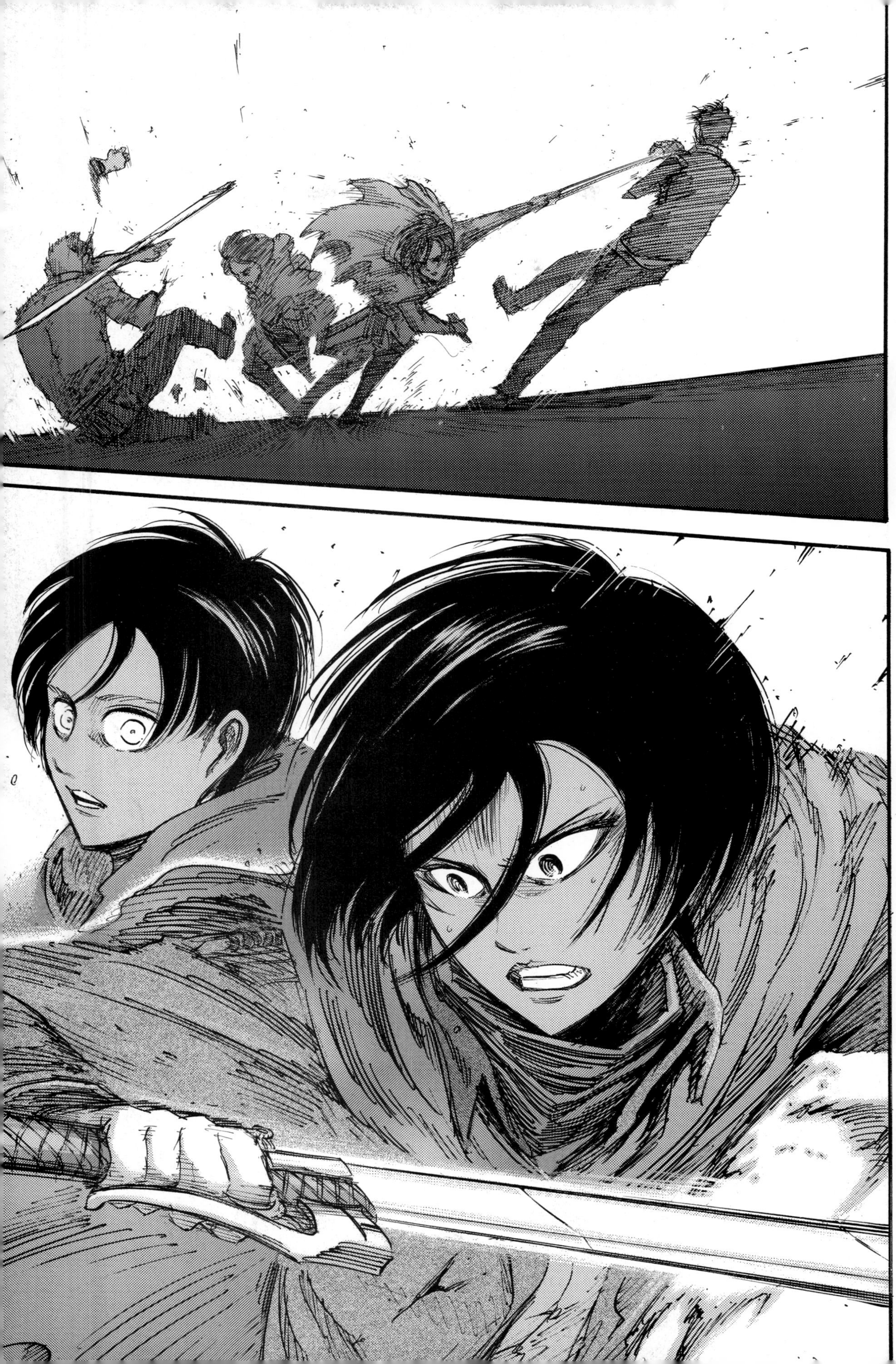

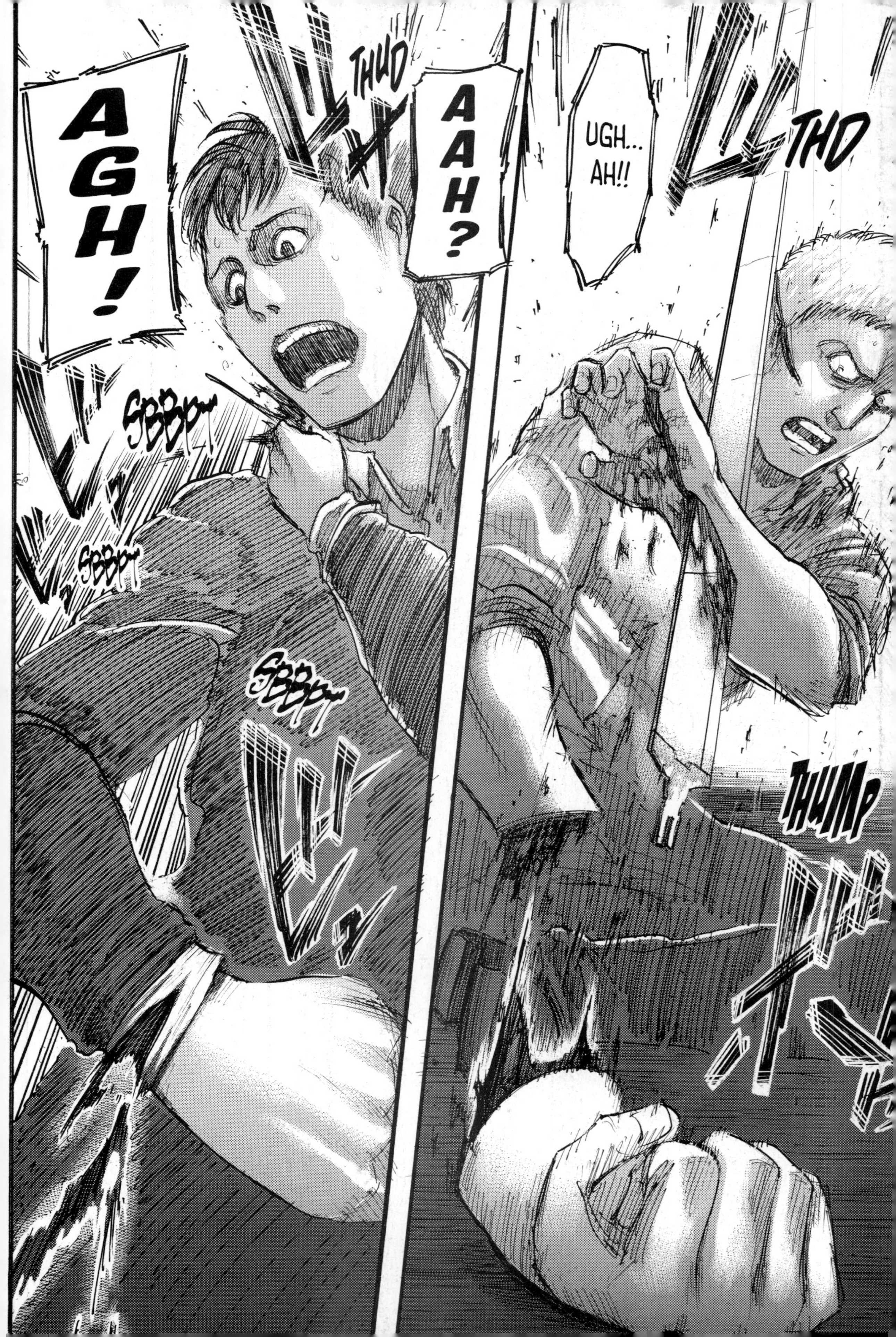
UGH... AH!!
THD
THUMP
AAH?
THUD
AGH!
SBBPT
SBBPT
SBBPT

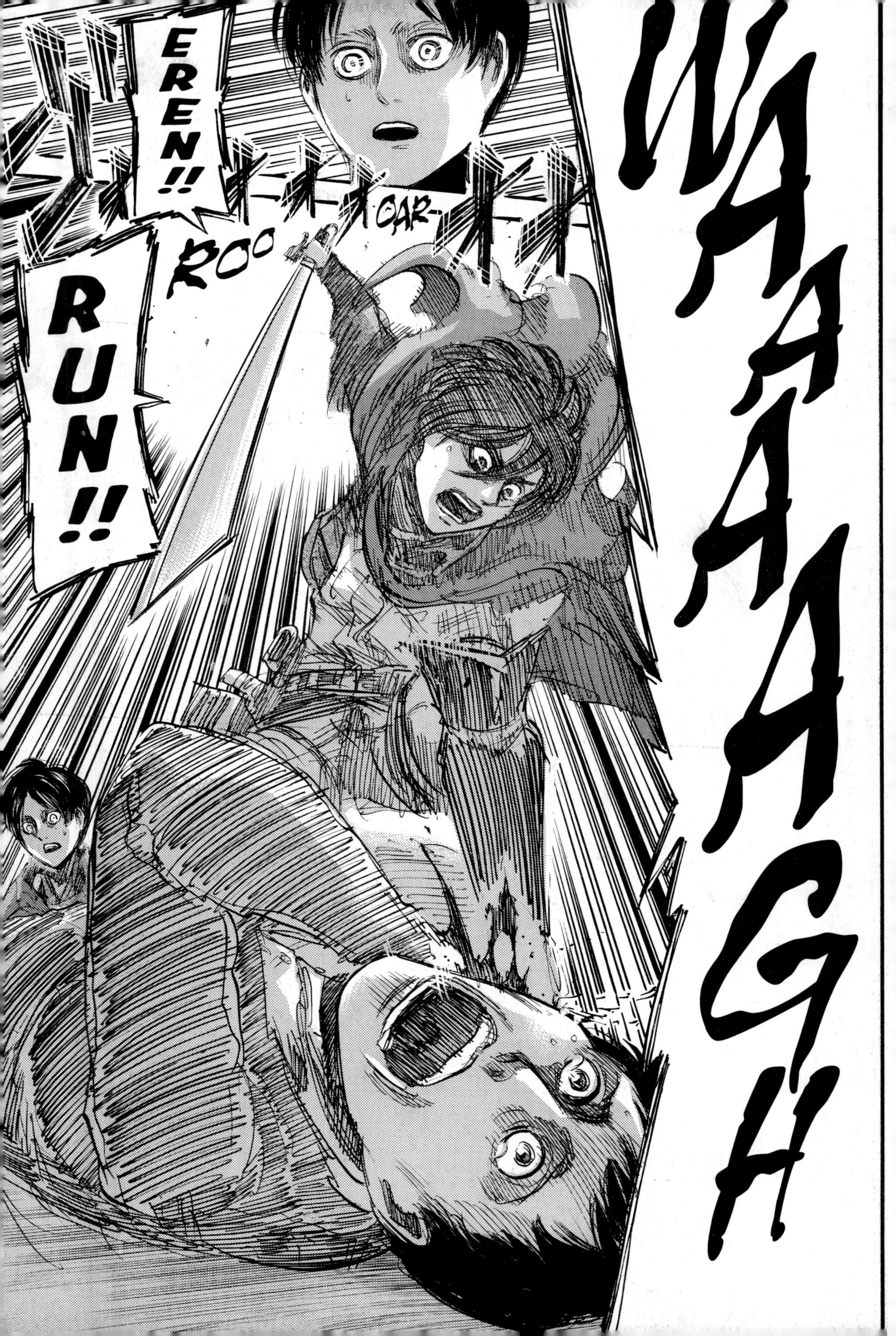
WAAAAGH!
EREN!!
RUN!!
ROO
OAR

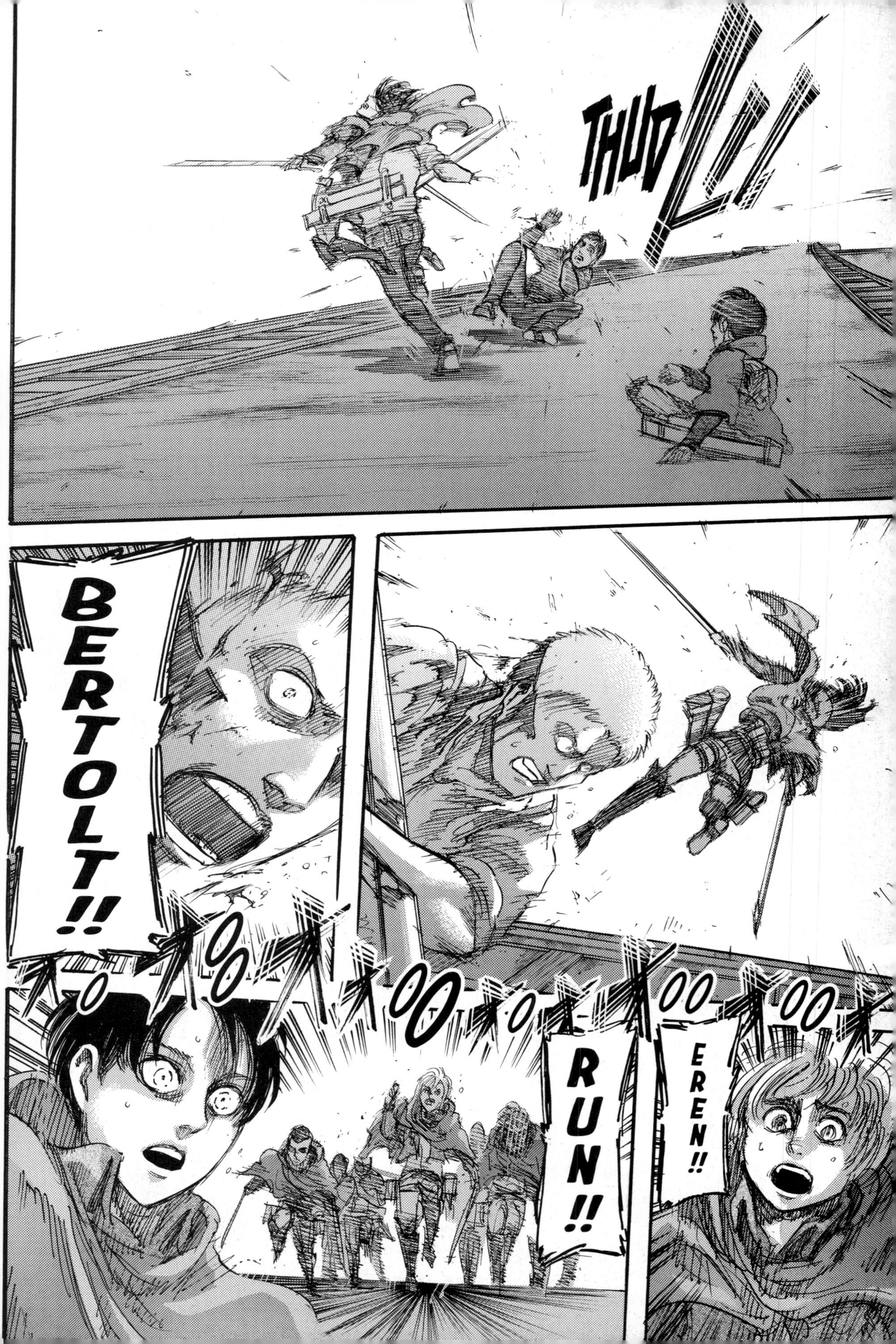
THUD
BERTOLT!!
OOOOOOOOOOO
EREN!!
RUN!!

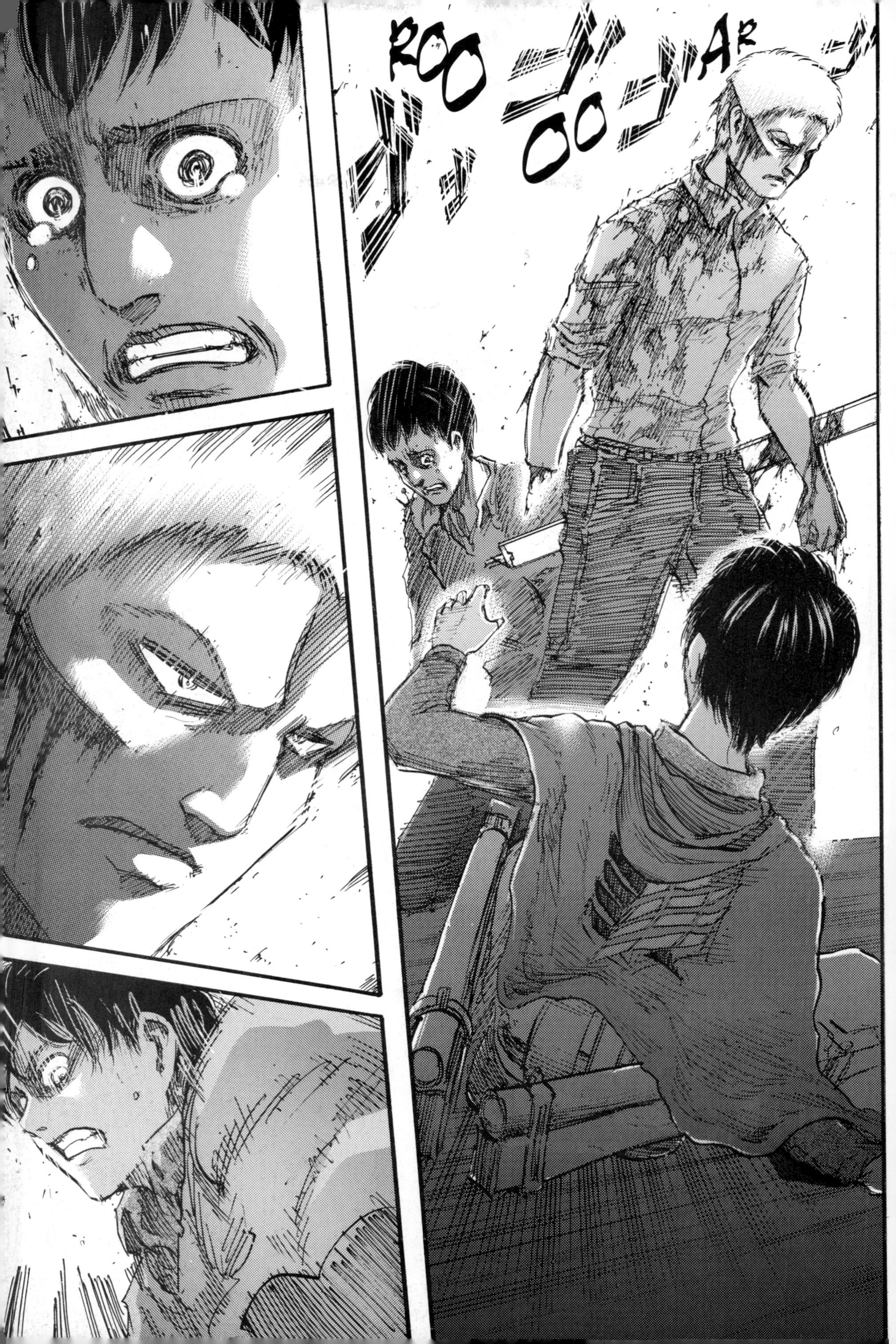
ROOOOAR

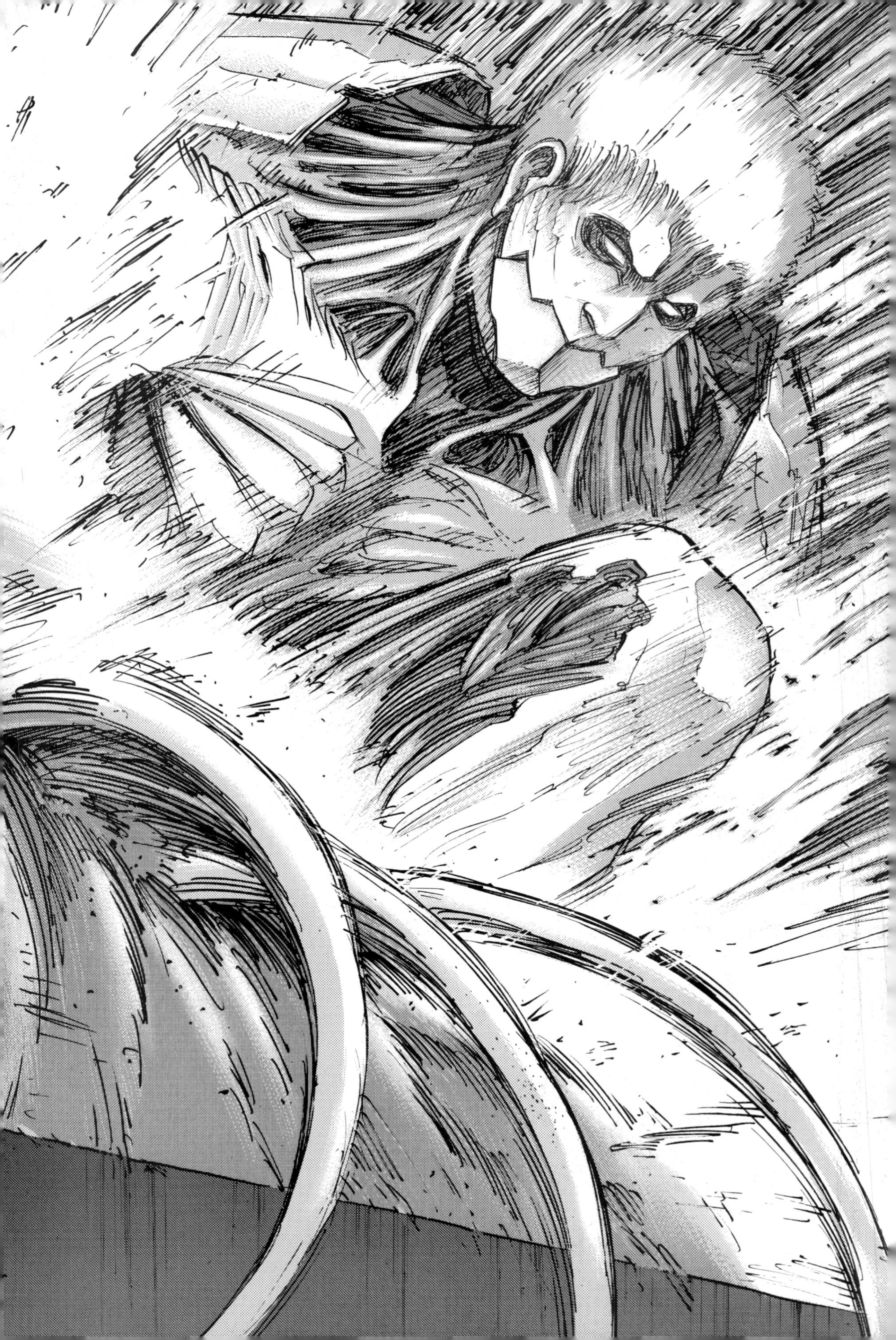

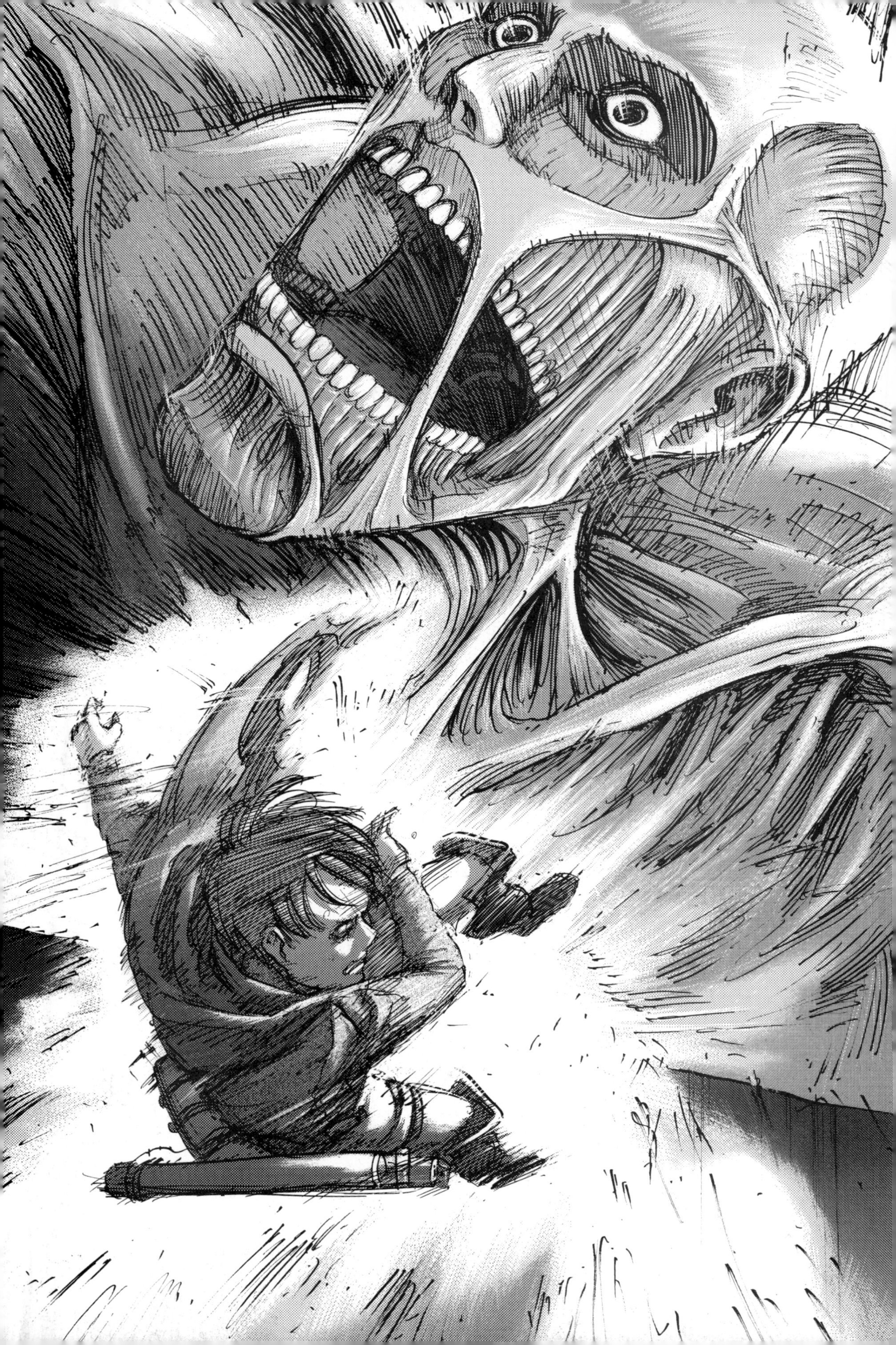

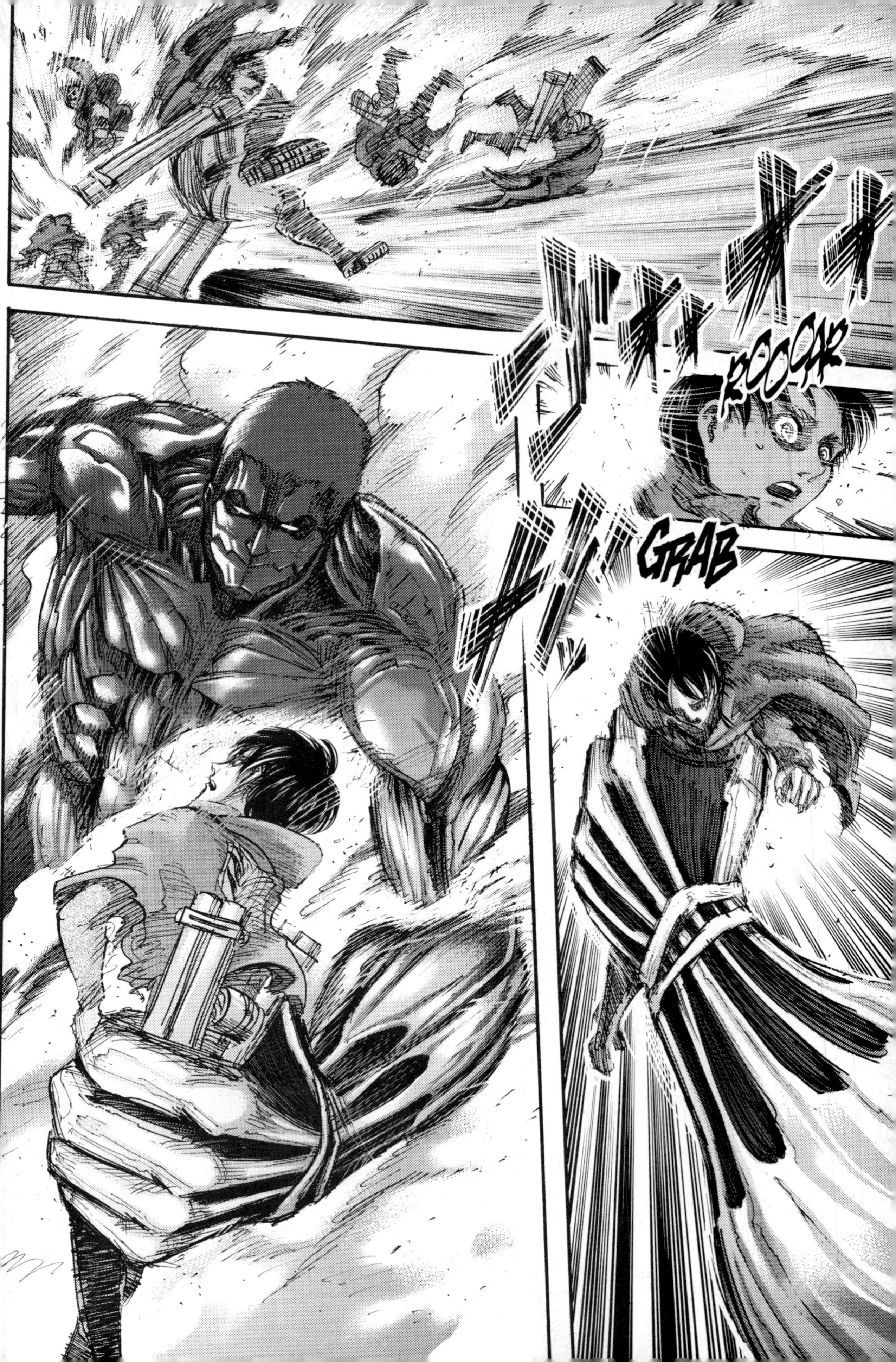
ROOAR
GRAB

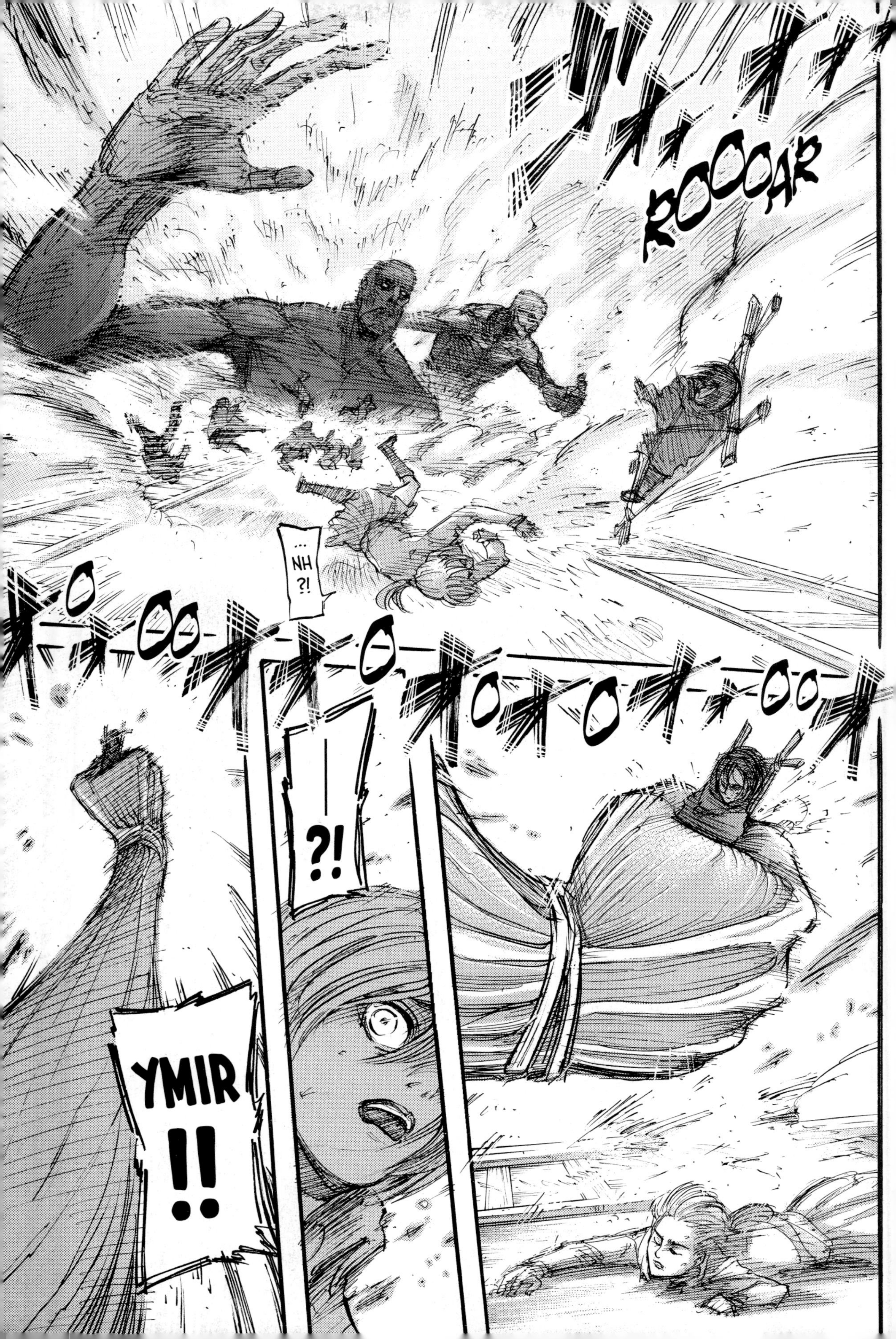
ROOOAR
...NH ?!
O OO O O O O OO
?!
YMIR !!

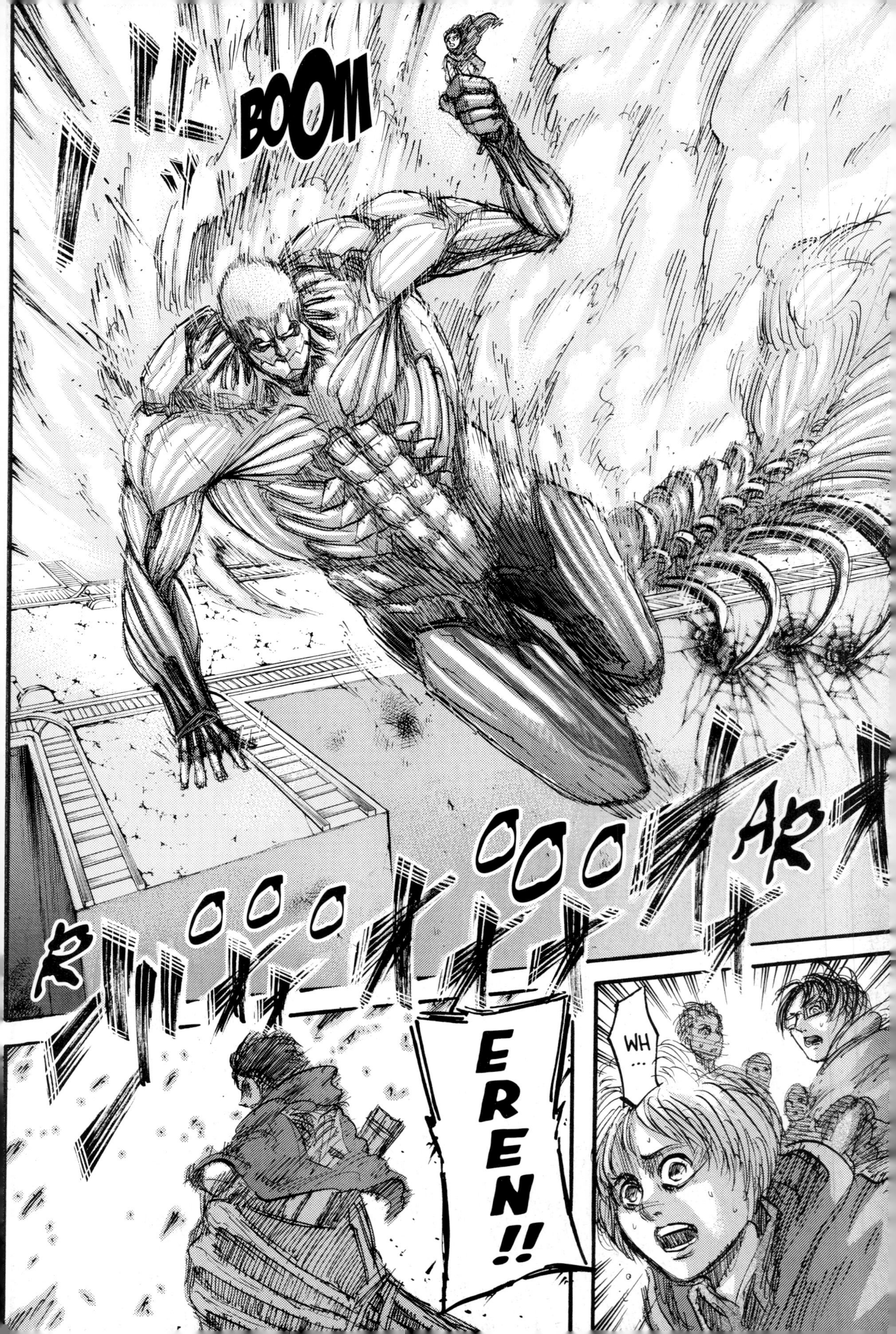
BOOM
ROOOOOOOAR
WH...
EREN!!

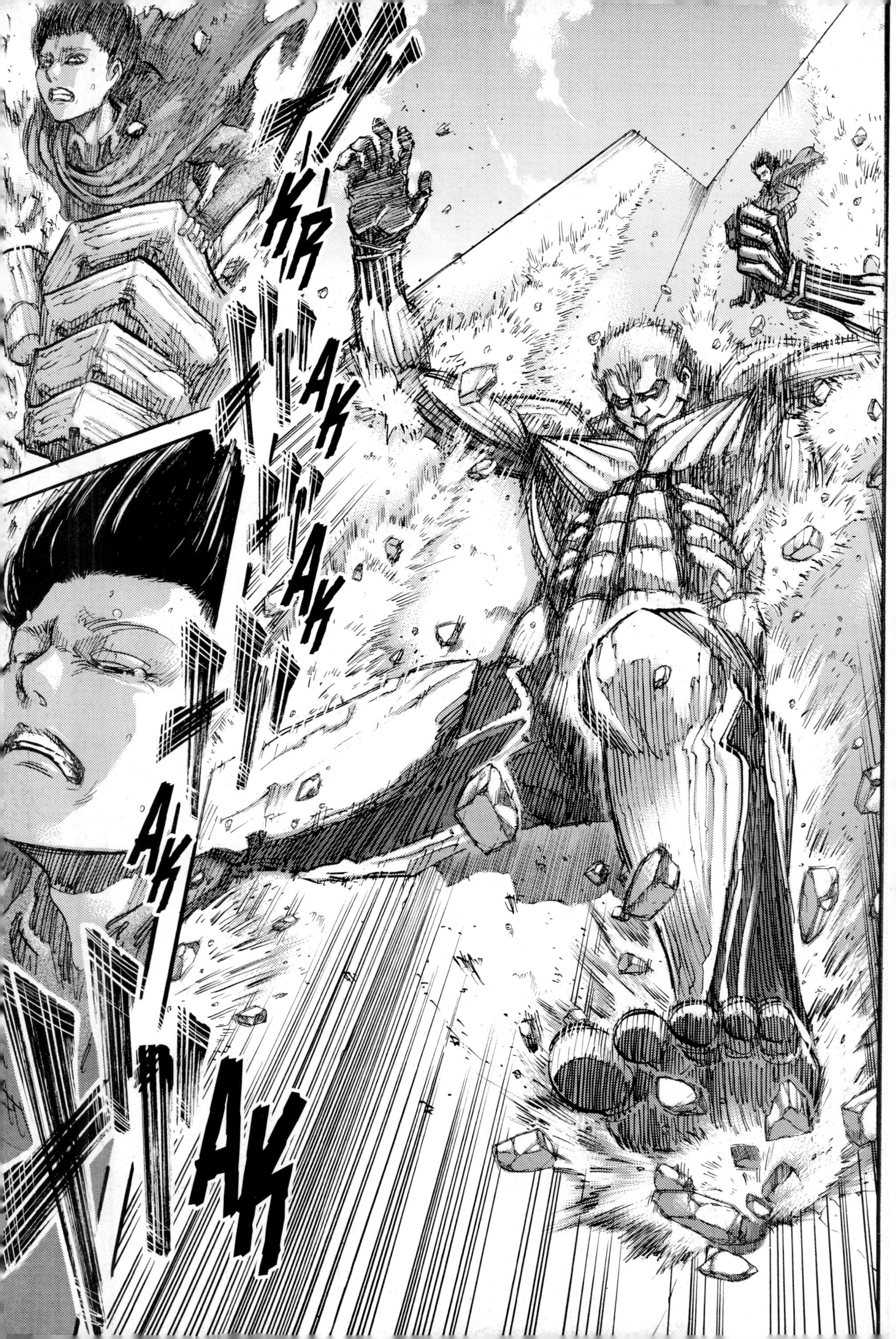
KRAK
AK
AK
AK

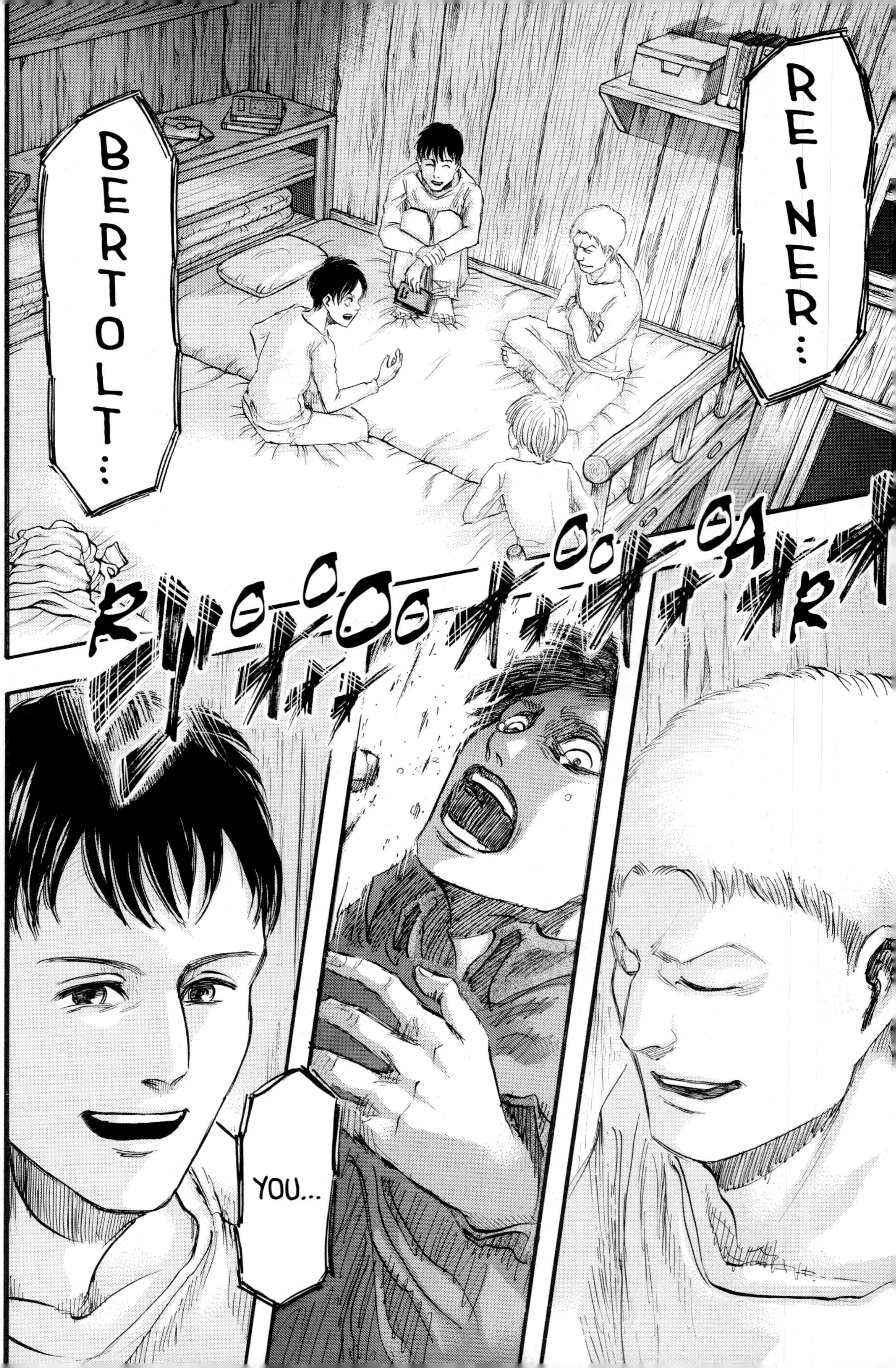
REINER...
BERTOLT...
YOU...

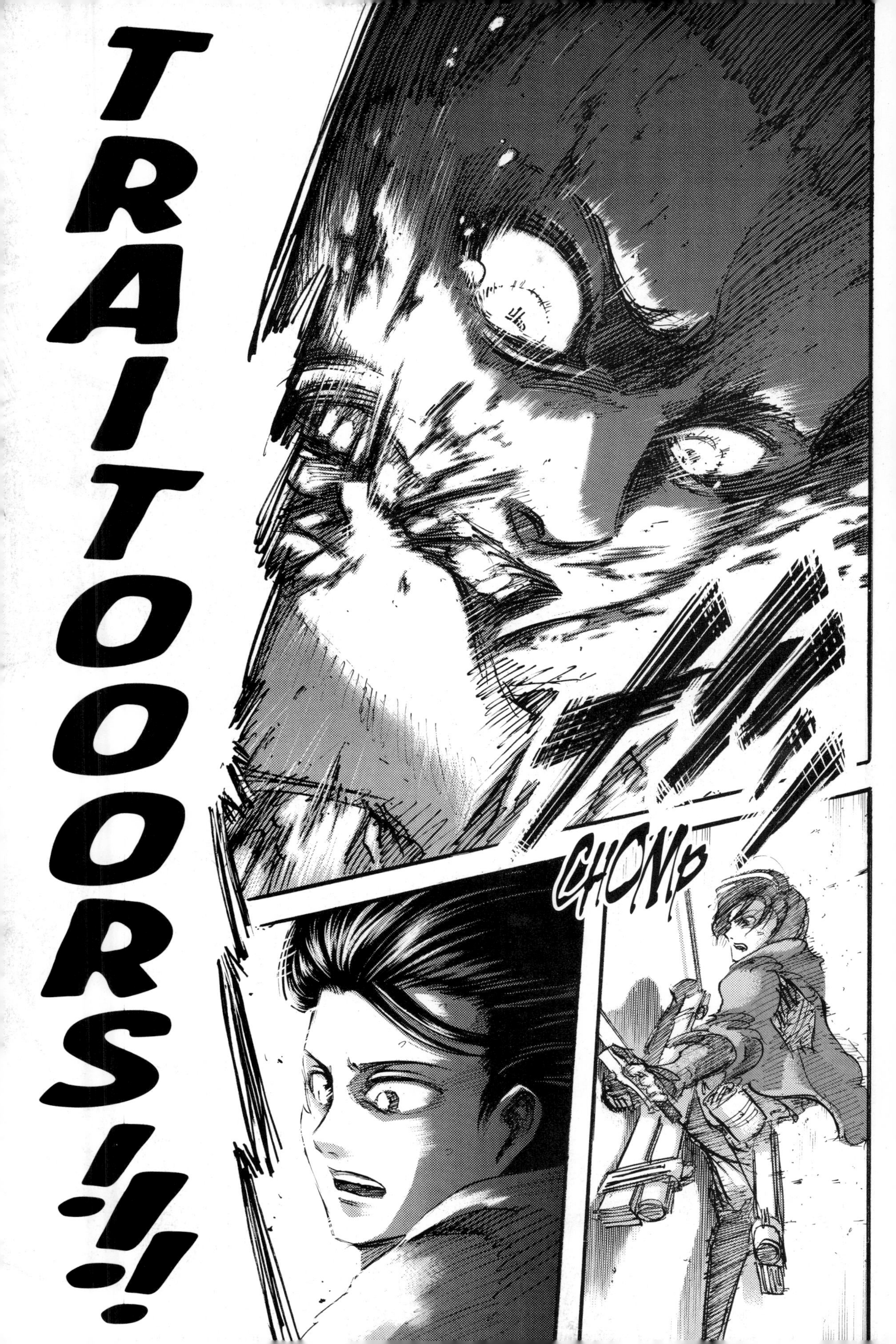
TRAITOOORS!!!
CHOMP

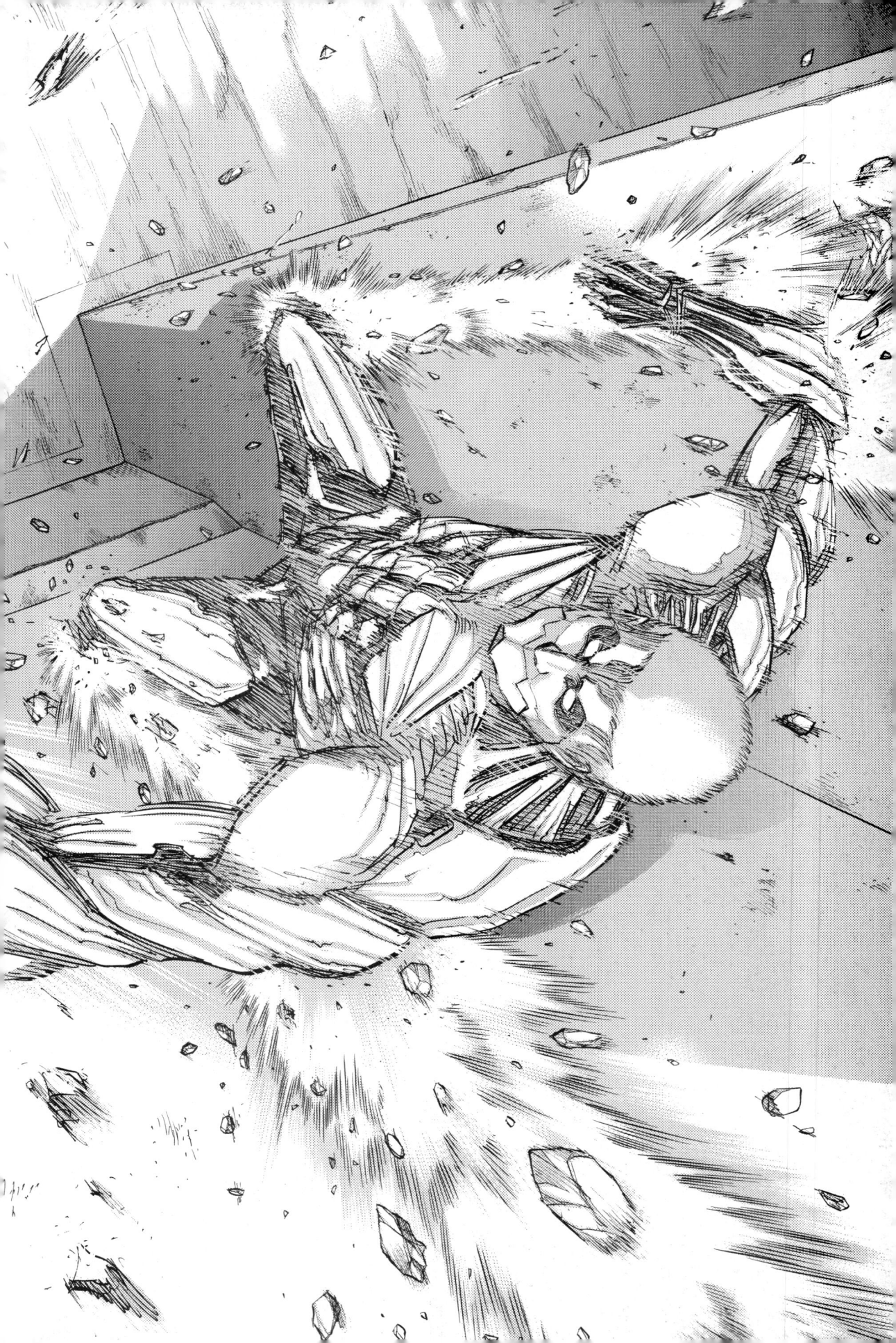

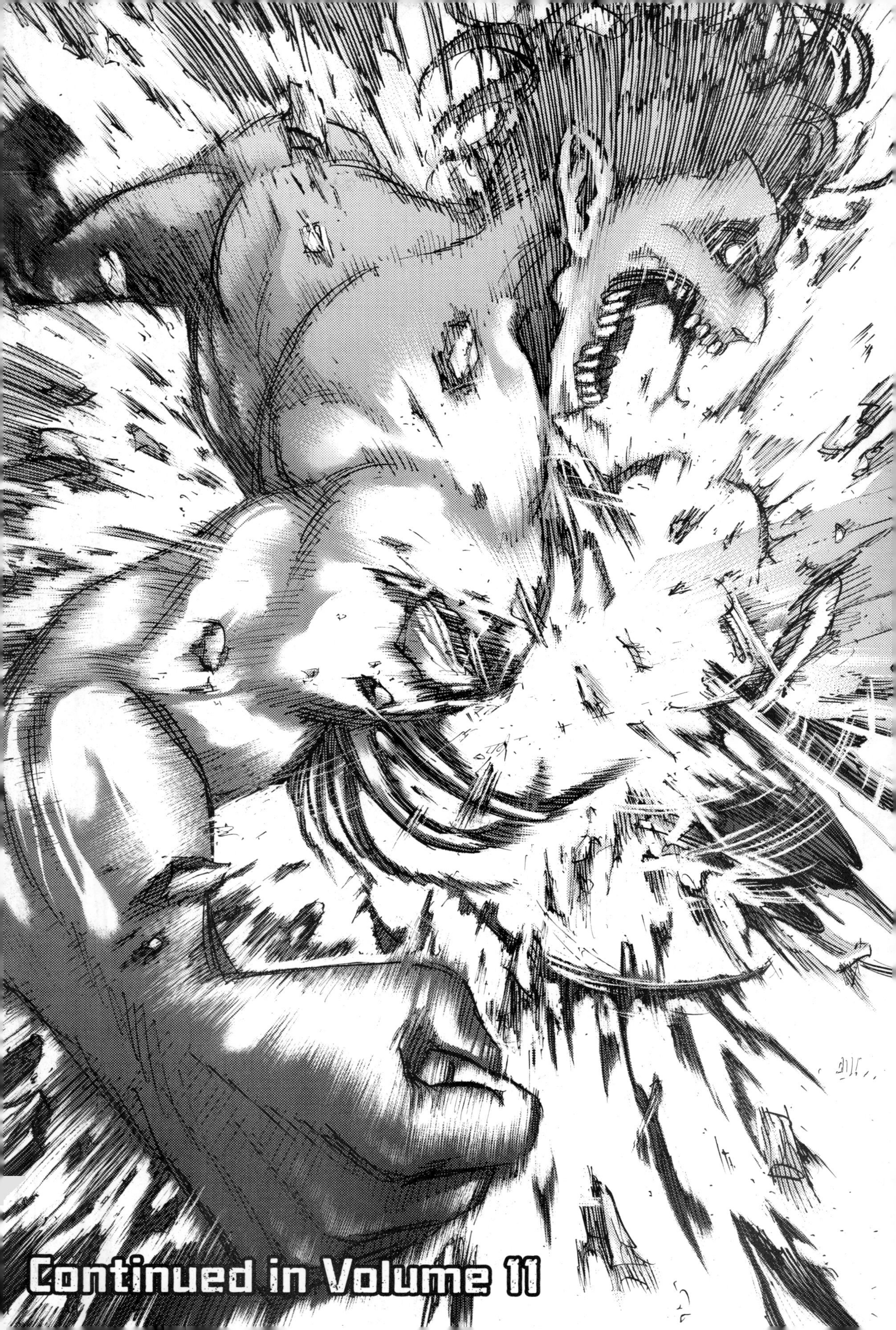
Continued in Volume 11

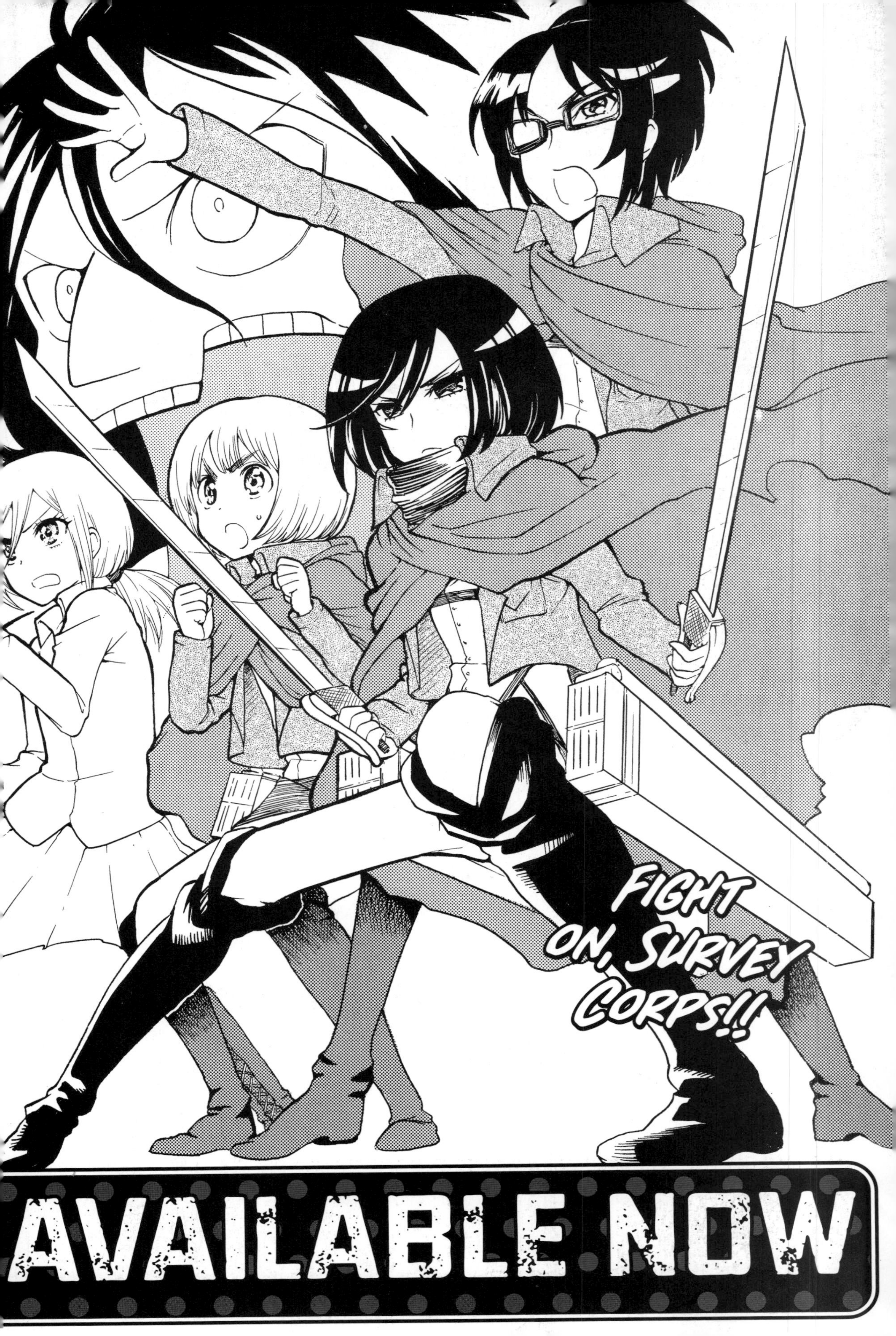
FIGHT ON, SURVEY CORPS!!
AVAILABLE NOW

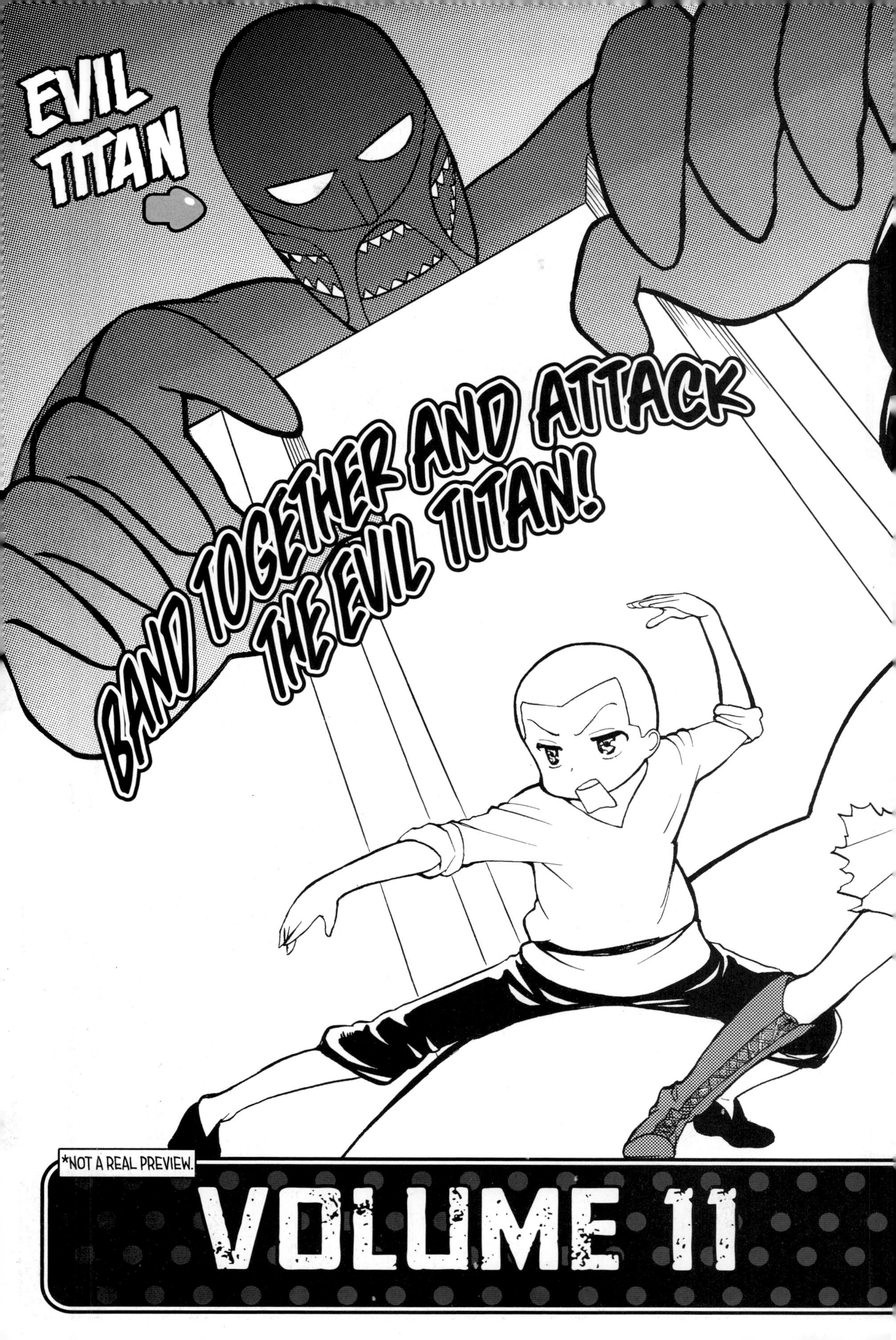
EVIL TITAN
BAND TOGETHER AND ATTACK THE EVIL TITAN!
*NOT A REAL PREVIEW.
VOLUME 11

Original *Attack on Titan* Drawings & Sketches

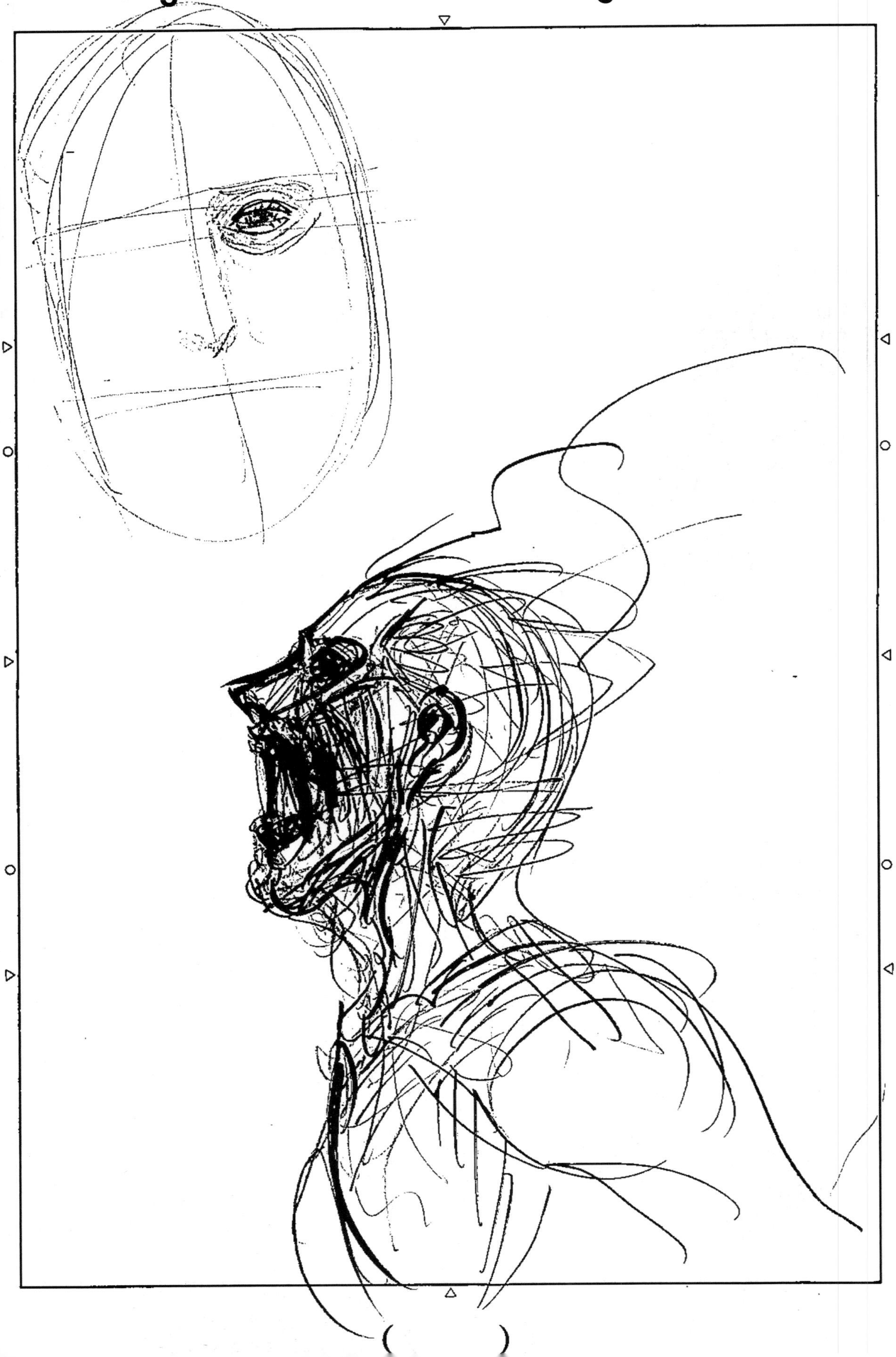

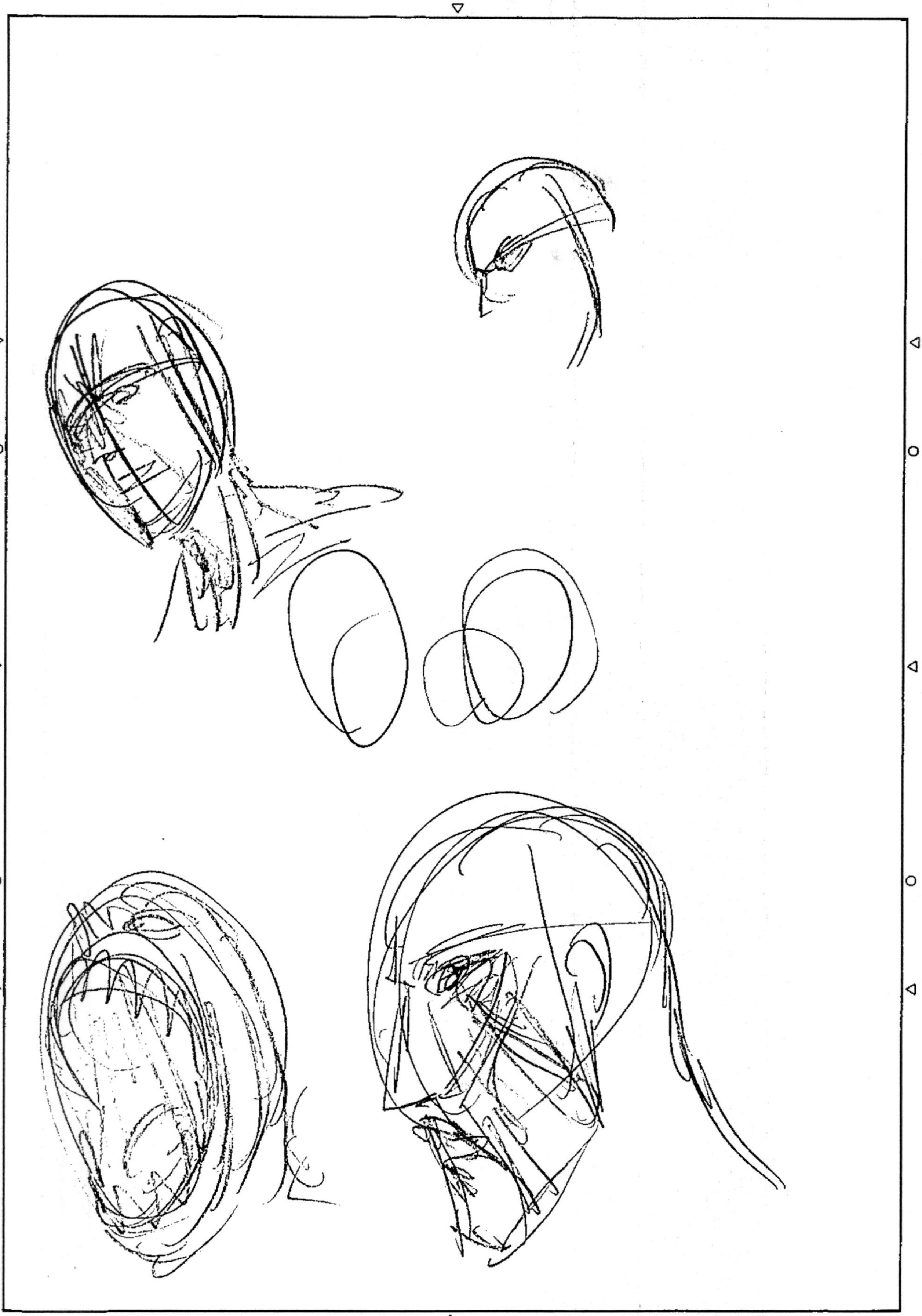

( )

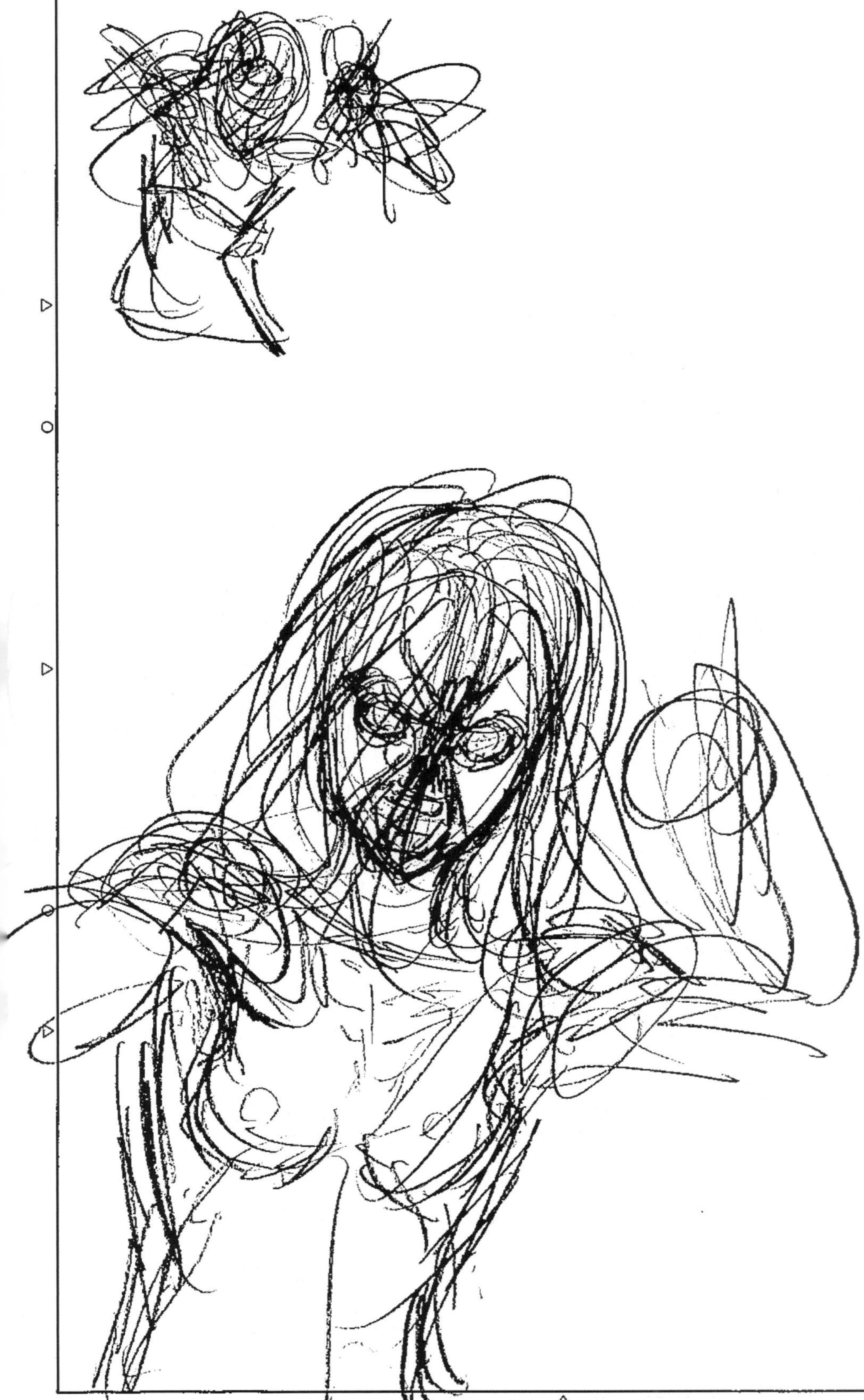

(　　)

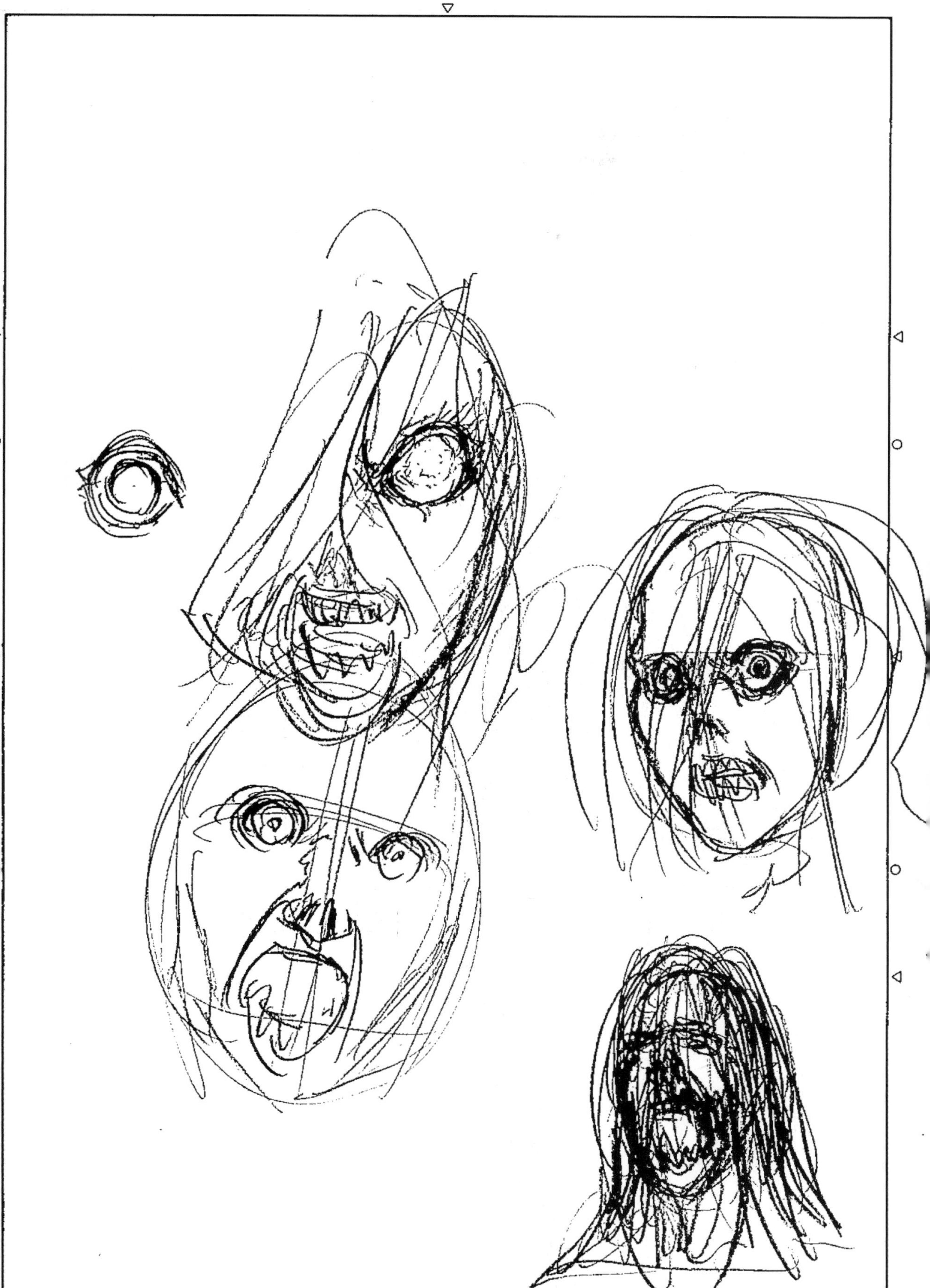

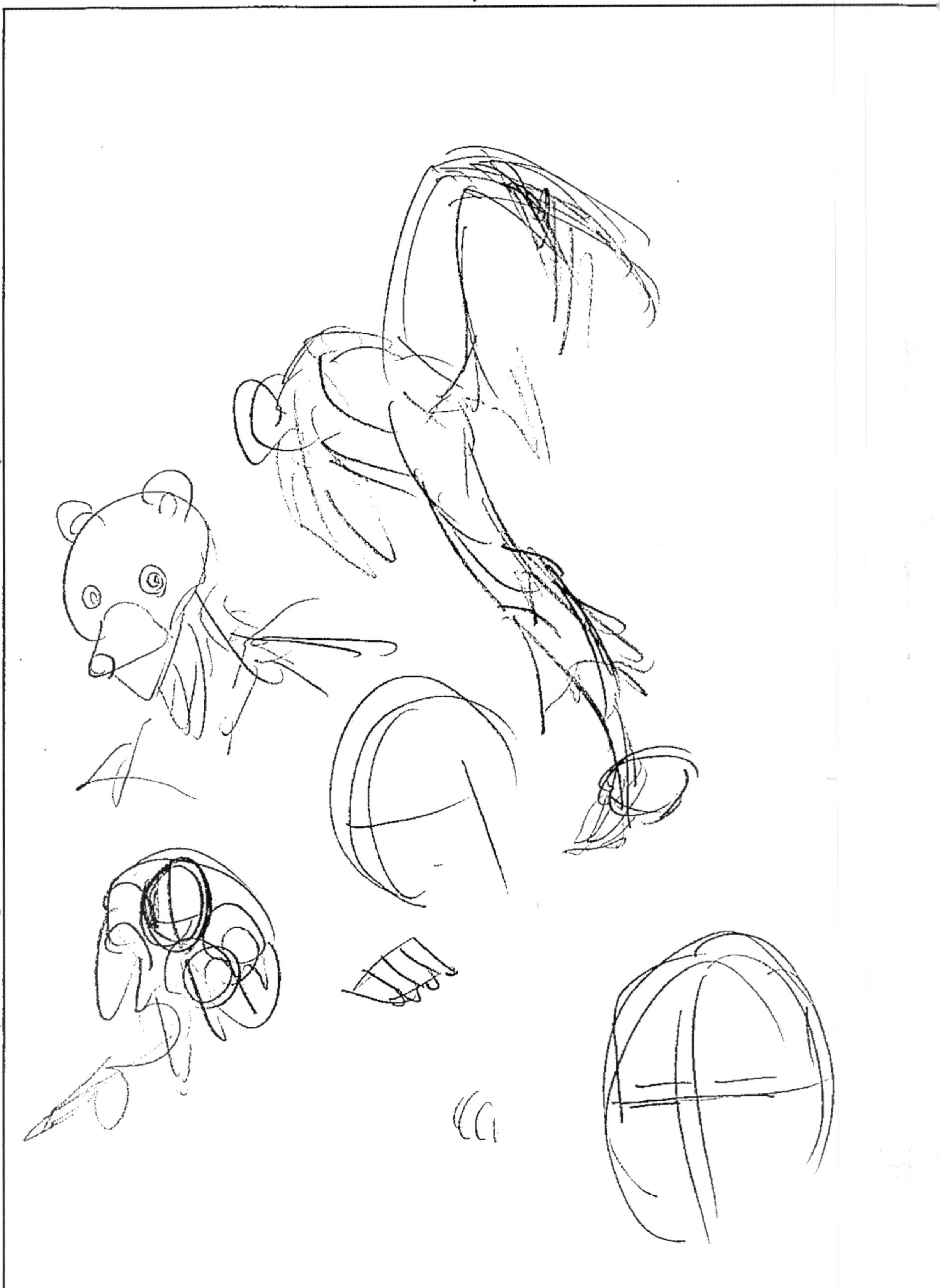

(　　　)

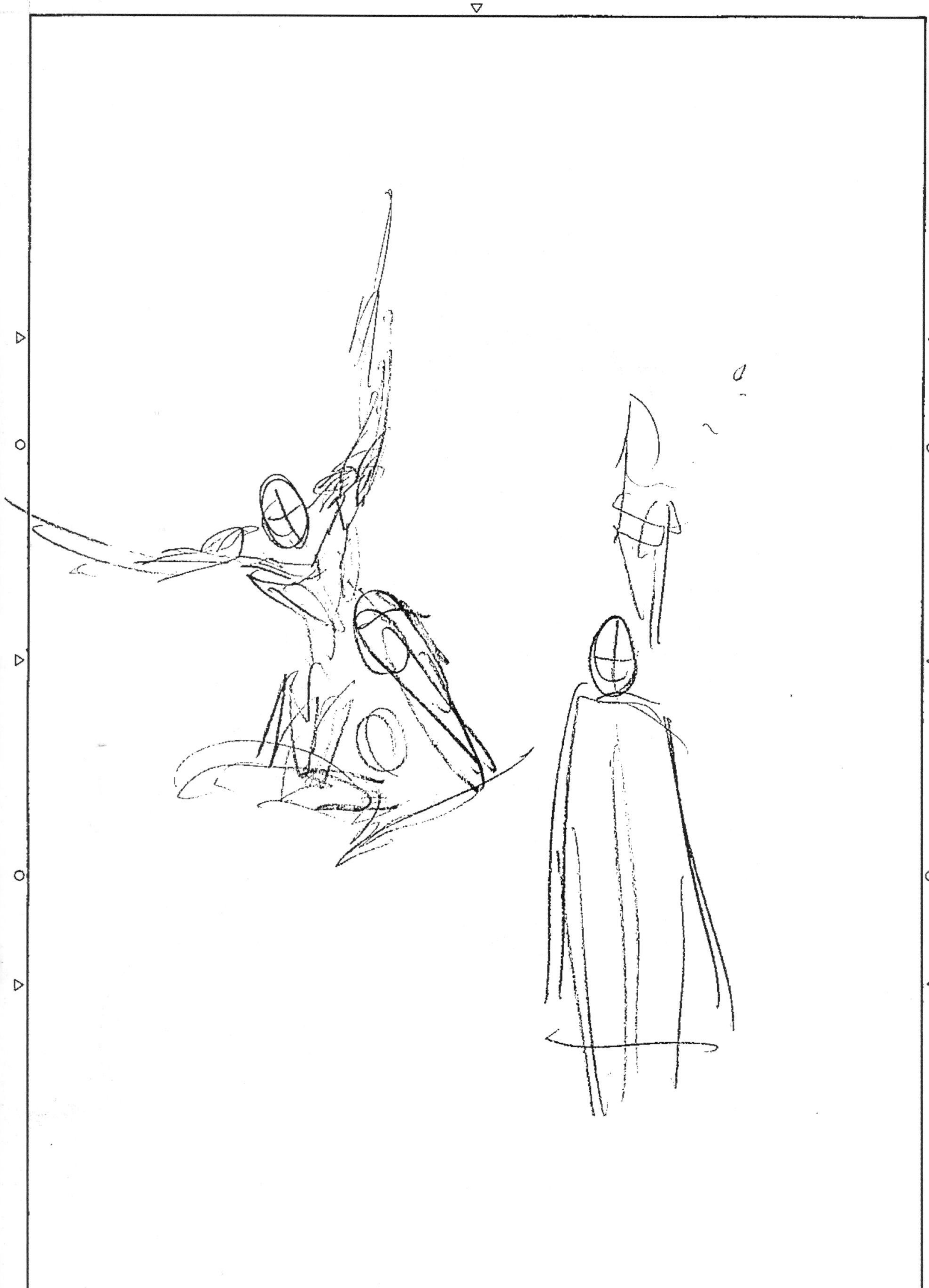

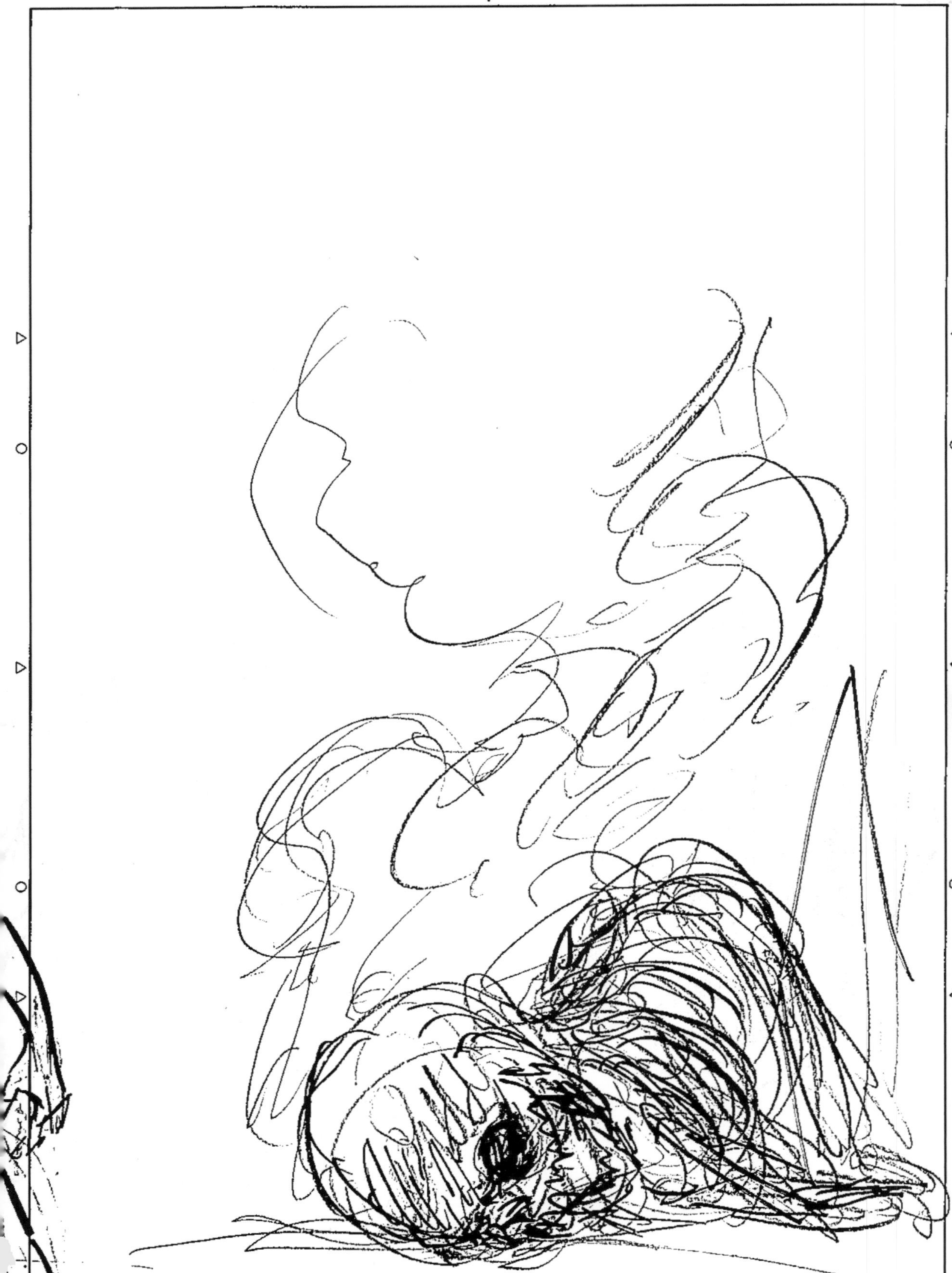

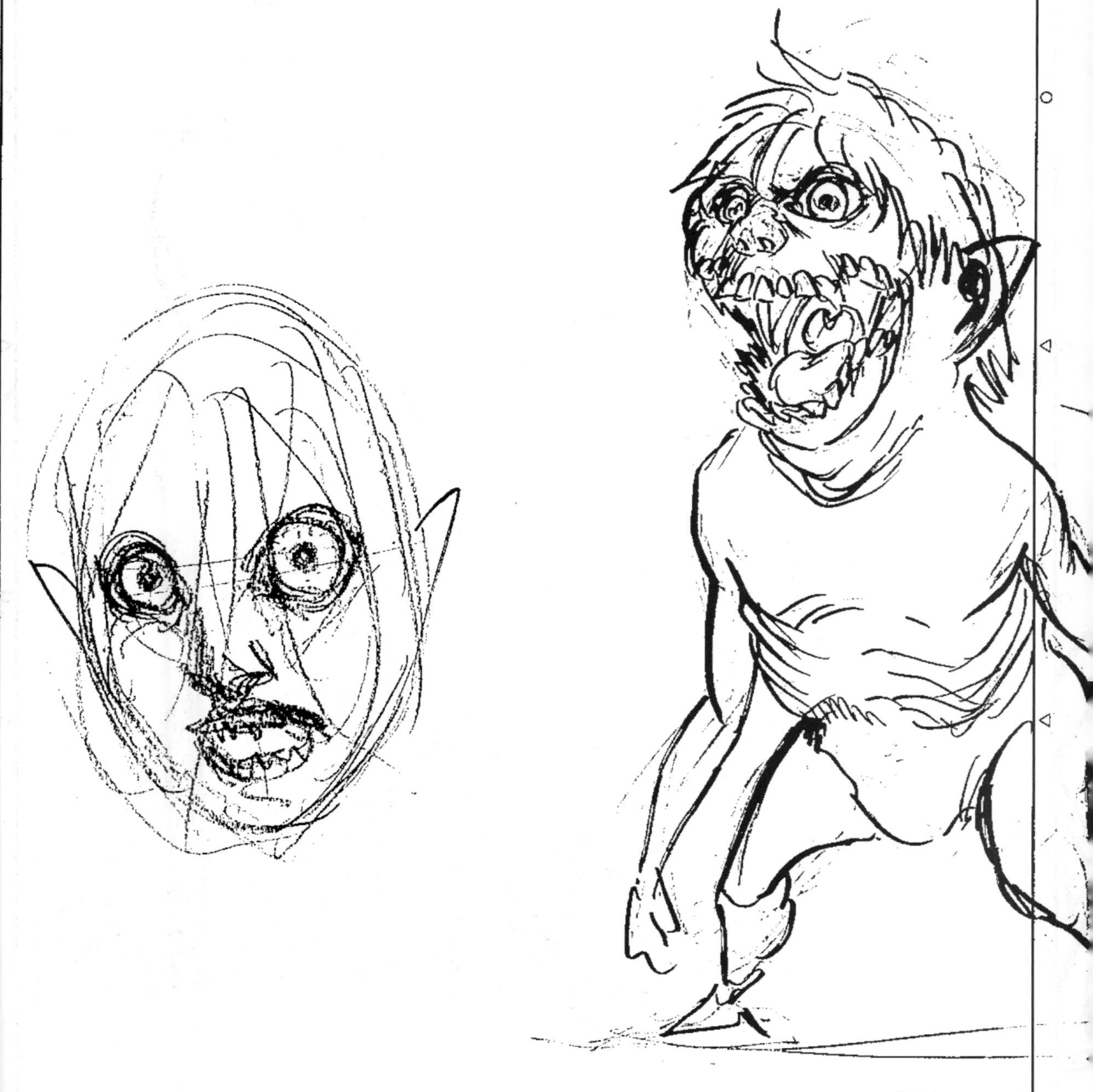

ATTACK on TITAN

Cover Art Gallery

The following pages contain the original cover images used for the individual volumes of Attack on Titan.

This book collects Vol. 6-10.

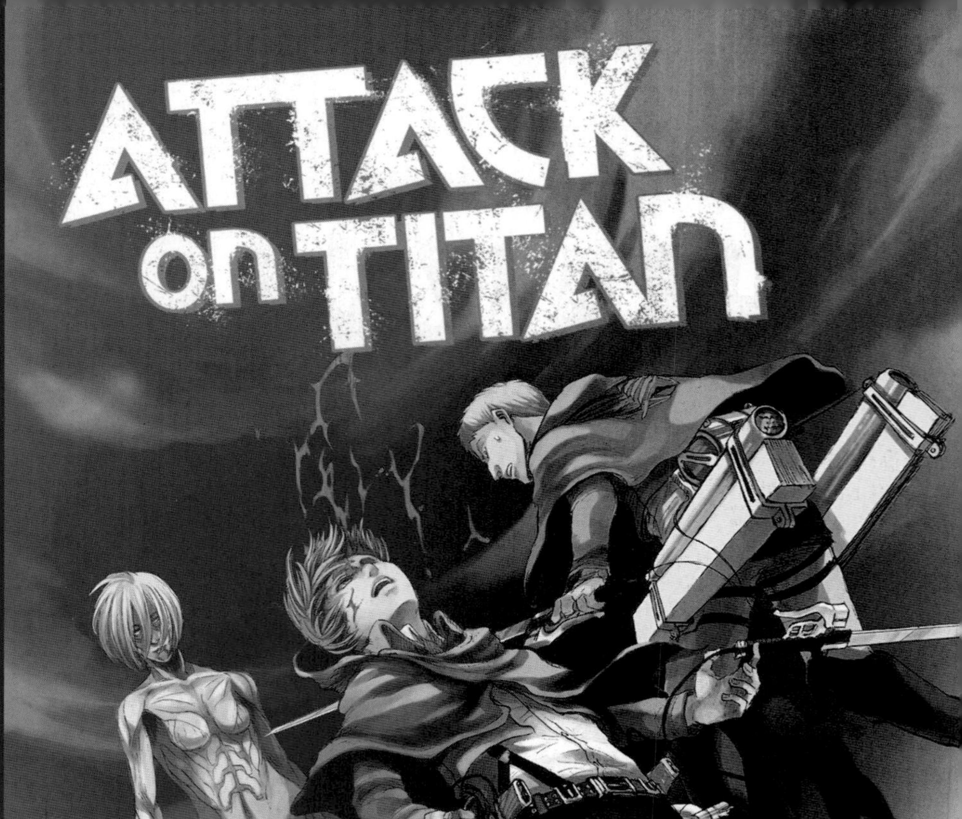
ATTACK on TITAN
6
HAJIME
ISAYAMA

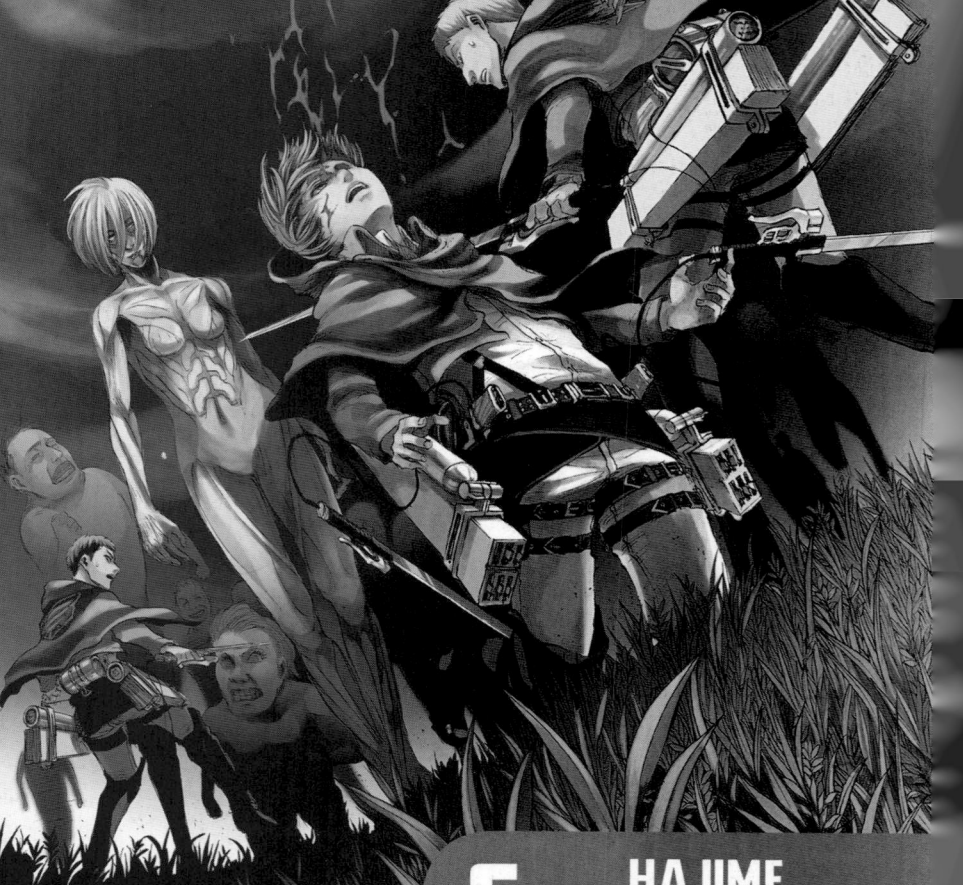

Vol. 7

ATTACK ON TITAN

7

HAJIME ISAYAMA

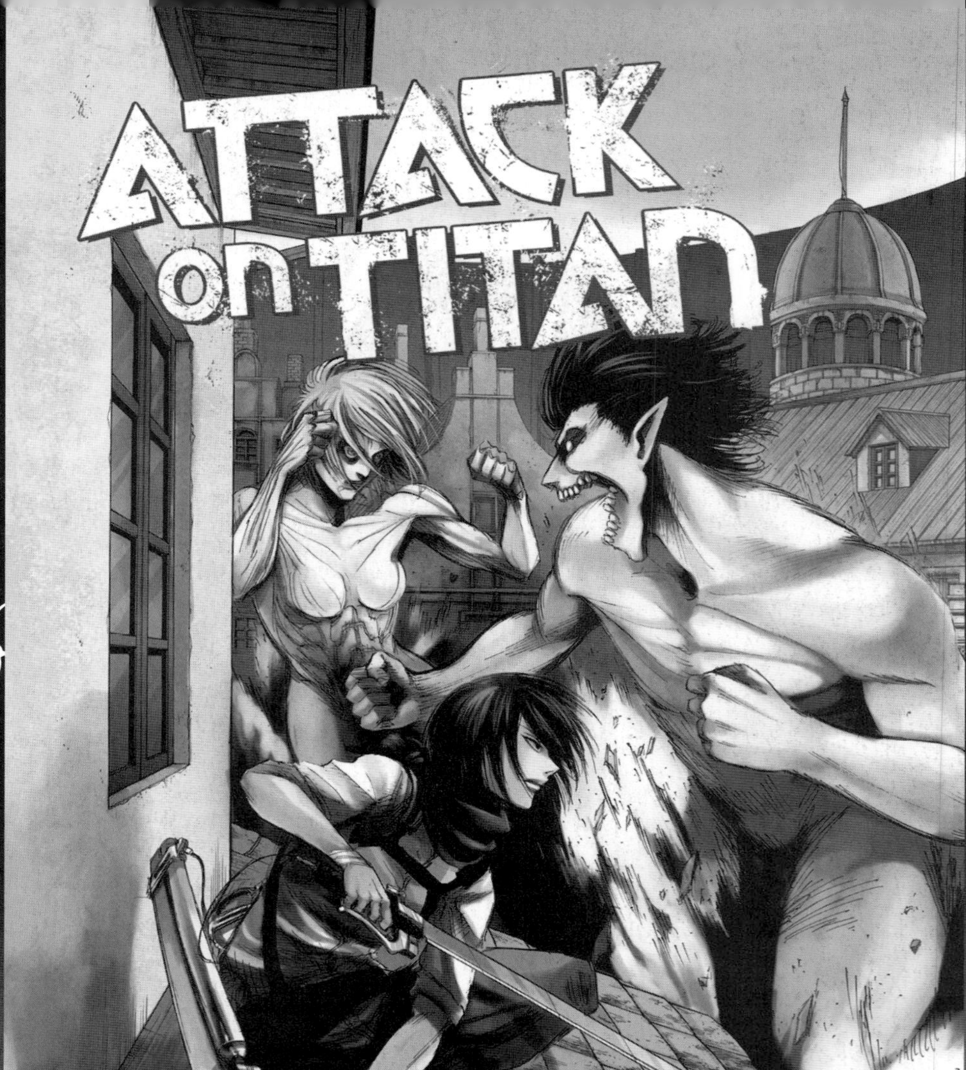
ATTACK on TITAN
8
HAJIME
ISAYAMA

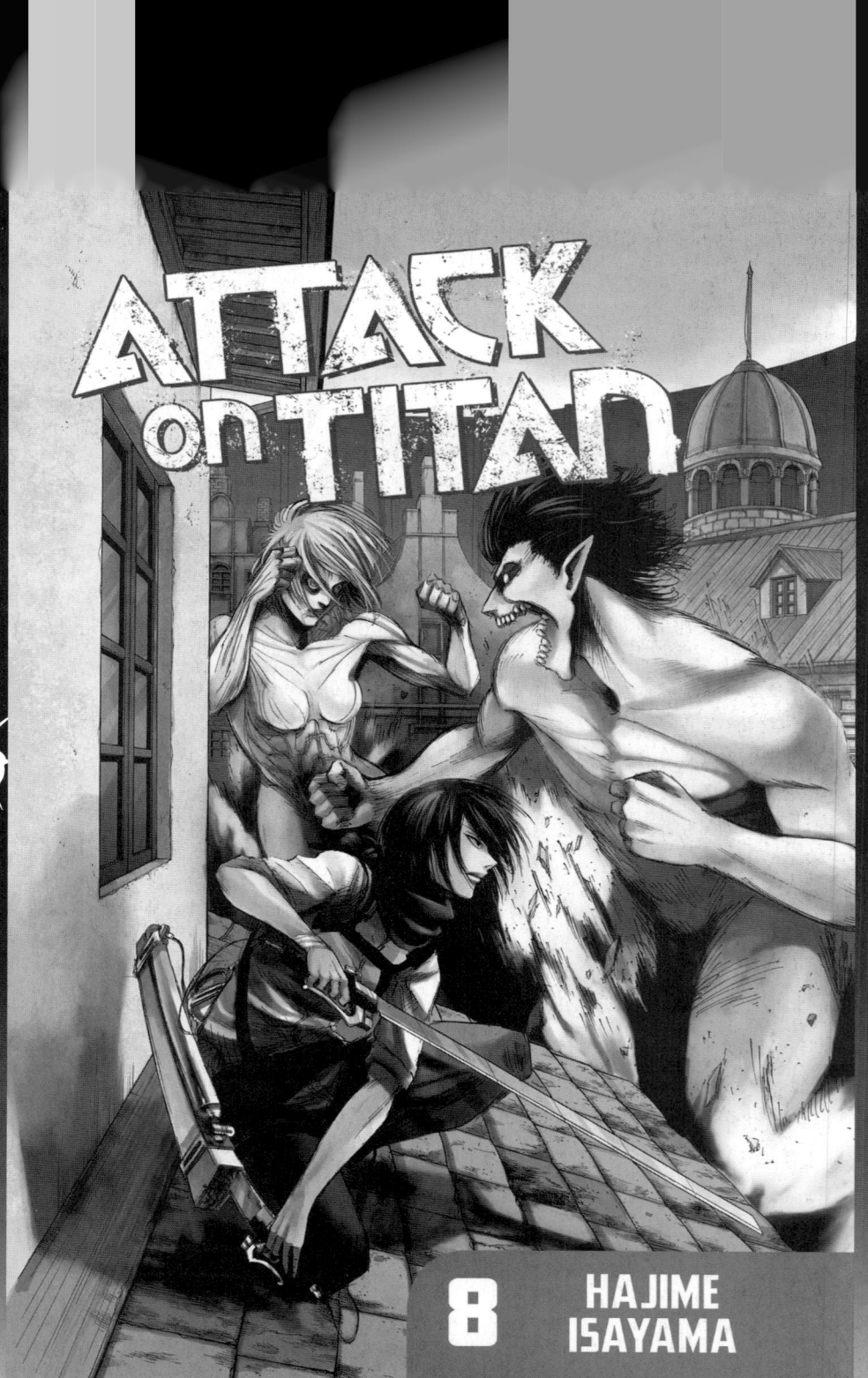

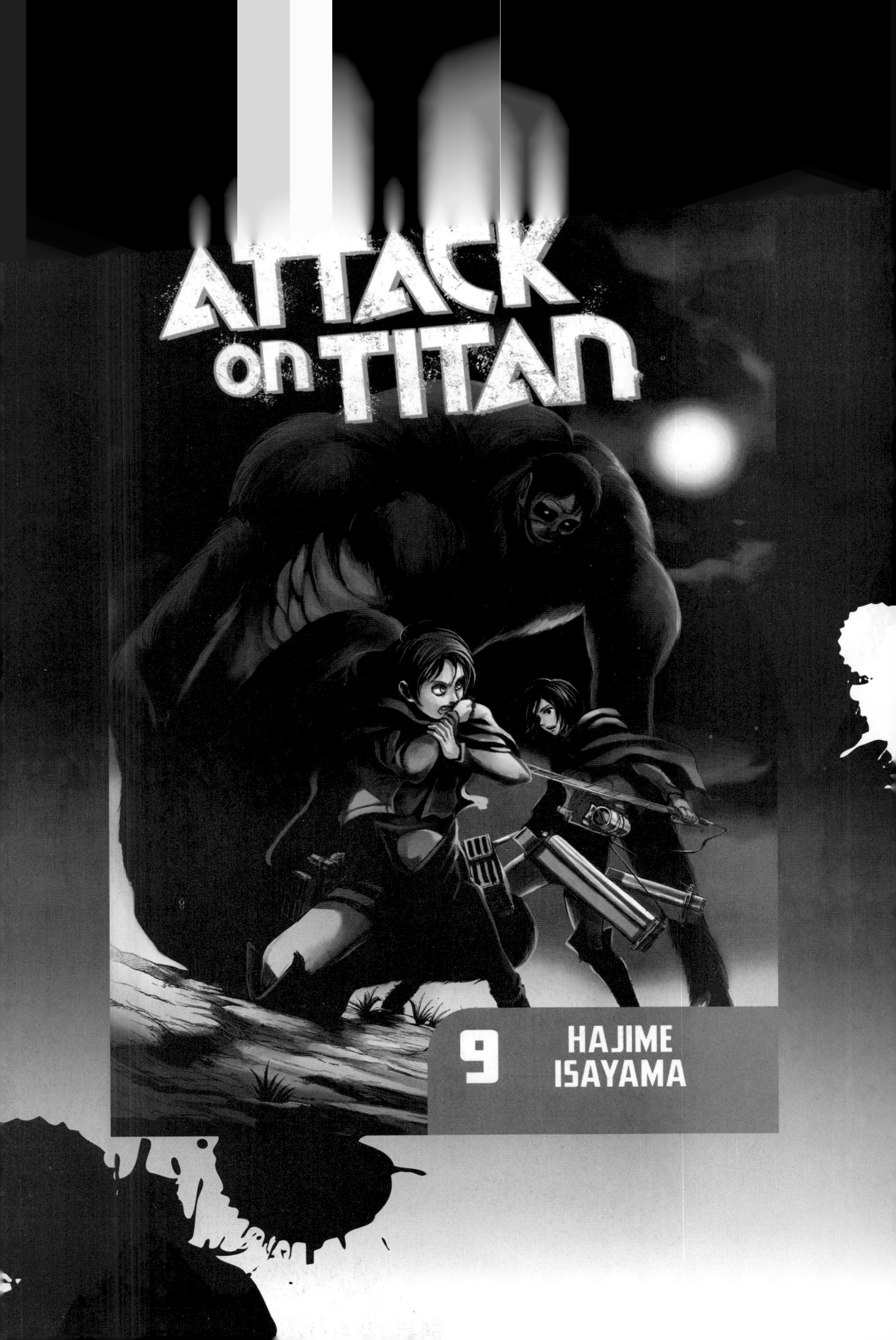
ATTACK on TITAN
9
HAJIME
ISAYAMA

ATTACK on TITAN
10
HAJIME ISAYAMA

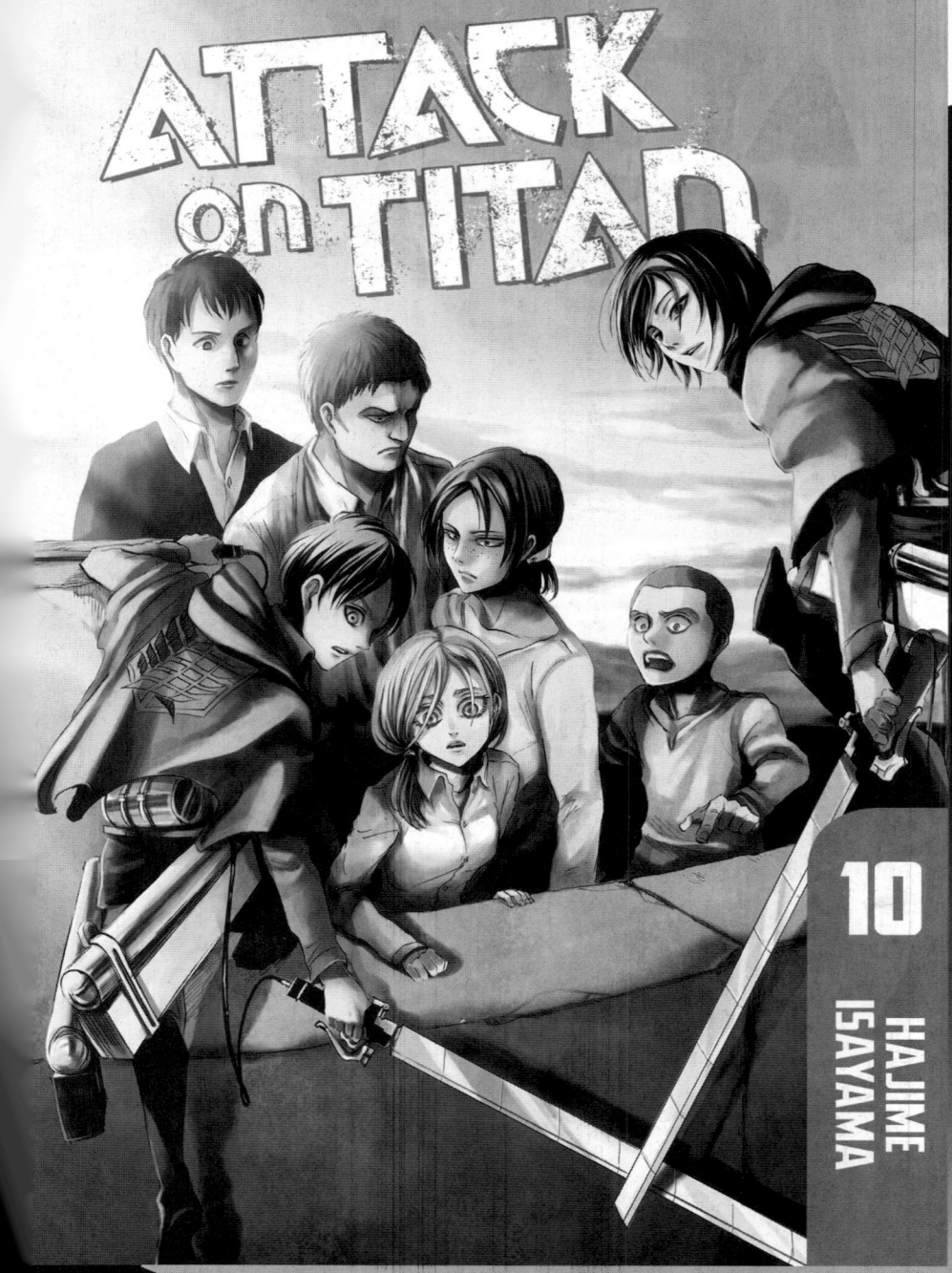

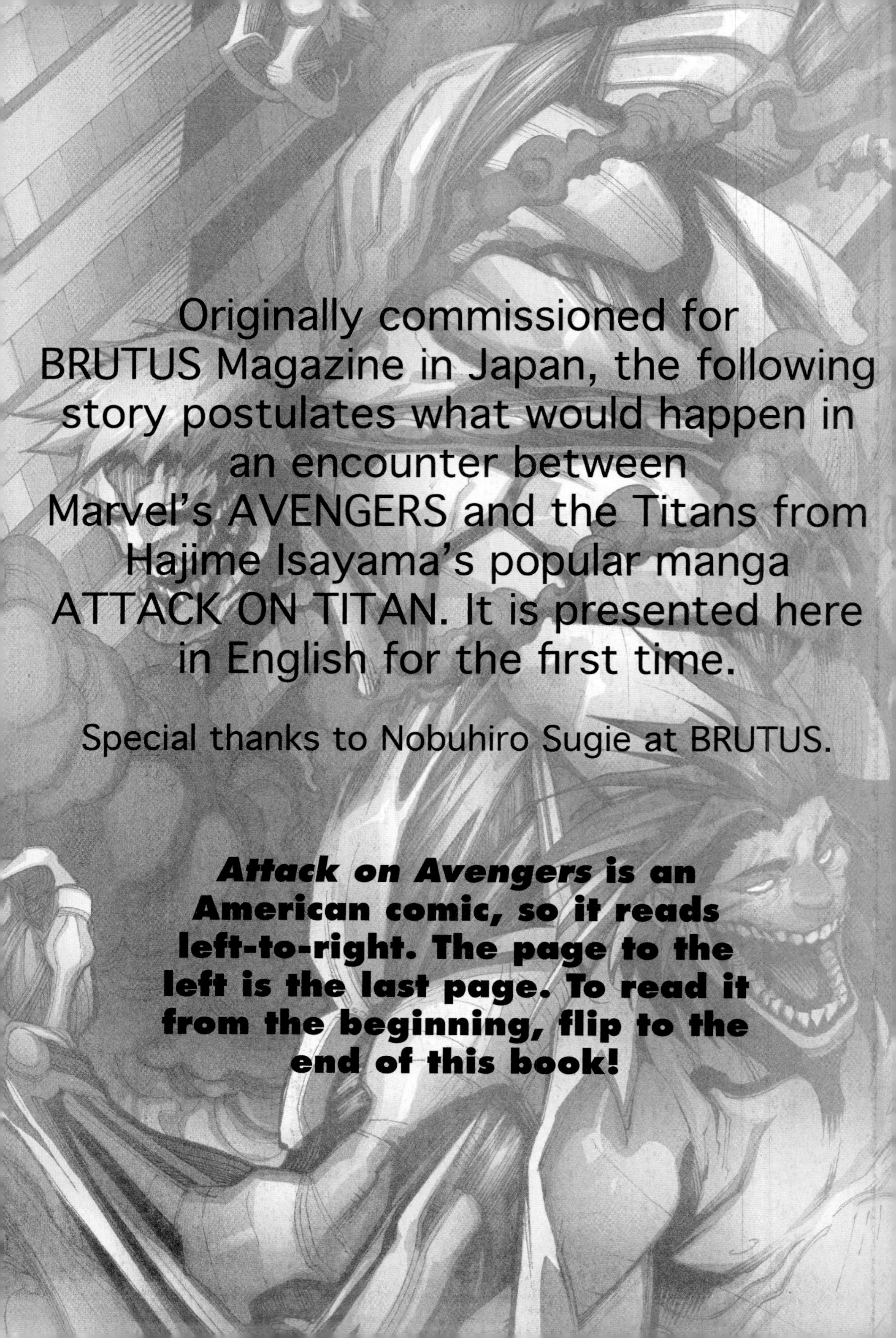

Originally commissioned for BRUTUS Magazine in Japan, the following story postulates what would happen in an encounter between Marvel's AVENGERS and the Titans from Hajime Isayama's popular manga ATTACK ON TITAN. It is presented here in English for the first time.

Special thanks to Nobuhiro Sugie at BRUTUS.

***Attack on Avengers* is an American comic, so it reads left-to-right. The page to the left is the last page. To read it from the beginning, flip to the end of this book!**

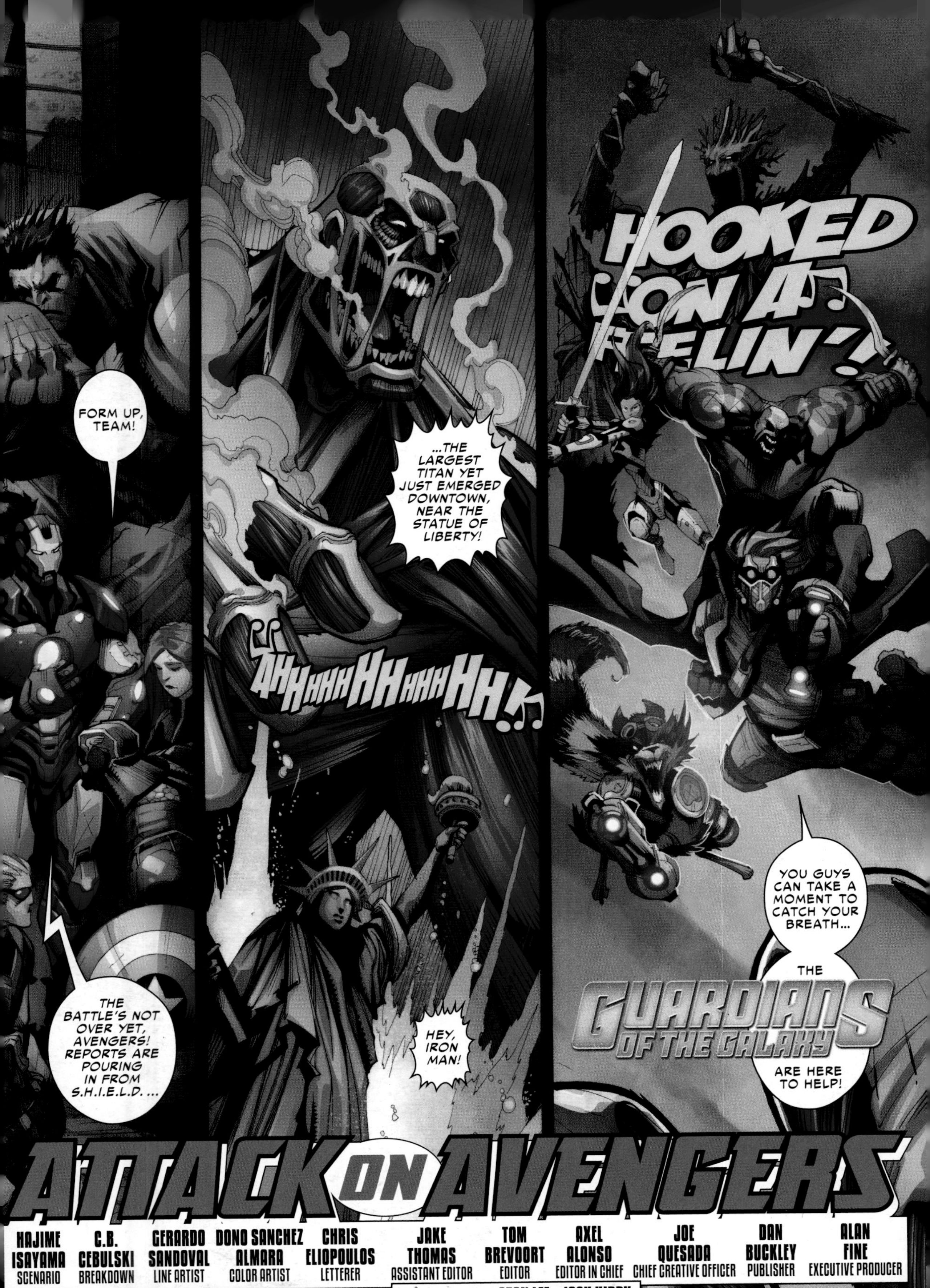
FORM UP, TEAM!
THE BATTLE'S NOT OVER YET, AVENGERS! REPORTS ARE POURING IN FROM S.H.I.E.L.D. ...
...THE LARGEST TITAN YET JUST EMERGED DOWNTOWN, NEAR THE STATUE OF LIBERTY!
AHHHHHHHHHHHHH!
HEY, IRON MAN!
HOOKED ON A
ELIN'!
YOU GUYS CAN TAKE A MOMENT TO CATCH YOUR BREATH...
THE GUARDIANS OF THE GALAXY ARE HERE TO HELP!
ATTACK ON AVENGERS
HAJIME ISAYAMA SCENARIO
C.B. CEBULSKI BREAKDOWN
GERARDO SANDOVAL LINE ARTIST
DONO SANCHEZ ALMARA COLOR ARTIST
CHRIS ELIOPOULOS LETTERER
JAKE THOMAS ASSISTANT EDITOR
TOM BREVOORT EDITOR
AXEL ALONSO EDITOR IN CHIEF
JOE QUESADA CHIEF CREATIVE OFFICER
DAN BUCKLEY PUBLISHER
ALAN FINE EXECUTIVE PRODUCER
AVENGERS CREATED BY STAN LEE & JACK KIRBY

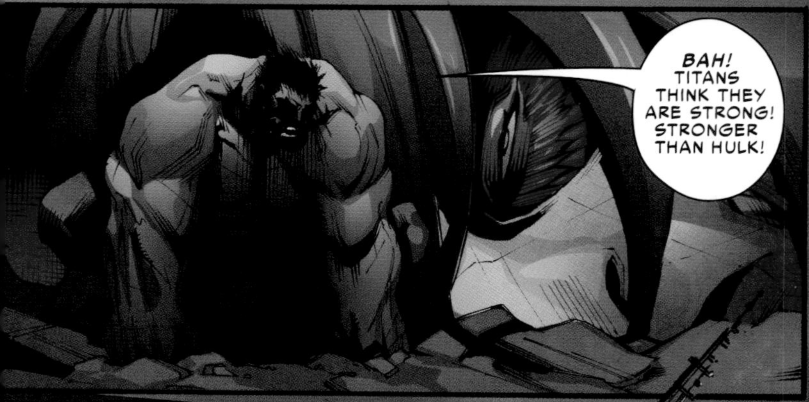
BAH! TITANS THINK THEY ARE STRONG! STRONGER THAN HULK!
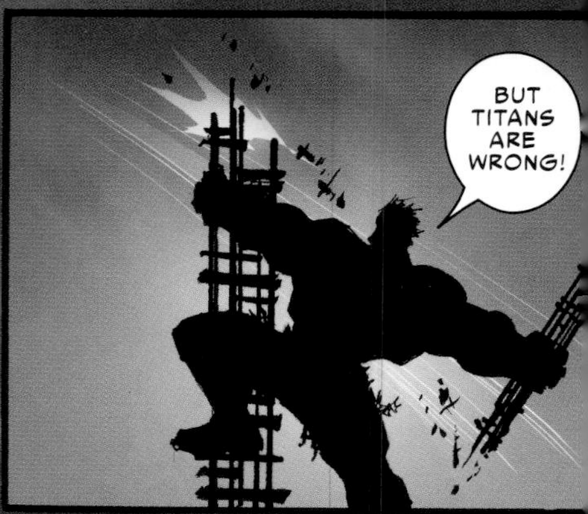
BUT TITANS ARE WRONG!
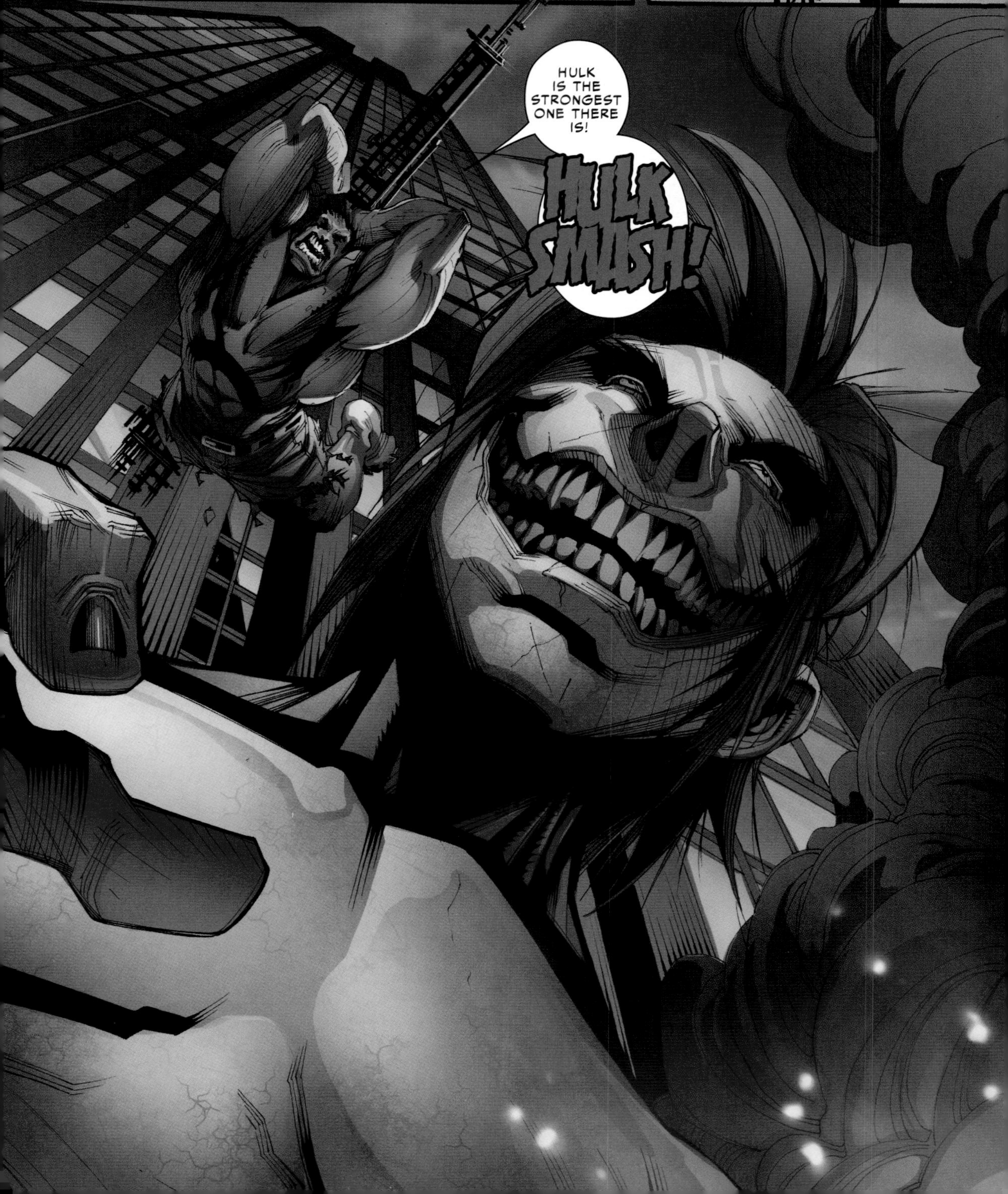
HULK IS THE STRONGEST ONE THERE IS!
HULK SMUSH!

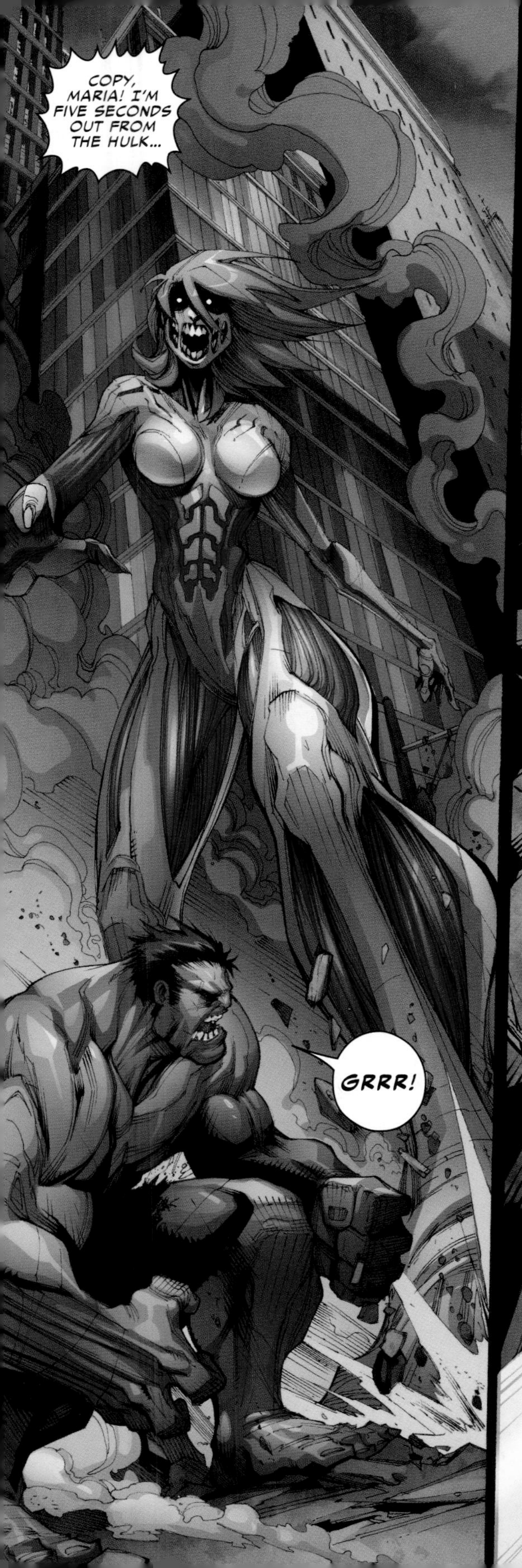
COPY, MARIA! I'M FIVE SECONDS OUT FROM THE HULK...
GRRR!
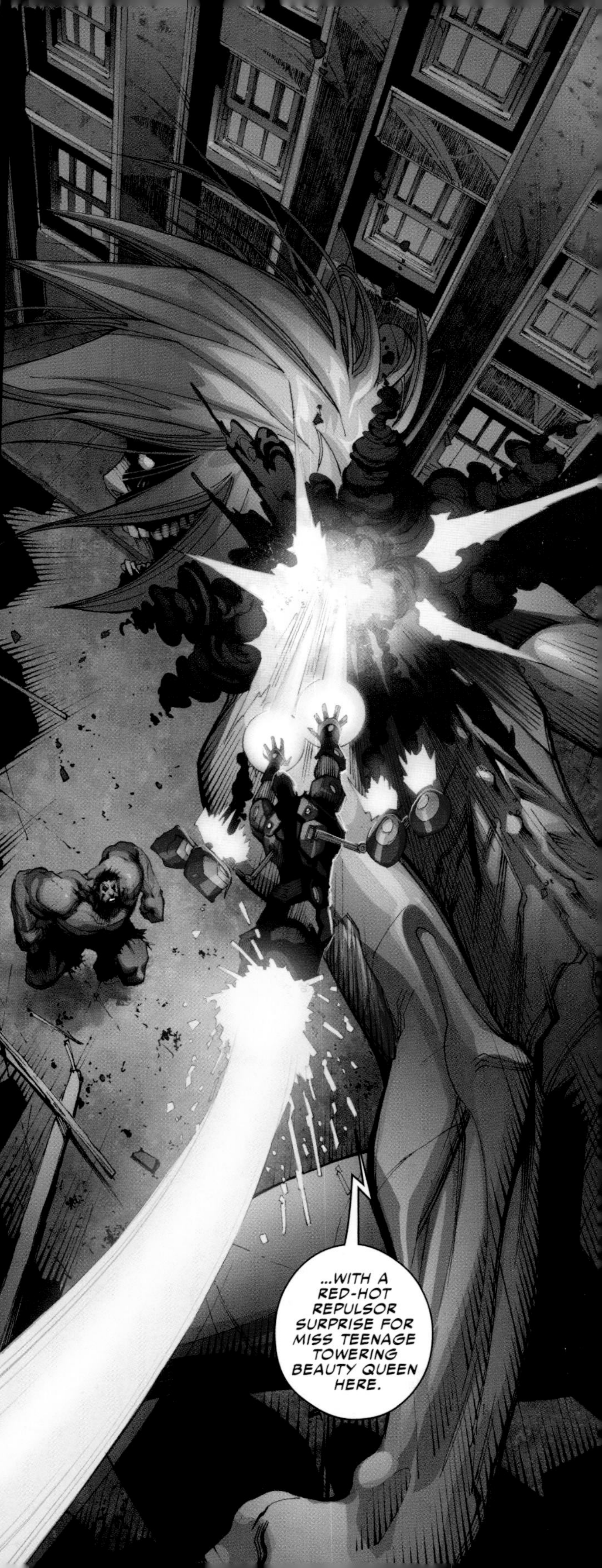
...WITH A RED-HOT REPULSOR SURPRISE FOR MISS TEENAGE TOWERING BEAUTY QUEEN HERE.

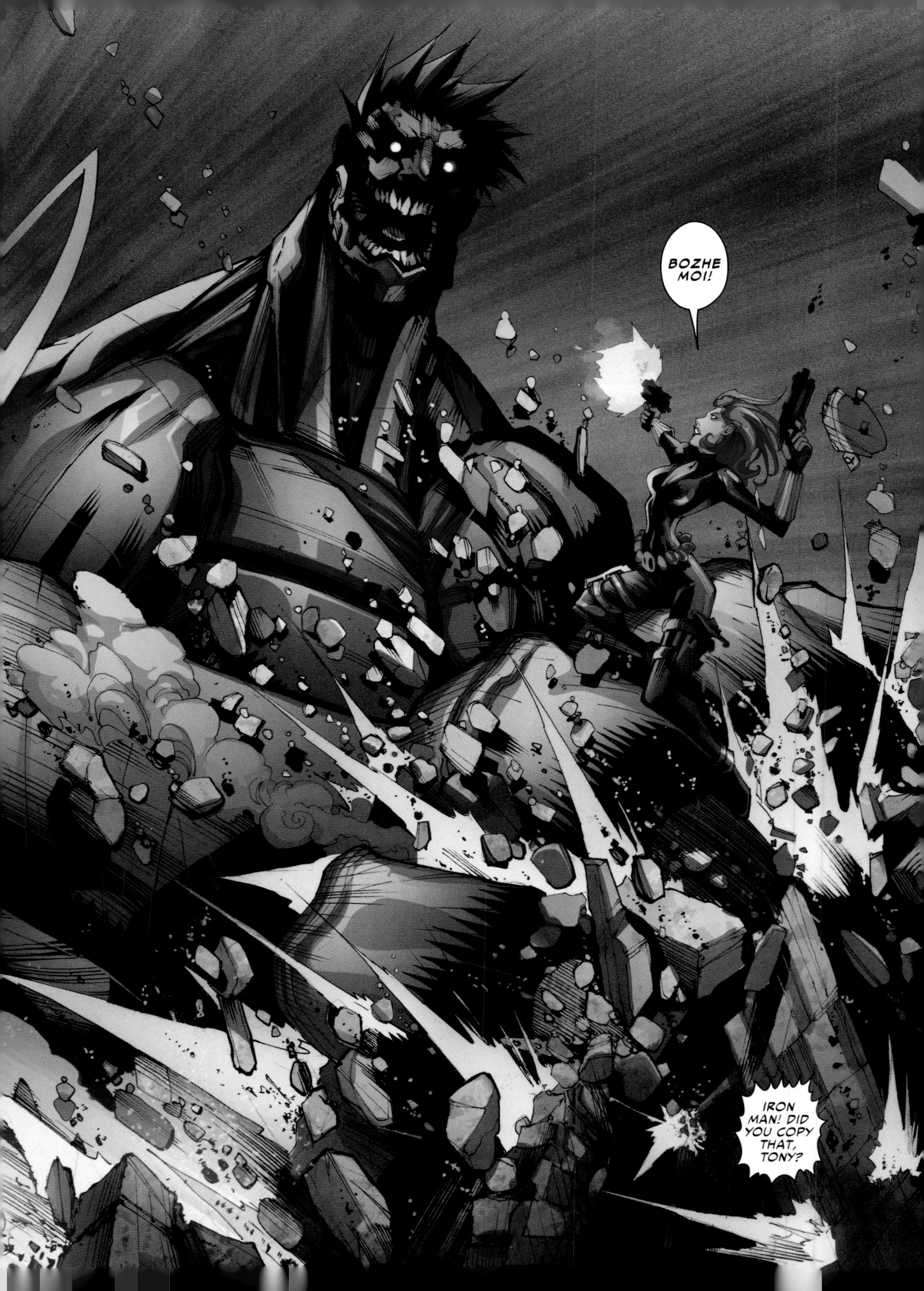
BOZHE MOI!
IRON MAN! DID YOU COPY THAT, TONY?

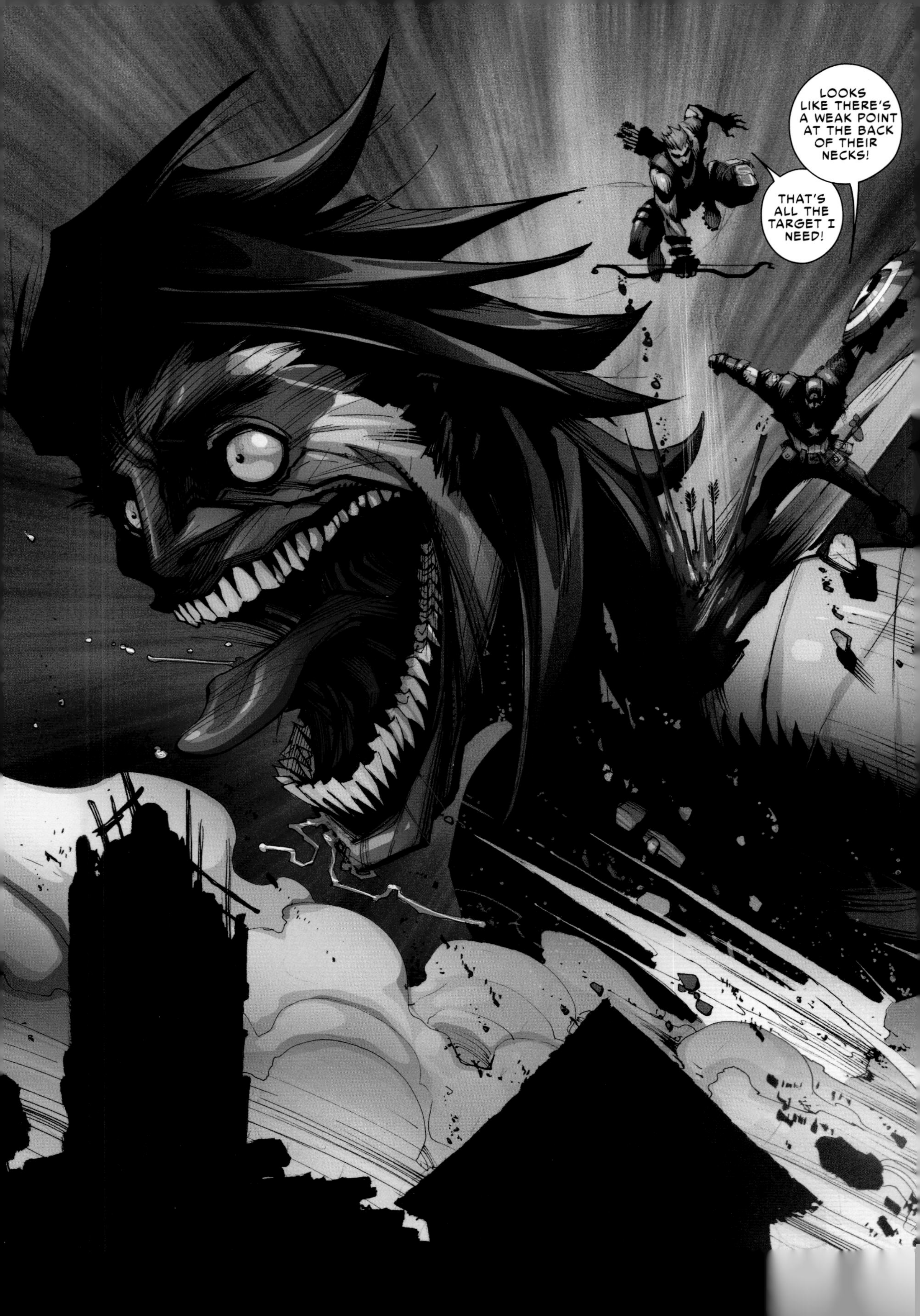
LOOKS LIKE THERE'S A WEAK POINT AT THE BACK OF THEIR NECKS!
THAT'S ALL THE TARGET I NEED!

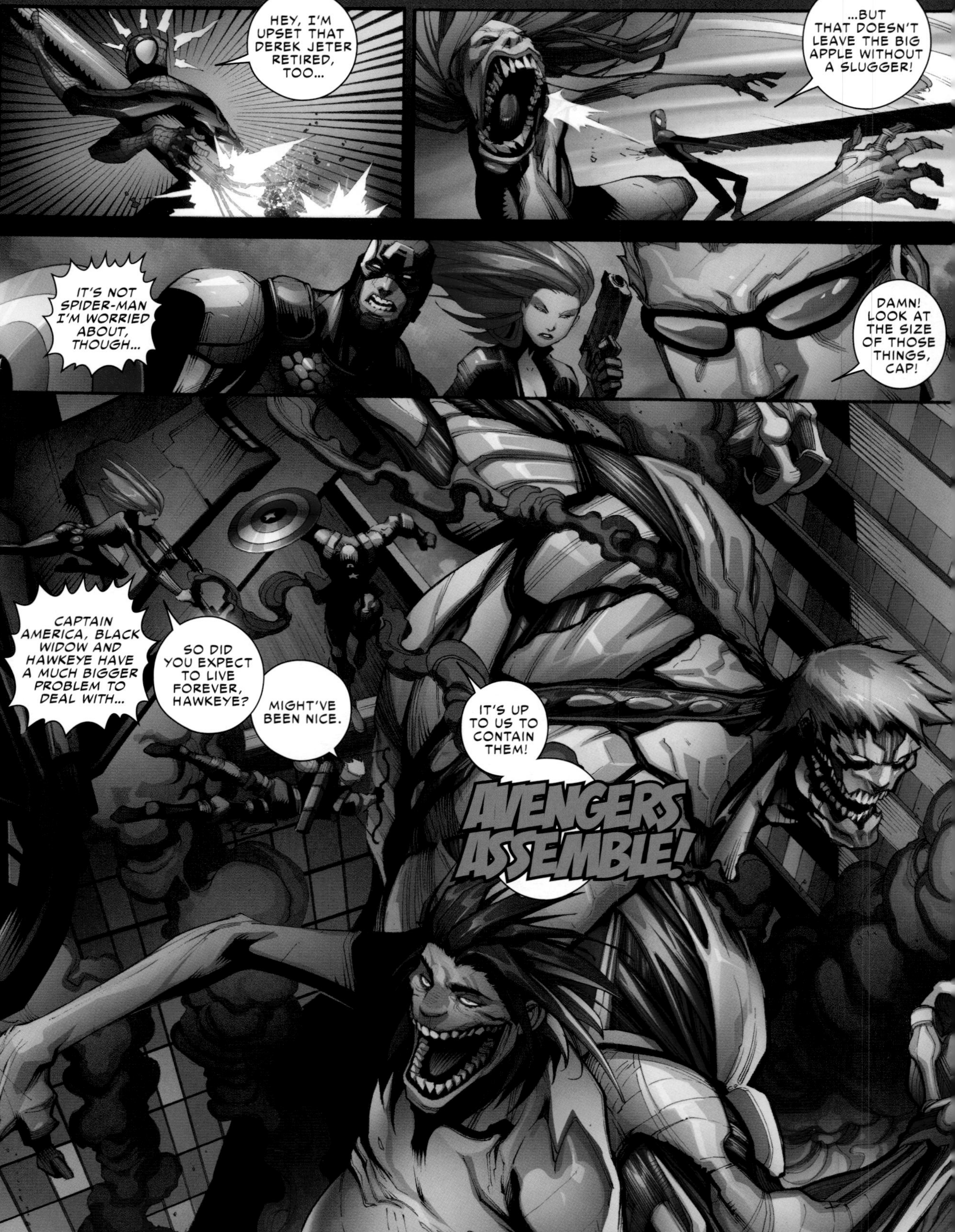
HEY, I'M UPSET THAT DEREK JETER RETIRED, TOO...
...BUT THAT DOESN'T LEAVE THE BIG APPLE WITHOUT A SLUGGER!
IT'S NOT SPIDER-MAN I'M WORRIED ABOUT, THOUGH...
DAMN! LOOK AT THE SIZE OF THOSE THINGS, CAP!
CAPTAIN AMERICA, BLACK WIDOW AND HAWKEYE HAVE A MUCH BIGGER PROBLEM TO DEAL WITH...
SO DID YOU EXPECT TO LIVE FOREVER, HAWKEYE?
MIGHT'VE BEEN NICE.
IT'S UP TO US TO CONTAIN THEM!
AVENGERS ASSEMBLE!

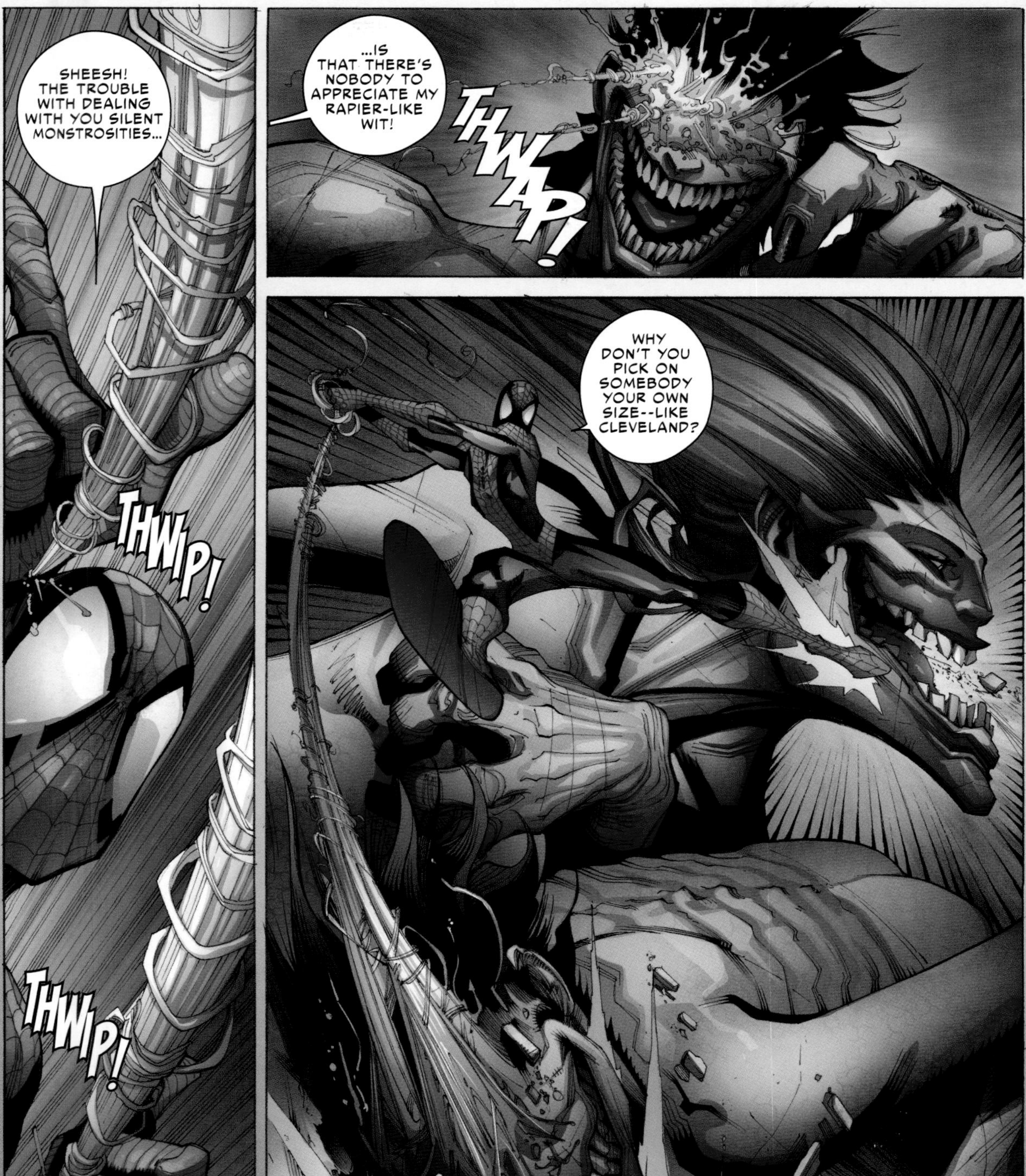
SHEESH! THE TROUBLE WITH DEALING WITH YOU SILENT MONSTROSITIES...
THWIP!
THWIP!
...IS THAT THERE'S NOBODY TO APPRECIATE MY RAPIER-LIKE WIT!
THWAP!
WHY DON'T YOU PICK ON SOMEBODY YOUR OWN SIZE--LIKE CLEVELAND?

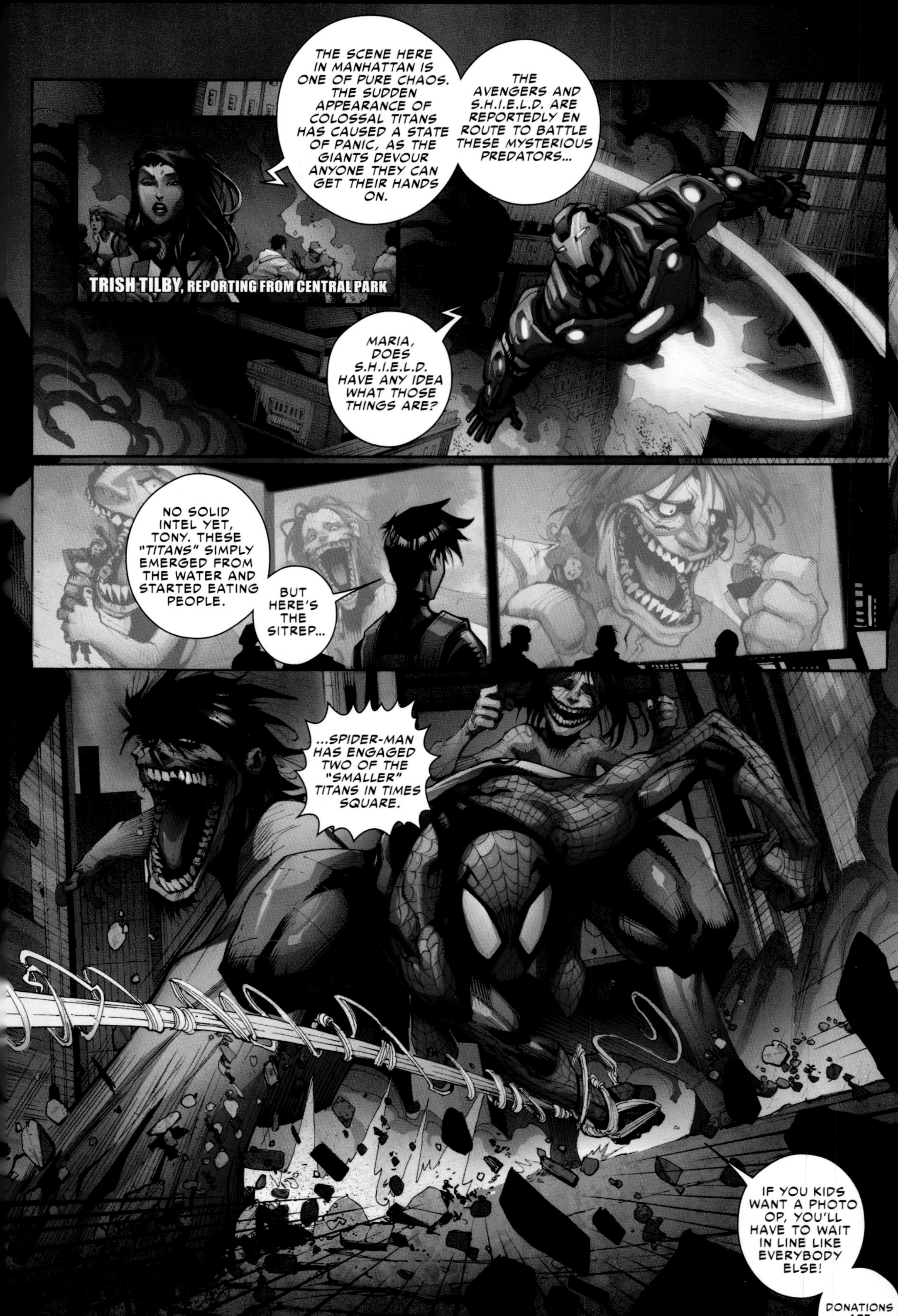
THE SCENE HERE IN MANHATTAN IS ONE OF PURE CHAOS. THE SUDDEN APPEARANCE OF COLOSSAL TITANS HAS CAUSED A STATE OF PANIC, AS THE GIANTS DEVOUR ANYONE THEY CAN GET THEIR HANDS ON.
THE AVENGERS AND S.H.I.E.L.D. ARE REPORTEDLY EN ROUTE TO BATTLE THESE MYSTERIOUS PREDATORS...
TRISH TILBY, REPORTING FROM CENTRAL PARK
MARIA, DOES S.H.I.E.L.D. HAVE ANY IDEA WHAT THOSE THINGS ARE?
NO SOLID INTEL YET, TONY. THESE "TITANS" SIMPLY EMERGED FROM THE WATER AND STARTED EATING PEOPLE.
BUT HERE'S THE SITREP...
...SPIDER-MAN HAS ENGAGED TWO OF THE "SMALLER" TITANS IN TIMES SQUARE.
IF YOU KIDS WANT A PHOTO OP, YOU'LL HAVE TO WAIT IN LINE LIKE EVERYBODY ELSE!
DONATIONS ARE OPTIONAL.